A Treasury of the

THEATRE

Volume One

WORLD DRAMA
FROM AESCHYLUS TO OSTROVSKY

Revised and expanded edition, edited by
JOHN GASSNER

SIMON AND SCHUSTER, NEW YORK

TWELFTH PRINTING

SBN 671-20137-9

LIBRARY OF CONGRESS CATALOG CARD NUMBER: 67-11743. MANUFACTURED IN THE UNITED STATES OF AMERICA

The editor and publishers of A TREASURY OF THE THEATRE are grateful to the following publishers, playwrights, and translators for permission to reprint many of the plays in this volume:

To W. W. Norton & Company, Inc., and Edith Hamilton for their consent to the inclusion of Edith Hamilton's translation of *Agamemnon* by Aeschylus. Copyright 1937 by W. W. Norton & Company, Inc., New York.

To John Gassner for his consent to the inclusion of his versions of *Oedipus the King* by Sophocles, the Brome *Abraham and Isaac, The Second Shepherds' Play,* and *Everyman.* Permission to perform these versions must be obtained from Mr. John Gassner, c/o Simon & Schuster, Inc., 1230 Sixth Avenue, New York, N.Y.

To Richmond Lattimore for his consent to the inclusion of his translation of *The Trojan Women* by Euripides, published in *Greek Plays in Modern Translation,* edited by Dudley Fitts, Dial Press, Inc., 1947. Copyright 1947 by Richmond Lattimore, Bryn Mawr, Pa.

To Random House, Inc., for their consent to the inclusion of *The Brothers* by Terence, printed in *The Complete Roman Drama,* edited by George E. Duckworth, 2 vols., 1942.

To Alfred A. Knopf, Inc., for their consent to the inclusion of *Sotoba Komachi,* a Noh play by Kwanami Kiyotsugu, as translated by Arthur Waley. Copyright 1922 by Arthur Waley.

To Angel Flores for his consent to the inclusion of *Fuente Ovejuna* by Lope de Vega, as translated by Angel Flores and Muriel Kittel. Permission to perform this version must be obtained from Mr. Angel Flores, Queens College, Flushing, N.Y.

To Random House, Inc., and Modern Library, Inc., for their consent to the inclusion of *Phaedra* by Jean Racine, as translated by Robert Henderson. Copyright 1931 by Modern Library, Inc., New York.

To James Laughlin and New Directions for their consent to the inclusion of the college edition of C. F. MacIntyre's translation of *Faust: Part 1,* by Johann Wolfgang von Goethe. Copyright 1949 by New Directions.

To Faber & Faber, Ltd., for their consent to the inclusion of *Danton's Death* by Georg Büchner, as translated by Stephen Spender and Goronwy Rees. Copyright by Faber & Faber, Ltd., London.

To George Rapall Noyes for his consent to the inclusion of *The Inspector* by Nikolai Gogol and *A Month in the Country* by Ivan Turgenev, the former as translated by John Laurence Seymour and George Rapall Noyes, the latter as translated by George Rapall Noyes, both in *Masterpieces of The Russian Drama,* published by O. Appleton and Company. Copyright 1933 by D. Appleton and Company, New York. Permission to perform these plays must be obtained from Mr. George R. Noyes, 1486 Greenwood Terrace, Berkeley 8, Calif.

To E. P. Dutton & Company, Inc., for their consent to the inclusion of *Maria Magdalena* by Friedrich Hebbel, as translated by Barker Fairley in the volume *Three Plays* by Friedrich Hebbel, in the Everyman's Library, E. P. Dutton & Company, Inc., New York.

To Penguin Books, Ltd., for their consent to the inclusion of Roger Lancelyn Green's translation of *The Searching Satyrs* from *Two Satyr Plays* (Penguin Classics).

To the University of Chicago Press for their consent to the inclusion of *The Bacchae* by Euripides, as translated by William Arrowsmith in *Complete Greek Tragedies, IV,* 1959.

To Bantam Books, Inc., for their consent to the inclusion of the following plays copyrighted by them: *The Cid* by Pierre Corneille, translated by Wallace Fowlie, reprinted from *Classical French Drama,* © 1962; *Mary Stuart* by Friedrich Schiller, translated by Theodore Lustig, reprinted from *Classical German Drama,* © 1963; *The Thunderstorm* by Alexander Ostrovsky, translated by Andrew MacAndrew, reprinted from *19th Century Russian Drama,* © 1963. The Editor also wishes to thank Bantam Books, Inc., for permission to include excerpts from his book *Medieval and Tudor Drama,* his version of *The Death of Pilate,* and Sister Mary Marguerite Butler's English version of Hrotsvitha's *Paphnutius.*

To Sister Mary Marguerite Butler of Mercy College, Detroit, for her consent to the inclusion of her translation of Hrotsvitha's *Paphnutius,* first published in *Medieval and Tudor Drama,* edited by John Gassner for Bantam Books, Inc.

To Samuel French, Inc.. for their consent to the inclusion of *The Portrait* by Flaminio Scala, as translated by Garrett H. Leverton. Copyright, 1932, by Samuel French, Inc. (In volume *Plays for the College Theatre.*) Copyright, 1960 (in renewal), by Samuel French, Inc.

To Edwin Honig for his consent to the inclusion of his translation of *The Cave of Salamanca,* published in his translations of Cervantes' *Interludes,* The New American Library (Signet Classic), 1964. Permission to perform this play must be obtained from Miss Toby Cole, 234 W. 44th St., New York.

To Edward and Elizabeth Huberman for consent to include their translation of Calderon's *Life Is a Dream,* and for the revisions Prof. Huberman made for me in the Bantam Books' text in which the translation was first printed, *Spanish Drama,* edited by Angel Flores, Bantam Books, Inc., 1962. Inquiries concerning performance rights to *Life Is a Dream,* copyright © 1963 by Edward and Elizabeth Huberman, should be addressed to Prof. Huberman, Rutgers University, Newark, N.J.

To Linda Asher for her consent to the inclusion of her translation of *Hernani,* first published in *The Genius of the French Theatre,* edited by Albert Bermel, The New American Library (Mentor), 1961.

CAUTION:

All the plays listed above are fully protected under the copyright laws of the United States of America, the British Empire including the Dominion of Canada, and all other countries, members of the Copyright Union. All rights including professional, amateur, motion picture, recitation, public reading, radio broadcasting, televised performance, and the rights of translation into foreign languages are strictly reserved in their present form. These plays are for the reading public only. All inquiries for such rights must be addressed to the copyright owners. Also see special cautions under acknowledgments.

For
Joseph Wood Krutch
and
Mark Van Doren

A Note on the Third Edition

In view of the considerable enlargement of *A Treasury of the Theatre* in this revision, a few explanations are in order.

A new section on various types of Western drama has been added. The present amplified edition should enlarge the reader's familiarity with the remarkable range of the dramatic medium and with the literature of several countries and periods. In the previous edition, which still constitutes Part I of this book, major periods of theatre from the fifth century B.C. to the beginning of the second half of the nineteenth century were covered. In Part II, perhaps less often read but historically important types of plays, such as *The Cid* and *Hernani* have been added, as well as some minor works that exemplify special aspects of the history of the theatre. Both parts of the book are divided into sections corresponding to theatrical eras; and each section has a special introduction noting the distinctive features of the period. These are followed by plays representative of the dramatic literature and theatre of the time and by introductions to each specific play and playwright. Many of these masterpieces are becoming increasingly familiar to the audiences that patronize university and community theatres throughout the country.

Readers who combine the divisions of Part I, Periods of World Drama (Aeschylus to Turgenev), with Part II, The Range of Western Drama (Sophocles to Ostrovsky), will have a comprehensive survey of the drama before Ibsen's major works. A chronology that coordinates the two parts has been devised to make the relationships instantly apparent. And because virtually every type of drama is represented, the instructor may now decide to organize his course around "tragedy," "farce," "comedy," and intermediate forms as well as by periods or by countries.

I advance no other claims for this volume except for my belief that it is not simply just another anthology of plays; and a conclusive reason for this will be found in the presence of more than a hundred and twenty thousand words of introductory material, which amounts to a short history of the drama before the modern period.

Finally, I cannot conclude this prefatory note without an appreciative salute to my wife Mollie Gassner for her part in this enterprise, and to my friend Stanley Burnshaw.

New Haven, Connecticut
January, 1967

JOHN GASSNER

Chronology

The purpose of this chart is to combine Parts I and II in a logical chronology that unifies the whole and may facilitate various teaching procedures.

Contents

CONTENTS

The Renaissance

The Seventeenth and Eighteenth Centuries

The Romantic and Early Realistic Drama

PART II. THE RANGE OF WESTERN DRAMA

Romantic Forms of Drama

Middle Class Drama

Introduction

I

MANY STRANDS are woven into the fiber of our theatrical heritage. In the course of some twenty-four hundred years graced by such masters as Sophocles, Shakespeare, and Molière, we acquired a dramatic literature of staggering proportions before entering the specifically modern period of the late nineteenth century with Ibsen, Strindberg, and Shaw.

Today our understanding of drama prevents us from considering any particular style as alien to our theatre simply because it fails to conform to modern realism. By exercising a modicum of imagination we can appreciate any kind of play, regardless of the antiquity of the theatrical convention in which it was first written. Sophocles' *Antigone* and *Oedipus the King* and Euripides' *Medea* and *The Trojan Women* can be as stirring on the twentieth-century stage as they must have been in the fifth century B.C. Shakespeare has been the most modern playwright of our English-speaking world, as well as of Germany and Russia. Molière is still the most vital master of the French drama despite the experiments of Cocteau, the metaphysics of Sartre, and the ironic fantasies of Giraudoux. Twentieth-century medicine may be more effective than the medical science of Hippocrates, and Einstein's physics may be more accurate than Newton's, but a play written in 1950 is not necessarily better than one written twenty-four centuries earlier.

The modern drama since about 1870 may have looked like a new phenomenon to its first proponents, but it was actually built upon the firm foundations laid down by earlier dramatists. On reflection, we find that it is not difficult to link Ibsen with Euripides, O'Neill with Aeschylus and Euripides, Shaw with Molière, Noel Coward with the authors of Roman comedy. Ever since the dramatic medium took shape, much of the world's experience and perception has been poured into it. As Edmund Burke wrote, "A history of the stage is no trivial thing to those who wish to study human nature in all shapes and positions." Moreover, although the dramatic form dictated by a stage convention provided the means for projecting the substance of characterization and thought, it is this substance that keeps a play alive. John Mason Brown has observed that "great plays are great for other reasons than that they are adapted to the stage. They soar above its physical limitations as the spirit of man transcends the body." And, at the same time, since the drama is written for public performance, good playwrights have always known how to make an impression upon people of considerable diversity of taste and culture. They learned how to capture attention by directly engaging the sensibility and understanding of their audience. We can respond profoundly or joyously to most masterpieces of the past once we leave our prepossessions or prejudices behind and let the play "act" upon us.

The question of what a play is becomes virtually irrelevant to us when we respond as a spectator either in the auditorium or in the study. Experience is presented instead of being described and explained; the description is present in the action of the human agent, the explanation in the state of mind that he reveals by his responses and decisions. We move with the play from incident to incident and from one response to another. We experience life directly as it proceeds from moment to moment. And in this way we not only participate in the lives and problems of the drama's agents but arrive at an understanding of their motives and conduct. Whether or not life has been imitated realistically or revealed imaginatively, it has been made more intense for us. And if we also derive any wisdom from the theatre, it has come directly from a shared experience.

Good theatre rarely presents difficulties to the spectator-participant. It certainly does not have to be explained to him. If explanations are often needed by the play reader, it is chiefly because he cannot adequately translate his reading into theatre. He has not formed the habit of reading creatively—that is, of visualizing events conveyed by dialogue and of finding out things for himself by observing the actions and reactions of the characters and hearing them speak. (And in a play, as in life, they will often misunderstand, rationalize, exaggerate, distort, or try to conceal the exact truth, for they do not speak with the detachment and omniscience claimed by an essayist or novelist.) Novels have accustomed the modern reader to being spoon-fed, so to speak. The novelists tell him all he needs to know and believe. Playwrights, on the other hand, treat him as an adult and invite him to make discoveries and draw conclusions. In the case of the older drama, moreover, he may believe himself handicapped by unfamiliarity with the kind of theatre for which the particular piece was written. Here he can, of course, help himself by reading about the stage conventions of the period. But he can sharpen his responses even more easily and surely if he will merely imagine the characters standing before him. What they say and do will make the play a direct experience for him even if he does not know how they were costumed and what kind of stage setting was used in the original performance of the work. Shakespeare's actors at his Globe Theatre, as well as Shakespearean actors of the next two centuries, wore the clothing of their own period instead of costumes of the time assigned in the play. In our own time, some of Shakespeare's plays have been clothed in modern dress. They have also been acted in the course of the years under sunlight, under gaslight, under electric lamps; on platforms, on formal stages with flats set at the sides in perspective, on solidly constructed settings, on revolving stages, and behind our familiar proscenium arches, which separate the actor from the audience as the staging at Shakespeare's Globe Theatre did not. Yet Shakespeare has remained Shakespeare whenever his unmutilated text has been properly spoken and competently acted. And in 1946 the Old Vic company did not have to erect an open-air theatre on the side of a hill and place the chorus in a dancing circle in order to allow Sophocles' *Oedipus the King* to exert its spell again. We are so willing to give ourselves up to stage illusion that we can be asked to imagine anything by way of physical setting, provided we are rewarded with absorbing human behavior and thought.

The object of these remarks, as the reader has no doubt suspected, is to bridge whatever impassable gulf he may imagine to exist between present and past theatre. In a very real sense, there is no such thing as "old drama." There is only well-written and ill-written, effectively realized and clumsily constructed, stimulating and unstimulating, pleasing and offensive drama.

II

Dramatic art has undergone much development since the fifth century B.C. But, although there is considerable continuity in the history of the art, there is also much discontinuity. Theatrical performance has been virtually uninterrupted since ancient times. Only certain periods, however, have produced drama of excellence and significance. Between such periods the theatre survived through revivals of old plays and effective performances of new though inferior plays. If the life of the theatre had depended solely on the production of masterpieces, it would have been extinguished long ago. And if talented performers had not kept the stage alive when the playwrights failed it, stageworthy plays of distinction might never have been written after Euripides died in 406 B.C. There would have been no medium for which one could write a play as anything but a literary exercise.

Dramatic excellence appears not only fitfully but often also very briefly. It was in evidence in Athens for a period of some seventy-five years, from about 475 to 400 B.C. We next find some distinction in Rome during the late third century and the first half of the second century B.C., although, if we are to believe the ancients and judge from fragments, Greece produced more or less distinguished comedies during the fourth century B.C. After a lapse of fourteen hundred years—except for a theatrical springtime in India that gave us such plays as *The Little Clay Cart* and *Shakuntala*—the world theatre again became fruitful when medieval drama attained some eminence. Then the Renaissance brought forth remarkable drama in Shakespeare's England and Lope de Vega's Spain, and the second half of the seventeenth century enriched us once more, chiefly with plays by Molière and Racine. The eighteenth century contributed, among others, Sheridan in England, Marivaux and Beaumarchais in France, and Goethe and Schiller in Germany. The early nineteenth century brought forth, amid much drama of uneven quality, a sparkling genius here and there in a Musset, Büchner, and Gogol. And around 1870, the modern drama began its ascent in France, Russia, and, most notably, Scandinavia.

It is to the theatre from its literary beginnings to the advent of Ibsen that this volume pays tribute. We are faced here, from the student's point of view, with certain problems, such as the choral nature of Greek drama, the epic flux of Elizabethan drama, the neoclassic rules of the unities, the grotesquerie of much romanticism, and the rising conventions of realism. We can also enrich our appreciations with as much scholarship as we care to collect. But the one absolute prerequisite for appreciation or gratification is a sensitivity to the play text and to the theatrical-visual possibilities inherent in its movement. For without this sensitivity our scholarship is barren, and with it the most valuable part of theatrical scholarship—an understanding of how the drama works its effects—is sure to follow. And when we have a sufficiency of this sensitivity, nothing in a good play is actually a problem at all—that is, until we try to stage the play. In that case everything becomes a problem, even in the most familiar kind of current realistic drama.

If we have an interest in the historical development of the theatre, we may also view its course in terms of types and forms. We can, then, observe a first period, when tragedy in the Greek world of the fifth century B.C. assumes distinctive shape as an orderly art of poetic dialogue and choral lyricism in a solvent of ritualistic spectacle; and when comedy rises to a high estate of lyricism and satirical extravaganza reminiscent of fertility rites of orgiastic release. The masters Aeschylus, Sophocles, Euripides, and Aristophanes create and grace this art. After the fifth century B.C., tragic art, which has by then ranged over a considerable area of possibilities (in heroic, psychological, symbolic, tragicomic and even romantic drama), enters upon a long period of stalemate and decline. And comedy, between the fourth and second centuries B.C. in Graeco-Roman society, becomes a more or less trim art of ordinary personal problems, social relationships, and manners, very much like the comic art of our own day.

After some fourteen centuries, we confront a second development of tragic art, medieval-religious in inspiration, epically episodic, and given to an admixture of realistic detail and supernatural marvels, as well as to a mingling of serious and comic matter. A few centuries later, however, during the Renaissance, we witness the rise of a thoroughly worldly kind of tragedy, full of the bustle of human desire on the part of extraordinary men bent upon self-realization or gratification of their "will-to-power." In Elizabethan England and Spain, an uncommon strenuousness bursts the seams of dramaturgy, disdains the constraints of time and place, and finds a single plot and a single mood altogether insufficient. A tragedy passionate, adventurous, and baroquely opulent in language and action mushrooms in the age of Marlowe, Shakespeare, and Lope de Vega. And comic art follows the same impulse in the dramatic forms of romance, fantasy, and idyll, of which such plays as *The Tempest, A Midsummer Night's Dream,* and *As You Like It* are representative; and in the forms of rough-hewn comedy of manners and obsessions ("humours"), of which Jonson's plays are examples.

Another century, the seventeenth, perfects a comedy of manners as elegant and urbane as it is pointed and astute—this largely through the collaboration of Molière with the spirit of Louis XIV's reign. Tragedy, at the same time, becomes shapely, reasoned, and severely dignified in the course of a similar collaboration between Racine and courtly life.

By the last quarter of the eighteenth century, however, the formal boundaries of comedy and tragedy begin to crumble, and out of the deterioration of the old forms come romantic tragedy, as loosely constructed as the Elizabethan play but without its driving energy; "melodrama," a vulgarization of tragic action; "middle-class tragedy," catastrophic in its conclusion but devoted to interests and characters that fall short of grandeur and call for a less than exalted form of dialogue, soon to become prose; and "sentimental comedy," in which sympathy displaces detachment and brittle wit yields to sentiment. By this time we are on the threshold of modern theatre, with its unheroic sociological and psychological plays and its great variety of dramatic styles.

We arrive at the age, in which we are still situated, when the stock characters of the older drama—rustics, "clowns," servants, and others of humble occupation —become citizens of the democratic world who receive the playwrights' full consideration as individuals; when a portion of common life is held to be more important than remarkable deeds; when the destiny of man is no longer considered the effect of a baleful star, a morally determined doom, or an act of independent will but the result of biological, psychological, and social coordinates; when, finally, the dramatist challenges society instead of remaining content to reflect it and makes the discussion of a problem or idea the spoke of his wheel of action.

In these last few paragraphs we may satisfy the historical conscience after a fashion. But, interesting as this history would be if it were rendered in detail, it concerns us here chiefly as evidence for the vitality of dramatic art, which has never exhausted its possibilities even if it has often exhausted our patience with the bumbling or shallowness of its practitioners and devotees. And the possibility of tracing through the theatre's varied course most of the thought of the centuries and most of the stirrings of civilization can be cited as further evidence. As an art that addresses itself not to isolated individuals but to a communion of spectators, the drama has represented, seriously or with amusement, humanity's maximum situations of tension, conflict, and crisis—in William Blake's words, "the contraries . . . without which there is no progression."

Still, to be as close to human concerns as the drama must be, since it is dependent upon the interest of large numbers of people rather than upon the favor of fastidious connoisseurs, it has had to follow rather than lead humanity. In following, it has not only assimilated thought rather than created it but has bent and twisted itself into many shapes. The fact is that dramatic art has been protean even in periods when standards seemed to be most firmly established, in fifth-century-B.C. Athens and seventeenth-century Paris. The plays with which we shall represent these and other ages in this volume do not sum up all the strategies of the dramatists of those times. Sophocles wrote idyllic tragicomedy in *Philoctetes* after having composed his *Antigone* and *Oedipus the King;* Euripides created romances after *The Trojan Women;* Shakespeare delivered *Cymbeline* and *The Tempest* after *Hamlet;* Molière performed farcical antics after the severities of *The Misanthrope*. In truth, we must realize that the drama has been unable to afford the purity or absoluteness of lyric and epic poetry, although it has itself been at its best a form of poetry. Playwrights have scaled the highest altitudes of poetic expression, but have also descended to "jigging veins" and to "such conceits as clownage keeps in pay." Mount Parnassus and all the market places of the world have been equally the province of the dramatists, and they have sometimes mistaken one for the other.

The history covered by the present anthology, then, is too multifarious—multifarious as it is vital—to be reduced to a single principle of unity. And no such principle is offered here. Certainly the plays have not been selected with the intention of supporting the editor's or anybody else's notion of what theatre is or should be. Theatre is construed here to be anything that has interested people who have congregated to witness a performance; drama, to be anything that has exerted an effect when performed. The plays presented in this anthology belong to "the republic of active literature," in Edmund Burke's apt phrase; a republic in which "anything goes." And this would be even more apparent if the present collection could be supplemented, as it should be, by twice the number of plays it has been feasible to include here.

PART I

PERIODS OF WORLD DRAMA

The Roman theatre at Orange (the best preserved in France) was built in the first or second century A.D. Its *frons scenae*, the highly decorated architectural façade that forms the background for the actors, is approximately 118 feet high and 338 feet long. From Durm, *Die Baustile*, Vol. II, 1905.

The Classic Age

The classic Greek theatre at Epidaurus. Note the orchestra, or dancing circle; the ruins of the *skene,* or permanent scene building behind the circle; and the rows of stone seats on three sides of the circle (see p. 6). *Opposite page* (top): *Oedipus the King* as directed by Tyrone Guthrie in 1955. Photo: Donald McKague, courtesy Stratford Shakespearean Festival Foundation of Canada.

The Classic Age

Greece was the cradle of the two civilized and civilizing arts of tragedy and comedy. It was on the Greek peninsula that they emerged out of ritual into art. In other ancient lands, dramatic art never lost its subordinate position with respect to magic and religion. In Greece, the ancestral tomb, the magic circle, and the temple became the theatre. The ancestral spirit became the living hero, the wraith of the primitive "vegetation spirit" assumed the body of a god, and the god took the shape of a man. Moreover, in Greece the god was displaced or made subordinate in the subject matter of the drama. Drawing upon the stories of local ancestors and upon the heroes of the Homeric epics (the *Iliad,* the *Odyssey,* and other narrative poetry long lost to the world), the playwrights assembled a cast of completely human characters who could be subjected to moral appraisal and psychological analysis.

In tragedy, these characters still wore the aura of their mythical and legendary origins—except when Euripides stripped them of their glory—and they retained the stature of historical figures from the heroic age. (The Greeks of the time tended to make no sharp distinction between legend and history.) Tragedians, after an early period, were restrained by convention from dealing with contemporary characters and events, except by implication. But in the exuberant Athenian comedy, the subject could be as fresh as today's news; the characters subjected to ridicule were contemporaries easily recognizable through the comic mask.

Even as Greek sculpture was the human figure frozen in the full bloom of limited perfection and not an abstracted, many-limbed, symbol-encrusted deity, so Greek theatre was man in movement. Even as Greek myth humanized the supernatural, so the Greek stage focused on the recognizable individual. The actor might still wear the mask of primitive rite, but he presented the individual in action and spoke for him with the identifiable voice of his pain and folly. The rites of man, rather than of god, were enacted in the Greek *theatron,* once a primitive dancing circle, and the drama performed was a human experience even when a god appeared among the cast. If in Greek tragedy the experience resembles a god's—that is, the rise and fall of a great spirit—it is not because the human being has been reduced but because he has been enlarged. And if he is decidedly less than a god in comedy, he is even more immediately recognizable as human in his littleness.

If not a trace had remained of the sculpture and architecture of Greece, we could have reconstructed a civilization from the fraction of Greek drama that has survived, just as we have been able to reconstruct an earlier civilization from the *Iliad* and *Odyssey.* Once the drama emerged from ritual and became an independent, man-directed art, it came to embrace all human complexities and interests. Drama, however, could transmute and transcend ritualistic magic only among a population that was unsubjugated by a priestly caste and unintimidated by the mysteries of the universe. The Greeks, intellectually and politically the freest people of the Mediterranean world, turned toward the life of reason and so became the first true humanists of Western civilization. It was reason that enabled them to accept a man-filled rather than a spirit-filled world and to translate every problem into human terms. As Edith Hamilton has said, the Greek artist "felt the real world completely sufficient for the demands of the spirit," and the real world provided all the wonders without which art becomes a dry and sterile convention. Moreover, the greatest of marvels to the Greeks was man. Sophocles said it long ago in the great chorus of his *Antigone:* "Wonders are there many—none more wonderful than man." He added, "His is speech and wind-swift thought."

Speech and thought were, indeed, the chief additions to the primitive rite and transformed it into drama. The earliest rites were undoubtedly pantomimic dances. These acquired "story content" from the myths developed in Greece, and, in time, the stories were translated into speech—into words of song—in addition to physical movement. These so-called *dithyrambs* were the first steps toward a literary drama, and both tragedy and comedy in the great fifth century B.C. retained the dance and the choral recitation as formal characteristics. Poetry of an extremely high order of excellence was, moreover, possible in Greece, because, by the beginning of the fifth century, Greece had already developed the lyric and choral poetic art for which Sappho and Pindar, respectively, are renowned. When dialogue was also introduced at about this time (the legendary founder of Greek tragedy, Thespis, is credited with this innovation), the dramatic form came into being. At the same time, too, "thought" entered the dancing circle, first through the content of myth and religion, then through inevitable reflections on the life of man as manifested by the legends of ancestral heroes, who had been objects of worship in tomb rites, and of the Homeric heroes whose sagas belonged to the cultural heritage. And, as the intellectual climate of Athens became more sharply defined, thought filtered into the dramatists' work in the form of moral, philosophical, and social inquiry. Even discursive reason or intellectual discussion penetrated into the drama, especially in the plays of Euripides, the Socratic tragedian.

THE CLASSIC HERITAGE IN DRAMA

Fifth-century Greek tragedy and comedy were the creation of Athens, then the cultural capital, as well as the leading political and commercial city-state, of Greece. Athens had assumed this leadership by repelling the Persian invasion of Europe and maintained its supremacy until its final defeat in the Peloponnesian War at the very end of the fifth century. The defeat was administered by Sparta, Athens' rival and its cultural antithesis—a militaristic, antidemocratic nation, averse to intellectual and artistic activity. Although tragedy continued to be written after the collapse of Athenian democracy, creativeness in this form of drama declined. The Greek world revived the Athenian plays continually without augmenting their number with new masterpieces; if any were actually written, which seems doubtful, they have not survived. (We retain, indeed, only a fraction of the tragedies written by the three major poets of the fifth century B.C., Aeschylus, Sophocles, and Euripides.) The specific Athenian form of comedy that we call Aristophanic, after the name of its greatest practitioner, also failed to survive the disaster. It became known to later generations as the "Old Comedy," and the "New Comedy" that took shape in the fourth century lost the exuberance and variety of its predecessor, as well as the latter's forthright topicality.

The Greek theatre, as developed in the golden age of Athenian civilization was not, however, created in vain. Its tragedies remain landmarks in the history of civilization and art, and as such they continue to represent an achievement by which tragic art can be measured. They could not be imitated successfully in Rome, for they grew out of a specific cultural context and they carried with them the mark of their origin in their specific formalism. The theatre for which they were written amalgamated quasi-religious and ethical tradition; it combined the communion of a rite with the communion of the Athenian life of reason. The Greek tragedies are, then, special in quality. But in their assumptions of human dignity and conscience, in the high valuation they place upon the human spirit, and in their sublimity, they possess universality—a universality, indeed, equaled in twenty-four centuries of theatre only by the high tragedies of Shakespeare.

Fifth-century tragic art did not provide a pattern for vital theatre even during the classic revival of the Renaissance. Literary imitations in post-Renaissance Europe re-created Greek choral tragedy, the most notable of these in English being Milton's *Samson Agonistes* and Swinburne's *Atalanta in Calydon,* but few of the re-creations were ever produced, and most of them were not even intended for stage production. In the case of the great poem *Samson Agonistes,* this is highly regrettable, since Milton captured not only the letter but the spirit of Greek tragedy. In our time, T. S. Eliot succeeded to some degree in making choral theatre in *Murder in the Cathedral,* but only with the aid of a Shavian prose apology by Becket's murderers which was magnificent in itself but alien to classic tragedy. The one

theatrically viable close re-creation was Racine's *Athalia,* a product of the reconciliation of the Hebraic and neoclassic elements that warred against each other in the soul of a seventeenth-century French poet. This play could not, of course, usher in a resuscitation of Greek tragic form, for the theatrical conditions of Greek theatre were never to recur in the world. It was in the form of opera and in the manner of so-called Senecan tragedy 'that the influence of Greek choral tragedy was most widely sustained in later times.

Poets and musicians of the Florentine nobleman Giovanni Bardi's circle of humanists gave an important impetus to the creation of opera by proceeding on the assumption that all the dialogue of Greek plays had been declaimed. They aimed at a form of music drama, the first product of their ambition being Rinuccini and Peri's *Dafne,* in 1597. When the elements of music and spectacle outweighed that of drama, true opera was born and found its first genius in Monteverdi.

Senecan tragedy was the product of a devolution of Greek tragedy in Roman times. After early imitations, of which no example survives, tragedy evidently found no popular audience in the debased theatre of imperial Rome. It became a literary exercise, apparently not intended for stage production. Nero's tutor, the Stoic philosopher Seneca, however, left nine imitations of an extremely rhetorical and sanguinary character. Greek drama having been largely forgotten in the Middle Ages, Seneca's plays came to be regarded after the thirteenth century as the only examples of classical drama. Extremely influential during the Renaissance, they set the standard for the later drama, promoted the use of soliloquy as an expository or dramatic device, gave sanction to melodramatic violence on the stage, and inaugurated the vogue of the "revenge play" type of tragedy which culminated in *Hamlet.*

As for Greek comedy, it may be said that its Aristophanic phase lives on mainly as a reminder of the power of intellectual and poetical playfulness. Its bright memory can stimulate us to an appreciation of how free and vigorous, how released from the limitations of drawing-room laughter, how wide-reaching and far-reaching comedy can be. Its more or less restrained equivalents were few before the nineteenth century (John Gay's *The Beggar's Opera* comes most readily to mind); they were few in the nineteenth century, too (the Gilbert and Sullivan operettas are the only memorable equivalents); and they are somewhat more abundant in our century, with such musical-comedy and musical-revue examples qualifying for acknowledgment as *Threepenny Opera, Of Thee I Sing, Call Me Mister,* and *Finian's Rainbow.* Greek comedy in its fourth-century phase of domestic "comedy of manners," however, started a dramatic *genre* which, although represented by only three surviving fragments of plays by Menander (342–291 B.C.), achieved coninuity in second- and third-century-B.C. Rome and has dominated the Western theatre ever since the beginning of the sixteenth century.

Since the New Comedy satirized men individually rather than collectively, it was nonpolitical and could be produced in undemocratic as well as democratic society. It also required from writers less genius, or intellectual penetration and poetic power, than talent —that is, talent for imitation of reality and for play construction. Aristophanic comedy had been sprawling and extravagant, whereas the dramatic form that succeeded it was a more or less tightly knit play. But classic New Comedy, too, incorporated the humanistic interest in man's life—in his emotions, personal complications, adjustments to other persons, morals, and manners.

Fourth-century-B.C. Greece found many writers equal to the pleasurable task of producing this type of drama and one genius, Menander—if we may arrive at a judgment from three incomplete plays recovered in our own time, and if we may credit the opinion of the Graeco-Roman world. Among the Romans who followed in his wake, Plautus developed farce and farce comedy and Terence created high comedy. After the second century B.C., the theatre of imperialistic Rome became debased and playwriting deteriorated. But comedy of manners was resuscitated during the Renaissance by translations, adaptations, and imitations, as well as supplemented by romantic comedies, such as Shakespeare's.

A long life was reserved, moreover, for the character types of Roman drama—for its lovers and obdurate fathers, clever or rascally servants, fatuous elders, cowardly braggarts, and hangers-on or parasites. Together, they constituted a Human Comedy. Italian improvisatory theatre of the sixteenth and seventeenth centuries (commedia dell' arte) displayed their descendants—doddering Pantalones, pedantic Dottores, rascally Arlecchinos, and various contemporary types of fool—at the crossroads and in the market places of Western Europe. Ben Jonson and other Elizabethans used these stereotypes for theatre of "humours," or idiosyncrasies, as well as for social satire. Molière domesticated and individualized them in the seventeenth-century theatre, and his successors have been translating them into recognizable personalities of European and American society ever since. We see, then, that the art of comedy is essentially a creation of the Greek theatre. The one modern addition has been a distinctive comedy of ideas, of which Shaw was the master and partly the creator.

FORMALISM AND THEATRICALITY

All surviving Greek plays were written for the theatre of Dionysus in Athens, and they were revived over a period of several centuries throughout the Mediterranean world in theatres that had more or less the same physical structure and abided by more or less the same stylization. It may be helpful, therefore, to glance at the Athenian theatre. It is also useful to know what relationship existed between stage production and audience, for without such a relationship there is neither living drama nor vital theatre.

As tragedy developed in the theatre of Dionysus, it acquired a distinctive form that determined the choral nature of the stage production. The general pattern of a Greek tragedy consists of an introductory scene (prologos), an entrance lyric by the chorus (parodos), a dramatic scene (episode), and then a choral ode (stasimon). As a rule, a tragedy has five episodes, separated by choral odes. In the final scene, in which the action is concluded, a messenger may report the catastrophe or a god may be brought on the stage to resolve the complications and throw light on future events. Then, usually, the chorus delivers its parting lines (concluding the exodos) and leaves the orchestra. The dramatic scenes are written in six-foot iambic verse, known as iambic trimeter (because counted in double feet), corresponding roughly to English blank verse, though Greek verse is "quantitative"— that is, it is measured by the length of the syllables rather than by accented syllables, as in English poetry. Contrary to later assumptions, the dialogue was intended to be spoken, not sung, and had no musical accompaniment, although occasionally the playwrights employed the anapestic meter that was delivered as recitative, similar to that which we have in modern opera. The choral odes, written in a variety of elaborate meters, were, however, sung and danced to and had an instrumental accompaniment. The choral ode, or stasimon, was antiphonal—that is, it was made up of a "turn" and "counterturn," of a series of lines of varying length constituting a strophe followed by an antistrophe of exactly the same metrical form. No rhyme was employed. Later, in the plays of Euripides, a simple solo song might be substituted for the choral ode. Occasionally, the chorus engaged in a lyric interchange (kommos) with an actor.

Greek plays were produced at quasi-religious celebrations after the democratic "tyrant" Pisistratus in 534 B.C. transferred the old rustic Dionysian festival of the fruits of the earth to the city of Athens. In the "City Dionysia," held at the end of March, the people acquired a splendid folk festival at which they could cement their interests and display the glories of their state to the visiting businessmen who filled the city at this time. An older but secondary celebration, held at the end of January and known as the Lenaea, or festival of the wine press, also began to include play contests. Here, in the main, comedies were produced. Later, other festivals in the towns and villages of Attica, known as the Rural Dionysia, began to favor dramatic productions, the most impressive being held in the Athenian seaport of Piraeus. Frequently these festivals, the Greek equivalent of the "road," revived plays that had been produced at the City Dionysia but could not be repeated in Athens—until an edict legalized the revival of plays by Aeschylus after his death.

The City Dionysia, considered so sacred that at first admission was free and minor violations of the law during the performances were punished as sacrilege, began elaborately with a procession of the ancient image of Dionysus along the road toward the village of Eleutherae and then back to Athens by torchlight. The image was then placed in or near the dancing circle (*orchestra*) of the theatre with appropriate rites. After a second day of dithyrambic events, consisting of contests by ten dancing and singing choruses of men and boys, fifty in each chorus, a day was devoted to comedies, with five playwrights competing; then came three days of tragic performances. Six days were consumed by the great spring festival of March-April, until it was contracted to five days during the Peloponnesian War (431–404 B.C.), when the Athenian drama attained its zenith. At that time, during the last three days, there were actually five performances daily: three tragedies and a burlesque, or "satyr play," in the morning, and one or two comedies in the afternoon. Three playwrights competed for the prize in tragedy, each with three tragedies and a satyr play. The plays were more or less related in subject matter, although only Aeschylus appears to have written strictly connected trilogies or tetralogies.

Actors were highly trained in Athens and played both male and female roles. Theirs was a highly honorable profession, and even so distinguished a citizen, as well as author, as Sophocles played leading parts until his voice proved too weak for the vast open-air Athenian theatre. Preparations for the contest were made some time before the festival. The plays were carefully selected by the first play-reader of the theatre, an official (*archon*) who also served as a casting director, since he chose the leading player, or protagonist, for each competing playwright. Wealthy citizens were designated to bear the expense of a chorus of twelve to fifteen men for tragedy (at first the chorus for each tragedy consisted of fifty, later of twelve, and still later of fifteen, men) and twenty-four for comedy, this being one of several state duties assigned to them until their impoverishment during the Peloponnesian War compelled the state to assume this burden. Rehearsals were arranged, the performance being staged, as a rule, by the playwright himself, and the chorus being placed under a trainer (*didascolos*); properties were purchased; and a "pipe" player was selected. Then, a few days before the performance, the playwrights, actors, and choruses presented themselves in a place adjoining the theatre to give a *proagon*. Here, in lieu of billboards, advertisements, and printed programs, they announced the titles of the plays, the authors'

names, and similar details. Immediately before the contest, the order of the contestants was determined by lot, and at the close of the contest the victors, judged by a committee also selected by lot, were crowned with garlands of ivy.

What the audience saw at a performance can be only roughly described, since stage production is the most mortal part of the theatre. But no doubt the artists of the Greek theatre strove for theatrical effect as ardently as any Max Reinhardt. An Athenian audience of the late fifth century B.C. saw performances which were theatrically colorful, diversified, and impressive. There is no foundation for the myth of extreme austerity foisted upon the Athenian theatre some twenty centuries later.

The masks, so frequently employed in primitive ritual, were not only a hallowed convention scrupulously retained by the Greek theatre but a powerful means of attracting attention, creating excitement, and expressing essential drama. They also helped to project the voice of the performer. And since the number of speaking actors was limited (to three in tragedy), the same actor could play several parts by merely changing his mask and costume. All the actors wore elongated grotesque masks of linen, cork, and wood, which grew larger and more curious with time. Although fairly stereotyped, representing general attributes such as cruelty, craftiness, and suffering, these disguises possessed considerable variety. Special masks would be required by mythological characters such as the horned Io, the multiple-eyed Argus, and the snaky-haired Furies and allegorical figures such as Death, Force, and Frenzy. That even some realism was attempted is shown by the report that at the conclusion of Sophocles' *Oedipus the King* the mask of the hero depicted a bloodstained countenance with mutilated eyes.

The familiar boots (*cothurni*), with their thickened, painted soles, and the high headdress (*onkos*) above the mask made the actors appear taller than life. A six-foot actor might be raised to seven and a half feet or more, so that he was prone to tumble ignominiously if he took an incautious step. Mantles of saffron, purple, and gold, and extravagant costumes, particularly in comedy, lent color; and padded clothing balanced the height effected by the boots and headdress. Characters were differentiated by means of the mask, the thickness of the boots, the quality of the garments, and such details as the crowns worn by kings, the turbans of Orientals, and the crutches that assisted old men across the stage.

Since the tragedians were heavily encumbered, their movements were necessarily slow and their gestures broad. It is not surprising, therefore that violent physical action was generally avoided, deaths occurring off stage and being recounted by a character known as the Messenger. Nevertheless, it was unlikely that the playgoer was bored by such static devices, for there was always more than enough movement in the chorus, in the orgiastic satyr plays which came at the close of the morning's tragedies. and, after 431 B.C., in the comedies that followed in the afternoon.

Facial play was of course concealed by the mask, but this, too, was no great loss in so vast a theatre as the Athenian. Nuances of emotion were for the most part expressed verbally, although mimetic gestures and expressive masks were of help. Fortunately, the acoustics of a Greek theatre were excellent, and the voice of the actor could be projected to the utmost tiers with the aid of the openmouthed mask that served as a sounding board. Actors were, in fact, chosen for their voices. Good actors were so greatly in demand that they soon commanded enormous salaries, and in later times, when playwriting talent had become scarce, acting assumed greater importance than the drama itself, so that it became customary to have contests among actors as well as playwrights.

The stage effect was vastly enhanced by the presence of the chorus, which marched in with aplomb from the wings (*parodoi*), remained thereafter "on stage" throughout the performance, and conversed with the actors from time to time. Every new scene was ushered in and followed by a chorus, and any amount of time could be assumed to have elapsed during the singing of the choral ode, or *stasimon*. Like the actors, the chorus was variously costumed and wore masks appropriate to the age, sex, and character of the persons represented. Especially varied was the costuming of the chorus in comedy, and the design of the clothing might contain considerable exaggeration for purposes of humor.

The chorus sang or chanted odes with appropriate, highly stylized movements. A dignified dance form called *emmelia* (harmony) accompanied the more stately odes, and a lively dance was associated with odes of ecstatic emotion or gladness. Much of the dancing was decidedly mimetic. One favorite dancer employed by Aeschylus was said to be famous for his ability to describe dramatic events by means of gestures.

Even when the chorus remained passive, it did not stand frozen in a tableau, as has been supposed. It continued to follow the story with descriptive movements conveying emotions of anxiety, terror, pity, hope, and exaltation. And the chorus did not always sing; it sometimes used recitative and even conversational speech in addressing the actors. Moreover, it did not always sing or speak in unison. During the murder of the king in *Agamemnon,* for example, the old men debate helplessly what to do and each member of the chorus voices his opinion. The odes were rendered with great distinctness, each note corresponding to a syllable, and were accompanied by a wood-wind instrument resembling our clarinet. Later, solos were added for greater effect and performers displayed their virtuosity in performing them, much to the distress of Athenian

purists. The use of a chorus in Greek drama had the disadvantages of slowing up and interrupting the dramatic portions of the play. But it gave occasion for great lyric poetry; it unified the play by carrying retrospective information; it added a reflective element, providing an observer's perspective on the events; and often it even contributed to the action, as in the last part of *Agamemnon.* Above all, the choral group, along with mute supernumeraries, greatly enriched the spectacular qualities of the Greek stage as it performed in the dancing circle, or *orchestra,* located between the spectators' seats on the hillside and the permanent setting, or *skene.*

It is no secret that in the open-air theatre of the fifth century B.C., much had to be imagined or reconstructed by the audience from the suggestive background of sky and landscape and the architectural façade of the scene building, in front of which much of the action transpired on a low platform. Nevertheless, there was no dearth of detail in the productions and, in time, devices and mechanical contraptions promoted illusion. A platform known as the *eccyclema,* a form of wagon-stage, was thrust out through the doors of the scene building, displaying an interior scene which we would nowadays show through a scrim curtain. A cranelike machine transported a god from the sky to some part of the scene building or acting area. (Since he came by way of the machine, he was "the god from the machine," or, in Latin, *deus ex machina*—a term that came to be applied to his occasional function of abruptly resolving the plot.) Sometimes, too, the gods were exhibited in heaven on a special platform (*theologeion*), and there could be such spectacular effects on the roof of the scene building as Medea's departure for Athens, after she has slain her children, in a chariot drawn by winged dragons. The stage setting was by no means as inadequate as might be imagined, for it could represent anything from the countryside to a building, such as a temple or palace, or a series of structures, since the stage building had wings (*paraskenia*) to the right and the left. Occasionally the background was suggestively changed within a single play with the aid of revolving painted prisms (*periakti*) set flush with the scene building on either side of the stage.

Audiences rose at dawn, ate heartily, and took provisions with them to the theatre. Sometimes the actors were pelted with an avalanche of fruit, and there is a case on record of one poor actor's being nearly stoned to death. What other annoyances plagued the anxious playwright and his players may be easily imagined. Some seventeen or eighteen thousand people packed into an auditorium from dawn to dusk cannot be expected to behave like soldiers at inspection.

As always, a spectacular production might camouflage the intrinsic merit of the dramatic composition, and a mediocre playwright who had a generous patron for his chorus would stand a better chance of winning the prize. *Oedipus the King,* long considered the greatest tragedy of antiquity, apparently lost first prize because its backer (*choregus*) was niggardly. The "angel" who has been the butt of so many jests of the theatre is a more venerable institution than many of us think.

Certainly neither the judges, who were not specialists, like our drama critics, nor the audiences interested themselves in the academic considerations of the unities of time, place, and action, which exercised critics during and after the Renaissance. When Aristotle declared in his *Poetics* that "tragedy endeavors, so far as possible, to confine itself to a single revolution of the sun or but slightly exceed the limit," he was merely making an observation, and a fairly elastic one, instead of laying down a law. There were practical reasons for this time limitation, since Greek tragedies were only as long as our long one-acters. That the Athenian playwrights should try to confine themselves to a single situation or to a series of events taking place in a short time was entirely natural. Nevertheless, they followed no hard and fast rules. As noted before, any amount of time could pass during the singing of a choral ode; Aeschylus, for example, violated the "unity of time" in his *Eumenides,* the sequel to *Agamemnon,* without the slightest scruple.

If the playwrights preferred a single locale, or "unity of place," it was because the physical conditions of their stage favored one-set plays. But here again they were not saddled with an inviolable law, as two-set plays such as the *Eumenides* and Sophocles' *Ajax* prove. Unity of action they may have observed, as so many writers have done, as a principle of good taste and order, although here, too, there were violations. (Aeschylus' *The Seven Against Thebes* is a case in point.) If the Greek playwrights did not clutter up their tragedies with "comic relief" or with extraneous clowning, one reason was probably the convention which enabled every tragedian to wind up his series of tragedies with a riotous and bawdy afterpiece, the so-called satyr play.

It is well to remember that a folk rite is not notable for restraint when it mobilizes the energies of a people. We should not be deceived, then, by the formal characteristics of Greek drama any more than by the retention of ritualistic elements in the Greek theatre. If the tragedies were subject to conventional or traditional restraints, and if they were permeated by the solemnities of a rite and by the sense of commonly held values that a rite implies, they involved all the resources of theatre action, recitation and song, dance, and spectacle. The tragedies were, besides, only one of the forms of drama presented at the theatre of Dionysus. The *élan vital,* or life force, was too strong among the Greeks for them to separate tears from laughter and mind from body. The satyr play afforded a release from tensions distinctly different from that provided by the purification, or catharsis, inherent in tragedy.

Comedy, moreover, had equal status with tragedy at the festival, and the comic theatre enjoyed unbounded freedom in fifth-century-B.C. Athens. For a long time it had been customary to celebrate Dionysus, who was the god of generation as well as of wine and vegetation, by means of masquerades and processions. Here, in these so-called "comuses," from which the word "comedy" is derived, was the sexual rite in full panoply, with the actors (at first unspecialized citizens) disguised as birds, cocks, horses, and dolphins, carrying aloft a huge phallus on a pole and singing and dancing suggestively. Social satire was added when a crude form of farce or mime was brought from Sicily and amalgamated with the native "comus," which had meanwhile pressed members of the audience into its service and transformed them into a comic chorus. Perhaps harking back to the primitive imitations of the struggle between the good season and the bad, as well as responding to the rapid development of tragedy, the chorus became divided into two bodies which expressed their rivalry by means of antiphonal song.

The comic processions, now on their way toward full-grown drama, soon came to be held in an *orchestra,* and were finally brought to Athens, where they were officially recognized in 486 B.C. They became afternoon performances at the City Dionysia, and comprised the most prominent feature of the related festival of Lenaea, where five comic poets competed for the prize. Sacred, not despite their connection with sexuality but because of it, the plays were supervised at the Lenaea by the same *archon basileus,* or king archon, who supervised the sacrosanct Eleusinian mysteries.

The art which reached its zenith in Aristophanes holds in solution most of the elements which we associate with comedy of any type. From the literal aspect of sexual ritual, Athenian comedy derived its comparative realism; and from early satire, its concern with the commonplace and the stupid. Hence its antiheroic attitude, which made Aristotle declare, "Comedy tends to represent the agents as worse than the men of present day." From the element of release present in sexual magic arose the addiction to unbridled fantasy and exaggerations of reality. Comedy has retained these features to various degrees throughout its venerable, if irreverent, course.

The specific pattern of the Old Comedy, however, has no modern parallels. The play opened with an expository scene in which a character conceived an odd plan, such as staging a sex strike or going down to Hades to bring back a dead poet because all the living ones are mediocre. Then the chorus, fantastically garbed in costumes frequently suggestive of

·vasps, frogs, clouds, and birds, and sometimes divided into two rival factions, made its entrance with a song (the *parados*). Once on the stage, the twenty-four members of the comic chorus remained there throughout the action, participating in it variously and enjoying many liberties. A high point was the contest, or *agon,* in which two characters representing opposite views or interests contended until one of them downed his rival—generally with a torrent of Rabelaisian argument and vituperation. Then, while the actors withdrew from the stage, the chorus faced the audience and, advancing toward it in military fashion, delivered itself of a long and highly charged harangue. This speech, known as the *parabasis,* voiced the playwright's views, sometimes even chaffed prominent personages in the audience, and called a spade a steam shovel. At the conclusion of the harangue, which could never have been permitted in an undemocratic community, the actors reappeared in a series of short scenes and the play was brought to a conclusion with a representation of the consequences entailed by the *agon.* Complexity might be added by means of two *parabases,* as in Aristophanes' *The Clouds* and *The Knights,* and variations in the general structure could be introduced by a freer treatment of the plot or by omitting the *parabasis* altogether, as in Aristophanes' last plays, *The Ecclesiazusae* and *Plutus.*

It was a gorgeous spectacle that the Athenians enjoyed as they watched the grotesquely dressed chorus and the extravagantly masked actors, sometimes made up to resemble some civic luminary, exposed as a fraud and nincompoop. Fantasy, whimsy, and undisguised buffoonery characterized the story that unfolded itself. Badinage, ribaldry, and scolding such as would put any fishwife to rout spiced the dialogue and the songs. And so the rites of spring and of man ended during each day of the Dionysian festival after 431 B.C. in a complete discharge of human energy and a rousing affirmation of the total man.

THE LATER CLASSIC THEATRE

Theatre spread throughout the Mediterranean world of the Greeks, who settled parts of Asia Minor, northeastern Africa, Sicily, and southern Italy. By the last third of the fifth century the physical theatre was fully established as an arrangement of rows of seats on the hillside, a dancing circle (*orchestra*) in front of this auditorium (in the middle of the *orchestra* stood the *thymele,* or altar of the theatre's patron god, Dionysus, and beside it were the musicians), side entrances (*parodoi*), a low platform or acting stage, and a rectangular scene building (*skene*), with side wings (*paraskenia*). The scene building, originally a wooden

hut for changing masks and costumes, became, after the fifth century, an imposing stage setting, with doorways pierced into the front wall and a colonnade of pillars or columns (a *proscenium*) between which painted panels (*pinakes*) were inserted. The scene building became more elaborate and the stage machinery more ingenious. When the new fourth-century style of comedy of manners came into vogue, requiring less grandeur and more realism, the height of the scene building was reduced and the façade became more detailed. Otherwise, the theatre remained unchanged.

When Rome finally began to erect permanent stone theatres after the second century B.C., however, some distinct departures were made from the Athenian and Hellenistic pattern. The Roman theatres were set on level ground rather than on hillsides; the dancing circle became a semicircle bounded by the stage; the side entrances to the stage became covered passages, called *vomitaria;* the stage area became deeper and more ornamental, and it was covered with a roof. And all the parts of the stage and auditorium constituted one structure, as in our theatres. (The Greek theatre had consisted of separate units—an architecturally distinct auditorium, a dancing circle separated from it, and a scene building separated from the dancing circle.) In the Roman theatre for which Plautus and Terence wrote, the stage was a long, narrow area representing, as a rule, a street, the background consisting of two or three city houses with doors opening on the street. By convention, the exit to the right led to the center of town or to the country and the exit to the left led to the harbor and foreign parts. A lane between two houses set at right angles to the street could provide an additional means of entering or leaving the scene of the action.

In the second century B.C., the Roman theatre still had some of the features of a communion, plays being presented on numerous more or less sacred civic occasions. But subsequently the connection with ritual was broken, and when this happened the actor lost caste; he was a mere entertainer, and the drama lost its vital connection with society. Gradually depleted of significance and vulgarized, dramatic art was in time overshadowed by gladiatorial shows, circuses, and nautical spectacles. The classic drama was dead long before Christianity abolished the classic theatre as a snare and a delusion and an abomination in the sight of the Lord. After the fall of the Roman Empire in the fifth century A.D., another six centuries were to elapse before a new drama could slowly take shape in medieval Europe. In the thirteenth century, a new theatrical art came out of the Christian communion. By then, however, Sophocles and Euripides had been dead for sixteen hundred years.

Aeschylus

(525–456 B.C.)

Tragedy, as those who respond to it know, is a majestic art. It is never more majestic than when its first high-souled poet, Aeschylus, shapes it monolithically out of passion-driven men and women. Whether he shows them in action or reflects upon them as a morally involved observer, he does so with a dignity rarely equaled by his successors, the rest of the noble brood of tragedians. For him the drama was a spiritual rite and not a momentary entertainment.

"Beneath this stone lies Aeschylus, son of Euphorion, the Athenian, who perished in the wheat-bearing land of Gela [Sicily]; of his prowess the groves of Marathon can speak, and the long-haired Persian who knew it well." Aeschylus' epitaph, which he may have composed himself, is a fitting summary of his Homeric character. Austere in temper and proud of his participation in the great battle in which Athenians repelled the Persian invasion (he probably participated also in the great naval battle of Salamis), the oldest of the Greek master drama-tists was closest in spirit to the heroic age which they all commemorated. He is said to have modestly claimed that his plays were only "crumbs gathered from Homer's banquet." As Athens, becoming a thriving emporium, relaxed its manners and reduced the power of the old martial families, Aeschylus, indeed, felt ill at ease in the city and removed himself to Sicily, where he died. The Athenians, in turn, venerated this conservative democrat and Marathon warrior, but tended to consider him a trifle archaic.

Aeschylus' mind was ever possessed with ethical problems, with questions of guilt, hereditary evil, and divine justice. Single plays were, indeed, too slight to contain his probings, and he expressed himself most effectively in trilogies. His trilogy on the fire-bringing Prometheus, of which only the first part, *Prometheus Bound,* has survived, dealt with nothing less than the question of universal moral order and the evolution of Zeus from an enemy to a merciful All-father of men. And the language of Aeschylus is altogether that of a rhapso-dist and a visionary poet. As one scholar has noted, "Aeschylus lives in a world of metaphor, and his metaphors are drawn from a wide range of sources in human life and the natural world." He strung together a variety of images and epithets, and com-pounded words lavishly in order to convey his far-reaching thought and rapt intuitions. No one but Aeschylus could have written the lines that convey the eerie, hypnotic visions of Cassandra in the *Agamemnon.* No other dramatist could have put together a series of geographical names and with them created the magic of distance and the excite-ment of drama, as he did in the opening of this tragedy. Aeschylus was a word-intoxicated, as well as a god-intoxicated, man.

Although he was the poet laureate of the Mara-thon generation and celebrated its victories in his early play *The Persians,* Aeschylus was not actually a martial poet but a mystic and a moralist, whose accents often recall the Old Testament prophets. Born in the sacred city of Eleusis and a member of one of the old aristocratic families, he was initiated into the famous Eleusinian mysteries. The temper of his mind was formed by these religious exercises. He is said to have claimed a visitation from the patron deity of both the theatre and the Eleusinian cult, Dionysus, who ordered him to write tragedies. As Aeschylus matured, he must have gravitated instinctively to the most religious literary activity of his time—the drama, which had by now risen from its obscure ritualistic beginnings to a position of great importance.

No one contributed more to the development of Greek tragedy than Aeschylus. In his youth the drama was primarily a choral affair, supplemented by some rudimentary action between the leader of the chorus and a single masked actor; such undoubt-edly were the lost plays of Thespis, who won the first dramatic contest. By adding a second actor, who could impersonate several characters, by ex-tending the action of the play, deepening character-ization, and intensifying the dramatic function of the chorus, Aeschylus became the world's first great dramatist, as he was also its first important show-man. (He is believed to have introduced the tradi-tional rich costumes and high boots of the Greek tragic theatre, and he is known to have employed spectacular effects, such as the gruesome masks of the Furies, which were said to have produced mis-carriages in the theatre of Dionysus. He also made a specialty of training choruses.) Before his death, Aeschylus enjoyed the satisfaction of seeing a theatre replete with action, movement, and color and knowing that it was largely his own creation.

Aeschylus' extant plays, seven in number out of a total of seventy-two or eighty-two, represent a steady progress toward dramatic complexity. The earliest of them, *The Suppliants* (c. 490 B.C.) and *The Persians,* were preponderantly choral, *The Per-sians* being little more than a paean of victory for the Greeks and a lament for the Persian dead. But *The*

Seven Against Thebes (467 B.C.) has a substantial plot based on the fatal struggle of the sons of Oedipus for the throne of Thebes; and Aeschylus' last plays, those of the Oresteian trilogy, reach dramatic heights almost unknown in the history of the theatre.

The *Oresteia,* written two years before Aeschylus' death, is the only complete trilogy that has survived. Its great first play, *Agamemnon,* retells the murder of the Homeric king by his wife, Clytemnestra. In the next play, *Choephoroe,* or *The Libation Pourers,* vengeance is wreaked on the murderess and her paramour by her children. The concluding drama, *Eumenides,* or *The Furies,* follows the destinies of Clytemnestra's son, Orestes, now a half-mad fugitive stained with his mother's blood. Like the prophets of old, Aeschylus believed that guilt perpetuates itself in succeeding generations. But in this trilogy he acknowledges the role of personal responsibility in human fate. Man's will collaborates in the shaping of his destiny, mysterious and weird though it be under the stars. From suffering, moreover, may come a healing wisdom, and justice must be tempered with mercy if life on earth is to be something other than a nightmare. Aeschylus' Greek reason, which has viewed the evil in his *Agamemnon* with dismay, prevails in the conclusion of his *Eumenides.* The sin of matricide and the law of retribution are voided; the avenging furies of conscience are placated and the primitive law of the blood feud is finally laid to rest. Life, which the poet has regarded with a shudder, attains at last the grace of God and humanity.

The *Agamemnon* represents Aeschylus at the peak of his dramatic and lyric power. Its protagonists are Homeric figures caught in a whirlpool of passion that is not of a day but of protracted ages of hereditary evil; Clytemnestra's murder of her husband and infidelity with Aegisthus, Agamemnon's cousin, stem from the past history of the crime-spattered family of Atreus. The play is violent, and it may well be presented as a telling refutation of the theory of classic restraint. But the moralist is close at hand to reflect on the events, and the great choruses transmute the sordid details of murder into absolute beauty. By virtue of the form, too—Greek choral drama was still austerely formal (773 lines out of a total of 1,673 belong to the chorus)—the domestic tragedy of a wife's slaying her husband fixes the mind on man's relation to moral order. Meaning is wrung from a spectacle, until a crime of passion becomes universal drama. Both as drama and poetry the *Agamemnon* possesses true sublimity. Here, and in the less satisfactory sequels which together with the *Agamemnon* constitute the Oresteian trilogy, Aeschylus sounded one of the great themes of tragedy. Both Sophocles and Euripides composed variations on it in their respective *Electra*'s. In twentieth-century America, in a world that Aeschylus could not have imagined even with his visionary power, the theme received three more or less notable treatments within less than two decades: Eugene O'Neill's psychoanalytical trilogy *Mourning Becomes Electra,* Robert Turney's *Daughters of Atreus,* and Robinson Jeffers' dramatic poem *The Tower Beyond Tragedy.*

AGAMEMNON

By Aeschylus

TRANSLATED FROM THE GREEK BY EDITH HAMILTON

CHARACTERS

AGAMEMNON	AEGISTHUS	SOLDIERS
CLYTEMNESTRA	CHORUS OF OLD MEN	TOWNSMEN
CASSANDRA	HERALD	SPEARSMEN
	ATTENDANTS	

The scene is laid in Argos before the palace of Agamemnon. An altar is in the center of the foreground. On the roof stands a Watchman. It is night.

WATCHMAN: Oh God, for an end to this weary work.
A year long I have watched here, head on arm,
crouched like a dog on Agamemnon's roof.
The stars of night have kept me company.
I know them all, and when they rise and set.
Those that bring winter's cold and summer's heat—
for they have power, those bright things in the sky.
And what I watch for is a beacon fire,[1]
a flash of flame to bring the word from Troy,
word that the town has fallen.
It's a woman's hope, for a woman is master here,
but her heart is as stout as ever was a man's.
No rest for me by night. I wander up and down.
My bed is wet with dew. Dreams keep away.
Fear is up here, not sleep. I never close my eyes.
Singing or whistling helps a sleepy man,
but if I try to make a sound I groan
for all the evil happenings down there.
Things once were right in this house, but no more.
Oh, for a bit of luck to free me now,
that fire to bring good news out of the night.
    [*A pause. He stands silent, watching. In the dark a spark of light is seen. It grows brighter, spreading into a blaze*]
A flame! Oh, see! It turns the dark to day.
There'll be dancing now and singing in the town.
Ho there! Ho there! O Agamemnon's Queen,
wake—wake.
Up from your bed— Quick, quick—and shout for joy.
Shout for the beacon light. Troy—Troy is taken.
The messenger has come, the fire signal.
    [*Lights and movement are seen within the palace*]
I'll start the dancing up here by myself.

[1] In the old stories the Greeks at Troy had arranged to have a long line of watchmen and fires ready to be lit which would carry the news from point to point, on to Greece, whenever Troy fell.

The dice have fallen well. I'll mark the score.
This beacon fire has thrown us three times six.
Oh, let me see my master home again,
and hold once more his dear hand in my own.
Those other things—no more of them. I put
a weight big as an ox upon my tongue.
And yet the very house, if it had voice,
would speak out clear—just as I too speak out
to those who know. To those who do not—why,
I lose my memory.
    [*Exit*]
    [Attendants *enter from the palace with torches, and kindle fire on the altar and sprinkle incense. Clytemnestra with Women in attendance enters and kneels before the altar. From the side a band of Old Men march in. They chant the chorus as they slowly march around the altar. During the song the day begins to dawn*]
CHORUS: The tenth year is this from the time Priam's foe,
the great adversary,
Agamemnon and Prince Menelaus,
with honor of scepter and honor of throne,
strong men, yoked together and brothers,
launched a thousand ships from this Argive land,[2]
a warrior band to carry help,
and they shouted a great shout, War!
So eagles scream as they circle aloft
or their feathered oars,
high over their nest on a lonely crag,
when the eaglets are stolen away.
And they grieve for their young
and the nest never more to be tended.
But in heaven above there is one who hears,
or Pan or Zeus or Apollo,
hears the shrill, screaming cry of the dwellers in air,
and slow-footed vengeance
he sends to those that transgress.
Even thus the Almighty who guards guest and host,
sent the children of Atreus[3] to Paris,
for a woman wooed of many men.
And many a struggle that weighs down the limbs,

[2] Greece.

[3] Atreus was the father of Agamemnon and Menelaus.

11

when the knee is bowed in the dust,
when the spear-shaft is shivered in the prelude of
    the fight,
he has sent to the Greek and the Trojan.
It is as it is. It shall end as it must.
Not by secret grief, not by secret gifts,
not by tears, can one make atonement
for altars without fire and the stubborn wrath of
    God.
But we, all unhonored for that we are old,
left behind when the host sailed to help,
weak as a child, we lean on our staves.
We are waiting.
When the marrow in the bones is young,
when a child's heart is lord within the breast,
war is far away—the aged are like children.
He that is exceeding old, when the leaf is withered,
walks the roads on three feet with his staff.
No better than a child,
he wanders, a dream—at noonday.

[As the Old Men *take their positions around the
altar, they approach nearer to* Clytemnestra. *She
does not appear to notice them*]

But you, Tyndarus' daughter,
Queen Clytemnestra, what thing is this?
What tidings, what news, has aroused you?
You have sent to the shrines. They have kindled the
    fires,
and the gods that guard the city,
gods of heaven and gods of hell,
gods of the market and gods of the field,
the sacrifice flames on their altars.
From one and another heaven-high
the fire is leaping
They have brought from the king's treasure holy oil,
thick unguents of myrrh and honey,
to coax the flame with a magic spell,
a pure and guileless persuasion.
Tell us of these things what is known
and what may be spoken.
Heal us now of our fear
that works in us thoughts of evil.
The light from your altars shows us hope,
hope that defends from consuming care,
from grief that eats away life.

[Clytemnestra *still takes no notice of them but
goes silently into the palace. The marching song,
in Greek tragedy sung as the chorus entered and
took their positions, comes here to an end, and
the chorus proper begins. They sing of the omen
shown to the two leaders of the army,* Agamemnon *and* Menelaus, *as they were starting for
Troy—two eagles that tore a hare to pieces*]

CHORUS: Power is mine to sing of a journey of
    heroes fate-driven.
Old though we are the spirit of God breathes in us
music's mighty persuasion.
How then the two,
the twin-throned strength of the young men of Hellas,
two with one purpose,

were sent with spear and with hand to seek vengeance
by a rushing bird to the land of Teucer.[4]
To the kings of ships came the kings of birds, one
    black and the other with tail white-feathered.
By the house of the king,
high toward the spear-hand where all could behold
    them,
two birds swooping together
tore at a pregnant hare and the brood of her young
    big within her.
Forever ended her swift coursing.
Sorrow, sing sorrow, but good shall prevail with
    power.

Calchas the wise, the host's seer, beholding two with
    one spirit,
Atreus' warrior sons, knew them for the eagles,
leaders and captains,
and thus he foretold the omen:
A time shall be
when these shall capture the city of Priam.
Before the towers,
sheep and oxen, the wealth of the people,
the fortune of war will ravage and slaughter.
Only may never our army, the great curb of Troy,
    be foredoomed by the anger of heaven.
For pity and wrath
move in the heart of Artemis[5] holy.
Winged hounds, eagles of Zeus,
slew a poor cowering creature, her unborn young
    slaughtered with her.
She loathes the feast the eagles made.
Sorrow, sing sorrow, but good shall prevail with
    power.

So gentle is she, loveliest,
to dewy youth,
fierce lions' tender sucklings,
the young of the beasts that roam the meadow,
nurslings of all wild forest creatures,
yet does she ask for the omen's fulfillment,
the signs from heaven, the good and the evil.
But I call upon God the healer,
Let her not send to the Greeks ill winds that will
    hold fast the ships from the sailing,
seeking to lay on her altar a victim abhorrent to
    offer,
worker of strife among kinsmen that spares not and
    fears not to murder.
For terrible, ever up-springing,

4 Troy. Teucer was the legendary first king of Troy.
5 The huntress and yet the protector too of wild animals. It was to her that Agamemnon sacrificed his
daughter, Iphigenia, to get favorable winds for the fleet
on its way to Troy, when they had long been weather-
bound. Symbolic utterances are, of course, not marked
by clarity. Here the eagles are the two Greek leaders and
the hare is Iphigenia. Then suddenly the symbol shifts
and Artemis is demanding the sacrifice of Iphigenia—
to expiate the death of the hare.

treachery waits in the house to avenge the old murder of children.[6]
These were the words of Calchas. With mightiest
blessings he spoke them,
omens of fate from the birds on the road to the house
of the chieftain.
So in accordance,
sorrow, sing sorrow, but good shall prevail with
power.

God—who is he? If that name he choose,
by it I will cry to him.
Nothing can I reach in thought,
all things searching to the depths,
nothing save God, if the load of vain care from my
spirit
I must cast and find the truth.

One first—who was great to them of old,
full of swollen blustering wrath,
now is as a tale that's told.
He who next came, went his way[7]
like a wrestler overthrown.
God—he who hails him in triumph as victor forever,
shall be led to understand.

Guide of mortal man to wisdom,
he who has ordained the law,
knowledge won through suffering.
Drop, drop—in our sleep, upon the heart
sorrow falls, memory's pain,
and to us, though against our very will,
even in our own despite,
comes wisdom
by the awful grace of God.

Then the leader of the ships,
prince of all the Grecian host,
spoke no word to blame the seer,
bent beneath
fortune's sudden stroke of doom.
When the ships could not sail, and the food
failed through all the Grecian camp
spread along the Thracian coast,
in Aulis where
waves roar with the ebb and flow.

And from the north
ever blew the storm wind.
It broke men's hearts.
Famine-struck they wandered
away to death.
It wasted ships,
spared not sheet nor cable.

[6] Atreus killed the children of Thyestes, his brother,
and served them to him at a banquet in revenge for
Thyestes' having seduced his wife.
[7] Two rulers of the gods preceded Zeus—whom
Aeschylus now calls Zeus and now God and who is to
him the supreme power behind all things, as unlike the
Zeus of the myths as possible.

The time dragged,
doubling itself in passing.
The slow delay
withered the flower of Grecian youth
But when to soothe the storm
a way of bitter evil,
weighting with sorrow the chieftains,
the prophet shrieked forth, calling upon
Artemis, queen,
so that the kings,
striking the ground,
scepter in hand,
could not hold a tear back—

The elder prince
lifted his voice in sorrow:
Heavy my load
if I refuse and obey not.
But heavy too
if I must slay
the joy of my house, my daughter.
A father's hands
stained in dark streams flowing with blood of a girl
slaughtered before the altar.
For me on every side is woe.
How desert my ship-mates?
Traitor to those who are with me?
Justice is with them when they seek
eagerly eager
wild winds to calm
even with blood,
blood of a girl.
And now may good befall us.

But when he bowed beneath the yoke of fortune,
shifting his sails to meet a wind of evil,
unholy, impious, bringing him to dare to think
what should not be thought of—
For men grow bold
when delusion leads them.
A frenzied counselor, that,
source of all sin.
The end—maddened he dared the deed,
slaying his child to help a war
waged for the sake of a woman,
ships to speed in their sailing.

And all her prayers—cries of Father, Father,
her maiden life,
these they held as nothing,
the warrior-judges, battle-mad.
Her father bade
with a prayer to lift her,
like a lamb, high above the altar.
Her garments wrapping her round,
falling forward,
her soul failed. Aloft they raised her,
binding her sweet lips with a curb,
stifling her cry of ill omen,
fraught with a curse to the king's house,
with force of bonds,

silent guards,
muffled might.

Upon the ground
fell her robe of saffron,
and from her eyes
sped an arrow
that pierced with pity those that slew her.
I see her there,
a picture clear before my eyes.
She strives to speak, as oftentimes,
her father near, at the banquet table,
she used to sing, the little maid,
pure voice raised,
honoring her father loved,
while in love
joining her, he poured the wine for blessing.

What then befell I did not see, I do not say.
The prophet's wiles failed not of fulfillment.
The scales of God
weigh to all
justice: those that suffer learn.
What shall be
slow time will show.
Never seek to know before.
Such seeking brings
grief too soon. For shining clear
will it dawn at sunrise.
        [Clytemnestra, *attended by her* Women, *enters*]
But now may good
come at last
after ill.
So she prays
who guards alone
this our land, a sure defense to her lord returning.
    LEADER OF THE CHORUS: I come to do you rever-
        ence, Clytemnestra.
For it is right to give the king's wife honor,
a woman on a throne a man left empty.
But if you know of good or only hope
to hear of good and so do sacrifice,
I pray you speak. Yet if you will, keep silence.
    CLYTEMNESTRA: With glad good tidings, so the
        proverb runs,
may dawn arise from the kind mother night.
For you shall learn a joy beyond all hope:
the Trojan town has fallen to the Greeks.
    LEADER: You say? I cannot hear—I cannot trust—
    CLYTEMNESTRA: I say the Greeks hold Troy. Do
        I speak clear?
    LEADER: Joy that is close to tears steals over me.
    CLYTEMNESTRA: Quite right. Such tears give proof
        of loyalty.
    LEADER: What warrant for these words? Some
        surety have you?
    CLYTEMNESTRA: I have. How not—unless the
        gods play tricks.
    LEADER: A fair persuasive dream has won your
        credence?

    CLYTEMNESTRA: I am not one to trust a mind
        asleep.
    LEADER: A wingless rumor then has fed your
        fancy?
    CLYTEMNESTRA: Am I some little child that you
        would mock at?
    LEADER: But when, *when,* tell us, was the city
        sacked?
    CLYTEMNESTRA: This night, I say, that now gives
        birth to dawn.
    LEADER: And what the messenger that came so
        swift?
    CLYTEMNESTRA: A god! The fire-god flashing
        from Mount Ida.
Beacon sped beacon on, couriers of flame.
First, Ida signaled to the island peak
of Lemnos, Hermes' rock, and swift from there
Athos, God's mountain, fired the great torch.
It leaped, it skimmed the sea, a might of moving light,
joy-bringing, golden shining, like a sun,
and sent the fiery message to Macistus.
Whose towers, then, in haste, not heedlessly
or like some drowsy watchman caught by sleep,
sped on the herald's task and flashed the beacon
afar, beyond the waters of Euripus,
to sentinels high on Messapius' hillside,
who fired in turn and sent the tidings onward,
touching with flame a heap of withered heather.
So, never dimmed but gathering strength, the splendor
over the levels of Asopus sprang,
lighting Cithaeron like the shining moon,
rousing a relay there of traveling flame.
Brighter beyond their orders given, the guards
kindled a blaze and flung afar the light.
It shot across the mere of Gorgopis.
It shone on Aegiplanctus' mountain height,
swift speeding on the ordinance of fire,
where watchers, heaping high the tinder wood,
sent darting onward a great beard of flame
that passed the steeps of the Saronic Gulf
and blazing leaped aloft to Arachnaeus,
the point of lookout neighbor to our town.
Whence it was flashed here to the palace roof,
A fire fathered by the flame on Ida.
Thus did they hand the torch on, one to other,
in swift succession finishing the course.
And he who ran both first and last is victor.
Such is my warrant and my proof to you:
my lord himself has sent me word from Troy.
    LEADER: The gods—oh, I will thank them soon in
        prayer.
But tell me clearly now once more your tale,
that I may know and wonder—
    CLYTEMNESTRA: Troy lies this day in the Achaeans'
        hands.[8]
I think within the town a great cry rises
that will not blend, as when into a cruse
one pours together oil and vinegar.

_____

[8] That is, the Greeks' hands.

Even so the cries of victor and of vanquished,
that differ as their lot is different.
For these have flung themselves on lifeless bodies
of husbands, brothers—little children cling
to the old dead who gave them life and sob
from throats no longer free, above their dearest.
While those—a night of roaming after battle
has set them hungry down to break their fast
on what the town affords, not in due order,
but as each man has drawn his lot by chance.
They are quartered in the captured homes of Troy,
no more beneath the open sky, delivered
from frost and dew, and there like happy men
all night they sleep without a sentinel.
Now, if they keep them clear of guilt to gods,
to shrines within the town and conquered land,
the captors shall not in their turn be captured—
if mad desire fall not on the army,
in greed for gain, to violate the holy.
For still before them lies the second lap
of their long course ere they can win safe home.
And though they wend their way unerringly,
what those dead suffered may yet work them ill,
—that pain[9] which never sleeps—and fresh woe
    come.
Such words you hear from me that am a woman.
But may good conquer, shining clear to all.
Of many blessings this joy I would choose.
        LEADER: Mistress, like some wise man you speak
            with wisdom,
and I who hear you judge your warrant good.
So that I turn to God to offer thanks
for deeds done that are price for all the toil.
        [Clytemnestra *enters the palace—the* Chorus *take
            their positions for the second choral song*]
        CHORUS: O all-ruling God and bounteous night,
great gifts of glory you bring us.
Who cast over Troy and her towered walls
a close-meshed net none could win way through,
none could leap beyond, never man, never child,
a snare that enslaved,
a doom that caught all in its clutches.
Heaven's Lord, who guards both guest and host,
I worship. These deeds were wrought by him.
Of old against Paris he bent his bow,
and the bolt fell neither short of the mark,
nor passed it, flying star-ward.

The blow God strikes, so say men ever.
They search out him and searching find him.
He wills and it is done. There spoke one saying:
God cares not when
men tread down
holy things inviolate
underfoot.
But who spoke thus
knew not God.
Our eyes have seen the price

the proud must pay in full
for daring deeds beyond man's daring.
When dwellings overflow with riches,
the greatest good
is not there:
wealth enough to keep away
misery,
and hearts that are wise to use it.
Gold is never a bulwark,
no defense to the haughty,
arrogance spurning out of sight
God's great altar of justice.

Temptation,
wickedly persuading,
destruction,
child of scheming mischief,
when they constrain what power can deliver?
No hiding place
covers sin.
It blazes forth
a light of death.
Metal base
when tested shows
black of grain.
A touchstone too is there
that tests men's lives and shows—
a child running after a bird on the wing,
to town and kin
a fool, a shame past bearing.
And if he prays,
no one hears,
not a god.
So too Paris once coming,
entered a friend's kind dwelling,
shamed the hand there that gave him food,
stealing away a woman.

And she—she left
clash of spears,
clang of shields,
to kith and kin,
gifts from her,
armored ships and sailors.
To Troy she brought in place of dower doom and
        death.
So swiftly through the gates did she go
to dare what none must dare. And deep they groaned,
the seers within
that house[10] abandoned, crying:
Alas—alas— A home, a home, the lord thereof.
Alas, a bed
pressed in love by one beloved.
In the house
one may see
silence, all alone,
dishonor borne without rebuke.
He longs for her

---

[9] Her own pain, which never permits her to forget her
daughter, sacrificed ten years ago.

[10] The house of Menelaus, after Helen—his wife—
had gone to Troy with Paris.

beyond the sea.
A ghost holds sway
where she once was mistress.
Beauty grown to him hateful,
grace of fair-fashioned statues.
Empty his eyes for want of her.
Lost all things that are lovely.

In dreams there come,
haunting him,
sweet fancies fond,
vain delight
bringing with them ever.
For vainly when the dreamer thinks to clasp his joy,
the vision slips through his hands and is lost.
It goes, a phantom swift, it vanishes
on wings that move
down the ways of slumber.
Within the house
these sorrows sit upon the hearth.
Nor they alone,
but woes surpassing even these.
For all who sped
forth to Troy,
joining company,
such grief as passes power to bear
in each man's home,
plain to see.
Many things
there to pierce a heart through.
Women know whom they sent forth,
but instead of the living,
back there comes to the house of each
armor, dust from the burning.

And War who trades
men for gold,
life for death,
holding scales
where the spear-points meet and clash,
to their beloved
back from Troy
he sends them dust
from the flame,
heavy dust,
dust wet with tears,
filling urns in seemly wise,
freight well stowed, the dust of men.
They make lament and speak each fair.
This one so wise in battle-lore,
that one fell nobly in the fight
and died—for whom? Another's wife.
So in silence the women speak.
So in secret a jealous pain
creeps toward the sons of Atreus.
Far away lie the victors,
near the walls of the Trojans,
fair young limbs in a hostile land,
foemen's earth for their burying.

A people's voice,

angered sore,
carries dread.
Those they curse,
lost and doomed must pay in full.
But dark fear now
shows me dim
dreadful shapes,
hid in night.
Men who shed the blood of men,
their ways are not unseen of God.
Black the spirits that avenge.
Or late or soon they lay him low
who prospers in unrighteousness.
His life a wavering shadow lost
in the unseen where none may help.
Overmuch fame a peril brings.
Heads carried high God's lightning strikes,
flame from his eyes, all-seeing.
Mine be good free from envy.
Not for me cities captured.
Neither let me a captive be,
holding my life from another.

A SINGLE MEMBER OF THE CHORUS: But tidings glad,
fire-spread,
throughout the town
swiftly go,
whether true or whether false
what man can know? A god, maybe, is tricking us.

ANOTHER: Yes. Who so childish, mind so shattered, that a flame,
a traveling fire
bearing news,
can set his heart
all a-fire, to sink and die
when another tale is told?

ANOTHER: Women we are not,
who before the truth is clear
give their trust to what they will.

ANOTHER: Credulous ever the mind of a woman is. leaping all bounds.
So swiftly it moves, so swiftly, too, pass
a woman's words.
News she spreads is short of life.

[A break in the action is presupposed here. Several days are assumed to have passed. The Chorus of Old Men have again assembled]

LEADER: Now we shall soon have knowledge of these fires,
these beacon-flames, these torches relayed on,
if they bring truth or only like to dreams
glad-seeming, visit us to cheat our sense.
A herald comes. I see him by the shore.
His brow is shaded by an olive-branch.
And, witness to his journey, see the dust,
the thirsty dust, twin-sister to the mire,
that fouls his dress and gives assurance clear
here is no voiceless messenger to speak
by kindling fires of mountain wood, and signs
of flame and smoke, but one who will speak out

and bid us plainly either to rejoice
or else— What else? I will not say the word.
To this of good we see may more good come.
  ANOTHER OLD MAN: Let him who prays not thus
    for land and town
reap in himself the fruit of evil thought.
  [Enter the Herald. His dress is travel-worn and
    stained]
  HERALD: O dear home of my fathers, Argos land!
Ten years have come and gone. This day I see you.
One hope come true of many hopes made shipwreck.
Oh, never did I think to die at home,
to have my share in that dear earth.
Now blessings, blessings on the land, the sun,
the land's most high king, Zeus, and Lord Apollo,
loosing no more against us his keen shafts.
Enough of hate you showed us by Scamander.[11]
Turn to us as of old, to save and heal.
Gods all, here met, to you I make my prayer.
Hermes, the herald, whom the heralds love,
the sovereign dead who sped us on our way,
kind welcome give these whom the spear has spared.
Oh, palace of our kings, beloved roof,
seats of the mighty, gods that front the sun,
if ever once in days of old, then now
look with glad eyes upon a king who comes
after long lapse of years to bring to you
and all here gathered, light in the dark night.
Receive him with due honor—Agamemnon.
Welcome him as is meet and right to do.
He took the mattock from the hand of Zeus, the
    just.
With it uprooted Troy, leveled her to a plain.
Dark are her altars, dark her shrines of gods.
The seed has perished out of all the land.
Such is the yoke he put upon Troy's neck,
our king, the elder of the sons of Atreus.
Blest of the gods he comes, the man most fit
of all men now alive to meet with honor.
For neither Paris nor his town that shared
with him his guilt, will ever boasting say
that what they did was more than what they suffered.
Judgment against him given for rape and theft,
his booty lost, he brought to utter ruin
his father's house so that the very place
knows it no more. Twice over Priam's sons
paid for the wrong they did.
  LEADER: Oh, herald from the host, we give you
    joy.
  HERALD: Joy truly—such that I could die content.
  LEADER: So much you longed for home and father-
    land?
  HERALD: So much that now my eyes are wet from
    joy.
  LEADER: Homesickness is a pleasant malady.
  HERALD: You mean? I cannot master that alone.
  LEADER: To long for those who long for you in
    turn—-

11 Apollo was on the Trojan side. The Scamander was
one of the rivers of Troy.

  HERALD: Our home then missed us who were sick
    for home?
  LEADER: So that our darkened minds could only
    grieve.
  HERALD: But why such weight of sorrow on your
    heart?
  LEADER: Long since I learned that silence physics
    pain.
  HERALD: No—tell me, with the prince gone did
    you fear?
  LEADER: Even as you said: death would be only
    joy—
  HERALD: Well ended now. And yet in those long
    years
a man might say the evil matched the good.
But who except a god can look to be
free from all trouble all his days on earth.
Trouble! If I should tell you how we lived—
No room on deck, and little more below.
All in the day's work, but we paid for it.
Ashore still worse, whatever men hate most.
Beds in the open, near the foeman's walls.
Forever rain or dew, the meadow dew.
Our very clothes were rotting from the wet.
Good for the lice—our hair was full of them.
The winters—well, if anyone would try
to say how cold it was—the birds fell dead.
And Ida's snow—enough to break your heart.
Hot, too, at noonday when upon his couch
the sea, windless and waveless, lay asleep.
But why complain? All trouble over now.
All over for the dead. They will not want
to live again—not they, never again.
And we who live will let them lie uncounted.
Why grieve now because fortune frowned on them?
A long good-by to trouble, so say I.
For us, we soldiers that are left alive,
the gain and not the loss weighs down the scale.
So that we make our boast to this day's sun,
as swift we fly across the land and sea:
"Troy at last captured, the Achaean fleet
has nailed these spoils of war up in the shrines,
paying the gods of Greece their ancient tribute."
And whoso hears must give the city glory,
the leaders too, and thank God for his grace,
who brought these things to pass. My tale is told.
  LEADER: Convinced. I own it. Such words win
    belief.
To learn is to be young, however old.
But news that makes me rich belongs yet more
to the king's house there—and to Clytemnestra.
  [As these words are spoken Clytemnestra enters]
  CLYTEMNESTRA: My triumph song I sang long
    since, when first
the fire-sped messenger came through the night,
proclaiming Ilium captive and laid low.
Some then spoke to me chiding. Beaconfires—
do these persuade you Troy is spoiled and sacked?
How like a woman, quickly light of heart.
They made me out a fool with wits astray.

Yet did I sacrifice, and everywhere,
throughout the town, one man and then another
followed a woman, joining in her praise,
echoing her triumph, and in all the shrines
they lulled to rest the fragrant spice-fed flames.
And now what need of words from me to you?
The king himself will tell me all the tale.
But that I best may hasten to give welcome
to him, my honored lord, as he returns—
for what so sweet in any woman's eyes,
a lamp in darkness, when, the gates flung wide,
her man, saved by God's grace, comes back from war—
take to my lord this message: bid him come
with all the speed he may, back to the town
that loves him, and within his palace find
the faithful wife he left there, through these years
a trusty watch-dog for him in his house,
foe to his foes, not changed in any wise,
on whom he set his seal, unbroken still
in the long lapse of time.
Pleasure from other men, a tarnished name,
these things are not for me. As easily
could I be taught to dye a bit of bronze.
    [*Exit* Clytemnestra]
    HERALD: Such ringing words when laden with the truth
are not amiss in a true woman's mouth.
    LEADER: Spoken for your ears, not for ours.
We are interpreters that understand too well.
But, herald, tell us, what of Menelaus?
Has he won home in safety, come with you?
A strong man he, one whom this land loves well.
    HERALD: There is no way to tell a pleasant false-hood
whose pleasure will endure as the days pass.
    LEADER: Good news if true—if not true then not good.
Evil when true is hard to cover up.
    HERALD: Swept away out of sight of all the fleet,
he and his ship. I do not speak a lie.
    LEADER: You saw him, then, set sail? or was he lost
in some great storm that threatened all the ships?
    HERALD: O master-bowman, you have hit the mark.
One word or two and all our trouble told.
    LEADER: Do sailors speak of him as dead or living?
What do men say who travel on the sea?
    HERALD: Not a man knows, not one to bring clear tidings.
He only saw, who quickens earth—the sun.
    LEADER: How rose, how passed, the storm? The gods were angered?
    HERALD: This day of happy omen let no tongue
that tells of evil, darken. Far apart
keep sorrow and the service due to God.
Of course, when to a town a grim-faced messenger
brings fearful tidings of an army fallen,
one common wound for all the folk to suffer,
and many men from many homes made victims
to the two-handled scourge the war-god loves,

a curse that points two ways, a bloody pair—
why then, a man packed full of such like troubles
will make his cry to hell and not to heaven.
But when one comes to bring his happy town
glad tidings of good peace, and safety won,
why mix the evil with the good?
Shall I tell you of the storm God's anger sent us?
For fire and sea took oath together, they
of old most bitter foes, and proved their bond
in ruin dealt the wretched ships of Argos.
At night a bitter evil of cruel waves
uprose and from the north the winds swept down.
Ship shattered against ship, so furiously
that evil shepherd, the wild hurricane,
drove them with roar of rain and thundering spray,
away—unseen—forever gone.
And when uprose the shining light of day
the sea had blossomed—on it floated thick
the flower of our host among the wreckage.
Ourselves, our ship, safe, not a timber sprung.
Someone, a god, no human, took the helm;
stole us away or begged us off from death.
Good Fortune boarded us, a willing shipmate.
Our anchor held against the foaming surf
that could not dash us on the rocky coast.
Saved from that hell of waters, when at last
the white day dawned it was beyond belief
we lived. Our darkened minds saw this alone,
this last calamity, the fleet shipwrecked.
Does one of them still draw the breath of life?
Then he is saying we are lost—why not?
As we in turn think it is so with them.
Good luck be with them. But for Menelaus,
look to see him returning first of all,
if anywhere a ray of sunshine finds him
alive and seeing the sweet light. God's plan.
Be sure he is not minded yet to bring the race to ruin.
There still is hope the prince will come back home.
Hearing these words, know that you hear the truth.
    [*Exit* Herald. *The* Chorus *take their position for another choral song*]
    CHORUS: Who was he who gave her name,
name so fearfully made true.
Was it one no man may see,
power dread,
knowing what had been foredoomed,
tongue that destiny controlled?
Calling her Helen, bride of strife,
bride of the spear—the spear she wielded.
Through the ships, through men, through her town she drove it.
Forth she stepped from her bower,
from the costly, broidered hangings,
by a mighty wind borne sea-ward.
And a host,
shield-bearing huntsmen, followed hot,
tracking the oar blades unseen footprints,
on to Simois'[12] shaded strand.

---

[12] The Simois was a river of Troy.

Oarsmen beached a boat there.
Blood was to flow in that quarrel.

Wrath of God that works his will
sped to Ilium a bride,
curse they called her when they knew,
when they paid
price in full for hearth defiled,
wrong to God who guards the hearth.
Singing aloud the marriage song
came they to honor bride and bridal,
upon whom the charge of the music lay,
near kin to the bridegroom.
But another song was taught them,
taught the ancient Trojan city,
and she groaned,
mourning in desolation deep
him who had sought the fatal bridal.
Desolation forevermore
dying children brought her,
blood that must flow to no purpose.

A man captured a lion's cub,
nursing still at its mother's breast,
reared it then in his dwelling.
Soft little thing in life's prelude,
gentle and fond of the children,
plaything the old took delight in,
holding it often in their arms,
fondling it like a little child.
Bright-eyed creature, it licked the hand
giving food for its hunger.

A day came when the lion cub
paid his price for the fostering care,
showed the strain he was bred from,
turning to kill in the sheep-folds.
Banquet unbidden he made him.
Blood in the court-yards was flowing,
anguish past bearing in the house,
slaughter and ruin far and wide.
Priest of death by the wrath of God,
death to those that had reared him.

So once there came
to the town of Ilium
what seemed
a very dream of peace,
the calm no wind stirs ever,
a rich man's
fragile, shining jewel,
soft eyes that glancing shot a dart,
flower of love that pierced men's hearts.
But she swerved sharp and she worked out
to a bitter end her bridal.
In her house base, to her friends base,
and she brought doom where she entered.
God—he avenged whom she wronged,
that bride of tears and accursèd.

An ancient word
fashioned long ago by men

speaks thus:
When prosperity
spreading waxes mighty,
it dies not
childless but leaves offspring.
Over much good grows rank apace,
evil crop for the race's reaping.
But alone I in my thought stand
and apart hold I from others.
It is sin only that breeds sin,
and the son is like to the father.
Blest house that harbors the good,
fairest sons are her portion.

But arrogance,
once grown old,
brings to birth
arrogance,
in the miseries of men
forever young. Her day of birth, or late or soon,
is fixed by fate.
Bold recklessness is her twin, irresistible,
none may wage war with, impious.
Curses to home and hearth,
black—like to the one who bore them.

But goodness shines,
giving light, in smoke-begrimed
hovels dim,
virtue there in honor held.
From gilded roofs that cover hands defiled with sin
she turns her eyes.
Where purity dwells, there she betakes herself.
Power of wealth she worships not,
counterfeit glory men love.
All to their haven guiding.
[*Enter* Agamemnon *in a chariot.* Cassandra *follows in another.* Attendants, Soldiers, Townsmen. *During the* Chorus' *speech of welcome,* Clytemnestra, *with* Attendants, *comes through the palace doors and stands on the steps*]
CHORUS: Come at last, O my king! Troy town is your spoil,
true son of your race.
How shall I greet you, how do you homage,
not over-passing, not falling short of,
due measure of praise.
Full many there are who give honor first
to fair seeming—the truth they regard not.
To heave a sigh when another fares ill,
all men are minded.
Sorrow that bites deep—
never a pang
reaches their heart's core.
And joy is feigned in the joy of a friend,
while a long-drawn face is constrained to smile.
But he who is wise to discern his flock,
a shepherd of men,
looks into false eyes and there finds
foul that seemed fair, and for friendship
adulation,

not wine but water.
When you marshaled the host in Helen's behalf,
through those days as I watched—
frank words be mine now—
dark were the colors that painted your portrait then.
A helmsman that could not steer his own mind,
   such a one as would bring
     boldness in vain
      while men lay dying.
Now deep from my heart and my heart's deepest love
   [13] .   .   .   .   .   .
Glad end can make toil to seem merry.
Time, wisest of teachers, will guide you to know
him who dealt justly, him who did evil,
of the men who guarded the town here.

AGAMEMNON: First Argos and my country's gods
   I greet,
as is their due who helped with me to bring
the host safe home and with me dealt out justice
to Priam's town. No ear to prayer or plea
did the gods give; not one whit wavering
they cast their votes into the urn of blood
for death, to Ilium and all therein.
The other urn, the merciful, was empty,
no hand to fill it, only hope stood by.
The smoke still shows where once a city was.
The whirlwind of blind doom is still alive.
From dying embers comes a breath of incense,
rich fragrance of the riches burning there.
Be mindful then of what you owe the gods
whose was the deed, when close about the town
we set our snares of wrath for Helen's sake.
The beast of Argos—him the wooden horse
gave birth to—set his teeth into his prey
and ground the town to powder. High they leaped,
that host of shield-armed men. The time of year
was near the setting of the Pleiades.[14]
Over the towered walls a lion sprang
that fed on flesh of men and lapped his fill
of blood of kings.
Thus to the gods I speak first, as is due.
Now, touching you, I heard and bear in mind
your words just spoken, and to all you said
I give assent. I am your advocate.
Few are the men to whom this is inborn,
to give full honor to a friend's good fortune.
But ill will settles on the heart, a poison,
and he who thus grows sick has double burdens,
a heavy heart for his own miseries
and grief to see the blessings of another.
I speak who know, for deeply I have learned
what friendship is—the semblance in a mirror,
a shadow's ghost—when men have seemed to be
all loyalty. Odysseus only—he
who sailed against his will—when once in harness,
pulled with me, proved a faithful yoke-fellow.
Alive or dead, this is his due from me.

[13] Here and on subsequent pages the ellipsis indicates a gap or an unintelligible passage in the MSS.

[14] A cluster of stars in the constellation of Taurus.

All else that bears upon the State, the gods,
we will consider in full conclave, there
appointing general councils of the people.
Where all goes well, to see that it endures.
Whatever needs a healing remedy,
give care that by kind use of knife or cautery
the mischief of the taint may be averted.
Now to my palace, to my home,
my hearth, where first the gods shall have my
   greeting,
who sent me forth and led me back again.
O Victory, now mine, be mine forever.
   [Clytemnestra *descends the steps of the palace
   followed by her* Waiting-women]
   CLYTEMNESTRA: My country-men, chief elders of
   our city,
it does not shame me to speak out to you
the love I bear my husband. Timid fears
die in us with long lapse of time.
I have not learned from others. No—I speak
of my own life, bitter to bear, the while
he lay beneath the walls of Ilium.
A woman sits at home—a man goes forth.
She first of all knows loneliness and terror,
forever giving ear to angry rumor.
First comes one messenger, then comes another,
and each with tidings worse than were the last,
shrieking calamity to house and household.
If he who now stands here had met with wounds
as many as report came pouring in,
no network were as full of holes as he.
If he had died the deaths they told to me—
so went the tale most often—separate bodies,
three at least, like Geryon of old,[15]
he would have needed, and a triple share
of earth for covering he must have claimed,
each body dying in a separate death.
Such tidings ever reaching me afresh,
so drove me on that others oftentimes
have loosed the tight-drawn halter from my neck.
And that is why the boy is not here with me,
as he should be, Orestes, in whom met
the pledges of our love. But do not think it strange.
One rears him who has raised his spear for you
in all good will, the Phocian Strophius.
He gave me warning of a twofold trouble,
your danger by the walls of Ilium,
and if the people so left leaderless,
a noisy rabble, should destroy the council.
For men are thus, they trample on the fallen.
Such is our nature—such excuse we plead.
But for myself—the river of my tears
has long run dry—not a drop left to me.
Through the sad watches of the night my eyes
grew dim with weeping, while the fires lit
against your coming ever died unheeded.
The light hum of the buzzing gnat would wake me
from dreams where I had seen more woes to you
than could be suffered in the time I slept.

[15] A monster with three bodies, slain by Hercules.

Such griefs I bore. But now, heart freed from grief,
I speak to him himself who is our safety,
the watch-dog of the fold, the stout ship's forestay,
the firm-based pillar of the lofty roof,
dear as the only son is to his father,
as land the sailor sees beyond his hope,
as day most fair to look on after storm,
to thirsty wayfarer a gushing stream.
Oh, sweet escape from stern necessity.
Thus do I greet him, name him, without fear
the gods may grudge my joy, so many sorrows
I bore of old. Now to me, dear beloved.
Down from your car—but not on common earth
shall your foot rest, my king, the foot that trod
Troy into dust. You women, to your task.
Why this delay? Cover the ground before him
as I gave order. Spread fair tapestries.
Straightway with purple let his path be paved.
—So justice lead him to a home unlooked for.
The rest my care that never sleeps will order
justly, with God and with fate's just decree.

[The Women *cover with purple stuffs the path
from the chariot to the palace door.* Agamemnon
does not move]

AGAMEMNON: Daughter of Leda, guardian of my
house,
long as my absence was so is your speech.
Nor is it seemly you should speak my praise.
Let other lips give me the honor due me.
And these things here—I will not be tricked out
in woman fashion. I am not foreign-bred
that you should grovel on the ground before me
with wide-mouthed noisy praise.
Cover my path—that would draw down upon me
God's jealousy, to whom alone belongs
such honor. For a mortal man to walk
on costly fineries is cause for dread.
I tell you, honor me as man, not god.
Foot rugs and fripperies—away with them.
Fame cries aloud of her own self. The gift
God gives the best is soberness of mind.
Count that alone a happy life which ends
while dear prosperity abides. If I
so fare in all things, courage will not fail me.

CLYTEMNESTRA: Tell me but this—if not against
your will—

AGAMEMNON: My will, be sure, shall never be
gainsayed.

CLYTEMNESTRA: Is it perhaps some vow fear drove
you to?

AGAMEMNON: What I have said I mean if ever man
did.

CLYTEMNESTRA: Would Priam so have done, had
he been victor?

AGAMEMNON: I do believe he would have walked
on purple.

CLYTEMNESTRA: While you stand off, afraid what
men may say—

AGAMEMNON: Ah, well—what men say is a mighty
power.

CLYTEMNESTRA: The man who stirs no ill will, stirs
no envy.

AGAMEMNON: A woman—and so eager for a fight!

CLYTEMNESTRA: To yield would well become a
happy victor.

AGAMEMNON: You too would be a victor? Over
me?

CLYTEMNESTRA: Yes. Yield to me—but of your
own free will.

AGAMEMNON: Well, have your way. Here then, my
hunting boots—
they did my feet good service—one of you,
quick, draw them off. And as I walk upon
this purple of the sea, may no far stroke
flashed with the jealous eye of God light on me.

[*He grumbles to himself while his boots are
drawn off*]

I hold it shame to waste the house's substance
by putting foot on stuffs that cost much silver.

[*As he resigns himself to the inevitable, it occurs
to him that the moment is a propitious one to
introduce an awkward subject,* Cassandra]

Enough of that. This girl you see, a stranger,
take her within, and kindly. He who rules
with gentleness, God looks upon with favor.
A slave's yoke no one bears of his own will.
She, chosen out of many goods and captives,
the flower of all, is mine—the army's gift.
Now, since you have subdued me to your will,
treading on purple I pass to my home.

[*He descends from the chariot and standing on
the purple waits for her a moment*]

CLYTEMNESTRA: There is the sea—and who shall
drain it dry?
—breeding in plenteousness and ever fresh
the purple dye men weigh out silver for.
Our house, thank God, has ample store of all,
and poverty it does not understand.
Purple enough I would have vowed to trample
beneath my feet if so the oracles
had bade me as a price for your return.
If the root lives, the tree will put forth green,
shade to the house against the dog-star's heat.
Even so you, coming back to hearth and home,
are sign that warmth has come in wintertime.
And when Zeus makes the wine from the sharp grape,
coolness is in the house where through the halls
the rightful lord once more goes in and out.

[*He turns and walks to the palace and enters it.
She follows him as far as the doors. Just when
she is about to go in she stops and breaks into a
brief intense prayer, as if she had forgotten that
anyone was near*]

God, God, fulfillment is with thee. Fulfill
my prayer. That which shall be fulfilled
in Thy care rests.

[*She goes into the palace*]

CHORUS: Why for me so steadfastly
hovers still this terror dark
at the portals of my heart prophetic?

Omen of evil I cry, all unbought and unbidden.
Cast it forth, a murky dream?
Ah, but throned within my heart
fear abides,
boldness fails,
faith that wins assurance broken.
    Time has grown old,
sand is heaped on cables cast
where they bound
ships to shore,
when the host put in from sea,
rushing on to Ilium.

Home they come. Mine eyes have seen.
    Other witness need I none.
Yet my heart, self-taught, within sings dirges.
Spirit of vengeance, your music is sung to no lyre.
Happy confidence of hope
once was mine, it fades and dies.
Heart that throbs,
breast that swells,
tides of pain that shake the spirit,
are you but fools?
Nay, you presage what shall be.
Yet I pray
these my words
be as lies that fall to naught,
never to fulfillment come.

Truly say men
nothing is sure.
Sickness or health—
they are neighbors.
Thin is the wall in between.
Ships holding their course yet are driven
where hides the reef. So fate sends
shipwreck to many a man unlooked for.
    Of the ship's load heave a part
overboard—the ship may live.
Cast away with measured aim
from the gathered wealth within,
all the house shall not go down
over-weighed, and sink the hull.
Famine comes, but the furrows are sown,
and the year will bring forth from God's bounteous
        store-house
gifts which stay the hunger pain.

But if once blood
fall to the ground,
dark tide of death,
it is ended.
Charms are there, magical spells,
to call back, to make live, what was murdered?

            .   .   .   .   .   .

Fate by fate God balances;
doom is crossed by other doom,
so ordained that each gives place.
Thus I muse, or else my thought
would outstrip my tongue to speak
what now whispers in the dark,

grief deep-piercing the heart without hope.
All too late is it now to unweave what is woven.
How see clear with mind aflame?
    [*As the choral song ends,* Clytemnestra *enters.
    She looks toward the chariot where* Cassandra
    is still seated]
    CLYTEMNESTRA: Down now and go within. To you
        I speak, Cassandra,
since to this house God in his grace has brought
    you,
where you may share his sacred rite and stand
with many another slave beside his altar
who is the guardian of all we own.
Down from the car—and be not over-proud.
Even Alcmena's son,[16] so goes the tale,
in days of long ago was sold and swallowed
the slaves' black bread. And, if one is a slave,
it is well to serve in an old family,
long used to riches. Every man
who reaps a sudden harvest past his hope,
is savage to his slaves beyond the rule.
From us expect such use as custom grants.
    [Cassandra *seems to hear nothing. The old men
    of the* Chorus *look pityingly at her and one of
    them speaks to her gently*]
    OLD MAN: It was to you she spoke. Her words are
        clear.
Now fate has caught you fast within her web.
Yield then, if yield you can. Not yet—not yet?
    CLYTEMNESTRA: Unless her speech is some strange
        foreign tongue
silly as swallows' twittering, my words
much reach her mind and move her to obey.
    ANOTHER OLD MAN: Go. What she bids is best. So
        stands the thing.
Obey her. Leave the chariot's high seat.
    CLYTEMNESTRA: There she sits fast. I have no time
        to waste
on such. Even now before the central hearth
the sheep stand ready for the sacrifice,
    [*She speaks with rising anger*]
—such joy as never did we hope to have.
You there, if you would have a part, make haste.
Have you no wit to catch my meaning? Speak.
If not with words, a gesture—like barbarians.
    LEADER: The strange maid needs some plain inter-
        preter.
She trembles like a wild thing newly caught.
    CLYTEMNESTRA: Quite mad. Her crazy thoughts
        are all she hears.
She has not learned—her town but lately captured—
to brook the curb yet. She must foam and bleed
and wear away her passion. Well—I go.
I will not waste more words to be defied.
    [*She enters the palace*]
    ANOTHER OLD MAN: No anger in me, I so pity her.
Poor thing, dismount. Come. Yield to what you must.
Take up your strange yoke now and carry it.
    [Cassandra *moves slowly down from the chariot.*
        16 Hercules.

She is dressed as a priestess. She seems not aware of the presence of the Old Men]

CASSANDRA: Oh, God, God! Apollo—Apollo—

ANOTHER: Why do you cry to him in misery?
Apollo gives no heed to those who mourn.

CASSANDRA: Oh, God, God! Apollo, Apollo!

ANOTHER: Again she cries dark words of evil omen
to him who has no place where sorrow is.

CASSANDRA: Apollo, Apollo, our guide,
guiding me
on to death.
Twice hast thou ruined me—now utterly.

ONE MAN: [*Softly to the rest of the* Chorus] Some
    prophecy of her own fate she speaks.
The thing within that is divine abides,
though in a slave.

CASSANDRA: Apollo, Apollo, our guide,
guiding me
on to death.
Where have you brought me—and to what a house—

ANOTHER: The house of Atreus' sons. What you
    would know
it is I will tell you, and will tell you true.

CASSANDRA: No—but a house God hates,
Murders and strangling deaths.
Kin striking down kin. Oh, they kill men here.
House that knows evil and evil—the floor drips red.

ANOTHER: [*Aside to the rest*] A hound on scent
    of blood, this stranger girl.
I think that she will find the thing she seeks.

CASSANDRA: Witness! The children cry,[17]
crying for wounds that bleed.
On—on they are leading me. I must go.
A father feasted—and the flesh his children's.

ANOTHER: We knew your strange prophetic power.
Prophets— Ah me. It is not such we need.

CASSANDRA: O God— O God— What would they
    bring to pass?
Is there a woe that this house knows not?
So great, so great the evil they would bring to pass.
Oh, dark deed, that love hates, beyond cure, beyond
    hope,
—and help stands far away.

ANOTHER: Such prophesyings pass my skill. What
    first
she spoke, I know—the whole town rings with it.

CASSANDRA: O woman, this—this is it you would
    do?
He who has lain in your bed, your lord?
The bath to cheer him—then— How tell the end?
So swift—see—it comes now. A hand there—a hand
    gropes.
Now—now—another hand—

ANOTHER: Not one word yet to clear my mind.
    First riddles,
then misty oracles—and not a clue.

CASSANDRA: Oh, look— Oh, terrible.
There—it is coming clear.

[17] She is speaking of the children Agamemnon's father
had killed and served to their father, his brother, to eat.

Net?—Net of death? Oh, truly.
The snare is she who lies with him. The blood—
it stains her too.
Furies who haunt the house,
shout, for your prey is here.
Death is due.
Doomed is he.

LEADER: What is this fury that you bid cry out
against the house? Such words bring me no cheer.
Back to my heart the blood
surges in fear pale as death.
    So fade
blood-drops ebbing slow,
    when they drip
where is a mortal wound,
    when the light
dims as life sinks low.
    Swift comes death.

CASSANDRA: What? What? Oh see— Oh see.
Hold the bull back—his mate
strikes— Black the horn that gores him.
In a tangle of raiment she caught him. Oh, cunning
    craft!
He falls— The bath— Water is all around,
but it is red— Oh, blood!
    Doom, ah, doom.
This is truth.

LEADER: I do not boast great skill in oracles,
but these things spell some mischief, to my mind.
And truly what of good
ever do prophets bring to men?
Craft of many words,
only through
evil your message speaks.
    Seers bring aye
terror, so to keep
men afraid.

CASSANDRA: Alas, alas! Oh, sad fate.
Poor woman— It is I.
Yes, it is I myself.
My pain that brims the cup.
This place—why did you bring me here? Oh, pity.
Only to die, to die, and not alone.

ANOTHER OLD MAN: Now is she mad of mood and
    by some god possessed.
Her words—wild they ring,
as for her fate she mourns. So wails
ever the bird with wings of brown,
musical nightingale,
crying O, Itys,[18] child,
lost to me, lost. In grief alone
rich, poor bird.

CASSANDRA: Ah me, ah me, her fate—sweet
melodist, singing bird.
They gave her wings, the gods.

[18] The son of Tereus, who violated Philomela, sister of
Tereus' wife, Procne. In revenge the two women slew
Itys and served him up as a meal to his father. Philomela
was subsequently transformed into a nightingale, Procne
into a swallow, and Tereus into a hawk.

They gave her life unmarred
by tears—sweet life. While I—for me there waits
a sword, sharp, sharp, that cuts, that cleaves apart—
    LEADER: Whence does it come, this woe, on-rush-
       ing, borne of God,
yet vain—anguish vain.
Terror you cry—ill-omened cry,
fearful, and yet a melody,
    music high,
      rings the strain.
Path that you follow, how
know you its bounds? Oh, ill
bodes your prophecy.
    CASSANDRA: Oh bridal, bridal—death
dealing to Paris and Paris' kin.
Scamander's stream,
waters my fathers drank,
once on your bank a girl,
sorrow-doomed, was reared,
tenderly cherished there.
Now to the river loud of lamentation,
the shores of pain, I go to prophesy.
    LEADER: What is this word that you speak,
word that is all too clear,
word to a new-born babe
    clear as day.
    Oh, sharp
    sorrow smites my heart,
    while your pain,
    bitter pain,
thrills as a sorrowful song,
    breaking the heart to hear.
    CASSANDRA: Oh, heavy-laden town,
worn unto death, unto death brought low.
Oh, dumb beasts slain,
offered to save her walls.
Many the flocks and herds
brought from pasture lands.
Nothing could they avail.
The town must suffer even as it has.
And this hot heart of mine must soon. . . .
    LEADER: Dark upon dark are your words.
New ill that follows old.
Oh—swiftly on you sweeps an evil thing,
crushing, weighing down,
    calling forth your cry,
    cry of death.
Desolate, weeping, you go.
Never the end see I.
    CASSANDRA: Now do I swear no more behind a veil
my truth shall hide like a new-wedded girl.
A shining wind shall blow strong to the sunrise,
and like a breaking wave lift to the light
something far greater than this pain of mine.
No longer will I speak in riddling words.
Be you my witnesses as I search out,
close on the scent, the trail of grievous things
in days long since.
For this house—ever through it sounds a chant

as of a choir singing with one voice,
not good to hear, a chant of evil words.
Drunken with blood, men's blood, to dare the more,
a band of revellers abides within,
of sister Furies—none may cast them out.
So seated in the house a song they sing,
of that first deed of wrong, and one by one
they spurn a brother's bed defiled[19] and him
who used it. Has my arrow missed or found
the mark? Prophet am I of lies, a babbler
from door to door? Give me your oath in witness
that I know this house, its evils old in story.
    AN OLD MAN: An oath you ask—a bond in honor
    bound?
No help there. Yet I marvel that one bred
beyond the sea, of foreign speech, should know
the truth as though her very eyes had seen it.
    CASSANDRA: Apollo gave to me my prophet spirit.
    ANOTHER: A god—and he desired you? Could
    that be?
    CASSANDRA: Time was I held it shame to speak
    of it.
    ANOTHER: Ah yes. Such feelings are for happy
    people.
    CASSANDRA: He wrestled with me and his breath
    was sweet.
    ANOTHER: You came to the getting of children as
    is fit?
    CASSANDRA: I swore to yield. I lied. I cheated
    him.
    ANOTHER: But you had then the gift of prophecy?
    CASSANDRA: And told my people all the woe to
    come.
    ANOTHER: A god—and did not smite you in his
    wrath?
    CASSANDRA: He did. I sinned—and no man more
    believed me.
    ANOTHER: To us you seem to speak the truth in-
    deed.
    CASSANDRA: It comes—it comes. Oh, misery.
The awful pain of prophecy—it comes,
a whirling wind of madness.
See them—those yonder by the wall—there—there—
so young—like forms that hover in a dream.
Children they seem—murdered by those they loved.
And in their hands is flesh— It is their own.
And inward parts— Oh, load most horrible.
I see it—and their father made his feast—
Vengeance, I say, from these is shaping still—
a lion's shape,[20] who never fights, who lurks
within a bed, until the master comes—
The master? Mine. The slave's yoke. I must bear it.
Lord of the ships who laid waste Ilium—
and yet not know that she-wolf's tongue.
She licks her lord's hand—fawns with pricking ear,
and bites at last, like secret death.

[19] When Thyestes seduced his brother's wife.
[20] She means Clytemnestra's lover. He is the son of
the man who was made to feast on his own children.

Such daring has a woman to kill a man?
How name her? Evil beast, a snake,
the monster crouching on the shore to prey on sailors,
the mother of hell, mad-raging, wild to war,
implacable, against her very own.
Her cry of joy—oh, woman daring all things,
joyful as men shout when the battle turns.
Her show of triumph for his home-coming—
Believe or not. Why do I longer care?
The thing that is to be shall be. And you
here standing, soon will in your pity call me
a prophet all too true.

LEADER: How once a father feasted on his children,
those words I understand, cold to my heart.
And terror holds me when she speaks no fancies
but what I know. All else she says I hear—
no more, I have no clue.

CASSANDRA: Then hear the truth.
Your eyes shall look on Agamemnon dead.

AN OLD MAN: Peace, wretched girl. Hush on your
    lips those words.

CASSANDRA: No peace is on my lips.

ANOTHER: If it must be—O God, not so—not so.

CASSANDRA: You pray. Their care is death.

ANOTHER: Who? Who is he who plots this cursèd
    thing?

CASSANDRA: You will not read my prophecy aright.

ANOTHER: Because I know the deed could not be
    done.

CASSANDRA: And yet I speak the Greek tongue—
    all too well.

ANOTHER: Greek are the oracles but none can
    read them.

CASSANDRA: Oh, strange! A flame—moving— It
    comes upon me.
Oh, terrible! Apollo! I see—I see—
A lioness—that walks upon two feet—
a wolf she lies with, the royal lion gone.
It is she will kill me. Pity me.
She brews a poison, and she swears
the vial of her wrath holds death for me.
I too must die because he brought me hither.
Her plan—and while she whets her sword for him.
Why then these gaudy things on head and throat?
They mock at me—the prophet's wreaths—the staff.
Down with you—now, before I die myself. Begone.
    [She tears off the adornments that mark her a
    prophet, and stamps on them]
You fall, and I myself shall follow soon.
Make rich in woe some other woman now.
See now. It is Apollo who has stripped me,
taken his prophet's robe. He watched while I was
    mocked,
still in his livery, reviled by friends
turned foes—one voice—no reason—to them all,
calling me vagrant, mountebank, a cheat,
a beggar. Wretched and starving I endured
The prophet now has done with me, his prophet.
It is he has brought me to this pass of death.

They slew my father on an altar stone.
For me a block waits hot with murdered blood.
Surely we shall not die unmarked of God.
Another[21] to avenge will come in turn,
to slay the one who bore him, to exact
blood for a father's blood. A wanderer,
outcast from home, he shall return at last
and crown the sins that blindly doomed his race.
A great oath has been sworn of God most high.
The fallen helpless corpse shall lead him home.
But I—why weep and pity such as these?
I, who once saw the town of Ilium
fare as she fared. And they that cast her down
have thus their end in the decrees of God.
So now I go to end as they have done.
I will endure to die. O gates of death,
my greeting. But—pray God, the blow strike home
quickly. No struggle. Death coming easily.
Blood ebbing gently and my eyes then closed.

LEADER: O woman, full of sorrows, full of wisdom,
you have spoken much. But if in very truth—
if death you see, how can you unafraid
go toward it like a dumb beast to the altar,
driven by the power of God?

CASSANDRA: There is no help, my friends, not any
    more.

AN OLD MAN: Yet he who dies last in some sort
    dies best—

CASSANDRA: The day is come. Small gain to me in
    flight.

ANOTHER: Steadfast in pain, O woman brave of
    heart.

CASSANDRA: None who are happy ever hear such
    praise.

ANOTHER: A brave death can make happy one who
    dies.

CASSANDRA: My father, you were brave, and brave
    your sons.
    [She moves toward the palace but starts back]

ANOTHER: What thing is there? What terror turns
    you back?

CASSANDRA: Oh, horror—

ANOTHER: [Frightened and angry] That cry—
    Within your own mind is the horror.

CASSANDRA: Death breathing from the door—
    blood, drop by drop—

ANOTHER: [Also angrily] How not? They are
    sacrificing at the hearth.

CASSANDRA: A breath as from a grave—

ANOTHER: [Remonstrating] The costly Tyrean in-
    cense! That? No, no.

CASSANDRA: Yet I am going, there within the house
    to weep
my own and Agamemnon's doom.
I have lived my life. Oh, friends, my terror is not
vain.

21 Orestes, who in the play following this returns and
kills Clytemnestra, his mother, because she killed his
father.

I am no silly bird that fears each bush.
When I am dead bear witness I spoke truth,
when a woman shall lie dead for me,[22] a woman,
and a man fall for a man who had an evil wife.
So I who am to die beg of your friendship.

OLD MAN: Oh wretched, those whom God tells
what shall be.

CASSANDRA: One last word more—but not to sing
my dirge.

O sun, O shining light
I shall not see again, I pray to you:
When they who murdered pay for what they did,
let them remember too this thing they did,
this easy thing, to kill a slave, a woman.
O world of men, what is your happiness?
A painted show. Comes sorrow and the touch—
a wet sponge—blots the painting out.
And this moves pity, sadder still than death.

[She enters the palace, and the Chorus take their
places for another song]

CHORUS: All unsatisfied are the hearts of men.
No house so great, when fortune comes knocking,
none so well-filled, the door
    bolted and barred,
    warns her away:
    "Enter no more. Enough."
So to the king did the high gods allow
to lay low Priam's town.
    And he came
    blest with honor of heaven.
Yet—if for the blood
shed in the years gone,
full price he must pay and must die for the dead
so that others who die may have vengeance—
Is there mortal hearing these things who will boast
fate gave him life
safe from all sorrow?

[A sudden cry from the palace]

VOICE: God! I am struck! My death blow. Here!
Within—

LEADER: Silence. A cry. Who is it done to death?

VOICE: O God! Again— Struck down again.

LEADER: Done the deed. That voice—I know it. He
who cried out was the king.

Now stand close and plan together. Safety— Is there
any way—

[The Old Men gather and debate confusedly]

FIRST SPEAKER: I give you straight my judgment.
Sound the call.

All citizens to the palace to give aid.

ANOTHER: No, no. Quick action now. Break in at
once.

Before they drop the dripping sword, convict them.

ANOTHER: Yes. Some such plan. I give my vote
to that.

Action and quick. No time now for delay.

ANOTHER: As clear as day. The first step to their
goal

[22] The woman she means is Clytemnestra and the
man is her lover, who will also be killed by Orestes.

to make themselves the masters of the state.

ANOTHER: While we wait here—wait till they
trample down

all that would hold them back. Their hands are
quick.

ANOTHER: If I knew what to say—what plan to
urge—

Let those give counsel who have strength to act.

ANOTHER: So I think too. There are no words I
know

to make the dead arise and live again.

ANOTHER: What? Drag our lives out in submission?
Yield

to rulers who have brought pollution on us?

ANOTHER: Intolerable. Far better let us die.

Death is a milder master than a tyrant.

ANOTHER: We have no witnesses. A groan we
heard.

We are not seers to know the man is dead.

ANOTHER: Clear facts first—then grow angry as
we will.

But guesswork is another thing from knowledge.

LEADER: We are agreed on this at least, to know
and quickly, what has happened to the king.

[As they press toward the door of the palace it
opens. The bodies of Agamemnon and Cassandra lie just within. Clytemnestra stands over
them. Blood stains are on her face and dress]

CLYTEMNESTRA: Words, endless words, I spoke to
serve my purpose.

Now I gainsay them all and feel no shame.
How can a woman work her hatred out
on him she hates and yet must seem to love,
how pile up ruin round him, fence the snare
too high to leap beyond—except by lies?
Long years ago I planned. Now it is done.
Old hatred ended. It was slow in coming,
but it came—
I stand here where I struck. So did I.
Nothing do I deny. I flung around him
a cloak, full folds, deadly folds. I caught him,
fish in a net. No way to run or fight.
Twice did I strike him and he cried out twice
and his limbs failed him and he fell, and there
I gave him the third stroke, an offering
to the god of hell who holds fast all his dead.
So there he lay and as he gasped, his blood
spouted and splashed me with black spray, a dew
of death, sweet to me as heaven's sweet rain drops
when the corn-land buds.
There stands the matter, ancient men of Argos.
Go now, and if you can, rejoice. For me,
I glory. Oh, if such a thing might be,
over the dead to pour thank-offerings,
over this dead it would be just and more.
So full of curses did he fill the cup
his house drank—but the dregs he drank himself.

LEADER: Oh, bold of tongue. We wonder at your
speech.

Loud words of boasting—and the man your husband.

CLYTEMNESTRA: Bring me to trial like any silly
     woman?
My heart is fearless, and you all well know
what I know. Curse me or bless me—either as you
     will—
all one to me. Look. This is Agamemnon,
my husband, dead, struck down by my right hand,
a righteous workman. So the matter stands.
     CHORUS: What evil thing, O you,
poisonous herb earth-grown, or a draught
drawn from the drifting sea,
put to your lips, has worked
     rage for this sacrifice,
     made you a thing accursed.
You have cast away and away shall you be cast,
     a thing of hate to your people.
     CLYTEMNESTRA: So now do you pass judgment on
          me? Exile—
the people's hate—cursed by men openly.
But he—you never spoke a word to cross him,
who cared no more than if a beast should die
when flocks are plenty in the fleecy fold,
and slew his daughter, dearest anguish borne
by me in travail—slew her for a charm
against the Thracian winds. Oh, never
would you drive him away from land and home,
a thing polluted. Now the deed is mine.
You are a stern judge then. I tell you plainly,
threaten what threats you will. I am content
that you shall rule if your hand prove the stronger.
But if God please the other way about,
you shall be taught, though late, the ways of wisdom.
     CHORUS: Proud in your thought alway.
Scornful the words on your lips.
     Deed of blood
stamped on the maddened mind,
stain on the brow so red,
plain for all eyes to see,
branding forever shame.
Doom of dishonor, the loss of all dear,
     and blow by blow
     paid in full for atonement.
     CLYTEMNESTRA: Hear me in turn. The oath I swear
          is holy.
By justice for my child now consummated,
by black, blind Doom, by all the powers of hell,
to whom I offered what I killed, I swear
hope does not tread the halls of fear for me
while on my hearth a fire is still kindled
by one now true in heart to me as ever,
Aegisthus, my sure shield of confidence.
Here lies the man who scorned me—me, his wife—
the fool and tool of every shameless woman
beneath Troy's walls. Here she lies too, his slave,
got by his spear, his sibyl bed-fellow,
his paramour—God's words upon her lips,
who rubbed the galley's benches at his side.
They have their due. he thus and she the same,
her swan-song sung. His lover—there she lies.
I in my soft bed lying, shall delight,

thinking of her, still more in its smooth softness.
     CHORUS: Would God that swift might come—
not after wracking pain,
not when sickness has wasted—
but swiftly come
borne by fate, unending
sleep everlasting. For he lies low now,
dearest defense to me, my master.
Much he bore
in a frail
woman's cause.
By a vile
woman's hand he fell at last.

O Helen, maddened of mind. Many men
     by a woman slain,
     many exceedingly.
Lives lost before Troy of her losing.
She wreathed for the last time her brow— Oh, that
     garland red,
as red as blood—it will not fade—and there within
is strife that has brought to death the master.
     CLYTEMNESTRA: Not death. Never pray for death—
          that must come—
though heavy your load.
Nor turn upon Helen your bitter wrath.
One woman—could she slay many a man?
Those lives so lost—were they lost at her hand?
That wound never closed—did she deal it?
     CHORUS: Spirit of evil now
fallen upon this house,
on two kings that were kindred,
the power you wield,
hands of women wrought it,
strong as their souls—to my heart it pierces.
     Over the body now exulting,
     croaking your song,
          raven-like,
     there you stand,
     hateful Spirit triumphant. . . .
     CLYTEMNESTRA: Now judged aright—so your lips
          speak truth.
It is he you name,
the spirit thrice-gorged with blood of the race.
From him it has come, the thirst to lap blood.
It dwells in their flesh. Before the old wound
can be healed, there is fresh blood oozing.
     CHORUS: Aye—he you tell of is great,
grievous in wrath—there within abiding.
Woe— Woe. All of evil the tale,
blinding doom never glutted.
Ah me. Ah me. God's work, God's will.
All springs from him. All moves in him.
What is brought to pass apart from God for mortals?
These deeds—his is the hand that wrought them.

Oh sorrow sore. O my King, O my King,
how shall I mourn you.
Or how speak from my heart that has loved you.
Caught fast in a web that a foul spider wove,
all unholy the death when your spirit fled.

So dies a slave—ah me. Like a slave you died,
by a crafty blow struck down.
Axe doubled-edged in a hand that spared not.
> CLYTEMNESTRA: This deed my work? It is mine
> you proclaim?
> Look then and know me.
Here is not Agamemnon's queen. Nay, not so,
no wife of this dead man am I. In her shape
    moves the avenger,
    ancient in anger.
The grim banquet of Atreus is paid for.
    Children were slaughtered.
    And a man offered up in requital.
> CHORUS: Guiltless—you—of this death?
Where is the one who will witness for you?
No— No. Yet I think another
worked with you, an avenger,
who rushes on where kin kill kin,
whose path is where dark blood flows fast,
where murdered children surely shall have vengeance,
that flesh served for a father's feasting.
> CLYTEMNESTRA: No! The traitorous craft of this
> man here dead
has brought down his house.
From his seed she sprang, that flower I bore
and wept for, Iphigenia slain.
Oh, a worthy deed and a worthy doom.
Will he boast in hell of the death he dealt,
now the score is paid
and the sword he slew with has slain him?
> CHORUS: As one astray
knows not where to turn him,
so do I wander witless
where path is none.
All my house is falling.
    I fear the storm.
    Crash of thunder shakes the walls.
    The rain beats down.
    Blood—a stream, not rain drops.

Ah me— Earth, Earth, would that you held me
now—ere I had seen
    him here defeated,
    slain thus in a bath silver-sided.
Who will make his grave? Who will make lament?
You? Will you dare who dared to kill him,
him who was yours?
    Now will you weep for him?
Deeds—deeds such as these—will you blot them out
by a tear? Will the dead take your offering?
Over the grave who will speak what is due him—
God-like king? Who with tears will mourn him,
and sorrow truly—heavy-laden?
> CLYTEMNESTRA: Not for you this care. Not for
> you is the task.
> Mine is it only.
Hands that he fell by and died by shall bury him.
Tears? Think you that we of his household will weep?
One—one will receive him in love where he goes,
    fitly—his daughter.

By the swift-flowing river of grief she will stand,
    welcome to bring him.
She will hold him, enfold him, and kiss him.
> CHORUS: Reproach in turn
meets reproach. I know not
who here can hold the balance.
The spoiler spoiled.
Kill—your life is forfeit.
God's law is sure.
He who wrongs, to him shall wrong
be done—in full.
From this house accursed
can any drive the seed of sin—uproot it?
No. The race fast-bound must seek its ruin.
> CLYTEMNESTRA: To this, then, you come—to the
> law of God.
Truth is your guide now.
But for me I will swear and join in a pact
with him—with the spirit that haunts this race.
Enough. What is done, bitter hard, must be borne.
No more. Let him go—go forth from this house,
wear down, waste away, other houses,
with his death-dealing curse.
I with but little shall find full contentment,
if I drive from these halls
that frenzy when brother kills brother.
> [Aegisthus *with* Attendants *enters triumphantly*]
> AEGISTHUS: O kindly light. O day that leads in
> justice.
Now I do know that gods on high behold
the woes of earth to help and to avenge,
now that I see him lie here in the web
woven by Furies—dear sight to my eyes.
His father's crafty hand wrought, and he pays.
Atreus, his father, ruler of the land,
his throne disputed by Thyestes—
my father, his own brother—cast
him out from home and city. In his misery,
after long years had passed,
he turned back, came a suppliant to his hearth,
and won at least this mercy for himself,
a promise that he should not die and stain with blood
his fathers' halls—not he himself. Ah, but
the godless father of the dead man here,
in greeting to my father, as when one
holds merry festival after sacrifice,
made him a feast—of his own children's flesh,
the feet, the fingers, broken off. . . .
So did he take in ignorance what then
he could not know—and fatal to the race,
as you will see, that feast has proved at last.
Poor wretch, when he had learned the deed abhor-
    rent,
he cried a great cry, falling back—spewed out
that flesh—cried out upon that house a doom
intolerable—the banquet board sent crashing
in token of his curse: "So perish all
born of this race."
And therefore is this dead man fallen here.
I planned the murder righteously,

I who, a little thing in swaddling clothes,
was cast out with my father, broken quite, at last.
But grown to manhood, justice led me back.
I was an exile, yet through me he died.
It was my hatred wove this cunning plot.
Now let death come. Why care when my own eyes
have seen him caught fast in the net of justice.

LEADER: Aegisthus, insult to grief I do detest.
Your plan, yours only, so you boast, this murder.
This piteous death your work. Justice still lives.
Your time will come, be sure, when there shall gather
from out the town all men to curse—throw stones—

AEGISTHUS: What! A poor oarsman at his lowly
post
deep in the ship, dares speak threats to the master?
Such words from you to me? Ah—you are old.
Gray hairs find learning bitter yet they must be taught
to be discreet, and bonds and hunger pain
are admirable teachers—physicians truly
to help the old to wisdom. You have eyes
and do not see things? Why kick
against the pricks? Your hurt alone—no more.

LEADER: [Turning from him to Clytemnestra] O
woman, waiting, watching in the house
for an army coming home from war. Their captain
came.
His bed you shamed—his death contrived, O woman.

AEGISTHUS: These too are words that shall be paid
with tears.
The opposite to Orpheus' tongue is yours.
He led all things by his enchanting song.
Your silly talk, that can but irritate,
shall lead you where you would not be.
You will be milder soon.

LEADER: You, master here in Argos—you, who
planned
a death and never dared to do it?

AEGISTHUS: To trick him was his wife's part. That
was clear.
All knew I was his enemy of old.
His goods are mine now. With gold a man can
rule.
I shall make trial of the people. Yoke
and heavily him who will not obey.
I'll have no trace-horse full of barley, running riot.
Hunger and hateful darkness, two who dwell
together, soon will see him tamed.

LEADER: Shame on your coward's soul who did not
kill
the man yourself but left him to a woman.
Oh, vile pollution of this land, polluting
the very gods. But yet Orestes lives.
Oh, may kind fortune lead him home again
to victory, to vengeance, on these two.

AEGISTHUS: Thus to speak, then, you are minded,
thus to do?

You shall be taught.
Ho there, men-at-arms, old comrades. Work for you
and to your hand.
[Spearsmen rush in and threaten the Chorus]

LEADER: Up, men all. Each one stand ready. Draw
now.
Sword in hand. Stand firm.

AEGISTHUS: Hand on hilt, I too am ready. Death
be judge. I am content.

LEADER: Death! Your word. We take the omen.
Gladly welcome it for you.
[A fight is imminent. Before they can come to
blows Clytemnestra hurries down the steps and
stands between the two bands. She turns to
Aegisthus]

CLYTEMNESTRA: Peace, oh peace, my best-beloved
No more evil now. Enough.
What is done will bring hard reaping, heavy harvest-
ing, not good.
Trouble in full measure here is. No more blood for
you and me.
Go your ways, old men, in honor. To your homes
now, everyone.
Destiny determined all here. Yield before you suffer
harm.
What we did was what was fated. Oh, if this could
be the end.
Sorely smitten though I am, brought low beneath
God's heavy hand,
these things I can bear. No more. A woman's word,
if men will hear.

AEGISTHUS: Let them go in peace, and safely sow
a crop of evil speech?
Casting sneering words against me, tempting for-
tune? Dangerous.
I forgive this insult—outrage? I their king now?
They shall learn—

LEADER: Evil men are never those the Argive breed
will cringe before—

AEGISTHUS: Wait. The days are near when I will
send for you and you will come.
[He turns away, lowering his spear]

LEADER: Never—if fate guides Orestes to come
home at last—at last.

AEGISTHUS: Well I know myself the exile's food to
feed the spirit—hope.

LEADER: Keep your course. Wax fat. Dishonor
justice. You have power—now.

AEGISTHUS: Know that folly always suffers. You
will pay full price to me.

LEADER: Cocks crow loudest to their hens—and
braggarts do the like, men say.

CLYTEMNESTRA: Dogs will bark. Who cares to
listen? What avails this foolish speech?
You and I are lords here. We two now will order
all things well.

Sophocles

(496?–406 B.C.)

Marathon and Salamis were remote memories when Sophocles reached the peak of his powers. Athens, having reaped the fruits of its leadership in the Persian wars, was the emporium and, in effect, the political capital of the Greek peninsula, as well as an overseas empire. The major part of Sophocles' long life, which virtually spanned the fifth century B.C., coincided with the high noon of Athens' glory as the cultural center of the Greek city-states. More than any other of the classic dramatists he reflected the taste and achievements of the Periclean age, perhaps the most luminous interval in the history of civilization.

Sophocles, the son of a prosperous armorer whom we should nowadays call a munitions magnate, was born in 496? B.C. at "White Colonus," a beautiful village about a mile northwest of Athens. Endowed with unusual physical beauty, a versatile actor until his voice proved too weak for the vast theatre of Dionysus, and a social lion, Sophocles enjoyed the favor of his city as few men did. He even attained the distinction of being made a more or less honorary general of the Athenian army. With characteristic good fortune, he won first prize in competition with the great Aeschylus the very first time he entered a play in the Athenian contest. He was twenty-eight at the time, and during the next sixty years he received more first prizes than any of his compeers. Sophocles became the legendary happy man of Hellas, and he was eulogized as such by his countrymen.

It is of course impossible to accept the idyllic Sophoclean legend without strong qualification. Sophocles lived to see the city he loved suffer many defeats at the hands of the Spartan Philistines. He died only a short time before Athens was crushed and Athenian democracy abolished. There is also an account of a somewhat sordid lawsuit between the aged Sophocles and his children. Certainly his plays reveal an acute awareness of human error and unreason, of the abysses of evil and suffering into which men can sink, and of the general instability of life. His *Ajax* is a painful study in humiliation, madness, and suicide. *Electra* presents an unrelenting picture of primitive vengeance. *Oedipus the King* is a tragedy of parricide, incest, suicide, and self-mutilation. And the *Antigone*, which culminates in a triple suicide, presents a welter of passion and conflict. Sophocles' serenity, which took the form of a love of order and moderation, seems to have been mingled later with a large measure of disenchantment. Unlike Aeschylus, he does not appear to have read any specific moral meaning into the universe; chance or blind fate is supreme in his world. "Human life," declares one of his choruses, "even in its utmost splendor hangs on the edge of a precipice."

Sophocles is nonetheless a true humanist. His work distills the quintessence of the tragic spirit because it is affirmative instead of depressing, exalting rather than debasing. Man's destiny may be horrible and men may often terrify us with their behavior. But man rises above his fate and his evil by the standards he acknowledges and uses in judging himself—namely, by the ideals he holds, no matter how miserably he violates them in practice when moved by the passions. Man is capable of arriving at self-knowledge and spiritual awakening. Men are shown accepting responsibility for their actions; they choose to follow a certain course at some point in the plot, they suffer the consequences, and they even acquiesce in their destiny. At the very least, they ultimately discern a pattern—an order or design—in their destiny; and this, too, frees them from total enslavement to their miseries. In one way or another, Sophocles' characters lift us above the estate of pain, of which they themselves are so keenly conscious, belonging as they do, in Edith Hamilton's felicitous phrase, to "the only genuine aristocracy known to the world—the aristocracy of passionate souls." When their struggle and suffering come to an end, they somehow leave the world, as John Mason Brown says, spiritually cross-ventilated. Sophocles' tragedies are, as Nietzsche was the first to point out, "the inevitable consequences of a glance into the secret and terrible things of nature. They are shining spots intended to heal the eye which dire night has seared." This noble playwright's hard-earned serenity is the direct reward of profoundly tragic insight.

It is the mark of Sophocles' genius that he was capable of disillusionment without cynicism or despair. He never surrendered his ideal of the dignity of man and his view of the idealizing power of art. The horror of life could not obscure for him its beauty and splendor. The cacophony of the universe could not submerge its natural and man-made music. As Matthew Arnold declared, Sophocles "saw life steadily, and saw it whole." In *Philoctetes* and *Oedipus at Colonus*, the fever of passion is finally stilled in resignation and magical wonder, and in all his surviving plays the humanity and the reasoning powers of man are set up against the anarchic power of instinct and nature. Man can create beauty and justice in his small world by ordering his own soul and learning to shun excess in any form—even an overzealous search for truths better left hidden, excessive remorse, and too great a despair when fate proves horrible. This, indeed, appears to be his attitude in *Oedipus the King.* In suffering, seemliness is all. And seemliness is, to a great degree, moderation. Oedipus is nobly immoderate in pursuing the facts of his case, and wrongly immoderate in blinding himself when he discovers them.

In a sense, Sophocles may strike modern Western man, who is romantically disposed in his view of life whether he be a minor poet or a businessman, as a cold and somewhat Philistine personality. But Sophocles gives this impression not because he is incapable of sympathy and warmth but because his cultivated mind and spirit—so Greek or Periclean that it will always be considered representative of ideal classicism—recoil from the "too large" and the "too much." He is the antithesis of the Faustian spirit. Edith Hamilton calls attention to the line in one of the choruses of *Antigone* which (literally translated) declares that "nothing that is vast enters into the life of mortals without a curse." The thought is very Greek, and it appears to have affected the Greeks' esthetic as well as moral sense. The temples are small and, with one known exception, the statues of gods are no larger than men. (Colossal statuary appeared later, in the Hellenistic period, after the conquests of the Macedonian Alexander the Great, when Asiatic and Egyptian influences were strong.) Edith Hamilton reminds us that "all Greek words that mean literally *boundless, indefinite, unlimited* have a bad connotation. The Greek liked what he could see clearly. The infinite was unpleasant to him." It also carried him too far beyond the humanly mensurable. As one of Sophocles' contemporaries, the humanistic philosopher Protagoras, announced, "Man is the measure of all things." And man is "small."

Nature is vast, and passion, which is a force of nature, exceeds humanistic bounds. Reason must rule man's course in life; it alone can establish and maintain boundaries of safety and sanity—provided of course that reason teaches us, as it did not teach Oedipus, to be reasonable, and provided, too, that reason teaches us, as it did not teach Oedipus, to recognize its limitations and not to expect it to unriddle every mystery. There are, as Oedipus learned to his dismay, tragic snares even in unqualified reliance upon our rational faculties, for these do not exercise unlimited control over the universe. Each of Sophocles' tragedies is precipitated by an access of human unreason and by some excess. Yet a Sophoclean hero is not ignominious; he is tragic. Oedipus is the victim of his noblest qualities: his self-confidence, masterfulness, and intensity. He may be snared by fate, but his self-destruction results from an excess of greatness in his constitution. If man consistently led a life of reason—which is not the

same thing as faith in the power of rationalism to solve all problems—perhaps there would be no such thing as tragedy.

There is always a supreme place for art in Sophocles' philosophy; substituting order for chaos of the emotions and of circumstance, art brings us the sustaining sweetness and light of beauty. Setting himself a craftsman's rather than a visionary's task, Sophocles cultivated dramaturgy more skillfully and earnestly than any of his contemporaries, maintaining balance in the structure of his work and insisting upon harmony between feeling and expression. To him belongs the credit for advancing Greek tragedy furthest as a dramatic art independent of primitive ritual. He reduced the choral narrative and lyric passages of classic tragedy, strove for concise and natural dialogue, added a third actor to enlarge the scope of dramatic complication, and ordered his situations on the principle of progressive action. Without scaling the lyric heights of Aeschylus or attempting the psychological and intellectual subtleties of Euripides, Sophocles created the most completely realized dramatic works of the ancient world.

Of the three great tragedies which Sophocles devoted to Oedipus and his family, the *Antigone,* produced in 441 B.C., was the first to be written. Thematically, however, it is the concluding part of his great saga of the Theban dynasty. The story begins in *Oedipus the King,* in which Oedipus discovers that he is a parricide and the husband of his mother. Then we see him finding hospitality and a grave in an Attic village, in the exquisite *Oedipus at Colonus,* the last play Sophocles lived to write. We witness, in *Antigone,* the tragedy of Oedipus' daughter, whose integrity and strength of will resemble her father's. Her two brothers have quarreled over their right to Oedipus' throne and slain each other, and power passes into the hands of their uncle Creon. Antigone defies Creon's verdict against the burial of the brother who laid siege to the city of Thebes and goes to her death, ending the immortal chronicle that Sophocles left as a legacy from himself and Athens.

The singular power of *Oedipus the King,* too overwhelming to require extended explication, has not faded after nearly twenty-four centuries. A memorable Old Vic production, with Laurence Olivier playing Oedipus, proved this to New York audiences shortly after the conclusion of the Second World War. This tragedy is a masterpiece of suspense, dramatic development, tragic irony, and characterization. One has every reason to marvel at the architectonics of the work, as well as at the power of the lean dialogue. We should be grossly in error, however, if we overlooked the poetry of the play, not only in its choruses but in its interweaving imagery of sight and blindness at various levels of meaning and in its formalism. The play is, in a sense, a rite dedicated to the mystery of human fate. Oedipus is a sacrifice to the dark powers, and for such a sacrifice the pattern of individual action interspersed with choral recitation, song, and dance movement is proper and significant.

A policy of containment is also served by the choral structure and by Sophocles' economical artistry. The coincidences that tangled Oedipus' life are excluded from the play. Here we have only the final result—the drama of discovery that moves with relentless logic, revealing the kind of man to whom the horror happened and locating the roots of his destiny in his character. In all respects, the artistic restraint of the formal pattern and of Sophocles' writing compensate for the "too much"—that is, the extreme anguish and horror—of the subject matter. Notable, too, are the tact and justice with which Oedipus is treated: If the evil that befell him is, in any ultimate sense, inexplicable (and Sophocles makes no attempt to explain it here), Oedipus remains nonetheless an extremely active sufferer. He may be the pawn of fate, but he is not its puppet.

He emerges from the pit dug for him by mystic powers or by "crass casualty," as Thomas Hardy would have said, a strong and impressive individual, willing to assume even more responsibility for his situation than we would assign to him, acquiescing in his further destiny, and worrying at the end for others, his daughters, rather than for himself. The reverberations that the legend can start in our unconscious minds are terrifying, and the fear runs deep into the primal self. As Sophocles treats his theme, nothing is spared us—neither the horror of incest nor that of the self-mutilation—which Freudians would call a symbolic form of castration. Nevertheless, the sorry story does not sully the quintessential man who is called Oedipus. An unmistakable magnificence lights him down his dark path, and through him the entire race of man is dignified. *Oedipus the King* is a full triumph of artistic power over the anarchy of life and a vindication of the healing and saving power of tragic art. Aristotle rightly considered Sophocles' play the ideal tragedy.

OEDIPUS THE KING

By Sophocles

AN ENGLISH VERSION BY JOHN GASSNER[1]

CHARACTERS

OEDIPUS, *King of Thebes*

A PRIEST OF ZEUS

CREON, *brother-in-law of Oedipus and Jocasta's brother*

TEIRESIAS, *blind prophet or seer of Thebes*

JOCASTA, *Queen of Thebes, wife of Oedipus and widow of Laius, the former king*

A MESSENGER FROM CORINTH, *an old shepherd*

A SHEPHERD, *formerly a slave in the palace of Thebes*

A SERVANT FROM THE PALACE, *who acts as a second messenger*

CHORUS, *senators or elders of the Theban state*

NONSPEAKING CHARACTERS

SUPPLIANTS, *old men, youths, and children*

ANTIGONE } *daughters of Oedipus and Jocasta*
ISMENE }

ATTENDANTS, SERVANTS, SUPPLIANTS

SCENE—*The royal palace of Thebes.*

In front of the columns, Suppliants *of various ages sit around the altars holding wreaths of branches.* Priests *stand among them, and at the main altar*

[1] With revisions suggested by Professor Dwight Durling.

The dialogue has been rendered in free verse in order to convey the lean and dramatic (occasionally even deliberately flat) quality of the original. I have tried to arrive at a simple, forthright, and stage-worthy style. I have also attempted to employ a language more direct than is usual in the old translations, closer to idiomatic speech, but still somewhat heightened. The choral odes are rendered in the irregular pattern of the original strophes and antistrophes. An attempt has been made to balance strophe and antistrophe by giving them the same number of lines and by making each successive line of the antistrophe approximate the length of the equivalent line of the strophe. (No rhyme has been used, but neither is there any rhyme in classic Greek verse.) The length of the line throughout this version is determined by the sense—whether literal, poetic, or dramatic. The break comes where it seems to me the breath would break, the voice would pause, or the inflection would rise with the sense, the feeling, the tone, or the tension. The reader should also note that the word Chorus is used both for a single speaker, the Leader of the Chorus in the dialogue, and for the Chorus as a whole reciting in unison. In staging the play, the director may, of course, take some liberties. Thus, if I were to stage the play, on page 49, during Oedipus' last appearance, I m ght consider employing two individual speakers—the Leader of the Chorus and a second, less sympathetic Elder of the Chorus. Then, again, I might decide to reject this procedure, in order to give the Chorus a strict unity and make it representative of "community." (See Francis Fergusson's *The Idea of a Theatre,* Chapter I, pp. 13–41. Although disagreement is possible with some of the points Mr. Fergusson raises, his chapter is the most searching analysis of *Oedipus the King* I have read.)—J. G.

stands the most reverend of these, the Priest of Zeus. *And now* Oedipus, *King of Thebes, comes out majestically through the central door.*

OEDIPUS: Children, youngest brood of Cadmus[2] the old,
why do you sit here with branches in your hand
while the air is heavy with incense
and the town rings with prayer and lament?
Deeming it unfit to hear the reason from a messenger,
I, Oedipus, on whom men rely,
have come myself to hear you out.
[*Turning to the* Priest of Zeus]
Tell me, venerable priest of Zeus,
you who can speak for these,
what do you want or fear?
Be sure I shall gladly help,
for hard of heart would I be
to have no pity for such suppliants.

PRIEST: Oedipus, ruler of my land,
you see our generations at the altar—
the nestlings here too weak to fly far,
the priesthood bent with age,
and the chosen young.
The rest sit with branches in the market-place,
before the twin altars to Pallas,
and by Ismenus who answers with fire.[3]
Our city—you yourself have seen!—
can no more lift prow out of the wave of death.
The blight lies on the blossom,
on the herds in pasture,
and on the women barren in labor.
The god who carries fire through the land,
the ferocious plague,
swoops down to empty the home of Cadmus
while the Grave grows more opulent with our weeping.

[2] The legendary founder of Thebes.
[3] An oracle which made signs by means of fire.

We, these children and I, do not call you a god.
But you are first among men
in the common chances of men,
and even when the contest
is with more than man.
For you came to Thebes and lifted the toll
we paid to the songstress sphinx:
we could tell you nothing, and no one taught you;
yet you prevailed—with the help, we think, of a
    god.
Now, Oedipus, the greatest of mortals,
we supplicate you to be savior again,
whether with the help of some god who whispers
    to you
or by your own wisdom as a man;
for I have learned this thing—
when men have proved themselves by former deeds,
they also prevail in present counsel.
Best of mortals,
lift up our estate once more.
Live up to your noble fame,
for now the land you rescued
calls you Savior.
Never let us remember of your reign
that as high as we rose with you
so low we were cast down thereafter.
Oh no, raise up our fallen city,
that it fail no more,
and bring us good fortune again.

If you are to rule this land, as you rule it now,
surely it is better to be the lord of men
than of a waste;
nor walled town nor ship has any worth
when no men live in it.
    OEDIPUS: Oh my poor children, known,
well known to me what brought you here!
I know you suffer,
and yet none among you can suffer as I:
Your pain comes to each one alone for himself,
and for none else, but I suffer for all:
for the city, for myself, and for you.
You do not rouse me, then, as one sunk in sleep;
be sure I have given many tears to this
and gone wide ways in the wandering of thought.
But the only recourse I knew I took:
I sent Menoeceus' son, Jocasta's brother,
to the Pythian house,[4] to hear from Apollo
by what word or deed I am to deliver you.
It troubles me to count the days Creon has been
    gone,
but when he comes I am no man of worth
if I fail to perform what God has ordered.
    PRIEST: In good season you have spoken, lord;
your servants signal that he is near.
    [Oedipus turns to see Creon approaching]
    OEDIPUS: Yes, and his face is bright.
O King Apollo, may the words he brings shine on
    us, too.

[4] The temple of Apollo.

    PRIEST: He brings good news; else he would not
    come
crowned with sprigs of bay.
    OEDIPUS: He can hear me now: Prince and kins-
    man,
Menoeceus' son, what news from the God?
    [Creon approaches Oedipus]
    CREON: Favorable news.—For even trouble hard
    to bear
is well, all well, if the issue be good.
    OEDIPUS: What says the oracle?
So far your words give us cause
for neither confidence nor despair.
    CREON: If you will hear me now, I am ready;
else let us go within.
    OEDIPUS: No, speak before them,
for the grief I bear is most for them.
    CREON: What the God has told I will then tell.
Phoebus, our lord, speaks plainly:
Drive out, he says, pollution,
defilement harbored in the land;
drive it out nor cherish it
until it prove past cure.
    OEDIPUS: And by what rite?
    CREON: Banish the guilty man, or let blood be
    shed
for bloodshed, since blood it is that brought
this storm of death upon the state.
    OEDIPUS: Who is the man for whom God decrees
    doom?
    CREON: King Laius was lord of Thebes before
    you held the helm—
    OEDIPUS: I know of him by hearsay;
I never knew him.
    CREON: He was slain.
The God commands punishment
for those who slew the King.
    OEDIPUS: And where are they? Where shall be
    found
the dim trace of an ancient crime?
    CREON: In this land, the God says.
What is sought for can be found;
only unheeded things escape.
    OEDIPUS: Was it in house, in field, or abroad
that Laius met death?
    CREON: To Delphi[5] he went who never came
    home.
    OEDIPUS: Had he companions who witnessed the
    deed?
    CREON: No, they perished, all but one
who fled; and of what he saw he had
but one thing to report as certain.
    OEDIPUS: The one thing might be the means
to discover all; if but a small beginning were made—
    CREON: He said that many robbers fell on them;
the deed was not done by a single hand.
    OEDIPUS: And how could robbers dare so far
unless bribed by someone in the city?
    CREON: We thought of that, ourselves.

[5] I.e., on a pilgrimage to Apollo's temple at Delphi.

But Laius was dead, and our trouble,
our *other* trouble, distracted us.
  OEDIPUS: What trouble was so great to hinder your
    search
when royalty was slain?
  CREON: The riddling sphinx.[6] It made us seek
an instant remedy for the instant thing
and let dark things go.
  OEDIPUS: Well, I will start afresh
and make dark things clear.
Right was Phoebus and right are you
to give this care to the dead man's cause,
and, as is meet, you shall find me
with you avenging country and God besides.
Not on behalf of one unknown but in my own
    interest,
as King, will I erase this stain,
for one who slew the old might slay the new;
I help myself in helping Laius.
Come, then, my children, rise from the altar-steps
and lift up your suppliant boughs,
and let the rest of Cadmus' seed be summoned here.
Say, nothing will be untried;
say, I will make a cleansing
and find for all Thebes, as God wills,
prosperity or grief.
  [Oedipus *goes into the palace with* Creon]
  PRIEST: My children, let us rise!
We came for this that the King promises,
and may God Phoebus, sender of the word, deliver
    us.
  [The Chorus, *composed of the* Elders of Thebes,
    now enters]
  CHORUS (1ST STROPHE): Oh, message of Zeus,
    whose words are sweet,
with what strange portent have you come
from the golden seat of Pytho[7]
to our glorious Theban home?
I am stretched as on the rack, and terror shakes me,
O Delian Healer,[8] to whom our pleas for help are
    sent,
and I stand in fear of what you may bring to pass:
new thing unknown or doom renewed in the cycle
    of years.
Speak to me of golden hope,
Immortal Voice.
  CHORUS (1ST ANTISTROPHE): I call upon you first,
    divine Athene, daughter of Zeus!
Then on your sister Artemis, the guardian of our
    land
who sits on her throne of fame

above the circled precinct of our market-place;
and on Phoebus, whose darts fly far.
Oh shine forth, averters of fate!
If ever before when destruction struck the state you
    came,
if ever you drove the fire of evil beyond our borders,
come to us now.
  CHORUS (2ND STROPHE): Numberless, alas, the
    griefs I bear,
the plague on all our host,
with no resource of mind a shield for our defense.
The fruit no longer sprung from the glorious land
and no woman rising relieved from birth-labor
by issue of a child.
And one by one you may see
flying away, like birds on swift wing,
life after life that hastens to the Evening Land.
  CHORUS (2ND ANTISTROPHE): By such unnumbered
    death the great town perishes:
unpitied her children lie upon the ground, spreading
    pestilence,
while the young wives and gray-haired mothers
uplift a wailing, some here, some there,
bent over the altar-edge suppliant and moaning.
Prayer to God the Healer rises
but intermingled with lament.
O golden Daughter of Zeus,
send bright-faced deliverance.
  CHORUS (3RD STROPHE): And grant that Ares[9] the
    Destroyer,
who neither with brass shield nor clamor of war
    racks me,
may speed from our land to the caverns of Amphi-
    trite[10]
below the wave
or to the Thracian sea where no haven is,
for whosoever escape the night
may find relief at last when the day-break comes.
O Zeus, Father, who wields the fire-fraught light-
    ning,
destroy Death with your bolt.
  CHORUS (3RD ANTISTROPHE): Next, Lycean King,
    Apollo, I were glad too
that the arrows from your bow-string of woven gold
winged forth in their might to confound the foe.
Yes, and that the beams of fire
Artemis[11] sends through the hills brought aid.
And I call the God
whose hair is bound with gold, flushed Bacchus
    with Maenad band,[12]
to draw near with his torch and defeat
the god unhonored among the gods.[13]
  [Oedipus *returns*]
  OEDIPUS: You are at prayer, and in answer,

[6] The Sphinx was a monster, half woman and half lion, who waylaid all passers and destroyed them after they failed to answer the riddle she proposed. For answering it successfully and causing the monster to destroy itself, Oedipus was rewarded with the throne of Thebes and the hand of Jocasta, the widowed queen of the city.
[7] Apollo—i.e., from Delphi, the seat of the oracle.
[8] Apollo.

[9] Mars, the war god.
[10] Wife of Poseidon and goddess of the sea.
[11] Diana, goddess of the moon.
[12] The women worshipers of Bacchus or Dionysus were called Bacchantes or Maenads.
[13] Ares, or Mars, the god of war and destruction.

if you will heed my words
and minister to your own disease,
you may hope for help and win relief.
These words I say who have been a stranger
to your report and to the deed,
for I were not now on the track of it
without your aid.
But made a citizen among you after the deed,
I now proclaim to all of Thebes:
Whoever among you knows the murderer
at whose hand King Laius died,
I command he tell the truth.
For though he fear blame, I say,
exempt shall he be from punishment
and leave the land unhurt,
enduring no other harm.
Or if anyone know the assassin
to be alien, of a foreign state,
let him not be silent,
for I will pay him a reward
and favor him forever.

But if he hold back from fear,
attempt to screen another or himself,
give ear to what I intend:
I order that no one in this land I rule
give shelter or speak word to the murderer
whoever he be,
nor make him partner to a prayer or a sacrifice,
nor serve him with water for his hand
in lustral rite.
And I command that the slayer
whosoever he be,
whether he alone be guilty or had confederates,
evilly, as he is evil, wear out his life
unblest in misery.
And for myself I pray:
If knowingly I succor him
as inmate of my household,
let me too endure the curse invoked on you.

This charge I lay upon you:
Make good my words—
for my sake,
for the sake of the God,
and for the sake of the land
so blasted and barren under wrathful Heaven.
For even without ordinance from God,
it was not right to leave the guilt unpurged
when one so noble, your own king, was dead.
You must search it out!
And now, since I hold the power he once held,
possess his marriage bed and wife,
and since, had his hope of issue not miscarried,
he and I would have had children from one mother
and so been bound by more ties still,
except that Fate came heavy upon his head—
on this account I, as for my own father,
will leave nothing unattempted
to ferret out those who shed his blood.
I will fight for the scions of Labdacus and Polydorus

and for the earlier ancestors, Cadmus and Agenor of
old.[14]
And for those who disobey me, I pray
the gods give them no harvest of earth and no fruit
of the womb;
waste be their lot—and a destiny still more dire.
But you, the loyal men of Cadmus who my intent
approve,
may Justice, our ally, and all the gods
forever proffer you their blessings.
    CHORUS: As you have put an oath upon me,
on oath, my King, I say:
I am not the slayer, nor knew him who slew.—
From Phoebus, himself, who set the quest, should
come the answer.
    OEDIPUS: You speak well,
but against their will
no man has the power to constrain the gods.
    CHORUS: I would propose, if I may, a second
course—
    OEDIPUS: —and I should listen to a third course,
too,
if it were proposed.
    CHORUS: Teiresias above all men
is known to see what Phoebus sees.
The clearest answer could come from him,
if one sought it.
    OEDIPUS: Not even this chance have I over-
looked:
Advised by Creon, I have twice sent for the seer;
I am perturbed he has not come.
    CHORUS: There are other reports besides:
faint, fading rumors to explore.
    OEDIPUS: What rumors? I am ready to weigh
every tale.
    CHORUS: Certain wayfarers, it was said, killed
Laius.
    OEDIPUS: That, too, I heard,
but he who saw it is himself unseen.
    CHORUS: But if he has a grain of fear in his heart
he will step forth, knowing your curse.
    OEDIPUS: My words will not frighten a man
who was not afraid to perform the deed.
    CHORUS: Then there is one to expose him, and he
comes:
Here they bring the godlike prophet
in whom truth lives.
    [Teiresias, led by a Boy, arrives]
    OEDIPUS: Teiresias, whose mind can search all
things,
the utterable and the unutterable alike,
secret of heaven and what lies on earth,
though you cannot see, you must know how the
plague
afflicts the land.
Our prophet, in you alone we find a protector,
the only savior.
Perhaps you have not been told,

[14] Labdacus was the father of Laius; Agenor was the
father of Cadmus; Cadmus was the father of Polydorus.

but Phoebus, when consulted, declared
we must discover the slayers of Laius
and slay or drive them out.
Do not, then, spare augury of birds
or any other form of divination you possess
to save yourself and the state,
and to save me and all who are defiled by the deed.
Man's noblest deed is to bring aid by what means
  he has,
and you alone can help.

  TEIRESIAS: O fate! How terrible it is to know
When nothing good can come of knowing.
I knew of the matter but it slipped out of mind;
else I would not have come.

  OEDIPUS: What now? How can you regret your
    coming?

  TEIRESIAS: Let me go home. You will bear your
    burden easier then,
and I mine, too.

  OEDIPUS: What! You have not spoken loyally or
    kindly,
giving no answer with strange words.

  TEIRESIAS: Because your own words miss the mark,
do not expect mine to hit it safely.

  OEDIPUS: For the love of God, if you know,
do not turn away.
We bend before you; we are your suppliants.

  TEIRESIAS: You ask only because you know noth-
    ing.
I will not reveal my grief—I call it mine, not yours.

  OEDIPUS: What do you know and refuse to tell?
You are a traitor if you allow the state to be
    destroyed.

  TEIRESIAS: Since I want no harm for you or myself,
why do you ask vain questions?
I will tell you nothing.

  OEDIPUS: Worst of traitors,
you would rouse a stone to wrath!
Will you never speak out, be stirred by nothing,
be obstinate to the end?

  TEIRESIAS: You see the fault in me but not in
    yourself.
So it is me you blame?

  OEDIPUS: Who would not take offense
hearing you flout the city?

  TEIRESIAS: It will come of itself—
the thing that must,
although I breathe no word.

  OEDIPUS: Since it must come,
surely you can tell me what it is!

  TEIRESIAS: I say no more. Storm at me if you
    will,
you'll hear no more.

  OEDIPUS: And being in such anger, I, for my
    part,
will hold back nothing, be sure.
I'll speak my thought:
Know then I suspect you of having plotted the
    deed yourself
and of having done it

short of killing with own hand;
and if you had eyesight,
I would declare the doing too your own.

  TEIRESIAS: Was it so?
Well then I charge you to abide by your own decree
and from this day on speak neither to me nor
    them,
being *yourself* the defiler of the land.

  OEDIPUS: So this is your taunt!
And you expect to go scot-free?

  TEIRESIAS: I *am* free,
for the truth has made me so.

  OEDIPUS: Tell me at least who is in league with
    you?
For surely this lie was not of your own making!

  TEIRESIAS: Yours is the blame,
who spurred me on to speak against my will.

  OEDIPUS: Speak again:
Perhaps I did not understand you.

  TEIRESIAS: Did you not understand at first hear-
    ing?
Or are you bent on provoking me again?

  OEDIPUS: No, I did not grasp your meaning.
Speak again!

  TEIRESIAS: I say that *you* are the murderer—
he whom you seek.

  OEDIPUS: Now at last, now you have spoken
    twice,
you shall rue your words.

  TEIRESIAS: Shall I speak on
and incense you more?

  OEDIPUS: Say what you will; it will be said in
    vain.

  TEIRESIAS: I say, then, you have lived in unsus-
    pected shame
with one who is your nearest,
and you do not yet see the plight you are in.

  OEDIPUS: And you expect to go on ranting
without smarting for it?

  TEIRESIAS: Yes, certainly, if there is strength in
    truth.

  OEDIPUS: Why, so there is—
except for you; you have no truth,
blind as you are in ears, in mind—and eyes.

  TEIRESIAS: Wretched man,
you utter taunts that everyone will soon heap
upon none other than yourself.

  OEDIPUS: Night, an endless night is your prison;
you cannot hurt me or any man who can see the
    sun.

  TEIRESIAS: No, it is not your doom to be hurt by
    me;
Apollo's is the work ahead,
and Apollo's work is enough.

  OEDIPUS: Are these inventions yours or Creon's?

  TEIRESIAS: Creon is not your enemy;
you are your own foe.

  OEDIPUS: Oh riches and dominion and the craft
surpassing others' craft in an envied life,
how deep is the source of jealousy

if for the sake of the power the city put into my
  hand,
a gift unsought by me.
trusty Creon, my old friend, creeps by stealth upon
  me,
seeks to unseat me,
and has suborned this quack and scheming juggler
who has an eye only for gain but whose divining skill
  is blind!

Yes, blind, I say:
For tell me, my prophet, when have you ever seen
  clear?
Where was your deliverance when the monster-
  woman wove dark song?
Surely the unriddling of the riddle
was not for a chance traveler like me
but for you with your skill of divination!
Yet no help came from you, neither from watching
  the flight of birds
nor talking to any god.

No, *I* came,
I the ignorant who had no miraculous aid.
I, by my own wit, made answer, untaught of birds,
and I stopped the monster's breath.
And now it is me you would thrust out,
thinking to stand by Creon's side when he takes the
  throne.
But *I* think you will regret your proffered purge for
  the land,
you and that other plotter;
and, dotard, you would have been punished already
if I had no regard for age however arrogant.

  CHORUS: O, Oedipus, to our mind,
both this man's words and your own
have been spoken in anger.
Our need is not for these recriminations,
but for guidance on how best to abide by God's
  command.

  TEIRESIAS: King though you be,
the right of reply, at least, belongs to us both;
I am your peer,
for I am Apollo's servant, not yours.
Nor will you find me in Creon's service.
And I tell you, who have taunted me with blindness,
you that have sight
do not see your plight, where you dwell,
and with whom.
You do not even know what stock you came from,
nor that, unknowing, you have been
foe to your own kin
both above the earth
and below, among the shades.
You, the double curse of mother and father,
shall leave your land one day in painful haste
with darkness on the eyes that now see so straight.

And what are the places that shall not hear your
  cry,

what Cithaeron-crag shall not resound with it soon,
when you have learned what marriage-song
wafted you on a fair voyage to a foul haven
in your own house!
What multitudinous evils you cannot guess
shall level you down to yourself
and to your own brood of children!
So heap all your scorn on Creon and my words,
but know this: no man shall be crushed
more utterly than you.

  OEDIPUS: Is this to be endured? Go quickly,
and my curse go with you.
Back from these walls of my home,
back to your own.

  TEIRESIAS: I should never have come had you not
    sent for me.

  OEDIPUS: You would have waited long to be
    called
if I had known you for a fool.

  TEIRESIAS: Yes, I am a fool to you
whose parents thought me wise.

  OEDIPUS: Parents, you say? Don't go!
Who were they? Who gave me birth?

  TEIRESIAS: This day shall give you both birth and
    ruin.

  OEDIPUS: Riddles, always riddles! You darken
    everything.

  TEIRESIAS: Does that disturb you
who were so adept at unriddling?

  OEDIPUS: Yes, cast it in my teeth,
that which lifted me high—

  TEIRESIAS: —and will soon bring you low!
Your fortune, Oedipus, has been your misfortune.

  OEDIPUS: If misfortune must befall me
for having saved the city,
I say I do not care.

  TEIRESIAS: Well, I will go then.
You, boy, lead me home.

  OEDIPUS: Yes, let him take you out of my
    sight.
Here you are only a hindrance and a trouble,
and when you are gone you will vex me no more.

  TEIRESIAS: I will go, having said what I came to
    say,
and not because I fear your anger, for you possess
no power to destroy me. But I tell you this now,
    King:
The man you have sought with threats and proclamation,
that man is here!
Believed to be of foreign birth, he shall soon be
  found
Theban-born, and he shall take no joy in the discovery.
Blind, he who still has sight,
a beggar, he who is still wealthy,
he shall turn his face toward an alien land,
tapping the ground before him with a staff.
And he shall be found at once
brother and father to the children in his house,

son and husband to the woman who bore him,
and fellow-sower in the bed of his father,
whom he slew.
Go into your palace and ponder upon all this—
and if I am proved wrong,
henceforth say that I have no skill in prophecy.
　　[Teiresias *departs, led by the* Boy, *while* Oedipus
　　goes into the palace]
　　CHORUS (1ST STROPHE): Who is he whom the
　　　　divine voice of the Delian rock
has pronounced guilty with red hands,
perpetrator of horrors no tongue dare name?
Now is his time to run faster than steeds that gallop
　　with the wind.
For upon him leaps the son of Zeus,[15]
armed with flame of lightning
and followed by the dread unerring Fates
that never tire in pursuit.
　　CHORUS (1ST ANTISTROPHE): For a word but now
　　　　blazed from snow-covered Parnassus
orders us to look for the unknown man who,
hidden in the wild-grown forest, slinks or roams,
fierce as a bull and forlorn, on a joyless path
through cave and crag to avoid
the doom pronounced at earth's central seat.
Yet that never-ending doom continues to follow and
　　to beat wings
over him in pursuit.
　　CHORUS (2ND STROPHE): In truth I am in dread
　　　　with darkest thought
aroused by the seer, the wise,
though I cannot approve or deny what he said.
I do not know what to say,
but I am uneasy with foreboding,
having no clear vision in the present or into the
　　future.
For never in past years or now did I hear
the house of Labdacus had reason
to fear hurt from a son of Polybus[16]
that I should arraign the good repute of Oedipus
to avenge the line of Labdacus for an unknown
　　crime.
　　CHORUS (2ND ANTISTROPHE): True, Zeus indeed
　　　　and Apollo are wise
and know the things of human concern,
but that a mere mortal man, though he be a seer,
can have certain knowledge above mine—
of this there is no clear proof.
One man may surpass another in wisdom,
yet until I see the prophet's word proved true
never will I agree when Oedipus is blamed;
for once the winged maiden[17] came against him
and he showed himself wise by the test and good to
　　the state.
So never shall verdict of mine turn against him to
　　accuse him of crime.
　　[Creon *appears and addresses the* Chorus]

[15] Apollo, or Phoebus.
[16] The supposed father of Oedipus.
[17] The Sphinx.

CREON: My fellow-citizens, having heard that
　　Oedipus makes a charge
against me that is vile, I come here indignant:
if in the present trouble he believes he was wronged
by me in some word or action,
then I willingly forego my term of years to come
rather than bear this blame.
For the rumor, having spread, wrongs me in all
　　respects
if I am considered a traitor by the populace,
by you and by all friends.
　　CHORUS: The reproach came, we think, under the
　　　　stress of anger,
not from the heart.
　　CREON: Has it not been said that I counseled the
　　　　seer to deliver falsehoods?
　　CHORUS: So it was said, though I cannot under-
　　　　stand to what purpose.
　　CREON: Did the king make his charge directly,
with steady eyes and a steadfast mind?
　　CHORUS: That I could not tell; it is my rule not
　　　　to look closely
at what my masters do. But here he is,
the lord of the house.
　　[Oedipus *comes out, in a rage*]
　　OEDIPUS: So, you have come with a bold face to
　　　　my house
who would make yourself assassin of its master
and brazen pilferer of his crown?
Come, tell me, in the name of all the gods,
what cowardice or dotage you found in Oedipus
that you dared to lay a plot against him.
How could you believe I would fail to notice
your creeping upon me by stealth
or, discovering your designs, I would not defend
　　myself?
Now was it not folly, this attempt of yours,
without a following, without a troop of friends, to
　　seize the throne?
It is a thing to be achieved, as you ought to know,
with followers and with support of wealth.
　　CREON: I beg you fairly to hear a fair reply and
　　　　then decide.
　　OEDIPUS: Are you so quick, then, to explain? You
　　　　should be forewarned,
I shall be slow to understand you;
I have found you a malignant enemy.
　　CREON: But hear my explanation—
　　OEDIPUS: Explain but this—this one thing:
Tell me you are not a villain.
　　CREON: You are not wise if you believe
unreasoning obstinacy is good.
　　OEDIPUS: And you are not sane if you believe
kinsmen who wrong kinsmen are not punished.
　　CREON: What you say is just, of course,
but what is my offense?
　　OEDIPUS: Did you or did you not advise me
to send for the canting prophet?
　　CREON: Yes, and I still believe I did right.
　　OEDIPUS: How long ago is it since Laius—

CREON: —since Laius . . . ? I do not understand—

OEDIPUS: —disappeared from men's sight by violence?

CREON: The count of years goes far into the past.

OEDIPUS: This seer of yours, did he practice his craft even then?

CREON: Yes. He was honored, as he is now.

OEDIPUS: Did he mention me at that time even once?

CREON: He did not. Never, certainly, in my presence.

OEDIPUS: And you never searched for the man who died?

CREON: We searched, of course; we discovered nothing.

OEDIPUS: Why did not this wise seer tell his story then?

CREON: It is not my wont to speak of things I do not know.

OEDIPUS: This much at least you know and will declare if you are wise—

CREON: What? If I know, I will make no denial.

OEDIPUS: That if he had not conspired with you, he would never have declared the King was slain by *me!*

CREON: You must know best whether this was said by him; but here I require enlightenment of you as you have required of me.

OEDIPUS: Learn this then: Never shall I be found guilty of the blood of Laius.

CREON: Learn this then! You have my sister to wife?

OEDIPUS: That there is no denying.

CREON: And she has equal rights with you in the state?

OEDIPUS: Yes, and she obtains everything she desires.

CREON: And I as a third owner of the land, am I not the equal of you two?

OEDIPUS: Ah!—and there, in that thought, appears the falseness of your friendship!

CREON: Not if you reason with yourself as I reason! Weigh this first: Would I rather choose burdensome sovereignty like yours and be uneasy with fear than equal power but power shared in untroubled peace? I am not by nature covetous of kingly rule but only of kingly worth, as befits a sober mind.

At present I have all needful things from you and none of your anxieties. But were I the ruler of the city, as you are now, I should have to do many things against my inclination. How would a throne, then, be pleasanter to me than painless sovereignty? I am not yet so bemused to want honors that afford no profit. Every man is my friend now. He greets me, and wishes me well. And whosoever has a boon to ask of you first he speaks with me to favor his cause. Why, then, should I exchange my life for yours? I should have to take leave of sense to want to dethrone you; I have no love for such designs at all, nor could I bear to act with one who plotted them. And for proof of this, first, go to Delphi and inquire if I did not report the oracle as it was given. Next, if you discover I plotted with the seer, seize me and slay me,— and do this, not with your sentence alone, but with mine, here given. But do not place guilt on me by conjecture, lacking all proof. It is not just to judge a bad man good and a good man bad; and to cast away a friend is like throwing away one's own life, which one values most. Ah well! only in time will you learn this thing, for time alone reveals the honest man while a single day is long enough to disclose the knave.

CHORUS: His words ring true, my King. Quick judgment is unsafe.

OEDIPUS: Quick? When a plotter moves against me I must be quick with counterplot; if I delay until he acts, he gains his ends and I miss mine.

CREON: What is it, then, you want? To expel me from my country?

OEDIPUS: By no means: I want your death, not banishment; to teach the world what danger there is in jealousy.

CREON: You speak as one resolved to believe nothing.

OEDIPUS: Because you deserve no belief.

CREON: You talk as one bereft of sense.

OEDIPUS: I have sense enough where my interest lies.

CREON: You should consider my interest too.

OEDIPUS: Never! You are false.

CREON: But if your judgment is mistaken?

OEDIPUS: Be that as it may, I must remain the ruler of this city.

CREON: But not if you rule wrongly.

OEDIPUS: This city is my city!

CREON: Yours only? The city is mine too.

CHORUS: Have done, my lords, have done! Here is Jocasta in good time; I see her coming whose voice will compose your quarrel.

[Jocasta *arrives*]

JOCASTA: Misguided men, for shame,

what has stirred up trouble among you
with strife of tongues while the land is so afflicted?
[*To* Oedipus]
Come into the palace,
and you, Creon, go home, go home;
push no mere nothing into a calamity.

CREON: Sister, your Oedipus threatens me:
he has only to decide whether to drive me from the
     city or kill me!

OEDIPUS: That is true! For I have found him out,
     finding him
conspiring against my person.

CREON: May I never know happiness and die
     accursed by God
if there is any truth in what you charge against
     me!

JOCASTA: Oedipus, in Heaven's name believe him,
first for the awful oath he has sworn by the gods,
and next for my sake and for the sake of all these
     men.

CHORUS: Hear her, our King. With wisdom reflect
     upon this
and be gracious, we pray you. Grant it.

OEDIPUS: What shall I grant?

CHORUS: Accept his word; he was never before
     found in folly,
and his oath is a weighty one.

OEDIPUS: Do you know what you ask?

CHORUS: Yes.

OEDIPUS: Declare it then.

CHORUS: Use no unproved conjecture against the
     man
who has been your friend and who has given his
     oath.

OEDIPUS: Then be very sure you know that in
     asking this
you call destruction or exile upon myself.

CHORUS: Oh no! By God the Sun, who stands
foremost in the heavens,
unblessed and accursed may I be,
cast in utter darkness, my lord,
if I have any such thought!
But the withering of the land wears down my un-
     happy heart
and this new trouble, strife between you,
is too heavy to bear.

OEDIPUS: Then let him go free,
though his freedom work my death or my doom
to be thrust out dishonored from Thebes.
Your lips, not his, have moved me to compassion.
But wherever he is he shall still have my hatred.

CREON: How sullen you are in yielding
and vehement in temper when moved!
Such natures are, not without justice,
the heaviest burden to themselves.

OEDIPUS: Will you not leave in peace and go
     away!

CREON: I will; but though you misjudge me, these
     men know I am innocent.
[Creon *leaves*. Oedipus *stands shaken with rage*]

CHORUS: O Lady, will you take him within?

JOCASTA: I will when I have learned what chanced.

CHORUS: A blind conjecture arose on one side,
bred of rash words;
and on the other side, the sting of injustice
brought strife.

JOCASTA: So both sides were wrong?

CHORUS: We think so.

JOCASTA: What was the story that started this?

CHORUS: Enough, enough!
Let it rest, now it has ended;
our land is vexed enough without it.

OEDIPUS: But do you see where your good purpose
has now carried you in blunting my anger?

CHORUS: King, I have said this before, and I say
     again:
I should be a madman, devoid of counsel, to put away
the man who steered a good course in my country's
     trouble
and who shall yet, may God grant it, lead us again
     to safety.

JOCASTA: In the name of the gods,
husband, I beg of you, what was the tale?
What put you in a rage? Tell me.

OEDIPUS: I will; I honor you more than I honor
     them:
Creon has laid a plot against me.

JOCASTA: Husband, be plainer—

OEDIPUS: He declares I am guilty of the blood of
     Laius.

JOCASTA: So? Did he say he heard it,
or does he claim to know it himself?

OEDIPUS: Neither: *He* keeps his own mouth un-
     soiled;
he made the rogue of a seer his mouthpiece.

JOCASTA: If that is all, prepare yourself to put it
     out of mind
at once. Listen to me and learn
that no one born of woman is capable of divination—
as I myself discovered:

To Laius once came an oracle—
I will not say directly from Apollo,
but from his ministers—
that he should die by the hand of a son
born of him and me.
But you must know that Laius, as reported,
was waylaid by robbers
where three highways meet,
and our child, who should have slain him,
if the oracle was true,
was barely three days old when Laius
pinned its ankles together
and had it cast out by servants
on a pathless mountain.
So Apollo did not bring it to pass
that the child should be the slayer of the man
and that Laius should suffer
the thing he dreaded—
death from the hand of the son.

The oracle was clear, yet was proved false, as you
    see.
So much then for the power of the seers!
What God desires us to know,
be sure he will reveal it himself.
    OEDIPUS: Oh wife, wife!
you cannot know what your report has done to me.
What anguish—
    JOCASTA: What disturbs you now?
    OEDIPUS: I thought I heard you say
Laius was slain where three roads meet—
    JOCASTA: Yes, so the report went and so it goes
    still.
    OEDIPUS: And where is this place, Jocasta?
    JOCASTA: In Phocis.
Two roads, one from Delphi and one from Daulia,
    meet.
    OEDIPUS: How long ago did all this happen?
    JOCASTA: The news was brought to the city
a short time before you became the king.
    OEDIPUS: O Zeus! what fate have you stored up
    for me?
    JOCASTA: What is troubling you?
    OEDIPUS: No! No questions yet! Tell me only
what sort of man was he? How tall was Laius?
How old?
    JOCASTA: He was no longer young—his hair was
    turning white,
and he was tall, his figure not unlike your own.
    OEDIPUS: I am a miserable man.
An ignorant man, Jocasta, I fear
I have laid myself under my own curse.
    JOCASTA: You terrify me, Oedipus. What are you
    saying?
    OEDIPUS: I have a misgiving the seer can see. Just
    that!
But you can make something plainer. Tell me—
    JOCASTA: What? Something makes me tremble,
yet I must answer.
    OEDIPUS: Did Laius have few attendants,
or did he travel with a host, as a prince should?
    JOCASTA: There were five of them, one a herald;
there was one carriage, for the King.
    OEDIPUS: All plain—too plain!
Who told you this, Jocasta?
    JOCASTA: The survivor who returned alone. A
    servant.
    OEDIPUS: Is he still in service?
    JOCASTA: No longer. When he found you king
    here on his return
in the place of Laius,
he touched my hand and petitioned me
to send him to the fields to pasture flocks.
He asked it as one who found himself ill at ease
in the city and would be far from it.
He deserved more than this consideration,
for, as slaves go, he was a worthy man.
I could not refuse his request.
    OEDIPUS: If only we could have him back here
    quickly!

    JOCASTA: He can be brought,
but why do you wish to see him?
    OEDIPUS: I fear, Jocasta, I have already said too
    much;
I must see him first.
    JOCASTA: He shall come, then.
But unburden your heart to me first;
I deserve your confidence.
    OEDIPUS: I shall not keep anything from you
since my forebodings have carried me so far.
In whom should I confide more,
passing through such a peril,
than you, my wife, who are dear to me?

My father, as you know, was Polybus of Corinth,
my mother, Merope, the Dorian,
and I was counted the first in the city.
Then something occurred—a startling thing,
although it should not have put me into such a pas-
    sion:
At the banquetboard, a man in his cups
said I was no true son of my mother and father.
For all my fury I checked my temper,
but the morning after, I went to my parents
and taxed them with it.
Their anger at the fellow who flung the taunt
was so great that I felt reassured;
yet the thing still galled me, for the rumor crept on.
So, unknown to father and mother, I went to Delphi.
Phoebus, it is true, left dark what I came to know,
but his answer was full of other things terrible to
    hear;
I was fated, he said, to defile my mother's bed
and bring forth a progeny intolerable to the light,
and to be my natural father's slayer, too.

So, having heard, I put Corinth far behind me,
thereafter measuring the way where the city lies
by the stars only,
seeking a place where I could never expect
the foretold infamies to be fulfilled.
But as I journeyed on
I found myself upon the very spot where, you say,
    Laius perished.

Worse still, when I was near those three roads,
I saw a herald advancing and a man in a carriage
    drawn by colts;
and both, the man in front and the old man,
wanted to edge me rudely off the road.
Enraged, I struck the man who thrust me aside,
whereupon the seated elder, biding time as I passed
    him,
leaned out and brought his goad with two tooth-
    points
down hard on my head.
I repaid the blow at once,
striking with my staff so hard that with one stroke
I rolled him out of the carriage into the road;
and then with my sword I struck down every man of
    them.

So, if there is reason to connect this nameless man
    with Laius,
you see before you a man more miserable than any
    man before.
For, then, what man could be more hated by the
    gods?—
a man whom no citizen and no stranger in Thebes
    may receive,
whom no man may welcome but must drive out of
    doors.
And none other than I, laid this curse on myself.

And hear me once more: If this is so,
with the hands that slew I pollute the bed
of him who was slain.
Am I not then loathsome and all unclean?

And think of it, it was only to be driven out of
    Thebes
that I had to flee before
in self-banishment, forsake my own people,
and never set foot again in Corinth my native city
lest I be fated to be yoked with my mother
and kill my father, the good Polybus who begot and
    reared me.

Would not a man then speak correctly who in judg-
    ing of this said
that a god of evil is my enemy?
Never, you pure and sacred majesties of Heaven,
    never
may I behold that day. Let me pass out of men's
    sight
before I see myself brought low by a destiny so vile.
    CHORUS: We, too, are fearful, Prince. Yet do not
      lose hope.
Await the man who saw the deed and can reveal all.
    OEDIPUS: Yes, I still hold on to hope until he
      arrives.
    JOCASTA: [*Troubled*] And when—when he ap-
      pears,
what will you ask him?
    OEDIPUS: I will tell you:
If his tale will tally with yours
I am clear at least of *this* disaster.
    JOCASTA: How so? What did you hear me say
that must tally?
    OEDIPUS: You were saying that he spoke of
    robbers.
Why, then, if he still speaks of several men,
I am not the slayer!
One is not the same as *many*.
But if he speaks of one man traveling alone,
then veritably the guilt leans toward me.
    JOCASTA: Of this be assured at least,
so the tale was told by him; he cannot revoke it
when the city, not I alone, heard him tell it so.
Yet even if he shifts from it, of this be sure—
he cannot make the death of Laius square with the
    prophecy.
Plain were Apollo's words:

Laius was to be slain by a son born of me.
And, after all, the poor thing never killed him
but died itself before! so henceforth
I do not mean to look to left or right
for fear of divination.
    OEDIPUS: You have reassured me, I think; yet
      send for the slave, I pray you.
See that it is done.
    JOCASTA: Since you desire this,
I will send someone quickly, to please you, as in
    everything.
And now let us go within.
    [Oedipus *and* Jocasta *go into the palace*]
    CHORUS (1ST STROPHE): Mine be a way of life
      that keeps
the holy purity of word and deed,
prescription of the laws that are sublime,
born in the regions of the sky,
whose only begetter is Olympian Zeus.

No mortal begot the laws
and no forgetfulness shall put them to sleep.
Ever-wakeful, the God lives great in them,
and He never grows old.
    CHORUS (1ST ANTISTROPHE): Pride begets the ty-
      rant,
and Insolence, puffed with vain wealth,
climbs and climbs to the topmost height
only to be flung down to horrible doom
where no foothold serves.
Only ambition that serves the whole state
is ever worthy and propitious,
and only rivalry that benefits all may God,
our defender, never quell.
    CHORUS (2ND STROPHE): But may an evil fate
      afflict
him who in ill-starred pride
proceeds with his arrogance by word or deed,
despising Justice
and the holy images of God.
May he be doomed
who seeks an advantage unfairly
and does not abstain from unholiness,
profaning inviolable things.

When such things are done what mortal may boast
he shall ward off the shafts of God from his life?
When such behavior is honored,
why, then, should we keep our sacred dance?
    CHORUS (2ND ANTISTROPHE): Never to the in-
      violate hearth
at the navel of the world,
nor to Abae's shrine or Olympia
will I go in prayer,
if the oracles are proved untrue
for each man's finger to point at with scorn.
No, Zeus, if you are rightly called King
of the world, let not this issue
leave your ever-deathless hands.

For already men set at nought

the old prophecy for Laius, now faded,
and nowhere does Apollo receive his due honor:
Worship vanishes from the earth.

[Jocasta *comes out of the palace with* Attendants]

JOCASTA: Princes of the land, it occurred to me
to visit the temples of the deities,
bringing in my hand these garlands and this incense.
For Oedipus lends his mind too much to alarms,
nor, like a sober person, measures
a new conjecture by past experience,
but is at the mercy of whoever speaks to him
of terrors at hand. I can do nothing with him.
So to Apollo I mean to go,
to you, Lycean God, to us the nearest,
a suppliant with offerings,
that you afford us some deliverance.
For now we are all frightened, seeing him, Oedipus,
helmsman of our ship, in fright.

[*A* Messenger *appears*]

MESSENGER: Strangers, may I learn of you, where
is the palace
of Oedipus the King? or better, where
is he himself, if you know?

AN ELDER OF THE CHORUS: Stranger, this is his
dwelling
and he is within;
and this lady is the mother of his children.

MESSENGER: May she be blessed in a happy home
since she is his queen.

JOCASTA: May you be blessed too for the kind
greeting.
Say what you have to seek or tell.

MESSENGER: Good news, my lady, to your house
and husband.

JOCASTA: What is your news? And from whom
have you come?

MESSENGER: From Corinth. What I am to say
will please you, if not without some pain.

JOCASTA: What can this mean, a double-faced
report?

MESSENGER: The people of the Isthmus, the
Corinthians,
intend to make him king.

JOCASTA: What! Does not Polybus, the old king,
still rule?

MESSENGER: No longer; he is death's subject in
the pit.

JOCASTA: The father of Oedipus is dead?

MESSENGER: May I be reft of life myself if my
report is untrue.

JOCASTA: [*To an* Attendant] Run, girl; tell your
master instantly.

[*The* Attendant *goes into the palace*]

O oracles of the gods, where are you now?
Oedipus fled long since from the man's presence,
fearing to become his murderer, and instead
the man has died a natural death; he was not killed
by Oedipus

[Oedipus *appears*]

OEDIPUS: [*Anxiously*] Jocasta, dear wife, why have
you sent for me?

JOCASTA: To hear this man speak.
And as you listen, mark well to what a pass
your dark oracles have come.

OEDIPUS: Who is this? And what does he say?

JOCASTA: He comes from Corinth
to report that Polybus, your father, is gone.

OEDIPUS: Is this true? Stranger,
let me have your news from your own mouth!

MESSENGER: To make the report plainer,
I tell you, King, that our king is dead.

OEDIPUS: Oh! Did he die by traitorous assault or by
illness?

MESSENGER: A light thing in the scale of life
brings the old to their rest.

OEDIPUS: Then he died, it seems, of illness.

MESSENGER: Yes, and of the long years he had
lived.

OEDIPUS: [*Triumphantly*] Oh, oh! Why should
one look to the hearth of Pytho
and to the birds that scream overhead
on whose showing I was to slay my father?
He is dead and already under earth,
and I have been here, not there, and have not put
my hand to the spear.—
Unless he died through longing
and in this sense is dead because of me.
So Polybus is gone,
and all those oracles as they stood
have been laid to rest with him in Hades,
and have been proved of no account.

JOCASTA: Did I not foretell all this?

OEDIPUS: You did, but my fear led me astray.

JOCASTA: And so let none of these predictions
weigh you down further.

OEDIPUS: Yet—yet how can I help still dreading my
mother's bed?

JOCASTA: Now, why should a man be so fearful
when he knows that Chance rules everything
and man foreknows nothing on earth?
To have a carefree mind is therefore best.
As for that mother marriage-bed—
have no fear of it, my dear.
Many men before have dreamed of such a marriage,
but he who gives no weight to these fantasies
is most at ease in his life.

OEDIPUS: All that you say would be well
if my mother were not living. But since she is alive
I have reason for my fears.

JOCASTA: Your father's death—does not this allay
them?

OEDIPUS: But my fear concerns the living.

MESSENGER: [*Puzzled*] Who is this, the woman
you dread?

OEDIPUS: Merope, old man, the consort of Polybus.

MESSENGER: But what disturbs you?

OEDIPUS: An oracle from the gods, appalling in
import.

MESSENGER: May it be told?
Or is it unlawful for another to know?

OEDIPUS: I may tell it.
The gods declared that I should marry my mother,
and with my own hands shed the blood of my
  father.
Corinth, my home, has not seen me for no other
  reason:
I have won great happiness here,
yet, you know, it is sweet to see the face of one's
  parents.

MESSENGER: This, then, was the fear that kept you
  away?

OEDIPUS: Old man, I did not want to slay my
  father!

MESSENGER: Why should I not then free you of this
  fear, my King,
since my coming here was well meant?

OEDIPUS: And a good reward would be yours.

MESSENGER: In truth, it was for this I came; mainly
that I should reap some favor on your return to the
  city.

OEDIPUS: [Frantically] Return? Oh no! Never!
I'll never go anywhere near my parents.

MESSENGER: O son, it is plain
you cannot know what you are doing.

OEDIPUS: In what way, old man? In God's name,
  tell me.

MESSENGER: That is, if I understand your reasons.

OEDIPUS: Yes, old man, these reasons hold me
  back—
I fear that Phoebus may somehow prove a true
  prophet.

MESSENGER: You fear to stain yourself with guilt
  through parents?

OEDIPUS: Even so—the thought appalls me.

MESSENGER: Then know your fears to be baseless.

OEDIPUS: But how—if I am their son?

MESSENGER: Because there is no blood-tie.

OEDIPUS: What are you saying? Was not Polybus
  my begetter?

MESSENGER: No more than I who speak to you,
or so much as I, in fact, and no more.

OEDIPUS: How, my own sire no more to me than
  a hireling?

MESSENGER: Yes. He did not beget you, no more
  than I.

OEDIPUS: Then why did he call me his son?

MESSENGER: Know this: he had you as a gift from
  me.

OEDIPUS: And he could love me so much, though
  I came from another's hand!

MESSENGER: His many seasons of childlessness
  drew him to you.

OEDIPUS: Was I an infant you found—or purchased?

MESSENGER: In Cithaeron's wooded valley—there
  I found you.

OEDIPUS: What took you up there?

MESSENGER: I tended flocks on the mountain.

OEDIPUS: You were a shepherd then, wandering
  for hire?

MESSENGER: But your preserver, my son, and I
  came in good time.

OEDIPUS: In good time? What was my plight?

MESSENGER: Your ankles might tell you.

OEDIPUS: Yes, that is an old affliction.

MESSENGER: I loosed you;
your ankles had been pierced and were pinned together.

OEDIPUS: Yes, I have borne a shameful mark on
  them from my cradle.

MESSENGER: And it is from this you bear the
  name of Oedipus
given to you for your swollen feet.[18]

OEDIPUS: Tell me this, by Heaven! Was it done by
  my father—or my mother?

MESSENGER: I have no knowledge of the deed.
He that gave you to me can tell you, I think.

OEDIPUS: What! You had me from another? You
  did not light on me yourself?

MESSENGER: Another shepherd gave you to me.

OEDIPUS: Who was he? Do you know him?

MESSENGER: I think the man belonged to Laius.

OEDIPUS: The king who ruled this city?

MESSENGER: The same. The man was a shepherd
  in his service.

OEDIPUS: Do you know whether he is alive? Can
  I see the man?

MESSENGER: You must know that best who live
  in this land.

OEDIPUS: [Addressing the crowd] Is there anyone
  present
who knows the herdsman of whom he speaks,
who has seen him in pasture or in the city?
If anyone knows, let him answer:
the hour has come for everything to be made
  clear.

CHORUS: The Corinthian speaks of no other, I
  think,
than the peasant you asked to see;
but Jocasta is the one who would know best.

OEDIPUS: Jocasta, do you remember him you sent
  for?
Are he and this herdsman one man?

JOCASTA: [Greatly troubled] Why ask of whom
  the Corinthian speaks?
Give no heed to this—waste no thought on it—
it is of no importance—

OEDIPUS: Importance? Can anything be more important!
With the clue close at hand,
should I not pursue the matter of my parentage
and let it come to light?

JOCASTA: Oedipus, for the sake of all the gods,
if you have any care for your own life, let the old
  things alone;
I am sick of all this—I have had enough!

[18] *Oidipous* (or Oedipus) was taken to mean "swellfoot" or club-foot

OEDIPUS: Have no fear, Jocasta. Even if I am
    proved a slave,
three times a slave, and if my mother were three-
    deep a slave,
you will not be considered a slave too.
    JOCASTA: Dearest, let me persuade you,
I beseech you, no more questions!
    OEDIPUS: Do not beseech me
to let the occasion slide; I must have light!
    JOCASTA: [*Desperately*] I have your interest at
        heart—my fears are for you—
my advice, my dear, is best.
    OEDIPUS: Then this best advice—
I am out of patience with it.
    JOCASTA: O Oedipus, Oedipus,
God keep you, ill-fated one, from learning who
    you are.
    OEDIPUS: Will someone go at once and fetch the
        herdsman,
and leave this woman to glory in her noble stock!
    JOCASTA: O miserable one, unhappy one—
that is all I can say—now and forever.
        [Jocasta *rushes into the palace in desperation*]
    CHORUS: Why has our lady run into the palace
wild with grief?
A premonition shakes me:
it was terror that sealed her lips.
    OEDIPUS: Let come what will.
Be my descent ever so lowly, I still must know.
Perhaps the woman, who is proud with a woman's
    towering pride,
finds my origin too humble for her.
As for me,
I hold myself to be the child of gracious Fortune,
and take no dishonor from this:
Fortune is the mother from whom I sprang,
and I call the months my brothers,
they that sometimes found me cast down
and then set high again.
With such a lineage,
I shall never be found ashamed
and falter in searching into my birth.
        [*The* Chorus *is filled with confidence on hearing*
        him]
    CHORUS (STROPHE): If I am a seer or wise of heart
        at all,
mountain nurse, Cithaeron,
you shall not fail by Heaven
to know at tomorrow's full moon
that Oedipus honors you as his foster-mother
and that you are honored in the dance by us
as one favored by our monarch.
Phoebus, to whom we call, favor these things
    too!
    CHORUS (ANTISTROPHE): Who was it, child? which
        of the ageless goddesses
bore you to Pan the father,
who roams the pasture hills?
Or was she bride to Phoebus? *He* the father?

Or to Cyllene's lord?[19] Or the Bacchantes'[20] god,
a dweller on the hill-tops, was it *He*
who received you his new-born joy from one
of the oreads[21] with whom he mostly sports?
        [Attendants *appear, leading a* Shepherd, *an old*
        man]
    OEDIPUS: [*To the Corinthian* Messenger] If I
        may guess, who never saw him,
here is your herdsman.
His ripe years measure with yours,
and the men who bring him are of my household.
But you, if you have seen him before, can tell me.
    CHORUS: I recognize him—
trustiest of the servants Laius had in his house.
    OEDIPUS: Now, Corinthian stranger:
Is it he?
    MESSENGER: This is the man.
    OEDIPUS: [*To the old* Shepherd] Well then—old
        man! Look at me!
Tell me—you served Laius?
    SHEPHERD: I was his slave.
Not bought by him, but reared in his house.
    OEDIPUS: Doing what work? What was your way
        of life?
    SHEPHERD: For the best part of my life I tended
        flocks.
    OEDIPUS: Where did they graze?
    SHEPHERD: Sometimes *on* Cithaeron, sometimes
        near the mountain.
    OEDIPUS: [*Pointing out the* Messenger] This man
        —do you recall having ever met him there?
    SHEPHERD: Not to say off-hand, from memory.
    MESSENGER: And no wonder, master!
But he will when I remind him. We kept pasture there
three half-years,
he with his two flocks, I with one.
They grazed together from spring-time to the rise of
    Arcturus in the fall.
Then I drove my sheep to our fold at home
and he brought his back to Laius.
        [*To the* Shepherd]
Was this so as I tell it or not?
    SHEPHERD: It was—but it was a long time ago.
    MESSENGER: And tell me now, do you remember
        giving me a boy,
an infant then, to rear as my own?
    SHEPHERD: [*Frightened*] What do you mean?
        Why do you ask me that?
    MESSENGER: [*Pointing to* Oedipus] Here is the
        man, my friend, who was then the child.
    SHEPHERD: [*Violently*] The plague take you! Hold
        your tongue!
    OEDIPUS: How now? You have no right to blame
        him.
The words that offend are yours.

[19] Hermes (or Mercury), said to have been born in
Cyllene.
[20] See footnote 12.
[21] Mountain nymphs.

SHEPHERD: Offend? How have I offended, master?

OEDIPUS: In not telling us about the child.

SHEPHERD: He busies himself with no business of his own.
He speaks without knowing.

OEDIPUS: Herdsman! if you will not speak to please me,
you shall be forced.

SHEPHERD: For God's love, master, do not harm an old man!

OEDIPUS: [To his Servants] Hold him fast; twist his arms behind him!

SHEPHERD: Wretch that I am! What do you want to know?

OEDIPUS: You gave him a child? The child he asks about?

SHEPHERD: I gave it. Would I had died before!

OEDIPUS: You will now, if you do not speak the truth.

SHEPHERD: And it will be worse with me if I speak it.

OEDIPUS: The fellow trifles with us still—evades the question . . .

SHEPHERD: [As the Servants twist his arms] No, no! I have told you that I gave him the child.

OEDIPUS: From whom did you have it?
Did someone give it to you,
or was it your own?

SHEPHERD: It was not mine.
Another gave it to me.

OEDIPUS: Which of these citizens? From whose home?

SHEPHERD: Master, I beg of you—
I beg you, do not ask it.

OEDIPUS: You are a dead man if I ask again.

SHEPHERD: It was a child, then—of the house of Laius.

OEDIPUS: A slave's child? Or born of the King's own family?

SHEPHERD: I stand on the knife-edge of dreadful words; I fear to speak.

OEDIPUS: And I, to hear. Yet I must!

SHEPHERD: The child was called his son;
but she within, your lady, could best say how that was.

OEDIPUS: Did she then give it to you?

SHEPHERD: So it was, my King.

OEDIPUS: For what purpose? Speak!

SHEPHERD: That I should do away with it.

OEDIPUS: Wretched woman! Her own child?

SHEPHERD: Yes, from fear of the evil prophecies.

OEDIPUS: What prophecies?

SHEPHERD: That he should kill his parents, it was said.

OEDIPUS: Why, then, did you give him to this old man?

SHEPHERD: Through pity, master.
I gave him the child,
thinking he would take it to another land, his own.

He did so but, alas, he saved it for the worst of sorrows.
For, if you are the man he says you are,
then surely you were born to great misery!

OEDIPUS: [Uttering the cry of a wounded animal]
Oh—oh—oh!
Everything is proved true—everything has come to pass!
Light of the sun,
never shall I look on you again,
I who am revealed
damned by the light I saw at birth,
damned by my marriage,
damned by the blood I shed.

[Oedipus rushes frantically into the palace]

CHORUS (1ST STROPHE): O generations of men,
how I account your lives no better
than not living at all!
Where is to be found the man
who attains more happiness than a mere seeming
and after the seeming, a falling away!
Yours is the fate that warns me—
luckless, unhappy Oedipus!—
to call no creature living on earth enviable.

CHORUS (1ST ANTISTROPHE): For this is he, o Zeus,
who speeding his bolt far beyond the rest
won the prize of all-engrossing prosperity.
He slew the darkly singing maiden,
her of the crooked talons;
he stood as a tower between death and our land,
and thereafter was called king,
received unrivaled honor
and next to none ruled great Thebes.

CHORUS (2ND STROPHE): But now, O Zeus, whose
is the story more grievous to hear,
and who is more yoked to misfortune
now his entire life is reversed?
O, renowned prince Oedipus,
who, on the nuptial bed,
sought the same source
as father that you had as son,
how could the soil your father sowed before
suffer you, unhappy one, in peace so long!

CHORUS (2ND ANTISTROPHE): Time, all-revealing,
that has found you
guilty without intent,
arraigns you now for a monstrous marriage
in which begetter and begotten are one.
O child of Laius,
I wish that I had never beheld your face!
True, I must lament your fate
with a dirge that pours from my lips,
and yet, though I got new life from you at first,[22]
you have dropped a great darkness on my eyes.

[A Servant rushes out of the palace]

SERVANT: O you, most honored in the land,

[22] Because Oedipus relieved Thebes of the Sphinx.
which destroyed its citizens.

what things you have to hear, what sights to see,
what sorrow to endure, if you still cherish
the house of Labdacus, true to your oath!
For neither the waves of Ister, I fear, nor Phasis[23]
can wash this house clean,
so many the evils it covers and shall soon disclose.
Yes, evils self-inflicted,
which are the worst to bear.

CHORUS: There was no lack of suffering before;
what report can cause more lamentation?

SERVANT: To tell the shortest tale,
our royal lady, Jocasta, is dead.

CHORUS: Unhappy woman! How did she die?

SERVANT: By her own hand.
It cannot be so terrible to you as to one who wit-
    nessed it,
but as far as I can tell, you shall hear:
When she passed into the vestibule, frantic,
she ran straight to the bedchamber
with her fingers tearing at her hair.
She dashed the doors shut behind her,
called upon dead Laius,
mindful of the begotten son
by whom, she said, he died
and by whom she bore unholy offspring.
So she bewailed the nuptial bed
on which she had brought forth a twofold brood—
a husband by her husband, and children by her
    son.
What happened next, how she died,
is more than I can tell, for Oedipus burst in
and we could not behold her end,
our eyes being fixed on him. For he went about raging
calling for a sword, and demanding
where he could find the wife who was no wife
but the mother-soil of both himself and his children.
And while he was raging, some power guided him
    to her;
for with a dreadful cry, as though led on,
he flung himself at the closed doors,
unhinging their bolts with his bare hands.

Going in after him, we saw the lady, her neck
in a twisted rope and swinging.
Then he, giving a dreadful cry,
loosed her halter and when she lay on the ground,
how awful the sequel we saw!
For tearing from the raiment the golden brooches
    of her robe,
he raised them high and struck them into his eyes,
calling out, as he smote:
"No longer, my eyes, shall you behold the horror
I suffered and performed! Too long
have you looked on those on whom you should not
    have looked
while failing to see what you should have seen.
Henceforth, therefore, be dark!"

[23] Ister or Istros, the lower reaches of the Danube;
Phasis, a river in eastern Asia that empties into the
Black Sea.

With words like these, not once but many times
he struck at his eyes with the lifted pins,
and at each blow the eyes streamed blood on his
    beard
like crimson rain.

These are the evils that from a two-fold source,
not one alone, but from woman and husband,
have burst forth. The fortune of the old house
was once a rare happiness, but in this hour
of shame and ruin, lamentation and death,
of all earthly suffering that can be named
nothing was spared.

CHORUS: Is he eased of his misery now and quiet?

SERVANT: He calls for someone to unbar the doors
and show him to all the Thebans as his father's
    slayer
and his mother's—but no, the unholy word shall not
    pass my lips.
He proposes to cast himself out of the land
and no longer to burden the house with his curse.
Yet he lacks strength and has no one to guide his
    steps,
for no one can bear to go near him.
But you will see for yourselves now, for the bolts
    are being drawn,
and he will come out, revealing
what even he who shrinks from the horror will pity.
    [Oedipus comes out of the palace, his eyes blood-
    stained and horrible]

CHORUS: O dreadful sight,
most dreadful that my eyes have ever looked
    upon!
Unhappy one, what madness came upon you?
Who is the demon, the foe to man,
that with a spring beyond mortal power
leaped upon your ill-fated life as its prey?
Hapless one, although there is more I would ask you
and I am drawn to you with pitying sorrow,
I cannot even bring myself to look again;
you fill me with such shuddering.

OEDIPUS: Wretched that I am! Oh! Oh!
Where am I going in my misery,
and where is my voice borne on the wings of air?
Fate, have you brought me so far?

CHORUS: To a destiny terrible to men's ears
and terrible to their sight!

OEDIPUS: Horror of darkness that envelops me!
Dreadful visitant, resistless and unspeakable,
whom a too fair breeze of fortune sped against me,
how my soul is stabbed, first by the present pain
and again by the memory of fearful deeds!

CHORUS: [Sympathetically] Amid troubles so
    many
you may well bear and mourn a two-fold pain.

OEDIPUS: Oh friend, you still are steadfast,
still ready to tend and to endure me,
a blind man!
Your presence is not hidden from me;
in my darkness I know your voice.

CHORUS: Yet, man of dreadful deed,
how could you bear to extinguish your sight?
What inhuman power drove you?
    OEDIPUS: Apollo, friends,
Apollo brought these woes to pass;
but it was my own hand that struck.
My own hand alone, man of misery that I am!
I did not want to see when sight could show me
    nothing good.
    CHORUS: It is true, alas.
    OEDIPUS: What was left to see?
What to love?
What greeting to hear with pleasure?
Hurry, lead me out of the land,
lead away the lost one, the most damned of men,
the man most abhorred by the gods.
    CHORUS: Unhappy equally in misfortune
and in too keen consciousness of horror,
it were better that you had never lived.
    OEDIPUS: A curse on the man who freed me in the
    pasture,
who unbound my feet
and saved me from death
and brought me to a life such as this.
Had I died then, on Cithaeron's slope,
I should have brought no grief
both to my friends and myself.
    CHORUS: I, too, could wish it had been so.
    OEDIPUS: I would not have come to shed my
    father's blood,
nor been known among men as my mother's husband.
But now I am forsaken by the gods,
the son of a defiled mother, and successor
in the bed of him who gave me miserable life.
If there is any evil that exceeds all evil,
that has been the fate of Oedipus.
    CHORUS: Yet I cannot say you have done well.
To have died would have been better than to be blind
    and living.
    OEDIPUS: I have done what I thought best; I'll
    have no counsel in this.
Had I retained my sight, with what eyes
in the land of shades underground
could I have looked on my father and my wretched
    mother—
those two against whom I have done such things
that no halter could punish the crime.
And would the children born to me
have been an endurable sight? Not to these eyes—
    never.
Nor could I look upon this city, with its citadel and
    shrines,
from which I cut myself off, I of Thebes the greatest,
when I myself pronounced the doom to drive him
    out,
the criminal revealed now by the gods as the hateful
    seed of Laius.
Bearing this stain upon me,
could I have looked with unaverted eyes on my
    people?

Never. And had there been some way
to seal the fountain of hearing, too,
I should have cast this wretched body into a still
    closer prison,
secure from all sound as well as sight,
for it is sweet to be beyond the stab of pain.

Oh, Cithaeron, why did you shelter me
who came to you an infant?
Why not have destroyed me at once,
leaving my birth unrevealed?
And you Polybus and Corinth
and the ancient house I called the home of my fathers,
how fair a nursling you fostered
and how foul a man
festered within the child,
doomed to be found evil and of evil birth.

And you crossroads—
hidden glen, thicket and narrow way
where the three paths met,
you that drank from my murdering hands
a father's blood,
do you still remember what you saw me do?

And, then, the deeds I went on to perform!
O, marriage, marriage,
You brought me forth,
then brought children to your child.
In a kinship of fathers, brothers, sons,
and of brides, wives, and mothers,
you compounded the foulest shame a man can know,
ghastly incest.
But no, it is unfit to utter what it is unfit to do!
Hurry, friends, and in God's name, hide me some-
    where beyond this land.
Or kill me;
or cast me into the sea where you may never look
    upon me again.

Approach; take hold of me.
Have no fear of contamination;
my plague will touch no one else.
    [Creon is seen approaching]
    CHORUS: No! Creon approaches in good time
to advise and perform what must be.
He is left sole guardian of the land.
    OEDIPUS: Creon! How shall I speak?
How can I request anything from him,
having proved unjust in what passed between us?
    [Creon appears with Attendants]
    CREON: I have come, Oedipus, not in mockery
nor with intended reproaches for past words.
But if you have no regard for the children of men,
respect, at least, the all-sustaining flame
of our Lord the Sun!
Spare Him the sight of naked pollution
that not earth, nor holy rain, nor light can
    welcome.
    [To the Attendants]
Come! Take him inside quickly.
It is seemly that kinsfolk alone

should see and hear a kinsman's grief.

OEDIPUS: For the God's sake, since you have come
    to me,
a man so vile, with so noble a spirit,
grant me one request.
For your own good I ask it, not for mine.

CREON: Ask what you wish.

OEDIPUS: Cast me out of this land,
speed me to a land where no man may greet me.

CREON: I should have done this, be sure,
if I had not wanted to learn first what the God de-
    crees.

OEDIPUS: Surely his oracle was clear—
to let the parricide and defiler die.

CREON: That was said.
But in our present plight it is well to ask the God
    again.

OEDIPUS: How can you expect a response from
    God
on behalf of so frightful a man as Oedipus?

CREON: Even you must now put your faith in the
    God.

OEDIPUS: Even so! And I entreat you
to order a burial that befits her who lies within;
she is your own,
for whom you should properly perform the rites.
But for me, never should my father's city
have to behold me dwelling in it while I live.

Let me go to the hills,
there where my mountain Cithaeron rises,
once appointed to be my tomb by mother and father.
Dying there,
I shall die as by their decree who rightly doomed
    me at my birth.

Yet I also know there is more to come.
Neither an illness nor anything else will destroy me.
I should never have been snatched from death there
but for a strange, still uncompleted, destiny.[24]

---

[24] Oedipus, according to Sophocles' later play, *Oedipus at Colonus,* was to be invested with a mysterious power after his present suffering. Creon was to try to bring him back to Thebes, in order that in dying and being buried there Oedipus should sanctify the land, or, as Oedipus says in the later tragedy, "that the city may escape unscathed" in a later war with Athens. Oedipus was to be endowed with some mystic power or magical *mana* to safeguard the land in which he might be buried. In *Oedipus at Colonus,* choosing to die on Athenian soil and to be buried in Sophocles' native village, Colonus (Sophocles having altered the old legend for reasons of patriotism), Oedipus blesses Athens and promises it safety in gratitude for the kind reception accorded him by Theseus, the legendary ruler of the Athenian state. A mysterious heavenly voice calls him, and his death is a mystic experience witnessed only by Theseus, who will not reveal what he saw. The Messenger in *Oedipus at Colonus* only reports:
"No fiery thunderbolt of the god removed him in that hour, nor any rising of storm from the sea, but either

Well, then, let my fate, whatever it be,
take me where it will! But my children, Creon!
My sons require none of your care,
being grown men who will not lack the means to
    live.
Creon, I pray you, take care of my daughters,[25]
my two poor unhappy girls,
who never ate at a separate table away from me or
    lacked my presence
and ever shared all things with me.
Grant them your protection.
And suffer me, if you will, to touch them
and share my grief with them.
Grant me this, Prince,
grant it, noble one,
that in touching them I may feel
they are with me, as when I still had my sight.

    [*Led out by* Servants, Antigone *and* Ismene, *the
    young daughters, come out of the palace,
    sobbing*]

OEDIPUS: [*Hearing them*] O heavenly powers, are
    those my children, sobbing?
Can it be that Creon, pitying me,
sends me the children, the dear ones?
Have you done that?

CREON: I have, seeing what joy you took in them
    before.
May they give you comfort.

OEDIPUS: Then a blessing be your reward.
May Heaven prove a kinder guide on your road of
    life[26]
than it was to me.
Oh, my children, where are you?
Come here—here to the hands of him
whose mother was your own,

---

a messenger from the gods, or the world of the dead, the nether adamant, riven for him in love, without pain; for the passing of the man was not with lamentation, or in sickness and suffering, but, above mortal's, wonderful." (Translation by Richard C. Jebb)

[25] There is tragic irony in this, as a Greek audience would have known. Creon was to condemn Antigone to death for burying one of her brothers, Polyneices, who besieged Thebes after being deprived of his royal rights by the other brother, Eteocles. Sophocles had dramatized this part of the Oedipus legend in his play *Antigone,* produced earlier. And there is, of course, further irony in the confidence with which Oedipus considers the future of his sons when, actually, they would soon engage in a furious rivalry that would end in their killing each other in a duel waged over the throne they inherit from Oedipus. (This rivalry is the subject of still another extant Greek tragedy that Sophocles' audience must have known—*The Seven Against Thebes,* by Aeschylus.)

[26] In the light of future events, known to Sophocles' audience, this wish adds more tragic irony to the play and sustains the point that man's life is full of uncertainties. Both Creon's wife and son were to kill themselves after Antigone's death; the son because he loved Antigone, the wife because her son was dead. See Sophocles' *Antigone.*

OEDIPUS THE KING

51

the hands that put out your father's once clear eyes,
which seeing nothing, understanding nothing,
brought him to her from whom he sprang
to become your father.
For you, too, I weep,
though I cannot see your faces,
knowing the bitter life men will make for you
in the days to come. For,
to what gathering of citizens will you go,
to what festival,
from which you will not come back in tears?
Where will be found the man
willing to assume the disgrace that clings to my
      offspring
and that would to yours?
For what reproach is lacking?
"Your father slew his father,
and planted you in the womb of his own being."
Such will be the taunts you must hear!
The man who would marry you does not live;
you must wither away in barrenness.

O Creon, son of Menoeceus, hear me!
You are the only father left to them,
both their parents lost—both!
Do not allow my children, who are your kinswomen
      too,
to wander about in beggary, unwed.[27]
Do not let them sink down to my misery.
Pity them when you see them forlorn,
so utterly forlorn in their young years.
Give me your promise with the touch of your hand!

And to you, my children,
I could give much counsel if you were older.
As it is, I can only make this prayer:
May you find some place where you can live in quiet,
and may you have a better life than your father's.

[27] In Sophocles' *Antigone*, Creon does betroth Antigone
to his son Haemon. But the consequences are tragic for
Creon.

CREON: Enough lamentation! Pass into the house,
      Oedipus.
OEDIPUS: I must obey, though it is hard.
CREON: To everything there is a season.
OEDIPUS: Know, then, on what conditions I go
      within.
CREON: Name them, and I shall know.
OEDIPUS: See to it that I am cast out of Thebes.
      Banish me!
CREON: That must be as the God decrees.
OEDIPUS: But surely you understand that I am
      hateful to the God!
CREON: If so, you will obtain your desire soon
      enough.
OEDIPUS: So you consent.
CREON: I have said as I mean.
OEDIPUS: [*Still holding on to his daughters*] Then
      it is time for me to be led within.
CREON: Go then, but let the children go.
OEDIPUS: [*Clinging passionately to them*] No, do
      not take them from me.
CREON: [*Severely*] Do not seek to be the master
      in everything,
for everything you mastered fell away from you.
      [Oedipus *is led into the palace by an* Attendant.
      Then Creon *goes in with* Antigone *and* Ismene,
      leaving the Chorus *outside*]
CHORUS: Dwellers in Thebes,
behold, this is Oedipus,
who unriddled the famous riddle
and was a man most notable.
What Theban did not envy his good fortune?
Yet behold into what a whirlwind of trouble he was
      hurled!

Therefore, with eyes fixed on the end destined for
      all,
count no one of the race of man happy
until he has crossed life's border free from pain.
      [*The* Chorus *retires*]

Euripides

(480–406 B.C.)

The Ibsen, as well as the Shaw, of the classic world was Euripides, youngest of Athens' master poets of tragedy. Aristotle, surveying the Greek drama many decades later, called him the most tragic of the poets. Certainly he was that in his power to evoke pity, although Sophocles and Aeschylus could evoke at least as much terror and provide a more thorough catharsis. But the qualities that have drawn the twentieth century most to Euripides are the attitude he brought to bear upon the familiar Greek subjects and heroes, his frame of mind, and the nature of his sympathies. It is hardly surprising that Euripides, the last and most modern of the great Greek tragic dramatists, should have been the least popular of them all during his life. He had a surplus of enemies in Athens and became the unfortunate butt of the comic poets. According to Aristophanes, the most devastating of them, Euripides was a lowborn panderer to popular taste and a cantankerous misogynist who insulted womanhood in his plays.

Actually, Euripides was born of aristocratic parents and in his youth held offices always reserved for the children of prominent citizens; and he treated women with more sympathy and understanding than did any other playwright before the fourth century B.C. However, he shocked his audiences with unconventional approaches to sexual and moral problems. He was a member of the unpopular peace party during the protracted and devastating Peloponnesian War and an articulate opponent of Athenian imperialism. And he was an innovator in dramatic style, intellectualizing it on one hand and intensifying its pathos on the other. This was tantamount to "modernizing" the old formal drama. He even inserted solos for singers into some plays and used music equivalent perhaps to what we call syncopation, by a composer who found it expedient to go into exile. Euripides was a faulty dramatist at times, as an experimental artist is apt to be, and he had the misfortune of becoming more radical in both art and thought precisely when Athens was becoming somewhat reactionary as a result of war hysteria.

In fifty years of writing, Euripides won only five prizes in the annual dramatic contests. He found it advisable to spend the last year and a half of his life in virtual exile at the court of Macedonia, where he died in 406 B.C. According to various legends, which may reflect the animosity of his detractors, he was torn to pieces by the king's hounds or killed by frenzied women in revenge for his aspersions on their sex. But the political refugee was more honored in death than in life. Sophocles, who outlasted him by a number of months, clothed his chorus in black as a mark of respect, and the Athenian state, still proud of its artists and men of letters, raised a cenotaph in his honor. Soon, too, the entire Hellenic world began to pay tribute to the playwright. Euripides became the most popular of the Greek dramatists, and after the fifth century B.C. his plays were performed regularly on the three continents of the Macedonian empire. It is probably for this reason that many more of his plays survived in copyists' manuscripts than did plays by Aeschylus and Sophocles.

Euripides, who approached ethical and political problems as a rationalist and a humanitarian, was aptly called by Nietzsche "the poet of esthetic Socratism." There were, in fact, stories current in Athens that Socrates aided in the composition of his plays. Certainly Euripides, like the great philosopher, paid scant respect to the polytheistic beliefs of his day. In his *Ion,* the god Phoebus is guilty of immorality and deception; and in his *Electra,* Apollo is openly criticized for having ordered Orestes to kill his mother. (Since the Delphic oracle was in disgrace with Athenians at the time for favoring the Spartan enemy, the poet could denounce Apollo with some safety.) In *The Trojan Women,* perhaps the most moving of all pacifist dramas, and in *Hecuba,* which condemns the malevolence of both victors and victims, Euripides made passionate attacks on the savagery of war. In *Hecuba* and *Iphigenia in Aulis* he went far toward deflating conventional heroism and demonstrating how closely it can approach cowardice and rank egotism. He was more disrespectful than any other tragic poet toward the heroes of the semi-sacred Homeric epics. In our time he might have been considered a "debunker."

It is also part of Euripides' modernity that, like Ibsen, Strindberg, and O'Neill, he displayed a keen interest in psychological problems. His findings, as a matter of fact, often harmonize with the observations of modern psychologists. Without, of course, employing any of our current labels, he treated the dangers of sexual repression in both *Electra* and *Hippolytus* and in *Medea* acknowledged the demoniacal power of overwrought feeling. He also explored the mechanisms of madness in his *Orestes* and hypnotic trances in his last tragedy, *The Bacchae.*

Euripides' characterizations were often realistic. Heroes such as Admetus, Jason, Agamemnon, and Achilles, held in popular esteem as paragons of manly virtue, appeared on the stage of Euripides as shoddy specimens of humanity. He treated common people with a sympathy and interest unusual in his time. And women, hitherto either idealized or ignored, filled his tragedies with their passions and problems. Approaching these characters sympathetically and with psychological penetration, Euripides succeeded in drawing many of the most poignantly real women in literature. His *Alcestis*, *Hippolytus*, *Medea*, and *Electra* are character studies that perplexed or outraged the Athenian playgoer with their slashing honesty.

Nevertheless, Euripides is not to be associated unreservedly with modern realistic writers and purveyors of problem plays. Some of his dramas, notably *Alcestis* and *The Bacchae*, have a *Midsummer Night's Dream* quality or breathe an air of mystery. And all his plays, irrespective of the problems they pose or the psychopathology they explore, are written poetically and formalistically. A Euripidean tragedy pours finite into infinite: the finite, realistic matter of the personal conflict into the infinite of poetic meaning and wonder. Primitive structural features in a number of the plays accentuate their poetic quality; their prologues and epilogues, in which deities introduce the action and make an appearance at the end (the well-known *deus ex machina* ending), produce the impression of a reality beyond the ordinary human complication. In so far as we can consider Euripides a realist, we must call him a poetic realist.

Medea is a powerful example of Euripides' interest in the heart of a woman, a subject generally shunned by Athenians. *Electra,* one of Euripides' last masterpieces, composed in 413 B.C., exemplifies many of his strongest qualities as a dramatist and a social thinker. It is, except for the *deus ex machina* at the end of the play, a profoundly realistic drama, which transforms a traditional heroine into a pathetically frustrated woman and condemns primitive morality. The play is Euripides' modern variant on the theme of the second part of the Oresteian trilogy by the then long dead Aeschylus. But it is *The Trojan Women* that engages our interest most today by its bitterness, its pathos, and, unfortunately, its immediacy.

All the tragedy of war is summoned before our eyes in Euripides' account of the fall of Troy and the fate of its women. Even the gods are appalled by the exhibition of man's inhumanity to man. Performed in 415 B.C., the theatrical season following a flagrant case of barbarity on the part of the Athenian forces (the violation of the neutrality of the island of Melos and the massacre of all the male inhabitants), Euripides' drama struck at Athens and its chauvinistic leaders. His *Palamedes*, another in the set of plays which included *The Trojan Women*, was also an exposé of evil, in which a just man is destroyed by a crafty politician, Odysseus. It is believed that in writing this play Euripides had in mind the exiling of the liberal philosopher Protagoras, for Athenian democracy, then staggering from reverses on the war fronts, had become intolerant and was looking for scapegoats among intellectuals. The "professors" were to blame because the Athenians were being defeated by the Spartans. By inculcating the habit of inquiry, they were said to have weakened morale. After the fall of Athens, Socrates was to be charged with the same crime and executed for it. Euripides, however, was loyal to his intellectual comrades.

It has often been maintained that *The Trojan Women* is one long lamentation and is static drama. If this were actually true, it is unlikely that it would be produced so often, although it is true that in our theatre, which does not use choruses effectively, the play may seem more languid than it is. It is episodic rather than static. But its episodes are held together by the theme and mount in pathos and intensity. "Wail for the world's woe" it does, but it does so through the struggles, though helpless ones, of women who have found sisters throughout the history of man's frequent relapse into savagery. *The Trojan Women* is a dirge for the world that even the Periclean civilization, in which Euripides had been cradled, had not succeeded in saving from war and inhumanity. Whatever stasis there may be in the play consists of finalities, as in the case of Synge's great one-acter, *Riders to the Sea*. The victims are already trapped; their fate has been decided; they are acted upon. Their role is only to react, which they do magnificently. There is little stasis in their situation, which moves from one outrage to another, and none whatsoever in their hearts, which beat fiercely, while the heart of the poet rages with them at the spectacle of bedeviled humanity. The last inhumanity he exhibits—the murder of Hector's infant —comes as a final testament of protest.

The emotions which Euripides whips up with these provocations do not, however, exhaust his artistry. He makes it plain in the herald's scene that he brings no blanket indictment against all humanity but only against its masters. He is an objective realist in the Helen of Troy scene—realist enough, indeed, to make the most tragic of his victims, Hecuba, exhibit a calculating vengefulness when she tries to prevail upon Menelaus to kill his wife. He is poet enough, too, to transmute suffering into song. And he is tragedian enough to lift us out of the morass of depression by the passionateness with which he endows the Trojan women. Moreover, there is evidence of human nobility in Hecuba's and Andromache's dignified conduct in connection with the death of Hector's child and in Cassandra's great speech as she looks beyond the present horror. In spite of everything that draws revulsion and deserves lament, man is no writhing maggot in Euripides' dramatic poem.

THE TROJAN WOMEN[1]

By Euripides

TRANSLATED FROM THE GREEK BY RICHMOND LATTIMORE

DRAMATIS PERSONAE

POSEIDON	MENELAOS	ANDROMACHE
ATHENE	TALTHYBIOS	ASTYANAX
HECUBA	KASSANDRA	HELEN

CHORUS OF TROJAN WOMEN

SCENE: *The action takes place shortly after the capture of Troy. All Trojan men have been killed, or have fled; all women and children are captives. The scene is an open space before the city, which is visible in the background, partly demolished, and smouldering. Against the walls are tents, or huts, which temporarily house the captive women. The entrance of the* Chorus *is made, in two separate groups which subsequently unite, from these buildings, as are those of* Kassandra *and* Helen. *The entrances of* Talthybios, Andromache, *and* Menelaos *are made from the wings. It is imaginable that the gods are made to appear high up, above the level of the other actors, as if near their own temples on the Citadel. As the play opens,* Hecuba *is prostrate on the ground (it is understood that she hears nothing of what the gods say).*

[*Enter* Poseidon]

POSEIDON: I am Poseidon. I come from the
    Aigaian depths
of the sea beneath whose waters Nereid choirs evolve
the intricate bright circle of their dancing feet.
For since that day when Phoibos Apollo and I laid
    down
on Trojan soil the close of these stone towers, drawn
    true
and straight, there has always been affection in my
    heart
unfading, for these Phrygians and for their city;
which smoulders now, fallen before the Argive
    spears,
ruined, sacked, gutted. Such is Athene's work, and
    his,
the Parnassian, Epeios of Phokis, architect
and builder of the horse that swarmed with inward
    steel,
that fatal bulk which passed within the battlements,
whose fame hereafter shall be loud among men un-
    born,

the Wooden Horse, which hid the secret spears
    within.
Now the gods' groves are desolate, their thrones of
    power
blood-spattered where beside the lift of the altar steps
of Zeus, Defender Priam was cut down and died.
The ships of the Achaians load with spoils of Troy
now, the piled gold of Phrygia. And the men of
    Greece
who made this expedition and took the city, stay
only for the favoring stern-wind now to greet their
    wives
and children after ten years' harvests wasted here.

The will of Argive Hera[2] and Athene won
its way against my will. Between them they broke
    Troy.
So I must leave my altars and great Ilion,
since once a city sinks into sad desolation
the gods' state sickens also, and their worship fades.
Skamandros' valley echoes to the wail of slaves,
the captive women given to their masters now,
some to Arkadia or the men of Thessaly
assigned, or to the lords of Athens, Theseus' strain;
while all the women of Troy yet unassigned are here
beneath the shelter of these walls, chosen to wait
the will of princes, and among them Tyndareus' child
Helen of Sparta, named—with right—a captive slave.

Nearby, beside the gates, for any to look upon
who has the heart, she lies face upward, Hecuba
weeping for multitudes her multitude of tears.
Polyxena, one daughter, even now was killed
in secrecy and pain beside Achilleus' tomb.
Priam is gone, their children dead; one girl is left,
Kassandra, reeling crazed at King Apollo's stroke,
whom Agamemnon, in despite of the gods' will
and all religion, will lead by force to his secret bed.

O city, long ago a happy place, good-bye;
good-bye, hewn bastions. Pallas, child of Zeus, did
    this.

[1] When Troy fell to the Greeks, the god Poseidon departed from the city which he had long loved. The men of Troy had been killed; the women, headed by aged Hecuba, Priam's queen, assembled before the walls of the burning town to await their departure into slavery.

[2] The Greek goddess who is the queen of heaven. Sister and wife of Zeus; called Juno by the Romans.

But for her hatred, you might stand strong-founded
  still.
  [Athene enters]
  ATHENE: August among the gods, O vast divinity,
closest in kinship to the father of all, may one
who quarreled with you in the past make peace, and
  speak?
  POSEIDON: You may, Lady Athene; for the strands
  of kinship
close drawn work no weak magic to enchant the
  mind.
  A HENE: I thank you for your gentleness, and
  bring you now
questions whose issue touches you and me, my lord.
  POSEIDON: Is this the annunciation of some new
  word spoken
by Zeus, or any other of the divinities?
  ATHENE: No; but for Troy's sake, on whose ground
  we stand, I come
to win the favor of your power, and an ally.
  POSEIDON: You hated Troy once; did you throw
  your hate away
and change to pity now its walls are black with fire?
  ATHENE: Come back to the question. Will you take
  counsel with me
and help me gladly in all that I would bring to pass?
  POSEIDON: I will indeed; but tell me what you wish
  to do.
Are you here for the Achaians' or the Phrygians'
  sake?
  ATHENE: For the Trojans, whom I hated such a
  short time since,
to make the Achaians' homecoming a thing of
  sorrow.
  POSEIDON: This is a springing change of sympathy.
  Why must
you hate too hard, and love too hard, your loves and
  hates?
  ATHENE: Did you not know they outraged my
  temple, and shamed me?
  POSEIDON: I know that Aias dragged Kassandra
  there by force.
  ATHENE: And the Achaians did nothing. They did
  not even speak.
  POSEIDON: Yet Ilion was taken by your strength
  alone.
  ATHENE: True; therefore help me. I would do
  some evil to them.
  POSEIDON: I am ready for anything you ask. What
  will you do?
  ATHENE: Make the home voyage a most unhappy
  coming home.
  POSEIDON: While they stay here ashore, or out on
  the deep sea?
  ATHENE: When they take ship from Ilion and set
  sail for home
Zeus will shower down his rainstorms and the weari-
  less beat
of hail, to make black the bright air with roaring
  winds.

He has promised my hand the gift of the blazing
  thunderbolt
to dash and overwhelm with fire the Achaian ships.
Yours is your own domain, the Aigaian crossing. Make
the sea thunder to the tripled wave and spinning surf,
cram thick the hollow Euboian fold with floating
  dead;[3]
that after this Greeks may learn to use with fear
my sacred places, and respect all gods beside.
  POSEIDON: This shall be done, and joyfully. It
  needs no long
discourse to tell you. I will shake the Aigaian Sea.
Mykonos' nesses[4] and the swine-back reefs of Delos,
the Kaphereian promontories, Skyros, Lemnos
shall take the washed up bodies of men drowned at
  sea.
Back to Olympos now, gather the thunderbolts
from your father's hands, then take your watcher's
  post, to wait
the chance, when the Achaian fleet puts out to sea.

That mortal who sacks fallen cities is a fool,
who gives the temples and the tombs, the hallowed
  places
of the dead to desolation. His own turn must come.
  [The Gods leave the stage, Hecuba seems to
  waken, and gets slowly to her feet as she speaks]
  HECUBA: Rise, stricken head from the dust;
lift up the throat. This is Troy, but Troy
and we, Troy's kings, are perished.
Stoop to the changing fortune.
Steer for the crossing and the death-god,
hold not life's prow on the course against
wave beat and accident.
Ah me,
what need I further for tears' occasion,
state perished, my sons, and my husband?
O massive pride that my fathers heaped
to magnificence, you meant nothing.
Must I be hushed? Were it better thus?
Should I cry a lament?
Unhappy, accursed,
limbs cramped, I lie
backed on earth's stiff bed.
O head, O temples
and sides; sweet, to shift,
let the tired spine rest
weight eased by the sides alternate,
against the strain of the tears' song
where the stricken people find music yet
in the song undanced of their wretchedness.

You ships' prows, that the fugitive
oars swept back to blessed Ilion
over the sea's blue water
by the placid harbors of Hellas
to the flute's grim beat

[3] Euboea is the largest island of Greece; it lies north-
east of Athens.
[4] A promontory, or cape.

and the swing of the shrill boat whistles;
you made the crossing, made fast ashore
the Egyptians' skill, the sea cables,
alas, by the coasts of Troy;
it was you, ships, that carried the fatal bride
of Menelaos, Kastor[5] her brother's shame,
the stain on the Eurotas.
Now she has killed
the sire of the fifty sons
Priam; me, unhappy Hecuba,
she drove on this reef of ruin.

Such state I keep
to sit by the tents of Agamemnon.
I am led captive
from my house, an old, unhappy woman,
my head struck pitiful.
Come then, sad wives of the Trojans
whose spears were bronze,
their daughters, brides of disaster,
let us mourn the smoke of Ilion.
And I, as among winged birds
the mother, lead out
the clashing cry, the song; not that song
wherein once long ago
when I held the sceptre of Priam
my feet were queens of the choir and led
the proud dance to the gods of Phrygia.

[*The* First Half-Chorus *comes out of the shelter at the back*]

1ST HALF-CHORUS: Hecuba, what are these cries?
What news now? For through the walls
I heard your pitiful weeping.
And fear shivered in the breasts
of the Trojan women, who within
sob out the day of their slavery.

HECUBA: My children, the ships of the Argives
will move today. The hand is at the oar.

1ST HALF-CHORUS: They will? Why? Ah me. Must
I take ship
so soon from the land of my fathers?

HECUBA: I know nothing. I look for disaster.

1ST HALF-CHORUS: Alas.
Poor women of Troy, torn from your homes,
bent to forced hard work.
The Argives push to the run home.

HECUBA: Oh
let her not come forth,
not now, my child
Kassandra, driven delirious
to shame us before the Argives;
not the mad one, to bring fresh pain to my pain
Ah no.
Troy, ill-starred Troy, this is the end;
your last sad people leave you now
still alive, and broken.

[*The* Second Half-Chorus *comes out of the shelter at the back*]

2ND HALF-CHORUS: Ah me. Shivering I left the tents
of Agamemnon to listen.
Tell us, our queen. Did the Argive council
decree our death?
Are the seamen manning the ships now,
oars ready for action?

HECUBA: My child, this was why I came, heart trembling
in the pale light of terror.

2ND HALF-CHORUS: Has a herald come from the Danaans?[6]
Whose wretched slave shall I be ordained?

HECUBA: You are near the lot now.

2ND HALF-CHORUS: Alas.
Who will lead me away? An Argive?
To an island home? To Phthiotis?
Unhappy, surely, and far from Troy

HECUBA: Ah,
whose wretched slave
shall I be? Where, in my gray age,
a faint drone,
poor image of a corpse,
weak shining among dead men? Shall
I stand and keep guard at their doors,
shall I nurse their children, I who in Troy
held state as a princess?

[*The two* Half-Choruses *now unite to form a single* Chorus]

CHORUS: Ah me, ah me. So pitiful
your shame and your lamentation.
No longer shall I turn the shifting design
of the shuttle at the looms of Ida.[7]
I shall look no more on the bodies of my sons.
No more. Shall I be a drudge, besides
being forced to the bed of Greek masters?
Night is a queen, but I curse her.
Must I draw the water of Peirene,
a servant at sacred springs?
Might I only be taken to the domain
of Theseus, the bright, the blessed!
Never to the whirl of Eurotas,[8]
detested, who gave us Helen,
not look with slave's eyes on the scourge
of Troy, Menelaos.

I have heard the rumor
of the hallowed ground by Peneios,
bright doorstone of Olympos,
deep burdened in beauty of flower and harvest.
There would I be next after the blessed,

[6] The Greeks

[7] A mountain sacred to Cybele (the Anatolian nature-goddess), located in Asia Minor, in Trojan territory. The chorus, we must remember, is composed of Trojan women.

[8] A river that crosses Sparta, the home of Helen and Menelaos (Menelaus), who were queen and king of Sparta.

[5] One of the twin sons of Leda by Zeus. He and Pollux, known as the Dioscuri, were later turned into stars (two bright stars of the constellation Gemini). They were Helen's (also Clytemnestra's) brothers.

the sacrosanct hold of Theseus.
And they say that the land of Aitna,
the Fire-God's keep against Punic men,
mother of Sicilian mountains, sounds
in the herald's cry for games' garlands;
and the land washed
by the streaming Ionian Sea.
that land watered by the loveliest
of rivers, Krathis, with the red-gold tresses
who draws from the depth of enchanted wells
blessings on a strong people.

See now, from the host of the Danaans
the herald, charged with new tidings, takes
the speed of his way toward us.
What message? What command? Since we count as
    slaves
even now in the Dorian kingdom.

[Talthybios enters, followed by a detail of armed
    soldiers]

TALTHYBIOS: Hecuba, incessantly my ways have
    led me to Troy
as the messenger of all the Achaian armament.
You know me from the old days, my lady; I am sent,
Talthybios, with new messages for you to hear.

HECUBA: This is it, beloved daughters of Troy; the
    thing I feared.

TALTHYBIOS: You are all given your masters now.
    Was this your dread?

HECUBA: Ah, yes. Is it Phthia, then? A city of
    Thessaly?
Tell me. The land of Kadmos?

TALTHYBIOS: All are allotted separately, each to a
    man.

HECUBA: Who is given to whom? Oh, is there any
    hope
left for the women of Troy?

TALTHYBIOS: I understand. Yet ask not for all, but
    for each apart.

HECUBA: Who was given my child? Tell me, who
    shall be lord
of my poor abused Kassandra?

TALTHYBIOS: King Agamemnon chose her. She
    was given to him.

HECUBA: Slave woman to that Lakedaimonian
    wife?
My unhappy child!

TALTHYBIOS: No. Rather to be joined with him in
    the dark bed of love.

HECUBA: She, Apollo's virgin, blessed in the privi-
    lege
the gold-haired god gave her, a life for ever unwed?

TALTHYBIOS: Love's archery and the prophetic
    maiden struck him hard.

HECUBA: Dash down, my daughter,
the keys of your consecration,
break the god's garlands to your throat gathered.

TALTHYBIOS: Is it not high favor to be brought to
    a king's bed?

HECUBA: My poor youngest, why did you take her

away from me?

TALTHYBIOS: You spoke now of Polyxena. Is it not
    so?

HECUBA: To whose arms did the lot force her?

TALTHYBIOS: She is given a guardianship, to keep
    Achilleus' tomb.

HECUBA: To watch, alas, my child? Over a tomb?
Tell me, is this their way,
some law, friend, established among the Greeks?

TALTHYBIOS: Speak of your child in words of bless-
    ing. She feels no pain.

HECUBA: What did that mean? Does she live in the
    sunlight still?

TALTHYBIOS: She lives her destiny, and her cares
    are over now.

HECUBA: The wife of bronze-embattled Hektor:
    tell me of her,
Andromache the forlorn. What shall she suffer
    now?

TALTHYBIOS: The son of Achilleus chose her. She
    was given to him.

HECUBA: And I, my aged strength crutched for
    support on staves,
whom shall I serve?

TALTHYBIOS: You shall be slave to Odysseus, lord
    of Ithaka.

HECUBA: Oh no, no!
Tear the shorn head,
rip nails through the folded cheeks.
Must I?
To be given as slave to serve that vile, that slippery
    man,
right's enemy, brute murderous beast,
that mouth of lies and treachery, that makes void
faith in things promised
and that which was beloved turns to hate. Oh, mourn,
daughters of Ilion, weep as one for me.
I am gone, doomed, undone,
O wretched, given
the worst lot of all.

CHORUS: I know your destiny now, Queen Hecuba.
    But mine?
What Hellene, what Achaian is my master now?

TALTHYBIOS: Men-at-arms, do your duty. Bring
    Kassandra forth
without delay. Our orders are to deliver her
to the general at once. And afterwards we can bring
to the rest of the princes their allotted captive
    women.
But see! What is that burst of a torch flame inside?
What can it mean? Are the Trojan women setting fire
to their chambers, at point of being torn from their
    land
to sail for Argos? Have they set themselves aflame
in longing for death? I know it is the way of freedom
in times like these to stiffen the neck against disaster.
Open, there, open; let not the fate desired by these,
dreaded by the Achaians, hurl their wrath on me.

HECUBA: You are wrong, there is no fire there. It
    is my Kassandra

whirled out on running feet in the passion of her
frenzy.
[Kassandra, *carrying a flaming torch, bursts
from the shelter*]
KASSANDRA: Lift up, heave up; carry the flame; I
bring fire of worship,
torches to the temple.
Io, Hymen,[9] my lord, Hymenaios.
Blessed the bridegroom.
Blessed am I indeed to lie at a king's side,
blessed the bride of Argos.
Hymen, my lord, Hymenaios.
Yours were the tears, my mother,
yours was the lamentation for my father fallen,
for your city so dear beloved,
but mine this marriage, my marriage,
and I shake out the torch-flare,
brightness, dazzle,
light for you, Hymenaios,
Hecate, light for you,
for the bed of virginity as man's custom ordains.

Let your feet dance, rippling the air; let go the
chorus,
as when my father's
fate went in blessedness.
O sacred circle of dance.
Lead now, Phoibos Apollo; I wear your laurel,
I tend your temple,
Hymen O Hymenaios.
Dance, mother, dance too; lead; let your feet
wind in the shifting pattern and follow mine,
keep the sweet step with me,
cry out the name Hymenaios
and the bride's name in the shrill
and the blessed incantation.
O you daughters of Phrygia robed in splendor,
dance for my wedding,
for the lord fate appointed to lie beside me.
CHORUS: Can you not, Queen Hecuba, stop this
bacchanal before
her light feet whirl her away into the Argive camp?
HECUBA: Fire God, in mortal marriages you lift
up your torch,
but here you throw a melancholy light, not seen
through my hopes that went so high in days gone
past. O child,
there was a time I dreamed you would not wed like
this,
not at the spear's edge, not under force of Argive
arms.
Let me take the light; crazed, passionate, you can not
carry
it straight enough, poor child. Your fate is intemperate
as you are, always. There is no relief for you.
[*Attendants come from the shelter. Hecuba gen-*

tly takes the torch from Kassandra *and gives it
to them to carry away*]
You Trojan women, take the torch inside, and change
to songs of tears this poor girl's marriage melodies.
KASSANDRA: O mother, star my hair with flowers of
victory.
I know you would not have it happen thus; and yet
this is a king I marry; then be glad; escort
the bride. Oh, thrust her strongly on. If Loxias[10]
is Loxias still, the Achaians' pride, great Agamemnon
has won a wife[11] more fatal than ever Helen was.
Since I will kill him; and avenge my brothers' blood
and my father's in the desolation of his house.
But I leave this in silence and sing not now the axe
to drop against my throat and other throats than
mine,
the agony of the mother murdered, brought to pass
from our marriage rites, and Atreus' house made
desolate.
I am ridden by God's curse still, yet I will step so far
out of my frenzy as to make plain this city's fate
as blessed beside the Achaians'. For one woman's
sake,
one act of love, these hunted Helen down and threw
thousands of lives away. Their general—clever
man—
in the name of a vile woman cut his darling down,
gave up for a brother the sweetness of children in his
house,
all to bring back that brother's wife, a woman who
went
of her free will, not caught in constraint of violence.
The Achaians came beside Skamandros' banks, and
died
day after day, though none sought to wrench their
land from them
nor their own towering cities. Those the War God
caught
never saw their sons again, nor were they laid to rest
decently in winding sheets by their wives' hands, but
lie
buried in alien ground; while all went wrong at home
as the widows perished, and barren couples raised
and nursed
the children of others, no survivor left to tend
the tombs, and what is left there, with blood sacrificed.
For such success as this congratulate the Greeks.
No, but the shame is better left in silence, for fear
my singing voice become the voice of wretchedness.
The Trojans have that glory which is loveliest:
they died for their own country. So the bodies of all
who took the spears were carried home in loving
hands,
brought, in the land of their fathers, to the embrace
of earth

[9] Hymen was the Greek god of marriage. He was celebrated with torches. "Io" was a Greek exclamation of joy
or exultation.

[10] Apollo, or Phoebus.
[11] Helen's sister, Clytemnestra, was Agamemnon's wife.
She murdered him on his return from Troy. See Aeschylus' *Agamemnon*, pages 11–29.

and buried becomingly as the rite fell due. The rest,
those Phrygians who escaped death in battle, day by
     day
came home to happiness the Achaians could not
     know;
their wives, their children. Then was Hektor's fate so
     sad?
You think so. Listen to the truth. He is dead and
     gone
surely, but with reputation, as a valiant man.
How could this be, except for the Achaians' coming?
Had they held back, none might have known how
     great he was.
The bride of Paris was the daughter of Zeus. Had he
not married her, fame in our house would sleep in
     silence still.
Though surely the wise man will forever shrink from
     war,
yet if war come, the hero's death will lay a wreath
not lustreless on the city. The coward alone brings
     shame.
Let no more tears fall, mother, for our land, nor for
this marriage I make; it is by marriage that I bring
to destruction those whom you and I have hated
     most.
  CHORUS: You smile on your disasters. Can it be
     that you
some day will illuminate the darkness of this song?
  TALTHYBIOS: Were it not Apollo who has driven
     wild your wits
I would make you sorry for sending the princes of
     our host
on their way home in augury of foul speech like this.
Now pride of majesty and wisdom's outward show
have fallen to stature less than what was nothing
     worth
since he, almighty prince of the assembled Hellenes,
Atreus' son beloved, has stooped—by his own will—
to find his love in a crazed girl. I, a plain man,
would not marry this woman or keep her as my slave.
You then, with your wits unhinged by idiocy,
your scolding of Argos and your Trojans glorified
I throw to the winds to scatter them. Come now with
     me
to the ships, a bride—and such a bride—for
     Agamemnon.

Hecuba, when Laertes' son calls you, be sure
you follow; if what all say who came to Ilion
is true, at the worst you will be a good woman's slave.
  KASSANDRA: That servant is a vile thing. Oh, how
     can heralds keep
their name of honor? Lackeys for despots be they, or
lackeys to the people, all men must despise them still.
You tell me that my mother must be slave in the
     house
of Odysseus? Where are all Apollo's promises
uttered to me, to my own ears, that Hecuba
should die in Troy? Odysseus I will curse no more,
poor wretch, who little dreams of what he must go

through when he will think Troy's pain and mine
     were golden grace
beside his own luck. Ten years he spent here, and ten
more years will follow before he at last comes home,
     forlorn
after the terror of the rock and the thin strait;
Charybdis;[12] and the mountain striding Cyclops,[13]
     who eats
men's flesh; the Ligurian witch who changes men to
     swine,
Kirkê;[14] the wreck of all his ships on the salt sea,
the lotus passion, the sacred oxen of the Sun
slaughtered, and dead flesh moaning into speech, to
     make
Odysseus listening shiver. Cut the story short:
he will go down to the water of death, and return
     alive
to reach home, and the thousand sorrows waiting
     there.

Why must I transfix each of Odysseus' labors one by
     one?
Lead the way, go quick to the house of death where
     I shall take my mate.
Lord of all the sons of Danaos, haughty in your mind
     of pride,
not by day, but evil in the evil night you shall find
     your grave
when I lie corpse-cold and naked next my husband's
     sepulchre,
piled in the ditch for animals to rip and feed on,
     beaten by
streaming storms of winter, I who wore Apollo's sac-
     raments.
Garlands of the god I loved so well, the spirit's dress
     of pride,
leave me, as I leave those festivals where once I was
     so gay.
See, I tear your adornments from my skin not yet
     defiled by touch,
throw them to the running winds to scatter, O lord
     of prophecy.
Where is this general's ship, then? Lead me where
     I must set my feet on board.
Wait the wind of favor in the sails; yet when the ship
     goes out
from this shore, she carries one of the three Furies
     in my shape.
Land of my ancestors, good-bye; O mother, weep no
     more for me.
You beneath the ground, my brothers, Priam, father
     of us all,
I will be with you soon and come triumphant to the
     dead below,
leaving at my back the wreckage of the house of
     Atreus.

[12] A female monster, a personification of a whirlpool
near Messina.
[13] One-eyed giants who lived in mountain caves.
[14] Better known as Circe; a sorceress in *The Odyssey*.

[Kassandra *is taken away by* Talthybios *and his soldiers.* Hecuba *collapses*]

CHORUS: Handmaids of aged Hecuba, can you not see
how your mistress, powerless to cry out, lies prone? Oh, take
her hand and help her to her feet, you wretched maids.
Will you let an aged helpless woman lie so long?

HECUBA: No. Let me lie where I have fallen. Kind acts, my maids,
must be unkind, unwanted. All that I endure
and have endured and shall, deserves to strike me down.
O gods! What wretched things to call on—gods!—for help
although the decorous action is to invoke their aid
when all our hands lay hold on is unhappiness.
No. It is my pleasure first to tell good fortune's tale,
to cast its count more sadly against disasters now.
I was a princess, who was once a prince's bride,
mother by him of sons preëminent, beyond
the mere numbers of them, lords of the Phrygian domain,
such sons for pride to point to as no woman of Troy,
no Hellene, none in the outlander's wide world might match.
And then I saw them fall before the spears of Greece,
and cut this hair for them, and laid it on their graves.
I mourned their father, Priam. None told me the tale
of his death. I saw it, with these eyes. I stood to watch
his throat cut, next the altar of the protecting god.
I saw my city taken. And the girls I nursed,
choice flowers to wear the pride of any husband's eyes,
matured to be dragged by hands of strangers from my arms.
There is no hope left that they will ever see me more,
no hope that I shall ever look on them again.
There is one more stone to key this arch of wretchedness:
I must be carried away to Hellas now, an old
slave woman, where all those tasks that wrack old age shall be
given me by my masters. I must work the bolt
that bars their doorway, I whose son was Hektor once;
or bake their bread; lay down these withered limbs to sleep
on the bare ground, whose bed was royal once; abuse
this skin once delicate the slattern's way, exposed
through robes whose rags will mock my luxury of long since.
Unhappy, O unhappy. And all this came to pass
and shall be, for the way one woman chose a man.
Kassandra, O daughter, whose excitements were the god's,
you have paid for your consecration now; at what a price!
And you, my poor Polyxena, where are you now?

Not here, nor any boy or girl of mine, who were
so many once, is near me in my unhappiness.
And you would lift me from the ground? What hope? What use?
Guide these feet long ago so delicate in Troy,
a slave's feet now, to the straw sacks laid on the ground
and the piled stones; let me lay down my head and die
in an exhaustion of tears. Of all who walk in bliss
call not one happy yet, until the man is dead.

[HECUBA, *after being led to the back of the stage, flings herself to the ground once more*]

CHORUS: Voice of singing, stay
with me now, for Ilion's sake;
take up the burden of tears,
the song of sorrow;
the dirge for Troy's death
must be chanted;
the tale of my captivity
by the wheeled stride of the fourfoot beast of the Argives,
the horse they left in the gates,
thin gold at its brows,
inward, the spears' high thunder.
Our people thronging
the rock of Troy let go the great cry:
'The war is over! Go down,
bring back the idol's enchanted wood
to the Maiden of Ilion, Zeus' daughter.'
Who stayed then? Not one girl, not one
old man, in their houses,
but singing for happiness
let the lurking death in.

And the generation of Troy
swept solid to the gates
to give the goddess
her pleasure: the colt immortal, unbroken,
the nest of Argive spears,
death for the children of Dardanos
sealed in the sleek hill pine chamber.
In the sling of the flax twist shipwise
they berthed the black hull
in the house of Pallas Athene
stone paved, washed now in the blood of our people
Strong, gay work
deep into black night
to the stroke of the Libyan lute
and all Troy singing, and girls'
light feet pulsing the air
in the kind dance measures;
indoors, lights everywhere,
torchflares on black
to forbid sleep's onset.

I was there also: in the great room
I danced the maiden of the mountains,
Artemis, Zeus' daughter.
When the cry went up, sudden,
bloodshot, up and down the city, to stun

the keep of the citadel. Children
reached shivering hands to clutch
at the mother's dress.
War stalked from his hiding place.
Pallas did this.
Beside their altars the Trojans
died in their blood. Desolate now,
men murdered, our sleeping rooms gave up
their brides' beauty
to breed sons for Greek men,
sorrow for our own country.

[*A wagon comes on the stage. It is heaped with
a number of spoils of war, in the midst of which
sits* Andromache *holding* Astyanax. *While the
Chorus continues speaking,* Hecuba *rises once
more*]

Hecuba look, I see her, rapt
to the alien wagon, Andromache,
close to whose beating breast clings
the boy Astyanax, Hektor's sweet child.
O carried away—to what land?—unhappy woman,
on the chariot floor, with the brazen arms
of Hektor, of Troy
captive and heaped beside you
torn now from Troy, for Achilleus' son
to hang in the shrines of Phthia.

ANDROMACHE: I am in the hands of Greek masters.
HECUBA: Alas
ANDROMACHE: Must the incantation
HECUBA: Ah me
ANDROMACHE: of my own grief win
  tears from you
HECUBA: It must—O Zeus
ANDROMACHE: my own dis-
  tress?
HECUBA: O my children
ANDROMACHE: once. No longer.
HECUBA: Lost, lost, Troy our dominion
ANDROMACHE: unhappy
HECUBA: and my lordly children.
ANDROMACHE: Gone, alas
HECUBA: they were mine
ANDROMACHE: sorrows only.
HECUBA: Sad destiny
ANDROMACHE: of our city
HECUBA: a wreck, and burning.
ANDROMACHE: Come back, O my husband.
HECUBA: Poor child, you invoke
a dead man; my son once
ANDROMACHE: my defender.
HECUBA: And you, whose death shamed the Acha-
  ians
ANDROMACHE: lord of us all once,
O patriarch, Priam,
HECUBA: take me to my death now.
ANDROMACHE: Longing for death drives deep;
HECUBA: O sor-
  rowful, such is our fortune
ANDROMACHE: lost our city

HECUBA: and our pain lies deep
  under pain piled over.
ANDROMACHE: We are the hated of God, since
  once your youngest escaping
Death, brought down Troy's towers in the arms of a
  worthless woman,
piling at the feet of Pallas the bleeding bodies of our
  young men
sprawled, kites' food, while Troy takes up the yoke
  of captivity.
HECUBA: O my city, my city forlorn
ANDROMACHE: abandoned,
  I weep this
HECUBA: miserable last hour
ANDROMACHE: of the house
  where I bore my children.
HECUBA: O my sons, this city and your mother are
  desolate of you.
Sound of lamentation and sorrow,
tears on tears shed. Home, farewell, since the dead
  have forgotten
all sorrows, and weep no longer.
CHORUS: They who are sad find somehow sweetness in tears, the song
of lamentation and the melancholy Muse.
ANDROMACHE: Hecuba, mother of the man whose
  spear was death
to the Argives, Hektor: do you see what they have
  done to us?
HECUBA: I see the work of gods who pile tower-
  high the pride
of those who were nothing, and dash present grandeur down.
ANDROMACHE: We are carried away, sad spoils,
  my boy and I; our life
transformed, as the aristocrat becomes the serf.
HECUBA: Such is the terror of necessity. I lost
Kassandra, roughly torn from my arms before you
  came.
ANDROMACHE: Another Aias to haunt your daughter? Some such thing
it must be. Yet you have lost still more than you yet
  know.
HECUBA: There is no numbering my losses. Infinitely
misfortune comes to outrace misfortune known before.
ANDROMACHE: Polyxena is dead. They cut your
  daughter's throat
to pleasure dead Achilleus' corpse, above his
  grave.
HECUBA: O wretched. This was what Talthybios
  meant, that speech
cryptic, incomprehensible, yet now so clear.
ANDROMACHE: I saw her die, and left this chariot
  seat to lay
a robe upon her body and sing the threnody.
HECUBA: Poor child, poor wretched, wretched darling, sacrificed,
but without pity, and in pain, to a dead man.

ANDROMACHE: She is dead, and this was death indeed; and yet to die
as she did was better than to live as I live now.

HECUBA: Child, no. No life, no light is any kind of death,
since death is nothing, and in life the hopes live still.

ANDROMACHE: O mother, our mother, hear me while I reason through
this matter fairly—might it even hush your grief?
Death, I am sure, is like never being born, but death
is better thus by far than to live a life of pain,
since the dead with no perception of evil feel no grief,
while he who was happy once, and then unfortunate,
finds his heart driven far from the old lost happiness.
She died; it is as if she never saw the light
of day, for she knows nothing now of what she suffered.
But I, who aimed the arrows of ambition high
at honor, and made them good, see now how far I fall,
I, who in Hektor's house worked out all custom that brings
discretion's name to women. Blame them or blame them not,
there is one act that swings the scandalous speech their way
beyond all else: to leave the house and walk abroad.
I longed to do it, but put the longing aside, and stayed
always within the enclosure of my own house and court.
The witty speech some women cultivate I would
not practice, but kept my honest inward thought, and made
my mind my only and sufficient teacher. I gave
my lord's presence the tribute of hushed lips, and eyes
quietly downcast. I knew when my will must have its way
over his, knew also how to give way to him in turn.
Men learned of this; I was talked of in the Achaian camp,
and reputation has destroyed me now. At the choice
of women, Achilleus' son picked me from the rest, to be
his wife: a lordly house, yet I shall be a slave.
If I dash back the beloved memory of Hektor
and open wide my heart to my new lord, I shall be
a traitor to the dead love, and know it; if I cling
faithful to the past, I win my master's hatred. Yet
they say one night of love suffices to dissolve
a woman's aversion to share the bed of any man.
I hate and loathe that woman who casts away the once
beloved, and takes another in her arms of love.
Even the young mare torn from her running mate and teamed
with another will not easily wear the yoke. And yet
this is a brute and speechless beast of burden, not
like us intelligent, lower far in nature's scale.
Dear Hektor, when I had you I had a husband, great

in understanding, rank, wealth, courage: all my wish.
I was a virgin when you took me from the house
of my father; I gave you all my maiden love, my first.
And now you are dead, and I must cross the sea, to serve,
prisoner of war, the slave's yoke on my neck, in Greece.
No, Hecuba; can you not see my fate is worse
than hers you grieve, Polyxena's? That one thing left
always while life lasts, hope, is not for me. I keep
no secret deception in my heart—sweet though it be
to dream—that I shall ever be happy any more.

CHORUS: You stand where I do in misfortune, and while you mourn
your own life, tell me what I, too, am suffering.

HECUBA: I have never been inside the hull of a ship, but know
what I know only by hearsay and from painted scenes,
yet think that seamen, while the gale blows moderately,
take pains to spare unnecessary work, and send
one man to the steering oar, another aloft, and crews
to pump the bilge from the hold. But when the water is troubled
and seas wash over the decks they lose their nerve, and let
her go by the run at the waves' will, leaving all to chance.
So I, in this succession of disasters, swamped,
battered by this storm immortally inspired, have lost
my lips' control and let them go, say anything
they will. Yet still, beloved child, you must forget
what happened with Hektor. Tears will never save you now.
Give your obedience to the new master; let your ways
entice his heart to make him love you. If you do
it will be better for all who are close to you. This boy,
my own son's child, might grow to manhood and bring back—
he alone could do it—something of our city's strength.
On some far day the children of your children might
come home, and build. There still may be another Troy.

But we say this, and others will speak also. See,
here is some runner of the Achaians come again.
Who is he? What news? What counsel have they taken now?

[Talthybios enters again with his escort]

TALTHYBIOS: O wife of Hektor, once the bravest man in Troy,
do not hate me. This is the will of the Danaans and
the kings. I wish I did not have to give this message.

ANDROMACHE: What can this mean, this hint of hateful things to come?

TALTHYBIOS: The council has decreed for your son—how can I say this?

ANDROMACHE: That he shall serve some other master than I serve?

TALTHYBIOS: No man of Achaia shall ever make this boy his slave.

ANDROMACHE: Must he be left behind in Phrygia, all alone?

TALTHYBIOS: Worse; horrible. There is no easy way to tell it.

ANDROMACHE: I thank your courtesy—unless your news be really good.

TALTHYBIOS: They will kill your son. It is monstrous. Now you know the truth.

ANDROMACHE: Oh, this is worse than anything I heard before.

TALTHYBIOS: Odysseus. He urged it before the Greeks, and got his way.

ANDROMACHE: This is too much grief, and more than anyone could bear.

TALTHYBIOS: He said a hero's son could not be allowed to live.

ANDROMACHE: Even thus may his own sons some day find no mercy.

TALTHYBIOS: He must be hurled from the battlements of Troy.

[He goes toward Andromache, who clings fast to her child, as if to resist]

No, wait!
Let it happen this way. It will be wiser in the end.
Do not fight it. Take your grief as you were born to take it,
give up the struggle where your strength is feebleness
with no force anywhere to help. Listen to me!
Your city is gone, your husband. You are in our power.
How can one woman hope to struggle against the arms
of Greece? Think, then. Give up the passionate contest.
                                                    This
will bring no shame. No man can laugh at your submission.
And please—I request you—hurl no curse at the Achaians
for fear the army, savage over some reckless word,
forbid the child his burial and the dirge of honor.
Be brave, be silent; out of such patience you can hope
the child you leave behind will not lie unburied here,
and that to you the Achaians will be less unkind.

ANDROMACHE: O darling child I loved too well for happiness,
your enemies will kill you and leave your mother forlorn.
Your own father's nobility, where others found
protection, means your murder now. The memory
of his valor comes ill-timed for you. O bridal bed,
O marriage rites that brought me home to Hektor's house
a bride, you were unhappy in the end. I lived
never thinking the baby I had was born for butchery
by Greeks, but for lordship over all Asia's pride of
earth.

Poor child, are you crying too? Do you know what they
will do to you? Your fingers clutch my dress. What use,
to nestle like a young bird under the mother's wing?
Hektor can not come back, not burst from underground
to save you, that spear of glory caught in the quick hand,
nor Hektor's fame, nor any strength of Phrygian arms.
Yours the sick leap head downward from the height, the fall
where none have pity, and the spirit smashed out in death.
O last and loveliest embrace of all, O child's
sweet fragrant body. Vanity in the end. I nursed
for nothing the swaddled baby at this mother's breast;
in vain the wrack of the labor pains and the long sickness.
Now once again, and never after this, come close
to your mother, lean against my breast and wind your arms
around my neck, and put your lips against my lips.

[She kisses Astyanax and relinquishes him]

Greeks! Your Greek cleverness is simple barbarity.
Why kill this child, who never did you any harm?
O flowering of the house of Tyndareus! Not his,
not God's daughter, never that, but child of many fathers
I say; the daughter of Vindictiveness, of Hate,
of Blood, Death; of all wickedness that swarms on earth.
I cry it aloud: Zeus never was your father, but you
were born a pestilence to all Greeks and the world beside.
Accursed; who from those lovely and accursed eyes
brought down to shame and ruin the bright plains of Troy.
Oh, seize him, take him, dash him to death if it must be done;
feed on his flesh if it is your will. These are the gods
who damn us to this death, and I have no strength to save
my boy from execution. Cover this wretched face
and throw me into the ship and that sweet bridal bed
I walk to now across the death of my own child.

[Talthybios gently lifts the child out of the wagon, which leaves the stage, carrying Andromache away]

CHORUS: Unhappy Troy! For the sweetness in one woman's arms'
embrace, unspeakable, you lost these thousands slain.

TALTHYBIOS: Come, boy, taken from the embrace beloved
of your mourning mother. Climb the high circle
of the towers your fathers built. There
end life. This was the order.
Take him.

[*He hands* Astyanax *to the guards, who lead him out*]

I am not the man
to do this. Some other
without pity, not as I ashamed,
should be herald of messages like this.

[*He goes out*]

HECUBA: O child of my own unhappy child,
shall your life be torn from your mother
and from me? Wicked. Can I help,
dear child, not only suffer? What help?
Tear face, beat bosom. This is all
my power now. O city,
O child, what have we left to suffer?
Are we not hurled
down the whole length of disaster?

CHORUS: Telamon, O king in the land where the
    bees swarm,
Salamis the surf-pounded isle where you founded
    your city
to front that hallowed coast where Athene broke
forth the primeval pale branch of olive,
wreath of the bright air and a glory on Athens the
    shining:
O Telamon, you came in your pride of arms
with Alkmena's archer[15]
to Ilion, our city, to sack and destroy it
on that age-old venture.

This was the first flower of Hellenic strength Herakles
    brought in anger
for the horses promised; and by Simoeis' calm
    waters[16]
checked the surf-wandering oars and made fast the
    ships' stern cables.
From which vessels came out the deadly bow hand,
death to Laomedon, as the scarlet wind of the flames
    swept over
masonry straight-hewn by the hands of Apollo.
This was a desolation of Troy
twice taken; twice in the welter of blood the walls
    Dardanian
went down before the red spear.

In vain, then, Laomedon's child,
you walk in delicate pride
by the golden pitchers
in loveliest servitude
to fill Zeus' wine cups;
while Troy your mother is given to the flame to eat,
and the lonely beaches
mourn, as sad birds sing
for the young lost,
for the sword hand and the children
and the aged women.
Gone now the shining pools where you bathed,
the fields where you ran

[15] Telamon, father of Ajax, accompanied Hercules, or
Herakles (referred to as "Alkmena's archer") on his
campaign.
[16] A river in the land of the Trojans in Asia Minor.

all desolate. And you
Ganymede,[17] go in grace by the thrones of God
with your young, calm smile even now
as Priam's kingdom
falls to the Greek spear.

O Love, Love, it was you
in the high halls of Dardanos,
the sky-daughters of melody beside you,
who piled the huge strength of Troy
in towers, the gods' own hands
concerned. I speak no more
against Zeus' name.
But the light men love, who shines
through the pale wings of morning,
balestar[18] on this earth now,
watched the collapse of tall towers:
Dawn. Her lord was of this land;
she bore his children,
Tithonos,[19] caught away by the golden car
and the starry horses,
who made our hopes so high.
For the gods loved Troy once.
Now they have forgotten.

[*Menelaos* comes on the stage, attended by a
    detail of armed soldiers*]

MENELAOS: O splendor of sunburst breaking forth
    this day, whereon
I lay my hands once more on Helen, my life. And yet
it is not, so much as men think, for the woman's
    sake
I came to Troy, but against that guest proved
    treacherous,
who pirate-like carried the woman from my house.
Since the gods have seen to it that *he* paid the penalty,
fallen before the Hellenic spear, his kingdom
    wrecked,
I come for *her* now, the wife once my own, whose
    name
I can no longer speak with any happiness,
to take her away. In this house of captivity
she is numbered among the other women of Troy, a
    slave.
And those men whose work with the spear has won
    her back
gave her to me, to kill, or not to kill, but lead
away to the land of Argos, if such be my pleasure.
And such it is; the death of Helen in Troy I will let
pass, have the oars take her by sea ways back to Greek
soil, and there give her over to execution;
blood penalty for friends who are dead in Ilion here.
Go to the house, my followers, and take her out;
no, drag her out; lay hands upon that hair so stained
with men's destruction. When the winds blow fair
    astern

[17] The handsome young cupbearer of the Olympian
gods.
[18] A star that brings evil (bale) to man.
[19] Brother of Priam and husband of Aurora, the dawn,
who granted him the dubious gift of immortality without
also giving him perpetual youth.

we will take ship again and bring her back to Hellas.

HECUBA: O power, who mount the world, wheel where the world rides,
O mystery of man's knowledge, whosoever you be,
Zeus named, nature's necessity or mortal mind,
I call upon you; for you walk the path none hears
yet bring all human action back to right at last.

MENELAOS: What can this mean? How strange a way to call on gods.

HECUBA: Kill your wife, Menelaos, and I will bless your name.
But keep your eyes away from her. Desire will win.
She looks enchantment, and where she looks homes are set fire;
she captures cities as she captures the eyes of men.
We have had experience, you and I. We know the truth.

[Men at arms bring Helen *roughly out of the shelter. She makes no resistance*]

HELEN: Menelaos, your first acts are argument of terror
to come. Your lackeys put their hands on me. I am dragged
out of my chambers by brute force. I know you hate
me; I am almost sure. And still there is one question
I would ask you, if I may. What have the Greeks decided
to do with me? Or shall I be allowed to live?

MENELAOS: You are not strictly condemned, but all the army gave
you into my hands, to kill you for the wrong you did.

HELEN: Is it permitted that I argue this, and prove
that my death, if I am put to death, will be unjust?

MENELAOS: I did not come to talk with you. I came to kill.

HECUBA: No. Menelaos, listen to her. She should not die
unheard. But give me leave to take the opposite case;
the prosecution. There are things that happened in Troy
which you know nothing of, and the long-drawn argument
will mean her death. She never can escape us now.

MENELAOS: This is a gift of leisure. If she wishes to speak
she may. But it is for your sake, understand, that I give
this privilege I never would have given to her.

HELEN: Perhaps it will make no difference if I speak well
or badly, and your hate will not let you answer me.
All I can do is to foresee the arguments
you will use in accusation of me, and set against
the force of your charges, charges of my own.
                                             First, then!
She mothered the beginning of all this wickedness.
For Paris was her child. And next to her the old king,

who would not destroy the infant Alexander,[20] that dream
of the firebrand's agony, has ruined Troy, and me.
This is not all; listen to the rest I have to say.
Alexander was the judge of the goddess trinity.
Pallas Athene would have given him power, to lead
the Phrygian arms on Hellas and make it desolate.
All Asia was Hera's promise, and the uttermost zones
of Europe for his lordship, if her way prevailed.
But Aphrodite, picturing my loveliness,
promised it to him for the word that her beauty surpassed
all others. Think what this means, and all the consequence.
Kypris[21] prevailed, and I was won in marriage: all
for Greek advantage. Asia is not your lord; you serve
no tyrant now, nor take the spear in his defense.
Yet Hellas' fortune was my own misfortune. I,
sold once for my body's beauty stand accused, who should
for what has been done wear garlands on my head.

                                             I know.
You will say all this is nothing to the immediate charge:
I did run away; I did go secretly from your house.
But when he came to me—call him any name you will:
Paris? or Alexander? or the spirit of blood
to haunt this woman?—he came with a goddess at his side;
no weak one. And you—it was criminal—took ship for Crete
and left me there in Sparta in the house, alone.

You see?
I wonder—and I ask this of myself, not you—
why *did* I do it? What made me run away from home
with the stranger, and betray my country and my hearth?
Challenge the goddess then, show your greater strength than Zeus'
who has the other gods in his power, and still is slave
to Aphrodite alone. Shall I not be forgiven?
Still you might have some show of argument against me.
When Paris was gone to the deep places of death, below
ground, and the immortal practice on my love was gone,
I should have come back to the Argive ships, left Troy.
I did try to do it, and I have witnesses,
the tower's gatekeepers and the sentinels on the wall,
who caught me again and again as I let down the rope

[20] Another name for Paris, of the Homeric epics.
[21] Cypris—another name for Aphrodite or Venus, the goddess of love.

from the battlements and tried to slip away to the
    ground.
For Deiphobos, my second husband: he took me
    away
by force and kept me his wife against the Phrygians'
    will.

O my husband, can you kill me now and think you
    kill
in righteousness? I was the bride of force. Before,
I brought their houses to the sorrow of slavery
instead of conquest. Would you be stronger than the
    gods?
Try, then. But even such ambition is absurd.
    CHORUS: O Queen of Troy, stand by your children
        and your country!
Break down the beguilement of this woman; since she
    speaks
well, and has done wickedly. This is dangerous.
    HECUBA: First, to defend the honor of the gods,
        and show
that the woman is a scandalous liar. I will not
believe it! Hera and the virgin Pallas Athene
could never be so silly and empty-headed that
Hera would sell Argos to the barbarians,
or Pallas let Athenians be the slaves of Troy.
They went to Ida in girlish emulation, vain
of their own loveliness? Why? Tell me the reason
    Hera
should fall so much in love with the idea of beauty.
To win some other lord more powerful than Zeus?
Or has Athene marked some god to be her mate,
she, whose virginity is a privilege won from Zeus,
who abjures marriage? Do not trick out your own
    sins
by calling the gods stupid. No wise man will believe
    you.
You claim, and I must smile to hear it, that Aphrodite
came at my son's side to the house of Menelaos;
who could have caught up you and your city of
    Amyklai[22]
and set you in Ilion, moving not from the quiet of
    heaven.
Nonsense. My son was handsome beyond all other
    men.
You looked at him, and sense went Cyprian[23] at the
    sight,
since Aphrodite is nothing but the human lust,
named rightly, since the word of lust begins the
    god's name.
You saw him in the barbaric spendor of his robes,
gorgeous with gold. It made your senses itch. You
    thought,
being queen only in Argos, in little luxury,
that once you got rid of Sparta for the Phrygian city
where gold streamed everywhere, you could let ex-
    travagance
run wild. No longer were Menelaos and his house

[22] Sparta.
[23] I.e., became overwhelmed with love.

sufficient to your spoiled luxurious appetites.
So much for that. You say my son took you away
by force. What Spartan heard you cry for help? You
    did
cry out? Or did you? Kastor, your brother, was there,
    a young
man, and his twin not yet caught up among the stars.
Then when you had reached Troy, and the Argives
    at your heels
came, and the agony of the murderous spears began,
when the reports came in that Menelaos' side
was winning, you would praise him, simply to make
    my son
unhappy at the strength of his love's challenger,
forgetting your husband when the luck went back to
    Troy.
You worked hard: not to make yourself a better
    woman,
but to make sure always to be on the winning side.
You claim you tried to slip away with ropes let
    down
from the ramparts, and this proves you stayed against
    your will?
Perhaps. But when were you ever caught in the
    strangling noose,
caught sharpening a dagger? Which any noble wife
would do, desperate with longing for her lord's return.
Yet over and over again I gave you good advice:
'Make your escape, my daughter; there are other
    girls
for my sons to marry. I will help you get away
to the ships of the Achaians. Let the Greeks, and us,
stop fighting.' So I argued, but you were not pleased.
Spoiled in the luxury of Alexander's house
you liked foreigners to kiss the ground before your
    feet.
All that impressed you.
                    And now you dare to come outside,
figure fastidiously arranged, to look upon
the same air as your husband, O abominable
heart, who should walk submissively in rags of robes,
shivering with anxiety, head Scythian-cropped,
your old impudence gone and modesty gained at last
by reason of your sinful life.
                    O Menelaos,
mark this, the end of my argument. Be true to your
high reputation and to Hellas. Grace both, and kill
Helen. Thus make it the custom toward all woman-
    kind
hereafter, that the price of adultery is death.
    CHORUS: Menelaos, keep the ancestral honor of
        your house.
Punish your wife, and purge away from Greece the
    stigma
on women. You shall seem great even to your
    enemies.
    MENELAOS: All you have said falls into line with
        my own thought.
This woman left my household for a stranger's bed
of her own free will, and all this talk of Aphrodite

is for pure show. Away, and face the stones of the
   mob.
Atone for the long labors of the Achaians in
the brief act of dying, and know your penance for my
   shame.
   [Helen *drops before him and embraces his
   knees*]
   HELEN: No, by your knees! I am not guilty of the
   mind's
infection, which the gods sent. Do not kill! Have
   pity!
   HECUBA: Be true to the memory of all your friends
   she murdered.
It is for them and for their children that I plead.
   [Menelaos *pushes* Helen *away*]
   MENELAOS: Enough, Hecuba. I am not listening to
   her now.
I speak to my servants: see that she is taken away
to where the ships are beached. She will make the
   voyage home.
   HECUBA: But let her not be put in the same ship
   with you.
   MENELAOS: What can you mean? That she is
   heavier than she was?
   HECUBA: A man in love once never is out of love
   again.
   MENELAOS: Sometimes; when the beloved's heart
   turns false to him.
Yet it shall be as you wish. She shall not be allowed
in the same ship I sail in. This was well advised.
And once in Argos she must die the vile death earned
by her vile life, and be an example to all women
to live temperately. This is not the easier way;
and yet her execution will tincture with fear
the lust of women even more depraved than she.
   [Helen *is led out*, Menelaos *following*]
   CHORUS: Thus, O Zeus, you betrayed all
to the Achaians: your temple
in Ilion, your misted altar,
the flame of the clotted sacraments,
the smoke of the skying incense,
Pergamon the hallowed,
the ivied ravines of Ida, washed
by the running snow. The utter
peaks that surprise the sun bolts,
shining and primeval place of divinity.

Gone are your sacrifices, the choirs'
glad voices singing to the gods
night long, deep into darkness;
gone the images, gold on wood
laid, the twelves of the sacred moons,
the magic Phrygian number.
Can it be, can it be, my lord, you have forgotten
from your throne high in heaven's
bright air, my city which is ruined
and the flame storm that broke it?

O my dear, my husband,
O wandering ghost
unwashed, unburied; the sea hull must carry me

in the flash of its wings' speed
to Argos, city of horses, where
the stone walls Cyclopian pasture in sky.[24]
The multitudes of our children stand
clinging to the gates and cry through their tears.
And one girl weeps:
'O mother, the Achaians take me away
lonely from your eyes
to the black ship
where the oars dip surf
toward Salamis the blessed,
or the peak between two seas
where Pelops' hold[25]
keeps the gates at the Isthmos.'

Oh that as Menelaos' ship
makes way through the mid-sea
the bright pronged spear immortal of thunder might
   smash it
far out in the Aigaian,[26]
as in tears, in bondage to Hellas
I am cut from my country;
as she holds the golden mirror
in her hands, girls' grace,
she, God's daughter.
Let him never come home again, to a room in
   Lakonia[27]
and the hearth of his fathers;
never more to Pitana's streets
and the bronze gates of the Maiden;[28]
since he forgave his shame
and the vile marriage, the sorrows
of great Hellas and the land
watered by Simoeis.[29]
   [Talthybios *returns. His men carry, laid on the
   shield of* Hektor, *the body of* Astyanax]
But see!
Now evils multiply in our land.
Behold, O pitiful wives
of the Trojans. This is Astyanax,
dead, dashed without pity from the towers, and borne
by the Danaans, who murdered him.
   TALTHYBIOS: Hecuba, one last vessel of Achilleus'
   son
remains, manned at the oar sweeps now, to carry back
to the shores of Phthiotis his last spoils of war.
Neoptolemos himself has put to sea. He heard
news of old Peleus in difficulty and the land
invaded by Akastos, son of Pelias.
Such news put speed above all pleasure of delay.

[24] The walls are made of massive stone, hence are
Cyclopian. The word "pasture" is here employed as an
intransitive verb.
[25] The fortress on the Peloponnesian peninsula, the
southern peninsula of Greece on which Sparta is situated.
[26] The Aegean Sea.
[27] Sparta.
[28] Athens had a sort of embassy, a temple of Athene
("the Maiden"), in Sparta.
[29] Helen brought suffering to both Hellas (Greece) and
the land watered by the river Simoeis—that is, Troy.

So he is gone, and took with him Andromache,
whose lamentations for her country and farewells
to Hektor's tomb as she departed brought these tears
crowding into my eyes. And she implored that you
bury this dead child, your own Hektor's son, who
     died
flung from the battlements of Troy. She asked as well
that the bronze-backed shield, terror of the Achaians
     once,
when the boy's father slung its defence across his
     side,
be not taken to the hearth of Peleus, nor the room
where the slain child's Andromache must be a bride
once more, to waken memories by its sight, but given
in place of the cedar coffin and stone-chambered
     tomb
for the boy's burial. He shall be laid in your arms
to wrap the body about with winding sheets, and
     flowers,
as well as you can, out of that which is left to you.
Since she is gone. Her master's speed prevented her
from giving the rites of burial to her little child.

The rest of us, once the corpse is laid out, and earth
is piled above it, must raise the mast tree, and go.
Do therefore quickly everything that you must do.
There is one labor I myself have spared you. As
we forded on our way here Skamandros' running
     water,
I washed the body and made clean the wounds. I go
now, to break ground and dig the grave for him, that
     my
work be made brief, as yours must be, and our tasks
     end
together, and the ships be put to sea, for home.

    HECUBA: Lay down the circled shield of Hektor
      on the ground:
a hateful thing to look at; it means no love to me.
      [Talthybios *and his escort leave. Two soldiers
      wait*]
Achaians! All your strength is in your spears, not in
the mind. What were you afraid of, that it made you
     kill
this child so savagely? That Troy, which fell, might be
raised from the ground once more? Your strength
     meant nothing, then.
When Hektor's spear was fortunate, and numberless
strong hands were there to help him, we were still
     destroyed.
Now when the city is fallen and the Phrygians slain,
this baby terrified you? I despise the fear
which is pure terror in a mind unreasoning.

O darling child, how mournful was this death. You
     might
have fallen fighting for your city, grown to man's
age, and married, and with the king's power like a
     god's,
and died happy, if there is any happiness here.
But no. You grew to where you could see and learn,
     my child,

yet your mind was not old enough to win advantage
of fortune. How wickedly, poor boy, your fathers'
     walls,
Apollo's handiwork, have crushed your pitiful head
tended and trimmed to ringlets by your mother's
     hand,
and the face she kissed once, where the brightness
     now is blood
shining through the torn bones—too horrible to say
     more.
O little hands, sweet likenesses of Hektor's once,
now you lie broken at the wrists before my feet;
and mouth beloved whose words were once so con-
     fident,
you are dead; and all was false, when you would lean
     across
my bed, and say: 'Mother, when you die I will cut
my long hair in your memory, and at your grave
bring companies of boys my age, to sing farewell.'
It did not happen; now I, a homeless, childless, old
woman must bury your poor corpse, which is so
     young.
Alas for all the tendernesses, my nursing care,
and all your slumbers gone. What shall the poet say,
what words will he inscribe upon your monument?
*Here lies a little child the Argives killed, because
they were afraid of him.* That? The epitaph of Greek
     shame.
You will not win your father's heritage, except
for this, which is your coffin now: the brazen shield.

O shield, who guarded the strong shape of Hektor's
     arm:
the bravest man of all, who wore you once, is dead.
How sweet the impression of his body on your sling,
and at the true circle of your rim the stain of sweat
where in the grind of his many combats Hektor
     leaned
his chin against you, and the drops fell from his
     brow!

Take up your work now; bring from what is left some
     robes
to wrap the tragic dead. The gods will not allow
us to do it right. But let him have what we can give.

That mortal is a fool who, prospering, thinks his life
has any strong foundation; since our fortune's course
of action is the reeling way a madman takes,
and no one person is ever happy all the time.
      [Hecuba's *handmaidens bring out from the shelter
      a basket of robes and ornaments. During the
      scene which follows, the body of* Astyanax *is
      being made ready for burial*]
    CHORUS: Here are your women, who bring you
      from the Trojan spoils
such as is left, to deck the corpse for burial.
    HECUBA: O child, it is not for victory in riding, won
from boys your age, not archery—in which acts our
     people
take pride, without driving competition to excess—

that your sire's mother lays upon you now these
     treasures
from what was yours before; though now the accursed
     of God,
Helen, has robbed you, she who has destroyed as well
the life in you, and brought to ruin all our house.
     CHORUS: My heart,
you touched my heart, you who were once
a great lord in my city.
     HECUBA: These Phrygian robes' magnificence you
          should have worn
at your marriage to some princess uttermost in pride
in all the East, I lay upon your body now.
And you, once so victorious and mother of
a thousand conquests, Hektor's huge beloved shield:
here is a wreath for you, who die not, yet are dead
with this body; since it is better far to honor you
than the armor of Odysseus the wicked and wise.
     CHORUS: Ah me.
Earth takes you, child;
our tears of sorrow.
Cry aloud, our mother.
     HECUBA: Yes
     CHORUS: the dirge of the dead
     HECUBA: ah me
     CHORUS: evils never to be forgotten.
     HECUBA: I will bind up your wounds with ban-
          dages, and be
your healer: a wretched one, in name alone, no use.
Among the dead your father will take care of you.
     CHORUS: Rip, tear your faces with hands
that beat like oars.
Alas.
     HECUBA: Dear women. . . .
     CHORUS: Hecuba, speak to us. We are yours. What
          did you cry aloud?
     HECUBA: The gods meant nothing except to make
          life hard for me,
and of all cities they chose Troy to hate. In vain
we gave them sacrifices. If the very hand
of God had gripped and crushed this city deep in
     the ground,
we should have disappeared in darkness, and not
     given
a theme for music, and the songs of men to come.
You may go now, and hide the dead in his poor tomb;
he has those flowers that are the right of the under-
     world.
I think it makes small difference to the dead, if they
are buried in the tokens of luxury. All this
is an empty glorification left for those who live.
     [The soldiers take up and carry away the body
          of Astyanax]
     CHORUS: Sad mother, whose hopes were so huge
for your life. They are broken now.
Born to high blessedness
and a lordly line
your death was horror.

But see, see

on the high places of Ilion
the torchflares whirling in the hands
of men. For Troy
some ultimate agony.
     [Talthybios comes back, with numerous men]
     TALTHYBIOS: I call to the captains who have orders
          to set fire
to the city of Priam: shield no longer in the hand
the shining flame. Let loose the fire upon it. So
with the citadel of Ilion broken to the ground
we can take leave of Troy, in gladness, and go home.

And I speak to you, in second figure of my orders.
Children of Troy, when the lords of the armament
     sound
the high echoing crash of the trumpet call, then go
to the ship of the Achaians, to be taken away
from this land. And you, unhappiest and aged
     woman,
go with them. For Odysseus' men are here, to whom
enslaved the lot exiles you from your native land.
     HECUBA: Ah, wretched me. So this is the unhappy
          end
and goal of all the sorrows I have lived. I go
forth from my country and a city lit with flames.
Come, aged feet; make one last weary struggle, that I
may hail my city in its affliction. O Troy, once
so huge over all Asia in the drawn wind of pride,
your very name of glory shall be stripped away.
They are burning you, and us they drag forth from
     our land
enslaved. O gods! Do I call upon those gods for help?
I cried to them before now, and they would not hear.
Come then, hurl ourselves into the pyre. How sweet
to die in the flaming ruins of our fathers' house!
     TALTHYBIOS: Unhappy creature, ecstatic in your
          sorrows! Men,
take her, spare not. She is Odysseus' property.
You have orders to deliver her into his hands.
     HECUBA: O sorrow.
Kronion, Zeus, lord of Phrygia,
prince of our house, have you seen
the dishonor done to the seed of Dardanos?[30]
     CHORUS: He has seen, but the great city
is a city no more, it is gone. There is no Troy.
     HECUBA: O sorrow.
Ilion flares.
The chambers of Pergamon[31] take fire,
the citadel and the wall's high places.
     CHORUS: Our city fallen to the spear
fades as smoke winged in the sky,
halls hot in the swept fire
and the fierce lances.
     HECUBA: O soil where my children grew.
     CHORUS: Alas.
     HECUBA: O children, hear me; it is your mother
          who calls.

[30] I.e., the Trojans, whose legendary ancestor was
Dardanos.
[31] Troy; or the citadel or acropolis of Troy.

CHORUS: They are dead you cry to. This is a dirge.

HECUBA: I lean my old body against the earth
and both hands beat the ground.

CHORUS: I kneel to the earth, take up
the cry to my own dead,
poor buried husband.

HECUBA: We are taken, dragged away

CHORUS: a cry of pain, pain

HECUBA: under the slave's roof

CHORUS: away from my country.

HECUBA: Priam, my Priam. Dead
graveless, forlorn,
you know not what they have done to me.

CHORUS: Now dark, holy death
in the brutal butchery closed his eyes

HECUBA: O gods' house, city beloved,

CHORUS: Alas,

HECUBA: you are given the red flame and the
spear's iron.

CHORUS: You will collapse to the dear ground and
be nameless.

HECUBA: Ash, matching the skyward smoke wing,
will pile and blot from my sight the house where I
lived once.
once.

CHORUS: Lost shall be the name of the land,
all gone, perished. Troy, city of sorrow,
is there no longer.

HECUBA: Did you see, did you hear?

CHORUS: The crash of the citadel.

HECUBA: The earth shook, riven

CHORUS: to engulf the city.

HECUBA: O
shaking, tremulous limbs
this is the way. Forward:
into the slave's life.

CHORUS: Mourn for the ruined city, then go away
to the ships of the Achaians.

[Hecuba *is led away, and all go out, leaving the
stage empty*]

Aristophanes

(446?–385? B.C.)

Aristophanes was one of the writers of comedy who scolded and amused Athens during the historically critical last quarter of the fifth century, and his plays are, indeed, the only surviving examples of the astringent comic form known to the classical world as the Old Comedy. The New Comedy, which took shape in the next century, is the familiar one of manners and intrigue that has dominated the theatre for the past twenty-three centuries. The Old Comedy, choral in form and festive in spirit, resembling an exuberantly erotic spring rite, called for the talents of a burlesque and revue specialist, a social critic, and a poet. Since Aristophanes was generously endowed with these talents, as well as with a lively imagination, he surpassed and survived all the other comic poets of the Attic age. He was the Mack Sennett, W. S. Gilbert, and George Bernard Shaw of his time, as well as the equal of Sophocles and Euripides as a lyric poet.

Although we know virtually nothing about Aristophanes' life, there is no reason to believe that he was not a very active and vocal member of the Athenian intelligentsia. Plato included him among the participants of his *Symposium* and invented a delightful parable on love for him. It is probable that Aristophanes had lively verbal tilts with Socrates and Euripides, and he may have actually been on more friendly terms with both men than his satires would suggest. Comic poets enjoyed great license in Athens and lampooning by them did not necessarily imply implacable hostility. It is certain, however, that Aristophanes did arouse the animosity of the popular political party and its leading demagogue, Cleon, with his comedy *Babylonians*, which criticized Athens' highhanded treatment of her allies. An effort was made to declare him a "foreigner" who had no right to comment on Athenian politics; and he would probably have been "sent back where he came from," had he not come from Athens.

Like Euripides, Aristophanes belonged to the minority peace party that sought to put an end to the Peloponnesian War, which was draining the resources of Athens. Unlike Euripides, however, he maintained a conservative position in politics, art, and philosophy. He regarded the war madness of the Athenians and their susceptibility to demagoguery with strong misgivings, but he also deplored the relaxed manners and morality of his times and placed some of the blame on the speculative sophistry of Socrates and the literary innovations and radicalism of Euripides. He longed for the good old days of plain living and high thinking that he himself

could never have known—the age of the Marathon warriors and of a democracy led by the best families of Athens.

One group of Aristophanes' plays constitutes a criticism of the prolongation of war with Sparta and advocates a cessation of hostilities. The first of these satires, *The Acharnians*, written in the sixth year of the Peloponnesian War (425 B.C.) is probably the first antiwar comedy of the European theatre. After alluding to the rapacity of popular leaders and representing the sufferings of the rural population from constant invasion of the countryside, Aristophanes had a hardheaded farmer conclude a private peace with Sparta on honorable terms. In a second comedy, *Peace*, produced four years later, he showed another farmer flying to Olympus in search of the long absent goddess of peace, liberating her from the dungeon in which the Greeks had imprisoned her and ushering in a golden age of good will and prosperity. In the twenty-first year of the war (411 B.C.), Aristophanes created his masterpiece *Lysistrata*, in which the women of Athens stage a successful sex strike in order to bring the men back to their senses. A fourth comedy, *The Birds*, a work of sheer fantasy, presents the adventures of two Athenians who abandon the city in the hope of finding a less contentious country than their own. They conceive the notion of getting the unoffending birds to build a community of their own between earth and heaven and to make themselves masters of both men and gods by intercepting the incense that the former send to the latter. The two men, having sprouted wings in the meantime, go through with their plans and build the new city of Cloudcuckooland, whereupon many human beings clamor for citizenship in the new state and the gods, relinquishing their royalty, submit to the new rulers. A fifth comedy, *The Wasps*, exposed the deterioration of Athenian life with a burlesque satire on the Athenians' passion for paid jury duty and litigation, and still another burlesque, *The Knights*, was a scintillating extravaganza on the chicanery of Cleon and other demagogues. According to tradition, Aristophanes played the role of Cleon himself, since no actor would venture to impersonate the politician.

The logic-chopping school of philosophers known as Sophists enjoyed considerable vogue in Aristophanes' time and he devoted an entire play, *The Clouds*, to the subject, making Socrates the scapegoat for all the excesses of pseudo intelligence and "sophistication." Since the intellectuals of the time interested themselves in feminism and communism—Plato's *Republic*, we may note, outlines a stratified communistic society with philosopher-kings at its head—Aristophanes devoted another play, *Ecclesiazusae,* to both topics. (It is even possible that this comedy was written after *The Republic* and was intended as a travesty on that book.) And since Euripides was the leader of the literary *avant-garde* and held advanced political views as well, Aristophanes made him the ludicrous hero of *Thesmophoriazusae* (*Women at the Festival of Demeter*), as well as an object of satire in *The Frogs.*

In all these works, Aristophanes gave rein to an abundant fancy and made liberal use of topical allusions and parody. Only toward the end of his life, after the military collapse of Athens in 404 B.C., did he moderate his vivacious style. By then, however, the Old Comedy was no longer in its prime; it was tapering off into an innocuous impersonal and unpolitical form, Middle Comedy. His last extant work, *Plutus,* produced in 388 B.C., conformed to the new fashion. Although the humor is distilled from a social problem—namely, the unequal distribution of wealth among men (Plutus, the god of wealth, distributes his blessings haphazardly because he is blind), the play has less brilliance and verve than the comedies which Aristophanes wrote under the fifth-century Athenian democracy. One of the ironies of literary history is that Aristophanes' genius could be sustained only by the liberal spirit and the rationalistic iconoclasm at which he had leveled some of his sharpest satire. More than he apparently ever realized, he was himself the supreme exponent of an age of intellectual inquiry and sophistication.

The Frogs, his prize-winning comedy of the year 405 B.C., is the first known literary satire in world literature. It is also the best one ever written, and it entitles its author to be considered the first brilliant literary critic in history. The butt of his more than usually good-natured satire is Euripides, whom he must have esteemed more highly than he generally pretended to do, since the god of the theatre, Dionysus, is impelled to go down to the underworld in search of a good dramatist once Euripides is dead. Aeschylus is the god's—and Aristophanes'—final choice, but Euripides is a strong contender with Aeschylus for the distinction of being selected for resuscitation. The incisiveness of Aristophanes' literary criticism must be apparent even to those who derive their knowledge of Greek drama solely from translations. Good taste, which is also a matter of manners and morals, is a major theme of the comedy. Mingled with appraisals of the tragic poets, moreover, are pleas for national unity and the recall of political exiles which serve comedy's function of recalling men to sanity. And hovering over all temporal matters, resolving all discords in a feeling of rollicking fellowship, are the music of comic verse and the laughter of a man who gives free rein to a general irreverence for gods and men alike. Permeating the fantasy, the buffoonery, and the literary debates of *The Frogs* is the spirit of urbane enlightenment which is not the least precious of the Greek theatre's legacies to civilization.

THE FROGS[1]

By Aristophanes

TRANSLATED FROM THE GREEK BY BENJAMIN BICKLEY ROGERS[2]

DRAMATIS PERSONAE

DIONYSUS (BACCHUS)
XANTHIAS, *servant and slave of Dionysus*
HERACLES
CHARON
AEACUS, *doorkeeper in Pluto's palace*
EURIPIDES
AESCHYLUS

PLUTO
DEAD MAN
PERSEPHONE'S MAID-SERVANT
TWO WOMEN SUTLERS
MUTES
CHORUS OF VOTARIES
FROGS

THE SCENE

A road, with a house in the background. Dionysus appears on foot, wearing a yellow robe and a lion's skin over part of his body; he also carries a club. His servant Xanthias accompanies him on a donkey, carrying luggage on a pole. Later, the house—that is, the scene building in the theatre of Dionysus—represents other palaces and temples. In the first scene it represents the home of Heracles.—J. G.

THE ARGUMENT

Dionysus, the patron of the stage, in despair at the decline of the dramatic art (which had lately been deprived of its best tragic authors, Sophocles and Euripides), determines to descend the infernal regions with the intention of procuring the release of Euripides. He appears accordingly, equipped for the expedition, with the lion's skin and club (in imitation of Heracles, whose success in a similar adventure has encouraged him to the attempt); he still retains, however, his usual effeminate costume, which forms a contrast with these heroic attributes. Xanthias, his slave (like Silenus, the mythologic attendant of Dionysus), is mounted upon an ass; but, in conformity with the practice of other human slaves when attending their mortal masters upon an earthly journey, he carries a certain pole upon his shoulder, at the ends of which the various packages, necessary for his master's accommodation, are suspended in equilibrio. The first scene (which, if it had not been the first, might perhaps have been omitted) contains a censure

of the gross taste of the audience (suitable to the character of Dionysus as patron of the stage) with allusions to some contemporary rival authors, who submitted to court the applause of the vulgar by mere buffoonery.—The argument between Dionysus and Xanthias, at the end of this scene, probably contains some temporary allusion now unknown, but is obviously, and in the first place, a humorous exemplification of the philosophical, verbal sophisms, not, in all probability, new, even then, but which were then, for the first time, introduced in Athens, and which may be traced from thence to the schoolmen of the middle ages. Xanthias carries the bundles *passivè* et *formaliter*, the ass carries them *activè* et *materialiter*.
—J. HOOKHAM FRERE

XANTHIAS: Shall I crack any of those old jokes, master,
At which the audience never fail to laugh?
DIONYSUS: Aye, what you will, except *I'm getting crushed:*
Fight shy of that: I'm sick of that already.
XANTHIAS: Nothing else smart?
DIONYSUS: Aye, save *my shoulder's aching.*
XANTHIAS: Come now, that comical joke?[3]
DIONYSUS: With all my heart.
Only be careful not to shift your pole,[4]
And—
XANTHIAS: What?
DIONYSUS: And vow that you've a belly-ache.
XANTHIAS: May I not say I'm overburdened so
That if none ease me, I must ease myself?
DIONYSUS: For mercy's sake, not till I'm going to vomit.
XANTHIAS: What! must I bear these burdens, and not make
One of the jokes Ameipsias and Lycis

[1] The play was written about half a year after the important naval battle of Arginusae (406 B.C.), at which slaves who participated in the Athenian victory received their freedom, an event to which Aristophanes refers with fervid patriotism. Both Sophocles and Euripides had recently died.

[2] I have made a few slight editorial changes in the text and in those annotations that are taken from Rogers and credited to him.—J. G.

[3] What the joke was is not told. Xanthias probably made an expressive gesture.

[4] ἀνάφορον is a yoke such as is used in carrying milk-pails.

73

And Phrynichus,[5] in every play they write,
Put in the mouths of all their burden-bearers?

DIONYSUS: Don't make them; no! I tell you when I see
Their plays, and hear those jokes, I come away
More than a twelvemonth older than I went.

XANTHIAS: O thrice unlucky neck of mine, which now
Is *getting crushed*, yet must not crack its joke!

DIONYSUS: Now is not this fine pampered insolence
When I myself, Dionysus, son of—Pipkin,[6]
Toil on afoot, and let this fellow ride,
Taking no trouble, and no burden bearing?

XANTHIAS: What, don't I bear?

DIONYSUS: How can you when you're riding?

XANTHIAS: Why, I bear these.

DIONYSUS: How?

XANTHIAS: Most unwillingly.

DIONYSUS: Does not the donkey bear the load you're bearing?

XANTHIAS: Not what I bear myself: by Zeus, not he.

DIONYSUS: How can you bear, when you are borne yourself?

XANTHIAS: Don't know: but anyhow *my shoulder's aching*.

DIONYSUS: Then since you say the donkey helps you not,
You lift him up and carry him in turn.

XANTHIAS: O hang it all! why didn't I fight at sea?[7]
You should have smarted bitterly for this.

DIONYSUS: Get down, you rascal; I've been trudging on
Till now I've reached the portal, where I'm going
First to turn in. Boy! Boy! I say there, Boy!

HERACLES: Who banged the door? How like a prancing Centaur
He drove against it! Mercy o' me, what's this?

DIONYSUS: Boy.

XANTHIAS: Yes.

DIONYSUS: Did you observe?

XANTHIAS: What?

DIONYSUS: How alarmed
He is.

XANTHIAS: Aye truly, lest you've lost your wits.

HERACLES: O by Demeter, I can't choose but laugh.
Biting my lips won't stop me. Ha! ha! ha!

DIONYSUS: Pray you, come hither, I have need of you.

HERACLES: I vow I can't help laughing, I can't help it.
A lion's hide upon a yellow silk,
A club and buskin! What's it all about?
Where were you going?

DIONYSUS: I was serving lately
Aboard the—Cleisthenes.[8]

HERACLES: And fought?

DIONYSUS: And sank
More than a dozen of the enemy's ships.

HERACLES: You two?

DIONYSUS: We two.

HERACLES: And then I awoke, and lo!

DIONYSUS: There as, on deck, I'm reading to myself
The *Andromeda*,[9] a sudden pang of longing
Shoots through my heart, you can't conceive how keenly.

HERACLES: How big a pang?

DIONYSUS: A small one, Molon's[10] size.

HERACLES: Caused by a woman?

DIONYSUS: No.

HERACLES: A boy?

DIONYSUS: No, no.

HERACLES: A man?

DIONYSUS: Ah! ah!

HERACLES: Was it for Cleisthenes?

DIONYSUS: Don't mock me, brother: on my life I am
In a bad way: such fierce desire consumes me.

HERACLES: Aye, little brother? how?

DIONYSUS: I can't describe it.
But yet I'll tell you in a riddling way.
Have you e'er felt a sudden lust for soup?

HERACLES: Soup! Zeus-a-mercy, yes, ten thousand times.

DIONYSUS: Is the thing clear, or must I speak again?

HERACLES: Not of the soup: I'm clear about the soup.

DIONYSUS: Well, just that sort of pang devours my heart
For lost Euripides.

HERACLES: A dead man too.

DIONYSUS: And no one shall persuade me not to go
After the man.

HERACLES: Do you mean below, to Hades?

DIONYSUS: And lower still, if there's a lower still.

HERACLES: What on earth for?

DIONYSUS: I want a genuine poet,
"For some are not, and those that are, are bad."[11]

HERACLES: What! does not Iophon[12] live?

DIONYSUS: Well, he's the sole
Good thing remaining, if even he is good.
For even of that I'm not exactly certain.

HERACLES: If go you must, there's Sophocles—he comes

[5] Ameipsias, Phrynichus, and Lycis were Athenian writers of comedy.

[6] A wine jar.

[7] Xanthias means "why didn't I fight in the sea battle of Arginusae and obtain my liberty, so that I wouldn't have to serve you?"

[8] An effeminate character. A coarse jest is intended here.

[9] A romantic play by Euripides.

[10] A tragic actor noted for his large body.

[11] From a play, *Oeneus*, by Euripides.

[12] A slur on the son of Sophocles who wrote tragedies. Aristophanes goes on to hint that the good parts were Sophocles' work.

Before Euripides—why not take *him?*
  DIONYSUS: Not till I've tried if Iophon's coin rings
    true
When he's alone, apart from Sophocles.
Besides, Euripides, the crafty rogue,
Will find a thousand shifts to get away,
But *he* was easy here, is easy there.
  HERACLES: But Agathon,[13] where is he?
  DIONYSUS: He has gone and left us.
A genial poet, by his friends much missed.
  HERACLES: Gone where?
  DIONYSUS: To join the blessed in their banquets.
  HERACLES: But what of Xenocles?[14]
  DIONYSUS: O he be hanged!
  HERACLES: Pythangelus?
  XANTHIAS: But never a word of me,
Not though my shoulder's chafed so terribly.
  HERACLES: But have you not a shoal of little
    songsters,
Tragedians by the myriad, who can chatter
A furlong faster than Euripides?
  DIONYSUS: Those be mere vintage-leavings, jab-
    berers, choirs
Of swallow-broods, degraders of their art,
Who get one chorus, and are seen no more,
The Muses' love once gained. But O, my friend,
Search where you will, you'll never find a true
Creative genius, uttering startling things.
  HERACLES: Creative? how do you mean?
  DIONYSUS: I mean a man
Who'll dare some novel venturesome conceit,
Air, Zeus's chamber, or *Time's foot,* or this,
'Twas not my mind that swore: my tongue com-
*   mitted*
A little perjury on its own account.[15]
  HERACLES: You like that style?
  DIONYSUS: Like it? I dote upon it.
  HERACLES: I vow it's ribald nonsense, and you
    know it.
  DIONYSUS: "Rule not my mind": you've got a
    house to mind.
  HERACLES: Really and truly though 'tis paltry stuff.
  DIONYSUS: Teach me to dine!
  XANTHIAS: But never a word of me.
  DIONYSUS: But tell me truly—'twas for this I came
Dressed up to mimic you—what friends received
And entertained you when you went below
To bring back Cerberus, in case I need them.
And tell me too the havens, fountains, shops,
Roads, resting-places, stews, refreshment-rooms,
Towns, lodgings, hostesses, with whom were found
The fewest bugs.
  XANTHIAS: But never a word of me.
  HERACLES: You are really game to go?
  DIONYSUS: O drop that, can't you?
And tell me this: of all the roads you know

13 An Athenian tragic poet, living at that time at the
Macedonian court.
14 A writer of inferior tragedies.
15 Here Aristophanes cites or parodies Euripidean lines.

Which is the quickest way to get to Hades?
I want one not too warm, nor yet too cold.
  HERACLES: Which shall I tell you first? which shall
    it be?
There's one by rope and bench: you launch away
And—hang yourself.
  DIONYSUS: No thank you: that's too stifling.
  HERACLES: Then there's a track, a short and
    beaten cut,
By pestle and mortar.
  DIONYSUS: Hemlock, do you mean?
  HERACLES: Just so.
  DIONYSUS: No, that's too deathly cold a way;
You have hardly started ere your shins get numbed.
  HERACLES: Well, would you like a steep and swift
    descent?
  DIONYSUS: Aye, that's the style: my walking
    powers are small.
  HERACLES: Go down to the Cerameicus.
  DIONYSUS: And do what?
  HERACLES: Climb to the tower's top pinnacle—
  DIONYSUS: And then?
  HERACLES: Observe the torch-race started, and
    when all
The multitude is shouting *Let them go,*
Let yourself go.
  DIONYSUS: Go! whither?
  HERACLES: To the ground.
  DIONYSUS: And lose, forsooth, two envelopes of
    brain.
I'll not try that.
  HERACLES: Which *will* you try?
  DIONYSUS: The way
You went yourself.
  HERACLES: A parlous voyage that,
For first you'll come to an enormous lake[16]
Of fathomless depth.
  DIONYSUS: And how am I to cross?
  HERACLES: An ancient mariner will row you over
In a wee boat, *so* big. The fare's two obols.[17]
  DIONYSUS: Fie! The power two obols have, the
    whole world through!
How came they thither!
  HERACLES: Theseus[18] took them down.
And next you'll see great snakes and savage monsters
In tens of thousands.
  DIONYSUS: You needn't try to scare me,
I'm going to go.
  HERACLES: Then weltering seas of filth
And ever-rippling dung: and plunged therein,
Whoso has wronged the stranger here on earth,
Or robbed his boylove of the promised pay,
Or swinged his mother, or profanely smitten

16 The Acherusian lake, the first passage to the world
below.
17 Charon's fee for ferrying the dead across the river
Styx, and the fee for admission to the theatre of Dionysus
in Athens.
18 The legendary hero of Athens who went down to
Hades.

His father's cheek, or sworn an oath forsworn,
Or copied out a speech of Morsimus.[19]

DIONYSUS: There too, perdie, should *he* be plunged, whoe'er
Has danced the sword-dance of Cinesias.

HERACLES: And next the breath of flutes will float around you,
And glorious sunshine, such as ours, you'll see,
And myrtle groves, and happy bands who clap
Their hands in triumph, men and women too.

DIONYSUS: And who are they?

HERACLES: The happy mystic bands.

XANTHIAS: And I'm the donkey in the mystery show.[20]
But I'll not stand it, not one instant longer.

HERACLES: Who'll tell you everything you want to know.
You'll find them dwelling close beside the road
You are going to travel, just at Pluto's gate.
And fare thee well, my brother.

DIONYSUS: And to you
Good cheer. [*To* Xanthias] Now sirrah, pick you up the traps.

XANTHIAS: Before I've put them down?

DIONYSUS: And quickly too.

XANTHIAS: No, prithee, no: but hire a body, one
They're carrying out, on purpose for the trip.

DIONYSUS: If I can't find one?

XANTHIAS: Then I'll take them.
[*A* Corpse, *wrapped in its grave-clothes, and lying on a bier, is carried across the stage*]

DIONYSUS: Good.
And see! they are carrying out a body now.
Hallo! you there, you deadman, are you willing
To carry down our little traps to Hades?

CORPSE: What are they?

DIONYSUS: These.

CORPSE: Two drachmas for the job?

DIONYSUS: Nay, that's too much.

CORPSE: Out of the pathway, you!

DIONYSUS: Beshrew thee, stop: may-be we'll strike a bargain.

CORPSE: Pay me two drachmas, or it's no use talking.

DIONYSUS: One and a half.

CORPSE: I'd liefer live again!

XANTHIAS: How absolute the knave is! He be hanged!
I'll go myself.

DIONYSUS: You're the right sort, my man.
Now to the ferry.

CHARON: Yoh, up! lay her to.

XANTHIAS: Whatever's that?

DIONYSUS: Why, that's the lake, by Zeus,
Whereof he spake, and yon's the ferry-boat.

XANTHIAS: Poseidon, yes, and that old fellow's Charon.

DIONYSUS: Charon! O welcome, Charon! welcome, Charon!

CHARON: Who's for the Rest—the rest from pain and ill?
Who's for the Lethe's plain? the Donkey-shearings?
Who's for Cerberia? Taenarum? or the Ravens?[21]

DIONYSUS: I.

CHARON: Hurry in.

DIONYSUS: But where are you going really?
In truth to the Ravens?

CHARON: Aye, for your behoof.
Step in.

DIONYSUS: [*To* Xanthias] Now, lad.

CHARON: A slave? I take no slave,
Unless he has fought for his bodyrights at sea.

XANTHIAS: I couldn't go. I'd got the eye-disease.

CHARON: Then fetch a circuit round about the lake.

XANTHIAS: Where must I wait?

CHARON: Beside the Withering Stone,
Hard by the Rest.

DIONYSUS: You understand?

XANTHIAS: Too well.
O, what ill omen crossed me as I started!

CHARON: [*To* Dionysus] Sit to the oar. [*Calling*]
Who else for the boat? Be quick.
[*To* Dionysus] Hi! what are you doing?

DIONYSUS: What am I doing? Sitting
On to the oar. You told me to, yourself.

CHARON: Now sit you there, you little Potgut.

DIONYSUS: So?

CHARON: Now stretch your arms full length before you.

DIONYSUS: So?

CHARON: Come, don't keep fooling; plant your feet, and now
Pull with a will.

DIONYSUS: Why, how am *I* to pull?
I'm not an oarsman, seaman, Salaminian.[22]
I can't!

CHARON: You can. Just dip your oar in once,
You'll hear the loveliest timing songs.

DIONYSUS: What from?

CHARON: Frog-swans, most wonderful.

DIONYSUS: Then give the word.

CHARON: Heave ahoy! heave ahoy!

FROGS: Brekekekex, ko-ax, ko-ax,[23]
Brekekekex, ko-ax, ko-ax!
We children of the fountain and the lake

[19] A tragedian ridiculed by Aristophanes in other plays too.

[20] Donkeys were used in the procession from Athens to the seat of the mystery rites, the city of Eleusis.

[21] Donkey-shearings: "nothingness" or death; Cerberia: the region of the three-headed dog of the underworld, Cerberus; Taenarum: an entrance to the underworld; the Ravens: curses.

[22] Anyone living on the island of Salamis was apt to be a good oarsman, as he had to row over to Athens.

[23] The ghosts of the dead frogs that used to croak in the Athenian marshlands now croak in the Acherusian lake of the underworld.

Let us wake
Our full choir-shout, as the flutes are ringing out,
Our symphony of clear-voiced song.
The song we used to love in the Marshland up above,
In praise of Dionysus to produce,
Of Nysaean Dionysus, son of Zeus,
When the revel-tipsy throng, all crapulous and gay,
To our precinct reeled along on the holy Pitcher Day,
Brekekekex, ko-ax, ko-ax.

DIONYSUS: O, dear! O, dear! now I declare
FROGS: I've got a bump upon my rump,
DIONYSUS: Brekekekex, ko-ax, ko-ax.
FROGS: But you, perchance, don't care.
DIONYSUS: Brekekekex, ko-ax, ko-ax.
Hang you, and your ko-axing too!
FROGS: There's nothing but ko-ax with you.
That is right, Mr. Busybody, right!
For the Muses of the lyre love us well;

And hornfoot Pan who plays
on the pipe his jocund lays;
And Apollo, Harper bright,
in our Chorus takes delight;
For the strong reed's sake
which I grow within my lake
To be girdled in his lyre's deep shell.
Brekekekex, ko-ax, ko-ax.

DIONYSUS: My hands are blistered very sore;
My stern below is sweltering so,
'Twill soon, I know, upturn and roar
Brekekekex, ko-ax, ko-ax.
O tuneful race, O pray give o'er,
O sing no more.
FROGS: Ah, no! ah, no!
Loud and louder our chant must flow.
Sing if ever ye sang of yore,
When in sunny and glorious days
Through the rushes and marsh-flags springing
On we swept, in the joy of singing
Myriad-diving roundelays.
Or when fleeing the storm, we went
Down to the depths, and our choral song
Wildly raised to a loud and long
Bubble-bursting accompaniment.
FROGS and DIONYSUS:
Brekekekex, ko-ax, ko-ax.
DIONYSUS: This timing song I take from you.
FROGS: That's a dreadful thing to do.
DIONYSUS: Much more dreadful, if I row
Till I burst myself, I trow.
FROGS and DIONYSUS:
Brekekekex, ko-ax, ko-ax.
Go, hang yourselves; for what care I?
FROGS: All the same we'll shout and cry,
Stretching all our throats with song,
Shouting, crying, all day long,
FROGS and DIONYSUS:
Brekekekex, ko-ax, ko-ax.
DIONYSUS: In this you'll never, never win.
FROGS: This you shall not beat us in.

DIONYSUS: No, nor ye prevail o'er me.
Never! never! I'll my song
Shout, if need be, all day long,
Until I've learned to master your ko-ax.
Brekekekex, ko-ax, ko-ax.
I thought I'd put a stop to your ko-ax.
CHARON: Stop! Easy! Take the oar and push her to.
Now pay your fare and go.
DIONYSUS: Here 'tis: two obols.
Xanthias! where's Xanthias? Is it Xanthias there?
XANTHIAS: Hoi, hoi!
DIONYSUS: Come hither.
XANTHIAS: Glad to meet you, master.
DIONYSUS: What have you there?
XANTHIAS: Nothing but filth and darkness.
DIONYSUS: But tell me, did you see the parricides
And perjured folk he mentioned?
XANTHIAS: Didn't you?
DIONYSUS: Poseidon, yes. Why look! [Pointing to the audience] I see them now.
What's the next step?
XANTHIAS: We'd best be moving on.
This is the spot where Heracles declared
Those savage monsters dwell.
DIONYSUS: O hang the fellow.
That's all his bluff: he thought to scare me off,
The jealous dog, knowing my plucky ways.
There's no such swaggerer lives as Heracles.
Why, I'd like nothing better than to achieve
Some bold adventure, worthy of our trip.
XANTHIAS: I know you would. Hallo! I hear a noise.
DIONYSUS: Where? what?
XANTHIAS: Behind us, there.
DIONYSUS: Get you behind.
XANTHIAS: No, it's in front.
DIONYSUS: Get you in front directly.
XANTHIAS: And now I see the most ferocious monster.
DIONYSUS: O, what's it like?
XANTHIAS: Like everything by turns.
Now it's a bull: now it's a mule: and now
The loveliest girl.
DIONYSUS: O, where? I'll go and meet her.
XANTHIAS: It's ceased to be a girl: it's a dog now.
DIONYSUS: It is Empusa![24]
XANTHIAS: Well, its face is all
Ablaze with fire.
DIONYSUS: Has it a copper leg?
XANTHIAS: A copper leg? yes, one; and one of cow dung.
DIONYSUS: O, whither shall I flee?
XANTHIAS: O, whither I?
DIONYSUS: My priest,[25] protect me, and we'll sup together.
XANTHIAS: King Heracles, we're done for.

[24] A hobgoblin that changed its shape frequently.
[25] A reference to the priest of Dionysus who presided at theatrical performances in Athens.

DIONYSUS: O, forbear,
Good fellow, call me anything but that.
    XANTHIAS: Well then, Dionysus.
    DIONYSUS: O, that's worse again.
    XANTHIAS: [*To the* Spectre] Aye, go thy way. O
    master, here, come here.
    DIONYSUS: O, what's up now?
    XANTHIAS: Take courage; all's serene.
And, like Hegelochus, we now may say
"Out of the storm there comes a new fine wether."[26]
Empusa's gone.
    DIONYSUS: Swear it.
    XANTHIAS: By Zeus she is.
    DIONYSUS: Swear it again.
    XANTHIAS: By Zeus.
    DIONYSUS: Again.
    XANTHIAS: By Zeus.
O dear, O dear, how pale I grew to see her,
But *he*, from fright has yellowed me all over.
    DIONYSUS: Ah me, whence fall these evils on my
    head?
Who is the god to blame for my destruction?
Air, Zeus's chamber, or the Foot of Time?
    [*A flute is played behind the scenes*]
Hist!
    XANTHIAS: What's the matter?
    DIONYSUS: Didn't you hear it?
    XANTHIAS: What?
    DIONYSUS: The breath of flutes.
    XANTHIAS: Aye, and a whiff of torches
Breathed o'er me too; a very mystic whiff.
    DIONYSUS: Then crouch we down, and mark what's
    going on.
    CHORUS: [*In the distance*] O Iacchus! O Iacchus!
    O Iacchus!
    XANTHIAS: I have it, master: 'tis those blessed
    Mystics,
Of whom he told us, sporting hereabouts.
They sing the Iacchus which Diagoras[27] made.
    DIONYSUS: I think so too: we had better both
    keep quiet
And so find out exactly what it is.
    [*The calling forth of Iacchus*]
    CHORUS: O Iacchus! power excelling,
          here in stately temples[28] dwelling,

[26] In the *Orestes* of Euripides. A reference to a slip
of the tongue by an Athenian actor, Hegelochus.

[27] The Chorus, which had chanted the frog songs off-
stage, now appears as a Chorus of Votaries (a Mystic
Chorus). Dionysus was called by the mystic name of
Iacchus at the Eleusinian Mysteries. The lyric poet
Diagoras wrote a hymn to Iacchus.

[28] Here the scene building represents the temples of
the Eleusinian deities, who were Persephone, Demeter,
and Iacchus. Soon the statue of Iacchus is brought out
and "the procession commences, the Chorus singing
hymns to the three deities, as they pass through the
Cerameicus, and out by the Eleusinian gate to the bridge
over the Cephisus, where a little chaffing takes place, and
whence they disappear from our sight on their way to
the flower-enamelled Thriasian plain."—B. B. ROGERS

O Iacchus! O Iacchus!
Come to tread this verdant level,
Come to dance in mystic revel,
Come whilst round thy forehead hurtles
Many a wreath of fruitful myrtles,
Come with wild and saucy paces
Mingling in our joyous dance,
Pure and holy, which embraces
        all the charms of all the Graces,
    When the mystic choirs advance.
    XANTHIAS: Holy and sacred queen, Demeter's
    daughter,
O, what a jolly whiff of pork breathed o'er me![29]
    DIONYSUS: Hist! and perchance you'll get some
    tripe yourself.
    [*The statue of Iacchus is brought out of the
    temple, and is welcomed by the* Chorus]
    CHORUS: Come, arise, from sleep awaking,
          come the fiery torches shaking,
    O Iacchus! O Iacchus!
Morning Star that shinest nightly.
Lo, the mead is blazing brightly,
Age forgets its years and sadness,
Agèd knees curvet for gladness,
Lift thy flashing torches o'er us,
Marshal all thy blameless train,
Lead, O lead the way before us;
        lead the lovely youthful Chorus
    To the marshy flowery plain.
    [*The warning-off of the profane*]
All evil thoughts and profane be still:
        far hence, far hence from our choirs depart,
Who knows not well what the Mystics tell,
        or is not holy and pure of heart;
Who ne'er has the noble revelry learned,
        or danced the dance of the Muses high;
Or shared in the Bacchic rites which old
        bull-eating Cratinus's[30] words supply;
Who vulgar coarse buffoonery loves,
        though all untimely the jests they make;
Or lives not easy and kind with all,
        or kindling faction forbears to slake,
But fans the fire, from a base desire
        some pitiful gain for himself to reap;
Or takes, in office, his gifts and bribes,
        while the city is tossed on the stormy deep;
Who fort or fleet to the foe betrays;
        or, a vile Thorycion, ships away
Forbidden stores from Aegina's shores,
        to Epidaurus across the Bay
Transmitting oar-pads and sails and tar,
        that curst collector of five per cents;
The knave who tries to procure supplies
        for the use of the enemy's armaments;

[29] Pigs were used as sacrifices at the initiation ceremonies of the Eleusinian mysteries.

[30] A comic poet who loved wine. He was Aristophanes'
successful competitor when he was a very old man, his
comedy receiving the prize in the same year that Aristophanes submitted his satire on Socrates, *The Clouds.*

The Cyclian singer who dares befoul
       the Lady Hecate's wayside shrine;
The public speaker who once lampooned
      in our Bacchic feasts would, with heart malign,
Keep nibbling away the Comedians' pay;—
      to these I utter my warning cry,
I charge them once, I charge them twice,
      I charge them thrice, that they draw not nigh
To the sacred dance of the Mystic choir.
      But *ye*, my comrades, awake the song,
The night-long revels of joy and mirth
      which ever of right to our feast belong.
  [The start of the procession]
  Advance, true hearts, advance!
  On to the gladsome bowers,
  On to the sward, with flowers
    Embosomed bright!
  March on with jest, and jeer, and dance,
  Full well ye've supped to-night.
  [The processional hymn to Persephone]
  March, chanting loud your lays,
  Your hearts and voices raising,
  The Saviour goddess praising
    Who vows she'll still
  Our city save to endless days,
  Whate'er Thorycion's will.
Break off the measure, and change the time;
      and now with chanting hymns adorn
Demeter, goddess mighty and high,
      the harvest-queen, the giver of corn.
  [The processional hymn to Demeter]
O Lady, over our rites presiding,
Preserve and succour thy choral throng,
And grant us all, in thy help confiding,
To dance and revel the whole day long;
And much in earnest, and much in jest,
Worthy thy feast, may we speak therein.
And when we have bantered and laughed our best,
The victor's wreath be it ours to win.

Call we now the youthful god,
      call him hither without delay,
Him who travels amongst his chorus,
      dancing along on the Sacred Way.
  [The processional hymn to Iacchus]
O, come with the joy of thy festival song,
O, come to the goddess, O, mix with our throng
Untired, though the journey be never so long.[31]
  O Lord of the frolic and dance,
  Iacchus, beside me advance!
For fun, and for cheapness, our dress thou hast rent,
Through thee we may dance to the top of our bent,
Reviling, and jeering, and none will resent.
  O Lord of the frolic and dance,
  Iacchus, beside me advance!
A sweet pretty girl I observed in the show,
Her robe had been torn in the scuffle, and lo,
There peeped through the tatters a bosom of snow.

[31] The twelve-mile journey from Athens to the holy
city of the mysteries, Eleusis.

  O Lord of the frolic and dance,
  Iacchus, beside me advance!
DIONYSUS: Wouldn't I like to follow on, and try
      A little sport and dancing?
XANTHIAS: Wouldn't I?
[The banter at the bridge of Cephisus]
CHORUS: Shall we all a merry joke
    At Archedemus[32] poke,
Who has not cut his guildsmen yet,[33] though seven
    years old;
    Yet up among the dead
    He is demagogue and head,
And contrives the topmost place of the rascaldom
    to hold?
    And Cleisthenes, they say,
    Is among the tombs all day,
Bewailing for his lover with a lamentable whine.
    And Callias,[34] I'm told,
    Has become a sailor bold,
And casts a lion's hide o'er his members feminine.
  DIONYSUS: Can any of you tell
  Where Pluto here may dwell,
For we, sirs, are two strangers who were never here
    before?
  CHORUS: O, then no further stray,
  Nor again inquire the way,
For know that ye have journeyed to his very
    entrance-door.
  DIONYSUS: Take up the wraps, my lad.
  XANTHIAS: Now is not this too bad?
Like "Zeus's Corinth,"[35] he "the wraps" keeps saying
    o'er and o'er.
  CHORUS: Now wheel your sacred dances through
    the glade with flowers bedight,
All ye who are partakers of the holy festal rite;
And I will with the women and the holy maidens go
Where they keep the nightly vigil, an auspicious light
    to show.
  [The departure for the Thriasian Plain]
  Now haste we to the roses,
  And the meadows full of posies,
  Now haste we to the meadows
    In our own old way,
  In choral dances blending,
  In dances never ending,
  Which only for the holy
    The Destinies array.
  O, happy mystic chorus,
  The blessed sunshine o'er us
  On us alone is smiling,
    In its soft sweet light:
  On us who strove for ever
  With holy, pure endeavour,
  Alike by friend and stranger

[32] The man who led attacks on the victorious leaders
of the naval battle of Arginusae.
[33] I.e., who has not yet proved his right to be considered an Athenian citizen.
[34] A worthless fellow.
[35] A redundant expression, considered ludicrous.

To guide our steps aright.
DIONYSUS: What's the right way to knock? I
wonder how
The natives here are wont to knock at doors.
XANTHIAS: No dawdling: taste the door. You've
got, remember,
The lion-hide and pride of Heracles.
DIONYSUS: Boy! boy!
AEACUS: Who's there?
DIONYSUS: I, Heracles the strong!
AEACUS: O, you most shameless desperate ruffian,
you!
O, villain, villain, arrant vilest villain!
Who seized our Cerberus by the throat, and fled,
And ran, and rushed, and bolted, haling off
The dog, my charge! But now I've got thee fast.
So close the Styx's inky-hearted rock,
The blood-bedabbled peak of Acheron
Shall hem thee in: the hell-hounds of Cocytus
Prowl round thee; whilst the hundred-headed Asp
Shall rive thy heart-strings: the Tartesian Lamprey[36]
Prey on thy lungs: and those Tithrasian Gorgons
Mangle and tear thy kidneys, mauling them,
Entrails and all, into one bloody mash.
I'll speed a running foot to fetch them hither.
XANTHIAS: Hallo! what now?
DIONYSUS: I've done it: call the god.
XANTHIAS: Get up, you laughing-stock; get up
directly,
Before you're seen.
DIONYSUS: What, *I* get up? I'm fainting.
Please dab a sponge of water on my heart.
XANTHIAS: Here! Dab it on.
DIONYSUS: Where is it?
XANTHIAS: Ye golden gods,
Lies your heart *there*?
DIONYSUS: It got so terrified
It fluttered down into my stomach's pit.
XANTHIAS: Cowardliest of gods and men!
DIONYSUS: The cowardliest? I?
What I, who asked you for a sponge, a thing
A coward never would have done!
XANTHIAS: What then?
DIONYSUS: A coward would have lain there wal-
lowing;
But I stood up, and wiped myself withal.
XANTHIAS: Poseidon! quite heroic.
DIONYSUS: 'Deed I think so.
But weren't *you* frightened at those dreadful threats
And shoutings?
XANTHIAS: Frightened? Not a bit. I cared not.
DIONYSUS: Come then, if you're so *very* brave a
man,
Will you be I, and take the hero's club
And lion's skin, since you're so monstrous plucky?
And I'll be now the slave, and bear the luggage.
XANTHIAS: Hand them across. I cannot choose but
take them.
And now observe the Xanthio-Heracles

[36] A delicacy, here used comically because intended
as a terrifying term by Aeacus.

If I'm a coward and a sneak like you.
DIONYSUS: Nay, you're the rogue from Melite's
own self.
And I'll pick up and carry on the traps.
[*A Maid-servant of Persephone enters*]
MAID: O welcome, Heracles! come in, sweetheart.
My Lady, when they told her, set to work,
Baked mighty loaves, boiled two or three tureens
Of lentil soup, roasted a prime ox whole,
Made rolls and honey-cakes. So come along.
XANTHIAS: [*Declining*] You are too kind.
MAID: I will not let you go.
I will not *let* you! Why, she's stewing slices
Of juicy bird's-flesh, and she's making comfits,
And tempering down her richest wine. Come, dear,
Come along in.
XANTHIAS: [*Still declining*] Pray thank her.
MAID: O you're jesting,
I shall not let you off: there's such a lovely
Flute-girl all ready, and we've two or three
Dancing-girls also.
XANTHIAS: Eh! what! Dancing-girls?
MAID: Young budding virgins, freshly tired and
trimmed.
Come, dear, come in. The cook was dishing up
The cutlets, and they are bringing in the tables.
XANTHIAS: Then go you in, and tell those dancing-
girls
Of whom you spake, I'm coming in Myself.
Pick up the traps, my lad, and follow me.
DIONYSUS: Hi! stop! you're not in earnest, just
because
I dressed you up, in fun, as Heracles?
Come, don't keep fooling, Xanthias, but lift
And carry in the traps yourself.
XANTHIAS: Why! what!
You are never going to strip me of these togs
You gave me!
DIONYSUS: Going to? No, I'm doing it now.
Off with that lion-skin.
XANTHIAS: Bear witness all,
The gods shall judge between us.
DIONYSUS: Gods, indeed!
Why, how could *you* (the vain and foolish thought!)
A slave, a mortal, act Alcmena's son?
XANTHIAS: All right then, take them; maybe, if
God will,
You'll soon require my services again.
CHORUS: This is the part of a dexterous clever
Man with his wits about him ever,
One who has travelled the world to see;
Always to shift, and to keep through all
Close to the sunny side of the wall;
Not like a pictured block to be,
Standing always in one position;
Nay but to veer, with expedition,
And ever to catch the favouring breeze,
This is the part of a shrewd tactician,
This is to be a—*Theramenes*![37]

[37] The shifty one, called "the Slipper," because the
slipper could be worn on either the left or the right foot

DIONYSUS: Truly an exquisite joke 'twould be,
Him with a dancing-girl to see,
Lolling at ease on Milesian rugs;
Me, like a slave, beside him standing,
Aught that he wants to his lordship handing;
Then as the damsel fair he hugs,
Seeing me all on fire to embrace her,
He would perchance (for there's no man baser),
Turning him round like a lazy lout,
Straight on my mouth deliver a facer,
Knocking my ivory choirmen out.

[*A Cook-shop Hostess and her partner,* Plathane, *enter*]

HOSTESS: O Plathane! Plathane! Here's that naughty man,
That's he who got into our tavern once,
And ate up sixteen loaves.
PLATHANE: O, so he is!
The very man.
XANTHIAS: Bad luck for somebody!
HOSTESS: O and, besides, those twenty bits of stew,
Half-obol pieces.
XANTHIAS: Somebody's going to catch it!
HOSTESS: That garlic too.
DIONYSUS: Woman, you're talking nonsense.
You don't know what you're saying.
HOSTESS: O, you thought
I shouldn't know you with your buskins on!
Ah, and I've not yet mentioned all that fish,
No, nor the new-made cheese: he gulped it down,
Baskets and all, unlucky that we were.
And when I just alluded to the price,
He looked so fierce, and bellowed like a bull.
XANTHIAS: Yes, that's his way: that's what he always does.
HOSTESS: O, and he drew his sword, and seemed quite mad.
PLATHANE: O, that he did.
HOSTESS: And terrified us so
We sprang up to the cockloft, she and I.
Then out he hurled, decamping with the rugs.
XANTHIAS: That's his way too; but something must be done.
HOSTESS: Quick, run and call my patron Cleon here!
PLATHANE: O, if you meet him, call Hyperbolus![38]
We'll pay you out to-day.
HOSTESS: O filthy throat,
O how I'd like to take a stone, and hack
Those grinders out with which you chawed my wares.
PLATHANE: I'd like to pitch you in the deadman's pit.[39]
HOSTESS: I'd like to get a reaping-hook and scoop
That gullet out with which you gorged my tripe.
But I'll to Cleon: he'll soon serve his writs;
He'll twist it out of you to-day, he will.

[38] They threaten him with the two warmongering Athenian demagogues detested and satirized by Aristophanes—Cleon and Hyperbolus.
[39] The pit into which criminals were cast in Athens.

DIONYSUS: Perdition seize me, if I don't love Xanthias.
XANTHIAS: Aye, aye, I know your drift: stop, stop that talking.
I won't be Heracles.
DIONYSUS: O, don't say so,
Dear, darling Xanthias.
XANTHIAS: Why, how can I,
A slave, a mortal, act Alcmena's son!
DIONYSUS: Aye, aye, I know you are vexed, and I deserve it,
And if you pummel me, I won't complain.
But if I strip you of these togs again,
Perdition seize myself, my wife, my children,
And, most of all, that blear-eyed Archedemus.
XANTHIAS: That oath contents me: on those terms I take them.
CHORUS: Now that at last you appear once more,
Wearing the garb that at first you wore,
Wielding the club and the tawny skin,
Now it is yours to be up and doing,
Glaring like mad, and your youth renewing,
Mindful of him whose guise you are in.
If, when caught in a bit of a scrape, you
Suffer a word of alarm to escape you,
Showing yourself but a feckless knave,
Then will your master at once undrape you,
Then you'll again be the toiling slave.
XANTHIAS: There, I admit, you have given to me a
Capital hint, and the like idea,
Friends, had occurred to myself before.
Truly if anything good befell
He would be wanting, I know full well,
Wanting to take to the togs once more.
Nevertheless, while in these I'm vested,
Ne'er shall you find me craven-crested,
No, for a dittany[40] look I'll wear,
Aye and methinks it will soon be tested,
Hark! how the portals are rustling there.

[*Aeacus and his* Assistants *return*]

AEACUS: Seize the dog-stealer, bind him, pinion him,
Drag him to justice!
DIONYSUS: Somebody's going to catch it.
XANTHIAS: [*Striking out*] Hands off! get away! stand back!
AEACUS: Eh? You're for fighting.
Ho! Ditylas, Sceblyas, and Pardocas,
Come hither, quick; fight me this sturdy knave.
DIONYSUS: Now isn't it a shame the man should strike
And he a thief besides?
AEACUS: A monstrous shame!
DIONYSUS: A regular burning shame!
XANTHIAS: By the Lord Zeus,
If ever I was here before, if ever
I stole one hair's-worth from you, let me die!
And now I'll make you a right noble offer,
Arrest my lad: torture him as you will,
And if you find I'm guilty, take and kill me.

[40] An acrid plant.

AEACUS: Torture him, how?

XANTHIAS: In any mode you please.
Pile bricks upon him: stuff his nose with acid:
Flay, rack him, hoist him; flog him with a scourge
Of prickly bristles: only not with this,
A soft-leaved onion, or a tender leek.

AEACUS: A fair proposal. If I strike too hard
And maim the boy, I'll make you compensation.

XANTHIAS: I shan't require it. Take him out and
    flog him.

AEACUS: Nay, but I'll do it here before your eyes.
Now then, put down the traps, and mind you speak
The truth, young fellow.

DIONYSUS: [In agony] Man! don't torture me!
I am a god. You'll blame yourself hereafter
If you touch me.

AEACUS: Hallo! What's that you are saying?

DIONYSUS: I say I'm Bacchus, son of Zeus, a god,
And he's the slave.

AEACUS: You hear him?

XANTHIAS: Hear him? Yes.
All the more reason you should flog him well.
For if he is a god, he won't perceive it.

DIONYSUS: Well, but you say that you're a god
    yourself.
So why not you be flogged as well as I?

XANTHIAS: A fair proposal. And be this the test,
Whichever of us two you first behold
Flinching or crying out—he's not the god.

AEACUS: Upon my word you're quite the gentle-
    man,
You're all for right and justice. Strip then, both.

XANTHIAS: How can you test us fairly?

AEACUS: Easily,
I'll give you blow for blow.

XANTHIAS: A good idea.
We're ready! Now! [Aeacus strikes him] see if you
    catch me flinching.

AEACUS: I struck you.

XANTHIAS: [Incredulously] No!

AEACUS: Well, it seems "no," indeed.
Now then I'll strike the other. [Strikes Dionysus]

DIONYSUS: Tell me when?

AEACUS: I struck you.

DIONYSUS: Struck me? Then why didn't I flinch?

AEACUS: Don't know, I'm sure. I'll try the other
    again.

XANTHIAS: And quickly too. Good gracious!

AEACUS: Why "good gracious"?
Not hurt you, did I?

XANTHIAS: No, I merely thought of
The Diomeian feast of Heracles.

AEACUS: A holy man! 'Tis now the other's turn.

DIONYSUS: Hi! Hi!

AEACUS: Hallo!

DIONYSUS: Look at those horsemen, look!

AEACUS: But why these tears?

DIONYSUS: There's such a smell of onions.

AEACUS: Then you don't mind it?

DIONYSUS: [Cheerfully]   Mind it? Not a bit.

AEACUS: Well, I must go to the other one again.

XANTHIAS: O! O!

AEACUS: Hallo!

XANTHIAS: Do pray pull out this thorn.

AEACUS: What does it mean? 'Tis this one's turn
    again.

DIONYSUS: [Shrieking] Apollo! Lord! [Calmly] of
Delos and of Pytho.

XANTHIAS: He flinched! You heard him?

DIONYSUS: Not at all; a jolly
Verse of Hipponax flashed across my mind.

XANTHIAS: You don't half do it: cut his flanks to
    pieces.

AEACUS: By Zeus, well thought on. Turn your
    belly here.

DIONYSUS: [Screaming] Poseidon!

XANTHIAS: There! he's flinching.

DIONYSUS: [Singing]   —who dost reign
    Amongst the Aegean peaks and creeks
    And o'er the deep blue main.

AEACUS: No, by Demeter, still I can't find out
Which is the god, but come ye both indoors;
My lord himself and Persephassa there,
Being gods themselves, will soon find out the truth.

DIONYSUS: Right! right! I only wish you had
    thought of that
Before you gave me those tremendous whacks.

[As the actors leave, the Chorus of Votaries
faces the audience and recites[41]]

CHORUS: Come, Muse, to our Mystical Chorus,
                O come to the joy of my song,
O see on the benches before us
            that countless and wonderful throng,
Where wits by the thousand abide,
            with more than a Cleophon's[42] pride—
On the lips of that foreigner base,
            of Athens the bane and disgrace,
    There is shrieking, his kinsman by race,
    The garrulous swallow of Thrace;
    From that perch of exotic descent,
    Rejoicing her sorrow to vent,
She pours to her spirit's content,
            a nightingale's woful lament,
That e'en though the voting be equal,[43]
            his ruin will soon be the sequel.

Well it suits the holy Chorus
            evermore with counsel wise
To exhort and teach the city;
            this we therefore now advise—
End the townsmen's apprehensions;
            equalize the rights of all;
If by Phrynichus's[44] wrestlings

41 This is a parabasis. See page 8.
42 A warmongering demagogue, whose mother was a
"foreigner," a Thracian. Hence the subsequent jibes at him.
43 This would result in his acquittal, according to
Athenian law.
44 One of the Four Hundred oligarchs, a leader of the
antidemocratic faction in Athens that tried to betray
Athens to its enemy, Sparta, in 411 B.C., during the last
years of the Peloponnesian War.

some perchance sustained a fall,
Yet to these 'tis surely open,
    having put away their sin,
For their slips and vacillations
    pardon at your hands to win.
Give your brethren back their franchise.
    Sin and shame it were that slaves,
Who have once with stern devotion
    fought your battle on the waves,
Should be straightway lords and masters,
    yea Plataeans[45] fully blown—
Not that this deserves our censure;
    there I praise you; there alone
Has the city, in her anguish,
    policy and wisdom shown—
Nay but these, of old accustomed
    on our ships to fight and win,
(They, their fathers too before them),
    these our very kith and kin,
You should likewise, when they ask you,
    pardon for their single sin.
O by nature best and wisest,
    O relax your jealous ire,
Let us all the world as kinsfolk
    and as citizens acquire,
All who on our ships will battle
    well and bravely by our side.
If we cocker up our city,
    narrowing her with senseless pride,
Now when she is rocked and reeling
    in the cradles of the sea,
Here again will after ages deem we acted brainlessly.

And O if I'm able to scan
    the habits and life of a man
Who shall rue his iniquities soon,
    not long shall that little baboon,
That Cleigenes shifty and small,
    the wickedest bathman of all,
Who adulterates earth—which is brought
    from the isle of Cimolus, and wrought
With nitre and lye into soap—[46]
Not long shall he vex us, I hope.
And this the unlucky one knows,
Yet ventures a peace to oppose,
And being addicted to blows
    he carries a stick as he goes,
Lest while he is tipsy and reeling,
    some robber his cloak should be stealing.
Often has it crossed my fancy,
    that the city loves to deal
With the very best and noblest
    members of her commonweal,
Just as with our ancient coinage,
    and the newly-minted gold.
Yea for these, our sterling pieces,
    all of pure Athenian mould,
All of perfect die and metal,
    all the fairest of the fair,
All of workmanship unequalled,
    proved and valued everywhere
Both amongst our own Hellenes
    and Barbarians far away,
These we use not: but the worthless
    pinchbeck coins of yesterday,
Vilest die and basest metal,
    now we always use instead.
Even so, our sterling townsmen,
    nobly born and nobly bred,
Men of worth and rank and mettle,
    men of honourable fame,
Trained in every liberal science,
    choral dance and manly game,
These we treat with scorn and insult,
    but the strangers newliest come,
Worthless sons of worthless fathers,
    pinchbeck townsmen, yellowy scum,
Whom in earlier days the city
    hardly would have stooped to use
Even for her scapegoat victims,
    these for every task we choose.
O unwise and foolish people,
    yet to mend your ways begin;
Use again the good and useful:
    so hereafter, if ye win
'Twill be due to this your wisdom:
    if ye fall, at least 'twill be
Not a fall that brings dishonour,
    falling from a worthy tree.[47]

AEACUS: By Zeus the Saviour, quite the gentleman
Your master is.

XANTHIAS: Gentleman? I believe you.
He's all for wine and women, is my master.

AEACUS: But not to have flogged you, when the
    truth came out
That you, the slave, were passing off as master!

XANTHIAS: He'd get the worst of that.

AEACUS: Bravo! that's spoken
Like a true slave: that's what I love myself.

XANTHIAS: You love it, do you?

AEACUS: Love it? I'm entranced
When I can curse my lord behind his back.

XANTHIAS: How about grumbling, when you have
    felt the stick,
And scurry out of doors?

AEACUS: That's jolly too.

XANTHIAS: How about prying?

AEACUS: That beats everything!

XANTHIAS: Great Kin-god Zeus! And what of over-
    hearing
Your master's secrets?

AEACUS: What? I'm mad with joy.

XANTHIAS: And blabbing them abroad?

AEACUS: O heaven and earth!
When I do that, I can't contain myself.

[45] Plataeans were granted Athenian citizenship in 427 B.C. for their loyalty to Athens.

[46] A vague charge of dishonesty or adulteration by tradesmen.

[47] If Athens must fall, it is better for it to do so after having tried to save itself by putting its reliance in the best men rather than the worst.

XANTHIAS: Phoebus Apollo! clap your hand in
  mine,
Kiss and be kissed: and prithee tell me this,
Tell me by Zeus, our rascaldom's own god,
What's all that noise within? What means this hub-
  bub
And row?
  AEACUS: That's Aeschylus and Euripides.
  XANTHIAS: Eh?
  AEACUS: Wonderful, wonderful things are going on.
The dead are rioting, taking different sides.
  XANTHIAS: Why, what's the matter?
  AEACUS: There's a custom here
With all the crafts, the good and noble crafts,
That the chief master of his art in each
Shall have his dinner in the assembly hall,[48]
And sit by Pluto's side.
  XANTHIAS: I understand.
  AEACUS: Until another comes, more wise than he
In the same art: then must the first give way.
  XANTHIAS: And how has this disturbed our Aeschy-
  lus?
  AEACUS: 'Twas he that occupied the tragic chair,
As, in his craft, the noblest.
  XANTHIAS: Who does now?
  AEACUS: But when Euripides came down, he kept
Flourishing off before the highwaymen,
Thieves, burglars, parricides—these form our mob
In Hades—till with listening to his twists
And turns, and pleas and counterpleas, they went
Mad on the man, and hailed him first and wisest:
Elate with this, he claimed the tragic chair
Where Aeschylus was seated.
  XANTHIAS: Wasn't he pelted?
  AEACUS: Not he: the populace clamoured out to
  try
Which of the twain was wiser in his art.
  XANTHIAS: You mean the rascals?
  AEACUS: Aye, as high as heaven!
  XANTHIAS: But were there none to side with
  Aeschylus?
  AEACUS: Scanty and sparse the good, [Regards the
  audience] the same as here.
  XANTHIAS: And what does Pluto now propose to
  do?
  AEACUS: He means to hold a tournament, and
  bring
Their tragedies to the proof.
  XANTHIAS: But Sophocles,
How came not he to claim the tragic chair?
  AEACUS: Claim it? Not he! When he came down,
  he kissed
With reverence Aeschylus, and clasped his hand,
And yielded willingly the chair to him.
But now he's going, says Cleidemides,[49]
To sit third-man: and then if Aeschylus win,

[48] The Public Hall in which Athens fed favorite citizens at public charge.
[49] Possibly Sophocles' favorite actor.

He'll stay content: if not, for his art's sake,
He'll fight to the death against Euripides.
  XANTHIAS: Will it come off?
  AEACUS: O yes, by Zeus, directly
And then, I hear, will wonderful things be done,
The art poetic will be weighed in scales.
  XANTHIAS: What! weigh out tragedy, like butcher's
  meat?
  AEACUS: Levels they'll bring, and measuring-tapes
  for words, . .
And moulded oblongs.[50]
  XANTHIAS: Is it bricks they are making?
  AEACUS: Wedges and compasses: for Euripides
Vows that he'll test the dramas, word by word.
  XANTHIAS: Aeschylus chafes at this, I fancy.
  AEACUS: Well,
He lowered his brows, upglaring like a bull.
  XANTHIAS: And who's to be the judge?
  AEACUS: There came the rub.
Skilled men were hard to find: for with the Athenians
Aeschylus, somehow, did not hit it off,
  XANTHIAS: Too many burglars, I expect, he
  thought.
  AEACUS: And all the rest, he said, were trash and
  nonsense
To judge poetic wits. So then at last
They chose your lord, an expert in the art.
But go we in: for when our lords are bent
On urgent business, that means blows for us.
  CHORUS: O surely with terrible wrath
            will the thunder-voiced monarch be filled,
When he sees his opponent beside him,
            the tonguester, the artifice-skilled,
Stand, whetting his tusks for the fight!
            O surely, his eyes rolling-fell
Will with terrible madness be fraught!
O then will be charging of plume-waving words
            with their wild-floating mane,
And then will be whirling of splinters,
      and phrases smoothed down with the plane,
When the man would the grand-stepping maxims,
            the language gigantic, repel
Of the hero-creator of thought.
There will his shaggy-born crest
            upbristle for anger and woe,
Horribly frowning and growling,
            his fury will launch at the foe
Huge-clamped masses of words,
            with exertion Titanic up-tearing
Great ship-timber planks for the fray.
But here will the tongue be at work,
            uncoiling, word-testing, refining,
Sophist-creator of phrases,
            dissecting, detracting, maligning,
Shaking the envious bits,
            and with subtle analysis paring
The lung's large labour away.

[50] For pressing clay into the shape of bricks.

[Pluto's *hall*. Pluto *is seated on a throne with* Dionysus, Aeschylus, *and* Euripides *standing before him*[51]]

EURIPIDES: Don't talk to me; I won't give up the chair,
I say I am better in the art than he.
DIONYSUS: You hear him, Aeschylus: why don't you speak?
EURIPIDES: He'll do the grand at first, the juggling trick
He used to play in all his tragedies.
DIONYSUS: Come, my fine fellow, pray don't talk too big.
EURIPIDES: I know the man, I've scanned him through and through,
A savage-creating stubborn-pulling fellow,
Uncurbed, unfettered, uncontrolled of speech,
Unperiphrastic, bombastiloquent.
AESCHYLUS: Hah! sayest thou so, child of the garden quean![52]
And this to *me*, thou chattery-babble-collector,
Thou pauper-creating rags-and-patches-stitcher?
Thou shalt abye it dearly!
DIONYSUS: Pray, be still;
Nor heat thy soul to fury, Aeschylus.
AESCHYLUS: Not till I've made you see the sort of man
This cripple-maker is who crows so loudly.
DIONYSUS: Bring out a ewe, a black-fleeced ewe, my boys:
Here's a typhoon about to burst upon us.[53]
AESCHYLUS: Thou picker-up of Cretan monodies,
Foisting thy tales of incest on the stage—
DIONYSUS: Forbear, forbear, most honoured Aeschylus;
And you, my poor Euripides, begone
If you are wise, out of this pitiless hail,
Lest with some heady word he crack your scull
And batter out your brain—less Telephus.[54]
And not with passion, Aeschylus, but calmly
Test and be tested. 'Tis not meet for poets
To scold each other, like two baking-girls.
But you go roaring like an oak on fire.
EURIPIDES: I'm ready, I! I don't draw back one bit.
I'll lash or, if he will, let him lash first
The talk, the lays, the sinews of a play:
Aye and my Peleus, aye and Aeolus,
And Meleager, aye and Telephus.

[51] We cannot tell whether the scene was changed here or whether Pluto was merely seated on a throne in front of the permanent scene building of the theatre of Dionysus.
[52] Euripides' mother was said to have sold greens—very probably a calumny. Also, a parody on a line by Euripides.
[53] The ewe was to be sacrificed in order to allay the approaching storm.
[54] A play by Euripides which Aristophanes regarded as absurd.

DIONYSUS: And what do *you* propose? Speak, Aeschylus.
AESCHYLUS: I could have wished to meet him otherwhere.
We fight not here on equal terms.
DIONYSUS: Why not?
AESCHYLUS: My poetry survived me:[55] his died with him:
He's got it here, all handy to recite.
Howbeit, if so you wish it, so we'll have it.
DIONYSUS: O bring me fire, and bring me frankincense.
I'll pray, or e'er the clash of wits begin,
To judge the strife with high poetic skill.
Meanwhile [*To the* Chorus] invoke the Muses with a song.
CHORUS: O Muses, the daughters divine
               of Zeus, the immaculate Nine,
Who gaze from your mansions serene
               on intellects subtle and keen,
When down to the tournament lists,
               in bright-polished wit they descend,
With wrestling and turnings and twists
               in the battle of words to contend,
O come and behold what the two
               antagonist poets can do,
Whose mouths are the swiftest to teach
               grand language and filings of speech:
For now of their wits is the sternest
               encounter commencing in earnest.
DIONYSUS: Ye two, put up your prayers before ye start.
AESCHYLUS: Demeter, mistress, nourisher of my soul,
O make me worthy of thy mystic rites!
DIONYSUS: [*To* Euripides] Now put on incense, you.
EURIPIDES: Excuse me, no;
My vows are paid to other gods than these.
DIONYSUS: What, a new coinage of your own?
EURIPIDES: Precisely.
DIONYSUS: Pray then to them, those private gods of yours.
EURIPIDES: Ether, my pasture, volubly-rolling tongue,
Intelligent wit and critic nostrils keen,
O well and neatly may I trounce his plays!
CHORUS: We also are yearning from these to be learning
          Some stately measure, some majestic grand
          Movement telling of conflicts nigh.
          Now for battle arrayed they stand,
          Tongues embittered, and anger high.
          Each has got a venturesome will,
          Each an eager and nimble mind;
          One will wield, with artistic skill,
          Clearcut phrases, and wit refined;

[55] Since Aeschylus' plays were allowed to be revived in Athens by special decree.

Then the other, with words defiant,
Stern and strong, like an angry giant
Laying on with uprooted trees,
Soon will scatter a world of these
Superscholastic subtleties.
DIONYSUS: Now then, commence your arguments,
      and mind you both display
True wit, not metaphors, nor things
      which any fool could say.
EURIPIDES: As for myself, good people all,
      I'll tell you by-and-by
My own poetic worth and claims;
      but first of all I'll try
To show how this portentous quack
      beguiled the silly fools
Whose tastes were nurtured, ere he came,
      in Phrynichus's schools.
He'd bring some single mourner on,
      seated and veiled, 'twould be
Achilles, say, or Niobe[56]
      —the face you could not see—
An empty show of tragic woe,
      who uttered not one thing.
DIONYSUS: 'Tis true.
EURIPIDES: Then in the Chorus came,
      and rattled off a string
Of four continuous lyric odes:
      the mourner never stirred.
DIONYSUS: I liked it too. I sometimes think
      that I those mutes preferred
To all your chatterers now-a-days.
EURIPIDES: Because, if you must know,
You were an ass.
DIONYSUS: An ass, no doubt;
      what made him do it though?
EURIPIDES: That was his quackery, don't you see,
      to set the audience guessing
When Niobe would speak; meanwhile,
      the drama was progressing.
DIONYSUS: The rascal, how he took me in!
      'Twas shameful, was it not?
[*To* Aeschylus] What makes you stamp and fidget so?
EURIPIDES: He's catching it so hot.
So when he had humbugged thus awhile,
      and now his wretched play
Was halfway through, a dozen words,
      great wild-bull words, he'd say,
Fierce Bugaboos, with bristling crests,
      and shaggy eyebrows too,
Which not a soul could understand.
AESCHYLUS: O heavens!
DIONYSUS: Be quiet, do.
EURIPIDES: But not one single word was clear.
DIONYSUS: St! don't your teeth be gnashing.

EURIPIDES: 'Twas all Scamanders, moated camps,
      and griffin-eagles flashing
In burnished copper on the shields,
      chivalric-precipice-high
Expressions, hard to comprehend.
DIONYSUS: Aye, by the Powers, and I
Full many a sleepless night have spent
      in anxious thought, because
I'd find the tawny cock-horse[57] out,
      what sort of bird it was!
AESCHYLUS: It was a sign, you stupid dolt,
      engraved the ships upon.
DIONYSUS: Eryxis I supposed it was,
      Philoxenus's son.
EURIPIDES: Now really should a cock be brought
      into a tragic play?
AESCHYLUS: You enemy of gods and men,
      what was *your* practice, pray?
EURIPIDES: No cock-horse in *my* plays, by Zeus,
      no goat-stag there you'll see,
Such figures as are blazoned forth
      in Median tapestry.
When first I took the art from you,
      bloated and swoln, poor thing,
With turgid gasconading words
      and heavy dieting,
First I reduced and toned her down,
      and made her slim and neat
With wordlets and with exercise
      and poultices of beet,
And next a dose of chatterjuice,
      distilled from books, I gave her,
And monodies she took, with sharp
      Cephisophon[58] for flavour.
I never used haphazard words,
      or plunged abruptly in;
Who entered first explained at large
      the drama's origin
And source.
AESCHYLUS: Its source, I really trust,
      was better than your own.
EURIPIDES: Then from the very opening lines
      no idleness was shown;
The mistress talked with all her might,
      the servant talked as much,
The master talked, the maiden talked,
      the beldame talked.
AESCHYLUS: For such
An outrage was not death your due?
EURIPIDES: No, by Apollo, no:
That was my democratic way.
DIONYSUS: Ah, let that topic go.
Your record is not there, my friend,
      particularly good.[59]

[56] He is referring to two lost tragedies of Aeschylus, the *Phrygians or the Ransom of Hector* and the *Niobe*. In the former, Achilles was introduced, wrapped in sullen gloom for the loss of Patroclus, and refusing all food and consolation. In the latter, Niobe was shown, dumb with sorrow for her six sons and six daughters, whom Apollo and Artemis had slain.—B. B. ROGERS

[57] He quotes a phrase from a now lost play by Aeschylus which described the figurehead of a ship.

[58] A slave of Euripides who was said to have assisted the playwright in his work.

[59] It is strange to find Euripides accused by Aristophanes of antidemocratic leanings. Rogers believes this refers to the fact that two of Euripides' students were active in the oligarchy of the Four Hundred.

EURIPIDES: Then next I taught all these to speak.

AESCHYLUS: You did so, and I would
That ere such mischief you had wrought,
                    your very lungs had split.

EURIPIDES: Canons of verse I introduced,
                    and neatly chiselled wit;
To look, to scan: to plot, to plan:
                    to twist, to turn, to woo:
On all to spy; in all to pry.

AESCHYLUS: You did: I say so too.

EURIPIDES: I showed them scenes of common life,
                    the things we know and see,
Where any blunder would at once
                    by all detected be.
I never blustered on, or took
                    their breath and wits away
By Cycnuses or Memnons[60] clad
                    in terrible array,
With bells upon their horses' heads,
                    the audience to dismay.
Look at *his* pupils, look at mine:
                    and there the contrast view.
Uncouth Megaenetus is his,
                    and rough Phormisius[61] too;
Great long-beard-lance-and-trumpet-men,
                    flesh-tearers with the pine: [62]
But natty smart Theramenes,
                    and Cleitophon are mine.

DIONYSUS: Theramenes? a clever man
                    and wonderfully sly:
Immerse him in a flood of ills,
                    he'll soon be high and dry,
"A Kian with a kappa, sir,
                    not Chian with a chi." [63]

EURIPIDES: I taught them all these knowing ways
By chopping logic in my plays,
And making all my speakers try
To reason out the How and Why.
So now the people trace the springs,
The sources and the roots of things,
And manage all their households too
Far better than they used to do,
Scanning and searching *What's amiss?*
And, *Why was that? And, How is this?*

DIONYSUS: Ay, truly, never now a man
Comes home, but he begins to scan;
And to his household loudly cries,
Why, where's my pitcher? What's the matter?
'Tis dead and gone my last year's platter.
Who gnawed these olives? Bless the sprat,
Who nibbled off the head of that?

---

[60] Allies of Priam in the Trojan War who wore rich trappings in battle.

[61] We do not know anything about Megaenetus, but Phormisius is known as a political figure.

[62] I.e., as barbaric as Sinis, the legendary robber, who tore men apart by tying them to pine trees which he bent down with his bare hands and then released. The line parodies Aeschylus' grand, Homeric style of writing.

[63] I.e., he changed his slogan or watchword very freely, depending upon which political party had the upper hand.

And where's the garlic vanished, pray,
I purchased only yesterday?
—Whereas, of old, our stupid youths
Would sit, with open mouths and eyes,
Like any dull-brained Mammacouths. [64]

CHORUS: "All this thou beholdest, Achilles our boldest." [65]
And what wilt thou reply? Draw tight the rein
Lest that fiery soul of thine
Whirl thee out of the listed plain,
Past the olives, and o'er the line.
Dire and grievous the charge he brings.
See thou answer him, noble heart,
Not with passionate bickerings.
Shape thy course with a sailor's art,
Reef the canvas, shorten the sails,
Shift them edgewise to shun the gales.
When the breezes are soft and low,
Then, well under control, you'll go
Quick and quicker to strike the foe.
O first of all the Hellenic bards
                    high loftily-towering verse to rear,
And tragic phrase from the dust to raise,
                    pour forth thy fountain with right good cheer.

AESCHYLUS: My wrath is hot at this vile mischance,
                    and my spirit revolts at the thought that I
Must bandy words with a fellow like *him:*
                    but lest he should vaunt that I can't reply—
Come, tell me what are the points for which
                    a noble poet our praise obtains.

EURIPIDES: For his ready wit, and his counsels sage,
                    and because the citizen folk he trains
To be better townsmen and worthier men.

AESCHYLUS: If then you have done the very reverse,
Found noble-hearted and virtuous men,
                    and altered them, each and all, for the worse,
Pray what is the meed you deserve to get?

DIONYSUS: Nay, ask not *him.* He deserves to die.

AESCHYLUS: For just consider what style of men
                    he received from me, great six-foot-high
Heroical souls, who never would blench
                    from a townsman's duties in peace or war;
Not idle loafers, or low buffoons,
                    or rascally scamps such as now they are.
But men who were breathing spears and helms,
                    and the snow-white plume in its crested pride,
The greave, and the dart, and the warrior's heart
                    in its sevenfold casing of tough bull-hide.

DIONYSUS: He'll stun me, I know, with his armoury-work;
                    this business is going from bad to worse.

EURIPIDES: And how did you manage to make them so grand,
                    exalted, and brave with your wonderful verse?

DIONYSUS: Come, Aeschylus, answer, and don't stand mute

---

[64] Blockhead.

[65] The opening line of Aeschylus' play *Myrmidons,* now lost.

in your self-willed pride and arrogant spleen.

AESCHYLUS: A drama I wrote with the War-god filled.

DIONYSUS: Its name?

AESCHYLUS: 'Tis the *Seven against Thebes* that I mean.
Which whoso beheld, with eagerness swelled
   to rush to the battlefield there and then.

DIONYSUS: O that was a scandalous thing you did!
  You have made the Thebans mightier men,
More eager by far for the business of war.
  Now, therefore, receive this punch on the head.

AESCHYLUS: Ah, *ye* might have practised the same yourselves,
   but ye turned to other pursuits instead.
Then next the *Persians* I wrote, in praise
  of the noblest deed that the world can show,
And each man longed for the victor's wreath,
   to fight and to vanquish his country's foe.

DIONYSUS: I was pleased, I own, when I heard their moan[66]
   for old Darius, their great king, dead;
When they smote together their hands, like this,
   and *Evir alake*[67] the Chorus said.

AESCHYLUS: Aye, such are the poet's appropriate works:
   and just consider how all along
From the very first they have wrought you good,
   the noble bards, the masters of song.
First, Orpheus taught you religious rites,
  and from bloody murder to stay your hands:
Musaeus healing and oracle lore;
   and Hesiod all the culture of lands,
The time to gather, the time to plough.
   And gat not Homer his glory divine
By singing of valour, and honour, and right,
   and the sheen of the battle-extended line,
The ranging of troops and the arming of men?

DIONYSUS: O ay, but he didn't teach *that,* I opine,
To Pantacles; when he was leading the show[68]
   I couldn't imagine what he was at,
He had fastened his helm on the top of his head,
   he was trying to fasten his plume upon that.

AESCHYLUS: But others, many and brave, he taught,
   of whom was Lamachus,[69] hero true;
And thence my spirit the impress took,
   and many a lion-heart chief I drew,
Patrocluses, Teucers, illustrious names;
   for I fain the citizen-folk would spur

To stretch themselves to *their* measure and height,
   whenever the trumpet of war they hear.
But Phaedras and Stheneboeas?[70] No!
   no harlotry business deformed my plays.
And none can say that ever I drew
   a love-sick woman in all my days.

EURIPIDES: For *you* no lot or portion had got
   in Queen Aphrodite.

AESCHYLUS: Thank Heaven for that.
But ever on you and yours, my friend,
   the mighty goddess mightily sat;
Yourself she cast to the ground at last.

DIONYSUS: O ay, that came uncommonly pat.
You showed how cuckolds are made, and lo,
  you were struck yourself by the very same fate.[71]

EURIPIDES: But say, you cross-grained censor of mine,
   how *my* Stheneboeas could harm the state.

AESCHYLUS: Full many a noble dame, the wife
   of a noble citizen, hemlock took,
And died, unable the shame and sin
   of your Bellerophon-scenes to brook.

EURIPIDES: Was then, I wonder, the tale I told
   of Phaedra's passionate love untrue?

AESCHYLUS: Not so: but tales of incestuous vice
  the sacred poet should hide from view,
Nor ever exhibit and blazon forth
   on the public stage to the public ken.
For boys a teacher at school is found,
   but we, the poets, are teachers of men.
We are *bound* things honest and pure to speak.

EURIPIDES: And to speak great Lycabettuses, pray,
And massive blocks of Parnassian rocks,
   is *that* things honest and pure to say?
In human fashion we ought to speak.

AESCHYLUS: Alas, poor witling, and can't you see
That for mighty thoughts and heroic aims,
   the words themselves must appropriate be?
And grander belike on the ear should strike
   the speech of heroes and godlike powers,
Since even the robes that invest their limbs
   are statelier, grander robes than ours.
Such was *my* plan: but when *you* began,
   you spoilt and degraded it all.

EURIPIDES: How so?

AESCHYLUS: Your kings in tatters and rags you dressed,
   and brought them on, a beggarly show,
To move, forsooth, our pity and ruth.

EURIPIDES: And what was the harm, I should like to know.

AESCHYLUS: No more will a wealthy citizen now
   equip for the state a galley of war.

[66] A reference to the doleful invocation of Darius, the deceased father of Xerxes, by the Persians in connection with their defeat by the Athenians in the Persian invasion of Greece. In Aeschylus' tragedy *The Persians,* which celebrated the defeat of the Persian host at Marathon and Salamis.

[67] Alas!

[68] Pantacles forgot to fasten the plume on his helmet before going into battle.

[69] One of the leaders of the Athenians' disastrous expedition against Sicily in the Peloponnesian War.

[70] Phaedra, the heroine of Euripides' *Hippolytus* (and of Racine's *Phaedra,* see pp. 413–429), desired her stepson. Stheneboea, the heroine of a lost tragedy by Euripides, was guilty of an adulterous passion.

[71] It was common report that one of his wives misconducted herself with Cephisophon: and some say that both his wives played him false.—B. B. ROGERS

He wraps his limbs in tatters and rags,
            and whines *he is poor, too poor by far.*
DIONYSUS: But under his rags he is wearing a vest,
            as woolly and soft as a man could wish.
Let him gull the state, and he's off to the mart;
            an eager, extravagant buyer of fish.
AESCHYLUS: Moreover to prate, to harangue, to debate,
            is now the ambition of all in the state.
Each exercise-ground is in consequence found
            deserted and empty: to evil repute
Your lessons have brought our youngsters, and taught
            our sailors to challenge, discuss, and refute
The orders they get from their captains and yet,
            when *I* was alive, I protest that the knaves
Knew nothing at all, save for rations to call,
            and to sing "Rhyppapae" as they pulled
                        through the waves.
DIONYSUS: And bedad to let fly from their sterns
    in the eye
        of the fellow who tugged at the undermost oar,
And a jolly young messmate with filth to besmirch,
            and to land for a filching adventure ashore;
But now they harangue, and dispute, and won't row
And idly and aimlessly float to and fro.
AESCHYLUS: Of what ills is he *not* the creator and cause?
Consider the scandalous scenes that he draws,
His bawds, and his panders, his women who give
        Give birth in the sacredest shrine,
Whilst others with brothers are wedded and bedded,
        And others opine
That "not to be living" is truly "to live."
And therefore our city is swarming to-day
With clerks and with demagogue-monkeys, who play
Their jackanape tricks at all times, in all places,
Deluding the people of Athens; but none
Has training enough in athletics to run
        With the torch in his hand at the races.
DIONYSUS: By the Powers, you are right! At the Panathenaea
I laughed till I felt like a potsherd to see a
Pale, paunchy young gentleman pounding along,
With his head butting forward, the last of the throng,
In the direst of straits; and behold at the gates,
The Ceramites[72] flapped him, and smacked him, and slapped him,
In the ribs, and the loin, and the flank, and the groin,
And still, as they spanked him, he puffed and he panted,
Till at one mighty cuff, he discharged such a puff
        That he blew out his torch and levanted.
CHORUS: Dread the battle, and stout the combat,
            mighty and manifold looms the war.
        Hard to decide is the fight they're waging,
        One like a stormy tempest raging,
One alert in the rally and skirmish,
            clever to parry and foin and spar.
        Nay but don't be content to sit

[72] Inhabitants of Cerameicus.

Always in one position only:
            many the fields for your keen-edged wit.
On then, wrangle in every way,
Argue, battle, be flayed and flay,
Old and new from your stores display,
Yea, and strive with venturesome daring
            something subtle and neat to say.

Fear ye this, that to-day's spectators
            lack the grace of artistic lore,
    Lack the knowledge they need for taking
    All the points ye will soon be making?
Fear it not: the alarm is groundless:
            that, be sure, is the case no more.
    All have fought the campaign ere this:
Each a book of the words is holding;
            never a single point they'll miss.
    Bright their natures, and now, I ween,
    Newly whetted, and sharp, and keen.
    Dread not any defect of wit,
Battle away without misgiving,
            sure that the audience, at least, are fit.
EURIPIDES: Well then I'll turn me to your pro-
    logues now,
Beginning first to test the first beginning
Of this fine poet's plays. Why he's obscure
Even in the enunciation of the facts.
DIONYSUS: Which of them will you test?
EURIPIDES: Many: but first
Give us that famous one from the Oresteia.[73]
DIONYSUS: St! Silence all! Now, Aeschylus, begin.
AESCHYLUS: *Grave Hermes, witnessing a father's power,*
Be thou my saviour and mine aid to-day,
For here I come and hither I return.
DIONYSUS: Any fault there?
EURIPIDES: A dozen faults and more.
DIONYSUS: Eh! why the lines are only three in all.
EURIPIDES: But every one contains a score of faults.
DIONYSUS: Now Aeschylus, keep silent; if you don't
You won't get off with three iambic lines.
AESCHYLUS: Silent for *him!*
DIONYSUS: If my advice you'll take.
EURIPIDES: Why, at first starting here's a fault skyhigh.
AESCHYLUS: [*To* Dionysus] You see your folly?[74]
DIONYSUS: Have your way; I care not.
AESCHYLUS: [*To* Euripides] What is my fault?
EURIPIDES: Begin the lines again.
AESCHYLUS: *Grave Hermes, witnessing a father's power*—
EURIPIDES: And this beside his murdered father's grave
Orestes speaks?
AESCHYLUS: I say not otherwise.

[73] The Oresteian trilogy (*Agamemnon*, see pp. 11–29,
The Libation Pourers, and *Eumenides*).
[74] I.e., in making me remain silent.

EURIPIDES: Then does he mean that when his father fell
By craft and violence at a woman's hand,
The god of craft was witnessing the deed?[75]

AESCHYLUS: It was not he: it was the Helper Hermes
He called the grave: and this he showed by adding
It was his sire's prerogative he held.

EURIPIDES: Why this is worse than all. If from his father
He held this office grave, why then——[76]

DIONYSUS: He was
A graveyard rifler on his father's side.

AESCHYLUS: Bacchus, the wine you drink is stale and fusty.[77]

DIONYSUS: Give him another: [To Euripides] you, look out for faults.

AESCHYLUS: *Be thou my saviour and mine aid to-day,*
For here I come, and hither I return.

EURIPIDES: The same thing twice says clever Aeschylus.

DIONYSUS: How twice?

EURIPIDES: Why, just consider: I'll explain.
"I come," says he; and "I return," says he:
It's the same thing, to "come" and to "return."

DIONYSUS: Aye, just as if you said, "Good fellow, lend me
A kneading trough: likewise, a trough to knead in."

AESCHYLUS: It is not so, you everlasting talker,
They're not the same, the words are right enough.

DIONYSUS: How so? inform me how you use the words.

AESCHYLUS: A man, not banished from his home, may "come"
To any land, with no especial chance.
A home-bound exile both "returns" and "comes."

DIONYSUS: O good, by Apollo!
What do you say, Euripides, to that?

EURIPIDES: I say Orestes never did "return."
He came in secret: nobody recalled him.

DIONYSUS: O good, by Hermes!
[Aside] I've not the least suspicion what he means.

EURIPIDES: Repeat another line.

DIONYSUS: Ay, Aeschylus,
Repeat one instantly: *you,* mark what's wrong.

AESCHYLUS: *Now on this funeral mound I call my father*
To hear, to hearken.

EURIPIDES: There he is again.
To "hear," to "hearken"; the same thing, exactly.

[75] Euripides gives the last three words of the line beginning *"Grave Hermes . . . "* a meaning which they can bear, "that dost survey *my* father's realm." He then asks why does Orestes at this solemn moment address Hermes as the surveyor of his father's realm. Does he mean that the god of craft was an onlooker, when Clytemnestra by craft destroyed her husband?—B. B. ROGERS

[76] Euripides misinterprets the words of Aeschylus.

[77] I.e., it makes you deliver stupid jests.

DIONYSUS: Aye, but he's speaking to the dead, you knave,
Who cannot hear us though we call them thrice.[78]

AESCHYLUS: And how do you make *your* prologues?

EURIPIDES: You shall hear;
And if you find one single thing said twice,
Or any useless padding, spit upon me.

DIONYSUS: Well, fire away: I'm all agog to hear
Your very accurate and faultless prologues.

EURIPIDES: *A happy man was Oedipus at first—*

AESCHYLUS: Not so, by Zeus; a most unhappy man.
Who, not yet born nor yet conceived, Apollo
Foretold would be his father's murderer.
How could *he* be a happy man at first?

EURIPIDES: *Then he became the wretchedest of men.*[79]

AESCHYLUS: Not so, by Zeus; he never ceased to be.
No sooner born, than they exposed the babe,
(And that in winter), in an earthen crock,
Lest he should grow a man, and slay his father.
Then with both ankles pierced and swoln, he limped
Away to Polybus: still young, he married
An ancient crone, and her his mother too.
Then scratched out both his eyes.

DIONYSUS: Happy indeed
Had he been Erasinides's colleague![80]

EURIPIDES: Nonsense; I say my prologues are firstrate.

AESCHYLUS: Nay then, by Zeus, no longer line by line
I'll maul your phrases: but with heaven to aid
I'll smash your prologues with a bottle of oil.

EURIPIDES: You mine with a bottle of oil?

AESCHYLUS: With only one.
You frame your prologues so that each and all
Fit in with a "bottle of oil," or "coverlet-skin,"
Or "reticule-bag." I'll prove it here, and now.

EURIPIDES: You'll prove it? You?

AESCHYLUS: I will.

DIONYSUS: Well then, begin.[81]

EURIPIDES: *Aegyptus, sailing with his fifty sons,*
As ancient legends mostly tell the tale,
Touching at Argos

AESCHYLUS: Lost his bottle of oil.

EURIPIDES: Hang it, what's that? Confound that bottle of oil!

DIONYSUS: Give him another: let him try again.

[78] The last call to the dead at a funeral.

[79] Both lines referring to Oedipus are the opening lines of a lost *Antigone* by Euripides.

[80] Erasinides, who won the naval battle of Arginusae, was ungratefully treated by the Athenian people.

[81] Euripides' prologues are being attacked in what follows by quotations from six of them. In the third line of each, the meter and grammar can be completed by the Greek words for which "Lost his bottle of oil" are used by the translator, Rogers. In each case, Aeschylus makes the meaning absurd by adding "Lost his bottle of oil."

EURIPIDES: *Bacchus, who, clad in fawnskins, leaps and bounds*
With torch and thyrsus in the choral dance
Along Parnassus
AESCHYLUS: Lost his bottle of oil.
DIONYSUS: Ah me, we are stricken[82]—with that bottle again!
EURIPIDES: Pooh, pooh, that's nothing. I've a prologue here,
He'll never tack his bottle of oil to this:
No man is blest in every single thing.
One is of noble birth, but lacking means.
Another, baseborn,
AESCHYLUS: Lost his bottle of oil.
DIONYSUS: Euripides!
EURIPIDES: Well?
DIONYSUS: Lower your sails, my boy;
This bottle of oil is going to blow a gale.
EURIPIDES: O, by Demeter, I don't care one bit;
Now from his hands I'll strike that bottle of oil.
DIONYSUS: Go on then, go: but ware the bottle of oil.
EURIPIDES: *Once Cadmus, quitting the Sidonian town,*
Agenor's offspring
AESCHYLUS: Lost his bottle of oil.
DIONYSUS: O pray, my man, buy off that bottle of oil,
Or else he'll smash our prologues all to bits.
EURIPIDES: I buy of *him?*
DIONYSUS: If *my* advice you'll take.
EURIPIDES: No, no, I've many a prologue yet to say,
To which he can't tack on his bottle of oil.
Pelops, the son of Tantalus, while driving
His mares to Pisa
AESCHYLUS: Lost his bottle of oil.
DIONYSUS: There! he tacked on the bottle of oil again.
O for Heaven's sake, pay him its price, dear boy;
You'll get it for an obol, spick and span.
EURIPIDES: Not yet, by Zeus; I've plenty of prologues left.
Oeneus once reaping
AESCHYLUS: Lost his bottle of oil.
EURIPIDES: Pray let me finish one entire line first.
Oeneus once reaping an abundant harvest,
Offering the first fruits
AESCHYLUS: Lost his bottle of oil.
DIONYSUS: What, in the act of offering? Fie! Who stole it?
EURIPIDES: O don't keep bothering! Let him try with this!
Zeus, as by Truth's own voice the tale is told,
DIONYSUS: No, he'll cut in with "Lost his bottle of oil!"
Those bottles of oil on all your prologues seem
To gather and grow, like styes upon the eye.

[82] Dionysus employs the words Agamemnon cries out when Clytemnestra is murdering him. See page 26.

Turn to his melodies now for goodness' sake.
EURIPIDES: O I can easily show that he's a poor
Melody-maker; makes them all alike.
CHORUS: What, O what will be done!
       Strange to think that he dare
       Blame the bard who has won,
       More than all in our days,
       Fame and praise for his lays,
       Lays so many and fair.
       Much I marvel to hear
       What the charge he will bring
       'Gainst our tragedy king;
       Yea for himself do I fear.
EURIPIDES: Wonderful lays! O yes, you'll see directly.
I'll cut down all his metrical strains to one.[83]
DIONYSUS: And I, I'll take some pebbles, and keep count.
[*A slight pause, during which the music of a flute is heard. The music serves as an accompaniment to the recitative*]
EURIPIDES: Lord of Phthia, Achilles, *why hearing the voice of the hero-dividing*
Hah! smiting! approachest thou not to the rescue?
We, by the lake who *abide, are adoring our ancestor Hermes.*
Hah! smiting! approachest thou not to the rescue?
DIONYSUS: O Aeschylus, twice art thou smitten!
EURIPIDES: Hearken to me, great king; yea, hearken *Atreides, thou noblest of all the Achaeans.*
Hah! smiting! approachest thou not to the rescue?
DIONYSUS: Thrice, Aeschylus, thrice art thou smitten!
EURIPIDES: Hush! the bee-wardens are here: they *will quickly the Temple of Artemis open.*
Hah! smiting! approachest thou not to the rescue?
I will expound (for *I know it*) the omen the chieftains encountered.
Hah! smiting! approachest thou not to the rescue?
DIONYSUS: O Zeus and King, the terrible lot of smitings!
I'll to the bath: I'm very sure my kidneys
Are quite inflamed and swoln with all these smitings.
EURIPIDES: Wait till you've heard another batch of lays
Culled from his lyre-accompanied melodies.
DIONYSUS: Go on then, go: but no more smitings, please.
EURIPIDES: How the twin-throned powers of *Achaea, the lords of the mighty Hellenes.*
O phlattothrattophlattothrat!

[83] Euripides accuses Aeschylus of having composed monotonous choral odes, because their lines tend to become Homeric hexameters. (And, indeed, Aeschylus was under Homer's influence.) Euripides then gives five illustrations of this tendency by quoting from the older poet's work and completing the first line by Aeschylus with the same Homeric hexameter.

Sendeth *the Sphinx, the unchancy, the chieftainness*
    bloodhound.
    O phlattothrattophlattothrat!
Launcheth fierce with brand *and hand the avengers*
    the terrible eagle.
    O phlattothrattophlattothrat!
So for the swift-*winged hounds of the air he provided*
    a booty.
    O phlattothrattophlattothrat!
    The throng down-bearing on Aias.
    O phlattothrattophlattothrat!
    DIONYSUS: Whence comes that phlattothrat? From
        Marathon,[84] or
Where picked you up these cable-twister's strains?
    AESCHYLUS: From noblest source for noblest ends[85]
        I brought them,
Unwilling in the Muses' holy field
The self-same flowers as Phrynichus to cull.
But *he* from all things rotten draws his lays,
From Carian flutings, catches of Meletus,[86]
Dance-music, dirges. You shall hear directly.
Bring me the lyre. Yet wherefore need a lyre
For songs like these? Where's she that bangs and
    jangles
Her castanets? Euripides's Muse,
Present yourself: fit goddess for fit verse.[87]
    DIONYSUS: The Muse herself can't be a wanton?
        No!
    AESCHYLUS: Halcyons, who by the ever-rippling[88]
Waves of the sea are babbling,
Dewing your plumes with the drops that fall
From wings in the salt spray dabbling.

Spiders, ever with twir-r-r-r-rling fingers
Weaving the warp and the woof,
Little, brittle, network, fretwork,
Under the coigns of the roof.

The minstrel shuttle's care.

Where in the front of the dark-prowed ships
Yarely the flute-loving dolphin skips.

Races here and oracles there.

And the joy of the young vines smiling,
And the tendril of grapes, care-beguiling.

[84] Aeschylus had fought against the Persians in the
memorable battle of Marathon and was highly regarded
as a "Marathon warrior."

[85] That is, from Homer's epics to noble Greek tragedy.

[86] A tragic poet who wrote erotic verse; later, one of
Socrates' accusers.

[87] An actor enters, personating a flaunting harlot, and
clashing oyster-shells together. Aeschylus hails him as
the Muse of Euripides.—B. B. ROGERS

[88] The lyrics of Euripides are now criticized as cor-
rupting the noble simplicity of the ancient metres, by
the introduction of affected novelties and dainty little
devices, like the tricks of a harlot, as Aeschylus says
below.—B. B. ROGERS
Aeschylus here parodies Euripides' style. The attack
on Euripides' alleged metrical effect is by now obscure.

O embrace me, my child, O embrace me.
[*To* Dionysus] You see this foot?[89]
    DIONYSUS: I do.
    AESCHYLUS: And this?
    DIONYSUS: And that one too.
    AESCHYLUS: [*To* Euripides] You, such stuff who
        compile,
    Dare my songs to upbraid;
    You, whose songs in the style
    Of Cyrene's embraces are made.[90]
So much for them: but still I'd like to show
The way in which your monodies are framed.[91]
    "O darkly-light mysterious Night,
    What may this Vision mean,
    Sent from the world unseen
    With baleful omens rife;
    A thing of lifeless life,
    A child of sable night,
    A ghastly curdling sight,
    In black funereal veils,
    With murder, murder in its eyes,
    And great enormous nails?
Light ye the lanterns, my maidens,
                and dipping your jugs in the stream,
Draw me the dew of the water,
                and heat it to boiling and steam;
So will I wash me away the ill effects of my dream.
    God of the sea!
    My dream's come true.
    Ho, lodgers, ho,
    This portent view.
    Glyce has vanished, carrying off my cock,
    My cock that crew!
    O Mania,[92] help! O Oreads of the rock
    Pursue! pursue!
For I, poor girl, was working within,
Holding my distaff heavy and full,
Twir-r-r-r-rling my hand as the threads I spin,
Weaving an excellent bobbin of wool;
Thinking 'To-morrow I'll go to the fair,
In the dusk of the morn, and be selling it there.'
But he to the blue upflew, upflew,
On the lightliest tips of his wings outspread;
To me he bequeathed but woe, but woe,
And tears, sad tears, from my eyes o'erflow,
Which I, the bereaved, must shed, must shed.
O children of Ida, sons of Crete,
Grasping your bows to the rescue come;
Twinkle about on your restless feet,

[89] Metrical foot, regarded as faulty.

[90] I.e., "you whose verses are as tricky as a harlot's—
the harlot Cyrene's—wiles."

[91] Aeschylus now improvises a lyrical monologue, in
the style and to a great extent in the very words of
Euripides. It is a satire on the trivial incidents around
which Euripides was accustomed to throw the grace and
dignity of tragic diction. A poor spinning girl has a bad
dream, and when she wakes finds that Glyce has ab-
sconded with her cock.—B. B. ROGERS

[92] A spinning girl comically related to an "oread" or
mountain nymph.

Stand in a circle around her home.
O Artemis, thou maid divine,
Dictynna, huntress, fair to see,
O bring that keen-nosed pack of thine,
And hunt through all the house with me.
O Hecate, with flameful brands,[93]
O Zeus's daughter, arm thine hands,
Those swiftliest hands, both right and left;
Thy rays on Glyce's cottage throw
That I serenely there may go,
And search by moonlight for the theft."
DIONYSUS: Enough of both your odes.
AESCHYLUS: Enough for me.
Now would I bring the fellow to the scales.
That, that alone, shall test our poetry now,
And prove whose words are weightiest, his or mine.
   DIONYSUS: Then both come hither, since I needs
     must weigh
The art poetic like a pound of cheese.
   [At this a scale is pushed into the scene]
   CHORUS: O the labour these wits go through!
O the wild, extravagant, new,
Wonderful things they are going to do!
Who but they would ever have thought of it?
Why, if a man had happened to meet me
Out in the street, and intelligence brought of it,
I should have thought he was trying to cheat me;
Thought that his story was false and deceiving.
That were a tale I could never believe in.
   DIONYSUS: Each of you stand beside his scale.
   [They do so]
   AESCHYLUS and EURIPIDES: We're here.
   DIONYSUS: And grasp it firmly whilst ye speak your
   lines,
And don't let go until I cry "cuckoo."
   [They keep the scale steady with a hand and
   then speak a line into it. They repeat their
   procedure for each new line]
   AESCHYLUS and EURIPIDES: Ready!
   DIONYSUS: Now speak your lines into the scale.
   EURIPIDES: *O that the Argo had not winged her*
   way—[94]
   AESCHYLUS: *River Spercheius, cattle-grazing*
   haunts—
   DIONYSUS: Cuckoo! let go. O look, by far the
   lowest
His scale sinks down.
   EURIPIDES: Why, how came that about?
   DIONYSUS: He threw a river in, like some wool-
   seller
Wetting his wool, to make it weigh the more.
But *you* threw in a light and wingèd word.
   EURIPIDES: Come, let him match another verse
   with mine.
   DIONYSUS: Each to his scale.
   AESCHYLUS and EURIPIDES: We're ready.

[93] Hecate, as connected with the moon, is always described as carrying lights in her hands.—B. B. ROGERS
[94] First line of the *Medea*. The other lines do not
appear in any plays that have survived.

   DIONYSUS: Speak your lines.
   EURIPIDES: *Persuasion's only shrine is eloquent*
   speech.
   AESCHYLUS: *Death loves not gifts, alone amongst*
   the gods.
   DIONYSUS: Let go, let go. Down goes his scale
   again.
He threw in Death, the heaviest ill of all.
   EURIPIDES: And I Persuasion, the most lovely
   word.
   DIONYSUS: A vain and empty sound, devoid of
   sense.
Think of some heavier-weighted line of yours,
To drag your scale down: something strong and big.
   EURIPIDES: Where have I got one? Where? Let's
   see.
   DIONYSUS: I'll tell you.
Achilles threw two singles and a four."[95]
Come, speak your lines: this is your last set-to.
   EURIPIDES: *In his right hand he grasped an iron-*
   clamped mace.
   AESCHYLUS: *Chariot on chariot, corpse on corpse*
   was hurled.
   DIONYSUS: There now! again he has done you.
   EURIPIDES: Done me? How?
   DIONYSUS: He threw two chariots and two corpses
   in;
Five-score Egyptians could not lift that weight.
   AESCHYLUS: No more of "line for line"; let him—
   himself,
His children, wife, Cephisophon—get in,
With all his books collected in his arms,
Two lines of mine shall overweigh the lot.
   DIONYSUS: Both are my friends; I can't decide
   between them:
I don't desire to be at odds with either:
One is so clever, one delights me so.
   PLUTO: Then you'll effect nothing for which you
   came?
   DIONYSUS: And how, if I decide?
   PLUTO: Then take the winner;
So will your journey not be made in vain.
   DIONYSUS: Heaven bless your Highness! Listen, I
   came down
After a poet.
   EURIPIDES: To what end?
   DIONYSUS: That so
The city, saved, may keep her choral games.
Now then, whichever of you two shall best
Advise the city, *he* shall come with me.
And first of Alcibiades,[96] let each

[95] This line appears to be from Euripides' *Telephus*,
in which he earned ridicule by showing the Homeric
heroes playing dice. Euripides deleted this scene later;
hence he hesitates to quote the line when Dionysus
proposes it.
[96] The "problem child" of Athens who alternately won
the favor and disfavor of the Athenians with his unstable
behavior. He was in exile for a second time when *The
Frogs* was written.

Say what he thinks; the city travails sore.

EURIPIDES: What does she think herself about him?

DIONYSUS: What?

She loves, and hates, and longs to have him back.
But give me *your* advice about the man.

EURIPIDES: I loathe a townsman who is slow to aid,
And swift to hurt, his town: who ways and means
Finds for himself, but finds not for the state.

DIONYSUS: Poseidon, but that's smart! [*To Aeschylus*] And what say *you?*

AESCHYLUS: 'Twere best to rear no lion in the state:
But having reared, 'tis best to humour him.

DIONYSUS: By Zeus the Saviour, still I can't decide.
One is so clever, and so clear the other.
But once again. Let each in turn declare
What plan of safety for the state ye've got.

EURIPIDES: First with Cinesias pair Cleocritus,[97]
Then let zephyrs waft them o'er the watery plain.

DIONYSUS: A funny sight, I own: but where's the sense?

EURIPIDES: If, when the fleets engage, they holding cruets
Should rain down vinegar in the foemen's eyes,
I know, and I can tell you.

DIONYSUS: Tell away.

EURIPIDES: When things, mistrusted now, shall trusted be,
And trusted things, mistrusted.

DIONYSUS: How! I don't
Quite comprehend. Be clear, and not so clever.

EURIPIDES: If we mistrust those citizens of ours
Whom now we trust, and those employ whom now
We don't employ, the city will be saved.
If on our present tack we fail, we surely
Shall find salvation in the opposite course.

DIONYSUS: Good, O Palamedes![98] Good, you genius you.
Is this *your* cleverness or Cephisophon's?

EURIPIDES: This is my own: the cruet-plan was his.

DIONYSUS: [*To Aeschylus*] Now, you.

AESCHYLUS: But tell me whom the city uses.
The good and useful?

DIONYSUS: What are you dreaming of?
She hates and loathes them.

AESCHYLUS: Does she love the bad?

DIONYSUS: Not love them, no: she uses them perforce.

AESCHYLUS: How can one save a city such as this,
Whom neither frieze nor woollen tunic suits?[99]

[97] An awkward, clumsy citizen who needs the graceful lightness of a Cinesias, a character in Aristophanes' popular comedy *The Birds*.

[98] Odysseus' rival in craftiness and an inventor. Euripides composed a tragedy, *Palamedes,* and presented him as a good man victimized by Odysseus, the wily politician.

[99] A proverbial saying about people who are satisfied neither with one alternative nor yet with the other.—
B. B. ROGERS

DIONYSUS: O, if to earth you rise, find out some way.

AESCHYLUS: There will I speak: I cannot answer here.

DIONYSUS: Nay, nay; send up your guerdon from below.

AESCHYLUS: When they shall count the enemy's soil their own,
And theirs the enemy's: when they know that ships
Are their true wealth, their so-called wealth delusion.

DIONYSUS: Aye, but the justices suck that down, you know.

PLUTO: Now then, decide.

DIONYSUS: I will; and thus I'll do it.
I'll choose the man in whom my soul delights.

EURIPIDES: O, recollect the gods by whom you swore
You'd take me home again; and choose your friends.

DIONYSUS: 'Twas my tongue swore; my choice is —Aeschylus.[100]

EURIPIDES: Hah! what have you done?

DIONYSUS: Done? Given the victor's prize
To Aeschylus; why not?

EURIPIDES: And do you dare
Look in my face, after that shameful deed?

DIONYSUS: What's shameful, if the audience think not so?[101]

EURIPIDES: Have you no heart? Wretch, would you leave me dead?

DIONYSUS: Who knows if death be life, and life be death,[102]
And breath be mutton broth, and sleep a sheepskin?

PLUTO: Now, Dionysus, come ye in.

DIONYSUS: What for?

PLUTO: And sup before ye go.

DIONYSUS: A bright idea.
In faith, I'm nowise indisposed for that.

[*The actors leave the scene*]

CHORUS: Blest the man who possesses a
              Keen intelligent mind.
         This full often we find.
         He, the bard of renown,
         Now to earth reascends,
         Goes, a joy to his town,
         Goes, a joy to his friends,
         Just because he possesses a
         Keen intelligent mind.
         Right it is and befitting,
         Not, by Socrates sitting,
         Idle talk to pursue,
         Stripping tragedy-art of
         All things noble and true.
         Surely the mind to school

[100] A dig at Euripides for an equivocal line, unfairly interpreted as a justification of violating one's promise—i.e., the tongue swore but the swearer is not bound by its promise.

[101] Another dig at Euripides' rationalism. A parody on one of his lines.

[102] A dig at Euripides' skepticism. Also a parody.

Fine-drawn quibbles to seek,
Fine-set phrases to speak,
Is but the part of a fool!
[Pluto *appears and he is seen bidding* Aes-
chylus *good-bye*]
PLUTO: Farewell then, Aeschylus, great and wise,
Go, save our state by the maxims rare
Of thy noble thought; and the fools chastise,
For many a fool dwells there.
[Pluto *hands him a rope*]
And *this* to Cleophon give, my friend,
And *this* to the revenue-raising crew,
Nicomachus, Myrmex,[103] next I send,
And *this* to Archenomus too.[104]
And bid them all that without delay,
To my realm of the dead they hasten away.
For if they loiter above, I swear
I'll come myself and arrest them there.
And branded and fettered the slaves shall go
With the vilest rascal in all the town,
Adeimantus, son of Leucolophus, down,
Down, down to the darkness below.
AESCHYLUS: I take the mission. This chair of mine

[103] An Athenian commander who, some months after
the production of *The Frogs*, betrayed the Athenian
fleet. Aristophanes' low opinion of him was then amply
justified.
[104] Evidently they embezzled the revenues they collected from the Athenian people—unless they were
simply unpopular, as all revenue officers are.

Meanwhile to Sophocles here commit,
(For I count him next in our craft divine,)
Till I come once more by thy side to sit.
But as for that rascally scoundrel there,
That low buffoon, that worker of ill,
O let him not sit in my vacant chair,
Not even against his will.
PLUTO: [*To the* Chorus] Escort him up with your
mystic throngs,
While the holy torches quiver and blaze.
Escort him up with his own sweet songs,
And his noble festival lays.
CHORUS: First, as the poet triumphant
is passing away to the light,
Grant him success on his journey,
ye powers that are ruling below.
Grant that he find for the city
good counsels to guide her aright;
So we at last shall be freed
from the anguish, the fear, and the woe,
Freed from the onsets of war.
Let Cleophon[105] now and his band
Battle, if battle they must,
far away in their own fatherland.

[105] Since the politician Cleophon twice dissuaded
Athens from arranging an honorable peace with Sparta
during the Peloponnesian War, he was thoroughly dis-
liked by Aristophanes, the author of three antiwar
comedies and numerous jibes at warmongering demagogues.

Plautus

(254?–184 B.C.)

The first important writer of Roman comedy, Titus Maccius Plautus, was a man of wide and not always fortunate experience. Leaving his poor parents in the Umbrian city of Sarsina, he apparently fought in his youth in the Roman legions. In time he became an actor in the native farces that edified Italian cities, playing a standard clown's part, "Maccus," for which he was evidently well suited if we are to believe that he was a paunchy, red-haired fellow with exceptionally large feet. He rose in the social scale for a time, becoming a merchant, but fell back even further than he had risen when his goods were lost at sea and he was reduced to wheeling a hand mill through the countryside and grinding corn for a living. (He is also said to have served as a baker's assistant.) For a long time this obscure man was known only by his nickname, Plautus, or "Splayfoot." It is certain that by the time he made his decision to become a playwright, about 204 B.C., he understood common Roman life as well as anyone could and was familiar with all the feints and resources of popular showmanship.

To this hard-won knowledge Plautus owed a considerable part of his success and fame. He wrote some hundred and thirty plays, of which twenty-one survive. Having become a man of letters, he also acquired Roman citizenship and the right to assume the customary three names borne by a gentleman. With a becoming sense of humor and perhaps some rueful recollections of his career, he named himself "Titus Clown Splayfoot," Titus Maccius Plautus.

Before he could win acceptance as a playwright, however, Plautus had to make one decisive adjustment to a new age in Roman civilization. He had to take into account a growing enthusiasm for the civilization of Greece. Greek culture was at a premium when, as a result of the conquest of the rival Carthaginian empire in the course of the first two Punic Wars (264–241 and 218–201 B.C.), Rome became empress of the Mediterranean world. Along with other Roman writers, Plautus could win a literary reputation only by following in the footsteps of the fourth-century Greeks, led by Menander, who had evolved a polished comedy of manners and domestic complications known as the New Comedy. The native forms of entertainment, in which Plautus had performed, had been crude, unliterary farces of rustic origin; pantomimic, burlesque, and probably lewd. The most developed of these, the so-called Atellan farces, employed stock character types—dolts, buffoons, senile old men, and avaricious fools, each bearing a standardized name such as Bucco, Dossennus, Pappus, and Maccus.

The New Comedy imposed a higher level of taste upon the formative Roman theatre. It set up a standard of literary excellence; Menander's style was frequently cited by authorities as a model for writers. Moreover, the New Comedy provided Roman authors of comedy with a good lesson in plot making or play construction. Indeed, Roman comedies, known as *palliata,* because the actors wore the standard Greek costume of a cloak, or *pallium* (as contrasted with the Roman toga), were fundamentally adaptations of Greek plays.

Plautus succeeded in mediating between the Hellenistic enthusiasm of Roman gentry and a craving for varied and rough entertainment by the populace. He domesticated the New Comedy by marrying it to native burlesque and popular realism. He provided recognizable Roman character types under the Greek cloak. He even introduced topical allusions in his plays, mentioning the various wars in which Rome engaged at the time and other current events, such as the imprisonment of the poet Naevius for satirizing the aristocracy and the repeal of a piece of "bluenose" legislation. The dialogue of Plautus was certainly no mere translation from the Greek and consisted of the rough-and-tumble colloquies of the Roman streets, markets, and military camps. In later times this was to be considered a blemish in his work, and Horace, writing in the refined age of Augustus Caesar, could reprove the generations that had favored the hearty jests and brisk verses of Plautus. There is no doubt that the actor-playwright made a specialty of broad humor and boisterous poetry. The Latin scholar F. A. Wright notes that this vigorous poetry tended to become "alliterative, assonant, accentual," very much like English, by contrast with the unaccented, quantitative, and decorous versification of the age of Vergil and Horace.

Plautus was, altogether, a masculine writer who supplied lusty entertainment for a people living in times of war and, in addition, turned out catchy tunes that the multitude could sing with relish. The audience must have also enjoyed the many epithets that he employed as names for his characters, such as Euclio Senex, Staphyla Anus, Eunomia Mulier, and Strobilus Servus, for which discreet English equivalents would be Old Skinflint, Mother Bunch, Mother Goodbody, and Whirl the Slave.

Among his milder plays is *The Captives,* in which a father recovers two lost sons. The recovery of a child lost by war, abduction, or shipwreck was a favorite subject of "New" and Roman comedy. This comedy is enlivened by the presence of a parasitical rogue, Ergasilus, who is never put out of countenance in his efforts to fasten himself on a patron. Other well-known and comparatively gentle comedies are *The Crock of Gold* (the source for Molière's *L'Avare,* or *The Miser*) and *Amphitruo,* which tells the amorous story of Jupiter's seduction of a virtuous woman with an impersonation of her husband. When Jean Giraudoux wrote his *Amphitryon 38* in 1935, it was by his count the thirty-eighth time that the famous tale had been reworked in literature.

Plautus wrote many more strenuous farce comedies and farces. Among the better known is *Miles Gloriosus,* or *The Braggart Soldier,* which provided the prototype of a vainglorious or cowardly military man for many later authors, including the creator of Falstaff. Also famous are the vivid comedies *Rudens,* or *The Slipknot,* and *Pseudolus,* or *The Trickster.* In these and other plays, Plautus pulled out many stops familiar to showmen from the times of Menander to those of George S. Kaufman. His audience probably palpitated to the sentimental situations of parents' finding their long lost children, of mothers' adhering to virtue while fathers wanted to sow stale oats, of slaves' serving their masters loyally, and of young men's overcoming obstacles to love.

Perhaps Plautus' best-known and most frequently imitated farce is *The Menaechmi,* in which the complications caused by identical twins are resourcefully protracted until all the fun has been extracted from the situation. More than in a number of other Plautian plays, plot is the sole preoccupation of the author. As usual, Plautus signals his story in advance, in order that the audience may never be in the dark as to the misunderstandings and so may enjoy "comic irony," or the pleasure of superiority over the characters. As usual, too, the characters identify themselves with the audience and impart their intentions and mistaken deductions by means of asides. In a play the very theme of which is confusion, these devices are indeed helpful. The audience settles down to the enjoyment of surface fun without serious expectations and with a feeling of being completely the master of the situation. It is never troubled by improbabilities because it knows the rules of the game and because the action rattles ahead incessantly in a crescendo. Here, moreover, there is such narrow "unity of time"—that is, the misunderstandings are of so short a duration—that the spectator is not affronted by coincidences, by the flagrant obtuseness of the characters, and by the fact that the two Menaechmi are identical not only in appearance but in other characteristics. *The Menaechmi* is playwriting on the most elementary level. If it has held the stage so long in its original form and in many transformations, this is because showmanship is the lowest common denominator of all drama.

Shakespeare's *Comedy of Errors* is the best-known adaptation of *The Menaechmi.* Shakespeare doubled the plot, using two sets of twins, and romanticized the material. But the theatre has played host to numerous other versions, including a musical one by Rodgers and Hart, *The Boys from Syracuse,* derived from Shakespeare's play.

THE MENAECHMI

By Plautus

DRAMATIS PERSONAE

MENAECHMUS OF EPIDAMNUM
OLD MAN, *father-in-law of Menaechmus*
PENICULUS, *a parasite, a hanger-on to Menaechmus*
SERVANT *of Menaechmus*
PHYSICIAN
CYLINDRUS, *a cook*
MENAECHMUS SOSICLES

MESSENIO, *servant of Menaechmus Sosicles*
WIFE *of Menaechmus of Epidamnum*
MAID-SERVANT *of Menaechmus of Epidamnum*
EROTIUM, *a courtezan, mistress of Menaechmus of Epidamnum*
SERVANTS *of Menaechmus of Epidamnum*

THE SCENE: *Epidamnum, a city of Macedonia*

PROLOGUE

Spectators;—first and foremost;—may all health
And happiness attend both you and me!
I bring you Plautus, with my tongue, not hand;
Give him, I pray, a fair and gentle hearing.
Now learn the argument, and lend attention:
I'll be as brief as may be.—'Tis the way
With poets in their comedies to feign
The business pass'd at Athens, so that you
May think it the more Graecian.—For our play,
I'll not pretend the incidents to happen
Where they do not: the argument is Graecian,
And yet it is not Attic, but Sicilian.—
So much by way of preface to our tale,
Which now I'll deal out to you in full measure,
Not as it were by bushels or by pecks,
But pour before you the whole granary;
So much am I inclined to tell the plot.
There was a certain merchant, an old man,
Of Syracuse. He had two sons were twins,
So like in form and feature, that the nurse
Could not distinguish them, who gave them suck,
Nor ev'n the mother that had brought them forth,
As one inform'd me, who had seen the children;
Myself ne'er saw them, don't imagine it.
When that the boys were sev'n years old, the father
Freighted a vessel with much store of merchandize.
Put one of them on board, and took the child
Along with him to traffic at Tarentum,
The other with his mother left at home.
When they arrived there at this same Tarentum,
It happen'd there were sports; and multitudes,
As they are wont at shows, were got together.
The child stray'd from his father in the crowd.
There chanc'd to be a certain merchant there,
An Epidamnian, who pick'd up the boy,
And bore him home with him to Epidamnum.
The father, on the sad loss of his boy,
'Took it to heart most heavily, and died
For grief of't, some days after, at Tarentum.

When news of this affair was brought to Syracuse
Unto the grandfather, how that the child
Was stolen, and the father dead with grief,
The good old man changes the other's name,
So much he lov'd the one that had been stolen:
Him that was left at home, he calls Menaechmus,
Which was the other's name; and by the same
The grandsire too was call'd; I do remember it
More readily, for that I saw him cry'd.
I now forewarn you, lest you err hereafter,
Both the twin brothers bear the self-same name.
Now must I foot it back to Epidamnum,
That I may clear this matter up exactly.
If any of you here have any business
At Epidamnum you want done, speak out,
You may command me;—but on this condition,
Give me the money to defray the charges.
He that don't give it, will be much mistaken;
Much more mistaken will he be that does.
   But now am I return'd whence I set forth,
Though yet I stand here in the self-same place.
This Epidamnian, whom I spoke of, he
Who stole that other boy, no children had
Except his riches, therefore he adopts
This stranger-boy, gave him a wife well-portioned,
And makes him his sole heir, before he died.
As he was haply going to the country,
After an heavy rain, trying to ford
A rapid river near unto the city,
Th' rapid river rap'd him off his legs,
And snatch'd him to destruction: a large fortune
Fell to the youth, who now lives here: the other,
Who dwells at Syracuse, is come to-day
To Epidamnum with a slave of his,
In quest of his twin brother. Now this city
   [*Pointing to the scenes*]
Is Epidamnum, while this play is acting;
And when another shall be represented,
'Twill be another place; like as our company
Are also wont to shift their characters.
While the same player at one time is a pimp,
And then a young gallant, an old curmudgeon,
A poor man, rich man, parasite, or priest.

ACT I. SCENE I.

[*Enter* Peniculus, *the parasite*]

PENICULUS: Our young men call me *Dishcloth,* for
    this reason,
Whene'er I eat, I wipe the tables clean.
Now in my judgment they act foolishly,
Who bind in chains their captives, and clap fetters
Upon their run-away slaves: for if you heap
Evil on evil to torment the wretch,
The stronger his desire is to escape.—
They'll free them from their chains by any means:
Load them with gifts, they file away the door,
Or knock the bolt out with a stone.—'Tis vain this:
But would you keep a man from 'scaping from you,
Be sure you chain him fast with meat and drink
And tie him by the beak to a full table.
Give him his fill, allow him meat and drink
At pleasure, in abundance, every day;
And I'll be sworn, although his crime be capital,
He will not run away: you'll easily
Secure him, while you bind him with these bonds.
They're wondrous supple these same belly-bonds,
The more you stretch them, they will bind the harder.
For instance, I'm now going to Menaechmus,
Most willingly I'm going to be bound,
According to his sentence past upon me.
Good soul! he's not content with giving us
A bare support and meagre sustenance,
But crams us even to satiety;
Gives us, as 'twere, new life, when dead with hunger.
O he's a rare physician: he's a youth
Of lordly appetite; he treats most daintily,
His table's bravely served; such heaps of dishes,
You must stand on your couch to reach the top.
Yet I've some days been absent from his house;
Homely I've liv'd at home with my *dear* friends,
For all I eat or buy is *dear* to me,
Yet they desert the very friends that rais'd them.
Now will I visit him; but the door opens:
And see! Menaechmus' self is coming forth.

SCENE II.

[*Enter* Menaechmus of Epidamnum, *with a robe,
    speaking to his* Wife *within*]

MENAECHMUS EPIDAMNUM: Were you not good for
    nothing, were you not
An ass, a stubborn idiot, what you see
Displeas'd your husband, would displease you too.
From this day forward, if you use me thus,
I'll turn you out of doors, and send you back
A widow to your father: for whenever
I would go forth, you hold me, call me back,
Ask where I'm going, what 'tis I'm about,
And what's my business, what I want abroad.
I've married sure some officer o' the customs,
I'm so examin'd—what I've done—what do—
Too kindly you've been treated hitherto;
I'll tell you how you shall be—Since I allow you
Maids, jewels, cloths, wool—Since you want for
    nothing,
If you were wife, you'd dread the·consequence,
And cease to watch your husband. So, that you
May watch me to some purpose, for your pains,
I'll dine abroad now with some trull or other.
    PENICULUS: [*Aside*] He means to gall his wife by
        what he says:
But me he spites; for if he dine abroad,
On me he recks his vengeance, not on her.
    MENAECHMUS EPIDAMNUM: Victoria! by my taunt-
        ings, I at length
Have driven her from the door.—Where, where are
    all
The intriguing husbands? why do they delay
To bring me gifts, and thank me for my prowess:—
I've stol'n this robe here of my wife's, and mean
To carry it to my mistress.—So we ought
To trick these crafty husband-watching dames:—
'Tis a fair action, this of mine, 'tis right,
'Tis pleasant faith, and admirably carried.
With plague enough, I've ta'en it from one plague
To give it to another.—Thus I've gain'd
A booty from the foe, without our loss.
    PENICULUS: [*Aloud*] What portion of the booty's
        mine, young Sir?
    MENAECHMUS EPIDAMNUM: Undone! I'm fall'n
        into an ambuscade.
    PENICULUS: You've lighted on a safeguard: never
        fear.
    MENAECHMUS EPIDAMNUM: Who's that?
    PENICULUS: 'Tis I.
    MENAECHMUS EPIDAMNUM: O my most welcome
        friend,
Save you.
    PENICULUS: And you.
    MENAECHMUS EPIDAMNUM: How fares it?
    PENICULUS: Let me take
My genius by the hand.
    MENAECHMUS EPIDAMNUM: You could not come
More opportune than now.
    PENICULUS: It is my way:
I know to hit each point and nick of time.
    MENAECHMUS EPIDAMNUM: Shall I acquaint you
        with a saucy prank?
    PENICULUS: Saucy? what cook has drest it? I shall
        know
If he has marr'd it when I see the relics.
    MENAECHMUS EPIDAMNUM: Now prithee tell me,
        have you never seen
The picture of an eagle bearing off
Jove's Ganymede, or *Venus* with *Adonis?*
    PENICULUS: Ay, many a time. But what are they
        to me?
    MENAECHMUS EPIDAMNUM: Look at me.—Do I
        bear resemblance to them?
    PENICULUS: What means that robe?

MENAECHMUS EPIDAMNUM: Say I'm a pleasant fellow.

PENICULUS: Where shall we dine?

MENAECHMUS EPIDAMNUM: Poh, say what I command you.

PENICULUS: Well then,—thou art a pleasant fellow.

MENAECHMUS EPIDAMNUM: What,
Canst add nought of thy own?

PENICULUS: Yes, joyous fellow.

MENAECHMUS EPIDAMNUM: Proceed.

PENICULUS: Not I, i'faith, unless I know
Why there's a falling out 'twixt you and Madam.
I take great care to have this from yourself.

MENAECHMUS EPIDAMNUM: Tell me without the knowledge of my wife,
Where shall we kill, where bury, time?

PENICULUS: Come, come;
You say right; I will dig its grave: the day's
Already half-expired.

MENAECHMUS EPIDAMNUM: 'Tis mere delay,
Your chattering thus.

PENICULUS: Knock out my only eye,
Menaechmus, if I speak one other word,
But what you bid.

MENAECHMUS EPIDAMNUM: Draw hither from the door.

PENICULUS: I will.

MENAECHMUS EPIDAMNUM: Draw hither.

PENICULUS: Well.

MENAECHMUS EPIDAMNUM: Come quickly hither,
Come from the lioness's den.

PENICULUS: 'Fore heav'n,
You'd make a dext'rous charioteer.

MENAECHMUS EPIDAMNUM: Why so?

PENICULUS: You look behind you, lest your wife should follow.

MENAECHMUS EPIDAMNUM: What say you now?

PENICULUS: What say I?—what you will
I say and unsay.

MENAECHMUS EPIDAMNUM: Were your nose to any thing,
Could you not make a shrewd guess by the smell?

PENICULUS: Aye, surely: the whole college, Sir, of Augurs
Have not so quick a scent at divination.

MENAECHMUS EPIDAMNUM: Come then, and smell this robe which I have here.
What does it smell of? [Holding it up] won't you take it? Hey-day!

PENICULUS: A woman's garment should be smelt at top;
The scent is else too strong for any nose.

MENAECHMUS EPIDAMNUM: Come, smell it here then, good Peniculus:—
How you make faces at it!

PENICULUS: I can't help it.

MENAECHMUS EPIDAMNUM: What does it smell of? answer.

PENICULUS: It smells strong
Of theft, of whore, and dinner.

MENAECHMUS EPIDAMNUM: I'm now going
To carry it to my mistress, my Erotium:
I'll bid her to provide a dinner for us,—
For me, for you, and for herself: we'll there
Carouse it till the morrow's morning star.

PENICULUS: O bravely spoken!—shall I knock?

MENAECHMUS EPIDAMNUM: You may.—
Yet hold a while.

PENICULUS: The cup was just at hand;
'Tis now a thousand paces off.

MENAECHMUS EPIDAMNUM: Knock softly.

PENICULUS: Are you afraid the door is made of crockery?

MENAECHMUS EPIDAMNUM: Hold, prithee hold:—
herself is coming forth.

PENICULUS: Oh, Sir, you look upon the sun: your eyes
Are blinded with her brightness.—

SCENE III.

[Enter Erotium]

EROTIUM: My *Menaechmus!*
My love! good morrow!

PENICULUS: Won't you welcome me too?

EROTIUM: You rank not in the number of my friends.

PENICULUS: Yet treat me as a supernumerary.

MENAECHMUS EPIDAMNUM: We mean to pitch a field with you today.

EROTIUM: Aye, that we will.

MENAECHMUS EPIDAMNUM: And prove, with pitcher fill'd,
Which is the mightier warrior at the bowl:
Yourself shall be commander; you shall choose,
Which you will pass the night with.—O my sweet,
When I look on you, how I loathe my wife!

EROTIUM: And yet you cannot choose, but you must wrap you
In some part of her gear.—Pray what is this?

MENAECHMUS EPIDAMNUM: A cast skin of my wife's to be slipt on
By thee, my rose-bud.

EROTIUM: You've the readiest way
To win preëminence in my affection,
From all that pay me suit.

PENICULUS: Right harlot this!
An harlot's sure to coax, whene'er she finds
There's any thing to get.—If you had loved him,
You would have bit his nose off by this time
With flobbering.—

MENAECHMUS EPIDAMNUM: Take my cloak, Peniculus;
For I must dedicate the spoils I've vow'd.

PENICULUS: Let's see't.

MENAECHMUS EPIDAMNUM: [Putting on the robe]
But prithee now, you'll afterwards
Dance in your robe.

PENICULUS: I dance in't?—

MENAECHMUS EPIDAMNUM: You are mad.

PENICULUS: Are you or I most mad?

MENAECHMUS EPIDAMNUM: Well, if you won't,
Then pull it off. I ran a mighty risk
In stealing of this robe: in my mind truly
Your Hercules ran not an equal hazard, when
He spoil'd the bold Hippolita of her girdle.
    [*Giving the robe to* Erotium]
Take it, since you alone of women living
Suit your affection gently unto mine.
True lovers should be thus disposed.

PENICULUS: Provided
They would run headlong into beggary.

MENAECHMUS EPIDAMNUM: 'Tis not a year past,
    since it stood me in
Four *minae* for my wife.

PENICULUS: Four *minae* then,
By your account, are plainly gone for ever.

MENAECHMUS EPIDAMNUM: Know you what I
    would have you do?

EROTIUM: I know;
And will take care according to your wish.

MENAECHMUS EPIDAMNUM: Let dinner be provided
    for us three;
Send to the market for some dainty morsel,
A gammon, some sow's kernels, a hog's cheek,
Or sausages, or something of that kind,
Which, when they're brought to table, may suggest
A kite-like appetite:—about it straight.

EROTIUM: I' faith I will.

MENAECHMUS EPIDAMNUM: We're going to the
    Forum,
We shall be here directly: while 'tis dressing,
We will amuse us with a whet i' th' interim.

EROTIUM: Come when you will, dear, all things
    shall be ready.

MENAECHMUS EPIDAMNUM: Quick, follow me.

PENICULUS: Yes, yes, I'll have an eye to you,
Close at your heels, I warrant; I'll not lose you,
Not for the wealth of all the gods.
    [*Exeunt* Menaechmus *and* Peniculus]

EROTIUM: Call forth
The cook Cylindrus, bid him come this instant.

SCENE IV.

[*Enter* Cylindrus]

EROTIUM: Take the hand-basket; and, d'ye mind?
    here are
Three pieces for you,—you have hold of them.

CYLINDRUS: I have.

EROTIUM: Go to the market and provide
Enough for three; now let there be sufficient,
And nought to spare.

CYLINDRUS: What kind of guests, pray, are they?

EROTIUM: I, and Menaechmus, and his parasite.

CYLINDRUS: Nay, there are ten then;—for the
    parasite
Will lay about him equal to eight men.

EROTIUM: I've told you what's the number of our
    guests:
You will provide accordingly.

CYLINDRUS: I warrant.
'Tis drest already: you've but to sit down.

EROTIUM: You'll come back quickly.

CYLINDRUS: I'll be here this instant.

ACT II. SCENE I.

[*Enter* Menaechmus Sosicles, *and* Messenio, *his
servant*]

MENAECHMUS SOSICLES: No greater joy have voy-
    agers, Messenio,
Than, from the deep far off, to spy out land.

MESSENIO: To speak the truth, 'tis still a greater
    joy
To find that land, when you arrive, your country.
But wherefore come we now to Epidamnum?
Must we go round each island like the sea?

MENAECHMUS SOSICLES: I am in quest of my twin
    brother.

MESSENIO: Good now,
When will there be an end of searching for him?
This is the sixth year since we set about it;
The Istrians, the Illyrians, the Massilians,
The Spaniards, the whole Adriatic gulf,
With farthest Greece, and each Italian coast,
That the sea washes, have we travers'd round.
Had we been looking for a needle, sure
We should have found it long ago, if visible.
So search we for a dead man 'mong the quick;
For we had found him long ago, if living.

MENAECHMUS SOSICLES: Would I could find out
    one, that might assure me
Of his own knowledge, that my brother's dead!
Then I'd forego my quest, not otherwise:
But, while I live, I'll never spare my pains,
Nor ever will desist from searching for him.
How dear he's to my heart, too well I feel—

MESSENIO: You in a bull-rush seek a knot—'tis
    vain:
Come, let's return; unless you mean to write
A book of voyages.

MENAECHMUS SOSICLES: No fine, subtle speeches,
Or you shall pay for't. Don't be impertinent.
None of your *freedoms*.

MESSENIO: By that single word
I know, I am a slave: 'tis briefly said,
Plainly, and fully:—yet I can't refrain
From speaking.—Mind me, Sir!—Our purse, look
    here,—
'Tis light enough, 'twon't make us sweat: now
    verily,—
If you return not home; when nothing's left,
You'll chase for this wild chase of your twin brother.
As for the people here, these Epidamnians,
They're errant debauchees, most potent drinkers;
Cheats, parasites abound here; and they say

Such wheedling harlotries are no where met with;
And therefore is this place call'd Epidamnum,
Because there's no one comes here, but says damn
    'em.
    MENAECHMUS SOSICLES: I'll look to that: give me
      the purse.
    MESSENIO: The purse?
What would you do with it?
    MENAECHMUS SOSICLES: I've apprehensions
'Bout you, from what you said.
    MESSENIO: What apprehensions?
    MENAECHMUS SOSICLES: Lest you should cry in
      Epidamnum, damn 'em.
You are a mighty lover of the wenches:
I'm cholerick, quite a madman when provok'd:
Now when I have the cash in my own hands,
'Twill guard against two harms; you'll not offend:
Nor I be angry with you.
    MESSENIO: Take and keep it.—
With all my soul.—

SCENE II.

[Cylindrus *entering*]
CYLINDRUS: I've marketed most rarely,
And to my mind: I warrant, I serve up
A dainty dinner to the guests.—But hold—
I see Menaechmus. Woe then to my back!
The guests are walking here before the door,
Ere I return from the market.—I'll accost them.
Save you, Menaechmus!
    MENAECHMUS SOSICLES: Save you! Do you know
      me?
    CYLINDRUS: No, to be sure! [*Ironically*] Where
      are the other guests?
    MENAECHMUS SOSICLES: What guests do you mean?
    CYLINDRUS: Your parasite.
    MENAECHMUS SOSICLES: My parasite?
Surely the man is mad.
    MESSENIO: Now say, my master,
Did I not tell you there were many cheats here?
    MENAECHMUS SOSICLES: Whom mean you by my
      parasite?
    CYLINDRUS: Why, *Dishcloth*.
    MESSENIO: See, see,—I have him safe here in the
      wallet.
    CYLINDRUS: Menaechmus, you are come too soon
      to dinner:
I am but now return'd from marketing.
    MENAECHMUS SOSICLES: What is the price, pray,
      of a hog for sacrifice?
    CYLINDRUS: A piece.
    MENAECHMUS SOSICLES: I'll give it: make a sacri-
      fice
At my expense; for sure you must be mad
To cross a stranger thus, whoe'er you are.
    CYLINDRUS: I am Cylindrus: know you not my
      name?

    MENAECHMUS SOSICLES: Or Cylinder, or Cullender;
    —begone:
I know you not, nor do I want to know you.
    CYLINDRUS: Your name's Menaechmus, that I
      know.
    MENAECHMUS SOSICLES: You talk
As one that's in his senses, calling me
Thus by my name. But where, pray, have you known
    me?
    CYLINDRUS: Where have I known you?—you, who
      have a wench here,
Erotium, my mistress.
    MENAECHMUS SOSICLES: I have not,
Nor know I who you are.
    CYLINDRUS: Not who I am?
I, who so oft have handed you the cup,
When you carous'd here.
    MESSENIO: O that I have nothing
To break his head with!
    MENAECHMUS SOSICLES: How? you've handed me
The cup? when till this day I never came
To Epidamnum, never set my eyes on't.
    CYLINDRUS: Will you deny it?
    MENAECHMUS SOSICLES: Yes, I must deny it.
    CYLINDRUS: Don't you live yonder?
    MENAECHMUS SOSICLES: Plague upon their heads
That live there!
    CYLINDRUS: Sure he's mad, to curse himself.
Hark'ye, Menaechmus?
    MENAECHMUS SOSICLES: What say you?
    CYLINDRUS: If you would
Take my advice, that piece you promised me,
Buy a hog with it for yourself to sacrifice:
For sure you are not in your perfect mind,
To curse yourself.
    MENAECHMUS SOSICLES: Thou'rt mad.—vexatious
      fellow!
    CYLINDRUS: In this wise will he often jest with me;
He's such a wag, he,—when his wife's not by.
    MENAECHMUS SOSICLES: Prithee now.
    CYLINDRUS: Prithee now, is this provision
Sufficient, what you see here, for you three?
Or would you have me to provide yet more,
For you, your parasite and wench?
    MENAECHMUS SOSICLES: What wench,
What parasite d'ye speak of?
    MESSENIO: Rascal! what
Provokes thee to molest him thus?
    CYLINDRUS: What business
Hast thou with me? I know thee not: I'm talking
To him I know.
    MESSENIO: You are not in your senses.
    CYLINDRUS: I'll get these ready out of hand:
      [*Pointing to the provisions*] then go not
Far from the door. Would you ought further with
    me?
    MENAECHMUS SOSICLES: Go hang yourself.
    CYLINDRUS: Go you and seat yourself,
While to the violence of Vulcan's rage
I these oppose—I'll in, and let Erotium

Know you are here, that she may fetch you in,
Rather than you should saunter here without doors.
    [*Goes in*]

SCENE III.

Menaechmus Sosicles *and* Messenio.

MENAECHMUS SOSICLES: So,—is he gone?—I find
    there is some truth
In what you told me.
    MESSENIO: Do but mind.—I fancy,
Some harlot dwells here; so this crackbrain said
Who went hence even now.
    MENAECHMUS SOSICLES: But I do marvel,
How he should know my name.
    MESSENIO: I' faith no wonder:
This is the way of courtezans: they send
Their lacqueys and their wenches to the port:
If any foreign ship arrive, to ask
Whose is it, what's its name? Then instantly
They set themselves to work, they stick like glue.
If they can lure some gull to their embraces,
They turn him out anon, undone and ruin'd.
A pirate vessel lurks within this port,
Which we in my opinion should beware of.
    MENAECHMUS SOSICLES: You counsel right.
    MESSENIO: It will be known at last
How right it is, if you as rightly follow it.
    MENAECHMUS SOSICLES: Softly a while: the door
    creaks: let us see
Who's coming forth.
    MESSENIO: Meanwhile I'll lay this down;
    [*Lays down his wallet on some oars*]
Pray keep it safe, ye water-treading oars.

SCENE IV.

    [*Enter* Erotium, *speaking to her servants within*]
    EROTIUM: Leave the door thus: I would not have
    it shut:
Begone: make ready: see that ev'ry thing
Be done that's wanting: lay the couches smooth,
Let the perfumes be set on fire. 'Tis neatness
Lures the fond lover's heart. A spruce appearance
Is damage to the lover, gain to us.
But where, where is he, whom the cook inform'd me
Was at the door? I see him, he's a gentleman,
From whom I draw much service and much profit;
And therefore I'm content, that he should hold,
As he deserves, with me, the highest place.
I'll go and speak to him. My life! my soul!
I marvel you should stand here at the door,
That's open to you more than is your own;
Your own it is.—Sweet, ev'ry thing is ready
Which you desir'd: nothing to stay you, love:
The dinner, which you order'd, we have got:
Then, whensoe'er you please, you may sit down.

MENAECHMUS SOSICLES: Whom does the woman
    speak to?
    EROTIUM: Why, to you.
    MENAECHMUS SOSICLES: What business have I ever
    had with you?
What business have I now?
    EROTIUM: 'Tis Venus' will,
I should prefer you before all my lovers;
Nor on your part unmerited, for you,
You only with your gifts enrich me.
    MENAECHMUS SOSICLES: Sure
This woman's either mad or drunk, Messenio,
Thus to accost a stranger so familiarly.
    MESSENIO: Such practices are common here, I
    told you.
These are but leaves; but if we tarry here
Three days, the trees themselves will tumble on you.
The courtezans here are all moneytraps.—
But suffer me to speak to her.—Heark ye, woman!
A word with you.
    EROTIUM: What is't?
    MESSENIO: Where did you know
This gentleman?
    EROTIUM: Where he has long known me:
In Epidamnum here.
    MESSENIO: In Epidamnum?
He never set his foot in't till to-day.
    EROTIUM: Ah! you are pleas'd to joke, my dear
    Menaechmus.
But prithee, sweet, come in; 'twere better for you.
    MENAECHMUS SOSICLES: 'Fore heav'n the woman
    calls me by my name.
I marvel what this means.
    MESSENIO: She smells the purse
Which you have there—
    MENAECHMUS SOSICLES: That's rightly put in mind.
Here take it. I shall know now if her love's
To me, or to the purse.
    EROTIUM: Let's in to dinner.
    MENAECHMUS SOSICLES: 'Tis a kind invitation, and
    I thank you.
    EROTIUM: Why did you bid me then to get a
    dinner?
    MENAECHMUS SOSICLES: I bid you get a dinner!
    EROTIUM: Yes, most certainly,
For you and for your parasite.
    MENAECHMUS SOSICLES: A plague!
What parasite?—Why sure the woman's crazy.
    EROTIUM: Peniculus.
    MENAECHMUS SOSICLES: Who's that Peniculus?
    EROTIUM: The parasite; in other words, the *Dish-
    cloth.*
    MENAECHMUS SOSICLES: O, what they wipe their
    shoes with?
    EROTIUM: He, I say,
Who came with you this morning, when you brought
    me
The robe that you had stolen from your wife.
    MENAECHMUS SOSICLES: How say you? I present
    you with a robe,

That I had stolen from my wife? art mad?
The woman sure, walks like a gelding, sleeping.
   EROTIUM: Why are you pleas'd to hold me for
     your sport?
And why do you deny what you have done?
   MENAECHMUS SOSICLES: What is it I deny? What
     have I done?
   EROTIUM: Given me a robe belonging to your wife.
   MENAECHMUS SOSICLES: I still deny it: I never had
     a wife,
Nor have I: neither have I set my foot
Within your doors, since I was born. I din'd
On ship-board, thence came hither, and here met you.
   EROTIUM: Ah! woe is me!—what ship is't you are
     talking of?
   MENAECHMUS SOSICLES: A wooden one, oft
     weather-beaten, oft
Bethump'd with mallets, like a tailor's pin-cushion
Peg close to peg.
   EROTIUM: I prithee, now have done
With jesting thus, and come along with me.
   MENAECHMUS SOSICLES: Some other man you
     mean, I know not whom,
Not me.
   EROTIUM: What! don't I know thee? not Menaech-
     mus,
The son of Moschus, who were born, thou say'st,
At Syracuse, in Sicily, where erst
Reign'd king Agathocles, and after Pinthia,
And next him Liparo, who by his death
The kingdom left to Hiero, now king.
   MENAECHMUS SOSICLES: 'Faith what you say is
     true.
   MESSENIO: O Jupiter!
Is she not come from thence, so well she knows you?
   MENAECHMUS SOSICLES: I can hold out no longer.
   MESSENIO: Stay, Sir, stay;
For if you cross her threshold, you're undone.
   MENAECHMUS SOSICLES: Be quiet: all is well: I
     will assent
To whatsoe'er she says, so I but get
Good entertainment, and a fair reception.
[*To* Erotium] For some time wittingly I have op-
     pos'd you,
Fearing this fellow here, lest he should tell
My wife concerning all—the robe and dinner:
Now when you please, we'll enter.
   EROTIUM: Then you do not
Stay for the parasite?
   MENAECHMUS SOSICLES: I neither stay,
Nor care a rush for him; nor would I have him
Be let in when he comes.
   EROTIUM: With all my heart.—
But do you know, sweet, what I'd have you do?
   MENAECHMUS SOSICLES: Command me what you
     will.
   EROTIUM: That robe you gave me
I'd have you carry it to the embroiderer's,
To be made up anew; with such additions,
As I shall order.

   MENAECHMUS SOSICLES: What you say is right:
So will it not be known; nor will my wife,
If she should see you with it in the street,
Know you have got it.
   EROTIUM: So then by and by,
Sweet, you shall take it with you, when you go.
   MENAECHMUS SOSICLES: I will.
   EROTIUM: Let's in now.
   MENAECHMUS SOSICLES: I'll attend you presently,
I would just speak a word with him.
    [Erotium *goes in*]

SCENE V.

Menaechmus Sosicles, Messenio.

   MENAECHMUS SOSICLES: Messenio!
Come hither.
   MESSENIO: What's the matter?
   MENAECHMUS SOSICLES: 'St!—shall I
Impart it to you?
   MESSENIO: What?
   MENAECHMUS SOSICLES: 'Tis such a chance.
   MESSENIO: What chance?
   MENAECHMUS SOSICLES: I know what you will
     say.
   MESSENIO: I say
So much the worse for you.
   MENAECHMUS SOSICLES: I have got it, boy:
I have already made a rare beginning.
Quick as you can, go carry these my shipmates
Directly to some place of entertainment.
Then come to me e'er sun-set.
   MESSENIO: Master! Master!
You're unacquainted with these harlotries.
   MENAECHMUS SOSICLES: Peace, prithee. If I play
     the fool, 'tis I,
Not you, shall suffer. Why, this woman here
Is a mere simpleton, an arrant ignorant,
As far I have prov'd her hitherto.—
She is our game, my boy.
   MESSENIO: 'Tis over with us.
   MENAECHMUS SOSICLES: Will you be gone?
   MESSENIO: He is undone, that's certain.
This pirate vessel has the boat in tow.
But I'm a fool, that I should seek to rule
My master: for he bought me to obey,
Not govern him. Come, follow me, that I
May wait upon him at the time he order'd.
    [*Exeunt*]

ACT III. SCENE I.

[*Enter* Peniculus, *the parasite*]
   PENICULUS: I have seen thirty years and more, yet
     never
Play'd I so foolish or so vile a trick
As I have done this day, in mixing with
The crowd in the assembly of the people.

Where while I stood staring about, Menaechmus
Gave me the slip, I fancy to his mistress;
Nor took me with him.—Gods confound the man!
First took it in his head, to institute
These meetings to engage the most engag'd.
'Twere better only to elect the idle
Who should be fined in case of non-attendance.
There are enough who eat their meals alone;
Who've nought to do, who nor invited are
Nor e'er invite.—These were the men to hold
Assemblies, and attend at the Comitia,[1]—
Had this been so, I had not lost my dinner.
Which he'd as sure have giv'n me, as I live.
I'll go however—Hope of the very scraps
Comforts my mind—but see, Menaechmus comes
From dinner, with a wreath—All's ta'en away,
And I come at a fine time indeed!

SCENE II.

[*Enter* Menaechmus Sosicles, *with a robe*]
MENAECHMUS SOSICLES: If I return it neatly fitted up,
[*Speaking to* Erotium *within*]
So that you scarce shall know it is the same,
And that this very day, shall you not then
Be satisfied?
    PENICULUS: [*Apart*] He's carrying the robe
To the embroiderer's—And dinner's done—
The wine drank off, and the poor parasite bilk'd.
By Hercules! if I put up with this,
And not revenge, I'm not the man I am.
Let's first see what he'll do, and then accost him.—
    MENAECHMUS SOSICLES: Immortal gods! is there a man on whom
You've in one day bestow'd more good, or one
Who less could hope for it? I've din'd, I've drank,
I've feasted with my mistress, have borne off
This robe, which she no more shall call her own.
    PENICULUS: [*Apart*] He speaks so softly, I can scarce distinguish
What 'tis he says: sure, now his belly's full,
He talks of me, and of my share at dinner.
    MENAECHMUS SOSICLES: She told me, I had given her the robe
And that I'd stol'n it from my wife: tho' I
Knew she was wrong, I seemingly assented
To all her story, as if both of us
Had been joint parties in the whole transaction,
Said as she said—What need of many words?
I never in my life have far'd so well,
And at so small expense.
    PENICULUS: I will accost him.
I'm out of patience till I quarrel with him.
    MENAECHMUS SOSICLES: Who is it that is coming to accost me?
    PENICULUS: Tell me, inconstant, lighter than a feather,

[1] Assembly.

Thou worst of men, most wicked of mankind,
Base man, deceiver, void of faith and honour!
Have I deserv'd this of thee? For what cause
Hast thou undone me? Say, have I deserv'd,
That thou should'st steal thyself away from me,
Now at the Forum? Thou hast buried too
The dinner in my absence, to the which
I was joint heir—How dare you serve me thus?
    MENAECHMUS SOSICLES: Prithee, young man, what hast to do with me?
Abusing thus a man thou dost not know—
You'd have me wreak this insult then hereafter?
    PENICULUS: You have done that already.
    MENAECHMUS SOSICLES: Answer me.
Tell me your name, young man.
    PENICULUS: Still mocking me?
As if you did not know my name?
    MENAECHMUS SOSICLES: In troth,
I know not till this day I ever saw thee,
Nor art thou known to me, who'er thou art,
It ill-becomes thee to be troublesome.
    PENICULUS: Not know me?
    MENAECHMUS SOSICLES: If I did, I'd not deny it.
    PENICULUS: Awake, Menaechmus.
    MENAECHMUS SOSICLES: 'Troth, I do not know,
That I'm asleep.
    PENICULUS: Not know your parasite?
    MENAECHMUS SOSICLES: Thy head is turn'd, young man, in my opinion.
    PENICULUS: Answer me, did you not this very day,
Steal from your wife that robe, and give't Erotium?
    MENAECHMUS SOSICLES: Neither have I a wife, nor robe have stol'n,
Nor given to Erotium.
    PENICULUS: Are you mad?
Have you your senses? Why the thing's apparent!
Did I not see you coming from the house,
The robe upon you?
    MENAECHMUS SOSICLES: Woe upon thy head!
'Cause you're a rogue, think you we all are such?
Say you, you saw me with this robe upon me?
    PENICULUS: I did, by Hercules!
    MENAECHMUS SOSICLES: Go, and be hang'd.
As you deserve, or else go purge your brain;
For thou'rt the veriest madman I e'er met with.
    PENICULUS: By Pollux' temple, nothing shall prevent me,
From telling to your wife, the whole that's pass'd.
And then shall all this scurril wit retort
Back on yourself. Nor shall you unreveng'd
Have swallow'd down my dinner.
    MENAECHMUS SOSICLES: What is this?
Shall ev'ry one I see, affront me thus?
But see, the door is opening.—

SCENE III.

[*Enter a* Maid-servant *of* Menaechmus of Epidamnum, *with a clasp*]

SERVANT: Erotium
Most earnestly entreats of her Menaechmus,
('Twill make it but one trouble,) to bear *this*
To the goldsmith, with her orders, that he add
An ounce more gold, and have it clean'd and mended.
 MENAECHMUS SOSICLES: This, and ought else that
   she would have me do,
Tell her I will take care to execute.
 SERVANT: But, do you know the clasp I'm speaking
   of?
 MENAECHMUS SOSICLES: I know it not; but see 'tis
   made of gold.
 SERVANT: 'Tis that, which sometimes since, you
   said you stole
And privately, from your wife's chest of drawers.
 MENAECHMUS SOSICLES: That's what I never did,
   by Hercules!
 SERVANT: What, don't you recollect it? then,
   return it.
 MENAECHMUS SOSICLES: Stay: I begin to recollect;
   it was
The same I gave your mistress.
 SERVANT: Yes, the same.
 MENAECHMUS SOSICLES: Where are the bracelets
   which I gave with it?
 SERVANT: You never gave them.
 MENAECHMUS SOSICLES: But I did, by Pollux!
And gave them both together.
 SERVANT: Shall I say,
You will take care—
 MENAECHMUS SOSICLES: Yes; and the robe and
   clasp
Shall be return'd together—
 SERVANT: Let me, Sir,
Beg you'd present me with a pair of earrings
Of gold, and of two piece value; that I may
Look well upon you, when you pay your visits.
 MENAECHMUS SOSICLES: It shall be done: give me
   the gold; I'll pay
Myself the fashion.
 SERVANT: No, I pray you, Sir,
Give it yourself, I'll be accountable.
 MENAECHMUS SOSICLES: I say, give me the gold—
 SERVANT: Another time.
I'll pay it back two-fold.
 MENAECHMUS SOSICLES: I have no money.
 SERVANT: But when you have, you'll pay the
   jeweller.
Any commands with me?
 MENAECHMUS SOSICLES: Yes, tell your mistress
I'll take great care of what she has order'd me—
   [*Exit* Servant]
Yes, soon as may be, I'll take care to sell them [*Aside*]
To the best bidder.—Is she now gone in?
She is, and shut the door. Sure all the gods
Befriend me, and heap favour upon favour.
Why do I stay when time and opportunity
Thus favours me in quitting this vile place,
This place of bawds and panders?
Haste thee, Menaechmus, then; use well thy feet,

And mend thy pace. Let me take off my wreath
And throw it to the left: that, if I'm follow'd,
They may suppose, I'm gone that way. I'll now
Find, if I can, my servant, and acquaint him
With what the gods are doing in my favour—[*Exit*]

ACT IV. SCENE I.

[*Enter the* Wife *of* Menaechmus of Epidamnum
   and Peniculus, *the parasite*]
 WIFE: And shall I tamely then submit to live
In marriage with a man, who filches from me
Whatever's in the house, and bears it off
A present to his mistress?
 PENICULUS: Hold your peace:
I will so order matters, that you shall
Surprise him in the fact. So follow me.
Crown'd with a wreath, and drunk, he bore away
The robe that he filch'd from you yesterday,
To the embroiderer's. But see, the wreath,
The very wreath he wore—Is it not true?
   [*Seeing the wreath on the ground*]
He's gone this way; and you may trace his steps.
And see, by Pollux' temple, he returns,
And opportunely; but without the robe.
 WIFE: How shall I treat him now?
 PENICULUS: How? Why as usual,
Most heartily abuse him.
 WIFE: Yes, I think so—
 PENICULUS: Let's stand aside, and watch him from
   our ambush.
   [*They retire*]

SCENE II.

[*Enter* Menaechmus of Epidamnum]
 MENAECHMUS EPIDAMNUM: How troublesome it is,
   thus to indulge
Ourselves in foolish customs! yet the great,
Those petty gods, too much come into it.
All wish to have a number of dependents,
But little care whether they're good or bad.
Their riches, not their qualities, they mind.
Honest and poor is bad.—Wicked and rich,
An honest man. Clients, that have regard
To neither law, nor common honesty,
Weary their patrons—Leave them a deposit,
They will deny the trust—Litigious,
Covetous, fraudulent, who've got their wealth
By usury or perjury—Their soul's
Still in their suits—A summons for defense
Once issu'd 'tis patron's summons too;
Who 'fore the people, praetor, commissary,
Must speak in their behalf, however wrong.
Thus was I plagu'd today by a dependent,
One of this sort, who would not let me do
Ought which I wanted in my own affairs:
Holding me close to his, he so detain'd me—

When I had battled for him 'fore the Aediles,[2]
With craft had pleaded his bad cause, had brought
To hard conditions his opponent, nay
Had more or less perplex'd the controversy,
And brought it e'en to making their deposits:
What does he do?—Why gives in bail—I never
Saw in all my life a villain more barefac'd
In all respects.—Three witnesses swore plumb,
And prov'd against him every accusation.
The gods confound him! for thus making me
Lose all my time: ay, and confound myself,
For having seen the Forum with these eyes!
The noblest day is lost: a dinner's order'd;
My mistress waits.—I know it, and as soon
As e'er I could, I've hast'ned from the Forum.
Doubtless she's angry with me; but the robe
Filch'd from my wife today, and sent to her,
Shall make all up.
    PENICULUS: What say you now?
    WIFE: Unhappy!
In having such a husband.—
    PENICULUS: Did you hear
Distinctly what he said?
    WIFE: Very distinctly.
    MENAECHMUS EPIDAMNUM: I shall do right, if I go
      in directly
And here refresh myself.
    WIFE: Wait but a little,
And I'll refresh you better. [*To him*] You shall pay;
Yes, and that you shall, by Castor! and with interest,
For that you filch'd from me, you've thus your due.
What, did you fancy you could play such tricks
In secret?
    MENAECHMUS EPIDAMNUM: What's the business,
      wife?
    WIFE: Ask that
Of me?
    MENAECHMUS EPIDAMNUM: Why, would you that
      I ask of him?
    PENICULUS: No soothing now. Go on.
    MENAECHMUS EPIDAMNUM: Say, why so pensive?
    WIFE: You can't but know the reason—
    PENICULUS: Yes, he knows.
But cunningly dissembles.
    MENAECHMUS EPIDAMNUM: What's the matter?
    WIFE: The robe.—
    MENAECHMUS EPIDAMNUM: The robe? what—
    WIFE: Ay, the robe.—
    PENICULUS: Why pale?
    MENAECHMUS EPIDAMNUM: I pale! unless the pale-
      ness of the robe
Has made me so.
    PENICULUS: I too am pale, because
You ate the supper, and ne'er thought of me.
To him again. [*To the* Wife]
    MENAECHMUS EPIDAMNUM: Won't you be silent?
    PENICULUS: No.
He nods to me to hold my tongue. [*To the* Wife]
    MENAECHMUS EPIDAMNUM: Not I,
    [2] Roman municipal officers.

By Hercules! I neither wink'd nor nodded.
    WIFE: I'm an unhappy woman!
    MENAECHMUS EPIDAMNUM: Why unhappy?
Explain—
    PENICULUS: A rare assurance, that denies
What yourself sees.—
    MENAECHMUS EPIDAMNUM: By Jove, and all the
      gods!
I nodded not.—Are you now satisfied?
    PENICULUS: And to be sure, she now will give you
      credit.
Go back again—
    MENAECHMUS EPIDAMNUM: And whither?
    PENICULUS: Whither else
But to th' embroiderer—Beyond all doubt
I think you ought—Go, and bring back the robe—
    MENAECHMUS EPIDAMNUM: What robe do you
      speak of?
    WIFE: Since he don't remember
What he has done, I have no more to say.
    MENAECHMUS EPIDAMNUM: Has any of the serv-
      ants been in fault?
Has any of the men or women slaves
Given you a saucy answer?—Say, speak out,
He shall not go unpunish'd.
    WIFE: Sure, you trifle.
    MENAECHMUS EPIDAMNUM: You're out of humour:
      that
I'm not quite pleas'd with.
    WIFE: You trifle still.
    MENAECHMUS EPIDAMNUM: Has any of the family
Done ought to make you angry?
    WIFE: Trifling still.
    MENAECHMUS EPIDAMNUM: Angry with me then—
    WIFE: Now you trifle not.
    MENAECHMUS EPIDAMNUM: 'Troth, I've done noth-
ing to deserve it of you.
    WIFE: Trifling again.
    MENAECHMUS EPIDAMNUM: What is it gives you
      pain?
Tell me, my dear.
    PENICULUS: He soothes you: civil creature!
    MENAECHMUS EPIDAMNUM: Can't you be quiet? I
      don't speak to you. [*To* Peniculus]
    WIFE: Off with your hand.
    PENICULUS: Ay, thus you're rightly serv'd—
      [*Aside*]
Dine then again in haste when I am absent
And rally me before the house when drunk!
A wreath too, on your head!
    MENAECHMUS EPIDAMNUM: By Pollux' temple!
I have not din'd to-day, nor have I once
Set foot within the house.
    PENICULUS: You dare deny it?
    MENAECHMUS EPIDAMNUM: I do, by Hercules!
    PENICULUS: Consummate impudence!
Did I not see you with a wreath of flowers,
Standing before the house here; when you said
My head was turn'd: when you denied you knew me,
And when you'd pass upon me for a stranger?

MENAECHMUS EPIDAMNUM: I do assure you, since
    I slip'd away
This morning from you, I've not been till now
At home.
    PENICULUS: I know you, Sir: But you knew not
I'd wherewithal to take revenge upon you.
I've told your wife the whole, by Hercules!
    MENAECHMUS EPIDAMNUM: What have you told?
    PENICULUS: I know not. Ask of her.
    MENAECHMUS EPIDAMNUM: What's this, my dear?
        What is it he has told you?
You answer not.—Why don't you say what 'tis?
    WIFE: As if you know not. Why, a robe has been
Stol'n from me in my house.
    MENAECHMUS EPIDAMNUM: A robe stol'n from
        you?
    WIFE: Do you ask me?
    MENAECHMUS EPIDAMNUM: In troth, I scarce
        should ask it,
Was I assur'd it was so.—
    PENICULUS: Wicked man!
How he dissembles! but you can't conceal it,
I know the whole affair; and I have told it
All to your wife.
    MENAECHMUS EPIDAMNUM: What is all this about?
    WIFE: Since you have lost all shame, and won't
        confess
The thing yourself, hearken to me, and hear it;
I'll tell you what has made me out of humour,
And everything has discover'd to me.
They have done well for *me*, they've stol'n my robe.
    MENAECHMUS EPIDAMNUM: Done well for *you* by
        stealing of your robe!
    PENICULUS: Observe his subterfuge: 'twas stol'n
        for her, [*Meaning* Erotium]
And not for *you:* Had it been stol'n for *you,*
It had been safe.
    MENAECHMUS EPIDAMNUM: I've nought to do with
        you.
But what say you? [*To his* Wife]
    WIFE: I say, I've lost from home
A robe.
    MENAECHMUS EPIDAMNUM: Who took it?
    WIFE: He who stole it, knows.
    MENAECHMUS EPIDAMNUM: And who is he?
    WIFE: One who is call'd Menaechmus.
    MENAECHMUS EPIDAMNUM: Spitefully done! And
        who is this Menaechmus?
    WIFE: Yourself, I say.
    MENAECHMUS EPIDAMNUM: What! I?
    WIFE: Yes, you.
    MENAECHMUS EPIDAMNUM: Who said so?
    WIFE: My self.
    PENICULUS: And I; and that you had carried it
Off to your mistress, to Erotium.
    MENAECHMUS EPIDAMNUM: I?
I give it her?
    PENICULUS: You, you, I say. Shall I
Go fetch an owl, to hoot in at your ears,
You, you? For we are both quite tir'd.

MENAECHMUS EPIDAMNUM: By Jove, and all the
    gods, I swear, my dear,
I never gave it her: Will that content you?
    PENICULUS: And I, I swear by Hercules! that we
Say nought but truth.
    MENAECHMUS EPIDAMNUM: I did not give it to her,
I only lent it.
    WIFE: 'Troth, I never lend
Your coat, nor cloak abroad. 'Tis right for women
To lend out women's garments; men, their own.
Won't you return my robe?
    MENAECHMUS EPIDAMNUM: The robe, I'll see
Shall be return'd—
    WIFE: 'Tis the best way.—For you
Shall never set a foot within your doors,
Unless you bring my robe.
    MENAECHMUS EPIDAMNUM: Not set a foot
Within my doors?
    PENICULUS: [*To the* Wife] What recompense for
        me,
Who have assisted you?
    WIFE: When you have had
A loss like mine, I'll do the same for you.
    PENICULUS: By Pollux' temple! that will never be;
For I have nought at home to lose. The gods
Confound you both, both of you, wife and husband!
I'll hie me to the Forum: for I find
'Tis now quite over with me in this family.
        [*Exeunt* Peniculus *and the* Wife, *severally*]
    MENAECHMUS EPIDAMNUM: My wife then thought
        she'd done a mighty matter,
In threatning thus, to shut me out of doors;
As if I had not a far better place,
Where I shall be admitted. Well, if I
Displease you, my dear wife, I must e'en bear it:
But I shall please Erotium; and she ne'er
Will shut me out, but rather shut me in.
Well, I'll go in, and pray her to return
The robe I just now gave her, and instead
Of that, I'll purchase her a better. Ho!
Who's porter here? Open the door, and call
Erotium hither.

SCENE III.

[*Enter* Erotium]
EROTIUM: Who inquires for me?
    MENAECHMUS EPIDAMNUM: 'Tis one, who to him-
        self is more enemy,
Than such to you.
    EROTIUM: My dear Menaechmus,
Do'st stand before the door? Follow me in.
    MENAECHMUS EPIDAMNUM: Stay here a little. Do
        you know the reason
I now come to you?
    EROTIUM: I know it very well:
'Tis to amuse yourself along with me.
    MENAECHMUS EPIDAMNUM: That robe I lately gave
        you, prithee, love,

Restore it.—For my wife hath been appris'd,
And knows the whole affair from first to last.
I'll buy one for you twice as rich, you'll like—
    EROTIUM: I gave it you but now, to carry it
To th' embroiderer's; with it, a bracelet
To give the jeweller to set a-new.
    MENAECHMUS EPIDAMNUM: You gave to me a
    bracelet, and the robe?
Never—For when I'd giv'n the robe to you,
I went directly to the market-place:
Now first return I; nor have seen you since.
    EROTIUM: I see through your design: because I
    trusted you,
You would deceive me; that 'tis you would do.
    MENAECHMUS EPIDAMNUM: I do not ask you for it
    to defraud you,
But tell you, that my wife knows all the affair.
    EROTIUM: Nor did I ask you for it: you yourself
Gave it me freely; as a gift, you gave it;
And now demand it back. Well, be it so:
Let it be yours, take it; make use of it,
You or your wife, preserve it as your eyes:
But don't deceive yourself; after this day
You never shall set foot within my doors,
Since you have treated with contempt a woman,
Who has not merited such usage from you.
Next time you come, be sure bring money with you,
You shall not have to visit me for nothing.
Henceforth find some one else to disappoint.
    MENAECHMUS EPIDAMNUM: You are too hasty—
    Hark you!—Stay—Come back.
    EROTIUM: Still are you there? and dare on my
    account
Still to return? [Exit]
    MENAECHMUS EPIDAMNUM: She's gone—has shut
    the door.
Now I'm turn'd out indeed; nor can I gain
Credit, or from my mistress or my wife.
I'll go, consult my friends in the affair.

SCENE IV.

[Enter Menaechmus Sosicles, with the robe]
    MENAECHMUS SOSICLES: 'Twas foolish in me when
    but now I trusted
My purse with all that's in it, to Messenio.
He has got, I doubt, into some brothel with it.
    [Enter the Wife of Menaechmus of Epidamnum]
    WIFE: I'll now see if my husband is come home.
But see, he's here! All's well, he brings my robe.
    MENAECHMUS SOSICLES: I wonder where Messenio
    can be got!
    WIFE: I'll go, and talk to him as he deserves.—
Art not asham'd, vile man, to appear before me,
And with this robe?
    MENAECHMUS SOSICLES: Why, what's the matter,
    woman?
What is't disturbs you!
    WIFE: Dare you, impudence!

Mutter a single word, or speak to me?
    MENAECHMUS SOSICLES: What have I done, I
    should not dare speak?
    WIFE: What! do you ask me? O, consummate im-
    pudence!
    MENAECHMUS SOSICLES: Did you ne'er hear, good
    woman, why the Grecians
Call'd Hecuba a bitch?
    WIFE: Not that I know of.
    MENAECHMUS SOSICLES: Because she did the same
    that you do now;
Threw out abuse on every one she saw:
And therefore, rightly did they call her bitch.
    WIFE: I cannot bear these scandalous reproaches:
I'd rather be a widow all my life,
Than bear these vile reflections you throw on me.
    MENAECHMUS SOSICLES: What is't to me, whether
    you live as married,
Or parted from your husband? Is it thus
The custom to sing out such idle stories
To strangers on their first arrival here?
    WIFE: What idle stories? No, I will not bear it,
I'd rather live a widow, than endure
Your humours any longer.
    MENAECHMUS SOSICLES: 'Troth, for me
Long as you please, you've leave to live a widow:
As long as Jupiter shall keep his kingdom.
    WIFE: You would not own but now, you stole that
    robe,
And now you hold it out before my eyes?
What, are you not asham'd?
    MENAECHMUS SOSICLES: By Hercules!
You are an impudent and wicked woman,
To dare to say this robe was stol'n from you;
When it was given me by another woman,
To get it alter'd for her.
    WIFE: Yes, by Castor!
I'll call my father hither, and lay open
All your base actions to him. Decius, go, [To a
    Servant]
Seek for my father, bring him with you; say,
'Tis proper he should come.—I'll tell him all
Your horrid usage.—
    MENAECHMUS SOSICLES: Are you in your senses?
What horrid usage?—
    WIFE: How you have filch'd from me
My robe, my gold, from me who are your wife,
And giv'n them to your mistress—Say I not
The very truth?—
    MENAECHMUS SOSICLES: I prithee, woman, say
Where I may sup, to charm me from your tongue.
I know not whom you take me for—For you,
I know as much of Parthaon.
    WIFE: Tho' you mock me,
You can't, by Pollux! serve my father so,
Who's just now coming hither—Look behind.
Say, do you know him?
    MENAECHMUS SOSICLES: Just as I know Chalcas.
The very day that I saw you, before
This day did I see him—

WIFE: Dar'st thou deny
That thou know'st me, deny thou know'st my father?
MENAECHMUS SOSICLES: I'd say the same thing,
did'st thou bring thy grandfather.
WIFE: By Castor! you are like yourself in all
things.

SCENE V.

[*Enter* Old Man]

OLD MAN: Fast, as my age permits, and as the
occasion
Calls, will I push my steps, and hasten forward.
How easily, I easily may guess.
My speed forsakes me; I'm beset with age;
I bear a weak, yet heavy laden body.
Old age is a sad pedlar; on his back
Carrying along a pack of grievances.
It would be tedious to recount them all;
But this affair I cannot well digest.
What should this matter be, which makes my
daughter
Want me to come to her in such a hurry?
She does not tell me what the business is,
What 'tis she wants, nor why she sends for me;
Yet I can give a shrewd guess, what it is:
I'm apt to think, some quarrel with her husband.
Such is their way, who of their portions proud,
Would keep their husbands under government.
Nor are the husbands often without fault.
But there are bounds how far a wife should go.
Nor does my daughter send to see her father,
But when some fault's committed, or perhaps
Some quarrel has arisen. What it is,
I soon shall know.—For, look, I see her then,
Before the door; and with her too, her husband,
Whose looks are pensive—'Tis as I suspected—
I'll call her.—
WIFE: I'll go meet him—Happiness
Attend you, father!
OLD MAN: That good will to you!
Am I come here to see things go on well?
Wherefore your order, that I should be sent for?
Why are you pensive, say? and what's the reason
Your husband keeps aloof in anger from you?
The reason I know not, but there has been
Some bickering between you—Who's in fault?
Tell in few words—No long discourse about it.—
WIFE: I am in nought to blame, be easy then
As to that point, my father. But I cannot
Live longer with him, nor stay longer here.
Therefore, I beg you take me hence away.
OLD MAN: Say, what's the matter?
WIFE: Matter? I am made
A laughing-stock.
OLD MAN: By whom?
WIFE: By him you've made
My husband.
OLD MAN: So! a quarrel! say, how often

I've warn'd you both, not to complain to me?
WIFE: How can I help it, Sir?
OLD MAN: What! ask you me?
WIFE: Yes, if you'll give me leave.
OLD MAN: How many times
Have I advis'd you to conform to your husband?
Never to watch his actions; where he goes,
Or what he is about.
WIFE: But he's in love,
Here in the neighbourhood, with a courtezan.
OLD MAN: He's wise in that: and by that care of
yours,
In thus observing him, I would advise him
To love still more.
WIFE: He drinks there, too.
OLD MAN: For you,
Think you he'll ever drink the less, or there,
Or elsewhere, as he likes? What impudence!
Do you insist, he never sup abroad,
Nor entertain a stranger at your house?
Would you, your husband should obey your pleasure?
You may as well require him to partake
Your work with you, and sit among the maids,
And card the wool.
WIFE: I find, Sir, I have brought you
No advocate for me, but for my husband.
Here stand you as a patron in my cause,
Yet plead for his.—
OLD MAN: Was he in ought to blame,
I should condemn him more than I do you.
But when I see he keeps you richly cloth'd,
Allows you servants, and a plenteous table,
A wife thus treated, should in my opinion
Bear towards him a more equal mind.
WIFE: But he
Pilfers my gold, my robe from out my chest;
Robs me, and carries to his courtezans
My richest ornaments.
OLD MAN: If he acts thus,
He acts amiss: if not, you act but ill,
When you accuse one that is innocent.
WIFE: Why, even at this very instant,
He has a bracelet, and a robe of mine,
Which he bore off here to this courtezan;
And now he finds I know it, brings them back.
OLD MAN: 'Tis right to know these matters from
himself:
I will accost, and speak to him. Say, Menaechmus,
What's your dispute? Give me at once to know it.
Why are you pensive? And why is your wife
In wrath against you?
MENAECHMUS SOSICLES: Whoso'er you are,
Whate'er's your name, I call great Jupiter,
And all the gods to witness—
OLD MAN: Why, and wherefore?
MENAECHMUS SOSICLES: That I this woman ne'er
have injur'd her,
Who raves about my stealing from her house
This robe, and bearing of it off. If ever
I've once set foot within her doors, I wish

I may become the veriest wretch alive.

OLD MAN: Have you your senses when you make
   that wish
Or, when deny that ever you set foot
Within that house, where you reside yourself?
O, of all madmen the most mad!

MENAECHMUS SOSICLES: Old man,
And do you say, that I inhabit here?

OLD MAN: Do you deny it?

MENAECHMUS SOSICLES: By Hercules, I do!

WIFE: 'Tis impudence to do so. But you mean,
Because you went this night elsewhere.

OLD MAN: Come hither,
Daughter—And you, [To him] what say you now?
This night went you from hence?

MENAECHMUS SOSICLES: Whither? for what, I pray
   you?

OLD MAN: I know not. I.

WIFE: 'Tis plain he banters you.

OLD MAN: [To her] What, can'st not hold thy
   tongue? Truly, Menaechmus,
You've jested long enough: now to the purpose.

MENAECHMUS SOSICLES: Pray, what have you to
   to do with me? what business?
Say whence you come; and who you are; and what
I've done to you, or to this woman here,
That ye thus tease me?—

WIFE: How his eyes shine! See!
A greenish colour spreads o'er all his temples,
O'er all his forehead. See his eyes! they sparkle!

MENAECHMUS SOSICLES: [Aside] Since they will
   have me mad, what can I do?
Better then feign a madness, I may thus
Fright them away.—

WIFE: Look how he yawns and stretches!
What shall I do, my father!

OLD MAN: Come this way,
As far off from him as you can, my child.

MENAECHMUS SOSICLES: Evoï, Evoï![3] Bacchus son
   of Jove,
Why dost thou call me to the wood to hunt?
I hear you, but I cannot stir from hence,
This woman on the left side, watches me
Like a mad dog; on t'other, this old goat,
Who often in his life has by false witness
Destroy'd the guiltless man.—

OLD MAN: Woe on thy life!

MENAECHMUS SOSICLES: See where Apollo from his
   oracle
Commands me to burn out both that woman's eyes,
With lighted torches.

WIFE: I'm undone, my father!
He threatens me, to burn out both my eyes.

MENAECHMUS SOSICLES: [Aside] Alas! they say
   I'm mad. They themselves
Are much more mad than I.

OLD MAN: Hark, you! my daughter!

WIFE: Your pleasure, Sir? What shall we do?

[3] A Greek exclamation of exhilaration—the cry of the
bacchants, worshipers of Bacchus, or Dionysus.

OLD MAN: Suppose
I call my servants quickly—I'll bring them, those
Shall carry him into the house, there bind him,
'Ere he make more disturbance.—

MENAECHMUS SOSICLES: On my word, [Aside]
Unless I take great care, they'll bear me off
By force into their house. Yes, thou hast order'd
   me,
Not to forbear the thrusting of my fists
Into her face, unless she marches off
Far from my sight, and goes and hangs herself.
Yes, yes, Apollo, I obey thy orders.

OLD MAN: Run home, my daughter, run into the
   house
Fast as you can, lest he belabour you.

WIFE: I fly. I pray you take good heed, my father,
That he escape not. An unhappy wife
Am I, to hear all this. [Exit]

MENAECHMUS SOSICLES: I've sent her off, [Aside]
Not ill. And now must I send after her
This more than filthy fellow, this old grey beard,
This totterer, this old Tithon, son of Cygnus—
'Tis they command that I should break his limbs,
   [Aloud]
His bones, his joints, with that same staff he carries.

OLD MAN: Touch, or come nearer me, and you'll
   repent it.

MENAECHMUS SOSICLES: Yes, I will do as you have
   order'd me,
Take up this two-edged axe, bone this old fellow,
And cut his bowels piece-meal.

OLD MAN: 'Troth, I must
Take care tho' of myself—I am afraid,
He'll do a mischief to me, as he threatens.

MENAECHMUS SOSICLES: Apollo! fast thou pour'st
   thy great behests—
Now thou command'st me, harness my wild steeds,
Fierce and untam'd; and now to mount my car
And crush in pieces this Getulian lion,
This stinking, toothless beast.—Now do I mount,
And now I shake the reins—I take the lash;
Now fly, my steeds, and let your sounding hoofs
Tell your swift course—Shew in the turn your speed.

OLD MAN: And dost thou threaten me with
   harness'd steeds?

MENAECHMUS SOSICLES: Again, Apollo! thou again
   command'st me
To rush upon yon fellow that stands there,
And murder him. But who is this, that by
My fluttering tresses plucks me from my car,
The dire commands revoking of Apollo?

OLD MAN: A sharp and obstinate distemper this!
Ye gods! is't possible, a man who seem'd
So well but now, should fall so suddenly
Into so strange a malady? Away,
I must make haste, and send for a physician. [Exit]

MENAECHMUS SOSICLES: What! are they gone? Are
   they both fled my sight?
Who forc'd me in my wits to feign the madman.
What hinders now, to 'mbark me, while I'm well?

I beg you, Sirs, [*To the spectators*] if the old man
    return,
Not to discover, down what street I took.— [*Exit*]

ACT V. SCENE I.

[*Enter* Old Man]
  OLD MAN: My limbs with fitting ache, my eyes with
    watering,
While this same Doctor from his patients comes.
Scarcely arriv'd at home, he's telling me,
He was oblig'd to set a broken leg
Of Aesculapius, and Apollo's arm.
I'm thinking whether I am bringing with me,
Or a physician, or a carpenter—
But see! he comes, tho' with an emmet's pace.

SCENE II.

[*Enter* Physician]
  PHYSICIAN: What did you say was his disorder,
    Sir?
Inform me, is he mad, or is he frantic?
Is it a lethargy, or is he dropsical?
  OLD MAN: I brought you hither to know that of
    you,
And that your art should cure him.
  PHYSICIAN: Nought more easy.
From this time, I engage he shall be well.
  OLD MAN: I'd have great care ta'en of in his cure.
  PHYSICIAN: My frequent visits oft will make me
    puff,
Such great care I shall take in curing him.
  OLD MAN: But see the man!
  PHYSICIAN: Let us observe his actions.

SCENE III.

[*Enter* Menaechmus of Epidamnum]
  MENAECHMUS EPIDAMNUM: This day has been un-
    lucky, and to me
Quite adverse—what I thought to have done in secret,
Has been discover'd by this parasite,
And brought both fear and infamy upon me.
He my Ulysses was, and my adviser;
Yet nought but evil heaps on me his king.
His thread of life, if I but live myself,
Will I cut off. How like a fool I talk!
His thread of life! His thread of life is mine;
He eats my victuals, lives at my expense.
Yes, I will be the death of him. Besides,
This wench has acted but in character,
The manner of them all. When I request her
To give me back the robe to give my wife,
She tells me, she already had return'd it.
'Troth, I'm unhappy!
  OLD MAN: Hear you what he says?

PHYSICIAN: He says he is unhappy.
  OLD MAN: Pray go nearer.
  PHYSICIAN: Save you, Menaechmus. Why do you
    bare your arms?
You know not how it helps on your disorder.
  MENAECHMUS EPIDAMNUM: Go, hang yourself.
    [*To the* Old Man]
  PHYSICIAN: What think you now?
  MENAECHMUS EPIDAMNUM: What think?
What can I think?
  PHYSICIAN: To work a cure requires
More than an acre of good hellebore.
Hark ye! Menaechmus?
  MENAECHMUS EPIDAMNUM: What would'st thou
    with me?
  PHYSICIAN: Answer to what I ask: Say, do you
    drink
White wine or red?
  MENAECHMUS EPIDAMNUM: Go, hang yourself.
  PHYSICIAN: I find
The mad fit just now coming on.
  MENAECHMUS EPIDAMNUM: Why not
Ask me as well the colour of my bread,
Whether I eat it purple, red, or yellow?
Whether eat scaly birds, or feather'd fish.
  OLD MAN: Hark! how deliriously he talks! or e'er
He grows stark staring mad, give him some potion.
  PHYSICIAN: Hold, stay a little, I shall further ques-
    tion him.
  OLD MAN: More idle talk will quite demolish him.
  PHYSICIAN: Tell me but this; do you ever find your
    eyes
Grow hard?
  MENAECHMUS EPIDAMNUM: Do you take me for a
    locust, fool?
  PHYSICIAN: Do you find your bowels make a noise
    sometimes?
  MENAECHMUS EPIDAMNUM: When I am full, my
    bowels make no noise:
They do, when I am hungry.—
  PHYSICIAN: By my troth,
In this he does not answer like a madman.
D'you sleep till day-light? When you go to bed,
D'you get to sleep with ease?
  MENAECHMUS EPIDAMNUM: My debts discharg'd,
I sleep with ease. May Jove and all the gods
Confound this questioner!
  PHYSICIAN: He 'gins to rave. [*Aside*]
Take heed of what you say.
  OLD MAN: In what he says,
He's much more moderate than he was but now.
'Tis but a while ago, he said, his wife
Was a mad bitch.
  MENAECHMUS EPIDAMNUM: What did I say?
  OLD MAN: You're mad,
I say.
  MENAECHMUS EPIDAMNUM: What, I?
  OLD MAN: You there, who threaten'd me,
You'd trample me beneath your horse's feet.
I saw you do it, and I will maintain it.

MENAECHMUS EPIDAMNUM: And I well know,
  you've stol'n Jove's sacred crown,
And for the fact have been confin'd in prison.
And when releas'd, you've been severely whip'd
Under a gibbet. And I know besides,
You've killed your father, and have sold your mother.
Think you I am so mad, I can't devise
The same abusive language against you,
As you can do 'gainst me?
OLD MAN: Doctor, I beg of you,
What you intend to do to him, do quickly.
Do you not see he's mad?
PHYSICIAN: 'Twere the best thing,
You know, to have him carried to my house.
OLD MAN: Do you think so?
PHYSICIAN: Why not? I there can treat him
As I think proper.
OLD MAN: Do just as you please.
PHYSICIAN: About some twenty days, you shall
  drink hellebore.
MENAECHMUS EPIDAMNUM: And you, some thirty
  days, shall be tied up,
And flog'd severely.
PHYSICIAN: Go, and call your men,
To bring him to my house.
OLD MAN: How many men
D'ye think will be sufficient?
PHYSICIAN: As I see him
So mad, not less than four.
OLD MAN: They shall be here
Immediately. Take care of him, good doctor.
PHYSICIAN: I'll home to get things ready that are
  wanting.
Go, bid your servants bring him to my house.
OLD MAN: I will take care that he shall soon be
  there.
PHYSICIAN: I am gone.
OLD MAN: Farewell.
  [Exeunt Physician and Old Man separately]
MENAECHMUS EPIDAMNUM: The father-in-law is
  gone,
And so's the doctor. Now I am alone.
How is it, Jove, these men will have me mad!
Since I was born, I've ne'er been sick one day.
Nor am I mad, nor do I seek for quarrels,
Nor stir up strifes. I'm well in health, and see
Others the same: I know men, and speak to them.
Is't not, that those who say that I am mad,
Are mad themselves? What shall I do? I would
Go home; but then my wife will not permit it.—
My mistress too will not admit me. This
All of it's ill. I'll e'en stay here till night,
And I may get admittance in the dark. [Stands apart]

SCENE IV.

[Enter Messenio]
MESSENIO: 'Tis on all hands allow'd to be the
  proof

Of a good servant, when he takes good care of,
Looks after, thinks of, and disposes rightly
His master's business. That, when he is absent,
Things may go on as well, or even better
Than when he's present. He whose heart is right,
Will think his back of greater consequence
Than is his gullet: Ay, and to his belly
Prefer his legs. He ought to bear in mind
The wages, servants good for nothing, idle,
Or wicked, from their masters' hands receive:
And these are, stripes and chains, the stocks, the
  mill,
Hard labour, cold and hunger. Such as these
Are the rewards of idleness. This evil
I'm terribly afraid of; therefore choose
Rather to do my duty, than neglect it.
Words I can bear, but stripes I hate. I rather
Like to eat that which has been ground by others,
Than grind myself what others are to eat.
I therefore execute my master's orders
Well; and with sober diligence I serve him:
This turns to my account—Let others act then
As best they think it for their interest,
I'll ever be that which I ought to be:
This fear I'll still retain, to keep me free
From fault; that wheresoe'er my master is,
I may be ready there to wait on him.
Those servants who have nothing done amiss,
Yet keep this fear, still make themselves of use
To their respective masters. But the servants
Who never live in fear of doing wrong,
Fear, when they've something done to merit punish-
  ment.
As for myself, I shan't live long in fear—
The time draws nigh, when master will reward me
For all the pains I have been at to serve him.
I've serv'd him so, as to consult my back.
Now that I've plac'd the servants, as he order'd,
And what they'd want i'th'inn, I'm come to meet him.
I'll now knock at the door, that he may know
I'm here, tho' doubtful whether I can bring him
Safe off from this vile house—I fear me much
Lest I should come after the battle's fought.

SCENE V.

[Enter Old Man, with Servants]
OLD MAN: [To the Servants] By gods and men, I
  here conjure you all
To take good care to execute the orders
Given you already; and I now repeat them.
See that man carried to the doctor's house;
On pain of both your sides and legs, obey me.
Be sure, each of you, not to heed his threats there.
Why stand you thus? why hesitate? e'en now
He ought to've been borne off. I'll go myself
Straight to the doctor: when you are got thither,
You'll find me there before you— [Exit]
MENAECHMUS EPIDAMNUM: I'm undone.

What is the matter? What do these men want,
That they run here so fast? What is't you want?
Why do you thus surround me? Why thus hale me?
Where would you carry me? Undone! help! help!
Aid me, ye Epidamnians! Let me go. [*To the* Servants]
  MESSENIO: Ye gods, what do I see! What men are these
Who thus unworthily are bearing off
My master?
    MENAECHMUS EPIDAMNUM: What, will no one dare to help me?
    MESSENIO: Master, I will, and boldly too.—What villainy!
Ye Epidamnians, thus to seize my master,
In the open street, by day-light, undisturb'd
By tumults in your city—A free man
He enter'd it—Then let him go, I say—
    MENAECHMUS EPIDAMNUM: Whoe'er you are, assist me, I beseech you,
Nor let them do such signal outrage on me.
    MESSENIO: Yes, I'll assist, defend, and succour you.
'Tis far more just, that I myself should perish,
Than suffer you to be thus treated, master:
Pluck out that fellow's eye, I beg of you,
Who holds you by the shoulder. I'll myself
Plant in these rascal chaps a crop of blows.
If you persist in bearing him away,
You'll find you'll have the worst of it. Let him go.
    MENAECHMUS EPIDAMNUM: I've got hold of the rascal's eye.
    MESSENIO: Why then,
Let in his head the socket strait appear.
Rogues! Rascals!
    SERVANTS: You'll murder us. Have mercy!
    MESSENIO: Let him go, then.
    MENAECHMUS EPIDAMNUM: What is't ye mean, you rascals!
By laying hands on me thus violently?
Curry the scoundrels with your blows.
    MESSENIO: Away,
Begone, go and be hang'd, ye rascals!
You there, that are the last to quit your hold,
Take this along with you as a reward— [*Strikes him*]
So, so: I think I've on this scoundrel's chaps
Written in red letters.—'Troth, I came in time
To your assistance, master.
    MENAECHMUS EPIDAMNUM: May the gods!
Whoe'er you are, be ever kind to you,
Young man. For without you, I ne'er had seen
The setting sun this day.
    MESSENIO: By Pollux! therefore,
If you do right, you'll give me, Sir, my freedom.
    MENAECHMUS EPIDAMNUM: Give you your freedom!
    MESSENIO: Out of doubt, my master,
Since I have sav'd your life.
    MENAECHMUS EPIDAMNUM: How's this! young man,

You are mistaken.
    MESSENIO: I mistaken! how?
    MENAECHMUS EPIDAMNUM: I swear by father Jupiter, I'm not
Your master.
    MESSENIO: Can you say so?
    MENAECHMUS EPIDAMNUM: I don't lie.
I never had a servant yet; I say,
Who ever did for me, what you have done?
    MESSENIO: If then you will not own me for your servant,
E'en let me go and have my liberty.
    MENAECHMUS EPIDAMNUM: As far as in my power, take your liberty,
And go where'er you please.
    MESSENIO: Then you command me?
    MENAECHMUS EPIDAMNUM: Yes sure, as far as I've a right to do so.
    MESSENIO: My patron, thanks!
    A SERVANT: I joy to see you free, Messenio.
    MESSENIO: In troth I well believe you.
By Hercules! I do. And now, my patron,
I beg, you'd lay on me the same commands
As when I was your servant. I'll live with you:
And, when you home return, go with you, Sir.
    MENAECHMUS EPIDAMNUM: No, by no means.
    MESSENIO: I'll go now to the inn,
And bring your goods and money to you straight:
The purse which has your money, is fast seal'd
Within the cloak-bag. I'll go bring it straight.
    MENAECHMUS EPIDAMNUM: Do so, and quickly.
    MESSENIO: Sir, I'll bring them back
In the same state as when you gave them me.
Wait for me here. [*Exit*]
    MENAECHMUS EPIDAMNUM: What I've to-day experienc'd
In many instances is most extraordinary.
Some of them say, that I am not the man
I am, and shut me out of doors. And here
A man insists upon't, ·he is my servant—
And I just now have given him his freedom.
He talks of bringing money to me straight;
Which if he does, I'll tell him he has liberty
To go from me whene'er it suits him best.
My father-in-law and the physician say
That I am mad. 'Tis strange what this should be:
It seems to me no other than a dream.
I'll now go to this courtezan, and see,
Tho' she is angry with me, if I can't
Prevail on her, to let me have the robe
To carry home, and give it to my wife. [*Exit*]

SCENE VI.

[*Enter* Menaechmus Sosicles *and* Messenio]
    MENAECHMUS SOSICLES: And do you dare affirm, audacious fellow,
That you have met me any where today,
When I had order'd you to meet me here?

MESSENIO: It is so true, that I not only met you;
But that e'en now, I freed you from four men,
Before this very house, who seiz'd on you,
And would have borne you off. You call'd on gods
And men for their assistance. I ran up,
And snatch'd you from them, notwithstanding all
On which account, as I had done you service,
You gave my freedom to me: After that,
You bade me go, and fetch your goods and money,
You've hasten'd on, fast as you could before,
To frustrate your own deeds—
    MENAECHMUS SOSICLES: And did I bid you
Depart a freeman?
    MESSENIO: Certainly.
    MENAECHMUS SOSICLES: And 'tis
Most certain, I'm as much a slave myself
As e'er I gave to you your liberty.

SCENE VII.

[*Enter* Menaechmus Epidamnum, *from* Erotium's *house*]
    MENAECHMUS EPIDAMNUM: Vile woman as you are! tho' you should swear
By all that's dear to you, that I this day
Bore off that robe and bracelet, yet you never,
No, never should convince me.
    MESSENIO: Gods immortal!
What is it that I see?
    MENAECHMUS SOSICLES: Why, what do you see?
    MESSENIO: Why, your resemblance, Sir, as in a mirror.
    MENAECHMUS SOSICLES: What is't you mean?
    MESSENIO: Your image, and as like
As possible.
    MENAECHMUS SOSICLES: 'Troth, if I know myself,
'Tis not unlike.
    MENAECHMUS EPIDAMNUM: Young man, who'er you are,
The gods preserve you! you have sav'd my life.
    MESSENIO: Young man, if 'tis not disagreeable,
Tell me your name?
    MENAECHMUS EPIDAMNUM: You have so much oblig'd me,
You cannot ask what I'd be slow to grant you,
My name's Menaechmus.
    MENAECHMUS SOSICLES: Mine's Menaechmus too.
    MENAECHMUS EPIDAMNUM: I'm a Sicilian, and of Syracuse.
    MENAECHMUS SOSICLES: I am the same: it is my native country—
    MENAECHMUS EPIDAMNUM: What's that I hear?
    MENAECHMUS SOSICLES: You hear the very truth.
    MESSENIO: I know this gentleman; he is my master.
I am his servant. But I thought myself
The other's servant. Sir, [*To* Menaechmus Sosicles] I thought him, you;
And by so doing, gave you some uneasiness.
If I have said ought foolish or imprudent,

I pray you pardon me.
    MENAECHMUS SOSICLES: You're mad, I think.
Don't you remember, that this very day
You disembark'd with me?
    MESSENIO: Nothing more just.
You are my master. Seek [*To* Menaechmus Epidamnum] another servant.
[*To* Menaechmus Sosicles] God save you, Sir! and you, [*To* Menaechmus Epidamnum] good' Sir, adieu!
This is, I say, Menaechmus.
    MENAECHMUS EPIDAMNUM: I say, I am.
    MENAECHMUS SOSICLES: What comedy is this? What! you Menaechmus!
    MENAECHMUS EPIDAMNUM: I am, Sir!—and my father's name was Moschus.
    MENAECHMUS SOSICLES: And are you then my father's son?
    MENAECHMUS EPIDAMNUM: I'm son
Of my own father, youth. I do not want
To claim your father, nor to take him from you.
    MESSENIO: Ye gods! confirm the unexpected hope
Which I'm conceiving. These, if I mistake not,
Are the twin brothers; for they both agree,
In owning the same father, the same country.
I'll call aside my master. Sir! Menaechmus!
    BOTH MEN: Whom is't you want?
    MESSENIO: I want but one of you.
But which of you came with me in the ship?
    MENAECHMUS EPIDAMNUM: Not I.
    MENAECHMUS SOSICLES: 'Twas I.
    MESSENIO: Why then, 'tis you I want.
Come this way.
    MENAECHMUS SOSICLES: Well, I'm here, what do you want?
    MESSENIO: That man is an impostor, Sir, or else
He's your twin brother. For I never saw
Two men, one like the other so exactly.
Water is, I assure you, not more like
To water, nor is milk more like to milk,
Than he is like to you, and you to him.
Besides, he owns himself of the same country,
And claims too the same father. Best accost him,
And ask him some few questions.
    MENAECHMUS SOSICLES: Your advice
Is right, by Hercules!—I thank you for it.
Beseech you, give me farther your assistance;
And, if you find us brothers, you shall have
Your freedom.
    MESSENIO: Sir, I hope I shall.
    MENAECHMUS SOSICLES: I hope
The same.
    MESSENIO: [*To* Menaechmus Epidamnum] What was't you said? I think it was
That you are call'd Menaechmus?
    MENAECHMUS EPIDAMNUM: Yes.
    MESSENIO: But he
Is call'd Menaechmus too.—In Sicily
You said that you were born, a citizen
Of Syracuse—Why there was he born too.

You've likewise said that Moschus was your father.
Why, Moschus was his father too. And now
Is't in the power of both of you to assist me;
And, in assisting me, to assist yourselves.

MENAECHMUS EPIDAMNUM: You have deserv'd so
much of me, that what
You ask, you may command. Free as I am
I'll serve you, just as if I was your slave.

MESSENIO: I hope you're just upon the point of
finding
That you're twin brothers, born at the same time,
Sons of one father, and one mother too.

MENAECHMUS EPIDAMNUM: You mention wonders.
Would you could effect
That which you've given assurance of—

MESSENIO: I can.
Come now. To that which I shall ask of you,
Both answer me.

MENAECHMUS EPIDAMNUM: Ask when you please,
I'll answer,
And not conceal one jot of what I know.

MESSENIO: Is then your name Menaechmus?
MENAECHMUS EPIDAMNUM: Yes, I own it.
MESSENIO: And yours the same?
MENAECHMUS SOSICLES: It is.
MESSENIO: You also say
Your father's name was Moschus.

MENAECHMUS EPIDAMNUM: Yes, I do.
MENAECHMUS SOSICLES: And mine the same.
MESSENIO: Are you of Syracuse?
MENAECHMUS EPIDAMNUM: Most certainly.
MESSENIO: And you?
MENAECHMUS SOSICLES: No doubt of it.
MESSENIO: Hitherto all the marks agree right well.
But let's go on. What's the most distant thing,
You recollect to have happened in your country?

MENAECHMUS EPIDAMNUM: The going with my
father to Tarentum
I'th' way of merchandising: in the crowd
My straying from my father; after that,
My being hither brought.

MENAECHMUS SOSICLES: Preserve me, Jupiter!
MESSENIO: Why is that exclamation? Hold your
peace.
[To Menaechmus Epidamnum] Say, when your
father from your country took you,
What was your age?

MENAECHMUS EPIDAMNUM: Seven years: for I
remember
Just at that time my teeth began to shed—
Nor from that time have I e'er seen my father.

MESSENIO: How many children had your father?
MENAECHMUS EPIDAMNUM: Two,
If I remember right.

MESSENIO: Were you or he
The elder?

MENAECHMUS EPIDAMNUM: We were both of the
same age.

MESSENIO: How can that be?—
MENAECHMUS EPIDAMNUM: We both were twins—

MENAECHMUS SOSICLES: The gods
Are pleas'd to bless me—
MESSENIO: If you interrupt me,
I'll say no more.
MENAECHMUS SOSICLES: Rather than so, I'm silent.
MESSENIO: Say, had you both one name?
MENAECHMUS EPIDAMNUM: Not so—My name
Was, as 'tis now, Menaechmus. But my brother
They named Sosicles.

MENAECHMUS SOSICLES: I own the proofs.
I cannot hold out longer. I'll embrace him.—
My brother, my twin brother, hail! 'Tis I
Am Sosicles.

MENAECHMUS EPIDAMNUM: If so, why were you
afterwards Menaechmus call'd?

MENAECHMUS SOSICLES: When afterwards we heard
You and your father both were dead, my grandfather
Changing my name, gave me the same as yours.

MENAECHMUS EPIDAMNUM: Well, I believe 'tis all
just as you say.
But in your turn now answer me.

MENAECHMUS SOSICLES: Your pleasure.
MENAECHMUS EPIDAMNUM: What was our mother's
name?

MENAECHMUS SOSICLES: 'Twas Theusimarche.
MENAECHMUS EPIDAMNUM: All this agree. Hail,
my unlook'd-for brother!
Whom after years of absence, I now see.

MENAECHMUS SOSICLES: The same all Hail! to you,
my dearest brother!
For whom I've search'd till now with so much pains,
And whom I now rejoice to have found at last.

MESSENIO: It was on this account, the courtezan
Then call'd you by his name, and taking you
For him, she ask'd you to her house to dinner.

MENAECHMUS EPIDAMNUM: 'Troth, I this day had
order'd at her house
A dinner, to my wife unknown, from whom
I filch'd a robe, and gave her as a present.

MENAECHMUS SOSICLES: Is this the robe you see me
have, my brother?

MENAECHMUS EPIDAMNUM: How came it in your
hands?

MENAECHMUS SOSICLES: A common woman
Invited me to dine, and said 'twas I
That gave it her—I ate a hearty dinner,
Drank freely, entertain'd myself with her,
And got this robe, this bracelet—

MENAECHMUS EPIDAMNUM: I'm glad, brother,
That you have fared so well on my account:
For when she ask'd you home to dinner with her,
'Twas me she took you for.

MESSENIO: What hinders then,
But, as you promis'd me, I should be free?

MENAECHMUS EPIDAMNUM: He asks but what is
right and just, my brother,
Do it on my account.

MENAECHMUS SOSICLES: Be free.
MENAECHMUS EPIDAMNUM: I joy,
Messenio. that you have obtain'd your freedom.

MESSENIO: You see a better hand than yours was wanting
To make me free for life.

MENAECHMUS SOSICLES: Since things are thus
As we could wish, let's both return together
To our native country.

MENAECHMUS EPIDAMNUM: As you please, my brother.
I'll make an auction, and sell all I have.
In the mean time, my brother, let's go in.

MENAECHMUS SOSICLES: With all my heart.

MESSENIO: Can you guess what I'd ask?

MENAECHMUS EPIDAMNUM: What is it?

MESSENIO: That you'd make me auctioneer.

MENAECHMUS EPIDAMNUM: 'Tis granted.

MESSENIO: Well, Sir, shall I then proclaim
The auction straight? and for what day?

MENAECHMUS EPIDAMNUM: The seventh.

MESSENIO: O yes!—O yes!—This, Sirs, is to give notice.—
The auction of Menaechmus will begin
The seventh of this month: when will be sold
Slaves, household goods, farms, houses, and—et cetera.
All may attend that will; and we sell all
For ready money. Sell his wife besides,
If any purchaser should offer. I scarce think
Our auction will amount to fifty times
A thousand sesterces.[4]
[To the spectators] Spectators, now
Adieu! and favour us with a loud applause.
     [Exeunt]

[4] A Roman silver coin used during the third century B.C., then worth two and a half asses.

Terence

(195?–159 B.C.)

Publius Terentius Afer was the educated man's Plautus, a writer of six high comedies that made him the Philip Barry of his age. He was a devoted follower of Greek models of literary taste and polish, so that to know the plays of Terence is also to know the Greek New Comedy as written by its fourth-century master, Menander; Julius Caesar admiringly called Terence a "half-Menander." With this successor to Plautus we come curiously close to the Augustan age of Roman refinement, which did not actually begin until about a century and a quarter after Terence's death. His dexterity in evolving a plot and his skill in shaping a character are accomplishments unapproached until his time and unequaled in Latin literature thereafter.

Terence was a native Carthaginian, the product of a Semitic civilization then dying out as a result of military conquest by Rome. Of either Negro or Berber extraction, he was brought to Rome as a slave in his youth but was educated in the household of a liberal senator and given his freedom. Handsome and refined, Terence was quickly received into the intellectual circle of the aristocracy and became a close friend of its leader, Scipio Africanus Minor. Influenced by his friends' fashionable taste for Greek learning and probably encouraged by the success of an older contemporary writer of high comedy, Caecilius Statius (219?–166? B.C.), also not a Roman, but a manumitted Gaul, Terence wrote like a Hellene for his Roman audiences.

Terence's first play, *Andria,* was produced in Rome in 166 B.C. He founded it on a comedy of the same title by Menander, and it appears to have received the approval of the influential Caecilius, to whom he is said to have read his manuscript. Nevertheless, Terence encountered sharp opposition from a rival playwright and the latter's clique on the grounds that he was guilty of *contaminatio*—that is, of taking liberties with the Greek original by mixing its plot with details taken from other plays. He was also accused of receiving assistance from his cultivated friends. The same charges were made against all his later work, and the accusation of *contaminatio* irked him as much as the competition he faced from popular forms of entertainment—side shows and rope-dancing interludes—to which the Roman masses were more susceptible than to high comedy. Terence wrote prologues to his plays justifying his free treatment of the original Greek comedies and his fusing the plots of several of these. This was, indeed, the method of playwriting which he consistently employed, although he probably invented scenes and characterizations himself. In his prologues he also embodied a plea for critical standards and good taste, hoping to lift the public up to his level.

Productions were difficult for Terence to obtain; his plays were put on mainly with the help of highly situated friends and of the leading actor of his time, Ambivius Turpio, who staged them with music specially written by a certain Flaccus, the gifted slave of the aristocrat Claudius. Lacking the rowdy humor and ingenious versification of Plautus, and departing from his contagious "song-and-dance" routine, Terence could not command immense popularity, although four of his plays won some favor and another, *The Eunuch,* became a popular success. But his urbanity marked a great advance in Roman playwriting. If, instead of following the direction in which he pointed, Rome returned to the farce comedies of Plautus with increased relish and turned, indeed, from all Greek-inspired comedy (*fabula palliata*) to a new, robust national comedy of Roman scenes and costumes (*fabula togata*), Terence is nonetheless an important figure in the European drama. His were the only comedies that the medieval world was to find morally acceptable, and the Renaissance considered his plays the most refined models for high comedy.

Terence wrote pithy natural speech addressed to cultivated ears. Relying on characterization to a great degree—despite the frequent presence of coincidence in his standardized, less than plausible plots—he set the first example of high comedy from which playwrights could learn anything, once the Greek originals had vanished. Dispensing with prefatory plot summaries, employing suspense in plot construction, and substituting development by dialogue for the more customary narrative monologues, he exemplified a new technique. Even his use of conventional asides advanced dramaturgy, because his were true soliloquies conveying the characters' thoughts instead of crude declamations to the audience. In his own time, consequently, Terence stood with the literary vanguard.

The plays of Terence won him considerable social standing, and it is not improbable that friends presented him with some property. He appears to have left an estate along the Appian Way to a daughter, who later married a Roman senator. Possibly with a view to acquiring more Greek plays for adaptation, Terence took a journey to Greece in 159 B.C., and he was never seen again. The circumstances of his death are not known.

Romantic sentiment prevails in the first Terentian comedy, *Andria,* or *The Woman of Andros,* in which a young lover succeeds in marrying the supposed sister of a courtesan in spite of his father's objections. (*Andria* served as the basis of Richard Steele's sentimental comedy *The Conscious Lovers,* 1722, as well as of Thornton Wilder's novel *The Woman of*

Andros.) Terence's next play, *The Self-Tormentor* (163 B.C.), contains greater emphasis on characterization, although it too is a comedy of love and intrigue resolved by a discovery. It was followed in 161 B.C. by the author's most successful, because most lively, work, *The Eunuch,* which, with Plautus' *Miles Gloriosus,* or *The Braggart Soldier,* provided the basis for the first fully realized pre-Shakespearean comedy, Nicholas Udall's *Ralph Roister Doister.* Although there is some salacious matter in the device of a young man posing as a eunuch in order to gain access into the house of the girl he intends to ravish, the effect of the writing is pleasant and exuberant. The play was certainly well suited to the occasion of the production, the feast in honor of Cybele, the Roman goddess of fertility. *Phormio,* produced at the Roman games in the same year, was almost as vivacious, largely as a result of the intrigues of the parasite Phormio, who is the most delightful stock character in classic comedy.

It is, however, in the last play, *Adelphi,* or *The Brothers,* produced in 160 B.C., that the Terentian vein of high comedy runs most purely. Although it has the usual plot of sentimental attachments and misunderstandings, the action is resolved by logic of characterization rather than by conventional farcical tricks and coincidences. The·substance of the writing, in fact, makes *The Brothers* the first extant "problem comedy" of European literature. The true subject is not the standardized romance but the question of what is the best policy to apply to youth—discipline or understanding tolerance. Two theories of education are contrasted by Terence, and the action demonstrates the validity of Terence's point of view, which favors tolerance. Among the later plays engendered by this work is Molière's *The School for Husbands.* We cannot overestimate the influence of this first known stress on an intellectual approach in comedy of manners upon the Western theatre that later produced Molière, Sheridan, Shaw, Barry, and Behrman. In spirit, *The Brothers* is hardly Roman at all; it is a late evocation of Greek humanism.

THE BROTHERS

By Terence

CHARACTERS IN THE PLAY

MICIO, *an aged Athenian*
DEMEA, *his brother, father of Aeschinus and Ctesipho*
SANNIO, *a pimp*
AESCHINUS, *son of Demea, adopted by Micio*
SYRUS, *slave of Micio and Aeschinus*
CTESIPHO, *son of Demea*
SOSTRATA, *an Athenian lady*

CANTHARA, *an old woman, servant of Sostrata*
GETA, *slave of Sostrata*
HEGIO, *an old man of Athens*
PAMPHILA, *daughter of Sostrata*
DROMO, *slave of Micio*
MUSIC GIRL
PARMENO, *a slave*

SCENE: *A street in Athens in front of the houses of* Micio *and* Sostrata. *The time is early morning*

DIDASCALIA

The Brothers of Terence. Acted at the Funeral Games in honour of Lucius Aemilius Paulus which were given by Quintus Fabius Maximus and Publius Cornelius Africanus. The chief actors were Lucius Ambivius Turpio and Lucius Atilius Praenestinus. It was set to music by Flaccus, slave of Claudius, to the accompaniment of Tyrian flutes. It is from the Greek of Menander and is the poet's sixth play. It was presented during the consulship of Marcus Cornelius Cethegus and Lucius Anicius Gallus (160 B.C.).

SUMMARY

Since Demea has two sons, he permits his brother Micio to adopt Aeschinus but he himself keeps Ctesipho. Demea was a harsh and strict father and when Ctesipho fell in love with a music girl his brother Aeschinus concealed it and took on himself the blame for the love affair; finally he took the music girl away from the pimp. Aeschinus had already seduced an impoverished Athenian girl and had promised to marry her. Demea upbraids him and is greatly vexed. Later, when the truth is revealed, Aeschinus marries the girl he has wronged and Ctesipho retains possession of the music girl.

PROLOGUE

When the poet found that his writings were likely to be attacked by malicious critics, and that his adversaries did all in their power to discredit the play we are now going to act, he resolved to give evidence regarding himself, and leave it to your judgment, whether what they reproach him with is worthy of praise or blame.

The *Synapothnescontes* is a comedy written by Diphilus. Plautus has rendered it into Latin, and called it *Commorientes*. In the Greek of Diphilus there is a youth, who, in the beginning of the play, takes a girl by force from a pimp. This Plautus has left untouched, and our poet has transferred it word for word into his *Brothers*, a new play that we are this day to act before you. Judge, therefore, whether this ought to be called a theft, or if it is not rather recovering what another's negligence has overlooked. For as to what these envious men allege, that some of our great men assist him, and are constantly writing with him; this, which they look upon as a mighty reproach, he regards as his greatest merit, that he has it in his power to please those, with whom you, and the whole people of Rome, are so much pleased; and whose services in war, in peace, and even in your private affairs, each one of you has used unreservedly, according to his need. As to what remains, do not expect now to hear from me the subject of the play; the two old men, who come on first, will partly explain it, and the rest will gradually appear in the representation. Do you, by a candid and impartial attention, encourage the poet to industry in writing.

ACT I. SCENE I.

[*Enter* Micio *from his house*]
MICIO: [*Calling within*] Storax! [*To himself, as there is no answer*] Well, Aeschinus didn't return last night from supper, nor any of the servants who went to meet him. It is, indeed, a true saying: if you are absent anywhere, or chance to stay longer than ordinary, better those things happen to you which your wife says, or fancies in her resentment, than what indulgent parents are apt to suspect. Your wife, if you are out late, fancies you have picked up a girl, or a girl you, or that you are at the tavern, or amusing yourself somewhere, and that you make yourself quite happy, while she is uneasy and pines at home. But for me now, what apprehensions am I under, because my son has not returned; how anxious, lest he may have caught cold, or had a fall, or broken some limb! Good

gods! That a man should set his mind so much upon anything, as to allow it to become dearer to him than he is to himself! Nor is this boy, indeed, my son, but my brother's, one who is of a temperament very different from mine. Even from my youth, I have courted ease, and the quiet enjoyments of a town life, and, what men of pleasure count a happiness, have always lived single. He again is quite the reverse of all this. He has lived in the country, being always sparing and laborious; he married, and had two sons. Of these, I have adopted the elder; bred him up from a child, kept him with me, and loved him as my own; he is now my whole delight, and what alone I hold dear; and I do all I can, too, that I may be equally dear to him. I give, I overlook things, I don't think it necessary to exert my authority on every occasion. In short, I have accustomed my son not to conceal from me those little extravagances natural to youth, which others are at so much pains to hide from their parents. For he who is accustomed to lie to, or deceive his father, will be more likely to cheat others. And I think it more prudent to hold children to their duty by the ties of kindness and honour, than by the restraints of fear. In this my brother and I differ widely, nor is he at all pleased with my manner. He often comes to me, loudly exclaiming, "What are you about, Micio? Why do you thus ruin the youth? Why does he drink? And why do you supply him with funds for all those extravagances? You indulge him too much in fine dress; you are quite silly in doing so." Why truly, he himself is much too severe, beyond what is either just or reasonable. And, in my judgment, he deceives himself greatly, to imagine that an authority established by force will be more lasting, or of greater weight, than one which is founded on friendship. For in this manner do I reason, and thus persuade myself to believe. He that does his duty from mere motives of fear will be upon his guard no longer than while he thinks there is danger of his being discovered, but if he can hope to escape notice, he returns to his natural bent; but where one is won over by kindness, he acts from inclination, strives to make a due return, and, present or absent, will be the same. This, indeed, is the part of a father, to accustom his son to do what is right, more from his own choice, than any fear of another; and here chiefly lies the difference between a father and a master. He who can't do this should admit that he doesn't know how to bring up children. But isn't this the very man of whom I was speaking? 'Tis the same; he seems vexed too, I can't think why. I believe, as usual, we shall have a quarrel. Demea, I am glad to see you so well.

SCENE II.

[*Enter* Demea *from the country*]

DEMEA: H'm! Just in time. You're the very man I was looking for.

MICIO: What makes you look so vexed?

DEMEA: Can you ask why? Do you know where our son Aeschinus is? Do you know now why I am vexed?

MICIO: [*Aside*] Didn't I say it would be so? [*To* Demea] What has he done?

DEMEA: What has he done? He is ashamed of nothing and afraid of nobody and thinks no law binding upon him. I pass over his former escapades; what an outrage he has just now perpetrated!

MICIO: Why, what has he done?

DEMEA: He has broken open a street-door and made his way into a strange house, has beaten the master of the house and all his people nearly to death, and carried away a woman he's in love with. Everybody declares that it is a most shameful thing. As I was coming here, Micio, you don't know how many people told me this story; all Athens is full of it. If the boy needs an example, doesn't he see his brother working away in the country thriftily and soberly? He does nothing of this sort. Now Micio, when I say this to him, I say it to you, for you are letting him go to the bad.

MICIO: There never is anything so unfair as an ignorant man, who thinks that nothing can be right except what he does himself.

DEMEA: What do you mean by that?

MICIO: I mean, Demea, that you take a wrong view of this. Believe me, it is not a monstrous crime for a young man to indulge in wine and women; it isn't, really; nor yet to break open street-doors. If neither you nor I did such things, it was because poverty did not permit us to do them; you now are taking credit to yourself for not having done what you could not afford to do. This is quite wrong, for had we had the means, we should have done these things; and if you were a sensible man, you would let that son of yours do so now, while he is of an age for such follies, rather than that he should do them all the same when he ought to be too old for them, when at last he has had the pleasure of putting you underground.

DEMEA: By Jupiter, you make me wild! Not a monstrous crime for a young man to do so?

MICIO: Listen, and don't din this into my ears. You have given me your son to be mine by adoption; he has become my son. Now, Demea, if he does wrong, that is my affair; I shall have to bear most of the expenses. Suppose that he makes love, drinks wine, perfumes himself: I shall pay for it. Suppose he keeps a mistress: well, as long as I find it convenient, I shall let him have money for her; if I don't find it convenient, perhaps he will find her door shut against him. Now, if he has broken open a street-door, it will have to be mended; if he has torn any clothes, they must be sewn up again; and, thanks be to the gods, I can afford to have these things done, and thus far they do not weigh heavily upon me. The long and the short of it is, either leave off interfering, or choose someone to arbitrate between us. I can show that you are more to blame than I.

DEMEA: Oh, dear me! Learn to be a father from those who really know what it is!

MICIO: You are his father according to nature; but in care of him, I am.

DEMEA: As if you cared at all for him!

MICIO: If you go on talking like that, I shall go away.

DEMEA: That you should act thus!

MICIO: How many times over am I to hear the same thing?

DEMEA: It is a matter of interest to me.

MICIO: So it is to me; but let us each look after our own part: you see to one brother, Demea, and I will see to the other; for if you look after both of them, it is much the same thing as asking back the son you gave to me.

DEMEA: Oh, Micio!

MICIO: That's my view of the matter.

DEMEA: Well, well, if you like it, let him squander, waste, and go to the devil; it's nothing to me. And if I ever hear another word—

MICIO: Why, Demea, are you getting into a passion again?

DEMEA: Don't you believe me? Do I ask you to give me back the son I gave you? I own it is hard; I am not a stranger to him; it would not be surprising if I were to interfere—well, I leave off interfering. You wish me to look after one of my sons; very good, I am looking after him, and I am thankful to heaven that he is such a son as I should wish. That one of yours will find out some day how wrong he has been. I do not want to say anything worse about him. [Demea departs]

MICIO: [To himself] What he says is not all true, yet there is some truth in it, and I myself am vexed at it somewhat, though I wouldn't show him that I was sorry for it; for he is the sort of man that, to try to appease him I must be careful to oppose and thwart him, and even then he does not take it kindly; but if I were to increase his anger or add fuel to it, why I should be as mad as he is. Yet, for all that, Aeschinus has not treated me quite properly by doing this. What courtesan is there in all Athens whom he has not been in love with, or to whom he has not made a present? Last of all, the other day, sick of them all, I believe, he said that he should like to marry. I hoped that he had sown his wild oats, and was glad of it; now, behold, he has begun afresh. But whatever it is that he has done, I should like to know about it and have a talk with him, if he's in the market place.

[Micio departs towards the forum. A short time is supposed to elapse before the next Act]

ACT II. SCENE I.

[Enter Aeschinus with a Music girl; Parmeno and other Slaves attend him. Sannio follows]

SANNIO: My countrymen, I beseech you, help an injured and innocent man. Assist one who is helpless.

AESCHINUS: [To the Girl] Take it easy, stand still here now. Why do you look behind you? There's no danger; he will never lay a finger on you while I'm here.

SANNIO: I'll get her back, in spite of all of you.

AESCHINUS: [To the Girl] Scoundrel as he is, he won't risk getting another thrashing today!

SANNIO: Aeschinus, listen to me, that you mayn't say you didn't know my ways. I am a slave-dealer.

AESCHINUS: I know that you are.

SANNIO: But the most honourable in my business that there ever was. Now I don't care a straw for what you will plead in your defence—that you are sorry for having committed this outrage upon me. Mark me, I'll stand out for my lawful rights, and it will not be by words alone that you will pay for the harm you have done me by deeds. I know your excuses—"Sorry it was done; will make an affidavit that you didn't deserve such ill-treatment," after I have been so shamefully misused!

AESCHINUS: [To the Slaves] Go on ahead quickly and open the door.

SANNIO: Then don't you pay any attention to what I say?

AESCHINUS: [To the Girl] Go into the house straightway.

SANNIO: But I won't let her go into the house.

AESCHINUS: Close up on that side, Parmeno; you are too far away; stand here close to him; there, that's where I want you to be. Now, mind you never take your eyes off mine, so that you may lose no time, when I give you the wink, in bringing your fist down on his jaw.

SANNIO: I should like him to try. [Lays hold of the Girl]

AESCHINUS: Here, mind what you're about. Let the girl go. [Parmeno hits Sannio in the face]

SANNIO: Oh, shame!

AESCHINUS: [To Sannio] He'll do it again, if you don't take care. [Parmeno hits Sannio again]

SANNIO: Oh, dear me!

AESCHINUS: I didn't wink to you to do it again; still, it's a fault on the right side. Now be off!

[Parmeno takes the Girl into Micio's house]

SANNIO: What's all this mean? Are you king in these parts, Aeschinus?

AESCHINUS: If I were, you would meet your deserts.

SANNIO: What have you to do with me?

AESCHINUS: Nothing.

SANNIO: What? Do you know who I am?

AESCHINUS: I don't want to know.

SANNIO: Have I meddled with any of your property?

AESCHINUS: It would have been the worse for you if you had.

SANNIO: Why should you have my slave, that I bought and paid for? Answer me.

AESCHINUS: You had better not abuse me in front of my own house; for if you go on making yourself a nuisance, I'll have you taken into the house and flogged there within an inch of your life.

SANNIO: Flog me, a free man!

AESCHINUS: That's what will be done.

SANNIO: O villain; and this is the place where they say that all men are free alike!

AESCHINUS: Now then, master slave-dealer, if you have quite done storming, be good enough to listen to me.

SANNIO: Have I been storming against you, or you against me?

AESCHINUS: Never mind that, come to the point.

SANNIO: What point? Where am I to come to?

AESCHINUS: Are you ready for me to tell you about your concern in this matter?

SANNIO: I am willing, provided that I get some of my rights.

AESCHINUS: Ho! Ho! Here's a slave-dealer bids me talk righteously!

SANNIO: I am a slave-dealer, I confess it, the ruin of all young men; I am a liar and a scoundrel; but still I have never done you any wrong.

AESCHINUS: No, that's the one thing that's left for you to do.

SANNIO: Pray, Aeschinus, return to what you began about.

AESCHINUS: You bought this girl for twenty minae; you shall be paid the same sum, and much good may it do you.

SANNIO: What if I refuse to sell her to you? Will you make me?

AESCHINUS: Not at all.

SANNIO: I was afraid that you would.

AESCHINUS: I don't believe that she is saleable, for I claim her as a free woman as the law directs in such cases. Now make your choice, whether you will take the money or think what defence you can make. I leave you to your reflections here, master slave-dealer, until I return. [Aeschinus *goes into the house*]

SANNIO: [*To himself*] Almighty Jove! I don't wonder at men being driven mad by outrage. He has dragged me out of my house, beaten me, and carried off my slave-girl against my will; he has bestowed more than five hundred blows upon me; and now, as the reward of his crimes, he expects to get her for no more than I gave for her. [*Ironically*] Well, since he has treated me so well, so be it; he has a right, no doubt. Why, I'm quite willing, provided he pays me the money for her. But I'm talking nonsense. When I say that I gave so much for her, he will straightway have witnesses ready to prove that I have sold her to him, and the money will be all moonshine. He'll say, "Call again tomorrow." Well, I could put up with that, too, if only he would pay, in spite of the injustice of it. But I know how things are: if you ply my trade, you must submit to outrages from young gentlemen and hold your tongue. I shall never be paid; it's no use for me to make these calculations.

SCENE II.

[*Enter* Syrus *from* Micio's *house*]

SYRUS: [*To his master within*] Say no more; I'll see the man myself; I'll make him glad to take the money, and declare that he has been well treated. [*To* Sannio] What's this I hear, Sannio, about your having been fighting with my master?

SANNIO: I never saw a more one-sided fight than that between him and me today, for I got beaten, and he beat me till we were both tired out.

SYRUS: Well, it was all your fault.

SANNIO: What ought I to have done?

SYRUS: You ought to have made allowances for the young gentleman.

SANNIO: What more could I have done; haven't I allowed him to hit me in the face?

SYRUS: Come, you understand what I mean. Sometimes the most profitable thing we can do is not to be overkeen after one's money.

SANNIO: The deuce it is!

SYRUS: You great goose, if you don't insist upon your rights just now, and let the young gentleman have his way, you surely cannot fear that you will not profit by so doing in the long run?

SANNIO: A bird in the hand is worth two in the bush.

SYRUS: You will never make a fortune; get along with you, Sannio, you don't understand how to entice men on.

SANNIO: I believe that is the best way, but I never was so cunning as not to prefer to get what I could in ready money.

SYRUS: Come, I know what you're thinking of; as if twenty minae made any difference to you, in comparison with doing my master a favour. Besides, they say you are on the point of setting sail for Cyprus.

SANNIO: [*Aside*] The devil!

SYRUS: That you have bought up a large cargo for that place, and hired a ship. Come, I know you're in two minds about it; when you return, I hope, you can still settle this affair.

SANNIO: I'm not going to stir from this place. [*Aside*] Confound it! This was what they were relying upon when they began.

SYRUS: [*Aside*] He's afraid. I've put a spoke in his wheel.

SANNIO: [*Aside*] What villainy! See how he has caught me just in the very nick of time. I've bought lots of slave-girls, and other merchandise besides, which I am going to take to Cyprus. Unless I get them there in time for the fair, it will be a dead loss. But if I drop this business now, and begin it again when I return from Cyprus, all's lost; the whole thing will have blown over. They will say, "Why didn't you come into court before? Why did you let him do it? Where were you?" So it is better to lose the money than either to wait here so long or to try to get it when I come back.

SYRUS: Well, have you finished reckoning up what you expect to make by your voyage?

SANNIO: Is this the way that Aeschinus ought to behave? To think that he should try to do such a thing; to expect to take this girl from me by main force.

SYRUS: [Aside] He is giving way. [Aloud] Now, Sannio, I've only one proposal to make; see whether it suits you. Rather than risk winning or losing it all, split the difference. He'll scrape up ten minae somehow.

SANNIO: Confound it, am I now to lose the principal as well as the interest? Has he no shame? He has loosened all my teeth; besides, my head is all bumps with his knocks; and is he going to cheat me as well? I won't leave this place.

SYRUS: Please yourself. Anything else before I go?

SANNIO: Yes, damn it! I beg you, Syrus, no matter what has been done, rather than go to law about it, let me have the bare price that I gave for the girl, anyway, my good Syrus. I know that you have not as yet profited by my friendship, but hereafter you will find me mindful of your kindness, and grateful.

SYRUS: I'll do my best. But I see Ctesipho there; he's pleased at getting his mistress.

SANNIO: What are you going to do about my request?

SYRUS: Wait a bit.

SCENE III.

[Enter Ctesipho, overjoyed]

CTESIPHO: [To himself] One is always pleased to be done a good turn in time of need, by anybody; much more pleasant is it when one whose duty it is does one good. My dear brother, what need is there for me to praise you now? I am quite sure that, however grandly I spoke of you, it would fall short of your real merit. I think that I have this great advantage over everybody else, that no one has so noble a gentleman for a brother.

SYRUS: Good day, Ctesipho.

CTESIPHO: Oh, Syrus, where is Aeschinus?

SYRUS: [Pointing to the house] There he is; he's waiting for you in the house.

CTESIPHO: Aha!

SYRUS: What is the matter?

CTESIPHO: The matter! Why, Syrus, I owe him my life for what he has done, the delightful fellow, who has thought nothing of his own disgrace compared with my interests. He has taken upon his own shoulders all the scandal, reproach, intrigue, and blame that belongs to me. He could do nothing more. What's that noise at the door?

SYRUS: Wait; he himself is coming out.

SCENE IV.

[Enter Aeschinus from Micio's house]

AESCHINUS: Where's that scoundrel?

SANNIO: [Aside] He is seeking me; is he bringing any money out with him? Confusion! I don't see any.

AESCHINUS: Oh, well met, Ctesipho; the very man I was looking for! How goes it? All is safely finished, so lay aside your gloom.

CTESIPHO: I do indeed lay it aside, because I have you for my brother. Oh, Aeschinus, my own brother, I am ashamed to praise you more to your face, for fear you should think I do it to flatter rather than because I am grateful to you.

AESCHINUS: Go on, goose; as if we didn't understand each other, Ctesipho. What I am sorry for is that we very nearly learned it too late, and that matters very nearly went so far that all the people in the world could not have helped you, if they had wanted.

CTESIPHO: I was ashamed to tell you.

AESCHINUS: That is folly, not shame. That you should have been on the point of leaving your native land all because of a trifle of money like that! Disgraceful! May heaven save us from such a fate!

CTESIPHO: I was wrong.

AESCHINUS: [To Syrus] And, pray, what terms does Sannio propose to us now?

SYRUS: He is quite reasonable now.

AESCHINUS: I'll go to the market place and pay him. Ctesipho, you go into the house to the girl.

SANNIO: Syrus, help me.

SYRUS: [To Aeschinus] Let us be going, for this man is in a hurry to go to Cyprus.

SANNIO: Yes; but not so much of a hurry as you wish. I have plenty of time to wait here.

SYRUS: You shall be paid, never fear.

SANNIO: But see that he pays me in full.

SYRUS: He will pay you in full; only hold your tongue and follow me this way.

SANNIO: I am following you.

[Aeschinus and Sannio depart. Syrus is detained by Ctesipho]

CTESIPHO: I say, Syrus.

SYRUS: What is it?

CTESIPHO: I entreat you, close your account with that loathsome villain as soon as may be, for fear that if he be made angrier than he is, my father may somehow get wind of this and I be ruined for ever.

SYRUS: You won't be, be of good cheer; go into the house and take your pleasure with her in the meantime, and tell them to lay the table for us and get things ready for dinner; as soon as I have transacted the business I will come home again with something to cook.

CTESIPHO: Do so, I pray you; after our success we will have a jolly day.

[Ctesipho goes into Micio's house; Syrus hurries after Aeschinus]

ACT III. SCENE I.

[Enter Sostrata from her house, followed by Canthara]

SOSTRATA: Pray, my dear nurse, what will happen now?

CANTHARA: What will happen, do you ask? All will go right, I hope.

SOSTRATA: My dear, her pains are just beginning to come upon her.

CANTHARA: You are as much afraid as if you had never seen a child born, never borne a child yourself.

SOSTRATA: Wretched woman that I am, I have no one, we are all alone, and Geta is not here. No one to send to the midwife, or to fetch Aeschinus.

CANTHARA: Heavens, he will be here soon, for he never misses a day without calling.

SOSTRATA: He is my only protection against my miseries.

CANTHARA: Mistress, after what has happened, things could not have turned out better than they have; since the girl has been violated, it is well that her seducer is such a fine young man, such a fine character and spirit, and belonging to so noble a family.

SOSTRATA: What you say is true; may the gods preserve him for us.

SCENE II.

[Enter Geta, hurrying in great excitement]

GETA: [To himself] Now this is a matter in which, if all mankind gave all the advice they could, and tried to find a remedy for this misfortune which has befallen me and my mistress and the daughter, they could give us no help. Oh, dear me! So many things suddenly threaten us on every side, from which there is no escape: violence, poverty, injustice, loneliness, disgrace. What a time we live in! What crimes are committed! What a vile race it is! What a wicked man he is!

SOSTRATA: [Aside to Canthara] Oh, dear me, why do I see Geta frightened and hurrying like this?

GETA: Neither honour, nor his plighted word, nor pity could hold him back or turn him from his purpose, nor yet the thought that the girl whom he had outraged was about to become a mother.

SOSTRATA: [Aside to Canthara] I don't quite understand what he's saying.

CANTHARA: Pray, Sostrata, let us go nearer to him.
[They approach]

GETA: Oh, dear! I am so hot with anger that I am scarcely in my right mind. I should like nothing better than to meet the whole of that household, that I might vent my rage upon them now, while the pain is fresh. I should not care how much I was punished if only I could take a thorough revenge upon them. First of all, I would choke the life out of the old man who begat the monster; then Syrus, the instigator of his wickedness! Oh, how I would mangle him! First, I would take him by the middle, hoist him up aloft, and bring his head down on to the ground, so that his brains bespattered the road. As

for the young man himself, I would first tear his eyes out, and then fling him down a cliff headfirst. The rest I would fall upon, beat them, dash them down, smash them, overthrow them. But why don't I tell my mistress this bad news straightway?

SOSTRATA: [To Canthara] Let us call him back. Geta!

GETA: Now, whoever you are, let me go my way.

SOSTRATA: It is I, Sostrata.

GETA: [Turning round] Where is she? It is you yourself that I am seeking, my mistress, it is you that I want; indeed, it's fortunate that you have fallen in with me.

SOSTRATA: What is it? Why are you in a flutter?

GETA: Oh, dear!

CANTHARA: Why are you in such a hurry, my good Geta? Wait and get your breath.

GETA: We are utterly—

SOSTRATA: What does that "utterly" mean?

GETA: Ruined. All's over with us.

SOSTRATA: Tell me, I beseech you, what the matter is?

GETA: By this time—

SOSTRATA: What is "by this time," Geta?

GETA: Aeschinus—

SOSTRATA: Well, what of him?

GETA: Is a stranger to our family.

SOSTRATA: What? Good gracious! Why so?

GETA: He has begun an amour with another woman.

SOSTRATA: Oh, miserable woman that I am!

GETA: And he makes no secret of it, but has carried her off from the slave-dealer in the sight of all men.

SOSTRATA: Is this proved to be true?

GETA: True! I saw it, Sostrata, with these very eyes.

SOSTRATA: Oh, poor wretch that I am! What is one now to believe, or whom should one believe? That our Aeschinus should have done this! He that was our very life, our only hope and help; he who used to swear that without her he could not live for one day; who used to say that he would set her child in his father's lap, and entreat him to let him marry her.

GETA: Mistress, dry your tears, and consider what we ought to do in this case. Are we to put up with his conduct, or shall we tell some one about it?

CANTHARA: Good gracious, man, are you in your right mind? Do you think that ours is a tale for anyone to hear?

GETA: I myself am against telling it. In the first place, what he has done shows that he doesn't care for us, and now, if we publish our story, I am quite sure he will contradict it, and then you will risk your good name and your daughter's prospects in life. Secondly, even if he admits the truth of our story, there's no point to letting him marry your daughter, since he loves another woman. So, in either case, you must hold your tongue.

SOSTRATA: Ah, but I won't; not a bit.

GETA: What will you do?

SOSTRATA: Publish the whole story.

CANTHARA: But, my dear Sostrata, just think what you are doing.

SOSTRATA: Matters can't be worse for us than they are; first of all she has no dowry, and then, too, her honour, her second dowry, is lost. I can't give her to anyone as a maid. If he disowns her, all that I shall have left to prove my story is the ring that he lost, which I have. Finally, as I am aware in my own mind that there has been nothing to blame in my conduct, Geta, that she has not received any money or anything else as compensation, and that neither of us has acted dishonourably, I'll try what the law will do for us.

GETA: Well, well, I agree; your suggestion is better.

SOSTRATA: Run as fast as you can and tell the whole story from the very beginning to Hegio, who was my Simulus' greatest friend, and was very fond of us.

GETA: Indeed, no one besides him takes any notice of us now. [Geta *departs*]

SOSTRATA: My good Canthara, do you haste to bring a midwife, so that she may be at hand when we want her.

[Canthara *departs;* Sostrata *goes into her house*]

SCENE III.

[*Enter* Demea, *much troubled*]

DEMEA: [*To himself*] Confusion! I have heard that my son Ctesipho took part with Aeschinus in this abduction. It would, indeed, be the last straw for me, if he is able to seduce the son who really is good for something, into mischief. Where am I to look for him? I suppose he has been carried off into some low dive; that profligate has led him away, I'm sure. Why, there I see Syrus going along. I will soon make out from him where he is. And yet Syrus is one of that gang; if he sees that I am looking for Ctesipho, the scoundrel will never tell me where he is. I won't let him see that I want to know.

[*Enter* Syrus *with a basket of provisions*]

SYRUS: [*To himself*] We told the old gentleman the whole story just as it happened from the outset. I never saw anyone better pleased.

DEMEA: [*Aside*] Great Jupiter, that the man should be such a fool!

SYRUS: He highly commended his son, and thanked me for having suggested the plan to him.

DEMEA: [*Aside*] I'm fit to burst with anger.

SYRUS: He counted out the money then and there, and gave us half a mina besides for our expenses. That has been laid out according to my ideas.

DEMEA: [*Aside*] Oh, yes, this is the man to entrust your business to, if you want it looked after properly! [*Advancing*]

SYRUS: Why, Demea, I didn't see you; how goes it?

DEMEA: How goes it! I am astounded at your proceedings.

SYRUS: Silly enough they are; to speak plainly,

ridiculous. [*He goes to the door and hands his basket to the cooks within*] Dromo, clean the fish all but that big eel; let him play in the water a little while; he shall be boned when I come back, but I don't want him killed till then.

DEMEA: Such atrocities as these!

SYRUS: Indeed, I don't approve of them myself, and I often cry out. [*To the cooks within*] Stephanio, mind you soak that salt fish thoroughly.

DEMEA: Good heavens! Is it his object to ruin his son, or does he think that it would be to his credit? Oh, dear me, I already seem to see the day when he will run away somewhere and enlist.

SYRUS: Indeed, Demea, this is true wisdom, not to see only what stares you in the face, but also what is to come.

DEMEA: Now then, is that music girl in your house now?

SYRUS: Yes, she's within.

DEMEA: Pray, is he going to keep her in his own house?

SYRUS: I believe he is; he's crazy enough to do it.

DEMEA: That such things should be done!

SYRUS: All the fault lies with his father's silly good-nature and criminal weakness.

DEMEA: I am ashamed of my brother and grieve for him.

SYRUS: Demea, I say this before your face as I would say it behind your back; there is too much, far too much difference between you and your brother. What a man you are, every inch a sage! He's a stupid fool! Would you have let your son do this?

DEMEA: Would I have let him? Wouldn't I have smelt a rat six months before he set about doing anything!

SYRUS: You need not tell me how sharp-sighted you are.

DEMEA: I hope I shall always be as sharp as I am now.

SYRUS: Each son is as his father would have him be.

DEMEA: What of mine? Have you seen him today?

SYRUS: Your son? [*Aside*] I'll send this old man off to the country. [*Aloud*] I think he's been working on your farm in the country for some time now.

DEMEA: Are you quite sure that he is there?

SYRUS: Why, I myself saw him off.

DEMEA: Capital! I was afraid he might be hanging about here.

SYRUS: And a fine rage he was in.

DEMEA: What about?

SYRUS: He quarrelled with his brother in the market place about this music girl.

DEMEA: Indeed?

SYRUS: Yes, he didn't mince matters; he came upon us all of a sudden when the money was being paid, and began to cry out, "Oh, Aeschinus, that you should behave so scandalously! That you should disgrace our family by such escapades!"

DEMEA: Oh, I weep with joy.

SYRUS: "It is not only this money," said he, "but your life that you are throwing away."

DEMEA: Long may he live; he, I hope, is a chip off the old block.

SYRUS: Quite.

DEMEA: Syrus, he's full of those wise saws.

SYRUS: Right. He had some one at home to learn them from.

DEMEA: I took care of that: I never lose an opportunity of instruction; I accustom him to virtue; in fact, I bid him look into all men's lives as into a mirror, and make others serve as examples to himself. I say to him, "Practise this."

SYRUS: Excellent!

DEMEA: "Avoid that."

SYRUS: A wise education!

DEMEA: I say, "Men praise this."

SYRUS: That's the way to teach.

DEMEA: "They disapprove of that."

SYRUS: You couldn't do better.

DEMEA: And moreover—

SYRUS: [Interrupting] Indeed, I have no leisure now to listen to you any longer, Demea. I have got some fish after my own heart; I must take care that they're not spoiled; for with us, Demea, this is as great a crime as it is with you, not to practise those noble precepts which you have just told us of, and I do my best to give my fellow-servants instruction after the same fashion, saying, "This is too salt"; "this is over-cooked"; "this is not properly cleaned"; "this is as it should be"; "bear this in mind another time." In fact, I bid them look into the dishes, Demea, as into a mirror, and tell them what they ought to do. I am aware that you think these pursuits of ours silly; but what are you to do? You must deal with a man according to his character. Have you anything further for me?

DEMEA: Only to pray that heaven may give you all better sense.

SYRUS: Are you going to the country?

DEMEA: Straightway.

SYRUS: Yes, indeed, what should you do here, where, if you did give good advice, no one would follow it. [Syrus goes into the house]

DEMEA: [To himself] Now I'm off to the country, because the boy I came here about has himself gone there: he is my only care; he belongs to me. As my brother wishes to have it so, he may look after the other one himself. [Looking down the street] But who is that I see in the distance? Is it not my fellow-tribesman, Hegio? If my eyes don't deceive me, it is he, indeed. Now there's a man who has been my friend from his youth up. Good heavens! We are not rich in citizens of his sort; he is of the good and honourable old school. It will be long ere the state suffers any injury from him. How pleased I am; I find life worth living even at the present day, when I see some remnants of that race still surviving. I'll wait for him here, that I may greet him and talk with him.

SCENE IV.

[Enter Hegio and Geta conversing]

HEGIO: By the immortal gods, this is a disgraceful action! What is it that you tell me?

GETA: The truth.

HEGIO: That such an ungentlemanly act should come from one of that family! By Jove, Aeschinus, you have shown little of your father's character in this!

DEMEA: [Aside] Of course, he must have heard about this music girl; the thing grieves him, though he is a stranger; but his father thinks nothing of it. Oh dear! I wish he were somewhere close by here, and could hear this.

HEGIO: Unless they behave properly, they shall not get away with it.

GETA: Hegio, our only hope is in you; we have no one beside you; you are our patron, our father. The old man, on his deathbed, entrusted us to your care. If you forsake us, we're lost.

HEGIO: Don't speak of such a thing. I won't desert you, nor could I, without disloyalty to my friend.

DEMEA: [Aside] I'll accost him. [Aloud] Hegio, my very best respects.

HEGIO: Well, you're the very man I was seeking; good day, Demea.

DEMEA: What is the matter?

HEGIO: That elder son of yours, Aeschinus, whom your brother adopted, has not behaved like a good man or like a gentleman.

DEMEA: What has he done?

HEGIO: You know my friend Simulus; he was about our own age?

DEMEA: Of course I knew him.

HEGIO: He has seduced his daughter.

DEMEA: Gracious heavens!

HEGIO: Wait, Demea, you haven't yet heard the worst part of it.

DEMEA: Why, is there anything worse?

HEGIO: Worse, indeed; for this might have been excused somehow; he was excited by the darkness, by passion, by wine, by youth; it is human nature. Now when he learned what he had done, he went of his own accord to the maiden's mother; he wept, prayed, and implored her, giving his word of honour and swearing that he would make her his wife. He was pardoned, the affair was hushed up, his word was believed. The girl became pregnant through his violence; this is the tenth month. Now, if you please, my young gentleman has carried off this music girl to live with him, and has deserted the other.

DEMEA: Are you sure of the truth of what you say?

HEGIO: There is the girl's mother, the girl herself, the thing itself; besides, here is Geta, not a bad slave as slaves go, and a hard-working one; he supports them, he alone maintains the whole household. Take him, put him in chains, and enquire into the matter.

GETA: Nay, put me to the torture if that isn't the

truth, Demea. Moreover, he won't deny it; bring him into my presence.

DEMEA: [*Aside*] I am ashamed. I don't know what to do, or what answer to give to him.

PAMPHILA: [*Within* Sostrata's *house*] Oh, dear me! I am in agonies. Juno, thou that bringest babes to light, save me, I beseech thee!

HEGIO: What's that? Can she be in labour?

GETA: She is indeed, Hegio.

HEGIO: Well, Demea, she now appeals to you to do of your own free will what the law can make you do. I hope that you will behave as becomes you in this matter; but, Demea, if you do not choose to do so, I will fight as hard as I can to protect her, and him who is gone. He was my kinsman; we were always together, both at home and in the wars; we endured bitter poverty together, and therefore I will struggle, and strive, and go to law, and lay down my very life sooner than desert his family.

DEMEA: I will talk to my brother, Hegio.

HEGIO: But, Demea, mind that you consider this point. You and your brother are powerful, rich, prosperous, and noble; but in proportion as life is easy to you, all the more ought you to judge things rightly and act righteously, if you wish to be esteemed honourable men. [*He turns towards* Sostrata's *door*]

DEMEA: Come back, come back; whatever is right shall be done.

HEGIO: That's what you ought to do. Geta, take me into the house to Sostrata.

[Hegio *and* Geta *go inside*]

DEMEA: [*To himself*] These things have not come to pass for want of my warnings. Please heaven, this may be the end of it all! But this excessive indulgence will certainly lead to some terrible mischief in the end. I will go and look for my brother, and pour all this into his ears. [Demea *departs towards the forum*]

SCENE V.

[*Re-enter* Hegio]

HEGIO: [*To* Sostrata *within*] Be of good cheer, Sostrata, and console the girl as well as you can. I will see Micio, if he's in the market place, and tell him the whole story, from beginning to end; then, if he is inclined to do his duty, he may do it; but if not, he shall give me his answer, and then I'll know without delay what steps I am to take. [Hegio *departs towards the forum*]

ACT IV. SCENE I.

[*Enter* Ctesipho *and* Syrus *from* Micio's *house*]

CTESIPHO: Did you say that my father went off to the country?

SYRUS: Long ago.

CTESIPHO: Pray tell me about it.

SYRUS: He is at his farm, and just about now, I fancy, he's engaged on some piece of work.

CTESIPHO: I trust so. I hope that, without doing himself any serious harm, he may so tire himself out that he won't be able to get out of bed for the whole of these next three days.

SYRUS: So be it; and better than that, if possible.

CTESIPHO: Yes; for I am desperately eager to pass all this day as I have begun it, in enjoyment; and the reason why I dislike this farm so much is that it is so near Athens. Now, if it had been further off, night would have overtaken him before he could have returned here. As it is, when he doesn't see me there, he will run back here, I am quite sure; he'll ask me where I have been; he'll say, "I haven't seen you the whole of this day." What answer am I to make?

SYRUS: Doesn't anything come into your head?

CTESIPHO: Nothing whatever.

SYRUS: So much the worse for you. Have you no dependent, no friend, no guest from abroad?

CTESIPHO: Yes, I have; what then?

SYRUS: Can't you say that you were attending to them?

CTESIPHO: When I wasn't attending to them? No, that won't do.

SYRUS: Yes, it will.

CTESIPHO: In the daytime, I grant you; but, Syrus, if I pass the night here, what reason can I give?

SYRUS: Dear me! How I wish it was the fashion to attend to one's friends by night as well as by day! But don't you trouble yourself, I know his ways perfectly; when he is at his angriest I can make him as quiet as a lamb.

CTESIPHO: How do you manage it?

SYRUS: He likes to hear your praises; I make a regular god of you in his mind. I tell him about your virtues.

CTESIPHO: My virtues?

SYRUS: Yes, yours; and straightway the tears roll down his cheeks for joy, as if he was a child. But look out!

CTESIPHO: What is it?

SYRUS: Talk of the devil!

CTESIPHO: Is it my father?

SYRUS: His very self.

CTESIPHO: O Syrus! What are we to do?

SYRUS: Run indoors directly, and I will see after him.

CTESIPHO: If he asks you, mind, you haven't seen me anywhere; do you hear?

SYRUS: Can't you hold your tongue?

[Ctesipho *goes inside*]

SCENE II.

[*Enter* Demea]

DEMEA: [*To himself*] Indeed I am an unlucky man; first of all I can't find my brother anywhere in the world, and besides that, while I was looking for my son, I saw a labourer from my farm who says that my son is not in the country. I don't know what to do.

CTESIPHO: [*Aside to* Syrus *from the house*] Syrus!

SYRUS: [*Aside to* Ctesipho] What's the matter?

CTESIPHO: [*Aside to* Syrus] Is he after me?

SYRUS: [*Aside to* Ctesipho] Yes.

CTESIPHO: [*Aside to* Syrus] I am lost!

SYRUS: [*Aside to* Ctesipho] No, keep your heart up.

DEMEA: What a mass of disaster this is! I can't get a right understanding of it, except on the supposition that I was born for nothing else but to endure miseries. I am the first to become aware of the misfortunes of the family: I learn the truth of them first; then, too, I am the first to bring the bad news to Micio; and I suffer alone for all that is done.

SYRUS: [*Aside*] He makes me laugh saying that he was the first to know, when he's the only man who knows nothing about it.

DEMEA: Now I've come back, I'll see whether my brother has come home.

CTESIPHO: [*Aside to* Syrus *from the house*] Syrus, pray take care he does not blunder straight in here.

SYRUS: [*Aside to* Ctesipho] Can't you be quiet. I'll take care.

CTESIPHO: [*Aside to* Syrus] I won't ever trust you to do that today; I'll lock myself in some room with the girl, that'll be the safest thing to do.

SYRUS: [*Aside to* Ctesipho] Come, I'll send him away.

DEMEA: Why, there's that scoundrel Syrus.

SYRUS: [*Pretending not to see* Demea] No, by heaven! If this sort of thing goes on, nobody can stay in this house. I should like to know how many masters I have; what misery this is!

DEMEA: What's he babbling about? What does he want? What are you saying, my good man? Is my brother at home?

SYRUS: What the devil do you mean by your "good man"? I am done for!

DEMEA: What's the matter with you?

SYRUS: The matter! Why, Ctesipho has thrashed me and that music girl almost to death.

DEMEA: Eh! What's that you tell me?

SYRUS: Why, see how he has split open my lip.

DEMEA: What did he do it for?

SYRUS: He says that it was by my advice that she was bought.

DEMEA: Didn't you say just now that you had seen him off to the country?

SYRUS: So I did, but after that he came back raving mad, and had no pity. He should have been ashamed to beat an old man like me; why, I carried him in my arms when he was only so big.

DEMEA: Well done, Ctesipho, you take after your father. Come, I count you a man.

SYRUS: What, do you praise him for it? Nay, if he is wise, he'll keep his fists to himself for the future.

DEMEA: He did bravely.

SYRUS: Oh, very bravely, to beat a wretched girl, and me, a slave, who dared not hit him back. Mighty bravely, indeed!

DEMEA: He could not have done better; like me, he saw that you were at the bottom of all this business. But is my brother at home?

SYRUS: No, he isn't.

DEMEA: I wonder where I can find him.

SYRUS: I know where he is, but I'll never tell you the place today.

DEMEA: Eh, what's that you say?

SYRUS: Just that.

DEMEA: You will have your head broken in a minute.

SYRUS: Well, I don't know the man's name, but I know where the place is.

DEMEA: Then tell me where the place is.

SYRUS: Do you know that colonnade at the butcher's shop down the street?

DEMEA: Of course I do.

SYRUS: When you've passed that, go straight up the street; when you've come there, there's a hill leading downwards; down that you go, and then there is a chapel on this side [*pointing*]; close by that there is a lane.

DEMEA: [*Looking*] Where?

SYRUS: [*Pointing*] There, where the great wild fig-tree stands.

DEMEA: I know.

SYRUS: Go that way.

DEMEA: But that lane is no thoroughfare.

SYRUS: True, by Jove! Why, what a fool I must be! I have made a mistake. You must come back to the colonnade again; indeed, this is a much shorter way, and less chance of your missing it. Do you know that house there, that belongs to the rich Cratinus?

DEMEA: Yes, I know it.

SYRUS: When you have passed it, turn to the left, go straight on that way till you come to Diana's temple, then to the right. Before you come to the city gate, just by the pond, there's a pounding-mill, and opposite a carpenter's shop; that's where he is.

DEMEA: What is he doing there?

SYRUS: He has ordered some benches to be made with oak legs, to stand the sun.

DEMEA: [*Sneering*] For you to lie upon and drink. Very well; I had better be off to him. [Demea *departs*]

SYRUS: Off with you, in heaven's name! I'll work you today as you deserve, you old fossil! [*Reflecting*] It's very wrong of Aeschinus not to come; our dinner is being spoiled. Ctesipho is thinking of nothing but his love; I must look out for myself. I'll go in and pick out the choicest morsel of all for myself, and then I'll linger over my wine for the rest of the day. [*He goes into the house*]

SCENE III.

[*Enter* Micio *and* Hegio, *conversing*]

MICIO: Hegio, I don't see anything in this for which I deserve such high praise. I am only doing my duty; I am repairing the fault which we have committed;

unless you used to reckon me among those who think that you are doing them an injury and abuse you if you complain of the wrong they have done you. Do you thank me because I don't act thus?

HEGIO: Oh, not at all; I never thought of you otherwise than as you are. But, Micio, I pray you, come with me to the girl's mother, and tell her yourself what you have told me, that all this suspicion arose on account of Aeschinus' brother and his music girl—

MICIO: Well, if you think it right, or that it needs doing, let us go.

HEGIO: You are right, for you will cheer up the woman, who is wasting away with sorrow and wretchedness, and you will have done your duty; still, if you don't wish to, I myself will tell her what you said.

MICIO: No, I'll go.

HEGIO: You are right. Somehow all those who are unsuccessful in life are prone to suspicion; they take everything as an insult, and believe that they are being slighted because they are helpless; so you are more likely to win their pardon if you defend yourself in person before them.

MICIO: What you say is true and proper.

HEGIO: Then come this way after me into the house.

MICIO: With all my heart.

[*They go into* Sostrata's *house*]

SCENE IV.

[*Enter* Aeschinus, *much troubled*]

AESCHINUS: [*To himself*] I am in terrible distress; so much trouble has come upon me all of a sudden that I don't know what to do with myself or how to act. My limbs quake with fear; my mind is stupefied with dread; my heart can form no plan. Heavens! How can I get myself out of this mess? I have become gravely suspected, and on very good grounds. Sostrata believes that I have bought this music girl for myself. The old woman told me this; she was going to fetch a midwife when I saw her. I straightway went to her and asked her how Pamphila was, whether her confinement was at hand and that was why she was fetching the midwife. She cried out, "Be off with you, Aeschinus; you have fooled us long enough; you have deceived us long enough with your fine professions." "Eh," says I, "pray what is all this?" "Good-bye," says she, "keep the girl you like best." I saw straightway what the women suspected, but still I restrained myself, for fear of telling that old chatterbox anything about my brother, and letting out the whole story. Now, what am I to do? Shall I tell them that the girl is my brother's mistress? That secret must not be breathed to anyone. And never mind that, for I think the secret may be kept; but I fear they would not believe the truth; so many circumstances point to the other as the real story. I myself carried off the girl; I paid the money for her; she was brought home to my house. I admit that I was wrong in that matter, not to have told my father the whole story of my love, and wrung permission from him to marry her. Hitherto I have been idling; now then, Aeschinus, my man, wake up. Now, first of all, I will go to the women and clear my character. Let me go up to the door. Oh, dear! I am always in a fright when I begin to knock at this door. [*Knocking*] Ho, there! It is Aeschinus. Open the door quick, somebody. Here is somebody coming out; I will stand aside here.

SCENE V.

[*Enter* Micio *from* Sostrata's *house*]

MICIO: [*To* Sostrata *within*] Do as I tell you, Sostrata; I will see Aeschinus, that he may know what has been done. But who is that who knocked?

AESCHINUS: [*Aside*] Heavens, it's my father! Confusion!

MICIO: Aeschinus!

AESCHINUS: [*Aside*] What is he doing here?

MICIO: Was it you who knocked at this door? [*Aside*] He doesn't answer. Why shouldn't I play with him for a while? It's right, seeing that he never chose to tell me anything about this. [*Aloud*] Do you give me no answer?

AESCHINUS: It wasn't that door, as far as I know.

MICIO: Indeed! I was wondering what business you could have here. [*Aside*] He blushes; all is well.

AESCHINUS: Tell me, pray, father, what business you have there.

MICIO: I have none. A friend just now brought me away from the market place as a witness.

AESCHINUS: What for?

MICIO: I'll tell you. Some poverty-stricken women live here; I don't suppose that you know them, indeed, I am quite sure you don't, for they have only lately moved into this house.

AESCHINUS: Well, what then?

MICIO: There is a young girl and her mother.

AESCHINUS: Yes, go on.

MICIO: The young girl has lost her father. This friend of mine is her next of kin, and is compelled by the law to marry her.

AESCHINUS: [*Aside*] The devil!

MICIO: [*Overhearing*] What's the matter?

AESCHINUS: Oh, nothing. I am all right. Go on.

MICIO: He is come to take her away with him, for he lives at Miletus.

AESCHINUS: What? To take the girl away with him?

MICIO: Yes.

AESCHINUS: What? All the way to Miletus?

MICIO: Just so.

AESCHINUS: [*Aside*] I feel as if I should faint. [*To* Micio] And what of the women? What do they say?

MICIO: What do you suppose they would say? Nothing at all. The mother did, indeed, make up a story that the girl had had a child by somebody else, some man or other, she didn't tell his name, and said that he came first, and that the girl ought not to marry my friend.

AESCHINUS: Well, don't you think that she was right to ask this?

MICIO: No.

AESCHINUS: What? "No?" And, father, is this man going to take her away?

MICIO: Why shouldn't he take her away?

AESCHINUS: Father, you have acted harshly and pitilessly, and even, to be plain, ungentlemanly.

MICIO: Why?

AESCHINUS: Do you ask me why? What do you suppose must be the feelings of that poor fellow, her former lover, who, unhappy man, perhaps is still desperately fond of her, when he has to stand by and see her carried off before his face and taken out of his sight? Father, it is a shameful thing to do.

MICIO: On what grounds do you say that? Who betrothed her to him? Who gave her to him? When was she married? Whom did she marry? Who gave his consent to these proceedings? Why did the man marry a girl who belonged to another?

AESCHINUS: Why, was such a great girl to sit at home waiting till her relative came to Athens from all that way off? That was what you should have urged, father, and pleaded.

MICIO: Absurd! Was I to plead against the interest of the man whom I had come to help as a witness? But what have we to do with this, Aeschinus, or what are these women to us? Let us be going. [As Aeschinus breaks down and weeps] What's the matter? Why are you in tears?

AESCHINUS: I beseech you, father, listen to me.

MICIO: I have heard all, Aeschinus, and I know all; I love you, and so I take all the more interest in your doings.

AESCHINUS: As I hope, father, that I shall deserve your love as long as I live, so I declare that I am deeply grieved at having committed this fault, and I am ashamed of myself in your sight.

MICIO: I verily believe you, for I know your honourable character; but I fear you are too remiss in this matter. In what city do you suppose that you are living? Here you have seduced a young lady whom you had no right to touch. This was your first sin, and a great one; a great sin, but after all, human nature. Many good men have done the same. But after that, pray did you ever think the matter over, or look forward on your own account to what would have to be done? If you were ashamed to tell me this story yourself, how was I to learn it? While you were hesitating, ten months have slipped away. You have, as far as in you lay, betrayed yourself and this poor girl and the child. What! Did you suppose that the gods would manage this business for you while you lay asleep, and that she would be brought home to you and installed in your bedroom without your taking any trouble about it? I hope you won't manage other business so negligently. Now

be of good cheer, she shall be your wife.

AESCHINUS: What?

MICIO: Be of good cheer, I say.

AESCHINUS: Father, I beseech you, are you mocking me?

MICIO: Mocking you? Why should I?

AESCHINUS: I don't know; but I am so terribly anxious that this should be true, that I am all the more inclined to doubt it.

MICIO: Go home, and pray to the gods that you may bring home your bride; off with you!

AESCHINUS: What? My bride already?

MICIO: Already.

AESCHINUS: What? Now?

MICIO: As soon as may be.

AESCHINUS: Father, may all the gods abhor me if I don't love you better than my own eyes.

MICIO: What? Better than her?

AESCHINUS: Just as much.

MICIO: [Smiling] That's very kind of you.

AESCHINUS: I say, where's that man from Miletus?

MICIO: He's gone; he's gone on board ship. But why do you linger here?

AESCHINUS: Father, you go and pray to the gods, rather than I, for I am quite sure that they will be more likely to hear your prayers, as you are a far better man than I.

MICIO: I'll go into the house to make what preparations are necessary; you, if you are wise, do as I have said. [Micio goes inside]

AESCHINUS: [To himself] What's this? Is this to be a father or to be a son? What more could he do for me if he were my brother or my bosom friend? Is he not a man to be loved? To be carried next one's heart? His kindness, however, has made me very anxious, for fear that through carelessness I may do something that will displease him. I must be on my guard. But why don't I go into the house, that I may not myself delay my own marriage? [Aeschinus goes inside]

SCENE VI.

[Enter Demea wearily]

DEMEA: [To himself] I have walked till I'm dead tired. Syrus, may great Jove confound you with your directions. I have crawled about all over the town—to the gate, to the pond; where haven't I been? There was no carpenter's shop there, and not a soul said he had seen my brother. Now I've made up my mind to wait for him in his house till he returns.

SCENE VII.

[Enter Micio from his house]

MICIO: [To Aeschinus within] I'll go and tell

them that there shall be no delay on our part.

DEMEA: Why, there's the man himself. I have long been seeking you, Micio.

MICIO: What for?

DEMEA: I bring you news of more outrageous wickedness done by that nice young man.

MICIO: More, eh?

DEMEA: Hanging matters.

MICIO: Oh, nonsense.

DEMEA: You don't know what sort of a man he is.

MICIO: Yes, I do.

DEMEA: Fool, you are mooning, thinking that I mean the affair of the music girl; but this is a rape committed on a young lady, a citizen of Athens.

MICIO: Yes, I know.

DEMEA: What? You know of it and you endure it?

MICIO: Why shouldn't I endure it?

DEMEA: Tell me, don't you cry out at it? Doesn't it drive you mad?

MICIO: No, it does not. I might have preferred—

DEMEA: There is a baby boy born.

MICIO: Heaven bless him!

DEMEA: The girl hasn't a penny.

MICIO: So I have heard.

DEMEA: And she is to be married without a dowry.

MICIO: Of course.

DEMEA: What's to be done now?

MICIO: What the occasion requires; the girl must be brought over from that house to this.

DEMEA: O Jupiter! Is that the way that you ought to take it?

MICIO: What more can I do?

DEMEA: What can you do? Why, if you are not really put out at this, at any rate it would be your duty to pretend that you are.

MICIO: Why, I have betrothed the girl to him; the whole affair is settled; the wedding is just going to take place. I have set them free from all fear; this was much more my duty.

DEMEA: But, Micio, do you approve of what he has done?

MICIO: No, not if I could alter it; but since I can't, I make the best of it. The life of man is like playing with dice: if you don't throw exactly what you want, you must use your wits to make shift with what you have thrown.

DEMEA: Make shift, indeed! By this use of your wits you have lost twenty minae for that music girl, whom you must now dispose of for nothing, if you can't sell her.

MICIO: I shall not; nor do I want to sell her.

DEMEA: Then what will you do with her?

MICIO: She will live with us.

DEMEA: Heavens and earth! A mistress and a wife in the same household?

MICIO: Why not?

DEMEA: Do you think you're in your right mind?

MICIO: I believe so.

DEMEA: So help me heaven, when I consider what a fool you are, I believe that you mean to keep her to give you music lessons!

MICIO: Why shouldn't she?

DEMEA: And will she give the bride music lessons too?

MICIO: Of course she will.

DEMEA: And you will dance "the ladies' chain" between them, I suppose?

MICIO: Very well.

DEMEA: Very well?

MICIO: Yes; and you shall join us, if need be.

DEMEA: Damn it! Aren't you ashamed of this?

MICIO: Now, Demea, just put away this ill temper of yours, and be merry and good-humoured, as you ought to be, on your son's wedding-day. I'll go and see the ladies, and then I'll come back here again. [Micio *goes into* Sostrata's *house*]

DEMEA: [*To himself*] Oh, Jupiter, what a life! What morals! What folly! A bride without a dowry is to be brought home; there's a music girl in the house; an extravagant establishment; a youth given over to debauchery, an old dotard. Why, the goddess of Salvation could not save this household, even if she wanted to.

ACT V. SCENE I.

[*Enter* Syrus *from the house*]

SYRUS: [*Drunk, talking to himself*] Faith, Syry, my boy, you've done finely for yourself and managed your part of the business sumptuously. Well, now that I've had a bellyful of all sorts of good things indoors, I've taken a fancy to a stroll out in front of the house here.

DEMEA: See, there's an instance of the way the household is kept in order.

SYRUS: Why, here's our old gentleman. How goes it? What are you so gloomy about?

DEMEA: Oh, you scoundrel!

SYRUS: Shut up! None of your jaw here, old wiseacre!

DEMEA: If you were my slave—

SYRUS: You'd have been a rich man, Demea, and have made your fortune.

DEMEA: I'd see that you were made a warning to all men.

SYRUS: What for? What harm have I done?

DEMEA: Do you ask me? Why, just at the very crisis, and after the worst of wrongdoing, you get drunk, you scoundrel, before things have even been quieted down, just as if you had done some good action.

SYRUS: [*Aside*] Oh, hell! I wish I'd stayed indoors.

SCENE II.

[Dromo *appears in the doorway*]

DROMO: Here, Syrus, Ctesipho wants you to come back.

SYRUS: Get along with you!

[Dromo *disappears*]

DEMEA: Ctesipho here! What's that he says?

SYRUS: Nothing.

DEMEA: Is Ctesipho here, scoundrel?

SYRUS: No.

DEMEA: Then why did he mention his name?

SYRUS: It's another man, a little parasite chap. Don't you know him?

DEMEA: I will directly. [*He approaches the door*]

SYRUS: What are you doing? Where are you going to? [*Catching hold of* Demea]

DEMEA: Let me go! [*Threatens him*]

SYRUS: I say, don't.

DEMEA: Will you take your hands off me, you villain, or do you prefer to have your brains knocked out here? [Demea *dashes into the house*]

SYRUS: He's gone. A damned unwelcome addition to their wine party, especially to Ctesipho. What am I to do now? Better get out of the way somewhere into a corner, and sleep off this drop of wine, until all these rows quiet down; that's what I'll do. [Syrus *goes inside unsteadily*]

SCENE III.

[*Enter* Micio *from* Sostrata's *house*]

MICIO: [*To Sostrata within*] We have everything ready, as I told you, Sostrata; so when you like— Why, who is that knocking so loud at my door?

[*Re-enter* Demea *from* Micio's *house*]

DEMEA: [*To himself*] Oh, dear me! What shall I do? What's to be done? How can I cry aloud and lament enough? O heavens, earth, and seas!

MICIO: [*Aside*] There you are! He has found out the whole story; you may be sure that that's what he's crying out about. There'll be a row. I must try to help.

DEMEA: See, there he is, the debaucher of both our sons!

MICIO: Pray restrain your passion and calm yourself.

DEMEA: I have restrained it. I am calm. I don't say another word of abuse. Let us look at the facts. Was it not arranged between us (you started the arrangement) that you were not to meddle with my son, and I was not to meddle with yours? Answer me.

MICIO: It was, I don't deny it.

DEMEA: Then why is he now drinking in your house? Why do you harbour my boy, Micio? Why do you buy a mistress for him? Isn't it fair that I should have as much rights over my son as you have over yours? Since I don't look after your son, don't you look after mine.

MICIO: What you say is not fair; no, it isn't; for it is an old proverb that friends have all things in common.

DEMEA: How clever! But this suggestion is a little late, isn't it?

MICIO: If you don't mind, Demea, listen while I say a few words. First of all, if you are vexed at the extravagance of your sons, pray bear these facts in mind. You, in the beginning, were going to bring up both your sons as your means permitted, because you supposed that your fortune would be enough for both of them, and of course you thought at that time that I should marry. Well, you keep on in that same old style now: pinch, scrape, and be stingy. Take care to leave them as large a fortune as ever you can, and glory in doing so. But let them use my fortune, which is available for them contrary to their expectations. Your property will not suffer thereby. What you get from me you may count as clear gain. If you would think these things over impartially, Demea, you would save both me and yourself and the boys much unpleasantness.

DEMEA: I pass over the expense; but their morals—

MICIO: Stay. I know; I was coming to that. There are many signs in people's characters whereby you may easily guess, when two of them are doing the same thing, how it will affect them, so that you can often say: "It will do this one no harm, it will do that one harm"; not because the thing that they are doing is different, but because their characters are different. Now by what I see of them, I am confident that they will turn out as we wish. I see that they are sensible, intelligent, high-minded, and fond of one another. You can see that they are gentlemen in thought and disposition; you can pull them in any day you please. Perhaps you are afraid that they are rather neglectful of business. Oh, my dear Demea, as we grow older we grow wiser about everything else, but the one vice which age brings to us, is that of being keener after money-making than we ought to be. Time will make them sharp enough at that.

DEMEA: Always provided, Micio, that your specious reasoning and easy good nature does not do them too much harm.

MICIO: Hush, I shall not do that. Now let us say no more about this business; be my guest today and clear your brow.

DEMEA: Well, it seems to be the fashion; I must do so; but at break of day I am off to the country with my son.

MICIO: Oh, tonight, for all I care; only do be cheerful today.

DEMEA: And I'll take that music girl away with me.

MICIO: Then you will have won your battle. By so doing you will quite gain your son's heart; only mind you keep her.

DEMEA: I will see to that: at the farm I'll make her cook and grind corn till she's all over ashes and smoke and flour; besides, I'll make her go gleaning under the noonday sun; I'll burn her as black as a coal.

MICIO: Right; now you seem to me to be showing good sense; and there I'd make him sleep with her, even if he doesn't want to.

DEMEA: Are you laughing at me? Well, you are lucky to be able to take it so. I feel—

MICIO: Now, no more of that.

DEMEA: Well, I'm just leaving off.

MICIO: Then come into the house, and let us spend this day as we ought.

[*They go into* Micio's *house. A short time is supposed to elapse before the next scene*]

SCENE IV.

[*Enter* Demea *from* Micio's *house*]

DEMEA: [*To himself*] No man ever lived in so well-regulated a fashion but what circumstances, years, and experience must continually present something new to him, and suggest something to him; so that you don't know what you once thought you knew, and cast away what you once supposed to be of the first importance. That is what's happened to me, for now, when my time is almost spent, I renounce the severe life that I have hitherto lived. Why do I do that? Because I have been taught by circumstances that nothing suits a man better than easygoing good nature. Anybody could tell this easily by comparing me and my brother. He has always spent his life at leisure, and in entertainments, in good humour, with unruffled temper, giving no man a harsh word, with a smile for everyone: he has lived to please himself, and has spent money on himself alone; well, all men speak well of him and love him. I, the countryman, rude, harsh, stingy, ill-tempered and self-willed—I married, and what wretchedness I went through. Sons were born: more trouble; and then, why, dear me! in trying to do the best I can for them, I have wasted all my life and manhood. Now, at the end of my days, what is my reward at their hands? Dislike; while that brother of mine has all a father's pleasures without the trouble. They are fond of him, and they run away from me. They tell him all their secrets, they love him, they are both at his house, and I am left alone. They hope that he will live, while of course they look forward to my death. Thus, for a small outlay, he has made them into his own sons, after I had brought them up with enormous trouble. I get all the pain, and he enjoys all the pleasure. Come, come now, let us try the other tack; let me see whether I can speak gently or behave kindly, since my brother challenges me to do so. I also demand to be loved and thought much of by my people; if that can be got by giving them presents and humouring their whim, I will not be behindhand. There will be a deficit in my exchequer, but that won't matter to me, seeing that I am the elder brother.

SCENE V.

[*Enter* Syrus *from* Micio's *house*]

SYRUS: Demea, your brother begs you to keep near the house.

DEMEA: Who's there? Oh, my good Syrus! How goes it? How's all with you?

SYRUS: Very well.

DEMEA: [*Aside*] I'm getting on capitally. There, for the first time in my life I have forced myself, against my true character, to add these three sayings, "My good," "how goes it?" and "how's all with you?" [*Aloud*] You are not a badly behaved slave, and I should be glad to do you some service.

SYRUS: Much obliged.

DEMEA: Indeed, Syrus, this is true, and facts will prove it to you before long.

SCENE VI.

[*Enter* Geta *from* Sostrata's *house*]

GETA: [*To* Sostrata *within*] I'm going across to our neighbours', ma'am, to see when they will be ready to fetch the young lady. [*Looking round*] Why, there is Demea! Good day, sir.

DEMEA: Oh, what's your name?

GETA: Geta.

DEMEA: Geta, I have today made up my mind that you are an invaluable fellow, for I think that the worth of a slave is thoroughly proved when he is zealous for his owner, as I have noticed you are, Geta, and for that I shall be pleased to be of service to you whenever I have an opportunity. [*Aside*] I am studying how to be amiable, and really making progress.

GETA: You are very good to think so.

DEMEA: [*Aside*] I am beginning with the mob and gradually winning their affections.

SCENE VII.

[*Enter* Aeschinus *from* Micio's *house*]

AESCHINUS: [*To himself*] They plague me to death, wanting to make such an ultra-solemn wedding of it; they are wasting the whole day with their preparations.

DEMEA: How goes it, Aeschinus?

AESCHINUS: Why, father, are you here?

DEMEA: Yes, your father both in will and in deed, who loves you more than his own eyes. Why don't you bring home your bride?

AESCHINUS: I want to, but I am waiting for flute-players and people to sing the wedding hymn.

DEMEA: Now, will you take the advice of an old man like me?

AESCHINUS: What do you advise?

DEMEA: Get rid of the wedding procession, hymns, torches, flute-players and all, and order this party-wall in the garden to be pulled down as soon as may be. Bring your bride through that way; throw the two houses into one. Bring her mother and all her household over to us.

AESCHINUS: Well said, my most charming father.

DEMEA: [Aside] Capital! I'm called charming already. My brother's house will become a thoroughfare; he will take a host of people into it, he will spend much money in entertaining them, there will be lots of expenses—well! what do I care? I am charming, and making myself popular. [To Aeschinus] Here, order old Croesus to pay you twenty minae straightway. Syrus, why don't you go and do what you are ordered?

SYRUS: What am I to do?

DEMEA: Pull down the wall. [To Geta, as Syrus goes inside] You go and bring the ladies through the garden.

GETA: May the gods bless you, Demea, for I see that you are a true well-wisher to our family.

DEMEA: I think that they deserve it. [To Aeschinus, as Geta goes into Sostrata's house] What do you say?

AESCHINUS: I quite agree.

DEMEA: It is much more proper than that she should be brought here along the public road, being ill and weak after childbirth.

AESCHINUS: Father, I never saw anything better arranged.

DEMEA: That's the way I always do arrange things; but see, here's Micio coming out of his house.

SCENE VIII.

[Enter Micio, somewhat upset]

MICIO: [To the men within who are pulling down the wall] My brother's orders, d'ye say? Where is my brother? [Seeing him] Are these your orders, Demea?

DEMEA: My orders are both in this and all other matters to make one household of it as far as may be, to cherish, help, and unite them.

AESCHINUS: Do so, father, I pray you.

MICIO: I think that we ought.

DEMEA: Nay, it's our duty so to do. In the first place, this bride has a mother.

MICIO: She has; what then?

DEMEA: An honest and discreet lady.

MICIO: So they say.

DEMEA: She's a trifle elderly.

MICIO: I know that she is.

DEMEA: She has long been too old to bear children, and she has no one to take care of her, a lone woman.

MICIO: [Aside] What is he driving at?

DEMEA: [To Micio] It is your duty to marry her, and [to Aeschinus] yours to see that he does so.

MICIO: Me marry!

DEMEA: Yes, you.

MICIO: Me?

DEMEA: Yes, you, I say.

MICIO: Nonsense.

DEMEA: [To Aeschinus] If you're a man, he'll do it.

AESCHINUS: Father, dear.

MICIO: What, you young donkey, are you giving ear to his proposals?

DEMEA: It is no use, you cannot help doing it.

MICIO: You're out of your mind.

AESCHINUS: Let me win your consent, father.

MICIO: You're mad; be off with you.

DEMEA: Come, do your son this favour.

MICIO: Are you in your right senses? Am I, in my sixty-fifth year, to become a bridegroom for the first time, and marry a decrepit old woman? Is that what you seriously propose that I should do?

AESCHINUS: Do it, father; I have promised them that you will.

MICIO: Promised, have you! Promise what is your own to give, my boy.

DEMEA: Come! Suppose he were to ask some greater favour of you.

MICIO: As if this wasn't the greatest of all!

DEMEA: Grant it.

AESCHINUS: Don't be cross.

DEMEA: Do it; promise you will do it.

MICIO: Leave me alone, can't you?

DEMEA: I won't, till you give your consent.

MICIO: This is assault and battery.

DEMEA: Behave generously, Micio.

MICIO: Although this marriage seems to me to be a mistaken, absurd, foolish proceeding, yet if you are so eager for it, let it take place.

AESCHINUS: You are right.

DEMEA: You deserve my affection; but—

MICIO: But what?

DEMEA: Now that I have got my wish, I will tell you.

MICIO: What next? What more am I to do?

DEMEA: The next of kin to these ladies, who is now a connection of ours, is Hegio, a poor man; it is our duty to do something for him.

MICIO: What are we to do?

DEMEA: There is a small piece of land here just outside the city, which you let out on hire. Let us give him the use of it.

MICIO: A small piece, d'ye call it?

DEMEA: If it were a big one, still you ought to do it; he has been like a father to her, he is a good man, and one of ourselves now; it is right to give it to him. Besides, I am now myself putting into practice the maxim which you, Micio, enunciated so wisely and so well a short time ago: "A vice common to all mankind is that of being too keen after money when we are old." It is our duty to put away this reproach from us; your maxim is a true one, and should be acted upon.

AESCHINUS: Dear father.

MICIO: Well, well, he shall have it, since Aeschinus so wishes it.

AESCHINUS: I am delighted.

DEMEA: Now you are truly my brother alike in body and in soul. [Aside] I am cutting his throat with his own sword.

SCENE IX.

[Enter Syrus]

SYRUS: I have done what you ordered, Demea.

DEMEA: You're an honest fellow; and now my opinion is that this day Syrus ought to be made a free man.

MICIO: Him a free man? Why, what for?

DEMEA: For many things.

SYRUS: Oh, dear Demea, you are indeed a good man. I have watched over both your sons for you ever since they were boys with the greatest care; I have taught them and admonished them, and always given them the best advice that I could.

DEMEA: The facts prove that you did; moreover, you can be trusted to buy fish for dinner, you can bring a courtesan into the house, and you can prepare a feast in the middle of the day. It requires no ordinary man to do this.

SYRUS: What a pleasant old gentleman!

DEMEA: Moreover, he helped today to buy the music girl. He managed the business, and he ought to be repaid for his trouble. The other slaves will be all the better for the example; besides, Aeschinus wishes it.

MICIO: [To Aeschinus] Do you wish it?

AESCHINUS: I do.

MICIO: Well, if you wish it: [To Syrus] Syrus, come here to me. [Strikes him with a stick] Be a free man.

SYRUS: 'Tis generously done: I return my thanks to you all; and to you in particular, Demea.

DEMEA: I rejoice at it.

AESCHINUS: And I too.

SYRUS: I believe it. I wish this my joy were complete, and that I might see my wife Phrygia free too.

DEMEA: An excellent woman, truly!

SYRUS: And the first that suckled my young master's son, your grandson today.

DEMEA: Indeed? Why, if she really was the first that suckled him, without any question she ought to be made free.

MICIO: What, for that?

DEMEA: For that: in fine, you shall have the price of her freedom from me.

SYRUS: May the gods ever grant you all your desires, Demea!

MICIO: Syrus, you've done nicely for yourself today.

DEMEA: Moreover, brother, if you'll do your duty, and let him have a little ready money to begin with, he'll soon repay it.

MICIO: Not this much. [Snapping his fingers]

AESCHINUS: He's an industrious honest fellow.

SYRUS: I'll return it, indeed; only let me have it.

AESCHINUS: Do, father.

MICIO: I'll consider it.

DEMEA: He'll do it.

SYRUS: O excellent man!

AESCHINUS: O delightful father!

MICIO: What means all this, brother? Whence this sudden change in your temper? What is this whim? What a hasty fit of prodigality!

DEMEA: I'll tell you, in order to make you realise that your passing for an easy agreeable man is not genuine, or founded on equity and good sense, but is due to your overlooking things, your indulgence, and giving them whatever they want. Now, Aeschinus, if I am, therefore, odious to you, because I don't wholly humour you in everything right or wrong, I'll concern myself with you no farther; squander, buy, do whatever you have a mind to. But if you had rather that I check and restrain you in pursuits, which, by reason of your youth, you are not aware of the consequences of, when passion misleads you or prompts you too far, and that I direct you, as occasion offers: behold me ready to do you that service.

AESCHINUS: Father, we submit to you entirely: you best know what is fit and proper. But how will you do with my brother?

DEMEA: I consent that he may have his girl, provided his follies end there.

AESCHINUS: That's well. [To the spectators] Give us your applause.

The Oriental Theatre

Above: A Noh stage. From M. C. Stopes and Joji Sakurai, *Plays of Old Japan:* . . ., 1913, courtesy E. P. Dutton & Co., Inc. *Left:* A Kabuki Theatre (17th century). Note the stage roof of the old temple type and the realistic properties. From Sheldon Cheney, *The Theatre*, Rev. ed., 1959, courtesy David McKay Co., Inc.

The Oriental Theatre

The plays of the Greeks and Romans constitute the classic drama of the Western theatre. There is also a classic drama of the East, upon which the Oriental theatre, with characteristic conservatism, has drawn more continuously than our stage has drawn upon its Greek and Roman heritage of plays. Oriental dramatic literature began to attract the West in the eighteenth century, and Voltaire and Goethe were among its early enthusiasts. At the turn of the nineteenth century, moreover, we began to look to the Eastern theatre for lessons in frank theatricality as contrasted with the facsimile renditions of life favored by the naturalistic stage. In the struggle for liberation from unimaginative realism, Western playwrights and stage directors welcomed Oriental styles of playwriting and stage production, with the result that these no longer seem to us hopelessly remote and esoteric.

Historical evidence points to the emergence of theatre in Egypt and the Near East several thousand years ago. It blossomed out of ritual, mainly in the form of passion plays or dramatic rites revolving around such vegetation and fertility gods as Osiris and Tammuz. But, apparently, theatre in Egypt, Mesopotamia, and Syria never obtained sufficient independence from ritual to provide a dramatic literature, as it did in Greece. The one masterly dramatic composition that we have from the Near East, the Book of Job, was never intended for the theatre, and it is more a symposium than a play. The ancient Hebrews, who might have given us drama of great literary distinction, were too disapproving of sympathetic magic and idolatry to develop a theatre. Only in Hebrew communities of the Hellenistic world, such as Alexandria after the fourth century B.C., is there any evidence of playwriting. It is from India and the Far East that we derive completely realized drama.

Eastern drama is the most theatrical we know because it was written for the most thoroughly stylized and convention-rooted theatres in the world. Here virtually every gesture and movement, every detail of costume and mask or masklike make-up, every color, and every stage prop was more or less symbolic. No one attempted to disguise the fact that the theatre was make-believe and that its effectiveness was dependent upon a willing suspension of disbelief on the part of the spectator. The latter was habituated to certain conventions and was familiar with the rules of the game being played upon the stage either in earnest or in jest.

In India, a simple platform in a palace hall or courtyard sufficed as a stage. No specific scenery was employed except for decorations and such furniture and props as seats, thrones, and chariots. A prologue made it plain to the audience that a play was going to be presented for its pleasure and edification. A multitude of rules concerning dialect and character types gave the work a traditional character. Convention afforded free range to the author's imagination; he could foreshorten parts of his story without regard to realistic requirements, and he could pile one incredible adventure upon another. He employed romances that satisfied the craving for storytelling which was widespread in the East. When men of talent, such as Kalidasa and the unknown author of *The Little Clay Cart,* applied themselves to this type of theatrical composition, they produced for their public and later generations in India a civilized and engagingly romantic drama that in time also charmed the West.

Stylization went even further in the Chinese theatre. On its platform stage, the actor might signify that he was riding a horse by merely flourishing a whip formally. He could indicate the crossing of a body of water by holding up a banner on which a few fish were painted. Symbolic details of his make-up and costuming identified him plainly as a character from whom a certain mode of behavior was to be expected, and the ubiquitous property man could supply the actor with furniture and stage properties in full view of the audience. No one felt any obligation to give the spectator the kind of stage illusion that the Western theatre began to provide once the Italian Renaissance had introduced painted scenery and perspective settings behind a proscenium arch. For the Chinese stage a playwright could spin out a legend, a moral story, or a romance as leisurely and episodic entertainment. This was distinctly drama for a worldly-wise, mildly disillusioned, and slow-paced civilization unagitated by the tragic sense of the Greeks, by the Elizabethan will effectuating itself in a storm of passion, by Ibsenite iconoclasm, or by the inner wranglings of a Strindberg or an O'Neill.

On the equally stylized Japanese stage appeared an entrancing form of drama, called the Noh play, which often did express a passionate view of life but in a manner that refined away the crudities of experience with imaginative formalism. And in the same theatre—on the popular, so-called *kabuki,* stage—proliferated an extravagantly active, melodramatic type of play that was boundlessly theatrical. But in Japan, too, stylization dominated dramatic art.

When we came to appreciate the freedom and flexibility of the Oriental stage, we began to adopt its stylization in our own plays and productions. A successful early use of Chinese motifs in America was George C. Hazelton and J. Harry Benrimo's *The Yellow Jacket;* its popularity came in 1912, at the peak of an "art theatre" movement inspired by French symbolists such as Maeterlinck and by imaginative theatrical artists such as Gordon Craig and

Max Reinhardt. A more distinguished and recent domestication of the Chinese style appeared in Thornton Wilder's New England drama *Our Town.* William Butler Yeats, ever eager to promote poetry and imagination, took his cue from the Japanese Noh play to write his series of one-acters *Four Plays for Dancers,* between 1917 and 1920. His desire that in these pieces (*At the Hawk's Well, The Only Jealousy of Emer, The Dreaming of the Bones,* and *Calvary*) "all may be as artificial as possible" made him require masks for the actors and demand that "the players must move a little stiffly and gravely like marionettes and, I think, to the accompaniment of drum taps." Stylization did not prevent him from writing, in these plays, some of the most forceful verse dialogue of his distinguished career. In 1922, the talented Russian stage director Vakhtangov gave a striking production in Oriental style of Gozzi's eighteenth-century romantic comedy *Princess Turandot;* and Vakhtangov imparted his policy of theatricalization to the Hebrew-language Habima theatre, which made a strong impression with such folk fantasies as *The Dybbuk* and *The Golem.* Among Central European playwrights, the poet-dramatist Bertolt Brecht availed himself of the Chinese conventions in writing didactic and, at the same time, poetic political plays.

Efforts along these lines, together with such adaptations from the Chinese as *Lute Song* (the fourteenth-century *Pi-pa-Ki,* as adapted by Sidney Howard and Will Irwin) and S. I. Hsiung's *Lady Precious Stream* (which had a long run in England), proved that Oriental dramatic art was no longer esoteric. The distance between East and West had narrowed considerably in other respects as well, and the East felt attracted to Western drama. In India, at the turn of the century, Rabindranath Tagore was turning out such plays as *Chitra* and *The King of the Dark Chamber,* which are indistinguishable from Maeterlinck's neoromantic dramas. Tolstoy, Ibsen, Strindberg, Shaw, and O'Neill exerted an influence on Japanese writers after 1900. Chinese intellectuals began to look askance at their classic drama and to favor Western realism.

Kalidasa

(5TH CENTURY?)

India's Shakespeare is Kalidasa, who was called the "Bridegroom of Poetry," a title which was well earned but is practically all that is known of him. Even his dates are uncertain. There is no doubt that he followed, rather than created, a tradition of playwriting and that he was the most gifted of the writers of India's classical period, which extended from about 350 to 800. He became a celebrated poet, noted for his descriptiveness and love of nature, as well as a dramatist. His extant poetry, especially *The Cloud Messenger,* is rich in observation and delicacy.

Kalidasa probably lived at the beginning of the fifth century, in a courtly age when Hindu writers reflected a relaxed view of life, a refined taste, and a playful disposition. The earlier dramatists may have been more vigorous; in one of the earliest Hindu plays, *The Little Clay Cart,* attributed by tradition to King Shudraka, there are political and realistic elements.

The first plays of Hindu drama, which had vague ritualistic beginnings, were mostly rudimentary dramatizations of mythology, abounding in pious sentiment and descriptions of gods and demigods such as Indra, Rama, and Krishna. According to an old Sanskrit text, the gods themselves originated Hindu drama, and in a sense the Hindu theatre, in its heyday between the fourth and eighth centuries, never outgrew its religious basis. The sacred epics, the *Mahabharata* and *Ramayana,* continued to be the playwrights' source books, and the themes of both appear in the work of the playwright Bhasa, who was mentioned by Kalidasa as a noteworthy predecessor. To this inspiration was added the penchant of the priestly caste for moral lessons and conversions to piety. Nature is celebrated in the plays because it conduces to plain living and high thinking in accordance with religious teachings.

The playwrights were untiring in their praise of the holiness of the Brahmin priests; especially admired were the hermits who had retired from the world to devote themselves to meditation and benevolence. Religion, it may be said, contributed the idyllic and idealistic elements in Hindu drama. Still, the plays of Kalidasa and of his less celebrated colleagues represent a shift from the priestly to the courtly domain. It is from the luxurious life of the courts that they derive their facetiousness, sophisticated naïveté, and buoyant humor. In later, more troubled times of civil wars and invasions, the Hindu dramatists, among whom the seventh- or eighth-century Bhavabhuti was pre-eminent, the humor vanishes and the style is less free and relaxed. The spirit is less buoyant. Evidently the accumulated rules for dramatic composition exert an oppressive influence.

In Kalidasa's time, the abysses of human fate and passion were not for the Hindu playwrights and their audiences. Their theatre was one of entertainment and fancy. Everything is possible in this type of drama. None of the unities is observed, time and place shift almost shamelessly; if the actor says that he is going somewhere, *presto,* he is there. Great variety prevails, representatives of various classes presenting a varied pattern of behavior and speaking and acting in accordance with their station. A king always has his *vidushaka,* or sportive servant, and his *vita,* or dignified counselor. The gods, the Brahmins, and royalty speak Sanskrit, the sacred and antiquated language of India, whereas the women and other less exalted personages employ dialects. Laughter and farcical byplay alternate with refined sentiment; poetry and prose intermingle; luxury and most idyllic simplicity appear side by side. A story is told, not in the straitlaced manner of realism but in the spirit of diversified and unconfined play.

For this kind of theatre, Kalidasa, with his remarkable descriptive faculty and lyrical power, was to the manner born. Three of his plays are extant—*Urvashi Won by Valor, Malavika and Agnimitra,* and *Shakuntala*—all romances of love and adventure steeped in fantasy and embroidered with euphuistic poetical language. *Shakuntala,* the most effective of the three comedies, epitomizes the Hindu theatre's effervescence of refined feeling and sophistication. The fancifulness of the play never palls; and its sentiment, present in generous proportions, does not cloy because it is offered with a grain of salt. What went on in the mind of the master as he pulled the strings of his play we cannot know; but in his comedies we see him as a gentle cynic for whom all the world was a stage and the men and women on it merely players.

Shakuntala, first translated into English in 1789 by the orientalist Sir William Jones, was enthusiastically received by the young romanticists of the time as welcome relief from the disciplines of rationalism and the neoclassic rules of the unities. On the European continent, the play won the admiration of Goethe, who used its device of a stage manager's prologue in *Faust,* and who wrote a fervid poem in appreciation of Kalidasa's masterpiece. The play is actually not remote from the tragicomedies and romances that became fashionable toward the end of Shakespeare's life.

SHAKUNTALA

By Kalidasa

TRANSLATED FROM THE SANSKRIT BY SIR MONIER MONIER-WILLIAMS

PERSONS OF THE DRAMA

DUSHYANTA, *King of India*

MATHAVYA, *the jester, friend, and companion of the King*

KANWA, *chief of the hermits, foster-father of Shakuntala*

SARNGARAVA ⎫ *two Brahmans, belonging to the*
SARADWATA ⎭ *hermitage of Kanwa*

MITRAVASU, *brother-in-law of the King, and superintendent of the city police*

JANKU *and* SUCHAKA, *two constables*

VATAYANA, *the chamberlain or attendant on the women's apartments*

SOMARATA, *the domestic priest*

KARABHAKA, *a messenger of the queen-mother*

RAIVATIKA, *the warder or doorkeeper*

SARVA-DAMANA, *afterwards* BHARATA, *a little boy, son of Dushyanta by Shakuntala*

KASYAPA, *a divine sage, progenitor of men and gods, son of Marichi, and grandson of Brahma*

MATALI, *charioteer of Indra*

SHAKUNTALA, *daughter of the sage Viswamitra and the nymph Menaka, foster-child of the hermit Kanwa*

PRIYAMVADA *and* ANASUYA, *female attendants, companions of Shakuntala*

GAUTAMI, *a holy matron, Superior of the female inhabitants of the hermitage*

VASUMATI, *the Queen of Dushyanta*

SANUMATI, *a nymph, friend of Shakuntala*

TARALIKA, *personal attendant of the Queen*

CHATURIKA, *personal attendant of the King*

VETRAVATI, *female warder or doorkeeper*

PARABHRITIKA *and* MADHUKARIKA, *maidens in charge of royal gardens*

SUVRATA, *a nurse*

ADITI, *wife of Kasyapa; granddaughter of Brahma through her father Daksha*

CHARIOTEER, FISHERMAN, OFFICERS, *and* HERMITS

PROLOGUE

BENEDICTION

Isa preserve you! he who is revealed
In these eight forms by man perceptible—
Water, of all creation's works the first;
The Fire that bears on high the sacrifice
Presented with solemnity to heaven;
The Priest, the holy offerer of gifts;
The Sun and Moon, those two majestic orbs,
Eternal marshalers of day and night;
The subtle Ether, vehicle of sound,
Diffused throughout the boundless universe;
The Earth, by sages called "The place of birth
Of all material essences and things";
And Air, which giveth life to all that breathe.

STAGE-MANAGER: [*After the recitation of the benediction, looking around the tiring-room*] Lady, when you have finished attiring yourself, come this way.

ACTRESS: [*Entering*] Here I am, Sir; what are your commands?

STAGE-MANAGER: We are here before the eyes of an audience of educated and discerning men; and have to represent in their presence a new drama composed by Kalidasa, called *Shakuntala; or, the Lost Ring*. Let the whole company exert themselves to do justice to their several parts.

ACTRESS: You, Sir, have so judiciously managed the cast of the characters, that nothing will be defective in the acting.

STAGE-MANAGER: Lady, I will tell you the exact state of the case.

No skill in acting can I deem complete,
Till from the wise the actor gain applause;
Know that the heart e'en of the truly skilful,
Shrinks from too boastful confidence in self.

ACTRESS: [*Modestly*] You judge correctly. And now, what are your commands?

STAGE-MANAGER: What can you do better than engage the attention of the audience by some captivating melody?

ACTRESS: Which among the seasons shall I select as the subject of my song?

STAGE-MANAGER: You surely ought to give the preference to the present summer season that has but recently commenced, a season so rich in enjoyment. For now

Unceasing are the charms of halcyon days,
When the cool bath exhilarates the frame;
When sylvan gales are laden with the scent
Of fragrant Patalas;[1] when soothing sleep
Creeps softly on beneath the deepening shade;
And when, at last, the dulcet calm of eve

[1] The seven or eight Hindu underworlds notable for sensual gratifications; also the semidivine creatures that inhabit these regions.

Entrancing steals o'er every yielding sense.

ACTRESS: I will:— [Sings]

Fond maids, the chosen of their hearts to please,
Entwine their ears with sweet Sirisha flowers,
Whose fragrant lips attract the kiss of bees
That softly murmur through the summer hours.

STAGE-MANAGER: Charmingly sung! The audience are motionless as statues, their souls riveted by the enchanting strain. What subject shall we select for representation, that we may ensure a continuance of their favor?

ACTRESS: Why not the same, Sir, announced by you at first? Let the drama called *Shakuntala; or, the Lost Ring,* be the subject of our dramatic performance.

STAGE-MANAGER: Rightly reminded!
For the moment I had forgotten it.
Your song's transporting melody decoyed
My thoughts, and rapt with ecstasy my soul;
As now the bounding antelope allures
The King Dushyanta on the chase intent.

[*Exeunt*]

ACT I.

SCENE—*A forest.*

[*Enter* King Dushyanta, *armed with a bow and arrow, in a chariot, chasing an antelope, attended by his* Charioteer]

CHARIOTEER: [*Looking at the deer, and then at the* King] Great Prince.
When on the antelope I bend my gaze,
And on your Majesty, whose mighty bow
Has its string firmly braced; before my eyes
The god that wields the trident seems revealed,
Chasing the deer that flies from him in vain.

KING: Charioteer, this fleet antelope has drawn us far from my attendants.
See! there he runs:
Aye and anon his graceful neck he bends
To cast a glance at the pursuing car;
And dreading now the swift-descending shaft,
Contracts into itself his slender frame;
About his path, in scattered fragments strewn,
The half-chewed grass falls from his panting mouth;
See! in his airy bounds he seems to fly,
And leaves no trace upon th' elastic turf.

[*With astonishment*]

How now! swift as is our pursuit, I scarce can see him.

CHARIOTEER: Sire, the ground here is full of hollows; I have therefore drawn in the reins and checked the speed of the chariot. Hence the deer has somewhat gained upon us. Now that we are passing over level ground, we shall have no difficulty in overtaking him.

KING: Loosen the reins, then.

CHARIOTEER: The King is obeyed. [*Drives the chariot at full speed*]
Great Prince, see! see!
Responsive to the slackened rein, the steeds,
Chafing with eager rivalry, career
With emulative fleetness o'er the plain;
Their necks outstretched, their waving plumes, that late
Fluttered above their brows, are motionless;
Their sprightly ears, but now erect, bent low;
Themselves unsullied by the circling dust
That vainly follows on their rapid course.

KING: [*Joyously*] In good sooth, the horses seem as if they would outstrip the steeds of Indra[2] and the Sun.
That which but now showed to my view minute
Quickly assumes dimension; that which seemed
A moment since disjoined in diverse parts,
Looks suddenly like one compacted whole;
That which is really crooked in its shape
In the far distance left, grows regular;
Wondrous the chariot's speed, that in a breath,
Makes the near distant and the distant near.
Now, Charioteer, see me kill the deer. [*Takes aim*]

A VOICE: [*Behind the scenes*] Hold, O King! this deer belongs to our hermitage. Kill it not! kill it not!

CHARIOTEER: [*Listening and looking*] Great King, some hermits have stationed themselves so as to screen the antelope at the very moment of its coming within range of your arrow.

KING: [*Hastily*] Then stop the horses.

CHARIOTEER: I obey. [*Stops the chariot*]
[*Enter a* Hermit, *and two others with him*]

HERMIT: [*Raising his hand*] This deer, O King, belongs to our hermitage. Kill it not! kill it not!
Now heaven forbid this barbèd shaft descend
Upon the fragile body of a fawn,
Like fire upon a heap of tender flowers!
Can thy steel bolts no meeter quarry find
Than the warm life-blood of a harmless deer?
Restore, great Prince, thy weapon to its quiver.
More it becomes thy arms to shield the weak,
Than to bring anguish on the innocent.

KING: 'Tis done. [*Replaces the arrow in its quiver*]

HERMIT: Worthy is this action of a
Prince, the light of Puru's race.
Well does this act befit a Prince like thee,
Right worthy is it of thine ancestry.
Thy guerdon be a son of peerless worth,
Whose wide dominion shall embrace the earth.

BOTH THE OTHER HERMITS: [*Raising their hands*] May heaven indeed grant thee a son, a sovereign of the earth from sea to sea!

KING: [*Bowing*] I accept with gratitude a Brahman's [benediction].

HERMIT: We came hither, mighty Prince, to collect sacrificial wood. Here on the banks of the Malini you may perceive the hermitage of the great sage

[2] The great national god of the Indo-Aryans.

Kanwa. If other duties require not your presence,
deign to enter and accept our hospitality.
When you behold our penitential rites
Performed without impediment by saints
Rich only in devotion, then with pride
Will you reflect:—Such are the holy men
Who call me Guardian; such the men for whom
To wield the bow I bare my nervous arm,
Scarred by the motion of the glancing string.

KING: Is the Chief of your Society now at home?

HERMIT: No; he has gone to Somatirtha to propitiate Destiny, which threatens his daughter Shakuntala with some calamity; but he has commissioned her in his absence to entertain all guests with hospitality.

KING: Good! I will pay her a visit. She will make me acquainted with the mighty sage's acts of penance and devotion.

HERMIT: And we will depart on our errand. [*Exit with his companions*]

KING: Charioteer, urge on the horses. We will at least purify our souls by a sight of this hallowed retreat.

CHARIOTEER: Your Majesty is obeyed. [*Drives the chariot with great velocity*]

KING: [*Looking all about him*] Charioteer, even without being told, I should have known that these were the precincts of a grove consecrated to penitential rites.

CHARIOTEER: How so?

KING: Do not you observe?
Beneath the trees, whose hollow trunks afford
Secure retreat to many a nestling brood
Of parrots, scattered grains of rice lie strewn.
Lo! here and there are seen the polished slabs
That serve to bruise the fruit of Ingudi.
The gentle roe-deer, taught to trust in man,
Unstartled hear our voices. On the paths
Appear the traces of bark-woven vests
Borne dripping from the limpid fount of waters.
And mark!
Laved are the roots of trees by deep canals,
Whose glassy waters tremble in the breeze;
The sprouting verdure of the leaves is dimmed
By dusky wreaths of upward curling smoke
From burnt oblations; and on new-mown lawns
Around our car graze leisurely the fawns.

CHARIOTEER: I observe it all.

KING: [*Advancing a little further*] The inhabitants of this sacred retreat must not be disturbed. Stay the chariot, that I may alight.

CHARIOTEER: The reins are held in. Your Majesty may descend.

KING: [*Alighting*] Charioteer, groves devoted to penance must be entered in humble attire. Take these ornaments. [*Delivers his ornaments and bow to the Charioteer*] Charioteer, see that the horses are watered, and attend to them until I return from visiting the inhabitants of the hermitage.

CHARIOTEER: I will. [*Exit*]

KING: [*Walking and looking about*] Here is the entrance to the hermitage. I will now go in.
[*Entering and feeling a throbbing sensation in his arm*]
Serenest peace is in this calm retreat,
By passion's breath unruffled; what portends
My throbbing arm? Why should it whisper here
Of happy love? Yet everywhere around us
Stand the closed portals of events unknown.

A VOICE: [*Behind the scenes*] This way, my dear companions; this way.

KING: [*Listening*] Hark! I hear voices to the right of yonder grove of trees. I will walk in that direction. [*Walking and looking about*] Ah! here are the maidens of the hermitage coming this way to water the shrubs, carrying water-pots proportioned to their strength. [*Gazing at them*] How graceful they look!
In palaces such charms are rarely ours;
The woodland plants outshine the garden flowers.
I will conceal myself in this shade and watch them.
[*Stands gazing at them*]
[*Enter Shakuntala, with her two female companions, employed in the manner described*]

SHAKUNTALA: This way, my dear companions; this way.

ANASUYA: Dear Shakuntala, one would think that Father Kanwa had more affection for the shrubs of the hermitage even than for you, seeing he assigns to you, who are yourself as delicate as the fresh-blown jasmine, the task of filling with water the trenches which encircle their roots.

SHAKUNTALA: Dear Anasuya, although I am charged by my good father with this duty, yet I cannot regard it as a task. I really feel a sisterly love for these plants. [*Continues watering the shrubs*]

KING: Can this be the daughter of Kanwa? The saintly man, though descended from the great Kasyapa, must be very deficient in judgment to habituate such a maiden to the life of the recluse.
The sage who would this form of artless grace
Inure to penance, thoughtlessly attempts
To cleave in twain the hard acacia's stem
With the soft edge of a blue lotus-leaf.
Well! concealed behind this tree, I will watch her without raising her suspicions. [*Conceals himself*]

SHAKUNTALA: Good Anasuya, Priyamvada has drawn this bark-dress too tightly about my chest. I pray thee, loosen it a little.

ANASUYA: I will. [*Loosens it*]

PRIYAMVADA: [*Smiling*] Why do you lay the blame on me? Blame rather your own blooming youthfulness which imparts fulness to your bosom.

KING: A most just observation!
This youthful form, whose bosom's swelling charms
By the bark's knotted tissue are concealed,
Like some fair bud close folded in its sheath,
Gives not to view the blooming of its beauty.
But what am I saying? In real truth this bark-dress, though ill-suited to her figure, sets it off like an ornament.

The lotus with the saivala entwined
Is not a whit less brilliant; dusky spots
Heighten the luster of the cold-rayed moon;
This lovely maiden in her dress of bark
Seems all the lovelier. E'en the meanest garb
Gives to true beauty fresh attractiveness.

SHAKUNTALA: [*Looking before her*] Yon Kesara-tree beckons to me with its young shoots, which, as the breeze waves them to and fro, appear like slender fingers. I will go and attend to it. [*Walks towards it*]

PRIYAMVADA: Dear Shakuntala, prithee, rest in that attitude one moment.

SHAKUNTALA: Why so?

PRIYAMVADA: The Kesara-tree, whilst your graceful form bends about its stem, appears as if it were wedded to some lovely twining creeper.

SHAKUNTALA: Ah! saucy girl, you are most appropriately named Priyam-vada ("Speaker of flattering things").

KING: What Priyamvada says, though complimentary, is nevertheless true. Verily,
Her ruddy lip vies with the opening bud;
Her graceful arms are as the twining stalks;
And her whole form is radiant with the glow
Of youthful beauty, as the tree with bloom.

ANASUYA: See, dear Shakuntala, here is the young jasmine, which you named "the Moonlight of the Grove," the self-elected wife of the mango-tree. Have you forgotten?

SHAKUNTALA: Rather will I forgot myself. [*Approaching the plant and looking at it*] How delightful is the season when the jasmine-creeper and the mango-tree seem thus to unite in mutual embraces! The fresh blossoms of the jasmine resemble the bloom of a young bride, and the newly-formed shoots of the mango appear to make it her natural protector. [*Continues gazing at it*]

PRIYAMVADA: Do you know, my Anasuya, why Shakuntala gazes so intently at the jasmine?

ANASUYA: No, indeed, I cannot imagine. I pray thee tell me.

PRIYAMVADA: She is wishing that as the jasmine is united to a suitable tree, so, in like manner, she may obtain a husband worthy of her.

SHAKUNTALA: Speak for yourself, girl; this is the thought in your own mind. [*Continues watering the flowers*]

KING: Would that my union with her were permissible! and yet I hardly dare hope that the maiden is sprung from a caste different from that of the Head of the hermitage. But away with doubt:
That she is free to wed a warrior-king
My heart attests. For, in conflicting doubts,
The secret promptings of the good man's soul
Are an unerring index of the truth.
However, come what may, I will ascertain the fact.

SHAKUNTALA: [*In a flurry*] Ah! a bee, disturbed by the sprinkling of the water, has left the young jasmine, and is trying to settle on my face. [*Attempts to drive it away*]

KING: [*Gazing at her ardently*] Beautiful! there is something charming even in her repulse.
Where'er the bee his eager onset plies,
Now here, now there, she darts her kindling eyes;
What love hath yet to teach, fear teaches now,
The furtive glances and the frowning brow.
[*In a tone of envy*]
Ah, happy bee! how boldly dost thou try
To steal the luster from her sparkling eye;
And in thy circling movements hover near,
To murmur tender secrets in her ear;
Or, as she coyly waves her hand, to sip
Voluptuous nectar from her lower lip!
While rising doubts my heart's fond hopes destroy,
Thou dost the fulness of her charms enjoy.

SHAKUNTALA: This impertinent bee will not rest quiet. I must move elsewhere. [*Moving a few steps off, and casting a glance around*] How now! he is following me here. Help! my dear friends, help! deliver me from the attacks of this troublesome insect.

PRIYAMVADA *and* ANASUYA: How can we deliver you? Call Dushyanta to your aid. The sacred groves are under the King's special protection.

KING: An excellent opportunity for me to show myself. Fear not—[*checks himself when the words are half-uttered. Aside*] But stay, if I introduce myself in this manner, they will know me to be the King. Be it so, I will accost them, nevertheless.

SHAKUNTALA: [*Moving a step or two further off*] What! it still persists in following me.

KING: [*Advancing hastily*] When mighty Puru's offspring sways the earth,
And o'er the wayward holds his threatening rod,
Who dares molest the gentle maids that keep
Their holy vigils here in Kanwa's grove?
[*All look at the* King, *and all are embarrassed*]

ANASUYA: Kind Sir, no outrage has been committed; only our dear friend here was teased by the the attacks of a troublesome bee. [*Points to* Shakuntala]

KING: [*Turning to* Shakuntala] I trust all is well with your devotional rites?
[Shakuntala *stands confused and silent*]

ANASUYA: All is well indeed, now that we are honored by the reception of a distinguished guest. Dear Shakuntala, go, bring from the hermitage an offering of flowers, rice, and fruit. This water that we have brought with us will serve to bathe our guest's feet.

KING: The rites of hospitality are already performed; your truly kind words are the best offering I can receive.

PRIYAMVADA: At least be good enough, gentle Sir, to sit down awhile, and rest yourself on this seat shaded by the leaves of the Sapta-parna tree.

KING: You, too, must all be fatigued by your employment.

ANASUYA: Dear Shakuntala, there is no impropriety in our sitting by the side of our guest; come, let us sit down here.

[All sit down together]

SHAKUNTALA: [Aside] How is it that the sight of this man has made me sensible of emotions inconsistent with religious vows?

KING: [Gazing at them all by turns] How charmingly your friendship is in keeping with the equality of your ages and appearance!

PRIYAMVADA: [Aside to Anasuya] Who can this person be, whose lively yet dignified manner, and polite conversation, bespeak him a man of high rank?

ANASUYA: I, too, my dear, am very curious to know. I will ask him myself. [Aloud] Your kind words, noble Sir, fill me with confidence, and prompt me to inquire of what regal family our noble guest is the ornament? what country is now mourning his absence? and what induced a person so delicately nurtured to expose himself to the fatigue of visiting this grove of penance?

SHAKUNTALA: [Aside] Be not troubled, O my heart, Anasuya is giving utterance to thy thoughts.

KING: [Aside] How now shall I reply? shall I make myself known, or shall I still disguise my real rank? I have it; I will answer her thus. [Aloud] I am the person charged by his Majesty, the descendant of Puru, with the administration of justice and religion; and am come to this sacred grove to satisfy myself that the rites of the hermits are free from obstruction.

ANASUYA: The hermits, then, and all the members of our religious society, have now a guardian.

[Shakuntala gazes bashfully at the King]

PRIYAMVADA and ANASUYA: [Perceiving the state of her feelings, and of the King's. Aside to Shakuntala] Dear Shakuntala, if Father Kanwa were but at home today——

SHAKUNTALA: [Angrily] What if he were?

PRIYAMVADA and ANASUYA: He would honor this our distinguished guest with an offering of the most precious of his possessions.

SHAKUNTALA: Go to! you have some silly idea in your minds. I will not listen to such remarks.

KING: May I be allowed, in my turn, to ask you maidens a few particulars respecting your friend?

PRIYAMVADA and ANASUYA: Your request, Sir, is an honor.

KING: The sage Kanwa lives in the constant practice of austerities. How, then, can this friend of yours be called his daughter?

ANASUYA: I will explain to you, Sir. You have heard of an illustrious sage of regal caste, Viswamitra, whose family name is Kausika.

KING: I have.

ANASUYA: Know that he is the real father of our friend. The venerable Kanwa is only her reputed father. He it was who brought her up, when she was deserted by her mother.

KING: "Deserted by her mother!" My curiosity is excited; pray let me hear the story from the beginning.

ANASUYA: You shall hear it, Sir. Some time since, this sage of regal caste, while performing a most severe penance on the banks of the river Godavari, excited the jealousy and alarm of the gods; insomuch that they despatched a lovely nymph named Menaka to interrupt his devotions.

KING: The inferior gods, I am aware, are jealous of the power which the practice of excessive devotion confers on mortals.

ANASUYA: Well, then, it happened that Viswamitra, gazing on the bewitching beauty of that nymph at a season when, spring being in its glory—[Stops short, and appears confused]

KING: The rest may be easily divined. Shakuntala, then, is the offspring of the nymph.

ANASUYA: Just so.

KING: It is quite intelligible.
How could a mortal to such charms give birth?
The lightning's radiance flashes not from earth.

[Shakuntala remains modestly seated with downcast eyes]

[Aside] And so my desire has really scope for its indulgence. Yet I am still distracted by doubts, remembering the pleasantry of her female companions respecting her wish for a husband.

PRIYAMVADA: [Looking with a smile at Shakuntala, and then turning towards the King] You seem desirous, Sir, of asking something further.

[Shakuntala makes a chiding gesture with her finger]

KING: You conjecture truly. I am so eager to hear the particulars of your friend's history, that I have still another question to ask.

PRIYAMVADA: Scruple not to do so. Persons who lead the life of hermits may be questioned unreservedly.

KING: I wish to ascertain one point respecting your friend.
Will she be bound by solitary vows
Opposed to love, till her espousals only?
Or ever dwell with these her cherished fawns,
Whose eyes, in luster vying with her own,
Return her gaze of sisterly affection?

PRIYAMVADA: Hitherto, Sir, she has been engaged in the practice of religious duties, and has lived in subjection to her foster-father; but it is now his fixed intention to give her away in marriage to a husband worthy of her.

KING: [Aside] His intention may be easily carried into effect.
Be hopeful, O my heart, thy harrowing doubts
Are past and gone; that which thou didst believe
To be as unapproachable as fire,
Is found a glittering gem that may be touched.

SHAKUNTALA: [Pretending anger] Anasuya, I shall leave you.

ANASUYA: Why so?

SHAKUNTALA: That I may go and report this impertinent Priyamvada to the venerable matron, Gautami.

ANASUYA: Surely, dear friend, it would not be

right to leave a distinguished guest before he has received the rites of hospitality, and quit his presence in this wilful manner.

[Shakuntala, *without answering a word, moves away*]

KING: [*Making a movement to arrest her departure, but checking himself. Aside*]

Ah! a lover's feelings betray themselves by his gestures.
When I would fain have stayed the maid, a sense
Of due decorum checked my bold design;
Though I have stirred not, yet my mien betrays
My eagerness to follow on her steps.

PRIYAMVADA: [*Holding Shakuntala back*] Dear Shakuntala, it does not become you to go away in this manner.

SHAKUNTALA: [*Frowning*] Why not, pray?

PRIYAMVADA: You are under a promise to water two more shrubs for me. When you have paid your debt, you shall go, and not before. [*Forces her to turn back*]

KING: Spare her this trouble, gentle maiden. The exertion of watering the shrubs has already fatigued her.
The water-jar has overtasked the strength
Of her slim arms; her shoulders droop, her hands
Are ruddy with the glow of quickened pulses;
E'en now her agitated breath imparts
Unwonted tremor to her heaving breast;
The pearly drops that mar the recent bloom
Of the Sirisha pendent in her ear,
Gather in clustering circles on her cheek;
Loosed is the fillet of her hair; her hand
Restrains the locks that struggle to be free.
Suffer me, then, thus to discharge the debt for you.

[*Offers a ring to* Priyamvada. *Both the maidens, reading the name* Dushyanta *on the seal, look at each other with surprise*]

KING: Nay, think not that I am King Dushyanta. I am only the King's officer, and this is the ring which I have received from him as my credentials.

PRIYAMVADA: The greater the reason you ought not to part with the ring from your finger. I am content to release her from her obligation at your simple request. [*With a smile*] Now, Shakuntala, my love, you are at liberty to retire, thanks to the intercession of this noble stranger, or rather of this mighty prince.

SHAKUNTALA: [*Aside*] My movements are no longer under my own control. [*Aloud*] Pray, what authority have you over me, either to send me away or keep me back?

KING: [*Gazing at* Shakuntala. *Aside*] Would I could ascertain whether she is affected towards me as I am towards her! At any rate, my hopes are free to indulge themselves. Because,
Although she mingles not her words with mine,
Yet doth her listening ear drink in my speech;
Although her eye shrinks from my ardent gaze,
No form but mine attracts its timid glances.

A VOICE: [*Behind the scenes*] O hermits, be ready to protect the animals belonging to our hermitage. King Dushyanta, amusing himself with hunting, is near at hand.
Lo! by the feet of prancing horses raised,
Thick clouds of moving dust, like glittering swarms
Of locusts, in the glow of eventide,
Fall on the branches of our sacred trees;
Where hang the dripping vests of woven bark,
Bleached by the waters of the cleansing fountain.
And see!
Scared by the royal chariot in its course,
With headlong haste an elephant invades
The hallowed precincts of our sacred grove;
Himself the terror of the startled deer,
And an embodied hindrance to our rites.
The hedge of creepers clinging to his feet,
Feeble obstruction to his mad career,
Is dragged behind him in a tangled chain;
And with terrific shock one tusk he drives
Into the riven body of a tree,
Sweeping before him all impediments.

KING: [*Aside*] Out upon it! my retinue are looking for me, and are disturbing this holy retreat. Well! there is no help for it; I must go and meet them.

PRIYAMVADA *and* ANASUYA: Noble Sir, we are terrified by the accidental disturbance caused by the wild elephant. Permit us to return to the cottage.

KING: [*Hastily*] Go, gentle maidens. It shall be our care that no injury happen to the hermitage.

[*All rise up*]

PRIYAMVADA *and* ANASUYA: After such poor hospitality, we are ashamed to request the honor of a second visit from you.

KING: Say not so. The mere sight of you, sweet maidens, has been to me the best entertainment.

SHAKUNTALA: Anasuya, a pointed blade of Kusa-grass has pricked my foot; and my bark-mantle is caught in the branch of a Kuruvaka-bush. Be so good as to wait for me until I have disentangled it. [*Exit with her two companions, after making pretexts for delay, that she may steal glances at the* King]

KING: I have no longer any desire to return to the city. I will therefore rejoin my attendants, and make them encamp somewhere in the vicinity of this sacred grove. In good truth, Shakuntala has taken such possession of my thoughts, that I cannot turn myself in any other direction.
My limbs drawn onward leave my heart behind,
Like silken pennon borne against the wind.

ACT II.

SCENE—*A plain on the skirts of the forest.*

[*Enter the jester Mathavya, in a melancholy mood*]

MATHAVYA: [*Sighing*] Heigh-ho! what an unlucky fellow I am! worn to a shadow by my royal friend's sporting propensities. "Here's a deer!" "There goes a boar!" "Yonder's a tiger!" This is the only burden of our talk, while in the heat of the meridian sun we toil on from jungle to jungle, wandering about in the paths of the woods, where the trees afford us no shelter. Are we thirsty? We have nothing to drink but the dirty water of some mountain stream mixed with dry leaves, which give it a most pungent flavor. Are we hungry? We have nothing to eat but roast game, which we must swallow down at odd times, as best we can. Even at night there is no peace to be had. Sleeping is out of the question, with joints all strained by dancing attendance upon my sporting friend; or if I do happen to doze, I am awakened at the very earliest dawn by the horrible din of a lot of rascally beaters and huntsmen, who must needs surround the wood before sunrise, and deafen me with their clatter. Nor are these my only troubles. Here's a fresh grievance, like a new boil rising upon an old one! Yesterday, while we were lagging behind, my royal friend entered yonder hermitage after a deer; and there, as ill-luck would have it, caught sight of a beautiful girl, called Shakuntala, the hermit's daughter. From that moment, not another thought about returning to the city! and all last night not a wink of sleep did he get for thinking of the damsel. What is to be done? At any rate I will be on the watch for him as soon as he has finished his toilet. [*Walking and looking about*] Oh! here he comes, attended by the Yavana women, with bows in their hands, and wearing garlands of wild flowers. What shall I do? I have it. I will pretend to stand in the easiest attitude for resting my bruised and crippled limbs. [*Stands leaning on a staff*]

[*Enter* King Dushyanta, *followed by a retinue, in the manner described*]

KING: True, by no easy conquest may I win her,
Yet are my hopes encouraged by her mien.
Love is not yet triumphant; but, methinks,
The hearts of both are ripe for his delights. [*Smiling*]
Ah! thus does the lover delude himself; judging of the state of his loved one's feelings by his own desires.
But yet,
The stolen glance with half-averted eye,
The hesitating gait, the quick rebuke
Addressed to her companion, who would fain
Have stayed her counterfeit departure; these
Are signs not unpropitious to my suit.
So eagerly the lover feeds his hopes,
Claiming each trivial gesture for his own.

MATHAVYA: [*Still in the same attitude*] Ah, friends, my hands cannot move to greet you with the usual salutation. I can only just command my lips to wish your Majesty victory.

KING: Why, what has paralyzed your limbs?

MATHAVYA: You might as well ask me how my eye comes to water after you have poked your finger into it.

KING: I don't understand you; speak more intelligibly.

MATHAVYA: Ah, my dear friend, is yonder upright reed transformed into a crooked plant by its own act, or by the force of the current?

KING: The current of the river causes it, I suppose.

MATHAVYA: Ay; just as you are the cause of my crippled limbs.

KING: How so?

MATHAVYA: Here are you living the life of a wild man of the woods in a savage unfrequented region, while your State-affairs are left to shift for themselves; and as for poor me, I am no longer master of my own limbs, but have to follow you about day after day in your chases after wild animals, till my bones are all crippled and out of joint. Do, my dear friend, let me have one day's rest.

KING: [*Aside*] This fellow little knows, while he talks in this manner, that my mind is wholly engrossed by recollections of the hermit's daughter, and quite as disinclined to the chase as his own.
No longer can I bend my well-braced bow
Against the timid deer; nor e'er again
With well-aimed arrows can I think to harm
These her beloved associates, who enjoy
The privilege of her companionship;
Teaching her tender glances in return.

MATHAVYA: [*Looking in the* King's *face*] I may as well speak to the winds, for any attention you pay to my requests. I suppose you have something on your mind, and are talking it over to yourself.

KING: [*Smiling*] I was only thinking that I ought not to disregard a friend's request.

MATHAVYA: Then may the King live for ever! [*Moves off*]

KING: Stay a moment, my dear friend. I have something else to say to you.

MATHAVYA: Say on, then.

KING: When you have rested, you must assist me in another business which will give you no fatigue.

MATHAVYA: Ah! In eating something nice, I hope.

KING: You shall know at some future time.

MATHAVYA: No time better than the present.

KING: What ho, there!

WARDER: [*Entering*] What are your Majesty's commands?

KING: O Raivatika, bid the General of the forces attend.

WARDER: I will, Sire. [*Exit and re-enters with the* General] Come forward, General; his Majesty is looking towards you, and has some order to give you.

GENERAL: [*Looking at the* King] Though hunting is known to produce ill effects, my royal master has derived only benefit from it. For
Like the majestic elephant that roams
O'er mountain wilds, so does the King display
A stalwart frame, instinct with vigorous life.
His brawny arms and manly chest are scored
By frequent passage of the sounding string;
Unharmed he bears the midday sun; no toil
His mighty spirit daunts; his sturdy limbs,
Stripped of redundant flesh, relinquish nought

Of their robust proportions, but appear
In muscle, nerve, and sinewy fiber cased.
[*Approaching the* King] Victory to the King! We
have tracked the wild beasts to their lairs in the
forest. Why delay, when everything is ready?

KING: My friend Mathavya here has been disparaging the chase, till he has taken away all my
relish for it.

GENERAL: [*Aside to* Mathavya] Persevere in your
opposition, my good fellow; I will sound the King's
real feelings, and humor him accordingly. [*Aloud*]
The blockhead talks nonsense, and your Majesty in
your own person furnishes the best proof of it. Observe, Sire, the advantage and pleasure the hunter
derives from the chase.

Freed from all grosser influences his frame
Loses its sluggish humors, and becomes
Buoyant, compact, and fit for bold encounter.
'Tis his to mark with joy the varied passions,
Fierce heats of anger, terror, blank dismay,
Of forest animals that cross his path.
Then what a thrill transports the hunter's soul
When, with unerring course, his driven shaft
Pierces the moving mark! Oh! 'tis conceit
In moralists to call the chase a vice;
What recreation can compare with this?

MATHAVYA: [*Angrily*] Away! tempter, away! The
King has recovered his senses, and is himself again.
As for you, you may, if you choose, wander about
from forest to forest, till some old bear seizes you by
the nose, and makes a mouthful of you.

KING: My good General, as we are just now in the
neighborhood of a consecrated grove, your panegyric
upon hunting is somewhat ill-timed, and I cannot
assent to all you have said. For the present.
All undisturbed the buffaloes shall sport
In yonder pool, and with their ponderous horns
Scatter its tranquil waters, while the deer,
Couched here and there in groups beneath the shade
Of spreading branches, ruminate in peace.
And all securely shall the herd of boars
Feed on the marshy sedge; and thou, my bow,
With slackened string, enjoy a long repose.

GENERAL: So please your Majesty, it shall be as
you desire.

KING: Recall, then, the beaters who were sent in
advance to surround the forest.
My troops must not be allowed to disturb this sacred
retreat, and irritate its pious inhabitants.
Know that within the calm and cold recluse
Lurks unperceived a germ of smothered flame,
All-potent to destroy; a latent fire
That rashly kindled bursts with fury forth;
As in the disc of crystal that remains
Cool to the touch, until the solar ray
Falls on its polished surface, and excites
The burning heat that lies within concealed.

GENERAL: Your Majesty's commands shall be
obeyed.

MATHAVYA: Off with you, you son of a slave! Your
nonsense won't go down here, my fine fellow.
[*Exit* General]

KING: [*Looking at his* Attendants] Here, women,
take my hunting-dress; and you, Raivatika, keep
guard carefully outside.

ATTENDANTS: We will, Sire. [*Exeunt*]

MATHAVYA: Now that you have got rid of these
plagues, who have been buzzing about us like so
many flies, sit down, do, on that stone slab, with
the shade of the tree as your canopy, and I will seat
myself by you quite comfortably.

KING: Go you, and sit down first.

MATHAVYA: Come along, then.
[*Both walk on a little way, and seat themselves*]

KING: Mathavya, it may be said of you that you
have never beheld anything worth seeing; for your
eyes have not yet looked upon the loveliest object in
creation.

MATHAVYA: How can you say so, when I see your
Majesty before me at this moment?

KING: It is very natural that every one should consider his own friend perfect; but I was alluding to
Shakuntala, the brightest ornament of these hallowed
groves.

MATHAVYA: [*Aside*] I understand well enough, but
I am not going to humor him. [*Aloud*] If, as you intimate, she is a hermit's daughter, you cannot lawfully ask her in marriage. You may as well then dismiss her from your mind, for any good the mere
sight of her can do.

KING: Think you that a descendant of the mighty
Puru could fix his affections on an unlawful object?
Though, as men say, the offspring of the sage,
The maiden to a nymph celestial owes
Her being, and by her mother left on earth,
Was found and nurtured by the holy man
As his own daughter, in this hermitage.
So, when dissevered from its parent stalk,
Some falling blossom of the jasmine, wafted
Upon the sturdy sun-flower, is preserved
By its support from premature decay.

MATHAVYA: [*Smiling*] This passion of yours for a
rustic maiden, when you have so many gems of
women at home in your palace, seems to me very like
the fancy of a man who is tired of sweet dates, and
longs for sour tamarinds as a variety.

KING: You have not seen her, or you would not
talk in this fashion.

MATHAVYA: I can quite understand it must require
something surpassingly attractive to excite the admiration of such a great man as you.

KING: I will describe her, my dear friend, in a
few words.
Man's all-wise Maker, wishing to create
A faultless form, whose matchless symmetry
Should far transcend Creation's choicest works,
Did call together by his mighty will,
And garner up in his eternal mind,

A bright assemblage of all lovely things;
And then, as in a picture, fashion them
Into one perfect and ideal form—
Such the divine, the wondrous prototype,
Whence her fair shape was moulded into being.

MATHAVYA: If that's the case, she must indeed throw all other beauties into the shade.

KING: To my mind she really does.
This peerless maid is like a fragrant flower,
Whose perfumed breath has never been diffused;
A tender bud, that no profaning hand
Has dared to sever from its parent stalk;
A gem of priceless water, just released
Pure and unblemished from its glittering bed.
Or may the maiden haply be compared
To sweetest honey, that no mortal lip
Has sipped; or, rather, to the mellowed fruit
Of virtuous actions in some former birth,
Now brought to full perfection! Lives the man
Whom bounteous heaven has destined to espouse her?

MATHAVYA: Make haste, then, to her aid; you have no time to lose, if you don't wish this fruit of all the virtues to drop into the mouth of some greasy-headed rustic of devout habits.

KING: The lady is not her own mistress, and her foster-father is not at home.

MATHAVYA: Well, but tell me, did she look at all kindly upon you?

KING: Maidens brought up in a hermitage are naturally shy and reserved; but for all that
She did look towards me, though she quick withdrew
Her stealthy glances when she met my gaze;
She smiled upon me sweetly, but disguised
With maiden grace the secret of her smiles.
Coy love was half unveiled; then, sudden checked
By modesty, left half to be divined.

MATHAVYA: Why, of course, my dear friend, you never could seriously expect that at the very first sight she would fall over head and ears in love with you, and without more ado come and sit in your lap.

KING: When we parted from each other, she betrayed her liking for me by clearer indications, but still with the utmost modesty.
Scarce had the fair one from my presence passed,
When, suddenly, without apparent cause,
She stopped, and, counterfeiting pain, exclaimed,
"My foot is wounded by this prickly grass."
Then, glancing at me tenderly, she feigned
Another charming pretext for delay,
Pretending that a bush had caught her robe
And turned as if to disentangle it.

MATHAVYA: I trust you have laid in a good stock of provisions, for I see you intend making this consecrated grove your game-preserve, and will be roaming here in quest of sport for some time to come.

KING: You must know, my good fellow, that I have been recognized by some of the inmates of the hermitage. Now I want the assistance of your fertile invention, in devising some excuse for going there again.

MATHAVYA: There is but one expedient that I can suggest. You are the King, are you not?

KING: What then?

MATHAVYA: Say you have come for the sixth part of their grain, which they owe you for tribute.

KING: No, no, foolish man; those hermits pay me a very different kind of tribute, which I value more than heaps of gold or jewels; observe,
The tribute which my other subjects bring
Must moulder into dust, but holy men
Present me with a portion of the fruits
Of penitential services and prayers—
A precious and imperishable gift.

A VOICE: [Behind the scenes] We are fortunate; here is the object of our search.

KING: [Listening] Surely those must be the voices of hermits, to judge by their deep tones.

WARDER: [Entering] Victory to the King! two young hermits are in waiting outside, and solicit an audience of your Majesty.

KING: Introduce them immediately.

WARDER: I will, my liege. [Goes out, and re-enters with two young Hermits] This way, Sirs, this way.

[Both the Hermits look at the King]

FIRST HERMIT: How majestic is his mien, and yet what confidence it inspires! But this might be expected in a King, whose character and habits have earned for him a title only one degree removed from that of a Sage.
In this secluded grove, whose sacred joys
All may participate, he deigns to dwell
Like one of us; and daily treasures up
A store of purest merit for himself,
By the protection of our holy rites.
In his own person wondrously are joined
Both majesty and saintlike holiness;
And often chanted by inspired bards,
His hallowed title of "Imperial Sage"
Ascends in joyous accents to the skies.

SECOND HERMIT: Bear in mind, Gautama, that this is the great Dushyanta, the friend of Indra.

FIRST HERMIT: What of that?

SECOND HERMIT: Where is the wonder if his nervous arm,
Puissant and massive as the iron bar
That binds a castle gateway, singly sways
The sceptre of the universal earth,
E'en to its dark-green boundary of waters?
Or if the gods, beholden to his aid
In their fierce warfare with the powers of hell,
Should blend his name with Indra's in their songs
Of victory, and gratefully accord
No lower meed of praise to his braced bow,
Than to the thunders of the god of heaven?

BOTH THE HERMITS: [Approaching] Victory to the King!

KING: [Rising from his seat] Hail to you both!

BOTH THE HERMITS: Heaven bless your Majesty! [*They offer fruits*]

KING: [*Respectfully receiving the offering*] Tell me, I pray you, the object of your visit.

BOTH THE HERMITS: The inhabitants of the hermitage, having heard of your Majesty's sojourn in our neighborhood, make this humble petition:—

KING: What are their commands?

BOTH THE HERMITS: In the absence of our Superior, the great sage Kanwa, evil demons are disturbing our sacrificial rites. Deign, therefore, accompanied by your charioteer, to take up your abode in our hermitage for a few days.

KING: I am honored by your invitation.

MATHAVYA: [*Aside*] Most opportune and convenient, certainly!

KING: [*Smiling*] Ho, there, Raivatika! Tell the charioteer from me to bring round the chariot with my bow.

WARDER: I will, sire. [*Exit*]

BOTH THE HERMITS: [*Joyfully*] Well it becomes
    the King by acts of grace
To emulate the virtues of his race.
Such acts thy lofty destiny attest;
Thy mission is to succor the distressed.

KING: [*Bowing to the* Hermits] Go first, reverend Sirs, I will follow you immediately.

BOTH THE HERMITS: May victory attend you! [*Exeunt*]

KING: My dear Mathavya, are not you full of longing to see Shakuntala?

MATHAVYA: To tell you the truth, though I was just now brimful of desire to see her, I have not a drop left since this piece of news about the demons.

KING: Never fear; you shall keep close to me for protection.

MATHAVYA: Well, you must be my guardian-angel, and act the part of a very Vishnu[3] to me.

WARDER: [*Entering*] Sire, the chariot is ready, and only waits to conduct you to victory. But here is a messenger named Karabhaka, just arrived from your capital, with a message from the Queen, your mother.

KING: [*Respectfully*] How say you? a messenger from the venerable Queen?

WARDER: Even so.

KING: Introduce him at once.

WARDER: I will, Sire. [*Goes out and re-enters with* Karabhaka] Behold the King. Approach.

KARABHAKA: Victory to the King! The Queen-mother bids me say that in four days from the present time she intends celebrating a solemn ceremony for the advancement and preservation of her son. She expects that your Majesty will honor her with your presence on that occasion.

KING: This places me in a dilemma. Here, on the one hand, is the commission of these holy men to be executed; and, on the other, the command of my

[3] The second god of the Hindu triumvirate (Brahma, the Creator, is the first), who has many "avatars," or incarnations, in the form of saviors.

revered parent to be obeyed. Both duties are too sacred to be neglected. What is to be done?

MATHAVYA: You will have to take up an intermediate position between the two, like King Trisanku, who was suspended between heaven and earth, because the sage Viswamitra commanded him to mount up to heaven, and the gods ordered him down again.

KING: I am certainly very much perplexed. For here,
Two different duties are required of me
In widely distant places; how can I
In my own person satisfy them both?
Thus is my mind distracted, and impelled
In opposite directions like a stream
That, driven back by rocks, still rushes on,
Forming two currents in its eddying course.
[*Reflecting*] Friend Mathavya, as you were my playfellow in childhood, the Queen has already received you like a second son; go you, then, back to her, and tell her of my solemn engagement to assist these holy men. You can supply my place in the ceremony, and act the part of a son to the Queen.

MATHAVYA: With the greatest pleasure in the world; but don't suppose that I am really coward enough to have the slightest fear of those trumpery demons.

KING: [*Smiling*] Oh, of course not; a great Brahman like you could not possibly give way to such weakness.

MATHAVYA: You must let me travel in a manner suitable to the King's younger brother.

KING: Yes, I shall send my retinue with you, that there may be no further disturbance in this sacred forest.

MATHAVYA: [*With a strut*] Already I feel quite like a young prince.

KING: [*Aside*] This is a giddy fellow, and in all probability he will let out the truth about my present pursuit to the women of the palace. What is to be done? I must say something to deceive him. [*Aloud to* Mathavya, *taking him by the hand*] Dear friend, I am going to the hermitage wholly and solely out of respect for its pious inhabitants, and not because I have really any liking for Shakuntala, the hermit's daughter. Observe:—
What suitable communion could there be
Between a monarch and a rustic girl?
I did but feign an idle passion, friend,
Take not in earnest what was said in jest.

MATHAVYA: Don't distress yourself; I quite understand.

[*Exeunt*]

PRELUDE TO ACT III.

SCENE—*The hermitage.*

[*Enter a* Young Brahman, *carrying bundles of Kusa-grass for the use of the sacrificing priest*]

YOUNG BRAHMAN: How wonderful is the power of

King Dushyanta! No sooner did he enter our hermitage, than we were able to proceed with our sacrificial rites, unmolested by the evil demons.
No need to fix the arrow to the bow;
The mighty monarch sounds the quivering string,
And, by the thunder of his arms dismayed,
Our demon foes are scattered to the wind.
I must now, therefore, make haste and deliver to the sacrificing priests these bundles of Kusa-grass, to be strewn round the altar. [*Walking and looking about; then addressing some one off the stage*] Why, Priyamvada, for whose use are you carrying that ointment of Usira-root and those lotus-leaves with fibers attached to them? [*Listening for her answer*] What say you?—that Shakuntala is suffering from fever produced by exposure to the sun, and that this ointment is to cool her burning frame? Nurse her with care, then, Priyamvada, for she is cherished by our reverend Superior as the very breath of his nostrils. I, for my part, will contrive that soothing waters, hallowed in the sacrifice, be administered to her by the hands of Gautami. [*Exit*]

ACT III.

SCENE—*The sacred grove.*

[*Enter* King Dushyanta, *with the air of one in love*]
  KING: [*Sighing thoughtfully*] The holy sage possesses magic power
In virtue of his penance; she, his ward,
Under the shadow of his tutelage,
Rests in security. I know it well;
Yet sooner shall the rushing cataract
In foaming eddies re-ascend the steep,
Than my fond heart turn back from its pursuit.
God of love! God of the flowery shafts! we lovers
are cruelly deceived by thee, and by the Moon, however deserving of confidence you may both appear.
For not to us do these thine arrows seem
Pointed with tender flowerets; not to us
Doth the pale Moon irradiate the earth
With beams of silver fraught with cooling dews;
But on our fevered frames the moonbeams fall
Like darts of fire, and every flower-tipt shaft
Of Kama,[4] as it probes our throbbing hearts,
Seems to be barbed with hardest adamant.
Adorable god of love! hast thou no pity for me?
    [*In a tone of anguish*]
How can thy arrows be so sharp when they are
pointed with flowers? Ah! I know the reason:
E'en now in thine unbodied essence lurks
The fire of Siva's[5] anger, like the flame
That ever hidden in the secret depths
Of ocean, smoulders there unseen. How else

    [4] The Hindu god of love.
    [5] The third member of the Hindu trinity, who represents the force of destruction (and restoration).

Could'st thou, all immaterial as thou art,
Inflame our hearts thus fiercely?—thou, whose form
Was scorched to ashes by a sudden flash
From the offended god's terrific eye.
Yet, methinks,
Welcome this anguish, welcome to my heart
These rankling wounds inflicted by the god,
Who on his scutcheon bears the monster-fish
Slain by his prowess; welcome death itself,
So that, commissioned by the lord of love,
This fair one be my executioner.
Adorable divinity! Can I by no reproaches excite
    your commiseration?
Have I not daily offered at thy shrine
Innumerable vows, the only food
Of thine ethereal essence? Are my prayers
Thus to be slighted? Is it meet that thou
Should'st aim thy shafts at thy true votary's heart,
Drawing thy bow-string even to thy ear?
[*Pacing up and down in a melancholy manner*]
Now that the holy men have completed their rites, and have no more need of my services, how shall I dispel my melancholy? [*Sighing*] I have but one resource. Oh for another sight of the idol of my soul! I will seek her. [*Glancing at the sun*] In all probability, as the sun's heat is now at its height, Shakuntala is passing her time under the shade of the bowers on the banks of the Malini, attended by her maidens. I will go and look for her there. [*Walking and looking about*] I suspect the fair one has but just passed by this avenue of young trees.
Here, as she tripped along, her fingers plucked
The opening buds; these lacerated plants,
Shorn of their fairest blossoms by her hand,
Seem like dismembered trunks, whose recent wounds
Are still unclosed; while from the bleeding socket
Of many a severed stalk, the milky juice
Still slowly trickles, and betrays her path.
    [*Feeling a breeze*]
What a delicious breeze meets me in this spot!
Here may the zephyr, fragrant with the scent
Of lotuses, and laden with the spray
Caught from the waters of the rippling stream,
Fold in its close embrace my fevered limbs.
[*Walking and looking about*] She must be somewhere in the neighborhood of this arbor of overhanging creepers enclosed by plantations of cane;
    [*Looking down*]
For at the entrance here I plainly see
A line of footsteps printed in the sand.
Here are the fresh impressions of her feet;
Their well-known outline faintly marked in front,
More deeply towards the heel; betokening
The graceful undulation of her gait.
I will peep through those branches.
    [*Walking and looking. With transport*]
Ah! now my eyes are gratified by an entrancing sight.
Yonder is the beloved of my heart reclining on a rock strewn with flowers, and attended by her two friends. How fortunate! Concealed behind the leaves

I will listen to their conversation, without raising their suspicions. [*Stands concealed, and gazes at them*]

[Shakuntala *and her two* Attendants, *holding fans in their hands, are discovered as described*]

PRIYAMVADA *and* ANASUYA: [*Fanning her. In a tone of affection*] Dearest Shakuntala, is the breeze raised by these broad lotus-leaves refreshing to you?

SHAKUNTALA: Dear friends, why should you trouble yourselves to fan me?

[Priyamvada *and* Anasuya *look sorrowfully at one another*]

KING: Shakuntala seems indeed to be seriously ill. [*Thoughtfully*] Can it be the intensity of the heat that has affected her? or does my heart suggest the true cause of her malady? [*Gazing at her passionately*] Why should I doubt it?
The maiden's spotless bosom is o'erspread
With cooling balsam; on her slender arm
Her only bracelet, twined with lotus-stalks,
Hangs loose and withered; her recumbent form
Betokens languor. Ne'er could noon-day sun
Inflict such fair disorder on a maid—
No, love, and love alone, is here to blame.

PRIYAMVADA: [*Aside to* Anasuya] I have observed, Anasuya, that Shakuntala has been indisposed ever since her first interview with King Dushyanta. Depend upon it, her ailment is to be traced to that source.

ANASUYA: The same suspicion, dear, has crossed my mind. But I will at once ask her and ascertain the truth. [*Aloud*] Dear Shakuntala, I am about to put a question to you. Your indisposition is really very serious.

SHAKUNTALA: [*Half rising from her couch*] What were you going to ask?

ANASUYA: We know very little about love-matters, dear Shakuntala; but for all that, I cannot help suspecting your present state to be something similar to that of the lovers we have heard about in romances. Tell us frankly what is the cause of your disorder. It is useless to apply a remedy, until the disease be understood.

KING: Anasuya bears me out in my suspicion.

SHAKUNTALA: [*Aside*] I am, indeed, deeply in love; but cannot rashly disclose my passion to these young girls.

PRIYAMVADA: What Anasuya says, dear Shakuntala, is very just. Why give so little heed to your ailment? Every day you are becoming thinner; though I must confess your complexion is still as beautiful as ever.

KING: Priyamvada speaks most truly.
Sunk is her velvet cheek; her wasted bosom
Loses its fulness; e'en her slender waist
Grows more attenuate; her face is wan,
Her shoulders droop;—as when the vernal blasts
Sear the young blossoms of the Madhavi,
Blighting their bloom; so mournful is the change,
Yet in its sadness, fascinating still,

Inflicted by the mighty lord of love
On the fair figure of the hermit's daughter.

SHAKUNTALA: Dear friends, to no one would I rather reveal the nature of my malady than to you; but I should only be troubling you.

PRIYAMVADA *and* ANASUYA: Nay, this is the very point about which we are so solicitous. Sorrow shared with affectionate friends is relieved of half its poignancy.

KING: Pressed by the partners of her joys and griefs,
Her much beloved companions, to reveal
The cherished secret locked within her breast,
She needs must utter it; although her looks
Encourage me to hope, my bosom throbs
As anxiously I listen for her answer.

SHAKUNTALA: Know then, dear friends, that from the first moment the illustrious Prince who is the guardian of our sacred grove presented himself to my sight—[*Stops short, and appears confused*]

PRIYAMVADA *and* ANASUYA: Say on, dear Shakuntala, say on.

SHAKUNTALA: Ever since that happy moment, my heart's affections have been fixed upon him, and my energies of mind and body have all deserted me, as you see.

KING: [*With rapture*] Her own lips have uttered the words I most longed to hear.
Love lit the flame, and Love himself allays
My burning fever, as when gathering clouds
Rise o'er the earth in summer's dazzling noon,
And grateful showers dispel the morning heat.

SHAKUNTALA: You must consent, then, dear friends, to contrive some means by which I may find favor with the King, or you will have ere long to assist at my funeral.

KING: Enough! These words remove all my doubts.

PRIYAMVADA: [*Aside to* Anasuya] She is far gone in love, dear Anasuya, and no time ought to be lost. Since she has fixed her affections on a monarch who is the ornament of Puru's line, we need not hesitate for a moment to express our approval.

ANASUYA: I quite agree with you.

PRIYAMVADA: [*Aloud*] We wish you joy, dear Shakuntala. Your affections are fixed on an object in every respect worthy of you. The noblest river will unite itself to the ocean, and the lovely Madhavi-creeper clings naturally to the mango, the only tree capable of supporting it.

KING: Why need we wonder if the beautiful constellation Visakha pines to be united with the Moon?

ANASUYA: By what stratagem can we best secure to our friend the accomplishment of her heart's desire both speedily and secretly?

PRIYAMVADA: The latter point is all we have to think about. As to "speedily," I look upon the whole affair as already settled.

ANASUYA: How so?

PRIYAMVADA: Did you not observe how the King betrayed his liking by the tender manner in which he gazed upon her, and how thin he has become the last few days, as if he had been lying awake thinking of her?

KING: [*Looking at himself*] Quite true! I certainly am becoming thin from want of sleep:
As night by night in anxious thought I raise
This wasted arm to rest my sleepless head,
My jewelled bracelet, sullied by the tears
That trickle from my eyes in scalding streams,
Slips towards my elbow from my shrivelled wrist.
Oft I replace the bauble, but in vain;
So easily it spans the fleshless limb
That e'en the rough and corrugated skin,
Scarred by the bow-string, will not check its fall.

PRIYAMVADA: [*Thoughtfully*] An idea strikes me, Anasuya. Let Shakuntala write a love-letter; I will conceal it in a flower, and contrive to drop it in the King's path. He will surely mistake it for the remains of some sacred offering, and will, in all probability, pick it up.

ANASUYA: A very ingenious device! It has my entire approval; but what says Shakuntala?

SHAKUNTALA: I must consider before I can consent to it.

PRIYAMVADA: Could you not, dear Shakuntala, think of some pretty composition in verse, containing a delicate declaration of your love?

SHAKUNTALA: Well, I will do my best; but my heart trembles when I think of the chances of a refusal.

KING: [*With rapture*] Too timid maid, here stands the man from whom
Thou fearest a repulse; supremely blessed
To call thee all his own. Well might he doubt
His title to thy love; but how could'st thou
Believe thy beauty powerless to subdue him?

PRIYAMVADA *and* ANASUYA: You undervalue your own merits, dear Shakuntala. What man in his senses would intercept with the skirt of his robe the bright rays of the autumnal moon, which alone can allay the fever of his body?

SHAKUNTALA: [*Smiling*] Then it seems I must do as I am bid. [*Sits down and appears to be thinking*]

KING: How charming she looks! My very eyes forget to wink, jealous of losing even for an instant a sight so enchanting.
How beautiful the movement of her brow,
As through her mind love's tender fancies flow!
And, as she weighs her thoughts, how sweet to trace
The ardent passion mantling in her face!

SHAKUNTALA: Dear girls, I have thought of a verse, but I have no writing-materials at hand.

PRIYAMVADA: Write the letters with your nail on this lotus-leaf, which is smooth as a parrot's breast.

SHAKUNTALA: [*After writing the verse*] Listen, dear friends, and tell me whether the ideas are appropriately expressed.

PRIYAMVADA *and* ANASUYA: We are all attention.

SHAKUNTALA: [*Reads*] I know not the secret thy bosom conceals,

Thy form is not near me to gladden my sight;
But sad is the tale that my fever reveals,
Of the love that consumes me by day and by night.

KING: [*Advancing hastily towards her*]
Nay, Love does but warm thee, fair maiden,—thy frame
Only droops like the bud in the glare of the noon;
But me he consumes with a pitiless flame,
As the beams of the day-star destroy the pale moon.

PRIYAMVADA *and* ANASUYA: [*Looking at him joyfully and rising to salute him*] Welcome, the desire of our hearts, that so speedily presents itself!

[*Shakuntala makes an effort to rise*]

KING: Nay, trouble not thyself, dear maiden.
Move not to do me homage; let thy limbs
Still softly rest upon their flowery couch,
And gather fragrance from the lotus-stalks,
Bruised by the fevered contact of thy frame.

ANASUYA: Deign, gentle Sir, to seat yourself on the rock on which our friend is reposing.

[*The King sits down. Shakuntala is confused*]

PRIYAMVADA: Any one may see at a glance that you are deeply attached to each other. But the affection I have for my friend prompts me to say something of which you hardly require to be informed.

KING: Do not hesitate to speak out, my good girl. If you omit to say what is in your mind, you may be sorry for it afterwards.

PRIYAMVADA: Is it not your special office as a King to remove the suffering of your subjects who are in trouble?

KING: Such is my duty, most assuredly.

PRIYAMVADA: Know, then, that our dear friend has been brought to her present state of suffering entirely through love for you. Her life is in your hands; take pity on her and restore her to health.

KING: Excellent maiden, our attachment is mutual. It is I who am the most honored by it.

SHAKUNTALA: [*Looking at* PRIYAMVADA] What do you mean by detaining the King, who must be anxious to return to his royal consorts after so long a separation?

KING: Sweet maiden, banish from thy mind the thought
That I could love another. Thou dost reign
Supreme, without a rival, in my heart,
And I am thine alone; disown me not,
Else must I die a second deadlier death,
Killed by thy words, as erst by Kama's shafts.

ANASUYA: Kind Sir, we have heard it said that kings have many favorite consorts. You must not, then, by your behavior towards our dear friend, give her relations cause to sorrow for her.

KING: Listen, gentle maiden, while in a few words I quiet your anxiety.
Though many beauteous forms my palace grace,
Henceforth two things alone will I esteem
The glory of my royal dynasty—
My sea-girt realm, and this most lovely maid.

PRIYAMVADA *and* ANASUYA: We are satisfied by your assurances.

PRIYAMVADA: [*Glancing on one side*] See, Anasuya, there is our favorite little fawn running about in great distress, and turning its eyes in every direction as if looking for its mother; come, let us help the little thing to find her.

[*Both move away*]

SHAKUNTALA: Dear friends, dear friends, leave me not alone and unprotected. Why need you both go?

PRIYAMVADA *and* ANASUYA: Unprotected! when the Protector of the world is at your side. [*Exeunt*]

SHAKUNTALA: What! have they both really left me?

KING: Distress not thyself, sweet maiden.
Thy adorer is at hand to wait upon thee.
Oh let me tend thee, fair one, in the place
Of thy dear friends; and with broad lotus fans
Raise cooling breezes to refresh thy frame;
Or shall I rather, with caressing touch,
Allay the fever of thy limbs, and soothe
Thy aching feet, beauteous as blushing lilies?

SHAKUNTALA: Nay, touch me not. I will not incur the censure of those whom I am bound to respect.

[*Rises and attempts to go*]

KING: Fair one, the heat of noon has not yet subsided, and thy body is still feeble.
How canst thou quit thy fragrant couch of flowers,
And from thy throbbing bosom cast aside
Its covering of lotus-leaves, to brave
With weak and fainting limbs the noonday heat?

[*Forces her to turn back*]

SHAKUNTALA: Infringe not the rules of decorum, mighty descendant of Puru. Remember, though I love you, I have no power to dispose of myself.

KING: Why this fear of offending your relations, timid maid? When your venerable foster-father hears of it, he will not find fault with you. He knows that the law permits us to be united without consulting him.
In Indra's heaven, so at least 'tis said,
No nuptial rites prevail, nor is the bride
Led to the altar by her future lord;
But all in secret does the bridegroom plight
His troth, and each unto the other vow
Mutual allegiance. Such espousals, too,
Are authorized on earth, and many daughters
Of royal saints thus wedded to their lords
Have still received their father's benison.

SHAKUNTALA: Leave me, leave me; I must take counsel with my female friends.

KING: I will leave thee when—

SHAKUNTALA: When?

KING: When I have gently stolen from thy lips
Their yet untasted nectar, to allay
The raging of my thirst, e'en as the bee
Sips the fresh honey from the opening bud.

[*Attempts to raise her face. Shakuntala tries to prevent him*]

A VOICE: [*Behind the scenes*] The loving birds, doomed by fate to nightly separation, must bid farewell to each other, for evening is at hand.

SHAKUNTALA: [*In confusion*] Great Prince, I hear the voice of the matron Gautami. She is coming this way to inquire after my health. Hasten and conceal yourself behind the branches.

KING: I will. [*Conceals himself*]

[*Enter* Gautami *with a vase in her hand, preceded by two* Attendants]

ATTENDANTS: This way, most venerable Gautami.

GAUTAMI: [*Approaching* Shakuntala] My child, is the fever of thy limbs allayed?

SHAKUNTALA: Venerable mother, there is certainly a change for the better.

GAUTAMI: Let me sprinkle you with this holy water, and all your ailments will depart. [*Sprinkling* Shakuntala's *head*] The day is closing, my child; come, let us go to the cottage.

[*They all move away*]

SHAKUNTALA: [*Aside*] Oh, my heart! thou didst fear to taste of happiness when it was within thy reach. Now that the object of thy desires is torn from thee, how bitter will be thy remorse, how distracting thine anguish! [*Moving on a few steps and stopping. Aloud*] Farewell! bower of creepers, sweet soother of my sufferings, farewell! may I soon again be happy under thy shade. [*Exit reluctantly with the others*]

KING: [*Returning to his former seat in the arbor. Sighing*] Alas! how many are the obstacles to the accomplishment of our wishes!
Albeit she did coyly turn away
Her glowing cheek, and with her fingers guard
Her pouting lips, that murmured a denial
In faltering accents, she did yield herself
A sweet reluctant captive to my will,
As eagerly I raised her lovely face;
But ere with gentle force I stole the kiss,
Too envious Fate did mar my daring purpose.
Whither now shall I betake myself? I will tarry for a brief space in this bower of creepers, so endeared to me by the presence of my beloved Shakuntala.

[*Looking round*]

Here printed on the flowery couch I see
The fair impression of her slender limbs;
Here is the sweet confession of her love,
Traced with her nail upon the lotus-leaf;
And yonder are the withered lily-stalks
That graced her wrist. While all around I view
Things that recall her image, can I quit
This bower, e'en though its living charm be fled?

A VOICE: [*In the air*] Great King.
Scarce is our evening sacrifice begun,
When evil demons, lurid as the clouds
That gather round the dying orb of day,
Cluster in hideous troops, obscene and dread,
About our altars, casting far and near
Terrific shadows, while the sacred fire
Sheds a pale luster o'er their ghostly shapes.

KING: I come to the rescue, I come. [*Exit*]

PRELUDE TO ACT IV.

SCENE—*The garden of the hermitage.*

[*Enter* Priyamvada *and* Anasuya *in the act of gathering flowers*]

ANASUYA: Although, dear Priyamvada, it rejoices my heart to think that Shakuntala has been happily united to a husband in every respect worthy of her, by the form of marriage prevalent among Indra's celestial musicians, nevertheless, I cannot help feeling somewhat uneasy in my mind.

PRIYAMVADA: How so?

ANASUYA: You know that the pious King was gratefully dismissed by the hermits on the successful termination of their sacrificial rites. He has now returned to his capital, leaving Shakuntala under our care; and it may be doubted whether, in the society of his royal consorts, he will not forget all that has taken place in this hermitage of ours.

PRIYAMVADA: On that score be at ease. Persons of his noble nature are not so destitute of all honorable feeling. I confess, however, that there is one point about which I am rather anxious. What, think you, will Father Kanwa say when he hears what has occurred?

ANASUYA: In my opinion, he will approve the marriage.

PRIYAMVADA: What makes you think so?

ANASUYA: From the first, it was always his fixed purpose to bestow the maiden on a husband worthy of her; and since heaven has given her such a husband, his wishes have been realized without any trouble to himself.

PRIYAMVADA: [*Looking at the flower-basket*] We have gathered flowers enough for the sacred offering, dear Anasuya.

ANASUYA: Well, then, let us now gather more, that we may have wherewith to propitiate the guardian-deity of our dear Shakuntala.

PRIYAMVADA: By all means.

[*They continue gathering*]

A VOICE: [*Behind the scenes*] Ho there! See you not that I am here!

ANASUYA: [*Listening*] That must be the voice of a guest announcing his arrival.

PRIYAMVADA: Surely, Shakuntala is not absent from the cottage. [*Aside*] Her heart at least is absent, I fear.

ANASUYA: Come along, come along; we have gathered flowers enough.

[*They move away*]

THE SAME VOICE: [*Behind the scenes*] Woe to thee, maiden, for daring to slight a guest like me!
Shall I stand here unwelcomed—even I,
A very mine of penitential merit,
Worthy of all respect? Shalt thou, rash maid,
Thus set at nought the ever sacred ties

Of hospitality? and fix thy thoughts
Upon the cherished object of thy love,
While I am present? Thus I curse thee, then—
He, even he of whom thou thinkest, he
Shall think no more of thee; nor in his heart
Retain thine image. Vainly shalt thou strive
To waken his remembrance of the past;
He shall disown thee, even as the sot,
Roused from his midnight drunkenness, denies
The words he uttered in his revellings.

PRIYAMVADA: Alas! alas! I fear a terrible misfortune has occurred. Shakuntala, from absence of mind, must have offended some guest whom she was bound to treat with respect. [*Looking behind the scenes*] Ah! yes; I see; and not less a person than the great sage Durvasas, who is known to be most irascible. He it is that has just cursed her, and is now retiring with hasty strides, trembling with passion, and looking as if nothing could turn him. His wrath is like a consuming fire.

ANASUYA: Go quickly, dear Priyamvada, throw yourself at his feet, and persuade him to come back, while I prepare a propitiatory offering for him, with water and refreshments.

PRIYAMVADA: I will. [*Exit*]

ANASUYA: [*Advancing hastily a few steps and stumbling*] Alas! alas! this comes of being in a hurry. My foot has slipped, and my basket of flowers has fallen from my hand. [*Stays to gather them up*]

PRIYAMVADA: [*Re-entering*] Well, dear Anasuya, I have done my best; but what living being could succeed in pacifying such a cross-grained, ill-tempered old fellow? However, I managed to mollify him a little.

ANASUYA: [*Smiling*] Even a little was much for him. Say on.

PRIYAMVADA: When he refused to turn back, I implored his forgiveness in these words: "Most venerable sage, pardon, I beseech you, this first offence of a young and inexperienced girl, who was ignorant of the respect due to your saintly character and exalted rank."

ANASUYA: And what did he reply?

PRIYAMVADA: "My word must not be falsified; but at the sight of the ring of recognition the spell shall cease." So saying, he disappeared.

ANASUYA: Oh! then we may breathe again; for, now I think of it, the King himself, at his departure, fastened on Shakuntala's finger, as a token of remembrance, a ring on which his own name was engraved. She has, therefore, a remedy for her misfortune at her own command.

PRIYAMVADA: Come, dear Anasuya, let us proceed with our religious duties.

[*They walk round*]

PRIYAMVADA: [*Looking off the stage*] See, Anasuya, there sits our dear friend, motionless as a statue, resting her face on her left hand, her whole mind absorbed in thinking of her absent husband.

She can pay no attention to herself, much less to a stranger.

ANASUYA: Priyamvada, let this affair never pass our lips. We must spare our dear friend's feelings. Her constitution is too delicate to bear much emotion.

PRIYAMVADA: I agree with you. Who would think of watering a tender jasmine with hot water?

ACT IV.

SCENE—*The neighborhood of the hermitage.*

[*Enter one of* Kanwa's *pupils just arisen from his couch at the dawn of day*]

PUPIL: My master, the venerable Kanwa, who is but lately returned from his pilgrimage, has ordered me to ascertain how the time goes. I have therefore come into the open air to see if it be still dark. [*Walking and looking about*] Oh! the dawn has already broken.

Lo! in one quarter of the sky, the Moon,
Lord of the herbs and night-expanding flowers,
Sinks towards his bed behind the western hills;
While in the east, preceded by the Dawn,
His blushing charioteer, the glorious Sun
Begins his course, and far into the gloom
Casts the first radiance of his orient beams.
Hail; co-eternal orbs, that rise to set,
And set to rise again; symbols divine
Of man's reverses, life's vicissitudes.

And now,
While the round Moon withdraws his looming disc
Beneath the western sky, the full-blown flower
Of the night-loving lotus sheds her leaves
In sorrow for his loss, bequeathing nought
But the sweet memory of her loveliness
To my bereaved sight; e'en as the bride
Disconsolately mourns her absent lord,
And yields her heart a prey to anxious grief.

ANASUYA: [*Entering abruptly*] Little as I know of the ways of the world, I cannot help thinking that King Dushyanta is treating Shakuntala very improperly.

PUPIL: Well, I must let my revered preceptor know that it is time to offer the burnt oblation. [*Exit*]

ANASUYA: I am broad awake, but what shall I do? I have no energy to go about my usual occupations. My hands and feet seem to have lost their power. Well, Love has gained his object; and Love only is to blame for having induced our dear friend, in the innocence of her heart, to confide in such a perfidious man. Possibly, however, the imprecation of Durvasas may be already taking effect. Indeed, I cannot otherwise account for the King's strange conduct, in allowing so long a time to elapse without even a letter; and that, too, after so many promises and protestations. I cannot think what to do unless we send him

the ring which was to be the token of recognition. But which of these austere hermits could we ask to be the bearer of it? Then, again, Father Kanwa has just returned from his pilgrimage; and how am I to inform him of Shakuntala's marriage to King Dushyanta, and her expectation of becoming soon a mother? I never could bring myself to tell him, even if I felt that Shakuntala had been in fault, which she certainly has not. What is to be done?

PRIYAMVADA: [*Entering joyfully*] Quick! quick! Anasuya! come and assist in the joyful preparations for Shakuntala's departure to her husband's palace.

ANASUYA: My dear girl, what can you mean?

PRIYAMVADA: Listen, now, and I will tell you all about it. I went just now to Shakuntala, to inquire whether she had slept comfortably—

ANASUYA: Well, well; go on.

PRIYAMVADA: She was sitting with her face bowed down to the very ground with shame, when Father Kanwa entered, and, embracing her, of his own accord offered her his congratulations. "I give thee joy, my child," he said, "we have had an auspicious omen. The priest who offered the oblation dropped it into the very center of the sacred fire, though thick smoke obstructed his vision. Henceforth thou wilt cease to be an object of compassion. This very day I purpose sending thee, under the charge of certain trusty hermits, to the King's palace; and shall deliver thee into the hands of thy husband, as I would commit knowledge to the keeping of a wise and faithful student."

ANASUYA: Who, then, informed the holy father of what passed in his absence?

PRIYAMVADA: As he was entering the sanctuary of the consecrated fire, an invisible being chanted a verse in celestial strains.

ANASUYA: [*With astonishment*] Indeed! pray repeat it.

PRIYAMVADA: [*Repeating the verse*]
Glows in thy daughter King Dushyanta's glory,
As in the sacred tree the mystic fire;
Let worlds rejoice to hear the welcome story,
And may the son immortalize the sire.

ANASUYA: [*Embracing* Priyamvada] Oh, my dear Priyamvada, what delightful news! I am pleased beyond measure; yet when I think that we are to lose our dear Shakuntala this very day, a feeling of melancholy mingles with my joy.

PRIYAMVADA: We shall find means of consoling ourselves after her departure. Let the dear creature only be made happy at any cost.

ANASUYA: Yes, yes, Priyamvada, it shall be so; and now to prepare the bridal array. I have always looked forward to this occasion, and some time since, I deposited a beautiful garland of Kesara flowers in a cocoa-nut box, and suspended it on a bough of yonder mango-tree. Be good enough to stretch out your hand and take it down, while I compound unguents and perfumes with this consecrated paste and these blades of sacred grass.

PRIYAMVADA: Very well.

[*Exit* Anasuya. Priyamvada *takes down the flowers*]

A VOICE: [*Behind the scenes*] Gautami, bid Sarngarava and the others hold themselves in readiness to escort Shakuntala.

PRIYAMVADA: [*Listening*] Quick, quick, Anasuya! They are calling the hermits who are to go with Shakuntala to Hastinapur.

ANASUYA: [*Re-entering with the perfumed unguents in her hand*] Come along then, Priyamvada! I am ready to go with you.

[*They walk away*]

PRIYAMVADA: [*Looking*] See! there sits Shakuntala, her locks arranged even at this early hour of the morning. The holy women of the hermitage are congratulating her, and invoking blessings on her head, while they present her with wedding-gifts and offerings of consecrated wild-rice. Let us join them.

[*They approach*]

[Shakuntala *is seen seated, with* Women *surrounding her, occupied in the manner described*]

FIRST WOMAN: [*To* Shakuntala] My child, may'st thou receive the title of "Chief-queen," and may thy husband delight to honor thee above all others!

SECOND WOMAN: My child, may'st thou be the mother of a hero!

THIRD WOMAN: My child, may'st thou be highly honored by thy lord!

[*Exeunt all the* Women, *excepting* Gautami, *after blessing* Shakuntala]

PRIYAMVADA *and* ANASUYA: [*Approaching*] Dear Shakuntala, we are come to assist you at your toilet, and may a blessing attend it!

SHAKUNTALA: Welcome, dear friends, welcome. Sit down here.

PRIYAMVADA *and* ANASUYA: [*Taking the baskets containing the bridal decorations, and sitting down*] Now, then, dearest, prepare to let us dress you. We must first rub your limbs with these perfumed unguents.

SHAKUNTALA: I ought indeed to be grateful for your kind offices, now that I am so soon to be deprived of them. Dear, dear friends, perhaps I shall never be dressed by you again. [*Bursts into tears*]

PRIYAMVADA *and* ANASUYA: Weep not, dearest; tears are out of season on such a happy occasion. [*They wipe away her tears and begin to dress her*]

PRIYAMVADA: Alas! these simple flowers and rude ornaments, which our hermitage offers in abundance, do not set off your beauty as it deserves.

[*Enter* Two Young Hermits, *bearing costly presents*]

BOTH HERMITS: Here are ornaments suitable for a queen.

[*The women look at them in astonishment*]

GAUTAMI: Why, Narada, my son, whence came these?

FIRST HERMIT: You owe them to the devotion of Father Kanwa.

GAUTAMI: Did he create them by the power of his own mind?

SECOND HERMIT: Certainly not; but you shall hear. The venerable sage ordered us to collect flowers for Shakuntala from the forest-trees; and we went to the wood for that purpose, when

Straightway depending from a neighboring tree
Appeared a robe of linen tissue, pure
And spotless as a moonbeam—mystic pledge
Of bridal happiness; another tree
Distilled a roseate dye wherewith to stain
The lady's feet; and other branches near
Glistened with rare and costly ornaments.
While, 'mid the leaves, the hands of forest-nymphs,
Vying in beauty with the opening buds,
Presented us with sylvan offerings.

PRIYAMVADA: [*Looking at Shakuntala*] The wood-nymphs have done you honor, indeed. This favor doubtless signifies that you are soon to be received as a happy wife into your husband's house, and are from this time forward to become the partner of his royal fortunes.

[Shakuntala *appears abashed*]

FIRST HERMIT: Come, Gautami; Father Kanwa has finished his ablutions. Let us go and inform him of the favor we have received from the deities who preside over our trees.

SECOND HERMIT: By all means.

[*Exeunt*]

PRIYAMVADA *and* ANASUYA: Alas! what are we to do? We are unused to such splendid decorations, and are at a loss how to arrange them. Our knowledge of painting must be our guide. We will dispose the ornaments as we have seen them in pictures.

SHAKUNTALA: Whatever pleases you, dear girls, will please me. I have perfect confidence in your taste.

[*They commence dressing her*]

[*Enter* Kanwa, *having just finished his ablutions*]

KANWA: This day my loved one leaves me, and my heart
Is heavy with its grief; the streams of sorrow,
Choked at the source, repress my faltering voice.
I have no words to speak; mine eyes are dimmed
By the dark shadows of the thoughts that rise
Within my soul. If such the force of grief
In an old hermit parted from his nursling,
What anguish must the stricken parent feel—
Bereft for ever of an only daughter. [*Advances towards* Shakuntala]

PRIYAMVADA *and* ANASUYA: Now, dearest Shakuntala, we have finished decorating you. You have only to put on the two linen mantles.

[Shakuntala *rises and puts them on*]

GAUTAMI: Daughter, see, here comes thy foster-father; he is eager to fold thee in his arms; his eyes swim with tears of joy. Hasten to do him reverence.

SHAKUNTALA: [*Reverently*] My father, I salute you.

KANWA: My daughter,

May'st thou be highly honored by thy lord,
E'en as Yayati Sarmishtha adored!
And, as she bore him Puru, so may'st thou
Bring forth a son to whom the world shall bow!

GAUTAMI: Most venerable father, she accepts your benediction as if she already possessed the boon it confers.

KANWA: Now come this way, my child, and walk reverently round these sacrificial fires.

[*They all walk round*]

KANWA: [*Repeats a prayer in the metre of the Rig-veda[6]*]

Holy flames, that gleam around
Every altar's hallowed ground;
Holy flames, whose frequent food
Is the consecrated wood,
And for whose encircling bed,
Sacred Kusa-grass is spread;
Holy flames, that waft to heaven
Sweet oblations daily given,
Mortal guilt to purge away,
Hear, oh hear me, when I pray—
Purify my child this day!

Now then, my daughter, set out on thy journey.
[*Looking on one side*] Where are thy attendants, Sarngarava and the others?

YOUNG HERMIT: [*Entering*] Here we are, most venerable father.

KANWA: Lead the way for thy sister.

SARNGARAVA: Come, Shakuntala, let us proceed.

[*All move away*]

KANWA: Hear me, ye trees that surround our hermitage!

Shakuntala ne'er moistened in the stream
Her own parched lips, till she had fondly poured
Its purest water on your thirsty roots;
And oft, when she would fain have decked her hair
With your thick-clustering blossoms, in her love
She robbed you not e'en of a single flower.
Her highest joy was ever to behold
The early glory of your opening buds;
Oh, then, dismiss her with a kind farewell.
This very day she quits her father's home,
To seek the palace of her wedded lord.

[*The note of a Koil[7] is heard*]

Hark! heard'st thou not the answer of the trees,
Our sylvan sisters, warbled in the note
Of the melodious Koil? they dismiss
Their dear Shakuntala with loving wishes.

VOICES IN THE AIR: Fare thee well, journey pleasantly on amid streams
Where the lotuses bloom, and the sun's glowing beams
Never pierce the deep shade of the wide-spreading trees,
While gently around thee shall sport the cool breeze;
Then light be thy footsteps and easy thy tread,

[6] One of the earliest sacred books of song and incantation of the Hindus.

[7] A Hindu or Eastern cuckoo.

Beneath thee shall carpets of lilies be spread;
Journey on to thy lord, let thy spirit be gay,
For the smiles of all Nature shall gladden thy way.

[*All listen with astonishment*]

GAUTAMI: Daughter! the nymphs of the wood, who love thee with the affection of a sister, dismiss thee with kind wishes for thy happiness. Take thou leave of them reverentially.

SHAKUNTALA: [*Bowing respectfully and walking on. Aside to her friend*] Eager as I am, dear Priyamvada, to see my husband once more, yet my feet refuse to move, now that I am quitting forever the home of my girlhood.

PRIYAMVADA: You are not the only one, dearest, to feel the bitterness of parting. As the time of separation approaches, the whole grove seems to share your anguish.

In sorrow for thy loss, the herd of deer
Forget to browse; the peacock on the lawn
Ceases its dance; the very trees around
Shed their pale leaves, like tears, upon the ground.

SHAKUNTALA: [*Recollecting herself*] My father, let me, before I go, bid adieu to my pet jasmine, the Moonlight of the Grove. I love the plant almost as a sister.

KANWA: Yes, yes, my child, I remember thy sisterly affection for the creeper. Here it is on the right.

SHAKUNTALA: [*Approaching the jasmine*] My beloved jasmine! most brilliant of climbing plants, how sweet it is to see thee cling thus fondly to thy husband, the mango-tree; yet, prithee, turn thy twining arms for a moment in this direction to embrace thy sister; she is going far away, and may never see thee again.

KANWA: Daughter, the cherished purpose of my heart

Has ever been to wed thee to a man
That should be worthy of thee; such a spouse
Hast thou thyself, by thine own merits, won.
To him thou goest, and about his neck
Soon shalt thou cling confidingly, as now
Thy favorite jasmine twines its loving arms
Around the sturdy mango. Leave thou it
To its protector—e'en as I consign
Thee to thy lord, and henceforth from my mind
Banish all anxious thought on thy behalf.
Proceed on thy journey, my child.

SHAKUNTALA: [*To Priyamvada and Anasuya*] To you, my sweet companions, I leave it as a keepsake. Take charge of it when I am gone.

PRIYAMVADA and ANASUYA: [*Bursting into tears*] And to whose charge do you leave us, dearest? Who will care for us when you are gone?

KANWA: For shame, Anasuya! dry your tears. Is this the way to cheer your friend at a time when she needs your support and consolation?

[*All move on*]

SHAKUNTALA: My father, see you there my pet deer, grazing close to the hermitage? She expects soon to fawn, and even now the weight of the little one she carries hinders her movements. Do not forget to send me word when she becomes a mother.

KANWA: I will not forget it.

SHAKUNTALA: [*Feeling herself drawn back*] What can this be, fastened to my dress? [*Turns round*]

KANWA: My daughter,
It is the little fawn, thy foster-child.
Poor helpless orphan! it remembers well
How with a mother's tenderness and love
Thou didst protect it, and with grains of rice
From thine own hand didst daily nourish it;
And, ever and anon, when some sharp thorn
Had pierced its mouth, how gently thou didst tend
The bleeding wound, and pour in healing balm.
The grateful nursling clings to its protectress,
Mutely imploring leave to follow her.

SHAKUNTALA: My poor little fawn! dost thou ask to follow an ungrateful wretch who hesitates not to desert her companions! When thy mother died, soon after thy birth, I supplied her place, and reared thee with my own hand; and now that thy second mother is about to leave thee, who will care for thee? My father, be thou a mother to her. My child, go back, and be a daughter to my father. [*Moves on, weeping*]

KANWA: Weep not, my daughter, check the gathering tear
That lurks beneath thine eyelid, ere it flow
And weaken thy resolve; be firm and true—
True to thyself and me; the path of life
Will lead o'er hill and plain, o'er rough and smooth,
And all must feel the steepness of the way;
Though rugged be thy course, press boldly on.

SARNGARAVA: Venerable Sire! the sacred precept is:—"Accompany thy friend as far as the margin of the first stream." Here, then, we are arrived at the border of a lake. It is time for you to give us your final instructions and return.

KANWA: Be it so; let us tarry for a moment under the shade of this fig-tree. [*They do so. Aside*] I must think of some appropriate message to send to his Majesty King Dushyanta. [*Reflects*]

SHAKUNTALA: [*Aside to* Anasuya] See, see, dear Anasuya, the poor female Chakravaka-bird, whom cruel fate dooms to nightly separation from her mate, calls to him in mournful notes from the other side of the stream, though he is only hidden from her view by the spreading leaves of the water-lily. Her cry is so piteous that I could almost fancy she was lamenting her hard lot in intelligible words.

ANASUYA: Say not so, dearest:
Fond bird! though sorrow lengthen out her night
Of widowhood, yet with a cry of joy
She hails the morning light that brings her mate
Back to her side. The agony of parting
Would wound us like a sword, but that its edge
Is blunted by the hope of future meeting.

KANWA: Sarngarava! when you have introduced Shakuntala into the presence of the King, you must give him this message from me:—

SARNGARAVA: Let me hear it, venerable father.

KANWA: This is it:—
Most puissant prince! we here present before thee
One thou art bound to cherish and receive
As thine own wife; yea, even to enthrone
As thine own queen—worthy of equal love
With thine imperial consorts. So much, Sire,
We claim of thee as justice due to us,
In virtue of our holy character,
In virtue of thine honorable rank,
In virtue of the pure spontaneous love
That secretly grew up 'twixt thee and her,
Without consent or privity of us.
We ask no more—the rest we freely leave
To thy just feeling and to destiny.

SARNGARAVA: A most suitable message! I will take care to deliver it correctly.

KANWA: And, now, my child, a few words of advice for thee. We hermits, though we live secluded from the world, are not ignorant of worldly matters.

SARNGARAVA: No, indeed. Wise men are conversant with all subjects.

KANWA: Listen, then, my daughter.
When thou reachest thy husband's palace, and art admitted into his family,
Honor thy betters; ever be respectful
To those above thee; and, should others share
Thy husband's love, ne'er yield thyself a prey
To jealousy; but ever be a friend,
A loving friend, to those who rival thee
In his affections. Should thy wedded lord
Treat thee with harshness, thou must never be
Harsh in return, but patient and submissive.
Be to thy menials courteous, and to all
Placed under thee, considerate and kind;
Be never self-indulgent, but avoid
Excess in pleasure; and, when fortune smiles,
Be not puffed up. Thus to thy husband's house
Wilt thou a blessing prove, and not a curse.
What thinks Gautami of this advice?

GAUTAMI: An excellent compendium, truly, of every wife's duties! Lay it well to heart, my daughter.

KANWA: Come, my beloved child, one parting embrace for me and for thy companions, and then we leave thee.

SHAKUNTALA: My father, must Priyamvada and Anasuya really return with you! They are very dear to me.

KANWA: Yes, my child; they, too, in good time, will be given in marriage to suitable husbands. It would not be proper for them to accompany thee to such a public place. But Gautami shall be thy companion.

SHAKUNTALA: [*Embracing him*] Removed from thy bosom, my beloved father, like a young tendril of the sandal-tree torn from its home in the western mountains, how shall I be able to support life in a foreign soil?

KANWA: Daughter, thy fears are groundless.
Soon shall thy lord prefer thee to the rank
Of his own consort; and unnumbered cares

Befitting his imperial dignity
Shall constantly engross thee. Then the bliss
Of bearing him a son—a noble boy,
Bright as the day-star, shall transport thy soul
With new delights, and little shalt thou reck
Of the light sorrow that afflicts thee now
At parting from thy father and thy friends.

[Shakuntala *throws herself at her foster-father's feet*]

KANWA: Blessings on thee, my child! May all my hopes of thee be realized!

SHAKUNTALA: [*Approaching her friends*] Come, my two loved companions, embrace me, both of you together.

PRIYAMVADA *and* ANASUYA: [*Embracing her*] Dear Shakuntala, remember, if the King should by any chance be slow in recognizing you, you have only to show him this ring, on which his own name is engraved.

SHAKUNTALA: The bare thought of it puts me in a tremor.

PRIYAMVADA *and* ANASUYA: There is no real cause for fear, dearest. Excessive affection is too apt to suspect evil where none exists.

SARNGARAVA: Come, lady, we must hasten on. The sun is rising in the heavens.

SHAKUNTALA: [*Looking towards the hermitage*] Dear father, when shall I ever see this hallowed grove again?

KANWA: I will tell thee; listen:—
When thou hast passed a long and blissful life
As King Dushyanta's queen, and jointly shared
With all the earth his ever-watchful care;
And hast beheld thine own heroic son,
Matchless in arms, united to a bride
In happy wedlock; when his aged sire,
Thy faithful husband, hath to him resigned
The helm of state; then, weary of the world,
Together with Dushyanta thou shalt seek
The calm seclusion of thy former home;
There amid holy scenes to be at peace,
Till thy pure spirit gain its last release.

GAUTAMI: Come, my child, the favorable time for our journey is fast passing. Let thy father return. Venerable Sire, be thou the first to move homewards, or these last words will never end.

KANWA: Daughter, detain me no longer. My religious duties must not be interrupted.

SHAKUNTALA: [*Again embracing her foster-father*] Beloved father, thy frame is much enfeebled by penitential exercises. Do not, oh! do not, allow thyself to sorrow too much on my account.

KANWA: [*Sighing*] How, O my child, shall my bereaved heart
Forget its bitterness, when, day by day,
Full in my sight shall grow the tender plants
Reared by thy care, or sprung from hallowed grain
Which thy loved hands have strewn around the door—

A frequent offering to our household gods?
Go, my daughter, and may thy journey be prosperous.

[*Exit* Shakuntala *with her escort*]

PRIYAMVADA *and* ANASUYA: [*Gazing after Shakuntala*] Alas! alas! she is gone, and now the trees hide our darling from our view.

KANWA: [*Sighing*] Well, Anasuya, your sister has departed. Moderate your grief, both of you, and follow me. I go back to the hermitage.

PRIYAMVADA *and* ANASUYA: Holy father, the sacred grove will be a desert without Shakuntala. How can we ever return to it?

KANWA: It is natural enough that your affection should make you view it in this light. [*Walking pensively on*] As for me, I am quite surprised at myself. Now that I have fairly dismissed her to her husband's house, my mind is easy; for, indeed,
A daughter is a loan—a precious jewel
Lent to a parent till her husband claim her.
And now that to her rightful lord and master
I have delivered her, my burdened soul
Is lightened, and I seem to breathe more freely.

[*Exeunt*]

ACT V.

SCENE—*A room in the palace.*

[King Dushyanta *and the jester* Mathavya *are discovered seated*]

MATHAVYA: [*Listening*] Hark! my dear friend, listen a minute, and you will hear sweet sounds proceeding from the music-room. Some one is singing a charming air. Who can it be? Oh! I know. The queen Hansapadika is practicing her notes, that she may greet you with a new song.

KING: Hush! Let me listen.

A VOICE: [*Sings behind the scenes*] How often hither didst thou rove, .
Sweet bee, to kiss the mango's cheek;
Oh! leave not, then, thy early love,
The lily's honey lip to seek.

KING: A most impassioned strain, truly!

MATHAVYA: Do you understand the meaning of the words?

KING: [*Smiling*] She means to reprove me, because I once paid her great attention, and have lately deserted her for the queen Vasumati. Go, my dear fellow, and tell Hansapadika from me that I take her delicate reproof as it is intended.

MATHAVYA: Very well. [*Rising from his seat*] But stay—I don't much relish being sent to bear the brunt of her jealousy. The chances are that she will have me seized by the hair of the head and beaten to a jelly. I would as soon expose myself, after a vow of celibacy, to the seductions of a lovely nymph, as encounter the fury of a jealous woman.

KING: Go, go; you can disarm her wrath by a civil speech; but give her my message.

MATHAVYA: What must be must be, I suppose. [*Exit*]

KING: [*Aside*] Strange! that song has filled me with a most peculiar sensation. A melancholy feeling has come over me, and I seem to yearn after some long-forgotten object of affection. Singular, indeed! but

Not seldom in our happy hours of ease,
When thought is still, the sight of some fair form,
Or mournful fall of music breathing low,
Will stir strange fancies, thrilling all the soul
With a mysterious sadness, and a sense
Of vague yet earnest longing. Can it be
That the dim memory of events long past,
Or friendships formed in other states of being,
Flits like a passing shadow o'er the spirit? [*Remains pensive and sad*]

[*Enter the* Chamberlain, *named* Vatayana]

CHAMBERLAIN: Alas! to what an advanced period of life have I attained!

Even this wand betrays the lapse of years;
In youthful days 'twas but a useless badge
And symbol of my office; now it serves
As a support to prop my tottering steps.

Ah me! I feel very unwilling to announce to the King that a deputation of young hermits from the sage Kanwa has arrived, and craves an immediate audience. Certainly, his Majesty ought not to neglect a matter of sacred duty, yet I hardly like to trouble him when he has just risen from the judgment-seat. Well, well; a monarch's business is to sustain the world, and he must not expect much repose; because—

Onward, for ever onward, in his car
The unwearied Sun pursues his daily course,
Nor tarries to unyoke his glittering steeds.
And, ever moving, speeds the rushing Wind
Through boundless space, filling the universe
With his life-giving breezes. Day and night,
The King of Serpents on his thousand heads
Upholds the incumbent earth; and even so,
Unceasing toil is aye the lot of kings,
Who, in return, draw nurture from their subjects.

I will therefore deliver my message. [*Walking and looking about*] Ah! here comes the King.

His subjects are his children; through the day,
Like a fond father, to supply their wants,
Incessantly he labors; wearied now,
The monarch seeks seclusion and repose;
E'en as the prince of elephants defies
The sun's fierce heat, and leads the fainting herd
To verdant pastures, ere his wayworn limbs
He yields to rest beneath the cooling shade.

[*Approaching*] Victory to the King! So please your Majesty, some hermits who live in a forest near the Snowy Mountains have arrived here, bringing certain women with them. They have a message to deliver from the sage Kanwa, and desire an audience. I await your Majesty's commands.

KING: [*Respectfully*] A message from the sage Kanwa, did you say?

CHAMBERLAIN: Even so, my liege.

KING: Tell my domestic priest Somarata to receive the hermits with due honor, according to the prescribed form. He may then himself introduce them into my presence. I will await them in a place suitable for the reception of such holy guests.

CHAMBERLAIN: Your Majesty's commands shall be obeyed. [*Exit*]

KING: [*Rising and addressing the* Warder] Vetravati, lead the way to the chamber of the consecrated fire.

WARDER: This way, Sire.

KING: [*Walking on, with the air of one oppressed by the cares of Government*] People are generally contented and happy when they have gained their desires; but kings have no sooner attained the object of their aspirations than all their troubles begin.

'Tis a fond thought that to attain the end
And object of ambition is to rest;
Success doth only mitigate the fever
Of anxious expectation; soon the fear
Of losing what we have, the constant care
Of guarding it, doth weary. Ceaseless toil
Must be the lot of him who with his hands
Supports the canopy that shields his subjects.

TWO HERALDS: [*Behind the scenes*] May the King be victorious!

FIRST HERALD: Honor to him who labors day by day

For the world's weal, forgetful of his own;
Like some tall tree that with its stately head
Endures the solar beam, while underneath
It yields refreshing shelter to the weary.

SECOND HERALD: Let but the monarch wield his threatening rod

And e'en the guilty tremble; at his voice
The rebel spirit cowers; his grateful subjects
Acknowledge him their guardian; rich and poor
Hail him a faithful friend—a loving kinsman.

KING: Weary as I was before, this complimentary address has refreshed me. [*Walks on*]

WARDER: Here is the terrace of the hallowed fire-chamber, and yonder stands the cow that yields the milk for the oblations. The sacred enclosure has been recently purified, and looks clean and beautiful. Ascend, Sire.

KING: [*Leans on the shoulders of his attendants, and ascends*] Vetravati, what can possibly be the message that the venerable Kanwa has sent me by these hermits?

Perchance their sacred rites have been disturbed
By demons, or some evil has befallen
The innocent herds, their favorites, that graze
Within the precincts of the hermitage;
Or haply, through my sins, some withering blight

Has nipped the creeping plants that spread their arms
Around the hallowed grove. Such troubled thoughts
Crowd through my mind, and fill me with misgiving.

WARDER: If you ask my opinion, Sire, I think the
hermits merely wish to take an opportunity to testify-
ing their loyalty, and are therefore come to offer
homage to your Majesty.

[*Enter the* Hermits *leading* Shakuntala, *attended
by* Gautami; *and in advance of them, the*
Chamberlain *and the* Domestic Priest]

CHAMBERLAIN: This way, reverend Sirs, this way.

SARNGARAVA: O Saradwata,
'Tis true the monarch lacks no royal grace,
Nor ever swerves from justice; true, his people,
Yea such as in life's humblest walks are found,
Refrain from evil courses; still to me,
A lonely hermit reared in solitude,
This throng appears bewildering, and I seem
To look upon a burning house, whose inmates
Are running to and fro in wild dismay.

SARADWATA: It is natural that the first sight of the
King's capital should affect you in this manner; my
own sensations are very similar.
As one just bathed beholds the man polluted;
As one late purified, the yet impure;
As one awake looks on the yet unawakened;
Or as the freeman gazes on the thrall,
So I regard this crowd of pleasure-seekers.

SHAKUNTALA: [*Feeling a quivering sensation in
her right eyelid, and suspecting a bad omen*] Alas!
what means this throbbing of my right eyelid?

GAUTAMI: Heaven avert the evil omen, my child!
May the guardian deities of thy husband's family
convert it into a sign of good fortune! [*Walks on*]

PRIEST: [*Pointing to the* King] Most reverend
Sirs, there stands the protector of the four classes of
the people, the guardian of the four conditions of the
priesthood. He has just left the judgment-seat, and is
waiting for you. Behold him!

SARNGARAVA: Great Brahman, we are happy in
thinking that the King's power is exerted for the pro-
tection of all classes of his subjects. We have not
come as petitioners—we have the fullest confidence
in the generosity of his nature.
The loftiest trees bend humbly to the ground
Beneath the teeming burden of their fruit;
High in the vernal sky the pregnant clouds
Suspend their stately course, and, hanging low,
Scatter their sparkling treasures o'er the earth;
And such is true benevolence; the good
Are never rendered arrogant by riches.

WARDER: So please your Majesty, I judge from the
placid countenance of the hermits that they have no
alarming message to deliver.

KING: [*Looking at* Shakuntala] But the lady
    there—
Who can she be, whose form of matchless grace
Is half concealed beneath her flowing veil?
Among the sombre hermits she appears

Like a fresh bud 'mid sear and yellow leaves.

WARDER: So please your Majesty, my curiosity is
also roused, but no conjecture occurs to my mind.
This at least is certain, that she deserves to be looked
at more closely.

KING: True; but it is not right to gaze at another
man's wife.

SHAKUNTALA: [*Placing her hand on her bosom.
Aside*] O my heart, why this throbbing? Remember
thy lord's affection, and take courage.

PRIEST: [*Advancing*] These holy men have been
received with all due honor. One of them has now a
message to deliver from his spiritual superior. Will
your Majesty deign to hear it?

KING: I am all attention.

HERMITS: [*Extending their hands*] Victory to the
King!

KING: Accept my respectful greeting.

HERMITS: May the desires of your soul be accomplished!

KING: I trust no one is molesting you in the prosecution of your religious rites.

HERMITS: Who dares disturb our penitential rites
When thou art our protector? Can the night
Prevail to cast her shadows o'er the earth
While the sun's beams irradiate the sky?

KING: Such, indeed, is the very meaning of my
title—"Defender of the Just." I trust the venerable
Kanwa is in good health. The world is interested in
his well-being.

HERMITS: Holy men have health and prosperity in
their own power. He bade us greet your Majesty, and,
after kind inquiries, deliver this message.

KING: Let me hear his commands.

SARNGARAVA: He bade us to say that he feels happy
in giving his sanction to the marriage which your
Majesty contracted with this lady, his daughter,
privately and by mutual agreement. Because,
By us thou art esteemed the most illustrious
Of noble husbands; and Shakuntala,
Virtue herself in human form revealed.
Great Brahma hath in equal yoke united
A bride unto a husband worthy of her;
Henceforth let none make blasphemous complaint
That he is pleased with ill-assorted unions.
Since, therefore, she expects soon to be the mother
of thy child, receive her into thy palace, that she
may perform, in conjunction with thee, the cere-
monies prescribed by religion on such an occasion.

GAUTAMI: So please your Majesty, I would add a
few words; but why should I intrude my sentiments
when an opportunity of speaking my mind has never
been allowed me?
She took no counsel with her kindred; thou
Didst not confer with thine, but all alone
Didst solemnize thy nuptials with thy wife.
Together, then, hold converse; let us leave you.

SHAKUNTALA: [*Aside*] Ah! how I tremble for my
lord's reply.

KING: What strange proposal is this?

SHAKUNTALA: [*Aside*] His words are like fire to me.

SARNGARAVA: What do I hear? Dost thou, then, hesitate? Monarch, thou art well acquainted with the ways of the world, and knowest that
A wife, however virtuous and discreet,
If she live separate from her wedded lord,
Though under shelter of her parent's roof,
Is mark for vile suspicion. Let her dwell
Beside her husband, though he hold her not
In his affection. So her kinsmen will it.

KING: Do you really mean to assert that I ever married this lady?

SHAKUNTALA: [*Despondingly. Aside*] O my heart, thy worst misgivings are confirmed.

SARNGARAVA: Is it becoming in a monarch to depart from the rules of justice, because he repents of his engagements?

KING: I cannot answer a question which is based on a mere fabrication.

SARNGARAVA: Such inconstancy is fortunately not common, except in men intoxicated by power.

KING: Is that remark aimed at me?

GAUTAMI: Be not ashamed, my daughter. Let me remove thy veil for a little space. Thy husband will then recognize thee. [*Removes her veil*]

KING: [*Gazing at* Shakuntala. *Aside*] What charms are here revealed before mine eyes!
Truly no blemish mars the symmetry
Of that fair form; yet can I ne'er believe
She is my wedded wife; and like a bee
That circles round the flower whose nectared cup
Teems with the dew of morning, I must pause
Ere eagerly I taste the proffered sweetness. [*Remains wrapped in thought*]

WARDER: How admirably does our royal master's behavior prove his regard for justice! Who else would hestitate for a moment when good fortune offered for his acceptance a form of such rare beauty?

SARNGARAVA: Great King, why art thou silent?

KING: Holy men, I have revolved the matter in my mind; but the more I think of it, the less able am I to recollect that I ever contracted an alliance with this lady. What answer, then, can I possibly give you when I do not believe myself to be her husband, and I plainly see that she is soon to become a mother?

SHAKUNTALA: [*Aside*] Woe! Woe! Is our very marriage to be called in question by my own husband? Ah me! is this to be the end of all my bright visions of wedded happiness?

SARNGARAVA: Beware!
Beware how thou insult the holy Sage!
Remember how he generously allowed
Thy secret union with his foster-child;
And how, when thou didst rob him of his treasure,
He sought to furnish thee excuse, when rather
He should have cursed thee for a ravisher.

SARADWATA: Sarngarava, speak to him no more.

Shakuntala, our part is performed; we have said all we have to say, and the King has replied in the manner thou hast heard. It is now thy turn to give him convincing evidence of thy marriage.

SHAKUNTALA: [*Aside*] Since his feeling towards me has undergone a complete revolution, what will it avail to revive old recollections? One thing is clear—I shall soon have to mourn my own widowhood. [*Aloud*] My revered husband— [*Stops short*] But no—I dare not address thee by this title, since thou hast refused to acknowledge our union. Noble descendant of Puru! It is not worthy of thee to betray an innocent-minded girl, and disown her in such terms, after having so lately and so solemnly plighted thy vows to her in the hermitage.

KING: [*Stopping his ears*] I will hear no more. Be such a crime far from my thoughts!
What evil spirit can possess thee, lady,
That thou dost seek to sully my good name
By base aspersions, like a swollen torrent,
That, leaping from its narrow bed, o'erthrows
The tree upon its bank, and strives to blend
Its turbid waters with the crystal stream?

SHAKUNTALA: If then, thou really believest me to be the wife of another, and thy present conduct proceeds from some cloud that obscures thy recollection, I will easily convince thee by this token.

KING: An excellent idea!

SHAKUNTALA: [*Feeling for the ring*] Alas! alas! woe is me! There is no ring on my finger! [*Looks with anguish at* Gautami]

GAUTAMI: The ring must have slipped off when thou wast in the act of offering homage to the holy water of Sachi's sacred pool, near Sakravatara.

KING: [*Smiling*] People may well talk of the readiness of woman's invention! Here is an instance of it.

SHAKUNTALA: Say, rather, of the omnipotence of fate. I will mention another circumstance, which may yet convince thee.

KING: By all means let me hear it at once.

SHAKUNTALA: One day, while we were seated in a jasmine-bower, thou didst pour into the hollow of thine hand some water, sprinkled by a recent shower in the cup of a lotus-blossom—

KING: I am listening; proceed.

SHAKUNTALA: At that instant, my adopted child, the little fawn, with soft, long eyes, came running towards us. Upon which, before tasting the water thyself, thou didst kindly offer some to the little creature, saying fondly:—"Drink first, gentle fawn." But she could not be induced to drink from the hand of a stranger; though immediately afterwards, when I took the water in my own hand, she drank with perfect confidence. Then, with a smile, thou didst say: "Every creature confides naturally in its own kind. You are both inhabitants of the same forest, and have learnt to trust each other."

KING: Voluptuaries may allow themselves to be

seduced from the path of duty by falsehoods such as these, expressed in honeyed words.

GAUTAMI: Speak not thus, illustrious Prince. This lady was brought up in a hermitage, and has never learnt deceit.

KING: Holy matron,
E'en in untutored brutes, the female sex
Is marked by inborn subtlety—much more
In beings gifted with intelligence.
The wily Koil, ere towards the sky
She wings her sportive flight, commits her eggs
To other nests, and artfully consigns
The rearing of her little ones to strangers.

SHAKUNTALA: [Angrily] Dishonorable man, thou judgest of others by thine own evil heart. Thou, at least, art unrivaled in perfidy, and standest alone— a base deceiver in the garb of virtue and religion— like a deep pit whose yawning mouth is concealed by smiling flowers.

KING: [Aside] Her anger, at any rate, appears genuine, and makes me almost doubt whether I am in the right. For indeed,
When I had vainly searched my memory,
And so with stern severity denied
The fabled story of our secret loves,
Her brows, that met before in graceful curves,
Like the arched weapon of the god of love,
Seemed by her frown dissevered; while the fire
Of sudden anger kindled in her eyes.

[Aloud] My good lady, Dushyanta's character is well known to all. I comprehend not your meaning.

SHAKUNTALA: Well do I deserve to be thought a harlot for having in the innocence of my heart, and out of the confidence I reposed in a Prince of Puru's race, entrusted my honor to a man whose mouth distils honey, while his heart is full of poison. [Covers her face with her mantle, and bursts into tears]

SARNGARAVA: Thus it is that burning remorse must ever follow rash actions which might have been avoided, and for which one has only one's self to blame.
Not hastily should marriage be contracted,
And specially in secret. Many a time,
In hearts that know not each the other's fancies,
Fond love is changed into most bitter hate.

KING: How now! Do you give credence to this woman rather than to me, that you heap such accusations on me?

SARNGARAVA: [Sarcastically] That would be too absurd, certainly. You have heard the proverb:—
Hold in contempt the innocent words of those
Who from their infancy have known no guile;
But trust the treacherous counsels of the man
Who makes a very science of deceit.

KING: Most veracious Brahman, grant that you are in the right, what end would be gained by betraying this lady?

SARNGARAVA: Ruin.

KING. No one will believe that a Prince of Puru's race would seek to ruin others or himself.

SARADWATA: This altercation is idle, Sarngarava. We have executed the commission of our preceptor; come, let us return.
[To the King] Shakuntala is certainly thy bride;
Receive her or reject her, she is thine.
Do with her, King, according to thy pleasure—
The husband o'er the wife is absolute.
Go on before us, Gautami.

[They move away]

SHAKUNTALA: What! is it not enough to have been betrayed by this perfidious man? Must you also forsake me, regardless of my tears and lamentations? [Attempts to follow them]

GAUTAMI: [Stopping] My son Sarngarava, see! Shakuntala is following us, and with tears implores us not to leave her. Alas! poor child, what will she do here with a cruel husband who casts her from him?

SARNGARAVA: [Turning angrily towards her] Wilful woman, dost thou seek to be independent of thy lord?

[Shakuntala trembles with fear]
Shakuntala!
If thou art really what the King proclaims thee,
How can thy father e'er receive thee back
Into his house and home? but if thy conscience
Be witness to thy purity of soul,
E'en should thy husband to a handmaid's lot
Condemn thee, thou may'st cheerfully endure it,
When ranked among the number of his household.
The duty therefore is to stay. As for us,
We must return immediately.

KING: Deceive not the lady, my good hermit, by any such expectations.
The moon expands the lotus of the night,
The rising sun awakens the lily; each
Is with his own contented. Even so
The virtuous man is master of his passions,
And from another's wife averts his gaze.

SARNGARAVA: Since thy union with another woman has rendered thee oblivious of thy marriage with Shakuntala, whence this fear of losing thy character for constancy and virtue?

KING: [To his domestic Priest] You must counsel me, revered Sir, as to my course of action. Which of the two evils involves the greater or less sin?
Whether by some dark veil my mind be clouded,
Or this designing woman speak untruly,
I know not. Tell me, must I rather be
The base disowner of my wedded wife,
Or the defiling and defiled adulterer?

PRIEST: [After deliberation] You must take an intermediate course.

KING: What course, revered Sir? Tell me at once.

PRIEST: I will provide an asylum for the lady in my own house until the birth of her child; and my reason, if you ask me, is this: Soothsayers have predicted that your first-born will have universal dominion. Now, if the hermit's daughter bring forth a son with the discus or mark of empire in the lines of his hand, you must admit her immediately into your royal apartments with great rejoicings; if not, then determine to send her back as soon as possible to her father.

KING: I bow to the decision of my spiritual adviser.

PRIEST: Daughter, follow me.

SHAKUNTALA: O divine earth, open and receive me into thy bosom!

[*Exit* Shakuntala *weeping, with the* Priest *and the* Hermits. *The* King *remains absorbed in thinking of her, though the curse still clouds his recollection*]

A VOICE: [*Behind the scenes*] A miracle! a miracle!

KING: [*Listening*] What has happened now?

PRIEST: [*Entering with an air of astonishment*] Great Prince, a stupendous prodigy has just occurred.

KING: What is it?

PRIEST: May it please your Majesty, so soon as Kanwa's pupils had departed,
Shakuntala, her eyes all bathed in tears,
With outstretched arms, bewailed her cruel fate—

KING: Well, well, what happened then?

PRIEST: When suddenly a shining apparition,
In female shape, descended from the skies,
Near the nymph's pool, and bore her up to heaven.

[*All remain motionless with astonishment*]

KING: My good priest, from the very first I declined having anything to do with this matter. It is now all over, and we can never, by our conjectures, unravel the mystery; let it rest; go, seek repose.

PRIEST: [*Looking at the* King] Be it so. Victory to the King! [*Exit*]

KING: Vetravati, I am tired out; lead the way to the bedchamber.

WARDER: This way, Sire.

[*They move away*]

KING: Do what I will, I cannot call to mind
That I did e'er espouse the sage's daughter;
Therefore I have disowned her; yet 'tis strange
How painfully my agitated heart
Bears witness to the truth of her assertion,
And makes me credit her against my judgment.

[*Exeunt*]

PRELUDE TO ACT VI.

SCENE—*A street.*

[*Enter the* King's *brother-in-law as* Superintendent *of the city police; and with him* Two Constables, *dragging a poor* Fisherman, *who has his hands tied behind his back*]

BOTH THE CONSTABLES: [*Striking the prisoner*] Take that for a rascally thief that you are; and now

tell us, sirrah, where you found this ring—aye, the King's own signet-ring. See, here is the royal name engraved on the setting of the jewel.

FISHERMAN: [*With a gesture of alarm*] Mercy! kind sirs, mercy! I did not steal it; indeed I did not.

FIRST CONSTABLE: Oh! then I suppose the King took you for some fine Brahman, and made you a present of it?

FISHERMAN: Only hear me. I am but a poor fisherman, living at Sakravatara—

SECOND CONSTABLE: Scoundrel, who ever asked you, pray, for a history of your birth and parentage?

SUPERINTENDENT: [*To one of the* Constables] Suchaka, let the fellow tell his own story from the beginning. Don't interrupt him.

BOTH CONSTABLES: As you please, master. Go on, then, sirrah, and say what you've got to say.

FISHERMAN: You see in me a poor man, who supports his family by catching fish with nets, hooks, and the like.

SUPERINTENDENT: [*Laughing*] A most refined occupation, certainly!

FISHERMAN: Blame me not for it, master.
The father's occupation, though despised
By others, casts no shame upon the son,
And he should not forsake it. Is the priest
Who kills the animal for sacrifice
Therefore deemed cruel? Sure a low-born man
May, though a fisherman, be tender-hearted.

SUPERINTENDENT: Well, well; go on with your story.

FISHERMAN: One day I was cutting open a large carp I had just hooked, when the sparkle of a jewel caught my eye, and what should I find in the fish's maw but that ring! Soon afterwards, when I was offering it for sale, I was seized by your honors. Now you know everything. Whether you kill me, or whether you let me go, this is the true account of how the ring came into my possession.

SUPERINTENDENT: [*To one of the* Constables] Well, Januka, the rascal emits such a fishy odor that I have no doubt of his being a fisherman; but we must inquire a little more closely into this queer story about the finding of the ring. Come, we'll take him before the King's household.

BOTH CONSTABLES: Very good, master. Get on with you, you cutpurse.

[*All move on*]

SUPERINTENDENT: Now attend, Suchaka; keep your guard here at the gate; and hark ye, sirrahs, take good care your prisoner does not escape, while I go in and lay the whole story of the discovery of this ring before the King in person. I will soon return and let you know his commands.

BOTH CONSTABLES: Go in, master, by all means; and may you find favor in the King's sight.

[*Exit* Superintendent]

FIRST CONSTABLE: [*After an interval*] I say, Januka, the Superintendent is a long time away.

SECOND CONSTABLE: Aye, aye; kings are not to be got at so easily. Folks must bide the proper opportunity.

FIRST CONSTABLE: Januka, my fingers itch to strike the first blow at this royal victim here. We must kill him with all the honors, you know. I long to begin binding the flowers round his head. [*Pretends to strike a blow at the* Fisherman]

FISHERMAN: You Honor surely will not put an innocent man to a cruel death.

SECOND CONSTABLE: [*Looking*] There's our Superintendent at last, I declare. See! he is coming towards us with a paper in his hand. We shall soon know the King's command; so prepare, my fine fellow, either to become food for the vultures, or to make acquaintance with some hungry cur.

SUPERINTENDENT: [*Entering*] Ho, there, Suchaka! set the fisherman at liberty, I tell you. His story about the ring is all correct.

FIRST CONSTABLE: Oh! very good, Sir; as you please.

SECOND CONSTABLE: The fellow had one foot in hell, and now here he is in the land of the living. [*Releases him*]

FISHERMAN: [*Bowing to the* Superintendent] Now, master, what think you of my way of getting a livelihood?

SUPERINTENDENT: Here, my good man, the King desired me to present you with this purse. It contains a sum of money equal to the full value of the ring. [*Gives him the money*]

FISHERMAN: [*Taking it and bowing*] His Majesty does me too great honor.

FIRST CONSTABLE: You may well say so. He might as well have taken you from the gallows to seat you on his state elephant.

SECOND CONSTABLE: Master, the King must value the ring very highly, or he would never have sent such a sum of money to this ragamuffin.

SUPERINTENDENT: I don't think he prizes it as a costly jewel so much as a memorial of some person he tenderly loves. The moment it was shown to him he became much agitated, though in general he conceals his feelings.

FIRST CONSTABLE: Then you must have done a great service—

SECOND CONSTABLE: Yes, to this husband of a fish-wife. [*Looks enviously at the* Fisherman]

FISHERMAN: Here's half the money for you, my masters. It will serve to purchase the flowers you spoke of, if not to buy me your good-will.

SECOND CONSTABLE: Well, now, that's just as it should be.

SUPERINTENDENT: My good fisherman, you are an excellent fellow, and I begin to feel quite a regard for you. Let us seal our first friendship over a glass of good liquor. Come along to the next wineshop, and we'll drink your health.

ALL: By all means.

[*Exeunt*]

ACT VI.

SCENE—*The garden of a palace.*

[*The nymph* Sanumati *is seen descending in a celestial car*]

SANUMATI: Behold me just arrived from attending in my proper turn at the nymph's pool, where I have left the other nymphs to perform their ablutions, whilst I seek to ascertain, with my own eyes, how it fares with King Dushyanta. My connection with the nymph Menaka has made her daughter Shakuntala dearer to me than my own flesh and blood; and Menaka it was who charged me with this errand on her daughter's behalf. [*Looking round in all directions*] How is it that I see no preparations in the King's household for celebrating the great vernal festival? I could easily discover the reason by my divine faculty of meditation; but respect must be shown to the wishes of my friend. How then shall I arrive at the truth? I know what I will do. I will become invisible, and place myself near those two maidens who are tending the plants in the garden. [*Descends and takes her station*]

[*Enter a* Maiden, *who stops in front of a mango-tree, and gazes at the blossom. Another* Maiden *is seen behind her*]

FIRST MAIDEN: Hail to thee, lovely harbinger of spring!
The varied radiance of thy opening flowers
Is welcome to my sight. I bid thee hail,
Sweet mango, soul of this enchanting season.

SECOND MAIDEN: Parabhritika, what are you saying there to yourself?

FIRST MAIDEN: Dear Madhukarika, am I not named after the Koil? and does not the Koil sing for joy at the first appearance of the mango-blossom?

SECOND MAIDEN: [*Approaching hastily, with transport*] What! is spring really come?

FIRST MAIDEN: Yes, indeed, Madhukarika, and with it the season of joy, love, and song.

SECOND MAIDEN: Let me lean upon you, dear, while I stand on tip-toe and pluck a blossom of the mango, that I may present it as an offering to the god of love.

FIRST MAIDEN: Provided you let me have half the reward which the god will bestow in return.

SECOND MAIDEN: To be sure you shall, and that without asking. Are we not one in heart and soul, though divided in body? [*Leans on her friend and plucks a mango-blossom*] Ah! here is a bud just bursting into flower. It diffuses a delicious perfume, though not yet quite expanded. [*Joining her hands reverentially*]
God of the bow, who with spring's choicest flowers
Dost point thy five unerring shafts; to thee
I dedicate this blossom; let it serve
To barb thy truest arrow; be its mark

Some youthful heart that pines to be beloved.
[*Throws down a mango-blossom*]
CHAMBERLAIN: [*Entering in a hurried manner, angrily*] Hold there, thoughtless woman. What are you about, breaking off those mango-blossoms, when the King has forbidden the celebration of the spring festival?
BOTH MAIDENS: [*Alarmed*] Pardon us, kind Sir, we have heard nothing of it.
CHAMBERLAIN: You have heard nothing of it? Why, all the vernal plants and shrubs, and the very birds that lodge in their branches, show more respect to the King's order than you do.
Yon mango-blossoms, though long since expanded,
Gather no down upon their tender crests;
The flower still lingers in the amaranth,
Imprisoned in its bud; the tuneful Koil,
Though winter's chilly dews be overpast,
Suspends the liquid volume of his song
Scarce uttered in his throat; e'en Love, dismayed,
Restores the half-drawn arrow to his quiver.
BOTH MAIDENS: The mighty power of King Dushyanta is not to be disputed.
FIRST MAIDEN: It is but a few days since Mitravasu, the King's brother-in-law, sent us to wait upon his Majesty; and, during the whole of our sojourn here, we have been entrusted with the charge of the royal pleasure-grounds. We are therefore strangers in this place, and heard nothing of the order till you informed us of it.
CHAMBERLAIN: Well then, now you know it, take care you don't continue your preparations.
BOTH MAIDENS: But tell us, kind Sir, why has the King prohibited the usual festivities? We are curious to hear, if we may.
SANUMATI: [*Aside*] Men are naturally fond of festive entertainments. There must be some good reason for the prohibition.
CHAMBERLAIN: The whole affair is now public; why should I not speak of it? Has not the gossip about the King's rejection of Shakuntala reached your ears yet?
BOTH MAIDENS: Oh yes, we heard the story from the King's brother-in-law, as far, at least, as the discovery of the ring.
CHAMBERLAIN: Then there is little more to tell you. As soon as the King's memory was restored by the sight of his own ring, he exclaimed: "Yes, it is all true. I remember now my secret marriage with Shakuntala. When I repudiated her, I had lost my recollection!" Ever since that moment, he has yielded himself a prey to the bitterest remorse.
He loathes his former pleasures; he rejects
The daily homage of his ministers;
On his lone couch he tosses to and fro,
Courting repose in vain. Whene'er he meets
The ladies of his palace, and would fain
Address them with politeness, he confounds
Their names; or, calling them "Shakuntala,"
Is straightway silent and abashed with shame.

SANUMATI: [*Aside*] To me this account is delightful.
CHAMBERLAIN: In short, the King is so completely out of his mind that the festival has been prohibited.
BOTH MAIDENS: Perfectly right.
A VOICE: [*Behind the scenes*] The King! the King! This way, Sire, this way.
CHAMBERLAIN: [*Listening*] Oh! here comes his Majesty in this direction. Pass on, maidens; attend to your duties.
BOTH MAIDENS: We will, sir. [*Exeunt*]
[*Enter* King Dushyanta, *dressed in deep mourning, attended by his jester*, Mathavya, *and preceded by* Vetravati]
CHAMBERLAIN: [*Gazing at the* King] Well, noble forms are certainly pleasing, under all varieties of outward circumstances. The King's person is as charming as ever, notwithstanding his sorrow of mind.
Though but a single golden bracelet spans
His wasted arm; though costly ornaments
Have given place to penitential weeds;
Though oft-repeated sighs have blanched his lips,
And robbed them of their bloom; though sleepless care
And carking thought have dimmed his beaming eye;
Yet does his form, by its inherent luster,
Dazzle the gaze; and, like a priceless gem
Committed to some cunning polisher,
Grow more effulgent by the loss of substance.
SANUMATI: [*Aside. Looking at the* King] Now that I have seen him, I can well understand why Shakuntala should pine after such a man, in spite of his disdainful rejection of her.
KING: [*Walking slowly up and down in deep thought*] When fatal lethargy o'erwhelmed my soul,
My loved one strove to rouse me, but in vain;
And now, when I would fain in slumber deep
Forget myself, full soon remorse doth wake me.
SANUMATI: [*Aside*] My poor Shakuntala's sufferings are very similar.
MATHAVYA: [*Aside*] He is taken with another attack of this odious Shakuntala-fever. How shall we ever cure him?
CHAMBERLAIN: [*Approaching*] Victory to the King! Great Prince, the royal pleasure-grounds have been put in order. Your Majesty can resort to them for exercise and amusement whenever you think proper.
KING: Vetravati, tell the worthy Pisuna, my prime minister, from me, that I am so exhausted by want of sleep that I cannot sit on the judgment-seat to-day. If any case of importance be brought before the tribunal, he must give it his best attention, and inform me of the circumstances by letter.
VETRAVATI: Your Majesty's commands shall be obeyed. [*Exit*]
KING: [*To the* Chamberlain] And you, Vatayana, may go about your own affairs.
CHAMBERLAIN: I will, Sire. [*Exit*]

MATHAVYA: Now that you have rid yourself of these troublesome fellows, you can enjoy the delightful coolness of your pleasure-ground without interruption.

KING: Ah! my dear friend, there is an old adage:—"When affliction has a mind to enter, she will find a crevice somewhere"; and it is verified in me.
Scarce is my soul delivered from the cloud
That darkened its remembrance of the past,
When lo! the heart-born deity of love
With yonder blossom of the mango barbs
His keenest shaft, and aims it at my breast.

MATHAVYA: Well, then, wait a moment; I will soon demolish Master Kama's arrow with a cut of my cane. [Raises his stick and strikes off the mango-blossom]

KING: [Smiling] That will do. I see very well the god of love is not a match for a Brahman. And now, my dear friend, where shall I sit down, that I may enchant my sight by gazing on the twining plants, which seem to remind me of the graceful shape of my beloved?

MATHAVYA: Don't you remember, you told your personal attendant, Chaturika, that you would pass the heat of the day in the jasmine-bower; and commanded her to bring the likeness of your queen Shakuntala, sketched with your own hand.

KING: True. The sight of her picture will refresh my soul. Lead the way to the arbor.

MATHAVYA: This way, Sire.
[Both move on, followed by Sanumati]

MATHAVYA: Here we are at the jasmine-bower. Look, it has a marble seat, and seems to bid us welcome with its offerings of delicious flowers. You have only to enter and sit down.
[Both enter and seat themselves]

SANUMATI: [Aside] I will lean against these young jasmines. I can easily, from behind them, glance at my friend's picture, and will then hasten to inform her of her husband's ardent affection. [Stands leaning against the creepers]

KING: Oh! my dear friend, how vividly all the circumstances of my union with Shakuntala present themselves to my recollection at this moment! But tell me now how it was that, between the time of my leaving her in the hermitage and my subsequent rejection of her, you never breathed her name to me? True, you were not by my side when I disowned her; but I had confided to you the story of my love, and you were acquainted with every particular. Did it pass out of your mind as it did out of mine?

MATHAVYA: No, no; trust me for that. But, if you remember, when you had finished telling me about it, you added that I was not to take the story in earnest, for that you were not really in love with a country girl, but were only jesting; and I was dull and thickheaded enough to believe you. But so fate decreed, and there is no help for it.

SANUMATI: [Aside] Exactly.

KING: [After deep thought] My dear friend, suggest some relief for my misery.

MATHAVYA: Come, come, cheer up; why do you give way? Such weakness is unworthy of you. Great men never surrender themselves to uncontrolled grief. Do not mountains remain unshaken even in a gale of wind?

KING: How can I be otherwise than inconsolable, when I call to mind the agonized demeanor of the dear one on the occasion of my disowning her?
When cruelly I spurned her from my presence,
She fain had left me; but the young recluse,
Stern as the Sage, and with authority
As from his saintly master, in a voice
That brooked not contradiction, bade her stay.
Then through her pleading eyes, bedimmed with tears,
She cast on me one long reproachful look,
Which like a poisoned shaft torments me still.

SANUMATI: [Aside] Alas! such is the force of self-reproach following a rash action. But his anguish only rejoices me.

MATHAVYA: An idea has just struck me. I should not wonder if some celestial being had carried her off to heaven.

KING: Very likely. Who else would have dared to lay a finger on a wife, the idol of her husband? It is said that Menaka, the nymph of heaven, gave her birth. The suspicion has certainly crossed my mind that some of her celestial companions may have taken her to their own abode.

SANUMATI: [Aside] His present recollection of every circumstance of her history does not surprise me so much as his former forgetfulness.

MATHAVYA: If that's the case, you will be certain to meet her before long.

KING: Why?

MATHAVYA: No father and mother can endure to see a daughter suffering the pain of separation from her husband.

KING: Oh! my dear Mathavya,
Was it a dream? or did some magic dire,
Dulling my senses with a strange delusion,
O'ercome my spirit? or did destiny,
Jealous of my good actions, mar their fruit,
And rob me of their guerdon? It is past,
Whate'er the spell that bound me. Once again
Am I awake, but only to behold
The precipice o'er which my hopes have fallen.

MATHAVYA: Do not despair in this manner. Is not this very ring a proof that what has been lost may be unexpectedly found?

KING: [Gazing at the ring] Ah! this ring, too, has fallen from a station not easily regained, and I offer it my sympathy. O gem,
The punishment we suffer is deserved,
And equal is the merit of our works,
When such our common doom. Thou didst enjoy
The thrilling contact of those slender fingers,
Bright as the dawn; and now how changed thy lot!

SANUMATI: [Aside] Had it found its way to the hand of any other person, then indeed its fate would have been deplorable.

MATHAVYA: Pray, how did the ring ever come upon her hand at all?

SANUMATI: [Aside] I myself am curious to know.

KING: You shall hear. When I was leaving my beloved Shakuntala that I might return to my own capital, she said to me, with tears in her eyes: "How long will it be ere my lord send for me to his palace and make me his queen?"

MATHAVYA: Well, what was your reply?

KING: Then I placed the ring on her finger, and thus addressed her:—
Repeat each day one letter of the name
Engraven on this gem; ere thou hast reckoned
The tale of syllables, my minister
Shall come to lead thee to thy husband's palace.
But, hard-hearted man that I was, I forgot to fulfil my promise, owing to the infatuation that took possession of me.

SANUMATI: [Aside] A pleasant arrangement! Fate, however, ordained that the appointment should not be kept.

MATHAVYA: But how did the ring contrive to pass into the stomach of that carp which the fisherman caught and was cutting up?

KING: It must have slipped from my Shakuntala's hand, and fallen into the stream of the Ganges, while she was offering homage to the water of Sachi's holy pool.

MATHAVYA: Very likely.

SANUMATI: [Aside] Hence it happened I suppose, that the King, always fearful of committing the least injustice, came to doubt his marriage with my poor Shakuntala. But why should affection so strong as his stand in need of any token of recognition?

KING: Let me now address a few words of reproof to this ring.

MATHAVYA: [Aside] He is going stark mad, I verily believe.

KING: Hear me, thou dull and undiscerning bauble! For so it argues thee, that thou could'st leave
The slender fingers of her hand, to sink
Beneath the waters. Yet what marvel is it
That thou should'st lack discernment? let me rather
Heap curses on myself, who, though endowed
With reason, yet rejected her I loved.

MATHAVYA: [Aside] And so, I suppose, I must stand here to be devoured by hunger, whilst he goes on in this sentimental strain.

KING: O forsaken one, unjustly banished from my presence, take pity on thy slave, whose heart is consumed by the fire of remorse, and return to my sight.

[Enter Chaturika hurriedly, with a picture in her hand]

CHATURIKA: Here is the Queen's portrait. [Shows the picture]

MATHAVYA: Excellent, my dear friend, excellent! The imitation of nature is perfect, and the attitude of the figures is really charming. They stand out in such bold relief that the eye is quite deceived.

SANUMATI: [Aside] A most artistic performance!

I admire the King's skill, and could almost believe that Shakuntala herself was before me.

KING: I own 'tis not amiss, though it portrays
But feebly her angelic loveliness.
Aught less than perfect is depicted falsely,
And fancy must supply the imperfection.

SANUMATI: [Aside] A very just remark from a modest man, whose affection is exaggerated by the keenness of his remorse.

MATHAVYA: Tell me:—I see three female figures drawn on the canvas, and all of them beautiful; which of the three is her Majesty Shakuntala?

SANUMATI: [Aside] If he cannot distinguish her from the others, the simpleton might as well have no eyes in his head.

KING: Which should you imagine to be intended for her?

MATHAVYA: She who is leaning, apparently a little tired, against the stem of that mango-tree, the tender leaves of which glitter with the water she has poured upon them. Her arms are gracefully extended; her face is somewhat flushed with the heat; and a few flowers have escaped from her hair, which has become unfastened, and hangs in loose tresses about her neck. That must be the queen Shakuntala, and the others, I presume, are her two attendants.

KING: I congratulate you on your discernment. Behold the proof of my passion;
My finger, burning with the glow of love,
Has left its impress on the painted tablet;
While here and there, alas! a scalding tear
Has fallen on the cheek and dimmed its brightness.
Chaturika, the garden in the background of the picture is only half-painted. Go, fetch the brush that I may finish it.

CHATURIKA: Worthy Mathavya, have the kindness to hold the picture until I return.

KING: Nay, I will hold it myself. [Takes the picture]

[Exit Chaturika]

My loved one came but lately to my presence
And offered me herself, but in my folly
I spurned the gift, and now I fondly cling
To her mere image; even as a madman
Would pass the waters of the gushing stream,
And thirst for airy vapors of the desert.

MATHAVYA: [Aside] He has been fool enough to forego the reality for the semblance, the substance for the shadow. [Aloud] Tell us, I pray, what else remains to be painted.

SANUMATI: [Aside] He longs, no doubt, to delineate some favorite spot where my Shakuntala delighted to ramble.

KING: You shall hear:—
I wish to see the Malini portrayed,
Its tranquil course by banks of sand impeded;
Upon the brink of a pair of swans; beyond,
The hills adjacent to Himalaya,
Studded with deer; and, near the spreading shade
Of some large tree, where 'mid the branches hang
The hermits' vests of bark, a tender doe.

Rubbing its downy forehead on the horn
Of a black antelope, should be depicted.

MATHAVYA: [Aside] Pooh! if I were he, I would fill
up the vacant spaces with a lot of grizzly-bearded old
hermits.

KING: My dear Mathavya, there is still a part of
Shakuntala's dress which I purposed to draw, but
find I have omitted.

MATHAVYA: What is that?

SANUMATI: [Aside] Something suitable, I suppose,
to the simple attire of a young and beautiful girl
dwelling in a forest.

KING: A sweet Sirisha blossom should be twined
Behind her ear, its perfumed crest depending
Towards her cheek; and, resting on her bosom,
A lotus-fiber necklace, soft and bright
As an autumnal moonbeam, should be traced.

MATHAVYA: Pray, why does the Queen cover her
lips with the tips of her fingers, bright as the blossom
of a lily, as if she were afraid of something? [Looking
more closely] Oh! I see; a vagabond bee, intent on
thieving honey from the flowers, has mistaken her
mouth for a rosebud, and is trying to settle upon it.

KING: A bee! drive off the impudent insect, will
you?

MATHAVYA: That's your business. Your royal
prerogative gives you power over all offenders.

KING: Very true. Listen to me, thou favorite guest
of flowering plants; why give thyself the trouble of
hovering here?
See where thy partner sits on yonder flower,
And waits for thee ere she will sip its dew.

SANUMATI: [Aside] A most polite way of warning
him off!

MATHAVYA: You'll find the obstinate creature is
not to be sent about his business so easily as you
think.

KING: Dost thou presume to disobey?
Now hear me:—
And thou but touch the lips of my beloved,
Sweet as the opening blossom, whence I quaffed
In happier days love's nectar, I will place thee
Within the hollow of yon lotus cup,
And there imprison thee for thy presumption.

MATHAVYA: He must be bold indeed not to show
any fear when you threaten him with such an awful
punishment. [Smiling, aside] He is stark mad, that's
clear; and I believe, by keeping him company, I am
beginning to talk almost as wildly. [Aloud] Look, it
is only a painted bee.

KING: Painted? impossible!

SANUMATI: [Aside] Even I did not perceive it; how
much less should he!

KING: Oh! my dear friend, why were you so ill-
natured as to tell me the truth?
While all entranced, I gazed upon her picture,
My loved one seemed to live before my eyes
Till every fiber of my being thrilled
With rapturous emotion. Oh! 'twas cruel
To dissipate the day-dream, and transform

The blissful vision to a lifeless image. [Sheds tears]

SANUMATI: [Aside] Separated lovers are very
difficult to please; but he seems more difficult than
usual.

KING: Alas! my dear Mathavya, why am I doomed
to be the victim of perpetual disappointment?
Vain is the hope of meeting her in dreams,
For slumber night by night forsakes my couch;
And now that I would fain assuage my grief
By gazing on her portrait here before me,
Tears of despairing love obscure my sight.

SANUMATI: [Aside] You have made ample amends
for the wrong you did Shakuntala in disowning her.

CHATURIKA: [Entering] Victory to the King! I was
coming along with the box of colors in my hand—

KING: What now?

CHATURIKA: When I met the queen Vasumati, attended by Taralika. She insisted on taking it from
me, and declared she would herself deliver it into
your Majesty's hands.

MATHAVYA: By what luck did you contrive to
escape her?

CHATURIKA: While her maid was disengaging her
mantle, which had caught in the branch of a shrub,
I ran away.

KING: Here, my good friend, take the picture and
conceal it. My attentions to the Queen have made
her presumptuous. She will be here in a minute.

MATHAVYA: Conceal the picture! conceal myself,
you mean. [Getting up and taking the picture] The
Queen has a bitter draught in store for you,
which you will have to swallow, as Siva did the
poison at the Deluge. When you are well quit of her,
you may send and call me from the Palace of Clouds,
where I shall take refuge. [Exit, running]

SANUMATI: [Aside] Although the King's affections
are transferred to another object, yet he respects his
previous attachments. I fear his love must be somewhat fickle.

VETRAVATI: [Entering with a despatch in her hand]
Victory to the King!

KING: Vetravati, did you observe the queen Vasumati coming in this direction?

VETRAVATI: I did; but when she saw that I had a
despatch in my hand for your Majesty, she turned
back.

KING: The Queen has too much regard for propriety to interrupt me when I am engaged with
State-affairs.

VETRAVATI: So please your Majesty, your prime
minister begs respectfully to inform you that he has
devoted much time to the settlement of financial calculations, and only one case of importance has been
submitted by the citizens for his consideration. He
has made a written report of the facts, and requests
your Majesty to cast your eyes over it.

KING: Hand me the paper.

[Vetravati delivers it]

[Reading]

What have we here? "A merchant named Dhanamitra, trading by sea, was lost in a late shipwreck. Though a wealthy trader, he was childless; and the whole of his immense property becomes by law forfeited to the king." So writes the minister. Alas! alas! for his childlessness! But surely, if he was wealthy, he must have had many wives. Let an inquiry be made whether any one of them is expecting to give birth to a child.

VETRAVATI: They say that his wife, the daughter of the foreman of a guild belonging to Ayodhya, has just completed the ceremonies usual upon such expectations.

KING: The unborn child has a title to its father's property. Such is my decree. Go, bid my minister proclaim it so.

VETRAVATI: [Going] I will, my liege.

KING: Stay a moment.

VETRAVATI: I am at your Majesty's service.

KING: Let there be no question whether he may or may not have left offspring;
Rather be it proclaimed that whosoe'er
Of King Dushyanta's subjects be bereaved
Of any loved relation, an it be not
That his estates are forfeited for crimes,
Dushyanta will himself to them supply
That kinsman's place in tenderest affection.

VETRAVATI: It shall be so proclaimed.
[Exit Vetravati, and re-enters after an interval]

VETRAVATI: Your Majesty's proclamation was received with acclamations of joy, like grateful rain at the right season.

KING: [Drawing a deep sigh] So, then, the property of rich men, who have no lineal descendants, passes over to a stranger at their decease. And such, alas! must be the fate of the fortunes of the race of Puru at my death; even as when fertile soil is sown with seed at the wrong season.

VETRAVATI: Heaven forbid!

KING: Fool that I was to reject such happiness when it offered itself for my acceptance!

SANUMATI: [Aside] He may well blame his own folly when he calls to mind his treatment of my beloved Shakuntala.

KING: Ah! Woe is me! when I forsook my wife—
My lawful wife—concealed within her breast
There lay my second self, a child unborn,
Hope of my race, e'en as the choicest fruit
Lies hidden in the bosom of the earth.

SANUMATI: [Aside] There is no fear of your race being cut off for want of a son.

CHATURIKA: [Aside to Vetravati] The affair of the merchant's death has quite upset our royal master, and caused him sad distress. Would it not be better to fetch the worthy Mathavya from the Palace of Clouds to comfort him?

VETRAVATI: A very good idea. [Exit]

KING: Alas! the shades of my forefathers are even now beginning to be alarmed, lest at my death they may be deprived of their funeral libations.
No son remains in King Dushyanta's place

To offer sacred homage to the dead
Of Puru's noble line; my ancestors
Must drink these glistening tears, the last libation
A childless man can ever hope to make them. [Falls
down in an agony of grief]

CHATURIKA: [Looking at him in consternation] Great King, compose yourself.

SANUMATI: [Aside] Alas! alas! though a bright light is shining near him, he is involved in the blackest darkness, by reason of the veil that obscures his sight. I will now reveal all, and put an end to his misery. But no; I heard the mother of the great Indra, when she was consoling Shakuntala, say that the gods will soon bring about a joyful union between husband and wife, being eager for the sacrifice which will be celebrated in their honor on the occasion. I must not anticipate the happy moment, but will return at once to my dear friend and cheer her with an account of what I have seen and heard. [Rises aloft and disappears]

A VOICE: [Behind the scenes] Help! help! to the rescue!

KING: [Recovering himself. Listening] Ha! I heard a cry of distress, and in Mathavya's voice too. What ho, there!

VETRAVATI: [Entering] Your friend is in danger; save him, great King.

KING: Who dares insult the worthy Mathavya?

VETRAVATI: Some evil demon, invisible to human eyes, has seized him, and carried him to one of the turrets of the Palace of Clouds.

KING: [Rising] Impossible! Have evil spirits power over my subjects, even in my private apartments? Well, well:—
Daily I seem less able to avert
Misfortune from myself, and o'er my actions
Less competent to exercise control;
How can I then direct my subjects' ways,
Or shelter them from tyranny and wrong?

A VOICE: [Behind the scenes] Halloo there! my dear friend; help! help!

KING: [Advancing with rapid strides] Fear nothing—

THE SAME VOICE: [Behind the scenes] Fear nothing, indeed! How can I help fearing when some monster is twisting back my neck, and is about to snap it as he would a sugar-cane?

KING: [Looking round] What ho, there! my bow!

SLAVE: [Entering with a bow] Behold your bow, Sire, and your arm-guard.
[The King snatches up the bow and arrows]

ANOTHER VOICE: [Behind the scenes]
Here, thirsting for thy life-blood, will I slay thee,
As a fierce tiger rends his struggling prey.
Call now thy friend Dushyanta to thy aid;
His bow is mighty to defend the weak;
Yet all its vaunted power shall be as nought.

KING: [With fury] What! dares he defy me to my face? Hold there, monster! Prepare to die, for your time is come. [*Stringing his bow*] Vetravati, lead the way to the terrace.

VETRAVATI: This way, Sire. [*They advance in haste*]

KING: [*Looking on every side*] How's this? there is nothing to be seen.

A VOICE: [*Behind the scenes*] Help! Save me! I can see you, though you cannot see me. I am like a mouse in the claws of a cat; my life is not worth a minute's purchase.

KING: Avaunt, monster! You may pride yourself on the magic that renders you invisible, but my arrow shall find you out. Thus do I fix a shaft
That shall discern between an impious demon,
And a good Brahman; bearing death to thee,
To him deliverance—even as the swan
Distinguishes the milk from worthless water. [*Takes aim*]

[*Enter* Matali *holding* Mathavya, *whom he releases*]

MATALI: Turn thou thy deadly arrows on the demons;
Such is the will of Indra; let thy bow
Be drawn against the enemies of the gods;
But on thy friends cast only looks of favor.

KING: [*Putting back his arrow*] What, Matali! Welcome, most noble charioteer of the mighty Indra.

MATHAVYA: So, here is a monster who thought as little about slaughtering me as if I had been a bullock for sacrifice, and you must e'en greet him with a welcome.

MATALI: [*Smiling*] Great Prince, hear on what errand Indra sent me into your presence.

KING: I am all attention.

MATALI: There is a race of giants, the descendants of Kalanemi, whom the gods find it difficult to subdue.

KING: So I have already heard from Narada.

MATALI: Heaven's mighty lord, who deigns to call thee "friend,"
Appoints thee to the post of highest honor,
As leader of his armies; and commits
The subjugation of this giant brood
To thy resistless arms, e'en as the sun
Leaves the pale moon to dissipate the darkness.
Let your Majesty, therefore, ascend at once the celestial car of Indra; and, grasping your arms, advance to victory.

KING: The mighty Indra honors me too highly by such a mark of distinction. But tell me, what made you act thus towards my poor friend Mathavya?

MATALI: I will tell you. Perceiving that your Majesty's spirit was completely broken by some distress of mind under which you were laboring, I determined to rouse your energies by moving you to anger. Because
To light a flame, we need but stir the embers;
The cobra, when incensed, extends his head
And springs upon his foe; the bravest men
Display their courage only when provoked.

KING: [*Aside to* Mathavya] My dear Mathavya,

the commands of the great Indra must not be left unfulfilled. Go you and acquaint my minister, Pisuna, with what has happened, and say to him from me:—
Dushyanta to thy care confides his realm—
Protect with all the vigor of thy mind
The interests of his people; while his bow
Is braced against the enemies of heaven.

MATHAVYA: I obey. [*Exit*]

MATALI: Ascend, illustrious Prince.
[*The King ascends the car*]
[*Exeunt*]

ACT VII.

SCENE—*The sky.*

[*Enter* King Dushyanta *and* Matali *in the car of Indra, moving in the air*]

KING: My good Matali, it appears to me incredible that I can merit such a mark of distinction for having simply fulfilled the behests of the great Indra.

MATALI: [*Smiling*] Great Prince, it seems to me that neither of you is satisfied with himself.
You underrate the services you have rendered,
And think too highly of the god's reward;
He deems it scarce sufficient recompense
For your heroic deeds on his behalf.

KING: Nay, Matali, say not so. My most ambitious expectations were more than realized by the honor conferred on me at the moment when I took my leave. For,
Tinged with celestial sandal, from the breast
Of the great Indra, where before it hung,
A garland of the ever-blooming tree
Of Nandana was cast about my neck
By his own hand; while, in the very presence
Of the assembled gods, I was enthroned
Beside their mighty lord, who smiled to see
His son Jayanta envious of the honor.

MATALI: There is no mark of distinction which your Majesty does not deserve at the hands of the immortals. See,
Heaven's hosts acknowledge thee their second savior;
For now thy bow's unerring shafts (as erst
The Lion-man's terrific claws) have purged
The empyreal sphere from taint of demons foul.

KING: The praise of my victory must be ascribed to the majesty of Indra.
When mighty gods make men their delegates
In martial enterprise, to them belongs
The palm of victory; and not to mortals.
Could the pale Dawn dispel the shades of night,
Did not the god of day, whose diadem
Is jewelled with a thousand beams of light,
Place him in front of his effulgent car?

MATALI: A very just comparison! [*Driving on*] Great King behold! the glory of thy fame has reached even to the vault of heaven.
Hark! yonder inmates of the starry sphere

Sing anthems worthy of thy martial deeds,
While with celestial colors they depict
The story of thy victories on scrolls
Formed of the leaves of heaven's immortal trees.

KING: My good Matali, yesterday, when I ascended the sky, I was so eager to do battle with the demons, that the road by which we were traveling towards Indra's heaven escaped my observation. Tell me, in which path of the seven winds are we now moving?

MATALI: We journey in the path of Parivaha—
The wind that bears along the triple Ganges
And causes Ursa's seven stars to roll
In their appointed orbits, scattering
Their several rays with equal distribution.
'Tis the same path that once was sanctified
By the divine impression of the foot
Of Vishnu, when, to conquer haughty Bali,[8]
He spanned the heavens in his second stride.

KING: This is the reason, I suppose, that a sensation of calm repose pervades all my senses. [Looking down at the wheels] Ah! Matali, we are descending towards the earth's atmosphere.

MATALI: What makes you think so?

KING: The car itself instructs me; we are moving
O'er pregnant clouds, surcharged with rain; below us
I see the moisture-loving Chatakas
In sportive flight dart through the spokes; the steeds
Of Indra glisten with the lightning's flash;
And a thick mist bedews the circling wheels.

MATALI: You are right; in a little while the chariot will touch the ground, and you will be in your own dominions.

KING: [Looking down] How wonderful the appearance of the earth as we rapidly descend!
Stupendous prospect! yonder lofty hills
Do suddenly uprear their towering heads
Amid the plain, while from beneath their crests
The ground receding sinks; the trees, whose stem
Seemed lately hid within their leafy tresses,
Rise into elevation, and display
Their branching shoulders; yonder streams, whose
    waters,
Like silver threads, were scarce, but now discerned,
Grow into mighty rivers; lo! the earth
Seems upward hurled by some gigantic power.

MATALI: Well described! [Looking with awe] Grand, indeed, and lovely is the spectacle presented by the earth.

KING: Tell me, Matali, what is the range of mountains which, like a bank of clouds illumined by the setting sun, pours down a stream of gold? On one side its base dips into the eastern ocean, and on the other side into the western.

MATALI: Great Prince, it is called "Golden-peak," and is the abode of the attendants of the god of wealth. In this spot the highest forms of penance are wrought out.
There Kasyapa, the great progenitor

Of demons and of gods, himself the offspring
Of the divine Marichi, Brahma's son,
With Aditi, his wife, in calm seclusion,
Does holy penance for the good of mortals.

KING: Then I must not neglect so good an opportunity of obtaining his blessing. I should much like to visit this venerable personage and offer him my homage.

MATALI: By all means. An excellent idea! [Guides the car to the earth]

KING: [In a tone of wonder] How's this?
Our chariot wheels move noiselessly. Around
No clouds of dust arise; no shock betokened
Our contact with the earth; we seem to glide
Above the ground, so lightly do we touch it.

MATALI: Such is the difference between the car of Indra and that of your Majesty.

KING: In which direction, Matali, is Kasyapa's sacred retreat?

MATALI: [Pointing] Where stands yon anchorite,
    towards the orb
Of the meridian sun, immovable
As a tree's stem, his body half-concealed
By a huge ant-hill. Round about his breast
No sacred cord is twined, but in its stead
A hideous serpent's skin. In place of necklace,
The tendrils of a withered creeper chafe
His wasted neck. His matted hair depends
In thick entanglement about his shoulders,
And birds construct their nests within its folds.

KING: I salute thee, thou man of austere devotion.

MATALI: [Holding in the reins of the car] Great Prince, we are now in the sacred grove of the holy Kasyapa—the grove that boasts as its ornament one of the five trees of Indra's heaven, reared by Aditi.

KING: This sacred retreat is more delightful than heaven itself. I could almost fancy myself bathing in a pool of nectar.

MATALI: [Stopping the chariot] Descend, mighty Prince.

KING: [Descending] And what will you do, Matali?

MATALI: The chariot will remain where I have stopped it. We may both descend. [Doing so] This way, great King. [Walking on] You see around you the celebrated region where the holiest sages devote themselves to penitential rites.

KING: I am filled with awe and wonder as I gaze.
In such a place as this do saints of earth
Long to complete their acts of penance; here,
Beneath the shade of everlasting trees,
Transplanted from the groves of Paradise,
May they inhale the balmy air, and need
No other nourishment; here may they bathe
In fountains sparkling with the golden dust
Of lilies; here, on jewelled slabs of marble,
In meditation rapt, may they recline;
Here, in the presence of celestial nymphs,
E'en passion's voice is powerless to move them.

MATALI: So true is it that the aspirations of the good and great are ever soaring upwards. [Turning *round and speaking off the stage*] Tell me, Vriddhasa-kalya, how is the divine son of Marichi now engaged? What sayest thou? that he is conversing with Aditi and some of the wives of the great sages, and that they are questioning him respecting the duties of a faithful wife?

KING: [*Listening*] Then we must await the holy father's leisure.

MATALI: [*Looking at the* King] If your Majesty will rest under the shade, at the foot of this Asoka-tree, I will seek an opportunity of announcing your arrival to Indra's reputed father.

KING: [*Remains under the tree*] As you think proper.

MATALI: Great King, I go. [*Exit*]

KING: [*Feeling his arm throb*] Wherefore this causeless throbbing, O mine arm?
All hope has fled for ever; mock me not
With presages of good, when happiness
Is lost, and nought but misery remains.

A VOICE: [*Behind the scenes*] Be not so naughty. Do you begin already to show a refractory spirit?

KING: [*Listening*] This is no place for petulance. Who can it be whose behavior calls for such a rebuke? [*Looking in the direction of the sound and smiling*] A child, is it? closely attended by two holy women. His disposition seems anything but child-like. See!
He braves the fury of yon lioness
Suckling its savage offspring, and compels
The angry whelp to leave the half-sucked dug,
Tearing its tender mane in boisterous sport.

[*Enter a* Child, *attended by* Two Women *of the hermitage, in manner described*]

CHILD: Open your mouth, my young lion, I want to count your teeth.

FIRST ATTENDANT: You naughty child, why do you tease the animals? Know you not that we cherish them in this hermitage as if they were our own children? In good sooth, you have a high spirit of your own, and are beginning already to do justice to the name Sarva-damana ("All-taming"), given you by the hermits.

KING: Strange! My heart inclines towards the boy with almost as much affection as if he were my own child. What can be the reason? I suppose my own childlessness makes me yearn towards the sons of others.

SECOND ATTENDANT: This lioness will certainly attack you if you do not release her whelp.

CHILD: [*Laughing*] Oh! indeed! let her come. Much I fear her, to be sure! [*Pouts his under-lip in defiance*]

KING: The germ of mighty courage lies concealed
Within this noble infant, like a spark
Beneath the fuel, waiting but a breath
To fan the flame and raise a conflagration.

FIRST ATTENDANT: Let the young lion go, like a dear child, and I will give you something else to play with.

CHILD: Where is it? Give it me first. [*Stretches out his hand*]

KING: [*Looking at his hand*] How's that? His hand exhibits one of those mystic marks which are the sure prognostic of universal empire. See!
His fingers stretched in eager expectation
To grasp the wished-for toy, and knit together
By a close-woven web, in shape resemble
A lotus blossom, whose expanding petals
The early dawn has only half unfolded.

SECOND ATTENDANT: We shall never pacify him by mere words, dear Suvrata. Be kind enough to go to my cottage, and you will find there a plaything belonging to Markandeya, one of the hermit's children. It is a peacock made of chinaware, painted in many colors. Bring it here for the child.

FIRST ATTENDANT: Very well. [*Exit*]

CHILD: No, no; I shall go on playing with the young lion. [*Looks at the* Female Attendant *and laughs*]

KING: I feel an unaccountable affection for this wayward child.
How blessed the virtuous parents whose attire
Is soiled with dust, by raising from the ground
The child that asks a refuge in their arms'
And happy are they while with lisping prattle,
In accents sweetly inarticulate,
He charms their ears; and with his artless smiles
Gladdens their hearts, revealing to their gaze
His pearly teeth just budding into view.

ATTENDANT: I see how it is. He pays me no manner of attention. [*Looking off the stage*] I wonder whether any of the hermits are about here. [*Seeing the* King] Kind Sir, could you come hither a moment and help me to release the young lion from the clutch of this child who is teasing him in boyish play?

KING: [*Approaching and smiling*] Listen to me, thou child of a mighty saint!
Dost thou dare show a wayward spirit here?
Here, in this hallowed region? Take thou heed
Lest, as the serpent's young defiles the sandal,
Thou bring dishonor on the holy Sage
Thy tender-hearted parent, who delights
To shield from harm the tenants of the wood.

ATTENDANT: Gentle Sir, I thank you; but he is not the Saint's son.

KING: His behavior and whole bearing would have led me to doubt it, had not the place of his abode encouraged the idea. [*Follows the* Child, *and takes him by the hand, according to the request of the Attendant*]
[*Aside*] I marvel that the touch of this strange child
Should thrill me with delight; if so it be,
How must the fond caresses of a son
Transport the father's soul who gave him being!

ATTENDANT: [*Looking at them both*] Wonderful! Prodigious!

KING: What excites your surprise, my good woman?

ATTENDANT: I am astonished at the striking resemblance between the child and yourself; and, what is still more extraordinary, he seems to have taken to you kindly and submissively, though you are a stranger to him.

KING: [*Fondling the* Child] If he be not the son of the great Sage, of what family does he come, may I ask?

ATTENDANT: Of the race of Puru.

KING: [*Aside*] What! are we, then, descended from the same ancestry? This, no doubt, accounts for the resemblance she traces between the child and me. Certainly it has always been an established usage among the princes of Puru's race,
To dedicate the morning of their days
To the world's weal, in palaces and halls,
'Mid luxury and regal pomp abiding;
Then, in the wane of life, to seek release
From kingly cares, and make the hallowed shade
Of sacred trees their last asylum, where
As hermits they may practice self-abasement,
And bind themselves by rigid vows of penance.
[*Aloud*] But how could mortals by their own power gain admission to this sacred region?

ATTENDANT: Your remark is just; but your wonder will cease when I tell you that his mother is the offspring of a celestial nymph, and gave him birth in the hallowed grove of Kasyapa.

KING: [*Aside*] Strange that my hopes should be again excited! [*Aloud*] But what, let me ask, was the name of the prince whom she deigned to honor with her hand?

ATTENDANT: How could I think of polluting my lips by the mention of a wretch who had the cruelty to desert his lawful wife?

KING: [*Aside*] Ha! the description suits me exactly. Would I could bring myself to inquire the name of the child's mother! [*Reflecting*] But it is against propriety to make too minute inquiries about the wife of another man.

FIRST ATTENDANT: [*Entering with the china peacock in her hand*] Sarva-damana, Sarva-damana, see, see, what a beautiful Shakunta ("bird").

CHILD: [*Looking round*] My mother! Where? Let me go to her.

BOTH ATTENDANTS: He mistook the word Shakunta for Shakuntala. The boy dotes upon his mother, and she is ever uppermost in his thoughts.

SECOND ATTENDANT: Nay, my dear child, I said: Look at the beauty of this Shakunta.

KING: [*Aside*] What! is his mother's name Shakuntala? But the name is not uncommon among women. Alas! I fear the mere similarity of a name, like the deceitful vapor of the desert, has once more raised my hopes only to dash them to the ground.

CHILD: Dear nurse, what a beautiful peacock! [*Takes the toy*]

FIRST ATTENDANT: [*Looking at the Child. In great distress*] Alas! alas! I do not see the amulet on his wrist.

KING: Don't distress yourself. Here it is. It fell off

while he was struggling with the young lion. [*Stoops to pick it up*]

BOTH ATTENDANTS: Hold! hold! Touch it not, for your life. How marvelous! He has actually taken it up without the slightest hesitation. [*Both raise their hands to their breasts and look at each other in astonishment*]

KING: Why did you try to prevent my touching it?

FIRST ATTENDANT: Listen, great Monarch. This amulet, known as "The Invincible," was given to the boy by the divine son of Marichi, soon after his birth, when the natal ceremony was performed. Its peculiar virtue is, that when it falls on the ground, no one except the father or mother of the child can touch it unhurt.

KING: And suppose another person touches it?

FIRST ATTENDANT: Then it instantly becomes a serpent, and bites him.

KING: Have you ever witnessed the transformation with your own eyes?

BOTH ATTENDANTS: Over and over again.

KING: [*With rapture. Aside*] Joy! joy! Are then my dearest hopes to be fulfilled? [*Embraces the* Child]

SECOND ATTENDANT: Come, my dear Suvrata, we must inform Shakuntala immediately of this wonderful event, though we have to interrupt her in the performance of her religious vows.

[*Exeunt*]

CHILD: [*To the* King] Don't hold me. I want to go to my mother.

KING: We will go to her together, and give her joy, my son.

CHILD: Dushyanta is my father, not you.

KING: [*Smiling*] His contradiction only convinces me the more.

[*Enter Shakuntala, in widow's apparel, with her long hair twisted into a single braid*]

SHAKUNTALA: [*Aside*] I have just heard that Sarva-damana's amulet has retained its form, though a stranger raised it from the ground. I can hardly believe in my good fortune. Yet why should not Sanumati's prediction be verified?

KING: [*Gazing at* Shakuntala] Alas! can this indeed be my Shakuntala?
Clad in the weeds of widowhood, her face
Emaciate with fasting, her long hair
Twined in a single braid, her whole demeanor
Expressive of her purity of soul;
With patient constancy she thus prolongs
The vow to which my cruelty condemned her.

SHAKUNTALA: [*Gazing at the King, who is pale with remorse*] Surely this is not like my husband; yet who can it be that dares pollute by the pressure of his hand my child, whose amulet should protect him from a stranger's touch?

CHILD: [*Going to his mother*] Mother, who is this man that has been kissing me and calling me his son?

KING: My best beloved, I have indeed treated thee most cruelly, but am now once more thy fond and affectionate lover. Refuse not to acknowledge me as thy husband.

SHAKUNTALA: [*Aside*] Be of good cheer, my heart. The anger of Destiny is at last appeased. Heaven regards thee with compassion. But is he in very truth my husband?

KING: Behold me, best and loveliest of women,
Delivered from the cloud of fatal darkness
That erst oppressed my memory. Again
Behold us brought together by the grace
Of the great lord of Heaven. So the Moon
Shines forth from dim eclipse, to blend his rays
With the soft lustre of his Rohini.

SHAKUNTALA: May my husband be victorious—
[*She stops short, her voice choked with tears*]

KING: O fair one, though the utterance of thy
    prayer
Be lost amid the torrent of thy tears,
Yet does the sight of thy fair countenance
And of thy pallid lips, all unadorned
And colorless in sorrow for my absence,
Make me already more than conqueror.

CHILD: Mother, who is this man?

SHAKUNTALA: My child, ask the deity that presides over thy destiny.

KING: [*Falling at* Shakuntala's *feet*] Fairest of women, banish from thy mind
The memory of my cruelty; reproach
The fell delusion that o'erpowered my soul,
And blame not me, thy husband; 'tis the curse
Of him in whom the power of darkness reigns,
That he mistakes the gifts of those he loves
For deadly evils. Even though a friend
Should wreathe a garland on a blind man's brow,
Will he not cast it from him as a serpent?

SHAKUNTALA: Rise, my own husband, rise. Thou wast not to blame. My own evil deeds, committed in a former state of being, brought down this judgment upon me. How else could my husband, who was ever of a compassionate disposition, have acted so unfeelingly? [*The* King *rises*] But tell me, my husband, how did the remembrance of thine unfortunate wife return to thy mind?

KING: As soon as my heart's anguish is removed, and its wounds are healed, I will tell thee all.
Oh! let me, fair one, chase away the drop
That still bedews the fringes of thine eye;
And let me thus efface the memory
Of every tear that stained thy velvet cheek,
Unnoticed and unheeded by thy lord,
When in his madness he rejected thee. [*Wipes away
    the tear*]

SHAKUNTALA: [*Seeing the signet-ring on his finger*] Ah! my dear husband, is that the Lost Ring?

KING: Yes; the moment I recovered it my memory was restored.

SHAKUNTALA: The ring was to blame in allowing itself to be lost at the very time when I was anxious to convince my noble husband of the reality of my marriage.

KING: Receive it back, as the beautiful twining-plant receives again its blossom in token of its reunion with the spring.

SHAKUNTALA: Nay; I can never more place confidence in it. Let my husband retain it.

[*Enter* Matali]

MATALI: I congratulate your Majesty. Happy are you in your reunion with your wife; happy are you in beholding the face of your own son.

KING: Yes, indeed. My heart's dearest wish has borne sweet fruit. But tell me, Matali, is this joyful event known to the great Indra?

MATALI: [*Smiling*] What is unknown to the gods? But come with me, noble Prince, the divine Kasyapa graciously permits thee to be presented to him.

KING: Shakuntala, take our child and lead the way. We will together go into the presence of the holy Sage.

SHAKUNTALA: I shrink from entering the august presence of the great Saint, even with my husband at my side.

KING: Nay; on such a joyous occasion it is highly proper. Come, come; I entreat thee.

[*All advance*]

[Kasyapa *is discovered seated on a throne with his wife* Aditi]

KASYAPA: [*Gazing at* Dushyanta. *To his wife*] O Aditi,
This is the mighty hero, King Dushyanta,
Protector of the earth; who, at the head
Of the celestial armies of thy son,
Does battle with the enemies of heaven.
Thanks to his bow, the thunderbolt of Indra
Rests from its work, no more the minister
Of death and desolation to the world,
But a mere symbol of divinity.

ADITI: He bears in his noble form all the marks of dignity.

MATALI: [*To* Dushyanta] Sire, the venerable progenitors of the celestials are gazing at your Majesty with as much affection as if you were their son. You may advance towards them.

KING: Are these, O Matali, the holy pair,
Offspring of Daksha and divine Marichi,
Children of Brahma's sons, by sages deemed
Sole fountain of celestial light, diffused
Through twelve effulgent orbs? Are these the pair
From whom the ruler of the triple world,
Sovereign of gods and lord of sacrifice,
Sprang into being? That immortal pair
Whom Vishnu, greater than the Self-existent,
Chose for his parents, when, to save mankind,
He took upon himself the shape of mortals?

MATALI: Even so.

KING: [*Prostrating himself*] Most august of beings! Dushyanta, content to have fulfilled the commands of your son Indra, offers you his adoration.

KASYAPA: My son, long may'st thou live, and happily may'st thou reign over the earth!

ADITI: My son, may'st thou ever be invincible in the the field of battle!

SHAKUNTALA: I also prostrate myself before you, most adorable Beings, and my child with me.

KASYAPA: My daughter,
Thy lord resembles Indra, and thy child
Is noble as Jayanta, Indra's son;
I have no worthier blessing left for thee,
May'st thou be faithful as the god's own wife!

ADITI: My daughter, may'st thou be always the object of thy husband's fondest love; and may thy son live long to be the joy of both his parents! Be seated.

[*All sit down in the presence of* Kasyapa]

KASYAPA: [*Regarding each of them by turns*]
Hail to the beautiful Shakuntala,
Hail to her noble son, and hail to thee,
Illustrious Prince—rare triple combination
Of virtue, wealth, and energy united.

KING: Most venerable Kasyapa, by your favor all my desires were accomplished even before I was admitted to your presence. Never was mortal so honored that his boon should be granted ere it was solicited. Because—
Bloom before fruit, the clouds before the rain,
Cause first and then effect, in endless sequence,
Is the unchanging law of constant nature;
But, ere the blessing issued from thy lips,
The wishes of my heart were all fulfilled.

MATALI: It is thus that the great progenitors of the world confer favors.

KING: Most reverend Sage, this thy handmaid was married to me by the Gandharva[9] ceremony, and after a time was conducted to my palace by her relations. Meanwhile a fatal delusion seized me; I lost my memory and rejected her, thus committing a grievous offence against the venerable Kanwa, who is of thy divine race. Afterwards the sight of this ring restored my faculties, and brought back to my mind all the circumstances of my union with his daughter. But my conduct still seems to me incomprehensible;
As foolish as the fancies of a man
Who, when he sees an elephant, denies
That 'tis an elephant; then afterwards,
When its huge bulk moves onward, hesitates;
Yet will not be convinced till it has passed
For ever from his sight, and left behind
No vestige of its presence save his footsteps.

KASYAPA: My son, cease to think thyself in fault. Even the delusion that possessed thy mind was not brought about by any act of thine. Listen to me.

KING: I am attentive.

KASYAPA: Know that when the nymph Menaka, the mother of Shakuntala, became aware of her daughter's anguish in consequence of the loss of the ring at the nymph's pool, and of thy subsequent rejection of her, she brought her and confided her to the care of Aditi. And I no sooner saw her than I ascertained by my divine faculty of meditation, that

⁹ One of the musicians of the Hindu gods.

thy repudiation of thy poor faithful wife had been caused entirely by the curse of Durvasas—not by thine own fault—and that the spell would terminate on the discovery of the ring.

KING: [*Drawing a deep breath*] Oh! what a weight is taken off my mind, now that my character is cleared of reproach.

SHAKUNTALA: [*Aside*] Joy! Joy! My revered husband did not, then, reject me without good reason, though I have no recollection of the curse pronounced upon me. But, in all probability, I unconsciously brought it upon myself, when I was so distracted on being separated from my husband soon after our marriage. For I now remember that my two friends advised me not to fail to show the ring in case he should have forgotten me.

KASYAPA: At last, my daughter, thou art happy, and hast gained thy heart's desire. Indulge, then, no feeling of resentment against thy consort. See, now,
Though he repulsed thee, 'twas the Sage's curse
That clouded his remembrance; 'twas the curse
That made thy tender husband harsh towards thee.
Soon as the spell was broken, and his soul
Delivered from its darkness, in a moment
Thou didst regain thine empire o'er his heart.
So on the tarnished surface of a mirror
No image is reflected, till the dust,
That dimmed its wonted luster, is removed.

KING: Holy father, see here the hope of my royal race. [*Takes his* Child *by the hand*]

KASYAPA: Know that he, too, will become the monarch of the whole earth. Observe,
Soon, a resistless hero, shall he cross
The trackless ocean, borne above the waves
In an aerial car; and shall subdue
The earth's seven sea-girt isles. Now has he gained,
As the brave tamer of the forest-beasts,
The title Sarva-damana; but then
Mankind shall hail him as King Bharata,
And call him the supporter of the world.

KING: We cannot but entertain the highest hopes of a child for whom your Highness performed the natal rites.

ADITI: My revered husband, should not the intelligence be conveyed to Kanwa, that his daughter's wishes are fulfilled, and her happiness complete? He is Shakuntala's foster-father. Menaka, who is one of my attendants, is her mother, and dearly does she love her daughter.

SHAKUNTALA: [*Aside*] The venerable matron has given utterance to the very wish that was in my mind.

KASYAPA: His penances have gained for him the faculty of omniscience, and the whole scene is already present to his mind's eye.

KING: Then most assuredly he cannot be very angry with me.

KASYAPA: Nevertheless, it becomes us to send him intelligence of this happy event, and hear his reply. What ho, there!

PUPIL: [*Entering*] Holy father, what are your commands?

KASYAPA: My good Galava, delay not an instant, but hasten through the air and convey to the venerable Kanwa, from me, the happy news that the fatal spell has ceased, that Dushyanta's memory is restored, that his daughter Shakuntala has a son, and that she is once more tenderly acknowledged by her husband.

PUPIL: Your Highness' commands shall be obeyed.
    [*Exit*]

KASYAPA: And now, my dear son, take thy consort and thy child, re-ascend the car of Indra, and return to thy imperial capital.

KING: Most holy father, I obey.

KASYAPA: And accept this blessing—
For countless ages may the god of gods,
Lord of the atmosphere, by copious showers
Secure abundant harvests to thy subjects;

And thou by frequent offerings preserve
The Thunderer's friendship. Thus, by interchange
Of kindly actions may you both confer
Unnumbered benefits on earth and heaven.

KING: Holy father, I will strive, as far as I am able, to attain this happiness.

KASYAPA: What other favor can I bestow on thee, my son?

KING: What other can I desire? If, however, you permit me to form another wish, I would humbly beg that the saying of the sage Bharata be fulfilled:
May kings reign only for their subjects' weal;
May the divine Saraswati, the source
Of speech, and goddess of dramatic art,
Be ever honored by the great and wise;
And may the purple self-existent god,
Whose vital Energy pervades all space,
From future transmigrations save my soul.
    [*Exeunt omnes*]

Kwanami Kiyotsugu

(1333–1384)

The prevalence of theatrical stylization in the Far East was not as conducive to distinction in playwriting as one might expect. Dramatic composition tended to be subordinated to purely theatrical effects, and the dramatist was too often apt to spin out yarns rather than to probe character or express personal insight or vision. In China, indeed, playwrights were regarded as writers of secondary rank, and the fastidious mandarin poets, whose verses enjoyed great esteem, refrained from writing for the theatre, scorning it as a vulgar entertainment. Although Chinese tragicomedies such as *The Circle of Chalk* and *The Story of the Lute* (*Pi-pa-Ki*) possess charm and deliver shrewd thrusts at human nature, they do not scale any peaks of dramatic art. And in Japan the popular theatre (*kabuki*) did not rise above lengthy, episodic melodramas by comparison with which Hollywood spectacles may be considered models of restraint. *Kabuki's* master playwright, Chikamatsu Monzayemon (1653–1724), won an enormous reputation by satisfying the popular appetite for sensationalism. Although some striking theatre will be found in individual scenes of his classic piece *The Battles of Kokusenya* (1710) and of his successor Takeda Izumo's account of the legendary forty-seven *ronins*, or outlaws, *Chusingura* (1748), it is difficult to derive any unified impression from these plays. Still less does it appear possible to esteem them as dramatic literature.

In Japan, however, dramatists of the period which corresponds to our Middle Ages achieved a measure of distinction by going to the opposite extreme of creating an ultrarefined drama known as the Noh play, in which expressive dancing is combined with a literary text. Although the dances may be performed at considerable—and to Western taste, monotonous—length, the written part of the play is often notable for dramatic compression. The Noh play is the theatrical counterpart of the exquisite in Japanese landscape painting and poetry. It is a distinctive form of composition, rather esoteric to the ordinary Western playgoer but extremely fascinating to the poet and the theatrical experimentalist because it stands at the furthest remove from realistic dramaturgy.

At first the plays were intended as popular entertainment, but they became caviar to the general. Eventually they were regarded as an exclusively aristocratic art. Japanese nobles did not consider it undignified to act in Noh plays along with professional actors, and they liked to recite favorite passages at banquets. Fastidious workmanship set this form of

drama apart from the grosser *kabuki* that captured popular support after the sixteenth century.

An outgrowth of primitive religious rites, the Noh play was largely the creation of two men of the fourteenth and fifteenth centuries—Kwanami Kiyotsugu (1333–1384) and Seami Motokiyo (1363–1444). We know very little about Kwanami beyond that he was a priest and performer who won the favor of the famous Shogun Yoshimitsu and that he was the father of Seami, acclaimed as the Shakespeare of his nation. Seami, who also wrote a considerable body of criticism, summarized the laws of the Noh, and the principle on which he laid the greatest stress was *yugen*—subtlety, or as he called it, "what lies beneath the surface." This subtlety was also possessed to the highest degree by Kwanami, who gave the Noh its artistic form. His work displays a remarkable talent for refinement and for an appealing pathos held in restraint by a highly developed sense of form.

The extant body of Noh drama consists of about eight hundred pieces, of which as many as two hundred and fifty have remained in repertory. They are of unequal merit and they differ in some other respects (for example, in some of the plays the protagonist is a ghost, in others a living person), but they all adhere to the same essential pattern. They exhibit extreme brevity of story and plot, formal augmentation of the verbal drama by dancing in the crucial section, and conformity to the conventions of the Noh theatre. The principals are the *shite*, or doer, who not only acts but sings and dances his part, and the *waki*, or wanderer, who goes in search of the main character or travels to a far place with some purpose of acquiring information or attaining redemption. The main actors are assisted by a chorus of eight or ten performers squatting on the right side of the stage and chanting to the accompaniment of an orchestra located at the back. In accordance with a convention, the chorus often speaks or recites in the first person for the actor while he is engaged in dancing the exacting climaxes of his story. The stage is virtually surrounded by the audience, and the only scenery, placed at the back of the platform, is a wooden panel on which a pine tree is painted. The actors enter the stage across a wooden bridge decorated with pine branches. The leading performers and their assistants are masked, and women's roles are played by men. The acting, speaking, and dancing are marked by formalism. The writing is also quite formal and is characterized by varying degrees of aristocratic preciosity.

Although the plays are uncannily mysterious in

mood, they suddenly flare into passion and activity, arriving at a climactic situation after very little exposition and development. The typical Noh piece begins with a brief moral or philosophical statement. Then the *waki* appears on the stage and announces his destination. He traverses a great distance in the course of a conventional travel song, at the conclusion of which he meets a stranger who turns out to be the hero or heroine of the piece. The latter, as a rule, explains his disappearance or his death, recalls and re-enacts decisive moments from his past, and, finally, vanishes. The recollection is vivid, often painful and tempestuous, and is made as immediate to the audience as the recalled experience.

A profoundly religious seriousness derived from Buddhism and its Japanese variants permeates many of the Noh plays. The world is understood to be ruled by moral law. This law decrees expiation in life and in death for every form of violence and arrogance, the punishment taking the form of continued bondage to the passions even in the ghostly life. Military heroes whose deeds are honored in national history are not exempt from this form of suffering, since they died with passion and violence in their hearts. Salvation is the attainment of *nirvana*—the annihilation of desire, detachment from the transitory things of the illusory world which the unredeemed call reality.

Many of the plays, such as Seami's *Atsumori* and *Tsunemasa*, deal with Japan's famous twelfth-century feudal wars between rival clans, the Taira and Minamoto families. When the plays were written, two or more centuries after these costly struggles for power, their history was sufficiently remote to point a Buddhist moral, although it was not the moral but the evocation of courtliness and feudal glory that attracted the aristocracy to the Noh plays.

Not all these plays, however, follow the heroic tradition. One of the most moving is Kwanami's *Sotoba Komachi,* in which a once arrogant court beauty is possessed by the ghost of the lover she had mistreated and expiates the sin of pride in her destitute and ravaged old age. Kwanami's little masterpiece is an affecting example of the Noh drama's remembrance of things past. The reader who submits to the mood and is not put off by the telescoping of time, which suggests the "montage" and "flashbacks" of motion pictures and the technique of modern expressionist theatre, will cherish *Sotoba Komachi* as lyric drama and imaginative theatre.

SOTOBA KOMACHI

By Kwanami Kiyotsugu

TRANSLATED FROM THE JAPANESE BY ARTHUR WALEY

PERSONS

A PRIEST OF THE KOYASAN
ONO NO KOMACHI

SECOND PRIEST
CHORUS

PRIEST: We who on shallow hills have built our home
In the heart's deep recess seek solitude.
[*Turning to the audience*]
I am a priest of the Koyasan. I am minded to go up to the Capital to visit the shrines and sanctuaries there.
The Buddha of the Past is gone.
And he that shall be Buddha has not yet come into the world.

SECOND PRIEST: In a dream-lull our lives are passed; all, all
That round us lies
Is visionary, void.
Yet got we by rare fortune at our birth
Man's shape, that is hard to get;
And dearer gift was given us, harder to win,
The doctrine of Buddha, seed of our Salvation.
And me this only thought possessed,
How I might bring that seed to blossom, till at last
I drew this sombre cassock across my back.
And knowing now the lives before my birth,
No love I owe
To those that to this life engendered me,
Nor seek a care (have I not disavowed
Such hollow bonds?) from child by me begot.
A thousand leagues
Is little road
To the pilgrim's feet.
The fields his bed,
The hills his home
Till the travel's close.

PRIEST: We have come so fast that we have reached the pine-woods of Abeno, in the country of Tsu. Let us rest in this place.
[*They sit down by the* Waki's *pillar*]

KOMACHI: Like a root-cut reed,
Should the tide entice,
I would come, I think; but now
No wave asks; no stream stirs.
Long ago I was full of pride;
Crowned with nodding tresses, halcyon locks,
I walked like a young willow delicately wafted
By the winds of Spring.
I spoke with the voice of a nightingale that has sipped the dew.

I was lovelier than the petals of the wild-rose open-stretched
In the hour before its fall.
But now I am grown loathsome even to sluts,
Poor girls of the people, and they and all men
Turn scornful from me.
Unhappy months and days pile up their score;
I am old; old by a hundred years.
In the City I fear men's eyes,
And at dusk, lest they should cry "Is it she?"
Westward with the moon I creep
From the cloud-high City of the Hundred Towers.
No guard will question, none challenge
Pilgrim so wretched: yet must I be walking
Hid ever in shadow of the trees.
Past the Lovers' Tomb,
And the Hill of Autumn
To the River of Katsura, the boats, the moonlight.
[*She shrinks back and covers her face, frightened at being known*]
Who are those rowing in the boats?
Oh, I am weary. I will sit on this tree-stump and rest awhile.

PRIEST: Come! The sun is sinking; we must hasten on our way. Look, look at that beggar there! It is a holy Stupa that she is sitting on! I must tell her to come off it.
Now then, what is that you are sitting on? Is it not a holy Stupa, the worshipful Body of Buddha? Come off it and rest in some other place.

KOMACHI: Buddha's worshipful body, you say? But I could see no writing on it, nor any figure carved. I thought it was only a tree-stump.

PRIEST: Even the little black tress on the hillside
When it has put its blossoms on
Cannot be hid;
And think you that this tree
Cut fivefold in the fashion of Buddha's holy form
Shall not make manifest its power?

KOMACHI: I too am a poor withered bough.
But there are flowers at my heart,
Good enough, maybe, for an offering.
But why is this called Buddha's body?

PRIEST: Hear then! This Stupa is the Body of the Diamond Lord. It is the symbol of his incarnation.

KOMACHI: And in what elements did he choose to manifest his body?

PRIEST: Earth, water, wind, fire and space.

KOMACHI: Of these five man also is compounded. Where then is the difference?

PRIEST: The forms are the same, but not the virtue.

KOMACHI: And what is the virtue of the Stupa?

PRIEST: "He that has looked once upon the Stupa, shall escape forever from the Three Paths of Evil."

KOMACHI: "One thought can sow salvation in the heart." Is that of less price?

SECOND PRIEST: If your heart has seen salvation, how comes it that you linger in the World?

KOMACHI: It is my body that lingers, for my heart left it long ago.

PRIEST: You have no heart at all, or you would have known the Body of Buddha.

KOMACHI: It was because I knew it that I came to see it!

SECOND PRIEST: And knowing what you know, you sprawled upon it without a word of prayer?

KOMACHI: It was on the ground already. What harm could it get by my resting on it?

PRIEST: It was an act of discord.

KOMACHI: Sometimes from discord salvation springs.

SECOND PRIEST: From the malice of Daiba. . . .[1]

KOMACHI: As from the Mercy of Kwannon.[2]

PRIEST: From the folly of Handoku. . . .[3]

KOMACHI: As from the wisdom of Monju.[4]

SECOND PRIEST: That which is called Evil

KOMACHI: Is Good.

PRIEST: That which is called Illusion

KOMACHI: Is Salvation.

SECOND PRIEST: For Salvation

KOMACHI: Cannot be planted like a tree.

PRIEST: And the Heart's Mirror

KOMACHI: Hangs in the void.

CHORUS: [*Speaking for* Komachi]
"Nothing is real.
Between Buddha and Man
Is no distinction, but a seeming of difference planned
For the welfare of the humble, the ill-instructed,
Whom he has vowed to save.
Sin itself may be the ladder of salvation."
So she spoke, eagerly; and the priests,
"A saint, a saint is this decrepit, outcast soul."
And bending their heads to the ground,
Three times did homage before her.

KOMACHI: I now emboldened
Recite a riddle, a jesting song.
"Were I in Heaven
The Stupa were an ill seat;
But here in the world without,

---

[1] A wicked disciple who in the end attained to Illumination.
[2] The Goddess of Mercy.
[3] A disciple so witless that he could not recite a single verse of Scripture.
[4] God of Wisdom.

What harm is done?"

CHORUS: The Priests would have rebuked her;
But they have found their match.

PRIEST: Who are you? Pray tell us the name you had, and we will pray for you when you are dead.

KOMACHI: Shame covers me when I speak my name; but if you will pray for me, I will try to tell you. This is my name; write it down in your prayer list: I am the ruins of Komachi, daughter of Ono no Yoshizane, Governor of the land of Dewa.

PRIESTS: Oh piteous, piteous! Is this
Komachi that once
Was a bright flower,
Komachi the beautiful, whose dark brows
Linked like young moons;
Her face white-farded ever;
Whose many, many damask robes
Filled cedar-scented halls?

KOMACHI: I made verses in our speech
And in the speech of the foreign Court.

CHORUS: The cup she held at the feast
Like gentle moonlight dropped its glint on her sleeve.
Oh how fell she from spendor,
How came the white of winter
To crown her head?
Where are gone the lovely locks, double-twined,
The coils of jet?
Lank wisps, scant curls wither now
On wilted flesh;
And twin-arches, moth-brows tinge no more
With the hue of far hills. "Oh cover, cover
From the creeping light of dawn
Silted seaweed locks that of a hundred years
Lack now but one.
Oh hide me from my shame."
    [Komachi *hides her face*]

CHORUS: [*Speaking for the* Priest] What is it you carry in the wallet string at your neck?

KOMACHI: Death may come to-day—or hunger to-morrow.
A few beans and a cake of millet:
That is what I carry in my bag.

CHORUS: And in the wallet on your back?

KOMACHI: A garment stained with dust and sweat.

CHORUS: And in the basket on your arm?

KOMACHI: Sagittaries white and black.

CHORUS: Tattered cloak.[5]

KOMACHI: Broken hat. . . .

CHORUS: She cannot hide her face from our eyes:
And how her limbs

KOMACHI: From rain and dew, hoar-frost and snow?

CHORUS: [*Speaking for* Komachi *while she mimes the action they describe*] Not rags enough to wipe the tears from my eyes!
Now, wandering along the roads
I beg an alms of those that pass.

---

[5] The words which follow suggest the plight of her lover Shosho when he traveled to her house "a hundred nights all but one," to cut his notch on the bench.

And when they will not give,
An evil rage, a very madness possesses me.
My voice changes.
Oh terrible!

KOMACHI: [*Thrusting her hat under the Priests'
noses and shrieking at them menacingly*] Grr! You
priests, give me something: give me something . . .
Ah!

PRIEST: What do you want?

KOMACHI: Let me go to Komachi.

[*The spirit of her lover Shosho has now entirely
possessed her: this "possession-scene" lasts very
much longer on the stage than the brief words
would suggest.* TRANSLATOR]

PRIEST: But you told us you were Komachi.
What folly is this you are talking?

KOMACHI: No, no. . . . Komachi was very beauti-
ful.
Many letters came to her, many messages,
Thick as raindrops out of a black summer sky.
But she sent no answer, not even an empty word.
And now in punishment she has grown old:
She has lived a hundred years—
I love her, oh I love her!

PRIEST: You love Komachi? Say then, whose spirit
has possessed you?

KOMACHI: There were many who set their hearts
on her,
But among them all
It was Shosho who loved her best,
Shii no Shosho of the Deep Grass.

CHORUS: [*Speaking for* Komachi, *i.e., for the spirit
of Shosho*]
The wheel goes back; I live again through the cycle
of my woes.
Again I travel to the shaft-bench.
The sun . . . what hour does he show?
Dusk. . . . Alone in the moonlight
I must go my way.
Though the watchmen of the barriers
Stand across my path,
They shall not stop me!

[*Attendants robe Komachi in the Court hat and
traveling-cloak of Shosho*]
Look, I go!

KOMACHI: Lifting the white skirts of my trailing
dress.

CHORUS: [*Speaking for* Komachi, *while she, dressed
as her lover Shosho, mimes the night-journey*]
Pulling down over my ears the tall, nodding hat,
Tying over my head the long sleeves of my hunting
cloak,
Hidden from the eyes of men,
In moonlight, in darkness,
On rainy nights I traveled; on windy nights,
Under a shower of leaves; when the snow was deep,

KOMACHI: And when water dripped at the roof-
eaves,—tok, tok . . .

CHORUS: Swiftly, swiftly coming and going, com-
ing and going . . .
One night, two nights, three nights,
Ten nights (and this was harvest night) . . .
I never saw her, yet I traveled;
Faithful as the cock who marks each day the dawn,
I carved my marks on the bench.
I was to come a hundred times;
There lacked but one . . .

KOMACHI: [*Feeling the death-agony of Shosho*] My
eyes dazzle. Oh the pain, the pain!

CHORUS: Oh the pain! and desperate,
Before the last night had come,
He died,—Shii no Shosho the Captain.

[*Speaking for* Komachi, *who is now no longer
possessed by Shosho's spirit*]
Was it his spirit that possessed me,
Was it his anger that broke my wits?
If this be so, let me pray for the life hereafter,
Where alone is comfort;
Piling high the sands
Till I be burnished as gold.[6]
See, I offer my flower to Buddha,[7]
I hold it in both hands.
Oh may He lead me into the Path of Truth,
Into the Path of Truth.

[6] The color of the saints in heaven.
[7] Her "heart-flower," *i.e.*, poetic talent.

The stage for the Passion Play produced at Valenciennes, France, in 1547. From the left the mansions represent: Paradise, Nazareth, the Temple, Jerusalem, a palace, the Golden Door, the sea, and Hell's Mouth. From a manuscript reproduced courtesy the Biblithèque Nationale. *Opposite page:* This detail from Denis von Alsloot, *The Triumph of Isabella,* 1615, suggests the type of pageant wagon used to stage the English cycle plays. Courtesy the Victoria and Albert Museum. Crown copyright.

The Medieval Drama

The Medieval Drama

There is no overwhelming literary distinction in medieval drama, and its authors possessed no music comparable to Dante's or Chaucer's. Yet there is a certain greatness in the drama. It conveys a grandeur of vision and faith. Although the authors often reduced divine matters to the lowest common denominator of ordinary behavior and feeling, they viewed earthly events under the aspect of heaven and eternity. Their ultimate subject is salvation. In those plays which form cycles tracing the history of man from the Creation to Doomsday, and in the French cycle *Les Miracles de Nostre-Dame,* which recounts the life and miracles of the Virgin, the scope is of epic magnitude. There is, besides, a greatness of stir about the entire enterprise associated with medieval drama. It affords the spectacle of an entire people growing and displaying its dramatic art as an act of communion. In the Middle Ages, as in the Athenian fifth century B.C., we find a community making a folk festival of the theatre, whether the plays were presented on fixed multiple stages or "stations" in the market place, as in France, or on pageant wagons driven in succession to places where people foregathered, as in England. The medieval plays constitute the most vital folk drama known to the Western world, whether these are "mystery" plays based on Biblical incidents, saint or "miracle" plays recounting the life of some saint or of the Virgin, or, later on, "moralities" imparting a lesson.

Since the medieval world of Western Europe was one spiritual community ruled by the Roman Catholic Church and nationalism was not yet a barrier between nations, the drama was essentially the same wherever it was produced. Practically the same types of plays were created in England, France, Holland, Italy, Spain, and other countries. Only local color and national taste or prejudice differentiated the writing. In France, for example, the Gallic spirit was already in evidence when one playwright found humor in the befuddlement of the elderly Joseph upon discovering that the Virgin had conceived. In England, the northern weather and the restiveness among the peasantry that flared into Wat Tyler's rebellion during Richard II's reign found vivid expression in *The Second Shepherds' Play.* And the German *Redentin Play* is strongly colored by anti-Semitism. In some countries the playwriting shows less of the folk spirit than in England. And there is less farce and demonology in the English religious plays than in their French and German counterparts.

Nevertheless, all medieval dramatic art manifests the folk spirit, and we must not underestimate its influence on the popular theatre of the Renaissance. The Middle Ages contributed substantially to the buoyancy of theatrical taste during the sixteenth and early seventeenth centuries—a buoyancy that manifested itself in the mingling of farcical and exalted matter and in the abundance of episodes in Marlowe's and Shakespeare's multiscened plays. Not enough notice has been taken of the medievalism of the "renaissance" theatre of England and Spain, which gave us Shakespeare and Lope de Vega and the popular platform stages for which they wrote.

THE RELIGIOUS PLAYS: MYSTERY AND MIRACLE

Medieval Europe created new forms of drama instead of continuing the dramatic traditions of the ancient world. A classic influence appears only in the academic exercises of the tenth-century Saxon nun Hrotsvitha, who patterned her saint plays after the comedies of Terence. In fact, except for the survival of an acting tradition in the performances of wandering actors or mimes, the theatre died with the Roman empire. Once again, European drama developed from ritualistic beginnings.

Although the church had been the obdurate enemy of the decadent classic stage, it inevitably promoted a theatre of its own, and it continued to influence the drama throughout the Middle Ages. Rudimentary dramatic rites appeared early in the form of pantomimic representations of the Nativity at Christmas and the Resurrection at Easter. By the ninth century, miniature Latin plays, known as tropes, arose when chanted dialogues were introduced into the wordless sequences of the mass at Easter, Christmas, and Epiphany and were chanted on the raised altar area of the churches.

In time, moreover, Biblical themes were treated by the priesthood at greater length, and the simple dialogued song was succeeded by a variety of liturgical one-act plays in Latin, frequently coalesced as cycles. Finally, the further elaboration of thematic material, the translation from Latin into the vernaculars, and the addition of realistic detail culminated in the fourteenth and fifteenth centuries in well-developed one-act episodes known as mystery plays. When strung together in Biblical sequence as cycles, they comprised a religious drama or Passion play of tremendous scope. It embraced heaven and hell, and it presented a sacred history of the world from the Creation to the Last Judgment.

The naïveté of many of the plays actually enhanced the general effect, and the crudities were negligible compared with the impressiveness of the great chronicle, which often required two or more days in performance. (Thus the complete Chester cycle in England contained twenty-five "pageants" or plays; the Wakefield or Townley, thirty-two; the York, forty-eight.) This was folk art of a high order; it was the work of anonymous authors who may have based their plays on Latin originals but were not impervious to the ordinary life of their audiences.

The history of the medieval theatre is, indeed, one of physical and figurative emergence from the church building. The higher clergy began to frown on the performances when these became too popular—that is, too realistic or boisterous; the productions, moreover, grew too spectacular for presentation within the confines of the altar area or the nave. At first, the stage was moved out to the church porch; *Adam*, an early French transitional work, appears to have been performed in front of the cathedral, since one of the stage directions has "God" entering and coming out of the church. Finally, the acting space was shifted to the market place and to other open-air areas of the medieval city, and control of the proceedings passed into the hands of the burghers, who, no doubt, influenced the dramatic treatment.

A great open-air drama festival arose in the fourteenth century throughout Western Europe. It became the principal event of the Corpus Christi holiday, established in 1311, and no effort or expense was spared by the thriving middle-class communities, which prided themselves on their ingenuity and ostentation. In France, the plays were produced by amateur groups, called *confréries*, on multiple stages or "stations" representing the different localities of the religious story. In many English cities each craft union or guild assumed responsibility for a different play and usually performed it on large pageant wagons at various places marked out with flags. (An exception is apparently the Coventry or "N. Towne" cycle of forty-three pageants, which is believed to have been performed on stationary sets by more professional actors than those supplied by the guilds from their own ranks.) Wagon succeeded wagon, each with its little drama, in a predetermined order, until the cycle was completed. Although the vogue of the plays declined rapidly during the Renaissance and Reformation owing to Protestant bias and the success of the secular drama, more or less adulterated Passion plays survived in the village of Oberammergau and elsewhere in Central Europe.

Four English cycles, fragments of other cycles, and individual plays have come down to us. They reveal differences in treatment of material and vary in merit. Some of them are commonplace; others are inspired and even memorable. Realistic and farcical elements enrich two of the plays that deal with Noah and the Deluge; in each, the patriarch is burdened with a stubborn or waspish wife and is not above engaging in a violent altercation with her. Glorious farce appears in the famous *Second Shepherds' Play* of the Wakefield cycle; here the journey of the shepherds to the manger is preceded by the invented tale of the thieving Mak, who steals a sheep and hides it in his wife's bed. Even social criticism enters into this work.

Originality and zest are less conspicuous in the serious plays, but some of them are heightened by tenderness and compassion. Thus the crucifixion scenes are permeated with pity and terror, and some of the Nativity plays are delicate and charming. The masterpiece among the serious English pieces, however, is undoubtedly the *Abraham and Isaac* preserved in a fifteenth-century manuscript at Brome Manor, Suffolk. Close to the original spirit of church drama, it is suffused with religious feeling and never deviates from its reverential mood. It is at the same time singularly human and touching; Abraham and Isaac are not frozen figures of antiquity but a tender father and a trusting child.

The Second Shepherds' Play is the masterpiece of medieval English farce, chiefly notable for its comic characterizations. There are no fewer than five realistically drawn and more or less individualized characters within the narrow compass of this one-acter. And among them is the elder cousin of both Falstaff and Autolycus, the sheep-stealing Mak, who has wits to live by in the hard world and a blithe impertinence with which to brazen things out when the pressure is on him. In *The Second Shepherds' Play*, the New Testament references to the Nativity lead to pure invention until the last episode, in which the shepherds follow the star to Bethlehem, and even here their adoration of the Christ child is in character. The Biblical theme has given rise to variations that belong to folk drama and folk realism. The shepherds are not of Israel but of the English countryside, and Judea is "not far" from England.

Actually the realism of the play is profoundly medieval—that is, it exists side by side with a sense of wonder and with unquestioning faith. Only when we take note of this fact and also remember that this little drama is part of a Passion play (the second of two shepherd plays in the Wakefield cycle) are we prepared to appreciate the remarkable artistry of the work. The grumblings of the shepherds over social injustice and domestic infelicity, Mak's complaints of poverty as well as his misbehavior, bad weather, gruff words—all dissolve into the mystery of the Nativity. Everything points to the necessity of redemption from suffering, sin, and error. It is not without reason that *The Second Shepherds' Play* has been called "perfect as a work of art" by Alfred William Pollard, one of the most careful students of medieval English drama.

MORALITIES

The medieval stage developed several types of drama that generally fell short of the distinction achieved by the best mystery plays, which dramatized Biblical situations. Nevertheless, two genres—the saint plays, and the so-called moralities—increased the scope of the theatre and furthered the development of the European drama. A third form—the independent farce, or *sotie*, such as the little French masterpiece *The Farce of the Worthy Master Pierre Pathelin*—served the public's interest in everyday life.

Saint plays, associated with celebrations of saints' days, satisfied medieval man's religious interest and his craving for marvels. Dramatizations of martyrdoms or miracles consequently appeared early in the Middle Ages, bringing numerous non-Biblical characters and situations into the theatre. These pieces were not much in vogue in England, but they enjoyed great popularity in France, which had, in addition to plays about the saints, a large cycle devoted to the miracles of the Virgin. In these works, too, there was a large element of human interest from the very start, as in *The Miracle of Theophilus,* written by the thirteenth-century minstrel Rutebeuf.

An important outgrowth of the religious drama, especially in England, was the morality play. Developing later, in the fifteenth century, the "moralities" were more original in invention and more complex in structure than either the mystery or the saint plays. The new dramatic form introduced moralization by means of didactic situations revolving around allegorical characters. Such abstract figures as Vice, Riches, Death, and Good-Deeds began to people the stage, which was in this case always stationary.

Humor was introduced in order to make the lesson more attractive, the devil and his mischief-loving assistant, known as the Vice, being singled out for considerable horseplay. Occasionally some degree of characterization appeared in the treatment of the personified virtues and vices. The plots were invented by the author rather than adapted from Biblical or legendary sources, and the treatment could be as free as the choice of the subject.

The themes were at first distinctly religious. Simple religious matter predominated in the early-fifteenth-century *Castle of Perseverance* and in *Everyman.* A fully equipped morality such as *The Castle of Perseverance* included several episodes: a conflict between the Virtues and the Vices for the possession of man's soul; the summons of Death; a debate between the Body and the Soul; and a debate of the Heavenly Graces.

Later, the didactic machinery of the moralities was put to the more controversial uses of religious disputation. Thus, in the early sixteenth century, Catholics and Protestants charged the morality drama with propaganda for their respective causes. Notable among these pieces are R. Wever's *Lusty Juventus,* in which the hero is converted to Protestantism, and Sir David Lyndsay's more comprehensive *Satire of the Three Estates,* in which the character "Pauper" cries out against the oppression he endures from "Landlord" and "Clergy." Finally, humanist propaganda began to appear in such a morality as *The Four Elements,* written by the great Sir Thomas More's brother-in-law John Rastell; this play intimates that theology must make way for science. John Redmond's plea for a humanist, antischolastic philosophy of education, *Wit and Science* (*c.* 1530), castigates ignorance and celebrates the romance between a student and Lady Science.

Moralities continued to be written even during the high noon of the Elizabethan stage. Marlowe was indebted to them for the general features of *Doctor Faustus.* Some specific morality elements in this drama are the Seven Deadly Sins and the comic devils. The highly popular Vice of the moralities is regarded as a prototype of many of the clowns so greatly favored in the theatre of Shakespeare's day. Nevertheless, this late type of medieval drama was, in the main, too crude and dull to stand comparison with the lusty new drama that had freed itself from the trammels of didacticism and was presenting rounded personages instead of abstract characters, often little more than personified attributes. Even before the blossoming of the Elizabethan stage, the moralities had encountered rivalry from popular farces and so-called interludes such as John Heywood's *The Four P's* and *The Play of the Weather.* Although the latter were hardly more than static debates performed on raised platforms in banquet halls, they had zest and humor, and they provided a welcome relief from didactic drama. The further triumph of Marlowe's and Shakespeare's theatre inevitably spelled extinction for the morality, although some of its elements, such as the aforementioned Vice and Seven Deadly Sins, survived.

Everyman (probably derived from the early Dutch *Elckerlijk*) alone was deservedly exempted from this fate. Written probably a few decades before the end of the fifteenth century, it was conceived early enough to be steeped in the spiritual values of the Middle Ages and to be free from the stridencies of religious controversy. The allegory is profoundly simple and fundamental. Its pathetically bewildered and lonely protagonist, significantly named "Everyman," is faced with the ultimate crisis of death and is overwhelmed by the most universal and least eradicable of human fears. The fascination of the play is attested by the popularity of Hugo von Hofmannsthal's twentieth-century German adaptation, *Jedermann,* staged originally by Reinhardt and produced annually at the Salzburg festival in Austria.

The Brome
ABRAHAM AND ISAAC

A MODERNIZED VERSION BY JOHN GASSNER

CHARACTERS

ABRAHAM   AN ANGEL
ISAAC   DOCTOR, *or teacher*

[*A hilly landscape.* Abraham *and* Isaac *are kneeling on a level piece of ground*][1]

ABRAHAM: Father of Heaven, omnipotent
With all my heart to thee I call.
Thou has given me both land and rent.
And my livelihood thou hast me sent.
  I thank thee highly evermore for all.

First of the earth thou madest Adam,
  And Eve also to be his wife;
All other creatures from these two came.
And now thou hast granted to me, Abraham,
  Here in this land to lead my life.

In my age thou has granted me this
  That this young child with me shall dwell.
I love nothing so much in this,
Except thine own self, dear Father of Bliss,
  As Isaac here, my own sweet son.

I who have many children mo'
  Love them not as half so well.
This fair sweet child he cheers me so
In every place wherever I do go,
  That of no affliction may I tell.

And therefore, Father of Heaven, I thee pray
  For his health and also for his grace.
Now, Lord, keep him both night and day
That never discomfort nor dismay
  Come to my child in any place.
  .[*Rising*]
Now come on, Isaac, my own sweet child,
  Go we home and take our rest.

ISAAC: Abraham, mine own father so mild,
To follow you I am full pleased,
  Both early and late.

ABRAHAM: Come on, sweet child. I love thee best
  Of all the children that ever I begot.
    [Abraham *and* Isaac *start on their homeward journey.* God *and an* Angel *appear*]
GOD: Mine angel, fast hie thee thy way,

[1] Brackets indicate interpolated stage directions; parentheses indicate stage directions found in the original text.

And unto middle-earth anon thou go—
Abram's heart now will I assay,
  Whether that he be steadfast or no.

Say I commanded him for to take
  Isaac, his young son that he loves so well,
And with his blood sacrifice he make,
  If any of my friendship he would feel.

Show him the way unto the hill
  Where that his sacrifice shall be.
I shall assay now his good will,
  Whether he loveth better his child or me.
All men shall take example by him
  My commandments how they shall keep.
    [*As the* Angel *descends,* Abraham, *moved in spirit, kneels again*]
ABRAHAM: Now, Father of Heaven, that formed everything,
  My prayers I make to thee again,
For this day a tender offering
  Here must I give to thee certain.
Ah, Lord God, almighty King,
  What manner of beast would'st thou fain?
If I had thereof true knowing,
  It should be done with all my main
    Full soon by me.
To do thy pleasure on a hill,
Verily, it is my will,
  Dear Father, God in Trinity!
    [*The* Angel *reaches* Abraham, *while* Isaac *has wandered off*]
ANGEL: Abraham, Abraham, be at rest!
  Our Lord commandeth thee to take
Isaac, thy young son whom thou lovest best,
  And with his blood that sacrifice thou make.

Into the Land of Vision do thou go,
  And offer thy child unto thy Lord;
I shall thee lead and show also.
  To God's behest, Abraham, accord,

And follow me upon this green!

ABRAHAM: Welcome to me be my Lord's command!
  And his word I will not withstand.

189

Yet Isaac, my young son in hand,
A full dear child to me has been.

I had rather, if God had been pleased,
    To have forborne all the goods that I have,
Than Isaac, my son, should be deceased,—
    So God in heaven my soul may save!

I have loved never a thing so much on earth,
    And now I must the child go kill!
Ah, Lord God, my conscience lacketh mirth!
And yet, my dear Lord, I am sore afeared
    To grudge anything against thy will.

I love my child as my life,
    But yet I love my God much more
For though my heart should make any strife,
Yet will I not spare for child or wife,
    But do after my dread Lord's lore.

Though I love my son never so well,
    Yet smite off his head soon I shall.
Ah, Father of Heaven! to thee I kneel—
A hard death my son shall feel,
    For to honor thee, Lord, withal!

ANGEL: Abraham, Abraham, this is well said,
    And all these commandments look that thou
        keep,—
But in thy heart be nothing dismayed.

ABRAHAM: Nay, nay, forsooth, I hold me well repaid
    To please my God to the best that I may.
For though my heart be heavily set
    To see the blood of my own dear son,
Yet for all that I will not let,
But Isaac, my son, I will go get,
    And come as fast as ever we can.
        [*The* Angel *departs and* Abraham *looks for his
        son*]
ABRAHAM: Now, Isaac, my own son dear,
    Where art thou, child? Speak to me.

ISAAC: My father, sweet father, I am here,
    And make my prayers to the Trinity.

ABRAHAM: Rise up, my child, and fast come hither,
    My gentle bairn that art so wise,
For we, too, child, must go together,
    And unto my Lord make sacrifice.
        [Isaac *rises and goes to him*]
ISAAC: I am full ready, my father, lo!
    Given to your hands, I stand right here;
And whatsoever ye bid me do, even so
    It shall be done with glad cheer,
        Full well and fine.

ABRAHAM: Ah, Isaac, my own son so dear,
    God's blessing I give thee, and mine.

Hold this faggot upon thy back,
    And I myself fire shall bring.

ISAAC: Father, all this here will I pack;
    I am full fain to do your bidding.

ABRAHAM: Ah, Lord of Heaven!
    [Abraham *looks up to heaven, and wrings his
    hands*]
This child's words all do wound my heart!
    [*Controlling himself and turning to* Isaac]
Now, Isaac, son, go we on our way
    Unto yon mount with all our main.

ISAAC: Go we, my dear father, as fast as I may;
    To follow you I am full fain,
        Although I be slender
    [Abraham *stops as they arrive at the mountain,
    his eyes fixed on heaven*]
ABRAHAM: Ah, Lord, my heart breaketh in twain
    This child's words, they be so tender!
        [*Again controlling himself*]
Ah, Isaac son, anon lay it down,
    No longer upon thy back it hold,
For I must make ready prayer soon
    To honor my Lord God as I was told.
        [Isaac *drops the faggots*]
ISAAC: Lo, my dear father, here it is.
    [*Moving close to him tenderly*]
To cheer you always I draw me near.
But, father, I marvel sore at this,
    Why ye make this heavy cheer,

And also, father, even more dread I—
    Where is your quick beast that ye should kill?
Both fire and wood we have ready nigh,
    But quick beast have we none on this hill.
        [*Anxiously*]
A quick beast, I wot well, must be slain,
    Your sacrifice to make.

ABRAHAM: Dread thee nought, my child, I would
        fain;
Our Lord will send me unto this place
    Some manner of beast for to take
        Through his command.

ISAAC: Yea, father, but my heart beginneth to quake
    To see that sharp sword in your hand.

Why bear ye your sword drawn so?
    Of your countenance I have much wonder.

ABRAHAM: [*Aside*] Ah, Father of Heaven! such is
        my woe,
This child here breaks my heart in sunder.

ISAAC: Tell me, my dear father, ere that ye cease—
    Bear ye your sword drawn for me?

ABRAHAM: Ah, Isaac! sweet son, peace, peace!
    For in truth thou break'st my heart in three!

ISAAC: Now truly, on something, father, ye think,
    That ye mourn thus more and more.

ABRAHAM: Ah, Lord of Heaven, let thy grace sink,
    For my heart was never half so sore!

ISAAC: I pray ye, father, that ye me know will let
    Whether I shall have any harm or no.

ABRAHAM: Alas, sweet son, I may not tell thee yet,
My heart is now so full of woe.

ISAAC: Dear father, I pray you, hide it not from me,
But some of your thought, I pray tell me.

ABRAHAM: Ah, Isaac, Isaac, I must kill thee!

ISAAC: Kill me, father? Alas, what have I done?

If I have trespassed against you aught,
With a rod ye may make me full mild;
And with your sharp sword kill me naught,
For in truth, father, I am but a child.

ABRAHAM: I am full sorry, son, thy blood for to spill,
But truly, child, I may not as I please.

ISAAC: Now I would to God my mother were here on
this hill.
She would kneel for me on both her knees
To save my life.
And since that my mother is not here,
I pray you, father, change your cheer,
And kill me not with your knife.

ABRAHAM: Forsooth, my son, save I thee kill,
I should grieve God right sore, I dread,
It is his commandment and also his will
That I should do this same deed.

He commanded me, son, for certain,
To make my sacrifice with thy blood.

ISAAC: And is it God's will that I should be slain?

ABRAHAM: Yea, truly, Isaac, my son so good;
And therefore my hands I wring!

ISAAC: Now father, against my Lord's will,
I will never grouch, loud or still.
He might a-sent me a better destiny,
If it had been his pleasure.

ABRAHAM: Forsooth, son, if not this deed I did,
Grievously displeased our Lord would be.

ISAAC: Nay, nay, father, God forbid
That ever ye should grieve him for me!

Ye have other children, one or two,
Which ye should love well in natural kind.
I pray you, father, make you no woe;
For, be I once dead and from you go,
I shall be soon out of your mind.

Therefore do our Lord's bidding,
And when I am dead, then pray for me.
But, good father, tell ye my mother nothing,
Say that I am in another country dwelling.

ABRAHAM: Ah, Isaac, Isaac, blessed mayest thou be!

My heart beginneth wildly to rise
To see the blood of thy blessed body!

ISAAC: Father, since it may be no other wise,
Let it pass over as well as I.

But, father, ere I go unto my death,
I pray you bless me with your hand.
[Isaac *kneels;* Abraham *places his hand on the
lad's head*]
ABRAHAM: Now Isaac, with all my breath
My blessing I give thee upon this land,
And God also thereto add his.
Isaac, Isaac, son, up thou stand,
Thy fair sweet mouth that I may kiss.

ISAAC: Now farewell, my own father so fine,
And greet well my mother on earth.
But I pray you, father, to hide my eyne
That I see not the stroke of your sharp sword
That my flesh shall defile.

ABRAHAM: Son, thy words make me to weep full sore;
Now, my dear son Isaac, speak no more.

ISAAC: Ah, my own dear father! wherefore?
We shall speak together here but a while.

And since that I must needs be dead,
Yet, my dear father, to you I pray,
Smite then but few strokes at my head
And make an end as soon as ye may,
And tarry not too long.

ABRAHAM: Thy meek words, child, do me dismay;
So "wellaway" must be my song,

Except alone for God's good will.
Ah! Isaac, my own sweet child,
Kiss me yet again upon this hill;
In all the world is none so mild!

ISAAC: Now, truly, father, all this tarrying,
It doth my heart but harm—
I pray you, father, make an ending.

ABRAHAM: Come up, sweet son, unto my arm.
[*He binds him*]
I must bind thy hands too
Although thou be never so mild.

ISAAC: Ah, mercy, father! Why should ye so do?

ABRAHAM: That thou should'st not stay me, my child.

ISAAC: Indeed nay, father, I will not stay you.
Do on, for me, your will;
And on the purpose that ye have set you,
For God's love, keep it steadfast still.

I am full sorry this day to die,
But yet I will not cause my God to grieve.
Do your desire for me hardily;
My fair sweet father, I do give you leave.

But, father, I pray you evermore,
Nothing to my mother tell,
If she wist it, she would weep full sore;
Indeed she loves me, father well,
God's good blessing may she have!

Now farewell, my mother so sweet,
We two are like no more to meet.

ABRAHAM: Ah! Isaac, Isaac, son, thou makest me grieve,
And with thy words thou so distemperest me.

ISAAC: Indeed, sweet father, I am sorry to grieve you;
I cry you mercy for what I have done,
And for all trespass ever I did do.
Now, dear father, forgive all I have done.—
God of Heaven be with me!

ABRAHAM: Ah! dear child, leave off thy moans!
In all thy life thou grieved me never once.
Now blessed be thou, body and bones,
That ever thou were bred and born;
Thou hast been to me child full good.
But in truth, child, though I mourn never so fast,
Yet must I needs here at the last
In this place shed all thy blood;

Therefore, my dear son, here shalt thou lie,—
[He places him on the altar]
Unto my work I must proceed.
In truth, I had as lief myself to die
If God were pleased with the deed
That I my own body should offer.

ISAAC: Ah, mercy, father, mourn ye no more;
Your weeping maketh my heart sore
That mine own death I am to suffer.

Your kerchief, father, about my eyes wind.

ABRAHAM: So I shall, my sweetest child on earth.

ISAAC: Now yet, good father, have this in mind,
And smite me not often with your sharp sword,
But hastily that it be sped.
("Here Abraham laid a cloth on Isaac's face, thus saying:")

ABRAHAM: Now farewell, my child so full of grace.

ISAAC: Ah, father, turn downward my face,
For of your sharp sword I am ever adread!
[Abraham looks up to heaven resignedly]

ABRAHAM: To do this deed I am full sorry,
But, Lord, thine behest I will not withstand.

ISAAC: Ah! Father of Heaven, to thee I cry;
Lord, receive me thou into thy hand!
[Abraham falters and pleads again]

ABRAHAM: Lo, now is the time come for certain,
That my sword in his neck shall bite.
Ah, Lord! my heart riseth there again,
I may not find it in my heart to smite.
My heart will not now thereto!
Ah, fain I would work my Lord's will,
But this young innocent lies so still,
I may not find it in my heart him to kill.
Oh, Father of Heaven! what shall I do?

ISAAC: Ah, mercy, father, why tarry ye so,
And let me lie there so long on this heath?
Now I would God the stroke were done also;
Father, heartily I pray you, shorten my woe,
And let me not wait thus for my death.

ABRAHAM: Now, heart, why would'st thou not break in three?

Yet shalt thou not make me to my God unmild.
I will no longer stay for thee,
For that my God aggrieved would be.
Now have thy stroke, my own dear child.
("Here Abraham drew his stroke, and the Angel took the sword in his hand suddenly")

ANGEL: I am an angel, thou mayest see blithe,
That from heaven to thee is sent.
Our Lord thanketh thee a hundred time
For the keeping of his commandment.

He knoweth thy will, and also thy heart,
That thou dreadst him above all thing;
And some of thy heaviness for to depart
A fair ram yonder I did bring;

He standeth, lo, among the briars tied.
Now, Abraham, amend thy mood,
For Isaac, thy young son, here by thy side
This day shall not shed his blood.

Go, make thy sacrifice with yon ram.
Now farewell, blessed Abraham,
For unto heaven I go now home,—
The way is full straight. . . .
Take up thy son now free!
[Exit]

ABRAHAM: Ah, Lord! I thank thee for thy great grace,
Now am I eased in diverse wise.
Arise up, Isaac, my dear son, arise,
Arise up, sweet child, and come to me!

ISAAC: Ah, mercy, father, why smite ye naught?
Ah, smite on, father, once with your knife.

ABRAHAM: Peace, my sweet son, and take no thought,
For our Lord of Heaven hath granted life
By his angel now,
That thou shalt not die this day, son, truly.

ISAAC: Ah, father, full glad then were I;
In truth, father— I say, I—wis,[2]
That this tale were true!

ABRAHAM: A hundred times, my son fair of hue,
For joy thy mouth now will I kiss.

ISAAC: Ah, my dear father Abraham,
Will not God be wroth that we do thus?

ABRAHAM: No, no! hardly, my sweet son!
For yon same ram he hath now sent
Hither down to us.
Yon beast shall die here in thy stead,
In the worship of our Lord, alone.
Go fetch him hither, my child, indeed.

ISAAC: Father I will go seize him by the head,
And bring yon beast with me anon.
[Isaac gets the ram]
Ah, sheep, sheep, blessed may thou be,
That ever thou wert sent down hither!
Thou shalt this day die for me,
In worship of the Holy Trinity.

2 Know.

Now come fast and go we together,
　　To my father of Heaven.
Though thou be never so gentle and good.
Yet I had liefer thou shed thy blood
　　In truth, sheep, than I!
　　[*He leads it to* Abraham]
Lo, father, I have brought here, full smart,
　　This gentle sheep, and him to you I give.
　　[*With a sigh of relief*]
But, Lord God, I thank thee with all my heart!
　　For I am glad that I shall live,
　　And kiss once more my dear mother!

ABRAHAM: Now be right merry, my sweet child,
For this quick beast, that is so mild,
　　Here I shall offer before all other.

ISAAC: And I will fast begin to blow;
　　This fire shall burn a full good speed.
　　[*Hesitating, however*]
But, father, if I stoop down low,
Ye will not kill me with your sword, I trow?

ABRAHAM: No, hardly, sweet son; have no dread.
　　My mourning is past!

ISAAC: Yea, but would that sword were sped—
　　For, father, it doth make me yet full ill aghast.
　　(*"Here* Abraham *made his offering, kneeling
　　and saying thus:"*)
ABRAHAM: Now, Lord God of Heaven in Trinity,
　　Almighty God omnipotent,
My offering I make in the worship of thee,
　　And with this quick beast I thee present.
　　Lord, receive thou mine intent,
As thou art God and ground of our grace.

GOD: Abraham, Abraham, well mayest thou speed,
　　And Isaac, thy young son, thee by!
Truly, Abraham, for this deed,
　　I shall multiply both your seed
　　As thick as stars be in the sky,
　　　Both of bigger and less.
And as thick as gravel in the sea,
　　So thick multiplied your seed shall be;
　　This grant I you for your goodness.

Of you shall come fruit unknown,
　　And ever be in bliss without end,
For ye dread me as God alone
And keep my commandments, every one.
　　My blessing I give wheresoever ye wend!

ABRAHAM: Lo, Isaac my son, how think ye
　　Of this work that we have wrought?
Full glad and blithe may we be
　　That 'gainst the will of God we muttered nought
　　On this fair heath.

ISAAC: Ah, father, I thank our Lord every deal
That my wit served me so weel
　　For God to fear more than my death.

ABRAHAM: Why, dear-worthy son, wert thou afraid?
　　Boldly, child, tell me thy lore.

ISAAC: Yea! by my faith, father, be it said,
　　I was never so afraid before,
　　As I have been on yon hill!
Ah, by my faith, father, I swear
I will nevermore come there,
　　Except it be against my will!

ABRAHAM: Yea, come on with me, my own sweet son,
　　And homeward fast let us be gone.

ISAAC: By my faith, father, thereto I agree!
I had never such good will to go home,
And to speak with my dear mother!

ABRAHAM: Ah, Lord of Heaven, I thank thee,
　　For now I may lead home with me
　　Isaac, my young son so free,
The gentlest child above all other,—
　　This may avowed be.
Now, go we forth, my blessed son.

ISAAC: I grant, father, let us be gone,
For, by my troth, were I home then,
I would never go out as thus again.
I pray God give us grace evermore true,
And all those that we be beholden to!
　　[Abraham *and* Isaac *go out. The* Doctor *enters*]
DOCTOR: Lo, now sovereigns and sirs, thus did we
　　show
This solemn story to great and small.
It is a good lesson for both learned and low,
　　And even for the wisest of us all,
　　Without any barring.
For this story showeth you deep
How to our best power we should keep
　　God's commandments without doubting.

Think ye, sirs, if God sent an angel,
　　And commanded you your child to slay,
By your truth, is there any of you
　　That would balk or gainsay?
How think ye now, sirs, thereby?

There be three or four or more, I trow,
And those women that weep so sorrowfully
　　When that their children from them die
　　As nature takes of our kind.
It is folly, as I may well avow,
Against God to grudge or to grieve so low;
For ye shall never see them mischiefed, well I know,
　　By land or water,—have this in mind!

And grudge not against our Lord God,
　　In wealth or woe whatever he you send,
Though ye be never so hard bestead;
　　For when he willeth, he may it amend,
His commandments truly if ye keep with good soul,
　　As this story hath now showed you before,
And faithfully serve him, while ye be whole,
　　That ye may please God both even and morn.
Now Jesu, that wore the crown of thorn,
　　Bring us all to heaven's bliss!

FINIS

THE SECOND SHEPHERDS' PLAY

A MODERNIZED VERSION BY JOHN GASSNER

CHARACTERS

FIRST SHEPHERD: COLL   MAK   THE VIRGIN MARY
SECOND SHEPHERD: GIB   MAK'S WIFE: GILL   THE INFANT CHRIST
THIRD SHEPHERD: DAW   AN ANGEL

*One unchanged setting, consisting of two huts—
one representing* Mak's *cottage and the other the
manger or stable of the Nativity. The space between
the two huts represents the moors or fields. The action occurs in Palestine, but only in name; actually
the local color of the play is drawn from the countryside of Wakefield, England.*

*The action is continuous; although scene divisions
have been added to the original text, there is no need
to drop curtains to indicate a lapse of time.*

SCENE I.

The moors.

1ST SHEPHERD: Lord, but these weathers are cold,
    and I am ill-wrapped!
Nearly numb of hand, so long have I napped;
My legs, they fold; my fingers are chapped.
It is not as I would, for I am all lapped
    In sorrow.
In storms and tempest,
Now in the east, now in the west,
Woe is him has never rest,
    Mid-day or morrow!

But we poor shepherds that walk on the moor,
In faith, we are near-hands out of the door.
No wonder, as it stands, if we be poor,
For the tilth of our lands lies as fallow as a floor,
    As ye ken.[1]
We are so lamed,
Overtaxed and blamed,[2]
We are made hand-tamed
    By these gentlery-men.

Thus they rob us of our rest, Our Lady them harry!
These men that are tied fast, their plough must tarry.
What men say is for the best, we find it contrary!
Thus are farming-men oppressed, in point to mis-
carry
    Alive:

[1] Know.
[2] Literally, "crushed."

Thus the lords hold us under,
Thus they bring us in blunder—
It were great wonder,
    If ever we should thrive.

Let man but get a painted sleeve or brooch nowa-
days,
Woe to one that grieves him or once gainsays;
No man dare reprove him that mastery has,
And yet may no man believe one word that he says—
    No letter!
He can make purveyance
With boast and braggance,
And all is through maintenance
    By men that are better.

There shall come a swain as proud as a po,[3]
And he must borrow my wain, my plow also
That I am full glad to grant before he go:
Thus live we in pain, anger, and woe,
    By night and day.
He must have if he wants it
Though I must do without it;
I were better off hanged
    Than once say him Nay!

It does me good as I walk thus by my own
Of this world for to talk in manner of moan.
To my sheep I will stalk and listen anon,
There abide on a ridge or sit on a stone
    Full soon.
For I think, pardie!
True men if they be,
We shall get more company
    Ere it be noon.

    [*A* Second Shepherd *appears on the moor, with-
    out at first noticing the* First Shepherd, *so ab-
    sorbed is he in his own thoughts*]
2ND SHEPHERD: *Benedicite*[4] and *Dominus!* what may
    this mean?
Why fares this world thus? Oft have we not seen:

[3] Peacock.
[4] He pronounces this, by contraction of the Latin for
"Bless you," as "Bencité."

194

Lord, these weathers are spiteful, and the winds are
        keen,
And the frosts so hideous they water my een:[5]
        No lie it be!
Now in dry, now in wet,
Now in snow, now in sleet,
When my shoes freeze to my feet,
        It is not at all easy.

But as far as I know, or yet as I go,
We poor wed men suffer much, we do;
We have sorrow then and then, it falls often so.
Poor Cappel, our hen, both to and fro
        She cackles,
But begin she to rock,
To groan or to cluck,
Woe is to him, our cock,
        For he is then in shackles!

These men that are wed have not all their will;
When they are set upon, they sigh full still.
God knows they are led full hard and full ill,
In bower or in bed they have their fill
        Beside.
My part have I found,
Know my lesson sound:
Woe is him that is bound,
        For he must abide.

But now late in our lives—marvel to me!
That I think my heart breaks such wonder to see:
That, as destiny drives, it should so be
That some men will have two wives, and some have
        three
        In store.
To some is woe that have any,
But so far as I see, I tell ye,
Woe is him that has many,
        For he feels sore.

[Addressing the audience]
But young men awooing, by God that you bought,
Beware of a wedding and mind in your thought
"Had I known" is a thing that serves you nought.
So much still mourning has wedding home brought
        And grief,
With many a sharp shower;
For ye may catch in an hour
What shall savor full sour
        As long as you live.

For, as ever read I scripture, I have her I keep near:
As sharp as a thistle, as rough as a briar;
She is browed like a bristle with sour-looking cheer.
Had she once wet her whistle, she could sing full
        clear
        Her Pater-Noster.
She is as great as a whale,
She has a gallon of gall;
By Him that died for us all,
        I would I had run till I lost her!

[5] Eyes.

[By now he has been observed by the First Shepherd, who rouses him from his meditations
roughly]
1ST SHEPHERD: God look over the row, you there,
        that deafly stand!
2ND SHEPHERD: [Startled] Yea, the devil in thy maw!
        —In tarrying, friend,
Saw you Daw about?
1ST SHEPHERD: Yes, on fallow land
I heard him blow. He comes here at hand
        Not far.
Stand still!
2ND SHEPHERD: Why?
1ST SHEPHERD: For he comes on, hope I.
1ST SHEPHERD: He will din us both a lie
        Unless we beware.

[A Third Shepherd, a boy called Daw, employed
by the First Shepherd, appears. The weather has
put him out of humor]
3RD SHEPHERD: Christ's cross me speed, and Saint
        Nicholas!
Thereof had I need: it is worse than it was!
Whoso could, take heed! and let the world pass!
It is ever in dread and brittle as glass,
        And slides.
This world fared never so,
With marvels more and more,
Now in weal, now in woe;
        And everything rides!

Was never since Noah's flood such floods seen,
Winds and rains so rude, and storms so keen;
Some stammered, some stood in doubt, as I ween.
Now God turn all to good! I say as I mean
        And ponder.
These floods, so they drown
Both fields and town
And bear all down—
        That it is a wonder.

We that walk in the nights our cattle to keep,
We see sudden sights when other men sleep—
        [Noticing that he is being observed by the other
        Shepherds]
But methinks my heart lightens, I see them peep.
Yea, you tall fellows!—I think I'll give my sheep
        A turn.
        [He is about to turn away, but changes his mind]
But this is ill intent,
For as I walk on this bent
I may lightly repent
        And stub my toes.

[Pretending to have just seen them]
Ah, sir, God you save, and you, master mine!
        [Coming up to them]
A drink fain would I have and somewhat to dine.
1ST SHEPHERD: Christ's curse, my knave, thou art a
        lazy swine!
2ND SHEPHERD: What, the boy pleases to rave? You'll
        wait on line
        When we have made it.

I'll drum on thy pate!
Though the knave comes late,
Yet is he in state
    To dine, if he had it.

3RD SHEPHERD: [*Grumbling*] Such servants as I, that
    sweats and swinks,[6]
Eats our bread dry, and that is ill, I thinks!
We are oft wet and weary when master-men winks,
Yet come full lately the dinners and the drinks.
    But neatly,
Both our dame and our sire,
When we have run in the mire,
They can nip us of our hire
    And pay us full lately.

But hear my oath: For the food that you serve, I
    say,
I shall do hereafter—work as you pay:
I shall work a little and a little play,
For yet my supper never on my stomach lay
    In the fields.
I won't complain, but a heap
With my staff I shall leap;
For a thing bought too cheap
    Nothing yields.

1ST SHEPHERD: Yea, thou wert a fool, lad, a-wooing
    to ride
With one that had but little for spending by his side.
2ND SHEPHERD: Peace, boy! And no more jangling
    I'll bide,
Or I shall make thee full sad, by heaven's King, beside,
    For thy gauds.[7]
Where are our sheep? Thy japes we scorn.
3RD SHEPHERD: Sir, this same day at morn
I left them in the corn
    When the bells rang Lauds.

They have pasture good, they cannot go wrong.
1ST SHEPHERD: That is right. By the rood, these
    nights are long!
Yet I would, ere we went, one gave us a song.
2ND SHEPHERD: So *I* thought as I stood—to cheer us
    along.
3RD SHEPHERD:
    I grant!
1ST SHEPHERD: Let me sing the tenory.
2ND SHEPHERD: And I the treble so high.
3RD SHEPHERD: Then the mean falls to me.
    Let's start the chant.

[*At this point,* Mak *appears, his cloak thrown
over his tunic*]
MAK: [*To himself*] Lord, for Thy names seven, that
    made the moon and stars on high
Well more than I reckon: Thy will, Lord, leaves me
    dry
And lacking, so that of my wits I am shy:

[6] Works. His speech is ungrammatical.
[7] Tricks or jests.

Now would God I were in heaven, for there no chil-
    dren cry
    So still.[8]
1ST SHEPHERD: [*Looking around*] Who is that pipes
    so poor?
MAK: [*Still grumbling to himself*] Would God knew
    how I endure:
A man that walks on the moor
    Without his will.

[*The* Shepherds *now recognize him as the thief
they know.* Mak *is startled, but pretends he does
not know them*]
2ND SHEPHERD: Mak, where have you been? Tell us
    tidings.
3RD SHEPHERD: Is *he* come, then let each one take
    heed to his things.
[*He takes* Mak's *cloak from him and shakes it,
to see whether* Mak *has stolen anything*]
MAK: [*Spluttering*] What! I be a yeoman, I tell ye, of
    the king's.
The self and same, sent from a great lording's
    And such.
Fie on you! Go hence
Out of my presence;
I must have reverence—
    You grieve me much!

1ST SHEPHERD: Why make ye it so quaint, Mak? You
    do wrong.
2ND SHEPHERD: Mak, play ye the saint? For this do
    ye long?
3RD SHEPHERD: I know the knave can deceive, the
    devil him hang!
MAK: I shall make complaint and get ye many a
    thwang
    At a word
When I tell my lord how ye do.
1ST SHEPHERD: [*Sarcastically*] But, Mak, is that true?
Come, that southern tooth unscrew[9]
    And set it in a turd.

2ND SHEPHERD: Mak, the devil in your eye, a stroke
    will I lend you.
[*He strikes him*]
3RD SHEPHERD: Mak, know ye not me? By God, I
    could beat ye too.
[*As he too is about to strike him,* Mak *draws
back and pretends to have just recognized the*
Shepherds]
MAK: God, look—you all three? Methought—how
    do you do?
Ye are a fair company.
1ST SHEPHERD: May we now recognize you?
2ND SHEPHERD:
    Blast your jest-dealing!
When a man so lately goes

[8] So continuously.
[9] In pretending to be in the king's service, the actor
playing Mak may have affected a Southern—that is,
London—accent.

What will good men suppose?
Ye have an ill name one knows
    For sheep-stealing.

MAK: And true as steel I am, know ye not?
But a sickness I feel that holds me full hot:
My belly fares not well, for it is out of estate.
3RD SHEPHERD: [*Unsympathetically*] Seldom lies the
    devil dead by the gate!
MAK: [*Ignoring the thrust*]
    Therefore,
Full sore am I and ill;
I stand stone-still,
I ate not a tittle
    This month and more.

1ST SHEPHERD: How fares thy wife? By my hood,
    tell us true.
MAK: She lies lolling by the road, by the fire too,
And a house full of brew she drinks well too.
Ill speed other things that she will shift
    To do.
Eats as fast as she can,
And each year that comes to man
She brings forth a brat—an'
    Some years, two.

But were I yet more gracious, and richer at will,
Eaten out of house and home I would be still.
Yet she is a foul dear, if ye come at her close;
None there is looks worse, as none knows
    Better than I.
Now will ye see what I proffer:
To give all in my coffer
And tomorrow next, to offer
    Mass-pence, should she die.

    [*The* Shepherds *have begun to feel drowsy during
    this recital*]
2ND SHEPHERD: So weary with watching is none in
    this shire:
I would sleep if it cost me a part of my hire.
3RD SHEPHERD: And I am cold and naked, and would
    have a fire.
1ST SHEPHERD: I am weary of walking, and I have
    run in the mire.
    [*To the* Second Shepherd]
    Keep the watch, you!
2ND SHEPHERD: Nay, I will lie down by,
For I must sleep or die.
3RD SHEPHERD: For sleep as good a man's son am I;
    It is my due.

    [*They begin to lie down to sleep. But the* Third
    Shepherd *eyes* Mak *suspiciously*]
3RD SHEPHERD: But, Mak, come hither; between us
    you shall lie down.
MAK: [*Unhappily*] But I may hinder your sleep and
    make you frown.
    [*The* Shepherds *force him down and compel him
    to stretch out among them, in order to prevent
    him from robbing them*]
    Ah well, no dread I heed:

From my head to my toe,
    [*Crossing himself*]
*Manus tuas commendo,
Pontio Pilato,*[10]
    Christ's cross me speed.

    [*Before long the* Three Shepherds *are in a deep
    sleep, and* Mak *disentangles himself and rises*]
MAK: Now were time for a man that lacks what he
    would
To stalk privily then into the fold
And nimbly to work, though not to be too bold,
For he might regret the bargain if it were told
    At the ending.
Now time for to work in the dell,
For he needs good counsel
That fain would fare well
    And has but little spending.

    [*He begins to work a spell on the sleepers, draw-
    ing a circle around them*]
But about you a circle round as the moon,
Till I have done what I will, till that it be noon—
That ye lie stone-still, until I am done;
And now I shall say thereto of good words a rune
    Anon:
*Over your heads my hand I light;
Out go your eyes, blind be your sight!*
And now that it may come out right
    I must shift on.

    [*He starts to leave in the direction of the sheep
    further down the field while the* Shepherds
    snore]
Lord, but they sleep hard—that may one hear . . .
Was I never shepherd, but now I will shear;
Though the flock be scared, yet shall I nip near;
I must draw hitherward and mend our cheer
    From sorrow.
    [*He spies a sheep that attracts him*]
A fat sheep, I daresay,
A good fleece, I dare lay;
Repay when I may—
    [*Seizing the animal*]
    But this will I *borrow*.

SCENE II.

Mak's *cottage: the exterior and the interior.
At first* Mak *stands outside and knocks at the door.
Later he enters and the action transpires inside.*

MAK: [*Knocking*] How, Gill, art thou in? Get us
    some light.
WIFE: Who makes such din this time of the night?
I am set for to spin: I think not I might
Rise a penny to win—a curse on him alight.
    So fares she,

[10] "Into your hands I commend myself, Pontius Pilate." The humor lies, of course, in the misquotation.

A housewife, I ween,
To be raced thus between.
In house may no work be seen
    Because of such small chores that be.

MAK: Good wife, open the door. Do ye not see what
    I bring?
WIFE: Then let thou draw the latch.
    [*As he enters*]
                    Ah! come in, my sweeting!
MAK: [*Grumpily*] Yea, and no thought for my long
    standing!
WIFE: [*Observing the sheep*] By the naked neck thou
    art like to get thy hanging.
MAK:
        Get away!
I am worthy my meat,
For in a pinch can I get
More than they that swink and sweat
    All day.

Thus it fell to my lot, Gill, I had such grace.
WIFE: It were a foul blot to be hanged for the case.
MAK: I have escaped oft from as narrow place.
WIFE: But so long goes the pot to the water, one
    says,
        At last
Comes it home broken.
MAK: Well I know the token;
But let it never be spoken!—
        But come and help fast.

    [Gill *helps to take the sheep in*]
I would it were slain and I sat down to eat:
This twelvemonth was I not so fain for sheep-meat.
WIFE: Come they ere it be slain and hear the sheep
    bleat—
MAK: Then might I be taken; cold's the sweat I am
    in, my sweet—
        Go, make fast
The outer door.
WIFE: [*Going to the door*]   Yes, Mak,
If they came at thy back—
MAK: Then got I from that pack
        The devil's own cast.

WIFE: [*Coming back*] A good jest I have spied, since
    thou hast none:
    [*Pointing to the cradle*]
Here shall we hide it till they be gone;
In the cradle may it abide. Let me alone,
And I shall lie beside in childbed and groan.
MAK:
        Well said!
And I shall say you are light
Of a man-child this night.
WIFE: How well it is, day bright,
        That ever I bred.

This is a good guise and a far cast:
A woman's advice, it helps at the last.
I shall care never who spies, so go thou fast!

MAK: [*Outside, walking in the fields toward the
    sleeping* Shepherds] If I do not come ere they
    rise, a cold blast
        Will blow; back to sleep
I go. Yet sleeps this company,
And I shall slip in privily
As it had never been me
        That carried their sheep.

SCENE III.

The moors.
Mak *slips in among the sleepers. The* Shepherds
begin to stir.

1ST SHEPHERD: [*Rising*] *Resurrex a mortruis:*[11] reach
    me a hand!
Judas carnas dominus! I may not well stand.
My foot sleeps, by Jesus, and I thirst—and
I thought that we laid us full near England.
2ND SHEPHERD: [*Rising*]
        Ah-ye!
Lord, I have slept well!
I am fresh as an eel,
As light I feel
    As leaf on tree.

3RD SHEPHERD: [*Awaking but dazed*] *Ben'cite* be
    herein; so my body quakes,
My heart is out of my skin with the noise it makes.
Who makes all this din, so my brow aches?
To the door will I win. Hark, fellows, who wakes?
        We were four:
See ye anywhere Mak now?
1ST SHEPHERD: We were up ere thou.
2ND SHEPHERD: Man, I give God a vow
        That he went nowhere.

3RD SHEPHERD: [*Troubled*] Methought he lay
    wrapped up in a wolf-skin.
1ST SHEPHERD: Many are thus wrapped now—that is,
    within!
2ND SHEPHERD: When we had long napped, me-
    thought with a gin[12]
A fat sheep he trapped without making a din.
3RD SHEPHERD: [*Pointing toward* Mak, *who pretends
    to be asleep*]
        Be still:
This dream makes thee wild,
It is but phantom, by the Holy Child![13]
1ST SHEPHERD: Now God turn all things mild,
        If it be His will.

[11] The unlettered shepherd is babbling Latin words he
has picked up imperfectly and makes no particular sense.
[12] Trick.
[13] An anachronism characteristic of naïve folk literature, since the Holy Child has not yet been born. In the
next few lines there are other anachronisms: "Christ's
Holy Name," "By Saint James," and "by Saint Steven"—
or Stephen.

[*The* Shepherds *rouse* Mak]

2ND SHEPHERD: Rise, Mak, for shame! Ye lie right
    long.
MAK: [*Stirring*] Now Christ's Holy Name, be it
    among
Us! What's this? By Saint James, I am not strong!
I hope I am the same—my neck has lain wrong
    All night!
    [*As they help him up*]
Many thanks! Since yester-even,
I swear by Saint Steven,
I was flayed by a dream, so driven
    That my heart was not right.

Methought my Gill began to croak, full sad
To labor well nigh at first cock—a lad
To add to our flock; and I never glad
To have more to provide, more than ever I had.
    Ah, my head!
A house full of young mouths—banes!
The devil knock out their brains!
Woe him that so many brats gains
    And so little bread.

I must go home, by your leave; to Gill, I thought.
But first look in my sleeve that I have stolen naught:
I am loth to grieve you or to take from you aught.
3RD SHEPHERD: Go forth, and ill may you thrive!
    [*Mak leaves*]
              Still I would we sought
    This morn
Whether we have all our store.
1ST SHEPHERD: Good! I will go before.
Let us meet.
2ND SHEPHERD: Where?
3RD SHEPHERD:
    At the crooked thorn.

SCENE IV.

Mak's *cottage.*

MAK: [*At his door*] Undo this door! Who is here?
    How long shall I stand?
WIFE: Who makes such a stir, to walk in the moon-
    waning?
MAK: Ah, Gill, what cheer? It is I, Mak, your hus-
    band.
WIFE: [*Grumpily*] Then see we here the devil him-
    self in a band,
    Sir Guile!
Lo, he comes with a noise about
As if he were held by the snout,
I may not do my work for that lout
    A hand-long while.

MAK: Will ye hear what noise she makes for an excuse
And does nothing but play about and stroke her toes!
WIFE: Why, who wanders, who wakes, who comes,
    who goes?

Who brews, who bakes—now who do you suppose?
    And more then
That it is pity to behold—
Now in hot, now in cold.
Full woefull is the household
    That lacks women.

But what end have ye made with the shepherds,
    Mak?
MAK: The last word that they said when I turned my
    back,
They would look that they had of their sheep all the
    pack;
I fear they will not be well pleased when they their
    sheep lack,
    Pardie!
But howso the sport goes
I'm the thief they'll suppose
And come with a full nose
    To cry out on me.

But thou must do as thou planned.
WIFE: They'll find me able!
I shall swaddle it right in my cradle.
When I sup with the Devil I use the long ladle!
I will lie down straightway. Come wrap me.
MAK: [*Doing so*]   I will.
WIFE: [*Sharply*]
    Behind!—
If Coll and his mate come, to our sorrow,
They will nip us full narrow.
MAK: But I may run and cry "Harrow"
    If the sheep they find.

WIFE: Listen close when they call—they will come
    anon.
Come and make ready all, and sing thou alone:
Sing "Lullay" you shall, for I must groan
And cry out by the wall on Mary and John
    As if sore.
Sing "Lullay" on fast
When you hear them at last,
And if I play a false cast
    Trust me no more!

SCENE V.

The moors, as the Shepherds *meet.*

3RD SHEPHERD: Ah, Coll, good morn: why sleep ye
    not?
1ST SHEPHERD: Alas, that ever was I born! We have
    a foul blot—
A fat wether have we lost.
3RD SHEPHERD: God forbid; say it not!
2ND SHEPHERD: Who should have done that harm?
    That were a foul spot.
1ST SHEPHERD:
    Some knave—beshrew!
I have sought with my dogs

All Horbury shrogs,[14]
And of fifteen hogs[15]
    I lack one ewe.

3RD SHEPHERD: Now trust me if ye will—by Saint
    Thomas of Kent!,
Either Mak or Gill a hand to it lent.
1ST SHEPHERD: Peace, man, be still: I watched when
    he went;
You slander him ill, you ought to repent
    With speed.
2ND SHEPHERD: Yet as ever I thrive or be,
Though the good Lord slay me,
I would say it were he
    That did the same deed.

3RD SHEPHERD: Go we thither then, I say, and let us
    run fleet;
Till I know the truth, may I never bread eat.
1ST SHEPHERD: Nor take drink in my head till with
    him I meet.
2ND SHEPHERD: I will take to no bed until I him greet,
    My brother!
One promise I will plight:
Till I get him in sight
I will never sleep one night
    Where I sleep another.

SCENE VI.

Mak's *cottage.*
Mak *is heard singing within, while* Gill *is heard
groaning as though she were delivering a child.*

3RD SHEPHERD: Will you hear how they hack away;
    our sir likes to croon.
1ST SHEPHERD: Heard I never none crack so clear
    out of tune.
Call on him!
2ND SHEPHERD: Mak, undo your door—soon!
MAK: Who is that spoke, as if it were noon
    Aloft?
Who is that, I say?
    [*He opens the door*]
3RD SHEPHERD: Good fellows you'd see, were it day.
MAK: As far as ye may,
    Friends, speak soft
Over a sick woman's head that is at malease;
I had sooner be dead than cause her dis-ease.
WIFE: Go to another place—I cannot breathe; please!
Each foot ye tread goes through my nose with a
    squeeze,
    Woe is me.
1ST SHEPHERD: Tell us, Mak, if ye may:
How fare ye, I say?
MAK: But are ye in this town today?—
    How fare *ye?*

[14] By this is meant the thickets of Horbury, about four
miles from Wakefield, where the play was given.
[15] Young sheep.

Ye have run in the mire and are wet a bit;
I shall make you a fire, if ye will sit.
    [*Pointing at his* Wife]
A nurse I would hire; think ye on it.
Well paid is my hire—my dream this is it,
    In season.
I have brats if ye knew
Many more than will do;
    [*With resignation*]
But, then, we must drink as we brew,
    And that is but reason!

I would ye dined ere you go; methinks that ye sweat.
2ND SHEPHERD: Nay, neither drink nor meat will
    mend us yet.
MAK: [*Innocently*] Why, sirs, what ails ye?
3RD SHEPHERD: Our sheep we must get
That was stolen. It is great loss that we met.
    [Mak *offers a drink*]
MAK:
    Sirs, drink!
Had I been near,
Someone should have bought it full dear.
1ST SHEPHERD: Marry, some men think that ye were.
    And that makes us think!

2ND SHEPHERD: Mak, some men think that it should
    be ye.
3RD SHEPHERD: Either you or your spouse, so say we.
MAK: Now if ye have suspicion against my Gill or me,
Come and search our house, and then may ye see
    Who had her,
Or if any sheep I got,
Either cow or stot.[16]
And Gill, my wife, rose not
    Here since she laid her.

If I am not true and loyal, to God I pray
    [*Pointing to the cradle, where the sheep—the al-
    leged child—is hidden*]
That *this* be the first meal I shall eat this day.
1ST SHEPHERD: Mak, as I may fare well, take
    heed, I say!
"He learned early to steal that could not say nay."
    [*The* Shepherds *start to search the room, but* Gill
    *waves them away when they approach the cradle
    near her*]
WIFE:
    I faint!
Out, thieves, from my dwelling!
Ye come to rob while I am swelling—
MAK: Your hearts should melt now she's yelling
    In plaint.

WIFE: Away, thieves, from my child; over him don't
    pore.
MAK: Knew ye how much she has borne, your hearts
    would be sore.
Ye do wrong, I warn you, thus to rummage before
[16] Bullock.

A woman that has suffered—but I say no more!

WIFE: [*Yelling*]
      Ah, my middle!
I pray to God so mild,
If I ever you beguiled,
That I *eat* this child
      That lies in this cradle.

MAK: [*Pretending concern for her*] Peace, woman, for God's pain, and cry not so:
Thou spill'st thy brain and fill'st me with woe.

2ND SHEPHERD: [*To the other* Two Shepherds] I think our sheep be slain; what find ye two?

3RD SHEPHERD: All this is in vain: we may as well go:
      [*Finding only rags of clothing as he searches*]
      Only tatters!
I can find no flesh,
Hard nor soft,
Salt nor fresh,
      But two bare platters.

[*But as he approaches the cradle and sniffs the air, he makes a grimace*]
Yet live cattle, as I may have bliss, nor tame nor wild,
None has smelled so strong as this—this child!

WIFE: [*Protesting*] Ah no, so God bless and give me joy, this child smells mild.

1ST SHEPHERD: We have aimed amiss: We were elsewhere beguiled.
      [*He is about to leave*]

2ND SHEPHERD: [*Also giving up the search*]
      Sir, we are done!
But sir—Our Lady him save!—
Is your child a lad?

MAK: [*Proudly*] Any lord might him have
      This child to his son.

When he wakens he has a grip that is a joy to see.

3RD SHEPHERD: Blessings on his hips, and happiness may he see.
But who were his godparents, will ye tell me?

MAK: [*Floundering*] Blessed be their lips!—

1ST SHEPHERD: [*Aside*] Now, what will the lie be?

MAK:
      So God them thank,—
Parkin and Gibbon Waller, be it said,
And gentle John Horne in good stead—
He that made the great riot spread,
      He with the big shank.

2ND SHEPHERD: [*Preparing to leave*] Mak, friends will we be, for we are all one.

MAK: [*Pretending to have been hurt by their suspicions*] We? Now I must hold back, for amends is there none.
Farewell, all three, and very glad to see you gone!
      [*The Shepherds* leave the house, and we see them outside]

3RD SHEPHERD: "Fair words may there be, but love is there none
      This year."

1ST SHEPHERD: [*To the* 2nd] Gave ye the child anything?

2ND SHEPHERD: No, not a farthing.

3RD SHEPHERD: Fast back will I fling:
      Await ye me here.

[*He goes back to* Mak's *cottage, the others following him*]
Mak, take it to no grief if I come to thy lad.

MAK: Nay, ye have grieved me much and made me sad.

3RD SHEPHERD: The child it will not grieve, thy little day-star so glad;
Mak, with your leave, let me give the child you have had
      But sixpence.

MAK: Nay, go away; he sleeps!

3RD SHEPHERD: Methinks, it peeps.[17]

MAK: When he wakens, he weeps;
      I pray you go hence.

[*The other* Shepherds *enter*]

3RD SHEPHERD: [*Coming closer*] Give me leave him to kiss and to lift up the clout.
      [*He lifts the cover a little*]
What the devil is this? He has a long snout!

1ST SHEPHERD: He is birth-marked amiss; let us not waste time hereabout.

2ND SHEPHERD: "From an ill-spun woof ever comes foul out."
      [*As he looks closer*]
      Ay—so!
He is like our sheep.

3RD SHEPHERD: How, Gib? May I peep?

1ST SHEPHERD: "Nature will still creep
      Where it may not go."

2ND SHEPHERD: This was a quaint trick and a far cast;
It was a high fraud!

3RD SHEPHERD: Yea, sirs, I am aghast!
Let's burn this bawd and bind her fast;
A false scold hangs at the last—
      So shalt thou.
      [*He has pulled the covers off*]
Will ye see how they swaddle
His four feet in the middle?
Saw I never in a cradle
      A hornèd lad ere now.

MAK: [*Who stands behind them and does not see the sheep uncovered; still attempting to brazen it out*]
Peace, bid I! And let be your fare;
I am he that him gat and yon woman him bare.[18]

1ST SHEPHERD: [*Mocking him*] What devil shall he be called, Mak? Lo, God! Mak's heir!

2ND SHEPHERD: An end to all jesting; now God give thee care
      I say!

[17] Whimpers.
[18] Bore.

[*As she is lying in bed, the* Wife *does not see that they have completely uncovered the sheep*]

WIFE: As pretty child is he
As sits on woman's knee;
A dilly-down, perdie,
    To make one gay.

3RD SHEPHERD: I know my sheep by the ear-mark—this good token.

MAK: I tell you, sirs, hear me: his nose was broken,
Since, as the priest told me, he was by witchcraft bespoken.

1ST SHEPHERD: This is false work and must be avenged; I have spoken:
    Get weapon!

WIFE: The child was taken by an elf—
I saw it myself.
When the clock struck twelve,
    Was he mis-shapen.

2ND SHEPHERD: Ye two are right deft, and belong in the same bed.

3RD SHEPHERD: Since they maintain their theft, let us do them dead.
    [*They seize* Mak]

MAK: [*Seeing the game is up*] If I trespass again, strike off my head.
I'll let you be the judge!

3RD SHEPHERD: [*To the others*]   Sirs, instead:
    For this trespass
We need neither curse nor spite,
Nor chide nor fight,
But take him forthright
    And toss him in canvas.
    [*They drag* Mak *outside and toss him lustily in a sheet while he yells with pain*]

SCENE VII.

The fields near Bethlehem in Judea.
We see the three Shepherds *again, weary after their sport with* Mak *and tired with walking.*

1ST SHEPHERD: Lord, how I am sore and like to burst in the breast!
In faith, I can stand no more, therefore will I rest.

2ND SHEPHERD: As a sheep of seven score Mak weighed in my fist;
To sleep anywhere methink I would list.

3RD SHEPHERD:
    Then I pray you,
Lie down on this green.

1ST SHEPHERD: [*Hesitating*] On these thefts to think I yet mean.

3RD SHEPHERD: Whereto should ye be worried lean?
    Do as I tell you.

[*They lie down to sleep; but they have barely done so when an* Angel *appears above. He first sings the hymn "Gloria in Excelsis," then addresses the* Shepherds]

ANGEL: Rise, herdsmen gentle, for now is He born
That shall take from the Fiend what Adam had lorn;[19]
That fiend to overthrow this night is He born;
God is made your Friend. Now at this morn,
    He commands,
To Bedlem[20] you go see:
There lies that divine He
In a crib that full poorly
    Betwixt two beasts stands.
    [*The* Angel *disappears*]

1ST SHEPHERD: This was a quaint voice that ever yet I heard.
It is a marvel to relate thus to be stirred.

2ND SHEPHERD: Of God's son of heaven, he spoke from above,
All the wood was in lightning as he spoke of love;
    I thought it fair.

3RD SHEPHERD: Of a child heard I tell
In Bedlem; I heard it well.
    [*Pointing to a star that has begun to blaze*]
Yonder star, above the dell:
    Let us follow him there.

2ND SHEPHERD: Say, what was his song? Heard ye how he sang it?
Three breves[21] to a long.

3RD SHEPHERD: Yes, marry, he thwacked it;
Was no crotchet wrong, nor nothing lacked it.

1ST SHEPHERD: For to sing it again right as he trilled it,
    I can, if I may.

2ND SHEPHERD: Let me see how ye croon,
Or do ye but bark at the moon?

3RD SHEPHERD: Hold your tongues! Have done!

1ST SHEPHERD:
    Hark after me, I say!
    [*They try to sing the hymn as best they can*]

2ND SHEPHERD: To Bedlem he bade that we should go;
I am troubled that we tarry too slow.

3RD SHEPHERD: Be merry and not sad: of mirth is our song, lo!
Everlasting glad in the rewards that will flow,
    No plaint may we make.

1ST SHEPHERD: Hie we thither, cheery,
Though we be wet and weary;
To that Child and that Lady
    Let us our way take.

2ND SHEPHERD: We find by the prophecy—let be your din!—
Of David and Isaiah, and more therein,
As prophesied by clergy, that on a virgin
Should He light and lie, to redeem our sin
    And slake it.
Our kind from woe

[19] Lost or forfeited.
[20] Bethlehem.
[21] A "breve" is equal to two whole notes; a "long" is equal to six whole notes; a "crotchet" is a quarter note.

To save—Isaiah said so.—
    "Ecce virgo
    Concipiet a child that is naked."[22]

3RD SHEPHERD: Full glad may we be, and await that
        day
That lovely day that He shall with His might sway.
Lord, well for me for once and for aye!
Might I but kneel on my knee some word for to say
        To that child.
But the angel said
In a crib is He laid,
He is poorly arrayed,
        So meek and mild.

1ST SHEPHERD: Patriarchs that have been, and
        prophets beforne,
They desired to have seen this Child that is born;
But *they* are gone full clean, from life forlorn—
It is *we* shall see him, ere it be morn
        By token.
When I see Him and feel,
Then shall I know full well
It is true as steel
        What prophets have spoken:

To so poor as we are that he would appear,
We the first to find and be his messenger!
2ND SHEPHERD: Go we now, let us fare: the place
        must be near.
3RD SHEPHERD: I am ready and eager: go we together
        To that Light!
Lord! if Thy will it be,
Though we are lowly all three,
Grant us of Thy glee,
        To comfort Thy wight.[23]
    [*They move on, following the star, to Beth-*
    lehem]

────────────────

SCENE VIII.

────────────────

The stable or manger in Bethlehem.
The Shepherds *enter and kneel before the* Virgin
and Child.

1ST SHEPHERD: Hail, comely and clean; hail, young
        child!
Hail, Maker, as I mean, born of maiden so mild!
Thou hast banned, I deem, the devil so wild;
The evil beguiler now goes beguiled.
    [*Pointing to the* Child]
        Lo, merry He is!

[22] "Behold, a virgin shall conceive." (Isaiah, 7:14).
[23] Creature.

Lo, he laughs, my sweeting,
A welcome greeting!
I have had my meeting—
    [*Offering the* Child *some cherries*]
        Have a bob of cherries?

2ND SHEPHERD: Hail, sovereign Saviour, for Thou
        hast us sought!
Hail, Nursling, leaf and flower, that all things hath
        wrought!
Hail, full of favor, that made all of nought!
    [*Offering a bird*]
Hail, I kneel and I cower.—A bird have I brought
        Without mar.
Hail, little, tiny mop,
Of our creed thou art the crop;
I would drink from thy cup,
        Little day-star.

3RD SHEPHERD: Hail, darling dear, full of godhead!
I pray Thee be near when that I have need.
Hail! Sweet is Thy cheer! And my heart would bleed
To see Thee sit here clothed so poor indeed,
        With no pennies.
Hail! Thy hand put forth to us all—
I bring thee but a ball;
Take and play with it withall,
        And go to the tennis.
THE VIRGIN MARY: The Father of heaven, God om-
        nipotent,
That set all aright, His son has He sent.
My name He chose forth, and on me His light spent;
And I conceived Him forthwith through His might as
        God meant:
        And now is the Child born.
May He keep you from woe!
I shall pray Him so.
Tell the glad news as ye go,
        And remember this morn.

1ST SHEPHERD: Farewell, Lady, so fair to behold
With thy child on thy knee.
2ND SHEPHERD: —But he lies full cold.—
Lord, it is well with me! Now we go, ye may behold.
3RD SHEPHERD: In truth, already it seems to be told
        Full oft
1ST SHEPHERD: What grace we have found.
2ND SHEPHERD: Come forth! Now are we won!
3RD SHEPHERD: To sing of it we're bound:
        Let us sing aloft!
    [*They leave the stable, singing*]

Explicit Pagina Pastorum
[*Here ends The Shepherds' Pageant*]

EVERYMAN

A MODERNIZED VERSION BY JOHN GASSNER

CHARACTERS

EVERYMAN	KINDRED	BEAUTY
GOD: ADONAI	GOODS	KNOWLEDGE
DEATH	GOOD-DEEDS	CONFESSION
MESSENGER	STRENGTH	ANGEL
FELLOWSHIP	DISCRETION	DOCTOR
COUSIN	FIVE-WITS	

Here Beginneth a Treatise How the High Father of Heaven Sendeth Death to Summon All Creatures to Come and Give Account of Their Lives in This World and Is in the Manner of a Moral Play.

PROLOGUE

MESSENGER: I pray you all give your audience,
And hear this matter with reverence,
By figure a moral play—
The *Summoning of Everyman* called it is,
That of our lives and ending shows
How transitory we be all our day.
This matter is wondrous precious,
But the intent of it is more gracious,
And sweet to bear away.
The story saith,—Man, in the beginning,
Look well, and take good heed to the ending,
Be you never so gay!
Ye think sin in the beginning full sweet,
Which in the end causeth the soul to weep,
When the body lieth in clay.
Here shall you see how Fellowship and Jollity,
And Strength, Pleasure, and Beauty,
Will fade from thee as flower in May.
For ye shall hear how our heaven's king
Calleth Everyman to a general reckoning.
Give audience, and hear what he doth say.

[God *appears and speaks*]
GOD: I perceive here in my majesty,
How that all creatures be to me unkind,
Living without dread in worldly prosperity.
Of spiritual sight the people be so blind,
Drowned in sin, they know me not for their God;
In worldly riches is all their mind,
They fear not my righteousness, the sharp rod;
My law that I showed, when I for them died,
They clean forget, and shedding of my blood red;
I hung between two, it cannot be denied;
To get them life I suffered to be dead;
I healed their feet, with thorns hurt was my head—
I could do no more than I did truly,

And now I see the people do clean forsake me.
They use the seven deadly sins damnable;
And pride, covetize, wrath, and lechery,
Now in the world be made commendable;
And thus they leave of angels the heavenly company;
Every man liveth so after his own pleasure,
And yet of their life they be nothing sure.
I see the more that I them forbear
The worse they be from year to year;
All that liveth impaireth fast,
Therefore I will in all the haste
Have a reckoning of Everyman's person
For if I leave the people thus alone
In their life and wicked tempests,
Verily they will become much worse than beasts;
For now one would by envy another eat up;
Charity they all do clean forget.
I hoped well that every man
In my glory should make his mansion,
And thereto I had them all elect;
But now I see, like traitors abject,
They thank me not for the pleasure that I to them meant,
Nor yet for their being that I them have lent;
I proffered the people great multitude of mercy,
And few there be that ask it heartily;
They be so cumbered with worldly riches,
That needs on them I must do justice,
On Everyman living without fear.
Where art thou, Death, thou mighty messenger?
[*Enter* Death]
DEATH: Almighty God, I am here at Thy will,
Thy commandment to fulfil.
GOD: Go thou to Everyman,
And show him in my name
A pilgrimage he must on him take,
Which he in no wise may escape;
And that he bring with him a sure reckoning
Without delay or any tarrying.
[God *withdraws*]
DEATH: Lord, I will in the world go, run over all,
And cruelly search out both great and small;

Every man I will beset that liveth beastly
Out of God's law, and dreadeth not folly.
He that loveth riches I will strike with my dart,
His sight to blind, and from heaven will him part,
Except that Alms be his good friend,
In hell for to dwell, world without end.
Lo, yonder I see Everyman walking;
Full little he thinketh on my coming.
His mind is on fleshly lusts and his treasure,
And great pain it shall cause him to endure
Before the Lord, heaven's King.
Everyman, stand still! whither art thou going
Thus gaily? Hast thou thy maker forgot?
   [*Enter* Everyman]
   EVERYMAN: Why askst thou?
Wouldest thou know?
   DEATH: Yea, sir, I will show you.
In great haste I am sent to thee
From God out of his majesty.
   EVERYMAN: What, sent to me?
   DEATH: Yea, certainly.
Though thou have forgot him here,
He thinketh on thee in the heavenly sphere,
As, ere we depart, thou shalt know.
   EVERYMAN: What desireth God of me?
   DEATH: That shall I show thee;
A reckoning he will needs have
Without any longer respite.
   EVERYMAN: To give a reckoning longer leisure I
     crave;
This blind matter troubleth my wit.
   DEATH: On thee thou must take a long journey.
Therefore thy book of accounts with thee bring;
For turn again thou canst not by no way,
And look thou be sure of thy reckoning:
For before God thou shalt answer, and show
Thy many bad deeds and good but a few;
How thou hast spent thy life, and in what wise,
Before the Great Lord of Paradise.
Make preparation that we be on the way,
For know thou well, thou shalt make none attorney.
   EVERYMAN: Full unready I am such reckoning to
     give,
I know thee not. What messenger art thou?
   DEATH: I am Death, that no man dreadeth.
That every man arrests and no man spareth;
For it is God's commandment
That all to me should be obedient.
   EVERYMAN: O Death, thou comest when I had
     thee least in mind;
In thy power it lieth me to save,
Yet of my goods will I give thee, if ye will be kind,
Yea, a thousand pound shalt thou have,
And defer this matter till another day!
   DEATH: Everyman, it may not be by no way;
I set not by gold, silver, nor riches,
Nor by pope, emperor, king, duke, nor princes,
For if I would receive gifts great,
All the world I might get;
But my custom is clean contrary.

I give thee no respite. Come hence, do not tarry!
   EVERYMAN: Alas, shall I have no longer respite?
I may say Death giveth no warning.
To think on thee it maketh my heart sick,
For all unready is my book of reckoning.
But twelve year if I might have abiding,
My counting book I would make so clear
That my reckoning I should not need to fear.
Wherefore, Death, I pray thee, for God's mercy,
Spare me till I be provided of remedy.
   DEATH: Thee availeth not to cry, weep, and pray,
But haste thee lightly that thou be gone the journey,
And prove thy friends if thou can.
For, know thou well, the tide abideth no man,
And in the world each living creature
For Adam's sin must die of nature.
   EVERYMAN: Death, if I should this pilgrimage take,
And my reckoning surely make,
Show me, for Saint Charity,
Should I not come again shortly?
   DEATH: No, Everyman. If thou be once there
Thou mayest nevermore come here,
Trust me verily.
   EVERYMAN: O Gracious God, in the high seat
     celestial,
Have mercy on me in this my need;
Shall I have no company from this vale terrestrial
Of mine acquaintance the way me to lead?
   DEATH: Yea, if any be so hardy,
That would go with thee and bear thee company.
Hie thee that be gone to God's magnificence,
Thy reckoning to give before his presence.
What, thinkest thou thy life is given thee,
And thy worldly goods also?
   EVERYMAN: I had thought so, verily.
   DEATH: Nay, nay, it was but lent thee!
For as soon as thou dost go,
Another awhile shall have it and then go therefro
Even as thou hast done.
Everyman, thou art mad. Thou hast thy wits five,
And here on earth will not amend thy life,
For suddenly do I come.
   EVERYMAN: O wretched caitiff, whither shall I flee,
That I might escape this endless sorrow!
Now, gentle Death, spare me till to-morrow,
That I may amend me
With good advisement.
   DEATH: Nay, thereto I will not consent,
Nor no man will I respite,
But to the heart suddenly I shall smite
Without any advisement.
And now out of thy sight I will me hie.
See thou make thee ready shortly,
For thou mayst say this is the day
That no man living may escape away.
   [Death *withdraws*]
   EVERYMAN: Alas, I may well weep with sighs deep.
Now have I no manner of company
To help me in my journey, and me to keep.
And also my writing is full unready!

What shall I do now for to excuse me?
I would to God I had never been begot!
To my soul a full great profit it would be.
For now I fear pains huge and hot.
The time passeth. Lord, help that all wrought!
For though I mourn it availeth nought.
The day passeth, and is almost gone.
I know not well what is to be done.
To whom were I best my complaint to make?
What if I to Fellowship thereof spake,
And showed him of this sudden chance?
For in him is all mine affiance,
We have in the world so many a day
Been good friends in sport and play.
I see him yonder, certainly—
I trust that he will bear me company.
Therefore to him will I speak to ease my sorrow.
  [Fellowship *enters*]
Well met, good Fellowship, and good morrow!
  FELLOWSHIP: Everyman, good morrow by this day.
Sir, why lookest thou so piteously?
If any thing be amiss, I pray thee, me say,
That I may help to remedy.
  EVERYMAN: Yea, good Fellowship, yea,
I am in great jeopardy.
  FELLOWSHIP: My true friend, show to me your
    mind;
I will not forsake thee, unto my life's end,
In the way of good company.
  EVERYMAN: That was well spoken, and lovingly.
  FELLOWSHIP: Sir, I must needs know your heavi-
    ness—
I have pity to see you in any distress.
If any have wronged you ye shall revenged be,
Though I on the ground be slain for thee,
Though that I know before that I should die.
  EVERYMAN: Verily, Fellowship, gramercy.
  FELLOWSHIP: Tush! by thy thanks I set not a
    straw.
Show me your grief and say no more.
  EVERYMAN: If I my heart should to you break,
And then you to turn your mind from me
And would not comfort me when you hear me speak,
Then should I ten times sorrier be.
  FELLOWSHIP: Sir, I say as I will do indeed.
  EVERYMAN: Then be you a good friend at need—
I have found you true here before.
  FELLOWSHIP: And so ye shall evermore.
For, in faith, if thou go to Hell,
I will not forsake thee by the way!
  EVERYMAN: Ye speak like a good friend, I believe
    you well.
I shall try to deserve it, I may.
  FELLOWSHIP: I speak of no deserving, by this day.
For he that will say and nothing do
Is not worthy with good company to go.
Therefore show me the grief of your mind,
As to your friend most loving and kind.
  EVERYMAN: I shall show you how it is:
Commanded I am to go a journey,

A long way, hard and dangerous,
And give a straight count without delay
Before the high judge Adonai.
Wherefore I pray you, bear me company,
As ye have promised, in this journey.
  FELLOWSHIP: This is matter indeed! Promise is
    duty,
But, if I should take such a voyage on me,
I know it well, it should be to my pain.
Also it maketh me afeard, for certain.
But let us take counsel here as well as we can,
For thy words would balk a strong man.
  EVERYMAN: Why, ye said, if I had need,
Ye would me never forsake, quick nor dead,
Though it were to Hell truly.
  FELLOWSHIP: So I said, certainly,
But from such pleasures set me aside, thee sooth to
    say!
And also, if we took such a journey,
When should we come again?
  EVERYMAN: Nay, never again till the day of doom.
  FELLOWSHIP: In faith, then I will not come there!
Who hath thee these tidings brought?
  EVERYMAN: Indeed, Death was with me here.
  FELLOWSHIP: Now, by God that all hath bought,
If Death were the messenger,
For no man living here to-day
Would I go that loathsome journey—
Nay, nor for the father that begat me!
  EVERYMAN: Ye promised otherwise, pardie.
  FELLOWSHIP: I know well I did say so truly.
And yet if thou wilt eat, and drink, and make good
    cheer,
Or haunt together women's lusty company,
I would not forsake you, while the day is clear,
Trust me verily!
  EVERYMAN: Yea, thereto ye would be ready—
To go to mirth, solace, and play,
Your mind will sooner apply
Than to bear me company in my far journey.
  FELLOWSHIP: Now, in good faith, I will not that
    way.
But if thou wilt murder, or any man kill,
In that I will help thee with a good will!
  EVERYMAN: O that is a simple advice indeed!
Gentle fellow, help me in my necessity—
We have loved long, and now I need,
And now, gentle Fellowship, remember me.
  FELLOWSHIP: Whether ye have loved me or no,
By Saint John, I will not with thee go.
  EVERYMAN: Yet I pray thee, take the labor, and
    do so much for me
To bring me forward, for Saint Charity,
And comfort me till I come without the town.
  FELLOWSHIP: Nay, if thou wouldst give me a new
    gown,
I will not a foot with thee go.
But if thou hadst tarried I would not have left thee so.
And so now, God speed thee in thy journey,
For from thee I will depart as fast as I may.

EVERYMAN: Whither away, Fellowship? will you forsake me?

FELLOWSHIP: Yea, by my fay, to God I bequeath thee.

EVERYMAN: Farewell, good Fellowship, for thee my heart is sore.

Adieu for ever, I shall see thee no more.

FELLOWSHIP: In faith, Everyman, farewell now at the end;

From you I will remember that parting is mourning.
[Exit Fellowship]

EVERYMAN: Alack! shall we thus depart indeed?

Our Lady, help, without any more comfort,

Lo, Fellowship forsaketh me in my most need:

For help in this world whither shall I resort?

Fellowship heretofore with me would merry make,

And now little sorrow for me doth he take.

It is said, in prosperity men friends may find

Which in adversity be full unkind.

Now whither for succor shall I flee,

Since that Fellowship hath forsaken me?

To my kinsmen I will truly,

Praying them to help me in my necessity.

I believe that they will do so,

For "kind will creep where it may not go."

I will go try, for yonder I see them go.

Where be ye now, my friends and kinsmen?
[Kindred and Cousin appear]

KINDRED: Here be we now at your commandment.

Cousin, I pray you show us your intent

In any wise, and not spare.

COUSIN: Yea, Everyman, and to us declare

If ye be disposed to go any whither,

For know you well we will live and die together.

KINDRED: In wealth and woe we will with you hold,

For with his kin a man may be bold.

EVERYMAN: Gramercy, my friends and kinsmen kind.

Now shall I show you the grief of my mind.

I was commanded by a messenger,

That is an High King's chief officer.

He bade me go a pilgrimage to my pain,

And I know well I shall never come again.

Also I must give a reckoning straight,

For I have a great enemy, that hath me in wait,

Which intendeth me for to hinder.

KINDRED: What account is that which ye must render?

That would I know.

EVERYMAN: Of all my works I must show

How I have lived and my days spent.

Also of ill deeds, that I have used

In my time, since life was me lent.

And of all virtues that I have refused.

Therefore I pray you go thither with me,

To help to make my account, for Saint Charity.

COUSIN: What, to go thither? Is that the matter?

Nay, Everyman, I had liefer fast bread and water

All this five year and more.

EVERYMAN: Alas, that ever I was born!

For now shall I never be merry

If you forsake me.

KINDRED: Ah, sir, what, ye be a merry man!

Take good heart to you, and make no moan.

But one thing I warn you, by Saint Anne,

As for me, ye shall go alone.

EVERYMAN: My Cousin, will you not with me go?

COUSIN: No, by our Lady, I have the cramp in my toe.

Wait not for me, for, so God me speed,

I will forsake you in your most need.

KINDRED: It availeth not us to entice.

You shall have my maid with all my heart;

She loveth to go to feasts, there to be nice,

And to dance, and abroad to start.

I will give her leave to help you in that journey,

If that you and she will agree.

EVERYMAN: Now show me the very effect of your mind—

Will you go with me, or abide behind?

KINDRED: Abide behind? yea, that I will if I may!

Therefore farewell until another day.

EVERYMAN: How should I be merry or glad?

For fair promises men to me make,

But when I have most need they me forsake.

I am deceived, alas—that maketh me sad.

COUSIN: Everyman, farewell now,

For verily I will not go with you.

Also of mine own an unready reckoning

I have to account; therefore I make tarrying.

Now, God keep thee, for now I go.
[Exit Kindred and Cousin]

EVERYMAN: Ah, Jesus, is all come hereto?

Lo, fair words make fools fain.

They promise and nothing will do certain.

My kinsmen promised me faithfully

For to abide with me steadfastly,

And now fast away do they flee.

Even so Fellowship promised me.

What friend were best for me to provide?

I lose my time here longer to abide.

Yet in my mind a thing there is—

All my life I have loved Riches;

If that my Goods now help me might,

It would make my heart full light.

I will speak to him in this distress.—

Where art thou, my Goods and Riches?

GOODS: Who calleth me? Everyman, what haste thou hast!

I lie here in corners, trussed and piled so high,

And in chests I am locked so fast,

Also sacked in bags, thou mayst see with thine eye,

I cannot stir; in packs low I lie.

What would ye have, lightly me say.

EVERYMAN: Come hither, Goods, in all the haste thou may,

For of counsel I must desire thee.

GOODS: Sir, if ye in the world have trouble or adversity,

That can I help you to remedy shortly.

EVERYMAN: It is another disease that grieveth me.
In this world it is not, I tell thee so.
I am sent for another way to go,
To give a straight account general
Before the highest Jupiter of all.
And all my life I have had joy and pleasure in thee.
Therefore I pray thee go with me,
For, peradventure, thou mayst before God Almighty
My reckoning help to clean and purify.
For it is said ever us among,
That money maketh all right that is wrong.
GOODS: Nay, Everyman, I sing another song,
I follow no man in such voyages.
For if I went with thee
Thou shouldst fare much the worse for me.
For because on me thou did bend thy mind,
Thy reckoning I have made blotted and blind,
That thine account thou canst not make truly—
And that hast thou for the love of me.
EVERYMAN: That would grieve me full sore,
When I should come to that fearful answer.
Up, let us go thither together.
GOODS: Nay, not so, I am too brittle, I may not
endure.
I will follow no man one foot, be ye sure.
EVERYMAN: Alas, I have loved thee, and had great
pleasure
All my life-days on goods and treasure.
GOODS: That is to thy damnation without ending;
For love of me is contrary to the love everlasting.
But if thou hadst loved me moderately,
And to the poor given part of me,
Then shouldst thou not in this dolor be,
Nor in this great sorrow and care.
EVERYMAN: Lo, now was I deceived ere I was
aware,
And all I may blame my misusing of time.
GOODS: What, thinkest thou that I am thine?
EVERYMAN: I had thought so.
GOODS: Nay, Everyman, I say no.
But for a while was I lent thee,
A season thou hast had me in prosperity.
My condition it is man's soul to kill—
If I save one, a thousand I do spill.
Thinkest thou that I will follow thee?
Nay, from this world, not verily.
EVERYMAN: I had thought otherwise.
GOODS: Therefore to thy soul Goods is a thief;
For when thou art dead, this is my game
Another to deceive in ways the same,
As I have done thee, and all to his soul's grief.
EVERYMAN: O false Goods, cursed thou be!
Thou traitor to God, that hast deceived me,
And snatched me in thy snare.
GOODS: Marry, thou brought thyself in care,
Whereof I am glad—
I must needs laugh; I cannot be sad.
EVERYMAN: Ah, Goods, thou hast had long my
heartly love;
I gave thee that which should be the Lord's above.

But wilt thou not go with me indeed?
I pray thee truth to say.
GOODS: No, so God me speed,
Therefore farewell, and have thou good day.
[Exit Goods]
EVERYMAN: O, to whom shall I make my moan
For to go with me in that heavy journey?
First Fellowship said he would with me be gone;
His words were very pleasant and gay,
But afterward he left me alone.
Then spake I to my kinsmen all in despair,
And they also gave me words fair.
They lacked no fair speaking,
But they forsook me in the ending.
Then went I to my Goods that I loved best,
In hope to have comfort, but there had I least.
For my Goods sharply did me tell
That he bringeth many into Hell.
Then of myself I was ashamed,
And so I am worthy to be blamed,
Thus may I well myself hate.
Of whom shall I now counsel take?
I think that I shall never speed
Till that I go to my Good-Deed,
But, alas, she is so weak,
That she can neither go nor speak.
Yet will I venture on her now.—
My Good-Deeds, where be you?
[Enter Good-Deeds]
GOOD-DEEDS: Here I lie cold in the ground.
Thy sins have me sore-bound
That I cannot stir.
EVERYMAN: O, Good-Deeds, I stand in fear;
I must pray you for counsel,
For help now would come right well.
GOOD-DEEDS: Everyman, I have understanding
That you be summoned account to make
Before Messias, of Jerusalem the King.
If you walk by me that journey with you I will take.
EVERYMAN: Therefore I come to you, my moan to
make—
I pray you, that ye will go with me.
GOOD-DEEDS: I would full fain, but I cannot stand,
verily.
EVERYMAN: Why, is there anything did you befall?
GOOD-DEEDS: Yea, sir, and I may thank you of all;
If ye had perfectly cheered me,
Your book of account now full ready would be.
Look, the books of your works and deeds, aye—
Oh, see how they under your feet lie,
Unto your soul's heaviness.
EVERYMAN: Our Lord Jesus, help me!
For one letter here I cannot see.
GOOD-DEEDS: There is a blind reckoning in time of
distress!
EVERYMAN: Good-Deeds, I pray you, help me in
this need,
Or else I am for ever damned indeed.
Therefore help me to make reckoning
Before the Redeemer of all thing,

That king is, and was, and ever shall.

GOOD-DEEDS: Everyman, I am sorry for your fall,
And fain would I help you, if I were able.

EVERYMAN: Good-Deeds, your counsel I pray you
give me.

GOOD-DEEDS: That shall I do verily.
Though that on my feet I may not go,
I have a sister that shall with you also,
Called Knowledge, which shall with you abide,
To help you to make that dreadful reckoning.

[Enter Knowledge]

KNOWLEDGE: Everyman, I will go with thee, and
be thy guide,
In utmost need to go by thy side.

EVERYMAN: In good condition I am now in every
thing,
And am wholly content with this good thing.
Thanked be God, my Creator!

GOOD-DEEDS: And when he hath brought thee there
Where thou shalt heal thee of thy smart,
Then go you with your reckoning and your Good-
Deeds together
For to make you joyful at heart
Before the blessed Trinity.

EVERYMAN: My Good-Deeds, gramercy;
I am well content, certainly,
With your words sweet.

KNOWLEDGE: Now go we together lovingly,
To Confession, that cleansing river.

EVERYMAN: For joy I weep. I would we were
there!
But, I pray you, give me cognition
Where dwelleth that holy man, Confession.

KNOWLEDGE: In the house of salvation.
We shall find him in that place
That shall comfort us by God's grace.

[Confession appears]

Lo, this is Confession; kneel down and ask mercy,
For he is in good conceit with God Almighty.

EVERYMAN: O glorious fountain that all unclean-
ness doth clarify,
Wash from me the spots of vices unclean,
That on me no sin may be seen.
I come with Knowledge for my redemption,
Repent with hearty and full contrition.
For I am commanded a pilgrimage to take,
And straight accounts before God to make.
Now, I pray you, Shrift, mother of Salvation,
Help my good deeds for my piteous exclamation.

CONFESSION: I know your sorrow well, Everyman.
Because with Knowledge ye come to me,
I will comfort you as well as I can,
And a precious jewel I will give thee,
Called penance, wise voider of adversity.
Therewith shall thy body chastised be,
With abstinence and perseverance in God's service.
Here shalt thou receive that scourge of me
Which is penance strong that you must endure,
To remember thy Saviour was scourged for thee
With sharp scourges, and suffered it patiently.

So must thou, ere thou escape that painful pil-
grimage;
Knowledge, keep him in this voyage,
And by that time Good-Deeds will be with thee.
And in any wise, be sure of mercy,
For your time draweth fast, if you will saved be.
Ask God mercy, and He will grant truly;
When with the scourge of penance man doth him
bind,
The oil of forgiveness then shall he find.

EVERYMAN: Thanked be God for his gracious
work!
For now I will my penance begin.
This hath rejoiced and lighted my heart,
Though the knots be painful and hard within.

KNOWLEDGE: Everyman, look that ye your penance
fulfil,
Whatever pain it to you be,
And Knowledge shall give you counsel at will.
How your accounts ye shall make clearly.

EVERYMAN: O eternal God, O heavenly figure,
O way of righteousness, O goodly vision,
Which descended down in a virgin pure
Because He would Everyman redeem,
Which Adam forfeited by his disobedience.
O blessed Godhead, elect and divine,
Forgive my grievous offence,
Here I cry Thee mercy in this presence.
O soul's treasure, O ransomer and redeemer
Of all the world, hope and leader,
Mirror of joy, and founder of mercy,
Which illumineth heaven and earth thereby,
Hear my clamorous complaint, though it late be,
Receive my prayers. Unworthy in this heavy life
Though I be, a sinner most abominable,
Yet let my name be written in Moses' table;
O Mary, pray to the Maker of everything,
To help me at my ending,
And save me from the power of my enemy,
For Death assaileth me strongly.
And, Lady, that I may by means of thy prayer
Of your Son's glory be the partaker,
By the pity of his Passion I it crave,
I beseech you, help my soul to save.—
Knowledge, give me the scourge of penance,
My flesh therewith shall give a quittance.
I will now begin, if God give me grace.

KNOWLEDGE: Everyman, God give you time and
space.
Thus I bequeath you into the hands of our Saviour,
Thus may you make your reckoning sure.

EVERYMAN: In the name of the blessed Trinity,
My body sore punished shall be.
Take this body for the sin of the flesh!
Thou that delightest to go gay and fresh,
And in the way of damnation didst me bring,
Now suffer therefore strokes and punishing.
Now of penance I will wade the water clear,
To save me from Purgatory, that sharp fire.

[Good-Deeds joins them]

GOOD-DEEDS: I thank God, now I can walk and go,
And am delivered of my sickness and woe.
Therefore with Everyman I will go, and not spare—
His good works I will help him to declare.

KNOWLEDGE: Now, Everyman, be merry and glad.
Your Good-Deeds cometh now, ye may not be sad.
Now is your Good-Deeds whole and sound,
Going upright upon the ground.

EVERYMAN: My heart is light, and shall be evermore,
Now I will smite faster than I did before.

GOOD-DEEDS: Everyman, pilgrim, my special friend,
Blessed be thou without end.
For thee is prepared the eternal glory.
Ye have me made whole and sound,
Therefore I will bide by thee in every round.

EVERYMAN: Welcome, my Good-Deeds! Now I
hear thy voice,
I weep for very sweetness of love.

KNOWLEDGE: Be no more sad, but ever rejoice,
God seeth thy living from his throne aloft.
Put on this garment which is so soft—
Wet with your tears it is.
Or else before God you may it miss,
When you to your journey's end shall come.

EVERYMAN: Gentle Knowledge, what is its name?

KNOWLEDGE: It is a garment of sorrow:
From pain it will divide you;
Contrition it is,
That getteth forgiveness;
It pleaseth God passing well.

GOOD-DEEDS: Everyman, will you wear it for your
heal?

[Everyman puts on the robe]

EVERYMAN: Now blessed be Jesu, Mary's Son!
For now have I on true contrition.
And let us go now without tarrying.
Good-Deeds, have we clear our reckoning?

GOOD-DEEDS: Yea, indeed I have it here.

EVERYMAN: Then I trust we need not fear;
Now, friends, let us not part in twain.

KNOWLEDGE: Nay, Everyman, that will we not,
certain.

GOOD-DEEDS: Yet must thou lead with thee
Three persons of great might.

EVERYMAN: Who should they be?

GOOD-DEEDS: Discretion and Strength they hight,
And thy Beauty may not abide behind.

KNOWLEDGE: Also you must call to mind
Your Five-Wits as for your counselors.

GOOD-DEEDS: You must have them ready at all
hours.

EVERYMAN: How shall I get them hither?

KNOWLEDGE: You must call them all together,
And they will hear you incontinent.

EVERYMAN: My friends, come hither and be
present,
Discretion, Strength, my Five-Wits, and Beauty.

[Discretion, Strength, Five-Wits and Beauty
enter]

BEAUTY: Here at your will we be all ready.
What will ye that we should do?

GOOD-DEEDS: That ye would with Everyman go,
And help him in his pilgrimage.
Advise you, will ye with him or not in that voyage?

STRENGTH: We will bring him all thither,
To his help and comfort, ye may believe me.

DISCRETION: So will we go with him all together.

EVERYMAN: Almighty God, loved mayest thou be,
I give thee laud that I have hither brought
Strength, Discretion, Beauty, and Five-Wits; I lack
nought!
And my Good-Deeds, with Knowledge clear,
All stay in my company at my will here;
I desire no more to my business.

STRENGTH: And I, Strength, will stand by you in
distress,
Though thou wouldest in battle fight on the ground.

FIVE-WITS: And though it were through the world
round,
We will not depart for sweet nor sour.

BEAUTY: No more will I unto death's hour,
Whatsoever thereof befall.

DISCRETION: Everyman, advise you first of all,
Go with a good advisement and deliberation.
We all give you virtuous monition
That all shall be well.

EVERYMAN: My friends, hearken what I will tell.
I pray God reward you in his heavenly sphere.
Now hearken, all that be here,
For I will make my testament
Here before every one present.
In alms half my good I will give with my hands
twain
In the way of charity, with good intent,
And the other half shall remain
In quiet to be returned where it ought to be.
This I do in despite of the fiend of hell,
To go quit of his peril
Ever after and this day.

KNOWLEDGE: Everyman, hearken what I say.
Go to priesthood, I advise,
And receive of him in any wise
The holy sacrament and ointment together,
Then shortly see ye turn again hither.
We will all await you here.

FIVE-WITS: Yea, Everyman, haste you that ye
ready be.
There is no emperor, king, duke, nor baron,
That of God hath commission,
As hath the least priest in the world's design.
For of the blessed sacraments pure and benign,
He beareth the keys and thereof hath the cure
For man's redemption, that is ever sure;
Which God for our soul's medicine
Gave us out of his heart with great pine.
Here in this transitory life, for thee and me,
The blessed sacraments seven there be,
Baptism, confirmation, with priesthood good,
And the sacrament of God's precious flesh and blood,

Marriage, the holy extreme unction, and penance;
These seven be good to have in remembrance,
Gracious sacraments of high divinity.
    EVERYMAN: Fain would I receive that holy body
And meekly to my spiritual father I will go.
    FIVE-WITS: Everyman, that is the best that ye can
      do.
God will you to salvation bring,
For priesthood exceedeth all other thing.
To us Holy Scripture they do teach,
And convert man from his sin heaven to reach;
God hath to them more power given,
Than to any angel that is in heaven.
With five words he may consecrate
God's body in flesh and blood to make,
And holdeth his maker between his hands,
The priest bindeth and unbindeth all bands,
Both in earth and in heaven,
He ministers all the sacraments seven.—
Though we kissed thy feet thou wert worthy,
Thou art surgeon that cureth sin deadly.
No remedy we find that is good
But only under priesthood.
Everyman, God gave priests that dignity,
And setteth them in his stead among us to be—
Thus be they above angels in degree.
    [Everyman *departs*]
    KNOWLEDGE: If priests be good it is so surely!
But when Jesus hanged on the cross with great smart
There he *gave*, out of his blessed heart,
The same sacrament in great torment:
He *sold* them not to us, that Lord Omnipotent!
Therefore Saint Peter, the apostle, doth say
That Jesu's curse have all they
Who God their Saviour do buy or sell,
Or for any money do take or tell.
Sinful priests have to sinners bad example been.
Their children sit by other men's fires, I have seen;
And some priests haunt women's company,
With unclean life, in lusts of lechery:
These be with sin made blind.
    FIVE-WITS: I trust to God no such may we find.
Therefore let us priesthood honor,
And follow their doctrine for our souls' succor.
We be their sheep, and they shepherds be
By whom we all are kept in surety.
Peace, for yonder I see Everyman come,
Who hath made true satisfaction.
    GOOD-DEEDS: Methinketh it is he indeed.
    [Everyman *returns*]
    EVERYMAN: Now Jesu all our labor speed,
I have received the sacrament for my redemption,
And then mine extreme unction.
Blessed be all they that counseled me to take it!
And now, friends, let us go without longer respite,
I thank God that ye have tarried so long.
Now set each of you on this rod your hand,
And shortly follow me.
I go before, there I would be, God be our guide!
    STRENGTH: Everyman, we will not from you go,

Till ye have gone this voyage long.
    DISCRETION: I, Discretion, will bide by you also.
    KNOWLEDGE: And though this pilgrimage be never
      so strong,
I will never part from you, too.
    EVERYMAN: I will be as sure by thee
As ever I stood by Judas Maccabee.
    [*They approach the grave*]
    EVERYMAN: Alas, I am so faint I may not stand,
My limbs under me do fold.
Friends, let us not turn again to this land,
Not for all the world's gold,
For into this cave must I creep
And turn to the earth and there sleep.
    BEAUTY: What, into this grave? Alas!
    EVERYMAN: Yea, there shall you consume more and
      less.
    BEAUTY: And what, should I smother here?
    EVERYMAN: Yea, by my faith, and never more
      appear.
In this world live no more we shall,
But in heaven before the highest lord of all.
    BEAUTY: I cross out all this, adieu by Saint John!
I take my cap in my lap and am gone.
    EVERYMAN: What, Beauty, whither will ye?
    BEAUTY: Peace, I am deaf! I look not behind me,
Not if thou would give me all the gold in thy chest
    [Beauty *departs*]
    EVERYMAN: Alas, in whom may I trust?
Beauty fast away doth hie—
She promised with me to live and die.
    STRENGTH: Everyman, I will thee also forsake
      and deny.
Thy game liketh me not at all.
    EVERYMAN: Why, then ye will forsake me all.
Sweet Strength, tarry a little space.
    STRENGTH: Nay, sir, by the rood of grace
I will hie me from thee first,
Though thou weep till thy heart burst.
    EVERYMAN: Ye would ever bide by me, ye said.
    STRENGTH: Yea, I have you far enough conveyed.
Ye be old enough, I understand,
Your pilgrimage to take on hand;
I repent me that I hither came.
    EVERYMAN: Strength, you to displease I am to
      blame;
Will you break promise that is debt?
    STRENGTH: In faith, I care not.
Thou art but a fool to complain,
You spend your speech and waste your brain—
Go thrust thee into the ground!
    EVERYMAN: I had thought surer I should have you
      found.
    [*Exit* Strength]
He that trusteth in his Strength
She deceiveth him at the length.
Both Strength and Beauty forsaking me,
Yet they promised me fair and lovingly.
    DISCRETION: Everyman, I will after Strength be
      gone,

As for me I will leave you alone.

EVERYMAN: Why, Discretion, will ye forsake me?

DISCRETION: Yea, in faith, I will go from thee,

For when Strength goeth before

I follow after evermore.

EVERYMAN: Yet, I pray thee, for the love of Trinity,

Look in my grave once piteously.

DISCRETION: Nay, so nigh will I not come.

Farewell, every one!

[*Exit* Discretion]

EVERYMAN: O all thing faileth, save God alone;

Beauty, Strength, and Discretion;

For when Death bloweth his blast

They all run from me full fast.

FIVE-WITS: Everyman, my leave now of thee I take;

I will follow the other, for here I thee forsake.

EVERYMAN: Alas! then may I wail and weep,

For I took you for my best friend.

FIVE-WITS: I will not longer thee keep.

Now farewell, and there an end.

[*Exit* Five-Wits]

EVERYMAN: O Jesu, help, all have forsaken me!

GOOD-DEEDS: Nay, Everyman, I will bide with thee,

I will not forsake thee indeed,

Thou shalt find me a good friend at need.

EVERYMAN: Gramercy, Good-Deeds, now may I true friends see.

They have forsaken me every one.

I loved them better than my Good-Deeds alone.

Knowledge, will ye forsake me also?

KNOWLEDGE: Yea, Everyman, when ye to death do go,

But not yet for no manner of danger.

EVERYMAN: Gramercy, Knowledge, with all my heart.

KNOWLEDGE: Nay, yet I will not from hence depart,

Till I be sure where ye shall come.

EVERYMAN: Methinketh, alas, that I must be on,

To make my reckoning and debts to pay,

For I see my time is nigh spent away.

Take example, all ye that this do hear or see,

How they that I loved best do forsake me,

Except my Good-Deeds that bideth truly.

GOOD-DEEDS: All earthly things are but vanity:

Beauty, Strength, and Discretion, do man forsake,

Foolish friends and kinsmen, that fair spake,

All flee save Good-Deeds, and he am I.

EVERYMAN: Have mercy on me, God most mighty;

And stand by me, thou Mother and Maid, holy Mary.

GOOD-DEEDS: Fear not, I will speak for thee.

EVERYMAN: Here I cry God mercy.

GOOD-DEEDS: Shorten our end, diminish our pain.

Let us go and never come again.

EVERYMAN: Into Thy hands, Lord, my soul I commend.

Receive it, Lord, that it be not lost!

As thou boughtest me, me so defend,

And rescue from the fiend's boast,

That I may appear with that blessed host

That shall be saved at the day of doom.

In manus tuas—of might's utmost

Forever—*commendo spiritum meum.*

[Everyman *and* Good-Deeds *enter the grave*]

KNOWLEDGE: Now hath he suffered that we all shall endure,

But Good-Deeds shall make all sure.

Now hath he made ending—

Methinketh that I hear angels sing

And make great joy and melody,

Where Everyman's soul received shall be.

[*An* Angel *appears*]

ANGEL: Come, excellent elect spouse to Jesu!

Hereabove thou shalt go

Because of thy singular virtue.

Now the soul is taken from the body so,

Thy reckoning is crystal-clear.

Now shalt thou into the heavenly sphere,

Unto which all ye shall come

That live well before the day of doom.

EPILOGUE

DOCTOR: This moral men may have in mind:

Ye hearers, take it of worth, old and young,

And forsake pride, for he deceiveth you in the end,

And remember Beauty, Five-Wits, Strength, and Discretion,

They all at the last do Everyman forsake,

Alone his Good-Deeds there doth he take.

But beware, if they be small

Before God, man hath no help at all.

No excuse may there be for Everyman—

Alas, what shall he do then?

For after death amends may no man make,

For then mercy and pity him forsake.

If his reckoning be not clear when he come,

God will say—*ite maledicti in ignem æternum.*

And he that hath his account whole and sound,

High in heaven he shall be crowned,

Unto which place God bring us all thither

That we may live body and soul together.

Thereto help blessed Trinity.

Amen, say ye, for Saint Charity.

Thus endeth this moral play of Everyman.

The Renaissance

A reconstruction by John C. Adams of the Globe Playhouse. The outer stage and "tiring house" are shown with the two inner-stage curtains closed (see p. 217). The Folger Library, Washington, D.C., photo: Wendell Kilmer.

The Renaissance

The surge of worldly and humanistic interest, the break with otherworldly medievalism, and the assertive—often blithe but sometimes deeply troubled —individualism associated with the Renaissance could hardly fail to be reflected in the theatre. In fact, the Renaissance determined the entire history of the stage and drama for centuries, and its influence is not yet exhausted. In many Western nations, it produced a polished court theatre; in some countries, it brought forth a vigorous popular theatre. As a result of a rich development in the fine arts, the Renaissance ushered in the illusionistic stage setting, which grew increasingly pictorial after the fifteenth century, moved farther and farther behind the proscenium arch—forming the picture-frame stage—and culminated after 1860 in realistic and naturalistic styles of production. And these developments, as one would expect, in turn altered styles of acting and playwriting.

Even more drastic and comprehensive than the innovations in theatrical staging were the changes consummated in dramatic literature. From the courtly theatre came a refinement of subjects, interests, and style of writing that made medieval comedy and farce seem intolerably crude. *As You Like It* and *A Midsummer Night's Dream,* not to mention the pastoral plays written in Italy by Tasso and Guarini, could not have been written for the medieval stage. From the gentlemen-scholars who redacted the Greek and Roman classics came an interest in the lost tradition of ancient drama and in classical myth and history as dramatic subjects. *Julius Caesar, Coriolanus,* and *Antony and Cleopatra* are only the culminations of this widening trend.

There also arose, to be sure, a concern with the interpretation and application of classical "rules," from Aristotle as well as Horace. At first proposed by scholars, the rule of the unities—of time, place, and action—acquired official sanction in France from the prime minister, Cardinal Richelieu, who made himself patron and arbiter of the arts. After 1640 the writers submitted or were forced into submission, with the result that a "neoclassic" drama came into being. Its hold upon the French theatre was not broken until the advent of Victor Hugo's *Hernani,* in 1830. In the most vital areas of Renaissance drama, professional playwrights generally ignored, resisted, or circumvented the rules. Only two of Shakespeare's many plays, *The Comedy of Errors* and *The Tempest,* were unified to the satisfaction of the humanist scholars. There is considerable difference, however, between even a free-flowing Elizabethan play, such as *Henry IV* or *Antony and Cleopatra,* and a medieval religious cycle consisting of numerous separate little plays. From the developed esthetic sense of the Renaissance came new concepts

of organization that made possible the writing of long and sustained plays. The advantages of unity of action and tone (unity of time and place matter less) are manifest in *Othello* and *Macbeth,* even though their author felt no allegiance to the rule of the classic unities.

Another and pre-eminent quality of the new drama was its literary excellence. Medieval drama reveals virtually no pride of authorship; the plays are, with very few exceptions, anonymous, and no one knows how many times the text was tampered with or how many casual redactions were responsible for the versions that have come down to us. The versification is generally rough; the *dolce stil nuovo,* the new, sweet style, does not appear in the medieval theatre. The custom of printing plays was not yet completely established. (Frequently Elizabethan plays were published long after they were first produced, probably to prevent piracy by a rival acting company.) Nevertheless, pride in authorship grew rapidly during the Renaissance, and playwrights thought of themselves as men of letters. They often took even more pride in their authorship of nondramatic literature. Many of them—Ariosto, Tasso, Marlowe, Shakespeare, and Jonson, among others—achieved independent distinction as poets. It is not unusual to find a Renaissance play— "minor" Elizabethan drama provides many examples —that one is tempted to dismiss as an extremely extravagant or botched piece of work, from which it is nonetheless possible to salvage passages of enduring poetry. Even in the great plays of Marlowe and Shakespeare, the word music is often the most impressive element. Although no one would call *Pericles* an indispensable item of the Shakespearean canon, one would have to be congenitally deaf to want to dispense with the description of the storm at sea, which contains such lines as

> The seaman's whistle
> Is as a whisper in the ears of death
> Unheard.

In the good plays, besides, the poetry is the carrier of the drama, so that all nuance of feeling and thought and all "action" save bare plot depend upon it. Poetry is the texture from which the great Renaissance play cannot be torn without destroying the whole. Without this verbal music and imagery, even *Hamlet, Othello, Macbeth, King Lear,* and *Antony and Cleopatra*—and each has its special music and imagery—would sink to the level of second-rate drama. Literature and drama become one creation and will always remain one experience in the best products of the Renaissance theatre.

The best Renaissance drama has, in addition to its literary merit, two qualities of greatness directly attributable to the age—rich individuality of characterization and humanistic meaning. Both are aspects of Renaissance humanism drawn from a revival of the classics and from the expanding interests and energies of the new age. The Copernican theory begins to dominate science and to conflict with religion—and its philosopher Giordano Bruno dies of it, at the stake. But there is no Copernican theory in the theatre. There, man is the center of the universe, more so than ever before. Moreover, he stands there not as a moral entity, attribute, or bundle of attributes but as the total man, complete with marrow, sinew, desire, will, and mind.

In Renaissance drama, the character's object is to effectuate himself in the world of desire, and his pursuit of it leads to pleasure on one hand and to tragedy on the other. The pleasure is elegant or rustic (we find both, for example, in *As You Like It*); or it is boisterous, as in the antics of Falstaff, Prince Hal, and their crew: or it turns to extravagance, inviting ridicule, as in Jonsonian "comedy of humours." The *élan vital*, or life force, is everywhere at work. Man pursues maid; maid pursues man. Maid pursues man openly, indeed, for the first time in two thousand years of theatre. Shakespeare's "mighty huntresses," to employ the Shavian designation, are on the springtime's traces. There is also capering and singing in the process, and there is lovers' banter, such as Benedick and Beatrice's in *Much Ado About Nothing*, as the sexes stand on fairly equal terms and let their intelligence be heard in wordplay.

Lovers or not, Renaissance characters are the creatures of their sense of worth. Even simple men have it and stand upon it—the Adam of *As You Like It*, the gravedigger of *Hamlet*, who speaks as man to man when he addresses the intellectual prince, and the peasants of Lope de Vega's *The Sheep Well* or Calderón's *The Mayor of Zalamea*, who punish aristocratic abuses of power. Among the nobility, the sense of honor leads to the extravagances of "cape and sword" Spanish drama, behind which, however, lies the genuine sense of the individual's worth as a gentleman. Self-valuation leads to gallant and desperate deeds and brings one to the extremities where passion rules. One step more in the scale of the playwright's values and passion leads to tragedy. In Renaissance drama, as is most apparent in Elizabethan plays, this becomes "tragedy of the will," for the dramatists had only to look about them to see a world in which men's struggles for self-realization and self-effectuation were frequently perilous to themselves and to others. Their efforts range from the lowest forms of "chiseling," or, as Robert Greene called it, "connycatching," to the extreme business ingenuities of a Volpone; from small political ambitions to the kingdom-shattering and soul-searing usurpation of a Macbeth. The will running riot almost destroys Lear's kingdom, the catastrophe having begun with nothing more than an old man's willfulness; and Hamlet's divided will has consequences almost as disastrous. Fate had also been rooted, more or less, in character during the first great age of tragedy, in Athens. But character had never before this time been taken over and activated so thoroughly by problems of the will.

As for the intellectual component which impregnates the new drama, it is to be found in many ways and many guises, for gone is the simple-mindedness of the folk characters and the single-mindedness of the Biblical characters or saints of the medieval plays. Something other than the delivery of sermons or the elaboration of a systematic philosophy is involved here. There is an intellectual ferment in the work. The intellect is now in the forefront of the stage, whether in the sharpness of an English, Spanish, or Italian clown or rogue, the euphuistically elaborate speech of a courtier, the tart tongue of a lover, the wit of a skeptical Mercutio, the cynicism of a villainous Iago, the ingenuities of an avenger such as Hieronymo of *The Spanish Tragedy*, the self-torment of a Hamlet, or the disillusionment and new-won humanity of the humbled and distracted Lear, who is given lines such as

Through tatter'd clothes small vices do appear;
    Robes and furr'd gowns hide all. Plate sin with
        gold,
And the strong lance of justice hurtless falls;
Arm it in rags, a pigmy's straw doth pierce it.

Lorenzo Valla, Pico della Mirandola, Leonardo da Vinci, Erasmus, Sir Thomas More, Montaigne, Machiavelli, and others had done some acute thinking, and the results of their thought and their habit of inquiry had been shaping the new age. Intellectual curiosity permeated the playwrights' characters, and the dialogue projected the subtleness of Renaissance thought. Ideas became part of a character's personality as in Hamlet and Faustus. Above all, thought became transmuted into image and metaphor. Many of the ideas, presented purely as ideas, might, indeed, have been banal. There is nothing strikingly original, for instance, in the Renaissance skepticism or fatalism to which Shakespeare appears to have helped himself quite generously. It is the poetically and dramatically transmuted article, as it appears in Hamlet's soliloquies and in some of Lear's ravings, that has genuine worth. There is a world of difference—to art, that is—between a parish report and Lear's

Poor naked wretches, whereso'er you are,
That bide the pelting of this pitiless storm,
How shall your houseless heads and unfed sides,
Your loop'd and window'd raggedness, defend you
From seasons such as these?

In some instances the translation of thought into

drama went so far that the intellectual was placed in the very center, the white-heat core, as in *Doctor Faustus* and *Hamlet*. In Marlowe's Faustus, indeed, we find the theatre's first extant hero of intellectual inquiry; and its self-immolated martyr, too.

Over the entire enterprise of theatre and drama, especially in Spain and England, there hung, moreover, a certain aura of magnitude. This went beyond the propensity toward representing heroic and splendid figures, and also beyond the distinct stature of such tragic characters as Hamlet, Macbeth, Othello, and Lear. On the visual side, sensationalism was sought. In Italy, this was most apparent in spectacular stage painting and machinery, mostly employed in opera and in the bustle of the popular, nonliterary theatre known as *commedia dell' arte;* in England and Spain, the striving for "effect" appeared in lavish costuming, stage processions, mimic battles, apparitions from trap doors, and mob scenes. There was a largeness, too, in the plots, passions, and conflicts. The plays were apt to surge and teem, to spread over much territory and time, to burst at the seams with plot and speech. The dramatic form had an epic extensiveness; it could not be packaged neatly and tied with ribbons. Here was a theatre of action, often reaching violence. It was also a theatre of rhetoric, in which even fustian had a place. When the artistry deteriorated, as in late Elizabethan tragedy (in Chapman, Marston, Tourneur, Webster, and Ford), it did so with an excess of passion and melodrama. All sorts of excesses of crabbed thought (in Chapman), of plot complication (in tragicomedy of the *Cymbeline* variety), of overelaboration and overrefinement (in John Fletcher), of obscenity (in Italian comedies such as Aretino's), of "honor" and intrigue (in Spanish "cape and sword" romanticism) marked and marred this theatre. It is the Renaissance growing into the "baroque" style—as it did in the titanic Michelangelo and later in Bernini, the master of sculptural movement—that we find on the stage. The drama that had started in the fifteenth century with little more than arid academic imitation became a riot of emotionalism and action.

SPAIN AND ENGLAND

The Renaissance drama that engages more than scholarly or purely theatrical interest came chiefly from two countries, England and Spain; countries geographically far from the starting point of the Renaissance, Italy, where the main artistic energies went into pictorial art and scenic display. Both England and Spain were also essentially removed from the white radiance of the High Renaissance, classic ideality being stained in these countries by a most unclassical lack of refinement in the energetic masses that supported the theatre. Elizabethan playwriting was delivered from academic and courtly restraint by a rough taste on the part of the Elizabethan

groundlings, to whom a good fight, a pungent jest, and a loud rhetoric were most welcome. The Spanish drama shared, especially during Lope de Vega's lifetime, the bustle and energy of a nation that had flung itself across the seas to become the greatest empire of the sixteenth century. Like Shakespeare and his English contemporaries, Lope de Vega and his Spanish contemporaries played a bold and wild gambit.

In both countries the open-air popular stage had priority over the enclosed courtly and "private" theatres during an important part of the period. The acting area of the popular theatre was still a platform, on three sides of which were spectators. In some respects, in fact, the medieval elements of popular drama—multiple scenes and the commingling of comic and serious matter—were retained. And in Spain, as a result of the Counter Reformation, a return to medieval religiosity made large claims, especially upon the second great Spanish playwright, Calderón de la Barca (1600–1681). The author of both "cape and sword" and peasant plays similar to Lope's, he began to write much religious and contemplative drama, including *autos,* or more or less allegorical pieces.

In Italy, playwriting first evolved chiefly as imitations of Plautus and Terence and then as astringent comedies of manners, contributed chiefly by three men of letters, Ariosto, Aretino, and Machiavelli. Among these plays, Machiavelli's cold satire on human imbecility, *Mandragola,* is the masterpiece. But a good deal of the best literary writing did not go into vital drama, and the liveliest dramatic art in Italy was nonliterary. It was created by the wandering *commedia dell' arte* actors, who merely pinned up synopses of plots backstage, employed memorized set speeches for certain standardized situations, and improvised the rest of the dialogue. In Spain, however, there arose a number of vigorous playwrights, who were soon overshadowed by Lope de Vega, the most energetic, as well as most distinguished, of all these dramatists. And Lope found an extremely talented associate and successor in Calderón, who became the leading playwright of the Catholic Counter Reformation and exerted considerable influence on continental European playwriting. Simultaneously in England, moreover, the drama underwent such rapid and memorable developments that the Elizabethan and Jacobean periods, from about 1580 to 1625, became the second great age of the theatre.

As Emerson observed, the Elizabethan stage was for its period "ballad, epic, newspaper, caucus, lecture, Punch, and library, at the same time." The universities and the court vied with one another in favoring stage productions. Strolling players drew appreciative auditors in the courtyards of large inns before special theatres were erected; choir boys of the Court Chapel and of St. Paul's were conscripted into the service of courtly comedies; large theatres were hastily constructed to accommodate the avid audiences. Productions were spectacular. No device was held to be too sensational if it aroused or sustained interest and excitement. The costuming of the actors was elaborate and costly, and the performances were enlivened with music, dancing, and acrobatics. Tragic situations alternated with grossly farcical ones; rhetoric, bombast, and blood flowed freely in the plays; battles and murders sparked the action; and prologues and epilogues harangued the audience and pleaded for applause. Audiences, composed chiefly of standees in the pit and spectators seated in the galleries, made a social occasion of playgoing; they were restive and excitable. Shakespeare and his colleagues wrote for a theatre that could not afford to be static.

The physical stage of the Elizabethans was the last place in the world where playwriting would tend to be stagnant. In the so-called popular theatres, action swirled continually, unconfined by scenery; the playwright had to depend to a considerable degree upon word pictures and verbal music to convey scenic effects—and also the time of day, since only natural lighting was possible in theatres that were open to the sky. (Only a portion of the stage and the balconies close to the wall of the building were covered with a thatched roof.) Painted scenery and artificial illumination by candles were used only in the completely roofed, higher-priced so-called "private theatres," whereas most of the vital drama of the period was originally written to be performed in the "popular theatres." In the latter, the stage consisted largely of an open platform. Most of the dramatic action took place on this platform, so that the acting area did not constitute a "box set" or "peephole stage" behind a proscenium arch.

The drama played on such a stage could not be a copy of real life but an emphatic projection of it. The style of writing, like the style of production, was therefore frankly theatrical instead of photographic. In this kind of theatre, poetry, rhetorical fireworks, soliloquies, asides, and a broad acting style were in place. They were "natural" in terms of the "theatricalist" medium, whereas they would be unnatural on the realistic stage. This was a theatre for a "presentational" rather than "representational" style of dramatic composition. On the platform, processions, court sessions, forest scenes, and battle scenes with rival armies rushing at each other from opposite sides were presented in rapid succession. A placard might be used to indicate the new locality, but very often the public gathered all it needed to know from the speeches, the furniture, the heraldic signs and banners carried by actors, and the action.

The fact that Elizabethan plays are formally divided into "scenes" means very little; there were no intervals between them, no scene endings with the stage "dimmed out" or the curtain dropped, as in modern stage production. There was, indeed, no curtain whatsoever in front of the platform to conceal changes of furniture and stage properties. The "dead" had to be carried off stage, in full sight of the audience, and the playwright had to be careful to justify the clearing of the stage with such a line as "Take up the bodies." Even the act divisions of the plays, mostly the work of post-Elizabethan editors, have no great significance. A production was not likely to have more than one intermission; and this was generally occupied with comic dances or "jigs" and acrobatics designed to keep the audience from straying out of the theatre.

Behind the platform stage, and separated from it by means of a curtain, or "arras," was a shallow "inner stage" which could localize the plot by indicating, for example, a boudoir. But the action rarely remained confined to this area. Behind the arras rose the wall of the "tiring house," or property and dressing room. It served as a permanent background, without having any localizing or true scenic function. Its doors, however, served as entrances and exits. On the second floor, moreover, stood a curtained shallow gallery or balcony, on which appropriate events, such as Juliet's balcony scene, could be played with some effect of illusion; or the gallery might be used for scenes occurring on the deck of a ship or on some height. Moving back and forth from outer to inner stage and balcony, the typical Elizabethan play traced a free and vigorous course. The audience's eyes traveled horizontally, across the platform, and vertically, up the gallery and toward a false ceiling, known as "the heavens," which gave the impression of a strip of sky; and the ear followed where the eye had nothing to perceive. Such was the popular Elizabethan theatre, still rather medieval in its multiple stage structure and subject to no restraint from the pseudo-Aristotelian rules for "unity" propounded by the scholars.

Playwriting for this stage underwent significant changes during the third quarter of the sixteenth century, when bold young intellectuals, most of them fresh from the universities, became professional playwrights. Combining classical with Italian and native influences, John Lyly, George Peele, and Robert Greene composed romantic comedies excelling in wit and gracefulness, while others of the fellowship, Thomas Kyd and Christopher Marlowe, advanced the cause of tragedy. Marlowe's contribution is especially noteworthy, for no one before Shakespeare achieved such exalted passion or created such dynamic personalities as the young author of *Tamburlaine, The Jew of Malta,* and *Doctor Faustus.* In these plays and in his masterpiece *Edward II,* Marlowe laid the foundations for Shakespearean tragedy. Especially influential was Marlowe's "mighty line" of blank verse, which provided Shakespeare with a powerful instrument for dramatic expression. When, in 1593, Marlowe's life was cut short at the age of twenty-nine in a tavern brawl, Shakespeare was still a novice in the theatre. In no respect an innovator, he observed the practice of his predecessors and contemporaries and simply bettered it. As Emerson wrote, "The greatest genius is the most indebted man." Shakespeare's work was the culmination of numerous tendencies in the multifarious fields of comedy, historical drama, tragedy, and romance, each of which he approached in due time.

During Shakespeare's active years in the theatre and for nearly a quarter of a century after his retirement from the theatre—that is, between 1598 and 1635—England had a great many other practicing playwrights. Among them were the redoubtable satirist Ben Jonson, the sultry tragedian John Webster, the gifted but short-lived Francis Beaumont and his collaborator John Fletcher, the genial Thomas Dekker, Thomas Middleton, Thomas Heywood, and Philip Massinger, best known for his comedy of acquisitiveness *A New Way to Pay Old Debts*. With Shakespeare's plays in the foreground, the dramatic works of these writers and of such colleagues as George Chapman, John Marston, Cyril Tourneur, and John Ford comprise the most varied and impressive collection of dramatic literature extant before the modern period.

That many of the Elizabethans were men of extraordinary talent no one can deny. But it is equally undeniable that most of them were sloppy craftsmen whose slipshod ways were encouraged by a lack of literary and theatrical discipline in their time. The romantic writers of the early nineteenth century and that incorrigible rhapsodist Algernon Swinburne, finding gorgeous flashes of poetic or dramatic genius in their work, sometimes overrated them. The English romanticists, who had no sound theatre of their own, often judged the so-called minor Elizabethans with slight reference to the requirements of completeness and logic in playwriting. In the extravagant efforts of the Elizabethan "noble brood," moreover, the later romanticists found justification for their own unrestrained imaginative flights. The inevitable reaction, toward the end of the nineteenth century, to such indiscriminate idealization went to the other extreme of denying many of Shakespeare's *confrères* or successors any merit whatsoever. Shaw, who dubbed John Webster a "Tussaud laureate," the poet laureate of waxworks, and baited the whole brotherhood mercilessly, was the bellwether of this reaction.

Although we can dismiss much of the "minor" work of the period, credit should not be withheld from fragments of superlative writing, and a number of plays—*Doctor Faustus, The Changeling, The White Devil, The Duchess of Malfi*—should be recognized as flawed but genuine masterpieces of tragic art. What the "minor Elizabethans" had in common with Shakespeare cannot be prized too highly in the theatre. They possessed a capacity for dramatic intensification and poetic expression granted only sparingly to the playwrights of later, tamer periods. If they lacked the workmanlike precision of many modern writers, their serious drama possessed something infinitely precious—inexhaustible passion and vigor. Their comedies, moreover, reflected a zest for life and a liveliness of observation too contagious and wholesome to be deprecated because the authors sometimes rode a "humour" or idiosyncrasy too hard or tried to cover too much ground in a single play. Comedies such as Jonson's best pieces, as well as *Eastward Ho!, The Knight of the Burning Pestle, The Shoemaker's Holiday*, and *A New Way to Pay Old Debts* still retain much of their original freshness.

Undoubtedly, the Renaissance theatre disintegrated partly as a result of its own excesses. But these became most flagrant when the society that had sustained the theatre was also in a state of deterioration—when Spain had entered upon a long period of stalemate and when the Stuart monarchy had begun to fall apart after the death of James I in 1625. The decree of the Puritan "Commonwealth" that snuffed out the theatre in 1649 by forbidding the performance of plays was only the death notice after the death. Since the theatre had by then lost most of its vigor in Spain, too, an important period of European drama was over. In the next period of creative playwriting, dominated by the culture of France under Louis XIV, discipline was the prevailing force, as it had not been when the floodgates of individualism were opened by the men of the Renaissance.

Christopher Marlowe

(1564–1593)

With the emergence of Christopher Marlowe the Western theatre entered upon its second age of greatness—the Elizabethan. This son of a Canterbury shoemaker and a clergyman's daughter responded with poetic intensity to Renaissance classicism and Elizabethan dynamism, and the result was the beginning of a vaulting dramatic art in England. Educated at the classically efficient King's School in his native town of Canterbury and at Cambridge University on scholarships, Marlowe became a classics-crammed bachelor of arts in 1584 and master of arts in 1587.

Although he had been expected to prepare himself for the church, Marlowe surrendered to worldliness and to the earth-centered and man-centered classic literature. His translation of Ovid's *Elegies* and his immature tragedy *Dido, Queen of Carthage* (completed by the satirist Thomas Nashe) were evidently started, if not actually completed, while he was still at Cambridge. And he did not wait for his master's degree before plunging into the active life favored by Elizabethan gentlemen. His frequent prolonged absences from Cambridge during his graduate-school period led the university authorities to suspect him of having traffic with the English Catholics in France, then believed to be conspiring against Queen Elizabeth. But the Queen's Privy Council ordered the dons to grant him the master's degree. According to a testimonial, dated June 29, 1587, "he had done her Majesty good service, and deserved to be rewarded for his good dealing." Evidently he had been employed in counterespionage at Rheims against the Catholic party, gathered there in anticipation of the invasion of England by the Spanish Armada. There is reason for also assuming postgraduate government employment from his association with Sir Francis Walsingham, who served the Queen not only as secretary but as chief of the secret service.

Settling in London in the summer of 1587, Marlowe entered upon the diversified life of the city, hobnobbing with intellectual aristocrats such as Sidney and Raleigh, as well as with the professional literati, and engaging in more or less forbidden speculations on religious questions. His volatile temper and associations were to cause him considerable trouble, so that the few remaining years of his life were marked by a succession of crises culminating in his murder. His inflammable spirit brought him to Newgate prison on a charge of homicide in 1592 and later led the London constabulary to put him under bond to keep the peace. He aroused the animosity of his fellow writers. The playwright Thomas Kyd, with whom he roomed one summer, denounced him on the grounds of a vile temper and antireligious sentiments, and Robert Greene wrote him a distinctly uncomplimentary admonition in the celebrated pamphlet *A Groatsworth of Wit Bought with a Million of Repentance*, which is better known for its apparent slurs on the young Shakespeare. Marlowe also had some decidedly disreputable companions, although he probably maintained an aristocratic fastidiousness with respect to them. One of these was a forger, another a spy, and a third a cutpurse; still another, Ingram Frizer, was notorious for shady transactions. Three of these associates were present at Marlowe's death at the age of twenty-nine, when, in a tavern brawl, Frizer drove a dagger into the poet's skull. The circumstances of Marlowe's death, once believed to have been merely an eight-hour debauch, appear to have been of a political character.[1]

Important, especially to the study of *Doctor Faustus,* is the fact that at the time of his death Marlowe was under investigation by the Privy Council on charges of atheism, which also involved Kyd and perhaps even the great courtier Raleigh. Although the accusations of intemperate blasphemy deposed by the informer Richard Baines may have been either partial or complete fabrications, it is certain that the poet held heterodox views. His spirit was at once speculative and daring. In nothing temperate, Marlowe wrote with fine excess that, especially in his early work, tended toward unruliness. In all but the last of his plays, *Edward II,* moreover, he was attracted to passion-driven, all-daring individuals who ride roughshod over established empires and beliefs. Marlowe was specially endowed for his historic role of bringing Promethean fire into the English tragic theatre. More than any of his contemporaries before Shakespeare, he introduced into Elizabethan drama the imagination and passion, the lambent rhetoric and poetry, and the fixation upon electrifying personalities that are its special attributes.

Marlowe made his mark in 1587 or 1588 with the production of *Tamburlaine*, a loose but impassioned chronicle of the Mongol conqueror Timur. In this vigorous epic drama, Marlowe epitomized the Renaissance cult of power in resounding terms. He not only dramatized the hero's search for "the sweet fruition of an earthly crown" but transfigured the empire conqueror's ambition into a romantic passion for the unattainable. The role was filled on the stage by the most popular actor of the time, the physically

[1] Consult Leslie Hotson's *The Death of Christopher Marlowe,* 1925, and S. A. Tannenbaum's *The Assassination of Christopher Marlowe,* 1928.

impressive Edward Alleyn, who also sustained the young author's next two tragedies. The play achieved an instant triumph, and Marlowe was encouraged to write a sequel, a second part, which added emotional depth to the story in spite of some tedious repetition of conquests.

The most important achievement in this two-part drama was Marlowe's use of his dramatic instrument—blank verse. The unrhymed iambic pentameter which had made its first appearance on the stage a quarter of a century earlier, in a "Senecan" exercise, *Gorboduc,* had been a stiff and lifeless medium. In *Tamburlaine,* Marlowe made it thunder and sing. And once having discovered its potency, he continued to adapt it to the dramatic needs of later plays, moderating its "swelling bombast," making it more expressive of dramatic feeling and action, and bringing it closer to normal speech. The young writer who fell early under the spell of Spenser's melodic stanzas and composed one of the most beautiful lyric narratives in the language, *Hero and Leander,* became the English theatre's first true poet.

From the epic style of *Tamburlaine* Marlowe turned to the more concentrated drama of *Doctor Faustus,* another tragedy of a rampant individualist, which was successfully produced in the winter of 1588–1589. Based on a German source which recounted the rise and fall of a medieval magician, the play became the tragedy of an extraordinary man destroyed by intellectual ambition. In *The Jew of Malta,* written between 1588 and 1592, Marlowe added to his list of Renaissance heroes a third protagonist, Barabas, who is neither a conqueror nor an intellectual but a merchant-prince, also intoxicated with the power and glory of this world. When Barabas is unjustly deprived of his wealth by the Christian rulers of Malta, he is, in addition, transformed into another familiar type of Elizabethan character—the implacable avenger. Barabas becomes a diabolical— or, as the Elizabethans would have said, a Machiavellian—figure when he devotes himself to weaving a furious intrigue of revenge that ultimately destroys him as well as those who injured him. Unfortunately, in spite of some superb writing, especially derisory wit, the garbled 1633 version that has come down to us is so ludicrously melodramatic in the later scenes that it invites T. S. Eliot's conjecture that *The Jew of Malta* should be regarded as an Elizabethan type of "serious" farce. Compared with Shakespeare's more humane and, in part, romantically congenial *Merchant of Venice,* the play, which deteriorates rapidly after its first act, is damaging evidence of Marlowe's want of discipline.

Even in *The Jew of Malta,* however, the poet was extending the range of his perception and sensibility, as shown in the opening scenes, in which Barabas is the victim of racial persecution. And in Marlowe's last play, *Edward II,* written shortly before his death, we find him mastering another Elizabethan dramatic form—the chronicle or history play. This work presents us with so sharp a departure from Marlovian thunder that we may wonder what further progress Marlowe might have made had he been granted a longer life. Edward, far from being a Renaissance superman, is a willful weakling, destroyed, like Richard II, by infirmity rather than strength of will. With this work, Marlowe moved into the field of complex human characterization that his successor, Shakespeare, was to make his special and lasting province. Here Marlowe's poetry is subdued by the requirements of conversation and trimmed down to the actual size of the characters. The climactic scene of Edward's murder moves us with its simple pathos rather than with tempestuous grandeur.

Marlowe sacrificed some of his young splendor and fire in writing *Edward II,* and he did not live long enough to bring to fruition an art of tragedy that would achieve complete humanization without a loss of tragic stature. The ripe fruit of Elizabethan tragedy, as well as of comedy, was to be gathered by one greater than the meteoric poet who was, in Drayton's words, given to raptures of "all air and fire" and "brave translunary things." Marlowe, however, left the novice Shakespeare—with whom he may have collaborated on *Henry VI, Richard III,* and *Titus Andronicus*—invaluable legacies in blank verse and vaulting tragedy.

In spite of flawed workmanship, *Doctor Faustus* —which has a magnificent beginning and ending but an uneven, episodic middle section—is Marlowe's most inspired, perhaps because most personally felt, tragedy. Faustus represents the passion for knowledge and for effectuation of the individual's will, the intellectual daring and yeasty ambition, of a typical "man of the Renaissance." The scholar who resorts to magic at the cost of his immortal soul may also be said to exemplify the dream of man's capacity for mastering nature, which Francis Bacon was soon to expound more soundly in *The Advancement of Learning* (1605), the *Novum Organum* (1620), and *The New Atlantis* (1622–1624). Marlowe presents this aspiration not merely in his plot but in the poetry and the specific imagery of his play, for a tragedy in Marlowe's hands is a species of poem, as it is in the work of Shakespeare.

Nevertheless, Marlowe's conception of Faustus is only partly affirmative. The play straddles the medieval and the modern worlds—magic and science, skepticism and faith, man unveiling the mysteries of nature and yet sensing a transgression in this ambition. For this reason, and also because he needed familiar symbols, Marlowe resorted to the medieval machinery of Vices and Virtues, angels and devils, Lucifer and brimstone. Along with the highly dramatic presentation of the divided Faustus, at once skeptical and believing, the morality-play devices serve to externalize the conflicts that Marlowe sensed in his times and, very probably, in himself. *Doctor Faustus* is both parable and tragedy.

THE TRAGICAL HISTORY OF DOCTOR FAUSTUS

By Christopher Marlowe

CHARACTERS

THE POPE
CARDINAL OF LORRAIN
THE EMPEROR OF GERMANY
DUKE OF VANHOLT
FAUSTUS
VALDES ⎫ *friends to Faustus*
CORNELIUS ⎭
WAGNER, *servant to Faustus*
CLOWN
ROBIN

RALPH
VINTNER
HORSE-COURSER
A KNIGHT
AN OLD MAN
SCHOLARS, FRIARS, *and* AT-
 TENDANTS
DUCHESS OF VANHOLT
LUCIFER
BELZEBUB

MEPHISTOPHILIS
GOOD ANGEL
EVIL ANGEL
THE SEVEN DEADLY SINS
DEVILS
SPIRITS *in the shapes of* ALEX-
 ANDER THE GREAT, *of his*
 PARAMOUR *and of* HELEN
CHORUS

[*Enter* Chorus]

CHORUS: Not marching now in fields of Thrasy-
  mene,
Where Mars did mate the Carthaginians;
Nor sporting in the dalliance of love,
In courts of kings where state is overturn'd;
Nor in the pomp of proud audacious deeds,
Intends our Muse to vaunt her heavenly verse:
Only this, gentlemen,—we must perform
The form of Faustus' fortunes, good or bad:
To patient judgments we appeal our plaud,
And speak for Faustus in his infancy.
Now is he born, his parents base of stock,
In Germany, within a town call'd Rhodes:
Of riper years, to Wittenberg he went,
Whereas his kinsmen chiefly brought him up.
So soon he profits in divinity,
The fruitful plot of scholarism grac'd,
That shortly he was grac'd with doctor's name,
Excelling all whose sweet delight disputes
In heavenly matters of theology;
Till swoln with cunning, of a self-conceit,
His waxen wings did mount above his reach,
And, melting, heavens conspir'd his overthrow;
For, falling to a devilish exercise,
And glutted now with learning's golden gifts,
He surfeits upon cursed necromancy;
Nothing so sweet as magic is to him,
Which he prefers before his chiefest bliss:
And this the man that in his study sits.
 [*Exit*]

SCENE I.

Faustus *discovered in his study.*

FAUSTUS: Settle thy studies, Faustus, and begin

To sound the depth of that thou wilt profess:
Having commenc'd, be a divine in show,
Yet level at the end of every art,
And live and die in Aristotle's works.
Sweet Analytics, 'tis thou hast ravish'd me!
Bene disserere est finis logices.[1]
Is, to dispute well, logic's chiefest end?
Affords this art no greater miracle?
Then read no more; thou hast attain'd that end:
A greater subject fitteth Faustus' wit:
Bid Economy farewell, and Galen[2] come,
Seeing, *Ubi desinit philosophus, ibi incipit medicus.*[3]
Be a physician, Faustus; heap up gold,
And be eternis'd for some wondrous cure:
Summum bonum medicinæ sanitas,
"The end of physic is our body's health."
Why, Faustus, hast thou not attain'd that end?
Is not thy common talk found aphorisms?
Are not thy bills hung up as monuments,
Whereby whole cities have escap'd the plague,
And thousand desperate maladies been eas'd?
Yet art thou still but Faustus, and a man.
Couldst thou make men to live eternally,
Or, being dead, raise them to life again,
Then this profession were to be esteem'd.
Physic, farewell! Where is Justinian?[4]
 [*Reads*]
*Si una eademque res legatur duobus, alter rem, alter
  valorem rei, etc.*[5]
A pretty case of paltry legacies!

 [1] "To argue well is the end of logic."
 [2] Second-century Greek physician.
 [3] "Where the philosopher stops, the physician begins."
 [4] Sixth-century ruler of the Eastern Roman Empire
under whom Roman law was codified.
 [5] "If one and the same thing is deeded to two people,
the one receives the thing, the other the value of the
thing, etc."

[*Reads*]

Exhæreditare filium non potest pater nisi, etc.[6]
Such is the subject of the Institute,[7]
And universal body of the law:
This study fits a mercenary drudge,
Who aims at nothing but external trash;
Too servile and illiberal for me.
When all is done, divinity is best:
Jerome's Bible, Faustus; view it well.
    [*Reads*]
Stipendium peccati mors est. Ha! *Stipendium, etc.*
"The reward of sin is death": that's hard.
    [*Reads*]
*Si pecasse negamus, fallimur, et nulla est in nobis
    veritas;*
"If we say that we have no sin, we deceive ourselves,
    and there's no truth in us."
Why, then, belike we must sin, and so consequently
    die:
Ay, we must die an everlasting death.
What doctrine call you this, *Che sera, sera,*
"What will be, shall be?" Divinity, adieu!
These metaphysics of magicians,
And necromantic books are heavenly;
Lines, circles, scenes, letters, and characters;
Ay, these are those that Faustus most desires.
O, what a world of profit and delight,
Of power, of honour, of omnipotence,
Is promis'd to the studious artisan!
All things that move between the quiet poles
Shall be at my command: emperors and kings
Are but obeyed in their several provinces,
Nor can they raise the wind, or rend the clouds;
But his dominion that exceeds in this,
Stretcheth as far as doth the mind of man;
Here, Faustus, tire thy brains to gain a deity.
A sound magician is a mighty god:
    [*Enter* Wagner]
Wagner, commend me to my dearest friends,
The German Valdes and Cornelius;
Request them earnestly to visit me.
    WAGNER: I will, sir.
    [*Exit*]
FAUSTUS: Their conference will be a greater help
    to me
Than all my labours, plod I ne'er so fast.
    [*Enter* Good Angel *and* Evil Angel]
GOOD ANGEL: O, Faustus, lay thy damned book
    aside,
And gaze not on it, lest it tempt thy soul,
And heap God's heavy wrath upon thy head!
Read, read the Scriptures:—that is blasphemy.
    EVIL ANGEL: Go forward, Faustus, in that famous
    art
Wherein all Nature's treasure is contain'd:
Be thou on earth as Jove is in the sky,
Lord and commander of these elements.
    [*Exeunt* Angels]
    6 "A father cannot disinherit his son, unless, etc."
    7 The Institutes of Justinian.

FAUSTUS: How am I glutted with conceit of this!
Shall I make spirits fetch me what I please,
Resolve me of all ambiguities,
Perform what desperate enterprise I will?
I'll have them fly to India for gold,
Ransack the ocean for orient pearl,
And search all corners of the new-found world
For pleasant fruits and princely delicates;
I'll have them read me strange philosophy.
And tell the secrets of all foreign kings;
I'll have them wall all Germany with brass,
And make swift Rhine circle fair Wertenberg;
I'll have them fill the public schools with silk,
Wherewith the students shall be bravely clad;
I'll levy soldiers with the coin they bring,
And chase the Prince of Parma from our land,
And reign sole king of all the provinces;
Yea, stranger engines for the brunt of war,
Than was the fiery keel at Antwerp's bridge,
I'll make my servile spirits to invent.
    [*Enter* Valdes *and* Cornelius]
Come, German Valdes and Cornelius,
And make me blest with your sage conference.
Valdes, sweet Valdes, and Cornelius,
Know that your words have won me at the last
To practise magic and concealed arts:
Yet not your words only, but mine own fantasy,
That will receive no object; for my head
But ruminates on necromantic skill.
Philosophy is odious and obscure;
Both law and physic are for petty wits;
Divinity is basest of the three,
Unpleasant, harsh, contemptible, and vile:
'Tis magic, magic, that hath ravish'd me.
Then, gentle friends, aid me in this attempt;
And I, that have with concise syllogisms
Gravell'd the pastors of the German church,
And made the flowering pride of Wittenberg
Swarm to my problems, as the infernal spirits
On sweet Musæus[8] when he came to hell,
Will be as cunning as Agrippa[9] was,
Whose shadow made all Europe honour him.
    VALDES: Faustus, these books, thy wit, and our
    experience,
Shall make all nations to canonise us.
As Indian Moors obey their Spanish lords,
So shall the spirits of every element
Be always serviceable to us three;
Like lions shall they guard us when we please;
Like Almain rutters[10] with their horsemen's staves;
Or Lapland giants, trotting by our sides;
Sometimes like women, or unwedded maids,
Shadowing more beauty in their airy brows
Than have the white breasts of the queen of love:
From Venice shall they drag huge argosies,

    8 The poet to whom Vergil refers in the *Aeneid*,
Book 6.
    9 Henry Cornelius Agrippa, the sixteenth-century
German physician and theologian.
    10 German riders.

And from America the golden fleece
That yearly stuffs old Philip's[11] treasury;
If learned Faustus will be resolute.

FAUSTUS: Valdes, as resolute am I in this
As thou to live: therefore object it not.

CORNELIUS: The miracles that magic will perform
Will make thee vow to study nothing else.
He that is grounded in astrology,
Enrich'd with tongues, well seen in minerals,
Hath all the principles magic doth require:
Then doubt not, Faustus, but to be renown'd,
And more frequented for this mystery
Than heretofore the Delphian oracle.
The spirits tell me they can dry the sea,
And fetch the treasure of all foreign wrecks,
Ay, all the wealth that our forefathers hid
Within the massy entrails of the earth:
Then tell me, Faustus, what shall we three want?

FAUSTUS: Nothing, Cornelius. O, this cheers my
soul!
Come, show me some demonstrations magical,
That I may conjure in some lusty grove,
And have these joys in full possession.

VALDES: Then haste thee to some solitary grove,
And bear wise Bacon's and Albertus' works,[12]
The Hebrew Psalter, and New Testament;
And whatsoever else is requisite
We will inform thee ere our conference cease.

CORNELIUS: Valdes, first let him know the words
of art;
And then, all other ceremonies learn'd,
Faustus may try his cunning by himself.

VALDES: First I'll instruct thee in the rudiments,
And then wilt thou be perfecter than I.

FAUSTUS: Then come and dine with me, and, after
meat,
We'll canvass every quiddity[13] thereof;
For, ere I sleep, I'll try what I can do:
This night I'll conjure, though I die therefore.

[Exeunt]

SCENE II.

Before Faustus' *house.*

[*Enter two* Scholars]

1ST SCHOLAR: I wonder what's become of Faustus,
that was wont to make our schools ring with *sic
probo.*[14]

2ND SCHOLAR: That shall we know, for see, here
comes his boy.

[*Enter* Wagner]

[11] Philip II of Spain, who sent the Armada against
England.
[12] Roger Bacon, the thirteenth-century philosopher who
combined theological with scholastic interests; Albertus
Magnus, the famous medieval philosopher.
[13] Every fine shade of meaning.
[14] "Thus I prove."

1ST SCHOLAR: How now, sirrah! where's thy
master?

WAGNER: God in heaven knows.

2ND SCHOLAR: Why, does not thou know?

WAGNER: Yes, I know; but that follows not.

1ST SCHOLAR: Go to, sirrah! leave your jesting, and
tell us where he is.

WAGNER: That follows not necessary by force of
argument, that you, being licentiates, should stand
upon: therefore acknowledge your error, and be attentive.

2ND SCHOLAR: Well, you will not tell thou knewest?

WAGNER: Have you any witness on't?

1ST SCHOLAR: Yes, sirrah, I heard you.

WAGNER: Ask my fellow if I be a thief.

2ND SCHOLAR: Well, you will not tell us?

WAGNER: Yes, sir, I will tell you; yet, if you were
not dunces, you would never ask me such a question,
for is not he *corpus naturale?* and is not that *mobile?*[15]
then wherefore should you ask me such a question?
But that I am by nature phlegmatic, slow to wrath,
and prone to lechery (to love, I would say), it were
not for you to come within forty foot of the place
of execution, although I do not doubt to see you both
hanged the next sessions. Thus having triumphed
over you, I will set my countenance like a precisian,
and begin to speak thus:—Truly, my dear brethren,
my master is within at dinner, with Valdes and Cornelius, as this wine, if it could speak, would inform
your worships: and so, the Lord bless you, preserve
you, and keep you, my dear brethren, my dear
brethren!

[*Exit*]

1ST SCHOLAR: Nay, then, I fear he has fallen into
that damned art for which they two are infamous
through the world.

2ND SCHOLAR: Were he a stranger, and not allied
to me, yet should I grieve for him. But, come, let us
go and inform the Rector, and see if he by his grave
counsel can reclaim him.

1ST SCHOLAR: O, but I fear me nothing can reclaim
him!

2ND SCHOLAR: You let us try what we can do.

[*Exeunt*]

SCENE III.

A grove.

[*Enter* Faustus *to conjure*]

FAUSTUS: Now that the gloomy shadow of the
earth,
Longing to view Orion's drizzling look,
Leaps from th' antarctic world unto the sky,
And dims the welkin with her pitchy breath,
Faustus, begin thine incantations,

[15] For is not he "physical body" and is not that
"movable"?

And try if devils will obey thy hest,
Seeing thou hast pray'd and sacrific'd to them.
Within this circle is Jehovah's name,
Forward and backward anagrammatis'd,
Th' abbreviated names of holy saints,
Figures of every adjunct to the heavens,
And characters of signs and erring stars,
By which the spirits are enforc'd to rise:
Then fear not, Faustus, but be resolute,
And try the uttermost magic can perform.—
    Sint mihi dei Acherontis propitii! Valeat numen
triplex Jehovæ! Ignei, aërii, aquatani spiritus, salvete!
Orientis princeps Belzebub, inferni ardentis monarcha,
et Demogorgon, propitiamus vos, ut appareat et sur-
gat Mephistophilis. Quid tu moraris? Per Jehovam,
Gehennam, et consecratum aquam quam nunc
spargo, signumque crucis quod nunc facio, et per
vota nostra, ipse nunc surgat nobis dicatus Mephis-
tophilis![16]
    [*Enter* Mephistophilis]
I charge thee to return, and change thy shape;
Thou art too ugly to attend on me:
Go, and return an old Franciscan friar;
That holy shape becomes a devil best.
    [*Exit* Mephistophilis]
I see there's virtue in my heavenly words:
Who would not be proficient in this art?
How pliant is this Mephistophilis,
Full of obedience and humility!
Such is the force of magic and my spells:
No, Faustus, thou art conjuror laureat,
That canst command great Mephistophilis.
    [*Reënter* Mephistophilis *like a Franciscan friar*]
    MEPHISTOPHILIS: Now, Faustus, what wouldst
      thou have me do?
    FAUSTUS: I charge thee wait upon me whilst I live,
To do whatever Faustus shall command,
Be it to make the moon drop from her sphere,
Or the ocean to overwhelm the world.
    MEPHISTOPHILIS: I am a servant to great Lucifer,
And may not follow thee without his leave;
No more than he commands must we perform.
    FAUSTUS: Did not he charge thee to appear to me?
    MEPHISTOPHILIS: No, I came hither of mine own
      accord.
    FAUSTUS: Did not my conjuring speeches raise
      thee? speak.
    MEPHISTOPHILIS: That was the cause, but yet *per*
      accidens;
For, when we hear one rack the name of God,
Abjure the Scriptures and his Saviour Christ,

We fly, in hope, to get his glorious soul;
Nor will we come, unless he use such means
Whereby he is in danger to be damn'd.
Therefore the shortest cut for conjuring
Is stoutly to abjure the Trinity,
And pray devoutly to the prince of hell.
    FAUSTUS: So Faustus hath
Already done; and holds this principle,
There is no chief but only Belzebub;
To whom Faustus doth dedicate himself.
This word "damnation" terrifies not him,
For he confounds hell in Elysium:
His ghost be with the old philosophers!
But, leaving these vain trifles of men's souls,
Tell me what is that Lucifer thy lord?
    MEPHISTOPHILIS: Arch-regent and commander of
      all spirits.
    FAUSTUS: Was not that Lucifer an angel once?
    MEPHISTOPHILIS: Yes, Faustus, and most dearly
      lov'd of God.
    FAUSTUS: How comes it, then, that he is prince
      of devils?
    MEPHISTOPHILIS: O, by aspiring pride and inso-
      lence;
For which God threw him from the face of heaven.
    FAUSTUS: And what are you that live with Lucifer?
    MEPHISTOPHILIS: Unhappy spirits that fell with
      Lucifer?
Conspir'd against our God with Lucifer,
And are for ever damn'd with Lucifer.
    FAUSTUS: Where are you damn'd?
    MEPHISTOPHILIS: In hell.
    FAUSTUS: How comes it, then, that thou art out of
      hell?
    MEPHISTOPHILIS: Why, this is hell, nor am I out
      of it.
Think'st thou that I, who saw the face of God,
And tasted the eternal joys of heaven,
Am not tormented with ten thousand hells,
In being depriv'd of everlasting bliss?
O, Faustus, leave these frivolous demands,
Which strike a terror to my fainting soul!
    FAUSTUS: What, is great Mephistophilis so pas-
      sionate
For being deprived of the joys of heaven?
Learn thou of Faustus manly fortitude
And scorn those joys thou never shalt possess.
Go bear these tidings to great Lucifer:
Seeing Faustus hath incurr'd eternal death
By desperate thoughts against Jove's deity,
Say, he surrenders up to him his soul,
So he will spare him four-and-twenty years,
Letting him live in all voluptuousness;
Having thee ever to attend on me,
To give me whatsoever I shall ask,
To tell me whatsoever I demand,
To slay mine enemies, and aid my friends,
And always be obedient to my will.
Go and return to mighty Lucifer,
And meet me in my study at midnight,

[16] "May the gods of Acheron be propitious to me!
May the tripartite [or three-formed] deity of Jehovah
prevail! Hail, spirits of fire, air, water! Prince of the East,
Belzebub, monarch of burning Hell, and Demogorgon, we
appease you, in order that Mephistophilis may appear
and rise. Why do you delay? By Jehovah, Gehenna, and
the holy water which I now sprinkle, and the sign of the
cross that I now make, and through our prayer, let
Mephistophilis, as summoned by us, arise at once!"

And then resolve me of thy master's mind.

MEPHISTOPHILIS: I will, Faustus.

[*Exit*]

FAUSTUS: Had I as many souls as there be stars,
I'd give them all for Mephistophilis.
By him I'll be great emperor of the world,
And make a bridge through the moving air,
To pass the ocean with a band of men;
I'll join the hills that bind the Afric shore,
And make that country continent to Spain,
And both contributory to my crown:
The Emperor shall not live but by my leave,
Nor any potentate of Germany.
Now that I have obtained what I desir'd,
I'll live in speculation of this art,
Till Mephistophilis return again.

[*Exit*]

SCENE IV.

A street.

[*Enter* Wagner *and* Clown]

WAGNER: Sirrah boy, come hither.

CLOWN: How, boy! swowns, boy! I hope you have seen many boys with such pickadevaunts as I have: boy, quotha!

WAGNER: Tell me, sirrah, hast thou any comings in?

CLOWN: Ay, and goings out too; you may see else.

WAGNER: Alas, poor slave! see how poverty jesteth in his nakedness! the villain is bare and out of service, and so hungry, that I know he would give his soul to the devil for a shoulder of mutton, though it were blood-raw.

CLOWN: How! my soul to the devil for a shoulder of mutton, though 'twere blood-raw! not so, good friend: by'r lady, I had need have it well roasted, and good sauce to it, if I pay so dear.

WAGNER: Well, wilt thou serve me, and I'll make thee go like *Qui mihi discipulus.*[17]

CLOWN: How, in verse?

WAGNER: No, sirrah; in beaten silk and staves-acre.

CLOWN: How, how, knaves-acre! ay, I thought that was all the land his father left him. Do you hear? I would be sorry to rob you of your living.

WAGNER: Sirrah, I say in staves-acre.

CLOWN: Oho, oho, staves-acre! why, then, belike, I were your man, I should be full of vermin.

WAGNER: So thou shalt, whether thou beest with me or no. But, sirrah, leave your jesting, and bind yourself presently unto me for seven years, or I'll turn all the lice about thee into familiars, and they shall tear thee in pieces.

CLOWN: Do you hear, sir? you may save that labour; they are too familiar with me already:

[17] An old Latin song.

swowns, they are as bold with my flesh as if they had paid for their meat and drink.

WAGNER: Well, do you hear, sirrah? hold, take these guilders.

[*Gives money*]

CLOWN: Gridirons! what be they?

WAGNER: Why, French crowns.

CLOWN: Mass, but for the name of French crowns, a man were as good have as many English counters. And what should I do with these?

WAGNER: Why, now, sirrah, thou art at an hour's warning, whensoever and wheresoever the devil shall fetch thee.

CLOWN: No, no; here, take your gridirons again.

WAGNER: Truly, I'll none of them.

CLOWN: Truly, but you shall.

WAGNER: Bear witness I gave them him.

CLOWN: Bear witness I give them you again.

WAGNER: Well, I will cause two devils presently to fetch thee away—Baliol and Belcher!

CLOWN: Let your Baliol and your Belcher come here, and I'll knock them, they were never so knocked since they were devils: say I should kill one of them, what would folks say? "Do ye see yonder tall fellow in the round slop? he has killed the devil." So I should be called Kill-devil all the parish over.

[*Enter two* Devils; *and the* Clown *runs up and down crying*]

WAGNER: Baliol and Belcher,—spirits, away!

[*Exeunt* Devils]

CLOWN: What, are they gone? a vengeance on them! they have vile long nails. There was a he-devil and a she-devil: I'll tell you how you shall know them; all he-devils has horns, and all she-devils has cloven feet.

WAGNER: Well, sirrah, follow me.

CLOWN: But, do you hear? if I should serve you, would you teach me to raise up Banios and Belcheos?

WAGNER: I will teach thee to turn thyself to anything, to a dog, or a cat, or a mouse, or a rat, or anything.

CLOWN: How! a Christian fellow to a dog, or a cat, a mouse, or a rat! no, no, sir; if you turn me into anything, let it be in the likeness of a little pretty frisking flea, that I may be here and there and everywhere.

WAGNER: Well, sirrah, come.

CLOWN: But, do you hear, Wagner?

WAGNER: How!—Baliol and Belcher!

CLOWN: O Lord! I pray, sir, let Banio and Belcher go sleep.

WAGNER: Villain, call me Master Wagner, and let thy left eye be diametarily fixed upon my right heel, with *quasi vestigias nostras insistere.*[18]

[*Exit*]

CLOWN: God forgive me, he speaks Dutch fustian. Well, I'll follow him; I'll serve him, that's flat.

[*Exit*]

[18] "As if to follow our footsteps."

SCENE V.

Faustus *discovered in his study.*

FAUSTUS: Now, Faustus, must
Thou needs be damn'd and canst thou not be
   sav'd:
What boots it, then, to think of God or heaven?
Away with such vain fancies, and despair;
Despair in God, and trust in Belzebub:
Now go not backward; no, Faustus, be resolute:
Why waver'st thou? O, something soundeth in mine
   ears,
"Abjure this magic, turn to God again!"
Ay, and Faustus will turn to God again.
To God? he loves thee not;
The god thou serv'st is thine own appetite,
Wherein is fix'd the love of Belzebub:
To him I'll build an altar and a church,
And offer lukewarm blood of new-born babes.
   [*Enter* Good Angel *and* Evil Angel]
   GOOD ANGEL: Sweet Faustus, leave that execrable
     art.
   FAUSTUS: Contrition, prayer, repentance—what of
     them?
   GOOD ANGEL: O, they are means to bring thee unto
     heaven!
   EVIL ANGEL: Rather illusions, fruits of lunacy,
That make men foolish that do trust them most.
   GOOD ANGEL: Sweet Faustus, think of heaven and
     heavenly things.
   EVIL ANGEL: No, Faustus; think of honour and of
     wealth.
   [*Exeunt* Angels]
   FAUSTUS: Of wealth!
Why, the signiory of Embden shall be mine.
When Mephistophilis shall stand by me,
What god can hurt thee, Faustus? thou art safe:
Cast no more doubts.—Come, Mephistophilis,
And bring glad tidings from great Lucifer;—
Is't not midnight?—come, Mephistophilis,
Veni, veni Mephistophile!
   [*Enter* Mephistophilis]
Now tell me what says Lucifer, thy lord?
   MEPHISTOPHILIS: That I shall wait on **Faustus**
     whilst he lives,
So he will buy my service with his soul.
   FAUSTUS: Already Faustus hath hazarded that for
     thee.
   MEPHISTOPHILIS: But, Faustus, thou must bequeath
     it solemnly,
And write a deed of gift with thine own blood;
For that security craves great Lucifer.
If thou deny it, I will back to hell.
   FAUSTUS: Stay, Mephistophilis, and tell me, what
     good will my soul do thy lord?
   MEPHISTOPHILIS: Enlarge his kingdom.
   FAUSTUS: Is that the reason why he tempts us
     thus?

   MEPHISTOPHILIS: *Solamen miseris socios habuisse*
     doloris.[19]
   FAUSTUS: Why, have you any pain that torture
     others!
   MEPHISTOPHILIS: As great as have the human souls
     of men.
But, tell me, Faustus, shall I have thy soul?
And I will be thy slave, and wait on thee,
And give thee more than thou hast wit to ask.
   FAUSTUS: Ay, Mephistophilis, I give it thee.
   MEPHISTOPHILIS: Then, Faustus, stab thy arm
     courageously,
And bind thy soul, that at some certain day
Great Lucifer may claim it as his own;
And then be thou as great as Lucifer.
   FAUSTUS: [*Stabbing his arm*] Lo, Mephistophilis,
     for love of thee
I cut mine arm, and with my proper blood
Assure my soul to be great Lucifer's,
Chief lord and regent of perpetual night!
View here the blood that trickles from mine arm,
And let it be propitious for my wish.
   MEPHISTOPHILIS: But, Faustus, thou must
Write it in manner of a deed of gift.
   FAUSTUS: Ay, so I will. [*Writes*] But, Mephis-
     tophilis,
My blood congeals, and I can write no more.
   MEPHISTOPHILIS: I'll fetch thee fire to dissolve it
     straight.
   [*Exit*]
   FAUSTUS: Why might the staying of my blood por-
     tend?
Is it unwilling I should write this bill?
Why streams it not, that I may write afresh?
Faustus gives to thee his soul: ah, there it stay'd!
Why shouldst thou not? is not thy soul thine
   own?
Then write again, *Faustus gives to thee his soul.*
   [*Reënter* Mephistophilis *with a chafer of coals*]
   MEPHISTOPHILIS: Here's fire; come, Faustus, set it
     on.
   FAUSTUS: So, now the blood begins to clear again;
Now will I make an end immediately.
   [*Writes*]
   MEPHISTOPHILIS: [*Aside*] O, what will not I do to
     obtain his soul!
   FAUSTUS: *Consummatum est;* this bill is ended,
And Faustus hath bequeathed his soul to Lucifer.
But what is this inscription on mine arm?
Homo, fuge: whither should I fly?
If unto God, he'll throw me down to hell.
My senses are deceiv'd; here's nothing writ:—
I see it plain; here in this place is writ,
Homo, fuge: yet shall not Faustus fly.
   MEPHISTOPHILIS: [*Aside*] I'll fetch him somewhat
     to delight his mind.
   [*Exit*]
   [*Reënter* Mephistophilis *with* Devils, *who give*

[19] "It is a comfort to the wretched to have companions
in their grief"—i.e., "Misery loves company."

crowns and rich apparel to Faustus, *dance, and then depart*]

FAUSTUS: Speak, Mephistophilis, what means this show?

MEPHISTOPHILIS: Nothing, Faustus, but to delight thy mind withal,

And to show thee what magic can perform.

FAUSTUS: But may I raise up spirits when I please?

MEPHISTOPHILIS: Ay, Faustus, and do greater things than these.

FAUSTUS: Then there's enough for a thousand souls.

Here, Mephistophilis, receive this scroll,
A deed of gift of body and of soul:
But yet conditionally that thou perform
All articles prescrib'd between us both.

MEPHISTOPHILIS: Faustus, I swear by hell and Lucifer

To effect all promises between us made!

FAUSTUS: Then hear me read them. [*Reads*] On these conditions following. First, that Faustus may be a spirit in form and substance. Secondly, that Mephistophilis shall be his servant, and at his command. Thirdly, that Mephistophilis shall do for him, and bring him whatsoever he desires. Fourthly, that he shall be in his chamber or house invisible. Lastly, that he shall appear to the said John Faustus, at all times, in what form or shape soever he please. I, John Faustus, of Wittenberg, Doctor, by these presents, do give both body and soul to Lucifer prince of the east, and his minister Mephistophilis: and furthermore grant unto them, that, twenty-four years being expired, the articles above-written inviolate, full power to fetch or carry the said John Faustus, body and soul, flesh, blood, or goods, into their habitation wheresoever. By me, John Faustus.

MEPHISTOPHILIS: Speak, Faustus, do you deliver this as your deed?

FAUSTUS: Ay, take it, and the devil give thee good on't!

MEPHISTOPHILIS: Now, Faustus, ask what thou wilt.

FAUSTUS: First will I question with thee about hell.
Tell me, where is the place that men call hell?

MEPHISTOPHILIS: Under the heavens.

FAUSTUS: Ay, but whereabout?

MEPHISTOPHILIS: Within the bowels of these elements,

Where we are tortur'd and remain for ever:
Hell hath no limits, nor is circumscrib'd
In one self place; for where we are is hell,
And where hell is, there must we ever be:
And, to conclude, when all the world dissolves,
And every creature shall be purified,
All places shall be hell that are not heaven.

FAUSTUS: Come, I think hell's a fable.

MEPHISTOPHILIS: Ay, think so still, till experience change thy mind.

FAUSTUS: Why, think'st thou, then, that Faustus shall be damn'd?

MEPHISTOPHILIS: Ay, of necessity, for here's the scroll

Wherein thou hast given thy soul to Lucifer.

FAUSTUS: Ay, and body too: but what of that?
Think'st thou that Faustus is so fond to imagine
That, after this life, there is any pain?
Tush, these are trifles and mere old wives' tales.

MEPHISTOPHILIS: But, Faustus, I am an instance to prove the contrary

For I am damn'd, and am now in hell.

FAUSTUS: How! now in hell!
Nay, an this be hell, I'll willingly be damn'd here:
What! walking, disputing, etc.
But, leaving off this, let me have a wife,
The fairest maid in Germany.

MEPHISTOPHILIS: How! a wife!
I prithee, Faustus, talk not of a wife.

FAUSTUS: Nay, sweet Mephistophilis, fetch me one, for I will have one.

MEPHISTOPHILIS: Well, thou wilt have one? Sit there till I come: I'll fetch thee a wife in the devil's name.

[*Exit*]

[*Reënter* Mephistophilis *with a* Devil *drest like a woman, with fireworks*]

MEPHISTOPHILIS: Tell me, Faustus, how dost thou like thy wife:

FAUSTUS: A plague on her!

MEPHISTOPHILIS: Tut, Faustus,
Marriage is but a ceremonial toy;
If thou lovest me, think no more of it.
She whom thine eyes shall like, thy heart shall have,
Be she as chaste as was Penelope,
As wise as Saba, or as beautiful
As was bright Lucifer before his fall.
Hold, take this book, peruse it thoroughly:
[*Gives book*]
The iterating of these lines brings gold;
The framing of this circle on the ground
Brings whirlwinds, tempests, thunder, and lightning;
Pronounce this thrice devoutly to thyself,
And men in armour shall appear to thee,
Ready to execute what thou desir'st.

FAUSTUS: Thanks, Mephistophilis: yet fain would I have a book wherein I might behold all spells and incantations, that I might raise up spirits when I please.

MEPHISTOPHILIS: Here they are in this book.
[*Turns to them*]

FAUSTUS: Now would I have a book where I might see all characters and planets of the heavens, that I might know their motions and dispositions.

MEPHISTOPHILIS: Here they are too.
[*Turns to them*]

FAUSTUS: Nay, let me have one book more,—and then I have done,—wherein I might see all plants, herbs and trees, that grow upon the earth.

MEPHISTOPHILIS: Here they be.

FAUSTUS: O, thou art deceived.

MEPHISTOPHILIS: Tut, I warrant thee.
[*Turns to them. Exeunt*]

SCENE VI.

A room in Faustus' *house.*

FAUSTUS: When I behold the heavens, then I repent,
And curse thee, wicked Mephistophilis,
Because thou hast depriv'd me of those joys.
MEPHISTOPHILIS: Why, Faustus,
Thinkest thou heaven is such a glorious thing?
I tell thee, 'tis not half so fair as thou,
Or any man that breathes on earth.
FAUSTUS: How prov'st thou that?
MEPHISTOPHILIS: 'Twas made for man, therefore is man more excellent.
FAUSTUS: If it were made for man, 'twas made for me:
I will renounce this magic and repent.
[*Enter* Good Angel *and* Evil Angel]
GOOD ANGEL: Faustus, repent; yet God will pity thee.
EVIL ANGEL: Thou art a spirit; God cannot pity thee.
FAUSTUS: Who buzzeth in mine ears I am a spirit?
Be I a devil, yet God may pity me;
Ay, God will pity me, if I repent.
EVIL ANGEL: Ay, but Faustus never shall repent.
[*Exeunt* Angels]
FAUSTUS: My heart's so harden'd, I cannot repent:
Scarce can I name salvation, faith, or heaven,
But fearful echoes thunder in mine ears,
"Faustus, thou art damn'd!" then swords, and knives,
Poison, guns, halters, and envenom'd steel
Are laid before me to despatch myself;
And long ere this I should have slain myself,
Had not sweet pleasure conquer'd deep despair.
Have not I made blind Homer sing to me
Of Alexander's love and Œnon's death?
And hath not he, that built the walls of Thebes
With ravishing sound of his melodious harp,
Made music with my Mephistophilis?
Why should I die, then, or basely despair!
I am resolv'd; Faustus shall ne'er repent.—
Come, Mephistophilis, let us dispute again,
And argue of divine astrology.
Tell me, are there many heavens above the moon?
Are all celestial bodies but one globe,
As is the substance of this centric earth?
MEPHISTOPHILIS: As are the elements, such are the spheres,
Mutually folded in each other's orb,
And, Faustus,
All jointly move upon one axletree,
Whose terminus is term'd the world's wide pole;
Nor are the names of Saturn, Mars, or Jupiter
Feign'd, but are erring stars.

FAUSTUS: But, tell me, have they all one motion, both *situ et tempore?*[20]
MEPHISTOPHILIS: All jointly move from east to west in twenty-four hours upon the poles of the world; but differ in their motion upon the poles of the zodiac.
FAUSTUS: Tush,
These slender trifles Wagner can decide:
Hath Mephistophilis no greater skill?
Who knows not the double motion of the planets?
The first is finish'd in a natural day;
The second thus; as Saturn in thirty years; Jupiter in twelve; Mars in four; the Sun, Venus, and Mercury in a year; the Moon in twenty-eight days. Tush, these are freshmen's suppositions. But, tell me, hath every sphere a dominion or *intelligentia?*
MEPHISTOPHILIS: Ay.
FAUSTUS: How many heavens or spheres are there?
MEPHISTOPHILIS: Nine; the seven planets, the firmament, and the empyreal heaven.
FAUSTUS: Well resolve me in this question; why have we not conjunctions, oppositions, aspects, eclipses, all at one time, but in some years we have more, in some less?
MEPHISTOPHILIS: *Per inæqualem motum respecta totius.*[21]
FAUSTUS: Well, I am answered. Tell me who made the world?
MEPHISTOPHILIS: I will not.
FAUSTUS: Sweet Mephistophilis, tell me.
MEPHISTOPHILIS: Move me not, for I will not tell thee.
FAUSTUS: Villain, have I not bound thee to tell me anything?
MEPHISTOPHILIS: Ay, that is not against our kingdom; but this is.
Think thou on hell, Faustus, for thou art damned.
FAUSTUS: Think, Faustus, upon God that made the world.
MEPHISTOPHILIS: Remember this.
[*Exit*]
FAUSTUS: Ay, go, accursed spirit, to ugly hell!
'Tis thou hast damn'd distressed Faustus' soul.
Is't not too late?
[*Reënter* Good Angel *and* Evil Angel]
EVIL ANGEL: Too late.
GOOD ANGEL: Never too late, if Faustus can repent.
EVIL ANGEL: If thou repent, devils shall tear thee in pieces.
GOOD ANGEL: Repent, and they shall never raze thy skin.
[*Exeunt* Angels]
FAUSTUS: Ah, Christ, my Saviour,
Seek to save distressed Faustus' soul!
[*Enter* Lucifer, Belzebub, *and* Mephistophilis]
LUCIFER: Christ cannot save thy soul, for he is just:

[20] "In place and time."
[21] "Because of their unequal motion in relation to the whole."

There's none but I have interest in the same.

FAUSTUS: O, who are thou that look'st so terrible?

LUCIFER: I am Lucifer.
And this is my companion-prince in hell.

FAUSTUS: O, Faustus, they are come to fetch away thy soul!

LUCIFER: We come to tell thee thou dost injure us;
Thou talk'st of Christ, contrary to thy promise:
Thou shouldst not think of God: think of the devil,
And of his dam too.

FAUSTUS: Nor will I henceforth: pardon me in this,
And Faustus vows never to look to heaven,
Never to name God, or to pray to Him,
To burn his Scriptures, slay his ministers,
And make my spirits pull his churches down.

LUCIFER: Do so, and we will highly gratify thee.
Faustus, we are come from hell to show thee some pastime: sit down, and thou shalt see all the Seven Deadly Sins appear in their proper shapes.

FAUSTUS: That sight will be as pleasing unto me,
As Paradise was to Adam, the first day
Of his creation.

LUCIFER: Talk not of Paradise nor creation; but mark this show: talk of the devil, and nothing else.—Come away!

[*Enter the* Seven Deadly Sins]

Now, Faustus, examine them of their several names and dispositions.

FAUSTUS: What art thou, the first?

PRIDE: I am Pride. I disdain to have any parents. But, fie, what a scent is here! I'll not speak another word, except the ground were perfumed, and covered with cloth of arras.

FAUSTUS: What art thou, the second?

COVETOUSNESS: I am Covetousness, begotten of an old churl, in an old leathern bag: and, might I have my wish, I would desire that this house and all the people in it were turned to gold, that I might lock you up in my good chest: O, my sweet gold!

FAUSTUS: What art thou, the third?

WRATH: I am Wrath. I had neither father nor mother: I leapt out of a lion's mouth when I was scarce half an hour old; and ever since I have run up and down the world with this case of rapiers, wounding myself when I had nobody to fight withal. I was born in hell; and look to it, for some of you shall be my father.

FAUSTUS: What art thou, the fourth?

ENVY: I am Envy, begotten of a chimney-sweeper and an oyster-wife. I cannot read, and therefore wish all books were burnt. I am lean with seeing others eat. O, that there would come a famine through all the world, that all might die, and I live alone! then thou shouldst see how fat I would be. But must thou sit, and I stand? come down, with a vengeance!

FAUSTUS: Away, envious rascal!—What art thou, the fifth?

GLUTTONY: Who, I, sir? I am Gluttony. My parents are all dead, and the devil a penny they have left me, but a bare pension, and that is thirty meals a day, and ten bevers,[22]—a small trifle to suffice nature. O, I come of a royal parentage! my grandfather was a Gammon of Bacon, my grandmother a Hogshead of Claret-wine; my godfathers were these, Peter Pickle-herring and Martin Martlemas-beef; O, but my godmother, she was a jolly gentlewoman, and well-beloved in every good town and city; her name was Mistress Margery March-beer. Now, Faustus, thou hast heard all my progeny; wilt thou bid me to supper?

FAUSTUS: No, I'll see thee hanged: thou wilt eat up all my victuals.

GLUTTONY: Then the devil choke thee!

FAUSTUS: Choke thyself, glutton!—What art thou, the sixth?

SLOTH: I am Sloth. I was begotten on a sunny bank, where I have lain ever since; and you have done me great injury to bring me from thence: let me be carried thither again by Gluttony and Lechery. I'll not speak another word for a king's ransom.

FAUSTUS: What are you, Mistress Minx, the seventh and last?

LECHERY: Who, I, sir? I am one that loves an inch of raw mutton better than an ell of fried stock-fish; and the first letter of my name begins with L.

FAUSTUS: Away, to hell, to hell!

[*Exeunt the* Sins]

LUCIFER: Now, Faustus, how dost thou like this?

FAUSTUS: O, this feeds my soul!

LUCIFER: Tut, Faustus, in hell is all manner of delight.

FAUSTUS: O, might I see hell, and return again,
How happy were I then!

LUCIFER: Thou shalt; I will send for thee at midnight.
In meantime take this book; peruse it thoroughly,
And thou shalt turn thyself into what shape thou wilt.

FAUSTUS: Great thanks, mighty Lucifer!
This will I keep as chary as my life.

LUCIFER: Farewell, Faustus, and think on the devil.

FAUSTUS: Farewell, great Lucifer.

[*Exeunt* Lucifer *and* Belzebub]

Come, Mephistophilis.

[*Exeunt*]

[*Enter* Chorus]

CHORUS: Learned Faustus,
To know the secrets of astronomy
Graven in the book of Jove's high firmament,
Did mount himself to scale Olympus' top,
Being seated in a chariot burning bright,
Drawn by the strength of yoky dragons' necks
He now is gone to prove cosmography,
And, as I guess, will first arrive in Rome,
To see the Pope and manner of his court,
And take some part of holy Peter's feast,

[22] Refreshments.

That to this day is highly solemnis'd.
   [*Exit*]

SCENE VII.

The Pope's *privy-chamber.*

[*Enter* Faustus *and* Mephistophilis]
FAUSTUS: Having now, my good Mephistophilis,
Pass'd with delight the stately town of Trier,
Environ'd round with airy mountaintops,
With walls of flint, and deep-entrenched lakes,
Not to be won by any conquering prince;
From Paris next, coasting the realm of France,
We saw the river Maine fall into Rhine,
Whose banks are set with groves of fruitful vines;
Then up to Naples, rich Campania,
Whose buildings fair and gorgeous to the eye,
The streets straight forth, and pav'd with finest brick,
Quarter the town in four equivalents:
There saw we learned Maro's golden tomb,
The way he cut, an English mile in length,
Through a rock of stone, in one night's space;
From thence to Venice, Padua, and the rest,
In one of which a sumptuous temple stands,
That threats the stars with her aspiring top.
Thus hitherto hath Faustus spent his time:
But tell me now what resting-place is this?
Hast thou, as erst I did command,
Conducted me within the walls of Rome?
   MEPHISTOPHILIS: Faustus, I have; and, because we
will not be unprovided, I have taken up his Holiness'
privy-chamber for our use.
   FAUSTUS: I hope his Holiness will bid us welcome.
   MEPHISTOPHILIS: Tut, 'tis no matter, man; we'll be
bold with his good cheer.
And now, my Faustus, that thou mayst perceive
What Rome containeth to delight thee with,
Know that this city stands upon seven hills
That underprop the groundwork of the same:
Just through the midst runs flowing Tiber's stream
With winding banks that cut it in two parts;
Over the which four stately bridges lean,
That make safe passage to each part of Rome:
Upon the bridge call'd Ponte Angelo
Erected is a castle passing strong,
Within whose walls such store of ordnance are,
And double cannons fram'd of carved brass,
As match the days within one complete year;
Besides the gates, and high pyramides,
Which Julius Caesar brought from Africa.
   FAUSTUS: Now, by the kingdoms of infernal rule,
Of Styx, of Acheron, and the fiery lake
Of ever-burning Phlegethon, I swear
That I do long to see the monuments
And situation of bright-splendent Rome:
Come, therefore, let's away.
   MEPHISTOPHILIS: Nay, Faustus, stay: I know you'd
    fain to see the Pope

And take some part of holy Peter's feast,
Where thou shalt see a troop of bald-pate friars,
Whose *summum bonum* is in belly-cheer.
   FAUSTUS: Well, I'm content to compass then some
    sport,
And by their folly make us merriment.
Then charm me, that I
May be invisible, to do what I please,
Unseen of any whilst I stay in Rome.
   [Mephistophilis *charms him*]
MEPHISTOPHILIS: So, Faustus; now
Do what thou wilt, thou shalt not be discern'd.
   [*Sound a sennet. Enter the* Pope *and the* Cardinal
    of Lorrain *to the banquet, with* Friars *attending*]
POPE: My lord of Lorrain, will't please you draw
near?
   FAUSTUS: Fall to, and the devil choke you, and you
spare!
   POPE: How now! who's that which spake?—Friars,
look about.
   1ST FRIAR: Here's nobody, if it like your Holiness.
   POPE: My lord, here is a dainty dish was sent me
from the Bishop of Milan.
   FAUSTUS: I thank you, sir.
   [*Snatches the dish*]
POPE: How now! who's that which snatched the
meat from me? will no man look?—My lord, this
dish was sent me from the Cardinal of Florence.
   FAUSTUS: You say true: I'll ha't.
   [*Snatches the dish*]
POPE: What, again!—My lord, I'll drink to your
grace.
   FAUSTUS: I'll pledge your grace.
   [*Snatches the cup*]
CARDINAL OF LORRAIN: My lord, it may be some
ghost, newly crept out of Purgatory, come to beg a
pardon of your Holiness.
   POPE: It may be so.—Friars, prepare a dirge to lay
the fury of this ghost.—Once again, my lord, fall to.
   [*The* Pope *crosses himself*]
FAUSTUS: What, are you crossing of yourself?
Well, use that trick no more, I would advise you.
   [*The* Pope *crosses himself again*]
Well, there's the second time. Aware the third;
I give you fair warning.
   [*The* Pope *crosses himself again, and* Faustus
    *hits him a box on the ear, and they all run
    away*]
Come on, Mephistophilis; what shall we do?
   MEPHISTOPHILIS: Nay, I know not: we shall be
cursed with bell, book, and candle.
   FAUSTUS: How! bell, book, and candle,—candle,
    book, and bell,—
Forward and backward, to curse Faustus to hell!
Anon you shall hear a hog grunt, a calf bleat, and an
    ass bray,
Because it is Saint Peter's holiday.
   [*Reënter all the* Friars *to sing the Dirge*]
1ST FRIAR: Come, brethren, let's about our business
with good devotion.

[*They sing*]

Cursed be he that stole away his Holiness' meat from
the table! *maledicat Dominus!*[23]

Cursed be he that struck his Holiness a blow on the
face! *maledicat Dominus!*

Cursed be he that took Friar Sandelo a blow on the
pate! *maledicat Dominus!*

Cursed be he that disturbeth our holy dirge! *maledicat
Dominus!*

Cursed be he that took away his Holiness' wine!
maledicat Dominus!

      Et omnes Sancti! Amen!

[*Mephistophilis and Faustus beat the Friars, and
fling fireworks among them; and so exeunt*]

[*Enter Chorus*]

CHORUS: When Faustus had with pleasure ta'en
    the view

Of rarest things, and royal courts of kings,
He stay'd his course, and so returned home;
Where such as bear his absence but with grief,
I mean his friends and near'st companions,
Did gratulate his safety with kind words,
And in their conference of what befell,
Touching his journey through the world and air,
They put forth questions of astrology,
Which Faustus answer'd with such learned skill
As they admir'd and wonder'd at his wit.
Now is his fame spread forth in every land:
Amongst the rest the Emperor is one,
Carolus the Fifth, at whose palace now
Faustus is feasted 'mongst his noblemen.
What there he did, in trial of his art,
I leave untold; your eyes shall see ['t] perform'd.

    [*Exit*]

SCENE VIII.

An inn-yard.

[*Enter Robin the Ostler, with a book in his hand*]

ROBIN: O, this is admirable! here I ha' stolen one of
Doctor Faustus' conjuring books, and i'faith, I mean
to search some circles for my own use. Now will I
make all the maidens in our parish dance at my
pleasure.

[*Enter Ralph, calling Robin*]

RALPH: Robin, prithee, come away; there's a
gentleman tarries to have his horse, and he would
have his things rubbed and made clean: he keeps
such a chafing with my mistress about it; and she
has set me to look thee out; prithee, come away.

ROBIN: Keep out, keep out, or else you are blown
up, you are dismembered, Ralph: keep out, for I am
about a roaring piece of work.

RALPH: Come, what doest thou with that same
book? thou canst not read?

ROBIN: Yes, my master and mistress shall find that
I can read, or else my art fails.

[23] "May the Lord curse him!"

RALPH: Why, Robin, what book is that?

ROBIN: What book! why, the most intolerable book
for conjuring that e'er was invented by any brimstone devil.

RALPH: Canst thou conjure with it?

ROBIN: I can do all these things easily with it;
first, I can make ·thee drunk with ippocras[24] at any
tavern in Europe for nothing; that's one of my conjuring works.

RALPH: Our Master Parson says that's nothing.

ROBIN: No more, sweet Ralph: let's go and make
clean our boots, which lie foul upon our hands, and
then to our conjuring in the devil's name.

    [*Exeunt*]

SCENE IX.

[*Enter Robin and Ralph with a silver goblet*]

ROBIN: Come, Ralph: did not I tell thee, we were
for ever made by this Doctor Faustus' book? *ecce,
signum!*[25] here's a simple purchase for horse-keepers:
our horses shall eat no hay as long as this lasts.

RALPH: But, Robin, here comes the Vintner.

ROBIN: Hush! I'll gull him supernaturally.

[*Enter Vintner*]

Drawer, I hope all is paid; God be with you!—Come,
Ralph.

VINTNER: Soft, sir; a word with you. I must yet
have a goblet paid from you, ere you go.

ROBIN: I a goblet, Ralph, I a goblet!—I scorn you;
and you are but a——, etc. I a goblet! search me.

VINTNER: I mean so, sir, with your favour.

    [*Searches Robin*]

ROBIN: How say you now?

VINTNER: I must say somewhat to your fellow.
You, sir!

ROBIN: Me, sir! me, sir! search your fill. [*Vintner
searches him*] Now, sir, you may be ashamed to
burden honest men with a matter of truth.

VINTNER: Well, one of you hath this goblet about
you.

ROBIN: You lie, drawer, 'tis afore me. [*Aside*]—
Sirrah you, I'll teach you to impeach honest men;—
stand by;—I'll scour you for a goblet;—stand aside
you had best, I charge you in the name of Belzebub.
[*Aside to Ralph*]—Look to the goblet, Ralph.

VINTNER: What mean you, sirrah?

ROBIN: I'll tell you what I mean. [*Reads from a
book*] *Sanctobulorum Periphrasticon*—nay, I'll tickle
you, Vintner. [*Aside to Ralph*]—Look to the goblet,
Ralph.—[*Reads*] *Polypragmos Belseborams framanto
pacostiphos tostu, Mephistophilis, etc.*[26]

    [*Enter Mephistophilis, sets squibs*[27] *at their backs,
and then exit. They run about*]

[24] A spiced wine.
[25] "Behold the mark!"
[26] The Latin here is nonsensical.
[27] Firecrackers.

VINTNER: *O nomine Domini!*[28] what meanest thou, Robin! thou hast no goblet.

RALPH: *Peccatum peccatorum!*[29] Here's thy goblet, good Vintner.

[*Gives the goblet to* Vintner, *who exit*]

ROBIN: *Misericordia pro nobis!*[30] what shall I do? Good devil, forgive me now, and I'll never rob thy library more.

[*Reënter* Mephistophilis]

MEPHISTOPHILIS: Monarch of hell, under whose black survey
Great potentates do kneel with awful fear,
Upon whose altars thousand souls do lie,
How am I vexed with these villains' charms?
From Constantinople am I hither come,
Only for pleasure of these damned slaves.

ROBIN: How, from Constantinople! you have had a great journey: will you take sixpence in your purse to pay for your supper, and be gone?

MEPHISTOPHILIS: Well, villains, for your presumption, I transform thee into an ape, and thee into a dog; and so be gone!

[*Exit*]

ROBIN: How, into an ape! that's brave: I'll have fine sport with the boys; I'll get nuts and apples enow.

RALPH: And I must be a dog.

ROBIN: I'faith, thy head will never be out of the pottage-pot.

[*Exeunt*]

SCENE X.

An apartment in the Emperor's *palace.*

[*Enter* Emperor, Faustus, *and a* Knight, *with* Attendants]

EMPEROR: Master Doctor Faustus, I have heard strange report of thy knowedge in the black art, how that none in my empire nor in the whole world can compare with thee for the rare effects of magic: they say thou has a familiar spirit, by whom thou canst accomplish what thou list. This, therefore, is my request, that thou let me see some proof of thy skill, that mine eyes may be witnesses to confirm what mine ears have heard reported: and here I swear to thee, by the honour of mine imperial crown, that, whatever thou doest, thou shalt be no ways prejudiced or endamaged.

KNIGHT: [*Aside*] I'faith, he looks much like a conjurer.

FAUSTUS: My gracious sovereign, though I must confess myself far inferior to the report men have published, and nothing answerable to the honour of your imperial majesty, yet, for that love and duty binds me thereunto, I am content to do whatsoever

28 "In the name of the Lord!"
29 "Sin of sins!"
30 "Mercy on us!"

your majesty shall command me.

EMPEROR: Then, Doctor Faustus, mark what I shall say.
As I was sometime solitary set
Within my closet, sundry thoughts arose
About the honour of mine ancestors,
How they had won by prowess such exploits,
Got such riches, subdu'd so many kingdoms,
As we that do succeed, or they that shall
Hereafter possess our throne, shall
(I fear me) ne'er attain to that degree
Of high renown and great authority:
Amongst which kings is Alexander the Great,
Chief spectacle of the world's pre-eminence,
The bright shining of whose glorious acts
Lightens the world with his reflecting beams,
It grieves my soul I never saw the man:
As when I hear but motion made of him,
If, therefore, thou, by cunning of thine art,
Canst raise this man from hollow vaults below,
Where lies entomb'd this famous conqueror,
And bring with him his beauteous paramour,
Both in their right shapes, gesture, and attire
They us'd to wear during their time of life,
Thou shalt both satisfy my just desire,
And give me cause to praise thee whilst I live.

FAUSTUS: My gracious lord, I am ready to accomplish your request, so far forth as by art and power of my spirit I am able to perform.

KNIGHT: [*Aside*] I'faith, that's just nothing at all.

FAUSTUS: But, if it like your grace, it is not in my ability to present before your eyes the true substantial bodies of those two deceased princes, which long since are consumed to dust.

KNIGHT: [*Aside*] Ay, marry, Master Doctor, now there's a sign of grace in you, when you will confess the truth.

FAUSTUS: But such spirits as can lively resemble Alexander and his paramour shall appear before your grace, in that manner that they both lived in, in their most flourishing estate; which I doubt not shall sufficiently content your imperial majesty.

EMPEROR: Go to, Master Doctor; let me see them presently.

KNIGHT: Do you hear, Master Doctor? you bring Alexander and his paramour before the Emperor!

FAUSTUS: How then, sir?

KNIGHT: I'faith, that's as true as Diana turned me to a stag.

FAUSTUS: Mephistophilis, be gone.

[*Exit* Mephistophilis]

KNIGHT: Nay, an you go to conjuring, I'll be gone.

[*Exit*]

FAUSTUS: I'll meet with you anon for interrupting me so.—Here they are, my gracious lord.

[*Reënter* Mephistophilis *with* Spirits *in the shapes of* Alexander *and his* Paramour]

EMPEROR: Master Doctor, I heard this lady, while she lived, had a wart or mole in her neck: how shall

I know whether it be so or no?

FAUSTUS: Your highness may boldly go and see.

EMPEROR: Sure, these are no spirits, but the true substantial bodies of those two deceased princes.

[*Exeunt* Spirits]

FAUSTUS: Wilt please your highness now to send for the knight that was so pleasant with me here of late?

EMPEROR: One of you call him forth.

[*Exit* Attendant]

[*Reënter the* Knight *with a pair of horns on his head*]

How now, sir knight! Feel on thy head.

KNIGHT: Thou damned wretch and execrable dog,
Bred in the concave of some monstrous rock,
How dar'st thou thus abuse a gentleman?
Villain, I say, undo what thou hast done!

FAUSTUS: O, not so fast, sir! there's no haste: but, good, are you remembered how you crossed me in my conference with the Emperor? I think I have met with you for it.

EMPEROR: Good Master Doctor, at my entreaty release him: he hath done penance sufficient.

FAUSTUS: My gracious lord, not so much for the injury he offereth me here in your presence, as to delight you with some mirth, hath Faustus worthily requited this injurious knight; which being all I desire, I am content to release him of his horns:—and, sir knight, hereafter speak well of scholars. Mephistophilis, transform him straight. [Mephistophilis *removes the horns*]—Now, my good lord, having done my duty, I humbly take my leave.

EMPEROR: Farewell, Master Doctor: yet, ere you go,
Expect from me a bounteous reward.

[*Exeunt* Emperor, Knight, *and* Attendants]

SCENE XI.

A fair and pleasant green.

FAUSTUS: Now, Mephistophilis, the restless course
That time doth run with calm and silent foot,
Shortening my days and thread of vital life,
Calls for the payment of my latest years:
Therefore, sweet Mephistophilis, let us
Make haste to Wittenberg.

MEPHISTOPHILIS: What, will you go on horseback or on foot?

FAUSTUS: Nay, till I'm past this fair and pleasant green, I'll walk on foot.

SCENE XII.

In or near the home of Faustus.

[*Enter a* Horse-Courser]

HORSE-COURSER: I have been all this day seeking one Master Fustian: mass, see where he is!—God save you, Master Doctor!

FAUSTUS: What, Horse-Courser! you are well met.

HORSE-COURSER: Do you hear, sir? I have brought you forty dollars for your horse.

FAUSTUS: I cannot sell him so: if thou likest him for fifty, take him.

HORSE-COURSER: Alas, sir, I have no more!—I pray you, speak for me.

MEPHISTOPHILIS: I pray you, let him have him: he is an honest fellow, and he has a great charge, neither wife nor child.

FAUSTUS: Well, come, give me your money [Horse-courser *gives* Faustus *the money*]: my boy will deliver him to you. But I must tell you one thing before you have him; ride him not into the water, at any hand.

HORSE-COURSER: Why, sir, will he not drink of all waters?

FAUSTUS: O, yes, he will drink of all waters; but ride him not into the water; ride him over hedge or ditch, or where thou wilt, but not into the water.

HORSE-COURSER: Well, sir.—Now am I made man for ever: I'll not leave my horse for forty: if he had but the quality of hey-ding-ding, hey-ding-ding, I'd make a brave living on him: he has a buttock as slick as an eel. [*Aside*]—Well, God b'wi'ye, sir: your boy will deliver him me: but, hark you, sir; if my horse be sick or ill at ease, you'll tell me what it is?

FAUSTUS: Away, you villain! what, dost think I am a horse-doctor?

[*Exit* Horse-Courser]

What art thou, Faustus, but a man condemn'd to die?
Thy fatal time doth draw to final end;
Despair doth drive distrust into my thoughts:
Confound these passions with a quiet sleep:
Tush, Christ did call the thief upon the Cross;
Then rest thee, Faustus, quiet in conceit.

[*Sleeps in his chair*]

[*Reënter* Horse-Courser, *all wet, crying*]

HORSE-COURSER: Alas, alas! Doctor Fustian, quotha? mass, Doctor Lopus was never such a doctor: has given me a purgation, has purged me of forty dollars; I shall never see them more. But yet, like an ass as I was, I would not be ruled by him, for he bade me I should ride him into no water: now I, thinking my horse had had some rare quality that he would not have had me know of, I, like a venturous youth, rid him into the deep pond at the town's end. I was no sooner in the middle of the pond, but my horse vanished away, and I sat upon a bottle of hay, never so near drowning in my life. But I'll seek out my doctor, and have my forty dollars again, or I'll make it the dearest horse!—O, yonder is his snipper-snapper. Do you hear? you, hey-pass, where's your master?

MEPHISTOPHILIS: Why, sir, what would you? you cannot speak with him.

HORSE-COURSER: But I will speak with him.

MEPHISTOPHILIS: Why, he's fast asleep: come

some other time.

HORSE-COURSER: I'll speak with him now, or I'll break his glass-windows about his ears.

MEPHISTOPHILIS: I tell thee, he has not slept this eight nights.

HORSE-COURSER: An he have not slept this eight weeks, I'll speak with him.

MEPHISTOPHILIS: See, where he is, fast asleep.

HORSE-COURSER: Ay, this is he.—God save you, Master Doctor, Master Doctor, Master Doctor Fustian! forty dollars, forty dollars for a bottle of hay!

MEPHISTOPHILIS: Why, thou seest he hears thee not.

HORSE-COURSER: So-ho, ho! So-ho, ho! [*In his ear*] No, will you not wake? I'll make you wake ere I go. [*Pulls* Faustus *by the leg, and pulls it away*] Alas! I am undone! what shall I do?

FAUSTUS: O, my leg, my leg;—Help, Mephistophilis! call the officers.—My leg, my leg!

MEPHISTOPHILIS: Come, villain, to the constable.

HORSE-COURSER: O Lord, sir, let me go, and I'll give you forty dollars more!

MEPHISTOPHILIS: Where be they?

HORSE-COURSER: I have none about me: come to my ostry, and I'll give them you.

MEPHISTOPHILIS: Be gone quickly.

[Horse-Courser *runs away*]

FAUSTUS: What, is he gone? farewell he! Faustus has his leg again, and the Horse-Courser, I take it, a bottle of hay for his labour: well, this trick shall cost him forty dollars more.

[*Enter* Wagner]

How now, Wagner! what's the news with thee?

WAGNER: Sir, the Duke of Vanholt doth earnestly entreat your company.

FAUSTUS: The Duke of Vanholt! an honourable gentleman, to whom I must be no niggard of my cunning.—Come, Mephistophilis, let's away to him.

[*Exeunt*]

SCENE XIII.

The court of the Duke of Vanholt.

[*Enter the* Duke of Vanholt, *the* Duchess, *and* Faustus]

DUKE: Believe me, Master Doctor, this merriment hath much pleased me.

FAUSTUS: My gracious lord, I am glad it contents you so well.—But it may be, madam, you take no delight in this. I have heard that women do long for some dainties or other: what is it, madam? tell me, and you shall have it.

DUCHESS: Thanks, good Master Doctor: and, for I see your courteous intent to pleasure me, I will not hide from you the thing my heart desires; and, were it now summer, as it is January and the dead time of the winter, I would desire no better meat than a dish of ripe grapes.

FAUSTUS: Alas, madam, that's nothing!—Mephistophilis, be gone. [*Exit* Mephistophilis] Were it a greater thing than this, so it would content you, you should have it.

[*Reënter* Mephistophilis *with grapes*]

Here they be, madam: wilt please you taste on them?

DUKE: Believe me, Master Doctor, this makes me wonder above the rest, that being in the dead time of winter and in the month of January, how you should come by these grapes.

FAUSTUS: If it like your grace, the year is divided into two circles over the whole world, that, when it is here winter with us, in the contrary circle it is summer with them, as in India, Saba, and farther countries in the east; and by means of a swift spirit that I have, I had them brought hither, as you see.—How do you like them, madam? be they good?

DUCHESS: Believe me, Master Doctor, they be the best grapes that e'er I tasted in my life before.

FAUSTUS: I am glad they content you so, madam.

DUKE: Come, madam, let us in, where you must well reward this learned man for the great kindness he hath showed to you.

DUCHESS: And so I will, my lord; and, whilst I live, rest beholding for this courtesy.

FAUSTUS: I humbly thank your grace.

DUKE: Come, Master Doctor, follow us, and receive your reward.

[*Exeunt*]

SCENE XIV.

A room in the house of Faustus.

[*Enter* Wagner]

WAGNER: I think my master means to die shortly,
For he hath given to me all his goods:
And yet, methinks, if that death were near,
He would not banquet, and carouse, and swill
Amongst the students, as even now he doth,
Who are at supper with such belly-cheer
As Wagner ne'er beheld in all his life.
See, where they come! belike the feast is ended.

[*Exit*]

[*Enter* Faustus *with two or three* Scholars, *and* Mephistophilis]

1ST SCHOLAR: Master Doctor Faustus, since our conference about fair ladies, which was the beautifulest in all the world, we have determined with ourselves that Helen of Greece was the admirablest lady that ever lived: therefore, Master Doctor, if you will do us that favour, as to let us see that peerless dame of Greece, whom all the world admires for majesty, we should think ourselves much beholding unto you.

FAUSTUS: Gentlemen,
For that I know your friendship is unfeign'd,
And Faustus' custom is not to deny
The just requests of those that wish him well,
You shall behold that peerless dame of Greece,

No otherways for pomp and majesty
Than when Sir Paris cross'd the seas with her,
And brought the spoils to rich Dardania.
Be silent, then, for danger is in words.
    [*Music sounds, and* Helen *passeth over the stage*]
    2ND SCHOLAR: Too simple is my wit to tell her praise,
Whom all the world admires for majesty.
    3RD SCHOLAR: No marvel though the angry Greeks pursu'd
With ten years' war the rape of such a queen,
Whose heavenly beauty passeth all compare.
    1ST SCHOLAR: Since we have seen the pride of Nature's works,
And only paragon of excellence,
Let us depart; and for this glorious deed
Happy and blest be Faustus evermore!
    FAUSTUS: Gentlemen, farewell: the same I wish to you.
    [*Exeunt* Scholars]
    [*Enter an* Old Man]
    OLD MAN: Ah, Doctor Faustus, that I might prevail
To guide thy steps unto the way of life,
By which sweet path thou mayst attain the goal
That shall conduct thee to celestial rest!
Break heart, drop blood, and mingle it with tears,
Tears falling from repentant heaviness
Of thy most vile and loathsome filthiness,
The stench whereof corrupts the inward soul
With such flagitious crimes of heinous sin
As no commiseration may expel,
But mercy, Faustus, of thy Saviour sweet,
Whose blood alone must wash away thy guilt.
    FAUSTUS: Where art thou, Faustus? wretch, what hast thou done?
Damn'd art thou, Faustus, damn'd; despair and die!
Hell calls for right, and with a roaring voice
Says, "Faustus, come; thine hour is almost come";
And Faustus now will come to do thee right.
    [Mephistophilis *gives him a dagger*]
    OLD MAN: Ah, stay, good Faustus, stay thy desperate steps!
I see an angel hovers o'er thy head,
And, with a vial full of precious grace,
Offers to pour the same into thy soul:
Then call for mercy, and avoid despair.
    FAUSTUS: Ah, my sweet friend, I feel
Thy words to comfort my distressed soul!
Leave me a while to ponder my sins.
    OLD MAN: I go, sweet Faustus; but with heavy cheer,
Fearing the ruin of thy hopeless soul.
    [*Exit*]
    FAUSTUS: Accursed Faustus, where is mercy now?
I do repent; and yet I do despair:
Hell strives with grace for conquest in my breast:
What shall I do to shun the snares of death?
    MEPHISTOPHILIS: Thou traitor, Faustus, I arrest thy soul
For disobedience to my sovereign lord.

Revolt, or I'll in piece-meal tear thy flesh.
    FAUSTUS: Sweet Mephistophilis, entreat thy lord
To pardon my unjust presumption,
And with my blood again I will confirm
My former vow I made to Lucifer.
    MEPHISTOPHILIS: Do it, then, quickly, with unfeigned heart,
Lest greater danger do attend thy drift.
    FAUSTUS: Torment, sweet friend, that base and crooked age,
That durst dissuade me from thy Lucifer,
With greatest torments that our hell affords.
    MEPHISTOPHILIS: His faith is great; I cannot touch his soul;
But what I may afflict his body with
I will attempt, which is but little worth.
    FAUSTUS: One thing, good servant, let me crave of thee,
To glut the longing of my heart's desire,
That I might have unto my paramour
That heavenly Helen which I saw of late,
Whose sweet embracings may extinguish clean
Those thoughts that do dissuade me from my vow,
And keep mine oath I made to Lucifer.
    MEPHISTOPHILIS: Faustus, this, or what else thou shalt desire,
Shall be perform'd in twinkling of an eye.
    [*Reënter* Helen]
    FAUSTUS: Was this the face that launch'd a thousand ships,
And burnt the topless towers of Ilium?—
Sweet Helen, make me immortal with a kiss.—
    [*Kisses her*]
Her lips suck forth my soul: see, where it flies!—
Come, Helen, come, give me my soul again.
Here will I dwell, for heaven is in these lips,
And all is dross that is not Helena.
I will be Paris, and for love of thee,
Instead of Troy, shall Wittenberg be sack'd;
And I will combat with weak Menelaus,
And wear thy colours on my plumed crest;
Yes, I will wound Achilles in the heel,
And then return to Helen for a kiss.
O, thou art fairer than the evening air
Clad in the beauty of a thousand stars;
Brighter art thou than flaming Jupiter
When he appear'd to hapless Semele;
More lovely than the monarch of the sky
In wanton Arethusa's azur'd arms;
And none but thou shalt be my paramour!
    [*Exeunt*]

SCENE XV.

A room in the Old Man's *house.*

[*Enter the* Old Man]
    OLD MAN: Accursed Faustus, miserable man,
That from thy soul exclud'st the grace of heaven,

And fly'st the throne of his tribunal-seat!
[*Enter* Devils]
Satan begins to sift me with his pride:
As in this furnace God shall try my faith,
My faith, vile hell, shall triumph over thee,
Ambitious fiends, see how the heavens smile
At your repulse, and laugh your state to scorn!
Hence, hell! for hence I fly unto my God.

[*Exeunt—on one side,* Devils, *on the other,*
Old Man]

SCENE XVI.

A room in the house of Faustus.

[*Enter* Faustus, *with* Scholars]
FAUSTUS: Ah, gentlemen!
1ST SCHOLAR: What ails Faustus?
FAUSTUS: Ah, my sweet chamber-fellow, had I
lived with thee, then had I lived still! but now I die
eternally. Look, comes he not? comes he not?
2ND SCHOLAR: What means Faustus?
3RD SCHOLAR: Belike he is grown into some sickness by being over-solitary.
1ST SCHOLAR: If it be so, we'll have physicians to
cure him.—'Tis but a surfeit; never fear, man.
FAUSTUS: A surfeit of deadly sin, that hath damned
both body and soul.
2ND SCHOLAR: Yet, Faustus, look up to heaven;
remember God's mercies are infinite.
FAUSTUS: But Faustus' offence can ne'er be pardoned: the serpent that tempted Eve may be saved,
but not Faustus. Ah, gentlemen, hear me with patience, and tremble not at my speeches! Though my
heart pants and quivers to remember that I have
been a student here these thirty years, O, would I
had never seen Wittenberg, never read book! and
what wonders I have done, all Germany can witness,
yea, all the world; for which Faustus hath lost both
Germany and the world, yea, heaven itself, heaven,
the seat of God, the throne of the bessed, the kingdom of joy; and must remain in hell for ever, hell, ah,
hell, for ever! Sweet friends, what shall become of
Faustus, being in hell for ever?
3RD SCHOLAR: Yet, Faustus, call on God.
FAUSTUS: On God, whom Faustus hath abjured!
on God, whom Faustus hath blasphemed! Ah, my
God, I would weep! but the devil draws in my tears.
Gush forth blood, instead of tears! yea, life and soul!
O, he stays my tongue! I would lift up my hands;
but see, they hold them, they hold them!
ALL: Who, Faustus?
FAUSTUS: Lucifer and Mephistophilis. Ah, gentle-
men, I gave them my soul for my cunning!
ALL: God forbid!
FAUSTUS: God forbade it, indeed; but Faustus
hath done it: for vain pleasure of twenty-four years
hath Faustus lost eternal joy and felicity. I writ them

a bill with mine own blood: the date is expired; the
time will come, and he will fetch me.
1ST SCHOLAR: Why did not Faustus tell us of this
before, that divines might have prayed for thee?
FAUSTUS: Oft have I thought to have done so; but
the devil threatened to tear me in pieces, if I named
God, to fetch both body and soul, if I once gave ear
to divinity: and now 'tis too late. Gentlemen, away,
lest you perish with me.
2ND SCHOLAR: O, what shall we do to save Faustus?
FAUSTUS: Talk not of me, but save yourselves, and
depart.
3RD SCHOLAR: God will strengthen me; I will stay
with Faustus.
1ST SCHOLAR: Tempt not God, sweet friend; but
let us into the next room, and there pray for him.
FAUSTUS: Ay, pray for me, pray for me; and what
noise soever ye hear, come not unto me, for nothing
can rescue me.
2ND SCHOLAR: Pray thou, and we will pray that
God may have mercy upon thee.
FAUSTUS: Gentlemen, farewell: if I live till morn-
ing, I'll visit you; if not, Faustus is gone to hell.
ALL: Faustus, farewell.
[*Exeunt* Scholars.—*The clock strikes eleven*]
FAUSTUS: Ah, Faustus.
Now hast thou but one bare hour to live,
And then thou must be damn'd perpetually!
Stand still, you ever-moving spheres of heaven,
That time may cease, and midnight never come;
Fair Nature's eye, rise, rise again, and make
Perpetual day; or let this hour be but
A year, a month, a week, a natural day,
That Faustus may repent and save his soul!
O lente, lente, currite noctis equi![31]
The stars move still, time runs, the clock will strike,
The devil will come, and Faustus must be damn'd.
O, I'll leap up to my God!—Who pulls me down?—
See, see, where Christ's blood streams in the firma-
ment!
One drop would save my soul, half a drop: ah, my
Christ!—
Ah, rend not my heart for naming of my Christ!
Yet will I call on him: O, spare me, Lucifer!—
Where is it now? 'tis gone: and see, where God
Stretcheth out his arm, and bends his ireful brows!
Mountains and hills, come, come, and fall on me,
And hide me from the heavy wrath of God!
No, no!
Then will I headlong run into the earth:
Earth, gape! O, no, it will not harbour me!
You stars that reign'd at my nativity,
Whose influence hath allotted death and hell,
Now draw up Faustus, like a foggy mist,
Into the entrails of yon labouring clouds,
That, when you vomit forth into the air,
My limbs may issue from your smoky mouths,
So that my soul may but ascend to heaven!

[31] "O, run softly, softly, horses of the night"—from
Ovid's *Amores.*

[The clock strikes the half-hour]
Ah, half the hour is past! 'twill all be past anon.
O God,
If thou wilt not have mercy on my soul,
Yet for Christ's sake, whose blood hath ransom'd me,
Impose some end to my incessant pain;
Let Faustus live in hell a thousand years,
A hundred thousand, and at last be sav'd!
O, no end is limited to damned souls!
Why wert thou not a creature wanting soul?
Or why is this immortal that thou hast?
Ah, Pythagoras' metempsychosis,[32] were that true,
This soul should fly from me, and I be chang'd
Unto some brutish beast! all beasts are happy,
For, when they die,
Their souls are soon dissolv'd in elements;
But mine must live still to be plagu'd in hell.
Curs'd be the parents that engender'd me!
No, Faustus, curse thyself, curse Lucifer
That hath depriv'd thee of the joys of heaven.
    [The clock strikes twelve]
O, it strikes, it strikes! Now, body, turn to air,
[32] Transmigration of souls.

EDITOR'S NOTE: The above edition agrees with the earliest
extant edition, the quarto of 1604. From the fourth edition, the
quarto of 1616, I reprint below the passages that possess literary
merit.
1. The CHORUS declares (Scene VI, p. 229, line 11 from end of
    scene) concerning "Learned Faustus" that
He views the clouds, the planets, and the stars,
The tropic zones, and quarters of the sky,
From the bright circle of the hornèd moon,
E'en to the height of Primum Mobile:
And whirling round with this circumference,
Within the concave compass of the pole;
From east to west his dragons swiftly glide,
And in eight days did bring him home again.
Not long he stayed within his quiet house,
To rest his bones after his weary toil,
But new exploits do hale him out again,
And mounted then upon a dragon's back,
That with his wings did part the subtle air,
He now is gone to prove cosmography,
That measures coasts, and kingdoms of the earth:
2. In Scene XIV (p. 235) an Old Man enters and pleads
  OLD MAN: O gentle Faustus, leave this damnèd art,
This magic, that will charm thy soul to hell,
And quite bereave thee of salvation.
Though thou hast now offended like a man,
Do not persévere in it like a devil;
Yet, yet, thou hast an amiable soul,
If sin by custom grow not into nature:
Then, Faustus, will repentance come too late,
Then thou art banish'd from the sight of heaven;
No mortal can express the pains of hell.
It may be this my exhortation
Seems harsh and all unpleasant; let it not,
For, gentle son, I speak it not in wrath,
Or envy of thee, but in tender love,
And pity of thy future misery.
4. In Scene XVI (p. 236, second column), after the Scholars
  leave Faustus and before his soliloquy that begins "Ah,
  Faustus," there is the following:
MEPHISTOPHILIS: Ay, Faustus, now thou hast no hope of
    heaven;
Therefore despair, think only upon hell,
For that must be thy mansion, there to dwell.
FAUST: O thou bewitching fiend, 'twas thy temptation
Hath robb'd me of eternal happiness.
MEPHISTOPHILIS: I do confess it, Faustus, and rejoice;
'Twas I, that when thou wert i' the way to heaven,
Damm'd up thy passage; when thou took'st the book,
To view the Scriptures, then I turn'd the leaves,
And led thine eye.
What, weep'st thou? 'tis too late, despair, farewell!

Or Lucifer will bear thee quick to hell!
    [Thunder and lightning]
O soul, be chang'd into little water-drops,
And fall into the ocean, ne'er be found!
    [Enter Devils]
My God, my God, look not so fierce on me!
Adders and serpents, let me breathe a while!
Ugly hell, gape not! come not, Lucifer!
I'll burn my books!—Ah, Mephistophilis!
    [Exeunt Devils with Faustus]
    [Enter Chorus]
  CHORUS: Cut is the branch that might have grown
    full straight,
    And burnèd is Apollo's laurel-bough,
That sometime grew within this learnèd man.
Faustus is gone: regard his hellish fall,
Whose fiendful fortune may exhort the wise,
Only to wonder at unlawful things,
Whose deepness doth entice such forward wits
To practise more than heavenly power permits.
    [Exit]
Terminat hora diem; terminat auctor opus.[33]
  [33] "The hour ends the day; the author ends his work."

Fools that will laugh on earth, must weep in hell.
    [Exit]
    [Enter the Good Angel and the Bad Angel at several doors]
GOOD ANGEL: Oh, Faustus, if thou hadst given ear to me,
Innumerable joys had follow'd thee.
But thou didst love the world.
  BAD ANGEL: Gavest ear to me,
And now must taste hell's pains perpetually.
  GOOD ANGEL: O what will all thy riches, pleasures, pomps,
Avail thee now?
  BAD ANGEL: Nothing but vex thee more,
To want in hell, that had on earth such store.
    [Music while the throne descends]
  GOOD ANGEL: O thou hast lost celestial happiness,
Pleasures unspeakable, bliss without end.
Hadst thou affected sweet divinity,
Hell, or the devil, had had no power on thee.
Hadst thou kept on that way, Faustus, behold,
In what resplendent glory thou hadst sit
In yonder throne, like those bright shining saints,
And triumphed over hell: that hast thou lost;
And now, poor soul, must thy good angel leave thee,
The jaws of hell are open to receive thee.
    [Exit]
    [Hell is discovered]
BAD ANGEL: Now, Faustus, let thine eyes with horror stare
Into that vast perpetual torture-house.
There are the Furies tossing damnèd souls
On burning forks; their bodies broil in lead;
There are live quarters broiling on the coals,
That ne'er can die: this ever-burning chair
Is for o'er-tortured souls to rest them in;
These that are fed with sops of flaming fire,
Were gluttons and loved only delicates,
And laugh'd to see the poor starve at their gates:
But yet all these are nothing; thou shalt see
Ten thousand tortures that more horrid be.
  FAUST: O, I have seen enough to torture me.
  BAD ANGEL: Nay, thou must feel them, taste the smart of all:
He that loves pleasure, must for pleasure fall:
And so I leave thee, Faustus, till anon;
Then wilt thou tumble in confusion.
    [Exit]
5. After "Exeunt Devils with Faustus" (p. 237, second col-
  umn) and before the Chorus enters, the Scholars return:
FIRST SCHOLAR: Come, gentlemen, let us go visit Faustus,
For such a dreadful night was never seen,
Since first the world's creation did begin.
Such fearful shrieks and cries were never heard:
Pray heaven the Doctor have escaped the danger.
  SECOND SCHOLAR: O help us heaven! see, here are Faustus'
    limbs,
All torn asunder by the hand of death. *[Exeunt]*

William Shakespeare

(1564–1616)

Praising Shakespeare has been a busy industry of long duration. It is an honorable one, since recognition of excellence argues some excellence in the perceiver. Appreciation is also the beginning of criticism if there is something to be appreciated, as there manifestly is in Shakespeare. But the ways of adoration are strewn with snares for the unwary.

George Bernard Shaw, for example, rightly deplored "bardolatry," ridiculing the centuries-old custom of the British theatre of glorifying Shakespeare with one breath while blowing away his dramatic structure and some of his best lines with another. (All the actor-managers after 1660—including the great David Garrick and the Victorian idol Sir Henry Irving—had "adapted" Shakespearean drama, distorting it and, in some cases, even substituting happy endings for the tragic ones. Only since the turn of our century has it been a principle of Shakespearean stage production to refrain from tampering with the texts. And even today the principle is frequently violated in practice, as there are still managements that consider themselves better playwrights and showmen than Shakespeare.)

Shaw's iconoclasm was also well advised when he objected to the habit of attributing philosophical virtues to Shakespeare that he did not possess while overlooking or failing to make the best use of virtues that he did possess. And contemporary criticism has followed suit by disparaging the tendency to attribute the thoughts of Shakespeare's characters to their author, on one hand, while treating the characters as human beings independent of his dramaturgy, on the other. Since charactermongering, along with turning Shakespearean dialogue into a guide-book for human conduct, became an obsession of Shakespearean criticism at the beginning of the nineteenth century, it is well to remember that the playwright's characters have reality only in the plays and that Shakespeare did not elaborate a unified world picture in his work.

In the matter of ideas, Shakespeare was, it is true, a ready assimilator. Skepticism may be traced through much of his work, and important characters express uncertainty about an afterlife; fatalism has many echoes in his tragedies; and the medieval-Elizabethan concept of "degree"—the political and moral principle that every individual, as well as class, has a particular place in the scheme of things—weaves some sort of pattern in his chronicle plays. Contemporary political, social, scientific, and psychological notions fill his pages. But no consistent outlook, except an intense concern with humanity, can be traced through his work. He was primarily a reflector, rather than a thinker. And the fluctuating Elizabethan age, which lacked the stable and comprehensive world view (Christian and Thomist) upon which Dante, for example, had been able to draw so securely in writing *The Divine Comedy,* could not supply Shakespeare with a steady and all-encompassing light. The age was empirical, and so was Shakespeare. It was interested in mankind's experiences rather than in systematizing them, and so was Shakespeare. He transcribed life instead of trying to define it. Since he was a practiced showman, he turned it into theatre. And since he was a superb poet, he succeeded in transfiguring life.

To view Shakespeare's plays as a fusion of poetry and drama, rather than as philosophy or a collection of character portraits, is the beginning of wisdom in Shakespearean appreciation and study. Such an approach is apt to guide us better through *Hamlet,* for example, than the innumerable special studies of the play, including those which advance the "Oedipus complex" theory made fashionable by Freud and his disciples. Our best recourse in reading the texts is to apply our maximum responsiveness to theatre and to poetry—provided, of course, that we can visualize a text and that we know enough to treat the verse as dramatic poetry, which conveys feeling and action in the cadence, rhythm, and pauses of the lines.

To undertake in a brief introduction an analysis of Shakespeare's artistry as a whole (or even of *Hamlet* alone) would be to attempt the impossible. The vast library on the subject would engage a reader's lifetime, and the flood of Shakespearean scholarship and criticism continues to rise without abatement. Mark Van Doren's *Shakespeare* will sharpen anybody's sensitivity to Shakespeare as a writer, and Harley Granville-Barker's *Prefaces to Shakespeare* soundly relate the plays to the theatre. For ready reference in the present volume, the reader can turn, if he wishes, to the bald summary of Shakespeare's plays on pages 1018–1021. As for generalizations concerning this work, they are numberless, and many are justly famous. Among the latter, the following include observations as conducive to a critical approach as they are applausive:

He was the man who of all modern, and perhaps ancient poets, had the largest, and most comprehensive soul. All the images of nature were still present to him, and he drew, not laboriously but luckily; when he describes anything, you more than see it, you feel it too. Those who accuse him to have wanted learning, give him the greater commendation: he was naturally learned; he needed not the spectacles of books to read nature; he looked inwards, and found her there. I cannot say he is everywhere alike; were he so, I should do him injury to compare him to the greatest of mankind.—JOHN DRYDEN

I remember the players that often mentioned it as an honor to Shakespeare that in his writings (whatsoever he penned) he never blotted out a line. My answer hath been, Would that he had blotted a thousand. . . . I loved the man and do honor his memory this side idolatry, as much as any.—BEN JONSON

Shakespeare, with the English man-of-war, lesser in bulk, but lighter in sailing, could turn with all tides, tack about, and take advantage of all winds, by the quickness of his wit and invention.—THOMAS FULLER

He was just like any other man, but that he was like all other men. He was the least of an egotist that it was possible to be.—WILLIAM HAZLITT

The greatest achievement possible to a man is full consciousness of his own feelings and thoughts, for this gives him the means of knowing intimately the hearts of others. . . . If we call Shakespeare one of the greatest of poets, we mean that few have perceived the world as accurately as he did, that few who have expressed their inner contemplation of it have given the reader deeper insight into its meaning and consciousness. . . . Shakespeare gets his effect by means of the living word. . . . Shakespeare's poems [i.e., plays] are a great animated fair. . . . In his plays Will and Necessity struggle to maintain an equilibrium; both contend powerfully, yet always so that the Will remains at a disadvantage. . . . The person, considered as a character, is under a certain necessity; he is constrained, appointed to a certain particular line of action [or status, Goethe might have said]; but as a human being he has a will, which is unconfined and universal in its demands. Thus arises an inner conflict, and Shakespeare is superior to all other writers in the significance with which he endows this conflict.—JOHANN WOLFGANG VON GOETHE

With the single exception of Homer, there is no eminent writer, not even Sir Walter Scott, whom I can despise so entirely as I despise Shakespeare when I measure my mind against his. . . . But I am bound to say that I pity the man who cannot enjoy Shakespeare. He has outlasted thousands of abler thinkers, and will outlast a thousand more. His gift of telling a story (provided some one else told it to him first); his enormous power over language, as conspicuous

in his senseless and silly abuse of it as in his miracles of expression; his humor; his sense of idiosyncratic character; and his prodigious fund of that vital energy which is, it seems, the true differentiating property behind the faculties, good, bad, or indifferent, of the man of genius, enable him to entertain us so effectively that the imaginary scenes and people he has created become more real to us than our actual life—at least until our knowledge and grip of actual life begins to deepen and glow beyond the common.—GEORGE BERNARD SHAW

The few established facts of Shakespeare's life are too well known to be repeated here in any detail. They indicate a successful and profitable career, but they throw only an indirect light, if any, on the nature of his genius. He was not long held by his native Stratford-on-Avon, where he received a grammar-school education, shared his family's financial vicissitudes, and married a woman of twenty-six when he was eighteen. He became the father of a daughter, Susanna, about six months after his marriage and of twins, Judith and Hamnet, less than two years later, early in 1585. By 1587 or 1588 he was settled in London, and there he remained, except for rare visits at home, until 1611. He appears to have found employment in the London theatre almost at once, serving it as an actor and writer. By 1592 he was already sufficiently successful to be regarded with envy by his fellow playwright Robert Greene and to be praised by another man of letters, Henry Chettle. Within two years he had also gained distinction as a poet with the two long poems *Venus and Adonis* and *The Rape of Lucrece* and won the patronage of the young Earl of Southampton, to whom the works were dedicated. Between 1594 and 1595 he became a member of the successful Lord Chamberlain's company of actors. He was an actor (we know that he played in Ben Jonson's *Every Man in His Humour* in 1598 and *Sejanus* in 1603), a shareholder in his company, and part owner of the famous Globe and Blackfriars theatres. He wrote plays steadily, suiting them to the talents of the great actor Richard Burbage and other members of the troupe. By 1598 he was already credited in a manual of English literature with the composition of twelve plays.

Shakespeare continued for another dozen or more years to write plays assiduously, while also composing the sonnet sequence for which he is most esteemed as a lyric poet (unless Leslie Hotson is correct in dating the sonnets earlier). His mastery of dramatic skill grew in several directions and his powers as a dramatic poet ripened steadily, not only in the great tragedies that deserved his highest flights of poetry but in the less ambitious and flawed plays which followed his major efforts. It is not to be supposed, however, that so practical a showman as Shakespeare, who had to meet the needs of his company and accommodate his pen to changes in public taste, could indulge in the luxury of pure self-expression as a playwright and climb from height to height uninterruptedly. It is also doubtful that he prized his playwriting as a bid for immortality, as he apparently did his sonnets. He was certainly not above composing potboilers such as *Pericles, Prince of Tyre* (1607–1608) and *Cymbeline* (1609–1610) after having written his towering tragedies. And, in spite of having outdistanced every other playwright of his times —and he must have had some intimations of this fact —he was not above collaborating with other writers, most notably with John Fletcher on *Henry VIII.*

Since Shakespeare's work reveals an amazing knowledge of humanity, it is not, finally, beside the point to remark on his worldliness. Contrary to romantic notions that genius is a delicate flower easily wilted by commerce with the world, Shakespeare prospered from his work; and he not only enjoyed his prosperity but tried to augment it with business dealings such as the buying and selling of property. He was listed as a large holder of corn and malt as early as 1598. He also shared the social ambitions of the average Elizabethan, applying for a gentleman's coat of arms in 1596, which was confirmed by the Herald's Office and extended to his father in 1599. And, after having bought himself in 1597 apparently the largest house in Stratford ("New Place"), he extended his holdings near the town in 1610. Retiring from the theatre, he spent the last years of his life as a country gentleman. In all probability, his emotions were involved in personal relationships (such as an affair with a court lady, the so-called dark lady of the sonnets) about which we know nothing with certainty, and he may well have been turned to unflattering and dismayed views of the human situation by such events as the execution of Essex and the sentencing of his patron-friend Southampton to imprisonment for life in 1600. His disenchanting or "dark" problem comedies (*All's Well That Ends Well, Troilus and Cressida,* and *Measure for Measure*) and his major tragedies came after the public upheavals of the Essex rebellion. If he had his private perturbations, however, it is plain that he settled down to making the best of the bad bargain that is life and to compensating it with flights of fancy. He continued to write—and in the then current fashions of tragicomedy and romance. And he continued to advance his material interests, tasting, to use a phrase by Thomas Mann, "the blisses of the commonplace." In all respects but his genius, Shakespeare, who created the most intensely alive characters of the world's stage, was certainly "like all other men."

EDITOR'S NOTE: For a helpful summary of the varied course of Shakespearian criticism in English since the seventeenth century one may consult *The Reader's Encyclopedia of Shakespeare,* edited by Oscar James Campbell and Edward G. Quinn (Thomas Y. Crowell Company, New York, 1966, pp. 155–163). A compendium of criticism in French and German as well as English, up to 1925, is Augustus J. Ralli's *A History of Shakespearian Criticism* in two volumes. Oxford University Press, London and New York, 1932, 1960; reprinted by the Humanities Press, New York, 1959.

HAMLET
Prince of Denmark

By William Shakespeare

DRAMATIS PERSONAE

CLAUDIUS, *King of Denmark*
HAMLET, *son to the former and nephew to the present King*
POLONIUS, *Lord Chamberlain*
HORATIO, *friend to Hamlet*
LAERTES, *son to Polonius*
VOLTIMAND
CORNELIUS
ROSENCRANTZ } *courtiers*
GUILDENSTERN
OSRIC
A GENTLEMAN
A PRIEST
FRANCISCO, *a soldier*

MARCELLUS
BERNARDO } *officers*
REYNALDO, *servant to Polonius*
PLAYERS
TWO CLOWNS, *grave-diggers*
FORTINBRAS, *Prince of Norway*
A CAPTAIN
ENGLISH AMBASSADORS
GHOST OF HAMLET'S FATHER
GERTRUDE, *Queen of Denmark and mother of Hamlet*
OPHELIA, *daughter to Polonius*
LORDS, LADIES, OFFICERS, SOLDIERS, SAILORS, MESSENGERS, *and other* ATTENDANTS

ACT I. SCENE I.

Elsinore. A platform before the castle.

[Francisco *at his post. Enter to him* Bernardo]
BERNARDO: Who's there?
FRANCISCO: Nay, answer me: stand, and unfold yourself.
BERNARDO: Long live the king!
FRANCISCO: Bernardo?
BERNARDO: He.
FRANCISCO: You come most carefully upon your hour.
BERNARDO: 'Tis now struck twelve; get thee to bed, Francisco.
FRANCISCO: For this relief much thanks: 'tis bitter cold,
And I am sick at heart.
BERNARDO: Have you had quiet guard?
FRANCISCO: Not a mouse stirring.
BERNARDO: Well, good-night.
If you do meet Horatio and Marcellus,
The rivals of my watch, bid them make haste.
FRANCISCO: I think I hear them.—Stand, ho! Who is there?
[Enter Horatio *and* Marcellus]
HORATIO: Friends to this ground.
MARCELLUS: And liegemen to the Dane.
FRANCISCO: Give you good-night.
MARCELLUS: O, farewell, honest soldier:
Who hath reliev'd you?
FRANCISCO: Bernardo has my place.

Give you good-night.
            [*Exit*]
MARCELLUS: Holla! Bernardo!
BERNARDO: Say.
What, is Horatio there?
HORATIO: A piece of him.
BERNARDO: Welcome, Horatio:—welcome, good Marcellus.
MARCELLUS: What, has this thing appear'd again to-night?
BERNARDO: I have seen nothing.
MARCELLUS: Horatio says 'tis but our fantasy,
And will not let belief take hold of him
Touching this dreaded sight, twice seen of us:
Therefore I have entreated him along
With us to watch the minutes of this night;
That, if again this apparition come
He may approve our eyes and speak to it.
HORATIO: Tush, tush, 'twill not appear.
BERNARDO: Sit down awhile,
And let us once again assail your ears,
That are so fortified against our story,
What we two nights have seen.
HORATIO: Well, sit we down,
And let us hear Bernardo speak of this.
BERNARDO: Last night of all,
When yon same star that's westward from the pole
Had made his course to illume that part of heaven
Where now it burns, Marcellus and myself,
The bell then beating one,—
MARCELLUS: Peace, break thee off; look where it comes again!
[*Enter* Ghost, *armed*]

241

BERNARDO: In the same figure, like the king that's dead.

MARCELLUS: Thou art a scholar; speak to it, Horatio.

BERNARDO: Looks it not like the king? mark it, Horatio.

HORATIO: Most like:—it harrows me with fear and wonder.

BERNARDO: It would be spoke to.

MARCELLUS: Question it, Horatio.

HORATIO: What art thou, that usurp'st this time of night,
Together with that fair and warlike form
In which the majesty of buried Denmark
Did sometimes march? by heaven I charge thee, speak!

MARCELLUS: It is offended.

BERNARDO: See, it stalks away!

HORATIO: Stay! speak, speak! I charge thee, speak!
  [Exit Ghost]

MARCELLUS: 'Tis gone, and will not answer.

BERNARDO: How now, Horatio! you tremble and look pale:
Is not this something more than fantasy?
What think you on't?

HORATIO: Before my God, I might not this believe
Without the sensible and true avouch
Of mine own eyes.

MARCELLUS: Is it not like the king?

HORATIO: As thou art to thyself:
Such was the very armor he had on
When he the ambitious Norway combated;
So frown'd he once when, in an angry parle,[1]
He smote the sledded Polacks on the ice.
'Tis strange.

MARCELLUS: Thus twice before, and just at this dead hour,
With martial stalk hath he gone by our watch.

HORATIO: In what particular thought to work I know not;
But, in the gross and scope of my opinion,
This bodes some strange eruption to our state.

MARCELLUS: Good now, sit down, and tell me, he that knows,
Why this same strict and most observant watch
So nightly toils the subject of the land;
And why such daily cast of brazen cannon,
And foreign mart for implements of war;
Why such impress of shipwrights, whose sore task
Does not divide the Sunday from the week;
What might be toward, that this sweaty haste
Doth make the night joint-laborer with the day:
Who is't that can inform me?

HORATIO: That can I;
At least, the whisper goes so. Our last king,
Whose image even but now appear'd to us,
Was, as you know, by Fortinbras of Norway,
Thereto prick'd on by a most emulate pride,
Dar'd to the combat; in which our valiant Hamlet,—

1 Parley, or conference.

For so this side of our known world esteem'd him,—
Did slay this Fortinbras; who, by a seal'd compact,
Well ratified by law and heraldry,
Did forfeit, with his life, all those his lands,
Which he stood seiz'd of,[2] to the conqueror:
Against the which, a moiety competent[3]
Was gagéd[4] by our king; which had return'd
To the inheritance of Fortinbras,
Had he been vanquisher; as by the same cov'nant,
And carriage of the article design'd,
His fell to Hamlet. Now, sir, young Fortinbras,
Of unimproved mettle hot and full,
Hath in the skirts of Norway, here and there,
Shark'd up a list of landless resolutes,
For food and diet, to some enterprise
That hath a stomach in't: which is no other,—
As it doth well appear unto our state,—
But to recover of us by strong hand,
And terms compulsatory, those foresaid lands
So by his father lost: and this, I take it,
Is the main motive of our preparations,
The source of this our watch, and the chief head
Of this post-haste and romage[5] in the land.

BERNARDO: I think it be no other, but e'en so:
Well may it sort that this portentous figure
Comes armed through our watch; so like the king
That was and is the question of these wars.

HORATIO: A mote it is to trouble the mind's eye.
In the most high and palmy state of Rome,
A little ere the mightiest Julius fell,
The graves stood tenantless, and the sheeted dead
Did squeak and gibber in the Roman streets:
As, stars with trains of fire and dews of blood,
Disasters in the sun; and the moist star,
Upon whose influence Neptune's empire stands,
Was sick almost to doomsday with eclipse:
And even the like precurse of fierce events,—
As harbingers preceding still the fates,
And prologue to the omen coming on,—
Have heaven and earth together demonstrated
Unto our climature and countrymen.—
But, soft, behold! lo, where it comes again!
  [Re-enter Ghost]
I'll cross it, though it blast me.—Stay, illusion!
If thou hast any sound or use of voice,
Speak to me:
If there be any good thing to be done,
That may to thee do ease, and grace to me,
Speak to me:
If thou art privy to thy country's fate,
Which, happily,[6] foreknowing may avoid,
O, speak!
Or if thou has uphoarded in thy life
Extorted treasure in the womb of earth,
For which, they say, you spirits oft walk in death,

2 Possessed.
3 A sufficient portion of his lands.
4 Engaged or pledged.
5 General activity.
6 Haply, or perhaps.

[*Cock crows*]
Speak of it:—stay, and speak!—Stop it, Marcellus.
　MARCELLUS: Shall I strike at it with my partisan?[7]
　HORATIO: Do, if it will not stand.
　BERNARDO:　　　　　　　　　'Tis here!
　HORATIO:　　　　　　　　　　　'Tis here!
　MARCELLUS: 'Tis gone!
　　[*Exit* Ghost]
We do it wrong, being so majestical,
To offer it the show of violence;
For it is, as the air, invulnerable,
And our vain blows malicious mockery.
　BERNARDO: It was about to speak when the cock
　　crew.
　HORATIO: And then it started like a guilty thing
Upon a fearful summons. I have heard,
The cock, that is the trumpet to the morn,
Doth with his lofty and shrill-sounding throat
Awake the god of day; and at his warning,
Whether in sea or fire, in earth or air,
The extravagant and erring spirit hies
To his confine: and of the truth herein
This present object made probation.[8]
　MARCELLUS: It faded on the crowing of the cock.
Some say that ever 'gainst that season comes
Wherein our Saviour's birth is celebrated,
The bird of dawning singeth all night long:
And then, they say, no spirit can walk abroad;
The nights are wholesome; then no planets strike,
No fairy takes, nor witch hath power to charm;
So hallow'd and so gracious is the time.
　HORATIO: So have I heard, and do in part believe.
But, look, the morn, in russet mantle clad,
Walks o'er the dew of yon high eastern hill:
Break we our watch up: and, by my advice,
Let us impart what we have seen to-night
Unto young Hamlet; for, upon my life,
This spirit, dumb to us, will speak to him:
Do you consent we shall acquaint him with it,
As needful in our loves, fitting our duty?
　MARCELLUS: Let's do't, I pray; and I this morning
　　know
Where we shall find him most conveniently.
　　[*Exeunt*]

SCENE II.

Elsinore. A room of state in the castle.

[*Enter the* King, Queen, Hamlet, Polonius,
Laertes, Voltimand, Cornelius, Lords, *and* At-
tendants]
　KING: Though yet of Hamlet our dear brother's
　　death
The memory be green; and that it us befitted
To bear our hearts in grief, and our whole kingdom
To be contracted in one brow of woe;

[7] Pike.
[8] Proof.

Yet so far hath discretion fought with nature
That we with wisest sorrow think on him,
Together with remembrance of ourselves.
Therefore our sometime sister, now our queen,
The imperial jointress of this warlike state,
Have we, as 'twere with defeated joy,—
With one auspicious and one dropping eye,
With mirth and funeral, and with dirge in marriage,
In equal scale weighing delight and dole,—
Taken to wife: nor have we herein barr'd
Your better wisdoms, which have freely gone
With this affair along:—for all, our thanks.
Now follows that you know, young Fortinbras,
Holding a weak supposal of our worth,
Or thinking by our late dear brother's death
Our state to be disjoint and out of frame,
Colleagued with the dream of his advantage,
He hath not fail'd to pester us with message,
Importing the surrender of those lands
Lost by his father, with all bonds of law,
To our most valiant brother. So much for him.—
Now for ourself, and for this time of meeting:
Thus much the business is:—we have here writ
To Norway, uncle of young Fortinbras,—
Who, impotent and bed-rid, scarcely hears
Of this his nephew's purpose,—to suppress
His further gait herein; in that the levies,
The lists, and full proportions, are all made
Out of his subject:—and we here despatch
You, good Cornelius, and you, Voltimand,
For bearers of this greeting to old Norway;
Giving to you no further personal power
To business with the king more than the scope
Of these dilated articles allow.
Farewell; and let your haste commend your duty.
　CORNELIUS *and* VOLTIMAND: In that and all things
　　will we show our duty.
　KING: We doubt it nothing: heartily farewell.
　　[*Exeunt* Voltimand *and* Cornelius]
And now, Laertes, what's the news with you?
You told us of some suit; what is't, Laertes?
You cannot speak of reason to the Dane,
And lose your voice: what wouldst thou beg, Laertes,
That shall not be my offer, nor thy asking?
The head is not more native to the heart,
The hand more instrumental to the mouth,
Than is the throne of Denmark to thy father.
What wouldst thou have, Laertes?
　LAERTES:　　　　　　　　Dread my lord,
Your leave and favor to return to France;
From whence though willingly I came to Denmark,
To show my duty in your coronation;
Yet now, I must confess, that duty done,
My thoughts and wishes bend again toward France.
And bow them to your gracious leave and pardon.
　KING: Have you your father's leave? What says
　　Polonius?
　POLONIUS: He hath, my lord, wrung from me my
　　slow leave
By laborsome petition; and at last

Upon his will I seal'd my hard consent:
I do beseech you, give him leave to go.
    KING: Take thy fair hour, Laertes; time be thine,
And thy best graces spend it at thy will!—
But now, my cousin Hamlet, and my son,—
    HAMLET: [*Aside*] A little more than kin, and less
    than kind.
    KING: How is it that the clouds still hang on you?
    HAMLET: Not so, my lord; I am too much i' the
    sun.
    QUEEN: Good Hamlet, cast thy nighted color off,
And let thine eye look like a friend on Denmark.
Do not for ever with thy vailed[9] lids
Seek for thy noble father in the dust:
Thou know'st 'tis common,—all that live must die,
Passing through nature to eternity.
    HAMLET: Ay, madam, it is common.
    QUEEN: If it be,
Why seems it so particular with thee?
    HAMLET: Seems, madam! nay, it is; I know not
    seems.
'Tis not alone my inky cloak, good mother,
Nor customary suits of solemn black,
Nor windy suspiration of forc'd breath,
No, nor the fruitful river in the eye,
Nor the dejected 'havior of the visage,
Together with all forms, moods, shows of grief,
That can denote me truly: these, indeed, seem;
For they are actions that a man might play:
But I have that within which passeth show;
These but the trappings and the suits of woe.
    KING: 'Tis sweet and cómmendable in your nature,
    Hamlet,
To give these mourning duties to your father:
But, you must know, your father lost a father;
That father lost, lost his; and the survivor bound,
In filial obligation, for some term
To do obsequious sorrow: but to persever
In obstinate condolement is a course
Of impious stubbornness; 'tis unmanly grief:
It shows a will most incorrect to heaven;
A heart unfortified, a mind impatient;
An understanding simple and unschool'd:
For what we know must be, and is as common
As any the most vulgar thing to sense,[10]
Why should we, in our peevish opposition,
Take it to heart? Fie! 'tis a fault to heaven,
A fault against the dead, a fault to nature,
To reason most absurd; whose common theme
Is death of fathers, and who still[11] hath cried,
From the first corse till he that died to-day,
This must be so. We pray you, throw to earth
This unprevailing woe; and think of us
As of a father: for let the world take note
You are the most immediate to our throne;
And with no less nobility of love
Than that which dearest father bears his son

Do I impart toward you. For your intent
In going back to school in Wittenberg,
It is most retrograde to our desire:
And we beseech you bend you to remain
Here, in the cheer and comfort of our eye,
Our chiefest courtier, cousin, and our son.
    QUEEN: Let not thy mother lose her prayers,
    Hamlet:
I pray thee, stay with us; go not to Wittenberg.
    HAMLET: I shall in all my best obey you, madam.
    KING: Why, 'tis a loving and a fair reply:
Be as ourself in Denmark.—Madam, come;
This gentle and unforc'd accord of Hamlet
Sits smiling to my heart: in grace whereof,
No jocund health that Denmark drinks to-day
But the great cannon to the clouds shall tell;
And the king's rouse[12] the heavens shall bruit[13] again,
Re-speaking earthly thunder. Come away.
    [*Exeunt all but* Hamlet]
    HAMLET: O, that this too too solid flesh would
    melt,
Thaw, and resolve itself into a dew!
Or that the Everlasting had not fix'd
His canon 'gainst self-slaughter! O God! O God!
How weary, stale, flat, and unprofitable
Seem to me all the uses of this world!
Fie on't! O fie! 'tis an unweeded garden,
That grows to seed; things rank and gross in nature
Possess it merely. That it should come to this!
But two months dead!—nay, not so much, not two:
So excellent a king; that was, to this,
Hyperion[14] to a satyr: so loving to my mother,
That he might not beteem the winds of heaven
Visit her face too roughly. Heaven and earth!
Must I remember? why, she would hang on him
As if increase of appetite had grown
By what it fed on: and yet, within a month,—
Let me not think on't,—Frailty, thy name is
    woman!—
A little month; or ere those shoes were old
With which she follow'd my poor father's body
Like Niobe, all tears;—why she, even she,—
O God! a beast, that wants discourse of reason,
Would have mourn'd longer,—married with mine
    uncle,
My father's brother; but no more like my father
Than I to Hercules: within a month;
Ere yet the salt of most unrighteous tears
Had left the flushing in her galled eyes,
She married:—O, most wicked speed, to post
With such dexterity to incestuous sheets!
It is not, nor it cannot come to good;
But break, my heart,—for I must hold my tongue!
    [*Enter* Horatio, Marcellus, *and* Bernardo]
    HORATIO: Hail to your lordship!
    HAMLET: I am glad to see you well:

[9] Downcast.
[10] Anything that is very commonly seen or heard.
[11] Ever, or always.
[12] Drink.
[13] Echo.
[14] The Greek sun god, the brightest and most beautiful of the gods.

Horatio,—or I do forget myself.

HORATIO: The same, my lord, and your poor servant ever.

HAMLET: Sir, my good friend; I'll change that
name with you:

And what make you from Wittenberg, Horatio?—
Marcellus?

MARCELLUS: My good lord,—

HAMLET: I am very glad to see you.—Good even,
sir.—

But what, in faith, make you from Wittenberg?

HORATIO: A truant disposition, good my lord.

HAMLET: I would not hear your enemy say so;

Nor shall you do mine ear that violence,

To make it truster of your own report

Against yourself: I know you are no truant.

But what is your affair in Elsinore?

We'll teach you to drink deep ere you depart.

HORATIO: My lord, I came to see your father's
funeral.

HAMLET: I pray thee, do not mock me, fellow-
student;

I think it was to see my mother's wedding.

HORATIO: Indeed, my lord, it follow'd hard upon.

HAMLET: Thrift, thrift, Horatio! the funeral-bak'd
meats

Did coldly furnish forth the marriage tables.

Would I had met my dearest foe[15] in heaven

Ere I had ever seen that day, Horatio!—

My father,—methinks I see my father.

HORATIO: Where, my lord?

HAMLET: In my mind's eye, Horatio.

HORATIO: I saw him once; he was a goodly[16] king.

HAMLET: He was a man, take him for all in all,

I shall not look upon his like again.

HORATIO: My lord, I think I saw him yester-
night.

HAMLET: Saw who?

HORATIO: My lord, the king your father.

HAMLET: The king my father!

HORATIO: Season your admiration[17] for awhile

With an attent ear, till I may deliver,

Upon the witness of these gentlemen,

This marvel to you.

HAMLET: For God's love, let me hear.

HORATIO: Two nights together had these gentlemen,

Marcellus and Bernardo, in their watch,

In the dead vast and middle of the night,

Been thus encounter'd. A figure like your father,

Arm'd at all points exactly, cap-a-pe,[18]

Appears before them, and with solemn march

Goes slow and stately by them: thrice he walk'd

By their oppress'd[19] and fear-surprised eyes,

Within his truncheon's length; whilst they, distill'd

[15] Worst enemy.
[16] Handsome.
[17] Astonishment.
[18] *Cap-a-pie*, from head to **toe**.
[19] Overwhelmed.

Almost to jelly with the act of fear,

Stand dumb, and speak not to him. This to me

In dreadful secrecy impart they did;

And I with them the third night kept the watch:

Where, as they had deliver'd, both in time,

Form of the thing, each word made true and good,

The apparition comes: I knew your father;

These hands are not more like.

HAMLET: But where was this?

MARCELLUS: My lord, upon the platform where we
watch'd.

HAMLET: Did you not speak to it?

HORATIO: My lord, I did;

But answer made it none: yet once methought

It lifted up its head, and did address

Itself to motion, like as it would speak:

But even then the morning cock crew loud,

And at the sound it shrunk in haste away,

And vanish'd from our sight.

HAMLET: 'Tis very strange.

HORATIO: As I do live, my honor'd lord, 'tis true;

And we did think it writ down in our duty

To let you know of it.

HAMLET: Indeed, indeed, sirs, but this troubles
me.

Hold you the watch to-night?

MARCELLUS *and* BERNARDO: We do, my lord.

HAMLET: Arm'd, say you?

MARCELLUS *and* BERNARDO: Arm'd, my lord.

HAMLET: From top to toe?

MARCELLUS *and* BERNARDO: My lord, from head to
foot.

HAMLET: Then saw you not his face?

HORATIO: O yes, my lord; he wore his beaver up.

HAMLET: What, look'd he frowningly?

HORATIO: A countenance more in sorrow than in
anger.

HAMLET: Pale or red?

HORATIO: Nay, very pale.

HAMLET: And fix'd his eyes upon you?

HORATIO: Most constantly.

HAMLET: I would I had been there.

HORATIO: It would have much amaz'd you.

HAMLET: Very like, very like. Stay'd it long?

HORATIO: While one with moderate haste might
tell[20] a hundred.

MARCELLUS *and* BERNARDO: Longer, longer.

HORATIO: Not when I saw't.

HAMLET: His beard was grizzled,—no?

HORATIO: It was, as I have seen it in his life,

A sable silver'd.

HAMLET: I will watch to-night;

Perchance 'twill walk again.

HORATIO: I warrant it will.

HAMLET: If it assume my noble father's person

I'll speak to it, though hell itself should gape

And bid me hold my peace. I pray you all,

If you have hitherto conceal'd this sight,

Let it be tenable in your silence still;

[20] Count.

And whatsoever else shall hap to-night,
Give it an understanding, but no tongue:
I will requite your loves. So, fare ye well:
Upon the platform, 'twixt eleven and twelve,
I'll visit you.
    ALL: Our duty to your honor.
    HAMLET: Your loves, as mine to you: farewell.
    [*Exeunt* Horatio, Marcellus, *and* Bernardo]
My father's spirit in arms; all is not well;
I doubt some foul play: would the night were come!
Till then sit still, my soul: foul deeds will rise,
Though all the earth o'erwhelm them, to men's eyes.
    [*Exit*]

SCENE III.

A room in Polonius' *house.*

[*Enter* Laertes and Ophelia]
    LAERTES: My necessaries are embark'd: farewell:
And, sister, as the winds give benefit,
And convoy[21] is assistant, do not sleep,
But let me hear from you.
    OPHELIA: Do you doubt that?
    LAERTES: For Hamlet, and the trifling of his favor,
Hold it a fashion and a toy in blood:
A violet in the youth of primy nature,
Forward, not permanent, sweet, not lasting,
The perfume and suppliance of a minute;
No more.
    OPHELIA: No more but so?
    LAERTES: Think it no more:
For nature, crescent,[22] does not grow alone
In thews and bulk; but as this temple[23] waxes,
The inward service of the mind and soul
Grows wide withal. Perhaps he loves you now;
And now no soil nor cautel[24] doth besmirch
The virtue of his will: but you must fear,
His greatness weigh'd, his will is not his own;
For he himself is subject to his birth:
He may not, as unvalu'd persons do,
Carve for himself; for on his choice depends
The safety and the health of the whole state;
And therefore must his choice be circumscrib'd
Unto the voice and yielding of that body
Whereof he is the head. Then if he says he loves
    you,
It fits your wisdom so far to believe it
As he in his particular act and place
May give his saying deed; which is no further
Than the main[25] voice of Denmark goes withal.
Then weigh what loss your honor may sustain
If with too credent ear you list his songs,
Or lose your heart, or your chaste treasure open

[21] Means of conveyance.
[22] Growing.
[23] Body.
[24] Deceit.
[25] Strong, or mighty.

To his unmaster'd importunity.
Fear it, Ophelia, fear it, my dear sister;
And keep within the rear of your affection,
Out of the shot and danger of desire.
The chariest maid is prodigal enough
If she unmask her beauty to the moon:
Virtue itself scapes not calumnious strokes:
The canker galls the infants of the spring
Too oft before their buttons be disclos'd;
And in the morn and liquid dew of youth
Contagious blastments are most imminent.
Be wary, then; best safety lies in fear:
Youth to itself rebels, though none else near.
    OPHELIA: I shall the effect of this good lesson keep
As watchman to my heart. But, good my brother,
Do not, as some ungracious pastors do,
Show me the steep and thorny way to heaven;
Whilst like a puff'd and reckless libertine,
Himself the primrose path of dalliance treads,
And recks not his own rede.[26]
    LAERTES: O, fear me not.
I stay too long:— but here my father comes.
    [*Enter* Polonius]
A double blessing is a double grace;
Occasion smiles upon a second leave.
    POLONIUS: Yet here, Laertes! aboard, aboard, for
    shame!
The wind sits in the shoulder of your sail,
And you are stay'd for. There,—my blessing with
    you!
    [*Laying his hand on* Laertes' *head*]
And these few precepts in thy memory
See thou charácter.[27] Give thy thoughts no tongue,
Nor any unproportion'd thought his act.
Be thou familiar, but by no means vulgar.
The friends thou hast, and their adoption tried,
Grapple them to thy soul with hoops of steel;
But do not dull thy palm with entertainment
Of each new-hatch'd, unfledg'd comrade. Beware
Of entrance to a quarrel; but, being in,
Bear't that the opposèd may beware of thee.
Give every man thine ear, but few thy voice:
Take each man's censure,[28] but reserve thy judgment.
Costly thy habit as thy purse can buy,
But not express'd in fancy; rich, not gaudy:
For the apparel oft proclaims the man;
And they in France of the best rank and station
Are most select and generous chief in that.
Neither a borrower nor a lender be:
For a loan oft loses both itself and friend;
And borrowing dulls the edge of husbandry.
This above all,—to thine own self be true;
And it must follow, as the night the day,
Thou canst not then be false to any man.
Farewell: my blessing season this in thee!
    LAERTES: Most humbly do I take my leave, my
    lord.

[26] Counsel.
[27] Engrave in your mind.
[28] Opinion.

POLONIUS: The time invites you; go, your servants tend.[29]

LAERTES: Farewell, Ophelia; and remember well
What I have said to you.

OPHELIA: 'Tis in my memory lock'd,
And you yourself shall keep the key of it.

LAERTES: Farewell. [*Exit*]

POLONIUS: What is't, Ophelia, he hath said to you?

OPHELIA: So please you, something touching the Lord Hamlet.

POLONIUS: Marry, well bethought:
'Tis told me he hath very oft of late
Given private time to you; and you yourself
Have of your audience been most free and bounteous:
If it be so,—as so 'tis put on me,
And that in way of caution,—I must tell you,
You do not understand yourself so clearly
As it behoves my daughter and your honor.
What is between you? give me up the truth.

OPHELIA: He hath, my lord, of late made many tenders
Of his affection to me.

POLONIUS: Affection! pooh! you speak like a green girl,
Unsifted in such perilous circumstance.
Do you believe his tenders,[30] as you call them?

OPHELIA: I do not know, my lord, what I should think.

POLONIUS: Marry, I'll teach you: think yourself a baby;
That you have ta'en these tenders for true pay,
Which are not sterling. Tender yourself more dearly;
Or,—not to crack the wind of the poor phrase,
Wronging it thus,—you'll tender me a fool.

OPHELIA: My lord, he hath impórtun'd me with love
In honorable fashion.

POLONIUS: Ay, fashion you may call it; go to, go to.

OPHELIA: And hath given countenance to his speech, my lord,
With almost all the holy vows of heaven:

POLONIUS: Ay, springes to catch woodcocks. I do know,
When the blood burns, how prodigal the soul
Lends the tongue vows: these blazes, daughter,
Giving more light than heat,—extinct in both,
Even in their promise, as it is a-making,—
You must not take for fire. From this time
Be somewhat scanter of your maiden presence;
Set your entreatments at a higher rate
Than a command to parley. For Lord Hamlet,
Believe so much in him, that he is young;
And with a larger tether may he walk
Than may be given you: in few, Ophelia,
Do not believe his vows; for they are brokers,[31]—

[29] Wait.
[30] Offers.
[31] Procurers.

Not of that die which their investments show,
But mere implorators of unholy suits,
Breathing like sanctified and pious bawds,
The better to beguile. This is for all,—
I would not, in plain terms, from this time forth,
Have you so slander any moment leisure
As to give words or talk with the Lord Hamlet.
Look to't, I charge you; come your ways.

OPHELIA: I shall obey, my lord.

[*Exeunt*]

SCENE IV.

The platform.

[*Enter* Hamlet, Horatio, *and* Marcellus]

HAMLET: The air bites shrewdly; it is very cold.

HORATIO: It is a nipping and an eager air.

HAMLET: What hour now?

HORATIO: I think it lacks of twelve.

MARCELLUS: No, it is struck.

HORATIO: Indeed? I heard it not: then it draws near the season
Wherein the spirit held his wont to walk.

[*A flourish of trumpets, and ordnance shot off within*]

What does this mean, my lord?

HAMLET: The king doth wake to-night, and takes his rouse,
Keeps wassail, and the swaggering upspring[32] reels;
And, as he drains his draughts of Rhenish down,
The kettle-drum and trumpet thus bray out
The triumph of his pledge.[33]

HORATIO: Is it a custom?

HAMLET: Ay, marry, is't:
But to my mind,—though I am native here,
And to the manner born,—it is a custom
More honor'd in the breach than the observance.
This heavy-headed revel east and west
Makes us traduc'd and tax'd of other nations:
They clepe us drunkards, and with swinish phrase
Soil our addition;[34] and, indeed, it takes
From our achievements, though perform'd at height,
The pith and marrow of our attribute.
So oft it chances in particular men
That, for some vicious mole of nature in them,
As in their birth,—wherein they are not guilty,
Since nature cannot choose his origin,—
By the o'ergrowth of some complexion,
Oft breaking down the pales and forts of reason;
Or by some habit, that too much o'erleavens
The form of plausive[35] manners;—that these men,—
Carrying, I say, the stamp of one defect,
Being nature's livery or fortune's star,—
Their virtues else,—be they as pure as grace,

[32] A dance.
[33] The glory of his toasts.
[34] Reputation.
[35] Pleasing.

As infinite as man may undergo,—
Shall in the general censure take corruption
From that particular fault: the dram of evil
Doth all the noble substance of a doubt
To his own scandal.

HORATIO: Look, my lord, it comes!
  [*Enter* Ghost]
  HAMLET: Angels and ministers of grace defend
us!—
Be thou a spirit of health or goblin damn'd,
Bring with thee airs from heaven or blasts from
  hell,
Be thy intents wicked or charitable,
Thou com'st in such a questionable shape
That I will speak to thee: I'll call thee Hamlet,
King, father, royal Dane: O, answer me!
Let me not burst in ignorance; but tell
Why thy canóniz'd bones, hearsèd in death,
Have burst their cerements; why the sepulchre,
Wherein we saw thee quietly in-urn'd,
Hath op'd his ponderous and marble jaws
To cast thee up again! What may this mean,
That thou, dead corse, again in còmplete steel,
Revisit'st thus the glimpses of the moon,
Making night hideous and we[36] fools of nature
So horridly to shake our disposition
With thoughts beyond the reaches of our souls?
Say, why is this? wherefore? what should we do?
      [Ghost *beckons* Hamlet]
  HORATIO: It beckons you to go away with it,
As if it some impartment did desire
To you alone.
  MARCELLUS: Look, with what courteous action
It waves you to a more removed ground:
But do not go with it.
  HORATIO: No, by no means.
  HAMLET: It will not speak; then will I follow it.
  HORATIO: Do not, my lord.
  HAMLET: Why, what should be the fear?
I do not set my life at a pin's fee;
And for my soul, what can it do to that,
Being a thing immortal as itself?
It waves me forth again;—I'll follow it.
  HORATIO: What if it tempt you toward the flood,
  my lord.
Or to the dreadful summit of the cliff
That beetles o'er his base into the sea,
And there assume some other horrible form,
Which might deprive your sovereignty of reason,
And draw you into madness? think of it:
The very place puts toys of desperation,
Without more motive, into every brain
That looks so many fathoms to the sea
And hears it roar beneath.
  HAMLET: It waves me still.—
Go on; I'll follow thee.
  MARCELLUS: You shall not go, my lord.
  HAMLET: Hold off your hands.
  HORATIO: Be rul'd; you shall not go.
[36] Us.

HAMLET: My fate cries out,
And makes each petty artery in this body
As hardy as the Némean lion's[37] nerve.—
  [Ghost *beckons*]
Still am I call'd;—unhand me, gentlemen;—[*Breaking
  from them*]
By heaven, I'll make a ghost of him that lets[38] me.
I say, away!—Go on; I'll follow thee.
      [*Exeunt* Ghost *and* Hamlet]
  HORATIO: He waxes desperate with imagination.
  MARCELLUS: Let's follow; 'tis not fit thus to obey
him.
  HORATIO: Have after.—To what issue will this
come?
  MARCELLUS: Something is rotten in the state of
Denmark.
  HORATIO: Heaven will direct it.
  MARCELLUS: Nay, let's follow him.
  [*Exeunt*]

SCENE V.

A more remote part of the platform.

  [*Enter* Ghost *and* Hamlet]
  HAMLET: Where wilt thou lead me? speak, I'll go
no further.
  GHOST: Mark me.
  HAMLET: I will.
  GHOST: My hour is almost come,
When I to sulphurous and tormenting flames
Must render up myself.
  HAMLET: Alas, poor ghost!
  GHOST: Pity me not, but lend thy serious hearing
To what I shall unfold.
  HAMLET: Speak; I am bound to hear.
  GHOST: So art thou to revenge, when thou shalt
hear.
  HAMLET: What?
  GHOST: I am thy father's spirit;
Doom'd for a certain term to walk the night,
And, for the day, confin'd to waste in fires
Till the foul crimes[39] done in my days of nature
Are burnt and purg'd away. But that I am forbid
To tell the secrets of my prison-house,
I could a tale unfold whose lightest word
Would harrow up thy soul; freeze thy young blood;
Make thy two eyes, like stars, start from their spheres;
Thy knotted and combined locks to part,
And each particular hair to stand on end,
Like quills upon the fretful porcupine:
But this eternal blazon[40] must not be

[37] The fierce lion that Hercules was called upon to slay
as one of his "twelve labors."
[38] Hinders.
[39] Rather, sins or faults.
[40] Disclosure of information concerning the other
world.

To ears of flesh and blood.—List, list, O, list!—
If thou didst ever thy dear father love,—
  HAMLET: O God!
  GHOST: Revenge his foul and most unnatural
    murder.
  HAMLET: Murder!
  GHOST: Murder—most foul, as in the best it is;
But this most foul, strange, and unnatural.
  HAMLET: Haste me to know't, that I, with wings
    as swift
As meditation or the thoughts of love,
May sweep to my revenge.
  GHOST: I find thee apt;
And duller shouldst thou be than the fat weed
That rots itself in ease on Lethe[41] wharf,
Wouldst thou not stir in this. Now, Hamlet,
'Tis given out that, sleeping in mine orchard,
A serpent stung me; so the whole ear of Denmark
Is by a forged process of my death
Rankly abus'd: but know, thou noble youth,
The serpent that did sting thy father's life
Now wears his crown.
  HAMLET: O my prophetic soul! mine uncle!
  GHOST: Ay, that incestuous, that adulterate beast,
With witchcraft of his wit, with traitorous gifts,—
O wicked wit and gifts that have the power
So to seduce!—won to his shameful lust
The will of my most seeming virtuous queen:
O Hamlet, what a falling-off was there!
From me, whose love was of that dignity
That it went hand in hand even with the vow
I made to her in marriage: and to decline
Upon a wretch whose natural gifts were poor
To those of mine!
But virtue, as it never will be mov'd,
Though lewdness court it in a shape of heaven;
So lust, though to a radiant angel link'd,
Will sate itself in a celestial bed
And prey on garbage.
But, soft! methinks I scent the morning air;
Brief let me be.—Sleeping within mine orchard,
My custom always in the afternoon,
Upon my sécure hour thy uncle stole,
With juice of cursed hebenon[42] in a vial,
And in the porches of mine ears did pour
The leperous distilment; whose effect
Holds such an enmity with blood of man
That, swift as quicksilver, it courses through
The natural gates and alleys of the body;
And with a sudden vigor it doth posset[43]
And curd, like eager[44] droppings into milk,
The thin and wholesome blood: so did it mine;
And a most instant tetter bark'd about,
Most lazar-like,[45] with vile and loathsome crust,

All my smooth body.
Thus was I, sleeping, by a brother's hand,
Of life, of crown, of queen, at once despatch'd:
Cut off even in the blossoms of my sin,
Unhousel'd, unanointed, unanel'd;
No reckoning made, but sent to my account
With all my imperfections on my head:
O, horrible! O, horrible! most horrible!
If thou hast nature in thee, bear it not;
Let not the royal bed of Denmark be
A couch for luxury[46] and damned incest.
But, howsoever thou pursu'st this act,
Taint not thy mind, nor let thy soul contrive
Against thy mother aught: leave her to heaven,
And to those thorns that in her bosom lodge,
To prick and sting her. Fare thee well at once!
The glowworm shows the matin to be near,
And 'gins to pale his uneffectual fire:
Adieu, adieu! Hamlet, remember me. [Exit]
  HAMLET: O all you host of heaven! O earth! what
    else?
And shall I couple hell?—O, fie!—Hold, my heart;
And you, my sinews, grow not instant old,
But bear me stiffly up.—Remember thee!
Ay, thou poor ghost, while memory holds a seat
In this distracted globe. Remember thee!
Yea, from the table of my memory
I'll wipe away all trivial fond[47] records,
All saws of books, all forms, all pressures past,
That youth and observation copied there;
And thy commandment all alone shall live
Within the book and volume of my brain,
Unmix'd with baser matter: yes, by heaven.—
O most pernicious woman!
O villain, villain, smiling, damned villain!
My tables,—meet it is I set it down,
That one may smile, and smile, and be a villain;
At least, I am sure, it may be so in Denmark:
    [Writing]
So, uncle, there you are. Now to my word;
It is, *Adieu, adieu! remember me:*
I have sworn't.
  HORATIO: [Within] My lord, my lord,—
  MARCELLUS: [Within]   Lord Hamlet,—
  HORATIO: [Within]   Heaven secure him!
  MARCELLUS: [Within] So be it!
  HORATIO: [Within] Illo, ho, ho, my lord!
  HAMLET: Hillo, ho, ho, boy! come, bird, come.[48]
    [Enter Horatio and Marcellus]
  MARCELLUS: How is't, my noble lord?
  HORATIO: What news, my lord?
  HAMLET: O, wonderful!
  HORATIO: Good my lord, tell it.
  HAMLET: No; you'll reveal it.
  HORATIO: Not I, my lord, by heaven.
  MARCELLUS: Nor I, my lord.

[41] The river of forgetfulness of the past, out of which
the dead drink.
[42] Ebony.
[43] Coagulate.
[44] Acid.
[45] Like a leper, whose skin is rough.

[46] Lechery.
[47] Foolish.
[48] Hamlet used the word "bird" because this is a
falconer's call.

HAMLET: How say you, then; would heart of man once think it?—

But you'll be secret?

HORATIO *and* MARCELLUS: Ay, by heaven, my lord.

HAMLET: There's ne'er a villain dwelling in all Denmark

But he's an arrant knave.

HORATIO: There needs no ghost, my lord, come from the grave

To tell us this.

HAMLET: Why, right; you are i' the right;
And so, without more circumstance at all,
I hold it fit that we shake hands and part:
You, as your business and desire shall point you,—
For every man has business and desire,
Such as it is;—and for mine own poor part,
Look you, I'll go pray.

HORATIO: These are but wild and whirling words, my lord.

HAMLET: I'm sorry they offend you, heartily;
Yes, faith, heartily.

HORATIO: There's no offence, my lord.

HAMLET: Yes, by Saint Patrick, but there is, Horatio,
And much offence too. Touching this vision here,—
It is an honest ghost, that let me tell you:
For you desire to know what is between us,
O'ermaster't as you may. And now, good friends,
As you are friends, scholars, and soldiers,
Give me one poor request.

HORATIO: What is't, my lord? we will.

HAMLET: Never make known what you have seen to-night.

HORATIO *and* MARCELLUS: My lord, we will not.

HAMLET: Nay, but swear't.

HORATIO: In faith,
My lord, not I.

MARCELLUS: Nor I, my lord, in faith.

HAMLET: Upon my sword.

MARCELLUS: We have sworn, my lord, already.

HAMLET: Indeed, upon my sword, indeed.

GHOST: [*Beneath*] Swear.

HAMLET: Ha, ha, boy! say'st thou so? art thou there, truepenny?—
Come on,—you hear this fellow in the cellarage,—
Consent to swear.

HORATIO: Propose the oath, my lord.

HAMLET: Never to speak of this that you have seen,
Swear by my sword.

GHOST: [*Beneath*] Swear.

HAMLET: *Hic et ubique?*[49] then we'll shift our ground.—
Come hither, gentlemen,
And lay your hands again upon my sword:
Never to speak of this that you have heard,
Swear by my sword.

GHOST: [*Beneath*] Swear.

HAMLET: Well said! old mole! canst work i' the earth so fast?

[49] Here and everywhere?

A worthy pioneer![50]—Once more remove, good friends.

HORATIO: O day and night, but this is wondrous strange!

HAMLET: And therefore as a stranger give it welcome.
There are more things in heaven and earth, Horatio,
Than are dreamt of in your philosophy.
But come;—
Here, as before, never, so help you mercy,
How strange or odd soe'er I bear myself,—
As I, perchance, hereafter shall think meet
To put an antic disposition on,—
That you, at such times seeing me, never shall,
With arms encumber'd[51] thus, or this headshake,
Or by pronouncing of some doubtful phrase,
As, *Well, well, we know;*—or, *We could, an if we would;*—
Or, *If we list to speak;*—or, *There be, an if they might;*—
Or such ambiguous giving out, to note
That you know aught of me:—this not to do,
So grace and mercy at your most need help you,
Swear.

GHOST: [*Beneath*] Swear.

HAMLET: Rest, rest, perturbed spirit!—So, gentlemen,
With all my love I do commend to you:
And what so poor a man as Hamlet is
May do, to express his love and friending to you,
God willing, shall not lack. Let us go in together;
And still your fingers on your lips, I pray.
The time is out of joint:—O cursed spite,
That ever I was born to set it right!—
Nay, come, let's go together.

[*Exeunt*]

ACT II. SCENE I.

A room in Polonius' *house.*

[*Enter* Polonius *and* Reynaldo]

POLONIUS: Give him this money and these notes, Reynaldo.

REYNALDO: I will, my lord.

POLONIUS: You shall do marvelous wisely, good Reynaldo,
Before you visit him, to make inquiry
On his behavior.

REYNALDO: My lord, I did intend it.

POLONIUS: Marry, well said; very well said. Look you, sir,
Inquire me first what Danskers[1] are in Paris;
And how, and who, what means, and where they keep,

[50] A soldier who digs trenches and undermines fortresses.

[51] Folded.

[1] Danes.

What company, at what expense; and finding,
By this encompassment and drift of question,
That they do know my son, come you more nearer
Than your particular demands will touch it:
Take you, as 'twere, some distant knowledge of him;
As thus, *I know his father and his friends,*
And in part him;—do you mark this, Reynaldo?

    REYNALDO: Ay, very well, my lord.

    POLONIUS: *And in part him;*—but, you may say,
    not well:
But if't be he I mean, he's very wild;
Addicted so and so; and there put on him
What forgeries you please; marry, none so rank
As may dishonor him; take heed of that;
But, sir, such wanton, wild, and usual slips
As are companions noted and most known
To youth and liberty.

    REYNALDO: As gaming, my lord.

    POLONIUS: Ay, or drinking, fencing, swearing,
    quarreling,
Drabbing:[2]—you may go so far.

    REYNALDO: My lord, that would dishonor him.

    POLONIUS: Faith, no; as you may season it in the
    charge.
You must not put another scandal on him,
That he is open to incontinency;
That's not my meaning: but breathe his faults **so**
    quaintly
That they may seem the taints of liberty;
The flash and outbreak of a fiery mind;
A savageness in unreclaimed blood,
Of general assault.

    REYNALDO: But, my good lord,—

    POLONIUS: Wherefore should you do this?

    REYNALDO: Ay, my lord,
I would know that.

    POLONIUS: Marry, sir, here's my drift;
And I believe it is a fetch of warrant:[3]
You laying these slight sullies on my son,
As 'twere a thing a little soil'd i' the working,
Mark you,
Your party in converse, him you would sound,
Having ever seen in the prenominate crimes
The youth you breathe of guilty, be assur'd
He closes with you in this consequence,
Good sir, or so; or *friend,* or *gentleman,*—
According to the phrase or the addition[4]
Of man and country.

    REYNALDO: Very good, my lord.

    POLONIUS: And then, sir, does he this,—he does,—
What was I about to say?—By the mass, I was
About to say something:—where did I leave?

    REYNALDO: At *closes in the consequence,*
At *friend or so,* and *gentleman.*

    POLONIUS: At—closes in the consequence,—ay,
    marry;
He closes with you thus:—*I know the gentleman;*

    [2] Going about with loose women.
    [3] A good device.
    [4] Form of address.

I saw him yesterday, or t'other day,
Or then, or then; with such, or such; and, as you say,
There was he gaming; there o'ertook in's rouse;
There falling out at tennis: or perchance,
I saw him enter such a house of sale,—
Videlicet, a brothel,—or so forth.—
See you now;
Your bait of falsehood takes this carp of truth:
And thus do we of wisdom and of reach,
With windlasses, and with assays of bias,
By indirections find directions out:
So, by my former lecture and advice,
Shall you my son. You have me, have you not?

    REYNALDO: My lord, I have.

    POLONIUS: God b' wi' you; fare you well.

    REYNALDO: Good my lord!

    POLONIUS: Observe his inclination in yourself.

    REYNALDO: I shall, my lord.

    POLONIUS: And let him ply his music.

    REYNALDO: Well, my lord.

    POLONIUS: Farewell!

    [*Exit* Reynaldo]
    [*Enter* Ophelia]
How now, Ophelia! what's the matter?

    OPHELIA: Alas, my lord, I have been so affrighted

    POLONIUS: With what, i' the name of God?

    OPHELIA: My lord, as I was sewing in my chamber,
Lord Hamlet,—with his doublet all unbrac'd;
No hat upon his head; his stockings foul'd,
Ungarter'd, and down-gyved[5] to his ankle;
Pale as his shirt; his knees knocking each other;
And with a look so piteous in purport
As if he had been loosed out of hell
To speak of horrors,—he comes before me.

    POLONIUS: Mad for thy love?

    OPHELIA: My lord, I do not know;
But truly I do fear it.

    POLONIUS: What said he?

    OPHELIA: He took me by the wrist, and held me
    hard;
Then goes he to the length of all his arm;
And with his other hand thus o'er his brow,
He falls to such perusal of my face
As he would draw it. Long stay'd he so;
At last,—a little shaking of mine arm,
And thrice his head thus waving up and down,—
He rais'd a sigh so piteous and profound
That it did seem to shatter all his bulk
And end his being; that done, he lets me go:
And, with his head over his shoulder turn'd,
He seem'd to find his way without his eyes;
For out o' doors he went without their help,
And to the last bended their light on me.

    POLONIUS: Come, go with me: I will go seek the
    king.
This is the very ecstasy[6] of love;
Whose violent property fordoes itself,[7]

    [5] Dangling like chains.
    [6] Madness.
    [7] Destroys itself.

And leads the will to desperate undertakings,
As oft as any passion under heaven
That does afflict our nature. I am sorry,—
What, have you given him any hard words of late?
    OPHELIA: No, my good lord; but, as you did command,
I did repel his letters, and denied
His access to me.
    POLONIUS: That hath made him mad.
I am sorry that with better heed and judgment
I had not quoted him: I fear'd he did but trifle,
And meant to wreck thee; but, beshrew my jealousy!
It seems it is as proper to our age
To cast beyond ourselves in our opinions
As it is common for the younger sort
To lack discretion. Come, go we to the king:
This must be known; which, being kept close, might move
More grief to hide than hate to utter love.
    [*Exeunt*]

SCENE II.

A room in the castle.

[*Enter* King, Queen, Rosencrantz, Guildenstern, *and* Attendants]
    KING: Welcome, dear Rosencrantz and Guildenstern!
Moreover that we much did long to see you,
The need we have to use you did provoke
Our hasty sending. Something have you heard
Of Hamlet's transformation; so I call it,
Since nor the exterior nor the inward man
Resembles that it was. What it should be,
More than his father's death, that thus hath put him
So much from the understanding of himself,
I cannot dream of: I entreat you both,
That being of so young days brought up with him,
And since so neighbor'd to his youth and humor,
That you vouchsafe your rest here in our court
Some little time: so by your companies
To draw him on to pleasures, and to gather,
So much as from occasion you may glean,
Whether aught, to us unknown, afflicts him thus,
That, open'd, lies within our remedy.
    QUEEN: Good gentlemen, he hath much talk'd of you;
And sure I am two men there are not living
To whom he more adheres. If it will please you
To show us so much gentry and good-will
As to expend your time with us awhile,
For the supply and profit of our hope,
Your visitation shall receive such thanks
As fits a king's remembrance.
    ROSENCRANTZ: Both your majesties
Might, by the sovereign power you have of us,
Put your dread pleasures more into command
Than to entreaty.

    GUILDENSTERN: We both obey,
And here give up ourselves, in the full bent,
To lay our service freely at your feet,
To be commanded.
    KING: Thanks, Rosencrantz and gentle Guildenstern.
    QUEEN: Thanks, Guildenstern and gentle Rosencrantz:
And I beseech you instantly to visit
My too-much-changed son.—Go, some of you,
And bring these gentlemen where Hamlet is.
    GUILDENSTERN: Heavens make our presence and our practices
Pleasant and helpful to him!
    QUEEN: Ay, amen!
    [*Exeunt* Rosencrantz, Guildenstern, *and some* Attendants]
    [*Enter* Polonius]
    POLONIUS: The ambassadors from Norway, my good lord,
Are joyfully return'd.
    KING: Thou still has been the father of good news.
    POLONIUS: Have I, my lord? Assure you, my good liege,
I hold my duty, as I hold my soul,
Both to my God and to my gracious king:
And I do think,—or else this brain of mine
Hunts not the trail of policy[8] so sure
As it hath us'd to do,—that I have found
The very cause of Hamlet's lunacy.
    KING: O, speak of that; that do I long to hear.
    POLONIUS: Give first admittance to the ambassadors;
My news shall be the fruit to that great feast.
    KING: Thyself do grace to them, and bring them in.
    [*Exit* Polonius]
He tells me, my sweet queen, that he hath found
The head and source of all your son's distemper.
    QUEEN: I doubt it is no other but the main,—
His father's death and our o'erhasty marriage.
    KING: Well, we shall sift him.
    [*Re-enter* Polonius, *with* Voltimand *and* Cornelius]
    Welcome, my good friends!
Say, Voltimand, what from our brother Norway?
    VOLTIMAND: Most fair return of greetings and desires.
Upon our first, he sent out to suppress
His nephew's levies; which to him appear'd
To be a preparation 'gainst the Polack;
But, better look'd into, he truly found
It was against your highness: whereat griev'd,—
That so his sickness, age, and impotence
Was falsely borne in hand,—sends out arrests
On Fortinbras; which he, in brief, obeys;
Receives rebuke from Norway; and, in fine,
Makes vows before his uncle never more
To give the assay of arms against your majesty.
Whereon old Norway, overcome with joy,
    [8] Statecraft.

Gives him three thousand crowns in annual fee;
And his commission to employ those soldiers,
So levied as before, against the Polack:
With an entreaty, herein further shown, [*gives a
    paper*]
That it might please you to give quiet pass
Through your dominions for this enterprise,
On such regards of safety and allowance
As therein are set down.
    KING: It likes us well;
And at our more consider'd time we'll read,
Answer, and think upon this business.
Meantime we thank you for your well-took labor:
Go to your rest; at night we'll feast together:
Most welcome home!
    [*Exeunt* Voltimand *and* Cornelius]
POLONIUS: This business is well ended.—
My liege, and madam,—to expostulate
What majesty should be, what duty is,
Why day is day, night night, and time is time,
Were nothing but to waste night, day, and time.
Therefore, since brevity is the soul of wit,
And tediousness the limbs and outward flourishes,
I will be brief:—your noble son is mad:
Mad call I it; for to define true madness,
What is't but to be nothing else but mad?
But let that go.
    QUEEN: More matter with less art.
    POLONIUS: Madam, I swear I use no art at all.
That he is mad, 'tis true 'tis pity;
And pity 'tis 'tis true: a foolish figure;
But farewell it, for I will use no art.
Mad let us grant him, then: and now remains
That we find out the cause of this effect;
Or rather say, the cause of this defect,
For this effect defective comes by cause:
Thus it remains, and the remainder thus.
Perpend.
I have a daughter,—have whilst she is mine,—
Who, in her duty and obedience, mark,
Hath given me this: now gather, and surmise
    [*Reads*]
*To the celestial, and my soul's idol, the most beauti-
fied Ophelia,—*
That's an ill phrase, a vile phrase,— *beautified* is a
    vile phrase: but you shall hear. Thus:
    [*Reads*]
In her excellent white bosom, these, &c.
    QUEEN: Came this from Hamlet to her?
    POLONIUS: Good madam, stay a while; I will be
    faithful.
    [*Reads*]
    Doubt thou the stars are fire;
       Doubt that the sun doth move;
    Doubt truth to be a liar;
       But never doubt I love.
*O dear Ophelia, I am ill at these numbers,
I have not art to reckon my groans: but that I love
    thee best, O most best, believe it. Adieu.
Thine evermore, most dear lady, whilst this ma-*

    chine is to him,   Hamlet
This, in obedience, hath my daughter show'd me:
And more above, hath his solicitings,
As they fell out by time, by means, and place,
All given to mine ear.
    KING: But how hath she
Receiv'd his love?
    POLONIUS: What do you think of me?
    KING: As of a man faithful and honorable.
    POLONIUS: I would fain prove so. But what might
    you think,
When I had seen this hot love on the wing,—
As I perceiv'd it, I must tell you that,
Before my daughter told me,—what might you,
Or my dear majesty your queen here, think,
If I had play'd the desk or table-book;[9]
Or given my heart a winking, mute and dumb;
Or look'd upon this love with idle sight;—
What might you think? No, I went round to work,
And my young mistress thus I did bespeak:
Lord Hamlet is a prince out of thy sphere;
This must not be: and then I precepts gave her,
That she should lock herself from his resort,
Admit no messengers, receive no tokens.
Which done, she took the fruits of my advice;
And he, repulsed,—a short tale to make,—
Fell into a sadness; then into a fast;
Thence to a watch; thence into a weakness;
Thence to a lightness; and, by this declension,
Into the madness wherein now he raves
And all we wail for.
    KING: Do you think 'tis this?
    QUEEN: It may be, very likely.
    POLONIUS: Hath there been such a time,—I'd fain
    know that,—
That I have positively said, *'Tis so,*
When it prov'd otherwise?
    KING: Not that I know.
    POLONIUS: Take this from this, if this be other-
    wise: [*Pointing to his head and shoulder*]
If circumstances lead me, I will find
Where truth is hid, though it were hid indeed
Within the center.
    KING: How may we try it further?
    POLONIUS: You know, sometimes he walks for
    hours together
Here in the lobby.
    QUEEN: So he does, indeed.
    POLONIUS: At such a time I'll loose my daughter
    to him:
Be you and I behind an arras[10] then;
Mark the encounter: if he love her not,
And be not from his reason fall'n thereon,
Let me be no assistant for a state,
But keep a farm and carters.
    KING: We will try it.
    QUEEN: But look, where sadly the poor wretch
    comes reading.

[9] Memorandum pad.
[10] Tapestry, hung some distance away from a wall.

POLONIUS: Away, I do beseech you, both away: I'll board[11] him presently:—O, give me leave.

[*Exeunt* King, Queen, *and* Attendants]

[*Enter* Hamlet, *reading*]

How does my good Lord Hamlet?

HAMLET: Well, God-a-mercy.

POLONIUS: Do you know me, my lord?

HAMLET: Excellent, excellent well; you're a fish-monger.

POLONIUS: Not I, my lord.

HAMLET: Then I would you were so honest a man.

POLONIUS: Honest, my lord!

HAMLET: Ay, sir; to be honest, as this world goes, is to be one man picked out of ten thousand.

POLONIUS: That's very true, my lord.

HAMLET: For if the sun breed maggots in a dead dog, being a god kissing carrion,—Have you a daughter?

POLONIUS: I have, my lord.

HAMLET: Let her not walk i' the sun: conception is a blessing; but not as your daughter may conceive:—friend, look to't.

POLONIUS: How say you by that?—[*Aside*] Still harping on my daughter:—yet he knew me not at first; he said I was a fishmonger: he is far gone, far gone: and truly in my youth I suffered much extremity for love; very near this. I'll speak to him again.—What do you read, my lord?

HAMLET: Words, words, words.

POLONIUS: What is the matter, my lord?

HAMLET: Between who?

POLONIUS: I mean, the matter that you read, my lord.

HAMLET: Slanders, sir: for the satirical slave says here that old men have gray beards; that their faces are wrinkled; their eyes purging thick amber and plum-tree gum; and that they have a plentiful lack of wit, together with most weak hams: all which, sir, though I most powerfully and potently believe, yet I hold it not honesty to have it thus set down; for you yourself, sir, should be old as I am, if, like a crab, you could go backward.

POLONIUS: [*Aside*] Though this be madness, yet there is method in't.—Will you walk out of the air, my lord?

HAMLET: Into my grave?

POLONIUS: Indeed, that is out o' the air.—[*Aside*] How pregnant[12] sometimes his replies are! a happiness that often madness hits on, which reason and sanity could not so prosperously be delivered of. I will leave him, and suddenly contrive the means of meeting between him and my daughter.—More honorable lord, I will most humbly take my leave of you.

HAMLET: You cannot, sir, take from me anything that I will more willingly part withal,—except my life, except my life, except my life.

POLONIUS: Fare you well, my lord.

HAMLET: These tedious old fools!

[11] Address.
[12] Ready, and clever.

[*Enter* Rosencrantz *and* Guildenstern]

POLONIUS: You go to seek the Lord Hamlet; there he is.

ROSENCRANTZ: [*To* Polonius] God save you, sir!

[*Exit* Polonius]

GUILDENSTERN: Mine honored lord!

ROSENCRANTZ: My most dear lord!

HAMLET: My excellent good friends! How dost thou, Guildenstern? Ah, Rosencrantz? Good lads, how do ye both?

ROSENCRANTZ: As the indifferent children of the earth.

GUILDENSTERN: Happy in that we are not over-happy; on fortune's cap we are not the very button.

HAMLET: Nor the soles of her shoe?

ROSENCRANTZ: Neither, my lord.

HAMLET: Then you live about her waist, or in the middle of her favors?

GUILDENSTERN: Faith, her privates we.

HAMLET: In the secret parts of fortune? O, most true; she is a strumpet. What's the news?

ROSENCRANTZ: None, my lord, but that the world's grown honest.

HAMLET: Then is doomsday near: but your news is not true. Let me question more in particular: what have you, my good friends, deserved at the hands of fortune, that she sends you to prison hither?

GUILDENSTERN: Prison, my lord!

HAMLET: Denmark's a prison.

ROSENCRANTZ: Then is the world one.

HAMLET: A goodly one; in which there are many confines, wards, and dungeons, Denmark being one o' the worst.

ROSENCRANTZ: We think not so, my lord.

HAMLET: Why, then, 'tis none to you; for there is nothing either good or bad, but thinking makes it so: to me it is a prison.

ROSENCRANTZ: Why, then, your ambition makes it one; 'tis too narrow for your mind.

HAMLET: O God, I could be bounded in a nutshell, and count myself a king of infinite space, were it not that I have bad dreams.

GUILDENSTERN: Which dreams, indeed, are ambition; for the very substance of the ambitious is merely the shadow of a dream.

HAMLET: A dream itself is but a shadow.

ROSENCRANTZ: Truly, and I hold ambition of so airy and light a quality that it is but a shadow's shadow.

HAMLET: Then are our beggars bodies, and our monarchs and outstretched heroes the beggars' shadows. Shall we to the court? for, by my fay, I cannot reason.

ROSENCRANTZ *and* GUILDENSTERN: We'll wait upon you.

HAMLET: No such matter: I will not sort you with the rest of my servants; for, to speak to you like an honest man, I am most dreadfully attended. But, in the beaten way of friendship, what make you at Elsinore?

ROSENCRANTZ: To visit you, my lord; no other occasion.

HAMLET: Beggar that I am, I am even poor in thanks; but I thank you: and sure, dear friends, my thanks are too dear a halfpenny. Were you not sent for? Is it your own inclining? Is it a free visitation? Come, deal justly with me: come, come; nay, speak.

GUILDENSTERN: What should we say, my lord?

HAMLET: Why, anything—but to the purpose. You were sent for; and there is a kind of confession in your looks, which your modesties have not craft enough to color: I know the good king and queen have sent for you.

ROSENCRANTZ: To what end, my lord?

HAMLET: That you must teach me. But let me conjure you, by the rights of our fellowship, by the consonancy of our youth, by the obligation of our ever-preserved love, and by what more dear a better proposer could charge you withal, be even and direct with me, whether you were sent for or no?

ROSENCRANTZ: What say you? [*To* Guildenstern]

HAMLET: [*Aside*] Nay, then, I have an eye of you. —If you love me, hold not off.

GUILDENSTERN: My lord, we were sent for.

HAMLET: I will tell you why; so shall my anticipation prevent your discovery, and your secrecy to the king and queen moult no feather. I have of late,—but wherefore I know not,—lost all my mirth, forgone all custom of exercises; and, indeed, it goes so heavily with my disposition that this goodly frame, the earth, seems to me a sterile promontory; this most excellent canopy, the air, look you, this brave o'erhanging firmament, this majestical roof fretted[13] with golden fire,—why, it appears no other thing to me than a foul and pestilent congregation of vapors. What a piece of work is man! How noble in reason! how infinite in faculties! in form and moving, how express and admirable! in action, how like an angel! in apprehension, how like a god! the beauty of the world! the paragon of animals! And yet, to me, what is this quintessence of dust? man delights not me; no, nor woman neither, though by your smiling you seem to say so.

ROSENCRANTZ: My lord, there was no such stuff in my thoughts.

HAMLET: Why did you laugh, then, when I said, *Man delights not me?*

ROSENCRANTZ: To think, my lord, if you delight not in man, what lenten entertainment[14] the players shall receive from you: we coted[15] them on the way; and hither are they coming, to offer you service.

HAMLET: He that plays the king shall be welcome, —his majesty shall have tribute of me; the adventurous knight shall use his foil and target; the lover shall not sigh gratis; the humorous[16] man shall end his part in peace; the clown shall make those laugh whose

lungs are tickled o' the sere;[17] and the lady shall say her mind freely, or the blank verse shall halt[18] for't.— What players are they?

ROSENCRANTZ: Even those you were wont to take delight in,—the tragedians of the city.

HAMLET: How chances it they travel? their residence, both in reputation and profit, was better both ways.

ROSENCRANTZ: I think their inhibition[19] comes by the means of the late innovation.

HAMLET: Do they hold the same estimation they did when I was in the city? Are they so followed?

ROSENCRANTZ: No, indeed, they are not.

HAMLET: How comes it? do they grow rusty?

ROSENCRANTZ: Nay, their endeavor keeps in the wonted pace; but there is, sir, an aery[20] of children, little eyases,[21] that cry out on the top of question, and are most tyrannically clapped for't: these are now the fashion; and so berattle the common stages,—so they call them,—that many wearing rapiers are afraid of goose-quills, and dare scarce come thither.

HAMLET: What, are they children? who maintains 'em? how are they escoted?[22] Will they pursue the quality[23] no longer than they can sing? will they not say afterwards, if they should grow themselves to common players,—as it is most like, if their means are no better,—their writers do them wrong, to make them exclaim against their own succession?

ROSENCRANTZ: Faith, there has been much to do on both sides; and the nation holds it no sin to tarre[24] them to controversy: there was for awhile no money bid for argument, unless the poet and the player went to cuffs in the question.

HAMLET: Is't possible?

GUILDENSTERN: O, there has been much throwing about of brains.

HAMLET: Do the boys carry it away?

ROSENCRANTZ: Ay, that they do, my lord; Hercules and his load[25] too.

HAMLET: It is not strange; for mine uncle is king of Denmark, and those that would make mouths at him while my father lived, give twenty, forty, fifty, an hundred ducats a-piece for his picture in little. 'Sblood, there is something in this more than natural, if philosophy could find it out.

[*Flourish of trumpets within*]

GUILDENSTERN: There are the players.

HAMLET: Gentlemen, you are welcome to Elsinore. Your hands, come: the appurtenance of welcome is

---

[13] A roof with fretwork.
[14] Poor reception.
[15] Passed.
[16] Eccentric.
[17] Whose lungs, for laughter, are easily tickled.
[18] Limp.
[19] Difficulty, preventing them from remaining in the capital.
[20] Aerie: brood of birds of prey.
[21] Young hawks; a reference to the boys' companies that became popular rivals of Shakespeare's company of players.
[22] Financially supported.
[23] Profession.
[24] Egg them on.
[25] The globe, or the world.

fashion and ceremony: let me comply with you in this garb; lest my extent[26] to the players, which, I tell you, must show fairly outward, should more appear like entertainment[27] than yours. You are welcome: but my uncle-father and aunt-mother are deceived.

GUILDENSTERN: In what, my dear lord?

HAMLET: I am but mad north-north-west: when the wind is southerly I know a hawk from a handsaw.

[*Enter* Polonius]

POLONIUS: Well be with you, gentlemen!

HAMLET: Hark you, Guildenstern;—and you too; —at each ear a hearer: that great baby you see there is not yet out of his swathing-clouts.

ROSENCRANTZ: Happily he's the second time come to them; for they say an old man is twice a child.

HAMLET: I will prophesy he comes to tell me of the players; mark it.—You say right, sir: o' Monday morning; 'twas so indeed.

POLONIUS: My lord, I have news to tell you.

HAMLET: My lord, I have news to tell you. When Roscius was an actor in Rome,—

POLONIUS: The actors are come hither, my lord.

HAMLET: Buzz, buzz!

POLONIUS: Upon mine honor,—

HAMLET: Then came each actor on his ass,—

POLONIUS: The best actors in the world, either for tragedy, comedy, history, pastoral, pastoral-comical, historical-pastoral, tragical-historical, tragical-comi-cal-historical-pastoral, scene individable,[28] or poem unlimited:[29] Seneca cannot be too heavy nor Plautus too light. For the law of writ and the liberty,[30] these are the only men.

HAMLET: O Jephthah, judge of Israel, what a treasure hadst thou!

POLONIUS: What a treasure had he, my lord?

HAMLET: Why—

> One fair daughter, and no more,
> The which he loved passing well.

POLONIUS: [*Aside*] Still on my daughter.

HAMLET: Am I not i' the right, old Jephthah?

POLONIUS: If you call me Jephthah, my lord, I have a daughter that I love passing well.

HAMLET: Nay, that follows not.

POLONIUS: What follows, then, my lord?

HAMLET: Why—

> As by lot, God wot,

and then, you know,

> It came to pass, as most like it was,—

26 Show of friendliness.
27 Welcome.
28 A play that observes the unities of time and place.
29 A typical multiscened Elizabethan type of drama, not restricted by the unities. Examples are *Hamlet, Macbeth, King Lear,* and virtually any other play by Shakespeare.
30 For the laws of the unities and for playwriting that is not so restricted.

the first row of the pious chanson will show you more; for look where my abridgement comes.

[*Enter four or five* Players]

You are welcome, masters; welcome, all:—I am glad to see thee well:—welcome, good friends.—O, my old friend! Thy face is valanced since I saw thee last; comest thou to beard me in Denmark?—What, my young lady and mistress! By'r lady, your ladyship is nearer heaven than when I saw you last, by the altitude of a chopine.[31] Pray God, your voice, like a piece of uncurrent gold, be not cracked within the ring.—Masters, you are all welcome. We'll e'en to't like French falconers, fly at anything we see: we'll have a speech straight: come, give us a taste of your quality; come, a passionate speech.

1ST PLAYER: What speech, my lord?

HAMLET: I heard thee speak me a speech once,—but it was never acted; or, if it was, not above once; for the play, I remember, pleased not the million; 'twas caviare to the general: but it was,—as I received it, and others whose judgments in such matters cried in the top of mine,—an excellent play, well digested in the scenes, set down with as much modesty as cunning. I remember, one said there were no sallets in the lines to make the matter savory, nor no matter in the phrase that might indite the author of affectation; but called it an honest method, as wholesome as sweet, and by very much more handsome than fine. One speech in it I chiefly loved: 'twas Æneas' tale to Dido; and thereabout of it especially where he speaks of Priam's slaughter: if it live in your memory, begin at this line;—let me see, let me see:—

> The rugged Pyrrhus, like the Hyrcanian beast,[32]

—it is not so:—it begins with Pyrrhus:—

> The rugged Pyrrhus,—he whose sable arms,
> Black as his purpose, did the night resemble
> When he lay couched in the ominous horse,—
> Hath now this dread and black complexion smear'd
> With heraldry more dismal; head to foot
> Now is he total gules; horridly trick'd
> With blood of fathers, mothers, daughters, sons,
> Bak'd and impasted with the parching streets,
> That lend a tyrannous and damned light
> To their vile murders: roasted in wrath and fire,
> And thus o'er-sized with coagulate gore,
> With eyes like carbuncles, the hellish Pyrrhus
> Old grandsire Priam seeks.—

So proceed you.

POLONIUS: 'Fore God, my lord, well spoken, with good accent and good discretion.

31 A wooden stilt more than a foot high used under a woman's shoe; a Venetian fashion introduced into England.
32 This speech is an example of the declamatory style of drama, which Shakespeare surely must have considered outmoded.

1ST PLAYER: Anon he finds him
Striking too short at Greeks; his antique sword,
Rebellious to his arm, lies where it falls,
Repugnant to command: unequal match'd,
Pyrrhus at Priam drives; in rage strikes wide;
But with the whiff and wind of his fell sword
The unnerved father falls. Then senseless Ilium,
Seeming to feel this blow, with flaming top
Stoops to his base; and with a hideous crash
Takes prisoner Pyrrhus' ear: for, lo! his sword,
Which was declining on the milky head
Of reverend Priam, seem'd i' the air to stick:
So, as a painted tyrant, Pyrrhus stood;
And, like a neutral to his will and matter,
Did nothing.
But as we often see, against some storm,
A silence in the heavens, the rack stand still,
The blood winds speechless, and the orb below
As hush as death, anon the dreadful thunder
Doth rend the region; so, after Pyrrhus' pause,
A roused vengeance sets him new a-work;
And never did the Cyclops' hammers fall
On Mars his armor, forg'd for proof eterne,
With less remorse than Pyrrhus' bleeding sword
Now falls on Priam.—
Out, out, thou strumpet, Fortune! All you gods,
In general synod, take away her power;
Break all the spokes and fellies from her wheel,
And bowl the round knave down the hill of heaven,
As low as to the fiends!
POLONIUS: This is too long.
HAMLET: It shall to the barber's, with your beard.
—Pr'ythee, say on.—He's for a jig, or a tale of
bawdry, or he sleeps:—say on; come to Hecuba.
1ST PLAYER: But who, O, who had seen the mobled
queen,—
HAMLET: *The mobled queen?*
POLONIUS: That's good; *mobled queen* is good.
1ST PLAYER: Run barefoot up and down, threaten-
ing the flames
With bissom rheum; a clout upon that head
Where late the diadem stood; and, for a robe,
About her lank and all o'er-teemed loins,
A blanket, in the alarm of fear caught up;—
Who this had seen, with tongue in venom steep'd,
'Gainst Fortune's state would treason have pro-
nounc'd:
But if the gods themselves did see her then,
When she saw Pyrrhus make malicious sport
In mincing with his sword her husband's limbs,
The instant burst of clamor that she made,—
Unless things mortal move them not at all,—
Would have made milch the burning eyes of heaven,
And passion in the gods.
POLONIUS: Look, whether he has not turn'd his
color, and has tears in's eyes.—Pray you, no more.
HAMLET: 'Tis well; I'll have thee speak out the
rest soon.—Good my lord, will you see the players
well bestowed? Do you hear, let them be well used;
for they are the abstracts and brief chronicles of the

time; after your death you were better have a bad
epitaph than their ill report while you live.
POLONIUS: My lord, I will use them according to
their desert.
HAMLET: Odd's bodikin, man, better: use every
man after his desert, and who should scape whipping?
Use them after your own honor and dignity: the less
they deserve the more merit is in your bounty. Take
them in.
POLONIUS: Come, sirs.
HAMLET: Follow him, friends: we'll hear a play
to-morrow.
[*Exit* Polonius *with all the* Players *but the* First]
Dost thou hear me, old friend; can you play the
Murder of Gonzago?
1ST PLAYER: Ay, my lord.
HAMLET: We'll ha't to-morrow night. You could,
for a need, study a speech of some dozen or sixteen
lines which I would set down and insert in't? could
you not?
1ST PLAYER: Ay, my lord.
HAMLET: Very well.—Follow that lord; and look
you mock him not.
[*Exit* First Player]
—My good friends, [*to* Rosencrantz *and* Guilden-
stern] I'll leave you till night: you are welcome to
Elsinore.
ROSENCRANTZ: Good my lord!
[*Exeunt* Rosencrantz *and* Guildenstern]
HAMLET: Ay, so God b' wi' ye!—Now I am alone.
O, what a rogue[33] and peasant slave am I!
Is it not monstrous that this player here,
But in a fiction, in a dream of passion,
Could force his soul so to his own conceit[34]
That from her working all his visage wan'd;
Tears in his eyes, distraction in's aspèct,
A broken voice, and his whole function suiting
With forms to his conceit? And all for nothing!
For Hecuba?
What's Hecuba to him or he to Hecuba,
That he should weep for her? What would he do,
Had he the motive and the cue for passion
That I have? He would drown the stage with tears,
And cleave the general ear with horrid speech;
Make mad the guilty, and appal the free;
Confound the ignorant, and amaze, indeed,
The very faculties of eyes and ears.
Yet I,
A dull and muddy-mettled rascal, peak,
Like John-a-dreams, unpregnant of my cause,
And can say nothing; no, not for a king
Upon whose property and most dear life
A damn'd defeat was made. Am I a coward?
Who calls me villain? breaks my pate across?
Plucks off my beard and blows it in my face?
Tweaks me by the nose? gives me the lie i' the throat,
As deep as to the lungs? who does me this, ha?
'Swounds, I should take it: for it cannot be

33 Wretched creature.
34 Conception

But I am pigeon-liver'd, and lack gall
To make oppression bitter; or ere this
I should have fatted all the region kites
With this slave's offal:—bloody, bawdy villain!
Remorseless, treacherous, lecherous, kindless villain!
O, vengeance!
Why, what an ass am I! This is most brave,
That I, the son of a dear father murder'd,
Prompted to my revenge by heaven and hell,
Must, like a whore, unpack my heart with words,
And fall a-cursing like a very drab,
A scullion!
Fie upon't! foh!—About, my brain! I have heard
That guilty creatures, sitting at a play,
Have by the very cunning of the scene
Been struck so to the soul that presently
They have proclaim'd their malefactions;
For murder, though it have no tongue, will speak
With most miraculous organ. I'll have these players
Play something like the murder of my father
Before mine uncle: I'll observe his looks;
I'll tent[35] him to the quick: if he but blench,
I know my course. The spirit that I have seen
May be the devil: and the devil hath power
To assume a pleasing shape; yea, and perhaps
Out of my weakness and my melancholy,—
As he is very potent with such spirits,—
Abuses me to damn me: I'll have grounds
More relative than this:—the play's the thing
Wherein I'll catch the conscience of the king. [*Exit*]

ACT III. SCENE I.

A room in the castle.

[*Enter* King, Queen, Polonius, Ophelia, Rosencrantz, *and* Guildenstern]

KING: And can you, by no drift of circumstance,
Get from him why he puts on this confusion,
Grating so harshly all his days of quiet
With turbulent and dangerous lunacy?
ROSENCRANTZ: He does confess he feels himself distracted;
But from what cause he will by no means speak.
GUILDENSTERN: Nor do we find him forward to be sounded;
But, with a crafty madness, keeps aloof
When we would bring him on to some confession
Of his true state.
QUEEN: Did he receive you well?
ROSENCRANTZ: Most like a gentleman.
GUILDENSTERN: But with much forcing of his disposition.
ROSENCRANTZ: Niggard of question; but, of our demands,
Most free in his reply.
QUEEN: Did you assay him
To any pastime?

[35] Probe.

ROSENCRANTZ: Madam, it so fell out that certain players
We o'er-raught on the way: of these we told him;
And there did seem in him a kind of joy
To hear of it: they are about the court;
And, as I think, they have already order
This night to play before him.
POLONIUS: 'Tis most true:
And he beseech'd me to entreat your majesties
To hear and see the matter.
KING: With all my heart; and it doth much content me
To hear him so inclin'd.
Good gentlemen, give him a further edge,
And drive his purpose on to these delights.
ROSENCRANTZ: We shall, my lord.
[*Exeunt* Rosencrantz *and* Guildenstern]
KING: Sweet Gertrude, leave us too;
For we have closely sent for Hamlet hither
That he, as 'twere by accident, may here
Affront Ophelia:
Her father and myself,—lawful espials,[1]—
Will so bestow ourselves that, seeing, unseen,
We may of their encounter frankly judge;
And gather by him, as he is behav'd,
If't be the affliction of his love or no
That thus he suffers for.
QUEEN: I shall obey you:—
And for your part, Ophelia, I do wish
That your good beauties be the happy cause
Of Hamlet's wildness: so shall I hope your virtues
Will bring him to his wonted way again,
To both your honors.
OPHELIA: Madam, I wish it may.
[*Exit* Queen]
POLONIUS: Ophelia, walk you here.—Gracious, so please you,
We will bestow ourselves.—[*To* Ophelia] Read on this book;
That show of such an exercise may color
Your loneliness.—We are oft to blame in this,—
'Tis too much prov'd,—that with devotion's visage
And pious action we do sugar o'er
The devil himself.
KING: [*Aside*] O, 'tis too true!
How smart a lash that speech doth give my conscience!
The harlot's cheek, beautied with plastering art,
Is not more ugly to the thing that helps it
Than is my deed to my most painted word:
O heavy burden!
POLONIUS: I hear him coming: let's withdraw, my lord.
[*Exeunt* King *and* Polonius]
[*Enter* Hamlet]
HAMLET: To be, or not to be,—that is the question:—
Whether 'tis nobler in the mind to suffer
The slings and arrows of outrageous fortune,

[1] Spies.

Or to take arms against a sea of troubles,
And by opposing end them?—To die,—to sleep,—
No more; and by a sleep to say we end
The heart-ache and the thousand natural shocks
That flesh is heir to,—'tis a consummation
Devoutly to be wish'd. To die,—to sleep;—
To sleep! perchance to dream:—ay, there's the rub;
For in that sleep of death what dreams may come,
When we have shuffled off this mortal coil,
Must give us pause: there's the respect
That makes calamity of so long life;
For who would bear the whips and scorns of time,
The oppressor's wrong, the proud man's contumely,
The pangs of déspis'd love, the law's delay,
The insolence of office, and the spurns
That patient merit of the unworthy takes,
When he himself might his quietus make
With a bare bodkin?[2] who would fardels[3] bear,
To grunt[4] and sweat under a weary life,
But that the dread of something after death,—
The undiscover'd country, from whose bourn[5]
No traveler returns,—puzzles the will,
And makes us rather bear those ills we have
Than to fly to others that we know not of?
Thus conscience does make cowards of us all;
And thus the native hue of resolution
Is sicklied o'er with the pale cast of thought;
And enterprises of great pith and moment,
With this regard, their currents turn awry,
And lose the name of action.—Soft you now!
The fair Ophelia.—Nymph, in thy orisons[6]
Be all my sins remember'd.

OPHELIA: Good my lord,
How does your honor for this many a day?

HAMLET: I humbly thank you; well, well, well.

OPHELIA: My lord, I have remembrances of yours,
That I have longed long to re-deliver;
I pray you, now receive them.

HAMLET: No, not I;
I never gave you aught.

OPHELIA: My honor'd lord, you know right well
    you did;
And with them, words of so sweet breath compos'd
As made the things more rich: their perfume lost,
Take these again; for to the noble mind
Rich gifts wax poor when givers prove unkind.
There, my lord.

HAMLET: Ha, ha! are you honest?

OPHELIA: My lord?

HAMLET: Are you fair?

OPHELIA: What means your lordship?

HAMLET: That if you be honest and fair, your
honesty should admit no discourse to your beauty.

OPHELIA: Could beauty, my lord, have better commerce than with honesty?

HAMLET: Ay, truly; for the power of beauty will
sooner transform honesty from what it is to a bawd
than the force of honesty can translate beauty into his
likeness: this was sometime a paradox, but now the
time gives it proof. I did love you once.

OPHELIA: Indeed, my lord, you made me believe so.

HAMLET: You should not have believed me; for
virtue cannot so inoculate our old stock but we shall
relish of it: I loved you not.

OPHELIA: I was the more deceived.

HAMLET: Get thee to a nunnery: why wouldst thou
be a breeder of sinners? I am myself indifferent[7]
honest; but yet I could accuse me of such things
that it were better my mother had not borne me: I am
very proud, revengeful, ambitious; with more offences
at my beck than I have thoughts to put them in,
imagination to give them shape, or time to act them
in. What should such fellows as I do crawling between heaven and earth? We are arrant knaves, all;
believe none of us. Go thy ways to a nunnery.
Where's your father?

OPHELIA: At home, my lord.

HAMLET: Let the doors be shut upon him, that he
may play the fool nowhere but in's own house.
Farewell.

OPHELIA: O, help him, you sweet heavens!

HAMLET: If thou dost marry, I'll give thee this
plague for thy dowry,—be thou as chaste as ice, as
pure as snow, thou shalt not escape calumny. Get
thee to a nunnery, go: farewell. Or, if thou wilt needs
marry, marry a fool; for wise men know well enough
what monsters you make of them. To a nunnery, go;
and quickly too. Farewell.

OPHELIA: O heavenly powers, restore him!

HAMLET: I have heard of your paintings too, well
enough; God has given you one face and you make
yourselves another: you jig, you amble, and you
lisp, and nickname God's creatures, and make your
wantonness your ignorance. Go to, I'll no more on't;
it hath made me mad. I say, we will have no more
marriages: those that are married already, all but
one, shall live; the rest shall keep as they are. To a
nunnery, go. [*Exit*]

OPHELIA: O, what a noble mind is here o'erthrown!
The courtier's, soldier's, scholar's eye, tongue, sword:
The expectancy and rose of the fair state,
The glass of fashion and the mould of form,
The observ'd of all observers,—quite, quite down!
And I, of ladies most deject and wretched
That suck'd the honey of his music vows,
Now see that noble and most sovereign reason,
Like sweet bells jangled, out of tune and harsh;
That unmatch'd form and feature of blown[8] youth
Blasted with ecstasy: O, woe is me,
To have seen what I have seen, see what I see!

[*Re-enter* King *and* Polonius]

KING: Love! his affections do not that way tend;
Nor what he spake, though it lack'd form a little,

[2] Stiletto.
[3] Burdens.
[4] Groan.
[5] Boundary.
[6] Prayers.

[7] Tolerably.
[8] Full-blown.

Was not like madness. There's something in his soul
O'er which his melancholy sits on brood;
And I do doubt[9] the hatch and the disclose
Will be some danger: which for to prevent,
I have in quick determination
Thus set it down:—he shall with speed to England
For the demand of our neglected tribute:
Haply, the seas and countries different,
With variable objects, shall expel
This something-settled matter in his heart;
Whereon his brains still beating puts him thus
From fashion of himself. What think you on't?
    POLONIUS: It shall do well: but yet do I believe
The origin and commencement of his grief
Sprung from neglected love.—How now, Ophelia!
You need not tell us what Lord Hamlet said;
We heard it all.—My lord, do as you please;
But if you hold it fit, after the play,
Let his queen mother all alone entreat him
To show his grief: let her be round with him;
And I'll be plac'd, so please you, in the ear
Of all their conference. If she finds him not,[10]
To England send him; or confine him where
Your wisdom best shall think.
    KING: It shall be so:
Madness in great ones must not unwatch'd go.
    [*Exeunt*]

<hr>

SCENE II.

<hr>

A hall in the castle.

[*Enter* Hamlet *and certain* Players]
    HAMLET: Speak the speech, I pray you, as I pro-
nounced it to you, trippingly on the tongue: but if
you mouth it, as many of your players do, I had as
lief the town-crier spoke my lines. Nor do not saw
the air too much with your hand, thus; but use all
gently: for in the very torrent, tempest, and, as I may
say, the whirlwind of passion, you must acquire and
beget a temperance that may give it smoothness. O,
it offends me to the soul, to hear a robustious periwig-
pated fellow tear a passion to tatters, to very rags, to
split the ears of the groundlings, who, for the most
part, are capable of nothing but inexplicable dumb
shows and noise: I could have such a fellow whipped
for o'erdoing Termagant;[11] it out-herods Herod:[12]
pray you, avoid it.
    1ST PLAYER: I warrant your honor.
    HAMLET: Be not too tame neither, but let your own
discretion be your tutor: suit the action to the word,
the word to the action; with this special observance,
that you o'erstep not the modesty of nature: for anything so overdone is from the purpose of playing,

    [9] Fear.
    [10] Does not find him out.
    [11] A violent pagan deity, supposedly Mohammedan.
    [12] Outrants the ranting Herod, who figures in medieval
drama.

whose end, both at the first and now, was and is, to
hold, as 'twere, the mirror up to nature; to show
virtue her own feature, scorn her own image, and the
very age and body of the time his form and pressure.
Now, this overdone or come tardy off, though it
make the unskilful laugh, cannot but make the judicious grieve; the censure of the which one must, in
your allowance, o'erweigh a whole theater of others.
O, there be players that I have seen play,—and heard
others praise, and that highly,—not to speak it profanely, that, neither having the accent of Christians,
nor the gait of Christian, pagan, nor man, have so
strutted and bellowed that I have thought some of
nature's journeymen had made men, and not made
them well, they imitated humanity so abominably.
    1ST PLAYER: I hope we have reformed that in-
differently with us, sir.
    HAMLET: O, reform it altogether. And let those
that play your clowns speak no more than is set down
for them: for there be of them that will themselves
laugh, to set on some quantity of barren spectators to
laugh too; though, in the meantime, some necessary
question of the play be then to be considered: that's
villainous, and shows a most pitiful ambition in the
fool that uses it. Go, make you ready.
    [*Exeunt* Players]
    [*Enter* Polonius, Rosencrantz, *and* Guildenstern]
How now, my lord! will the king hear this piece of
work?
    POLONIUS: And the queen, too, and that presently.
    HAMLET: Bid the players make haste.
    [*Exit* Polonius]
Will you two help to hasten them?
    ROSENCRANTZ *and* GUILDENSTERN: We will, my
    lord. [*Exeunt*]
    HAMLET: What, ho, Horatio!
    [*Enter* Horatio]
    HORATIO: Here, sweet lord, at your service.
    HAMLET: Horatio, thou art e'en as just a man
As e'er my conversation cop'd withal.
    HORATIO: O, my dear lord,—
    HAMLET: Nay, do not think I flatter;
For what advancement may I hope from thee,
That no revénue hast, but thy good spirits,
To feed and clothe thee? Why should the poor be
    flatter'd?
No, let the candied tongue lick ábsurd pomp;
And crook the pregnant hinges of the knee
Where thrift may follow fawning. Dost thou hear?
Since my dear soul was mistress of her choice,
And could of men distinguish, her election
Hath seal'd thee for herself: for thou hast been
As one, in suffering all, that suffers nothing;
A man that Fortune's buffets and rewards
Hast ta'en with equal thanks: and bless'd are those
Whose blood and judgment are so well commingled
That they are not a pipe for Fortune's finger
To sound what stop she please. Give me that man
That is not passion's slave, and I will wear him
In my heart's core, ay, in my heart of heart,

As I do thee.—Something too much of this.—
There is a play to-night before the king;
One scene of it comes near the circumstance
Which I have told thee of my father's death:
I pr'ythee, when thou see'st that act a-foot,
Even with the very comment of thy soul
Observe mine uncle: if this his occulted guilt
Do not itself unkennel in one speech,
It is a damned ghost that we have seen;
And my imaginations are as foul
As Vulcan's stithy.[13] Give him heedful note:
For I mine eyes will rivet to his face;
And, after, we will both our judgments join
In censure of his seeming.
    HORATIO: Well, my lord:
If he steal aught the whilst this play is playing,
And scape detecting, I will pay the theft.
    HAMLET: They are coming to the play; I must be
idle:[14]
Get you a place.
    [*Danish march. A flourish. Enter* King, Queen,
      Polonius, Ophelia, Rosencrantz, Guildenstern,
      and others]
    KING: How fares our cousin Hamlet?
    HAMLET: Excellent, i'faith; of the chameleon's
dish:[15] I eat the air, promise-crammed: you cannot
feed capons so.
    KING: I have nothing with this answer, Hamlet;
these words are not mine.
    HAMLET: No, nor mine now. [*To* Polonius] My
lord, you played once i'the university, you say?
    POLONIUS: That did I, my lord, and was accounted
a good actor.
    HAMLET: And what did you enact?
    POLONIUS: I did enact Julius Cæsar: I was killed i'
the Capitol; Brutus killed me.
    HAMLET: It was a brute part of him to kill so
capital a calf there.—Be the players ready.
    ROSENCRANTZ: Ay, my lord; they stay upon your
patience.
    QUEEN: Come hither, my good Hamlet, sit by me.
    HAMLET: No, good mother, here's metal more at-
tractive.
    POLONIUS: O, ho! do you mark that? [*To the* King]
    HAMLET: Lady, shall I lie in your lap? [*Lying down
at* Ophelia's *feet*]
    OPHELIA: No, my lord.
    HAMLET: I mean, my head upon your lap?
    OPHELIA: Ay, my lord.
    HAMLET: Do you think I meant country matters?
    OPHELIA: I think nothing, my lord.
    HAMLET: That's a fair thought to lie between
maids' legs.
    OPHELIA: What is, my lord?
    HAMLET: Nothing.
    OPHELIA: You are merry, my lord.
    HAMLET: Who, I?

[13] Smithy.
[14] Foolish.
[15] Chameleons were supposed to live on air.

    OPHELIA: Ay, my lord.
    HAMLET: O, your only jig-maker. What should a man
do but be merry? for, look you, how cheerfully my
mother looks, and my father died within's two hours.
    OPHELIA: Nay, 'tis twice two months, my lord.
    HAMLET: So long? Nay, then, let the devil wear
black, for I'll have a suit of sables. O heavens! die
two months ago, and not forgotten yet? Then there's
hope a great man's memory may outlive his life half
a year: but, by'r lady, he must build churches, then;
or else shall he suffer not thinking on, with the
hobby-horse, whose epitaph is, *For, O, for, O, the
hobby-horse is forgot.*
    [*Trumpets sound. The dumb show enters*]
    [*Enter a* King *and a* Queen, *very lovingly; the*
    Queen *embracing him and he her. She kneels,
    and makes show of protestation unto him. He
    takes her up, and declines his head upon her
    neck: lays him down upon a bank of flowers:
    she, seeing him asleep, leaves him. Anon
    comes in a fellow, takes off his crown, kisses
    it, and pours poison in the* King's *ears, and exit.
    The* Queen *returns; finds the* King *dead, and
    makes passionate action. The* Poisoner, *with
    some two or three* Mutes, *comes in again, seem-
    ing to lament with her. The dead body is carried
    away. The* Poisoner *woos the* Queen *with gifts:
    she seems loth and unwilling awhile, but in the
    end accepts his love*]
    [*Exeunt*]
    OPHELIA: What means this, my lord?
    HAMLET: Marry, this is miching mallecho;[16] it
means mischief.
    OPHELIA: Belike this show imports the argument
of the play.
    [*Enter* Prologue]
    HAMLET: We shall know by this fellow: the players
cannot keep counsel; they'll tell all.
    OPHELIA: Will he tell us what this show meant?
    HAMLET: Ay, or any show that you'll show him:
be not you ashamed to show, he'll not shame to tell
you what it means.
    OPHELIA: You are naught, you are naught: I'll
mark the play.
    PROLOGUE: *For us, and for our tragedy,
        Here stooping to your clemency,
        We beg your hearing patiently.*
    HAMLET: Is this a prologue, or the posy[17] of a ring?
    OPHELIA: 'Tis brief, my lord.
    HAMLET: As woman's love.
    [*Enter a* King *and a* Queen]
    PROLOGUE KING: *Full thirty times hath Phœbus'
        cart gone round*
Neptune's salt wash and Tellus' orbed ground,[18]
And thirty dozen moons with borrow'd sheen
About the world have times twelve thirties been,
Since love our hearts, and Hymen did our hands

[16] A sneaking misdeed.
[17] Motto or inscription.
[18] The globe.

Unite commutual in most sacred bands.
 PROLOGUE QUEEN: So many journeys may the sun
  and moon
Make us again count o'er ere love be done!
But, woe is me, you are so sick of late,
So far from cheer and from your former state
That I distrust you.[19] Yet, though I distrust,
Discomfort you, my lord, it nothing must:
For women's fear and love holds quantity,[20]
In neither aught, or in extremity.
Now, what my love is, proof hath made you know;
And as my love is siz'd, my fear is so:
Where love is great, the littlest doubts are fear;
Where little fears grow great, great love grows there.
 PROLOGUE KING: Faith, I must leave thee, love, and
  shortly too;
My operant powers their functions leave[21] to do:
And thou shalt live in this fair world behind,
Honor'd, belov'd; and haply one as kind
For husband shalt thou,—
 PROLOGUE QUEEN: O, confound the rest!
Such love must needs be treason in my breast:
In second husband let me be accurst!
None wed the second but who kill'd the first.
 HAMLET: [Aside] Wormwood, wormwood.
 PROLOGUE QUEEN: The instances that second mar-
  riage move
Are base respects of thrift, but none of love:
A second time I kill my husband, dead,
When second husband kisses me in bed.
 PROLOGUE KING: I do believe you think what now
  you speak;
But what we do determine oft we break.
Purpose is but the slave to memory;
Of violent birth, but poor validity:
Which now, like fruit unripe, sticks on the tree;
But fall unshaken when they mellow be.
Most necessary 'tis that we forget
To pay ourselves what to ourselves is debt:
What to ourselves in passion we propose,
The passion ending, doth the purpose lose.
The violence of either grief or joy
Their own enactures with themselves destroy:
Where joy most revels grief doth most lament;
Grief joys, joy grieves, on slender accident.
This world is not for aye; nor 'tis not strange
That even our loves should with our fortunes change;
For 'tis a question left us yet to prove
Whether love lead fortune or else fortune love.
The great man down, you mark his favorite flies;
The poor advanc'd makes friends of enemies.
And hitherto doth love on fortune tend:
For who not needs shall never lack a friend;
And who in want a hollow friend doth try,
Directly seasons him his enemy.
But, orderly to end where I begun,—
Our wills and fates do so contráry run

19 Worry about you.
20 Correspond in degree.
21 Cease.

That our devices still are overthrown;
Our thoughts are ours, their ends none of our own:
So think thou wilt no second husband wed;
But die thy thoughts when thy first lord is dead.
 PROLOGUE QUEEN: Nor earth to me give food, nor
  heaven light!
Sport and repose lock from me day and night!
To desperation turn my trust and hope!
An anchor's[22] cheer in prison be my scope!
Each opposite, that blanks the face of joy,
Meet what I would have well, and it destroy!
Both here and hence, pursue me lasting strife,
If, once a widow, ever I be wife!
 HAMLET: If she should break it now! [To Ophelia]
 PROLOGUE KING: 'Tis deeply sworn. Sweet, leave me
  here awhile;
My spirits grow dull, and fain I would beguile.
The tedious day with sleep. [Sleeps]
 PROLOGUE QUEEN: Sleep rock thy brain,
And never come mischance between us twain! [Exit]
 HAMLET: Madam, how like you this play?
 QUEEN: The lady doth protest too much, methinks.
 HAMLET: O, but she'll keep her word.
 KING: Have you heard the argument? Is there no
offence in't?
 HAMLET: No, no, they do but jest, poison in jest;
no offence i' the world.
 KING: What do you call the play?
 HAMLET: The Mouse-trap. Marry, how? Tropi-
cally.[23] This play is the image of a murder done in
Vienna: Gonzago is the duke's name: his wife, Bap-
tista: you shall see anon; 'tis a knavish piece of
work: but what o' that? your majesty, and we that
have free souls, it touches us not: let the galled jade
wince, our withers are unwrung.
 [Enter Lucianus]
This is one Lucianus, nephew to the king.
 OPHELIA: You are a good chorus, my lord.
 HAMLET: I could interpret between you and your
love, if I could see the puppets dallying.
 OPHELIA: You are keen, my lord, you are keen.
 HAMLET: It would cost you a groaning to take off
my edge.
 OPHELIA: Still better, and worse.
 HAMLET: So you must take your husbands.—Be-
gin, murderer; pox, leave thy damnable faces and
begin. Come:—*The croaking raven doth bellow for
revenge.*
 LUCIANUS: Thoughts black, hands apt, drugs fit,
  and time agreeing;
Confederate season, else no creature seeing;
Thou mixture rank, of midnight weeds collected,
With Hecate's ban[24] thrice blasted, thrice infected,
Thy natural magic and dire property
On wholesome life usurp immediately.
 [Pours the poison into the sleeper's ears]

22 Anchorite's, or hermit's.
23 Figuratively, or metaphorically; by means of a
"trope."
24 The spell of the goddess of witchcraft.

HAMLET: He poisons him i' the garden for's estate. His name's Gonzago: the story is extant, and writ in choice Italian: you shall see anon how the murderer gets the love of Gonzago's wife.

OPHELIA: The king rises.

HAMLET: What, frighted with false fire!

QUEEN: How fares my lord?

POLONIUS: Give o'er the play.

KING: Give me some light:—away!

ALL: Lights, lights, lights!

[*Exeunt all but* Hamlet *and* Horatio]

HAMLET: Why, let the stricken deer go weep,
The hart ungallèd play;
For some must watch, while some must sleep:
So runs the world away.—
Would not this, sir, and a forest of feathers,
If the rest of my fortunes turn Turk with me,
With two Provencial roses on my razed shoes,
Get me a fellowship in a cry[25] of players, sir?

HORATIO: Half a share.

HAMLET: A whole one, I.
For thou dost know, O Damon dear,
This realm dismantled was
Of Jove himself; and now reigns here
A very, very—pajock.[26]

HORATIO: You might have rhymed.

HAMLET: O good Horatio, I'll take the ghost's word for a thousand pound. Didst perceive?

HORATIO: Very well, my lord.

HAMLET: Upon the talk of the poisoning,—

HORATIO: I did very well note him.

HAMLET: Ah, ha!—Come, some music! come, the recorders!—
For if the king like not the comedy,
Why, then, belike,—he likes it not, perdy. Come, some music!

[*Re-enter* Rosencrantz *and* Guildenstern]

GUILDENSTERN: Good my lord, vouchsafe me a word with you.

HAMLET: Sir, a whole history.

GUILDENSTERN: The king, sir,—

HAMLET: Ay, sir, what of him?

GUILDENSTERN: Is, in his retirement, marvelous distempered.

HAMLET: With drink, sir?

GUILDENSTERN: No, my lord, rather with choler.

HAMLET: Your wisdom should show itself more richer to signify this to his doctor; for, for me to put him to his purgation would perhaps plunge him into far more choler.

GUILDENSTERN: Good my lord, put your discourse into some frame, and start not so wildly from my affair.

HAMLET: I am tame, sir:—pronounce.

GUILDENSTERN: The queen, your mother, in most great affliction of spirit, hath sent me to you.

HAMLET: You are welcome.

GUILDENSTERN: Nay, good my lord, this courtesy is

25 Company.
26 Peacock.

not of the right breed. If it shall please you to make me a wholesome answer, I will do your mother's commandment: if not, your pardon and my return shall be the end of my business.

HAMLET: Sir, I cannot.

GUILDENSTERN: What, my lord?

HAMLET: Make you a wholesome answer; my wit's diseas'd: but, sir, such answer as I can make, you shall command; or, rather, as you say, my mother: therefore no more, but to the matter: my mother, you say,—

ROSENCRANTZ: Then thus she says: your behavior hath struck her into amazement and admiration.

HAMLET: O wonderful son, that can so astonish a mother!—But is there no sequel at the heels of this mother's admiration?

ROSENCRANTZ: She desires to speak with you in her closet[27] ere you go to bed.

HAMLET: We shall obey, were she ten times our mother. Have you any further trade with us?

ROSENCRANTZ: My lord, you once did love me.

HAMLET: So I do still, by these pickers and stealers.[28]

ROSENCRANTZ: Good, my lord, what is your cause of distemper? you do, surely, bar the door upon your own liberty if you deny your griefs to your friend.

HAMLET: Sir, I lack advancement.

ROSENCRANTZ: How can that be, when you have the voice of the king himself for your succession in Denmark?

HAMLET: Ay, but *While the grass grows,*—the proverb is something musty.

[*Re-enter the* Players, *with recorders*]

O, the recorders:—let me see one.—To withdraw with you:—why do you go about to recover the wind of me, as if you would drive me into a toil?

GUILDENSTERN: O, my lord, if my duty be too bold, my love is too unmannerly.

HAMLET: I do not well understand that. Will you play upon this pipe?

GUILDENSTERN: My lord, I cannot.

HAMLET: I pray you.

GUILDENSTERN: Believe me, I cannot.

HAMLET: I do beseech you.

GUILDENSTERN: I know no touch of it, my lord.

HAMLET: 'Tis as easy as lying: govern these ventages[29] with your finger and thumb, give it breath with your mouth, and it will discourse most eloquent music. Look you, these are the stops.

GUILDENSTERN: But these cannot I command to any utterance of harmony; I have not the skill.

HAMLET: Why, look you now, how unworthy a thing you make of me! You would play upon me; you would seem to know my stops; you would pluck out the heart of my mystery; you would sound me from my lowest note to the top of my compass: and there is much music, excellent voice, in this little organ;

27 Boudoir.
28 Fingers.
29 Holes.

yet cannot you make it speak. 'Sblood, do you think that I am easier to be played on than a pipe? Call me what instrument you will, though you can fret me you cannot play upon me.

[*Enter* Polonius]

God bless you, sir!

POLONIUS: My lord, the queen would speak with with you, and presently.

HAMLET: Do you see yonder cloud that's almost in shape of a camel?

POLONIUS: By the mass, and 'tis like a camel indeed.

HAMLET: Methinks it is like a weasel.

POLONIUS: It is backed like a weasel.

HAMLET: Or like a whale?

POLONIUS: Very like a whale.

HAMLET: Then will I come to my mother by and by.—They fool me to the top of my bent.—I will come by and by.

POLONIUS: I will say so.

HAMLET: By and by is easily said.

[*Exit* Polonius]

Leave me, friends.

[*Exeunt* Rosencrantz, Guildenstern, Horatio, *and* Players]

'Tis now the very witching time of night,
When churchyards yawn, and hell itself breathes out
Contagion to this world: now could I drink hot blood,
And do such bitter business as the day
Would quake to look on. Soft! now to my mother.—
O heart, lose not thy nature; let not ever
The soul of Nero[30] enter this firm bosom:
Let me be cruel, not unnatural:
I will speak daggers to her, but use none;
My tongue and soul in this be hypocrites,—
How in my words soever she be shent,
To give them seals never, my soul, consent! [*Exit*]

SCENE III.

A room in the castle

[*Enter* King, Rosencrantz, *and* Guildenstern]

KING: I like him not; nor stands it safe with us
To let his madness range. Therefore prepare you;
I your commission will forthwith despatch,
And he to England shall along with you:
The terms of our estate may not endure
Hazard so dangerous as doth hourly grow
Out of his lunacies.

GUILDENSTERN: We will ourselves provide:
Most holy and religious fear it is
To keep those many many bodies safe
That live and feed upon your majesty.

ROSENCRANTZ: The single and peculiar life is bound,
With all the strength and armor of the mind,

30 Nero killed his mother, a crime of which Hamlet does not want to be guilty.

To keep itself from 'noyance; but much more
That spirit upon whose weal depend and rest
The lives of many. The cease of majesty
Dies not alone; but like a gulf doth draw
What's near it with it: it is a massy wheel,
Fix'd on the summit of the highest mount,
To whose huge spokes ten thousand lesser things
Are mortis'd and adjoin'd; which, when it falls,
Each small annexment, petty consequence,
Attends the boisterous ruin. Never alone
Did the king sigh, but with a general groan.

KING: Arm you, I pray you, to this speedy voyage;
For we will fetters put upon this fear,
Which now goes too free-footed.

ROSENCRANTZ *and* GUILDENSTERN: We will haste us.

[*Exeunt* Rosencrantz *and* Guildenstern]

[*Enter* Polonius]

POLONIUS: My lord, he's going to his mother's closet:
Behind the arras I'll convey myself
To hear the process; I'll warrant she'll tax him home:[31]
And, as you said, and wisely was it said,
'Tis meet that some more audience than a mother,
Since nature makes them partial, should o'erhear
The speech, of vantage. Fare you well, my liege:
I'll call upon you ere you go to bed,
And tell you what I know.

KING: Thanks, dear my lord.

[*Exit* Polonius]

O, my offence is rank, it smells to heaven;
It hath the primal eldest curse upon't,—
A brother's murder!—Pray can I not,
Though inclination be as sharp as will:
My stronger guilt defeats my strong intent;
And, like a man to double business bound,
I stand in pause where I shall first begin,
And both neglect. What if this cursed hand
Were thicker than itself with brother's blood,—
Is there not rain enough in the sweet heavens
To wash it white as snow? Whereto serves mercy
But to confront the visage of offence?
And what's in prayer but this twofold force,—
To be forestalled ere we come to fall,
Or pardon'd being down? Then I'll look up;
My fault is past. But, O, what form of prayer
Can serve my turn? Forgive me my foul murder?—
That cannot be; since I am still possess'd
Of those effects for which I did the murder,—
My crown, mine own ambition, and my queen.
May one be pardon'd and retain the offence?[32]
In the corrupted currents of this world
Offence's gilded hand may shove by justice;
And oft 'tis seen the wicked prize itself
Buys out the law: but 'tis not so above;
There is no shuffling,—there the action lies
In his true nature; and we ourselves compell'd,
Even to the teeth and forehead of our faults,

31 Reprove him properly.

32 That is. the gains won by the offense.

To give in evidence. What then? what rests?[33]
Try what repentance can: what can it not?
Yet what can it when one can not repent?
O wretched state! O bosom black as death!
O limed[34] soul, that, struggling to be free,
Art more engag'd! Help, angels! make assay:
Bow, stubborn knees; and, heart, with strings of
    steel,
Be soft as sinews of the new-born babe!
All may be well. [*Retires and kneels*]
    [*Enter* Hamlet]
  HAMLET: Now might I do it pat, now he is pray-
    ing;
And now I'll do't—and so he goes to heaven;
And so am I reveng'd:—that would be scann'd:
A villain kills my father; and for that,
I, his sole son, do this same villain send
To heaven.
O, this is hire and salary, not revenge.
He took my father grossly, full of bread;
With all his crimes broad blown, as flush as May;
And how his audit stands who knows save heaven?
But in our circumstance and course of thought
'Tis heavy with him: and am I, then, reveng'd,
To take him in the purging of his soul,
When he is fit and season'd for his passage?
No.
Up, sword; and know thou a more horrid hent:[35]
When he is drunk, asleep, or in his rage;
Or in the incestuous pleasure of his bed;
At gaming, swearing; or about some act
That has no relish of salvation in't;—
Then trip him, that his heels may kick at heaven;
And that his soul may be as damn'd and black
As hell, whereto it goes. My mother stays:
This physic but prolongs thy sickly days. [*Exit*]
    [*The* King *rises and advances*]
  KING: My words fly up, my thoughts remain below:
Words without thoughts never to heaven go. [*Exit*]

SCENE IV.

Another room in the castle.

    [*Enter* Queen *and* Polonius]
  POLONIUS: He will come straight. Look you lay
    home to him:
Tell him his pranks have been too broad to bear with,
And that your grace hath screen'd and stood between
Much heat and him. I'll silence me e'en here.
Pray you, be round with him.
  HAMLET: [*Within*] Mother, mother, mother!
  QUEEN: I'll warrant you:
Fear me not:—withdraw, I hear him coming.
    [Polonius *goes behind the arras*]
    [*Enter* Hamlet]

[33] Remains.
[34] Snared.
[35] Opportunity.

  HAMLET: Now, mother, what's the matter?
  QUEEN: Hamlet, thou hast thy father much of-
    fended.
  HAMLET: Mother, you have my father much
    offended.
  QUEEN: Come, come, you answer with an idle
    tongue.
  HAMLET: Go, go, you question with a wicked
    tongue.
  QUEEN: Why, how now, Hamlet!
  HAMLET: What's the matter now?
  QUEEN: Have you forgot me?
  HAMLET: No, by the rood, not so:
You are the queen, your husband's brother's wife;
And,—would it were not so!—you are my mother.
  QUEEN: Nay, then, I'll set those to you that can
    speak.
  HAMLET: Come, come, and sit you down; you shall
    not budge;
You go not till I set you up a glass
Where you may see the inmost part of you.
  QUEEN: What wilt thou do? thou wilt not murder
    me?—
Help, help, ho!
  POLONIUS: [*Behind*] What, ho! help, help, help!
  HAMLET: How now! a rat? [*Draws*]
Dead, for a ducat, dead! [*Makes a pass through the
    arras*]
  POLONIUS: [*Behind*] O, I am slain! [*Falls and dies*]
  QUEEN: O me, what hast thou done?
  HAMLET: Nay, I know not:
Is it the king? [*Draws forth* Polonius]
  QUEEN: O, what a rash and bloody deed is this!
  HAMLET: A bloody deed!—almost as bad, good
    mother,
As kill a king and marry with his brother.
  QUEEN: As kill a king!
  HAMLET: Ay, lady, 'twas my word.—
Thou wretched, rash, intruding fool, farewell! [*To
    Polonius*]
I took thee for thy better: take thy fortune;
Thou find'st to be too busy is some danger.—
Leave wringing of your hands: peace; sit you down,
And let me wring your heart: for so I shall,
If it be made of penetrable stuff;
If damned custom have not braz'd it so
That it is proof and bulwark against sense.
  QUEEN: What have I done, that thou dar'st wag
    thy tongue
In noise so rude against me?
  HAMLET: Such an act
That blurs the grace and blush of modesty;
Calls virtue hypocrite; takes off the rose
From the fair forehead of an innocent love,
And sets a blister there; makes marriage-vows
As false as dicers' oaths: O, such a deed
As from the body of contraction plucks
The very soul, and sweet religion makes
A rhapsody of words: heaven's face doth glow;
Yea, this solidity and compound mass,

With tristful[36] visage, as against the doom,
Is thought-sick at the act.
    QUEEN: Ah me, what act,
That roars so loud, and thunders in the index?
    HAMLET: Look here upon this picture and on
        this,—
The counterfeit presentment of two brothers.
See what grace was seated on this brow;
Hyperion's curls; the front of Jove himself;
An eye like Mars, to threaten and command;
A station like the herald Mercury
New-lighted on a heaven-kissing hill;
A combination and a form, indeed,
Where every god did seem to set his seal,
To give the world assurance of a man:
This was your husband.—Look you now, what fol-
    lows:
Here is your husband, like a mildew'd ear
Blasting his wholesome brother. Have you eyes?
Could you on this fair mountain leave to feed,
And batten on this moor? Ha! have you eyes?
You cannot call it love; for at your age
The hey-day in the blood is tame, it's humble,
And waits upon the judgment: and what judgment
Would step from this to this? Sense, sure, you have,
Else could you not have motion: but sure that
    sense
Is apoplex'd: for madness would not err;
Nor sense to ecstasy was ne'er so thrill'd
But it reserv'd some quantity of choice
To serve in such a difference. What devil was't
That thus hath cozen'd you at hoodman-blind?[37]
Eyes without feeling, feeling without sight,
Ears without hands or eyes, smelling sans all,
Or but a sickly part of one true sense
Could not so mope.
O shame! where is thy blush! Rebellious hell,
If thou canst mutine in a matron's bones,
To flaming youth let virtue be as wax,
And melt in her own fire: proclaim no shame
When the compulsive ardor gives the charge,
Since frost itself as actively doth burn,
And reason panders[38] will.
    QUEEN: O Hamlet, speak no more:
Thou turn'st mine eyes into my very soul;
And there I see such black and grained spots
As will not leave their tinct.[39]
    HAMLET: Nay, but to live
In the rank sweat of an enseamed bed,
Stew'd in corruption, honeying and making love
Over the nasty sty,—
    QUEEN: O, speak to me no more;
These words like daggers enter in mine ears;
No more, sweet Hamlet.
    HAMLET: A murderer and a villain;
A slave that is not twentieth part the tithe

[36] Gloomy.
[37] Tricked you at blindman's buff.
[38] Becomes subservient to.
[39] As will not yield up their color.

Of your precedent lord; a vice of kings;[40]
A cutpurse of the empire and the rule,
That from a shelf the precious diadem stole,
And put it in his pocket!
    QUEEN: No more.
    HAMLET: A king of shreds and patches,—
    [*Enter* Ghost]
Save me, and hover o'er me with your wings,
You heavenly guards!—What would your gracious
    figure?
    QUEEN: Alas, he's mad!
    HAMLET: Do you not come your tardy son to
    chide,
That, laps'd in time and passion, lets go by
The important acting of your dread command?
O, say!
    GHOST: Do not forget: this visitation
Is but to whet thy almost blunted purpose.
But, look, amazement on thy mother sits:
O, step between her and her fighting soul,—
Conceit in weakest bodies strongest works,—
Speak to her, Hamlet.
    HAMLET: How is it with you, lady?
    QUEEN: Alas, how is't with you,
That you do bend your eye on vacancy,
And with the incorporal air do hold discourse?
Forth at your eyes your spirits wildly peep;
And, as the sleeping soldiers in the alarm,
Your bedded hair, like life in excrements,[41]
Starts up and stands on end. O gentle son,
Upon the heat and flame of thy distemper
Sprinkle cool patience. Whereon do you look?
    HAMLET: On him, on him! Look you, how pale he
    glares!
His form and cause conjoin'd, preaching to stones,
Would make them capable.—Do not look upon me;
Lest with this piteous action you convert
My stern effects: then what I have to do
Will want true color; tears perchance for blood.
    QUEEN: To whom do you speak this?
    HAMLET: Do you see nothing there?
    QUEEN: Nothing at all; yet all that is I see.
    HAMLET: Nor did you nothing hear?
    QUEEN: No, nothing but ourselves.
    HAMLET: Why, look you there! look, how it steals
    away!
My father, in his habit as he liv'd!
Look, where he goes, even now, out at the portal!
    [*Exit* Ghost]
    QUEEN: This is the very coinage of your brain:
This bodiless creation ecstasy
Is very cunning in.
    HAMLET: Ecstasy!
My pulse, as yours, doth temperately keep time.
And makes as healthful music: it is not madness
That I have utter'd: bring me to the test,
And I the matter will re-word; which madness
Would gambol from. Mother, for love of grace,

[40] A buffoon among kings. The "Vice" in morality plays.
[41] In outgrowths or extremities.

Lay not that flattering unction to your soul,
That not your trespass, but my madness speaks:
It will but skin and film the ulcerous place,
Whilst rank corruption, mining all within,
Infects unseen. Confess yourself to Heaven;
Repent what's past; avoid what is to come;
And do not spread the compost on the weeds,
To make them ranker. Forgive me this my virtue;
For in the fatness[42] of these pursy times
Virtue itself of vice must pardon beg,
Yea, curb and woo for leave to do him good.
    QUEEN: O Hamlet, thou hast cleft my heart in
      twain.
    HAMLET: O, throw away the worser part of it,
And live the purer with the other half.
Good-night: but go not to mine uncle's bed;
Assume a virtue, if you have it not.
That monster custom, who all sense doth eat,
Of habits devil, is angel yet in this,—
That to the use of actions fair and good
He likewise gives a frock or livery
That aptly is put on. Refrain to-night;
And that shall lend a kind of easiness
To the next abstinence: the next more easy;
For use almost can change the stamp of nature,
And either curb the devil, or throw him out
With wondrous potency. Once more, good-night:
And when you are desirous to be bless'd,
I'll blessing beg of you.—For this same lord [*point-
ing to* Polonius]
I do repent: but Heaven hath pleas'd it so,
To punish me with this, and this with me,
That I must be their[43] scourge and minister.
I will bestow him, and will answer well
The death I gave him. So, again, good-night.—
I must be cruel only to be kind:
Thus bad begins and worse remains behind.—
One word more, good lady.
    QUEEN: What shall I do?
    HAMLET: Not this, by no means, that I bid you do:
Let the bloat king tempt you again to bed;
Pinch wanton on your cheek; call you his mouse;
And let him, for a pair of reechy kisses,
Or paddling in your neck with his damn'd fingers,
Make you to ravel all this matter out,
That I essentially am not in madness,
But mad in craft. 'Twere good you let him know;
For who that's but a queen, fair, sober, wise,
Would from a paddock,[44] from a bat, a gib,
Such dear concernings hide? who would do so?
No, in despite of sense and secrecy,
Unpeg the basket on the house's top,
Let the birds fly, and, like the famous ape,
To try conclusions, in the basket creep,
And break your own neck down.
    QUEEN: Be thou assur'd, if words be made of
      breath

42 Corruption.
43 Heaven's, or the heavens'.
44 Paddock: toad; gib: tomcat.

And breath of life, I have not life to breathe
What thou hast said to me.
    HAMLET: I must to England; you know that?
    QUEEN: Alack,
I had forgot: 'tis so concluded on.
    HAMLET: There's letters seal'd: and my two school-
      fellows,—
Whom I will trust as I will adders fang'd,
They bear the mandate; they must sweep my way,
And marshal me to knavery. Let it work;
For 'tis the sport to have the engineer
Hoist with his own petard: and't shall go hard
But I will delve one yard below their mines,
And blow them at the moon: O, 'tis most sweet,
When in one line two crafts directly meet.—
This man shall set me packing:
I'll lug the guts into the neighbor room.—
Mother, good-night.—Indeed, this counsellor
Is now most still, most secret, and most grave,
Who was in life a foolish prating knave.
Come, sir, to draw toward an end with you:—
Good-night, mother.
    [*Exeunt severally;* Hamlet *dragging out* Polo-
    nius]

ACT IV. SCENE I.

A room in the castle.

[*Enter* King, Queen, Rosencrantz, *and* Guilden-
stern]
    KING: There's matter in these sighs, these prófound
      heaves:
You must translate: 'tis fit we understand them.
Where is your son?
    QUEEN: Bestow this place on us a little while.
    [*To* Rosencrantz *and* Guildenstern, *who go out*]
Ah, my good lord, what have I seen to-night!
    KING: What, Gertrude? How does Hamlet?
    QUEEN: Mad as the sea and wind, when both con-
      tend
Which is the mightier: in his lawless fit,
Behind the arras hearing something stir,
He whips his rapier out, and cries, *A rat, a rat!*
And, in this brainish apprehension,[1] kills
The unseen good old man.
    KING: O heavy deed!
It had been so with us had we been there:
His liberty is full of threats to all;
To you yourself, to us, to every one.
Alas, how shall this bloody deed be answer'd?
It will be laid to us, whose providence
Should have kept short, restrain'd, and out of haunt
This mad young man: but so much was our love,
We would not understand what was most fit;
But, like the owner of a foul disease,
To keep it from divulging, let it feed
Even on the pith of life. Where is he gone?
    1 Mad notion.

QUEEN: To draw apart the body he hath kill'd:
O'er whom his very madness, like some ore
Among a mineral of metals base,
Shows itself pure; he weeps for what is done.
    KING: O Gertrude, come away!
The sun no sooner shall the mountains touch
But we will ship him hence: and this vile deed
We must, with all our majesty and skill,
Both countenance and excuse.—Ho, Guildenstern!
    [*Exeunt* Rosencrantz *and* Guildenstern]
Friends both, go join you with some further aid:
Hamlet in madness hath Polonius slain,
And from his mother's closet hath he dragg'd him:
Go seek him out; speak fair, and bring the body
Into the chapel. I pray you, haste in this.
    [*Exeunt* Rosencrantz *and* Guildenstern]
Come, Gertrude, we'll call up our wisest friends;
And let them know both what we mean to do
And what's untimely done: so haply slander,—
Whose whisper o'er the world's diameter,
As level as the cannon to his blank,
Transports his poison'd shot,—may amiss our name,
And hit the woundless air.—O, come away!
My soul is full of discord and dismay.
    [*Exeunt*]

SCENE II.

Another room in the castle.

    [*Enter* Hamlet]
    HAMLET: Safely stowed.
    ROSENCRANTZ and GUILDENSTERN: [*Within*] Hamlet! Lord Hamlet!
    HAMLET: What noise? who calls on Hamlet?
O, here they come.
    [*Enter* Rosencrantz *and* Guildenstern]
    ROSENCRANTZ: What have you done, my lord, with the dead body?
    HAMLET: Compounded it with dust, whereto 'tis kin.
    ROSENCRANTZ: Tell us where 'tis, that we may take it thence,
And bear it to the chapel.
    HAMLET: Do not believe it.
    ROSENCRANTZ: Believe what?
    HAMLET: That I can keep your counsel, and not mine own. Besides, to be demanded of a sponge!—what replication should be made by the son of a king?
    ROSENCRANTZ: Take you me for a sponge, my lord?
    HAMLET: Ay, sir; that soaks up the king's countenance, his rewards, his authorities. But such officers do the king best service in the end: he keeps them, like an ape, in the corner of his jaw; first mouthed, to be last swallowed: when he needs what you have gleaned, it is but squeezing you, and, sponge, you shall be dry again.
    ROSENCRANTZ: I understand you not, my lord.

HAMLET: I am glad of it: a knavish speech sleeps in a foolish ear.
    ROSENCRANTZ: My lord, you must tell us where the body is, and go with us to the king.
    HAMLET: The body is with the king, but the king is not with the body. The king is a thing,—
    GUILDENSTERN: A thing, my lord!
    HAMLET: Of nothing: bring me to him.
Hide fox, and all after.
    [*Exeunt*]

SCENE III.

Another room in the castle.

    [*Enter* King, *attended*]
    KING: I have sent to seek him, and to find the body.
How dangerous is it that this man goes loose!
Yet must not we put the strong law on him:
He's lov'd of the distracted multitude,
Who like not in their judgment, but their eyes;
And where 'tis so, the offender's scourge is weigh'd,
But never the offence. To bear all smooth and even,
This sudden sending him away must seem
Deliberate pause: diseases desperate grown
By desperate appliance are reliev'd,
Or not at all.
    [*Enter* Rosencrantz]
How now! what hath befallen!
    ROSENCRANTZ: Where the dead body is bestow'd, my lord,
We cannot get from him.
    KING: But where is he?
    ROSENCRANTZ: Without, my lord; guarded, to know your pleasure.
    KING: Bring him before us.
    ROSENCRANTZ: Ho, Guildenstern! bring in my lord.
    [*Enter* Hamlet *and* Guildenstern]
    KING: Now, Hamlet, where's Polonius?
    HAMLET: At supper.
    KING: At supper! where?
    HAMLET: Not where he eats, but where he is eaten: a certain convocation of politic worms are e'en at him. Your worm is your only emperor for diet: we fat all creatures else to fat us, and we fat ourselves for maggots: your fat king and your lean beggar is but variable service,—two dishes, but to one table: that's the end.
    KING: Alas, alas!
    HAMLET: A man may fish with the worm that hath eat of a king, and eat of the fish that hath fed of that worm.
    KING: What dost thou mean by this?
    HAMLET: Nothing but to show you how a king may go a progress through the guts of a beggar.
    KING: Where is Polonius?
    HAMLET: In heaven; send thither to see: if your messenger find him not there, seek him i' the other

place yourself. But, indeed, if you find him not within this month, you shall nose him as you go up the stairs into the lobby.

KING: Go seek him there. [*To some* Attendants]

HAMLET: He will stay till ye come.

[*Exeunt* Attendants]

KING: Hamlet, this deed, for thine especial safety,—

Which we do tender, as we dearly grieve
For that which thou hast done,—must send thee hence
With fiery quickness: therefore prepare thyself;
The bark is ready, and the wind at help,
The associates tend, and everything is bent
For England.

HAMLET: For England!

KING: Ay, Hamlet.

HAMLET: Good.

KING: So is it, if thou knew'st our purposes.

HAMLET: I see a cherub that sees them.—But, come; for England!—Farewell, dear mother.

KING: Thy loving father, Hamlet.

HAMLET: My mother: father and mother is man and wife; man and wife is one flesh; and so, my mother.—Come, for England! [*Exit*]

KING: Follow him at foot; tempt him with speed aboard;

Delay it not; I'll have him hence to-night:
Away! for everything is seal'd and done
That else leans on the affair, pray you, make haste.

[*Exeunt* Rosencrantz *and* Guildenstern]

And, England, if my love thou hold'st at aught,—
As my great power thereof may give thee sense,
Since yet thy cicatrice looks raw and red
After the Danish sword, and thy free awe
Pays homage to us,—thou mayst not coldly set
Our sovereign process; which imports at full,
By letters conjuring to that effect,
The present death of Hamlet. Do it, England;
For like the hectic in my blood he rages,
And thou must cure me: till I know 'tis done,
Howe'er my haps, my joys will ne'er begin. [*Exit*]

SCENE IV.

A plain in Denmark.

[*Enter* Fortinbras, *and* Forces *marching*]

FORTINBRAS: Go, from me greet the Danish king:
Tell him that, by his license, Fortinbras
Craves the conveyance of a promis'd march
Over his kingdom. You know the rendezvous,
If that his majesty would aught with us,
We shall express our duty in his eye,
And let him know so.

CAPTAIN: I will do't, my lord.

FORTINBRAS: Go softly on.

[*Exeunt* Fortinbras *and* Forces]
[*Enter* Hamlet, Rosencrantz, Guildenstern, &c.]

HAMLET: Good sir, whose powers are these?

CAPTAIN: They are of Norway, sir.

HAMLET: How purpos'd, sir, I pray you?

CAPTAIN: Against some part of Poland.

HAMLET: Who commands them, sir?

CAPTAIN: The nephew to old Norway, Fortinbras.

HAMLET: Goes it against the main of Poland, sir, Or for some frontier?

CAPTAIN: Truly to speak, and with no addition,
We go to gain a little patch of ground
That hath in it no profit but the name.
To pay five ducats, five, I would not farm it;
Nor will it yield to Norway or the Pole
A ranker[2] rate should it be sold in fee.

HAMLET: Why, then the Polack never will defend it.

CAPTAIN: Yes, it is already garrison'd.

HAMLET: Two thousand souls and twenty thousand ducats

Will not debate the question of this straw:
This is the imposthume[3] of much wealth and peace,
That inward breaks, and shows no cause without
Why the man dies.—I humbly thank you, sir.

CAPTAIN: God b' wi' you, sir. [*Exit*]

ROSENCRANTZ: Will't please you go, my lord?

HAMLET: I'll be with you straight. Go a little before.

[*Exeunt all but* Hamlet]

How all occasions do inform against me,
And spur my dull revenge! What is a man,
If his chief good and market of his time
Be but to sleep and feed? a beast, no more.
Sure he that made us with such large discourse,[4]
Looking before and after, gave us not
That capability and godlike reason
To fust[5] in us unus'd. Now, whether it be
Bestial oblivion or some craven scruple
Of thinking too precisely on the event,—
A thought which, quarter'd, hath but one part wisdom
And ever three parts coward,—I do not know
Why yet I live to say, *This thing's to do;*
Sith[6] I have cause, and will, and strength, and means
To do't. Examples, gross as earth, exhort me:
Witness this army, of such mass and charge,
Led by a delicate and tender prince;
Whose spirit, with divine ambition puff'd,
Makes mouths at the invisible event,
Exposing what is mortal and unsure
To all that fortune, death, and danger dare,
Even for an egg-shell. Rightly to be great
Is not to stir without great argument,
But greatly to find quarrel in a straw
When honor's at the stake. How stand I, then,
That have a father kill'd, a mother stain'd,
Excitements of my reason and my blood,

2 Dearer.
3 Ulcer.
4 Reasoning faculty.
5 Grow musty.
6 Since.

And let all sleep? while, to my shame, I see
The imminent death of twenty thousand men,
That, for a fantasy and trick of fame,
Go to their graves like beds; fight for a plot
Whereon the numbers cannot try the cause,
Which is not tomb enough and continent[7]
To hide the slain?—O, from this time forth,
My thoughts be bloody, or be nothing worth! [*Exit*]

SCENE V.

Elsinore. A room in the castle.

[*Enter* Queen *and* Horatio]
QUEEN: I will not speak with her.
HORATIO: She is importunate; indeed, distract:
Her mood will needs be pitied.
QUEEN: What would she have?
HORATIO: She speaks much of her father; says she
hears
There's tricks i' the world; and hems, and beats her
heart;
Spurns enviously at straws; speaks things in doubt,
That carry but half sense: her speech is nothing,
Yet the unshapéd use of it doth move
The hearers to collection; they aim at it,
And botch the words up fit to their own thoughts;
Which, as her winks, and nods, and gestures yield
them,
Indeed would make one think there might be thought,
Though nothing sure, yet much unhappily.
'Twere good she were spoken with; for she may
strew
Dangerous conjectures in ill-breeding minds.
QUEEN: Let her come in.
[*Exit* Horatio]
To my sick soul, as sin's true nature is,
Each toy seems prologue to some great amiss:
So full of artless jealousy is guilt,
It spills itself in fearing to be spilt.
[*Re-enter* Horatio *and* Ophelia]
OPHELIA: Where is the beauteous majesty of Den-
mark?
QUEEN: How now, Ophelia!
OPHELIA: [*Sings*]
     How should I your true love know
          From another one?
     By his cockle hat and staff,
          And his sandal shoon.

QUEEN: Alas, sweet lady, what imports this song?
OPHELIA: Say you? nay, pray you, mark.
     [*Sings*]
     He is dead and gone, lady,
          He is dead and gone;
     At his head a grass green turf,
          At his heels a stone.

[7] Container.

QUEEN: Nay, but, Ophelia,—
OPHELIA: Pray you, mark.
     [*Sings*]
     White his shroud as the mountain snow,

[*Enter* King]
QUEEN: Alas, look here, my lord.
OPHELIA: [*Sings*]
          Larded with sweet flowers;
     Which bewept to the grave did go
          With true-love showers.

KING: How do you, pretty lady?
OPHELIA: Well, God 'ild[8] you! They say the owl
was a baker's daughter. Lord, we know what we are,
but know not what we may be. God be at your table!
KING: Conceit upon her father.
OPHELIA: Pray you, let's have no words of this; but
when they ask you what it means, say you this:
     [*Sings*]
     To-morrow is Saint Valentine's day
          All in the morning betime,
     And I a maid at your window,
          To be your Valentine.

     Then up he rose, and donn'd his clothes,
          And dupp'd the chamber-door;
     Let in the maid, that out a maid
          Never departed more.

KING: Pretty Ophelia!
OPHELIA: Indeed, la, without an oath, I'll make
an end on't;
     [*Sings*]
     By Gis[9] and by Saint Charity,
          Alack, and fie for shame!
     Young men will do't, if they come to't;
          By cock, they are to blame.

     Quoth she, before you tumbled me,
          You promis'd me to wed.
     So would I ha' done, by yonder sun,
          An thou hadst not come to my bed.

KING: How long hath she been thus?
OPHELIA: I hope all will be well. We must be pa-
tient: but I cannot choose but weep, to think they
should lay him i' the cold ground. My brother shall
know of it: and so I thank you; for your good coun-
sel.—Come, my coach!—Good-night, ladies; good-
night, sweet ladies; good-night, good-night. [*Exit*]
KING: Follow her close; give her good watch, I
pray you.
[*Exit* Horatio]
O, this is the poison of deep grief; it springs
All from her father's death. O Gertrude, Gertrude,
When sorrows come, they come not single spies,
But in battalions! First, her father slain:
Next, your son gone; and he most violent author
Of his own just remove: the people muddied,

[8] Yield you—that is, reward you.
[9] A contraction for "by Jesus."

Thick and unwholesome in their thoughts and
　　whispers
For good Polonius' death; and we have done but
　　greenly
In hugger-mugger[10] to inter him: poor Ophelia
Divided from herself and her fair judgment,
Without the which we are pictures, or mere beasts:
Last, and as much containing as all these,
Her brother is in secret come from France;
Feeds on his wonder, keeps himself in clouds,
And wants not buzzers to infect his ear
With pestilent speeches of his father's death;
Wherein necessity, of matter beggar'd,
Will nothing stick our person to arraign
In ear and ear. O my dear Gertrude, this,
Like to a murdering piece,[11] in many places
Gives me superfluous death.
　　　[A noise within]
　　QUEEN:　　　Alack, what noise is this?
　　KING: Where are my Switzers?[12] let them guard the
　　　door.
　　　[Enter a Gentleman]
What is the matter?
　　GENTLEMAN:　　　Save yourself, my lord:
The ocean, overpeering of his list,
Eats not the flats with more impetuous haste
Than young Laertes, in a riotous head,
O'erbears your officers. The rabble call him lord;
And, as the world were now but to begin,
Antiquity forgot, custom not known,
The ratifiers and props of every word,
They cry, Choose we, Laertes shall be king!
Caps, hands, and tongues applaud it to the clouds,
Laertes shall be king, Laertes king!
　　QUEEN: How cheerfully on the false trail they cry!
O, this is counter, you false Danish dogs!
　　KING: The doors are broke.
　　　[Noise within]
　　　[Enter Laertes armed; Danes following]
　　LAERTES: Where is this king?—Sirs, stand you all
　　　without.
　　DANES: No, let's come in.
　　LAERTES:　　　I pray you, give me leave.
　　DANES: We will, we will. [They retire without the
　　　door]
　　LAERTES: I thank you:—keep the door.—O thou
　　　vile king,
Give me my father!
　　QUEEN:　　　Calmly, good Laertes.
　　LAERTES: That drop of blood that's calm proclaims
　　　me bastard;
Cries cuckold to my father; brands the harlot
Even here, between the chaste unsmirched brow
Of my true mother.
　　KING: What is the cause, Laertes,
That thy rebellion looks so giant-like?—
Let him go, Gertrude; do not fear our person:

10 In great secrecy and haste.
11 A cannon.
12 Bodyguard of Swiss mercenaries.

There's such divinity doth hedge a king,
That treason can but peep to what it would,
Acts little of his will.—Tell me, Laertes,
Why thou art thus incens'd.—Let him go, Ger-
　　trude:—
Speak, man.
　　LAERTES: Where is my father?
　　KING:　　　Dead.
　　QUEEN:　　　　　　But not by him.
　　KING: Let him demand his fill.
　　LAERTES: How came he dead? I'll not be juggled
　　　with:
To hell, allegiance! vows, to the blackest devil!
Conscience and grace, to the profoundest pit!
I dare damnation:—to this point I stand,—
That both the worlds I give to negligence,
Let come what comes; only I'll be reveng'd
Most thoroughly for my father.
　　KING:　　　　　Who shall stay you?
　　LAERTES: My will, not all the world:
And for my means, I'll husband them so well,
They shall go far with little.
　　KING:　　　　Good Laertes,
If you desire to know the certainty
Of your dear father's death, is't writ in your revenge
That, sweepstake, you will draw both friend and foe,
Winner or loser?
　　LAERTES: None but his enemies.
　　KING:　　　Will you know them, then?
　　LAERTES: To his good friends thus wide I'll ope my
　　　arms;
And, like the kind life-rendering pelican,[13]
Repast them with my blood.
　　KING:　　　Why, now you speak
Like a good child and a true gentleman.
That I am guiltless of your father's death,
And am most sensible in grief for it,
It shall as level to your judgment pierce
As day does to your eye.
　　DANES: [Within] Let her come in.
　　LAERTES: How now! what noise is that?
　　　[Re-enter Ophelia, fantastically dressed with
　　　straws and flowers]
O heat, dry up my brains! tears seven times salt
Burn out the sense and virtue of mine eyes!—
By heaven, thy madness shall be paid by weight
Till our scale turn the beam. O rose of May!
Dear maid, kind sister, sweet Ophelia!—
O heavens! is't possible a young maid's wits
Should be as mortal as an old man's life!
Nature is fine in love; and where 'tis fine
It sends some precious instance of itself
After the thing it loves.
　　OPHELIA: [Sings]
　　　They bore him barefac'd on the bier;
　　　Hey no nonny, nonny, hey nonny;
　　　And on his grave rain'd many a tear,—
　　　Fare you well, my dove!

13 The pelican mother was believed to draw blood from
itself to feed its young.

LAERTES: Hadst thou thy wits, and didst persuade revenge,
It could not move thus.

OPHELIA: You must sing, *Down-a-down, an you call him a-down-a.* O, how the wheel becomes it! It is the false steward, that stole his master's daughter.

LAERTES: This nothing's more than matter.

OPHELIA: There's rosemary, that's for remembrance; pray, love, remember: and there is pansies that's for thoughts.

LAERTES: A document in madness,—thoughts and remembrance fitted.

OPHELIA: There's fennel for you, and columbines: —there's rue for you; and here's some for me:—we may call it herb-grace o' Sundays:—O, you must wear your rue with a difference.—There's a daisy:— I would give you some violets, but they withered all when my father died:—they say, he made a good end,—

[*Sings*]
   For bonny sweet Robin is all my joy,—

LAERTES: Thoughts and affliction, passion, hell itself,
She turns to favor and to prettiness.

OPHELIA: [*Sings*]
      And will he not come again?
      And will he not come again?
         No, no, he is dead,
         Go to thy death-bed,
      He never will come again.

      His beard was as white as snow
      All flaxen was his poll:
         He is gone, he is gone,
         And we cast away moan:
      God ha' mercy on his soul!

And of all Christian souls, I pray God.—God b' wi' ye. [*Exit*]

LAERTES: Do you see this, O God?

KING: Laertes, I must commune with your grief,
Or you deny me right. Go but apart,
Make choice of whom your wisest friends you will,
And they shall hear and judge 'twixt you and me:
If by direct or by collateral hand
They find us touch'd, we will our kingdom give,
Our crown, our life, and all that we call ours,
To you in satisfaction; but if not,
Be you content to lend your patience to us,
And we shall jointly labor with your soul
To give it due content.

LAERTES: Let this be so;
His means of death, his óbscure burial,—
No trophy, sword, nor hatchment[14] o'er his bones
No noble rite nor formal ostentation,—
Cry to be heard, as 'twere from heaven to earth,
That I must call't in question.

[14] A tablet with coat of arms.

KING: So you shall;
And where the offence is, let the great axe fall.
I pray you, go with me.
   [*Exeunt*]

SCENE VI.

Another room in the castle.

[*Enter* Horatio *and a* Servant]

HORATIO: What are they that would speak with me?

SERVANT: Sailors, sir: they say they have letters for you.

HORATIO: Let them come in.—
   [*Exit* Servant]
I do not know from what part of the world
I should be greeted, if not from Lord Hamlet.
   [*Enter* Sailors]

1ST SAILOR: God bless you, sir.

HORATIO: Let him bless thee too.

1ST SAILOR: He shall, sir, an't please him. There's a letter for you, sir; it comes from the ambassador that was bound for England; if your name be Horatio, as I am let to know it is.

HORATIO: [*Reads*] *Horatio, when thou shalt have overlooked this, give these fellows some means to the king: they have letters for him. Ere we were two days old at sea, a pirate of very warlike appointment gave us chase. Finding ourselves too slow of sail, we put on a compelled valor; and in the grapple I boarded them; on the instant they got clear of our ship; so I alone became their prisoner. They have dealt with me like thieves of mercy: but they knew what they did; I am to do a good turn for them. Let the king have the letters I have sent; and repair thou to me with as much haste as thou wouldst fly death. I have words to speak in thine ear will make thee dumb; yet are they much too light for the bore of the matter. These good fellows will bring thee where I am. Rosencrantz and Guildenstern hold their course for England: of them I have much to tell thee. Farewell. He that thou knowest thine.* Hamlet
Come, I will give you way for these your letters;
And do't the speedier, that you may direct me
To him from whom you brought them.
   [*Exeunt*]

SCENE VII.

Another room in the castle.

[*Enter* King *and* Laertes]

KING: Now must your conscience my acquittance seal,
And you must put me in your heart for friend,
Sith you have heard, and with a knowing ear,
That he which hath your noble father slain
Pursu'd my life.

LAERTES: It well appears:—but tell me
Why you proceeded not against these feats,
So crimeful and so capital in nature,
As by your safety, wisdom, all things else,
You mainly were stirr'd up.

KING: O, for two special reasons;
Which may to you, perhaps, seem much unsinew'd,
But yet to me they are strong. The queen his mother
Lives almost by his looks; and for myself,—
My virtue or my plague, be it either which,—
She's so conjunctive to my life and soul,
That, as the star moves not but in his sphere,
I could not but by her. The other motive,
Why to a public count I might not go,
Is the great love the general gender bear him;
Who, dipping all his faults in their affection,
Would, like the spring that turneth wood to stone,
Convert his gyves to graces; so that my arrows,
Too slightly timber'd for so loud a wind,
Would have reverted to my bow again,
And not where I had aim'd them.

LAERTES: And so have I a noble father lost;
A sister driven into desperate terms,—
Whose worth, if praises may go back again,
Stood challenger on mount of all the age
For her perfections:—but my revenge will come.

KING: Break not your sleeps for that: you mus.
    not think
That we are made of stuff so flat and dull
That we can let our beard be shook with danger,
And think it pastime. You shortly shall hear more:
I lov'd your father, and we love ourself;
And that, I hope, will teach you to imagine,—
    [Enter a Messenger]
How now! what news?

MESSENGER: Letters, my lord, from Hamlet:
This to your majesty; this to the queen.

KING: From Hamlet! Who brought them?

MESSENGER: Sailors, my lord, they say; I saw
    them not:
They were given me by Claudio,—he receiv'd them
Of him that brought them.

KING: Laertes, you shall hear them.—Leave us.
    [Exit Messenger]
[Reads] High and mighty,—You shall know I am set
naked on your kingdom. To-morrow shall I beg leave
to see your kingly eyes: when I shall, first asking
your pardon thereunto, recount the occasions of my
sudden and more strange return.   Hamlet
What should this mean? Are all the rest come back?
Or is it some abuse,[15] and no such thing?

LAERTES: Know you the hand?

KING: 'Tis Hamlet's character:[16]—Naked,—
And in a postscript here, he says, alone.
Can you advise me?

LAERTES: I am lost in it, my lord. But let him
    come;
It warms the very sickness in my heart,

[15] Ruse.
[16] Handwriting.

That I shall live, and tell him to his teeth,
Thus diddest thou.

KING: If it be so, Laertes,—
As how should it be so? how otherwise?—
Will you be rul'd by me?

LAERTES: Ay, my lord:
So you will not o'errule me to a peace.

KING: To thine own peace. If he be now return'd,—
As checking at his voyage, and that he means
No more to undertake it,—I will work him
To an exploit, now ripe in my device,
Under the which he shall not choose but fall:
And for his death no wind of blame shall breathe;
But even his mother shall uncharge the practice
And call it accident.

LAERTES: My lord, I will be rul'd;
The rather if you could devise it so
That I might be the organ.

KING: It falls right.
You have been talk'd of since your travel much,
And that in Hamlet's hearing, for a quality
Wherein they say you shine: your sum of parts
Did not together pluck such envy from him
As did that one; and that, in my regard,
Of the unworthiest siege.

LAERTES: What part is that, my lord?

KING: A very riband in the cap of youth,
Yet needful too; for youth no less becomes
The light and careless livery that it wears
Than settled age his sables and his weeds,
Importing health and graveness.—Two months since,
Here was a gentleman of Normandy,—
I've seen myself, and serv'd against, the French,
And they can well on horseback: but this gallant
Had witchcraft in't; he grew unto his seat;
And to such wondrous doing brought his horse,
As he had been incorps'd and demi-natur'd[17]
With the brave beast: so far he topp'd my thought,
That I, in forgery of shapes and tricks,[18]
Come short of what he did.

LAERTES: A Norman was't?

KING: A Norman.

LAERTES: Upon my life, Lamond.

KING: The very same.

LAERTES: I know him well: he is the brooch,
    indeed,
And gem of all the nation.

KING: He made confession of you;
And gave you such a masterly report
For art and exercise in your defence,
And for your rapier most especially,
That he cried out, 'twould be a sight indeed
If one could match you: the scrimers[19] of their na-
    tion,
He swore, had neither motion, guard, nor eye,
If you oppos'd them. Sir, this report of his

[17] Made as one body and formed into half man, half
horse—or centaur.
[18] In imagining tricks of horsemanship.
[19] Fencers.

Did Hamlet so envenom with his envy,
That he could nothing do but wish and beg
Your sudden coming o'er, to play with him.
Now, out of this,—

LAERTES: What out of this, my lord?

KING: Laertes, was your father dear to you?
Or are you like the painting of a sorrow,
A face without a heart?

LAERTES: Why ask you this?

KING: Not that I think you did not love your
   father;
But that I know love is begun by time;
And that I see, in passages of proof,[20]
Time qualifies the spark and fire of it.
There lives within the very flame of love
A kind of wick or snuff that will abate it;
And nothing is at a like goodness still;
For goodness, growing to a pleurisy,[21]
Dies in his own too much: that we would do
We should do when we would; for this *would*
   changes,
And hath abatements and delays as many
As there are tongues, or hands, or accidents;
And then this *should* is like a spendthrift sigh
That hurts by easing. But to the quick o' the
   ulcer:—
Hamlet comes back: what would you undertake
To show yourself your father's son in deed
More than in words?

LAERTES: To cut his throat i' the church.

KING: No place, indeed, should murder sanc-
   tuarize;
Revenge should have no bounds. But, good
   Laertes,
Will you do this, keep close within your chamber.
Hamlet return'd shall know you are come home:
We'll put on those shall praise your excellence,
And set a double varnish on the fame
The Frenchman gave you; bring you, in fine, to-
   gether,
And wager on yours heads: he, being remiss,[22]
Most generous, and free from all contriving,
Will not peruse the foils; so that, with ease,
Or with a little shuffling, you may choose
A sword unbated, and, in a pass of practice,
Requite him for your father.

LAERTES: I will do't it:
And, for that purpose, I'll anoint my sword.
I bought an unction of a mountebank,
So mortal that but dip a knife in it,
Where it draws blood no cataplasm so rare,[23]
Collected from all simples that have virtue
Under the moon, can save the thing from death
That is but scratch'd withal: I'll touch my point
With this contagion, that, if I gall him slightly,
It may be death.

---

[20] The evidence of experience.
[21] Plethora, an excess of blood.
[22] Unguarded and free from suspicion.
[23] No poultice, however remarkably efficacious.

KING: Let's further think of this;
Weigh what convenience both of time and means
May fit us to our shape: if this should fail,
And that our drift look through our bad perform-
   ance,
'Twere better not assay'd: therefore this project
Should have a back or second, that might hold
If this should blast in proof. Soft! let me see:—
We'll make a solemn wager on your cunnings,—
I ha't:
When in your motion you are hot and dry,—
As make your bouts more violent to that end,—
And that he calls for drink, I'll have prepar'd him
A chalice for the nonce;[24] whereon but sipping,
If he by chance escape your venom'd stuck
Our purpose may hold there.

[*Enter* Queen]

                How now, sweet queen!

QUEEN: One woe doth tread upon another's heel,
So fast they follow:—your sister's drown'd, Laertes.

LAERTES: Drown'd! O, where?

QUEEN: There is a willow grows aslant a brook,
That shows his hoar leaves in the glassy stream;
There with fantastic garlands did she come
Of crowflowers, nettles, daisies, and long purples,
That liberal shepherds give a grosser name,
But our cold maids do dead men's fingers call
   them.
There, on the pendant boughs her coronet weeds
Clambering to hang, an envious[25] sliver broke;
When down her weedy trophies and herself
Fell in the weeping brook. Her clothes spread
   wide;
And, mermaid-like, awhile they bore her up:
Which time she chanted snatches of old tunes;
As one incapable of her own distress,
Or like a creature native and indu'd
Unto that element: but long it could not be
Till that her garments, heavy with their drink,
Pull'd the poor wretch from her melodious lay
To muddy death.

LAERTES: Alas, then, she is drown'd?

QUEEN: Drown'd, drown'd.

LAERTES: Too much of water hast thou, poor
   Ophelia,
And therefore I forbid my tears: but yet
It is our trick; nature her custom holds,
Let shame say what it will: when these are gone,
The woman will be out.[26]—Adieu, my lord:
I have a speech of fire, that fain would blaze,
But that this folly douts it.[27] [*Exit*]

KING: Let's follow, Gertrude;
How much I had to do to calm his rage!
Now fear I this will give it start again;
Therefore let's follow.

[*Exeunt*]

---

[24] Purpose.
[25] Malicious.
[26] That is, "I shall be ruthless."
[27] Drowns it.

ACT V. SCENE I.

A churchyard.

[*Enter two* Clowns[1] *with spades, &c.*]

1ST CLOWN: Is she to be buried in Christian burial that wilfully seeks her own salvation?

2ND CLOWN: I tell thee she is; and therefore make her grave straight: the crowner[2] hath sat on her, and finds it Christian burial.

1ST CLOWN: How can that be, unless she drowned herself in her own defence?

2ND CLOWN: Why, 'tis found so.

1ST CLOWN: It must be *se offendendo;*[3] it cannot be else. For here lies the point: if I drown myself wittingly, it argues an act: and an act hath three branches; it is to act, to do, and to perform: argal,[4] she drowned herself wittingly.

2ND CLOWN: Nay, but hear you, goodman delver,—

1ST CLOWN: Give me leave. Here lies the water; good: here stands the man; good: if the man go to this water and drown himself, it is, will he, nill he, he goes,—mark you that: but if the water come to him and drown him, he drowns not himself: argal, he that is not guilty of his own death shortens not his own life.

2ND CLOWN: But is this law?

1ST CLOWN: Ay, marry, is't; crowner's quest law.

2ND CLOWN: Will you ha' the truth on't? If this had not been a gentlewoman she should have been buried out of Christian burial.

1ST CLOWN: Why, there thou say'st: and the more pity that great folks should have countenance in this world to drown or hang themselves more than their even-Christian.[5]—Come, my spade. There is no ancient gentlemen but gardeners, ditchers, and grave-makers; they hold up Adam's profession.

2ND CLOWN: Was he a gentleman?

1ST CLOWN: He was the first that ever bore arms.

2ND CLOWN: Why, he had none.

1ST CLOWN: What, art a heathen? How dost thou understand the Scripture? The Scripture says, Adam digged: could he dig without arms? I'll put another question to thee: if thou answerest me not to the purpose, confess thyself,[6]—

2ND CLOWN: Go to.

1ST CLOWN: What is he that builds stronger than either the mason, the shipwright, or the carpenter?

2ND CLOWN: The gallows-maker; for that frame outlives a thousand tenants.

1ST CLOWN: I like thy wit well, in good faith: the gallows does well; but how does it well? it does well

to those that do ill: now thou dost ill to say the gallows is built stronger than the church: argal, the gallows may do well to thee. To't again, come.

2ND CLOWN: Who builds stronger than a mason, a shipwright, or a carpenter?

1ST CLOWN: Ay, tell me that, and unyoke.

2ND CLOWN: Marry, now I can tell.

1ST CLOWN: To't.

2ND CLOWN: Mass, I cannot tell.

[*Enter Hamlet and* Horatio, *at a distance*]

1ST CLOWN: Cudgel thy brains no more about it, for your dull ass will not mend his pace with beating; and when you are asked this question next, say a grave-maker; the houses that he makes last till doomsday. Go, get thee to Yaughan: fetch me a stoup of liquor.

[*Exit* Second Clown]

[*Digs and sings*]

In youth, when I did love, did love,
  Methought it was very sweet,
To contract, O, the time, for, ah, my behove,[7]
  O, methought there was nothing meet.

HAMLET: Has this fellow no feeling of his business, that he sings at grave-making?

HORATIO: Custom hath made it in him a property of easiness.

HAMLET: 'Tis e'en so: the hand of little employment hath the daintier sense.

1ST CLOWN: [*Sings*]

But age, with his stealing steps,
  Hath claw'd me in his clutch,
And hath shipp'd me intil the land,
  As if I had never been such.

[*Throws up a skull*]

HAMLET: That skull had a tongue in it, and could sing once: how the knave joels[8] it to the ground, as if it were Cain's jawbone, that did the first murder! This might be the pate of a politician, which this ass now o'erreaches; one that would circumvent God, might it not?

HORATIO: It might, my lord.

HAMLET: Or of a courtier; which could say, *Good-morrow, sweet lord! How dost thou, good lord?* This might be my lord such-a-one, that praised my lord such-a-one's horse, when he meant to beg it,—might it not?

HORATIO: Ay, my lord.

HAMLET: Why, e'en so: and now my Lady Worm's; chapless,[9] and knocked about the mazard[10] with a sexton's spade: here's fine revolution, an we had the trick to see't. Did these bones cost no more the breeding but to play at loggats[11] with 'em? Mine ache to think on't.

---

[1] Rustic fellows.
[2] Coroner.
[3] In self-offense; he means *se defendendo*, in self-defense.
[4] He means *ergo*, therefore.
[5] Fellow Christian.
[6] "Confess thyself an ass," perhaps.

[7] Behoof, or advantage.
[8] Throws.
[9] Without a lower jaw.
[10] Head.
[11] A game in which small pieces of wood are hurled at a stake.

1ST CLOWN: [*Sings*]
     A pick-axe and a spade, a spade,
        For and a shrouding sheet:
     O, a pit of clay for to be made
        For such a guest is meet.

[*Throws up another*]

HAMLET: There's another: why may not that be the skull of a lawyer? Where be his quiddits[12] now, his quillets,[13] his cases, his tenures, and his tricks? why does he suffer this rude knave now to knock him about the sconce with a dirty shovel, and will not tell him of his action of battery? Hum! This fellow might be in's time a great buyer of land, with his statutes, his recognizances, his fines, his double vouchers, his recoveries: is this the fine of his fines, and the recovery of his recoveries, to have his fine pate full of fine dirt? will his vouchers vouch him no more of his purchases, and double ones too, than the length and breadth of a pair of indentures? The very conveyances of his lands will hardly lie in this box; and must the inheritor himself have no more, ha?

HORATIO: Not a jot more, my lord.

HAMLET: Is not parchment made of sheep-skins?

HORATIO: Ay, my lord, and of calf-skins too.

HAMLET: They are sheep and calves which seek out assurance in that. I will speak to this fellow.— Whose grave's this, sir?

1ST CLOWN: Mine, sir.—[*Sings*]
     O, a pit of clay for to be made
        For such a guest is meet.

HAMLET: I think it be thine indeed; for thou liest in't.

1ST CLOWN: You lie out on't, sir, and therefore it is not yours: for my part, I do not lie in't, and yet it is mine.

HAMLET: Thou dost lie in't, to be in't, and say it is thine: 'tis for the dead, not for the quick; therefore thou liest.

1ST CLOWN: 'Tis a quick lie, sir: 'twill away again from me to you.

HAMLET: What man dost thou dig it for?

1ST CLOWN: For no man, sir.

HAMLET: What woman, then?

1ST CLOWN: For none, neither.

HAMLET: Who is to be buried in't?

1ST CLOWN: One that was a woman, sir; but, rest her soul, she's dead.

HAMLET: How absolute the knave is! we must speak by the card, or equivocation will undo us. By the Lord, Horatio, these three years I have taken note of it; the age is grown so picked[14] that the toe of the peasant comes so near the heel of the courtier, he galls his kibe.[15]—How long hast thou been a gravemaker?

1ST CLOWN: Of all the days i' the year, I came to't

12 "Whatnesses"—that is, hair-splittings.
13 Quibbling distinctions.
14 Refined or educated.
15 Rubs and irritates the chilblain sore on the courtier's heel.

that day that our last King Hamlet o'ercame Fortinbras.

HAMLET: How long is that since?

1ST CLOWN: Cannot you tell that? every fool can tell that: it was the very day that young Hamlet was born,—he that is mad, and sent into England.

HAMLET: Ay, marry, why was he sent into England?

1ST CLOWN: Why, because he was mad: he shall recover his wits there; or, if he do not, it's no great matter there.

HAMLET: Why?

1ST CLOWN: 'Twill not be seen in him there; there the men are as mad as he.

HAMLET: How came he mad?

1ST CLOWN: Very strangely, they say.

HAMLET: How strangely?

1ST CLOWN: Faith, e'en with losing his wits.

HAMLET: Upon what ground?

1ST CLOWN: Why, here in Denmark: I have been sexton here, man and boy, thirty years.

HAMLET: How long will a man lie i' the earth ere he rot?

1ST CLOWN: Faith, if he be not rotten before he die,—as we have many pocky corses now-a-days, that will scarce hold the laying in,—he will last you some eight year or nine year: a tanner will last you nine year.

HAMLET: Why he more than another?

1ST CLOWN: Why, sir, his hide is so tanned with his trade that he will keep out water a great while; and your water is a sore decayer of your whoreson dead body. Here's a skull now; this skull has lain in the earth three-and-twenty years.

HAMLET: Whose was it?

1ST CLOWN: A whoreson mad fellow's it was: whose do you think it was?

HAMLET: Nay, I know not.

1ST CLOWN: A pestilence on him for a mad rogue! 'a poured a flagon of Rhenish on my head once. This same skull, sir, was Yorick's skull, the king's jester.

HAMLET: This?

1ST CLOWN: E'en that.

HAMLET: Let me see. [*Takes the skull*]—Alas, poor Yorick!—I knew him, Horatio; a fellow of infinite jest, of most excellent fancy: he hath borne me on his back a thousand times; and now, how abhorred in my imagination it is! my gorge rises at it. Here hung those lips that I have kissed I know not how oft. Where be your gibes now? your gambols? your songs? your flashes of merriment, that were wont to set the table on a roar? Not one now, to mock your own grinning? quite chap-fallen? Now get you to my lady's chamber, and tell her, let her paint an inch thick, to this favor[16] she must come; make her laugh at that.—Pr'ythee, Horatio, tell me one thing.

HORATIO: What's that, my lord?

HAMLET: Dost thou think Alexander looked o' this fashion i' the earth?

HORATIO: E'en so.

16 Face.

HAMLET: **And smelt so? pah!** [*Throws down the skull*]

HORATIO: E'en so, my lord.

HAMLET: To what base uses we may return, Horatio! Why may not imagination trace the noble dust of Alexander till he find it stopping a bung-hole?

HORATIO: 'Twere to consider too curiously to consider so.

HAMLET: No, faith, not a jot; but to follow him thither with modesty enough, and likelihood to lead it: as thus; Alexander died, Alexander was buried, Alexander returneth into dust; the dust is earth; of earth we make loam; and why of that loam whereto he was converted might they not stop a beer-barrel?

Imperious Caesar, dead and turn'd to clay,
Might stop a hole to keep the wind away:
O, that that earth which kept the world in awe
Should patch a wall to expel the winter's flaw!—

But soft! but soft! aside.—Here comes the king.
  [*Enter* Priests, *&c., in procession; the corpse of*
  Ophelia, Laertes *and* Mourners *following;* King,
  Queen, *their* Trains, *&c.*]
The queen, the courtiers: who is that they follow?
And with such maimed rites? This doth betoken
The corse they follow did with desperate hand
Fordo its own life: 'twas of some estate.
Couch we awhile and mark. [*Retiring with* Horatio]

LAERTES: What ceremony else?

HAMLET: That is Laertes,
A very noble youth: mark.

LAERTES: What ceremony else?

1ST PRIEST: Her obsequies have been as far enlarg'd
As we have warrantise: her death was doubtful,
And, but that great command o'ersways the order,
She should in ground unsanctified have lodg'd
Till the last trumpet; for charitable prayers,
Shards, flints, and pebbles, should be thrown on her,
Yet here she is allowed her virgin rites,
Her maiden strewments, and the bringing home
Of bell and burial.

LAERTES: Must there no more be done?

1ST PRIEST: No more be done:
We should profane the service of the dead
To sing a *requiem,* and such rest to her
As to peace-parted souls.

LAERTES: Lay her i' the earth;—
And from her fair and unpolluted flesh
May violets spring!—I tell thee, churlish priest,
A ministering angel shall my sister be
When thou liest howling.

HAMLET: What, the fair Ophelia!

QUEEN: Sweets to the sweet: farewell! [*Scattering flowers*]
I hop'd thou shouldst have been my Hamlet's wife;
I thought thy bride-bed to have deck'd, sweet maid,
And not have strew'd thy grave.

LAERTES: O, treble woe
Fall ten times treble on that cursed head

Whose wicked deed thy most ingenious sense
Depriv'd thee of!—Hold off the earth awhile,
Till I have caught her once more in mine arms:
  [*Leaps into the grave*]
Now pile your dust upon the quick and dead,
Till of this flat a mountain you have made,
To o'er-top old Pelion[17] or the skyish head
Of blue Olympus.

HAMLET: [*Advancing*] What is he whose grief
Bears such an emphasis? whose phrase of sorrow
Conjures the wandering stars, and makes them stand
Like wonder-wounded hearers? this is I, Hamlet the
      Dane. [*Leaps into the grave*]

LAERTES: The devil take thy soul! [*Grappling with him*]

HAMLET: Thou pray'st not well.
I pr'ythee, take thy fingers from my throat;
For, though I am not splenetive and rash,
Yet have I in me something dangerous,
Which let thy wiseness fear: away thy hand.

KING: Pluck them asunder.

QUEEN: Hamlet! Hamlet!

ALL: Gentlemen,—

HORATIO: Good my lord, be quiet.
  [*The* Attendants *part them, and they come out of
  the grave*]

HAMLET: Why, I will fight with him upon this theme
Until my eyelids will no longer wag.

QUEEN: O my son, what theme?

HAMLET: I lov'd Ophelia; forty thousand brothers
Could not, with all their quantity of love,
Make up my sum.—What wilt thou do for her?

KING: O, he is mad, Laertes.

QUEEN: For love of God, forbear him.

HAMLET: 'Swounds, show me what thou'lt do:
Woul't weep? woul't fight? woul't fast? woul't tear thyself?
Woul't drink up eisel?[18] eat a crocodile?
I'll do't.—Dost thou come here to whine?
To outface me with leaping in her grave?
Be buried quick[19] with her, and so will I:
And, if thou prate of mountains, let them throw
Millions of acres on us, till our ground,
Singeing his pate against the burning zone,[20]
Make Ossa[21] like a wart! Nay, an thou'lt mouth,
I'll rant as well as thou.

QUEEN: This is mere madness:
And thus awhile the fit will work on him;
Anon, as patient as the female dove,
When that her golden couplets are disclos'd,[22]
His silence will sit drooping.

HAMLET: Hear you, sir;
What is the reason that you use me thus?
I lov'd you ever: but it is no matter;

17 A mountain in Greece.
18 Vinegar.
19 Alive.
20 The fiery zone of the celestial sphere.
21 A high mountain in Greece.
22 When the golden twins are hatched.

Let Hercules himself do what he may,
The cat will mew, and dog will have his day. [*Exit*]
   KING: I pray thee, good Horatio, wait upon him.—
     [*Exit* Horatio]
     [*To* Laertes]
Strengthen your patience in our last night's speech;
We'll put the matter to the present push.—
Good Gertrude, set some watch over your son.—
This grave shall have a living monument:
An hour of quiet shortly shall we see;
Till then, in patience our proceeding be.
     [*Exeunt*]

SCENE II.

A hall in the castle.

     [*Enter* Hamlet *and* Horatio]
   HAMLET: So much for this, sir: now let me see the
     other;
You do remember all the circumstance?
   HORATIO: Remember it, my lord!
   HAMLET: Sir, in my heart there was a kind of
     fighting
That would not let me sleep: methought I lay
Worse than the mutines in the bilboes.[23] Rashly,
And prais'd be rashness for it,—let us know,
Our indiscretion sometimes serves us well,
When our deep plots do fail: and that should teach
   us
There's a divinity that shapes our ends,
Rough-hew them how we will.
   HORATIO: This is most certain.
   HAMLET: Up from my cabin,
My sea-gown scarf'd about me, in the dark
Grop'd I to find out them: had my desire;
Finger'd their packet; and, in fine, withdrew
To mine own room again: making so bold,
My fears forgetting manners, to unseal
Their grand commission; where I found, Horatio,
O royal knavery! an exact command,—
Larded with many several sorts of reasons,
Importing Denmark's health and England's too,
With, ho! such bugs[24] and goblins in my life,—
That, on the supervise, no leisure bated,
No, not to stay the grinding of the axe,
My head should be struck off.
   HORATIO: Is't possible?
   HAMLET: Here's the commission: read it at more
     leisure.
But wilt thou hear me how I did proceed?
   HORATIO: I beseech you.
   HAMLET: Being thus benetted round with vil-
     lainies,—
Ere I could make a prologue to my brains,
They had begun the play,—I sat me down;
Devis'd a new commission; wrote it fair:

[23] Mutineers in the iron stocks on board ship.
[24] Bugbears.

I once did hold it, as our statists do,
A baseness to write fair, and labor'd much
How to forget that learning; but, sir, now
It did me yeoman's service. Wilt thou know
The effect of what I wrote?
   HORATIO: Ay, good my lord.
   HAMLET: An earnest conjuration from the king,—
As England was his faithful tributary;
As love between them like the palm might flourish;
As peace should still her wheaten garland wear
And stand a comma[25] 'tween their amities;
And many such like as's of great charge,—
That, on the view and know of these contents,
Without debatement further, more or less,
He should the bearers put to sudden death,
Not shriving-time allow'd.
   HORATIO: How was this seal'd?
   HAMLET: Why, even in that was heaven ordinant.
I had my father's signet in my purse,
Which was the model of that Danish seal:
Folded the writ up in form of the other;
Subscrib'd it; gav't the impression; plac'd it safely,
The changeling never known. Now, the next day
Was our sea-fight; and what to this was sequent
Thou know'st already.
   HORATIO: So Guildenstern and Rosencrantz go to't.
   HAMLET: Why, man, they did make love to this
     employment;
They are not near my conscience; their defeat
Does by their own insinuation[26] grow:
'Tis dangerous when the baser nature[27] comes
Between the pass and fell[28] incensed points
Of mighty opposites.
   HORATIO: Why, what a king is this!
   HAMLET: Does it not, think'st thee, stand me now
     upon,[29]—
He that hath kill'd my king and whor'd my mother;
Popp'd in between the election and my hopes;
Thrown out his angle for my proper life,
And with such cozenage,[30]—is't not perfect con-
     science
To quit him with this arm? and is't not to be damn'd,
To let this canker of our nature come
In further evil?
   HORATIO: It must be shortly known to him from
     England
What is the issue of the business there.
   HAMLET: It will be short: the interim is mine;
And a man's life's no more than to say One.
But I am very sorry, good Horatio,
That to Laertes I forgot myself;
For by the image of my cause I see
The portraiture of his: I'll court his favors:
But, sure, the bravery[31] of his grief did put me

[25] Link.
[26] By their own "sticking their noses" into the business.
[27] Men of lower rank.
[28] Fierce.
[29] That is, "Don't you think it is my duty?"
[30] Deceit.
[31] Ostentation

Into a towering passion.

HORATIO: Peace; who comes here?

[*Enter* Osric]

OSRIC: Your lordship is right welcome back to Denmark.

HAMLET: I humbly thank you, sir.—Dost know this water-fly?

HORATIO: No, my good lord.

HAMLET: Thy state is the more gracious; for 'tis a vice to know him. He hath much land, and fertile: let a beast be lord of beasts, and his crib shall stand at the king's mess: 'tis a chough;[32] but, as I say, spacious in the possession of dirt.

OSRIC: Sweet lord, if your lordship were at leisure, I should impart a thing to you from his majesty.

HAMLET: I will receive it with all diligence of spirit. Put your bonnet to his right use; 'tis for the head.

OSRIC: I thank your lordship, 'tis very hot.

HAMLET: No, believe me, 'tis very cold; the wind is northerly.

OSRIC: It is indifferent cold, my lord, indeed.

HAMLET: Methinks it is very sultry and hot for my complexion.

OSRIC: Exceedingly, my lord; it is very sultry,—as't were,—I cannot tell how.—But, my lord, his majesty bade me signify to you that he has laid a great wager on your head. Sir, this is the matter,—

HAMLET: I beseech you, remember,—

[Hamlet *moves him to put on his hat*]

OSRIC: Nay, in good faith; for mine ease, in good faith. Sir, here is newly come to court Laertes; believe me, an absolute gentleman, full of most excellent differences, of very soft society and great showing: indeed, to speak feelingly of him, he is the card or calendar of gentry, for you shall find in him the continent of what part a gentleman would see.

HAMLET: Sir, his definement suffers no perdition in you;—though, I know, to divide him inventorially would dizzy the arithmetic of memory, and yet but yaw neither, in respect of his quick sail. But, in the verity of extolment, I take him to be a soul of great article; and his infusion of such dearth[33] and rareness as, to make true diction of him, his semblable is his mirror; and who else would trace him, his umbrage,[34] nothing more.

OSRIC: Your lordship speaks most infallibly of him.

HAMLET: The concernancy, sir? why do we wrap the gentleman in our more rawer breath?

OSRIC: Sir?

HORATIO: Is't not possible to understand in another tongue? You will do't sir, really.

HAMLET: What imports the nomination[35] of this gentleman?

OSRIC: Of Laertes?

HORATIO: His purse is empty already; all's golden words are spent.

HAMLET: Of him, sir.

OSRIC: I know, you are not ignorant,—

HAMLET: I would you did, sir; yet, in faith, if you did, it would not much approve me.[36]—Well, sir.

OSRIC: You are not ignorant of what excellence Laertes is,—

HAMLET: I dare not confess that, lest I should compare with him in excellence; but to know a man well were to know himself.

OSRIC: I mean, sir, for his weapon; but in the imputation laid on him by them, in his meed he's unfellowed.[37]

HAMLET: What's his weapon?

OSRIC: Rapier and dagger.

HAMLET: That's two of his weapons: but, well.

OSRIC: The king, sir, hath wagered with him six Barbary horses: against the which he has imponed,[38] as I take it, six French rapiers and poniards, with their assigns, as girdle, hangers, and so: three of the carriages, in faith, are very dear to fancy, very responsive to the hilts, most delicate carriages, and of very liberal conceit.

HAMLET: What call you the carriages?

HORATIO: I knew you must be edified by the margent ere you had done.[39]

OSRIC: The carriages, sir, are the hangers.

HAMLET: The phrase would be more german to the matter if we could carry cannon by our sides: I would it might be hangers till then. But, on: six Barbary horses against six French swords, their assigns, and three liberal conceited carriages; that's the French bet against the Danish: why is this imponed, as you call it?

OSRIC: The king, sir, hath laid, that in a dozen passes between you and him he shall not exceed you three hits: he hath laid on twelve for nine; and it would come to immediate trial if your lordship would vouchsafe the answer.

HAMLET: How if I answer no?

OSRIC: I mean, my lord, the opposition of your person in trial.[40]

HAMLET: Sir, I will walk here in the hall: if it please his majesty, it is the breathing time of day with me: let the foils be brought, the gentleman willing, and the king hold his purpose, I will win for him if I can; if not, I will gain nothing but my shame and the odd hits.

OSRIC: Shall I re-deliver you[41] e'en so?

HAMLET: To this effect, sir; after what flourish your nature will.

[32] He shall have his trough at the king's table: he is a chattering fool.

[33] Rareness, or excellence.

[34] Shadow.

[35] Naming.

[36] If you, who are a fool, thought me not ignorant, that would not be particularly to my credit.

[37] In his worth he has no equal.

[38] Staked.

[39] Informed by a note in the margin of your instructions.

[40] That is, the presence of your person as Laertes' opponent in the fencing contest.

[41] Carry back your answer.

OSRIC: I commend my duty to your lordship.

HAMLET: Yours, yours.

[*Exit* Osric]

He does well to commend it himself; there are no tongues else for's turn.

HORATIO: This lapwing runs away with the shell on his head.[42]

HAMLET: He did comply with his dug before he sucked it.[43] Thus has he,—and many more of the same bevy, that I know the drossy age dotes on,— only got the tune of the time, and outward habit of encounter; a kind of yesty collection,[44] which carries them through and through the most fanned and winnowed opinions; and do but blow them to their trial, the bubbles are out.

[*Enter a Lord*]

LORD: My lord, his majesty commended him to you by young Osric, who brings back to him that you attend him in the hall: he sends to know if your pleasure hold to play with Laertes, or that you will take longer time.

HAMLET: I am constant to my purposes; they follow the king's pleasure: if his fitness speaks, mine is ready; now or whensoever, provided I be so able as now.

LORD: The king and queen and all are coming down.

HAMLET: In happy time.

LORD: The queen desires you to use some gentle entertainment to Laertes before you fall to play.

HAMLET: She well instructs me.

[*Exit* Lord]

HORATIO: You will lose this wager, my lord.

HAMLET: I do not think so; since he went into France I have been in continual practice: I shall win at the odds. But thou wouldst not think how ill all's here about my heart: but it is no matter.

HORATIO: Nay, good my lord,—

HAMLET: It is but foolery; but it is such a kind of gain-giving[45] as would perhaps trouble a woman.

HORATIO: If your mind dislike anything, obey it: I will forestall their repair hither, and say you are not fit.

HAMLET: Not a whit, we defy augury: there's a special providence in the fall of a sparrow. If it be now, 'tis not to come; if it be not to come, it will be now; if it be not now, yet it will come: the readiness is all. Since no man has aught of what he leaves, what is't to leave betimes?[46]

[*Enter* King, Queen, Laertes, Lords, Osric, *and* Attendants *with foils, &c.*]

KING: Come, Hamlet, come, and take this hand from me.

[*The* King *puts* Laertes' *hand into* Hamlet's]

HAMLET: Give me your pardon, sir: I have done you wrong:

But pardon't, as you are a gentleman.

This presence knows, and you must needs have heard,

How I am punish'd with sore distraction.

What I have done,

That might your nature, honor, and exception

Roughly awake, I here proclaim was madness.

Was't Hamlet wrong'd Laertes? Never Hamlet:

If Hamlet from himself be ta'en away,

And when he's not himself does wrong Laertes,

Then Hamlet does it not, Hamlet denies it.

Who does it, then? His madness: if't be so,

Hamlet is of the faction that is wrong'd;

His madness is poor Hamlet's enemy.

Sir, in this audience,

Let my disclaiming from a purpos'd evil

Free me so far in your most generous thoughts

That I have shot mine arrow o'er the house

And hurt my brother.

LAERTES: I am satisfied in nature,

Whose motive, in this case, should stir me most

To my revenge: but in my terms of honor

I stand aloof; and will no reconcilement

Till by some elder masters of known honor

I have a voice and precedent of peace

To keep my name ungor'd. But till that time

I do receive your offer'd love like love,

And will not wrong it.

HAMLET: I embrace it freely;

And will this brother's wager frankly play.[47]—

Give us the foils; come on.

LAERTES: Come, one for me.

HAMLET: I'll be your foil, Laertes; in mine ignorance

Your skill shall, like a star in the darkest night,

Stick fiery off indeed.

LAERTES: You mock me, sir.

HAMLET: No, by this hand.

KING: Give them the foils, young Osric. Cousin Hamlet,

You know the wager?

HAMLET: Very well, my lord;

Your grace hath laid the odds o' the weaker side.

KING: I do not fear it; I have seen you both;

But since he's better'd, we have therefore odds.

LAERTES: This is too heavy, let me see another.

HAMLET: This likes me well. These foils have all a length?

[*They prepare to play*]

OSRIC: Ay, my good lord.

KING: Set me the stoups of wine upon that table,—

If Hamlet give the first or second hit,

Or quit in answer of the third exchange,

Let all the battlements their ordnance fire;

The king shall drink to Hamlet's better breath;

---

[42] This precocious fellow is like a lapwing that starts running when it is barely out of the shell.

[43] He paid compliments to his mother's breast before he sucked it.

[44] Yeasty or frothy affair.

[45] Misgiving.

[46] What does an early death matter?

[47] Fence with a heart free from resentment.

And in the cup an union[48] shall he throw,
Richer than that which four successive kings
In Denmark's crown have worn. Give me the cups;
And let the kettle[49] to the trumpet speak,
The trumpet to the cannoneer without,
The cannons to the heavens, the heavens to earth,
Now the king drinks to Hamlet.—Come, begin;—
And you, the judges, bear a wary eye.

HAMLET: Come on, sir.

LAERTES: Come, my lord.
        [*They play*]

HAMLET: One.

LAERTES: No.

HAMLET: Judgment.

OSRIC: A hit, a very palpable hit.

LAERTES: Well;—again.

KING: Stay, give me a drink.—Hamlet, this pearl is
    thine;
Here's to thy health.—
        [*Trumpets sound, and cannon shot off within*]
Give him the cup.

HAMLET: I'll play this bout first; set it by awhile.—
Come.—Another hit; what say you?
        [*They play*]

LAERTES: A touch, a touch, I do confess.

KING: Our son shall win.

QUEEN: He's fat, and scant of breath.—
Here, Hamlet, take my napkin, rub thy brows:
The queen carouses to thy fortune, Hamlet.

HAMLET: Good madam!

KING: Gertrude, do not drink.

QUEEN: I will, my lord; I pray you, pardon me.

KING: [*Aside*] It is the poison'd cup; it is too late.

HAMLET: I dare not drink yet, madam; by and by.

QUEEN: Come, let me wipe thy face.

LAERTES: My lord, I'll hit him now.

KING: I do not think't.

LAERTES: [*Aside*] And yet 'tis almost 'gainst my
    conscience.

HAMLET: Come, for the third, Laertes: you but
    dally;
I pray you, pass with your best violence:
I am afeard you make a wanton of me.

LAERTES: Say you so? come on.
        [*They play*]

OSRIC: Nothing, neither way.

LAERTES: Have at you now!
        [*Laertes wounds Hamlet; then, in scuffling, they
        change rapiers, and Hamlet wounds Laertes*]

KING: Part them; they are incens'd.

HAMLET: Nay, come, again.
        [*The Queen falls*]

OSRIC: Look to the queen there, ho!

HORATIO: They bleed on both sides.—How is it,
    my lord?

OSRIC: How is't, Laertes?

LAERTES: Why, as a woodcock to my own springe,
    Osric;

[48] A pearl.
[49] Kettledrum.

I am justly kill'd with mine own treachery.

HAMLET: How does the queen?

KING: She swoons to see them bleed.

QUEEN: No, no, the drink, the drink,—O my dear
    Hamlet,—
The drink, the drink!—I am poison'd. [*Dies*]

HAMLET: O villainy!—Ho! let the door be lock'd:
Treachery! seek it out.
        [*Laertes falls*]

LAERTES: It is here, Hamlet: Hamlet, thou art
    slain;
No medicine in the world can do thee good;
In thee there is not half an hour of life;
The treacherous instrument is in thy hand,
Unbated and envenom'd: the foul practice
Hath turn'd itself on me; lo, here I lie,
Never to rise again: thy mother's poison'd:
I can no more:—the king, the king's to blame.

HAMLET: The point envenom'd too!—
Then venom to thy work. [*Stabs the* King]

OSRIC *and* LORDS: Treason! treason!

KING: O, yet defend me, friends; I am but hurt.

HAMLET: Here, thou incestuous, murderous,
    damned Dane,
Drink off this potion.—Is thy union here?
Follow my mother.
        [*King dies*]

LAERTES: He is justly serv'd;
It is a poison temper'd by himself.—
Exchange forgiveness with me, noble Hamlet:
Mine and my father's death come not upon thee,
Nor thine on me! [*Dies*]

HAMLET: Heaven make thee free of it! I follow
    thee.—
I am dead, Horatio.—Wretched queen, adieu!—
You that look pale and tremble at this chance,
That art but mutes or audience to this act,
Had I but time,—as this fell sergeant, death,
Is strict in his arrest,—O, I could tell you,—
But let it be.—Horatio, I am dead;
Thou liv'st; report me and my cause aright
To the unsatisfied.[50]

HORATIO: Never believe it:
I am more an antique Roman than a Dane,—
Here's yet some liquor left.

HAMLET: As thou'rt a man,
Give me the cup; let go; by heaven, I'll have't.—
O good Horatio, what a wounded name,
Things standing thus unknown, shall live behind me!
If thou didst ever hold me in thy heart,
Absent thee from felicity awhile,
And in this harsh world draw thy breath in pain,
To tell my story.—
        [*March afar off, and shot within*]
                What warlike noise is this?

OSRIC: Young Fortinbras, with conquest come
    from Poland,
To the ambassadors of England gives
This warlike volley.

[50] The uninformed.

HAMLET:　　　　O, I die, Horatio;
The potent poison quite o'er-crows my spirit:
I cannot live to hear the news from England;
But I do prophesy the election lights
On Fortinbras: he has my dying voice;
So tell him, with the occurrents, more and less,
Which have solicited.[51]—The rest is silence. [*Dies*]
　　HORATIO: Now cracks a noble heart.—Good-night,
　　　　sweet prince,
And flights of angels sing thee to thy rest!
Why does the drum come hither?
　　　　[*March within. Enter* Fortinbras, *the* English
　　　　　Ambassadors, *and others*]
　　FORTINBRAS: Where is this sight?
　　HORATIO:　　　What is it you would see?
If aught of woe or wonder, cease your search.
　　FORTINBRAS: This quarry cries on havoc.[52]—O
　　　　proud death,
What feast is toward in thine eternal cell,
That thou so many princes at a shot
So bloodily hast struck?
　　1ST AMBASSADOR:　　The sight is dismal;
And our affairs from England come too late:
The ears are senseless that should give us hearing,
To tell him his commandment is fulfill'd,
That Rosencrantz and Guildenstern are dead:
Where should we have our thanks?
　　HORATIO:　　　　Not from his mouth,
Had it the ability of life to thank you:
He never gave commandment for their death.
But since, so jump[53] upon this bloody question,
You from the Polack wars, and you from England,

[51] So tell him, together with the events, more or less,
that have brought on this tragic affair.
[52] This collection of dead bodies cries out havoc.
[53] Opportunely.

Are here arriv'd, give order that these bodies
High on a stage be placed to the view;
And let me speak to the yet unknowing world
How these things came about: so shall you hear
Of carnal, bloody, and unnatural acts;
Of accidental judgments, casual slaughters;
Of deaths put on by cunning and forc'd cause;
And, in this upshot, purposes mistook
Fall'n on the inventors' heads: all this can I
Truly deliver.
　　FORTINBRAS:　　Let us haste to hear it,
And call the noblest to the audience.
For me, with sorrow I embrace my fortune:
I have some rights of memory in this kingdom,[54]
Which now to claim my vantage doth invite me.
　　HORATIO: Of that I shall have also cause to speak,
And from his mouth whose voice will draw on
　　more:
But let this same be presently perform'd,
Even while men's minds are wild: lest more mis-
　　chance
On plots and errors happen.
　　FORTINBRAS:　　　Let four captains
Bear Hamlet like a soldier to the stage;
For he was likely, had he been put on,[55]
To have prov'd most royally: and, for his passage,
The soldier's music and the rites of war
Speak loudly for him.—
Take up the bodies.—Such a sight as this
Becomes the field, but here shows much amiss.
Go, bid the soldiers shoot.
　　　[*A dead march*]
　　　[*Exeunt, bearing off the dead bodies: after which
　　　　a peal of ordnance is shot off*]

[54] I have some unforgotten rights to this kingdom.
[55] Tested by succession to the throne.

Ben Jonson

(1573–1637)

Ben Jonson, who loved a good fight and a good book almost equally, was the Elizabethan's angry man. In his opinion, art had a mission, and it was comedy's particular one to castigate erring humanity. The comic poet, he declared, must "scourge those apes," his contemporaries; reveal "the time's deformity"; and dethrone "prodigious ignorance." Jonson was by no means an unbending moralist incapable of cheer and good humor. A brilliant conversationalist, he cherished good fellowship and imbibed the intoxicating life of London with huge relish. No man of letters in his day gave so good an impersonation of John Bull while retaining an Elizabethan elegance of fancy and sentiment for the proper occasion of a song, a tribute to a contemporary, an allegory, or a court "masque." He was a sensitive lyricist as well as a slashing satirist, and he was made poet laureate of England. In his own day, indeed, he was a more important literary figure than Shakespeare. He could also provide workmanlike, if somewhat arid, tragedies: *Catiline* and *Sejanus*. His was, indeed, a spacious spirit, ruggedly English and at the same time extremely respectful to classical learning. But his special gift was for a type of comedy which whirled like a rough wind through the scented garden of Elizabethan romantic comedy.

Jonson had more than the usual share of just grievances against fate and circumstance. Born in Westminster a month after his father died leaving his mother penniless, saddled with an unsympathetic stepfather, forced to labor in the latter's brickyard, and impelled to enlist as a soldier in the Netherlands, he approached playwriting with a definite chip on his shoulder. In his youth he was favored only in one particular: he was an apt scholar. The learned antiquarian William Camden consequently took an interest in him and gave him the foundation for an excellent classical education. Although Jonson never attended a university, he became one of the most erudite literary men of his time.

After five years of obscurity following his return to London from the Netherlands in 1592, Jonson, who may have worked as an actor for a time, emerged as a professional collaborator on plays. In 1597 he collaborated on a now lost play, *The Isle of Dogs*, and was imprisoned for a brief period when the work was found offensive by the authorities. The clouds lifted for him for a short time in 1598, when his *Every Man in His Humour* was received with enthusiasm. It was produced by Shakespeare's company, the Lord Chamberlain's men, with a distinguished cast which included Burbage, Shakespeare, and the famous clown Will Kemp. But before the year was out Jonson had experienced another of his typical reverses. He was convicted of manslaughter, branded on the thumb, and imprisoned for killing an actor, Gabriel Spenser, in a duel.

This second encounter with the law was also of brief duration, and he resumed his profession in the fall of 1599 with a second comedy, *Every Man out of His Humour*. It was followed by a series of comedies, tragedies, and other kinds of writing, which established their author as one of the luminaries of the English stage and letters. In 1613 he traveled to France as tutor to Sir Walter Raleigh's son and had a riotous time in Paris; and in 1618 he visited Scotland, where he enjoyed the unstinted hospitality of the poet Drummond of Hawthornden, who kept an interesting record of his conversation. Oxford University made him an honorary master of arts and James I offered him knighthood, which Jonson declined. He received generous gifts from wealthy patrons as well as a royal pension from James I, collected a convivial and admiring group of writers about himself, and was accorded burial in Westminster Abbey upon his death in 1637. (He was buried in a vertical position—not, however, as a special distinction for upright conduct but in order to save space.)

Jonson seems to have had a positive talent for getting into trouble. He became involved at the turn of the sixteenth century in a virulent feud with the playwrights Dekker and Marston, whom he satirized in the *Poetaster*. He was thrown into prison again in 1605 for his part in the writing of the breezy comedy *Eastward Ho!*, which was allegedly disrespectful to Elizabeth's Stuart successor, James I. He narrowly escaped the indignity of having his ears and nose clipped at that time, in accordance with an Elizabethan penal custom. After the loss of his valuable library in a fire in 1623 and the death of his patron James I in 1625, he found it expedient to return to the theatre, from which he had been virtually retired for years; but, although he wrote several new plays, they did not advance his fortunes. In 1628 he suffered a paralytic stroke, and he never managed to complete his beautifully written play *The Sad Shepherd*. After having collaborated with the scenic artist Inigo Jones on court masques for many years, he quarreled with the latter and in consequence lost royal patronage in 1630. His old age was darkened by poverty and disease.

Drawing upon Roman comedy of manners and upon a large fund of realistic observation, Jonson created in his early plays, *Every Man in His Humour* and *Every Man out of His Humour,* a type of social satire, "comedy of humours," which differed from the genial romantic comedies of Greene and Shakespeare as winter differs from summer. The method is caricature, with a particular foible brought to the foreground as the essence of each individual's character and made to serve as a badge of identification —if not, indeed, as a substitute for the total personality. It is noteworthy, however, that Jonson's genius went a long way beyond mere inventory of current idiosyncrasies or "humours." Volpone, in the comedy that bears his name, is not merely a personified idiosyncrasy but a clever man among whose carnal appetites is a consuming rage for wealth. It determines his course of action, but it does not deter him from seeking gratification with the wife of one of his dupes. And the pleasure of exercising his cleverness and making fools of those who share his avarice without possessing his intelligence is perhaps as great as his hunger for their possessions. Jonson gave full expression to his comic genius in a series of three satires—*Volpone* (1606), *The Alchemist* (1610), and *Bartholomew Fair* (1614). These abound in shrewdly drawn characters and possess a fairly unified comic situation or intrigue. Here, as T. S. Eliot has pointed out, "Jonson behaved as

the great creative mind that he was: he created his own world . . ."—a world of "great caricature" and "non-Euclidean humanity," which Eliot also rightly calls "a titanic show."

Nowhere in Jonson's work is evil so sinister and nowhere is it flayed so mercilessly as in *Volpone.* Europe has wittier and more graceful comedies than this *reductio ad absurdum* of avarice but few so sustained and perhaps none so drastic. (For later treatments of the same theme we may turn to Molière's *The Miser,* Henry Becque's *The Vultures,* and Lillian Hellman's *The Little Foxes.*) Jonson's genius, which is at its zenith in this satire, is, in fact, saturnine, and no writer of comedy after Aristophanes ever raised indignation to so fine an art. The author of *Volpone* was England's most formidable satirist before the advent of Jonathan Swift. If Jonson was not the only playwright of his day to write mordant comedy—even "gentle" Shakespeare had his period of the "dark comedies"—no one else moved so steadily and unerringly toward his target. His strength lay to a large degree in his inclination to follow a single direction unrelentingly. His artistry can scarcely fail to impress, even if there are times, especially in *Volpone,* when one could wish for a more congenial companion.

VOLPONE

or The Fox

By Ben Jonson

DRAMATIS PERSONAE

VOLPONE, *a magnifico*
MOSCA, *his parasite*
VOLTORE, *an advocate*
CORBACCIO, *an old gentleman*
CORVINO, *a merchant*
BONARIO, *son to Corbaccio*
SIR POLITICK WOULD-BE, *a knight*
PEREGRINE, *a gentleman traveler*
NANO, *a dwarf*
CASTRONE, *a eunuch*

ANDROGYNO, *an hermaphrodite*
GREGE (*or Mob*)
COMMANDADORI, *officers of justice*
MERCATORI, *three merchants*
AVOCATORI, *four magistrates*
NOTARIO, *the register*

LADY POLITICK WOULD-BE, *Sir Politick's wife*
CELIA, *Corvino's wife*

SERVITORI, SERVANTS, TWO WAITING-WOMEN, &C.

THE SCENE: *Venice*

ACT I. SCENE I.

A room in Volpone's *house.*

[*Enter* Volpone *and* Mosca]
VOLPONE: Good morning to the day; and next, my
   gold!
Open the shrine, that I may see my saint.
   [Mosca *withdraws the curtain, and discovers
   piles of gold, plate, jewels, etc.*]
Hail the world's soul, and mine! more glad than is
The teeming earth to see the longed-for sun
Peep through the horns of the celestial Ram,
Am I, to view thy splendor darkening his;
That lying here, amongst my other hoards,
Show'st like a flame by night, or like the day
Struck out of chaos, when all darkness fled
Unto the centre. O thou son of Sol,
But brighter than thy father, let me kiss,
With adoration, thee, and every relic
Of sacred treasure in this blessed room.
Well did wise poets, by thy glorious name,
Title that age which they would have the best;
Thou being the best of things, and far transcending
All style of joy, in children, parents, friends,
Or any other walking dream on earth:
Thy looks when they to Venus did ascribe,
They should have given her twenty thousand Cupids;
Such are thy beauties and our loves! Dear saint,
Riches, the dumb god, that giv'st all men tongues,
That canst do nought, and yet mak'st men do all
   things;
The price of souls; even hell, with thee to boot,
Is made worth heaven. Thou art virtue, fame,

Honor, and all things else. Who can get thee,
He shall be noble, valiant, honest, wise——
   MOSCA: And what he will, sir. Riches are in for-
   tune
A greater good than wisdom is in nature.
   VOLPONE: True, my beloved Mosca. Yet I glory
More in the cunning purchase of my wealth,
Than in the glad possession, since I gain
No common way; I use no trade, no venture;
I wound no earth with ploughshares, fat no beasts
To feed the shambles; have nó mills for iron,
Oil, corn, or men, to grind them into powder:
I blow no subtle glass, expose no ships
To threat'nings of the furrow-faced sea;
I turn no monies in the public bank,
No usurer private.
   MOSCA: No sir, nor devour
Soft prodigals. You shall have some will swallow
A melting heir as glibly as your Dutch
Will pills of butter, and ne'er purge for it;
Tear forth the fathers of poor families
Out of their beds, and coffin them alive
In some kind clasping prison, where their bones
May be forthcoming, when the flesh is rotten:
But your sweet nature doth abhor these courses;
You loathe the widow's or the orphan's tears
Should wash your pavements, or their piteous cries
Ring in your roofs, and beat the air for vengeance.
   VOLPONE: Right, Mosca; I do loathe it.
   MOSCA: And, besides, sir,
You are not like the thresher that doth stand
With a huge flail, watching a heap of corn,
And, hungry, dares not taste the smallest grain,
But feeds on mallows, and such bitter herbs;
Nor like the merchant, who hath filled his vaults
With Romagnia, and rich Candian wines,
Yet drinks the lees of Lombard's vinegar:

You will not lie in straw, whilst moths and worms
Feed on your sumptuous hangings and soft beds;
You know the use of riches, and dare give now
From that bright heap, to me, your poor observer,
Or to your dwarf, or your hermaphrodite,
Your eunuch, or what other household trifle
Your pleasure allows maintenance——

VOLPONE: Hold thee, Mosca, [*gives him money*]
Take of my hand; thou strik'st on truth in all,
And they are envious term thee parasite.
Call forth my dwarf, my eunuch, and my fool,
And let them make me sport. [*Exit* Mosca] What
    should I do,
But cocker up my genius, and live free
To all delights my fortune calls me to?
I have no wife, no parent, child, ally,
To give my substance to; but whom I make
Must be my heir; and this makes men observe me:
This draws new clients daily to my house,
Women and men of every sex and age,
That bring me presents, send me plate, coin, jewels
With hope that when I die (which they expect
Each greedy minute) it shall then return
Tenfold upon them; whilst some, covetous
Above the rest, seek to engross me whole,
And counter-work the one unto the other,
Contend in gifts, as they would seem in love:
All which I suffer, playing with their hopes,
And am content to coin them into profit,
And look upon their kindness, and take more,
And look on that; still bearing them in hand,
Letting the cherry knock against their lips,
And draw it by their mouths, and back again.——
How now!

[*Re-enter* Mosca *with* Nano, Androgyno, *and*
    Castrone]

NANO: "Now, room for fresh gamesters, who do
    will you to know,
They do bring you neither play nor university show;
And therefore do intreat you that whatsoever they
    rehearse,
May not fare a whit the worse, for the false pace of
    the verse.
If you wonder at this, you will wonder more ere we
    pass,
For know, here is enclosed the soul of Pythagoras,[1]
That juggler divine, as hereafter shall follow;
Which soul, fast and loose, sir, came first from
    Apollo,
And was breathed into Æthalides, Mercurius his
    son,
Where it had the gift to remember all that ever was
    done.
From whence it fled forth, and made quick trans-
    migration
To goldy-locked Euphorbus, who was killed in good
    fashion,

[1] What follows is a series of fantastic ruminations on
the transmigration of souls, the doctrine of Pythagoras in
classic times.

At the siege of old Troy, by the cuckold of Sparta.
Hermotimus was next (I find it in my charta),
To whom it did pass, where no sooner it was missing,
But with one Pyrrhus of Delos it learned to go a-fish-
    ing;
And thence did it enter the sophist of Greece.
From Pythagore, she went into a beautiful piece,
Hight Aspasio, the meretrix; and the next toss of
    her
Was again of a whore, she became a philosopher,
Crates the cynick, as itself doth relate it:
Since kings, knights, and beggars, knaves, lords, and
    fools gat it,
Besides ox and ass, camel, mule, goat, and brock,
In all which it hath spoke, as in the cobbler's cock.
But I come not here to discourse of that matter,
Or his one, two, or three, or his great oath, *By Quater!*
His musics, his trigon, his golden thigh,
Or his telling how elements shift; but I
Would ask, how of late thou hast suffered translation,
And shifted thy coat in these days of reformation.

ANDROGYNO: Like one of the reformed, a fool, as
    you see,
Counting all old doctrine heresy.

NANO: But not on thine own forbid meats has thou
    ventured?

ANDROGYNO: On fish, when first a Carthusian I en-
    tered.

NANO: Why, then thy dogmatical silence hath left
    thee?

ANDROGYNO: Of that an obstreperous lawyer bereft
    me.

NANO: O wonderful change, when sir lawyer for-
    sook thee!
For Pythagore's sake, what body then took thee?

ANDROGYNO: A good dull mule.

NANO: And how! by that means
Thou wert brought to allow of the eating of beans?

ANDROGYNO: Yes.

NANO: But from the mule into whom didst thou
    pass?

ANDROGYNO: Into a very strange beast, by some
    writers called an ass;
By others a precise, pure, illuminate brother
Of those devour flesh, and sometimes one another:
And will drop you forth a libel, or a sanctified lie,
Betwixt every spoonful of a nativity-pie.

NANO: Now quit thee, for heaven, of that profane
    nation,
And gently report thy next transmigration.

ANDROGYNO: To the same that I am.

NANO: A creature of delight,
And, what is more than a fool, an hermaphrodite!
Now, prithee, sweet soul, in all thy variation,
Which body wouldst thou choose to keep up thy sta-
    tion?

ANDROGYNO: Troth, this I am in: even here would
    I tarry.

NANO: 'Cause here the delight of each sex thou
    canst vary!

ANDROGYNO: Alas, those pleasures be stale and for-
saken;
No, 'tis your fool wherewith I am so taken,
The only one creature that I can call blessed;
For all other forms I have proved most distressed.
NANO: Spoke true, as thou wert in Pythagoras still,
This learned opinion we celebrate will,
Fellow eunuch, as behoves us, with all our wit and
art,
To dignify that whereof ourselves are so great and
special a part."
VOLPONE: Now, very, very pretty; Mosca, this
Was thy invention?
MOSCA: If it please my patron,
Not else.
VOLPONE: It doth, good Mosca.
MOSCA: Then it was, sir.
  [Nano *and* Castrone *sing*]
  Fools, they are the only nation
  Worth men's envy or admiration;
  Free from care or sorrow-taking,
  Selves and others merry making:
  All they speak or do is sterling.
  Your fool he is your great man's darling,
  And your ladies' sport and pleasure;
  Tongue and bauble are his treasure.
  E'en his face begetteth laughter,
  And he speaks truth free from slaughter;
  He's the grace of every feast,
  And sometimes the chiefest guest;
  Hath his trencher and his stool,
  When wit waits upon the fool.
    O, who would not be
    He, he, he?
  [*Knocking without*]
VOLPONE: Who's that? Away! [*Exeunt* Nano *and*
Castrone] Look, Mosca. Fool, begone!
  [*Exit* Androgyno]
MOSCA: 'Tis Signior Voltore, the advocate; I know
him by his knock.
VOLPONE: Fetch me my gown,
My furs, and night-caps; say my couch is changing.
And let him entertain himself awhile
Without i' the gallery. [*Exit* Mosca] Now, now my
clients
Begin their visitation! Vulture, kite,
Raven, and gorcrow, all my birds of prey,
That think me turning carcase, now they come:
I am not for them yet.
  [*Re-enter* Mosca, *with the gown, &c.*]
                How now! the news?
MOSCA: A piece of plate, sir.
VOLPONE: Of what bigness?
MOSCA: Huge,
Massy, and antique, with your name inscribed.
And arms engraven.
VOLPONE: Good! and not a fox
Stretched on the earth, with fine delusive sleights,
Mocking a gaping crow? ha, Mosca!
MOSCA: Sharp, sir.

VOLPONE: Give me my furs. [*Puts on his sick dress*]
Why dost thou laugh so, man?
MOSCA: I cannot choose, sir, when I apprehend
What thoughts he has without now, as he walks:
That this might be the last gift he should give;
That this would fetch you; if you died to-day,
And gave him all, what he should be to-morrow;
What large return would come of all his ventures;
How he should worshipped be, and reverenced;
Ride with his furs, and foot-cloths; waited on
By herds of fools and clients; have clear way
Made for his mule, as lettered as himself;
Be called the great and learned advocate:
And then concludes, there's nought impossible.
VOLPONE: Yes, to be learned, Mosca.
MOSCA: O, no: rich
Implies it. Hood an ass with reverend purple,
So you can hide his two ambitious ears,
And he shall pass for a cathedral doctor.
VOLPONE: My caps, my caps, good Mosca. Fetch
him in.
MOSCA: Stay, sir; your ointment for your eyes.
VOLPONE: That's true;
Dispatch, dispatch: I long to have possession
Of my new present.
MOSCA: That, and thousands more,
I hope to see you lord of.
VOLPONE: Thanks, kind Mosca.
MOSCA: And that, when I am lost in blended dust,
And hundreds such as I am, in succession—
VOLPONE: Nay, that were too much, Mosca.
MOSCA: You shall live
Still to delude these harpies.
VOLPONE: Loving Mosca!
'Tis well: my pillow now, and let him enter.
  [*Exit* Mosca]
Now, my feigned cough, my phtisic, and my gout,
My apoplexy, palsy, and catarrhs,
Help, with your forced functions, this my posture,
Wherein, this three year, I have milked their hopes.
He comes; I hear him—Uh! [*coughing*] uh! uh! uh!
    O——
  [*Re-enter* Mosca, *introducing* Voltore *with a
  piece of plate*]
MOSCA: You still are what you were, sir. Only you,
Of all the rest, are he commands his love,
And you do wisely to preserve it thus,
With early visitation, and kind notes
Of your good meaning to him, which, I know,
Cannot but come most grateful. Patron! sir!
Here's Signior Voltore is come——
VOLPONE: [*Faintly*] What say you?
MOSCA: Sir, Signior Voltore is come this morning
To visit you.
VOLPONE: I thank him.
MOSCA: And hath brought
A piece of antique plate, bought of St. Mark,
With which he here presents you.
VOLPONE: He is welcome.
Pray him to come more often.

MOSCA: Yes.

VOLTORE: What says he?

MOSCA: He thanks you, and desires you to see him
often.

VOLPONE: Mosca.

MOSCA: My patron!

VOLPONE: Bring him near, where is he?
I long to feel his hand.

MOSCA: The plate is here, sir.

VOLTORE: How fare you, sir?

VOLPONE: I thank you, Signior Voltore;
Where is the plate? mine eyes are bad.

VOLTORE: [*Putting it into his hands*] I'm sorry
To see you still thus weak.

MOSCA: [*Aside*] That he's not weaker.

VOLPONE: You are too munificent.

VOLTORE: No, sir; would to heaven,
I could as well give health to you, as that plate!

VOLPONE: You give, sir, what you can; I thank
you.
Your love
Hath taste in this, and shall not be unanswered:
I pray you see me often.

VOLTORE: Yes, I shall, sir.

VOLPONE: Be not far from me.

MOSCA: Do you observe that, sir?

VOLPONE: Hearken unto me still; it will concern
you.

MOSCA: You are a happy man, sir; know your good.

VOLPONE: I cannot now last long——

MOSCA: You are his heir, sir.

VOLTORE: Am I?

VOLPONE: I feel me going: Uh! uh! uh! uh!
I'm sailing to my port, Uh! uh! uh! uh!
And I am glad I am so near my haven.

MOSCA: Alas, kind gentleman! Well, we must all
go——

VOLTORE: But, Mosca——

MOSCA: Age will conquer.

VOLTORE: Pray thee, hear me;
Am I inscribed his heir for certain?

MOSCA: Are you!
I do beseech you, sir, you will vouchsafe
To write me in your family. All my hopes
Depend upon your worship: I am lost
Except the rising sun do shine on me.

VOLTORE: It shall both shine, and warm thee,
Mosca.

MOSCA: Sir,
I am a man that hath not done your love
All the worst offices: here I wear your keys,
See all your coffers and your caskets locked,
Keep the poor inventory of your jewels,
Your plate, and monies; am your steward, sir,
Husband your goods here.

VOLTORE: But am I sole heir?

MOSCA: Without a partner, sir: confirmed this
morning:
The wax is warm yet, and the ink scarce dry
Upon the parchment.

VOLTORE: Happy, happy me!
By what good chance, sweet Mosca?

MOSCA: Your desert, sir;
I know no second cause.

VOLTORE: Thy modesty
Is not to know it; well, we shall requite it.

MOSCA: He ever liked your course, sir; that first
took him.
I oft have heard him say how he admired
Men of your large profession, that could speak
To every cause, and things mere contraries,
Till they were hoarse again, yet all be law;
That, with most quick agility, could turn,
And return; make knots, and undo them;
Give forked counsel; take provoking gold
On either hand, and put it up; these men,
He knew, would thrive with their humility.
And, for his part, he thought he should be blest
To have his heir of such a suffering spirit,
So wise, so grave, of so perplexed a tongue,
And loud withal, that would not wag, nor scarce
Lie still, without a fee; when every word
Your worship but lets fall, is a chequine!² —
[*Knocking without*]
Who's that? one knocks; I would not have you seen,
sir.
And yet—pretend you came, and went in haste;
I'll fashion an excuse—and, gentle sir,
When you do come to swim in golden lard,
Up to the arms in honey, that your chin
Is borne up stiff with fatness of the flood,
Think on your vassal; but remember me:
I have not been your worst of clients.

VOLTORE: Mosca!——

MOSCA: When will you have your inventory
brought, sir?
Or see a copy of the Will?—Anon!
I'll bring them to you, sir. Away, begone,
Put business in your face.
[*Exit* Voltore]

VOLPONE: [*Springing up*] Excellent Mosca!
Come hither, let me kiss thee.

MOSCA: Keep you still, sir.
Here is Corbaccio.

VOLPONE: Set the plate away:
The vulture's gone, and the old raven's come.

MOSCA: Betake you to your silence, and your sleep.
Stand there and multiply. [*Putting the plate to the
rest*] Now we shall see
A wretch who is indeed more impotent
Than this can feign to be; yet hopes to hop
Over his grave.
[*Enter* Corbaccio]
Signior Corbaccio!
You're very welcome, sir.

CORBACCIO: How does your patron?

MOSCA: Troth, as he did, sir; no amends.

CORBACCIO: What! mends he?

MOSCA: No, sir: he's rather worse.

² Sequin: a coin.

CORBACCIO: That's well. Where is he?

MOSCA: Upon his couch, sir, newly fall'n asleep.

CORBACCIO: Does he sleep well?

MOSCA: No wink, sir, all this night,
Nor yesterday; but slumbers.

CORBACCIO: Good! he should take
Some counsel of physicians: I have brought him
An opiate here, from mine own doctor.

MOSCA: He will not hear of drugs.

CORBACCIO: Why? I myself
Stood by while it was made, saw all the ingredients;
And know it cannot but mostly gently work:
My life for his, 'tis but to make him sleep.

VOLPONE: [Aside] Ay, his last sleep, if he would
take it.

MOSCA: Sir,
He has no faith in physic.

CORBACCIO: Say you, say you?

MOSCA: He has no faith in physic: he does think
Most of your doctors are the greater danger,
And worse disease, to escape. I often have
Heard him protest that your physician
Should never be his heir.

CORBACCIO: Not I his heir?

MOSCA: Not your physician, sir.

CORBACCIO: O, no, no, no.
I do not mean it.

MOSCA: No, sir, nor their fees
He cannot brook: he says they flay a man
Before they kill him.

CORBACCIO: Right, I do conceive you.

MOSCA: And then they do it by experiment;
For which the law not only doth absolve them,
But gives them great reward: and he is loth
To hire his death so.

CORBACCIO: It is true, they kill
With as much license as a judge.

MOSCA: Nay, more;
For he but kills, sir, where the law condemns,
And these can kill him too.

CORBACCIO: Ay, or me;
Or any man. How does his apoplex?
Is that strong on him still?

MOSCA: Most violent.
His speech is broken, and his eyes are set,
His face drawn longer than 'twas wont——

CORBACCIO: How! how!
Stronger than he was wont?

MOSCA: No, sir; his face
Drawn longer than 'twas wont.

CORBACCIO: O, good!

MOSCA: His mouth
Is ever gaping, and his eyelids hang.

CORBACCIO: Good.

MOSCA: A freezing numbness stiffens all his joints,
And makes the color of his flesh like lead.

CORBACCIO: 'Tis good.

MOSCA: His pulse beats slow, and dull.

CORBACCIO: Good symptoms still.

MOSCA: And from his brain——

CORBACCIO: I conceive you; good.

MOSCA: Flows a cold sweat, with a continual
rheum,
Forth the resolved corners of his eyes.

CORBACCIO: Is't possible? Yet I am better, ha!
How does he with the swimming of his head?

MOSCA: O, sir, 'tis past the scotomy;[3] he now
Hath lost his feeling, and hath left to snort:
You hardly can perceive him, that he breathes.

CORBACCIO: Excellent, excellent! sure I shall outlast him:
This makes me young again, a score of years.

MOSCA: I was a-coming for you, sir.

CORBACCIO: Has he made his Will?
What has he given me?

MOSCA: No, sir.

CORBACCIO: Nothing! ha?

MOSCA: He has not made his Will, sir.

CORBACCIO: Oh, oh, oh!
What then did Voltore, the lawyer, here?

MOSCA: He smelt a carcase, sir, when he but heard
My master was about his testament;
As I did urge him to it for your good——

CORBACCIO: He came unto him, did he? I thought
so.

MOSCA: Yes, and presented him this piece of plate.

CORBACCIO: To be his heir?

MOSCA: I do not know, sir.

CORBACCIO: True:
I know it too.

MOSCA: [Aside] By your own scale, sir.

CORBACCIO: Well,
I shall prevent him yet. See, Mosca, look
Here I have brought a bag of bright chequines,
Will quite weigh down his plate.

MOSCA: [Taking the bag] Yea, marry, sir.
This is true physic, this your sacred medicine;
No talk of opiates to this great elixir!

CORBACCIO: 'Tis aurum palpabile, if not potabile.

MOSCA: It shall be ministered to him in his bowl

CORBACCIO: Ay, do, do, do.

MOSCA: Most blessed cordial!
This will recover him.

CORBACCIO: Yes, do, do, do.

MOSCA: I think it were not best, sir.

CORBACCIO: What?

MOSCA: To recover him.

CORBACCIO: O, no, no, no; by no means.

MOSCA: Why, sir, this
Will work some strange effect, if he but feel it.

CORBACCIO: 'Tis true, therefore forbear; I'll take
my venture:
Give me it again.

MOSCA: At no hand: pardon me:
You shall not do yourself that wrong, sir. I
Will so advise you, you shall have it all.

CORBACCIO: How?

MOSCA: All, sir; 'tis your right, your own; no man
Can claim a part: 'tis yours without a rival,

[3] Dizziness.

Decreed by destiny.

   CORBACCIO: How, how, good Mosca?

   MOSCA: I'll tell you, sir. This fit he shall recover.

   CORBACCIO: I do conceive you.

   MOSCA: And on first advantage

Of his gained sense, will I re-importune him

Unto the making of his testament:

And show him this. [*Pointing to the money*]

   CORBACCIO: Good, good.

   MOSCA: 'Tis better yet,

If you will hear, sir.

   CORBACCIO: Yes, with all my heart.

   MOSCA: Now would I counsel you, make home
      with speed;

There, frame a Will; whereto you shall inscribe

My master your sole heir.

   CORBACCIO: And disinherit

My son!

   MOSCA: O, sir, the better: for that color

Shall make it much more taking.

   CORBACCIO: O, but color?

   MOSCA: This Will, sir, you shall send it unto me.

Now, when I come to inforce, as I will do,

Your cares, your watchings, and your many prayers,

Your more than many gifts, your this day's present,

And last, produce your Will; where, without thought,

Or least regard, unto your proper issue,

A son so brave, and highly meriting,

The stream of your diverted love hath thrown you

Upon my master, and made him your heir:

He cannot be so stupid, or stone-dead,

But out of conscience and mere gratitude——

   CORBACCIO: He must pronounce me his?

   MOSCA: 'Tis true.

   CORBACCIO: This plot

Did I think on before.

   MOSCA: I do believe it.

   CORBACCIO: Do you not believe it?

   MOSCA: Yes, sir.

   CORBACCIO: Mine own project.

   MOSCA: Which, when he hath done, sir——

   CORBACCIO: Published me his heir?

   MOSCA: And you so certain to survive him——

   CORBACCIO: Ay.

   MOSCA: Being so lusty a man——

   CORBACCIO: 'Tis true.

   MOSCA: Yes, sir——

   CORBACCIO: I thought on that too. See, how he
      should be

The very organ to express my thoughts!

   MOSCA: You have not only done yourself a
      good——

   CORBACCIO: But multiplied it on my son.

   MOSCA: 'Tis right, sir.

   CORBACCIO: Still, my invention.

   MOSCA: 'Las, sir! heaven knows,

It hath been all my study, all my care,

(I e'en grow gray withal,) how to work things——

   CORBACCIO: I do conceive, sweet Mosca.

   MOSCA: You are he

For whom I labor here.

   CORBACCIO: Ay, do, do, do:

I'll straight about it. [*Going*]

   MOSCA: [*Aside*] Rook go with you, raven!

   CORBACCIO: I know thee honest.

   MOSCA: You do lie, sir!

   CORBACCIO: And——

   MOSCA: Your knowledge is no better than your
      ears, sir.

   CORBACCIO: I do not doubt to be a father to thee.

   MOSCA: Nor I to gull my brother of his blessing.

   CORBACCIO: I may have my youth restored to me,
      why not?

   MOSCA: Your worship is a precious ass!

   CORBACCIO: What sayest thou?

   MOSCA: I do desire your worship to make haste,
      sir.

   CORBACCIO: 'Tis done, 'tis done; I go. [*Exit*]

   VOLPONE: [*Leaping from his couch*] O, I shall
      burst!

Let out my sides, let out my sides——

   MOSCA: Contain

Your flux of laughter, sir: you know this hope

Is such a bait, it covers any hook.

   VOLPONE: O, but thy working, and thy placing it!

I cannot hold; good rascal, let me kiss thee:

I never knew thee in so rare a humor.

   MOSCA: Alas, sir, I but do as I am taught;

Follow your grave instructions; give them words;

Pour oil into their ears, and send them hence.

   VOLPONE: 'Tis true, 'tis true. What a rare punish-
      ment.

Is avarice to itself!

   MOSCA: Ay, with our help, sir.

   VOLPONE: So many cares, so many maladies,

So many fears attending on old age.

Yea, death so often called on, as no wish

Can be more frequent with them, their limbs faint,

Their senses dull, their seeing, hearing, going,

All dead before them; yea, their very teeth,

Their instruments of eating, failing them:

Yet this is reckoned life! nay, here was one,

Is now gone home, that wishes to live longer!

Feels not his gout, nor palsy; feigns himself

Younger by scores of years, flatters his age

With confident belying it, hopes he may

With charms like Æson, have his youth restored;

And with these thoughts so battens, as if fate

Would be as easily cheated on as he,

And all turns air! [*Knocking within*] Who's that
      there, now? a third!

   MOSCA: Close, to your couch again; I hear his
      voice.

It is Corvino, our spruce merchant.

   VOLPONE: [*Lies down as before*] Dead.

   MOSCA: Another bout, sir, with your eyes. [*Anoint-
      ing them*] Who's there?

      [*Enter* Corvino]

Signior Corvino! come most wished for! O,

How happy were you, if you knew it, now!

CORVINO: Why? what? wherein?

MOSCA: The tardy hour is come, sir.

CORVINO: He is not dead?

MOSCA: Not dead, sir, but as good;
He knows no man.

CORVINO: How shall I do then?

MOSCA: Why, sir?

CORVINO: I have brought him here a pearl.

MOSCA: Perhaps he has
So much remembrance left as to know you, sir:
He still calls on you; nothing but your name
Is in his mouth. Is your pearl orient, sir?

CORVINO: Venice was never owner of the like.

VOLPONE: [Faintly] Signior Corvino!

MOSCA: Hark.

VOLPONE: Signior Corvino.

MOSCA: He calls you; step and give it him—He's
here, sir.
And he has brought you a rich pearl.

CORVINO: How do you, sir?
Tell him it doubles the twelve caract.

MOSCA: Sir,
He cannot understand, his hearing's gone;
And yet it comforts him to see you——

CORVINO: Say
I have a diamond for him, too.

MOSCA: Best show it, sir;
Put it into his hands: 'tis only there
He apprehends: he has his feeling yet.
See how he grasps it!

CORVINO: 'Las, good gentleman!
How pitiful the sight is!

MOSCA: Tut, forget, sir.
The weeping of an heir should still be laughter
Under a visor.

CORVINO: Why, am I his heir?

MOSCA: Sir, I am sworn, I may not show the Will
Till he be dead; but here has been Corbaccio,
Here has been Voltore, here were others too,
I cannot number 'em, they were so many;
All gaping here for legacies: but I,
Taking the vantage of his naming you,
Signior Corvino, Signior Corvino, took
Paper, and pen, and ink, and there I asked him
Whom he would have his heir! Corvino. Who
Should be executor? Corvino. And
To any question he was silent to,
I still interpreted the nods he made,
Through weakness, for consent: and sent home th'
others,
Nothing bequeathed them, but to cry and curse.

CORVINO: O, my dear Mosca. [They embrace] Does
he not perceive us?

MOSCA: No more than a blind harper. He knows
no man,
No face of friend, nor name of any servant,
Who 'twas that fed him last, or gave him drink:
Not those he had begotten, or brought up,
Can he remember.

CORVINO: Has he children?

MOSCA: Bastards,
Some dozen, or more, that he begot on beggars,
Gypsies, and Jews, and black-moors, when he was
drunk.
Knew you not that, sir? 'tis the common fable.
The dwarf, the fool, the eunuch, are all his;
He's the true father of his family,
In all save me:—but he has given them nothing.

CORVINO: That's well, that's well! Art sure he does
not hear us?

MOSCA: Sure, sir! why, look you, credit your own
sense.
[Shouts in Volpone's ear]
The pox approach, and add to your diseases,
If it would send you hence the sooner, sir,
For your incontinence, it hath deserved it
Thoroughly and thoroughly, and the plague to
boot!—
You may come near, sir.—Would you would once
close
Those filthy eyes of yours, that flow with slime,
Like two frog-pits; and those same hanging cheeks,
Covered with hide instead of skin—Nay, help,
sir——
That look like frozen dish-clouts set on end!

CORVINO: [Aloud] Or like an old smoked wall, on
which the rain
Ran down in streaks!

MOSCA: Excellent, sir! speak out:
You may be louder yet; a culverin⁴
Discharged in his ear would hardly bore it.

CORVINO: His nose is like a common sewer, still
running.

MOSCA: 'Tis good! And what his mouth!

CORVINO: A very draught.

MOSCA: O, stop it up——

CORVINO: By no means.

MOSCA: Pray you, let me:
Faith I could stifle him rarely with a pillow
As well as any woman that should keep him.

CORVINO: Do as you will; but I'll begone.

MOSCA: Be so;
It is your presence makes him last so long.

CORVINO: I pray you use no violence.

MOSCA: No, sir! why?
Why should you be thus scrupulous, pray you, sir?

CORVINO: Nay, at your discretion.

MOSCA: Well, good sir, be gone.

CORVINO: I will not trouble you now to take my
pearl.

MOSCA: Puh! nor your diamond. What a needless
care.
Is this afflicts you? Is not all here yours?
Am not I here, whom you have made your creature?
That owe my being to you?

CORVINO: Grateful Mosca!
Thou art my friend, my fellow, my companion,
My partner, and shalt share in all my fortunes.

MOSCA: Excepting one.

⁴ A long cannon.

CORVINO: What's that?

MOSCA: Your gallant wife, sir.

   [*Exit* Corvino]

Now he is gone: we had no other means
To shoot him hence but this.

   VOLPONE: My divine Mosca!

Thou hast to-day outgone thyself.

   [*Knocking within*]

   Who's there?

I will be troubled with no more. Prepare
Me music, dances, banquets, all delights;
The Turk is not more sensual in his pleasures
Than will Volpone. [*Exit* Mosca] Let me see; a pearl!
A diamond! plate! chequines! Good morning's pur-
   chase.
Why, this is better than rob churches, yet;
Or fat, by eating, once a month, a man——

   [*Re-enter* Mosca]

Who is't?

   MOSCA: The beauteous Lady Would-be, sir,

Wife to the English knight, Sir Politick Would-be
(This is the style, sir, is directed me),
Hath sent to know how you have slept to-night,
And if you would be visited?

   VOLPONE: Not now:

Some three hours hence.

   MOSCA: I told the squire so much.

   VOLPONE: When I am high with mirth and wine;
   then, then:

'Fore heaven, I wonder at the desperate valor
Of the bold English, that they dare let loose
Their wives to all encounters!

   MOSCA: Sir, this knight

Had not his name for nothing, he is *politick*,
And knows, howe'er his wife affect strange airs,
She hath not yet the face to be dishonest:
But had she Signior Corvino's wife's face——

   VOLPONE: Hath she so rare a face?

   MOSCA: O, sir, the wonder,

The blazing star of Italy! a wench
Of the first year, a beauty ripe as harvest!
Whose skin is whiter than a swan all over,
Than silver, snow, or lilies; a soft lip,
Would tempt you to eternity of kissing!
And flesh that melteth in the touch to blood!
Bright as your gold, and lovely as your gold!

   VOLPONE: Why had not I known this before?

   MOSCA: Alas, sir,

Myself but yesterday discovered it.

   VOLPONE: How might I see her?

   MOSCA: O, not possible;

She's kept as warily as is your gold;
Never does come abroad, never takes air
But at a window. All her looks are sweet,
As the first grapes or cherries, and are watched
As near as they are.

   VOLPONE: I must see her.

   MOSCA: Sir,

There is a guard of spies ten thick upon her,
All his whole household; each of which is set

Upon his fellow, and have all their charge,
When he goes out, when he comes in, examined.

   VOLPONE: I will go see her, though but at her
   window.

   MOSCA: In some disguise then.

   VOLPONE: That is true; I must

Maintain mine own shape still the same: we'll think.

   [*Exeunt*]

ACT II. SCENE I.

St. Mark's Place; a retired corner before Corvino's
house.

   [*Enter* Sir Politick Would-be, *and* Peregrine]

   SIR POLITICK: Sir, to a wise man, all the world's
   his soil:

It is not Italy, nor France, nor Europe,
That must bound me, if my fates call me forth.
Yet I protest, it is no salt desire
Of seeing countries, shifting a religion,
Nor any disaffection to the state
Where I was bred, and unto which I owe
My dearest plots, hath brought me out; much less
That idle, antique, stale, grey-headed project
Of knowing men's minds and manners, with Ulysses!
But a peculiar humor of my wife's
Laid for this height of Venice, to observe,
To quote, to learn the language, and so forth——
I hope you travel, sir, with license?

   PEREGRINE: Yes.

   SIR POLITICK: I dare the safelier converse——How
   long, sir,

Since you left England?

   PEREGRINE: Seven weeks.

   SIR POLITICK: So lately!

You have not been with my lord ambassador?

   PEREGRINE: Not yet, sir.

   SIR POLITICK: Pray you, what news, sir, vents our
   climate?

I heard last night a most strange thing reported
By some of my lord's followers, and I long
To hear how 'twill be seconded.

   PEREGRINE: What was't, sir?

   SIR POLITICK: Marry, sir, of a raven that should
   build

In a ship royal of the king's.

   PEREGRINE: This fellow,

Does he gull me, trow? or is gulled? [*Aside*] Your
   name, sir?

   SIR POLITICK: My name is Politick Would-be.

   PEREGRINE: O, that speaks him. [*Aside*]

A knight, sir?

   SIR POLITICK: A poor knight, sir.

   PEREGRINE: Your lady

Lies here in Venice, for intelligence
Of tires and fashions, and behavior,
Among the courtezans? the fine Lady Would-be?

SIR POLITICK: Yes, sir; the spider and the bee oft-times
Suck from one flower.
    PEREGRINE: Good Sir Politick,
I cry you mercy; I have heard much of you:
'Tis true, sir, of your raven.
    SIR POLITICK: On your knowledge?
    PEREGRINE: Yes, and your lion's whelping in the
    Tower.
    SIR POLITICK: Another whelp?
    PEREGRINE: Another, sir.
    SIR POLITICK: Now heaven!
What prodigies be these? The fires at Berwick!
And the new star! these things concurring, strange,
And full of omen! Saw you those meteors?
    PEREGRINE: I did, sir.
    SIR POLITICK: Fearful! Pray you, sir, confirm me,
Were there three porpoises seen above the bridge,
As they give out?
    PEREGRINE: Six, and a sturgeon, sir.
    SIR POLITICK: I am astonished.
    PEREGRINE: Nay, sir, be not so;
I'll tell you a greater prodigy than these.
    SIR POLITICK: What should these things portend?
    PEREGRINE: The very day
(Let me be sure) that I put forth from London,
There was a whale discovered in the river,
As high as Woolwich, that had waited there,
Few know how many months, for the subversion
Of the Stode fleet.
    SIR POLITICK: Is't possible? believe it,
'Twas either sent from Spain, or the archduke's:
Spinola's whale, upon my life, my credit!
Will they not leave these projects? Worthy sir,
Some other news.
    PEREGRINE: Faith, Stone the fool is dead,
And they do lack a tavern fool extremely.
    SIR POLITICK: Is Mass Stone dead?
    PEREGRINE: He's dead, sir; why, I hope
You thought him not immortal?—[Aside] O, this
    knight,
Were he well known, would be a precious thing
To fit our English stage: he that should write
But such a fellow, should be thought to feign
Extremely, if not maliciously.
    SIR POLITICK: Stone dead!
    PEREGRINE: Dead—Lord! how deeply, sir, you ap-
    prehend it!
He was no kinsman to you?
    SIR POLITICK: That I know of.
Well! that same fellow was an unknown fool.
    PEREGRINE: And yet you knew him, it seems?
    SIR POLITICK: I did so. Sir,
I knew him one of the most dangerous heads
Living within the state, and so I held him.
    PEREGRINE: Indeed, sir?
    SIR POLITICK: While he lived, in action,
He has received weekly intelligence,
Upon my knowledge, out of the Low Countries,
For all parts of the world, in cabbages;

And those dispensed again to ambassadors,
In oranges, musk-melons, apricots,
Lemons, pome-citrons, and such-like; sometimes
In Colchester oysters, and your Selsey cockles.
    PEREGRINE: You make me wonder.
    SIR POLITICK: Sir, upon my knowledge.
Nay, I've observed him, at your public ordinary,
Take his advertisement from a traveler,
A concealed statesman, in a trencher of meat;
And instantly, before the meal was done,
Convey an answer in a tooth-pick.
    PEREGRINE: Strange!
How could this be, sir?
    SIR POLITICK: Why, the meat was cut
So like his character, and so laid as he
Must easily read the cypher.
    PEREGRINE: I have heard,
He could not read, sir.
    SIR POLITICK: So 'twas given out,
In policy, by those that did employ him:
But he could read, and had your languages.
And to't, as sound a noddle——
    PEREGRINE: I have heard, sir,
That your baboons were spies, and that they were
A kind of subtle nation near to China.
    SIR POLITICK: Ay, ay, your Mamaluchi. Faith,
    they had
Their hand in a French plot or two; but they
Were so extremely given to women, as
They made discovery of all: yet I
Had my advices here, on Wednesday last,
From one of their own coat, they were returned,
Made their relations, as the fashion is,
And now stand fair for fresh employment.
    PEREGRINE: Heart! This Sir Pol will be ignorant
    of nothing. [Aside]
It seems, sir, you know all.
    SIR POLITICK: Not all, sir; but
I have some general notions. I do love
To note and to observe: though I live out,
Free from the active torrent, yet I'd mark
The currents and the passages of things,
For mine own private use; and know the ebbs
And flows of state.
    PEREGRINE: Believe it, sir, I hold
Myself in no small tie unto my fortunes,
For casting me thus luckily upon you,
Whose knowledge, if your bounty equal it,
May do me great assistance, in instruction
For my behavior, and my bearing, which
Is yet so rude and raw.
    SIR POLITICK: Why? came you forth
Empty of rules for travel?
    PEREGRINE: Faith, I had
Some common ones, from out that vulgar grammar,
Which he that cried Italian to me, taught me.
    SIR POLITICK: Why, this it is that spoils all our
    brave bloods,
Trusting our hopeful gentry unto pedants,
Fellows of outside, and mere bark. You seem

To be a gentleman of ingenuous race:——
I not profess it, but my fate hath been
To be, where I have been consulted with,
In this high kind, touching some great men's sons,
Persons of blood and honor.——

[*Enter* Mosca *and* Nano *disguised, followed by persons with materials for erecting a stage*]

PEREGRINE: Who be these, sir?

MOSCA: Under that window, there 't must be. The same.

SIR POLITICK: Fellows, to mount a bank. Did your instructor
In the dear tongues, never discourse to you
Of the Italian mountebanks?

PEREGRINE: Yes, sir.

SIR POLITICK: Why,
Here you shall see one.

PEREGRINE: They are quacksalvers,
Fellows that live by venting oils and drugs.

SIR POLITICK: Was that the character he gave you of them?

PEREGRINE: As I remember.

SIR POLITICK: Pity his ignorance.
They are the only knowing men of Europe!
Great general scholars, excellent physicians,
Most admired statesmen, profest favorites,
And cabinet counselors to the greatest princes;
The only languaged men of all the world!

PEREGRINE: And, I have heard, they are most lewd impostors;
Made all of terms and shreds; no less beliers
Of great men's favors, than their own vile med'cines;
Which they will utter upon monstrous oaths;
Selling that drug for twopence, ere they part,
Which they have valued at twelve crowns before.

SIR POLITICK: Sir, calumnies are answered best with silence.
Yourself shall judge.—Who is it mounts, my friends?

MOSCA: Scoto of Mantua, sir.

SIR POLITICK: Is't he? Nay, then
I'll proudly promise, sir, you shall behold
Another man than has been phant'sied to you.
I wonder yet, that he should mount his bank,
Here in this nook, that has been wont t' appear
In face of the Piazza!—Here he comes.

[*Enter* Volpone, *disguised as a mountebank doctor, and followed by a crowd of people*]

VOLPONE: Mount, zany. [*To* Nano]

MOB: Follow, follow, follow, follow!

SIR POLITICK: See how the people follow him! he's a man
May write ten thousand crowns in bank here. Note,
[Volpone *mounts the stage*]
Mark but his gesture:—I do use to observe
The state he keeps in getting up.

PEREGRINE: 'Tis worth it, sir.

VOLPONE: "Most noble gentlemen, and my worthy patrons! It may seem strange that I, your Scoto Mantuano, who was ever wont to fix my bank in the face of the public Piazza, near the shelter of the Portico to the Procuratia, should now, after eight months' absence from this illustrious city of Venice, humbly retire myself into an obscure nook of the Piazza."

SIR POLITICK: Did not I now object the same?

PEREGRINE: Peace, sir.

VOLPONE: "Let me tell you: I am not, as your Lombard proverb saith, cold on my feet; or content to part with my commodities at a cheaper rate than I am accustomed: look not for it. Nor that the calumnious reports of that impudent detractor, and shame to our profession (Alessandro Buttone, I mean), who gave out, in public, I was condemned a sforzato to the galleys, for poisoning the Cardinal Bembo's—cook, hath at all attached, much less dejected me. No, no, worthy gentlemen; to tell you true, I cannot endure to see the rabble of these ground ciarlitani,[5] that spread their cloaks on the pavement, as if they meant to do feats of activity, and then come in lamely, with their mouldy tales out of Boccaccio, like stale Tabarine, the fabulist: some of them discoursing their travels, and of their tedious captivity in the Turk's galleys, when, indeed, were the truth known, they were the Christian's galleys, where very temperately they eat bread, and drink water, as a wholesome penance, enjoined them by their confessors, for base pilferies."

SIR POLITICK: Note but his bearing, and contempt of these.

VOLPONE: "These turdy-facy-nasty-paty-lousy-fartical rogues, with one poor groat's-worth of unprepared antimony, finely wrapt up in several scartoccios,[6] are able, very well, to kill their twenty a week, and play; yet these meagre, starved spirits, who have half stopt the organs of their minds with earthy oppilations, want not their favorers among your shriveled salad-eating artisans, who are overjoyed that they may have their half-per'th of physic; though it purge them into another world, it makes no matter."

SIR POLITICK: Excellent! have you heard better language, sir?

VOLPONE: "Well, let them go. And, gentlemen, honorable gentlemen, know, that for this time, our bank, being thus removed from the clamors of the canaglia, shall be the scene of pleasure and delight; for I have nothing to sell, little or nothing to sell."

SIR POLITICK: I told you, sir, his end.

PEREGRINE: You did so, sir.

VOLPONE: "I protest, I, and my six servants, are not able to make of this precious liquor, so fast as it is fetched away from my lodging by gentlemen of your city; strangers of the Terra-firma; worshipful merchants; ay, and senators too: who, ever since my arrival, have detained me to their uses, by their splendidous liberalities. And worthily; for, what avails

[5] Charlatans.
[6] Folds of paper.

your rich man to have his magazines stuft with mos-
cadelli, or of the purest grape, when his physicians
prescribe him, on pain of death, to drink nothing but
water cocted with aniseeds? O, health! health! the
blessing of the rich! the riches of the poor! who can
buy thee at too dear a rate, since there is no enjoying this world without thee? Be not then so sparing
of your purses, honorable gentlemen, as to abridge
the natural course of life——"

PEREGRINE: You see his end.

SIR POLITICK: Ay, is't not good?

VOLPONE: "For when a humid flux, or catarrh, by
the mutability of air, falls from your head into an
arm or shoulder, or any other part; take you a ducket,
or your chequine of gold, and apply to the place
affected: see what good effect it can work. No, no,
'tis this blessed unguento, this rare extraction, that
hath only power to disperse all malignant humors,
that proceed either of hot, cold, moist, or windy
causes——"

PEREGRINE: I would he had put in dry too.

SIR POLITICK: Pray you observe.

VOLPONE: "To fortify the most indigest and crude
stomach, ay, were it of one that, through extreme
weakness, vomited blood, applying only a warm napkin to the place, after the unction and fricace;[7]—for
the vertigine in the head, putting but a drop into your
nostrils, likewise behind the ears; a most sovereign
and approved remedy; the mal caduco, cramps, con-
vulsions, paralysies, epilepsies, tremor-cordia, retired
nerves, ill vapors of the spleen, stopping of the liver,
the stone, the strangury, hernia ventosa, iliaca passio;
stops a dysenteria immediately; easeth the torsion of
the small guts; and cures melancholia hypondriaca,
being taken and applied, according to my printed
receipt. [*Pointing to his bill and his vial*] For this is
the physician, this the medicine; this counsels, this
cures; this gives the directions, this works the effect;
and, in sum, both together may be termed an abstract
of the theorick and practick in the Æsculapian art.
'Twill cost you eight crowns. And,—Zan Fritada,
prithee sing a verse extempore in honor of it."

SIR POLITICK: How do you like him, sir?

PEREGRINE: Most strangely, I!

SIR POLITICK: Is not his language rare?

PEREGRINE: But alchemy,
I never heard the like; or Broughton's books.

[*Nano sings*]
Had old Hippocrates, or Galen,
That to their books put med'cines all in,
But known this secret, they had never
(Of which they will be guilty ever)
Been murderers of so much paper,
Or wasted many a hurtless taper;
No Indian drug had e'er been famed,
Tobacco, sassafras not named;
Ne yet of guacum one small stick, sir,
Nor Raymund Lully's great elixir.

[7] Salve rubbed into the skin.

Ne had been known the Danish Gonswart,
Or Paracelsus, with his long sword.

PEREGRINE: All this, yet, will not do; eight crowns
is high.

VOLPONE: "No more.—Gentlemen, if I had but
time to discourse to you the miraculous effects of this
my oil, surnamed Oglio del Scoto; with the countless
catalogue of those I have cured of the aforesaid, and
many more diseases; the patents and privileges of all
the princes and commonwealths of Christendom; or
but the depositions of those that appeared on my
part, before the signiory of the Sanita and most
learned College of Physicians; where I was authorized, upon notice taken of the admirable virtues of
my medicaments, and mine own excellency in matter
of rare and unknown secrets, not only to disperse
them publicly in this famous city, but in all the
territories, that happily joy under the government of
the most pious and magnificent states of Italy. But
may some other gallant fellow say, O, there be divers
that make profession to have as good, and as experi-
mented receipts as yours: indeed, very many have
assayed, like apes, in imitation of that, which is
really and essentially in me, to make of this oil;
bestowed great cost in furnaces, stills, alembecks,
continual fires, and preparation of the ingredients (as
indeed there goes to it six hundred several simples,
besides some quantity of human fat, for the conglu-
tination, which we buy of the anatomists), but when
these practitioners come to the last decoction, blow,
blow, puff, puff, and all flies in fumo: ha, ha, ha!
Poor wretches! I rather pity their folly and indiscretion, than their loss of time and money; for these may
be recovered by industry: but to be a fool born, is a
disease incurable.

"For myself, I always from my youth have endeavored to get the rarest secrets, and book them,
either in exchange, or for money: I spared nor cost
nor labor, where anything was worthy to be learned.
And, gentlemen, honorable gentlemen, I will undertake, by virtue of chemical art, out of the honorable
hat that covers your head, to extract the four elements; that is to say, the fire, air, water, and earth,
and return you your felt without burn or stain. For,
whilst others have been at the Balloo,[8] I have been at
my book; and am now past the craggy paths of study,
and come to the flowery plains of honor and reputation."

SIR POLITICK: I do assure you, sir, that is his aim.

VOLPONE: "But to our price——"

PEREGRINE: And that withal, Sir Pol.

VOLPONE: "You all know, honorable gentlemen, I
never valued this ampulla, or vial, at less than eight
crowns; but for this time, I am content to be deprived
of it for six; six crowns is the price, and less in
courtesy I know you cannot offer me; take it or leave
it, howsoever, both it and I am at your service. I ask
you not as the value of the thing, for then I should

[8] A game of ball.

demand of you a thousand crowns, so the Cardinals Montalto, Fernese, the great Duke of Tuscany, my gossip, with divers other princes, have given me; but I despise money. Only to show my affection to you, honorable gentlemen, and your illustrious State here, I have neglected the messages of these princes, mine own offices, framed my journey hither, only to present you with the fruits of my travels.—Tune your voices once more to the touch of your instruments, and give the honorable assembly some delightful recreation."

PEREGRINE: What monstrous and most painful circumstance
Is here, to get some three or four gazettes,
Some threepence in the whole! for that 'twill come to.

[Nano *sings*]
You that would last long, list to my song,
Make no more coil, but buy of this oil.
Would you be ever fair and young?
Stout of teeth, and strong of tongue?
Tart of palate? quick of ear?
Sharp of sight? of nostril clear?
Moist of hand? and light of foot?
Or, I will come nearer to't,
Would you live free from all diseases?
Do the act your mistress pleases,
Yet fright all aches from your bones?
Here's a med'cine for the nones.

VOLPONE: "Well, I am in a humor at this time to make a present of the small quantity my coffer contains; to the rich in courtesy, and to the poor for God's sake. Wherefore now mark: I asked you six crowns; and six crowns, at other times, you have paid me; you shall not give me six crowns, nor five, nor four, nor three, nor two, nor one; nor half a ducat; no, nor a moccinigo.[9] Sixpence it will cost you, or six hundred pound—expect no lower price, for, by the banner of my front, I will not bate a bagatine,[10]—that I will have, only, a pledge of your loves, to carry something from amongst you, to show I am not contemned by you. Therefore, now, toss your handkerchiefs, cheerfully, cheerfully; and be advertised, that the first heroic spirit that deigns to grace me with a handkerchief, I will give it a little remembrance of something, beside, shall please it better than if I had presented it with a double pistolet."

PEREGRINE: Will you be that *heroic spark*, Sir Pol?

[Celia, *at a window above, throws down her handkerchief*]
O, see! the window has prevented you.

VOLPONE: "Lady, I kiss your bounty; and for this timely grace you have done your poor Scoto of Mantua, I will return you, over and above my oil, a secret of that high and inestimable nature, shall make you for ever enamored on that minute, wherein your eye first descended on so mean, yet not altogether to be despised, an object. Here is a powder concealed in this paper, of which, if I should speak

[9] A small coin.
[10] *Bagatino,* a Venetian copper of low value.

to the worth, nine thousand volumes were but as one page, that page as a line, that line as a word; so short is this pilgrimage of man (which some call life) to the expressing of it. Would I reflect on the price? why, the whole world is but as an empire, that empire as a province, that province as a bank, that bank as a private purse to the purchase of it. I will only tell you; it is the powder that made Venus a goddess (given her by Apollo), that kept her perpetually young, cleared her wrinkles, firmed her gums, filled her skin, colored her hair; from her derived to Helen, and at the sack of Troy unfortunately lost: till now, in this our age, it was as happily recovered, by a studious antiquary, out of some ruins of Asia, who sent a moiety of it to the court of France (but much sophisticated), wherewith the ladies there now color their hair. The rest, at this present, remains with me; extracted to a quintessence: so that, wherever it but touches, in youth it perpetually preserves, in age restores the complexion; seats your teeth, did they dance like virginal jacks, firm as a wall: makes them white as ivory, that were black as——"

[*Enter* Corvino]

CORVINO: Spite o' the devil, and my shame! come down, here;
Come down;—No house but mine to make your scene?
Signior Flaminio, will you down, sir? down?
What, is my wife your Franciscina, sir?
No windows on the whole Piazza, here,
To make your properties, but mine? but mine? [*Beats away* Volpone, Nano, &c.]
Heart! ere to-morrow I shall be new christened,
And called the Pantalone di Besogniosi,
About the town.

PEREGRINE: What should this mean, Sir Pol?

SIR POLITICK: Some trick of state, believe it; I will home.

PEREGRINE: It may be some design on you.

SIR POLITICK: I know not.
I'll stand upon my guard.

PEREGRINE: It is your best, sir.

SIR POLITICK: This three weeks, all my advices, all my letters,
They have been intercepted.

PEREGRINE: Indeed, sir!
Best have a care.

SIR POLITICK: Nay, so I will.

PEREGRINE: This knight,
I may not lose him, for my mirth, till night.

[*Exeunt*]

SCENE II.

A room in Volpone's *house.*

[*Enter* Volpone *and* Mosca]
VOLPONE: O, I am wounded!
MOSCA: Where, sir?

VOLPONE: Not without;
Those blows were nothing: I could bear them ever.
But angry Cupid, bolting from her eyes,
Hath shot himself into me like a flame;
Where now he flings about his burning heat,
As in a furnace an ambitious fire,
Whose vent is stopt. The fight is all within me.
I cannot live, except thou help me, Mosca;
My liver melts, and I, without the hope
Of some soft air, from her refreshing breath,
Am but a heap of cinders.
    MOSCA: 'Las, good sir,
Would you had never seen her!
    VOLPONE: Nay, would thou
Hadst never told me of her!
    MOSCA: Sir, 'tis true;
I do confess I was unfortunate,
And you unhappy; but I'm bound in conscience,
No less than duty, to effect my best
To your release of torment, and I will, sir.
    VOLPONE: Dear Mosca, shall I hope?
    MOSCA: Sir, more than dear,
I will not bid you to despair of aught
Within a human compass.
    VOLPONE: O, there spoke
My better angel. Mosca, take my keys,
Gold, plate, and jewels, all's at thy devotion;
Employ them how thou wilt: nay, coin me too:
So thou in this but crown my longings, Mosca.
    MOSCA: Use but your patience.
    VOLPONE: So I have.
    MOSCA: I doubt not
To bring success to your desires.
    VOLPONE: Nay, then,
I not repent me of my late disguise.
    MOSCA: If you can horn him, sir, you need not.
    VOLPONE: True:
Besides, I never meant him for my heir.
Is not the color of my beard and eyebrows
To make me known?
    MOSCA: No jot.
    VOLPONE: I did it well.
    MOSCA: So well, would I could follow you in mine,
With half the happiness! and yet I would
Escape your epilogue. [*Aside*]
    VOLPONE: But were they gulled
With a belief that I was Scoto?
    MOSCA: Sir,
Scoto himself could hardly have distinguished!
I have not time to flatter you now, we'll part:
And as I prosper, so applaud my art.
    [*Exeunt*]

SCENE III.

A room in Corvino's *house.*

[*Enter* Corvino, *with his sword in his hand, drag-ging in* Celia]

CORVINO: Death of mine honor, with the city's
    fool!
A juggling, tooth-drawing, prating mountebank!
And at a public window! where, whilst he,
With his strained action, and his dole of faces,
To his drug-lecture draws your itching ears,
A crew of old, unmarried, noted letchers,
Stood leering up like satyrs: and you smile
Most graciously, and fan your favors forth,
To give your hot spectators satisfaction!
What, was your mountebank their call? their whistle?
Or were you enamored on his copper rings,
His saffron jewel, with the toad-stone in't,
Or his embroidered suit, with the cope-stitch,
Made of a herse cloth? or his old tilt-feather?
Or his starched beard! Well you shall have him,
    yes!
He shall come home, and minister unto you
The fricace for the mother. Or, let me see,
I think you'd rather mount; would you not mount?
Why, if you'll mount, you may; yes, truly, you may!
And so you may be seen, down to the foot.
Get you a cittern,[11] Lady Vanity,
And be a dealer with the virtuous man;
Make one: I'll but protest myself a cuckold,
And save your dowry. I'm a Dutchman, I!
For if you thought me an Italian,
You would be damned ere you did this, you whore!
Thou'dst tremble, to imagine, that the murder
Of father, mother, brother, all thy race,
Should follow, as the subject of my justice.
    CELIA: Good sir, have patience.
    CORVINO: What couldst thou propose
Less to thyself, than in this heat of wrath,
And stung with my dishonor, I should strike
This steel into thee, with as many stabs
As thou wert gazed upon with goatish eyes?
    CELIA: Alas, sir, be appeased! I could not think
My being at the window should more now
Move your impatience than at other times.
    CORVINO: No! not to seek and entertain a parley
With a known knave, before a multitude!
You were an actor with your handkerchief,
Which he most sweetly kist in the receipt,
And might, no doubt, return it with a letter,
And point the place where you might meet; your
    sister's,
Your mother's, or your aunt's might serve the turn.
    CELIA: Why, dear sir, when do I make these
    excuses
Or ever stir abroad, but to the church?
And that so seldom——
    CORVINO: Well, it shall be less;
And thy restraint before was liberty,
To what I now decree: and therefore mark me.
First, I will have this bawdy light dammed up;
And till't be done, some two or three yards off,
I'll chalk a line; o'er which if thou but chance
To set thy desperate foot, more hell, more horror,

[11] A lutelike instrument.

More wild remorseless rage shall seize on thee,
Than on a conjuror that had heedless left
His circle's safety ere his devil was laid.
Then here's a lock which I will hang upon thee,
And, now I think on't, I will keep thee backwards;
Thy lodging shall be backwards; thy walks back-
    wards;
Thy prospect, all be backwards; and no pleasure,
That thou shalt know but backwards: nay, since you
    force
My honest nature, know, it is your own,
Being too open, makes me use you thus:
Since you will not contain your subtle nostrils
In a sweet room, but they must snuff the air
Of rank and sweaty passengers.
    [*Knocking within*]
    One knocks.
Away, and be not seen, pain of thy life;
Nor look toward the window; if thou dost—
Nay, stay, hear this—let me not prosper, whore,
But I will make thee an anatomy,
Dissect thee mine own self, and read a lecture
Upon thee to the city, and in public.
Away!—
    [*Exit* Celia]
    [*Enter* Servant]
    Who's there?
    SERVANT: 'Tis Signior Mosca, sir.
    CORVINO: Let him come in. [*Exit* Servant] His
      master's dead; there's yet
Some good to help the bad.
    [*Enter* Mosca]
           My Mosca, welcome!
    I guess your news.
    MOSCA: I fear you cannot, sir.
    CORVINO: Is't not his death?
    MOSCA: Rather the contrary.
    CORVINO: Not his recovery.
    MOSCA: Yes, sir.
    CORVINO: I am cursed,
I am bewitched, my crosses meet to vex me.
How? how? how? how?
    MOSCA: Why, sir, with Scoto's oil;
Corbaccio and Voltore brought of it,
Whilst I was busy in an inner room——
    CORVINO: Death! that damned mountebank! but
      for the law
Now, I could kill the rascal: it cannot be
His oil should have that virtue. Have not I
Known him a common rogue, come fiddling in
To the osteria,[12] with a tumbling whore,
And, when he has done all his forced tricks, been
    glad
Of a poor spoonful of dead wine, with flies in't?
It cannot be. All his ingredients
Are a sheep's gall, a roasted bitch's marrow,
Some few sod earwigs, pounded caterpillars,
A little capon's grease, and fasting spittle:
I know them to a dram.
    [12] Hostelry.

    MOSCA: I know not, sir;
But some on't, there, they poured into his ears,
Some in his nostrils, and recovered him:
Applying but the fricace.
    CORVINO: Pox o' that fricace!
    MOSCA: And since, to seem the more officious
And flatt'ring of his health, there, they have had,
At extreme fees, the college of physicians
Consulting on him, how they might restore him;
Where one would have a cataplasm of spices,
Another a flayed ape lapped to his breast,
A third would have it a dog, a fourth an oil,
With wild cats' skins: at last, they all resolved
That to preserve him, was no other means
But some young woman must be straight sought
    out,
Lusty, and full of juice, to sleep by him;
And to this service most unhappily,
And most unwillingly, am I now employed,
Which here I thought to pre-acquaint you with,
For your advice, since it concerns you most;
Because I would not do that thing might cross
Your ends, on whom I have my sole dependence,
    sir;
Yet, if I do it not, they may delate
My slackness to my patron, work me out
Of his opinion; and there all your hopes,
Ventures, or whatsoever, are all frustrate!
I do but tell you, sir. Besides, they are all
Now striving who shall first present him; therefore—
I could entreat you, briefly conclude somewhat;
Prevent them if you can.
    CORVINO: Death to my hopes,
This is my villainous fortune! Best to hire
Some common courtezan.
    MOSCA: Ay, I thought on that, sir;
But they are all so subtle, full of art—
And age again doting and flexible,
So as—I cannot tell—we may, perchance,
Light on a quean may cheat us all.
    CORVINO: 'Tis true.
    MOSCA: No, no: it must be one that has no tricks,
    sir,
Some simple thing, a creature made unto it;
Some wench you may command. Have you no kins-
    woman?
Odso—Think, think, think, think, think, think, think,
    sir.
One o' the doctors offered there his daughter.
    CORVINO: How!
    MOSCA: Yes, Signior Lupo, the physician.
    CORVINO: His daughter!
    MOSCA: And a virgin, sir. Why, alas,
He knows the state of's body, what it is;
That nought can warm his blood, sir, but a fever;
Nor any incantation raise his spirit:
A long forgetfulness hath seized that part.
Besides, sir, who shall know it? some one or two—
    CORVINO: I pray thee give me leave.
    [*Walks aside*] If any man

But I had had this luck—The thing in't self,
I know, is nothing—Wherefore should not I
As well command my blood and my affections
As this dull doctor? In the point of honor,
The cases are all one of wife and daughter. [*Aside*]
   MOSCA: I hear him coming.
   CORVINO: She shall do't: 'tis done.
Slight! if this doctor, who is not engaged,
Unless 't be for his counsel, which is nothing,
Offer his daughter, what should I, that am
So deeply in? I will prevent him: Wretch!
Covetous wretch!—Mosca, I have determined.
   MOSCA: How, sir?
   CORVINO: We'll make all sure. The party you wot of
Shall be mine own wife, Mosca.
   MOSCA: Sir, the thing,
But that I would not seem to counsel you,
I should have motioned to you, at the first:
And make your count, you have cut all their throats.
Why, 'tis directly taking a possession!
And in his next fit, we may let him go.
'Tis but to pull the pillow from his head,
And he is throttled: it had been done before
But for your scrupulous doubts.
   CORVINO: Ay, a plague on't,
My conscience fools my wit! Well, I'll be brief,
And so be thou, lest they should be before us:
Go home, prepare him, tell him with what zeal
And willingness I do it: swear it was
On the first hearing, as thou mayst do, truly,
Mine own free motion.
   MOSCA: Sir, I warrant you,
I'll so possess him with it, that the rest
Of his starved clients shall be banished all;
And only you received. But come not, sir,
Until I send, for I have something else
To ripen for your good, you must not know't.
   CORVINO: But do not you forget to send now.
   MOSCA: Fear not. [*Exit*]
   CORVINO: Where are you, wife? my Celia! wife!
   [*Re-enter* Celia]
      —What, blubbering?
Come, dry those tears. I think thou thought'st me
   in earnest;
Ha! by this light I talked so but to try thee:
Methinks, the lightness of the occasion
Should have confirmed thee. Come, I am not jealous.
   CELIA: No!
   CORVINO: Faith I am not, I, nor never was;
It is a poor unprofitable humor.
Do not I know, if women have a will,
They'll do 'gainst all the watches of the world,
And that the fiercest spies are tamed with gold?
Tut, I am confident in thee, thou shalt see't;
And see I'll give thee cause too, to believe it.
Come kiss me. Go, and make thee ready straight,
In all thy best attire, thy choicest jewels,
Put them all on, and, with them, thy best looks:
We are invited to a solemn feast,
At old Volpone's, where it shall appear

How far I am free from jealousy or fear.
   [*Exeunt*]

<hr>

ACT III. SCENE I.

<hr>

A street.

   [*Enter* Mosca]
   MOSCA: I fear I shall begin to grow in love
With my dear self, and my most prosperous parts,
They do so spring and burgeon; I can feel
A whimsy in my blood: I know not how,
Success hath made me wanton. I could skip
Out of my skin now, like a subtle snake,
I am so limber. O! your parasite
Is a most precious thing, dropt from above,
Not bred 'mongst clods and clodpoles, here on earth.
I muse, the mystery was not made a science,
It is so liberally profest! Almost
All the wise world is little else, in nature,
But parasites or sub-parasites. And yet
I mean not those that have your bare town-art,
To know who's fit to feed them; have no house,
No family, no care, and therefore mould
Tales for men's ears, to bait that sense; or get
Kitchen-invention, and some stale receipts
To please the belly, and the groin; nor those,
With their court dog-tricks, that can fawn and fleer,
Make their revenue out of legs and faces,
Echo my lord, and lick away a moth:
But your fine elegant rascal, that can rise
And stoop, almost together, like an arrow;
Shoot through the air as nimbly as a star;
Turn short as doth a swallow; and be here,
And there, and here, and yonder, all at once;
Present to any humor, all occasion;
And change a visor swifter than a thought!
This is the creature had the art born with him;
Toils not to learn it, but doth practice it
Out of most excellent nature: and such sparks
Are the true parasites, others but their zanies.
   [*Enter* Bonario]
Who's this? Bonario, old Corbaccio's son?
The person I was bound to seek. Fair sir,
You are happily met.
   BONARIO: That cannot be by thee.
   MOSCA: Why, sir?
   BONARIO: Nay, pray thee know thy way, and leave
   me:
I would be loth to interchange discourse
With such a mate as thou art.
   MOSCA: Courteous sir,
Scorn not my poverty.
   BONARIO: Not I, by heaven;
But thou shalt give me leave to hate thy baseness.
   MOSCA: Baseness!
   BONARIO: Ay; answer me, is not thy sloth
Sufficient argument? thy flattery?
Thy means of feeding?

MOSCA: Heaven be good to me!
These imputations are too common, sir,
And easily stuck on virtue when she's poor.
You are unequal to me, and however
Your sentence may be righteous, yet you are not,
That, ere you know me, thus proceed in censure:
St. Mark bear witness 'gainst you, 'tis inhuman.
    [*Weeps*]
    BONARIO: What! does he weep? The sign is soft
        and good:
I do repent me that I was so harsh. [*Aside*]
    MOSCA: 'Tis true, that, swayed by strong necessity,
I am enforced to eat my careful bread
With too much obsequy; 'tis true, beside,
That I am fain to spin mine own poor raiment
Out of my mere observance, being not born
To a free fortune: but that I have done
Base offices, in rending friends asunder,
Dividing families, betraying counsels,
Whispering false lies, or mining men with praises,
Trained their credulity with perjuries,
Corrupted chastity, or am in love
With mine own tender ease, but would not rather
Prove the most rugged and laborious course,
That might redeem my present estimation,
Let me here perish, in all hope of goodness.
    BONARIO: This cannot be a personated passion.
        [*Aside*]
I was to blame, so to mistake thy nature;
Prithee forgive me: and speak out thy business.
    MOSCA: Sir, it concerns you; and though I may
        seem
At first to make a main offence in manners,
And in my gratitude unto my master;
Yet for the pure love which I bear all right,
And hatred of the wrong, I must reveal it.
This very hour your father is in purpose
To disinherit you——
    BONARIO: How!
    MOSCA: And thrust you forth,
As a mere stranger to his blood: 'tis true, sir.
The work no way engageth me, but, as
I claim an interest in the general state
Of goodness and true virtue, which I hear
To abound in you; and for which mere respect,
Without a second aim, sir, I have done it.
    BONARIO: This tale hath lost thee much of the late
        trust
Thou hadst with me; it is impossible:
I know not how to lend it any thought,
My father should be so unnatural.
    MOSCA: It is a confidence that well becomes
Your piety; and formed, no doubt, it is
From your own simple innocence: which makes
Your wrong more monstrous and abhorred. But, sir,
I now will tell you more. This very minute,
It is, or will be doing; and if you
Shall be but pleased to go with me, I'll bring you,
I dare not say where you shall see, but where
Your ear shall be a witness of the deed;

Hear yourself written bastard, and profest
The common issue of the earth.
    BONARIO: I am mazed!
    MOSCA: Sir, if I do it not, draw your just sword,
And score your vengeance on my front and face;
Mark me your villain: you have too much wrong,
And I do suffer for you, sir. My heart
Weeps blood in anguish——
    BONARIO: Lead; I follow thee.
        [*Exeunt*]

SCENE II.

A room in Volpone's *house.*

    [*Enter* Volpone]
VOLPONE: Mosca stays long, methinks.—Bring
    forth your sports,
And help to make the wretched time more sweet.
    [*Enter* Nano, Androgyno, *and* Castrone]
    NANO: "Dwarf, fool, and eunuch, well met here
        we be.
A question it were now, whether of us three,
Being all the known delicates of a rich man,
In pleasing him, claim the precedency can?"
    CASTRONE: "I claim for myself."
    ANDROGYNO: "And so doth the fool."
    NANO: " 'Tis foolish indeed: let me set you both to
        school.
First for your dwarf, he's little and witty,
And everything, as it is little, is pretty;
Else why do men say to a creature of my shape,
So soon as they see him, It's a pretty little ape?
And why a pretty ape, but for pleasing imitation
Of greater men's actions, in a ridiculous fashion?
Beside, this feat body of mine doth not crave
Half the meat, drink, and cloth, one of your bulks
    will have.
Admit your fool's face be the mother of laughter,
Yet, for his brain, it must always come after;
And though that do feed him, it's a pitiful case,
His body is beholding to such a bad face."
    [*Knocking within*]
VOLPONE: Who's there? my couch; away! look!
    Nano, see:
    [*Exeunt* Androgyno *and* Castrone]
Give me my caps first—go, inquire.
    [*Exit* Nano]
    Now, Cupid
Send it be Mosca, and with fair return!
    NANO: [*Within*] It is the beauteous madam—
VOLPONE: Would-be—is it?
    NANO: The same.
VOLPONE: Now torment on me! Squire her in;
For she will enter, or dwell here for ever:
Nay, quickly. [*Retires to his couch*] That my fit were
    past! I fear
A second hell too, that my loathing this
Will quite expel my appetite to the other:

Would she were taking now her tedious leave.
Lord, how it threats me what I am to suffer!
      [*Re-enter* Nano *with* Lady Politick Would-be]
   LADY POLITICK: I thank you, good sir. Pray you
      signify
Unto your patron I am here.—This band
Shows not my neck enough.—I trouble you, sir;
Let me request you bid one of my women
Come hither to me. In good faith, I am drest
Most favorably to-day! It is no matter:
'Tis well enough.
      [*Enter* 1st Waiting-woman]
                  Look, see these petulant things,
How they have done this!
   VOLPONE: I do feel the fever
Entering in at mine ears; O, for a charm,
To fright it hence! [*Aside*]
   LADY POLITICK: Come nearer: is this curl
In his right place, or this? Why is this higher
Than all the rest? You have not washed your eyes
      yet!
Or do they not stand even in your head?
Where is your fellow? call her.
      [*Exit* 1st Woman]
   NANO: Now, St. Mark
Deliver us! anon she'll beat her women,
Because her nose is red.
      [*Re-enter* 1st *with* 2nd Woman]
   LADY POLITICK: I pray you view.
This tire, forsooth: are all things apt, or no?
   1ST WOMAN: One hair a little here sticks out, for-
      sooth.
   LADY POLITICK: Does't so, forsooth, and where was
      your dear sight,
When it did so, forsooth! What now! bird-
      eyed?
And you, too? Pray you, both approach and mend it.
Now, by that light I muse you are not ashamed!
I, that have preached these things so oft unto you,
Read you the principles, argued all the grounds,
Disputed every fitness, every grace,
Called you to counsel of so frequent dressings.
   NANO: More carefully than of your fame or honor.
      [*Aside*]
   LADY POLITICK: Made you acquainted what an
      ample dowry
The knowledge of these things would be unto you,
Able alone to get you noble husbands
At your return: and you thus to neglect it!
Besides, you seeing what a curious nation
The Italians are, what will they say of me?
The English lady cannot dress herself.
Here's a fine imputation to our country!
Well, go your ways, and stay in the next room.
This focus was too coarse, too; it's no matter—
Good sir, you'll give them entertainment?
      [*Exeunt* Nano *and* Waiting-women]
   VOLPONE: The storm comes toward me.
   LADY POLITICK: [*Goes to the couch*] How does my
      Volpone?

   VOLPONE: Troubled with noise, I cannot sleep; I
      dreamt
That a strange fury entered now my house,
And, with the dreadful tempest of her breath,
Did cleave my roof asunder.
   LADY POLITICK: Believe me, and I
Had the most fearful dream, could I remember't——
   VOLPONE: Out on my fate! I have given her the
      occasion
How to torment me: she will tell me hers. [*Aside*]
   LADY POLITICK: Methought the golden mediocrity,
Polite, and delicate——
   VOLPONE: O, if you do love me,
No more: I sweat, and suffer, at the mention
Of any dream; feel how I tremble yet.
   LADY POLITICK: Alas, good soul! the passion of the
      heart.
Seed-pearl were good now, boiled with syrup of
      apples,
Tincture of gold, and coral, citron-pills,
Your elicampane root, myrobalanes——
   VOLPONE: Ah me, I have ta'en a grasshopper by
      the wing! [*Aside*]
   LADY POLITICK: Burnt silk and amber. You have
      muscadel
Good in the house——
   VOLPONE: You will not drink, and part?
   LADY POLITICK: No, fear not that. I doubt we shall
      not get
Some English saffron, half a dram would serve;
Your sixteen cloves, a little musk, dried mints;
Bugloss,[13] and barley-meal——
   VOLPONE: She's in again!
Before I feigned diseases, now I have one. [*Aside*]
   LADY POLITICK: And these applied with a right
      scarlet cloth.
   VOLPONE: Another flood of words! a very torrent!
      [*Aside*]
   LADY POLITICK: Shall I, sir, make you a poultice?
   VOLPONE: No, no, no.
I'm very well, you need prescribe no more.
   LADY POLITICK: I have a little studied physic; but
      now
I'm all for music, save, in the forenoons,
An hour or two for painting. I would have
A lady, indeed, to have all letters and arts,
Be able to discourse, to write, to paint,
But principal, as Plato holds, your music,
And so does wise Pythagoras, I take it,
Is your true rapture: when there is concent[14]
In face, in voice, and clothes: and is, indeed,
Our sex's chiefest ornament.
   VOLPONE: The poet
As old in time as Plato, and as knowing,
Says that your highest female grace is silence.
   LADY POLITICK: Which of your poets? Petrarch, or
      Tasso, or Dante?
Guarini, Ariosto? Aretine?

[13] A plant: the European hawkweed.
[14] Harmony.

Cieco di Hadria? I have read them all.

VOLPONE: Is everything a cause to my destruction?
[*Aside*]

LADY POLITICK: I think I have two or three of them
about me.

VOLPONE: The sun, the sea, will sooner both stand
still

Than her eternal tongue! nothing can scape it.
[*Aside*]

LADY POLITICK: Here's Pastor Fido——

VOLPONE: Profess obstinate silence;

That's now my safest. [*Aside*]

LADY POLITICK: All our English writers,
I mean such as are happy in the Italian,
Will deign to steal out of this author, mainly;
Almost as much as from Montagnié:
He has so modern and facile a vein,
Fitting the time, and catching the court-ear!
Your Petrarch is more passionate, yet he,
In days of sonnetting, trusted them with much
Dante is hard, and few can understand him.
But for a desperate wit, there's Aretine;
Only his pictures are a little obscene——
You mark me not.

VOLPONE: Alas, my mind's perturbed.

LADY POLITICK: Why, in such cases, we must cure
ourselves.

Make use of our philosophy——

VOLPONE: Oh me!

LADY POLITICK: And as we find our passions do
rebel,

Encounter them with treason, or divert them,
By giving scope unto some other humor
Of lesser danger: as, in politic bodies,
There's nothing more doth overwhelm the judg-
ment,
And cloud the understanding, than too much
Settling and fixing, and, as 'twere, subsiding
Upon one object. For the incorporating
Of these same outward things, into that part,
Which we call mental, leaves some certain fæces
That stop the organs, and, as Plato says,
Assassinate our knowledge.

VOLPONE: Now, the spirit
Of patience help me! [*Aside*]

LADY POLITICK: Come, in faith, I must
Visit you more a days; and make you well:
Laugh and be lusty.

VOLPONE: My good angel save me! [*Aside*]

LADY POLITICK: There was but one sole man in all
the world

With whom I e'er could sympathize; and he
Would lie you, often, three, four hours together
To hear me speak; and be sometimes so rapt,
As he would answer me quite from the purpose,
Like you, and you are like him, just. I'll discourse,
An't be but only, sir, to bring you a sleep,
How we did spend our time and loves together,
For some six years.

VOLPONE: Oh, oh, oh, oh, oh, oh!

LADY POLITICK: For we were coætanei, and brought
up——

VOLPONE: Some power, some fate, some fortune
rescue me! [*Enter* Mosca]

MOSCA: God save you, madam!

LADY POLITICK: Good sir.

VOLPONE: Mosca! Welcome,
Welcome to my redemption.

MOSCA: Why, sir?

VOLPONE: Oh,
Rid me of this my torture, quickly, there;
My madam with the everlasting voice:
The bells, in time of pestilence, ne'er made
Like noise, or were in that perpetual motion!
The Cock-pit comes not near it. All my house,
But now, steamed like a bath with her thick
breath,
A lawyer could not have been heard; nor scarce
Another woman, such a hail of words
She has let fall. For hell's sake, rid her hence.

MOSCA: Has she presented?

VOLPONE: Oh, I do not care!
I'll take her absence upon any price,
With any loss.

MOSCA: Madam——

LADY POLITICK: I have brought your patron
A toy, a cap here, of mine own work.

MOSCA: 'Tis well.
I had forgot to tell you I saw your knight,
Where you would little think it.——

LADY POLITICK: Where?

MOSCA: Marry,
Where yet, if you make haste, you may apprehend
him,
Rowing upon the water in a gondole,
With the most cunning courtezan of Venice.

LADY POLITICK: Is't true?

MOSCA: Pursue them, and believe your eyes:
Leave me to make your gift.
[*Exit* Lady Politick *hastily*]
I knew 'twould take:
For, lightly, they that use themselves most licence,
Are still most jealous.

VOLPONE: Mosca, hearty thanks,
For thy quick fiction, and delivery of me.
Now to my hopes, what sayst thou?
[*Re-enter* Lady Politick Would-be]

LADY POLITICK: But do you hear, sir?——

VOLPONE: Again! I fear a paroxysm.

LADY POLITICK: Which way
Rowed they together?

MOSCA: Toward the Rialto.

LADY POLITICK: I pray you lend me your dwarf

MOSCA: I pray you take him.
[*Exit* Lady Politick]
Your hopes, sir, are like happy blossoms, fair,
And promise timely fruit, if you will stay
But the maturing; keep you at your couch,
Corbaccio will arrive straight, with the Will;
When he is gone, I'll tell you more. [*Exit*]

VOLPONE: My blood,
My spirits are returned; I am alive
And, like your wanton gamester at primero,[15]
Whose thought had whispered to him, not go less,
Methinks I lie, and draw——for an encounter.
[*The scene closes upon* Volpone]

SCENE III.

The passage leading to Volpone's *chamber.*

[*Enter* Mosca *and* Bonario]
MOSCA: Sir, here concealed [*shows him a closet*]
    you may hear all. But, pray you,
Have patience, sir [*knocking within*]—the same's
    your father knocks:
I am compelled to leave you. [*Exit*]
BONARIO: Do so.—Yet
Cannot my thought imagine this a truth. [*Goes into
    the closet*]

SCENE IV.

Another part of the same.

[*Enter* Mosca *and* Corvino, Celia *following*]
MOSCA: Death on me! you are come too soon, what
    meant you?
Did not I say I would send?
CORVINO: Yes, but I feared
You might forget it, and then they prevent us.
MOSCA: Prevent! Did e'er man haste so for his
    horns?
A courtier would not ply it so for a place. [*Aside*]
Well, now there is no helping it, stay here;
I'll presently return. [*Exit*]
CORVINO: Where are you, Celia?
You know not wherefore I have brought you hither?
CELIA: Not well, except you told me.
CORVINO: Now I will:
Hark hither.
    [*Exeunt*]

SCENE V.

A closet opening into a gallery.

[*Enter* Mosca *and* Bonario]
MOSCA: Sir, your father hath sent word,
It will be half an hour ere he come;
And therefore, if you please to walk the while
Into that gallery—at the upper end,
There are some books to entertain the time:
And I'll take care no man shall come unto you, sir.
BONARIO: Yes, I will stay there——I do doubt this
    fellow. [*Aside, and exit*]
[15] An old card game.

MOSCA: [*Looking after him*] There; he is far
    enough; he can hear nothing:
And for his father, I can keep him off. [*Exit*]

SCENE VI.

Volpone's *chamber.* Volpone *on his couch.* Mosca
sitting by him.

[*Enter* Corvino, *forcing in* Celia]
CORVINO: Nay, now, there is no starting back, and
    therefore,
Resolve upon it: I have so decreed.
It must be done. Nor would I move't afore,
Because I would avoid all shifts and tricks,
That might deny me.
CELIA: Sir, let me beseech you,
Affect not these strange trials; if you doubt
My chastity, why, lock me up for ever;
Make me the heir of darkness. Let me live
Where I may please your fears, if not your trust.
CORVINO: Believe it, I have no such humor, I.
All that I speak I mean; yet I'm not mad;
Not horn-mad, you see? Go to, show yourself
Obedient, and a wife.
CELIA: O heaven!
CORVINO: I say it,
Do so.
CELIA: Was this the train?
CORVINO: I've told you reasons;
What the physicians have set down; how much
It may concern me; what my engagements are;
My means, and the necessity of those means
For my recovery: wherefore, if you be
Loyal, and mine, be won, respect my venture.
CELIA: Before your honor?
CORVINO: Honor! tut, a breath:
There's no such thing in nature; a mere term
Invented to awe fools. What is my gold
The worse for touching, clothes for being looked on?
Why, this 's no more. An old decrepit wretch,
That has no sense, no sinew; takes his meat
With others' fingers: only knows to gape
When you do scald his gums; a voice, a shadow;
And what can this man hurt you?
CELIA: Lord! what spirit
Is this hath entered him? [*Aside*]
CORVINO: And for your fame,
That's such a jig; as if I would go tell it,
Cry it on the Piazza! who shall know it
But he that cannot speak it, and this fellow,
Whose lips are in my pocket? Save yourself
(If you'll proclaim't, you may), I know no other
Should come to know it.
CELIA: Are heaven and saints then nothing?
Will they be blind or stupid?
CORVINO: How!
CELIA: Good sir,
Be jealous still, emulate them; and think

What hate they burn with toward every sin.
    CORVINO: I grant you: if I thought it were a sin
I would not urge you. Should I offer this
To some young Frenchman, or hot Tuscan blood
That had read Aretine, conned all his prints,
Knew every quirk within lust's labyrinth,
And were profest critic in lechery;
And I would look upon him, and applaud him,
This were a sin: but here, 'tis contrary,
A pious work, mere charity for physic,
And honest polity, to assure mine own.
    CELIA: O heaven! canst thou suffer such a change?
    VOLPONE: Thou art mine honor, Mosca, and my
      pride
My joy, my tickling, my delight! Go bring them.
    MOSCA: [Advancing] Please you draw near, sir.
    CORVINO: Come on, what——
You will not be rebellious? by that light——
    MOSCA: Sir,
Signior Corvino, here, is come to see you.
    VOLPONE: Oh!
    MOSCA: And hearing of the consultation had,
So lately, for your health, is come to offer,
Or rather, sir, to prostitute——
    CORVINO: Thanks, sweet Mosca.
    MOSCA: Freely, unasked, or unintreated——
    CORVINO: Well.
    MOSCA: As the true fervent instance of his love,
His own most fair and proper wife; the beauty
Only of price in Venice——
    CORVINO: 'Tis well urged.
    MOSCA: To be your comfortress, and to preserve
      you.
    VOLPONE: Alas, I am past, already! Pray you,
      thank him
For his good care and promptness; but for that,
'Tis a vain labor e'en to fight 'gainst heaven;
Applying fire to stone—uh, uh, uh, uh! [Coughing]
Making a dead leaf grow again. I take
His wishes gently, though; and you may tell him
What I have done for him: marry, my state is hope-
    less.
Will him to pray for me; and to use his fortune
With reverence when he comes to't.
    MOSCA: Do you hear, sir?
Go to him with your wife.
    CORVINO: Heart of my father!
Wilt thou persist thus? come, I pray thee come.
Thou seest 'tis nothing, Celia. By this hand
I shall grow violent. Come, do't, I say.
    CELIA: Sir, kill me, rather: I will take down poison,
Eat burning coals, do anything——
    CORVINO: Be damned!
Heart, I will drag thee hence home by the hair;
Cry thee a strumpet through the streets; rip up
Thy mouth unto thine ears; and slit thy nose,
Like a raw rochet!—Do not tempt me: come,
Yield, I am loth—Death! I will buy some slave
Whom I will kill, and bind thee to him alive!
And at my window hang you forth, devising

Some monstrous crime, which I, in capital letters,
Will eat into thy flesh with aquafortis,
And burning corsives, on this stubborn breast.
Now, by the blood thou hast incensed, I'll do it!
    CELIA: Sir, what you please, you may, I am your
      martyr.
    CORVINO: Be not thus obstinate, I have not de-
      served it:
Think who it is intreats you. Prithee, sweet;—
Good faith, thou shalt have jewels, gowns, attires,
What thou wilt think, and ask. Do but go kiss him.
Or touch him but. For my sake. At my suit—
This once. No! not! I shall remember this.
Will you disgrace me thus? Do you thirst my un-
    doing?
    MOSCA: Nay, gentle lady, be advised.
    CORVINO: No, no.
She has watched her time. Ods precious, this is
    scurvy,
'Tis very scurvy; and you are——
    MOSCA: Nay, good sir.
    CORVINO: An arrant locust—by heaven, a locust!—
Whore, crocodile, that hast thy tears prepared,
Expecting how thou'lt bid them flow——
    MOSCA: Nay, pray you, sir!
She will consider.
    CELIA: Would my life would serve
To satisfy——
    CORVINO: 'Sdeath! if she would but speak to
      him,
And save my reputation, it were somewhat;
But spitefully to affect my utter ruin!
    MOSCA: Ay, now you have put your fortune in her
      hands.
Why i'faith, it is her modesty, I must quit her.
If you were absent, she would be more coming;
I know it: and dare undertake for her.
What woman can before her husband? pray you,
Let us depart, and leave her here.
    CORVINO: Sweet Celia,
Thou mayst redeem all yet; I'll say no more:
If not, esteem yourself as lost. Nay, stay there. [Shuts
    the door and exit with Mosca]
    CELIA: O God, and his good angels! whither,
      whither.
Is shame fled human breasts? that with such ease,
Men dare put off your honors, and their own?
Is that, which ever was a cause of life,
Now placed beneath the basest circumstance,
And modesty an exile made, for money?
    VOLPONE: Ay, in Corvino, and such earth-fed
      minds, [leaping from his couch]
That never tasted the true heaven of love.
Assure thee, Celia, he that would sell thee,
Only for hope of gain, and that uncertain,
He would have sold his part of Paradise
For ready money, had he met a cope-man.[16]
Why art thou mazed to see me thus revived?
Rather applaud thy beauty's miracle;
    [16] Chapman or merchant.

'Tis thy great work: that hath, not now alone,
But sundry times raised me, in several shapes,
And, but this morning, like a mountebank,
To see thee at thy window: ay, before
I would have left my practice, for thy love,
In varying figures, I would have contended
With the blue Proteus, or the horned flood.
Now art thou welcome.

    CELIA: Sir!

    VOLPONE: Nay, fly me not.
Nor let thy false imagination
That I was bed-rid, make thee think I am so:
Thou shalt not find it. I am now as fresh,
As hot, as high, and in as jovial plight
As, when, in that so celebrated scene,
At recitation of our comedy,
For entertainment of the great Valois,
I acted young Antinous; and attracted
The eyes and ears of all the ladies present,
To admire each graceful gesture, note, and footing.
    [Sings]

        Come, my Celia, let us prove
        While we can, the sports of love,
        Time will not be ours forever,
        He, at length, our good will sever;
        Spend not then his gifts in vain:
        Suns that set may rise again;
        But if once we lose this light,
        'Tis with us perpetual night.
        Why should we defer our joys?
        Fame and rumor are but toys.
        Cannot we delude the eyes
        Of a few poor household spies?
        Or his easier ears beguile,
        Thus removed by our wile?
        'Tis no sin love's fruits to steal;
        But the sweet thefts to reveal:
        To be taken, to be seen,
        These have crimes accounted been.

    CELIA: Some serene blast me, or dire lightning strike
This my offending face!

    VOLPONE: Why droops my Celia?
Thou hast, in the place of a base husband found
A worthy lover: use thy fortune well,
With secrecy and pleasure. See, behold,
What thou art queen of; not in expectation,
As I feed others: but possessed and crowned.
See, here, a rope of pearl; and each more orient
Than the brave Ægyptian queen caroused:
Dissolve and drink them. See, a carbuncle,
May put out both the eyes of our St. Mark;
A diamond would have bought Lollia Paulina,
When she came in like star-light, hid with jewels,
That were the spoils of provinces, take these
And wear, and lose them; yet remains an earring
To purchase them again, and this whole state.
A gem but worth a private patrimony,
Is nothing; we will eat such at a meal.
The heads of parrots, tongues of nightingales,

The brains of peacocks, and of estriches,[17]
Shall be our food, and, could we get the phœnix,
Though nature lost her kind, she were our dish.

    CELIA: Good sir, these things might move a mind affected
With such delights; but I, whose innocence
Is all I can think wealthy, or worth th' enjoying,
And which, once lost, I have nought to lose beyond it,
Cannot be taken with these sensual baits:
If you have conscience——

    VOLPONE: 'Tis the beggar's virtue;
If thou hast wisdom, hear me, Celia.
Thy baths shall be the juice of July-flowers,
Spirit of roses, and of violets,
The milk of unicorns, and panthers' breath
Gathered in bags, and mixed with Cretan wines.
Our drink shall be prepared gold and amber;
Which we will take until my roof whirl round
With the vertigo: and my dwarf shall dance,
My eunuch sing, my fool make up the antic,
Whilst we, in changed shapes, act Ovid's tales,
Thou, like Europa now, and I like Jove,
Then I like Mars, and thou like Erycine:
So of the rest, till we have quite run through,
And wearied all the fables of the gods.
Then will I have thee in more modern forms,
Attired like some sprightly dame of France,
Brave Tuscan lady, or proud Spanish beauty;
Sometimes unto the Persian sophy's[18] wife;
Or the grand signior's mistress; and for change,
To one of our most artful courtezans,
Or some quick Negro, or cold Russian;
And I will meet thee in as many shapes:
Where we may so transfuse our wandering souls
Out at our lips, and score up sums of pleasures,
    [Sings]

        That the curious shall not know
        How to tell them as they flow;
        And the envious, when they find
        What their number is, be pined.

    CELIA: If you have ears that will be pierced—or eyes
That can be opened—a heart that may be touched—
Or any part that yet sounds man above you—
If you have touch of holy saints—or heaven—
Do me the grace to let me 'scape—if not,
Be bountiful and kill me. You do know,
I am a creature, hither ill betrayed,
By one whose shame I would forget it were:
If you will deign me neither of these graces,
Yet feed your wrath, sir, rather than your lust
(It is a vice comes nearer manliness),
And punish that unhappy crime of nature,
Which you miscall my beauty: flay my face,
Or poison it with ointments for seducing
Your blood to this rebellion. Rub these hands
With what may cause an eating leprosy,
E'en to my bones and marrow: anything

    [17] Ostriches.
    [18] Persian ruler.

That may disfavor me, save in my honor—
And I will kneel to you, pray for you, pay down
A thousand hourly vows, sir, for your health;
Report, and think you virtuous——
    VOLPONE: Think me cold,
Frozen, and impotent, and so report me?
That I had Nestor's hernia, thou wouldst think.
I do degenerate, and abuse my nation,
To play with opportunity thus long;
I should have done the act, and then have parleyed.
Yield, or I'll force thee. [*Seizes her*]
    CELIA: O! just God!
    VOLPONE: In vain——
    BONARIO: [*Rushing in*] Forbear, foul ravisher!
    libidinous swine!
Free the forced lady, or thou diest, impostor.
But that I'm loth to snatch thy punishment
Out of the hand of justice, thou shouldst yet
Be made the timely sacrifice of vengeance,
Before this altar and this dross, thy idol.——
Lady, let's quit the place, it is the den
Of villainy; fear nought, you have a guard:
And he ere long shall meet his just reward.
    [*Exeunt* Bonario *and* Celia]
    VOLPONE: Fall on me, roof, and bury me in ruin!
Become my grave, that wert my shelter! O!
I am unmasked, unspirited, undone,
Betrayed to beggary, to infamy——
    [*Enter* Mosca *wounded and bleeding*]
    MOSCA: Where shall I run, most wretched shame of
    men,
To beat out my unlucky brains?
    VOLPONE: Here, here.
What! dost thou bleed?
    MOSCA: O, that his well-driven sword
Had been so courteous to have cleft me down
Unto the navel, ere I lived to see
My life, my hopes, my spirits, my patron, all
Thus desperately engaged by my error!
    VOLPONE: Woe on thy fortune!
    MOSCA: And my follies, sir.
    VOLPONE: Thou hast made me miserable.
    MOSCA: And myself, sir,
Who would have thought he would have hearkened
    so?
    VOLPONE: What shall we do?
    MOSCA: I know not; if my heart
Could expiate the mischance, I'd pluck it out.
Will you be pleased to hang me, or cut my throat?
And I'll requite you, sir. Let's die like Romans,
Since we have lived like Grecians.
    [*Knocking within*]
    VOLPONE: Hark! who's there?
I hear some footing; officers, the saffi,
Come to apprehend us! I do feel the brand
Hissing already at my forehead; now
Mine ears are boring.
    MOSCA: To your couch, sir, you.
Make that place good, however. [Volpone *lies down
    as before*] Guilty men

Suspect what they deserve still.
    [*Enter* Corbaccio]
Signior Corbaccio!
    CORBACCIO: Why, how now, Mosca?
    MOSCA: O, undone, amazed, sir.
Your son, I know not by what accident,
Acquainted with your purpose to my patron,
Touching your Will, and making him your heir,
Entered our house with violence, his sword drawn,
Sought for you, called you wretch, unnatural,
Vowed he would kill you.
    CORBACCIO: Me!
    MOSCA: Yes, and my patron.
    CORBACCIO: This act shall disinherit him indeed:
Here is the Will.
    MOSCA: 'Tis well, sir.
    CORBACCIO: Right and well:
Be you as careful now for me.
    [*Enter* Voltore *behind*]
    MOSCA: My life, sir,
Is not more tendered; I am only yours.
    CORBACCIO: How does he? will he die shortly,
    think'st thou?
    MOSCA: I fear
He'll outlast May.
    CORBACCIO: To-day?
    MOSCA: No, last out May, sir.
    CORBACCIO: Couldst thou not give him a dram?
    MOSCA: O, by no means, sir.
    CORBACCIO: Nay, I'll not bid you.
    VOLTORE: [*Coming forward*] This is a knave,
    I see.
    MOSCA: [*Seeing* Voltore] How! Signior Voltore!
    [*Aside*] did he hear me?
    VOLTORE: Parasite!
    MOSCA: Who's that?—O, sir, most timely wel-
    come—
    VOLTORE: Scarce,
To the discovery of your tricks, I fear.
You are his, *only?* and mine also, are you not?
    MOSCA: Who? I sir!
    VOLTORE: You, sir. What device is this
About a Will?
    MOSCA: A plot for you, sir.
    VOLTORE: Come,
Put not your foists upon me; I shall scent them.
    MOSCA: Did you not hear it?
    VOLTORE: Yes, I hear Corbaccio
Hath made your patron there his heir.
    MOSCA: 'Tis true,
By my device, drawn to it by my plot,
With hope——
    VOLTORE: Your patron should reciprocate?
And you have promised?
    MOSCA: For your good I did, sir.
Nay, more, I told his son, brought, hid him here,
Where he might hear his father pass the deed;
Being persuaded to it by this thought, sir,
That the unnaturalness, first, of the act,
And then his father's oft disclaiming in him

(Which I did mean t' help on), would sure enrage
    him
To do some violence upon his parent,
On which the law should take sufficient hold,
And you be stated in a double hope:
Truth be my comfort, and my conscience,
My only aim was to dig you a fortune
Out of these two old rotten sepulchres——
    VOLTORE: I cry thee mercy, Mosca.
    MOSCA: Worth your patience,
And your great merit, sir. And see the change!
    VOLTORE: Why, what success?
    MOSCA: Most hapless! you must help, sir.
Whilst we expected the old raven, in comes
Corvino's wife, sent hither by her husband—
    VOLTORE: What, with a present?
    MOSCA: No, sir, on visitation
(I'll tell you how anon); and staying long,
The youth he grows impatient, rushes forth,
Seizeth the lady, wounds me, makes her swear
(Or he would murder her, that was his vow)
To affirm my patron to have done her rape:
Which how unlike it is, you see! and hence,
With that pretext he's gone, to accuse his father,
Defame my patron, defeat you——
    VOLTORE: Where is her husband?
Let him be sent for straight.
    MOSCA: Sir, I'll go fetch him.
    VOLTORE: Bring him to the Scrutineo.
    MOSCA: Sir, I will.
    VOLTORE: This must be stopt.
    MOSCA: O you do nobly, sir.
Alas, 'twas labored all, sir, for your good;
Nor was there want of counsel in the plot:
But fortune can, at any time, o'erthrow
The projects of a hundred learned clerks, sir.
    CORBACCIO: [Listening] What's that?
    VOLTORE: Wilt please you, sir, to go along?
    [Exit Corbaccio, followed by Voltore]
    MOSCA: Patron, go in, and pray for our success.
    VOLPONE: [Rising from his couch] Need makes
    devotion: heaven your labor bless!
    [Exeunt]

ACT IV. SCENE I.

A street.

    [Enter Sir Politick Would-be and Peregrine]
    SIR POLITICK: I told you, sir, it was a plot; you see
What observation is! You mentioned me
For some instructions: I will tell you, sir
(Since we are met here in this height of Venice),
Some few particulars I have set down,
Only for this meridian, fit to be known
Of your crude traveler; and they are these.
I will not touch, sir, at your phrase, or clothes,
For they are old.
    PEREGRINE: Sir, I have better.

    SIR POLITICK: Pardon,
I meant, as they are themes.
    PEREGRINE: O, sir, proceed:
I'll slander you no more of wit, good sir.
    SIR POLITICK: First, for your garb, it must be grave
    and serious,
Very reserved and locked; not tell a secret
On any terms, not to your father: scarce
A fable, but with caution: make sure choice
Both of your company and discourse; beware
You never speak a truth——
    PEREGRINE: How!
    SIR POLITICK: Not to strangers,
For those be they you must converse with most;
Others I would not know, sir, but at distance.
So as I still might be a saver in them:
You shall have tricks else past upon you hourly.
And then, for your religion, profess none,
But wonder at the diversity of all;
And, for your part, protest, were there no other
But simply the laws o' th' land, you could content
    you.
Nic. Machiavel and Monsieur Bodin, both
Were of this mind. Then must you learn the use
And handling of your silver fork at meals,
The metal of your glass (these are main matters
With your Italian); and to know the hour
When you must eat your melons and your figs.
    PEREGRINE: Is that a point of state too?
    SIR POLITICK: Here it is:
For your Venetian, if he see a man
Preposterous in the least, he has him straight;
He has; he strips him. I'll acquaint you, sir,
I now have lived here 'tis some fourteen months:
Within the first week of my landing here,
All took me for a citizen of Venice,
I knew the forms so well——
    PEREGRINE: [Aside] And nothing else.
    SIR POLITICK: I had read Contarene,[19] took me a
    house,
On which the law would take sufficient hold,
Dealt with my Jews to furnish it with movables—
Well, if I could but find one man, one man
To mine own heart, whom I durst trust, I would——
    PEREGRINE: What, what, sir?
    SIR POLITICK: Make him rich; make him a fortune:
He should not think again. I would command it.
    PEREGRINE: As how?
    SIR POLITICK: With certain projects that I have;
Which I may not discover.
    PEREGRINE: If I had
But one to wager with, I would lay odds now,
He tells me instantly. [Aside]
    SIR POLITICK: One is, and that
I care not greatly who knows, to serve the state
Of Venice with red herrings for three years,
And at a certain rate, from Rotterdam,

[19] Probably Gasparo Contarini (1483–1542), Venetian
cardinal and diplomat who tried to reconcile Protestants
and Catholics at the Diet of Ratisbon, 1541.

Where I have correspondence. There's a letter,
Sent me from one o' the states, and to that purpose:
He cannot write his name, but that's his mark.
  PEREGRINE: He is a chandler?
  SIR POLITICK: No, a cheese-monger.
There are some others too with whom I treat
About the same negotiation;
And I will undertake it: for 'tis thus.
I'll do't with ease, I have cast it all. Your hoy[20]
Carries but three men in her, and a boy;
And she shall make me three returns a year:
So if there come but one of three, I save;
If two, I can defalk:—but this is now,
If my main project fail.
  PEREGRINE: Then you have others?
  SIR POLITICK: I should be loth to draw the subtle
    air
Of such a place, without my thousand aims.
I'll not dissemble, sir: where'er I come,
I love to be considerative; and 'tis true,
I have at my free hours thought upon
Some certain goods unto the state of Venice,
Which I do call *my Cautions;* and, sir, which
I mean, in hope of pension, to propound
To the Great Council, then unto the Forty,
So to the Ten. My means are made already——
  PEREGRINE: By whom?
  SIR POLITICK: Sir, one that though his place be
    obscure,
Yet he can sway, and they will hear him. He's
A commandador.
  PEREGRINE: What! a common serjeant?
  SIR POLITICK: Sir, such as they are, put it in their
    mouths,
What they should say, sometimes; as well as greater:
I think I have my notes to show you—— [*Searching
    his pockets*]
  PEREGRINE: Good sir.
  SIR POLITICK: But you shall swear unto me, on
    your gentry,
Not to anticipate——
  PEREGRINE: I, sir!
  SIR POLITICK: Nor reveal
A circumstance——My paper is not with me.
  PEREGRINE: O, but you remember, sir.
  SIR POLITICK: My first is
Concerning tinder-boxes. You must know,
No family is here without its box.
Now, sir, it being so portable a thing,
Put case, that you or I were ill affected
Unto the state, sir; with it in our pockets,
Might not I go into the Arsenal,
Or you come out again, and none the wiser?
  PEREGRINE: Except yourself, sir.
  SIR POLITICK: Go to, then. I therefore
Advertise to the state, how fit it were
That none but such as were known patriots,
Sound lovers of their country, should be suffered
To enjoy them in their houses; and even those

[20] A small coasting vessel.

Sealed at some office, and at such a bigness
As might not lurk in pockets.
  PEREGRINE: Admirable!
  SIR POLITICK: My next is, how to inquire, and be
    resolved,
By present demonstration, whether a ship,
Newly arrived from Soria, or from
Any suspected part of all the Levant,
Be guilty of the plague: and where they use
To lie out forty, fifty days, sometimes,
About the Lazaretto,[21] for their trial;
I'll save that charge and loss unto the merchant,
And in an hour clear the doubt.
  PEREGRINE: Indeed, sir!
  SIR POLITICK: Or——I will lose my labor.
  PEREGRINE: My faith, that's much.
  SIR POLITICK: Nay, sir, conceive me. It will cost me
    in onions,
Some thirty livres——
  PEREGRINE: Which is one pound sterling.
  SIR POLITICK: Beside my waterworks: for this I do,
    sir.
First, I bring in your ship 'twixt two brick walls;
But those the state shall venture. On the one
I strain me a fair tarpauling, and in that
I stick my onions, cut in halves; the other
Is full of loopholes, out of which I thrust
The noses of my bellows; and those bellows
I keep, with waterworks, in perpetual motion,
Which is the easiest matter of a hundred.
Now, sir, your onion, which doth naturally
Attract the infection, and your bellows blowing
The air upon him, will show instantly,
By his changed color, if there be contagion;
Or else remain as fair as at the first.
Now it is known, 'tis nothing.
  PEREGRINE: You are right, sir.
  SIR POLITICK: I would I had my note.
  PEREGRINE: Faith, so would I:
But you have done well for once, sir.
  SIR POLITICK: Were I false,
Or would be made so, I could show you reasons
How I could sell this state now to the Turk,
Spite of their galleys, or their—— [*Examining his
    papers*]
  PEREGRINE: Pray you, Sir Pol.
  SIR POLITICK: I have them not about me.
  PEREGRINE: That I feared:
They are there, sir.
  SIR POLITICK: No, this is my diary,
Wherein I note my actions of the day.
  PEREGRINE: Pray you let's see, sir. What is here?
    Notandum,
    [*Reads*]
"A rat had gnawn my spur-leathers; notwithstanding,
I put on new, and did go forth; but first
I threw three beans over the threshold. Item,
I went and bought two toothpicks, whereof one

[21] A place for the confinement of persons suffering
from contagious diseases.

I burst immediately, in a discourse
With a Dutch merchant, 'bout ragion del stato.
From him I went and paid a moccinigo
For piecing my silk stockings; by the way
I cheapened sprats; and at St. Mark's I urined."

Faith these are politic notes!
   SIR POLITICK: Sir, I do slip
No action of my life, but thus I quote it.
   PEREGRINE: Believe it, it is wise!
   SIR POLITICK: Nay, sir, read forth.
     [*Enter, at a distance,* Lady Politick Would-be,
     Nano, *and two* Waiting-women]
   LADY POLITICK: Where should this loose knight be,
     trow? sure he's housed.
   NANO: Why, then he's fast.
   LADY POLITICK: Ay, he plays both with me.
I pray you stay. This heat will do more harm
To my complexion than his heart is worth.
(I do not care to hinder, but to take him.)
How it comes off! [*Rubbing her cheeks*]
   1ST WOMAN: My master's yonder.
   LADY POLITICK: Where?
   2ND WOMAN: With a young gentleman.
   LADY POLITICK: That same's the party;
In man's apparel! Pray you, sir, jog my knight:
I will be tender to his reputation,
However he demerit.
   SIR POLITICK: [*Seeing her*] My lady!
   PEREGRINE: Where?
   SIR POLITICK: 'Tis she indeed, sir; you shall know
     her. She is,
Were she not mine, a lady of that merit,
For fashion and behavior; and for beauty
I durst compare——
   PEREGRINE: It seems you are not jealous,
That dare commend her.
   SIR POLITICK: Nay, and for discourse——
   PEREGRINE: Being your wife, she cannot miss that.
   SIR POLITICK: [*Introducing* Peregrine] Madam,
Here is a gentleman, pray you, use him fairly;
He seems a youth, but he is——
   LADY POLITICK: None.
   SIR POLITICK: Yes one
Has put his face as soon into the world——
   LADY POLITICK: You mean, as early? but to-day?
   SIR POLITICK: How's this?
   LADY POLITICK: Why, in this habit, sir; you appre-
     hend me:
Well, Master Would-be, this doth not become you;
I had thought the door, sir, of your good name
Had been more precious to you; that you would not
Have done this dire massacre on your honor;
One of your gravity, and rank besides!
But knights, I see, care little for the oath
They make to ladies; chiefly their own ladies.
   SIR POLITICK: Now, by my spurs, the symbol of my
     knighthood——
   PEREGRINE: [*Aside*] Lord, how his brain is hum-
     bled for an oath!

   SIR POLITICK: I reach you not.
   LADY POLITICK: Right, sir, your policy
May bear it through thus. [*To* Peregrine] Sir, a word
     with you.
I would be loth to contest publicly
With any gentlewoman, or to seem
Froward, or violent, as the courtier says;
It comes too near rusticity in a lady,
Which I would shun by all means: and however
I may deserve from Master Would-be, yet
T' have one fair gentlewoman thus be made
The unkind instrument to wrong another,
And one she knows not, ay, and to perséver;
In my poor judgment, is not warranted
From being a solecism in our sex,
If not in manners.
   PEREGRINE: How is this!
   SIR POLITICK: Sweet madam,
Come nearer to your aim.
   LADY POLITICK: Marry, and will, sir.
Since you provoke me with your impudence,
And laughter of your light land-syren here,
Your Sporus, your hermaphrodite——
   PEREGRINE: What's here?
Poetic fury and historic storms!
   SIR POLITICK: The gentleman, believe it, is of
     worth
And of our nation.
   LADY POLITICK: Ay, your Whitefriars nation.[22]
Come, I blush for you, Master Would-be, I;
And am ashamed you should have no more forehead,
Than thus to be the patron, or St. George,
To a lewd harlot, a base fricatrice,
A female devil, in a male outside.
   SIR POLITICK: Nay,
An you be such a one, I must bid adieu
To your delights. The case appears too liquid. [*Exit*]
   LADY POLITICK: Ay, you may carry't clear, with
     your state-face!
But for your carnival concupiscence,
Who here is fled for liberty of conscience,
From furious persecution of the marshal,
Her will I dis'ple.
   PEREGRINE: This is fine, i' faith!
And do you use this often? Is this part
Of your wit's exercise, 'gainst you have occasion?
Madam——
   LADY POLITICK: Go to, sir.
   PERERGINE: Do you hear me, lady?
Why, if your knight have set you to beg shirts.
Or to invite me home, you might have done it
A nearer way by far.
   LADY POLITICK: This cannot work you
Out of my snare.
   PEREGRINE: Why, am I in it, then?
Indeed your husband told me you were fair,
And so you are; only your nose inclines,
That side that's next the sun, to the queen-apple.

   [22] Various types of social outcasts resided in Whitefriars, London.

LADY POLITICK: This cannot be endured by any
patience.
[*Enter* Mosca]
MOSCA: What is the matter, madam?
LADY POLITICK: If the senate
Right not my quest in this, I will protest them
To all the world no aristocracy.
MOSCA: What is the injury, lady?
LADY POLITICK: Why, the callet²³
You told me of, here I have ta'en disguised.
MOSCA: Who? this! what means your ladyship? the
creature
I mentioned to you is apprehended now,
Before the senate; you shall see her——
LADY POLITICK: Where?
MOSCA: I'll bring you to her. This young gentle-
man,
I saw him land this morning at the port.
LADY POLITICK: Is't possible! how has my judgment
wandered?
Sir, I must, blushing, say to you, I have erred;
And plead your pardon.
PEREGRINE: What, more changes yet!
LADY POLITICK: I hope you have not the malice to
remember
A gentlewoman's passion. If you stay
In Venice here, please you to use me, sir——
MOSCA: Will you go, madam?
LADY POLITICK: Pray you, sir, use me; in faith,
The more you see me the more I shall conceive
You have forgot our quarrel.
[*Exeunt* Lady Would-be, Mosca, Nano, *and* Wait-
ing-women]
PEREGRINE: This is rare!
Sir Politick Would-be? no, Sir Politick Bawd,
To bring me thus acquainted with his wife!
Well, wise Sir Pol, since you have practised thus
Upon my freshman-ship, I'll try your salt-head,
What proof it is against a counter-plot. [*Exit*]

SCENE II.

The Scrutineo, or senate house.

[*Enter* Voltore, Corbaccio, Corvino, *and* Mosca]
VOLTORE: Well, now you know the carriage of the
business,
Your constancy is all that is required
Unto the safety of it.
MOSCA: Is the lie
Safely conveyed amongst us? is that sure?
Knows every man his burden?
CORVINO: Yes.
MOSCA: Then shrink not.
CORVINO: But knows the advocate the truth?
MOSCA: O, sir,
By no means; I devised a formal tale,
²³ Common harlot.

That salved your reputation. But be valiant, sir.
CORVINO: I fear no one but him that this his plead-
ing
Should make him stand for a co-heir——
MOSCA: Co-halter!
Hang him; we will but use his tongue, his noise,
As we do croaker's here.
CORVINO: Ay, what shall he do?
MOSCA: When we have done, you mean?
CORVINO: Yes.
MOSCA: Why, we'll think:
Sell him for mummia: he's half dust already.
Do you not smile, [*to* Voltore] to see this buffalo,
How he doth sport it with his head? I should,
If all were well and past. [*Aside*] Sir, [*to* Corbaccio]
only you
And he that shall enjoy the crop of all,
And these not know for whom they toil.
CORBACCIO: Ay, peace.
MOSCA: [*Turning to* Corvino] But you shall eat it.
Much! [*Aside*] Worshipful sir, [*to* Voltore]
Mercury sit upon your thundering tongue,
Or the French Hercules, and make your language
As conquering as his club, to beat along,
As with a tempest, flat, our adversaries;
But much more yours, sir.
VOLTORE: Here they come, have done.
MOSCA: I have another witness, if you need, sir, I
can produce.
VOLTORE: Who is it?
MOSCA: Sir, I have her.
[*Enter* Avocatori, *and take their seats,* Bonario,
Celia, Notario, Commandadori, Saffi, *and other
Officers of Justice*]
1ST AVOCATORE: The like of this the senate never
heard of.
2ND AVOCATORE: 'Twill come most strange to them
when we report it.
4TH AVOCATORE: The gentlewoman has been ever
held
Of unreproved name.
3RD AVOCATORE: So has the youth.
4TH AVOCATORE: The more unnatural part that of
his father.
2ND AVOCATORE: More of the husband.
1ST AVOCATORE: I do not know to give
His act a name, it is so monstrous!
4TH AVOCATORE: But the impostor, he's a thing
created
To exceed example!
1ST AVOCATORE: And all after-times!
2ND AVOCATORE: I never heard a true voluptuary
Described but him.
3RD AVOCATORE: Appear yet those were cited?
NOTARIO: All but the old magnifico, Volpone.
1ST AVOCATORE: Why is not he here?
MOSCA: Please your fatherhoods,
Here is his advocate: himself so weak,
So feeble——
4TH AVOCATORE: Who are you?

BONARIO: His parasite,
His knave, his pander. I beseech the court
He may be forced to come, that your grave eyes
May bear strong witness of his strange impostures.

VOLTORE: Upon my faith and credit with your virtues,
He is not able to endure the air.

2ND AVOCATORE: Bring him, however.

3RD AVOCATORE: We will see him.

4TH AVOCATORE: Fetch him.

VOLTORE: Your fatherhoods' fit pleasures be obeyed;
[Exeunt Officers]
But sure, the sight will rather move your pities
Than indignation. May it please the court,
In the mean time, he may be heard in me:
I know this place most void of prejudice,
And therefore crave it, since we have no reason
To fear our truth should hurt our cause.

3RD AVOCATORE: Speak free.

VOLTORE: Then know, most honored fathers, I must now
Discover to your strangely abused ears,
The most prodigious and most frontless piece
Of solid impudence, and treachery,
That ever vicious nature yet brought forth
To shame the state of Venice. This lewd woman,
That wants no artificial looks or tears
To help the vizor she has now put on,
Hath long been known a close adulteress
To that lascivious youth there; not suspected,
I say, but known, and taken in the act
With him; and by this man, the easy husband,
Pardoned; whose timeless bounty makes him now
Stand here, the most unhappy, innocent person,
That ever man's own goodness made accused.
For these not knowing how to owe a gift
Of that dear grace, but with their shame; being placed
So above all powers of their gratitude,
Began to hate the benefit; and in place
Of thanks, devise to extirpe the memory
Of such an act: wherein I pray your fatherhoods
To observe the malice, yea, the rage of creatures
Discovered in their evils: and what heart
Such take, even from their crimes:—but that anon
Will more appear.—This gentleman, the father,
Hearing of this foul fact, with many others,
Which daily struck at his too tender ears,
And grieved in nothing more than that he could not
Preserve himself a parent (his son's ills
Growing to that strange flood), at last decreed
To disinherit him.

1ST AVOCATORE: These be strange turns!

2ND AVOCATORE: The young man's fame was ever fair and honest.

VOLTORE: So much more full of danger is his vice,
That can beguile so under shade of virtue.
But, as I said, my honored sires, his father
Having this settled purpose, by what means
To him betrayed, we know not, and this day

Appointed for the deed; that parricide,
I cannot style him better, by confederacy
Preparing this his paramour to be there,
Entered Volpone's house (who was the man,
Your fatherhoods must understand, designed
For the inheritance), there sought his father:—
But with what purpose sought he him, my lords?
I tremble to pronounce it, that a son
Unto a father, and to such a father,
Should have so foul, felonious intent!
It was to murder him: when being prevented
By his more happy absence, what then did he?
Not check his wicked thoughts; no, now new deeds
(Mischief doth never end where it begins);
An act of horror, fathers! he dragged forth
The aged gentleman that had there lain bed-rid
Three years and more, out of his innocent couch,
Naked upon the floor, there left him; wounded
His servant in the face; and with this strumpet,
The stale to his forged practice, who was glad
To be so active—(I shall here desire
Your fatherhoods to note but my collections,
As most remarkable—) thought at once to stop
His father's ends, discredit his free choice
In the old gentleman, redeem themselves,
By laying infamy upon this man,
To whom, with blushing, they should owe their lives.

1ST AVOCATORE: What proofs have you of this?

BONARIO: Most honored fathers,
I humbly crave there be no credit given
To this man's mercenary tongue.

2ND AVOCATORE: Forbear.

BONARIO: His soul moves in his fee.

3RD AVOCATORE: O, sir.

BONARIO: This fellow,
For six sols more would plead against his Maker.

1ST AVOCATORE: You do forget yourself.

VOLTORE: Nay, nay, grave fathers,
Let him have scope: can any man imagine
That he will spare his accuser, that would not
Have spared his parent?

1ST AVOCATORE: Well, produce your proofs.

CELIA: I would I could forget I were a creature.

VOLTORE: Signior Corbaccio!
[Corbaccio comes forward]

4TH AVOCATORE: What is he?

VOLTORE: The father.

2ND AVOCATORE: Has he had an oath?

NOTARIO: Yes.

CORBACCIO: What must I do now?

NOTARIO: Your testimony's craved.

CORBACCIO: Speak to the knave?
I'll have my mouth first stopt with earth; my heart
Abhors his knowledge: I disclaim in him.

1ST AVOCATORE: But for what cause?

CORBACCIO: The mere portent of nature!
He is an utter stranger to my loins.

BONARIO: Have they made you to this?

CORBACCIO: I will not hear thee,
Monster of men, swine, goat, wolf, parricide!

Speak not, thou viper.

BONARIO: Sir, I will sit down,
And rather wish my innocence should suffer
Than I resist the authority of a father.

VOLTORE: Signior Corvino!

[Corvino *comes forward*]

2ND AVOCATORE: This is strange.

1ST AVOCATORE: Who's this?

NOTARIO: The husband.

4TH AVOCATORE: Is he sworn?

NOTARIO: He is.

3RD AVOCATORE: Speak then.

CORVINO: This woman, please your fatherhoods, is
a whore,
Of most hot exercise, more than a partrich,
Upon record——

1ST AVOCATORE: No more.

CORVINO: Neighs like a jennet.

NOTARIO: Preserve the honor of the court.

CORVINO: I shall,
And modesty of your most reverend ears.
And I hope that I may say these eyes
Have seen her glued unto that piece of cedar,
That fine well timbered gallant: and that here
The letters may be read, thorough the horn,
That makes the story perfect.

MOSCA: Excellent! sir.

CORVINO: [*Aside to* Mosca] There is no shame in
this now, is there?

MOSCA: None.

CORVINO: Or if I said, I hoped that she were on-
ward
To her damnation, if there be a hell
Greater than whore and woman; a good Catholic
May make the doubt.

3RD AVOCATORE: His grief hath made him frantic.

1ST AVOCATORE: Remove him hence.

2ND AVOCATORE: Look to the woman.

[Celia *swoons*]

CORVINO: Rare!
Prettily feigned again!

4TH AVOCATORE: Stand from about her.

1ST AVOCATORE: Give her the air.

3RD AVOCATORE: [*To* Mosca] What can you say?

MOSCA: My wound,
May it please your wisdoms, speaks for me, received
In aid of my good patron, when he mist
His sought-for father, when that well-taught dame
Had her cue given her to cry out, A rape!

BONARIO: O most laid impudence!
Fathers——

3RD AVOCATORE: Sir, be silent;
You had your hearing free, so must they theirs.

2ND AVOCATORE: I do begin to doubt the imposture
here.

4TH AVOCATORE: This woman has too many moods.

VOLTORE: Grave fathers,
She is a creature of a most profest
And prostituted lewdness.

CORVINO: Most impetuous,
Unsatisfied, grave fathers!

VOLTORE: May her feignings
Not take your wisdoms: but this day she baited
A stranger, a grave knight, with her loose eyes,
And more lascivious kisses. This man saw them
Together on the water, in a gondola.

MOSCA: Here is the lady herself, that saw them too,
Without; who then had in the open streets
Pursued them, but for saving her knight's honor.

1ST AVOCATORE: Produce that lady.

2ND AVOCATORE: Let her come.

[*Exit* Mosca]

4TH AVOCATORE: These things,
They strike with wonder.

3RD AVOCATORE: I am turned a stone.

[*Re-enter* Mosca *with* Lady Would-be]

MOSCA: Be resolute, madam.

LADY POLITICK: Ay, this same is she. [*Pointing to*
Celia]
Out, thou camelion harlot! now thine eyes
Vie tears with the hyæna. Dar'st thou look
Upon my wronged face? I cry your pardons,
I fear I have forgettingly transgrest
Against the dignity of the court——

2ND AVOCATORE: No, madam.

LADY POLITICK: And been exorbitant——

2ND AVOCATORE: You have not, lady.

4TH AVOCATORE: These proofs are strong.

LADY POLITICK: Surely, I had no purpose
To scandalize your honors, or my sex's.

3RD AVOCATORE: We do believe it.

LADY POLITICK: Surely you may believe it.

2ND AVOCATORE: Madam, we do.

LADY POLITICK: Indeed you may; my breeding
Is not so coarse——

4TH AVOCATORE: We know it.

LADY POLITICK: To offend
With pertinancy——

3RD AVOCATORE: Lady——

LADY POLITICK: Such a presence!
No surely.

1ST AVOCATORE: We well think it.

LADY POLITICK: You may think it.

1ST AVOCATORE: Let her o'ercome. What witnesses
have you,
To make good your report?

BONARIO: Our consciences.

CELIA: And heaven, that never fails the innocent.

4TH AVOCATORE: These are no testimonies.

BONARIO: Not in your courts,
Where multitude and clamor overcomes.

1ST AVOCATORE: Nay, then you do wax insolent.

[*Re-enter* Officers, *bearing* Volpone *on a couch*]

VOLTORE: Here, here.
The testimony comes that will convince,
And put to utter dumbness their bold tongues!
See here, grave fathers, here's the ravisher,
The rider on men's wives, the great impostor,

The grand voluptuary! Do you not think
These limbs should affect venery? or these eyes
Covet a concubine? pray you mark these hands;
Are they not fit to stroke a lady's breasts?
Perhaps he doth dissemble!
    BONARIO: So he does.
    VOLTORE: Would you have him tortured?
    BONARIO: I would have him proved.
    VOLTORE: Best try him then with goads, or burning
      irons;
Put him to the strappado; I have heard
The rack hath cured the gout; faith, give it him,
And help him of a malady; be courteous.
I'll undertake, before these honored fathers,
He shall have yet as many left diseases,
As she has known adulterers, or thou strumpets.
O, my most equal hearers, if these deeds,
Acts of this bold and most exorbitant strain,
May pass with sufferance, what one citizen
But owes the forfeit of his life, yea, fame,
To him that dares traduce him? which of you
Are safe, my honored fathers? I would ask,
With leave of your grave fatherhoods, if their plot
Have any face or color like to truth?
Or if, unto the dullest nostril here,
It smell not rank, and most abhorred slander?
I crave your care of this good gentleman,
Whose life is much endangered by their fable;
And as for them, I will conclude with this,
That vicious persons, when they're hot, and fleshed
In impious acts, their constancy abounds:
Damned deeds are done with greatest confidence.
    1ST AVOCATORE: Take them to custody, and sever
      them.
    2ND AVOCATORE: 'Tis pity two such prodigies should
      live.
    1ST AVOCATORE: Let the old gentleman be returned
      with care.
      [*Exeunt* Officers *with* Volpone]
I'm sorry our credulity hath wronged him.
    4TH AVOCATORE: These are two creatures!
    3RD AVOCATORE: I've an earthquake in me.
    2ND AVOCATORE: Their shame, even in their cradles,
      fled their faces.
    4TH AVOCATORE: [*To* Voltore] You have done a
      worthy service to the state, sir,
In their discovery.
    1ST AVOCATORE: You shall hear, ere night,
What punishment the court decrees upon them.
      [*Exeunt* Avocatori, Notario, *and* Officers *with*
      Bonario *and* Celia]
    VOLTORE: We thank your fatherhoods. How like
      you it?
    MOSCA: Rare.
I'd have your tongue, sir, tipt with gold for this;
I'd have you be the heir to the whole city;
The earth I'd have want men ere you want living:
They're bound to erect your statue in St. Mark's.
Signior Corvino, I would have you go

And show yourself that you have conquered.
    CORVINO: Yes.
    MOSCA: It was much better that you should profess
Yourself a cuckold thus, than that the other
Should have been proved.
    CORVINO: Nay, I considered that:
Now it is her fault.
    MOSCA: Then it had been yours.
    CORVINO: True; I do doubt this advocate still.
    MOSCA: I' faith,
You need not, I dare ease you of that care.
    CORVINO: I trust thee, Mosca. [*Exit*]
    MOSCA: As your own soul, sir.
    CORBACCIO: Mosca!
    MOSCA: Now for your business, sir.
    CORBACCIO: How! have you business?
    MOSCA: Yes, yours, sir.
    CORBACCIO: O, none else.
    MOSCA: None else, not I.
    CORBACCIO: Be careful then.
    MOSCA: Rest you with both your eyes, sir.
    CORBACCIO: Dispatch it.
    MOSCA: Instantly.
    CORBACCIO: And look that all,
Whatever, be put in, jewels, plate, moneys,
Household stuff, bedding, curtains.
    MOSCA: Curtain-rings, sir:
Only the advocate's fee must be deducted.
    CORBACCIO: I'll pay him now; you'll be too
      prodigal.
    MOSCA: Sir, I must tender it.
    CORBACCIO: Two chequines is well.
    MOSCA: No, six, sir.
    CORBACCIO: 'Tis too much.
    MOSCA: He talked a great while;
You must consider that, sir.
    CORBACCIO: Well, there's three——
    MOSCA: I'll give it him.
    CORBACCIO: Do so, and there's for thee. [*Exit*]
    MOSCA: Bountiful bones! What horrid strange of-
    ence
Did he commit 'gainst nature, in his youth,
Worthy this age? [*Aside*] You see, sir, [*to* Voltore]
how I work
Unto your ends: take you no notice.
    VOLTORE: No,
I'll leave you. [*Exit*]
    MOSCA: All is yours, the devil and all:
Good advocate!—Madam, I'll bring you home.
    LADY POLITICK: No, I'll go see your patron.
    MOSCA: That you shall not:
I'll tell you why. My purpose is to urge
My patron to reform his will, and for
The zeal you have shown to-day, whereas before
You were but third or fourth, you shall be now
Put in the first; which would appear as begged
If you were present. Therefore——
    LADY POLITICK: You shall sway me.
      [*Exeunt*]

ACT V. SCENE I.

A room in Volpone's *house.*

[*Enter* Volpone]
VOLPONE: Well, I am here, and all this brunt is
      past.
I ne'er was in dislike with my disguise
Till this fled moment: here 'twas good, in private;
But in your public,—*cave*[24] whilst I breathe
'Fore God, my left leg 'gan to have the cramp,
And I apprehended straight some power had struck
      me
With a dead palsy. Well! I must be merry,
And shake it off. A many of these fears
Would put me into some villainous disease,
Should they come thick upon me: I'll prevent 'em.
Give me a bowl of lusty wine, to fright
This humor from my heart. [*Drinks*] Hum, hum,
      hum!
'Tis almost gone already: I shall conquer.
Any device now of rare ingenious knavery,
That would possess me with a violent laughter,
Would make me up again. [*Drinks again*] So, so, so,
      so!
This heat is life; 'tis blood by this time:—Mosca!
      [*Enter* Mosca]
MOSCA: How now, sir? does the day look clear
      again?
Are we recovered, and wrought out of error,
Into our way, to see our path before us?
Is our trade free once more?
      VOLPONE: Exquisite Mosca!
MOSCA: Was it not carried learnedly?
      VOLPONE: And stoutly:
Good wits are greatest in extremities.
      MOSCA: It were folly beyond thought to trust
Any grand act unto a cowardly spirit:
You are not taken with it enough, methinks.
      VOLPONE: O, more than if I had enjoyed the
      wench:
The pleasure of all woman-kind's not like it.
      MOSCA: Why, now you speak, sir. We must here
      be fixed;
Here we must rest; this is our masterpiece;
We cannot think to go beyond this.
      VOLPONE: True,
Thou hast played thy prize, my precious Mosca.
      MOSCA: Nay, sir,
To gull the court——
      VOLPONE: And quite divert the torrent
Upon the innocent.
      MOSCA: Yes, and to make
So rare a music out of discords——
      VOLPONE: Right.
That yet to me's the strangest, how thou hast borne it!
That these, being so divided amongst themselves,
Should not scent somewhat, or in me or thee,

24 Beware!

Or doubt their own side.
      MOSCA: True, they will not see't,
Too much light blinds them, I think. Each of them
Is so possest and stuft with his own hopes
That anything unto the contrary,
Never so true, or never so apparent,
Never so palpable, they will resist it——
      VOLPONE: Like a temptation of the devil.
      MOSCA: Right, sir.
Merchants may talk of trade, and your great signiors
Of land that yields well; but if Italy
Have any glebe more fruitful than these fellows,
I am deceived. Did not your advocate rare?
      VOLPONE: O.—"My most honored fathers, my
      grave fathers,
Under correction of your fatherhoods,
What face of truth is here? If these strange deeds
May pass, most honored fathers"—I had much ado
To forbear laughing.
      MOSCA: It seemed to me, you sweat, sir.
      VOLPONE: In troth, I did a little.
      MOSCA: But confess, sir,
Were you not daunted?
      VOLPONE: In good faith, I was
A little in a mist, but not dejected;
Never but still myself.
      MOSCA: I think it, sir.
Now, so truth help me, I must needs say this, sir,
And out of conscience for your advocate,
He has taken pains, in faith, sir, and deserved,
In my poor judgment, I speak it under favor,
Not to contrary you, sir, very richly—
Well—to be cozened.
      VOLPONE: Troth, and I think so too,
By that I heard him in the latter end.
      MOSCA: O, but before, sir: had you heard him first
Draw it to certain heads, then aggravate,
Then use his vehement figures—I looked still
When he would shift a shirt; and doing this
Out of pure love, no hope of gain——
      VOLPONE: 'Tis right.
I cannot answer him Mosca, as I would,
Not yet; but for thy sake, at thy entreaty,
I will begin, even now—to vex them all,
This very instant.
      MOSCA: Good sir.
      VOLPONE: Call the dwarf
And eunuch forth.
      MOSCA: Castrone, Nano!
      [*Enter* Castrone *and* Nano]
NANO: Here.
      VOLPONE: Shall we have a jig now?
      MOSCA: What you please, sir.
      VOLPONE: Go,
Straight give out about the streets, you two,
That I am dead; do it with constancy,
Sadly, do you hear? impute it to the grief
Of this late slander.
      [*Exeunt* Castrone *and* Nano]
      MOSCA: What do you mean, sir?

VOLPONE: O,
I shall have instantly my Vulture, Crow,
Raven, come flying hither, on the news,
To peck for carrion, my she-wolf, and all,
Greedy, and full of expectation——

    MOSCA: And then to have it ravished from their
      mouths!

    VOLPONE: 'Tis true. I will have thee put on a gown,
And take upon thee, as thou wert mine heir;
Show them a Will. Open that chest, and reach
Forth one of those that has the blanks; I'll straight
Put in thy name.

    MOSCA: It will be rare, sir. [*Gives him a paper*]

    VOLPONE: Ay,
When they ev'n gape, and find themselves de-
    luded——

    MOSCA: Yes.

    VOLPONE: And thou use them scurvily!
Dispatch, get on thy gown.

    MOSCA: [*Putting on a gown*] But what, sir, if they
    ask
After the body?

    VOLPONE: Say, it was corrupted.

    MOSCA: I'll say it stunk, sir; and was fain to have it
Coffined up instantly, and sent away.

    VOLPONE: Anything; what thou wilt. Hold, here's
    my Will.
Get thee a cap, a count-book, pen and ink,
Papers afore thee; sit as thou wert taking
An inventory of parcels: I'll get up
Behind the curtain, on a stool, and hearken:
Sometime peep over, see how they do look,
With what degrees their blood doth leave their faces.
O, 'twill afford me a rare meal of laughter!

    MOSCA: [*Putting on a cap, and setting out the
    table, &c.*] Your advocate will turn stark dull
    upon it.

    VOLPONE: It will take off his oratory's edge.

    MOSCA: But your clarissimo, old roundback, he
Will crump you like a hog-louse, with the touch.

    VOLPONE: And what Corvino?

    MOSCA: O, sir, look for him,
To-morrow morning, with a rope and dagger,
To visit all the streets; he must run mad,
My lady too, that came into the court,
To bear false witness for your worship——

    VOLPONE: Yes,
And kissed me 'fore the fathers, when my face
Flowed all with oils——

    MOSCA: And sweat, sir. Why, your gold
Is such another med'cine, it dries up
All those offensive savours! it transforms
The most deformed, and restores them lovely,
As 'twere the strange poetical girdle. Jove
Could not invent t' himself a shroud more subtle
To pass Acrisius' guards. It is the thing
Makes all the world her grace, her youth, her beauty.

    VOLPONE: I think she loves me.

    MOSCA: Who? the lady, sir?
She's jealous of you.

    VOLPONE: **Dost thou say so?**
    [*Knocking within*]

    MOSCA: Hark,
There's some already.

    VOLPONE: Look.

    MOSCA: It is the Vulture;
He has the quickest scent.

    VOLPONE: I'll to my place,
Thou to thy posture. [*Goes behind the curtain*]

    MOSCA: I am set.

    VOLPONE: But, Mosca,
Play the artificer now, torture them rarely.
    [*Enter* Voltore]

    VOLTORE: How now, my Mosca?

    MOSCA: [*Writing*] "Turkey carpets, nine——'

    VOLTORE: Taking an inventory! that is well.

    MOSCA: "Two suits of bedding, tissue——"

    VOLTORE: Where's the Will?
Let me read the while.
    [*Enter* Servants *with* Corbaccio *in a chair*]

    CORBACCIO: So, set me down,
And get you home.
    [*Exeunt* Servants]

    VOLTORE: Is he come now, to trouble us!

    MOSCA: "Of cloth of gold, two more——"

    CORBACCIO: Is it done, Mosca?

    MOSCA: "Of several velvets, eight——"

    VOLTORE: I like his care.

    CORBACCIO: Dost thou not hear?
    [*Enter* Corvino]

    CORVINO: Ha! is the hour come, Mosca?

    VOLPONE: [*Peeping over the curtain*] Ay, now
    they muster.

    CORVINO: What does the advocate here,
Or this Corbaccio?

    CORBACCIO: What do these here?
    [*Enter* Lady Politick Would-be]

    LADY POLITICK: Mosca!
Is his thread spun?

    MOSCA: "Eight chests of linen——"

    VOLPONE: O,
My fine Dame Would-be, too!

    CORVINO: Mosca, the Will,
That I may show it these, and rid them hence.

    MOSCA: "Six chests of diaper, four of damask."—
    There
    [*Gives them the Will carelessly, over his
    shoulder*]

    CORBACCIO: Is that the Will?

    MOSCA: "Down-beds, and bolsters——"

    VOLPONE: Rare!
Be busy still. Now they begin to flutter:
They never think of me. Look, see, see, see!
How their swift eyes run over the long deed,
Unto the name, and to the legacies,
What is bequeathed them there——

    MOSCA: "Ten suits of hangings——"

    VOLPONE: Ay, in their garters, Mosca. Now their
    hopes
Are at the gasp.

VOLTORE: Mosca the heir.

CORBACCIO: What's that?

VOLPONE: My advocate is dumb; look to my
    merchant,
He has heard of some strange storm, a ship is lost,
He faints; my lady will swoon. Old glazen-eyes,
He hath not reached his despair yet.

CORBACCIO: All these
Are out of hope; I am, sure, the man. [*Takes the
    Will*]

CORVINO: But, Mosca——

MOSCA: "Two cabinets——"

CORVINO: Is this in earnest?

MOSCA: "One
Of ebony——"

CORVINO: Or do you but delude me?

MOSCA: "The other, mother of pearl"—
I am very busy.
Good faith, it is a fortune thrown upon me——
"Item, one salt of agate"—not my seeking.

LADY POLITICK: Do you hear, sir?

MOSCA: "A perfumed box"—Pray you forbear,
You see I'm troubled—"made of an onyx——"

LADY POLITICK: How!

MOSCA: To-morrow or next day, I shall be at
    leisure
To talk with you all.

CORVINO: Is this my large hope's issue?

LADY POLITICK: Sir, I must have a fairer answer.

MOSCA: Madam!
Marry, and shall: pray you, fairly quit my house.
Nay, raise no tempest with your looks; but hark you,
Remember what your ladyship offered me
To put you in an heir; go to, think on it:
And what you said e'en your best madams did
For maintenance; and why not you? Enough.
Go home, and use the poor Sir Pol, your knight, well,
For fear I tell some riddles; go, be melancholy.
    [*Exit* Lady Politick Would-be]

VOLPONE: O, my fine devil!

CORVINO: Mosca, pray you a word.

MOSCA: Lord! will not you take your dispatch
    hence yet?
Methinks, of all, you should have been the example.
Why should you stay here? with what thought, what
    promise?
Hear you; do you not know, I know you an ass,
And that you would most fain have been a wittol[25]
If fortune would have let you? that you are
A declared cuckold, on good terms? This pearl,
You'll say, was yours? right: this diamond?
I'll not deny't, but thank you. Much here else?
It may be so. Why, think that these good works
May help to hide your bad. I'll not betray you;
Although you be but extraordinary,
And have it only in title, it sufficeth:
Go home, be melancholy too, or mad.
    [*Exit* Corvino]

25 A complaisant cuckold.

VOLPONE: Rare Mosca! how his villainy becomes
    him!

VOLTORE: Certain he doth delude all these for me.

CORBACCIO: Mosca, the heir!

VOLPONE: O, his four eyes have found it.

CORBACCIO: I am cozened, cheated, by a parasite
    slave;
Harlot, thou hast gulled me.

MOSCA: Yes, sir. Stop your mouth,
Or I shall draw the only tooth is left.
Are not you he, that filthy covetous wretch,
With the three legs, that here, in hope of prey,
Have, any time this three years, snuffed about,
With your most groveling nose, and would have hired
Me to the poisoning of my patron, sir:
Are not you he that have to-day in court
Professed the disinheriting of your son?
Perjured yourself? Go home, and die, and stink;
If you but croak a syllable, all comes out:
Away, and call your porters! [*Exit* Corbaccio] Go,
    go, stink.

VOLPONE: Excellent varlet!

VOLTORE: Now, my faithful Mosca,
I find thy constancy——

MOSCA: Sir!

VOLTORE: Sincere.

MOSCA: [*Writing*] "A table
Of porphyry"—I marle[26] you'll be thus troublesome.

VOLTORE: Nay, leave off now, they are gone.

MOSCA: Why, who are you?
What! who did send for you? O, cry you mercy,
Reverend sir! Good faith, I am grieved for you,
That any chance of mine should thus defeat
Your (I must needs say) most deserving travails:
But I protest, sir, it was cast upon me,
And I could almost wish to be without it,
But that the will o' the dead must be observed.
Marry, my joy is that you need it not;
You have a gift, sir (thank your education),
Will never let you want, while there are men,
And malice, to breed causes. Would I had
But half the like, for all my fortune, sir!
If I have any suits, as I do hope,
Things being so easy and direct, I shall not,
I will make bold with your obstreperous aid,
Conceive me—for your fee, sir. In mean time,
You that have so much law, I know have the con-
    science
Not to be covetous of what is mine.
Good sir, I thank you for my plate; 'twill help
To set up a young man. Good faith, you look
As you were costive;[27] best go home and purge, sir.
    [*Exit* Voltore]

VOLPONE: [*Comes from behind the curtain*] Bid
him eat lettuce well. My witty mischief,
Let me embrace thee. O that I could now
Transform thee to a Venus!—Mosca, go,

26 An obsolete contraction of "marvel."

27 Constipated.

Straight take my habit of clarissimo,
And walk the streets; be seen, torment them more:
We must pursue, as well as plot. Who would
Have lost this feast?
    MOSCA: I doubt it will lose them.
    VOLPONE: O, my recovery shall recover all.
That I could now but think on some disguise
To meet them in, and ask them questions:
How I would vex them still at every turn!
    MOSCA: Sir, I can fit you.
    VOLPONE: Canst thou?
    MOSCA: Yes, I know
One o' the commandadori, sir, so like you;
Him will I straight make drunk, and bring you his
    habit.
    VOLPONE: A rare disguise, and answering thy
    brain!
O, I will be a sharp disease unto them.
    MOSCA: Sir, you must look for curses——
    VOLPONE: Till they burst;
The Fox fares ever best when he is curst.
    [Exeunt]

SCENE II.

A hall in Sir Politick's *house.*

    [*Enter* Peregrine *disguised, and three* Mer-
    chants]
PEREGRINE: Am I enough disguised?
1ST MERCHANT: I warrant you.
PEREGRINE: All my ambition is to fright him only.
2ND MERCHANT: If you could ship him away,
    'twere excellent.
3RD MERCHANT: To Zant, or to Aleppo!
PEREGRINE: Yes, and have his
Adventures put i' the Book of Voyages,
And his gulled story registered for truth.
Well, gentlemen, when I am in a while,
And that you think us warm in our discourse,
Know your approaches.
    1ST MERCHANT: Trust it to our care.
    [*Exeunt* Merchants]
    [*Enter* Waiting-woman]
PEREGRINE: Save you, fair lady! Is Sir Pol within?
WOMAN: I do not know, sir.
PEREGRINE: Pray you say unto him
Here is a merchant, upon urgent business,
Desires to speak with him.
    WOMAN: I will see, sir. [*Exit*]
PEREGRINE: Pray you.
I see the family is all female here.
    [*Re-enter* Waiting-woman]
    WOMAN: He says, sir, he has weighty affairs of
    state,
That now require him whole; some other time
You may possess him.

PEREGRINE: Pray you say again,
If those require him whole, these will exact him,
Whereof I bring him tidings. [*Exit* Woman] What
    might be
His grave affair of state now! how to make
Bolognian sausages here in Venice, sparing
One o' the ingredients?
    [*Re-enter* Waiting-woman]
WOMAN: Sir, he says, he knows
By your word *tidings*, that you are no statesman,
And therefore wills you stay.
    PEREGRINE: Sweet, pray you return him;
I have not read so many proclamations,
And studied them for words, as he has done——
But—here he deigns to come.
    [*Exit* Woman]
    [*Enter* Sir Politick Would-be]
    SIR POLITICK: Sir, I must crave
Your courteous pardon. There hath chanced to-day
Unkind disaster 'twixt my lady and me;
And I was penning my apology,
To give her satisfaction, as you came now.
    PEREGRINE: Sir, I am grieved I bring you worse
    disaster:
The gentleman you met at the port to-day,
That told you he was newly arrived——
    SIR POLITICK: Ay, was
A fugitive punk?
    PEREGRINE: No, sir, a spy set on you:
And he has made relation to the senate,
That you profest to him to have a plot
To sell the State of Venice to the Turk.
    SIR POLITICK: O me!
    PEREGRINE: For which warrants are signed by this
    time,
To apprehend you, and to search your study
For papers——
    SIR POLITICK: Alas, sir, I have none, but notes
Drawn out of play-books——
    PEREGRINE: All the better, sir.
    SIR POLITICK: And some essays. What shall I do?
    PEREGRINE: Sir, best
Convey yourself into a sugar-chest:
Or, if you could lie round, a frail[28] were rare.
And I could send you aboard.
    SIR POLITICK: Sir, I but talked so,
For discourse sake merely.
    [*Knocking within*]
    PEREGRINE: Hark! they are there.
    SIR POLITICK: I am a wretch, a wretch!
    PEREGRINE: What will you do, sir?
Have you ne'er a currant-butt to leap into?
They'll put you to the rack; you must be sudden.
    SIR POLITICK: Sir, I have an ingine——
    3RD MERCHANT: [*Within*] Sir Politick Would-be!
    2ND MERCHANT: [*Within*] Where is he?
    SIR POLITICK: That I have thought upon before
    time.

[28] A basket made of rushes.

PEREGRINE: What is it?

SIR POLITICK: I shall ne'er endure the torture.
Marry, it is, sir, of a tortoise-shell,
Fitted for these extremities: pray you, sir, help me.
Here I've a place, sir, to put back my legs,
Please you to lay it on, sir, [*lies down while* Peregrine
  places the shell upon him]—with this cap,
And my black gloves. I'll lie, sir, like a tortoise,
Till they are gone.

PEREGRINE: And call you this an ingine?

SIR POLITICK: Mine own device——Good sir, bid
  my wife's women
To burn my papers.
  [*Exit* Peregrine]
  [*The three* Merchants *rush in*]

1ST MERCHANT: Where is he hid?

3RD MERCHANT: We must,
And will sure find him.

2ND MERCHANT: Which is his study?
  [*Re-enter* Peregrine]

1ST MERCHANT: What
Are you, sir?

PEREGRINE: I am a merchant, that came here
To look upon this tortoise?

3RD MERCHANT: How!

1ST MERCHANT: St. Mark!
What beast is this?

PEREGRINE: It is a fish.

2ND MERCHANT: Come out here!

PEREGRINE: Nay, you may strike him, sir, and tread
  upon him:
He'll bear a cart.

1ST MERCHANT: What, to run over him?

PEREGRINE: Yes, sir.

3RD MERCHANT: Let's jump upon him.

2ND MERCHANT: Can he not go?

PEREGRINE: He creeps, sir.

1ST MERCHANT: Let's see him creep.

PEREGRINE: No, good sir, you will hurt him.

2ND MERCHANT: Heart, I will see him creep, or
  prick his guts.

3RD MERCHANT: Come out here!

PEREGRINE: Pray you, sir.—Creep a little. [*Aside
  to* Sir Politick Would-be]

1ST MERCHANT: Forth.

2ND MERCHANT: Yet farther.

PEREGRINE: Good sir!—Creep.

2ND MERCHANT: We'll see his legs.
  [*They pull off the shell and discover him*]

3RD MERCHANT: Ods so, he has garters!

1ST MERCHANT: Ay, and gloves!

2ND MERCHANT: Is this
Your fearful tortoise?

PEREGRINE: [*Discovering himself*] Now, Sir Pol,
  we are even;
For your next project I shall be prepared:
I am sorry for the funeral of your notes, sir.

1ST MERCHANT: 'Twere a rare motion to be seen
  in Fleetstreet.

2ND MERCHANT: Ay, in the Term.

1ST MERCHANT: Or Smithfield, in the fair.

3RD MERCHANT: Methinks 'tis but a melancholy
  sight.

PEREGRINE: Farewell, most politic tortoise!
  [*Exeunt* Peregrine *and* Merchants]
  [*Re-enter* Waiting-woman]

SIR POLITICK: Where's my lady?
Knows she of this?

WOMAN: I know not, sir.

SIR POLITICK: Enquire.—
O, I shall be the fable of all feasts,
The freight of the gazetti,[29] ship-boys' tale;
And, which is worst, even talk for ordinaries.

WOMAN: My lady's come most melancholy home,
And says, sir, she will straight to sea, for physic.

SIR POLITICK: And I, to shun this place and clime
  for ever,
Creeping with house on back, and think it well
To shrink my poor head in my politic shell.
  [*Exeunt*]

SCENE III.

A room in Volpone's *house.*

[*Enter* Mosca *in the habit of a clarissimo, and*
  Volpone *in that of a commandadore*]

VOLPONE: Am I then like him?

MOSCA: O, sir, you are he;
No man can sever you.

VOLPONE: Good.

MOSCA: But what am I?

VOLPONE: 'Fore heaven, a brave clarissimo; thou
  becom'st it!
Pity thou wert not born one.

MOSCA: If I hold
My made one, 'twill be well. [*Aside*]

VOLPONE: I'll go and see
What news first at the court. [*Exit*]

MOSCA: Do so. My Fox
Is out of his hole, and ere he shall re-enter,
I'll make him languish in his borrowed case,
Except he come to composition with me.—
Androgyno, Castrone, Nano!
  [*Enter* Androgyno, Castrone, *and* Nano]

ALL: Here.

MOSCA: Go, recreate yourselves abroad; go,
  sport.—
  [*Exeunt*]
So, now I have the keys, and am possest.
Since he will needs be dead afore his time,
I'll bury him, or gain by him: I am his heir,
And so will keep me, till he share at least.
To cozen him of all, were but a cheat
Well placed: no man would construe it a sin:
Let his sport pay for't. This is called the Fox-trap.
  [*Exit*]

[29] Gazettes or newspapers.

SCENE IV.

A street.

[*Enter* Corbaccio *and* Corvino]
CORBACCIO: They say the court is set.
CORVINO: We must maintain
Our first tale good, for both our reputations.
CORBACCIO: Why, mine's no tale: my son would
    there have killed me.
CORVINO: That's true, I had forgot:—[*aside*] mine
    is, I'm sure.
But for your Will, sir.
CORBACCIO: Ay, I'll come upon him
For that hereafter, now his patron's dead.
    [*Enter* Volpone]
VOLPONE: Signior Corvino! and Corbaccio! sir,
Much joy unto you.
CORVINO: Of what?
VOLPONE: The sudden good
Dropt down upon you——
CORBACCIO: Where?
VOLPONE: And none knows how,
From old Volpone, sir.
CORBACCIO: Out, arrant knave!
VOLPONE: Let not your too much wealth, sir, make
    you furious.
CORBACCIO: Away, thou varlet.
VOLPONE: Why, sir?
CORBACCIO: Dost thou mock me?
VOLPONE: You mock the world, sir; did you not
    change Wills?
CORBACCIO: Out, harlot!
VOLPONE: O! belike you are the man,
Signior Corvino? faith, you carry it well;
You grow not mad withal; I love your spirit;
You are not over-leavened with your fortune.
You should have some would swell now, like a wine-
    fat,
With such an autumn—Did he give you all, sir?
CORVINO: Avoid, you rascal!
VOLPONE: Troth, your wife has shown
Herself a very woman; but you are well,
You need not care, you have a good estate,
To bear it out, sir, better by this chance:
Except Corbaccio have a share.
CORBACCIO: Hence, varlet.
VOLPONE: You will not be acknown, sir; why, 'tis
    wise.
Thus do all gamesters, at all games, dissemble:
No man will seem to win. [*Exeunt* Corvino *and* Cor-
    baccio] Here comes my vulture,
Heaving his beak up in the air, and snuffing.
    [*Enter* Voltore]
VOLTORE: Outstript thus, by a parasite! a slave,
Would run on errands, and make legs for crumbs.
Well, what I'll do——
VOLPONE: The court stays for your worship.
I e'en rejoice, sir, at your worship's happiness,

And that it fell into so learned hands,
That understand the fingering——
    VOLTORE: What do you mean?
VOLPONE: I mean to be a suitor to your worship,
For the small tenement, out of reparations,
That, at the end of your long row of houses,
By the Piscaria: it was, in Volpone's time,
Your predecessor, ere he grew diseased,
A handsome, pretty, customed bawdyhouse
As any was in Venice, none dispraised;
But fell with him: his body and that house
Decayed together.
    VOLTORE: Come, sir, leave your prating.
VOLPONE: Why, if your worship give me but your
    hand,
That I may have the refusal, I have done.
'Tis a mere toy to you, sir; candle-rents;
As your learned worship knows——
    VOLTORE: What do I know?
VOLPONE: Marry, no end of your wealth, sir; God
    decrease it!
    VOLTORE: Mistaking knave! what, mock'st thou my
    misfortune? [*Exit*]
    VOLPONE: His blessing on your heart, sir; would
    'twere more!——
Now to my first again, at the next corner. [*Exit*]

SCENE V.

Another part of the street.

[*Enter* Corbaccio *and* Corvino;—Mosca *passes
    over the stage, before them*]
CORBACCIO: See, in our habit! see the impudent
    varlet!
CORVINO: That I could shoot mine eyes at him, like
    gun-stones!
    [*Enter* Volpone]
VOLPONE: But is this true, sir, of the parasite?
CORBACCIO: Again, to afflict us! monster!
VOLPONE: In good faith, sir,
I'm heartily grieved, a beard of your grave length
Should be so over-reached. I never brooked
That parasite's hair; methought his nose should cozen:
There still was somewhat in his look, did promise
The bane of a clarissimo.
    CORBACCIO: Knave——
    VOLPONE: Methinks
Yet you, that are so traded in the world,
A witty merchant, the fine bird, Corvino,
That have such moral emblems on your name,
Should not have sung your shame, and dropt your
    cheese,
To let the Fox laugh at your emptiness.
    CORVINO: Sirrah, you think the privilege of the
    place,
And your red saucy cap, that seems to me
Nailed to your jolt-head with those two chequines,

Can warrant your abuses; come you hither:
You shall perceive, sir, I dare beat you; approach.
   VOLPONE: No haste, sir, I do know your valor well,
Since you durst publish what you are, sir.
   CORVINO: Tarry,
I'd speak with you.
   VOLPONE: Sir, sir, another time——
   CORVINO: Nay, now.
   VOLPONE: O lord, sir! I were a wise man,
Would stand the fury of a distracted cuckold.
     [*As he is running off, re-enter* Mosca]
   CORBACCIO: What, come again!
   VOLPONE: Upon 'em, Mosca; save me.
   CORBACCIO: The air's infected where he breathes.
   CORVINO: Let's fly him.
     [*Exeunt* Corvino *and* Corbaccio]
   VOLPONE: Excellent basilisk! turn upon the vulture.
     [*Enter* Voltore]
   VOLTORE: Well, flesh-fly, it is summer with you
now;
Your winter will come on.
   MOSCA: Good advocate,
Prithee not rail, nor threaten out of place thus;
Thou'lt make a solecism, as madam says.
Get you a biggin[30] more; your brain breaks loose.
     [*Exit*]
   VOLTORE: Well, sir.
   VOLPONE: Would you have me beat the insolent
slave,
Throw dirt upon his first good clothes?
   VOLTORE: This same
Is doubtless some familiar.
   VOLPONE: Sir, the court,
In troth, stays for you. I am mad, a mule
That never read Justinian, should get up,
And ride an advocate. Had you no quirk
To avoid gullage, sir, by such a creature?
I hope you do but jest; he has not done it:
'Tis but confederacy to blind the rest.
You are the heir.
   VOLTORE: A strange, officious,
Troublesome knave! thou dost torment me.
   VOLPONE: I know——
It cannot be, sir, that you should be cozened;
'Tis not within the wit of man to do it;
You are so wise, so prudent; and 'tis fit
That wealth and wisdom still should go together.
     [*Exeunt*]

SCENE VI.

The Scrutineo, or senate house.

[*Enter* Avocatori, Notario, Bonario, Celia, Corbaccio, Corvino, Commandadori, Saffi, &c.]
1ST AVOCATORE: Are all the parties here?
NOTARIO: All but the advocate.
2ND AVOCATORE: **And here he comes.**

[30] Nightcap.

[*Enter* Voltore *and* Volpone]
   1ST AVOCATORE: Then bring them forth to sentence.
   VOLTORE: O, my most honored fathers, let your
mercy
Once win upon your justice, to forgive——
I am distracted——
   VOLPONE: What will he do now? [*Aside*]
   VOLTORE: O,
I know not which to address myself to first;
Whether your fatherhoods, or these innocents——
   CORVINO: Will he betray himself? [*Aside*]
   VOLTORE: Whom equally
I have abused, out of most covetous ends——
   CORVINO: The man is mad!
   CORBACCIO: What's that?
   CORVINO: He is possest.
   VOLTORE: For which, now struck in conscience
here I prostrate
Myself at your offended feet, for pardon.
   1ST, 2ND AVOCATORI: Arise.
   CELIA: O heaven, how just thou art!
   VOLTORE: I am caught
In mine own noose—— [*Aside*]
   CORVINO: [*To* Corbaccio] Be constant, sir; nought
now
Can help but impudence.
   1ST AVOCATORE: Speak forward.
   COMMANDADORI: Silence!
   VOLTORE: It is not passion in me, reverend fathers,
But only conscience, conscience, my good sires,
That makes me now tell truth. That parasite,
That knave, hath been the instrument of all.
   1ST AVOCATORE: Where is that knave? fetch him.
   VOLPONE: I go. [*Exit*]
   CORVINO: Grave fathers,
This man's distracted; he confest it now:
For, hoping to be old Volpone's heir,
Who now is dead——
   3RD AVOCATORE: How!
   2ND AVOCATORE: Is Volpone dead?
   CORVINO: Dead since, grave fathers.
   BONARIO: O sure vengeance!
   1ST AVOCATORE: Stay,
Then he was no deceiver.
   VOLTORE: O no, none:
This parasite, grave fathers.
   CORVINO: He does speak
Out of mere envy, 'cause the servant's made
The thing he gaped for: please your fatherhoods,
This is the truth, though I'll not justify
The other, but he may be some-deal faulty.
   VOLTORE: Ay, to your hopes, as well as mine.
   Corvino:
But I'll use modesty. Pleaseth your wisdoms,
To view these certain notes, and but confer them;
And as I hope favor, they shall speak clear truth.
   CORVINO: The devil has entered him!
   BONARIO: Or bides in you.
   4TH AVOCATORE: We have done ill, by a public
officer

To send for him, if he be heir.

2ND AVOCATORE: For whom?

4TH AVOCATORE: Him that they call the parasite.

3RD AVOCATORE: 'Tis true,
He is a man of great estate, now left.

4TH AVOCATORE: Go you, and learn his name, and
   say the court
Entreats his presence here, but to the clearing
Of some few doubts.
   [*Exit* Notary]

2ND AVOCATORE: This same's a labyrinth!

1ST AVOCATORE: Stand you unto your first report?

CORVINO: My state,
My life, my fame——

BONARIO: Where is it?

CORVINO: Are at the stake.

1ST AVOCATORE: Is yours so too?

CORBACCIO: The advocate's a knave,
And has a forked tongue——

2ND AVOCATORE: Speak to the point.

CORBACCIO: So is the parasite too.

1ST AVOCATORE: This is confusion.

VOLTORE: I do beseech your fatherhoods, read
   but those—[*Giving them papers*]

CORVINO: And credit nothing the false spirit hath
   writ:
It cannot be but he's possest, grave fathers.
   [*The scene closes*]

SCENE VII.

A street.

   [*Enter* Volpone]

VOLPONE: To make a snare for mine own neck!
   and run
My head into it, wilfully! with laughter!
When I had newly scaped, was free and clear,
Out of mere wantonness! O, the dull devil
Was in this brain of mine when I devised it,
And Mosca gave it second; he must now
Help to sear up this vein, or we bleed dead.
   [*Enter* Nano, Androgyno, *and* Castrone]
How now! who let you loose? whither go you now?
What, to buy gingerbread, or to drown kitlings?

NANO: Sir, Master Mosca called us out of doors,
And bid us all go play, and took the keys.

ANDROGYNO: Yes.

VOLPONE: Did Master Mosca take the keys? why,
   so!
I'm farther in. These are my fine conceits!
I must be merry, with a mischief to me!
What vile wretch was I, that could not bear
My fortune soberly? I must have my crochets,
And my conundrums! Well, go you, and seek him:
His meaning may be truer than my fear.
Bid him, he straight come to me to the court;
Thither will I, and, if't be possible,
Unscrew my advocate, upon new hopes:

When I provoked him, then I lost myself.
   [*Exeunt*]

SCENE VIII.

The Scrutineo, or senate house.

   [Avocatori, Bonario, Celia, Corbaccio, Corvino,
   Commandadori, Saffi, &c., *as before*]

1ST AVOCATORE: These things can ne'er be recon-
   ciled. He here [*showing the papers*]
Professeth that the gentleman was wronged,
And that the gentlewoman was brought thither,
Forced by her husband, and there left.

VOLTORE: Most true.

CELIA: How ready is heaven to those that pray!

1ST AVOCATORE: But that
Volpone would have ravished her, he holds
Utterly false, knowing his impotence.

CORVINO: Grave fathers, he's possest; again, I say,
Possest: nay, if there be possession, and
Obsession, he has both.

3RD AVOCATORE: Here comes our officer.
   [*Enter* Volpone]

VOLPONE: The parasite will straight be here, grave
   fathers.

4TH AVOCATORE: You might invent some other
   name, sir varlet.

3RD AVOCATORE: Did not the notary meet him?

VOLPONE: Not that I know.

4TH AVOCATORE: His coming will clear all.

2ND AVOCATORE: Yet it is misty.

VOLTORE: May't please your fatherhoods——

VOLPONE: [*Whispers to* Voltore] Sir, the parasite
Willed me to tell you that his master lives;
That you are still the man; your hopes the same;
And this was only a jest——

VOLTORE: How?

VOLPONE: Sir, to try
If you were firm, and how you stood affected.

VOLTORE: Art sure he lives?

VOLPONE: Do I live, sir?

VOLTORE: O me!
I was too violent.

VOLPONE: Sir, you may redeem it.
They said you were possest: fall down, and seem so:
I'll help to make it good. [*Voltore falls*] God bless
   the man!——
Stop your wind hard, and swell—See, see, see, see!
He vomits crooked pins! his eyes are set,
Like a dead hare's hung in a poulterer's shop!
His mouth's running away! Do you see, signior?
Now it is in his belly.

CORVINO: Ay, the devil!

VOLPONE: Now in his throat.

CORVINO: Ay, I perceive it plain.

VOLTORE: 'Twill out, 'twill out! stand clear. See
   where it flies,
In shape of a blue toad, with a bat's wings!

Do you not see it, sir?

CORBACCIO: What? I think I do.

CORVINO: 'Tis too manifest.

VOLPONE: Look! he comes to himself!

VOLTORE: Where am I?

VOLPONE: Take good heart, the worst is past, sir.
You are dispossest.

1ST AVOCATORE: What accident is this!

2ND AVOCATORE: Sudden, and full of wonder!

3RD AVOCATORE: If he were
Possest, as it appears, all this is nothing.

CORVINO: He has been often subject to these fits.

1ST AVOCATORE: Show him that writing:—do you
know it, sir?

VOLPONE: [Whispers to Voltore] Deny it, sir, forswear it; know it not.

VOLTORE: Yes, I do know it well, it is my hand;
But all that it contains is false.

BONARIO: O practice!

2ND AVOCATORE: What maze is this!

1ST AVOCATORE: Is he not guilty then,
Whom you there name the parasite?

VOLTORE: Grave fathers,
No more than his good patron, old Volpone.

4TH AVOCATORE: Why, he is dead.

VOLTORE: O no, my honored fathers,
He lives——

1ST AVOCATORE: How! lives?

VOLTORE: Lives.

2ND AVOCATORE: This is subtler yet!

3RD AVOCATORE: You said he was dead.

VOLTORE: Never.

3RD AVOCATORE: You said so.

CORVINO: I heard so.

4TH AVOCATORE: Here comes the gentleman; make
him way.
[Enter Mosca]

3RD AVOCATORE: A stool.

4TH AVOCATORE: A proper man; and were Volpone
dead,
A fit match for my daughter. [Aside]

3RD AVOCATORE: Give him way.

VOLPONE: Mosca, I was almost lost; the advocate
Had betrayed all; but now it is recovered;
All's on the hinge again——Say I am living. [Aside
to Mosca]

MOSCA: What busy knave is this!—Most reverend
fathers,
I sooner had attended your grave pleasures,
But that my order for the funeral
Of my dear patron did require me——

VOLPONE: Mosca! [Aside]

MOSCA: Whom I intend to bury like a gentleman.

VOLPONE: Ay, quick, and cozen me of all. [Aside]

2ND AVOCATORE: Still stranger!
More intricate!

1ST AVOCATORE: And come about again!

4TH AVOCATORE: It is a match, my daughter is
bestowed. [Aside]

MOSCA: Will you give me half? [Aside to Volpone]

VOLPONE: First I'll be hanged.

MOSCA: I know
Your voice is good, cry not so loud.

1ST AVOCATORE: Demand.
The advocate.—Sir, did you not affirm
Volpone was alive?

VOLPONE: Yes, and he is;
This gentleman told me so.—[Aside to Mosca]
Thou shalt have half.

MOSCA: Whose drunkard is this same? speak, some
that know him:
I never saw his face.—[Aside to Volpone] I cannot
now
Afford it you so cheap.

VOLPONE: No!

1ST AVOCATORE: What say you?

VOLTORE: The officer told me.

VOLPONE: I did, grave fathers,
And will maintain he lives, with mine own life,
And that this creature [points to Mosca] told me.—
[Aside] I was born
With all good stars my enemies.

MOSCA: Most grave fathers,
If such an insolence as this must pass
Upon me, I am silent; 'twas not this
For which you sent, I hope.

2ND AVOCATORE: Take him away.

VOLPONE: Mosca!

3RD AVOCATORE: Let him be whipt.

VOLPONE: Wilt thou betray me?
Cozen me?

3RD AVOCATORE: And taught to bear himself
Toward a person of his rank.

4TH AVOCATORE: Away.
[The Officers seize Volpone]

MOSCA: I humbly thank your fatherhoods.

VOLPONE: Soft, soft: Whipt!
And lose all that I have! If I confess,
It cannot be much more. [Aside]

4TH AVOCATORE: Sir, are you married?

VOLPONE: They'll be allied anon; I must be resolute;
The Fox shall here uncase. [Throws off his disguise]

MOSCA: Patron!

VOLPONE: Nay, now
My ruin shall not come alone; your match
I'll hinder sure: my substance shall not glue you,
Nor screw you into a family.

MOSCA: Why, patron!

VOLPONE: I am Volpone, and this is my knave;
[pointing to Mosca]
This [to Voltore], his own knave; this [to Corbaccio],
avarice's fool;
This [to Corvino], a chimera of wittol, fool, and
knave:
And, reverend fathers, since we all can hope
Nought but a sentence, let's not now despair it.
You hear me brief.

CORVINO: May it please your fatherhoods——

COMMANDADORI: Silence.

1ST AVOCATORE: The knot is now undone by
    miracle.

2ND AVOCATORE: Nothing can be more clear.

3RD AVOCATORE: Or can more prove
These innocent.

1ST AVOCATORE: Give them their liberty.

BONARIO: Heaven could not long let such gross
    crimes be hid.

2ND AVOCATORE: If this be held the highway to get
    riches,
May I be poor!

3RD AVOCATORE: This is not the gain, but torment.

1ST AVOCATORE: These possess wealth, as sick men
    possess fevers,
Which trulier may be said to possess them.

2ND AVOCATORE: Disrobe that parasite.

CORVINO and MOSCA: Most honored fathers——

1ST AVOCATORE: Can you plead aught to stay the
    course of justice?
If you can, speak.

CORVINO and VOLTORE: We beg favor.

CELIA: And mercy.

1ST AVOCATORE: You hurt your innocence, suing
    for the guilty.
Stand forth; and first the parasite. You appear
T'have been the chiefest minister, if not plotter,
In all these lewd impostures, and now, lastly,
Have with your impudence abused the court,
And habit of a gentleman of Venice,
Being a fellow of no birth or blood:
For which our sentence is, first, thou be whipt;
Then live a perpetual prisoner in our galleys.

VOLPONE: I thank you for him.

MOSCA: Bane to thy wolfish nature!

1ST AVOCATORE: Deliver him to the saffi. [Mosca
    is carried out] Thou, Volpone,
By blood and rank a gentleman, canst not fall
Under like censure; but our judgment on thee
Is, that thy substance all be straight confiscate
To the hospital of the Incurabili:
And since the most was gotten by imposture,
By feigning lame, gout, palsy, and such diseases,
Thou art to lie in prison, cramp'd with irons,
Till thou be'st sick and lame indeed. Remove him.

[He is taken from the bar]

VOLPONE: This is called mortifying of a Fox.

1ST AVOCATORE: Thou, Voltore, to take away the
    scandal,
Thou hast given all worthy men of thy profession,
Art banished from their fellowship, and our state.
Corbaccio!—bring him near. We here possess
Thy son of all thy state, and confine thee
To the monastery of San Spirito;
Where, since thou knewest not how to live well here,
Thou shalt be learned to die well.

CORBACCIO: Ha! what said he?

COMMANDADORI: You shall know anon, sir.

1ST AVOCATORE: Thou, Corvino, shalt
Be straight embarked from thine own house, and
    rowed
Round about Venice, through the grand canale,
Wearing a cap, with fair long ass's ears,
Instead of horns! and so to mount, a paper
Pinned on thy breast, to the Berlina.[31]

CORVINO: Yes,
And have mine eyes beat out with stinking fish,
Bruised fruit, and rotten eggs—'tis well. I am glad
I shall not see my shame yet.

2ND AVOCATORE: And to expiate
Thy wrongs done to thy wife, thou art to send her
Home to her father, with her dowry trebled:
And these are all your judgments.

ALL: Honored fathers——

1ST AVOCATORE: Which may not be revoked. Now
    you begin,
When crimes are done, and past, and to be punished
To think what your crimes are: away with them.
Let all that see these vices thus rewarded,
Take heart, and love to study 'em. Mischiefs feed
Like beasts, till they be fat, and then they bleed.

[Exeunt]

[Volpone comes forward]
"The seasoning of a play is the applause.
Now, though the Fox be punished by the laws,
He yet doth hope, there is no suffering due,
For any fact which he hath done 'gainst you;
If there be, censure him; here he doubtful stands.
If not, fare jovially, and clap your hands." [Exit]

[31] A pillory.

John Webster

(1575?–1638?)

John Webster, the most powerful dramatic poet after Shakespeare, was a misfit in his day and is still shunned more or less as a monstrosity by those who dislike too strong a reminder of human deviltry. For them the opprobrious use of the term "melodrama" is a ready defense against his kind of tragedy, and his own excesses help to convict him. But Webster's work is the last frontier of Shakespearean tragedy. When he composed his masterpiece, *The Duchess of Malfi*, Elizabethan drama had already given ground to the rather flaccid romanticism of Beaumont and Fletcher. During the first six years of their collaboration (1608–1614) Francis Beaumont and John Fletcher wrote such creditable plays as the well-known *Philaster* and that pleasant parody on the theatre *The Knight of the Burning Pestle*. But facility took control, sentimentality triumphed over tragedy, and a contrived plot displaced serious characterizations and sharp appraisals of the human condition.

John Webster fought a brief and losing battle for Jacobean or late Elizabethan high tragedy. All England was beginning to be divided into two hostile camps—the Puritans, who regarded the theatre as an abomination in the sight of the Lord, and the court, which encouraged playwrights to dissipate the vigor for which the Elizabethan theatre is renowned. "Webster," in the words of his inspired champion Rupert Brooke, "appears even mistier and grander than he really is, because he is the last of Earth, looking over a sea of saccharine."

Though Webster wrote for nearly twenty years, practically nothing is known about him except that he lived in the late sixteenth and early seventeenth centuries and collaborated industriously with Dekker, Heywood, Chapman, and other playwrights as a hireling of the manager Henslowe. Such plays as Dekker's *Northward Ho!* and *Westward Ho!* were probably merely doctored by Webster, and he may have contributed more substantially to Marston's *Malcontent* and Rowley's *A Cure for a Cuckold*. He probably wrote the best part of a strong Roman drama, *Appius and Virginia*, on which he collaborated with Thomas Heywood. Toiling for Henslowe argues poverty, and it appears that this morose playwright never enjoyed much success in the theatre. Everything else that may be said about him with some certainty must be derived from his plays. From these we may conclude that he looked at humanity with mixed feelings of cynicism and horror and that he was morbidly obsessed with death.

Webster was much possessed by death
And saw the skull beneath the skin,

runs the verse of T. S. Eliot. Webster's two dirges, "Call for the robin redbreast and the wren" and "Hark, now everything is still" are among the most nobly macabre poems in English literature.

Of the three plays which are entirely his own, the last, *The Devil's Law Case* (1620), can be dismissed as an unsuccessful attempt to write in the fashionable tragicomic vein of Fletcher. Webster's tragic genius, which was as narrow as the point of a flame, would not let him be much more than a hack writer in the foreign, though not unfrequented, field of lighter drama. Two tragedies, *The White Devil*, a drama of illicit passion probably performed in 1609 and printed in 1612, and *The Duchess of Malfi*, produced about 1612 and first published in 1623, represent his chief claim to recognition. Together with *The Changeling* (1622), by Middleton and Rowley, and *'Tis Pity She's a Whore* (published in 1633), by John Ford, Webster's two major works are last testaments of the Elizabethan-Jacobean tragic spirit.

Webster's plays were not suited for performance in the centuries that followed their first production, although his tragedies were adapted in the early eighteenth century. But the English romanticists felt a kinship to him. Charles Lamb's tribute to *The Duchess of Malfi* was generous and just: "To move a horror skilfully, to touch a soul to the quick, to lay upon fear as much as it can bear, to wean and weary a life till it is ready to drop, and then step in with mortal instruments to take its last forfeit: this only a Webster can do." In our time, universities have performed his tragedies, and the Phoenix Society of London gave *The Duchess* a notable production in 1919. An inadequate New York production in 1947, with Elisabeth Bergner playing the Duchess, won no esteem for the play.

Although *The White Devil* is a more original and energetic play, Webster reached the zenith of his flawed but formidable art, according to many of his admirers, in *The Duchess of Malfi*. Only Shakespeare and, to some extent, Marlowe equal the tragic utterance of this grotesque and technically weak but touching play, which piles terror upon terror and attains sublimity in defiance of all the rules of good taste. In stripping the mask from power and sanctimony the play may perhaps be said to point a moral, to constitute a kind of *reductio ad absurdum* of Renaissance ruthlessness and individualism. But it is essentially a timeless nightmare in which "human beings are writhing grubs in an immense night"; though, as the author of this statement, Rupert Brooke, did not observe, the night is of their own making. However, in looking into Webster's world, which he himself called a "deep pit of darkness," we should be observing his and tragedy's power only partly if we did not see certain triumphs of the human spirit from time to time—in the nobility of the victimized Duchess who dared to marry a man beneath her in station, in men's ultimate power to distinguish between good and evil, and in the realization that there is a retributive justice in the world and in our consciences. The last words of the good woman's brother and tormentor, Duke Ferdinand, are

> Whether we fall by ambition, blood, or lust,
> Like diamonds we are cut with our own dust;

and the concluding scene looks forward to a re-establishment of sanity and humane order. In the forged language of Webster's lines and in the direction of both his thought and action he creates terror for the sake of enlightenment and not for mere sensationalism. He gives us the melodrama of life rather than that of the stage, and he indicates what humanity should be by showing what it should not be. He is a tragic poet rather than a "melodramatist."

Webster's talent bears a close resemblance to Shakespeare's genius in the latter's mature tragedies, especially *King Lear*. Webster sounded the same note of despair concerning humanity. He also possessed some of Shakespeare's sharp discrimination between good and evil; he brought an almost puritanical or, at least, old Roman moral sense to his characterization. Above all, the author of *The Duchess of Malfi* was a master of turbulent passion and extreme anguish. He combined horror with pathos, and he expressed both with remarkably concentrated tension in dramatic poetry which, at its best, is surpassed only by Shakespeare's mature blank verse. Webster's plot may be snarled, but his vision is clear.

THE DUCHESS OF MALFI

By John Webster

DRAMATIS PERSONAE

FERDINAND, *Duke of Calabria*
THE CARDINAL, *his brother*
ANTONIO BOLOGNA, *steward of the household to the Duchess*
DELIO, *his friend*
DANIEL DE BOSOLA, *gentleman of the horse to the Duchess*
CASTRUCCIO
MARQUIS OF PESCARA
COUNT MALATESTI

RODERIGO
SILVIO
GRISOLAN
DOCTOR
DUCHESS OF MALFI
CARIOLA, *her woman*
JULIA, *Castruccio's wife, and the Cardinal's mistress*
OLD LADY, LADIES, AND CHILDREN
SEVERAL MADMEN, PILGRIMS, EXECUTIONERS, OFFICERS, ATTENDANTS, &C.

SCENE: *Malfi, Rome, and Milan*

ACT I. SCENE I.

The presence-chamber in the Duchess' *palace at Malfi.*

[*Enter* Antonio *and* Delio]

DELIO: You are welcome to your country, dear Antonio;
You have been long in France, and you return
A very formal Frenchman in your habit:
How do you like the French court?

ANTONIO: I admire it:
In seeking to reduce both state and people
To a fixed order, their judicious king
Begins at home; quits first his royal palace
Of flattering sycophants, of dissolute
And infamous persons,—which he sweetly terms
His master's master-piece, the work of Heaven:
Considering duly that a prince's court
Is like a common fountain, whence should flow
Pure silver drops in general, but if't chance
Some cursed example poison't near the head,
Death and diseases through the whole land spread.
And what is't makes this blessed government
But a most provident council, who dare freely
Inform him the corruption of the times?
Though some o' the court hold it presumption
To instruct princes what they ought to do,
It is a noble duty to inform them
What they ought to foresee.—Here comes Bosola,
The only court-gall; yet I observe his railing
Is not for simple love of piety:
Indeed, he rails at those things which he wants;
Would be as lecherous, covetous, or proud,
Bloody, or envious, as any man,
If he had means to be so.—Here's the cardinal.

[*Enter the* Cardinal *and* Bosola]

BOSOLA: I do haunt you still.

CARDINAL: So.

BOSOLA: I have done you better service than to be slighted thus. Miserable age, where only the reward of doing well is the doing of it!

CARDINAL: You enforce your merit too much.

BOSOLA: I fell into the galleys in your service; where, for two years together, I wore two towels instead of a shirt, with a knot on the shoulder, after the fashion of a Roman mantle. Slighted thus! I will thrive some way: blackbirds fatten best in hard weather; why not I in these dog-days?

CARDINAL: Would you could become honest!

BOSOLA: With all your divinity do but direct me the way to it. I have known many travel far for it, and yet return as arrant knaves as they went forth, because they carried themselves always along with them. [*Exit* Cardinal] Are you gone? Some fellows, they say, are possessed with the devil, but this great fellow were able to possess the greatest devil, and make him worse.

ANTONIO: He hath denied thee some suit?

BOSOLA: He and his brother are like plum-trees that grow crooked over standing-pools; they are rich and o'er-laden with fruit, but none but crows, pies, and caterpillars feed on them. Could I be one of their flattering panders, I would hang on their ears like a horseleech, till I were full, and then drop off. I pray, leave me. Who would rely upon these miserable dependancies, in expectation to be advanced to-morrow? what creatures ever fed worse than hoping Tantalus?[1] nor ever died any man more fearfully than he had hoped for a pardon. There are rewards for hawks and dogs when they have done us service; but for a soldier that hazards his limbs in a battle, nothing but a kind of geometry is his last supportation.

DELIO: Geometry!

BOSOLA: Ay, to hang in a fair pair of slings, take

[1] Legendary king whose punishment it was in the lower world to be unable to slake his thirst and allay his hunger.

his latter swing in the world upon an honorable pair of crutches, from hospital to hospital. Fare ye well, sir: and yet do not you scorn us; for places in the court are but like beds in the hospital, where this man's head lies at that man's foot, and so lower and lower. [*Exit*]

DELIO: I knew this fellow seven years in the galleys
For a notorious murder; and 'twas thought
The cardinal suborned it: he was released
By the French general, Gaston de Foix,
When he recovered Naples.

ANTONIO: 'Tis great pity
He should be thus neglected: I have heard
He's very valiant. This foul melancholy
Will poison all his goodness; for, I'll tell you,
If too immoderate sleep be truly said
To be an inward rust into the soul,
It then doth follow want of action
Breeds all black malcontents; and their close rearing,
Like moths in cloth, do hurt for want of wearing.

DELIO: The presence 'gins to fill: you promised me
To make me the partaker of the natures
Of some of your great courtiers.

ANTONIO: The lord cardinal's,
And other strangers' that are now in court?
I shall.—Here comes the great Calabrian duke.

[*Enter Ferdinand, Castruccio, Silvio, Roderigo, Grisolan, and Attendants*]

FERDINAND: Who took the ring oftenest?

SILVIO: Antonio Bologna, my lord.

FERDINAND: Our sister duchess' great-master of her household? give him the jewel.—When shall we leave this sportive action, and fall to action indeed?

CASTRUCCIO: Methinks, my lord, you should not desire to go to war in person.

FERDINAND: Now for some gravity:—why, my lord?

CASTRUCCIO: It is fitting a soldier arise to be a prince, but not necessary a prince descend to be a captain.

FERDINAND: No?

CASTRUCCIO: No, my lord; he were far better do it by a deputy.

FERDINAND: Why should he not as well sleep or eat by a deputy? this might take idle, offensive, and base office from him, whereas the other deprives him of honor.

CASTRUCCIO: Believe my experience, that realm is never long in quiet where the ruler is a soldier.

FERDINAND: Thou toldest me thy wife could not endure fighting.

CASTRUCCIO: True, my lord.

FERDINAND: And of a jest she broke of a captain she met full of wounds: I have forgot it.

CASTRUCCIO: She told him, my lord, he was a pitiful fellow, to lie, like the children of Ismael, all in tents.[2]

FERDINAND: Why, there's a wit were able to undo

[2] A play upon the word "tent," which means also a bandage.

all the surgeons o' the city; for although gallants should quarrel, and had drawn their weapons, and were ready to go to it, yet her persuasions would make them put up.

CASTRUCCIO: That she would, my lord.—How do you like my Spanish gennet?

RODERIGO: He is all fire.

FERDINAND: I am of Pliny's opinion,[3] I think he was begot by the wind; he runs as if he were ballasted with quicksilver.

SILVIO: True, my lord, he reels from the tilt often.

RODERIGO *and* GRISOLAN: Ha! ha! ha!

FERDINAND: Why do you laugh? methinks you that are courtiers should be my touchwood, take fire when I give fire; that is, laugh but when I laugh, were the subject never so witty.

CASTRUCCIO: True, my lord: I myself have heard a very good jest, and have scorned to seem to have so silly a wit as to understand it.

FERDINAND: But I can laugh at your fool, my lord.

CASTRUCCIO: He cannot speak, you know, but he makes faces: my lady cannot abide him.

FERDINAND: No?

CASTRUCCIO: Nor endure to be in merry company; for she says too much laughing, and too much company, fills her too full of the wrinkle.

FERDINAND: I would, then, have a mathematical instrument made for her face, that she might not laugh out of compass.—I shall shortly visit you at Milan, Lord Silvio.

SILVIO: Your grace shall arrive most welcome.

FERDINAND: You are a good horseman, Antonio: you have excellent riders in France: what do you think of good horsemanship?

ANTONIO: Nobly, my lord: as out of the Grecian horse issued many famous princes, so out of brave horsemanship arise the first sparks of growing resolution that raise the mind to noble action.

FERDINAND: You have bespoke it worthily.

SILVIO: Your brother, the lord cardinal, and sister duchess.

[*Re-enter Cardinal, with Duchess, Cariola, and Julia*]

CARDINAL: Are the galleys come about?

GRISOLAN: They are, my lord.

FERDINAND: Here's the Lord Silvio is come to take his leave.

DELIO: Now, sir, your promise; what's that cardinal?
I mean his temper? they say he's a brave fellow,
Will play his five thousand crowns at tennis, dance,
Court ladies, and one that hath fought single combats.

ANTONIO: Some such flashes superficially hang on him for form; but observe his inward character: he is a melancholy churchman; the spring in his face is nothing but the engendering of toads; where he is jealous of any man, he lays worse plots for them

[3] Pliny the Elder (23–79 A.D.), Roman naturalist, whose *Historia Naturalis* was a source of information and misinformation until the rise of modern science.

than ever was imposed on Hercules, for he strews
in his way flatterers, panders, intelligencers, atheists,
and a thousand such political monsters. He should
have been Pope; but instead of coming to it by the
primitive decency of the church, he did bestow bribes
so largely and so impudently as if he would have
carried it away without Heaven's knowledge. Some
good he hath done—

DELIO: You have given too much of him. What's
his brother?

ANTONIO: The duke there? a most perverse and
turbulent nature;
What appears in him mirth is merely outside;
If he laugh heartily, it is to laugh
All honesty out of fashion.

DELIO: Twins?

ANTONIO: In quality.
He speaks with others' tongues, and hears men's
suits
With others' ears; will seem to sleep o' the bench
Only to entrap offenders in their answers;
Dooms men to death by information;
Rewards by hearsay.

DELIO: Then the law to him
Is like a foul black cobweb to a spider,—
He makes it his dwelling and a prison
To entangle those shall feed him.

ANTONIO: Most true:
He never pays debts unless they be shrewd turns,
And those he will confess that he doth owe.
Last, for his brother there, the cardinal,
They that do flatter him most say oracles
Hang at his lips; and verily I believe them,
For the devil speaks in them.
But for their sister, the right noble duchess,
You never fixed your eye on three fair medals
Cast in one figure, of so different temper.
For her discourse, it is so full of rapture,
You only will begin then to be sorry
When she doth end her speech, and wish, in wonder,
She held it less vain-glory to talk much,
Than your penance to hear her: whilst she speaks,
She throws upon a man so sweet a look,
That it were able to raise one to a galliard⁴
That lay in a dead palsy, and to dote
On that sweet countenance; but in that look
There speaketh so divine a continence
As cuts off all lascivious and vain hope.
Her days are practised in such noble virtue,
That sure her nights, nay, more, her very sleeps,
Are more in Heaven than other ladies' shrifts.
Let all sweet ladies break their flattering glasses,
And dress themselves in her.

DELIO: Fie, Antonio,
You play the wire-drawer with her commendations.

ANTONIO: I'll case the picture up: only thus much;
All her particular worth grows to this sum,—
She stains the time past, lights the time to come.

CARIOLA: You must attend my lady in the gallery,

⁴ A dance.

Some half an hour hence.

ANTONIO: I shall.
[Exeunt Antonio and Delio]

FERDINAND: Sister, I have a suit to you.

DUCHESS: To me, sir?

FERDINAND: A gentleman here, Daniel de Bosola,
One that was in the galleys—

DUCHESS: Yes, I know him.

FERDINAND: A worthy fellow he is: pray, let me
entreat for
The provisorship of your horse.⁵

DUCHESS: Your knowledge of him
Commends him and prefers him.

FERDINAND: Call him hither.
[Exit Attendant]
We are now upon parting. Good Lord Silvio,
Do us commend to all our noble friends
At the leaguer.⁶

SILVIO: Sir, I shall.

FERDINAND: You are for Milan?

SILVIO: I am.

DUCHESS: Bring the caroches.⁷ We'll bring you
down to the haven.
[Exeunt Duchess, Silvio, Castruccio, Roderigo,
Grisolan, Cariola, Julia, and Attendants]

CARDINAL: Be sure you entertain that Bosola
For your intelligence: I would not be seen in't;
And therefore many times I have slighted him
When he did court our furtherance, as this morning.

FERDINAND: Antonio, the great-master of her
household,
Had been far fitter.

CARDINAL: You are deceived in him:
His nature is too honest for such business.—
He comes: I'll leave you. [Exit]
[Re-enter Bosola]

BOSOLA: I was lured to you.

FERDINAND: My brother, here, the cardinal, could
never
Abide you.

BOSOLA: Never since he was in my debt.

FERDINAND: May be some oblique character in your
face
Made him suspect you.

BOSOLA: Doth he study physiognomy?
There's no more credit to be given to the face
Than to a sick man's urine, which some call
The physician's whore because she cozens him.
He did suspect me wrongfully.

FERDINAND: For that
You must give great men leave to take their times.
Distrust doth cause us seldom be deceived:
You see the oft shaking of the cedar-tree
Fastens it more at root.

BOSOLA: Yet, take heed;
For to suspect a friend unworthily

⁵ Stewardship of her horses; perhaps command of her
cavalry.
⁶ Camp; from the German *Lager*.
⁷ Stately carriages.

Instructs him the next way to suspect you,
And prompts him to deceive you.
  FERDINAND: There's gold.
  BOSOLA: So:
What follows? never rained such showers as these
Without thunderbolts i' the tail of them: whose throat
    must I cut?
  FERDINAND: Your inclination to shed blood rides
    post
Before my occasion to use you. I give you that
To live i' the court here, and observe the duchess;
To note all the particulars of her havior,
What suitors do solicit her for marriage,
And whom she best affects. She's a young widow:
I would not have her marry again.
  BOSOLA: No, sir?
  FERDINAND: Do not you ask the reason; but be
    satisfied
I say I would not.
  BOSOLA: It seems you would create me
One of your familiars.
  FERDINAND: Familiar! what's that?
  BOSOLA: Why, a very quaint invisible devil in flesh,
An intelligencer.
  FERDINAND: Such a kind of thriving thing
I would wish thee; and ere long thou mayest arrive
At a higher place by't.
  BOSOLA: Take your devils,
Which hell calls angels; these cursed gifts would make
You a corrupter, me an impudent traitor;
And should I take these, they'd take me to hell.
  FERDINAND: Sir, I'll take nothing from you that I
    have given:
There is a place that I procured for you
This morning, the provisorship o' the horse;
Have you heard on't?
  BOSOLA: No.
  FERDINAND: 'Tis yours: is't not worth thanks?
  BOSOLA: I would have you curse yourself now, that
    your bounty
(Which makes men truly noble) e'er should make me
A villain. O, that to avoid ingratitude
For the good deed you have done me, I must do
All the ill man can invent! Thus the devil
Candies all sins o'er; and what Heaven terms vile,
That names he complimental.
  FERDINAND: Be yourself;
Keep your old garb of melancholy; 'twill express
You envy those that stand above your reach,
Yet strive not to come near 'em: this will gain
Access to private lodgings, where yourself
May, like a politic dormouse—
  BOSOLA: As I have seen some
Feed in a lord's dish, half asleep, not seeming
To listen to any talk; and yet these rogues
Have cut his throat in a dream. What's my place?
The provisorship o' the horse? say, then, my corrup-
    tion
Grew out of horse-dung: I am your creature.
  FERDINAND: Away!

  BOSOLA: Let good men, for good deeds, covet good
    fame,
Since place and riches oft are bribes of shame:
Sometimes the devil doth preach. [Exit]
  [Re-enter Duchess, Cardinal, and Cariola]
  CARDINAL: We are to part from you; and your own
    discretion
Must now be your director.
  FERDINAND: You are a widow:
You know already what man is; and therefore '
Let not youth, high promotion, eloquence—
  CARDINAL: No,
Nor any thing without the addition, honor,
Sway your high blood.
  FERDINAND: Marry! they are most luxurious[8]
Will wed twice.
  CARDINAL: O, fie!
  FERDINAND: Their livers are more spotted
Than Laban's sheep.
  DUCHESS: Diamonds are of most value,
They say, that have passed through most jewelers'
    hands.
  FERDINAND: Whores by that rule are precious.
  DUCHESS: Will you hear me?
I'll never marry.
  CARDINAL: So most widows say;
But commonly that motion lasts no longer
Than the turning of an hour-glass: the funeral
    sermon
And it end both together.
  FERDINAND: Now hear me:
You live in a rank pasture, here, i' the court;
There is a kind of honey-dew that's deadly;
'Twill poison your fame; look to't: be not cunning;
For they whose faces do belie their hearts
Are witches ere they arrive at twenty years,
Ay, and give the devil suck.
  DUCHESS: This is terrible good counsel.
  FERNINAND: Hypocrisy is woven of a fine small
    thread,
Subtler than Vulcan's engine:[9] yet, believe't,
Your darkest actions, nay, your privat'st thoughts,
Will come to light.
  CARDINAL: You may flatter yourself,
And take your own choice; privately be married
Under the eves of night—
  FERDINAND: Think't the best voyage
That e'er you made; like the irregular crab,
Which, though't goes backward, thinks that it **goes**
    right
Because it goes its own way; but observe,
Such weddings may more properly be said
To be executed than celebrated.
  CARDINAL: The marriage night
Is the entrance into some prison.
  FERDINAND: And those joys,
Those lustful pleasures, are like heavy **sleeps**
Which do fore-run man's mischief.
  [8] Lecherous.
  [9] The net which held Mars and Venus.

CARDINAL: Fare you well.
Wisdom begins at the end: remember it. [*Exit*]
DUCHESS: I think this speech between you both
    was studied,
It came so roundly off.
FERDINAND: You are my sister;
This was my father's poniard, do you see?
I'd be loth to see't look rusty, 'cause 'twas his.
I would have you give o'er these chargeable revels:
A visor and a mask are whispering-rooms
That were never built for goodness;—fare ye well;—
And women like that part which, like the lamprey,
Hath never a bone in't.
DUCHESS: Fie, sir!
FERDINAND: Nay,
I mean the tongue; variety of courtship:
What cannot a neat knave with a smooth tale
Make a woman believe? Farewell, lusty widow. [*Exit*]
DUCHESS: Shall this move me? If all my royal
    kindred
Lay in my way unto this marriage,
I'd make them my low footsteps: and even now,
Even in this hate, as men in some great battles,
By apprehending danger, have achieved
Almost impossible actions (I have heard soldiers say
    so),
So I through frights and threatenings will assay
This dangerous venture. Let old wives report
I winked and chose a husband.—Cariola,
To thy known secrecy I have given up
More than my life—my fame.
CARIOLA: Both shall be safe;
For I'll conceal this secret from the world
As warily as those that trade in poison
Keep poison from their children.
DUCHESS: Thy protestation
Is ingenious and hearty: I believe it.
Is Antonio come?
CARIOLA: He attends you.
DUCHESS: Good, dear soul,
Leave me; but place thyself behind the arras,
Where thou mayst overhear us. Wish me good speed;
For I am going into a wilderness
Where I shall find nor path nor friendly clue
To be my guide.
    [Cariola *goes behind the arras*[10]]
    [*Enter* Antonio]
            I sent for you: sit down;
Take pen and ink, and write: are you ready?
ANTONIO: Yes.
DUCHESS: What did I say?
ANTONIO: That I should write somewhat.
DUCHESS: O, I remember.
After these triumphs and this large expense,
It's fit, like thrifty husbands, we inquire
What's laid up for to-morrow.
ANTONIO: So please your beauteous excellence.
DUCHESS: Beauteous!
Indeed, I thank you: I look young for your sake;
    [10] The curtain of the Elizabethan inner stage.

You have ta'en my cares upon you.
ANTONIO: I'll fetch your grace
The particulars of your revenue and expense.
DUCHESS: O, you are
An upright treasurer: but you mistook;
For when I said I meant to make inquiry
What's laid up for to-morrow, I did mean
What's laid up yonder for me.
ANTONIO: Where?
DUCHESS: In Heaven.
I am making my will (as 'tis fit princes should,
In perfect memory), and, I pray, sir, tell me,
Were not one better make it smiling, thus,
Than in deep groans and terrible ghastly looks,
As if the gifts we parted with procured
That violent distraction?
ANTONIO: O, much better.
DUCHESS: If I had a husband now, this care were
    quit:
But I intend to make you overseer.
What good deed shall we first remember? say.
ANTONIO: Begin with that first good deed began i'
    the world
After man's creation, the sacrament of marriage:
I'd have you first provide for a good husband;
Give him all.
DUCHESS: All!
ANTONIO: Yes, your excellent self.
DUCHESS: In a winding-sheet?
ANTONIO: In a couple.
DUCHESS: Saint Winifred, that were a strange will!
ANTONIO: 'Twere stranger if there were no will in
    you
To marry again.
DUCHESS: What do you think of marriage?
ANTONIO: I take't, as those that deny purgatory,
It locally contains or Heaven or hell;
There's no third place in't.
DUCHESS: How do you affect it?
ANTONIO: My banishment, feeding my melancholy,
Would often reason thus.
DUCHESS: Pray, let's hear it.
ANTONIO: Say a man never marry, nor have chil-
    dren,
What takes that from him? only the bare name
Of being a father, or the weak delight
To see the little wanton ride a-cock-horse
Upon a painted stick, or hear him chatter
Light a taught starling.
DUCHESS: Fie, fie, what's all this?
One of your eyes is blood-shot; use my ring to't,
They say 'tis very sovereign: 'twas my wedding-ring,
And I did vow never to part with it
But to my second husband.
ANTONIO: You have parted with it now.
DUCHESS: Yes, to help your eye-sight.
ANTONIO: You have made me stark blind.
DUCHESS: How?
ANTONIO: There is a saucy and ambitious devil
Is dancing in this circle.

DUCHESS: Remove him.

ANTONIO: How?

DUCHESS: There needs small conjuration, when your finger
May do it: thus; is it fit?

[*She puts the ring upon his finger; he kneels*]

ANTONIO: What said you?

DUCHESS: Sir,
This goodly roof of yours is too low built;
I cannot stand upright in't nor discourse,
Without I raise it higher: raise yourself;
Or, if you please, my hand to help you: so. [*Raises him*]

ANTONIO: Ambition, madam, is a great man's madness,
That is not kept in chains and close-pent rooms,
But in fair lightsome lodgings, and is girt
With the wild noise of prattling visitants,
Which makes it lunatic beyond all cure.
Conceive not I am so stupid but I aim
Whereto your favors tend: but he's a fool
That, being a-cold, would thrust his hands i' the fire
To warm them.

DUCHESS: So, now the ground's broke,
You may discover what a wealthy mine
I make you lord of.

ANTONIO: O my unworthiness!

DUCHESS: You were ill to sell yourself:
This darkening of your worth is not like that
Which tradesmen use i' the city; their false lights
Are to rid bad wares off: and I must tell you,
If you will know where breathes a complete man
(I speak it without flattery), turn your eyes,
And progress through yourself.

ANTONIO: Were there nor Heaven nor hell,
I should be honest: I have long served virtue,
And ne'er ta'en wages of her.

DUCHESS: Now she pays it.
The misery of us that are born great!
We are forced to woo, because none dare woo us;
And as a tyrant doubles with his words,
And fearfully equivocates, so we
Are forced to express our violent passions
In riddles and in dreams, and leave the path
Of simple virtue, which was never made
To seem the thing it is not. Go, go brag
You have left me heartless: mine is in your bosom:
I hope 'twill multiply love there. You do tremble:
Make not your heart so dead a piece of flesh,
To fear more than to love me. Sir, be confident:
What is't distracts you? This is flesh and blood, sir;
'Tis not the figure cut in alabaster
Kneels at my husband's tomb. Awake, awake, man!
I do here put off all vain ceremony,
And only do appear to you a young widow
That claims you for her husband, and, like a widow,
I use but half a blush in't.

ANTONIO: Truth speak for me;
I will remain the constant sanctuary
Of your good name.

DUCHESS: I thank you, gentle love:
And 'cause you shall not come to me in debt,
Being now my steward, here upon your lips
I sign your *Quietus est.*[11] This you should have begged now:
I have seen children oft eat sweetmeats thus,
As fearful to devour them too soon.

ANTONIO: But for your brothers?

DUCHESS: Do not think of them:
All discord without this circumference
Is only to be pitied, and not feared:
Yet, should they know it, time will easily
Scatter the tempest.

ANTONIO: These words should be mine,
And all the parts you have spoke, if some part of it
Would not have savored flattery.

DUCHESS: Kneel.

[Cariola *comes from behind the arras*]

ANTONIO: Ha!

DUCHESS: Be not amazed; this woman's of my counsel:
I have heard lawyers say, a contract in a chamber
Per verba presenti is absolute marriage.

[*She and* Antonio *kneel*]

Bless, Heaven, this sacred gordian, which let violence
Never untwine!

ANTONIO: And may our sweet affections, like the spheres,
Be still in motion!

DUCHESS: Quickening, and make
The like soft music!

ANTONIO: That we may imitate the loving palms,
Best emblem of a peaceful marriage,
That never bore fruit, divided!

DUCHESS: What can the church force more?

ANTONIO: That fortune may not know an accident,
Either of joy or sorrow, to divide
Our fixèd wishes!

DUCHESS: How can the church build faster?
We now are man and wife, and 'tis the church
That must but echo this.—Maid, stand apart:
I now am blind.

ANTONIO: What's your conceit in this?

DUCHESS: I would have you lead your fortune by the hand
Unto your marriage bed
(You speak in me this, for we now are one):
We'll only lie, and talk together, and plot
To appease my humorous kindred; and if you please,
Like the old tale in Alexander and Lodowick,[12]
Lay a naked sword between us, keep us chaste.
O, let me shroud my blushes in your bosom,
Since 'tis the treasury of all my secrets!

[11] Discharge.

[12] The heroes of an English ballad based on the medieval tale *Amis and Amiloun*; extraordinarily faithful friends who look alike. One friend marries a princess in behalf of the other but places a naked sword between himself and the bride in the marriage bed.

[*Exeunt* Duchess *and* Antonio]

CARIOLA: Whether the spirit of greatness or of
   woman
Reign most in her, I know not; but it shows
A fearful madness: I owe her much of pity. [*Exit*]

ACT II. SCENE I.

An apartment in the palace of the Duchess.

[*Enter* Bosola *and* Castruccio]

BOSOLA: You say you would fain be taken for an
eminent courtier?

CASTRUCCIO: 'Tis the very main of my ambition.

BOSOLA: Let me see: you have a reasonable good
face for't already, and your nightcap expresses your
ears sufficient largely. I would have you learn to twirl
the strings of your band with a good grace, and in a
set speech, at the end of every sentence, to hum
three or four times, or blow your nose till it smart
again, to recover your memory. When you come to
be a president in criminal causes, if you smile upon
a prisoner, hang him but if you frown upon him and
threaten him, let him be sure to scape the gallows.

CASTRUCCIO: I would be a very merry president.

BOSOLA: Do not sup o' nights; 'twill beget you an
admirable wit.

CASTRUCCIO: Rather it would make me have a good
stomach to quarrel; for they say, your roaring boys[13]
eat meat seldom, and that makes them so valiant. But
how shall I know whether the people take me for an
eminent fellow?

BOSOLA: I will teach a trick to know it: give out
you lie a-dying, and if you hear the common people
curse you, be sure you are taken for one of the
prime nightcaps.[14]

[*Enter an* Old Lady]
You come from painting now.

OLD LADY: From what?

BOSOLA: Why, from your scurvy face-physic. To
behold thee not painted inclines somewhat near a
miracle; these in thy face here were deep ruts and
foul sloughs the last progress.[15] There was a lady in
France that, having had the small-pox, flayed the skin
off her face to make it more level; and whereas before
she looked like a nutmeg-grater, after she resembled
an abortive hedge-hog.

OLD LADY: Do you call this painting?

BOSOLA: No, no, but you call it careening of an
old morphewed lady, to make her disembogue[16]
again: there's rough-cast phrase to your plastic.

OLD LADY: It seems you are well acquainted with
my closet.

BOSOLA: One would suspect it for a shop of witchcraft, to find in it the fat of serpents, spawn of

[13] Bullies.
[14] Lawyers.
[15] As though a state procession had driven across it.
[16] Morphewed: scaly; disembogue: empty.

snakes, Jews' spittle, and their young children's
ordure; and all these for the face. I would sooner
eat a dead pigeon taken from the soles of the feet
of one sick of the plague than kiss one of you fasting.
Here are two of you, whose sin of your youth is the
very patrimony of the physician; makes him renew
his footcloth with the spring, and change his high-
priced courtezan with the fall of the leaf. I do wonder
you do not loathe yourselves. Observe my meditation
now.
What thing is in this outward form of man
To be beloved? We account it ominous,
If nature do produce a colt, or lamb,
A fawn, or goat, in any limb resembling
A man, and fly from't as a prodigy:
Man stands amazed to see his deformity
In any other creature but himself.
But in our own flesh, though we bear diseases
Which have their true names only ta'en from beasts,—
As the most ulcerous wolf and swinish measle,—
Though we are eaten up of lice and worms,
And though continually we bear about us
A rotten and dead body, we delight
To hide it in rich tissue: all our fear,
Nay, all our terror, is lest our physician
Should put us in the ground to be made sweet.—
Your wife's gone to Rome: you two couple, and get
you to the wells at Lucca to recover your aches. I
have other work on foot.

[*Exeunt* Castruccio *and* Old Lady]
I observe our duchess
Is sick a-days, she pukes, her stomach seethes,
The fins of her eye-lids look most teeming blue,
She wanes i' the cheek, and waxes fat i' the flank,
And, contrary to our Italian fashion,
Wears a loose-bodied gown: there's somewhat in't.
I have a trick may chance discover it,
A pretty one; I have bought some apricocks,
The first our spring yields.

[*Enter* Antonio *and* Delio]

DELIO: And so long since married!
You amaze me.

ANTONIO: Let me seal your lips for ever:
For, did I think that any thing but the air
Could carry these words from you, I should wish
You had no breath at all.—Now, sir, in your con-
   templation?
You are studying to become a great wise fellow.

BOSOLA: O, sir, the opinion of wisdom is a foul
tether that runs all over a man's body: if simplicity
direct us to have no evil, it directs us to a happy
being; for the subtlest folly proceeds from the subtlest wisdom: let me be simply honest.

ANTONIO: I do understand your inside.

BOSOLA: Do you so?

ANTONIO: Because you would not seem to appear
   to the world
Puffed up with your preferment, you continue
This out-of-fashion melancholy: leave it, leave it.

BOSOLA: Give me leave to be honest in any phrase,

in any compliment whatsoever. Shall I confess myself
to you? I look no higher than I can reach: they are
the gods that must ride on winged horses. A lawyer's
mule of a slow pace will both suit my disposition and
business; for, mark me, when a man's mind rides
faster than his horse can gallop, they quickly both
tire.

ANTONIO: You would look up to Heaven, but I
think
The devil, that rules i' the air, stands in your light.

BOSOLA: O, sir, you are lord of the ascendant, chief
man with the duchess; a duke was your cousin-
german[17] removed. Say you are lineally descended
from King Pepin, or he himself, what of this? search
the heads of the greatest rivers in the world, you shall
find them but bubbles of water. Some would think the
souls of princes were brought forth by some more
weighty cause than those of meaner persons: they are
deceived, there's the same hand to them; the like passions sway them; the same reason that makes a vicar
to go to law for a tithe-pig, and undo his neighbors,
makes them spoil a whole province, and batter down
goodly cities with the cannon.

[Enter Duchess and Ladies]

DUCHESS: Your arm, Antonio: do I not grow fat?
I am exceeding short-winded.—Bosola,
I would have you, sir, provide for me a litter;
Such a one as the Duchess of Florence rode in.

BOSOLA: The duchess used one when she was great
with child.

DUCHESS: I think she did.—Come hither, mend my
ruff;
Here, when? thou art such a tedious lady; and
Thy breath smells of lemon-pills; would thou hadst
done!
Shall I swoon under thy fingers! I am
So troubled with the mother![18]

BOSOLA: [Aside] I fear too much.

DUCHESS: I have heard you say that the French
courtiers
Wear their hats on 'fore the king.

ANTONIO: I have seen it.

DUCHESS: In the presence?

ANTONIO: Yes.

DUCHESS: Why should not we bring up that
fashion!
'Tis ceremony more than duty that consists
In the removing of a piece of felt:
Be you the example to the rest o' the court;
Put on your hat first.

ANTONIO: You must pardon me:
I have seen, in colder countries than in France,
Nobles stand bare to the prince; and the distinction
Methought showed reverently.

BOSOLA: I have a present for your grace.

DUCHESS: For me, sir?

BOSOLA: Apricocks, madam.

DUCHESS: O, sir, where are they?

17 First cousin.
18 Hysteria.

I have heard of none to-year.

BOSOLA: [Aside] Good; her color rises.

DUCHESS: Indeed, I thank you: they are wondrous
fair ones.
What an unskilful fellow is our gardener!
We shall have none this month.

BOSOLA: Will not your grace pare them?

DUCHESS: No: they taste of musk, methinks; indeed they do.

BOSOLA: I know not: yet I wish your grace had
pared 'em.

DUCHESS: Why?

BOSOLA: I forgot to tell you, the knave gardener,
Only to raise his profit by them the sooner,
Did ripen them in horse-dung.

DUCHESS: O, you jest—
You shall judge: pray taste one.

ANTONIO: Indeed, madam,
I do not love the fruit.

DUCHESS: Sir, you are loth
To rob us of our dainties: 'tis a delicate fruit;
They say they are restorative.

BOSOLA: 'Tis a pretty art,
This grafting.

DUCHESS: 'Tis so; bettering of nature.

BOSOLA: To make a pippin grow upon a crab,
A damson[19] on a blackthorn.—[Aside] How greedily
she eats them!
A whirlwind strike off these bawd farthingales![20]
For, but for that and the loose-bodied gown,
I should have discovered apparently
The young springal cutting a caper in her belly.

DUCHESS: I thank you, Bosola: they are right good
ones,
If they do not make me sick.

ANTONIO: How now, madam!

DUCHESS: This green fruit and my stomach are not
friends:
How they swell me!

BOSOLA: [Aside] Nay, you are too much swelled
already.

DUCHESS: O, I am in an extreme cold sweat!

BOSOLA: I am very sorry.

DUCHESS: Lights to my chamber!—O good Antonio, I fear I am undone!

DELIO: Lights there, lights!
[Exeunt Duchess and Ladies.—Exit, on the other
side, Bosola]

ANTONIO: O my trusty Delio, we are lost!
I fear she's fall'n in labor; and there's left
No time for her remove.

DELIO: Have you prepared
Those ladies to attend her? and procured
That politic safe conveyance for the midwife
Your duchess plotted?

ANTONIO: I have.

DELIO: Make use, then, of this forced occasion:
Give out that Bosola hath poisoned her

19 Plum.
20 Hooped petticoats.

With these apricocks; that will give some color
For her keeping close.

ANTONIO: Fie, fie, the physicians
Will then flock to her.

DELIO: For that you may pretend
She'll use some prepared antidote of her own,
Lest the physicians should re-poison her.

ANTONIO: I am lost in amazement: I know not what
    to think on't.
    [Exeunt]

SCENE II.

A hall in the same palace.

[Enter Bosola]

BOSOLA: So, so, there's no question but her techiness and most vulturous eating of the apricocks are apparent signs of breeding.
    [Enter an Old Lady]
Now?

OLD LADY: I am in haste, sir.

BOSOLA: There was a young waiting-woman had a monstrous desire to see the glass-house—

OLD LADY: Nay, pray let me go.

BOSOLA: And it was only to know what strange instrument it was should swell up a glass to the fashion of a woman's belly.

OLD LADY: I will hear no more of the glass-house. You are still abusing women?

BOSOLA: Who, I? no; only, by the way now and then, mention your frailties. The orange-tree bears ripe and green fruit and blossoms all together; and some of you give entertainment for pure love, but more for more precious reward. The lusty spring smells well; but drooping autumn tastes well. If we have the same golden showers that rained in the time of Jupiter the thunderer, you have the same Danaës[21] still, to hold up their laps to receive them. Didst thou never study the mathematics?

OLD LADY: What's that, sir?

BOSOLA: Why to know the trick how to make a many lines meet in one centre. Go, go, give your foster-daughters good counsel: tell them, that the devil takes delight to hang at a woman's girdle, like a false rusty watch, that she cannot discern how the time passes.
    [Exit Old Lady]
    [Enter Antonio, Roderigo, and Grisolan]

ANTONIO: Shut up the court-gates.

RODERIGO: Why, sir? what's the danger?

ANTONIO: Shut up the posterns presently, and call
All the officers o' the court.

GRISOLAN: I shall instantly. [Exit]

ANTONIO: Who keeps the key o' the park-gate?

[21] Jupiter (or Zeus) wooed the maiden Danaë by transforming himself into a golden shower which dropped into her lap.

RODERIGO: Forobosco.

ANTONIO: Let him bring't presently.
    [Re-enter Grisolan with Servants]

1ST SERVANT: O, gentlemen o' the court, the foul treason!

BOSOLA: [Aside] If that these apricocks should be
    poisoned now,
Without my knowledge!

1ST SERVANT: There was taken even now a Switzer[22] in the duchess' bed-chamber—

2ND SERVANT: A Switzer!

1ST SERVANT: With a pistol in his great cod-piece.[23]

BOSOLA: Ha, ha, ha!

1ST SERVANT: The cod-piece was the case for't.

2ND SERVANT: There was a cunning traitor: who would have searched his cod-piece?

1ST SERVANT: True, if he had kept out of the ladies' chambers: and all the moulds of his buttons were leaden bullets.

2ND SERVANT: O wicked cannibal! a firelock in's cod-piece!

1ST SERVANT: 'Twas a French plot, upon my life.

2ND SERVANT: To see what the devil can do!

ANTONIO: Are all the officers here?

SERVANTS: We are.

ANTONIO: Gentlemen,
We have lost much plate you know; and but this
    evening
Jewels, to the value of four thousand ducats,
Are missing in the duchess' cabinet.
Are the gates shut?

SERVANTS: Yes.

ANTONIO: 'Tis the duchess' pleasure
Each officer be locked into his chamber
Till the sun-rising; and to send the keys
Of all their chests and of their outward doors
Into her bed-chamber. She is very sick.

RODERIGO: At her pleasure.

ANTONIO: She entreats you take't not ill: the innocent
Shall be the more approved by it.

BOSOLA: Gentlemen o' the wood-yard, where's your
    Switzer now?

1ST SERVANT: By this hand, 'twas credibly reported by one o' the black guard.
    [Exeunt all except Antonio and Delio]

DELIO: How fares it with the duchess?

ANTONIO: She's exposed
Unto the worst of torture, pain and fear.

DELIO: Speak to her all happy comfort.

ANTONIO: How I do play the fool with mine own
    danger!
You are this night, dear friend, to post to Rome:
My life lies in your service.

DELIO: Do not doubt me.

[22] Swiss.
[23] An ornamented flap concealing the opening in the breeches.

ANTONIO: O, 'tis far from me: and yet fear presents me
Somewhat that looks like danger.
DELIO: Believe it,
'Tis but the shadow of your fear, no more:
How superstitiously we mind our evils!
The throwing down salt, or crossing of a hare,
Bleeding at nose, the stumbling of a horse,
Or singing of a cricket, are of power
To daunt whole man in us. Sir, fare you well:
I wish you all the joys of a blessed father;
And, for my faith, lay this unto your breast,—
Old friends, like old swords, still are trusted best.
  [Exit]
  [Enter Cariola]
CARIOLA: Sir, you are the happy father of a son:
Your wife commends him to you.
ANTONIO: Blessed comfort!—
For Heaven's sake tend her well: I'll presently
Go set a figure for's nativity.
  [Exeunt]

SCENE III.

The court of the same palace.

[Enter Bosola, with a dark lantern]
BOSOLA: Sure I did hear a woman shriek: list, ha!
And the sound came, if I received it right,
From the duchess' lodgings. There's some stratagem
In the confining all our courtiers
To their several wards: I must have part of it;
My intelligence will freeze else. List, again!
It may be 'twas the melancholy bird,
Best friend of silence and of solitariness,
The owl, that screamed so.—Ha! Antonio!
  [Enter Antonio]
ANTONIO: I heard some noise.—Who's there? what art thou? speak.
BOSOLA: Antonio, put not your face nor body
To such a forced expression of fear:
I am Bosola, your friend.
ANTONIO: Bosola!—
[Aside] This mole does undermine me.—Heard you not
A noise even now?
BOSOLA: From whence?
ANTONIO: From the duchess' lodging.
BOSOLA: Not I: did you?
ANTONIO: I did, or else I dreamed.
BOSOLA: Let's walk towards it.
ANTONIO: No: it may be 'twas
But the rising of the wind.
BOSOLA: Very likely.
Methinks 'tis very cold, and yet you sweat:
You look wildly.
ANTONIO: I have been setting a figure
For the duchess' jewels.

BOSOLA: Ah, and how falls your question?
Do you find it radical?[24]
ANTONIO: What's that to you?
'Tis rather to be questioned what design,
When all men were commanded to their lodgings,
Makes you a night-walker.
BOSOLA: In sooth, I'll tell you:
Now all the court's asleep, I thought the devil
Had least to do here; I came to say my prayers;
And if it do offend you I do so,
You are a fine courtier.
ANTONIO: [Aside] This fellow will undo me.—
You gave the duchess apricocks to-day:
Pray Heaven they were not poisoned!
BOSOLA: Poisoned! A Spanish fig
For the imputation.
ANTONIO: Traitors are ever confident
Till they are discovered. There were jewels stol'n too:
In my conceit, none are to be suspected
More than yourself.
BOSOLA: You are a false steward.
ANTONIO: Saucy slave, I'll pull thee up by the roots.
BOSOLA: May be the ruin will crush you to pieces.
ANTONIO: You are an impudent snake indeed, sir:
Are you scarce warm, and do you show your sting?
You libel well, sir.
BOSOLA: No, sir: copy it out,
And I will set my hand to't.
ANTONIO: [Aside] My nose bleeds.
One that were superstitious would count
This ominous, when it merely comes by chance:
Two letters, that are wrote here for my name,
Are drowned in blood!
Mere accident.—For you, sir, I'll take order
I' the morn you shall be safe:—[Aside] 'tis that must color
Her lying-in:—sir, this door you pass not:
I do not hold it fit that you come near
The duchess' lodgings, till you have quit yourself.—
[Aside] The great are like the base, nay, they are the same,
When they seek shameful ways to avoid shame. [Exit]
BOSOLA: Antonio hereabout did drop a paper:—
Some of your help, false friend:—O, here it is.
What's here? a child's nativity calculated! [Reads]
"The duchess was delivered of a son, 'tween the
hours twelve and one in the night, *Anno Dom.* 1504,"
—that's this year—"*decimo nono Decembris,*"—
that's this night,—"taken according to the meridian
of Malfi,"—that's our duchess: happy discovery!—
"The lord of the first house being combust in the
ascendant, signifies short life; and Mars being in a
human sign, joined to the tail of the Dragon, in the
eighth house, doth threaten a violent death. *Cætera
non scrutantur.*"[25]
Why, now 'tis most apparent: this precise fellow
Is the duchess' bawd:—I have it to my wish!
This is a parcel of intelligency

[24] Fit to be judged.
[25] The rest is not investigated.

Our courtiers were cased up for: it needs must follow
That I must be committed on pretence
Of poisoning her; which I'll endure, and laugh at.
If one could find the father now! but that
Time will discover. Old Castruccio
I' the morning posts to Rome: by him I'll send
A letter that shall make her brothers' galls
O'erflow their livers. This was a thrifty way.
Though lust do mask in ne'er so strange disguise,
She's oft found witty, but is never wise. [*Exit*]

SCENE IV.

An apartment in the palace of the Cardinal *at Rome.*

[*Enter* Cardinal *and* Julia]
CARDINAL: Sit: thou art my best of wishes. Prithee, tell me
What trick didst thou invent to come to Rome
Without thy husband.
    JULIA: Why, my lord, I told him
I came to visit an old anchorite
Here for devotion.
    CARDINAL: Thou art a witty false one,—
I mean, to him.
    JULIA: You have prevailed with me
Beyond my strongest thoughts: I would not now
Find you inconstant.
    CARDINAL: Do not put thyself
To such a voluntary torture, which proceeds
Out of your own guilt.
    JULIA: How, my lord!
    CARDINAL: You fear
My constancy, because you have approved
Those giddy and wild turnings in yourself.
    JULIA: Did you e'er find them?
    CARDINAL: Sooth, generally for women,
A man might strive to make glass malleable,
Ere he should make them fixèd.
    JULIA: So, my lord.
    CARDINAL: We had need go borrow that fantastic glass
Invented by Galileo the Florentine
To view another spacious world i' the moon,
And look to find a constant woman there.
    JULIA: This is very well, my lord.
    CARDINAL: Why do you weep?
Are tears your justification? the self-same tears
Will fall into your husband's bosom, lady,
With a loud protestation that you love him
Above the world. Come, I'll love you wisely,
That's jealousy; since I am very certain
You cannot make me cuckold.
    JULIA: I'll go home
To my husband.
    CARDINAL: You may thank me, lady,
I have taken you off your melancholy perch,
Bore you upon my fist, and showed you game,

And let you fly at it.—I pray thee, kiss me.—
When thou wast with thy husband, thou wast watched
Like a tame elephant:—still you are to thank me:—
Thou hadst only kisses from him and high feeding;
But what delight was that? 'twas just like one
That hath a little fingering on the lute,
Yet cannot tune it:—still you are to thank me.
    JULIA: You told me of a piteous wound i' the heart
And a sick liver, when you wooed me first,
And spake like one in physic.
    CARDINAL: Who's that?—
    [*Enter* Servant]
Rest firm, for my affection to thee,
Lightning moves slow to't.
    SERVANT: Madam, a gentleman,
That's come post from Malfi, desires to see you.
    CARDINAL: Let him enter: I'll withdraw. [*Exit*]
    SERVANT: He says
Your husband, old Castruccio, is come to Rome,
Most pitifully tired with riding post. [*Exit*]
    [*Enter* Delio]
    JULIA: [*Aside*] Signior Delio! 'tis one of my old suitors.
    DELIO: I was bold to come and see you.
    JULIA: Sir, you are welcome.
    DELIO: Do you lie here?
    JULIA: Sure, your own experience
Will satisfy you no: our Roman prelates
Do not keep lodging for ladies.
    DELIO: Very well:
I have brought you no commendations from your husband,
For I know none by him.
    JULIA: I hear he's come to Rome.
    DELIO: I never knew man and beast, of a horse and a knight,
So weary of each other: if he had had a good back,
He would have undertook to have borne his horse,
His breech was so pitifully sore.
    JULIA: Your laughter
Is my pity.
    DELIO: Lady, I know not whether
You want money, but I have brought you some.
    JULIA: From my husband?
    DELIO: No, from mine own allowance.
    JULIA: I must hear the condition, ere I be bound to take it.
    DELIO: Look on't, 'tis gold: hath it not a fine color?
    JULIA: I have a bird more beautiful.
    DELIO: Try the sound on't.
    JULIA: A lute-string far exceeds it:
It hath no smell, like cassia or civet;
Nor is it physical, though some fond doctors
Persuade us seethe't in cullises.[26] I'll tell you,
This is a creature bred by—
    [*Re-enter* Servant]
    SERVANT: Your husband's come,
Hath delivered a letter to the Duke of Calabria

[26] Strong broths. The old recipe-books recommend "pieces of gold" among the ingredients.

That, to my thinking, hath put him out of his wits.
[*Exit*]
JULIA: Sir, you hear:
Pray, let me know your business and your suit
As briefly as can be.
DELIO: With good speed: I would wish you,
At such time as you are non-resident
With your husband, my mistress.
JULIA: Sir, I'll go ask my husband if I shall,
And straight return your answer. [*Exit*]
DELIO: Very fine!
Is this her wit, or honesty, that speaks thus?
I heard one say the duke was highly moved
With a letter sent from Malfi. I do fear
Antonio is betrayed: how fearfully
Shows his ambition now! unfortunate fortune!
They pass through whirlpools, and deep woes do
shun,
Who the event weigh ere the action's done. [*Exit*]

SCENE V.

Another apartment in the same palace.

[*Enter* Cardinal *and* Ferdinand *with a letter*]
FERDINAND: I have this night digged up a man-
drake.
CARDINAL: Say you?
FERDINAND: And I am grown mad with't.
CARDINAL: What's the prodigy?
FERDINAND: Read there,—a sister damned: she's
loose i' the hilts;
Grown a notorious strumpet.
CARDINAL: Speak lower.
FERDINAND: Lower!
Rogues do not whisper't now, but seek to publish't
(As servants do the bounty of their lords)
Aloud; and with a covetous searching eye,
To mark who note them. O, confusion seize her!
She hath had most cunning bawds to serve her turn,
And more secure conveyances for lust
Than towns of garrison for service.
CARDINAL: Is't possible?
Can this be certain?
FERDINAND: Rhubarb, O, for rhubarb
To purge this choler! here's the cursèd day
To prompt my memory; and here't shall stick
Till of her bleeding heart I make a sponge
To wipe it out.
CARDINAL: Why do you make yourself
So wild a tempest?
FERDINAND: Would I could be one,
That I might toss her palace 'bout her ears,
Root up her goodly forests, blast her meads,
And lay her general territory as waste
As she hath done her honors.
CARDINAL: Shall our blood,
The royal blood of Arragon and Castile,
Be thus attainted?

FERDINAND: Apply desperate physic:
We must not now use balsamum, but fire,
The smarting cupping-glass, for that's the mean
To purge infected blood, such blood as hers.
There is a kind of pity in mine eye,—
I'll give it to my handkercher; and now 'tis here,
I'll bequeath this to her bastard.
CARDINAL: What to do?
FERDINAND: Why, to make soft lint for his mother's
wounds,
When I have hewed her to pieces.
CARDINAL: Cursèd creature!
Unequal nature, to place women's hearts
So far upon the left side!
FERDINAND: Foolish men,
That e'er will trust their honor in a bark
Made of so slight weak bulrush as is woman,
Apt every minute to sink it!
CARDINAL: Thus
Ignorance, when it hath purchased honor,
It cannot wield it.
FERDINAND: Methinks I see her laughing—
Excellent hyena! Talk to me somewhat quickly,
Or my imagination will carry me
To see her in the shameful act of sin.
CARDINAL: With whom?
FERDINAND: Happily with some strong-thighed
bargeman,
Or one o' the woodyard that can quoit the sledge
Or toss the bar, or else some lovely squire
That carries coals up to her privy lodgings.
CARDINAL: You fly beyond your reason.
FERDINAND: Go to, mistress!
'Tis not your whore's milk that shall quench my wild
fire,
But your whore's blood.
CARDINAL: How idly shows this rage, which car-
ries you,
As men conveyed by witches through the air,
On violent whirlwinds! this intemperate noise
Fitly resembles deaf men's shrill discourse,
Who talk aloud, thinking all other men
To have their imperfection.
FERDINAND: Have not you
My palsy?
CARDINAL: Yes, but I can be angry
Without this rupture: there is not in nature
A thing that makes man so deformed, so beastly,
As doth intemperate anger. Chide yourself.
You have divers men who never yet expressed
Their strong desire of rest but by unrest,
By vexing of themselves. Come, put yourself
In tune.
FERDINAND: So I will only study to seem
The thing I am not. I could kill her now,
In you, or in myself; for I do think
It is some sin in us Heaven doth revenge
By her.
CARDINAL: Are you stark mad?
FERDINAND: I would have their bodies

Burnt in a coal-pit with the ventage stopped,
That their cursed smoke might not ascend to Heaven
Or dip the sheets they lie in in pitch or sulphur,
Wrap them in't, and then light them like a match;
Or else to boil their bastard to a cullis,
And give't his lecherous father to renew
The sin of his back.
    CARDINAL: I'll leave you.
    FERDINAND: Nay, I have done.
I am confident, had I been damned in hell,
And should have heard of this, it would have put me
Into a cold sweat. In, in; I'll go sleep.
Till I know who leaps my sister, I'll not stir:
That known, I'll find scorpions to string my whips,
And fix her in a general eclipse.
    [*Exeunt*]

ACT III. SCENE I.

An apartment in the palace of the Duchess.

    [*Enter* Antonio *and* Delio]
    ANTONIO: Our noble friend, my most belovèd
    Delio!
O, you have been a stranger long at court;
Came you along with the Lord Ferdinand?
    DELIO: I did, sir: and how fares your noble
    duchess?
    ANTONIO: Right fortunately well: she's an excel-
    lent
Feeder of pedigrees; since you last saw her,
She hath had two children more, a son and daughter.
    DELIO: Methinks 'twas yesterday: let me but wink,
And not behold your face, which to mine eye
Is somewhat leaner, verily I should dream
It were within this half hour.
    ANTONIO: You have not been in law, friend Delio,
Nor in prison, nor a suitor at the court,
Nor begged the reversion of some great man's place,
Nor troubled with an old wife, which doth make
Your time so insensibly hasten.
    DELIO: Pray, sir, tell me,
Hath not this news arrived yet to the ear
Of the lord cardinal?
    ANTONIO: I fear it hath:
The Lord Ferdinand, that's newly come to court,
Doth bear himself right dangerously.
    DELIO: Pray, why?
    ANTONIO: He is so quiet that he seems to sleep
The tempest out, as dormice do in winter:
Those houses that are haunted are most still
Till the devil be up.
    DELIO: What say the common people?
    ANTONIO: The common rabble do directly say
She is a strumpet.
    DELIO: And your graver heads
Which would be politic, what censure they?
    ANTONIO: They do observe I grow to infinite pur-
    chase,

The left hand way, and all suppose the duchess
Would amend it, if she could; for, say they,
Great princes, though they grudge their officers
Should have such large and unconfinèd means
To get wealth under them, will not complain,
Lest thereby they should make them odious
Unto the people; for other obligation
Of love or marriage between her and me
They never dream of.
    DELIO: The Lord Ferdinand
Is going to bed.
    [*Enter* Duchess, Ferdinand, *and* Attendants]
    FERDINAND: I'll instantly to bed,
For I am weary.—I am to bespeak
A husband for you.
    DUCHESS: For me, sir! pray, who is't?
    FERDINAND: The great Count Malatesti.
    DUCHESS: Fie upon him!
A count! he's a mere stick of sugar-candy;
You may look quite through him. When I choose
A husband, I will marry for your honor.
    FERDINAND: You shall do well in't.—How is't,
    worthy Antonio?
    DUCHESS: But, sir, I am to have private conference
    with you
About a scandalous report is spread
Touching mine honor.
    FERDINAND: Let me be ever deaf to't:
One of Pasquil's paper bullets,[27] court-calumny,
A pestilent air, which princes' palaces
Are seldom purged of. Yet say that it were true,
I pour it in your bosom, my fixed love
Would strongly excuse, extenuate, nay, deny
Faults, were they apparent in you. Go, be safe
In your own innocency.
    DUCHESS: [*Aside*] O blessed comfort!
This deadly air is purged.
    [*Exeunt* Duchess, Antonio, Delio, *and* At-
    tendants]
    FERDINAND: Her guilt treads on
Hot-burning coulters.
    [*Enter* Bosola]
              Now, Bosola,
How thrives our intelligence?
    BOSOLA: Sir, uncertainly:
'Tis rumored she hath had three bastards, but
By whom we may go read i' the stars.
    FERDINAND: Why, some
Hold opinion all things are written there.
    BOSOLA: Yes, if we could find spectacles to read
    them.
I do suspect there hath been some sorcery
Used on the duchess.
    FERDINAND: Sorcery! to what purpose?
    BOSOLA: To make her dote on some desertless
    fellow
She shames to acknowledge.
    FERDINAND: Can your faith give way
To think there's power in potions or in charms,
    [27] Scurrilous verses.

To make us love whether we will or no?
BOSOLA: Most certainly.
FERDINAND: Away! these are mere gulleries, horrid
things,
Invented by some cheating mountebanks
To abuse us. Do you think that herbs or charms
Can force the will? Some trials have been made
In this foolish practice, but the ingredients
Were lenitive poisons, such as are of force
To make the patient mad; and straight the witch
Swears by equivocation they are in love.
The witchcraft lies in her rank blood. This night
I will force confession from her. You told me
You had got, within these two days, a false key
Into her bed-chamber.
BOSOLA: I have.
FERDINAND: As I would wish.
BOSOLA: What do you intend to do?
FERDINAND: Can you guess?
BOSOLA: No.
FERDINAND: Do not ask, then:
He that can compass me, and know my drifts,
May say he hath put a girdle 'bout the world,
And sounded all her quicksands.
BOSOLA: I do not
Think so.
FERDINAND: What do you think, then, pray?
BOSOLA: That you are
Your own chronicle too much, and grossly
Flatter yourself.
FERDINAND: Give me thy hand; I thank thee:
I never gave pension but to flatterers,
Till I entertainèd thee. Farewell.
That friend a great man's ruin strongly checks,
Who rails into his belief all his defects.
[*Exeunt*]

SCENE II.

The bed-chamber of the Duchess.

[*Enter* Duchess, Antonio, *and* Cariola]
DUCHESS: Bring me the casket hither, and the
glass.—You get no lodging here tonight, my lord.
ANTONIO: Indeed, I must persuade one.
DUCHESS: Very good:
I hope in time 'twill grow into a custom,
That noblemen shall come with cap and knee
To purchase a night's lodging of their wives.
ANTONIO: I must lie here.
DUCHESS: Must! you are a lord of misrule.
ANTONIO: Indeed, my rule is only in the night.
DUCHESS: To what use will you put me?
ANTONIO: We'll sleep together.
DUCHESS: Alas,
What pleasure can two lovers find in sleep!
CARIOLA: My lord, I lie with her often; and I know
She'll much disquiet you.
ANTONIO: See, you are complained of.

CARIOLA: For she's the sprawling'st bedfellow.
ANTONIO: I shall like her the better for that.
CARIOLA: Sir, shall I ask you a question?
ANTONIO: Ay, pray thee, Cariola.
CARIOLA: Wherefore still, when you lie with my
lady,
Do you rise so early?
ANTONIO: Laboring men
Count the clock oftenest, Cariola,
Are glad when their task's ended.
DUCHESS: I'll stop your mouth. [*Kisses him*]
ANTONIO: Nay, that's but one; Venus had two soft
doves
To draw her chariot; I must have another—
[*She kisses him again*]
When wilt thou marry, Cariola?
CARIOLA: Never, my lord.
ANTONIO: O, fie upon this single life! forego it.
We read how Daphne, for her peevish flight,
Became a fruitless bay-tree; Syrinx turned
To the pale empty reed; Anaxarete
Was frozen into marble: whereas those
Which married, or proved kind unto their friends,
Were by a gracious influence transhaped
Into the olive, pomegranate, mulberry,
Became flowers, precious stones, or eminent stars.
CARIOLA: This is a vain poetry: but I pray you
tell me,
If there were proposed me, wisdom, riches, and
beauty,
In three several young men, which should I choose.
ANTONIO: 'Tis a hard question: this was Paris'
case,
And he was blind in't, and there was great cause;
For how was't possible he could judge right,
Having three amorous goddesses in view,
And they stark naked? 'twas a motion
Were able to benight the apprehension
Of the severest counsellor of Europe.
Now I look on both your faces so well formed,
It puts me in mind of a question I would ask.
CARIOLA: What is't?
ANTONIO: I do wonder why hard-favored ladies,
For the most part, keep worse-favored waiting-
women
To attend them, and cannot endure fair ones.
DUCHESS: O, that's soon answered.
Did you ever in your life know an ill painter
Desire to have his dwelling next door to the shop
Of an excellent picture-maker? 'twould disgrace
His face-making, and undo him. I prithee,
When were we so merry?—My hair tangles.
ANTONIO: Pray thee, Cariola, let's steal forth the
room,
And let her talk to herself: I have divers times
Served her the like, when she hath chafed extremely.
I love to see her angry. Softly, Cariola.
[*Exeunt* Antonio *and* Cariola]
DUCHESS: Doth not the color of my hair 'gin to
change?

When I wax gray, I shall have all the court
Powder their hair with arras,[28] to be like me.
You have cause to love me; I entered you into my
    heart
Before you would vouchsafe to call for the keys.
    [*Enter* Ferdinand *behind*]
We shall one day have my brothers take you nap-
    ping;
Methinks his presence, being now in court,
Should make you keep your own bed; but you'll
    say
Love mixed with fear is sweetest. I'll assure you,
You shall get no more children till my brothers
Consent to be your gossips.[29] Have you lost your
    tongue?
'Tis welcome:
For know, whether I am doomed to live or die,
I can do both like a prince.
        FERDINAND: Die, then, quickly! [*Giving her a
            poniard*]
Virtue, where art thou hid? what hideous thing
Is it that doth eclipse thee?
    DUCHESS: Pray, sir, hear me.
    FERDINAND: Or is it true thou art but a bare name,
And no essential thing?
    DUCHESS: Sir,—
    FERDINAND: Do not speak.
    DUCHESS: No, sir:
I will plant my soul in mine ears, to hear you.
    FERDINAND: O most imperfect light of human
        reason,
That mak'st us so unhappy to foresee
What we can least prevent! Pursue thy wishes,
And glory in them: there's in shame no comfort
But to be past all bounds and sense of shame.
    DUCHESS: I pray, sir, hear me: I am married.
    FERDINAND: So!
    DUCHESS: Happily, not to your liking: but for
        that,
Alas, your shears do come untimely now
To clip the bird's wing that's already flown!
Will you see my husband?
    FERDINAND: Yes, if I could change
Eyes with a basilisk.
    DUCHESS: Sure, you came hither
By his confederacy.
    FERDINAND: The howling of a wolf
Is music to thee, screech-owl: prithee, peace.—
Whate'er thou art that hast enjoyed my sister,
For I am sure thou hear'st me, for thine own sake
Let me not know thee. I came hither prepared
To work thy discovery; yet am now persuaded
It would beget such violent effects
As would damn us both. I would not for ten millions
I had beheld thee: therefore use all means
I never may have knowledge of thy name;
Enjoy thy lust still, and a wretched life,
On that condition.—And for thee, vile woman,

[28] Orrisroot—the rootstock of irises, used in perfumes.
[29] Godparents.

If thou do wish thy lecher may grow old
In thy embracements, I would have thee build
Such a room for him as our anchorites
To holier use inhabit. Let not the sun
Shine on him till he's dead; let dogs and monkeys
Only converse with him, and such dumb things
To whom nature denies use to sound his name;
Do not keep a paraquito, lest she learn it;
If thou do love him, cut out thine own tongue,
Lest it bewray him.
    DUCHESS: Why might not I marry?
I have not gone about in this to create
Any new world or custom.
    FERDINAND: Thou art undone;
And thou hast ta'en that massy sheet of lead
That hid thy husband's bones, and folded it
About my heart.
    DUCHESS: Mine bleeds for't.
    FERDINAND: Thine! thy heart!
What should I name't unless a hollow bullet
Filled with unquenchable wild-fire?
    DUCHESS: You are in this
Too strict; and were you not my princely brother,
I would say, too wilful: my reputation
Is safe.
    FERDINAND: Dost thou know what reputation is?
I'll tell thee,—to small purpose, since the instruction
Comes now too late.
Upon a time Reputation, Love, and Death,
Would travel o'er the world; and it was concluded
That they should part, and take three several ways.
Death told them, they should find him in great bat-
    tles,
Or cities plagued with plagues: Love gives them
    counsel
To inquire for him 'mongst unambitious shepherds,
Where dowries were not talked of, and sometimes
'Mongst quiet kindred that had nothing left
By their dead parents: "Stay," quoth Reputation,
"Do not forsake me; for it is my nature,
If once I part from any man I meet,
I am never found again." And so for you:
You have shook hands with Reputation,
And made him invisible. So, fare you well:
I will never see you more.
    DUCHESS: Why should only I,
Of all the other princes of the world,
Be cased up, like a holy relic? I have youth
And a little beauty.
    FERDINAND: So you have some virgins
That are witches. I will never see thee more. [*Exit*]
        [*Re-enter* Antonio *with a pistol, and* Cariola]
    DUCHESS: You saw this apparition?
    ANTONIO: Yes: we are
Betrayed. How came he hither? I should turn
This to thee, for that.
    CARIOLA: Pray, sir, do; and when
That you have cleft my heart, you shall read there
Mine innocence.
    DUCHESS: That gallery gave him entrance.

ANTONIO: I would this terrible thing would come again,
That, standing on my guard, I might relate
My warrantable love.—
    [*She shows the poniard*]
                Ha! what means this?
DUCHESS: He left this with me.
ANTONIO: And it seems did wish
You would use it on yourself.
DUCHESS: His action
Seemed to intend so much.
ANTONIO: This hath a handle to't,
As well as a point: turn it towards him,
And so fasten the keen edge in his rank gall.
    [*Knocking within*]
How now! who knocks? more earthquakes?
DUCHESS: I stand
As if a mine beneath my feet were ready
To be blown up.
CARIOLA: 'Tis Bosola.
DUCHESS: Away!
O misery! methinks unjust actions
Should wear these masks and curtains, and not we.
You must instantly part hence: I have fashioned it already.
    [*Exit* Antonio]
    [*Enter* Bosola]
BOSOLA: The duke your brother is ta'en up in a whirlwind;
Hath took horse, and 's rid post to Rome.
DUCHESS: So late?
BOSOLA: He told me, as he mounted into the saddle,
You were undone.
DUCHESS: Indeed, I am very near it.
BOSOLA: What's the matter?
DUCHESS: Antonio, the master of our household,
Hath dealt so falsely with me in 's accounts:
My brother stood engaged with me for money
Ta'en up of certain Neapolitan Jews,
And Antonio lets the bonds be forfeit.
BOSOLA: Strange!—[*Aside*] This is cunning.
DUCHESS: And hereupon
My brother's bills at Naples are protested
Against.—Call up our officers.
BOSOLA: I shall. [*Exit*]
    [*Re-enter* Antonio]
DUCHESS: The place that you must fly to is Ancona:
Hire a house there; I'll send after you
My treasure and my jewels. Our weak safety
Runs upon enginous[30] wheels: short syllables
Must stand for periods. I must now accuse you
Of such a feignèd crime as Tasso calls
Magnanima menzogna, a noble lie,
'Cause it must shield our honors.—Hark! they are coming.
    [*Re-enter* Bosola *and* Officers]
ANTONIO: Will your grace hear me?
[30] Rapid.

DUCHESS: I have got well by you; you have yielded me
A million of loss: I am like to inherit
The people's curses for your stewardship.
You had the trick in audit-time to be sick,
Till I had signed your quietus;[31] and that cured you
Without help of a doctor.—Gentlemen,
I would have this man be an example to you all;
So shall you hold my favor; I pray, let him;
For h'as done that, alas, you would not think of,
And, because I intend to be rid of him,
I mean not to publish.—Use your fortune elsewhere.
ANTONIO: I am strongly armed to brook my over-throw,
As commonly men bear with a hard year:
I will not blame the cause on't; but do think
The necessity of my malevolent star
Procures this, not her humor. O, the inconstant
And rotten ground of service! you may see,
'Tis even like him, that in a winter night,
Takes a long slumber o'er a dying fire,
A-loth to part from't; yet parts thence as cold
As when he first sat down.
DUCHESS: We do confiscate,
Towards the satisfying of your accounts,
All that you have.
ANTONIO: I am all yours; and 'tis very fit
All mine should be so.
DUCHESS: So, sir, you have your pass.
ANTONIO: You may see, gentlemen, what 'tis to serve
A prince with body and soul. [*Exit*]
BOSOLA: Here's an example for extortion: what moisture is drawn out of the sea, when foul weather comes, pours down, and runs into the sea again.
DUCHESS: I would know what are your opinions
Of this Antonio.
2ND OFFICER: He could not abide to see a pig's head gaping: I thought your grace would find him a Jew.
3RD OFFICER: I would you had been his officer, for your own sake.
4TH OFFICER: You would have had more money.
1ST OFFICER: He stopped his ears with black wool, and to those came to him for money said he was thick of hearing.
2ND OFFICER: Some said he was an hermaphrodite, for he could not abide a woman.
4TH OFFICER: How scurvy proud he would look when the treasury was full! Well, let him go.
1ST OFFICER: Yes, and the chippings of the butterfly after him, to scour his gold chain.
DUCHESS: Leave us.
    [*Exeunt* Officers]
What do you think of these?
BOSOLA: That these are rogues that in 's prosperity,
But to have waited on his fortune, could have wished
His dirty stirrup rivetted through their noses.

[31] Here, death certificate; reminds us of the playful use of *Quietus,* Act I, Scene I.

And followed after's mule, like a bear in a ring;
Would have prostituted their daughters to his lust;
Made their first-born intelligencers; thought none
    happy
But such as were born under his blest planet,
And wore his livery: and do these lice drop off now?
Well, never look to have the like again:
He hath left a sort of flattering rogues behind him;
Their doom must follow. Princes pay flatterers
In their own money: flatterers dissemble their vices,
And they dissemble their lies; that's justice.
Alas, poor gentleman!
    DUCHESS: Poor! he hath amply filled his coffers.
    BOSOLA: Sure, he was too honest. Pluto, the god of
        riches,
When he's sent by Jupiter to any man,
He goes limping, to signify that wealth
That comes on God's name comes slowly; but when
    he's sent
On the devil's errand, he rides post and comes in by
    scuttles.[32]
Let me show you what a most unvalued jewel
You have in a wanton humor thrown away,
To bless the man shall find him. He was an excellent
Courtier and most faithful; a soldier that thought it
As beastly to know his own value too little
As devilish to acknowledge it too much.
Both his virtue and form deserved a far better for-
    tune:
His discourse rather delighted to judge itself than
    show itself:
His breast was filled with all perfection,
And yet it seemed a private whispering-room,
It made so little noise of't.
    DUCHESS: But he was basely descended.
    BOSOLA: Will you make yourself a mercenary
        herald,
Rather to examine men's pedigrees than virtues?
You shall want him:
For know an honest statesman to a prince
Is like a cedar planted by a spring;
The spring bathes the tree's root, the grateful tree
Rewards it with his shadow: you have not done so.
I would sooner swim to the Bermoothes[33] on
Two politicians' rotten bladders, tied
Together with an intelligencer's heartstring,
Than depend on so changeable a prince's favor.
Fare thee well, Antonio! since the malice of the
    world
Would needs down with thee, it cannot be said yet
That any ill happened unto thee, considering thy fall
Was accompanied with virtue.
    DUCHESS: O, you render me excellent music!
    BOSOLA: Say you?
    DUCHESS: This good one that you speak of is my
husband.
    BOSOLA: Do I not dream! can this ambitious age
Have so much goodness in't as to prefer

[32] A quick run.
[33] Bermudas.

A man merely for worth, without these shadows
Of wealth and painted honors? possible?
    DUCHESS: I have had three children by him.
    BOSOLA: Fortunate lady!
For you have made your private nuptial bed
The humble and fair seminary of peace.
No question but many an unbeneficed scholar
Shall pray for you for this deed, and rejoice
That some preferment in the world can yet
Arise from merit. The virgins of your land
That have no dowries shall hope your example
Will raise them to rich husbands. Should you want
Soldiers, 'twould make the very Turks and Moors
Turn Christians, and serve you for this act.
Last, the neglected poets of your time,
In honor of this trophy of a man,
Raised by that curious engine, your white hand,
Shall thank you, in your grave, for't; and make that
More reverend than all the cabinets
Of living princes. For Antonio.
His fame shall likewise flow from many a pen,
When heralds shall want coats to sell to men.
    DUCHESS: As I taste comfort in this friendly speech,
So would I find concealment.
    BOSOLA: O, the secret of my prince,
Which I will wear on the inside of my heart!
    DUCHESS: You shall take charge of all my coin
        and jewels
And follow him; for he retires himself
To Ancona.
    BOSOLA: So.
    DUCHESS: Whither, within few days,
I mean to follow thee.
    BOSOLA: Let me think:
I would wish your grace to feign a pilgrimage
To our Lady of Loretto, scarce seven leagues
From fair Ancona; so may you depart
Your country with more honor, and your flight
Will seem a princely progress, retaining
Your usual train about you.
    DUCHESS: Sir, your direction
Shall lead me by the hand.
    CARIOLA: In my opinion,
She were better progress to the baths at Lucca,
Or go visit the Spa
In Germany; for, if you will believe me,
I do not like this jesting with religion,
This feignèd pilgrimage.
    DUCHESS: Thou art a superstitious fool:
Prepare us instantly for our departure.
Past sorrows, let us moderately lament them;
For those to come, seek wisely to prevent them.
        [Exeunt Duchess and Cariola]
    BOSOLA: A politician is the devil's quilted anvil;
He fashions all sins on him, and the blows
Are never heard: he may work in a lady's chamber,
As here for proof. What rests but I reveal
All to my lord? O, this base quality
Of intelligencer! why, every quality i' the world
Prefers but gain or commendation:

Now for this act I am certain to be raised,
And men that paint weeds to the life are praised.
 [*Exit*]

SCENE III.

An apartment in the Cardinal's *palace at Rome.*

[*Enter* Cardinal, Ferdinand, Malatesti, Pescara,
 Delio, *and* Silvio]
CARDINAL: Must we turn soldier, then?
MALATESTI: The emperor,
Hearing your worth that way, ere you attained
This reverend garment, joins you in commission
With the right fortunate soldier the Marquis of Pes-
 cara,
And the famous Lannoy.
CARDINAL: He that had the honor
Of taking the French king prisoner?
MALATESTI: The same.
Here's a plot drawn for a new fortification
At Naples.
FERDINAND: This great Count Malatesti, I perceive,
Hath got employment?
DELIO: No employment, my lord;
A marginal note in the muster-book, that he is
A voluntary lord.
FERDINAND: He's no soldier.
DELIO: He has worn gunpowder in's hollow tooth
for the toothache.
SILVIO: He comes to the leaguer[34] with a full intent
To eat fresh beef and garlic, means to stay
Till the scent be gone, and straight return to court.
DELIO: He hath read all the late service
As the city chronicle relates it;
And keeps two pewterers going, only to express
Battles in model.
SILVIO: Then he'll fight by the book.
DELIO: By the almanac, I think,
To choose good days and shun the critical;
That's his mistress' scarf.
SILVIO: Yes, he protests
He would do much for that taffeta.
DELIO: I think he would run away from a battle,
To save it from taking prisoner.
SILVIO: He is horribly afraid
Gunpowder will spoil the perfume on't.
DELIO: I saw a Dutchman break his pate once
For calling him pot-gun; he made his head
Have a bore in't like a musket.
SILVIO: I would he had made a touchhole to't.
He is indeed a guarded sumpter-cloth,
Only for the remove of the court.
 [*Enter* Bosola]
PESCARA: Bosola arrived! what should be the busi-
 ness?
Some falling-out amongst the cardinals.
These factions amongst great men, they are like
 ³⁴ Camp.

Foxes, when their heads are divided,
They carry fire in their tails, and all the country
About them goes to wreck for't.
SILVIO: What's that Bosola?
DELIO: I knew him in Padua—a fantastical scholar,
like such who study to know how many knots was
in Hercules' club, of what color Achilles' beard was,
or whether Hector were not troubled with the tooth-
ache. He hath studied himself half blear-eyed to
know the true symmetry of Cæsar's nose by a shoe-
ing-horn; and this he did to gain the name of a
speculative man.
PESCARA: Mark Prince Ferdinand:
A very salamander lives in's eye,
To mock the eager violence of fire.
SILVIO: That cardinal hath made more bad faces
with his oppression than ever Michael Angelo made
good ones: he lifts up's nose, like a foul porpoise
before a storm.
PESCARA: The Lord Ferdinand laughs.
DELIO: Like a deadly cannon
That lightens ere it smokes.
PESCARA: These are your true pangs of death,
The pangs of life, that struggle with great statesmen.
DELIO: In such a deformed silence witches whisper
their charms.
CARDINAL: Doth she make religion her riding-
 hood
To keep her from the sun and tempest?
FERDINAND: That,
That damns her. Methinks her fault and beauty,
Blended together, show like leprosy,
The whiter, the fouler. I make it a question
Whether her beggarly brats were ever christened.
CARDINAL: I will instantly solicit the state of
 Ancona
To have them banished.
FERDINAND: You are for Loretto:
I shall not be at your ceremony; fare you well.—
Write to the Duke of Malfi, my young nephew
She had by her first husband, and acquaint him
With's mother's honesty.
BOSOLA: I will.
FERDINAND: Antonio!
A slave that only smelled of ink and counters,
And never in's life looked like a gentleman,
But in the audit-time.—Go, go presently,
Draw me out an hundred and fifty of our horse,
And meet me at the fort-bridge.
 [*Exeunt*]

SCENE IV.

The shrine of Our Lady of Loretto.

[*Enter* Two Pilgrims]
1ST PILGRIM: I have not seen a goodlier shrine
 than this;
Yet I have visited many.

2ND PILGRIM: The Cardinal of Arragon
Is this day to resign his cardinal's hat:
His sister duchess likewise is arrived
To pay her vow of pilgrimage. I expect
A noble ceremony.
    1ST PILGRIM: No question.—They come.
      [*Here the ceremony of the* Cardinal's *instalment,
      in the habit of a soldier, is performed by his
      delivering up his cross, hat, robes, and ring, at
      the shrine, and the investing of him with sword,
      helmet, shield, and spurs; then* Antonio, *the*
      Duchess, *and their* Children, *having presented
      themselves at the shrine, are, by a form of ban-
      ishment in dumb-show expressed towards them
      by the* Cardinal *and the state of Ancona, ban-
      ished: during all which ceremony, this ditty is
      sung, to very solemn music, by divers church-
      men*]
Arms and honors deck thy story,
To thy fame's eternal glory!
Adverse fortune ever fly thee;
No disastrous fate come nigh thee!
I alone will sing thy praises,
Whom to honor virtue raises;
And thy study, that divine is,
Bent to martial discipline is.
Lay aside all those robes lie by thee;
Crown thy arts with arms, they'll beautify thee.
O worthy of worthiest name, adorned in this manner,
Lead bravely thy forces on under war's warlike ban-
    ner!
O, mayst thou prove fortunate in all martial courses!
Guide thou still by skill in arts and forces!
Victory attend thee nigh, whilst fame sings loud thy
    powers;
Triumphant conquest crown thy head, and blessings
    pour down showers!
      [*Exeunt all except the* Two Pilgrims]
    1ST PILGRIM: Here's a strange turn of state! who
    would have thought
So great a lady would have matched herself
Unto so mean a person? yet the cardinal
Bears himself much too cruel.
    2ND PILGRIM: They are banished.
    1ST PILGRIM: But I would ask what power hath
    this state
Of Ancona to determine of a free prince?
    2ND PILGRIM: They are a free state, sir, and her
    brother showed
How that the Pope, fore-hearing of her looseness,
Hath seized into the protection of the church
The dukedom which she held as dowager.
    1ST PILGRIM: But by what justice?
    2ND PILGRIM: Sure, I think by none,
Only her brother's instigation.
    1ST PILGRIM: What was it with such violence he
    took
Off from her finger?
    2ND PILGRIM: 'Twas her wedding-ring;
Which he vowed shortly he would sacrifice

To his revenge.
    1ST PILGRIM: Alas, Antonio!
If that a man be thrust into a well,
No matter who sets hand to't, his own weight
Will bring him sooner to the bottom. Come, let's
    hence.
Fortune makes this conclusion general,
All things do help the unhappy man to fall.
    [*Exeunt*]

SCENE V.

Near Loretto.

    [*Enter* Duchess, Antonio, Children, Cariola, *and*
    Servants]
DUCHESS: Banished Ancona!
ANTONIO: Yes, you see what power
Lightens in great men's breath.
    DUCHESS: Is all our train
Shrunk to this poor remainder?
    ANTONIO: These poor men,
Which have got little in your service, vow
To take your fortune: but your wiser buntings,[35]
Now they are fledged, are gone.
    DUCHESS: They have done wisely.
This puts me in mind of death: physicians thus,
With their hands full of money, use to give o'er
Their patients.
    ANTONIO: Right the fashion of the world:
From decayed fortunes every flatterer shrinks;
Men cease to build where the foundation sinks.
    DUCHESS: I had a very strange dream tonight.
    ANTONIO: What was't?
    DUCHESS: Methought I wore my coronet of state,
And on a sudden all the diamonds
Were changed to pearls.
    ANTONIO: My interpretation
Is, you'll weep shortly; for to me the pearls
Do signify your tears.
    DUCHESS: The birds that live i' the field
On the wild benefit of nature live
Happier than we; for they may choose their mates,
And carol their sweet pleasures to the spring.
    [*Enter* Bosola *with a letter*]
BOSOLA: You are happily o'erta'en.
DUCHESS: From my brother?
BOSOLA: Yes, from the Lord Ferdinand your
    brother
All love and safety.
    DUCHESS: Thou dost blanch mischief,
Wouldst make it white. See, see, like to calm weather
At sea before a tempest, false hearts speak fair
To those they intend most mischief.
[*Reads*] "Send Antonio to me; I want his head in a
    business."
A politic equivocation!

[35] A bird that resembles a lark but does not possess its
voice.

He doth not want your counsel, but your head;
That is, he cannot sleep till you be dead.
And here's another pitfall that's strewed o'er
With roses; mark it, 'tis a cunning one:
[*Reads*] "I stand engaged for your husband for
several debts at Naples: let not that trouble him; I
had rather have his heart than his money":—
And I believe so too.

    BOSOLA: What do you believe?

    DUCHESS: That he so much distrusts my husband's
      love,
He will by no means believe his heart is with him
Until he sees it: the devil is not cunning enough
To circumvent us in riddles.

    BOSOLA: Will you reject that noble and free league
Of amity and love which I present you?

    DUCHESS: Their league is like that of some politic
      kings,
Only to make themselves of strength and power
To be our after-ruin: tell them so.

    BOSOLA: And what from you?

    ANTONIO: Thus tell him; I will not come.

    BOSOLA: And what of this?

    ANTONIO: My brothers have dispersed
Blood-hounds abroad; which till I hear are muzzled,
No truce, though hatched with ne'er such politic
    skill,
Is safe, that hangs upon our enemies' will.
I'll not come at them.

    BOSOLA: This proclaims your breeding:
Every small thing draws a base mind to fear,
As the adamant draws iron. Fare you well, sir:
You shall shortly hear from's. [*Exit*]

    DUCHESS: I suspect some ambush:
Therefore by all my love I do conjure you
To take your eldest son, and fly towards Milan.
Let us not venture all this poor remainder
In one unlucky bottom.

    ANTONIO: You counsel safely.
Best of my life, farewell, since we must part:
Heaven hath a hand in't; but no otherwise
Then as some curious artist takes in sunder
A clock or watch, when it is out of frame,
To bring't in better order.

    DUCHESS: I know not which is best,
To see you dead, or part with you.—Farewell, boy:
Thou art happy that thou hast not understanding
To know thy misery; for all our wit
And reading brings us to a truer sense
Of sorrow.—In the eternal church, sir,
I do hope we shall not part thus.

    ANTONIO: O, be of comfort!
Make patience a noble fortitude,
And think not how unkindly we are used:
Man, like to cassia,[36] is proved best being bruised.

    DUCHESS: Must I, like a slave-born Russian,
Account it praise to suffer tyranny?
And yet, O Heaven, thy heavy hand is in't!
I have seen my little boy oft scourge his top,

    [36] A medicinal bark.

And compared myself to't: naught made me e'er
Go right but Heaven's scourge-stick.

    ANTONIO: Do not weep:
Heaven fashioned us of nothing, and we strive
To bring ourselves to nothing.—Farewell, Cariola,
And thy sweet armful.—If I do never see thee more,
Be a good mother to your little ones,
And save them from the tiger: fare you well.

    DUCHESS: Let me look upon you once more, for
      that speech
Came from a dying father: your kiss is colder
Than that I have seen an holy anchorite
Give to a dead man's skull.

    ANTONIO: My heart is turned to a heavy lump of
      lead,
With which I sound my danger: fare you well.
    [*Exeunt* Antonio *and his* Son]

    DUCHESS: My laurel is all withered.

    CARIOLA: Look, madam, what a troop of armèd
      men
Make towards us.

    DUCHESS: O, they are very welcome:
When Fortune's wheel is over-charged with princes,
The weight makes it move swift: I would have my
    ruin
Be sudden.
    [*Re-enter* Bosola *visarded, with a* Guard]
      I am your adventure,[37] am I not?

    BOSOLA: You are: you must see your husband no
      more.

    DUCHESS: What devil art thou that counterfeit'st
      Heaven's thunder?

    BOSOLA: Is that terrible? I would have you tell me
      whether
Is that note worse that frights the silly birds
Out of the corn, or that which doth allure them
To the nets? you have hearkened to the last too much.

    DUCHESS: O misery! like to a rusty o'ercharged
      cannon,
Shall I never fly in pieces?—Come, to what prison?

    BOSOLA: To none.

    DUCHESS: Whither, then?

    BOSOLA: To your palace.

    DUCHESS: I have heard
That Charon's boat serves to convey all o'er
The dismal lake, but brings none back again.

    BOSOLA: Your brothers mean you safety and pity.

    DUCHESS: Pity!
With such a pity men preserve alive
Pheasants and quails, when they are not fat enough
To be eaten.

    BOSOLA: These are your children?

    DUCHESS: Yes.

    BOSOLA: Can they prattle?

    DUCHESS: No;
But I intend, since they were born accursed,
Curses shall be their first language.

    BOSOLA: Fie, madam!
Forget this base, low fellow,—

    [37] Quarry.

DUCHESS: Were I a man,
I'd beat that counterfeit face into thy other.
    BOSOLA: One of no birth.
    DUCHESS: Say that he was born mean,
Man is most happy when's own actions
Be arguments and examples of his virtue.
    BOSOLA: A barren, beggarly virtue.
    DUCHESS: I prithee, who is greatest? can you tell?
Sad tales befit my woe: I'll tell you one.
A salmon, as she swam unto the sea,
Met with a dog-fish, who encounters her
With this rough language: "Why art thou so bold
To mix thyself with our high state of floods,
Being no eminent courtier, but one
That for the calmest and fresh time o' the year
Dost live in shallow rivers, rank'st thyself
With silly smelts and shrimps? and darest thou
Pass by our dog-ship without reverence?"
"O!" quoth the salmon, "sister, be at peace:
Thank Jupiter we both have passed the net!
Our value never can be truly known,
Till in the fisher's basket we be shown:
I' the market then my price may be the higher,
Even when I am nearest to the cook and fire."
So to great men the moral may be stretched;
Men oft are valued high, when they're most
        wretched.—
But come, whither you please. I am armed 'gainst
        misery;
Bent to all sways of the oppressor's will:
There's no deep valley but near some great hill.
    [Exeunt]

ACT IV. SCENE I.

An apartment in the Duchess' *palace at Malfi.*

    [Enter Ferdinand and Bosola]
    FERDINAND: How doth our sister duchess bear
        herself
In her imprisonment?
    BOSOLA: Nobly: I'll describe her.
She's sad as one long used to't, and she seems
Rather to welcome the end of misery
Than shun it; a behavior so noble
As gives a majesty to adversity:
You may discern the shape of loveliness
More perfect in her tears than in her smiles:
She will muse four hours together; and her silence,
Methinks, expresseth more than if she spake.
    FERDINAND: Her melancholy seems to be fortified
With a strange disdain.
    BOSOLA: 'Tis so; and this restraint,
Like English mastiffs that grow fierce with tying,
Makes her too passionately apprehend
Those pleasures she's kept from.
    FERDINAND: Curse upon her!
I will no longer study in the book

Of another's heart. Inform her what I told you. [Exit]
    [Enter Duchess]
    BOSOLA: All comfort to your grace!
    DUCHESS: I will have none.
Pray thee, why dost thou wrap thy poisoned pills
In gold and sugar?
    BOSOLA: Your elder brother, the Lord Ferdinand,
Is come to visit you, and sends you word,
'Cause once he rashly made a solemn vow
Never to see you more, he comes i' the night;
And prays you gently neither torch nor taper
Shine in your chamber: he will kiss your hand,
And reconcile himself; but for his vow
He dares not see you.
    DUCHESS: At his pleasure.—
Take hence the lights.—He's come.
    [Enter Ferdinand]
    FERDINAND: Where are you?
    DUCHESS: Here, sir.
    FERDINAND: This darkness suits you well.
    DUCHESS: I would ask your pardon.
    FERDINAND: You have it;
For I account it the honorabl'st revenge,
Where I may kill, to pardon.—Where are your cubs?
    DUCHESS: Whom?
    FERDINAND: Call them your children;
For though our national law distinguish bastards
From true legitimate issue, compassionate nature
Makes them all equal.
    DUCHESS: Do you visit me for this?
You violate a sacrament o' the church
Shall make you howl in hell for't.
    FERDINAND: It had been well,
Could you have lived thus always; for, indeed,
You were too much i' the light:—but no more:
I come to seal my peace with you. Here's a hand
    [Gives her a dead man's hand]
To which you have vowed much love; the ring upon't
You gave.
    DUCHESS: I affectionately kiss it.
    FERDINAND: Pray, do, and bury the print of it in
        your heart.
I will leave this ring with you for a love-token;
And the hand as sure as the ring; and do not doubt
But you shall have the heart too: when you need a
        friend,
Send it to him that owned it; you shall see
Whether he can aid you.
    DUCHESS: You are very cold:
I fear you are not well after your travel.—
Ha! lights!—O, horrible!
    FERDINAND: Let her have lights enough. [Exit]
    DUCHESS: What witchcraft doth he practice, that he
        hath left
A dead man's hand here?
    [Here is discovered, behind a traverse,[38] the
        artificial figures of Antonio and his Children,
        appearing as if they were dead]
    [38] A curtain.

BOSOLA: Look you, here's the piece from which
    'twas ta'en.
He doth present you this sad spectacle,
That, now you know directly they are dead,
Hereafter you may wisely cease to grieve
For that which cannot be recoverèd.
    DUCHESS: There is not between Heaven and earth
    one wish
I stay for after this: it wastes me more
Than were't my picture, fashioned out of wax,
Stuck with a magical needle, and then buried
In some foul dunghill; and yond's an excellent
    property
For a tyrant, which I would account mercy.
    BOSOLA: What's that?
    DUCHESS: If they would bind me to that lifeless
    trunk,
And let me freeze to death.
    BOSOLA: Come, you must live.
    DUCHESS: That's the greatest torture souls feel in
    hell,
In hell, that they must live, and cannot die.
Portia,[39] I'll new kindle thy coals again,
And revive the rare and almost dead example
Of a loving wife.
    BOSOLA: O, fie! despair? remember
You are a Christian.
    DUCHESS: The church enjoins fasting:
I'll starve myself to death.
    BOSOLA: Leave this vain sorrow.
Things being at the worst begin to mend: the bee
When he hath shot his sting into your hand,
May then play with your eyelid.
    DUCHESS: Good comfortable fellow,
Persuade a wretch that's broke upon the wheel
To have all his bones new set; entreat him live
To be executed again. Who must despatch me?
I account this world a tedious theater,
For I do play a part in't 'gainst my will.
    BOSOLA: Come, be of comfort; I will save your life.
    DUCHESS: Indeed, I have not leisure to tend
So small a business.
    BOSOLA: Now, by my life, I pity you.
    DUCHESS: Thou art a fool, then,
To waste thy pity on a thing so wretched
As cannot pity itself. I am full of daggers.
Puff, let me blow these vipers from me.
    [Enter Servant]
What are you?
    SERVANT: One that wishes you long life.
    DUCHESS: I would thou wert hanged for the hor-
    rible curse
Thou hast given me: I shall shortly grow one
Of the miracles of pity. I'll go pray;—
No, I'll go curse.
    BOSOLA: O, fie!

[39] Brutus' wife, who committed suicide by casting burning coals into her mouth and choking herself with them
after the death of Brutus at Philippi.

    DUCHESS: I could curse the stars.
    BOSOLA: O, fearful.
    DUCHESS: And those three smiling seasons of the
    year
Into a Russian winter: nay, the world
To its first chaos.
    BOSOLA: Look you, the stars shine still.
    DUCHESS: O, but you must
Remember, my curse hath a great way to go.—
Plagues, that make lanes through largest families,
Consume them!—
    BOSOLA: Fie, lady!
    DUCHESS: Let them, like tyrants,
Never be remembered but for the ill they have done;
Let all the zealous prayers of mortified
Churchmen forget them!—
    BOSOLA: O, uncharitable!
    DUCHESS: Let Heaven a little while cease crown-
    ing martyrs,
To punish them!—
Go, howl them this, and say, I long to bleed:
It is some mercy when men kill with speed. [Exit]
    [Re-enter Ferdinand]
    FERDINAND: Excellent, as I would wish; she's
    plagued in art:
These presentations are but framed in wax
By the curious master in that quality,
Vincentio Lauriola, and she takes them
For true substantial bodies.
    BOSOLA: Why do you do this?
    FERDINAND: To bring her to despair.
    BOSOLA: Faith, end here,
And go no farther in your cruelty:
Send her a penitential garment to put on
Next to her delicate skin, and furnish her
With beads and prayer-books.
    FERDINAND: Damn her! that body of hers,
While that my blood ran pure in 't, was more worth
Than that which thou wouldst comfort, called a soul.
I will send her masks of common courtezans,
Have her meat served up by bawds and ruffians,
And, 'cause she'll needs be mad, I am resolved
To remove forth the common hospital
All the mad-folk, and place them near her lodging;
There let them practice together, sing and dance,
And act their gambols to the full o' the moon:
If she can sleep the better for it, let her.
Your work is almost ended.
    BOSOLA: Must I see her again?
    FERDINAND: Yes.
    BOSOLA: Never.
    FERDINAND: You must.
    BOSOLA: Never in mine own shape;
That's forfeited by my intelligence
And this last cruel lie: when you send me next,
The business shall be comfort.
    FERDINAND: Very likely;
Thy pity is nothing of kin to thee. Antonio
Lurks about Milan: thou shalt shortly thither,

To feed a fire as great as my revenge,
Which never will slack till it have spent his fuel:
Intemperate agues make physicians cruel.
    [*Exeunt*]

SCENE II.

Another room in the Duchess' *lodging.*

    [*Enter* Duchess *and* Cariola]
    DUCHESS: What hideous noise was that?
    CARIOLA: 'Tis the wild consort
Of madmen, lady, which your tyrant brother
Hath placed about your lodging: this tyranny,
I think, was never practiced till this hour.
    DUCHESS: Indeed, I thank him: nothing but noise
    and folly
Can keep me in my right wits; whereas reason
And silence make me stark mad. Sit down;
Discourse to me some dismal tragedy.
    CARIOLA: O, 'twill increase your melancholy.
    DUCHESS: Thou art deceived:
To hear of greater grief would lessen mine.
This is a prison?
    CARIOLA: Yes, but you shall live
To shake this durance off.
    DUCHESS: Thou art a fool:
The robin-redbreast and the nightingale
Never live long in cages.
    CARIOLA: Pray, dry your eyes.
What think you of, madam?
    DUCHESS: Of nothing;
When I muse thus, I sleep.
    CARIOLA: Like a madman, with your eyes open?
    DUCHESS: Dost thou think we shall know one
    another
In the other world?
    CARIOLA: Yes, out of question.
    DUCHESS: O, that it were possible we might
But hold some two days' conference with the dead!
From them I should learn somewhat, I am sure,
I never shall know here. I'll tell thee a miracle;
I am not mad yet, to my cause of sorrow:
The Heaven o'er my head seems made of molten
    brass,
The earth of flaming sulphur, yet I am not mad.
I am acquainted with sad misery
As the tanned galley-slave is with his oar;
Necessity makes me suffer constantly,
And custom makes it easy. Who do I look like now?
    CARIOLA: Like to your picture in the gallery,
A deal of life in show, but none in practice;
Or rather like some reverend monument
Whose ruins are even pitied.
    DUCHESS: Very proper;
And Fortune seems only to have her eyesight
To behold my tragedy.—How now!
What noise is that?
    [*Enter* Servant]

    SERVANT: I am come to tell you
Your brother hath intended you some sport.
A great physician, when the Pope was sick
Of a deep melancholy, presented him
With several sorts of madmen, which wild object
Being full of change and sport, forced him to laugh,
And so the imposthume[40] broke: the self-same cure
The duke intends on you.
    DUCHESS: Let them come in.
    SERVANT: There's a mad lawyer; and a secular
    priest;
A doctor that hath forfeited his wits
By jealousy; an astrologian
That in his works said such a day o' the month
Should be the day of doom, and, failing of't,
Ran mad; an English tailor crazed i' the brain
With the study of new fashions; a gentleman-usher
Quite beside himself with care to keep in mind
The number of his lady's salutations
Or "How do you" she employed him in each morn-
    ing;
A farmer, too, an excellent knave in grain,
Mad 'cause he was hindered transportation:
And let one broker that's mad loose to these,
You'd think the devil were among them.
    DUCHESS: Sit, Cariola.—Let them loose when you
    please,
For I am chained to endure all your tyranny.
    [*Enter* Madmen]
    [*Here this song is sung to a dismal kind of music
    by a* Madman]
    O, let us howl some heavy note,
      Some deadly doggèd howl,
    Sounding as from the threatening throat
      Of beasts and fatal fowl!
    As ravens, screech-owls, bulls, and bears,
      We'll bell, and bawl our parts,
    Till irksome noise have cloyed your ears
      And còrrosived your hearts.
    At last, whenas our quire wants breath,
      Our bodies being blest,
    We'll sing, like swans, to welcome death,
      And die in love and rest.
    1ST MADMAN: Doom's-day not come yet! I'll draw
it nearer by a perspective, or make a glass that shall
set all the world on fire upon an instant. I cannot
sleep; my pillow is stuffed with a litter of porcupines.
    2ND MADMAN: Hell is a mere glass-house, where
the devils are continually blowing up women's souls
on hollow irons, and the fire never goes out.
    3RD MADMAN: I will lie with every woman in my
parish the tenth night; I will tythe them over like
haycocks.
    4TH MADMAN: Shall my pothecary out-go me be-
cause I am a cuckold? I have found out his roguery;
he makes alum of his wife's urine, and sells it to
Puritans that have sore throats with overstraining.
    1ST MADMAN: I have skill in heraldry.
    2ND MADMAN: Hast?
    40 Ulcer.

1ST MADMAN: You do give for your crest a wood-cock's head with the brains picked out on't; you are a very ancient gentleman.

3RD MADMAN: Greek is turned Turk: we are only to be saved by the Helvetian translation.[41]

1ST MADMAN: Come on, sir, I will lay the law to you.

2ND MADMAN: O, rather lay a corrosive: the law will eat to the bone.

3RD MADMAN: He that drinks but to satisfy nature is damned.

4TH MADMAN: If I had my glass here, I would show a sight should make all the women here call me mad doctor.

1ST MADMAN: What's he? a rope-maker?

2ND MADMAN: No, no, no, a snuffling knave that, while he shows the tombs, will have his hand in a wench's placket.

3RD MADMAN: Woe to the caroche that brought home my wife from the masque at three o'clock in the morning! it had a large feather-bed in it.

4TH MADMAN: I have pared the devil's nails forty times, roasted them in raven's eggs, and cured agues with them.

3RD MADMAN: Get me three hundred milch-bats, to make possets to procure sleep.

4TH MADMAN: All the college may throw their caps at me: I have made a soap-boiler costive;[42] it was my masterpiece.

[Here a dance of Eight Madmen, with music answerable thereto; after which, Bosola, like an Old Man, enters]

DUCHESS: Is he mad too?

SERVANT: Pray, question him. I'll leave you.

[Exeunt Servant and Madmen]

BOSOLA: I am come to make thy tomb.

DUCHESS: Ha! my tomb!
Thou speak'st as if I lay upon my deathbed,
Gasping for breath: dost thou perceive me sick?

BOSOLA: Yes, and the more dangerously, since thy sickness is insensible.

DUCHESS: Thou art not mad, sure: dost know me?

BOSOLA: Yes.

DUCHESS: Who am I?

BOSOLA: Thou art a box of worm-seed, at best but a salvatory of green mummy. What's this flesh? a little crudded[43] milk, fantastical puff-paste. Our bodies are weaker than those paper-prisons boys use to keep flies in; more contemptible, since ours is to preserve earth-worms. Didst thou ever see a lark in a cage? Such is the soul in the body: this world is like her little turf of grass, and the Heaven o'er our heads, like her looking-glass, only gives us a miserable knowledge of the small compass of our prison.

DUCHESS: Am not I thy duchess?

BOSOLA: Thou art some great woman, sure, for riot

[41] The Genevan Bible, a translation made by Puritan exiles in 1560.
[42] Constipated.
[43] Curdled.

begins to sit on thy forehead (clad in grey hairs) twenty years sooner than on a merry milkmaid's. Thou sleepest worse than if a mouse should be forced to take up her lodging in a cat's ear: a little infant that breeds its teeth, should it lie with thee, would cry out, as if thou wert the more unquiet bedfellow.

DUCHESS: I am Duchess of Malfi still.

BOSOLA: That makes thy sleeps so broken:
Glories, like glow-worms, afar off shine bright,
But looked to near, have neither heat nor light.

DUCHESS: Thou art very plain.

BOSOLA: My trade is to flatter the dead, not the living;
I am a tomb-maker.

DUCHESS: And thou comest to make my tomb?

BOSOLA: Yes.

DUCHESS: Let me be a little merry:—of what stuff wilt thou make it?

BOSOLA: Nay, resolve me first, of what fashion?

DUCHESS: Why do we grow fantastical in our death-beds? do we affect fashion in the grave?

BOSOLA: Most ambitiously. Princes' images on their tombs do not lie, as they were wont, seeming to pray up to Heaven; but with their hands under their cheeks, as if they died of the toothache: they are not carved with their eyes fixed upon the stars; but as their minds were wholly bent upon the world, the self-same way they seem to turn their faces.

DUCHESS: Let me know fully therefore the effect
Of this thy dismal preparation,
This talk fit for a charnel.

BOSOLA: Now I shall:——

[Enter Executioners, with a coffin, cords, and a bell]

Here is a present from your princely brothers;
And may it arrive welcome, for it brings
Last benefit, last sorrow.

DUCHESS: Let me see it:
I have so much obedience in my blood,
I wish it in their veins to do them good.

BOSOLA: This is your last presence-chamber.

CARIOLA: O my sweet lady!

DUCHESS: Peace; it affrights not me.

BOSOLA: I am the common bellman,
That usually is sent to condemned persons
The night before they suffer.

DUCHESS: Even now thou said'st
Thou wast a tomb-maker.

BOSOLA: 'Twas to bring you
By degrees to mortification. Listen.

Hark, now every thing is still
The screech-owl and the whistler shrill
Call upon our dame aloud,
And bid her quickly don her shroud!
Much you had of land and rent;
Your length in clay's now competent:
A long war disturbed your mind;
Here your perfect peace is signed.
Of what is't fools make such vain keeping?

Sin their conception, their birth weeping,
Their life a general mist of error,
Their death a hideous storm of terror.
Strew your hair with powders sweet,
Don clean linen, bathe your feet,
And (the foul fiend more to check)
A crucifix let bless your neck:
'Tis now full tide 'tween night and day;
End your groan, and come away.

CARIOLA: Hence, villains, tyrants, murderers! alas!
What will you do with my lady?—Call for help.
DUCHESS: To whom? to our next neighbors? they
are mad-folks.
BOSOLA: Remove that noise.
DUCHESS: Farewell, Cariola.
In my last will I have not much to give:
A many hungry guests have fed upon me;
Thine will be a poor reversion.[44]
CARIOLA: I will die with her.
DUCHESS: I pray thee, look thou giv'st my little
boy
Some syrup for his cold, and let the girl
Say her prayers ere she sleep.
[Cariola *is forced out by the* Executioners]
Now what you please:
What death?
BOSOLA: Strangling; here are your executioners.
DUCHESS: I forgive them:
The apoplexy, catarrh, or cough o' the lungs
Would do as much as they do.
BOSOLA: Doth not death fright you?
DUCHESS: Who would be afraid on't,
Knowing to meet such excellent company
In the other world?
BOSOLA: Yet, methinks,
The manner of your death should much afflict you:
This cord should terrify you.
DUCHESS: Not a whit:
What would it pleasure me to have my throat cut
With diamonds? or to be smotherèd
With cassia? or to be shot to death with pearls?
I know death hath ten thousand several doors
For men to take their exists; and 'tis found
They go on such strange geometrical hinges,
You may open them both ways; any way, for Heaven
sake,
So I were out of your whispering. Tell my brothers
That I perceive death, now I am well awake,
Best gift is they can give or I can take.
I would fain put off my last woman's fault,
I'd not be tedious to you.
1ST EXECUTIONER: We are ready.
DUCHESS: Dispose my breath how please you; but
body
Bestow upon my women, will you?
1ST EXECUTIONER: Yes.
DUCHESS: Pull, and pull strongly, for your able
strength

[44] Residue.

Must pull down Heaven upon me:—
Yet stay; Heaven-gates are not so highly arched
As princes' palaces; they that enter there.
Must go upon their knees. [*Kneels*]—Come, violent
death,
Serve for mandragora to make me sleep!—
Go tell my brothers, when I am laid out,
They then may feed in quiet.
[*The* Executioners *strangle the* Duchess]
BOSOLA: Where's the waiting woman?
Fetch her: some other strangle the children.
[Cariola *and* Children *are brought in by the*
Executioners; *who presently strangle the* Chil-
dren]
Look you, there sleeps your mistress.
CARIOLA: O, you are damned
Perpetually for this! My turn is next,
Is't not so ordered?
BOSOLA: Yes, and I am glad
You are so well prepared for't.
CARIOLA: You are deceived, sir,
I am not prepared for't, I will not die;
I will first come to my answer, and know
How I have offended.
BOSOLA: Come, despatch her.—
You kept her counsel; now you shall keep ours.
CARIOLA: I will not die, I must not; I am contracted
To a young gentleman.
1ST EXECUTIONER: Here's your wedding-ring.
CARIOLA: Let me but speak with the duke; I'll dis-
cover
Treason to his person.
BOSOLA: Delays:—throttle her.
1ST EXECUTIONER: She bites and scratches.
CARIOLA: If you kill me now,
I am damned; I have not been at confession
This two years.
BOSOLA: [*To* Executioners] When?
CARIOLA: I am quick with child.
BOSOLA: Why, then,
Your credit's saved.
[*The* Executioners *strangle* Cariola]
Bear her into the next room;
Let these lie still.
[*Exeunt the* Executioners *with the body of*
Cariola]
[*Enter* Ferdinand]
FERDINAND: Is she dead?
BOSOLA: She is what
You'd have her. But here begin your pity. [*Shows
the* Children *strangled*]
Alas, how have these offended?
FERDINAND: The death
Of young wolves is never to be pitied.
BOSOLA: Fix your eye here.
FERDINAND: Constantly.
BOSOLA: Do you not weep?
Other sins only speak; murder shrieks out:
The element of water moistens the earth,
But blood flies upwards and bedews the heavens.

FERDINAND: Cover her face; mine eyes dazzle: she
  died young.

BOSOLA: I think not so; her infelicity
Seemed to have years too many.

FERDINAND: She and I were twins;
And should I die this instant, I had lived
Her time to a minute.

BOSOLA: It seems she was born first:
You have bloodily approved the ancient truth,
That kindred commonly do worse agree
Than remote strangers.

FERDINAND: Let me see her face
Again. Why didst not thou pity her? what
An excellent honest man mightst thou have been,
If thou hadst borne her to some sanctuary!
Or, bold in a good cause, opposed thyself,
With thy advancèd sword above thy head,
Between her innocence and my revenge!
I bade thee, when I was distracted of my wits,
Go kill my dearest friend, and thou hast done't.
For let me but examine well the cause:
What was the meanness of her match to me?
Only I must confess I had a hope,
Had she continued widow, to have gained
An infinite mass of treasure by her death:
And what was the main cause? her marriage,
That drew a stream of gall quite through my heart.
For thee, as we observe in tragedies
That a good actor many times is cursed
For playing a villain's part, I hate thee for't,
And, for my sake, say, thou hast done much ill well.

BOSOLA: Let me quicken your memory, for I per-
  ceive
You are falling into ingratitude: I challenge
The reward due to my service.

FERDINAND: I'll tell thee
What I'll give thee.

BOSOLA: Do.

FERDINAND: I'll give thee a pardon
For this murder.

BOSOLA: Ha!

FERDINAND: Yes, and 'tis
The largest bounty I can study to do thee.
By what authority didst thou execute
This bloody sentence?

BOSOLA: By yours.

FERDINAND: Mine! was I her judge?
Did any ceremonial form of law
Doom her to not-being? did a còmplete jury
Deliver her conviction up i' the court?
Where shalt thou find this judgment registered,
Unless in hell? See, like a bloody fool,
Thou'st forfeited thy life, and thou shalt die for't.

BOSOLA: The office of justice is perverted quite
When one thief hangs another. Who shall dare
To reveal this?

FERDINAND: O, I'll tell thee;
The wolf shall find her grave, and scrape it up,
Not to devour the corpse, but to discover
The horrid murder

BOSOLA: You, not I, shall quake for't.

FERDINAND: Leave me.

BOSOLA: I will first receive my pension.

FERDINAND: You are a villain.

BOSOLA: When your ingratitude
Is judge, I am so.

FERDINAND: O horror,
That not the fear of him which binds the devils
Can prescribe man obedience!—
Never look upon me more.

BOSOLA: Why, fare thee well.
Your brother and yourself are worthy men:
You have a pair of hearts are hollow graves,
Rotten, and rotting others; and your vengeance,
Like two chained bullets, still goes arm in arm:
You may be brothers; for treason, like the plague,
Doth take much in a blood. I stand like one
That long hath ta'en a sweet and golden dream:
I am angry with myself, now that I wake.

FERDINAND: Get thee into some unknown part o'
  the world,
That I may never see thee.

BOSOLA: Let me know
Wherefore I should be thus neglected. Sir,
I served your tyranny, and rather strove
To satisfy yourself than all the world:
And though I loathed the evil, yet I loved
You that did counsel it; and rather sought
To appear a true servant than an honest man.

FERDINAND: I'll go hunt the badger by owl-light.
'Tis a deed of darkness. [Exit]

BOSOLA: He's much distracted. Off, my painted
  honor!
While with vain hopes our faculties we tire,
We seem to sweat in ice and freeze in fire.
What would I do, were this to do again?
I would not change my peace of conscience
For all the wealth of Europe.—She stirs; here's
  life:—
Return, fair soul, from darkness, and lead mine
Out of this sensible hell:—she's warm, she
  breathes:—
Upon thy pale lips I will melt my heart,
To store them with fresh color.—Who's there!
Some cordial drink!—Alas! I dare not call:
So pity would destroy pity.—Her eye opes,
And Heaven in it seems to ope, that late was shut,
To take me up to mercy.

DUCHESS: Antonio!

BOSOLA: Yes, madam, he is living;
The dead bodies you saw were but feigned statues:
He's reconciled to your brothers; the Pope hath
  wrought
The atonement.

DUCHESS: Mercy! [Dies]

BOSOLA: O, she's gone again! there the cords of
  life broke.
O sacred innocence, that sweetly sleeps
On turtles' feathers, whilst a guilty conscience
Is a black register wherein is writ

All our good deeds and bad, a perspective
That shows us hell! That we cannot be suffered
To do good when we have a mind to it!
This is manly sorrow;
These tears, I am very certain, never grew
In my mother's milk: my estate has sunk
Below the degree of fear: where were
These penitent fountains while she was living?
O, they were frozen up! Here is a sight
As direful to my soul as is the sword
Unto a wretch has slain his father. Come,
I'll bear thee hence,
And execute thy last will; that's deliver
Thy body to the reverend dispose
Of some good women: that the cruel tyrant
Shall not deny me. Then I'll post to Milan,
Where somewhat I will speedily enact
Worth my dejection. [*Exit*]

ACT V. SCENE I.

A public place in Milan.

[*Enter* Antonio *and* Delio]
ANTONIO: What think you of my hope of recon-
cilement
To the Arragonian brethren?
DELIO: I misdoubt it;
For though they have sent their letters of safe-
conduct
For your repair to Milan, they appear
But nets to entrap you. The Marquis of Pescara,
Under whom you hold certain land in cheat,[45]
Much 'gainst his noble nature hath been moved
To seize those lands; and some of his dependents
Are at this instant making it their suit
To be invested in your revenues.
I cannot think they mean well to your life
That do deprive you of your means of life,
Your living.
ANTONIO: You are still an heretic
To any safety I can shape myself.
DELIO: Here comes the marquis: I will make my-
self
Petitioner for some part of your land,
To know whither it is flying.
ANTONIO: I pray do.
[*Enter* Pescara]
DELIO: Sir, I have a suit to you.
PESCARA: To me?
DELIO: An easy one:
There is the citadel of Saint Bennet,
With some demesnes, of late in the possession
Of Antonio Bologna,—please you bestow them on
me.
PESCARA: You are my friend; but this is such a suit,
Nor fit for me to give, nor you to take.
DELIO: No, sir?
[45] Subject to escheat.

PESCARA: I will give you ample reason for't
Soon in private:—here's the cardinal's mistress.
[*Enter* Julia]
JULIA: My lord, I am grown your poor petitioner,
And should be an ill beggar, had I not
A great man's letter here, the cardinal's,
To court you in my favor. [*Gives a letter*]
PESCARA: He entreats for you
The citadel of Saint Bennet, that belonged
To the banished Bologna.
JULIA: Yes.
PESCARA: I could not have thought of a friend I
could rather
Pleasure with it: 'tis yours.
JULIA: Sir, I thank you;
And he shall know how doubly I am engaged
Both in your gift, and speediness of giving
Which makes your grant the greater. [*Exit*]
ANTONIO: How they fortify
Themselves with my ruin!
DELIO: Sir, I am
Little bound to you.
PESCARA: Why?
DELIO: Because you denied this suit to me, and
gave't
To such a creature.
PESCARA: Do you know what it was?
It was Antonio's land; not forfeited
By course of law, but ravished from his throat
By the cardinal's entreaty: it were not fit
I should bestow so main a piece of wrong
Upon my friend; 'tis a gratification
Only due to a strumpet, for it is injustice.
Shall I sprinkle the pure blood of innocents
To make those followers I call my friends
Look ruddier upon me? I am glad
This land, ta'en from the owner by such wrong,
Returns again unto so foul an use
As salary for his lust. Learn, good Delio,
To ask noble things of me, and you shall find
I'll be a noble giver.
DELIO: You instruct me well.
ANTONIO: Why, here's a man now would fright
impudence
From sauciest beggars.
PESCARA: Prince Ferdinand's come to Milan,
Sick, as they give out, of an apoplexy;
But some say 'tis a frenzy: I am going
To visit him. [*Exit*]
ANTONIO: 'Tis a noble old fellow.
DELIO: What course do you mean to take, Antonio?
ANTONIO: This night I mean to venture all my
fortune,
Which is no more than a poor lingering life,
To the cardinal's worst of malice: I have got
Private access to his chamber; and intend
To visit him about the mid of night,
As once his brother did our noble duchess.
It may be that the sudden apprehension
Of danger,—for I'll go in mine own shape,—

When he shall see it fraight with love and duty,
May draw the poison out of him, and work
A friendly reconcilement: if it fail,
Yet it shall rid me of this infamous calling;
For better fall once than be ever falling.

DELIO: I'll second you in all danger; and, howe'er,
My life keeps rank with yours.

ANTONIO: You are still my loved and best friend.

[Exeunt]

SCENE II.

A gallery in the Cardinal's palace at Milan.

[Enter Pescara and Doctor]

PESCARA: Now, doctor, may I visit your patient?

DOCTOR: If't please your lordship: but he's instantly
To take the air here in the gallery
By my direction.

PESCARA: Pray thee, what's his disease?

DOCTOR: A very pestilent disease, my lord,
They call lycanthropia.

PESCARA: What's that?
I need a dictionary to't.

DOCTOR: I'll tell you.
In those that are possessed with't there o'erflows
Such melancholy humor they imagine
Themselves to be transformed into wolves;
Steal forth to churchyards in the dead of night,
And dig dead bodies up: as two nights since
One met the duke 'bout midnight in a lane
Behind Saint Mark's church, with the leg of a man
Upon his shoulder; and he howled fearfully;
Said he was a wolf, only the difference
Was, a wolf's skin was hairy on the outside,
His on the inside; bade them take their swords,
Rip up his flesh, and try: straight I was sent for,
And, having ministered to him, found his grace
Very well recovered.

PESCARA: I am glad on't.

DOCTOR: Yet not without some fear
Of a relapse. If he grow to his fit again,
I'll go a nearer way to work with him
Than ever Paracelsus[46] dreamed of; if
They'll give me leave, I'll buffet his madness out of
    him.
Stand aside; he comes.

[Enter Ferdinand, Cardinal, Malatesti, and
    Bosola]

FERDINAND: Leave me.

MALATESTI: Why doth your lordship love this
solitariness?

FERDINAND: Eagles commonly fly alone; they are
crows, daws, and starlings that flock together. Look,
what's that follows me?

MALATESTI: Nothing, my lord.

FERDINAND: Yes.

[46] Physician and alchemist (1493?-1541).

MALATESTI: 'Tis your shadow.

FERDINAND: Stay it; let it not haunt me.

MALATESTI: Impossible, if you move, and the sun
shine.

FERDINAND: I will throttle it. [Throws himself
down on his shadow]

MALATESTI: O, my lord, you are angry with
nothing.

FERDINAND: You are a fool: how is't possible I
should catch my shadow, unless I fall upon't? When
I go to hell, I mean to carry a bribe; for, look you,
good gifts evermore make way for the worst persons.

PESCARA: Rise, good my lord.

FERDINAND: I am studying the art of patience.

PESCARA: 'Tis a noble virtue.

FERDINAND: To drive six snails before me from
this town to Moscow; neither use goad nor whip to
them, but let them take their own time;—the patient'st man i' the world match me for an experiment;
—and I'll crawl after like a sheep-biter.

CARDINAL: Force him up.

[They raise him]

FERDINAND: Use me well, you were best. What
I have done, I have done: I'll confess nothing.

DOCTOR: Now let me come to him.—Are you mad,
my lord? are you out of your princely wits?

FERDINAND: What's he?

PESCARA: Your doctor.

FERDINAND: Let me have his beard sawed off, and
his eyebrows filed more civil.

DOCTOR: I must do mad tricks with him, for that's
the only way on't.—I have brought your grace a
salamander's skin to keep you from sun-burning.

FERDINAND: I have cruel sore eyes.

DOCTOR: The white of a cockatrix's egg is present
remedy.

FERDINAND: Let it be a new laid one, you were
    best.—
Hide me from him: physicians are like kings,—
They brook no contradiction.

DOCTOR: Now he begins to fear me: now let me
alone with him.

CARDINAL: How now! put off your gown!

DOCTOR: Let me have some forty urinals filled
with rose-water: he and I'll go pelt one another with
them.—Now he begins to fear me.—Can you fetch
a frisk, sir?—Let him go, let him go, upon my peril:
I find by his eye he stands in awe of me; I'll make
him as tame as a dormouse.

FERDINAND: Can you fetch your frisks, sir!—I will
stamp him into a cullis, flay off his skin, to cover
one of the anatomies[47] this rogue hath set i' the cold
yonder in Barber-Surgeon's[48] hall.—Hence, hence!
you are all of you like beasts for sacrifice: there's
nothing left of you but tongue and belly, flattery and
lechery. [Exit]

PESCARA: Doctor, he did not fear you thoroughly.

[47] Skeletons.

[48] The surgeons or barber-surgeons were given the
bodies of four executed criminals each year.

DOCTOR: True; I was somewhat too forward.

BOSOLA: Mercy upon me, what a fatal judgment
Hath fall'n upon this Ferdinand!

PESCARA: Knows your grace
What accident hath brought unto the prince
This strange distraction?

CARDINAL: [Aside] I must feign somewhat.—Thus
they say it grew.
You have heard it rumored, for these many years
None of our family dies but there is seen
The shape of an old woman, which is given
By tradition to us to have been murdered
By her nephews for her riches. Such a figure
One night, as the prince sat up late at's book,
Appeared to him; when crying out for help,
The gentlemen of's chamber found his grace
All on a cold sweat, altered much in face
And language: since which apparition,
He hath grown worse and worse, and I much fear
He cannot live.

BOSOLA: Sir, I would speak with you.

PESCARA: We'll leave your grace,
Wishing to the sick prince, our noble lord,
All health of mind and body.

CARDINAL: You are most welcome.
[Exeunt Pescara, Malatesti, and Doctor]
Are you come? so.—[Aside] This fellow must not
know
By any means I had intelligence
In our duchess' death; for, though I counselled it,
The full of all the engagement seemed to grow
From Ferdinand.—Now, sir, how fares our sister?
I do not think but sorrow makes her look
Like to an oft-dyed garment: she shall now
Taste comfort from me. Why do you look so wildly?
O, the fortune of your master here the prince
Dejects you; but be you of happy comfort:
If you'll do one thing for me I'll entreat,
Though he had a cold tombstone o'er his bones,
I'd make you what you would be.

BOSOLA: Any thing;
Give it me in a breath, and let me fly to't:
They that think long small expedition win,
For musing much o' the end cannot begin.
[Enter Julia]

JULIA: Sir, will you come in to supper?

CARDINAL: I am busy; leave me.

JULIA: [Aside] What an excellent shape hath that
fellow! [Exit]

CARDINAL: 'Tis thus. Antonio lurks here in Milan:
Inquire him out, and kill him. While he lives,
Our sister cannot marry; and I have thought
Of an excellent match for her. Do this, and style me
Thy advancement.

BOSOLA: But by what means shall I find him out?

CARDINAL: There is a gentleman called Delio
Here in the camp, that hath been long approved
His loyal friend. Set eye upon that fellow;
Follow him to mass; may be Antonio,
Although he do account religion
But a school-name, for fashion of the world
May accompany him; or else go inquire out
Delio's confessor, and see if you can bribe
Him to reveal it. There are a thousand ways
A man might find to trace him; as to know
What fellows haunt the Jews for taking up
Great sums of money, for sure he's in want;
Or else to go to the picture-makers, and learn
Who bought her picture lately: some of these
Happily may take.

BOSOLA: Well, I'll not freeze i' the business:
I would see that wretched thing, Antonio,
Above all sights i' the world.

CARDINAL: Do, and be happy. [Exit]

BOSOLA: This fellow doth breed basilisks in's
eyes,
He's nothing else but murder; yet he seems
Not to have notice of the duchess' death.
'Tis his cunning: I must follow his example;
There cannot be a surer way to trace
Than that of an old fox.
[Re-enter Julia]

JULIA: So, sir, you are well met.

BOSOLA: How now!

JULIA: Nay, the doors are fast enough:
Now, sir, I will make you confess your treachery.

BOSOLA: Treachery!

JULIA: Yes, confess to me
Which of my women 'twas you hired to put
Love-powder into my drink?

BOSOLA: Love-powder!

JULIA: Yes, when I was at Malfi.
Why should I fall in love with such a face else?
I have already suffered for thee so much pain,
The only remedy to do me good
Is to kill my longing.

BOSOLA: Sure, your pistol holds
Nothing but perfumes or kissing-comfits.[49]
Excellent lady!
You have a pretty way on't to discover
Your longing. Come, come, I'll disarm you,
And arm you thus: yet this is wondrous strange.

JULIA: Compare thy form and my eyes together,
You'll find my love no such great miracle.
Now you'll say
I am wanton: this nice modesty in ladies
Is but a troublesome familiar
That haunts them.

BOSOLA: Know you me, I am a blunt soldier.

JULIA: The better:
Sure, there wants fire where there are no lively sparks
Of roughness.

BOSOLA: And I want compliment.

JULIA: Why, ignorance
In courtship cannot make you do amiss,
If you have a heart to do well.

BOSOLA: You are very fair.

[49] Perfumed sugar-plums, for sweetening the breath.

JULIA: Nay, if you lay beauty to my charge,
I must plead unguilty.

BOSOLA: Your bright eyes
Carry a quiver of darts in them sharper
Than sunbeams.

JULIA: You will mar me with commendation,
Put yourself to the charge of courting me,
Whereas now I woo you.

BOSOLA: [Aside] I have it, I will work upon this
  creature.—
Let us grow most amorously familiar:
If the great cardinal now should see me thus,
Would he not count me a villain?

JULIA: No; he might count me a wanton,
Not lay a scruple of offence on you;
For if I see and steal a diamond,
The fault is not i' the stone, but in me the thief
That purloins it. I am sudden with you:
We that are great women of pleasure use to cut off
These uncertain wishes and unquiet longings,
And in an instant join the sweet delight
And the pretty excuse together. Had you been i' the
  the street,
Under my chamber-window, even there
I should have courted you.

BOSOLA: O, you are an excellent lady!

JULIA: Bid me do somewhat for you presently
To express I love you.

BOSOLA: I will; and if you love me,
Fail not to effect it.
The cardinal is grown wondrous melancholy;
Demand the cause, let him not put you off
With feigned excuse; discover the main ground on't.

JULIA: Why would you know this?

BOSOLA: I have depended on him,
And I hear that he is fall'n in some disgrace
With the emperor: if he be, like the mice
That forsake falling houses, I would shift
To other dependance.

JULIA: You shall not need
Follow the wars: I'll be your maintenance.

BOSOLA: And I your loyal servant: but I cannot
Leave my calling.

JULIA: Not leave an ungrateful
General for the love of a sweet lady!
You are like some cannot sleep in feather-beds,
But must have blocks for their pillows.

BOSOLA: Will you do this?

JULIA: Cunningly.

BOSOLA: To-morrow I'll expect the intelligence.

JULIA: To-morrow! get you into my cabinet;
You shall have it with you. Do not delay me,
No more than I do you: I am like one
That is condemned; I have my pardon promised,
But I would see it sealed. Go, get you in:
You shall see me wind my tongue about his heart
Like a skein of silk.
        [Exit Bosola]
        [Re-enter Cardinal]

CARDINAL: Where are you?
        [Enter Servants]

SERVANTS: Here.

CARDINAL: Let none, upon your lives, have con-
ference
With the Prince Ferdinand, unless I know it.—
[Aside] In this distraction he may reveal
The murder.
        [Exeunt Servants]
        Yond's my lingering consumption:
I am weary of her, and by any means
Would be quit of.

JULIA: How now, my lord! what ails you?

CARDINAL: Nothing.

JULIA: O, you are much altered:
Come, I must be your secretary, and remove
This lead from off your bosom: what's the matter?

CARDINAL: I may not tell you.

JULIA: Are you so far in love with sorrow
You cannot part with part of it? or think you
I cannot love your grace when you are sad
As well as merry? or do you suspect
I, that have been a secret to your heart
These many winters, cannot be the same
Unto your tongue?

CARDINAL: Satisfy thy longing,—
The only way to make thee keep my counsel
Is, not to tell thee.

JULIA: Tell your echo this,
Or flatterers, that like echoes still report
What they hear though most imperfect, and not me;
For if that you be true unto yourself,
I'll know.

CARDINAL: Will you rack me?

JULIA: No, judgment shall
Draw it from you: it is an equal fault,
To tell one's secrets unto all or none.

CARDINAL: The first argues folly.

JULIA: But the last tyranny.

CARDINAL: Very well: why, imagine I have com-
mitted
Some secret deed which I desire the world
May never hear of.

JULIA: Therefore may not I know it?
You have concealed for me as great a sin
As adultery. Sir, never was occasion
For perfect trial of my constancy
Till now: sir, I beseech you—

CARDINAL: You'll repent it.

JULIA: Never.

CARDINAL: It hurries thee to ruin: I'll not tell thee.
Be well advised, and think what danger 'tis
To receive a prince's secrets: they that do,
Had need have their breasts hooped with adamant
To contain them. I pray thee, yet be satisfied;
Examine thine own frailty; 'tis more easy
To tie knots than unloose them: 'tis a secret
That, like a lingering poison, may chance lie
Spread in thy veins, and kill thee seven year hence.

JULIA: Now you dally with me.

CARDINAL: No more; thou shalt know it.
By my appointment the great Duchess of Malfi
And two of her young children, four nights since,
Were strangled.

JULIA: O Heaven! sir, what have you done!

CARDINAL: How now? how settles this? think you
     your bosom
Will be a grave dark and obscure enough
For such a secret?

JULIA: You have undone yourself, sir.

CARDINAL: Why?

JULIA: It lies not in me to conceal it.

CARDINAL: No?
Come, I will swear you to't upon this book.

JULIA: Most religiously.

CARDINAL: Kiss it.
     [She kisses the book]
Now you shall never utter it; thy curiosity
Hath undone thee: thou'rt poisoned with that book;
Because I knew thou couldst not keep my counsel,
I have bound thee to't by death.
     [Re-enter Bosola]

BOSOLA: For pity-sake, hold!

CARDINAL: Ha, Bosola!

JULIA: I forgive you
This equal piece of justice you have done;
For I betrayed your counsel to that fellow:
He overheard it; that was the cause I said
It lay not in me to conceal it.

BOSOLA: O foolish woman,
Couldst not thou have poisoned him?

JULIA: 'Tis weakness,
Too much to think what should have been done.
     I go,
I know not whither. [Dies]

CARDINAL: Wherefore com'st thou hither?

BOSOLA: That I might find a great man like your-
     self,
Not out of his wits as the Lord Ferdinand,
To remember my service.

CARDINAL: I'll have thee hewed in pieces.

BOSOLA: Make not yourself such a promise of that
     life
Which is not yours to dispose of.

CARDINAL: Who placed thee here?

BOSOLA: Her lust, as she intended.

CARDINAL: Very well:
Now you know me for your fellow-murderer.

BOSOLA: And wherefore should you lay fair mar-
     ble colors
Upon your rotten purposes to me?
Unless you imitate some that do plot great treasons,
And when they have done, go hide themselves i' the
     graves
Of those were actors in't?

CARDINAL: No more; there is
A fortune attends thee.

BOSOLA: Shall I go sue to Fortune any longer?

'Tis the fool's pilgrimage.

CARDINAL: I have honors in store for thee.

BOSOLA: There are many ways that conduct to
     seeming honor,
And some of them very dirty ones.

CARDINAL: Throw to the devil
Thy melancholy. The fire burns well;
What need we keep a stirring of't, and make
A greater smother? Thou wilt kill Antonio?

BOSOLA: Yes.

CARDINAL: Take up that body.

BOSOLA: I think I shall
Shortly grow the common bier for churchyards.

CARDINAL: I will allow thee some dozen of at-
     tendants
To aid thee in the murder.

BOSOLA: O, by no means. Physicians that apply
horse-leeches to any rank swelling use to cut off
their tails, that the blood may run through them the
faster: let me have no train when I go to shed blood,
lest it make me have a greater when I rid to the
gallows.

CARDINAL: Come to me after midnight, to help to
     remove
That body to her own lodging: I'll give out
She died o' the plague; 'twill breed the less inquiry
After her death.

BOSOLA: Where's Castruccio, her husband?

CARDINAL: He's rode to Naples, to take possession
Of Antonio's citadel.

BOSOLA: Believe me, you have done a very happy
     turn.

CARDINAL: Fail not to come: there is the master-
     key
Of our lodgings; and by that you may conceive
What trust I plant in you.

BOSOLA: You shall find me ready.
     [Exit Cardinal]
O poor Antonio, though nothing be so needful
To thy estate as pity, yet I find
Nothing so dangerous; I must look to my footing:
In such slippery ice-pavements men had need
To be frost-nailed well, they may break their necks.
The precedent's here afore me. How this man
Bears up in blood! seems fearless! Why, 'tis well:
     else;
Security some men call the suburbs of hell,
Only a dead wall between. Well, good Antonio,
I'll seek thee out; and all my care shall be
To put thee into safety from the reach
Of these most cruel biters that have got
Some of thy blood already. It may be,
I'll join with thee in a most just revenge:
The weakest arm is strong enough that strikes
With the sword of justice. Still methinks the duchess
Haunts me: there, there!—'Tis nothing but my
     melancholy.
O Penitence, let me truly taste thy cup,
That throws men down only to raise them up! [Exit]

SCENE III.

A fortification at Milan.

[*Enter* Antonio *and* Delio]

DELIO: Yond's the cardinal's window. This forti-
fication
Grew from the ruins of an ancient abbey;
And to yond side o' the river lies a wall,
Piece of a cloister, which in my opinion
Gives the best echo that you ever heard,
So hollow and so dismal, and withal
So plain in the distinction of our words,
That many have supposed it is a spirit
That answers.

ANTONIO: I do love these ancient ruins.
We never tread upon them but we set
Our foot upon some reverend history:
And, questionless, here in this open court,
Which now lies naked to the injuries
Of stormy weather, some men lie interred
Loved the church so well, and gave so largely to't,
They thought it should have canopied their bones
Till doomsday; but all things have their end:
Churches and cities, which have diseases like to men,
Must have like death that we have.

ECHO: "Like death that we have."

DELIO: Now the echo hath caught you.

ANTONIO: It groaned, methought, and gave
A very deadly accent.

ECHO: "Deadly accent."

DELIO: I told you 'twas a pretty one: you may
make it
A huntsman, or a falconer, a musician,
Or a thing of sorrow.

ECHO: "A thing of sorrow."

ANTONIO: Ay, sure, that suits it best.

ECHO: "That suits it best."

ANTONIO: 'Tis very like my wife's voice.

ECHO: "Ay, wife's voice."

DELIO: Come, let us walk further from't.
I would not have you go to the cardinal's to-night:
Do not.

ECHO: "Do not."

DELIO: Wisdom doth not more moderate wasting
sorrow
Than time: take time for't; be mindful of thy safety.

ECHO: "Be mindful of thy safety."

ANTONIO: Necessity compels me:
Make scrutiny throughout the passages
Of your own life, you'll find it impossible
To fly your fate.

ECHO: "O, fly your fate."

DELIO: Hark! the dead stones seem to have pity
on you,
And give you good counsel.

ANTONIO: Echo, I will not talk with thee,
For thou art a dead thing.

ECHO: "Thou art a dead thing."

ANTONIO: My duchess is asleep now,
And her little ones, I hope sweetly: O Heaven,
Shall I never see her more?

ECHO: "Never see her more."

ANTONIO: I marked not one repetition of the echo
But that; and on the sudden a clear light
Presented me a face folded in sorrow.

DELIO: Your fancy merely.

ANTONIO: Come, I'll be out of this ague,
For to live thus is not indeed to live;
It is a mockery and abuse of life:
I will not henceforth save myself by halves;
Lose all, or nothing.

DELIO: Your own virtues save you!
I'll fetch your eldest son, and second you:
It may be that the sight of his own blood
Spread in so sweet a figure may beget
The more compassion. However, fare you well.
Though in our miseries Fortune have a part,
Yet in our noble sufferings she hath none:
Contempt of pain, that we may call our own.

[*Exeunt*]

SCENE IV.

An apartment in the Cardinal's *palace.*

[*Enter* Cardinal, Pescara, Malatesti, Roderigo,
and Grisolan]

CARDINAL: You shall not watch to-night by the
sick prince;
His grace is very well recovered.

MALATESTI: Good my lord, suffer us.

CARDINAL: O, by no means;
The noise, and change of object in his eye,
Doth more distract him: I pray, all to bed;
And though you hear him in his violent fit,
Do not rise, I entreat you.

PESCARA: So, sir; we shall not.

CARDINAL: Nay, I must have you promise
Upon your honors, for I was enjoined to't
By himself; and he seemed to urge it sensibly.

PESCARA: Let our honors bind this trifle.

CARDINAL: Nor any of your followers.

MALATESTI: Neither.

CARDINAL: It may be, to make trial of your
promise.
When he's asleep, myself will rise and feign
Some of his mad tricks, and cry out for help,
And feign myself in danger.

MALATESTI: If your throat were cutting,
I'd not come at you, now I have protested against
it.

CARDINAL: Why, I thank you.

GRISOLAN: 'Twas a foul storm to-night.

RODERIGO: The Lord Ferdinand's chamber shook
like an osier.

MALATESTI: 'Twas nothing but pure kindness in the devil,
To rock his own child.

[*Exeunt all except the* Cardinal]

CARDINAL: The reason why I would not suffer these
About my brother, is, because at midnight
I may with better privacy convey
Julia's body to her own lodging. O, my conscience!
I would pray now; but the devil takes away my heart
For having any confidence in prayer.
About this hour I appointed Bosola
To fetch the body: when he hath served my turn,
He dies. [*Exit*]

[*Enter* Bosolo]

BOSOLA: Ha! 'twas the cardinal's voice; I heard him name
Bosola and my death. Listen; I hear one's footing.

[*Enter* Ferdinand]

FERDINAND: Strangling is a very quiet death.

BOSOLA: [*Aside*] Nay, then, I see I must stand upon my guard.

FERDINAND: What say you to that? whisper softly; do you agree to't? So; it must be done i' the dark: the cardinal would not for a thousand pounds the doctor should see it. [*Exit*]

BOSOLA: My death is plotted; here's the consequence of murder.
We value not desert nor Christian breath,
When we know black deeds must be cured with death.

[*Enter* Antonio *and* Servant]

SERVANT: Here stay, sir, and be confident, I pray:
I'll fetch you a dark lantern. [*Exit*]

ANTONIO: Could I take him at his prayers,
There were hope of pardon.

BOSOLA: Fall right, my sword!—[*Stabs him*]
I'll not give thee so much leisure as to pray.

ANTONIO: O, I am gone! Thou hast ended a long suit
In a minute.

BOSOLA: What art thou?

ANTONIO: A most wretched thing,
That only have thy benefit in death,
To appear myself.

[*Re-enter* Servant, *with a lantern*]

SERVANT: Where are you, sir?

ANTONIO: Very near my home.—Bosola!

SERVANT: O, misfortune!

BOSOLA: Smother thy pity, thou art dead else.—Antonio!
The man I would have saved 'bove mine own life!
We are merely the stars' tennis-balls, struck and bandied
Which way please them.—O good Antonio,
I'll whisper one thing in thy dying ear
Shall make thy heart break quickly! thy fair duchess and two sweet children—

ANTONIO: Their very names
Kindle a little life in me.

BOSOLA: Are murdered.

ANTONIO: Some men have wished to die
At the hearing of sad things; I am glad
That I shall do't in sadness:[50] I would not now
Wish my wounds balmed nor healed, for I have no use
To put my life to. In all our quest of greatness,
Like wanton boys, whose pastime is their care,
We follow after bubbles blown in the air.
Pleasure of life, what is't? only the good hours
Of an ague; merely a preparative to rest,
To endure vexation. I do not ask
The process of my death; only commend me
To Delio.

BOSOLA: Break, heart!

ANTONIO: And let my son fly the courts of princes. [*Dies*]

BOSOLA: Thou seem'st to have loved Antonio?

SERVANT: I brought him hither,
To have reconciled him to the cardinal.

BOSOLA: I do not ask thee that.
Take him up, if thou tender thine own life,
And bear him where the lady Julia
Was wont to lodge.—O, my fate moves swift;
I have this cardinal in the forge already;
Now I'll bring him to the hammer. O direful misprision![51]
I will not imitate things glorious,
No more than base; I'll be mine own example.—
On, on, and look thou represent, for silence,
The thing thou bear'st.

[*Exeunt*]

SCENE V.

Another apartment in the same.

[*Enter* Cardinal, *with a book*]

CARDINAL: I am puzzled in a question about hell:
He says, in hell there's one material fire,
And yet it shall not burn all men alike.
Lay him by. How tedious is a guilty conscience!
When I look into the fish-ponds in my garden,
Methinks I see a thing armed with a rake,
That seems to strike at me.

[*Enter* Bosola, *and* Servant *bearing* Antonio's body]

Now, art thou come?
Thou look'st ghastly:
There sits in thy face some great determination
Mixed with some fear.

BOSOLA: Thus it lightens into action:
I am come to kill thee.

CARDINAL: Ha!—Help! our guard!

BOSOLA: Thou art deceived;
They are out of thy howling.

CARDINAL: Hold; and I will faithfully divide

50 In earnest.
51 Mistake.

Revenues with thee.

BOSOLA: Thy prayers and proffers
Are both unseasonable.

CARDINAL: Raise the watch! we are betrayed!

BOSOLA: I have confined your flight:
I'll suffer your retreat to Julia's chamber,
But no further.

CARDINAL: Help! we are betrayed!

[*Enter, above*, Pescara, Malatesti, Roderigo, *and* Grisolan]

MALATESTI: Listen.

CARDINAL: My dukedom for rescue!

RODERIGO: Fie upon his counterfeiting!

MALATESTI: Why, 'tis not the cardinal.

RODERIGO: Yes, yes, 'tis he:
But I'll see him hanged ere I'll go down to him.

CARDINAL: Here's a plot upon me; I am assaulted!
    I am lost,
Unless some rescue.

GRISOLAN: He doth this pretty well;
But it will not serve to laugh me out of mine honor.

CARDINAL: The sword's at my throat!

RODERIGO: You would not bawl so loud then.

MALATESTI: Come, come, let's go
To bed: he told us thus much aforehand.

PESCARA: He wished you should not come at him; but,
The accent of the voice sounds not in jest:
I'll down to him, howsoever, and with engines believe't,
Force ope the doors. [*Exit above*]

RODERIGO: Let's follow him aloof,
And note how the cardinal will laugh at him.

[*Exeunt, above*, Malatesti, Roderigo, *and* Grisolan]

BOSOLA: There's for you first,
'Cause you shall not unbarricade the door
To let in rescue. [*Kills the* Servant]

CARDINAL: What cause hast thou to pursue my life?

BOSOLA: Look there.

CARDINAL: Antonio!

BOSOLA: Slain by my hand unwittingly.
Pray, and be sudden: when thou killed'st thy sister,
Thou took'st from Justice her most equal balance,
And left her naught but her sword.

CARDINAL: O, mercy!

BOSOLA: Now it seems thy greatness was only outward;
For thou fall'st faster of thyself than calamity
Can drive thee. I'll not waste longer time; there!
    [*Stabs him*]

CARDINAL: Thou hast hurt me.

BOSOLA: Again! [*Stabs him again*]

CARDINAL: Shall I die like a leveret,[52]
Without any resistance?—Help, help, help!
I am slain!

[*Enter* Ferdinand]

FERDINAND: The alarum! give me a fresh horse;
Rally the vaunt-guard, or the day is lost.

[52] A hare in its first year.

Yield, yield! I give you the honor of arms,
Shake my sword over you; will you yield?

CARDINAL: Help me; I am your brother!

FERDINAND: The devil!
My brother fight upon the adverse party!
    [*He wounds the* Cardinal, *and, in the scuffle, gives* Bosola *his death-wound*]
There flies your ransom.

CARDINAL: O justice!
I suffer now for what hath former bin:
Sorrow is held the eldest child of sin.

FERDINAND: Now you're brave fellows. Cæsar's fortune was harder than Pompey's; Cæsar died in the arms of prosperity, Pompey at the feet of disgrace. You both died in the field. The pain's nothing: pain many times is taken away with the apprehension of greater, as the toothache with the sight of the barber that comes to pull it out: there's philosophy for you.

BOSOLA: Now my revenge is perfect.—Sink, thou main cause [*Kills* Ferdinand]
Of my undoing!—The last part of my life
Hath done me best service.

FERDINAND: Give me some wet hay; I am broken-winded.
I do account this world but a dog kennel:
I will vault credit and affect high pleasures
Beyond death.

BOSOLA: He seems to come to himself,
Now he's so near the bottom.

FERDINAND: My sister, O my sister! there's the cause on't.
Whether we fall by ambition, blood, or lust,
Like diamonds we are cut with our own dust. [*Dies*]

CARDINAL: Thou hast thy payment too.

BOSOLA: Yes, I hold my weary soul in my teeth;
'Tis ready to part from me. I do glory
That thou, which stood'st like a huge pyramid
Begun upon a large and ample base,
Shalt end in a little point, a kind of nothing.

[*Enter below*, Pescara, Malatesti, Roderigo, *and* Grisolan]

PESCARA: How now, my lord!

MALATESTI: O sad disaster!

RODERIGO: How comes this?

BOSOLA: Revenge for the Duchess of Malfi murdered
By the Arragonian brethren; for Antonio
Slain by this hand; for lustful Julia
Poisoned by this man; and lastly for myself,
That was an actor in the main of all
Much 'gainst mine own good nature, yet i' the end
Neglected.

PESCARA: How now, my lord!

CARDINAL: Look to my brother:
He gave us these large wounds, as we were struggling
Here i' the rushes. And now, I pray, let me
Be laid by and never thought of. [*Dies*]

PESCARA: How fatally, it seems, he did withstand
His own rescue!

MALATESTI: Thou wretched thing of blood,

How came Antonio by his death?
BOSOLA: In a mist; I know not how:
Such a mistake as I have often seen
In a play. O, I am gone!
We are only like dead walls or vaulted graves,
That, ruined, yield no echo. Fare you well.
It may be pain, but no harm, to me to die
In so good a quarrel. O, this gloomy world!
In what a shadow, or deep pit of darkness,
Doth womanish and fearful mankind live!
Let worthy minds ne'er stagger in distrust
To suffer death or shame for what is just:
Mine is another voyage. [Dies]
PESCARA: The noble Delio, as I came to the palace,
Told me of Antonio's being here, and showed me
A pretty gentleman, his son and heir.

[Enter Delio and Antonio's Son]
MALATESTI: O sir, you come too late!
DELIO: I heard so, and
Was armed for't, ere I came. Let us make noble use
Of this great ruin; and join all our force
To establish this young hopeful gentleman
In's mother's right. These wretched eminent things
Leave no more fame behind 'em, than should one
Fall in a frost, and leave his print in snow;
As soon as the sun shines, it ever melts,
Both form and matter. I have ever thought
Nature doth nothing so great for great men
As when she's pleased to make them lords of truth:
Integrity of life is fame's best friend,
Which nobly, beyond death, shall crown the end.
[Exeunt]

Lope de Vega

(1562–1635)

The theatre of Spain to which Lope de Vega began to give his fabulous energies in 1585 had been developing for some three quarters of a century. It had already emerged from the medieval miracle-play period, although Spain still harbored religious drama to a greater extent than other countries of Europe. (Both Lope and his successor Calderón wrote sacred one-acters, or *autos.*) Before Lope, the stage had the usual Renaissance crop of more or less academic imitations of classic drama. But the sixteenth century was, from the start, the age of political and economic expansion in Spain. Under Charles V, the nation became the leading power in Europe and the Western hemisphere, and an energetic popular theatre flourished before, as well as during, Lope's career. Dramas of lively and occasionally salacious intrigue abounded. The goldsmith turned actor, Lope de Rueda (1510–1565?), was a leader among writers of romantic comedy who drew upon the stories, or *novelle,* of Italy, which also supplied subjects to Elizabethan playwrights. (One of his pieces, *Los engañados,* or *The Deceived,* bears a resemblance to Shakespeare's *Twelfth Night,* having the same ultimate source.) Another playwright, Juan de la Cueva (1550?–1610?), introduced variety of versification and developed the vastly popular plotty and romantic "cape and sword" (*capa y espada*) drama of love and adventure.

Well formed, too, were the conventions of staging, which resembled those of Shakespeare's time. Not until the seventeenth century did painted scenery and stage machinery begin to supersede the platform stage set in open-air theatres of Madrid and Seville known as *corrales.* And it was with regret, in fact, that Lope de Vega viewed the subsidence of the freely moving stage action that swirled before its audience at the command of poets rather than stage carpenters. It was poetry that conjured up most of the stage illusion throughout the greater part of Lope's career. Moreover, the phrasing of Lope's complaint that "the poets avail themselves of the carpenters and the auditors of their eyes" is significant. Lope, like Shakespeare, counted upon his audience's ears.

Lope's personality is a relevant factor in his particular contribution to the theatre. He is a representative Spaniard of his country's expansive "golden age" of explorers and empire-building conquistadors. He is also a representative "man of the Renaissance" by virtue of his adventurous spirit and vaulting self-confidence. Born on November 25, 1562, the man whose resounding full name was Lope Félix de Vega Carpio was a contemporary of Marlowe and Shakespeare, although he outlived both of them. Marlowe was a fractious youngster and Shakespeare a sedate bourgeois by comparison with the great lover, soldier, careerist, and author of some 2,200 short and long plays, four or five hundred of which have survived; this, in addition to numerous lyrics, fulsome epics, an autobiography, and miscellaneous religious writings. He was a greater romantic figure than "stout Cortez"; a more impressive—and more fortunate—phenomenon than the Spanish Armada, which he joined. His great contemporary, Cervantes, facetiously referred to him as the "Monster of Nature."

The son of Asturian peasants who were living in Madrid when he was born, Lope began reading Latin and composing verse at the age of five, was a student at the Imperial College at fourteen, and by then was already an adept in fencing, dancing, music, and literature. Prompted by the desire for adventure, he left school and wandered over northwestern Spain with a classmate. By the time he reached fifteen, he was also a soldier, having fought in an expedition against Portugal. Shortly after this campaign, he was taken in tow by the prominent Bishop of Ávila, who sent him to the University of Alcalá to complete his education. Here he took his bachelor's degree at seventeen. He was then also on the verge of taking the tonsure, but his heart had acquired other, non-religious interests that were to become chronic with him. In a letter explaining why he did not become a priest, he wrote waggishly, "I fell blindly in love, God forgive it; I am married now, and he that is so ill off fears nothing!"

After embarking on a naval expedition, he went on to Madrid to work in the theatre and won the interest of the influential Madrid stage producer Jerónimo Velázquez. He also took the latter's daughter Elena away from her actor husband, celebrating her under the name of Filis in ballads and receiving as a reward her heart and her jewelry. Five years later, he renounced both the lady and her father, whom he lampooned mercilessly after refusing him his plays. As the result of a libel suit, he was imprisoned for a short time and then exiled from the kingdom of Castile for two years. He went to Valencia, but three months later returned to Madrid and eloped with Isabel de Urbina, the daughter of a powerful courtier; shortly after their marriage he left her to join the Spanish Armada. His galleon, the *San Juan,* was one of the few ships to return from the fateful expedition. Since the voyage back to Cádiz took some six months, he made good use of his enforced leisure to compose a long romance. A month later he was back in Valencia, writing plays for a living, supplying several managers at the same time. His wife had died by this time, and he turned to a new love, the actress Micaela de Luján, who bore him four children. He wrote numerous sonnets to her and remained more or less constant for a while, but in 1598 he married the daughter of a prosperous pork merchant, who brought him a comfortable dowry. In the year 1605 his wife gave him a son and his former wife gave him a daughter.

In 1610, after having attained prosperity from his writings and won patrons among the aristocracy, he settled his family in Madrid, and when his wife died in 1613 he devotedly brought all his children under the same paternal roof. He next turned to the church, becoming an official, or "familiar," of the Inquisition. This step did not, however, deter him from both continuing to write secular plays and continuing to have liaisons, of which two are recorded—one with an uninhibited actress whom he described as *la loca*, or the mad one, and another with his "Amarilis," a young married woman who enlarged his paternity when he was close to sixty. Only after the death of the latter, in 1632, and of his talented son Lopito, who was lost at sea, did the by now aged playwright give himself up to piety. And even then his lifetime habit of excess had not left him. During the three years before his death, on August 27, 1635, he used to scourge himself until the walls of his room were flecked with blood.

No single play can convey the inexhaustible vitality of Lope de Vega, who would have been the world's greatest dramatist if his artistry had matched his fecundity. In playwriting he was surely "so wide as a church-door" but by no means "so deep as a well." The bulk of his work consisted of hastily composed comedies and tragicomedies of intrigue, romance, and conflicts of honor and love. His verse and dramaturgy, even in the plays that have commended themselves to the theatre beyond Spain, were facile rather than fully crystallized; his characterization, vivid rather than extensive or profound. But the least that can be said for a good example of "cape and sword" drama such as *A Certainty for Doubt* is that it has the surge of passion and will that affords exciting theatre. Lope comprehended the complexities of human behavior even if he made too little use of them. There was certainly no want of experience and intelligence in his endowment.

Much more than an irrepressible plot grinder, Lope

viewed the manners and conventions of his time with an easy skepticism, as we may see in such a comedy as *The Gardener's Dog*. In this play the difference in station between a lady and her lover is dissolved by the simple expedient of his getting himself a fictitious family tree, and she is entirely willing to accept the fiction so long as it wins general credence. Lope was too clever a man to confuse social forms with feeling, and he was, naturally, too conversant with human impulses and contradictions not to view them with a lively indulgence. He created, indeed, a veritable, if limited, "human comedy" in his work, and the stage historian Allardyce Nicoll has even found it possible to point out anticipations of the Pirandellian contrast between "what is" and "what seems," between reality and illusion, in some of Lope's plays written between 1600 and 1634—*The Prize for Good Speech, Belisa's Tricks, There's Method in 't,* and *The Lunatics of Valencia.*

Lope's singular achievement for us, however, appears in two peasant plays that have had much currency in our time, *The King the Greatest Alcalde* and *Fuente Ovejuna,* or *The Sheep Well.* Both contain much modern realism in effective combination with a democratic idealism that we should not have expected from the Spain of Philip II. Both pieces, it is true, are presented as episodes from earlier Spanish history and are marked by a complimentary view of monarchy as the champion of the common man against the overbearing feudal aristocracy. (There is, indeed, a certain degree of historical evidence for this view, since the early kings sought to check the power of the nobles.) More important, however, is the fact that Lope endows the peasantry with wholesome vitality and a rugged sense of honor. The plays flare into vigorous self-assertiveness by the peasants and culminate in the punishment of the villainous noblemen by the commoners they have abused. The king, by ultimately carrying out the wishe_ of the peasants or pardoning their refractory behavior, sets his seal on their revolt. By these means, Lope succeeded in representing the mettlesome spirit of the Spanish people and at the same time paying homage to royalty. In *Fuente Ovejuna,* Lope has also performed the feat—and a modern one it is—of creating a "collective hero" by treating the village of Fuente Ovejuna as the protagonist of the play. And he has done this without failing to individualize his peasant characters and to endow them with uncommon impressiveness.

FUENTE OVEJUNA[1]

By Lope de Vega

TRANSLATED FROM THE SPANISH BY ANGEL FLORES AND MURIEL KITTEL

DRAMATIS PERSONAE

QUEEN ISABELLA OF CASTILE
KING FERDINAND OF ARAGON
RODRIGO TÉLLEZ GIRÓN, *Maestre of the religious and military Order of Calatrava*
FERNÁN GÓMEZ DE GUZMÁN, *Comendador Mayor of the Order of Calatrava*
DON MANRIQUE
A JUDGE
TWO COUNCILMEN OF CIUDAD REAL
ORTUÑO } *servants of the Comendador*
FLORES }
ESTEBAN } *Mayors of Fuente Ovejuna*
ALONSO }

LAURENCIA }
JACINTA } *peasant girls*
PASCUALA }
JUAN ROJO, *Councilman of Fuente Ovejuna, a peasant*
ANOTHER COUNCILMAN OF FUENTE OVEJUNA
FRONDOSO }
MENGO } *peasants*
BARRILDO }
LEONELO, *Licentiate of Law*
CIMBRANOS, *a soldier*
A BOY
PEASANTS, MEN AND WOMEN
MUSICIANS

TIME: 1476

ACT I.

Hall of the Maestre *of the Order of Calatrava, in Almagro.*

[*Enter the* Comendador *and his servants,* Flores *and* Ortuño]

COMENDADOR: Does the Maestre know that I am here?

FLORES: He does, my lord.

ORTUÑO: The Maestre is becoming more mature.

COMENDADOR: Does he know that I am Fernán Gómez de Guzmán?

FLORES: He's only a boy—you mustn't be surprised if he doesn't.

COMENDADOR: Nevertheless he must know that I am the Comendador.

ORTUÑO: There are those who advise him to be discourteous.

COMENDADOR: That will win him little love. Courtesy is the key to good will, while thoughtless discourtesy is the way to make enemies.

ORTUÑO: If we but realized how it makes us hated and despised by everyone we would rather die than be discourteous.

FLORES: What a nuisance discourtesy is: among equals it's foolish and toward inferiors it's tyrannical. In this case it only means that the boy has not learned what it is to be loved.

COMENDADOR: The obligation he took upon himself when he accepted his sword and the Cross of Calatrava was placed on his breast should have been enough to teach him courtesy.

[1] This play has also been translated under the title *The Sheep Well*.

FLORES: If you have been prejudiced against him you'll soon get to know him.

ORTUÑO: Why don't you leave if you're in doubt?

COMENDADOR: I wish to see what he is like.

[*Enter the* Maestre *of Calatrava and retinue*]

MAESTRE: Pardon me, Fernán Gómez de Guzmán; I only just heard that you had come. Forgive me if I have kept you waiting.

COMENDADOR: I have come to you with a very reasonable request that both my love for you and my rank entitle me to make—for you are the Maestre of Calatrava and I your Comendador and your servant.

MAESTRE: I did not know of your welcome arrival —let me embrace you again.

COMENDADOR: You owe me a great deal; I have risked my life to settle your many difficulties. I even managed to persuade the Pope to increase your age.

MAESTRE: That is true, and by the holy cross which we both proudly bear on our breasts I shall repay you in love, and honor you as my own father.

COMENDADOR: I am satisfied that you will.

MAESTRE: What news of the war?

COMENDADOR: Listen carefully, and I will tell you where your duty lies.

MAESTRE: I am listening; tell me.

COMENDADOR: Maestre Don Rodrigo Téllez Girón, I need hardly remind you how your brave father resigned his high position as Maestre[2] to you eight years ago, and appointed Don Juan Pacheco, the Grand Maestre of Santiago,[3] to be your coadjutor, nor how kings and comendadors confirmed and swore

[2] Office and dignity of a Master of the Order.

[3] Religious and military order founded in the twelfth century.

to his act, and the Pope and his successor Paul agreed to it in their bulls; no, what I have come to tell you is this: now that Pacheco is dead and you, in spite of your youth, have sole control of the government, now is the time for you to take up arms for the honor of your family. Since the death of Henry IV your relatives have supported the cause of Don Alonso, King of Portugal, who claims the throne of Castile through his wife Juana. Ferdinand, the great prince of Aragon, makes a similar claim through his wife Isabella. But your relatives do not consider Ferdinand's rights to be as clear as those of Juana—who is now in your cousin's power. So I advise you to rally the knights of Calatrava in Almagro and to capture Ciudad Real, which stands on the frontier between Andalusia and Castile. You will not need many men, because the enemy can count only on their neighbors and a few noblemen who support Isabella and consider Ferdinand their legitimate king. It will be wonderful if you, Rodrigo, if you, a youth, can astonish those who say that this cross is too heavy for your young shoulders. Emulate the counts of Urueña from whom you spring, and who from the height of their fame seem to shower upon you the laurels they have won; emulate the marquises of Villena and those other captains who are so numerous that the wings of fame are not strong enough to bear them. Unsheathe your white sword, dye it red in battle till it matches the cross upon your breast. For I cannot call you the Maestre of the Red Cross as long as your sword is white: both the sword you bear and the cross you wear must be red. And you, mighty Girón, must add the crowning glory to the immortal fame of your ancestors.

MAESTRE: Fernán Gómez, you may be sure that I side with my family in this dispute, for I am convinced that they are right. And as I translate my conviction into action at Ciudad Real you will see me tearing the city walls down with the violence of a thunderbolt. I know that I am young—but do not think that my courage died with my uncle's death. I will unsheathe my white sword and its brilliance shall become the color of the cross, bathed in red blood.

But tell me, where do you live, and do you have any soldiers?

COMENDADOR: A few—but they are faithful and they will fight like lions. I live in Fuente Ovejuna,[4] where the people are skilled in agriculture and husbandry rather than in the arts of war.

MAESTRE: And you live there, you say?

COMENDADOR: I do. I chose a house on my estate to stay in during these troubled times. Now see that all your people go into action with you—let no man stay behind!

MAESTRE: You shall see me today on horseback, bearing my lance on high.

[4] A town in the province of Córdoba; it belonged in feudal title to the Order of Calatrava.

A public square in Fuente Ovejuna.

[*Enter* Laurencia *and* Pascuala]

LAURENCIA: I hoped he would never come back.

PASCUALA: I must say I thought you'd be more distressed at the news.

LAURENCIA: I hoped to God I'd never see him again.

PASCUALA: I have seen women just as adamant as you, Laurencia, if not more so—and yet, underneath, their hearts were as soft as butter.

LAURENCIA: Well, is there an oak tree as hard as I am?

PASCUALA: Be careful. No one should boast that he'll never thirst for water.

LAURENCIA: But I do. And I'll maintain it against the world. What good would it do me to love Fernán? Do you think I would marry him?

PASCUALA: Of course not.

LAURENCIA: Well then, I condemn infamy. Too many girls hereabouts have trusted the Comendador only to be ruined by him.

PASCUALA: All the same it will be a miracle if you escape him.

LAURENCIA: You don't understand, Pascuala. He has been after me for a month now, but he has only been wasting his time. His emissary, Flores, and that blustering fool Ortuño have come to show me a blouse, a necklace, a hat, and have told me so many wonderful stories about their lord and master that they have succeeded in frightening me but not in moving my heart.

PASCUALA: Where did they talk to you?

LAURENCIA: Down there by the brook, about six days ago.

PASCUALA: It looks as if they are trying to deceive you, Laurencia.

LAURENCIA: Deceive me?

PASCUALA: If not you, then the priest.

LAURENCIA: I may be a young chicken, but I'm too tough for his highness. Pascuala, I would far rather put a slice of ham on the fire in the early morning and eat it with my homemade bread and a glass of wine stolen from my mother, and then at noon to smell a piece of beef boiling with cabbage and eat it ravenously, or, if I have had a trying day, marry an eggplant to some bacon; and in the evening, while cooking the supper, go and pick a handful of grapes from the vines (God save them from the hail) and afterwards dine on chopped meat with oil and pepper, and so happily to bed murmuring "Lead us not into temptation"—I would much rather this than all the wiles and tricks of scoundrels. For after all, all they want after giving us so much trouble is their pleasure at night and our sorrow in the morning.

PASCUALA: You are right, Laurencia, for as soon as they tire of love they are more ungrateful than the sparrows are to the peasants. In winter when the fields are frozen hard the sparrows fly down from the roofs, and saying "Sweet Sweet" hop right on to the dining table for crumbs, but as soon as the cold is over and the fields are again in bloom they no longer come down saying "Sweet Sweet" but stay hopping on the roof, mocking us with their calls. Men are the same; when they need us nothing can be sweeter than they—we are their life, their soul, their heart, their all—but as soon as they tire of us their sweetness disappears and their wooing phrases become a mockery.

LAURENCIA: The moral of which is: trust no man, Pascuala.

PASCUALA: That's what I say.

[*Enter* Mengo, Barrildo, *and* Frondoso]

FRONDOSO: You are wrong, Barrildo, in this argument.

BARRILDO: Well never mind, here's somebody who will settle the matter.

MENGO: Let's have an understanding before we reach them: if I'm right, then each of you gives me a present as a reward.

BARRILDO: All right. But if you lose, what will you give?

MENGO: I'll give my boxwood rebec,[5] which I value more than a barn.

BARRILDO: That's fine.

FRONDOSO: Let's approach them. God bless you, fair ladies.

LAURENCIA: You call us ladies, Frondoso?

FRONDOSO: We want to keep up with the times. In these days all bachelors are licentiates;[6] the blind are one-eyed; the cross-eyed merely squint; and the lame have only a sprained ankle. The unscrupulous are called honest; the ignorant, clever; and the braggart, brave. A large mouth is described as luscious, a small eye as sharp. The pettifogger is called diligent; the busybody, charming; the charlatan, sympathetic; the deadly bore, gallant. The cowardly become valiant; the hard-headed, vivacious; coxcombs are comrades; fools, broad-minded; malcontents, philosophers. Baldness is identified with authority, foolish chatter with wit. People with tumors have only a slight cold, and those who are arrogant are circumspect; the shifty are constant; and the humpbacked, just slightly bent. This, in short—the enumeration could go on indefinitely—was the sort of thing I did in calling you ladies. I merely followed the fashion of the day.

LAURENCIA: In the city, Frondoso, such words are used in courtesy; discourteous tongues use a severer and more acrimonious vocabulary.

FRONDOSO: I should like to hear it.

LAURENCIA: It's the very opposite of yours. The serious-minded are called bores; the unfortunate, lucky; the even-tempered, melancholy; and anyone who expresses disapproval is hateful. Those who offer good advice are importunate; the liberal-minded are dull-witted; the just, unjust; and the pious, weak-

kneed. In this language the faithful become inconstant; the courteous, flatterers; the charitable, hypocrites; and the good Christians, frauds. Anyone who has won a well-deserved reward is called fortunate; truth becomes impudence; patience, cowardice; and misfortune, retribution. The modest woman is foolish; the beautiful and chaste, unnatural; and the honorable woman is called . . . But enough! This reply should be sufficient.

MENGO: You little devil!

LAURENCIA: What an elegant expression.

MENGO: I bet the priest poured handfuls of salt on her when he christened her.

LAURENCIA: What was the argument that brought you here, if we may ask?

FRONDOSO: Listen, Laurencia.

LAURENCIA: Speak.

FRONDOSO: Lend me your ear, Laurencia.

LAURENCIA: Lend it to you? Why, I'll give it to you right now.

FRONDOSO: I trust your discretion.

LAURENCIA: Well, what was the wager about?

FRONDOSO: Barrildo and I wagered against Mengo.

LAURENCIA: And what does Mengo claim?

BARRILDO: It is something that he insists on denying, although it is plainly a fact.

MENGO: I deny it because I know better.

LAURENCIA: But what is it?

BARRILDO: He claims that love does not exist.

LAURENCIA: Many people think that.

BARRILDO: Many people do, but it's foolish. Without love not even the world could exist.

MENGO: I don't know how to philosophize; as for reading, I wish I could! But I say that if the elements of Nature live in eternal conflict, then our bodies, which receive from them food, anger, melancholy, phlegm, and blood, must also be at war with each other.

BARRILDO: The world here and beyond, Mengo, is perfect harmony. Harmony is pure love, for love is complete agreement.

MENGO: As far as the natural world goes, I do not deny it. There is love which rules all things through an obligating inter-relationship. I have never denied that each person has love proportionate to his humour[7]—my hand will protect me from the blow aimed at my face, my foot will protect me from harm by enabling me to flee danger, my eyelids will protect my eyes from threatening specks—such is love in nature.

PASCUALA: What are you trying to prove, then?

MENGO: That individuals love only themselves.

PASCUALA: Pardon me, Mengo, for telling you that you lie. For it is a lie. The intensity with which a man loves a woman or an animal its mate . . .

MENGO: I call that self-love, not love. What is love?

LAURENCIA: A desire for beauty.

[5] A musical instrument.

[6] Bachelors of arts pretend to be masters of arts.

[7] His inclination, supposedly determined by an excess of glandular secretions.

MENGO: And why does love seek beauty?

LAURENCIA: To enjoy it.

MENGO: That's just what I believe. Is not such enjoyment selfish?

LAURENCIA: That's right.

MENGO: Therefore a person seeks that which brings him joy.

LAURENCIA: That is true.

MENGO: Hence there is no love but the kind I speak of, the one I pursue for my personal pleasure, and which I enjoy.

BARRILDO: One day the priest said in a sermon that there was a man named Plato who taught how to love, and that this man loved only the soul and the virtues of the beloved.

PASCUALA: You have raised a question which the wise men in their schools and academies cannot solve.

LAURENCIA: He speaks the truth; do not try to refute his argument. Be thankful, Mengo, that Heaven made you without love.

MENGO: Are you in love?

LAURENCIA: I love my honor.

FRONDOSO: May God punish you with jealousy.

BARRILDO: Who has won the wager then?

PASCUALA: Go to the sacristan with your dispute, for either he or the priest will give you the best answer. Laurencia does not love deeply, and as for me, I have little experience. How are we to pass judgment?

FRONDOSO: What can be a better judgment than her disdain?

[Enter Flores]

FLORES: God be with you!

PASCUALA: Here is the Comendador's servant.

LAURENCIA: His goshawk, you mean. Where do you come from, my good friend?

FLORES: Don't you see my soldier's uniform?

LAURENCIA: Is Don Fernán coming back?

FLORES: Yes, the war is over, and though it has cost us some blood and some friends, we are victorious.

FRONDOSO: Tell us what happened.

FLORES: Who could do that better than I? I saw everything. For his campaign against this city (which is now called Ciudad Real—Royal City), the valiant Maestre raised an army of two thousand brave infantry from among his vassals and three hundred cavalry from laymen and friars. For even those who belong to Holy Orders are obliged to fight for their emblem of the red cross—provided, of course, that the war is against the Moors. The high-spirited youth rode out to battle wearing a green coat embroidered with golden scrolls; the sleeves were fastened with six hooks, so that only his gauntlets showed beneath them. His horse was a dappled roan, bred on the banks of the Betis,[8] drinking its waters and grazing on its lush grass. Its tailpiece was decorated with buckskin straps, the curled panache with white knots that

matched the snowflakes covering its mane. Our lord, Fernán Gómez, rode at the Maestre's side on a powerful honey-colored horse with black legs and mane and a white muzzle.[9] Over a Turkish coat of mail he wore a magnificent breast-and-back plate with orange fringes and resplendent with gold and pearls. His white plumes seemed to shower orange blossoms on his bronze helmet. His red and white band flashed on his arm as he brandished an ash tree for a lance, making himself feared even in Granada. The city rushed to arms; the inhabitants apparently did not come out to fight but stayed within the city walls to defend their property. But in spite of the strong resistance the Maestre entered the city. He ordered the rebels and those who had flagrantly dishonored him to be beheaded, and the lower classes were gagged and whipped in public. He remained in the city and is so feared and loved that people prophesy great things for him. They say that a young man who has fought so gloriously and punished so severely all in a short time must one day fall on fertile Africa like a thunderbolt, and bring many blue moons under the red cross. He made so many gifts to the Comendador and his followers that he might have been disposing of his own estate rather than despoiling a city. But now the music sounds. The Comendador comes. Welcome him with festivity, for good will is one of the most precious of a victor's laurels.

[Enter the Comendador and Ortuño. Musicians. Juan Rojo, Esteban, and Alonso, elders of the town]

[They sing]

Welcome, Comendador,
Conqueror of lands and men!
Long live the Guzmanes!
Long live the Girones!
In peacetime gracious,
Gentle his reasoning,
When fighting the Moors
Strong as an oak.
From Ciudad Real
He comes victorious,
Bearing to Fuente Ovejuna
Its banners in triumph.
Long live Fernán Gómez,
Long live the hero!

COMENDADOR: Citizens of Fuente Ovejuna, I am most grateful to you for the love you show me.

ALONSO: It is but a small part of the love we feel, and no matter how great our love it is less than you deserve.

ESTEBAN: Fuente Ovejuna and its elders, whom you have honored with your presence, beg you to accept a humble gift. In these carts, Sir, we bring you an expression of gratitude rather than a display of wealth. There are two baskets filled with earthenware; a flock of geese that stretch their heads out of

___
[8] I.e., an Andalusian horse.

[9] Considered of good breed

their nets to praise your valor in battle; ten salted hogs, prize specimens, more precious than amber; and a hundred pairs of capons and hens, which leave the cocks of the neighboring villages desolate. You will find no arms, no horses, no harnesses studded with pure gold. The only gold is the love your vassals feel towards you. And for purity you could find nothing greater than those twelve skins of wine. That wine could give warmth and courage to your soldiers even unclothed in the dead of winter; it will be as important as steel in the defense of your walls. I leave unmentioned the cheese and other victuals: they are a fitting tribute from our people to you. May you and yours enjoy our gifts.

COMENDADOR: I am very grateful to you for all of them. Go now and rest.

ESTEBAN: Feel at home in this town, my lord! I wish the reeds of mace and sedge that we placed on our doors to celebrate your triumphs were oriental pearls. You deserve such tribute and more.

COMENDADOR: Thank you, gentlemen. God be with you.

ESTEBAN: Singers, sing again.

    [*They sing*]

        Welcome, Comendador,
        Conqueror of lands and men!

    [*Exeunt* Elders *and* Musicians]

COMENDADOR: You two wait.

LAURENCIA: What is your lordship's pleasure?

COMENDADOR: You scorned me a few days ago, didn't you?

LAURENCIA: Is he speaking to you, Pascuala?

PASCUALA: I should say not—not to me!

COMENDADOR: I am talking to you, beautiful wildcat, and to the other girl too. Are you not mine, both of you?

PASCUALA: Yes, sir, to a certain extent.

COMENDADOR: Go into the house. There are men inside, so you need not fear.

LAURENCIA: If the elders accompany us—I am the daughter of one of them—it will be all right for us to go in too, but not otherwise.

COMENDADOR: Flores!

FLORES: Sir?

COMENDADOR: Why do they hesitate to do what I command?

FLORES: Come along, girls, come right in.

LAURENCIA: Let me go!

FLORES: Come in, girl, don't be silly.

PASCUALA: So that you can lock us in? No thank you!

FLORES: Come on. He wants to show you his spoils of war.

COMENDADOR: [*Aside to* Ortuño] Lock the door after them. [*Exit*]

LAURENCIA: Flores, let us pass.

ORTUÑO: Aren't you part of the gifts of the village?

PASCUALA: That's what you think! Out of my way, fool, before I . . .

FLORES: Leave them alone. They're too unreasonable.

LAURENCIA: Isn't your master satisfied with all the meat given him today?

ORTUÑO: He seems to prefer yours.

LAURENCIA: Then he can starve!

    [*Exeunt* Laurencia *and* Pascuala]

FLORES: A fine message for us to bring! He'll swear at us when we appear before him empty-handed.

ORTUÑO: That's a risk servants always run. When he realizes the situation he'll either calm down or else leave at once.

Chamber of the Catholic Kings, in Medina del Campo.

[*Enter* King Ferdinand of Aragon, Queen Isabella, Manrique, *and* Attendants]

ISABELLA: I think it would be wise to be prepared, Your Majesty—especially since Don Alfonso of Portugal is encamped there. It is better for us to strike the first blow than to wait for the enemy to attack us.

KING: We can depend on Navarre and Aragon for assistance, and I'm trying to reorganize things in Castile so as to ensure our success there.

ISABELLA: I'm sure your plan will succeed.

MANRIQUE: Two councilmen from Ciudad Real seek audience with Your Majesty.

KING: Let it be granted them.

[*Enter two* Councilmen *of Ciudad Real*]

1ST COUNCILMAN: Most Catholic King of Aragon, whom God has sent to Castile to protect us, we appear as humble petitioners before you to beg the assistance of your great valor for our city of Ciudad Real. We are proud to consider ourselves your vassals, a privilege granted us by a royal charter but which an unkind fate threatens to take away. Don Rodrigo Téllez Girón, famous for the valiant actions that belie his youth, and ambitious to augment his power, recently laid close siege to our city. We prepared to meet his attack with bravery, and resisted his forces so fiercely that rivers of blood streamed from our innumerable dead. He finally conquered us—but only because of the advice and assistance given him by Fernán Gómez. Girón remains in possession of our city, and unless we can remedy our disaster soon we will have to acknowledge ourselves his vassals against our will.

KING: Where is Fernán Gómez now?

2ND COUNCILMAN: In Fuente Ovejuna, I think. That is his native town and his home is there. But the truth is, his subjects are far from contented.

KING: Do you have a leader?

2ND COUNCILMAN: No, we have none, Your Majesty. Not one nobleman escaped imprisonment, injury, or death.

ISABELLA: This matter requires swift action, for

delay will only work to the advantage of the impudent Girón. Furthermore the King of Portugal will soon realize that he can use him to gain entry to Extremadura, and so cause us much damage.

KING: Don Manrique, leave at once with two companies. Be relentless in avenging the wrongs this city has suffered. Let the Count of Cabra go with you. The Cordovan is recognized by everyone as a brave soldier. This is the best plan for the moment.

MANRIQUE: I think the plan is an excellent one. As long as I live, his excesses shall be curbed.

ISABELLA: With your help we are sure to succeed.

The countryside near Fuente Ovejuna.

[*Enter* Laurencia *and* Frondoso]

LAURENCIA: You are very stubborn, Frondoso. I left the brook with my washing only half wrung out, so as to give no occasion for gossip—yet you persist in following me It seems that everyone in town is saying that you are running after me and I after you. And because you are the sort of fellow who struts about and shows off his clothes, which are more fashionable and expensive than other people's, all the girls and boys in the countryside think there must be something between us. They are all waiting for the day when Juan Chamorro will put down his flute and lead us to the altar. I wish they would occupy their minds with things that are more their business—why don't they imagine that their granaries are bursting with red wheat, or that their winejars are full of dregs? Their gossip annoys me, but not so much that it keeps me awake at night.

FRONDOSO: Your disdain and beauty are so great, Laurencia, that when I see you and listen to you I fear they will kill me. You know that my only wish is to become your husband: is it fair then to reward my love in this way?

LAURENCIA: I know no other way.

FRONDOSO: Can you feel no pity for my troubled mind, no sympathy for my sad condition when you know I cannot eat or drink or sleep for thinking of you? Is it possible that such a gentle face can hide so much unkindness? Heavens! you'll drive me mad.

LAURENCIA: Why don't you take medicine for your condition, Frondoso?

FRONDOSO: You are the only medicine I need, Laurencia. Come with me to the altar, and let us live like turtle doves, billing and cooing, after the church has blessed us.

LAURENCIA: You had better ask my uncle, Juan Rojo. I'm not passionately in love with you . . . but there is hope that I might be in time.

FRONDOSO: Oh—here comes the Comendador!

LAURENCIA: He must be hunting deer. Hide behind these bushes.

FRONDOSO: I will. But I'll be full of jealousy.

[*Enter the* Comendador]

COMENDADOR: This is good luck. My chase of the timid fawn has led me to a lovely doe instead.

LAURENCIA: I was resting a bit from my washing. By your lordship's leave I'll return to the brook.

COMENDADOR: Such disdain, fair Laurencia, is an insult to the beauty Heaven gave you; it turns you into a monster. On other occasions you have succeeded in eluding my desires—but now we are alone in these solitary fields where no one can help you. Now, with no one to witness, you cannot be so stubborn and so proud, you cannot turn your face away without loving me. Did not Salustiana, the wife of Pedro Redondo, surrender to me—and Martín del Pozo's wife, too, only two days after her wedding?

LAURENCIA: These women, sir, had had others before you, and knew the road to pleasure only too well. Many men have enjoyed *their* favors. Go, pursue your deer, and God be with you. You persecute me so that were it not for the cross you wear I should think you were the devil.

COMENDADOR: You little spitfire! [*Aside*] I had better put my bow down and take her by force.

LAURENCIA: What? . . . What are you doing? Are you mad?

[*Enter* Frondoso, *who picks up the bow*]

COMENDADOR: Don't struggle. It won't help you.

FRONDOSO: [*Aside*] I'll pick up his bow, but I hope I don't have to use it.

COMENDADOR: Come on, you might as well give in now.

LAURENCIA: Heaven help me now!

COMENDADOR: We are alone. Don't be afraid.

FRONDOSO: Generous Comendador, leave the girl alone. For much as I respect the cross on your breast, it will not stop me from aiming this bow at you if you do not let her go.

COMENDADOR: You dog, you peasant slave!

FRONDOSO: There's no dog here. Laurencia, go quickly now.

LAURENCIA: Take care of yourself, Frondoso.

FRONDOSO: Run . . .

[*Exit* Laurencia]

COMENDADOR: What a fool I was to put down my sword so as not to frighten my quarry!

FRONDOSO: Do you realize, Sir, that I have only to touch this string to bring you down like a bird?

COMENDADOR: She's gone. You damned, treacherous villain. Put that bow down, put it down, I say.

FRONDOSO: Put it down? Why? So that you can shoot me? No, love is deaf, remember, and hears nothing when it comes into its own.

COMENDADOR: Do you think a knight surrenders to a peasant? Shoot, you villain, shoot and be damned, or I'll break the laws of chivalry.

FRONDOSO: No, not that. I'm satisfied with my station in life, and since I must preserve my life, I'll take your bow with me. [*Exit*]

COMENDADOR: What a strange experience! But I'll avenge this insult and remove this obstacle . . . But to let him go! My God, how humiliating!

ACT II.

The Plaza of Fuente Ovejuna.

[*Enter* Esteban *and* 1st Councilman]

ESTEBAN: I don't think any more grain should be taken out of our community granaries, even though they are full right now. It's getting late in the year, and the harvest looks poor. I think it's better to have provisions stored up in case of emergency——though I know some people have other ideas.

1ST COUNCILMAN: I agree with you. And I've always tried to administer the land along such peaceable ways.

ESTEBAN: Well, let's tell Fernán Gómez what we think about it. We shouldn't let those astrologers, who are so ignorant of the future, persuade us that they know all the secrets that are only God's business. They pretend to be as learned as the theologians the way they mix up the past and the future——but if you ask them anything about the immediate present they are completely at a loss. Do they have the clouds and the course of the sun, the moon, and the stars locked up at home that they can tell us what is happening up there and what is going to bring us grief? At seed time they levy tax on us; give us just so much wheat, oats and vegetables, pumpkins, cucumbers, mustard . . . Then they tell us someone has died, and later we discover it happened in Transylvania; they tell us that wine will be scarce and beer plentiful——somewhere in Germany; that cherries will freeze in Gascony, or hordes of tigers will prowl through Hircania.[10] Their final prophecy is that whether we sow or not the year will end in December!

[*Enter the licentiate* Leonelo *and* Barrildo]

LEONELO: You won't be awarded the hickory stick to beat the other students with, for it's already been won by somebody else.

BARRILDO: How did you get on at Salamanca?

LEONELO: That's a long story.

BARRILDO: You must be a very learned man by now.

LEONELO: No, I'm not even a barber. The things I was telling you about happen all the time in the school I was at.

BARRILDO: At least you are a scholar now.

LEONELO: Well, I've tried to learn things that are important.

BARRILDO: Anyone who has seen so many printed books is bound to think he is wise.

LEONELO: Froth and confusion are the chief results of so much reading matter. Even the most voracious reader gets sick of seeing so many titles. I admit that printing has saved many talented writers from oblivion, and enshrined their works above the ravages of time. Printing circulates their books and makes

[10] The lions of Hircania were supposed to be extraordinarily fierce.

them known. Gutenberg, a famous German from Mainz, is responsible for this invention. But many men who used to have a high reputation are no longer taken seriously now that their works have been printed. Some people put their ignorance in print, passing it off as wisdom; others inspired by envy write down their crazy ideas and send them into the world under the name of their enemies.

BARRILDO: That's a disgraceful practice.

LEONELO: Well, it's natural for ignorant people to want to discredit scholars.

BARRILDO: But in spite of all this, Leonelo, you must admit that printing is important.

LEONELO: The world got on very well without it for a good many centuries——and no Saint Jerome or Saint Augustine has appeared since we have had it.

BARRILDO: Take it easy, Leonelo. You're getting all worked up about this printing business.

[*Enter* Juan Rojo *and another* Peasant]

JUAN ROJO: Four farms put together would not raise one dowry, if they're all like the one we've just seen. It's obvious that both the land and the people are in a state of chaos.

PEASANT: What's the news of the Comendador?—— don't get excited now.

JUAN ROJO: How he tried to take advantage of Laurencia in this very field!

PEASANT: That lascivious brute! I'd like to see him hanging from that olive tree! . . .

[*Enter* Comendador, Ortuño, *and* Flores]

COMENDADOR: Good day to you all!

COUNCILMAN: Your Lordship!

COMENDADOR: Please don't get up.

ESTEBAN: You sit down, my lord. We would rather stand.

COMENDADOR: Do sit down.

ESTEBAN: Honor can only be rendered by those who have it themselves.

COMENDADOR: Sit down, and let us talk things over calmly.

ESTEBAN: Has your Lordship seen the hound I sent you?

COMENDADOR: Mayor, my servants are all amazed by its great speed.

ESTEBAN: It really is a wonderful animal. It can overtake any culprit or coward who is trying to escape.

COMENDADOR: I wish you would send it after a hare that keeps eluding me.

ESTEBAN: I'd be glad to. Whereabouts is this hare?

COMENDADOR: It's your daughter.

ESTEBAN: My daughter!

COMENDADOR: Yes.

ESTEBAN: But is she worth your while?

COMENDADOR: Intervene in my favor, Mayor, for God's sake.

ESTEBAN: What has she done?

COMENDADOR: She's determined to hurt me——while the wife of a nobleman here in town is dying for an opportunity to see me.

ESTEBAN: Then she would do wrong——and you do

yourself no good to talk so flippantly.

COMENDADOR: My, my, what a circumspect peasant! Flores, give him a copy of the *Politics* and tell him to read Aristotle.

ESTEBAN: My lord, the town's desire is to live peaceably under you. You must remember that there are many honorable persons living in Fuente Ove-juna.

LEONELO: Did you ever hear such impudence as this Comendador's?

COMENDADOR: Have I said anything to offend you, Councilman?

COUNCILMAN: Your pronouncements are unjust, my lord, and not worth uttering. It is unfair to try to take away our honor.

COMENDADOR: Honor? Do you have honor? Listen to the saintly friars of Calatrava!

COUNCILMAN: Some people may boast of the cross you awarded them, but their blood is not as pure as you may think.

COMENDADOR: Do I sully mine by mixing it with yours?

COUNCILMAN: Evil will sully it rather than cleanse it.

COMENDADOR: However that may be, your women are honored by it.

ESTEBAN: Such words are dishonorable.

COMENDADOR: What boors these peasants are! Ah, give me the cities, where nobody hinders the pleasures of lofty men. Husbands are glad when we make love to their wives.

ESTEBAN: They certainly should not be. Do you expect us to suffer such tribulations as readily? There is a God in the cities too, and punishment falls swiftly.

COMENDADOR: Get out of here!

ESTEBAN: Are you talking to us?

COMENDADOR: Get off the Plaza immediately. I don't want to see any of you around here.

ESTEBAN: We're going.

COMENDADOR: Not in a group like that . . .

FLORES: I beg of you to control yourself.

COMENDADOR: These peasants will gossip in groups behind my back.

ORTUÑO: Have a little patience.

COMENDADOR: I marvel that I have so much. Let each man go alone to his own house.

LEONELO: Good Heavens! Will the peasants stomach that?

ESTEBAN: I'm going this way.

[*Exeunt* Peasants]

COMENDADOR: What do you think of those fellows?

ORTUÑO: You don't seem to be able to hide your emotions, yet you refuse to sense the ill feeling around you.

COMENDADOR: But are these fellows my equals?

FLORES: It's not a question of equality.

COMENDADOR: Is that peasant to keep my bow unpunished?

FLORES: Last night I thought I saw him by Lau-rencia's door and I gave him a slash from ear to ear—but it was someone else.

COMENDADOR: I wonder where that Frondoso is now?

FLORES: They say he's around.

COMENDADOR: So that's it. The villain who tried to murder me is allowed to go about scot free.

FLORES: Don't worry. Sooner or later he'll fall into the snare like a stray bird, or be caught on the hook like a fish.

COMENDADOR: But imagine—a peasant, a boy, to threaten me with my own crossbow, me, a captain whose sword made Cordova and Granada tremble! Flores, the world is coming to an end!

FLORES: Blame it on love.

ORTUÑO: I suppose you spared him for friendship's sake.

COMENDADOR: I have acted out of friendship, Ortuño, else I should have ransacked the town in a couple of hours. However, I plan to withhold my vengeance until the right moment arrives. And now —what news of Pascuala?

FLORES: She says she's about to get married.

COMENDADOR: Is she going to that length?

FLORES: In other words, she's sending you to where you'll be paid in cash.

COMENDADOR: What about Olalla?

ORTUÑO: Her reply is charming.

COMENDADOR: She's a gay young thing. What does she say?

ORTUÑO: She says her husband follows her around all the time because he's jealous of my messages and your visits, but as soon as she manages to allay his fears you'll be the first to see her.

COMENDADOR: Fine! Keep an eye on the old man.

ORTUÑO: You'd better be careful.

COMENDADOR: What news from Inés?

FLORES: Which Inés?

COMENDADOR: The wife of Antón.

FLORES: She's ready when you are. I spoke to her in her backyard, through which you may go whenever you wish.

COMENDADOR: Easy girls I love dearly and repay poorly. Flores, if they only knew their worth! . . .

FLORES: To conquer without a struggle nullifies the joy of victory. A quick surrender impairs the pleasure of love making. But, as the philosophers say, there are women as hungry for men as form is for matter, so you shouldn't be surprised if things are the way they are.

COMENDADOR: A man who is maddened by love congratulates himself when girls fall easily to him, but later he regrets it. For however much we desire things we soon forget them, even the most thoughtful of us, if we have gotten them cheaply.

[*Enter* Cimbranos, *a soldier*]

CIMBRANOS: Is the Comendador here?

ORTUÑO: Don't you see him before you?

CIMBRANOS: Oh, valiant Fernán Gómez! Change your green cap for your shining helmet, and your cloak for a coat of mail! For the Maestre of Santiago[11] and the Count of Cabra are attacking Rodrigo Girón, and laying siege to Ciudad Real in the name of the Queen of Castile. All that we won at so much cost in blood and men may soon be lost again. Already the banners of Aragon with their castles, lions and bars, can be seen above the high towers of the city. Though the King of Portugal has paid homage to Girón, the Maestre of Calatrava may have to return to Almagro in defeat. Mount your horse, my lord, your presence alone will force the enemy back to Castile.

COMENDADOR: Stop. That's enough. Ortuño, order a trumpet to sound at once in the Plaza. Tell me, how many soldiers do I have?

ORTUÑO: Fifty, I believe, sir.

COMENDADOR: Order them to horse.

CIMBRANOS: Ciudad Real will fall to the King if you do not hurry.

COMENDADOR: Never fear, that shall not happen!

[*Exeunt all*]

Open country near Fuente Ovejuna.

[*Enter* Mengo, Laurencia, *and* Pascuala, *running*]

PASCUALA: Please don't leave us.

MENGO: Why? What are you afraid of?

LAURENCIA: Well, Mengo, we prefer to go to the village in groups when we don't have a man to go with us. We're afraid of meeting the Comendador.

MENGO: What a cruel and importunate devil that man is.

LAURENCIA: He never stops pestering us.

MENGO: I wish God would strike him with a thunderbolt and put an end to his wickedness.

LAURENCIA: He's a bloodthirsty beast that poisons and infects the whole countryside.

MENGO: I hear that in trying to protect you, here in the meadow, Frondoso aimed his crossbow at the Comendador.

LAURENCIA: I used to hate men, Mengo, but since that day I've looked at them with different eyes. Frondoso acted so gallantly! But I'm afraid it may cost him his life.

MENGO: He'll be forced to leave the village.

LAURENCIA: I keep telling him to go away, although I love him dearly now. But he answers all such counsel with anger and contempt—and all the while the Comendador threatens to hang him by the feet.

PASCUALA: I'd like to see that Comendador carried off by the plague!

MENGO: I'd rather kill him with a mean stone. By God, if I threw a stone at him that I have up at the sheep-fold, it would hit him so hard it would crush his skull in. The Comendador is more vicious than that old Roman, Sabalus.

LAURENCIA: You mean Heliogabalus, who was more wicked than a beast.

[11] Don Manrique.

MENGO: Well, Galván or whoever it was—I don't know too much about history—the Comendador surpasses him in wickedness. Can anyone be more despicable than Fernán Gómez?

PASCUALA: No one can compare with him. You'd think he'd sucked his cruelty from a tigress.

[*Enter* Jacinta]

JACINTA: If friendship means anything, in God's name help me now!

LAURENCIA: What's happened, Jacinta, my friend?

PASCUALA: Both of us are your friends.

JACINTA: Some of the Comendador's attendants are trying to take me to him. They're on their way to Ciudad Real, but they're acting more like villains than soldiers.

LAURENCIA: May God protect you, Jacinta! If the Comendador is bold with you he'll be cruel to me. [*Exit*]

PASCUALA: Jacinta, I'm not a man, so I can't defend you. [*Exit*]

MENGO: But I have both strength and reputation. Stand beside me, Jacinta.

JACINTA: Have you any arms?

MENGO: Yes, those that Nature gave me.

JACINTA: I wish you were armed.

MENGO: Never mind, Jacinta. There are plenty of stones around here.

[*Enter* Flores *and* Ortuño]

FLORES: So you thought you could get away from us, did you?

JACINTA: Mengo, I'm dead with fear.

MENGO: Gentlemen, this is a poor peasant girl . . .

ORTUÑO: Oh, have you decided to defend young women?

MENGO: I'm merely asking for mercy. I'm her relative, and I hope to be able to keep her near me.

FLORES: Kill him off!

MENGO: By God, if you make me mad and I take out my sling, your life will be in danger!

[*Enter the* Comendador *and* Cimbranos]

COMENDADOR: What's all this? Do I have to get off my horse for some petty quarrel?

FLORES: You ought to destroy this miserable village for all the joy it brings you. These wretched peasants have dared to challenge our arms.

MENGO: My lord, if injustice can move you to pity, punish these soldiers who in your name are forcing this girl to leave her husband and honest parents. Grant me permission to take her home.

COMENDADOR: I will grant them permission to punish you. Drop that sling!

MENGO: My lord!

COMENDADOR: Flores, Ortuño, Cimbranos, tie his hands with it.

MENGO: Is this your justice?

COMENDADOR: What do Fuente Ovejuna and its peasants think of me?

MENGO: My lord, how have I or Fuente Ovejuna offended you?

FLORES: Shall I kill him?

COMENDADOR: Don't soil your arms with such trash. Keep them for better things.

ORTUÑO: What are your orders?

COMENDADOR: Flog him. Tie him to that oak tree and beat him with the reins.

MENGO: Pity, my lord, have pity, for you are a nobleman!

COMENDADOR: Flog him till the rivets fall from the leather.

MENGO: My God. For such ugly deeds, uglier punishments!

[Exeunt]

COMENDADOR: Now my girl, why were you running away? Do you prefer a peasant to a nobleman?

JACINTA: Can you restore the honor which your attendants have taken from me in bringing me to you?

COMENDADOR: Do you mean to say your honor has been lost because I wanted to take you away?

JACINTA: Yes. For I have an honest father who, if he does not equal you in birth, surpasses you in virtue.

COMENDADOR: All these troubles around this village, where peasants defy their betters, scarcely help to soothe my temper. Come along here now!

JACINTA: With whom?

COMENDADOR: With me.

JACINTA: You had better think over what you're doing.

COMENDADOR: I have thought it over, and it's so much the worse for you. Instead of keeping you for myself, I shall give you to my whole army.

JACINTA: No power on earth can inflict such an outrage on me while I live.

COMENDADOR: Get a move on now, girl.

JACINTA: Sir, have pity!

COMENDADOR: There is no pity.

JACINTA: I appeal from your cruelty to divine justice.

[Exit Comendador, hauling her out]

Esteban's house.

[Enter Laurencia and Frondoso]

LAURENCIA: Are you not aware of your danger, that you dare to come here?

FRONDOSO: My daring is proof of my love for you. From that hill I saw the Comendador riding away, and since I have complete confidence in you all my fear left with him. I hope he never comes back!

LAURENCIA: Don't curse him—for the more one wishes a person to die the longer he lives.

FRONDOSO: In that case may he live a thousand years, and so by wishing him well let's hope his end will be certain . . . Tell me, Laurencia, has my fondness for you affected you at all? Is my loyalty safely entrusted? You know that the entire village thinks we are made for each other. Won't you forget your modesty and say definitely yes or no?

LAURENCIA: My answer to you and to the village is—yes!

FRONDOSO: I could kiss your feet for such an answer! You give me new life . . . let me tell you now how much I love you.

LAURENCIA: Save your compliments and speak to my father, Frondoso, for that's the important thing now. Look, there he comes with my uncle. Be calm and confident, Frondoso, for this meeting will determine whether I'm to be your wife or no.

FRONDOSO: I put my trust in God.

[Laurencia hides herself]

[Enter Esteban and the Councilman]

ESTEBAN: The Comendador's visit has aroused the whole town. His behavior was most regrettable, to say the least. Everybody was shocked, and poor Jacinta is bearing the brunt of his madness.

COUNCILMAN: Before long Spain will be rendering obedience to the Catholic Kings, as they are called. The Maestre of Santiago has been appointed Captain General, and is already coming on horseback to free Ciudad Real from Girón . . . I'm very sorry about Jacinta, who is an honest girl.

ESTEBAN: The Comendador also had Mengo flogged.

COUNCILMAN: Yes. His flesh is blacker than ink or a black cloth.

ESTEBAN: Please, no more—it makes my blood boil when I think of his disgusting behavior and reputation. What good is my Mayor's staff against that?

COUNCILMAN: It was his servants who did it. Why should you be so upset?

ESTEBAN: Shall I tell you something else? I have been told that one day Pedro Redondo's wife was found down there in the depth of the valley. He had abused her and then turned her over to his soldiers.

COUNCILMAN: Listen, I hear something . . . Who's there?

FRONDOSO: It is I, Frondoso, waiting for permission to come in.

ESTEBAN: You need no permission, Frondoso, to enter my house. You owe your life to your father, but your upbringing to me. I love you like my own son.

FRONDOSO: Sir, trusting that love, I want to ask a favor. You know whose son I am.

ESTEBAN: Did that crazy Fernán Gómez hurt you?

FRONDOSO: Not a little.

ESTEBAN: My heart told me so.

FRONDOSO: You have shown me so much affection that I feel free to make a confession to you. I love Laurencia, and wish to become her husband. Forgive me if I have been too hasty. I'm afraid I've been very bold.

ESTEBAN: You have come just at the right moment, Frondoso, and you will prolong my life, for this touches the fear nearest my heart. I thank God that you have come to save my honor, and I thank you for your love and the purity of your intentions. But I think it only right to tell your father of this first. As soon as he approves I will give my consent too. How happy I shall be if this marriage takes place.

COUNCILMAN: You should ask the girl about him before you accept him.

ESTEBAN: Don't worry about that. The matter is settled; for they discussed it beforehand, I'm sure. If you like, Frondoso, we might talk about the dowry, for I'm planning to give you some *maravedíes*.[12]

FRONDOSO: I'm not concerned about that. I don't need a dowry.

COUNCILMAN: You should be grateful that he doesn't ask you for it in wineskins.

ESTEBAN: I'll ask Laurencia what she would like to do and then let you know.

FRONDOSO: That's fair. It's a good idea to consult everybody concerned.

ESTEBAN: Daughter! . . . Laurencia!

LAURENCIA: Yes, father.

ESTEBAN: You see how quickly she replies. Laurencia, come here a minute. What would you say if your friend Gila were to marry Frondoso, who is as honest a young man as one could find in Fuente Ovejuna?

LAURENCIA: Is Gila thinking of getting married?

ESTEBAN: Why yes, if someone can be found who would be a worthy match for her.

LAURENCIA: My answer is yes.

ESTEBAN: I would say yes too—except that Gila is ugly, and it would be much better if Frondoso became your husband, Laurencia.

LAURENCIA: In spite of your years, you are still a flatterer, father.

ESTEBAN: Do you love him?

LAURENCIA: I am fond of him, and he returns my affection, but you were saying . . .

ESTEBAN: Shall I say yes to him?

LAURENCIA: Yes, say it for me, sir.

ESTEBAN: I? Well, then I have the keys. It's settled then. Let's go to his father.

COUNCILMAN: Yes, let's go.

ESTEBAN: What shall we tell him about the dowry, son? I can afford to give you 4000 *maravedíes*.

FRONDOSO: Do you want to offend me, sir?

ESTEBAN: Come, come, my boy, you'll get over that attitude in a day or two. Even if you don't need it now, a dowry will come in handy later on.

[*Exeunt* Esteban *and* Councilman]

LAURENCIA: Tell me, Frondoso, are you happy?

FRONDOSO: Happy? I'm afraid I'll go crazy with so much joy and happiness. My heart is so overflowing that my eyes are swimming with joy when I look at you, Laurencia, and realize that you, sweet treasure, will be mine.

[*Exeunt*]

[12] Coins.

Meadow near Ciudad Real.

[*Enter the* Maestre, *the* Comendador, Flores, *and* Ortuño]

COMENDADOR: Fly, sir! There's no hope for us.

MAESTRE: The walls were weak and the enemy strong.

COMENDADOR: They have paid dearly for it, though, in blood and lives.

MAESTRE: And they will not be able to boast that our banner of Calatrava is among their spoils. That alone would have been enough to honor their enterprise.

COMENDADOR: Your plans are ruined now, Girón.

MAESTRE: What can I do if Fate in its blindness raises a man aloft one day only to strike him down the next?

VOICES BACKSTAGE: Victory for the Kings of Castile!

MAESTRE: They're decorating the battlements with lights now, and hanging out pennants of victory from the windows in the high towers.

COMENDADOR: They do that because they have paid heavily in blood—it's really more a sign of tragedy than a celebration.

MAESTRE: Fernán Gómez, I'm going back to Calatrava.

COMENDADOR: And I to Fuente Ovejuna. Now you have to think of either defending your relatives or paying homage to the Catholic King.

MAESTRE: I'll write to you about my plans.

COMENDADOR: Time will tell you what to do.

MAESTRE: Ah, years full of the bitterness of time's betrayals!

[*Exeunt*]

A meadow near Fuente Ovejuna.

[*Enter the wedding train:* Musicians, Mengo, Frondoso, Laurencia, Pascuala, Barrildo, Esteban, *and* Juan Rojo]

MUSICIANS: Long live the bride and groom! Many long and happy years to them.

MENGO: It has not been very difficult for you to sing.

BARRILDO: You could have done better yourself, couldn't you?

FRONDOSO: Mengo knows more about whippings now than songs.

MENGO: Don't be surprised if I tell you that there's someone in the valley to whom the Comendador . . .

BARRILDO: Don't say it. That brutal assassin has assailed everyone's honor.

MENGO: It was bad enough for a hundred soldiers to whip me that day when all I had was a sling. It must have been unbearable for that man to whom they gave an enema of dye and herbs—I won't mention his name, but he was an honorable man.

BARRILDO: It was done in jest, I suppose . . .

MENGO: This was no joke. Enemas are desirable sometimes, but I would rather die than undergo one like that.

FRONDOSO: Please sing us a song—if you have anything worth listening to.

MENGO:

> God grant the bride and groom long life
> Free from envy and jealous strife,
> And when their span of years is past,
> May they be united at the last.
> God grant the bride and groom long life!

FRONDOSO: Heaven curse the poet who conceived such a poem!

BARRILDO: It was rather a sloppy job.

MENGO: This makes me think of something about the whole crew of poets. Have you see a baker making crullers? He throws the pieces of dough into the boiling oil until the pot is full. Some buns come out puffed up, others twisted and funnily shaped, some lean to the left, others to the right, some are well fried, others are burnt. Well, I think of a poet composing his verses in much the same way that the baker works on his dough. He hastily throws words into his pot of paper, confident that the honey will conceal what may turn out ridiculous or absurd. But when he tries to sell his poem no one wants it and the confectioner is forced to eat it himself.

BARRILDO: Stop your foolishness now, and let the bride and groom speak.

LAURENCIA: Give us your hands to kiss.

JUAN ROJO: Do you ask to kiss my hand, Laurencia? You and Frondoso had better ask to kiss your father's first.

ESTEBAN: Rojo, I ask Heaven's blessing on her and her husband for ever.

FRONDOSO: Give us your blessing, both of you.

JUAN ROJO: Let the bells ring, and everyone celebrate the union of Laurencia and Frondoso.

MUSICIANS:

> To the valley of Fuente Ovejuna
> Came the maid with the flowing hair.
> A knight of Calatrava
> Followed her to the valley here.
> Amid the shrubs she hid herself,
> Disturbed by shame and fear.
> With the branches she covered herself,
> Feigning she had not seen him,
> But the knight of Calatrava drew near:
> "Why are you hiding, fair maiden,
> Know you not that my keen desire
> Can pierce the thickest wall?"
> She made curtains of the branches
> Confused by shame and fear.
> But love passes sea and mountain:
> "Why are you hiding, fair maiden,
> Know you not that my keen desire
> Can pierce the thickest wall?"

[Enter the Comendador, Flores, Ortuño, and Cimbranos]

COMENDADOR: Silence! You will all remain quietly where you are.

JUAN ROJO: This is not a game, my lord, and your orders will be obeyed. Won't you join us? Why do you come in such a bellicose manner? Are you our conqueror? But what am I saying . . .

FRONDOSO: I'm a dead man. Heaven help me!

LAURENCIA: Quickly, Frondoso, escape this way.

COMENDADOR: No. Arrest him, and tie him up.

JUAN ROJO: Yield to them, my boy, and go quietly to prison.

FRONDOSO: Do you want them to kill me?

JUAN ROJO: Why?

COMENDADOR: I am not a man to murder people without reason. If I were, these soldiers would have run him through by now. I'm ordering him to be taken to jail where his own father will pronounce sentence on him.

PASCUALA: Sir, a wedding is in progress here now.

COMENDADOR: What is that to me? Is he the only person in town who counts?

PASCUALA: If he offended you, pardon him, as becomes your rank.

- COMENDADOR: Pascuala, it is nothing that concerns me personally. He has offended the Maestre Téllez Girón, whom God preserve. He acted counter to his orders and his honor, and must be punished as an example. Otherwise others may rebel too. Don't you know that one day this boy aimed a crossbow at the very heart of the Comendador, Mayor? Loyal vassals you are indeed!

ESTEBAN: As his father-in-law I feel I must come to his defence. I think it only natural that a man, especially a man in love, should challenge you for trying to take away his girl—what else could he do?

COMENDADOR: You are a fool, Mayor.

ESTEBAN: In your opinion, my lord!

COMENDADOR: I had no intention of taking away his girl—for she was not his.

ESTEBAN: You had the thought, and that is enough. There are kings in Castile who are drawing up new rules to prevent disorder. And they will do wrong if, after the wars, they tolerate in the towns and country districts such powerful men wearing those huge crosses on their chests. Those crosses were meant for royal breasts, and only kings should wear them.

COMENDADOR: Wrest the mayor's staff from him!

ESTEBAN: Take it, sir, it is yours to keep.

COMENDADOR: I'll strike him with it as if he were an unbroken horse.

ESTEBAN: You are my lord, and I must bear it: strike, then.

PASCUALA: Shame on you! Striking an old man!

LAURENCIA: You strike him because he is my father—what injury do you avenge in this way?

COMENDADOR: Arrest her, and let ten soldiers guard her.

[Exeunt Comendador and his men]

ESTEBAN: May Heaven visit justice upon him!
[*Exit*]

PASCUALA: The wedding has become a mourning.
[*Exit*]

BARRILDO: Is there not one of us who can speak?

MENGO: I've already had a sound whipping and I'm covered with wales—let someone else anger him this time.

JUAN ROJO: Let us all take counsel.

MENGO: I advise everybody to keep quiet. He made my posterior look like a piece of salmon.
[*Exeunt*]

ACT III.

A room in the Town Hall of Fuente Ovejuna.

[*Enter* Esteban, Alonso, *and* Barrildo]

ESTEBAN: Has everybody come to the meeting?

BARRILDO: Some people are absent.

ESTEBAN: Then our danger is more serious.

BARRILDO: Nearly all the town has been warned.

ESTEBAN: With Frondoso imprisoned in the tower, and my daughter Laurencia in such peril, if God, in his mercy, does not come to our help . . .

[*Enter* Juan Rojo *and the* Councilman]

JUAN ROJO: What are you shouting about, Esteban? Don't you know secrecy is all important now?

ESTEBAN: I wonder I'm not shouting even louder!

[*Enter* Mengo]

MENGO: I want to join in this meeting.

ESTEBAN: With tears streaming down my beard, I ask you, honest farmers, what funeral rites can we give to a country without honor—a country that is lost? And if our honor is indeed lost, which of us can perform such rites, when there is not one among us who has not been dishonored? Answer me now, is there anyone here whose life, whose deep life of honor, is still intact? Are we not all of us in mourning for each other now? If all is lost, what is there to wait for? What is this misfortune that has overtaken us?

JUAN ROJO: The blackest ever known . . . But it has just been announced that the Kings of Castile have concluded a victorious peace, and will soon arrive in Cordova. Let us send two Councilmen to that city to kneel at their feet and ask their help.

BARRILDO: But King Ferdinand, who has conquered so many enemies, is still busy making war, and will not be able to help us now while he's in the midst of battles. We must find some other way out.

COUNCILMAN: If you want my opinion, I suggest we leave the town.

JUAN ROJO: But how can we do that on such short notice?

MENGO: If I understand the situation at all, this meeting will cost us a good many lives.

COUNCILMAN: The mast of patience has been torn from us, and now we are a ship driven before a storm of fear. They have brutally abducted the daughter of the good man who rules our community, and unjustly broken the staff of office over his head. What slave was ever treated worse?

JUAN ROJO: What do you want the people to do?

COUNCILMAN: Die, or give death to the tyrants, for we are many and they are few.

BARRILDO: What? Raise our weapons against our lord and master!

ESTEBAN: Except for God, the King's our only lord and master, not these inhuman, barbarous men. If God is behind our rightful anger, what have we to lose?

MENGO: Let us be a little more cautious. I'm here to speak for the humblest peasants who always have to bear the brunt of any trouble—and I want to represent their fears prudently.

JUAN ROJO: Our misfortunes have prepared us to sacrifice our lives, so what are we waiting for? Our houses and vineyards have been burned down. They are tyrants and we must have our revenge.

[*Enter* Laurencia, *her hair dishevelled*]

LAURENCIA: Let me come in, for I sorely need the advice of men! Do you know me?

ESTEBAN: God in Heaven, is that my daughter?

JUAN ROJO: Don't you recognize your Laurencia?

LAURENCIA: Yes, I am Laurencia, but so changed that looking at me you still doubt it.

ESTEBAN: My daughter!

LAURENCIA: Don't call me your daughter!

ESTEBAN: Why not, my dear? Why not?

LAURENCIA: For many reasons—but chiefly because you let me be carried off by tyrants, by the traitors who rule over us, without attempting to avenge me. I was not yet Frondoso's wife, so you cannot say my husband should have defended me; this was my father's duty as long as the wedding had not been consummated; just as a nobleman about to purchase a jewel need not pay for it if it is lost while still in the merchant's keeping. From under your very eyes, Fernán Gómez dragged me to his house, and you let the wolf carry the sheep like the cowardly shepherd you are. Can you conceive what I suffered at his hands?— the daggers pointed at my breast, the flatteries, threats, insults, and lies used to make my chastity yield to his fierce desires? Does not my bruised and bleeding face, my dishevelled hair tell you anything? Are you not good men?—not fathers and relatives? Do not your hearts sink to see me so grievously betrayed? . . . Oh, you are sheep, how well named the village of Fuente Ovejuna, Sheep Well. Give me weapons and let me fight, since you are but things of stone or metal, since you are but tigers—no, not tigers, for tigers fiercely attack those who steal their offspring, killing the hunters before they can escape. You were born timid rabbits; you are infidels, not Spaniards. Chicken-hearted, you permit other men to abuse your women. Put knitting in your scabbards—what need have you of swords? By the living God, I swear that your women will avenge those tyrants and stone you all, you spinning girls, you sodomites, you effeminate cowards. Tomorrow deck yourselves in our bonnets and skirts, and beautify yourselves with our cosmetics. The Comendador will hang Frondoso from a merlon of the tower, without let or trial, and presently he will string you all up. And I shall be glad—you race of half-men—that this honorable town will be rid of effeminates, and the age of Amazons will return, to the eternal amazement of the world.

ESTEBAN: Daughter, I will not stay to hear such names. I shall go now, even if I have to fight the whole world.

JUAN ROJO: I will go with you, in spite of the enemy's power.

COUNCILMAN: We shall die together.

BARRILDO: Let us hang a cloth from a stick to fly in the wind, and death to the traitors.

JUAN ROJO: What shall our orders be?

MENGO: To kill the Comendador without order. To rally the whole town around us: let us all agree to kill the tyrants.

ESTEBAN: Take with you swords, lances, crossbows, pikes, and sticks.

MENGO: Long live the Kings, our only lords and masters!

ALL: Long live the Kings!

MENGO: Death to the traitor tyrants!

ALL: Death to the tyrants!

[Exeunt all but Laurencia]

LAURENCIA: Go—God will be with you! Come, women of the town, your honor will be avenged—rally round me!

[Enter Pascuala, Jacinta, and Other Women]

PASCUALA: What is happening? What are you shouting about?

LAURENCIA: Can't you see how they're on their way to kill Fernán Gómez? Every man, boy, and child is rushing furiously to do his duty. Is it fair that the men alone should have the glory of a day like this, when we women have the greater grievances?

JACINTA: Tell us your plans then.

LAURENCIA: I propose that we all band together and perform a deed that will shake the world. Jacinta, your great injury will be our guide.

JACINTA: No more than yours.

LAURENCIA: Pascuala, you be our standard bearer.

PASCUALA: I'll be a good one. I'll put a cloth on a lance and we'll have a flag in the wind.

LAURENCIA: There's no time for that. We'll wave our caps for banners.

PASCUALA: Let's appoint a captain.

LAURENCIA: We don't need one.

PASCUALA: Why not?

LAURENCIA: Because when my courage is up, we don't need any Cids or Rodamontes.[13]

[Exeunt]

Hall in the castle of the Comendador.

[Enter Frondoso, *his hands tied,* Flores, Cimbranos, Ortuño, *and the* Comendador]

COMENDADOR: I want him hung by the cord that binds his wrists, so that his punishment may be the more severe.

FRONDOSO: How this will add to your descendants' honor, my lord!

COMENDADOR: Hang him from the highest merlon.

FRONDOSO: It was never my intention to kill you.

FLORES: Do you hear that noise outside?

[Alarum]

COMENDADOR: What can it be?

FLORES: It looks as if the villagers are planning to stay your sentence, my lord.

ORTUÑO: They are breaking down the doors!

[Alarum]

COMENDADOR: The door of my house? The seat of the Commandry?

FRONDOSO: The whole town is here!

JUAN ROJO: [Within] Break them down, smash them in, burn, destroy!

ORTUÑO: It's hard to stop a riot once it gets started.

COMENDADOR: The town against me!

FLORES: And their fury has driven them to tear down all the doors.

COMENDADOR: Untie him. And you, Frondoso, go and calm down the peasant mayor.

FRONDOSO: I'm going, Sir—love has spurred them to action. [Exit]

MENGO: [Within] Long live Ferdinand and Isabella, and down with the tyrants!

FLORES: In God's name, my lord, don't let them find you here.

COMENDADOR: If they persist—why, this room is strong and well protected. They will soon turn back.

FLORES: When villages with a grievance decide to rise against their rulers they never turn back until they have shed blood and taken their revenge.

COMENDADOR: We'll face this mob with our weapons, using this door as a portcullis.[14]

FRONDOSO: [Within] Long live Fuente Ovejuna!

COMENDADOR: What a leader! I'll take care of his bravery!

FLORES: My lord, I marvel at yours.

[Enter Esteban *and the* Peasants]

ESTEBAN: There's the tyrant and his accomplices! Long live Fuente Ovejuna, death to the tyrants!

COMENDADOR: Wait, my people!

ALL: Wrongs never wait.

[13] Famous Spanish and Italian leaders.
[14] Grating over the gateway of a fortress.

COMENDADOR: Tell me your wrongs, and, on a knight's honor, I'll set them right.

ALL: Long live Fuente Ovejuna! Long live King Ferdinand! Death to bad Christians and traitors!

COMENDADOR: Will you not hear me? It is I who address you, I, your lord.

ALL: Our lords are the Catholic Kings.

COMENDADOR: Wait.

ALL: Long live Fuente Ovejuna, and death to Fernán Gómez!

[*Exeunt all*]

[*Enter* Laurencia, Pascuala, Jacinta, *and* Other Women, *armed*]

LAURENCIA: You brave soldiers, no longer women, wait here in this place of vantage.

PASCUALA: Only women know how to take revenge. We shall drink the enemy's blood.

JACINTA: Let us pierce his corpse with our lances.

PASCUALA: Agreed.

ESTEBAN: [*Within*] Die, treacherous Comendador!

COMENDADOR: I die. O God, in Thy clemency, have mercy on me!

BARRILDO: [*Within*] Here's Flores.

MENGO: Get that scoundrel! He's the one who gave me a thousand whippings.

FRONDOSO: [*Within*] I shan't consider myself avenged until I've pulled out his soul.

LAURENCIA: There's no excuse for not going in.

PASCUALA: Calm yourself. We had better guard the door.

BARRILDO: [*Within*] I am not moved. Don't come to me with tears now, you fops.

LAURENCIA: Pascuala, I'm going in; I don't care to keep my sword in its scabbard. [*Exit*]

BARRILDO: [*Within*] Here's Ortuño.

FRONDOSO: [*Within*] Slash his face!

[*Enter* Flores, *fleeing, pursued by* Mengo]

FLORES: Pity, Mengo! I'm not to blame!

MENGO: O no? Not for being a pimp, you scoundrel, not for having whipped me?

PASCUALA: Mengo, give him to us women, we'll . . . Hurry, Mengo!

MENGO: Fine, you can have him—no punishment could be worse!

PASCUALA: We'll avenge the whippings he gave you.

MENGO: That's fine!

JACINTA: Come on, death to the traitor!

FLORES: To die at the hands of women!

JACINTA: Don't you like it?

PASCUALA: Is that why you're weeping?

JACINTA: Die, you panderer to his pleasures!

PASCUALA: Die, you traitor!

FLORES: Pity, women, *pity!*

[*Enter* Ortuño, *pursued by* Laurencia]

ORTUÑO: You know I have had nothing at all to do with it . . .

LAURENCIA: I know you! Come on, women, dye your conquering weapons in their vile blood.

PASCUALA: I'll die killing!

ALL: Long live Fuente Ovejuna! Long live King Ferdinand!

[*Exeunt all*]

Room of the Catholic Kings, at Toro.

[*Enter* King Ferdinand, Queen Isabella, *and the* Maestre Don Manrique]

MANRIQUE: We planned our attack so well that we carried it out without any setback. There was little resistance—even if they had tried to organize any, it would have been weak. Cabra has remained there to guard the place in case of counter-attack.

KING: That was a wise decision, and I am glad that he is in charge of operations. Now we can be sure that Alfonso, who is trying to seize power in Portugal, will not be able to harm us. It is fortunate that Cabra is stationed there and that he is making a good show, for in this way he protects us from any danger and, by acting as a loyal sentinel, works for the good of the kingdom.

[*Enter* Flores, *wounded*]

FLORES: Catholic King Ferdinand, upon whom Heaven has bestowed the Crown of Castile, excellent gentleman that you are—listen to the worst cruelty that a man could ever behold from sunrise to sunset.

KING: Calm yourself!

FLORES: Supreme Sovereign, my wounds forbid me to delay in reporting my sad case, for my life is ebbing away. I come from Fuente Ovejuna, where, with ruthless heart, the inhabitants of that village have deprived their lord and master of his life. Fernán Gómez has been murdered by his perfidious subjects, indignant vassals who dared attack him for but a trivial cause. The mob called him tyrant and inflamed by the power of the epithet committed this despicable crime: they broke into his house and having no faith that he, a perfect gentleman, would right all their wrongs, would not listen to him, but with impatient fury pierced his chest which bore the cross of Calatrava with a thousand cruel wounds and threw him from the lofty windows onto the pikes and lances of the women in the street below. They carried him away, dead, and competed with one another in pulling his beard and hair, and recklessly slashing his face. In fact their constantly growing fury was so great, that some cuts went from ear to ear. They blotted out his coat-of-arms with their pikes and loudly proclaimed that they wanted to replace it with your royal coat-of-arms since those of the Comendador offended them. They sacked his house as if it were the enemy's and joyfully divided the spoils among themselves. All this I witnessed from my hiding place, for my cruel fate did not grant me death at such a time. Thus I remained all day in hiding until nightfall, when I was able to slip

away furtively to come to render you this account.
Sire, since you are just, see that a just punishment
is administered to the brutal culprits who have perpetrated such an outrage.

KING: You may rest assured that the culprits will
not go without due punishment. The unfortunate
event is of such magnitude that I am astonished; I
will send a judge to investigate the case and punish
the culprits as an example to all. A captain will accompany him for his protection, for such great offence requires exemplary punishment. In the meantime your wounds will be cared for.

[Exeunt]

[Enter Peasants, both men and women, with
Fernán Gómez' head on a lance]

MUSICIANS: [Sing]
Long live Isabella and Ferdinand
And death to the tyrants!

BARRILDO: Sing us a song, Frondoso.

FRONDOSO: Here goes, and if it limps let some
critic fix it.

Long live fair Isabella
And Ferdinand of Aragon.
He is made for her
And she is meant for him.
May St. Michael guide them
To Heaven by the hand . . .
Long live Isabella and Ferdinand
And death to the tyrants!

LAURENCIA: Now it's your turn, Barrildo.

BARRILDO: Listen to this, for I've been working on
it.

PASCUALA: If you say it with feeling, it's going to
be good.

BARRILDO:
Long live the famous kings
For they are victorious.
They'll be our lords
Happy and glorious.
May they conquer always
All giants and dwarfs . . .
And death to the tyrants!

MUSICIANS: [Sing]
Long live Isabella and Ferdinand
And death to the tyrants!

LAURENCIA: Now it's your turn, Mengo.

FRONDOSO: Yes, Mengo.

MENGO: I'm a most gifted poet, you know.

PASCUALA: You mean a poet with a bruised backside.

MENGO:
I was whipped on a Sunday morning
My back still feels the pain
But the Christian Kings are coming
There'll be no tyrants here again.

MUSICIANS: Long live the Kings!

ESTEBAN: Take away that head!

MENGO: He has the face of one who has been
hanged.

[Juan Rojo brings in a scutcheon with the royal
arms]

COUNCILMAN: The scutcheon has arrived.

ESTEBAN: Let's see it.

JUAN ROJO: Where shall we place it?

COUNCILMAN: Here, in the Town Hall.

ESTEBAN: What a beautiful scutcheon!

BARRILDO: What joy!

FRONDOSO: A new day is dawning for us, and that's
our sun.

ESTEBAN:
Long live Castile and Leon
And the bars of Aragon.
Down with tyranny!

People of Fuente Ovejuna, listen to the words of
an old man whose life has been blameless. The Kings
will want to investigate what has happened, and this
they will do soon. So agree now among yourselves on
what to say.

FRONDOSO: What is your advice?

ESTEBAN: To die saying Fuente Ovejuna and nothing else.

FRONDOSO: That's fine! Fuente Ovejuna did it!

ESTEBAN: Do you want to answer in that way?

ALL: Yes.

ESTEBAN: Well then, I'd like to play the role of
questioner—let's rehearse! Mengo, pretend that you
are the one being grilled.

MENGO: Can't you pick on someone else, someone
more emaciated?

ESTEBAN: But this is all make believe.

MENGO: All right, go ahead!

ESTEBAN: Who killed the Comendador?

MENGO: Fuente Ovejuna did it!

ESTEBAN: You dog, I'm going to torture you.

MENGO: I don't care—even if you kill me.

ESTEBAN: Confess, you scoundrel.

MENGO: I am ready to confess.

ESTEBAN: Well, then, who did it?

MENGO: Fuente Ovejuna.

ESTEBAN: Bind him tighter.

MENGO: That will make no difference.

ESTEBAN: To hell with the trial then!

[Enter the Councilman]

COUNCILMAN: What are you doing here?

FRONDOSO: What has happened, Cuadrado?

COUNCILMAN: The questioner is here.

ESTEBAN: Send him in.

COUNCILMAN: A captain is with him.

ESTEBAN: Who cares? Let the devil himself come
in: you know your answer.

COUNCILMAN: They are going around town arrest-
ing people.

ESTEBAN: There's nothing to fear. Who killed the
Comendador, Mengo?

MENGO: Who? Fuente Ovejuna.

[Exeunt]

Room of the Maestre of Calatrava, *at Almagro.*

[*Enter the* Maestre *and a* Soldier]

MAESTRE: What a horrible thing to have happened! Melancholy as his end. I could murder you for bringing me such news.

SOLDIER: Sir, I'm but a messenger. I did not intend to annoy you.

MAESTRE: That a town should become so fierce and wrathful, that it would dare to do such a thing! It's incredible! I'll go there with a hundred men and raze the town to the ground, blotting out even the memory of its inhabitants.

SOLDIER: Calm yourself, Sir. They have given themselves up to the King and the most important thing for you is not to enrage him.

MAESTRE: How can they give themselves up to the King? Are they not the vassals of the Comendador?

SOLDIER: That, Sir, you'll have to thrash out with the King.

MAESTRE: Thrash it out? No, for the King placed the land in his hands and it is the King's. He is the Sovereign Lord and as such I recognize him. The fact that they have given themselves up to the King soothes my anger. My wisest course is to see him, even if I am at fault. He will pardon me on account of my youth. I am ashamed to go—but my honor demands that I do so and I shall not forget my dignity.

[*Enter* Laurencia]

LAURENCIA:

Loving, to suspect one's love will suffer pain
Becomes an added suffering of love;
To fear that pain great harm to him may prove
Brings new torture to the heart again.

Devotion, watching eagerly, would fain
Give way to worry, worm of love;
For the heart is rare that does not bend or move
When fear his threat on the belov'd has lain.

I love my husband with a love that does not tire;
But now I live and move beneath
The fear that fate may take away his breath.
His good is all the end of my desire.

If he is present, certain is my grief;
If he is absent, certain is my death.

[*Enter* Frondoso]

FRONDOSO: Laurencia!

LAURENCIA: My dear husband! How do you dare to come here?

FRONDOSO: Does my loving care for you give you such worries?

LAURENCIA: My love, take care of yourself. I am afraid something may happen to you.

FRONDOSO: It would displease God, Laurencia, if I made you unhappy.

LAURENCIA: You have seen what has happened to your friends and the ferocious rage of that judge. Save yourself, and fly from danger!

FRONDOSO: Would you expect cowardice from me? Do not advise me to escape. It is inconceivable that in order to avoid harm I should forego seeing you and betray my friends and my own blood at this tragic moment.

[*Cries within*]

I hear cries. If I am not mistaken, they are from someone put to the torture. Listen carefully!

[*The* Judge *speaks, within, and is answered*]

JUDGE: Tell me the truth, old man.

FRONDOSO: Laurencia, they are torturing an old man!

LAURENCIA: What cruelty!

ESTEBAN: Let me go a moment.

JUDGE: Let him go. Now, tell me, who murdered Fernán?

ESTEBAN: Fuente Ovejuna killed him.

LAURENCIA: Father, I will make your name immortal!

FRONDOSO: What courage!

JUDGE: Take that boy. Pup, speak up! I know you know. What? You refuse? Tighten the screws.

BOY: Fuente Ovejuna, Sir.

JUDGE: By the life of the King, I'll hang the lot of you, you peasants, with my own hands! Who killed the Comendador?

FRONDOSO: They're racking the child, and he answers that way . . .

LAURENCIA: What a brave village!

FRONDOSO: Brave and strong.

JUDGE: Put that woman, over there, in the chair. Tighten it up!

LAURENCIA: He's blind with rage.

JUDGE: You see this chair, peasants, this means death to you all! Who killed the Comendador?

PASCUALA: Fuente Ovejuna, Sir.

JUDGE: Tighter!

FRONDOSO: I hadn't imagined . . .

LAURENCIA: Pascuala will not tell him, Frondoso.

FRONDOSO: Even the children deny it!

JUDGE: They seem to be delighted. Tighter!

PASCUALA: Merciful God!

JUDGE: Tighter, you bastard! Are you deaf?

PASCUALA: Fuente Ovejuna killed him.

JUDGE: Bring me someone a bit bigger—that fat one, half stripped already!

LAURENCIA: Poor Mengo! That must be Mengo!

FRONDOSO: I'm afraid he'll break down.

MENGO: Oh . . . Oh . . .

JUDGE: Give it to him!

MENGO: Oh . . .

JUDGE: Need any help?

MENGO: Oh . . . Oh . . .

JUDGE: Peasant, who killed the Comendador?

MENGO: Oh . . . I'll tell, Sir . . .

JUDGE: Release him a bit.

FRONDOSO: He's confessing!

JUDGE: Now, hard, on the back!

MENGO: Wait, I'll tell all . . .

JUDGE: Who killed him?

MENGO: Sir, Fuente Ovejuna.

JUDGE: Did you ever see such scoundrels? They make fun of pain. The ones I was surest of lie most emphatically. Dismiss them: I'm exhausted.

FRONDOSO: Oh, Mengo, God bless you! I was stiff with fear—but you have rid me of it.

[Enter Mengo, Barrildo, and the Councilman]

BARRILDO: Long live Mengo!

COUNCILMAN: Well he may . . .

BARRILDO: Mengo, bravo!

FRONDOSO: That's what I say.

MENGO: Oh . . . Oh . . .

BARRILDO: Drink and eat, my friend . . .

MENGO: Oh . . . Oh . . . What's that?

BARRILDO: Sweet cider.

MENGO: Oh . . . Oh . . .

FRONDOSO: Something for him to drink!

BARRILDO: Right away!

FRONDOSO: He quaffs it well! That's better, now.

LAURENCIA: Give him a little more.

MENGO: Oh . . . Oh . . .

BARRILDO: This glass, for me.

LAURENCIA: Solemnly he drinks it!

FRONDOSO: A good denial gets a good drink.

BARRILDO: Want another glass?

MENGO: Oh . . . Oh . . . Yes, yes.

FRONDOSO: Drink it down; you deserve it.

LAURENCIA: A drink for each turn of the rack.

FRONDOSO: Cover him up, he'll freeze to death.

BARRILDO: Want some more?

MENGO: Three more. Oh . . . Oh . . .

FRONDOSO: He's asking for the wine . . .

BARRILDO: Yes, there's a boy, drink deep. What's the matter now?

MENGO: It's a bit sour. Oh, I'm catching cold.

FRONDOSO: Here, drink this, it's better. Who killed the Comendador?

MENGO: Fuente Ovejuna killed him . . .

[Exeunt Mengo, Barrildo, and the Councilman]

FRONDOSO: He deserves more than they can give him. But tell me, my love, who killed the Comendador?

LAURENCIA: Little Fuente Ovejuna, my dear.

FRONDOSO: Who did?

LAURENCIA: You bully, you torturer! I say Fuente Ovejuna did it.

FRONDOSO: What about me? How do I kill you?

LAURENCIA: With love, sweet love, with lots of love.

Room of the Kings, at Tordesillas.

[Enter the King and Queen]

ISABELLA: I did not expect to find you here, but my luck is good.

KING: The pleasure of seeing you lends new glory to my eyes. I was on my way to Portugal and I had to stop here.

ISABELLA: Your Majesty's plans are always wise.

KING: How did you leave Castile?

ISABELLA: Quiet and peaceful.

KING: No wonder, if you were the peacemaker.

[Enter Don Manrique]

MANRIQUE: The Maestre of Calatrava, who has just arrived, begs audience.

ISABELLA: I wanted very much to see him.

MANRIQUE: I swear, Madame, that although young in years, he is a most valiant soldier.

[Exit Don Manrique, and enter the Maestre]

MAESTRE: Rodrigo Téllez Girón, Maestre of Calatrava, who never tires of praising you, humbly kneels before you and asks your pardon. I admit that I have been deceived and that, ill-advised, I may have transgressed in my loyalty to you. Fernán's counsel deceived me and for that reason I humbly beg forgiveness. And if I am deserving of this royal favor, I pledge to serve you from now on; in the present campaign which you are undertaking against Granada, where you are now going, I promise to show the valor of my sword. No sooner will I unsheathe it, bringing fierce suffering to the enemy, than I will hoist my red crosses on the loftiest merlon of the battlements. In serving you I will employ five hundred soldiers, and I promise on my honor nevermore to displease you.

KING: Rise, Maestre. It is enough that you have come for me to welcome you royally.

MAESTRE: You are a consolation to a troubled soul.

ISABELLA: You speak with the same undaunted courage with which you act.

MAESTRE: You are a beautiful Esther, and you a divine Xerxes.[15]

[Enter Manrique]

MANRIQUE: Sir, the judge you sent to Fuente Ovejuna has returned and he asks to see you.

KING: [To the Maestre] Be the judge of these aggressors.

MAESTRE: If I were not in your presence, Sire, I'd certainly teach them how to kill Comendadores.

KING: That is no longer necessary.

ISABELLA: God willing, I hope this power lies with you.

[Enter Judge]

JUDGE: I went to Fuente Ovejuna, as you commanded, and carried out my assignment with special care and diligence. After due investigation, I cannot produce a single written page of evidence, for to my question: "Who killed the Comendador?" the people answered with one accord: "Fuente Ovejuna did it." Three hundred persons were put to torture, quite ruthlessly, and I assure you, Sire, that I could get no more out of them than this. Even children, only ten years old, were put to the rack, but to no avail— neither did flatteries nor deceits do the least good.

15 Esther was the wife of Xerxes, king of Persia in the fifth century B.C.

And since it is so hopeless to reach any conclusion: either you must pardon them all or kill the entire village. And now the whole town has come to corroborate in person what they have told me. You will be able to find out from them.

KING: Let them come in.

[*Enter the two Mayors,* Esteban *and* Alonso, Frondoso, *and* Peasants, *men and women*]

LAURENCIA: Are those the rulers?

FRONDOSO: Yes, they are the powerful sovereigns of Castile.

LAURENCIA: Upon my faith, they are beautiful! May Saint Anthony bless them!

ISABELLA: Are these the aggressors?

ESTEBAN: Fuente Ovejuna, Your Majesty, who humbly kneel before you, ready to serve you. We have suffered from the fierce tyranny and cruelty of the dead Comendador, who showered insults upon us—and committed untold evil. He was bereft of all mercy, and did not hesitate to steal our property and rape our women.

FRONDOSO: He went so far as to take away from me this girl, whom Heaven has granted to me and who has made me so blissful that no human being can compete with me in joy. He snatched her away to his house on my wedding night, as if she were his property, and if she had not known how to protect herself, she, who is virtue personified, would have paid dearly, as you can well imagine.

MENGO: Is it not my turn to talk? If you grant me permission you will be astonished to learn how he treated me. Because I went to defend a girl whom his insolent servants were about to abuse, that perverse Nero handled me so roughly that he left my posterior like a slice of salmon. Three men beat my buttocks so relentlessly that I believe I still bear some wales. To heal my bruises I have had to use more powders and myrtle-berries than my farm is worth.

ESTEBAN: Sire, we want to be your vassals. You are our King and in your defence we have borne arms. We trust in your clemency and hope that you believe in our innocence.

KING: Though the crime is grave, I am forced to pardon it since no indictment is set down. And since I am responsible for you, the village will remain under my jurisdiction until such time as a new Comendador appears to inherit it.

FRONDOSO: Your Majesty speaks with great wisdom. And at this point, worthy audience, ends the play FUENTE OVEJUNA.

Opposite page: The theatre of Bordeaux opened in 1780. It illustrates the development of the *picture-frame* stage in the late neoclassic French theatre. Note the wide forestage, or *apron,* on which most of the action occurred; the deep stage area containing the scenery, which consisted of a backdrop and painted flats arranged one behind the other in narrowing perspective; and the orchestra, or *parterre,* in which there were still no seats for the public (see pp. 385–387). Courtesy Pierre Beres, Inc.

Left: Molière. From Luciene Dubeche, *Histoire générale du Théâtre. Above: The School for Scandal.* An engraving published October 1, 1851, showing Sir Peter and Lady Teazle with Farren as Sir Peter. Theatre Collection, Library and Museum of the Performing Arts at Lincoln Center.

The Seventeenth and Eighteenth Centuries

The Seventeenth and Eighteenth Centuries

THE RULES

The popular theatre of the Renaissance, especially in Spain and England, had been supercharged with violence and had grown dangerously diffuse. As the failure of many Elizabethan and Jacobean plays proved, the merit of vitality could not always compensate deficiencies in logic, credibility, and organization. For all the narrow academicism that vitiates Sir Philip Sidney's criticism of the theatre of his great age in his *Apologie for Poetrie,* he managed to sum up as early as 1581 (although the *Apologie* was not published until 1595) the dangers that tended to undermine the Renaissance drama or to transform it into a species of rambling romance.

". . . You shall have Asia on the one side, and Afric of the other, and so many other under-kingdoms, that the player, when he cometh in, must ever begin telling where he is, or else the tale will not be conceived. Now ye shall have three ladies walk to gather flowers, and then we must believe the stage to be a garden. By and by we hear news of shipwreck in the same place, and then we are to blame, if we accept it not for a rock. Upon the back of that, comes out a hideous monster, with fire and smoke, and then the miserable beholders are bound to take it for a cave. While in the meantime, two armies fly in, represented with four swords and bucklers, and then what hard heart will not receive it for a pitched field?

"Now, of time they are much more liberal. For ordinary it is that two young princes fall in love; after many traverses, she is got with child, delivered of a fair boy; he is lost, groweth a man, falls in love, and is ready to get another child, and all this in two hours' space: which how absurd it is in sense, even sense may imagine, and art hath taught, and all ancient examples justified. . . ."

By reaction and by contrast, the second half of the seventeenth century, especially in France, came to favor a form of playwriting with fewer plot complications. This tendency was to reassert itself, after 1870, in much naturalistic, poetic, symbolist, psychological, and discussion drama—after both the academic practice of the late seventeenth century and the Romantic reaction of the early nineteenth century had outworn their specific value. It is consequently a mistake to dismiss the seventeenth-century reaction to Elizabethanism as inconsequential to the development of the drama. The defense of so-called neoclassicism by John Dryden in 1668, for example, was fundamentally sound when he told his readers that the drama could have action without plottiness: ". . . 'Tis a great mistake in us to believe the French present no part of the action on the stage; every alteration or crossing of a design, every new-sprung passion, and turn of it, is a part of the action, and much the noblest, except we conceive nothing to be action till the players come to blows; as if the painting of the hero's mind were not more properly the poet's work than the strength of his body. . . ."

Taste in the drama swung—and swung often dogmatically—toward concentration and regulation of creativeness. The ideal of the theatre of the period known as the neoclassic was restraint by common sense and reason, as well as by rules of dramatic unity ascribed to Aristotle and by a principle of "decorum" derived from Horace and acclaimed in the name of good taste. Passionless tragedy, of course, is a contradiction in terms. So is unanimated comedy. It is obvious that an age represented by such masters as Racine and Molière, whose work epitomizes French tragedy and universal comedy for millions, could not have "liquidated" passionateness and liveliness.

That is not to say that pundits and self-appointed censor-critics did not attempt such liquidation, especially when prescribing for tragedy. France was the center of civilization after 1640, and the efforts of the statesmen Mazarin and Richelieu and of Louis XIV resulted in an absolute monarchy dedicated to the maintenance of order and stability in all walks of life. Order was also imposed on the stage, and Richelieu's interest in bringing the arts under control (culminating in the creation of the French Academy), combined with the teaching of Renaissance scholars and French critics, forced two principles upon dramatic composition in France—the rule of the "unities" of time, place, and action and the test of good sense or moderation. One short period, not exceeding twenty-four hours, was prescribed for the action of a play, in order that the discrepancy between actual and "stage" time should not strain credulity; there was to be one place for the action, instead of a dozen or more localities, as in *Antony and Cleopatra;* and there was to be only one plot, instead of two or more. Aristotle's authority was cited for these rules, although the only unity on which the Greek philosopher's *Poetics* had actually insisted was unity of action. The real authority for the rules lay in the century's ideal of orderliness.

This principle could, and did, become an incubus rather than a guardian angel. But while the ideal had vitality it proved a challenge to artistry. If by temperament Racine could accommodate himself easily to the "rules," so much the better. If you have an aptitude for sonneteering, you do not write poorer sonnets because a sonnet has formal requirements. Passion is intensified in Racine's plays by the very fact that it has formal confines which it threatens to rend apart with its nuclear energy. Racine expressed the aims of neoclassic dramatic art most concisely when he quoted Horace in the preface to *Bérénice:* "Whatever you write, it must be simple and it must be one." Taking pride, moreover, in avoiding "stage tricks as astonishing as they would be false to nature" and in not allowing characters to do something "out of sheer caprice," he set exacting standards for his art.

Concentration was also Molière's ideal for comedy. In his satire he is sure of his marksmanship because he concentrates its fire. And it is characteristic of Molière's genius, as well as of the irrepressible spirit of comedy, that for him orderliness was a matter of tact rather than of conformity to pedantic rules. In his *Critique of the School for Wives,* he declared, "I should like to know whether the great rule of all rules is not to please; and whether a play which attains this has not followed a good method." Nor was he inclined to submit to any other form of arbitrary regulation, writing in his preface to *Tartuffe,* "If it be the aim of comedy to correct man's vices, then I do not see for what reason there should be a privileged class. Such a one is, in the State, decidedly more dangerous in its consequences than any other, and we have seen that the stage possesses a great virtue as a corrective medium." Neither the prevailing aristocratic taste nor the rules of unity of Louis XIV's France could restrain Molière more than his own taste and temperament disposed him to restrain himself.

NEOCLASSIC TRAGEDY

A new classicism arose in France during the reign of Louis XIV. The classicism of the Renaissance had been chiefly Roman in inspiration, but now the superiority of Greek art came to be acknowledged. Not fully understood, and adulterated by French courtly taste and bias, Greek classicism was made an ideal or was cited as authority for any artistic ideals that the age developed. The two classicisms of Rome and Greece blended with French elements to produce a standard for art that has been aptly called "neoclassic."

The first important French tragedian, Pierre Corneille (1606–1684), started out as an individualist and romanticist in *The Cid* (1636), a drama of tempestuous love crossed by a girl's sense of duty to her father, who had been slain by her lover in a duel. But soon Corneille came to include more and more Roman sturdiness verging on stiffness, a Roman sense of duty, and a tragic awareness of the clash between the private passions and social or spiritual obligations. Beginning with his *Horace* and *Cinna* in 1640, he became the poet of the claims and restraints of society upon the individual. Corneille wrote true heroic drama. Man's sense of having a place in the scheme of things requires of him a sense of honor and responsibility. With this sense of obligation, man is Man, and when he sacrifices his passions or his life to principle he makes a sacrifice to his ideal conception of himself. Corneille's work suffered, however, from too much stiffness and moralizing grandeur. It does not properly represent the rich sensibility and the graceful mobility of the classic French spirit, which is best expressed by the genius of Corneille's younger contemporary Jean Racine.

In the work of Racine (1639–1699) appeared a keen understanding of passion as the great threat to happiness and stability. His *Andromache, Britannicus,* and *Phaedra* are superb examples of tragedy in which reason and order are upheld in the midst of emotional chaos. The superficial classicism of the Greek and Roman subjects in plays such as these is imbued with the deeper classicism of the "golden mean" and the cultivation of rationality that Greece contributed to Western civilization. Racine's blending of this attitude with the puritanical Catholic sectarianism known as Jansenism and with courtly taste (as when he introduced in *Phaedra* a romantic attachment that was absent in its Greek model, *Hippolytus*) made his classicism more alive than an academic imitation of Greek tragedy would have been. The modern French critic Jules Lemaître aptly described his genius as "the genius of our race—order, reason, measured sentiment, and force underlying gracefulness." Lemaître might have added "power of analysis"—for Racine's tragic art involves considerable reasoning as well as reason. A passion in his plays is always broken up into its elements and analyzed in the very process of being presented.

A more exacting kind of tragic theatre than the neoclassic has never emanated from the human mind, and when mediocre playwrights worked within its confines the results were arid. Talentless writers found neoclassicism a sedative rather than a stimulant. French playwrights, especially after the end of Louis XIV's age, which sustained Racine's talent, could provide only the empty shell of neoclassic tragedy. Not even so talented a man of letters as Voltaire could do more, even though he wrote many plays and filled them with the advanced ideas of eighteenth-century rationalism. Elsewhere on the Continent, more or less talented poets were also unable to achieve mastery in this cramping style. And in England, only John Dryden's neoclassic redaction of *Antony and Cleopatra* under the title *All for Love* (1678) rose sufficiently above mediocrity or artificiality. Had neoclassicism also exerted a limiting effect on the sister art of comedy, the disadvantages of the classicist revival would have greatly exceeded its advantages. Fortunately, however, the neoclassic stage was able to sustain a great deal of inspired laughter from the time of Molière to the time of Beaumarchais and Sheridan.

COMEDY

The greatest achievements in comedy for nearly a century and a half came from the play of the essentially rationalistic mind on the gregarious nature of the human species. Any deviation from established manners, such as the extravagant behavior of characters in the comedies of Molière and the Restoration playwrights, makes a man an object of laughter. This, of course, presupposes a belief that established society is a desideratum, that it has reached the peak of possible development, and that it is not subject to drastic change. To violate its dictates is consequently to fly in the face of reason and is punishable with ridicule—a condign and severe punishment, since ridicule excludes us, if not physically certainly psychologically, from good society. Any surrender to unrealistic desire or extreme attitudes disposes us to ridiculous behavior—behavior contrary to human nature and to the norms established by the community. Excess of any sort—except a socially sanctioned excess (as of skepticism and philandering among the gentlemen of the Restoration)—confuses the mind and may even blind the heart. An elderly man who wants to marry a very young girl (as in Molière's *The School for Wives*), a merchant who loves his wealth too much (as in *The Miser*), a rich bourgeois consumed with a desire to push himself into aristocratic society (as in *The Would-be Gentleman*), a man who is overeager to welcome piety and too trusting to question its genuineness (as in *Tartuffe*), and, to be sure, even a person too inflexibly noble (as in *The Misanthrope*)—all ride for a fall. So the facts of reality, which are facts of reason, decree.

This view of life is rationalistic, and rationalism was the key to much of the thinking, including the philosophy and science, of the second half of the seventeenth century, when Molière left his mark and the Restoration playwrights their scratches on the theatre. It is, we recall, the century of mathematical progress, when even the devout Pascal started out as a mathematician and so God-intoxicated a man as Spinoza demonstrated his ethics "in the manner of geometry."

In a period so concerned with social norms, especially in the work of writers endowed with a sense of humor, rationalism was not to be carried to its logical conclusion. Even the skeptical philosopher Descartes did not drive his philosophy to such consistent extremes as to fly in the face of theology and get himself into trouble that would prevent him from pursuing philosophy undisturbed. Reasonableness—or, as the French called it, *bon sens*—was the practical and the comedic conclusion derived from the disposition of the time. Rarely did skepticism become cynicism, and even more rarely did it translate itself into active iconoclasm. Individualistic revolt was reserved for the later age of Romanticism. Revolt was not good manners. It is difficult to be revolutionary and urbane at the same time. (The Puritans had not been urbane and they cut off Charles I's head.) A revolutionary situation was long in the making in France, but the Voltaires and Diderots of the eighteenth century who contributed to the intellectual ferment of the French Revolution would not have recognized their way of life in the Reign of Terror.

The great apostle of "Reason" during the Revolution was Robespierre. Voltaire would have found him no gentleman but a monomaniac.

The age also made much use of the term "nature," but clipped its hedges into formal shapes. Nature was something that the rationalists liked to see tamed and the later romanticists preferred in a wild state. It may be assumed that an elderly man's infatuation with a young girl, as in Molière's *The School for Wives,* is a fact of nature, but to Molière, who himself had married a woman many years his junior and was tormented by jealousy, it was unnatural and thus absurd. Although he knew only too well that the provocations to impatience with human behavior and to social protest are numerous, Molière reflected his age in deploring the violence of Alceste's reactions in *The Misanthrope.* Until the floodgates of revolution were opened in America and France during the last quarter of the eighteenth century, too keen an awareness of evil was considered a vice rather than a virtue. It unnerved one; it ruined one's temper and spoiled one's happiness. It was also bad taste to make too much of evil, because it interfered with normal relations among men and led to the making of extravagant or "unnatural" demands on them.

Urbanity to so profound a man as Molière was not ignorance but a necessary defense against extremism and folly. It was a necessary condition for getting on with one's fellowmen, which was his modest ideal for man in society. And it was society that his age prized most—an ideal that is not necessarily specious, if one considers society to be the requisite condition for civilization. Other times and other kinds of men had raised and were again to raise the questions: What kind of society and what kind of civilization? What kind of man is produced? To whom does he owe his first allegiance—to his society or to his God? And what are the rival claims of Caesar and God? And the rival claims of social conformity and private conscience? But it is precisely such questions that might lead to disturbance and excess. The age would have none of this, if it could help it. And the writers of comedy *could* help it—unless, like the Restoration's William Wycherley and unlike Molière or Congreve, they occasionally, for reasons of circumstance or temper, lost control of their pens.

Whether these generalizations apply accurately to any but the most masterly comedies of the period can be questioned. They cannot, in fact, cover a century and a half of playwriting. The sentimental comedies of Richard Steele also belong to the eighteenth century. High comedy was achieved only at special times in the theatre of the period under consideration—and in special hands.

The quality of laughter of such plays as *The Misanthrope,* Congreve's *The Way of the World*, and Sheridan's *The School for Scandal* can perhaps be summed up most simply by George Meredith's reflections on the comic spirit in his famous essay. "If you detect the ridicule" in humanity, he writes, "and your kindliness is chilled by it, you are slipping into the grasp of satire." If, in dealing with the ridiculous individual, "you laugh all around him, tumble him, roll him about, deal him a smack, and drop a tear on him . . . it is the spirit of Humor that is moving you." You serve the pure comic spirit and write high comedy not by "sharply driving into the quivering sensibilities," which is satire, and not by "comforting them and tucking them up," which is humor, but in retaining a cool detachment, productive of laughter that is "impersonal and of unrivaled politeness, nearer a smile, often no more than a smile."

For most writers as for most other people, this is an almost impossible requirement. During Molière's lifetime, he was the only one in France who met it; and after him, only Le Sage, the author of the famous novel of roguery *Gil Blas*, came close to meeting it, with his comedy of political corruption *Turcaret* (1709). The next effective playwright, Marivaux (1688-1763), signaled a turn in the temper of comic writing. His comedies, among which *The Game of Love and Chance* (*Le Jeu de l'amour et du hasard*) is still in repertory at the Comédie Française, are romantic, genial, and almost benevolent. The play of sentiment receives his warm, if also amused and urbane, regard. He carries us some distance from Molière, although he, too, is on the side of reason and "nature." Finally, just as the age came to a close, it found a prodigal genius in Beaumarchais (1732-1799). Politician, adventurer, munitions contractor to the American Revolution, and playwright, Beaumarchais mediates in his best play, *The Marriage of Figaro*, between the comedy of aristocratic society and the spirit of the democratic Revolution. *Figaro* was at first suppressed by Louis XVI, and its *première* in 1784, a mere five years before the fall of the monarchy, caused a riot. "What have you done to merit this splendor?" Figaro the servant asks the master who is trying to seduce Figaro's bride. "You made the effort to be born, and that is all. You are a very ordinary fellow, while I, an obscure man in the crowd, required more wit and knowledge to rise in the world than has been invested in recent years in the government of all the Spanish provinces." Figaro's words may have tolled the death knell of feudalism and the tocsin of the insurgent middle class in France. They also announced the end of genuine high comedy in France for half a century, or if we except the special romantic genius of Alfred de Musset, for an entire century—that is, until the advent of Henry Becque, who found another seemingly fixed society upon which to play with an imperturbable comic spirit.

ENGLISH COMEDY

High "comedy of manners" came into vogue throughout Europe after 1660. In Denmark,

Molière found a rather Teutonically blunt disciple in Ludwig Holberg (1684-1754), whose best-known play, *Erasmus Montanus*, submits pedantry to some caustic laughter. In Russia, the playwright Fonvizin wrote an earthy piece, *The Brigadier General*, which derives humor from the manners of the landed gentry. In both instances, however, we miss the finished style and natural urbanity of Molière. The most polished artistry on the Continent was that of the Venetian Carlo Goldoni (1707-1793), whose best-known play, *La Locandiera*, or *The Mistress of the Inn*, remains a fresh comedy of lively encounters between a sensible woman of the people and her suitors. Yet Goldoni was more facile than incisive. And significantly, for not only France but all Europe was changing, Goldoni was routed from the stage by his rival Carlo Gozzi (1722-1806), whose staples were the fairy tale and romantic drama, such as the well-known Chinese comedy *Turandot*. Goldoni went to France and died in poverty in 1793 after losing the subsidy he had received from Louis XVI before the Revolution.

In England, from the Restoration of the Stuart monarchy in 1660 to 1700, upper-class comedy, nourished by the effervescent aristocracy of the "Merry Monarch" Charles II, had a flourishing career. A century later the Victorian and liberal historian Macaulay waxed indignant when he recorded the antics of the fashionable Restoration set. "Profligacy," he wrote, "was the badge of a cavalier and a high churchman. Decency was associated with conventicles and calves' heads."

Compounded of old and new styles of comic writing (native late Elizabethan, Spanish, and French), "Restoration Comedy" was comedy of manners, even if the manners tended to be gross and sometimes downright indecent. A society was observed, if only by way of caricature; a norm of sophistication was assumed, and deviations from it were reprehended with ridicule. And the ridicule, although frequently as heartless as it was monotonous, and although dependent upon stereotypes of fops, philanderers, and betrayed husbands, often rose to the estate of wit. If the plots, frequently doubled or trebled, tended to be snarled, they were largely excuses for shrewd bursts of clever dialogue that became dazzling in the plays of one expert, William Congreve.

The first specialists in Restoration comedy, the poet John Dryden and the Cavalier playwright George Etherege (1635?-1691), laid down the general lines of the assault on fashionable folly and unfashionable crudity. The dialogue was written in prose (Molière generally put his final versions into verse); the neoclassic unities of time and place were observed, although more loosely than in France; "type" and "class" characters predominated; and actual life was not so much represented as exaggerated for purposes of entertainment. Etherege had a vigorous successor and social critic in William Wycherley (1640?-1715), who was less inclined than his contemporaries to take a detached view of his society and is still remembered for his last plays, *The Country Wife* (1675) and *The Plain Dealer* (1676). After a number of uninspired years had elapsed, the busy architect Sir John Vanbrugh (1664–1726) contributed comedies which are sharper than most plays of the period. Vanbrugh, in turn, was overshadowed by the master of the Restoration mode, William Congreve, whose *Love for Love* and *The Way of the World* represent the peak of "artificial" comedy in English.

After Congreve, the short-lived but gifted George Farquhar (1677?–1707), from Ireland, turned out the pleasant comedies *The Recruiting Officer* (1706) and *The Beaux' Stratagem* (1707), which held the English and American stage for an uncommonly long time. (*The Beaux' Stratagem* could still delight London during the season of 1949–1950.) But with Farquhar's plays the specific Restoration style came to an end, making way for a new vogue—sentimental, moralizing comedy, which glutted the theatres throughout the eighteenth century. During the first half of the century, however, the comic spirit flared up in John Gay's *The Beggar's Opera* (1728) and in the farces of the great novelist Henry Fielding, especially in his literary burlesque *Tom Thumb the Great* (1730). And during the last quarter of the century the stage acquired some fresh gaiety with Oliver Goldsmith's *She Stoops to Conquer* (1773), and the art of high comedy was recovered by Richard Brinsley Sheridan in *The Rivals, The Critic,* and *The School for Scandal*. When the last-mentioned piece was produced in 1777, however, the Revolution was already in progress in America, and in England, too, the old, stable society that had sustained the rationalistic comedy of manners was succumbing to a philosophy of change and to a romantic revolt in the arts.

Molière

(1622–1673)

Most modern writers of comedy, from Congreve and Goldoni to the latest practitioners in Paris, London, or New York, are the lineal descendants of Jean Baptiste Poquelin, better known as Molière. Although not strictly an innovator in a field already explored by the playwrights of ancient Rome and of the Italian *commedia dell' arte* of the fifteenth and sixteenth centuries, Molière, by perfecting critical comedy and sharpening its edge, became the most influential dramatist next to Shakespeare.

Circumstances, education, and experience conspired to make Molière a man of the world and a master of the theatre. Born in 1622, the son of Louis XIV's private upholsterer, he spent his formative years close to the court, received a nobleman's education, conversed with scholars and philosophers, and later studied law at Orléans. The professions did not attract him, but the theatre did, his interest having been aroused early by Italian comedy in Paris and by his training in rhetoric, elocution, and Latin drama at the Jesuit Collège de Clermont. He joined a theatrical troupe as an amateur in 1643, partly because he was attracted to an actress, and soon became a professional actor, helping to found the Illustre Théâtre company and assuming the stage name of Molière. Several years later, his group failed in Paris. Sharing its vicissitudes out of choice rather than necessity, he then spent twelve years in the provinces as an itinerant player and also as company playwright. His wanderings in the wilderness disciplined him. He learned that it was the theatre's first condition of success to excite and entertain; that there was only one mortal sin on the stage—dullness. After obtaining for his acting troupe the helpful patronage of the Duc d'Anjou, Molière returned to Paris the foremost comedian of his time, as well as a budding dramatist of unrivaled resourcefulness.

The young playwright's development thereafter was in the direction of greater depth and more solid craftsmanship. Although he never actually revolted against the stable society of his time and continued to compose light farces for the edification of the court, he was by disposition an untiring critic of men and manners. Some of his plays, such as *The Would-be Gentleman* and *Georges Dandin*, satirized the social climbing of the bourgeoisie. The professional pietists and the aristocrats of the age saw themselves pilloried in *Tartuffe* and *The Misanthrope*, respectively. And a variety of human foibles—miserliness, affectation, pedantry, senile infatuation, and general fatuousness—served as subjects for detached laughter in many of his other works. From *The Affected Misses* (*Les Précieuses ridicules*), his first Parisian satire on the pseudo sophistication of the smart set, in 1659, to *The Imaginary Invalid*, his last comedy, thirteen years later, Molière maintained an uninterrupted attack on contemporary vices and follies.

It is to be noted, too, that the age collaborated unstintedly with its satirist. "It was a boon to the comic poet," wrote George Meredith. "He had that lively quicksilver world of the animalcule passions, the huge pretensions, the placid absurdities, under his eyes in full activity; vociferous quacks and snapping dupes, hypocrites, posturers, extravagants, pedants, rose-pink ladies and mad grammarians, sonneteering marquises, high-flying mistresses, plain-minded maids, interthreading as in a loom, noisy as at a fair."

The nobility was sometimes aroused against Molière, social cliques were annoyed at him, and his clerical enemies succeeded in delaying for five years the production of his satire on religious hypocrisy, *Tartuffe*. Nevertheless, up to his death in 1673, his company and his comedies ruled the French stage, and his equanimity remained generally impervious to attacks and misfortunes. His sense of humor, sorely tried by an unhappy marriage with an actress many years his junior, never quite abandoned him. Though he sometimes argued with his critics, he was free from acrimony and continued to supplement his caricatures with fresh and spirited characters. The young lovers in his plays qualify as some of the most agreeable creations of the comic theatre.

Molière's masterpiece, *The Misanthrope*, was produced in 1666, at the peak of the "golden age" of Louis XIV. Court life was at the height of its elegance when Molière laid bare its pretences and foibles. His satire is so sharp and his references to injustice and corruption are so direct that we must conclude that he was emotionally involved in his observations and that it was only with some effort that he succeeded in maintaining the equipoise that ensures success in the fine art of writing high comedy. *The Misanthrope* is comedy of manners; it provides, indeed, a veritable cross section of upper-class society. But the intense revulsion and protest of Molière's comic hero Alceste suggest a modern social consciousness that threatens to burst the confines of neoclassic humor. It is significant that the famous Restoration-period adaptation of *The Misanthrope*, Wycherley's *The Plain Dealer*, is a bitter drama, and that some modern readers have found Molière's play too serious to be considered unalloyed comedy. Molière's own audiences apparently also found it too serious when it was first performed. And, practiced showman that he was, Molière applied his skill to the fashioning of more marketable comedies—the sprightly, semifarcical *Physician in Spite of Himself*, the broad comedy of social-climbing *The Would-be Gentleman,* the delightful travesty on avarice *The Miser,* the pellucid satire on pedantry and pseudo intellectualism *The Learned Ladies,* and the burlesque on hypochondria and medical charlatanism *The Imaginary Invalid.* Never again was Molière to expose the total area of social relations, including social injustice, in a play. But the same quality of comprehensive and incisive satire that militated against the success of *The Misanthrope* in his own day also made it the most durable and significant of his plays.

At the same time, it is apparent to a close reader of *The Misanthrope* that in this play Molière did not depart from the fundamental principles of high comedy. His laughter is still the laughter of reason, and it is directed as unerringly against the misanthropic Alceste's overintense protest as against the follies that provoke him. If reason cannot fail to unmask social error and wrong, neither can it fail to repudiate extreme indignation and demands for greater integrity than should be expected of fallible humanity. So runs the argument of the comic spirit exemplified by Molière, who makes the *raisonneur* Philinte declare, "I take men quietly just as they are. . . . My mind is no more shocked at seeing a man a rogue, unjust, or selfish than at seeing vultures eager for prey, mischievous apes, or fury-lashed wolves." It is a point of view not precisely complimentary to the human species, but it fully expresses the disenchanted comic equanimity which we associate with the urbane author of *The Misanthrope.* Here comic wisdom is wrung from the same social realities that were to yield plays of violent social protest and conflict when the democratic spirit of the late nineteenth and the twentieth centuries committed Europe to a philosophy of social transformation that was inacceptable to the age of Louis XIV. *The Misanthrope* is a rare work and a genuine high comedy precisely because it manages to balance the follies of society against the absurdity of monomaniacally fighting against them, the frailty of the human species against the mistake of not making allowances for it.

THE MISANTHROPE

By Molière

TRANSLATED FROM THE FRENCH BY HENRI VAN LAUN

DRAMATIS PERSONAE

ALCESTE, *in love with Célimène*
PHILINTE, *his friend*
ORONTE, *in love with Célimène*
CÉLIMÈNE, *beloved by Alceste*
ÉLIANTE, *her cousin*
ARSINOÉ, *Célimène's friend*

ACASTE ⎱ *marquises*
CLITANDRE ⎰
BASQUE, *servant to Célimène*
DUBOIS, *servant to Alceste*
AN OFFICER OF THE MARÉCHAUSSÉE

SCENE: *At Paris, in Célimène's house*

ACT I. SCENE I.

Philinte, Alceste.

PHILINTE: What is the matter? What ails you?

ALCESTE: [*Seated*] Leave me, I pray.

PHILINTE: But, once more, tell me what strange whim . . .

ALCESTE: Leave me, I tell you, and get out of my sight.

PHILINTE: But you might at least listen to people, without getting angry.

ALCESTE: I choose to get angry, and I do not choose to listen.

PHILINTE: I do not understand you in these abrupt moods, and although we are friends, I am the first . . .

ALCESTE: [*Rising quickly*] I, your friend? Lay not that flattering unction to your soul. I have until now professed to be so; but after what I have just seen of you, I tell you candidly that I am such no longer; I have no wish to occupy a place in a corrupt heart.

PHILINTE: I am then very much to be blamed from your point of view, Alceste?

ALCESTE: To be blamed? You ought to die from very shame; there is no excuse for such behavior, and every man of honor must be disgusted at it. I see you almost stifle a man with caresses, show him the most ardent affection, and overwhelm him with protestations, offers, and vows of friendship. Your ebullitions of tenderness know no bounds; and when I ask you who that man is, you can scarcely tell me his name; your feelings for him, the moment you have turned your back, suddenly cool; you speak of him most indifferently to me. Zounds! I call it unworthy, base, and infamous, so far to lower one's self as to act contrary to one's own feelings, and if, by some mischance, I had done such a thing, I should hang myself at once out of sheer vexation.

PHILINTE: I do not see that it is a hanging matter at all; and I beg of you not to think it amiss if I ask you to show me some mercy, for I shall not hang myself, if it be all the same to you.

ALCESTE: That is a sorry joke.

PHILINTE: But, seriously, what would you have people do?

ALCESTE: I would have people be sincere, and that, like men of honor, no word be spoken that comes not from the heart.

PHILINTE: When a man comes and embraces you warmly, you must pay him back in his own coin, respond as best you can to his show of feeling, and return offer for offer, and vow for vow.

ALCESTE: Not so. I cannot bear so base a method, which your fashionable people generally affect; there is nothing I detest so much as the contortions of these great time-and-lip servers, these affable dispensers of meaningless embraces, these obliging utterers of empty words who view every one in civilities, and treat the man of worth and the fop alike. What good does it do if a man heaps endearments on you, vows that he is your friend, that he believes in you, is full of zeal for you, esteems and loves you, and lauds you to the skies, when he rushes to do the same to the first rapscallion he meets? No, no, no heart with the least self-respect cares for esteem so prostituted; he will hardly relish it, even when openly expressed, when he finds that he shares it with the whole universe. Preference must be based on esteem, and to esteem every one is to esteem no one. Since you abandon yourself to the vices of the times, zounds! you are not the man for me. I decline this over-complaisant kindness, which uses no discrimination. I like to be distinguished; and, to cut the matter short, the friend of all mankind is no friend of mine.

PHILINTE: But when we are of the world, we must conform to the outward civilities which custom demands.

391

ALCESTE: I deny it. We ought to punish pitilessly that shameful pretence of friendly intercourse. I like a man to be a man, and to show on all occasions the bottom of his heart in his discourse. Let that be the thing to speak, and never let our feelings be hidden beneath vain compliments.

PHILINTE: There are many cases in which plain speaking would become ridiculous, and could hardly be tolerated. And, with all due allowance for your unbending honesty, it is as well to conceal your feelings sometimes. Would it be right or decent to tell thousands of people what we think of them? And when we meet with some one whom we hate or who displeases us, must we tell him so openly?

ALCESTE: Yes.

PHILINTE: What! Would you tell old Emilia that it ill becomes her to set up for a beauty at her age, and that the paint she uses disgusts everyone?

ALCESTE: Undoubtedly.

PHILINTE: Or Dorilas, that he is a bore, and that there is no one at court who is not sick of hearing him boast of his courage, and the lustre of his house?

ALCESTE: Decidedly so.

PHILINTE: You are jesting.

ALCESTE: I am not jesting at all; and I would not spare any one in that respect. It offends my eyes too much; and whether at court or in town, I behold nothing but what provokes my spleen. I become quite melancholy and deeply grieved to see men behave to each other as they do. Everywhere I find nothing but base flattery, injustice, self-interest, deceit, roguery. I cannot bear it any longer; I am furious; and my intention is to break with all mankind.

PHILINTE: This philosophical spleen is somewhat too savage. I cannot but laugh to see you in these gloomy fits, and fancy that I perceive in us two, brought up together, the two brothers described in *The School for Husbands,*[1] who . . .

ALCESTE: Good Heavens! drop your insipid comparisons.

PHILINTE: Nay, seriously, leave off these vagaries. The world will not alter for all your meddling. And as plain speaking has such charms for you, I shall tell you frankly that this complaint of yours is as good as a play, wherever you go, and that all those invectives against the manners of the age, make you a laughing stock to many people.

ALCESTE: So much the better, zounds! so much the better. That is just what I want. It is a very good sign, and I rejoice at it. All men are so odious to me, that I should be sorry to appear rational in their eyes.

PHILINTE: But do you wish harm to all mankind?

ALCESTE: Yes, I have conceived a terrible hatred for them.

PHILINTE: Shall all poor mortals, without exception, be included in this aversion? There are some, even in the age in which we live . . .

ALCESTE: No, they are all alike; and I hate all

[1] An earlier play by Molière.

men: some, because they are wicked and mischievous; others because they lend themselves to the wicked, and have not that healthy contempt with which vice ought to inspire all virtuous minds. You can see how unjustly and excessively complacent people are to that bare-faced scoundrel with whom I am at law. You may plainly perceive the traitor through his mask; he is well known everywhere in his true colors; his rolling eyes and his honeyed tones impose only on those who do not know him. People are aware that this low-bred fellow, who deserves to be pilloried, has, by the dirtiest jobs, made his way in the world; and that the splendid postion he has acquired makes merit repine and virtue blush. Yet whatever dishonorable epithets may be launched against him everywhere, nobody defends his wretched honor. Call him a rogue, an infamous wretch, a confounded scoundrel if you like, all the world will say "yea," and no one contradicts you. But for all that, his bowing and scraping are welcome everywhere; he is received, smiled upon, and wriggles himself into all kinds of society; and, if any appointment is to be secured by intriguing, he will carry the day over a man of the greatest worth. Zounds! these are mortal stabs to me, to see vice parleyed with; and sometimes I feel suddenly inclined to fly into a wilderness far from the approach of men.

PHILINTE: Great Heaven! let us torment ourselves a little less about the vices of our age, and be a little more lenient to human nature. Let us not scrutinize it with the utmost severity, but look with some indulgence at its failings. In society, we need virtue to be more pliable. If we are too wise, we may be equally to blame. Good sense avoids all extremes, and requires us to be soberly rational. This unbending and virtuous stiffness of ancient times shocks too much the ordinary customs of our own; it requires too great perfection from us mortals; we must yield to the times without being too stubborn; it is the height of folly to busy ourselves in correcting the world. I, as well as yourself, notice a hundred things every day which might be better managed, differently enacted; but whatever I may discover at any moment, people do not see me in a rage like you. I take men quietly just as they are; I accustom my mind to bear with what they do; and I believe that at court, as well as in the city, my phlegm is as philosophical as your bile.

ALCESTE: But this phlegm, good sir, you who reason so well, could it not be disturbed by anything? And if perchance a friend should betray you; if he forms a subtle plot to get hold of what is yours; if people should try to spread evil reports about you, would you tamely submit to all this without flying into a rage?

PHILINTE: Ay, I look upon all these faults of which you complain as vices inseparably connected with human nature; in short, my mind is no more shocked at seeing a man a rogue, unjust, or selfish, than at seeing vultures eager for prey, mischievous apes, or fury-lashed wolves.

ALCESTE: What! I should see myself deceived, torn to pieces, robbed, without being . . . Zounds! I shall say no more about it; all this reasoning is beside the point!

PHILINTE: Upon my word, you would do well to keep silence. Rail a little less at your opponents, and attend a little more to your suit.

ALCESTE: That I shall not do; that is settled long ago.

PHILINTE: But whom then do you expect to solicit for you?

ALCESTE: Whom? Reason, my just right, equity.

PHILINTE: Shall you not pay a visit to any of the judges?

ALCESTE: No. Is my cause unjust or dubious?

PHILINTE: I am agreed on that; but you know what harm intrigues do, and . . .

ALCESTE: No. I am resolved not to stir a step. I am either right or wrong.

PHILINTE: Do not trust to that.

ALCESTE: I shall not budge an inch.

PHILINTE: Your opponent is powerful, and by his underhand work, may induce . . .

ALCESTE: It does not matter.

PHILINTE: You will make a mistake.

ALCESTE: Be it so. I wish to see the end of it.

PHILINTE: But . . .

ALCESTE: I shall have the satisfaction of losing my suit.

PHILINTE: But after all . . .

ALCESTE: I shall see by this trial whether men have sufficient impudence, are wicked, villainous, and perverse enough to do me this injustice in the face of the whole world.

PHILINTE: What a strange fellow!

ALCESTE: I could wish, were it to cost me ever so much, that, for the fun of the thing, I lost my case.

PHILINTE: But people will really laugh at you, Alceste, if they hear you go on in this fashion.

ALCESTE: So much the worse for those who will.

PHILINTE: But this rectitude, which you exact so carefully in every case, this absolute integrity in which you intrench yourself, do you perceive it in the lady you love? As for me, I am astonished that, appearing to be at war with the whole human race, you yet, notwithstanding everything that can render it odious to you, have found aught to charm your eyes. And what surprises me still more, is the strange choice your heart has made. The sincere Éliante has a liking for you, the prude Arsinoé looks with favor upon you, yet your heart does not respond to their passion; whilst you wear the chains of Célimène, who sports with you, and whose coquettish humor and malicious wit seem to accord so well with the manner of the times. How comes it that, hating these things as mortally as you do, you endure so much of them in that lady? Are they no longer faults in so sweet a charmer? Do not you perceive them, or if you do, do you excuse them?

ALCESTE: Not so. The love I feel for this young widow does not make me blind to her faults, and, notwithstanding the great passion with which she has inspired me, I am the first to see, as well as to condemn, them. But for all this, do what I will, I confess my weakness, she has the art of pleasing me. In vain I see her faults; I may even blame them; in spite of all, she makes me love her. Her charms conquer everything, and, no doubt, my sincere love will purify her heart from the vices of our times.

PHILINTE: If you accomplish this, it will be no small task. Do you believe yourself beloved by her?

ALCESTE: Yes, certainly! I should not love her at all, did I not think so.

PHILINTE: But if her love for you is so apparent, how comes it that your rivals cause you so much uneasiness?

ALCESTE: It is because a heart, deeply smitten, claims all to itself; I come here only with the intention of telling her what, on this subject, my feelings dictate.

PHILINTE: Had I but to choose, her cousin Éliante would have all my love. Her heart, which values yours, is stable and sincere; and this more compatible choice would have suited you better.

ALCESTE: It is true; my good sense tells me so every day; but good sense does not always rule love.

PHILINTE: Well, I fear much for your affections; and the hope which you cherish may perhaps . . .

SCENE II.

Oronte, Alceste, Philinte.

ORONTE: [To Alceste] I have been informed yonder, that Éliante and Célimène have gone out to make some purchases. But as I heard that you were here, I came to tell you, most sincerely, that I have conceived the greatest regard for you, and that, for a long time, this regard has inspired me with the most ardent wish to be reckoned among your friends. Yes; I like to do homage to merit; and I am most anxious that a bond of friendship should unite us. I suppose that a zealous friend, and of my standing, is not altogether to be rejected. [All this time Alceste has been musing, and seems not to be aware that Oronte is addressing him. He looks up only when Oronte says to him]—It is to you, if you please, that this speech is addressed.

ALCESTE: To me, sir?

ORONTE: To you. Is it in any way offensive to you?

ALCESTE: Not in the least. But my surprise is very great; and I did not expect that honor.

ORONTE: The regard in which I hold you ought not to astonish you, and you claim it from the whole world.

ALCESTE: Sir . . .

ORONTE: Our whole kingdom contains nothing above the dazzling merit which people discover in you.

ALCESTE: Sir . . .

ORONTE: Yes; for my part, I prefer you to the most important in it.

ALCESTE: Sir . . .

ORONTE: May Heaven strike me dead, if I lie! And, to convince you, on this very spot, of my feelings, allow me, sir, to embrace you with all my heart, and to solicit a place in your friendship. Your hand, if you please. Will you promise me your friendship?

ALCESTE: Sir . . .

ORONTE: What! you refuse me?

ALCESTE: Sir, you do me too much honor; but friendship is a sacred thing, and to lavish it on every occasion is surely to profane it. Judgment and choice should preside at such a compact; we ought to know more of each other before engaging ourselves; and it may happen that our dispositions are such that we may both of us repent of our bargain.

ORONTE: Upon my word! that is wisely said; and I esteem you all the more for it. Let us therefore leave it to time to form such a pleasing bond; but, meanwhile, I am entirely at your disposal. If you have any business at court, every one knows how well I stand with the King; I have his private ear; and, upon my word, he treats me in everything with the utmost intimacy. In short, I am yours in every emergency; and, as you are a man of brilliant parts, and to inaugurate our charming amity, I come to read you a sonnet which I made a little while ago, and to find out whether it be good enough for publicity.

ALCESTE: I am not fit, sir, to decide such a matter. You will therefore excuse me.

ORONTE: Why so?

ALCESTE: I have the failing of being a little more sincere in those things than is necessary.

ORONTE: The very thing I ask; and I should have reason to complain, if, in laying myself open to you that you might give me your frank opinion, you should deceive me, and disguise anything from me.

ALCESTE: If that be the case, sir, I am perfectly willing.

ORONTE: *Sonnet* . . . It is a sonnet . . . *Hope* . . . It is to a lady who flattered my passion with some hope. *Hope* . . . They are not long, pompous verses, but mild, tender and melting little lines. [*At every one of these interruptions he looks at* Alceste]

ALCESTE: We shall see.

ORONTE: Hope . . . I do not know whether the style will strike you as sufficiently clear and easy, and whether you will approve of my choice of words.

ALCESTE: We shall soon see, sir.

ORONTE: Besides, you must know that I was only a quarter of an hour in composing it.

ALCESTE: Let us hear, sir; the time signifies nothing.

ORONTE: [*Reads*] *Hope, it is true, oft gives relief,*
Rocks for a while our tedious pain,
But what a poor advantage, Phillis,
When nought remains, and all is gone!

PHILINTE: I am already charmed with this little bit.

ALCESTE: [*Softly to* Philinte] What! do you mean to tell me that you like this stuff?

ORONTE: *You once showed some complaisance,*
But less would have sufficed,
You should not take that trouble
To give me nought but hope.

PHILINTE: In what pretty terms these thoughts are put!

ALCESTE: How now! you vile flatterer, you praise this rubbish!

ORONTE: *If I must wait eternally,*
My passion, driven to extremes,
Will fly to death.
Your tender cares cannot prevent this,
Fair Phillis, aye we're in despair,
When we must hope for ever.

PHILINTE: The conclusion is pretty, amorous, admirable.

ALCESTE: [*Softly, and aside to* Philinte] A plague on the conclusion! I wish you had concluded to break your nose, you poisoner to the devil!

PHILINTE: I never heard verses more skilfully turned.

ALCESTE: [*Softly, and aside*] Zounds! . . .

ORONTE: [*To* Philinte] You flatter me, and you are under the impression perhaps . . .

PHILINTE: No, I am not flattering at all.

ALCESTE: [*Softly, and aside*] What else are you doing, you wretch?

ORONTE: [*To* Alceste] But for you, you know our agreement. Speak to me, I pray, in all sincerity.

ALCESTE: These matters, sir, are always more or less delicate, and every one is fond of being praised for his wit. But I was saying one day to a certain person, who shall be nameless, when he showed me some of his verses, that a gentleman ought at all times to exercise a great control over that itch for writing which sometimes attacks us, and should keep a tight rein over the strong propensity which one has to display such amusements; and that, in the frequent anxiety to show their productions, people are frequently exposed to act a very foolish part.

ORONTE: Do you wish to convey to me by this that I am wrong in desiring . . .

ALCESTE: I do not say that exactly. But I told him that writing without warmth becomes a bore; that there needs no other weakness to disgrace a man; that, even if people, on the other hand, had a hundred good qualities, we view them from their worst sides.

ORONTE: Do you find anything to object to in my sonnet?

ALCESTE: I do not say that. But, to keep him from writing, I set before his eyes how, in our days, that desire had spoiled a great many very worthy people.

ORONTE: Do I write badly? Am I like them in any way?

ALCESTE: I do not say that. But, in short, I said to him: What pressing need is there for you to rhyme, and what the deuce drives you into print? If we can pardon the sending into the world of a badly-written book, it will only be in those unfortunate men who write for their livelihood. Believe me, resist your temptations, keep these effusions from the public, and do not, how much soever you may be asked, forfeit the reputation which you enjoy at court of being a man of sense and a gentleman, to take, from the hands of a greedy printer, that of a ridiculous and wretched author. That is what I tried to make him understand.

ORONTE: This is all well and good, and I seem to understand you. But I should like to know what there is in my sonnet to . . .

ALCESTE: Candidly, you had better put it in your closet. You have been following bad models, and your expressions are not at all natural. Pray what is—*Rocks for a while our tedious pain?* And what, *When nought remains, and all is gone?* What, *You should not take that trouble to give me nought but hope?* And what, *Phillis, aye we're in despair when we must hope for ever?* This figurative style, that people are so vain of, is beside all good taste and truth; it is only a play upon words, sheer affectation, and it is not thus that nature speaks. The wretched taste of the age is what I dislike in this. Our forefathers, unpolished as they were, had a much better one; and I value all that is admired now-a-days far less than an old song which I am going to repeat to you:

Had our great monarch granted me
His Paris large and fair;
And I straightway must quit for aye
The love of my true dear;
Then would I say, King Hal, I pray,
Take back your Paris fair,
I love much mo my dear, I trow,
I love much mo my dear.

This versification is not rich, and the style is antiquated; but do you not see that it is far better than all those trumpery trifles against which good sense revolts, and that in this, passion speaks from the heart?

Had our great monarch granted me
His Paris large and fair;
And I straightway must quite for aye
The love of my true dear;
Then would I say, King Hal, I pray,
Take back your Paris fair,
I love much mo my dear, I trow,
I love much mo my dear.

This is what a really loving heart would say. [*To Philinte, who is laughing*] Yes, master wag, in spite of all your wit, I care more for this than for all the florid pomp and the tinsel which everybody is admiring now-a-days.

ORONTE: And I, I maintain that my verses are very good.

ALCESTE: Doubtless you have your reasons for thinking them so; but you will allow me to have mine, which, with your permission, will remain independent.

ORONTE: It is enough for me that others prize them.

ALCESTE: That is because they know how to dissemble, which I do not.

ORONTE: Do you really believe that you have such a great share of wit?

ALCESTE: If I praised your verses, I should have more.

ORONTE: I shall do very well without your approbation.

ALCESTE: You will have to do without it, if it be all the same.

ORONTE: I should like much to see you compose some on the same subject, just to have a sample of your style.

ALCESTE: I might, perchance, make some as bad; but I should take good care not to show them to any one.

ORONTE: You are mighty positive; and this great sufficiency . . .

ALCESTE: Pray, seek some one else to flatter you, and not me.

ORONTE: But, my little sir, drop this haughty tone.

ALCESTE: In truth, my big sir, I shall do as I like.

PHILINTE: [*Coming between them*] Stop, gentlemen! that is carrying the matter too far. Cease, I pray.

ORONTE: Ah! I am wrong, I confess; and I leave the field to you. I am your servant, sir, most heartily.

ALCESTE: And I, sir, am your most humble servant.

SCENE III.

Philinte, Alceste.

PHILINTE: Well! you see. By being too sincere, you have got a nice affair on your hands; I saw that Oronte, in order to be flattered . . .

ALCESTE: Do not talk to me.

PHILINTE: But . . .

ALCESTE: No more society for me.

PHILINTE: Is it too much . . .

ALCESTE: Leave me alone.

PHILINTE: If I . . .

ALCESTE: Not another word.

PHILINTE: But what . . .

ALCESTE: I will hear no more.

PHILINTE: But . . .

ALCESTE: Again?

PHILINTE: People insult . . .

ALCESTE: Ah! Zounds! this is too much. Do not dog my steps.

PHILINTE: You are making fun of me; I shall not leave you.

ACT II. SCENE I.

Alceste, Célimène.

ALCESTE: Will you have me speak candidly to you, Madam? Well, then, I am very much dissatisfied with your behavior. I am very angry when I think of it; and I perceive that we shall have to break with each other. Yes; I should only deceive you were I to speak otherwise. Sooner or later a rupture is unavoidable; and if I were to promise the contrary a thousand times, I should not be able to bear this any longer.

CÉLIMÈNE: Oh, I see! it is to quarrel with me, that you wished to conduct me home?

ALCESTE: I do not quarrel. But your disposition, Madam, is too ready to give any first comer an entrance into your heart. Too many admirers beset you; and my temper cannot put up with that.

CÉLIMÈNE: Am I to blame for having too many admirers? Can I prevent people from thinking me amiable? and am I to take a stick to drive them away, when they endeavor by tender means to visit me?

ALCESTE: No, Madam, there is no need for a stick, but only a heart less yielding and less melting at their love-tales. I am aware that your good looks accompany you, go where you will; but your reception retains those whom your eyes attract; and that gentleness, accorded to those who surrender their arms, finishes on their hearts the sway which your charms began. The too agreeable expectation which you offer them increases their assiduities towards you; and your complacency, a little less extended, would drive away the great crowd of so many admirers. But tell me, at least, Madam, by what good fortune Clitandre has the happiness of pleasing you so mightily? Upon what basis of merit and sublime virtue do you ground the honor of your regard for him? Is it by the long nail on his little finger that he has acquired the esteem which you display for him? Are you, like all the rest of the fashionable world, fascinated by the dazzling merit of his fair wig? Do his great rolls make you love him? Do his many ribbons charm you? Is it by the attraction of his great German breeches that he has conquered your heart, whilst at the same time he pretended to be your slave? Or have his manner of smiling, and his falsetto voice, found out the secret of moving your feelings?

CÉLIMÈNE: How unjustly you take umbrage at him! Do not you know why I countenance him; and that he has promised to interest all his friends in my lawsuit?

ALCESTE: Lose your lawsuit, Madam, with patience, and do not countenance a rival whom I detest.

CÉLIMÈNE: But you are getting jealous of the whole world.

ALCESTE: It is because the whole world is so kindly received by you.

CÉLIMÈNE: That is the very thing to calm your frightened mind, because my good-will is diffused over all: you would have more reason to be offended if you saw me entirely occupied with one.

ALCESTE: But as for me, whom you accuse of too much jealousy, what have I more than any of them, Madam, pray?

CÉLIMÈNE: The happiness of knowing that you are beloved.

ALCESTE: And what grounds has my lovesick heart for believing it?

CÉLIMÈNE: I think that, as I have taken the trouble to tell you so, such an avowal ought to satisfy you.

ALCESTE: But who will assure me that you may not, at the same time, say as much to everybody else perhaps?

CÉLIMÈNE: Certainly, for a lover, this is a pretty amorous speech, and you make me out a very nice lady. Well! to remove such a suspicion, I retract this moment everything I have said; and no one but yourself shall for the future impose upon you. Will that satisfy you?

ALCESTE: Zounds! why do I love you so! Ah! if ever I get heart-whole out of your hands, I shall bless Heaven for this rare good fortune. I make no secret of it; I do all that is possible to tear this unfortunate attachment from my heart; but hitherto my greatest efforts have been of no avail; and it is for my sins that I love you thus.

CÉLIMÈNE: It is very true that your affection for me is unequaled.

ALCESTE: As for that, I can challenge the whole world. My love for you cannot be conceived; and never, Madam, has any man loved as I do.

CÉLIMÈNE: Your method, however, is entirely new, for you love people only to quarrel with them; it is in peevish expression alone that your feelings vent themselves; no one ever saw such a grumbling swain.

ALCESTE: But it lies with you alone to dissipate this ill-humor. For mercy's sake let us make an end of all these bickerings; deal openly with each other, and try to put a stop . . .

SCENE II.

Célimène, Alceste, Basque.

CÉLIMÈNE: What is the matter?
BASQUE: Acaste is below.
CÉLIMÈNE: Very well! bid him come up.

SCENE III.

Célimène, Alceste.

ALCESTE: What! can one never have a little private conversation with you? You are always ready to receive company; and you cannot, for a single instant, make up your mind to be "not at home."

CÉLIMÈNE: Do you wish me to quarrel with Acaste?

ALCESTE: You have such regard for people, which I by no means like.

CÉLIMÈNE: He is a man never to forgive me, if he knew that his presence could annoy me.

ALCESTE: And what is that to you, to inconvenience yourself so . . .

CÉLIMÈNE: But, good Heaven! the amity of such as he is of importance; they are a kind of people who, I do not know how, have acquired the right to be heard at court. They take their part in every conversation; they can do you no good, but they may do you harm; and, whatever support one may find elsewhere, it will never do to be on bad terms with these very noisy gentry.

ALCESTE: In short, whatever people may say or do, you always find reasons to bear with every one; and your very careful judgment . . .

SCENE IV.

Alceste, Célimène, Basque.

BASQUE: Clitandre is here, too, Madam.

ALCESTE: Exactly so. [*Wishes to go*]

CÉLIMÈNE: Where are you running to?

ALCESTE: I am going.

CÉLIMÈNE: Stay.

ALCESTE: For what?

CÉLIMÈNE: Stay.

ALCESTE: I cannot.

CÉLIMÈNE: I wish it.

ALCESTE: I will not. These conversations only weary me; and it is too bad of you to wish me to endure them.

CÉLIMÈNE: I wish it, I wish it.

ALCESTE: No, it is impossible.

CÉLIMÈNE: Very well, then; go, begone; you can do as you like.

SCENE V.

Éliante, Philinte, Acaste, Clitandre, Alceste, Célimène, Basque.

ÉLIANTE: [*To* Célimène] Here are the two marquises coming up with us. Has anyone told you?

CÉLIMÈNE: Yes. [*To* Basque] Place chairs for everyone. [Basque *places chairs, and goes out*] [*To* Alceste] You are not gone?

ALCESTE: No; but I am determined, Madam, to have you make up your mind either for them or for me.

CÉLIMÈNE: Hold your tongue.

ALCESTE: This very day you shall explain yourself.

CÉLIMÈNE: You are losing your senses.

ALCESTE: Not at all. You shall declare yourself.

CÉLIMÈNE: Indeed!

ALCESTE: You must take your stand.

CÉLIMÈNE: You are jesting, I believe.

ALCESTE: Not so. But you must choose. I have been too patient.

CLITANDRE: Egad! I have just come from the Louvre,[2] where Cléonte, at the levee, made himself very ridiculous. Has he not some friend who could charitably enlighten him upon his manners?

CÉLIMÈNE: Truth to say, he compromises himself very much in society; everywhere he carries himself with an air that is noticed at first sight, and when after a short absence you meet him again, he is still more absurd than ever.

ACASTE: Egad! Talk of absurd people, just now, one of the most tedious ones was annoying me. That reasoner, Damon, kept me, if you please, for a full hour in the broiling sun, away from my sedan-chair.

CÉLIMÈNE: He is a strange talker, and one who always finds the means of telling you nothing with a great flow of words. There is no sense at all in his tittle-tattle, and all that we hear is but noise.

ÉLIANTE: [*To* Philinte] This beginning is not bad; and the conversation takes a sufficiently agreeable turn against our neighbors.

CLITANDRE: Timante, too, Madam, is another original.

CÉLIMÈNE: He is a complete mystery from top to toe, who throws upon you, in passing, a bewildered glance, and who, without having anything to do, is always busy. Whatever he utters is accompanied with grimaces; he quite oppresses people by his ceremonies. To interrupt a conversation, he has always a secret to whisper to you, and that secret turns out to be nothing. Of the merest molehill he makes a mountain, and whispers everything in your ear, even to a "good-day."

ACASTE: And Geralde, Madam?

CÉLIMÈNE: That tiresome story-teller! He never comes down from his nobleman's pedestal; he continually mixes with the best society, and never quotes any one of minor rank than a Duke, Prince, or Princess. Rank is his hobby, and his conversation is of nothing but horses, carriages, and dogs. He *thee's* and *thou's* persons of the highest standing, and the word *Sir* is quite obsolete with him.

CLITANDRE: It is said that he is on the best of terms with Bélise.

CÉLIMÈNE: Poor silly woman, and the dreariest company! When she comes to visit me, I suffer from martyrdom; one has to rack one's brain perpetually to find out what to say to her; and the impossibility of her expressing her thoughts allows the conversation to drop every minute. In vain you try to overcome her stupid silence by the assistance of the most commonplace topic; even the fine weather, the rain, the heat and the cold are subjects, which, with her, are soon exhausted. Yet for all that, her calls, unbearable enough, are prolonged to an insufferable

[2] The Louvre, now a famous museum in Paris, was then a royal palace.

length; and you may consult the clock, or yawn twenty times, but she stirs no more than a log of wood.

ACASTE: What think you of Adraste?

CÉLIMÈNE: Oh! What excessive pride! He is a man positively puffed out with conceit. His self-importance is never satisfied with the court, against which he inveighs daily; and whenever an office, a place, or a living is bestowed on another, he is sure to think himself unjustly treated.

CLITANDRE: But young Cléon, whom the most respectable people go to see, what say you of him?

CÉLIMÈNE: That it is to his cook he owes his distinction, and to his table that people pay visits.

ÉLIANTE: He takes pains to provide the most dainty dishes.

CÉLIMÈNE: True; but I should be very glad if he would not dish up himself. His foolish person is a very bad dish, which, to my thinking, spoils every entertainment which he gives.

PHILINTE: His uncle Damis is very much esteemed; what say you to him, Madam?

CÉLIMÈNE: He is one of my friends.

PHILINTE: I think him a perfect gentleman, and sensible enough.

CÉLIMÈNE: True; but he pretends to too much wit, which annoys me. He is always upon stilts, and, in all his conversations, one sees him laboring to say smart things. Since he took it into his head to be clever, he is so difficult to please that nothing suits his taste. He must needs find mistakes in everything that one writes, and thinks that to bestow praise does not become a wit, that to find fault shows learning, that only fools admire and laugh, and that, by not approving of anything in the works of our time, he is superior to all other people. Even in conversations he finds something to cavil at, the subjects are too trivial for his condescension; and, with arms crossed on his breast, he looks down from the height of his intellect with pity on what everyone says.

ACASTE: Drat it! his very picture.

CLITANDRE: [To Célimène] You have an admirable knack of portraying people to the life.

ALCESTE: Capital, go on, my fine courtly friends. You spare no one, and everyone will have his turn. Nevertheless, let but any one of those persons appear, and we shall see you rush to meet him, offer him your hand, and, with a flattering kiss, give weight to your protestations of being his servant.

CLITANDRE: Why this to us? If what is said offends you, the reproach must be addressed to this lady.

ALCESTE: No, gadzooks! it concerns you; for your assenting smiles draw from her wit all these slanderous remarks. Her satirical vein is incessantly recruited by the culpable incense of your flattery; and her mind would find fewer charms in raillery, if she discovered that no one applauded her. Thus it is that to flatterers we ought everywhere to impute the vices which are sown among mankind.

PHILINTE: But why do you take so great an interest in those people, for you would condemn the very things that are blamed in them?

CÉLIMÈNE: And is not this gentleman bound to contradict? Would you have him subscribe to the general opinion; and must he not everywhere display the spirit of contradiction with which Heaven has endowed him? Other people's sentiments can never please him. He always supports a contrary idea, and he would think himself too much of the common herd, were he observed to be of any one's opinion but his own. The honor of gainsaying has so many charms for him, that he very often takes up the cudgels against himself; he combats his own sentiments as soon as he hears them from other folks' lips.

ALCESTE: In short, Madam, the laughters are on your side; and you may launch your satire against me.

PHILINTE: But it is very true, too, that you always take up arms against everything that is said; and that your avowed spleen cannot bear people to be praised or blamed.

ALCESTE: 'Sdeath! spleen against mankind is always seasonable, because they are never in the right, and I see that, in all their dealings, they either praise impertinently, or censure rashly.

CÉLIMÈNE: But . . .

ALCESTE: No, Madam, no, though I were to die for it, you have pastimes which I cannot tolerate; and people are very wrong to nourish in your heart this great attachment to the very faults which they blame in you.

CLITANDRE: As for myself, I do not know; but I openly acknowledge that hitherto I have thought this lady faultless.

ACASTE: I see that she is endowed with charms and attractions; but the faults which she has have not struck me.

ALCESTE: So much the more have they struck me; and far from appearing blind, she knows that I take care to reproach her with them. The more we love any one, the less we ought to flatter her. True love shows itself by overlooking nothing; and, were I a lady, I would banish all those mean-spirited lovers who submit to all my sentiments, and whose mild complacencies every moment offer up incense to my vagaries.

CÉLIMÈNE: In short, if hearts were ruled by you we ought, to love well, to relinquish all tenderness, and make it the highest aim of perfect attachment to rail heartily at the persons we love.

ÉLIANTE: Love, generally speaking, is little apt to put up with these decrees, and lovers are always observed to extol their choice. Their passion never sees aught to blame in it, and in the beloved all things become lovable. They think their faults perfections, and invent sweet terms to call them by. The pale one vies with the jessamine in fairness; another, dark enough to frighten people, becomes an adorable brunette; the lean one has a good shape and is lithe; the stout one has a portly and majestic bearing; the slattern, who has few charms, passes under the name of a careless beauty; the giantess seems a very goddess in their sight; the dwarf is an epitome of all the wonders of Heaven; the proud one has a soul worthy of a diadem; the artful brims with wit; the silly one is very good-natured; the chatterbox is good tempered; and the silent one modest and reticent. Thus a passionate swain loves even the very faults of those of whom he is enamored.

ALCESTE: And I maintain that . . .

CÉLIMÈNE: Let us drop the subject, and take a turn or two in the gallery. What! are you going, gentlemen?

CLITANDRE *and* ACASTE: No, no, Madam.

ALCESTE: The fear of their departure troubles you very much. Go when you like, gentlemen; but I tell you beforehand that I shall not leave until you leave.

ACASTE: Unless it inconveniences this lady, I have nothing to call me elsewhere the whole day.

CLITANDRE: I, provided I am present when the King retires, I have no other matter to call me away.

CÉLIMÈNE: [*To* Alceste] You only joke, I fancy.

ALCESTE: Not at all. We shall soon see whether it is me of whom you wish to get rid.

SCENE VI.

Alceste, Célimène, Éliante, Acaste, Philinte, Clitandre, Basque.

BASQUE: [*To* Alceste] There is a man downstairs, sir, who wishes to speak to you on business which cannot be postponed.

ALCESTE: Tell him that I have no such urgent business.

BASQUE: He wears a jacket with large plaited skirts embroidered with gold.

CÉLIMÈNE: [*To* Alceste] Go and see who it is, or else let him come in.

SCENE VII.

Alceste, Célimène, Éliante, Acaste, Philinte, Clitandre, a Guard of the Maréchaussée.[3]

ALCESTE: [*Going to meet the* Guard] What may be your pleasure? Come in, sir.

GUARD: I would have a few words privately with you, sir.

ALCESTE: You may speak aloud, sir, so as to let me know.

GUARD: The Marshals of France, whose commands I bear, hereby summon you to appear before them immediately, sir.

ALCESTE: Whom? Me, sir?

GUARD: Yourself.

ALCESTE: And for what?

[3] The police force of the period.

PHILINTE: [*To* Alceste] It is this ridiculous affair between you and Oronte.

CÉLIMÈNE: [*To* Philinte] What do you mean?

PHILINTE: Oronte and he have been insulting each other just now about some trifling verses which he did not like; and the Marshals wish to nip the affair in the bud.

ALCESTE: Well, I shall never basely submit.

PHILINTE: But you must obey the summons: come, get ready.

ALCESTE: How will they settle this between us? Will the edict of these gentlemen oblige me to approve of the verses which are the cause of our quarrel? I will not retract what I have said; I think them abominable.

PHILINTE: But with a little milder tone . . .

ALCESTE: I will not abate one jot; the verses are execrable.

PHILINTE: You ought to show a more accommodating spirit. Come along.

ALCESTE: I shall go, but nothing shall induce me to retract.

PHILINTE: Go and show yourself.

ALCESTE: Unless an express order from the King himself commands me to approve of the verses which cause all this trouble, I shall ever maintain, egad, that they are bad, and that a fellow deserves hanging for making them. [*To* Clitandre *and* Acaste *who are laughing*] Hang it! gentlemen, I did not think I was so amusing.

CÉLIMÈNE: Go quickly whither you are wanted.

ALCESTE: I am going, Madam; but shall come back here to finish our discussion.

ACT III. SCENE I.

Clitandre, Acaste.

CLITANDRE: My dear marquis, you appear mightily pleased with yourself; everything amuses you, and nothing discomposes you. But really and truly, think you, without flattering yourself, that you have good reasons for appearing so joyful?

ACASTE: Egad, I do not find, on looking at myself, any matter to be sorrowful about. I am wealthy, I am young, and am descended from a family which, with some appearance of truth, may be called noble; and I think that, by the rank which my lineage confers upon me, there are very few offices to which I might not aspire. As for courage, which we ought especially to value, it is well known—this without vanity—that I do not lack it; and people have seen me carry on an affair of honor in a manner sufficiently vigorous and brisk. As for wit, I have some, no doubt; and as for good taste, to judge and reason upon everything without study; at "first nights," of which I am very fond, to take my place as a critic upon the stage, to give my opinion as a judge, to applaud, and point out the best passages by repeated bravoes, I am sufficiently adroit; I carry myself well, and am good-looking, have particularly fine teeth, and a good figure. I believe, without flattering myself, that, as for dressing in good taste, very few will dispute the palm with me. I find myself treated with every possible consideration, very much beloved by the fair sex; and I stand very well with the King. With all that, I think, dear marquis, that one might be satisfied with oneself anywhere.

CLITANDRE: True. But, finding so many easy conquests elsewhere, why come you here to utter fruitless sighs?

ACASTE: I? Zounds! I have neither the wish nor the disposition to put up with the indifference of any woman. I leave it to awkward and ordinary people to burn constantly for cruel fair maidens, to languish at their feet, and to bear with their severities, to invoke the aid of sighs and tears, and to endeavor, by long and persistent assiduities, to obtain what is denied to their little merit. But men of my stamp, marquis, are not made to love on trust, and be at all the expenses themselves. Be the merit of the fair ever so great, I think, thank Heaven, that we have our value as well as they; that it is not reasonable to enthrall a heart like mine without its costing them anything; and that, to weigh everything in a just scale, the advances should be, at least, reciprocal.

CLITANDRE: Then you think that you are right enough here, marquis?

ACASTE: I have some reason, marquis, to think so.

CLITANDRE: Believe me, divest yourself of this great mistake: you flatter yourself, dear friend, and are altogether self-deceived.

ACASTE: It is true. I flatter myself, and am, in fact, altogether self-deceived.

CLITANDRE: But what causes you to judge your happiness to be complete?

ACASTE: I flatter myself.

CLITANDRE: Upon what do you ground your belief?

ACASTE: I am altogether self-deceived.

CLITANDRE: Have you any sure proofs?

ACASTE: I am mistaken, I tell you.

CLITANDRE: Has Célimène made you any secret avowal of her inclinations?

ACASTE: No, I am very badly treated by her.

CLITANDRE: Answer me, I pray.

ACASTE: I meet with nothing but rebuffs.

CLITANDRE: A truce to your raillery; and tell me what hope she has held out to you.

ACASTE: I am the rejected, and you are the lucky one. She has a great aversion to me, and one of these days I shall have to hang myself.

CLITANDRE: Nonsense. Shall we two, marquis, to adjust our love affairs, make a compact together? Whenever one of us shall be able to show a certain proof of having the greater share in Célimène's heart, the other shall leave the field free to the supposed conqueror, and by that means rid him of an obstinate rival.

ACASTE: Egad! you please me with these words,

and I agree to that from the bottom of my heart. But, hush.

SCENE II.

Célimène, Acaste, Clitandre.

CÉLIMÈNE: What! here still?

CLITANDRE: Love, Madam, detains us.

CÉLIMÈNE: I hear a carriage below. Do you know whose it is?

CLITANDRE: No.

SCENE III.

Célimène, Acaste, Clitandre, Basque.

BASQUE: Arsinoé, Madam, is coming up to see you.

CÉLIMÈNE: What does the woman want with me?

BASQUE: Éliante is downstairs talking to her.

CÉLIMÈNE: What is she thinking about, and what brings her here?

ACASTE: She has everywhere the reputation of being a consummate prude, and her fervent zeal . . .

CÉLIMÈNE: Psha, downright humbug. In her inmost soul she is as worldly as any; and her every nerve is strained to hook some one, without being successful, however. She can only look with envious eyes on the accepted lovers of others; and in her wretched condition, forsaken by all, she is for ever railing against the blindness of the age. She endeavors to hide the dreadful isolation of her home under a false cloak of prudishness; and to save the credit of her feeble charms, she brands as criminal the power which they lack. Yet a swain would not come at all amiss to the lady; and she has even a tender hankering after Alceste. Every attention that he pays me, she looks upon as a theft committed by me, and as an insult to her attractions; and her jealous spite, which she can hardly hide, breaks out against me at every opportunity, and in an underhand manner. In short, I never saw anything, to my fancy, so stupid. She is impertinent to the last degree . . .

SCENE IV.

Arsinoé, Célimène, Clitandre, Acaste.

CÉLIMÈNE: Ah! what happy chance brings you here, Madam? I was really getting uneasy about you.

ARSINOÉ: I have come to give you some advice as a matter of duty.

CÉLIMÈNE: How very glad I am to see you!
[*Exeunt* Clitandre *and* Acaste, *laughing*]

SCENE V.

Arsinoé, Célimène.

ARSINOÉ: They could not have left at a more convenient opportunity.

CÉLIMÈNE: Shall we sit down?

ARSINOÉ: It is not necessary. Friendship, Madam, must especially show itself in matters which may be of consequence to us; and as there are none of greater importance than honor and decorum, I come to prove to you, by an advice which closely touches your reputation, the friendship which I feel for you. Yesterday I was with some people of rare virtue, where the conversation turned upon you; and there, your conduct, which is causing some stir, was unfortunately, Madam, far from being commended. That crowd of people, whose visits you permit, your gallantry and the noise it makes, were criticized rather more freely and more severely than I could have wished. You can easily imagine whose part I took. I did all I could to defend you. I exonerated you, and vouched for the purity of your heart, and the honesty of your intentions. But you know there are things in life which one cannot well defend, although one may have the greatest wish to do so; and I was at last obliged to confess that the way in which you lived did you some harm; that, in the eyes of the world, it had a doubtful look; that there was no story so ill-natured as not to be everywhere told about it; and that, if you liked, your behavior might give less cause for censure. Not that I believe that decency is in any way outraged. Heaven forbid that I should harbor such a thought! But the world is so ready to give credit to the faintest shadow of a crime, and it is not enough to live blameless one's self. Madam, I believe you to be too sensible not to take in good part this useful counsel, and not to ascribe it only to the inner promptings of an affection that feels an interest in your welfare.

CÉLIMÈNE: Madam, I have a great many thanks to return you. Such counsel lays me under an obligation; and, far from taking it amiss, I intend this very moment to repay the favor, by giving you an advice which also touches your reputation closely; and as I see you prove yourself my friend by acquainting me with the stories that are current of me, I shall follow so nice an example, by informing you what is said of you. In a house the other day, where I paid a visit, I met some people of exemplary merit, who, while talking of the proper duties of a well spent life, turned the topic of the conversation upon you, Madam. There your prudishness and your too fervent zeal were not at all cited as a good example. This affectation of a grave demeanor, your eternal conversations on wisdom and honor, your mincings and mouthings at the slightest shadows of indecency, which an innocent though ambiguous word may convey, that lofty esteem in which you hold yourself, and those pitying glances which you cast upon all, your frequent lectures and your acrid censures on things which are pure and harmless; all this, if I may speak frankly to you, Madam, was blamed unanimously. What is the good, said they, of this modest mien and this prudent exterior, which is belied by all the rest? She says her prayers with the utmost exactness; but she beats her servants and pays them no wages. She displays great fervor in every place of devotion; but she paints and wishes to appear handsome. She covers the nudities in her pictures; but loves the reality. As for me, I undertook your defence against everyone, and positively assured them that it was nothing but scandal; but the general opinion went against me, as they came to the conclusion that you would do well to concern yourself less about the actions of others, and take a little more pains with your own; that one ought to look a long time at one's self before thinking of condemning other people; that when we wish to correct others, we ought to add the weight of a blameless life; and that even then, it would be better to leave it to those whom Heaven has ordained for the task. Madam, I also believe you to be too sensible not to take in good part this useful counsel, and not to ascribe it only to the inner promptings of an affection that feels an interest in your welfare.

ARSINOÉ: To whatever we may be exposed when we reprove, I did not expect this retort, Madam, and, by its very sting, I see how my sincere advice has hurt your feelings.

CÉLIMÈNE: On the contrary, Madam; and, if we were reasonable, these mutual counsels would become customary. If honestly made use of, they would to a great extent destroy the excellent opinion people have of themselves. It depends entirely on you whether we shall continue this trustworthy practice with equal zeal, and whether we shall take great care to tell each other, between ourselves, what we hear, you of me, I of you.

ARSINOÉ: Ah! Madam, I can hear nothing said of you. It is in me that people find so much to reprove.

CÉLIMÈNE: Madam, it is easy, I believe, to blame or praise everything; and everyone may be right, according to their age and taste. There is a time for gallantry, there is one also for prudishness. One may out of policy take to it, when youthful attractions have faded away. It sometimes serves to hide vexatious ravages of time. I do not say that I shall not follow your example, one of these days. Those things come with old age; but twenty, as everyone well knows, is not an age to play the prude.

ARSINOÉ: You certainly pride yourself upon a very small advantage, and you boast terribly of your age. Whatever difference there may be between your years and mine, there is no occasion to make such a tremendous fuss about it; and I am at a loss to know, Madam, why you should get so angry, and what makes you goad me in this manner.

CÉLIMÈNE: And I, Madam, am at an equal loss to know why one hears you inveigh so bitterly against me everywhere. Must I always suffer for your vexations? Can I help it, if people refuse to pay you any attentions? If men will fall in love with me, and will persist in offering me each day those attentions of which your heart would wish to see me deprived, I cannot alter it, and it is not my fault. I leave you the field free, and do not prevent you from having charms to attract people.

ARSINOÉ: Alas! and do you think that I would trouble myself about this crowd of lovers of which you are so vain, and that it is not very easy to judge at what price they may be attracted now-a-days? Do you wish to make it be believed, that, judging by what is going on, your merit alone attracts this crowd; that their affection for you is strictly honest, and that it is for nothing but your virtue that they all pay you their court? People are not blinded by those empty pretences; the world is not duped in that way; and I see many ladies who are capable of inspiring a tender feeling, yet who do not succeed in attracting a crowd of beaux; and from that fact we may draw our conclusion that those conquests are not altogether made without some great advances; that no one cares to sigh for us, for our handsome looks only; and that the attentions bestowed on us are generally dearly bought. Do not therefore pull yourself up with vain-glory about the trifling advantages of a poor victory; and moderate slightly the pride on your good looks, instead of looking down upon people on account of them. If I were at all envious about your conquests, I dare say that I might manage like other people; be under no restraint, and thus show plainly that one may have lovers, when one wishes for them.

CÉLIMÈNE: Do have some then, Madam, and let us see you try it; endeavor to please by this extraordinary secret; and without . . .

ARSINOÉ: Let us break off this conversation, Madam, it might excite too much both your temper and mine; and I would have already taken my leave, had I not been obliged to wait for my carriage.

CÉLIMÈNE: Please stay as long as you like, and do not hurry yourself on that account, Madam. But instead of wearying you any longer with my presence, I am going to give you some more pleasant company. This gentleman, who comes very opportunely, will better supply my place in entertaining you.

SCENE VI.

Alceste, Célimène, Arsinoé.

CÉLIMÈNE: Alceste, I have to write a few lines, which I cannot well delay. Please to stay with this lady; she will all the more easily excuse my rudeness.

SCENE VII.

Alceste, Arsinoé.

ARSINOÉ: You see, I am left here to entertain you, until my coach comes round. She could have devised no more charming treat for me, than such a conversation. Indeed, people of exceptional merit attract the esteem and love of every one; and yours has undoubtedly some secret charm, which makes me feel interested in all your doings. I could wish that the court, with a real regard to your merits, would do more justice to your deserts. You have reason to complain; and it vexes me to see that day by day nothing is done for you.

ALCESTE: For me, Madam? And by what right could I pretend to anything? What service have I rendered to the State? Pray, what have I done, so brilliant in itself, to complain of the court doing nothing for me?

ARSINOÉ: Not everyone whom the State delights to honor, has rendered signal services; there must be an opportunity as well as the power; and the abilities which you allow us to perceive, ought . . .

ALCESTE: For Heaven's sake, let us have no more of my abilities, I pray. What would you have the court to do? It would have enough to do, and have its hands full, to discover the merits of people.

ARSINOÉ: Sterling merit discovers itself. A great deal is made of yours in certain places; and let me tell you that, not later than yesterday, you were highly spoken of in two distinguished circles, by people of very great standing.

ALCESTE: As for that, Madam, everyone is praised now-a-days, and very little discrimination is shown in our times. Everything is equally endowed with great merit, so that it is no longer an honor to be lauded. Praises abound, they throw them at one's head, and even my valet is put in the gazette.

ARSINOÉ: As for me, I could wish that, to bring yourself into greater notice, some place at court might tempt you. If you will only give me a hint that you seriously think about it, a great many engines might be set in motion to serve you; and I know some people whom I could employ for you, and who would manage the matter smoothly enough.

ALCESTE: And what should I do when I got there, Madam? My disposition rather prompts me to keep away from it. Heaven, when ushering me into the world, did not give me a mind suited for the atmosphere of a court. I have not the qualifications necessary for success, nor for making my fortune there. To be open and candid is my chief talent; I possess not the art of deceiving people in conversation; and he who has not the gift of concealing his thoughts, ought not to stay long in those places. When not at court, one has not, doubtless, that standing, and the advantage of those honorable titles which it bestows now-a-days; but, on the other hand, one has not the vexation of playing the silly fool. One has not to bear a thousand galling rebuffs; one is not, as it were, forced to praise the verses of Mister so-and-so, to laud Madam such and such, and to put up with the whims of some ingenious marquis.

ARSINOÉ: Since you wish it, let us drop the subject of the court: but I cannot help grieving for your amours; and, to tell you my opinions candidly on that head, I could heartily wish your affections better bestowed. You certainly deserve a much happier fate, and she who has fascinated you is unworthy of you.

ALCESTE: But in saying so, Madam, remember, I pray, that this lady is your friend.

ARSINOÉ: True. But really my conscience revolts at the thought of suffering any longer the wrong that is done to you. The position in which I see you afflicts my very soul, and I caution you that your affections are betrayed.

ALCESTE: This is certainly showing me a deal of good feeling, Madam, and such information is very welcome to a lover.

ARSINOÉ: Yes, for all Célimène is my friend, I do not hesitate to call her unworthy of possessing the heart of a man of honor; and hers only pretends to respond to yours.

ALCESTE: That is very possible, Madam, one cannot look into the heart; but your charitable feelings might well have refrained from awakening such a suspicion as mine.

ARSINOÉ: Nothing is easier than to say no more about it, if you do not wish to be undeceived.

ALCESTE: Just so. But whatever may be openly said on this subject is not half so annoying as hints thrown out; and I for one would prefer to be plainly told that only which could be clearly proved.

ARSINOÉ: Very well! and that is sufficient; I can fully enlighten you upon this subject. I will have you believe nothing but what your own eyes see. Only have the kindness to escort me as far as my house; and I will give you undeniable proof of the faithlessness of your fair one's heart; and if, after that, you can find charms in anyone else, we will perhaps find you some consolation.

ACT IV. SCENE I.

Éliante, Philinte.

PHILINTE: No, never have I seen so obstinate a mind, nor a reconciliation more difficult to effect. In vain was Alceste tried on all sides; he would still maintain his opinion; and never, I believe, has a more curious dispute engaged the attention of those gentlemen. "No, gentlemen," exclaimed he, "I will not retract, and I shall agree with you on every point, except on this one. At what is Oronte offended? and with what does he reproach me? Does it reflect upon his honor that he cannot write well? What is my opinion to him, which he has altogether wrongly construed? One may be a perfect gentleman, and write bad verses; those things have nothing to do with honor. I take him to be a gallant man in every way; a man of standing, of merit, and courage, anything you like, but he is a wretched author. I shall praise, if you wish, his mode of living, his lavishness, his skill in riding, in fencing, in dancing; but as to praising his verses, I am his humble servant; and if one has not the gift of composing better, one ought to leave off rhyming altogether, unless condemned to it on forfeit of one's life." In short, all the modification they could with difficulty obtain from him, was to say, in what he thought a much gentler tone—"I am sorry, sir, to be so difficult to please; and out of regard to you, I could wish, with all my heart, to have found your sonnet a little better." And they compelled them to settle this dispute quickly with an embrace.

ÉLIANTE: He is very eccentric in his doings; but I must confess that I think a great deal of him; and the candor upon which he prides himself has something noble and heroic in it. It is a rare virtue now-a-days, and I, for one, should not be sorry to meet with it everywhere.

PHILINTE: As for me, the more I see of him, the more I am amazed at that passion to which his whole heart is given up. I cannot conceive how, with a disposition like his, he has taken it into his head to love at all; and still less can I understand how your cousin happens to be the person to whom his feelings are inclined.

ÉLIANTE: That shows that love is not always produced by compatibility of temper; and in this case, all the pretty theories of gentle sympathies are belied.

PHILINTE: But do you think him beloved in return, to judge from what we see?

ÉLIANTE: That is a point not easily decided. How can we judge whether it be true she loves? Her own heart is not so very sure of what it feels. It sometimes loves, without being quite aware of it, and at other times thinks it does, without the least grounds.

PHILINTE: I think that our friend will have more trouble with this cousin of yours than he imagines; and to tell you the truth, if he were of my mind, he would bestow his affections elsewhere; and by a better choice, we should see him, Madam, profit by the kind feelings which your heart evinces for him.

ÉLIANTE: As for me, I do not mince matters, and I think that in such cases we ought to act with sincerity. I do not run counter to his tender feelings; on the contrary, I feel interested in them; and, if it depended only on me, I would unite him to the object of his love. But if, as it may happen in love affairs, his affections should receive a check, and if Célimène should respond to the love of any one else, I could easily be prevailed upon to listen to his addresses, and I should have no repugnance whatever to them on account of their rebuff elsewhere.

PHILINTE: Nor do I, from my side, oppose myself, Madam, to the tender feelings which you entertain for him; and he himself, if he wished, could inform you what I have taken care to say to him on that score. But if, by the union of those two, you should be prevented from accepting his attentions, all mine would endeavor to gain that great favor which your kind feelings offer to him; only too happy, Madam, to have them transferred to myself, if his heart could not respond to yours.

ÉLIANTE: You are in the humor to jest, Philinte.

PHILINTE: Not so, Madam, I am speaking my inmost feelings. I only wait the opportune moment to offer myself openly, and am wishing most anxiously to hurry its advent.

SCENE II.

Alceste, Éliante, Philinte.

ALCESTE: Ah, Madam! obtain me justice, for an offence which triumphs over all my constancy.

ÉLIANTE: What ails you? What disturbs you?

ALCESTE: This much ails me, that it is death to me to think of it; and the upheaving of all creation would less overwhelm me than this accident. It is all over with me . . . My love . . . I cannot speak.

ÉLIANTE: Just endeavor to be composed.

ALCESTE: Oh, just Heaven; can the odious vices of the basest minds be joined to such beauty?

ÉLIANTE: But, once more, what can have . . .

ALCESTE: Alas! All is ruined! I am! I am betrayed! I am stricken to death. Célimène . . . would you credit it! Célimène deceives me and is faithless.

ÉLIANTE: Have you just grounds for believing so?

PHILINTE: Perhaps it is a suspicion, rashly conceived; and your jealous temper often harbors fancies . . .

ALCESTE: Ah! 'Sdeath, please to mind your own business, sir. [To Éliante] Her treachery is but too certain, for I have in my pocket a letter in her own handwriting. Yes, Madam, a letter, intended for Oronte, has placed before my eyes my disgrace and her shame; Oronte, whose addresses I believed she avoided, and whom, of all my rivals, I feared the least.

PHILINTE: A letter may deceive by appearances, and is sometimes not so culpable as may be thought.

ALCESTE: Once more, sir, leave me alone, if you please, and trouble yourself only about your own concerns.

ÉLIANTE: You should moderate your passion; and the insult . . .

ALCESTE: You must be left to do that, Madam; it is to you that my heart has recourse to-day to free itself from this goading pain. Avenge me on an ungrateful and perfidious relative who basely deceives such constant tenderness. Avenge me for an act that ought to fill you with horror.

ÉLIANTE: I avenge you? How?

ALCESTE: By accepting my heart. Take it, Madam, instead of the false one; it is in this way that I can avenge myself upon her; and I shall punish her by the sincere attachment, and the profound love, the respectful cares, the eager devotions, the ceaseless attentions which this heart will henceforth offer up at your shrine.

ÉLIANTE: I certainly sympathize with you in your sufferings, and do not despise your proffered heart; but the wrong done may not be so great as you think, and you might wish to forego this desire for revenge. When the injury proceeds from a beloved object, we form many designs which we never execute; we may find as powerful a reason as we like to break off the connection, the guilty charmer is soon again innocent; all the harm we wish her quickly vanishes, and we know what a lover's anger means.

ALCESTE: No, no, Madam, no. The offence is too cruel; there will be no relenting, and I have done with her. Nothing shall change the resolution I have taken, and I should hate myself for ever loving her again. Here she comes. My anger increases at her approach. I shall taunt her with her black guilt, completely put her to the blush, and, after that, bring you a heart wholly freed from her deceitful attractions.

SCENE III.

Célimène, Alceste.

ALCESTE: [Aside] Grant, Heaven, that I may control my temper.

CÉLIMÈNE: [Aside] Ah! [To Alceste] What is all this trouble that I see you in, and what means those long-drawn sighs, and those black looks which you cast at me?

ALCESTE: That all the wickedness of which a heart is capable is not to be compared to your perfidy; that neither fate, hell, nor Heaven in its wrath, ever produced anything so wicked as you are.

CÉLIMÈNE: These are certainly pretty compliments, which I admire very much.

ALCESTE: Do not jest. This is no time for laughing. Blush rather, you have cause to do so; and I have undeniable proofs of your treachery. This is what the agitations of my mind prognosticated; it was not without cause that my love took alarm; by these frequent suspicions, which were hateful to you, I was trying to discover the misfortune which my eyes have beheld; and in spite of all your care and your skill in dissembling, my star foretold me what I had to fear. But do not imagine that I will bear unavenged this slight of being insulted. I know that we have no command over our inclinations, that love will everywhere spring up spontaneously, that there is no entering a heart by force, and that every soul is free to name its conqueror: I should thus have no reason to complain if you had spoken to me without dissembling, and rejected my advances from the very beginning; my heart would then have been justified in blaming fortune alone. But to see my love encouraged by a deceitful avowal on your part, is an action so treacherous and perfidious, that it cannot meet with too great a punishment; and I can allow my resentment to do anything. Yes, yes; after such an outrage, fear everything; I am no longer myself, I am mad with rage. My senses, struck by the deadly blow with which you kill me, are no longer governed by reason; I give way to the outbursts of a just wrath, and am no longer responsible for what I may do.

CÉLIMÈNE: Whence comes, I pray, such a passion? Speak! Have you lost your senses?

ALCESTE: Yes, yes, I lost them when, to my misfortune, I beheld you and thus took the poison which kills me, and when I thought to meet with some sincerity in those treacherous charms that bewitched me.

CÉLIMÈNE: Of what treachery have you to complain?

ALCESTE: Ah! how double-faced she is! how well she knows how to dissemble! But I am fully prepared with the means of driving her to extremities. Cast your eyes here and recognize your writing. This picked-up note is sufficient to confound you, and such proof cannot easily be refuted.

CÉLIMÈNE: And this is the cause of your perturbation of spirits?

ALCESTE: You do not blush on beholding this writing!

CÉLIMÈNE: And why should I blush?

ALCESTE: What! You add boldness to craft! Will you disown this note because it bears no name?

CÉLIMÈNE: Why should I disown it, since I wrote it.

ALCESTE: And you can look at it without becoming confused at the crime of which its style accuses you!

CÉLIMÈNE: You are, in truth, a very eccentric man.

ALCESTE: What! you thus out-brave this convincing proof! And the contents so full of tenderness for Oronte, need have nothing in them to outrage me, or to shame you?

CÉLIMÈNE: Oronte! Who told you that this letter is for him?

ALCESTE: The people who put it into my hands this day. But I will even suppose that it is for some one else. Has my heart any less cause to complain of yours? Will you, in fact, be less guilty towards me?

CÉLIMÈNE: But if it is a woman to whom this letter is addressed, how can it hurt you, or what is there culpable in it?

ALCESTE: Hem! The prevarication is ingenious, and the excuse excellent. I must own that I did not expect this turn; and nothing but that was wanting to convince me. Do you dare to have recourse to such palpable tricks? Do you think people entirely destitute of common sense? Come, let us see a little by what subterfuge, with what air, you will support so palpable a falsehood; and how you can apply to a woman every word of this note which evinces so much tenderness! Reconcile, if you can, to hide your deceit, what I am about to read. . . .

CÉLIMÈNE: It does not suit me to do so. I think it ridiculous that you should take so much upon yourself, and tell me to my face what you have the daring to say to me!

ALCESTE: No, no, without flying into a rage, take a little trouble to explain these terms.

CÉLIMÈNE: No, I shall do nothing of the kind, and it matters very little to me what you think upon the subject.

ALCESTE: I pray you, show me, and I shall be satisfied, if this letter can be explained as meant for a woman.

CÉLIMÈNE: Not at all. It is for Oronte; and I will have you believe it. I accept all his attentions gladly; I admire what he says, I like him, and I shall agree to whatever you please. Do as you like, and act as you think proper; let nothing hinder you and do not harass me any longer.

ALCESTE: [Aside] Heavens! can anything more cruel be conceived, and was ever heart treated like mine? What! I am justly angry with her, I come to complain, and I am quarreled with instead! My grief and my suspicions are excited to the utmost, I am allowed to believe everything, she boasts of everything; and yet, my heart is still sufficiently mean not to be able to break the bonds that hold it fast, and not to arm itself with a generous contempt for the ungrateful object of which it is too much enamored. [To Célimène] Perfidious woman, you know well how to take advantage of my great weakness, and to employ for your own purpose that excessive, astonishing, and fatal love which your treacherous looks have inspired! Defend yourself at least from this crime that overwhelms me, and stop pretending to be guilty. Show me, if you can, that this letter is innocent; my affection will even consent to assist you. At any rate, endeavor to appear faithful, and I shall strive to believe you such.

CÉLIMÈNE: Bah, you are mad with your jealous frenzies, and do not deserve the love which I have for you. I should much like to know what could compel me to stoop for you to the baseness of dissembling; and why, if my heart were disposed towards another, I should not say so candidly. What! does the kind assurance of my sentiments towards you not defend me sufficiently against all your suspicions? Ought they to possess any weight at all with such a guarantee? Is it not insulting me even to listen to them? And since it is with the utmost difficulty that we can resolve to confess our love, since the strict honor of our sex, hostile to our passion, strongly opposes such a confession, ought a lover who sees such an obstacle overcome for his sake, doubt with impunity our avowal? And is he not greatly to blame in not assuring himself of the truth of that which is never said but after a severe struggle with oneself? Begone, such suspicions deserve my anger, and you are not worthy of being cared for.

I am silly, and am vexed at my own simplicity in still preserving the least kindness for you. I ought to place my affections elsewhere, and give you a just cause for complaint.

ALCESTE: Ah! you traitress! mine is a strange infatuation for you; those tender expressions are, no doubt, meant only to deceive me. But it matters little, I must submit to my fate; my very soul is wrapt up in you; I will see to the bitter end how your heart will act towards me, and whether it will be black enough to deceive me.

CÉLIMÈNE: No, you do not love me as you ought to love.

ALCESTE: Indeed! Nothing is to be compared to my exceeding love; and, in its eagerness to show itself to the whole world, it goes even so far as to form wishes against you. Yes, I could wish that no one thought you handsome, that you were reduced to a miserable existence; that Heaven, at your birth, had bestowed upon you nothing; that you had no rank, no nobility, no wealth, so that I might openly proffer my heart, and thus make amends to you for the injustice of such a lot; and that, this very day, I might have the joy and the glory of seeing you owe everything to my love.

CÉLIMÈNE: This is wishing me well in a strange way! Heaven grant that you may never have occasion . . . But here comes Monsieur Dubois curiously decked out.

SCENE IV.

Célimène, Alceste, Dubois.

ALCESTE: What means this strange attire, and that frightened look? What ails you?

DUBOIS: Sir . . .

ALCESTE: Well?

DUBOIS: The most mysterious event.

ALCESTE: What is it?

DUBOIS: Our affairs are turning out badly, sir.

ALCESTE: What?

DUBOIS: Shall I speak out?

ALCESTE: Yes, do, and quickly.

DUBOIS: Is there no one there?

ALCESTE: Curse your trifling! Will you speak?

DUBOIS: Sir, we must beat a retreat.

ALCESTE: What do you mean?

DUBOIS: We must steal away from this quietly.

ALCESTE: And why?

DUBOIS: I tell you that we must leave this place.

ALCESTE: The reason?

DUBOIS: You must go, sir, without staying to take leave.

ALCESTE: But what is the meaning of this strain?

DUBOIS: The meaning is, sir, that you must make yourself scarce.

ALCESTE: I shall knock you on the head to a cer-

tainty, booby, if you do not explain yourself more clearly.

DUBOIS: A fellow, sir, with a black dress, and as black a look, got as far as the kitchen to leave a paper with us, scribbled over in such a fashion that Old Nick himself could not have read it. It is about your law-suit, I make no doubt; but the very devil, I believe, could not make head nor tail of it.

ALCESTE: Well! what then? What has the paper to do with the going away of which you speak, you scoundrel?

DUBOIS: I must tell you, sir, that, about an hour afterwards, a gentleman who often calls, came to ask for you quite eagerly, and not finding you at home, quietly told me, knowing how attached I am to you, to let you know . . . Stop a moment, what the deuce is his name?

ALCESTE: Never mind his name, you scoundrel, and tell me what he told you.

DUBOIS: He is one of your friends, in short, that is sufficient. He told me that for your very life you must get away from this, and that you are threatened with arrest.

ALCESTE: But how! has he not specified anything?

DUBOIS: No. He asked me for ink and paper, and has sent you a line from which you can, I think, fathom the mystery!

ALCESTE: Hand it over then.

CÉLIMÈNE: What can all this mean?

ALCESTE: I do not know; but I am anxious to be informed. Have you almost done, devil take you?

DUBOIS: [After having fumbled for some time for the note] After all, sir, I have left it on your table.

ALCESTE: I do not know what keeps me from . . .

CÉLIMÈNE: Do not put yourself in a passion, but go and unravel this perplexing business.

ALCESTE: It seems that fate, whatever I may do, has sworn to prevent my having a conversation with you. But, to get the better of her, allow me to see you again, Madam, before the end of the day.

ACT V. SCENE I.

Alceste, Philinte.

ALCESTE: I tell you, my mind is made up about it.

PHILINTE: But, whatever this blow may be, does it compel you . . .

ALCESTE: You may talk and argue till doomsday if you like, nothing can avert me from what I have said. The age we live in is too perverse, and I am determined to withdraw altogether from intercourse with the world. What! when honor, probity, decency, and the laws are all against my adversary; when the equity of my claim is everywhere cried up; when my mind is at rest as to the justice of my cause, I meanwhile see myself betrayed by its issue! What! I have got justice on my side, and I lose my case! A wretch, whose scandalous history is well known, comes off triumphant by the blackest falsehood! All good faith yields to his treachery! He finds the means of being in the right, whilst cutting my throat! The weight of his dissimulation, so full of cunning, overthrows the right and turns the scales of justice! He obtains even a decree of court to crown his villainy. And, not content with the wrong he is doing me, there is abroad in society an abominable book, of which the very reading is to be condemned, a book that deserves the utmost severity, and of which the scoundrel has the impudence to proclaim me the author. Upon this, Oronte is observed to mutter, and tries wickedly to support the imposture! He, who holds an honorable position at court, to whom I have done nothing without having been sincere and candid, who came to ask me in spite of myself of my opinion of some of his verses; and because I treat him honestly, and will not betray either him or truth, he assists in overwhelming me with a trumped-up crime. Behold him now my greatest enemy! And I shall never obtain his sincere forgiveness, because I did not think that his sonnet was good! 'Sdeath! to think that mankind is made thus! The thirst for fame induces them to do such things! This is the good faith, the virtuous zeal, the justice and the honor to be found amongst them! Let us begone; it is too much to endure the vexations they are devising; let us get out of this wood, this cut-throat hole; and since men behave towards each other like real wolves, wretches, you shall never see me again as long as I live.

PHILINTE: I think you are acting somewhat hastily; and the harm done is not so great as you would make it out. Whatever your adversary dares to impute to you has not had the effect of causing you to be arrested. We see his false reports defeating themselves, and this action is likely to hurt him much more than you.

ALCESTE: Him? he does not mind the scandal of such tricks as these. He has a license to be an arrant knave; and this event, far from damaging his position, will obtain him a still better standing to-morrow.

PHILINTE: In short, it is certain that little notice has been taken of the report which his malice spread against you; from that side you have already nothing to fear; and as for your law-suit, of which you certainly have reason to complain, it is easy for you to bring the trial on afresh, and against this decision . . .

ALCESTE: No, I shall leave it as it is. Whatever cruel wrong this verdict may inflict, I shall take particular care not to have it set aside. We see too plainly how right is maltreated in it, and I wish to go down to posterity as a signal proof, as a notorious testimony of the wickedness of the men of our age. It may indeed cost me twenty thousand francs, but at the cost of twenty thousand francs I shall have the right of railing against the iniquity of human nature, and of nourishing an undying hatred of it.

PHILINTE: But after all . . .

ALCESTE: But after all, your pains are thrown away. What can you, sir, say upon this head? Would you have the assurance to wish, to my face, to excuse the villainy of all that is happening?

PHILINTE: No, I agree with you in all that you say. Everything goes by intrigue, and by pure influence. It is only trickery which carries the day in our time, and men ought to act differently. But is their want of equity a reason for wishing to withdraw from their society? All human failings give us, in life, the means of exercising our philosophy. It is the best employment for virtue; and if probity reigned everywhere, if all hearts were candid, just, and tractable, most of our virtues would be useless to us, inasmuch as their functions are to bear, without annoyance, the injustice of others in our good cause; and just in the same way as a heart full of virtue . . .

ALCESTE: I know that you are a most fluent speaker, sir; that you always abound in fine arguments; but you are wasting your time, and all your fine speeches. Reason tells me to retire for my own good. I cannot command my tongue sufficiently; I cannot answer for what I might say, and should very probably get myself into a hundred scrapes. Allow me, without any more words, to wait for Célimène. She must consent to the plan that brings me here. I shall see whether her heart has any love for me; and this very hour will prove it to me.

PHILINTE: Let us go upstairs to Éliante, and wait her coming.

ALCESTE: No, my mind is too harassed. You go and see her, and leave me in this little dark corner with my black care.

PHILINTE: That is strange company to leave you in; I will induce Éliante to come down.

SCENE II.

Célimène, Oronte, Alceste.

ORONTE: Yes, Madam, it remains for you to consider whether, by ties so dear, you will make me wholly yours. I must be absolutely certain of your affection: A lover dislikes to be held in suspense upon such a subject. If the ardor of my affection has been able to move your feelings, you ought not to hesitate to let me see it; and the proof, after all, which I ask of you, is not to allow Alceste to wait upon you any longer; to sacrifice him to my love, and, in short, to banish him from your house this very day.

CÉLIMÈNE: But why are you so incensed against him; you, whom I have so often heard speak of his merits?

ORONTE: There is no need, Madam, of these explanations; the question is, what are your feelings? Please to choose between the one or the other; my resolution depends entirely upon yours.

ALCESTE: [*Coming out of his corner*] Yes, this gentleman is right, Madam, you must make a choice; and his request agrees perfectly with mine. I am equally eager, and the same anxiety brings me here. My love requires a sure proof. Things cannot go on any longer in this way, and the moment has arrived for explaining your feelings.

ORONTE: I have no wish, sir, in any way to disturb, by an untimely affection, your good fortune.

ALCESTE: And I have no wish, sir, jealous or not jealous, to share aught in her heart with you.

ORONTE: If she prefers your affection to mine . . .

ALCESTE: If she has the slightest inclination towards you . . .

ORONTE: I swear henceforth not to pretend to it again.

ALCESTE: I peremptorily swear never to see her again.

ORONTE: Madam, it remains with you now to speak openly.

ALCESTE: Madam, you can explain yourself fearlessly.

ORONTE: You have simply to tell us where your feelings are engaged.

ALCESTE: You may simply finish the matter, by choosing between us two.

ORONTE: What! you seem to be at a loss to make such a choice.

ALCESTE: What! your heart still wavers, and appears uncertain!

CÉLIMÈNE: Good Heavens, how out of place is this persistence, and how very unreasonable you both show yourselves! It is not that I do not know whom to prefer, nor is it my heart that wavers. It is not at all in doubt between you two; and nothing could be more quickly accomplished than the choice of my affections. But to tell the truth, I feel too confused to pronounce such an avowal before you; I think that disobliging words ought not to be spoken in people's presence; that a heart can give sufficient proof of its attachment without going so far as to break with everyone; and gentler intimations suffice to inform a lover of the ill success of his suit.

ORONTE: No, no, I do not fear a frank avowal; for my part I consent to it.

ALCESTE: And I demand it; it is just its very publicity that I claim, and I do not wish you to spare my feelings in the least. Your great study has always been to keep friends with everyone; but no more trifling, no more uncertainty. You must explain yourself clearly, or I shall take your refusal as a verdict; I shall know, for my part, how to interpret your silence, and shall consider it as a confirmation of the worst.

ORONTE: I owe you many thanks, sir, for this wrath, and I say in every respect as you do.

CÉLIMÈNE: How you weary me with such a whim! Is there any justice in what you ask? And have I not told you what motive prevents me? I will be judged by Éliante, who is just coming.

SCENE III.

Éliante, Philinte, Célimène, Oronte, Alceste.

CÉLIMÈNE: Good cousin, I am being persecuted here by people who have concerted to do so. They both demand, with the same warmth, that I should declare whom my heart has chosen, and that, by a decision which I must give before their very faces, I should forbid one of them to tease me any more with his attentions. Say, has ever such a thing been done?

ÉLIANTE: Pray, do not consult me upon such a matter. You may perhaps address yourself to a wrong person, for I am decidedly for people who speak their mind.

ORONTE: Madam, it is useless for you to decline.

ALCESTE: All your evasions here will be badly supported.

ORONTE: You must speak, you must, and no longer waver.

ALCESTE: You need do no more than remain silent.

ORONTE: I desire but one word to end our discussions.

ALCESTE: To me your silence will convey as much as speech.

SCENE IV.

Arsinoé, Célimène, Éliante, Alceste, Philinte, Acaste, Clitandre, Oronte.

ACASTE: [*To* Célimène] We have both come, by your leave, Madam, to clear up a certain little matter with you.

CLITANDRE: [*To* Oronte *and* Alceste] Your presence happens fortunately, gentlemen; for this affair concerns you also.

ARSINOÉ: [*To* Célimène] No doubt you are surprised at seeing me here, Madam; but these gentlemen are the cause of my intrusion. They both came to see me, and complained of a proceeding which I could not have credited. I have too high an opinion of your kindness of heart ever to believe you capable of such a crime; my eyes even have refused to give credence to their strongest proofs, and in my friendship, forgetting trivial disagreements, I have been induced to accompany them here, to hear you refute this slander.

ACASTE: Yes, Madam, let us see, with composure, how you will manage to bear this out. This letter has been written by you, to Clitandre.

CLITANDRE: And this tender epistle you have addressed to Acaste.

ACASTE: [*To* Oronte *and* Alceste] This writing is not altogether unknown to you, gentlemen, and I have no doubt that her kindness has before now made you familiar with her hand. But this is well worth the trouble of reading.

"*You are a strange man to condemn my live-*

*liness of spirits, and to reproach me that I am
never so merry as when I am not with you. Nothing could be more unjust; and if you do not come
very soon to ask my pardon for this offence, I
shall never forgive you as long as I live. Our great
hulking booby of a Viscount.*" He ought to have
been here. "*Our great hulking booby of a Viscount, with whom you begin your complaints, is
a man who would not at all suit me; and ever
since I watched him for full three-quarters of an
hour spitting in a well to make circles in the water,
I never could have a good opinion of him. As for
the little Marquis . . .*" that is myself, ladies and
gentlemen, be it said without the slightest vanity,
. . . "*as for the little Marquis, who held my hand
yesterday for a long while, I think that there is
nothing so diminutive as his whole person, and his
sole merit consists in his cloak and sword. As to
the man with the green shoulder knot.*" [*To* Alceste] It is your turn now, sir. "*As to the man with
the green shoulder knot, he amuses me sometimes
with his bluntness and his splenetic behavior; but
there are hundreds of times when I think him the
greatest bore in the world. Respecting the man
with the big waistcoat . . .*" [*To* Oronte] This is
your share. "*Respecting the man with the big
waistcoat, who has thought fit to set up as a wit,
and wishes to be an author in spite of everyone, I
cannot even take the trouble to listen to what he
says; and his prose bores me just as much as his
poetry. Take it for granted that I do not always
enjoy myself so much as you think; and that I
wish for you, more than I care to say, amongst all
the entertainments to which I am dragged; and
that the presence of those we love is an excellent
relish to our pleasures.*"

CLITANDRE: Now for myself.

"*Your Clitandre, whom you mention to me, and
who has always such a quantity of soft expressions
at his command, is the last man for whom I could
feel any affection. He must be crazed in persuading himself that I love him; and you are so too in
believing that I do not love you. You had better
change your fancies for his, and come and see
me as often as you can, to help me in bearing the
annoyance of being pestered by him.*"

This shows the model of a lovely character, Madam;
and I need not tell you what to call it. It is enough. We
shall, both of us, show this admirable sketch of your
heart everywhere and to everybody.

ACASTE: I might also say something, and the subject is tempting; but I deem you beneath my anger;
and I will show you that little marquises can find
worthier hearts than yours to console themselves.

SCENE V.

Célimène, Éliante, Arsinoé, Alceste, Oronte,
Philinte.

ORONTE: What! Am I to be pulled to pieces in this
fashion, after all that you have written to me? And
does your heart, with all its semblance of love, plight
its faith to all mankind by turns! Bah, I have been
too great a dupe, but I shall be so no longer. You
have done me a service, in showing yourself in your
true colors to me. I am the richer by a heart which
you thus restore to me, and find my revenge in your
loss. [*To* Alceste] Sir, I shall no longer be an obstacle to your flame, and you may settle matters with
this lady as soon as you please.

SCENE VI.

Célimène, Éliante, Arsinoé, Alceste, Philinte.

ARSINOÉ: [*To* Célimène] This is certainly one of
the basest actions which I have ever seen; I can no
longer be silent, and feel quite upset. Has any one
ever seen the like of it? I do not concern myself
much in the affairs of other people, but this gentleman [*pointing to* Alceste], who has staked the whole
of his happiness on you, an honorable and deserving
man like this, and who worshipped you to madness,
ought he to have been . . .

ALCESTE: Leave me, I pray you, Madam, to manage
my own affairs; and do not trouble yourself unnecessarily. In vain do I see you espouse my quarrel. I am
unable to repay you for this great zeal; and if ever
I intended to avenge myself by choosing some one
else, it would not be you whom I would select.

ARSINOÉ: And do you imagine, sir, that I ever harbored such a thought, and that I am so very anxious
to secure you? You must be very vain, indeed, to
flatter yourself with such an idea. Célimène's leavings
are a commodity, of which no one needs be so very
much enamored. Pray, undeceive yourself, and do
not carry matters with so high a hand. People like
me are not for such as you. You will do much better
to remain dangling after her skirts, and I long to
see so beautiful a match.

SCENE VII.

Célimène, Éliante, Alceste, Philinte.

ALCESTE: [*To* Célimène] Well! I have held my
tongue, notwithstanding all I have seen, and I have
let everyone have his say before me. Have I controlled myself long enough? and will you now
allow me . . .

CÉLIMÈNE: Yes, you may say what you like; you
are justified when you complain, and you may reproach me with anything you please. I confess that I
am in the wrong; and overwhelmed by confusion I do
not seek by any idle excuse to palliate my fault. The
anger of the others I have despised; but I admit my
guilt towards you. No doubt, your resentment is

just; I know how culpable I must appear to you, that everything speaks of my treachery to you and that, in short, you have cause to hate me. Do so, I consent to it.

ALCESTE: But can I do so, you traitress? Can I thus get the better of all my tenderness for you? And although I wish to hate you with all my soul, shall I find a heart quite ready to obey me? [*To* Éliante *and* Philinte] You see what an unworthy passion can do, and I call you both as witnesses of my infatuation. Nor, truth to say, is this all, and you will see me carry it out to the bitter end, to show you that it is wrong to call us wise, and that in all hearts there remains still something of the man. [*To* Célimène] Yes, perfidious creature, I am willing to forget your crimes. I can find, in my own heart, an excuse for all your doings, and hide them under the name of a weakness into which the vices of the age betrayed your youth, provided your heart will second the design which I have formed of avoiding all human creatures, and that you are determined to follow me without delay into the solitude in which I have made a vow to pass my days. It is by that only, that, in everyone's opinion, you can repair the harm done by your letters, and that, after the scandal which every noble heart must abhor, it may still be possible for me to love you.

CÉLIMÈNE: What! I renounce the world before I grow old, and bury myself in your wilderness!

ALCESTE: If your affection responds to mine what need the rest of the world signify to you? Am I not sufficient for you?

CÉLIMÈNE: Solitude is frightful to a widow of twenty. I do not feel my mind sufficiently grand and strong to resolve to adopt such a plan. If the gift of my hand can satisfy your wishes, I might be induced to tie such bonds; and marriage . . .

ALCESTE: No. My heart loathes you now, and this refusal alone effects more than all the rest. As you are not disposed, in those sweet ties, to find all in all in me, as I would find all in all in you, begone, I refuse your offer, and this much-felt outrage frees me for ever from your unworthy toils.

SCENE VIII.

Éliante, Alceste, Philinte.

ALCESTE: [*To* Éliante] Madam, your beauty is adorned by a hundred virtues; and I never saw anything in you but what was sincere. For a long while I thought very highly of you; but allow me to esteem you thus for ever, and suffer my heart in its various troubles not to offer itself for the honor of your acceptance. I feel too unworthy, and begin to perceive that Heaven did not intend me for the marriage bond; that the homage of only the remainder of a heart unworthy of you would be below your merit, and that in short . . .

ÉLIANTE: You may pursue this thought. I am not at all embarrassed with my hand; and here is your friend, who, without giving me much trouble, might possibly accept it if I asked him.

PHILINTE: Ah! Madam, I ask for nothing better than that honor, and I could sacrifice my life and soul for it.

ALCESTE: May you, to taste true contentment, preserve for ever these feelings towards each other! Deceived on all sides, overwhelmed with injustice, I will fly from an abyss where vice is triumphant, and seek out some small secluded nook on earth, where one may enjoy the freedom of being an honest man.

PHILINTE: Come, Madam, let us leave nothing untried to deter him from the design on which his heart is set.

Jean Racine

(1639–1699)

It is difficult to assess, or even to describe, the character of the playwright who was able to turn the neoclassic restrictions on the drama into an artistic advantage, for Jean Racine was a complex man, both in harmony and disharmony with his times and his talents.

Born in 1639 of good family, Racine was left an orphan at the age of four and was brought up by fanatically religious relatives of the puritanical Catholic sect called the Jansenists. At the Jansenist monastery of Port Royal, he steeped himself in the Greek and Latin classics, as well as in romances. Wavering at college between law and theology, he finally decided in favor of the latter; yet upon graduation he chose the pursuit of literature—and the most graceful and worldly literature Europe had known. He also gave himself up to the gay courtly life of Paris, fell into dissolute company, and cast ridicule on the Port Royalists. He seemed to be completely at home in high society, won a subsidy of sorts from Louis XIV, and gained the valuable friendship of Boileau, the leading critic of the day. He sold his first tragedy quickly to the famous Hôtel de Bourgogne company, and his second play, *Thébaïde*, was produced by Molière in 1664. In this work and in its successor, *Alexander the Great* (1665), he made successful trial flights as a poet and playwright.

Two years later, he found his métier. In his early work he had written in the heroic vein of the elder dramatist Pierre Corneille, had neglected the love element in his material, and had dazzled his audience with displays of noble action. But in 1667, in *Andromache*, a drama of passion and destructive jealousy, he took the feminine heart for his field of observation and love for his subject. He made himself the popular tragedian of an age in which concern with the tender relations and the art of gallantry was extraordinarily fashionable. With equal talent he accommodated himself to the rules that had been drawn for the stage—the rules of the "unities." He formed his plots into climaxes that presented only the highest moments of intensity in a tragic life, revealing the rest of the story only through the light shed upon it by the dramatic crisis. And by dint of this dramaturgic concentration he developed a deep-thrusting psychological art, valid and convincing in penetration and yet in no way hampered by strict observation of the unities of time, place, and action.

As Professor Paul Landis has written, "what happens is of less importance than the mental reactions of the characters. In fact, the action is practically confined to the mind. Once this is realized, it becomes clear that the 'room in the palace of Pyrrhus' is simply a place where tortured souls display their strength and agony. Any room would have done as well, and the very poverty of the scene helps to concentrate the attention upon the psychological analysis." Corneille, Racine's senior, had no such talent for concentration because his temperament was less psychologically directed. When Corneille tried to conform to the "rules" in his famous romantic drama *The Cid*, he found it necessary to create the most crowded day in theatrical history and thereby to strain credibility; his later work, in which he attempted to avoid diffuseness, suffered from rigidity. Racine, on the other hand, moved easily within the narrowest confines. His dramatic compositions seem inactive only because movement of the mind is less obvious than physical movement and because we tend to confuse action with incident. Professor Landis reminds us of a story told by Abbé Dimnet about a teacher who, upon hearing a pupil say that he preferred Victor Hugo's tragedies to Racine's because "there is more life in them," muttered, "More bustle."

In the work of Racine, French classicism became an instrument of remarkable dramatic effectiveness. Combining consummate craftsmanship with explosive emotional power, Racine composed a series of tragedies that have reigned supreme on the French stage. Much is made of their beauty of design and of the flawlessness of their dramatic poetry, which has been a boon to French actresses and a bane to readers dependent on translations. The esthetic gratification provided by these qualities is indisputable. But Racine's power as a playwright derives largely from his insight into feminine personality and from his wholesome respect for the power of evil. He possessed an uncanny sense of dramatic intensification, and his inner world is always seething. Evidently the Jansenist view of life left its mark even upon his courtly outlook. Essentially, Racine could not help regarding human nature as corrupt. Mankind, for all its surface nobility, is possessed by evil impulses; and tragedy, according to this dramatist, is the victory of the passions over reason and order. This is especially pronounced in the case of female characters; six of Racine's nine tragedies are named after classical and Biblical characters who have been aptly described as "fair women full of Attic grace but who lack the grace of God." And since women dominated the courtly world of Louis XIV, Racine had many models for his heroines.

411

His first success, with the production of *Andromache*, was followed by such other triumphs of art as *Phaedra, Bérénice,* and *Britannicus,* the last a brilliant presentation of a critical situation that decides Nero upon the course of life that made him notorious in history. Nevertheless, wounded in self-esteem, as well as motivated by increasing pietism, Racine retired from the theatre at the peak of his career. Abandoning the court, he retired to the Jansenist stronghold of Port Royal and married a simple, pious woman who apparently had never read a line of his work. His last tragedies, *Esther* and *Athalia,* the latter especially notable for its choral poetry and surging conflict, dealt with Biblical themes and were written for production by Madame de Maintenon's fashionable religious school for girls. Racine died in 1699, a penitent man in an age that gloried in worldliness and sophistication.

Phaedra, based on Euripides' famous tragedy *Hippolytus,* is Racine's most powerful study of passion. It is a rational demonstration of the irrational—which is one of the methods of writing tragedy. Ever since its first production in 1677, this play has been regarded as the summit of French tragic art and has been played to applause by such eminent actresses as Rachel and Sarah Bernhardt. Unfortunately the English Channel and the North Atlantic still seem natural barriers to a proper production and appreciation of Racine in the English-speaking world. Perhaps no amount of explanation will be convincing to those who are unresponsive to *Phaedra,* let alone some of Racine's other tragedies, the merits of which lie even deeper below the surface. A knowledge of the French language alone will not suffice; it may lead to the realization that Racine is a great poet without proving that he is also a great dramatist. Superlative acting alone can do that, unless the reader has the imaginative perception to act out the play for himself. In that case he will find in the fluctuation of feelings all the action he needs. When this action is experienced, moreover, the universality of the play will also acquire the "meaning" of Racinian tragedy which Francis Fergusson has so aptly defined as "the eternal plight of reason."

PHAEDRA

By Jean Racine

TRANSLATED FROM THE FRENCH BY ROBERT HENDERSON

CHARACTERS

THESEUS, *son of Ægeus and King of Athens*
PHAEDRA, *wife of Theseus and daughter of Minos and Pasiphaë*
HIPPOLYTUS, *son of Theseus and Antiope, Queen of the Amazons*[1]
ARICIA, *princess of the blood royal of Athens*

OENONE, *nurse of Phædra*
THERAMENES, *tutor of Hippolytus*
ISMENE, *friend of Aricia*
PANOPE, *waiting-woman of Phædra*
GUARDS

The scene is laid in Trœzen, a town of the Peloponnesus.

ACT I.

[*Enter* Hippolytus *and* Theramenes]
HIPPOLYTUS: My mind is settled, dear Theramenes,
And I must stay no more in lovely Trœzen,
Racking my soul in doubt and mortal anguish.
I am ashamed of my long idleness.
Look you, my father gone six months and more—
One so dear gone,—and to what fate befallen
I do not know, nor do I know what corner
Of all the wide earth hides him!
    THERAMENES: Ah, my prince,—
And where, then, would you seek him? I have sailed
Over the seas on either side of Corinth.
Where Acheron is lost among the Shades
I asked, indeed, if aught were known of Theseus!
And to content you, I have gone to Elis,
Rounded Tœnarus, sailed to the far waters
Where Icarus once fell. What newer hope? . . .
Under what favored sky would you think now
To trace his footsteps? Who knows if your father
Wishes the secret of his absence known?
Perhaps while we are trembling for his life
The hero calmly plots a fresh intrigue,
And only waits till the deluded lady—

HIPPOLYTUS: Peace, good Theramenes! Respect his name.
The waywardness of youth is his no longer,
And nothing so unworthy should detain him.
Now for a long time, Phædra has held that heart
Inconstant once, and she need fear no rival.
And if I seek him, it is but my duty.
I leave a place I dare no longer see!
    THERAMENES: Indeed! When, prince, did you begin to dread
These peaceful haunts, so dear to happy childhood,
Where I have often known you rather stay
Than face the tumult and the pomp of Athens?
What danger do you shun? Or is it grief?
    HIPPOLYTUS: All things are changed. That happy past is gone.
Since then, the gods sent Phædra!
    THERAMENES: Now I see!
It is the queen whose sight offends you. Yes,—
For with a step-dame's spite she schemed your exile
At her first sight of you. But then, her hatred
Is somewhat milder, if not wholly vanished.
A dying woman—one who longs for death!
What danger can she bring upon your head?
Weary of life, and weary of herself,—
Sick with some ill she will not ever speak of,—
Can Phædra then lay plots?—
    HIPPOLYTUS: I do not fear
The hatred of the queen. There is another
From whom I fly, and that is young Aricia,
The sole survivor of an impious race.
    THERAMENES: What! You become her persecutor, too?
The gentle sister of the cruel sons
Of Pallas, did not share their perfidy.
Why should you hate such charming innocence?
    HIPPOLYTUS: If it were hate, I should not need to fly.
    THERAMENES: Then will you tell me what your flying means?
Is this the proud Hippolytus I see?

---

[1] The story of Hippolytus was one of the myths of Greece. The son of Theseus by the Amazon Hippolyte, he attracted the love of his stepmother, Phædra. He was destroyed by Poseidon at the request of Theseus after Phædra had falsely accused Hippolytus of having made advances to her. Euripides wrote two plays about Phædra and Hippolytus, treating the story as a tragedy of the revenge of Aphrodite, conceived as the natural force of love. Hippolytus was presented as disinterested in love. Therefore, nature hits back at him through the passion of Phædra and destroys him. Racine based his play on the second and only extant Euripidean version, the *Hippolytus*. Racine's departures from Euripides are extremely important. He employs no symbolism, he does not give us an antisexual Hippolytus, and he concentrates on Phædra as passion-wrecked woman.

413

Love's fiercest foe alive?—the fiercest hater
Of Theseus' well-worn yoke?—Now can it be
That Venus, scorned, will justify your father?
And is Hippolytus, like other mortals,
To bow, perforce, and offer incense to her?—
And can he love? . . .

HIPPOLYTUS: My friend, you must not ask me.
You who have known my heart through all my
   life,
And know it to be proud and most disdainful,—
You will not ask that I should shame myself
By now disowning all that I professed.
My mother was an Amazon,—my wildness,
Which you think strange, I suckled at her breast,
And as I grew, why, Reason did approve
What Nature planted in me. Then you told me
The story of my father, and you know
How, often, when I listened to your voice
I kindled, hearing of his noble acts,—
And you would tell how he brought consolation
To mortals for the absence of Alcides,
And how he cleared the roads of monsters,—rob-
   bers,—
Procrustes, Cercyron, Sciro, Sinnis slain,
Scattered the Epidaurian giant's bones,
And how Crete ran with blood of the Minotaur![2]
But when you told me of less glorious deeds,—
Troth plighted here and there and everywhere,
Young Helen stolen from her home at Sparta,
And Peribœa's tears in Salamis,
And many other trusting ones deceived,
Whose very names he cannot now remember,—
Lone Ariadne, crying to the rocks,—
And last of all this Phædra, bound to him
By better ties,—You know that with regret
I heard, and urged that you cut short the tale.
I had been happier, could I erase
This one unworthy part of his bright story
Out of my memory. Must I in turn
Be made love's slave, and brought to bend so low?
It is the more contemptible in me,
For no such brilliance clings about my name
As to the name of Theseus,—no monsters quelled
Have given me the right to share his weakness.
And if I must be humbled for my pride,
Aricia should have been the last to tame me!
Was I not mad that I should have forgotten
Those barriers which must keep us far apart
Eternally? For by my father's order
Her brothers' blood must never flow again
In a child of hers. He dreads a single shoot
From any stock so guilty, and would bury
Their name with her; so even to the tomb
No torch of Hymen[3] may be lit for her.
Shall I espouse her rights against my father,
Provoke his wrath, launch on a mad career?—

[2] Theseus destroyed the Cretan bull-monster, the Minotaur, who each year devoured seven youths and seven
maidens sent by Athens to Crete as a tribute.

[3] The god of marriage, symbolized by burning torches.

THERAMENES: But if your time has come, dear
   prince, the gods
Will care but little for your guiding reason.
Theseus would shut your eyes;—he but unseals them.
His hatred kindles you to burn, rebellious,
And only lends his enemy new charms.
Then, too, why should you fear a guiltless passion?
Do you not dare this once to try its sweetness,
Rather than follow such a hair-drawn scruple?—
Afraid to stray where Hercules has wandered?
What heart so stout that Venus has not won it?
And you, so long her foe, where would you be
Had your own mother, always scorning love,
Never been moved with tenderness for Theseus?
What good to act a pride you do not feel?
If you are changed, confess it! For some time
You have been seldom seen urging the car
With wild delight, rapid, along the shore,
Or, skillful in the art that Neptune taught,
Making th' unbroken steed obey the bit.
The forest has flung back our shouts less often.
A secret burden, cast upon your spirits,
Has dimmed your eye.—Can I then doubt your love?
It is in vain that you conceal your hurt.
Tell me, has not Aricia touched your heart?

HIPPOLYTUS: Theramenes, I go to find my father.

THERAMENES: Will you not see the queen before
   you leave?

HIPPOLYTUS: So I intend. And you may tell her so.
Yes, I will see her, since it is my duty.
But what new ill vexes her dear Œnone?

   [Enter Œnone]

OENONE: Alas, my lord, what grief was e'er like
   mine?
The queen has almost touched the gates of death.
It is in vain I watch her night and day,
In my very arms this secret malady
Is killing her—her mind is all disordered.
She rises from her bed, weary yet restless,
Pants for the outer air, yet she commands me
That none should see her in her misery.
She comes!

HIPPOLYTUS: That is enough. I shall not vex her
Nor make her see the face of one she hates.

   [Exeunt Hippolytus and Theramenes. Enter
   Phædra]

PHAEDRA: Yes, this is far enough. Stay here,
   Œnone.
My strength is failing. I must rest a little.
I am dazzled with the light; it has been long
Since I have seen it. Ah, my trembling knees
Are failing me—

OENONE: Dear Heaven, I would our tears
Might bring relief.

PHAEDRA: And how these clumsy trinkets,
These veils oppress me! Whose officious hand
Tied up these knots, and gathered all these coils
Over my brow? All things conspire against me
And would distress me more!

OENONE: That which you wish

This moment, frets you next! Did you not ask
A minute past, that we should deck you out,
Saying you felt your energy return,
Saying you sickened of your idleness,
And wished to go and see the light of day?
You sought the sun, and now you see it here,—
And now you would be hidden from its shining!

PHAEDRA: O splendid author of a hapless race,—
You whom my mother boasted as her father,—
Well may my blush to see me in such plight.
For the last time I look on thee, O Sun!

OENONE: So! And are you still in love with
death?
Will you not ever make your peace with life,
And leave these cruel accents of despair?

PHAEDRA: I wish that I were seated in the forest.
When may I follow with delighted eye,
Through glorious dust, flying in full career,—
A chariot?—

OENONE: Madam?

PHAEDRA: Have I lost my wits?
What did I say? Where am I? Ah, and where
Do my vain wishes wander? For the gods
Have made me mad! And now I blush, Œnone,—
I hide my face, for you have seen too clearly
The grief and shame, that, quite in spite of me,
Will overflow my eyes.

OENONE: If you must blush,
Blush at the silence that inflames your grief.
Deaf to my voice, you will not have my care.
Then will you have no pity on yourself,
But let your life be ended in mid-course?
What evil spell has drained its fountains dry?
Night-shadows thrice have darkened all the heavens
Since sleep came to your eyes, and now three times
The dawn has chased the darkness back again
Since your pale lips knew food. You faint, are
languid,—
What awful purpose have you in your heart?
How do you dare attempt to lose your life
And so offend the gods who gave it you,—
And so prove false to Theseus and your marriage?—
Yes, and betray your most unhappy children,
Bending their necks yourself, beneath the yoke?
That day, be sure, which robs them of their mother
Will give his high hopes back to the stranger's son,—
To that proud enemy of you and yours,
Born of an Amazon,—Hippolytus!—

PHAEDRA: You gods!

OENONE: Ah, this is a reproach to move you!

PHAEDRA: Unhappy one, what name have your lips
spoken?

OENONE: Your anger is most just, and it is well
That hated name can rouse such rage! Then live,
And hear again the claims of love and duty!
Live, then,—and stop this son of Scythia
From crushing down your children by his sway,
Ruling the noblest offspring of the gods,—
The purest blood of Greece! Never delay!
Death threatens every moment! Now restore

Your shattered strength, while the dim torch of life
Burns, and can yet be fanned into a flame.

PHAEDRA: I have endured its guilt and shame too
long.

OENONE: Why? What remorse is gnawing at your
heart?
What crime can have disturbed you so? Your hands
Have not been stained with the blood of innocence.

PHAEDRA: No, I thank Heaven my hands are free
from stain,—
I would my soul were innocent as they!

OENONE: Why then, what awful plan have you
been scheming,
At which your conscience still should be afraid?

PHAEDRA: Have I not said enough? Spare me the
rest!
I die to save myself a full confession.

OENONE: Die, then,—keep a silence more than
human!—
But seek some other hand to close your eyes,
For I will go before you to the Shades.
There are a thousand highways always open,
And since you have so little faith in me,
I'll go the shortest! When has my love failed you?
Remember, in my arms you lay, new-born.
For you I left my country and my children,—
And is this payment for my service to you?

PHAEDRA: What will you gain from words that
are so bitter?
Were I to speak, horror would freeze your blood.

OENONE: What can you say more terrible to me
Than to behold you die before my eyes?

PHAEDRA: If you should know my sin, I still should
die,
But with guilt added—

OENONE: Oh, my dearest lady,
By all the tears that I have wept for you,
By these poor knees I clasp, now ease my mind
From doubt and torture!

PHAEDRA: As you wish. Then rise.

OENONE: I hear you. Speak.

PHAEDRA: Ah, how shall I begin?

OENONE: Leave off your fears,—you hurt me with
distrust.

PHAEDRA: O malice of great Venus! Into what madness,
What wild distractions, did she cast my mother!

OENONE: Let them be blotted from all memory,
Buried in silence, for all times to come.

PHAEDRA: My sister, Ariadne, what was the love
Which brought you death, forsaken on lone shores?

OENONE: Madam, what deep pain is it prompts reproaches
Thus against all your kin—?

PHAEDRA: It is her will—
It is the will of Venus, and I perish,
Last and least happy of a family
Where all were wretched!

OENONE: Do you love?

PHAEDRA: I feel

All of its fever—
  OENONE: Ah! For whom?
  PHAEDRA: Now hear
The final horror. Yes, I love. My lips
Tremble to name him.
  OENONE: Whom?
  PHAEDRA: And do you know him?—
He whom I tortured long,—the Amazon's son!
  OENONE: Hippolytus! Great gods!
  PHAEDRA: Yes, you have named him.
  OENONE: Blood freezes in my veins! O cursed race!
Ill-omened journey! Land of misery,
Why did we ever reach these dangerous shores?
  PHAEDRA: My wound is not a new one. Scarcely
    had I
Been bound to Theseus by our marriage tie,
With peace and happiness seeming so well secured,
Until at Athens I saw my enemy.
I looked, I first turned pale, then blushed to see him,
And all my soul was in the greatest turmoil;
A mist made dim my sight, and my voice faltered,
And now my blood ran cold, then burned like fire.
In all my fevered body I could feel
Venus, whose fury had pursued so many
Of my sad race. I sought to shun her torments
With fervent vows. I built a shrine for her,
And there, 'mid many victims did I seek
The reason I had lost; but all for nothing.
I found no remedy for pain of love!
I offered incense vainly on her altars,
I called upon her name, and while I called her,
I loved Hippolytus, always before me!
And when I made her altars smoked with victims,
'Twas for a god whose name I dared not utter,—
And still I fled his presence, only to find him—
(The worst of horrors)—in his father's features!
At last I raised revolt against myself,
And stirred my courage up to persecute
The enemy I loved. To banish him
I wore a harsh and jealous step-dame's manner,
And ceaselessly I clamored for his exile,
Till I had torn him from his father's arms!
I breathed once more, Œnone. In his absence
The days passed by less troubled than before—
Innocent days! I hid my bitter grief,
Submitted to my husband, cherished the fruits
Of our most fatal marriage,—and in vain!
Again I saw the one whom I had banished,
Brought here by my own husband, and again
The old wound bled. And now it is not love
Hid in my heart, but Venus in her might
Seizing her prey. Justly I fear my sin!
I hate my life, and hold my love in horror.
I die:—I would have kept my name unsullied,
Burying guilty passion in the grave;
But I have not been able to refuse you;
You weep and pray, and so I tell you all,
And I shall be content, if as I perish,
You do not vex me with unjust reproaches,
Nor vainly try to snatch away from death

The last faint sparks of life, yet lingering!
  [Enter Panope]
  PANOPE: I wish that I might hide sad tidings from
    you,
But 'tis my duty, madam, to reveal them.
The hand of death has seized your peerless husband.
You are the last to hear it.
  OENONE: What is this?
  PANOPE: The queen begs Heaven for the safe re-
    turn
Of Theseus, but she trusts, indeed, in vain—
She is deceived. Hippolytus, his son,
Has learned from vessels newly come to port
That Theseus is dead.
  PHAEDRA: Oh gods!
  PANOPE: At Athens
Opinions are divided; some would have it
Your child should rule, and some, despite the law,
Are bold, and dare support the stranger's son,
While one presuming faction, it is said,
Would crown Aricia, and the house of Pallas.
I thought it well to warn you of this danger.
Hippolytus is ready, now, to start,
And if he chance to show himself in Athens,
The crowd, I fear, will follow in his lead.
  OENONE: It is enough. The queen has heard your
    message,
And she will not neglect your timely warning.
  [Exit Panope]
Dear lady, I had almost ceased from urging
That you should wish to live. I thought to follow
My mistress to that tomb from which my pleading
Had failed to turn her,—but this new misfortune
Changes the aspect of affairs, and prompts us
To take fresh measures. Madam, Theseus is gone,
And you must fill his place. He leaves a son,—
Slave if you die, but if you live, a king!
Upon whom can he lean, but you, his mother?
There is no hand but yours to dry his tears.
Live then, for him, or else his guiltless weeping
Will move the gods to wrath against his mother.
Live, for no blame is in your passion now.
The king is dead, you bear the bonds no longer
Which made your love a thing of crime and horror.
You need no longer dread Hippolytus,
For you may see him, now, without reproach.
Perhaps, if he is certain of your hatred,
He means to lead the rebels. Undeceive him!
Soften his callous heart, and bend his pride!
King of this fertile land, his portion lies
Here in his Trœzen, yet he knows the laws,—
They give your son these walls Minerva built,
Aye, and protects,—but if a common foe
Threatens you both, you had best be united.
For you must thwart Aricia!
  PHAEDRA: I consent.
Yes, I will live, if life can yet be mine,—
If my affection for a son has power
To rouse my sinking heart, at such a dangerous hour!
  [Exeunt]

ACT II.

[*Enter* Aricia *and* Ismene]

ARICIA: Hippolytus has asked to see me here?
Hippolytus has asked to bid farewell?
'Tis true, Ismene? You are not deceived?

ISMENE: This is the first result of Theseus' death,
And you may look to see from every side
Hearts that he kept away, now turning to you.
Aricia soon shall find all Greece low-bending
To do her homage.

ARICIA: Then it is not only
An idle tale? Am I a slave no longer?
Have I no enemies?

ISMENE: The gods, Aricia,
Trouble your peace no more, for Theseus' soul
Is with your brothers, now.

ARICIA: Does rumor tell
How Theseus died?

ISMENE: Tales most incredible
Are spread. Some say that, seizing a new bride,
The faithless man was swallowed by the waves.
Others have said, and this report prevails,
That he, together with Pirithous,
Went to the world below, seeking the shores
Of Cocytus, showing his living self
To the pale ghosts, but could not leave the gloom,
For they who enter there abide forever.

ARICIA: Can I believe a mortal may descend
Into that gulf before his destined hour?
What lure could ever overcome its terrors?

ISMENE: Nay, he is dead; 'tis only you who doubt
it.
The men of Athens all bewail his loss.
Trœzen already hails Hippolytus,
And Phædra, fearing for her children's rights,
Asks counsel of such friends as share her troubles,
Here in this palace!

ARICIA: Will Hippolytus
Prove kinder than his father, make my chains light,
And pity my misfortunes?

ISMENE: Yes, I think so.

ARICIA: Indeed, I think you do not know him well,
Or you would not believe a heart so hard
Could ever pity, or could look on me
As one not sharing in the scorn he feels
For all our sex. Does he not still avoid
Whatever place we go?

ISMENE: I know the stories
Of proud Hippolytus, but I have seen him
When he was near to you, and watched to see
How one supposed so cold would bear himself.
I found his manners not at all like those
Which I had looked to see, for in his face
Was great confusion, at your slightest glance.
He could not turn his languid eyes away,
But still looked back again to gaze at you.
Love is a word that may offend his pride,
But though the tongue deny it, looks betray!

ARICIA: How eagerly my heart hears what you say,
Though it may be delusion, dear Ismene!
Did it seem possible to you, who know me,
That I, poor toy of unrelenting fate,
Fed upon bitter tears by night and day,
Could ever taste the maddening draught of love?
I am the last frail offspring of my race—
My royal race, the Children of the Earth,
And of them, I alone survive war's fury.
Yes, I have lost six brothers, in their youth,—
Mown by the sword, cut off in their first flower!
They were the hope of an illustrious house.
Earth drank their blood with sorrow; it was kin
To his whom she brought forth. And well you know,
Since then, no heart in Greece could sigh for me,
Lest, by a sister's flame, her brothers' ashes
Might chance to blaze again. And, too, you know
How I disdained the cautions of my captor,
His care, and his suspicion, and you know
How often I have thanked the king's injustice,
Since I had never loved the thought of love.
He happily confirmed my inclinations,—
But then, I never yet had seen his son!
It is not merely that my eye is caught,
And that I love him for his grace and beauty,—
Charms which he does not know, or seems to
scorn,—
I love him for a kind of wealth that's rarer.
He has his father's virtues, not his faults.
I love, and I must grant it, that high pride
Which never stooped beneath the yoke of love.
Phædra gains little glory from a lover
Free of his sighs; I am too proud, I think,
To share devotion with a thousand others,
Or enter in a door that's never shut.
But to make one who never stooped before
Bend his proud neck,—to pierce a heart of stone,
And bind one captive, whom his chains astonish,
Who struggles vainly in his pleasant bonds,—
That takes my fancy, and I long for it.
The god of strength was easier disarmed
Than this Hippolytus, for Hercules
Yielded so often to the eyes of beauty
That he made triumph cheap. But, dear Ismene,
I take too little heed of a resistance
Which I may never quell. If I am humbled,
And if I find defeat, then you will hear me
Speak ill of that same pride I so admire!
What! can he love? And have I been so happy
That I have bent—?

ISMENE: He comes,—and you shall hear him.

[*Enter* Hippolytus]

HIPPOLYTUS: Lady, before you go, it is my duty
To tell you of the changes of your fortune.
What I have feared is true; my sire is dead.
Yes, his long stay was what I had supposed it.
For only death, which came to end his labors,
Could keep him hidden from the world so long.
The gods at last have doomed Alcides' friend—
His friend, and his successor. Since your hatred

I think will grant his virtues, it can hear
Some praise for him, without resenting it,
Knowing that it is due. I have one hope
To soothe me in my sorrow. I can free you.
Now I revoke the laws, whose strictness moved me
To pity for you; you are your own mistress
Of heart and hand. Here in my heritage,
In Trœzen, here where Pittheus once reigned,
And where I now am king, by my own right,
I leave you free, free as myself,—and more.

ARICIA: Your kindness is too great; it overcomes
me.

A goodness which will pay disgrace with honor
Can give a greater force than you would think
To the harsh laws from which you would release me.

HIPPOLYTUS: Athens, not knowing how to fill the
throne

Left empty, speaks of you, and then of me,
And then of Phædra's son.

ARICIA: Of me, my lord?

HIPPOLYTUS: I know that by the law it is not mine,
For Greece reproaches me my foreign mother.
But if my brother were my only rival,
My rights are clearly truer ones than his,
So that I should not care for twists of the law.
There is a juster claim to check my boldness.
I yield my place to you, or rather, grant
That you should have it,—you should hold the
sceptre,

Bequeathed to you from Earth's great son, Erectheus.
It came, then, to Ægeus, and the city
Which was protected and increased by him
Was glad to welcome such a king as Theseus,
Leaving your luckless brothers out of mind.
Now Athens calls you back within her walls.
Long strife has cost her groans enough already,
Her fields are glutted with your kinsmen's blood,
Fattening those same furrows whence it sprang.
I will rule here in Trœzen; Phædra's son
Has his rich kingdom waiting him in Crete.
Athens is yours, and I will do my best
To bring to you the votes which are divided
Between us two.

ARICIA: I fear a dream deceives me.

For I am stunned, my lord, at what I hear.
Am I, indeed, awake? Can I believe
Such generosity as this? What god
Has put it in your heart? Well you deserve
That fame you have, yet it falls short of you.
For me, you will be traitor to yourself!
Was it not grace enough never to hate me,
To have been free so long from enmity,
Which some have harbored—

HIPPOLYTUS: Hate you? I to hate you?
However darkly you have seen my pride,
Did you suppose a monster gave me birth?
What savagery, what hatred, full of venom
Would not become less evil, seeing you?
Could I resist this charm which caught my soul—

ARICIA: Why, what is this, sir?

HIPPOLYTUS: I have said too much
Not to say more. No prudence can resist
The violence of passion. Now, at last,
Silence is broken. I must tell you now
The secret that my heart can hold no longer.
You see before you an unhappy victim
Of hasty pride,—a prince who begs compassion.
For I was long the enemy of love.
I mocked his fetters, I despised his captives,
And while I pitied these poor, shipwrecked mortals,
I watched the storms, and seemed quite safe on land.
And now I find that I have such a fate,
And must be tossed upon a sea of troubles!
My boldness is defeated in a moment,
And all my boasted pride is humbleness.
For nearly six months past, ashamed, despairing,
Carrying with me always that sharp arrow
Which tears my heart, I struggle quite in vain
To free me, both from you and from myself.
I leave your presence;—leaving, I find you near,
And in the forest's darkness see your form.
Black night, no less than daylight brings the vision
Of charms that I avoid. All things conspire
To make Hippolytus your slave. The fruit
Of all my sighs is only that I cannot
Find my own self again. My bow, my spear,
Please me no longer. I have quite forgotten
My chariot, and the teaching of the Sea God.
The woods can only echo back my groans,
Instead of flinging back those joyous shouts
With which I urged my horses. Hearing this,
A tale of passion so uncouth, you blush
At your own handiwork. These are wild words
With which I offer you my heart, a captive
Held, strangely, by a silken jess.[4] And yet
The off'ring should be dearer to your eyes,
Since such words come as strangers to my lips.
Nor do not scorn my vows, so poorly spoken
Since, but for you, they never had been formed.

[*Enter* Theramenes]

THERAMENES: My lord, I came to tell you of the
queen.

She comes to seek you.

HIPPOLYTUS: Me?

THERAMENES: And what she wishes
I do not know. I speak at her request,
For she would talk with you before you go.

HIPPOLYTUS: What shall I say to her? Can she
expect—?

ARICIA: You cannot, noble prince, refuse to hear
her,

Though you are sure she is your enemy.
There is a shade of pity due her tears.

HIPPOLYTUS: Shall we part so? And will you let me
leave you

Not knowing if I have offended you,—
The goddess I adore,—with all this boldness?
Of if this heart, which I now leave with you—

4 A short strap of silk tied to the leg of a hawk in
hawking.

ARICIA: Go now, my prince, and do whatever deeds
Your generosity would have you do.
Make Athens own my sceptre. All these gifts
I will accept. But the high throne of Empire
Is not the thing most precious to my eyes!
    [*Exeunt* Aricia *and* Ismene]
HIPPOLYTUS: Friend, are we ready?—But the queen is coming.
See that the ship is trimmed and fit to sail.
Hurry, gather the crew, and hoist the signal,
And then return, the sooner to release me
From a most irksome meeting.
    [*Exit* Theramenes. *Enter* Phædra *and* Œnone]
PHAEDRA: [*To* Œnone] Look, I see him!
My blood forgets to flow,—tongue will not speak
What I have come to say!
    OENONE: Think of your son.
And think that all his hopes depend on you.
    PHAEDRA: They tell me that you leave us, hastily.
I come to add my own tears to your sorrow,
And I would plead my fears for my young son.
He has no father, now; 'twill not be long
Until the day that he will see my death,
And even now, his youth is much imperiled
By a thousand foes. You only can defend him.
And in my inmost heart, remorse is stirring,—
Yes, and fear, too, lest I have shut your ears
Against his cries; I fear that your just anger
May, before long, visit on him that hatred
His mother earned.
    HIPPOLYTUS: Madam, you need not fear.
Such malice is not mine.
    PHAEDRA: I should not blame you
If you should hate me; I have injured you.
So much you know;—you could not read my heart.
Yes, I have tried to be your enemy,
For the same land could never hold us both.
In private and abroad I have declared it;—
I was your enemy! I found no peace
Till seas had parted us; and I forbade
Even your name to be pronounced to me.
And yet, if punishment be meted out
Justly, by the offense;—if only hatred
Deserves a hate, then never was there woman
Deserved more pity, and less enmity.
    HIPPOLYTUS: A mother who is jealous for her children
Will seldom love the children of a mother
Who came before her. Torments of suspicion
Will often follow on a second marriage.
Another would have felt that jealousy
No less than you; perhaps more violently.
    PHAEDRA: Ah, prince, but Heaven made me quite exempt
From what is usual, and I can call
That Heaven as my witness! 'Tis not this—
No, quite another ill devours my heart!
    HIPPOLYTUS: This is no time for self-reproaching, madam.
Perhaps your husband still beholds the light,

Perhaps he may be granted safe return
In answer to our prayers; his guarding god
Is Neptune, whom he never called in vain.
    PHAEDRA: He who has seen the mansions of the dead
Returns not thence. Since Theseus has gone
Once to those gloomy shores, we need not hope,
For Heaven will not send him back again.
Prince, there is no release from Acheron;—
It is a greedy maw,—and yet I think
He lives and breathes in you,—and still I see him
Before me here; I seem to speak to him—
My heart—! Oh, I am mad! Do what I will,
I cannot hide my passion.
    HIPPOLYTUS: Yes, I see
What strange things love will do, for Theseus, dead,
Seems present to your eyes, and in your soul
A constant flame is burning.
    PHAEDRA: Ah, for Theseus
I languish and I long, but not, indeed,
As the Shades have seen him, as the fickle lover
Of a thousand forms, the one who fain would ravish
The bride of Pluto,—but one faithful, proud,
Even to slight disdain,—the charm of youth
That draws all hearts, even as the gods are painted,—
Or as yourself. He had your eyes, your manner,—
He spoke like you, and he could blush like you,
And when he came across the waves to Crete,
My childhood home, worthy to win the love
Of Minos' daughters,—what were you doing then?
Why did my father gather all these men,
The flower of Greece, and leave Hippolytus?
Oh, why were you too young to have embarked
On board the ship that brought your father there?
The monster would have perished at your hands,
Despite the windings of his vast retreat.
My sister would have armed you with the clue
To guide your steps, doubtful within the maze.—
But no—for Phædra would have come before her,
And love would first have given me the thought,
And I it would have been, whose timely aid
Had taught you all the labyrinthine ways!
The care that such a dear life would have cost me!
No thread could satisfy my lover's fears.
I would have wished to lead the way myself,
And share the peril you were sure to face.
Yes, Phædra would have walked the maze with you,—
With you come out in safety, or have perished!
    HIPPOLYTUS: Gods! What is this I hear? Have you forgotten
That Theseus is my father and your husband?
    PHAEDRA: Why should you fancy I have lost remembrance
And that I am regardless of my honor?
    HIPPOLYTUS: Forgive me, madam! With a blush I own
That I mistook your words, quite innocent.
For very shame I cannot see you longer—
Now I will go—

PHAEDRA: Ah, prince, you understood me,—
Too well, indeed! For I had said enough.
You could not well mistake. But do not think
That in those moments when I love you most
I do not feel my guilt. No easy yielding
Has helped the poison that infects my mind.
The sorry object of divine revenge,
I am not half so hateful to your sight
As to myself. The gods will bear me witness,—
They who have lit this fire within my veins,—
The gods who take their barbarous delight
In leading some poor mortal heart astray!
Nay, do you not remember, in the past,
How I was not content to fly?—I drove you
Out of the land, so that I might appear
Most odious—and to resist you better
I tried to make you hate me—and in vain!
You hated more, and I loved not the less,
While your misfortunes lent you newer charms.
I have been drowned in tears and scorched by fire!
Your own eyes might convince you of the truth
If you could look at me, but for a moment!
What do I say? You think this vile confession
That I have made, is what I meant to say?
I did not dare betray my son. For him
I feared,—and came to beg you not to hate him.
This was the purpose of a heart too full
Of love for you to speak of aught besides.
Take your revenge, and punish me my passion!
Prove yourself worthy of your valiant father,
And rid the world of an offensive monster!
Does Theseus' widow dare to love his son?
Monster indeed! Nay, let her not escape you!
Here is my heart! Here is the place to strike!
It is most eager to absolve itself!
It leaps impatiently to meet your blow!—
Strike deep! Or if, indeed, you find it shameful
To drench your hand in such polluted blood,—
If that be punishment too mild for you,—
Too easy for your hate,—if not your arm,
Then lend your sword to me.—Come! Give it
    now!—
    OENONE: What would you do, my lady? Oh, just
    gods!
But someone comes;—go quickly. Run from shame.
You cannot fly, if they should find you thus.
    [Exeunt Phædra and Œnone. Enter Thera-
    menes]
    THERAMENES: Is that the form of Phædra that I
    see
Go hurrying? What are these signs of sorrow?
Where is your sword? Why are you pale and shaken?
    HIPPOLYTUS: Friend, let us fly. Indeed, I am con-
    fused
With greatest horror and astonishment.
Phædra—but no; gods, let this dreadful secret
Remain forever buried and unknown.
    THERAMENES: The ship is ready if you wish to
    sail,
But Athens has already cast her vote.

Their leaders have consulted all the tribes.
Your brother is elected;—Phædra wins!
    HIPPOLYTUS: Phædra?
    THERAMENES: A herald bringing a commission
Has come from Athens, placing the reins of power
In Phædra's hands. Her son is king.—
    HIPPOLYTUS: O gods,—
O ye who know her, is it thus, indeed,
That ye reward her virtue?
    THERAMENES: Meanwhile rumor
Is whispering that Theseus is not dead,—
That there are those who saw him in Epirus,—
But I have searched, and I know all too well—
    HIPPOLYTUS: No matter. Let no chances be neg-
    lected.
This rumor must be hunted to its source,
And if it be not worthy of belief
Let us then sail, and at whatever cost,
We'll trust the sceptre to deserving hands.
    [Exeunt]

ACT III.

[Enter Phædra and Œnone]
    PHAEDRA: Ah, let them take away the worthless
    honors
They bring to me;—why urge that I should see them?
What flattery can soothe my wounded heart?
Far rather hide me. I have said too much.
My madness bursting like a stream in flood,
I spoke what never should have reached his ears.
Oh gods! The way he heard me! How reluctant
To take my meaning,—dull and cold as marble,
And only eager for a quick retreat!
And how his blushes made my shame the deeper!
Why did you turn me from the death I sought?
Ah, when his sword was pointed at my breast,
Did he grow pale?—or try to snatch it from me?
That I had touched it was enough for him
To make it seem forever horrible,
And to defile whatever hand should hold it.
    OENONE: When you will brood upon your bitter
    grief,
You only fan a fire that must be quenched.
Would it not more become the blood of Minos
To find you peace in cares that are more noble?—
And in defiance of this wretch, who flies
From what he hates, reign on the throne you're of-
fered?
    PHAEDRA: I reign?—And shall I hold the rod of
    empire,
When reason can no longer reign in me?
When I have lost control of mine own senses?
When I do gasp beneath a shameful yoke?
When I am dying?—
    OENONE: Fly!
    PHAEDRA: I cannot leave him.
    OENONE: You dare not fly from one you dared to
    banish?

PHAEDRA: That time is past. He knows how I am frenzied,
For I have overstepped my modesty,
And blazoned out my shame before his eyes.
Against my will, hope crept into my heart.
Did you not call my failing powers to me?
Was it not you, yourself, called back my soul
Which fluttered on my lips, and with your counsel
Lent me new life? Who told me I might love him?
OENONE: Blame me or blame me not for your misfortunes,—
What could I not have done if it would save you?
But if your anger ever was aroused
By insult, can you pardon him his scorn?
How cruel were his eyes, severe and fixed,
Surveying you, half prostrate at his feet!
How hateful, then, his savage pride appeared!
Why did not Phædra see as I saw them?
PHAEDRA: This pride that you detest may yield to time.
The rudeness of the forest clings about him,
For he was bred there by the strictest laws.
Love is a word he never knew before.
Perhaps it was surprise that stunned him so;—
There was much vehemence in all I said.
OENONE: Remember that his mother was barbaric—
PHAEDRA: She was a Scythian, but she learned to love.
OENONE: He has a bitter hate for all our sex.
PHAEDRA: Well, then no rival ever rules his heart.
Your counsel comes a little late, Œnone.
Now you must serve my madness, not my reason.
Love cannot find a way into his heart,
So let us take him where he has more feeling.
The lure of power seemed somewhat to touch him.
He could not hide that he was drawn to Athens,—
His vessels' prows were pointed there already,
With sails all set to run before the breeze.
Go, and on my behalf, touch his ambition,—
Dazzle his eyes with prospects of the crown.
The sacred diadem shall grace his brow,—
My highest honor is to set it there,
And he shall have the power I cannot keep.
He'll teach my son how men are ruled.— It may be
That he will deign to be a father to him.
He shall control both son and mother;—try him,—
Try every means to move him, for your words
Should meet more favor than my own could find.
Urge him with groans and tears,—say Phædra's dying,
Nor blush to speak in pleading terms with him.
My last hope is in you,—do what you will,
I'll sanction it,—the issue is my fate!
    [Exit Œnone]
    PHAEDRA: [Alone] Venus implacable, thou seest me ashamed,
And I am sore confounded. Have I not
Been humbled yet enough? Can cruelty
Stretch farther still? Thine arrows have struck home!

It is thy victory! Wouldst gain new triumphs?—
Then seek an enemy more obdurate,—
Hippolytus neglects thee, braves thine anger.
He never bows his knee before thine altars.
Thy name offends his proud, disdainful hearing.
Our interests are alike,—avenge thyself,
Force him to love—But what is this, Œnone?
Already back? Then it must be he hates me,
And will not hear you speak—
    [Enter Œnone]
    OENONE: Yes, you must stifle
A love that's vain, and best call back your virtue.
The king we thought was dead will soon appear
Here to your eyes. Yes, Theseus will be here,
For he has come again. The eager people
Are hastening to see him. I had gone
As you commanded, seeking for the prince,
When all the air was torn,—a thousand shouts—
    PHAEDRA: My husband living! 'Tis enough, Œnone.
I owned a passion that dishonors him.
He is alive. I wish to know no more.
    OENONE: What is it?
    PHAEDRA: What I prophesied to you,—
What you refused to hear, while with your weeping
You overcame repentance. Had I died
I had deserved some pity, earlier.
I took your counsel, and I die dishonored.
    OENONE: You die?
    PHAEDRA: Just heavens! What I have done today!
My husband comes, and with him comes his son,
And I shall see the witness of my passion,
The object of my most adulterous flame
Watch with what face I make his father welcome,
Knowing my heart is big with sighs he scorned,
And my eyes wet with tears that could not move him.
Will his respect for Theseus make him hide it?—
Conceal my madness?—not disgrace his father?
And do you think he can repress the horror
Which he must have for me? A fruitless silence!
I know my treason, and I lack the boldness
Of those abandoned women, who can feel
Tranquillity in crime,—can show a forehead
All unashamed. I know my madness well,
Recall it all. I think that these high roofs
And all these walls can speak. They will accuse me.
They only wait until my husband comes,
And then they will reveal my perfidy.
'Tis death alone can take away this horror.
Is it so great an ill to cease to live?
Death holds no fear for those in misery.
I tremble only for the name I leave,—
My son's sad heritage. The blood of Jove
Might justly swell the pride of those who boast it,
But what a heavy weight a mother's guilt
Leaves for her children! Yes, I dread that scorn
For my disgrace, which will be cast on them
With too much truth. I tremble when I think
How they will never dare to raise their heads,
Crushed with that curse.—

OENONE: Nay, do not doubt my pity.
There never was a juster fear than yours.
Then why do you expose them to this shame?
And why must you accuse yourself, destroying
The one hope left. It will be said of Phædra
That she well knows of her own perfidy,
That she has fled from out her husband's sight,—
And proud Hippolytus may well rejoice
That, dying, you should lend his tale belief.
What answer can I make him? It will be
For him, a story easy to deny,
And I shall hear him, while triumphantly
He tells your shame to every open ear.
Why, I had sooner Heaven's fire consumed me!
Deceive me not! And do you love him still?
What think you now of this contemptuous prince?

PHAEDRA: As of a monster fearful to mine eyes!

OENONE: Why do you give him easy victory?
You are afraid! Dare to accuse him first!
Say he is guilty of the charge he brings
This day against you. Who shall say it's false?
All things conspire against him. In your hands
His sword, which he most happily forgot,—
Your present trouble, and your past distress,—
Your warnings to his father,—and his exile
Which you accomplished with your earnest prayers—

PHAEDRA: So! You would have me slander innocence!

OENONE: My zeal asks nothing from you but your
silence.
I also tremble. I am loath to do it.
I'd face a thousand deaths more willingly.
But since, without this bitter deed, I lose you,
And since, for me, your life outweighs all else,
Why, I will speak. Theseus, however angry,
Will do no worse than banish him again.
A father, punishing, remains a father.
His anger will be soothed with easy penance.
But even if some guiltless blood be spilt,
Is not your honor of a greater worth,—
A treasure far too precious to be risked?
You must submit, no matter what is needful,
For when your reputation is at stake,
Then you must sacrifice your very conscience.
But someone comes. 'Tis Theseus—

PHAEDRA: Look, I see
Hippolytus most stern, and in his eyes
There is my ruin written. I am helpless.
My fate is yours. Do with it as you will.

[Enter Theseus, Hippolytus and Theramenes]

THESEUS: Fortune will fight no longer with my
wishes,
But to your arms it brings me back—

PHAEDRA: Wait, Theseus.
Nay, do not hurry to profane caresses
One time so sweet, which I am now not worthy
Even to taste of, for you have been wronged.
Fortune has proved most spiteful. In your absence
It has not spared your wife. I am not fit
To meet you tenderly, and from this time

I only care how I shall bear my shame.

[Exeunt Phædra and Œnone]

THESEUS: Strange welcome for your father, is it
not?
What does it mean, my son?

HIPPOLYTUS: Why, only Phædra
Can solve that mystery. If I can move you
By any wish, then let me never see her.
Hippolytus begs leave to disappear,—
To leave the home that holds your wife, forever.

THESEUS: You, my son! Leave me?

HIPPOLYTUS: 'Twas not I who sought her.
You were the one to lead her to these shores!
My lord, at your departure you thought fit
To leave Aricia and the queen in Trœzen,
And I, myself, was charged with their protection.
But now, what cares will need to keep me here?
My idle youth has shown what skill it has
Over such petty foes as roam the woods.
May I not leave this life of little glory,
Of ease—and dip my spear in nobler blood?
Before you reached my age, more than one tyrant
More than one monster had already felt
The force of your good arm. You had succeeded
In whipping insolence; you had removed
All of the dangers lurking on our coasts.
The traveler no longer feared for outrage,
And Hercules, himself, who knew your deeds,
Relied on you, and rested from his labors.
But I—the son of such a noble father,—
I am unknown, and I am far behind
Even my mother's footsteps. Let my courage
Have scope to act. If there is yet some monster
Escaped from you, then let me seek for glory,
Bringing the spoils to you; or let it be
That memory of death well met with courage
Shall keep my name a living one,—shall prove
To all the world I am my father's son.

THESEUS: Why, what is this? What terror can have
seized you?
What makes my kindred fly before my face?
If I return to find myself so feared,
To find so little welcome in my home,
Then why did Heaven free me from my prison?
My only friend, misled by his own passion,
Set out to rob the tyrant of Epirus,—
To rob him of his wife! Regretfully
I gave the lover aid. Fate blinded us,—
Myself as well as him. The tyrant seized me,
Defenseless and unarmed. With tears I saw
Pirithous cast forth to be devoured
By savage beasts, that lapped the blood of men.
He shut me in a gloomy cave, far down,
Deep in the earth, near to the realm of Pluto.
I lay six months, before the gods had pity,
Then I escaped the eyes that guarded me.
I purged the world of this, its enemy,
And he, himself has fed his monsters' hunger.
But when I come, with an expectant joy,
When I draw close to all that is most precious

Of what the gods have left me,—when my soul
Looks for its happiness in these dear places,
Then I am welcomed only with a shudder,
With turning from me, and with hasty flight.
And since it seems that I inspire such terror,
Would I were still imprisoned in Epirus!
Phædra complains that I have suffered outrage.
Who has betrayed me? Speak! Was I avenged?
Why was I not? Has Greece, to whom mine arm
Has often brought good help, sheltered my foe?
You do not answer. Is it that my son,—
My own son—has he joined mine enemies?
I'll enter, for I cannot bear to wonder.
I'll learn at once the culprit and the crime,
And Phædra must explain her trouble to me. [*Exit*]
    HIPPOLYTUS: What mean these words? They freeze
      my very blood!
Will Phædra, in her frenzy, blame herself,—
Make sure of her destruction? And the king,—
What will he say? O gods! The fatal poison
That love has spread through all my father's house!
I burn with fires his hatred disapproves.
How changed he finds me from the son he knew!
My mind is much alarmed with dark forebodings,
But surely innocence need never fear.
Come, let us go, and in some other place
Consider how I best may move my father
To make him tender, and to tell a love
Troubled, but never vanquished, by his frown.
    [*Exeunt*]

ACT IV.

[*Enter* Theseus *and* Œnone]
THESEUS: Ah, what is this I hear? Presumptuous
    traitor!
And would he have disgraced his father's honor?
With what relentless footsteps Fate pursues me!
I know not where I go, nor where I am!
My kindest love, how very ill repaid!
Bold scheme! Oh most abominable thought!
A wretch who did not shrink from violence
To reach the object of his evil passion!
I know this sword,—it served to arm his fury,—
The sword I gave him for a nobler use!
And could the sacred ties of blood not stop him?
And Phædra,—was she loath to have him punished?
She held her silence. Was it to spare his guilt?
    OENONE: Only to spare a most unhappy father.
She knew it shameful that her eyes had kindled
So infamous a love,—had prompted him
To such a crime,—and Phædra would have died.
I saw her raise her arm, and ran to save her.
To me alone you owe it that she lives.
And since I pity her, and pity you
I came, unwilling, to explain her tears.
    THESEUS: The traitor! Well indeed might he turn
    pale!

It was for fear he trembled when he saw me!
I was amazed that he should show no gladness.
The coldness of his greeting chilled my love.
But was this guilty passion that consumes him
Declared before I banished him from Athens?
    OENONE: Remember, sire, how Phædra urged it on
    you.
It was illicit love that caused her hatred.
    THESEUS: And then this flame burst out again at
    Trœzen?
    OENONE: Sire, I have told you all there is. The
    queen
Is left to bear her grief alone too long.
Let me now leave you. I will wait on her.
    [*Exit. Enter* Hippolytus]
    THESEUS: Ah, there he is! Great gods! That noble
    manner
Might well deceive an eye less fond than mine!
Why should the sacred mark of virtue shine
Bright on the forehead of an evil wretch?
Why should the blackness of a traitor's heart
Not show itself by sure and certain signs?
    HIPPOLYTUS: My father, may I ask what fatal
    cloud
Has troubled so the face of majesty?
Dare you not trust this secret to your son?
    THESEUS: Traitor, how dare you show yourself
    before me?
Monster, whom Heaven's bolts have spared too long!
A last survivor of that robber band
Whereof I cleansed the earth, your brutal lust
Scorned to respect even my marriage bed!
And now you dare,—my hated foe,—to come
Here to my presence, here where all things are filled
And foul with infamy, instead of seeking
Some unknown land, that never heard my name.
Fly, traitor, fly! Stay not to tempt my wrath!
I scarce restrain it. Do not brave my hatred.
I have been shamed forever; 'tis enough
To be the father of so vile a son,
Without your death, to stain indelibly
The splendid record of my noble deeds.
Fly! And unless you yearn for punishment
To make you yet another villain slain,
Take heed that this sun, shining on us now
Shall see your foot no more upon this soil.
I say it once again,—fly!—and in haste!
Rid all my realms of your detested person.
On thee,—on thee, great Neptune, do I call!
If once I cleared thy shores of murderers,
Remember, then, thy promise to reward me
For these good deeds, by granting my first prayer.
I was held long in close captivity.
I did not then demand thy mighty aid,
For I have saved so great a privilege
To use in greatest need. That time is come.
And now I ask, avenge a wretched father!
I leave this traitor subject to thy wrath.
I ask that thou shouldst quench his fires in blood,
And by thy fury, I will judge thy favor!

HIPPOLYTUS: Phædra accuses me of wanton passion!
A final horror to confuse my soul!
Such blows, unlooked for, falling all at once,
Have crushed me, choked me, struck me into silence!
THESEUS: Traitor, you thought that in a timid silence
Phædra would cover your brutality.
But, though you fled, you still should not have left her
Holding the sword that seals your condemnation.
Or rather, to complete your perfidy,
You should have robbed her both of speech and life!
HIPPOLYTUS: Most justly angered at so black a lie,
I might be pardoned, should I speak the truth.
But it concerns your honor to conceal it.
Welcome that reverence which stops my tongue,
And, without seeking to increase your troubles,
Look closely at my life, as it has been.
Great crimes come never singly; they are linked
To sins that went before. Who once has sinned,
May, at the last, do greater violence
To all that men hold sacred. Vice, like virtue,
Grows in small steps, and no true innocence
Can ever fall at once to deepest guilt.
No man of virtue, in a single day,
Can turn himself to treason, murder, incest!
I am the son of one both chaste and brave.
I have not proved unworthy of my birth.
Pittheus, one by all men reckoned wise,
Deigned to instruct me, when I left her keeping.
I do not wish to boast upon my merits,
But if I may lay claim to any virtue,
I think I have displayed, beyond all else,
That I abhor those sins with which you charge me.
Look you, Hippolytus is known in Greece
As one so continent he's thought austere,
And all men know how I abstain, unbending.
The daylight is not purer than my heart.
Then how could I, if burning so profanely,—
THESEUS: Villain, it is that very pride condemns you!
I see the hateful reason for your coldness,
For only Phædra charmed your shameless eyes.
Your heart, quite cold to other witcheries,
Refused the pure flame of a lawful love.
HIPPOLYTUS: No, father, I have hidden it too long.
This heart has not disdained its sacred flame.
Here, at your feet, I'll tell my real offense.
I love, and love, indeed, where you forbid it.
My heart's devotion binds me to Aricia,—
The child of Pallas has subdued your son!
Her I adore, rebellious to your laws.
For her alone I breathe my ardent sighs.
THESEUS: You love her? Gods! But no,—I see the truth.
You play this crime to justify yourself.
HIPPOLYTUS: Sir, for six months I kept me from her presence,
And still I love her. I have come to tell it,—

Trembling I come—! Can nothing free your mind
Of such an error? Can my oaths not soothe you?
By Heaven—Earth,—by all the powers of Nature—
THESEUS: The wicked will not ever shrink from lying.
Be still, and spare me tiresome vows and pleadings,
Since your false virtue knows no other way.
HIPPOLYTUS: Although you think it false and insincere,
Phædra has cause enough to know it true.
THESEUS: Ah, how your boldness rouses all my anger!
HIPPOLYTUS: What is my term and place of banishment?
THESEUS: Were you beyond the Pillars of Alcides,[5]
Your perjured presence still were far too near me!
HIPPOLYTUS: What friends will pity me, if you forsake me
And think me guilty of so vile a crime?
THESEUS: Go seek for friends who praise adultery,
And look for those who clap their hands at incest!—
Low traitors, lawless,—steeped in infamy,—
Fit comforters for such an one as you!
HIPPOLYTUS: Are incest and adultery the words
Which you will cast at me? I hold my peace.
Yet think what mother Phædra had—remember
Her blood, not mine, is tainted with these horrors!
THESEUS: So then! Before my eyes your rage bursts out,
And loses all restraint. Go from my sight!—
This last time I will say it,—traitor, go!
And do not wait until a father's anger
Drives you away in public execration!
[Exit Hippolytus]
THESEUS: [Alone] Wretch! Thou must meet inevitable ruin!
Neptune has sworn by Styx,—an oath most dreadful
Even to gods,—and he will keep his promise.
Thou canst not ever flee from his revenge.
I loved thee, and in spite of this offense
My heart is moved by what I see for thee.
Nay, but thy doom is but too fully earned.
Had father ever better cause for rage?
O you just gods, who see my crushing grief,
Why was I cursed with such an evil son?
[Enter Phædra]
PHAEDRA: I come to you, my lord, in proper dread,
For I have heard your voice raised high in anger,
And much I fear that deeds have followed threats.
Oh, spare your child, if there is still some time!
Respect your race, your blood, I do beseech you.
I would not hear that blood cry from the earth!
Save me the horror and the lasting shame
Of having caused his father's hand to shed it!
THESEUS: No, madam, I am free from such a stain.
But still the wretch has not escaped my vengeance.
The hand of an Immortal holds his doom,

[5] Pillars of Hercules—the two promontories at the eastern end of Gibraltar, supposedly set there by Hercules when he went there to seek the oxen of Geryon.

And pledges his destruction. 'Tis a debt
That Neptune owes me. You shall be avenged.
    PHAEDRA: A debt to you? Prayers made in anger—
    THESEUS: Fear not.
They will not fail. But join your prayers to mine,
And paint his crimes for me in all their blackness,
To fan my sluggish wrath to whitest heat.
You do not know of all his villainy.
His rage against you feeds itself on slanders.
Your words, he says, are full of all deceit.
He says Aricia has his heart and soul,
That he loves only her—
    PHAEDRA: Aricia?—
    THESEUS: Yes.
He said it to my face:—an idle pretext!
A trick I am not caught by. Let us hope
That Neptune does swift justice. I am going
Now to his altars, urging he keep his oath. [*Exit*]
    PHAEDRA: [*Alone*] So he is gone! What words have
    struck mine ears?
What smothered fires are burning in my heart?
What fatal stroke falls like a thunder-bolt?
Stung with remorse that would not give me peace,
I tore myself from out Œnone's arms
And hurried here to help Hippolytus,
With all my soul and strength. Who knows, indeed,
But that new-found repentance might have moved
    me
To speak in accusation of myself?—
And if my voice had not been choked with shame,
Perhaps I might have told the frightful truth.
Hippolytus can feel—but not for me!
Aricia has his heart, his plighted word!
You gods! I thought his heart could not be touched
By any love, when, deaf to all my tears,
He armed his eye with scorn, his brow with threats.
I thought him strong against all other women,
And yet another has prevailed upon him!
She tamed his pride, and she has gained his favor!
Perhaps he has a heart that's quick to melt,
And I alone am she he cannot bear!
Then shall I charge myself with his protection?
    [*Enter Œnone*]
    PHAEDRA: Dear nurse, and do you know what I
    have learned?
    OENONE: No, but in truth I come with trembling
    limbs.
I dreaded what you planned when you went out,
And fear of fatal madness turned me pale.
    PHAEDRA: Who would have thought it, nurse? I had
    a rival.
    OENONE: A rival?
    PHAEDRA: Yes, he loves. I cannot doubt it.
This wild Hippolytus I could not tame,—
Who scorned to be admired, and who was wearied
With lovers' sighs,—this tiger whom I dreaded
Fawns on the hand of one who broke his pride.
Aricia found the entrance to his heart!
    OENONE: Aricia?
    PHAEDRA: 'Tis a torture yet untried!

Now for what other pains am I reserved?
All I have suffered,—ecstasies of passion,
Longings and fears, the horrors of remorse,
The shame of being spurned with contumely,
Were feeble tastes of what is now my torment.
They love each other! By what secret charm
Have they deceived me? When and where and how
Did they contrive to meet? You knew it all,—
And why, then, was I kept from knowing of it?
You never told me of their stolen hours
Of love and of delight. Have they been seen
Talking together often?—did they seek
The forest shadows? Ah, they had full freedom
To be together. Heaven watched their sighs.
They loved,—and never felt that they were guilty.
The morning sun shone always clear for them,
While I,—an outcast from the face of Nature,
Shunned the bright day, and would have hid myself,—
Death the one god whom I dared ask for aid!
I waited for the freedom of the grave.
My woe was fed with bitterness, and watered
With many tears. It was too closely watched.
I did not dare to weep without restraint,
And knowing it a solace perilous,
I feared it, and I hid my mortal terror
Beneath a face most tranquil. Oftentimes
I stopped my tears, and made myself to smile—
    OENONE: What fruit can they desire from fruitless
    love?
For they can meet no more.
    PHAEDRA: That love will stay,
And it will stay forever. While I speak—
O dreadful thought—they laugh and scorn my mad-
    ness
And my distracted heart. In spite of exile,
In spite of that which soon must come to part them,
They make a thousand oaths to bind their union.
Œnone, can I bear this happiness
Which so insults me? I would have your pity.
Yes, she must be destroyed. My husband's fury
Against her hated race shall be renewed.
The punishment must be a heavy one.
Her guilt outruns the guilt of all her brothers.
I'll plead with Theseus, in my jealousy,—
What do I say? Oh, have I lost my senses?
Is Phædra jealous? Will she, then, go begging
For Theseus' help? He lives,—and yet I burn.
For whom? Whose heart is this I claim as mine?
My hair stands up with horror at my words,
And from this time, my guilt has passed all bounds!
Hypocrisy and incest breathe at once
Through all I do. My hands are ripe for murder,
To spill the guiltless blood of innocence.
Do I still live, a wretch, and dare to face
The holy Sun, from whom I have my being?
My father's father was the king of gods;
My race is spread through all the universe.—
Where can I hide? In the dark realms of Pluto?
But there my father holds the fatal urn.
His hands award the doom irrevocable.—

Minos is judge of all the ghosts in hell.
And how his awful shade will start and shudder
When he shall see his daughter brought before him,
And made confess such many-colored sins,
Such crimes, perhaps, as hell itself knows not!
O father, what will be thy words at seeing
So dire a sight? I see thee drop the urn,
Turning to seek some punishment unheard of,—
To be, thyself, mine executioner!
O spare me! For a cruel deity
Destroys thy race. O look upon my madness,
And in it see her wrath. This aching heart
Gathers no fruit of pleasure from its crime.
It is a shame which hounds me to the grave,
And ends a life of misery in torment.

    OENONE: Ah, madam, drive away this groundless
      fear.
Look not so hard upon a little sin.
You love. We cannot conquer destiny.
Why, you were drawn as by a fatal charm;—
Is that a marvel we have never seen?
Has love, then, come to triumph over you,
And no one else? By nature man is weak.
You are a mortal,—bow to mortal fortune.
You chafe against a yoke that many others
Have borne before you. They upon Olympus,—
The very gods themselves, who make us tremble
For our poor sins, have burned with lawless passions.

    PHAEDRA: What words are these? What counsels
      do you give me?
Why will you still pour poison in mine ears?
You have destroyed me. You have brought me back
When I should else have left the light of day.
You made me to forget my solemn duty,
And see Hippolytus, whom I had shunned.
What have you done? Why did those wicked lips
Slander his faultless life with blackest lies?
It may be you have murdered him. By now
The prayer unholy of a heartless father
May have been granted. I will have no words!
Go, monster! Leave me to my sorry fate.
May the just gods repay you properly,
And may your punishment remain forever
To strike with fear, all such as you, who strive
To feed the frailty of the great with cunning,
To push them to the very brink of ruin
To which their feet incline,—to smooth the path
Of guilt. Such flatterers the gods, in anger,
Bestow on kings as their most fatal gift! [Exit]

    OENONE: [Alone] O gods! What is there I've not
      done to serve her?
And this is the reward that I have won! [Exit]

ACT V.

[Enter Hippolytus and Aricia]
    ARICIA: Can you keep silent in this mortal danger?
Your father loves you. Will you leave him so—
When he is thus deceived? If you are cruel,—

If, in your heart, you will not see my tears,
Why then, content,—and do not ever see me.
Abandon poor Aricia,—but at least
If you must go, make sure your life is safe.
Defend your honor from a shameful stain,
And force your father to recall his prayers.
There still is time. Why, for a mere caprice,
Should you leave open way for Phædra's slanders?
Let Theseus know the truth.

    HIPPOLYTUS: Could I say more
And not expose him to a great disgrace?
How should I dare, by speaking what I know,
To make my father's brow blush red with shame?
You only know the hateful mystery.
I have not showed my heart to any other
But you and Heaven. Judge, then, if I love you,
Since you have seen I could not hide from you
All I would fain have hidden from myself!
Remember under what a seal I spoke.
Forget what I have said, if that may be,
And never let so pure a mouth give voice
To such a secret. Let us trust to Heaven
To give me justice, for the gods are just.
For their own honor they will clear the guiltless.
The time will come for Phædra to be punished.
She cannot always flee the shame she merits.
I ask no other favor than your silence.
In all besides, I give my wrath free scope.
Make your escape from this captivity,
Be bold, and come with me upon my flight.
Oh, do not stay on this accursèd soil
Where virtue breathes the air of pestilence.
To hide your leaving, take the good advantage
Of all this turmoil, roused by my disgrace.
I promise you the means of flight are ready.
You have, as yet, no other guards than mine.
Defenders of great strength will fight our quarrel.
Argos has open arms, and Sparta calls us.
Let us appeal for justice to our friends,
And let us not stand by while Phædra joins us
Together in one ruin, driving us
Down from the throne,—and swells her son's posses-
    sions
By robbing us. Come, take this happy chance.
What fear can hold you back? You seem to pause.
Only your better fortune makes me urge
That we be bold. When I am all a-fire,
Why are you ice? Are you afraid to follow
One who is banished?

    ARICIA: Ah, but such an exile
Would be most dear to me. For with what joy
I'd live, if I could link my fate to yours,
And be forgot by all the world. But still
We are not bound by that sweet tie together.
Then how am I to steal away with you?
I know the strictest honor need not stop me
From seeking freedom from your father's hands,
For this, indeed, is not my parents' home,
And flight is lawful, when one flies from tyrants.
But you, sir, love me, and my virtue shrinks—

HIPPOLYTUS: No, no! To me your honor is as dear
As it is to yourself. A nobler purpose
Brings me to you. I ask you leave your foes
And follow with your husband. That same Heaven
Which sends these woes, sets free the pledge between
    us
From human hands. There are not always torches
To light the face of Hymen. Come with me—
Beside the gates of Trœzen is a temple,
Amid the ancient tombs of princes, buried.
They who are false can never enter there,
And there no mortal dares make perjured oaths,
For instant punishment will come on guilt.
There is not any stronger check to falsehood
Than what is present there,—fear of a death
That cannot be escaped. There we shall go,
If you consent, and swear eternal love,
And call the god who watches there to witness
Our solemn vows, and ask his guarding care.
I will invoke the holiest of powers—
The chaste Diana and the Queen of Heaven,—
Yes, all the gods, who know my inmost heart,
Will answer for my sacred promises.
    ARICIA: Here is the king. Away—make no delay.
I linger yet a while to hide my flight.
Go you, and leave me with some trusted one
To lead my timid footsteps to your side.
    [Exit Hippolytus. Enter Theseus and Ismene]
    THESEUS: O gods, throw light upon my troubled
        mind!
Show me the truth which I am seeking here.
    ARICIA: [To Ismene] Be ready, dear Ismene, for
        our flight.
    [Exit Ismene]
    THESEUS: Your color changes, and you seem con-
        fused.
Madam,—what dealing had my son with you?
    ARICIA: Sire, he was bidding me his last farewell.
    THESEUS: It seems your eyes can tame that stub-
        born pride,
And the first sighs he breathes are paid to you.
    ARICIA: I cannot well deny the truth; he has not
Inherited your hatred and injustice,—
He does not treat me as a criminal.
    THESEUS: That is to say,—he swore eternal love.
Do not depend on such a fickle heart.
He swore as much to others, long before.
    ARICIA: He, Sire?
    THESEUS: You stop the roving of his taste.
How should you bear so vile a partnership?
    ARICIA: And how can you endure that wicked
        slanders
Should make so pure a life seem black as pitch?
How do you know so little of his heart?
Do you so ill distinguish innocence
From the worst guilt? What mist before your eyes
Can make them blind to such an open virtue?
Ah! 'Tis too much to let false tongues defame him!
Repent! Call back again your fatal prayers.
Oh, be afraid, lest Heaven in its justice

Hate you enough to hear your wish and grant it!
The gods, in anger, often take our victims,—
And oftentimes they punish us with gifts!
    THESEUS: No, it is vain to seek to hide his guilt.
Your love is blind to his depravity.
But I have witnesses beyond reproach,—
Tears I have seen,—true tears, that may be trusted.
    ARICIA: Take heed, my lord. Although your mighty
        hand
Has rid the world of many beasts and monsters,
You have not slain them all,—there's one alive!—
Your son, himself, forbids that I say more,
And since I know how much he still reveres you,
I know that I should cause him much distress
If I should dare to finish. I shall act
Like reverence,—and to be silent,—leave you. [Exit]
    THESEUS: [Alone] What is there in her mind?
        What hidden meaning
Lurks in a speech begun, then broken short?
Would both deceive me with a vain pretense?
Have they conspired to put me to this torture?
And yet, for all that I am most severe,
What plaintive voice is crying in my heart?
I have a secret pity that disturbs me.
Œnone must be questioned, once again,
For I must see this crime in clearer light.
Guards, bid Œnone come to me,—alone.
    [Enter Panope]
    PANOPE: I do not know the purpose of the queen,
Yet, seeing her distress, I fear the worst;—
Despair most fatal, painted on her features,—
Death's pallor is already in her face.
Œnone, shamed and driven from her sight,
Has thrown herself into the ocean's depths.
What moved her to so rash a deed, none knows,
And now the waves forever hide her from us.
    THESEUS: What is it that you say?
    PANOPE: Her sad fate adds
New trouble to the queen's tempestuous soul.
Sometimes, to soothe her secret pain, she clasps
Her children to her, bathes them with her tears,—
Then suddenly forgets her mother's love,
And thrusts them from her with a look of horror.
She wanders back and forth with doubtful steps,
Her eyes look vacantly, and will not know us.
She wrote three times, and thrice she changed her
    mind,
And tore the letter when it scarce was started.
Be willing then to see her, Sire,—to help her. [Exit]
    THESEUS: Œnone dead, and Phædra bent on dying?
Oh, call my son to me again, great Heaven!
Let him defend himself, for I am ready
To hear him, now. Oh, haste not to bestow
Thy fatal bounty, Neptune. Rather my prayers
Should stay unheard forever. Far too soon
I raised too cruel hands, and I believed
Lips that may well have lied! Ah, what may follow?
    [Enter Theramenes]
    THESEUS: 'Tis you, Theramenes? Where is my son?
I gave him to your keeping in his childhood,—

But why should tears be flowing from thine eyes?
How is it with my son—?
  THERAMENES: You worry late.
It is a vain affection. He is dead.
  THESEUS: O gods!
  THERAMENES: Yes, I have seen the very flower
Of all mankind cut down; and I am bold
To say that never man deserved it less.
  THESEUS: My son! My son is dead! When I was
    reaching
My arms to him again, then why should Heaven
Hasten his doom? What sudden blow was this?
  THERAMENES: When we had scarcely passed the
    gates of Trœzen,—
He, silent in his chariot, his guards
Downcast and silent, too, all ranged around him,—
He turned his steeds to the Mycenian road,
And, lost in thought, allowed the reins to lie
Loose on their backs, and his high-mettled chargers,
One time so eager to obey his voice,
Now seemed to know his sadness and to share it.
Then, coming from the sea, a frightful cry
Shatters the troubled air with sudden discord;
And groaning from the bosom of the earth
Answers the crying of that fearful voice.
It froze the blood within our very hearts!
Our horses hear, and stand with bristling manes.
Meanwhile there rises on the watery plain
A mountain wave, mighty, with foaming crest.
It rolls upon the shore, and as it breaks
It throws before our eyes a raging monster.
Its brow is armed with terrifying horns
And all its body clothed with yellow scales.
In front it is a bull, behind, a dragon,
Turning and twisting in impatient fury.
It bellows till the very shores do tremble.
The sky is struck with horror at the sight.
The earth in terror quakes; breath of the beast
Poisons the air. The very wave that brought it
Runs back in fear. All fly, forgetting courage
Which cannot help,—and in a nearby temple
Take refuge,—all but brave Hippolytus.
A hero's worthy son, he stays his horses,
Seizes his darts, and rushing forward, hurls
A missile with sure aim, and wounds the beast
Deep in the flank. It springs, raging with pain,
Right to the horses' feet, and roaring, falls,
Writhes in the dust, shows them his fiery throat,
And covers them with flame and smoke and blood.
Fear lends them wings; deaf to his voice for once,
Heeding no curb, the horses race away.
Their master tires himself in futile efforts.
Each courser's bit is red with blood and foam.
Some say a god, in all this wild disorder,
Is seen, pricking their dusty flanks with goads.
They rush to jagged rocks, urged by this terror.
The axle crashes, and the hardy youth
Sees his car broken, shattered into bits.
He himself falls, entangled in the reins.—
Forgive my grief. That cruel sight will be

For me, the source of never-ending tears.
I saw thy luckless son,—I saw him, Sire,
Dragged by those horses that his hands had fed.
He could not stop their fierce career,—his cries
But added to their terror. All his body
Was soon a mass of wounds. Our anguished cries
Filled the whole plain. At length the horses slackened.
They stopped close by the ancient tombs which mark
The place where lie the ashes of his fathers.
I ran there panting, and behind me came
His guard, along a track fresh-stained with blood,
Reddening all the rocks; locks of his hair
Hung dripping in the briers,—gory triumphs!
I came and called him. Stretching out his hand,
He opened dying eyes, soon to be closed.
"The gods have robbed me of a guiltless life."
I heard him say, "Take care of sad Aricia,
When I am dead. Friend, if my father mourn
When he shall know his son's unhappy fate,—
One accused falsely,—then, to give me peace,
Tell him to treat his captive tenderly,
And to restore—" The hero's breath had failed,
And in my arms there lay a mangled body,—
A thing most piteous, the bleeding spoil
Of Heaven's wrath,—his father could not know him.
  THESEUS: Alas, my son:—my hope, now lost for-
    ever!
The gods are ruthless. They have served me well,
And I am left to live a life of anguish
And of a great remorse.
  THERAMENES: And then Aricia,
Flying from you, came timidly to take him
To be her husband, there, before the gods.
And coming close, she saw the grass, all reeking,
All bloody red, and (sad for a lover's eyes!)
She saw him, lying there, disfigured, pale,—
And for a time she knew not her misfortune.
She did not know the hero she adores.
She looked and asked, "Where is Hippolytus?"
Only too sure, at last, that he was lying
Before her there, with sad eyes, silently
Reproaching Heaven, she groaned, and shuddering
Fell fainting, all but lifeless, at his feet.
Ismene, all in tears, knelt down beside her,
And called her back to life, a life of nothing
But sense of pain. And I to whom the light
Is only darkness, now, come to discharge
The duty he imposed on me: to tell you
His last desire,—a melancholy task.—
But here his mortal enemy is coming.
  [Enter Phædra and Guards]
  THESEUS: Madam, you've triumphed, and my son
    is killed!
Ah, but what room have I for fear! How justly
Suspicion racks me that in blaming him
I erred! But he is dead; accept your victim,
Rightly or wrongly slain. Your heart may leap.
For me, my eyes shall be forever blind.
Since you have said it, I'll believe him guilty.
His death is cause enough for me to weep.

It would be folly, should I seek a light
Which could not bring him back to soothe my grief,
And which might only make me more unhappy.
I will go far from you and from this shore,
For here the vision of my mangled son
Would haunt my memory, and drive me mad.
I wish I might be banished from the world,
For all the world must rise in judgment on me.
Even my glory weights my punishment,
For if I bore a name less known to men,
'Twere easier to hide me. Ah, I mourn
And hate all prayers the gods have granted me.
Nor will I ever go to them again
With useless pleadings. All that they can give
Is far outweighed by what they took from me.
    PHAEDRA: My lord, I cannot hear you and be silent.
I must undo the wrong that he has suffered,—
Your son was innocent.
    THESEUS: Unhappy father!
And I condemned him for a word of yours!
You think I can forgive such cruelty—?
    PHAEDRA: Moments are precious to me; let me
      speak.
'Twas I who cast an eye of lawless passion
On chaste and dutiful Hippolytus.
The gods had lit a baleful fire in me,
And vile Œnone's cunning did the rest.
She feared Hippolytus,—who knew my madness,—
Would tell you of that passion which he hated.
And so she took advantage of my weakness
And hastened, that she might accuse him first.
She has been punished now, but all too lightly.

She sought to flee my anger,—cast herself
Into the waves. The sword had long since cut
My thread of life, but still I heard the cry
Of slandered innocence, and I determined
To die a slower way, and first confess
My penitence to you. There is a poison
Medea brought to Athens,[6] in my veins.
The venom works already in my heart.
A strange and fatal chill is spreading there.
I see already, through a gathering mist,
The husband whom I outrage with my presence.
Death veils the light of Heaven from mine eyes,
And gives it back its purity, defiled.
    PANOPE: She dies, my lord.
    THESEUS: I would the memory
Of her disgraceful deed might perish with her!
Ah! I have learned too late! Come, let us go,
And with the blood of mine unhappy son
Mingle our tears,—embrace his dear remains,
Repenting deeply for a hated prayer.
Let him have honor such as he deserves,
And, to appease his sore-offended spirit,
No matter what her brothers' guilt has been,
From this day forth, Aricia is my daughter.
    [*Exeunt*]

FINIS

[6] The poison with which Medea destroyed Jason's bride
in Corinth. After perpetrating this deed, as well as killing
her own children by Jason, Medea fled to Athens.

William Congreve

When Voltaire visited England, he made a point of paying his respects to William Congreve, then long retired from the stage. Congreve told his admirer that playwriting had been a youthful indiscretion and that he preferred to be considered a gentleman. Voltaire, appalled at such self-disparagement, declared: "If you had been merely a gentleman, I should not have come to see you." Voltaire's point was, of course, well taken. But Congreve would have been a less effective writer of Restoration comedy if he had been less attached to the courtly world. Perhaps he would not have written plays at all if he had not enjoyed the fashionable set and assimilated its sophistication. Congreve came honorably by the title of "Phoebus Apollo of the Mall."

Born in England in 1670 of a family of Cavaliers which had fought for King Charles against the Puritan Roundheads, he was at an early age taken by his father, a military officer, to Ireland. Here he attended the fashionable Kilkenny School, known as the Eton of Irish gentlemen, and Trinity College in Dublin, where Jonathan Swift, his senior by three years, was also a student. Returning to England in 1691, Congreve enrolled as a law student at the Inner Temple, but renounced all thought of the profession a year later, when he wrote a novel of intrigue, *Incognita,* and became the protégé of England's literary arbiter John Dryden, who recognized him as a youth of uncommon promise. Congreve mingled with society and its men of letters, nearly all of whom were devotees of the theatre that the Puritans had padlocked for many years as an ungodly institution and that the middle classes still shunned. It was for this stage, patronized by the select few, that he began to write when, at the age of twenty-one, he composed his first play, *The Old Bachelor.* Corrected and polished by Dryden and the experienced older dramatist Thomas Southerne (1659–1746), the play was performed at Drury Lane in 1693 by the famous Restoration acting couple Betterton and Mrs. Bracegirdle. Graced with these advantages and possessing dialogue of superior quality, *The Old Bachelor* was singularly successful and established its young author's reputation about town.

In November of the same year, Congreve had a second and superior play, *The Double Dealer,* on the boards of the Drury Lane. Although it did not fare as well as his maiden effort, it won unstinted praise from Dryden in a commendatory poem to the published work:

Heaven that but once was prodigal before,
To Shakespeare gave as much; she could not give
him more.

With so much encouragement from the dictator of taste, Congreve could not fail to exert his best efforts, and the result was his liveliest comedy, *Love for Love.* Betterton produced it with such success at his newly built New Theatre that he made a contract with the author whereby the latter was to supply him with a play every year. Congreve failed to do this, but he did give Betterton two pieces: a somber tragedy, *The Mourning Dove,* better remembered for Samuel Johnson's high praise of one of its passages than for its merit as drama, and a second comic masterpiece, *The Way of the World.*

By 1700, when *The Way of the World* was written, Restoration comedy had already been soundly trounced by the Anglican churchman Jeremy Collier in his pamphlet, *A Short View of the Immorality and Profaneness of the English Stage* (1698), and Congreve had come out second-best in a rejoinder, *Amendments on Mr. Collier's False and Imperfect Citations.* The new play, actually less subject to criticism on moral grounds than his earlier comedies, failed to win popularity, and its discouraged author gave up writing for the stage. He spent the last twenty-nine years of his life as a "gentleman," living on the bounty of government sinecures as commissioner for licensing hackney coaches, commissioner of wine licenses, and secretary to the island of Jamaica. He enjoyed the friendship of Henrietta, the daughter of the great Duke of Marlborough, and of such men of prominence as Swift, Addison, Steele, and Arbuthnot. He was singled out for very special distinction when Alexander Pope dedicated to him his enormously popular translation of the *Iliad.* To the younger generation, indeed, Congreve was himself a classic. When he died, in 1729, he was accorded burial in Westminster Abbey.

The failure of the initial production of *The Way of the World* is explainable on grounds other than a change in taste ushered in by Jeremy Collier's tract. The plot is complicated, and it requires perhaps more attentiveness from the spectator or the reader than it deserves. Nevertheless, the masterful artistry of the work won increasing appreciation. Though less consistently sprightly than *Love for Love,* it is considered Congreve's best play. It contains the most brilliant comic dialogue written before the advent of Wilde and Shaw. And in Congreve's parade of clever caricatures appear two of the best-drawn characters of English high comedy, Mirabell and Millamant. George Meredith could rightly call the former "the sprightliest male figure in English comedy" and he might with equal justice have considered the vivacious Millamant a worthy descendant of the Beatrice of *Much Ado About Nothing*.

Love and intrigue are the substance of the play in a context of fashionable Restoration society. That the love of Mirabell and Millamant never degenerates into sentimentality and wears a defense of banter and wit is the measure of Congreve's adult view of men and women. There is delight in the very fact that the lovers know the "way of the world" and are at home in it. There is even a touch of Ibsenite or Shavian modernism in their insistence upon a marriage of equals grounded in mutual respect and independence. It is probably for this reason, as well as because of the sophistication and frankness of Congreve's writing, that *The Way of the World* had no particular vogue until the twentieth century.

Referring to Restoration comedy as a whole, Charles Lamb wrote that he could "never connect those sports of a witty fancy in any shape with any result to be drawn from them to imitation in real life. They are a world of themselves, almost as much as fairy land." What validity there is to this statement—and it applies in some measure to Congreve's carefree urbanity in general and to his boldest caricatures—is contradicted by such characters as Millamant and Mirabell. If Lamb, living when he did, could not connect *them* in any way with "real life," it is because he evidently knew too little about Restoration and could know nothing about twentieth-century "society." Lamb's gentle disposition would not have allowed him to recognize an accord with real men and women even if he had found it in his day. Even that late-Victorian critic William Archer, who translated and defended Ibsen, could only grumble that "Congreve regards life from a standpoint of complete ethical indifference."

Congreve's comedies are always cited as supreme examples of "artificial comedy." We may wonder whether the term does not conceal as much as it reveals—especially in the case of *The Way of the World*. More reality pertains to the lovers, the country squire Sir Wilfull Witwoud, and other characters than is generally conceded by those who are merely dazzled by the author's surface of wit, plot intrigue, and levity. It does not necessarily follow, besides, that an author conveys no grasp of reality because he employs an unrealistic play technique or a heightened style. And, at least to modern taste, Congreve's habit of preferring a good discussion now and then to inconsequential plot is actually a relief from artifice. The theatre had, and continued to have, a superfluity of plots like Congreve's. It had, and continued to have, too few conversations and discussions like his.

THE WAY OF THE WORLD

By William Congreve

DRAMATIS PERSONAE

FAINALL, *in love with Mrs. Marwood*
MIRABELL, *in love with Mrs. Millamant*
WITWOUD ⎱ *followers of Mrs. Millamant*
PETULANT ⎰
SIR WILFULL WITWOUD, *half-brother to Witwoud, and nephew to Lady Wishfort*
WAITWELL, *servant to Mirabell*
LADY WISHFORT, *enemy to Mirabell, for having falsely pretended love to her*
MRS. MILLAMANT, *a fine Lady, niece to Lady Wish-*

fort, and loves Mirabell
MRS. MARWOOD, *friend to Mr. Fainall, and likes Mirabell*
MRS. FAINALL, *daughter to Lady Wishfort, and wife to Fainall, formerly friend to Mirabell*
FOIBLE, *woman to Lady Wishfort*
MINCING, *woman to Mrs. Millamant*
BETTY, *waiting-maid at a chocolate-house*
PEG, *maid to Lady Wishfort*
COACHMEN, DANCERS, FOOTMEN, AND ATTENDANTS

SCENE: *London*

The time equal to that of the representation

ACT I. SCENE I.

A chocolate-house.

[Mirabell *and* Fainall *rising from cards.* Betty *waiting*]

MIRABELL: You are a fortunate man, Mr. Fainall!

FAINALL: Have we done?

MIRABELL: What you please: I'll play on to entertain you.

FAINALL: No, I'll give you your revenge another time, when you are not so indifferent; you are thinking of something else now, and play too negligently; the coldness of a losing gamester lessens the pleasure of the winner. I'd no more play with a man that slighted his ill fortune than I'd make love to a woman who undervalued the loss of her reputation.

MIRABELL: You have a taste extremely delicate, and are for refining on your pleasures.

FAINALL: Prithee, why so reserved? Something has put you out of humor.

MIRABELL: Not at all: I happen to be grave to-day, and you are gay; that's all.

FAINALL: Confess, Millamant and you quarreled last night after I left you; my fair cousin has some humors that would tempt the patience of a Stoic. What, some coxcomb came in, and was well received by her, while you were by?

MIRABELL: Witwoud and Petulant; and what was worse, her aunt, your wife's mother, my evil genius; or to sum up all in her own name, my old Lady Wishfort came in.

FAINALL: Oh, there it is then! She has a lasting passion for you, and with reason.—What, then my wife was there?

MIRABELL: Yes, and Mrs. Marwood, and three or four more, whom I never saw before. Seeing me, they all put on their grave faces, whispered one another; then complained aloud of the vapors, and after fell into a profound silence.

FAINALL: They had a mind to be rid of you.

MIRABELL: For which reason I resolved not to stir. At last the good old lady broke through her painful taciturnity with an invective against long visits. I would not have understood her, but Millamant joining in the argument, I rose, and, with a constrained smile, told her I thought nothing was so easy as to know when a visit began to be troublesome. She reddened, and I withdrew, without expecting her reply.

FAINALL: You were to blame to resent what she spoke only in compliance with her aunt.

MIRABELL: She is more mistress of herself than to be under the necessity of such a resignation.

FAINALL: What! though half her fortune depends upon her marrying with my lady's approbation?

MIRABELL: I was then in such a humor, that I should have been better pleased if she had been less discreet.

FAINALL: Now, I remember, I wonder not they were weary of you; last night was one of their cabal nights; they have 'em three times a-week, and meet by turns at one another's apartments, where they come together like the coroner's inquest, to sit upon the murdered reputations of the week. You and I are excluded; and it was once proposed that all the male sex should be excepted; but somebody moved that, to avoid scandal, there might be one man of the community; upon which motion Witwoud and Petulant were enrolled members.

MIRABELL: And who may have been the foundress of this sect? My Lady Wishfort, I warrant, who publishes her detestation of mankind; and full of the vigor of fifty-five, declares for a friend and ratafia;[1] and let posterity shift for itself, she'll breed no more.

FAINALL: The discovery of your sham addresses to her, to conceal your love to her niece, has provoked this separation; had you dissembled better, things might have continued in the state of nature.

MIRABELL: I did as much as man could, with any reasonable conscience; I proceeded to the very last act of flattery with her, and was guilty of a song in her commendation. Nay, I got a friend to put her into a lampoon and compliment her with the imputation of an affair with a young fellow, which I carried so far, that I told her the malicious town took notice that she was grown fat of a sudden; and when she lay in of a dropsy, persuaded her she was reported to be in labor. The devil's in't, if an old woman is to be flattered further, unless a man should endeavor downright personally to debauch her; and that my virtue forbade me. But for the discovery of this amour I am indebted to your friend, or your wife's friend, Mrs. Marwood.

FAINALL: What should provoke her to be your enemy, unless she has made you advances which you have slighted? Women do not easily forgive omissions of that nature.

MIRABELL: She was always civil to me till of late.— I confess I am not one of those coxcombs who are apt to interpret a woman's good manners to her prejudice, and think that she who does not refuse 'em everything, can refuse 'em nothing.

FAINALL: You are a gallant man, Mirabell; and though you may have cruelty enough not to satisfy a lady's longing, you have too much generosity not to be tender of her honor. Yet you speak with an indifference which seems to be affected, and confesses you are conscious of a negligence.

MIRABELL: You pursue the argument with a distrust that seems to be unaffected, and confesses you are conscious of a concern for which the lady is more indebted to you than is your wife.

FAINALL: Fie, fie, friend! if you grow censorious I must leave you.—I'll look upon the gamesters in the next room.

MIRABELL: Who are they?

FAINALL: Petulant and Witwoud.—[To Betty] Bring me some chocolate. [Exit]

MIRABELL: Betty, what says your clock?

BETTY: Turned of the last canonical hour, sir. [Exit]

MIRABELL: How pertinently the jade answers me!—[Looking on his watch]—Ha! almost one o'clock!—Oh, y'are come!

[Enter Footman]

Well, is the grand affair over? You have been something tedious.

1 A liqueur flavored with fruits.

FOOTMAN: Sir, there's such coupling at Pancras[2] that they stand behind one another, as 'twere in a country dance. Ours was the last couple to lead up; and no hopes appearing of dispatch; besides, the parson growing hoarse, we were afraid his lungs would have failed before it came to our turn; so we drove round to Duke's-place,[3] and there they were rivetted in a trice.

MIRABELL: So, so, you are sure they are married.

FOOTMAN: Married and bedded, sir; I am witness.

MIRABELL: Have you the certificate?

FOOTMAN: Here it is, sir.

MIRABELL: Has the tailor brought Waitwell's clothes home, and the new liveries?

FOOTMAN: Yes, sir.

MIRABELL: That's well. Do you go home again, d'ye hear, and adjourn the consummation till further orders. Bid Waitwell shake his ears, and Dame Partlet rustle up her feathers, and meet me at one o'clock by Rosamond's Pond, that I may see her before she returns to her lady; and as you tender your ears be secret. [Exit]

SCENE II.

The same.

[Mirabell, Fainall, *and* Betty]

FAINALL: Joy of your success, Mirabell; you look pleased.

MIRABELL: Aye; I have been engaged in a matter of some sort of mirth, which is not yet ripe for discovery. I am glad this is not a cabal night. I wonder, Fainall, that you who are married, and of consequence should be discreet, will suffer your wife to be of such a party.

FAINALL: Faith, I am not jealous. Besides, most who are engaged are women and relations; and for the men, they are of a kind too contemptible to give scandal.

MIRABELL: I am of another opinion. The greater the coxcomb, always the more the scandal: for a woman who is not a fool can have but one reason for associating with a man who is one.

FAINALL: Are you jealous as often as you see Witwoud entertained by Millamant?

MIRABELL: Of her understanding I am, if not of her person.

FAINALL: You do her wrong; for, to give her her due, she has wit.

MIRABELL: She has beauty enough to make any man think so; and complaisance enough not to contradict him who shall tell her so.

FAINALL: For a passionate lover, methinks you are a man somewhat too discerning in the failings of your mistress.

2 The Church of St. Pancras.

3 One of several places where irregular marriages were made.

MIRABELL: And for a discerning man, somewhat too passionate a lover; for I like her with all her faults; nay, like her for her faults. Her follies are so natural, or so artful, that they become her; and those affectations which in another woman would be odious, serve but to make her more agreeable. I'll tell thee, Fainall, she once used me with that insolence, that in revenge I took her to pieces; sifted her, and separated her failings; I studied 'em, and got 'em by rote. The catalogue was so large, that I was not without hopes one day or other to hate her heartily: to which end I so used myself to think of 'em, that at length, contrary to my design and expectation, they gave me every hour less and less disturbance; till in a few days it became habitual to me to remember 'em without being displeased. They are now grown as familiar to me as my own frailties; and in all probability, in a little time longer, I shall like 'em as well.

FAINALL: Marry her, marry her! Be half as well acquainted with her charms, as you are with her defects, and my life on't, you are your own man again.

MIRABELL: Say you so?

FAINALL: Aye, aye, I have experience: I have a wife, and so forth.

[Enter Messenger]

MESSENGER: Is one squire Witwoud here?

BETTY: Yes, what's your business?

MESSENGER: I have a letter for him, from his brother Sir Wilfull, which I am charged to deliver into his own hands.

BETTY: He's in the next room, friend—that way.

[Exit Messenger]

MIRABELL: What, is the chief of that noble family in town, Sir Wilfull Witwoud?

FAINALL: He is expected to-day. Do you know him?

MIRABELL: I have seen him. He promises to be an extraordinary person; I think you have the honor to be related to him.

FAINALL: Yes; he is half-brother to this Witwoud by a former wife, who was sister to my Lady Wishfort, my wife's mother. If you marry Millamant, you must call cousins too.

MIRABELL: I had rather be his relation than his acquaintance.

FAINALL: He comes to town in order to equip himself for travel.

MIRABELL: For travel! Why, the man that I mean is above forty.

FAINALL: No matter for that; 'tis for the honor of England, that all Europe should know we have blockheads of all ages.

MIRABELL: I wonder there is not an act of parliament to save the credit of the nation, and prohibit the exportation of fools.

FAINALL: By no means; 'tis better as 'tis. 'Tis better to trade with a little loss, than to be quite eaten up with being overstocked.

MIRABELL: Pray, are the follies of this knight-errant, and those of the squire his brother, anything related?

FAINALL: Not at all; Witwoud grows by the knight, like a medlar grafted on a crab. One will melt in your mouth, and t'other set your teeth on edge; one is all pulp, and the other all core.

MIRABELL: So one will be rotten before he be ripe, and the other will be rotten without ever being ripe at all.

FAINALL: Sir Wilfull is an odd mixture of bashfulness and obstinacy.—But when he's drunk he's as loving as the monster in *The Tempest,* and much after the same manner. To give t'other his due, he has something of good nature, and does not always want wit.

MIRABELL: Not always: but as often as his memory fails him, and his commonplace of comparisons. He is a fool with a good memory, and some few scraps of other folks' wit. He is one whose conversation can never be approved, yet it is now and then to be endured. He has indeed one good quality, he is not exceptious; for he so passionately affects the reputation of understanding raillery, that he will construe an affront into a jest; and call downright rudeness and ill language satire and fire.

FAINALL: If you have a mind to finish his picture, you have an opportunity to do it at full length. Behold the original!

[Enter Witwoud]

WITWOUD: Afford me your compassion, my dears! Pity me, Fainall! Mirabell, pity me!

MIRABELL: I do, from my soul.

FAINALL: Why, what's the matter?

WITWOUD: No letters for me, Betty?

BETTY: Did not a messenger bring you one but now, sir?

WITWOUD: Aye, but no other?

BETTY: No, sir.

WITWOUD: That's hard, that's very hard.—A messenger! a mule, a beast of burden! he has brought me a letter from the fool my brother, as heavy as a panegyric in a funeral sermon, or a copy of commendatory verses from one poet to another: and what's worse, 'tis as sure a forerunner of the author, as an epistle dedicatory.

MIRABELL: A fool, and your brother, Witwoud!

WITWOUD: Aye, aye, my half-brother. My half-brother he is; no nearer, upon honor.

MIRABELL: Then 'tis possible he may be but half a fool.

WITWOUD: Good, good, Mirabell, *le drôle!* Good, good; hang him, don't let's talk of him.—Fainall, how does your lady? Gad, I say anything in the world to get this fellow out of my head. I beg pardon that I should ask a man of pleasure, and the town, a question at once so foreign and domestic. But I talk like an old maid at a marriage; I don't know what I say: but she's the best woman in the world.

FAINALL: 'Tis well you don't know what you say,

or else your commendation would go near to make me either vain or jealous.

WITWOUD: No man in town lives well with a wife but Fainall.—Your judgment, Mirabell.

MIRABELL: You had better step and ask his wife, if you would be credibly informed.

WITWOUD: Mirabell?

MIRABELL: Aye.

WITWOUD: My dear, I ask ten thousand pardons—gad, I have forgot what I was going to say to you!

MIRABELL: I thank you heartily, heartily.

WITWOUD: No, but prithee excuse me: my memory is such a memory.

MIRABELL: Have a care of such apologies, Witwoud; for I never knew a fool but he affected to complain, either of the spleen or his memory.

FAINALL: What have you done with Petulant?

WITWOUD: He's reckoning his money—my money it was.—I have no luck to-day.

FAINALL: You may allow him to win of you at play: for you are sure to be too hard for him at repartee; since you monopolize the wit that is between you, the fortune must be his of course.

MIRABELL: I don't find that Petulant confesses the superiority of wit to be your talent, Witwoud.

WITWOUD: Come, come, you are malicious now, and would breed debates.—Petulant's my friend, and a very honest fellow, and a very pretty fellow, and has a smattering—faith and troth, a pretty deal of an odd sort of a small wit: nay, I'll do him justice. I'm his friend, I won't wrong him neither.—And if he had any judgment in the world, he would not be altogether contemptible. Come, come, don't detract from the merits of my friend.

FAINALL: You don't take your friend to be over-nicely bred?

WITWOUD: No, no, hang him, the rogue has no manners at all, that I must own: no more breeding than a bum-bailiff, that I grant you—'tis pity, faith; the fellow has fire and life.

MIRABELL: What, courage?

WITWOUD: Hum, faith I don't know as to that, I can't say as to that. Yes, faith, in a controversy, he'll contradict anybody.

MIRABELL: Though 'twere a man whom he feared, or a woman whom he loved.

WITWOUD: Well, well, he does not always think before he speaks—we have all our failings: you are too hard upon him, you are, faith. Let me excuse him—I can defend most of his faults, except one or two: one he has, that's the truth on't; if he were my brother, I could not acquit him—that, indeed, I could wish were otherwise.

MIRABELL: Aye, marry, what's that, Witwoud?

WITWOUD: O pardon me!—Expose the infirmities of my friend!—No, my dear, excuse me there.

FAINALL: What, I warrant he's unsincere, or 'tis some such trifle.

WITWOUD: No, no; what if he be? 'tis no matter for that, his wit will excuse that: a wit should no

more be sincere, than a woman constant; one argues a decay of parts, as t'other of beauty.

MIRABELL: Maybe you think him too positive?

WITWOUD: No, no, his being positive is an incentive to argument, and keeps up conversation.

FAINALL: Too illiterate?

WITWOUD: That! that's his happiness: his want of learning gives him the more opportunities to show his natural parts.

MIRABELL: He wants words?

WITWOUD: Aye: but I like him for that now; for his want of words gives me the pleasure very often to explain his meaning.

FAINALL: He's impudent?

WITWOUD: No, that's not it.

MIRABELL: Vain?

WITWOUD: No.

MIRABELL: What! He speaks unseasonable truths sometimes, because he has not wit enough to invent an evasion?

WITWOUD: Truths! ha! ha! ha! No, no; since you will have it—I mean, he never speaks truth at all—that's all. He will lie like a chambermaid, or a woman of quality's porter. Now that is a fault.

[Enter Coachman]

COACHMAN: Is Master Petulant here, mistress?

BETTY: Yes.

COACHMAN: Three gentlewomen in a coach would speak with him.

FAINALL: O brave Petulant! three!

BETTY: I'll tell him.

COACHMAN: You must bring two dishes of chocolate and a glass of cinnamon-water.

[Exeunt Betty and Coachman]

WITWOUD: That should be for two fasting strumpets, and a bawd troubled with the wind. Now you may know what the three are.

MIRABELL: You are very free with your friend's acquaintance.

WITWOUD: Aye, aye, friendship without freedom is as dull as love without enjoyment, or wine without toasting. But to tell you a secret, these are trulls whom he allows coach-hire, and something more, by the week, to call on him once a day at public places.

MIRABELL: How!

WITWOUD: You shall see he won't go to 'em, because there's no more company here to take notice of him.—Why, this is nothing to what he used to do: before he found out this way, I have known him call for himself.

FAINALL: Call for himself! What dost thou mean?

WITWOUD: Mean! Why, he would slip you out of this chocolate-house, just when you had been talking to him—as soon as your back was turned—whip he was gone!—then trip to his lodging, clap on a hood and scarf, and a mask, slap into a hackney-coach, and drive hither to the door again in a trice, where he would send in for himself; that I mean, call for himself, wait for himself; nay, and what more, not finding himself, sometimes leave a letter for himself.

MIRABELL: I confess this is something extraordinary.—I believe he waits for himself now, he is so long a-coming: Oh! I ask his pardon.

[Enter Petulant and Betty]

BETTY: Sir, the coach stays.

PETULANT: Well, well; I come.—'Sbud, a man had as good be a professed midwife as a professed whoremaster, at this rate! To be knocked up and raised at all hours, and in all places! Pox on 'em, I won't come!—D'ye hear, tell 'em I won't come—let 'em snivel and cry their hearts out.

FAINALL: You are very cruel, Petulant.

PETULANT: All's one, let it pass: I have a humor to be cruel.

MIRABELL: I hope they are not persons of condition that you use at this rate.

PETULANT: Condition! condition's a dried fig, if I am not in humor!—By this hand, if they were your —a—a—your what d'ye-call-'ems themselves, they must wait or rub off, if I want appetite.

MIRABELL: What d'ye-call-'ems! What are they, Witwoud?

WITWOUD: Empresses, my dear: by your what-d'ye-call-'ems he means sultana queens.

PETULANT: Aye, Roxolanas.

MIRABELL: Cry you mercy!

FAINALL: Witwoud says they are—

PETULANT: What does he say th' are?

WITWOUD: I? Fine ladies, I say.

PETULANT: Pass on, Witwoud.—Hark'ee, by this light, his relations: two coheiresses his cousins, and an old aunt, who loves caterwauling better than a conventicle.

WITWOUD: Ha! ha! ha! I had a mind to see how the rogue would come off.—Ha! ha! ha! Gad, I can't be angry with him, if he had said they were my mother and my sisters.

MIRABELL: No!

WITWOUD: No; the rogue's wit and readiness of invention charm me. Dear Petulant!

BETTY: They are gone, sir, in great anger.

PETULANT: Enough, let 'em trundle. Anger helps complexion, saves paint.

FAINALL: This continence is all dissembled; this is in order to have something to brag of the next time he makes court to Millamant, and swears he has abandoned the whole sex for her sake.

MIRABELL: Have you not left off your impudent pretensions there yet? I shall cut your throat some time or other, Petulant, about that business.

PETULANT: Aye, aye, let that pass—there are other throats to be cut.

MIRABELL: Meaning mine, sir?

PETULANT: Not I—I mean nobody—I know nothing: but there are uncles and nephews in the world —and they may be rivals. What, then! All's one for that.

MIRABELL: How! hark'ee, Petulant, come hither—explain, or I shall call your interpreter.

PETULANT: Explain! I know nothing. Why, you have an uncle, have you not, lately come to town, and lodges by my Lady Wishfort's?

MIRABELL: True.

PETULANT: Why, that's enough—you and he are not friends; and if he should marry and have a child you may be disinherited, ha?

MIRABELL: Where hast thou stumbled upon all this truth?

PETULANT: All's one for that; why, then, say I know something.

MIRABELL: Come, thou art an honest fellow, Petulant, and shalt make love to my mistress, thou sha't, faith. What hast thou heard of my uncle?

PETULANT: I? Nothing, I. If throats are to be cut, let swords clash! snug's the word, I shrug and am silent.

MIRABELL: Oh, raillery, raillery! Come, I know thou art in the women's secrets.—What, you're a cabalist; I know you stayed at Millamant's last night, after I went. Was there any mention made of my uncle or me? Tell me. If thou hadst but good nature equal to thy wit, Petulant, Tony Witwoud, who is now thy competitor in fame, would show as dim by thee as a dead whiting's eye by a pearl of orient; he would no more be seen by thee, than Mercury is by the sun. Come, I'm sure thou wo't tell me.

PETULANT: If I do, will you grant me common sense then for the future?

MIRABELL: Faith, I'll do what I can for thee, and I'll pray that Heaven may grant it thee in the meantime.

PETULANT: Well, hark'ee.

[Mirabell and Petulant talk apart]

FAINALL: Petulant and you both will find Mirabell as warm a rival as a lover.

WITWOUD: Pshaw! pshaw! that she laughs at Petulant is plain. And for my part, but that it is almost a fashion to admire her, I should—hark'ee—to tell you a secret, but let it go no further—between friends, I shall never break my heart for her.

FAINALL: How!

WITWOUD: She's handsome; but she's a sort of an uncertain woman.

FAINALL: I thought you had died for her.

WITWOUD: Umh—no—

FAINALL: She has wit.

WITWOUD: 'Tis what she will hardly allow anybody else: now, demme, I should hate that, if she were as handsome as Cleopatra. Mirabell is not so sure of her as he thinks for.

FAINALL: Why do you think so?

WITWOUD: We stayed pretty late there last night, and heard something of an uncle to Mirabell, who is lately come to town—and is between him and the best part of his estate. Mirabell and he are at some distance, as my Lady Wishfort has been told; and you know she hates Mirabell worse than a quaker hates a parrot, or than a fishmonger hates a hard frost.[4] Whether this uncle has seen Mrs. Millamant or not, I cannot say, but there were items of such a treaty being in embryo; and if it should come to life, poor Mirabell would be in some sort unfortunately fobbed, i'faith.

FAINALL: 'Tis impossible Millamant should hearken to it.

WITWOUD: Faith, my dear, I can't tell; she's a woman, and a kind of humorist.

MIRABELL: And this is the sum of what you could collect last night?

PETULANT: The quintessence. Maybe Witwoud knows more, he staid longer. Besides, they never mind him; they say anything before him.

MIRABELL: I thought you had been the greatest favorite.

PETULANT: Aye, tête-à-tête, but not in public, because I make remarks.

MIRABELLE: You do?

PETULANT: Aye, aye; pox, I'm malicious, man! Now he's soft you know; they are not in awe of him—the fellow's well-bred; he's what you call a what-d'ye-call-'em, a fine gentleman; but he's silly withal.

MIRABELL: I thank you, I know as much as my curiosity requires.—Fainall, are you for the Mall?[5]

FAINALL: Aye, I'll take a turn before dinner.

WITWOUD: Aye, we'll all walk in the Park; the ladies talked of being there.

MIRABELL: I thought you were obliged to watch for your brother Sir Wilfull's arrival.

WITWOUD: No, no; he comes to his aunt's, my Lady Wishfort. Pox on him! I shall be troubled with him, too; what shall I do with the fool?

PETULANT: Beg him for his estate, that I may beg you afterwards: and so have but one trouble with you both.

WITWOUD: Oh, rare Petulant! Thou art as quick as fire in a frosty morning: thou shalt to the Mall with us, and we'll be very severe.

PETULANT: Enough, I'm in a humor to be severe.

MIRABELL: Are you? Pray, then, walk by yourselves: let not us be accessory to your putting the ladies out of countenance with your senseless ribaldry, which you roar out aloud as often as they pass by you; and when you have made a handsome woman blush, then you think you have been severe.

PETULANT: What, what! Then let 'em either show their innocence by not understanding what they hear, or else show their discretion by not hearing what they would not be thought to understand.

MIRABELL: But hast not thou then sense enough to know that thou oughtest to be most ashamed thy-self, when thou hast put another out of countenance?

PETULANT: Not I, by this hand!—I always take blushing either for a sign of guilt, or ill breeding.

MIRABELL: I confess you ought to think so. You are in the right, that you may plead the error of your judgment in defence of your practice.

Where modesty's ill manners, 'tis but fit
That impudence and malice pass for wit.

[*Exeunt*]

ACT II. SCENE I.

St. James's Park.

[Mrs. Fainall *and* Mrs. Marwood]

MRS. FAINALL: Aye, aye, dear Marwood, if we will be happy, we must find the means in ourselves, and among ourselves. Men are ever in extremes; either doting or averse. While they are lovers, if they have fire and sense, their jealousies are insupportable; and when they cease to love (we ought to think at least) they loathe; they look upon us with horror and distaste; they meet us like the ghosts of what we were, and as such, fly from us.

MRS. MARWOOD: True, 'tis an unhappy circumstance of life, that love should ever die before us; and that the man so often should outlive the lover. But say what you will, 'tis better to be left than never to have been loved. To pass our youth in dull indifference, to refuse the sweets of life because they once must leave us, is as preposterous as to wish to have been born old, because we one day must be old. For my part, my youth may wear and waste, but it shall never rust in my possession.

MRS. FAINALL: Then it seems you dissemble an aversion to mankind, only in compliance to my mother's humor?

MRS. MARWOOD: Certainly. To be free; I have no taste of those insipid dry discourses, with which our sex of force must entertain themselves, apart from men. We may affect endearments to each other, profess eternal friendships, and seem to dote like lovers; but 'tis not in our natures long to persevere. Love will resume his empire in our breasts; and every heart, or soon or late, receive and readmit him as its lawful tyrant.

MRS. FAINALL: Bless me, how have I been deceived! Why, you profess a libertine.

MRS. MARWOOD: You see my friendship by my freedom. Come, be as sincere, acknowledge that your sentiments agree with mine.

MRS. FAINALL: Never!

MRS. MARWOOD: You hate mankind?

MRS. FAINALL: Heartily, inveterately.

MRS. MARWOOD: Your husband?

MRS. FAINALL: Most transcendently; aye, though I say it, meritoriously.

---

[4] A parrot talks a great deal and Quakers believe in silent meditation at their services; cold weather makes a fishmonger's business difficult.

[5] The promenade in St. James's Park, London.

MRS. MARWOOD: Give me your hand upon it.

MRS. FAINALL: There.

MRS. MARWOOD: I join with you; what I have said has been to try you.

MRS. FAINALL: Is it possible? Dost thou hate those vipers, men?

MRS. MARWOOD: I have done hating 'em, and am now come to despise 'em; the next thing I have to do, is eternally to forget 'em.

MRS. FAINALL: There spoke the spirit of an Amazon, a Penthesilea![6]

MRS. MARWOOD: And yet I am thinking sometimes to carry my aversion further.

MRS. FAINALL: How?

MRS. MARWOOD: Faith, by marrying; if I could but find one that loved me very well, and would be thoroughly sensible of ill usage, I think I should do myself the violence of undergoing the ceremony.

MRS. FAINALL: You would not make him a cuckold?

MRS. MARWOOD: No; but I'd make him believe I did, and that's as bad.

MRS. FAINALL: Why, had not you as good do it?

MRS. MARWOOD: Oh! if he should ever discover it, he would then know the worst, and be out of his pain; but I would have him ever to continue upon the rack of fear and jealousy.

MRS. FAINALL: Ingenious mischief! would thou wert married to Mirabell.

MRS. MARWOOD: Would I were!

MRS. FAINALL: You change color.

MRS. MARWOOD: Because I hate him.

MRS. FAINALL: So do I; but I can hear him named. But what reason have you to hate him in particular?

MRS. MARWOOD: I never loved him; he is, and always was, insufferably proud.

MRS. FAINALL: By the reason you give for your aversion, one would think it dissembled; for you have laid a fault to his charge, of which his enemies must acquit him.

MRS. MARWOOD: Oh, then it seems you are one of his favorable enemies! Methinks you look a little pale, and now you flush again.

MRS. FAINALL: Do I! I think I am a little sick o' the sudden.

MRS. MARWOOD: What ails you?

MRS. FAINALL: My husband. Don't you see him? He turned short upon me unawares, and has almost overcome me.

[Enter Fainall and Mirabell]

MRS. MARWOOD: Ha! ha! ha! He comes opportunely for you.

MRS. FAINALL: For you, for he has brought Mirabell with him.

FAINALL: My dear!

MRS. FAINALL: My soul!

FAINALL: You don't look well to-day, child.

MRS. FAINALL: D'ye think so?

[6] The queen of the Amazons who fought against the Greeks as a Trojan ally.

MIRABELL: He is the only man that does, madam.

MRS. FAINALL: The only man that would tell me so at least; and the only man from whom I could hear it without mortification.

FAINALL: Oh, my dear, I am satisfied of your tenderness; I know you cannot resent anything from me; especially what is an effect of my concern.

MRS. FAINALL: Mr. Mirabell, my mother interrupted you in a pleasant relation last night; I would fain hear it out.

MIRABELL: The persons concerned in that affair have yet a tolerable reputation.—I am afraid Mr. Fainall will be censorious.

MRS. FAINALL: He has a humor more prevailing than his curiosity, and will willingly dispense with the hearing of one scandalous story, to avoid giving an occasion to make another by being seen to walk with his wife. This way, Mr. Mirabell, and I dare promise you will oblige us both.

[Exeunt Mrs. Fainall and Mirabell]

FAINALL: Excellent creature! Well, sure if I should live to be rid of my wife, I should be a miserable man.

MRS. MARWOOD: Aye!

FAINALL: For having only that one hope, the accomplishment of it, of consequence, must put an end to all my hopes; and what a wretch is he who must survive his hopes! Nothing remains when that day comes, but to sit down and weep like Alexander, when he wanted other worlds to conquer.

MRS. MARWOOD: Will you not follow 'em?

FAINALL: Faith, I think not.

MRS. MARWOOD: Pray let us; I have a reason.

FAINALL: You are not jealous?

MRS. MARWOOD: Of whom?

FAINALL: Of Mirabell.

MRS. MARWOOD: If I am, is it inconsistent with my love to you that I am tender of your honor?

FAINALL: You would intimate, then, as if there were a fellow-feeling between my wife and him.

MRS. MARWOOD: I think she does not hate him to that degree she would be thought.

FAINALL: But he, I fear, is too insensible.

MRS. MARWOOD: It may be you are deceived.

FAINALL: It may be so. I do now begin to apprehend it.

MRS. MARWOOD: What?

FAINALL: That I have been deceived, madam, and you are false.

MRS. MARWOOD: That I am false! What mean you?

FAINALL: To let you know I see through all your little arts.—Come, you both love him; and both have equally dissembled your aversion. Your mutual jealousies of one another have made you clash till you have both struck fire. I have seen the warm confession reddening on your cheeks, and sparkling from your eyes.

MRS. MARWOOD: You do me wrong.

FAINALL: I do not. 'Twas for my ease to oversee and wilfully neglect the gross advances made him by my wife; that by permitting her to be engaged, I might continue unsuspected in my pleasures; and take you oftener to my arms in full security. But could you think, because the nodding husband would not wake, that e'er the watchful lover slept?

MRS. MARWOOD: And wherewithal can you reproach me?

FAINALL: With infidelity, with loving another, with love of Mirabell.

MRS. MARWOOD: 'Tis false! I challenge you to show an instance than can confirm your groundless accusation. I hate him.

FAINALL: And wherefore do you hate him? He is insensible, and your resentment follows his neglect. An instance! the injuries you have done him are a proof: your interposing in his love. What cause had you to make discoveries of his pretended passion? To undeceive the credulous aunt, and be the officious obstacle of his match with Millamant?

MRS. MARWOOD: My obligations to my lady urged me; I had professed a friendship to her; and could not see her easy nature so abused by that dissembler.

FAINALL: What, was it conscience, then? Professed a friendship! Oh, the pious friendships of the female sex!

MRS. MARWOOD: More tender, more sincere, and more enduring than all the vain and empty vows of men, whether professing love to us or mutual faith to one another.

FAINALL: Ha! ha! ha! You are my wife's friend, too.

MRS. MARWOOD: Shame and ingratitude! Do you reproach me? You, you upbraid me? Have I been false to her, through strict fidelity to you, and sacrificed my friendship to keep my love inviolate? And have you the baseness to charge me with the guilt, unmindful of the merit? To you it should be meritorious, that I have been vicious: and do you reflect that guilt upon me, which should lie buried in your bosom?

FAINALL: You misinterpret my reproof. I meant but to remind you of the slight account you once could make of strictest ties, when set in competition with your love to me.

MRS. MARWOOD: 'Tis false, you urged it with deliberate malice! 'Twas spoken in scorn, and I never will forgive it.

FAINALL: Your guilt, not your resentment, begets your rage. If yet you loved, you could forgive a jealousy: but you are stung to find you are discovered.

MRS. MARWOOD: It shall be all discovered. You too shall be discovered; be sure you shall. I can but be exposed.—If I do it myself I shall prevent your baseness.

FAINALL: Why, what will you do?

MRS. MARWOOD: Disclose it to your wife; own what has passed between us.

FAINALL: Frenzy!

MRS. MARWOOD: By all my wrongs I'll do't!—I'll publish to the world the injuries you have done me, both in my fame and fortune! With both I trusted you, you bankrupt in honor, as indigent of wealth.

FAINALL: Your fame I have preserved: your fortune has been bestowed as the prodigality of your love would have it, in pleasures which we both have shared. Yet, had not you been false, I had ere this repaid it—'tis true—had you permitted Mirabell with Millamant to have stolen their marriage, my lady had been incensed beyond all means of reconcilement: Millamant had forfeited the moiety of her fortune; which then would have descended to my wife; and wherefore did I marry, but to make lawful prize of a rich widow's wealth, and squander it on love and you?

MRS. MARWOOD: Deceit and frivolous pretence!

FAINALL: Death, am I not married? What's pretence? Am I not imprisoned, fettered? Have I not a wife? nay a wife that was a widow, a young widow, a handsome widow; and would be again a widow, but that I have a heart of proof, and something of a constitution to bustle through the ways of wedlock and this world! Will you yet be reconciled to truth and me?

MRS. MARWOOD: Impossible. Truth and you are inconsistent: I hate you, and shall for ever.

FAINALL: For loving you?

MRS. MARWOOD: I loathe the name of love after such usage; and next to the guilt with which you would asperse me, I scorn you most. Farewell!

FAINALL: Nay, we must not part thus.

MRS. MARWOOD: Let me go.

FAINALL: Come, I'm sorry.

MRS. MARWOOD: I care not—let me go—break my hands, do—I'd leave 'em to get loose.

FAINALL: I would not hurt you for the world. Have I no other hold to keep you here?

MRS. MARWOOD: Well, I have deserved it all.

FAINALL: You know I love you.

MRS. MARWOOD: Poor dissembling!—Oh, that—well, it is not yet—

FAINALL: What? What is it not? What is it not yet? It is not yet too late—

MRS. MARWOOD: No, it is not yet too late—I have that comfort.

FAINALL: It is, to love another.

MRS. MARWOOD: But not to loathe, detest, abhor mankind, myself, and the whole treacherous world.

FAINALL: Nay, this is extravagance.—Come, I ask your pardon—no tears—I was to blame, I could not love you and be easy in my doubts. Pray forbear—I believe you; I'm convinced I've done you wrong; and anyway, every way will make amends. I'll hate my wife yet more, damn her! I'll part with her, rob her of all she's worth, and we'll retire somewhere, anywhere, to another world. I'll marry thee—be pacified.—'Sdeath they come, hide your face, your tears—you have a mask, wear it a moment. This way, this way—be persuaded.

[*Exeunt*]

SCENE II.

The same.

[Mirabell *and* Mrs. Fainall]

MRS. FAINALL: They are here yet.

MIRABELL: They are turning into the other walk.

MRS. FAINALL: While I only hated my husband, I could bear to see him; but since I have despised him, he's too offensive.

MIRABELL: Oh, you should hate with prudence.

MRS. FAINALL: Yes, for I have loved with indiscretion.

MIRABELL: You should have just so much disgust for your husband, as may be sufficient to make you relish your lover.

MRS. FAINALL: You have been the cause that I have loved without bounds, and would you set limits to that aversion of which you have been the occasion? Why did you make me marry this man?

MIRABELL: Why do we daily commit disagreeable and dangerous actions? To save that idol, reputation. If the familiarities of our loves had produced that consequence of which you were apprehensive, where could you have fixed a father's name with credit, but on a husband? I knew Fainall to be a man lavish of his morals, an interested and professing friend, a false and a designing lover; yet one whose wit and outward fair behavior have gained a reputation with the town enough to make that woman stand excused who has suffered herself to be won by his addresses. A better man ought not to have been sacrificed to the occasion; a worse had not answered to the purpose. When you are weary of him, you know your remedy.

MRS. FAINALL: I ought to stand in some degree of credit with you, Mirabell.

MIRABELL: In justice to you, I have made you privy to my whole design, and put it in your power to ruin or advance my fortune.

MRS. FAINALL: Whom have you instructed to represent your pretended uncle?

MIRABELL: Waitwell, my servant.

MRS. FAINALL: He is an humble servant to Foible, my mother's woman, and may win her to your interest.

MIRABELL: Care is taken for that—she is won and worn by this time. They were married this morning.

MRS. FAINALL: Who?

MIRABELL: Waitwell and Foible. I would not tempt any servant to betray me by trusting him too far. If your mother, in hopes to ruin me, should consent to marry my pretended uncle, he might, like Mosca in *The Fox*,[7] stand upon terms; so I made him sure beforehand.

MRS. FAINALL: So if my poor mother is caught in a contract, you will discover the imposture betimes, and release her by producing a certificate of her gallant's former marriage?

MIRABELL: Yes, upon condition that she consent to my marriage with her niece, and surrender the moiety of her fortune in her possession.

MRS. FAINALL: She talked last night of endeavoring at a match between Millamant and your uncle.

MIRABELL: That was by Foible's direction, and my instruction, that she might seem to carry it more privately.

MRS. FAINALL: Well, I have an opinion of your success; for I believe my lady will do anything to get a husband; and when she has this, which you have provided for her, I suppose she will submit to anything to get rid of him.

MIRABELL: Yes, I think the good lady would marry anything that resembled a man, though 'twere no more than what a butler could pinch out of a napkin.

MRS. FAINALL: Female frailty! We must all come to it, if we live to be old, and feel the craving of a false appetite when the true is decayed.

MIRABELL: An old woman's appetite is depraved like that of a girl—'tis the green sickness of a second childhood; and, like the faint offer of a latter spring, serves but to usher in the fall, and withers in an affected bloom.

MRS. FAINALL: Here's your mistress.

[*Enter* Mrs. Millamant, Witwoud, *and* Mincing]

MIRABELL: Here she comes, i'faith, full sail, with her fan spread and her streamers out, and a shoal of fools for tenders; ha, no, I cry her mercy!

MRS. FAINALL: I see but one poor empty sculler; and he tows her woman after him.

MIRABELL: [*To* Mrs. Millamant] You seem to be unattended, madam—you used to have the *beau monde*[8] throng after you; and a flock of gay fine perukes hovering around you.

WITWOUD: Like moths about a candle.—I had like to have lost my comparison for want of breath.

MRS. MILLAMANT: Oh, I have denied myself airs to-day, I have walked as fast through the crowd.

WITWOUD: As a favorite just disgraced; and with as few followers.

MRS. MILLAMANT: Dear Mr. Witwoud, truce with your similitudes; for I'm as sick of 'em—

WITWOUD: As a physician of a good air.—I cannot help it, madam, though 'tis against myself.

MRS. MILLAMANT: Yet, again! Mincing, stand between me and his wit.

WITWOUD: Do, Mrs. Mincing, like a screen before a great fire.—I confess I do blaze to-day; I am too bright.

MRS. FAINALL: But, dear Millamant, why were you so long?

MRS. MILLAMANT: Long! Lord, have I not made violent haste; I have asked every living thing I met for you; I have inquired after you, as after a new fashion.

WITWOUD: Madam, truce with your similitudes.—

[7] *Volpone,* a comedy by Ben Jonson (see pp. 285–323). Mosca, Volpone's servant, doublecrosses his master.

[8] The fashionable world.

No, you met her husband, and did not ask him for her.

MRS. MILLAMANT: By your leave, Witwoud, that were like inquiring after an old fashion, to ask a husband for his wife.

WITWOUD: Hum, a hit! a hit! a palpable hit! I confess it.

MRS. FAINALL: You were dressed before I came abroad.

MRS. MILLAMANT: Aye, that's true.—Oh, but then I had—Mincing, what had I? Why was I so long?

MINCING: O mem, your la'ship stayed to peruse a packet of letters.

MRS. MILLAMANT: Oh, aye, letters—I had letters —I am persecuted with letters—I hate letters.—Nobody knows how to write letters, and yet one has 'em, one does not know why. They serve one to pin up one's hair.

WITWOUD: Is that the way? Pray, madam, do you pin up your hair with all your letters? I find I must keep copies.

MRS. MILLAMANT: Only with those in verse, Mr. Witwoud; I never pin up my hair with prose.—I think I tried once, Mincing.

MINCING: O mem, I shall never forget it.

MRS. MILLAMANT: Aye, poor Mincing tift and tift all the morning.

MINCING: Till I had the cramp in my fingers, I'll vow, mem: and all to no purpose. But when your la'ship pins it up with poetry, it sits so pleasant the next day as anything, and is so pure and so crips.

WITWOUD: Indeed, so crips?

MINCING: You're such a critic, Mr. Witwoud.

MRS. MILLAMANT: Mirabell, did you take exception last night? Oh, aye, and went away.—Now I think on't I'm angry—no, now I think on't I'm pleased—for I believe I gave you some pain.

MIRABELL: Does that please you?

MRS. MILLAMANT: Infinitely; I love to give pain.

MIRABELL: You would affect a cruelty which is not in your nature; your true vanity is in the power of pleasing.

MRS. MILLAMANT: Oh, I ask you pardon for that —one's cruelty is one's power; and when one parts with one's cruelty, one parts with one's power; and when one has parted with that, I fancy one's old and ugly.

MIRABELL: Aye, aye, suffer your cruelty to ruin the object of your power, to destroy your lover— and then how vain, how lost a thing you'll be! Nay, 'tis true: you are no longer handsome when you've lost your lover; your beauty dies upon the instant; for beauty is the lover's gift; 'tis he bestows your charms—your glass is all a cheat. The ugly and the old, whom the looking-glass mortifies, yet after commendation can be flattered by it, and discover beauties in it; for that reflects our praises, rather than your face.

MRS. MILLAMANT: Oh, the vanity of these men! —Fainall, d'ye hear him? If they did not commend us, we were not handsome! Now you must know they could not commend one, if one was not handsome. Beauty the lover's gift!—Lord, what is a lover, that it can give? Why, one makes lovers as fast as one pleases, and they live as long as one pleases, and they die as soon as one pleases: and then, if one pleases, one makes more.

WITWOUD: Very pretty. Why, you make no more of making of lovers, madam, than of making so many card-matches.

MRS. MILLAMANT: One no more owes one's beauty to a lover, than one's wit to an echo. They can but reflect what we look and say; vain empty things if we are silent or unseen, and want a being.

MIRABELL: Yet to those two vain empty things you owe the two greatest pleasures of your life.

MRS. MILLAMANT: How so?

MIRABEL: To your lover you owe the pleasure of hearing yourselves praised; and to an echo the pleasure of hearing yourselves talk.

WITWOUD: But I know a lady that loves talking so incessantly, she won't give an echo fair play; she has that everlasting rotation of tongue, that an echo must wait till she dies, before it can catch her last words.

MRS. MILLAMANT: Oh, fiction!—Fainall, let us leave these men.

MIRABELL: [Aside to Mrs. Fainall] Draw off Witwoud.

MRS. FAINALL: Immediately.—I have a word or two for Mr. Witwoud.

[Exeunt Mrs. Fainall and Witwoud]

MIRABELL: I would beg a little private audience, too.—You had the tyranny to deny me last night; though you knew I came to impart a secret to you that concerned my love.

MRS. MILLAMANT: You saw I was engaged.

MIRABELL: Unkind! You had the leisure to entertain a herd of fools; things who visit you from their excessive idleness; bestowing on your easiness that time which is the encumbrance of their lives. How can you find delight in such society? It is impossible they should admire you, they are not capable: or if they were, it should be to you as a mortification; for sure to please a fool is some degree of folly.

MRS. MILLAMANT: I please myself: besides, sometimes to converse with fools is for my health.

MIRABELL: Your health! Is there a worse disease than the conversation of fools?

MRS. MILLAMANT: Yes, the vapors; fools are physic for it, next to asafœtida.

MIRABELL: You are not in a course of fools?

MRS. MILLAMANT: Mirabell, if you persist in this offensive freedom, you'll displease me.—I think I must resolve, after all, not to have you; we shan't agree.

MIRABELL: Not in our physic, it may be.

MRS. MILLAMANT: And yet our distemper, in all likelihood, will be the same; for we shall be sick of one another. I shan't endure to be reprimanded nor instructed: 'tis so dull to act always by advice, and so tedious to be told of one's faults—I can't bear it. Well, I won't have you, Mirabell,—I'm resolved—I think—you may go.—Ha! ha! ha! What would you give, that you could help loving me?

MIRABELL: I would give something that you did not know I could not help it.

MRS. MILLAMANT: Come, don't look grave, then. Well, what do you say to me?

MIRABELL: I say that a man may as soon make a friend by his wit, or a fortune by his honesty, as win a woman by plain dealing and sincerity.

MRS. MILLAMANT: Sententious Mirabell!—Prithee, don't look with that violent and inflexible wise face, like Solomon at the dividing of the child in an old tapestry hanging.

MIRABELL: You are merry, madam, but I would persuade you for a moment to be serious.

MRS. MILLAMANT: What, with that face? No, if you keep your countenance, 'tis impossible I should hold mine. Well, after all, there is something very moving in a lovesick face. Ha! ha! ha!—Well, I won't laugh, don't be peevish—Heigho! now I'll be melancholy, as melancholy as a watch-light. Well, Mirabell, if ever you will win me woo me now.—Nay, if you are so tedious, fare you well—I see they are walking away.

MIRABELL: Can you not find in the variety of your disposition one moment—

MRS. MILLAMANT: To hear you tell me Foible's married, and your plot like to speed—no.

MIRABELL: But how came you to know it?

MRS. MILLAMANT: Without the help of the devil, you can't imagine; unless she should tell me herself. Which of the two it may have been I will leave you to consider; and when you have done thinking of that, think of me. [Exit]

MIRABELL: I have something more.—Gone!—Think of you? To think of a whirlwind, though't were in a whirlwind, were a case of more steady contemplation; a very tranquillity of mind and mansion. A fellow that lives in a windmill, has not a more whimsical dwelling than the heart of a man that is lodged in a woman. There is no point of the compass to which they cannot turn, and by which they are not turned; and by one as well as another; for motion, not method, is their occupation. To know this, and yet continue to be in love, is to be made wise from the dictates of reason, and yet persevere to play the fool by the force of instinct.—Oh, here come my pair of turtles!—What, billing so sweetly! Is not Valentine's Day over with you yet?

[Enter Waitwell and Foible]

Sirrah, Waitwell, why sure you think you were married for your own recreation, and not for my conveniency.

WAITWELL: Your pardon, sir. With submission, we have indeed been solacing in lawful delights; but still with an eye to business, sir. I have instructed her as well as I could. If she can take your directions as readily as my instructions, sir, your affairs are in a prosperous way.

MIRABELL: Give you joy, Mrs. Foible.

FOIBLE: Oh, 'las, sir. I'm so ashamed!—I'm afraid my lady has been in a thousand inquietudes for me. But I protest, sir, I made as much haste as I could.

WAITWELL: That she did indeed, sir. It was my fault that she did not make more.

MIRABELL: That I believe.

FOIBLE: But I told my lady as you instructed me, sir, that I had a prospect of seeing Sir Rowland your uncle; and that I would put her ladyship's picture in my pocket to show him; which I'll be sure to say has made him so enamored of her beauty, that he burns with impatience to lie at her ladyship's feet, and worship the original.

MIRABELL: Excellent Foible! Matrimony has made you eloquent in love.

WAITWELL: I think she has profited, sir, I think so.

FOIBLE: You have seen Madam Millamant, sir?

MIRABELL: Yes.

FOIBLE: I told her, sir, because I did not know that you might find an opportunity; she had so much company last night.

MIRABELL: Your diligence will merit more—in the meantime—[Gives money]

FOIBLE: O dear sir, your humble servant!

WAITWELL: Spouse.

MIRABELL: Stand off, sir, not a penny!—Go on and prosper, Foible—the lease shall be made good, and the farm stocked, if we succeed.

FOIBLE: I don't question your generosity, sir: and you need not doubt of success. If you have no more commands, sir, I'll be gone; I'm sure my lady is at her toilet, and can't dress till I come.—Oh, dear, I'm sure that [looking out] was Mrs. Marwood that went by in a mask! If she has seen me with you I'm sure she'll tell my lady. I'll make haste home and prevent her. Your servant, sir.—B'w'y, Waitwell. [Exit]

WAITWELL: Sir Rowland, if you please.—The jade's so pert upon her preferment she forgets herself.

MIRABELL: Come, sir, will you endeavor to forget yourself, and transform into Sir Rowland?

WAITWELL: Why, sir, it will be impossible I should remember myself.—Married, knighted, and attended all in one day! 'tis enough to make any man forget himself. The difficulty will be how to recover my acquaintance and familiarity with my former self, and fall from my transformation to a reformation into Waitwell. Nay, I shan't be quite the same Waitwell neither; for now, I remember me, I'm married, and can't be my own man again.

Aye, there's my grief; that's the sad change of life,
To lose my title, and yet keep my wife.

[Exeunt]

ACT III. SCENE I.

A room in Lady Wishfort's *house.*

[Lady Wishfort *at her toilet,* Peg *waiting*]

LADY WISHFORT: Merciful! No news of Foible yet?

PEG: No, madam.

LADY WISHFORT: I have no more patience.—If I have not fretted myself till I am pale again, there's no veracity in me! Fetch me the red—the red, do you hear, sweetheart?—An arrant ash-color, as I am a person! Look you how this wench stirs!—Why dost thou not fetch me a little red? Didst thou not hear me, mopus?[9]

PEG: The red ratafia, does your ladyship mean, or the cherry-brandy?

LADY WISHFORT: Ratafia, fool! No, fool. Not the ratafia, fool—grant me patience!—I mean the Spanish paper, idiot—complexion, darling. Paint, paint, paint, dost thou understand that, changeling, dangling thy hands like bobbins before thee? Why dost thou not stir, puppet? Thou wooden thing upon wires!

PEG: Lord, madam, your ladyship is so impatient! —I cannot come at the paint, madam; Mrs. Foible has locked it up, and carried the key with her.

LADY WISHFORT: A pox take you both!—Fetch me the cherry-brandy then.

[*Exit* Peg]

I'm as pale and as faint, I look like Mrs. Qualmsick, the curate's wife, that's always breeding.—Wench, come, come, wench, what art thou doing? sipping, tasting?—Save thee, dost thou not know the bottle?

[*Re-enter* Peg *with a bottle and china cup*]

PEG: Madam, I was looking for a cup.

LADY WISHFORT: A cup, save thee! and what a cup hast thou brought!—Dost thou take me for a fairy, to drink out of an acorn? Why didst thou not bring thy thimble? Hast thou ne'er a brass thimble clinking in thy pocket with a bit of nutmeg?—I warrant thee. Come, fill, fill!—So—again.—[*Knocking at the door*]—See who that is.—Set down the bottle first—here, here, under the table.—What, wouldst thou go with the bottle in thy hand, like a tapster? As I am a person, this wench has lived in an inn upon the road, before she came to me, like Maritornes the Asturian in *Don Quixote!*—No Foible yet?

PEG: No, madam; Mrs. Marwood.

LADY WISHFORT: Oh, Marwood; let her come in.— Come in, good Marwood.

[*Enter* Mrs. Marwood]

MRS. MARWOOD: I'm surprised to find your ladyship in dishabille at this time of day.

LADY WISHFORT: Foible's a lost thing; has been abroad since morning, and never heard of since.

MRS. MARWOOD: I saw her but now, as I came masked through the park, in conference with Mirabell.

[9] Fool.

LADY WISHFORT: With Mirabell!—You call my blood into my face, with mentioning that traitor. She durst not have the confidence! I sent her to negotiate an affair, in which, if I'm detected, I'm undone. If that wheedling villain has wrought upon Foible to detect me, I'm ruined. O my dear friend, I'm a wretch of wretches if I'm detected.

MRS. MARWOOD: O madam, you cannot suspect Mrs. Foible's integrity!

LADY WISHFORT: Oh, he carries poison in his tongue that would corrupt integrity itself! If she has given him an opportunity, she has as good as put her integrity into his hands. Ah, dear Marwood, what's integrity to an opportunity?—Hark! I hear her!—dear friend, retire into my closet, that I may examine her with more freedom.—You'll pardon me, dear friend; I can make bold with you.—There are books over the chimney—Quarles and Prynne, and *The Short View of the Stage*, with Bunyan's works, to entertain you.[10]—[*To* Peg]—Go, you thing, and send her in.

[*Exeunt* Mrs. Marwood *and* Peg]

[*Enter* Foible]

LADY WISHFORT: O Foible, where hast thou been? What has thou been doing?

FOIBLE: Madam, I have seen the party.

LADY WISHFORT: But what hast thou done?

FOIBLE: Nay, 'tis your ladyship has done, and are to do; I have only promised. But a man so enamored —so transported!—Well, here it is, all that is left; all that is not kissed away.—Well, if worshiping of pictures be a sin—poor Sir Rowland, I say.

LADY WISHFORT: The miniature has been counted like—but hast thou not betrayed me, Foible? Hast thou not detected me to that faithless Mirabell?— What hadst thou to do with him in the Park? Answer me, has he got nothing out of thee?

FOIBLE: [*Aside*] So the devil has been beforehand with me. What shall I say?—[*Aloud*]—Alas, madam, could I help it, if I met that confident thing? Was I in fault? If you had heard how he used me, and all upon your ladyship's account, I'm sure you would not suspect my fidelity. Nay, if that had been the worst, I could have borne; but he had a fling at your ladyship, too; and then I could not hold; but i'faith I gave him his own.

LADY WISHFORT: Me? What did the filthy fellow say?

FOIBLE: O madam! 'tis a shame to say what he said —with his taunts and his fleers, tossing up his nose. Humph! (says he) what, you are a-hatching some plot (says he), you are so early abroad, or catering (says he), ferreting for some disbanded officer, I warrant.—Half-pay is but thin subsistence (says he) —well, what pension does your lady propose? Let me

[10] Quarles and Prynne were religious poets of the time; *The Short View of the Stage* was Jeremy Collier's pamphlet attacking the immorality of the Restoration stage; John Bunyan was the author of the allegory *The Pilgrim's Progress.*

see (says he), what, she must come down pretty deep now, she's superannuated (says he) and—

LADY WISHFORT: Odds my life, I'll have him, I'll have him murdered! I'll have him poisoned! Where does he eat?—I'll marry a drawer to have him poisoned in his wine. I'll send for Robin from Locket's[11] immediately.

FOIBLE: Poison him! poisoning's too good for him. Starve him, madam, starve him: marry Sir Rowland, and get him disinherited. Oh, you would bless yourself to hear what he said!

LADY WISHFORT: A villain! Superannuated!

FOIBLE: Humph (says he), I hear you are laying designs against me too (says he) and Mrs. Millamant is to marry my uncle (he does not suspect a word of your ladyship); but (says he) I'll fit you for that. I warrant you (says he) I'll hamper you for that (says he); you and your old frippery too (says he); I'll handle you—

LADY WISHFORT: Audacious villain! Handle me! would he durst!—Frippery! old frippery! Was there ever such a foul-mouthed fellow? I'll be married to-morrow, I'll be contracted to-night.

FOIBLE: The sooner the better, madam.

LADY WISHFORT: Will Sir Rowland be here, sayest thou? when, Foible?

FOIBLE: Incontinently, madam. No new sheriff's wife expects the return of her husband after knighthood with that impatience in which Sir Rowland burns for the dear hour of kissing your ladyship's hand after dinner.

LADY WISHFORT: Frippery! superannuated frippery! I'll frippery the villain; I'll reduce him to frippery and rags! a tatterdemalion! I hope to see him hung with tatters, like a Long-lane penthouse[12] or a gibbet thief. A slander-mouthed railer! I warrant the spendthrift prodigal's in debt as much as the million lottery, or the whole court upon a birthday. I'll spoil his credit with his tailor. Yes, he shall have my niece with her fortune, he shall.

FOIBLE: He! I hope to see him lodge in Ludgate first, and angle into Blackfriars for brass farthings with an old mitten.

LADY WISHFORT: Aye, dear Foible; thank thee for that, dear Foible. He has put me out of all patience. I shall never recompose my features to receive Sir Rowland with any economy of face. This wretch has fretted me that I am absolutely decayed. Look, Foible.

FOIBLE: Your ladyship has frowned a little too rashly, indeed, madam. There are some cracks discernible in the white varnish.

LADY WISHFORT: Let me see the glass.—Cracks, sayest thou?—why, I am errantly flayed—I look like an old peeled wall. Thou must repair me, Foible,

before Sir Rowland comes, or I shall never keep up to my picture.

FOIBLE: I warrant you, madam, a little art at once made your picture like you; and now a little of the same art must make you like your picture. Your picture must sit for you, madam.

LADY WISHFORT: But art thou sure Sir Rowland will not fail to come? Or will he not fail when he does come? Will he be importunate, Foible, and push? For if he should not be importunate, I shall never break decorums—I shall die with confusion, if I am forced to advance.—Oh, no, I can never advance!—I shall swoon if he should expect advances. No, I hope Sir Rowland is better bred than to put a lady to the necessity of breaking her forms. I won't be too coy, neither.—I won't give him despair—but a little disdain is not amiss; a little scorn is alluring.

FOIBLE: A little scorn becomes your ladyship.

LADY WISHFORT: Yes, but tenderness becomes me best—a sort of dyingness—you see that picture has a sort of a—ha, Foible! a swimmingness in the eye—yes, I'll look so—my niece affects it; but she wants features. Is Sir Rowland handsome? Let my toilet be removed—I'll dress above. I'll receive Sir Rowland here. Is he handsome? Don't answer me. I won't know; I'll be surprised, I'll be taken by surprise.

FOIBLE: By storm, madam, Sir Rowland's a brisk man.

LADY WISHFORT: Is he! Oh, then he'll importune, if he's a brisk man. I shall save decorums if Sir Rowland importunes. I have a mortal terror at the apprehension of offending against decorums. Oh, I'm glad he's a brisk man. Let my things be removed, good Foible. [Exit]

[Enter Mrs. Fainall]

MRS. FAINALL: Oh, Foible, I have been in a fright, lest I should come too late! That devil Marwood saw you in the Park with Mirabell, and I'm afraid will discover it to my lady.

FOIBLE: Discover what, madam!

MRS. FAINALL: Nay, nay, put not on that strange face, I am privy to the whole design, and know that Waitwell, to whom thou wert this morning married, is to personate Mirabell's uncle, and as such, winning my lady, to involve her in those difficulties from which Mirabell only must release her, by his making his conditions to have my cousin and her fortune left to her own disposal.

FOIBLE: O dear madam, I beg your pardon. It was not my confidence in your ladyship that was deficient; but I thought the former good correspondence between your ladyship and Mr. Mirabell might have hindered his communicating this secret.

MRS. FAINALL: Dear Foible, forget that.

FOIBLE: O dear madam, Mr. Mirabell is such a sweet, winning gentleman—but your ladyship is the pattern of generosity.—Sweet lady, to be so good! Mr. Mirabell cannot choose but be grateful. I find your ladyship has his heart still. Now, madam, I can safely tell your ladyship our success; Mrs. Marwood

---

[11] The waiter at the popular Locket's restaurant, in London.

[12] Long Lane was filled with low buildings (penthouses) in which old clothes were sold.

had told my lady; but I warrant I managed myself; I turned it all for the better. I told my lady that Mr. Mirabell railed at her; I laid horrid things to his charge, I'll vow; and my lady is so incensed that she'll be contracted to Sir Rowland to-night, she says; I warrant I worked her up, that he may have her for asking for, as they say of a Welsh maidenhead.

MRS. FAINALL: O rare Foible!

FOIBLE: Madam, I beg your ladyship to acquaint Mr. Mirabell of his success. I would be seen as little as possible to speak to him: besides, I believe Madam Marwood watches me.—She has a month's mind; but I know Mr. Mirabell can't abide her.—John!—[calls] remove my lady's toilet.—Madam, your servant: my lady is so impatient, I fear she'll come for me if I stay.

MRS. FAINALL: I'll go with you up the backstairs, lest I should meet her.

[Exeunt]

SCENE II.

Lady Wishfort's closet.

[Mrs. Marwood alone]

MRS. MARWOOD: Indeed, Mrs. Engine, is it thus with you? Are you become a go-between of this importance? Yes, I shall watch you. Why this wench is the passe-partout, a very master-key to everybody's strong-box. My friend Fainall, have you carried it so swimmingly? I thought there was something in it; but it seems 'tis over with you. Your loathing is not from a want of appetite, then, but from a surfeit. Else you could never be so cool to fall from a principal to be an assistant; to procure for him! A pattern of generosity that, I confess. Well, Mr. Fainall, you have met with your match.—O man, man! woman, woman, the devil's an ass: if I were a painter, I would draw him like an idiot, a driveler with a bib and bells: man should have his head and horns, and woman the rest of him. Poor simple fiend!—"Madam Marwood has a month's mind, but he can't abide her."—'Twere better for him you had not been his confessor in that affair, without you could have kept his counsel closer. I shall not prove another pattern of generosity: he has not obliged me to that with those excesses of himself! and now I'll have none of him. Here comes the good lady, panting ripe; with a heart full of hope, and a head full of care, like any chemist upon the day of projection.[13]

[Enter Lady Wishfort]

LADY WISHFORT: Oh dear, Marwood, what shall I say for this rude forgetfulness?—but my dear friend is all goodness.

MRS. MARWOOD: No apologies, dear madam, I have been very well entertained.

LADY WISHFORT: As I'm a person, I am in a very

[13] The completion of an experiment.

chaos to think I should so forget myself: but I have such an olio of affairs, really I know not what to do.—Foible!—[Calls] I expect my nephew, Sir Wilfull, every moment, too.—Why, Foible!—He means to travel for improvement.

MRS. MARWOOD: Methinks Sir Wilfull should rather think of marrying than traveling, at his years. I hear he is turned of forty.

LADY WISHFORT: Oh, he's in less danger of being spoiled by his travels—I am against my nephew's marrying too young. It will be time enough when he comes back, and has acquired discretion to choose for himself.

MRS. MARWOOD: Methinks Mrs. Millamant and he would make a very fit match. He may travel afterwards. 'Tis a thing very usual with young gentlemen.

LADY WISHFORT: I promise you I have thought on't—and since 'tis your judgment, I'll think on't again. I assure you I will; I value your judgment extremely. On my word, I'll propose it.

[Enter Foible]

LADY WISHFORT: Come, come, Foible—I had forgot my nephew will be here before dinner—I must make haste.

FOIBLE: Mr. Witwoud and Mr. Petulant are come to dine with your ladyship.

LADY WISHFORT: Oh, dear, I can't appear till I'm dressed.—Dear Marwood, shall I be free with you again, and beg you to entertain 'em? I'll make all imaginable haste. Dear friend, excuse me.

SCENE III.

A room in Lady Wishfort's house.

[Mrs. Marwood, Mrs. Millamant, and Mincing]

MRS. MILLAMANT: Sure never anything was so unbred as that odious man!—Marwood, your servant.

MRS. MARWOOD: You have a color; what's the matter?

MRS. MILLAMANT: That horrid fellow, Petulant, has provoked me into a flame: I have broken my fan.—Mincing, lend me yours; is not all the powder out of my hair?

MRS. MARWOOD: No. What has he done?

MRS. MILLAMANT: Nay, he has done nothing; he has only talked—nay, he has said nothing neither; but he has contradicted everything that has been said. For my part, I thought Witwoud and he would have quarreled.

MINCING: I vow, mem, I thought once they would have fit.

MRS. MILLAMANT: Well, 'tis a lamentable thing, I swear, that one has not the liberty of choosing one's acquaintance as one does one's clothes.

MRS. MARWOOD: If we had that liberty, we should be as weary of one set of acquaintance, though never so good, as we are of one suit though never so fine. A fool and a doily stuff would now and then find days of grace, and be worn for variety.

MRS. MILLAMANT: I could consent to wear 'em, if they would wear alike; but fools never wear out—they are such *drap de Berri*[14] things without one could give 'em to one's chambermaid after a day or two!

MRS. MARWOOD: 'Twere better so indeed. Or what think you of the playhouse? A fine gay glossy fool should be given there, like a new masking habit, after the masquerade is over, and we have done with the disguise. For a fool's visit is always a disguise; and never admitted by a woman of wit, but to blind her affair with a lover of sense. If you would but appear barefaced now, and own Mirabell, you might as easily put off Petulant and Witwoud as your hood and scarf. And indeed, 'tis time, for the town has found it; the secret is grown too big for the pretence. 'Tis like Mrs. Primly's great belly; she may lace it down before, but it burnishes on her hips. Indeed, Millamant, you can no more conceal it than my Lady Strammel can her face; that goodly face, which in defiance of her Rhenish wine tea, will not be comprehended in a mask.

MRS. MILLAMANT: I'll take my death, Marwood, you are more censorious than a decayed beauty, or a discarded toast.—Mincing, tell the men they may come up.—My aunt is not dressing here; their folly is less provoking than your malice.

[*Exit* Mincing]

The town has found it! what has it found? That Mirabell loves me is no more a secret than it is a secret that you discovered it to my aunt, or than the reason why you discovered it is a secret.

MRS. MARWOOD: You are nettled.

MRS. MILLAMANT: You're mistaken. Ridiculous!

MRS. MARWOOD: Indeed, my dear, you'll tear another fan, if you don't mitigate those violent airs.

MRS. MILLAMANT: Oh, silly! ha! ha! ha! I could laugh immoderately. Poor Mirabell! His constancy to me has quite destroyed his complaisance for all the world beside. I swear, I never enjoined it him to be so coy—If I had the vanity to think he would obey me, I would command him to show more gallantry—'tis hardly well-bred to be so particular on one hand, and so insensible on the other. But I despair to prevail, and so let him follow his own way. Ha! ha! ha! pardon me, dear creature, I must laugh, ha! ha! ha! though I grant you 'tis a little barbarous, ha! ha! ha!

MRS. MARWOOD: What pity 'tis so much fine raillery, and delivered with so significant gesture, should be so unhappily directed to miscarry!

MRS. MILLAMANT: Ha! dear creature, I ask your pardon—I swear I did not mind you.

MRS. MARWOOD: Mr. Mirabell and you both may think it a thing impossible, when I shall tell him by telling you—

MRS. MILLAMANT: O dear, what? for it is the same thing if I hear it—ha! ha! ha!

[14] Coarse cloth.

MRS. MARWOOD: That I detest him, hate him, madam.

MRS. MILLAMANT: O madam, why so do I—and yet the creature loves me, ha! ha! ha! How can one forbear laughing to think of it.—I am a sibyl if I am not amazed to think what he can see in me I'll take my death, I think you are handsomer—and within a year or two as young—if you could but stay for me, I should overtake you—but that cannot be.—Well, that thought makes me melancholic.—Now, I'll be sad.

MRS. MARWOOD: Your merry note may be changed sooner than you think.

MRS. MILLAMANT: D'ye say so? Then I'm resolved I'll have a song to keep up my spirits.

[*Re-enter* Mincing]

MINCING: The gentlemen stay but to comb, madam, and will wait on you.

MRS. MILLAMANT: Desire Mrs.—that is in the next room to sing the song I would have learned yesterday.—You shall hear it, madam—not that there's any great matter in it—but 'tis agreeable to my humor.

SONG

"Love's but the frailty of the mind,
  When 'tis not with ambition joined;
A sickly flame, which, if not fed, expires,
And feeding, wastes in self-consuming fires.

" 'Tis not to wound a wanton boy
  Or amorous youth, that gives the joy;
But 'tis the glory to have pierced a swain,
For whom inferior beauties sighed in vain.

"Then I alone the conquest prize,
  When I insult a rival's eyes!
If there's delight in love, 'tis when I see
That heart, which others bleed for, bleed for me."

[*Enter* Petulant *and* Witwoud]

MRS. MILLAMANT: Is your animosity composed, gentlemen?

WITWOUD: Raillery, raillery, madam; we have no animosity—we hit off a little wit now and then, but no animosity.—The falling out of wits is like the falling out of lovers: we agree in the main,[15] like treble and bass.—Ha, Petulant?

PETULANT: Aye, in the main—but when I have a humor to contradict—

WITWOUD: Aye, when he has a humor to contradict, then I contradict, too. What, I know my cue. Then we contradict one another like two battledores; for contradictions beget one another like Jews.

PETULANT: If he says black's black—if I have a humor to say 'tis blue—let that pass—all's one for that. If I have a humor to prove it, it must be granted.

[15] The tenor—the middle—part, with which the other two parts are supposed to harmonize.

WITWOUD: Not positively must—but it may—it may.

PETULANT: Yes, it positively must, upon proof positive.

WITWOUD: Aye, upon proof positive it must; but upon proof presumptive it only may.—That's a logical distinction now, madam.

MRS. MARWOOD: I perceive your debates are of importance, and very learnedly handled.

PETULANT: Importance is one thing, and learning's another; but a debate's a debate, that I assert.

WITWOUD: Petulant's an enemy to learning; he relies altogether on his parts.

PETULANT: No, I'm no enemy to learning; it hurts not me.

MRS. MARWOOD: That's a sign indeed it's no enemy to you.

PETULANT: No, no, it's no enemy to anybody but them that have it.

MRS. MILLAMANT: Well, an illiterate man's my aversion: I wonder at the impudence of any illiterate man to offer to make love.

WITWOUD: That I confess I wonder at too.

MRS. MILLAMANT: Ah! to marry an ignorant that can hardly read or write.

PETULANT: Why should a man be any further from being married, though he can't read, than he is from being hanged? The ordinary's paid for setting the psalm, and the parish priest for reading the ceremony. And for the rest which is to follow in both cases, a man may do it without book—so all's one for that.

MRS. MILLAMANT: D'ye hear the creature?—Lord, here's company, I'll be gone. [Exit]

[Enter Sir Wilfull Witwoud in a riding dress, followed by Footman]

WITWOUD: In the name of Bartlemew and his fair,[16] what have we here?

MRS. MARWOOD: 'Tis your brother, I fancy. Don't you know him?

WITWOUD: Not I.—Yes, I think it is he—I've almost forgot him; I have not seen him since the Revolution.[17]

FOOTMAN: [To Sir Wilfull] Sir, my lady's dressing. Here's company; if you please to walk in, in the meantime.

SIR WILFULL: Dressing! What, it's but morning here I warrant, with you in London; we should count it towards afternoon in our parts, down in Shropshire. —Why then, belike, my aunt han't dined yet, ha, friend?

FOOTMAN: Your aunt, sir?

SIR WILFULL: My aunt, sir! Yes, my aunt, sir, and your lady, sir; your lady is my aunt, sir.—Why, what

[16] The fair of St. Bartholomew was held in Smithfield every August.

[17] The so-called bloodless revolution of 1688, when James II, the last Stuart king, fled from England and William and Mary became joint rulers of the country.

dost thou not know me, friend? why then send somebody hither that does. How long hast thou lived with thy lady, fellow, ha?

FOOTMAN: A week, sir; longer than anybody in the house, except my lady's woman.

SIR WILFULL: Why then belike thou dost not know thy lady, if thou seest her, ha, friend?

FOOTMAN: Why, truly, sir, I cannot safely swear to her face in a morning, before she is dressed. 'Tis like I may give a shrewd guess at her by this time.

SIR WILFULL: Well, prithee try what thou canst do; if thou canst not guess, inquire her out, dost hear, fellow? and tell her, her nephew, Sir Wilfull Witwoud, is in the house.

FOOTMAN: I shall, sir.

SIR WILFULL: Hold ye, hear me, friend; a word with you in your ear; prithee who are these gallants?

FOOTMAN: Really, sir, I can't tell; here come so many here, 'tis hard to know 'em all. [Exit]

SIR WILFULL: Oons, this fellow knows less than a starling; I don't think a' knows his own name.

MRS. MARWOOD: Mr. Witwoud, your brother is not behindhand in forgetfulness—I fancy he has forgot you too.

WITWOUD: I hope so—the devil take him that remembers first, I say.

SIR WILFULL: Save you, gentlemen and lady!

MRS. MARWOOD: For shame, Mr. Witwoud; why don't you speak to him?—And you, sir.

WITWOUD: Petulant, speak.

PETULANT: And you, sir.

SIR WILFULL: No offence, I hope. [Salutes Mrs. Marwood]

MRS. MARWOOD: No, sure, sir.

WITWOUD: This is a vile dog, I see that already. No offence! ha! ha! ha! To him; to him, Petulant, smoke him.

PETULANT: It seems as if you had come a journey, sir; hem, hem. [Surveying him round]

SIR WILFULL: Very likely, sir, that it may seem so.

PETULANT: No offence, I hope, sir.

WITWOUD: Smoke the boots, the boots; Petulant, the boots: ha! ha! ha!

SIR WILFULL: May be not, sir; thereafter, as 'tis meant, sir.

PETULANT: Sir, I presume upon the information of your boots.

SIR WILFULL: Why, 'tis like you may, sir: if you are not satisfied with the information of my boots, sir, if you will step to the stable, you may inquire further of my horse, sir.

PETULANT: Your horse, sir! your horse is an ass, sir!

SIR WILFULL: Do you speak by way of offence, sir?

MRS. MARWOOD: The gentleman's merry, that's all, sir.—[Aside] S'life, we shall have a quarrel betwixt an horse and an ass before they find one another out. —[Aloud] You must not take anything amiss from your friends, sir. You are among your friends here, though it may be you don't know it.—If I am not mistaken, you are Sir Wilfull Witwoud.

SIR WILFULL: Right, lady; I am Sir Wilfull Witwoud, so I write myself; no offence to anybody, I hope; and nephew to the Lady Wishfort of this mansion.

MRS. MARWOOD: Don't you know this gentleman, sir?

SIR WILFULL: Hum! what, sure 'tis not—yea by'r Lady, but 'tis—s'heart, I know not whether 'tis or no—yea, but 'tis, by the Rekin. Brother Anthony! what Tony, i'faith! what, dost thou not know me? By'r Lady, nor I thee, thou art so becravated, and so beperiwigged.—S'heart, why dost not speak? art thou overjoyed?

WITWOUD: Odso, brother, is it you? your servant, brother.

SIR WILFULL: Your servant! why yours, sir. Your servant again—s'heart, and your friend and servant to that—and a —and a—flap-dragon for your service, sir! and a hare's foot and a hare's scut for your service, sir! an you be so cold and so courtly.

WITWOUD: No offence, I hope, brother.

SIR WILFULL: S'heart, sir, but there is, and much offence!—A pox, is this your inns o' court breeding, not to know your friends and your relations, your elders and your betters?

WITWOUD: Why, brother Wilfull of Salop, you may be as short as a Shrewsbury-cake, if you please. But I tell you 'tis not modish to know relations in town: you think you're in the country, where great lubberly brothers slabber and kiss one another when they meet, like a call of serjeants—and 'tis not the fashion here; 'tis not indeed, dear brother.

SIR WILFULL: The fashion's a fool; and you're a fop, dear brother. S'heart, I've suspected this—by'r Lady, I conjectured you were a fop, since you began to change the style of your letters, and write on a scrap of paper gilt round the edges, no bigger than a *subpœna*. I might expect this when you left off, "Honored brother"; and "hoping you are in good health," and so forth—to begin with a "Rat me, knight, I'm so sick of a last night's debauch"—'ods heart, and then tell a familiar tale of a cock and a bull, and a whore and a bottle, and so conclude.— You could write news before you were out of your time, when you lived with honest Pimple Nose the attorney of Furnival's Inn—you could entreat to be remembered then to your friends round the reckan.[18] We could have gazettes, then, and Dawks' Letter, and the Weekly Bill, till of late days.

PETULANT: S'life, Witwoud, were you ever an attorney's clerk? of the family of the Furnivals? Ha! ha! ha!

WITWOUD: Aye, aye, but that was but for a while: not long, not long. Pshaw! I was not in my own power then; an orphan, and this fellow was my guardian; aye, aye, I was glad to consent to that, man, to come to London: he had the disposal of

[18] Rackan, or chain.

me then. If I had not agreed to that, I might have been bound 'prentice to a felt-maker in Shrewsbury; this fellow would have bound me to a maker of felts.

SIR WILFULL: S'heart, and better than to be bound to a maker of fops; where, I suppose, you have served your time; and now you may set up for yourself.

MRS. MARWOOD: You intend to travel, sir, as I'm informed.

SIR WILFULL: Belike I may, madam. I may chance to sail upon the salt seas, if my mind hold.

PETULANT: And the wind serve.

SIR WILFULL: Serve or not serve, I shan't ask licence of you, sir; nor the weathercock your companion: I direct my discourse to the lady, sir—'Tis like my aunt may have told you, madam—yes, I have settled my concerns, I may say now, and am minded to see foreign parts. If an how that the peace holds, whereby that is, taxes abate.

MRS. MARWOOD: I thought you had designed for France at all adventures.

SIR WILFULL: I can't tell that; 'tis like I may, and 'tis like I may not. I am somewhat dainty in making a resolution—because when I make it I keep it. I don't stand shill I, shall I, then; if I say't, I'll do't; but I have thoughts to tarry a small matter in town, to learn somewhat of your lingo first, before I cross the seas. I'd gladly have a spice of your French as they say, whereby to hold discourse in foreign countries.

MRS. MARWOOD: Here's an academy in town for that use.

SIR WILFULL: There is? 'Tis like there may.

MRS. MARWOOD: No doubt you will return very much improved.

WITWOUD: Yes, refined, like a Dutch skipper from a whale-fishing.

[*Enter* Lady Wishfort *and* Fainall]

LADY WISHFORT: Nephew, you are welcome.

SIR WILFULL: Aunt, your servant.

FAINALL: Sir Wilfull, your most faithful servant.

SIR WILFULL: Cousin Fainall, give me your hand.

LADY WISHFORT: Cousin Witwoud, your servant; Mr. Petulant, your servant—nephew, you are welcome again. Will you drink anything after your journey, nephew; before you eat? dinner's almost ready.

SIR WILFULL: I'm very well, I thank you, aunt— however, I thank you for your courteous offer. S'heart I was afraid you would have been in the fashion, too, and have remembered to have forgot your relations. Here's your cousin Tony, belike, I mayn't call him brother for fear of offence.

LADY WISHFORT: Oh, he's a *railleur*, nephew—my cousin's a wit: and your great wits always rally their best friends to choose. When you have been abroad, nephew, you'll understand raillery better.

[Fainall *and* Mrs. Marwood *talk apart*]

SIR WILFULL: Why then let him hold his tongue

in the meantime; and rail when that day comes.

[Enter Mincing]

MINCING: Mem, I am come to acquaint your la'ship that dinner is impatient.

SIR WILFULL: Impatient! why then belike it won't stay till I pull off my boots.—Sweetheart, can you help me to a pair of slippers?—My man's with his horses, I warrant.

LADY WISHFORT: Fie, fie, nephew! you would not pull off your boots here?—Go down into the hall—dinner shall stay for you.—My nephew's a little unbred, you'll pardon him, madam.—Gentlemen, will you walk?—Marwood—

MRS. MARWOOD: I'll follow you, madam—before Sir Wilfull is ready.

[Exeunt all but Mrs. Marwood and Fainall]

FAINALL: Why then, Foible's a bawd, an arrant, rank, match-making bawd: and I, it seems, am a husband, a rank husband; and my wife a very arrant, rank wife—all in the way of the world. 'Sdeath, to be a cuckold by anticipation, a cuckold in embryo! sure I was born with budding antlers, like a young satyr or a citizen's child. 'Sdeath! to be outwitted—to be out-jilted—out-matrimony'd!—If I had kept my speed like a stag, 'twere somewhat—but to crawl after, with my horns, like a snail, and be outstripped by my wife—'tis scurvy wedlock.

MRS. MARWOOD: Then shake it off; you have often wished for an opportunity to part—and now you have it. But first prevent their plot—the half of Millamant's fortune is too considerable to be parted with, to a foe, to Mirabell.

FAINALL: Damn him! that had been mine—had you not made that fond discovery—that had been forfeited, had they been married. My wife had added luster to my horns by that increase of fortune; I could have worn 'em tipped with gold, though my forehead had been furnished like a deputy-lieutenant's hall.

MRS. MARWOOD: They may prove a cap of maintenance to you still, if you can away with your wife. And she's no worse than when you had her.—I dare swear she had given up her game before she was married.

FAINALL: Hum! that may be.

MRS. MARWOOD: You married her to keep you; and if you contrive to have her keep you better than you expected, why should you not keep her longer than you intended?

FAINALL: The means, the means.

MRS. MARWOOD: Discover to my lady your wife's conduct; threaten to part with her!—my lady loves her, and will come to any composition to save her reputation. Take the opportunity of breaking it, just upon the discovery of this imposture. My lady will be enraged beyond bounds, and sacrifice niece, and fortune, and all, at that conjuncture. And let me alone to keep her warm; if she should flag in her part, I will not fail to prompt her.

FAINALL: Faith, this has an appearance.

MRS. MARWOOD: I'm sorry I hinted to my lady to endeavor a match between Millamant and Sir Wilfull; that may be an obstacle.

FAINALL: Oh, for that matter, leave me to manage him: I'll disable him for that; he will drink like a Dane; after dinner, I'll set his hand in.

MRS. MARWOOD: Well, how do you stand affected towards your lady?

FAINALL: Why, faith, I'm thinking of it.—Let me see—I am married already, so that's over: my wife has played the jade with me—well, that's over too: I never loved her, or if I had, why that would have been over too by this time—jealous of her I cannot be, for I am certain; so there's an end of jealousy: weary of her I am, and shall be—no, there's no end of that—no, no, that were too much to hope. Thus far concerning my repose; now for my reputation. As to my own, I married not for it, so that's out of the question; and as to my part in my wife's—why, she had parted with hers before; so bringing none to me, she can take none from me; 'tis against all rule of play, that I should lose to one who has not wherewithal to stake.

MRS. MARWOOD: Besides, you forget, marriage is honorable.

FAINALL: Hum, faith, and that's well thought on; marriage is honorable as you say; and if so, wherefore should cuckoldom be a discredit, being derived from so honorable a root?

MRS. MARWOOD: Nay, I know not; if the root be honorable, why not the branches?

FAINALL: So, so, why this point's clear—well, how do we proceed?

MRS. MARWOOD: I will contrive a letter which shall be delivered to my lady at the time when that rascal who is to act Sir Rowland is with her. It shall come as from an unknown hand—for the less I appear to know of the truth, the better I can play the incendiary. Besides, I would not have Foible provoked if I could help it—because you know she knows some passages—nay, I expect all will come out—but let the mine be sprung first, and then I care not if I am discovered.

FAINALL: If the worst comes to the worst—I'll turn my wife to grass—I have already a deed of settlement of the best part of her estate; which I wheedled out of her; and that you shall partake at least.

MRS. MARWOOD: I hope you are convinced that I hate Mirabell now; you'll be no more jealous?

FAINALL: Jealous! no—by this kiss—let husbands be jealous; but let the lover still believe; or if he doubt, let it be only to endear his pleasure, and prepare the joy that follows, when he proves his mistress true. But let husbands' doubts convert to endless jealousy; or if they have belief, let it corrupt to superstition and blind credulity. I am single, and will herd no more with 'em. True, I wear the badge, but I'll disown the order. And since I take my leave of 'em, I care not if I leave 'em a common motto to their common crest:

All husbands must or pain or shame endure;
The wise too jealous are, fools too secure.

[Exeunt]

ACT IV. SCENE I.

A room in Lady Wishfort's house.

[Lady Wishfort and Foible]

LADY WISHFORT: Is Sir Rowland coming, sayest thou, Foible? And are things in order?

FOIBLE: Yes, madam, I have put wax lights in the sconces, and placed the footmen in a row in the hall, in their best liveries, with the coachman and postilion to fill up the equipage.

LADY WISHFORT: Have you pulvilled[19] the coachman and postilion, that they may not stink of the stable when Sir Rowland comes by?

FOIBLE: Yes, madam.

LADY WISHFORT: And are the dancers and the music ready, that he may be entertained in all points with correspondence to his passion?

FOIBLE: All is ready, madam.

LADY WISHFORT: And—well—how do I look, Foible?

FOIBLE: Most killing well, madam.

LADY WISHFORT: Well, and how shall I receive him? in what figure shall I give his heart the first impression? there is a great deal in the first impression. Shall I sit?—no, I won't sit—I'll walk—aye, I'll walk from the door upon his entrance; and then turn full upon him—no, that will be too sudden. I'll lie,—aye, I'll lie down—I'll receive him in my little dressing-room, there's a couch—yes, yes, I'll give the first impression on a couch.—I won't lie neither, but loll and lean upon one elbow: with one foot a little dangling off, jogging in a thoughtful way—yes—and then as soon as he appears, start, aye, start and be surprised, and rise to meet him in a pretty disorder—yes—oh, nothing is more alluring than a levee from a couch, in some confusion: it shows the foot to advantage, and furnishes with blushes, and recomposing airs beyond comparison. Hark! there's a coach.

FOIBLE: 'Tis he, madam.

LADY WISHFORT: Oh, dear!—Has my nephew made his addresses to Millamant? I ordered him.

FOIBLE: Sir Wilfull is set in to drinking, madam, in the parlor.

LADY WISHFORT: Odds my life, I'll send him to her. Call her down, Foible; bring her hither. I'll send him as I go—when they are together, then come to me, Foible, that I may not be too long alone with Sir Rowland. [Exit]

[Enter Mrs. Millamant and Mrs. Fainall]

FOIBLE: Madam, I stayed here, to tell your ladyship that Mr. Mirabell has waited this half-hour for

[19] Poured sachet powder on.

an opportunity to talk with you: though my lady's orders were to leave you and Sir Wilfull together. Shall I tell Mr. Mirabell that you are at leisure?

MRS. MILLAMANT: No—what would the dear man have? I am thoughtful, and would amuse myself—bid him come another time.

"There never yet was woman made
Nor shall, but to be cursed."

[Repeating, and walking about]
That's hard!

MRS. FAINALL: You are very fond of Sir John Suckling[20] to-day, Millamant, and the poets.

MRS. MILLAMANT: He? Aye, and filthy verses—so I am.

FOIBLE: Sir Wilfull is coming, madam. Shall I send Mr. Mirabell away?

MRS. MILLAMANT: Aye, if you please, Foible, send him away—or send him hither—just as you will, dear Foible.—I think I'll see him—shall I? Aye, let the wretch come.

[Exit Foible]

"Thyrsis, a youth of the inspired train."[21]

[Repeating]
Dear Fainall, entertain Sir Wilfull—thou hast philosophy to undergo a fool, thou art married and hast patience—I would confer with my own thoughts.

MRS. FAINALL: I am obliged to you, that you would make me your proxy in this affair; but I have business of my own.

[Enter Sir Wilfull]

MRS. FAINALL: O Sir Wilfull, you are come at the critical instant. There's your mistress up to the ears in love and contemplation; pursue your point now or never.

SIR WILFULL: Yes; my aunt will have it so—I would gladly have been encouraged with a bottle or two, because I'm somewhat wary at first before I am acquainted.—[This while Millamant walks about repeating to herself] But I hope, after a time, I shall break my mind—that is, upon further acquaintance —so for the present, cousin, I'll take my leave—if so be you'll be so kind to make my excuse, I'll return to my company—

MRS. FAINALL: Oh, fie, Sir Wilfull! What, you must not be daunted.

SIR WILFULL: Daunted! no, that's not it, it is not so much for that—for if so be that I set on't, I'll do't. But only for the present, 'tis sufficient till further acquaintance, that's all—your servant.

MRS. FAINALL: Nay, I'll swear you shall never lose so favorable an opportunity, if I can help it. I'll leave you together, and lock the door. [Exit]

SIR WILFULL: Nay, nay, cousin—I have forgot my gloves—what d'ye do?—S'heart, a'has locked the door indeed, I think—nay, Cousin Fainall, open the door—pshaw, what a vixen trick is this?—Nay, now

[20] A spirited Cavalier poet (1609–1642).
[21] A line from the poet Edmund Waller (1606–1687).

a'has seen me too.—Cousin, I made bold to pass through as it were—I think this door's enchanted!

MRS. MILLAMANT: [*Repeating*]

"I prithee spare me, gentle boy,
Press me no more for that slight toy."

SIR WILFULL: Anon? Cousin, your servant.

MRS. MILLAMANT: [*Repeating*]

"That foolish trifle of a heart."

Sir Wilfull!

SIR WILFULL: Yes—your servant. No offence, I hope, cousin.

MRS. MILLAMANT: [*Repeating*]

"I swear it will not do its part,
Though thou dost thine, employest thy power and
    art."

Natural, easy Suckling!

SIR WILFULL: Anon? Suckling! no such suckling neither, cousin, nor stripling: I thank Heaven, I'm no minor.

MRS. MILLAMANT: Ah, rustic, ruder than Gothic!

SIR WILFULL: Well, well, I shall understand your lingo one of these days, cousin; in the meanwhile I must answer in plain English.

MRS. MILLAMANT: Have you any business with me, Sir Wilfull?

SIR WILFULL: Not at present, cousin—yes, I make bold to see, to come and know if that how you were disposed to fetch a walk this evening, if so be that I might not be troublesome, I would have sought a walk with you.

MRS. MILLAMANT: A walk! what then?

SIR WILFULL: Nay, nothing—only for the walk's sake, that's all.

MRS. MILLAMANT: I nauseate walking; 'tis a country diversion; I loathe the country, and everything that relates to it.

SIR WILFULL: Indeed! ha! Look ye, look ye, you do? Nay, 'tis like you may—here are choice of pastimes here in town, as plays and the like; that must be confessed indeed.

MRS. MILLAMANT: *A l'étourdie!*[22] I hate the town too.

SIR WILFULL: Dear heart, that's much—ha! that you should hate 'em both! Ha! 'tis like you may; there are some can't relish the town, and others can't away with the country—'tis like you may be one of those, cousin.

MRS. MILLAMANT: Ha! ha! ha! yes, 'tis like I may. —You have nothing further to say to me?

SIR WILFULL: Not at present, cousin.—'Tis like when I have an opportunity to be more private—I may break my mind in some measure—I conjecture you partly guess—however, that's as time shall try —but spare to speak and spare to speed, as they say.

22 Madly.

MRS. MILLAMANT: If it is of no great importance, Sir Wilfull, you will oblige me to leave me; I have just now a little business—

SIR WILFULL: Enough, enough, cousin: yes, yes, all a case—when you're disposed: now's as well as another time; and another time as well as now. All's one for that—yes, yes, if your concerns call you, there's no haste; it will keep cold, as they say.— Cousin, your servant—I think this door's locked.

MRS. MILLAMANT: You may go this way, sir.

SIR WILFULL: Your servant; then with your leave I'll return to my company. [*Exit*]

MRS. MILLAMANT: Aye, aye; ha! ha! ha!

"Like Phœbus sung the no less amorous boy."[23]

[*Enter Mirabell*]

MIRABELL: *"Like Daphne she, as lovely and as coy."* Do you lock yourself up from me, to make my search more curious? or is this pretty artifice contrived to signify that here the chase must end, and my pursuits be crowned? For you can fly no further.

MRS. MILLAMANT: Vanity! no—I'll fly, and be followed to the last moment. Though I am upon the very verge of matrimony, I expect you should solicit me as much as if I were wavering at the grate of a monastery, with one foot over the threshold. I'll be solicited to the very last, nay, and afterwards.

MIRABELL: What, after the last?

MRS. MILLAMANT: Oh, I should think I was poor and had nothing to bestow, if I were reduced to an inglorious ease, and freed from the agreeable fatigues of solicitation.

MIRABELL: But do not you know, that when favors are conferred upon instant and tedious solicitation, that they diminish in their value, and that both the giver loses the grace, and the receiver lessens his pleasure?

MRS. MILLAMANT: It may be in things of common application; but never sure in love. Oh, I hate a lover that can dare to think he draws a moment's air, independent of the bounty of his mistress. There is not so impudent a thing in nature, as the saucy look of an assured man, confident of success. The pedantic arrogance of a very husband has not so pragmatical an air. Ah! I'll never marry, unless I am first made sure of my will and pleasure.

MIRABELL: Would you have 'em both before marriage? or will you be contented with the first now, and stay for the other till after grace?

MRS. MILLAMANT: Ah! don't be impertinent.—My dear liberty, shall I leave thee? my faithful solitude, my darling contemplation, must I bid you then adieu? Ay-h adieu—my morning thoughts, agreeable wakings, indolent slumbers, all ye *douceurs*, ye *sommeils du matin*,[24] adieu?—I can't do't, 'tis more than impossible—positively, Mirabell, I'll lie abed in a morning as long as I please.

23 Also by Waller.
24 Sweetnesses, morning naps.

MIRABELL: Then I'll get up in a morning as early as I please.

MRS. MILLAMANT: Ah! idle creature, get up when you will—and d'ye hear, I won't be called names after I'm married; positively I won't be called names.

MIRABELL: Names!

MRS. MILLAMANT: Aye, as wife, spouse, my dear, joy, jewel, love, sweetheart, and the rest of that nauseous cant, in which men and their wives are so fulsomely familiar—I shall never bear that—good Mirabell, don't let us be familiar or fond, nor kiss before folks, like my Lady Fadler and Sir Francis: nor go to Hyde Park together the first Sunday in a new chariot, to provoke eyes and whispers, and then never to be seen there together again; as if we were proud of one another the first week, and ashamed of one another ever after. Let us never visit together, nor go to a play together; but let us be very strange and well-bred: let us be as strange as if we had been married a great while; and as well-bred as if we were not married at all.

MIRABELL: Have you any more conditions to offer? Hitherto your demands are pretty reasonable.

MRS. MILLAMANT: Trifles!—As liberty to pay and receive visit to and from whom I please; to write and receive letters, without interrogatories or wry faces on your part; to wear what I please; and choose conversation with regard only to my own taste; to have no obligation upon me to converse with wits that I don't like, because they are your acquaintance: or to be intimate with fools, because they may be your relations. Come to dinner when I please; dine in my dressing-room when I'm out of humor, without giving a reason. To have my closet inviolate; to be sole empress of my tea-table, which you must never presume to approach without first asking leave. And lastly, wherever I am, you shall always knock at the door before you come in. These articles subscribed, if I continue to endure you a little longer, I may by degrees dwindle into a wife.

MIRABELL: Your bill of fare is something advanced in this latter account.—Well, have I liberty to offer conditions—that when you are dwindled into a wife, I may not be beyond measure enlarged into a husband?

MRS. MILLAMANT: You have free leave; propose your utmost, speak and spare not.

MIRABELL: I thank you.—*Imprimis*[25] then, I covenant, that your acquaintance be general; that you admit no sworn confidant, or intimate of your own sex; no she-friend to screen her affairs under your countenance, and tempt you to make trial of a mutual secrecy. No decoy-duck to wheedle you a fop-scrambling to the play in a mask—then bring you home in a pretended fright, when you think you shall be found out—and rail at me for missing the play, and disappointing the frolic which you had to pick me up, and prove my constancy.

[25] "First," as in a legal document.

MRS. MILLAMANT: Detestable *imprimis!* I go to the play in a mask!

MIRABELL: *Item*, I article, that you continue to like your own face, as long as I shall: and while it passes current with me, that you endeavor not to new-coin it. To which end, together with all vizards for the day, I prohibit all masks for the night, made of oiled-skins, and I know not what—hogs' bones, hares' gall, pig-water, and the marrow of a roasted cat. In short, I forbid all commerce with the gentlewoman in what d'ye call it court. *Item*, I shut my doors against all bawds with baskets, and pennyworths of muslin, china, fans, atlases, etc.—*Item*, when you shall be breeding—

MRS. MILLAMANT: Ah! name it not.

MIRABELL: Which may be presumed with a blessing on our endeavors—

MRS. MILLAMANT: Odious endeavors!

MIRABELL: I denounce against all strait lacing, squeezing for a shape, till you mould my boy's head like a sugar-loaf, and instead of a man-child, make me father to a crooked billet. Lastly, to the dominion of the tea-table I submit—but with proviso, that you exceed not in your province; but restrain yourself to native and simple tea-table drinks, as tea, chocolate, and coffee: as likewise to genuine and authorized tea-table talk—such as mending of fashions, spoiling reputations, railing at absent friends, and so forth—but that on no account you encroach upon the men's prerogative, and presume to drink healths, or toast fellows; for prevention of which I banish all foreign forces, all auxiliaries to the tea-table, as orange-brandy, all aniseed, cinnamon, citron, and Barbadoes waters, together with ratafia, and the most noble spirit of clary—but for cowslip wine, poppy water, and all dormitives, those I allow.—These provisoes admitted, in other things I may prove a tractable and complying huband.

MRS. MILLAMANT: O horrid provisoes! filthy strong-waters! I toast fellows! odious men! I hate your odious provisoes.

MIRABELL: Then we are agreed! Shall I kiss your hand upon the contract? And here comes one to be a witness to the sealing of the deed.

[*Enter* Mrs. Fainall]

MRS. MILLAMANT: Fainall, what shall I do? shall I have him? I think I must have him.

MRS. FAINALL: Aye, aye, take him, take him, what should you do?

MRS. MILLAMANT: Well then—I'll take my death I'm in a horrid fright—Fainall, I shall never say it —well—I think—I'll endure you.

MRS. FAINALL: Fie! fie! have him, have him, and tell him so in plain terms: for I am sure you have a mind to him.

MRS. MILLAMANT: Are you? I think I have—and the horrid man looks as if he thought so too—well, you ridiculous thing you, I'll have you—I won't be kissed, nor I won't be thanked—here kiss my hand though.—So, hold your tongue now, don't say a word.

MRS. FAINALL: Mirabell, there's a necessity for your obedience; you have neither time to talk nor stay. My mother is coming; and in my conscience if she should see you, would fall into fits, and maybe not recover time enough to return to Sir Rowland, who, as Foible tells me, is in a fair way to succeed. Therefore spare your ecstacies for another occasion, and slip down the back-stairs, where Foible waits to consult you.

MRS. MILLAMANT: Aye, go, go. In the meantime I suppose you have said something to please me.

MIRABELL: I am all obedience. [Exit]

MRS. FAINALL: Yonder Sir Wilfull's drunk, and so noisy that my mother has been forced to leave Sir Rowland to appease him; but he answers her only with singing and drinking—what they may have done by this time I know not; but Petulant and he were upon quarreling as I came by.

MRS. MILLAMANT: Well, if Mirabell should not make a good husband, I am a lost thing, for I find I love him violently.

MRS. FAINALL: So it seems; for you mind not what's said to you.—If you doubt him, you had best take up with Sir Wilfull.

MRS. MILLAMANT: How can you name that superannuated lubber? foh!

[Enter Witwoud]

MRS. FAINALL: So, is the fray made up, that you have left 'em?

WITWOUD: Left 'em? I could stay no longer—I have laughed like ten christenings—I am tipsy with laughing—if I had stayed any longer I should have burst—I must have been let out and pieced in the sides like an unsized camlet.—Yes, yes, the fray is composed; my lady came in like a *nolle prosequi,*[26] and stopped the proceedings.

MRS. MILLAMANT: What was the dispute?

WITWOUD: That's the jest; there was no dispute. They could neither of 'em speak for rage, and so fell a-sputtering at one another like two roasting apples.

[Enter Petulant, *drunk*]

WITWOUD: Now, Petulant, all's over, all's well. Gad, my head begins to whim it about—why dost thou not speak? thou art both as drunk and as mute as a fish.

PETULANT: Look you, Mrs. Millamant—if you can love me, dear nymph—say it—and that's the conclusion—pass on, or pass off—that's all.

WITWOUD: Thou hast uttered volumes, folios, in less than *decimo sexto,*[27] my dear Lacedemonian. Sirrah, Petulant, thou art an epitomizer of words.

PETULANT: Witwoud—you are an annihilator of sense.

[26] "Unwilling to prosecute"—a legal entry to the effect that the plaintiff is unwilling to press his charge.
[27] A tiny volume.

WITWOUD: Thou art a retailer of phrases; and dost deal in remnants of remnants, like a maker of pincushions—thou art in truth (metaphorically speaking) a speaker of shorthand.

PETULANT: Thou art (without a figure) just one-half of an ass, and Baldwin yonder, thy half-brother, is the rest.—A Gemini of asses split would make just four of you.

WITWOUD: Thou dost bite, my dear mustard seed; kiss me for that.

PETULANT: Stand off!—I'll kiss no more males—I have kissed your twin yonder in a humor of reconciliation, till he [*hiccups*] rises upon my stomach like a radish.

MRS. MILLAMANT: Eh! filthy creature! what was the quarrel?

PETULANT: There was no quarrel—there might have been a quarrel.

WITWOUD: If there had been words enow between 'em to have expressed provocation, they had gone together by the ears like a pair of castanets.

PETULANT: You were the quarrel.

MRS. MILLAMANT: Me!

PETULANT: If I have a humor to quarrel, I can make less matters conclude premises.—If you are not handsome, what then, if I have a humor to prove it? If I shall have my reward, say so; if not, fight for your face the next time yourself—I'll go sleep.

WITWOUD: Do, wrap thyself up like a wood-louse, and dream revenge—and hear me, if thou canst learn to write by to-morrow morning, pen me a challenge.—I'll carry it for thee.

PETULANT: Carry your mistress' monkey a spider! —Go flea dogs, and read romances!—I'll go to bed to my maid. [*Exit*]

MRS. FAINALL: He's horribly drunk.—How came you all in this pickle?

WITWOUD: A plot! a plot! to get rid of the night —your husband's advice; but he sneaked off.

SCENE II.

The dining-room in Lady Wishfort's *house.*

[Sir Wilfull *drunk,* Lady Wishfort, Witwoud, Mrs. Millamant, *and* Mrs. Fainall]

LADY WISHFORT: Out upon't, out upon't! At years of discretion, and comport yourself at this rantipole rate!

SIR WILFULL: No offence, aunt.

LADY WISHFORT: Offence! as I'm a person, I'm shamed of you—foh! how you stink of wine! D'ye think my niece will ever endure such a Borachio! you're an absolute Borachio.[28]

SIR WILFULL: Borachio?

LADY WISHFORT: At a time when you should com-

[28] A villain in Shakespeare's *Much Ado About Nothing.*

mence an amour, and put your best foot foremost—

SIR WILFULL: S'heart, an you grutch me your liquor, make a bill—give me more drink, and take my purse—[*Sings*]

"*Prithee fill me the glass,*
  Till it laugh in my face,
With ale that is potent and mellow;
  He that whines for a lass,
  Is an ignorant ass,
For a bumper has not its fellow."

But if you would have me marry my cousin—say the word, and I'll do't—Wilfull will do't, that's the word—Wilfull will do't, that's my crest—my motto I have forgot.

LADY WISHFORT: My nephew's a little overtaken, cousin—but 'tis with drinking your health.—O' my word you are obliged to him.

SIR WILFULL: *In vino veritas,* aunt.—If I drunk your health to-day, cousin—I am a Borachio. But if you have a mind to be married, say the word, and send for the piper; Wilfull will do't. If not, dust it away, and let's have 'tother round.—Tony! Odds heart, where's Tony!—Tony's an honest fellow; but he spits after a bumper, and that's a fault—[*Sings*]

"*We'll drink, and we'll never ha' done, boys,*
  Put the glass then around with the sun, boys,
Let Apollo's example invite us;
  For he's drunk every night,
  And that makes him so bright,
That he's able next morning to light us."

The sun's a good pimple, an honest soaker; he has a cellar at your Antipodes. If I travel, aunt, I touch at your Antipodes.—Your Antipodes are a good, rascally sort of topsy-turvy fellows: if I had a bumper, I'd stand upon my head and drink a health to 'em.—A match or no match, cousin with the hard name?—Aunt, Wilfull will do't. If she has her maidenhead, let her look to't; if she has not, let her keep her own counsel in the meantime, and cry out at the nine months' end.

MRS. MILLAMANT: Your pardon, madam, I can stay no longer—Sir Wilfull grows very powerful. Eh! how he smells! I shall be overcome, if I stay.—Come, cousin.

[*Exeunt* Mrs. Millamant *and* Mrs. Fainall]

LADY WISHFORT: Smells! He would poison a tallow-chandler and his family! Beastly creature, I know not what to do with him!—Travel, quotha! aye, travel, travel, get thee gone, get thee gone, get thee but far enough, to the Saracens, or the Tartars, or the Turks!—for thou art not fit to live in a Christian commonwealth, thou beastly pagan!

SIR WILFULL: Turks, no; no Turks, aunt: your Turks are infidels, and believe not in the grape. Your Mahometan, your Mussulman, is a dry stinkard—no offence, aunt. My map says that your Turk is not so honest a man as your Christian. I cannot find by the

map that your Mufti is orthodox—whereby it is a plain case, that orthodox is a hard word, aunt, and [*hiccups*] Greek for claret.—[*Sings*]

"*To drink is a Christian diversion,*
  Unknown to the Turk or the Persian:
Let Mahometan fools
Live by heathenish rules,
And be damned over tea-cups and coffee.
  But let British lads sing,
  Crown a health to the king,
And a fig for your sultan and sophy!"

Ah, Tony!

[*Enter* Foible, *who whispers to* Lady Wishfort]

LADY WISHFORT: [*Aside to* Foible] Sir Rowland impatient? Good lack! what shall I do with this beastly tumbril?—[*Aloud*] Go lie down and sleep, you sot! —or, as I'm a person, I'll have you bastinadoed with broomsticks.—Call up the wenches.

SIR WILFULL: Ahey! wenches, where are the wenches?

LADY WISHFORT: Dear Cousin Witwoud, get him away, and you will bind me to you inviolably. I have an affair of moment that invades me with some precipitation—you will oblige me to all futurity.

WITWOUD: Come, knight.—Pox on him, I don't know what to say to him.—Will you go to a cock-match?

SIR WILFULL: With a wench, Tony! Is she a shake-bag, sirrah? Let me bite your cheek for that.

WITWOUD: Horrible! he has a breath like a bag-pipe!—Aye, aye; come, will you march, my Salopian?

SIR WILFULL: Lead on, little Tony—I'll follow thee, my Anthony, my Tantony, sirrah, thou shalt be my Tantony, and I'll be thy pig. [*Sings*]

"*And a fig for your sultan and sophy.*"

[*Exeunt* Sir Wilfull *and* Witwoud]

LADY WISHFORT: This will never do. It will never make a match—at least before he has been abroad.

[*Enter* Waitwell, *disguised as* Sir Rowland]

LADY WISHFORT: Dear Sir Rowland, I am confounded with confusion at the retrospection of my own rudeness!—I have more pardons to ask than the pope distributes in the year of jubilee. But I hope, where there is likely to be so near an alliance, we may unbend the severity of decorums, and dispense with a little ceremony.

WAITWELL: My impatience, madam, is the effect of my transport; and till I have the possession of your adorable person, I am tantalized on the rack; and do but hang, madam, on the tenter of expectation.

LADY WISHFORT: You have excess of gallantry, Sir Rowland, and press things to a conclusion with a most prevailing vehemence.—But a day or two for decency of marriage—

WAITWELL: For decency of funeral, madam! The delay will break my heart—or, if that should fail, I shall be poisoned. My nephew will get an inkling of my designs, and poison me—and I would willingly starve him before I die—I would gladly go out of the world with that satisfaction.—That would be some comfort to me, if I could but live so long as to be revenged on that unnatural viper!

LADY WISHFORT: Is he so unnatural, say you? Truly I would contribute much both to the saving of your life, and the accomplishment of your revenge.—Not that I respect myself, though he has been a perfidious wretch to me.

WAITWELL: Perfidious to you!

LADY WISHFORT: O Sir Rowland, the hours that he has died away at my feet, the tears that he has shed, the oaths that he has sworn, the palpitations that he has felt, the trances and the tremblings, the ardors and the ecstasies, the kneelings and the risings, the heart-heavings and the handgrippings, the pangs and the pathetic regards of his protesting eyes!—Oh, no memory can register!

WAITWELL: What, my rival! is the rebel my rival? —a' dies.

LADY WISHFORT: No, don't kill him at once, Sir Rowland, starve him gradually, inch by inch.

WAITWELL: I'll do't. In three weeks he shall be barefoot; in a month out at knees with begging an alms.—He shall starve upward and upward, till he has nothing living but his head, and then go out in a stink like a candle's end upon a save-all.

LADY WISHFORT: Well, Sir Rowland, you have the way—you are no novice in the labyrinth of love— you have the clue.—But as I am a person, Sir Rowland, you must not attribute my yielding to any sinister appetite, or indigestion of widowhood; nor impute my complacency to any lethargy of continence.—I hope you do not think me prone to any iteration of nuptials—

WAITWELL: Far be it from me—

LADY WISHFORT: If you do, I protest I must recede —or think that I have made a prostitution of decorums; but in the vehemence of compassion, and to save the life of a person of so much importance—

WAITWELL: I esteem it so.

LADY WISHFORT: Or else you wrong my condescension.

WAITWELL: I do not, I do not!

LADY WISHFORT: Indeed you do.

WAITWELL: I do not, fair shrine of virtue!

LADY WISHFORT: If you think the least scruple of carnality was an ingredient,—

WAITWELL: Dear madam, no. You are all camphor and frankincense, all chastity and odor.

LADY WISHFORT: Or that—

[Enter Foible]

FOIBLE: Madam, the dancers are ready; and there's one with a letter, who must deliver it into your own hands.

LADY WISHFORT: Sir Rowland, will you give me leave? Think favorably, judge candidly, and conclude you have found a person who would suffer racks in honor's cause, dear Sir Rowland, and will wait on you incessantly. [Exit]

WAITWELL: Fie, fie!—What a slavery have I undergone! Spouse, hast thou any cordial? I want spirits.

FOIBLE: What a washy rogue art thou, to pant thus for a quarter of an hour's lying and swearing to a fine lady!

WAITWELL: Oh, she is an antidote to desire! Spouse, thou wilt fare the worse for't—I shall have no appetite to iteration of nuptials this eight-and-forty hours.—By this hand I'd rather be a chairman in the dog-days—than act Sir Rowland till this time tomorrow.

[Re-enter Lady Wishfort, with a letter]

LADY WISHFORT: Call in the dancers.—Sir Rowland, we'll sit, if you please, and see the entertainment. [A dance] Now, with your permission, Sir Rowland, I will peruse my letter.—I would open it in your presence, because I would not make you uneasy. If it should make you uneasy, I would burn it.—Speak, if it does—but you may see the superscription is like a woman's hand.

FOIBLE: [Aside to Waitwell] By Heaven! Mrs. Marwood's, I know it.—My heart aches—get it from her.

WAITWELL: A woman's hand! no, madam, that's no woman's hand, I see that already. That's somebody whose throat must be cut.

LADY WISHFORT: Nay, Sir Rowland, since you give me a proof of your passion by your jealousy, I promise you I'll make a return, by a frank communication.—You shall see it—we'll open it together— look you here.—[Reads]—"Madam, though unknown to you"—Look you there, 'tis from nobody that I know—"I have that honor for your character, that I think myself obliged to let you know you are abused. He who pretends to be Sir Rowland, is a cheat and a rascal."—Oh, Heavens! what's this?

FOIBLE: [Aside] Unfortunate! all's ruined!

WAITWELL: How, how, let me see, let me see!— [Reads] "A rascal, and disguised and suborned for that imposture,"—O villainy! O villainy!—"by the contrivance of—"

LADY WISHFORT: I shall faint, I shall die, oh!

FOIBLE: [Aside to Waitwell] Say 'tis your nephew's hand—quickly, his plot, swear it, swear it!

WAITWELL: Here's a villain! Madam, don't you perceive it, don't you see it?

LADY WISHFORT: Too well, too well! I have seen too much.

WAITWELL: I told you at first I knew the hand.— A woman's hand! The rascal writes a sort of a large hand; your Roman hand—I saw there was a throat to be cut presently. If he were my son, as he is my nephew, I'd pistol him!

FOIBLE: O treachery!—But are you sure, Sir Rowland, it is his writing?

WAITWELL: Sure! am I here? Do I live? Do I love this pearl of India? I have twenty letters in my pocket from him in the same character.

LADY WISHFORT: How!

FOIBLE: Oh, what luck it is, Sir Rowland, that you

were present at this juncture!—This was the business that brought Mr. Mirabell disguised to Madam Millamant this afternoon. I thought something was contriving, when he stole by me and would have hid his face.

LADY WISHFORT: How, how!—I heard the villain was in the house indeed; and now I remember, my niece went away abruptly, when Sir Wilfull was to have made his addresses.

FOIBLE: Then, then, madam, Mr. Mirabell waited for her in her chamber! but I would not tell your ladyship to discompose you when you were to receive Sir Rowland.

WAITWELL: Enough, his date is short.

FOIBLE: No, good Sir Rowland, don't incur the law.

WAITWELL: Law! I care not for law. I can but die, and 'tis in a good cause.—My lady shall be satisfied of my truth and innocence, though it cost me my life.

LADY WISHFORT: No, dear Sir Rowland, don't fight; if you should be killed I must never show my face; or hanged—oh, consider my reputation, Sir Rowland!—No, you shan't fight—I'll go in and examine my niece; I'll make her confess. I conjure you, Sir Rowland, by all your love, not to fight.

WAITWELL: I am charmed, madam, I obey. But some proof you must let me give you; I'll go for a black box, which contains the writings of my whole estate, and deliver that into your hands.

LADY WISHFORT: Aye, dear Sir Rowland, that will be some comfort, bring the black box.

WAITWELL: And may I presume to bring a contract to be signed this night? may I hope so far?

LADY WISHFORT: Bring what you will; but come alive, pray come alive. Oh, this is a happy discovery!

WAITWELL: Dead or alive I'll come—and married we will be in spite of treachery; aye, and get an heir that shall defeat the last remaining glimpse of hope in my abandoned nephew. Come, my buxom widow:

Ere long you shall substantial proofs receive,
That I'm an errant knight—

FOIBLE: [*Aside*]   *Or errant knave.*
[*Exeunt*]

ACT V. SCENE I.

A room in Lady Wishfort's *house.*

[Lady Wishfort *and* Foible]

LADY WISHFORT: Out of my house, out of my house, thou viper! thou serpent, that I have fostered! thou bosom traitress, that I raised from nothing!—Begone! begone! begone!—go! go!—That I took from washing of old gauze and weaving of dead hair, with a bleak blue nose over a chafing-dish of starved embers, and

dining behind a traverse rag, in a shop no bigger than a bird-cage!—Go, go! starve again, do, do!

FOIBLE: Dear Madam, I'll beg pardon on my knees.

LADY WISHFORT: Away! out! out!—Go, set up for yourself again!—Do, drive a trade, do, with your three-pennyworth of small ware, flaunting upon a pack-thread, under a brandy-seller's bulk, or against a dead wall by a ballad-monger! Go, hang out an old frisoneer-gorget, with a yard of yellow colbertine[29] again! Do; an old gnawed mask, two rows of pins, and a child's fiddle; a glass necklace with the beads broken, and a quilted night-cap with one ear! Go, go, drive a trade!—These were your commodities, you treacherous trull! this was the merchandise you dealt in when I took you into my house, placed you next myself, and made you governante of my whole family! You have forgot this, have you, now you have feathered your nest?

FOIBLE: No, no, dear madam. Do but hear me, have but a moment's patience, I'll confess all. Mr. Mirabell seduced me; I am not the first that he has wheedled with his dissembling tongue; your ladyship's own wisdom has been deluded by him; then how should I, a poor ignorant, defend myself? O madam, if you knew but what he promised me, and how he assured me your ladyship should come to no damage!—Or else the wealth of the Indies should not have bribed me to conspire against so good, so sweet, so kind a lady as you have been to me.

LADY WISHFORT: No damage! What, to betray me, and marry me to a cast servingman! to make me a receptacle, an hospital for a decayed pimp! No damage! O thou frontless impudence, more than a big-bellied actress!

FOIBLE: Pray, do but hear me, madam; he could not marry your ladyship, madam.—No, indeed, his marriage was to have been void in law, for he was married to me first, to secure your ladyship. He could not have bedded your ladyship; for if he had consummated with your ladyship, he must have run the risk of the law, and been put upon his clergy.[30]—Yes, indeed, I inquired of the law in that case before I would meddle or make.

LADY WISHFORT: What, then, I have been your property, have I? I have been convenient to you, it seems!—While you were catering for Mirabell, I have been broker for you! What, have you made a passive bawd of me?—This exceeds all precedent; I am brought to fine uses, to become a botcher of second-hand marriages between Abigails and Andrews!—I'll couple you!—Yes, I'll baste you together, you and your Philander! I'll Duke's-place you, as I am a person! Your turtle is in custody already: you shall coo in the same cage, if there be a constable or warrant in the parish. [*Exit*]

FOIBLE: Oh, that ever I was born! Oh, that I was

[29] Frisoneer-gorget: A collar made of waste silk; colbertine: French lace.

[30] Forced to plead benefit of clergy to escape capital punishment.

ever married!—A bride!—aye, I shall be a Bridewell-bride.[31]—Oh!

[*Enter* Mrs. Fainall]

MRS. FAINALL: Poor Foible, what's the matter?

FOIBLE: O madam, my lady's gone for a constable. I shall be had to a justice, and put to Bridewell to beat hemp. Poor Waitwell's gone to prison already.

MRS. FAINALL: Have a good heart, Foible; Mirabell's gone to give security for him. This is all Marwood's and my husband's doing.

FOIBLE: Yes, yes; I know it, madam: she was in my lady's closet, and overheard all that you said to me before dinner. She sent the letter to my lady; and that missing effect, Mr. Fainall laid this plot to arrest Waitwell, when he pretended to go for the papers; and in the meantime Mrs. Marwood declared all to my lady.

MRS. FAINALL: Was there no mention made of me in the letter? My mother does not suspect my being in the confederacy? I fancy Marwood has not told her, though she has told my husband.

FOIBLE: Yes, madam; but my lady did not see that part; we stifled the letter before she read so far —Has that mischievous devil told Mr. Fainall of your ladyship, then?

MRS. FAINALL: Aye, all's out—my affair with Mirabell—everything discovered. This is the last day of our living together, that's my comfort.

FOIBLE: Indeed, madam; and so 'tis a comfort if you knew all—he has been even with your ladyship, which I could have told you long enough since, but I loved to keep peace and quietness by my goodwill. I had rather bring friends together, than set 'em at distance: but Mrs. Marwood and he are nearer related than ever their parents thought for.

MRS. FAINALL: Sayest thou so, Foible? Canst thou prove this?

FOIBLE: I can take my oath of it, madam; so can Mrs. Mincing. We have had many a fair word from Madam Marwood, to conceal something that passed in our chamber one evening when you were at Hyde Park; and we were thought to have gone a-walking, but we went up unawares; though we were sworn to secrecy, too. Madam Marwood took a book and swore us upon it, but it was but a book of poems. So long as it was not a bible-oath, we may break it with a safe conscience.

MRS. FAINALL: This discovery is the most opportune thing I could wish.—Now, Mincing!

[*Enter* Mincing]

MINCING: My lady would speak with Mrs. Foible, mem. Mr. Mirabell is with her; he has set your spouse at liberty, Mrs. Foible, and would have you hide yourself in my lady's closet till my old lady's anger is abated. Oh, my old lady is in a perilous passion at something Mr. Fainall has said; he swears, and my old lady cries. There's a fearful hurricane, I vow. He says, mem, how that he'll have my lady's fortune made over to him, or he'll be divorced.

[31] A house-of-correction bride.

MRS. FAINALL: Does your lady or Mirabell know that?

MINCING: Yes, mem; they have sent me to see if Sir Wilfull be sober, and to bring him to them. My lady is resolved to have him, I think, rather than lose such a vast sum as six thousand pounds.—Oh, come, Mrs. Foible, I hear my old lady.

MRS. FAINALL: Foible, you must tell Mincing that she must prepare to vouch when I call her.

FOIBLE: Yes, yes, madam.

MINCING: Oh, yes, mem, I'll vouch anything for your ladyship's service, be what it will.

[*Exeunt*]

SCENE II.

Another room in Lady Wishfort's *house.*

[Mrs. Fainall, Lady Wishfort, *and* Mrs. Marwood]

LADY WISHFORT: Oh, my dear friend, how can I enumerate the benefits that I have received from your goodness! To you I owe the timely discovery of the false vows of Mirabell; to you I owe the detection of the impostor Sir Rowland. And now you are become an intercessor with my son-in-law, to save the honor of my house, and compound for the frailties of my daughter. Well, friend, you are enough to reconcile me to the bad world, or else I would retire to deserts and solitudes, and feed harmless sheep by groves and purling streams. Dear Marwood, let us leave the world, and retire by ourselves and be shepherdesses.

MRS. MARWOOD: Let us first dispatch the affair in hand, madam. We shall have leisure to think of retirement afterwards. Here is one who is concerned in the treaty.

LADY WISHFORT: Oh, daughter, daughter! is it possible thou shouldst be my child, bone of my bone, and flesh of my flesh, and, as I may say, another me, and yet transgress the most minute particle of severe virtue? Is it possible you should lean aside to iniquity, who have been cast in the direct mould of virtue? I have not only been a mould but a pattern for you, and a model for you, after you were brought into the world.

MRS. FAINALL: I don't understand your ladyship.

LADY WISHFORT: Not understand! Why, have you not been naught? have you not been sophisticated? Not understand! here I am ruined to compound for your caprices and your cuckoldoms. I must pawn my plate and my jewels, and ruin my niece, and all little enough—

MRS. FAINALL: I am wronged and abused, and so are you. 'Tis a false accusation, as false as hell, as false as your friend there, aye, or your friend's friend, my false husband.

MRS. MARWOOD: My friend, Mrs. Fainall! your husband my friend! what do you mean?

MRS. FAINALL: I know what I mean, madam, and so do you; and so shall the world at a time convenient.

MRS. MARWOOD: I am sorry to see you so passionate, madam. More temper would look more like innocence. But I have done. I am sorry my zeal to serve your ladyship and family should admit of misconstruction, or make me liable to affronts. You will pardon me, madam, if I meddle no more with an affair in which I am not personally concerned.

LADY WISHFORT: O dear friend, I am so ashamed that you should meet with such returns!—[*To* Mrs. Fainall] You ought to ask pardon on your knees, ungrateful creature! she deserves more from you than all your life can accomplish.—[*To* Mrs. Marwood] Oh, don't leave me destitute in this perplexity!—no, stick to me, my good genius.

MRS. FAINALL: I tell you, madam, you are abused. —Stick to you! aye, like a leech, to suck your best blood—she'll drop off when she's full. Madam, you shan't pawn a bodkin, nor part with a brass counter, in composition for me. I defy 'em all. Let 'em prove their aspersions; I know my own innocence, and dare stand a trial. [*Exit*]

LADY WISHFORT: Why, if she should be innocent, if she should be wronged after all, ha?—I don't know what to think—and I promise you her education has been unexceptionable—I may say it; for I chiefly made it my own care to initiate her very infancy in the rudiments of virtue, and to impress upon her tender years a young odium and aversion to the very sight of men: aye, friend, she would ha' shrieked if she had but seen a man, till she was in her teens. As I am a person 'tis true—she was never suffered to play with a male child, though but in coats; nay, her very babies were of the feminine gender. Oh, she never looked a man in the face but her own father, or the chaplain, and him we made a shift to put upon her for a woman, by the help of his long garments, and his sleek face, till she was going in her fifteen.

MRS. MARWOOD: 'Twas much she should be deceived so long.

LADY WISHFORT: I warrant you, or she would never have borne to have been catechized by him; and have heard his long lectures against singing and dancing, and such debaucheries; and going to filthy plays, and profane music-meetings, where the lewd trebles squeak nothing but bawdy, and the basses roar blasphemy. Oh, she would have swooned at the sight or name of an obscene play-book!—and can I think, after all this, that my daughter can be naught? What, a whore? and thought it excommunication to set her foot within the door of a playhouse! O dear friend, I can't believe it, no, no! As she says, let him prove it, let him prove it.

MRS. MARWOOD: Prove it, madam! What, and have your name prostituted in a public court! Yours and your daughter's reputation worried at the bar by a pack of bawling lawyers! To be ushered in with an O yes of scandal; and have your case opened by an old fumbling lecher in a quoif[32] like a man-midwife; to bring your daughter's infamy to light; to be a theme for legal punsters and quibblers by the statute; and become a jest against a rule of court, where there is no precedent for a jest in any record—not even in doomsday-book; to discompose the gravity of the bench, and provoke naughty interrogatories in more naughty law Latin; while the good judge, tickled with the proceeding, simpers under a gray beard, and fidgets off and on his cushion as if he had swallowed cantharides,[33] or sat upon cow-itch!—

LADY WISHFORT: Oh, 'tis very hard!

MRS. MARWOOD: And then to have my young revelers of the Temple[34] take notes, like 'prentices at a conventicle; and after talk it over again in commons, or before drawers in an eating-house.

LADY WISHFORT: Worse and worse!

MRS. MARWOOD: Nay, this is nothing; if it would end here 'twere well. But it must, after this, be consigned by the shorthand writers to the public press; and from thence be transferred to the hands, nay into the throats and lungs of hawkers, with voices more licentious than the loud flounder-man's: and this you must hear till you are stunned; nay, you must hear nothing else for some days.

LADY WISHFORT: Oh, 'tis insupportable! No, no, dear friend, make it up, make it up; aye, aye, I'll compound. I'll give up all, myself and my all, my niece and her all—anything, everything for composition.

MRS. MARWOOD: Nay, madam, I advise nothing, I only lay before you, as a friend, the inconveniences which perhaps you have overseen. Here comes Mr. Fainall; if he will be satisfied to huddle up all in silence, I shall be glad. You must think I would rather congratulate than condole with you.

[*Enter* Fainall]

LADY WISHFORT: Aye, aye, I do not doubt it, dear Marwood; no, no, I do not doubt it.

FAINALL: Well, madam, I have suffered myself to be overcome by the importunity of this lady your friend; and am content you shall enjoy your own proper estate during life, on condition you oblige yourself never to marry, under such penalty as I think convenient.

LADY WISHFORT: Never to marry!

FAINALL: No more Sir Rowlands; the next imposture may not be so timely detected.

MRS. MARWOOD: That condition, I dare answer, my lady will consent to without difficulty; she has already but too much experienced the perfidiousness of men.—Besides, madam, when we retire to our pastoral solitude we shall bid adieu to all our thoughts.

LADY WISHFORT: Aye, that's true; but in case of necessity, as of health, or some such emergency—

[32] Legal costume, which had a hood or coif.
[33] A medicine for blistering the patient.
[34] The Inns of Court, which law students attended.

FAINALL: Oh, if you are prescribed marriage, you shall be considered; I only will reserve to myself the power to choose for you. If your physic be wholesome, it matters not who is your apothecary. Next, my wife shall settle on me the remainder of her fortune, not made over already; and for her maintenance depend entirely on my discretion.

LADY WISHFORT: This is most inhumanly savage; exceeding the barbarity of a Muscovite husband.

FAINALL: I learned it from his Czarish majesty's retinue, in a winter evening's conference over brandy and pepper, amongst other secrets of matrimony and policy, as they are at present practiced in the northern hemisphere. But this must be agreed unto, and that positively. Lastly, I will be endowed, in right of my wife, with that six thousand pounds, which is the moiety of Mrs. Millamant's fortune in your possession; and which she has forfeited (as will appear by the last will and testament of your deceased husband, Sir Jonathan Wishfort) by her disobedience in contracting herself against your consent or knowledge; and by refusing the offered match with Sir Wilfull Witwoud, which you, like a careful aunt, had provided for her.

LADY WISHFORT: My nephew was *non compos,* and could not make his addresses.

FAINALL: I come to make demands—I'll hear no objections.

LADY WISHFORT: You will grant me time to consider?

FAINALL: Yes, while the instrument is drawing, to which you must set your hand till more sufficient deeds can be perfected: which I will take care shall be done with all possible speed. In the meanwhile I'll go for the said instrument, and till my return you may balance this matter in your own discretion. [*Exit*]

LADY WISHFORT: This insolence is beyond all precedent, all parallel: must I be subject to this merciless villain?

MRS. MARWOOD: 'Tis severe indeed, madam, that you should smart for your daughter's wantonness.

LADY WISHFORT: 'Twas against my consent that she married this barbarian, but she would have him, though her year was not out.—Ah! her first husband, my son Languish, would not have carried it thus. Well, that was my choice, this is hers: she is matched now with a witness.—I shall be mad!—Dear friend, is there no comfort for me? must I live to be confiscated at this rebel rate?—Here come two more of my Egyptian plagues too.

[*Enter* Mrs. Millamant *and* Sir Wilfull Witwoud]

SIR WILFULL: Aunt, your servant.

LADY WISHFORT: Out, caterpillar, call not me aunt! I know thee not!

SIR WILFULL: I confess I have been a little in disguise, as they say.—S'heart! and I'm sorry for't. What would you have? I hope I have committed no offence, aunt—and if I did I am willing to make satisfaction; and what can a man say fairer? If I have broke anything I'll pay for't, an it cost a pound. And so let that content for what's past, and make no more words. For what's to come, to pleasure you I'm willing to marry my cousin. So pray let's all be friends, she and I are agreed upon the matter before a witness.

LADY WISHFORT: How's this, dear niece? Have I any comfort? Can this be true?

MRS. MILLAMANT: I am content to be a sacrifice to your repose, madam; and to convince you that I had no hand in the plot, as you were misinformed, I have laid my commands on Mirabell to come in person, and be a witness that I give my hand to this flower of knighthood: and for the contract that passed between Mirabell and me, I have obliged him to make resignation of it in your ladyship's presence; he is without, and awaits your leave for admittance.

LADY WISHFORT: Well, I'll swear I am something revived at this testimony of your obedience: but I cannot admit that traitor.—I fear I cannot fortify myself to support his appearance. He is as terrible to me as gorgon; if I see him I fear I shall turn to stone, and petrify incessantly.

MRS. MILLAMANT: If you disoblige him, he may resent your refusal, and insist upon the contract still. Then 'tis the last time he will be offensive to you.

LADY WISHFORT: Are you sure it will be the last time?—If I were sure of that—shall I never see him again?

MRS. MILLAMANT: Sir Wilfull, you and he are to travel together, are you not?

SIR WILFULL: S'heart, the gentleman's a civil gentleman, aunt, let him come in; why, we are sworn brothers and fellow-travelers.—We are to be Pylades and Orestes, he and I.—He is to be my interpreter in foreign parts. He has been over-seas once already; and with proviso that I marry my cousin, will cross 'em once again, only to bear me company.—S'heart, I'll call him in, an I set on't once, he shall come in; and see who'll hinder him. [*Goes to the door and hems*]

MRS. MARWOOD: This is precious fooling, if it would pass; but I'll know the bottom of it.

LADY WISHFORT: O dear Marwood, you are not going?

MRS. MARWOOD: Not far, madam; I'll return immediately. [*Exit*]

[*Enter* Mirabell]

SIR WILFULL: Look up, man, I'll stand by you; 'sbud an she do frown, she can't kill you; besides—harkee—she dare not frown desperately, because her face is none of her own. S'heart, an she should, her forehead would wrinkle like the coat of a cream-cheese; but mum for that, fellow-traveler.

MIRABELL: If a deep sense of the many injuries I have offered to so good a lady, with a sincere remorse, and a hearty contrition, can but obtain the least glance of compassion, I am too happy.—Ah, madam, there was a time!—but let it be forgotten—

I confess I have deservedly forfeited the high place I once held of sighing at your feet. Nay, kill me not, by turning from me in disdain.—I come not to plead for favor; nay, not for pardon; I am a suppliant only for pity—I am going where I never shall behold you more—

SIR WILFULL: How, fellow-traveler! you shall go by yourself then.

MIRABELL: Let me be pitied first, and afterwards forgotten.—I ask no more.

SIR WILFULL: By'r Lady, a very reasonable request, and will cost you nothing, aunt! Come, come, forgive and forget, aunt. Why, you must, an you are a Christian.

MIRABELL: Consider, madam, in reality, you could not receive much prejudice; it was an innocent device; though I confess it had a face of guiltiness—it was at most an artifice which love contrived; and errors which love produces have ever been accounted venial. At least think it is punishment enough, that I have lost what in my heart I hold most dear, that to your cruel indignation I have offered up this beauty, and with her my peace and quiet; nay, all my hopes of future comfort.

SIR WILFULL: An he does not move me, would I may never be o' the quorum!—an it were not as good a deed as to drink, to give her to him again, I would I might never take shipping!—Aunt, if you don't forgive quickly, I shall melt, I can tell you that. My contract went no farther than a little mouth glue, and that's hardly dry—one doleful sigh more from my fellow-traveler, and 'tis dissolved.

LADY WISHFORT: Well, nephew, upon your account —Ah, he has a false insinuating tongue!—Well sir, I will stifle my just resentment at my nephew's request.—I will endeavor what I can to forget, but on proviso that you resign the contract with my niece immediately.

MIRABELL: It is in writing, and with papers of concern; but I have sent my servant for it, and will deliver it to you, with all acknowledgments for your transcendent goodness.

LADY WISHFORT: [Aside] Oh, he has witchcraft in his eyes and tongue!—When I did not see him, I could have bribed a villain to his assassination; but his appearance rakes the embers which have so long lain smothered in my breast.

SCENE III.

The same.

[Lady Wishfort, Mrs. Millamant, Sir Wilfull, Mirabell, Fainall, *and* Mrs. Marwood]

FAINALL: Your date of deliberation, madam, is expired. Here is the instrument; are you prepared to sign?

LADY WISHFORT: If I were prepared, I am not im-powered. My niece exerts a lawful claim, having matched herself by my direction to Sir Wilfull.

FAINALL: That sham is too gross to pass on me— though 'tis imposed on you, madam.

MRS. MILLAMANT: Sir, I have given my consent.

MIRABELL: And, sir, I have resigned my pretensions.

SIR WILFULL: And, sir, I assert my right: and will maintain it in defiance of you, sir, and of your instrument. S'heart, an you talk of an instrument, sir, I have an old fox by my thigh that shall hack your instrument of ram vellum to shreds, sir! It shall not be sufficient for a *mittimus*[35] or a tailor's measure. Therefore withdraw your instrument, sir, or by'r Lady, I shall draw mine.

LADY WISHFORT: Hold, nephew, hold!

MRS. MILLAMANT: Good Sir Wilfull, respite your valor.

FAINALL: Indeed! Are you provided of your guard, with your single beef-eater there? but I'm prepared for you, and insist upon my first proposal. You shall submit your own estate to my management, and absolutely make over my wife's to my sole use, as pursuant to the purport and tenor of this other covenant. —I suppose, madam, your consent is not requisite in this case; nor, Mr. Mirabell, your resignation; nor, Sir Wilfull, your right.—You may draw your fox if you please, sir, and make a bear-garden flourish somewhere else: for here it will not avail. This, my Lady Wishfort, must be subscribed, or your darling daughter's turned adrift, like a leaky hulk, to sink or swim, as she and the current of this lewd town can agree.

LADY WISHFORT: Is there no means, no remedy to stop my ruin? Ungrateful wretch! dost thou not owe thy being, thy subsistence, to my daughter's fortune?

FAINALL: I'll answer you when I have the rest of it in my possession.

MIRABELL: But that you would not accept of a remedy from my hands—I own I have not deserved you should owe any obligation to me; or else perhaps I could advise—

LADY WISHFORT: Oh, what? what? To save me and my child from ruin, from want, I'll forgive all that's past; nay, I'll consent to anything to come, to be delivered from this tyranny.

MIRABELL: Aye, madam; but that is too late, my reward is intercepted. You have disposed of her who only could have made me a compensation for all my services; but be it as it may, I am resolved I'll serve you! you shall not be wronged in this savage manner.

LADY WISHFORT: How! dear Mr. Mirabell, can you be so generous at last! But it is not possible. Harkee, I'll break my nephew's match; you shall have my niece yet, and all her fortune, if you can but save me from this imminent danger.

MIRABELL: Will you? I'll take you at your word. I ask no more. I must have leave for two criminals to appear.

[35] "We send"—a writ or warrant for imprisonment.

LADY WISHFORT: Aye, aye, anybody, anybody!

MIRABELL: Foible is one, and a penitent.

[*Enter* Mrs. Fainall, Foible, *and* Mincing]

MRS. MARWOOD: Oh, my shame! [Mirabell *and* Lady Wishfort *go to* Mrs. Fainall *and* Foible] These corrupt things are brought hither to expose me.

[*To* Fainall]

FAINALL: If it must all come out, why let 'em know it; 'tis but the way of the world. That shall not urge me to relinquish or abate one tittle of my terms; no, I will insist the more.

FOIBLE: Yes, indeed, madam, I'll take my bible-oath of it.

MINCING: And so will I, mem.

LADY WISHFORT: O Marwood, Marwood, art thou false? my friend deceive me! hast thou been a wicked accomplice with that profligate man?

MRS. MARWOOD: Have you so much ingratitude and injustice to give credit against your friend, to the aspersions of two such mercenary trulls?

MINCING: Mercenary, mem? I scorn your words. 'Tis true we found you and Mr. Fainall in the blue garret; by the same token, you swore us to secrecy upon Messalina's[36] poems. Mercenary! No, if we would have been mercenary, we should have held our tongues; you would have bribed us sufficiently.

FAINALL: Go, you are an insignificant thing!— Well, what are you the better for this; is this Mr. Mirabell's expedient? I'll be put off no longer.—You thing, that was a wife, shall smart for this! I will not leave thee wherewithal to hide thy shame; your body shall be naked as your reputation.

MRS. FAINALL: I despise you, and defy your malice! —you have aspersed me wrongfully—I have proved your falsehood—go you and your treacherous—I will not name it, but starve together—perish!

FAINALL: Not while you are worth a groat, indeed, my dear.—Madam, I'll be fooled no longer.

LADY WISHFORT: Ah, Mr. Mirabell, this is small comfort, the detection of this affair.

MIRABELL: Oh, in good time—your leave for the other offender and penitent to appear, madam.

[*Enter* Waitwell *with a box of writings*]

LADY WISHFORT: O Sir Rowland!—Well, rascal!

WAITWELL: What your ladyship pleases. I have brought the black box at last, madam.

MIRABELL: Give it me.—Madam, you remember your promise.

LADY WISHFORT: Aye, dear sir.

MIRABELL: Where are the gentlemen?

WAITWELL: At hand, sir, rubbing their eyes—just risen from sleep.

FAINALL: 'Sdeath, what's this to me? I'll not wait your private concerns.

[*Enter* Petulant *and* Witwoud]

PETULANT: How now? What's the matter? Whose hand's out?

[36] Roman empress (d. 48 A.D.) notorious for her licentiousness.

WITWOUD: Heyday! what, are you all got together, like players at the end of the last act?

MIRABELL: You may remember, gentlemen, I once requested your hands as witnesses to a certain parchment.

WITWOUD: Aye, I do, my hand I remember—Petulant set his mark.

MIRABELL: You wrong him, his name is fairly written, as shall appear.—You do not remember, gentlemen, anything of what that parchment contains?—[*Undoing the box*]

WITWOUD: No.

PETULANT: Not I; I writ, I read nothing.

MIRABELL: Very well, now you shall know.— Madam, your promise.

LADY WISHFORT: Aye, aye, sir, upon my honor.

MIRABELL: Mr. Fainall, it is now time that you should know that your lady, while she was at her own disposal, and before you had by your insinuations wheedled her out of a pretended settlement of the greatest part of her fortune—

FAINALL: Sir! pretended!

MIRABELL: Yes, sir. I say that this lady while a widow, having it seems received some cautions respecting your inconstancy and tyranny of temper, which from her own partial opinion and fondness of you she could never have suspected—she did, I say, by the wholesome advice of friends, and of sages learned in the laws of this land, deliver this same as her act and deed to me in trust, and to the uses within mentioned. You may read if you please— [*holding out the parchment*] though perhaps what is written on the back may serve your occasions.

FAINALL: Very likely, sir. What's here?—Damnation! [*Reads*] "A deed of conveyance of the whole estate real of Arabella Languish, widow, in trust to Edward Mirabell."—Confusion!

MIRABELL: Even so, sir; 'tis the way of the world, sir, of the widows of the world. I suppose this deed may bear an elder date than what you have obtained from your lady.

FAINALL: Perfidious fiend! then thus I'll be revenged. [*Offers to run at* Mrs. Fainall]

SIR WILFULL: Hold, sir! Now you may make your bear-garden flourish somewhere else, sir.

FAINALL: Mirabell, you shall hear of this, sir, be sure you shall.—Let me pass, oaf! [*Exit*]

MRS. FAINALL: Madam, you seem to stifle your resentment; you had better give it vent.

MRS. MARWOOD: Yes, it shall have vent—and to your confusion; or I'll perish in the attempt. [*Exit*]

LADY WISHFORT: O daughter, daughter! 'Tis plain thou hast inherited thy mother's prudence.

MRS. FAINALL: Thank Mr. Mirabell, a cautious friend, to whose advice all is owing.

LADY WISHFORT: Well, Mr. Mirabell, you have kept your promise—and I must perform mine.— First, I pardon, for your sake, Sir Rowland there, and Foible; the next thing is to break the matter to my nephew—and how to do that—

MIRABELL: For that, madam, give yourself no trouble; let me have your consent. Sir Wilfull is my friend; he has had compassion upon lovers, and generously engaged a volunteer in this action, for our service; and now designs to prosecute his travels.

SIR WILFULL: S'heart, aunt, I have no mind to marry. My cousin's a fine lady, and the gentleman loves her, and she loves him, and they deserve one another; my resolution is to see foreign parts—I have set on't—and when I'm set on't I must do't. And if these two gentlemen would travel too, I think they may be spared.

PETULANT: For my part, I say little—I think things are best off or on.

WITWOUD: I'gad, I understand nothing of the matter; I'm in a maze yet, like a dog in a dancing-school.

LADY WISHFORT: Well, sir, take her, and with her all the joy I can give you.

MRS. MILLAMANT: Why does not the man take me? Would you have me give myself to you over again?

MIRABELL: Aye, and over and over again; [*kisses her hand*] I would have you as often as possibly I can. Well, Heaven grant I love you not too well, that's all my fear.

SIR WILFULL: S'heart, you'll have time enough to toy after you're married; or if you will toy now, let us have a dance in the meantime, that we who are not lovers may have some other employment besides looking on.

MIRABELL: With all my heart, dear Sir Wilfull. What shall we do for music?

FOIBLE: Oh, sir, some that were provided for Sir Rowland's entertainment are yet within call.

[*A dance*]

LADY WISHFORT: As I am a person, I can hold out no longer; I have wasted my spirits so to-day already, that I am ready to sink under the fatigue; and I cannot but have some fears upon me yet, that my son Fainall will pursue some desperate course.

MIRABELL: Madam, disquiet not yourself on that account; to my knowledge his circumstances are such he must of force comply. For my part, I will contribute all that in me lies to a reunion; in the meantime, madam—[*to* Mrs. Fainall] let me before these witnesses restore to you this deed of trust: it may be a means, well-managed, to make you live easily together.

From hence let those be warned, who mean to wed;
Lest mutual falsehood stain the bridal bed;
For each deceiver to his cost may find
That marriage-frauds too oft are paid in kind.

[*Exeunt omnes*]

Richard Brinsley Sheridan

(1751–1816)

Richard Brinsley Sheridan was the ablest successor to Congreve and the only other master of English high comedy of manners before Wilde and Shaw. Brilliant conversationalist and man about town, close friend of the Prince of Wales and an associate of distinguished political figures, later one of England's famous orators, and David Garrick's successor in the management of the government-licensed Drury Lane Theatre, Sheridan was completely at home both in the theatre and in the social world which nourishes comedy. Fortune favored him often, although not so lavishly as Byron thought when he wrote in his diary that "whatever Sheridan has done or chosen to do has been, *par excellence,* always the *best* of its kind."

Sheridan was exceedingly well descended for a playwright. He was the Dublin-born grandson of an erudite and clever friend of Dean Swift, as well as the son of the actor and fashionable elocutionist Thomas Sheridan and a talented woman who won a reputation with three comedies and two novels, the first written when she was fifteen. He was educated at Harrow and then, instead of attending a university, was trained by his father in oratory. When the family moved to Bath, the young Sheridan was let loose upon the most fashionable town of eighteenth-century England. Bath by itself could have supplied him with all the material for such comedies of manners as *The Rivals* and *The School for Scandal.*

In Bath, moreover, Sheridan gained the first of his public victories, wooing and winning the most coveted beauty of the time, Elizabeth Linley, the talented singer to whom many men of fashion addressed themselves. Even George III was not insensible to her charms; Horace Walpole reported in a letter that the King "ogles her as much as he dares to do in so holy a place as an oratorio." The marriage was not formally completed with the consent of Miss Linley's father, a noted composer, and with the benefit of the Anglican clergy until an elopement and a "French marriage" at Dunkirk had taken place and Sheridan had fought two duels with a persistent married rival. Sheridan's marital adventures were the talk of "society."

Now properly married (1773), Sheridan turned to the theatre for a living. He wrote *The Rivals* in 1774 at the suggestion of the manager of Covent Garden. The first performance, in January 1775, was a dismal failure, owing to imperfections in the play, wretched acting, and a hissing clique. But Sheridan withdrew the comedy at once and within ten days succeeded in revising it and getting it performed properly, winning a complete victory. To reward one of his actors, the confident author immediately wrote a two-act farce, *St. Patrick's Day, or The Scheming Lieutenant,* for a benefit performance for him to star in. The play was inconsequential, but it had cost Sheridan only two days' labor, and it was successfully performed a number of times in 1775. For Covent Garden and possibly as a reward to his father-in-law, Thomas Linley, who composed the score, the twenty-four-year-old prodigy wrote the opera *The Duenna.* Its success later in that year eclipsed even that of *The Beggar's Opera.* Next, in 1776, Sheridan became part owner and manager of the Drury Lane. For its acting company he adapted the Restoration playwright Vanbrugh's comedy *The Relapse* under the title *A Trip to Scarborough* and wrote *The School for Scandal;* both were produced successfully in 1777. Two years later he wrote the literary burlesque *The Critic,* which proved a popular successor to the earlier distinguished satires on the drama Lord Buckingham's *The Rehearsal* (1671) and Fielding's *Tom Thumb the Great* (1730).

Within four years Sheridan had made himself the most successful English playwright of his time, and for many years his popularity in the English theatre was destined to be second only to Shakespeare's. But by 1779 he had begun to look for another career upon which to leave the impress of his talents. He chose politics, and entered the House of Commons in 1780. Here he remained for thirty-two years, resigning in 1812 only because the debts he had contracted by his improvident ways and his losses in the theatre prevented him from defraying his election expenses. In Parliament, Sheridan distinguished himself generally and scored a resounding success in 1787 and 1788 with two speeches in connection with the impeachment and trial of Warren Hastings. No less an authority than Burke called his famous six-hour speech against Hastings in 1787 "the most astonishing effort of eloquence, argument, and wit united, of which there is any record or tradition."

The latter part of Sheridan's career was marred by misfortunes. His wife died in 1792, and his remarriage three years later brought him only unhappiness and financial distress. Drury Lane suffered from mismanagement, one of its productions—a Shakespearean forgery—was a costly failure, and the playhouse burned down in 1807. His debts were a source of continual harassment; a sheriff was in Sheridan's apartment at the time of his death in 1816. But he was less daunted by his financial difficulties than might be imagined, and they did not lessen his repute in a nation so appreciative of his talents that it placed his remains in Westminster Abbey.

Sheridan's reputation rests most securely on his two high comedies *The Rivals* and *The School for Scandal*. They represent a final and successful effort to recover high comedy for the British stage after three quarters of a century of reaction against the amoralism and obscenities of the Restoration playwrights. It was unfortunate only that the victory was a temporary one and was followed by the further deterioration of English drama until the last decades of the next century. Sheridan managed to revive a good deal of the Restoration's aptitude for witty comedy of manners while simplifying its plot intrigues and avoiding its indelicacies. He departed conspicuously from the eighteenth-century theatre's habit of moralizing and substituting sentimentality for satiric comedy.

Of the two plays, *The Rivals* provides more exuberance and ready "theatre," and its Mrs. Malaprop is an immortal comic figure. But *The School for Scandal* is the more carefully wrought play. It approaches pure comedy of manners more closely than any work written after Congreve's *The Way of the World*. Sheridan set himself the objective of not merely conventionally exposing hypocrisy, incarnate in Joseph Surface, but of mocking the vogue of sententiousness and the parade of edifying moral sentiments in a society notable for neither sincerity nor morality. Had he made Joseph less villainous and his brother Charles less virtuous, Sheridan might have written an even better play. He would then have scaled completely the altitudes of the detached mind toward which masters of the art of high comedy aspire. It is probable that he could have attained those heights if he had worked some seventy-five years earlier. Had he written during the Restoration period, he would certainly have insisted less upon Charles Surface's natural goodness of heart. But it is doubtful whether *The School for Scandal* would, then, have held the stage as long as it did.

THE SCHOOL FOR SCANDAL

By Richard Brinsley Sheridan

DRAMATIS PERSONAE

SIR PETER TEAZLE	CARELESS	LADY TEAZLE
SIR OLIVER SURFACE	SNAKE	LADY SNEERWELL
SIR HARRY BUMPER	CRABTREE	MRS. CANDOUR
SIR BENJAMIN BACKBITE	ROWLEY	MARIA
JOSEPH SURFACE	MOSES	GENTLEMEN, MAID, *and*
CHARLES SURFACE	TRIP	SERVANTS

SCENE: *London*

A PORTRAIT;

ADDRESSED TO MRS. CREWE, WITH THE COMEDY OF
THE SCHOOL FOR SCANDAL
By R. B. Sheridan, Esq.

Tell me, ye prime adepts in Scandal's school,
Who rail by precept, and detract by rule,
Lives there no character, so tried, so known,
So deck'd with grace, and so unlike your own,
That even you assist her fame to raise,
Approve by envy, and by silence praise!
Attend!—a model shall attract your view—
Daughters of calumny, I summon you!
You shall decide if this a portrait prove,
Or fond creation of the Muse and Love.
Attend, ye virgin critics, shrewd and sage,
Ye matron censors of this childish age,
Whose peering eye and wrinkled front declare
A fix'd antipathy to young and fair;
By cunning, cautious; or by nature, cold,—
In maiden madness, virulently bold;—
Attend, ye skill'd to coin the precious tale,
Creating proof, where innuendos fail!
Whose practised memories, cruelly exact,
Omit no circumstance, except the fact!—
Attend, all ye who boast,—or old or young,—
The living libel of a slanderous tongue!
So shall my theme, as far contrasted be,
As saints by fiends or hymns by calumny.
Come, gentle Amoret (for 'neath that name
In worthier verse is sung thy beauty's fame),
Come—for but thee who seek the Muse? and while
Celestial blushes check thy conscious smile,
With timid grace and hesitating eye,
The perfect model which I boast supply:—
Vain Muse! couldst thou the humblest sketch create
Of her, or slightest charm couldst imitate—
Could thy blest strain in kindred colours trace
The faintest wonder of her form and face—
Poets would study the immortal line,
And Reynolds own his art subdued by thine;
That art, which well might added lustre give

To nature's best and heaven's superlative:
On Granby's cheek might bid new glories rise,
Or point a purer beam from Devon's eyes!
Hard is the task to shape that beauty's praise,
Whose judgment scorns the homage flattery pays?
But praising Amoret we cannot err,
No tongue o'ervalues Heaven, or flatters her!
Yet she by fate's perverseness—she alone
Would doubt our truth, nor deem such praise her
  own!
Adorning fashion, unadorn'd by dress,
Simple from taste, and not from carelessness;
Discreet in gesture, in deportment mild,
Not stiff with prudence, nor uncouthly wild:
No state has Amoret; no studied mien;
She frowns no goddess, and she moves no queen,
The softer charm that in her manner lies
Is framed to captivate, yet not surprise;
It justly suits the expression of her face,—
'Tis less than dignity, and more than grace!
On her pure cheek the native hue is such,
That, form'd by Heaven to be admired so much,
The hand divine, with a less partial care,
Might well have fixed a fainter crimson there,
And bade the gentle inmate of her breast—
Inshrined Modesty—supply the rest.
But who the peril of her lips shall paint?
Strip them of smiles—still, still all words are faint!
But moving Love himself appears to teach
Their action, though denied to rule her speech;
And thou who seest her speak, and dost not hear,
Mourn not her distant accents 'scape thine ear;
Viewing those lips, thou still may'st make pretence
To judge of what she says, and swear 'tis sense:
Clothed with such grace, with such expression
  fraught,
They move in meaning, and they pause in thought!
But dost thou farther watch, with charm'd surprise,
The mild irresolution of her eyes.
Curious to mark how frequent they repose,
In brief eclipse and momentary close—
Ah! seest thou not an ambush'd Cupid there,
Too tim'rous of his charge, with jealous care
Veils and unveils those beams of heavenly light,

Too full, too fatal else, for mortal sight?
Nor yet, such pleasing vengeance fond to meet,
In pard'ning dimples hope a safe retreat.
What though her peaceful breast should ne'er allow
Subduing frowns to arm her altered brow,
By Love, I swear, and by his gentle wiles,
More fatal still the mercy of her smiles!
Thus lovely, thus adorn'd, possessing all
Of bright or fair that can to woman fall,
The height of vanity, might well be thought
Prerogative in her, and Nature's fault.
Yet gentle Amoret, in mind supreme
As well as charms, rejects the vainer theme;
And, half mistrustful of her beauty's store,
She barbs with wit those darts too keen before:—
Read in all knowledge that her sex should reach,
Though Greville, or the Muse, should deign to teach,
Fond to improve, nor timorous to discern
How far it is a woman's grace to learn;
In Millar's dialect she would not prove
Apollo's priestess, but Apollo's love,
Graced by those signs which truth delights to own,
The timid blush, and mild submitted tone:
Whate'er she says, though sense appear throughout,
Displays the tender hue of female doubt;
Deck'd with that charm, how lovely wit appears,
How graceful science, when that robe she wears!
Such too her talents, and her bent of mind,
As speak a sprightly heart by thought refined:
A taste for mirth, by contemplation school'd,
A turn for ridicule, by candour ruled,
A scorn of folly, which she tries to hide;
An awe of talent, which she owns with pride!

Peace, idle Muse! no more thy strain prolong,
But yield a theme, thy warmest praises wrong;
Just to her merit, though thou canst not raise
Thy feeble verse, behold th' acknowledged praise
Has spread conviction through the envious train,
And cast a fatal gloom o'er Scandal's reign!
And lo! each pallid hag, with blister'd tongue,
Mutters assent to all thy zeal has sung—
Owns all the colours just—the outline true:
Thee my inspirer, and my model—CREWE!

PROLOGUE

Written by Mr. Garrick
A School for Scandal! tell me, I beseech you,
Needs there a school this modish art to teach you?
No need of lessons now, the knowing think;
We might as well be taught to eat and drink.
Caused by a dearth of scandal, should the vapours
Distress our fair ones—let them read the papers;
Their powerful mixtures such disorders hit;
Crave what you will—there's *quantum sufficit.*
"Lord!" cries my Lady Wormwood (who loves tattle,
And puts much salt and pepper in her prattle),
Just risen at noon, all night at cards when threshing
Strong tea and scandal—"Bless me, how refreshing!

Give me the papers, Lisp—how bold and free! [*Sips*]
Last night Lord L. [*Sips*] *was caught with Lady D.*
For aching heads what charming sal volatile! [*Sips*]
If Mrs. B. will still continue flirting,
We hope she'll DRAW, *or we'll* UNDRAW *the curtain.*
Fine satire, poz—in public all abuse it,
But, by ourselves [*Sips*], our praise we can't refuse it.
Now, Lisp, read you—there, at that dash and star."
"Yes, ma'am—*A certain Lord had best beware,*
Who lives not twenty miles from Grosvenor Square;
For should he Lady W. find willing,
Wormwood is bitter"——"Oh! that's me! the villain!
Throw it behind the fire, and never more
Let that vile paper come within my door."
Thus at our friends we laugh, who feel the dart;
To reach our feelings, we ourselves must smart.
Is our young bard so young, to think that he
Can stop the full spring-tide of calumny?
Knows he the world so little, and its trade?
Alas! the devil's sooner raised than laid.
So strong, so swift, the monster there's no gagging:
Cut Scandal's head off, still the tongue is wagging.
Proud of your smiles once lavishly bestow'd,
Again our young Don Quixote takes the road;
To show his gratitude he draws his pen,
And seeks his hydra, Scandal, in his den.
For your applause all perils he would through—
He'll fight—that's write—a cavalliero true,
Till every drop of blood—that's ink—is spilt for you.

ACT I. SCENE I.

Lady Sneerwell's *dressing-room.*
Lady Sneerwell *discovered at her toilet;* Snake *drinking chocolate.*

LADY SNEERWELL: The paragraphs, you say, Mr. Snake, were all inserted?

SNAKE: They were, madam; and, as I copied them myself in a feigned hand, there can be no suspicion whence they came.

LADY SNEERWELL: Did you circulate the report of Lady Brittle's intrigue with Captain Boastall?

SNAKE: That's in as fine a train as your ladyship could wish. In the common course of things, I think it must reach Mrs. Clackitt's ears within four-and-twenty hours; and then, you know, the business is as good as done.

LADY SNEERWELL: Why, truly, Mrs. Clackitt has a very pretty talent, and a great deal of industry.

SNAKE: True, madam, and has been tolerably successful in her day. To my knowledge, she has been the cause of six matches being broken off, and three sons being disinherited; of four forced elopements, and as many close confinements; nine separate maintenances, and two divorces. Nay, I have more than once traced her causing a *tête-à-tête* in the "Town and Country Magazine," when the parties, perhaps, had never seen each other's face before in the course of their lives.

LADY SNEERWELL: She certainly has talents, but her manner is gross.

SNAKE: 'Tis very true. She generally designs well, has a free tongue and a bold invention; but her colouring is too dark, and her outlines often extravagant. She wants that delicacy of tint, and mellowness of sneer, which distinguish your ladyship's scandal.

LADY SNEERWELL: You are partial, Snake.

SNAKE: Not in the least; everybody allows that Lady Sneerwell can do more with a word or look than many can with the most laboured detail, even when they happen to have a little truth on their side to support it.

LADY SNEERWELL: Yes, my dear Snake; and I am no hypocrite to deny the satisfaction I reap from the success of my efforts. Wounded myself, in the early part of my life, by the envenomed tongue of slander, I confess I have since known no pleasure equal to the reducing others to the level of my own injured reputation.

SNAKE: Nothing can be more natural. But, Lady Sneerwell, there is one affair in which you have lately employed me, wherein, I confess, I am at a loss to guess your motives.

LADY SNEERWELL: I conceive you mean with respect to my neighbour, Sir Peter Teazle, and his family?

SNAKE: I do. Here are two young men, to whom Sir Peter has acted as a kind of guardian since their father's death; the eldest possessing the most amiable character, and universally well spoken of—the youngest, the most dissipated and extravagant young fellow in the kingdom, without friends or character: the former an avowed admirer of your ladyship, and apparently your favourite; the latter attached to Maria, Sir Peter's ward, and confessedly beloved by her. Now, on the face of these circumstances, it is utterly unaccountable to me, why you, the widow of a city knight, with a good jointure,[1] should not close with the passion of a man of such character and expectations as Mr. Surface; and more so why you should be so uncommonly earnest to destroy the mutual attachment subsisting between his brother Charles and Maria.

LADY SNEERWELL: Then, at once to unravel this mystery, I must inform you that love has no share whatever in the intercourse between Mr. Surface and me.

SNAKE: No!

LADY SNEERWELL: His real attachment is to Maria or her fortune; but, finding in his brother a favoured rival, he has been obliged to mask his pretensions, and profit by my assistance.

SNAKE: Yet still I am more puzzled why you should interest yourself in his success.

LADY SNEERWELL: Heavens! how dull you are!

[1] Settlement of an estate.

Cannot you surmise the weakness which I hitherto, through shame, have concealed even from you? Must I confess that Charles—that libertine, that extravagant, that bankrupt in fortune and reputation—that he it is for whom I am thus anxious and malicious, and to gain whom I would sacrifice everything?

SNAKE: Now, indeed, your conduct appears consistent; but how came you and Mr. Surface so confidential?

LADY SNEERWELL: For our mutual interest. I have found him out a long time since. I know him to be artful, selfish, and malicious—in short, a sentimental knave; while with Sir Peter, and indeed with all his acquaintance, he passes for a youthful miracle of prudence, good sense, and benevolence.

SNAKE: Yes; yet Sir Peter vows he has not his equal in England; and, above all, he praises him as a man of sentiment.

LADY SNEERWELL: True; and with the assistance of his sentiment and hypocrisy he has brought Sir Peter entirely into his interest with regard to Maria; while poor Charles has no friend in the house—though, I fear, he has a powerful one in Maria's heart, against whom we must direct our schemes.

[Enter Servant]

SERVANT: Mr. Surface.

LADY SNEERWELL: Show him up.

[Exit Servant]

He generally calls about this time. I don't wonder at people giving him to me for a lover.

[Enter Joseph Surface]

JOSEPH SURFACE: My dear Lady Sneerwell, how do you do to-day? Mr. Snake, your most obedient.

LADY SNEERWELL: Snake has just been rallying me on our mutual attachment; but I have informed him of our real views. You know how useful he has been to us; and, believe me, the confidence is not ill-placed.

JOSEPH SURFACE: Madam, it is impossible for me to suspect a man of Mr. Snake's sensibility and discernment.

LADY SNEERWELL: Well, well, no compliments now; but tell me when you saw your mistress, Maria—or, what is more material to me, your brother.

JOSEPH SURFACE: I have not seen either since I left you; but I can inform you that they never meet. Some of your stories have taken a good effect on Maria.

LADY SNEERWELL: Ah, my dear Snake! the merit of this belongs to you. But do your brother's distresses increase?

JOSEPH SURFACE: Every hour. I am told he has had another execution in the house yesterday. In short, his dissipation and extravagance exceed anything I have ever heard of.

LADY SNEERWELL: Poor Charles!

JOSEPH SURFACE: True, madam; notwithstanding his vices, one can't help feeling for him. Poor Charles! I'm sure I wish it were in my power to be of any essential service to him; for the man who does not share in the distresses of a brother, even though merited by his own misconduct, deserves——

LADY SNEERWELL: O Lud! you are going to be moral, and forget that you are among friends.

JOSEPH SURFACE: Egad, that's true! I'll keep that sentiment till I see Sir Peter. However, it is certainly a charity to rescue Maria from such a libertine, who, if he is to be reclaimed, can be so only by a person of your ladyship's superior accomplishments and understanding.

SNAKE: I believe, Lady Sneerwell, here's company coming; I'll go and copy the letter I mentioned to you. Mr. Surface, your most obedient.

JOSEPH SURFACE: Sir, your very devoted.

[Exit Snake]

Lady Sneerwell, I am very sorry you have put any farther confidence in that fellow.

LADY SNEERWELL: Why so?

JOSEPH SURFACE: I have lately detected him in frequent conference with old Rowley, who was formerly my father's steward, and has never, you know, been a friend of mine.

LADY SNEERWELL: And do you think he would betray us?

JOSEPH SURFACE: Nothing more likely: take my word for't, Lady Sneerwell, that fellow hasn't virtue enough to be faithful even to his own villainy. Ah, Maria!

[Enter Maria]

LADY SNEERWELL: Maria, my dear, how do you do? What's the matter?

MARIA: Oh! there's that disagreeable lover of mine, Sir Benjamin Backbite, has just called at my guardian's, with his odious uncle, Crabtree; so I slipped out, and ran hither to avoid them.

LADY SNEERWELL: Is that all?

JOSEPH SURFACE: If my brother Charles had been of the party, madam, perhaps you would not have been so much alarmed.

LADY SNEERWELL: Nay, now you are severe; for I dare swear the truth of the matter is, Maria heard you were here. But, my dear, what has Sir Benjamin done, that you should avoid him so?

MARIA: Oh, he has done nothing—but 'tis for what he has said: his conversation is a perpetual libel on all his acquaintance.

JOSEPH SURFACE: Ay, and the worst of it is, there is no advantage in not knowing him; for he'll abuse a stranger just as soon as his best friend: and his uncle's as bad.

LADY SNEERWELL: Nay, but we should make allowance; Sir Benjamin is a wit and a poet.

MARIA: For my part, I own, madam, wit loses its respect with me, when I see it in company with malice. What do you think, Mr. Surface?

JOSEPH SURFACE: Certainly, madam; to smile at the jest which plants a thorn in another's breast is to become a principal in the mischief.

LADY SNEERWELL: Psha! there's no possibility of being witty without a little ill-nature: the malice of a good thing is the barb that makes it stick. What's your opinion, Mr. Surface?

JOSEPH SURFACE: To be sure, madam; that conversation, where the spirit of raillery is suppressed, will ever appear tedious and insipid.

MARIA: Well, I'll not debate how far scandal may be allowable; but in a man, I am sure, it is always contemptible. We have pride, envy, rivalship, and a thousand motives to depreciate each other; but the male slanderer must have the cowardice of a woman before he can traduce one.

[Re-enter Servant]

SERVANT: Madam, Mrs. Candour is below, and, if your ladyship's at leisure, will leave her carriage.

LADY SNEERWELL: Beg her to walk in.

[Exit Servant]

Now, Maria, here is a character to your taste; for, though Mrs. Candour is a little talkative, everybody knows her to be the best-natured and best sort of woman.

MARIA: Yes, with a very gross affectation of good nature and benevolence, she does more mischief than the direct malice of old Crabtree.

JOSEPH SURFACE: I'faith that's true, Lady Sneerwell: whenever I hear the current running against the characters of my friends, I never think them in such danger as when Candour undertakes their defence.

LADY SNEERWELL: Hush!—here she is!

[Enter Mrs. Candour]

MRS. CANDOUR: My dear Lady Sneerwell, how have you been this century?—Mr. Surface, what news do you hear?—though indeed it is no matter, for I think one hears nothing else but scandal.

JOSEPH SURFACE: Just so, indeed, ma'am.

MRS. CANDOUR: Oh, Maria! child,—what, is the whole affair off between you and Charles? His extravagance, I presume—the town talks of nothing else.

MARIA: I am very sorry, ma'am, the town has so little to do.

MRS. CANDOUR: True, true, child: but there's no stopping people's tongues. I own I was hurt to hear it, as I indeed was to learn, from the same quarter, that your guardian, Sir Peter, and Lady Teazle have not agreed lately as well as could be wished.

MARIA: 'Tis strangely impertinent for people to busy themselves so.

MRS. CANDOUR: Very true, child; but what's to be done? People will talk—there's no preventing it. Why, it was but yesterday I was told that Miss Gadabout had eloped with Sir Filagree Flirt. But, Lord! there's no minding what one hears; though, to be sure, I had this from very good authority.

MARIA: Such reports are highly scandalous.

MRS. CANDOUR: So they are, child—shameful, shameful! But the world is so censorious, no character escapes. Lord, now who would have suspected your friend, Miss Prim, of an indiscretion? Yet such is the ill-nature of people, that they say her uncle stopped her last week, just as she was stepping into the York mail with her dancing-master.

MARIA: I'll answer for't there are no grounds for that report.

MRS. CANDOUR: Ah, no foundation in the world, I dare swear: no more, probably, than the story circulated last month, of Mrs. Festino's affair with Colonel Cassino—though, to be sure, that matter was never rightly cleared up.

JOSEPH SURFACE: The license of invention some people take is monstrous indeed.

MARIA: 'Tis so; but, in my opinion, those who report such things are equally culpable.

MRS. CANDOUR: To be sure they are; tale-bearers are as bad as the tale-makers—'tis an old observation, and a very true one: but what's to be done, as I said before? how will you prevent people from talking? To-day, Mrs. Clackitt assured me, Mr. and Mrs. Honeymoon were at last become mere man and wife, like the rest of their acquaintance. She likewise hinted that a certain widow, in the next street, had got rid of her dropsy and recovered her shape in a most surprising manner. And at the same time Miss Tattle, who was by, affirmed, that Lord Buffalo had discovered his lady at a house of no extraordinary fame; and that Sir Harry Bouquet and Tom Saunter were to measure swords on a similar provocation. But, Lord, do you think I would report these things! No, no! tale-bearers, as I said before, are just as bad as the tale-makers.

JOSEPH SURFACE: Ah! Mrs. Candour, if everybody had your forbearance and good nature!

MRS. CANDOUR: I confess, Mr. Surface, I cannot bear to hear people attacked behind their backs; and when ugly circumstances come out against our acquaintances I own I always love to think the best. By-the-by, I hope 'tis not true that your brother is absolutely ruined?

JOSEPH SURFACE: I am afraid his circumstances are very bad indeed, ma'am.

MRS. CANDOUR: Ah!—I heard so—but you must tell him to keep up his spirits; everybody almost is in the same way: Lord Spindle, Sir Thomas Splint, Captain Quinze, and Mr. Nickit—all up, I hear, within this week; so, if Charles is undone, he'll find half his acquaintance ruined too, and that, you know, is a consolation.

JOSEPH SURFACE: Doubtless, ma'am—a very great one.

[Re-enter Servant]

SERVANT: Mr. Crabtree and Sir Benjamin Backbite. [Exit]

LADY SNEERWELL: So, Maria, you see your lover pursues you; positively you shan't escape.

[Enter Crabtree and Sir Benjamin Backbite]

CRABTREE: Lady Sneerwell, I kiss your hand. Mrs. Candour, I don't believe you are acquainted with my nephew, Sir Benjamin Backbite? Egad, ma'am he has a pretty wit, and is a pretty poet too. Isn't he, Lady Sneerwell?

SIR BENJAMIN: Oh, fie, uncle!

CRABTREE: Nay, egad it's true: I back him at a rebus or a charade against the best rhymer in the kingdom. Has your ladyship heard the epigram he wrote last week on Lady Frizzle's feather catching fire?—Do, Benjamin, repeat it, or the charade you made last night extempore at Mrs. Drowzie's conversazione.[2] Come now; your first is the name of a fish, your second a great naval commander, and——

SIR BENJAMIN: Uncle, now—pr'ythee——

CRABTREE: I'faith, ma'am, 'twould surprise you to hear how ready he is at all these sort of things.

LADY SNEERWELL: I wonder, Sir Benjamin, you never publish anything.

SIR BENJAMIN: To say truth, ma'am, 'tis very vulgar to print; and, as my little productions are mostly satires and lampoons on particular people, I find they circulate more by giving copies in confidence to the friends of the parties. However, I have some elegies, which, when favoured with this lady's smiles, I mean to give the public. [Pointing to Maria]

CRABTREE: [To Maria] 'Fore heaven, ma'am, they'll immortalize you—you will be handed down to posterity, like Petrarch's Laura, or Waller's Sacharissa.

SIR BENJAMIN: [To Maria] Yes, madam, I think you will like them, when you shall see them on a beautiful quarto page, where a neat rivulet of text shall meander through a meadow of margin. 'Fore Gad, they will be the most elegant things of their kind!

CRABTREE: But, ladies, that's true—have you heard the news?

MRS. CANDOUR: What, sir, do you mean the report of——

CRABTREE: No, ma'am, that's not it.—Miss Nicely is going to be married to her own footman.

MRS. CANDOUR: Impossible!

CRABTREE: Ask Sir Benjamin.

SIR BENJAMIN: 'Tis very true, ma'am: everything is fixed, and the wedding liveries bespoke.

CRABTREE: Yes—and they do say there were pressing reasons for it.

LADY SNEERWELL: Why, I have heard something of this before.

MRS. CANDOUR: It can't be—and I wonder any one should believe such a story of so prudent a lady as Miss Nicely.

SIR BENJAMIN: O Lud! ma'am, that's the very reason 'twas believed at once. She has always been so cautious and so reserved, that everybody was sure there was some reason for it at bottom.

MRS. CANDOUR: Why, to be sure, a tale of scandal is as fatal to the credit of a prudent lady of her stamp as a fever is generally to those of the strongest constitutions. But there is a sort of puny sickly reputation, that is always ailing, yet will outlive the robuster characters of a hundred prudes.

SIR BENJAMIN: True, madam, there are valetudi-

2 A meeting for discussion of literature.

narians in reputation as well as constitution, who, being conscious of their weak part, avoid the least breath of air, and supply their want of stamina by care and circumspection.

MRS. CANDOUR: Well, but this may be all a mistake. You know, Sir Benjamin, very trifling circumstances often give rise to the most injurious tales.

CRABTREE: That they do, I'll be sworn, ma'am. Did you ever hear how Miss Piper came to lose her lover and her character last summer at Tunbridge?—Sir Benjamin, you remember it?

SIR BENJAMIN: Oh, to be sure!—the most whimsical circumstance.

LADY SNEERWELL: How was it, pray?

CRABTREE: Why, one evening, at Mrs. Ponto's assembly, the conversation happened to turn on the breeding Nova Scotia sheep in this country. Says a young lady in company, I have known instances of it; for Miss Letitia Piper, a first cousin of mine, had a Nova Scotia sheep that produced her twins. "What!" cries the Lady Dowager Dundizzy (who you know is as deaf as a post), "has Miss Piper had twins?" This mistake, as you may imagine, threw the whole company into a fit of laughter. However, 'twas the next morning everywhere reported, and in a few days believed by the whole town, that Miss Letitia Piper had actually been brought to bed of a fine boy and girl: and in less than a week there were some people who could name the father, and the farm-house where the babies were put to nurse.

LADY SNEERWELL: Strange, indeed!

CRABTREE: Matter of fact, I assure you. O Lud! Mr. Surface, pray is it true that your uncle, Sir Oliver, is coming home?

JOSEPH SURFACE: Not that I know of, indeed, sir.

CRABTREE: He has been in the East Indies a long time. You can scarcely remember him, I believe? Sad comfort, whenever he returns, to hear how your brother has gone on!

JOSEPH SURFACE: Charles has been imprudent, sir, to be sure; but I hope no busy people have already prejudiced Sir Oliver against him. He may reform.

SIR BENJAMIN: To be sure he may; for my part I never believed him to be so utterly void of principle as people say; and though he has lost all his friends, I am told nobody is better spoken of by the Jews.

CRABTREE: That's true, egad, nephew. If the old Jewry was a ward, I believe Charles would be an alderman: no man more popular there, 'fore Gad! I hear he pays as many annuities as the Irish tontine;[3] and that, whenever he is sick, they have prayers for the recovery of his health in all the synagogues.

SIR BENJAMIN: Yet no man lives in greater splendour. They tell me, when he entertains his friends he will sit down to dinner with a dozen of his own securities; have a score of tradesmen in the ante-chamber, and an officer behind every guest's chair.

JOSEPH SURFACE: This may be entertainment to

[3] An annuity shared by a group of persons.

you, gentlemen, but you pay very little regard to the feelings of a brother.

MARIA: [Aside] Their malice is intolerable! [Aloud] Lady Sneerwell, I must wish you a good morning: I'm not very well. [Exit]

MRS. CANDOUR: O dear! she changes colour very much.

LADY SNEERWELL: Do, Mrs. Candour, follow her; she may want your assistance.

MRS. CANDOUR: That I will, with all my soul, ma'am.—Poor dear girl, who knows what her situation may be! [Exit]

LADY SNEERWELL: 'Twas nothing but that she could not bear to hear Charles reflected on, notwithstanding their difference.

SIR BENJAMIN: The young lady's penchant is obvious.

CRABTREE: But, Benjamin, you must not give up the pursuit for that: follow her, and put her into good humour. Repeat her some of your own verses. Come, I'll assist you.

SIR BENJAMIN: Mr. Surface, I did not mean to hurt you; but depend on't your brother is utterly undone.

CRABTREE: O Lud, ay! undone as ever man was—can't raise a guinea.

SIR BENJAMIN: And everything sold, I'm told, that was movable.

CRABTREE: I have seen one that was at his house. Not a thing left but some empty bottles that were overlooked, and the family pictures, which I believe are framed in the wainscots.

SIR BENJAMIN: And I'm very sorry also to hear some bad stories against him. [Going]

CRABTREE: Oh, he has done many mean things, that's certain.

SIR BENJAMIN: But, however, as he's your brother—— [Going]

CRABTREE: We'll tell you all another opportunity.

[Exeunt Crabtree and Sir Benjamin]

LADY SNEERWELL: Ha, ha! 'tis very hard for them to leave a subject they have not quite run down.

JOSEPH SURFACE: And I believe the abuse was no more acceptable to your ladyship than to Maria.

LADY SNEERWELL: I doubt her affections are further engaged than we imagine. But the family are to be here this evening, so you may as well dine where you are, and we shall have an opportunity of observing further; in the meantime, I'll go and plot mischief, and you shall study sentiment.

[Exeunt]

SCENE II.

A room in Sir Peter Teazle's house.

[Enter Sir Peter Teazle]

SIR PETER: When an old bachelor marries a young wife, what is he to expect? 'Tis now six months since Lady Teazle made me the happiest of men—and I have been the most miserable dog ever since! We tift a little going to church, and fairly quarrelled before the bells had done ringing. I was more than once nearly choked with gall during the honeymoon, and had lost all comfort in life before my friends had done wishing me joy. Yet I chose with caution— a girl bred wholly in the country, who never knew luxury beyond one silk gown, nor dissipation above the annual gala of a race ball. Yet she now plays her part in all the extravagant fopperies of fashion and the town, with as ready a grace as if she never had seen a bush or a grass-plot out of Grosvenor Square! I am sneered at by all my acquaintance, and paragraphed in the newspapers. She dissipates my fortune, and contradicts all my humours; yet the worst of it is, I doubt I love her, or I should never bear all this. However, I'll never be weak enough to own it.

[*Enter* Rowley]

ROWLEY: Oh! Sir Peter, your servant: how is it with you, sir?

SIR PETER: Very bad, Master Rowley, very bad. I meet with nothing but crosses and vexations.

ROWLEY: What can have happened since yesterday?

SIR PETER: A good question to a married man!

ROWLEY: Nay, I'm sure, Sir Peter, your lady can't be the cause of your uneasiness.

SIR PETER: Why, has anybody told you she was dead?

ROWLEY: Come, come, Sir Peter, you love her, notwithstanding your tempers don't exactly agree.

SIR PETER: But the fault is entirely hers, Master Rowley. I am, myself, the sweetest-tempered man alive, and hate a teasing temper; and so I tell her a hundred times a day.

ROWLEY: Indeed!

SIR PETER: Ay; and what is very extraordinary, in all our disputes she is always in the wrong! But Lady Sneerwell, and the set she meets at her house, encourage the perverseness of her disposition. Then, to complete my vexation, Maria, my ward, whom I ought to have the power of a father over, is determined to turn rebel too, and absolutely refuses the man whom I have long resolved on for her husband; meaning, I suppose, to bestow herself on his profligate brother.

ROWLEY: You know, Sir Peter, I have always taken the liberty to differ with you on the subject of these two young gentlemen. I only wish you may not be deceived in your opinion of the elder. For Charles, my life on't! he will retrieve his errors yet. Their worthy father, once my honoured master, was, at his years, nearly as wild a spark; yet, when he died, he did not leave a more benevolent heart to lament his loss.

SIR PETER: You are wrong, Master Rowley. On their father's death, you know, I acted as a kind of guardian to them both, till their uncle Sir Oliver's liberality gave them an early independence: of course, no person could have more opportunities of judging

of their hearts, and I was never mistaken in my life. Joseph is indeed a model for the young men of the age. He is a man of sentiment, and acts up to the sentiments he professes; but, for the other, take my word for't, if he had any grain of virtue by descent, he has dissipated it with the rest of his inheritance. Ah! my old friend, Sir Oliver, will be deeply mortified when he finds how part of his bounty has been misapplied.

ROWLEY: I am sorry to find you so violent against the young man, because this may be the most critical period of his fortune. I came hither with news that will surprise you.

SIR PETER: What! let me hear.

ROWLEY: Sir Oliver is arrived, and at this moment in town.

SIR PETER: How! you astonish me! I thought you did not expect him this month.

ROWLEY: I did not: but his passage has been remarkably quick.

SIR PETER: Egad, I shall rejoice to see my old friend. 'Tis sixteen years since we met. We have had many a day together: but does he still enjoin us not to inform his nephews of his arrival?

ROWLEY: Most strictly. He means, before it is known, to make some trial of their dispositions.

SIR PETER: Ah! There needs no art to discover their merits—however, he shall have his way; but, pray, does he know I am married?

ROWLEY: Yes, and will soon wish you joy.

SIR PETER: What, as we drink health to a friend in consumption! Ah, Oliver will laugh at me. We used to rail at matrimony together, but he has been steady to his text. Well, he must be soon at my house, though—I'll instantly give orders for his reception. But, Master Rowley, don't drop a word that Lady Teazle and I ever disagree.

ROWLEY: By no means.

SIR PETER: For I should never be able to stand Noll's jokes; so I'll have him think, Lord forgive me! that we are a very happy couple.

ROWLEY: I understand you:—but then you must be very careful not to differ while he is in the house with you.

SIR PETER: Egad, and so we must—and that's impossible. Ah! Master Rowley, when an old bachelor marries a young wife, he deserves—no—the crime carries its punishment along with it.

[*Exeunt*]

ACT II. SCENE I.

A room in Sir Peter Teazle's *house.*

[*Enter* Sir Peter *and* Lady Teazle]

SIR PETER: Lady Teazle, Lady Teazle, I'll not bear it!

LADY TEAZLE: Sir Peter, Sir Peter, you may bear it or not, as you please; but I ought to have my own way in everything, and what's more, I will too. What though I was educated in the country, I know very well that women of fashion in London are accountable to nobody after they are married.

SIR PETER: Very well, ma'am, very well; so a husband is to have no influence, no authority?

LADY TEAZLE: Authority! No, to be sure:—if you wanted authority over me, you should have adopted me, and not married me: I am sure you were old enough.

SIR PETER: Old enough!—ay, there it is! Well, well, Lady Teazle, though my life may be made unhappy by your temper, I'll not be ruined by your extravagance!

LADY TEAZLE: My extravagance! I'm sure I'm not more extravagant than a woman of fashion ought to be.

SIR PETER: No, no, madam, you shall throw away no more sums on such unmeaning luxury. 'Slife! to spend as much to furnish your dressing-room with flowers in winter as would suffice to turn the Pantheon into a greenhouse, and give a *fête champêtre*[4] at Christmas.

LADY TEAZLE: And am I to blame, Sir Peter, because flowers are dear in cold weather? You should find fault with the climate, and not with me. For my part, I'm sure I wish it was spring all the year round, and that roses grew under our feet!

SIR PETER: Oons! madam—if you had been born to this, I shouldn't wonder at your talking thus; but you forget what your situation was when I married you.

LADY TEAZLE: No, no, I don't; 'twas a very disagreeable one, or I should never have married you.

SIR PETER: Yes, yes, madam, you were then in somewhat a humbler style—the daughter of a plain country squire. Recollect, Lady Teazle, when I saw you first sitting at your tambour,[5] in a pretty figured linen gown, with a bunch of keys at your side, your hair combed smooth over a roll, and your apartment hung round with fruits in worsted, of your own working.

LADY TEAZLE: Oh, yes! I remember it very well, and a curious life I led. My daily occupation to inspect the dairy, superintend the poultry, make extracts from the family receipt-book, and comb my aunt Deborah's lapdog.

SIR PETER: Yes, yes, ma'am, 'twas so indeed.

LADY TEAZLE: And then, you know, my evening amusements! To draw patterns for ruffles, which I had not the materials to make up; to play Pope Joan[6] with the Curate; to read a sermon to my aunt; or to be stuck down to an old spinet to strum my father to sleep after a fox-chase.

SIR PETER: I am glad you have so good a memory. Yes, madam, these were the recreations I took you from; but now you must have your coach—*vis-à-vis*

4 An open-air entertainment.
5 Frame for embroidering.
6 A card game.

—and three powdered footmen before your chair; and, in the summer, a pair of white cats to draw you to Kensington Gardens. No recollection, I suppose, when you were content to ride double, behind the butler, on a docked coach-horse?

LADY TEAZLE: No—I swear I never did that; I deny the butler and the coach-horse.

SIR PETER: This, madam, was your situation; and what have I done for you? I have made you a woman of fashion, of fortune, of rank—in short, I have made you my wife.

LADY TEAZLE: Well, then, and there is but one thing more you can make me to add to the obligation, that is——

SIR PETER: My widow, I suppose?

LADY TEAZLE: Hem! Hem!

SIR PETER: I thank you, madam—but don't flatter yourself; for, though your ill-conduct may disturb my peace of mind, it shall never break my heart, I promise you: however, I am equally obliged to you for the hint.

LADY TEAZLE: Then why will you endeavour to make yourself so disagreeable to me, and thwart me in every little elegant expense?

SIR PETER: 'Slife, madam, I say, had you any of these little elegant expenses when you married me?

LADY TEAZLE: Lud, Sir Peter! would you have me be out of the fashion?

SIR PETER: The fashion, indeed! what had you to do with the fashion before you married me?

LADY TEAZLE: For my part, I should think you would like to have your wife thought a woman of taste.

SIR PETER: Ay—there again—taste! Zounds! madam, you had no taste when you married me!

LADY TEAZLE: That's very true, indeed, Sir Peter! and, after having married you, I should never pretend to taste again, I allow. But now, Sir Peter, since we have finished our daily jangle, I presume I may go to my engagement at Lady Sneerwell's?

SIR PETER: Ay, there's another precious circumstance—a charming set of acquaintance you have made there!

LADY TEAZLE: Nay, Sir Peter, they are all people of rank and fortune, and remarkably tenacious of reputation.

SIR PETER: Yes, egad, they are tenacious of reputation with a vengeance; for they don't choose anybody should have a character but themselves! Such a crew! Ah! many a wretch has rid on a hurdle who has done less mischief than these utterers of forged tales, coiners of scandal, and clippers of reputation.

LADY TEAZLE: What, would you restrain the freedom of speech?

SIR PETER: Ah! they have made you just as bad as any one of the society.

LADY TEAZLE: Why, I believe I do bear a part with a tolerable grace. But I vow I bear no malice against the people I abuse: when I say an ill-natured thing, 'tis out of pure good humour; and I take it for granted they deal exactly in the same manner with me. But, Sir Peter, you know you promised to come to Lady Sneerwell's too.

SIR PETER: Well, well, I'll call in just to look after my own character.

LADY TEAZLE: Then, indeed, you must make haste after me or you'll be too late. So good-bye to ye. [Exit]

SIR PETER: So—I have gained much by my intended expostulation! Yet with what a charming air she contradicts everything I say, and how pleasantly she shows her contempt for my authority! Well, though I can't make her love me, there is great satisfaction in quarrelling with her; and I think she never appears to such advantage as when she is doing everything in her power to plague me. [Exit]

SCENE II.

A room in Lady Sneerwell's house.
Lady Sneerwell, Mrs. Candour, Crabtree, Sir Benjamin Backbite, and Joseph Surface, discovered.

LADY SNEERWELL: Nay, positively, we will hear it.
JOSEPH SURFACE: Yes, yes, the epigram, by all means.

SIR BENJAMIN: O plague on't, uncle! 'tis mere nonsense.

CRABTREE: No, no; 'fore Gad, very clever for an extempore!

SIR BENJAMIN: But, ladies, you should be acquainted with the circumstance. You must know, that one day last week, as Lady Betty Curricle was taking the dust in Hyde Park, in a sort of duodecimo phaeton,[7] she desired me to write some verses on her ponies; upon which, I took out my pocket-book, and in one moment produced the following:—

Sure never were seen two such beautiful ponies;
Other horses are clowns, but these macaronies:[8]
To give them this title I am sure can't be wrong.
Their legs are so slim, and their tails are so long.

CRABTREE: There, ladies, done in the smack of a whip, and on horseback too.

JOSEPH SURFACE: A very Phoebus, mounted—indeed, Sir Benjamin!

SIR BENJAMIN: Oh dear, sir!—trifles—trifles.—
[Enter Lady Teazle and Maria]

MRS. CANDOUR: I must have a copy.

LADY SNEERWELL: Lady Teazle, I hope we shall see Sir Peter?

LADY TEAZLE: I believe he'll wait on your ladyship presently.

LADY SNEERWELL: Maria, my love, you look grave. Come, you shall sit down to piquet with Mr. Surface.

MARIA: I take very little pleasure in cards—however, I'll do as your ladyship pleases.

[7] A carriage.
[8] Affected young men of fashion.

LADY TEAZLE: I am surprised Mr. Surface should sit down with her; I thought he would have embraced this opportunity of speaking to me before Sir Peter came. [Aside]

MRS. CANDOUR: Now, I'll die; but you are so scandalous, I'll forswear your society.

LADY TEAZLE: What's the matter, Mrs. Candour?

MRS. CANDOUR: They'll not allow our friend Miss Vermillion to be handsome.

LADY SNEERWELL: Oh, surely she is a pretty woman.

CRABTREE: I am very glad you think so, ma'am.

MRS. CANDOUR: She has a charming fresh colour.

LADY TEAZLE: Yes, when it is fresh put on.

MRS. CANDOUR: Oh, fie! I'll swear her colour is natural: I have seen it come and go!

LADY TEAZLE: I dare swear you have, ma'am: it goes off at night, and comes again in the morning.

SIR BENJAMIN: True, ma'am, it not only comes and goes; but, what's more, egad, her maid can fetch and carry it!

MRS. CANDOUR: Ha! ha! ha! how I hate to hear you talk so! But surely, now, her sister is, or was, very handsome.

CRABTREE: Who? Mrs. Evergreen? O Lord! she's six-and-fifty if she's an hour!

MRS. CANDOUR: Now positively you wrong her; fifty-two or fifty-three is the utmost—and I don't think she looks more.

SIR BENJAMIN: Ah! there's no judging by her looks, unless one could see her face.

LADY SNEERWELL: Well, well, if Mrs. Evergreen does take some pains to repair the ravages of time, you must allow she effects it with great ingenuity; and surely that's better than the careless manner in which the widow Ochre caulks her wrinkles.

SIR BENJAMIN: Nay, now, Lady Sneerwell, you are severe upon the widow. Come, come, 'tis not that she paints so ill—but, when she has finished her face, she joins it on so badly to her neck, that she looks like a mended statue, in which the connoisseur may see at once that the head's modern, though the trunk's antique!

CRABTREE: Ha! ha! ha! Well said, nephew!

MRS. CANDOUR: Ha! ha! ha! Well, you make me laugh; but I vow I hate you for it. What do you think of Miss Simper?

SIR BENJAMIN: Why, she has very pretty teeth.

LADY TEAZLE: Yes; and on that account, when she is neither speaking nor laughing (which very seldom happens), she never absolutely shuts her mouth, but leaves it always on ajar, as it were—thus. [Shows her teeth]

MRS. CANDOUR: How can you be so ill-natured?

LADY TEAZLE: Nay, I allow even that's better than the pains Mrs. Prim takes to conceal her losses in front. She draws her mouth till it positively resembles the aperture of a poor's-box, and all her words appear to slide out edge-wise, as it were—thus: How do you do, madam? Yes, madam.

LADY SNEERWELL: Very well, Lady Teazle; I see you can be a little severe.

LADY TEAZLE: In defence of a friend it is but justice. But here comes Sir Peter to spoil our pleasantry.

[*Enter* Sir Peter Teazle]

SIR PETER: Ladies, your most obedient. [*Aside*] Mercy on me, here is the whole set! a character dead at every word, I suppose.

MRS. CANDOUR: I am rejoiced you are come, Sir Peter. They have been so censorious—and Lady Teazle as bad as any one.

SIR PETER: That must be very distressing to you, Mrs. Candour, I dare swear.

MRS. CANDOUR: Oh, they will allow good qualities to nobody; not even good nature to our friend Mrs. Pursy.

LADY TEAZLE: What, the fat dowager who was at Mrs. Quadrille's last night?

MRS. CANDOUR: Nay, her bulk is her misfortune; and, when she takes so much pains to get rid of it, you ought not to reflect on her.

LADY SNEERWELL: That's very true, indeed.

LADY TEAZLE: Yes, I know she almost lives on acids and small whey; laces herself by pulleys; and often, in the hottest noon in summer, you may see her on a little squat pony, with her hair plaited up behind like a drummer's and puffing round the Ring on a full trot.

MRS. CANDOUR: I thank you, Lady Teazle, for defending her.

SIR PETER: Yes, a good defence, truly.

MRS. CANDOUR: Truly, Lady Teazle is as censorious as Miss Sallow.

CRABTREE: Yes, and she is a curious being to pretend to be censorious—an awkward gawky, without any one good point under heaven.

MRS. CANDOUR: Positively you shall not be so very severe. Miss Sallow is a near relation of mine by marriage, and, as for her person, great allowance is to be made; for, let me tell you, a woman labours under many disadvantages who tries to pass for a girl of six-and-thirty.

LADY SNEERWELL: Though, surely, she is handsome still—and for the weakness in her eyes, considering how much she reads by candle-light, it is not to be wondered at.

MRS. CANDOUR: True; and then as to her manner, upon my word I think it is particularly graceful, considering she never had the least education; for you know her mother was a Welsh milliner, and her father a sugar-baker at Bristol.

SIR BENJAMIN: Ah! you are both of you too good-natured!

SIR PETER: Yes, damned good-natured! This their own relation! mercy on me! [*Aside*]

MRS. CANDOUR: For my part, I own I cannot bear to hear a friend ill-spoken of.

SIR PETER: No, to be sure.

SIR BENJAMIN: Oh! you are of a moral turn.

Mrs. Candour and I can sit for an hour and hear Lady Stucco talk sentiment.

LADY TEAZLE: Nay, I vow Lady Stucco is very well with the dessert after dinner; for she's just like the French fruit one cracks for mottoes—made up of paint and proverb.

MRS. CANDOUR: Well, I will never join in ridiculing a friend; and so I constantly tell my cousin Ogle, and you all know what pretensions she has to be critical on beauty.

CRABTREE: Oh, to be sure! she has herself the oddest countenance that ever was seen; 'tis a collection of features from all the different countries of the globe.

SIR BENJAMIN: So she has, indeed—an Irish front——

CRABTREE: Caledonian locks——

SIR BENJAMIN: Dutch nose——

CRABTREE: Austrian lips——

SIR BENJAMIN: Complexion of a Spaniard——

CRABTREE: And teeth *à la Chinoise*——

SIR BENJAMIN: In short, her face resembles a table d'hôte at Spa—where no two guests are of a nation——

CRABTREE: Or a congress at the close of a general war—wherein all the members, even to her eyes, appear to have a different interest, and her nose and her chin are the only parties likely to join issue.

MRS. CANDOUR: Ha! ha! ha!

SIR PETER: Mercy on my life!—a person they dine with twice a week! [*Aside*]

LADY SNEERWELL: Go—go—you are a couple of provoking toads.

MRS. CANDOUR: Nay, but I vow you shall not carry the laugh off so—for give me leave to say, that Mrs. Ogle——

SIR PETER: Madam, madam, I beg your pardon—there's no stopping these good gentlemen's tongues. But when I tell you, Mrs. Candour, that the lady they are abusing is a particular friend of mine, I hope you'll not take her part.

LADY SNEERWELL: Ha! ha! ha! well said, Sir Peter! but you are a cruel creature—too phlegmatic yourself for a jest, and too peevish to allow wit in others.

SIR PETER: Ah, madam, true wit is more nearly allied to good nature than your ladyship is aware of.

LADY TEAZLE: True, Sir Peter: I believe they are so near akin that they can never be united.

SIR BENJAMIN: Or rather, madam, I suppose them man and wife, because one seldom sees them together.

LADY TEAZLE: But Sir Peter is such an enemy to scandal, I believe he would have it put down by parliament.

SIR PETER: 'Fore heaven, madam, if they were to consider the sporting with reputation of as much importance as poaching on manors, and pass an act for the preservation of fame, I believe many would thank them for the bill.

LADY SNEERWELL: O Lud! Sir Peter; would you deprive us of our privileges?

SIR PETER: Ay, madam; and then no person should be permitted to kill characters and run down reputations, but qualified old maids and disappointed widows.

LADY SNEERWELL: Go, you monster!

MRS. CANDOUR: But, surely, you would not be quite so severe on those who only report what they hear?

SIR PETER: Yes, madam, I would have law merchant for them too; and in all cases of slander currency, whenever the drawer of the lie was not to be found, the injured parties should have a right to come on any of the indorsers.

CRABTREE: Well, for my part, I believe there never was a scandalous tale without some foundation.

LADY SNEERWELL: Come, ladies, shall we sit down to cards in the next room?

[Enter Servant, who whispers to Sir Peter]

SIR PETER: I'll be with them directly. [Exit Servant] I'll get away unperceived. [Aside]

LADY SNEERWELL: Sir Peter, you are not going to leave us?

SIR PETER: Your ladyship must excuse me; I'm called away by particular business. But I leave my character behind me. [Exit]

SIR BENJAMIN: Well—certainly, Lady Teazle, that lord of yours is a strange being: I could tell you some stories of him would make you laugh heartily if he were not your husband.

LADY TEAZLE: Oh, pray don't mind that; come, do let's hear them.

[Exeunt all but Joseph Surface and Maria]

JOSEPH SURFACE: Maria, I see you have no satisfaction in this society.

MARIA: How is it possible I should? If to raise malicious smiles at the infirmities or misfortunes of those who have never injured us be the province of wit or humour, heaven grant me a double portion of dulness!

JOSEPH SURFACE: Yet they appear more ill-natured than they are; they have no malice at heart.

MARIA: Then is their conduct still more contemptible; for, in my opinion, nothing could excuse the intemperance of their tongues but a natural and uncontrollable bitterness of mind.

JOSEPH SURFACE: Undoubtedly, madam; and it has always been a sentiment of mine, that to propagate a malicious truth wantonly is more despicable than to falsify from revenge. But can you, Maria, feel thus for others, and be unkind to me alone? Is hope to be denied the tenderest passion?

MARIA: Why will you distress me by renewing this subject?

JOSEPH SURFACE: Ah, Maria! you would not treat me thus, and oppose your guardian, Sir Peter's will, but that I see that profligate Charles is still a favoured rival.

MARIA: Ungenerously urged! But, whatever my sentiments are for that unfortunate young man, be

assured I shall not feel more bound to give him up, because his distresses have lost him the regard even of a brother.

JOSEPH SURFACE: Nay, but, Maria, do not leave me with a frown: by all that's honest, I swear——
[Kneels]
[Re-enter Lady Teazle behind]
[Aside] Gad's life, here's Lady Teazle. [Aloud to Maria] You must not—no, you shall not—for, though I have the greatest regard for Lady Teazle——

MARIA: Lady Teazle!

JOSEPH SURFACE: Yet were Sir Peter to suspect——

LADY TEAZLE: [Coming forward] What is this, pray? Do you take her for me?—Child, you are wanted in the next room.——
[Exit Maria]
What is all this, pray?

JOSEPH SURFACE: Oh, the most unlucky circumstance in nature! Maria has somehow suspected the tender concern I have for your happiness, and threatened to acquaint Sir Peter with her suspicions, and I was just endeavouring to reason with her when you came in.

LADY TEAZLE: Indeed! but you seemed to adopt a very tender mode of reasoning—do you usually argue on your knees?

JOSEPH SURFACE: Oh, she's a child, and I thought a little bombast——but, Lady Teazle, when are you to give me your judgment on my library, as you promised?

LADY TEAZLE: No, no; I begin to think it would be imprudent, and you know I admit you as a lover no farther than fashion requires.

JOSEPH SURFACE: —True—a mere Platonic cicisbeo,[9] what every wife is entitled to.

LADY TEAZLE: Certainly, one must not be out of the fashion. However, I have so many of my country prejudices left, that, though Sir Peter's ill humour may vex me ever so, it never shall provoke me to——

JOSEPH SURFACE: The only revenge in your power. Well, I applaud your moderation.

LADY TEAZLE: Go—you are an insinuating wretch! But we shall be missed—let us join the company.

JOSEPH SURFACE: But we had best not return together.

LADY TEAZLE: Well, don't stay; for Maria shan't come to hear any more of your reasoning, I promise you. [Exit]

JOSEPH SURFACE: A curious dilemma, truly, my politics have run me into! I wanted, at first, only to ingratiate myself with Lady Teazle, that she might not be my enemy with Maria; and I have, I don't know how, become her serious lover. Sincerely I begin to wish I had never made such a point of gaining so very good a character, for it has led me into so many cursed rogueries that I doubt I shall be exposed at last. [Exit]

[9] Gallant of a married woman.

SCENE III.

A room in Sir Peter Teazle's *house.*

[*Enter* Sir Oliver Surface *and* Rowley]

SIR OLIVER: Ha! ha! ha! so my old friend is married, hey?—a young wife out of the country. Ha! ha! ha! that he should have stood bluff to old bachelor so long, and sink into a husband at last!

ROWLEY: But you must not rally him on the subject, Sir Oliver; 'tis a tender point, I assure you, though he has been married only seven months.

SIR OLIVER: Then he has been just half a year on the stool of repentance!—Poor Peter! But you say he has entirely given up Charles—never sees him, hey?

ROWLEY: His prejudice against him is astonishing, and I am sure greatly increased by a jealousy of him with Lady Teazle, which he has industriously been led into by a scandalous society in the neighborhood, who have contributed not a little to Charles's ill name. Whereas the truth is, I believe, if the lady is partial to either of them, his brother is the favourite.

SIR OLIVER: Ay, I know there are a set of malicious, prating, prudent gossips, both male and female, who murder characters to kill time, and will rob a young fellow of his good name before he has years to know the value of it. But I am not to be prejudiced against my nephew by such, I promise you! No, no; if Charles has done nothing false or mean, I shall compound for his extravagance.

ROWLEY: Then, my life on't, you will reclaim him. Ah, sir, it gives me new life to find that your heart is not turned against him, and that the son of my good old master has one friend, however, left.

SIR OLIVER: What! shall I forget, Master Rowley, when I was at his years myself? Egad, my brother and I were neither of us very prudent youths; and yet, I believe, you have not seen many better men than your old master was?

ROWLEY: Sir, 'tis this reflection gives me assurance that Charles may yet be a credit to his family. But here comes Sir Peter.

SIR OLIVER: Egad, so he does! Mercy on me, he's greatly altered, and seems to have a settled married look! One may read husband in his face at this distance.

[*Enter* Sir Peter Teazle]

SIR PETER: Ha! Sir Oliver—my old friend! Welcome to England a thousand times!

SIR OLIVER: Thank you, thank you, Sir Peter! and i'faith I am glad to find you well, believe me!

SIR PETER: Oh! 'tis a long time since we met—fifteen years, I doubt, Sir Oliver, and many a cross accident in the time.

SIR OLIVER: Ay, I have had my share. But, what! I find you are married, hey, my old boy? Well, well, it can't be helped; and so—I wish you joy with all my heart!

SIR PETER: Thank you, thank you, Sir Oliver.—

Yes, I have entered into—the happy state; but we'll not talk of that now.

SIR OLIVER: True, true, Sir Peter; old friends should not begin on grievances at first meeting. No, no, no.

ROWLEY: [*Aside to* Sir Oliver] Take care, pray, sir.

SIR OLIVER: Well, so one of my nephews is a wild rogue, hey?

SIR PETER: Wild! Ah! my old friend, I grieve for your disappointment there; he's a lost young man, indeed. However, his brother will make you amends; Joseph is, indeed, what a youth should be—everybody in the world speaks well of him.

SIR OLIVER: I am sorry to hear it; he has too good a character to be an honest fellow. Everybody speaks well of him! Psha! then he has bowed as low to knaves and fools as to the honest dignity of genius and virtue.

SIR PETER: What, Sir Oliver! do you blame him for not making enemies?

SIR OLIVER: Yes, if he has merit enough to deserve them.

SIR PETER: Well, well—you'll be convinced when you know him. 'Tis edification to hear him converse; he professes the noblest sentiments.

SIR OLIVER: Oh, plague of his sentiments! If he salutes me with a scrap of morality in his mouth, I shall be sick directly. But, however, don't mistake me, Sir Peter; I don't mean to defend Charles's errors: but, before I form my judgment of either of them, I intend to make a trial of their hearts; and my friend Rowley and I have planned something for the purpose.

ROWLEY: And Sir Peter shall own for once he has been mistaken.

SIR PETER: Oh, my life on Joseph's honour!

SIR OLIVER: Well—come, give us a bottle of good wine, and we'll drink the lads' health, and tell you our scheme.

SIR PETER: *Allons,* then!

SIR OLIVER: And don't, Sir Peter, be so severe against your old friend's son. Odds my life! I am not sorry that he has run out of the course a little: for my part, I hate to see prudence clinging to the green suckers of youth; 'tis like ivy round a sapling, and spoils the growth of the tree.

[*Exeunt*]

ACT III. SCENE I.

A room in Sir Peter Teazle's *house.*

[*Enter* Sir Peter Teazle, Sir Oliver Surface, *and* Rowley]

SIR PETER: Well, then, we will see this fellow first, and have our wine afterwards. But how is this, Master Rowley? I don't see the jet of your scheme.

ROWLEY: Why, sir, this Mr. Stanley, whom I was speaking of, is nearly related to them by their mother.

He was once a merchant in Dublin, but has been ruined by a series of undeserved misfortunes. He has applied, by letter, since his confinement, both to Mr. Surface and Charles: from the former he has received nothing but evasive promises of future service, while Charles has done all that his extravagance has left him power to do; and he is, at this time, endeavouring to raise a sum of money, part of which, in the midst of his own distresses, I know he intends for the service of poor Stanley.

SIR OLIVER: Ah, he is my brother's son.

SIR PETER: Well, but how is Sir Oliver personally to——

ROWLEY: Why, sir, I will inform Charles and his brother that Stanley has obtained permission to apply personally to his friends; and, as they have neither of them ever seen him, let Sir Oliver assume his character, and he will have a fair opportunity of judging, at least, of the benevolence of their dispositions: and believe me, sir, you will find in the youngest brother one who, in the midst of folly and dissipation, has still, as our immortal bard expresses it,—

"a heart to pity, and a hand
Open as day, for melting charity."

SIR PETER: Psha! What signifies his having an open hand or purse either, when he has nothing left to give? Well, well, make the trial, if you please. But where is the fellow whom you brought for Sir Oliver to examine, relative to Charles's affairs?

ROWLEY: Below, waiting his commands, and no one can give him better intelligence.—This, Sir Oliver, is a friendly Jew, who, to do him justice, has done everything in his power to bring your nephew to a proper sense of his extravagance.

SIR PETER: Pray let us have him in.

ROWLEY: Desire Mr. Moses to walk upstairs. [Calls to Servant]

SIR PETER: But, pray, why should you suppose he will speak the truth?

ROWLEY: Oh, I have convinced him that he has no chance of recovering certain sums advanced to Charles but through the bounty of Sir Oliver, who he knows is arrived; so that you may depend on his fidelity to his own interests. I have also another evidence in my power, one Snake, whom I have detected in a matter little short of forgery, and shall shortly produce to remove some of your prejudices, Sir Peter, relative to Charles and Lady Teazle.

SIR PETER: I have heard too much on that subject.

ROWLEY: Here comes the honest Israelite.

[Enter Moses]

—This is Sir Oliver.

SIR OLIVER: Sir, I understand you have lately had great dealings with my nephew Charles.

MOSES: Yes, Sir Oliver, I have done all I could for him; but he was ruined before he came to me for assistance.

SIR OLIVER: That was unlucky, truly; for you have had no opportunity of showing your talents.

MOSES: None at all; I hadn't the pleasure of knowing his distresses till he was some thousands worse than nothing.

SIR OLIVER: Unfortunate, indeed! But I suppose you have done all in your power for him, honest Moses?

MOSES: Yes, he knows that. This very evening I was to have brought him a gentleman from the City,[10] who does not know him and will, I believe, advance him some money.

SIR PETER: What, one Charles has never had money from before?

MOSES: Yes, Mr. Premium, of Crutched Friars, formerly a broker.

SIR PETER: Egad, Sir Oliver, a thought strikes me! —Charles, you say, does not know Mr. Premium?

MOSES: Not at all.

SIR PETER: Now then, Sir Oliver, you may have a better opportunity of satisfying yourself than by an old romancing tale of a poor relation: go with my friend Moses, and represent Premium, and then, I'll answer for it, you'll see your nephew in all his glory.

SIR OLIVER: Egad, I like this idea better than the other, and I may visit Joseph afterwards as old Stanley.

SIR PETER: True—so you may.

ROWLEY: Well, this is taking Charles rather at a disadvantage, to be sure. However, Moses, you understand Sir Peter, and will be faithful.

MOSES: You may depend upon me. [Looks at his watch] This is near the time I was to have gone.

SIR OLIVER: I'll accompany you as soon as you please, Moses—— But hold! I have forgot one thing —how the plague shall I be able to pass for a Jew?

MOSES: There's no need—the principal is Christian.

SIR OLIVER: Is he? I'm very sorry to hear it. But, then again, an't I rather too smartly dressed to look like a money-lender?

SIR PETER: Not at all; 'twould not be out of character, if you went in your carriage—would it, Moses?

MOSES: Not in the least.

SIR OLIVER: Well, but how must I talk? there's certainly some cant of usury and mode of treating that I ought to know.

SIR PETER: Oh, there's not much to learn. The great point, as I take it, is to be exorbitant enough in your demands. Hey, Moses?

MOSES: Yes, that's a very great point.

SIR OLIVER: I'll answer for't I'll not be wanting in that. I'll ask him eight or ten per cent. on the loan, at least.

MOSES: If you ask him no more than that, you'll be discovered immediately.

SIR OLIVER: Hey! what, the plague! how much then?

MOSES: That depends upon the circumstances. If he appears not very anxious for the supply, you should require only forty or fifty per cent.; but if

[10] The commercial center of Greater London.

you find him in great distress, and want the moneys very bad, you may ask double.

SIR PETER: A good honest trade you're learning, Sir Oliver!

SIR OLIVER: Truly I think so—and not unprofitable.

MOSES: Then, you know, you haven't the moneys yourself, but are forced to borrow them for him of a friend.

SIR OLIVER: Oh! I borrow it of a friend, do I?

MOSES: And your friend is an unconscionable dog: but you can't help that.

SIR OLIVER: My friend an unconscionable dog, is he?

MOSES: Yes, and he himself has not the moneys by him, but is forced to sell stocks at a great loss.

SIR OLIVER: He is forced to sell stocks at a great loss, is he? Well, that's very kind of him.

SIR PETER: I'faith, Sir Oliver—Mr. Premium, I mean—you'll soon be master of the trade. But, Moses! would not you have him run out a little against the annuity bill? That would be in character, I should think.

MOSES: Very much.

ROWLEY: And lament that a young man now must be at years of discretion before he is suffered to ruin himself?

MOSES: Ay, great pity!

SIR PETER: And abuse the public for allowing merit to an act whose only object is to snatch misfortune and imprudence from the rapacious grip of usury, and give the minor a chance of inheriting his estate without being undone by coming into possession.

SIR OLIVER: So, so—Moses shall give me further instructions as we go together.

SIR PETER: You will not have much time, for your nephew lives hard by.

SIR OLIVER: Oh, never fear! my tutor appears so able, that though Charles lived in the next street, it must be my own fault if I am not a complete rogue before I turn the corner. [Exit with Moses]

SIR PETER: So, now, I think Sir Oliver will be convinced: you are partial, Rowley, and would have prepared Charles for the other plot.

ROWLEY: No, upon my word, Sir Peter.

SIR PETER: Well, go bring me this Snake, and I'll hear what he has to say presently. I see Maria, and want to speak with her. [Exit Rowley] I should be glad to be convinced my suspicions of Lady Teazle and Charles were unjust. I have never yet opened my mind on this subject to my friend Joseph—I am determined I will do it—he will give me his opinion sincerely.

[Enter Maria]

So, child, has Mr. Surface returned with you?

MARIA: No, sir; he was engaged.

SIR PETER: Well, Maria, do you not reflect, the more you converse with that amiable young man, what return his partiality for you deserves?

MARIA: Indeed, Sir Peter, your frequent importu-

nity on this subject distresses me extremely—you compel me to declare, that I know no man who has ever paid me a particular attention whom I would not prefer to Mr. Surface.

SIR PETER: So—here's perverseness! No, no, Maria, 'tis Charles only whom you would prefer. 'Tis evident his vices and follies have won your heart.

MARIA: This is unkind, sir. You know I have obeyed you in neither seeing nor corresponding with him: I have heard enough to convince me that he is unworthy my regard. Yet I cannot think it culpable, if, while my understanding severely condemns his vices, my heart suggests pity for his distresses.

SIR PETER: Well, well, pity him as much as you please; but give your heart and hand to a worthier object.

MARIA: Never to his brother!

SIR PETER: Go, perverse and obstinate! But take care, madam; you have never yet known what the authority of a guardian is: don't compel me to inform you of it.

MARIA: I can only say, you shall not have just reason. 'Tis true, by my father's will, I am for a short period bound to regard you as his substitute; but must cease to think you so, when you would compel me to be miserable. [Exit]

SIR PETER: Was ever man so crossed as I am, everything conspiring to fret me! I had not been involved in matrimony a fortnight, before her father, a hale and hearty man, died, on purpose, I believe, for the pleasure of plaguing me with the care of his daughter. [Lady Teazle sings without] But here comes my helpmate! She appears in great good humour. How happy I should be if I could tease her into loving me, though but a little!

[Enter Lady Teazle]

LADY TEAZLE: Lud! Sir Pete, I hope you haven't been quarrelling with Maria? It is not using me well to be ill humoured when I am not by.

SIR PETER: Ah, Lady Teazle, you might have the power to make me good humoured at all times.

LADY TEAZLE: I am sure I wish I had; for I want you to be in a charming sweet temper at this moment. Do be good humoured now, and let me have two hundred pounds, will you?

SIR PETER: Two hundred pounds; what, an't I to be in a good humour without paying for it! But speak to me thus, and i'faith there's nothing I could refuse you. You shall have it; but seal me a bond for the repayment.

LADY TEAZLE: Oh, no—there—my note of hand will do as well. [Offering her hand]

SIR PETER: And you shall no longer reproach me with not giving you an independent settlement. I mean shortly to surprise you; but shall we always live thus, hey?

LADY TEAZLE: If you please, I'm sure I don't care how soon we leave off quarrelling, provided you'll own you were tired first.

SIR PETER: Well—then let our future contest be, who shall be most obliging.

LADY TEAZLE: I assure you, Sir Peter, good nature becomes you. You look now as you did before we were married, when you used to walk with me under the elms, and tell me stories of what a gallant you were in your youth, and chuck me under the chin, you would; and ask me if I thought I could love an old fellow, who would deny me nothing—didn't you?

SIR PETER: Yes, yes, and you were as kind and attentive——

LADY TEAZLE: Ay, so I was, and would always take your part, when my acquaintance used to abuse you, and turn you into ridicule.

SIR PETER: Indeed!

LADY TEAZLE: Ay, and when my cousin Sophy has called you a stiff, peevish old bachelor, and laughed at me for thinking of marrying one who might be my father, I have always defended you, and said, I didn't think you so ugly by any means, and that you'd make a very good sort of a husband.

SIR PETER: And you prophesied right; and we shall now be the happiest couple——

LADY TEAZLE: And never differ again?

SIR PETER: No, never—though at the same time, indeed, my dear Lady Teazle, you must watch your temper very seriously; for in all our little quarrels, my dear, if you recollect, my love, you always began first.

LADY TEAZLE: I beg your pardon, my dear Sir Peter: indeed, you always gave the provocation.

SIR PETER: Now, see, my angel! take care—contradicting isn't the way to keep friends.

LADY TEAZLE: Then, don't you begin it, my love!

SIR PETER: There, now! you—you are going on. You don't perceive, my life, that you are just doing the very thing which you know always makes me angry.

LADY TEAZLE: Nay, you know if you will be angry without any reason, my dear——

SIR PETER: There! now you want to quarrel again.

LADY TEAZLE: No, I'm sure I don't: but, if you will be so peevish——

SIR PETER: There now! who begins first?

LADY TEAZLE: Why, you, to be sure. I said nothing—but there's no bearing your temper.

SIR PETER: No, no, madam: the fault's in your own temper.

LADY TEAZLE: Ay, you are just what my cousin Sophy said you would be.

SIR PETER: Your cousin Sophy is a forward, impertinent gipsy.

LADY TEAZLE: You are a great bear, I am sure, to abuse my relations.

SIR PETER: Now may all the plagues of marriage be doubled on me, if ever I try to be friends with you any more!

LADY TEAZLE: So much the better.

SIR PETER: No, no, madam: 'tis evident you never cared a pin for me, and I was a madman to marry you—a pert, rural coquette, that had refused half the honest 'squires in the neighbourhood!

LADY TEAZLE: And I am sure I was a fool to marry you—an old dangling bachelor, who was single at fifty, only because he never could meet with any one who would have him.

SIR PETER: Ay, ay, madam; but you were pleased enough to listen to me: you never had such an offer before.

LADY TEAZLE: No! didn't I refuse Sir Tivy Terrier, who everybody said would have been a better match? for his estate is just as good as yours, and he has broke his neck since we have been married.

SIR PETER: I have done with you, madam! You are an unfeeling, ungrateful—but there's an end of everything. I believe you capable of everything that is bad. Yes, madam, I now believe the reports relative to you and Charles, madam. Yes, madam, you and Charles are, not without grounds——

LADY TEAZLE: Take care, Sir Peter! you had better not insinuate any such thing! I'll not be suspected without cause, I promise you.

SIR PETER: Very well, madam! very well! a separate maintenance as soon as you please. Yes, madam, or a divorce! I'll make an example of myself for the benefit of all old bachelors. Let us separate, madam.

LADY TEAZLE: Agreed! agreed! And now, my dear Sir Peter, we are of a mind once more, we may be the happiest couple, and never differ again, you know: ha! ha! ha! Well, you are going to be in a passion, I see, and I shall only interrupt you—so, bye! bye! [Exit]

SIR PETER: Plagues and tortures! can't I make her angry either! Oh, I am the most miserable fellow! But I'll not bear her presuming to keep her temper: no! she may break my heart, but she shan't keep her temper. [Exit]

SCENE II.

A room in Charles Surface's house.

[Enter Trip, Moses, and Sir Oliver Surface]

TRIP: Here, Master Moses! if you'll stay a moment; I'll try whether—what's the gentleman's name?

SIR OLIVER: Mr. Moses, what is my name? [Aside to Moses]

MOSES: Mr. Premium.

TRIP: Premium—very well. [Exit, taking snuff]

SIR OLIVER: To judge by the servants, one wouldn't believe the master was ruined. But what!—sure, this was my brother's house?

MOSES: Yes, sir; Mr. Charles bought it of Mr. Joseph, with the furniture, pictures, &c., just as the old gentleman left it. Sir Peter thought it a piece of extravagance in him.

SIR OLIVER: In my mind, the other's economy in telling it to him was more reprehensible by half.

[*Re-enter* Trip]

TRIP: My master says you must wait, gentlemen: he has company, and can't speak with you yet.

SIR OLIVER: If he knew who it was wanted to see him, perhaps he would not send such a message?

TRIP: Yes, yes, sir; he knows you are here—I did not forget little Premium: no, no, no.

SIR OLIVER: Very well; and I pray, sir, what may be your name?

TRIP: Trip, sir; my name is Trip, at your service.

SIR OLIVER: Well, then, Mr. Trip, you have a pleasant sort of place here, I guess?

TRIP: Why, yes—here are three or four of us pass our time agreeably enough; but then our wages are sometimes a little in arrear—and not very great either —but fifty pounds a year, and find our own bags and bouquets.

SIR OLIVER: Bags and bouquets! halters and bastinadoes! [*Aside*]

TRIP: And *à propos,* Moses, have you been able to get me that little bill discounted?

SIR OLIVER: Wants to raise money, too!—mercy on me! Has his distresses too, I warrant, like a lord, and affects creditors and duns. [*Aside*]

MOSES: 'Twas not to be done, indeed, Mr. Trip.

TRIP: Good lack, you surprise me! My friend Brush has indorsed it, and I thought when he put his name at the back of a bill 'twas the same as cash.

MOSES: No, 'twouldn't do.

TRIP: A small sum—but twenty pounds. Hark'ee, Moses, do you think you couldn't get it me by way of annuity?

SIR OLIVER: An annuity! ha! ha! a footman raise money by way of annuity! Well done, luxury, egad! [*Aside*]

MOSES: Well, but you must insure your place.

TRIP: Oh, with all my heart! I'll insure my place, and my life too, if you please.

SIR OLIVER: It's more than I would your neck. [*Aside*]

MOSES: But is there nothing you could deposit?

TRIP: Why, nothing capital of my master's wardrobe has dropped lately; but I could give you a mortgage on some of his winter clothes, with equity of redemption before November—or you shall have the reversion of the French velvet, or a post-obit on the blue and silver;—these, I should think, Moses, with a few pair of point ruffles, as a collateral security—hey, my little fellow?

MOSES: Well, well.

[*Bell rings*]

TRIP: Egad, I heard the bell! I believe, gentlemen, I can now introduce you. Don't forget the annuity, little Moses! This way, gentlemen, I'll insure my place, you know.

SIR OLIVER: [*Aside*] If the man be a shadow of the master, this is the temple of dissipation indeed!

[*Exeunt*]

SCENE III.

Another room in the same.

Charles Surface, Sir Harry Bumper, Careless, *and* Gentlemen, *discovered drinking.*

CHARLES SURFACE: 'Fore heaven, 'tis true!—there's the great degeneracy of the age. Many of our acquaintance have taste, spirit, and politeness; but plague on't they won't drink.

CARELESS: It is so, indeed, Charles! they give in to all the substantial luxuries of the table, and abstain from nothing but wine and wit. Oh, certainly society suffers by it intolerably! for now, instead of the social spirit of raillery that used to mantle over a glass of bright Burgundy, their conversation is become just like the Spa-water they drink, which has all the pertness and flatulency of champagne, without its spirit or flavour.

1ST GENTLEMAN: But what are they to do who love play better than wine?

CARELESS: True! there's Sir Harry diets himself for gaming, and is now under a hazard regimen.

CHARLES SURFACE: Then he'll have the worst of it. What! you wouldn't train a horse for the course by keeping him from corn? For my part, egad, I'm never so successful as when I am a little merry: let me throw on a bottle of champagne, and I never lose —at least I never feel my losses, which is exactly the same thing.

2ND GENTLEMAN: Ay, that I believe.

CHARLES SURFACE: And, then, what man can pretend to be a believer in love, who is an abjurer of wine? 'Tis the test by which the lover knows his own heart. Fill a dozen bumpers to a dozen beauties, and she that floats at the top is the maid that has bewitched you.

CARELESS: Now then, Charles, be honest, and give us your real favourite.

CHARLES SURFACE: Why, I have withheld her only in compassion to you. If I toast her, you must give a round of her peers, which is impossible—on earth.

CARELESS: Oh, then we'll find some canonised vestals or heathen goddesses that will do, I warrant!

CHARLES SURFACE: Here then, bumpers, you rogues! bumpers! Maria! Maria——

SIR HARRY: Maria who?

CHARLES SURFACE: Oh, damn the surname—'tis too formal to be registered in Love's calendar—but now, Sir Harry, beware, we must have beauty superlative.

CARELESS: Nay, never study, Sir Harry: we'll stand to the toast, though your mistress should want an eye, and you know you have a song will excuse you.

SIR HARRY: Egad, so I have! and I'll give him the song instead of the lady. [*Sings*]

Here's to the maiden of bashful fifteen;
  Here's to the widow of fifty;
Here's to the flaunting extravagant quean,
  And here's to the housewife that's thrifty.

Chorus.   Let the toast pass,—
Drink to the lass,
I'll warrant she'll prove an excuse for a glass.

Here's to the charmer whose dimples we prize;
Now to the maid who has none, sir;
Here's to the girl with a pair of blue eyes,
And here's to the nymph with but one, sir.

Chorus.   Let the toast pass,—
Drink to the lass,
I'll warrant she'll prove an excuse for a glass.

Here's to the maid with a bosom of snow:
Now to her that's as brown as a berry:
Here's to the wife with a face full of woe,
And now to the damsel that's merry.

Chorus.   Let the toast pass,—
Drink to the lass,
I'll warrant she'll prove an excuse for a glass.

For let 'em be clumsy, or let 'em be slim,
Young or ancient, I care not a feather;
So fill a pint bumper quite up to the brim,
So fill up your glasses, nay, fill to the brim,
And let us e'en toast them together.

Chorus.   Let the toast pass,—
Drink to the lass,
I'll warrant she'll prove an excuse for a glass.

ALL: Bravo! Bravo!

[*Enter* Trip, *and whispers to* Charles Surface]

CHARLES SURFACE: Gentlemen, you must excuse me a little.—Careless, take the chair, will you?

CARELESS: Nay, pr'ythee, Charles, what now? This is one of your peerless beauties, I suppose, dropped in by chance?

CHARLES SURFACE: No, faith! To tell you the truth, 'tis a Jew and a broker, who are come by appointment.

CARELESS: Oh, damn it! let's have the Jew in.

1ST GENTLEMAN: Ay, and the broker too, by all means.

2ND GENTLEMAN: Yes, yes, the Jew and the broker.

CHARLES SURFACE: Egad, with all my heart!—Trip, bid the gentlemen walk in. [*Exit* Trip] Though there's one of them a stranger, I can tell you.

CARELESS: Charles, let us give them some generous Burgundy, and perhaps they'll grow conscientious.

CHARLES SURFACE: Oh, hang 'em, no! wine does but draw forth a man's natural qualities; and to make them drink would only be to whet their knavery.

[*Re-enter* Trip, *with* Sir Oliver Surface *and* Moses]

CHARLES SURFACE: So, honest Moses; walk in, pray, Mr. Premium—that's the gentleman's name, isn't it, Moses?

MOSES: Yes, sir.

CHARLES SURFACE: Set chairs, Trip.—Sit down, Mr. Premium.—Glasses, Trip. [Trip *gives chairs and glasses, and exit*] Sit down, Moses.—Come, Mr. Pre-

mium, I'll give you a sentiment; here's *Success to usury!*—Moses, fill the gentleman a bumper.

MOSES: Success to usury! [*Drinks*]

CARELESS: Right, Moses—usury is prudence and industry, and deserves to succeed.

SIR OLIVER: Then here's—All the success it deserves! [*Drinks*]

CARELESS: No, no, that won't do! Mr. Premium, you have demurred at the toast, and must drink it in a pint bumper.

1ST GENTLEMAN: A pint bumper, at least.

MOSES: Oh, pray, sir, consider—Mr. Premium's a gentleman.

CARELESS: And therefore loves good wine.

2ND GENTLEMAN: Give Moses a quart glass—this is mutiny, and a high contempt for the chair.

CARELESS: Here, now for't! I'll see justice done, to the last drop of my bottle.

SIR OLIVER: Nay, pray, gentlemen—I did not expect this usage.

CHARLES SURFACE: No, hang it, you shan't; Mr. Premium's a stranger.

SIR OLIVER: Odd! I wish I was well out of their company. [*Aside*]

CARELESS: Plague on 'em then! if they won't drink, we'll not sit down with them. Come, Harry, the dice are in the next room.—Charles, you'll join us when you have finished your business with the gentlemen?

CHARLES SURFACE: I will! I will!

[*Exeunt* Sir Harry Bumper *and* Gentlemen; Careless *following*]

Careless.

CARELESS: [*Returning*] Well!

CHARLES SURFACE: Perhaps I may want you.

CARELESS: Oh, you know I am always ready: word, note, or bond, 'tis all the same to me. [*Exit*]

MOSES: Sir, this is Mr. Premium, a gentleman of the strictest honour and secrecy; and always performs what he undertakes. Mr. Premium, this is——

CHARLES SURFACE: Psha! have done. Sir, my friend Moses is a very honest fellow, but a little slow at expression: he'll be an hour giving us our titles. Mr. Premium, the plain state of the matter is this: I am an extravagant young fellow who wants to borrow money; you I take to be a prudent old fellow, who has got money to lend. I am blockhead enough to give fifty per cent. sooner than not have it! and you, I presume, are rogue enough to take a hundred if you can get it. Now, sir, you see we are acquainted at once, and may proceed to business without further ceremony.

SIR OLIVER: Exceeding frank, upon my word. I see, sir, you are not a man of many compliments.

CHARLES SURFACE: Oh, no, sir! plain dealing in business I always think best.

SIR OLIVER: Sir, I like you the better for it. However, you are mistaken in one thing; I have no money to lend, but I believe I could procure some of a friend; but then he's an unconscionable dog. Isn't he, Moses? And must sell stock to accommodate you. Mustn't he, Moses?

MOSES: Yes, indeed! You know I always speak the truth, and scorn to tell a lie!

CHARLES SURFACE: Right. People that speak truth generally do. But these are trifles. Mr. Premium. What! I know money isn't to be bought without paying for't!

SIR OLIVER: Well, but what security could you give? You have no land, I suppose?

CHARLES SURFACE: Not a mole-hill, nor a twig, but what's in the bough-pots out of the window!

SIR OLIVER: Nor any stock, I presume?

CHARLES SURFACE: Nothing but live stock—and that's only a few pointers and ponies. But pray, Mr. Premium, are you acquainted at all with any of my connections?

SIR OLIVER: Why, to say the truth, I am.

CHARLES SURFACE: Then you must know that I have a devilish rich uncle in the East Indies, Sir Oliver Surface, from whom I have the greatest expectations?

SIR OLIVER: That you have a wealthy uncle, I have heard; but how your expectations will turn out is more, I believe, than you can tell.

CHARLES SURFACE: Oh, no!—there can be no doubt. They tell me I'm a prodigious favourite, and that he talks of leaving me everything.

SIR OLIVER: Indeed! this is the first I've heard of it.

CHARLES SURFACE: Yes, yes, 'tis just so. Moses knows 'tis true; don't you, Moses?

MOSES: Oh, yes, I'll swear to't.

SIR OLIVER: Egad, they'll persuade me presently I'm at Bengal. [Aside]

CHARLES SURFACE: Now I propose, Mr. Premium, if it's agreeable to you, a post-obit on Sir Oliver's life: though at the same time the old fellow has been so liberal to me, that I give you my word, I should be very sorry to hear that anything had happened to him.

SIR OLIVER: Not more than I should, I assure you. But the bond you mention happens to be just the worst security you could offer me—for I might live to a hundred and never see the principal.

CHARLES SURFACE: Oh, yes, you would! the moment Sir Oliver dies, you know, you would come on me for the money.

SIR OLIVER: Then I believe I should be the most unwelcome dun you ever had in your life.

CHARLES SURFACE: What! I suppose you're afraid that Sir Oliver is too good a life?

SIR OLIVER: No, indeed I am not; though I have heard he is as hale and healthy as any man of his years in Christendom.

CHARLES SURFACE: There again, now, you are misinformed. No, no, the climate has hurt him considerably, poor uncle Oliver. Yes, yes, he breaks apace, I'm told—and is so much altered lately that his nearest relations would not know him.

SIR OLIVER: No! Ha! ha! ha! so much altered lately that his nearest relations would not know him! Ha! ha! ha! egad—ha! ha! ha!

CHARLES SURFACE: Ha! ha!—you're glad to hear that, little Premium?

SIR OLIVER: No, no, I'm not.

CHARLES SURFACE: Yes, yes, you are—ha! ha! ha!—you know that mends your chance.

SIR OLIVER: But I'm told Sir Oliver is coming over; nay, some say he has actually arrived.

CHARLES SURFACE: Psha! sure I must know better than you whether he's come or not. No, no, rely on't he's at this moment at Calcutta. Isn't he, Moses?

MOSES: Oh, yes, certainly.

SIR OLIVER: Very true, as you say, you must know better than I, though I have it from pretty good authority. Haven't I, Moses?

MOSES: Yes, most undoubted!

SIR OLIVER: But, sir, as I understand you want a few hundreds immediately, is there nothing you could dispose of?

CHARLES SURFACE: How do you mean?

SIR OLIVER: For instance, now, I have heard that your father left behind him a great quantity of massy old plate.

CHARLES SURFACE: O Lud, that's gone long ago. Moses can tell you how better than I can.

SIR OLIVER: [Aside] Good lack! all the family race-cups and corporation-bowls! [Aloud] Then it was also supposed that his library was one of the most valuable and compact.

CHARLES SURFACE: Yes, yes, so it was—vastly too much so for a private gentleman. For my part, I was always of a communicative disposition, so I thought it a shame to keep so much knowledge to myself.

SIR OLIVER: [Aside] Mercy upon me! learning that had run in the family like an heir-loom! [Aloud] Pray, what has become of the books?

CHARLES SURFACE: You must inquire of the auctioneer, Master Premium, for I don't believe even Moses can direct you.

MOSES: I know nothing of books.

SIR OLIVER: So, so, nothing of the family property left, I suppose?

CHARLES SURFACE: Not much, indeed; unless you have a mind to the family pictures. I have got a room full of ancestors above: and if you have a taste for old paintings, egad, you shall have 'em a bargain!

SIR OLIVER: Hey! what the devil! sure, you wouldn't sell your forefathers, would you?

CHARLES SURFACE: Every man of them, to the best bidder.

SIR OLIVER: What! your great-uncles and aunts?

CHARLES SURFACE: Ay, and my great-grandfathers and grandmothers too.

SIR OLIVER: [Aside] Now I give him up! [Aloud] What the plague, have you no bowels for your own kindred? Odd's life! do you take me for Shylock in the play, that you would raise money of me on your own flesh and blood?

CHARLES SURFACE: Nay, my little broker, don't be angry: what need you care, if you have your money's worth?

SIR OLIVER: Well, I'll be the purchaser: I think I can dispose of the family canvas. [*Aside*] Oh, I'll never forgive him this! never!

[*Re-enter* Careless]

CARELESS: Come, Charles, what keeps you?

CHARLES SURFACE: I can't come yet. I'faith, we are going to have a sale above stairs, here's little Premium will buy all my ancestors!

CARELESS: Oh, burn your ancestors!

CHARLES SURFACE: No, he may do that afterwards, if he pleases. Stay, Careless, we want you: egad, you shall be auctioneer—so come along with us.

CARELESS: Oh, have with you, if that's the case. I can handle a hammer as well as a dice box; going! going!

SIR OLIVER: Oh, the profligates! [*Aside*]

CHARLES SURFACE: Come, Moses, you shall be appraiser, if we want one. Gad's life, little Premium, you don't seem to like the business?

SIR OLIVER: Oh, yes, I do, vastly! Ha! ha! ha! yes, yes, I think it a rare joke to sell one's family by auction—ha! ha! [*Aside*] Oh, the prodigal!

CHARLES SURFACE: To be sure! when a man wants money, where the plague should he get assistance, if he can't make free with his own relations?

[*Exeunt*]

SIR OLIVER: I'll never forgive him; never! never!

ACT IV. SCENE I.

A picture room in Charles Surface's *house.*

[*Enter* Charles Surface, Sir Oliver Surface, Moses, *and* Careless]

CHARLES SURFACE: Walk in, gentlemen, pray walk in;—here they are, the family of the Surfaces, up to the Conquest.[11]

SIR OLIVER: And, in my opinion, a goodly collection.

CHARLES SURFACE: Ay, ay, these are done in the true spirit of portrait-painting; no *volontière grâce* or expression. Not like the works of your modern Raphaels, who give you the strongest resemblance, yet contrive to make your portrait independent of you; so that you may sink the original and not hurt the picture. No, no; the merit of these is the inveterate likeness—all stiff and awkward as the originals, and like nothing in human nature besides.

SIR OLIVER: Ah! we shall never see such figures of men again.

CHARLES SURFACE: I hope not. Well, you see, Master Premium, what a domestic character I am; here I sit of an evening surrounded by my family. But come, get to your pulpit, Mr. Auctioneer; here's

[11] Up to the Norman Conquest; a humorous way of saying that the whole family is there, as a family tracing its line to the Norman Conquest would have a great many members.

an old gouty chair of my grandfather's will answer the purpose.

CARELESS: Ay, ay, this will do. But, Charles, I haven't a hammer; and what's an auctioneer without his hammer?

CHARLES SURFACE: Egad, that's true. What parchment have we here? Oh, our genealogy in full. [*Taking pedigree down*] Here, Careless, you shall have no common bit of mahogany, here's the family tree for you, you rogue! This shall be your hammer, and now you may knock down my ancestors with their own pedigree.

SIR OLIVER: What an unnatural rogue!—an *ex post facto* parricide! [*Aside*]

CARELESS: Yes, yes, here's a list of your generation indeed;—faith, Charles, this is the most convenient thing you could have found for the business, for 'twill not only serve as a hammer, but a catalogue into the bargain. Come, begin—A-going, a-going, a-going!

CHARLES SURFACE: Bravo, Careless! Well, here's my great uncle, Sir Richard Ravelin, a marvellous good general in his day, I assure you. He served in all the Duke of Marlborough's wars, and got that cut over his eye at the battle of Malplaquet. What say you, Mr. Premium? look at him—there's a hero! not cut out of his feathers, as your modern clipped captains are, but developed in wig and regimentals, as a general should be. What do you bid?

SIR OLIVER: [*Aside to* Moses] Bid him speak.

MOSES: Mr. Premium would have you speak.

CHARLES SURFACE: Why, then, he shall have him for ten pounds, and I'm sure that's not dear for a staff-officer.

SIR OLIVER: [*Aside*] Heaven deliver me! his famous uncle Richard for ten pounds! [*Aloud*] Very well, sir, I take him at that.

CHARLES SURFACE: Careless, knock down my uncle Richard.—Here now, is a maiden sister of his, my great-aunt Deborah, done by Kneller, in his best manner, and esteemed a very formidable likeness. There she is, you see, a shepherdess feeding her flock. You shall have her for five pounds ten—the sheep are worth the money.

SIR OLIVER: [*Aside*] Ah! poor Deborah! a woman who set such a value on herself! [*Aloud*] Five pounds ten—she's mine.

CHARLES SURFACE: Knock down my aunt Deborah! Here, now, are two that were a sort of cousins of theirs.—You see, Moses, these pictures were done some time ago, when beaux wore wigs, and the ladies their own hair.

SIR OLIVER: Yes, truly, head-dresses appear to have been a little lower in those days.

CHARLES SURFACE: Well, take that couple for the same.

MOSES: 'Tis a good bargain.

CHARLES SURFACE: Careless!—This, now, is a grandfather of my mother's, a learned judge, well known on the western circuit.—What do you rate him at, Moses?

MOSES: Four guineas.

CHARLES SURFACE: Four guineas! Gad's life, you don't bid me the price of his wig.—Mr. Premium, you have more respect for the woolsack; do let us knock his lordship down at fifteen.

SIR OLIVER: By all means.

CARELESS: Gone.

CHARLES SURFACE: And there are two brothers of his, William and Walter Blunt, Esquires, both members of Parliament, and noted speakers; and, what's very extraordinary, I believe, this is the first time they were ever bought or sold.

SIR OLIVER: That is very extraordinary, indeed! I'll take them at your own price, for the honour of Parliament.

CARELESS: Well said, little Premium! I'll knock them down at forty.

CHARLES SURFACE: Here's a jolly fellow—I don't know what relation, but he was mayor of Norwich: take him at eight pounds.

SIR OLIVER: No, no; six will do for the mayor.

CHARLES SURFACE: Come, make it guineas, and I'll throw you the two aldermen there into the bargain.

SIR OLIVER: They're mine.

CHARLES SURFACE: Careless, knock down the mayor and aldermen. But, plague on't! we shall be all day retailing in this manner; do let us deal wholesale: what say you, little Premium? Give me three hundred pounds for the rest of the family in the lump.

CARELESS: Ay ay, that will be the best way.

SIR OLIVER: Well, well, anything to accommodate you; they are mine. But there is one portrait which you have always passed over.

CARELESS: What, that ill-looking little fellow over the settee?

SIR OLIVER: Yes, sir, I mean that; though I don't think him so ill-looking a little fellow, by any means.

CHARLES SURFACE: What, that? Oh; that's my uncle Oliver! 'Twas done before he went to India.

CARELESS: Your uncle Oliver! Gad, then you'll never be friends, Charles. That, now to me, is as stern a looking rogue as ever I saw; an unforgiving eye, and a damned disinheriting countenance! an inveterate knave, depend on't. Don't you think so, little Premium?

SIR OLIVER: Upon my soul, sir, I do not; I think it is as honest a looking face as any in the room, dead or alive. But I suppose uncle Oliver goes with the rest of the lumber?

CHARLES SURFACE: No, hang it! I'll not part with poor Noll. The old fellow has been very good to me, and, egad, I'll keep his picture while I've a room to put it in.

SIR OLIVER: [Aside] The rogue's my nephew after all!— [Aloud] But, sir, I have somehow taken a fancy to that picture.

CHARLES SURFACE: I'm sorry for't, for you certainly will not have it. Oons, haven't you got enough of them?

SIR OLIVER: [Aside] I forgive him everything! [Aloud] But, sir, when I take a whim in my head, I don't value money. I'll give you as much for that as for all the rest.

CHARLES SURFACE: Don't tease me, master broker; I tell you I'll not part with it, and there's an end of it.

SIR OLIVER: [Aside] How like his father the dog is. [Aloud] Well, well, I have done. [Aside] I did not perceive it before, but I think I never saw such a striking resemblance. [Aloud] Here is a draught for your sum.

CHARLES SURFACE: Why, 'tis for eight hundred pounds!

SIR OLIVER: You will not let Sir Oliver go?

CHARLES SURFACE: Zounds! no! I tell you, once more.

SIR OLIVER: Then never mind the difference, we'll balance that another time. But give me your hand on the bargain; you are an honest fellow, Charles—I beg pardon, sir, for being so free.—Come, Moses.

CHARLES SURFACE: Egad, this is a whimsical old fellow!—But hark'ee, Premium, you'll prepare lodgings for these gentlemen.

SIR OLIVER: Yes, yes, I'll send for them in a day or two.

CHARLES SURFACE: But hold; do now send a genteel conveyance for them, for, I assure you, they were most of them used to ride in their own carriages.

SIR OLIVER: I will, I will—for all but Oliver.

CHARLES SURFACE: Ay, all but the little nabob.

SIR OLIVER: You're fixed on that?

CHARLES SURFACE: Peremptorily.

SIR OLIVER: [Aside] A dear extravagant rogue! [Aloud] Good day!—Come, Moses. [Aside] Let me hear now who dares call him profligate! [Exit with Moses]

CARELESS: Why, this is the oddest genius of the sort I ever met with!

CHARLES SURFACE: Egad, he's the prince of brokers, I think. I wonder how the devil Moses got acquainted with so honest a fellow.—Ha! here's Rowley.—Do, Careless, say I'll join the company in a few moments.

CARELESS: I will—but don't let that old blockhead persuade you to squander any of that money on old musty debts, or any such nonsense; for tradesmen, Charles, are the most exorbitant fellows.

CHARLES SURFACE: Very true, and paying them is only encouraging them.

CARELESS: Nothing else.

CHARLES SURFACE: Ay, ay, never fear. [Exit Careless] So! this was an odd old fellow, indeed. Let me see, two-thirds of these five hundred and thirty odd pounds are mine by right. 'Fore Heaven! I find one's ancestors are more valuable relations than I took them for!—Ladies and gentlemen, your most obedient and very grateful servant. [Bows ceremoniously to the pictures]

[Enter Rowley]

Ha! old Rowley! egad, you are just come in time to take leave of your old acquaintance.

ROWLEY: Yes, I heard they were a-going. But I wonder you can have such spirits under so many distresses.

CHARLES SURFACE: Why, there's the point! my distresses are so many, that I can't afford to part with my spirits; but I shall be rich and splenetic, all in good time. However, I suppose you are surprised that I am not more sorrowful at parting with so many near relations; to be sure, 'tis very affecting; but you see they never move a muscle, so why should I?

ROWLEY: There's no making you serious a moment.

CHARLES SURFACE: Yes, faith, I am so now. Here, my honest Rowley, here, get me this changed directly, and take a hundred pounds of it immediately to old Stanley.

ROWLEY: A hundred pounds! Consider only——

CHARLES SURFACE: Gad's life, don't talk about it! poor Stanley's wants are pressing, and, if you don't make haste, we shall have some one call that has a better right to the money.

ROWLEY: Ah! there's the point! I never will cease dunning you with the old proverb——

CHARLES SURFACE: *Be just before you're generous.* —Why, so I would if I could; but Justice is an old hobbling beldame, and I can't get her to keep pace with Generosity, for the soul of me.

ROWLEY: Yet, Charles, believe me, one hour's reflection——

CHARLES SURFACE: Ay, ay, it's very true; but, hark'ee, Rowley, while I have, by Heaven I'll give; so, damn your economy! and now for hazard.

[*Exeunt*]

SCENE II.

Another room in the same.

[*Enter* Sir Oliver Surface *and* Moses]

MOSES: Well, sir, I think, as Sir Peter said, you have seen Mr. Charles in high glory; 'tis great pity he's so extravagant.

SIR OLIVER: True, but he would not sell my picture.

MOSES: And loves wine and women so much.

SIR OLIVER: But he would not sell my picture.

MOSES: And games so deep.

SIR OLIVER: But he would not sell my picture. Oh, here's Rowley.

[*Enter* Rowley]

ROWLEY: So, Sir Oliver, I find you have made a purchase——

SIR OLIVER: Yes, yes, our young rake has parted with his ancestors like old tapestry.

ROWLEY: And here has he commissioned me to re-deliver you part of the purchase-money—I mean, though, in your necessitous character of old Stanley.

MOSES: Ah! there is the pity of all: he is so damned charitable.

ROWLEY: And I left a hosier and two tailors in the hall, who, I'm sure, won't be paid, and this hundred would satisfy them.

SIR OLIVER: Well, well, I'll pay his debts, and his benevolence too. But now I am no more a broker, and you shall introduce me to the elder brother as old Stanley.

ROWLEY: Not yet awhile; Sir Peter, I know, means to call there about this time.

[*Enter* Trip]

TRIP: Oh, gentlemen, I beg pardon for not showing you out; this way—Moses, a word. [*Exit with* Moses]

SIR OLIVER: There's a fellow for you! Would you believe it, that puppy intercepted the Jew on our coming, and wanted to raise money before he got to his master!

ROWLEY: Indeed.

SIR OLIVER: Yes, they are now planning an annuity business, Ah, Master Rowley, in my days servants were content with the follies of their masters, when they were worn a little threadbare; but now they have their vices, like their birthday clothes, with the gloss on.

[*Exeunt*]

SCENE III.

A library in Joseph Surface's *house.*

[*Enter* Joseph Surface *and* Servant]

JOSEPH SURFACE: No letter from Lady Teazle?

SERVANT: No, sir.

JOSEPH SURFACE: [*Aside*] I am surprised she has not sent, if she is prevented from coming. Sir Peter certainly does not suspect me. Yet I wish I may not lose the heiress, through the scrape I have drawn myself into with the wife; however, Charles's imprudence and bad character are great points in my favour.

[*Knocking without*]

SERVANT: Sir, I believe that must be Lady Teazle.

JOSEPH SURFACE: Hold! See whether it is or not, before you go to the door: I have a particular message for you if it should be my brother.

SERVANT: 'Tis her ladyship, sir; she always leaves the chair at the milliner's in the next street.

JOSEPH SURFACE: Stay, stay: draw that screen before the window—that will do;—my opposite neighbour is a maiden lady of so curious a temper. [Servant *draws the screen, and exit*] I have a difficult hand to play in this affair. Lady Teazle has lately suspected my views on Maria; but she must by no means be let into that secret,—at least, till I have her more in my power.

[*Enter* Lady Teazle]

LADY TEAZLE: What sentiment in soliloquy now? Have you been very impatient? O Lud! don't pretend to look grave. I vow I couldn't come before.

JOSEPH SURFACE: O madam, punctuality is a

species of constancy very unfashionable in a lady of quality. [*Places chairs, and sits after* Lady Teazle *is seated*]

LADY TEAZLE: Upon my word, you ought to pity me. Do you know Sir Peter is grown so ill-natured to me of late, and so jealous of Charles too—that's the best of the story, isn't it?

JOSEPH SURFACE: I am glad my scandalous friends keep that up. [*Aside*]

LADY TEAZLE: I am sure I wish he would let Maria marry him, and then perhaps he would be convinced; don't you, Mr. Surface?

JOSEPH SURFACE: [*Aside*] Indeed I do not. [*Aloud*] Oh, certainly I do! for then my dear Lady Teazle would also be convinced how wrong her suspicions were of my having any design on the silly girl.

LADY TEAZLE: Well, well, I'm inclined to believe you. But isn't it provoking, to have the most ill-natured things said at one? And there's my friend Lady Sneerwell has circulated I don't know how many scandalous tales of me, and all without any foundation, too; that's what vexes me.

JOSEPH SURFACE: Ay, madam, to be sure, that is the provoking circumstance—without foundation; yes, yes, there's the mortification, indeed; for, when a scandalous story is believed against one, there certainly is no comfort like the consciousness of having deserved it.

LADY TEAZLE: No, to be sure, then I'd forgive their malice; but to attack me, who am really so innocent, and who never say an ill-natured thing of anybody— that is, of any friend; and then Sir Peter, too, to have him so peevish, and so suspicious, when I know the integrity of my own heart—indeed 'tis monstrous!

JOSEPH SURFACE: But, my dear Lady Teazle, 'tis your own fault if you suffer it. When a husband entertains a groundless suspicion of his wife, and withdraws his confidence from her, the original compact is broken, and she owes it to the honour of her sex to endeavour to outwit him.

LADY TEAZLE: Indeed! So that, if he suspects me without cause, it follows, that the best way of curing his jealousy is to give him reason for't?

JOSEPH SURFACE: Undoubtedly—for your husband should never be deceived in you: and in that case it becomes you to be frail in compliment to his discernment.

LADY TEAZLE: To be sure, what you say is very reasonable, and when the consciousness of my innocence——

JOSEPH SURFACE: Ah, my dear madam, there is the great mistake; 'tis this very conscious innocence that is of the greatest prejudice to you. What is it makes you negligent of forms, and careless of the world's opinion? why, the consciousness of your own innocence. What makes you thoughtless in your conduct, and apt to run into a thousand little imprudences? why, the consciousness of your own innocence. What makes you impatient of Sir Peter's temper, and out-

rageous at his suspicions? why, the consciousness of your innocence.

LADY TEAZLE: 'Tis very true!

JOSEPH SURFACE: Now, my dear Lady Teazle, if you would but once make a trifling *faux pas*, you can't conceive how cautious you would grow, and how ready to humour and agree with your husband.

LADY TEAZLE: Do you think so?

JOSEPH SURFACE: Oh, I'm sure on't; and then you would find all scandal would cease at once, for—in short, your character at present is like a person in a plethora, absolutely dying from too much health.

LADY TEAZLE: So, so; then I perceive your prescription is, that I must sin in my own defence, and part with my virtue to preserve my reputation?

JOSEPH SURFACE: Exactly so, upon my credit, ma'am.

LADY TEAZLE: Well, certainly this is the oddest doctrine, and the newest receipt for avoiding calumny!

JOSEPH SURFACE: An infallible one, believe me. Prudence, like experience, must be paid for.

LADY TEAZLE: Why, if my understanding were once convinced——

JOSEPH SURFACE: Oh, certainly, madam, your understanding should be convinced. Yes, yes— Heaven forbid I should persuade you to do anything you thought wrong. No, no, I have too much honour to desire it.

LADY TEAZLE: Don't you think we may as well leave honour out of the argument? [*Rises*]

JOSEPH SURFACE: Ah, the ill effects of your country education, I see, still remain with you.

LADY TEAZLE: I doubt they do, indeed; and I will fairly own to you, that if I could be persuaded to do wrong, it would be by Sir Peter's ill-usage sooner than your honourable logic, after all.

JOSEPH SURFACE: Then, by this hand, which he is unworthy of—— [*Taking her hand*]

[*Re-enter* Servant]

'Sdeath, you blockhead—what do you want?

SERVANT: I beg your pardon, sir, but I thought you would not choose Sir Peter to come up without announcing him.

JOSEPH SURFACE: Sir Peter!—Oons—the devil!

LADY TEAZLE: Sir Peter! O Lud; I'm ruined! I'm ruined!

SERVANT: Sir, 'twasn't I let him in.

LADY TEAZLE: Oh! I'm quite undone! What will become of me? Now, Mr. Logic—Oh! mercy, sir, he's on the stairs—I'll get behind here—and if ever I'm so imprudent again—— [*Goes behind the screen*]

JOSEPH SURFACE: Give me that book. [*Sits down.* Servant *pretends to adjust his chair*]

[*Enter* Sir Peter Teazle]

SIR PETER: Ay, ever improving himself. Mr. Surface, Mr. Surface—— [*Pats* Joseph *on the shoulder*]

JOSEPH SURFACE: Oh, my dear Sir Peter, I beg your pardon. [*Gaping, throws away the book*] I have been dozing over a stupid book. Well, I am much obliged to you for this call. You haven't been here, I believe, since I fitted up this room. Books, you know, are the only things I am a coxcomb in.

SIR PETER: 'Tis very neat indeed. Well, well, that's proper; and you can make even your screen a source of knowledge—hung, I perceive, with maps.

JOSEPH SURFACE: Oh, yes, I find great use in that screen.

SIR PETER: I dare say you must, certainly, when you want to find anything in a hurry.

JOSEPH SURFACE: Ay, or to hide anything in a hurry either. [Aside]

SIR PETER: Well, I have a little private business——

JOSEPH SURFACE: [To Servant] You need not stay.

SERVANT: No, sir. [Exit]

JOSEPH SURFACE: Here's a chair, Sir Peter—I beg——

SIR PETER: Well, now we are alone, there is a subject, my dear friend, on which I wish to unburden my mind to you—a point of the greatest moment to my peace; in short, my good friend, Lady Teazle's conduct of late has made me very unhappy.

JOSEPH SURFACE: Indeed! I am very sorry to hear it.

SIR PETER: Yes, 'tis but too plain she has not the least regard for me; but, what's worse, I have pretty good authority to suppose that she has formed an attachment to another.

JOSEPH SURFACE: Indeed! you astonish me!

SIR PETER: Yes! and, between ourselves, I think I've discovered the person.

JOSEPH SURFACE: How! you alarm me exceedingly.

SIR PETER: Ay, my dear friend, I knew you would sympathize with me!

JOSEPH SURFACE: Yes, believe me, Sir Peter, such a discovery would hurt me just as much as it would you.

SIR PETER: I am convinced of it. Ah! it is a happiness to have a friend whom we can trust even with one's family secrets. But have you no guess who I mean?

JOSEPH SURFACE: I haven't the most distant idea. It can't be Sir Benjamin Backbite!

SIR PETER: Oh, no! what say you to Charles?

JOSEPH SURFACE: My brother! impossible!

SIR PETER: Oh, my dear friend, the goodness of your own heart misleads you. You judge of others by yourself.

JOSEPH SURFACE: Certainly, Sir Peter, the heart that is conscious of its own integrity is ever slow to credit another's treachery.

SIR PETER: True; but your brother has no sentiment—you never hear him talk so.

JOSEPH SURFACE: Yet I can't but think Lady Teazle herself has too much principle.

SIR PETER: Ay; but what is principle against the flattery of a handsome, lively young fellow?

JOSEPH SURFACE: That's very true.

SIR PETER: And then, you know, the difference of our ages makes it very improbable that she should have any great affection for me; and if she were to be frail, and I were to make it public, why the town would only laugh at me, the foolish old bachelor, who had married a girl.

JOSEPH SURFACE: That's true, to be sure—they would laugh.

SIR PETER: Laugh! ay, and make ballads, and paragraphs, and the devil knows what of me.

JOSEPH SURFACE: No, you must never make it public.

SIR PETER: But then again—that the nephew of my old friend, Sir Oliver, should be the person to attempt such a wrong, hurts me more nearly.

JOSEPH SURFACE: Ay, there's the point. When ingratitude barbs the dart of injury, the wound has double danger in it.

SIR PETER: Ay—I, that was, in a manner, left his guardian: in whose house he had been so often entertained; who never in my life denied him—my advice!

JOSEPH SURFACE: Oh, 'tis not to be credited! There may be a man capable of such baseness, to be sure; but, for my part, till you can give me positive proofs, I cannot but doubt it. However, if it should be proved on him, he is no longer a brother of mine—I disclaim kindred with him: for the man who can break the laws of hospitality, and tempt the wife of his friend, deserves to be branded as the pest of society.

SIR PETER: What a difference there is between you! What noble sentiments!

JOSEPH SURFACE: Yet I cannot suspect Lady Teazle's honour.

SIR PETER: I am sure I wish to think well of her, and to remove all ground of quarrel between us. She has lately reproached me more than once with having made no settlement on her; and, in our last quarrel, she almost hinted that she should not break heart if I was dead. Now, as we seem to differ in our ideas of expense, I have resolved she shall have her own way, and be her own mistress in that respect for the future; and, if I were to die, she will find I have not been inattentive to her interest while living. Here, my friend, are the drafts of two deeds, which I wish to have your opinion on. By one, she will enjoy eight hundred a year independent while I live; and, by the other, the bulk of my fortune at my death.

JOSEPH SURFACE: This conduct, Sir Peter, is indeed truly generous.— [Aside] I wish it may not corrupt my pupil.

SIR PETER: Yes, I am determined she shall have no cause to complain, though I would not have her acquainted with the latter instance of my affection yet awhile.

JOSEPH SURFACE: Nor I, if I could help it. [Aside]

SIR PETER: And now, my dear friend, if you please, we will talk over the situation of your hopes with Maria.

JOSEPH SURFACE: [Softly] Oh, no, Sir Peter; another time, if you please.

SIR PETER: I am sensibly chagrined at the little progress you seem to make in her affections.

JOSEPH SURFACE: [*Softly*] I beg you will not mention it. What are my disappointments when your happiness is in debate! [*Aside*] 'Sdeath, I shall be ruined every way!

SIR PETER: And though you are averse to my acquainting Lady Teazle with your passion, I'm sure she's not your enemy in the affair.

JOSEPH SURFACE: Pray, Sir Peter, now oblige me. I am really too much affected by the subject we have been speaking of to bestow a thought on my own concerns. The man who is entrusted with his friend's distresses can never——

[*Re-enter* Servant]

Well, sir?

SERVANT: Your brother, sir, is speaking to a gentleman in the street, and says he knows you are within.

JOSEPH SURFACE: 'Sdeath, blockhead, I'm not within—I'm out for the day.

SIR PETER: Stay—hold—a thought has struck me:—you shall be at home.

JOSEPH SURFACE: Well, well, let him up. [*Exit* Servant] He'll interrupt Sir Peter, however. [*Aside*]

SIR PETER: Now, my good friend, oblige me, I entreat you. Before Charles comes, let me conceal myself somewhere, then do you tax him on the point we have been talking, and his answer may satisfy me at once.

JOSEPH SURFACE: Oh, fie, Sir Peter! would you have me join in so mean a trick?—to trepan my brother too?

SIR PETER: Nay, you tell me you are sure he is innocent; if so, you do him the greatest service by giving him an opportunity to clear himself, and you will set my heart at rest. Come, you shall not refuse me: [*Going up*] here, behind the screen will be— Hey! what the devil! there seems to be one listener here already—I'll swear I saw a petticoat!

JOSEPH SURFACE: Ha! ha! ha! Well, this is ridiculous enough. I'll tell you, Sir Peter, though I hold a man of intrigue to be a most despicable character, yet you know, it does not follow that one is to be an absolute Joseph either! Hark'ee, 'tis a little French milliner, a silly rogue that plagues me; and having some character to lose, on your coming, sir, she ran behind the screen.

SIR PETER: Ah, a rogue—— But, egad, she has overheard all I have been saying of my wife.

JOSEPH SURFACE: Oh, 'twill never go any farther, you may depend upon it!

SIR PETER: No! then, faith let her hear it out.— Here's a closet will do as well.

JOSEPH SURFACE: Well, go in there.

SIR PETER: Sly rogue! sly rogue! [*Goes into the closet*]

JOSEPH SURFACE: A narrow escape, indeed! and a curious situation I'm in, to part man and wife in this manner.

LADY TEAZLE: [*Peeping*] Couldn't I steal off?

JOSEPH SURFACE: Keep close, my angel!

SIR PETER: [*Peeping*] Joseph, tax him home.

JOSEPH SURFACE: Back, my dear friend!

LADY TEAZLE: [*Peeping*] Couldn't you lock Sir Peter in?

JOSEPH SURFACE: Be still, my life!

SIR PETER: [*Peeping*] You're sure the little milliner won't blab?

JOSEPH SURFACE: In, in, my dear Sir Peter!— 'Fore Gad, I wish I had a key to the door.

[*Enter* Charles Surface]

CHARLES SURFACE: Holla! brother, what has been the matter? Your fellow would not let me up at first. What! have you had a Jew or a wench with you?

JOSEPH SURFACE: Neither, brother, I assure you.

CHARLES SURFACE: But what has made Sir Peter steal off? I thought he had been with you.

JOSEPH SURFACE: He was, brother; but, hearing you were coming, he did not choose to stay.

CHARLES SURFACE: What! was the old gentleman afraid I wanted to borrow money of him!

JOSEPH SURFACE: No, sir: but I am sorry to find, Charles, you have lately given that worthy man grounds for uneasiness.

CHARLES SURFACE: Yes, they tell me I do that to a great many worthy men. But how so, pray?

JOSEPH SURFACE: To be plain with you, brother, he thinks you are endeavouring to gain Lady Teazle's affections from him.

CHARLES SURFACE: Who, I? O Lud! not I, upon my word.—Ha! ha! ha! ha! so the old fellow has found out that he has got a young wife, has he?—or, what is worse, Lady Teazle has found out she has an old husband?

JOSEPH SURFACE: This is no subject to jest on, brother. He who can laugh——

CHARLES SURFACE: True, true, as you were going to say—then, seriously, I never had the least idea of what you charge me with, upon my honour.

JOSEPH SURFACE: Well, it will give Sir Peter great satisfaction to hear this. [*Raising his voice*]

CHARLES SURFACE: To be sure, I once thought the lady seemed to have taken a fancy to me; but, upon my soul, I never gave her the least encouragement. Besides, you know my attachment to Maria.

JOSEPH SURFACE: But sure, brother, even if Lady Teazle had betrayed the fondest partiality for you——

CHARLES SURFACE: Why, look'ee, Joseph, I hope I shall never deliberately do a dishonourable action; but if a pretty woman was purposely to throw herself in my way—and that pretty woman married to a man old enough to be her father——

JOSEPH SURFACE: Well!

CHARLES SURFACE: Why, I believe I should be obliged to borrow a little of your morality, that's all. But, brother, do you know now that you surprise me exceedingly, by naming me with Lady Teazle; for i'faith, I always understood you were her favourite.

JOSEPH SURFACE: Oh, for shame, Charles! This retort is foolish.

CHARLES SURFACE: Nay, I swear I have seen you exchange such significant glances——

JOSEPH SURFACE: Nay, nay, sir, this is no jest.

CHARLES SURFACE: Egad, I'm serious! Don't you remember one day, when I called here——

JOSEPH SURFACE: Nay, pr'ythee, Charles——

CHARLES SURFACE: And found you together——

JOSEPH SURFACE: Zounds, sir, I insist——

CHARLES SURFACE: And another time, when your servant——

JOSEPH SURFACE: Brother, brother, a word with you! [*Aside*] Gad, I must stop him.

CHARLES SURFACE: Informed, I say, that——

JOSEPH SURFACE: Hush! I beg your pardon, but Sir Peter has overheard all we have been saying. I knew you would clear yourself, or I should not have consented.

CHARLES SURFACE: How, Sir Peter! Where is he?

JOSEPH SURFACE: Softly, there! [*Points to the closet*]

CHARLES SURFACE: Oh, 'fore Heaven, I'll have him out. Sir Peter come forth!

JOSEPH SURFACE: No, no——

CHARLES SURFACE: I say, Sir Peter, come into court. [*Pulls in* Sir Peter] What! my old guardian!—What! —turn inquisitor, and take evidence, incog.? Oh, fie! Oh, fie!

SIR PETER: Give me your hand, Charles—I believe I have suspected you wrongfully; but you mustn't be angry with Joseph—'twas my plan!

CHARLES SURFACE: Indeed!

SIR PETER: But I acquit you. I promise you I don't think near so ill of you as I did. What I have heard has given me great satisfaction.

CHARLES SURFACE: Egad, then, 'twas lucky you didn't hear any more. Wasn't it, Joseph?

SIR PETER: Ah! you would have retorted on him.

CHARLES SURFACE: Ah, ay, that was a joke.

SIR PETER: Yes, yes, I know his honour too well.

CHARLES SURFACE: But you might as well have suspected him as me in this matter, for all that. Mightn't he, Joseph?

SIR PETER: Well, well, I believe you.

JOSEPH SURFACE: Would they were both out of the room! [*Aside*]

SIR PETER: And in future, perhaps, we may not be such strangers.

[*Re-enter* Servant *and whispers to* Joseph Surface]

SERVANT: Lady Sneerwell is below, and she says she will come up.

JOSEPH SURFACE: Gentlemen, I beg pardon—I must wait on you downstairs; here's a person come on particular business.

CHARLES SURFACE: Well, you can see him in another room. Sir Peter and I have not met a long time, and I have something to say to him.

JOSEPH SURFACE: [*Aside*] They must not be left together. [*Aloud*] I'll send Lady Sneerwell away, and return directly. [*Aside to* Sir Peter] Sir Peter, not a word of the French milliner.

SIR PETER: [*Aside to* Joseph Surface] I! not for the world!— [*Exit* Joseph Surface] Ah, Charles, if you associated more with your brother, one might indeed hope for your reformation. He is a man of sentiment. Well, there is nothing in the world so noble as a man of sentiment.

CHARLES SURFACE: Psha! he is too moral by half; and so apprehensive of his good name, as he calls it, that I suppose he would as soon let a priest into his house as a wench.

SIR PETER: No, no,—come, come,—you wrong him. No, no, Joseph is no rake, but he is no such saint either, in that respect. [*Aside*] I have a great mind to tell him—we should have such a laugh at Joseph.

CHARLES SURFACE: Oh, hang him! he's a very anchorite, a young hermit!

SIR PETER: Hark'ee—you must not abuse him: he may chance to hear of it again, I promise you.

CHARLES SURFACE: Why, you won't tell him?

SIR PETER: No—but—this way. [*Aside*] Egad, I'll tell him. [*Aloud*] Hark'ee, have you a mind to have a good laugh at Joseph?

CHARLES SURFACE: I should like it of all things.

SIR PETER: Then, i'faith, we will! I'll be quit with him for discovering me. He had a girl with him when I called. [*Whispers*]

CHARLES SURFACE: What! Joseph? you jest.

SIR PETER: Hush!—a little French milliner—and the best of the jest is—she's in the room now.

CHARLES SURFACE: The devil she is!

SIR PETER: Hush! I tell you. [*Points to the screen*]

CHARLES SURFACE: Behind the screen! Odds life, let's unveil her!

SIR PETER: No, no, he's coming:—you shan't, indeed!

CHARLES SURFACE: Oh, egad, we'll have a peep at the little milliner!

SIR PETER: Not for the world!—Joseph will never forgive me.

CHARLES SURFACE: I'll stand by you——

SIR PETER: Odds, here he is!

[Charles Surface *throws down the screen*]
[*Re-enter* Joseph Surface]

CHARLES SURFACE: Lady Teazle, by all that's wonderful!

SIR PETER: Lady Teazle, by all that's damnable!

CHARLES SURFACE: Sir Peter, this is one of the smartest French milliners I ever saw. Egad, you seem all to have been diverting yourselves here at hide and seek, and I don't see who is out of the secret. Shall I beg your ladyship to inform me? Not a word!— Brother, will you be pleased to explain this matter? What! is Morality dumb too?—Sir Peter, though I found you in the dark, perhaps you are not so now! All mute! Well—though I can make nothing of the affair, I suppose you perfectly understand one another; so I'll leave you to yourselves. [*Going*]

Brother, I'm sorry to find you have given that worthy man grounds for so much uneasiness.—Sir Peter! there's nothing in the world so noble as a man of sentiment! [*Exit*]

JOSEPH SURFACE: Sir Peter—notwithstanding—I confess—that appearances are against me—if you will afford me your patience—I make no doubt—but I shall explain everything to your satisfaction.

SIR PETER: If you please, sir.

JOSEPH SURFACE: The fact is, sir, that Lady Teazle, knowing my pretensions to your ward Maria—I say, sir, Lady Teazle, being apprehensive of the jealousy of your temper—and knowing my friendship to the family—she, sir, I say—called here—in order that—I might explain these pretensions—but on your coming—being apprehensive—as I said—of your jealousy—she withdrew—and this, you may depend on it, is the whole truth of the matter.

SIR PETER: A very clear account, upon my word; and I dare swear the lady will vouch for every article of it.

LADY TEAZLE: For not one word of it, Sir Peter!

SIR PETER: How! don't you think it worth while to agree in the lie?

LADY TEAZLE: There is not one syllable of truth in what that gentleman has told you.

SIR PETER: I believe you, upon my soul, ma'am!

JOSEPH SURFACE: [*Aside to* Lady Teazle] 'Sdeath, madam, will you betray me?

LADY TEAZLE: Good Mr. Hypocrite, by your leave, I'll speak for myself.

SIR PETER: Ay, let her alone, sir; you'll find she'll make out a better story than you, without prompting.

LADY TEAZLE: Hear me, Sir Peter!—I came here on no matter relating to your ward, and even ignorant of this gentleman's pretensions to her. But I came, seduced by his insidious arguments, at least to listen to his pretended passion, if not to sacrifice your honour to his baseness.

SIR PETER: Now, I believe, the truth is coming, indeed!

JOSEPH SURFACE: The woman's mad!

LADY TEAZLE: No, sir; she has recovered her senses, and your own arts have furnished her with the means.—Sir Peter, I do not expect you to credit me—but the tenderness you expressed for me, when I am sure you could not think I was a witness to it, has penetrated so to my heart, that had I left the place without the shame of this discovery, my future life should have spoken the sincerity of my gratitude. As for that smooth-tongued hypocrite, who would have seduced the wife of his too credulous friend, while he affected honourable addresses to his ward—I behold him now in a light so truly despicable, that I shall never again respect myself for having listened to him. [*Exit*]

JOSEPH SURFACE: Notwithstanding all this, Sir Peter, Heaven knows——

SIR PETER: That you are a villain! and so I leave you to your conscience.

JOSEPH SURFACE: You are too rash, Sir Peter; you shall hear me. The man who shuts out conviction by refusing to——

[*Exeunt* Sir Peter *and* Joseph Surface, *talking*]

ACT V. SCENE I.

The library in Joseph Surface's *house.*

[*Enter* Joseph Surface *and* Servant]

JOSEPH SURFACE: Mr. Stanley! and why should you think I would see him? you must know he comes to ask something.

SERVANT: Sir, I should not have let him in, but that Mr. Rowley came to the door with him.

JOSEPH SURFACE: Psha! blockhead! to suppose that I should now be in a temper to receive visits from poor relations!—Well, why don't you show the fellow up?

SERVANT: I will, sir.—Why, sir, it was not my fault that Sir Peter discovered my lady——

JOSEPH SURFACE: Go, fool! [*Exit* Servant] Sure Fortune never played a man of my policy such a trick before! My character with Sir Peter, my hopes with Maria, destroyed in a moment! I'm in a rare humour to listen to other people's distresses! I shan't be able to bestow even a benevolent sentiment on Stanley.—So! here he comes, and Rowley with him. I must try to recover myself, and put a little charity into my face, however. [*Exit*]

[*Enter* Sir Oliver Surface *and* Rowley]

SIR OLIVER: What! does he avoid us? That was he, was it not?

ROWLEY: It was, sir. But I doubt you are come a little too abruptly. His nerves are so weak, that the sight of a poor relation may be too much for him. I should have gone first to break it to him.

SIR OLIVER: Oh, plague of his nerves! Yet this is he whom Sir Peter extols as a man of the most benevolent way of thinking!

ROWLEY: As to his way of thinking, I cannot pretend to decide; for, to do him justice, he appears to have as much speculative benevolence as any private gentleman in the kingdom, though he is seldom so sensual as to indulge him in the exercise of it.

SIR OLIVER: Yet he has a string of charitable sentiments at his fingers' ends.

ROWLEY: Or, rather, at his tongue's end, Sir Oliver; for I believe there is no sentiment he has such faith in as that *Charity begins at home.*

SIR OLIVER: And his, I presume, is of that domestic sort which never stirs abroad at all.

ROWLEY: I doubt you'll find it so;—but he's coming. I mustn't seem to interrupt you; and you know, immediately as you leave him, I come in to announce your arrival in your real character.

SIR OLIVER: True; and afterwards you'll meet me at Sir Peter's.

ROWLEY: Without losing a moment. [*Exit*]

SIR OLIVER: I don't like the complaisance of his features.

[*Re-enter* Joseph Surface]

JOSEPH SURFACE: Sir, I beg you ten thousand pardons for keeping you a moment waiting.—Mr. Stanley, I presume.

SIR OLIVER: At your service.

JOSEPH SURFACE: Sir, I beg you will do me the honour to sit down—I entreat you, sir.

SIR OLIVER: Dear sir—there's no occasion. [*Aside*] Too civil by half!

JOSEPH SURFACE: I have not the pleasure of knowing you, Mr. Stanley; but I am extremely happy to see you look so well. You were nearly related to my mother, I think, Mr. Stanley?

SIR OLIVER: I was, sir; so nearly that my present poverty, I fear, may do discredit to her wealthy children, else I should not have presumed to trouble you.

JOSEPH SURFACE: Dear sir, there needs no apology: he that is in distress, though a stranger, has a right to claim kindred with the wealthy. I am sure I wish I was one of that class, and had it in my power to offer you even a small relief.

SIR OLIVER: If your uncle, Sir Oliver, were here, I should have a friend.

JOSEPH SURFACE: I wish he was, sir, with all my heart: you should not want an advocate with him, believe me, sir.

SIR OLIVER: I should not need one—my distresses would recommend me. But I imagined his bounty would enable you to become the agent of his charity.

JOSEPH SURFACE: My dear sir, you were strangely misinformed. Sir Oliver is a worthy man, a very worthy man; but avarice, Mr. Stanley, is the vice of age. I will tell you, my good sir, in confidence, what he has done for me has been a mere nothing; though people, I know, have thought otherwise, and, for my part, I never chose to contradict the report.

SIR OLIVER: What! has he never transmitted you bullion—rupees—pagodas?

JOSEPH SURFACE: Oh, dear sir, nothing of the kind! No, no; a few presents now and then—china, shawls, congou tea, Avadavats,[12] and Indian crackers—little more, believe me.

SIR OLIVER: Here's gratitude for twelve thousand pounds!—Avadavats and Indian crackers! [*Aside*]

JOSEPH SURFACE: Then, my dear sir, you have heard, I doubt not, of the extravagance of my brother; there are very few would credit what I have done for that unfortunate young man.

SIR OLIVER: Not I, for one! [*Aside*]

JOSEPH SURFACE: The sums I have lent him! Indeed I have been exceeding to blame; it was an amiable weakness; however, I don't pretend to defend it—and now I feel it doubly culpable, since it has deprived me of the pleasure of serving you, Mr. Stanley, as my heart dictates.

SIR OLIVER: [*Aside*] Dissembler! [*Aloud*] Then, sir, you can't assist me?

[12] Small Indian songbirds.

JOSEPH SURFACE: At present, it grieves me to say, I cannot; but, whenever I have the ability, you may depend upon hearing from me.

SIR OLIVER: I am extremely sorry——

JOSEPH SURFACE: Not more than I, believe me; to pity, without the power to relieve, is still more painful than to ask and be denied.

SIR OLIVER: Kind sir, your most obedient humble servant.

JOSEPH SURFACE: You leave me deeply affected, Mr. Stanley.—William, be ready to open the door. [*Calls to* Servant]

SIR OLIVER: O, dear sir, no ceremony.

JOSEPH SURFACE: Your very obedient.

SIR OLIVER: Your most obsequious.

JOSEPH SURFACE: You may depend upon hearing from me, whenever I can be of service.

SIR OLIVER: Sweet sir, you are too good.

JOSEPH SURFACE: In the meantime I wish you health and spirits.

SIR OLIVER: Your ever grateful and perpetual humble servant.

JOSEPH SURFACE: Sir, yours as sincerely.

SIR OLIVER: [*Aside*] Charles!—you are my heir. [*Exit*]

JOSEPH SURFACE: This is one bad effect of a good character; it invites application from the unfortunate, and there needs no small degree of address to gain the reputation of benevolence without incurring the expense. The silver ore of pure charity is an expensive article in the catalogue of a man's good qualities; whereas the sentimental French plate I use instead of it makes just as good a show, and pays no tax.

[*Re-enter* Rowley]

ROWLEY: Mr. Surface, your servant: I was apprehensive of interrupting you, though my business demands immediate attention, as this note will inform you.

JOSEPH SURFACE: Always happy to see Mr. Rowley. [*Aside. Reads the letter*] Sir Oliver Surface!—My uncle arrived!

ROWLEY: He is, indeed: we have just parted—quite well, after a speedy voyage, and impatient to embrace his worthy nephew.

JOSEPH SURFACE: I am astonished!—William! stop Mr. Stanley, if he's not gone. [*Calls to* Servant]

ROWLEY: Oh! he's out of reach, I believe.

JOSEPH SURFACE: Why did you not let me know this when you came in together?

ROWLEY: I thought you had particular business. But I must be gone to inform your brother, and appoint him here to meet your uncle. He will be with you in a quarter of an hour.

JOSEPH SURFACE: So he says. Well, I am strangely overjoyed at his coming. [*Aside*] Never, to be sure, was anything so damned unlucky!

ROWLEY: You will be delighted to see how well he looks.

JOSEPH SURFACE: Oh! I'm overjoyed to hear it. [*Aside*]—Just at this time!

ROWLEY: I'll tell him how impatiently you expect him.

JOSEPH SURFACE: Do, do; pray give my best duty and affection. Indeed, I cannot express the sensations I feel at the thought of seeing him. [*Exit* Rowley] Certainly his coming just at this time is the cruellest piece of ill fortune. [*Exit*]

SCENE II.

A room in Sir Peter Teazle's *house.*

[*Enter* Mrs. Candour *and* Maid]

MAID: Indeed, ma'am, my lady will see nobody at present.

MRS. CANDOUR: Did you tell her it was her friend Mrs. Candour?

MAID: Yes, ma'am; but she begs you will excuse her.

MRS. CANDOUR: Do go again; I shall be glad to see her, if it be only for a moment, for I am sure she must be in great distress. [*Exit* Maid] Dear heart, how provoking! I'm not mistress of half the circumstances! We shall have the whole affair in the newspapers, with the names of the parties at length, before I have dropped the story at a dozen houses.

[*Enter* Sir Benjamin Backbite]

Oh, dear Sir Benjamin! you have heard, I suppose——

SIR BENJAMIN: Of Lady Teazle and Mr. Surface——

MRS. CANDOUR: And Sir Peter's discovery——

SIR BENJAMIN: Oh, the strangest piece of business, to be sure!

MRS. CANDOUR: Well, I never was so surprised in my life. I am so sorry for all parties, indeed.

SIR BENJAMIN: Now, I don't pity Sir Peter at all: he was so extravagantly partial to Mr. Surface.

MRS. CANDOUR: Mr. Surface! Why, 'twas with Charles Lady Teazle was detected.

SIR BENJAMIN: No, no, I tell you: Mr. Surface is the gallant.

MRS. CANDOUR: No such thing! Charles is the man. 'Twas Mr. Surface brought Sir Peter on purpose to discover them.

SIR BENJAMIN: I tell you I had it from one——

MRS. CANDOUR: And I have it from one——

SIR BENJAMIN: Who had it from one, who had it——

MRS. CANDOUR: From one immediately——But here comes Lady Sneerwell; perhaps she knows the whole affair.

[*Enter* Lady Sneerwell]

LADY SNEERWELL: So, my dear Mrs. Candour, here's a sad affair of our friend Lady Teazle!

MRS CANDOUR: Ay, my dear friend, who would have thought——

LADY SNEERWELL: Well, there is no trusting to appearances; though indeed, she was always too lively for me.

MRS. CANDOUR: To be sure, her manners were a a little too free; but then she was so young!

LADY SNEERWELL: And had, indeed, some good qualities.

MRS. CANDOUR: So she had, indeed. But have you heard the particulars?

LADY SNEERWELL: No; but everybody says that Mr. Surface——

SIR BENJAMIN: Ay, there; I told you Mr. Surface was the man.

MRS. CANDOUR: No, no: indeed the assignation was with Charles.

LADY SNEERWELL: With Charles! You alarm me, Mrs. Candour.

MRS. CANDOUR: Yes, yes: he was the lover. Mr. Surface, to do him justice, was only the informer.

SIR BENJAMIN: Well, I'll not dispute with you, Mrs. Candour; but, be it which it may, I hope that Sir Peter's wound will not——

MRS. CANDOUR: Sir Peter's wound! Oh, mercy! I didn't hear a word of their fighting.

LADY SNEERWELL: Nor I, a syllable.

SIR BENJAMIN: No! what, no mention of the duel?

MRS. CANDOUR: Not a word.

SIR BENJAMIN: Oh, yes: they fought before they left the room.

LADY SNEERWELL: Pray let us hear.

MRS. CANDOUR: Ay, do oblige us with the duel.

SIR BENJAMIN: "*Sir*," says Sir Peter, immediately after the discovery, "*you are a most ungrateful fellow.*"

MRS. CANDOUR: Ay, to Charles——

SIR BENJAMIN: No, no—to Mr. Surface—"*a most ungrateful fellow; and old as I am, sir,*" says he, "*I insist on immediate satisfaction.*"

MRS. CANDOUR: Ay, that must have been to Charles; for 'tis very unlikely Mr. Surface should fight in his own house.

SIR BENJAMIN: 'Gad's life, ma'am, not at all—"*giving me immediate satisfaction.*"—On this, ma'am, Lady Teazle, seeing Sir Peter in such danger, ran out of the room in strong hysterics, and Charles after her, calling out for hartshorn and water; then, madam, they began to fight with swords——

[*Enter* Crabtree]

CRABTREE: With pistols, nephew—pistols! I have it from undoubted authority.

MRS. CANDOUR: Oh, Mr. Crabtree, then it is all true!

CRABTREE: Too true, indeed, madam, and Sir Peter is dangerously wounded——

SIR BENJAMIN: By a thrust in second quite through his left side——

CRABTREE: By a bullet lodged in the thorax.

MRS. CANDOUR: Mercy on me! Poor Sir Peter!

CRABTREE: Yes, madam; though Charles would have avoided the matter, if he could.

MRS. CANDOUR: I knew Charles was the person.

SIR BENJAMIN: My uncle, I see, knows nothing of the matter.

CRABTREE: But Sir Peter taxed him with the basest ingratitude——

SIR BENJAMIN: That I told you, you know——

CRABTREE: Do, nephew, let me speak!—and insisted on immediate——

SIR BENJAMIN: Just as I said——

CRABTREE: Odds life, nephew, allow others to know something too! A pair of pistols lay on the bureau (for Mr. Surface, it seems, had come home the night before late from Salthill, where he had been to see the Montem with a friend, who has a son at Eton), so, unluckily, the pistols were left charged.

SIR BENJAMIN: I heard nothing of this.

CRABTREE: Sir Peter forced Charles to take one, and they fired, it seems, pretty nearly together. Charles's shot took effect, as I tell you, and Sir Peter's missed; but, what is very extraordinary, the ball struck against a little bronze Shakspeare that stood over the fireplace, grazed out of the window at a right angle, and wounded the postman, who was just coming to the door with a double letter from Northamptonshire.

SIR BENJAMIN: My uncle's account is more circumstantial, I confess; but I believe mine is the true one for all that.

LADY SNEERWELL: [Aside] I am more interested in this affair than they imagine, and must have better information. [Exit]

SIR BENJAMIN: Ah! Lady Sneerwell's alarm is very easily accounted for.

CRABTREE: Yes, yes, they certainly do say—but that's neither here nor there.

MRS. CANDOUR: But, pray, where is Sir Peter at present?

CRABTREE: Oh! they brought him home, and he is now in the house, though the servants are ordered to deny him.

MRS. CANDOUR: I believe so, and Lady Teazle, I suppose, attending him.

CRABTREE: Yes, yes; and I saw one of the faculty enter just before me.

SIR BENJAMIN: Hey! who comes here?

CRABTREE: Oh, this is he: the physician, depend on't.

MRS. CANDOUR: Oh, certainly! it must be the physician; and now we shall know.

[Enter Sir Oliver Surface]

CRABTREE: Well, doctor, what hopes?

MRS. CANDOUR: Ay, doctor, how's your patient?

SIR BENJAMIN: Now, doctor, isn't it a wound with a small-sword?

CRABTREE: A bullet lodged in the thorax, for a hundred!

SIR OLIVER: Doctor! a wound with a small-sword! and a bullet in the thorax?—Oons! are you mad, good people?

SIR BENJAMIN: Perhaps, sir, you are not a doctor?

SIR OLIVER: Truly, I am to thank you for my degree, if I am.

CRABTREE: Only a friend of Sir Peter's, then, I presume. But, sir, you must have heard of his accident?

SIR OLIVER: Not a word!

CRABTREE: Not of his being dangerously wounded?

SIR OLIVER: The devil he is!

SIR BENJAMIN: Run through the body——

CRABTREE: Shot in the breast——

SIR BENJAMIN: By one Mr. Surface——

CRABTREE: Ay, the younger.

SIR OLIVER: Hey! what the plague! you seem to differ strangely in your accounts: however, you agree that Sir Peter is dangerously wounded.

SIR BENJAMIN: Oh, yes, we agree in that.

CRABTREE: Yes, yes, I believe there can be no doubt in that.

SIR OLIVER: Then, upon my word, for a person in that situation, he is the most imprudent man alive; for here he comes, walking as if nothing at all was the matter.

[Enter Sir Peter Teazle]

Odds heart, Sir Peter! you are come in good time, I promise you; for we had just given you over!

SIR BENJAMIN: [Aside to Crabtree] Egad, uncle, this is the most sudden recovery!

SIR OLIVER: Why, man! what do you do out of bed with a small-sword through your body, and a bullet lodged in your thorax?

SIR PETER: A small-sword and a bullet?

SIR OLIVER: Ay; these gentlemen would have killed you without law or physic, and wanted to dub me a doctor, to make me an accomplice.

SIR PETER: Why, what is all this?

SIR BENJAMIN: We rejoice, Sir Peter, that the story of the duel is not true, and are sincerely sorry for your other misfortune.

SIR PETER: So, so; all over the town already. [Aside]

CRABTREE: Though, Sir Peter, you were certainly vastly to blame to marry at your years.

SIR PETER: Sir, what business is that of yours?

MRS. CANDOUR: Though, indeed, as Sir Peter made so good a husband, he's very much to be pitied.

SIR PETER: Plague on your pity, ma'am! I desire none of it.

SIR BENJAMIN: However, Sir Peter, you must not mind the laughing and jests you will meet with on the occasion.

SIR PETER: Sir, sir! I desire to be master in my own house.

CRABTREE: 'Tis no uncommon case, that's one comfort.

SIR PETER: I insist on being left to myself: without ceremony, I insist on your leaving my house directly!

MRS. CANDOUR: Well, well, we are going; and depend on't, we'll make the best report of it we can. [Exit]

SIR PETER: Leave my house!

CRABTREE: And tell how hardly you've been treated. [*Exit*]

SIR PETER: Leave my house!

SIR BENJAMIN: And how patiently you bear it. [*Exit*]

SIR PETER: Fiends! vipers! furies! Oh! that their own venom would choke them!

SIR OLIVER: They are very provoking indeed, Sir Peter.

[*Enter* Rowley]

ROWLEY: I heard high words: what has ruffled you, sir?

SIR PETER: Psha! what signifies asking? Do I ever pass a day without my vexations?

ROWLEY: Well, I'm not inquisitive.

SIR OLIVER: Well, Sir Peter, I have seen both my nephews in the manner we proposed.

SIR PETER: A precious couple they are!

ROWLEY: Yes, and Sir Oliver is convinced that your judgment was right, Sir Peter.

SIR OLIVER: Yes, I find Joseph is indeed the man, after all.

ROWLEY: Ay, as Sir Peter says, he is a man of sentiment.

SIR OLIVER: And acts up to the sentiments he professes.

ROWLEY: It certainly is edification to hear him talk.

SIR OLIVER: Oh, he's a model for the young men of the age! But how's this, Sir Peter? you don't join us in your friend Joseph's praise, as I expected.

SIR PETER: Sir Oliver, we live in a damned wicked world, and the fewer we praise the better.

ROWLEY: What! do you say so, Sir Peter, who were never mistaken in your life?

SIR PETER: Psha! plague on you both! I see by your sneering you have heard the whole affair. I shall go mad among you!

ROWLEY: Then, to fret you no longer, Sir Peter, we are indeed acquainted with it all. I met Lady Teazle coming from Mr. Surface's so humbled, that she deigned to request me to be her advocate with you.

SIR PETER: And does Sir Oliver know all this?

SIR OLIVER: Every circumstance.

SIR PETER: What, of the closet and the screen, hey?

SIR OLIVER: Yes, yes, and the little French milliner. Oh, I have been vastly diverted with the story! ha! ha! ha!

SIR PETER: 'Twas very pleasant.

SIR OLIVER: I never laughed more in my life, I assure you: ha! ha! ha!

SIR PETER: Oh, vastly diverting! ha! ha! ha!

ROWLEY: To be sure, Joseph with his sentiments! ha! ha! ha!

SIR PETER: Yes, his sentiments! ha! ha! ha! Hypocritical villain!

SIR OLIVER: Ay, and that rogue Charles to pull Sir Peter out of the closet: ha! ha! ha!

SIR PETER: Ha! ha! 'twas devilish entertaining, to be sure!

SIR OLIVER: Ha! ha! ha! Egad, Sir Peter, I should like to have seen your face when the screen was thrown down: ha! ha!

SIR PETER: Yes, my face when the screen was thrown down: ha! ha! ha! Oh, I must never show my head again!

SIR OLIVER: But come, come, it isn't fair to laugh at you neither, my old friend; though, upon my soul, I can't help it.

SIR PETER: Oh, pray don't restrain your mirth on my account: it does not hurt me at all! I laugh at the whole affair myself. Yes, yes, I think being a standing jest for all one's acquaintance a very happy situation. Oh, yes, and then of a morning to read the paragraphs about Mr. S——, Lady ——, and Sir P——, will be so entertaining!

ROWLEY: Without affectation, Sir Peter, you may despise the ridicule of fools. But I see Lady Teazle going towards the next room; I am sure you must desire a reconciliation as earnestly as she does.

SIR OLIVER: Perhaps my being here prevents her coming to you. Well, I'll leave honest Rowley to mediate between you; but he must bring you all presently to Mr. Surface's where I am now returning, if not to reclaim a libertine, at least to expose hypocrisy.

SIR PETER: Ah, I'll be present at your discovering yourself there with all my heart; though 'tis a vile unlucky place for discoveries.

ROWLEY: We'll follow.

[*Exit* Sir Oliver Surface]

SIR PETER: She is not coming here, you see, Rowley.

ROWLEY: No, but she has left the door of that room open, you perceive. See, she is in tears.

SIR PETER: Certainly a little mortification appears very becoming in a wife. Don't you think it will do her good to let her pine a little?

ROWLEY: Oh, this is ungenerous in you!

SIR PETER: Well, I know not what to think. You remember the letter I found of hers evidently intended for Charles!

ROWLEY: A mere forgery, Sir Peter! laid in your way on purpose. This is one of the points which I intend Snake shall give you conviction of.

SIR PETER: I wish I were once satisfied of that. She looks this way. What a remarkably elegant turn of the head she has. Rowley, I'll go to her.

ROWLEY: Certainly.

SIR PETER: Though, when it is known that we are reconciled, people will laugh at me ten times more.

ROWLEY: Let them laugh, and retort their malice only by showing them you are happy in spite of it.

SIR PETER: I'faith, so I will! and, if I'm not mistaken, we may yet be the happiest couple in the country.

ROWLEY: Nay, Sir Peter, he who once lays aside suspicion——

SIR PETER: Hold, Master Rowley! if you have any regard for me, never let me hear you utter anything like a sentiment: I have had enough of them to serve me the rest of my life.

[*Exeunt*]

SCENE III.

The library in Joseph Surface's *house.*

[*Enter* Joseph Surface *and* Lady Sneerwell]

LADY SNEERWELL: Impossible! Will not Sir Peter immediately be reconciled to Charles, and of course no longer oppose his union with Maria? The thought is distraction to me.

JOSEPH SURFACE: Can passion furnish a remedy?

LADY SNEERWELL: No, nor cunning either. Oh, I was a fool, an idiot, to league with such a blunderer!

JOSEPH SURFACE: Surely, Lady Sneerwell, I am the greatest sufferer; yet you see I bear the accident with calmness.

LADY SNEERWELL: Because the disappointment doesn't reach your heart; your interest only attached you to Maria. Had you felt for her what I have for that ungrateful libertine, neither your temper nor hypocrisy could prevent your showing the sharpness of your vexation.

JOSEPH SURFACE: But why should your reproaches fall on me for this disappointment?

LADY SNEERWELL: Are you not the cause of it? Had you not a sufficient field for your roguery in imposing Sir Peter, and supplanting your brother, but you must endeavour to seduce his wife? I hate such an avarice of crimes; 'tis an unfair monopoly, and never prospers.

JOSEPH SURFACE: Well, I admit I have been to blame. I confess I deviated from the direct road of wrong, but I don't think we're so totally defeated either.

LADY SNEERWELL: No!

JOSEPH SURFACE: You tell me you have made a trial of Snake since we met, and that you still believe him faithful to us?

LADY SNEERWELL: I do believe so.

JOSEPH SURFACE: And that he has undertaken, should it be so necessary, to swear and prove, that Charles is at this time contracted by vows and honour to your ladyship, which some of his former letters to you will serve to support?

LADY SNEERWELL: This, indeed, might have assisted.

JOSEPH SURFACE: Come, come; it is not too late yet.

[*Knocking at the door*]

But hark! this is probably my uncle, Sir Oliver: retire to that room; we'll consult further when he's gone.

LADY SNEERWELL: Well, but if he should find you out too.

JOSEPH SURFACE: Oh, I have no fear of that. Sir Peter will hold his tongue for his own credit's sake—and you may depend on it I shall soon discover Sir Oliver's weak side!

LADY SNEERWELL: I have no diffidence of your abilities! only be constant to one roguery at a time.

JOSEPH SURFACE: I will, I will!

[*Exit* Lady Sneerwell]

So! 'tis confounded hard, after such bad fortune, to be baited by one's confederate in evil. Well, at all events, my character is so much better than Charles's, that I certainly—hey!—what—this is not Sir Oliver, but old Stanley again. Plague on't that he should return to tease me just now! I shall have Sir Oliver come and find him here—and—

[*Enter* Sir Oliver Surface]

Gad's life, Mr. Stanley, why have you come back to plague me at this time? You must not stay now, upon my word.

SIR OLIVER: Sir, I hear your uncle Oliver is expected here, and though he has been so penurious to you, I'll try what he'll do for me.

JOSEPH SURFACE: Sir, 'tis impossible for you to stay now, so I must beg——Come any other time, and I promise you, you shall be assisted.

SIR OLIVER: No: Sir Oliver and I must be acquainted.

JOSEPH SURFACE: Zounds, sir! then I insist on your quitting the room directly.

SIR OLIVER: Nay, sir——

JOSEPH SURFACE: Sir, I insist on't!—Here, William! show this gentleman out. Since you compel me, sir, not one moment—this is such insolence. [*Going to push him out*]

[*Enter* Charles Surface]

CHARLES SURFACE: Heyday! what's the matter now? What the devil have you got hold of my little broker here? Zounds, brother, don't hurt little Premium. What's the matter, my little fellow?

JOSEPH SURFACE: So! he has been with you, too, has he?

CHARLES SURFACE: To be sure he has. Why, he's as honest a little——But sure, Joseph, you have not been borrowing money too, have you?

JOSEPH SURFACE: Borrowing! no! But, brother, you know we expect Sir Oliver here every——

CHARLES SURFACE: O Gad, that's true! Noll mustn't find the little broker here, to be sure.

JOSEPH SURFACE: Yet, Mr. Stanley insists——

CHARLES SURFACE: Stanley! why his name's Premium.

JOSEPH SURFACE: No, sir, Stanley.

CHARLES SURFACE: No, no, Premium.

JOSEPH SURFACE: Well, no matter which—but——

CHARLES SURFACE: Ay, ay, Stanley or Premium, 'tis the same thing, as you say; for I suppose he goes by half a hundred names, besides A. B. at the coffee-house.[13]

[13] Eighteenth-century coffeehouses were fashionable meeting places.

[*Knocking*]

JOSEPH SURFACE: 'Sdeath! here's Sir Oliver at the door. Now I beg, Mr. Stanley——

CHARLES SURFACE: Ay, ay, and I beg, Mr. Premium——

SIR OLIVER: Gentlemen——

JOSEPH SURFACE: Sir, by heaven you shall go!

CHARLES SURFACE: Ay, out with him, certainly.

SIR OLIVER: This violence——

JOSEPH SURFACE: Sir, 'tis your own fault.

CHARLES SURFACE: Out with him, to be sure.

[*Both forcing* Sir Oliver *out*]

[*Enter* Sir Peter *and* Lady Teazle, Maria, *and* Rowley]

SIR PETER: My old friend, Sir Oliver—hey! What in the name of wonder!—here are dutiful nephews—assault their uncle at his first visit!

LADY TEAZLE: Indeed, Sir Oliver, 'twas well we came in to rescue you.

ROWLEY: Truly it was; for I perceive, Sir Oliver, the character of old Stanley was no protection to you.

SIR OLIVER: Nor of Premium either: the necessities of the former could not extort a shilling from that benevolent gentleman; and with the other I stood a chance of faring worse than my ancestors, and being knocked down without being bid for.

JOSEPH SURFACE: Charles!

CHARLES SURFACE: Joseph!

JOSEPH SURFACE: 'Tis now complete!

CHARLES SURFACE: Very.

SIR OLIVER: Sir Peter, my friend, and Rowley too —look on that elder nephew of mine. You know what he has already received from my bounty; and you also know how gladly I would have regarded half my fortune as held in trust for him? judge, then, my disappointment in discovering him him to be destitute of truth, charity, and gratitude!

SIR PETER: Sir Oliver, I should be more surprised at this declaration, if I had not myself found him to be mean, treacherous, and hypocritical.

LADY TEAZLE: And if the gentleman pleads not guilty to these, pray let him call me to his character.

SIR PETER: Then, I believe, we need add no more: if he knows himself, he will consider it as the most perfect punishment that he is known to the world.

CHARLES SURFACE: If they talk this way to Honesty, what will they say to me, by-and-by? [*Aside*]

[Sir Peter, Lady Teazle, *and* Maria *retire*]

SIR OLIVER: As for that prodigal, his brother, there——

CHARLES SURFACE: Ay, now comes my turn: the damned family pictures will ruin me! [*Aside*]

JOSEPH SURFACE: Sir Oliver—uncle, will you honour me with a hearing?

CHARLES SURFACE: Now, if Joseph would make one of his long speeches, I might recollect myself a little. [*Aside*]

SIR OLIVER: [*To* Joseph Surface] I suppose you would undertake to justify yourself?

JOSEPH SURFACE: I trust I could.

SIR OLIVER: [*To* Charles Surface] Well, sir!—and you could justify yourself too, I suppose?

CHARLES SURFACE: Not that I know of, Sir Oliver.

SIR OLIVER: What!—Little Premium has been let too much into the secret, I suppose?

CHARLES SURFACE: True, sir; but they were family secrets, and should not be mentioned again, you know.

ROWLEY: Come, Sir Oliver, I know you cannot speak of Charles's follies with anger.

SIR OLIVER: Odd's heart, no more I can; nor with gravity either. Sir Peter, do you know the rogue bargained with me for all his ancestors; sold me judges and generals by the foot, and maiden aunts as cheap as broken china.

CHARLES SURFACE: To be sure, Sir Oliver, I did make a little free with the family canvas, that's the truth on't. My ancestors may rise in judgment against me, there's no denying it; but believe me sincere when I tell you—and upon my soul I would not say so if I was not—that if I do not appear mortified at the exposure of my follies, it is because I feel at this moment the warmest satisfaction at seeing you, my liberal benefactor.

SIR OLIVER: Charles, I believe you. Give me your hand again: the ill-looking little fellow over the settee has made your peace.

CHARLES SURFACE: Then, sir, my gratitude to the original is still increased.

LADY TEAZLE: [*Advancing*] Yet, I believe, Sir Oliver, here is one whom Charles is still more anxious to be reconciled to. [*Pointing to* Maria]

SIR OLIVER: Oh, I have heard of his attachment there; and, with the young lady's pardon, if I construe right—that blush——

SIR PETER: Well, child, speak your sentiments.

MARIA: Sir, I have little to say, but that I shall rejoice to hear that he is happy; for me, whatever claim I had to his attention, I willingly resign to one who has a better title.

CHARLES SURFACE: How, Maria!

SIR PETER: Heyday! what's the mystery now? While he appeared an incorrigible rake, you would give your hand to no one else; and now that he is likely to reform I'll warrant you won't have him.

MARIA: His own heart and Lady Sneerwell know the cause.

CHARLES SURFACE: Lady Sneerwell!

JOSEPH SURFACE: Brother, it is with great concern I am obliged to speak on this point, but my regard to justice compels me, and Lady Sneerwell's injuries can no longer be concealed. [*Opens the door*]

[*Enter* Lady Sneerwell]

SIR PETER: So! another French milliner! Egad, he has one in every room in the house, I suppose!

LADY SNEERWELL: Ungrateful Charles! Well may you be surprised, and feel for the indelicate situation your perfidy has forced me into.

CHARLES SURFACE: Pray, uncle, is this another plot of yours? For, as I have life, I don't understand it.

JOSEPH SURFACE: I believe, sir, there is but the evidence of one person more necessary to make it extremely clear.

SIR PETER: And that person, I imagine, is Mr. Snake.—Rowley, you were perfectly right to bring him with us, and pray let him appear.

ROWLEY: Walk in, Mr. Snake.

[Enter Snake]

I thought his testimony might be wanted; however, it happens unluckily, that he comes to confront Lady Sneerwell, not to support her.

LADY SNEERWELL: A villain! Treacherous to me at last! Speak, fellow, have you too conspired against me?

SNAKE: I beg your ladyship ten thousand pardons: you paid me extremely liberally for the lie in question; but I unfortunately have been offered double to speak the truth.

LADY SNEERWELL: The torments of shame and disappointment on you all! [Going]

LADY TEAZLE: Hold, Lady Sneerwell—before you go, let me thank you for the trouble you and that gentleman have taken, in writing letters from me to Charles, and answering them yourself; and let me also request you to make my respects to the scandalous college, of which you are president, and inform them, that Lady Teazle, licentiate, begs leave to return the diploma they granted her, as she leaves off practice, and kills characters no longer.

LADY SNEERWELL: You too, madam!—provoking —insolent! May your husband live these fifty years! [Exit]

SIR PETER: Oons! what a fury!

LADY TEAZLE: A malicious creature, indeed!

SIR PETER: What! not for her last wish?

LADY TEAZLE: Oh, no!

SIR OLIVER: Well, sir, and what have you to say now?

JOSEPH SURFACE: Sir, I am so confounded, to find that Lady Sneerwell could be guilty of suborning Mr. Snake in this manner, to impose on us all, that I know not what to say: however, lest her revengeful spirit should prompt her to injure my brother, I had certainly better follow her directly. [Exit]

SIR PETER: Moral to the last drop!

SIR OLIVER: Ay, and marry her, Joseph, if you can. Oil and vinegar!—egad, you'll do very well together.

ROWLEY: I believe we have no more occasion for Mr. Snake at present?

SNAKE: Before I go, I beg pardon once for all, for whatever uneasiness I have been the humble instrument of causing to the parties present.

SIR PETER: Well, well, you have made atonement by a good deed at last.

SNAKE: But I must request of the company, that it shall never be known.

SIR PETER: Hey! what the plague! are you ashamed of having done a right thing once in your life?

SNAKE: Ah, sir, consider—I live by the badness of my character; and, if it were once known that I had been betrayed into an honest action, I should lose every friend I have in the world.

SIR OLIVER: Well, well—we'll not traduce you by saying anything in your praise, never fear.

[Exit Snake]

SIR PETER: There's a precious rogue!

LADY TEAZLE: See, Sir Oliver, there needs no persuasion now to reconcile your nephew and Maria.

SIR OLIVER: Ay, ay, that's as it should be, and, egad, we'll have the wedding to-morrow morning.

CHARLES SURFACE: Thank you, dear uncle.

SIR PETER: What, you rogue! don't you ask the girl's consent first?

CHARLES SURFACE: Oh, I have done that a long time—a minute ago—and she has looked yes.

MARIA: For shame, Charles!—I protest, Sir Peter, there has not been a word——

SIR OLIVER: Well, then, the fewer the better: may your love for each other never know abatement.

SIR PETER: And may you live as happily together as Lady Teazle and I intend to do!

CHARLES SURFACE: Rowley, my old friend, I am sure you congratulate me; and I suspect that I owe you much.

SIR OLIVER: You do, indeed, Charles.

ROWLEY: If my efforts to serve you had not succeeded you would have been in my debt for the attempt—but deserve to be happy—and you overrepay me.

SIR PETER: Ay, honest Rowley always said you would reform.

CHARLES SURFACE: Why as to reforming, Sir Peter, I'll make no promises, and that I take to be a proof that I intend to set about it. But here shall be my monitor—my gentle guide.—Ah! can I leave the virtuous path those eyes illumine?

Though thou, dear maid, shouldst wave thy beauty's sway,
Thou still must rule, because I will obey:
An humble fugitive from Folly view,
No sanctuary near but Love and you:
[To the audience] You can, indeed, each anxious fear remove,
For even Scandal dies, if you approve.

[Exeunt omnes]

EPILOGUE

By Mr. Colman

LADY TEAZLE: I, who was late so volatile and gay,
Like a trade-wind must now blow all one way,
Bend all my cares, my studies, and my vows,
To one dull rusty weathercock—my spouse!
So wills our virtuous bard—the motley Bayes
Of crying epilogues and laughing plays!

Old bachelors, who marry smart young wives,
Learn from our play to regulate your lives:
Each bring his dear to town, all faults upon her—
London will prove the very source of honour.
Plunged fairly in, like a cold bath it serves,
When principles relax, to brace the nerves:
Such is my case; and yet I must deplore
That the gay dream of dissipation's o'er.
And say, ye fair! was ever lively wife,
Born with a genius for the highest life,
Like me untimely blasted in her bloom,
Like me condemn'd to such a dismal doom?
Save money—when I just knew how to waste it!
Leave London—just as I began to taste it!
   Must I then watch the early crowing cock,
The melancholy ticking of a clock;
In a lone rustic hall for ever pounded,
With dogs, cats, rats, and squalling brats surrounded?
With humble curate can I now retire,
(While good Sir Peter boozes with the squire),
And at backgammon mortify my soul,
That pants for loo, or flutters at a vole.[14]
Seven's the main! Dear sound that must expire,
Lost at hot cockles round a Christmas fire;
The transient hour of fashion too soon spent,
Farewell the tranquil mind, farewell content![15]
Farewell the plumèd head, cushion'd tête,[16]
That takes the cushion from its proper seat!
That spirit-stirring drum!—card drums I mean,
Spadille—odd trick—pam—basto—king and queen!
And you, ye knockers, that, with brazen throat,
The welcome visitors' approach denote;

Farewell all quality of high renown,
Pride, pomp, and circumstance of glorious town!
Farewell! your revels I partake no more,
And Lady Teazle's occupation's o'er!
All this I told our bard; he smiled, and said 'twas clear,
I ought to play deep tragedy next year.
Meanwhile he drew wise morals from his play,
And in these solemn periods stalk'd away:—
"Bless'd were the fair like you; her faults who stopp'd,
And closed her follies when the curtain dropp'd!
No more in vice or error to engage,
Or play the fool at large on life's great stage."

14 "Loo" and "vole" were card games.
15 This and the next ten lines constitute a parody on *Othello*, Act III, Scene III, lines 348–357. Othello speaks the lines upon being told by Iago that Desdemona is unfaithful:

Farewell the tranquil mind! farewell content!
Farewell the plumed troop, and the big wars
That make ambition virtue! O, farewell!
Farewell the neighing steed and the shrill trump,
The spirit-stirring drum, th' ear-piercing fife,
The royal banner, and all quality,
Pride, pomp, and circumstance of glorious war!
And O ye mortal engines whose rude throats
Th' immortal Jove's dread clamours counterfeit,
Farewell! Othello's occupation's gone.

Sheridan's audience would have recognized this as a parody and would have enjoyed his skill as a parodist.
16 Head, in French.

The Romantic and Early Realistic Drama

A Month in the Country. Act I from the Moscow Art Theatre's 1909 production. Stanislavsky in the role of Rakitin may be seen at the left. From *Moscow Art Theatre, 1898–1917*. Moscow, 1955.

The Romantic and Early Realistic Drama

THE ROMANTIC SPIRIT

The release from the cool discipline of eighteenth-century reason and the rigor of neoclassic rules amounted to a major revolution in European drama. The discipline actually deteriorated early, when sentimental comedy came into vogue during the eighteenth century. Only the shell of high comedy remained in the second half of the century, except for the work of a Sheridan or a Beaumarchais. Sentimental comedy was very nearly a contradiction in terms in exalting feeling and sentiment as the first considerations in comic art. But vaster changes were in the making during the last quarter of the century, and the most important of these took the form of an aggressive assertion of individuality.

The struggles of a unique individual, heroically at odds with conventions and his environment, absorbed the attention of playwrights. As for dramatic form, the rule of the unities was challenged, and plays became as unlimited in time, place, and action as their characters were free from the demands of "decorum." Nature, wild and untamed, came to be represented in stage settings, although these did not differ radically from those in vogue since the Renaissance. (The stage set still consisted of painted flats arranged in perspective and closed at the back of the stage by a painted backdrop.) Nature in man, equally wild and untamed, was represented in the dramatic conflicts of the plays. Since observation of men in orderly contemporary society, moreover, was apt to be tame and, above all, since it was not likely to fill the spectator with a sense of wonder, the dramatists turned to situations of social disorder and to the romantic past.

The favorite period was, indeed, the Middle Ages, by then wrapped in mist and remembered as an age full of heroic personalities, adventure, and magic. Two of the most important plays of Goethe, *Goetz von Berlichingen* and *Faust,* deal respectively with a feudal baron and a "magician." On the stage, the desire to represent earlier periods resulted in an antiquarianism of backgrounds and costumes even as the new interest in nature resulted in the painting of natural scenery. "Drawing room" drama and "drawing room" stage settings seemed equally obsolete to the romanticists. Dramatists broke with the dramatic art of Corneille, Racine, and Molière. The only dramatic art with which the romanticists first identified themselves was the Elizabethan. (Later, writers such as Schiller and Goethe also turned to classic drama, but only to romanticize it in the end.) They discarded the French classicists and made a cult of Shakespeare.

In France, romanticism was held in check by the great reputation and undisputed talent of the dramatists of Louis XIV's time. Moreover, the vast social turmoil of the Revolution of 1789 was identified with Roman and Greek republicanism, and consequently there was less inclination to sunder ties with classicism in art. And the Napoleonic empire which followed the French Republic also favored classicism to a degree; the "little corporal" turned emperor was Julius Caesar and Augustus Caesar in modern dress. Although the romantic afflatus became strong in nondramatic literature, it did not exert its spell in the French theatre until 1830, when Victor Hugo thrust his grandiose drama of Spanish honor and passion, *Hernani,* upon the stage. Before that year, the romantic tendencies in France were "sentimentalism," in the form of *comédie larmoyante,* or tearful comedy, and "liberalism," in the form of a demand for *drame bourgeoise,* or serious plays about middle-class figures, expressed chiefly by the eighteenth-century philosopher Denis Diderot.

In England, romanticism found a popular outlet in extravagant melodramas, such as Matthew Gregory Lewis' *The Castle Spectre* and *Rugantino,* and in poetic plays less qualified for stage production, such as Shelley's *The Cenci* and Byron's *Cain.* The poets' plays, including the more successfully theatrical ones by James Sheridan Knowles (*Virginius,* 1820, and *William Tell,* 1825), had little effect. The British stage was overrun with melodramas for the greater part of the century. Its sole claim to distinction came from the inspired performances of romantic actors, chiefly in Shakespearean roles. To the most exciting of these artists, Edmund Kean, who made his debut at Drury Lane in 1814, Coleridge paid the supreme (and typically romantic) tribute of saying that watching him act was "like reading Shakespeare by flashes of lightning."

In time, romanticism swept through Europe, and surely not the least important romantic plays were those produced by the man who was to become the father of modern realism, the Scandinavian Henrik Ibsen. But it was in Germany that distinguished romantic drama flourished first and most successfully. The soil was seeded by the critical writings of the great critic Gotthold Ephraim Lessing, who fought French classicism and championed Shakespeare in *Hamburg Dramaturgy,* a collection of essays written between April 1767 and November 1768. He called for freedom in dramatic art with such statements as: "The only unpardonable fault of a tragic poet is this, that he leaves us cold; if he interests us, he may do as he likes with the little mechanical rules." Besides, although his own playwriting was permeated with eighteenth-century rationalism, his idealism, especially in his drama of "natural religion" and religious tolerance *Nathan the Wise,* prefigured the romantic idealism of the later German writers—most notably that of Schiller and the young Goethe.

Nathan the Wise was first published in 1779 By

then the first phase of romantic revolt was in full swing in Germany. In 1776, a young poet, Friedrich Maximilian von Klinger, had written an extravagantly impassioned play, *Sturm und Drang,* or *Storm and Stress.* It gave its name to the entire movement which, much to the dismay of the temperate Lessing, unleashed all the pent-up romanticism of the new generation. The new movement found two young men of genius, Johann Wolfgang von Goethe and Friedrich von Schiller. The former aroused excitement with a historical play about a baron's attempt to uphold the dying ideals of chivalry, *Goetz von Berlichingen* (1773); the latter contributed an electrifying Robin Hood drama of youthful rebellion, *The Robbers* (1782). Goethe became Germany's most celebrated writer, Schiller its ablest playwright. Both men later acquired disciplines unknown to most of their contemporaries and successors, although the work of neither was free from serious defects. Their plays, supplemented by the uneven but often fascinating efforts of Heinrich von Kleist, the Austrian Franz Grillparzer, Georg Büchner, and Friedrich Hebbel, comprise the most impressive collection of romantic drama in Europe.

It is difficult, nevertheless, to form a clear picture of the romantic movement in drama from about 1770 to 1835, because it consisted of many facets not always easy to reconcile. We must resort to bald summary, indeed, in trying to make some sense of the confusing tendencies of an age that experienced several political revolutions, many social changes, and numerous artistic ventures: (1) The desire to experience excitement at all costs led to the creation of melodrama on both literary and nonliterary levels. The most popular "melodramatist" was the German playwright August Friedrich Ferdinand von Kotzebue, author of numerous undistinguished plays that held the stage in many countries. In England alone twenty-two of his plays were produced in adaptation. Melodrama, "that bourgeois offspring of the romantic drama," as Zola called it, captured the stage. We also observe the passion for the weird and the grotesque culminating in Victor Hugo's writing—especially in *The King Amuses Himself* (1832), which provided the plot of Verdi's opera *Rigoletto*—as well as in Alfred de Musset's superior *Fantasio.* (2) The interest in romantic situations, often combined with liberal or democratic idealism, resulted in the composition of numerous historical plays. Notable among these were Schiller's *Maria Stuart, The Maid of Orleans* (that is, Joan of Arc), *Don Carlos,* and *Wilhelm Tell;* Goethe's *Goetz von Berlichingen* and *Egmont;* and Karl Gutzkow's *Uriel Acosta,* the tragedy of an intellectual's revolt against Jewish orthodoxy. (3) The glorification of individuality produced the already described Storm and Stress drama, including plays about the outlaw and rebel against society, such as Schiller's *The Robbers* and Hugo's *Hernani.* Genius, misunderstood and misprized or exposed to suffering by inner tension, was also a subject, as in Goethe's *Torquato Tasso* and Alfred de Vigny's *Chatterton.* (4) Interest in the individual's personal aspirations gave rise to philosophical and moral drama such as Goethe's *Faust* and, later on, Ibsen's *Brand* and *Peer Gynt.* (5) Concern with the individual's sensibility resulted in perceptive treatments of love by Musset and in studies of psychological twists, such as Heinrich von Kleist's *Penthesilea* and *The Prince of Homburg.* (6) The common man appeared on the stage as a grotesque figure, as a psychological problem, or as an appealing victim of tyranny.

Hugo's famous 1827 preface to his play *Cromwell,* along with the battle between romantics and classicists that raged in Paris for some hundred nights in 1830 over his drama *Hernani,* gave expression to most of the aspirations of the romantic theatre. "Let us take a hammer to poetic systems," Hugo wrote. "Let us throw down the old plastering that conceals the façade of art. There are neither rules nor models; or, rather, there are no rules other than the general laws of nature." Inevitably, he opposed the classic "unities" as unnecessary restraints to the dramatic imagination and demanded a departure from the narratives, descriptions, and tableaux of French classic drama, calling instead for the active drama of "scenes." Nature, moreover, not only refuses to submit to a rationalist or classical order, but it knows no such thing as the decorum of Louis XIV's court ideals. For Hugo, announcing the gospel of romanticism in drama, life was a fitful array of contrasts of ugliness and beauty, loveliness and hatefulness, appearance and reality. The royal character may combine outward majesty and inner corruption, and the criminal, the former convict Jean Valjean of *Les Misérables,* may be moved by noble impulses. The clown may provoke laughter while his heart breaks. The monstrosity, the deformed Quasimodo of *Notre Dame de Paris,* may entertain a passion belying his ugly exterior.

Art, released from a formalism that limits it to socially stabilized concepts—nobility is a prerogative of royalty and of a good figure or clownage is a mean estate, for example—must be free to stir us with the strangeness and wonder, the grotesque and paradoxical qualities, of "nature." Medieval civilization, Hugo believed, understood and expressed the mixed character of reality in legend, romance, literary phantasmagoria, and the fine arts; the world of contrasts was epitomized in the fairy tale *Beauty and the Beast,* which classic antiquity could not have produced. Hugo conveniently forgot the centaurs and satyrs, the Silenuses and Polyphemuses of Greece. He had in view only the version of classicism nucleated in the French classicism against which he was breaking lances.

Art, in short, must be hospitable to all phases of reality—that is, to the "truth." "It will realize," wrote Hugo, "that everything in creation is not humanely *beautiful,* that the ugly exists beside the beautiful, the unshapely beside the graceful, the grotesque on the reverse of the sublime, evil with good, darkness with light. It will ask itself if the narrow and relative sense of the artist should prevail over the infinite, absolute sense of the Creator. . . . It will set about doing as nature does, mingling in its creations—but without confounding them . . . the body and the soul, the beast and the intellect; for the starting point of religion is always the starting point of poetry. All things are connected."

Although this doctrine could hardly have startled Shakespeare and other Elizabethans or the earlier romantic poets of Germany and England, it was new enough in the pseudo-classic French theatre of 1830 to sound like a revelation. If the stress which Hugo placed on local color was also not new, he nonetheless presented a challenging contrast to the abstract universality of place in a tragedy by Racine or his successors. "People," Hugo wrote, "are beginning to understand in our day that exact localization is one of the first elements of reality. The speaking or acting characters are not the only ones who engrave on the minds of spectators a faithful representation of the facts. The place where this or that catastrophe occurred becomes a terrible and inseparable witness thereof. . . . The local color should not be on the surface of the drama, but in its substance, in the very heart of the work."

Here, then, in the preface to *Cromwell,* was the romanticists' Book of Revelations, announcing a new heaven and a new earth in dramatic literature. Curiously, many of Hugo's phrases could have been lifted bodily to announce also another revelation never intended by the young Hugo, for whom the drama was to be a "complete poetry" more lyrical even than Shakespeare's. Half a century later, realists calling themselves "naturalists" were to substitute for poetic local color a realistic local color of environment; for "grotesqueness," an ugliness of ordinary reality. By 1880 the theatre was playing host to a "truth," a "nature," and a *Beauty and the Beast* in commonplace life that Hugo's followers in 1830 would have found a dismaying antithesis to their quest for ardors and sublimities.

FORMATIVE REALISM

An explosion scatters fragments in all directions, and it is perhaps most accurate to think of the romantic movement as an explosive theatricalization of the drama. The general result was imaginativeness in dramatic writing, a loosening of formal structure, and, concurrently, the opening up of a variety of possibilities in dramatic expression. Almost everything was tried. In this way the stage was also cleared for multifarious modern expository, analytical, and psychological writing.

After 1830, indeed, romanticism developed phases that merged haphazardly into modern drama. For example, one German playwright, Georg Büchner,

in some respects belongs more to the expressionist theatre of the early nineteen-twenties than to the eighteen-thirties, when he wrote his plays. Historical drama became analytical and critical. The supreme early example is Büchner's *Danton's Death* (1835); it was followed by Hebbel's attempt to treat historical subjects as conflicts of ideas. Musset's plays harked back to Marivaux' eighteenth-century sentimental comedies but also foreshadowed a modern analysis of love. Hugo's interest in the grotesque anticipated the late nineteenth century's naturalistic presentations of the sordid aspects of reality. In comedy, a good deal of realism penetrated the work of even those playwrights whose serious plays were intensely romantic.

In much romantic writing, the liberal point of view prefigured social criticism in realistic drama. Indeed, in some early plays a critical attitude began to assume many of the attributes of realism. We see this especially in Nikolai Gogol's social satire *The Inspector* (1834–1836). The anti-Philistine approach to social situations (and most romanticists loathed the middle class and, anticipating Matthew Arnold, considered it Philistine and pharisaical) resulted in Hebbel's realistic middle-class drama *Maria Magdalena* (1844). Even romantic situations were in time clothed with an outward realism of detail, as in some of the work of the French showman Eugène Scribe and of the English playwright T. W. Robertson. Romantic situations were also used, after 1850, in combination with problem drama or social theses, by Alexandre Dumas *fils* and Émile Augier.

A tentative realism shaped itself early in the second half of the nineteenth century, while romanticism lost whatever vitality it had once possessed. In Germany, *Maria Magdalena* was followed by Otto Ludwig's relentless drama *The Forester* (1850), in which a stubbornly righteous forester and the owner of the forest engage in a hard and destructive struggle. In Russia, realism grew naturally in plays by Alexander Ostrovski and the great Ivan Turgenev and appeared in quite well-developed form after 1850 without actually having any program; by comparison with Ostrovski's *The Thunderstorm* (1860) and Turgenev's *A Month in the Country,* the plays of Dumas *fils* and Augier are artificial and arid. The stage, too, responded to a growing interest in the everyday world and in factuality; the wings gave way to a set composed of three walls, and the scenery became solid.

In some instances, it is, indeed, difficult to make a distinct chronological division between a romantic and a realistic period. Genius does not heed the historians' rules. Officially, according to them, modern dramatic realism does not come into existence before Ibsen's *A Doll's House,* in 1879, or, at the earliest, before Émile Zola's naturalistic *Thérèse Raquin,* in 1873. *The Inspector* would have been a distinguished example of "realistic" social satire if it had been written in 1884 or 1914 instead of in 1834; and *A Month in the Country,* written in 1849, could just as well have been created by Chekhov in 1898 and would have been acclaimed as an excellent product of modern realism if it had been written in 1948.

All that can be said without fear of inaccuracy is that a concerted effort to create modern realistic drama throughout Europe did not make its appearance before the eighteen-seventies. When it did, it developed a theory and a program, and it acquired an influential master in Henrik Ibsen. When we have come that far in a review of the world's drama, however, we are ready for the second volume of this *Treasury of the Theatre.*

CONCLUSIONS

In nineteenth-century drama, before the advent of Zola and Ibsen, we observe a division of impulse that was to be repeated, in a sense, during the latter-day history of the theatre. We may describe this division as a conflict between imagination and verisimilitude. The romanticists gave primacy to the imaginative recreation of experience, the realists to the faithful rendering of the "facts" of ordinary life. *Faust* and *Maria Magdalena* represent this polarity.

The prime weakness of the romantic playwrights lay not in their poetry but in their disinclination to let the complete physical and emotional man stand in the foreground. Unlike Shakespeare, who let "ideas" emanate from multidimensional characters, the pure romanticists tended to turn people into concepts and to halt the action of their characters in order to embroider sentiments and principles. The trouble with these writers was that they wanted to be philosophers rather than playwrights. Their talent, moreover, was self-centered and subjective. They were better lyricists than dramatists.

The deficiency of the realists lay in their narrow view of reality. The trouble with the realistic playwrights was that they wanted to be photographers. And, to a degree, they too wanted to be philosophers or, more commonly, moralists.

Fortunately, the romantic and realistic playwrights did not always conform to the logical pattern of "all-spirit" or "all-matter." There were romanticists such as Musset and Büchner, who represented a real world. And in time the theatre was to acquire realists of the fellowship of Ibsen, Strindberg, and Chekhov, who were to re-create the world instead of merely copying it. In their best work, as foreshadowed by Turgenev's *A Month in the Country,* there appeared an autonomous world compounded of their special observation and feeling and their special insight and thought.

Johann Wolfgang von Goethe

(1749–1832)

Johann Wolfgang von Goethe is not only the chief literary figure of Germany but one of the greatest writers of all time. He applied his genius to almost all forms of literature, including the drama, for which, in spite of his experience as the director of the court theatre of Weimar, he had only a wayward talent. He never developed a sure grasp of dramatic composition; and if he had developed it, he would in all probability have quickly relinquished it in order to launch into philosophical discussions or to indulge his supreme talent for poetry. Nor were correctives at hand in the feeble German theatre to turn Goethe into an accomplished playwright. If, nevertheless, his contributions to the theatre were far from negligible, and if one of his plays, *Faust,* is the outstanding dramatic work of the romantic movement, the reason lies in his singular power of self-expression and in his happy choice of subjects. Faust's insatiable thirst for experience, for example, epitomizes European romanticism. It is with good reason that the venturesomeness of Western man in all fields of human activity and his insatiable desire for self-realization have been called "Faustian."

Goethe was himself the major modern representative of the "Faustian man." The son of patrician parents in Frankfort on the Main, he was carefully educated at home by his father, went to the University of Leipzig at the age of sixteen to study law, interrupted his legal studies to dabble in art, suffered from strange maladies, fell in love twice, felt the call of spiritualism, interested himself in alchemy, and exhibited all the instabilities of a young and romantic nature. Obeying his practical-minded father, he resumed and completed his law studies. But he fell in love again and came under the influence of the romantic critic Herder, who awakened his interest in folk poetry, nature worship and its French apostle Rousseau, sentimental literature as written by Laurence Sterne and Oliver Goldsmith, and Shakespearean drama.

Although Goethe began to practice law in Frankfort in 1771, he quickly won a reputation with lyric poetry; with the very stormy Storm and Stress drama *Goetz von Berlichingen,* begun in 1771 and completed in 1773; and with a short sentimental novel, *The Sorrows of Werther,* published in 1774. *Werther* captivated Europe with the story of the unhappy love and suicide of a morbid personality. Also in 1774, Goethe wrote *Clavigo,* a psychologically probing, if less than satisfactory, drama of a broken love affair similar to his own with the parson's daughter Friederike Brion, whom he left out of fear that a settled life would impair his genius. And in 1775 he created a minor scandal with his first version of another play, *Stella,* in which the hero solves the problem of loving two women equally well by living with both of them in the same household.

At the height of his popularity as Germany's leading romanticist, Goethe accepted an invitation from the young ruler of the German principality of Weimar to join his court. Goethe arrived there on November 7, 1775. He became the luminary of the little duchy and was loaded with honors by the Duke of Weimar. Here he could write as he pleased without concern for financial considerations. But another practical side of his character asserted itself in Weimar and he assumed a staggering number of official duties as member of the Privy Council, president of the Chamber of Finance, supervisor of roads, and the like. A passion for drawing all activities and interests into the orbit of his life seized Goethe, and everything became grist for his romantic search for self-expression. He even turned to science, making some small contribution to evolutionary theory with his discovery of the intermaxillary bone in the human jaw, propounding geological and botanical theories, and disputing Newton's theory of colors. As a result, Goethe's purely literary work suffered a diminution for years; he started many writings, including *Faust,* and completed none.

In October 1786, however, Goethe made a memorable journey to Italy, which released his pent-up creative energy. After his return to Weimar, he relinquished most of his ministerial duties; wrote noteworthy poetry, *The Roman Elegies;* completed three plays, *Egmont, Iphigenia in Tauris,* and *Torquato Tasso;* and in 1790 published a version of *Faust.* He also became director of the Weimar court theatre. From that time until his death (on March 22, 1832), while still pursuing scientific studies, he wrote more distinguished poetry, the *Wilhelm Meister* novels, and a famous autobiography.

Faust, which had germinated in Goethe's mind ever since his twentieth year, and on which he continued to work throughout the rest of his life, grew by accretion. He completed Part One in 1808 and Part Two in 1831. *Faust* is the testament of a long lifetime, and it reflects the experience and thought of one of the world's most completely developed literary personalities. The two parts of *Faust* comprise an amazingly comprehensive dramatic poem rich in insight and wisdom and studded with marvelous poetry and a number of highly dramatic scenes. The work as a whole is uneven and hangs together only loosely, even if it is philosophically connected as the story of a man's search for self-realization through the varied experiences of a lifetime's aspiration and experiment. Part Two is a miscellany of many scraps of fantastication and drama; its most potent idea appears in the realization that Faust, who sought to penetrate nature's inmost secrets, ultimately finds the greatest contentment in practical endeavors to create a busy and happy community. Part One, however, manages to hold together as a more or less integrated drama and contains many nuggets of characterization and dramatic situation.

Faust is a representative romantic work in its scope, as well as in its combination of lyric and dramatic and of comic and tragic elements. It gives, moreover, the full literary expression to the romantic philosophy which glorifies life as a search for fulfillment and as a vast adventure into the knowable and the unknowable worlds. Whereas Marlowe's Faustus is doomed to perdition, Goethe's Faust is saved by the redeeming quality of his continual dissatisfaction, experimentation, and striving. Opposed to him, in Goethe's work, is not a conventional devil but an incarnation of every unromantic and cynical attitude. Faust is the insatiable yea-sayer to life's possibilities; Mephistopheles is the nay-sayer who denies that life has any possibilities other than shallow and passing gratification. The struggle between Faust and Mephistopheles is the central conflict of Goethe's work. Salvation resides in man's refusal to accept contentment and in his unremitting effort to fulfill the highest promptings of the human spirit. If his grasp exceeds his reach, he is nonetheless redeemed by his aspiration. Beyond this affirmation even romanticism could not go.

Although only Part One of *Faust* constitutes a more or less satisfactory play, the reader must bear in mind the plan of the entire play if even Part One is to be gratifying. Obviously a drama that begins with wagers in heaven and on earth concerning man's moral destiny cannot come to a satisfactory conclusion with the death of a seduced girl. The dramaturgic shortcomings of Part Two dispose us, unfortunately, to lean too heavily on Part One for an appreciation of *Faust* as dramatic art. The blame devolves upon Goethe, who failed to confine himself to one limited objective—that of writing a *play*. But the blame is ours if we ignore the scope of Goethe's creative imagination.

In relying upon Part One, then, we must not only bear in mind the rest of Faust's story but note particularly those scenes in which the "Faustian" quest is announced, debated, and demonstrated. Since Faust, the protagonist, and Mephistopheles, the antagonist, do not know—and cannot know—what will follow or what solution will eventuate, Part One is the drama of the first stages of an experiment. It constitutes a play the essential theme of which is the question whether Faust, the essential romantic man, can find clarification and peace in his human career. By the same token, the play is also a dramatic statement that this question is the sum and essence of the human condition. Part Two, which should provide an answer to the question, is a wayward chronicle and concludes with a categorical—and operatic!—assurance of salvation. As Goethe declared in a suppressed epilogue and as Santayana has reminded us, the total work "is like human life: it has a beginning, it has an end; but it has no totality, it is not one whole." But in Part One the "beginning," the quest, at least, can be discerned distinctly.

FAUST[1]

Part One

By Johann Wolfgang von Goethe

TRANSLATED FROM THE GERMAN BY C. F. MAC INTYRE

CHARACTERS

THEATRICAL MANAGER
DRAMATIC POET
JESTER
MEPHISTOPHELES, *evil angel*
FAUST, *a scholar*
WAGNER, *servant and companion of Faust*
FROSCH ⎫
BRANDER ⎪
SIEBEL ⎬ *drinking companions*
ALTMAYER ⎭
MARGARET *or* GRETCHEN
MARTHA, *Margaret's neighbor*

LILYBETH, *Margaret's friend*
VALENTINE, *Margaret's brother*
THE LORD
ARCHANGELS
SPIRITS
WITCHES, SORCERERS, ETC.
APES
CHORUS OF ANGELS
CHORUS OF WOMEN
CHORUS OF DISCIPLES
APPRENTICES, SERVANT GIRLS, STUDENTS, PEASANTS, ETC.

PROLOGUE AT THE THEATRE

[*A* Manager, *a* Dramatic Poet *and a* Jester]

MANAGER: You two who have stood by me so often in need and trouble, tell me what you hope for in Germany from our undertaking. I wish very much to please the crowd, especially because it lives and lets live. The posts and boards are erected and everyone looks for a big time. They're seated already, with raised eyebrows, patiently waiting to be astonished. I know how to soothe the people's spirit, but I've never been so embarrassed; it's true they've never been used to the best, but they've read a great deal. How shall we arrange it that everything will be fresh and new and pleasant, even though instructive? For really I like to see the crowd rushing toward our show, and wave after wave forcing itself through the narrow gate of grace, in bright day; already before four o'clock they're pushing toward the box office, breaking their necks for a ticket, as if, in a famine, they wanted bread from the baker. It's only the poet who works this miracle on such various people. My friend, do it today!

POET: Oh, don't talk to me of that motley crowd, for a glimpse of them scares off my inspiration. Hide from me that surging multitude which sucks us against our will into the whirlpool. No, lead me to a quiet heavenly corner where pure joy blos-

¹ A new American version of the translation by C. F. MacIntyre, prepared by the translator in collaboration with James Laughlin.

soms for the poet, where love and friendship, by the hand of God, create and foster blessings for the heart. Ah, what has sprung forth from us there, what the lips stammered timidly, now failing or maybe succeeding, then swallowed by the power of the mad moment. Often, only after it has lasted for years does it look like a perfect creation. What dazzles is born for the moment, the real thing is never lost to posterity.

JESTER: If only I didn't have to hear so much about posterity! Just suppose I were to talk about it, who would make fun for us now? The people want it and ought to have it. The presence of a fine young man is always worth something, it seems to me. The man who knows how to put himself across agreeably will never be worsted by the caprice of the public; he wants a big audience so that he can be more sure of stirring it up. So be ready and give them a model performance. Let Fancy come with her chorus of Reason, Understanding, Feeling, and Passion, but mind that you let some Foolishness be heard.

MANAGER: But the most important thing is a lot of action! The people come to see things happen; that's what they like. If a lot is spun before their eyes, so that they can stare with surprise, in the long run you've succeeded, and you're a made man. You can only get volume through volume. Everybody chooses something to his liking. If you have a new show give it out in bits! With a hash like that you can't help but have a run. It's easy to dish it out as fast as invented. Why give it whole when the public will pick it to pieces anyhow?

POET: You don't feel how bad such hack-work is! How little it becomes the real artist! The botches of these gentlemen seem to have set up a standard for you.

MANAGER: Such a reproach doesn't worry me. A man who wants to do his work right must have the best tools. Remember: you have soft wood to split, and notice whom you're writing for! If one fellow goes to the theatre out of sheer boredom, another comes stuffed from a too-full table. And what's still worse: many come from reading the newspapers. They go to a play absent-mindedly as to a masquerade, moved only by curiosity. The women put on a show with themselves and their clothes and join the cast for nothing. What are you dreaming about in your ivory tower? How does one cheer up a full house? Look at your backers closely! Half of them are cold, the other half are coarse. Some hope for a card-game after the play, others are going out for a wild night with a tart. You poor fools, why do you worry the Muses for such an end? I tell you, only give them more and more, and always more, and you'll never miss. Try to mystify them, for to satisfy them is a hard job. What's the matter now? Are you pleased or hurt?

POET: Go on, and look for another slave! Is the poet to laugh off foolishly for your sake the highest right which nature has given him—that of being a man? How does he stir all hearts? And transcend every element? Isn't it because of the harmony which springs from his heart and which draws the world back into itself? When nature, indifferently twisting, feeds the thread's endless length to the spindle; when the discordant crowd of creatures jangles annoyingly—who then shall divide the ever-flowing monotonous series and give them life so that they move in rhythm? Who calls the isolated to the common consecration where it chimes in glorious agreement? Who lets the storm rage in the passions? The evening sunset glow in thoughtful minds? Who pours out the fairest flowers of spring on the path of the beloved? Who twines the meaningless green leaves to wreaths of honor for all deserts? Who assures Olympus? Unites the gods? The strength of man revealed in the poet.

JESTER: Use these fine powers then, push forward your poetry as one carries on a love-affair. By accident you are attracted, your passion grows, you linger, and by and by you are entangled. Happiness increases, then is upset; you are delighted, then comes the sorrow; and before you know it, it's a romantic novel. Let us give such a play! Get hold of life in all its variety. Everyone lives it, but not many understand it. Take hold of it where you will, it's always interesting. Give them colorful pictures and little clarity, much error but a spark of truth—that's how the best drink's brewed which refreshes and props up the world. The flower of youth will assemble at your play and listen to the revelation; every tender spirit will suck melancholy nourish-ment from your work; then soon this spectator and soon that one is stirred up until each sees what he has in his own heart. They are still ready to weep and to laugh; they still honor the flight of fancy and rejoice in illusions. With the person who is mature, nothing can be done; but he who is growing will always be grateful.

POET: Then give me those times again when I was still developing; when a fountain of crowding songs gushed forth, fresh and uninterrupted; when mist veiled the world from me and the bud still promised a miracle as I picked the thousand flowers that richly filled the valleys. I had nothing, but still it was enough, the yearning for truth and the delight in illusion. Give me back those untamed impulses, the deep and painful happiness, the strength of hatred, the power of love—give me back my youth!

JESTER: My friend, you may need youth when enemies press you in conflict, when the prettiest girls passionately embrace you, when far away the crown of the swift race beckons from the difficult goal, when after the violent whirling dance you drink away the night. But to play the harp with grace and spirit, to wander along gaily toward a self-set goal—that is the duty of older men, and we reverence you no less on that account. Age does not, as man says, make us childish, but it finds us truly childlike still.

MANAGER: We've talked enough, now let me see results; while you're exchanging compliments something useful could be done. What's the good of talking about being in the mood? It never comes to a man who dilly-dallies. If poetry is your job make it obey you. You know what we need—strong stuff—so brew some at once! What you don't do today won't be done tomorrow, and not a day should be wasted. Be resolute and grasp what is possible. Then you don't dare let it go and keep on working because you must. You know that on the German stage everyone tries what he wants to; therefore, don't spare either stage-sets or mechanical effects. Use the big and the little lights of the skies, be spendthrift of the stars; there's plenty of water, fire, rock-backdrops, animals, and birds. So on this narrow stage show the whole circle of creation, and travel with reasonable speed from Heaven through the world to Hell.

PROLOGUE IN HEAVEN

[The Lord, *the* Heavenly Host, *and later* Mephistopheles. *The three* Archangels *come forward and speak*]

RAPHAEL: The sun sings in the ancient major,
in song-match with its brother-spheres,
and finishes its ordained journey
with thunder-crash about their ears.
Its face gives strength to all the angels

though none of them can fathom why;
the inconceivably great work shines,
new as on the founding day.

GABRIEL: And swift, past understanding swift,
the splendor of the earth whirls past,
changing the paradisial brightness
for the night's deepness, shuddering, vast.
Broadly the ocean currents, foaming
out of the depths, are tossed and swirled,
and rocks and water hurtle onward
forever with the racing worlds.

MICHAEL: And tempests bluster in a wager,
from sea to land, from land to sea,
raging, forging an encoiling
chain of deepest energy.
A dazzling desolation is flaming
with thundering strokes along the way.
But, Lord, your messengers must honor
the gentle power of your day.

ALL THREE: This vision gives the angels power
though none of them can fathom you;
and all your wonderful creations
are splendid as on their first day.

MEPHISTOPHELES: Since you, O Lord, once more
approach and ask
how we are getting on, and since you used
to see me gladly, I have taken the risk
and come among your servants; but I can't
make pretty speeches, though the crowd here scoff
and scorn me, lest my pathos make you laugh—
if long ago you'd not dispensed with laughter.
I don't know how the suns and worlds are turned,
I only see how men will plague themselves.
The little earth-god's stamped in the old way
and is as odd as on creation day.
He'd be much better, Lord, if you'd not let
him have the merest glimpse of heavenly light
which he calls reason, using it at best
only to grow more bestial than the beasts.
He seems to me—I hope I'm not improper—
exactly like a spindly-legg'd grasshopper
that flits and flies and jumps,
then landing in the grass, will always sing
the same old worn-out song.
I wish that he were lost forever in the grass!
He digs his nose in every sort of trash.

THE LORD: And is there nothing else you want to
say?
Do you come here only to lodge complaints?
Is there nothing at all upon the earth that suits you?

MEPHISTOPHELES: No, Lord! I find things there,
as always, pretty bad.

Men grieve me so with the days of their lamenting,
I even hate to plague them with my torments.

THE LORD: Do you know Faust?
MEPHISTOPHELES: The Doctor?
THE LORD: He's my servant!
MEPHISTOPHELES: He serves you very strangely
then, indeed.

For nothing earthly will he eat or drink, the fool.
A yeasty yearning has driven him so far,
he's only half-aware that he is mad.
He wants from the sky the fairest star,
and from earth the highest joy that's to be had;
yet everything near and everything far
can never satisfy his deeply stirred desire.

THE LORD: Since, though confused, he serves me
still,
I'll lead him soon toward a clearer view.
The gardener knows that when the branches green,
soon fruit and flowers will show what time can do.

MEPHISTOPHELES: What will you bet? You'd lose
him yet
if you let me lead him gently down my street!

THE LORD: As long as he lives on earth,
I'll not forbid your trying.
Man is doomed to err as long as he is striving.

MEPHISTOPHELES: Thank you. Because I always
hate
to get involved with the dead and dying.
I'd rather have the fresh and rounded cheeks.
I'm never at home to a corpse.
I prefer, like a cat, to play with a mouse that squeaks.

THE LORD: Very well then. It shall be as you
wish.
Pervert this soul from its first source,
lead him—if you can get hold of him—
along your downward path; but when you lose
stand up and admit defeat.
A good man, struggling in his darkness,
will always be aware of the true course.

MEPHISTOPHELES: Good, Lord, and it won't take
me long!
I'll not be worried about this wager!
But when I win, please let me take
my triumph fully. He must gorge on dust,
and love it, like my aunt, the celebrated snake.

THE LORD: Do as you will. I give you a free
hand.
I have no hatred for the like of you.
Among destroyers, you must understand,
the rogue's the least offensive of the lot.
Man's active spirit easily falls asleep;
he's much too readily seduced by sloth.
Therefore, I gladly give him a companion
who prods and twists and must act as a devil.
[Turning to the Good Angels] But you, who are the
real sons of The Lord,
rejoice in beauty's live dominions.
May the Becoming, which eternally moves and lives,
surround you with the friendly walls of love!
To all that wavers you must minister,
basing it firmly in enduring thoughts.
      [The heavens close and the Angels go out]
MEPHISTOPHELES: [Alone] I like to see the Old
Boy now and then,
and I take care not to cross him by a word.
It's very decent of so great a lord
to gossip with the Devil like a man.

PART ONE

NIGHT

[Faust *sits restlessly at his desk in a high-vaulted, narrow, Gothic room*]
FAUST: Now I have studied philosophy,
medicine and the law,
and unfortunately, theology,
wearily sweating, yet I stand now,
poor fool, no wiser than I was before;
I am called Master, even Doctor,
and for these last ten years have led
my students by the nose—up, down,
crosswise and crooked. Now I see
that we know nothing finally.

This burns my heart, but I know, at least,
that I'm cleverer than all the conceited pedagogues,

the doctors, masters, clerks, and priests;
I am not troubled by doubts or scruples,
I'm not afraid of Hell or the Devil—
but, in return, all joy has been torn from me.

I don't presume to know anything now,
nor imagine I can teach anyone
how he can grow better. I have no
property, I haven't any money,
no decorations, or glories of this earth—
not even a dog would want to live like me.

Therefore I've turned to magic,
hoping a spirit will give me power
to fathom some of the secrets
so that I need no longer say, with sour sweat,
things that I don't know anything about;
so I may learn the fabric of the world,
see all the seeds, watch the wheels run,
and stop this rummaging around with words.

O radiant full moon, if only for the last time
you were looking down on my misery!
So many midnights when I've watched
beside my desk, over the books and papers,
you have appeared, my melancholy friend!
If I could only go along the mountain tops
under your friendly light,
ride round the mountain caverns with the spirits,
float over the meadows in your glimmering,
purged of the smoke of knowledge,
and bathe myself back to health in your dew!

Alas, am I still stuck in this prison?
This damned damp hole in the wall
where the sweet light of heaven
breaks gloomily through the painted panes!

Shut in by this heap of worm-gnawed
dust-covered books, that reach to the high arches
where smoke-stained paper clings;
cluttered with glassware and boxes,
with instruments stacked on all sides,

and crammed with inherited rubbish—
this is your world! Or what is called a world!

And do you still wonder why your heart
is cramped with fear?
Why this inexplicable hurt
represses all your lust for life?
Instead of living nature
in which God created man,
you're surrounded by smoke and rot,
animals' skeletons and dead men's bones.

Escape from this! Bestir yourself!
Move into the wider realm.
Is not this mysterious book by Nostradamus[2]
sufficient company for you?
You'll understand the stars' procession,
and when Nature has instructed you,
the strength of your own soul will be revealed
as spirit speaks to spirit.
All this dry plodding never can explain
the holy symbols to you. Hover about me,
spirits, and answer if you hear me!
[*He opens the book and sees the sign of the Mácrocosm*[3]]
Oh, what delight thrills through me
from this sudden sight!
I feel a young and holy zest for life flow,
newly glowing, through my veins and nerves.
Was it a god who drew these signs
which still my inner ravings,
fill my wretched heart with joy,
and with mysterious impulses unveil
the powers of nature around me?
Am I a god? All becomes clearer to me!
I see in these pure lines
creative nature lying open before my soul.
Now I begin to understand what the sage means:
'The world of spirits is not closed;
but your senses are shut, your heart is dead!
Up, neophyte, and undismayed
bathe your mortality in the morning light!'
[*He gazes at the sign*]
How everything moves toward the whole;
each in the other works and lives,
like seraphs climbing up and down,
passing to one another golden buckets!
On blessed fragrant wings
pressing from heaven through earth,
all sounding through the All with harmony!

What a great spectacle! But, yet, it's nothing more!
Eternal nature, where shall I grasp you?
Where are you, breasts, you springs of life
on which hang heaven and earth,
toward which the parched heart presses?

[2] Famous French astrologer of the sixteenth century.
[3] Literally, "Great World" (Greek)—the name given
by the astrologers to the universe as a whole. The sign is
a geometrical figure intended to provide Faust with a
beatific vision of the design or harmony of the universe.

You flow, you suckle—must I do without you?
    [*He leafs through the book impatiently and finds*
       the sign of the Earth-Spirit]
How differently this symbol works on me!
Spirit of the Earth, you are nearer to me;
already I feel my powers increasing,
already I glow as if I'd drunk new wine.
I have the courage to venture into the world,

to bear the woe and joy of earth,
to tussle with storms,
and not to fear the crash of shipwreck.
Clouds gather above me—
the moon now hides her light—
the lamp goes out!
Mists rise!—red gleams dart
round my head—cold horror
is dropping from the arches to seize me!
Spirit whom I implored, I feel you near me.
Unveil yourself!
You're tearing at my heart!
My senses burst
with strange new feelings!
My heart is utterly yielded to you!
Come! You must come! Although it costs my life!
    [*He seizes the book and mysteriously speaks the*
      spell. The Spirit *appears in a red flame*]
    SPIRIT: Who calls me?
    FAUST: [*Turning away*] Terrible apparition!
    SPIRIT: Powerfully you have summoned me;
long have you sucked for nourishment from my
    sphere,
and now—
    FAUST: I can't endure you!
    SPIRIT: Breathlessly, you prayed to behold me,
to hear my voice, to see my face;
the strong petitions of your soul have touched me—
and here I am! What pitiful terror
now overwhelms this superman! Where is the soul's
    cry?
Where is this mind that conceived a world within,
bore it and cherished it, joyously trembling,
and puffed itself up to rival us spirits?
Where are you, Faust, whose voice I heard,
who drove yourself toward me with all your strength?
Is this you, encompassed by my breath,
who tremble in your inmost being,
a worm that wriggles away in fear?
    FAUST: O flame-form, must I yield to you?
I am Faust! I am your equal!
    SPIRIT: Like the swirling of life, the storm of
    action,
I rise and fall,
moving here and there!
I am the womb and the tomb,
an eternal ocean,
a changing, glowing
life in ferment:
thus working on the roaring loom of time,
I weave God's living garment.

    FAUST: O active spirit, how near I feel to you!
You who swirl round the whole wide world.
    SPIRIT: You resemble the spirit which you compre-
    hend,
not me! [*The* Spirit *vanishes*]
    FAUST: [*Overpowered*] Not you?
Whom then?
I, the image of godhead,
yet not so much as you?
    [*There is a knock*]
O death! I know it—that's my assistant!
My greatest chance will come to nothing!
This boring plodder will destroy
the abundance of these revelations!
    [Wagner, *ready for bed, in a nightcap and*
    dressing gown, comes in with a lamp. Faust
    turns round impatiently]
    WAGNER: Excuse me! I heard you declaiming;
You're reading a part from some Greek tragedy?
That is an art from which I'd like to profit,
for nowadays everyone should know about it.
I've often heard it said that people
skilled in acting can instruct a parson.
    FAUST: Yes, if the preacher is an actor,
as happens very often in these times.
    WAGNER: When one's so cooped up in his little
    study
and scarcely sees the world on a holiday,
and as though through a telescope, it's so far away—
how can he ever persuade or lead anybody?
    FAUST: Unless you feel it, you will never achieve it.
If it doesn't flow from your soul
with natural easy power,
your listeners will not believe it.
You can sit down and paste phrases together by the
    hour,
cook up a little stew from others' feasts;
you can blow up miserable flames
from your heap of ashes
that will amaze children and monkeys—
if such little triumphs please your taste—
but you'll never move others, heart to heart,
unless your speech comes from your own heart.
    WAGNER: But orators depend for success
on elocution, and there I'm far behind.
    FAUST: Seek only honest gain.
Don't be a jingling jester!
Common sense and understanding
can go far with little art.
If you've something serious to say,
the words will come to you.
Glib tongues frill up their hash of knowledge
for mankind in polished speeches
that are no more than vaporous winds
rustling the fallen leaves in autumn.
    WAGNER: O God, art is so long!
And life so short.
Often during my philological studies
I lose heart and courage.
How hard it is to earn the means

to reach the sources!
And before a man can get half-way,
generally he dies, poor devil!

FAUST: Is parchment then the blessed spring
whose water quenches your thirst forever?
What does not burst from your own soul
will never refresh you.

WAGNER: Excuse me! It is the greatest pleasure
to put oneself in the spirit of the ages,
for by comparison with wise men before us
we see how far our own time has advanced.

FAUST: Oh yes, up to the stars! My friend,
the past is a book of seven seals, and what
you call the spirit of the times, in the end,
is merely the spirit of those gentlemen
in whom the times are mirrored.
And often as not they're a pretty sad lot!
At the first glance one runs away.
The garbage cans, the attics, the high-flown political
    dramas
have been raked for the proper didactic maxims
for the marionettes to mouth.

WAGNER: But the world, the mind and heart of
    men!
Everyone yearns to learn about them.

FAUST: To learn about them, yes, after a fashion.
But who dares call the child by its right name?
The few who know anything about it
are foolish not to guard it in their hearts;
those who have shown the rabble their feelings and
    thoughts
have been finally crucified or burned at the stake.
But it's late, my friend, and we'd better
break off for tonight.

WAGNER: I'd have liked to go right on, wide-awake
and talking here so learnedly with you.
But tomorrow's the first day of Easter vacation,
and maybe you'll answer another question or two.
I've been so eager and busy and patient;
I know a lot already, but I'd like to be omniscient.
    [He goes out]

FAUST: [Alone] How can anyone clinging to such
    trash
keep any hope in his head?
With greedy hands he digs for treasure,
and is happy when he finds earthworms!
How could the voice of such a man dare sound
here where a host of spirits hovered round me?
But I must thank you, this once,
poorest son of earth, for what you've done.
You tore me loose from the despair
that had almost driven me to frenzy.
The apparition was so huge a giant,
that I felt like a dwarf.

I, the image of godhead, who thought myself
near to the mirror of eternal truth,
enjoying myself in heaven's clear radiance
and stripping off all mortality;
I, more than a cherub, I, whose free strength

already dreamed it flowed through the veins of nature
and dared presume to enjoy
the creative life of gods—I must do penance for that.
A word of thunder swept me far away.

I dare not liken myself to you!
If I had the power to draw you,
I would have no strength to hold you.
In that happy instant you were near me
I felt myself so small, and yet so great . . .
ruthlessly you thrust me back
into humanity's ambiguous fate.
Who will teach me? What must I avoid?
Shall I yield to impulse and ask the spirits' help?
Alas, our acts, as well as our sufferings,
cramp the course of our lives.

Things—alien and ever more foreign—
intrude on the mind's most noble conceptions.
When we achieve some good here in our world,
we call the better merely deceit and illusion.
The glorious aspirations that made us alive
turn torpid in the earthly turmoil.

Though fancy once with daring hopeful flight
expanded toward infinity, now a speck
of space contents her when joy after joy
founders in the great maelstrom of time.
Anxiety nests deeply in the heart,
working her sorrow in secret;
restlessly she cradles herself, disturbing
joy and peace, with new masks veiling
her face, or else appearing
as house and property, as wife and child,
as fire, water, poison and dagger.
You worry about so many things which may not
    happen
and weep for things you may never lose.

I am not like the gods! I feel that so deeply;
I am the worm that crawls in dust,
lives there and must feed on dust, and dies,
crushed and buried under the wanderer's heel.

Is it not dust that cramps this lofty wall
with a hundred shelves around me?
This rubbish with a thousand trifles
that stifle me in this world of moths?
Shall I find here what I lack?
Shall I, perhaps, read in a thousand books
that everywhere men plague themselves,
with only here and there one happy man?

Why are you grinning at me, hollow skull, unless
that in your brain, confused like mine, once lived
something that sought bright day, desiring truth,
yet in the heavy dusk went miserably astray?
Surely this apparatus mocks me with its wheels,
rollers, cogs, and tackle. I stood at the gateway;
these should have been the key. The wards
are intricately made, but move no bolts.

Mysterious even in the light of day,

nature will never let her veil be stolen,
and what she will not show your mind
you'll not get out of her with screws and levers.
These ancient tools that I have never used
are here because my father needed them.
This scroll of parchment has been stained with smoke
since first the lamp was lighted on this desk.
Better if I had squandered my slight possessions,
than to be sweating here now with this worthless
    burden.
What you inherit from your father
must first be earned before it's yours.
What you don't use becomes a heavy load;
the moment creates the tool to serve its need.

But why is now my gaze drawn to that spot?
Can that flask be a magnet to my eyes?
What is this sudden gentle radiance
like moonlight drifting through the woods at night?

Hail, precious phial! With awe
I take you down and honor man's cunning art.
Essence of kindly opiates,
extract of subtle and deadly agents,
now give your favor to your master!
I see you and my pain is soothed;
I grasp you, and at once my struggles are calmed;
the flood-tide of the spirit ebbs away.
I am shown the path above the ocean
where mirror-waters glisten at my feet;
a new day lures me to new shores.

On light wings a fiery chariot hovers,
gliding toward me. I feel ready
to pierce new pathways in the ether,
into new spheres of action without limits.
Exalted existence, godlike delight!
Can I, no better than a worm, deserve them?
Firmly resolved, I turn my back
to the bright sun of earth. Be bold to burst open
the gates past which others would gladly go slinking!
Now it is time to show that man's dignity
vies with the high gods, and will not tremble
before that dark cavern where phantasy, self-damned,
lives among torments; then on to the passage
whose narrow mouth flames with all Hell's seething.
Serenely determine to take this final step
though you risk the danger of plunging to nothing-
    ness.

Come down, pure crystal goblet, from your case.
For many years I have not thought of you.
You shone at gay ancestral feasts
and used to cheer the solemn guests
when one touched you to another for a toast.
The elaborate images carved and wrought on you—
it was the drinker's task to rhyme on them
and drain your bowl with one long drink.
Now they recall those nights of youth.

Now I shall never pass you gaily to my neighbor,
or show my wit off on your art.

Here is a juice that quickly makes men drunk.
I pour the brown stream in the cup.
I have prepared it, now I choose it
and take the final drink with all my will,
a solemn festal pledge to Easter morning!
    [*He raises the goblet to his lips. But, as he does
    so, there comes the sound of chimes and a
    chorus of voices*]
    CHORUS OF ANGELS: Christ is arisen!
        Joy to the mortal
        whom baneful, insidious,
        inherited failings
        of earth had entwined.
    FAUST: With that deep resonance, what bright
    sound
now forcibly pulls the goblet from my lips?
Those booming bells, do they announce the first glad
    hour
of Easter? Is the choir already singing
the hymn of consolation
which through the night of the tomb
rang from the angels' lips, pledging a new covenant?
    CHORUS OF WOMEN: With myrrh and spices
        we tenderly tended him.
        We, his most faithful ones,
        laid him away;
        in swathings and grave clothes
        we cleanly wrapped him.
        Alas! for we find now
        Christ is not here.
    CHORUS OF ANGELS: Christ is arisen!
        Blest is the loving one
        who has transcended
        the wholesome and chastening
        trials that beset him!
    FAUST: Gentle and mighty music of heaven,
why do you seek me here in the dust?
Ring rather to soft-hearted men.
I hear your message, but I lack belief.
Miracle is the darling child of faith.
I dare not struggle up to those high spheres
where the glad tidings ring;
and yet from childhood I was used
to these same sounds, and now they call me back
    to life.
In other times the kiss of heavenly love
fell on me in the solemn Sabbath stillness;
the full chimes rang prophetically;
a prayer was ardent pleasure; a longing,
sweet, unfathomable, drove me through woods and
    fields,
and while I shed a thousand burning tears,
I felt a new world rise within me.
This song announced the happy sports of youth,
the free and joyous festival of spring;
now memory with childlike feelings keeps me
from this last decisive step.
Oh, ring, sweet heavenly songs! Ring out!
My tears flow and earth has me back again!
    CHORUS OF DISCIPLES: He who was buried

is risen already,
alive and sublimely
exalted on high.
To the joy of becoming,
to the gladness of creation,
now he is near.
But here down on earth
we stand in affliction.
He has left us, who loved us,
we pine for him here.
Master, we weep for you,
weep for your happiness!

CHORUS OF ANGELS: Christ is arisen
from the womb of corruption.
Joyfully loosen
yourselves from your bonds!
If you live, praising him,
showing all love to him,
with brotherly feasting,
journeying and preaching,
promising joy,
the master will be near you,
the master is here!

OUTSIDE THE TOWN GATE

[*Various classes of people are promenading*]
APPRENTICES: Why do you go that way?
OTHERS: We're off to the Hunters' Lodge.
THE FIRST: We're going down to the mill.
ANOTHER: I'd rather go to the inn by the water.
THE SECOND: The road there is not very pretty.
OTHERS: What will you do?
THE THIRD: I'll just go along with the rest.
THE FOURTH: Come up to Burgdorf. You'll find
    there
the prettiest girls and the strongest beer,
and there's always something doing.
THE FIFTH: Well, you're too much for me!
Does your hide itch for a third beating?
I'm afraid of the place.
I'll not go there.
A SERVANT GIRL: No, no! I'm going back to town.
A SECOND: We'll surely find him there by the pop-
    lars.
THE FIRST: Well isn't that a piece of luck for me!
He'll walk with you, he'll dance
with no one else but you.
What good will all your fun do me?
THE SECOND: Today he's not alone.
He said that Curly would come with him.
A STUDENT: Wow! look at that pair just going
    by!
Come on, brother, let's try to pick them up.
Beer with a head, tobacco that bites,
and a girl like that will suit my appetite.
A BURGHER'S DAUGHTER: Just watch those good
    looking boys!
Now aren't they awful?

When they could have the best society,
they'd rather chase after those housemaids!
THE SECOND STUDENT: Don't go so fast! Here come
a couple of really nice looking girls.
That one there lives next door to me
and I like her a lot. They look shy,
but they'll let us go along with them.
THE FIRST STUDENT: No, brother, thanks, but I
    don't like them tame.
Quick! or we'll lose the ones we want to get.
The arm that wields a broom on Saturday
on Sunday always snuggles you the best!
A BURGHER: I don't like our new mayor. Since the
    election
he acts like a dictator. And what has he done
for the city? Every day it's getting worse.
We're regimented and taxed as never before.
A BEGGAR: [*Singing*] Sweet ladies and kind gentle-
    men,
        red-cheeked, in such fine clothes,
        be gracious and remember me,
        take pity on my woes.
        Don't let me grind my organ in vain!
        Only the generous are gay.
        A time when people celebrate
        should be my harvest-day.
A SECOND BURGHER: It's fine on a Sunday or holi-
    day
to sit snugly and talk of war and the noise of battles;
how they're fighting down in Turkey, far away.
You stand by the tavern window and empty your
    bottle
and look at the river where gay boats glide past;
then go home at evening, happy, and praising peace.
A THIRD: That's right, neighbor, no foreign inter-
    vention!
Let them crack each others' heads open.
However things go there, we'd better
stay at home and stick to the old customs.
A BAWDY OLD WOMAN: [*To the* Burghers' Daugh-
    ters] So smartly dressed! Oh, the gay young
    blood!
Who could resist falling in love with you?
Now I know exactly—don't act so shocked—
just how to manage the thing that you'd like.
THE GIRL: Hurry up, Agatha! We must be careful
not to be seen in public with a witch.
But just last Hallowe'en she showed me
my future lover, real as flesh and blood.
THE OTHER GIRL: She called up mine, too, in a
    crystal:
he was a soldier, marching with his troop.
Since then I've looked around for him everywhere,
But so far I haven't been able to find him.
CHORUS OF SOLDIERS MARCHING PAST: Castles with
    mighty walls,
        towers, and battlements,
        girls who are haughty
        and scornful and hard—
        we'd like to win all of them!

Daring's the doing,
and great the reward.

Hear how the trumpets
woo us to pleasure,
and coax us to peril.
Oh what a life it is!
Oh what a storm!
Castles and girls as well
yield in the end.
Daring's the doing,
great the reward!
And the soldiers go marching
away down the road.
     [Faust *and* Wagner *enter*]
     FAUST: Now spring's reviving glance has freed
the ice from stream and river.
The valley turns green with the joy of hope.
Old winter, growing impotent, crawls back
to the rough mountains; as he flees, he hurls
fitful gusts of icy-kerneled sleet
in streaks on the green meadows.
But the sun allows no whiteness;
growth and creation stir and strive
to cover everything with color.
And since the landscape still lacks flowers, the sun
must use the color of peoples' clothes instead.
Turn round and from this hill-top
look at the town. Now from the towered
gloomy gateway streams a motley swarm
eager to sun themselves today.
They celebrate the resurrection
of the Lord; for they themselves
are newly risen from the tenements,
from the damp rooms and the press
of mills and factories, from the weight
of roofs and gables and the stifling
crush of alleys, from the solemn
venerable gloom of churches—
now they come out into the sunlight.
See how lively now the crowd
scatters through the fields and gardens,
while, up and down, there on the river
bob the merry little row-boats,
and the last skiff, over-laden
and almost sinking, pushes off.

Even from the mountain pathways
bright-colored dresses are shining.
Already I hear the bustle of the village.
Here's the heaven of the people;
rich and poor are happy and shouting.
Here I feel, and dare feel, like a man.
     WAGNER: It's an honor to go walking with you,
          Doctor,
and also profitable; but I wouldn't care
to lose myself alone here, since I'm opposed
to everything that's vulgar. Fiddling, shouting,
and nine-pins are noises that I hate.
The people riot, driven by the Devil,
and call it joy and think it's music.

     [*There are* Peasants *under a linden tree, dancing
     and singing*]
     THE PEASANTS: The shepherd was all dressed up
          for the dance,
          with wreath and ribbons and leather pants,
          and he was making a show.
     Already under the linden tree
     the crowd was dancing crazily.
     Jukey! Jukey!
     Jubilo!
     So went the fiddle-bow.

     As he pushed swiftly through the swirl,
     he bumped a pretty peasant girl
     sharply with his elbow.
     The jolly maiden turned around
     and said, 'Well, you're a clumsy clown!'
     Jukey! Jukey!
     Jubilo!
     'And your behavior's low.'

     Then in a circle, twirling swift,
     they danced to the right, they danced to the
          left—
     and the skirts whirled out and rose.
     They got red and they got warm,
     and rested, puffing, arm in arm.
     Jukey! Jukey!
     Jubilo!
     Hip against elbow.

     'Don't be familiar! How many men
     wheedle and lie to their sweethearts, then
     off and away they go!'
     But he coaxed her aside with flattery
     while the music rang round the linden tree:
     Jukey! Jukey!
     Jubilo!
     Oh, the shouts and that fiddle-bow!
     AN OLD PEASANT: Doctor, it is good of you
not to disdain today
to come among us farmers,
though you're a great scholar.
Pray take the finest tankard,
brimming with our freshest draught.
May it quench your thirst, and each drop
be a day added to your life.
     FAUST: I take it gladly, this refreshing drink;
here's to your health and many thanks!
     [*The people gather round him*]
     OLD PEASANT: You have kindly come to share
our happy day, as long ago
in evil times you helped us here.
There's many a man stands here alive
saved by your father from the rage
of the hot fever when he stopped
the pestilence. A young man then,
you went in every stricken house;
many a corpse was carried out,
but you kept well and bore hard trials.
The Helper yonder helped the helper here.

ALL: Long life to this well-proven man,
long may he live and help us!
FAUST: Bow down to Him above
Who teaches and sends help! [*He goes on with
Wagner*]
WAGNER: O great man, what a feeling
all this honor from the crowd must give you!
Happy is he who from his skill
can gain such benefits! Each father calls
his boy to look at you. The people rush up
and stand around you, asking questions.
The dancers stop, the fiddle's still.
They stand in rows to watch you pass;
throw their caps in the air. And almost
get on their knees, as if you were the sacred Host.
FAUST: A few steps farther, to that stone.
We'll rest after our walk. How many times
I've brooded here, tortured myself with prayers
and fastings, rich in hope and firm in faith;
with sighs and tears, wringing my hands, I thought
to force the Lord in heaven to end the plague.
The crowd's applause now sounds like scorn.
If they could read my mind, they'd see
how little both father and son deserve their praise.

My father was an obscure gentleman
who loved, quite honestly, in his odd way
to ponder on nature and her sacred workings,
with a crank's unsystematic zeal.
He shut himself in the black kitchen
with a group of expert alchemists,
seeking by many a recipe
to make the incompatibles agree.

There the red Lion, a brisk chaser,
married the Lily in a lukewarm bath,
and both above the open flame
were tortured from one bride-chamber to another.
Then, if the young queen appeared
with varied colors in the glass retort,
that was the medicine! The patients died;
and no one asked: 'Who recovered?'
Thus, with Hell's electuaries,[4]
we brought more destruction than the plague
among these mountains and valleys.
I have poisoned many thousands;
they pined away from our drugs, yet I must live
to hear the reckless murderers praised.
WAGNER: Why let it worry you? Does not the good
man
fulfill his duty when he practices
skilfully and scrupulously the art
transmitted to him? If in your youth you honor
your father, you will gladly learn from him.
If in your manhood you carry this knowledge farther,
maybe your son will reach a higher goal.
FAUST: Oh, happy the man with any hope
of rising out of error's ocean!
You need just what you do not know,
and what you really know is worthless.

4 Medicines.

But let us not embitter this blessed hour
with melancholy thoughts.
See how the green-encircled huts
shine in the glow of the evening sun.
The day is over; the sun yields and hastens
onward to quicken new life. Oh, that wings
could lift me from the earth to follow,
struggling in the sun-wake! I would see
beneath my feet the silent world
glowing in the eternal evening;
each peak on fire, each valley calm,
the silver brooks flowing to golden rivers.
And the wild mountain with its gorges
could not check my godlike flight.
Already the ocean with its sun-warmed bays
broadens beneath my astonished eye.
Yet finally the sun appears to sink;
and a new instinct awakens.
I hurry onward to drink his eternal light,
the day before me, and the night behind,
the sky above, the waves below—
a splendid dream until the sun fades out.

Ah, if only the wings that raise the spirit
might be brothered by strong earthly wings!
Man is born with a desire
that drives his feeling upward, onward,
when overhead, lost in blue space,
the skylark sings his quavering song;
when over the craggy fir-topped heights
he sees the out-spread eagle soaring,
or the crane struggling homeward
over lakes and swampy moors.
WAGNER: I've often had strange whims myself,
but never such an urge as that.
You soon get bored with fields and forests;
I'll never envy any bird his flight.
How differently the spirit's pleasures bear us,
from page to page, through volume after volume.
Then winter nights are cheerful and friendly,
warm delight steals through the bones,
and ah, when you unroll some precious parchment,
Heaven itself comes down to you!
FAUST: You know the one impulse only.
It's better if you never learn the other.
Alas, there are two souls that live in me
and one would like to leave its brother;
one with gripping organs clings to earth
with a rough and hearty lust;
the other rises powerfully from the dirt
up toward the region of the great forefathers.
If there are lordly spirits in the air
roaming between the earth and sky,
let them come down from the golden atmosphere
and lead me to a new, more vivid life!
Yes, if I had a magic cloak to carry me
to foreign lands, I would not trade it
for the richest robes, or for the mantle of a king.
WAGNER: Do not invoke the much-feared throng
of demons

that rush about the murky air,
preparing evils, thousands of them, for mankind
from every quarter of the sky.
Out of the North the sharp-toothed ghosts
sweep down on you with tongues like arrows;
out of the East they come to quench
their thirst and feed upon your lungs;
if the Southwind swirls them up from the desert,
pouring heat-waves on your skull,
then the West will send its swarm, reviving you first
    with rain,
then drowning you and the fields and meadows.
Being full of mischief, they love to listen;
they gladly obey, for they like to betray you,
pretending to be sent from Heaven,
and lisping like angels, while they lie.
But let us go. The world turns gray,
the air grows cool, the fog blows in.
Only at evening can you really value home—
But why do you stand like that and look amazed?
What is it fascinates you in the twilight?

    FAUST: Do you see that black dog sneaking
through the stubble and the grain?

      WAGNER: I saw him long ago. It seemed unim-
      portant.

      FAUST: Look at him closely. What kind of animal
      is it?

      WAGNER: It's a poodle, sniffing after
the footsteps of his master, as they all do.

      FAUST: But see in what wide-spirals
he stalks us, always coming closer.
And unless my eyes deceive me,
a fiery whirlpool is following his path.

      WAGNER: I don't see anything except a plain black
      poodle.
It must be just an optical illusion.

      FAUST: It seems to me he's drawing magic nooses
around our feet to make a snare.

      WAGNER: All that I notice is that he jumps uncer-
      tainly about
because he sees two strangers, not his master.

      FAUST: The circle narrows. Now he's getting near.

      WAGNER: You see! It's nothing but a dog. No
      spectre there.
He snarls and hesitates, crawls on his belly
and wags his tail—all common canine habits.

      FAUST: Here, boy! here! Come here!

      WAGNER: It's only a stupid poodle. You stand still,
and he'll sit up and beg; you speak and he jumps up
    on you.
Lose something, and he'll hunt for it
or jump into the water for your stick.

      FAUST: You're right. I don't find any traces
of the supernatural. It is just his training.

      WAGNER: A well-trained dog can win a learned
      man.
He's worth your favor, for it's clear
that he's a scholar of the students,
who have taught him tricks.

    [*They enter the city gates*]

FAUST'S STUDY

[Faust *comes in with the poodle*]
FAUST: I have left the fields and meadows
    hidden deeply in the veil of night
    that wakens the true soul with holy
    and prophetic shudderings. Now violent
    actions
    and the wild impulses are asleep;
    love for mankind revives,
    and the love of God is stirring in the heart.

Be quiet, poodle, don't run back and forth!
What are you sniffing at there by the threshold?
Lie down behind the stove, I'll give you
my best cushion. Up there on the hillside
your games amused me; now I'll keep you here
if you can act like a quiet and welcome guest.

    Ah, when the lamp again burns friendly
    in our little study,
    then all glows bright within us,
    in the heart that understands itself.
    Reason begins to speak again, hope blooms;
    we yearn then for the springs of life,
    and long to attain its very source.

Stop growling, poodle!
That brutish noise is not in tune
with the holy tones that fill my soul.
We are used to men who jeer at what
they do not understand, who grumble
at the beautiful and good which often are difficult.
Must dogs snarl at them, too?

But now, although I want it, I no longer feel
that inner peacefulness.
Why must the stream run dry so soon and leave us
thirsting once again? I have gone through it all so
    often.
And yet, this want can be relieved. We learn
to prize the supernatural; we yearn for revelation
which never burned more beautifully, more nobly,
than here in the New Testament. Now I must open
the original text, with this my honest purpose,
once and for all, to turn the holy scripture
into my own beloved German.
    [*He opens the book and begins*]
It is written: 'In the beginning was the *Word!*'
I'm stopped already. Who will help me further?
I cannot possibly rate the *Word* so highly.
I must translate it otherwise,
if I am rightly enlightened by the spirit.
It is written: 'In the beginning was the *Thought!*'
Consider the first line well,
lest the pen write too hastily.
Is it the *Thought* that works and creates all?
Should it not be: 'In the beginning was the *Power!*'
Yet, even as I write it down,
I feel I can not let that stand.
The spirit helps me! Suddenly I have it,
and confidently write: 'In the beginning was the
Deed!'

Poodle, if I must share this room with you,
then stop that growling,
and that howling!
I can't stand a companion who's a nuisance.
One of us must leave.
I hate to withdraw
my hospitality, but the door is open.
The way is free.
But what is this I see?
Can such things happen naturally?
Is it shadow or reality?
How my poodle grows long and broad!
He swells with power.
That's no dog's form!
What phantom have I brought into the house?
Now he looks like a hippopotamus
with fiery eyes and a terrible jaw of teeth.
Ah, now I'm sure of you!
Solomon's Key[5] is good
for creatures of such Hellish blood!

SPIRITS: [*In the corridor*] Someone is caught in
there!
> Don't follow. Stay safe here!
> Like a fox in a gin,
> Hell's lynx quakes within.
> But take care!
> Hover here, hover there,
> up and down.
> Soon he'll be free.
> If you can serve him,
> help now to save him;
> for he has done
> good turns for everyone.

FAUST: I cannot meet this beast until
I quell him with the Spell of Four:[6]

> Let salamander glow
> and undine coil,
> sylph disappear
> and goblin toil!

Who is ignorant
of the four elements,
their potencies
and properties,
shall never master
the spirits.

> Vanish in flames, salamander!
> undines,
> flow gurgling together.
> Sylphs,
> be bright as meteors.
> Incubus, to all in-doors
> be helpful; incubus,
> come forth and put an end to this!

[5] *Clavicula Salomonis,* a conjurer's book containing spells for evoking and exorcising spirits.
[6] The "formula of four" for dealing with a spirit of nature—the formula of the four elements of nature: earth, air, fire, and water.

None of the four
is in the beast.
He lies at rest
and grins at me.
I haven't hurt him yet;
now he shall hear me conjure
with a mightier sorcery.
> [*He shows the beast a crucifix*]
> Are you a fugitive from Hell?
> Behold this sign!
> To this the black hosts
> of Hell bow down.

He swells up now, with bristling hair.

> Rejected creature,
> can you read this symbol?
> Sign of the uncreated,
> the unnamable.
> Him through all realms diffused,
> Who was wantonly spear-pierced?

Forced by my spells behind the stove,
he's swelling like an elephant.
Now he fills the room completely,
he's about to dissolve in vapor.
Don't rise to the ceiling!
Lie down at your master's feet!
You see I don't threaten vainly.
I'll scorch you with holy fire!
Do not wait
for the triple-glowing light!
Do not wait
for the full strength of my arts!
> [Mephistopheles *comes from behind the stove while the mist vanishes. He is dressed like a traveling scholar*]

MEPHISTOPHELES: Why all the noise?
How may I serve you, Sir?
FAUST: So that was the poodle's kernel!
A vagabond scholar! It makes me laugh.
MEPHISTOPHELES: I salute you, learned Sir.
You certainly made me sweat.
FAUST: What is your name?
MEPHISTOPHELES: Now that seems to me rather
petty
in one so scornful of the Word,
one who is sceptical of appearances,
and looks only for the depths of being.
FAUST: We can usually recognize the identity
of such gentlemen as you by the name,
which shows itself all too plainly
when they call you the God of Flies, the Destroyer,
the Liar. So then, who are you?
MEPHISTOPHELES: A part of that power
which always wills evil and always works good.
FAUST: What does that riddle mean?
MEPHISTOPHELES: I am the spirit that always
denies! A good thing, too,
for all that exists deserves to be destroyed.
It would be much better if nothing were ever created.

So I'm everything that you call sin and destruction,
in short, evil—these are my proper element.

FAUST: You call yourself a part, yet stand there whole.

MEPHISTOPHELES: I speak the modest truth. Though man,

that silly little microcosm,
commonly thinks himself an entity.
I am part of the part that at first was all,
part of the darkness that gave birth to light,
that supercilious light which now disputes
with Mother Night her ancient rank and realm,
and yet can not succeed; however much it struggles,
it sticks to matter and can't get free.
Light flows from substance, makes it beautiful;
solids can check its path, so I hope it won't be long
till light and the world-stuff are destroyed together.

FAUST: Now I understand your important duties!
You can't destroy things quite wholesale,
So you've started on a smaller scale.

MEPHISTOPHELES: And really I haven't got far with it.

In spite of all I've undertaken
I can't get under the skin of this fat world,
this something that opposes the nothing.
Earth-quakes, tidal-waves, hurricanes, fires—no use,
the land and sea remain as calm as ever.
And that damned trash, the race of beasts and men—?
I can't get at them either, as I'd like.
How many of them I've buried!
Yet always there's fresh new blood
to go on circulating, on and on,
until I'm almost crazy! For out of the waters,
and out of the earth and the air,
thousands of seeds are unfolding everywhere,
in drouth and moisture, in heat and cold.
If I hadn't reserved fire for myself
I'd certainly have very little.

FAUST: You dare to raise your cold devil's fist,
clenched vainly in malice,
against the ever-working, healing, creative power?
Try something else, you wayward son of Chaos!

MEPHISTOPHELES: We'll take the matter under advisement

and consider it at our next meeting.
And now, may I go?

FAUST: I don't see why you ask.
I've just now made your acquaintance.
Visit me when you wish.
Here is the door, there is the window,
and there's the old reliable chimney.

MEPHISTOPHELES: To tell the truth, I can't leave,
there's a little obstacle: the swan-foot-print[7]
of the incubus on your threshold.

[7] This incubus, called the "drude" in German mythology, had swan's feet. Her foot, a magical symbol in the form of a five-pointed star, called the "pentagram," was carved or painted on the threshold in order to ward off evil spirits.

FAUST: So the pentagram's[7] giving you trouble?
But tell me, you son of Hell,
if that stops you, how did you get in?
What was it tricked a devil like you?

MEPHISTOPHELES: Just look closely! It's not well drawn;

the angle pointing out is not connected.

FAUST: A lucky accident! I've got you prisoner?
A splendid opportunity for me!

MEPHISTOPHELES: The poodle didn't see it when he jumped in;

but things look different now.
In fact, the Devil can't get out.

FAUST: But why not through the window?

MEPHISTOPHELES: Oh, that's just one of those things: a law for spirits

and demons—wherever they steal in they must go out.
We can choose the first but are bound by the second.

FAUST: Then even Hell itself has laws?
I think that's fine, because some binding pact
might be arranged between us.

MEPHISTOPHELES: What's promised you'll enjoy in full.

Nothing shall be pinched from it.
But the matter's not so easily settled.
We'll talk it over next time. For the present,
with your permission, I'll withdraw.

FAUST: But stay a moment and tell me some good news.

MEPHISTOPHELES: Let me go now! I'll come back soon;

then you can question me to your heart's content.

FAUST: I set no trap for you. You walked into the meshes.

Let him who's caught the Devil hold him!
He won't be caught so soon a second time.

MEPHISTOPHELES: If it will please you, I'm prepared

to stay—on one condition:
to pass the time I'll demonstrate
my art as a magician.

FAUST: I'd like that. Anything you wish,
but make it something pleasant.

MEPHISTOPHELES: My friend, you'll get more from this hour

to delight your senses than you could get
in a year of academic monotony.
All that the dainty spirits sing,
and all their pretty pictures,
are not mere empty sorcery.
They'll tickle your nose, refresh your palate,
and finally ravish your feelings.
It doesn't require rehearsal,
and so, since we're all ready, then let's go!

SPIRITS: Vanish, O gloomy
arches above us!
Let the blue ether gaze
tenderly down on us.
Let the black cumulus

clouds scud away from us!
Little stars glitter,
and milder suns shine.
Ethereal beauty
of bright sons of heaven,
wavering, lean to us,
hovering over us;
and wistful yearning
comes following after.
Fluttering ribbons
of the bright garments
cover the countryside,
cover the arbors
where dreaming lovers
swear love forever.
Leaves, what a wealth of leaves!
Tendrils still budding!
Heavily grape-clusters
fall in the must-vats.
How the juice gushes now,
crushed out by presses,
falling in torrents
of red-foaming wine,
purling round purest gems,
leaving the hills behind,
spreading in lakes and ponds,
bathing in pleasure
the flanks of green hillocks.
Now all the birds come
and drink it with joy,
then fly toward the sunlight,
fly to bright islands
that dance on the waves.
We hear in a chorus
voices rejoicing,
and over the meadows
see dancers amusing
themselves in the open.
People are climbing
over the mountains;
and some are sailing
over the water;
others are flying:
all move toward living,
all toward the distant
earth loving stars
blessed and kind.

MEPHISTOPHELES: He sleeps! Well done, my deli-
cate airy rascals!
Your lullaby has really made him sleep.
I am indebted to you for this concert.
You're not the man yet who can hold the Devil!
Weave sweet phantom-forms around him;
plunge him in the ocean of delusion.
And now I need some sharp rat-teeth
to splinter this magic threshold.
But I shan't have to conjure long.
Already one comes scampering to obey me.

The lord of mice and rats,

bed-bugs, flies, frogs and lice,
orders you to come. Be bold
and gnaw this threshold for him
as soon as he's smeared a spot with oil—
here you come hopping. Start your work.
The point at the edge there has me caught.
Another nibble, and the trick is done.
Now, Faust, dream on until we meet again.
FAUST: [Awakening] Have I been deceived again
and led astray?
Can such a throng of spirits disappear?
Was it a lying dream that the Devil was here,
and *was* it a poodle that ran away?

FAUST'S STUDY

[Faust *and* Mephistopheles]
FAUST: Who knocks? Come in! Who's bothering
me again?
MEPHISTOPHELES: Just me.
FAUST: Come in!
MEPHISTOPHELES: You must ask three times.
FAUST: Come in, then!
MEPHISTOPHELES: I like you this way.
I hope we'll hit it off together!
Here I am, come to chase away your wild moods,
gotten up as a nobleman in a red doublet trimmed
with gold,
with a stiff silk cloak, a cock's feather
in my hat, and a long pointed sword.
I advise you to dress the same way.
Then we may travel easily,
while you discover what life can be.
FAUST: Whatever the clothes, I still would feel the
pain
of this earth's narrow life. I am too old
for play, too young to live without desire.
What more can the world allow me? Renounce!
You must renounce! That's the eternal song
every man hears ringing in his ear,
singing hoarsely every hour,
his whole life long.
I wake at dawn with horror; I could weep
bitterly, to see another day
which in its course will not fulfill one wish, not one:
a day that lessens with capricious disappointments
all my anticipated pleasures.
A day that checks my creative power
with a thousand grinning goblins of life.
Then when night sinks down, I must stretch out
on a bed of desperation that gives me no rest;
for even there wild dreams will frighten me.
The god who lives within can stir me deeply,
can sit like a king, throned on my own strength,
but has no power over external things;
and so, existence is a burden,
death wished-for, and life hated.
MEPHISTOPHELES: And yet death's never a wholly
welcome guest.

FAUST: Happy that man whose brow death winds
with bloody laurels in the splendor of victory;
or he who is taken in a girl's arms
after the nimble maddening dance.
Oh, would that I had fallen dead,
overcome by the might of the great spirit!

    MEPHISTOPHELES: Yet, wasn't there someone on
      a certain night
who didn't drink the brown juice from the jug?

    FAUST: It seems, you like to spy.

    MEPHISTOPHELES: I'm not omniscient, but I do
      know many things.

    FAUST: Although a sweet familiar tone drew me
from dreadful frenzy and deceived the remnant
of childhood's feelings with echoes of happy times,
now I curse all that holds the soul with lures
and hocus-pocus, all that confines it with blinding
    flattery
to this cave of gloom. I curse above all
that false self-exaltation with which the mind
befuddles itself. Cursed be the blinding
of illusion that wraps our senses.
A curse on cheating dreams,
obsessions of glory and desire for an immortal name.
Cursed be all flattering possessions, like wife and
    child,
servant and plough. Damned be Mammon
when he incites us to rash acts
with hopes of wealth, or when he softens our beds
for futile pleasures. Cursed be the balsam-juice
of the grape, and the delights of love.
Accursed be hope and faith and, above all, patience!

    CHORUS OF SPIRITS: [*Off-stage*] Woe, woe!
      You have destroyed
      the splendid world
      with a mighty fist.
      It is shattered, and falls!
      A demi-god broke it!
      We carry the fragments
      back to the nothingness.
      We make lamentation
      over lost beauty.
      O mighty one
      among earth's sons,
      build it again, build it greater,
      build it within yourself!
      Begin the new way of life
      brightly, more cheerfully,
      and new songs will praise it!

    MEPHISTOPHELES: These little fellows
      belong to my faction.
      Hear how they shrewdly
      advise you to act
      and enjoy yourself.
      Try the wide world;
      abandon this solitude,
      which dries up the brain
      and stagnates the blood.

Stop playing with your grief

which, like a vulture, eats your life.
The worst society will let you feel
that you're a man among men.
And yet I don't mean that you should
be thrust among the stupid masses.
I'm not a high ranking devil, but if you'd like
to try your luck with me in a new life,
I'll gladly put myself at your disposal—
go where you will, do what you'd like to do,
be your companion—and if I suit you,
I'll be your servant and your slave.

    FAUST: What must I do for you in return?

    MEPHISTOPHELES: The debt can be handled on
      quite a long term.

    FAUST: No, no! The Devil is an egoist
and certainly not inclined to help
anyone for God's charity. State your conditions
    clearly;
a servant like you must be expensive.

    MEPHISTOPHELES: I'll bind myself to your service
      here
and do everything you ask of me;
Then when we meet over *yonder,* you shall do
as much for me as I've done for you.

    FAUST: What lies beyond doesn't worry me.
Suppose you break this world to bits, another may
    arise.
My joy springs from this earth,
this sun shines on my sorrows.
When I leave here, let come what must.
What do I care about it now, if hereafter
men hate or love, or if in those other spheres
there be an Above or a Below?

    MEPHISTOPHELES: In this mood you'll go far.
Commit yourself, and in the days to come
I'll use my arts for your pleasure.
I'll give you things that no man ever saw.

    FAUST: Poor devil, what have you to give?
Was ever the ambitious spirit of man
understood by one of your kind?
If you have food—it never satisfies;
you have red gold—that's fickle as mercury
and runs from the hands; a game—nobody wins;
a girl—right in my arms
she would make eyes at someone else;
suppose you give the godlike joy of honor—
it vanishes like a meteor!
Show me the fruit that rots before it's picked,
and trees that grow green again each day!

    MEPHISTOPHELES: I'm not afraid of such demands,
I can bring you such treasures without trouble.
But, my friend, the time will come
when we shall want to feast in peace.

    FAUST: If I ever rest on a lazy bed of ease,
then let me die at once. If you can beguile me
with blandishments, satisfy me with what I am,
or deceive me with pleasure,
let that be my last day. I'll bet on that!

    MEPHISTOPHELES: Taken!

    FAUST: Yes, taken and taken again!

If ever I say to any moment:
'Linger—you are so wonderful!'
Then you may throw me in chains.
I'll be ready for the earth.
Then let the death-bells toll, you'll be released.
The clock may stand still, the hands drop down,
and time come to an end, for all of me!

MEPHISTOPHELES: Consider this carefully. We'll
not forget it.

FAUST: Stand on your legal rights.
My action is not rash. I'll not regret it.
As soon as I stagnate, I become a slave.
So what does it matter whose I am?

MEPHISTOPHELES: I'll begin my service at once.
Tonight
at the faculty dinner. But one thing more:
to provide for contingencies,
give me a couple of lines.

FAUST: O you pedant, to want a written statement!
Did you never know a man who kept his word?
Isn't it enough that my spoken word
rules all my days until eternity?
Doesn't the world go raging in all its currents,
and would a promise bind me?

Yes, man has a fixation on this illusion;
and who would like to rid himself of it?
Happy is he who has the pure truth in him.
He will regret no sacrifice that keeps it.
But a parchment, signed and sealed, is a ghost
that everybody fears. The word dies on the pen,
and wax and leather remain our masters. Spirit of
evil,
what do you want of me: bronze, marble, vellum,
paper?
Shall I write with chisel, engraving tool, or goose-
quill?
I let you have your choice.

MEPHISTOPHELES: Come now! Don't get excited,
and oratorical!
A scrap of paper is enough for me,
and a little drop of blood to sign it.

FAUST: If this will satisfy you fully,
then let's carry out the farce.

MEPHISTOPHELES: Blood is a very special kind of
juice.

FAUST: Don't worry. I'll not break the bargain.
The goal of all my struggling's been just this
that I now promise. I aspired too high.
I'm merely on the level of the Devil.
The mighty spirit has scorned me;
nature has closed herself to me.
The thread of thought is broken;
and long ago all knowledge made me sick.
Let me put out my burning passion
in sloughs of lechery!
Let every wonder be made ready
that hides behind magic veils.
Let us throw ourselves into the rush of time,

into the swirls of chance, where pain and pleasure,
success and disappointment,
change and shift as luck goes:
restless activity's the only thing for man.

MEPHISTOPHELES: Neither moderation nor goal
is set for you.
You can sample and nibble at everything;
and snatch at things as you fly past.
And may you prosper in your pleasures,
but start at once and don't be timid!

FAUST: Listen! It's not a question of joy.
I vow myself to excitement, intoxication,
the bitterest pleasures, amorous hatred,
and stirring remorse. My heart, now free
of the longing for learning, shall close itself
to no future pain. I mean to enjoy
in my innermost being all that is offered to mankind,
to seize the highest and the lowest,
to mix all kinds of good and evil,
and thus expand my Self till it includes
the spirit of all men—and, with them,
I shall be ruined and perish in the end.

MEPHISTOPHELES: Listen to me, for I have chewed
this same tough food for many thousand years:
from cradle to coffin there's no man
who can digest this ancient sour dough.
You can believe me that this world was made
to suit a god who dwells in eternal light.
He has cast us devils into darkness;
for you it's enough to have only night and day.

FAUST: But I will!

MEPHISTOPHELES: A proper answer!
But I'm still troubled by one thing:
time is short and art is long.
I'd think you'd let yourself be instructed.
Associate yourself with a poet
and let him gallop through the fields of thought
and heap all noble qualities on your honored head:
the lion's courage, the stag's speed,
the fiery Italian blood,
the Northman's fortitude;
let him solve for you the secret that binds
cunning with magnanimity, and teaches you
how, with the instincts of youth's hot desires,
to fall in love according to a plan.
I'd like myself to met with such man,
and I'd name him Sir Microcosm.

FAUST: But what am I if I should fail to gain
the crown of mankind for which I struggle
with all my senses?

MEPHISTOPHELES: In the end, you are exactly—
what you are.
Put on a wig with a million curls,
put the highest heeled boots on your feet,
yet you remain in the end just what you are.

FAUST: I feel how every effort has been in vain
to encompass human wisdom in my head,
and when I sit down finally
no new strength comes to me,
and I'm not taller by a hair or any nearer to infinity.

MEPHISTOPHELES: My dear man, these things seem
  to you
just as they do to others.
We must manage more cleverly
before the joys of life escape us.
Damn it all! You must use hands and feet,
and head and sex to gain your ends!
And because I enjoy all these in play,
are they in any way less mine?
If I can hire six stallions,
is not all their power mine?
I dash away and act as big
as if I had two dozen legs.
Quick now, give up this idle pondering!
And let's be off into the great wide world!
I tell you: the fool who speculates on things
is like some animal on a dry heath,
led by an evil fiend in endless circles,
while fine green pastures lie on every side.
  FAUST: When do we start?
  MEPHISTOPHELES: As soon as we can.
This place is a torment.
What sort of life is it where a man
bores both himself and his students?
Leave that to your neighbor, Doctor Paunch!
Why should you slave to thresh out that old straw?
The best you know you can't show to the boys.
Right now I hear one at the door.
  FAUST: It's quite impossible for me to see him.
  MEPHISTOPHELES: The poor boy's waited so long
    already,
he mustn't go away uncomforted.
Come, give me your doctor's gown and hood.
This mask will suit me wonderfully. [*He changes his
    clothes*]
Go now and leave it to my wits!
A quarter-hour is all I'll need,
in which time go get ready for our trip!
    [Faust *goes out*]
  MEPHISTOPHELES: [*In the doctor's gown*] Scoff at
    all knowledge and despise
reason and science, those flowers of mankind.
Let the father of all lies
with dazzling necromancy make you blind,
then I'll have you unconditionally—
fate gave him a spirit that's ever pressing forward,
uncurbed; his rash impulses overleap
the joys of earth. I'll drag him through the wild life,
through the flat wasteland. I'll let him flounder,
stiffen, stick fast, and food and drink
shall bait his insatiate sense,
hovering before his greedy lips.
Vainly he'll beg me for refreshment,
and even if he hadn't given himself to the Devil,
he'd still be ruined in the end.
    [*A* Student *enters*]
  STUDENT: I've been here just a little while
and come, full of devotion,
to meet and know a man of whom
the world speaks with such reverence.

MEPHISTOPHELES: I'm flattered by your courtesy.
You see a man like any other.
Have you already been around elsewhere?
  STUDENT: Please, sir, assist me. I have come
with the best intentions, good health, and a little
  money.
My mother didn't like to have me leave her;
I want to learn something here that's practical.
  MEPHISTOPHELES: That's fine. You've come to the
    right place.
  STUDENT: But honestly I don't like it here at all
and would love to get away from these walls and
  halls
and these narrow gloomy lecture-rooms.
I feel so cramped: no grass, no trees—
and on a bench in the auditorium
I cannot think and I am deaf and dumb.
  MEPHISTOPHELES: That comes with practice; as a
    child at first
unwillingly receives the mother's breast,
but soon takes to the feeding eagerly;
so you, nursed on the breasts of wisdom,
will satisfy your thirst more gladly every day.
  STUDENT: I'll hang with joy about her neck!
But only tell me the best means to use.
  MEPHISTOPHELES: Before proceeding, you must
    tell me:
what subject will you chose?
  STUDENT: I want to be very learned and under-
    stand
the secrets of the earth and of the firmament—
the natural sciences, that is to say!
  MEPHISTOPHELES: You're starting out on the right
    paths,
but you mustn't let any distraction lead you astray.
  STUDENT: I'm set upon it, body and soul;
but I'd like some time to play
in freedom and not have to study
during the summer holidays!
  MEPHISTOPHELES: Use your time well. It glides
    away so swiftly, .
but system will teach you how to conserve it.
My friend, take logic. There your spirit's deftly
laced in the tight Spanish boot.[8]
Thereafter you'll proceed more circumspectly,
crawling down the road of reason, but never veer,
like a will o' the wisp, and criss-cross here and there.
Each day you'll learn that what required no thought
for its performance, as when you eat and drink,
must now be done in order—one, two, three!
And really in these thinking-mills
it's like a masterpiece worked on a weaver's loom:
one treadle moves like a thousand threads on spools;
the humming shuttles dart from side to side;
threads flow invisibly; one stroke
will tie a thousand knots—then the philosopher steps
  in
and shows you that it must be so:
the first was thus and the second so;
    [8] An instrument of torture.

therefore the third and fourth are likewise so;
but if it weren't for the first and second,
the third and fourth just never could have been.
Everywhere the scholars praise
this sort of thing, but never become weavers.
The man who wants to know
organic truth and describe it well
seeks first to drive the living spirit out;
he's got the parts in hand there,
it's merely the breath of life that's lacking.
The chemists call it *encheiresin naturae*[9]
and mock themselves and don't know how or why.

STUDENT: I don't quite understand you.

MEPHISTOPHELES: You'll get the hang of it by and by.
Everything will be simplified
after it's properly classified.

STUDENT: I'm all confused from what you've said,
as if a mill-wheel were turning in my brain.

MEPHISTOPHELES: Then, before studying any further,
you must try metaphysics; but take care
to grasp the deepest meanings and explore
what isn't suitable for human brains.
There's always a pompous word to serve
for what we may or may not understand.
See that throughout the first semester
you follow the routine most carefully.
When the chimes ring in the tower,
be at class punctually—don't miss a day.
Be well prepared for five long lectures;
study each paragraph so well
that you can check up on the teacher;
don't let him put in a syllable
that isn't in the book.
And busily write down his every word
as though the Holy Ghost were dictating to you!

STUDENT: That you won't have to tell me more than once!
I think that's very good advice.
What one gets down in black and white in notes
he can carry home to comfort him at night.

MEPHISTOPHELES: Now you must choose your major subject.

STUDENT: The study of law does not seem too attractive.

MEPHISTOPHELES: I can't hold that against you, I admit,
for I know well just how that matter stands.
The statutes and the laws are handed on
like some disease that never ends,
stealthily creeping from race to race.
Reason turns nonsense; beneficence becomes a plague.
It's too bad that you're a grandchild, my lad.
But of natural rights, unfortunately,
there's never any question.

STUDENT: You have increased my own aversion for the law.
The students you teach are lucky indeed.

[9] Nature's procedure.

Maybe I'd like to study theology.

MEPHISTOPHELES: I wouldn't want to be leading you astray,
but in the subject matter of this field
it's difficult to keep on the right track;
there's so much poison hidden here
it's hard to tell it from the medicine.
You'll find it's best to have just one professor
and swear by the master's words. In general,
stick fast to words, and through that trusty gateway
you'll get into the temple of assurance.

STUDENT: But there ought to be some idea behind a word.

MEPHISTOPHELES: Of course! But don't torment yourself too much.
Just where the idea's lacking a word pops up.
Words are splendid weapons for fighting;
with words you can prepare a system;
words are grand to put your faith in—
and you can't take anything from one.

STUDENT: Excuse me if I ask too many questions;
but won't you please make some suggestions for the study
of medicine? Three years go by so quickly
and, God, the field's so wide!
If only I could get a pointer
then I could grope my way ahead.

MEPHISTOPHELES: [Aside] I'm bored with this dry tone
and now I'll really play the Devil again.

[Aloud] The spirit of medicine is easily comprehended;
you study through the macrocosm and microcosm,
but in the end let it all go, as pleases God.
In vain you rummage learnedly far and wide;
each one learns only what he can;
but he who seizes the instant boldly,
he is the clever one!
Now you, you're pretty well built
and will not be lacking in daring.
As long as you thoroughly trust yourself,
all the simple souls will have confidence in you.
Above all, learn how to manage the women:
all their eternal Ah's and Oh's
of a thousand sorts
can be cured at a single point.
And if you act discreetly,
you'll keep them all under your thumb.
First, your M. D. will give them confidence
that your skill and learning are immense.
Right at the start you can fumble them here and there,
when another man would have to coax for years.
Learn how to press the pulse in the little wrist
and with fiery furtive glances slip
your arm around her slender hips
to see how tightly she is laced.

STUDENT: Already it seems better!
Now I begin to see the where and how.

MEPHISTOPHELES: My friend, all theory is gray,
and the golden tree of life is green.
STUDENT: I swear to you it's like a dream.
May I return another time and trouble you
to expound your system to the bottom?
MEPHISTOPHELES: I'll do all that I can for you and
    more.
STUDENT: I cannot possibly leave
until I get your autograph.
I wonder if you'd be so kind.
MEPHISTOPHELES: With pleasure. [*He writes in
    the book and returns it*]
STUDENT: [*Reading*] Eritis sicut Deus, scientes
    bonum et malum[10]
[*He closes the book reverently and goes out*]
MEPHISTOPHELES: Just follow the old proverb and
    my cousin the snake;
and in spite of your likeness to God,
your soul will soon be quaking!
    [Faust *comes in*]
FAUST: Where do we go from here?
MEPHISTOPHELES: Wherever you please. First we
    can see
the world of little people, then the great.
With pleasure and profit
you can crib through the course.
FAUST: But admit that it's pretty hard to be
a man of the world, with a beard as long as mine.
I lack the *savoir vivre*. I won't succeed.
I never did know how to get around;
indeed, I feel so small before most other men,
that often I could sink into the dirt.
MEPHISTOPHELES: Time will take care of that, my
    friend.
Gain some self-confidence and you'll know how to
    live.
FAUST: But how shall we get away from here?
Where have you a coach, driver and horses?
MEPHISTOPHELES: We only need to spread this
    cloak
and it will carry us through the sky.
Of course, upon this daring journey
your baggage must be very light.
A puff of hydrogen which I'll prepare
will hoist us quickly to the upper regions.
Congratulations on your new career!

AUERBACH'S CELLAR IN LEIPSIC

[*A lively drinking party is in progress*]
FROSCH: Will no one drink? Nobody laugh?
I'll teach you how to make faces!
Today you're all like soggy straw,
but usually you're all ablaze.
BRANDER: And you're to blame; you've given us
neither nonsense or bawdiness.
FROSCH: [*Pouring a glass of wine over his head*]
    There now! You've both.

10 You shall be as God, knowing good and evil.

BRANDER: You double-swine!
FROSCH: You asked for it! And there it is!
SIEBEL: Throw all brawlers out of doors!
Swill and shout and sing the chorus!
Hurray, hurrah, and heidy ho!
ALTMAYER: Damn you, shut up! Bring me some
    cotton.
He's broken my ear-drum.
SIEBEL: When the ceiling echoes back the song,
then you can feel that rolling bass.
FROSCH: That's right! Put out the man who doesn't
    like it!
Oh! tara lara lay!
ALTMAYER: Oh! tara lara lay!
FROSCH: That's the right tune. Let's go.
    [*He sings*]
        The darling Roman Empire, oh,
        what holds the thing together?
BRANDER: That's a nasty song! To hell with politics!
No more of that. And thank God every day
that you weren't born to rule
the Roman Empire. You can bet I'm glad
I'm not the Kaiser or his chancellor!
But we must have a chief, so let's elect a Pope.
You know the one essential quality
that turns the scale and raises up a man.
FROSCH: [*Singing*] Soar to the sky, O nightingale,
    and greet my love ten thousand times!
SIEBEL: No songs to girls! I can't stand that.
FROSCH: Just try to stop me! Greetings and kisses
    to my girl!
    [*He sings*]
        Unbolt the door in the quiet night.
        Unbolt the door. My love sleeps light.
        But now it's dawn so bolt it tight!
SIEBEL: Yes, sing! Go on and brag of her!
I'll have my turn for laughter soon.
She led me on—I followed, but
she'll do the same to you. She needs a goblin
to play with her at a dark cross-road.
An old he-goat galloping from the Brocken[11]
may bleat Good Night to her! A flesh and blood
lover is far too good for that little bitch.
The only greeting she'll get from me
is when I bash in her window.
BRANDER: [*Pounding on the table*] Quiet, all you,
    and listen to me.
Admit I know what's what. We've got
some lovesick fellows sitting here.
And I must give them something cheerful
to make them feel a little better.
So here's a brand new song. Now open up
and bear down on the choruses.
    [*He sings*]
        In a nest in the cellar lived a rat
        that fed on butter, grease, and lard
        till she achieved a paunch as fat

11 The mountain to which witches ride on the backs of
devils on Walpurgis Night, the eve of May Day. The
devils take the form of rams, he-goats, and other animals.

as Doctor Luther's, round and hard.
The cook smeared poison out one night—
and the rat's world soon grew small and tight,
as though she had love in her belly.

CHORUS: [*Shouting*] As though she had love in her belly!

BRANDER: The rat raced here, the rat raced there,
she lapped up puddle-water,
tore up the whole house, everywhere,
but nothing made her better.
She hopped and leaped in agony
as though she had love in her belly!

CHORUS: As though she had love in her belly!

BRANDER: Driven by torment to the light,
she ran about the kitchen,
fell on the hearth and gasped and lay,
most piteously twitching.
Then laughed the poisoner: Bless my soul!
she's whistling now on the final hole—
as though she had love in her belly!

CHORUS: As though she had love in her belly!

SIEBEL: How these dull birds amuse themselves!
It strikes me it's a mighty art
to sprinkle poison for the poor old rats!

BRANDER: So you like them, do you?

ALTMAYER: Misfortune has turned tame and mild
this old pot-gut with the shiny skull.
He looks at the bloated rat and sees
his portrait, lifelike as could be.

[*Faust and* Mephistopheles *come in*]

MEPHISTOPHELES: First now I must introduce you
to some lively fellows who'll amuse you.
Here you can see how pleasant life can be
when every day's a holiday.
With slender wit and plenty of leisure
each man dances his little round,
like kittens chasing their tails for pleasure.
And while no hang-overs spoil their fun,
and the host lets the little bills run on,
they are happy and free from worry.

BRANDER: These gentlemen are traveling.
You can see that from their foreign air;
they've not been here in town an hour.

FROSCH: You're right. But my Leipsic's the place
for me!
It's a little Paris and gives its people refinement.

SIEBEL: Who do you guess these strangers are?

FROSCH: Just let me at them! Over a full glass
I'll pull the worms of fact
from the fellow's nose like a baby's tooth.
They appear to me to be noblemen,
they look so proud and discontented.

BRANDER: They're phonies, I'll bet you.

ALTMAYER: Maybe so.

FROSCH: Watch me. I'll screw their secret out.

MEPHISTOPHELES: [*To* Faust] These little sods
here wouldn't suspect
the Devil if he had them by the neck!

FAUST: Good evening, gentlemen!

SIEBEL: And we return the compliment with thanks.

[*Softly, as he looks at* Mephistopheles *from the side*]
Why does the rascal limp with his left foot?

MEPHISTOPHELES: May we sit here? Instead of a
decent drink,
which can't be had, we'll have good company.

ALTMAYER: You're spoiled, or used to the best, I
guess.

FROSCH: Have you just come from Rippach?
Did you dine with Master Hans[12] tonight?

MEPHISTOPHELES: Today we went by without stopping,
but the last time we spoke to him
he talked a lot about his relatives
and gave us many greetings to bring you! [*He bows
to* Frosch]

ALTMAYER: [*Softly*] There now! He understands
what you're up to!

SIEBEL: A clever customer!

FROSCH: Just wait a minute. I'll get him soon.

MEPHISTOPHELES: Unless I'm wrong, I heard just
now
some well-trained voices singing a chorus.
The arches here must make fine echoes.

FROSCH: Perhaps you're a virtuoso.

MEPHISTOPHELES: I'd like to sing but I haven't the
voice.

ALTMAYER: Give us a song.

MEPHISTOPHELES: All you want of them.

SIEBEL: But let it be new as a nail!

MEPHISTOPHELES: We've recently returned from
Spain,
that lovely country of song and wine.
[*He sings*]
    Once on a time a monarch
    had a flea, a giant one . . .

FROSCH: Hear that! You understand? A flea!
A neat little customer, not for me!

MEPHISTOPHELES: [*Singing*] Once on a time a
monarch
    had a flea, a giant one,
    which he loved no less fondly
    than if it were his son.
    He called the royal tailor,
    the tailor to him came.
    "Measure Milord for a coat
    and breeches to match the same!"

BRANDER: Don't forget to tell the tailor
he must really measure carefully;
if he wants to keep his head
those trousers will have to be a good fit!

MEPHISTOPHELES: [*Singing*] Soon in silk and
velvet
    the flea was grandly dressed;
    he had ribbons on his clothing
    and a cross upon his chest.
    He became a high official
    and wore a gorgeous star.

[12] Hans Arsch, the fictitious hero of a student's joke,
which is not too delicate.

He found jobs for his relations
at court, and they went far.

Of course, the lords and ladies
were exceedingly provoked.
The queen and her maid-in-waiting
were pinched and plagued and poked;
but didn't dare to crack them
or scratch them off at night.
But we can smother and crunch them
as soon as they start to bite.

CHORUS: [*Shouting*] We can smother and crunch
them
as soon as they start to bite!

FROSCH: Bravo! bravo! That was fine.

SIEBEL: The same to every flea!

BRANDER: Squash them with your finger-tips.

ALTMAYER: Hurray for wine and liberty!

MEPHISTOPHELES: I'd like to drink to freedom myself,
if your wine were only a little bit better.

SIEBEL: You'd better not let us hear that again!

MEPHISTOPHELES: If the landlord wouldn't be
offended,
I'd like to stand you, as my guests,
a round of the best drinks from *our* cellar.

SIEBEL: Just bring them on. I'll take the blame.

FROSCH: Give us a good drink, and we'll praise
you.
But see that it's not too small.
For if you want my judgment,
I must have a real mouthful.

ALTMAYER: [*Aside*] I've smelled it out. They're
from the Rhine.

MEPHISTOPHELES: Bring me an auger.

BRANDER: What will you do with that?
Have you got some kegs outside the door?

ALTMAYER: [*Aside*] The landlord's tool-box is back
there.

MEPHISTOPHELES: [*Taking the auger, to* Frosch]
Tell me, what's your favorite wine?

FROSCH: What do you mean? Have you several
kinds?

MEPHISTOPHELES: I'll give each of you what he
likes best.

ALTMAYER: [*To* Frosch] Ah ha! already you're
smacking your lips.

FROSCH: Good. If I can choose, I'll take Rhine
wine,
the best gift of our fatherland.

MEPHISTOPHELES: [*As he bores a hole in the
table's edge at* Frosch's *place*] Get wax and
make some stoppers at once.

ALTMAYER: Ridiculous! This is some sleight of
hand.

MEPHISTOPHELES: [*To* Brander] And you?

BRANDER: I'd like champagne, and with plenty of
sparkle!

[*Mephistopheles bores. Meanwhile stoppers are
made and the holes plugged*]

BRANDER: You can't steer clear of everything that's
foreign.
Often the best things come from far away.
A German hates the French with all his heart
and yet he gladly drinks their wine.

SIEBEL: [*As* Mephistopheles *approaches his place*]
I must admit, I don't like sour.
Give me a glass of something really sweet.

MEPHISTOPHELES: [*As he bores*] Just wait a minute, and Tokay will pour.

ALTMAYER: No, gentlemen! Look me in the eye!
You're pulling our legs.

MEPHISTOPHELES: No, no, with noble guests like
you
that would be going too far.
But speak up quickly!
What kind of wine do you want?

ALTMAYER: Anything. Only, hurry with it.

MEPHISTOPHELES: [*After the holes have been
bored and plugged, with strange gestures*] Clustered grapes the vine has borne,
and the billy goat wears horns.
The stalks are food, the sap is new,
the wooden table can give wine too.
Gaze deeply in nature and believe!
Here is a miracle achieved!

Pull corks and fill your glasses to the top!
[*As each draws a stopper, the wine asked for
flows into his glass*]

ALL: Beautiful fountain, may it never stop flowing!

MEPHISTOPHELES: Be careful not to spill a drop!
[*They drink freely*]

ALL: [*Singing*] We're all as gay as cannibals,
or as five hundred sows!

MEPHISTOPHELES: See how they lap it and like it!
They're doing fine.

FAUST: I'd like to go now.

MEPHISTOPHELES: First you must see
their splendid bestiality.
[Siebel, *drinking carelessly, spills some wine on
the floor. It bursts into flames*]

SIEBEL: Help! Fire! Help! Hell's burning!

MEPHISTOPHELES: [*As he charms the flame*] Be
quiet, friendly element!
[*To* Siebel] This time is was just a drop of purga-
torial fire.

SIEBEL: What's this? Just wait! We'll pay you back!
It seems you don't know who we are.

FROSCH: Just think again before you try it a second
time!

ALTMAYER: We'd better pack him off on the quiet!

SIEBEL: What, sir? Do you dare insult us
with this outrageous hocus-pocus?

MEPHISTOPHELES: Shut up, you old wine-keg!

SIEBEL: You broom-stick, you!
You dare insult us!

BRANDER: Just wait! Blows will fall here, black and
blue!

[Altmayer *draws a cork from the table and flames leap forth*]

ALTMAYER: I'm burning! I'm burning!

SIEBEL: It's sorcery!

Hit him! He's anybody's game!

[*They draw knives and attack* Mephistopheles]

MEPHISTOPHELES: [*With solemn gestures*] False images and words,
    ensnare their senses and change the scene.
    Be here . . . be there!

[*They stand amazed and look at one another*]

ALTMAYER: Where am I? What a lovely land!

FROSCH: Vineyards! Am I seeing things?

SIEBEL: And these beautiful bunches of grapes!

BRANDER: Look at these vine branches

under the spreading leaves!

[*He seizes* Siebel *by the nose. The others, with raised knives, do the same*]

MEPHISTOPHELES:[*With more gestures*] Illusion take the veils from their eyes!
    And you, see how the Devil plays a trick!

[*He vanishes with* Faust. *The drinkers come to their senses, startled*]

SIEBEL: What happened?

ALTMAYER: How did we get this way?

FROSCH: Was that your nose?

BRANDER: [*To* Siebel] And I have hold of yours!

ALTMAYER: Somebody knocked me out.

Get me a chair. I'm going to faint.

FROSCH: Can anybody tell me just what happened?

SIEBEL: Where has he gone? When I find him,

he'll not get off alive.

ALTMAYER: I saw him riding a cask through the tavern door,

but my feet stuck to the floor, heavy as lead.

[*Turning to the table*] I wonder if the wine still flows.

SIEBEL: It was all fake and deception.

FROSCH: I thought I was drinking wine.

BRANDER: And weren't those real grapes either?

ALTMAYER: Can you believe in miracles? Who knows?

THE WITCH'S KITCHEN

[*A big cauldron hangs over a fire on a low hearth. In the rising vapor various forms appear. A* She-Ape *is skimming the broth. The* He-ape *and their* Young Ones *are sitting nearby. The walls and ceiling are covered with fantastic witches' apparatus.* Faust *and* Mephistopheles *come in*]

FAUST: This crazy sorcery disgusts me. Promise me

I'll recover in this chaos of madness.

Must I ask help from this old hag?

And can this messy cookery take thirty years

from my body? Too bad you know nothing better!

I've neither heart nor hope for this.

Have nature and some noble mind

been able to find no other formula?

MEPHISTOPHELES: My friend, you're talking sense again.

There is a natural method for recapturing youth;

but that's in another book, in a curious chapter.

FAUST: I want to know it.

MEPHISTOPHELES: Good! The remedy requires no money,

physician nor magic. Just go out in the field

and begin to dig and plough.

Keep your whole life within a little circle,

eat simple food, live with the beasts as a beast,

don't be too proud to dung the field you reap.

That's the best method, believe me,

to keep yourself young at eighty.

FAUST: But I'm not used to that sort of thing.

I can't even dig with a spade.

The narrow life doesn't suit me.

MEPHISTOPHELES: Then you must try the witch.

FAUST: Will no one do but this old hag?

Can't you yourself work up a brew?

MEPHISTOPHELES: Now, wouldn't that be a pretty pastime!

In the same time I could build a thousand bridges.

It isn't science or art alone;

it takes lots of patience to do this work.

A quiet spirit keeps busy with it for years;

for only time produces the fermentation.

And everything about it is a wonderful business!

The Devil taught her how to brew it,

yet the Devil alone isn't able to make it.

[*He sees the animals*] Look! What an ornamental pair!

That's the slavey. And there's the house-boy.

[*To the* Apes] The old lady isn't at home, it seems?

THE APES: She's at a party!

She flew up the chimney!

Out of the house.

MEPHISTOPHELES: How long is she usually off on a revel?

THE APES: As long as it takes us to warm our paws.

MEPHISTOPHELES: [*To* Faust] What do you think of these dainty creatures?

FAUST: I never saw anything so absurd!

MEPHISTOPHELES: No—a little discourse with such beasts

can prove amusing indeed.

[*To the* Apes] Now tell me, you damned puppets,

what are you stirring there in the porridge pot?

THE APES: We're cooking some waterish beggars' soup.

MEPHISTOPHELES: You'll have plenty of customers for that.

HE-APE: [*Making up to* Mephistopheles] Oh, roll the dice
    that can make me rich,
    and let me win!
    My luck's so bad,
    but if I had money
    then I'd have brains.

MEPHISTOPHELES: This monkey here would love to bet
in any kind of lottery.

[*The* Young Apes *have been playing with a big globe, which they now roll forward*]

HE-APE: This is the world.
    It rises and falls
    and continually whirls.
    It rings like glass—
    how soon it breaks!
    It's hollow inside.
    Here it shines bright,
    and here even more.
    Now me, I'm lively!
    But, my dear son,
    you keep away—
    you too must die!
    It's made of clay
    and will crumble to bits.

MEPHISTOPHELES: What good's that sieve?

HE-APE: [*Taking it down*] If you were a thief,
    I could tell it at once.

[*He runs to the* She-Ape *and lets her look through it*]
    Look through the sieve.
    Do you recognize The Thief
    but dare not name him?

MEPHISTOPHELES: [*Going toward the fire*] And what's this pot?

THE APES: The silly idiot
    doesn't know the pot!
    He doesn't know the kettle!

MEPHISTOPHELES: You ill-bred brute!

HE-APE: Take the whisk-broom to it
    and settle down on the settle!

[*He makes* Mephistopheles *sit down*]

FAUST: [*Who has been looking in a mirror, now approaching, then drawing back from it*]
What do I see? What a heavenly picture
shows itself in this magic mirror!
O love, lend me your swiftest wings
and lead me straight to her.
But alas, when I move forward from this spot
and try to approach, she fades away in mist,
this lovely image of a woman.
Is it possible that she can be so beautiful?
Do I not see in this reclining body
the very essence of heaven?
"Earth has not anything more fair."

MEPHISTOPHELES: Why, naturally, if God worked
    six whole days
and shouted Bravo! at the finish,
he must have done something pretty impressive.
For the present gaze your fill. I know
exactly where to spy out just such a treasure.
And happy the man whose luck it is
to lead her home as his bride.

[Faust *continues to look at the mirror.* Mephistopheles *is stretched on the bench and plays with the broom*]

I sit here like a king on his throne.
Here is my sceptre, but where's the crown?

[*The* Apes, *who have been playing pranks, bring him a crown and shriek*]

THE APES: Just be so good,
    as with sweat and blood
    to glue this crown together!

[*They fight for the crown. It breaks and they dance with the pieces*]
    Now it's done for and broke,
    we talk and we look,
    we listen and make verses.

FAUST: [*Before the mirror*] God, I'm almost crazy!

MEPHISTOPHELES: [*Pointing to the* Apes] It makes even me a little bit dizzy.

THE APES: If the rhyme goes well
    and fits, who can tell
    but there may be some thought in it?

FAUST: My heart begins to burn.
Quick! Let's get away from here.

MEPHISTOPHELES: Well, at least it's good to learn
some poets are sincere.

[*The kettle, neglected by the* She-Ape, *boils over. A great flame leaps up, and the* Witch *comes down the chimney, shrieking*]

THE WITCH: Aouw! Aouw!
You damned beast! You sow!
You've forgotten the kettle and burned me!
Damned beast!

[*She sees the visitors*]
    What is this here?
    Who are you?
    What do you want?
    How did you sneak in?
    Let the torture of fire
    burn your bones!

[*She dips the ladle in the pot and throws flames at everyone. The* Apes *whimper*]

MEPHISTOPHELES: [*Turning the brush end for end and smashing the glassware and pots*] Be broken in two!
    I'll spatter your stew!
    The glass is broken,
    but it's all a joke.
    You carcass, it's only the time
    and beat of your rhyme!

[*As the* Witch *steps back in anger and horror*]
Don't you know me, skeleton, scarecrow?
Don't you recognize your lord and master?
Why don't I give you a beating,
and crush you and your ape-spirits?
Have you no longer any respect for the scarlet jacket?
Did you never see the cock's feather before?
Is this face disguised? Must I tell you my name?

THE WITCH: Master, pardon my raw greeting!
But I don't see the horse's hoof.
And where are your two ravens?

MEPHISTOPHELES: This time you can get away with it.

It's been a long while, I'll admit,
since we have seen each other.
And then, since culture has taken a lick at the
    world,
the Devil's also been touched up a bit.
The phantom of the North is seen no longer.
Can you detect any horns or tail or claws?
And as for the hoof, which I can't quite spare,
it would prejudice people against me;
therefore, I do as many a buck has done
and have worn false calves for many years.

    THE WITCH: [Dancing] I almost go out of my
        head
when I see Squire Satan here again!

    MEPHISTOPHELES: I forbid you, woman, to call me
        by that name!

    THE WITCH: Why so? Has it done you any harm?

    MEPHISTOPHELES: It's long been buried in the
        book of fabies,
but men have grown no better:
They're free of the Evil One, but the evil ones re-
    main.
Just call me Baron; that's all right.
I'm merely a cavalier like any other.
If you've any doubt about my noble blood,
just look at the splendid coat-of-arms I bear! [He
    makes an indecent gesture]

    THE WITCH: [Laughing immoderately] Ha! ha!
        That's your old self:
the same old rascal you always were!

    MEPHISTOPHELES: [To Faust] My friend, learn
        this:
the way to handle witches.

    THE WITCH: Now tell me, gentlemen, how can I
        oblige you?

    MEPHISTOPHELES: A good glass of your famous
        liquor.
The very oldest, if you please!
For age puts double strength in it.

    THE WITCH: Gladly! I've got here a bottle
from which I sometimes tipple myself.
It's lost at last all trace of stink.
I'll give you a little glass of it with pleasure.
    [Softly, to Mephistopheles] But if this man drinks
      it unprepared,
he will not live an hour, as you know.

    MEPHISTOPHELES: He's a good friend and will
        thrive on it.
I don't begrudge him your kitchen's best.
Draw your circle and speak your spells,
and let him have a good full cup.

    [With fantastic gestures the Witch makes a cir-
    cle and puts curious things in it. Meanwhile the
    glasses ring and the kettle makes music. Finally
    she brings a large book and arranges the Apes
    to serve as a lectern and hold torches. She
    beckons Faust to approach]

    FAUST: [To Mephistopheles] What's all this crazy
        apparatus?
I've seen this frantic nonsense and trickery before

and have always despised them.

    MEPHISTOPHELES: It's a sort of mummery. She's
        only joking.
Don't be so particular.
She's like a doctor with her hocus-pocus
that makes the potion work the miracle. [He gets
        Faust into the circle]

    THE WITCH: [With great emphasis, declaiming
      from the book] Watch me and then
        from one get ten,
        drop two, then three,
        make it even, see!
        Now you are rich.
        Then drop the four.
        From five and six,
        so says the witch,
        make seven and eight.
        Then all's complete.
        And nine is one,
        and ten is none.
    That is the witch's multiplication-table!

    FAUST: The old girl is raving in a delirium.

    MEPHISTOPHELES: There's a lot more yet where
        that came from.
I know it well; the whole book sounds the same.
And I have lost much time on it, because
the perfect contradiction remains
as much a mystery to the wise as to the fools.
My friend, the art is old and new.
It's been the custom in all ages
through three and one, and one and three,
to hide the truth and propagandize error.
Untroubled, they chatter and teach it in the schools—
and why concern yourself with idiots?
When he hears words man's likely to believe
that they convey ideas and have meaning.

    THE WITCH: [Continuing] The exalted skill
      of science still
      from the world is well-concealed.
      Who doesn't think
      gets in a wink
      the whole affair revealed.

    FAUST: What craziness is that she is drooling?
My head is almost splitting.
I seem to hear a hundred thousand fools
speaking in one vast chorus.

    MEPHISTOPHELES: Enough, O excellent sibyl!
Give us the panacea
and fill the cup to the rim.
This little drink won't hurt my friend:
he's taken many honorary degrees
and plenty of good gulps with them.

    [With much ceremony, the Witch pours the
    elixir. As Faust raises the cup to his lips, a
    little flame rises]

    MEPHISTOPHELES: Bottoms up! Quickly! It will do
your heart a lot of good. For shame!
You're the Devil's intimate friend,
yet you're afraid of a little fire?

    [The Witch breaks the ring. Faust comes out]

MEPHISTOPHELES: Now, hurry! You should not rest.

THE WITCH: May this little swallow do you good!

MEPHISTOPHELES: [*To the* Witch] If I can do a favor for you,
you need only mention it on Walpurgis Night.

THE WITCH: Here's a song! Whenever you sing it,
you'll get a remarkable reaction.

MEPHISTOPHELES: [*To* Faust] Hurry! And let me guide you. You must sweat
to make its power work through your whole body.
And then I'll teach you how to pass
your time in noble idleness.
Soon you'll feel, with pleasant surprise
how Cupid stirs in you and sets things going.

FAUST: Just one more glimpse in that looking-glass!
That woman's image was magnificent!

MEPHISTOPHELES: No, no! Soon you'll see the very model
of beauty in solid human flesh.
[*Aside*] With that drink in your belly,
you'll think you're seeing Helen of Troy
in every woman you meet.

A STREET

[Faust *sees* Margaret[13] *going by*]

FAUST: Beautiful lady, I wonder if I may
offer my arm to escort you anywhere?

MARGARET: I'm neither a lady, nor am I pretty,
and I know my own way home. [*She goes out*]

FAUST: By heaven! that's a lovely child!
I've never seen one like that before.
Modest and virtuous, unspoiled,
and yet with some snap in her too.
Her lips were red, her cheeks were bright—
Will I ever forget
how my heart jumped, how she dropped her eyes?
Even her curtness filled me with ecstasy.

[Mephistopheles *enters*]

FAUST: Listen! You must get that girl for me!

MEPHISTOPHELES: Which one?

FAUST: The one that just went by.

MEPHISTOPHELES: Oh, that one! She was just coming from the priest,
and he absolved her of every sin.
I sneaked up close behind the box;
she's the most innocent little thing,
with less than nothing to confess.
I have no power over her.

FAUST: Yet she must be fourteen or more.

MEPHISTOPHELES: You talk like any libertine
who wants each tender flower, and imagines
she has nothing that can't be picked;
but it doesn't always turn out like that.

FAUST: Come off your perch. Don't preach again
to me of morals. I tell you, short and plain:

13 Goethe also calls her Gretchen in some of the later scenes.

unless that girl with her fresh young blood
sleeps in my arms tonight, our contract's void.

MEPHISTOPHELES: Hold on now. Think what may and might happen.
Allow me at least a fortnight
to feel around for an opportunity.

FAUST: If I had seven hours, I'd have no need
for the Devil's help. I could seduce
the little creature by myself.

MEPHISTOPHELES: You talk like any French roué.
Buck up. Don't be downhearted.
Why do you want to enjoy her right away?
The pleasure isn't half so great
as if, with various softening tricks,
you slowly mold her and get her ready,
just as they do in Italian stories.

FAUST: I've appetite enough without all that.

MEPHISTOPHELES: Yet, without jesting or joking
I tell you that this young beauty
can't be had so easily.
It depends less on passion than on cunning.

FAUST: Get me something that belongs to that angel.
Lead me to her room, or bring me the kerchief
from her breast, or her garter for my love's delight!

MEPHISTOPHELES: So that you'll see how willingly
I work to remedy your pain and gloom,
I'l take you, without losing an instant,
right into her bedroom itself.

FAUST: And I'll see her? I'll have her?

MEPHISTOPHELES: No! She'll be visiting a neighbor.
But you can pasture your hope on the perfume
and dream of future joys, alone in her room.

FAUST: Can't we go now?

MEPHISTOPHELES: It's still too early.

FAUST: Get me a little present for her.
[Faust *goes out*]

MEPHISTOPHELES: What! Gifts so soon? That's gallant.
Oh, you'll surely get her.
I know of several caches of ancient treasure.
But I'll have to reconnoitre them a bit. [*He goes out*]

EVENING. A NEAT LITTLE ROOM

[Margaret *is braiding and putting up her hair*]

MARGARET: I'd give a penny if I knew
who that was I saw today.
He looked so gallant, like a nobleman.
That was plain from his manner,
and explains his being so forward.

[*She goes out.* Faust *and* Mephistopheles *enter*]

MEPHISTOPHELES: Come in! But quietly. Come in!

FAUST: [*After a silence*] Leave me here alone, I beg you.

MEPHISTOPHELES: [*Snooping around*] Not every girl keeps things so tidy. [*He goes out*]

FAUST: [*Looking around*] Welcome, sweet twilight glow
that permeates this blessed place.
Seize my heart, sweet pains of love that live
in yearning on the dews of hope.
Around me breathes the feeling
of calmness, order and contentment.
In this poverty what plenty;
in this narrow cell what happiness!
[*He sit down in the arm chair by the bed*]
In times long past this chair with open arms
received all joy and sorrow!
How often children must have played
around this father-throne!
Perhaps here my darling,
grateful for some Christmas gift,
piously kissed grandfather's wrinkled hand
with her full childish lips.
I feel the spirit of order and fulness
instructing her daily, like a mother,
to lay the table cloth and spread it smoothly,
to strew the sand in patterns on the floor.
Her darling hands have turned this cottage
into a paradise. And here—
[*He raises the bed-curtain*]
What makes me tremble so?
Here I could linger many an hour.
Here nature lightly created in dreams
this little native angel.
Here lay the child, with warm life
filling her tender body,
and here by pure and holy molding
the image of a goddess was created.

And you! What brings you here?
How deeply I am stirred.
What do you want? Why is your heart so heavy?
Unhappy Faust, I no longer understand you.

Is this enchantment's fragrance that surrounds me?
I was driven by lust for immediate pleasure,
yet now I am softly dissolved in a dream of love!
Are we playthings for every gust of wind?

And if she came in right now,
how you'd do penance for this sacrilege!
How the bragging Jack would grow small
and lie melting, at her feet!

MEPHISTOPHELES: [*Entering*] Quickly! I see her
coming below.
FAUST: Away from this! I'll never return.
MEPHISTOPHELES: Here's a fairly heavy box of
jewels
that I got in a certain place.
Just put it in the chest at once.
I swear to you, she'll lose her mind over it.
I put enough little trinkets in it for you
to win any woman. And certainly
a girl's a girl and fun is always fun!
FAUST: I don't know. Should I?
MEPHISTOPHELES: Why do you hesitate?

Or maybe you'd like to keep the things yourself.
Then I advise your lustfulness to waste
no more of this sweet daylight and my trouble.
I hope you're not a miser.
I scratch my head, I rub my hands—
[*He puts the box in the chest and locks it*]
Come on. Hurry! All this to turn
the sweet young ninny's fancy to you—
yet you look as though you had to go
to the lecture room where, gray and incarnate,
Physics and Metaphysics had come to life before you.
Come on!
[*They go out.* Margaret *enters with a lamp*]
MARGARET: It's so close and stuffy here,
[*She opens a window*] yet outside it's not so warm.
I feel so—I don't know how—
but I wish mother would come home.
Now I'm trembling all over—
I'm just a fearful silly woman.
[*While she undresses she sings*]
There was a king in Thule,
faithful to the grave,
to whom his dying sweetheart
a golden goblet gave.

There was nothing he liked better,
he drained it at every feast;
he wept while he was drinking,
but he held the goblet fast.

When he felt death nearing,
he tallied his towns and lands,
consigned them to his successor,
but he kept the cup in his hands.

He sat at the royal banquet,
and his knights sat, knee to knee,
in the tall ancestral chamber
in the castle there by the sea.

Drinking his life's passion,
the aged drunkard stood,
and he hurled the holy goblet
down into the flood.

He watched it plunging and drinking
till the water brimmed the top.
His eyelids closed and he never
drank another drop.
[*She opens the chest and sees the jewel box*]
How did this pretty box get here?
I certainly locked the chest.
It's very strange. What can be in it?
Maybe someone left it as a pledge
and mother made a loan on it.
Here's a little key on a ribbon.
I think I'll open it.
What's this! O God in heaven! Look!
I've never seen such things in all my life:
jewels a noble lady might wear on a high feast day.
I wonder how this chain would look on me?
And whose can they be?

[*She puts on the chain and looks in the glass*]
If only these ear-rings were mine!
I look entirely different with them on.
What good are beauty and young blood?
It's fine if you can have them, but just the same
people let you alone or praise you in half-pity.
Everyone strives for gold,
everyone clings to gold.
Alas, we poor folk!

A STREET

[Faust *is walking back and forth in meditation*]
MEPHISTOPHELES: [*Entering*] By all rejected love!
    By the fires of hell!
I wish I knew something worse to swear by!
    FAUST: What's the matter? What's pinching you?
I never saw such a face in all my life.
    MEPHISTOPHELES: I'd like to give myself to the
        Devil,
if I weren't the Devil myself!
    FAUST: Have you gone crazy?
It certainly suits you to rave like a maniac!
    MEPHISTOPHELES: Imagine this! A priest has car-
        ried off
the jewels I brought to Margaret. Listen!
The mother saw them and got scared at once.
The woman has a nose!
She's always sniffling her prayer-book,
whiffing at everything till she's sure
whether its pure or naughty;
and she knew very well when she smelled the gems
that very little holiness clung to them.
'My child,' says she, 'ill-gotten goods
snare the soul and suck out the blood.
We'll give them to God's mother,
and she'll shower down manna on us.'
Little Maggie made a wry face
and thought: 'A gift horse is all right;
there can be no great impiety
in whoever it was who brought these things.'
But mother called a priest. He came,
saw how things lay, and circumspectly said:
'You've reasoned as you should.
He wins the most who learns to tame his greed.
The Church has a strong stomach,
she has gobbled many lands and realms,
yet never suffered surfeit from it,
or greasy qualms. My daughters, for illegal goods
I recommend the Church's sound digestion.'
    FAUST: That's the way they always do,
and a Jew or a king can do it as well.
    MEPHISTOPHELES: With that, he swept rings, chain,
        and brooch,
like so many mushrooms, into his pouch,
hardly thanking them any more
than if it had been a basketful of nuts.
He promised them both a heavenly reward
and left them feeling very righteous.

    FAUST: And Margaret?
    MEPHISTOPHELES: Has the fidgets now,
doesn't know what she want to do.
She thinks of the jewels night and day,
but more about him who brought them.
    FAUST: The little darling's trouble hurts me.
Get her some new trinkets at once.
The others weren't much, anyway.
    MEPHISTOPHELES: You think getting them is child's
        play?
    FAUST: Do what I tell you.
And stick close to her neighbor.
Don't get soft! Be a real devil,
and bring another box of jewels.
    MEPHISTOPHELES: Yes, gracious sir, with all my
        heart.
    [Faust *goes out*]
Such a love-sick fool would puff out the sun,
moon and stars, in thin air, to make sport
for his lady-love. [*He leaves*]

THE NEIGHBOR'S HOUSE

[Martha *is alone*]
MARTHA: God pardon my poor husband!
He did not behave too well by me.
Off into the world he's gone,
leaving me alone in the straw.
I never crossed or bothered him;
God knows how well I petted him!
[*She weeps*] Maybe he's dead—How terrible!—
If I only had his death-certificate!
    [Margaret *comes in*]
MARGARET: Martha!
MARTHA: Margaret, what's the trouble?
MARGARET: My knees are almost giving away!
Just now I found another little box
in my dresser, made of ebony,
and the things in it are more expensive
and wonderful than the others were.
MARTHA: You mustn't say anything to your mother;
she'd take them to the confessional like the others.
MARGARET: But look now! Just look!
MARTHA: [*Putting the things on* Margaret] You
        lucky creature!
MARGARET: But I wouldn't dare be seen with them
at church or on the street, or anywhere.
MARTHA: Whenever you want to you can bring
your treasures here and try them on;
parade before the mirror for an hour,
and in that way we'll have our fun.
Then on some big occasion, like a feast,
you can show off one piece, to start with:
a chain at first, then a pearl at your ear—
your mother won't notice, or we'll make up a story.
MARGARET: But who could have brought them
        both?
Things that are right don't happen this way.
    [*Someone knocks*]

O God, that must be mother!

MARTHA: [*Peeking through the curtains*] It's a
strange man. Come in.
[Mephistopheles *come in*]

MEPHISTOPHELES: If I have been a little free in
walking in,
I pray you ladies to pardon me.
[*He steps back respectfully from* Margaret]
Is this where Mrs. Martha Schwerdtlein lives?

MARTHA: That's me. What is it that you want?

MEPHISTOPHELES: [*Softly to her*] I know you now
and that's enough.
You've such distinguished company.
So please excuse the liberty I've taken;
I'll call again this afternoon.

MARTHA: [*Aloud*] Think, child—of all things in
the world—
This gentleman takes you for a well-born lady!

MARGARET: I am poor and of humble blood.
Heavens, the gentleman is too kind:
The jewels are not mine.

MEPHISTOPHELES: It isn't merely all this finery;
you've a distinguished look and a certain air.
I'm glad that you will let me stay.

MARTHA: What is your business? I want very
much—

MEPHISTOPHELES: I wish I had more cheerful news
for you.
I hope you won't make me repent it.
Your husband's dead, and sent you a last greeting.

MARTHA: He's dead? That faithful heart! Oh! Oh!
My husband's dead! Let me die too!

MARGARET: Dear Martha, don't be so upset!

MEPHISTOPHELES: You must hear the mournful
story.

MARGARET: I never want to fall in love at all.
A loss like this would kill me.

MEPHISTOPHELES: Joy must have sorrow and
sorrow, joy.

MARTHA: Tell me about his last days.

MEPHISTOPHELES: He lies buried in Padua,
near the Church of St. Anthony
in holy ground that has been consecrated
for cool and eternal rest.

MARTHA: Did you bring nothing else but this
news?

MEPHISTOPHELES: Oh yes, one last request that's
very serious:
you should have three hundred masses sung for him.
Aside from this, my pocket's empty.

MARTHA: What! Not a souvenir or a medal
Such as every journeyman keeps in his bag?
A token he will not part with,
even though he's hungry or has to beg?

MEPHISTOPHELES: Madam, I'm very sorry from
my heart;
he really didn't squander all his money.
He felt sincere repentance for his faults
and lamented his misfortunes even more.

MARGARET: Oh, why must men be so unfortunate?

I shall say many a prayer for him.

MEPHISTOPHELES: You're ready to be married now
yourself.
You are a child who's worthy of being loved.

MARGARET: Oh no, not for a long time still.

MEPHISTOPHELES: If not a husband, then a handsome beau.
For it is one of heaven's greatest gifts
to hold a loved one in one's arms.

MARGARET: That's not the custom in this town.

MEPHISTOPHELES: Custom or not, it's often done!

MARTHA: Oh, tell me more!

MEPHISTOPHELES: I stood by his death-bed—
it was a little better than manure,
being half-rotten straw. He died a Christian,
and felt that he had left too much unsettled.
'Oh, how I hate myself!' he cried. 'I left my wife
and my business. Ah, the memory strikes me dead.
If only she'd forgive me in this life!—'

MARTHA: [*Weeping*] The good man! I forgave him
long ago.

MEPHISTOPHELES: '—Though she, God knows,
was more to blame than I!'

MARTHA: A lie! And right on the brink of the
grave!

MEPHISTOPHELES: In his last agonies his senses
wandered,
if I'm anything of a connoisseur.
'There was no time in life for play,' he cried.
'First the children, then to get them bread,
and bread in the broadest sense,
and never time to eat my share in peace.'

MARTHA: Did he forget my love's fidelity,
my drudgery for him, day and night?

MEPHISTOPHELES: Oh, no! He mentioned all that
tenderly.
'When I left Malta how I prayed
for my wife and the little tots!' he said.
'And heaven blessed us. We were lucky.
Our vessel captured a Turkish merchantman
which carried a treasure of the mighty Sultan.
For my bravery I got a share of it.'

MARTHA: How much? Where is it? Do you think
he buried it?

MEPHISTOPHELES: Who knows where the four
winds carried it?
When he was a stranger in Naples
a pretty tart adopted him as her friend
and gave him such loving devotion that he didn't
get rid of her little gift till his blessed end.

MARTHA: The villain! stealing from his children,
and all our misery and need
couldn't restrain him from this evil living!

MEPHISTOPHELES: But think: because of it he's
dead.
If I were in your place, I'd mourn
a decent year for him and then
look around for another love.

MARTHA: O God! A man like my first man
I'll never find on earth again!

And so good-hearted, though he never stayed home,
but liked strange women and foreign liquor
and never could let the wicked dice alone.

MEPHISTOPHELES: There, there, all could have gone on well

if he had overlooked some little slips
of yours. On such a basis, isn't it possible
that you and I might trade lovers' rings?

MARTHA: It amuses the gentleman to joke.

MEPHISTOPHELES: [Aside] I'd better get away in time.

She'd hold the Devil himself to his word.
[To Margaret] How are things going with your heart, my dear?

MARGARET: What do you mean, Sir?

MEPHISTOPHELES: [Aside] You innocent sweet thing!

[Aloud] Farewell, ladies!

MARGARET: Good-by.

MARTHA: Tell me quickly before you go:
I wish I had a witness to where and how
my dear man died and was buried.
I've always liked things to be right
and want to read about it in the weekly paper.

MEPHISTOPHELES: Well, my good woman, what two witnesses will swear

is everywhere considered valid evidence.
And I've a good friend who, I know,
will go right with us to the judge and testify.
I'll bring him here.

MARTHA: Oh yes, please do!

MEPHISTOPHELES: And this young lady will she still be here?

He's a fine lad who's traveled widely
and knows how to pay the ladies his respect.

MARGARET: I'm afraid he'd make me blush for shame.

MEPHISTOPHELES: You wouldn't need to blush before a king.

MARTHA: We'll expect you gentlemen this evening
in the garden back of the house.

A STREET

[Faust is with Mephistopheles]

FAUST: How is it going? Have you made some progress?

MEPHISTOPHELES: Fine! So you're all on fire for her.

Gretchen will soon be yours.
Tonight you'll see her at Neighbor Martha's.
Now there's a woman, if ever there was one,
made to play the gypsy and procuress.

FAUST: That's good!

MEPHISTOPHELES: But she'll want something for her trouble.

FAUST: Well, one good turn deserves another.

MEPHISTOPHELES: We'll have to witness a certificate

that her husband's remains
lie in holy ground in Padua.

FAUST: Clever! But first we'll have to go there!

MEPHISTOPHELES: Sancta Simplicitas![14] There's no need to do that;

just sign the deposition as though you knew it.

FAUST: If that's the way it is, you must give up the plan.

MEPHISTOPHELES: Oh, you righteous and holy man!

Is this the first time in your life
you've told a lie? Haven't you defined,
with pompous words and brash effrontery,
God, the world, and living things, and man—
what stirs in his heart and runs through his mind?
And if you want to take it up, confess
you know just as much of Mr. Schwerdtlein's death
as you really do of things like those.

FAUST: Once and for all, you're a sophist and a liar.

MEPHISTOPHELES: Yes, if you don't look any deeper.

But tomorrow, will you not yourself
deceive poor little Margaret, in all honor,
swearing your whole soul's love to her?

FAUST: Yes, and with all my heart.

MEPHISTOPHELES: That's perfectly splendid!

Then you pledge her eternal love and faith,
whispering about one all-absorbing passion—
will that too come from your heart?

FAUST: Stop this! It will! When I feel this great emotion,

this tumult, and try to name it, but cannot;
when my mind searches the world for words
to call this flame that burns me,
this thing that must be eternal—is that nothing
but a devilish playing with lies?

MEPHISTOPHELES: And still I'm right!

FAUST: Just hear me out, I pray, and spare my lungs.

A man determined to be right who has a tongue
will always have the final word. But come,
I'm sick of talking. And besides, what makes you right
is that I cannot act in any other way.

A GARDEN

[Margaret on Faust's arm, with Martha and Mephistopheles, walking back and forth]

MARGARET: I feel you're only sparing me
and stooping to make me feel ashamed.
A traveler gets used to accommodating
himself good-naturedly. I know very well
my poor words can't amuse a man of the world.

FAUST: A glance, a word from you are worth

[14] Sacred simplicity!—words spoken by the martyr of Protestantism John Huss when he was being burned at the stake and saw an ignorant old woman throwing a piece of wood into the flames.

more than all the wisdom of this world. [*He kisses
her hand*]

MARGARET: Don't put yourself out!
Why should you want to kiss
a hand as rough and coarse as mine?
I've so much work to do at home,
and mother is so exacting, too.
[*They walk on*]

MARTHA: And are you always on the go?

MEPHISTOPHELES: Alas, my duties and business
drive me on!
With what regret we leave so many places,
and yet we can't stay always in one spot!

MARTHA: It's all very fine in your active years
to galavant around the world,
but it's not so good when the evil days draw near
and the bachelor slips toward the brink
of the grave alone: that's not so pleasant.

MEPHISTOPHELES: It makes me shudder merely
to think of it.

MARTHA: Then, worthy sir, consider it in time.
[*They go on*]

MARGARET: Yes, out of sight is out of mind.
It's easy enough for you to flatter.
You can find so many friends more sensible
than I.

FAUST: Believe me, my dear, what men call sense
is often just pretence and narrow-mindedness.

MARGARET: What do you mean?

FAUST: Oh, I mean that innocence and simplicity
so seldom know their worth.
That meekness and lowliness, the highest gifts
of loving bountiful nature—

MARGARET: If only you'll remember me a little;
I shall have time enough to think of you.

FAUST: You're often alone, then?

MARGARET: Yes, our household is very small
but still it must be looked after. We've no servant:
I have to cook, sweep, knit, and do the sewing,
run all the errands, early and late, and mother
is so particular about everything!
Not that she has to skimp herself—
we could make more show than many others;
for father left us a nice little property:
a little house and garden outside the town.
But now my life is quiet.
My brother is a soldier;
my little sister is dead.
I had my blessed trials with the child!
Yet I would gladly go through it all again,
because I loved her so.

FAUST: She was an angel if she was like you.

MARGARET: I brought her up and she was fond
of me.
My father died before she came.
Mother lay sick to death. We gave her up.
But slowly she recovered, little by little.
But she couldn't dream of nursing the poor little
worm,
and so I raised her myself,

on milk and water. So she really was mine!
She nestled in my arms, played in my lap,
she was friendly and kicked and grew.

FAUST: You've certainly felt the purest happiness.

MARGARET: But many a heavy hour too.
The little one's cradle stood at night
beside my bed, and if she stirred, I wakened;
sometimes I had to give her a drink, sometimes
take her in bed with me; then, if she wouldn't hush,
get out of bed and dance her up and down
around the room; early each morning
I was up, doing the washing in the tubs,
going to market, doing the cooking.
And so it went, each day was like the last.
I'm not always too cheerful;
but it makes me like my supper and my bed.
[*They walk on*]

MARTHA: We women are badly off. It's hard
to bring a bachelor to his senses.

MEPHISTOPHELES: Till I met you I hadn't heard
anyone so convincing.

MARTHA: But tell me: have you never found anyone
to whom your heart felt bound?

MEPHISTOPHELES: The proverb is so true:
a man's own hearth and a good wife
are better than gold and pearls.

MARTHA: I mean, have you never been stirred by
a passion?

MEPHISTOPHELES: I've been entertained everywhere most cordially.

MARTHA: I wanted to say: were you ever serious,
ever?

MEPHISTOPHELES: One shouldn't ever trifle with
the ladies.

MARTHA: Ah, you don't understand me!

MEPHISTOPHELES: I'm so sorry! But I do understand
that you're very kindly disposed to me.
[*They go on*]

FAUST: You knew me again, you little angel,
as soon as I came in the garden?

MARGARET: Didn't you see it? I lowered my eyes.

FAUST: And do you forgive the freedom—
my boldness when I tried to talk to you
as you came out of church?

MARGARET: I was upset. It never happened before,
and no one could say one bad thing about me.
I thought: has he seen something in my manner
that is immodest or unbecoming?
It seemed to strike him all at once: that girl
is easy to flirt with. But I must admit,
I don't know what but something in me began at once
to take your part, and I was very angry
with myself because I couldn't be angrier with you.

FAUST: You darling!

MARGARET: Just a minute! [*She picks a star-flower
and strips off the petals slowly*]

FAUST: What's that? A posy?

MARGARET: No, it's only a game.

FAUST: What game?

MARGARET: Go away. You'd laugh at me. [*She pulls off the petals*]

FAUST: What are you murmuring?

MARGARET: [*Under her breath*] He loves me . . . he loves me not.

FAUST: Heaven is in your face!

MARGARET: [*Pulling off the last petals joyfully*] He loves me . . . not . . . loves me . . . not . . . he loves me!

FAUST: Yes, child! Let this flower's decision be the gods' oracle to you. He loves you! You understand what that means? He loves you! [*He takes her hands*]

MARGARET: It makes me tremble.

FAUST: Don't shudder! Look at me. Let our hands say what can't be said. To give yourself up wholly and feel joy that must last forever! Forever! . . . Its end would be desperation. No, no end! No end! [*Margaret presses his hands, frees herself and runs off. He stands thoughtfully a moment and then follows*]

MARTHA: [*Entering*] It's almost night.

MEPHISTOPHELES: Yes, and we must leave.

MARTHA: I'd ask you to stay longer, but this is a wicked place. Nobody is ever too busy to stare at his neighbor's comings and goings. A woman gets talked about, no matter how she acts. But where are our love-birds?

MEPHISTOPHELES: They fluttered up the path there.

Like summer butterflies!

MARTHA: He seems to like her.

MEPHISTOPHELES: And she him. It's the way of the world.

A Garden House

[Margaret *runs in and hides behind the door, with her finger at her lips, and looking through the crack*]

MARGARET: He's coming!

[Faust *enters*]

FAUST: Ah, you rascal, you're teasing me! I've got you now. [*He kisses her*]

MARGARET: [*Returning his kiss*] Dearest, I love you with all my heart! [*Mephistopheles knocks*]

FAUST: [*Provoked*] Who's there?

MEPHISTOPHELES: A friend!

FAUST: You're a beast!

MEPHISTOPHELES: It's time to go.

MARTHA: [*Coming*] It's really getting late, Sir.

FAUST: Can't I take you home?

MARGARET: Mother wouldn't . . . no, good-by!

FAUST: Must I leave you? Good-by!

MARTHA: Adieu!

MARGARET: Till we meet soon!

[Faust *and* Mephistopheles *go out*]

MARGARET: Dear God, was there ever such a man? What things he thinks about! I stand before him, all ashamed, and just say 'yes' to everything. I'm a poor ignorant girl and I don't know what he sees in me. [*She goes out*]

Forest and Cavern

[Faust *is alone*]

FAUST: Spirit sublime, you gave me, gave me all I asked for. Not for nothing did you turn your face to me out of the fire. And for my kingdom you gave me glorious nature, the power to feel and enjoy her, not merely in cold astonished visits; but you allowed me to look deep within her, as one looks into the heart of a friend. You lead the procession of living creatures before me, and teach me to know my brothers in the silent thickets, in the air and water. And when the storm in the forest roars and creaks, when the giant fir tree crashes down, crushing the neighboring branches and trunks; when the hills rumble with hollow thunder; then you lead me to the sheltered cavern and show me myself, and in my mind deep and secret wonders are revealed. Before my eyes the pure moon rises, softening everything, and from rock-walls, out of damp bushes, the silver phantoms of a bygone world drift before me, to temper the stern delight of contemplation. Oh, I know now that for man there is no perfection. With this joy leading me nearer and nearer to the gods, you gave me a companion whom I can no longer spare, though scornfully and coldly, he degrades me before myself and with a word-breath changes your gifts to nothing. Busily he fans a raging fire in my heart for that beautiful image. So from desire I stagger toward enjoyment, and in getting that I languish again for desire. [*Mephistopheles enters*]

MEPHISTOPHELES: Won't you have had enough of this life soon? In the long run how can it please you? It was all right to try it once, but soon now we ought to be getting along to something new.

FAUST: I wish you had other things to do than plague me on a happy day.

MEPHISTOPHELES: All right, all right, I'll gladly let you be; you wouldn't dare say that in earnest. A companion so crazy, cross and ungracious certainly wouldn't be much of a loss.

All day you're a handful! And never from your looks
can I get any idea what you like or don't.
  FAUST: Now isn't that just the tone!
He wants to be thanked for having bored me.
    MEPHISTOPHELES: You miserable earthling, before
      I came
how well did you manage your life?
For a time I saved you
from all this rubbish of the imagination;
if it were not for me then long ago
you'd have walked off this earth-ball.
Why do you sit in these caves and fissures like an owl,
sucking your food from dripping stones
and wet moss like a toad?
A fine and pleasant pastime!
The Doctor still sticks in your bones.
  FAUST: Can you not understand the new life-
      energy
this roaming in the wasteland has given me?
If you could guess what it means to me,
you'd be devil enough, I suppose, to begrudge me it.
    MEPHISTOPHELES: A super-natural pleasure!
To lie in the night dew on a mountain side,
to embrace heaven and earth in ecstasy,
to puff yourself up to godhead size
and wallow through earth's marrow with prescient
      force,
to feel the six days' creation within yourself,
to enjoy in your haughty power I don't know what,
now to flood everything with a surge of love,
your earthly nature completely transcended,
and then the ultimate intuition . . .
[*With a flippant gesture*] I mustn't say how you
      will achieve it!
  FAUST: You're rotten!
    MEPHISTOPHELES: So, you don't like it!
Well, you have the right to say so.
I mustn't mention to the modest ear
the very thing the chaste heart can't forbear.
But, to be brief, I can't deny you the pleasure
of deluding yourself with occasional evasions;
but you can't hold out much longer.
You're already exhausted, and if it goes on like
      this
you'll be driven to madness, or anguish and horror.
So enough! Your little darling's waiting,
shut up by herself and feeling sad.
She's thinking about you constantly;
she's overpoweringly in love with you.
At first your passion overflowed,
like a torrent swollen with melting snow;
you poured it into her heart—but now
your little brook has run quite dry again.
Instead of sitting enthroned in the woods,
shouldn't your lordship reward
the little monkey for her devotion?
Now time is dragging pitifully for her;
she stands by the window and watches the clouds
drifting over the old town-walls.
'If only I were a little bird!' so runs her song

the whole day long and half the night.
Sometimes she is lively, but more often troubled,
sometimes she's quite wept-out,
then calm again, or so she seems,
and always love-sick for you.
  FAUST: You serpent! You snake!
    MEPHISTOPHELES: [*Aside*] That's right! But I'll
      catch you yet!
  FAUST: Get out, you reprobate!
Don't mention that lovely creature!
Don't stir up desire for her sweet body
in my half-mad senses again!
    MEPHISTOPHELES: What *do* you want, then? She
      thinks you've left her,
and more or less, that's what you've done.
  FAUST: No, I am near her even now,
and if I were ever so far away,
I could never forget or lose her.
I even envy the Holy Sacrament
when her lips touch it.
    MEPHISTOPHELES: Very good, my friend! I've often
      envied you
those little twins that feed among the roses.
  FAUST: You pimp, get out!
    MEPHISTOPHELES: All right! Swear at me, I have
      to laugh.
When God fashioned boy and girl,
he knew the duty of this noblest profession
was to arrange the opportunity for meeting.
Let's get along now. It's agony!
You're going to your sweetheart's room,
not to your death!
  FAUST: What is the heavenly joy that's in her arms?
Let me be warm upon her breast!
Am I not always feeling her distress?
Am I not homeless and a fugitive?
A monster without aim or peace,
roaring like a cataract from crag to crag,
with greedy rage toward the abyss?
While she, with vague and childish feelings,
in a tiny hut on a little Alpine meadow by the stream,
with all her homely problems
is locked in her little world.
And I, with God's hate on me, was still not satisfied
to grip the rocks and break them into pieces!
No, I must undermine her, and destroy her peace!
O Hell, do you demand this sacrifice?
Now help me, demon, to shorten the time of anguish!
May that which is doomed to happen happen soon!
Let her fate crash down on me
and hurl us both together to one ruin!
    MEPHISTOPHELES: What's all this seething and fire-
      works about?
You fool, go in and comfort her!
Whenever a pin-head sees no way out,
he imagines at once it's the end of everything.
Live dangerously and you live right!
You've played the devil already with quite a flair,
and there's nothing in this world that's more absurd
than a devil who can't make up his mind.

GRETCHEN'S ROOM

GRETCHEN: [*Alone, at her spinning wheel*] My
peace is gone—
   my heart is sore—
   I shall find it never,
   no, never more.

Where I don't have him
it's a grave for me.
And all the world
becomes gall to me.

Oh my poor head
is dazed and numb;
and my poor brains
are dull and dumb.

My peace is gone—
My heart is sore—
I shall find it never,
no, never more.

From my window
I watch for him;
I only go walking
to look for him.

His manly walk,
his noble ways,
the smile of his mouth,
the power of his eyes,

and the way he talks,
his magic speech,
the touch of his hand,
the kiss of his lips!

My peace is gone—
my heart is sore—
I shall find it never,
no, never more.

My heart would follow
wherever he goes.
If I could embrace him
and hold him close,

and kiss and kiss him
as much as I wish
and finally die
beneath his kiss.

MARTHA'S GARDEN

[Margaret *and* Faust *are together*]
MARGARET: Promise me, Henry!
FAUST: If I can.
MARGARET: Tell me: what do you think about
   religion?
You're a loving, wonderful man,
but it seems to me you don't think much about it.
   FAUST: Let's leave that, child. You know I'm fond
   of you;

I'd give my flesh and blood for those I love,
and I'd never rob anyone of his feelings and faith.
   MARGARET: That's not enough. You must believe!
   FAUST: Must I?
   MARGARET: Oh, if I had the power to change you!
You don't even honor the Holy Sacrament.
   FAUST: I do honor it.
   MARGARET: Yes, but you don't partake of it.
How long since you have been to mass or confession?
Do you believe in God?
   FAUST: My dear, who dares to say:
I believe in God?
Question any priest or philosopher,
and his answer will seem to mock you.
   MARGARET: So you don't believe?
   FAUST: Don't misunderstand me, my love.
Who dares name him?
Who can declare:
I believe in him?
Who can feel
and be bold enough to say:
I don't believe in him?
Does not the all-encompassing,
the all-supporting,
embrace and uphold us,
you, me, and Himself?
Does not the sky arch over us?
Does not the earth stand firmly below us?
Do not the eternal stars arise,
looking down kindly upon us?
When we gaze in each other's eyes,
is there not a surging in your heart and head,
formed by the eternal mystery,
invisibly and visibly about you!
Fill your great heart with that,
and when you're wholly overcome by the feeling,
then call it what you will:
call it joy, or heart, or love, or God!
I have no name for it!
Feeling is everything;
the name is sound and smoke
beclouding the glow of heaven.
   MARGARET: All that is fine and true.
The preacher talks very much the same,
only with slightly different words.
   FAUST: All hearts beneath the light of day
say it everywhere, each in his own tongue;
then why not I in mine?
   MARGARET: That sounds all right, and yet
there's something warped about it.
Like that, you're not a Christian.
   FAUST: Dear child!
   MARGARET: It's worried me so long
to see you in such company.
   FAUST: How so?
   MARGARET: That man who comes with you,
deep in my soul, I hate him.
Nothing in all my life has stabbed me to the heart
like his repulsive face.
   FAUST: My darling, don't be afraid of him.

MARGARET: His presence chills my blood.
Toward everyone else I feel good will;
but, though I long to see you,
he fills me with a secret horror—
and I think he's a scoundrel too,
though God forgive me, if I do him an injustice!

FAUST: But there must be a few such odd fish in the world.

MARGARET: I wouldn't want to live with a man like him!
When he comes to the door
he always looks mocking and half-way angry.
You can see he has sympathy for nothing.
It's written on his forehead
that he can love no one.
I feel so happy in your arms,
so happy and yielding and warm,
but when he comes, my heart is suddenly shut.

FAUST: You're a foreboding little angel!

MARGARET: It overcomes me so
that when we meet him, I even feel
as if I didn't love you any more.
And when he's near me, I can never pray.
And that eats into my heart.
Henry, you must feel it too.

FAUST: It's just a prejudice!

MARGARET: I must go now.

FAUST: Can we never spend a little hour of peace
close to each other, body and soul?

MARGARET: If only I slept by myself!
I'd gladly leave the door unbolted for you tonight;
but mother's a light sleeper,
and if she found us out,
it would kill me.

FAUST: You angel, don't worry about that.
Here is a little bottle. Three drops of this
mixed in her drink and she will sleep
the deep sleep that pleases nature.

MARGARET: There's nothing I wouldn't do for you.
But will it hurt her?

FAUST: Darling, would I give it to you if it would?

MARGARET: O best of men, when I look at you,
something makes me do what you want.
I've done so much for you already:
there's almost nothing left that I can do.

[She leaves. Mephistopheles enters]

MEPHISTOPHELES: Well, has the little monkey gone?

FAUST: Spying again?

MEPHISTOPHELES: I heard it all in great detail.
The Doctor has been catechized!
I hope it will do him a lot of good.
Girls nowadays are keen on knowing
if a man is pious and simple in the old way.
They think: if he gives in there, he'll yield to us too.

FAUST: Monster, you cannot understand
how this true-loving soul,
filled with her faith, which quite alone
assures her of salvation,
can suffer awful anguish
if she thinks her lover is damned.

MEPHISTOPHELES: You transcendental sensualist,
a little minx is leading you by the nose.

FAUST: You vile abortion of dung and fire!

MEPHISTOPHELES: And how she knows her physiognomies!
When she's near me, she feels—she doesn't know what.
She finds a hidden meaning behind my mask.
She feels I'm surely a spirit,
perhaps the Devil himself!
Now, about tonight—?

FAUST: What's that to you?

MEPHISTOPHELES: Never mind. I get my pleasure from it too!

AT THE WELL

[Gretchen and Lilybeth have come to fill pitchers]

LILYBETH: You heard about Barbara?

GRETCHEN: Not a word. I don't go out very much.

LILYBETH: But it's true, for Sibyl told me today!
She's finally made a fool of herself,
with all her affectations.

GRETCHEN: How do you mean?

LILYBETH: It smells!
She's feeding two when she eats and drinks.

GRETCHEN: Ah!

LILYBETH: At last she's got what was coming to her.
How long she's been hanging on to that fellow!
All that parading about with him,
in the dance halls and around the town,
always trying to show herself off,
while he was treating her with wine
and little pastries. She was so vain
about her looks. And all her shameless behavior
in taking the presents he gave her.
With all her kissing and petting,
finally she's lost that little virgin flower.

GRETCHEN: Poor thing!

LILYBETH: So you still pity her?
When girls like us were at the spinning-wheel
and our mothers wouldn't let us go out at night,
she was with her lover in the dark hall,
and the hours weren't too long on the bench by the door.
She's got to humble herself now
and do penance at church in the sinner's shirt!

GRETCHEN: But he'll marry her, surely.

LILYBETH: He'd be a fool! A slick fellow
like him can get along anywhere.
He's gone already.

GRETCHEN: That isn't right!

LILYBETH: If she should get him, you can be sure
the boys would tear off her bridal-wreath
and strew chopped straw for shame at her door! [She goes out]

GRETCHEN: [*Starting homeward*] Once, how boldly
    I'd have run down
any girl that got herself in trouble!
My tongue would have found hard words
for her sins, to smear them black and blacker
and still not black enough.
And I'd have blessed myself
and been so good and smug—
but now we're tarred with the same brush!
Yet—all that led to it, O God,
it was so good! It was so sweet!

BY THE TOWN WALL

[Gretchen *is putting flowers in vases before the
image of the Mater Dolorosa which stands in
a niche*]
GRETCHEN: O rich-in-sorrow,
turn your face
graciously to my distress!

With the sword in your heart
and a thousand hurts,
you are gazing up where your son lies dead.

You look to the father
and sigh to him
the pain in you and the pain in him.

Who feels
the grief
in my body and bones?
How my heart is afraid
and trembles and yearns
you only know, and you alone!

Wherever I go,
what woe, what woe, what woe
I carry with me!
And when I'm alone
I weep, I weep, I weep
till my heart is broken.

My tears fell and wet
the pots by my window
when this morning early
I broke you these blossoms.

When the sun shone early,
so bright in my bedroom,
I sat on my bed,
awake with my misery.

Help me! And save me
from death and disgrace!
Turn your eyes toward me,
O my sister in sorrow!

NIGHT
IN THE STREET IN FRONT OF GRETCHEN'S HOUSE

[Valentine, *a soldier,* Gretchen's *brother, is standing in the street*]

VALENTINE: Often at some drinking-party
when my companions would boast
about their sweethearts,
praising them drunkenly
and washing the words down with full cups,
I'd sit there, head propped on my elbows,
complacently listening to their bragging,
and smile at ease and stroke my beard,
then take a full glass in my hand
and say: Each man to his own taste!
But is there one in all the land
like my faithful Gretchen,
one worthy to stand by my sister?
'None! That's right!' Clink, clink!
'She's the best of all the girls in town!'
And all the braggarts would sit there, dumb.
But now!—I could tear out my hair
and knock my head against the walls!
With nasty names, they thumb their noses,
and any bastard dares insult me!
Like a bankrupt debtor, I must sit,
and be the butt of every joke,
sweating to smash them into bits—
yet I can't call them liars.
Who comes there? Who is sneaking near?
Unless I'm wrong, there are two. If it's he,
he'll never leave here alive.
    [Faust *and* Mephistopheles *come along*]
FAUST: As from the window of the chancel there
the glow of the eternal lamp flames upward,
glimmering weaker and weaker at the sides,
while darkness presses round; so gloom
makes night in my thoughts.
MEPHISTOPHELES: And I'm a yearning tom-cat
sneaking up fire-escapes and creeping stealthily
along the tops of walls.
I feel virtuous but thievish,
and a bit like a ram,
for premonitions of Walpurgis Night
are spooking through my body.
It's just two days away, and then
you'll see what keeps a man awake.
FAUST: Isn't that some buried treasure that I see
glinting and rising in the air?
MEPHISTOPHELES: Soon you can have the pleasure
of lifting the kettle out.
Not long ago I peeked in
and it's full of lion-dollars.
FAUST: And no jewelry, or perhaps a ring,
as a present for the girl?
MEPHISTOPHELES: I think I did see some such
        thing,
a sort of rope of pearls.
FAUST: That's good! I don't like going there
without some little gift for her.
MEPHISTOPHELES: Really, it ought not to annoy
        you
to get some pleasures free.
Now the sky is glowing, full of stars,
you'll hear a musical masterpiece;

I'll sing a moral song to her
and make a fool of her through the ear.
[*He sings, playing on a zither*]
What do you there
by your true-love's door,
Ophelia dear,
at break of day?

Ah, let it alone,
you'll go as a maid,
but when you come out
you'll not be one.

Take care of yourself!
If the deed is done,
why, then Good-night,
poor little thing!

For your own sake
don't steal or take
any love unless
you've got a ring.
VALENTINE: [*Coming forward*] What are you
after? By the body and blood!
You damned rat-catcher!
To the devil with your zither!
Then I'll send the singer after it!
MEPHISTOPHELES: He's broken my zither! It's no
good now.
VALENTINE: And next I'll smash your skull!
MEPHISTOPHELES: [*To* Faust] Stand fast, Doctor!
Keep cool!
Stick tight to me. I'll help you.
Out with your feather-duster!
You thrust! I'll parry!
VALENTINE: Parry that!
MEPHISTOPHELES: And why not!
VALENTINE: And that!
MEPHISTOPHELES: Yes indeed!
VALENTINE: I think it's the Devil who's fighting me!
What's that? He's got my hand.
MEPHISTOPHELES: [*To* Faust] Let him have it.
VALENTINE: [*Falling*] Aaah!
MEPHISTOPHELES: Now the fool's tamed!
But quick! We've got to vanish.
Already someone's yelling Murder!
I get along splendidly with the police,
but in penal court the blood-ban's hard to manage.
MARTHA: [*At her window*] Help! Help!
GRETCHEN: [*At hers*] Bring a light!
MARTHA: They're cursing and scuffling, shouting
and fighting!
[*A crowd gathers*]
PEOPLE: Someone's been killed already!
MARTHA: [*Coming out*] Where did the murderers
go?
GRETCHEN: [*Coming out*] Who lies there?
PEOPLE: Your mother's son.
GRETCHEN: Almighty God! How horrible!
VALENTINE: I'm dying. That is quickly said
and quicker for me to do.

Why do you women stand there and howl?
Come here and listen to me.
[*They gather round him*]
Listen, Gretchen. You're still young;
but you've not been smart enough.
You've managed your business badly.
Confidentially, I've got
a sister who's become a whore!
Well, be a real one then.
GRETCHEN: My brother! God! Such words to me?
VALENTINE: Just leave God out of this!
What's done, unfortunately, is done,
and what's to come will surely come.
You started with one, on the sly;
but others will follow soon enough
and when you've had a dozen,
then the whole town can have you.

When shame is born, how secretly
she is brought into the world;
over her head and ears
the veils of night are drawn.
Oh yes, you'd like to murder her,
but she gets so bold when she starts to grow
that she goes out naked in daytime,
and though she's gotten no lovelier,
the more loathsome that she looks,
the more she seeks the light of day.

Already I foresee the time
when every decent person in the town
will turn away from you, you slut,
as though you were a rotting carcass.
And then your heart will despair
when they look you in the eyes.
You'll never wear a golden chain!
You'll never stand near the altar in church!
Or enjoy yourself on the dancing floor,
dressed in a pretty lace collar.
In some dark corner of misery
you'll hide among beggars and cripples,
and even though God may pardon you,
on earth you shall be damned!
MARTHA: Commend your soul to the grace of God.
Must you add slander to your burden?
VALENTINE: If I could reach your withered body,
you shameless, coupling pimp,
then I might get full pardon
for all the sins of my life!
GRETCHEN: My brother! what agony!
VALENTINE: I tell you: no more tears!
When you first lost your honor
you gave my heart its death-blow.
Now I go, like an honest soldier,
through the sleep of death to God.

IN THE CATHEDRAL
SERVICE, ORGAN, AND CHOIR

[Gretchen *stands among many people. An* Evil
Spirit *is behind her*]

THE EVIL SPIRIT: How different, Gretchen, it was once

when you, still innocent,
came here to the altar
and prattled your prayer
from the well-worn little book,
half in childish play,
half with God in your heart!
Gretchen, what are you thinking?
What crime is brooding
in your heart?
Are you praying for your mother's soul,
who slept, because of you,
into the long, long torment?
Whose blood is that on your threshold?
—And underneath your heart
what stirs, quickening already,
torturing you and itself
with its ominous presence?

GRETCHEN: O God!

If I could be free of these thoughts
that go through me, back and forth,
accusing me!

CHORUS: *Dies irae, dies illa*
solvet saeclum in favilla.[15]

[*There is organ music*]

THE EVIL SPIRIT: Wrath seizes you!

The trumpet sounds!
The graves quake!

And your heart,
recreated,
trembles forth
from the peace of ashes
toward fiery torment!

GRETCHEN: I wish I were outside!

I feel as if the organ
throttled my breath,
and the anthem had loosened
the depths of my heart.

CHORUS: *Judex ergo cum sedebit,*
quidquid latet adparebit,
nil inultum remanebit.[16]

GRETCHEN: It is so close here!

The walls and pillars
oppress me! The ceiling
crushes me! . . . I must have air!

THE EVIL SPIRIT: Hide yourself!

Sin and shame cannot be hidden.
Air? Light?

Woe unto you!

CHORUS: *Quid sum miser tunc dicturus?*
Quem patronum rogaturus?
Cum vix justus sit securus.[17]

[15] Day of wrath, day that shall scatter the world to ashes.

[16] When the judge shall take his seat, what is hidden shall appear, nothing shall be unavenged.

[17] What shall I, the wretched, say then? Whom appeal to for protection? The just man barely shall be safe.

THE EVIL SPIRIT: The transfigured spirits

turn away from you.
The pure ones shudder
to reach you their hands.
Woe!

CHORUS: *Quid sum miser tunc dicturus?*

GRETCHEN: Neighbor! Your smelling salts! [*She faints*]

WALPURGIS NIGHT
THE HARZ MOUNTAINS IN THE NEIGHBORHOOD OF
SCHIERKE AND ELEND

[Faust *and* Mephistopheles]

MEPHISTOPHELES: Wouldn't you love to have a broomstick?

I wish I were straddling a good stout ram.
Our goal is still a long way off.

FAUST: As long as I still feel fresh on my legs,

this knotty staff's enough.
Why should you want to shorten the way?—
To wander through this labyrinth of valleys,
to climb these rocks where springs gush,
spitting spray forever: these are the pleasures
that make the path spicy!
Spring stirs the birches,
even the fir trees feel it already;
ought not the season to work in our bodies?

MEPHISTOPHELES: Really, I don't feel a thing. It's winter

in my bones, and I would rather
snow and frost lay on my pathway.
How drearily the lop-sided disk
of the red moon rises with its belated glow!
And it's bad illumination too! At every step
you crack your shins against a stone or stump!
Let me call a Jack o' Lantern.
There's one blazing away so cheerfully.
Ho, there friend! Won't you help us?
You're burning yourself out for no reason.
Be so kind as to light our way upward!

JACK O' LANTERN: Out of respect, I hope I shall succeed

in restraining my vacillating disposition.
It's our nature to go zigzag.

MEPHISTOPHELES: Ah, well, he's trying to imitate mankind.

But go ahead now, in the Devil's name!
Or I'll blow your flicker-flame life out.

JACK O' LANTERN: I plainly see you're the master of the place

and shall readjust myself to suit the situation.
But remember: the mountain is bewitched tonight;
and if a will o' the wisp is to guide you correctly,
you mustn't take his directions too exactly.

[*All three, singing in turn, as they climb*]

MEPHISTOPHELES: In the dream-and-magic-spheres

we have entered, it appears.

**Lead us well and get our praises
when we soon succeed in climbing
to the wide and desert places.**

JACK O' LANTERN: Through the trees that grow
here thickly
see us rush and pass them quickly.
All the cliffs bow down before us,
and the long rock-snouts snore for us.
How they puff and blow!

FAUST: Through the stones and through the
grasses
streams and little brooklets pass us.
Do I hear singing on the air
and the charming lover's prayer,
voices of our heavenly days?
What we love and long to seize!
And the echo chimes and rhymes
like a saga of old times.

MEPHISTOPHELES: Uhu! Shuhu! Can you hear?
Lapwing, owl, and jay are near.
It is late for them to waken!
Are those newts there in the bracken?—
their bodies are fat but their legs are long!
How the tangled tree-roots throng
like serpents through the stones and soil
twined in marvelous coil on coil,
stretching out to catch and grip
like the tentacles of a polyp,
reaching from a rocky lair
for an unsuspecting wanderer.
Mice of every color and shade
scamper through the heathery glade.
And glowworms crowd in swarms to fly
a bewildering escort in the sky.

FAUST: Tell me if we stay or go,
everything is whirling so!
Rocks and trees are making faces
and the firefly darts and chases,
seems to multiply and grow.

MEPHISTOPHELES: Hold my coat-tail tightly!
Here's a midway ridge. From here
people can see with astonishment
how Evil burns inside the mountain.

FAUST: How strangely a troubled dawn-like red
glimmers through the gorges!
In the chasms of the abyss it darts its gleams.
Reek is rising, vapor is drifting,
and a glow burns through the fog-veil,
creeping like a slender thread
till its bursts out like a spring.
Its hundred veins, twisting a long way,
are knotted through the valley,
here, compressed in a sharp elbow,
then suddenly spread far and wide.
Now sparks are sputtering
like scattered golden sand!
Look how the rocky walls are kindled
and blazing to their highest peaks.

MEPHISTOPHELES: Didn't Mammon light his
palace

marvellously for the revel?
You're lucky that you got to see it.
Already I hear the rowdy guests approaching.

FAUST: How the whirlwind is raging!
It's almost breaking my neck!

MEPHISTOPHELES: Cling tightly to these rocky ribs,
or you'll be hurled into the chasm.
Mist thickens the night.
Hear how the forest crashes!
The owls are flying away in terror.
Listen! the pillars of the eternal
green palace are splintering.
Branches moan and are broken!
Tree trunks groan mightily,
creeping roots gaping.
Then in fearful confusion
they're hurtled together,
crashing over each other.
Through the wreck-cluttered chasms
the air howls and hisses.

You hear those voices in the sky?
Near and far, down the mountain ridges
flows a furious incantation!

THE WITCHES: [In a chorus] Up to the Brocken
the witches speed,
the stubble is yellow, green is the seed.
A thronging crowd will gather there,
with Old Nick sitting high in the air.
So over stock and stone we go;
the witch breaks wind and the goat lets go.

A VOICE: Old lecherous Baubo is coming now,
riding along on a mother-sow.

THE CHORUS: Honor her now who is worthy of
honor!
Forward, Dame Baubo, to lead the rout!
A tough old sow with her mother upon her,
and the witches dancing a roundabout.

A VOICE: Which road did you come by?

ANOTHER VOICE: I came by Ilsenstein.
There I peeked in an owl's eyes,
and she stared in mine.

ANOTHER VOICE: Oh, go to Hell!
Why do you ride so fast?

ANOTHER VOICE: She has gored me.
Look at the wound!

THE WITCHES' CHORUS: The road is long, the road
is broad.
Did you ever see such a crazy crowd?
The broom it scratches, the pitch-fork pokes,
the mother pops open, but baby chokes.

A HALF-CHORUS OF SORCERERS: We creep along like
a snail in her house;
the women are in the lead.
For, when we're hell-bent on a carouse,
the female is always ahead.

THE OTHER HALF: That's not the way it goes,
exactly.
With a thousand steps a woman must creep;
no matter how she hurries quickly,

the man can make it with a leap!

A VOICE: [*From above*] Come along, come along, from Rocky Lake!

VOICES: [*From below*] We'd love to fly with you up there.

We scour ourselves, all white and bare;
but we're barren still, as we always were.

BOTH CHORUSES: The stars have fled, the wind is still,

the dreary moon is glad to retire.
The magic chorus, whizzing wildly,
sputters a thousand sparks of fire.

A VOICE: [*From below*] Stop! Stop!

A VOICE: [*From above*] Who calls down there from the stone-abyss?

A VOICE: [*From below*] Take me with you, oh, take me too!

Three long centuries I've been climbing,
and still I can't get to the top.
I want to be with my own kind.

BOTH CHORUSES: We ride the broom and the walking-stick,

we ride the pitch-fork and the buck;
whoever can't find a steed today
is lost and will never get away.

HALF-WITCH: [*Below*] I've been tottering on for such a long time;

but the others are all so far ahead.
At home I've neither rest nor peace,
and even here I still can't find them.

WITCHES' CHORUS: There's a magic salve puts pluck in a hag.

You can make a sail from any old rag.
A trough can be a wonderful boat.
But who doesn't now, will never float.

BOTH CHORUSES: And when we finally get up there,

We'll cover the ground and fill the air;
The mountain heather's farthest reaches
will be swarming with us spooks and witches.
[*They alight*]

MEPHISTOPHELES: They shove and jostle, push and clatter,

They hiss and swirl, and rattle and rush!
They glow, spray sparks and stink and flare!
Truly a world of the witches.
Keep close or we'll be separated.
Where are you?

FAUST: [*In the distance*] Here!

MEPHISTOPHELES: Already torn away?

I'll have to claim my house-rights here.
Attention! Squire Voland[18] the Seducer is here.
Make room, good people, if you please, make room!
Here, Doctor, hold me tightly.
In one leap we'll leave this mob,
that's even too mad for me.
Something shines there, gleaming weirdly,
luring me to this thicket. Let's slip in.

FAUST: Spirit of contradiction! Yes, I'll follow you.

[18] A name for the Devil.

I still think that you've done it cleverly;
we're on the Brocken for Walpurgis Night,
yet we arrange to draw apart
and watch things from the side.

MEPHISTOPHELES: Look! what many-colored flames!

That's a jolly little club there.
In a little circle you're never alone.

FAUST: I'd rather be up there. Already I see

the glow and the swirling smoke.
There the crowd streams toward the Evil One;
and many a riddle will be untied.

MEPHISTOPHELES: And many will be knotted, too.

Let the great world riot and rave;
we'll hide a while here, on the quiet.
It's an old saw that from large worlds
we make the little ones. But look—
the younger witches go naked and bare,
while the old ones cover up cleverly.
Be friendly to them, for my sake;
it isn't much bother, and it can be fun.
I hear the sound of their instruments!
What a damned noise! But we've got to get used to it.
Come on! Come on! We'd better start.
I'll go ahead and make the introductions—
and, incidentally, this ratifies our bond.
What do you say, my friend? Up here
there's lots of space. You can't see the end.
A hundred fires are burning, rows of them;
they dance and chatter, cook and drink, make love;
where will you find it better, tell me that.

FAUST: Now when you introduce us at this revel, will you present yourself as devil or magician?

MEPHISTOPHELES: Really, I'm used to going incognito,

but on a gala day we sport our orders.
I haven't got the Garter to set me up,
but here the horse's hoof is held in high esteem.
You see the snail there, crawling toward us,
she's smelled me out with searching feelers.
I can't disguise myself here as I would like to.
But come, let's go from fire to fire.
I am the pander and you be the wooer.
[*To a group by a dying fire*] Venerable gentlemen, why are you in the rear?
If I found you in the middle of the party,
with riot and revelry around you,
I'd praise you; but you're enough alone at home.

A GENERAL: Who now can trust the nations?

No matter what we've done for them,
the fickle people, like women,
give the prize to younger men.

A MINISTER: Man stands so far from justice now;

I praise the good old times;
when we had all the power,
those were the golden days.

A PARVENU: Really, we aren't exactly dumb,

though often we did things we shouldn't;
but now the world whirls round and round,
just when we want to hold it.

AN AUTHOR: Who is there now will read a book,
that's written with real intelligence?
And the younger generation
is getting cockier than ever.

MEPHISTOPHELES: [*Who suddenly looks very old*]
I feel mankind is ripe for Judgment Day,
and never again will I climb up the Brocken.
My little keg is dripping less,
and the world, like me, is on the wane.

A HUCKSTER-WITCH: Gentlemen, stop! Don't pass
    me by.
This is your opportunity!
Inspect my little stock with care.
You'll find here vast variety;
in all the world there's no such shop.
There's nothing here that hasn't done
malicious evil to somebody.
There is no dagger here that's not drawn blood;
no goblet that's not poured destructive poison
into some healthy body. And each jewel
has bought some lovely female person.
There's not a sword here that's not cut a pact
or stabbed an enemy in the back.

MEPHISTOPHELES: Now, aunty, you don't under-
    stand the times.
What's done is gone! What's gone is done!
Stock up your booth with something new,
for only novelties can please our taste.

FAUST: I'll lose my wits if I don't watch out.
Now this is what I really call a fair!

MEPHISTOPHELES: The whole swirl struggles to
    get to the top;
you think you're pushing but you're being shoved.

FAUST: Who is that there?

MEPHISTOPHELES: Look at her closely!
That's Lilith.

FAUST: Who?

MEPHISTOPHELES: 'Of Adam's first wife Lilith it is
    said . . .'
beware of her beautiful hair—
she's famous for it!
When a young fellow falls for it,
he doesn't soon get loose—she has him.

FAUST: Look at that couple, the hag and the girl!
They've done some pretty good whirls and leaps.

MEPHISTOPHELES: No one can rest a minute to-
night.
Here's another dance starting. Let's get in it!

FAUST: [*Dancing with the* Girl] Once I had a
    lovely dream:
    I dreamt that on an apple tree,
    I saw two pretty apples gleam—
    I climbed for them most eagerly.

THE PRETTY WITCH: These little apples have seduced
    man since the days of Eden.
    I want to treat you as you're used,
    and am I glad you need them!

MEPHISTOPHELES: [*With the* Old Witch] Once I
    had a bawdy dream

of an old tree that was split.
It had a——— ——— ———
that pleased me quite a bit.

THE OLD WITCH: It gives me pleasure to salute
    the knight who bears the horse's foot.
    Let him get ready a proper cork
    if a large———doesn't cramp his work.

THE PROCTOPHANTASMIST:[19] Damned rabble! How
    dare you!
Haven't I proved conclusively
that ghosts don't have ordinary feet—?
But here you're dancing like mortals!

THE PRETTY WITCH: [*Dancing*] Then what is he
    doing at our ball?

FAUST: Oh, that fellow gets around everywhere.
While others dance, he judges all their steps.
If he doesn't find them sound,
they're as good as never taken.
What riles him most is when we go ahead;
but if we just keep going in a circle—
like him with his old windmill—
he's sure to think it quite all right,
especially if you consult him with respect!

THE PROCTOPHANTASMIST: Are you still here? This
    is unheard-of!
Vanish at once! This nonsense has been cleared up!
This devil-pack just won't observe the law.
We are so wise, yet ghosts can still haunt Tegel.[20]
How long I've tried to clean away this folly!
But everything's still dirty. It's impossible!

THE PRETTY WITCH: Oh, stop boring us!

THE PROCTOPHANTASMIST: I tell you spirits to your
    face,
I'll not put up with this spectral despotism;
my spirit can't endure it.
    [*The dancing continues*]
I see that I will not succeed today,
but I always carry a copy of my *Travels,*
and hope before I make my final tour,
I'll overcome the devils and the poets.

MEPHISTOPHELES: Now he'll sit down in the near-
    est puddle,
for he knows his trouble and how to cure it:
the leeches at his bum will phlebotomize his muddle,
and he'll recover from these spirits and from spirit.

[*To* Faust, *who has stopped dancing*] But why did
    you let that pretty piece go
who sang so sweetly while she was dancing?

FAUST: Because right in the middle of her song
out of her mouth sprang a little red mouse!

MEPHISTOPHELES: That was all right. Don't be
    alarmed!
It doesn't matter as long it wasn't gray.
And when you're on this kind of a date, why worry?

[19] Friedrich Nicolai, who published in 1799 a paper on
ghosts and the curative power of leeches. He also wrote
several travel books and professed himself the leader of
the "Age of Enlightenment."
[20] A place near Berlin.

FAUST: And I saw too—
MEPHISTOPHELES: What?
FAUST: Mephistopheles, can't you see
that beautiful girl there, standing alone
and far away? Slowly she drags herself along,
as if her feet were chained. It seems to me,
she's very like my Gretchen.
   MEPHISTOPHELES: Now let that one alone! She's
   no good!
In fact, it's a magic image, lifeless, a phantom.
It's bad luck to meet her.
That rigid stare would 'thick men's blood with cold'
and almost turn you into stone.
Haven't you ever heard about Medusa?
   FAUST: Truly, they are the eyes of a dead girl,
unclosed by any loving hand.
That is the breast that Gretchen gave me.
That is the sweet body I enjoyed.
   MEPHISTOPHELES: It's sorcery, deluded simpleton!
Every man sees in her his own beloved!
   FAUST: What joy and what torture!
I cannot leave this vision.
How strangely that one scarlet thread,
no thicker than the blade of a knife,
adorns her lovely neck!
   MEPHISTOPHELES: That's right! I see it too.
She can cary her own head away, under her arm,
for Perseus[21] sliced it off.
You've always this hankering for illusion!
But come, let's climb this little hill.
It's as lively as the Prater Park in Vienna.
And unless someone's put a spell on me,
I really see a theatre. What's going on?
   A STAGE-HAND: The play will soon begin: a brand-
   new piece,
the last of a series of seven,
for here it's the custom
to put them on in batches.
A dilettante wrote it,
and dilettanti act in it.
Excuse me, gentlemen, I've got to go,
with dilettantish joy, to hoist the curtain.
   MEPHISTOPHELES: I'm glad to find you on the
   Brocken,
for you belong here, that's certain.

WALPURGIS NIGHT'S DREAM, OR THE GOLDEN
WEDDING OF OBERON AND TITANIA. INTERMEZZO

MANAGER OF THE THEATRE: Hardy sons of
  Mieding,
   for once we'll rest today.
   A misty valley is our scene
   and a mountain old and gray.
A HERALD: Fifty years must be well-passed
   before a wedding's golden.

[21] Perseus cut off the monster Gorgon's head.

When the quarrel has been patched up,
   I'm most to gold beholden.
OBERON: If you're spirits, round me here,
   appear to me straightway!
   The great king and his lady queen
   are pledged anew today.
PUCK: Comes now Puck and whimsically
   steps in a gay rhythm;
   several hundred come behind him,
   all rejoicing with him.
ARIEL: In tones of heavenly purity
   Ariel starts his song;
   the hideous and the lovely both
   the sound will draw along.
OBERON: Couples that would be serene,
   watch our demonstration:
   people love each other more
   after a separation.
TITANIA: If he sulks and she has crotchets,
   quickly send them forth:
   her to noon's meridian,
   him to the far North.
THE WHOLE ORCHESTRA: [*Fortissimo*] Fly-snouts
  and gnat-noses
   with all of their relations,
   tree-frogs and crickets in the grass,
   these are our musicians.
A SOLO: Heigh, here comes the bag-pipe now,
   like a soap bubble it blows!
   Listen to the Schnicka-schneck
   through its snubby nose.
A SPIRIT JUST TAKING FORM: With little wings and
  a spider's foot
   and the paunch of a toad this beast
   will never grow into anything
   that makes a rhyme at least!
A PAIR OF POETASTERS: Little steps and lofty
  leapings
   through the fragrant dew and honey:
   although your tripping's neat enough,
   you'll not get in the money.
AN INQUISITIVE TRAVELER: Isn't this a masquerade?
   Can I trust my sight?
   Is it Oberon the fairy-god
   whom I see here tonight?
AN ORTHODOX: No claws and certainly no tail!
   But it seems to be on the level:
   along with all the gods of Greece
   they've, also got the Devil!
A NORTHERN ARTIST: I understand but sketchily
   the meaning of these revels;
   but meanwhile I prepare myself
   for my Italian travels.
A PURIST: Alas, misfortune's brought me here
   where all grows lewd and lewder.
   in all this horde of witches
   only two wear powder.
A YOUNG WITCH: Oh powder here is like a skirt—

for gray hags fagged and shoddy.
Naked I ride my Billy-goat
and sport a bawdy body.

MATRON: We won't begin to call you names
because we're too well bred;
but though you're young and lovely now
one day you'll rot instead.

THE ORCHESTRA LEADER: Fly-snouts and gnat-
noses,
avoid this naked creature!
Tree-frogs and crickets in the grass,
keep time—that's the main feature!

A WEATHER-VANE, TO ONE SIDE: There is no better
company,
the brides are what they should be,
and handsome bachelors, man for man,
as promising as they could be.

A WEATHER-VANE, TO THE OTHER SIDE: And if
earth doesn't open up
to swallow them, pell-mell,
I swear that I will quickly jump
down to the depths of Hell.

XENIA: Here we buzz, like little bugs
with tiny sharpened scissors,
to honor Satan, our papa—
we're his sincerest praisers.

HENNINGS: See now how this mob naively
lets loose their little passions.
But at the end they'll all declare
they had the best intentions.

MUSAGET (Leader of the Muses): Oh, gladly
would I lose myself
among the crowd of witches;
For I could do that better far
than regiment the Muses.

QUONDAM 'GENIUS OF THE AGE': With good connections you'll arrive.
Come on, they'll never pass us.
The Brocken has a top as wide
as Germany's Parnassus.

AN INQUISITIVE TRAVELER: Tell me: who's this
solemn pedant
with haughty foot-steps shuffling?
He whiffs and sniffles all he can—
'For Jesuits he's snuffling.'

A CRANE: In waters clear I love to fish
and also in mud puddles;
that's why you see this godly man
consorting with the devils.

A MAN OF THE WORLD: For pious people seeking
grace
all things may be a vehicle;
Even up here on the Brocken
they'll set up a conventicle.

A DANCER: [As a group of Philosopher-Herons
approaches, dancing] Is that another chorus
there?
I hear a distant thrumming—
Don't get excited! In the reeds

the herons are at their drumming.

A DANCING-MASTER: How each man hoists a nimble leg
yet somehow gets his clearance.
The cripple leaps, the clumsy hop,
none question the appearance.

A FIDDLER: The rascal-pack is full of hate,
they'd tear each other to tatters;
but as Orpheus' playing calmed the beasts,
so the bag-pipe smooths out matters.

A DOGMATIST: I'll let no critic scream me down,
or doubts lead me astray.
The Devil must exist or else
how comes he here today?

AN IDEALIST: The phantasy within my brain
is acting like a bully.
Really, if I am all I see
today, I'm very silly.

A REALIST: This business is a pain to me
and irks me much already;
for the first time I am standing here
on feet that are not steady.

A SUPERNATURALIST: With satisfaction I am here
and take pleasure in their merits;
seeing the devils here, I'm sure
there also are good spirits.

A SCEPTIC: They chase and trace the little flames
and fancy they're near treasure;
Devil and Doubtful rhyme (almost!),
so I'm at the right place here.

THE ORCHESTRA LEADER: Frogs in the leaves and
crickets in the grass,
you dilettantes pernicious,
fly-noses and you beaks of gnats,
remember, you're musicians!

THE VERSATILE: Sans souci, we call this army
of us care-free creatures;
when we can travel no more a-foot,
we just up-end our statures.

THE NE'ER-DO-WELLS: We've chiseled many a little
piece,
as the good Lord permitted.
But we have danced our shoes through now
and must run on, bare-footed.

IGNES FATUI: We have come up from the swamp
where we originated;
here in rows we're dancing now,
gallants illuminated.

METEORITE: Out of the heights I have shot down
through nebular and star-light.
Now I lie twisted in the grass,
and who will help me upright?

THE HEAVY ONES: Make way and give us room
about.
Let all the grass be trodden!
The spirits come, and though they're ghosts,
their bodies are all sodden.

PUCK: Don't come trampling here, obesely
like an elephant's calf!

Let the clumsiest fellow here be
sturdy Puck himself!
ARIEL: If loving nature gave you wings
and Mind their use proposes,
follow the airy road I take
up to the hill of roses.
THE ORCHESTRA: [*Pianissimo*] The mist-veil and
the train of clouds
brightly above are glowing.
Air in leaves and breeze in branches—
all away are blowing.

A GLOOMY DAY IN A FIELD

[Faust *and* Mephistopheles]

FAUST: In misery! Desperate! Pitifully wandering all this long time on earth, and now imprisoned! That lovely ill-fated being, shut in a dungeon like a criminal, and exposed to horrible tortures! It has come to this! To this!—Perfidious, contemptible demon, to have concealed this from me!—Stop! Stand there, and roll your hellish eyes in their sockets with rage! Stand and defy me with your unendurable presence! In prison! In irreparable extremity! Given up to evil spirits and to mankind which damns without mercy! And you, you cradled me all this while in insipid dissipations, and hid from me her growing anguish and let her perish without help!

MEPHISTOPHELES: She's not the first one.

FAUST: You dog! Detestable brute!—O Infinite Spirit, turn this vermin back into that dog-shape in which he liked to trot before me, the unsuspecting wanderer, rolling at my feet, or leaping on my shoulders when I fell down. Turn him back again to his favorite form, so that he can crawl on his belly in the sand while I kick him—the depraved creature!—Not the first one!—God's wounds! Can the human spirit conceive that more than one being has sunk into these depths of wretchedness, and that the first one, writhing in the agony of death, was not enough to expiate the guilt of all others in the eyes of the eternal pardoner! Her misery cuts clean to the marrow of my life; yet you grin coolly at the doom of thousands!

MEPHISTOPHELES: Here we are again at our wits' end, where human reason snaps. Why do you try to join up with us, if you can't go through with it? You want to fly, but you get dizzy! Did we intrude on you, or you on us?

FAUST: Don't gnash your hungry fangs at me! You make me sick!—Glorious and Mighty Spirit who condescended to manifest yourself to me, you who know my heart and my soul, why did you chain me to this miscreant who feeds on suffering and gluts himself on destruction?

MEPHISTOPHELES: Is that all now?

FAUST: Save her, or you'll be sorry! May you suffer an awful curse for thousands of years!

MEPHISTOPHELES: I cannot loosen the avenger's chains, nor shoot back his bolts.—Save her!—Who was it ruined her, you or I?

[Faust *looks wildly about*]

Do you want to seize the thunder? It's a good thing, you miserable mortals can't do it! It's the tyrant's nature to smash the innocent bystander into bits; it helps him out of the mess.

FAUST: Take me to her! She must be freed!

MEPHISTOPHELES: And what of the dangers you lay yourself open to? Did it ever occur to you that you're guilty of murder in that town? Avenging furies hover over the place where a man has been slain, and they lurk in waiting for the return of the killer.

FAUST: That, too, from you? All the murder and death of a world be upon you, monster! Lead me there, I tell you, and set her free!

MEPHISTOPHELES: I'll take you there, and I'll tell you what I *can* do! Am I all-powerful in heaven or on earth? I'll muddle the jailer's brains while you get the keys and lead her out. A human hand must do it. I'll stand on guard. The magic horses are ready. I'll carry you off. That much I can do.

FAUST: Then hurry!

NIGHT
IN THE OPEN COUNTRY

[Faust *and* Mephistopheles *are galloping on black horses*]

FAUST: What are they doing there at the Ravenstone gibbet?

MEPHISTOPHELES: I wouldn't know what their cookery's concocting.

FAUST: They're soaring and swooping, bowing and scraping.

MEPHISTOPHELES: It's the witches' union holding a meeting.

FAUST: They're making a magic spell.

MEPHISTOPHELES: Come on! Come along!

A DUNGEON

[Faust, *with a bunch of keys and a lamp, is standing before an iron door*]

FAUST: A feeling of awe runs through me—
such as I have not felt for a long time;
all the misery of mankind grips me.
Here she lives behind these damp walls,
yet her crime was only a dear illusion.
You hesitate to go to her?
You fear to see her again?
On now! Your irresolution draws death nearer.

[*He takes hold of the lock. There is singing within*]

My mother, the whore,
she murdered me!
My father, the villain,
has eaten me.
My wee little sister

gathered my bones
and hid them away
beneath cool stones;
then I turned into a pretty bird.
Fly away! fly away!

FAUST: [*Unlocking the door*] She does not dream that her lover is listening,
that he hears the chains rattling and the straw rustling. [*He goes in*]

MARGARET: [*Hiding in the bed*] They're coming for me! Oh bitter death!

FAUST: [*Softly*] Hush, hush! I've come to free you.

MARGARET: [*Throwing herself before him*] If you're a man, take pity on my misery!

FAUST: Your cries will waken the guard! [*He starts to unlock the fetters*]

MARGARET: [*On her knees*] Executioner, who gave you this power?
It's only midnight, yet you come for me.
Have pity on me and let me live!
Is not tomorrow morning soon enough?

[*She stands up*] I'm still so young, so young!
Yet soon to die!
And I was beautiful—that was my ruin.
My lover was near, but now he's far away.
The wreath is torn and the blossoms are scattered.
Don't clutch me so roughly!
Spare me! What have I done to you?
Don't let me beg you in vain.
I've never seen you before in all my life!

FAUST: Can I endure this agony?

MARGARET: Now I'm completely in your power.
Only first, let me suckle my baby again.
I cuddled it to me all night long;
but they took it away to hurt me,
and now they say I've murdered it.
And I'll never be happy again.
They sing songs about me! It's wicked of the people!
There's an old tale that ends so . . .
but why do they mix me up in it?

FAUST: [*Throwing himself at her feet*] Your lover lies at your feet,
come to free you from this misery and anguish.

MARGARET: [*Throwing herself beside him*] Oh, let us kneel and call to the saints!
See, under these steps,
under the threshold
Hell is seething!
The Evil One
in a fearful rage
is making a hub-bub!

FAUST: [*Aloud*] Margaret! Margaret!

MARGARET: [*Listening*] That was my lover's voice!
[*She jumps up. The chains fall off*]
Where is he? I heard him call me.
I am free! No one can stop me!
I will go to him and lie close to him!
He called 'Margaret!' He stood on the threshold,
and through the shrieking and the clatter of Hell,

through the angry scoffings of the devils,
I recognized that sweet and tender voice.

FAUST: It is I!

MARGARET: You! Oh, say it again! [*She embraces him*]
It is he! It is he! Where now is all my misery?
The suffering in this dungeon? The chains?
It is you come to save me!
I am saved!—
I see the street again where I first met you,
and the garden
where I waited for you with Martha.

FAUST: [*Urging her to leave*] Come now! Come!

MARGARET: Oh, wait!
I want to stay here, just with you! [*She caresses him*]

FAUST: Hurry!
If you don't hurry,
we shall have to pay for it dearly.

MARGARET: What? Can't you kiss any more?
My love, we were only parted a little while,
and yet you have forgotten how to kiss?
Why am I so afraid in your arms?
Just a word or look from you
made heaven come down to me,
and you used to kiss me
as though you wanted to smother me.
Kiss me! Or I'll kiss you! [*She embraces him*]

Oh, your lips are cold and silent.
Where has your love hidden?
Who has stolen it from me? [*She turns away from him*]

FAUST: Come, follow me! Darling, be brave!
I love you more than ever before;
but follow me, I beg you.

MARGARET: [*Turning to him*] And is it you? And is it really you?

FAUST: Of course. But come!

MARGARET: You undo the chains,
and you hold me close to you again.
How is it that you aren't afraid of me?—
And do you really know whom you're setting free?

FAUST: Come! It's almost daylight.

MARGARET: I have killed my mother,
I have drowned my child.
Wasn't it given to you and me?
To you too—It *is* you! I can hardly believe it.
Give me your hand! It isn't a dream!
Your dear hand!—But, oh, it's wet!
Wipe it off! It seems to me
that there's blood on it.
O God, what have you done?
Put up your sword, I beg you!

FAUST: Forget what is past.
You're torturing me!

MARGARET: No, you must go on living!
I'll tell you about their graves.
You must see to them
the first thing in the morning.
Give the best place to mother;

put my brother close by.
Put me a little to one side—
only not too far away!
And the baby on my right breast.
No one else will ever lie beside me!
It was a dear sweet joy
to be close beside you.
But it isn't like that any more.
Now it's as if I must force myself toward you,
and you were thrusting me away.
And yet it's you, and you seem so good and kind.

FAUST: If you feel this, then come!
MARGARET: Out there?
FAUST: To freedom.
MARGARET: If the grave is there

and death lurks for me, then I'll come!
From here to the eternal bed of rest
but farther not one step—
Are you going?
O Henry, if I could only go with you!

FAUST: You can if you will. The door is open.
MARGARET: I dare not go out. There is nothing for
me to hope.

What would it help if I fled? They're waiting to catch
me.
It's miserable to have to beg,
and worse with an evil conscience!
It is miserable having to wander in a strange land.
And finally I'd be caught!

FAUST: I'll stay with you.
MARGARET: Quickly! Quickly!

Save your poor child.
Run! Straight up the path
along the brook,
over the foot-bridge,
into the woods,
to the left where the plank
is in the pond.
Seize it quickly!
It's trying to keep afloat,
it is still struggling.
Save it! Save it!

FAUST: Think! Please think!

One step and you're free!

MARGARET: If we were only beyond the hill!

My mother sits there on a stone—
it's as if a cold hand had me by the hair!
My mother sits there on a stone
and wags her head.
She doesn't beckon, she doesn't nod. Her head is so
heavy.

She has slept so long, and will never waken.
She slept so that we could enjoy ourselves,
and those were happy times!

FAUST: My begging and my words are no help.

I must carry you away.

MARGARET: Let me go! I'll not be forced!

Don't take hold of me so murderously!
Didn't I once do everything you wanted?

FAUST: Dearest, it will soon be dawn!
MARGARET: Dawn! Soon daylight! My last day is
breaking;

it was to have been my wedding-day!
Don't tell a soul you've been with Margaret already.
Alas my virgin's wreath
is a thing of the past now!
We'll see each other again,
but not at the dance.
The crowd presses nearer. No one speaks.
The square and the streets
can't hold them all.
The bell tolls, the judge's staff is broken.
They seize me and bind me!
I'm taken to the bloody block.
Each one imagines above his own neck
the sharp sword trembling over mine.
The world lies hushed as a grave.

FAUST: I wish I had never been born!
MEPHISTOPHELES: [*Appearing outside*] Come! Or
you're lost.

This futile hesitation! This wavering and babbling!
My horses are shuddering
because the day is breaking.

MARGARET: What rises there from the ground?

It is he! He! Oh, send him away!
What does he want in this holy place?
He wants me!

FAUST: You shall live!
MARGARET: I give myself up to the judgment of
God!

MEPHISTOPHELES: [*To* Faust] Come along! Or
I'll leave you in the lurch with her!

MARGARET: Father, I am yours! Save me!

Angels and hosts of heaven,
gather your forces around me! Protect me!
Henry—I am afraid for you!

MEPHISTOPHELES: She is judged and doomed!
A VOICE: [*From above*] She is saved!
MEPHISTOPHELES: [*To* Faust] Come with me!
[*They vanish*]
MARGARET'S VOICE: [*From within, dying away*]
Henry! Henry!

Alfred de Musset

(1810–1857)

Everything in Alfred de Musset's background and experience conspired to make him the representative of flamboyant French romanticism; and his youthful poetic genius, of course, joined the conspiracy. Yet the special excellence that distinguished him as a dramatist, rather than as a poet and a public figure, consists in qualities of economy, grace, and wit that belonged to the eighteenth century, if indeed they are not endowments that talent can display at any time. Musset was able to produce some of the least perishable, because least disorderly and perfervid, plays of the romantic movement, as well as to make the only original contribution to French comedy between Molière's death and the rise of Becque in the eighteen-eighties.

A descendant of the old nobility, Musset was reared in an atmosphere of veneration for Napoleon. He enjoyed a sheltered boyhood, and was given every opportunity to develop his poetic inclinations. Introduced in his green years to the society of literary men, such as Scribe and Hugo, he found himself in the swim of the romantic movement by the time he was eighteen. He made his first successful attempts at writing in 1828, about the time when the elder Alexandre Dumas' romantic drama *Henry III and His Court* was produced by the Théâtre Français (now the Comédie Française) and Hugo's first play, *Cromwell,* was published along with a preface that renounced classicism and laid down the romantic program for the theatre. His published verses having been lauded by distinguished contemporaries, including the great critic Sainte-Beuve, Musset plunged into the less productive but equally exhilarating life of a young man about town. He was bent, as he declared in excusing his follies, to learn everything by "experience." It was at this time, in 1829, that he also published a translation of De Quincey's *Confessions of an Opium Eater,* with additions of his own. He acquired a reputation for dissipation and became the great lover whose tempestuous affair with George Sand gave him notoriety. In 1833, his romantic writings and conduct had won him so much admiration in romantic circles that after his Byronic poem *Rolla* appeared, "a young stranger picked up the end of a cigar that Musset threw away in the street and reverently wrapped it up like a relic." At the end of that year, Musset, having already expressed some rueful disenchantment with life in his little play *Fantasio,* made a journey with George Sand to Italy which culminated in a devastating quarrel and resulted in the publication of books by both lovers giving their respective and contradictory views of the stormy affair. Musset returned to his family in 1834, bringing with him, as he wrote, "a sick frame, a crushed soul, and a bleeding heart."

The first fruit of his experience with George Sand was *No Trifling with Love (On ne badine pas avec l'amour).* Poems, plays, and prose work such as his gloomy novel *Confession* flowed freely from his sharpened and yet also somewhat chastened sensibilities between 1834 and 1839. But illness in 1840 reduced his literary output, and he produced nothing of note for many years. He suffered from heart disease, and his intemperate habits aggravated his condition. He lived long enough to see some of his plays produced (1847–1849), to write a few short ones, to start a few unfinished projects (including a play for Rachel, the greatest actress of the age), and to be made a member of the French Academy (1851). But he worked only intermittently; his efforts to recover health by traveling during the years 1854–1856 were unsuccessful, and he succumbed to his disease on May 1, 1857, at Saint-Cloud.

Musset was nineteen when he wrote his brother, "I am aware of the presence of two selves in myself, one that acts and another that observes." This self-analysis is particularly relevant to his dramatic work. Although he wrote some immature frantic pieces, he was generally able to stand at some distance from his vagaries and passions. He proved himself a master of romantic irony, reversing situations to bring out the obtuseness and perversity of people in love and the incalculableness of the passion. In one of the earliest of his stage pieces, *The Follies of Marianne* (*Les Caprices de Marianne,* 1833), for example, a woman capriciously fixes her love on the one man who cannot love her while rejecting and causing the death of the youth who is desperately enamored of her. The play is also the first example of Musset's ability to blend comic and sentimental complications. In *The Chandler,* a brittle but brilliant comedy, an officer of dragoons prevails upon a married woman to attach a young clerk to herself as her gallant in order to conceal the officer's own clandestine relationship with her. The young man is to be their "chandler," and is expected to "carry the candle" to their affair. Before long, however, it is the dragoon who becomes the "chandler" to the woman and the clerk. In *Fantasio,* Musset presents all the possibilities of a romance between a gallant and a princess, but interposes the impediment of disenchantment and detachment on the part of the young man. Here Musset inverts the role of a Byronic hero, so that for once Byronism nullifies an attachment instead of engendering it. And in *No Trifling with Love,* Musset develops a situation that should lead to a comic resolution but actually leads to a catastrophe, because it is unsafe to trifle with the human heart.

A rueful insight permeates these and other plays, as it also permeates and transforms a good deal of the dialogue that would otherwise seem no more than an echo of romantic sentiment. Musset succeeds in involving and detaching us simultaneously, of depicting feelings and at the same time analyzing them—or, more accurately, of presenting them to us for analysis by exposing their contradictions. Musset expressed an ambivalence toward romantic matter that is as modern and fresh today as it was in 1835. It is not surprising, then, that on one hand the plays could command little popularity during the vogue of romanticism and that on the other hand they have outlasted plays such as *Hernani,* which were once very successful but which exist on only one level of romantic interest.

Musset's originality is stamped upon the form of his dramatic work. His best plays are short. Some of these, called *proverbes dramatiques,* are brief dramatizations of maxims or popular saws. Although he did not create this epigrammatic form, which had had some vogue on the amateur stage and was known as *comédie-proverbe,* he gave it a special penetration, delicacy, and loveliness. In some of these pieces, economy becomes actual daintiness of form and style, as in the miniature masterpiece *A Door Should Be Open or Shut* (*Il faut qu'une porte soit ouverte ou fermée*), which is an excellent example of the brevity of his wit. Moreover, in these *proverbes,* as well as in comedies that are not actually elaborations of some aphorism, he did not hesitate to override the classic boundaries between comedy and tragedy.

No Trifling with Love, whose literally translated title would be "One Does Not Trifle with Love," is a distinguished example of a *proverbe dramatique.* It is written with stylized charm, and it even contains the formal feature of a chorus. Yet the writing and the characterization are remarkably natural. One finds oneself on the comfortable level of comedy as two young lovers become increasingly capricious; yet we also sense a deepening of feelings as the play progresses, and we are finally shocked, as are the two lovers, into a sudden awareness of tragedy. The jest we are following turns into earnest, and the lightness of the writing shades into darkness. Absorbed by the egotism of young love and pride, the lovers have been playing with another person's life, and the irony lies in our awareness and their unawareness of the risk they are taking. Everything in this little drama is exquisitely sketched, yet the delicate lines weave a firm net of circumstance. Nor does Musset's consummate artistry fail him at the end. A few lines are all he needs to establish the further ironic fact that the death of a common girl, whose feelings had never figured in their calculations, is the one impassable gulf between the lovers. Only Henry James might have written this denouement as well. (As a matter of fact, he did—in the superb novel, *The Wings of the Dove.*)

In *No Trifling with Love,* Musset made human drama out of a comedy of paradoxes that would have been delightful if it had remained nothing more, and he filled the nutshell of a lovers' tiff with the large substance of life itself. To have been able to accomplish this while writing what seems on the surface a mere comedy of sentiment is evidence of a unique talent. Musset's life and poems reflected the passions and aberrations of the romanticists, but as a writer of plays he had no contemporaries, and as yet he has had no successors. Time had to elapse and an exceptionally sensitive stage production had to materialize before so unconventional a play as *No Trifling with Love* could be appreciated. Although published in 1834, it was first staged on November 18, 1861, at the Théâtre Français, with Coquelin speaking the "Young Chorus," the famous actor Delaunay playing Perdican, and the gifted Mlle. Favart interpreting the exacting role of Camille.

NO TRIFLING WITH LOVE

By Alfred de Musset

TRANSLATED FROM THE FRENCH BY RAOUL PELLISSIER

CHARACTERS

THE BARON
PERDICAN, *his son*
MASTER BLAZIUS, *Perdican's tutor*
MASTER BRIDAINE, *parish priest*

CAMILLE, *the Baron's niece*
DAME PLUCHE, *her governess*
ROSETTE, *foster-sister of Camille*
PEASANTS, SERVANTS, ETC.

ACT I. SCENE I.

[*A village green before the château*]

THE CHORUS: Gently rocked on his prancing mule, Master Blazius advances through the blossoming corn-flowers; his clothes are new, his writing-case hangs by his side. Like a chubby baby on a pillow, he rolls about on top of his protuberant belly, and with his eyes half closed mumbles a paternoster into his double chin. Welcome, Master Blazius; you come for the vintage-time in the semblance of an ancient amphora.

MASTER BLAZIUS: Let those who wish to learn an important piece of news first of all bring me here a glass of new wine.

CHORUS: Here is our biggest bowl: drink, Master Blazius; the wine is good; you shall speak afterward.

BLAZIUS: You are to know, my children, that young Perdican, our signor's son, has just attained his majority, and that he has taken his doctor's degree at Paris. This very day he comes home to the château with his mouth full of such fine flowery phrases, that three-quarters of the time you do not know how to answer him. His charming person is just all one golden book; he can not see a blade of grass on the ground without giving you the Latin name for it; and when it blows or when it rains he tells you plainly the reason why. You will open your eyes as wide as the gate there to see him unroll one of the scrolls he has illuminated in ink of all colors, all with his own hands, and not a word said to anybody. In short, he is a polished diamond from top to toe, and that is the message I am bringing to my lord the Baron. You perceive that does some credit to me, who have been his tutor since he was four years old; so now, my good friends, bring a chair and let me just get off this mule without breaking my neck; the beast is a trifle restive, and I should not be sorry to drink another drop before going in.

CHORUS: Drink, Master Blazius, and recover your wits. We saw little Perdican born, and once you said he is coming, we did not need to hear such a long story about him. May we find the child in the grown man's heart!

BLAZIUS: On my word the bowl is empty; I did not think I had drunk it all. Good-by! As I trotted along the road I got ready two or three unpretending phrases that will please my lord; I will go and pull the bell. [*Exit*]

CHORUS: Sorely jolted on her panting ass, Dame Pluche mounts the hill. Her frightened groom belabors the poor animal with all his might, while it shakes its head with a thistle in its jaws. Her long lean legs jerk with anger, whilst her bony hands string off her beads. Good-day to you, Dame Pluche; you come like the fever with the wind that colors the leaves.

DAME PLUCHE: A glass of water, you rabble; a glass of water and a little vinegar.

CHORUS: Where do you come from, Pluche, my darling? Your false hair is covered with dust; there's a wig spoiled; and your chaste gown is tucked up to your venerable garters.

PLUCHE: Know, boors, that the fair Camille, your master's niece, arrives at the château to-day. She left the convent by my lord's express orders to come and enter on possession of her mother's rich estate, in due time and place, as much is to be done. Her education, thank God, is finished, and those who see her will have the fortune to inhale the fragrance of a glorious flower of goodness and piety. Never was there anything so pure, so lamblike, so dovelike, as that dear novice; the Lord God of heaven be her guide: Amen. Stand aside, you rabble; I fancy my legs are swollen.

CHORUS: Smooth yourself down, honest Pluche, and when you pray to God ask for rain; our corn is as dry as your shanks.

PLUCHE: You have brought me water in a bowl that smells of the kitchen. Give me a hand to help me down. You are a pack of ill-mannered boobies. [*Exit*]

CHORUS: Let us put on our Sunday best, and wait till the Baron sends for us. Either I am greatly mistaken, or there is to be some jolly merry-making to-day.

SCENE II.

[*The* Baron's *drawing-room. Enter the* Baron, Master Bridaine, *and* Master Blazius]

THE BARON: Master Bridaine, you are my friend: let me introduce Master Blazius, my son's tutor. My son yesterday, at eight minutes past twelve, noon, was exactly twenty-one years old. He has taken his degree, and passed in four subjects. Master Blazius, I introduce to you Master Bridaine, priest of the parish, and my friend.

BLAZIUS: [*Bowing*] Passed in four subjects, your lordship: literature, philosophy, Roman law, canon law.

BARON: Go to your room, my dear Blazius; my son will not be long in appearing. Arrange your dress a little, and return when the bell rings.

[*Exit* Master Blazius]

BRIDAINE: Shall I tell you what I am thinking, my lord? Your son's tutor smells strongly of wine.

BARON: It is impossible!

BRIDAINE: I am as sure as I am alive. He spoke to me very closely just now. He smells terribly of wine.

BARON: No more of this. I repeat, it is impossible.

[*Enter* Dame Pluche]

There you are, good Dame Pluche! My niece is with you, no doubt?

PLUCHE: She is following me, my lord. I preceded her by a few steps.

BARON: Master Bridaine, you are my friend. I present to you Dame Pluche, my niece's governess. My niece, yesterday at seven o'clock P.M., attained the age of eighteen years. She is leaving the best convent in France. Dame Pluche, I present to you Master Bridaine, priest of the parish, and my friend.

PLUCHE: [*Bowing*] The best convent in France, my lord; and, I may add, the best Christian in the convent.

BARON: Go, Dame Pluche, and repair the disorder you are in. My niece will be here shortly, I hope. Be ready at the dinner-hour.

[*Exit* Dame Pluche]

BRIDAINE: That old lady seems full of unction.

BARON: Full of unction and compunction, Master Bridaine. Her virtue is unassailable.

BRIDAINE: But the tutor smells of wine. I am absolutely certain of it.

BARON: Master Bridaine, there are moments when I doubt your friendship. Are you setting yourself to contradict me? Not a word more on that matter. I have formed the project of marrying my son to my niece. They are a couple made for one another. Their education has stood me in six thousand crowns.

BRIDAINE: It will be necessary to obtain a dispensation.

BARON: I have it, Bridaine; it is in my study on the table. Oh, my friend, let me tell you now that I am full of joy. You know I have always detested solitude. Nevertheless, the position I occupy and the seriousness of my character compel me to reside in this château for three months every summer and winter. It is impossible to insure the happiness of men in general, and one's vassals in particular, without sometimes giving one's valet the stern order to admit no one. How austere and irksome is the statesman's retirement! and what pleasure may I not hope to find in mitigating, by the presence of my wedded children, the melancholy gloom to which I have been inevitably a prey since the King saw fit to appoint me collector!

BRIDAINE: Will the marriage be performed here or at Paris?

BARON: That is just what I expected, Bridaine. I was certain you would ask that. Well, then, my friend—what would you say if those very hands—yes, Bridaine, your own hands—do not look at them so deprecatingly—were destined solemnly to bless the happy realization of my dearest dreams? Eh?

BRIDAINE: I am silent; gratitude seals my lips.

BARON: Look out of this window; do you not see my servants crowding to the gate? My two children are arriving at the same moment: it is the happiest combination. I have arranged things in such a way that all is foreseen; my niece will be introduced by this door on the left, my son by the door on the right. What do you say to that? It will be the greatest delight to me to see how they will address one another, and what they will say. Six thousand crowns is no trifle, there's no mistake about that. Besides, the children loved each other tenderly from the cradle. Bridaine, I have an idea—

BRIDAINE: What?

BARON: During dinner, without seeming to mean anything by it—you understand, my friend?—while emptying some merry glass—you know Latin, Bridaine?

BRIDAINE: *Ita ædepol*, by Jove, I should think so.

BARON: I should be very pleased to see you put the lad through his paces—discreetly of course—before his cousin: that can not fail to produce a good effect. Make him speak a little Latin; not exactly during dinner, that would spoil our appetites, and as for me, I do not understand a word of it: but at dessert, do you see?

BRIDAINE: If you do not understand a word of it, my lord, probably your niece is in the same plight.

BARON: All the more reason. Would you have a woman admire what she understands? Where were you brought up, Bridaine? That is a lamentable piece of reasoning.

BRIDAINE: I do not know much about women; but it seems to me difficult to admire what one does not understand.

BARON: Ah, Bridaine, I know them; I know the charming indefinable creatures! Be convinced that they love to have dust in their eyes, and the faster one throws, the wider they strain them to catch more.

[*Enter on one side* Perdican, Camille *on the other*]

Good day, children; good day, my dear Camille, and you, my dear Perdican: kiss me and kiss each other.

PERDICAN: Good day, father, and you, my darling cousin. How delightful; how happy I am!

CAMILLE: How do you do, uncle? and you, cousin?

PERDICAN: How tall you are, Camille, and beautiful as the day!

BARON: When did you leave Paris, Perdican?

PERDICAN: Wednesday, I think—or Tuesday. Why, you are transformed into a woman! So I am a man, am I? It seems only yesterday I saw you only so high.

BARON: You must both be tired; it is a long journey, and the day is hot.

PERDICAN: Oh dear no! Look how pretty Camille is, father.

BARON: Come, Camille, give your cousin a kiss.

CAMILLE: Pardon me.

BARON: A compliment is worth a kiss. Give her a kiss, Perdican.

PERDICAN: If my cousin draws back when I hold out my hand, I will say to you in my turn: pardon me. Love may steal a kiss, friendship never.

CAMILLE: Neither friendship nor love should accept anything but what they can give back.

BARON. [*To* Master Bridaine] This is an ill-omened beginning, eh?

BRIDAINE: [*To the* Baron] Too much modesty is a fault, no doubt; but marriage does away with a deal of scruples.

BARON: [*To* Master Bridaine] I am shocked—I am hurt. That answer displeased me. Pardon me! Did you see that she made a show of crossing herself? Come here, and let me speak to you. It pains me to the last degree. This moment, that was to be so sweet, is wholly spoiled for me. I am vexed, annoyed. The devil take it; it is a regular bad business.

BRIDAINE. Say a few words to them; look at them turning their backs on each other.

BARON: Well, children, what in the world are you thinking of? What are you doing there, Camille, in front of that tapestry?

CAMILLE: [*Looking at a picture*] That is a fine portrait, uncle. Is it not a great-aunt of ours?

BARON: Yes, my child, it is your great-grandmother —or, at least, your great-grandfather's sister: for the dear lady never contributed—except, I believe, in prayers—to the augmentation of the family. She was a pious woman, upon my honor.

CAMILLE: Oh yes, a saint. She is my great-aunt Isabel. How that nun's dress becomes her!

BARON: And you, Perdican, what are you about before that flower-pot?

PERDICAN: That's a charming flower, father. It is a heliotrope.

BARON: Are you joking? It is no bigger than a fly.

PERDICAN: That little flower no bigger than a fly is worth having all the same.

BRIDAINE: No doubt the doctor is right. Ask him what sex or what class it belongs to, of what elements it consists, whence it gets its sap and its color: he will throw you into ecstasies with a description of the phenomena of yonder sprig, from its root to its flower.

PERDICAN: I do not know so much about it, your reverence. I think it smells good, that is all.

SCENE III.

[*Before the château. Enter the* Chorus]

CHORUS: Several things amuse us and excite our curiosity. Come, friends, sit down under this walnut tree. Two formidable eaters are this moment present at the château—Master Bridaine and Master Blazius. Have you not noticed this—that when two men, closely alike, equally fat and fond of drink, with the same vices and the same passions, come to a meeting by some chance, it follows of necessity that they shall either adore or abominate each other? For the same reason that opposites attract, that a tall lean man will like a short round one, that fair people court the dark, and *vice versa,* I foresee a secret struggle between the tutor and the priest. Both are armed with equal impudence, each has a barrel for a belly; they are not only gluttons, but epicures; both will quarrel at table for quality as well as quantity. If the fish is small, what is to be done? And in any case a carp's tongue can not be divided, and a carp can not have two tongues.

Then both are chatterers; but if the worst should come to the worst, they can talk at once and neither listen to the other. Already Master Bridaine has wanted to put several pedantic questions to young Perdican, and the tutor scowled. It is distasteful to him that his pupil should appear to be examined by any one but himself. Again, one is as ignorant as the other. Again, they are priests, the pair of them: one will parade his benefice, the other will plume himself on the tutorship. Master Blazius is the son's confessor, Master Bridaine the father's. I see them already, elbows on the table, cheeks inflamed, eyes starting out of their heads, shaking their double chins in a paroxysm of hatred. They eye each other from head to foot; they begin the battle with petty skirmishes; soon war is declared; shots are exchanged; volleys of pedantry cross in midair; and, to cap all, between them frets Dame Pluche, repulsing them on either side with her sharp-pointed elbows.

Now that dinner is over, the château gate is opened. The company are coming out; let us step aside out of the way.

[*Exeunt. Enter the* Baron *and* Dame Pluche]

BARON: Venerable Pluche, I am pained.

PLUCHE: Is it possible, my lord?

BARON: Yes, Pluche, possible. I had calculated for a long time past—I had even set it down in black and white on my tablets—that this day was to be the most enjoyable of my life. Yes, my good madame, the most enjoyable. You are not unaware that my plan was to marry my son to my niece. It was decided, arranged—I had mentioned it to Bridaine—and I see, I fancy I see, that these children speak to each other with coolness; they have not said a word to each other.

PLUCHE: There they come, my lord. Are they advised of your projects?

BARON: I dropped a few hints to each of them in private. I think it would be well, since they are thrown together now, that we should sit down under this propitious shade and leave them to themselves for a moment.

[*He withdraws with* Dame Pluche. *Enter* Camille *and* Perdican]

PERDICAN: Do you know, Camille, it was not a bit nice of you to refuse me a kiss?

CAMILLE: I am always like that; it is my way.

PERDICAN: Will you take my arm for a stroll in the village?

CAMILLE: No, I am tired.

PERDICAN: Would it not please you to see the meadow again? Do you remember our boating excursions? Come, we will go down as far as the mill; I will take the oars, and you the tiller.

CAMILLE: I do not feel the least inclined for it.

PERDICAN: You cut me to the heart. What! not one remembrance, Camille? Not a heart-throb for our childhood, for all those kind, sweet past days, so full of delightful sillinesses? You will not come and see the path we used to go by to the farm?

CAMILLE: No, not this evening.

PERDICAN: Not this evening! But when? Our whole life lies there.

CAMILLE: I am not young enough to amuse myself with my dolls, nor old enough to love the past.

PERDICAN: What do you mean by that?

CAMILLE: I mean that recollections of childhood are not to my taste.

PERDICAN: They bore you?

CAMILLE: Yes, they bore me.

PERDICAN: Poor child; I am sincerely sorry for you.

[*Exit in opposite directions*]

BARON: [*Entering with* Dame Pluche] You see and you hear, my excellent Pluche. I expected the softest harmony; and I feel as if I were attending a concert where the violin is playing "My heart it sighs," while the flute plays "Long live King Henry." Think of the frightful discord such a combination would produce! Yet that is what is going on in my heart.

PLUCHE: I must admit it is impossible for me to blame Camille, and to my mind nothing is in worse taste than boating excursions.

BARON: Are you serious?

PLUCHE: My lord, a young lady who respects herself does not risk herself on water.

BARON: But remark, pray Dame Pluche, that her cousin is to marry her, and that thenceforward——

PLUCHE: The proprieties forbid steering; and it is indelicate to leave *terra firma* alone with a young man.

BARON: But I repeat— I tell you——

PLUCHE: That is my opinion——

BARON: Are you mad? Really you would make me say— There are certain expressions that I do not choose—that are repugnant to me. You make me want— Really, if I did not control myself— Pluche, you are a stupid person— I do not know what to think of you.

[*Exeunt*]

SCENE IV.

[*A village green*. The Chorus. Perdican]

PERDICAN: Good day, friends; do you know me?

CHORUS: My lord, you are like a child we loved dearly.

PERDICAN: Was it not you who took me on your back to cross the streams of your meadows, who danced me on your knees, who took me up behind you on your sturdy horses, who crowded closer sometimes round your tables to make room for me at the farm supper?

CHORUS: We remember, my lord. You were certainly the naughtiest rogue and the finest boy on earth.

PERDICAN: Why do you not kiss me then, instead of saluting me like a stranger?

CHORUS: God bless you, child of our hearts. Each of us would like to take you in his arms; but we are old, my lord, and you are a man.

PERDICAN: Yes, it is ten years since I saw you; and in a single day all beneath the sun changes. I have grown some feet toward heaven; you have bowed some inches toward the grave. Your heads have whitened, your steps grown slower; you can no longer lift from the ground your child of long ago. So it is my turn now to be your father—father of you who were fathers to me.

CHORUS: Your return is a happier day than your birth. It is sweeter to recover what we love than to embrace a new-born babe.

PERDICAN: So this is my dear valley: my walnut trees, my green paths, my little fountain. Here are my past days still full of life; here is the mysterious world of my childhood's dreams. Home, ah home!—incomprehensible word. Can man be born just for a single corner of the earth, there to build his nest, and there to live his day?

CHORUS: We hear you are a learned man, my lord.

PERDICAN: Yes, I hear that too. Knowledge is a fine thing, lads. These trees and this meadow find a voice to teach the finest knowledge of all—how to forget what one knows.

CHORUS· There has been many a change during your absence. Girls are married, boys are gone to the army.

PERDICAN: You shall tell me all about it. I expect a deal of news; but to tell the truth, I do not care to hear it yet. How small this pool is; formerly it seemed immense. I had carried away an ocean and forests in my mind: I come back to find a drop of water and blades of grass. But who can that girl be, singing at her lattice behind those trees?

CHORUS: It is Rosette, your cousin Camille's foster-sister.

PERDICAN: [*Stepping forward*] Come down quick, Rosette, and come here.

ROSETTE: [*Entering*] Yes, my lord.

PERDICAN: You saw me from your window, and you did not come, you wicked girl! Give me that hand of yours, quick now, and those cheeks to be kissed.

ROSETTE: Yes, my lord.

PERDICAN: Are you married, little one? They told me so.

ROSETTE: Oh, no!

PERDICAN: Why? There is not a prettier girl than you in the village. We'll find you a match, child.

CHORUS: My lord, she wants to die a maid.

PERDICAN: Is that true, Rosette?

ROSETTE: Oh, no!

PERDICAN: Your sister Camille is come! Have you seen her?

ROSETTE: She has not come this way yet.

PERDICAN: Be off quick, and put on your new dress, and come to supper at the château.

SCENE V.

[*A large room. Enter the* Baron *and* Master Blazius]

BLAZIUS: A word in your ear, my lord. The priest of your parish is a drunkard.

BARON: Shame! it is impossible.

BLAZIUS: I am certain of it. He drank three bottles of wine at dinner.

BARON: That is excessive.

BLAZIUS: And on leaving table he trampled on the flower-beds.

BARON: On the beds. You confound me. This is very strange. Drink three bottles of wine at dinner and trample on the flower-beds. Incomprehensible! And why did he not keep to the path?

BLAZIUS: Because he walked crooked.

BARON: [*Aside*] I begin to think Bridaine was right. This fellow Blazius smells shockingly of wine.

BLAZIUS: Besides, he ate enormously; his utterance was thick.

BARON: Indeed I remarked that myself.

BLAZIUS: He delivered himself of a few Latin phrases; they were so many blunders. My lord, he is a depraved character.

BARON: [*Aside*] Ugh! The odor of this fellow Blazius is past endurance. Understand, Mr. Tutor, that I am engaged with something very different from this, and that I do not concern myself with what is eaten or what is drunk here. I am not a major-domo.

BLAZIUS: Please God, I will never displease you, my lord. Your wine is good.

BARON: There is good wine in my cellars.

[*Enter* Master Bridaine]

BRIDAINE: My lord, your son is out there on the green with all the ragamuffins of the village at his heels.

BARON: It is impossible.

BRIDAINE: I saw it with my own eyes. He was picking up pebbles to make ducks and drakes.

BARON: Ducks and drakes! My brain begins to reel. Here are all my ideas turning upside down. Bridaine, the report you bring me is absurd. It is unheard of that a Doctor of Laws should make ducks and drakes.

BRIDAINE: Go to the window, my lord; you will see with your own eyes.

BARON: [*Aside*] Good heavens! Blazius was right. Bridaine walks crooked.

BRIDAINE: Look, my lord, there he is beside the pond. He has his arm round a peasant girl.

BARON: A peasant girl! Does my son come here to debauch my vassals? His arm round a peasant, and all the rowdies in the village round! I feel myself taking leave of my senses.

BRIDAINE: That calls for retribution.

BARON: All is lost—irretrievably lost. I am lost. Bridaine staggers, Blazius reeks with wine, and my son seduces all the girls in the village while playing ducks and drakes. [*Exit*]

ACT II. SCENE I.

[*A garden. Enter* Master Blazius *and* Perdican]

BLAZIUS: My lord, your father is in despair.

PERDICAN: Why so?

BLAZIUS: You are aware that he had formed a plan of uniting you to your cousin Camille.

PERDICAN: Well, I ask no better!

BLAZIUS: Nevertheless, the Baron thinks he perceives an incompatibility in your characters.

PERDICAN: That is unlucky. I can not remodel mine.

BRAZIUS: Will you allow this to make the match impossible?

PERDICAN: I tell you once more I ask no better than to marry Camille. Go and find the Baron and tell him so.

BLAZIUS: My lord, I withdraw; here comes your cousin.

[*Exit* Blazius. *Enter* Camille]

PERDICAN: Up already. cousin? I stick to what I said yesterday; you are ever so pretty!

CAMILLE: Let us be serious, Perdican. Your father wants to make a match between us. I do not know what you think of it, but I consider it right to forewarn you that I have made up my mind on the matter.

PERDICAN: The worse for me, if you dislike me.

CAMILLE: No more than any one else; I do not intend to marry. There is nothing in that to wound your pride!

PERDICAN: I do not deal in pride: I care for neither its joys nor its pains.

CAMILLE: I came here to enter on possession of my mother's property; to-morrow I go back to my convent.

PERDICAN: Well, you play fair. Shake hands and let us be good friends!

CAMILLE: I do not like demonstrations.

PERDICAN: [*Taking her hand*] Give me your hand, Camille, I beg of you. What do you fear of me? You do not choose that we should be married. Very well! let us not marry. Is that a reason for hating one another? Are we not brother and sister? When your mother enjoined this marriage in her will, she wished that our friendship should be unending, that is all she wished. Why marry? There is your hand, there is mine, and to keep them united thus to our last sigh, do you think we need a priest? We need none but God.

CAMILLE: I am very glad my refusal leaves you unconcerned.

PERDICAN: I am not unconcerned, Camille. Your love would have given me life, but your friendship shall console me for the lack of it. Do not leave the château to-morrow. Yesterday you refused to stroll round the garden with me, because you saw in me a husband you would not accept. Stay here a few days; let me hope that our past life is not dead for ever in your heart.

CAMILLE: I am bound to leave.

PERDICAN: Why?

CAMILLE: That is my secret.

PERDICAN: Do you love another?

CAMILLE: No; but I will go.

PERDICAN: Is it irrevocable?

CAMILLE: Yes, irrevocable.

PERDICAN: Well! adieu. I should have liked to sit with you under the chestnuts in the little wood, and chat like kind friends for an hour or two. But if you do not care for that, let us say no more. Good-by, my child.

[*Exit* Perdican. *Enter* Dame Pluche]

CAMILLE: Is all ready, Dame Pluche? Shall we start to-morrow? Has my guardian finished his accounts?

PLUCHE: Yes, dear unspotted dove. The Baron called me a stupid person yesterday, and I am delighted to go.

CAMILLE: Stay; here is a line you will take to Lord Perdican, before dinner, from me.

PLUCHE: O Lord of heaven! Is it possible? You writing a note to a man——

CAMILLE: Am I not to be his wife? Surely I may write to my fiancé.

PLUCHE: Lord Perdican has just left this spot. What can you have to write? Your fiancé; heaven have pity on us! Can it be true that you are forgetting Jesus?

CAMILLE: Do what I tell you, and make all ready for my departure.

[*Exeunt*]

SCENE II.

[*The dining-room; servants setting the table. Enter* Master Bridaine]

BRIDAINE: Yes, it is a certainty, they will give him the place of honor again to-day. This chair on the Baron's right that I have filled so long will be the tutor's prize. Wretch that I am! A mechanical ass, a brazen drunkard gets me banished to the lower end of the table. The butler will pour for him the first glass of Malaga, and when the dishes reach me they will be half cold; all the tid-bits will be eaten up; not a cabbage nor a carrot left round the partridges. Holy Catholic Church! To give him that place yesterday—well that was intelligible. He had just arrived, and was sitting down to that table for the first time since many a long year. Heavens, how he drank! No, he will leave me nothing but bones and chicken's claws. I will not endure this affront. Farewell, venerable arm-chair in which many and many a time I have thrown myself back stuffed with juicy dishes! Farewell, sealed bottles; farewell, matchless savor of venison done to a turn! Farewell, splendid board, noble dining-hall; I shall say grace here no longer. I return to my vicarage; they shall not see me confounded among the mob of guests; and, like Cæsar, I will rather be first in the village than second in Rome.

SCENE III.

[*A field in front of a cottage. Enter* Rosette *and* Perdican]

PERDICAN: Since your mother is out, come for a little walk.

ROSETTE: Do you think all these kisses do me any good?

PERDICAN: What harm do you see in them? I would kiss you before your mother. Are you not Camille's sister? Am I not your brother just as I am hers?

ROSETTE: Words are words. and kisses are kisses.

I am no better than a fool, and I find it out too, as soon as I have something to say. Fine ladies know what it means if you kiss their right hand, or if you kiss the left. Their fathers kiss them on the forehead; their mothers on the cheeks; and their lovers on the lips. Now everybody kisses me on both cheeks, and that vexes me.

PERDICAN: How pretty you are, child!

ROSETTE: All the same, you must not be angry with me for that. How sad you seem this morning! So your marriage is broken off?

PERDICAN: The peasants of your village remember they loved me; the dogs in the poultry yard and the trees in the wood remember it too; but Camille does not remember. And your marriage, Rosette—when is it to be?

ROSETTE: Do not let us talk of that, if you please? Talk of the weather, of the flowers here, of your horses, of my caps.

PERDICAN: Of whatever you please, of whatever can cross your lips without robbing them of that heavenly smile. [He kisses her]

ROSETTE: You respect my smile, but you do not spare my lips much, it seems to me. Why, do look; there is a drop of rain fallen on my hand, and yet the sky is clear.

PERDICAN: Forgive me.

ROSETTE: What have I done to make you weep?

[Exeunt]

SCENE IV.

[The château. Enter Master Blazius and the Baron]

BLAZIUS: My lord, I have a strange thing to tell you. A few minutes ago I chanced to be in the pantry—I mean in the gallery; what should I be doing in the pantry? Well, I was in the gallery. I had happened to find a decanter—I mean a jug of water. How was I to find a decanter in the gallery? Well, I was just drinking a drop of wine—I mean a glass of water—to pass the time, and I was looking out of the window between two flower vases that seemed to me to be in a modern style, though they are copied from the Etruscan.

BARON: What an intolerable manner of talking you have adopted, Blazius! Your speeches are inexplicable.

BLAZIUS: Listen to me, my lord; lend me a moment's attention. Well, I was looking out of the window. In heaven's name, do not grow impatient. It concerns the honor of the family.

BARON: The family! This is incomprehensible. The honor of the family, Blazius? Do you know there are thirty-seven males of us, and nearly as many females, in Paris and in the country?

BLAZIUS: Allow me to continue. Whilst I was drinking a drop of wine—I mean a glass of water—

to hasten tardy digestion, would you believe I saw Dame Pluche passing under the window out of breath?

BARON: Why out of breath, Blazius? That is unwonted.

BLAZIUS: And beside her, red with anger, your niece Camille.

BARON: Who red with anger—my niece or Dame Pluche?

BLAZIUS: Your niece, my lord.

BARON: My niece red with anger? It is unheard of! And how do you know it was with anger? She might have been red for a thousand reasons. No doubt she had been chasing butterflies in my flowergarden.

BLAZIUS: I can not be positive about that—that may be; but she was exclaiming with vigor, "Go! Find him. Do as you are bid! You are a fool! I will have it!" And she rapped with her fan the elbow of Dame Pluche, who gave a jump in the clover at each exclamation.

BARON: In the clover! And what did the governess reply to my niece's vagaries? for such conduct merits that description.

BLAZIUS: The governess replied: "I will not go! I did not find him. He is making love to the villagers, to silly girls. I am too old to begin to carry love-letters. Thank God, I have kept my hands clean up till now." And while she spoke she was crumpling up in her fingers a scrap of paper folded in four.

BARON: I do not understand at all; my ideas are becoming totally confused. What reason could Dame Pluche have for crumpling a paper folded in four, while she gave jumps in the clover? I can not lend credence to such enormities.

BLAZIUS: Do you not clearly understand, my lord, what that indicated?

BARON: No, upon my honor, my friend; no, I do not understand a word of it, good or bad. All this seems to be a piece of ill-regulated conduct, but equally devoid of motive and excuse.

BLAZIUS: It means that your niece has a clandestine correspondence.

BARON: What are you saying? Do you reflect of whom you are speaking? Weigh your words, Abbé!

BLAZIUS: I might weigh them in the heavenly scales that are to weigh my soul at the last judgment, without finding a single syllable of them that does not ring true. Your niece has a clandestine correspondence.

BARON: But reflect, my friend, that it is impossible.

BLAZIUS: Why should she have entrusted a letter to her governess? Why should she have exclaimed, "Find him!" while the other sulked and petted?

BARON: And to whom was this letter addressed?

BLAZIUS: That is exactly the question—the *hic jacet lepus*.[1] To whom was this letter addressed? To a man who is making love to a silly girl. Now a man who publicly courts a silly girl may be evi-

[1] Here lies the hare.

dently suspected of being himself born to herd geese. Nevertheless, it is impossible that your niece, with the education she has received, should be captivated by such a man. That is what I tell you, and that is why, saving your presence, I do not understand a word of it any more than you.

BARON: Good heavens! My niece declared to me this morning that she refused her cousin Perdican's hand. Can she be in love with a gooseherder? Step into my study. Since yesterday I have experienced such violent shocks that I can not collect my ideas.

[*Exeunt*]

SCENE V.

[*A fountain in a wood. Enter* Perdican, *reading a note*]

PERDICAN: "Be at the little fountain at noon." What does that mean? Such coldness; so positive and cruel a refusal; such unfeeling pride; and, to crown all, a rendezvous. If it is to talk business, why choose such a spot? Is it a piece of coquetry? This morning, as I walked with Rosette, I heard a stir in the brushwood. I thought it was a doe's tread. Is there some plot in this?

[*Enter* Camille]

CAMILLE: Good day, cousin. I thought, rightly or wrongly, that you left me sadly this morning. You took my hand in spite of me. I come to ask you to give me yours. I refused you a kiss—here it is for you. [*Kissing him*] Now then, you said you would like to have a friendly chat with me. Sit down then, and let us talk. [*She sits down*]

PERDICAN: Was it a dream, or do I dream again now?

CAMILLE: You thought it odd to get a note from me, did you not? I am changeable; but you said one thing this morning that was very true: "Since we part, let us part good friends." You do not know the reason of my leaving, and I have come here to tell you. I am going to take the veil.

PERDICAN: Is it possible? Is it you, Camille, that I see reflected in this fountain, sitting on the daisies, as in the old days?

CAMILLE: Yes, Perdican, it is I. I have come to live over again one half-hour of the past life. I seemed to you rude and haughty. That is easily understood; I have renounced the world. Yet, before I leave it, I should like to hear your opinion. Do you think I am right to turn nun?

PERDICAN: Do not question me on the subject, for I shall never turn monk.

CAMILLE: In the ten years almost that we have lived separated from each other you have begun the experience of life. I know the man you are; and a heart and brain like yours must have learned much in a little while. Tell me, have you had mistresses?

PERDICAN: Why so?

CAMILLE: Answer me, I beg of you, without bashfulness and without affectation.

PERDICAN: I have had.

CAMILLE: Did you love them?

PERDICAN: With all my heart.

CAMILLE: Where are they now? Do you know?

PERDICAN: These are odd questions, upon my word. What would you have me say? I am neither their husband nor their brother. They went where it pleased them.

CAMILLE: There must needs have been one you preferred to all others. How long did you love the one you loved best?

PERDICAN: You are a queer girl. Do you want to turn father confessor?

CAMILLE: I ask of you as a favor to answer me sincerely. You are far from a libertine, and I believe that your heart is honest. You must have inspired love, for you are worth it; and you would not have abandoned yourself to a whim. Answer me, I beg.

PERDICAN: On my honor, I do not remember.

CAMILLE: Do you know a man who has loved only one woman?

PERDICAN: There are such, certainly.

CAMILLE: Is he one of your friends? Tell me his name.

PERDICAN: I have no name to tell you; but I believe there are men capable of loving once, and once only.

CAMILLE: How often can an honorable man love?

PERDICAN: Do you want to make me repeat a litany, or are you repeating a catechism yourself?

CAMILLE: I want to get information, and to learn whether I do right or wrong to take the veil. If I married you, would you not be bound to answer all my questions frankly, and lay your heart bare for me to see? I have a great regard for you, and I count you superior by nature and education to many other men. I am sorry you have forgotten the things I question you about. Perhaps if I knew you better I should grow bolder.

PERDICAN: What are you driving at? Go on. I will answer.

CAMILLE: Answer my first question then. Am I right to stay in the convent?

PERDICAN: No!

CAMILLE: Then I should do better to marry you?

PERDICAN: Yes.

CAMILLE: If the priest of your parish breathed on a glass of water, and told you it was a glass of wine, would you drink it as such?

PERDICAN: No!

CAMILLE: If the priest of your parish breathed on you, and told me that you would love all your life, should I do right to believe him?

PERDICAN: Yes, and no.

CAMILLE: What would you advise me to do the day I saw you loved me no longer?

PERDICAN: To take a lover.

CAMILLE: What shall I do next the day my lover loves me no longer?

PERDICAN: Take another.

CAMILLE: How long will that go on?

PERDICAN: Till your hairs are gray, and then mine will be white.

CAMILLE: Do you know what the cloisters are, Perdican? Did you ever sit a whole day long on the bench of a nunnery?

PERDICAN: Yes, I have.

CAMILLE: I have a friend, a sister, thirty years old, who at fifteen had an income of five hundred thousand crowns. She is the most beautiful and noble creature that ever walked on earth. She was a peeress of the parliament,[2] and had for a husband one of the most distinguished men in France. Not one of the faculties that ennoble humanity had been left uncultivated in her, and like a sapling of some choice stock all her buds had branched. Love and happiness will never set their crown of flowers on a fairer forehead. Her husband deceived her; she loved another man, and she is dying of despair.

PERDICAN: That is possible.

CAMILLE: We share the same cell, and I have passed whole nights in talking of her sorrows. They have almost become mine: that is strange, is it not? I do not quite know how it comes to pass. When she spoke to me of her marriage, when she painted the intoxication of the first days, and then the tranquillity of the rest, and how at last the whole had taken wings and flown; how in the evening she sat down at the chimney-corner, and he by the window, without a word said between them; how their love had languished, and how every effort to draw close again only ended in quarrels; how little by little a strange figure came and placed itself between them, and glided in amid their sufferings; it was still myself that I saw acting while she spoke. When she said, "There I was happy," my heart leaped; when she added, "There I wept," my tears flowed. But fancy a thing stranger still. I ended by creating an imaginary life for myself. It lasted four years. It is needless to tell by how many reflected lights, how many doublings on myself all this came about. What I wanted to tell you as a curiosity is that all Louise's tales, all the phantoms of my dreams, bore your likeness.

PERDICAN: My likeness—mine?

CAMILLE: Yes—and that is natural; you were the only man I had known. In all truth I loved you, Perdican.

PERDICAN: How old are you, Camille?

CAMILLE: Eighteen.

PERDICAN: Go on, go on; I am listening.

CAMILLE: There are two hundred women in our convent. A small number of these women will never know life; all the rest are waiting for death. More than one of them left the convent as I leave it to-day, virgin and full of hopes. They returned after a little

[2] In pre-Revolutionary France, a feudal council and court; later, the chief court of a province.

while old and blasted. Every day some of them die in our dormitories, and every day fresh ones come to take the place of the dead on the hair mattresses. Strangers who visit us admire the calm and order of the house; they look attentively at the whiteness of our veils; but they ask themselves why we lower them over our eyes. What do you think of these women, Perdican? Are they wrong or are they right?

PERDICAN: I can not tell.

CAMILLE: There were some of them who counseled me to remain unmarried. I am glad to be able to consult you. Do you believe these women would have done better to take a lover, and counsel me to do the same?

PERDICAN: I can not tell.

CAMILLE: You promised to answer me.

PERDICAN: I am absolved, as a matter of course, from the promise. I do not believe it is you who are speaking.

CAMILLE: That may be; there must be great absurdities in all my ideas. It may well be that I have learned by rote, that I am only an ill-taught parrot. In the gallery there is a little picture that represents a monk bending over a missal; through the gloomy bars of his cell slides a feeble ray of sunlight, and you catch sight of an Italian inn, in front of which dances a goatherd. Which of these two men has more of your esteem?

PERDICAN: Neither one nor the other, and both. They are two men of flesh and blood; there is one that reads and one that dances; I see nothing else in it. You are right to turn nun.

CAMILLE: A minute ago you told me no.

PERDICAN: Did I say no? That is possible.

CAMILLE: So you advise me to do it?

PERDICAN: So you believe in nothing?

CAMILLE: Lift your head, Perdican. Who is the man that believes in nothing?

PERDICAN: [Rising] Here is one: I do not believe in immortal life. My darling sister, the nuns have given you their experience, but believe me it is not yours; you will not die without loving.

CAMILLE: I want to love, but I do not want to suffer. I want to love with an undying love, and to swear vows that are not broken. Here is my lover. [Showing her crucifix]

PERDICAN: That lover does not exclude others.

CAMILLE: For me, at least, he shall exclude them. Do not smile, Perdican. It is ten years since I saw you, and I go to-morrow. In ten years more, if we meet again, we will again speak of this. I did not wish your memory to picture me as a cold statue; for lack of feeling leads to the point I have reached. Listen to me. Return to life; and so long as you are happy, so long as you love as men can love on earth, forget your sister Camille; but if ever it chances to you to be forgotten, or yourself to forget; if the angel of hope abandons you when you are alone, with emptiness in your heart, think of me, who shall be praying for you.

PERDICAN: You are a proud creature; take care of yourself.

CAMILLE: Why?

PERDICAN: You are eighteen, and you do not believe in love.

CAMILLE: Do you believe in it, you who speak to me? There you are, bending beside me knees that have worn themselves on the carpets of your mistresses, whose very names you forget. You have wept tears of joy and tears of despair; but you knew that the spring water was more constant than your tears, and would be always there to wash your swollen eyelids. You follow your vocation of young man, and you smile when one speaks to you of women's lives blasted; you do not believe that love can kill, since you have loved and live. What is the world then? It seems to me that you must cordially despise the women who take you as you are, and who dismiss their last lover to draw you to their arms with another's kisses on their lips. A moment ago I was asking you if you had loved. You answered me like a traveler whom one might ask had he been in Italy or in Germany, and who should say, "Yes, I have been there"; then should think of going to Switzerland or the first country you may name. Is your love a coinage then, that it can pass like this from hand to hand till the day of death? No, not even a coin; for the tiniest gold piece is better than you, and whatever hand it may pass to, still keeps its stamp.

PERDICAN: How beautiful you are, Camille, when your eyes grow bright!

CAMILLE: Yes, I am beautiful; I know it. Compliment-mongers will teach me nothing new. The cold nun who cuts my hair off will perhaps turn pale at her work of mutilation; but it shall not change into rings and chains to go the round of the boudoirs. Not a strand of it shall be missing from my head when the steel passes there. I ask only one snap of the scissors, and when the consecrating priest draws on my finger the gold ring of my heavenly spouse, the tress of hair I give him may serve him for a cloak.

PERDICAN: Upon my word, you are angry.

CAMILLE: I did wrong to speak; my whole life is on my lips. Oh, Perdican, do not scoff; it is all deathly sad.

PERDICAN: Poor child, I let you speak, and I have a good mind to answer you one word. You speak to me of a nun who appears to me to have a disastrous influence upon you. You say that she has been deceived, that she herself has been false, and that she is in despair. Are you sure that if her husband or her lover came back, and stretched his hand to her through the grating of the convent parlor, she would not give him hers?

CAMILLE: What do you say? I did not understand.

PERDICAN: Are you sure that if her husband or her lover came, and bade her suffer again, she would answer, no?

CAMILLE: I believe it.

PERDICAN: There are two hundred women in your convent, and most of them have in the recesses of their hearts deep wounds. They have made you touch them, and they have dyed your maiden thoughts with drops of their blood. They have lived, have they not? And they have shown you shudderingly their life's road. You have crossed yourself before their scars as you would before the wounds of Jesus. They have made a place for you in their doleful processions, and you press closer to these fleshless bodies with a religious dread when you see a man pass. Are you sure that if the man passing were he who deceived them, he for whom they weep and suffer, he whom they curse as they pray to God—are you sure that at sight of him they would not burst their fetters to fly to their past misfortunes, and to press their bleeding breasts against the poniard that scarred them? Oh, child! do you know the dreams of these women who tell you not to dream? Do you know what name they murmur when the sighs issuing from their lips shake the sacramental host as it is offered to them? These women who sit down by you with swaying heads to pour into your ear the poison of their tarnished age, who clang among the ruins of your youth the tocsin of their despair, and strike into your crimson blood the chill of their tombs, do you know who they are?

CAMILLE: You frighten me. Anger is gaining upon you too.

PERDICAN: Do you know what nuns are, unhappy girl? Do they who represent to you men's love as a lie, know that there is a worse thing still—the lie of a divine love? Do they know that they commit a crime when they come whispering to a maiden, woman's talk? Ah! how they have schooled you! How clearly I divined all this when you stopped before the portrait of our old aunt! You wanted to go without pressing my hand; you would not revisit this wood, nor this poor little fountain that looks at us bathed in tears; you were a renegade to the days of your childhood, and the mask of plaster the nuns have placed on your cheeks refused me a brother's kiss. But your heart beat; it forgot its lesson, for it has not learned to read, and you returned to sit on this turf where now we are. Well, Camille, these women said well. They put you in the right path. It may cost me my life's happiness, but tell them from me—heaven is not for them.

CAMILLE: Nor for me, is it?

PERDICAN: Farewell, Camille. Return to your convent; and when they tell you one of their hideous stories that have poisoned your nature, give them the answer: "All men are liars, fickle, chatterers, hypocrites, proud or cowardly, despicable, sensual; all women faithless, tricky, vain, inquisitive, and depraved." The world is only a bottomless cesspool, where the most shapeless sea-beasts climb and writhe on mountains of slime. But there is in the world a thing holy and sublime—the union of two of these beings, imperfect and frightful as they are. One is often deceived in love, often wounded, often unhappy; but one loves, and on the brink of the grave one turns to look back and says: I have suffered often, sometimes I have been mistaken, but I have loved. It is I who have lived, and not a spurious being bred of my pride and my sorrow. [*Exit*]

ACT III. SCENE I.

[*The front of the château. Enter the* Baron *and* Master Blazius]

BARON: Independently of your drunkenness, you are a worthless fellow, Master Blazius. My servants see you enter the pantry furtively; and when you are accused of having stolen my wine, in the most pitiable manner you think to justify yourself by accusing my niece of a clandestine correspondence.

BLAZIUS: But, my lord, pray remember——

BARON: Leave the house, Abbé, and never appear before me again. It is unreasonable to act as you do, and my self-respect constrains me never to pardon you as long as I live.

[*Exit* Baron. Master Blazius *follows. Enter* Perdican]

PERDICAN: I should like to know if I am in love. On the one hand, there is that fashion of questioning me, a trifle bold for a girl of eighteen. On the other, the ideas that these nuns have stuffed into her head will not be set right without trouble. Besides, she is to go to-day. Confound it! I love her; there is not a doubt of it. After all, who knows! Perhaps she was repeating a lesson; and besides, it is clear she does not trouble her head about me. On the other hand again, her prettiness is all very well; but that does not alter the fact that she has much too decided a manner and too curt a tone. My only plan is to think no more of it. It is plain I do not love her. There is no doubt she is pretty; but why can I not put yesterday's talk out of my head? Upon my word, my wits were wandering all last night. Now where am I going? Ah, I am going to the village. [*Exit*]

SCENE II.

[*A road. Enter* Master Bridaine]

BRIDAINE: What are they doing now? Alas! there is twelve o'clock. They are at table. What are they eating? What are they not eating? I saw the cook cross the village with a huge turkey. The scullion carried the truffles, with a basket of grapes.

[*Enter* Master Blazius]

BLAZIUS: Oh, unforeseen disgrace! here I am turned out of the château, and, in consequence, from the dinner-table. I shall never drink the wine in the pantry again.

BRIDAINE: I shall never see the dishes smoke again. Never again before the blaze of that noble hearth shall I warm my capacious belly.

BLAZIUS: Why did a fatal curiosity prompt me to listen to the conversation between Dame Pluche and the niece? Why did I report all I saw to the Baron?

BRIDAINE: Why did an idle pride remove me from that honorable dinner when I was so kindly welcomed? What mattered to me the seat on the right or seat on the left?

BLAZIUS: Alas! I was tipsy, it must be admitted, when I committed this folly.

BRIDAINE: Alas! the wine had mounted to my head when I was guilty of this rashness.

BLAZIUS: Yonder is the Vicar, I think.

BRIDAINE: It is the tutor in person.

BLAZIUS: Oh! oh! Vicar, what are you doing here?

BRIDAINE: I? I am going to dinner. Are you not coming?

BLAZIUS: Alas, Master Bridaine, intercede for me; the Baron has dismissed me. I falsely accused Mademoiselle Camille of having a clandestine correspondence; and yet, God is my witness that I saw, or thought I saw, Dame Pluche in the clover. I am ruined, Vicar.

BRIDAINE: What do you tell me?

BLAZIUS: Alas! alas! the truth. I am in utter disgrace for stealing a bottle.

BRIDAINE: What has this talk of stolen bottles to do, sir, with a clover patch and correspondence?

BLAZIUS: I entreat you to plead my cause. I am honorable, my Lord Bridaine. O worshipful Lord Bridaine, I am yours to command.

BRIDAINE: O fortune! is it a dream? Shall I then be seated on yon blessed chair?

BLAZIUS: I shall be grateful to you would you hear my story and kindly excuse me, your worship, my dear Vicar.

BRIDAINE: That is impossible, sir; it has struck twelve, and I am off to dinner. If the Baron complains of you, that is your business. I do not intercede for a sot. [*Aside*] Quick, fly to the gate: swell, my stomach. [*Exit running*]

BLAZIUS: [*Alone*] Wretched Pluche! it is you shall pay for them all; yes, it is you are the cause of my ruin, shameless woman, vile go-between, it is to you I owe my disgrace. Holy University of Paris! I am called sot! I am undone if I do not get hold of a letter, and if I do not prove to the Baron that his niece has a correspondence. I saw her writing at her desk this morning. Patience! here comes news!

[*Dame Pluche passes carrying a letter*]
Pluche, give me that letter.

PLUCHE: What is the meaning of this? It is a letter of my mistress's that I am going to post in the village.

BLAZIUS: Give it to me, or you are a dead woman.

PLUCHE: I dead! Dead?

BLAZIUS: Yes, dead, Pluche; give me that paper.

[*They fight. Enter* Perdican]

PERDICAN: What is this? What are you about, Blazius? Why are you molesting this woman?

PLUCHE: Give me back the letter. He took it from me, my lord. Justice!

BLAZIUS: She is a go-between, my lord. That letter is a billet-doux.

PLUCHE: It is a letter of Camille's, my lord— your fiancée's.

BLAZIUS: It is a billet-doux to a gooseherder.

PLUCHE: You lie, Abbé. Let me tell you that.

PERDICAN: Give me that letter. I understand nothing about your quarrel; but as Camille's fiancé, I claim the right to read it. [*Reads*] "To Sister Louise, at the Convent of ——." Leave me, Dame Pluche; you are a worthy woman, and Master Blazius is a fool. Go to dinner; I undertake to put this letter in the post.

[*Exeunt* Master Blazius *and* Dame Pluche]

PERDICAN: [*Alone*] That it is a crime to open a letter I know too well to be guilty of it. What can Camille be saying to this sister? Am I in love after all? What empire has this strange girl gained over me that the line of writing on this address should make my hand shake? That's odd; Blazius in his struggle with Dame Pluche has burst the seal. Is it a crime to unfold it? No matter, I will put everything just as it was. [*Opens the letter and reads*] "I am leaving today, my dear, and all has happened as I had foreseen. It is a terrible thing; but that poor young man has a dagger in his heart; he will never be consoled for having lost me. Yet I have done everything in the world to disgust him with me. Gòd will pardon me for having reduced him to despair by my refusal. Alas! my dear, what could I do? Pray for me; we shall meet again to-morrow, and forever. Yours with my whole soul—CAMILLE." Is it possible? That is how Camille writes! That is how she speaks of me! I in despair at her refusal! Oh! Good heavens, if that were true it would be easily seen; what shame could there be in loving? She does everything in the world, she says, to disgust me, and I have a dagger in my heart. What reason can she have to invent such a romance? Is it then true—the thought that I had to-night? Oh women! This poor Camille has great piety perhaps. With a willing heart she gives herself to God, but she has resolved and decreed that she would leave me in despair. That was settled between the two friends before she left the convent. It was decided that Camille was going to see her cousin again, that they would wish her to marry him, that she would refuse, and that the cousin would be in despair. It is so interesting for a young girl to sacrifice to God the happiness of a cousin! No, no, Camille, I do not love you, I am not in despair, I have not a dagger in my heart, and I will prove it to you. Yes, before you leave this you shall know that I love another. Here, my good man!

[*Enter a* Peasant]

Go to the château; tell them in the kitchen to send a servant to take this note to Mademoiselle Camille. [*He writes*]

PEASANT: Yes, my lord. [*He goes out*]

PERDICAN: Now for the other. Ah! I am in despair. Here! Rosette, Rosette! [*He knocks at a door*]

ROSETTE: [*Opening it*] Is it you, my lord? Come in, my mother is here.

PERDICAN: Put on your prettiest cap, Rosette, and come with me.

ROSETTE: Where?

PERDICAN: I will tell you. Ask leave of your mother, but make haste.

ROSETTE: Yes, my lord. [*She goes into the house*]

PERDICAN: I have asked Camille for another rendezvous, and I am sure she will come; but, by heaven, she will not find what she expects there. I mean to make love to Rosette before Camille herself.

SCENE III.

[*The little wood. Enter* Camille *and the* Peasant]

PEASANT: I am going to the château with a letter for you, mademoiselle. Must I give it to you, or must I leave it in the kitchen, as Lord Perdican told me?

CAMILLE: Give it me.

PEASANT: If you would rather I took it to the château, it is not worth while waiting here.

CAMILLE: Give it me, I tell you.

PEASANT: As you please. [*Gives the letter*]

CAMILLE: Stop. There is for your trouble.

PEASANT: Much obliged. I may go, may I not?

CAMILLE: If you like.

PEASANT: I am going, I am going. [*Exit*]

CAMILLE: [*Reading*] Perdican asks me to say good-by to him before leaving, near the little fountain where I brought him yesterday. What can he have to say to me? Why, here is the fountain, and I am on the spot. Ought I to grant this second rendezvous? Ah! [*Hides behind a tree*] There is Perdican coming this way with my foster-sister. I suppose he will leave her. I am glad that I shall not seem to be the first to arrive.

[*Enter* Perdican *and* Rosette, *and sit down*]

CAMILLE: [*Hidden, aside*] What is the meaning of this? He is making her sit down beside him. Does he ask me for a rendezvous to come there and talk with another girl? I am curious to know what he says to her.

PERDICAN: [*Aloud, so that* Camille *hears*] I love you, Rosette. You alone, out of all the world, have forgotten nothing of our good days that are past. You are the only one who remembers the life that is no more. Share my new life. Give me your heart, sweet child. There is the pledge of our love. [*Putting his chain on her neck*]

ROSETTE: Are you giving me your gold chain?

PERDICAN: Now look at this ring. Stand up and let us come near the fountain. Do you see us both in the spring leaning on each other? Do you see your lovely eyes near mine, your hand in mine? Watch how all that is blotted out. [*Throwing his ring into the water*] Look how our image has disappeared. There it is coming back little by little. The troubled water regains its tranquillity. It trembles still. Great black rings float over its surface. Patience. We are reappearing. Already I can make out again your arms entwined in mine. One minute more and there will not be a wrinkle left in your pretty face. Look! It was a ring that Camille gave me.

CAMILLE: [*Aside*] He has thrown my ring into the water.

PERDICAN: Do you know what love is, Rosette? Listen! the wind is hushed; the morning rain runs pearling over the parched leaves that the sun revives. By the light of heaven, by this sun we see, I love you! You will have me, will you not? No one has tarnished your youth! No one has distilled into your crimson blood the dregs of jaded veins! You do not want to turn nun? There you stand, young and fair, in a young man's arms. O Rosette, Rosette, do you know what love is?

ROSETTE: Alas, Doctor, I will love you as best I can.

PERDICAN: Yes, as best you can; and that will be better, doctor though I am, and peasant though you are, than these pale statues can love, fashioned by nuns, their heads where their hearts should be, who leave the cloisters to come and spread through life the damp atmosphere of their cells. You know nothing; you could not read in a book the prayer that your mother taught you as she learned it from her mother. You do not even understand the sense of the words you repeat when you kneel at your bedside; but you understand that you are praying, and that is all God wants.

ROSETTE: How speak you, my lord!

PERDICAN: You can not read; but you can tell what these woods and meadows say, their warm rivers and fair harvest-covered fields, and all this nature radiant with youth. You recognize all these thousands of brothers and me as one of them. Rise up; you shall be my wife, and together we shall strike root into the vital currents of the almighty world.

SCENE IV.

[*Enter the* Chorus]

CHORUS: Certainly there is something strange going on at the château. Camille has refused to marry Perdican. She is to return to the convent from which she came. But I think his lordship, her cousin, has consoled himself with Rosette. Alas! the poor girl does not know the risk she runs in listening to the speeches of a gallant young nobleman.

[*Enter* Dame Pluche]

PLUCHE: Quick! quick! saddle my ass.

CHORUS: Will you pass away like a beautiful dream, venerable lady? Are you going to bestride anew so soon that poor beast who is so sad to bear your weight?

PLUCHE: Thank God, my sweet rabble, I shall not die here!

CHORUS: Die far from here, Pluche, my darling; die unknown in some unwholesome cavern. We will pray for your worshipful resurrection.

PLUCHE: Here comes my mistress. [*To* Camille, *who enters*] Dear Camille, all is ready for our start; the Baron has rendered his account, and they have pack-saddled my ass.

CAMILLE: Go to the devil, you and your ass too! I shall not start to-day. [*Exit*]

CHORUS: What can this mean? Dame Pluche is pale with anger; her false hair tries to stand on end, her chest whistles, and her fingers stretch out convulsively.

PLUCHE: Lord God of heaven! Camille swore!

[*Exit* Pluche]

SCENE V.

[*Enter the* Baron *and* Master Bridaine]

BRIDAINE: My lord, I must speak to you in private. Your son is making love to a village girl.

BARON: It is absurd, my friend.

BRIDAINE: I distinctly saw him passing in the heather with her on his arm. He was bending his head to her ear and promising to marry her.

BARON: This is monstrous.

BRIDAINE: You may be convinced of it. He made her a considerable present that the girl showed her mother.

BARON: Heavens, Bridaine, considerable? In what way considerable?

BRIDAINE: In weight and importance. It was the gold chain he used to wear in his cap.

BARON: Let us step into my study. I do not know what to think of it.

[*Exeunt*]

SCENE VI.

[Camille's *room. Enter* Camille *and* Dame Pluche]

CAMILLE: He took my letter, you say?

PLUCHE: Yes, my child; he undertook to put it in the post.

CAMILLE: Go to the drawing-room, Dame Pluche, and do me the kindness to tell Perdican that I expect him here.

[*Exit* Dame Pluche]

He read my letter, that is a certainty. His scene in the wood was a retaliation, like his love for Rosette. He wished to prove to me that he loved another girl, and to play at unconcern in spite of his vexation. Could he be in love with me by any chance? [*She lifts the tapestry*] Are you there, Rosette?

ROSETTE: [*Entering*] Yes; may I come in?

CAMILLE: Listen to me, my child. Is not Lord Perdican making love to you?

ROSETTE: Alas! yes.

CAMILLE: What do you think of what he said to you this morning?

ROSETTE: This morning? Where?

CAMILLE: Do not play the hypocrite. This morning at the fountain in the little wood.

ROSETTE: You saw me there?

CAMILLE: Poor innocent! No, I did not see you. He made you fine speeches, did he not? I would wager he promised to marry you.

ROSETTE: How do you know that?

CAMILLE: What matter how? I know it. Do you believe in his promises, Rosette?

ROSETTE: Why, how could I help it? He deceive me? Why should he?

CAMILLE: Perdican will not marry you, my child.

ROSETTE: Alas! I can not tell.

CAMILLE: You are in love with him, poor girl. He will not marry you; and for proof, you shall have it. Go behind this curtain. You need only keep your ears open, and come when I call you.

[*Exit* Rosette]

CAMILLE: [*Alone*] Can it be that I, who thought I was doing an act of vengeance, am doing an act of humanity? The poor girl's heart is caught.

[*Enter* Perdican]

Good morning, cousin. Please sit down.

PERDICAN: What a toilette, Camille. Whose scalp are you after?

CAMILLE: Yours perhaps. I am sorry I could not come to the rendezvous you asked for; had you anything to say to me?

PERDICAN: [*Aside*] A good-sized fib that, on my life, for a spotless lamb. I saw her listening to the conversation behind a tree. [*Aloud*] I have nothing to say to you but a farewell, Camille. I thought you were starting; yet your horse is in the stable, and you do not look as if you were dressed for traveling.

CAMILLE: I like discussion. I am not very sure that I did not want to quarrel with you again.

PERDICAN: What is the use in quarreling when it is impossible to make friends again? The pleasure of disputes is in making peace.

CAMILLE: Are you convinced that I do not wish to make it?

PERDICAN: Do not laugh at me; I am no match for you there.

CAMILLE: I should like a flirtation. I do not know whether it is that I have a new dress on, but I want to amuse myself. You proposed going to the village; let us go. I am ready; let us take the boat. I want to picnic on the grass, or to take a stroll in the forest. Will it be moonlight this evening? That is odd; you have not the ring I gave you on your finger.

PERDICAN: I have lost it.

CAMILLE: Then that is why I found it. There, Perdican; here it is for you.

PERDICAN: Is it possible? Where did you find it?

CAMILLE: You are looking to see if my hands are wet, are you not? Indeed, I spoiled my convent dress to get this little child's plaything out of the fountain. That is why I have put on another, and I tell you it has changed me. Come, put that on your finger.

PERDICAN: You got this ring out of the water, Camille, at the risk of falling in yourself. Is this a dream? There it is. It is you who are putting it on my finger. Ah, Camille, why do you give it me back, this sad pledge of a happiness that exists no longer? Speak, coquette; speak, rash girl. Why do you go? Why do you stay? Why do you change aspect and color from hour to hour, like the stone of this ring at every ray of the sun?

CAMILLE: Do you know the heart of women, Perdican? Are you sure of their inconstancy, and do you know whether they really change in thought when they change in words sometimes? Some say no. Undoubtedly we often have to play a part, often lie. You see I am frank. But are you sure that the whole woman lies when her tongue lies? Have you reflected well on the nature of this weak and passionate being, on the sternness with which she is judged, and on the rules that are imposed on her? And who knows whether, forced by the world into deceit, this little brainless being's head may not take a pleasure in it, and. lie sometimes for pastime or for folly, as she does for necessity?

PERDICAN: I understand nothing of all this, and I never lie. I love you, Camille. That is all I know.

CAMILLE: You say that you love me, and that you never lie——

PERDICAN: Never.

CAMILLE: Yet here is one who says that that sometimes happens to you. [*She raises the tapestry. Rosette is seen in the distance fainting on a chair*] What answer will you make to this child, Perdican, when she demands an account of your words? If you never lie, how comes it then that she fainted on hearing you tell me that you love me? I leave you with her. Try to restore her. [*She attempts to leave*]

PERDICAN: One moment, Camille. Listen to me.

CAMILLE: What would you tell me? It is to Rosette you should speak. I do not love you. I did not go out of spite and fetch this unhappy child from the shelter of her cottage, to make a bait and a plaything of her. I did not rashly repeat before her burning words addressed to another woman. I did not feign to hurl to the winds for her sake the remembrance of a cherished friendship. I did not put my chain on her neck. I did not tell her I would marry her.

PERDICAN: Listen to me, listen to me.

CAMILLE: Did you not smile a moment ago when I told you I had not been able to go to the fountain? Well. Yes, I was there, and I heard all. But God is my witness, I would not care to have spoken as you spoke there. What will you do with that girl yonder, now when she comes with your passionate kisses on her lips and shows you, weeping, the wound you have dealt her? You wished to be revenged on me—did you not?—and to punish me for a letter written to my convent. You wished to loosen, at whatever cost, any shaft that could reach me, and you counted it as nothing to pierce this child with your poisoned arrow, provided it struck me behind her. I had boasted of having inspired some love in you, of leaving you some regret for me. So that wounded you in your noble pride! Well, learn it from my lips. You love me—do you hear?—but you will marry that girl, or you are a coward.

PERDICAN: Yes, I will marry her.

CAMILLE: And you will do well.

PERDICAN: Right well, and far better than if I married you yourself. Why so hot, Camille? This child has fainted. We shall easily restore her. A flask of vinegar is all that is needed. You wished to prove to me that I had lied once in my life. That is possible, but I think you are bold to determine at what moment. Come, help me to aid Rosette.

[Exeunt]

SCENE VII.

[The Baron and Camille]

BARON: If that takes place, I shall run mad.

CAMILLE: Use your authority.

BARON: I shall run mad, and I shall refuse my consent, that's certain.

CAMILLE: You ought to speak to him, and make him listen to reason.

BARON: This will throw me into despair for the whole carnival, and I shall not appear once at court. It is a disproportioned marriage. Nobody ever heard of marrying one's cousin's foster-sister; that passes all kinds of bounds.

CAMILLE: Send for him, and tell him flatly that you do not like the marriage. Believe me, it is a piece of madness, and he will not resist.

BARON: I shall be in black this winter, be assured of that.

CAMILLE: But speak to him, in heaven's name.

This is a freak of his; perhaps it is too late already; if he has spoken of it, he will carry it out.

BARON: I am going to shut myself up, that I may abandon myself to my sorrow. Tell him, if he asks for me, that I have shut myself up, and that I am abandoning myself to my sorrow at seeing him wed a nameless girl. [Exit]

CAMILLE: Shall I not find a man of sense here? Upon my word, when you look for one, the solitude becomes appalling.

[Enter Perdican]

Well, cousin, and when is the wedding to be?

PERDICAN: As soon as possible; I have mentioned it already to the notary, the priest, and all the peasants.

CAMILLE: You really think, then, that you will marry Rosette?

PERDICAN: Assuredly.

CAMILLE: What will your father say?

PERDICAN: Whatever he pleases; I choose to marry this girl; it is an idea for which I am indebted to you, and I stand to it. Need I repeat to you the hackneyed commonplaces about my birth and hers? She is young and pretty, and she loves me; it is more than one needs to be trebly happy. Whether she has brains or not, I might have found worse. People will raise an outcry, and a laugh; I wash my hands of them.

CAMILLE: There is nothing laughable in it; you do very well to marry her. But I am sorry for you on one account: people will say you married her out of spite.

PERDICAN: You sorry for that? Oh, no!

CAMILLE: Yes, I am really sorry for it. It injures a young man to be unable to resist a moment's annoyance.

PERDICAN: Be sorry then; for my part, it is all one to me.

CAMILLE: But you do not mean it; she is nobody.

PERDICAN: She will be somebody then, when she is my wife.

CAMILLE: You will tire of her before the notary has put on his best coat and his shoes, to come here; your gorge will rise at the wedding breakfast, and the evening of the ceremony you will have her hands and feet cut off, as they do in the "Arabian Nights," because she smells of *ragoût*.

PERDICAN: No such thing, you will see. You do not know me. When a woman is gentle and affectionate, fresh, kind, and beautiful, I am capable of contenting myself with that; yes, upon my word, even to the length of not caring to know if she speaks Latin.

CAMILLE: It is a pity there was so much money spent on teaching it to you: it is three thousand crowns lost.

PERDICAN: Yes; they would have done better to give it to the poor.

CAMILLE: You will take charge of it, for the poor in spirit, at least.

PERDICAN: And they will give me in exchange the kingdom of heaven, for it is theirs.

CAMILLE: How long will this sport last?

PERDICAN: What sport?

CAMILLE: Your marriage with Rosette.

PERDICAN: A very little while: God has not made man a lasting piece of work: thirty or forty years at the most.

CAMILLE: I look forward to dancing at your wedding.

PERDICAN: Listen to me, Camille, this tone of raillery is out of place.

CAMILLE: I like it too well to leave it.

PERDICAN: Then I leave you, for I have enough of you for the moment.

CAMILLE: Are you going to your bride's home?

PERDICAN: Yes, this instant.

CAMILLE: Give me your arm; I am going there too.

[Enter Rosette]

PERDICAN: Here you are, my child. Come, I want to present you to my father.

ROSETTE: [Kneeling down] My lord, I am come to ask a favor of you. All the village people I spoke to this morning told me that you loved your cousin, and that you only made love to me to amuse both of you; I am laughed at as I pass, and I shall not be able to find a husband in the country, now that I have been the laughing-stock of the neighborhood. Allow me to give you the necklace you gave me, and to live in peace with my mother.

CAMILLE: You are a good girl, Rosette; keep the necklace. It is I who give it you, and my cousin will take mine in its place. As for a husband, do not trouble your head for that; I undertake to find one for you.

PERDICAN: Certainly there is no difficulty about that. Come, Rosette, come and let me take you to my father.

CAMILLE: Why? It is useless.

PERDICAN: Yes, you are right; my father would receive us ill; we must let the first moment of his surprise pass by. Come with me; we will go back to the green. A good joke indeed that it should be said I do not love you, when I am marrying you. By Jove, we will silence them. [Exit with Rosette]

CAMILLE: What can be happening in me? He takes her away with a very tranquil air. That is odd; my head seems to be swimming. Could he marry her in good earnest? Ho! Dame Pluche, Dame Pluche! Is no one here?

[Enter a Footman]

Run after Lord Perdican; make haste, and tell him to come here again, I want to speak to him.

[Exit Footman]

What in the world is all this? I can bear no more; my feet refuse to support me.

[Re-enter Perdican]

PERDICAN: You asked for me, Camille?

CAMILLE: No—no——

PERDICAN: Truly you are pale; what have you to say to me? You recalled me to speak to me.

CAMILLE: No—no—— O Lord God! [Exit]

SCENE VIII.

[An oratory.[3] Enter Camille. She throws herself at the foot of the altar]

CAMILLE: Have you abandoned me, O my God? You know when I came here I had promised to be faithful to you. When I refused to become the bride of another than you, I thought I spoke in singleness of heart, before you and before my conscience. You know it, O my Father! Do not reject me now. Ah, why do you make truth itself a liar? Why am I so weak? Ah, unhappy girl that I am; I can pray no more!

[Enter Perdican]

PERDICAN: Pride, most fatal of men's counselors, why didst thou come between this girl and me? Yonder is she, pale and affrighted, pressing on the unfeeling stone her heart and her face. She might have loved me. We were born for one another. Wherefore camest thou on our lips, O Pride, when our hands were about to join——?

CAMILLE: Who followed me? Who speaks beneath this vault? Is it you, Perdican?

PERDICAN: Blind fools that we are; we love each other. What were we dreaming, Camille? What vain words, what wretched follies passed between us like a pestilent wind? Which wished to deceive the other? Alas, this life is in itself so sad a dream; why should we confound it further with fancies of our own? Oh, my God, happiness is a pearl so rare in this ocean of a world. Thou, Heavenly Fisherman, hadst given it us; Thou hadst fetched it for us from the depths of the abyss, this priceless jewel; and we, like spoiled children that we are, made a plaything of it. The green path that led us toward each other sloped so gently, such flowery shrubs surrounded it, it merged in so calm a horizon—and vanity, light talking, and anger must cast their shapeless rocks on this celestial way, which would have brought us to thee in a kiss. We must do wrong, for we are of mankind. O blind fools! We love each other——!

CAMILLE: Yes, we love each other, Perdican. Let me feel it on your heart. The God who looks down on us will not be offended. It is by His will that I love you. He has known it these fifteen years.

PERDICAN: Dear one, you are mine.

[He kisses her. A great cry is heard from behind the altar]

---

[3] A small chapel for private devotions.

CAMILLE: It is my foster-sister's voice.

PERDICAN: How does she come here? I had left her on the staircase when you sent to bring me back. She must have followed me unobserved.

CAMILLE: Come out into the gallery; the cry was from there.

PERDICAN: What is this I feel? I think my hands are covered with blood.

CAMILLE: The poor child must have spied on us. She has fainted again. Come, let us bring her help. Alas! it is all cruel——

PERDICAN: No, truly, I will not go in. I feel a deadly chill that paralyzes me. Go you, Camille, and try to restore her.

[*Exit* Camille]

I beseech you, my God, do not make me a murderer. You see what is happening. We are two senseless children. We played with life and death, but our hearts are pure. Do not kill Rosette, O righteous God! I will find her a husband; I will repair my fault. She is young; she will be happy. Do not do that, O God! You may yet bless four of your children.

[*Enter* Camille]

Well, Camille, what is it?

CAMILLE: She is dead. Farewell, Perdican!

Georg Büchner

(1813–1837)

The brevity of many promising careers in the romantic movement has often been noted. One of the briefest was that of Georg Büchner, who died in his twenty-fourth year. He may be called the Chatterton of German literature, although the epithet is no description of his singular creativeness. His work was, indeed, so meager and at the same time so unusual that although he found two contemporary admirers in the playwright Gutzkow and the poet Herwegh, his reputation was posthumous and long delayed. His collected works were first published forty-two years after his death, and only after a lapse of another thirty years did this edition, carefully revised, win any attention. His memorable fragment *Woyzeck* was first staged in 1913 and his only full-length drama, *Danton's Death,* in 1916. He became known almost entirely through Max Reinhardt's production of *Danton* and Alban Berg's modernist opera *Wozzeck* (1925).

Büchner was born on October 17, 1813, near Darmstadt, the son of a surgeon in Napoleon's army who later became a medical officer of the duchy of Hesse-Darmstadt. The boy grew up under the vigilant eye of a disillusioned and unorthodox yet staunchly antiliberal martinet who had no sympathy for his son's literary aspirations. It was from his father, however, that the young writer acquired the naturalistic views which differentiate his work from that of other writers of the period. His scientific bent, indeed, asserted itself early, in a school where the classics dominated the curriculum. Büchner left Darmstadt to prepare himself for medicine at the University of Strasbourg and then at Giessen. After an exciting interlude as a writer and political revolutionary, he earned a doctorate in science and was given a lectureship in comparative anatomy at the University of Zurich. By then his revolutionary ardor had cooled and he had a distinguished scientific career ahead of him when he succumbed to brain fever.

Büchner might not have turned to literature at all but for the democratic "Young Germany" movement of the eighteen-thirties, which attracted many young idealists, including the poet Heinrich Heine, the playwright Karl Gutzkow, and Karl Marx. During his two-year term of study at Strasbourg he evinced slight interest in politics; he took a poet's pleasure in nature, an intellectual's interest in discussion, and a lover's delight in a young woman, a parson's daughter, to whom he became engaged in 1834. But he had no sooner gone to Giessen to continue his studies than he was drawn into an underground circle by a liberal Protestant clergyman. Büchner became an active conspirator and journalist in behalf of the movement, writing and circulating in 1834 a semisocialistic pamphlet, *The Hessian Courier,* later considered one of the most brilliant political brochures in the German language. The pamphlet fell into the hands of the authorities, his underground Society for the Rights of Man was betrayed, arrests followed, and Büchner found it expedient to leave Giessen.

He returned home, was interrogated there by the police, and lived under constant fear of imprisonment. It was during this crisis in his young life that he completed *Danton's Death* during the year 1835, writing it feverishly, on his father's laboratory table. The play arose from his own involvement in a revolutionary movement and from his voracious reading of histories of the French Revolution of 1789, although Büchner's objective account is anything but the work of a zealot. (To *Danton's Death* he brought a naturalist's perceptions and an idealist's views on the irrational courses that a revolutionary struggle should not follow.) Patrols were watching the house while he finished his work.

Fortunately, Büchner was able to escape to Strasbourg, whose authorities hesitated to extradite political prisoners, and it was here that he wrote his short comedy *Leonce and Lena,* a combination of whimsy and satire on the aristocracy, and his naturalistic *Woyzeck* fragment, a gripping drama of a conscript driven to desperation by jealousy and humiliation. He wrote a third play, *Pietro Aretino,* evidently even more trenchantly naturalistic, since his shocked fiancée, the parson's daughter, destroyed it after his death as an indecent piece of writing. To sustain himself he also translated two of Victor Hugo's plays, *Maria Tudor* and *Lucrezia Borgia,* and started a novel, *Lenz,* intended for serialization in Gutzkow's newspaper *The Telegraph* but left uncompleted when the periodical was suppressed. And in Strasbourg he also completed his doctoral dissertation, on the strength of which he obtained his appointment to the University of Zurich.

The furthest reaches of Büchner's talents appear in *Woyzeck* and *Danton's Death.* Responding with precocious alertness to the tensions of his age and situation, he wove a modern fabric of thought and sensibility in his work. Taking advantage of the freedom of dramatic form introduced by romanticism, moreover, he wrote staccato drama, surcharged with action and feeling, in brief and seemingly disjointed scenes often crude but also extremely effective. The form and style of both *Woyzeck* and

Danton's Death bear a strong resemblance to motion-picture montage and to the surging expressionism of such twentieth-century plays as O'Neill's *The Hairy Ape* and Toller's *Man and the Masses*. Büchner may consequently be regarded as both a naturalist and an expressionist well in advance of his time. He was, besides, an anachronism among the romantic idealists of the age, especially after losing his revolutionary ardor. His point of view is the antiromantic, deterministic one of later-nineteenth-century mechanistic science. "Individuals," he wrote in a fascinating letter, "are so much surf on a wave, greatness the sheerest accident, the strength of genius a puppet play—a child's struggle against an iron law."

Danton's Death projects this fatalistic view and exhibits Büchner's curiously modern dramaturgy. If the play betrays the haste of its writing and the immaturity of its author, it is, nonetheless, a probing and profoundly troubling historical tragedy. Measured by conventional standards, it is chaotic; read unimaginatively, it is ambiguous and confusing. But its form is its substance. Büchner captured the swirling character of a great upheaval in which ideals and ambitions, humanity and inhumanity, justice and injustice, became hopelessly tangled. In such a whirl of events, the individual who tries to retain his equilibrium is helplessly tossed about and driven into a state of apathy and despair, as Danton is, or into hypomanic excesses, as the mob-man is. At the same time, two powerful individuals, Danton and Robespierre, are locked in conflict, and the protagonist, the great Danton, is a profoundly tragic figure in his defiant isolation. The creator of a revolution becomes its prisoner and ultimately its prey. Here, then, we have a tragic hero whose struggle is both personal and historical, and whose destiny is both individually and historically determined. *Danton's Death,* which treats a theme that could hardly have been more immediate if it had been written in 1950, is in all respects a modern tragedy involving man and the masses, revolutionists and the questionable fruits of revolution.

DANTON'S DEATH

By Georg Büchner

TRANSLATED FROM THE GERMAN BY STEPHEN SPENDER AND GORONWY REES

CHARACTERS

GEORGES DANTON[1]
LEGENDRE
CAMILLE DESMOULINS[2]
HÉRAULT-SÉCHELLES
LACROIX } deputies
PHILIPPEAU
FABRE D'EGLANTINE
MERCIER
THOMAS PAYNE [PAINE]
ROBESPIERRE
SAINT-JUST
BARÈRE } members of the Committee of Public Safety
COLLOT D'HERBOIS
BILLAUD-VARENNES
CHAUMETTE, *Procurator of the Paris Commune*
DILLON, *a general*

FOUQUIER-TINVILLE, *public prosecutor*
AMAR
VOULAND } *members of the Committee of Security*
HERMAN
DUMAS } *presidents of the Revolutionary Tribunal*
PARIS, *friend to Danton*
SIMON, *a prompter*
LAFLOTTE
JULIE, *Danton's wife*
LUCILE, *wife of Camille Desmoulins*
ADELAIDE
MARION } *prostitutes*
ROSALIE
MEN AND WOMEN OF THE PEOPLE, PROSTITUTES, EXECUTIONERS, ETC.

ACT I. SCENE I.

[Hérault-Séchelles, Ladies (*at a card table*). Danton, Julie, *a little apart,* Danton *on a stool at Julie's feet*]

DANTON: See the pretty lady, how cleverly she shuffles the cards! Yes, really, she understands! They say she deals hearts to her husband and diamonds to everyone else. She has clumsy legs and she's apt to fall; her husband carries the bumps on his forehead, he thinks they're bumps of humor and laughs them off. You could make a man fall in love with lies.

JULIE: Do you believe in me?

DANTON: How do I know? We know little of one another. We are thick-skinned, our hands reach out to each other but it's waste of time, leather rubs against leather—we are very lonely.

JULIE: You know me, Danton.

[1] Georges Jacques Danton (1759–1794), the French revolutionary leader, lawyer, and founder of the revolutionary Cordelier club, who assumed leadership of the French Revolution and became minister of justice under the Republic. In that capacity and as a member of the Committee of Public Safety, he introduced repressive measures against the enemies of the Republic and the moderate Girondist faction. But he lost power late in 1793 to Robespierre and the extremist elements of the Revolution, was imprisoned and tried, and was guillotined on April 5, 1794.

[2] Desmoulins (1760–1794) was a brilliant pamphleteer of the French Revolution.

DANTON: Yes, what one calls knowing. You have dark eyes and curly hair and a delicate complexion and always call me 'Dear George.' But there, there! [*Touching her eyes and her forehead*] What lies behind them? Look, our senses are gross. Know each other! We'd have to break open our skulls and pick out the thoughts from our brain-boxes.

A LADY: [*To* Hérault] What are you doing with your fingers?

HÉRAULT: Nothing.

LADY: Don't stick your thumbs in like that, it's unbearable.

HÉRAULT: You see, it has a peculiar significance.

DANTON: No, Julie, I love you like the grave.

JULIE: [*Turning away*] Oh!

DANTON: No, listen. They say that in the grave there is peace, and that the grave and peace are one. If that is so, then lying in your lap I am already under the earth. Sweet grave, your lips are funeral bells, your voice my death knell, your breast the mound above me, and your heart my coffin.

LADY: [*To* Hérault] You've lost.

HÉRAULT: It was a lover's adventure, that cost money like all the others.

LADY: Then you declared your love like a deaf mute—with your fingers.

HÉRAULT: And why not? People even say that they are easiest to understand. I had an affair with a queen, my fingers were princes bewitched into spiders, and you, madam, were the fairy; but it went badly, the queen was always pregnant, and every minute gave birth to a knave. I wouldn't let my daughter play such games; kings and queens lie on top of each other so shamelessly, and the knaves come close behind.

[*Enter* Camille Desmoulins *and* Philippeau]

HÉRAULT: What sad eyes, Philippeau! Have you torn a hole in your red cap? Has St. Jacob[3] frowned on you? Did it rain during the executions? Or did you get a bad place and see nothing?

CAMILLE: You parody Socrates. Do you know what the divine philosopher asked Alcibiades, when he found him sad and depressed? 'Have you lost your shield on the battle-field? Have you been beaten in a race or a duel? Has someone sung better or struck the lyre better than you?' What classical Republicans! Take some of our guillotine romanticism against it!

PHILIPPEAU: To-day another twenty victims have fallen. We made a mistake, the Hébertists[4] were only sent to the guillotine because they weren't systematic enough, and perhaps because the Decemvirs[5] thought they were lost, if for over a week men existed who were even more feared than they.

HÉRAULT: They'd like to send us back to the stone age. Saint-Just wouldn't mind if we crawled on all fours, so that the lawyer from Arras could give us school-caps and benches and a God Almighty after the mechanism of the Geneva watchmaker.

PHILIPPEAU: They wouldn't shrink from hanging on a few noughts to Marat's figures for the proscriptions. How long must we remain dirty and bloody like new-born children, have coffins for cradles and heads for dolls? We must advance. The Committee of Clemency must be set up, the expelled deputies must be reinstated.

HÉRAULT: The Revolution has entered the period of reorganization.—The Revolution must end, and the Republic must begin.—In our Constitution right must take the place of duty, happiness the place of virtue, protection the place of punishment. Every individual must count, and be able to assert his own nature. He may be reasonable or unreasonable, educated or uneducated, good or bad—it's no concern of the State's. We are all fools and no one has the right to impose his own particular folly on any one else.—Every one must be allowed to enjoy himself in his own way, so long as he does not enjoy himself at the expense of others and does not interfere with their pleasure. The individuality of the majority must be revealed in the form of the State.

CAMILLE: The Constitution should be a transparent veil, clinging closely to the body of the People. It

must answer to every throb of their veins, every tension of the muscles, every pulse of desire. The body may be fair or foul, it has the right to be what it is, and we have no right to cut its clothes to our measure.—We will rap over the knuckles those who wish to throw a nun's hood over the naked shoulders of France, loveliest of sinners.—We want naked Gods Bacchantes, Olympic games, roses in our hair, sparkling wine, heaving breasts and singing lips; oh, wicked, limb-loosening Love!—We don't want to prevent the Romans from sitting in the corner and cooking roots; but we'll have no more gladiatorial games. The divine Epicurus and Venus with the lovely buttocks shall be the door-keepers of the Republic, instead of St. Marat and St. Chalier. Danton, you will make the attack in the Convention!

DANTON: I shall, thou wilt, he will. If we live till then, as the old women say. After an hour sixty minutes will have passed, isn't that so, my boy?

CAMILLE: What do you mean? That goes without saying.

DANTON: Oh, it all goes without saying. And who is to put all these fine things into action?

PHILIPPEAU: We, and all honest men.

DANTON: That 'and' in between is a long word, it holds us rather far apart; there's a long distance to cover and Honesty will be out of breath before we meet. And when we do!—you can lend money to honest men, you can be godfather to their children and marry them to your daughters, but that's all.

CAMILLE: If you know that, why did you begin the struggle?

DANTON: Those people annoyed me. I couldn't look at those swaggering Catos, without giving them a kick. That is my nature. [*Rises*]

JULIE: You're going?

DANTON: [*To* Julie] I must get out of here; they rub me up the wrong way again with their politics. [*On his way out*] Between the door and the door-post I will prophesy unto you; the Statue of Liberty has not yet been cast, the furnace is glowing, and we can still all burn our fingers. [*Exit*]

CAMILLE: Leave him alone! Do you think he can keep his hands off if it comes to action?

HÉRAULT: No, but only to kill time, as one plays chess.

SCENE II.

[*A street*. Simon. *His* Wife]

SIMON: [*Beats his* Wife] You old pimp, you wrinkled pill, you maggotty apple of sin.

WIFE: Help, help!

PEOPLE: [*Running in*] Pull them apart, pull them apart!

SIMON: Unhand me, Romans! I'll batter these bones to bits! You vestal virgin!

WIFE: Me a vestal virgin? I'll say I am.

---

[3] A reference to the ultrarevolutionary Jacobin Club, which clamored for the execution of suspected enemies of the French Republic.

[4] Followers of Jacques-René Hébert (1757–1794); an extremist faction of the French Revolution that was crushed by Robespierre.

[5] A body of ten magistrates in ancient Rome. The reference here is to the French Committee of Public Safety, which, led by Robespierre, ruled the French Republic.

SIMON: **Thus** from thy shoulders I tear off thy robe, and **naked** in the sun display thine arse. You whore's bed, lust breeds in every wrinkle of your body.

[*They are separated*]

1ST CITIZEN: What's the matter?

SIMON: Where is the virgin? Speak! No, I can't say virgin. The maiden? No, not that either. The woman, the wife! Oh, not even that! There's only one other name; oh, it chokes me! I've no breath to say it.

2ND CITIZEN: Lucky you haven't, or it would stink of brandy.

SIMON: Aged Virginius, veil your hoary head—the raven shame sits upon it and pecks at your eyes. Give me a knife, Romans! [*He sinks to the ground*]

WIFE: Ah, usually he's a good man, but he can't carry much drink; brandy gives him an extra leg.

2ND CITIZEN: Then he must walk on three.

WIFE: No, he falls down.

2ND CITIZEN: Quite right, first he walks on three legs, then falls over the third until the third itself falls down again.

SIMON: You're the vampire's tongue that sucks my warmest heart's blood.

WIFE: Just leave him alone; now's the time he always get sentimental; it'll soon be over.

1ST CITIZEN: But what's up?

WIFE: Well, it was like this, you see. I was sitting on a stone in the sun, warming myself, you see— we've got no firewood, you see—

2ND CITIZEN: Use your husband's nose—

WIFE: —and my daughter had gone down to the corner—she's a fine girl and supports her parents.

SIMON: There, she confesses!

WIFE: You Judas, would you have a pair of trousers to put on if the young gentlemen didn't take theirs off with her? You brandy cask, do you want to thirst when the fountain ceases to flow?—We work with all our limbs, why not with that one? Her mother did, when she brought her into the world, and it gave her pain; can't she get something for her mother with it, eh? and does it give her pain, eh? You idiot!

SIMON: Ha, Lucretia! A knife, give me a knife, Romans! Ha, Appius Claudius!

1ST CITIZEN: Yes, a knife, but not for the poor whore! What has she done? Nothing! Her hunger whores and begs. A knife for the people who buy the flesh of our wives and daughters! Woe to those who whore with the daughters of the people! Your stomachs are empty, theirs are filled to bursting; you have holes in your coats, they have warm clothes; you have horny hands, theirs are soft as silk. *Ergo,* you toil and they do nothing; *ergo,* you earn your bread and they have stolen it; *ergo,* when you want a few coppers of your stolen property you must whore and beg; *ergo,* they are thieves, and we must cut off their heads.

3RD CITIZEN: They have no blood in their veins but what they have sucked out of ours. They told us: kill the aristocrats, they are wolves! We hanged the aristocrats from the lantern. They said to us: the veto[6] devours your bread. We killed the veto. They said to us: the Girondins are starving you. We sent the Girondins to the guillotine. But they have taken the dead men's clothes and we go naked and freeze as before. We will peel the skin from their bones to make trousers for ourselves, we will melt down their fat and make soup out of it. Forward! Death to all who have no holes in their clothes!

1ST CITIZEN: Death to all who can read and write!

2ND CITIZEN: Death to all who go abroad!

ALL: Death, death!

[*A Young Man is dragged on*]

VOICES: He's got a handkerchief! An aristocrat! To the lantern! to the lantern!

2ND CITIZEN: What? He doesn't wipe his nose with his fingers? To the lantern!

[*A lantern is let down*]

YOUNG MAN: Gentlemen!

2ND CITIZEN: There are no gentlemen here! To the lantern!

SOME: [*Sing*]

> Who lie in the earth
> Are eaten by worms,
> Better hang in the air
> Than rot in the grave.

YOUNG MAN: Mercy!

3RD CITIZEN: Only a game with a hempen noose round your neck! It only takes a minute, we're kinder-hearted than you. Our life is murder by hard labor; for sixty years we hang by the rope and struggle, but we'll cut ourselves loose.—To the lantern!

YOUNG MAN: I don't care, it won't help you to see any clearer.

CROWD: Bravo, bravo!

SOME VOICES: Let him go!

[*He disappears*]

[*Enter* Robespierre, *followed by* Women *and* Sans-Culottes]

ROBESPIERRE: What's wrong, citizens?

3RD CITIZEN: What's wrong? The few drops of blood shed in August and September have not made the cheeks of the people red. The guillotine is too slow. We need a hailstorm.

1ST CITIZEN: Our wives and children cry for bread, we want to feed them with the flesh of aristocrats. Death to all with no holes in their clothes!

ALL: Death, death!

ROBESPIERRE: In the name of the law!

1ST CITIZEN: What is the law?

ROBESPIERRE: The will of the people.

1ST CITIZEN: We are the people, and our will is there should be no law; *ergo,* our will is the law, *ergo,* in the name of the law there is no law, *ergo,* death!

VOICES: Silence for Aristides! silence for the Incorruptible!

6 The king's veto on legislation before Louis XVI was overthrown by the French Revolution.

A WOMAN: Hear the Messiah, who is sent to elect and to judge; he will strike the wicked with the edge of the sword. His eyes are the eyes of election, his hands are the hands of judgment.

ROBESPIERRE: Poor, virtuous People! You do your duty, you sacrifice your enemies. People, thou art great! In flashes of lightning and in thunder thou art revealed. But my people, your blows must not wound your own body; you murder yourself in your fury. You can fall only through your own strength; your enemies know it well. Your legislators watch over you, they will guide your hands; their eyes are unerring, your hands are inescapable. Come with me to the Jacobin Club! Your brothers will open their arms to you, we will hold a bloody assize on our enemies.

MANY VOICES: To the Jacobins! Long live Robespierre!

[All off]

SIMON: Alas, abandoned! [He tries to rise]

WIFE: There! [Supports him]

SIMON: Ah, my Baucis, you heap coals of fire on my head.

WIFE: Now stand up.

SIMON: You turn away? Can you forgive me, Portia? Did I strike you? It was not my hand, it was not my arm, my madness did it.

Then Hamlet did it not; Hamlet denies it.
His madness is poor Hamlet's enemy.

Where is our daughter, where is my Susie?

WIFE: There, on the corner!

SIMON: Let us go to her! Come, my virtuous spouse!

[Exeunt]

SCENE III.

[The Jacobin Club]

A CITIZEN FROM LYONS: Our brothers in Lyons have sent us to pour out their bitter anger on your breast. We do not know if the tumbril that carried Ronsin to the guillotine was the hearse of Liberty; but we do know that since that day Chalier's murderers have trod the earth as safely as if no grave were waiting for them. Have you forgotten that Lyons is a stain upon the earth of France which must be covered by the limbs of traitors? Have you forgotten that this whore of kings has only the waters of the Rhone in which to wash her scabs? Have you forgotten that the flood tide of the Revolution must wash Pitt's Mediterranean fleet aground on the corpses of aristocrats? Your compassion is murdering the Revolution. The breath of an aristocrat is the death rattle of Freedom. Only a coward dies for the Republic; a Jacobin kills for her. I warn you; if we no longer find in you the energy of the men of the 10th of August, of September, and the 31st of May, there remains for us, as for the patriot Gaillard, only the dagger of Cato.[7]

[Applause and confused cries]

A JACOBIN: We will drink the cup of Socrates with you!

LEGENDRE: [Springs to the tribune] We have no need to turn our eyes to Lyons. In the last few days the people who wear silken clothes, who ride in carriages, who sit in boxes at the theatre and speak like the dictionary of the Academy have carried their heads firmly on their shoulders. They are witty and say Marat and Chalier should be given a second martyrdom and be guillotined in effigy.

[Sensation throughout the assembly]

SOME VOICES: They are dead men, their tongues have guillotined them.

LEGENDRE: The blood of these saints be upon them! I ask the members of the Committee of Public Safety here present, since when have their ears become so deaf—

COLLOT D'HERBOIS: [Interrupting] And I ask you, Legendre, whose voice gives breath to such thoughts, so that they come to life and dare to speak? The time has come to tear off the mask. Listen to me! The cause is accusing its effect, the voice its echo, the premise its conclusion. The Committee of Public Safety is more logical than that, Legendre. Be calm! The busts of these saints will remain undisturbed and like heads of Medusa they will turn the traitors to stone.

ROBESPIERRE: I demand the tribune!

THE JACOBINS: Silence, silence for the Incorruptible!

ROBESPIERRE: We waited only for the cries of dissatisfaction which resounded on every side before we spoke. Our eyes were open, we saw the enemy arm and rise, but we did not sound the alarm; we let the people watch over itself, and the people has not slumbered, the people has rushed to arms. We allowed the enemy to come out of hiding, we allowed him to advance; now he stands free and unconcealed in the light of day, and every stroke will find its mark; he is dead as soon as you have seen him.

I have said it to you before; the internal enemies of the Republic have fallen into two groups, like two

[7] The 10th of August: date of the attack on the Tuileries palace during the French Revolution; the 31st of May: date of the defeat of the moderate Girondin faction, which opposed the massacre of aristocrats, refused to vote for the execution of Louis XVI, and on May 31, 1793, staged an unsuccessful *coup* against the extremist leadership of the Revolution; September: a reference to the slaughter of prisoners by a band of revolutionists paid by the Paris Commune as a result of an invasion of the Prussian army, which tried to quell the French Revolution; Gaillard: a citizen of Lyons who stabbed himself upon learning of the arrest of his Hébertist leader, General Ronsin, by the Committee of Public Safety, which ruled France; Cato: conspirator against Julius Caesar, with Brutus and Cassius, who killed himself when the republican cause was defeated.

armies. Under different flags and by different ways they march towards the same goal. One of these factions is no more. In its affectation and madness it tried to set aside as worn-out weaklings the most proven patriots, so as to deprive the Republic of its strongest arms. They declared war on God and on Property, to create a diversion in favor of the Kings. They parodied the sublime drama of the Revolution, so as to discredit it by calculated excesses. The triumph of Hébert would have transformed the Republic into chaos, and despotism would have been satisfied. The sword of the law has struck down the traitor. But what do the foreigners care, so long as they have criminals of another brand through whom to achieve the same end? We have accomplished nothing, so long as a second faction remains to be destroyed.

That faction is the opposite of the first. They force us to be weak, their battle-cry is: Mercy! They wish to rob the People of its weapons, and the strength to use these weapons, so as to hand the people over naked and enfeebled to the Kings.

The weapon of the Republic is the Terror, the strength of the Republic is Virtue—Virtue because without it the Terror is pernicious, the Terror because without it Virtue is powerless. The Terror is the consequence of Virtue, the Terror is nothing else than swift, strong, and unswerving Justice. They say that the Terror is an instrument of dictatorship and that our Government therefore resembles a dictatorship. Granted! but only as the sword in the hand of Freedom's heroes resembles the sabre with which the satellites of tyrants are armed. If a tyrant rules his brutish subjects through terror he is, as a tyrant, justified; destroy the enemies of freedom through terror and as the founders of the Republic you are no less justified. The Revolutionary Government is the dictatorship of freedom against tyranny.

Certain people shout 'Mercy on the Royalists!' Mercy for criminals? No! Mercy for the innocent, mercy for the weak, mercy for the unfortunate, mercy for Mankind! Only the law-abiding citizen deserves protection by society.

In a republic only republicans are citizens, royalists and foreigners are enemies. To punish the oppressors of mankind is mercy; to pardon them is barbarism. Every display of false sensibility seems to me a sigh that flies to England or to Austria.

But they are not content to disarm the People; they even try to poison the purest sources of its strength by Vice. Of all attacks on Freedom, that is the subtlest, the most dangerous, the most loathsome. Only the most hellish Machiavellianism—but no! I will not say that such a plan could be misbegotten in a human mind! It may not be intentional, but the intention is beside the point, the effect is the same, the danger equally great. Vice is the brand of Cain on the forehead of Aristocracy. In a republic it is not merely a moral but a political offence. The libertine is the political opponent of freedom, and is the more

dangerous the greater the services he seems to perform. The most dangerous citizen is he who finds it easier to wear out a dozen red caps than to do a single good action.

You will find it easy to understand me, if you think of people who once lived in attics and now ride in carriages and fornicate with ci-devant[8] countesses and duchesses. We may well ask: have they plundered the People or have they pressed the golden hands of the Kings, when we see the People's law-givers parading with all the vices and luxury of the former courtiers, when we see these counts and marquesses of the Revolution marrying rich wives, giving magnificent banquets, gambling, keeping servants, and wearing costly clothes? We may well be astonished when we hear of their wit, their culture, and their good taste. A short time ago one of them gave a shameful parody of Tacitus, I could answer out of Sallust and travesty Catiline; but I imagine there is nothing more for me to add, the portrait is complete.

No compromise, no truce with men who thought only of exploiting the people, who hope to carry out their plans with impunity, to whom the Republic is a speculation and the Revolution a trade! Terrified by the mounting tide of examples, they now softly seek to mitigate our justice. One might think that each of them said to himself: 'We are not virtuous enough to employ such terror. Philosophic law-givers, have pity on our weakness! I dare not say to you that I am vicious; so I say to you rather: be not pitiless!'

Be calm, virtuous People, be calm, you patriots! Tell your comrades in Lyons: the sword of the law does not rust in the hands to which you have entrusted it!—We shall set the Republic a great example.

[*General applause*]

MANY VOICES: Long live the Republic! Long live Robespierre!

PRESIDENT: The session is closed.

SCENE IV.

[*A street*]

LACROIX: What have you done, Legendre? Do you realize whose head you've thrown down with those busts of yours?

LEGENDRE: A few dandies, and some elegant women, that's all.

LACROIX: You're a suicide, a shadow who murders his original and with it himself.

LEGENDRE: I don't understand.

LACROIX: I thought Collot spoke clearly enough.

LEGENDRE: What does that matter? It was as if a champagne bottle burst. He was drunk again.

LACROIX: Fools, babes, and—well?—drunkards tell the truth. Whom do you think Robespierre meant by Catiline?

[8] Former; that is, before the French Revolution abolished titles of nobility.

LEGENDRE: Well?

LACROIX: The thing's simple. The atheists and the extremists have been sent to the guillotine; but the people are no better off, they go barefoot in the streets and want to make shoes out of the skins of aristocrats. The thermometer of the guillotine must not fall; a few degrees lower and the Committee of Public Safety can make its bed on the Place de la Révolution.

LEGENDRE: What has all this to do with my busts?

LACROIX: Still don't you see? You have made the counter-revolution known officially, you've forced the Committee to take energetic measures, you've directed their hands. The people is a Minotaur that must be fed with corpses every week if it is not to eat the Committee alive.

LEGENDRE: Where is Danton?

LACROIX: How should I know? He's trying to discover the Venus de Medici piecemeal in all the tarts in the Palais Royal; he's making mosaics, as he says. God knows what limb he's got to now. What a pity that Nature cuts up beauty into so many pieces, like Medea with her brothers, and deposits it in fragments in people's bodies.—Let's go to the Palais Royal.

SCENE V.

[*A room*. Danton, Marion]

MARION: No, don't touch me! At your feet like this. I'll tell you a story.

DANTON: Your lips have better uses.

MARION: No, let me alone for once.—I came of a good family. My mother was a clever woman and brought me up carefully. She always told me that modesty is a great virtue. When people came to the house and began to speak of certain things she sent me out of the room; if I asked what they meant she said I ought to be ashamed of myself; if she gave me a book to read, there were almost always some pages I had to leave out. But I could read as much as I liked of the Bible; every page of it was holy. There were some things in it I couldn't understand. I couldn't ask any one; I brooded over myself. Then the Spring came, and all around me something was happening, something I had no share in. A strange atmosphere surrounded me; it almost stifled me. I looked at my own body; sometimes I felt as if there were two of me, and then again I melted into one. In those days a young man came to visit us; he was handsome and often said silly things to me; I didn't quite know what they meant, but I couldn't help laughing. My mother made him come often; it suited us both. In the end we couldn't see why we shouldn't just as well lie beside each other between the sheets as sit beside each other on two chairs. It gave me more pleasure than his conversation and I didn't see why I should be allowed the smaller and denied the

greater. We did it secretly. That went on. But I was like a sea that swallowed everything and sank deeper and deeper into itself. For me only my opposite existed, all men melted into one body. It was my nature, who can get beyond that? In the end he noticed. One morning he came and kissed me as if he was going to suffocate me; his arms closed tightly round my neck, I was in terrible fear. Then he released me, laughed and said he had nearly done a stupid thing. He said I need only keep my dress and use it, it would soon wear out by itself; he didn't want to spoil my fun for me too soon, and after all it was the only thing I had. Then he went away; I still didn't know what he meant. In the evening I was sitting at the window; I am very sensitive and my only hold on everything around me is through feeling; I sank into the waves of the sunset. Then a crowd came down the street, children ran ahead, women watched from the windows. I looked down; they carried him past in a basket, the moon shone on his pale forehead, his curls were wet—he had drowned himself. I had to cry. It was the one break in my whole being. Other people have Sundays and weekdays, they work for six days and pray on the seventh, once a year they have a birthday and feel sentimental, and every year they look forward to New Year. All that means nothing to me; for me there are no dates, no changes. I am always one thing only, an unbroken longing and desire, a flame, a stream. My mother died of grief; people point their fingers at me. That is stupid. Only one thing matters, what people enjoy, whether it's the body, or holy images, wine, flowers, or toys; the feeling is the same; those who enjoy most, pray most.

DANTON: Why can't I gather your beauty into myself, embrace it completely?

MARION: Danton, your lips have eyes.

DANTON: I wish I were part of the air, to bathe you in my flood and break myself on every wave of your beautiful body.

[*Enter* Lacroix, Adelaide, Rosalie]

LACROIX: [*Remains in the doorway*] I must laugh, I must laugh.

DANTON: [*Suspiciously*] Well?

LACROIX: I was thinking about the street.

DANTON: And?

LACROIX: In the street two dogs—a mastiff and an Italian poodle—were having a go at each other.

DANTON: What does that matter?

LACROIX: It just occurred to me and I couldn't help laughing. It was so edifying. The girls were watching from the windows; people ought to be more careful and not let them sit in the sun. The flies tickle their hands and that puts ideas into their heads. —Legendre and I have visited nearly every cell here, and the nuns of the Revelation through the Flesh clung to our coat tails and demanded a blessing. Legendre is administering penance to one of them, but he'll have to fast a month for it himself. Here are two priestesses of the body I've brought with me.

MARION: Good day, Mlle Adelaide, good day, Mlle Rosalie.

ROSALIE: It's a long time since we had the pleasure.

MARION: I was sorry not to see you.

ADELAIDE: Oh God, we're busy night and day.

DANTON: [To Rosalie] What slender hips you've acquired, little one.

ROSALIE: Oh, one improves every day.

LACROIX: What's the difference between an ancient and a modern Adonis?

DANTON: And Adelaide's become spiritually suggestive; it's a piquant change. Her face looks like a fig leaf which she holds before her whole body. Such a fig-tree gives a refreshing shade in so crowded a street.

ADELAIDE: I'd be a cattle truck, if Monsieur—

DANTON: I understand; only don't be angry, my girl.

LACROIX: Listen! A modern Adonis is torn not by a boar but by sows. He receives his wound not in the thigh but the parts, and from his blood no roses blossom but buds of mercury shoot up.

DANTON: Mlle Rosalie is a restored torso, of which only the hips and feet are antique. She's a magnetic needle, and what the pole of the head repels the pole of the feet attracts; the center is an equator where every one crossing the line for the first time needs to be ducked in mercury.

LACROIX: Two sisters of mercy; each works in a hospital, that is, in her own body.

ROSALIE: Aren't you ashamed of yourselves? Our ears are burning.

ADELAIDE: You ought to have more manners!

[Exeunt Rosalie and Adelaide]

DANTON: Good night, pretty children.

LACROIX: Good night, mercury mines.

DANTON: I'm sorry for them, they've lost their supper.

LACROIX: Listen, Danton, I've come from the Jacobins.

DANTON: Is that all?

LACROIX: The delegation from Lyons read a proclamation, as if there was nothing left for them but to wrap themselves in a toga. Every one made a face as if to say to his neighbor: 'Paetus,[9] it doesn't hurt.' Legendre cried that there were some who wished to destroy the busts of Marat and Chalier. I think he wants to paint himself red again. He's come through the Terror with a whole skin and the children tug at his coat in the streets.

DANTON: And Robespierre?

LACROIX: Tapped his fingers on the tribune and said: Virtue must rule through Terror. The phrase gives me a pain in the neck.

DANTON: It saws the planks for the guillotine.

LACROIX: And Collot cried as if possessed that the masks must be torn off.

DANTON: The faces will come away with them.

[Enter Paris]

LACROIX: What is it, Fabricius?

PARIS: From the Jacobins I went to Robespierre; I demanded an explanation. He tried to look like Brutus sacrificing his children, generalized about duty and said that in the defence of freedom he had no scruples and would make every sacrifice—himself, his brothers, his friends.

DANTON: That's perfectly clear; one has only to reverse the order and he comes underneath and holds out the ladder for his friends. We ought to thank Legendre, he has made them speak out.

LACROIX: The Hébertists aren't dead yet, and the people are starving; that is a terrible lever. The scale of blood must not grow lighter or it will lift the Committee of Public Safety to the lantern. They need ballast, they need one heavy head.

DANTON: I know, I know—the Revolution is like Saturn and devours her own children. [After a pause] And yet, they will not dare.

LACROIX: Danton, you're a dead saint; but the Revolution has no use for relics, it threw the limbs of kings into the gutter and all the holy images out of the churches. Do you think they'd leave you standing as a monument?

DANTON: My name! The People!

LACROIX: Your name! You're a moderate, and so am I and so are Camille, Philippeau, Hérault. To the people moderation is the same as weakness; they kill every one who lags behind. The tailors in the Section of Red Caps would feel all Roman history in their needles if the Man of September[10] had become a moderate compared with them.

DANTON: Perfectly true; and besides—the People is a child who smashes everything to see what's inside.

LACROIX: And in any case, Danton, as Robespierre says, we are vicious; that is, we enjoy ourselves. The People are virtuous, that is, they do not enjoy themselves, because work dulls their organs of pleasure; they don't drink because they have no money, and they don't go to brothels because their breath stinks of cheese and herrings and the girls are disgusted by it.

DANTON: They hate the pleasure-loving, as eunuchs hate men.

LACROIX: They call us rogues, and [in Danton's ear] between ourselves there's something in what they say. Robespierre and the masses will be virtuous, Saint-Just will write a novel, Barère will cut a Carmagnole[11] and wrap the Convention in a mantle of blood and—I see it all.

DANTON: You're dreaming. They had no courage without me, they'll have none against me. The Revolution is not yet ended, they may still need me; they'll hang me up in the Arsenal.

[9] Arria, wife of Paetus, was condemned to death by the Roman emperor Claudius but killed herself first, declaring, "Paete, non dolet"—"Paetus, it doesn't hurt."

[10] Robespierre.

[11] A revolutionary song to which the populace danced in 1793.

LACROIX: We must act.

DANTON: A way will be found.

LACROIX: A way will be found when we are lost.

MARION: [*To* Danton] Your lips have grown cold, your words have choked your kisses.

DANTON: [*To* Marion] So much time wasted! It's not worth the trouble! [*To* Lacroix] To-morrow I'll go to Robespierre; I'll make him angry, he can't keep his mouth shut then. So to-morrow! Good night, my friends, good night! Many thanks!

LACROIX: Get out, my good friends, get out! Good night, Danton! A girl's legs will be your guillotine, the Mound of Venus your Tarpeian Rock.

[*Exit with* Paris]

SCENE VI.

[*A room.* Robespierre, Danton, Paris]

ROBESPIERRE: I tell you, any one who falls on my arm when I draw the sword is my enemy—his motive's beside the point; a man who hinders me from defending myself kills me just as much as if he attacked me.

DANTON: Where self-defence ends, murder begins; I see no reason that forces us to go on killing.

ROBESPIERRE: The social revolution is not yet ended; to carry out a revolution by halves is to dig your own grave. Aristocracy is not yet dead; the healthy forces of the people must take the place of this completely degenerate class. Vice must be punished, Virtue must rule through the Terror.

DANTON: I do not understand the word punishment.—You and your virtue, Robespierre! You have not taken money, you have no debts, you haven't slept with women, you've always worn a respectable suit and have never been drunk. Robespierre, you're appallingly righteous. I'd be ashamed to walk between heaven and earth for thirty days with the same moral expression, merely for the miserable pleasure of finding others less virtuous than myself.—Isn't there something within you which sometimes whispers, softly, secretly: you lie, you lie?

ROBESPIERRE: My conscience is clear.

DANTON: Conscience is a mirror before which a monkey torments himself; every one gets himself up as best he can and goes out to take his pleasure in his own way. It's not worth the trouble to make a fuss about it. Every one has the right to protect himself if some one else spoils his fun. Have you the right to turn the guillotine into a washtub for other people's dirty linen and use their heads as cakes of soap for washing their dirty clothes, merely because your coat has always been brushed and clean? Yes, you can defend yourself if they spit on it and want to tear it to rags; but so long as they leave you in peace, what business is it of yours? If they don't trouble about the way they carry on, does that give you the right to lock them up in the tomb? Are you

God's policeman? And if you're not able to look on, like your good God Himself, then hold your handkerchief before your eyes.

ROBESPIERRE: You deny Virtue?

DANTON: And Vice. All men are hedonists, some crude and some sensitive; Christ was the most sensitive of all; that is the only difference between men I've been able to discover. Every one acts according to his nature, that is, he does what does him good. —It's a shame, isn't it, Incorruptible, to tread on your corns like this?

ROBESPIERRE: Danton, at certain moments Vice is High Treason.

DANTON: But you musn't suppress it, for God's sake don't, it would be ungrateful; you owe it too much, by contrast I mean.—But to speak in your terms, our blows must be of service to the Republic, we musn't strike innocent and guilty alike.

ROBESPIERRE: Who says that an innocent man has been struck?

DANTON: Did you hear that, Fabricius? Not one innocent man dead! [*He goes; on his way out, to* Paris] There's not a moment to lose, we must show ourselves to the people.

[*Exeunt* Danton *and* Paris]

ROBESPIERRE: [*Alone*] Let him go! He wants to halt the wild horses of the Revolution at a brothel, like a coachman with his tame hacks. They'll have enough strength to drag him to the guillotine.

To tread on my corns!—To speak in my terms!— Stop! Stop! Is that it?—They will say his gigantic figure threw me so much into the shade that I had to get him out of the sun.—What if they're right?—Is it so necessary? Yes, yes, the Republic! He must go. It's laughable, how my thoughts suspect each other. —He must go. A man who stands still in a crowd that presses forward is as much of an obstacle as if he opposed it; he'll be trampled under foot.

We will not allow the ship of the Revolution to run aground on the shallow scruples and mudbanks of these people; we must cut off the hand which dares to hold it back—yes, and even if he tries to hang on by his teeth!

Away with a clique that has stolen the clothes of the dead aristocrats and inherited their sores!

No Virtue! Virtue one of my corns! In my terms! —How that always comes back to me!—Why can't I get away from the thought? Always he points a bloody finger there, there! I may wrap as many bandages as I like around it, but the blood still pulses through.— [*After a pause*] I don't know what it is in me that denies the pretence. [*He goes to the window*]

Night snores over the earth and tosses in wild dreams. Thoughts, desires, hardly conscious, confused and formless, that timidly hide away from the light of day, now take form and raiment and steal into the silent house of dreams. They open the doors, look out of the windows, they half become flesh, limbs stretch themselves in sleep, the lips murmur. —And is not our waking a clearer dream? Are we not sleep-walkers? Are not our actions those of our dreams, only more precise, defined and brought to completion? Who will blame us for that? In one hour the mind performs more acts of thought than the sluggish organism of our body can carry out in years. The sin is in our thoughts. Whether the thought becomes action, whether the body carries it out, is mere chance.

[*Enter* Saint-Just]

ROBESPIERRE: Help, who's there in the dark? Help, lights, lights!

SAINT-JUST: Do you know my voice?

ROBESPIERRE: Oh, you, Saint-Just!

[*A* Maid *brings lights*]

SAINT-JUST: Were you alone?

ROBESPIERRE: Danton had just left.

SAINT-JUST: I met him on the way in the Palais Royal. He was making his revolutionary face, speaking in epigrams, and fraternizing with the *sans-culottes;* the whores clustered around his legs and the crowd stood still and whispered to each other what he had said.—We shall lose the benefit of the attack. Must you delay any longer? We shall act without you; our minds are made up.

ROBESPIERRE: What do you want to do?

SAINT-JUST: Summon the Legislative Committee, the Committee of Security, and the Committee of Public Safety to a solemn session.

ROBESPIERRE: Very formal.

SAINT-JUST: We must bury the great corpse decently, like priests, not murderers. It mustn't be torn to pieces, all the limbs must be there.

ROBESPIERRE: Speak more clearly.

SAINT-JUST: We must bury him in full armor, and sacrifice his horses and slaves on the tomb. Lacroix—

ROBESPIERRE: An absolute scoundrel, formerly barrister's clerk, now Lieutenant-General of France. Go on.

SAINT-JUST: Hérault-Séchelles.

ROBESPIERRE: A lovely head.

SAINT-JUST: He was the finely engraved capital letter of the Constitution; we've no need of such ornaments any more, he shall be obliterated.—Philippeau. —Camille.

ROBESPIERRE: Him too?

SAINT-JUST: [*Gives him a paper*] I thought as much. Read that.

ROBESPIERRE: Oh, 'Le Vieux Cordelier.' Is that all? He's a child, he laughs at you.

SAINT-JUST: [*Points to a passage*] Read that; read that!

ROBESPIERRE: [*Reads*] 'This bloody Messiah, Robespierre, on his calvary between the two thieves, Couthon and Collot, to whom he sacrifices and himself is not sacrificed. The holy sisters of the guillotine stand at his feet like Mary and Magdalene. Saint-Just lies in his bosom like John the Beloved Apostle and imparts to the Convention the apocalyptic revelations of the Master; he carries his head like a monstrance.'

SAINT-JUST: I'll make him carry his like Saint-Denis.

ROBESPIERRE: [*Reads on*] 'Must we believe that the Messiah's neat frock coat is France's winding-sheet, that his thin fingers twitching on the tribune are the knives of the guillotine?—And you, Barère —who once said money would be minted on the Place de la Révolution! But enough—I will not delve into that old sack. He is a widow, who already has had six husbands and helped to bury them all. But what can be done? That is his talent—to see death in people's faces, like Hippocrates, six months before they die. Who wants to sit with corpses and smell their decay?' You too then, Camille?—Away with them! Quickly! Only dead men never return. Have you the indictment ready?

SAINT-JUST: It's not difficult. You gave the hints in the Jacobins.

ROBESPIERRE: I wanted to frighten them.

SAINT-JUST: I need only carry out your threats. Forgers shall give them meat and foreigners drink— they'll die of their meal, I give you my word.

ROBESPIERRE: Quickly then, to-morrow! No long death struggle! I've grown sensitive in the last few days.—Only be quick.

[*Exit* Saint-Just]

[*Alone*] Yes, a bloody Messiah, who sacrifices and is not sacrificed.—He redeemed men with His blood, and I redeem them with their own. He made them sin against Him and I take the sin upon myself. He had the pleasure of suffering and I have the torments of the hangman. Who denied himself most, He or I? —And yet there's something of folly in that thought —Why must we always look towards Him? Truly the Son of Man is crucified in each of us, and we all wrestle in bloody sweat in the Garden of Gethsemane, but not one of us redeems the others by his wounds.

My Camille!—They are all leaving me—all is waste and empty—I am alone.

ACT II. SCENE I.

[*A room.* Danton, Lacroix, Philippeau, Paris, Camille Desmoulins]

CAMILLE: Quickly, Danton, we have no time to lose!

DANTON: [*Dressing*] But time loses us. How tedious drawing on the shirt first and then the trousers over it, and evening for bed and then creaking out again in the morning, and always setting one foot in front of the other; there's no prospect at all of its ever being any different. That's very sad, and that millions have already done so, and that millions will do again, and that over and above all, we consist of two halves which both do the same thing, so that everything happens double—that is very sad.

CAMILLE: You speak absolutely like a child.

DANTON: The dying often become childish.

LACROIX: You fall into ruin by your delay and you drag all your friends with you. Inform the cowards that it's time for them to rally around you, summon them from the valleys as well as from the hills; shriek over the tyranny of the Committee, speak of daggers, invoke Brutus, then you'll terrify the spectators and collect round you even those who were threatened as accomplices of Hébert's. You must give yourself over to your anger. At least don't let us die disarmed and thrown in the mud, like the shameful Hébert.

DANTON: You have a bad memory, you called me a dead saint. You were more in the right than you yourself thought. I have been to the Sections, they were respectful but like undertakers. I am a relic, and relics are thrown into the gutter; you were right.

LACROIX: Why have you let things come to this?

DANTON: To this? Yes, indeed, finally it bored me, always going round in the same coat and knitting my brow into the same wrinkles! It's so pitiful! To be such a miserable instrument, on which one string always gives out one note! It's not to be borne. I wanted to make myself comfortable. I've succeeded; the Revolution sets me at rest, but in a different way from what I thought.

What else can one rely on? Our whores might take it up with the nuns of the guillotine. I can think of nothing else. You can figure it all out on your fingers. The Jacobins have declared that virtue is on the agenda; the Cordeliers call me Hébert's hangman; the Commune does penance. The Convention—that might still have been a way!—but there was a 31st of May, they wouldn't soften willingly. Robespierre is the dogma of the Revolution which can't be struck out. In any case it wouldn't work. We haven't made the Revolution, the Revolution made us.

And even if it worked—I'd rather be guillotined than guillotine. I've had enough of it, why should we men fight with each other? We should sit down side by side and have peace. A mistake was made in the creating of us; something's lacking in us, I don't know the name for it, but we won't be able to burrow it out of each other's entrails, so why break our bodies over it? Enough, we're sick alchemists.

CAMILLE: Said with more pathos, it would run: how long will humanity in everlasting hunger devour its own limbs? Or how long shall we shipwrecked beings on a wreck suck the blood from each other's veins in unquenchable thirst? Or how long must we algebraists in flesh, in our search for the unknown, ever-withheld x, write our sums with mutilated limbs?

DANTON: You are a powerful echo.

CAMILLE: You think so?—A pistol shot resounds just like a thunderclap. So much the better for you, you should have me always by you.

PHILIPPEAU: And France remains with her hangmen?

DANTON: What of it? The people enjoy themselves just the same. They are unhappy; can a man ask more to make him compassionate, noble, virtuous, witty, or never bored?—Does it matter whether they die on the guillotine or from fever or from old age? The first is even preferable; they tread with supple limbs behind the scenes, and are able to gesticulate prettily as they go off, and hear the spectators clap. It's very proper and suits us who always stand on the stage, even though finally we're stabbed in earnest.

It's quite right that the length of life should be reduced a little; the coat was too long, our limbs couldn't fill it out. Life becomes an epigram, that's good; for who has breath and spirit enough for an epic in fifty or sixty cantos? It's time one started drinking one's little elixir out of tubs not out of liqueur glasses, so long as one still fills one's mouth full; otherwise one could scarcely make the few drops run together in the clumsy vessel.

But finally I have to cry out that the effort is too great for me, life is not worth the trouble one takes to hold on to it.

PARIS: Then fly, Danton!

DANTON: Can you take your country with you on the soles of your shoes? And finally—and that's the chief thing: they won't dare. [*To* Camille] Come, my boy, I tell you, they won't dare. Adieu, adieu!

[*Exeunt* Danton *and* Camille]

PHILIPPEAU: There he goes.

LACROIX: And doesn't believe a word of what he said. Nothing but laziness! He'd sooner be guillotined than make a speech.

PARIS: What's to be done?

LACROIX: Go home and like Lucretia[12] study some honest matter.

SCENE II.

[*A promenade.* Passers-by]

A CITIZEN: My good Jacqueline—I mean to say Korn . . . I meant . . . Cor. . . .

SIMON: Cornelia, citizen, Cornelia.

CITIZEN: My good Cornelia has blessed me with a little boy.

SIMON: Has borne a son to the Republic.

CITIZEN: The Republic? That sounds too universal: one might say. . . .

SIMON: That's exactly it; the particular and the universal must. . . .

CITIZEN: Ah yes, that's what my wife says too.

BALLAD-SINGER: [*Sings*]
  What is then, what is then
  A joy and pleasure for all men?

CITIZEN: Ah, but the names; I can't get them right.

SIMON: Christen him Pike, Marat!

BALLAD-SINGER:
  In spite of care, in spite of sorrow
  Toil and sweat from early morrow
  Till the day is past again.

[12] Roman matron who stabbed herself after having been violated by the tyrant Tarquin.

CITIZEN: I should like three; there's something about the number three, something useful and something right; now I have it: Plough, Robespierre. And then the third?

SIMON: Pike.

CITIZEN: Thank you, neighbor; Pike, Plough, Robespierre, three pretty names, that sounds well.

SIMON: I tell you, the breast of your Cornelia will, like the udder of the Roman she-wolf—no, that's no good. Romulus was a tyrant, that's no good.

[Citizen *and* Simon *walk inside*]

A BEGGAR: [*Sings*] 'A handful of earth and a little moss!' Dear sirs, lovely ladies!

1ST GENTLEMAN: Work, you lout, you look quite well-nourished.

2ND GENTLEMAN: [*Gives him money*] There, he has a hand like silk. Shameless.

BEGGAR: Sir, where did you get your coat from?

2ND GENTLEMAN: Work, work! You can have the same; I will give you work. come with me, I live. . . .

BEGGAR: Sir, why did you work?

2ND GENTLEMAN: Fool, in order to have the coat.

BEGGAR: You've tortured yourself, in order to have a pleasure; for a coat like that's a pleasure, a tramp does that as well.

2ND GENTLEMAN: Certainly. It's the only way.

BEGGAR: If only I were a fool then. It cancels itself out. The sun shines warm on the corner, and things go easily. [*He sings*] 'A handful of earth and a little moss.'

ROSALIE: [*To* Adelaide] Hurry along, there comes the soldiers! We haven't had anything warm in our bodies since yesterday.

BEGGAR: 'Is once upon this earth my final lot!' Ladies and Gentlemen!

SOLDIER: Halt! Where are you going, my children? [*To* Rosalie] How old are you?

ROSALIE: Just as old as my litle finger.

SOLDIER: You're very sharp.

ROSALIE: And you're very blunt.

SOLDIER: Then I'd better sharpen myself on you.

[*He sings*]

Christina, my Christina,

Does the pain hurt you sore,

Hurt you sore, hurt you sore, hurt you sore?

ROSALIE: [*Sings*]

Oh no, Mister Soldier,

I'd gladly have some more,

Have some more, have some more, have some more.

[*Enter* Danton *and* Camille]

DANTON: Isn't it a merry scene?—I scent something in the atmosphere, it's as though the sun hatched out lechery. Wouldn't one like to spring into the middle of it, tear off one's trousers and take them from behind like dogs in the street?

[*Both walk aside*]

YOUNG GENTLEMAN: Ah, Madame, the sound of a bell, the evening light on the trees, the twinkling of a star. . . .

MADAME: The scent of a flower, the natural pleasures, this pure enjoyment of nature! [*To her daughter*] See, Eugénie, only virtue has eyes for this!

EUGÉNIE: [*Kisses her mother's hand*] Ah, Mamma, I see only you!

MADAME: Good child.

YOUNG GENTLEMAN: [*Whispers in* Eugénie's *ear*] Do you see the pretty lady with the old gentleman over there?

EUGÉNIE: I know her.

YOUNG GENTLEMAN: They say her barber has done her hair *à l'enfant*.

EUGÉNIE: [*Laughing*] Naughty gossip!

YOUNG GENTLEMAN: The old gentleman walks beside her, he sees the bud swell and carries it into the sun and thinks that he is the thundery shower which has made it grow.

EUGÉNIE: How improper! I feel like going red!

YOUNG GENTLEMAN: That could make me go white.

DANTON: [*To* Camille] Only don't expect me to be serious. I fail to understand why the people don't stand still in the street and laugh in each other's faces. I mean they must laugh up to the windows and out of the graves, and Heaven must burst, and Earth must waltz round with laughter.

[*Exeunt* Danton *and* Camille]

1ST GENTLEMAN: I assure you, an extraordinary discovery. Through it, all the technical arts assume an altogether different physiognomy. Humanity hurries with giant strides towards its high destiny.

2ND GENTLEMAN: Have you seen the new play? A Babylonian tower, a maze of arches, steps, gangways, and all blown up so light and brave into the air. One grows dizzy at every step. A bizarre head! [*He stands thoughtful*]

1ST GENTLEMAN: What is it?

2ND GENTLEMAN: Oh nothing! Your hand, sir. The puddles, look! Thank you, thank you, I can hardly get past: that might be very dangerous.

1ST GENTLEMAN: Surely you weren't afraid?

2ND GENTLEMAN: Yes, the earth is a thin crust; I mean I might fall through, where there's a hole like that.

One must go carefully, one might fall through. But go to the Theatre, that's what I advise.

SCENE III.

[*A room.* Danton, Camille, Lucile]

CAMILLE: I tell you, if they don't have wooden copies of everything scattered in theatres, concert halls, and art exhibitions, people have neither eyes nor ears for it. Let some one cut out a marionette, so that you see the string it's tugged by hanging down, and with its joints cracking out a five-foot blank verse at every step—what a character, what consistency! Let him take a little feeling, a sentence, an idea, and dress it in jacket and trousers, give it hands and feet, paint its face and let the thing moan its way through three acts until finally it's married or shoots itself dead—an ideal! Let him fiddle out an opera which reproduces the floating and sinking of human life as a bird warbler does the nightingale—behold art!

Turn the people out of the theatre on to the street —behold pitiful reality! They forget their Lord God Almighty on account of his bad imitators. Of creation, the glowing, roaring, lightening, newly born in them each moment, they hear and see nothing. They go into the theatre, read poems and novels, and make grimaces like the faces they find in them, and say to God's creations, 'How commonplace!' The Greeks knew what they were saying when they told how Pygmalion's statue came to life but bore no children.

DANTON: And the artists treat nature like David, who, when the murdered bodies were thrown out of La Force[13] on to the streets in September, cold-bloodedly drew them and said: I snatch the last spasms of life from these scoundrels. [*He is called outside*]

CAMILLE: What have you to say, Lucile?

LUCILE: Nothing, I so like watching you talk.

CAMILLE: Do you listen as well?

LUCILE: Why, certainly!

CAMILLE: Am I in the right? Did you know what I was saying?

LUCILE: No, really not.

[Danton *comes back*]

CAMILLE: What's the matter?

DANTON: The Committee of Public Safety has decided on my arrest. I've been warned and offered a place where I can take refuge.

They want my head; they can have it, for all I care. I'm sick of these vexations. Let them take it, what does it matter? I'll know how to die with courage: it's easier than living.

CAMILLE: Danton, there's still time!

DANTON: Impossible—but I shouldn't have thought . . .

CAMILLE: Your laziness!

DANTON: I'm not lazy, but tired; the soles of my feet burn me.

CAMILLE: Where will you go?

DANTON: Yes, who knows where?

CAMILLE: Seriously, where?

DANTON: For a walk, my boy, for a walk. [*Exit*]

LUCILE: Camille—

CAMILLE: Quiet, dear child!

LUCILE: When I think that they . . . this head . . .! Camille, dear, it's nonsense, I'm crazy, aren't I?

CAMILLE: Quiet, Danton and I are not one person!

LUCILE: The earth is broad and there are many things on it—then why always this one thing? Who would take it from me? It would be outrageous. And what do they want it for?

CAMILLE: I tell you again: you need not be disturbed! I spoke yesterday with Robespierre: he was friendly. We're a little on edge, that's true; different points of view, nothing else.

[13] A prison in which royalists were imprisoned.

LUCILE: Go to see him.

CAMILLE: We sat together on the same school bench. He was always sombre and lonely. I alone sought him out and made him laugh sometimes. He has always shown a great affection for me. I'll go.

LUCILE: So swiftly, my friend? Go! Come! Only this [*She kisses him*] and this! Go! Go!

[*Exit* Camille]

These are wicked times. Sometimes things happen like that. Who knows the way out? One must restrain oneself.

[*Sings*]

> Oh, parting, parting, parting,
> Who of parting had thought?

Why does that, of all things, run through my head? It's bad that it should come of its own like that.— When he went out it seemed to me as though he could never come back again and must always go further away from me, ever further.

How empty this room is! The windows are open, as though a corpse had lain in here. I can't stand being up here any longer. [*Exit*]

SCENE IV.

[*A field.* Danton]

DANTON: I can go no further. In this silence, I will make no noise with the chattering of my footsteps and the panting of my breath. [*He sits down. After a pause*] I've been told of an illness which makes one lose one's memory. There is something of that in death. Then sometimes the hope comes to me that it is still more powerful and makes one lose everything.—Oh, if that were so!—Then I'd run like a Christian to rescue an enemy, that is, my memory. —This place should be safe, yes, for my memory but not for me: the grave gives me more safety, it gives me at least forgetting. It would kill my memory. But here my memory lives and kills me. I or it? The answer is easy. [*He gets up and turns round*] I flirt with death, it is very pleasant to make eyes at her through lorgnettes from a distance.

Actually, I have to laugh at the whole business. There's a sense of permanence in me which says: to-morrow and the day after to-morrow and so on and on, and everything will be as it is now. This is just a false alarm to frighten me; they'd never dare! [*Exit*]

SCENE V.

[*A room. Night*]

DANTON: [*At a window*] Will it never stop? Will

the light never cease glowing and the echoes never be up to date? Will it never be still and dark, so that we no longer listen to and watch each other's filthy sins?——September!

JULIE: [*Calls from within*] Danton! Danton!

DANTON: Eh!

JULIE: [*Enters*] What did you call out?

DANTON: Did I call?

JULIE: You spoke of filthy sins and then you groaned: September!

DANTON: I, I? No, I didn't speak, I hardly thought anything—they were only quite gentle, secret thoughts.

JULIE: You are trembling, Danton.

DANTON: And have I no cause for trembling, when the walls chatter so? If my body is so jarred that my fitful thoughts speak madly with lips of stone? That's strange.

JULIE: George, my own George.

DANTON: Yes, Julie, it's very strange. I'd better not think any more, if my thoughts immediately speak. Julie, there are thoughts for which there should be no ears. It's bad that they should cry out like children at their birth; it's bad.

JULIE: God preserve your reason, George. George, do you recognize me?

DANTON: Yes, why not? You're a human being and then a woman and finally my wife, and the earth has five continents, Europe, Asia, Africa, America, Australia, and twice two makes four. You see, I'm in my senses. . . . Didn't I cry out September? Didn't you say something of the sort?

JULIE: Yes, Danton, I heard it through all the rooms.

DANTON: When I went to the window—[*He looks out*] the town is quiet, all the lights out.

JULIE: A child is crying near by.

DANTON: When I went to the window—through all the streets it cried out and shrieked: September!

JULIE: You were dreaming, Danton: pull yourself together!

DANTON: Dreaming? Yes, I dreamed; but that was different. I'll tell you quickly what—my poor head is weak—quickly. Good, now I have it. Under me the globe panted in its rotation; I had laid hold of it like a wild horse, with giant limbs I clutched into its mane and gripped its flanks, my head bent backwards, my hair streaming over the abyss; so I was dragged along. Then I called out in terror and I awoke. I sprang to the window—and there I heard it, Julie.

What is it that the word wants? Why that of all words? What have I to do with it? Why does it stretch out its bloody hands to me? I never struck it. —Oh, help me, Julie, my brain is numb. Wasn't it in September, Julie?

JULIE: The kings were within forty hours of Paris . . .

DANTON: The fortresses had fallen, the aristocrats were in the city . . .

JULIE: The Republic was lost.

DANTON: Yes, lost. We couldn't let our enemies stab us in the back, we should have been fools, two enemies on a single plank; we or they, the stronger would push the weaker under, isn't that right?

JULIE: Yes, yes.

DANTON: We killed them, that was no murder, it was civil war.

JULIE: You saved the fatherland.

DANTON: Yes, I did, it was self-defence, we did what we had to do. The Man on the Cross made it so easy for himself: 'It must needs be that offences come; but woe to that man by whom the offence cometh.'—It must; that was this must! Who will curse the hand on which the curse of 'must' has fallen? Who spoke that 'must,' who? What is it in us that whores, lies, steals, and murders?

We're puppets drawn by unknown powers on wire; nothing, nothing in ourselves—the swords with which spirits fight—only one doesn't see the hands, as in fairy tales.—Now I'm quiet.

JULIE: Perfectly quiet, dear heart?

DANTON: Yes, Julie, come to bed!

SCENE VI.

[*A street before* Danton's *house.* Simon. *Citizens armed as soldiers*]

SIMON: How late is it in the night?

1ST CITIZEN: What in the night?

SIMON: How late is the night?

1ST CITIZEN: As late as between sunset and sunrise.

SIMON: Rogue, what time is it?

1ST CITIZEN: Look at your watch-dial, it's the time when the pendulum swings to and fro between the sheets.

SIMON: We must up! Forward, citizens! We answer with our heads for it! Dead or living! He has strong limbs! I will go first, citizens. Clear the way for freedom.—Take care of my wife! I will bequeath a crown of acorns to her!

1ST CITIZEN: A crown of acorns! Enough acorns must fall in her lap every day without that.

SIMON: Onward, citizens, you will have deserved well of the fatherland!

2ND CITIZEN: I wish the fatherland would deserve well of us. For all the holes we've made in other people's bodies not a single one has yet closed up in our trousers.

1ST CITIZEN: Do you want your fly-buttons closed up? Ha, ha, ha!

THE OTHERS: Ha, ha, ha!

SIMON: Forward, forward.

[*They crowd into* Danton's *house*]

SCENE VII.

[*The National Convention. A group of* Deputies]

LEGENDRE: Will the execution of deputies never cease? Who is safe if Danton falls?

A DEPUTY: What's to be done?

ANOTHER: He must be heard before the bar of the Convention. The success of this method is certain. What could they oppose to his voice?

ANOTHER: Impossible. A decree prevents us.

LEGENDRE: It must either be withdrawn or an exception allowed. I will propose the motion; I count on your support.

THE PRESIDENT: The session is opened.

LEGENDRE: [*Ascends the tribune*] Four members of the National Convention were arrested during the past night. I know that Danton is one of them, the names of the remainder I do not know. Nevertheless, whoever they are, I demand that they be heard before the bar.

Citizens, I make this declaration: I hold Danton to be as innocent as myself, and I don't believe that any accusation can be made against me. I will attack no member of the Committee of Security or of the Committee of Public Safety, but well-founded reasons leave me afraid lest private hatred and private passions may deprive Liberty of men who have done her the greatest services. The man who through his energy saved France in the year 1792 deserves to be heard; he should be allowed to clear himself, if he is charged with high treason.

[*Great excitement*]

SOME VOICES: We support Legendre's motion.

A DEPUTY: We are here in the name of the people; without the will of those who voted for us, no one can deprive us of our places.

ANOTHER: Your words stink of corpses; you have taken them out of the mouths of the Girondists. Do you want privilege? The knife of the law sweeps over all heads.

ANOTHER: We cannot allow our committees to send our lawgivers from the sanctuary of the law to the guillotine.

ANOTHER: Crime has no sanctuary, only crowned criminals find one on the throne.

ANOTHER: Only thieves appeal to their right of sanctuary.

ANOTHER: Only murderers fail to recognize it.

ROBESPIERRE: Such disorder, unknown for so long in this assembly, shows that great matters are under discussion. To-day will decide whether a few men will benefit by it to win a victory over their country. —How can you so far deny your fundamental principles as to grant a few individuals to-day that which yesterday you refused Chabot, Delaunay, and Fabre? What is the meaning of this discrimination in favor of a few men? Why should I concern myself with the complimentary speeches which people pay to themselves and their friends? Only too many experiences have shown us how much they are worth. We do not ask whether a man has brought to completion this or that task of patriotism; we ask after his whole political career.—Legendre appears to be ignorant of the names of the arrested men; the whole Convention knows them. His friend Lacroix is one of them. Why does Legendre seem ignorant of this? Because he knows that only shamelessness could defend Lacroix. Danton alone he named, because he thinks that a privilege has attached itself to this name. No, we want no privileges, we want no idols.

[*Applause*]

What is there in Danton that places him before Lafayette, before Dumouriez, before Brissot, Fabre, Chabot, Hébert? What does one say of these that one cannot also say of him? And did you spare them? Through what service has he earned precedence over his fellow citizens? Perhaps because certain betrayed individuals, and others who had not let themselves be betrayed, had ranged themselves behind him, so that in his train they might run into the arms of power and fortune? The more he has betrayed those patriots who put trust in him, the more energetic must he find the strength of the friends of liberty.

They wish to inspire you with fear at the misuse of a power which you yourselves have exercised. They whine over the despotism of the Committees, as though the trust which the people have placed in you, and which you have handed over to these committees, were not a sure guarantee of your patriotism. They pretend that everybody is trembling. But I tell you that whoever at this moment trembles is guilty, because innocence never trembles before public vigilance.

[*General applause*]

They've tried to frighten me too; they gave me to understand that the danger, if it neared Danton, could also reach as far as me. They wrote to me that Danton's friends held me besieged, believing that the memory of an old association, a blind faith in a simulated virtue could induce me to restrain my ardor and my passion for liberty.—So I declare that nothing will stop me, not even should Danton's danger become my own. We all need a certain courage and a certain grandeur of soul. Only criminals and vulgar spirits fear to see those who resemble them fall at their side, because if a troop of accomplices no longer stuck to them, they would see themselves exposed in the light of truth. But if there are spirits such as these in this assembly, so also are there those who are heroic. The number of scoundrels is not great; we have only to lop off a few heads and the country is saved.

[*Applause*]

I demand that Legendre's motion be rejected.

[*The* Delegates *rise together as a sign of general approbation*]

SAINT-JUST: There seem to be in this assembly a few sensitive ears which cannot hear the word 'blood' with equanimity. A few general observations on the relations between nature and history should convince them that we are not crueller than Nature or than Time. Nature follows quietly and irresistibly her laws; Man is destroyed, wherever he comes in conflict with them. An alteration in the ingredients of the air, a flaring up of the tellurian fires, a vacillation in the balance of masses of water, and an epidemic, a volcanic eruption, a flood bury thousands. What is the result? A meaningless, on the whole, scarcely noticeable alteration of physical nature, which would have passed by scarcely leaving a trace, if corpses did not lie in its path.

I ask you: shall moral nature be more considerate than physics in making her revolutions? Shall not an idea, just as well as a law of physics, annihilate that which opposes it? Above all, shall an experience which alters the whole configuration of moral nature, which means humanity, not dare to wade through blood? The spirit of the world uses our arms in the spiritual sphere just as in the physical it uses volcanoes and floods. What difference does it make whether one dies now through an epidemic or through the Revolution?

The strides of humanity are slow; one can only count them by centuries; behind each one rise the graves of generations. To arrive at the simplest invention and fundamental truth has cost the lives of millions who died on the way. Is it not then simply that in a time where the pace of history is faster, more men lose their breath?

We conclude quickly and simply: since all men were created in the same circumstances, all are equal, apart from those differences which Nature herself has made. Therefore every one has merits but none has privileges, either as individuals or as a smaller or larger class of individuals.—Every link in this argument translated into reality has killed its men. The 14th of July, the 10th of August, the 31st of May are its punctuation marks. It required four years to be carried out in the physical world, and under ordinary conditions it would have required centuries and been punctuated by generations. Is it so miraculous that the stream of the Revolution at every stop, at every new bend, discharges its corpses?

We still have a few inferences to add to our proposition; shall a few hundred corpses prevent us from making them? Moses led his people through the Red Sea and into the desert, till the old corrupted generation had been annihilated, before he founded the new state. Legislators! We have neither Red Sea nor desert, but we have war and the guillotine.

The Revolution is like the daughter of Pelias; she dismembers humanity to make it young. Humanity comes out of the cauldron of blood, like earth out of the waters of the deluge, to raise itself with primordial limbs, as though it were first created.

[*Long-sustained applause, some* Deputies *rise in enthusiasm*]
We call upon all the secret enemies of tyranny, who in Europe and the whole globe carry under their cloaks the dagger of Brutus, to share with us this exalted moment.
[*The* Spectators *and the* Deputies *join in singing the 'Marseillaise'*]

ACT III. SCENE I.

[*The Luxembourg. A hall with* Prisoners. Chaumette, Payne, Mercier, Hérault-Séchelles, *and other* Prisoners]

CHAUMETTE: [*Takes* Payne's *arm*] Listen, Payne, that might be it. Before it came over me so clearly, to-day I have a headache; help me a little with your arguments, it seems to me quite uncannily difficult.

PAYNE: Come, come, philosopher Anaxagoras, I will catechize thee.—There is no God, for either God made the world, or he did not. If he did not create it, then the world contained its origins in itself, and there is no God, since God is only God through the fact that he contains the origins of all being. Now God cannot have created the world; for creation must either be eternal like God, or it must have a beginning. If it had a beginning, God must have created it at a certain point in time. Thus God, having rested for an eternity, must once suddenly have become active, and must therefore have undergone an alteration in himself, which made him apply the conception of time, both of which conflict with the nature of God's being. Thus it is impossible for God to have created the world. Now since we know very clearly that we exist or at least that our own ego exists and that, in accordance with what I have just told you, it also must have origins in itself or in something not itself which is not God, then it follows that there is no God. *Quod erat demonstrandum.*

CHAUMETTE: Yes, indeed, that gives me light again. I thank you, I thank you.

MERCIER: Wait, Payne! Supposing though that creation were eternal?

PAYNE: Then it ceases to be creation any more, it becomes one with God or an attribute of him, as Spinoza said, then God is present in everything, in thee, my worthiest philosopher Anaxagoras, and in me. That wouldn't be so bad, but you must admit that it's not saying much for the heavenly majesty if the Lord God Almighty gets a headache in each one of us, or leprosy, or is buried alive, or at least experiences a very unpleasant impression of these things.

MERCIER: But surely there must be a first cause?

PAYNE: Who denies it? But who insists that this first cause must be that which we think of as God— that is to say, as perfection? Do you hold that the world is perfect?

MERCIER: No.

PAYNE: Then how do you arrive at an imperfect effect from a perfect cause?—Voltaire dared displease Gods as little as kings, and for that reason he did. He who has nothing except his reasoning, yet who does not know how or does not dare to use it consistently, is a blunderer.

MERCIER: Against that, I ask can a perfect cause have a perfect effect, which means—can something perfect create something perfect? Is it not impossible, because the created thing can never contain its origin within itself, which indeed, as you say, appertains to perfection?

CHAUMETTE: Be quiet! Be quiet!

PAYNE: Calm yourself, philosopher! You are quite right; but if God once starts creating, then if he can only create imperfect things he would have done better to leave well alone. Isn't it very human of us that we can only think of God as creating? Since we must always stir and shake ourselves, only in order that we may ever be saying to ourselves that we exist! But must we ascribe to God as well this sickening need?—Must we, if our spirit is sunk in a being harmoniously at rest with itself in eternal blessedness, at once assume that it stretches out a finger over the table and kneads homunculi[14] of bread—through immeasurable need for love, as we secretly whisper in each other's ears? Must we do all this merely to make ourselves the sons of God? I prefer a lesser father, at least I will not be able to say afterwards that he let me be educated beneath his rank in the manger or amongst the slaves.

Do away with imperfection: then alone can you demonstrate God—Spinoza tried it. One can deny evil but not pain, only the understanding can accept God, the feeling rebels against him. Mark well, Anaxagoras, why do I suffer? That is the rock of atheism. The least twinge of pain, stir it only an atom, rends your creation from top to bottom.

MERCIER: And morality?

PAYNE: First you prove God from morality and then morality from God. A nice vicious circle that licks its own hindquarters. What do you want with your morality? I don't know whether there is an intrinsic good or evil and have no need to alter my way of life on that account. I act according to my nature; what suits it is good for me and I do it, and what is bad for it is bad for me and I don't do it and take sides against it when it lies in my way. You can be virtuous, as they call it, and arm yourself against so-called vice, without being obliged on that account to despise your opponents, which is a very sad feeling to have!

CHAUMETTE: True, very true!

HÉRAULT: O, philosopher Anaxagoras,[15] one can also say since God is everything, he must also be his own opposite, that's to say perfect and imperfect, evil

[14] Manikins.
[15] Chaumette had assumed the name Anaxagoras.

and good, blessed and suffering; the result would admittedly then be nil, it would cancel itself out, we should end with nothing.—Rejoice, you emerge victorious, you can pray undisturbed to Madame Momoro[16] as nature's masterpiece; at least she's left you a crown of roses in the groin.

CHAUMETTE: Gentlemen, I give you my heartiest thanks. [Exit]

PAYNE: He still has no trust, he'll still give himself extreme unction, set his feet towards Mecca, and have himself circumcised, in order to lose no opportunity.

[Danton, Lacroix, Camille, Philippeau are brought in]

HÉRAULT: [Runs to Danton and embraces him] Good morning! No—I should say—Good night! I can't ask how you slept? How will you sleep?

DANTON: Well, well. One must go laughing to bed.

MERCIER: [To Payne] These mastiffs with wings of doves! He's the evil genius of the Revolution, he defied his mother but she was stronger than he.

PAYNE: His life and his death are equal misfortunes.

LACROIX: [To Danton] I hadn't thought that you'd be here so soon.

DANTON: I knew, I was warned.

LACROIX: And you said nothing?

DANTON: To what? An apoplexy is the best death. Would you care to be ill first? And I thought they'd never dare. [To Hérault] It's better to lie down in the earth than to walk on it with corns. I'd rather have her as a cushion than as a footstool.

HÉRAULT: At least we won't have warts on our fingers when we stroke the cheeks of the pretty lady putrefaction.

CAMILLE: Only don't trouble yourself, you can hang your tongue out as far as your neck, but still you can't lick the death-sweat from your brow. O Lucile! That is a great affliction.

[The Prisoners crowd around the newcomers]

DANTON: [To Payne] What you did for the good of your country, I have tried to do for mine. I was less fortunate; they send me to the scaffold; for my own part, I won't trip.

MERCIER: [To Danton] The blood of the twenty-two drowns you.

A PRISONER: [To Hérault] The power of the people and the power of reason are one.

ANOTHER: [To Camille] Well, General Procurator of the Lanterns,[17] your improvements in the lighting of the streets have not made France any lighter.

ANOTHER: Leave him alone. His are the lips which spoke the word pity. [He embraces Camille; several other Prisoners follow his example]

PHILIPPEAU: We are priests who have prayed with

[16] An opera singer who was made Goddess of Reason by the Revolution. She was Chaumette's mistress.
[17] A reference to the stringing up of royalists by the revolutionary mobs.

the dying. We have been infected and die of the same epidemic.

A FEW VOICES: The blow that falls on you, kills us all.

CAMILLE: Gentlemen, I grieve deeply that our efforts were so fruitless; I go to the scaffold, because my eyes were wet at the fate of a few unfortunate ones.

SCENE II.

[*A room.* Fouquier-Tinville, Herman]

FOUQUIER: All prepared?

HERMAN: It will be difficult; if Danton weren't amongst them it would be easy.

FOUQUIER: He must open the ball.

HERMAN: He will frighten the jury, he's the scarecrow of the Revolution.

FOUQUIER: The jury must will it.

HERMAN: I thought of a way, but it would violate the letter of the law.

FOUQUIER: Only say it!

HERMAN: We don't draw by lot, but pick out our stalwarts.

FOUQUIER: That must be done—that will provide a good bonfire. There are nineteen of them. They're cleverly mixed together. The four forgers, then a few bankers and foreigners. That's a piquant tribunal. The people need such. Good then, let's have reliable people. Who, for example?

HERMAN: Leroi, he is deaf, so he hears nothing the accused say. With him there, Danton can scream himself hoarse.

FOUQUIER: Very good. Go on.

HERMAN: Vilatte and Lumière, the one sits in the pub all day, and the other's always asleep. Both only open their mouths to say the word 'Guilty!' Girard makes it a principle that no one can clear himself once he's been put before the Tribunal. Renaudin. . . .

FOUQUIER: He too? He once helped get some parsons off.

HERMAN: Don't worry, a few days ago he came to me and demanded that all the condemned should be bled before their execution to make them a little pale; the defiant look of most of them annoys him.

FOUQUIER: Very good. Then I shall rely on you.

HERMAN: Leave it to me!

SCENE III.

[*The Luxembourg. A corridor.* Lacroix, Danton, Mercier, *and other* Prisoners *pacing to and fro*]

LACROIX: [*To a* Prisoner] What, so many unfortunates, and in such a wretched situation?

PRISONER: Have the guillotine carts never told you that Paris is a slaughterhouse?

MERCIER: Isn't it so, Lacroix? Equality swings its sickle over all heads, the lava of revolution flows; the guillotine makes Republicans. The gallery clap and the Romans rub their hands; but they don't hear in every one of these words the death rattle of a victim. Follow your slogans to the point at which they become incarnate. Stare around you, you have said it all, it is a mimic translation of your words. These grief-stricken people, their hangmen, and their guillotines are your speeches turned to life. You build your system, as Bajazet[18] his pyramids, from the heads of men.

DANTON: You're right! To-day one works out everything in human flesh. That is the curse of our time. My body also will be used now.

It's exactly a year since I established the Revolutionary Tribunal. I pray forgiveness of God and humanity for it; I wished to anticipate a new September massacre, I hoped to save the innocent, but this slow murder with its formalities is more cruel and just as inescapable. Gentlemen, I hoped to have you all out of this place.

MERCIER: Oh, we shall all get out of it!

DANTON: Now I am with you; Heaven knows how it will end!

SCENE IV.

[*The Revolutionary Tribunal*]

HERMAN: [*To* Danton] Your name, citizen?

DANTON: The Revolution names my name. My dwelling will soon be in nothing and my name in the Pantheon of history.

HERMAN: Danton, the Convention accuses you of having conspired with Mirabeau, with Dumouriez, with Orleans, with the Girondists, with the foreigners, and with the factions of Louis XVII.

DANTON: My voice, which I have so often raised for the people's cause, will easily refute this calumny. The wretches who accuse me should appear here, and I will cover them with shame. The Committee should present themselves here; I shall only answer in front of them. I need them as prosecutors and as witnesses. They ought to show themselves.

Apart from all this, what concern have I with you and your accusations? I have told you already: the void will soon be my sanctuary. To me life is a load, they may tear it away from me, I long to shake it off.

HERMAN: Danton, audacity is the mark of crime, calm the mark of innocence.

DANTON: Private audacity is doubtless blameworthy, but that national audacity which I have so often shown, with which I have so often fought for freedom, is the most meritorious of all the virtues. That is my audacity, that is what, for the good

18 The Turkish sultan who conquered Asia Minor in 1396 and was defeated by Tamerlane in 1402.

of the Republic, I use here against my miserable accusers. Can I control myself when I see myself calumniated in so shameful a manner? No one can expect cool pleading from a revolutionary like me. Men of my stamp are inestimable in revolutions, the genius of freedom hovers on their brows.

[*Signs of applause amongst the audience*]

I am accused of having conspired with Mirabeau, with Dumouriez, with Orleans, of having sat at the feet of sick despots; I am called upon to make my answer before inescapable, unbending justice! You, cowering Saint-Just, will be responsible to posterity for this blasphemy.

HERMAN: I call upon you to answer calmly; think of Marat, he came before his judges with awe.

DANTON: You have laid hands on my whole life; for that reason it rises and faces you. I will bury you under the weight of each one of my deeds.

I am not proud of this. Fate controlled our arms, but only powerful natures are her instruments.—On the field of Mars I declared war on the monarchy, I struck it on the 10th of August, on the 21st of January I killed it and threw the head of a king as a gauntlet to kings.

[*Repeated signs of applause; he becomes the accuser*]

When I throw a glance at this shameful document, I feel my whole being quiver. Who then are those who had to force Danton to show himself on that memorable 10th of August? Who are the privileged beings from whom he borrowed his energy?—My accusers should appear! I am quite in my senses when I make this demand! I will expose these worthless scoundrels and cast them back into the nothing out of which they have crawled.

HERMAN: [*Rings a bell*] Don't you hear the bell?

DANTON: The voice of a man who defends his honor and his life must cry louder than your bell.

In September I fed the young brood of the Revolution with the dismembered bodies of the aristocrats. My voice has forged weapons for the People from the gold of the aristocrats and the rich. My voice was the hurricane which drowned the satellites of despotism under waves of bayonets.

[*Loud applause*]

HERMAN: Danton, your voice is exhausted. You are too violently moved. You will conclude your defence next time. You need rest.—The session is ended.

DANTON: Now you still know Danton—a few hours more and he will slumber in the arms of fame.

SCENE V.

[*The Luxembourg. A cell.* Dillon, Laflotte, *a Gaoler*]

DILLON: Fool, don't shine your nose in my face like that. Ha, ha, ha!

LAFLOTTE: Keep your mouth shut, your sickle moon has a stinking halo! Ha, ha, ha, ha!

GAOLER: Ha, ha, ha! Do you think, sir, that you could read by your light? [*He shows the writing on a paper which he holds in his hand*]

DILLON: Give it to me!

GAOLER: Sir, my sickle moon has ebbed.

LAFLOTTE: Your trousers look as if it were the flood.

GAOLER: No, they draw water. [*To* Dillon] She has waned at your sun, sir; you must give me that which makes you fiery again, if you wish to see.

DILLON: There, knave! Clear out!

[*Gives him money. Exit* Gaoler]

DILLON: [*Reads*] Danton has terrified the tribunal, the jury hesitated, the audience muttered. The crowd was extraordinary. The people pressed round the Palace of Justice and stood right up to the benches. A handful of gold, an arm to strike—hm! hm! [*He walks to and fro and drinks from time to time from a glass*] If only I had one foot on the pavement, I wouldn't allow myself to be struck down like this. Yes, only one foot on the pavement.

LAFLOTTE: And one in the tumbrils.

DILLON: You think so? A couple of strides still lie between, long enough to cover with the corpses of the Committee. The time has come at last when right-thinking people should lift their heads.

LAFLOTTE: [*To himself*] So that it's easier to cut them off. Go on, old man, only a few glasses more and I'll be floating.

DILLON: The rascals, the fools, in the end they'll guillotine themselves. [*He paces to and fro*]

LAFLOTTE: [*Aside*] One could love life again properly, like a child, if one gave it to oneself. But that doesn't often happen, to commit incest with chance and become one's own father. Father and child at the same time. A crazy Oedipus!

DILLON: You don't fodder the people with corpses. Let the wives of Danton and Camille throw banknotes among the people, that's better than heads.

LAFLOTTE: [*Aside*] Unlike Oedipus, I won't tear my eyes out; I may need them to weep for the good general.

DILLON: Hands on Danton! Who's safe after that? Fear will unite them.

LAFLOTTE: [*Aside*] Yes, he's lost. What does it matter then if I tread on a corpse in order to clamber out of the grave?

DILLON: Only a foot on the pavement. I will find enough people, old soldiers, Girondists, ci-devants; we'll break open the prisons, we must come to terms with the prisoners.

LAFLOTTE: Cetainly it smells a little of treachery. What does it matter? I should like to try that myself; until now I've been too one-sided. One gets remorse, that too is a change; it isn't so unpleasant to smell one's own stink. The prospect of the guillotine has begun to bore me; to wait so long for the thing! I have been through it at least twenty times in my mind.

There's nothing spicy about it any longer. It's become quite vulgar.

DILLON: A letter must be got through to Danton's wife.

LAFLOTTE: [*Aside*] And then—it isn't death I fear but the pain. It might hurt, who can guarantee it doesn't? True they say it only lasts a moment; but pain has a finer measure for time; it splits up a fraction of a second. No, pain's the only sin, and suffering the only burden; I will stay virtuous.

DILLON: Listen, Laflotte, where is that fellow gone to? I have money, it must succeed. We must strike while the iron is hot; my plan is ready.

LAFLOTTE: At once, at once! I know the turnkey, I'll speak to him; you can count on me, general. We'll get out of this hole [*to himself, going out*] to go into another: I into the broadest, the world—he into the narrowest, the grave.

SCENE VI.

[*The Committee of Public Safety.* Saint-Just, Barère, Collot d'Herbois, Billaud-Varennes]

BARÈRE: What does Fouquier write?

SAINT-JUST: The second hearing is over. The prisoners demand the appearance of several members of the Convention and the Committee of Public Safety; they appeal to the people against the silencing of witnesses. The excitement seems to be indescribable. Danton parodied Jupiter and shook his locks.

COLLOT: The easier for Samson to shear them.

BARÈRE: We mustn't show ourselves, the fishwives and rag-collectors might find us less imposing.

BILLAUD: The people have an instinct for letting themselves be trodden on, even if it's only with glances: these insolent physiognomies please them. Such expressions are more awe-inspiring than a nobleman's coat of arms; the fine aristocracy of those who despise humanity sits on them. Every one whom it disgusts to be looked at up and down, should help to smash them in.

BARÈRE: He is like the horned Siegfried. The blood of the Septembrists has made him invulnerable.— What does Robespierre say?

SAINT-JUST: He behaves as though he had something to say. The jury must declare themselves sufficiently instructed and close the debate.

BARÈRE: Impossible—that would never do.

SAINT-JUST: They must be done away with—at any price—even if we have to throttle them with our hands. 'Dare!' Danton mustn't have taught us that word in vain. The Revolution won't stumble over their bodies; but if Danton stays alive—he will seize her by the skirt and he has something in his face as though he might rape liberty. [*He is called away*]

[*The* Gaoler *enters*]

GAOLER: Some prisoners in St. Pélagie lie dying; they are asking for a doctor.

BILLAUD: Unnecessary; so much the less trouble for the executioner.

GAOLER: There are pregnant women amongst them—

BILLAUD: So much the better. Their children will need no coffins.

BARÈRE: The consumption of an aristocrat spares the Tribunal a session. Any medicine would be counter-revolutionary.

COLLOT: [*Taking up a paper*] A petition! A woman's name!

BARÈRE: Yes, from one of those who are compelled to choose between the plank of a guillotine and the bed of a Jacobin. Those who, like Lucretia, die at the loss of their honor, but somewhat later than the Roman . . . in childbirth or of old age. Perhaps it may not be so unpleasant to drive a Tarquin out of the virtuous Republic of a virgin.

COLLOT: She is too old. Madame desires death, she knows how to express herself, prison lies on her like the lid of a coffin. She's been there four weeks. The answer's easy. [*He writes and reads out*] 'Citizeness, you have not yet wished long enough for death.'

BARÈRE: Well said! But Collot, it's not good that the guillotine begins to laugh; the people aren't afraid of it any more; one mustn't make oneself so familiar.

[Saint-Just *returns*]

SAINT-JUST: I have just received a denunciation. There is a conspiracy in the prison; a young man called Laflotte has discovered all. He was in the same cell as Dillon. Dillon got drunk and blabbed.

BARÈRE: He cuts his own neck off with his bottle; that's happened often enough before.

SAINT-JUST: Danton's and Camille's wives must scatter money amongst the people; Dillon will break out; the prisoners will be freed; the Convention will be blown up.

BARÈRE: Fairy stories!

SAINT-JUST: We'll send them to sleep with these fairy tales. I hold the proofs in my hands; add to them the impudence of the accused, the muttering of the people, the dismay of the jury; I'll make a report.

BARÈRE: Yes, go, Saint-Just, and spin your periods, where every comma is the stroke of a sword and every period a head struck off.

SAINT-JUST: The Convention must decree that the Tribunal carry through the session without interruption and that it exclude from the proceedings any witness who shows contempt for the judges or who creates a scene causing disturbance.

BARÈRE: You have the revolutionary instinct; that sounds quite moderate and yet it will achieve its purpose. They cannot be silent; Danton is bound to cry out.

SAINT-JUST: I count on your support. In the Convention there are people as ill as Danton who fear the same cure. They've gained courage, they'll scream about the irregular procedure . . .

BARÈRE: [*Interrupting him*] I'll say to them: in

Rome the consul who discovered the Catiline conspiracy and punished the criminals with instant death was accused of irregular procedure. Who were his accusers?

COLLOT: [*With pathos*] Go, Saint-Just, the lava of revolution flows! Liberty will suffocate in her embrace those weaklings who wished to fertilize her mighty womb; the majesty of the people will appear in thunder and lightning, as Jupiter to Semele, and change them into ashes. Go, Saint-Just, we will help you; the thunderbolt must strike on the heads of cowards.

[Saint-Just *exit*]

BARÈRE: Did you hear the word 'Cure'? They'll end by making the guillotine a specific against syphilis. They don't fight the moderates, they fight vice.

BILLAUD: Until now our ways have gone together.

BARÈRE: Robespierre will make the Revolution a hall for preaching moral sermons and use the guillotine as a pulpit.

BILLAUD: Or as a hassock.

COLLOT: On which finally he'll not stand but lie.

BARÈRE: That will happen easily enough. The world would be topsy turvy if the so-called wrongdoers were hanged by the so-called righteous folk.

COLLOT: [*To* Barère] When do you return to Clichy?

BARÈRE: When the doctor stops visiting me.

COLLOT: Doesn't a star stand over the place, under whose beams the marrow of your spine will be quite dried up?

BILLAUD: Soon the pretty fingers of that charming Demaly will tear it out of its sheath, and make it hang down over his back as a pigtail.

BARÈRE: [*Shrugs his shoulders*] Pooh! Virtue should know nothing of those things.

BILLAUD: He's an impotent free-mason.

[Billaud *and* Collot *exeunt*]

BARÈRE: The monster! 'You have not yet wished long enough for death!' These words should have withered the tongue that spoke them.

And I? When the Septembrists broke into the prisons, a prisoner seized his knife, joined with the assassins, and plunged it into the breast of a priest; he was saved! Who could object to that? Shall I now go join with the murderers or sit on the Committee of Public Safety? Shall I use the guillotine or a pocket knife? It's the same situation only under rather more complex circumstances; the fundamentals are the same.—And dare he murder one, two, or three or even more of us? Where does it end? There come the barleycorns, do two make a heap, or three, or four, or how many? Come, my conscience, come, my chicken, cluck, cluck, cluck, here's your fodder.

Yet—if I also were a prisoner? If I were suspected, it would be the same thing, my death would be certain. Come, my conscience, you and I still carry on all right! [*Exit*]

SCENE VII.

[*The Conciergerie, a prison in Paris.* Lacroix, Danton, Philippeau, Camille]

LACROIX: You have shrieked well, Danton; had you taken such pains earlier with your life, things would be different now. You realize now, don't you, when death comes so shamelessly close to one, and has such stinking breath, and becomes more and more importunate?

CAMILLE: If only she'd ravish one, and tear her prize from the hot limbs with fighting and struggle! But with such formality, like a marriage with an old woman, with the contracts set out, with the witnesses called, with the amens said, and then with the counterpane lifted up when, with her cold limbs, she creaks slowly into bed.

DANTON: Would it were a fight so that arms and teeth clutched at each other! But I feel as though I'd fallen into a mill-shaft and that my limbs were slowly and systematically being wrenched off by the cold physical power. To be killed so mechanically!

CAMILLE: And then to lie there, alone, cold, stiff, in the damp vapor of putrefaction. Perhaps death slowly torments the life out of one's fibres, with the knowledge, perhaps, that one's falling to pieces.

PHILIPPEAU: Quiet, my friend. We are like the meadow saffron which first bears seed after the winter. We only distinguish ourselves from flowers which are transplanted because in the attempt we stink a little. Is that so bad?

DANTON: An edifying prospect! From one manure heap to another. Isn't that the theistic theory of classes? From first to second, second to third and so on? I've had enough of the school bench, I've got piles on my seat like an ape from sitting on it.

PHILIPPEAU: Then what would you like?

DANTON: Rest.

PHILIPPEAU: Rest is in God.

DANTON: In nothingness. What can you sink back in which is more restful than nothingness, and if the highest peace is God, isn't nothingness God? But I'm an atheist; that accursed phrase! Something cannot become nothing! And I am something, that is the trouble! Creation has made itself so broad, nothing is empty. Everything full of multitude. Nothingness has killed itself, creation is its wound, we are the drops of its blood, the world is the grave in which it decomposes. That sounds mad but there's some truth in it.

CAMILLE: The world's the eternal Jew, nothingness is death, but that's impossible. Oh, not to be able to die, as the song goes!

DANTON: We are all buried alive and set aside like kings in threefold or fourfold coffins, under the sky, in our houses, in our coats and shirts. We scratch for fifty years on our coffin lids. If one could believe in annihilation! Yes, that would be a help.—There is no hope in death. It is only a simpler form of laziness, whilst life is one that is more complex, more organized. That's the whole difference! But it's exactly this form of indolence which I've been accustomed to; the devil knows how I'll get used to another.

O, Julie, if I could go alone! If she would leave me in solitude! And if I could fall to pieces utterly, dissolve entirely—then I would be a handful of tormented dust—every one of my atoms could only find peace in her. I cannot die, no, I cannot die. We aren't struck down yet. We must shriek, they must tear every drop of life-blood out of my limbs.

LACROIX: We must stand by our demands. Our accusers and the Committee must appear before the Tribunal.

SCENE VIII.

[*A room.* Fouquier-Tinville, Amar, Vouland]

FOUQUIER: I no longer know what answer to make: they are demanding a commission.

AMAR: We've got the scoundrels—here you have what you want. [*Hands* Fouquier *a paper*]

VOULAND: That will satisfy them.

FOUQUIER: Certainly. We needed it.

AMAR: Quickly then, so that we rid ourselves of this affair and of them. . . .

SCENE IX.

[*The Revolutionary Tribunal*]

DANTON: The Republic is in danger and is not instructed of it. We call upon the people; my voice is still strong enough to speak the funeral oration of the Committee. I repeat—we demand a commission; we have important matters to reveal. I will re-establish myself in the citadel of reason, I will break through with the cannons of truth and pulverize my enemies.

[*Signs of applause*]

[*Enter* Fouquier-Tinville, Amar, *and* Vouland]

FOUQUIER: Silence in the name of the Republic and in the name of the law! The Convention decrees: in view of the fact that signs of mutiny have been shown in the prisons; in view of the fact that the wives of Danton and Camille distribute money amongst the people and that General Dillon has plotted to escape and put himself at the head of an insurrection to free the accused; lastly, in view of the fact that they themselves have endeavored to provoke disturbances and to insult the Tribunal: the Tribunal will be empowered to carry out its inquiry without interruption and to exclude any of the accused who shall ignore the respect due to the law.

DANTON: I ask all here whether we have derided the Tribunal, the People or the Convention?

VOICES: No! No!

CAMILLE: Miserable wretches, they wish to murder my Lucile!

DANTON: One day the truth will be known. I see a great misfortune overwhelming France. It is dictatorship; it has torn off its veils, it carries its head high, it strides over our bodies. [*Pointing at* Amar *and* Vouland] See there the cowardly murderers, see the ravens of the Committee of Public Safety! I accuse Robespierre, Saint-Just, and their hangmen of high treason. They want to suffocate the Republic in blood. The ruts of their guillotine carts are the roads by which the foreign armies will thrust into the heart of the Fatherland.

How long will the footprints of liberty be graves? You need bread and you are thrown heads! You thirst, and they make you lap up the blood from the steps of the guillotine!

[*Great emotion amongst the audience, cries of applause*]

MANY VOICES: Long live Danton! Down with the Committee!

[*The* Prisoners *are led away by force*]

SCENE X.

[*A square in front of the Palace of Justice. A crowd*]

VOICES: Down with the Committee! Long live Danton!

1ST CITIZEN: Yes, that's right. Heads instead of bread, blood instead of wine.

WOMEN: The guillotine is a bad mill and Samson a bad baker. We want bread, bread!

2ND CITIZEN: Your bread—Danton's devoured it. His head will give bread to all of you. He was right.

1ST CITIZEN: Danton was with us on the 10th of August. Danton was with us in September. Where were the people who make accusations against him?

2ND CITIZEN: And Lafayette was with you in Versailles, and was a traitor just the same.

1ST CITIZEN: Who says that Danton is a traitor?

2ND CITIZEN: Robespierre.

1ST CITIZEN: Then Robespierre is a traitor!

2ND CITIZEN: Who says that?

1ST CITIZEN: Danton.

2ND CITIZEN: Danton has beautiful clothes, Danton has a beautiful house, Danton has a beautiful wife, he bathes himself in Burgundy, eats pheasants off silver plates and sleeps with your wives and daughters when he's drunk. Danton was poor like you. Where does it all come from? The King bought it for him, hoping Danton would save his crown for him. The Duke of Orleans made him a present of it, hoping he would *steal* the crown for *him*. The foreigner gave it to him, hoping he would betray you all. What has Robespierre got? The virtuous Robespierre! You all know him.

ALL: Long live Robespierre! Down with Danton!
Down with the traitor.

ACT IV. SCENE I.

[*A room.* Julie, *a Boy*]
JULIE: It's all over. They trembled before him.
They kill him out of fear. Go! I have seen him for
the last time; tell him I could not see him as he is
now. [*Gives him a lock of hair*] There, give him
this and tell him he will not go alone—he will understand. And come back quickly, I will read his look
in your eyes.

SCENE II.

[*A street.* Dumas, *a Citizen*]
CITIZEN: How can they condemn so many unfor-
tunates to death after such a trial?
DUMAS: Indeed it's extraordinary; but revolu-
tionaries have a sense other men lack, and their
instinct never betrays them.
CITIZEN: It's the instinct of the tiger.—You have
a wife?
DUMAS: Soon I shall have had one.
CITIZEN: So it's true?
DUMAS: The Revolutionary Tribunal will pro-
nounce our divorce; the guillotine will divide us from
bed and board.
CITIZEN: You are a monster!
DUMAS: Idiot! You admire Brutus?
CITIZEN: With all my soul.
DUMAS: Must one be a Roman consul and be able
to hide one's head in a toga, to sacrifice one's dearest
to the Fatherland? I shall wipe my eyes with the
sleeve of my red coat; that's the only difference.
CITIZEN: That is horrible!
DUMAS: Go, you don't understand me.
[*Exeunt*]

SCENE III.

[*The Conciergerie.* Lacroix, Hérault-Séchelles *on
one bed,* Danton, Camille *on another*]
LACROIX: One's hair grows long, and one's finger-
nails, really one's ashamed of oneself.
HÉRAULT: Take care what you're doing, you sneeze
sand all over my face!
LACROIX: And don't tread on my feet, my dear
fellow, I've got corns.
HÉRAULT: You've got lice too.
LACROIX: Ah! If I only were free of the worms.
HÉRAULT: Anyhow, sleep well! We must see how
we get on with each other, there's not much room.

—Don't scratch me with your nails in your sleep!—
So!—Don't pull at the shroud like that, it's cold
down there!
DANTON: Yes, Camille, to-morrow we're worn out
shoes, thrown into the lap of the beggar woman
Earth.
CAMILLE: The cowhide which Plato says the
angels make slippers out of, when they grope their
way about the earth. But there's more to come hereafter.—My Lucile!
DANTON: Be calm, my boy!
CAMILLE: How can I? What do you think, Danton? Can I? They can't lay their hands on her, it's
impossible! The light of beauty that pours from her
lovely body can't be put out. Look, the Earth would
not dare to bury her; it would arch itself above her,
the damp of the grave would sparkle like dew on her
eyelashes, crystals would shoot up like flowers about
her limbs and bright springs murmur to her in sleep.
DANTON: Sleep, my boy, sleep.
CAMILLE: Listen, Danton, between ourselves, it's
so miserable to have to die. And it does no good.
I'll still steal from life a last look from her pretty
eyes, I will have my eyes open.
DANTON: They will stay open anyhow. Samson[19]
does not close one's eyes. Sleep is more merciful.
Sleep, my boy, sleep!
CAMILLE: Lucile, your kisses play tricks upon my
lips, every kiss becomes a dream, my eyelids drop
and close fast upon it.
DANTON: Will the clock not be quiet? With every
tick it pushes the walls closer round me, till they're
as close as a coffin—I read such a story as a child,
my hair stood on end. Yes, as a child! It wasn't
worth their trouble to fatten me up and keep me
warm. Only work for the gravediggers!

I feel as if I stank already. My dear body, I will
hold my nose and pretend you're a woman sweating
and stinking after a dance and pay you compliments.
We've often passed the time together in other ways.

To-morrow you're a broken violin; the melody is
played out. To-morrow you're an empty bottle; the
wine is finished but hasn't made me drunk and
I go soberly to bed—lucky people who can still get
tight. To-morrow you're a worn-out pair of trousers;
you'll be thrown into the wardrobe and the moths
will eat you, you may smell as much as you like.

Ugh, it's no good! Yes, it is miserable to have to
die. Death mimics birth, and dying we're as helpless
and naked as new-born children. Of course, we're
given a shroud for swaddling-clothes, but how will
that help? In the grave we can whimper just as well
as in the cradle.

Camille! He's asleep; [*bends over him*] a dream
plays between his eyelashes. I will not brush the
golden dew of sleep from his eyes.

[*Rises and goes to the window*] I shall not go
alone; I thank you, Julie! And yet I should have
liked to die differently, without any effort, as a star

[19] Famous executioner during the French Revolution.

falls, as a note expires, kissing itself dead with its own lips, as a ray of light buries itself in the clear stream.—

Like glimmering tears the stars are sprinkled through the night; there must be some great sorrow in the eyes from which they fall.

CAMILLE: Oh! [*He has sat up and reaches towards the ceiling*]

DANTON: What is it, Camille?

CAMILLE: Oh, Oh!

DANTON: [*Shakes him*] Do you want to scratch the roof down.

CAMILLE: Oh you, you, hold me, speak to me!

DANTON: You're trembling in every limb, there's sweat on your forehead.

CAMILLE: It is you, it is me—so! This is my hand! Yes, now I remember. Oh Danton, it was terrible!

DANTON: What was?

CAMILLE: I lay between dream and waking. Then the roof disappeared, and the moon sank into the room, close and thick, my arm took hold of it. The roof of heaven with its lights had sunk lower, I knocked on it, I touched the stars, I reeled like a drunken man under the roof of ice. It was terrible, Danton.

DANTON: The lamp throws a round shadow on the ceiling, that's what you saw.

CAMILLE: As for me, it doesn't need much to make me lose my scrap of reason. Madness grasped me by the hair. [*He rises*] I won't sleep any more, I don't want to go mad. [*He reaches for a book*]

DANTON: What are you taking?

CAMILLE: The 'Night Thoughts.'[20]

DANTON: Do you want to die beforehand? I'll take 'La Pucelle.'[21] I'll steal away from life not as from a praying-desk but as from the bed of a sister of mercy. Life is a whore; she fornicates with the whole world.

SCENE IV.

[*Before the Conciergerie. A* Gaoler, *two* Carters *with tumbrils,* Women]

GAOLER: Who said you were to come here?

1ST CARTER: I'm not To-Come-Here, what a curious name.

GAOLER: Fool, who gave you the commission?

1ST CARTER: I don't get any commission, nothing except ten sous a head.

2ND CARTER: The villain takes the bread out of my mouth.

1ST CARTER: What do you call your bread? [*Pointing to the window of the prisoners*] That's food for worms.

2ND CARTER: My children are worms too, and

[20] *Night Thoughts on Life, Death, and Immortality,* a long reflective poem in blank verse by Edward Young.
[21] *La Pucelle,* a narrative poem by Voltaire about Joan of Arc.

they also want their share. Oh, things are going badly with our business and yet we're the best carters.

1ST CARTER: Why's that?

2ND CARTER: Who is the best carter?

1ST CARTER: He who carries furthest and fastest.

2ND CARTER: Well, donkey, who can carry further than to carry you out of the world, and who can carry faster than one who does it in quarter of an hour! It's exactly a quarter of an hour from here to the Place de la Révolution.

GAOLER: Quickly, you villains! Nearer to the door; make way, my girl!

1ST CARTER: Don't move! A man doesn't go round a girl, he always goes through her.

2ND CARTER: I'll bet he does; you can drive your cart and horses through her, you'll find the ruts easy; but you'll have to go into quarantine when you come out.

[*They drive forward*]

2ND CARTER: [*To the* Women] What are you staring at?

A WOMAN: We're waiting for old customers.

2ND CARTER: Do you mean my cart is going to be turned into a brothel? It's a respectable cart, it carried the King and all the fine gentlemen of Paris to the scaffold.

[*Lucile enters. She sits on a stone under the prisoners' window*]

LUCILE: Camille! Camille!

[*Camille appears at the window*]

LUCILE: Listen, Camille, you make me laugh with that long coat of stone and that iron mask before your face; can't you bend down? Where are your arms?—I'll entice you, sweet bird.

[*Sings*]

    Two stars stand in the sky
      Shining brighter than the moon,
    One shines at my darling's window
      The other at her door.

Come, come, my friend! Softly up the steps, they're all asleep. The moon has helped me to wait. But you can't get through the door, your clothes are impossible. The joke's gone too far, give it up. You don't move, why don't you speak to me? You frighten me.

Listen, the people say that you must die, and they make such serious faces over it. Die! I can't help laughing at their faces. Die! What kind of a word is that? Tell me, Camille. Die! I will think it over. There it is, there! I'll run after it, come, sweet friend, help me catch it, come, come! [*She runs away*]

CAMILLE: [*Calls*] Lucile, Lucile!

SCENE V.

[*The Conciergerie.* Danton, *at a window which looks into the next room.* Camille, Philippeau, Lacroix, Hérault]

DANTON: You're quiet now, Fabre.

A VOICE: [*From within*] As death.

DANTON: Do you know what we are doing now?

A VOICE: Well?

DANTON: What you've done all your life; making verses—*des vers.*[22]

CAMILLE: [*To himself*] Madness sat behind her eyes. More people have gone mad already. It's the way of the world. What can we do? We wash our hands of them.—It is better so.

DANTON: I leave everything in terrible confusion. Not one of them knows how to govern. Things might still be managed if I left Robespierre my whores and Couthon my legs.

LACROIX: We'd have turned liberty into a whore!

DANTON: And what else is it? Liberty and whores are the most cosmopolitan things under the sun. Liberty will now prostitute herself decently in the marriage bed of the lawyer from Arras. But I think she will be a Clytemnestra to him; I don't give him more than six months' respite, I drag him with me.

CAMILLE: [*To himself*] Heaven help her to some comfortable *idée fixe!* The universal *idée fixe* which is called good sense is intolerably boring. The happiest man would be he who could persuade himself that he was God the Father, the Son, and the Holy Ghost.

LACROIX: The fools will cry 'Long live the Republic!' as we pass by.

DANTON: What does it matter? The deluge of the Revolution may carry our corpses where it likes; with our fossilized bones men can always break the heads of all kings.

HÉRAULT: Yes, so long as there's a Samson to use our jaw-bones.

DANTON: They bear the brand of Cain.

LACROIX: Nothing shows more clearly that Robespierre is a Nero than that he was never so friendly to Camille as two days before his arrest. Isn't it so, Camille?

CAMILLE: What does it matter, so far as I'm concerned?—[*To himself*] What an attractive thing she has made of madness. Why must I go away now? We'd have laughed over it together, have nursed it and kissed it.

DANTON: If History once opens her vaults, Despotism may still suffocate from the vapors of our corpses.

HÉRAULT: We stank quite sufficiently in our lifetime.—These are phrases for posterity, aren't they, Danton; they have nothing to do with us.

CAMILLE: He makes a face, as if it ought to turn to stone and be dug up by posterity as an antique.

That isn't worth the trouble either, to pull faces and put on red and speak with a good accent; once in a while we should take off the masks, then we should see everywhere, as in a room of mirrors, the one, primeval, toothless, everlasting sheep's head, no

more and no less. The differences are not so big, we are all villains and angels, fools and geniuses, and indeed all of them in one; the four find plenty of room in one body, they are not so large as people pretend. Sleep, digest, breed children—every one does that; other things are only variations in different keys on the same theme. And yet men have to walk on tiptoes and make faces, still they have to be embarrassed in front of each other. We have all eaten ourselves sick at the same table and have now got the gripes; why do you hold your napkins before your faces? Scream and cry as the fancy takes you! But don't make such virtuous and such witty and such heroic and such brilliant grimaces. After all, we know each other; spare yourselves the trouble.

HÉRAULT: Yes, Camille, let us sit beside each other and scream; nothing stupider than pressing your lips together if something is hurting you.—Greeks and Gods screamed, Romans and Stoics made heroic grimaces.

DANTON: The second were as good Epicureans as the first. They gave themselves a very comforting self-respect. It's not so bad to drape your toga and look around to see if you throw a long shadow. What should we aim at? To hide our shame with laurel leaves, rose wreaths or vine leaves or to show the ugly thing openly and let it be licked by the dogs?

PHILIPPEAU: My friends, one need not stand very high above the earth to see nothing more of all the confused flux and glimmer and have one's eye filled by a few great godlike outlines. There is an ear for which the clamor and discordance which deafen us are a stream of harmonies.

DANTON: But we are the poor musicians and our bodies the instruments. Do the ugly sounds that are ground out of them only exist so that rising higher and higher and finally softly echoing they expire in a voluptuous sigh in the ear of heaven?

HÉRAULT: Are we sucking-pigs which are whipped to death for princely tables, so that their flesh is tastier?

DANTON: Are we children, roasted in the glowing Moloch arms of this world and tickled with rays of light so that the Gods may enjoy their laugh?

CAMILLE: Is the air with its golden eyes a dish full of golden carp that stands on the table of the blissful Gods, and the blissful Gods laugh eternally, and the fish die eternally, and the Gods rejoice eternally at the play of color in the death struggle.

DANTON: The world is chaos. The Nothing is its too fertile Deity.

[*Enter the* Gaoler]

GAOLER: Gentlemen, you may go, the carriages wait at the door.

PHILIPPEAU: Good night, my friends! Let us quietly draw over our heads the great coverlet, under which all hearts burn out and all eyes close.

[*They embrace each other*]

HÉRAULT: [*Takes* Camille's *arm*] Rejoice, Camille, we shall have a good night. The clouds hang in the

---

[22] Fabre d'Eglantine had made verses or poems, but now would make *vers*, worms, since he is dying in prison. A mordant pun.

calm evening sky like a burnt-out Olympus with the fading sinking forms of the Gods.

[*They leave*]

SCENE VI.

[*A room*]

JULIE: The people ran into the street, now all is quiet. I should not like to keep him waiting a moment. [*She takes out a phial*] Come, dearest priest, whose amen sends us to bed. [*Goes to the window*] It is so lovely to say good-bye; now I have only to close the door behind me. [*Drinks*]

One would like to stand like this forever.—The sun has gone down. The earth's features were so sharp in her light, but now her face is as calm and grave as a dying woman's.—How beautifuliy the evening light plays about her forehead and her cheeks.—Paler and paler she becomes, like a corpse she drives downwards on the flood of the air. Will no arm seize her by the golden hair and take her from the stream and bury her?

I go softly. I do not kiss her, so that no breath, no sigh may wake her from her slumber.—Sleep, sleep! [*Dies*]

SCENE VII.

[*Place de la Révolution. The tumbrils are driven on and halt at the guillotine.* Men *and* Women *sing and dance the Carmagnole. The* Prisoners *sing the Marseillaise*]

WOMAN: [*With* Children] Make room, make room! The children are crying, they're hungry. I must make them watch, so they'll be quiet. Make room!

A WOMAN: Hey, Danton, now you can go to bed with the worms.

ANOTHER: Hérault, I'll get myself a wig made from your lovely hair.

HÉRAULT: I haven't enough bush to cover so denuded a Mound of Venus.

CAMILLE: Damned witches! You shall still cry: may the mountains fall upon us.

A WOMAN: The mountain has fallen on you, or rather you've fallen beneath it.

DANTON: [*To* Camille] Quiet, my boy! You've shouted yourself hoarse.

CAMILLE: [*Gives the* Driver *money*] There, old Charon, your cart is a fine platter!—Gentlemen, I shall serve myself first. This is a classical banquet; we lie in our places and scatter a little blood as a libation. Adieu, Danton!

[*He ascends the scaffold, the* Prisoners *follow him one by one,* Danton *last*]

LACROIX: [*To the people*] You kill us on the day when you've lost your reason; you'll kill them on the day you recover it.

SOME VOICES: That's been said before; how tiresome!

LACROIX: The tyrants will break their necks over our graves.

HÉRAULT: [*To* Danton] He thinks his corpse a breeding-ground of Freedom.

PHILIPPEAU: [*On the scaffold*] I forgive you; I hope that your hour of death may be no bitterer than mine.

HÉRAULT: I knew it! He has to reach into his bosom once more to show the people down there that he has clean linen.

FABRE: Good luck, Danton! I die twice over.

DANTON: Adieu, my friend! The guillotine is the best doctor.

HÉRAULT: [*Tries to embrace* Danton] Ah, Danton, I can't even make a joke. The time has come.

[*An* Executioner *separates them*]

DANTON: [*To the* Executioner] Do you wish to be more cruel than death? Can you prevent our heads from kissing at the bottom of the basket?

SCENE VIII.

[*A street*]

LUCILE: And yet there's something serious in it. I must think about it. I'm beginning to understand a little.

To die—to die!—Yet everything may live, yes, everything, the little fly there, the birds. Why not he? The river of life would cease to flow if but one drop were spilled. The earth would have a wound from such a blow.

Everything moves, the clocks tick, the bells peal, the people run, the water flows, and everything else goes on except there, there—! No, it shall not happen, no, I will sit upon the ground and scream, so that everything will stand still in fear, everything come to a stop, nothing moves any more. [*She sits down, covers her eyes, and gives one cry. Then after a pause she gets up*] It doesn't help, everything remains as before; the houses, the street, the wind blows, the clouds pass.—We have to bear it.

[*Some* Women *come down the street*]

1ST WOMAN: A handsome man, Hérault!

2ND WOMAN: When he stood at the triumphal arch at the Feast of the Constitution, I thought to myself, he'd look well on the guillotine, that's what I said. It was a presentiment, as you might say.

3RD WOMAN: Yes, one must see people under all conditions; it's a good thing dying's become so public. [*They pass by*]

LUCILE: My Camille! Where shall I look for you now?

SCENE IX.

[*Place de la Révolution. Two* Executioners *at work on the guillotine*]

1ST EXECUTIONER: [*Stands on the guillotine and sings*]

> And when home go I
> The moon shines so shy. . . .

2ND EXECUTIONER: Hey, hallo! Will you finish soon?

1ST EXECUTIONER: In a minute!

[*Sings*]

> Shines in my old father's window—
> Boy, where have you been for so long?

Hey, give us my coat.

[*They go singing away*]

> And when home go I
> The moon shines so shy. . . .

LUCILE: [*Enters and sits on the steps of the guillotine*] I lay myself in your lap, quiet angel of death.

[*Sings*]

> There is a reaper, his name is Death,
> Has power from Almighty God. . . .

Dear cradle, who lulled my Camille to sleep, who stifled him beneath your roses. You bells of death, whose sweet tongue sang him to the grave.

[*Sings*]

> Hundreds of thousands without number
> Fall beneath the sickle only.

[*Enter a* Patrol]

A CITIZEN: Hey, who goes there?

LUCILE: Long live the King!

CITIZEN: In the name of the Republic!

[*She is surrounded by the watch and taken away*]

Nikolai Gogol

(1809–1852)

Although Nikolai Vasilevich Gogol was Russia's first great novelist and short-story writer, he also occupies an honorable position in the theatre, chiefly on the strength of his broad satire *The Inspector*. He had predecessors as far back as the second half of the eighteenth century in Fonvizin, author of two satiric comedies, and in Kapnist, whose *Chicane* exposed the Russian law courts. He was also preceded by Alexander Griboyedov, whose *Woe from Wit* resembles Molière's satire *The Misanthrope* with its scorn for society. But Gogol wrote realistic prose whereas his predecessors wrote verse, and it was in prose realism that the later Russian drama excelled. When in the eighteen-thirties he applied his special talent for realistic-grotesque fiction to the stage, he made an important contribution to playwriting.

To the historian of the drama, Gogol stands at the crossroads. His sense of the grotesque places him among the romanticists; his keen observation of social reality, among the realists. But his talent, a unique one that cannot be subsumed under any label, reflects a complex personality that never found a clear definition for itself. He was exuberant, yet also disenchanted; gay, yet often depressed. He had a large bump of irreverence in his nature and liked farce and burlesque; nevertheless, he also possessed a poet's sensitivity and fancy and a vein of mysticism not to be found in the plays. Perhaps the best description of Gogol's work as a whole was given by Prince D. S. Mirsky: "He has an abnormally sensitive eye for the details of real life, but he uses these realistic details to construct monsters as impossible as unicorns and griffins, which yet seem more alive than if they were real."

Gogol's dramatic writing appeared in the midst of his activity as a writer of fiction. He was born in a Ukrainian village of Cossack stock; his father was a man of standing who held an honorary post as regimental secretary of the Ukrainian army. After being tutored at home by a theological student, Gogol was sent to a school of the "Higher Sciences," but instead of studying science he first learned to draw and then became absorbed in literature. After completing his course, he went to St. Petersburg (1829) to become a government clerk. But he gave up his employment quickly, traveled in Europe, and tried to become an actor. Failing to realize his ambition, he became a teacher of Russian literature and later a professor of Russian history. But he never made a success of anything but literature, and even literature did not entirely satisfy his complex, unstable personality. After 1831, he attracted much attention with his humorous yet also pathetic stories, among which *The Cloak,* an account of the humiliations of a government clerk, became justly famous. Since it was the first notable piece of realistic fiction in Russia, it exerted a strong influence on later writers, as Dostoevsky was to remember, many decades later, when he declared that all Russian writers came out of Gogol's "cloak." He also won great popularity with the stirring prose epic of Cossack life *Taras Bulba* (1832). Finally, he turned to a large project, the writing of a novel of manners about provincial Russian society, *Dead Souls,* in which bitterness and despair mingle with grotesque humor. The first part of this work is, indeed, one of the masterpieces of modern fiction; the second is only a fragment. Overcome with a sense of guilt and despair, Gogol became a religious mystic and burned his manuscript. He died under a cloud of pathological melancholy.

Marriage, Gogol's first play, was begun in 1832 but completed ten years later. It is a riotous farce of no particular importance. He also began a trenchant play, *The Gamblers,* in 1836, which he finished in 1842. It is a short work but a remarkably observant picaresque comedy of scoundrels who outsmart one another. Caricature, satire, and sharp naturalistic detail are combined in this, one of the least known of his writings. Gogol also left a dramatic fragment, *The Order of St. Vladimir, Third Class,* which he decided not to finish after realizing that a satire on St. Petersburg government circles could not be produced in Russia.

Gogol's masterpiece, *The Inspector* (translated also under other titles—*Revizor, The Inspector General,* and *The Government Inspector*), was begun by him in 1834 and produced on April 19, 1836, with the consent of Emperor Nicholas I, who attended the *première* but later regretted his tolerance. It proved to be a devastating satire on bureaucratic corruption in provincial Russia, and represented a great step in that country toward realistic social drama. Gogol was not actually a liberal or a democrat in any political sense, but there is no doubt that he was keenly aware of the frailties of the human species and the imperfections of the society he knew. "Do not blame the mirror," he wrote in adding a little motto to the published version, "when it is your face that is crooked." *The Inspector* has been kept alive, however, not merely by the relevance of the theme but by the liveliness of the writing. Its realism is not literal but imaginative and extravagant. Its broad and salty dialogue is realistic in the best sense; that is, it sounds authentic, even if it is not intended as a strict transcript of ordinary conversation, since the prime object is to ridicule the provincial bureaucracy. Gogol painted life as a realist but employed the brush-strokes of a caricaturist. *The Inspector* became one of the most frequently revived plays of the Russian theatre for the simplest of good reasons—it was unfailingly entertaining.

Although Gogol, who had difficulties with official censorship in Russia, could not have foreseen that he had opened up a new vein of realistic comedy, *The Inspector* foreshadowed the vogue of social and political satire in the second half of the nineteenth century and in the twentieth century. In 1851, Balzac's *Mercadet,* a sharply satirical study of dishonest business dealings, was to be produced. In 1868, Ibsen was to write his first political comedy, *The League of Youth,* and in 1882, his famous satire on vested interests *An Enemy of the People.* From then on there was never to be any dearth of comic and satiric encounters between playwrights and the political life. American comedies such as *State of the Union* and *Born Yesterday,* produced at about the mid-point of our century, can also be said to have come out of Gogol's "cloak."

THE INSPECTOR[1]

By Nikolai Gogol

TRANSLATED FROM THE RUSSIAN BY JOHN LAURENCE SEYMOUR AND GEORGE RAPALL NOYES

CHARACTERS[2]

ANTON ANTONOVICH SKVOZNIK-DMUKHANOVSKY, *chief of police*
ANNA ANDREYEVNA, *his wife*
MARYA ANTONOVNA, *his daughter*
LUKA LUKICH HLOPOV, *superintendent of schools*
HIS WIFE
AMMOS FEDOROVICH LYAPKIN-TYAPKIN, *judge*
ARTEMY FILIPPOVICH ZEMLYANIKA, *supervisor of charitable institutions*
IVAN KUZMICH SHPEKIN, *postmaster*
PETR IVANOVICH DOBCHINSKY ⎱ *landed proprietors liv-*
PETR IVANOVICH BOBCHINSKY ⎰ *ing in the town*
IVAN ALEXANDROVICH HLESTAKOV, *an official from St. Petersburg*
OSIP, *his servant*

CHRISTIAN IVANOVICH GIBNER, *district physician*
FEDOR ANDREYEVICH LYULYUKOV ⎫ *retired officials, re-*
IVAN LAZAREVICH RASTAKOVSKY ⎬ *spected person-*
STEPAN IVANOVICH KOROBKIN ⎭ *ages in the town*
STEPAN ILYICH UKHOVERTOV, *police captain*
SVISTUNOV ⎫
PUGOVITSYN ⎬ *policemen*
DERZHIMORDA ⎭
ABDULIN, *a merchant*
FEVRONYA PETROVA POSHLEPKIN, *wife of a locksmith*
WIDOW OF A SERGEANT
MISHKA, *servant of the chief of police*
INN SERVANT
MEN AND WOMEN GUESTS, MERCHANTS, TOWNSFOLK, PETITIONERS

CHARACTERS AND COSTUMES

(Notes for the Actors)

The Chief of Police[3] *has grown old in the service and is, in his own way, anything but a stupid man. Although a bribe-taker, he behaves with marked dignity; he is rather serious, and is even somewhat inclined to moralize; he speaks neither loudly nor softly, much nor little. His every word is significant. His features are harsh and coarse, such as are common in people who have advanced with difficulty from the lowest ranks. The change from fear to joy, from servility to arrogance, is very sudden, as in the case*

[1] This play has also been translated under the titles *The Inspector General, Revizor,* and *The Government Inspector.*

[2] Several of these names have grotesque associations; the following translations may serve: Skvoznik-Dmukhanovsky, Rascal-Puftug; Hlopov, Bedbug; Lyapkin-Tyapkin, Bungle-Steal; Zemlyanika, Strawberry; Hlestakov, Whippersnapper; Lyulyukov, Halloo; Rastakovsky, Say-Yes; Korobkin, Woodenhead; Ukhovertov, Earwig; Svistunov, Whistle; Pugovitsyn, Buttons; Derzhimorda, Holdyourmug; Abdulin, Tatar; Poshlepkin (pronounced Po-shlyop'kin), Draggletail. Fedor is pronounced Fyŏ'dor; Fedorovich, Fyŏ'do-ro-vich; Shpekin, Shpyŏ'kin; Ukhovertov, U-kho-vyŏr'toff; Petr, Pyŏtr (one syllable).

[3] The office of *gorodnichy,* or chief of city police, existed from 1775 to 1862. The *gorodnichy* was appointed by the imperial authorities in St. Petersburg and was responsible to them. His duties were far more extensive than those of the chief of police of an American or an English city. The title *city manager* might suggest them more accurately. In some translations he is called *the mayor.*

of a man with crudely developed personal traits. He is dressed in the usual manner, in his uniform with frogs, wearing high boots with spurs. His hair is cut short and shows gray streaks.

Anna Andreyevna, *his wife, is a provincial coquette, still in middle life, brought up half on novels and albums, half on bustling about her housekeeping supplies and supervising her maids. She is very inquisitive, and on occasion displays vanity. Sometimes she gets the upper hand of her husband simply because he is unable to answer her, but this power extends only to trifles and consists of curtain lectures and nagging. During the course of the play she changes her costume four times.*

Hlestakov *is a young man twenty-three years old, very thin and lean; he is rather stupid, and, as they say, rattle-headed, one of those people who in their offices are called hopelessly "dumb." He speaks and acts without any reflection. He is incapable of focusing his attention on any thought whatsoever. His speech is abrupt, and the words fly out of his mouth quite unexpectedly. The more sincerity and simplicity the actor puts into this rôle, the better he will play it. He is dressed fashionably.*

Osip *is the usual sort of elderly manservant. He talks seriously, and has a rather condescending air; he is inclined to moralize, and likes to sermonize his master behind his back. His voice is almost unchanging: in conversation with his master he assumes a severe, abrupt, and even rather rude expression. He is cleverer than his master, and therefore grasps a situation more quickly; but he does not like to talk much, and is a silent rascal. He wears a gray or blue frock coat, much worn.*

Bobchinsky and Dobchinsky *are both short and stubby and very inquisitive, extraordinarily like each other: both are slightly corpulent; both speak very fast with an extraordinary amount of gesticulation.* Dobchinsky *is a little taller and more serious than* Bobchinsky, *but* Bobchinsky *is more expansive and lively than* Dobchinsky.

Lyapkin-Tyapkin, *the Judge, is a man who has read five or six books, and is consequently something of a freethinker. He is very fond of conjectures, and therefore gives much weight to his every word. The actor who plays the rôle must always preserve a knowing expression of countenance. He speaks in a bass voice with a prolonged drawl, with a sound of wheezing and strangling, like an old clock, which first squeaks and then strikes.*

Zemlyanika, *the Supervisor of Charitable Institutions, is a very stout, awkward, and clumsy man, but for all that a schemer and a rogue. He is very officious and bustling.*

The Postmaster *is simple-hearted to the point of naïveté.*

The remaining rôles require no special explanations: their prototypes may be found in almost any community.

The actors should pay particular attention to the last scene. The last speech should produce upon all a sudden electric shock. The whole group should strike its pose in a twinkling. A cry of astonishment should be uttered by all the women at once, as if proceeding from a single bosom. From a disregard of these remarks may result a total loss of effect.

ACT I. SCENE I.

A room in the house of the Chief of Police.
Chief of Police, Supervisor of Charitable Institutions, Superintendent of Schools, Judge, Police Captain, District Physician, *and two* Sergeants of Police.

CHIEF OF POLICE: I have invited you here, gentlemen, in order to communicate to you a most unpleasant piece of news: a government inspector is coming to visit us.

AMMOS FEDOROVICH: What, an inspector?

ARTEMY FILIPPOVICH: What, an inspector?

CHIEF OF POLICE: An inspector from Petersburg, incognito. And furthermore, with secret instructions.

AMMOS FEDOROVICH: Well, I declare!

ARTEMY FILIPPOVICH: As if we didn't have troubles enough already!

LUKA LUKICH: Oh, my God, and with secret instructions too!

CHIEF OF POLICE: I had a sort of presentiment. All last night I kept dreaming about two most extraordinary rats. Honest, I've never seen any like them: black, and awfully big. They came, sniffled about, and went away again. And now I'm going to read you a letter that I've received from Andrey Ivanovich Chmykhov, whom you know, Artemy Filippovich. Here's what he writes: "My dear friend, godfather, and benefactor," [*He mutters in an undertone, rapidly glancing over the letter*] . . . "and to inform you." Ah, here it is! "I hasten to inform you, by the way, that an official has arrived with instructions to inspect the whole province and especially our district. [*Raising his fingers significantly*] I have found this out from most reliable people, although he is representing himself as a private individual. Knowing as I do that you, like everybody else, are liable to your little failings, because you're a smart chap and don't like to miss anything that fairly swims into your hands . . ." [*After a pause*] Well, this is a friendly party. . . . "I advise you to take precautions, because he may arrive at any moment, if he hasn't already, and isn't living somewhere around now, incognito. . . . Yesterday I . . ." Well, next there's some family matters: "Cousin Anna Kirilovna has come to see us with her husband; Ivan Kirilovich has grown very stout, and he plays on the fiddle all the time . . ." and so forth, and so on. Now there's a fix for you!

AMMOS FEDOROVICH: Yes, and such an unusual fix; absolutely extraordinary! There's something up.

LUKA LUKICH: But why on earth, Anton Antonovich, what's this for? Why send an inspector here?

CHIEF OF POLICE: What for? Evidently it's fate. [*Sighing*] Up to this time, thanks be to God, they've poked into other people's business; but now it's our turn.

AMMOS FEDOROVICH: I think, Anton Antonovich, that in this case it's for a subtle and more political reason. Here's what it means: Russia . . . yes . . . Russia's going to war; and the ministry, you see, has sent the official to find out if there's any treason brewing.

CHIEF OF POLICE: Where do you get that stuff? Aren't you the smart man! Treason in a provincial town! Is this a frontier town? Why, you can gallop away from here for three years without reaching a foreign country.

AMMOS FEDOROVICH: No, I tell you, you don't understand . . . you don't . . . The authorities have subtle ideas: even if it is a long distance, they aren't taking any chances.

CHIEF OF POLICE: Whether they are or not, gentlemen, I've warned you. See here: I've made, for my part, some kind of arrangements, and I advise you to do the same. Especially you, Artemy Filippovich! No doubt the passing official will want first of all to inspect the charitable institutions belonging to your department, and therefore you'd better see that everything's in decent shape: the nightcaps had better be clean, and the patients had better not look like blacksmiths, as they usually do, in their little home circle.

ARTEMY FILIPPOVICH: Come, that's all right. They can put on clean nightcaps if you want.

CHIEF OF POLICE: Yes. And also above each bed write up in Latin or some such language—here, that's your job, Christian Ivanovich—the name of each disease, when the person was taken ill, and the day of the week and month. . . . And it's a bad thing that your patients smoke such strong tobacco that a fellow always begins to sneeze as soon as he goes in. Yes, and it would be better if there were fewer of 'em: people will attribute it right off to bad supervision or to the doctor's lack of skill.

ARTEMY FILIPPOVICH: Oh, so far as the doctoring goes, Christian Ivanovich and I have taken our measures: the closer you get to nature, the better; we don't use expensive medicines. Man's a simple creature: if he's going to die, he dies; if he's going to get well, he gets well. And besides it would be hard for Christian Ivanovich to consult with them: he doesn't know a word of Russian.

[Christian Ivanovich *utters a sound somewhat like the letter "e" and a little like "a"*]

CHIEF OF POLICE: I'd also advise you, Ammos Fedorovich, to pay some attention to the courthouse. There in the hall where the petitioners usually appear, the janitors have started raising domestic geese and goslings, and they all duck under your feet as you walk. Of course it's praiseworthy for every man to look after his domestic enterprises, and why shouldn't a janitor? Only in such a place, you know, it's hardly suitable. . . . I meant to bring that to your attention before, but somehow I forgot it.

AMMOS FEDOROVICH: Well, I'll order them all taken away to my kitchen this very day. Come to dinner if you want to.

CHIEF OF POLICE: Besides that it's a bad thing that you have all kinds of rubbish drying up right in the court room, and a hunter's whip right over the cupboard where the documents are kept. I know that you like hunting, but all the same you'd better remove it for a while; and then, when the government inspector has gone away, you can hang it up there again. And your assessor likewise . . . of course, he's a well-informed man, but he smells exactly as if he'd just come out of a distillery—and that's no good either. I've been going to speak to you about that for some time back; but I was distracted, I don't remember how. There's a remedy against that smell, if, as he says, it's actually natural to him: he can be advised to eat onions or garlic or something else. In that case Christian Ivanovich might help out with some drugs.

[Christian Ivanovich *utters the same sound*]

AMMOS FEDOROVICH: No, it's impossible to drive it out. He says that in his childhood his nurse bumped him and that since that time he smells a little of vodka.

CHIEF OF POLICE: Well, I only brought it to your notice. So far as internal arrangements go and what Andrey Ivanovich calls in his letter little failings, I can't say anything, and it would be queer to talk about them, for there's no man who hasn't some weaknesses or other. Why, God himself has fixed it like that, and the Voltairians make a great mistake to say anything to the contrary.

AMMOS FEDOROVICH: And what do you presume to call failings, Anton Antonovich? There are sins and sins. I tell everybody openly that I take bribes—but what kind of bribes? Wolfhound puppies. That's absolutely another matter.

CHIEF OF POLICE: Well, puppies or anything else—it's bribes, all the same.

AMMOS FEDOROVICH: Indeed not, Anton Antonovich. Here, for instance, if a man accepts a fur coat worth five hundred rubles, or a shawl for his wife . . .

CHIEF OF POLICE: Well, and what if you do accept only wolfhound puppies as bribes? To make up for it, you don't believe in God; you never go to church; but I am at least firm in the faith, and I go to church every Sunday. But you . . . Oh, I know you: if you begin to talk about the creation of the world, my hair simply stands on end.

AMMOS FEDOROVICH: But you see I reasoned it out for myself, with my own intellect.

CHIEF OF POLICE: Well, in some cases it's worse to have too much intellect than to have none at all. However, I merely wanted to mention the district court; but to tell the truth, I doubt that any one will ever take a peep at it; it's such an enviable place, God Himself must protect it. Now, as for you, Luka Lukich, as supervisor of educational institutions, you'd better take special care of the teachers. Of course they're learned people, educated in various colleges; but they have very strange ways, naturally inseparable from their learned calling. One of them, for instance, the one with the fat face . . . I don't remember his name . . . when he gets on the platform can't do without making faces, like this [*Making a grimace*] and then begins to iron out his beard with his hand, from under his cravat. Of course, when he pulls a snout like that at one of his pupils, it doesn't matter much, and it may even be necessary for all I can say; but judge for yourself if he should do it to a visitor—that would be awful: the government inspector or whoever it was might consider it personal, and the devil knows what might come of it.

LUKA LUKICH: Surely, but what can I do with him? I've spoken to him about it several times already. Here, just a few days ago, when our marshal of nobility happened to drop in on the class, he cut such a mug as I've never seen before. Of course he did it with the best heart in the world, but I got called down: "Why," says they, "are our young people being exposed to the contagion of freethinking?"

CHIEF OF POLICE: I ought also to mention your history teacher. His head's full of learning, that's evident, and he's picked up information by the ton; only he gets so hot in his explanations that there's no understanding him. I once listened to him: well, while he was talking about the Assyrians and the Babylonians, it was all right; but when he got as far as Alexander of Macedon I can't tell you what came over him. Damme if I didn't think there was a fire!

He ran down from the platform, and banged a chair against the door with all his might. Of course, Alexander of Macedon was a hero; but why smash the chairs over him? It causes a loss to the treasury.

LUKA LUKICH: Yes, he's hot-headed. I've remarked the fact to him several times already. . . . He says, "Just as you please: for science I won't spare life itself."

CHIEF OF POLICE: Yes, such is the inexplicable law of the Fates: a wise man is either a drunkard or he makes such faces that you've got to carry out the holy ikons.[4]

LUKA LUKICH: God save us from serving in the educational line! A fellow's afraid of everybody: all sorts of people interfere, and they all want to show that they're educated, too.

CHIEF OF POLICE: But all this wouldn't amount to anything—it's that damned incognito! He'll look in all of a sudden with an "Oh, here you are, sweethearts! And who's the judge here?" he'll say.—"Lyapkin-Tyapkin."—"All right, hand over Lyapkin-Tyapkin! And who's the supervisor of charitable institutions?" —"Zemlyanika."—"Well, hand over Zemlyanika!"— That's what's bad!

SCENE II.

The same and the Postmaster.

POSTMASTER: Will you explain, gentlemen, what sort of official is coming, and why?

CHIEF OF POLICE: But haven't you heard?

POSTMASTER: I heard something from Petr Ivanovich Bobchinsky. He just called on me at the post office.

CHIEF OF POLICE: Well, then, what do you think about it?

POSTMASTER: What do I think? I think we're going to war with the Turks.

AMMOS FEDOROVICH: Right-o! That's exactly what I thought.

CHIEF OF POLICE: Yes, but you're both talking through your hat!

POSTMASTER: Sure, it's war with the Turks. The French keep spoiling everything.

CHIEF OF POLICE: War with the Turks, your grandmother! *We're* going to be in a mess, not the Turks. We know that already; I have a letter.

POSTMASTER: If that's so, then there's not going to be war with the Turks.

CHIEF OF POLICE: Well, then, how about you, Ivan Kuzmich?

POSTMASTER: About me? How about you, Anton Antonovich?

CHIEF OF POLICE: Well, what about me? I'm not afraid: that is, only a little. . . . The merchants and

the townspeople make me uneasy. They say that I'm somewhat hard-boiled; but if I've ever taken anything from anybody, God knows it was without the least ill-feeling. I even think [*Taking him by the arm and leading him aside*], I even think there may have been some private denunciation of me. Otherwise why in the world send the inspector to us? Now listen here, Ivan Kuzmich, hadn't you better, for our mutual benefit, just unseal and read every letter that arrives at the post office, both incoming and outgoing? You know, just in case there should be some sort of denunciation, or simply, correspondence. If there isn't, of course you can seal them up again; or, so far as that goes, you can even deliver them opened.

POSTMASTER: I know, I know. . . . Don't try to teach me. I do it already, not as a precaution, but more out of curiosity; I'm deadly fond of finding out what's new in the world. I tell you, it's most interesting reading. There are piles of letters that you'll thoroughly enjoy, certain passages are so descriptive . . . and they're so instructive . . . lots better than the *Moscow News*.

CHIEF OF POLICE: Well, tell me, haven't you ever come across anything about some such official from Petersburg?

POSTMASTER: No, absolutely nothing about any one from Petersburg, but there's a lot said about those from Kostroma and Saratov. However, it's a pity that *you* don't read the letters: there are some corking places in them. Not long ago a lieutenant was writing to a friend and he described a ball in the most playful way . . . it was awfully good: "My life, my dear friend, is being passed in the empyrean," he says; "there are lots of young ladies; the band is playing; the standard gallops by. . . ." He described it all with very great feeling. I kept the letter out just on purpose. Do you want me to read it to you?

CHIEF OF POLICE: Well, this is hardly the time for it. So you'll do me the favor, Ivan Kuzmich, if you accidentally come across a complaint or a denunciation, to keep it back without any question.

POSTMASTER: With the greatest of pleasure.

AMMOS FEDOROVICH: Look out, or you'll catch it for that, sometime!

POSTMASTER: Great Scott!

CHIEF OF POLICE: Never mind, never mind. It would be another story if you were to make anything public out of it; but you see, this is a family matter.

AMMOS FEDOROVICH: Yes, a nasty mess has been brewed! I admit I was going to call on you, Anton Antonovich, to make you a present of a little bitch. She's a sister to the dog you know. You've doubtless heard that Cheptovich and Varkhovinsky have started a lawsuit, so that now I'm living in luxury: I course hares now on one man's land, now on the other's.

CHIEF OF POLICE: Holy Saints, I don't care anything about your hares now! I can't get that damned incognito out of my head. You wait until the door opens, and then suddenly—

---

[4] To avoid shocking them.

SCENE III.

The same, with Dobchinsky *and* Bobchinsky, *who both come in panting.*

BOBCHINSKY: An extraordinary event!

DOBCHINSKY: What unexpected news!

ALL: Why, what is it?

DOBCHINSKY: A most unforeseen affair. We went into the inn—

BOBCHINSKY: [*Interrupting*] Petr Ivanovich and I went into the inn—

DOBCHINSKY: [*Interrupting*] Hey, if you please, Petr Ivanovich, I'll tell it!

BOBCHINSKY: Hey yourself, let me . . . let me, let me . . . you haven't got the right style. . . .

DOBCHINSKY: But you'll get all balled up and won't remember everything.

BOBCHINSKY: I'll remember, by George, I'll remember! Only don't mix in, let me tell it; don't meddle! Gentlemen, please tell Petr Ivanovich not to interfere!

CHIEF OF POLICE: Yes, for God's sake, tell us what's up! My heart's in my mouth. Be seated, gentlemen; take chairs! Petr Ivanovich, here's a chair for you.

[*All seat themselves around the two* Petr Ivanoviches]

Well now, what's up?

BOBCHINSKY: Allow me, allow me; I'll tell everything in order. No sooner had I had the pleasure of leaving you after you had got all upset over the receipt of that letter—yes, sir—than I just dropped in . . . now, please don't interrupt, Petr Ivanovich! I already know all, all, all about it, sir! So, as you'll be kind enough to see, I dropped in on Korobkin. But not finding Korobkin at home, I turned in at Rastakovsky's; and not finding Rastakovsky, I went straight to Ivan Kuzmich in order to communicate to him the news you had received; and then, going away from there, I met Petr Ivanovich—

DOBCHINSKY: [*Interrupting*] Near the stall where they sell meat pies.

BOBCHINSKY: Near the stall where they sell meat pies. Yes, I met up with Petr Ivanovich; and I said to him, "Have you heard the news that Anton Antonovich has received in a trustworthy letter?" But Petr Ivanovich had already heard about it from your housekeeper, Avdotya, who had been sent, I don't know what for, to Filipp Antonovich Pochechuyev's.

DOBCHINSKY: [*Interrupting*] For a little keg for French brandy.

BOBCHINSKY: [*Pushing his hands aside*] For a little keg for French brandy. So Petr Ivanovich and I went to Pochechuyev's. . . . For heaven's sake, Petr Ivanovich, don't interrupt; please don't interrupt! . . . We went to Pochechuyev's, and on the way Petr Ivanovich said to me: "Let's stop," he says, "at the inn. I haven't had anything in my stomach since morning, and it's simply flopping about. . . ." Yes, sir, Petr Ivanovich's belly was. . . . "But they've just brought some fresh salmon into the inn," he says, "and we'll take a snack." Well, no sooner were we in the hotel, when suddenly a young man—

DOBCHINSKY: [*Interrupting*] Not bad-looking, in civilian clothes. . . .

BOBCHINSKY: Not bad-looking, in civilian clothes, was walking up and down the room with such a thoughtful expression on his face and in his actions, and here [*Putting his hand over his forehead*] much of everything, very much. I had a sort of presentiment, and I says to Petr Ivanovich: "There's more in this than meets the eye." Yes, I did. But Petr Ivanovich beckoned to me with his finger and we called the innkeeper, sir, the innkeeper Vlas. His wife was confined three weeks ago; and such a smart boy, too, he's going to take care of the inn just like his daddy. Well, having called Vlas, Petr Ivanovich asked him on the quiet: "Who's that young man?" he says. And Vlas answered, "Why that . . ." Hey, don't interrupt, Petr Ivanovich; please don't interrupt; you won't be able to tell it, God knows you won't: you lisp. I know you've got a tooth in your head that whistles. . . . "That young man," he says, "is an official." Yes, sir. "He's come from Petersburg," says Vlas, "and his name is Ivan Alexandrovich Hlestakov, sir; and he's going," says Vlas, "into the Province of Saratov; and," he says, "he's certainly acting queer: this is the second week he's been here, he never goes outside of the tavern; he orders everything on account; and he won't pay a kopek." As soon as he had told me that, I saw through it at once. "Aha!" I said to Petr Ivanovich—

DOBCHINSKY: No, Petr Ivanovich, it was I who said "Aha!"

BOBCHINSKY: You said it first, but I said it next. "Aha!" said Petr Ivanovich and I. "But why has he come here if he's headed for the Province of Saratov?"—Yes, sir. And so he must be that official.

CHIEF OF POLICE: Who? What official?

BOBCHINSKY: Why, that there official that you received the notice about, the government inspector.

CHIEF OF POLICE: [*Frightened*] What the deuce are you saying? That can't be he!

DOBCHINSKY: Yes, it is! He doesn't pay and he doesn't go. How could it be anybody else? And his traveling papers are made out for Saratov.

BOBCHINSKY: It's he; it's he, by God, it's he. . . . And what an observing fellow: he inspected everything. He even noticed that Petr Ivanovich and I were eating salmon, chiefly because Petr Ivanovich, on account of his stomach . . . well, yes, he even took a look in our plates. I fairly shivered with fright.

CHIEF OF POLICE: O Lord, forgive us sinners! Where's he staying?

DOBCHINSKY: In number five, under the staircase.

BOBCHINSKY: In the very same room where those traveling officers had a fight last year.

CHIEF OF POLICE: Has he been here long?

DOBCHINSKY: Just two weeks. He came on the day of St. Vasily of Egypt.

CHIEF OF POLICE: Two weeks! [*Aside*] Holy Saints and Martyrs, get us out of this! In these two weeks the sergeant's wife has been beaten up! No provisions have been issued to the prisoners! The streets are like a dramshop, such filth! Oh, shame! Disgrace! [*He clutches at his head*]

ARTEMY FILIPPOVICH: What do you think, Anton Antonovich: shall we go in a body to the hotel?

AMMOS FEDOROVICH: No, no! Let the Chief of Police go first, then the clergy, and the merchants—isn't that the way it is in the book, *The Deeds of John the Mason?*[5]

CHIEF OF POLICE: No, no, please leave it to me. Difficult situations have occurred in my life, but they have turned out all right, and I have even been thanked. Maybe God will get us off this time. [*Turning to* Bobchinsky] You say he's a young man?

BOBCHINSKY: He is; not much over twenty-three or four.

CHIEF OF POLICE: All the better: you can smell out a young one quicker. It's fierce when it's an old devil; but a young one is all on the surface. Get your own business fixed up, gentlemen; but I'll go by myself, or maybe with Petr Ivanovich here, privately, just for a walk, to inquire whether the transient strangers are suffering any annoyances. Hey, Svistunov!

SVISTUNOV: What, sir?

CHIEF OF POLICE: Go call the police captain right away—but no, I need you. Tell some one outside to go for him as quickly as possible, and then come back here.

[*The* Sergeant of Police *runs out at full speed*]

ARTEMY FILIPPOVICH: Let's go, let's go, Ammos Fedorovich! There may be some trouble, for a fact.

AMMOS FEDOROVICH: Aw, what are you afraid of? Put clean nightcaps on the patients, and cover up your tracks.

ARTEMY FILIPPOVICH: To hell with your nightcaps! I ordered oatmeal porridge served to the patients, but all the same the corridors stink so of cabbage that you have to hold your nose!

AMMOS FEDOROVICH: Well, I'm easy for my part. As a matter of fact, whoever 'll look into a district court? But if he does happen to glance at any paper, he'll lose all joy in life. Here I've been sitting on the judge's bench for fifteen years, and if I merely look at a report, all I can do is wave my hand! Solomon himself couldn't make out what's truth in it and what isn't.

[*The* Judge, *the* Supervisor of Charitable Institutions, *the* Superintendent of Schools, *and the* Postmaster *go out, and at the door encounter the returning* Sergeant of Police]

[5] The Freemasons were prohibited in Russia as a society dangerous to the government. Apparently the freethinking judge refers to a masonic book.

SCENE IV.

Chief of Police, Bobchinsky, Dobchinsky, *and* Sergeant of Police.

CHIEF OF POLICE: Well, is the cab waiting?

SERGEANT OF POLICE: Yes, sir.

CHIEF OF POLICE: Go down to the street . . . or no, stop! Go bring in . . . But where are the others? Are you just alone? I certainly ordered Prokhorov to be here. Where's Prokhorov?

SERGEANT OF POLICE: Prokhorov is in a private house, but he can hardly be put on the job now.

CHIEF OF POLICE: Why not?

SERGEANT OF POLICE: Because they carried him in this morning dead drunk. They've soused him with two tubs of water, but so far he hasn't sobered up.

CHIEF OF POLICE: [*Clutching his head*] Oh, my God, my God! Hurry into the street; or no, run first to my room—d'you hear?—and bring me my sword and my new hat. Well, Petr Ivanovich, let's be going!

BOBCHINSKY: Me too, me too! Let me go, too, Anton Antonovich!

CHIEF OF POLICE: No, no, Petr Ivanovich, you simply can't! It's bad form, and there's not room enough in the cab.

BOBCHINSKY: Never mind, never mind; I'll manage; I'll run along behind on my own prongs. I'd just like to peep through a chink in the door to see how he behaves. . . .

CHIEF OF POLICE: [*To the* Policeman, *who hands him his sword*] Run right off and get the patrolmen, and have each of them take . . . How my sword has been scratched! That damned cheat of a merchant, Abdulin: he sees that the Chief of Police has nothing but an old sword, but he won't send me a new one. Oh, what a sly gang! As it is, I think those swindlers are getting complaints ready now to yank out from under their coat-tails. Have every patrolman grab a street—deuce take it—I mean a broom—and tell 'em to sweep the whole street that leads to the inn, and sweep it clean. . . . D'you hear? And look out, you; oh, I know you! You're mighty chummy with everybody, but you'll steal spoons and stick 'em in your leggings! Look out; I've got sharp ears! . . . What did you do to the merchant Chernyayev, ha? He gave you two yards of cloth for your uniform, but you swiped the whole bolt. Look out! You take tips too big for your rank! Now, get out!

SCENE V.

The same and Police Captain.

CHIEF OF POLICE: Ah, Stepan Ilyich! Say, for God's sake, where've you been hiding out? Whoever heard the like!

POLICE CAPTAIN: Why, I was right outside the gates.

CHIEF OF POLICE: Well, listen here, Stepan Ilyich!

An official has come from Petersburg. What arrangements have you made out there?

POLICE CAPTAIN: Why, just as you ordered. I sent Police Sergeant Pugovitsyn with the patrolmen to clean the sidewalk.

CHIEF OF POLICE: But where's Derzhimorda?

POLICE CAPTAIN: Derzhimorda has gone off on the fire wagon.

CHIEF OF POLICE: And Prokhorov's drunk?

POLICE CAPTAIN: He is.

CHIEF OF POLICE: How did you happen to allow that?

POLICE CAPTAIN: Why, God knows. Yesterday there was a fight in the suburbs; he went out to restore order, and came back drunk.

CHIEF OF POLICE: Well, listen, here's your job: Police Sergeant Pugovitsyn . . . he's tall, so you can post him on the bridge for the sake of law and order. Then clear away the old fence next to the shoemaker's as quick as you can, and put up a straw waymark as if surveyors were doing some leveling. The more pulling-down there is, the more it shows activity on the part of the governor of the town. Oh, my God! I had forgotten that there's about forty cartloads of every sort of rubbish heaped up against that fence! What a rotten town! You no sooner set up a monument of some kind, or simply a fence, than people bring on all manner of rubbish, the devil knows where from! [He sighs] And if that traveling official asks the people in service whether they're satisfied, have 'em say, "We're satisfied with everything, your Honor." And if any one is not satisfied, I'll give him something afterwards to be dissatisfied about! . . . Ow, ow, ow, I'm a sinner, a sinner in many ways! [He picks up the cardboard hatbox instead of his hat] Just grant, O Lord, that I may get all this off my hands as quickly as possible, and I'll set up such a candle as was never lighted before; I'll make every brute of a merchant contribute a hundred pounds of wax. Oh, my God, my God! Let's go, Petr Ivanovich! [He attempts to put on the box instead of his hat]

POLICE CAPTAIN: Anton Antonovich, that's the box, not your hat.

CHIEF OF POLICE: [Throwing away the box] Box, is it? Oh, to hell with it! And if they ask why the church for the almshouse hasn't been built, for which an appropriation was made five years ago, don't forget to say that it was started, but it burned down. I even presented a report on the matter. Even so I suppose some idiot out of sheer stupidity will forget and say that it wasn't ever started. Yes, and tell Derzhimorda not to be too free with his fists; he's always making people see stars in the name of law and order, innocent and guilty alike. Let's go, let's go, Petr Ivanovich! [He goes out, but returns] And don't let the soldiers out on the street without a stitch on; that dirty garrison will put on their uniforms just over their shirts, but with absolutely nothing below! . . .

[They all go out]

SCENE VI.

Anna Andreyevna *and* Marya Antonovna, *who come in running.*

ANNA ANDREYEVNA: Where are they? Where are they? Oh, my heavens! . . . [Opening the door] Husband! Antosha, Anton! [To her daughter, speaking quickly] It's your fault, it's all because of you! You would be rummaging for a pin or a neckerchief. [She runs to the window and calls out] Anton, where are you going? Who's come? A government inspector? With a mustache! What sort of mustache?

VOICE OF THE CHIEF OF POLICE: I'll tell you later, dearie.

ANNA ANDREYEVNA: Later? What d'you know about that! Later! I don't want to wait till later. . . . Tell me in a word; what is he, a colonel? Ha? [With indifference] He's gone! I'll remember that against you! And this girl keeps saying, "Mamma dear, mamma, wait a minute, I'm pinning my neckerchief behind; I'll come right away." Here's your right away for you! And so we haven't found out a thing! Always your darned primping! You heard that the postmaster was here, and you had to go and prink before the mirror, twisting this way and that! She imagines that he's courting her; but he's making faces at you as soon as you turn your back.

MARYA ANTONOVNA: Well, what's to be done, mamma? It's all the same! We'll find out everything in two hours.

ANNA ANDREYEVNA: In two hours! I most humbly thank you! There's an obliging answer! I wonder you never thought of saying that we'd know better yet in a month! [Leaning out of the window] Hey, Avdotya! Ha? What? Avdotya, haven't you heard that somebody has arrived? . . . You haven't? What a blockhead! He waved you off? Well, let him, you might have pumped him all the same. You couldn't find that out! Your head's full of nonsense—nothing but your beaux. Ha? They went away in a hurry? Well, you could have run after the cab. Now get along with you this minute! Listen: run and ask where they've gone; and find out everything; who the newcomer is and what he's like, d'you hear? Peek through a crack and find out everything: and what kind of eyes he has, black or not; and come back this minute, d'you hear? Hurry up, hurry up, hurry up, hurry up!

[She keeps shouting until the curtain falls, both of them still standing at the window]

ACT II. SCENE I.

A small room at the inn. A bed, a table, a trunk, an empty bottle, top-boots, a clothes-brush, and other objects.

Osip alone.

OSIP: [*Lying on his master's bed*] Devil take me; I'm so hungry that there's a continual rumbling in my stomach as though the whole regiment were beginning to blow their trumpets. I s'pose we'll never get home, and that's all there is to it. What do you want me to do? You came here two months ago, all the way from Petersburg! You squandered your dough on the road, my boy, and now you sit with your tail between your legs and keep cool. There would have been plenty of money for fares; but no, you had to spread yourself in every town! [*Taking him off*] "Hey, Osip, run along and look up the best room for me, and order the best dinner possible. I can't eat a poor dinner; I have to have the best." That would be all right if he were really something decent, but he's just a junior clerk. You get acquainted with some traveler or other—then out with the cards, and first you know you're cleaned out! Bah! I'm sick of such a life! To be sure, it's better in the country: although there's not much society, there's less anxiety; you get yourself a woman and spend your life lying on the sleeping-shelf of the stove and eating meat pies. Of course if anybody wanted to argue about it and get at the truth, living in Petersburg is best of all. If one only had money, life would be very fine and polished: there are theatres, with dancing dogs, and everything you like. All conversation's smart 'n elegant, second only to that of the nobility. You walk into the Shchukin Bazaar, and the clerks shout "Honorable sir!" at you. Crossing on the ferry boat you sit down with an official. If you want company, walk into a shop: there a military man will tell you about the camp, and explain just what each star means, so that you can see it all as plain as your hand before your face. An old officer's wife will stroll in; and such a pretty housemaid may peep in. . . . Tra, la, la! [*He bursts out laughing and shakes his head*] Very gallant manners, deuce take it! You never hear an impolite word; every one addresses you as an equal. If you get tired of walking, you take a cab and sit back like a gentleman; and if you don't want to pay the cabby, never mind: every house has front and rear gates, and you can slip through so fast no devil can follow you up. Only one thing is bad: you eat swell one day, but the next you may croak with hunger, like now, for instance. But he's always to blame. What's to be done with him? His dad will send him money, but instead of hanging on to it—nothing of the kind; off he goes on a spree. He rides in cabs, gets a theatre ticket every day, and then at the end of a week he sends me to the old-clothes shop to sell his new dress-coat. Sometimes he'll sell even his last shirt so that he's nothing to put on but his frock-coat and his overcoat. . . . That's the truth, by God! And such fine English cloth, too! One coat cost him one hundred and fifty rubles, but the old clo' dealer got it from him for twenty. As for the trousers, there's nothing to be said: they go for nothing. And why? Because he won't attend to business. Instead of going to his work, he strolls up and down the Nevsky Prospect and plays cards. If the old gentleman should find out—wow! He wouldn't consider the fact that you're an official, but he'd snatch up your little shirt-tail and give you such a hiding that you'd rub yourself for four days. If you're in the service, do your work. Here's the innkeeper now who says he won't give us anything more to eat until we pay for what we've had; but what if we don't pay? [*Sighing*] Oh Lord, my God, if only I had some cabbage soup, good or bad! I think I could gobble up the world. There's a knock; that's him coming, sure. [*He hops off the bed in a hurry*]

SCENE II.

Osip *and* Hlestakov.

HLESTAKOV: Here, take this. [*He gives* Osip *his hat and cane*] So you've been lolling on the bed again?

OSIP: Why should I? Haven't I ever seen a bed before?

HLESTAKOV: You're lying, you were lolling! You see, it's all mussed up.

OSIP: What should I muss it for? Don't you suppose I know what a bed is? I have legs; I know how to stand up. What's your bed to me?

HLESTAKOV: [*Walking about the room*] See if there's any tobacco in the bag yonder.

OSIP: How could there be any? You smoked up the last four days ago.

HLESTAKOV: [*Walks about and purses up his lips in a variety of ways, finally speaking in a loud and determined voice*] Listen! . . . Hey, Osip!

OSIP: What do you want?

HLESTAKOV: [*In a loud, but not so determined voice*] You go down there.

OSIP: Where?

HLESTAKOV: [*In a voice quite lacking in determination, softer, and almost entreating*] Downstairs, to the bar . . . and tell them to . . . to send me my dinner.

OSIP: Oh no, I don't want to.

HLESTAKOV: How dare you, blockhead!

OSIP: Why, because it'll be all the same; even if I go, we won't get anything. The boss said he wouldn't give us any more dinners.

HLESTAKOV: How does he dare not give us any? That's nonsense.

OSIP: "I'm going to the Chief of Police," says he; "the gentleman hasn't paid anything for three weeks. You and your master are swindlers," he says, "and your master's a rascal. We've seen spongers and scoundrels like you before."

HLESTAKOV: And I'll bet you're happy, you brute, to be telling me all that now.

OSIP: He says: "A fellow like that will come, live high, run up a bill, and afterwards there's no driving him out. I'm not going to joke," he says; "I'm going to complain straight off and have him taken to the police station and then to jail."

HLESTAKOV: Well, that's enough, you blockhead! Get along with you and tell him! What a vulgar animal!

OSIP: It would be better for me to call the proprietor up here to you.

HLESTAKOV: Why call the proprietor? Go yourself and tell him.

OSIP: But really, sir . . .

HLESTAKOV: Well then, deuce take you, call the proprietor!

[Osip *goes out*]

SCENE III.

Hlestakov *alone*.

HLESTAKOV: It's awful how hungry I am! I thought that if I'd just take a walk my appetite would go; but no, damned if it would! If I hadn't gone on a spree at Penza, I'd have had the money to get home. That infantry captain hooked me for fair: he plays wonderful faro, the cheat! We sat down for a quarter of an hour in all, and he fleeced me clean. All the same I was crazy to have another go at him, but I didn't have the opportunity. What a rotten hick town! In their lousy shops they won't sell a thing on credit. I call that simply mean. [*He begins to whistle an air from "Robert the Devil," then "The Red Sarafan," and finally no particular tune*] Nobody'll come.

SCENE IV.

Hlestakov, Osip, *and an* Inn Servant.

SERVANT: The proprietor told me to ask for your orders.

HLESTAKOV: Good day, my boy! How's your health?

SERVANT: Good, thank God.

HLESTAKOV: Well, how are things with the inn: everything going all right?

SERVANT: Yes, thank God, everything's all right.

HLESTAKOV: Many travelers?

SERVANT: Yes, enough.

HLESTAKOV: Listen, my boy, they haven't brought me my dinner yet, so please hurry up and bring it as quickly as possible; you see, I have something to attend to directly after dinner.

SERVANT: But the boss said he wasn't going to send up anything more. He came near going to the Chief of Police to-day with a complaint.

HLESTAKOV: But why complain? Just consider, my boy, what's the use? You see, I've got to eat. Otherwise I might get thin. I'm awfully hungry; and I'm not joking either.

SERVANT: Exactly, sir. But he said, "I shan't give him anything to eat until he's paid for what he's had." That's what his answer was.

HLESTAKOV: Well, you reason with him; talk him over.

SERVANT: What in the world shall I say to him?

HLESTAKOV: You put it to him seriously that I need to eat. The money is another matter. . . . He thinks that if a peasant like him can go without eating for a day, other people can. What an idea!

SERVANT: All right, I'll tell him.

SCENE V.

Hlestakov *alone*.

HLESTAKOV: It's rotten, all the same, if he won't give me anything at all to eat. I never was so hungry in my life. I wonder whether I could raise something on my clothes? Could I sell my trousers? No, I'd rather go hungry than not go home in my Petersburg suit. It's a pity that Joachim[6] wouldn't rent me a carriage. It would have been fine, confound it all, to drive up like a swell to some neighboring landowner's front door, with lanterns, and Osip behind in livery. I can imagine how excited they'd all get! "Who's there? What does he want?" And the footman would go in [*Drawing himself up straight like a footman*] and announce: "Ivan Alexandrovich Hlestakov, from Petersburg; will you receive him?" They, country bumpkins as they are, don't even know what "will you receive him?" means. When any goose of a landowner goes to see them, he wallows straight into the parlor like a bear. I'd go up to some good-looking young daughter and say, "Madam, how happy I . . ." [*He rubs his hands and scrapes with one foot*] Fah! [*Spitting*] I'm sick at my stomach, I'm so hungry.

SCENE VI.

Hlestakov, Osip, *then the* Servant.

HLESTAKOV: Well, what now?

OSIP: They're bringing dinner.

HLESTAKOV: [*Clapping his hands and making a slight jump in his chair*] Hurrah, they're bringing dinner!

SERVANT: [*With plates and a napkin*] This is the last dinner the proprietor will send.

HLESTAKOV: Oh, the proprietor, the proprietor! . . . I spit on your proprietor! What have you got there?

SERVANT: Soup and roast.

HLESTAKOV: What, only two courses?

6 A celebrated horse and carriage dealer of St. Petersburg.

SERVANT: That's all, sir.

HLESTAKOV: What trash is this? I won't accept it. You tell him that this is the limit! . . . That's not enough.

SERVANT: No, the boss says that it's a lot.

HLESTAKOV: But why isn't there any sauce?

SERVANT: There isn't any sauce.

HLESTAKOV: Why isn't there any? I saw them preparing a lot of it myself when I passed by the kitchen. And in the dining-room this morning there were two rather short fellows eating salmon and a lot of other things.

SERVANT: Well, there is some, of course, and there isn't.

HLESTAKOV: What d'you mean, isn't?

SERVANT: There just ain't.

HLESTAKOV: And salmon, and fish, and cutlets?

SERVANT: They're for better people, sir.

HLESTAKOV: Oh, you blockhead!

SERVANT: Yes, sir.

HLESTAKOV: You contemptible little swine! Why do they eat when I don't? Why, damn it all, can't I do as they do? Aren't they travelers just like me?

SERVANT: Why, everybody knows that they ain't.

HLESTAKOV: What are they, then?

SERVANT: The regular sort! Everybody knows: they pay their bills!

HLESTAKOV: I don't care to argue with you, you blockhead. [He helps himself to soup and begins to eat] What kind of soup is this? You've just poured water into the tureen: it hasn't any taste; it merely stinks. I don't want this soup; bring me some other.

SERVANT: I'll remove it, sir. The proprietor said, "If he doesn't want it, he needn't have it."

HLESTAKOV: [Protecting the food with his hands] Well, well, well . . . leave it, you blockhead! You may be used to treating other people like that; but I'm not that sort, my boy. . . . I advise you not to act like that with me. . . . [He eats] My God, what soup! [He continues eating] I think no man on earth to date has ever eaten such soup: there's some kind of feathers swimming around in it instead of grease! [He cuts the chicken in the soup] Ow, ow, ow, what a bird! Give me the roast! There, Osip, there's a little soup left; take it yourself. [He carves the roast] What kind of roast is this? This is no roast.

SERVANT: Why, what is it?

HLESTAKOV: The devil knows what it is, but it's not roast. It's roasted ax instead of ox. [He eats] Swindlers, riffraff! What stuff they hand you! Your jaw begins to ache if you swallow a single bite. [He picks his teeth with his finger] Rascals! It's just like bark—you can't pull it out anyhow; and your teeth will turn black after such dishes. Swindlers! [Wiping his mouth with his napkin] Isn't there anything more?

SERVANT: No.

HLESTAKOV: Riffraff! Rascals! And not even a little sauce or a pudding. Grafters! They simply fleece travelers.

[The Servant and Osip collect the dishes and carry them away]

SCENE VII.

Hlestakov, later Osip.

HLESTAKOV: Really, I feel as if I hadn't eaten a thing: I've just whetted my appetite. If I had any small change, I'd send to the market for a bun.

OSIP: [Coming in] The Chief of Police has come on some errand; he's making inquiries and asking about you.

HLESTAKOV: [Frightened] Well, I declare! Has that brute of an innkeeper managed to complain already? What if he really drags me to jail! What then? I suppose, if he did it in a gentlemanly manner, I might . . . But no, no, I won't! There in town officers and people are strolling about, and I purposely played the swell and exchanged winks with a tradesman's daughter. . . . No, I won't. . . . But how in the world did he dare? What does he take me for, anyhow, a merchant or an artisan? [He adopts a bold manner and straightens up] I'll go right to him and say, "How dare you? How dare . . . ?"

[The door-handle turns; Hlestakov turns pale and shrinks]

SCENE VIII.

Hlestakov, Chief of Police, and Dobchinsky.
Upon entering the room, the Chief of Police stands still. He and Hlestakov stare at each other wide-eyed in fright for several moments.

CHIEF OF POLICE: [Recovering somewhat and standing at attention] Please accept my greetings!

HLESTAKOV: [Bowing] And mine to you, sir.

CHIEF OF POLICE: Pardon me. . . .

HLESTAKOV: Oh, certainly. . . .

CHIEF OF POLICE: It is my duty as the chief official of the town to see that travelers and members of the nobility experience no inconvenience. . . .

HLESTAKOV: [At first stammering a little, but finally speaking loudly] But what's to be done? . . . It's not my fault. . . . I'll pay, honest. . . . They'll send me some money from the country.

[Bobchinsky peeks in at the door]
He's more to blame: he sends me beef as tough as a wooden beam; as for soup, the devil knows what he slops into it; I should have thrown it out the window. He starves me out for days at a time. . . . And such queer tea: it smells of fish, but not of tea. Why should I? . . . What an idea!

CHIEF OF POLICE: [Losing courage] Pardon me, I'm really not to blame. There's always good beef in our market. Dealers from Holmogory[7] supply it, sober men and well-behaved. I don't know where he could get such as you describe. But if anything is not just right . . . Permit me to propose that I remove you to other lodgings.

HLESTAKOV: No, I won't. I know what you mean by other lodgings—the jail. But what right have you? How dare you? . . . Look here, I . . . I'm in the government service in Petersburg. [*Growing bolder*] I, I, I . . .

CHIEF OF POLICE: [*Aside*] Oh, Lord my God, how angry he is! He's found out everything, those damned merchants have told him!

HLESTAKOV: [*More bravely*] Even if you came with a whole regiment, I wouldn't go. I'll go straight to the Minister! [*Striking the table with his fist*] What's the matter with you, anyway?

CHIEF OF POLICE: [*Drawing himself up straight and trembling in every limb*] Have mercy; don't ruin me! Consider my wife, my little children! . . . Don't make a man wretched!

HLESTAKOV: No, I won't go. The idea! What's all that to me? Because you have a wife and children, I have to go to jail—that's grand!

[*Bobchinsky peeks through the door, then hides in fright*]

No, I humbly thank you, I won't go!

CHIEF OF POLICE: [*Trembling*] It's my inexperience, God knows, just my inexperience. The insufficiency of my income . . . Please, sir, judge for yourself: my official salary doesn't even buy our tea and sugar. If I've taken a few bribes, they were mere trifles, something or other for the table or for a suit of clothes. And as for the sergeant's widow who keeps a shop, whom I'm supposed to have flogged, that's all slander, God knows it is. All that was thought up by my enemies; they're people who are ready to make an attempt on my life.

HLESTAKOV: What of it? I have nothing to do with them. . . . [*Meditating*] Still, I don't know why you're talking about your enemies and some sergeant's widow or other. A sergeant's widow is quite another matter, but you won't dare to flog me; you're a long way from that job! . . . The idea! What a chap you are! . . . I'll pay, I'll pay the money, but I haven't it now. I'm sticking around here because I haven't a kopek.

CHIEF OF POLICE: [*Aside*] Oh, a sly trick! What a hint! He makes things hazy, and you can take 'em as you please! There's no knowing how to get at him. Well, I'll make a stab at it, no matter what happens. What will be, will be. I'll take a shot at random. [*Aloud*] If you're really needing money or something else, I'm ready to help you this very minute. It's my duty to assist travelers.

HLESTAKOV: Lend me, do lend me some! I'll settle with the dirty innkeeper at once. I owe him only about two hundred rubles, a little more or less.

[7] A small town in the province of Archangel, noted for its cattle.

CHIEF OF POLICE: [*Producing some notes*] Exactly two hundred rubles, but don't trouble to count them.

HLESTAKOV: [*Taking the money*] I thank you heartily. I'll return the amount at once from the country. . . . This was a sudden embarrassment. . . . I see that you are a gentleman. Now things are very different.

CHIEF OF POLICE: [*Aside*] Well, thank God, he took the money! Now I think everything will go smoothly. I slipped him four hundred instead of two.

HLESTAKOV: Hey, Osip!

[*Osip comes in*]

Call that waiter here! [*To the Chief of Police and Dobchinsky*] But why are you standing? Do me the favor to be seated! [*To Dobchinsky*] Do please sit down.

CHIEF OF POLICE: Oh, no, we're all right standing.

HLESTAKOV: Do please be seated. Now I see perfectly your candor and cordiality; I admit that at first I thought you had come to . . . [*To Dobchinsky*] Sit down!

[*The Chief of Police and Dobchinsky sit down. Bobchinsky peeps through the door and listens*]

CHIEF OF POLICE: [*Aside*] I'll have to be more daring. He wants us to consider him as traveling incognito. Very good, we can fake, too; we'll pretend we haven't the least idea who he is. [*Aloud*] While strolling about on my official duties with Petr Ivanovich Dobchinsky here, a landed proprietor of the vicinity, I came into the inn on purpose to inquire whether the travelers were being well entertained; because I'm not like some police chiefs who don't care about anything. Aside from my duty, out of a Christian love of humanity, I want every mortal to be given a good reception; and here, as if to reward me, chance has afforded me this pleasant acquaintance.

HLESTAKOV: I also am very glad. I confess that except for you, I should have had to stay here a long time: and I absolutely didn't know how I could pay.

CHIEF OF POLICE: [*Aside*] Why, how you talk! He didn't know how he was going to pay! [*Aloud*] And may I venture to inquire where you are going?

HLESTAKOV: I'm going to my own village in the province of Saratov.

CHIEF OF POLICE: [*Aside, with an ironical expression of countenance*] To Saratov, he? And he doesn't blush! Oh, one needs a sharp ear with him! [*Aloud*] You have undertaken a good task. Concerning the road, they say that while, on the one hand, there is unpleasantness because of the delay for horses, on the other, it's a distraction for the mind. I suppose that you're traveling chiefly for your own pleasure?

HLESTAKOV: No, my father wants to see me. The old gentleman is angry because so far I've not been promoted in Petersburg. He thinks that you've only to go there and they'll stick the Vladimir ribbon in your buttonhole. No—I'd like to send *him* to bustle about in the office!

CHIEF OF POLICE: [*Aside*] Listen to the yarns he's spinning! He's even tangling up his old daddy! [*Aloud*] And shall you be gone long?

HLESTAKOV: Indeed, I don't know. You see, my father is obstinate and silly, the old duffer, stubborn as a post. I shall say to him right out: "Whether you like it or not, I can't live away from Petersburg. And why, as a matter of fact, must I ruin my life among peasants? Nowadays a man's needs are quite different: my soul thirsts for enlightenment."

CHIEF OF POLICE: [*Aside*] How well he strings it together! He lies and lies and never trips himself. And he's such an insignificant little fellow, I think I could squash him with my finger nail. Well, just hold on! I'll make you blab yet. I'll make you talk some more. [*Aloud*] Your remark is quite correct. What can you do in the wilderness? Now, take it here, for instance: you work all night long; you labor for your fatherland; you spare yourself in no way; but as for your reward, no one knows when you'll get it. [*He glances about the room*] It strikes me this room is a little damp?

HLESTAKOV: A beastly room, and the bugs surpass any I've ever seen: they bite like bulldogs.

CHIEF OF POLICE: You don't say! Such a cultured guest, and he suffers, from what?—from worthless bugs that should never have been born into the world! Isn't it also a little dark in this room?

HLESTAKOV: Yes, quite dark. The proprietor has introduced the custom of not allowing candles. Sometimes when I want to do something, to read a little, or if I take a fancy to compose something, I can't: it's dark, always dark.

CHIEF OF POLICE: Might I ask you—? But no, I'm unworthy.

HLESTAKOV: Why, what is it?

CHIEF OF POLICE: No, no, I'm unworthy; I'm unworthy.

HLESTAKOV: But what in the world is it?

CHIEF OF POLICE: I might venture . . . At my house there's a room that would just suit you: light, and quiet. . . . But no, I realize that it would be too great an honor for me. . . . Don't be angry! Honest to God, I offered it only in the simplicity of my soul.

HLESTAKOV: On the contrary, I'll accept with pleasure, if you please. It would be much more agreeable for me in a private home than in this dump.

CHIEF OF POLICE: How glad I shall be! And how glad my wife will be, too! That's my disposition, hospitable from my childhood, especially if the guest is a man of culture. Don't think I'm saying this in flattery: no, I haven't that vice; I am expressing myself out of the fullness of my heart.

HLESTAKOV: I thank you heartily. I'm the same: I don't like two-faced people. I'm delighted with your candor and cordiality; and I confess I ask nothing more than to be shown devotion and respect, respect and devotion.

SCENE IX.

The same and the Inn Servant, *introduced by* Osip. Bobchinsky *continues peeking through the door.*

SERVANT: Did you send for me, sir?

HLESTAKOV: Yes; bring me my bill.

SERVANT: I handed it to you long ago for the second time.

HLESTAKOV: I don't remember your stupid bills. Tell me: how much is it?

SERVANT: On the first day you ordered dinner; on the second you just ate a little kippered salmon; and then you began to order everything on credit.

HLESTAKOV: Blockhead! He's begun to reckon it all over again. What does it come to in all?

CHIEF OF POLICE: Don't trouble yourself; he can wait. [*To the* Servant] Go away; the money'll be sent down.

HLESTAKOV: Yes, indeed; just so.

[*He puts away the money. The* Servant *goes out;* Bobchinsky *peeks through the door*]

SCENE X.

Chief of Police, Hlestakov, Dobchinsky.

CHIEF OF POLICE: Now wouldn't you like to inspect some of the institutions in our town, the charitable ones and others?

HLESTAKOV: What is there to see?

CHIEF OF POLICE: So you can see how things go with us . . . what sort of order . . .

HLESTAKOV: With great pleasure; I'm ready.

[Bobchinsky *sticks his head through the door*]

CHIEF OF POLICE: Also, if you wish it, we can go next to the district school to see how the sciences are taught there.

HLESTAKOV: Yes, let's do so.

CHIEF OF POLICE: Then, if you want to visit the prison and the city jails, you will see how we treat criminals.

HLESTAKOV: But why the city jails? We'd better inspect the charitable institutions.

CHIEF OF POLICE: Just as you please. How do you intend to go: in your own carriage, or with me in a cab?

HLESTAKOV: Well, I think I'd better go with you in a cab.

CHIEF OF POLICE: [*To* Dobchinsky] Well, Petr Ivanovich, there'll be no place for you.

DOBCHINSKY: Never mind; I'm all right.

CHIEF OF POLICE: [*Softly to* Dobchinsky] Listen: you run lickety-split and carry two notes, one to Zemlyanika at the hospital and the other to my wife. [*To* Hlestakov] May I venture to ask your permission to write in your presence a line to my wife, bidding her prepare for the reception of an honored guest?

HLESTAKOV: Certainly. . . . Here's the ink; but as for paper, I don't know . . . How about the back of this bill?

CHIEF OF POLICE: I'll write on that. [*He writes, meanwhile talking to himself*] Now we'll see how things will go after lunch and a big-bellied bottle! We have some provincial Madeira—not much to look at, but it'll knock an elephant off its feet. If I could only find out what sort of fellow he is, and how much I need to be afraid of him.

[*Having written, he hands the notes to* Dobchinsky, *who approaches the door; but at that moment the door falls off its hinges, and Bobchinsky, who has been listening on the other side, flies into the room with it. All utter exclamations.* Bobchinsky *picks himself up*]

HLESTAKOV: I hope you didn't hurt yourself anywhere?

BOBCHINSKY: Not at all, not at all, sir, not the least derangement, sir; only a little scratch over my nose. I'll run over to Christian Ivanovich; he has some kind of little plaster, sir, and it'll soon get well.

CHIEF OF POLICE: [*To* Hlestakov, *after making a reproachful sign to* Bobchinsky] That's nothing, sir. If you please, we'll go now. And I'll tell your servant to bring your trunk over. [*To* Osip] My good fellow, just bring everything over to my house, to the Police Chief's residence—any one will show you the way. After you, sir. [*He permits* Hlestakov *to go out first and follows him; then, turning around, he speaks reproachfully to* Bobchinsky] That's you all over! You couldn't find any other place to fall! And there you sprawled like the devil knows what!

[*He goes out,* Bobchinsky *after him. The curtain falls*]

ACT III. SCENE I.

The same room as in Act I.
Anna Andreyevna *and* Marya Antonovna *are standing at the window in the same positions.*

ANNA ANDREYEVNA: Well now, we've been waiting a whole hour, and all the time you with your silly primping: you were all dressed, but no! you still had to rummage! . . . I shouldn't have listened to her at all. What an annoyance! As if on purpose, there's not a soul about! It's as if everything had died.

MARYA ANTONOVNA: But really, mamma, in two minutes we'll find out everything. Avdotya must be back soon. [*She looks out of the window and exclaims*] Oh, mamma, mamma! Some one's coming, there at the end of the street!

ANNA ANDREYEVNA: Where is he? You're always having crazy notions. Well, sure enough. But who is it? Medium-sized . . . in a dress coat. . . . Who can it be? Ha! Isn't that annoying! Who in the world can it be?

MARYA ANTONOVNA: It's Dobchinsky, mamma!

ANNA ANDREYEVNA: Dobchinsky, my foot! You're always imagining things! . . . It can't be Dobchinsky. [*She waves her handkerchief*] Hey, you, come here! Hurry up!

MARYA ANTONOVNA: Really, mamma, it is Dobchinsky.

ANNA ANDREYEVNA: There you go, always quarreling! I tell you it's *not* Dobchinsky.

MARYA ANTONOVNA: Aha, mamma, what did I tell you? You see, it *is* Dobchinsky.

ANNA ANDREYEVNA: Well, yes, it's Dobchinsky; I see now—why are you arguing about it? [*Shouting out of the window*] Hurry up, hurry up; you're too slow! Well, where are they? Huh? Go ahead and talk from where you are. What? Very severe? Huh? And my husband? Where's my husband? [*Leaning slightly out of the window, with vexation*] What a boob: until he gets into the very room, he won't tell a thing!

SCENE II.

The same and Dobchinsky.

ANNA ANDREYEVNA: Now, please tell me: well, aren't you ashamed? I relied on you as a decent man. They all rode off in a hurry, and you after them; and I can't get a sensible word from anybody since. Aren't you ashamed? I christened your Johnny and your Lizzie, and then you act like that with me!

DOBCHINSKY: Heavens, godmother, I ran so fast to prove my respect for you that I can't catch my breath. My respects, Marya Antonovna.

MARYA ANTONOVNA: How do you do, Petr Ivanovich.

ANNA ANDREYEVNA: Well, what's the news? Tell me what happened and how.

DOBCHINSKY: Anton Antonovich has sent you a note.

ANNA ANDREYEVNA: But what's the man like? Is he a general?

DOBCHINSKY: No, he's not a general; but he's not inferior to one in education and elegant manners.

ANNA ANDREYEVNA: Aha! Then he must be the one they wrote to my husband about.

DOBCHINSKY: The very same. I was the first to discover the fact, along with Petr Ivanovich.

ANNA ANDREYEVNA: Well, tell us what happened and how.

DOBCHINSKY: Well, thank God, everything is all right. At first he wanted to treat Anton Antonovich rather rough; yes, he did. He got angry and said that everything was bad at the inn, that he wouldn't go to his house, and wouldn't go to jail on his account; but afterwards, when he found out Anton Antonovich's innocence, and had talked a little more to the point with him, he changed his attitude all at once, and, thank God, everything came out fine. Now they've gone to have a look at the charitable institutions. . . . I admit that Anton Antonovich was thinking that there had been some secret denunciation; I was a little bit scared myself.

ANNA ANDREYEVNA: What have you to be afraid of? You're not in the service.

DOBCHINSKY: Well, you know how it is when a bigwig talks: you feel scared.

ANNA ANDREYEVNA: Oh, the idea! . . . That's all nonsense. Now tell us: what's he like? Is he old or young?

DOBCHINSKY: Young—a young man, about twenty-three years old; but he talks just like an old man. "By all means," he says, "I'll go there, and there, too" . . . [*Waving his hands*] and he says it all so grandly. "I like to write and to read," he says, "but I'm annoyed by the darkness of the room."

ANNA ANDREYEVNA: But what does he look like? Is he light or dark-complexioned?

DOBCHINSKY: No, more of a chestnut. And he has such quick eyes, like some little animal's; they're positively disconcerting.

ANNA ANDREYEVNA: Well, what's he written me in this note? [*She reads*] "I hasten to inform you, my dear, that my situation was altogether lamentable; but trusting in God's clemency, item, for two salted cucumbers and for half a portion of caviar, twenty-five kopeks—" [*Pausing*] I don't understand a thing: what's this about pickles and caviar?

DOBCHINSKY: Oh, Anton Antonovich just wrote that on a piece of scratch paper to save time: some sort of bill had been written on it.

ANNA ANDREYEVNA: Oh, I see. [*Continuing her reading*] "But trusting in God's clemency, it looks as if everything would come out all right. Hurry and get a room ready for an important guest, the one hung with yellow wall paper; you needn't go to any extra trouble for dinner because we're going to have a bite at the hospital, with Artemy Filippovich, but order a lot of wine; tell the dealer Abdulin to send his very best; if he doesn't, I'll overhaul his whole cellar. Kissing your little hand, sweetheart, I remain your Anton Skvoznik-Dmukhanovsky." . . . Oh, good heavens! We'll have to hurry! Hey, who's there? Mishka?

DOBCHINSKY: [*Running to the door and shouting*] Mishka! Mishka! Mishka!

    [Mishka *comes in*]

ANNA ANDREYEVNA: Listen: run to the merchant Abdulin . . . wait, I'll give you a note. [*She sits down at the table and writes a note, talking meanwhile*] Give this note to the coachman, Sidor, and have him run to the merchant Abdulin's and get some wine. You yourself go at once and get the room in fine shape for a guest. Put up a bed and a washstand, and so forth.

DOBCHINSKY: Well, Anna Andreyevna, I'll hurry off now to see how the inspection's going on.

ANNA ANDREYEVNA: Go along, go along! I'm not keeping you!

SCENE III.

Anna Andreyevna *and* Marya Antonovna.

ANNA ANDREYEVNA: Now, Mashenka, we'll have to see about the way we're dressed. He's a Petersburg dandy; God forbid he should laugh at anything! The most becoming thing you can put on is your blue dress with the little flounces.

MARYA ANTONOVNA: Fudge, mamma, the blue! I don't like it at all! Lyapkin-Tyapkin's daughter wears blue, and so does Zemlyanika's. No, I'd better put on my flowered dress.

ANNA ANDREYEVNA: The flowered dress! . . . Really, you're saying that to be spiteful. The other'll be much better, because I want to wear my straw-colored; I'm very fond of straw color.

MARYA ANTONOVNA: Oh, mamma, it doesn't become you at all!

ANNA ANDREYEVNA: It doesn't become me?

MARYA ANTONOVNA: No, it doesn't; I'll bet anything you please, it doesn't; you've got to have dark eyes to wear straw color.

ANNA ANDREYEVNA: Well, upon my word! And haven't I got dark eyes? As dark as can be. What nonsense she's talking! How can they be otherwise when I always tell my fortune by the queen of clubs?

MARYA ANTONOVNA: Why, mamma! You usually tell it by the queen of hearts!

ANNA ANDREYEVNA: Nonsense, absolute nonsense! I never was the queen of hearts! [*She hastily goes out with* Marya Antonovna *and continues talking in the wings*] What's she imagining now! The queen of hearts! Heaven knows what she means!

    [*After they have gone out a door opens, and* Mishka *is seen throwing out some trash. Through another door* Osip *comes in with a trunk on his head*]

SCENE IV.

Mishka *and* Osip.

OSIP: Which way?

MISHKA: This way, uncle, this way!

OSIP: Wait, let me get my breath first. Oh, what a dog's life! Every load seems heavy on an empty belly.

MISHKA: Well, uncle, what d'you say? Will the general be here soon?

OSIP: What general?

MISHKA: Why, your master.

OSIP: My master? Is he a general?

MISHKA: Well, isn't he?

OSIP: He is a general something or other, all right.

MISHKA: Is that more or less than a real general?

OSIP: More. Much more!

MISHKA: You don't say! That's why they've kicked up such a rumpus.

OSIP: Listen, my boy; I see you're a smart fellow; just get me something to eat!

MISHKA: There's nothing ready for you yet, uncle. You aren't going to eat common chow, but when your boss sits down to the table, they'll give you the same as he gets.

OSIP: What kind of common food have you got?

MISHKA: Cabbage soup, porridge, and pies.

OSIP: Give us your cabbage soup, porridge, and pies! That's all right, I'll eat everything. Well, let's carry in the trunk. Is there another way out?

MISHKA: Yes.

[*They carry the trunk into a room at one side*]

SCENE V.

The Policemen *open both wings of the door.* Hlestakov *comes in, after him the* Chief of Police, *the* Supervisor of Charitable Institutions, *the* Superintendent of Schools, Dobchinsky *and* Bobchinsky, *the latter with a plaster on his nose. The* Chief of Police *shows the* Policemen *a piece of paper on the floor; they run to pick it up, bumping each other at full speed.*

HLESTAKOV: Very good institutions. I'm delighted that you show visitors everything in the town. They didn't show me anything in the other towns.

CHIEF OF POLICE: In other towns, I venture to inform you, the city managers and the other officials are more concerned about their own profit; but here, I may say, there is no other thought but to deserve by good order and vigilance the attention of the authorities.

HLESTAKOV: The lunch was very good. I quite overate myself. Do you fare like that every day?

CHIEF OF POLICE: That was especially for our welcome guest.

HLESTAKOV: I'm fond of eating. That's what we live for: to cull the flowers of pleasure. What was that fish called?

ARTEMY FILIPPOVICH: [*Running up*] Aberdeen cod, sir.

HLESTAKOV: Very tasty. Where was it we had lunch—in the hospital?

ARTEMY FILIPPOVICH: Just so, sir, in the charity hospital.

HLESTAKOV: I remember, I remember, there were some beds there. Have the patients all recovered? It seems to me there weren't many.

ARTEMY FILIPPOVICH: About ten remain, no more; the rest have all got well. That's the way it's arranged: such order! From the time I undertook the management—incredible as it may seem to you—all of them have been getting well, like flies.[8] A patient can hardly enter the hospital before he's cured, not so much by the medicines as by the reliability of the management.

CHIEF OF POLICE: The obligations of a chief of police are, I venture to inform you, simply headbreaking! So many different things devolve on him, concerning sanitation alone, repairs, and reconstruction . . . in a word, the wisest man might find himself in a quandary; but, thanks be to God, everything is coming out splendidly. Any other police chief, of course, would look out for his own profit; but—would you believe it?—even when I lie down to sleep I think: "O Lord my God, how can I bring it to pass that the authorities may perceive my zeal and be satisfied?" . . . Whether they will reward me or not is, of course, up to them; but at least I shall be at peace in my own heart. When there is order everywhere in the city, the streets swept clean, the people under arrest well cared for, and few drunkards . . . why, what more can I do? And in truth, I want no honors. Of course, honors are alluring, but compared to virtue, they are all ashes and vanity.

ARTEMY FILIPPOVICH: [*Aside*] Oho, the grafter, how thick he spreads it! God gave him a gift for it!

HLESTAKOV: That is true. I admit that I myself like to philosophize once in a while: I toss things off sometimes in prose, sometimes in verse.

BOBCHINSKY: [*To Dobchinsky*] Correct, all correct, Petr Ivanovich! Such remarks . . . one can see he's studied the sciences.

HLESTAKOV: Tell me, please, don't you ever have any amusements or social gatherings—where one might, for instance, play a game of cards?

CHIEF OF POLICE: [*Aside*] Aha, my boy, we know what windowpane you're pebbling now! [*Aloud*] God forbid! There's not even a rumor about such social gatherings here! I've never had cards in my hands; I don't even know how to play cards. I never could even look at them calmly; and if I ever happen to catch sight of such a thing as a king of diamonds, such disgust comes over me that I simply have to spit. It happened once that to amuse the children I built a little house of cards, but afterwards I had the damnedest dreams all night long. Deuce take them! How can people kill such precious time with them?

LUKA LUKICH: [*Aside*] But you cleaned me out of a hunded rubles yesterday, you scoundrel!

CHIEF OF POLICE: I could use that time better in the service of the state.

HLESTAKOV: However, you put it too strongly. . . . All depends upon the way in which you look at the thing. If, for instance, you pass when you ought to raise your ante . . . then, of course . . . No, I disagree: sometimes playing is very tempting.

[8] The humor lies in the reference to the usual Russian phrase "They die like flies."

SCENE VI.

The same, Anna Andreyevna, *and* Marya Antonovna.

CHIEF OF POLICE: I venture to present my family: my wife and daughter.

HLESTAKOV: [*Making a bow*] How fortunate I am, madam, to have, as it were, the pleasure of seeing you.

ANNA ANDREYEVNA: It is even more agreeable for us to see such a personage.

HLESTAKOV: [*Strutting*] Pardon me, madam, quite the contrary: my pleasure is greater.

ANNA ANDREYEVNA: How can that be, sir! You are pleased to say that out of compliment. Won't you please be seated?

HLESTAKOV: Merely to stand beside you is happiness: nevertheless, if such be unmistakably your wish, I shall be seated. How happy I am at last to be sitting beside you!

ANNA ANDREYEVNA: Really, sir, I cannot take that compliment to myself. . . . I suppose that after the capital, a tour of the country has seemed very unpleasant?

HLESTAKOV: Exceedingly unpleasant. Accustomed to live, *comprenez-vous,* in society and suddenly to find oneself on the road: dirty eating-houses, the darkness of ignorance . . . I confess, that were it not for this circumstance [*Glancing at* Anna Andreyevna *and posing*] which has compensated me for everything . . .

ANNA ANDREYEVNA: Indeed, how unpleasant it must have been for you.

HLESTAKOV: However, madam, at this minute it is very pleasant for me.

ANNA ANDREYEVNA: Oh, really, sir! You do me too much honor. I do not deserve it.

HLESTAKOV: Why do you not deserve it? You do deserve it, madam.

ANNA ANDREYEVNA: I live in the country. . . .

HLESTAKOV: But the country also has its hillocks and its streamlets. . . . Of course, who'd compare it with Petersburg? Oh, Petersburg! What a life, truly! You may think that I am only a copying clerk; but no, I'm on a friendly footing with the chief of my department. He'll clap me on the shoulder and say, "Come have dinner with me, my boy!" I drop in at the office for two minutes, only long enough to say how things are to be done. And there the copy-clerk, poor rat, goes scribbling away with his pen, tr, tr. . . . They even wanted to make me a collegiate assessor;[9] but I thought, what for? And the porter flies up the stairs after me with a brush: "If you please, Ivan Alexandrovich," he says, "I'll clean your boots." [*To the* Chief of Police] Why are you standing, gentlemen? Please be seated.

[9] The eighth rank in the Russian service; Hlestakov is in the fourteenth!

CHIEF OF POLICE, ARTEMY FILIPPOVICH, *and* LUKA LUKICH: [*Speaking together*] Our rank is such that we can stand. We'll just stand. Please don't disturb yourself.

HLESTAKOV: All rank aside, I beg you to be seated.

[*The* Chief of Police *and all sit down*]
I don't like ceremony. On the contrary, I try and try to slip through unnoticed. But it's impossible to hide oneself, quite impossible! I can hardly go out anywhere but they begin saying, "There goes Ivan Alexandrovich!" Once they even took me for the commander-in-chief: the soldiers jumped out of the guardrooms and presented arms. Afterwards an officer with whom I am well acquainted said to me: "Well, my boy, we positively took you for the commander-in-chief."

ANNA ANDREYEVNA: You don't say!

HLESTAKOV: I'm acquainted with the pretty actresses. You see, I've writen a few theatrical sketches. . . . I often see literary people. I'm on friendly terms with Pushkin. I often say to him, "Well, now Pushkin, my boy, how goes it?" "Oh, so-so, old chap," he'll reply, "just so-so. . . ." He's a great character!

ANNA ANDREYEVNA: And so you even write? How delightful it must be to be an author! Do you really contribute to the magazines?

HLESTAKOV: Yes, I contribute to the magazines. Besides, my works are numerous: *The Marriage of Figaro, Robert the Devil, Norma.*[10] I don't even remember all their titles. And it was all by accident: I didn't want to write, but the theatre management said, "Please write something, old boy." So I thought to myself, "Well, go ahead, old fellow." And then all of a sudden, one evening, I think it was, I wrote the whole thing and astonished everybody. I have extraordinary ease in thinking. Everything that has appeared under the name of Baron Brambeus[11]—*The Frigate Hope,*[12] and the *Moscow Telegraph*[13] . . . I wrote all that.

ANNA ANDREYEVNA: You don't say! And so you were Brambeus?

HLESTAKOV: Of course; I correct all their articles. Smirdin[14] pays me forty thousand for doing it.

ANNA ANDREYEVNA: I dare say *Yury Miloslavsky*[15] is your work also.

HLESTAKOV: Yes, that's my work.

ANNA ANDREYEVNA: I guessed it at once.

MARYA ANTONOVNA: But, mamma, it says on the binding that it was written by Mr. Zagoskin.

ANNA ANDREYEVNA: There you go: I knew that you'd argue even here.

HLESTAKOV: Oh, yes, that is true: that is Zago-

[10] Operas by Mozart, Meyerbeer, and Bellini.
[11] Pseudonym of the popular author Sienkowski (1800-1858).
[12] A novel by Bestuzhev.
[13] A newspaper.
[14] A noted St. Petersburg publisher.
[15] A famous historical novel.

skin's; but there's another *Yury Miloslavsky,* and that's mine.

ANNA ANDREYEVNA: Well, it's certain that I read yours. So well written!

HLESTAKOV: I confess that I exist by literature. Mine is the foremost house in Petersburg. It's even known as Ivan Alexandrovich's house. [*Turning to all present*] Do me the favor, ladies and gentlemen, to come to see me when you are in Petersburg. I also give balls.

ANNA ANDREYEVNA: I suppose that balls there must be given with remarkable taste and magnificence?

HLESTAKOV: It's simply beyond description. On the table, for instance, is a watermelon—a watermelon costing seven hundred rubles. Soup ready in the tureen has come directly from Paris by steamer; raise the lid and there's a fragrant steam the like of which you can't find in nature. I go to balls every day. We've formed our own whist club: the Minister of Foreign Affairs, the French Ambassador, the English, the German Ambassadors, and I. We nearly kill ourselves playing; really, you never saw anything like it. As I run up the stairs to my fourth-story apartment, I just say to the cook: "Here, Mavrushka, my overcoat! . . ." What am I lying about! I quite forgot that I live on the second floor. My staircase alone is worth . . . But it would be curious to glance into my hall before I'm awake mornings: counts and princes jostle each other and hum there like bees, you can hear nothing but buzz, buzz. . . . Sometimes even the Minister . . . [*The* Chief of Police *and others timidly rise from their chairs*] My mail even comes addressed to "Your Excellency." Once I was even the director of a department. It's strange: the director went away—no one knows where. Well, naturally there was a lot of talk as to who should occupy the post. Many of the generals applied eagerly and got it, but when they started to work, it was no go—too hard. The job looks easy enough, but just examine it; why, it's the very deuce! Afterwards they saw there was nothing to do but give it to me. And that very minute they sent messengers through the streets, messengers, messengers, and messengers . . . you can imagine for yourself: thirty-five thousand messengers! What a situation, I ask you! "Ivan Alexandrovich, go take charge of the department!" I confess that I felt somewhat uneasy. I came out in my dressing gown. I wanted to decline, but I thought, this will get to the tsar; and then, there's the service record! . . . "Very well, gentlemen, I accept the post," I said; "I accept it," I said; "So be it," I said; "I accept; only look out for me; I have sharp ears! You know me. . . ." And that's the way it was: it used to be, when I walked through the department, as if an earthquake had struck them: every one was trembling and shaking like a leaf.

[*The* Chief of Police *and the others shake with fear;* Hlestakov *grows more excited*]
Oh, I don't like to joke; I gave them all a bawling-out. The Council of State itself is afraid of me. And why

not, indeed? Because I'm that kind of man. I don't care for anybody. . . . I tell 'em all, "I know my business; shut up!" I go everywhere, everywhere! I drive to the Palace every day. Why, to-morrow they're going to make me a field-mar— [*He slips and almost sprawls upon the floor, but the officials respectfully support him*]

CHIEF OF POLICE: [*Approaching, trembling in every limb, and striving to speak out*] You—your—your . . .

HLESTAKOV: [*In a rapid, abrupt tone*] What is it?

CHIEF OF POLICE: You—your—

HLESTAKOV: [*In the same tone*] I can't make out anything; it's all nonsense.

CHIEF OF POLICE: You . . . your . . . your Excellency, don't you wish to rest? . . . Here's your room, and everything that you need.

HLESTAKOV: Rest—bosh! All right. I'm willing to have a rest. Your lunch, gentlemen, was good. . . . I'm satisfied, I'm satisfied. . . . [*Declaiming*] Aberdeen! Aberdeen cod! [*He goes into a side room, followed by the* Chief of Police]

SCENE VII.

The same without Hlestakov *and the* Chief of Police.

BOBCHINSKY: [*To* Dobchinsky] There's a man for you, Petr Ivanovich! That's what I call a man! Never in my life have I been in the presence of so important a personage; I all but died of fright. What do you think his rank may be, Petr Ivanovich?

DOBCHINSKY: I think almost a general.

BOBCHINSKY: And I think a general isn't fit to pull off his boots; but if he's a general, he's a generalissimo. Did you hear how he squashed the Council of State? Let's be quick and tell Ammos Fedorovich and Korobkin. Good-by, Anna Andreyevna!

DOBCHINSKY: [*To* Anna Andreyevna] Good-by, godmother!

[*They both go out*]

ARTEMY FILIPPOVICH: [*To* Luka Lukich] It's simply terrifying, but just why, you can't tell, yourself. We haven't even got into our uniforms. Well, do you suppose he'll send off a report to Petersburg when he wakes up?

[*They go out thoughtfully along with the* Superintendent of Schools, *saying as they go*]
Good-by, madam!

SCENE VIII.

Anna Andreyevna *and* Marya Antonovna.

ANNA ANDREYEVNA: Oh, what a charming man!

MARYA ANTONOVNA: Oh, what a darling!

ANNA ANDREYEVNA: But what refinement in everything he does! You can see at once he's a Petersburg swell. His manners, and all that. . . . Oh, how nice! I'm crazy over young men like him! I simply lose my head over them. And moreover, he took a fancy to me; I noticed that he kept glancing my way.

MARYA ANTONOVNA: Why, mamma, he was looking at me!

ANNA ANDREYEVNA: I'll thank you to be off with your nonsense. It's quite out of place here.

MARYA ANTONOVNA: No, mamma, really!

ANNA ANDREYEVNA: Well, I declare! God forbid we should quarrel about it! That will do! Why should he look at you? What reason would he have for looking at you?

MARYA ANTONOVNA: Really, mamma, he kept looking at me. First when he began to talk about literature, he gave me a look; and then when he was telling about how he played whist with the ambassadors, he looked at me again.

ANNA ANDREYEVNA: Well, maybe, once or twice, but that's all it amounted to. "Oh, I'll just take a look at her!" he said to himself.

SCENE IX.

The same and the Chief of Police.

CHIEF OF POLICE: [*Coming in on tiptoes*] Sh, sh!

ANNA ANDREYEVNA: What is it?

CHIEF OF POLICE: I'm sorry I got him drunk. What if half he says is true? [*Reflecting*] And why shouldn't it be true? When he's on a spree, a man brings everything to the surface: whatever is in his heart is on his tongue. Of course, he lied a little; but unless you lie a little bit, no conversation is possible. He plays cards with the Ministers and drives to the Palace. . . . And so really, the more you think about it . . . the devil knows who he is. . . . I don't know what's going on in my head; it's as if I were either standing on a sort of steeple or were just about to be hanged.

ANNA ANDREYEVNA: And I felt absolutely no timidity whatever; I simply saw in him an educated, high-toned man of the world, and his rank was nothing to me.

CHIEF OF POLICE: That's the way with you women! That word "women" sums it all up! They always fall for fiddle-faddle! They wise-crack about anything that comes into their noddles. They get off with a whipping, but the husband's as good as dead. You, sweet soul, behaved as familiarly with him as if he were another Dobchinsky.

ANNA ANDREYEVNA: I advise you not to be uneasy on that score. We know a thing or two. . . . [*Glancing at her daughter*]

CHIEF OF POLICE: [*To himself*] Well, what's the use of talking to you women! . . . Here's a fix, in-

deed! I haven't yet been able to get over my fright. [*He opens the door and speaks off stage*] Mishka! Call Police Sergeants Svistunov and Derzhimorda: they're outside the gate somewhere or other. [*After a brief silence*] Everything in the world has turned queer; you might expect a man to be something to look at; but such a lean, skinny fellow—how are you going to know who he is? If a man's military, the fact shows plainly enough; but when he puts on a dress coat, he's like a fly with his wings pulled off. He whooped it up such a long time at the inn a while ago, and faked up such a lot of fairy tales and bunk that you'd never make sense of it in a lifetime. But then he finally gave in. He even blabbed more than he needed to. Evidently he's a young man.

SCENE X.

The same and Osip.
They all run to meet him, beckoning.

ANNA ANDREYEVNA: Come here, my good fellow.

CHIEF OF POLICE: Sh! . . . Well, what about it? Is he asleep?

OSIP: Not yet; he's stretching a bit.

ANNA ANDREYEVNA: Listen; what's your name?

OSIP: Osip, madam.

CHIEF OF POLICE: [*To his wife and daughter*] That'll do for you! [*To* Osip] Well now, my boy, have they fed you well?

OSIP: They have, I thank you heartily; very well indeed.

ANNA ANDREYEVNA: Tell me: an awful lot of counts and princes call on your master, don't they?

OSIP: [*Aside*] What shall I say? If they've fed me well now, they'll do even better later. [*Aloud*] Yes, even counts come.

MARYA ANTONOVNA: My dear Osip, how good-looking your master is!

ANNA ANDREYEVNA: And please tell us, Osip, how he . . .

CHIEF OF POLICE: Oh, please stop! You only mix me up with such silly talk. Now then, my friend! . . .

ANNA ANDREYEVNA: What rank has your master?

OSIP: Oh, he has the usual thing.

CHIEF OF POLICE: Oh, my God, you keep asking such silly questions! You won't let me get in a word to the point. Now, my friend, what sort of man is your master? . . . Strict? Does he like to bawl people out or doesn't he?

OSIP: Yes, he likes to have things orderly. He sees to it that everything around him is kept ship-shape.

CHIEF OF POLICE: I like your face very much. My friend, you must be a good fellow. Now, what—?

ANNA ANDREYEVNA: Listen, Osip, does your master wear his uniform at home?

CHIEF OF POLICE: Really, that'll do, chatterboxes that you are! This is a serious business: it's a question of a man's life. [*To* Osip] Well, now, my friend, I like you very much. When traveling there's no harm, you know, in taking an extra little glass of tea —the weather has turned cooler—so here's a couple of rubles for tea.

OSIP: [*Taking the money*] Thank you very much, sir! God grant you the best of health! I'm a poor man, and you've helped me.

CHIEF OF POLICE: Good, good, the pleasure is mine. Now what, my friend—?

ANNA ANDREYEVNA: Listen, Osip, what kind of eyes does your master like best?

MARYA ANTONOVNA: Osip, dear, what a darling little nose your master has!

CHIEF OF POLICE: Oh, stop! Let me! . . . [*To* Osip] Now please tell me, my boy: to what does your master pay the most attention, that is, what pleases him most in traveling?

OSIP: What he likes depends on circumstances. Most of all he likes to be well received; he likes good entertainment.

CHIEF OF POLICE: Good entertainment?

OSIP: Yes, sir. Now take me, for instance, I'm only a serf, but he sees that I'm well treated, too. Darned if he doesn't! Sometimes when we go to a place, he'll say: "Well, Osip, did they treat you well?" "Badly, your Honor!" "Hm," he'll say, "he's a bad host, Osip. Remind me of that when I get home." "Aha," I think to myself [*Waving his hand*]; "I should worry; I'm a plain man."

CHIEF OF POLICE: Very good, you're talking sense. There, I've given you something for tea; here's something more for biscuits.

OSIP: Why do you favor me, your Honor? [*He pockets the money*] I'll drink your health.

ANNA ANDREYEVNA: Come to me, Osip, and I'll give you something, too.

MARYA ANTONOVNA: Osip, dear, take your master a kiss from me!

[Hlestakov *is heard coughing in the next room*]

CHIEF OF POLICE: Sh! . . . [*Rising upon tiptoe, and finishing the scene in a subdued voice*] God forbid your making any noise! Go to your own rooms— you've said enough. . . .

ANNA ANDREYEVNA: Let's go, Mashenka! I told you that I noticed something in our guest that only we two can talk about.

CHIEF OF POLICE: Oh, they'll talk enough! I think if I went to listen to them, I'd have to stuff my ears. [*Turning to* Osip] Now, my friend. . . .

SCENE XI.

The same, Derzhimorda, *and* Svistunov.

CHIEF OF POLICE: Sh! You stamp with your boots like bow-legged bears! You make a thumping like dumping a ton of rocks out of a cart! Where the devil have you been?

DERZHIMORDA: I was acting on your orders. . . .

CHIEF OF POLICE: Sh! [*Putting his hand over the Policeman's mouth*] You croak like a crow! [*Imitating him*] "I was acting on your orders!" Roaring like an empty barrel! [*To* Osip] Now, my friend, run along and get everything ready for your master. Command everything there is in the house.

[Osip *goes out*]

As for you two, go stand on the doorstep and don't move! And don't let any outsider into the house, especially tradesmen! If you let in a single one, I'll . . . Only see to it that if any one comes with a complaint or even looks as if he had a complaint to present against me, throw him out on his neck! Sock it to him! Like that! [*Illustrating a kick*] Do you get me? Sh . . . sh. . . . [*He goes out on tiptoe after the* Policemen]

ACT IV. SCENE I.

The same room in the house of the Chief of Police.

Enter carefully, almost on tiptoe, Ammos Fedorovich, Artemy Filippovich, *the* Postmaster, Luka Lukich, Dobchinsky, *and* Bobchinsky *in full dress uniforms. The whole scene proceeds in an undertone.*

AMMOS FEDOROVICH: [*Arranging them all in a semicircle*] For God's sake, gentlemen, make a circle as quickly as possible and put on your best manner! Confound him, he rides to the Palace and bawls out the Council of State! Draw up in military order; it must be in military order. You run over to that side, Petr Ivanovich; and you, Petr Ivanovich, stand right here.

[*Both* Petr Ivanoviches *run on tiptoe*]

ARTEMY FILIPPOVICH: If you're willing, Ammos Fedorovich, we ought to undertake something or other.

AMMOS FEDOROVICH: Just what exactly?

ARTEMY FILIPPOVICH: Everybody knows what.

AMMOS FEDOROVICH: Slip him something?

ARTEMY FILIPPOVICH: Well, yes, slip him something.

AMMOS FEDOROVICH: It's dangerous, deuce take it! He might raise Cain—a government man like him! But how about an offering on the part of the nobility for a memorial of some sort?

POSTMASTER: Or say this: "Here is some money left unclaimed at the post office."

ARTEMY FILIPPOVICH: Look out that he doesn't send *you* away somewhere by post! Listen: things aren't done like that in a well-regulated state. Why is there a whole squadron of us here? We should introduce ourselves one by one; and then, between man and man, everything is fixed, and nothing leaks out. That's the way it's done in a well-regulated society! Now you'll be the first to begin, Ammos Fedorovich.

AMMOS FEDOROVICH: It would be better for you: our august guest broke bread in your establishment.

ARTEMY FILIPPOVICH: It would be still better for you, Luka Lukich, as the enlightener of youth.

LUKA LUKICH: I can't, I can't, gentlemen! I confess I was so brought up that if I have to talk with a man one rank higher than mine, I get heart failure and my tongue seems to stick in the mud. No, gentlemen, you really must relieve me!

ARTEMY FILIPPOVICH: Yes, Ammos Fedorovich, there's no one but you. You have only to say a word, and Cicero fairly flies off your tongue!

AMMOS FEDOROVICH: What are you talking about! Cicero! See here, what have you thought up! What if I do get carried away sometimes, talking about my house dogs or my hunting hounds? . . .

ALL: [Surrounding him] No, not only about dogs; you can talk about the Tower of Babel, too. . . .[16] No, Ammos Fedorovich, don't abandon us, be a father to us! . . . No, Ammos Fedorovich!

AMMOS FEDOROVICH: Let me be, gentlemen!

[At this moment steps and coughing are heard in Hlestakov's room. All vie with each other in their haste to reach the door, crowding and trying to get out, which they do only with some squeezing. A few exclamations are heard in undertones]

VOICE OF BOBCHINSKY: Ow! Petr Ivanovich, you stepped on my foot, Petr Ivanovich!

VOICE OF ARTEMY FILIPPOVICH: Let me out, gentlemen! you've squeezed me as flat as a soul in Purgatory!

[A few gasping exclamations of "Ow! ow!" are heard; finally all have been pushed out, and the room remains empty]

SCENE II.

Hlestakov alone, entering sleepy-eyed.

HLESTAKOV: I think I must have snored properly. Where did they get such mattresses and feather beds? I fairly perspired. They must have slipped me something strong at lunch yesterday; my head still goes bang. So far as I can see, a fellow can spend his time agreeably here. I like cordiality; and I admit I like it best of all when people gratify me out of sheer kind-heartedness rather than for their personal interest. The Chief of Police's daughter isn't half bad to look at, and even her mamma might perhaps . . . Well, I don't know, but I sure like this life.

[16] The allusion is to the Judge's skepticism.

SCENE III.

Hlestakov and the Judge (Ammos Fedorovich).

AMMOS FEDOROVICH: [Upon entering, stops, and says to himself] My God, my God! Make this come out right! My knees will hardly hold me up. [Aloud, drawing himself up, and grasping his sword-hilt] I have the honor to introduce myself: Judge of the local District Court, Collegiate Assessor Lyapkin-Tyapkin.

HLESTAKOV: I beg you to sit down. So you're the Judge here?

AMMOS FEDOROVICH: In 1816 I was elected to a three-year term by the will of the nobility and I have held the post ever since.

HLESTAKOV: It's profitable to be Judge, isn't it?

AMMOS FEDOROVICH: After three terms I was presented with the order of Vladimir of the Fourth Class, with the commendation of the authorities. [Aside] The money is in my fist, and my fist is on fire!

HLESTAKOV: I like the Vladimir. Now the Anna of the Third Class isn't so good.

AMMOS FEDOROVICH: [Little by little thrusting forward his closed fist, aside] O Lord God! I don't know where I'm sitting. It's as if I had live coals under me.

HLESTAKOV: What have you got in your hand?

AMMOS FEDOROVICH: [Flustered, and letting some notes fall to the floor] Nothing, sir.

HLESTAKOV: Nothing, you say? I see you've dropped some money.

AMMOS FEDOROVICH: [Trembling all over] Not at all, sir! [Aside] O God, here I am in the dock, and they're bringing up the police cart to get me!

HLESTAKOV: [Picking it up] Yes, it's money.

AMMOS FEDOROVICH: [Aside] Well, it's all over! I'm lost and done for!

HLESTAKOV: I say, won't you lend it to me?

AMMOS FEDOROVICH: [Hastily] Certainly, why not, sir? . . . With the greatest pleasure. [Aside] Now, bolder, bolder! Pull me through, Most Holy Mother!

HLESTAKOV: On the road, you know, I spent every kopek, on this and that. . . . Of course, I'll send it to you at once from my country home.

AMMOS FEDOROVICH: Please, sir, the idea! It's honor enough without repayment. . . . Of course, in my poor, weak way, by zeal and diligent service of the authorities . . . I shall always strive to deserve . . . [He rises from his chair and draws himself up to an attitude of attention] I won't venture to disturb you longer by my presence. Have you no orders for me?

HLESTAKOV: What sort of orders?

AMMOS FEDOROVICH: I considered that you might have some orders for the local District Court.

HLESTAKOV: What for? I haven't any need of it at present; no, there's nothing. Thank you very much.

AMMOS FEDOROVICH: [Bowing and going out, aside] The town is ours!

HLESTAKOV: [*When alone*] The Judge is a good fellow!

SCENE IV.

Hlestakov *and the* Postmaster, *who, clad in his uniform, stands at attention, hand on sword.*

POSTMASTER: I have the honor to introduce myself: Postmaster and Court Councilor Shpekin.

HLESTAKOV: Ah, do come in! I'm very fond of pleasant society. Be seated. I suppose you live here all the time?

POSTMASTER: Just so, sir.

HLESTAKOV: I like this little town. Of course, it's not very populous; but what of that? It's not the capital. It's not the capital, is it?

POSTMASTER: That's perfectly true.

HLESTAKOV: You find *bong tong*[17] only in the capital, where there are no provincial geese. What's your opinion: isn't that right?

POSTMASTER: Quite right, sir. [*Aside*] I see he's not a bit haughty: he asks about everything.

HLESTAKOV: You'll have to admit, I suppose, that it's possible to live happily even in a small town?

POSTMASTER: Just so, sir.

HLESTAKOV: In my opinion all one needs is to be respected and sincerely liked—isn't that right?

POSTMASTER: Absolutely right.

HLESTAKOV: I confess I'm glad that you're of my opinion. Of course they call me peculiar, but that's the kind of disposition I have. [*Looking into the* Postmaster's *eyes and speaking to himself*] Why not ask this postmaster for a loan? [*Aloud*] A strange sort of thing has happened to me: I got entirely cleaned out on the road. Couldn't you lend me three hundred rubles?

POSTMASTER: Why, certainly; I'd consider it the greatest pleasure. Here you are, sir. I'm heart and soul at your service.

HLESTAKOV: I'm much obliged. I confess I hate like hell to deny myself anything when traveling; and why should I? How does that strike you?

POSTMASTER: Just so, sir. [*He rises and stands at attention, hand on sword*] I won't venture to disturb you any longer by my presence. . . . Have you perchance some remarks to make upon the management of the post office?

HLESTAKOV: No, nothing.

[*The* Postmaster *bows and goes out*]

HLESTAKOV: [*Lighting a cigar*] The Postmaster, it seems to me, is also a nice fellow; at any rate, he's obliging. I like such people.

---

[17] A corruption of the French *bon ton*—good taste, or elegance.

SCENE V.

Hlestakov *and* Luka Lukich, *who is almost pushed through the door. Behind him a voice says, half aloud,* "What are you afraid of?"

LUKA LUKICH: [*Drawing himself up in trepidation and holding tight to his sword*] I have the honor to introduce myself: Superintendent of Schools and Titular Councilor Hlopov.

HLESTAKOV: Oh, pleased to meet you. Sit down, sit down. Have a cigar? [*Handing him a cigar*]

LUKA LUKICH: [*Undecidedly, to himself*] Well, I declare! I didn't expect this. Shall I take it or not?

HLESTAKOV: Go ahead, take it; that's a good cigar. Of course it's not like those you get in Petersburg. There, my dear man, I used to smoke little cigars at twenty-five rubles the hundred—they simply make you want to kiss your hand after smoking. Here's a candle; have a light! [*He holds out a candle to him*]

[Luka Lukich *tries to light his cigar and trembles all over*]

HLESTAKOV: But that's the wrong end!

LUKA LUKICH: [*Dropping the cigar in his fright, spitting, and waving his hand; aside*] Devil take everything! My damned timidity has ruined me!

HLESTAKOV: Well, I see you don't care for cigars. I confess they're my weakness. Also, where the fair sex is concerned, I simply can't be indifferent. How about you? Which do you like better, brunettes or blondes?

[Luka Lukich *finds himself in utter bewilderment as to what to say*]

HLESTAKOV: No, tell me frankly which: brunettes or blondes?

LUKA LUKICH: I don't venture to judge.

HLESTAKOV: No, no, now, don't offer excuses! I wish positively to find out your taste.

LUKA LUKICH: I venture to inform you . . . [*Aside*] Well, I myself don't know what I'm saying.

HLESTAKOV: Ah, ha! You don't want to say! I believe some little brunette has got you into a slight embarrassment. Admit it now: hasn't she?

[Luka Lukich *remains silent*]

HLESTAKOV: Ah, ha! You blushed! You see! You see! Why don't you talk?

LUKA LUKICH: I got scared, your Hon— . . . Excel— . . . Gra— . . . [*Aside*] My damned tongue has betrayed me!

HLESTAKOV: Got scared? Well, there is something in my eyes that inspires timidity. At least I know there's not a woman who can hold out against them, is there?

LUKA LUKICH: Quite right, sir.

HLESTAKOV: A very strange thing has happened to me: on the road I got cleaned out. Couldn't you lend me three hundred rubles?

LUKA LUKICH: [*To himself, clutching at his pocket*]

What a fix if I haven't got it! I have! I have! [*He produces and tremblingly hands over the notes*]

HLESTAKOV: Thanks ever so much.

LUKA LUKICH: [*Drawing himself up, hand on sword*] I won't venture to disturb you longer by my presence.

HLESTAKOV: Good-by.

LUKA LUKICH: [*Hurries out almost running, speaking aside*] Well, thank God! Here's hoping he won't peep in on the classes!

SCENE VI.

Hlestakov *and* Artemy Filippovich, *who draws himself up, hand on sword.*

ARTEMY FILIPPOVICH: I have the honor to present myself: the Supervisor of Charitable Institutions, Court Councilor Zemlyanika.

HLESTAKOV: How do you do? Pray be seated.

ARTEMY FILIPPOVICH: I had the honor of escorting you, and of receiving you personally in the charitable institutions entrusted to my care.

HLESTAKOV: Ah, yes, I remember. You treated me to a very good lunch.

ARTEMY FILIPPOVICH: I'm happy to do my best in the service of my country.

HLESTAKOV: I like good cooking; I admit it's my weakness. . . . Tell me, please, weren't you a little shorter in height yesterday? It seems so to me.

ARTEMY FILIPPOVICH: It may well be. [*A brief silence*] I may say that I spare nothing, and zealously fulfill my duties. [*He draws his chair nearer and speaks in a lower voice*] The Postmaster here does absolutely nothing: all the business is greatly neglected: the mail is kept back—you can find it out for yourself. The Judge also, who was here before I came, does nothing but course hares; he keeps dogs in the court rooms, and his behavior, if I may admit it in your presence—of course, for the good of my country, I must do it, although he's both a relative and a friend of mine—his behavior is most reprehensible. There's a certain landowner here named Dobchinsky, whom you have seen; and no sooner does this Dobchinsky go out of his house somewhere, than the Judge goes over to sit with his wife, and I'm ready to swear . . . And you have only to look at the children: there's not one that looks like Dobchinsky, but every one of them, even the little girl, is the spit'n image of the Judge.

HLESTAKOV: You don't say so! I never thought of it.

ARTEMY FILIPPOVICH: Then there's the Superintendent of Schools. . . . I don't know how the authorities could entrust him with such a responsibility: he's worse than a Jacobin, and he inspires in the youth such radical principles that it's hard even to express them. Don't you want me to put all this on paper for you?

HLESTAKOV: Yes, put it on paper. I'd be much pleased. You know, when I'm bored I like to read over something amusing. . . . What is your name? I've quite forgotten.

ARTEMY FILIPPOVICH: Zemlyanika.

HLESTAKOV: Ah, yes, Zemlyanika. And tell me, please, have you any children?

ARTEMY FILIPPOVICH: I should say so, sir! Five of them, two grown up.

HLESTAKOV: You don't say! Grown up! And what are they? . . . How do you . . . ?

ARTEMY FILIPPOVICH: Do you wish to ask what their names are?

HLESTAKOV: Yes, what are their names?

ARTEMY FILIPPOVICH: Nikolay, Ivan, Elizaveta, Marya, and Perepetuya.

HLESTAKOV: That's nice.

ARTEMY FILIPPOVICH: I won't venture to disturb you any longer by my presence, depriving you of time dedicated to your sacred duties. . . . [*He bows and is about to go out*]

HLESTAKOV: [*Accompanying him*] No, that's all right. That was all very funny, what you were telling me. Come and see me again. I enjoy it so much. [*He returns, and opening the door, calls after him*] Hey, you! What's your name? I keep forgetting your name.

ARTEMY FILIPPOVICH: Artemy Filippovich.

HLESTAKOV: Do me a favor, Artemy Filippovich! A queer thing has happened to me: I got quite cleaned out on the road. Haven't you some money you could lend me—say four hundred rubles?

ARTEMY FILIPPOVICH: Yes.

HLESTAKOV: Well, how opportune! I thank you heartily.

SCENE VII.

Hlestakov, Bobchinsky, *and* Dobchinsky.

BOBCHINSKY: I have the honor to introduce myself: Petr Ivanovich Bobchinsky, a resident of this town.

DOBCHINSKY: Petr Ivanovich Dobchinsky, a landowner.

HLESTAKOV: Ah, yes, I've seen you before. I think you had a fall: well, how's your nose?

BOBCHINSKY: First rate! Don't feel any anxiety, please; it's quite well and dried up.

HLESTAKOV: I'm glad it's healed. I'm very glad. . . . [*Suddenly and abruptly*] Have you any money on you?

DOBCHINSKY: What do you mean, money?

HLESTAKOV: Lend me a thousand rubles.

BOBCHINSKY: Good Lord, I haven't such a sum. But haven't you, Petr Ivanovich?

DOBCHINSKY: I haven't it about me, because my money, if you care to know, has been deposited with the Charitable Board.

HLESTAKOV: Well, if you haven't a thousand, a hundred will do.

BOBCHINSKY: [*Rummaging in his pockets*] Haven't you a hundred rubles, Petr Ivanovich? I have only forty altogether, in notes.

DOBCHINSKY: [*Looking in his bill-fold*] Twenty-five rubles in all.

BOBCHINSKY: Just take a better look, Petr Ivanovich. I know there's a hole in your right-hand pocket, and really, something may have fallen through.

DOBCHINSKY: No, really, there's nothing in the hole.

HLESTAKOV: Well, it's all the same. I just asked. Good: sixty-five rubles will do. . . . That's all right. [*He takes the money*]

DOBCHINSKY: I venture to ask your help about a very delicate matter.

HLESTAKOV: What is it?

DOBCHINSKY: It's a thing of very great delicacy, sir: my eldest son, you see, was born before my marriage. . . .

HLESTAKOV: Yes?

DOBCHINSKY: Of course, that's only so to speak, sir, because he was born absolutely the same as if in wedlock; and I afterwards fixed everything up properly by the lawful bonds of matrimony, sir. And so, you see, I now want him to be my son entirely, that is, legally, sir, and to bear my name, Dobchinsky, sir.

HLESTAKOV: Very good, let him; that's all right.

DOBCHINSKY: I shouldn't have troubled you, but I'm sorry for the boy, who has such talents. He fills us with the greatest hopes: he can repeat different poems by heart; and if he happens to get hold of a pocket knife, he makes a little cab right off, as skillfully as a juggler, sir. Petr Ivanovich here knows all about it.

BOBCHINSKY: Yes, he has great talents.

HLESTAKOV: Very good, very good. I'll see about it. . . . I'll speak to . . . I have hopes . . . that can all be done; yes, yes. . . . [*Turning to Bobchinsky*] Haven't *you* something to say to me?

BOBCHINSKY: Why, yes, I have a very humble petition.

HLESTAKOV: Well, what about?

BOBCHINSKY: I humbly beg you, when you return to Petersburg, to say to all those various grandees, senators, and admirals, "Your Grace," or, "Your Excellency, there lives in such-and-such a town a certain Petr Ivanovich Bobchinsky." Just tell them that there is such a person as Petr Ivanovich Bobchinsky.

HLESTAKOV: Very well.

BOBCHINSKY: And likewise, if you should meet the tsar, just say to him, "Your Imperial Majesty, in such-and-such a town there lives a certain Petr Ivanovich Bobchinsky."

HLESTAKOV: Very well.

DOBCHINSKY: Excuse me for troubling you with my presence.

BOBCHINSKY: Excuse me for troubling you with my presence.

HLESTAKOV: That's all right! That's all right! It was a pleasure. [*He shows them out*]

SCENE VIII.

Hlestakov, *alone.*

HLESTAKOV: There are a good many functionaries here. And, by the way, it strikes me that they take me for an important government official. I really threw dust in their eyes yesterday. What foolishness! I believe I'll write all about it to Tryapichkin in Petersburg; he'll write a little satire and take them off first-rate. Hey, Osip! Bring me paper and ink.

[Osip *glances in at the door, saying,* "Right away"]

And if Tryapichkin ever gets his tooth into anybody, let that man look out! He won't spare his own father for the sake of a lampoon, and he likes money, too. However, these officials are good fellows; it's a great point in their favor that they lent me money. I might as well see how much I've got. Here's three hundred from the Judge; three hundred from the Postmaster, six hundred, seven hundred, eight hundred. . . . What a greasy note! Eight hundred, nine hundred! Oho! more than a thousand! . . . Now, then, captain, just let me get at you now! We'll see who's who!

SCENE IX.

Hlestakov, *and* Osip *with ink and paper.*

HLESTAKOV: Well, you blockhead, do you see how they receive and entertain me? [*He begins to write*]

OSIP: Yes, thank God! Only do you want me to tell you something, Ivan Alexandrovich?

HLESTAKOV: What?

OSIP: Get away from here! By Heaven, it's time!

HLESTAKOV: [*Writing*] What nonsense! Why?

OSIP: Because. Deuce take 'em all! We've bummed two days here, and that's enough. Why tie up with 'em any longer. Spit on 'em! Before you know it some one else may arrive. . . . Yes, Ivan Alexandrovich, by Heavens! There are some splendid horses here—they'd give us a fine ride.

HLESTAKOV: [*Writing*] No, I'd like to stay here a little longer. Wait till to-morrow.

OSIP: But why to-morrow? Good God, let's skip, Ivan Alexandrovich! Although it's a great honor for you, all the same you know that we'd better be off quick; they've really taken you for some one else. . . . And your dad will be peeved because you've dawdled so long. Really, we'd have a grand ride! They'd furnish you tiptop horses here.

HLESTAKOV: [*Writing*] Well, all right. But first take this letter and get an order for post horses. And see to it that they're good horses! Tell the drivers that I'll give them a ruble apiece if they'll bowl along as if I were a special courier and sing songs! [*He continues writing*] I imagine Tryapichkin will die laughing. . . .

OSIP: I'll send the letter by the house servant, sir; but I'd better attend to our packing to save time.

HLESTAKOV: [*Writing*] All right, only bring me a candle.

OSIP: [*Goes out and speaks behind the scene*] Hey, listen, my boy! Take this letter to the post office and tell the Postmaster to frank it; and have them send my master their best troika of post horses; tell 'em my master won't be paying the fee, because it's at the government's expense. And tell 'em to look lively or the master'll be angry. Wait, the letter isn't ready yet.

HLESTAKOV: [*Continuing to write*] I'm curious to know whether he lives on Post Office Street or Gorokhovaya Street. He likes to change his lodgings frequently without paying up. I'll take a chance on addressing him at Post Office Street. [*He folds up the letter and addresses it*]

    [Osip *brings in a candle.* Hlestakov *seals the letter. At the same time the voice of* Derzhimorda *is heard outside*]

DERZHIMORDA: Where're you going, whiskers? I tell you I can't admit anybody.

HLESTAKOV: [*Handing* Osip *the letter*] There, take it away.

VOICES OF MERCHANTS: Let us in, please! You can't refuse; we've come on business.

DERZHIMORDA: Go away! Go away! He's not receiving; he's asleep.

    [*The noise increases*]

HLESTAKOV: What's going on there, Osip? Go see what the noise is about.

OSIP: [*Looking out of the window*] Some merchants want to come in, but the policemen won't let 'em. They're waving some papers; they really want to see you.

HLESTAKOV: [*Going to the window*] What do you want, my good men?

VOICES OF MERCHANTS: We appeal to your kindness. Give orders to receive our petitions, your Honor.

HLESTAKOV: Let 'em in, let 'em in! Let 'em come. Osip, tell 'em to come in.

    [Osip *goes out*]

HLESTAKOV: [*Accepts the petitions through the window, unrolls one of them and reads*] "To his Honorable Excellency the Minister of Finance from the merchant Abdulin." . . . What the devil! There's no such rank!

SCENE X.

Hlestakov, *and the* Merchants, *who carry a basket of wine and loaf sugar.*

HLESTAKOV: What do you want, my good men?

MERCHANTS: We humbly implore your favor.

HLESTAKOV: But what do you want?

MERCHANTS: Don't ruin us, sir! We are suffering insults for no cause at all.

HLESTAKOV: From whom?

ONE OF THE MERCHANTS: All from the Chief of Police of this town. There never was such a Chief of Police, your Honor. He invents such insults as are beyond description. He has ruined us with billeting, until we want to hang ourselves. And his behavior is simply awful. He'll seize a man by the beard and say, "Ha, you Tatar!" By Heaven, he does! It isn't as though we hadn't shown him respect; we always do the regular thing, giving him cloth for his dear wife's clothes and his daughter's—we don't object to that. But, bless you, that's not enough for him; oh, no! He walks into the shop and takes anything he can lay his hands on. He'll see a piece of cloth and say, "Hey, my dear fellow, that's a fine piece of cloth; just send it over to me." Well, you take it over—and there's pretty close to forty yards in the piece.

HLESTAKOV: Is it possible? Why, what a swindler he is!

MERCHANTS: By Heaven, nobody can remember such a chief of police. You have to hide everything in the shop when you catch sight of him. And that's not saying that he takes only delicacies; oh, no! Dried prunes that have been lying in the barrel seven years and my own clerks wouldn't eat, he'll put away by the pocketful. His name day's St. Anthony's,[18] and on that day we take him seems like everything he needs; but no, we've got to keep it up; he says St. Onufry's his name day too. What can we do? We bring him stuff on St. Onufry's also.

HLESTAKOV: He's a regular highwayman!

MERCHANT: I'll say! And just try to say no to him, and he'll quarter a whole regiment on you. And if you object, he'll have the doors locked on you. "I'm not going to subject you to corporal punishment," he says, "or put you to the torture—that's forbidden by law," he says; "but you're going to eat salted herrings, my man."[19]

HLESTAKOV: Oh, what a swindler! Why, he ought to be sent to Siberia!

MERCHANTS: We don't care where your Honor packs him off to; any place'll do so long as it's far from us. Don't scorn our bread and salt, father: we beg to present you with this loaf sugar and this basket of wine.

[18] In Russia the day of the saint for whom a person is named is a family holiday.

[19] To produce excessive thirst. This indirect form of torture was employed, to extort confession, by the secret police.

HLESTAKOV: No, don't think of such a thing; I accept absolutely no bribes. But, for instance, if you should propose to lend me three hundred rubles—well, that would be another matter: I can accept loans.

MERCHANTS: Please do, your Honor! [*Taking out money*] But why three hundred? You had better take five; only help us!

HLESTAKOV: Thanks. I have nothing to say against a loan; I'll take it.

MERCHANTS: [*Handing him the money on a silver tray*] And please take the tray with it.

HLESTAKOV: Well, you can throw the tray in.

MERCHANTS: [*Bowing*] And for once you might take the sugar.

HLESTAKOV: Oh, no, I never take any bribes. . . .

OSIP: Your Honor, why not take it? Do! Everything comes in good on the road. Just hand over the sugar and the sack. Give us everything; it'll all come in useful. What's that—a rope? Give us the rope, too; a rope is useful in traveling; the wagon may break down or something, and you'll have to tie it up.

MERCHANTS: Just do us the favor, your Grace! If you don't help us out as we ask you to, we shan't know what to do: we might as well hang ourselves.

HLESTAKOV: Without fail! without fail! I'll do my best.

[*The* Merchants *go out*]

A WOMAN'S VOICE: [*Outside*] No, don't you dare refuse to admit me! I'll complain to him himself! Stop shoving so hard!

HLESTAKOV: Who's there? [*Going to the window*] What's the matter, my good woman?

VOICES OF TWO WOMEN: We beseech your favor, sir! Please hear us, your Honor!

HLESTAKOV: [*Out of the window*] Let her in.

SCENE XI.

Hlestakov, *the* Locksmith's Wife, *and the* Sergeant's Widow.

LOCKSMITH'S WIFE: [*Bowing down to his feet*] I implore your favor. . . .

SERGEANT'S WIDOW: I implore your favor. . . .

HLESTAKOV: Who are you, my good women?

SERGEANT'S WIDOW: I'm the widow of Sergeant Ivanov.

LOCKSMITH'S WIFE: I'm the wife of a locksmith of the town, Fevronya Petrova Poshlepkin, sir.

HLESTAKOV: Wait; speak one at a time. What do you want?

LOCKSMITH'S WIFE: I implore your aid against the Chief of Police! May God send him every evil! May his children, and he, the swindler, and his uncles and his aunts, prosper in nothing they ever do!

HLESTAKOV: Why?

LOCKSMITH'S WIFE: He sent my husband away as a soldier, and it wasn't our turn, the scoundrel! And it's against the law, too, he being a married man.

HLESTAKOV: How could he do that?

LOCKSMITH'S WIFE: He did it, the scoundrel, he did it! May God smite him in this world and the next! May every misfortune visit him and his aunt, too, if he has one, and if his father's living, the rascal, may he croak or choke himself forever—such a scoundrel he is! He ought to have taken the tailor's son, who's a drunkard anyway; but his parents made him a handsome present; so he jumped on the son of Mrs. Panteleyev, the shopkeeper; but Mrs. Panteleyev sent his wife three pieces of cloth, and so he came to me. "What good's your husband to you?" says he. "He's no use to you." As if I didn't know whether he's any use or not; that's my business—the scoundrel! "He's a thief," says he; "although he hasn't stolen anything yet, it's all the same," he says; "he will; and anyway he'll be sent as a recruit next year." How can I manage without my husband—the scoundrel! I'm a weak woman, and you're a villain! May none of your relatives ever see the light of God! And if you have a mother-in-law, may she—!

HLESTAKOV: All right, all right. [*He shows the old woman out. Then to the other woman*] And you, now?

LOCKSMITH'S WIFE: [*Going*] Don't forget, honored sir! Be merciful to me!

SERGEANT'S WIDOW: I've come to complain against the Chief of Police, sir.

HLESTAKOV: Well, what about? Put it in a few words.

SERGEANT'S WIDOW: He beat me up, sir!

HLESTAKOV: How?

SERGEANT'S WIDOW: By mistake, your Honor! Some of our peasant women were fighting in the market, but the police didn't get there soon enough, so they nabbed me, and reported me: I couldn't sit down for two days.

HLESTAKOV: Well, what's to be done about it, now?

SERGEANT'S WIDOW: Of course, there's nothing to be done now. But you can make him pay damages for making the mistake. I can't turn my back on my own luck, and the money would help me a lot just now.

HLESTAKOV: Well, well, run along, run along; I'll see to it.

[*Several hands containing petitions are thrust through the window*]

What next? [*Approaching the window*] I don't want them! I don't want them! There's no use! There's no use! [*Going away*] They make me tired, deuce take 'em! Don't let 'em in, Osip!

OSIP: [*Shouting out the window*] Go away, go away! He hasn't time now! Come back to-morrow!

[*The door opens and there appears a strange figure in a frieze overcoat, unshaven, with a swollen lip and bandaged cheek; behind him several others appear in perspective*]

OSIP: Get out, get out! Where'd you come from?

[*He gives the first one a push in the belly and forces his own way out into the passage with him, slamming the door behind him*]

SCENE XII.

Hlestakov *and* Marya Antonovna.

MARYA ANTONOVNA: Oh!

HLESTAKOV: What are you afraid of, young lady?

MARYA ANTONOVNA: No, I wasn't frightened.

HLESTAKOV: [*Posing*] It is most gratifying to me, young lady, that you should take me for a man who . . . May I be so bold as to ask you where you were going?

MARYA ANTONOVNA: Well, really, I wasn't going anywhere.

HLESTAKOV: And why weren't you, if I may ask?

MARYA ANTONOVNA: I thought mamma might be here. . . .

HLESTAKOV: No, I'd like to know why you weren't going anywhere.

MARYA ANTONOVNA: I've disturbed you. You were engaged with important matters.

HLESTAKOV: [*Posing*] Your eyes are more important than mere business. . . . You couldn't possibly disturb me, not in any manner whatsoever; on the contrary, you only bring me pleasure.

MARYA ANTONOVNA: You're talking in Petersburg style.

HLESTAKOV: To such a beautiful creature as you. Dare I be so happy as to offer you a chair? But no, you need, not a chair but a throne.

MARYA ANTONOVNA: Really, I don't know . . . I thing I ought to be going. [*She sits down*]

HLESTAKOV: What a beautiful fichu you have on!

MARYA ANTONOVNA: You men are flatterers; you just want to laugh at us provincials.

HLESTAKOV: How I should like to be your fichu, young lady, that I might embrace your lily-white neck.

MARYA ANTONOVNA: I'm sure I don't know what you're talking about: a little fichu. . . . What strange weather we're having to-day!

HLESTAKOV: But your lips, young lady, are better than any kind of weather!

MARYA ANTONOVNA: You keep talking like that! . . . I'd better ask you to write me some verses in my autograph album, as a souvenir. You surely know a lot of them.

HLESTAKOV: For your sake, young lady, I'll do anything you want. Command me, what sort of verses do you wish?

MARYA ANTONOVNA: Oh, any kind . . . such as . . . good ones . . . and new.

HLESTAKOV: But what are verses! I know a lot of them.

MARYA ANTONOVNA: Just say over the kind you're going to write for me.

HLESTAKOV: Why say them? I know them without doing that.

MARYA ANTONOVNA: I'm so fond of poetry.

HLESTAKOV: Well, I know a lot of different poems. For instance, I might write this for you:

O man, who in thine hour of grief
Against thy God in vain complainest. . . .[20]

And there are others. . . . I can't recall them now; however, that's all right. Instead I had better present you with my love, which your eyes have . . . [*Moving his chair nearer*]

MARYA ANTONOVNA: Love! I don't understand love! . . . I have never known what love is. . . . [*She moves her chair away*]

HLESTAKOV: Why do you move your chair away? It would be better for us to sit close together.

MARYA ANTONOVNA: [*Moving away*] Why close together? We're as well off at a distance.

HLESTAKOV: [*Moving nearer*] Why at a distance? We're as well off nearer.

MARYA ANTONOVNA: [*Moving away*] But why is that?

HLESTAKOV: [*Moving nearer*] It just seems to you that we're close; but you ought to imagine we're far apart. How happy I should be, young lady, if I could only hold you in my embrace.

MARYA ANTONOVNA: [*Looking out the window*] I wonder what that was that flew by. Was it a magpie or some other bird?

HLESTAKOV: [*Kissing her shoulder and looking out the window*] That was a magpie.

MARYA ANTONOVNA: [*Rising in indignation*] No, this is too much! . . . Such impudence! . . .

HLESTAKOV: [*Detaining her*] Forgive me, young lady, I did it from love, only from love.

MARYA ANTONOVNA: You consider me only a common provincial girl. . . . [*She tries to get away*]

HLESTAKOV: [*Continues to detain her*] From love, truly, only from love. I was only joking, Marya Antonovna; don't be angry. I'm ready to beg forgiveness on my knees. [*He falls upon his knees*] Forgive me, please forgive me! You see, I'm on my knees.

SCENE XIII.

The same and Anna Andreyevna.

ANNA ANDREYEVNA: [*Seeing* Hlestakov *on his knees*] Oh, what a scene!

HLESTAKOV: [*Rising*] Oh, the deuce!

[20] The opening lines of an ode by Lomonosov (1708?-1765). Hlestakov recalls a scrap of an old-fashioned poet that he learned at school!

ANNA ANDREYEVNA: [*To her daughter*] What does this mean, young lady? What sort of behavior is this?

MARYA ANTONOVNA: Mamma, I . . .

ANNA ANDREYEVNA: Go away at once, do you hear? Go away, go away! Don't you dare show yourself before my eyes.

[Marya Antonovna *goes out in tears*]
Pardon me, but I confess I was carried away by astonishment. . . .

HLESTAKOV: [*Aside*] She's also rather appetizing, not half bad-looking. [*Throwing himself upon his knees*] Madam, you see, I am consumed with love.

ANNA ANDREYEVNA: What, on your knees? Oh, please get up. The floor is anything but clean.

HLESTAKOV: No, upon my knees, absolutely upon my knees, I wish to know my fate. Is it life or death?

ANNA ANDREYEVNA: I beg your pardon, but I still don't entirely understand your words. If I am not mistaken, you are declaring your sentiments regarding my daughter.

HLESTAKOV: No, I am in love with you. My life hangs by a hair. If you do not crown my constant love, then I am unworthy of earthly existence. With flames in my bosom I beseech your hand.

ANNA ANDREYEVNA: Permit me to remark that I am —well, as they say . . . married.

HLESTAKOV: That's nothing! In love that makes no difference. Even Karamzin says, "The laws condemn it."[21] We shall flee to the shade of the streams! . . . Your hand, I ask your hand.

SCENE XIV.

The same and Marya Antonovna, *who comes in running.*

MARYA ANTONOVNA: Mamma, papa says for you to . . . [*Seeing* Hlestakov *on his knees, cnd exclaiming*] Oh, what a scene!

ANNA ANDREYEVNA: Well, what's the matter with you! What did *you* come in for? What flightiness! She runs in like a cat in a fit! Well, what have you found that's so surprising? What have you thought up? Really, you act like a three-year-old child. No one in the world would ever think she was eighteen years old. I don't know when you'll have any more sense, or when you'll behave like a well-brought-up girl, or when you'll know what good principles and propriety are.

MARYA ANTONOVNA: [*Through her tears*] Really, mamma, I didn't know . . .

ANNA ANDREYEVNA: You always have wheels in your head; you pattern after Lyapkin-Tyapkin's daughters! Much good it does you to imitate them! You needn't copy them. There are other models for

[21] Quoted from some verses in the romance, *Bornholm Island*, by Karamzin (1766–1826).

you—you have your mother, for example. That's the example you ought to follow!

HLESTAKOV: [*Seizing the daughter's hand*] Anna Andreyevna, do not oppose our felicity, bless our constant love!

ANNA ANDREYEVNA: [*Astonished*] And so you're in love with *her*?

HLESTAKOV: Decide! Is it life or death?

ANNA ANDREYEVNA: There, you see, you little fool, you see: all on your account, you rubbish, our guest was on his knees; and you had to run in like a chicken with its head off. I really ought to refuse my consent: you're unworthy such good fortune.

MARYA ANTONOVNA: I won't do it again, mamma; really, I won't do it again.

SCENE XV.

The same and the Chief of Police, *who enters out of breath.*

CHIEF OF POLICE: Your Excellency, don't ruin me, don't ruin me!

HLESTAKOV: What's the matter?

CHIEF OF POLICE: The merchants have been complaining to your Excellency. I assure you on my honor that not half of what they say is true. They're the ones who cheat and overreach the people. The sergeant's widow lied to you, saying I'd flogged her; she's lying, by God, she's lying! She flogged herself.

HLESTAKOV: Damn the sergeant's widow; I've nothing to do with her!

CHIEF OF POLICE: Don't believe it, don't believe it! . . . They're all liars! Not even a baby would believe them. They're known for liars all over town. And so far as swindling goes, I venture to inform you that they are swindlers such as the earth has never produced before.

ANNA ANDREYEVNA: Do you know the honor that Ivan Alexandrovich has done us? He is asking for our daughter's hand.

CHIEF OF POLICE: What in the world! . . . You've gone crazy, my dear! Don't be angry, your Excellency; she's a little bit off, and her mother was the same.

HLESTAKOV: But I actually am asking for her hand. I'm in love.

CHIEF OF POLICE: I can't believe it, your Excellency!

ANNA ANDREYEVNA: But when you're told so!

HLESTAKOV: I'm not joking you. . . . I may go mad from love.

CHIEF OF POLICE: I don't dare believe it; I'm unworthy of such an honor.

HLESTAKOV: Yes, if you do not agree to give me Marya Antonovna's hand, then I'm ready to do the devil knows what. . . .

CHIEF OF POLICE: I can't believe it! Your Excellency is having his joke!

ANNA ANDREYEVNA: Oh, what a blockhead you are! When he's explaining it to you?

CHIEF OF POLICE: I can't believe it!

HLESTAKOV: Give her, give her to me! I'm a desperate man, ready for anything: when I shoot myself, you'll be put on trial!

CHIEF OF POLICE: Oh, my God! I'm really not to blame, in intention or in fact! Please don't be angry! Just act as your Honor wishes! My poor head, really . . . I don't know myself what's going on. I've made a bigger blockhead of myself than ever.

ANNA ANDREYEVNA: Well, give 'em your blessing!

[Hlestakov *approaches him with* Marya Antonovna]

CHIEF OF POLICE: May God bless you! It's not my fault!

[Hlestakov *kisses* Marya Antonovna. *The* Chief of Police *watches them*]

What the devil! They really are! [*Wiping his eyes*] They're kissing! Holy Saints, they're kissing! They're actually engaged! [*Shouting and prancing with joy*] Hey, Anton! Hey, Anton! Aha, Police Chief! That's the way it's turned out!

SCENE XVI.

The same and Osip.

OSIP: The horses are ready.

HLESTAKOV: Oh, all right. . . . In a minute.

CHIEF OF POLICE: What, sir? Are you leaving?

HLESTAKOV: Yes, I am.

CHIEF OF POLICE: But when? . . . That is . . . you hinted something about a wedding, didn't you?

HLESTAKOV: Oh, as to that . . . It's only for a minute—just a day with my uncle. He's a rich old man—and to-morrow I'll be back.

CHIEF OF POLICE: We dare not detain you and we hope for your prosperous return.

HLESTAKOV: Why, of course, of course, I'll be right back. Good-by, my love. . . . No, I simply cannot express myself! Good-by, my darling! [*He kisses her hand*]

CHIEF OF POLICE: But don't you need anything for traveling? You were somewhat short of money, weren't you?

HLESTAKOV: Oh, no, what for? [*Upon reflection*] However, if you wish.

CHIEF OF POLICE: How much would you like?

HLESTAKOV: Well, you gave me two hundred, that is, not two hundred, but four—I don't want to profit by your mistake—so perhaps you'd be willing to let me have as much again, to make an even eight hundred.

CHIEF OF POLICE: At once! [*He takes it from his pocketbook*] Fortunately I have it in brand-new bills.

HLESTAKOV: Ah, yes. [*He takes the notes and looks at them*] That's fine. They say that new notes bring good luck.

CHIEF OF POLICE: Just so, sir.

HLESTAKOV: Good-by, Anton Antonovich! I'm much obliged for your hospitality. I confess from the bottom of my heart, I've never had such a kind reception. Good-by, Anna Andreyevna! Good-by, my darling Marya Antonovna!

[*They go out*]

[*Voices behind the scenes*]

HLESTAKOV'S VOICE: Good-by, Marya Antonovna, my soul's angel!

VOICE OF THE CHIEF OF POLICE: What's this? You're going by the public post?

HLESTAKOV'S VOICE: Yes, I'm used to it. Springs give me the headache.

DRIVER'S VOICE: Whoa!

VOICE OF THE CHIEF OF POLICE: Then at least let me spread something on the seat: a rug, for instance. Won't you let me give you a little rug?

HLESTAKOV'S VOICE: No, what for? That's needless; still, you might let them bring a rug.

VOICE OF THE CHIEF OF POLICE: Hey, Avdotya! Run to the storeroom and bring out the best rug—the Persian one with the blue ground. Hurry!

DRIVER'S VOICE: Whoa!

VOICE OF THE CHIEF OF POLICE: When may we expect you back?

HLESTAKOV'S VOICE: To-morrow or the day after.

OSIP'S VOICE: Ah, is that the rug? Well, give it here; fold it like this. Now put some hay on this side.

DRIVER'S VOICE: Whoa!

OSIP'S VOICE: Here on this side! Here! That'll do! Good! That'll be fine. [*Slapping his hand on the rug*] Now, sit down, your Honor!

HLESTAKOV'S VOICE: Good-by, Anton Antonovich!

VOICE OF THE CHIEF OF POLICE: Good-by, your Excellency!

WOMEN'S VOICES: Good-by, Ivan Alexandrovich!

HLESTAKOV'S VOICE: Good-by, mamma!

DRIVER'S VOICE: Giddap, my beauties!

[*The harness bells jingle; the curtain falls*]

ACT V. SCENE I.

The same room.

The Chief of Police, Anna Andreyevna, *and* Marya Antonovna.

CHIEF OF POLICE: Well, Anna Andreyevna, what about it? Would you ever have expected it? What a rich prize, hang it all! Now, admit it candidly: you never even dreamed of such luck! From being a mere police chief's wife suddenly to . . . oh, the deuce! . . . to make connections with such a devil as this!

ANNA ANDREYEVNA: Not at all; I knew it all the

time. It seems wonderful to you, because you're an ordinary man and have never seen decent people.

CHIEF OF POLICE: I'm a decent man myself, dear. On the other hand, really, when you think of it, Anna Andreyevna, what fine birds you and I have become! Ha, Anna Andreyevna? We'll fly high, deuce take it! Just wait, now I'll pepper those guys for presenting petitions and denunciations! Hey, who's there?

[*A policeman comes in*]

Oh, it's you, Ivan Karpovich. Call the merchants in, my boy. I'll give it to them, the rascals! To complain about *me!* Nothing but a damned bunch of Jews! Just wait, sweethearts! Up to date I've merely warmed your breeches, but now I'll tan your whole hides! Write down the name of every man who came to peach on me, and, above all, the scribblers who fixed up their petitions for them. And you can announce so they'll all know it, what an honor God has bestowed on the Chief of Police, who is marrying his daughter to no ordinary man, but to one whose like can't be found on earth, a man who can do everything, everything, everything! Announce it so they'll all know it. Shout it to the whole population! Ring the bells, dammit! This is a regular holiday.

[*The policeman goes out*]

That's the way, Anna Andreyevna, huh? What'll we do now, where shall we live: here or in Petersburg?

ANNA ANDREYEVNA: In Petersburg, of course. How could we stay here!

CHIEF OF POLICE: Well, if it's to be Petersburg, so be it; but it wouldn't be so bad here. And I suppose the police business may go to hell, huh, Anna Andreyevna?

ANNA ANDREYEVNA: Of course; what's a police job!

CHIEF OF POLICE: Don't you think, Anna Andreyevna, I may now land a swell title? He's chummy with all the ministers and goes to the Palace, so he may get me promoted in time to a generalship. What do you think, Anna Andreyevna, may I get to be a general?

ANNA ANDREYEVNA: Sure, of course you may.

CHIEF OF POLICE: It's damned nice to be a general! They hang decorations across your breast! Which ribbon is better, Anna Andreyevna, the red or the blue?

ANNA ANDREYEVNA: Of course the blue is best.

CHIEF OF POLICE: Eh? So that's what you fancy. Well, the red's nice, too. Why do I want to be a general? Because if it happens that you travel anywhere, messengers and adjutants gallop ahead everywhere, shouting, "Horses!" And at the posting stations they won't give any to any one else; all have to wait: all those titular councilors, captains, police chiefs—and you don't give a snap of your fingers. You dine somewhere at a governor's, and there a police chief has to stand! He, he, he! [*He laughs himself into a perspiration*] That's what's so attractive, damn it!

ANNA ANDREYEVNA: You always like everything vulgar. You must remember that we've got to change our whole manner of living, that your acquaintances won't be like the dog fancier Judge with whom you course hares, or like Zemlyanika; on the contrary, your acquaintances will be from the most refined society, counts and swells. . . . Though I'm really scared on your account: you'll let slip occasionally some word that simply isn't heard in polite society.

CHIEF OF POLICE: What of it? A word doesn't hurt.

ANNA ANDREYEVNA: It was all right while you were a police chief; but in Petersburg life will be quite different.

CHIEF OF POLICE: Yes; they say that there are two kinds of fish there, sea-eels and sparlings, which simply make your mouth water when you begin to eat.

ANNA ANDREYEVNA: He's always thinking about fish! I want to be sure that our house is the swellest in the capital, and I want such an odor of ambergris in my drawing-room that there'll be no going into it: you'll simply have to shut your eyes. [*She shuts her eyes and sniffs*] Oh, how nice!

SCENE II.

The same and the Merchants.

CHIEF OF POLICE: Ah, how are you, you flock of hawks!

MERCHANTS: [*Bowing*] We wish you good health, sir!

CHIEF OF POLICE: Well, darlings, how are you? How's trade, eh? What, you tea-swilling cloth-stretchers, you'll complain, will you? You arch-rascals, you dirty brutes, you swollen swindlers, you'll complain, will you? Well, did you get much? They thought they'd have me thrown in the jug! . . . Do you know, I'll swear by seven devils and one witch that . . .

ANNA ANDREYEVNA: Oh, good Heavens, Antosha, what words you use!

CHIEF OF POLICE: [*Greatly displeased*] Words don't matter now. Do you know that that very official to whom you complained is marrying my daughter? Do you? What d'you say now? Now I'll fix you! . . . You deceive people. . . . You make a contract with the government and swindle it out of a hundred thousand by supplying rotten cloth, and then you donate twenty yards and expect to be rewarded for it! And if they found it out, you'd catch it! . . . He struts along, belly foremost: he's a merchant; nobody must touch him! "We don't give way even to the nobility," he says. As for a nobleman . . . Bah, you pigs' mugs! . . . A nobleman studies the sciences; and if they beat him at school, it's to some purpose, so that he'll learn something useful. But what about you? You begin with rascalities, and you're beaten by the master because you don't know how to cheat. While still little brats, before you know your Lord's

Prayer, you give short measure; and when you've developed a belly and lined your pockets with money, how you do put on airs! Oh, you're wonders, I'll say! Because you empty sixteen samovars a day, you put on airs, do you? I spit on you and your conceit!

MERCHANTS: [*Bowing*] We're at fault, Anton Antonovich!

CHIEF OF POLICE: Complain, will you? But who helped you swindle when you built the bridge and charged twenty thousand for lumber when you didn't use a hundred rubles' worth? I helped you, you old billy goat![22] Have you forgotten that? If I had peached on you for that, I could have sent you to Siberia. What d'you say, ha?

ONE OF THE MERCHANTS: God knows we're guilty, Anton Antonovich! The devil misled us. We swear never to complain again. Demand any satisfaction you please, only don't be angry!

CHIEF OF POLICE: Don't be angry! And now you're wallowing at my feet. And why? Because I've got the upper hand; but if you had even the least advantage, you scum, you'd trample me in the very mud, and roll a log over me.

MERCHANTS: [*Bowing to his feet*] Don't ruin us, Anton Antonovich!

CHIEF OF POLICE: "Don't ruin us!" Now it's "Don't ruin us!" But what was it before? I could . . . [*Waving his hand*] Well, God forgive you! That'll do! I'm not vindictive; only see that you look sharp from now on! I'm not marrying my daughter to any ordinary noble: let your congratulations be . . . d'you understand? Don't try to wriggle out of it with a chunk of dried sturgeon or a loaf of sugar. . . . Now, go to the devil!

[*The* Merchants *go out*]

SCENE III.

The same, Ammos Fedorovich, Artemy Filippovich, *and later* Rastakovsky.

AMMOS FEDOROVICH: [*Still in the door*] Can I believe the rumors, Anton Antonovich? Has this unusual good luck really struck you?

ARTEMY FILIPPOVICH: I have the honor to ^ongratulate you upon your unusual good fortune. I rejoiced with all my soul when I heard about it. [*He goes to kiss* Anna Andreyevna's *hand*] Anna Andreyevna! [*He goes to kiss* Marya Antonovna's *hand*] Marya Antonovna!

RASTAKOVSKY: [*Entering*] I congratulate Anton Antonovich! May God prolong your life and that of the new pair, and give you a numerous posterity of grandchildren and great-grandchildren! Anna Andreyevna! [*Going to kiss her hand*] Marya Antonovna! [*Going to kiss her hand*]

[22] At the date of the play, only the lower classes wore beards.

SCENE IV.

The same, Korobkin *and his wife, and* Lyulyukov.

KOROBKIN: I have the honor to congratulate Anton Antonovich! Anna Andreyevna! [*Going to kiss her hand*] Marya Antonovna! [*Going to kiss her hand*]

KOROBKIN'S WIFE: I congratulate you from my soul, Anna Andreyevna, upon your new happiness!

LYULYUKOV: I have the honor to congratulate you, Anna Andreyevna. [*He goes to kiss her hand, then turning towards the spectators, he makes a clicking sound with his tongue with an air of bravado*] Marya Antonovna, I have the honor to congratulate you! [*He goes to kiss her hand and turns to the spectators with the same bravado*]

SCENE V.

A number of guests in frock coats and swallowtails come up first to kiss the hand of Anna Andreyevna, *saying her name, then to* Marya Antonovna, *saying hers.* Bobchinsky *and* Dobchinsky *push their way forward.*

BOBCHINSKY: I have the honor to congratulate you!

DOBCHINSKY: Anton Antonovich, I have the honor to congratulate you!

BOBCHINSKY: Upon this prosperous event!

DOBCHINSKY: Anna Andreyevna!

BOBCHINSKY: Anna Andreyevna!

[*Both go up to kiss her hand at the same time and knock their heads together*]

DOBCHINSKY: Marya Antonovna! [*He goes to kiss her hand*] I have the honor to congratulate you. You will be very, very happy; you will walk in cloth of gold and eat all sorts of delicate soups, and pass your time very entertainingly.

BOBCHINSKY: [*Interrupting*] Marya Antonovna, I have the honor to congratulate you! May God give you all kinds of riches and gold and a baby boy no bigger than that! [*Showing with his hand*] So small he can sit on the palm of your hand, yes, ma'am; and all the time he'll cry wa, wa, wa!

SCENE VI.

Still more guests come to kiss the ladies' hands, among them Luka Lukich *and his* Wife.

LUKA LUKICH: I have the honor. . . .

LUKA LUKICH'S WIFE: [*Running forward*] I congratulate you, Anna Andreyevna! [*They kiss*] I was so delighted, truly. They told me, "Anna Andreyevna is marrying off her daughter." "Oh, my goodness," I thought to myself; and I was so delighted that I said to my husband, "Listen, Luky-duky, here's a new happiness for Anna Andreyevna!" "Well," I thought, "thank God!" And I said to him, "I'm so beside myself with joy that I'm burning with impatience to declare it personally to Anna Andreyevna." . . . "Oh, good heavens!" I thought to myself, "Anna Andreyevna was just waiting for a good match for her daughter, and now see what fate has done: it has all happened exactly as she wished." And truly, I was so glad that I couldn't speak. I wept and wept; why, I fairly sobbed. Luka Lukich even said, "Nastenka, what are you sobbing about?" "Luky-duky," I said, "I don't know, myself; the tears are just flowing in a stream."

CHIEF OF POLICE: I humbly beg you to be seated, ladies and gentlemen! Hey, Mishka, bring in some more chairs here!

[*The guests sit down*]

SCENE VII.

The same, the Police Captain, *and* Sergeants of Police.

POLICE CAPTAIN: I have the honor to congratulate you, your Honor, and to wish you prosperity and long life!

CHIEF OF POLICE: Thanks, thanks! I beg you to sit down, gentlemen!

[*The guests sit down*]

AMMOS FEDOROVICH: Now please tell us, Anton Antonovich, how all this started, the whole thing, step by step.

CHIEF OF POLICE: The course of the affair was extraordinary: he was kind enough to make the proposal in person.

ANNA ANDREYEVNA: Very respectfully, and in the most refined manner. He put everything extraordinarily well. "It's only out of respect for your virtues, Anna Andreyevna," he said. And he's such a handsome, well-bred man, of the most aristocratic manners. "Believe me, Anna Andreyevna," he said, "my life isn't worth a kopek; I'm doing this only because I respect your rare qualities."

MARYA ANTONOVNA: Why, mamma, he said that to me!

ANNA ANDREYEVNA: Stop it! You don't know anything about it. Don't mix into everything! "I'm astonished, Anna Andreyevna," he says. Then he launched forth into the most flattering words . . . and when I wanted to say, "We really don't dare hope for such an honor," he suddenly fell upon his knees and said in the most aristocratic style: "Anna Andreyevna, don't make me wretched! Please consent to reciprocate my feelings, or I shall let death end it all."

MARYA ANTONOVNA: Really, mamma, he said that about me. . . .

ANNA ANDREYEVNA: Yes, of course . . . it was about you, also. . . . I don't deny it at all.

CHIEF OF POLICE: As it was he frightened me; he said he would shoot himself. "I'll shoot myself, I'll shoot myself!" he said.

NUMEROUS GUESTS: Really, you don't say!

AMMOS FEDOROVICH: Well I declare!

LUKA LUKICH: It was surely fate that brought this to pass.

ARTEMY FILIPPOVICH: Not fate, old man, fate's too flighty a bird: his merits have done it. [*Aside*] Luck always comes to such swine as he!

AMMOS FEDOROVICH: If you want him, I'll give you that pup you were bargaining for, Anton Antonovich.

CHIEF OF POLICE: No, I've no use for pups now.

AMMOS FEDOROVICH: Well, if you don't want him, we can agree on another dog.

KOROBKIN'S WIFE: Oh, Anna Andreyevna, how glad I am of your happiness! You simply can't imagine!

KOROBKIN: And where, if I may ask, is our eminent guest now? I heard that he had gone away for some reason.

CHIEF OF POLICE: Yes, he has left for one day, on a very important matter.

ANNA ANDREYEVNA: To see his uncle and ask his blessing.

CHIEF OF POLICE: To ask his blessing; but to-morrow . . . [*He sneezes, and is greeted by a din of good wishes*] Thanks very much! But to-morrow he'll be back. . . . [*He sneezes again; renewed chorus of good wishes; the following people speak louder than the others*]

POLICE CAPTAIN: We wish you good health, your Honor!

BOBCHINSKY: A hundred years and a sack of gold!

DOBCHINSKY: God prolong your days forever and ever!

ARTEMY FILIPPOVICH: May you croak!

KOROBKIN'S WIFE: The devil take you!

CHIEF OF POLICE: I humbly thank you! I wish you the same.

ANNA ANDREYEVNA: We're planning to live in Petersburg now. I confess that in this town there's an atmosphere that's too . . . well, countrified! . . . I confess it's very disagreeable. . . . And my husband —he'll be made a general there.

CHIEF OF POLICE: Yes, and I admit, ladies and gentlemen, deuce take it, that I'd like awfully to be a general.

LUKA LUKICH: God grant you may be!

RASTAKOVSKY: What is impossible for man is possible for God.

AMMOS FEDOROVICH: A big ship travels far.[23]

ARTEMY FILIPPOVICH: Your merits deserve the honor.

AMMOS FEDOROVICH: [*Aside*] That will be the

[23] Russian proverb.

limit, if they actually make him a general! A general-ship will suit him like a saddle on a cow! But no, it's a far cry from this to that. There are men here more respectable than you that aren't generals yet.

ARTEMY FILIPPOVICH: [*Aside*] And so he's crawling into a general's boots! What the devil! But there's no telling; he may get to be a general. The devil knows he's got conceit enough for it. [*Turning to him*] Don't forget us then, Anton Antonovich.

AMMOS FEDOROVICH: And if anything should happen—for instance, some emergency in our affairs—don't deny us your patronage!

KOROBKIN: Next year I shall take my son to the capital to enter the government service. Please do us the favor to grant him your protection; be like a father to an orphan child.

CHIEF OF POLICE: I'm quite ready, for my part, to do what I can.

ANNA ANDREYEVNA: Antosha, you're always ready to make promises. In the first place, you'll have no time to think about that. How can you, and why should you, burden yourself with such promises?

CHIEF OF POLICE: Why not, my dear? Sometimes one can do something.

ANNA ANDREYEVNA: Of course one can; but one can't patronize all the small fry.

KOROBKIN'S WIFE: Do you hear how she's treating us?

A WOMAN GUEST: Yes, she was always like that. I know her. Let her sit at the table and she'll put her feet on it.[24]

SCENE VIII.

The same and the Postmaster, *who enters out of breath, with an unsealed letter in his hand.*

POSTMASTER: An astonishing thing, ladies and gentlemen! The official whom we took to be the government inspector, was not the inspector at all.

ALL: What—not the inspector?

POSTMASTER: Absolutely not; I've learned from this letter.

CHIEF OF POLICE: What's that? What's that? From what letter?

POSTMASTER: Why, from his own letter. They brought me a letter to the post office. I glanced at the address and saw, "Post Office Street." I was stupefied. "Well," I thought to myself, "he's surely found some irregularity in the post office and is notifying the authorities." So I took and opened it.

CHIEF OF POLICE: How did you dare?

POSTMASTER: I don't know; some supernatural power inspired me. I was about to call a messenger to dispatch it by express; but such curiosity as I have never felt before overcame me. I couldn't let it go; I simply couldn't! I was just drawn to open it. In one

[24] Russian proverb.

ear I seemed to hear, "Don't unseal it! You'll croak on the spot!" But in the other some demon kept whispering, "Open it, open it, open it!" And when I pressed the wax, a fire ran through my veins; and when I unsealed it, I was frozen, by Heaven I was. My hands shook, and all went black before my eyes.

CHIEF OF POLICE: But how did you dare open the letter of such an august emissary?

POSTMASTER: But that's just the point; he ain't an emissary and he ain't august!

CHIEF OF POLICE: Well, what do you think he *is?*

POSTMASTER: A mere nobody; the devil knows what he is.

CHIEF OF POLICE: [*Testily*] What do you mean? How dare you call him a nobody and the devil knows who? I'll have you arrested!

POSTMASTER: Who? You?

CHIEF OF POLICE: Yes, I!

POSTMASTER: You ain't the size!

CHIEF OF POLICE: Don't you know that he is marrying my daughter, that I'm to be a dignitary myself, and that I can bundle you off to Siberia?

POSTMASTER: Oh, Anton Antonovich! What's Siberia? Siberia's far away. I'd better read you the letter. Ladies and gentlemen, shall I read the letter?

ALL: Read it, read it!

POSTMASTER: [*Reading*] "I hasten to inform you, my dear Tryapichkin, what wonders are happening to me. On the road I was cleaned out by an infantry captain, with the result that the innkeeper was going to have me jailed. Then all of a sudden, because of my Petersburg countenance and clothes, the whole town took me for a Governor-General. And now I'm living at the Police Chief's, enjoying myself, and flirting desperately with his wife and daughter. I haven't yet decided which one to begin with—I think the mother, because she seems to be ready to go the limit. Do you remember how hard up we used to be, and dined by being foxy; and how once a confectioner grabbed me by the collar because of some pastry we had eaten, telling him to charge it to the King of England? Now it's the other way round. Everybody lends me money, all I want. They're terrific freaks: you'd die laughing at them. I know you write articles; stick them in your contributions. In the first place, there's the Police Chief, as stupid as a gray jackass. . . ."

CHIEF OF POLICE: It can't be! It isn't there!

POSTMASTER: [*Showing the letter*] Read it yourself.

CHIEF OF POLICE: [*Reading*] "As a gray jackass." It can't be! You wrote that yourself!

POSTMASTER: How was I to write it?

ARTEMY FILIPPOVICH: Read it!

LUKA LUKICH: Read it!

POSTMASTER: [*Continuing his reading*] "the Police Chief—as stupid as a gray jackass. . . ."

CHIEF OF POLICE: Oh, damn you! Do you have to repeat it? As if we didn't know it was there!

POSTMASTER: [*Continuing his reading*] Hm . . . hm . . . hm . . . hm . . . "a gray jackass. The Postmaster is also a nice chap. . . ." [*Stopping*] Well, then he goes on to express himself rather indecently about me.

CHIEF OF POLICE: No, read it!

POSTMASTER: What for?

CHIEF OF POLICE: What the devil! If you're reading it, read it! Read it all!

ARTEMY FILIPPOVICH: Here, just let me read it. [*Putting on his spectacles and reading*] "The Postmaster is the exact image of our department janitor, Mikheyev; and the rascal must be just such another old soak."

POSTMASTER: [*To the spectators*] Well, he's a contemptible brat who needs a hiding; that's all!

ARTEMY FILIPPOVICH: [*Continuing*] "The Supervisor of Charitable Insti . . . tu . . . tu . . ." [*He begins to stammer*]

KOROBKIN: Why are you stopping?

ARTEMY FILIPPOVICH: The writing is illegible . . . however, I can see he's a scamp.

KOROBKIN: Give it to me! I think I have better eyes. [*Taking hold of the letter*]

ARTEMY FILLIPOVICH: [*Holding on to it*] No, we can skip that part; further on one can make it out.

KOROBKIN: Come on, I can do it.

ARTEMY FILIPPOVICH: If it has to be read, I'll do it myself: further on, really, it's quite legible.

POSTMASTER: No, read it all! So far everything has been read.

ALL: Give him the letter, Artemy Filippovich, give him the letter! [*To Korobkin*] Read it!

ARTEMY FILIPPOVICH: All right. [*Giving the letter*] Here, if you please . . . [*Covering part with his finger*] Read from here on. [*All gather around him*]

POSTMASTER: Read it, read it! Nonsense! Read it all!

KOROBKIN: [*Reading*] "The Supervisor of Charitable Institutions, Zemlyanika, is a regular pig in a nightcap."

ARTEMY FILIPPOVICH: [*To the spectators*] It isn't even witty! A pig in a nightcap! When did a pig ever have a nightcap?

KOROBKIN: [*Continuing*] "The Superintendent of Schools reeks of onions from head to foot."

LUKA LUKICH: [*To the spectators*] By God, I never had an onion in my mouth!

AMMOS FEDOROVICH: [*Aside*] Thank God, at least there's nothing about me!

KOROBKIN: [*Reading*] "The Judge . . ."

AMMOS FEDOROVICH: Now I'll catch it . . . [*Aloud*] Ladies and gentlemen, I think the letter's rather long. Devil take it, why read such trash?

LUKA LUKICH: No!

POSTMASTER: No, read it!

ARTEMY FILIPPOVICH: No, just read it!

KOROBKIN: [*Continuing*] "The Judge, Lyapkin-Tyapkin, is *movay tone*[25] in the highest degree. . . ." [*Stopping*] That must be a French word.

AMMOS FEDOROVICH: The devil knows what it means! It's all right if it's nothing but swindler, but it may mean something worse!

KOROBKIN: [*Continuing*] "But after all they're a hospitable and kindhearted lot. Good-by, my dear Tryapichkin. I myself, following your example, want to become a writer. It's a bore to live like this, my boy; one needs food for one's soul. I see that exactly what I need is something lofty to occupy me. Write to me in the Saratov Province, to the village of Podkatilovka." [*He turns over the letter and reads the address*] "To Ivan Vasilyevich Tryapichkin, Esquire, Third Floor, Number Ninety-seven, turning to the right from the yard entrance, Post Office Street, St. Petersburg."

ONE OF THE LADIES: What an unexpected setback!

CHIEF OF POLICE: He's as good as cut my throat! I'm killed. I'm simply killed dead. I can see absolutely nothing in front of me but pigs' snouts instead of faces. . . . Get him back, get him back! [*He waves his arm*]

POSTMASTER: How can we get him back? It's just my luck to have ordered the superintendent to give him the fastest horses; and the devil put me up to sending similar orders ahead.

KOROBKIN'S WIFE: This is certainly confusion worse confounded!

AMMOS FEDOROVICH: But, damn it, gentlemen, he borrowed three hundred rubles from me!

ARTEMY FILIPPOVICH: Three hundred from me, too.

POSTMASTER: [*Sighing*] Oh, and three hundred from me!

BOBCHINSKY: And from me and Petr Ivanovich, sixty-five, sir, in notes, yes, sir!

AMMOS FEDOROVICH: [*Shrugging his shoulders in perplexity*] How did this happen, gentlemen? How in the world did we make such a mistake?

CHIEF OF POLICE: [*Striking his brow*] How could I, how could I, old blockhead that I am! Stupid old ram! I've outlived my good sense! . . . Thirty years I've been in the service; not a merchant, not a contractor has been able to impose on me; I've fooled swindlers upon swindlers; sharpers and rascals who could fool the whole world I have hooked neatly! I've bamboozled three governors! . . . What are governors! [*Waving his hand*] Governors aren't worth mentioning!

ANNA ANDREYEVNA: But this can't be, Antosha; he's betrothed to Mashenka.

CHIEF OF POLICE: [*Angrily*] Betrothed! A cat and a fiddle! Betrothed indeed! She dares to throw the engagement in my face! . . . [*In desperation*] Here, just look—all the world, all Christianity, all of you— just see how the Police Chief has made a fool of himself! Blockhead that he is! the old blockhead, the

___
[25] A corruption of the French *mauvais ton*—vulgarity.

old scoundrel! [*Threatening himself with his fist*] Oh, you thick-nosed imbecile! To take a lounge-lizard, a rag, for a man of importance! And there he skims along the road with his bells jingling! He'll spread the story all over the earth! And I'll not only be a laughingstock, but some quill-driver, some paper-spoiler will be found to put me in a comedy! That's what hurts! He won't spare my rank or my calling; and they'll all show their teeth in a grin and clap their hands. What are you laughing at? You're laughing at yourselves! . . . Damn you! . . . [*He stamps on the floor in his rage*] I'd like to do the same to all scribblers! Bah, you quill-drivers, you damned Liberals! You devil's brood! I'd like to tie you all in a knot and grind you to powder, and ram you into the devil's cap! . . . [*He strikes out with his fist and stamps on the floor. After a brief silence*] I simply can't get over it. Indeed it's true that when God wants to punish a man, he takes away his reason first. Now, what was there in that weathercock like a government inspector? Absolutely nothing! Not even half a finger's length of resemblance; but suddenly everybody shouts, "The inspector, the government inspector!" Now, who was the first to let out the notion that he was the government inspector? Speak up!

ARTEMY FILIPPOVICH: [*Shrugging his shoulders*] I couldn't tell you how it happened if my life depended on it! It's as if a fog had descended upon us and the devil had misled us.

AMMOS FEDOROVICH: Who started it? There's who: those two smart Alecks! [*Pointing to* Dobchinsky *and* Bobchinsky]

BOBCHINSKY: Not at all! Not me! I never even thought . . .

DOBCHINSKY: I didn't do anything, absolutely not . . .

ARTEMY FILIPPOVICH: Of course you did.

LUKA LUKICH: It stands to reason. They ran in from the tavern like two lunatics, yelling: "He's come! He's come! and he doesn't pay anything! . . ." They found a rare bird!

CHIEF OF POLICE: Naturally, it was you. You town scandal-mongers, you damned liars!

ARTEMY FILIPPOVICH: May the devil take you with your inspectors and your yarns!

CHIEF OF POLICE: You just snoop about the town and mess things up, you damned chatterboxes! You scatter scandals, you bobtailed magpies!

AMMOS FEDOROVICH: You damned bunglers!

LUKA LUKICH: Dunces!

ARTEMY FILIPPOVICH: Pot-bellied little shrimps! [*They all surround them*]

BOBCHINSKY: By God, it wasn't I, it was Petr Ivanovich!

DOBCHINSKY: It was not, Petr Ivanovich, you said it first. . . .

BOBCHINSKY: Certainly not; you were the first yourself.

LAST SCENE.

The same and a Gendarme.

GENDARME: The official who has come from Petersburg by imperial order demands your instant appearance before him. He is stopping at the inn.

[*The words just pronounced strike all like a thunderbolt. A sound of astonishment escapes from the lips of all the ladies at once; the whole group, having suddenly changed its position, remains as if petrified*]

DUMB SHOW

The Chief of Police *stands in the midst like a post, his arms outspread and his head tilted backwards; on the right his wife and his daughter appear on the verge of rushing towards him; beyond them the* Postmaster, *transformed into a question mark, is turned towards the spectators; beyond him* Luka Lukich, *in the most innocent bewilderment; beyond him, at the very edge of the scene, three lady guests are leaning towards each other with the most sarcastic expressions of countenance, aimed directly at the* Police Chief's *family. On the* Police Chief's *left stands* Zemlyanika, *his head inclined somewhat to one side, as if he were listening to something; beyond him, the* Judge, *with outspread arms, almost squatting on the floor, and making movements of the lips as if about to whistle or say, "So you see what you've come to, old lady!" Beyond him is* Korobkin, *turned towards the spectators, with one eye cocked and a derisive gesture towards the* Chief of Police; *beyond him, on the extreme side,* Dobchinsky *and* Bobchinsky *make movements of their hands towards each other, their mouths open, and regarding each other with bulging eyes. The other guests simply stand like statues. For nearly a minute and a half the group remains in this position.*

THE CURTAIN FALLS

Friedrich Hebbel

(1813–1863)

Friedrich Hebbel mediated the claims of romanticism and realism in the theatre, and his life prepared him for the role. He experienced extreme poverty and learned at first hand the hard fact that man is subject to environment. But he managed to surmount his circumstances after his thirtieth year, married a celebrated Viennese actress, and gained the favor of princes.

Born to a poor Holstein bricklayer, Hebbel was mistreated in childhood by his embittered parent. After losing his father at the age of fourteen, he first found employment in a menial capacity and later worked as a clerk in the local police court. He also tried to become an actor, picked up some education as a charity student, and at the late age of twenty-three became an ill-prepared and poverty-stricken university student at Heidelberg. Here, in 1836, he formed a liaison with a seamstress which lasted many years, until he achieved some measure of literary success and married in 1846. He began to hew out a literary career for himself in 1840 with the Biblical drama *Judith,* but he remained in straitened circumstances until 1843, when King Christian VIII of Denmark was prevailed upon to grant him an annual stipend.

After this turn in his fortunes, Hebbel, who had often gone hungry and was long unable to overcome his fear of poverty, went to Paris and became a man of the world. Here he completed his masterpiece *Maria Magdalena.* He then went to the south of France, traveled to Italy, and in 1845 made an effort to establish himself in the Viennese theatre. Here he finally won success with *Maria Magdalena* in 1848, the year of the European democratic revolutions; and in 1849 he had another successful production with *Judith,* his wife, the court actress Christine Enghaus, playing the title role. Although his *Herod and Mariamne* was a failure in the same year, Hebbel was by now a writer of considerable importance in Central Europe. His next play, *Agnes Bernauer,* opened in Munich in 1852 and was well received; his last plays, *Gyges and His Ring,* finished in 1854, and the *Nibelung* trilogy, completed in 1860, increased his reputation. The king of Bavaria granted him the Order of Maximilian for the trilogy, and in 1863, while Hebbel lay dying, he was granted the high distinction of the Schiller Prize by Prussia.

Hebbel is a precursor of modern dramatists both as a writer of historical drama and as the author of the most thoroughgoing example of "bourgeois" or middle-class tragedy before the advent of Ibsen. In his historical plays, he was scrupulously probing. He gave attention to psychological processes, as in his study of pathologically extreme jealousy in *Herod and Mariamne.* He was also adept at linking private drama to the social milieu, interpreting the struggles between characters, as well as the struggles within them, as a conflict between two principles at war with each other in society. Under the influence of the philosopher Hegel, this dramatist made his characters represent a struggle between an old order and a new one, an established social attitude and a formative one.

The clash between the two points of view constituted historical necessity and produced personal tragedy. In *Gyges and His Ring,* for example, Kandaules, the king of Lydia, manifests a conventional view of masculine prerogatives and a disregard of the rights of both woman and the individual. Conflict is precipitated when he insists on showing his queen, Rhodope, disrobed in order to display the charms in which he takes proprietary pride. Rhodope, representing a rising consciousness of individuality, considers herself deeply wronged and destroys him.

With the historical view, Hebbel combined other philosophical attitudes, as was his wont. The vengeful woman may be said to represent Nature, and Nature punishes those who would unveil her. Invariably, however, society is more than a background; it is an impediment or a categorical imperative, against which the individual's destiny works itself out; and generally, the individual's will is found to be secondary to social forces in importance. In *Agnes Bernauer,* a prince finds it necessary to renounce his love for a low-born heroine in the interests of the state, and the noble Agnes is presented as a tragic victim of social necessity.

In verse drama, unfortunately, Hebbel was severe, crabbed, and awkward. He was exacting and impressive rather than attractive and appealing. His importance in the history of the modern theatre resides less in his having written completely successful plays than in his having found new ways of giving significance to the drama, whether romantic or realistic. He stood at the crossroads between romantic historical drama and modern social drama, and the ideas he tried to embody in his plays and made explicit in his diaries (*Hebbels Tagebücher*) foreshadow the analytical modernism of Ibsen, Strindberg, and Shaw.

Hebbel's notes on drama are well worth reading. One of these insists on the necessity of dramatizing reality as a process of change: "It is an error to assert that only the completed thing is suitable material for the dramatist. His proper subject, on the contrary, is the *becoming* of things—all that is coming to birth as a result of conflicting elements of reality." According to Hebbel, the dramatist's task was "not to relate new *stories,* but to present new *relations.*" He went so far as to maintain that "all characters must be in the right." The question in mature drama is not who is good and who is bad but what important principles or ideas are involved in a dramatic conflict. "Ideas," he wrote, "are to drama what counterpoint is to music; they are in themselves nothing, but they underlie everything the drama represents." It was, in short, imperative for the serious playwright to view dramatic conflicts as historical or historically determined processes.

Interest in historical processes, fortunately, also led Hebbel to the life of his own times in *Maria Magdalena;* and in this play, completed in Paris in 1844, he was not only more successfully a playwright but also more directly a predecessor of the modern drama that became dominant three decades later. In *Maria Magdalena* we have another conflict working itself out within a social context by means of the social attitudes held or reflected by the characters. And since these are middle-class people, Hebbel wrote the play in prose and invested it with the moral code and the interests of middle-class society. As a result, *Maria Magdalena* does not suffer from the remoteness and laboriousness we find in its author's historical plays. The language is very much more natural, the action swifter. Although Hebbel employed the now old-fashioned device of soliloquies, he came close to writing naturalistic drama. He also anticipated Ibsen and his successors, who generally dramatized a large social problem in a domestic situation, by projecting his social conflict through a middle-class home environment which is represented in a process of disintegration. And the sympathy he expresses for Clara, along with his criticism of the pharisaical point of view, places Hebbel in the company of both the romantic and the later realistic critics of middle-class society and its values. *Maria Magdalena* is indisputably a landmark in the evolution of modern drama.

MARIA MAGDALENA

By Friedrich Hebbel

TRANSLATED FROM THE GERMAN BY BARKER FAIRLEY

DRAMATIS PERSONAE

ANTHONY, *a joiner*
HIS WIFE
CLARA, *his daughter*
KARL, *his son*
LEONARD
A SECRETARY

WOLFRAM, *a merchant*
ADAM, *a bailiff*
SECOND BAILIFF
BOY
MAID

THE SCENE: *A town of moderate size*

ACT I. SCENE I.

Room in the master-joiner's house.
Clara. *Her* Mother.

CLARA: Your wedding-dress? Oh, how well it suits you! It might have been made to-day!

MOTHER: Yes, child, the fashion runs on, till it can't get any further, and has to turn back. This dress has gone out of fashion ten times already, and has always come in again.

CLARA: But not quite, this time, mother. The sleeves are too wide. Don't be cross with me now!

MOTHER: [*Smiling*] No, I should be *you* if I were!

CLARA: And so that's what you looked like! But surely you wore a garland, too?

MOTHER: I should think so! Why else do you suppose I tended the myrtle-bush in the flower-pot all these years?

CLARA: I've asked you so many times, and you would never put it on. You always said, "It's not my wedding-dress now, it's my shroud, and not to be played with." I began at last to hate the sight of it, hanging all white there, because it made me think of your death and of the day when the old women would pull it over your head. What've you put it on for, to-day, then?

MOTHER: When you're as ill as I've been, and don't know whether you'll get better or not, lots of things go round in your head. Death is more terrible than people think. Death is bitter-hard. He darkens the world, he blows out all the lights, one after another, that gleam so bright and gay all round us. The dear eyes of husband and children cease to shine, and it grows dim on every side. But death sets a light in the heart, and there it grows clear, and you can see lots—lots that you can't bear to see. . . .

I don't know what wrong I've done. I've trodden God's path, and worked in the house as well as I could. I've brought up your brother and you in the fear of the Lord, and eked out what your father earned with the sweat of his brow. And I always managed to have a penny to spare for the poor. If I did turn one away at times because I was cross-tempered, or because there were too many of them, it was no misfortune for him, for I was sure to call him back and do him double. But what's all that worth! We tremble just the same when the last hour threatens. We cringe like worms. We pray to God for our lives, like a servant asking his master to let him do a spoiled job over again, so as not to come short on pay-day.

CLARA: Do stop that, mother dear, it exhausts you.

MOTHER: Child, it does me good. Am I not strong and healthy again? Didn't God simply call me to make me see that my garment was not yet spotless and pure, and didn't He let me turn back at the mouth of the grave, and give me time to adorn myself for the heavenly bridal? He was not as lenient as that to those seven virgins in the Gospel that I made you read to me last night. That's why I've put this dress on to-day, to go to holy communion in. I wore it on the day when I made my best and purest vows. Let it remind me of those I didn't keep.

CLARA: You are talking just as you did in your illness!

SCENE II.

KARL: [*Enters*] Good-morning, mother. Now, Clara, how would you fancy me, suppose I weren't your brother?

CLARA: A gold chain? Where've you got that?

KARL: What do I toil and sweat for? Why do I

636

work two hours longer than the others every night? I *like* your cheek.

MOTHER: Quarrelling on a good Sunday morning? For shame, Karl.

KARL: Mother, haven't you got a couple of shillings for me?

MOTHER: I've only got money for housekeeping.

KARL: Well, give me some of that. I won't grumble if the pancakes are a bit thin for the next fortnight. You've done it many a time before. I know that. When you were saving up for Clara's white dress, there was nothing tasty on the table for months. I closed my eyes to it, but I knew very well that a new hat or some showpiece was on the way. Let me have the benefit of it for a change.

MOTHER: You are impudent.

KARL: Well, I've no time now, or else——[*going*].

MOTHER: Where are you going?

KARL: I won't tell you. Then you won't need to blush when the old grizzly asks where I've gone. Tell him you don't know. I don't want your money either. It's a good job there's water in more wells than one. [*Aside*] They always think the worst of me at home, anyway. Why shouldn't I keep them on the tremble, just for fun? Why should I tell them that I shall have to go to church now, unless somebody helps me out?

SCENE III.

CLARA: What does that mean?

MOTHER: Oh, he grieves me to the heart. Yes, your father's right. That's the outcome of it. When he was still a curly-headed boy, he used to ask so sweetly for his piece of sugar, and now he demands money of me just as insolently. I wonder whether he really wouldn't want the money, if I had refused him the sugar. It worries me often. I don't believe he even loves me. Did you ever once see him crying when I was sick?

CLARA: I saw very little of him; scarcely ever, except at meal times. He had a better appetite than I had!

MOTHER: [*Quickly*] That's natural; his work is hard.

CLARA: Of course. Men are like that, too. They are more ashamed of their tears than of their sins. They don't mind showing a clenched fist, but a weeping eye, no! Father's just the same. The afternoon they opened your vein and no blood came, he was sobbing away at his bench. It went right through me. But when I went up to him and stroked him on the cheek, what do you think he said? "See if you can't get this damned shaving out of my eye. There's so much to do and I'm not getting on with it at all."

MOTHER: [*Smiling*] Yes, yes.—I never see Leonard now. How is that?

CLARA: Let him stay away.

MOTHER: I hope you don't see him anywhere except at home here.

CLARA: Do I stay too long when I go to the well at night, that you start suspecting me?

MOTHER: I don't say that. But it was only to keep him from hanging about after you at night in all weathers, that I let him come into the house at all. My mother wouldn't allow that sort of thing, either.

CLARA: I never see him at all.

MOTHER: Have you been sulking with each other? I don't dislike him. He's so steady. If only he *was* somebody! In my time he wouldn't have had to wait long. The gentlefolk used to be as crazy after a good clerk as a lame man after a crutch, for a good clerk was rare then. He was useful to small people like us, too. One day he would compose a New Year's greeting from son to father, and would get as much for the gold lettering alone as would buy a child a doll. The next day the father would send for him, and have him read it aloud to him, secretly, with the door locked, lest he should be caught unawares, and show his ignorance. That meant double pay. Clerks were top-dog then, and raised the price of beer. But it's different now. We old people, who can neither read nor write, are the laughing-stocks of nine-year-old boys. The world's getting cleverer every day. Perhaps the time will come when we shall be ashamed if we can't walk the tight-rope.

CLARA: There goes the church bell.

MOTHER: Well, child, I will pray for you. And as for this Leonard of yours, love him as he loves God, neither more nor less. That's what my old mother said to me when she was leaving this world, and giving me her blessing. I've kept it long enough and now I'll pass it on to you.

CLARA: [*Giving her a bunch of flowers*] There!

MOTHER: I'm sure that came from Karl.

CLARA: [*Nods, then aside*] I wish it did! If anything is to give her real pleasure, it's got to come from him.

MOTHER: Oh, he's a good boy and loves his mother. [*Goes*]

CLARA: [*Looking after her through the window*] There she goes. Three times I dreamed she lay in her coffin, and now—— Oh these malicious dreams, they clothe themselves in our fears to terrify our hopes. I'll never give heed to a dream again. I'll never again take pleasure in a good one, and then I won't have to worry about the evil one that follows it. How firm and sure is her step! She's already near the church-yard. I wonder who'll be the first to meet her—not that it matters, but——[*starting in terror*]. The grave-digger! He has just dug a grave and is climbing out of it. She's nodded to him, and is looking down into the dark hole with a smile. Now she's thrown the flowers in, and is going into church. [*Music is heard*] They're singing: "Now thank we all our God." [*Folding her hands*] Yes! yes! If mother had died, I'd never have been happy again, for—— [*looking towards heaven*]. But Thou art gracious,

Thou art merciful! I wish I had a faith like the Catholics, so that I could give Thee something. I would empty my money-box and buy Thee a lovely golden heart and wreathe it with roses. Our clergyman says that gifts are nothing in Thy eyes, for all is Thine, and we should not try to give Thee what Thou hast. But then, everything in the house belongs to father, and yet he's pleased when I buy him a kerchief with his own money, and embroider it neatly and put it on his plate on his birthday. Yes, he honours me by wearing it on special holidays, Christmas or Whitsuntide. Once I saw a tiny little Catholic girl bringing her cherries to the altar. How I loved to see her! They were the first of the year, and I could see how she longed to eat them. But still she fought against her innocent desire, and threw them down quickly to make an end of temptation. The priest, saying Mass, had just raised the chalice, and looked frowningly at her, and the child hurried away terrified, but the Virgin over the altar smiled down so tenderly, as if she would have liked to step out of her frame, run after the child, and kiss her. I did it for her. There's Leonard. Ah!

SCENE IV.

LEONARD: [*Outside*] Are you dressed?

CLARA: Why so tender, so thoughtful? I'm not a princess.

LEONARD: [*Coming in*] I didn't think you were alone. As I went past, I thought I saw Barbara from next-door at the window.

CLARA: That's why, then, is it?

LEONARD: You are always cross. A fellow can stay away for a fortnight; it can have rained and shone again ten times over; but each time I see *you*, there's always the same old cloud on your face.

CLARA: It used to be so different.

LEONARD: Yes, indeed! If you'd always looked as you do now, we'd never have been good friends.

CLARA: What does it matter?

LEONARD: Oh, you feel as free of me as that, do you? It suits me all right. So [*meaningly*] that toothache of yours the other day was a false alarm?

CLARA: Oh Leonard, you'd no right to do it!

LEONARD: No right to bind what is dearest to me—yourself—by the last bond of all? And just when I stood in danger of losing it! Do you think I didn't see you exchanging quiet glances with the secretary? That was a nice holiday for me! I take you to a dance and——

CLARA: You never stop worrying me. I looked at him, of course. Why should I deny it? but only because of the moustache he's grown at college. It——[*she breaks off*].

LEONARD: Suits him so well, eh? That's what you mean. Oh, you women! You like the mark of the soldier even in the silliest caricature. The little round-faced fop—I hate him! I don't conceal it; he's stood in my way with you long enough;—with that forest of hair in the middle of his face, he looks like a white rabbit trying to hide in a thicket.

CLARA: I haven't praised him yet. You don't need to start running him down.

LEONARD: You still seem to take a warm interest in him.

CLARA: We played together as children, and after that—you know all about it.

LEONARD: Oh yes, I know. That's just the trouble.

CLARA: Well, surely it was natural for me, seeing him again for the first time after so long, to look at him and wonder at——

LEONARD: Why did you blush then, when he looked at you?

CLARA: I thought he was looking to see if the wart on my left cheek had got any bigger. You know I always think that when anybody stares at me, and it makes me blush. The wart seems to grow, whenever it's looked at!

LEONARD: That may be. But it troubled me, and I said to myself: "I'll test her this very night. If she really wants to be my wife, she knows that she's running no risks. If she says No——"

CLARA: Oh, you spoke a wicked, wicked word, when I pushed you away, and jumped up from the seat. The moon that had shone, for my help, right into the arbour, wrapped herself cunningly in the wet clouds. I tried to hurry away, but something held me back. At first I thought it was you, but it was the rose-tree, whose thorns had caught my dress like teeth. You reviled me, until I could no longer trust my own heart. You stood before me, like one demanding a debt. And I—— O God!

LEONARD: I can't regret it. I know that it was the only way of keeping you. Your old love had opened its eyes and I could not close them fast enough.

CLARA: When I got home, I found my mother ill, dangerously ill. Smitten down suddenly, as if by an unseen hand. Father had wanted to send for me, but she wouldn't let him, because of spoiling my pleasure. Imagine how I felt, when I heard that! I kept out of the way. I didn't dare to touch her; I trembled. She thought it was just a child's concern, and motioned me to go to her. When I went up to her slowly, she pulled me down and kissed my desecrated mouth. I gave way altogether, I wanted to confess to her. I wanted to tell her what I thought and felt: "*I'm* to blame for your lying there like that." I did so, too, but tears and sobs choked my words; she took father's hand and said, looking at me so happily—"What a tender heart!"

LEONARD: She's well again now. I came to congratulate her, and—what do you think?

CLARA: And what?

LEONARD: To ask your father for your hand in marriage!

CLARA: Ah!

LEONARD: Isn't that all right?

CLARA: Right? It would be the death of me, if I were not soon your wife. But you don't know my father. He doesn't know why we're in a hurry. He can't know, and we can't tell him. And he's told me a hundred times that he will only give me, as he puts it, to a man who has both love in his heart and bread in his cupboard. He will say, "Wait a year or two, my son," and then what will you answer?

LEONARD: Why, you little silly, that difficulty's all over. I've got the job, I'm cashier now.

CLARA: You're cashier? And what about the other candidate, the parson's nephew?

LEONARD: He came drunk into the exam., bowed to the stove instead of to the mayor, and knocked three cups off the table when he sat down. You know how hot-tempered the old boy is. "Sir!" he began, but he bit his lips and controlled himself, although his eyes flashed through his spectacles like two snakes ready to spring, and all his face was working. Then came the arithmetic and ha! ha! my opponent used a system of tables he had invented himself, and got quite original results. "He's all astray," said the mayor, and held out his hand to me with a glance that told me the job was mine. I put it reverently to my lips, although it stank of tobacco, and here's the appointment, signed and sealed.

CLARA: That's a——

LEONARD: Surprise, eh? Well, it's not altogether an accident. Why do you think I never turned up here for a whole fortnight?

CLARA: How do I know? I should think because we quarrelled on that last Sunday.

LEONARD: I was cunning enough to bring that little quarrel about on purpose, so that I might stay away without causing you too much surprise.

CLARA: I don't understand you.

LEONARD: I dare say not. I made use of the time in paying court to that little humpbacked niece of the mayor's, who has so much weight with him. She's his right hand, just as the bailiff's his left. Don't misunderstand me! I didn't say pleasant things to her directly, except for a compliment on her hair, which is red, as you know. I only said a few things, that pleased her, about you.

CLARA: About me?

LEONARD: Yes, why should I keep it back? It was all done with the best intentions. You talk as if I had never been in earnest about you, as if—— Enough! That affair lasted till I'd got *this* in my hand, and she'll know which way I meant it, the credulous little man-mad fool, when she hears the banns read in church.

CLARA: Leonard!

LEONARD: Child! Child! Just you be as harmless as a dove, and I'll be wise as a serpent. Then we shall fulfil the words of the Gospel, for man and wife are but one. [*He laughs*] And it wasn't altogether an accident either, that young Herrmann was drunk at the most important moment of his life. I'm sure you never heard that he went in for boozing!

CLARA: Not a word.

LEONARD: That made it all the easier. Three glasses did it. Two chums of mine went up to him and clapped him on the back. "Can we congratulate you?" "Not yet." "Oh, but it's all settled beforehand. Your uncle——" And then—"drink, pretty creature, drink!" When I was on my way here this morning, he was standing by the river looking gloomily over the parapet of the bridge. I grinned and nodded, and asked him whether he'd dropped anything into the water. "Yes," said he, without looking up, "and perhaps it's as well for me to jump in after it."

CLARA: You wretch! Get out of my sight!

LEONARD: Yes? [*Pretending to go*]

CLARA: O my God, and I am chained to this man!

LEONARD: Don't be childish. Just one word more in confidence. Has your father still got that two hundred pounds with the apothecary?

CLARA: I know nothing about it.

LEONARD: You know nothing about so important a matter?

CLARA: Here comes father.

LEONARD: You understand, the apothecary is supposed to be going bankrupt. That's why I asked.

CLARA: I must go into the kitchen. [*Goes*]

LEONARD: [*Alone*] In that case there's nothing to be got here. I can well believe it, for, if an extra letter happened to get on old Anthony's gravestone by mistake, his ghost would walk till it was scratched out. That's the sort of man he is. He'd think it dishonest to own more of the alphabet than was due to him.

SCENE V.

[*Enter* Anthony]

ANTHONY: Good morning, Mr. Cashier. [*Takes his hat off and puts on a woollen cap*] Will you allow an old man to keep his head covered?

LEONARD: You've heard, then——

ANTHONY: Heard last night. When I was on my way, in the evening, to measure the old miller for his last abode, I heard two good friends of yours railing against you. So I said to myself "Leonard, at any rate, hasn't broken his neck!" I got particulars at the dead man's house from the sexton, who had arrived there before me, to console the widow, and to get drunk at the same time.

LEONARD: And yet you let Clara wait till I told her?

ANTHONY: If you weren't in a hurry to give her the pleasure, why should I be? I don't light any candles in my house except my own. Then I know that nobody can come and blow them out, just when we're enjoying them.

LEONARD: You surely don't think that I——

ANTHONY: Think? About you? About anybody? I shape planks with my tools, I'll admit, but never a man with my thoughts. I got over that sort of folly long ago. When I see a tree in leaf, I say to myself: It'll soon be in bloom. And when it's in bloom: Now it'll bear fruit. I don't get taken in there, so I stick to the old custom. But I think nothing about men, nothing at all, neither bad nor good. So that when they disappoint first my fears and then my hopes, I don't need to go red and white in turn. I simply get knowledge and experience out of them, and I take the cue from my pair of eyes. They can't think either, they just see. I thought I knew all about you already, but now you're here again, I have to admit that I only half knew you.

LEONARD: Master Anthony, you've got it the wrong way about. A tree depends on wind and weather, but a man has rule and law inside of him.

ANTHONY: Do you think so? Ah, we old men owe a lot to death, for letting us knock about so long among you young fellows and giving us the chance to get educated. Once upon a time the world was foolish enough to believe that the father was there to educate the son. Now, it's the other way. The son has to put the finishing touches on his father, lest the old simpleton should disgrace himself in the grave before the worms. Thank God, I've an excellent teacher in this boy, Karl, of mine; he wages ruthless war upon my prejudices, and doesn't spoil the old fellow with too much indulgence. Only this morning, for instance, he's taught me two new lessons. And very skilfully too, without so much as opening his mouth, without even showing himself; in fact, just by not doing so. In the first place, he has shown me that you don't need to keep your word; secondly, that it's unnecessary to go to church and freshen up your memory of God's commandments. Last night he promised me he'd go, and I counted on it, for I thought, "He'll surely want to thank the Creator for sparing his mother's life." But he wasn't there, and I was quite comfortable in my pew, which indeed is a bit small for two. I wonder how he'd like it, if I were to act on this new lesson of his at once, and break my word to him? I promised him a new suit on his birthday, and so I have a good chance of seeing what pleasure he would take in a ready pupil. But—prejudice, prejudice! I shan't do it.

LEONARD: Perhaps he wasn't well——

ANTHONY: That may be. I only need to ask my wife. She'll be sure to tell me he's sick. She tells me the truth about everything on earth except that boy. And even if he isn't sick—there you young men have the pull over us old folks again. You can do your devotions anywhere; you can say your prayers when you're out bird-snaring, or taking a walk, or even in a public-house. " 'Our Father, which art in Heaven'— Good-morning, Peter, coming to the dance to-night? —'Hallowed be Thy Name'—Yes, you may smile, Katherine, but you'll see—'Thy will be done'—By God, I'm not shaved yet,' "—and so on to the end, when you pronounce your own blessing, since you're just as much a man as the parson, and there's as

much virtue in a blue coat as in a black. I've nothing against it. If you want to insert seven drinks between the seven petitions, what does it matter? I can't prove to any one that beer and religion don't go together. Perhaps it will get into the prayer-book some day, as a new way of taking communion. But I, old sinner that I am, am not strong enough to follow the fashion. I can't catch devotion in the street, as if it were a cockchafer. The twittering of sparrows and swallows cannot take the place of the organ for me. If my heart is to be uplifted, I must first hear the heavy iron church-doors clang behind me, and imagine they are the gates of the world. The high walls with their narrow windows, that only let the bright bold light of the world filter dimly through, must close in upon me, and in the distance I must see the dead-house with the walled-in skull. Well—better is better.

LEONARD: You take it too seriously.

ANTHONY: Without doubt. And I must admit as an honest man that it didn't work to-day. I lost the mood for worship when I was in church, because of the empty seat beside me, and found it again outside, under the pear-tree in my garden. You are surprised? See, I was going home sad and depressed, like a man that's had his harvest spoilt; for children are just like land, you sow good seeds and get tares in return. I stood still under the pear-tree, that the caterpillars have devoured. "Yes," I thought, "my boy is like this tree, bare and empty." Then I seemed to get thirsty, and felt as if I must go to the inn and have a drink. I was deceiving myself. It wasn't beer that I wanted. I wanted to find my boy and rate him, and I knew for certain I should find him there. I was just going, when the wise old tree dropped a juicy pear at my feet, as if to say: Quench your thirst with that, and don't insult me by comparing me with your knave of a son. I thought better of it, ate the pear and went home.

LEONARD: Do you know that the apothecary is going bankrupt?

ANTHONY: It doesn't concern me.

LEONARD: Not at all?

ANTHONY: Yes, it does! I am a Christian, and the man has children.

LEONARD: He has more creditors than children. Children are creditors too, in a way.

ANTHONY: Lucky the man who has neither the one nor the other!

LEONARD: But I thought you yourself——

ANTHONY: That's settled long ago.

LEONARD: You're a cautious man. Of course, you called in your money—as soon as you saw that the old herbalist was going downhill.

ANTHONY: Yes, I've no need to tremble at losing what I lost long ago.

LEONARD: You're joking.

ANTHONY: It's a fact.

CLARA: [Looking in] Did you call, father?

ANTHONY: Are your ears burning already? We weren't talking about you.

CLARA: The newspaper! [*Goes*]

LEONARD: You're a philosopher.

ANTHONY: What does that mean?

LEONARD: You can control yourself.

ANTHONY: I sometimes wear a millstone round my neck instead of a collar. That has stiffened my backbone!

LEONARD: Let him who can do likewise!

ANTHONY: Whoever has so worthy a helper, as I appear to have in you, can surely dance under his burden. Why, you've gone quite pale! There's sympathy for you!

LEONARD: I hope you don't mistake me.

ANTHONY: Certainly not. [*Rapping on a cupboard*] Funny thing that you can't see through wood, isn't it?

LEONARD: I don't understand you.

ANTHONY: How foolish grandfather Adam was to take Eve, although she was stark naked and didn't even bring a fig-leaf with her. We two, you and I, would have whipped her out of paradise for a vagabond. Don't you think so?

LEONARD: You are annoyed at your son. I came to ask for your daughter's——

ANTHONY: Stop! Perhaps I might not say "No."

LEONARD: I hope you won't. And I'll tell you what I think. Even the holy patriarchs did not despise their wives' dowries. Jacob loved Rachel and courted her for seven years, but he was pleased, too, with the fat rams and ewes that he earned in her father's service. It does him no disgrace, to my mind, and I don't wish to shame him by doing better. I should like to have seen your daughter bring twenty pounds with her. Naturally. It would have been all the better for her, for when a girl brings her bed with her, she doesn't need to start carding wool and spinning yarn. But she hasn't got it, and what does it matter? We'll taken Lenten soup for Sunday's dinner, and feast on our Sunday joint at Christmas. We can manage that way.

ANTHONY: [*Shakes his hand*] You speak well, and the Lord approves your words. So I'll try to forget that my daughter put a cup for you on the tea-table every evening, and you never came for a fortnight. And now that you're going to be my son-in-law, I'll tell you where my two hundred pounds have gone.

LEONARD: [*Aside*] So he has lost them. Well, I shan't need to take any sauce from the old werewolf, when he's my father-in-law.

ANTHONY: I had a hard time when I was young. I wasn't born a prickly hedgehog any more than you were, but I've turned into one by degrees. At first all my prickles were turned inside and people for fun used to nip my smooth sensitive skin and laugh when I shrank back, because the points went into my heart and bowels. But that wouldn't do for me. I turned my skin inside out and now the prickles get into their fingers, and I have peace.

LEONARD: [*Aside*] The devil's own peace, I should think!

ANTHONY: My father never rested night and day, and worked himself into his grave when he was only thirty. My poor mother made a living, as best she could, with her spinning-wheel. I grew up without any schooling. When I got bigger and still could earn nothing, I should have liked at the least to go without eating. But if I did pretend to be sick at dinner-time and push my plate back, what was the good? My stomach was too much for me at supper-time, and I had to be well again. My greatest sorrow was my own clumsiness. I would quarrel with myself over it, as if I was to blame, as if I had provided myself in the womb with nothing but wolf's teeth and deliberately left behind me every useful craft and quality. I was fit to blush when the sun shone on me. As soon as I was confirmed, the man they buried yesterday, old Master Gebhardt, came into our little room. He wrinkled his brow and twisted his face, as he always did when he had something good in his mind; then he said to my mother: "Have you brought this boy into the world to eat your head off?" I was just about to cut myself a slice of bread, but I felt so ashamed that I quickly put the loaf back in the cupboard. My mother was annoyed at his words. She stopped her wheel, and retorted hotly that her son was a good boy. "Well, we shall see," replied old Gebhardt, "if he wants, he can come now, just as he stands, into my workshop. I want no apprentice money. He'll get his food, and I'll see to his clothes, too. And if he's willing to get up early and go to bed late, he'll get a chance now and then of earning a little money for his old mother." Mother began to cry and I began to dance, and when at last we started to speak, the old man closed his ears and motioned to me to come. I didn't need to put my hat on, because I hadn't got one. I followed him without even saying good-bye to my mother, and when I got half-an-hour off on my first Sunday to go and see, he sent her half a ham with me. God's peace on his grave! I can still hear him, in that half-angry way of his: "By Gosh, under your coat with it, for fear my wife should see!"

LEONARD: You can weep, then?

ANTHONY: [*Wiping his eyes*] Yes, I hardly dare let myself think of that. However well the source of tears in me is stopped up, that opens it afresh every time. Well, it's a good thing, too. If ever I get dropsy, there'll be the less water to tap off. [*Changing his tone*] What do you think? If you went on a Sunday afternoon to smoke a pipe with the man you owed everything to, and found him all dazed and confused, with a knife in his hand, the very knife you had cut him his bread with hundreds of times, and bleeding at the throat and holding a cloth to the wound in terror——

LEONARD: Is *that* how his end came?

ANTHONY: And if you came in time to save him and help him, not just by taking his knife from him and binding up his wound, but by giving him a dirty two hundred pounds you'd saved up, all in secret, because else he wouldn't take it,—what would you do?

LEONARD: Being a free man without wife or child, I'd sacrifice the money.

ANTHONY: And if you had ten wives, like the Turks, and as many children as were promised to Father Abraham, and you had only a minute to decide in, you'd—well, anyway you're going to be my son-in-law. Now you know where the money is. I can tell you to-day because my old master was buried yesterday. A month ago I'd have kept it to myself on my deathbed. I put the IOU under the dead man's head before they nailed up his coffin. If I could write, I would have put "Honourably paid" at the bottom, but all I could do in my ignorance was to tear the paper lengthways. Now he'll sleep in peace, and I hope I shall too, when I stretch myself some day by his side.

SCENE VI.

MOTHER: [Comes in quickly] Do you know me still?

ANTHONY: [Pointing to the wedding-dress] The frame has kept well, but the picture's gone a bit. There seem to have been a lot of spiders' webs on it. Well. the time was long enough!

MOTHER: Haven't I a frank husband? But I don't need to praise him in particular. Frankness is the virtue of all husbands.

ANTHONY: Are you sorry that you had more gilt on you at twenty than at fifty?

MOTHER: Certainly not. If it weren't so, I'd be ashamed of us both.

ANTHONY: Well there, give me a kiss. I have had a shave and I'm in a better temper than usual.

MOTHER: I'll say "Yes" just to see if you still know how to kiss. It's a long time since you thought of trying.

ANTHONY: Dear old mother. I won't wish that you should close my eyes. It's a hard task, and I'll do it for you instead. I'll do you that last service of love. But you must give me time, do you hear? Time to prepare and steel myself, and not make a mess of it. It's far too soon yet.

MOTHER: Thank God, we are to be together a little longer.

ANTHONY: I hope so, indeed. Why your cheeks are quite rosy again!

MOTHER: A queer little man, that new grave-digger. He was digging a grave, as I was going to church this morning. I asked him whom it was for. "For whom God will," says he, "perhaps for myself. I might have the same experience as my grandfather. He once had got an extra grave ready, and that night when he was going home from the inn, he fell in and broke his neck."

LEONARD: [Who has been reading the paper all the time] The fellow doesn't belong to this town; he can tell us any lies he likes.

MOTHER: I asked him why he didn't wait till there was an order for a grave. "I'm invited to a wedding to-day," he said, "and I'm prophet enough to know that I shall feel it in my head to-morrow morning. Then somebody's sure to have gone and died, just to spite me, and that would mean getting up early without finishing my sleep."

ANTHONY: "You fathead," I'd have said, "what if the grave doesn't fit?"

MOTHER: That's what I said. But he can shake out sharp answers as quick as the devil can shake out fleas. "I've made it to fit Weaver John," says he, "he's as big as King Saul, head and shoulders above everybody else. So anybody can come that likes— he won't find his house too small for him. And if it's too big, it'll hurt no one but me. I'm an honourable man and won't charge for an inch over the coffin-length." I threw my flowers in, and said, "Now it's occupied."

ANTHONY: I think the fellow was only joking, but that's bad enough. Digging graves in advance is like setting death-traps. The scoundrel ought to be sacked for it. [To Leonard, who is reading] Any news? Is some kind creature looking for a poor widow who could do with a few pounds? Or is it the other way about, the widow looking for the friend that will give her them?

LEONARD: There's news of a jewel-robbery. Funny thing! It shows that, although times are bad, there are still people among us that own jewels.

ANTHONY: A jewel-robbery! At whose house?

LEONARD: At Wolfram's, the merchant's.

ANTHONY: Wolfram's—impossible! That's where Karl went to polish a desk a few days ago.

LEONARD: They were stolen from the desk, right enough.

MOTHER: [To Anthony] May God forgive you for saying that!

ANTHONY: You're right. It was a base thought.

MOTHER: I must say, that to your son you're only half a father.

ANTHONY: We won't talk about that to-day, wife.

MOTHER: Do you think he must be bad, just because he's different from you?

ANTHONY: Where is he now? It's long past dinner-time. I'll wager the food is all boiled away or dried up, because Clara has secret orders not to set the table till he comes.

MOTHER: Where do you think he is? At most he'll be playing skittles. He has to go to the farthest alley, so that you won't find him, and then of course it takes him a long time to get back. I don't know what you have against the game; it's harmless enough.

ANTHONY: Against the game? I've nothing at all against it. Fine gentlemen must have their amusements. But for the kings of spades and diamonds, real kings would often find time heavy on their hands. And if there were no skittles—who knows?—dukes and princes might be rolling our heads about. But there's no worse folly for a working man than to waste his hard-earned money on games. What a man has laboured for by the sweat of his brow, that he should honour and value highly, unless he wants to lose his balance altogether and grow to despise his honest work. How it hurts me to throw away a shilling!

[*Door bell rings*]

MOTHER: There he comes.

SCENE VII.

[*Enter* Bailiff Adam *and* Second Bailiff]

ADAM: [*To* Anthony] Now you may go and pay your bet. *People in red coats with blue facings* [*with emphasis*] would never come into *your* house! Eh? Well, here you have two of us. [*To* Second Bailiff] Why don't you keep your hat on, as I do? Who's going to stand on ceremony, when he's among his equals?

ANTHONY: Equals, you cur?

ADAM: You're right, we're not among equals. Knaves and thieves are not our equals! [*Pointing to the cupboard*] Open that! And then three paces back! Don't juggle anything out of it.

ANTHONY: What! What!

CLARA: [*Bringing cloth for dinner*] Should I—— [*stops*].

ADAM: [*Showing a paper*] Can you read writing?

ANTHONY: How should I, when my schoolmaster couldn't?

ADAM: Well, listen! Your son has been stealing jewels. We've got the thief already. Now we are going to search the house.

MOTHER: Jesus!—[*falls down; dies*].

CLARA: Oh, mother, mother! Look at her eyes!

LEONARD: I'll fetch a doctor.

ANTHONY: No need.—That's the last face. I've seen it hundreds of times. Good-night, Teresa. You died when you heard it. That shall be put on your grave-stone.

LEONARD: Perhaps I'd better—— [*going*]. How awful! But it's a good thing for me. [*Goes out*]

ANTHONY: [*Takes out his keys and throws them on the floor*] There! Open up! Drawers and cup-boards! Bring me an axe! I've lost the key of the chest! Oho! Knaves and thieves, eh! [*Pulls out his pockets*] I don't find anything here!

SECOND BAILIFF: Master Anthony, compose your-self! Everybody knows you're the honestest man in the town.

ANTHONY: Is that so? [*Laughing*] Yes, I've used up all the honesty there was in the family. Poor boy! There was none left for him. She, too—[*pointing to the dead body*]—was far too respectable. Who knows whether my daughter—— [*Suddenly to* Clara] What do you think, my innocent child?

CLARA: Oh, father!

SECOND BAILIFF: [*To* Adam] Have you no sym-pathy?

ADAM: Sympathy? Am I feeling in the old man's pockets? Am I making him take his socks off and turn up his boots? I meant to begin with that, for I hate him, as I never hated, since that affair at the inn, when he—— You know the story and you'd have been insulted too, if you'd any self-respect in you. [*To* Clara] Where's your brother's room?

CLARA: [*Pointing*] At the back.

[Bailiffs *go off*]

Father, he's innocent! He must be! He's your son, and he's my brother!

ANTHONY: Innocent, when he's murdered his mother? [*Laughs*]

GIRL: [*With letter to* Clara] From Mr. Leonard. [*Goes out*]

ANTHONY: You don't need to read it. He's deserted you. [*Claps his hands*] Bravo, you rascal!

CLARA: [*After reading*] My God, he has!

ANTHONY: Never mind him.

CLARA: But, father, I must!

ANTHONY: Must! Must! What do you mean? Are you——

[Bailiffs *return*]

ADAM: [*Maliciously*] Seek and ye shall find!

SECOND BAILIFF: [*To* Adam] What are you think-ing about? Was it true, then?

ADAM: Hold your jaw. [*Both go out*]

ANTHONY: He's innocent, and you, you——

CLARA: Oh, father, you're awful!

ANTHONY: [*Takes her by the hand, very gently*] My daughter, Karl is a bungler after all. He killed his mother, but what of that? His father's left alive. You help him out! You can't expect him to do it all by himself. You finish *me* off! The old tree looks pretty knotty yet, doesn't it? But it's shaking already. It won't give you much trouble to fell it. You don't need an axe. You've a pretty face. I've never praised you before, but let me tell you now, to give you courage and confidence. Your eyes and nose and mouth are sure to please; you turn into—you under-stand!—but it seems to me you're that way al-ready.

CLARA: [*Almost demented, flings herself with up-raised arms at the dead woman's feet, and calls out like a child*] Oh, mother, mother!

ANTHONY: Take the hand of the dead and swear to me that you are as you should be.

CLARA: I—swear—that—I—will—never—bring—shame—upon—you.

ANTHONY: Good. [*Puts his hat on*] It's a fine day. We'll run the gauntlet, up street and down street.

[*Goes out*]

ACT II. SCENE I.

SCENE—*Same.*
[Anthony *gets up from table.* Clara *begins to clear away dishes*]

ANTHONY: Have you still no appetite?

CLARA: I've had enough, father.

ANTHONY: Enough of nothing!

CLARA: I had a bite in the kitchen.

ANTHONY: A poor appetite means a bad conscience. Well, we shall see. Or was there poison in the soup, as I dreamed last night, a bit of wild hemlock that was plucked with the other herbs by mistake? That would be a wise thing for you to do.

CLARA: Almighty God!

ANTHONY: Forgive me, I—— To the devil with that pale, suffering look of yours, stolen from the Mother of Christ! Young people should look rosy. There's only one man who has the right to parade a face like that, and he doesn't do it. Ho! A box on the ears for every man that says "Uh" when he cuts his finger. Nobody has the right to now, for here's a man that—— Self-praise is no recommendation, but what did I do, when our neighbour was going to nail the lid on your mother's coffin?

CLARA: You snatched the hammer from him and did it yourself, and said, "This is my masterpiece." The choir-master, who was singing the funeral-hymn at the door with the choristers, thought you'd gone mad.

ANTHONY: Mad! [*Laughs*] Mad! Ay, ay, it's a wise man that cuts his own throat when the time comes. Mine seems to be too tough, or else—— A man lives in his corner of the world, and imagines he's sitting by the fireside in a comfortable inn, when suddenly some one puts a light on the table, and behold, he's in a robber's den, and it goes bang! bang! on all sides. But no matter. Luckily my heart's made of stone.

CLARA: So it is, father.

ANTHONY: What do you know about it? Do you think you have any right to join your curses to mine, because that clerk of yours left you in the lurch? Some one else will take you for a walk on Sunday afternoons, some one else will tell you that your cheeks are red and your eyes are blue, some one else will make you his wife, if you deserve it. But when you've borne your burden honourably for thirty years, without complaining, when you've patiently endured suffering and bereavement and all manner of misfortune, and then your son, who should be making a soft pillow for you in your old age, comes and heaps disgrace on you, till you feel like calling to the earth, "Swallow me, if you can stomach me, for I am more foul than you"—*then* you may pour out all the curses that I am holding back; then you may tear your hair and beat your breast. That's the privilege you shall have over me, since you're a woman.

CLARA: Oh, Karl!

ANTHONY: I often wonder what I shall do when I see him again, when he comes in some evening before we've got the lamp lit, with his head shaved, prison-fashion, and stutters out "Good-evening" with his hand glued to the door-latch. I shall do something, I know, but what? [*Grinding his teeth*] And if they keep him ten years, he'll find me still. I shall live till then, I know that. Mark you, Death! From now on I'm a stone to your scythe. Sooner shall it be shattered in your hands, than move me an inch.

CLARA: [*Taking his hand*] Father, do lie down for half an hour.

ANTHONY: To dream you are in childbed, eh? And jump up and lay hold of you and then remember, and say I didn't know what I was doing? Thank you, no. My sleep has dismissed its magician and hired a prophet instead, who shows me fearful things with his bloody fingers. I don't know how it is. Anything seems possible to me now. Ugh! The future makes me shudder, like a glass of water seen through a microscope—is that right, Mr. Choirmaster, you've spelt it for me often enough? I did that once at the fair in Nürnberg, and couldn't take a drink the whole day after it. I saw our Karl last night with a pistol in his hand. When I looked at him more closely, he fired. I heard a cry, but I couldn't see anything for smoke. When the smoke cleared, there was no split skull to be seen, but in the meantime my fine son had become a rich man. He was standing counting gold pieces from one hand into the other, and his face—devil take me if a man could look more placid, if he had slaved all day and just locked up his work-shop. We might look out for that. We might first sit in judgment, and then go ourselves before the greatest judge of all.

CLARA: Do calm yourself!

ANTHONY: Cure yourself, you mean. Why am I sick? Give me the healing draught, physician! Your brother is the worst of sons. You be the best of daughters. Here I stand before the world like a worthless bankrupt. I owed it a worthy man, to take the place of this invalid here, and I've pawned off a rogue on it. You be the woman your mother was. Then people will say: "It wasn't the parents' fault that the boy went wrong, for the daughter is going the right road and leads the way for others." [*With fearful coldness*] And I'll do my share. I'll make it easier for you than the others. The moment I see people pointing their fingers at you,—I shall—[*passing his finger over his throat*] shave myself, and, this I'll swear, I shall shave myself away altogether. You can say a fright did it—a horse ran away in the street, or the cat knocked a chair over, or a mouse ran up my legs. Those that know me will have their doubts, because I'm not particularly nervous, but what does it matter? I can't go on living in a world where only sympathy keeps people from spitting when they see me.

CLARA: Merciful God, what shall I do?

ANTHONY: Nothing at all, my child. I'm too hard on you. I know it well. Nothing at all. Just stay as you are and it will be all right. I've suffered such injustice that I must practise it, or go under altogether, when it takes hold of me. I was crossing the road just now when Small-pox John came along, that vagabond I had locked up years ago, after he'd robbed me three times. There was a time when the wretch didn't dare to look at me, but now he walks up coolly and holds out his hand. I wanted to box his ears, but thought better of it and didn't even spit. Aren't we cousins of a week's standing? And isn't it right for relations to greet one another? Our good man, the parson, came to see me yesterday, and said a man was responsible for nobody but himself, and it was unchristian arrogance in me to make myself answerable for my son, or else Adam would have to take it as much to heart as I. O God, I well believe that it doesn't disturb the arch-father's peace in paradise, when one of his great-great-grandchildren goes robbing and murdering, but didn't he tear his hair over Cain? No, no, it is too much! At times I feel like looking to see if my shadow hasn't gone blacker. I can bear anything, and I've proved it, anything but disgrace. Put as much weight round my neck as you like, but don't cut through the nerve that holds me together.

CLARA: But, father, Karl hasn't confessed to it yet, and they didn't find anything on him.

ANTHONY: What do I care about that? I went round the town, and inquired about his debts in all the pubs. I found that he owed more than he'd have earned from me in a quarter-year, even if he'd worked three times as hard as he did. Now I know why he used to work two hours later at night than I did, and got up earlier, too. But he saw it was no good. It was too much trouble, or it took too long, so he seized the opportunity when it came.

CLARA: You always think the worst of Karl. You always did. Do you remember how——?

ANTHONY: You talk just like your mother. And I'll answer you as I used to answer her—by saying nothing.

CLARA: And what if Karl gets off? What if they find the jewels again?

ANTHONY: Then I'd hire a lawyer, and I'd sell my last shirt to find out whether the mayor had the right to imprison the son of an honourable man, or not. If so, I'd submit, for if it can happen to anybody, I must put up with it, even though I had to pay a thousand times dearer than others. It was fate, and when God strikes me, I fold my hands and say: "O Lord, thou knowest why." But if it was not so, if that man with the gold chain round his neck overstepped himself, because he couldn't think of anything except that the merchant who lost the jewels was his brother-in-law, then we'd see whether there's a hole in the law. The king knows full well that he must justly repay the obedience and loyalty of his subjects, and would wish least of all to be unfair

to the smallest of them. We'll see then whether he'll stop the hole up for us. But this is all nonsense. It's as easy for your mother to rise from her grave as for that boy to clear himself. I've had no comfort from him, and never shall have. So remember what *you* owe me. Keep your word and then I won't have to keep mine. [*Goes, and turns back*] I shan't be home till late. I'm going to see the old wood-cutter in the hills. He's the only man who looks me in the face as he used to, because he knows nothing yet of my shame. He's deaf. They can't tell him anything without shrieking themselves hoarse, and then he mixes it all up and never gets the truth of it. [*Goes out*]

SCENE II.

CLARA: [*Alone*] O God, O God, have mercy! Have mercy on this old man! Take me! It's the only way to help him. Look! The sunshine lies so golden on the street that the children snatch at it. The birds fly about. Flowers and plants are never weary of growing. Everything lives and wants to live. Thousands of sick people tremble before Thee at this hour, O Death! Those who called to thee in the oppression of the night, because their pain was more than they could bear, now once more find comfort in their beds. To thee I call! Spare him whose soul shrinks furthest from thee! Let him live until this lovely world again seems grey and desolate. Take me for him! I will not shudder at thy chilly hand. I will seize it bravely, and follow thee more gladly than ever any child of man has followed thee before.

SCENE III.

WOLFRAM: [*Enters*] Good morning, Miss Clara, isn't your father at home?

CLARA: He's just gone out.

WOLFRAM: I came to—my jewels have turned up!

CLARA: O father, if only you were here! There are his spectacles! He's forgotten them. If only he'd notice it and come back! How did you find them? Where? At whose house?

WOLFRAM: My wife—Tell me frankly, Miss Clara, did you ever hear anything strange about my wife?

CLARA: I did.

WOLFRAM: That she—[*tapping his forehead*]. What?

CLARA: That she's a bit wrong in the head? Yes.

WOLFRAM: [*Bursting into anger*] My God! My God! All in vain! I've never let a servant go, that I've once taken into my house. I've paid each one double wages and winked at all sorts of carelessness, to purchase their silence, and yet—Oh the false, ungrateful creatures! Oh my poor children! 'Twas for your sakes alone that I tried to conceal it.

CLARA: Don't blame your servants. They're innocent enough. Ever since that day the house next door was burned down, when your wife stood at the open window and laughed and clapped and puffed her cheeks and blew at the flames to fan them, people have had to choose between calling her a she-devil or a madwoman. And hundreds of people saw that.

WOLFRAM: That is true. Well, since the whole town knows my misfortune, it would be folly to ask you to keep it quiet. Listen to me, then. This theft, that your brother is in prison for, was due to insanity.

CLARA: Your own wife ——

WOLFRAM: I've known for a long time that she, who once was the noblest and kindest of women, had turned malicious and spiteful. She rejoices when she sees an accident, if a maid breaks a glass or cuts her finger. But I only discovered to-day, when it was too late, that she steals things about the house, hides money, and destroys papers. I had lain down on the bed and was just dozing off, when I saw her come quietly up to me and stare at me to see if I was asleep. I closed my eyes tight, and then she took my keys out of my waistcoat, that I'd hung over the chair, opened the desk, took some money out, locked the desk again, and put the key back. I was horrified, but I controlled myself and kept quiet. She left the room and I went after her on tip-toe. She went right to the top of the house and threw the money into an old chest of my grandfather's that stood empty there. Then she looked nervously about her on all sides, and hurried away without seeing me. I lit a candle and looked through the chest, and found there my youngest daughter's doll, a pair of the maid's slippers, an account book, some letters and unfortunately—or God be praised, which?—right at the bottom I found the jewels!

CLARA: Oh my poor mother! It is too shameful!

WOLFRAM: God knows, I'd sacrifice the trinkets if I could undo what's done. But I'm not to blame. Much as I honour your father, it was natural for me to suspect your brother. He had polished the desk, and the jewels disappeared with him. I noticed it almost immediately, because I had to get some papers out of the very drawer they were in. But I had no intention of taking severe steps against him. I informed bailiff Adam, and asked him to investigate the matter secretly; but he would not hear of caution. He said it was his duty to report the case at once and he was going to do it. Your brother was a boozer and a borrower, and the bailiff had so much weight with the mayor that he could get him to do anything he wanted. The man seems to be incensed against your father in the extreme. I don't know why. I simply couldn't calm him down. He stuffed his fingers in his ears and shouted as he ran, "If you'd made me a present of the jewels I wouldn't be as pleased as I am now!"

CLARA: The bailiff once set his glass down beside

father's in the inn, and nodded to him to clink with him. Father pulled his away and said: "People in red coats with blue facings used once to have to drink out of wooden cans, and they used to have to stand outside at the window, or, if it rained, in the doorway; and they had to take their hats off, when the landlord served them, and if they wanted to clink with any one, they waited till old Fallmeister came along." O God, O God! Anything can happen in this world! Mother paid for that with her death.

WOLFRAM: Offend no one, and bad men least of all. Where's your father?

CLARA: Gone to see the wood-cutter in the hills.

WOLFRAM: I'll ride out and look for him. I've already been at the mayor's, but didn't find him at home. If I had, your brother would have been here by this time. However, the secretary sent a messenger at once. You'll see him before night. [*Goes out*]

SCENE IV.

CLARA: [*Alone*] Now I ought to be glad. O God! And all I can think of is—"It's only you now." And yet I feel as if I'm bound to think of something soon that will put it all right again.

SCENE V.

SECRETARY: [*Entering*] Good-day.

CLARA: [*Grasping chair as if falling*] He! Oh, if only he hadn't come back——

SECRETARY: Your father's not at home?

CLARA: No.

SECRETARY: I've brought good news. Your brother, Miss—Oh, Clara, I can't go on talking in this stiff way to you, with all the old tables and cupboards and chairs around me; my old acquaintances, that we played among when we were children. Good-day, you there! [*Nodding to a cupboard*] How are you? You haven't changed.—I should think they'd put their heads together and laugh at me for a fool if I don't call you "Clara" as I used to.[1] If you don't like it just think—"The poor chap's dreaming, I'll wake him up—I'll go up to him and show him [*with a toss of head*] I'm not a little girl now"—that was your mark when you were eleven [*pointing to a mark on the door*]—"but a proper grown-up, that can reach the sugar when it's put on the side-board." Do you remember? That was the spot, that was the stronghold, safe from us, even when it stood unlocked. When the sugar was there, we used to play at catching flies, because we couldn't bear to let them, flying about so merrily, get at what we couldn't reach!

CLARA: I thought people forgot all those things

_____

[1] *German:* Ich muss "du" zu dir sagen.

when they had to study hundreds and thousands of books.

SECRETARY: They do forget! I wonder what don't people forget over Justinian and Gaius! Boys, that kick against the A B C so obstinately, know why they do it. They have a sort of feeling that, if they leave the spelling-book alone, they'll never get at cross-purposes with the Bible. It's disgraceful how they tempt the innocent souls with the red cock, and the basket of eggs, till they say A of their own accord —and then there's no holding them! They tear down hill from A to Z, and on and on, till they are in the midst of *Corpus Juris* and realise to their horror what a desert they've been enticed into by those cursèd twenty-six letters, which they first used in their play to make tasty, sweet-scented words like "cherry" and "rose."

CLARA: And what happens then? [*Absently without interest*]

SECRETARY: That depends on temperament. Some work their work through, and come out again into the light of day after three or four years. They're a bit thin and pale, but you can't blame them for that. I belong to them. Others lie down in the middle of the wood. They only want to rest, but they very seldom get up again. One of my own friends has drunk his beer under the shade of the "Lex Julia" for three years. He chose the place on account of the name. It recalls pleasant memories. Others get desperate and turn back. They are the biggest fools of all, for they're only allowed out of one thicket on condition that they plunge straight into another. And there are some there that never come to an end at all! [*Aside*] What stuff a fellow will talk, when he has something in his mind and can't get it out!

CLARA: Everybody is merry and jolly to-day. It must be the fine weather.

SECRETARY: Yes, in weather like this owls fall out of their nests, bats kill themselves, because they feel that the devil made them. The mole bores down into the earth till he loses his way and is stifled, unless he can eat through to the other side and come out in America! To-day every ear of corn puts out a double shoot, and every poppy goes twice as red as usual, if only for shame at not being so. Why should man remain behind? Is he to rob God of the one tribute that this world pays Him, a bright face and a clear eye, that reflects and glorifies all this splendour? Indeed, when I see these lazy-bones crawling out of their houses in the mornings with their brows all wrinkled, and glowering at heaven as if it were a sheet of blotting paper, I often think: "It'll rain soon. God will have to let down His curtain of clouds; He's bound to, so as not to be annoyed by such grimaces." Such fellows ought to be prosecuted as thwarters of holidays and destroyers of harvests. How should you give thanks for life, except by living? Rejoice, bird! else you don't deserve to have a throat!

CLARA: That is true, so true. It makes me want to cry.

SECRETARY: I wasn't saying it against you. I can understand your being a bit down this last week. I know your old man. But, God be praised, I can make you happy again and that's what I'm here for. You'll see your brother again to-night. People won't point their fingers at him, but at those who threw him into prison. Does that earn me a kiss, a sisterly one, if it can't be any other? Or should we play blind-man's-buff for it? If I don't catch you in ten minutes, I'll go without and take a slap on the cheek into the bargain.

CLARA: [*To herself*] I feel as if I'd suddenly grown a thousand years old and time had stopped still over my head. I can't go back and I can't go forward. Oh, this immovable sunshine and all the gaiety about me!

SECRETARY: You don't answer. Of course, I'd forgotten. You're engaged. O girl, why did you do that by me? And yet, have I any right to complain? She is all that's dear and good. All that's dear and good should have reminded me of her. And yet for years she was as good as dead to me. In return she has—— If only it were a *man* whom one could honour and respect! But this Leonard——

CLARA: [*Suddenly hearing the name*] I must go to him. That's it! I'm no longer the sister of a thief! O God, what do I want? He will, he must! Unless he's a very devil, all will be as it was. [*In horror*] As it was. [*To* Secretary] Don't be offended, Frederick.—What makes my legs so heavy all at once?

SECRETARY: Are you going?

CLARA: To see Leonard, where else? I've only this one path to go in all the world.

SECRETARY: You love him then?

CLARA: [*Excitedly*] Love him? It is him or death. Are you surprised that I choose him? I wouldn't do it if I were thinking of myself alone.

SECRETARY: Him or death? Why, girl, this sounds like despair.

CLARA: Don't drive me mad. Don't speak to me! You! I love you! There! There! I'll shout it at you, as if I were already wandering beyond the grave, where no one blushes, where they all sliak past one another, cold and naked, because that terrible, holy nearness of God has laid bare the thoughts of each one down to the roots.

SECRETARY: Me? You still love me? Clara, I suspected it when I saw you outside in the garden.

CLARA: Did you? He did, too. [*Dully, as if alone*] He stood before me. He or I? Oh, my heart, my cursed heart! To prove to him and to myself that it wasn't so, or to crush it if it were so, I did what I now——[*bursting into tears*] O God in Heaven, I would have pity if I were Thou and Thou were I!

SECRETARY: Clara, be my wife! I came to you to look you in the eyes in the old way. If you had not understood my look, I would have gone away and said nothing. Now I offer you all that I am and all that I have. It's little, but it can grow. I'd have been here long ago, only your mother was ill—and then she died.

[Clara *laughs madly*]

Have courage, girl! You gave him your word. Is that on your mind? And I must say it's a devil of a nuisance. How could you——?

CLARA: Oh! Go on asking me how things combine to drive a poor girl mad! Sneers and mockery on all sides when you had gone to college and never wrote. "She's thinking about him." "She thinks his fun was meant seriously." "Does she get letters from him?" And then mother: "Stick to your equals." "Pride goes before a fall." "Leonard's a fine young man; everybody is surprised that you turn your back on him." And then my own heart: "If he's forgotten you, show him that you too——" O God!

SECRETARY: I am to blame, I know. Well, what's hard is not therefore impossible. I'll get you free. Perhaps——

CLARA: Get me free!—Read that! [*throwing him Leonard's letter*]

SECRETARY: [*Reading*] As cashier—your brother—thief—very sorry—I have no choice in view of my office. [*To Clara*] Did he write that the day your mother died? Why, he goes on to express his sympathy at her sudden death!

CLARA: Yes, he did.

SECRETARY: May be be— Dear God, the cats and snakes and other monsters that slipped through your fingers at the creation pleased Beelzebub, so that he made them after you. But he decked them out better than you did. He gave them human form. Now they stand shoulder to shoulder with mankind, and we don't recognise them till they begin to spit and scratch. [*To Clara*] Very good! Excellent! [*Tries to embrace her*] Come! For eternity. With this kiss——

CLARA: [*Sinks into his arms*] No, not for ever. Don't let me fall,—but no kiss.

SECRETARY: Girl, you don't love him, you've got your word back.

CLARA: [*Dully, drawing herself up again*] And yet I must go to him; I must go down on my knees to him and stutter: "Look at my father's white hairs; take me!"

SECRETARY: Unhappy one, do I understand?

CLARA: Yes!

SECRETARY: That's too much for any man. To have to lower one's eyes before *him*—a fellow that's only fit to be spat on. [*Pressing Clara to him*] You poor, poor child!

CLARA: Go, now go!

SECRETARY: [*To himself, broodingly*] Or shoot the dog dead that knows it. If he only had pluck! If he'd only show himself! Could I force him? I wouldn't fear to meet him.

CLARA: I beg you——

SECRETARY: [*Going out*] After dark! [*Turns round and seizes Clara's hand*] Girl, here you stand—[*Turning away*] Thousands of her sex would have cunningly concealed it, only to murmur it into one's ear in some hour of sweet forgetfulness. I feel what I owe you. [*Goes out*]

SCENE VI.

CLARA: [*Alone*] Close, close, my heart! Crush in upon thyself. Let not a drop of blood escape, to fire anew the waning life in my veins. There again something like a hope arose in thee. I realise it now. I thought [*laughing*]—"That's too much for any man." And if—isn't it too much for you? Would you have courage to seize a hand that——? No, no, you would not have such base courage. You would have to bolt yourself into your prison, if they tried to open the gate from without. For ever—Oh, why does it stop, why doesn't it go on grinding for ever, why is there a pause now and then? That's why it seems so long. The tortured one thinks he is having a rest because the torturer has to stop and take breath; you breathe again, like a drowning man in the waves, when the whirlpool that is sucking him down, throws him up again, only to lay hold of him afresh. All he gains from it is a redoubled death-struggle.

"Well, Clara." Yes, father, I'll go, I'll go! Your daughter won't drive you to suicide. I shall soon be his wife, or—O God, no! I'm not begging for happiness, I'm begging for misery, the deepest misery—surely you'll grant me my misery. Away!—where is the letter? [*Taking it*] There are three wells on the road to him. Let me stop at none of them. You have no right to, yet. [*Goes out*]

ACT III. SCENE I.

Leonard's *room*.

LEONARD: [*Writing at a table covered with documents*] There's the sixth sheet since dinner. How fine a man feels when he does his duty! Anybody could come into the room that liked, even the king himself—I would stand up, but I would not be embarrassed. Except for one man, that old joiner. But at bottom he can't trouble me much. Poor Clara! I'm sorry for her. It disturbs me to think of her. If it hadn't been for that one cursed evening. It was more jealousy than love that excited me, and I'm sure she was only yielded to refute my reproaches, for she was as cold as death towards me. She has bad times ahead of her, and I shall have a lot of worry, too. Let each bear his lot. Above all things, I must make sure of that little humpbacked girl and not let her escape me when the storm breaks. Then I shall have the mayor on my side and need fear nothing.

SCENE II.

CLARA: [*Enters*] Good-evening, Leonard.

LEONARD: Clara? [*Aside*] I didn't expect this.

[*Aloud*] Didn't you get my letter? Oh—perhaps your father's sent you to pay the rates. How much is it? [*Turning leaves in a journal*] I ought to know it without looking it up.

CLARA: I've come to give you your letter back. Here it is. Read it again.

LEONARD: [*Reads it very seriously*] It's quite a sensible letter. How can a man, who's in charge of public money, marry into a family that—[*swallowing a word*] your brother belongs to?

CLARA: Leonard!

LEONARD: Perhaps the whole town's wrong? Your brother isn't in prison? Never been in prison? You're not the sister of—of your brother?

CLARA: Leonard, I'm my father's daughter. I don't come as the sister of an innocent man whose name has already been cleared—that's my brother;—nor as a girl who shudders at unmerited shame—for [*in a low voice*] I shudder more at you—I come in the name of the old man who gave me life.

LEONARD: What do you want?

CLARA: Can you ask? Oh, if only I were free to go! My father will cut his throat if I—marry me!

LEONARD: Your father——

CLARA: He has sworn it. Marry me!

LEONARD: Hand and throat are close cousins. They won't damage one another. Don't worry about that.

CLARA: He has sworn it.—Marry me, and then kill me—and I'll thank you more for the one than the other.

LEONARD: Do you love me? Did your heart tell you to come? Am I the man without whom you can't live or die?

CLARA: Answer that yourself.

LEONARD: Can you swear that you love me? That you love me as a girl should love the man who is to be bound to her for life?

CLARA: No, I can't swear that. But this I can swear. That whether I love you or not, you shall never know. I'll serve you, I'll work for you. You don't need to feed me. I'll keep myself. I'll sew and spin in the nighttime for other people. I'll go hungry if I've no work to do. I'll eat my own flesh rather than go to my father and let him notice anything. If you strike me because your dog isn't handy, or you've done away with him, I'll swallow my own tongue rather than utter a sound that could let it out to the neighbours. I can't promise you that my skin shall not show the marks of your lash, but I'll lie about it, I'll say that I ran my head against the cupboard or that the floor was too much polished and I slipped on it. I'll do it before anybody has time to ask me where the blue marks came from. Marry me—I shan't live long. And if it lasts too long for you, and you can't afford to divorce me, buy some poison at the chemist's and put it down as if it were for the rats. I'll take it without even a sign from you, and when I'm dying I'll tell the neighbours I thought it was crushed sugar.

LEONARD: Well, if you expect me to do all that, you won't be surprised if I say no.

CLARA: May God, then, not look upon me too hardly, if I come before He calls me. If it meant only me, I'd bear it; take it patiently, as well-deserved punishment for I don't know what, if people trampled on me in my misery, instead of helping me. I would love my child, even if it bore this man's features. I would weep so before its helpless innocence, that it would not curse and despise its mother when it was older and wiser. But I'm not the only one. And when the judge asks me on the last day "Why did you kill yourself?" it will be an easier question to answer than "Why did you drive your father to it?"

LEONARD: You talk as if you were the first woman and the last. Thousands before you have gone through this and borne it. Thousands after you will get into your plight and accept their fate. Are they all so low, that you want to go away in a corner by yourself? They had fathers too, who invented heaps of new curses when they heard of it, and talked about death and murder. They were ashamed of themselves later on, and did penance for their curses and blasphemies. Why! they sat down and rocked the child, or fanned the flies off him!

CLARA: Oh, I can well believe that you don't understand how anybody in the world should keep his oath!

SCENE III.

BOY: [*Enters*] I've brought some flowers. I haven't to say who's sent them.

LEONARD: Oh, what lovely flowers! [*Strikes his brow*] The devil! That's stupid! *I* should have sent some! How am I to get out of it? I don't know much about these things, and the little girl will notice it; she has nothing else to think about. [*Takes the flowers*] But I won't keep them all. [*To* Clara] These mean remorse and shame, don't they? Didn't you once tell me that?

[Clara *nods*]

LEONARD: [*To the* Boy] Look here, boy. These are for me. I put them here, you see, over my heart. These red ones here, that burn like a glowing fire, you can take back. Do you understand? When my apples are ripe you can come again.

BOY: That's a long time yet! [*Goes out*]

SCENE IV.

LEONARD: Yes, Clara, you talked about keeping one's word, and just because I *am* a man of my word, I am compelled to answer as I do. I broke with you a week ago. You can't deny it. There lies the letter. [*He passes the letter; she takes it mechanically*] I had good reason to; your brother—you say he's been cleared. I'm glad to hear it. In the course of this week I have made promises elsewhere. I had a perfect right to, because you didn't protest at the right time against my letter. In my own mind I was as free as before the law. Now you've come, but I've already given my word and taken somebody else's, yes—[*aside*] I wish it were so!—she's in the same condition as you.—I'm sorry for you—[*stroking back her hair,* Clara *passive, as if she did not notice it*], but you'll understand that the mayor is not to be trifled with.

CLARA: [*Absently*] Trifled with!

LEONARD: Now, you're getting sensible. And as for your father, you can tell him straight to his face that he's to blame for it all. Don't stare at me like that, don't shake your head; it is so, my girl, it is so! Just tell him so; he'll understand and keep quiet, I'll answer for it. [*Aside*] When a man gives away his daughter's dowry, he needn't be surprised if she's left on the shelf. It puts my back up to think of it, and almost makes me wish the old boy was here to be lectured to. Why do I have to be cruel? Simply because he was a fool! Whatever happens, he's responsible for it, that's clear. [*To* Clara] Would you like me to talk to him, myself? I'll risk a black eye for your sake and go to him. He can be as rude as he likes, he can throw the boot-tree at me, but he'll have to swallow the truth, in spite of the belly-ache it gives him, and leave you in peace. Be assured of that. Is he at home?

CLARA: [*Standing up straight*] Thank you. [*Going*]

LEONARD: Should I come across with you? I'm not afraid.

CLARA: I thank you as I would thank a snake that had entwined itself around me, and then left me of its own accord to follow other game. I know that I've been stung, and am only released because it doesn't seem worth while to suck the bit of marrow out of my bones. But I thank you in spite of it, for now I shall have a quiet death. Yes, it is no mockery! I thank you. I feel as if I had seen through your heart into the abyss of hell, and whatever may be my lot in the terrors of eternity, I shall have no more to do with *you,* and that's a comfort! And just as the unhappy creature bitten by a snake is not blamed for opening his veins in horror and disgust and letting his poisoned life well quickly away, so it may be that God of His grace will take pity on me when He sees you and what you've made of me.—If I had no *right* ever to do such a thing, how should I be *able* to do it?—One thing more: my father knows nothing of this, he doesn't suspect, and in order that he may never know, I shall leave this world tonight. If I thought that *you*—— [*Takes a step wildly towards him*] But that's folly. Nothing could suit you better than to see them all stand and shake their heads and vainly ask why it happened.

LEONARD: Such things do happen. What's to be done? Clara!

CLARA: Away, away! He can speak! [*Going*]

LEONARD: Do you think I believe you?

CLARA: No!

LEONARD: If you kill yourself, you kill your child, too.

CLARA: Rather both than kill my father! I know you can't amend sin with sin. But what I do now, comes on my head alone. If I put the knife in his hand, it affects him as well as me. *I* get it in any case. That gives me courage and strength in all my anguish. It'll go well with you on this earth. [*Goes out*]

SCENE V.

LEONARD: [*Alone*] I must marry her! Yet why must I? She's going to do a mad trick to keep her father from doing a mad trick. What need is there for me to stop her by doing a madder trick still? I can't agree to it, not until I see the man before me who'll anticipate me by doing the maddest trick of all, and if he thinks as I do, there'll be no end to the business. That sounds quite clear,—and yet—I must go after her! There's some one at the door. Thank God! Nothing's worse than quarrelling with your own thoughts. A rebellion in your head, when you beget snake after snake and each one devours the other or bites off its tail, is the worst kind of all.

SCENE VI.

SECRETARY: [*Enters*] Good-evening.

LEONARD: The secretary! To what do I owe the honour of——

SECRETARY: You'll soon see, my boy.[2]

LEONARD: You're very familiar.[2] We *were* at school together, of course——

SECRETARY: And perhaps we shall die together. [*Producing pistols*] Do you know how to use these things?

LEONARD: I don't understand you.

SECRETARY: [*Cocks one*] Do you see? That's the way you do it. Then you aim at me, so, and fire.

LEONARD: What are you talking about?

SECRETARY: One of us two has got to die. Die!

LEONARD: Die?

SECRETARY: You know why.

LEONARD: By God, I don't.

SECRETARY: Never mind. You'll remember when you breathe your last.

LEONARD: I haven't the faintest idea.

SECRETARY: Now just come to your senses. Or else I might shoot you down for a mad dog that has bitten what is dearest to me, without knowing what I was doing;—as it is I've got to treat you as an equal for half an hour.

²Using "du."

LEONARD: Don't talk so loud. If any one heard you——

SECRETARY: If any one could hear, you'd have called out long ago. Well?

LEONARD: If it's on the girl's account, I can marry her. I'd half made up my mind to, when she was here.

SECRETARY: She's been and gone again, without seeing you on your knees in remorse and contrition? Come! Come!

LEONARD: I beg you! I will do anything you wish. I'll get engaged to her to-night.

SECRETARY: Either I do that or nobody. And if the world depended on it, you shan't touch the hem of her garment again. Come with me. Into the woods! Look here, I'll take you by the arm and if you make so much as a sound on the road, I'll——[*raising a pistol*]. Believe me. Anyhow we'll take the back way through the gardens, to keep you out of temptation.

LEONARD: One's mine; give it me.

SECRETARY: So that you can throw it away and force me to let you run away, or murder you, what? Have patience till we get to the spot, then I'll divide squarely with you.

LEONARD: [*Accidentally knocks his glass off the table when going out*] Shall I never drink again?

SECRETARY: Buck up, boy, you may come off all right. God and the devil are forever fighting for the world, it seems. Who knows which is master? [*Takes his arm; both go out*]

SCENE VII.

Room in Anthony's *house. Evening.*

KARL: [*Enters*] No one at home! If I didn't know the rat-hole under the threshold where they keep the key, when they all go out, I wouldn't have been able to get in. Well, that wouldn't have mattered. I could run round the town twenty times and imagine there was no greater pleasure in the world than using your legs. Let's have a light. [*Lights up*] The matches are just where they used to be, I'll bet, because in this house we've got twice ten commandments. "Put your hat on the third nail, not the fourth." "You must be sleepy at half-past nine." "You've no right to be chilly before Martinmas and no right to sweat after it." And that's on a level with "Thou shalt fear God and love Him." I'm thirsty. [*Calls*] Mother! Phew! I'd forgotten she'd gone where there's no waiters to serve you. I didn't blubber in that gloomy cell when I heard them ringing the bell for her; but—you redcoat! You didn't let me have my last throw in the skittle-alley, although I'd the ball in my hand. I won't give you time to breathe your last, when I find you by yourself. And that may be to-night. I know where to find you at ten o'clock. And then off to sea! What keeps Clara out? I'm as hungry as I'm thirsty. To-

day's Thursday. They've had veal broth. If it was winter, there'd have been cabbage; white cabbage up to Shrove Tuesday and green after. That's as certain as that Thursday comes after Wednesday and that it can't say to Friday, "Take my place, my feet are tired."

SCENE VIII.

[Clara *enters*]

KARL: At last! You shouldn't do so much kissing. Where four red lips get baked together, there's a bridge for the devil to cross. What have you got there?

CLARA: Where? What?

KARL: Where? What? In your hand.

CLARA: Nothing.

KARL: Nothing! Is it secrets? [*Snatches* Leonard's *letter from her*] Give it to me! When your father's out, your brother's your guardian.

CLARA: I kept the thing in my hand, and yet the wind is so strong that it is blowing slates off the roofs. As I went past the church, one fell right at my feet. I nearly fell over it. "O God," I thought, "one more" —and stood still. It would have been so beautiful. They'd have buried me and said it was an accident. But I hoped in vain for a second.

KARL: [*Who has read the letter*] Damnation! I'll smash the arm of the man that wrote that. Fetch me a bottle of wine! Or is the money-box empty?

CLARA: There's one bottle left in the house. I bought it secretly and hid it for mother's birthday. It was to have been tomorrow——[*turns away*].

KARL: Give it to me.

[Clara *brings the wine*]

KARL: [*Drinking quickly*] Now we might begin again—planing, sawing, and hammering, and then eating, drinking, and sleeping between-whiles to be able to go on planing and sawing and hammering. And a-bending of the knee on Sundays into the bargain: O God, I thank Thee for letting me plane and saw and hammer! [*Drinks*] Long live every dog that doesn't bite on the chain! [*Drinks again*] Here's to him again!

CLARA: Karl, don't drink so much. Father says there's the devil in wine.

KARL: And the parson says there's God in it. [*Drinks*] We'll see who's right. The bailiff came here. How did he behave?

CLARA: He behaved as if he were in a thieves' den. Mother fell down and died the moment he opened his mouth.

KARL: Good! If you hear in the morning that he's been found dead, don't curse the murderer.

CLARA: But, Karl, you won't——

KARL: I'm not the only enemy he's got. He's been attacked many a time. It would be no easy matter to spot the right man, unless he leaves his hat or his stick lying. [*Drinks*] Whoever he is, I wish him luck.

CLARA: You're talking——

KARL: Don't you like the idea? Leave it alone, then. You won't see me for a long time again.

CLARA: [*Shuddering*] No.

KARL: No! Do you know already that I'm going to sea? Do my thoughts crawl on my forehead for you to read them? Or has the old man been raving in his usual fashion and threatening to lock me out? Bah! That would be much the same as if the warder had said to me——"You can't stay in prison any longer; I'll throw you out where you'll be free."

CLARA: You don't understand me.

KARL: [*Sings*]

"The good ship puffs its sails, oh,
And merrily blows the breeze."

Yes, truly, I'm not bound to the joiner's bench any longer. Mother's dead. There's nobody now to stop me from eating fish after every storm. Besides, I've wanted it ever since I was a boy. Out into the world! I shall never get on here, or not until I have it proved to me that Fortune no longer favours the man that boldly risks his life, the man that throws away the copper he gets from the great treasury, to see whether she'll take it from him, or give it back to him gilded.

CLARA: And will you leave father alone? He's sixty now.

KARL: Alone? Aren't you staying with him?

CLARA: I?

KARL: Yes, you, his favourite! What nonsense have you got in your head that you ask such questions? I don't begrudge him his pleasure. He'll be freed from his eternal worry, when I go. So why shouldn't I? We simply don't suit each other. Things can't be too narrow for him. He'd like to clench his fist and creep inside of it. I'd like to burst my skin like baby's clothes, if I could! [*Sings*]

"The anchor's lightly lifted,
The rudder's quickly shifted,
Away she flies with ease."

Tell me now, did he doubt my guilt for a moment? Didn't he comfort himself as usual with his over-wise: "I expected it. I always thought as much. It had to come to that." If *you'd* done it, he'd have killed himself. I'd like to see him if you went the woman's way. He'd feel as if he was with child him-self,—with the devil, too.

CLARA: Oh, how that tears my heart! I must go!

KARL: What do you mean?

CLARA: I must go into the kitchen—what else? [*Clutches at her brow*] Yes, that's what I came home to do. [*Goes out*]

KARL: She seems very queer! [*Sings*]

"There comes a daring seabird
With greetings from the West."

CLARA: [*Comes in again*] The last thing's done now. Father's evening jug is by the fire. When I closed the kitchen door behind me and realised I should never go in again, I shivered to the very soul. So shall I leave this room, so this house, and so the world.

KARL: [*Sings, walking up and down. Clara in back-ground*]

"The sun it flames down daily
And the little fishes gaily
Do sport around their guest."

CLARA: Why don't I do it then? Shall I never do it? Shall I put it off from day to day? Just as I'm putting it off now, from minute to minute—yes, away then, away! And yet I stay here. I feel as if hands were raised in my womb, as if eyes—— [*Sits down on a chair*] What does this mean? Am I too weak to do it? Well, am I strong enough to see my father with his throat cut? [*Standing up*] No! No!—Our Father, which art in Heaven—Hallowed be Thy kingdom. O God, my poor head! I can't even pray. Karl! Karl! Help me!

KARL: What's wrong?

CLARA: The Lord's Prayer. [*Recollects*] I felt as if I was in the water and sinking, and had forgotten to pray. I— [*Suddenly*] Forgive us our trespasses, as we forgive them that trespass against us. That's it. Yes! Yes! Of course I forgive him. I'd forgotten all about him. Good-night, Karl.

KARL: Are you going to bed so early? Good-night!

CLARA: [*Like a child, going through the Lord's Prayer*] Forgive us——

KARL: You might get me a drink of water first—but it must be cold.

CLARA: [*Quickly*] I'll fetch it from the well.

KARL: Well, if you like; it isn't far.

CLARA: Thanks! Thanks! That was the only thing that troubled me. The deed itself was bound to be-tray me. Now they will say—"She's had an accident. She fell in."

KARL: Take care, though; they haven't nailed that plank on yet.

CLARA: Why, the moon's up! O God, I only come to save my father from coming. Forgive me as I—Be gracious, gracious—— [*Goes out*]

SCENE IX.

KARL: [*Sings*]

"I'd spring into it gladly,
It's where I'd live and die."

Yes, but first— [*Looking at clock*] What time is it? Nine.

"I'm far from being hoary,
And travelling's my glory—
But whither? What care I?"

SCENE X.

ANTHONY: [*Enters*] I owed you an apology for something, but if I excuse you for making debts secretly, and pay them for you into the bargain, I may be let off.

KARL: The one's good and the other is unnecessary. If I sell my Sunday clothes I can satisfy the people myself, that want a few shillings from me. When I'm a sailor—[*aside*] there, it's out!—I shan't want them.

ANTHONY: What talk is this?

KARL: It's not the first time you've heard it, but say what you like, my mind's made up this time.

ANTHONY: Well, you're old enough, that's true.

KARL: Just because I'm old enough, I don't crow about it. But to my mind, fish and fowl shouldn't quarrel as to whether it's better in the air or in the water. One thing more. Either you'll never see me again, or you'll clap me on the shoulder and tell me I did right.

ANTHONY: We'll wait and see. I don't need to pay off the man I'd engaged to do your work. What more is there in it?

KARL: Thank you!

ANTHONY: Tell me. Did the bailiff really take you right through the town to the mayor's, instead of taking the shortest road?

KARL: Up street and down street, and over the market place, like a Shrove Tuesday ox. But take my word for it—I shall pay him out before I go.

ANTHONY: I can't blame you, but I forbid you to do it.

KARL: Ho!

ANTHONY: I won't let you out of my sight. If you tried to lay hands on him, I'd help the fellow myself.

KARL: I thought you, too, were fond of mother.

ANTHONY: I'll prove that I was.

SCENE XI.

SECRETARY: [*Comes in weak and tottering, pressing a scarf to his breast*] Where's Clara? Thank God I came here again. Where is she? [*Sinks into a chair*]

KARL: She went to— Why, isn't she back yet? Her talk—I am afraid—— [*Goes out*]

SECRETARY: She is avenged. The wretch lies—— But I too—— Why, O God! Now I can't——

ANTHONY: What's wrong? What's the matter with you?

SECRETARY: It'll soon be over. Don't turn your daughter out. Give me your hand on it. Do you hear? Don't turn her out, if she——

ANTHONY: This is strange talk. Why should I——? Oh, I'm beginning to see! Perhaps I wasn't unjust to her?

SECRETARY: Give me your hand on it.

ANTHONY: No! [*Puts both hands in his pockets*] But I'll stand out of her way. She knows that. I've told her so.

SECRETARY: [*In horror*] You have—unhappy man, now I begin to understand you!

KARL: [*Rushes in*] Father, father, there's some one in the well! If only it isn't——

ANTHONY: Bring the big ladder! Bring ropes and hooks! What are you tarrying for? Quick! Even if it's the bailiff!

KARL: Everything's there already. The neighbours were there before me. If only it isn't Clara!

ANTHONY: Clara? [*Clutching at a table*]

KARL: She went to get some water, and they found her handkerchief.

SECRETARY: Now I know why the bullet struck me. It is Clara.

ANTHONY: Go and see. [*Sits down*] I can't. [*Karl goes out*] And yet—— [*Stands up again*] If I understand you properly [*to Secretary*] it's quite right.

KARL: [*Comes back*] Clara's dead. Her head's all broken in by the edge of the well, when she—— Father, she didn't fall in, she jumped in. A girl saw her.

ANTHONY: Let her think well before she speaks. It is too dark for her to have seen that for certain.

SECRETARY: Do you doubt it? You'd like to, but you can't. Just think of what you said to her. You sent her out on the road to death, and I, I'm to blame that she didn't turn back. When you suspected her misfortune, you thought of the tongues that would hiss at it, but not of the worthlessness of the snakes that own them. You said things to her that drove her to despair. And I, instead of folding her in my arms, when she opened her heart to me in nameless terror, thought of the knave that might mock at me, and ——I made myself dependent on a man who was *worse* than I, and I'm paying for it with my life. And you, too, though you stand there like a rock, you too will say some day, "Daughter, I wish you had not spared me the head-shakes and shoulder-shruggings of the Pharisees; it humiliates me more, that you are not here to sit by my deathbed and wipe the sweat of anguish from my brow."

ANTHONY: She has spared me nothing. They saw her.

SECRETARY: She did what she could. You were not worthy that she should succeed.

ANTHONY: Or she, perhaps!

[*Noises without*]

KARL: They're bringing her. [*Going*]

ANTHONY: [*Standing immovable till the end, calls him back*] Into the back room with her, where her mother lay.

SECRETARY: I must go to meet her. [*Tries to get up and falls*] Oh, Karl!

[*Karl helps him out*]

ANTHONY: I don't understand the world any more. [*Stands thinking*]

Ivan Turgenev

(1818–1883)

Although Ivan Sergyeevich Turgenev was primarily a novelist, he also belongs to the theatre. It is a curious circumstance, indeed, that most of the important Russian playwrights came to the drama only after having made distinguished contributions to realistic fiction. The theatre was more drastically censored than published literature, and it was, besides, easier for a writer to be realistic on paper than in writing for a stage that first adopted realistic production styles in the late eighteen-nineties, when the Moscow Art Theatre was established. It is probably because modern Russian writers wrote novels and stories and had little firsthand acquaintance with the theatre that their plays are marked by so much naturalness. When Western European playwrights such as Dumas *fils* and Augier had serious intentions —and these were so serious that most of the plays were more or less theses—they resorted to artificial dramaturgy because, except for their moralism, they thought of "theatre" first of all. The Russian playwrights thought of life first. Consequently, Russian authors moved toward the naturalistic ideal of uncontrived dramaturgy earlier than did the playwrights of Western Europe. This is particularly true of the few plays in which Turgenev anticipates the quiet artistry and sensitive characterization of Chekhov.

Turgenev was one of the earliest and most important novelists who made realism their province. He was also the first major novelist to attract attention beyond the borders of Russia, winning the approval of French writers and Henry James. He did not, indeed, put anything into his plays that he did not present better in his novels and stories—except for his play *A Month in the Country,* a masterpiece which holds its own in any comparison with his fiction.

Turgenev was born of aristocratic parents on an estate in the province of Orel and in his boyhood acquired an intimate knowledge of the life of the peasantry and the landed gentry. After a year at the University of Moscow, he completed his studies at the University of St. Petersburg (1837). From there he went to the University of Berlin for three years of graduate work in philosophy, literature, and history; he spent his vacations in European travel. He took a degree in philosophy at St. Petersburg in 1842, but instead of pursuing a scholarly career he assumed a government position for two years. By then, however, his passion for literature was fully aroused. Having already published verse and obtained the **approval** of the famous Russian critic

Belinsky, Turgenev devoted the rest of his life to writing. Wealthy and endowed with a handsome figure and polished manners, he became a man of the world as well as a man of lettters. He spent most of his time abroad after 1856, hobnobbing with Western writers and artists and maintaining a romantic relation with a French opera singer, whom he followed from country to country. He died in Paris on September 3, 1883.

Turgenev's first important work was a collection of stories and sketches of country life, *A Sportsman's Sketches,* which he had started to write in 1847. Published in 1852, the collection made a powerful impression with its realism and its exposure of the evils of serfdom. Although he wrote with literary tact and with moderation, there could be no doubt concerning his sincerity. When he inherited an enormous estate with some two thousand male serfs, he emancipated them and enabled them to acquire independent farms on the land. *A Sportsman's Sketches* became the *Uncle Tom's Cabin* of Russian literature and promoted the abolition of serfdom in Russia. Next, Turgenev wrote his first novel, *Rudin* (1865), a study of a futile intellectual, and followed it with another portrait of a Russian Hamlet in a provincial setting, *A Nest of Gentlefolk* (1859). He became, indeed, the objective transcriber of the decay of the Russian landed gentry and the flounderings of the young intelligentsia, in his masterpiece *Fathers and Sons* (1862) as well as in *Smoke* (1867) and *Virgin Soil* (1872). With these and other novels and stories, written with great sensitivity, disciplined artistry, and exquisite style, Turgenev made himself one of the masters of realism, even if he never touched the turbid depths of Dostoevsky and never attained Tolstoy's Olympian power.

Although Turgenev had no particular confidence in his capabilities as a playwright, he was attracted to the theatre. He hoped that though his plays might not be satisfactory for the stage, they might afford interest to readers of his nondramatic writings. His self-judgment proved too modest, however, in the case of *A Month in the Country,* which was successfully produced by the Moscow Art Theatre in 1909 and the Theatre Guild in 1930. He wrote about a dozen short and long plays early in his literary career. The pleasant one-act comedy *The Lady from the Provinces* (1851, produced by the Moscow Art Theatre in 1912), with its theme of a provincial woman's efforts to get to Moscow, suggests Chekhov's great play *The Three Sisters. Broke* is an amusing sketch of a shiftless young country squire's difficulties with his creditors, and *Where It Is Thin, There It Breaks* portrays an intellectual Hamlet who cannot bring himself to the point of wooing the girl he loves and consequently loses her to a more resolute friend. A noteworthy full-length comedy of manners, *The Bachelor,* revolves about the efforts of a middle-aged man to marry off his ward, who chooses him instead of the young snobs of the province. The girl, Maria, is a characterization that would be a credit to any playwright. Turgenev, indeed, was at his best in drawing women, especially women who are more sensible and energetic than men and make an effort to relieve the frustration of their lives.

Frustration is also the theme of *A Month in the Country,* and it is exemplified on different levels of characterization and environment with a sensitivity worthy of Chekhov. It is a study of boredom, jealousy, heartbreak, and the renunciations or compromises that life enforces upon human beings. It is tragic in a new way in European drama, in that it ends in a partial stalemate, anticipating in this respect the drama of attrition that later became Chekhov's special province. Life seethes beneath the surface, explodes with a demand for self-realization, then sinks back into a partly numb existence for most of the characters. It is hardly surprising that the play should have won the interest of Chekhov and of the Moscow Art Theatre's Stanislavsky.

A Month in the Country, written in 1849, is in all respects a work of modern inner realism—"inner" because, although the provincial background is meticulously observed and the characters give us an impression of complete authenticity, Turgenev is primarily interested in his characters' feelings and state of mind. The play exemplifies its author's explanation of his writing in general: "What do I care whether a woman perspires in the middle of her back or under her arms? I do not care how or where she sweats; I want to know how she thinks." Moreover, although less conspicuously than Chekhov, Turgenev employs a style of composition that has been well described as "centrifugal." The life in the characters draws them away from service to the plot. The persons in the play are absorbed in themselves or in other characters—who, in turn, may be absorbed only in themselves or in someone other than the individual who is interested in them. If they clash it is because their desires conflict and not because a situation has been contrived. Given their character and circumstances, they often meet only tangentially and then fly apart. And the elements of the play run parallel instead of meeting in one entanglement of plot. They blend, of course, but they blend into a picture of life as it is for real people rather than for puppets of a stage contrivance. Character is plot in *A Month in the Country.*

A MONTH IN THE COUNTRY

By Ivan Turgenev

TRANSLATED FROM THE RUSSIAN BY GEORGE RAPALL NOYES

CHARACTERS

ARKADY SERGEICH ISLAYEV, *a rich landowner, thirty-six years old*

NATALYA PETROVNA (NATASHA), *his wife, twenty-nine years old*

KOLYA, *their son, ten years old*

VERA (VEROCHKA[1]), *a protégée of the family, seventeen years old*

ANNA SEMENOVNA[2] ISLAYEV, *mother of ISLAYEV, fifty-eight years old*

LIZAVETA BOGDANOVNA, *a companion, thirty-seven years old*

ADAM IVANOVICH SCHAAF, *a German tutor, forty-five years old*

MIKHAYLO ALEXANDROVICH RAKITIN, *a friend of the family, thirty years old*

ALEXEY NIKOLAYEVICH BELYAYEV, *a student, teacher of KOLYA, twenty-one years old*

AFANASY IVANOVICH BOLSHINTSOV, *a neighbor, forty-eight years old*

IGNATY ILYICH SHPIGELSKY, *a doctor, forty years old*

MATVEY, *a servant, forty years old*

KATYA, *a maid, twenty years old*

The action takes place on Islayev's *estate, about 1840. There is a lapse of one day between Acts I and II, II and III, and IV and V.*

ACT I.

A drawing-room. On the right a card table and door to the study. Center, a door to the hall. On the left, two windows and a round table. In the corners of the room are couches. At the card table Anna Semenovna, Lizaveta Bogdanovna, and Schaaf are playing preference. At the round table are seated Natalya Petrovna and Rakitin. Natalya is embroidering on canvas. Rakitin has a book in his hands. The wall clock points to three.

SCHAAF: Hearts.

ANNA SEMENOVNA: Once more! My dear sir, you will beat us all to nothing.

SCHAAF: [*Phlegmatically*] Eight on hearts.

ANNA SEMENOVNA: [*To* Lizaveta Bogdanovna] What a man! There's no playing with him.

[Lizaveta Bogdanovna *smiles*]

NATALYA PETROVNA: [*To Rakitin*] Why have you stopped? Go on reading.

RAKITIN: [*Slowly raising his head*] "Monte Cristo se redressa haletant. . . ." Natalya Petrovna, are you interested?

NATALYA PETROVNA: Not a bit.

RAKITIN: Why are we reading this, then?

NATALYA PETROVNA: This is why. The other day a lady said to me, "Haven't you read Monte Cristo? You ought to read it; it is charming." At the time I

[1] An affectionate diminutive.

[2] Pronounced Se-myŏ′no-vna.

made her no reply, but now I can tell her I have read it and did not find it charming at all.

RAKITIN: Very well, if you have already convinced yourself. . . .

NATALYA PETROVNA: Oh, how lazy you are!

RAKITIN: I am ready to go on, certainly. [*He finds the place where he has stopped*] "Se redressa haletant, et . . ."

NATALYA PETROVNA: [*Interrupting him*] Have you seen Arkady to-day?

RAKITIN: I met him at the dam. Your men are repairing it. He was explaining something to the workmen, and to make it clearer, he waded into the sand up to his knees.

NATALYA PETROVNA: He takes hold of everything with too much enthusiasm—tries too hard. That's his failing. What do you think about it?

RAKITIN: I agree with you.

NATALYA PETROVNA: How tiresome! You always agree with me. Go on reading.

RAKITIN: Ah, so you want me to quarrel with you. All right.

NATALYA PETROVNA: I do! . . . I do! . . . I want you to have a will of your own. Read on, I tell you.

RAKITIN: I obey. [*Applies himself to the book again*]

SCHAAF: On hearts.

ANNA SEMENOVNA: What! Once more? This is unbearable. [*To* Natalya Petrovna] Natasha! Natasha!

NATALYA PETROVNA: What?

ANNA SEMENOVNA: Just imagine! Schaaf has been beating us all to pieces. He keeps saying seven or eight on hearts.

SCHAAF: Zis time, seven once more.

ANNA SEMENOVNA: Do you hear? This is awful.

NATALYA PETROVNA: Yes. Awful. [*To* Schaaf] Well, you can have them!

ANNA SEMENOVNA: [*To* Natalya Petrovna] But where's Kolya?

NATALYA PETROVNA: He's gone walking with the new teacher.

ANNA SEMENOVNA: Ah, Lizaveta Bogdanovna, I call you.

RAKITIN: [*To* Natalya Petrovna] With what teacher?

NATALYA PETROVNA: Oh, yes. I forgot to tell you. While you were gone we hired a new teacher.

RAKITIN: In place of Dufour?

NATALYA PETROVNA: No. A Russian teacher. The princess will send us a Frenchman from Moscow.

RAKITIN: What kind of a man is he—this Russian? Old?

NATALYA PETROVNA: No. Young. However, we have taken him only for the summer months.

RAKITIN: Oh, a general tutor.

NATALYA PETROVNA: Yes. That's what they call it, I believe. And, let me tell you, Rakitin, you like to observe people, to analyze them, to study their natures. . . .

RAKITIN: Good gracious! Why do you . . . ?

NATALYA PETROVNA: Yes, yes. . . . Observe him carefully. I like him. He's slender and well-built. He has a merry glance and a confident expression—you will see. To be sure, he is a little clumsy, and in your eyes, that's a drawback.

RAKITIN: Natalya Petrovna, you are frightfully hard on me to-day.

NATALYA PETROVNA: Joking aside, just observe him. It seems to me that he may turn out a splendid man. However, Lord knows!

RAKITIN: You arouse my curiosity.

NATALYA PETROVNA: Really? [*Pensively*] Go on reading.

RAKITIN: "Se redressa haletant, et . . ."

NATALYA PETROVNA: [*Suddenly looking around*] Where is Vera? I haven't seen her since morning. [*With a smile to Rakitin*] Drop that book! I see we shan't be able to read to-day. You'd better tell me some story or other.

RAKITIN: Very well. What shall I tell you? You know I have spent some days with the Krinitsyns. Just imagine! Our young people already are being bored.

NATALYA PETROVNA: How did you manage to observe that?

RAKITIN: Is it possible to conceal boredom? You can conceal anything else, but not boredom.

NATALYA PETROVNA: [*With a glance at him*] Can you conceal everything else?

RAKITIN: [*After a short silence*] I think so.

NATALYA PETROVNA: [*Lowering her eyes*] So, what did you do at the Krinitsyns'?

RAKITIN: Nothing at all. Being bored with friends is an awful thing. You feel at ease, you are not embarrassed, you like them, you have nothing to be vexed at, but still boredom torments you, and your heart is silly enough to ache as if it were hungry.

NATALYA PETROVNA: Probably you are often bored with friends.

RAKITIN: As if you yourself did not know what it means to be with a person whom you love and of whom you are tired!

NATALYA PETROVNA: [*Slowly*] Whom you love—that is a great word. You speak somewhat mysteriously.

RAKITIN: Mysteriously? Why mysteriously?

NATALYA PETROVNA: Yes. That's your failing. Do you know, Rakitin, of course you are a very clever man, but . . . [*stopping*] sometimes you and I converse as if we were weaving lace. . . . And have you watched people weaving lace? They do it in stuffy rooms, without moving from the spot. Lace is a beautiful thing, but a swallow of fresh water on a hot day is far better.

RAKITIN: Natalya Petrovna, to-day you—

NATALYA PETROVNA: What?

RAKITIN: To-day you are angry at me for some reason.

NATALYA PETROVNA: Oh, you shrewd men! How little penetration you have even if you are shrewd! . . . No. I am not angry at you.

ANNA SEMENOVNA: Oh, at last he's caught. He has to pay a fine. [*To* Natalya Petrovna] Natasha, our villain has had to pay a fine.

SCHAAF: [*Sourly*] Lissafet Bogdanovna is to blame.

LIZAVETA BOGDANOVNA: [*Crossly*] Excuse me. How was I to know that Anna Semenovna had no hearts?

SCHAAF: In ze future I vill not call Lissafet Bogdanovna.

ANNA SEMENOVNA: [*To* Schaaf] But how is she to blame?

SCHAAF: [*Repeats in exactly the same voice*] In ze future I vill not call Lissafet Bogdanovna.

LIZAVETA BOGDANOVNA: What do I care? The idea!

RAKITIN: The more I watch you, Natalya Petrovna, the more I find your face strange to-day.

NATALYA PETROVNA: [*With a certain curiosity*] Really?

RAKITIN: It's true I observe a definite change in you.

NATALYA PETROVNA: In that case, will you be so kind—you know me—guess the nature of that change that has taken place in me. What is it?

RAKITIN: Well, just wait a moment. . . .

[Kolya *suddenly runs in noisily from the hall, straight to* Anna Semenovna]

KOLYA: Grandma! Grandma! Just look what I have. [*He shows her a bow and arrows*] Just look!

ANNA SEMENOVNA: Show them to me, my darling. Oh, what a spendid bow! Who made it for you?

KOLYA: He did! He did! [*He points at* Belyayev, *who has stopped at the door of the hall*]

ANNA SEMENOVNA: Oh, how nicely it is made.

KOLYA: I've shot from it at a tree, grandma, and I hit it twice. [*He jumps up and down*]

NATALYA PETROVNA: Show it to me, Kolya.

KOLYA: [*Runs to her and talks while* Natalya Petrovna *examines the bow*] Oh, *maman,* how splendidly Alexey Nikolayevich climbs trees! He's going to teach me to swim, too. He's going to teach me everything. [*He jumps up and down*]

NATALYA PETROVNA: [*To* Belyayev] I'm very grateful to you for your attention to Kolya—

KOLYA: [*Interrupting her excitedly*] I'm so fond of him, *maman*—so very fond of him.

NATALYA PETROVNA: [*Stroking* Kolya *on the head*] My boy is a little bit pampered. Try to change him into a strong and vigorous lad. [*Belyayev bows*]

KOLYA: Alexey Nikolayevich, come on to the stable. We'll take some bread to Favorit.

BELYAYEV: Come on.

ANNA SEMENOVNA: [*To* Kolya] Come here and kiss me first.

KOLYA: [*Running away*] Later, grandma, later. [*Runs off into the hall;* Belyayev *follows him*]

ANNA SEMENOVNA: [*Following* Kolya *with her eyes*] What a charming child! [*To* Schaaf *and* Lizaveta Bogdanovna] Is he not?

LIZAVETA BOGDANOVNA: Yes, indeed.

SCHAAF: [*After a short silence*] I pass.

NATALYA PETROVNA: [*With a certain animation*] Well, how did he strike you?

RAKITIN: Who?

NATALYA PETROVNA: [*After a short silence*] That— Russian teacher.

RAKITIN: Oh, excuse me. I quite forgot. I was so occupied with the question that you put to me.

[Natalya Petrovna *looks at him with a hardly perceptible, mocking smile*]

However, his face . . . is really . . . Yes, he has a nice face. I like him, only he seems very bashful.

NATALYA PETROVNA: Yes.

RAKITIN: [*Glancing at her*] But, nevertheless, I cannot make up my mind. . . .

NATALYA PETROVNA: What if you and I took him in hand, Rakitin. Do you wish to? Let us finish his education. This is a splendid chance for sober, sedate people like you and me! We are very sedate, aren't we?

RAKITIN: This young man interests you. If he knew it—he would feel flattered.

NATALYA PETROVNA: Oh, believe me, not at all! You can't judge of him by what—people like us would do in his place. He's not at all like us, Rakitin. That's the trouble, my friend. We study ourselves with great diligence and then imagine that we know men.

RAKITIN: Another man's soul is a dark forest. But why these hints? Why do you keep teasing me to-day?

NATALYA PETROVNA: Whom should we tease if not our friends? And you are my friend—you know it.

[*Presses his hand.* Rakitin *smiles and his face brightens*] You are my old friend.

RAKITIN: I'm only afraid that you may grow tired of that old friend.

NATALYA PETROVNA: [*Laughing*] We grow tired only of good things.

RAKITIN: Maybe. . . . Only that makes it no easier for them.

NATALYA PETROVNA: Stop it. [*Lowering her voice*] As if you did not know . . . *ce que vous êtes pour moi.*

RAKITIN: Natalya Petrovna, you are playing with me as a cat with a mouse. . . . But the mouse does not complain.

NATALYA PETROVNA: Oh, poor little mouse!

ANNA SEMENOVNA: Twenty kopeks from you, Adam Ivanovich. . . . Aha!

SCHAAF: In ze future I vill not call Lissafet Bogdanovna.

MATVEY: [*Entering from the hall and announcing*] Ignaty Ilyich has arrived.

SHPIGELSKY: [*Entering after him*] Doctors are not announced.

[Matvey *goes out*]

My most humble respects to the whole family. [*Goes to* Anna Semenovna *and kisses her hand*] Good day, madam. I trust you are winning?

ANNA SEMENOVNA: Winning! I had hard work to come out even. . . . Thank the Lord for that! It's all owing to this villain. [*Points to* Schaaf]

SHPIGELSKY: [*To* Schaaf] Adam Ivanovich, with ladies! That is not nice. . . . I'm ashamed of you!

SCHAAF: [*Muttering through his teeth*] Wiz ladies, wiz ladies. . . .

SHPIGELSKY: [*Going up to the round table on the left*] Good day, Natalya Petrovna! Good day, Mikhaylo Alexandrovich!

NATALYA PETROVNA: Good day, doctor! How are you?

SHPIGELSKY: I like that question very much. . . . So *you* are well. How am I getting along? A respectable doctor is never ill. He just suddenly up and dies. . . . Ha! ha!

NATALYA PETROVNA: Sit down. I am well, to be sure—but I'm not in good spirits. . . . And even that is ill health.

SHPIGELSKY: [*Sitting down beside* Natalya Petrovna] Permit me to feel your pulse. [*He feels it*] Ah, those nerves, those nerves. . . . You take too little exercise, Natalya Petrovna. You laugh too little. . . . That's the trouble. Mikhaylo Alexandrovich, what are you looking at? Now, I can prescribe white drops.

NATALYA PETROVNA: I'm not averse to laughing. . . . [*With animation*] Now, doctor, you have a spiteful tongue. I'm honestly very fond of you for that quality and respect you for it. . . . Tell me something funny. Mikhaylo Alexandrovich insists upon talking seriously to-day.

SHPIGELSKY: [*Looking stealthily at* Rakitin] Evidently it is not only the nerves that suffer, but you have a slight effusion of bile.

NATALYA PETROVNA: Oh, you are singing the same song! Observe as much as you wish, doctor, but not aloud. We all know that you are frightfully penetrating. . . . You are both very penetrating.

SHPIGELSKY: I agree.

NATALYA PETROVNA: Tell us something funny.

SHPIGELSKY: I agree. I never thought of expecting you all of a sudden to want me to tell a story. Let me take a pinch of snuff. [*He takes one*]

NATALYA PETROVNA: What preparations!

SHPIGELSKY: But, my dear madam, Natalya Petrovna, please consider there are different sorts of funny stories. It depends on the person. In the case of your neighbor, Mr. Hlopushkin, you only have to raise one finger and he explodes into laughter and wheezes and weeps. . . . But you . . . Well, permit me. Do you know Platon Vasilyevich Verinitsyn?

NATALYA PETROVNA: I think I know him, or I have heard of him.

SHPIGELSKY: He has an insane sister. In my opinion, either both of them are insane or both of them in their right mind, because there is absolutely no difference between brother and sister, but that is not the point. Fate always, fate always, fate, fate everywhere. Verinitsyn has a daughter, a sallow girl, you know, with pale eyes, a little red nose, and yellow lips—in a word, a very amiable girl. She plays the piano and lisps, too. So everything is as it should be. She has two hundred serfs,[3] and her aunt has one hundred and fifty. Her aunt is still alive and will live a long time, as all insane people are long-lived. But still there is a remedy for every grief. She has made a will in favor of her niece. Only yesterday I, with my own hands, poured cold water on her head, and I had absolutely no reason to do so, because there is utterly no possibility of curing her. Well, so then, Verinitsyn has a daughter—not the worst match in the world. He began to take her into society; suitors began to make their appearance. Among others, there was a certain Perekuzov, an anæmic young fellow, timid, but of excellent principles. So the father liked our Perekuzov, and the daughter liked him too. Then where was the hindrance, you say? Let them be married, and good luck to them! And really everything went finely. Mr. Verinitsyn, Platon Vasilyevich, was already beginning to tap Mr. Perekuzov on the stomach, this way, you know, and to pat him on the shoulder, when suddenly, from somewhere or other, an officer turned up—Ardalion Protobekasov. At the ball of the Marshal of the Nobility he saw Verinitsyn's daughter. He danced three polkas with her, and he said to her, probably rolling his eyes like this, "Oh, how unhappy I am!" And the young lady immediately fell for it. Then there were tears, sighs, and "ohs."

[3] A landed proprietor's wealth was reckoned by the number of serfs that he owned

She wouldn't look at Perekuzov, wouldn't talk to Perekuzov—she had spasms at the mere word "marriage." Good Lord my God, what a story! "Well," thinks Verinitsyn, "if it's Protobekasov, then Protobekasov it must be. It's lucky that he, too, is a man of property." They invite Protobekasov and say, "Do us the honor." Protobekasov does them the honor. Protobekasov arrives, hangs around, falls in love, finally offers his hand and heart. What do you think about it? Does the Verinitsyn girl immediately agree with joy? Not much! God forbid! Again tears, sighs, spasms! The father is clean stuck: "What's this anyway? What does she want?" And what do you think she answers him? "I don't know, dad," says she, "whether I love this man or the other one." "What's that?" "Honest to God, I don't know, and I'd better not marry either one, but just love him." Verinitsyn, of course, immediately had a fit, and the suitors, also, didn't know what was up, but she held her ground! Pray consider what miracles take place in these parts.

NATALYA PETROVNA: I don't see anything surprising in this. . . . As if it were impossible to love two men at once!

RAKITIN: Ah, you think . . .

NATALYA PETROVNA: [*Slowly*] I think— However, I don't know. Maybe this proves only that you love neither one of them.

SHPIGELSKY: [*Taking snuff and looking first at* Natalya Petrovna *and then at* Rakitin] That's it. That's it.

NATALYA PETROVNA: [*To* Shpigelsky *with animation*] Your story is very good, but nevertheless you didn't make me laugh.

SHPIGELSKY: But, my dear madam, who could ever make you laugh now, if you please? You don't need that now.

NATALYA PETROVNA: What do I need?

SHPIGELSKY: [*With an affectedly submissive air*] The Lord only knows!

NATALYA PETROVNA: Oh, how tiresome you are! No better than Rakitin!

SHPIGELSKY: That is a great honor, if you please.

[Natalya Petrovna *makes an impatient movement*]

ANNA SEMENOVNA: [*Rising from her place*] Well, at last! . . . [*Sighs*] I've sat still so long that my joints are stiff.

[Lizaveta Bogdanovna *and* Schaaf *also rise*] O—oh!

NATALYA PETROVNA: [*Rises and goes to them*] You must like sitting still for so long.

[Shpigelsky *and* Rakitin *rise*]

ANNA SEMENOVNA: [*To* Schaaf] You owe seventy kopeks, my dear sir.

[Schaaf *bows stiffly*]

You can't give us orders all the time. [*To* Natalya Petrovna] You seem to be pale to-day, Natasha. Are you well? Shpigelsky, is she well? . . .

SHPIGELSKY: [*Who has been whispering with* Rakitin] Oh, perfectly.

ANNA SEMENOVNA: That's right. . . . But I'll go and rest a bit before dinner. I'm tired to death! Liza, come on. Oh, my joints, my joints! . . .

[*She goes into the hall with* Lizaveta Bogdanovna. Natalya Petrovna *accompanies her to the door.* Shpigelsky, Rakitin, *and* Schaaf *remain in the foreground*]

SHPIGELSKY: [*To* Schaaf, *offering his snuff box*] Well, Adam Ivanovich, *wie befinden Sie sik?*

SCHAAF: [*Taking snuff with dignity*] Very vell. And how are you?

SHPIGELSKY: Thank you kindly. . . . So, so. [*To* Rakitin *in a low voice*] Don't you really know what the matter is with Natalya Petrovna to-day?

RAKITIN: I honestly don't know.

SHPIGELSKY: Well, if *you* don't know . . . [*He turns aside and goes to meet* Natalya Petrovna, *who returns from the door*] I have a small bit of business with you, Natalya Petrovna.

NATALYA PETROVNA: [*Going to the window*] Really? What?

SHPIGELSKY: I need to speak with you alone.

NATALYA PETROVNA: Really? You frighten me!

[Rakitin *meanwhile has taken* Schaaf's *arm and is walking back and forth with him and is whispering something to him in German.* Schaaf *laughs, and says in a low voice:* "Ja, ja, ja! Ja wohl, ja wohl! Sehr gut"]

SHPIGELSKY: [*Lowering his voice*] This matter really concerns others besides yourself.

NATALYA PETROVNA: [*Looking into the garden*] What do you mean?

SHPIGELSKY: This is how the matter stands. One of my acquaintances asked me to find out . . . so to speak . . . your intentions with regard to your protégée . . . Vera Alexandrovna.

NATALYA PETROVNA: My intentions?

SHPIGELSKY: That is, to speak frankly . . . my acquaintance—

NATALYA PETROVNA: Is he making a proposal for her?

SHPIGELSKY: Quite so.

NATALYA PETROVNA: Are you joking?

SHPIGELSKY: Not at all, madam.

NATALYA PETROVNA: [*Laughing*] But pray consider, she is still a child. What a strange commission!

SHPIGELSKY: Why strange, Natalya Petrovna? My acquaintance—

NATALYA PETROVNA: You're a splendid man of business, Shpigelsky. And who is your acquaintance?

SHPIGELSKY: [*Smiling*] Permit me, permit me, you have not yet told me anything positive with regard to—

NATALYA PETROVNA: Stop, doctor. Vera is still a child. You know that yourself, Mr. Diplomat. [*Turning around*] By the way, here she is.

[Vera *and* Kolya *run in from the hall*]

KOLYA: [*Running to* Rakitin] Rakitin, tell 'em to give us some glue, some glue!

NATALYA PETROVNA: [*To* Vera] Where do you come from? [*Patting her on the cheek*] How flushed you are!

VERA: From the garden. . . .

[Shpigelsky *bows to her*]

How do you do, Ignaty Ilyich?

RAKITIN: [*To* Kolya] What do you want glue for?

KOLYA: I must have it! I must have it! . . . Alexey Nikolayevich is making a kite for us. . . . Tell 'em! . . .

RAKITIN: [*About to ring the bell*] Wait, right away.

SCHAAF: *Erlauben Sie.* . . . Mr. Kolya hass not hat hiss lesson to-day. [*Takes* Kolya *by the hand*] *Kommen Sie!*

KOLYA: [*In a melancholy tone*] *Morgen, Herr Schaaf, morgen.*

SCHAAF: *"Morgen, Morgen, nur nicht heute, sagen alle faule Leute." Kommen Sie!* [Kolya *resists*]

NATALYA PETROVNA: [*To* Vera] Who have you been walking with for so long? I haven't seen you since morning.

VERA: With Alexey Nikolayevich . . . with Kolya. . . .

NATALYA PETROVNA: Ah. [*Turning*] Kolya, what does this mean?

KOLYA: [*Lowering his voice*] Mr. Schaaf . . . Mamma dear.

RAKITIN: [*To* Natalya Petrovna] They are making a kite outside, and in here he's due for a lesson.

SCHAAF: [*With a feeling of dignity*] *Gnädige Frau* . . .

NATALYA PETROVNA: [*Sternly to* Kolya] Kindly be obedient. You have had enough for to-day. Go with Mr. Schaaf.

SCHAAF: [*Leading* Kolya *into the hall*] *Es ist unerhört!*

KOLYA: [*Whispering to* Rakitin *as he leaves*] All the same, tell 'em to get the glue.

[Rakitin *nods*]

SCHAAF: [*Pulling at* Kolya] *Kommen Sie, mein Herr.*

[*Goes out into the hall with him;* Rakitin *follows them*]

NATALYA PETROVNA: [*To* Vera] Sit down. You must be tired. [*She sits down herself*]

VERA: [*Sitting down*] Not at all.

NATALYA PETROVNA: [*With a smile to* Shpigelsky] Shpigelsky, look at her. Isn't she tired?

SHPIGELSKY: But that does Vera Alexandrovna good.

NATALYA PETROVNA: I do not say . . . [*To* Vera] Well, what have you been doing in the garden?

VERA: Playing, running. At first we watched them building the dam, and then Alexey Nikolayevich climbed a tree for a squirrel—way, way up, and he began to shake the top of the tree. . . . We all felt very scared. . . . At last the squirrel fell, and Trezor almost caught it, but it got away.

NATALYA PETROVNA: [*Looking at* Shpigelsky *with a smile*] And then?

VERA: And then Alexey Nikolayevich made a bow for Kolya, and so quickly! . . . And then he stole up to our cow in the meadow and all of a sudden jumped on her back. . . . The cow was scared and began to run and kick, and he just laughed. [*She laughs herself*] And then Alexey Nikolayevich wanted to make a kite for us and so we came here.

NATALYA PETROVNA: [*Patting her on the cheek*] You're a child, a child, a perfect child. Aren't you?—What do you think about it, Shpigelsky?

SHPIGELSKY: [*Speaks slowly, watching* Natalya Petrovna] I agree with you.

NATALYA PETROVNA: That's right.

SHPIGELSKY: But this does no harm. . . . On the contrary. . . .

NATALYA PETROVNA: Do you think so? [*To* Vera] Well, did you have a very good time?

VERA: Yes. . . . Alexey Nikolayevich is so amusing.

NATALYA PETROVNA: So that's it. [*After a short silence*] Vera, how old are you?

[Vera *looks at her with a certain amazement*] You're a child, a child.

[Rakitin *comes in from the hall*]

SHPIGELSKY: [*Fussily*] Oh, I forgot. . . . Your coachman is ill . . . and I haven't seen him yet.

NATALYA PETROVNA: What's the matter with him?

SHPIGELSKY: Fever. However, there's no great danger.

NATALYA PETROVNA: [*Calling after him*] Are you dining with us, doctor?

SHPIGELSKY: If you'll permit me. [*Goes out into the hall*]

NATALYA PETROVNA: *Mon enfant, vous feriez bien de mettre une autre robe pour le dîner. . . .*

[Vera *rises*]

Come to my room. [*Kisses her on the forehead*] A child! A child!

[Vera *kisses her hand and goes into the study*]

RAKITIN: [*In a low voice to* Vera, *winking*] I've sent everything necessary to Alexey Nikolayevich.

VERA: [*Whispering*] Thank you, Mikhaylo Alexandrovich. [*Goes out*]

RAKITIN: [*Approaching* Natalya Petrovna, *who stretches out her hand to him. He immediately seizes it*] At last we're alone. . . . Natalya Petrovna, tell me what is the matter with you?

NATALYA PETROVNA: Nothing, Michel, nothing. And if there was anything, it is all over now. Sit down. [Rakitin *sits down beside her*] This happens to everybody. Little clouds pass over the sky. Why are you looking at me in this way?

RAKITIN: I'm looking at you. . . . I'm happy.

NATALYA PETROVNA: [*Smiling in reply to him*] Open the window, Michel. How fine it is in the garden.

[Rakitin *gets up and opens the window*]

Greetings, wind! [*She laughs*] The wind seems to have been waiting for a chance to break in. [*She looks around*] How it has taken possession of the whole room! . . . You can't drive it out now.

RAKITIN: Now you're as soft and quiet as an evening after a thunderstorm.

NATALYA PETROVNA: [*Pensively repeating his last words*] "After a thunderstorm." . . .

RAKITIN: [*Shaking his head*] One was gathering.

NATALYA PETROVNA: Really? [*Looking at him after a short silence*] Let me tell you, Michel, I cannot imagine a kinder man than yourself. Honestly.

[Rakitin *tries to stop her*]

No, don't hinder me from expressing myself. You are sympathetic, affectionate, faithful. You do not betray one. I am indebted to you in many ways.

RAKITIN: Natalya Petrovna, why do you say this to me at this particular moment?

NATALYA PETROVNA: I don't know. I feel gay. I'm taking a bit of relaxation. Don't forbid me to chatter.

RAKITIN: [*Pressing her hand*] You are kind as an angel.

NATALYA PETROVNA: [*Laughing*] This morning you would not have said that! . . . But listen to me, Michel. You know me, you must excuse me. Our relations are so pure, so sincere, and yet they are not entirely natural.—You and I have a right to look straight in the eyes, not only of Arkady, but of all the world. Yes, but . . . [*Falls into meditation*] that is why I am sometimes troubled and depressed and cross. I am ready like a child to vent my vexation upon another person, especially upon you. . . . This preference does not make you angry?

RAKITIN: [*With animation*] On the contrary. . . .

NATALYA PETROVNA: Yes. Sometimes it's pleasant to torture a person whom you love . . . whom you love. You see that I, like Tatyana, can say, "Why dissemble?"[4]

RAKITIN: Natalya Petrovna, you—

NATALYA PETROVNA: [*Interrupting him*] Yes . . . I love you. But let me tell you, Rakitin, do you know that occasionally it seems strange to me. I love you, and that feeling is so clear, so peaceful. . . . It does not excite me . . . I am warmed by it, but . . . [*With animation*] You never have caused me to weep, and I apparently should— [*Interrupting herself*] What does this mean?

RAKITIN: [*Somewhat sadly*] Such a question demands no answer.

NATALYA PETROVNA: [*Pensively*] Yet you and I are old acquaintances.

RAKITIN: Four years. Yes. We're old friends. . . .

NATALYA PETROVNA: Friends. No, you are more than a friend to me.

RAKITIN: Natalya Petrovna, do not touch on that

4 A reference to Pushkin's poem *Eugene Onegin.*

question. I fear for my happiness—that it may vanish under your hands.

NATALYA PETROVNA: No . . . no . . . no! The whole thing is that you are too kind. You humor me too much. . . . You have spoiled me. . . . You are too kind. . . . Do you hear?

RAKITIN: [*With a smile*] I hear.

NATALYA PETROVNA: [*Looking at him*] I don't know how you . . . I wish no other happiness. . . . Many people might envy me. [*She stretches out both hands to him*] Is that not true?

RAKITIN: I am in your power. . . . Do with me as you wish.

[*From the hall is heard* Islayev's *voice:* "So you have sent for him."]

NATALYA PETROVNA: [*Rising quickly*] It is he. I cannot see him now. . . . Good-by! [*She goes out into the study*]

RAKITIN: [*Gazing after her*] What does this mean? Is it the beginning of the end, or absolutely the end? [*After a short silence*] Or the beginning?

[Islayev *comes in with a troubled air and takes off his hat*]

ISLAYEV: Good day, Michel![5]

RAKITIN: We've seen each other before to-day.

ISLAYEV: Oh, excuse me! . . . I have been absorbed in business. [*Paces the room*] It is queer. The Russian peasant is very clever, very quick to understand; I respect the Russian peasant. . . . And yet sometimes you tell him something—tell him, and explain. . . . Everything seems clear, but nothing comes of it. The Russian peasant hasn't that . . . that . . .

RAKITIN: Are you still bothering with the dam?

ISLAYEV: That . . . so to speak . . . hasn't that love for his work. That's the point. He hasn't a love for it. He won't let you explain your meaning fully— "I understand, sir . . ." and yet he understood nothing at all. Look at a German—that's another story. The Russian has no patience.— With all that, I respect him. . . . But where is Natasha? Don't you know?

RAKITIN: She was here just now.

ISLAYEV: And what time is it? It must be time for dinner. I've been on my legs since morning. I've loads of work . . . and yet I haven't looked at the building operations to-day. Time does pass so. It's simply terrific—you can't get anywhere!

[Rakitin *smiles*]

You're laughing at me, I see. . . . But what's to be done, friend? Each to his own business. I'm a matter-of-fact man, born to be a landlord and nothing more. There was a time when I had dreams of something else, but I missed fire, friend. I burnt my fingers— like that!— Why is it Belyayev doesn't come?

RAKITIN: Who is Belyayev?

[5] In Russia friends greet each other and shake hands on their first meeting each day. It is a breach of etiquette to repeat the salutation later.

ISLAYEV: Our new teacher, the Russian. He's a queer lad, but he'll get used to things. He's not a stupid fellow. I asked him to-day to see how the building was getting on.

[Belyayev *comes in*]

Oh, here he is! Well, how about it? How are they getting along there? They aren't doing a thing, I suppose. Are they?

BELYAYEV: Yes. They are at work.

ISLAYEV: Have they finished the second frame?

BELYAYEV: They have begun on the third.

ISLAYEV: And about the beams? Did you tell them?

BELYAYEV: I did.

ISLAYEV: Well, and what did they say?

BELYAYEV: They say they never have done it in any other fashion.

ISLAYEV: Hm! Is Ermil, the carpenter, there?

BELYAYEV: Yes.

ISLAYEV: Oh! . . . Well, thank you. [Natalya Petrovna *comes in*] Oh, good day, Natasha!

RAKITIN: How is it that to-day you are bidding everybody good day twenty times over?

ISLAYEV: I tell you I got deep in business. Oh, by the way, I haven't shown you my new winnowing fan. Come on, please; it's worth seeing. Just imagine! It makes a hurricane, a regular hurricane. We'll have time before dinner. . . . Want to?

RAKITIN: All right.

ISLAYEV: And Natasha—won't you come with us?

NATALYA PETROVNA: The idea of my understanding anything about your winnowing fans!—You two go on alone and see that you don't get delayed.

ISLAYEV: [*Going out with* Rakitin] We'll be back directly.

[Belyayev *is about to follow them*]

NATALYA PETROVNA: [*To* Belyayev] Where are you going, Alexey Nikolayevich.

BELYAYEV: I . . . . I . . .

NATALYA PETROVNA: However, if you wish to take a walk—

BELYAYEV: No, I've been in the open air all the morning.

NATALYA PETROVNA: Well, in that case, sit down here. . . . Sit down here. [*She points to a chair*] You and I have not yet had a real conversation, Alexey Nikolayevich; we've not yet got acquainted.

[Belyayev *bows and sits down*]

And I want to get acquainted with you.

BELYAYEV: I . . . . that is very flattering to me.

NATALYA PETROVNA: [*With a smile*] Now you are afraid of me again; I see that. But wait! You will learn to know me and you will stop being afraid of me. Tell me . . . tell me how old you are.

BELYAYEV: Twenty-one, madam.

NATALYA PETROVNA: Are your parents living?

BELYAYEV: My mother is dead; my father is living.

NATALYA PETROVNA: And did your mother pass away long ago?

BELYAYEV: Yes, madam.

NATALYA PETROVNA: But, do you remember her?

BELYAYEV: Of course I remember her.

NATALYA PETROVNA: And is your father living in Moscow?

BELYAYEV: No, madam, in the country.

NATALYA PETROVNA: Well, have you brothers and sisters?

BELYAYEV: One sister.

NATALYA PETROVNA: Do you love her very much?

BELYAYEV: Yes, I do. She is much younger than I.

NATALYA PETROVNA: And what's her name?

BELYAYEV: Natalya.

NATALYA PETROVNA: [*With animation*] Natalya? That's queer! My name is Natalya also. [*She pauses*] And you love her very much?

BELYAYEV: Yes, madam.

NATALYA PETROVNA: Tell me, how do you find my Kolya?

BELYAYEV: He's a very charming boy.

NATALYA PETROVNA: Isn't he? And so affectionate! He's already become attached to you.

BELYAYEV: I try to do my best. . . . I am glad . . .

NATALYA PETROVNA: Now you see, Alexey Niko-layevich, of course I should like to make a man of action out of him. I don't know whether I shall succeed in that, but at any rate I want him always to remember with pleasure the time of his childhood. Let him grow up at liberty—that is the main thing. I myself was educated otherwise, Alexey Nikolaye-vich. My father, although not an ill-tempered man, was irritable and stern. . . . Every one in the house, beginning with mamma, was afraid of him. My mother and I used to cross ourselves secretly every time we were summoned to him. Sometimes my father would undertake to caress me, but even in his embraces, I remember, I felt faint all over. My brother grew up, and perhaps you have heard of his rupture with father. . . . I shall never forget that awful day. . . . I remained my father's obedient daughter to the very end. . . . He called me his comfort, his Antigone—he was blind during the last years of his life. But his most tender caresses could not efface from my mind the first impressions of my youth. . . . I was afraid of him, the blind old man, and in his presence I never felt myself free. . . . The traces of this timidity, of this long constraint, perhaps have not yet completely disappeared. . . . I know that at first glance I appear . . . what shall I call it? . . . cold, possibly. . . . But I notice that I am telling you of myself, instead of speaking to you of Kolya. I just want to say that I know of my own experience how good it is for a child to grow up at liberty. . . . Now I think that in your childhood you did not suffer from constraint.

BELYAYEV: How can I tell you? . . . Of course, no one constrained me . . . no one paid any attention to me.

NATALYA PETROVNA: [*Timidly*] But perhaps, your father—

BELYAYEV: He had no interest in the matter. He was always riding round to our neighbors . . . on business. Or maybe not on business, but . . . He made his living through them, I may say, . . . through his services to them. .

NATALYA PETROVNA: Oh, and so no one attended to your education?

BELYAYEV: To tell the truth, no one. However, probably you've noticed that already. I am only too conscious of my own defects.

NATALYA PETROVNA: Perhaps . . . but on the other hand— [*She stops and continues with a certain confusion*] Oh, by the way, was it you, Alexey Niko-layevich, who was singing in the garden yesterday?

BELYAYEV: When?

NATALYA PETROVNA: In the evening, near the pond.

BELYAYEV: Yes. [*Hastily*] I did not think . . . the pond is so far from here . . . I did not think that it could be heard here.

NATALYA PETROVNA: And you seem to be excusing yourself? You have a very pleasant, sonorous voice, and you sing so well. Have you studied music?

BELYAYEV: Not a bit. I sing by ear . . . only simple songs.

NATALYA PETROVNA: You sing them splendidly. I shall ask you sometime . . . not now . . . but when you and I get better acquainted, when we become intimate. You see, Alexey Nikolayevich, we shall certainly become intimate, shan't we? I feel confidence in you. My chatter may prove it. . . .

[*She stretches out her hand to him in order that he may press it.* Belyayev *takes it indecisively and has a certain perplexity in knowing what to do with that hand; he kisses it.* Natalya Pe-trovna *blushes and withdraws her hand. At that moment* Shpigelsky *enters from the hall, stops and takes a step backward.* Natalya Petrovna *rises quickly,* Belyayev *also*]

NATALYA PETROVNA: [*In confusion*] Oh, is that you, doctor? Alexey Nikolayevich and I are here. [*She stops*]

SHPIGELSKY: [*In a loud, casual tone*] Just imagine, Natalya Petrovna, what things are going on in your household! I went into your servants' room and asked for your sick coachman. Lo and behold! My invalid was sitting at the table and consuming pancakes and onions at full speed. After this you can quit studying medicine and relying on disease as an innocent source of income!

NATALYA PETROVNA: [*With a forced smile*] Oh, really . . .

[Belyayev *is about to go*]

Alexey Nikolayevich, I forgot to tell you. . . .

[Vera *runs in from the hall*]

VERA: Alexey Nikolayevich, Alexey Nikolayevich! [*She suddenly stops at the sight of* Natalya Petrovna]

NATALYA PETROVNA: [*With a certain surprise*] What's all this? What do you want?

VERA: [*Blushing and lowering her eyes; points to* Belyayev] They're calling him.

NATALYA PETROVNA: Who?

VERA: Kolya. That is, Kolya asked me about the kite.

NATALYA PETROVNA: Oh! [*In a low voice to* Vera] On n'entre pas comme cela dans une chambre. . . . Cela ne convient pas. [*Turning to* Shpigelsky] Well, what time it, doctor? Your watch is always right. . . . Is it time for dinner?

SHPIGELSKY: Just a moment, please. [*Takes his watch from his pocket*] Now . . . now . . . I may report, it's twenty minutes past four.

NATALYA PETROVNA: So you see, it's time.

[*Goes to the mirror and adjusts her hair; meanwhile* Vera *whispers something to* Belyayev. *They both laugh.* Natalya Petrovna *sees them in the mirror.* Shpigelsky *takes a sidelong glance at her*]

BELYAYEV: [*Laughing softly*] Really?

VERA: [*Nodding and also in a low voice*] Yes, yes, she just fell.

NATALYA PETROVNA: [*With an affected indifference, turning to* Vera] What's that? Who fell?

VERA: [*Confused*] No . . . Alexey Nikolayevich had made a swing, and then nurse took it into her head—

NATALYA PETROVNA: [*Without waiting for the end of the answer, to* Shpigelsky] Oh, by the way, Shpigelsky, come here. [*She leads him aside and again turns to* Vera] Did she hurt herself?

VERA: Oh, no.

NATALYA PETROVNA: That's good. And yet, Alexey Nikolayevich, you make a mistake to—

MATVEY: [*Enters from the hall and announces*] Dinner is served.

NATALYA PETROVNA: Oh, where is Arkady Sergeich? He and Mikhaylo Alexandrovich will be late again.

MATVEY: They are already in the dining-room.

NATALYA PETROVNA: And mamma?

MATVEY: She is in the dining-room also.

NATALYA PETROVNA: Oh, very well. Come on! [*Pointing to* Belyayev] Vera, allez en avant avec monsieur.

[Matvey *goes out, followed by* Belyayev *and* Vera]

SHPIGELSKY: [*To* Natalya Petrovna] Did you wish to say anything to me?

NATALYA PETROVNA: Oh, yes! To be sure. . . . Now you see . . . I'll speak to you later about . . . about your proposal.

SHPIGELSKY: In regard to . . . Vera Alexandrovna?

NATALYA PETROVNA· Yes. I'll think it over. . . . I'll think it over.

[*Both go out into the hall*]

ACT II.

A garden. On the right and left, under the trees, benches. Center, a raspberry patch. Katya *and* Matvey *come in from the right.* Katya *has a basket in her hands.*

MATVEY: Well, then, Katerina Vasilyevna. Will you please explain yourself? I earnestly beg you to.

KATYA: Why really, Matvey Egorych . . .

MATVEY: You know only too well, Katerina Vasilyevna, what my attitude is towards you. Of course, I am older than you. There is no dispute about that, but all the same I can still look out for myself. I am still in the very prime of life, and also, as you perfectly well know, I am of a gentle disposition, so what more do you want?

KATYA: Believe me, Matvey Egorych, I appreciate it very much. I am very grateful, Matvey Egorych. . . . But you see . . . I think I had better wait.

MATVEY: But what shall we wait for, pray, Katerina Vasilyevna? Formerly, if you will permit me to remark, you did not talk in this way, and as for showing you due respect, I think I may vouch for myself. You will receive such respect, Katerina Vasilyevna, that you could ask for nothing better. Besides that, I don't drink, and I have never heard any reproaches from the gentlefolk.

KATYA: Really, Matvey Egorych, I don't know what to say to you. . . .

MATVEY: Oh, Katerina Vasilyevna, a little while ago you began to be . . .

KATYA: [*With a slight blush*] A little while ago? Why so?

MATVEY: I really don't know. . . . Only before . . . before you behaved quite differently towards me.

KATYA: [*Looking hastily off stage*] Look out! . . . The German is coming.

MATVEY: [*With vexation*] Plague take him, the long-nosed donkey! . . . But I'll have further conversation with you later.

[*Goes out to the right.* Katya *also is about to go into the raspberry patch.* Schaaf *comes in from the left with a fishing rod on his shoulder*]

SCHAAF: [*Calling after* Katya] Vere to, vere to, Caterin?

KATYA: [*Stopping*] They told me to pick some raspberries, Adam Ivanovich.

SCHAAF: Raspberriess? . . . Raspberriess are a pleasant fruit. You luf raspberriess?

KATYA: Yes, I do.

SCHAAF: Hee, hee! . . . I do . . . I do too. I luf every zing zat you luf. [*Seeing that she is about to leave*] Oh, Caterin, vait a bit.

KATYA: No time. . . . The housekeeper will scold me.

SCHAAF: Oh, zat's all right. Now I am going to . . . [*Pointing to his fishing rod*] I am going vat you say, you understand, fishing, zat is, catching fish. You like zem, fish?

KATYA: Yes.

SCHAAF: Eh, hee, hee! So do I. So do I. And let me tell you, Caterin. . . . In German zere is a song [*Sings*] Cathrinchen, Cathrinchen, wie lieb' ich dich so sehr! Zat iss in Russian: Oh, Caterin, Caterin, you are pretty, I luf you. [*Tries to embrace her with one arm*]

KATYA: Stop! Stop! Aren't you ashamed! . . . And here comes the mistress! [*Takes refuge in the raspberry patch*]

SCHAAF: [*Assuming a stern air, in a low voice*] Das ist dumm. . . .

[*Natalya Petrovna comes in from the right, arm in arm with* Rakitin]

NATALYA PETROVNA: [*To* Schaaf] Oh, Adam Ivanovich, are you going fishing?

SCHAAF: Yoost so!

NATALYA PETROVNA: And where is Kolya?

SCHAAF: Mit Lissafet Bogdanovna. . . . A lesson on ze piano. . . .

NATALYA PETROVNA: Oh! [*Looking around*] Are you alone here?

SCHAAF: Yes, ma'am.

NATALYA PETROVNA: Haven't you seen Alexey Nikolayevich?

SCHAAF: Not at all.

NATALYA PETROVNA: [*After a pause*] Let's go on together, Adam Ivanovich, shan't we? We'll watch you fish.

SCHAAF: I am very glat.

RAKITIN: [*In a low voice to* Natalya Petrovna] What an idea!

NATALYA PETROVNA: [*To* Rakitin] Come on, come on, beau ténébreux.

[*All three go out to the right*]

KATYA: [*Cautiously putting her head out of the raspberry patch*] They have gone. [*She comes out, pauses for a moment, and falls to thinking*] That German! . . . [*Sighs, and again begins to pick raspberries, humming in a low voice*]

The fire does not burn, the pitch does not boil
But there boils and there burns my eager heart. . . .

Matvey Egorych was certainly right! [*Continues to hum*]

But there boils and there burns my eager heart;
And not for my father, not for my mother dear . . .

[*Stops singing and exclaims*] What huge raspberries! [*Continues to hum*]

Not for my father, not for my mother dear . . .

How hot it is! Absolutely suffocating. [*Continues to hum*]

Not for my father, not for my mother dear:
It boils and it burns—

[*Suddenly she looks around, stops singing, and half hides herself behind a bush.* Belyayev *and* Verochka *come in from the left.* Belyayev *has a kite in his hands*]

BELYAYEV: [*Walking past the raspberry patch, to* Katya] Why do you stop, Katya? [*He sings*]

But it boils and burns for a maiden fair.

KATYA: [*Blushing*] That's not the way *we* sing it.

BELYAYEV: Well, how do you?

[Katya *laughs and does not answer*] What are you doing, picking raspberries? Let me try some.

KATYA: [*Giving him the basket*] Take 'em all.

BELYAYEV: Why all of them? . . . Vera Alexandrovna, will you have some? [*Both* Vera *and he take some from the basket*] Well, that's enough. [*Tries to give back the basket to* Katya]

KATYA: [*Pushing away his hand*] Take 'em all, take 'em.

BELYAYEV: No, thank you, Katya. [*He gives her back the basket*] Thank you. [*To* Vera] Vera Alexandrovna, let's sit down on the bench. [*Pointing to the kite*] We must tie on the tail. You'll help me. [*They both go and sit down on the bench.* Belyayev *hands her the kite*] That's the way. Now look out, hold it straight. [*He begins to tie on the tail*] What are you doing?

VERA: Put that away! I can't see you.

BELYAYEV: And what do you want to see me for?

VERA: I mean, I want to see how you tie on the tail.

BELYAYEV: Oh, well, stand still. [*He arranges the kite so that she can see him*] Katya, why don't you sing? Go ahead.

[*In a moment* Katya *begins to hum in a low voice*]

VERA: Tell me, Alexey Nikolayevich, do you sometimes fly kites in Moscow too?

BELYAYEV: No time for kites in Moscow! Hold the cord! . . . That's the way. Do you think we haven't anything else to do in Moscow?

VERA: What do you do in Moscow?

BELYAYEV: What do we do? We study and listen to the professors.

VERA: What do they teach you?

BELYAYEV: Everything.

VERA: You must be a very good student. Best of all of them.

BELYAYEV: No, not very good. Very far from the best. I'm lazy.

VERA: Why are you lazy?

BELYAYEV: Lord knows! I must have been born so.

VERA: [*After a pause*] Well, have you some student friends in Moscow?

BELYAYEV: Of course. Oh, that cord isn't strong enough.

VERA: And do you love them?

BELYAYEV: Certainly! . . . Don't you love your friends among the boys?

VERA: Among the boys? I haven't any friends among them.

BELYAYEV: I meant to say, your girl friends.

VERA: [Slowly] Yes.

BELYAYEV: You have girl friends?

VERA: Yes, only—I don't know why—for some time I haven't been thinking much about them. I haven't even anwered Liza Moshnin and she so urged me in her last letter.

BELYAYEV: What do you mean by saying that you haven't any boy friends? . . . Where do I come in?

VERA: [With a smile] Oh, you . . . you are another story. [After a pause] Alexey Nikolayevich!

BELYAYEV: What?

VERA: Do you write poetry?

BELYAYEV: No. Why do you ask?

VERA: No special reason. [After a pause] In our pension one young lady wrotes verses.

BELYAYEV: [Pulling a knot with his teeth] Well, well, were they good ones?

VERA: I don't know. She used to read them to us and we wept.

BELYAYEV: Why did you weep?

VERA: For sorrow. We were so sorry for her!

BELYAYEV: Were you educated in Moscow?

VERA: Yes, at Mrs. Bolus's. Natalya Petrovna took me from there last year.

BELYAYEV: Do you love Natalya Petrovna?

VERA: Yes, she is so kind. I love her very much.

BELYAYEV: [With a grin] And you are afraid of her, I suppose?

VERA: [Also with a grin] A little bit.

BELYAYEV: [After a pause] And who put you in the pension?

VERA: Natalya Petrovna's mother, who is now dead. I grew up in her house. I am an orphan.

BELYAYEV: [Letting his hands fall] You are an orphan? And you don't remember either your father or your mother?

VERA: No.

BELYAYEV: And my mother is dead, too. We are both of us orphans. What can we do about it? But anyhow we needn't be cast down.

VERA: They say that orphans make friends with each other very quickly.

BELYAYEV: [Looking into her eyes] Really, what do you think about it?

VERA: [Also looking into his eyes with a smile] I think they do.

BELYAYEV: [Laughing, and again applying himself to the kite] I should like to know how long I have been in these parts.

VERA: To-day is the twenty-eighth day.

BELYAYEV: What a memory you have! Well, here's the kite finished. Just see what a tail! We must go for Kolya.

KATYA: [Coming up to them with a basket] Will you have some more raspberries?

BELYAYEV: No, thank you, Katya.

[Katya silently moves away]

VERA: Kolya is with Lizaveta Bogdanovna.

BELYAYEV: They must like to keep a child indoors in such weather.

VERA: Lizaveta Bogdanovna would just be in our way.

BELYAYEV: I am not talking about her.

VERA: [Hastily] Kolya couldn't come with us without her. . . . By the way, she spoke of you in a very complimentary fashion yesterday.

BELYAYEV: Really!

VERA: You don't like her?

BELYAYEV: Plague take her. Let her take snuff, and much good may it do her! . . . Why are you sighing?

VERA: [After a pause] I don't know. How bright the sky is!

BELYAYEV: Is that what makes you sigh? [Silence] Maybe you feel lonesome.

VERA: Me, lonesome? No! I never know myself why I sigh. . . . I am not lonesome at all. On the contrary . . . [After a pause] . . . I don't know. I probably am not in perfect health. Yesterday I went upstairs for a book and all of a sudden—just imagine! —I sat down on a step and began to cry . . . God knows why . . . and for a long time after tears kept coming into my eyes. What does that mean? And yet I feel very well.

BELYAYEV: That is because you are growing. You are growing up. Such things happen. . . . That's true: yesterday evening your eyes looked swollen.

VERA: Did you notice it?

BELYAYEV: Certainly.

VERA: You notice everything.

BELYAYEV: Oh, no! . . . Not everything.

VERA: [Pensively] Alexey Nikolayevich . . .

BELYAYEV: What?

VERA: [After a pause] What was it that I wanted to ask you anyway? I've really forgotten what I wanted to ask.

BELYAYEV: You are so absent-minded.

VERA: No . . . but . . . oh, yes! Here's what I wanted to ask you. You were telling me you have a sister?

BELYAYEV: Yes.

VERA: Tell e, am I like her?

BELYAYEV: Oh no! You are a lot nicer than she.

VERA: Impossible! Your sister . . . I should lik to be in her place.

BELYAYEV: What? You would like to be in our littl house now?

VERA: I didn't mean that. . . . Is your house a little one?

BELYAYEV: Very little. . . . Not like this one here.

VERA: But what's the use of so many rooms?

BELYAYEV: What's the use of them? You'll find out in due time what the use of rooms is.

VERA: In due time? . . . When?

BELYAYEV: When you become a housewife yourself.

VERA: [*Pensively*] Do you think so?

BELYAYEV: You will see. [*After a pause*] Well then, shall we go for Kolya, Vera Alexandrovna? Shall we?

VERA: Why don't you call me Verochka?

BELYAYEV: And can you really call me Alexey?

VERA: Why not? . . . [*With a sudden start*] Oh!

BELYAYEV: What's the matter?

VERA: [*In a low voice*] Natalya Petrovna is coming this way.

BELYAYEV: [*Also in a low voice*] Where?

VERA: [*Indicating with her head*] Along the path there with Mikhaylo Alexandrovich.

BELYAYEV: [*Rising*] Let's go to Kolya. . . . He must have finished his lesson by this time.

VERA: Come on! Otherwise I'm afraid she'll scold me.

[*They both rise and go out quickly to the left. Katya again hides in the raspberry patch. Natalya Petrovna and Rakitin come in from the right*]

NATALYA PETROVNA: [*Stopping*] I think that's Mr. Belyayev going out with Verochka.

RAKITIN: Yes, it's they.

NATALYA PETROVNA: They seem to be running away from us.

RAKITIN: Perhaps.

NATALYA PETROVNA: [*After a pause*] However, I don't think that Verochka ought . . . to be alone with a young man in the garden in this way. . . . Of course she's a child but all the same it isn't proper. I'll tell her.

RAKITIN: How old is she?

NATALYA PETROVNA: Seventeen. She's already seventeen. . . . How warm it is to-day! I'm tired. Let's sit down.

[*They both sit down on the bench where* Vera *and* Belyayev *have been sitting*]

. . . Has Shpigelsky gone?

RAKITIN: Yes.

NATALYA PETROVNA: You made a mistake not to keep him. I don't know how that man got the idea of becoming a country doctor. . . . He's very amusing. He makes me laugh.

RAKITIN: But I imagine that you are not in a laughing humor to-day.

NATALYA PETROVNA: Why do you think so?

RAKITIN: Just a fancy!

NATALYA PETROVNA: Is it because to-day I dislike everything sentimental? Oh yes, I forewarn you: to-day absolutely nothing can touch my emotions. . . . But that doesn't keep me from laughing. . . . Besides, I needed to have a talk with Shpigelsky.

RAKITIN: May I inquire—what about?

NATALYA PETROVNA: No, you may not. Anyhow, you know everything that I think . . . that I do. That's tiresome.

RAKITIN: Excuse me! . . . I did not suppose . . .

NATALYA PETROVNA: I should like to conceal at least some one little thing from you.

RAKITIN: Good gracious. From your words I might infer that I knew everything. . . .

NATALYA PETROVNA: [*Interrupting him*] And don't you?

RAKITIN: You seem to enjoy laughing at me.

NATALYA PETROVNA: So really don't you know everything that goes on within me? In that case I don't congratulate you. Impossible! A man observes me from morning till evening—

RAKITIN: What's that? A reproach?

NATALYA PETROVNA: A reproach? [*After a pause*] I now see clearly: you are not a man of penetration.

RAKITIN: Perhaps not. . . . But since I observe you from morning till evening, permit me to make one remark to you. . . .

NATALYA PETROVNA: In regard to me? Pray do so.

RAKITIN: You won't be angry with me?

NATALYA PETROVNA: Oh, no! I should like to be, but I shan't.

RAKITIN: For some time, Natalya Petrovna, you have been in a sort of constantly irritated condition and this irritation of yours is involuntary, from within. You seem to be struggling with yourself, seem to be in perplexity. Before my trip to the Krinitsyns' I did not observe this. It is of recent date with you.

[Natalya Petrovna *draws figures on the ground with her parasol*]

Sometimes you sigh so deeply . . . just as a weary, a very weary person sighs, a person who never has a chance to take a rest.

NATALYA PETROVNA: What conclusion do you form from that, Mr. Observer?

RAKITIN: None at all. . . . But this disquiets me.

NATALYA PETROVNA: Thank you humbly for your sympathy.

RAKITIN: And besides—

NATALYA PETROVNA: [*With a certain impatience*] Please let's change the subject.

[*Silence*]

RAKITIN: You don't intend to take a ride anywhere to-day?

NATALYA PETROVNA: No.

RAKITIN: Why not? The weather's fine.

NATALYA PETROVNA: I'm too lazy. [*Silence*] Tell me. . . . You are acquainted with Bolshintsov?

RAKITIN: Our neighbor, Afanasy Ivanovich?

NATALYA PETROVNA: Yes.

RAKITIN: What a question! Only day before yesterday you and I were playing preference with him.

NATALYA PETROVNA: What kind of a man is he, I should like to know.

RAKITIN: Bolshintsov?

NATALYA PETROVNA: Yes, yes, Bolshintsov.

RAKITIN: Well, I must confess, I never expected this.

NATALYA PETROVNA: [*With impatience*] What didn't you expect?

RAKITIN: That you would ever ask me about Bolshintsov! He is a stupid, fat, heavy man, and yet one can't say anything bad about him.

NATALYA PETROVNA: He is by no means so stupid and so heavy as you think.

RAKITIN: Maybe. I confess I haven't studied that gentleman with any great attention.

NATALYA PETROVNA: [*Ironically*] You haven't been observing *him*?

RAKITIN: [*With a forced smile*] How did you get that idea?

NATALYA PETROVNA: Just a fancy! [*Again a silence*]

RAKITIN: Look, Natalya Petrovna, how beautiful that dark-green oak is against the dark-blue sky! It is all bathed in the sunbeams—and what vivid colors! . . . How much indomitable life and force there is in it, especially when you compare it with that young birch. . . . The birch seems already to vanish in the radiance; its little leaves gleam with a sort of moist luster, as if they were melting, and yet the birch also is beautiful. . . .

NATALYA PETROVNA: Let me tell you, Rakitin. I long ago noticed this trait in you: You have a very keen sense for the so-called beauties of nature, and you speak of them very elegantly, very cleverly . . . so elegantly, so cleverly, that I imagine nature ought to be inexpressibly grateful to you for your aptly-turned expressions. You pay court to it as a perfumed marquis with red-heeled shoes does to a pretty peasant girl. . . . Only here's the trouble: it occasionally seems to me that nature could not in the least understand or appreciate your acute observations, just as the peasant girl would not understand the elegant courtesies of the marquis. Nature is far simpler, even coarser, than you suppose, because, thank God, it is healthy. . . . Birches do not melt and do not faint away like nervous ladies.

RAKITIN: *Quelle tirade!* Nature is healthy. That is, in other words, I am a sickly creature.

NATALYA PETROVNA: You are not the only sickly creature. Both you and I are by no means healthy.

RAKITIN: Oh, I know very well that method of telling another person the most unpleasant things in the most inoffensive fashion. . . . Instead of telling him straight to his face, for instance: "My boy, you are stupid," you merely have to remark to him with a good-natured smile, "You see, both of us are stupid."

NATALYA PETROVNA: Are you taking offense? Stop! What nonsense! I only meant that both of us . . . you don't like the word "sickly" . . . that both of us are old, very old.

RAKITIN: Why old? That's not my opinion of myself.

NATALYA PETROVNA: Well, anyway, listen to me. Here you and I are sitting now . . . perhaps on the very same bench on which a quarter of an hour ago there were sitting . . . two genuinely young creatures.

RAKITIN: Belyayev and Verochka? Of course they are younger than we are. . . . Between us and them there is a few years' difference, that is all. . . . But that doesn't make us old yet awhile.

NATALYA PETROVNA: The difference between us is not in years alone.

RAKITIN: Oh, I understand. You envy their . . naïveté and freshness and innocence . . . in a word, their stupidity. . . .

NATALYA PETROVNA: You think so? Ah! You think they are stupid? I see that you regard every one as stupid to-day. No, you don't understand me. And besides . . . stupid! Where's the harm in that? What's the use of intellect when it isn't amusing? . . . There's nothing more wearisome than melancholy intellect.

RAKITIN: Hm. . . . Why won't you say straight out, without beating around the bush, that I don't amuse you? That's what you really mean. . . . And why do you make intellect in general suffer for my sins?

NATALYA PETROVNA: You take everything wrong. . . .

[Katya *comes out of the raspberry patch*]
Well, have you picked the raspberries, Katya?

KATYA: Yes, madam.

NATALYA PETROVNA: Show them to me. . . .
[Katya *comes up to her*]
Splendid raspberries! What a bright color! . . . But your cheeks are still brighter.
[Katya *smiles and lowers her eyes*]
Well, go along.
[Katya *goes out*]

RAKITIN: There is one more young creature to your taste.

NATALYA PETROVNA: To be sure. [*She rises*]

RAKITIN: Where are you going?

NATALYA PETROVNA: In the first place I want to see what Verochka is doing. It's time for her to be going indoors. . . . And in the second place I must confess that I don't specially like our conversation. It would be better for a while to cut short our discussion of nature and youth.

RAKITIN: Maybe you would like to have a walk alone?

NATALYA PETROVNA: To tell the truth, I should. We'll soon see each other again. . . . All the same, we part friends, do we not? [*Extends her hand to him*]

RAKITIN: Of course. [*Presses her hand*]

NATALYA PETROVNA: *Au revoir.* [*She opens her parasol and goes out to the left*]

RAKITIN: [*Walks for some time back and forth*] What's the matter with her? [*After a pause*] Just a caprice. Caprice? I've never before thought her capricious. On the contrary, I don't know a woman of more equable temper. What's the reason? . . . [*He paces back and forth again and suddenly stops*] Oh, how ridiculous people are who have only one thought in their head, one aim, one occupation in life! . . . Take me, for example. She told the truth: from morning till evening you observe trifles and so you become trifling yourself. . . . That's all true, but I can't live without her. In her presence I am more than happy. This feeling cannot be called mere happiness. I belong to her entirely. To part from her would be just as difficult for me, without any exaggeration, as to part with life itself. What's the matter with her? What is the meaning of that inner emotion, that involuntary bitterness of expression. Am I not beginning to bore her? Hm. [*He sits down*] I have never deceived myself. I know very well in what way she loves me, but I hoped that this calm feeling would in the course of time . . . I hoped! Have I the right, may I dare to hope? I confess my position is ridiculous enough . . . almost contemptible. [*After a pause*] Well, what's the use of such words? She's an honorable woman and I am not a Lovelace. [*With a bitter smile*] Unfortunately. [*Rising quickly*] Well, that's enough! I must get all this nonsense out of my head. [*Walking up and down*] What a splendid day this is! [*After a pause*] How cleverly she wounded me! . . . My "aptly-turned expressions"! . . . She is very, very shrewd, especially when she is out of spirits. And what a sudden adoration for simplicity and innocence! . . . That Russian teacher! . . . She often speaks to me of him. I confess I don't see anything special in him. He is simply a student like other students. Is it possible that she . . . ? Impossible! She is out of spirits. . . . She doesn't know herself what she wants, and so she scratches me. Even children beat their nurse. . . . What a happy comparison! But I don't want to hinder her. When this attack of uneasiness and disquiet is over she will be the first to laugh at that lanky fledgling, at that unspoiled youth. . . . Your explanation is not bad, Mikhaylo Alexandrovich, my friend. But is it correct? The Lord knows! We'll see later. It has often happened, my dear fellow, that after long debate with yourself, you have suddenly had to renounce all suppositions and surmises, fold your arms calmly and wait humbly to see what would happen. And meanwhile, confess that you are in a decidedly embarrassing and bitter position. . . . Such is your trade now. . . . [*Looking around*] But here he comes himself, our unspoiled youth. . . . He has arrived just in time . . . I haven't had a single conversation with him worth mentioning. Let's see what sort of man he is.

[Belyayev *comes in from the left*]

Oh, Alexey Nikolayevich, have you been walking in the fresh air?

BELYAYEV: Yes.

RAKITIN: That is to say, we must confess the air to-day isn't altogether fresh: it's frightfully hot. But here under these linden trees in the shade it's bearable enough. [*After a pause*] Have you seen Natalya Petrovna?

BELYAYEV: I just met her. . . . She and Vera Alexandrovna have gone into the house.

RAKITIN: But wasn't it Vera Alexandrovna that I saw here a half hour ago?

BELYAYEV: Yes. . . . I was strolling with her.

RAKITIN: Ah! [*Takes his arm*] Well, how do you like life in the country?

BELYAYEV: I like the country. The only trouble is that the hunting here is poor.

RAKITIN: Are you a sportsman?

BELYAYEV: Yes. And you?

RAKITIN: I? No, I must confess I am a poor shot. I am too lazy.

BELYAYEV: And I am lazy too . . . only not about walking.

RAKITIN: Oh! Are you lazy about reading?

BELYAYEV: No, I like to read. I am lazy about working for a long time at a stretch; I am especially lazy about applying myself continuously to one and the same subject.

RAKITIN: [*Smiling*] As for instance, conversing with the ladies?

BELYAYEV: Oh! You are laughing at me. . . . I am generally afraid of the ladies.

RAKITIN: [*Slightly confused*] Why did you think . . . ? Why should I make fun of you?

BELYAYEV: Just a fancy. Where's the harm! [*After a pause*] Tell me, where can I get powder here?

RAKITIN: In the town, I think. They sell it there under the name of poppy seed. Do you need good powder?

BELYAYEV: No, musket powder will do. I don't want to shoot. I want to make some fireworks.

RAKITIN: What, do you know how?

BELYAYEV: I do. And I have already chosen a place on the other side of the pond. I've heard that next week will come the name day[6] of Natalya Petrovna, and so fireworks would be appropriate.

RAKITIN: Natalya Petrovna will be much pleased at such an attention on your part. . . . She likes you, Alexey Nikolayevich, let me tell you.

BELYAYEV: That is very flattering for me. . . . Oh, by the way, Mikhaylo Alexandrovich, I think you receive a magazine. Could you lend it to me?

RAKITIN: Certainly, with pleasure. . . . It contains good poetry.

BELYAYEV: I'm not fond of poetry.

RAKITIN: Why not?

BELYAYEV: I just am not. Humorous poetry seems to me forced; and besides, there is very little of it. . . . And sentimental verse . . . Somehow I don't believe in it.

RAKITIN: Do you prefer stories?

BELYAYEV: Yes. I like good stories. . . . But critical articles, those are what take hold of me.

RAKITIN: Why so?

BELYAYEV: A man of heart writes those.

RAKITIN: And you yourself do not cultivate literature?

BELYAYEV: Oh, no! What's the use of writing if God has given you no talent? It only makes people laugh. And besides, here is what is surprising; here is what you must explain to me, if you please: Some-

⁹ The day on which a child is named.

times a man seems clever, but when he takes up a pen you have to call the fire department. No, what's the use of our writing? Lord help us to understand what other people write!

RAKITIN: Let me tell you, Alexey Nikolayevich, not many young men have as much common sense as you have.

BELYAYEV: Thank you humbly for the compliment. [*After a pause*] I have selected a place for the fireworks the other side of the pond, because I know how to make Roman candles that burn on water.

RAKITIN: That must be very beautiful. Excuse me, Alexey Nikolayevich . . . but permit me to ask you . . . do you know French?

BELYAYEV: No. I translated a novel of Paul de Kock, *The Milkmaid of Montfermel*—maybe you have heard of it—for fifty rubles paper money, but I don't know a word of French. Just imagine, I translated *quatre-vingt-dix*[7] as four twenty ten! . . . Poverty, you know, forced me to. But I'm sorry. I should like to know French. I should like to read George Sand in French. But that pronunciation! How can you expect me to manage it? *An, on, in, un.* . . . Isn't it awful?

RAKITIN: Well, we can help that trouble.

BELYAYEV: Permit me to inquire what time it is?

RAKITIN: [*Looking at his watch*] Half past one.

BELYAYEV: Why is it that Lizaveta Bogdanovna is keeping Kolya at the piano for so long? . . . I think he must want awfully to have a run.

RAKITIN: [*In a kind tone*] But yet people must study, Alexey Nikolayevich.

BELYAYEV: [*With a sigh*] It's not for you to say that, Mikhaylo Alexandrovich, or for me to listen to it. . . . Of course not everybody should be as shiftless as I.

RAKITIN: Oh, stop!

BELYAYEV: I know very well what I am talking about.

RAKITIN: But, on the contrary, I know quite as well—I am convinced—that the very quality which you regard as a defect in yourself, your lack of constraint, your ease of manner, is what makes you liked by people.

BELYAYEV: By whom, for example?

RAKITIN: Well, by Natalya Petrovna, for instance.

BELYAYEV: Natalya Petrovna? But I do not feel myself at ease with her, as you say.

RAKITIN: Oh, really?

BELYAYEV: And finally, if you please, Mikhaylo Alexandrovich, is not education the matter of first importance for a man? It is easy for you to speak. . . . I really don't understand you. . . . [*Suddenly stopping*] What's that? I thought I heard a rail[8] call in the garden. [*Is about to leave*]

RAKITIN: Perhaps. . . . But where are you going?

BELYAYEV: For my gun.

[7] Ninety, in French.
[8] A bird.

[*He goes off to the left*. Natalya Petrovna *meets him. Seeing him, she smiles suddenly*]

NATALYA PETROVNA: Where are you going, Alexey Nikolayevich?

BELYAYEV: I . . .

RAKITIN: For his gun. . . . He heard a rail in the garden. . . .

NATALYA PETROVNA: No, please don't shoot in the garden. . . . Let the poor bird live. . . . Besides that, you may scare grandmother.

BELYAYEV: I obey.

NATALYA PETROVNA: [*Laughing*] Oh, Alexey Nikolayevich, aren't you ashamed? "I obey." What an expression! . . . How can you speak that way? But wait, Mikhalyo Alexandrovich and I will attend to your education. Yes, yes. . . . We have already spoken of you several times. . . . We have a conspiracy against you. I warn you. Will you permit me to attend to your education?

BELYAYEV: Why . . . I . . . .

NATALYA PETROVNA: In the first place, don't be so bashful. That is not becoming to you at all. Yes, we will take charge of you. [*Pointing to* Rakitin] He and I are old people—and you are a young man. . . . Isn't that so? You'll see how well everything turns out. You will attend to Kolya and I . . . and we will attend to you.

BELYAYEV: I shall be very grateful to you.

NATALYA PETROVNA: That's right. What were you talking about here with Mikhaylo Alexandrovich?

RAKITIN: [*Smiling*] He was telling me how he translated a French book without knowing a word of French.

NATALYA PETROVNA: Well, then, we'll teach you French too. And by the way, what have you done with your kite?

BELYAYEV: I took it to my room. It seemed to me that you . . . did not like it.

NATALYA PETROVNA: [*With a certain confusion*] How did you get that idea? Because I said to Verochka . . . because I took Verochka into the house? No, that . . . no, you made a mistake. [*With animation*] However, let me tell you: Kolya must have finished his lesson by this time. Let's go and get him and Verochka and the kite, will you? And we'll all go to the meadow together. Shall we?

BELAYEV: With pleasure, Natalya Petrovna.

NATALYA PETROVNA: That's fine! Well, come on, come on! [*Stretches out her hand to him*] Oh, take my hand! How clumsy you are! Come on, hurry up!

[*They go out quickly to the left*]

RAKITIN: [*Gazing after them*] What animation . . . what gayety! I have never seen such an expression on her face. And what a sudden change! [*After a pause*] *Souvent femme varie.* . . . But I . . . it is evident that to-day I don't suit her. That's clear. [*After a pause*] Well, we'll see what comes next. [*Slowly*] Is it possible that . . . ? [*Waves his hand*] Impossible! . . . But that smile, that affable, soft, radiant expression! . . . Oh, Lord forbid that I should experience the torments of jealousy, especially senseless jealousy! [*Looking around*] Bah, bah, bah! . . . And what brought *them*?

[*From the left* Shpigelsky *and* Bolshintsov *come in.* Rakitin *goes to meet them*]

How do you do, gentlemen. . . . I must confess, Shpigelsky, I didn't expect you to-day. [*Shakes hands with them*]

SHPIGELSKY: And I, myself . . . I myself had no such idea. . . . But you see, I called on him [*Pointing to* Bolshintsov] and he was already sitting in his carriage, starting for this house. Well, I immediately turned right-about-face and came back here.

RAKITIN: Well, you are welcome.

BOLSHINTSOV: I was really preparing to—

SHPIGELSKY: [*Shutting him off*] The servants told us that the ladies and gentlemen were in the garden. . . . At any rate, there was no one in the drawing-room.

RAKITIN: But didn't you meet Natalya Petrovna?

SHPIGELSKY: When?

RAKITIN: Why, just now.

SHPIGELSKY: No, we didn't come straight from the house. Afanasy Ivanovich wanted to see whether there were any mushrooms in the grove.

BOLSHINTSOV: [*Perplexed*] I . . .

SHPIGELSKY: Well, we know that you are a great lover of birch mushrooms. So Natalya Petrovna has gone indoors. Well, then we may return.

BOLSHINTSOV: Of course.

RAKITIN: But she went indoors to call all of them to go for a walk. . . . I think they were going to fly the kite.

SHPIGELSKY: Oh, splendid. In such weather you must stroll about the country.

RAKITIN: You can stay here. . . . I'll go and tell her that you've arrived.

SHPIGELSKY: But why trouble yourself? . . . Pray don't, Mikhaylo Alexandrovich.

RAKITIN: Oh, I need to go there anyway.

SHPIGELSKY: Oh, well, in that case, we won't detain you. . . . Without ceremony, you know. . . .

RAKITIN: Good-by for the moment, gentlemen. [*Goes out to the left*]

SHPIGELSKY: Good-by. [*To* Bolshintsov] Well, Afanasy Ivanovich?

BOLSHINTSOV: [*Interrupting him*] How did you get that idea about mushrooms, Ignaty Ilyich? . . . I'm astonished. What mushrooms?

SHPIGELSKY: I suppose I ought to have said that my friend Afanasy Ivanovich got scared, and didn't want to come the straight road, but begged to take a bypath.

BOLSHINTSOV: That's the truth. . . . But all the same, mushrooms! . . . I don't know. Maybe I'm mistaken. . . .

SHPIGELSKY: You're certainly mistaken, my friend. Here's what you had better reflect on. You see, you and I have come here. We've done what you wished. Look out that you don't make a fizzle of it!

BOLSHINTSOV: But, Ignaty Ilyich, you . . . you told me that . . . That is, I should like to know positively what answer . . .

SHPIGELSKY: My most respected Afanasy Ivanovich! From your village to this place is at least ten miles. Every half mile at least you have asked me the same question three times over. . . . Isn't that enough for you? Now listen, I'll humor you just this last time. Here's what Natalya Petrovna told me: "I . . ."

BOLSHINTSOV: [*Nodding*] Yes.

SHPIGELSKY: [*With vexation*] "Yes" . . . well, why "Yes"? I haven't said anything to you yet. . . . "I am little acquainted with Mr. Bolshinstov," she told me, "but he seems to me a good man. On the other hand, I have no intention of putting pressure on Verochka, and so let him come to see us, and if he wins—"

BOLSHINTSOV: "Wins"? Did she say "wins"?

SHPIGELSKY: "If he wins her regard, Anna Semenovna and I will not interpose objections."

BOLSHINTSOV: "Will not interpose objections"? Is that what she said? "Will not interpose objections"?

SHPIGELSKY: Oh, yes, yes, yes. What a queer man you are. "We will not interpose objections to their happiness."

BOLSHINTSOV: Hm.

SHPIGELSKY: "To their happiness." Yes, but observe, Afanasy Ivanovich, what your problem is now. . . . Now you need to convince Vera Alexandrovna herself that a marriage with you will be happiness for her. You need to win her regard.

BOLSHINTSOV: [*Blinking*] Yes, yes. Win . . . To be sure, I agree with you.

SHPIGELSKY: You insisted that I should bring you here to-day. . . . Well, let's see how you will get down to work.

BOLSHINTSOV: Get down to work? Yes, yes, I must get down to work; I must win her regard. Only here's the point, Ignaty Ilyich. . . . I must confess to you my single weakness, since you are my best friend. I desired, as you have said, to have you bring me here to-day.

SHPIGELSKY: You didn't desire it. You demanded it. You demanded it insistently.

BOLSHINTSOV: Well, let's suppose so. . . . I agree with you. But just see here. At home I really . . . at home I was ready for everything, I think, but now timidity overcomes me.

SHPIGELSKY: But why are you timid?

BOLSHINTSOV: [*Looking at him in an embarrassed fashion*] The risk.

SHPIGELSKY: Wha-at?

BOLSHINTSOV: The risk. It's a great risk. Ignaty Ilyich, I must confess to you that . . .

SHPIGELSKY: [*Interrupting him*] "As to your best friend." I know, I know. . . . Next?

BOLSHINTSOV: Quite so. I agree with you. I must confess to you, Ignaty Ilyich, that I . . . that in general, I have had only slight contact with the female sex in general, so to speak. I confess to you openly, Ignaty Ilyich, that I simply cannot imagine what you can talk about with a person of the female sex, and besides that, all alone . . . especially with a girl.

SHPIGELSKY: You surprise me! I don't know what you *can't* talk about with a person of the female sex, especially with a girl, and especially all alone.

BOLSHINTSOV: Yes, but you . . . consider what a difference there is between you and me. Now, on this occasion, I should like to ask your help, Ignaty Ilyich. They say that in these matters it is the first step that counts. So couldn't you tell me something to serve as an introduction to the conversation? Some little word. Something pleasant, in the nature of a remark, for instance—and then I'll go to meet them. After that, I'll manage it myself, somehow.

SHPIGELSKY: I can't tell you any little word, Afanasy Ivanovich, because no word will be of any use to you. . . . But I can give you some advice, if you wish.

BOLSHINTSOV: Be kind enough to do so, sir. . . . And as for my gratitude . . . You know . . .

SHPIGELSKY: Stop, stop! Am I driving a bargain with you?

BOLSHINTSOV: [*Lowering his voice*] You may rest easy about that team of three horses.

SHPIGELSKY: Oh, do stop! Now you see, Afanasy Ivanovich. . . . Without any dispute, you are a splendid man in all respects . . .

[Bolshintsov *makes a slight bow*]

a man of excellent qualities.

BOLSHINTSOV: Oh, pray don't!

SHPIGELSKY: And, besides, I believe you have three hundred serfs.

BOLSHINTSOV: Three hundred and twenty.

SHPIGELSKY: Not mortgaged.

BOLSHINTSOV: I am not a single kopek in debt.

SHPIGELSKY: Well, you see, I told you you were a most excellent man, and a suitor of the finest kind. Well then, you say yourself that you have associated little with ladies. . . .

BOLSHINTSOV: [*With a sigh*] Quite so. I might say, Ignaty Ilyich, that from my childhood I have avoided the female sex.

SHPIGELSKY: [*With a sigh*] Well, there, you see. In a husband that's not a vice. Quite the contrary. But still in some cases—for instance, at the first confession of love, it's indispensable to be able to say at least something. . . . Isn't that so?

BOLSHINTSOV: I quite agree with you.

SHPIGELSKY: And then, possibly Vera Alexandrovna may think that you don't feel well, and nothing more. Besides that, your figure, although it's presentable in every respect, is not of the sort, you know, that elicits instant admiration, and that's required nowadays.

BOLSHINTSOV: [*With a sigh*] That's required nowadays.

SHPIGELSKY: At least, the girls like it. Well, and

then, your years! . . . In a word, you and I can't hope to succeed by our personal attractions. So you needn't think about any pleasant remarks. That's a poor support. But you have another support which is far more firm and dependable. That's your personal qualities, my most excellent Afanasy Ivanovich, and your three hundred and twenty serfs. In your place, I should simply say to Vera Alexandrovna . . .

BOLSHINTSOV: All alone?

SHPIGELSKY: Oh, all alone, by all means.— "Vera Alexandrovna,"

[*By the movements of* Bolshintsov's *lips you can see that in a whisper he repeats every word after* Shpigelsky]

"I love you, and I ask for your hand. I am a good, simple man, of gentle disposition, and far from poor. With me, you will be at complete liberty. I will try to suit you in every way, and pray make inquiries about me. Pray devote a little more attention to me than you have previously, and give me what answer you choose, and when you choose. I am ready to wait, and shall even regard that as a pleasure."

BOLSHINTSOV: [*Pronouncing aloud the last word*] "Pleasure." Yes, yes, yes. . . . I agree with you. Only here's the point, Ignaty Ilyich. I think that you were pleased to employ the words, "of gentle disposition." So I am a man of gentle disposition?

SHPIGELSKY: Well, aren't you a man of gentle disposition?

BOLSHINTSOV: Ye-es. . . . But all the same, it seems to me . . . Will that be proper, Ignaty Ilyich? Wouldn't it be better to say, for instance . . . ?

SPHIGELSKY: For instance?

BOLSHINTSOV: For instance . . . for instance . . . [*After a pause*] However, it may do to say "of gentle disposition."

SHPIGELSKY: Oh, Afanasy Ivanovich, listen to me. The more simply you express yourself, the fewer ornamentations you introduce into your speech, the better things will go, believe me; and above all, don't insist, Afanasy Ivanovich, don't insist. Vera Alexandrovna is still very young. You may scare her. . . . Give her time to consider your proposal thoroughly. . . . And one more point! . . . I almost forgot. You see, you have permitted me to give you advice. . . . Sometimes it happens, my dear Afanasy Ivanovich, that you say "duin" and "noo." Of course, why not? You can do it. But you know, the word "doing" and the word "new" are rather more usual. They are in better usage, so to speak. And then, I remember once in my presence you called a certain hospitable landowner a "bonzhiban." You remarked, "What a bonzhiban he is." It's a fine word, but unfortunately, it doesn't mean anything. You know, I myself am not any too strong in the French dialect, but I know that much. Avoid eloquence, and I warrant your success. [*Looking around*] But here they are! They are all coming this way.

[Bolshintsov *is about to withdraw*]

Where are you going? For mushrooms again?
[Bolshintsov *smiles, blushes, and holds his ground*]
The main thing is not to be timid!

BOLSHINTSOV: [*Hastily*] But Vera Alexandrovna doesn't know anything about it yet.

SHPIGELSKY: Of course not.

BOLSHINTSOV: At any rate, I rely on you. [*Blows his nose*]

[*From the left there come in* Natalya Petrovna, Vera, Belyayev *with the kite,* Kolya, *and following them,* Rakitin *and* Lizaveta Bogdanovna. Natalya Petrovna *is in high spirits*]

NATALYA PETROVNA: [*To* Bolshintsov *and* Shpigelsky] Oh, how do you do, gentlemen! How do you do, Shpigelsky! I didn't expect to see you to-day, but I'm always glad to see you. How do you do, Afanasy Ivanovich!

[Bolshintsov *bows with a certain confusion*]

SHPIGELSKY: [*To* Natalya Petrovna, *indicating* Bolshintsov] You see, this gentleman insisted on bringing me here.

NATALYA PETROVNA: [*Laughing*] I am much obliged to him. . . . But do you need to be forced to come to see us?

SHPIGELSKY: Not at all. But . . . I left here only this morning. . . . Just think. . . .

NATALYA PETROVNA: Oh, you have got mixed up, you have got mixed up, Mr. Diplomat!

SHPIGELSKY: It is very pleasant for me, Natalya Petrovna, to see you in such a gay mood, if I observe correctly.

NATALYA PETROVNA: And you think it necessary to remark on that? . . . But is that such a rare occurrence with me?

SHPIGELSKY: Oh, no indeed. . . . But . . .

NATALYA PETROVNA: *M. le diplomate,* you are getting more and more mixed up.

KOLYA: [*Who has all this time been impatiently hovering about* Belyayev *and* Vera] But, mamma, when are we going to fly the kite?

NATALYA PETROVNA: Whenever you please. . . . Alexey Nikolayevich—and you, too, Verochka—let's go to the meadow. [*Turning to the rest of the group*] Gentlemen, I don't think that this will be very interesting for you. Lizaveta Bogdanovna, and you, too, Mr. Rakitin, I commend to you our good friend, Afanasy Ivanovich.

RAKITIN: But why do you think, Natalya Petrovna, that we shall not be interested?

NATALYA PETROVNA: You are clever people. . . . This may seem to you a silly frolic. . . . However, as you wish. We won't hinder you from following us. . . . [*To* Belyayev *and* Verochka] Come on!

[Natalya Petrovna, Vera, Belyayev *and* Kolya *go out on the right*]

SHPIGELSKY: [*Looking with a certain amazement at* Rakitin. *To* Bolshintsov] My good friend, Afanasy Ivanovich, offer your arm to Lizaveta Bogdanovna.

BOLSHINTSOV: [*Hastily*] With great pleasure. . . .
[*Takes* Lizaveta Bogdanovna's *arm*]

SHPIGELSKY: [*To* Rakitin] And you and I will go together, if you will allow me, Mikhaylo Alexandrovich. [*Takes his arm*] You see how they are running down the path by the trees. Come on, let's see how they fly the kite, even if we are clever people. . . . Afanasy Ivanovich, won't you go in front?

BOLSHINTSOV: [*To* Lizaveta Bogdanovna, *as they walk off*] To-day . . . the weather . . . is . . . quite pleasant . . . one may say.

LIZAVETA BOGDANOVNA: [*Coquettishly*] Oh, very!

SHPIGELSKY: [*To* Rakitin] But I need to talk over something with you, Mikhaylo Alexandrovich. . . .
[Rakitin *suddenly laughs*]
What are you laughing at?

RAKITIN: Oh . . . nothing! . . . It amuses me that we've fallen into the rear guard.

SHPIGELSKY: The vanguard may very easily, you know, become the rear guard. . . . Everything depends on a change of direction.

[*They all go off on the right*]

ACT III.

The same setting as in Act I. From the hall door Rakitin *and* Shpigelsky *come in.*

SHPIGELSKY: Well, then, Mikhaylo Alexandrovich, help me out, if you please.

RAKITIN: But how can I help you, Ignaty Ilyich?

SHPIGELSKY: How? Just consider. Just understand my situation, Mikhaylo Alexandrovich. I am really only a third party in this matter, of course. I may say that I acted merely from a desire to be of service. . . . My kind heart will be my ruin yet!

RAKITIN: [*Laughing*] Well, your ruin is still a long way off.

SHPIGELSKY: [*Also laughing*] Can't tell about that yet, but my position is certainly embarrassing. I brought Bolshintsov here according to Natalya Petrovna's desire, and I informed him of her answer, with her permission. And now, on one side, they look askance at me, as if I had done something silly, and on the other hand, Bolshintsov won't give me any rest. They avoid him, and won't talk to me.

RAKITIN: Why did you want to take up this matter, Ignaty Ilyich? You see, just between ourselves, Bolshintsov is simply stupid.

SHPIGELSKY: "Between ourselves," you say! What news you are giving me! How long is it since only clever people have been getting married? You can ruin the business of fools in everything else, but you ought not to do so in the marrying line. You say, I took up this affair. . . . Not at all. This is how the matter came about. My friend asked me to put in a word for him. Well, should I have refused him? I am a kind man. I don't know how to refuse. I carried out my friend's commission, and they replied: "We thank you humbly. Don't trouble about the matter any more." I understood, and I didn't trouble them any more. Then, all of a sudden, they made a proposal to me themselves, and urged me, so to speak. . . . I submitted, and now they are discontented with me. How am I to blame in this?

RAKITIN: Who ever said that you were to blame? . . . I am surprised at just one thing: Why are you taking so much trouble?

SHPIGELSKY: Why? . . . Why? The man won't give me any rest.

RAKITIN: Oh, don't say that! . . .

SHPIGELSKY: And, besides, he is my old, old friend.

RAKITIN: [*With a distrustful smile*] Well, that's different.

SHPIGELSKY: [*Also smiling*] However, I won't dissemble to you. . . . Nobody can deceive *you*. Well, yes . . . he promised me. My side horse has gone lame, and so he promised me—

RAKITIN: Another side horse?

SHPIGELSKY: No, I must confess, a whole team of three.

RAKITIN: You ought to have said that long ago!

SHPIGELSKY: [*With animation*] But please don't think . . . I wouldn't have agreed on any consideration to mediate in such a matter—that is completely against my nature—

[Rakitin *smiles*]

if I did not know Bolshintsov as the most honorable of men. . . . However, even now, I am anxious for only one thing: let them give me a decisive answer, yes or no.

RAKITIN: Has the matter reached that point?

SHPIGELSKY: How can you imagine that? . . . I am not talking about marriage, but about permission to make visits here. . . .

RAKITIN: But who can forbid that?

SHPIGELSKY: Forbid it, you say! Of course, for any other person. . . . But Bolshintsov is a timid man, an innocent soul, straight from the Golden Age of Astræa.[9] He is almost like a baby sucking his thumb. . . . He has little self-confidence. He needs to be encouraged a bit. Besides that, his intentions are the most honorable.

RAKITIN: And his horses are good?

SHPIGELSKY: And his horses are good. [*Takes snuff and offers the snuff box to* Rakitin] Will you have some?

RAKITIN: No, I thank you.

SHPIGELSKY: That's the way it is, Mikhaylo Alexandrovich. I don't want to deceive you, you see, and what's the use? The whole matter is as clear as a bell. A man of honorable principles, and a man of property, of gentle disposition . . . if he suits, all right. If he doesn't suit, then tell him so.

[9] The goddess of justice, the last to leave the earth at the end of the Golden Age; later, the constellation Virgo.

RAKITIN: All that's fine, I suppose, but how do I come in? I really don't see how *I* can help you.

SHPIGELSKY: Oh, Mikhaylo Alexandrovich, don't I know that Natalya Petrovna esteems you highly, and even sometimes takes your advice. . . . Really, Mikhaylo Alexandrovich, [*Putting his arm around him*] be my friend. Put in a word for me.

RAKITIN: And do you think he is a good husband for Verochka?

SHPIGELSKY: [*Assuming a serious air*] I am convinced of it. You don't believe it. . . . Well, you'll see. In the marrying game, as you know yourself, the principal thing is a solid character, and there is nothing solider than Bolshintsov. [*Looking around*] But I think that here comes Natalya Petrovna herself. . . . My friend, my father, my benefactor! Two roans as side horses, and a dark brown for the center! Will you make efforts?

RAKITIN: [*Smiling*] Well, all right, all right.

SHPIGELSKY: See to it! I rely on you. [*Takes refuge in the hall*]

RAKITIN: [*Gazing after him*] What an intriguer that doctor is! Vera . . . and Bolshintsov! . . . And yet why not? There are worse marriages than that. I'll fulfill his commission, and what follows is none of my affair.

[*He turns around.* Natalya Petrovna *comes in from the study and stops when she sees him*]

NATALYA PETROVNA: [*Indecisively*] Is that . . . you? . . . I thought you were in the garden.

RAKITIN: You seem displeased.

NATALYA PETROVNA: [*Interrupting him*] Oh, don't say that! [*Coming to the front of the stage*] Are you alone here?

RAKITIN: Shpigelsky has just left.

NATALYA PETROVNA: [*Slightly frowning*] Oh, that district Talleyrand! . . . What was he saying to you? Is he still hanging around here?

RAKITIN: That district Talleyrand, as you call him, is evidently not in favor with you to-day. . . . But I think that yesterday . . .

NATALYA PETROVNA: He is ridiculous. He is amusing, to be sure, but . . . but he doesn't mind his own business. . . . That's unpleasant. . . . And besides, with all his servility, he is very insolent and importunate. . . . He is a great cynic.

RAKITIN: [*Approaching her*] Yesterday you did not speak of him in any such tone.

NATALYA PETROVNA: Possibly. [*With animation*] So what was he telling you?

RAKITIN: He was telling me . . . about Bolshintsov.

NATALYA PETROVNA: Oh? About that stupid man?

RAKITIN: Yesterday you spoke differently of him, too.

NATALYA PETROVNA: [*With a forced smile*] Yesterday isn't to-day.

RAKITIN: For most men. . . . But evidently my case is different.

NATALYA PETROVNA: [*Lowering her eyes*] How so?

RAKITIN: For me, to-day is the same as yesterday.

NATALYA PETROVNA: [*Extending her hand to him*] I understand your reproach, but you are mistaken. Yesterday, I should not have confessed that you had any cause to blame me.

[Rakitin *is about to stop her*]

Do not reply to me. I know, and you know, what I mean. . . . And to-day I confess it. To-day I have thought over many things. . . . Believe me, Michel, whatever stupid thoughts may occupy me, whatever I may say, whatever I may do, I rely on no one so much as on you. [*Lowering her voice*] I do not love . . . any one as I love you. . . . [*After a short pause*] Do you not believe me?

RAKITIN: I believe you, but to-day you seem sad. . . . What's the matter with you?

NATALYA PETROVNA: [*Not listening to him, continues*] Only, I have become convinced of one thing, Rakitin. I cannot answer for myself on any occasion, and I can vouch for nothing. Often we do not understand our own past, and how can we answer for the future? You cannot put chains on the future.

RAKITIN: That's true.

NATALYA PETROVNA: [*After a long silence*] Listen, I want to be frank with you. Perhaps I shall slightly wound you . . . but I know that my reticence would wound you still more. I confess to you, Michel: that young student—that Belyayev—has produced a rather strong impression upon me.

RAKITIN: [*In a low voice*] I knew it.

NATALYA PETROVNA: Oh, you noticed it? Long ago?

RAKITIN: Only yesterday.

NATALYA PETROVNA: Ah!

RAKITIN: The day before yesterday, you remember, I was talking to you about the change that had occurred in you. . . . At that time I did not yet know to what to ascribe it. But yesterday, after our conversation . . . and out there in the meadow . . . if you could have seen yourself! I did not recognize you. You seemed to have become another woman. You laughed, you skipped, you frolicked like a little girl. Your eyes glittered, your cheeks glowed—and with what trustful curiosity, with what joyous attention you gazed at him, how you smiled! [*Glancing at her*] And even now your face lights up at the mere recollection. [*He turns away*]

NATALYA PETROVNA: No, Rakitin, for the Lord's sake, do not turn away from me. . . . Listen: why exaggerate? This man has infected me with his youth—that's all. I myself was never young, Michel. Never from my childhood until now. . . . You know my whole life. . . . All this was so unwonted that it went to my head like wine, but I know it will pass away just as quickly as it came. . . . It's hardly worth speaking of. [*After a pause*] Only do not turn away from me. Do not withdraw your hand from me. . . . Help me!

RAKITIN: [*In a low voice*] Help you! . . . A cruel word! [*Aloud*] You do not know, yourself, Natalya Petrovna, what is occurring within you. You are convinced that it is not worth talking of, and yet you ask for help. . . . Evidently you feel that you need it!

NATALYA PETROVNA: That is . . . I . . . I appeal to you as a friend.

RAKITIN: [*Bitterly*] Yes . . . I am ready to justify your confidence. . . . But permit me to collect myself a bit.

NATALYA PETROVNA: Collect yourself? But are you threatened by any . . . unpleasantness? Has anything changed?

RAKITIN: [*Bitterly*] Oh, no! Everything is as formerly.

NATALYA PETROVNA: Well, what are you thinking of, Michel? It's impossible that you can suppose . . . ?

RAKITIN: I don't suppose anything.

NATALYA PETROVNA: It's impossible that you so despise me that—

RAKITIN: Stop, for the Lord's sake. We had better talk about Bolshintsov. The doctor expects an answer with regard to Verochka, you know.

NATALYA PETROVNA: [*Gloomily*] You are angry with me.

RAKITIN: I? Oh, no! But I am sorry for you.

NATALYA PETROVNA: Well, that is genuinely irritating. Michel, aren't you ashamed?

[Rakitin *is silent. She shrugs her shoulders and continues with irritation*]

You say the doctor expects an answer? But who asked him to meddle?

RAKITIN: He assured me that you did yourself.

NATALYA PETROVNA: [*Interrupting him*] Perhaps, perhaps. . . . Although I think I said nothing positive to him. . . . Besides, I may change my intentions. And now—good Heavens!—what difference does it make? Shpigelsky interests himself in affairs of every sort, and in that trade he ought not to succeed every time.

RAKITIN: He only desires to know what answer . . .

NATALYA PETROVNA: What answer? . . . [*After a pause*] Michel, stop! Give me your hand. Why this indifferent glance, this cold courtesy? . . . How am I to blame? Just think, is all this my fault? I came to you in the hopes of getting some good advice. I did not hesitate a single moment. I did not think of dissembling with you. And you . . . I see that I was wrong to be so open with you. . . . It would never have entered your head. You suspected nothing. You deceived me. And now, the Lord knows what you think.

RAKITIN: I? The idea!

NATALYA PETROVNA: Give me your hand. . . . [*He does not move. She continues with a somewhat offended air*] Do you turn away from me for good and all? Look out, it will be so much the worse for you. However, I don't blame you. . . . [*Bitterly*] You are jealous!

RAKITIN: I have no right to be jealous, Natalya Petrovna. . . . What an idea!

NATALYA PETROVNA: [*After a pause*] As you wish.

And as for Bolshintsov, I have not yet spoken to Verochka.

RAKITIN: I can send her to you directly.

NATALYA PETROVNA: Why directly? . . . However, as you choose.

RAKITIN: [Going toward the door of the study] Then will you have me send her?

NATALYA PETROVNA: Michel, for the last time! . . . You have just told me that you are sorry for me. . . . So, are you sorry for me? Is it possible that . . . ?

RAKITIN: [Coldly] Shall I send her?

NATALYA PETROVNA: [With vexation] Yes!

[Rakitin goes into the study. Natalya Petrovna for some time remains motionless. She sits down, takes a book from the table, opens it, and drops it in her lap]

And that man! What does this mean? He! . . . And he . . . And yet I relied on him. And Arkady? I didn't even remember him! [Straightening up] I see it's time to stop all this.

[Vera comes in from the study]

Yes, it's time.

VERA: [Timidly] You asked for me, Natalya Petrovna?

NATALYA PETROVNA: [Looking around quickly] Ah, Verochka! Yes, I asked for you.

VERA: [Coming up to her] Are you well?

NATALYA PETROVNA: Yes. Why do you ask?

VERA: It seemed to me . . .

NATALYA PETROVNA: No, I'm all right. I'm a little heated. . . . That's all. Sit down.

[Vera sits down]

Listen, Vera, you aren't busy with anything at present?

VERA: No.

NATALYA PETROVNA: I ask you because I need to talk with you . . . to talk seriously. Now, you see, my darling, hitherto you have seemed a mere child, but now you are seventeen. You are clever. . . . It's time for you to be thinking of your future. You know I love you as a daughter. My house will always be your house. . . . But, all the same, in the eyes of other people, you are an orphan, you are not rich. In the course of time you may grow tired of living constantly with people not your own. Listen, should you like to be a housewife, mistress of your own house?

VERA: [Slowly] I don't understand you, Natalya Petrovna.

NATALYA PETROVNA: [After a pause] I am asked for your hand.

[Vera with amazement looks at Natalya Petrovna]

You didn't expect that? I confess that I myself find it rather strange. You are still so young. . . . I need not tell you that I have no intention of putting pressure upon you. . . . In my opinion, it is still early for you to marry. I only thought it my duty to inform you. . . .

[Vera suddenly covers her face with her hands]

Vera, what does this mean? You are weeping. [Takes her by the hand] You are trembling all over? . . . Is it possible that you are afraid of me, Vera?

VERA: [In a choking voice] I am in your power, Natalya Petrovna.

NATALYA PETROVNA: [Removing Vera's hands from her face] Vera, aren't you ashamed to weep? Aren't you ashamed to say that you are in my power? Who do you take me for? I am speaking to you as to a daughter, and you . . . [Vera kisses her hands] So? Are you in my power? Then please laugh right off. . . . I command you to. . . .

[Vera smiles through her tears]

That's the way. [Natalya Petrovna embraces her with one arm, and draws her to her] Vera, my child, behave toward me as you would toward your mother, or, no, rather imagine that I am your older sister. And now, let's talk together about all these marvelous things. . . . Will you?

VERA: I am ready.

NATALYA PETROVNA: Well, then, listen. . . . Move up nearer. That's the way. In the first place, since you are my sister, let's suppose that I need not assure you that you are here at home. Such eyes are always at home. Therefore, it ought not to enter your head that you can be a burden to anybody in the world, and that they want to get rid of you. . . . Do you hear? But now, one fine day your sister comes to you and says, "Just imagine, Vera, they are making proposals for you." Well, what will you reply to that? That you are still very young, that you don't even think of marriage?

VERA: Yes, madam.

NATALYA PETROVNA: Don't say, "Yes, madam." Do sisters say, "Yes, madam" to each other?

VERA: [Smiles] Well, yes.

NATALYA PETROVNA: Your sister agrees with you. They refuse the suitor and the matter is over. But if the suitor is a good man with property, if he is ready to wait, if he merely asks permission to see you occasionally in the hope that in time you will like him . . .

VERA: And who is this suitor?

NATALYA PETROVNA: Oh, you are curious. You don't guess?

VERA: No.

NATALYA PETROVNA: You have seen him to-day.

[Vera blushes all over]

To be sure, he isn't very handsome, and not very young. . . . Bolshintsov.

VERA: Afanasy Ivanovich?

NATALYA PETROVNA: Yes, Afanasy Ivanovich.

VERA: [Looks for some time at Natalya Petrovna. She suddenly begins to laugh and then stops] You aren't joking?

NATALYA PETROVNA: [Smiling] No. . . . But I see that Bolshintsov has no further business here. If you had wept at his name, he might still have hopes, but you laugh. There's only one thing left for him, to go home, and the Lord help him!

VERA: Excuse me. . . . But I really never expected . . . At his age, do men still marry?

NATALYA PETROVNA: What do you think? How old is he? He isn't fifty yet. He is in the very prime of life.

VERA: Perhaps . . . but he has such a queer face.

NATALYA PETROVNA: Well, we won't speak of him any more. He is dead and buried. . . . Let him stay so! However, this much is plain. A girl of your age cannot like a man such as Bolshintsov. . . . All of you want to marry for love, and not from interested motives. Is that not true?

VERA: But, Natalya Petrovna . . . did you not yourself marry Arkady Sergeich for love?

NATALYA PETROVNA: [*After a pause*] Of course I married him for love. [*After another pause, and clasping* Vera's *hands*] But Vera . . . I just called you a little girl . . . but little girls are right.

[Vera *lowers her eyes*]

Well, then, the matter is decided. Bolshintsov is dismissed. I must confess I myself should not greatly enjoy seeing his puffy old countenance alongside your fresh little face, although, after all, he is a very good man. So you see how wrong it was of you to be afraid of me. How quickly everything was settled! . . . [*With a reproach*] Really, you have behaved with me as if I were your benefactress! You know how I hate that word.

VERA: [*Embracing her*] Pardon me, Natalya Petrovna.

NATALYA PETROVNA: That's right! You are really not afraid of me?

VERA: No, I love you. I am not afraid of you.

NATALYA PETROVNA: Well, thank you. So now we are great friends, and hide nothing from each other. Well, what if I were to ask you: "Verochka, whisper to me: Do you refuse, then, to marry Bolshintsov merely because he is very much older than you, and not at all good-looking?"

VERA: Well, isn't that enough, Natalya Petrovna?

NATALYA PETROVNA: I don't dispute it, but isn't there any other reason?

VERA: I don't know him at all.

NATALYA PETROVNA: Quite true, but you do not answer my question.

VERA: There is no other reason.

NATALYA PETROVNA: Really? In that case, I should advise you to reflect a bit more. I know that it is hard to fall in love with Bolshintsov . . . but I repeat to you, he is a good man. Now, if you had fallen in love with some other man . . . well, then matters would be different. But your heart is still silent, is it not?

VERA: [*Timidly*] What?

NATALYA PETROVNA: You do not yet love any one?

VERA: I love you . . . and Kolya. I also love Anna Semenovna.

NATALYA PETROVNA: No, I am not talking about that kind of love; you don't understand me. . . . For instance, of the various young men whom you may have met in our house, or when visiting, is it possible that you do not care for a single one?

VERA: No, I like several of them, but . . .

NATALYA PETROVNA: For instance, I noticed that at the evening party at the Krinitsyns', you danced three times with that tall officer. . . . What's his name?

VERA: With an officer?

NATALYA PETROVNA: Yes, he has a large mustache.

VERA: Oh, that man? No, I don't care for him.

NATALYA PETROVNA: Well, how about Shalansky?

VERA: Shalansky is a good man, but he . . . I think he has no use for me.

NATALYA PETROVNA: Why so?

VERA: He . . . He seems to think more of Liza Velsky.

NATALYA PETROVNA: [*Glancing at her*] . . . Ah, you noticed that? [*After a pause*] Well, Rakitin?

VERA: I am very fond of Mikhaylo Alexandrovich. . . .

NATALYA PETROVNA: Yes, as a brother. Well, how about Belyayev?

VERA: [*Blushing*] Alexey Nikolayevich? I like Alexey Nikolayevich.

NATALYA PETROVNA: [*Observing* Vera] Yes, he is a good man, only he is so shy with every one.

VERA: [*Artlessly*] No . . . he is not shy with me.

NATALYA PETROVNA: Ah!

VERA: He talks with me. Perhaps the reason why you think that, is that he . . . he is afraid of you. He has not yet learned to know you.

NATALYA PETROVNA: But how do you know that he is afraid of me?

VERA: He told me so.

NATALYA PETROVNA: Ah, he told you so? . . . So he is franker with you than with other people?

VERA: I don't know how he behaves toward others, but with me . . . perhaps because we are both orphans. . . . And besides, in his eyes, I am a child.

NATALYA PETROVNA: You think so? I also like him very much. Probably he has a very kind heart.

VERA: Oh, awfully kind! If you only knew! . . . Everybody in the house likes him. He is so friendly. He talks to everybody. He is ready to help everybody. Day before yesterday he carried a poor old woman in his arms from the road to the hospital. . . . Once he picked a flower for me from such a steep ravine that I just shut my eyes for fear he might fall and hurt himself, but he's so very active! You yourself, yesterday, in the meadow, could see how active he was.

NATALYA PETROVNA: Yes, that is true.

VERA: Do you remember when he was running after the kite, what a broad ditch he jumped across? But that was nothing for him.

NATALYA PETROVNA: And, really, did he pick a flower for you from a dangerous place? Evidently he loves you.

VERA: [*After a pause*] And he is always gay, always in good spirits.

NATALYA PETROVNA: Well, that seems strange! Why in my presence he is—?

VERA: [*Interrupting her*] But I tell you that he doesn't know you. Just wait, I'll tell him. I'll tell him that he needn't be afraid of you—isn't that true? —that you are so kind. . . .

NATALYA PETROVNA: [*With a forced laugh*] Thanks.

VERA: Wait, you'll see. . . . And he takes my advice, in spite of my being younger than he.

NATALYA PETROVNA: I didn't know that you and he were such friends. . . . But look out, Vera; be cautious. Of course he is a splendid young man . . . but you know at your age . . . this isn't proper. People may gossip. I reminded you of this yesterday —do you remember?—in the garden.

[*Vera lowers her eyes*]

On the other hand, I do not wish to hinder your inclinations. I have too much confidence in you and in him. . . . But all the same, do not be angry with me, my darling, for my straitlaced ways. This is what old people like me are for—to bore young people with advice. With advice and instruction. However, I am wrong in saying all this. It is true, is it not, you like him—and nothing more?

VERA: [*Timidly raising her eyes*] He . . .

NATALYA PETROVNA: Now you are looking at me again as you did before. Is that the way to look at a sister? Listen, Verochka, bend down to me. . . . [*Caressing her*] Well, if your sister, your real sister, were to ask you in a whisper, "Verochka, do you really love no one, are you sure?" What should you answer her?

[*Vera looks in perplexity at Natalya Petrovna*]

These eyes wish to tell me something. . . .

[*Vera suddenly presses her face against the bosom of Natalya Petrovna. Natalya Petrovna turns pale, and after a pause continues*]

Do you love him? Tell me, do you love him?

VERA: [*Not raising her head*] Oh, I don't know myself what is the matter with me.

NATALYA PETROVNA: Poor little girl! You are in love.

[*Vera presses still closer to the bosom of Natalya Petrovna*]

You are in love. . . . And he, what about him, Vera?

VERA: [*Still not raising her head*] Why do you ask me? . . . I don't know. . . . Maybe. . . . I don't know. . . . I don't know. . . .

[*Natalya Petrovna trembles and remains motionless. Vera raises her head and suddenly notices a change on Natalya Petrovna's face*]

Natalya Petrovna, what is the matter with you?

NATALYA PETROVNA: [*Coming to herself*] Nothing is the matter with me. Why do you ask? Nothing at all.

VERA: You are so pale, Natalya Petrovna. . . . What is the matter with you? Permit me, I'll ring. [*She rises*]

NATALYA PETROVNA: No, no, don't ring. . . . It's nothing. . . . It will pass. There, it's past, already.

VERA: Permit me at least to call somebody.

NATALYA PETROVNA: No indeed. I . . . I . . . want to be left alone. Leave me. Do you hear? We'll have a talk later. Go away.

VERA: You are not angry with me, Natalya Petrovna?

NATALYA PETROVNA: I? What for? Not at all. On the contrary, I am grateful to you for your confidence. . . . Only leave me, please, now.

[*Vera tries to take her hand, but Natalya Petrovna turns away, as if she did not notice Vera's movement*]

VERA: [*With tears in her eyes*] Natalya Petrovna!

NATALYA PETROVNA: Leave me, I beg of you.

[*Vera slowly goes off to the study. Natalya Petrovna remains alone for some time, motionless*]

Now everything is clear to me. . . . These children love each other. [*She stops and passes her hand over her face*] Well, so much the better. God grant them happiness! [*Laughing*] And I . . . I might have thought . . . [*She stops again*] She blurted it out very quickly. . . . I confess I never suspected. . . . I confess this news overwhelmed me. . . . But just wait. It isn't all over yet. Good Heavens, what am I saying? What is the matter with me? I don't recognize myself. What have I come to? [*After a pause*] What am I doing? I am trying to marry a poor little girl . . . to an old man! . . . I send the doctor as a messenger. . . . He guesses what is up and hints at it. . . . Arkady . . . Rakitin . . . and I . . . [*She trembles and suddenly raises her head*] But what does this mean, really? Am I jealous of Vera? Am I . . . am I in love with him? [*After a pause*] And do you still doubt it? You are in love, unhappy woman! How this happened, I do not know. It is as if I had been given poison. . . . Suddenly all is crushed, shattered, swept away. . . . He is afraid of me. . . . Everybody is afraid of me. What does he care for me? . . . What use has he for such a creature as I? He is young, and she is young. And I? [*Bitterly*] How can he appreciate me? They are both stupid, as Rakitin says. Oh, how I hate that clever man! And Arkady, my kind, trustful Arkady! My God! My God! This will kill me! [*Rises*] Really, it seems to me that I am going mad. Why exaggerate? Well, yes, I am overwhelmed. . . . This is a new thing to me. This is the first time that I . . . Yes, the first time! I am in love now for the first time! [*She sits down again*] He must go away. Yes, and Rakitin, too. It's time for me to come to my senses. I have permitted myself to take one step, and see what has happened. Here's what I have come to. And what is it that I like in him? [*Meditates*] So here it is, that frightful emotion. . . . Arkady! Yes, I will run to his embrace. I will implore him to forgive me, to defend me, to save me— he . . . and no one else. All other men are strangers to me, and must remain strangers. . . . But, is it possible . . . is it possible there is no other means? That little girl, she is only a child. She may have been mistaken. This is all childishness, after all. . . . Why did I . . . ? I will have an explanation with him myself. I will ask him . . . [*With a reproach*] Ah, ha? Do you still have hope? Do you still desire to have hope? And what do I hope for! Good God, do not let me despise myself!

[*She leans her head on her hands.* Rakitin *comes in from the study, pale and agitated*]

RAKITIN: [*Going up to* Natalya Petrovna] Natalya Petrovna! . . . [*She does not move. To himself*] What can have happened between her and Vera? [*Aloud*] Natalya Petrovna!

NATALYA PETROVNA: [*Raising her head*] You, is it? Ah, you.

RAKITIN: Vera Alexandrovna told me that you were not well. I . . .

NATALYA PETROVNA: [*Turning aside*] I am well. . . . How did she get that idea?

RAKITIN: No, Natalya Petrovna, you are not well. Just look at yourself.

NATALYA PETROVNA: Well, maybe. . . . But what's that to you? What do you want? Why did you come here?

RAKITIN: [*In voice full of feeling*] I'll tell you why I came here. I came here to beg your forgiveness. A half-hour ago I was unspeakably stupid and harsh to you. . . . Forgive me! You see, Natalya Petrovna, however modest may be the desires and . . . and the hopes of a man, it is hard for him not to lose control of himself for a moment, when they suddenly spring up within him; but I now have come to myself. I understand my position, and my fault, and I wish for only one thing, your forgiveness. [*He sits down quietly beside her*] Look at me. . . . Pray do not turn away from me. Before you is your former Rakitin, your friend, a man who demands nothing but the permission to serve as a support, to use your own words. . . . Do not deprive me of your confidence—let me serve you—and forget that once on a time I . . . Forget everything that may have offended you.

NATALYA PETROVNA: [*Who has been looking fixedly at the floor all this time*] Yes, yes. [*Stopping*] Oh, pardon me, Rakitin! I did not hear anything of what you were saying to me.

RAKITIN: [*Sadly*] I was saying . . . I was begging your forgiveness, Natalya Petrovna. I was asking you whether you would permit me to remain your friend.

NATALYA PETROVNA: [*Slowly turning toward him, and putting both her hands on his shoulders*] Tell me, Rakitin, what is the matter with me?

RAKITIN: [*After a pause*] You are in love.

NATALYA PETROVNA: [*Slowly repeating after him*] I am in love. . . . But this is madness, Rakitin. This is impossible. Can it happen so suddenly? You say I am in love. [*She becomes silent*]

RAKITIN: Yes, you are in love, poor woman. . . . Do not deceive yourself.

NATALYA PETROVNA: [*Without looking at him*] What is there left for me to do now?

RAKITIN: I am ready to tell you, Natalya Petrovna, if you will promise me——

NATALYA PETROVNA: [*Interrupting him, and still not looking at him*] You know that that little girl, Vera, loves him. . . . They are in love with each other.

RAKITIN: In that case, there is one further reason——

NATALYA PETROVNA: [*Again interrupting him*] I long ago suspected this, but just now she confessed the whole story to me . . . just now.

RAKITIN: [*In a low voice, as if to himself*] Poor woman!

NATALYA PETROVNA: [*Passing her hand over her face*] Well, at all events . . . it is time for me to come to my senses. I think you wish to say something to me. . . . Advise me, for God's sake, Rakitin, what I should do.

RAKITIN: I am ready to advise you, Natalya Petrovna, but under one condition.

NATALYA PETROVNA: Tell me what it is.

RAKITIN: Promise me that you will not suspect my intentions. Tell me that you believe in my disinterested desire to aid you. And you must aid me also. Your confidence will give me strength. Otherwise, you had better permit me to be silent.

NATALYA PETROVNA: Speak. Speak.

RAKITIN: You do not doubt me!

NATALYA PETROVNA: Speak.

RAKITIN: Well, then, listen. He must go away.

[Natalya Petrovna *looks at him in silence*] Yes, he must go away. I will not speak to you of your husband . . . of your duty. From me these words . . . would be out of place. . . . But these children love each other. You yourself told me that just now. Then imagine yourself now as standing between them. . . . You will perish!

NATALYA PETROVNA: He must go away. . . . [*After a pause*] And you? You will remain?

RAKITIN: [*Confused*] I? . . . I? . . . [*After a pause*] I too must go away. For your peace, for your happiness, for the happiness of Verochka, both he . . . and I . . . we both must go away forever.

NATALYA PETROVNA: Rakitin . . . I have sunk so low that I . . . I was almost ready to marry that poor little girl, an orphan, entrusted to me by my mother . . . to marry her to a stupid, ridiculous old man! . . . I did not have the courage, Rakitin; the words died on my lips when she laughed, in reply to my proposal. . . . But I made a conspiracy with that doctor. I permitted him to smile in a knowing way. I endured those smiles, those courtesies of his, his hints. . . . Oh, I feel that I am on the edge of an abyss! Save me!

RAKITIN: Natalya Petrovna, you see that I was right. . . . [*She is silent. He hastily continues*] He must go away. . . . We must both go away. . . . There is no other salvation.

NATALYA PETROVNA: [*Wearily*] But what shall I live for after that?

RAKITIN: Good heavens! Has it come to this? . . . Natalya Petrovna, you will recover, believe me. . . . This will all pass off. How can you ask what you will live for?

NATALYA PETROVNA: Yes, yes, what shall I live for when every one is deserting me?

RAKITIN: But . . . your family . . .

[*Natalya Petrovna lowers her eyes*]

Listen. If you wish, after his departure I can remain for a few days more . . . in order to . . .

NATALYA PETROVNA: [*Gloomily*] Ah! I understand you. You count on habit, on our former friendship. . . . You hope that I shall come to my senses, that I shall return to you, do you not? I understand you.

RAKITIN: [*Blushing*] Natalya Petrovna! Why do you insult me?

NATALYA PETROVNA: [*Bitterly*] I understand you. . . . But you deceive yourself.

RAKITIN: What? After your promises? After what I have done for you, for you alone, for your happiness, and finally, for your position in the world?

NATALYA PETROVNA: Ah, is it long since you have taken such care of it? Why have you never spoken to me of that subject before?

RAKITIN: [*Rising*] Natalya Petrovna, I shall leave here to-day—at once. And you will never see me again. [*Is about to go*]

NATALYA PETROVNA: [*Stretching out her hands to him*] Michel, forgive me. I do not know myself what I am saying. . . . You see what a position I am in. Forgive me!

RAKITIN: [*Quickly returning to her and taking her hands*] Natalya Petrovna! . . .

NATALYA PETROVNA: Ah, Michel, I cannot tell you what torment I suffer! [*Leans on his shoulder and presses her handkerchief to her eyes*] Help me! Without you I shall perish!

[*At this moment the door of the hall opens, and Islayev and Anna Semenovna come in*]

ISLAYEV: [*In a loud voice*] I have also been of the opinion . . . [*He stops in amazement at the sight of Rakitin and Natalya Petrovna. Natalya Petrovna looks around and quickly walks out into the study. Rakitin does not stir, but is extremely abashed*]

ISLAYEV: [*To Rakitin*] What does this mean? What sort of scene is this?

RAKITIN: Oh! . . . Nothing. . . . This . . .

ISLAYEV: Is Natalya Petrovna ill?

RAKITIN: No. . . . But . . .

ISLAYEV: But why should she run out so suddenly? What were you talking about together? She seemed to be weeping. . . . You were comforting her. . . . What does this mean?

RAKITIN: Nothing at all.

ANNA SEMENOVNA: Let me ask you why this is nothing at all, Mikhaylo Alexandrovich? [*After a pause*] I'll go and see. [*Is about to go into the study*]

RAKITIN: [*Stopping her*] No, you had better leave her in peace, now; I beg of you.

ISLAYEV: But what does all this mean? Tell me, pray!

RAKITIN: Nothing, I swear to you. Listen, I promise you both that I will explain everything this very day. I give you my word. But just now, please, if you have confidence in me, do not ask me anything, and do not trouble Natalya Petrovna.

ISLAYEV: All right. . . . Only this is surprising. This is not like Natasha. This is something unusual.

ANNA SEMENOVNA: Above all, what could make Natasha weep, and why did she go out? . . . Are we strangers?

RAKITIN: What are you saying? How can you!— But listen: I must confess, we had not finished our conversation. . . . I must ask you . . . both of you . . . to leave us alone for a little while.

ISLAYEV: Well, well! So you had a secret?

RAKITIN: A secret. . . . But you will learn it.

ISLAYEV: [*After meditation*] Come on, mamma! . . . Let's leave them. Let them finish their mysterious conversation.

ANNA SEMENOVNA: But . . .

ISLAYEV: Come on, come on! You have heard him promise to explain everything.

RAKITIN: You may rest at peace.

ISLAYEV: [*Coldly*] Oh, I am perfectly at peace! [*To Anna Semenovna*] Come on.

[*They both go out*]

RAKITIN: [*Gazing after them and going quickly to the door of the study*] Natalya Petrovna! . . . Natalya Petrovna! . . . Come out, I beg of you!

NATALYA PETROVNA: [*Coming out of the study. She is very pale*] What did they say?

RAKITIN: Nothing. Calm yourself. . . . They were really a trifle surprised. Your husband thought that you were not well. He noticed your agitation. . . .

[*Natalya Petrovna sits down*]

I told him . . . I asked him not to disturb you . . . to leave us alone.

NATALYA PETROVNA: And he agreed?

RAKITIN: Yes. I must confess that I had to promise him that I would explain everything to-morrow. . . . Why did you go out?

NATALYA PETROVNA: [*Bitterly*] Why! . . . But what will you tell him?

RAKITIN: I . . . I will think up something. . . . That's not the question now. . . . We must take advantage of this postponement. You see, this cannot continue in the same way. . . . You are not in a condition to bear such agitations. . . . They are unworthy of you. . . . I, myself . . . But that is not what we were speaking of. Only be firm, and I will attend to the matter. Listen. You agree with me?

NATALYA PETROVNA: In what?

RAKITIN: As to the necessity . . . of our departure? Do you agree? In that case there is no delaying. If you will permit me, I will talk things over immediately myself with Belyayev. . . . He is a gentleman. He will understand.

NATALYA PETROVNA: You wish to talk things over with him? You? . . . But what can you say to him?

RAKITIN: [*Confused*] I . . .

NATALYA PETROVNA: [*After a pause*] Listen, Rakitin. Don't you think that we both seem out of our senses? . . . I was frightened. I frightened you. And perhaps the whole thing is just nonsense.

RAKITIN: What?

NATALYA PETROVNA: Honestly, what are you and I doing? A while ago, as I think of it, everything was so calm, so peaceful in this house . . . and all of a sudden, what has happened? On my word, we've all gone mad. Really, we've played the fool long enough! . . . Now we'll begin to live as we used to. . . . And you will have no need to explain things to Arkady. I myself will tell him of our misdeeds, and he and I will laugh at them together. I do not need a mediator between my husband and myself.

RAKITIN: Natalya Petrovna, now you *are* frightening me. You are smiling, but you are pale as death. . . . Do at least remember what you were telling me a quarter of an hour ago.

NATALYA PETROVNA: There's a lot to remember! However, I see how the matter stands. . . . You yourself raised this storm . . . in order at least not to drown alone.

RAKITIN: Again! Again suspicion, again reproach, Natalya Petrovna! . . . The Lord help you! . . . But you are tormenting me. Or do you repent your frankness?

NATALYA PETROVNA: I repent nothing.

RAKITIN: Then how shall I understand you?

NATALYA PETROVNA: [*With animation*] Rakitin, if you say even a word to Belyayev about me, or as coming from me, I shall never forgive you.

RAKITIN: Oh, so that's it! . . . Be at peace, Natalya Petrovna, I not only shall say nothing to Mr. Belyayev, but I shall not even say good-by to him when I leave here. I have no intention of forcing my services on people.

NATALYA PETROVNA: [*With some confusion*] But perhaps you think that I have changed my opinion with regard to . . . his departure?

RAKITIN: I don't think anything at all.

NATALYA PETROVNA: On the contrary, I am so convinced of the necessity of his departure, as you term it, that I, myself, have decided to dismiss him. [*After a pause*] Yes, I will dismiss him myself.

RAKITIN: You?

NATALYA PETROVNA: Yes, I, and immediately. I beg you to send him to me.

RAKITIN: What? Right away?

NATALYA PETROVNA: Right away. I beg you to do so, Rakitin. You see, I am now calm. Besides, I am now at liberty. I must take advantage of this. . . . I shall be very grateful to you. I will cross-examine him.

RAKITIN: But may I remark that he won't tell you anything! He himself confessed to me that he felt embarrassed in your presence.

NATALYA PETROVNA: [*Suspiciously*] Ah, you have already spoken with him about me?

[*Rakitin shrugs his shoulders*]

Well, excuse me, excuse me, Michel, but send him to me. You will see that I shall dismiss him, and everything will be over. Everything will pass by and be forgotten like a bad dream. Please send him to me. It is absolutely necessary for me to have a final talk with him. You will be content with me. Please!

RAKITIN: [*Who all the time has kept his eyes fixed upon her: coldly and sadly*] Very well, your desires shall be fulfilled. [*He goes to the door of the hall*]

NATALYA PETROVNA: [*Calls after him*] Thank you, Michel.

RAKITIN: [*Turning around*] Oh, don't thank me, at any rate! [*He quickly goes out into the hall*]

NATALYA PETROVNA: [*Alone, after a pause*] He is a gentleman. . . . But is it possible that I ever loved him? [*Rising*] He is right: the teacher must leave. But how shall I dismiss him? I only wish to know whether he really likes that little girl. Perhaps that is all nonsense. How could I have become so agitated? . . . What is the use of all these bursts of emotion? Well, now there is no help for it! I want to know what he will say to me. But he must leave . . . without fail . . . without fail. . . . Perhaps he will refuse to answer me, seeing that he is afraid of me. . . . Well, so much the better. I have no need to converse much with him. . . . [*Puts her hand to her forehead*] But my head aches. Shan't I postpone it until to-morrow? That would be better. To-day I keep thinking that I am being observed. . . . What have I come to! No, it is better to finish it up all at once. . . . One more final effort and I am free! . . . Oh, yes! . . . I thirst for freedom and peace.

[*Belyayev comes in from the hall*]

It is he. . . .

BELYAYEV: [*Going up to her*] Natalya Petrovna, Mikhaylo Alexandrovich told me that you desired to see me.

NATALYA PETROVNA: [*With a certain effort*] Quite so. . . . I need to have . . . an explanation with you.

BELYAYEV: An explanation?

NATALYA PETROVNA: [*Without looking at him*] Yes, an explanation. [*After a pause*] Permit me to tell you, Alexey Nikolayevich, that I . . . that I am dissatisfied with you.

BELYAYEV: May I inquire the reason?

NATALYA PETROVNA: Listen to me. . . . I . . . I really don't know how to begin. . . . At all events I must forewarn you that my displeasure does not proceed from any neglect of duty . . . on your part. . . . On the contrary, I have liked your conduct with Kolya.

BELYAYEV: But what can be the reason?

NATALYA PETROVNA: [*Glancing at him*] You have no cause for alarm. Your fault is not of any great importance. You are young, and probably have never lived in another person's house. You could not foresee . . .

BELYAYEV: But, Natalya Petrovna . . .

NATALYA PETROVNA: You wish to know what the trouble is? I understand your impatience. Well, I must inform you that Verochka . . . [*With a glance at him*] Verochka has confessed everything to me.

BELYAYEV: [*Amazed*] Vera Alexandrovna? What could Vera Alexandrovna confess to you? And how do I come in?

NATALYA PETROVNA: Don't you really know what she could confess? Don't you guess?

BELYAYEV: I? Not a bit.

NATALYA PETROVNA: In that case, pardon me. If you really don't guess—I must ask your forgiveness. I really thought . . . I was mistaken. But permit me to remark to you . . . I don't believe you. I understand what makes you speak in that way. . . . I greatly respect your modesty.

BELYAYEV: I absolutely do not understand you, Natalya Petrovna.

NATALYA PETROVNA: Really? Is it possible that you think that you can make me believe that you have not noticed the affection of that child Verochka for you?

BELYAYEV: The affection of Vera Alexandrovna for me? I don't even know what to reply to you. . . . Good gracious, I think I have always behaved with Vera Alexandrovna as—

NATALYA PETROVNA: As with every one else, I suppose? [*After a slight pause*] However it may be, whether you really do not know it, or whether you are pretending you do not know, here's the point: that little girl is in love with you. She herself has confessed it to me. Well, now I ask you as an honorable man what you intend to do.

BELYAYEV: [*Amazed*] What I intend to do?

NATALYA PETROVNA: [*Folding her arms*] Yes.

BELYAYEV: All this is so unexpected, Natalya Petrovna.

NATALYA PETROVNA: [*After a pause*] Alexey Nikolayevich, I see . . . I haven't taken hold of this affair correctly. You don't understand me. You think I am angry with you, and I . . . and I . . . am just a little excited. . . . And this is very natural. Calm yourself. Let us sit down.

[*They both sit down*]

I will be frank with you, Alexey Nikolayevich. And on your side, pray show a little less reserve toward me. Honestly, you are wrong in holding aloof from me. Vera loves you. . . . Of course you are not to blame for that. I am ready to suppose that you are not to blame for that. . . . But you see, Alexey Nikolayevich, she is an orphan, my protégée. . . . I am responsible for her, for her future, for her happiness. She is still young, and I am convinced that the feeling you have inspired in her may soon vanish. . . . At her years, love doesn't last for long.

But you understand that it was my duty to forewarn you. And, moreover, it is always dangerous to play with fire . . . and I don't doubt that you, since you now know her affection for you, will alter your behavior toward her, will avoid meetings and walks in the garden. . . . Is not that the case? I may rely upon you, I am sure. . . . With another man I should have been afraid of so direct an explanation.

BELYAYEV: Natalya Petrovna, believe me, I am able to appreciate—

NATALYA PETROVNA: I tell you that I have confidence in you. . . . Besides, this will all remain a secret between us two.

BELYAYEV: I confess to you, Natalya Petrovna, all that you have told me seems to me so strange. . . . Of course I do not dare to disbelieve you, but—

NATALYA PETROVNA: Listen, Alexey Nikolayevich, all that I have just now told you I . . . I have said on the supposition that on your side there is nothing . . . [*Interrupting herself*] Because in any other case . . . Of course, I am still little acquainted with you, but I already know you well enough to see no reason for opposing your intentions. You are not rich . . . but you are young. You have a future, and when two people love each other . . . I repeat to you, I regarded it as my duty to forewarn you, as an honorable man, with regard to the consequences of your acquaintance with Vera. But if you . . .

BELYAYEV: [*With perplexity*] I really don't know what you mean, Natalya Petrovna.

NATALYA PETROVNA: [*Hastily*] Oh, believe me, I do not require a confession from you. Even without it . . . I shall understand from your conduct how the matter stands. [*With a glance at him*] However, I must tell you that Vera thought that on your side you were not entirely indifferent to her.

BELYAYEV: [*After a pause. Rising*] Natalya Petrovna, I see that I cannot remain in your house.

NATALYA PETROVNA: [*Flashing up*] I think that you might have waited for me to discharge you myself. [*She rises*]

BELYAYEV: You have been frank with me. . . . Permit me also to be frank with you. I do not love Vera Alexandrovna. At least, I do not love her in the way you suppose.

NATALYA PETROVNA: But have I . . . ? [*She stops*]

BELYAYEV: And if Vera Alexandrovna has come to like me; if it appears to her that I, too, as you say, am not indifferent to her, I do not wish to deceive her. I will tell the whole story to her herself, the whole truth. But after such an explanation, you will understand yourself, Natalya Petrovna, it will be hard for me to remain here. My position would be too embarrassing. I will not tell you how hard it is for me to leave your house, but there is nothing else for me to do. I shall always remember you with gratitude. . . . Permit me to withdraw. . . . I shall have the honor of bidding you farewell later.

NATALYA PETROVNA: [*With feigned indifference*]

As you wish . . . but I confess I did not expect this. . . . This was not at all the reason why I wished to have an explanation with you. . . . I only wished to forewarn you. . . . Vera is still a child. . . . Perhaps I have attached too much importance to all this. I see no necessity for your departure. However, as you wish.

BELYAYEV: Really, Natalya Petrovna . . . it is impossible for me to remain here longer.

NATALYA PETROVNA: Evidently it is very easy for you to bid us farewell!

BELYAYEV: No, Natalya Petrovna, it is not easy.

NATALYA PETROVNA: I am not accustomed to retain persons against their will . . . but I confess this is very unpleasant to me.

BELYAYEV: [*With a certain indecision*] Natalya Petrovna . . . I should not like to cause you the least unpleasantness. . . . I will remain.

NATALYA PETROVNA: [*Suspiciously*] Ah! . . . [*After a pause*] I did not expect that you would change your decision so quickly. . . . I am grateful to you, but . . . permit me to think. Perhaps you are right. Perhaps it is really necessary for you to leave. I will think it over and inform you. . . . You will permit me to leave you in uncertainty until this evening?

BELYAYEV: I am ready to wait as long as you please. [*He bows and is about to leave*]

NATALYA PETROVNA: You promise me . . .

BELYAYEV: [*Stopping*] What?

NATALYA PETROVNA: I think that you wish to have an explanation with Vera. I do not know whether that will be proper. However, I will inform you of my decision. I begin to think that it is really necessary for you to leave. Good-by for the present.

[Belyayev *bows for a second time and goes out into the hall*]

NATALYA PETROVNA: [*Gazes after him*] I am calm. He does not love her. . . . [*Pacing up and down the room*] So instead of dismissing him, I was the one to retain him? He remains here. . . . But what shall I tell Rakitin? What have I done? [*After a pause*] And what right did I have to publish abroad the love of that poor little girl? . . . How could I? I myself enticed a confession from her . . . a half-confession, and then I behaved so pitilessly, so harshly! [*Covers her face with her hands*] Perhaps he was beginning to love her. What right did I have to trample that budding flower? . . . But after all, did I trample it? Perhaps he deceived me. . . . And I wished to deceive him! . . . Oh, no! He has too much fineness for that. . . . He is not like me! And why was I in such a hurry? Why did I blurt it all out at once? [*Sighing*] What didn't I do? If I could have foreseen! . . . How cunning I was! What lies I told him! . . . And he! How boldly and freely he spoke! . . . I bowed before him. . . . That is a man! I never knew him before. . . . He must leave. . . . If he remains . . . I feel I shall come to such a pass

that I shall lose all self-respect. . . . He must leave or I am lost! I will write him before he has a chance to see Vera. He must leave! [*She goes out quickly into the study*]

ACT IV.

A large, empty hall. The walls are bare. The floor is of uneven stones. Six brick columns, whitewashed, and in poor repair, support the ceiling, three on each side. On the left are two open windows and a door into the garden. On the right is a door to a corridor which leads to the main house. In the center is an iron door, which leads to the storehouse. Near the first column at the right is a green garden bench. In one corner are several spades, watering pots, and flower pots. It is evening. The red beams of the sun fall on the floor through the windows.

KATYA: [*Entering from a door on the right, goes quickly to the window, and for some time looks into the garden*] No, he is not to be seen. And they told me that he had gone to the hothouse. So, he cannot have come out from there yet. I'll wait till he passes by. He must come by that path. [*She sighs and leans against the window*] They say that he is going away. [*Sighs again*] How can we live without him? . . . Poor young lady! How she begged me! . . . Well, why shouldn't I be of service to her? Let her have a talk with him for the last time! How warm it is to-day! And I think the rain is beginning to patter. [*Again looks out of the window and suddenly moves back*] But aren't they coming here? . . . They certainly are. Oh, Heavens! [*She starts to run away, but before she can reach the door of the corridor, there enter from the garden Shpigelsky and Lizaveta Bogdanovna. Katya hides behind the column*]

SHPIGELSKY: [*Brushing off his hat*] We may wait here till the shower is over. It will pass soon.

LIZAVETA BOGDANOVNA: I suppose so.

SHPIGELSKY: [*Looking around*] What kind of structure is this? Is it a storehouse?

LIZAVETA BOGDANOVNA: [*Pointing to the iron door*] No, the storehouse is there. They call this a hall. The father of Arkady Sergeich built it when he returned from abroad.

SHPIGELSKY: Oh, I see what this means. This is Venice, pray observe! [*Sitting down on the bench*] Let's sit here.

[Lizaveta Bogdanovna *sits down*]

And you must agree, Lizaveta Bogdanovna, that that shower came at the wrong moment. It interrupted our interview at the most delicate point.

LIZAVETA BOGDANOVNA: [*Lowering her eyes*] Ignaty Ilyich . . .

SHPIGELSKY: But no one can hinder us from renewing our conversation. . . . By the way, you say that Anna Semenovna is out of sorts to-day?

LIZAVETA BOGDANOVNA: Yes, she is. She even had dinner in her own room.

SHPIGELSKY: Well, well! What a misfortune! I declare!

LIZAVETA BOGDANOVNA: This morning she found Natalya Petrovna in tears . . . with Mikhaylo Alexandrovich. . . . He, of course, is a friend of the family, but all the same . . . However, Mikhaylo Alexandrovich promised to explain everything.

SHPIGELSKY: Ah! Well, she is quite wrong in being agitated. Mikhaylo Alexandrovich, in my opinion, was never a dangerous man, and now he is less so than ever.

LIZAVETA BOGDANOVNA: Why so?

SHPIGELSKY: Well, you see, he talks too cleverly. Some people are subject to a rash, but these clever men are subject to too much wagging of the tongue. In the future, Lizaveta Bogdanovna, don't be afraid of people who talk a lot. They aren't dangerous. But those who are generally silent, and have a dash of madness, and a lot of temperament, and broad craniums—those people are dangerous.

LIZAVETA BOGDANOVNA: [*After a pause*] Tell me, is Natalya Petrovna really ill?

SHPIGELSKY: Just as ill as you and I.

LIZAVETA BOGDANOVNA: She didn't eat anything at dinner.

SHPIGELSKY: Other things than illness take away the appetite.

LIZAVETA BOGDANOVNA: Did you dine with Bolshintsov?

SHPIGELSKY: Yes, I did. . . . I went to call on him. And I came back solely on your account, I swear.

LIZAVETA BOGDANOVNA: Oh, stop! Let me tell you, Ignaty Ilyich, Natalya Petrovna is angry at you for some reason. . . . At table she expressed herself about you in no flattering terms.

SHPIGELSKY: Really? Evidently fine ladies don't like it when men like me have keen eyes. You must act according to their wishes and help them—and pretend into the bargain that you don't understand them. That's their kind! But we'll see later. And Rakitin, I suppose, is hanging his head, too?

LIZAVETA BOGDANOVNA: Yes. To-day he seems to be a little bit off his balance.

SHPIGELSKY: Hm! And Vera Alexandrovna? And Belyayev?

LIZAVETA BOGDANOVNA: Every one. Absolutely every one is out of sorts. I really can't think what's the matter with all of them to-day.

SHPIGELSKY: If you know too much, you will grow old too soon, Lizaveta Bogdanovna. Well, anyway, deuce take 'em! Let's talk about our own affair. The shower, you see, hasn't stopped yet. . . . Will you?

LIZAVETA BOGDANOVNA: [*Lowering her eyes affectedly*] What are you asking me, Ignaty Ilyich?

SHPIGELSKY: Oh, Lizaveta Bogdanovna, let me inquire of you: Why do you want to be so affected and lower your eyes all of a sudden in this fashion? You and I are not young people any longer! These ceremonies, these tendernesses, these sighs—all such things are unbecoming to us. Let's speak calmly and to the point, as befits people of our years. And so here's the question: We like each other . . . at least I presume that you like me. . . .

LIZAVETA BOGDANOVNA: [*With slight affectation*] Ignaty Ilyich, really. . . .

SHPIGELSKY: Well, yes, yes, all right. For you, as a woman, it's proper, I suppose . . . in a way . . . [*With a gesture*] to beat about the bush like this, so to speak. Well, then, we like each other, and in other regards we are also well suited. Of course I must admit that I myself am not of high birth. But then, you also are not of gentle origin. I am not a rich man, otherwise I should . . . [*Grins*] But I have a fair practice, my patients don't all die, and you, according to your own account, have fifteen thousand in cash. That's all not so bad, you see. Besides, I imagine that you are tired of an eternal existence as a governess. And the perpetual fussing with an old woman, and playing preference with her, and humoring her—that also cannot be gay. On my side, I am not exactly bored with a bachelor life, but I am getting old. My cooks are plundering me. And so, all these circumstances harmonize with each other. But here's where the difficulty comes in, Lizaveta Bogdanovna. We don't know each other at all: that is, to be more exact, you don't know me. . . . I do know you. Your character is well known to me. I don't say that you have no defects. Since you are an old maid, you have soured a bit, but there's no harm in that. For a good man, a wife is like soft wax, but I desire that you, too, should be acquainted with me before our marriage, otherwise maybe you'll begin to complain of me later. I don't want to deceive you.

LIZAVETA BOGDANOVNA: [*With dignity*] But it seems to me, Ignaty Ilyich, that I also have had a chance to observe your character.

SHPIGELSKY: You? Oh, stop it! . . . That's not a woman's business. For instance, I warrant, you think that I'm a man of gay disposition, a jolly fellow, don't you?

LIZAVETA BOGDANOVNA: You have always seemed to me a very genial man.

SHPIGELSKY: That's the point. You see how easy it is to make a mistake. Because I play the fool to other people, tell them funny stories, and pay court to them, you immediately assumed that I was really a jolly fellow. If I had no need for them, those strangers, I wouldn't even look at them. . . . And even so, whenever I can—without any great danger, you know —I hold those very people up to ridicule. . . . However, I don't deceive myself. I know that some people, who need my services at every step, and who are bored when I am gone, nevertheless think they have the right to despise me. But I give them as good as I get. Now take Natalya Petrovna, for instance. . . .

You think that I don't see through her? [*Taking her off*] "My dear doctor, I really am very fond of you. . . . You have such a sharp tongue. . . ." Hee, hee! Coo, dovey, coo! Oh, those fine ladies! They smile at you, and they screw up their eyes this way—and condescending contempt is written on their faces. . . . They scorn men like me, but what can you do about it! I understand why she is giving a poor report of me to-day. Really, these fine ladies are a surprising lot of people! Because they wash themselves every day with cologne, and speak with a certain carelessness, as if they were dropping words— "You can pick 'em up," they tell you—they imagine that you can't catch 'em by the tail. Well, can't you, though! They are just such mortals as all the rest of us sinners.

LIZAVETA BOGDANOVNA: Ignaty Ilyich, you surprise me.

SHPIGELSKY: I knew I should surprise you. You see I'm not a jolly man at all, possibly not even a very kind man. . . . But I do not wish to pass in your eyes for something that I have never been. However much I show off before the gentlefolk, no one ever saw me a buffoon, and no one ever slapped my face. I may say that they are even a bit afraid of me. They know that I bite. Once, three years ago, a certain gentleman, a country squire, was foolish enough at table to stick a radish into my hair. What do you think happened? Immediately—without getting excited, you know—in the most courteous fashion, I challenged him to a duel. My squire almost got paralysis with terror. My host made him apologize. The effect was startling. . . . I must confess I knew in advance that he wouldn't fight. So you see, Lizaveta Bogdanovna, I have a huge amount of self-esteem—but so it is. I have also no great talent, and I had only a helter-skelter education. I am a poor doctor. I have no need of dissembling to you, and if you ever fall ill here, it is not I who will treat you. If I had talent and education, I should hurry off to the capital. But for the inhabitants of these parts, of course, no better doctor is necessary. As for my personal character, I must forewarn you, Lizaveta Bogdanovna: at home I am glum, silent and exacting. I do not get angry when people humor me and show respect to me. I like to have them note my habits and give me tasty food, but all the same I am not jealous and not stingy, and in my absence you can do anything you choose. Any romantic love between us you need not expect. But nevertheless, I imagine you will find it possible to live under one roof with me, so long as you humor me and don't weep in my presence—I can't stand that! And I don't pick quarrels. There's my whole confession. Well, what will you say now?

LIZAVETA BOGDANOVNA: What can I say to you, Ignaty Ilyich? . . . If you have not purposely blackened yourself—

SHPIGELSKY: But how did I blacken myself? Do not forget that another man in my place would calmly

have kept quiet about his own defects, seeing that you had noticed nothing. But after the marriage is over—after the marriage it's too late. But I am too proud for that.

[Lizaveta Bogdanovna *glances at him*]

Yes, yes, too proud. . . . Why won't you look at me? I have no intention of deceiving my future wife and lying to her, not for a hundred thousand, to say nothing of fifteen. But I will bow down humbly to a stranger for the sake of a sack of flour. Such is my character. . . . To a stranger I grin and I think within me: "What a blockhead, my boy, to be caught with such a bait!" But with you I say what I think. That is, if you will permit me, I do not tell you everything that I think, but at any rate, I don't deceive you. I must seem to you a great freak, to be sure. But just wait, sometime I will tell you the story of my life. You will be surprised that I am still so well preserved. I don't think that in your childhood you ate off of gold plates. But nevertheless, my darling, you can't understand what genuine hardpan poverty is like. . . . However, I will tell you all this at some other time. Now, then, you had better think over what I have had the honor to report to you. . . . Think over this little matter well by yourself, and then give me your decision. So far as I have been able to observe, you are a woman of good judgment. You . . . By the way, how old are you?

LIZAVETA BOGDANOVNA: I . . . I . . . am thirty.

SHPIGELSKY: [*Calmly*] That's not true. You are all of forty.

LIZAVETA BOGDANOVNA: [*Flushing up*] Not forty at all, but thirty-six.

SHPIGELSKY: That's more than thirty, anyway. Well, you must lose this habit, Lizaveta Bogdanovna . . . the more so, as a married woman is by no means old at thirty-six. You also make a mistake in taking snuff. [*Rising*] But I think the shower has stopped.

LIZAVETA BOGDANOVNA: [*Also rising*] Yes, it has.

SHPIGELSKY: So you will give me the answer in a few days?

LIZAVETA BOGDANOVNA: I will tell you my decision to-morrow.

SHPIGELSKY: Well, I like that. . . . That's sensible. So sensible! Good for you, Lizaveta Bogdanovna. Well, give me your hand. Let's go in the house.

LIZAVETA BOGDANOVNA: [*Giving him her hand*] Come on!

SHPIGELSKY: And, by the way, I haven't kissed it. . . . And that's obligatory, I think. . . . Let this be done at all hazards! [*Kisses her hand.* Lizaveta Bogdanovna *blushes*] There now! [*He goes toward the garden door*]

LIZAVETA BOGDANOVNA: [*Stopping*] So you think, Ignaty Ilyich, that Mikhaylo Alexandrovich is really not a dangerous man?

SHPIGELSKY: That's what I think.

LIZAVETA BOGDANOVNA: Let me tell you, Ignaty Ilyich, it seems to me that Natalya Petrovna for some time . . . It seems to me that Mr. Belyayev . . .

She is paying attention to him, isn't she? And Verochka, what do you think about her? Wasn't that the reason that to-day—

SHPIGELSKY: [*Interrupting her*] I forgot to tell you one thing, Lizaveta Bogdanovna: I myself am awfully curious, but I can't stand curious women. Let me explain. In my opinion, a wife should be curious and observant—that is really useful for her husband—but only with outsiders. You understand me? With outsiders. However, if you insist on knowing my opinion about Natalya Petrovna, Vera Alexandrovna, Mr. Belyayev, and in general, the inhabitants of this house, just listen while I sing you a song. I have a wretched voice, but don't expect too much.

LIZAVETA BOGDANOVNA: [*With surprise*] A song!

SHPIGELSKY: Listen, first stanza! [*Sings first verse*]

Grandma had a little goat, gray goat;
Grandma had a little goat, gray goat:
Hey hey! ha ha! a little goat!
Hey hey! ha ha! a little goat!

Second stanza! [*Sings*]

Goatie wished to roam the woods, the woods;
Goatie wished to roam the woods, the woods:
Hey hey! ha ha! to roam the woods!
Hey hey! ha ha! to roam the woods!

LIZAVETA BOGDANOVNA: But I really don't understand.

SHPIGELSKY: Listen! Third stanza! [*Sings*]

Great gray wolves ate up the goat, the goat;
Great gray wolves ate up the goat, the goat:
[*Cutting a caper*]
Hey hey! ha ha! ate up the goat!
Hey hey! ha ha! ate up the goat!

And now, let's come on. By the way, I must have a talk with Natalya Petrovna. I don't think she'll bite me. If I'm not mistaken, I'm still necessary to her. Come on!

[*They go out into the garden*]

KATYA: [*Cautiously emerging from behind the column*] I thought they'd never go! How spiteful that doctor is! . . . He talked and talked, how he talked! And how he does sing! I'm afraid that meanwhile Alexey Nikolayevich may have returned to the house . . . and they needed to come to this very spot! [*Goes to the window*] So Lizaveta Bogdanovna will be a doctor's wife. . . . [*Laughing*] What a woman! . . . Well, I don't envy her. . . . [*Looking out of the window*] The grass looks as if it had been washed. . . . What a lovely fragrance! . . . It's from the cherry tree. Ah, so here he comes! [*After waiting a moment*] Alexey Nikolayevich! . . . Alexey Nikolayevich!

BELYAYEV: [*Off stage*] Who is calling me? Oh, is that you, Katya? [*Comes up to the window*] What do you want?

KATYA: Come in here. . . . I want to tell you something.

BELYAYEV: Oh, all right. [*He goes away from the window and in a moment comes in at the door*] Here I am.

KATYA: You didn't get wet in the shower?

BELYAYEV: No. . . . I was sitting in the hothouse with Potap. . . . Is he your uncle or something of the sort?

KATYA: Yes, he's my uncle.

BELYAYEV: How pretty you are to-day!

[*Katya smiles and lowers her eyes. He takes a peach out of his pocket*]

Will you have it?

KATYA: [*Declining*] Thank you kindly. . . . Eat it yourself.

BELYAYEV: But did I decline when you brought me some raspberries yesterday? Take it. I picked it for you. . . . Honest.

KATYA: Well, thank you. [*Takes the peach*]

BELYAYEV: That's right. Well then, what did you want to tell me?

KATYA: The young lady . . . Vera Alexandrovna . . . asked me. . . . She wants to see you.

BELYAYEV: Oh! Well, I'll go to her directly.

KATYA: No. She is coming here herself. She wants to have a talk with you.

BELYAYEV: [*With marked amazement*] She wants to come here?

KATYA: Yes, here. Here, you know. . . . Nobody comes here. Here you won't be interrupted. [*Sighing*] She loves you very much, Alexey Nikolayevich. . . . She is so kind. Now I'll go for her, shall I? And you'll wait here?

BELYAYEV: Of course, of course.

KATYA: Right away. [*She goes off and stops*] Alexey Nikolayevich, is it true, as they say, that you are leaving us?

BELYAYEV: I? No. . . . Who told you that?

KATYA: Then you are not leaving? Well, thank Heaven! [*With confusion*] I'll return directly [*She goes out by the door leading to the house*]

BELYAYEV: [*Remains motionless for some time*] What marvels! Marvels are certainly happening to me. I confess I never expected this. . . . Vera loves me. . . . Natalya Petrovna knows it. . . . Vera herself confessed everything to her. . . . Marvels! Vera is such a dear, kind child. But . . . but what does this note mean, for instance? [*Takes out of his pocket a small bit of paper*] From Natalya Petrovna . . . written in pencil: "Do not go away. Do not decide on anything until I have discussed matters with you." What does she want to talk over with me? [*After a pause*] What stupid thoughts come into my head! I confess all this disturbs me extremely. If any one had told me a month ago that I . . . I . . . I can't recover my senses after that conversation with Natalya Petrovna. Why is my heart beating so fast? Now it's Vera that wants to see me. What shall I tell her! At any rate, I will find out what the matter is. . . . Perhaps Natalya Petrovna is angry with me. . . . But why? [*He looks at the note again*] All this is strange, very strange.

[*The door quietly opens. He quickly hides the note. Vera and Katya appear on the threshold. He goes up to them. Vera is very pale. She does not raise her eyes and does not move from the spot*]

KATYA: Don't be afraid, young lady, go up to him. I'll stand guard. . . . Don't be afraid. [*To Belyayev*] Oh, Alexey Nikolayevich! [*She closes the window, goes into the garden, and shuts the door behind her*]

BELYAYEV: Vera Alexandrovna, you wanted to see me. Come here. Sit down here. [*He takes her arm and leads her to the bench. Vera sits down*] That's the way. [*Looking at her with surprise*] Have you been crying?

VERA: [*Without raising her eyes*] That's nothing. I've come to ask your forgiveness, Alexey Nikolayevich.

BELYAYEV: What for?

VERA: I heard that you had . . . an unpleasant explanation with Natalya Petrovna. . . . You are going away. . . . You have been discharged.

BELYAYEV: Who told you that?

VERA: Natalya Petrovna herself. . . . I met her after your explanation with her. . . . She told me that you yourself did not care to stay with us longer. But I think that she discharged you.

BELYAYEV: Tell me, do the people in the house know it?

VERA: No . . . only Katya. . . . I had to tell her. . . . I wanted to speak with you and to ask your forgiveness. But please just imagine how hard this must be for me. I am the cause of it all, Alexey Nikolayevich; I am the only one to blame.

BELYAYEV: You, Vera Alexandrovna?

VERA: I didn't expect it at all. . . . Natalya Petrovna . . . However, I excuse her. And you must excuse me. . . . This morning I was a stupid child, but now . . . [*She stops*]

BELYAYEV: There is nothing decided yet, Vera Alexandrovna. . . . Maybe I shall stay.

VERA: [*Sadly*] You say that nothing is decided, Alexey Nikolayevich. . . . No, everything is decided; everything is ended. You see how you are behaving to me now. But do you remember—only yesterday in the garden. . . . [*After a pause*] Ah, I see, Natalya Petrovna has told you everything.

BELYAYEV: [*Confused*] Vera Alexandrovna . . .

VERA: She has told you everything; I can see that. . . . She wanted to catch me, and I was just silly enough to throw myself into her net. . . . But she betrayed herself too. . . . Anyhow I am not a child any longer. [*Lowering her voice*] Oh, no!

BELYAYEV: What do you mean?

VERA: [*Glancing at him*] Alexey Nikolayevich, do you really want to leave us yourself?

BELYAYEV: Yes.

VERA: Why? [*Belyayev is silent*] You do not answer me?

BELYAYEV: Vera Alexandrovna, you were not mistaken. Natalya Petrovna did tell me everything.

VERA: [*In a weak voice*] What, for instance?

BELYAYEV: Vera Alexandrovna, it is really impossible . . . for me. . . . You understand me.

VERA: Perhaps she told you that I was in love with you?

BELYAYEV: [*Indecisively*] Yes.

VERA: [*Quickly*] But that's not true.

BELYAYEV: [*Taken aback*] What?

VERA: [*Covering her face with her hands and whispering through her fingers in a choked voice*] At any rate, I didn't tell her that. I don't remember. [*Raising her head*] Oh, how cruelly she acted toward me! And you . . . Is that why you wanted to leave?

BELYAYEV: Vera Alexandrovna, consider yourself. . . .

VERA: [*Glancing at him*] He doesn't love me! [*Again covers her face*]

BELYAYEV: [*Sitting down near her and taking her hands*] Give me your hand. . . . Listen, there must be no misunderstanding between us. I love you as a sister. I love you because I cannot help loving you. Pardon me if I . . . Never in my life have I been in such a position. . . . I don't want to hurt your feelings. . . . I will not dissemble to you. I know that you have come to like me, that you have come to love me. . . . But judge for yourself what the result of this may be. I am only twenty years old, and I haven't a penny. Please do not be angry with me. I really do not know what to say to you.

VERA: [*Removing her hands from her face and looking at him*] As if I had demanded anything! Good Heavens! But why do you act so cruelly, so mercilessly? [*She stops*]

BELYAYEV: I did not wish to grieve you, Vera Alexandrovna.

VERA: I do not blame you, Alexey Nikolayevich. How are you to blame? I am the only one to blame. . . . That is why I am punished. I do not blame even her. I know that she is a good woman, but she could not restrain herself. . . . She lost her self-control.

BELYAYEV: [*With perplexity*] Lost her self-control?

VERA: [*Turning to him*] Natalya Petrovna is in love with you, Belyayev.

BELYAYEV: What?

VERA: She is in love with you.

BELYAYEV: What are you saying?

VERA: I know what I am saying. To-day has aged me. . . . I am no longer a child, believe me. She took upon herself to be jealous . . . of me! [*With a bitter smile*] How do you like that?

BELYAYEV: But that is impossible!

VERA: Impossible! . . . But why did she suddenly form the idea of marrying me to that gentleman, what's his name, Bolshintsov? Why did she send the doctor to me? Why did she herself try to persuade me? Oh, I know what I am saying! If you could have seen, Belyayev, how her face changed when I told her! . . . Oh, you cannot imagine how cunningly, how craftily, she extorted this confession from me. . . . Yes, she loves you. That is only too clear.

BELYAYEV: You are mistaken, Vera Alexandrovna, I assure you.

VERA: No, I am not mistaken. Believe me, I am not mistaken. If she does not love you, why did she torture me so? What have I done to her? [*Bitterly*] Jealousy excuses everything! But what is the use of talking! . . . Even now, why does she dismiss you? . . . She thinks that you . . . that you and I . . . Oh, she may be at ease! You may remain here! [*She covers her face with her hands*]

BELYAYEV: She has not yet discharged me, Vera Alexandrovna. . . . I have already told you that nothing is yet decided.

VERA: [*Suddenly raising her head and looking at him*] Really?

BELYAYEV: Yes. . . . But why are you looking at me in this way?

VERA: [*As if to herself*] Ah, I understand. . . . Yes, yes. . . . She . . . she herself still has hopes. [*The door to the corridor opens suddenly and on the threshold appears* Natalya Petrovna. *She stops at the sight of* Vera *and* Belyayev]

BELYAYEV: What are you saying?

VERA: Yes, everything is clear to me now. . . . She has come to herself. She understands that I am not dangerous to her. And really, what do I amount to? I am a stupid girl, and she—!

BELYAYEV: How can you think, Vera Alexandrovna . . . ?

VERA: And anyway, who knows? Perhaps she is right. . . . Perhaps you do love her.

BELYAYEV: I?

VERA: [*Rising*] Yes, you. Why do you blush?

BELYAYEV: I, Vera Alexandrovna?

VERA: Do you love her? Can you fall in love with her? . . . You do not answer my question.

BELYAYEV: But consider: what do you wish me to reply to you? You are so excited, Vera Alexandrovna. . . . Calm yourself, for Heaven's sake!

VERA: [*Turning away from him*] You behave toward me as if I were a child. . . . You do not even think me worth a serious answer. . . . You simply want to get rid of me. . . . You are comforting me! [*She is about to leave, but suddenly stops at the sight of* Natalya Petrovna] Natalya Petrovna!

[Belyayev *looks around quickly*]

NATALYA PETROVNA: [*Making a few steps forward*] Yes, it is I. [*She speaks with a certain effort*] I have come for you, Verochka.

VERA: [*Slowly and coldly*] Why did you think of coming to this place of all others? So you have been looking for me?

NATALYA PETROVNA: Yes, I have been looking for you. You are indiscreet, Verochka. . . . I have

already cautioned you several times. . . . And you, Alexey Nikolayevich, you have forgotten your promise. . . . You have deceived me.

VERA: Oh, do stop, Natalya Petrovna; do please stop!

[Natalya Petrovna *looks at her with amazement*]

You needn't talk to me as you would to a child any longer. [*Lowering her voice*] I am a woman from this day forward. . . . I am just as much a woman as you.

NATALYA PETROVNA: [*In confusion*] Vera!

VERA: [*Almost in a whisper*] He did not deceive you. . . . It was not he who sought for this interview with me. He is not in love with me, you know that. You have no occasion to be jealous.

NATALYA PETROVNA: [*With rising amazement*] Vera!

VERA: Believe me! . . . Do not be crafty any more. These crafty devices are of no further use to you now. . . . I see through them now. Believe me that I do. Natalya Petrovna, I am no longer your protégée whom you watch over [*With irony*] as an elder sister. . . . [*Moving toward her*] I am your rival.

NATALYA PETROVNA: Vera, you forget yourself.

VERA: Perhaps. . . . But who has brought me to this pass? I do not understand myself how I dare to speak to you in this way. . . . Perhaps I am speaking thus because I no longer have any hopes, because you have been good enough to trample me in the dust. . . . And you succeeded in doing so . . . completely. But listen to me: I do not intend to dissemble with you, if you do not with me. . . . Be sure of that. I have told him everything. [*Indicating* Belyayev]

NATALYA PETROVNA: What could you tell him?

VERA: What? [*With irony*] Why, everything that I have been able to observe. You hoped to learn everything from me without giving yourself away. You made a mistake, Natalya Petrovna. You were too confident of your own strength.

NATALYA PETROVNA: Vera, Vera, recollect yourself.

VERA: [*In a whisper and coming still nearer to her*] Tell me that I made a mistake. . . . Tell me that you do not love him. . . . He has told me that he does not love me! [Natalya Petrovna *is silent with amazement.* Vera *remains immovable for some time, and suddenly puts her hand to her brow*] Natalya Petrovna, forgive me! . . . I . . . do not know myself . . . what is the matter with me. Pardon me; be indulgent to me. [*She bursts into tears and quickly goes out by the corridor door. A pause*]

BELYAYEV: [*Going up to* Natalya Petrovna] I may assure you, Natalya Petrovna . . .

NATALYA PETROVNA: [*Looking fixedly at the floor and stretching out her hand toward him*] Stop, Alexey Nikolayevich. Really . . . Vera is right. . . . It is time . . . it is time for me to stop dissembling.

I have done her wrong and done you wrong. You have the right to despise me.

[Belyayev *makes an involuntary movement*]
I have lowered myself in my own eyes. I have left only one means of again winning your regard: frankness, complete frankness, whatever may be the consequences. Besides that, I now see you for the last time, and now speak to you for the last time. I love you. [*She gazes fixedly at him*]

BELYAYEV: You, Natalya Petrovna!

NATALYA PETROVNA: Yes, I. I love you. Vera was not deceived and did not deceive you. I fell in love with you the very first day of your arrival, but I recognized this myself only yesterday. I do not intend to justify my conduct. . . . It was unworthy of me . . . but at least you now can understand, can excuse me. Yes, I was jealous of Vera. Yes, in my thoughts I married her to Bolshintsov in order to remove her from myself and from you. Yes, I took advantage of my greater age, of my position in society, to find out her secret and—of course I didn't expect this—I betrayed myself. I love you, Belyayev, but be sure of this, only pride forces this confession from me. . . . The farce that I have played up till now has at last disgusted me. You cannot remain here. . . . However, after what I have just told you, it will doubtless be very embarrassing for you in my presence, and you yourself will wish to withdraw from here as quickly as may be. I am convinced of that. This conviction has given me boldness. I confess I did not wish you to carry away a bad memory of me. Now you know everything. . . . Perhaps I have hindered you. Perhaps if all this had not happened, you would have fallen in love with Verochka. . . . I have only one excuse, Alexey Nikolayevich. . . . All this was beyond my power. [*She becomes silent. She says all this in a rather even and calm voice, without looking at* Belyayev. *He is silent. She continues with a certain agitation, still without looking at him*] You do not answer me? . . . However, I understand that. You have nothing to tell me. The position of a man who does not love but who receives a declaration of love is altogether too difficult. I thank you for your silence. Believe me: when I told you . . . that I loved you . . . I was not dissembling . . . as I had been before. I did not count on anything. On the contrary, I wished finally to throw off the mask, to which, I may assure you, I was not accustomed. . . . And finally, why should I coquette and dissemble any longer when all is known? Why should I play the hypocrite any more when there is no one to deceive? All is ended between us. I will not detain you any longer. You may leave here without saying a word to me, without even bidding me farewell. I shall not even regard that as a discourtesy. On the contrary, I shall be grateful to you. There are occasions in which delicacy is out of place . . . worse than rudeness. Evidently it was not fated for us to understand each other. Farewell! No, it was

not fated for us to understand each other . . . but at least I hope that now, in your eyes, I have ceased to be an oppressive, secretive, and cunning creature. . . . Farewell forever!

[Belyayev *in agitation tries to say something, but cannot*]
You are not leaving?

BELYAYEV: [*Bowing, is about to leave, but after a short struggle with himself returns*] No, I cannot leave.

[Natalya Petrovna *for the first time looks at him*]
I cannot leave in this way! . . . Listen, Natalya Petrovna, you have just told me . . . you do not desire me to carry away an unfavorable memory of you, and for my part I do not wish you to remember me as a man who . . . Good Heavens! I do not know how to express myself! . . . Natalya Petrovna, excuse me. . . . I do not know how to speak with ladies. . . . Up till now I have known . . . women of an altogether different sort. You say that we are not fated to understand each other, but consider: could I, a simple, almost uneducated boy—could I even think of any intimacy with you? Remember who you are and who I am! Remember: could I even think. . . ? With your education. . . . But why do I speak of education? . . . Look at me. . . . This old coat and your fragrant garments! . . . Consider! Yes, I was afraid of you, and I am afraid of you now! . . . Without any exaggeration I looked upon you as a higher being . . . and at the same time . . . you, you tell me that you love me. You, Natalya Petrovna, love me! . . . I feel my heart beating within me as it has never beat in my life. It beats not from amazement only. It is not my self-conceit that is flattered. . . . Why so! . . . It is not a question of self-conceit now . . . but I . . . I cannot leave in this way, if you will permit me to say so.

NATALYA PETROVNA: [*After a pause, as if to herself*] What have I done?

BELYAYEV: Natalya Petrovna, believe me, please, for God's sake! . . .

NATALYA PETROVNA: [*In a changed voice*] Alexey Nikolayevich, if I did not know you as a gentleman, as a man to whom falsehood is impossible, I should think the Lord knows what. Perhaps I should repent my own frankness. But I believe you. I do not wish to hide my feelings from you. I thank you for what you have just now told me. Now I know why we have not become intimate. . . . And so it was not my own personality, it was nothing in me that repelled you. . . . It was only my position. . . . [*Stopping*] All this makes things better, of course. . . . And now it will be easier for me to part with you . . . farewell! [*She is about to leave*]

BELYAYEV: [*After a pause*] I know, Natalya Petrovna, that I cannot stay here. . . . But I cannot make you understand all that is going on within me. You love me! . . . It is terrible for me even to pronounce those words! . . . All this is so new to me. . . . It seems to me that I see you, hear you, for the first time. But I feel one thing. It is indispensable for me to go away. . . . I feel that I cannot be responsible for anything that may happen.

NATALYA PETROVNA: [*In a feeble voice*] Yes, Belyayev, you must go away. . . . Now, after this explanation, you must go away. . . . But is it really possible, notwithstanding all that I have done? . . . Oh, believe me, if I had suspected even distantly all that you have told me, that confession would have died within me. . . . I merely wished to put an end to all the misunderstandings. I wished to repent, to punish myself. I wished once for all to snap the last thread. If I could have imagined—! [*She covers her face with her hands*]

BELYAYEV: I believe you, Natalya Petrovna, I believe you. But I myself, a quarter of an hour ago . . . did I imagine? . . . Only to-day, during the time of our last meeting before dinner, did I feel for the first time something unusual, something unwonted, as if some one's hand were gripping my heart; and I felt such ardent warmth in my bosom. . . . Really, formerly I held myself aloof from you, as it were, I even seemed to dislike you, but when you told me to-day that Vera Alexandrovna thought . . . [*He pauses*]

NATALYA PETROVNA: [*With an involuntary smile of happiness on her lips*] Enough, enough, Belyayev. We must not think of that. We must not forget that we are speaking to each other for the last time . . . that you leave to-morrow.

BELYAYEV: Oh, yes! I shall leave to-morrow. I may still leave now. . . . All this will pass. . . . You see, I do not wish to exaggerate. . . . I am going. . . . And then as God wills! I shall carry away with me one memory; I shall remember eternally that you loved me. . . . But how is it that I never knew you before? . . . Here you are looking at me now. . . . Is it possible that I ever tried to avoid your glance? . . . Is it possible that I ever felt timidity in your presence?

NATALYA PETROVNA: [*With a smile*] You just now told me that you were afraid of me.

BELYAYEV: I? [*After a pause*] To be sure. . . . I am surprised at myself. . . . Do I—I speak so boldly to you? I do not recognize myself.

NATALYA PETROVNA: And you are not deceiving yourself?

BELYAYEV: In what?

NATALYA PETROVNA: In thinking that you love me? [*With a shudder*] Oh, Heavens, what am I doing? Listen, Belyayev. . . . Come to my aid. . . . No woman ever found herself in such a position before. I have no more strength, truly. . . . Perhaps it is better thus. Everything has been cut off at one blow. But we, at least, have come to understand each other. . . . Give me your hand—and farewell forever!

BELYAYEV: [*Taking her hand*] Natalya Petrovna

. . . I do know what to say to you in farewell. . . . My heart is so full. . . . God grant you . . . ! [*He stops and presses her hand to his lips*] Farewell! [*He is about to leave by the door into the garden*]

NATALYA PETROVNA: [*Gazing after him*] Belyayev!

BELYAYEV: [*Turning around*] Natalya Petrovna!

NATALYA PETROVNA: [*After a considerable pause, in a weak voice*] Remain!

BELYAYEV: What?

NATALYA PETROVNA: Remain! And let God pass judgment on us! [*She buries her head in her hands*]

BELYAYEV: [*Quickly approaching her and stretching out his hands to her*] Natalya Petrovna!

[*At that moment the door into the garden opens and Rakitin appears on the threshold. He looks at them both for some time and suddenly approaches them*]

RAKITIN: [*In a loud voice*] They are looking for you everywhere, Natalya Petrovna. [*Natalya Petrovna and Belyayev glance around*]

NATALYA PETROVNA: [*Removing her hands from her face and seeming to come to herself*] Ah, is that you? Who is looking for me?

[*Belyayev, confused, bows to Natalya Petrovna and is about to leave*]

Are you going, Alexey Nikolayevich? . . . Don't forget, you know—

[*He bows to her a second time and goes out into the garden*]

RAKITIN: Arkady is looking for you. . . . I confess I didn't expect to find you here. . . . But as I was passing by . . .

NATALYA PETROVNA: [*With a smile*] You heard our voices. . . . I met Alexey Nikolayevich here . . . and I had a long explanation with him. . . . To-day is evidently a day of explanations, but now we can go to the house. [*She is about to leave by the corridor door*]

RAKITIN: [*With some agitation*] May I inquire . . . what decision? . . .

NATALYA PETROVNA: [*Pretending to be surprised*] What decision? . . . I don't understand you.

RAKITIN: [*After a long silence, in a gloomy voice*] In that case I understand everything.

NATALYA PETROVNA: Well, so it is. . . . Again mysterious hints! Well, yes, I have had an explanation with him, and now everything is straightened out again. . . . Those were trifles, exaggerations. . . . Everything that you and I have been speaking of is all childishness. We must forget it now.

RAKITIN: I am not cross-examining you, Natalya Petrovna.

NATALYA PETROVNA: [*Forcing herself to speak casually*] What was it I wanted to tell you? . . . I don't remember. It's all the same. Come on. All that is over now. . . . It's all past.

RAKITIN: [*Looking at her fixedly*] Oh, it's all over. And how vexed you are with yourself now, most likely . . . because of your frankness to-day!

NATALYA PETROVNA: [*Turning away from him*] Rakitin. . . . [*He again glances at her. She evidently does not know what to say*] You haven't spoken with Arkady yet?

RAKITIN: By no means. . . . I haven't yet managed to prepare myself. . . . You understand that I need to make up something.

NATALYA PETROVNA: How unbearable this is! What do they want of me? They follow after me at every step. Really, Rakitin, I feel ashamed to see you.

RAKITIN: Oh, don't be disturbed, Natalya Petrovna. . . . Why should you be? This is all in the natural course of things. But one can see that Mr. Belyayev is still a novice! And why was he so confused? Why did he run away? . . . However, in the course of time . . . [*In a low, hurried voice*] you will both learn how to dissemble. [*Aloud*] Come on.

[*Natalya Petrovna is about to come up to him, but stops. At that moment the voice of Islayev is heard just outside the garden door: "He came this way, you say?" After these words, Islayev and Shpigelsky come in*]

ISLAYEV: To be sure, there he is.—Bah, bah, bah! And Natalya Petrovna is here too! [*Coming up to her*] What's this? A continuation of to-day's explanation?—Evidently it's an important subject.

RAKITIN: I met Natalya Petrovna here.

ISLAYEV: Met her? [*Looking around*] What a frequented place, to be sure!

NATALYA PETROVNA: But you came here yourself.

ISLAYEV: I came here because . . . [*He stops*]

NATALYA PETROVNA: You were looking for me?

ISLAYEV: [*After a pause*] Yes, I was looking for you. Would you not like to come back to the house? Tea is ready. It will be dark soon.

NATALYA PETROVNA: [*Taking his hand*] Come on, then.

ISLAYEV: [*Looking around*] And we can make this hall into two good rooms for the gardeners—or another servant's room—what do you think about it, Shpigelsky?

SHPIGELSKY: Of course.

ISLAYEV: Come on through the garden, Natasha. [*He goes out by the door into the garden. During the course of all this scene, he has not once glanced at Rakitin. On the threshold he half turns around*] Well, folks, come on and have tea. [*He goes out with Natalya Petrovna*]

SHPIGELSKY: [*To Rakitin*] Well, Mikhaylo Alexandrovich, come on! . . . Give me your hand. . . . Evidently fate has cast us into the rear guard.

RAKITIN: [*Testily*] Oh, Mr. Doctor, permit me to tell you, I am decidedly sick of you.

SHPIGELSKY: [*With affected good humor*] But I am sick of myself, Mikhaylo Alexandrovich, if you did but know it!

[*Rakitin smiles involuntarily*]

Come on. come on.

[*They both go out by the door into the garden*]

ACT V.

The scene is the same as in Acts I and III. Morning. Islayev is sitting at his desk looking over papers. He rises suddenly.

ISLAYEV: No, I absolutely can't work to-day. It's as if a nail were run through my head. [*Pacing the room*] I must confess I didn't expect this. I didn't expect that I should be disturbed . . . as I am now. . . . What shall I do then? . . . That's the problem. [*Falls to thinking and suddenly calls*] Matvey!

MATVEY: [*Coming in*] What will you have, sir?

ISLAYEV: Call my overseer . . . and tell the diggers to wait for me at the dam. . . . Go along!

MATVEY: Yes, sir. [*Goes out*]

ISLAYEV: [*Going to the table again. Running through his papers*] Yes, that's the problem.

ANNA SEMENOVNA: [*Coming in and approaching Islayev*] Arkasha!

ISLAYEV: Oh, is that you, mamma? How are you feeling?

ANNA SEMENOVNA: [*Sitting down on the couch*] I am well, thank Heaven! [*Sighing*] I'm well. [*Sighing still louder*] Thank Heaven! [*Seeing that Islayev does not listen to her, she gives a very vigorous sigh, with a slight groan*]

ISLAYEV: You are sighing. . . . What's the matter with you?

ANNA SEMENOVNA: [*Again sighing, but this time more gently*] Oh, Arkasha, as if you didn't know what I am sighing about.

ISLAYEV: What do you mean?

ANNA SEMENOVNA: [*After a pause*] I am your mother, Arkasha. Of course you are already a grown man, and a man of sense. But all the same, I am your mother. That is a great word, mother!

ISLAYEV: Oh, please explain yourself!

ANNA SEMENOVNA: You know what I am hinting at, my dear. Your wife Natasha . . . Of course, she is a splendid woman—and her conduct up till now has been most exemplary . . . but she is still so young, Arkasha! And youth . . .

ISLAYEV: I understand what you mean. . . . It seems to you that her relations with Rakitin—

ANNA SEMENOVNA: God forbid! I wasn't thinking of that at all.

ISLAYEV: You didn't let me finish my speech. . . . It seems to you that her relations with Rakitin . . . are not quite . . . plain. . . . Those mysterious conversations, those tears—all that seems to you strange.

ANNA SEMENOVNA: Well, Arkasha, did he finally tell you what those conversations of theirs were about? . . . He hasn't told me anything.

ISLAYEV: I haven't cross-examined him, and he evidently is in no great hurry to gratify my curiosity.

ANNA SEMENOVNA: So what do you intend to do now?

ISLAYEV: I, mamma? Nothing at all.

ANNA SEMENOVNA: Nothing?

ISLAYEV: Certainly. Nothing.

ANNA SEMENOVNA: [Rising] I confess that I am surprised. Of course you are the master in your own house, and you know better than I what's good and what's bad. However, consider what consequences . . .

ISLAYEV: Really, mamma, you are quite wrong in being disturbed.

ANNA SEMENOVNA: My dear, I am a mother. . . . But, however, as you think best. [After a pause] I came to see you, I must confess, with the intention of offering my services as mediator.

ISLAYEV: [With animation] No. In this matter, I must ask you not to trouble yourself, mamma. . . . Please oblige me!

ANNA SEMENOVNA: As you wish, Arkasha; as you wish. I won't say a word more. I have forewarned you, I have done my duty. But now—my lips are sealed. [A short silence]

ISLAYEV: You aren't going anywhere to-day?

ANNA SEMENOVNA: But I merely felt obliged to forewarn you. You are too trustful, my dear boy. You judge every one by yourself! Believe me, true friends are very rare in these times!

ISLAYEV: [With impatience] Mamma! . . .

ANNA SEMENOVNA: Well, I am silent, I am silent! And why should an old woman like me mix in? I suppose I have outlived my wits! And I was brought up on other principles and I tried to teach them to you. . . . Well, well, attend to your business. I won't hinder you. . . . I am going. [She goes to the door and stops] Well, then? . . . Well, as you wish, as you wish. [She goes out]

ISLAYEV: [Gazing after her] Why is it that people who really love you like to put each and every one of their fingers in your wound? And yet they are convinced that this makes it easier for you—that's what's amusing! However, I don't blame mother. Her intentions, I know, are of the best, and how can she help giving advice? But that is not the point. . . . [Sitting down] How shall I act? [After reflecting, he rises] Ah, the simplest way is the best! Diplomatic finesse doesn't suit me. . . . I am the first to get entangled in it.

[He rings the bell. Matvey comes in]

Is Mikhaylo Alexandrovich in the house? Do you know?

MATVEY: He is. I just saw him in the billiard room.

ISLAYEV: Ah! Then ask him to come to see me.

MATVEY: Very well, sir. [He goes out]

ISLAYEV: [Walking back and forth] I am not used to such perplexities. . . . I hope they won't be often repeated. . . . Although I am of a strong build, I couldn't stand this for long. [Putting his hand to his breast] Ah! . . .

[Rakitin comes in from the hall in some confusion]

RAKITIN: Did you call me?

ISLAYEV: Yes. . . . [After a pause] Michel, you owe me something.

RAKITIN: I?

ISLAYEV: Certainly. Have you forgotten your promise about . . . Natasha's tears . . . and in general? . . . You remember how mother and I found you. . . . You told me then that there was a secret between Natasha and yourself that you wished to explain to me.

RAKITIN: Did I say secret?

ISLAYEV: Yes.

RAKITIN: But what secret can there be between us? We were just talking.

ISLAYEV: What about? And why was she weeping?

RAKITIN: You know, Arkady . . . moments occur in the life of a woman . . . even the happiest . . .

ISLAYEV: Wait a bit, Rakitin. You can't act this way—I can't see you in such a position. . . . Your confusion is more embarrassing for me than for yourself. [Taking him by the hand] You see, you and I are old friends. . . . You have known me from childhood. . . . I am unable to dissemble. . . . And you have always been frank with me. Give me permission to ask you one question. . . . I give you my word of honor that I will not doubt the sincerity of your answer. You are in love with my wife, aren't you? [Rakitin glances at Islayev] You understand me? You love her . . . well, in a word, you love my wife with the sort of love that is hard to confess to a husband?

RAKITIN: [After a pause. In a hoarse voice] Yes. I love your wife with that sort of love.

ISLAYEV: [Also after a pause] Thank you for your frankness, Michel. You are a gentleman. Well, anyway, what shall we do now? Sit down and let's consider this matter together.

[Rakitin sits down. Islayev paces the room]

I know Natasha. I know her value. But I also know my own value. I am not your equal, Michel . . . don't interrupt me, please! . . . I am not your equal. You're a finer man. In a word, you're more clever. You're more clever. You're a finer man. In a word, a more pleasing person than I. I am a simple fellow. Natasha loves me, I think, but she has eyes. . . . Well, in a word, she must like you. And so here's what I'll tell you further. I have long remarked your mutual regard for each other. . . . But I have also been confident of you both—and so far nothing has come to light. . . . Oh, I don't know how to speak of it! [He stops] But after the scene yesterday, after your second meeting in the evening, what can I think? If it were only I who had found you! But witnesses were involved in the case; mamma, and that rascal Shpigelsky. . . . Well, what have you to say, Michel?

RAKITIN: You are quite right, Arkady.

ISLAYEV: That's not the question. . . . But what's to be done? I must tell you, Michel, that though I am a simple man, I have this much sense: I know that it isn't a good thing to embitter another man's life, and there are cases when it is sinful to insist on one's own rights. I didn't read that in books, my friend. . . . Conscience tells me so. If I must give you freedom . . . Well, then I'll do so. Only we must think this over. It's too important.

RAKITIN: [*Rising*] I have thought it over already.

ISLAYEV: Well?

RAKITIN: I must be leaving. . . . I am going away.

ISLAYEV: [*After a pause*] Do you think so? . . . To leave us for good and all?

RAKITIN: Yes.

ISLAYEV: [*Again beginning to pace the room*] What . . . what is this you propose! But perhaps you are right. It will be hard for us without you. . . . Lord knows, perhaps this won't lead to the desired end. . . . But you can see things better; you can judge best. I think that you have the right idea. You are dangerous to me, my boy. [*With a mournful smile*] Yes . . . you are dangerous to me. So what I have just said . . . in regard to freedom—but really, I could not live after that! For me to exist without Natasha . . . [*He waves his hand*] And one thing further, my boy. For some time, especially during these last few days, I have noticed a great change in her. She has given indications of a certain deep, constant agitation, which alarms me. Is not that true? I am not mistaken, am I?

RAKITIN: [*Bitterly*] Oh, no! You are not mistaken.

ISLAYEV: Well, there, you see! And so you are going away?

RAKITIN: Yes.

ISLAYEV: Hm. And how suddenly this load was shaken off! And really, did you need to be so confused when mother and I found you?

MATVEY: [*Coming in*] The overseer has come.

ISLAYEV: Let him wait.

[*Matvey goes out*]

Michel, you aren't going to leave us for long, are you? All this is nonsense, my boy!

RAKITIN: I really don't know. . . . I think . . . for a long time.

ISLAYEV: Well, you don't take me for an Othello, do you? Really, since the world was made, I don't think any such conversation has ever taken place between two friends! I cannot part with you in this way.

RAKITIN: [*Pressing his hand*] You will inform me when it is possible for me to return.

ISLAYEV: But we have no one to replace you here! Certainly not Bolshintsov!

RAKITIN: There are other people here.

ISLAYEV: Who? Krinitsyn? That dandy? Belyayev is of course a good fellow . . . but he is as far below you as he is below the stars of heaven.

RAKITIN: [*Caustically*] You think so? You don't know him, Arkady. . . . You just pay attention to him. . . . I advise you to. . . . Do you hear? He is a very . . . very remarkable fellow!

ISLAYEV: Bah! You and Natasha were always going to attend to his education. [*Glancing at the door*] Ah, here he comes himself, I think. . . . [*Hastily*] And so, my dear fellow, this is decided, you are leaving us . . . for a short time . . . in a day or two. . . . There is no need of haste. We must prepare Natasha. . . . I'll calm mother down. . . . And God grant you happiness! You have moved a stone from my heart. . . . Embrace me, my dear fellow. [*He hastily embraces him, and turns toward Belyayev, who has just come in*] Ah, is that you? Well . . . well . . . how are you?

BELYAYEV: First rate, Arkady Sergeich.

ISLAYEV: Well, where's Kolya?

BELYAYEV: He is with Mr. Schaaf.

ISLAYEV: Ah, fine! [*Taking his hat*] Well, gentlemen, good-by. I haven't made my daily rounds to-day. I haven't been either at the dam or at the new building. . . . Why, I haven't even looked over my papers. [*Tucks them under his arm*] Good-by for the moment! Matvey, Matvey, come on with me! [*He goes out*]

[*Rakitin remains in the foreground, buried in thought*]

BELYAYEV: [*Coming up to* Rakitin] How do you feel to-day, Mikhaylo Alexandrovich?

RAKITIN: Thank you. As usual. And how are you?

BELYAYEV: I am well.

RAKITIN: That's evident!

BELYAYEV: Why so?

RAKITIN: Why, just . . . by your face. . . . Ah, so you've put on a new frock coat to-day. . . . And what's this I see? A flower in your buttonhole?

[Belyayev, *blushing, pulls it out*]

But why should you, why should you, pray? . . . It looks very nice. [*After a pause*] By the way, Alexey Nikolayevich, if you need anything . . . I am going to town to-morrow.

BELYAYEV: To-morrow?

RAKITIN: Yes . . . and from there, perhaps, to Moscow.

BELYAYEV: [*With surprise*] To Moscow? But I think you told me only yesterday that you intended to stay here about a month.

RAKITIN: Yes . . . but business . . . circumstances have occurred.

BELYAYEV: And are you leaving for a long time?

RAKITIN: I don't know. . . . Maybe for a long time.

BELYAYEV: Permit me to inquire: Does Natalya Petrovna know of your intention?

RAKITIN: No. Why do you ask me about her in particular?

BELYAYEV: Why? [*With some confusion*] No special reason.

RAKITIN: [*After a pause, and looking round*] Alexey Nikolayevich, I think that there is no one in the room except ourselves. Isn't it strange that we are playing a comedy to each other, eh? What do you think about it?

BELYAYEV: I don't understand you, Mikhaylo Alexandrovich.

RAKITIN: Really? You actually don't understand why I am going away?

BELYAYEV: No.

RAKITIN: That's queer. . . . However, I am ready to believe you. Possibly you really don't know the reason. . . . Do you want me to tell you why I am leaving?

BELYAYEV: Pray do.

RAKITIN: You see, Alexey Nikolayevich—by the way, I rely on your discretion—you found me with Arkady Sergeich just now. . . . He and I had a rather important conversation, and in consequence of that very conversation I have decided to go away. Do you know why? I am telling you all this because I regard you as a gentleman. . . . He fancies that I . . . that I am in love with Natalya Petrovna. What do you think of that, eh? Isn't it really rather a strange idea? But I am thankful to him that he didn't begin to dissemble and keep watch of us, but that he addressed himself to me frankly and directly. Well now, tell me what should you have done in my place? Of course, his suspicions have no foundation, but they cause him anxiety. . . . For the peace of his friends, a gentleman should know how . . . sometimes, to sacrifice . . . his own pleasure. And that is the reason I am going away. . . . I am convinced that you will approve my decision; will you not? Is it not true that you . . . that you would have acted in just the same way in my place? You, too, would have gone away?

BELYAYEV: [After a pause] Perhaps.

RAKITIN: I am very glad to hear that. . . . Of course, I don't dispute that in my intention of withdrawing there is a comic side; it is as if I regarded myself as a dangerous person. But you see, Alexey Nikolayevich, the honor of a woman is such an important matter. . . . And besides—of course I don't say this in reference to Natalya Petrovna—but I have known women who were pure and innocent in heart, genuine children in their intellect, who in consequence of that very purity and innocence were more likely than any others to give way to a sudden infatuation. . . . And then, who knows? An excess of caution does no harm in such cases, so much the more that— By the way, Alexey Nikolayevich, perhaps you still have the notion that love is the highest good on earth.

BELYAYEV: [Coldly] I have not experienced that emotion, but I think that to be loved by a woman whom you love must be a great happiness.

RAKITIN: God grant that you long preserve such a pleasant conviction! In my opinion, Alexey Nikolayevich, every love, whether it be happy or unhappy, is a genuine misery when you give yourself up to it entirely. . . . Just wait! You will perhaps find out in the future how those tender little hands know how to torture, with what caressing persistency they tear your heart to bits. . . . Just wait! You will find out how much burning hatred lies hidden under the most ardent love! You will remember me when, as a sick man thirsts for health, you thirst for peace, for the most nonsensical, the most commonplace peace; when you envy every man who is free and has no cares. . . . Just wait! You will learn what it means to belong to a skirt, what it means to be enslaved, to be infected, and how shameful and tormenting is that slavery! . . . You will learn, finally, what trifles are purchased at so high a price. . . . But why am I saying all this to you? You will not believe me now. The thing is that your approval is very pleasant to me. Yes, yes. In such cases, one should be cautious.

BELYAYEV: [Who all this time has gazed fixedly at Rakitin] Thank you for the lesson, Mikhaylo Alexandrovich, although I did not need it.

RAKITIN: [Taking his hand] Excuse me, please. I had no intention . . . I am not in a position to give lessons to any man whatsoever. . . . I merely got started talking.

BELYAYEV: [With slight irony] Without any reason?

RAKITIN: [Slightly confused] That's just it: without any special reason. I merely wished . . . Up to this time, Alexey Nikolayevich, you have had no opportunity of studying women. Women are a very peculiar kind of people.

BELYAYEV: Of whom are you speaking?

RAKITIN: Well, of no one in particular.

BELYAYEV: Of all women in general, I suppose?

RAKITIN: [With a forced smile] Yes, maybe. I really don't know for what reason I have fallen into this instructive tone, but permit me, in saying farewell, to give you one good piece of advice. [Stopping and waving his hand] Oh, but anyhow, who am I to give advice! Pray excuse my chatter.

BELYAYEV: On the contary, on the contrary.

RAKITIN: Well then, so you don't need anything from town?

BELYAYEV: No, I thank you. But I am sorry that you are going away.

RAKITIN: I thank you humbly. . . . Pray believe that I, also . . .

[From the door of the study come out Natalya Petrovna and Vera. Vera is very sad and pale] I have been very glad to make your acquaintance. [He again presses his hand]

NATALYA PETROVNA: [Gazes at both for some time, and goes up to them] How do you do, gentlemen!

RAKITIN: [Turning around quickly] How do you do, Natalya Petrovna! . . . How do you do, Vera Alexandrovna! . . .

[Belyayev bows slightly to Natalya Petrovna and Vera. He is confused]

NATALYA PETROVNA: [To Rakitin] What in the world are you up to?

RAKITIN: Oh, nothing.

NATALYA PETROVNA: Vera and I have been strolling in the garden. It's so nice out of doors to-day. . . . The lindens have such a sweet fragrance. We strolled all the time under the lindens. . . . It's pleasant in the shade to listen to the humming of the bees over your head. . . . [*Timidly to* Belyayev] We hoped to meet you there. [Belyayev *is silent*]

RAKITIN: [*To* Natalya Petrovna] Ah, so you are interested in the beauties of nature to-day. . . . [*After a pause*] Alexey Nikolayevich could not go into the garden. . . . He has put on his new frock coat to-day.

BELYAYEV: [*With a slight flash of temper*] Of course: it's naturally the only frock coat I have, and in the garden I might tear it. Is that what you mean?

RAKITIN: [*Reddening*] Oh, no! . . . I didn't mean that at all.

[Vera *goes silently to the couch on the right, sits down, and takes up some work.* Natalya Petrovna *smiles in a constrained fashion to* Belyayev. *There is a short and rather oppressive silence.* Rakitin *continues with biting carelessness*]

Oh, yes, I forgot to tell you, Natalya Petrovna, that I am going away to-day.

NATALYA PETROVNA: [*With some agitation*] You are going away? Where to?

RAKITIN: To town. . . . On business.

NATALYA PETROVNA: I hope not for long.

RAKITIN: As business demands.

NATALYA PETROVNA: Be sure to come back soon. [*To* Belyayev, *without looking at him*] Alexey Nikolayevich, were those your drawings that Kolya was showing me? Were they your work?

BELYAYEV: Yes . . . I . . . trifles.

NATALYA PETROVNA: On the contrary, they are very charming. You have talent.

RAKITIN: I see that you are discovering new excellences every day in Mr. Belyayev.

NATALYA PETROVNA: [*Coldly*] Possibly. . . . So much the better for him. [*To* Belyayev] Probably you have still other drawings. You will show them to me? [Belyayev *bows*]

RAKITIN: [*Who all this time seems to be on pins and needles*] However, I recollect that it is time for me to be packing. . . . Good-by for the moment. [*He goes to the door of the hall*]

NATALYA PETROVNA: [*Calling after him*] But you will come back to say good-by to us?

RAKITIN: Of course.

BELYAYEV: [*After hesitating slightly*] Wait, Mikhaylo Alexandrovich. I'll go with you. I want to say a couple of words to you.

RAKITIN: Ah!

[They both go out into the hall. Natalya Petrovna remains in the middle of the stage. After waiting a short time she sits down at the left]

NATALYA PETROVNA: [*After a short pause*] Vera!

VERA: [*Without raising her head*] What do you wish?

NATALYA PETROVNA: For the Lord's sake, Vera, don't act so with me! . . . For the Lord's sake, Vera . . . Verochka! . . .

[Vera *says nothing.* Natalya Petrovna *rises,*

crosses the stage, and quietly kneels before her. Vera *tries to raise her, turns away, and hides her face*]

NATALYA PETROVNA: [*Speaks, still kneeling*] Vera, forgive me. Don't cry, Vera. I have done you wrong. I am to blame. Is it possible that you cannot forgive me?

VERA: [*Through her tears*] Please get up, please do!

NATALYA PETROVNA: I shall not get up, Vera, until you forgive me. It is hard for you . . . but consider . . . is it easier for me? . . . Consider, Vera! . . . You know everything. . . . Between us there is only this difference, that you have done me no wrong at all and I . . .

VERA: [*Bitterly*] Only that difference! No, Natalya Petrovna, between us there is another difference. . . . To-day you are so soft, so kind, so caressing. . . .

NATALYA PETROVNA: [*Interrupting her*] Because I feel my own guilt.

VERA: Really? Only for that reason?

NATALYA PETROVNA: [*Rising and sitting down beside her*] But what other reason can there be?

VERA: Natalya Petrovna, do not torture me any more. Do not question me.

NATALYA PETROVNA: [*With a sigh*] Vera, I see that you cannot forgive me.

VERA: To-day you are so good and so soft because you feel that you are loved.

NATALYA PETROVNA: [*Confused*] Vera?

VERA: [*Turning toward her*] Well, isn't that the truth?

NATALYA PETROVNA: [*Sadly*] Believe me, both of us are equally unfortunate.

VERA: He loves you!

NATALYA PETROVNA: Vera, why should we desire to torture each other? It is time for both of us to come to our senses. Remember in what a position I am, in what a position we both are. Remember that our secret and the wrong that I have done you are already known to two persons here. . . . [*Stopping*] Vera, instead of tormenting each other by suspicions and reproaches, would it not be better for both of us to think how to find a way out of this hard position . . . how to save ourselves! Do you think that I can bear these agitations, these anxieties? Have you forgotten who I am? But you are not listening to me.

VERA: [*Pensively gazing at the floor*] He loves you. . . .

NATALYA PETROVNA: He is going away, Vera.

VERA: [*Turning around*] Oh, let me alone! . . . [Natalya Petrovna *looks at her with indecision. At that moment the voice of* Islayev *is heard in the study:* "Natasha! Oh, Natasha! Where are you?"]

NATALYA PETROVNA: [*Rising quickly and going to the door of the study*] I am here. What do you wish?

VOICE OF ISLAYEV: Come here, I want to tell you something.

NATALYA PETROVNA: **Right away.**

[*She returns to* Vera *and extends her hand to her.* Vera *does not move.* Natalya Petrovna *sighs and goes out into the study*]

VERA: [*Alone, after a pause*] He loves her! . . . And I must remain in her house! . . . Oh, that is too much.

[*She covers her face with her hands, and remains motionless. From the door leading into the hall peers the head of* Shpigelsky. *He cautiously looks around and comes up on tiptoe to* Vera, *who does not notice him*]

SHPIGELSKY: [*After standing in front of her with arms folded and with a biting smile on his countenance*] Vera Alexandrovna! . . . Oh, Vera Alexandrovna!

VERA: [*Raising her head*] Who is that? Is it you, doctor?

SHPIGELSKY: Well, my young lady, are you not feeling well?

VERA: No, I'm all right.

SHPIGELSKY: Let me feel your pulse. [*Feels her pulse*] Hm! Why so fast? Oh, my young lady, my young lady! . . . You are not listening to me. . . . But I think that I sincerely wish you happiness.

VERA: [*Looking at him with decision*] Ignaty Ilyich!

SHPIGELSKY: [*Quickly*] I am listening, Vera Alexandrovna. . . . What an expression there is on your face: good gracious! . . . I am listening.

VERA: That Mr. . . . Bolshintsov, your acquaintance—is he really a good man?

SHPIGELSKY: My friend Bolshintsov? A most excellent, a most honorable man . . . the mold and pattern of virtue!

VERA: He isn't bad-tempered?

SHPIGELSKY: The kindest sort of man. He isn't really a man, he is just soft dough. All you have to do is to take him and knead him. You couldn't find another man as kind as he in all the world, by daylight, with a candle. He's a dove and not a man.

VERA: Do you vouch for him?

SHPIGELSKY: [*Putting one hand on his heart and raising the other on high*] As I would for myself!

VERA: In that case, you may tell him . . . that I am ready to marry him.

SHPIGELSKY: [*With joyous amazement*] Well, really?

VERA: Only, as quickly as possible—do you hear? —As quickly as possible.

SHPIGELSKY: To-morrow, if you wish. . . . By all means! Good for you, Vera Alexandrovna! Splendid girl! I'll gallop away for him right off, and won't I make him happy! . . . What an unexpected turn things have taken. He is fairly infatuated with you, Vera Alexandrovna.

VERA: [*Impatiently*] I am not inquiring of you about that, Ignaty Ilyich.

SHPIGELSKY: As you choose, Vera Alexandrovna, as you choose. Only you'll be happy with him; you'll thank me, you'll see. . . . [Vera *again makes an impatient move*] Well, I am silent. I am silent . . . So I may tell him?

VERA: You may, you may.

SHPIGELSKY: Very good. Then I'll set out right off. Good-by for a while. [*Listening*] By the way, some one's coming in here. [*He goes into the study, and on the threshold makes a grimace of amazement for his own benefit*] Good-by for the moment. [*He goes out*]

VERA: [*Gazing after him*] Anything in the world rather than remain here! . . . [*She rises*] Yes, I have decided. I will not remain in this house, not under any consideration. I can't endure her gentle look, her smiles; I can't see how her whole being seems refreshed, how she revels in her own happiness. . . . For she is happy, however she may pretend to be sad and melancholy. . . . Her caresses are more than I can stand. . . .

[Belyayev *appears from the hall door. He looks around and goes up to* Vera]

BELYAYEV: [*In a low voice*] Vera Alexandrovna, are you alone?

VERA: [*Looks around, shudders, and after a short pause utters the word*] Yes.

BELYAYEV: I am glad you are alone. . . . Otherwise I should not have come here. I have come to bid you farewell, Vera Alexandrovna.

VERA: Farewell?

BELYAYEV: Yes, I am going away.

VERA: You are going away? You, too, are going away?

BELYAYEV: Yes. . . . I, too. [*With intense internal agitation*] You see, Vera Alexandrovna, it is impossible for me to remain here. My presence has already been the cause of many troubles here. Besides the fact that, without myself knowing how, I have disturbed your peace of mind, and the peace of mind of Natalya Petrovna, I have also broken up old ties of friendship. Thanks to me, Mr. Rakitin is leaving here, and you have quarreled with your benefactress. . . . It is time to put a stop to all this. After my departure I hope that all will calm down again and return to its former quiet routine. . . . Turning the heads of rich ladies and young girls is not my line. . . . You will forget me, and perhaps in time you will be surprised how all this could have happened. . . . Even now it surprises me. . . . I do not wish to deceive you, Vera Alexandrovna: I am afraid, I am alarmed at the thought of staying here. . . . I cannot be responsible for anything. . . . You know I am not accustomed to such things as this. I feel embarrassed. . . . It seems to me that every one is looking at me. . . . And finally, it will be impossible for me . . . now . . . with both of you. . . .

VERA: Oh, don't be anxious about me! I shan't remain here long.

BELYAYEV: Why so?

VERA: That's my secret, but I shan't hinder you. You may be sure of that.

BELYAYEV: Well, then, you see, how can I help departing? Judge for yourself. I seem to have brought the plague into this house; every one is fleeing from here. . . . Is it not better for me alone to disappear while there is still time? I had a long conversation with Mr. Rakitin just now. . . . You can't imagine how much bitterness there was in his words. . . . And he was right in making fun of my new frock coat. . . . He was right. Yes, I must depart. Believe me, Vera Alexandrovna, I can hardly wait for the moment when I shall be rushing along the highway in a carriage. . . . I am suffocating here; I want fresh air. I am exhausted; I have a sense of bitterness, and at the same time, of relief, just like a man who is setting out on a long sea voyage. He is loth to part with his friends, he feels oppressed; and at the same time, the sea ripples so merrily, the wind blows so freshly in his face, that the blood involuntarily leaps in his veins, however heavy his heart may be. . . . Yes, I am going away without fail. I shall return to Moscow to my companions. I shall set to work.

VERA: So you love her, Alexey Nikolayevich. You love her, and yet you are going away.

BELYAYEV: Oh, don't, Vera Alexandrovna! Why do you say that? Do you not see that all is ended? It flashed up and went out like a spark. Let us part friends. It is time. I have come to myself. I wish you health and happiness. Sometime we shall see each other again. . . . I shall never forget you, Vera Alexandrovna. . . . I have become very fond of you, believe me! . . . [He presses her hand, and hastily adds] Give this note to Natalya Petrovna from me.

VERA: [Looking at him in confusion] A note?

BELYAYEV: Yes. . . . I cannot bid her farewell.

VERA: But are you going off right away?

BELYAYEV: Right away. . . . I have told no one about this . . . with the exception of Mikhaylo Alexandrovich. He approves my decision. From here I shall go immediately on foot to Petróvskoye. In Petróvskoye I shall wait for Mikhaylo Alexandrovich, and together we shall go to town. From town I shall write. They will send me my things. You see, everything has been arranged. . . . By the way, you may read that note. There are only two words in it.

VERA: [Taking the note from him] And are you really going away?

BELYAYEV: Yes, yes. . . . Give her this note and tell her— No, don't tell her anything. What's the use? [Listening] They are coming here. Good-by. . . .
[He rushes to the door, stops for a moment on the threshold, then runs out. Vera remains with the note in her hand. Natalya Petrovna comes in]

NATALYA PETROVNA: [Going up to Vera] Verochka! [Looking at her and stopping] What is the matter with you?

[Vera silently extends the note to her] A note? From whom?

VERA: [In a hoarse voice] Read it.

NATALYA PETROVNA: You alarm me. [She reads the note to herself, suddenly presses both hands to her face, and falls into a chair]
[A long pause]

VERA: [Approaching her] Natalya Petrovna!

NATALYA PETROVNA: [Not removing her hands from her face] He is going away! . . . He did not even wish to say good-by to me! . . . Oh, to you he at least said good-by!

VERA: [Sadly] He did not love me.

NATALYA PETROVNA: [Removing her hands and rising] But he has no right to go away in such fashion. . . . I wish . . . He can't do it. . . . Who permitted him to break off so stupidly? . . . This amounts to contempt. . . . I . . . How does he know that I should never have decided . . . ? [She drops into a chair] My God, my God!

VERA: Natalya Petrovna, you yourself told me just now that he must leave. . . . Recollect!

NATALYA PETROVNA: You are happy now. . . . He is going away. . . . Now you and I are in the same position. . . . [Her voice breaks]

VERA: You just said to me, Natalya Petrovna . . . These are your own words: "Instead of torturing each other, would it not be better for both of us to think how to escape from this position, how to save ourselves?" . . . Now we are saved.

NATALYA PETROVNA: [Turning away from her, almost with hatred] Ah!

VERA: I understand you, Natalya Petrovna. . . . Do not be disturbed. . . . I shall not long hamper you by my presence. It is impossible for us to live together.

NATALYA PETROVNA: [Starting to extend her hand to her, and dropping it on her knees] Why do you say that, Verochka? . . . Is it possible that you, too, wish to leave me? Yes, you are right. We are saved now. All is ended. . . . Everything is again quite normal.

VERA: [Coldly] Don't be disturbed, Natalya Petrovna.

[Vera gazes at her sadly. Islayev comes out of the study]

ISLAYEV: [After looking for some time at Natalya Petrovna, in a low voice to Vera] Does she know that he is going away?

VERA: [Perplexed] Yes. She knows.

ISLAYEV: [To himself] But why is he leaving so soon? [Aloud] Natasha! [He takes her hand. She raises her head] It is I, Natasha. [She strives to smile] You are not well, my darling? I should advise you to lie down . . . really.

NATALYA PETROVNA: I am perfectly well, Arkady. . . . This is nothing at all.

ISLAYEV: But you are pale. . . . Really, listen to me. . . . Take a bit of rest.

NATALYA PETROVNA: Oh, very well. [She tries to rise, but cannot]

ISLAYEV: [Helping her] There, you see! [She leans

on his arm] Do you want me to see you to your room?

NATALYA PETROVNA: Oh, I am not yet so weak as that! Come on, Vera!

[*She goes toward the study.* Rakitin *comes in from the hall.* Natalya Petrovna *stops*]

RAKITIN: I have come, Natalya Petrovna—

ISLAYEV: [*Interrupting him*] Ah, Michel, come here! [*Leading him aside. In a low voice, with vexation*] Why did you tell her everything right away? You know I asked you not to, I think! What was the use of hurrying? . . . I found her here in such agitation.

RAKITIN: [*With amazement*] I don't understand you.

ISLAYEV: You have told Natasha that you are going away.

RAKITIN: Then you suppose that this was what caused her agitation?

ISLAYEV: Shh!— She is looking at us. [*Aloud*] Aren't you going to your room, Natasha?

NATALYA PETROVNA: Yes. . . . I am going.

RAKITIN: Good-by, Natalya Petrovna!

[Natalya Petrovna *takes hold of the door knob and makes no reply*]

ISLAYEV: [*Putting his hand on* Rakitin's *shoulder*] Natasha does not know that this is one of the best men. . . .

NATALYA PETROVNA: [*With a sudden burst of emotion*] Yes, I know he is a splendid man. All of you are splendid men . . . all of you . . . all of you . . . and yet—

[*She suddenly covers her face with her hands, pushes the door with her knee, and quickly goes out.* Vera *follows her.* Islayev *sits down silently at the table and rests his head on his hands*]

RAKITIN: [*After looking at him for some time, shrugging his shoulders with a bitter smile: to himself*] What a position I am in! Splendid, I must say! Really, it is quite refreshing. And what a farewell after four years of love! It's fine, very fine; serves the chatterbox right. But, thank God, it's all for the best. It was time to stop these morbid, these feverish relations. [*Aloud to* Islayev] Well, Arkady, good-by!

ISLAYEV: [*Raising his head. He has tears in his eyes*] Good-by, my friend—but this . . . isn't very easy. I didn't expect this, friend. It was like a thunderstorm on a clear day. Well, things will come out all right. And all the same, thank you, thank you! You are a true friend!

RAKITIN: [*To himself*] This is too much. [*Abruptly*] Good-by. [*He is about to go into the hall.* Shpigelsky *comes running in and meets him*]

SHPIGELSKY: What's this? They told me that Natalya Petrovna was not feeling well.

ISLAYEV: [*Rising*] Who told you?

SHPIGELSKY: The girl . . . the chambermaid.

ISLAYEV: No, it's of no importance, doctor. I think you'd better not trouble Natasha now.

SHPIGELSKY: Very well! [*To* Rakitin] They say that you are going to town.

RAKITIN: Yes, on business.

SHPIGELSKY: Oh, on business!

[*At that moment there burst in together from the hall* Anna Semenovna, Lizaveta Bogdanovna, Kolya, *and* Schaaf]

ANNA SEMENOVNA: What's this? What's all this? What's the matter with Natasha?

KOLYA: What's the matter with mamma? What's the matter with her?

ISLAYEV: Nothing is the matter with her. . . . I saw her a moment ago. What's the matter with you?

ANNA SEMENOVNA: But really, Arkasha, we've been told that Natasha was not feeling well.

ISLAYEV: And you were quite wrong in believing it.

ANNA SEMENOVNA: Why are you getting so excited, Arkasha? Our sympathy is perfectly natural.

ISLAYEV: Of course! . . . Of course!

RAKITIN: However, it is time for me to be going.

ANNA SEMENOVNA: Are you leaving?

RAKITIN: Yes, I am leaving.

ANNA SEMENOVNA: [*To herself*] Ah! Well, now I understand.

KOLYA: [*To* Islayev] Papa.

ISLAYEV: What do you want?

KOLYA: Why has Alexey Nikolayevich gone off?

ISLAYEV: Gone off where?

KOLYA: I don't know. . . . He kissed me, put on his cap, and walked off. . . . And now it's the time for our Russian lesson.

ISLAYEV: Probably he will come back right away. . . . However, we can send for him.

RAKITIN: [*In a low voice*] Don't send for him, Arkady; he won't come back.

[Anna Semenovna *tries to hear what is being said.* Shpigelsky *whispers with* Lizaveta Bogdanovna]

ISLAYEV: What does this mean?

RAKITIN: He is leaving also.

ISLAYEV: Leaving? Where is he going?

RAKITIN: To Moscow.

ISLAYEV: What? To Moscow? Well, are all of you going crazy to-day?

RAKITIN: [*In a still lower voice*] Between us two . . . Verochka fell in love with him. . . . Well, as an honorable man, he decided to withdraw.

[Islayev, *spreading out his hands, drops into a chair*]

Why . . . you understand now.

ISLAYEV: I? I don't understand anything. My head is in a whirl. This is all beyond anybody's understanding. Everybody is flying away helter-skelter, like partridges, and all because they are honorable men. . . . And all this, all of a sudden, on one and the same day.

ANNA SEMENOVNA: [*Coming up to him from one side*] But what's this? Mr. Belyayev, you say . . .

ISLAYEV: [*Shouting nervously*] That's all right, mother, that's all right! Mr. Schaaf, will you please take care of Kolya now instead of Mr. Belyayev. Will you kindly take him away!

SCHAAF: Very vell. [*Takes* Kolya *by the hand*]

KOLYA: But, papa—

ISLAYEV: [*Shouting*] Go away, go away!

[Schaaf *leads* Kolya *away*]

I'll see you off, Rakitin. . . . I'll order my horse saddled, and I'll wait for you at the dam. . . . And you, mamma, for the present, for God's sake, don't trouble Natasha—nor you either, doctor! . . . Matvey, Matvey! [*He goes out hastily*]

[Anna Semenovna *sits down with an air of grief and dignity.* Lizaveta Bogdanovna *takes her stand behind her.* Anna Semenovna *raises her eyes to Heaven as if desirous of withdrawing from everything that is happening around her*]

SHPIGELSKY: [*Stealthily and craftily to* Rakitin] Well, Mikhaylo Alexandrovich, won't you permit me to take you to the highway with my new team of three?

RAKITIN: Ah! . . . Have you already got your horses?

SHPIGELSKY: [*Modestly*] I have had a talk with Vera Alexandrovna. . . . Then you will permit me?

RAKITIN: Very well! [*He bows to* Anna Semenovna] Anna Semenovna, I have the honor. . . .

ANNA SEMENOVNA: [*As majestically as ever, without rising*] Good-by, Mikhaylo Alexandrovich. . . . I wish you a happy journey.

RAKITIN: Thank you humbly. Good-by Lizaveta Bogdanovna. [*He bows to her, and she curtsies in reply. He goes out into the hall*]

SHPIGELSKY: [*Taking* Anna Semenovna's *hand in order to kiss it*] Good-by, madam.

ANNA SEMENOVNA: [*With less majesty, but still sternly*] Ah, are you too going away, doctor?

SHPIGELSKY: Yes. . . . My patients, you know, need . . . And besides, you see, my presence is not required here. [*While bowing, he winks craftily to* Lizaveta Bogdanovna, *who answers him with a smile*] Good-by. [*He runs out after* Rakitin]

[Anna Semenovna *lets him go out, and folding her arms, slowly turns to* Lizaveta Bogdanovna]

ANNA SEMENOVNA: What do you think of all this, my dear? Eh?

LIZAVETA BOGDANOVNA: [*Sighing*] I really don't know what to tell you, Anna Semenovna.

ANNA SEMENOVNA: Have you heard? Belyayev also is leaving.

LIZAVETA BOGDANOVNA: [*Sighing once more*] Oh, Anna Semenovna, perhaps I, too, shall not be staying here for very long. . . . I am going away too.

[Anna Semenovna *looks at her with inexpressible amazement.* Lizaveta Bogdanovna *stands before her without raising her eyes*]

PART II

THE RANGE OF WESTERN DRAMA

Types and Styles of Western Theatre

EVEN IF WE LIMIT OURSELVES to the theatre before its present-day chaos in the arts, even if we confine ourselves to the occidental drama, with which we are presumably somewhat familiar, we are likely to be overwhelmed with a profusion of dramatic forms and styles. In the preceding sections of the present collection of plays, we encountered quite a number of these, and this not so much by design as by necessity in tracing historical developments. Classic fifth century B.C. Greek tragedy and Aristophanic comedy, Roman comedy based on fourth-century Greek models, and types of medieval renaissance, neoclassic, romantic, and early realistic drama came under our purview as we moved up to the modern theatre. But in this survey we left out a number of genres the reader may know only by hearsay unless he has specialized in some foreign language, period, or field. The section following will fill some lacunae in his literary and theatrical background.

Not all gaps can be closed in Part II, and it may be wise to refrain from attempting to fill in all of them in any case, lest we lose sight of the trees for the woods. But important types or styles of Western drama are added here, while others are briefly described in the introductions to this and the previous sections of the book. Thus plays that can be loosely defined as Dionysian have a special interest for us when we turn to the Greek theatre; Senecan tragedy when we consider Roman and later Renaissance drama; "saint" and "miracle" plays in the Middle Ages; *commedia dell' arte,* interludes or "entremésés," and masques during the Renaissance and seventeenth century; "middle-class drama" in the eighteenth century and later; and so on.

Since relevance to the history and practice of Western drama is a major consideration in the following section, and in the book as a whole, there is no attempt to supplement the brief section in oriental drama on pages 138–183. Theatre in the East has indeed produced a large variety of dramatic forms, but few of these have made any impression on Western playwrights, and only one of these, the Japanese Noh play, has attracted literary imitation. Moreover, this has been the case only in the twentieth century, mainly due to the efforts of the Irish poet William Butler Yeats to create formal poetic drama utilizing masks and choruses in some distinguished short plays such as *At the Hawks Well* (1917), *Calvary* (1920), and *A Full Moon in March* (1935).

A few minor forms of Western drama represented in this part of the book had at least local and temporal sway. This was the case when the *masque* came into vogue in the Italian Renaissance and attained literary distinction in seventeenth-century England. If no literary claims can be made for the scenarios of another Renaissance type of theatre, the *commedia dell' arte,* they were nevertheless an important part of the theatre of their age, and an important influence on the work of one of the masters of European playwriting, Molière. Efforts to continue the *commedia dell' arte* in literary form have been made even in the twentieth century. Two examples are Edna St. Vincent Millay's masterly one-act harlequinade *Aria da Capo* and the Spanish Nobel Prize laureate Jacinto Benavente's *Bonds of Interest,* the play chosen, after World War I, by the Theatre Guild to open some four decades of basically distinguished theatre in the United States.

Other dramatic forms had a sufficiently wide influence to clearly justify representation here even if the specific work that gave the main impetus to that influence is more or less dated. When that is the case, it will be found that the particular work —say, *The London Merchant* or *Hernani*—reveals both faults and attractions quite intrinsic to the very genre it represents. Such work may crudely accentuate the faults that later, and even contemporary, pieces written in the same vein manage to conceal or soften with some degree of sophistication or more timely idiom. Thus, there is a common denominator between Lillo's "middle-class tragedy" *The London Merchant* and dramas of antisocial middle-class conduct by Ibsen (*Pillars of Society* or *John Gabriel Borkman*), and Arthur Miller (*All My Sons*), not to mention numerous plays by less well-known authors. There is also a common denominator between some of Maxwell Anderson's verse tragedies of the nineteen-thirties (*Elizabeth the Queen, Mary of Scotland*) and Hugo's *Hernani* and other romantic plays of the eighteen-thirties, not to mention Schiller's *Mary Stuart* of the year 1800. And there are works like *The Beggar's Opera* (John Gay) and, for that matter, *Mary Stuart* that play well long after their original production and hardly "date" at all except in the opinion of fanatical followers of a "new wave," for whom even a decade is long enough to outdate works of some distinction.

Dramatic writing is extraordinarily susceptible to external pressures such as the *Zeitgeist,* or time-spirit, and the nature and conditions of the theatre for which they are written. Important factors in the success or failure, vogue or lack of vogue, of plays are the genres into which they naturally or historically fall as well as the styles of writing involved in them. These genres, many of them represented in *both* parts of the present volume in either their primal or full-blown state, are essential to an appreciation of the theatre and its literature.

Variant Classic Forms

The Roman theatre of Aspendos, showing the *frons scenae,* or stage façade, in front of which, on the raised platform, the actors performed (see p. 8). Other features are the roof over the stage and the entrance (left), one of the two *vomitaria*. Since the stage is connected with the auditorium (note the rows of seats at the left), the theatre is, unlike the theatre of Epidaurus, a single unit.

Variant Classic Forms

DIONYSIAN THEATRE: SATYR PLAY AND TRAGEDY

Although the content of classic tragedy usually revolved around someone other than Dionysus, the name for this type of theatre is appropriate. The Athenians, in their fifth-century, B.C. theatre, traced tragedy (as did Aristotle in his fourth-century B.C. treatise, *The Poetics*) to the dithyrambic courses performed in honor of Dionysus at the great spring festival, the City Dionysia. This theatre was, moreover, sacred to Dionysus, and disorders in its precincts during the performances were not mere infractions of law; they were acts of blasphemy.

Dionysus, according to his *cultus* and mythology, was a fertility god, probably of Thracian origin. He was also celebrated as the spirit and the giver of wine and regarded by imaginative extension as the god of ecstatic emotion and erotic release. At the City Dionysia festival (the first official production in Athens occurred in 534 B.C.), the statue of the god was brought in with great pomp, male sexual symbols or *phalli* were carried in the procession honoring him, and sacrifices were performed. Then, by torchlight, the statue was borne into the theatre so that the god might attend the dramatic performances with their riualistic characteristics—the great choral sections, and the masks that were used regardless of whether the play's content was tragic or comic.

In the numerous extant plays in which he does not appear as a character the relationship between Dionysus and Dionysian theatre is, for the most part, found under the surface. It is apparent in their formalistic style and structure, in the more or less liturgical performances they required, and in the wild, emotional spirit of the subject matter.[1] Dionysus does appear as an important character twice in extent Greek drama: in a comedy, *The Frogs* (pages 71–95) usually regarded as Aristophanes' masterpiece, and in a tragedy, *The Bacchae* (pages 721–738) invariably ranked among the finest works of Euripides.

The Dionysian influence is particularly obvious and strongly marked in a riotous type of farce known as the *satyr play*, of which two examples have come down to us: Sophocles' *Ichneutai* (*The Searching Satyrs, The Seachers*, or *The Trackers*) and Euripides' *Cyclops*. The former is a somewhat amputated text, but is still sufficiently intact to be entertaining and read with pleasure (see pages 710–718)). In these satyr plays, semisacred burlesque pieces, Dionysus

does not appear, but his spirit of lively release is vividly represented by Silenus, a folklore figure who is at some time in his scanty history drawn into the company of Dionysus, travels and fights by his side, frolics continually, and makes and imbibes wine. (As a water-spirit, it became his duty to keep the vines well watered and thus he acquired a legendary taste for wine.) And Silenus is accompanied by the minor nature-deities, the satyrs, sometimes regarded as his children and presented as a raffish, licentious, bibulous, rather cowardly lot. Their brutish features have some resemblance to horses and other animals; they are drawn with bristly hair, pointed ears, and tails. Plainly these burlesque characters are related to fertility rites, one of the main origins of early drama, and they illustrate, as Roger Lancelyn Green, the translator of the two extant satyr plays puts it, "the desire and the pursuit of fecundity" combining the Dionysian elements of riot and magic or, as it were, magic-making riot. In *The Bacchae* or *Bacchants* (in which Dionysus does appear) the same spirit is represented by the wild women called *maenads* or *bacchants*, whose behavior is scandalously uninhibited as they go into a frenzy or ecstasy while celebrating the divinity of Bacchus, one of the names of Dionysus.

This tragedy, and the two aforementioned satyr plays, are the only directly Dionysian plays that have come down from classic times, although it was customary in the fifth-century Dionysian festival theatre for playwrights to top off their programs of three tragedies with satyr-plays. Even the august tragedian Aeschylus staged them at the conclusion of his mighty trilogies, and he apparently attempted to provide some thematic connection between the tragic and "satyric" types of plays. Tragedy and folkfarce maintained a congenial coexistence on the Athenian stage. Greece, indeed, provides us with fine relics of this primitive type of drama; but relics that were literary enough to entice the poet Shelley into attempting a free translation in 1819 of *The Cyclops*, Euripides' satyr-play version of the Polyphemus episode in the *Odyssey*.[2]

SENECAN TRAGEDY

If Latin tragedy lost its vogue at an early period during the Roman Republic (only fragments have survived), it secured a place in the history of the theatre when Western Europe inherited the nine plays written by Seneca.[3] Seneca, the stoic philosopher of Nero's time, was the inventor and sole practi-

[1] Liturgical performances are also required for the religion-inspired classic works of the Orient and modern European dramas, whether of pagan inspiration like many of Yeats' plays, patterned after the Japanese Noh theatre, or Christian in orientation as in T. S. Eliot's *Murder in the Cathedral* and *The Family Reunion*.

[2] *The Collected Poetical Works of Percy Bysshe Shelley.* New York: Oxford University Press, 1919, pp. 696–712.
[3] Actually ten plays were attributed to him, but the tenth was certainly not his.

tioner of the form of theatre now appropriately called Senecan tragedy. And, although it seems almost certain his plays were intended for recitation rather than for enactment on the stage, his work is important to us because of its influence on dramatists of the Renaissance. The Senecan ingredients of their work consist of the revenge *motif,* the ghost that clamors for vengeance upon some malefactor, and the messenger technique, the use of a minor character to bring reports onstage of bloody deeds perpetrated offstage. Senecan, too, are some of the stylistic features, such as the effects of rhetoric and sententiousness.[4] And it should be remembered that Greek tragedy was vitually unknown until late in the Renaissance.

Seneca, F. L. Lucas noted in his *Seneca and Elizabethan Tragedy,* "was near enough to Renaissance exuberance to appeal to it as a model; classic enough, when taken as a model, to impose upon it a wholesome sense of structure and style." The five-act structure for tragedy, established in Europe long after the Middle Ages can be traced to Seneca.

His influence can be traced even in Shakespeare's writings. And not merely in his apprentice work such as *Richard III* and *Titus Andronicus,* but even in *Hamlet,* which along with Thomas Kyd's *The Spanish Tragedy* belongs to the genre of "revenge tragedy."

All Seneca's plays had been translated into English by 1581, before Marlowe, Kyd, and Shakespeare had

[4] In English, the best known of the distinctly imitative pieces is *Gorboduc* (1561–1562), also considered historically important for the first dramatic use of blank verse in English.

been heard of. "His work is little remembered," writes Lucas, "still less regarded now. But if you seek his memorial, look round on the tragic stage of England, France, and Italy." Thomas Nashe charged that writers in England who "read Seneca by candlelight were copying whole Hamlets, I should say handfuls of tragical speeches." T. S. Eliot remarked " . . . Dante had behind him an Aquinas and Shakespeare behind him a Seneca." and that "Without [Seneca's] bombast we should not have had *King Lear.*"

An excellent summary of the Elizabethan playwrights' indebtedness to Seneca's example will be found in Fredson Thayer Bowers' *Elizabethan Revenge Tragedy* (Princeton University Press, 1966), p. 75:

They were delighted with his rhetoric, for they were still so intellectually young as to be impressed by bombast and flamboyance. Introspection had become a national trait, and fed agreeably on the elaborate Senecan philosophizing, with its spice of stoicism suitable to a hard-bitten age. The long Senecan descriptions were suited for imitation on the bare English stage. Finally, Seneca's emphasis on sensationalism, on physical horrors to stimulate emotion, appealed to the English taste, for blood and horror on the stage could not be offensive to the spectators at cruel executions. Ghosts were accepted as fact, and forewarnings were everyday affairs. . . . Except for his classical subject-matter and his rigid classical form involving the use of choruses, there was no single element of Seneca that could not be accepted immediately by the spectator in the pit.

Sophocles and The Searching Satyrs

It is perhaps significant that Sophocles' sole surviving satyr play was performed about the same time as Sophocles' profound tragedy *Antigone*. At the very peak of Attic civilization the Dionysian release from serious concerns, which was also a prompt release from the shattering tensions of classic Greek tragedy, remained *de rigeur* in the Theatre of Dionysus.[1]

The satyr-plays were brief; Greek tragedies were short enough by our standards for full drama (shorter than two acts of *Hamlet*, writes the Greek scholar Moses Hadas), but the satyric drama was even shorter. Still, like a good modern one-act play it reflected in its stylized and concentrated action respectable artistic potentialities. A talented writer could revel in the essentially frolicsome nature or sportiveness produced not merely by its plot but by the chorus of disreputable satyrs led by their inebriated putative father, Silenus. The diction, which gave the writer greater freedom than did tragedy, even introduced colloquialism into the formal theatre of myth and epic. And the productions included a lively and indecorous choral dance called the *sikinnis*.

That so great an artist as Sophocles should have applied his poetic and dramatic talent to the genre is not at all surprising. He was, of course, required to write satyr plays in order to conclude each set of three tragedies submitted for production to the *archon,* or public official, in charge of the annual spring festival at which they were intended to be performed.[2] Moreover, the satyr play was traditional, and the conservative Sophocles was not one to flout tradition. It had religious sanction, and the worldly Sophocles was at ease with orthodoxy. It provided ample opportunities for theatrical display, especially in costuming, and for lyricism, which was enriched in all the Athenian performances with music and dancing. Sophocles, like the other Athenian tragedians, would appreciate these advantages and endeavor to make the best use of them. Finally, any writer of Greek tragedy, a very austere form of drama, might welcome the abandon of the satyric

(not to be confused by us with "satiric") form; and Sophocles might well have relished opportunities for exercising his sense of humor.[3]

If, as seems possible, Sophocles used the seventh-century "Homeric" *Hymn to Hermes* as the springboard for his *Searching Satyrs,* he could not but have taken delight in it. (The curious student will find an entrancing English version of this long narrative poem by Shelley entitled *Homer's Hymn to Mercury,* published in *Posthumous Poems* in 1824.) The fabulous roguery of the infant Hermes (the patron god of thieves—one of his various attributes in Greek mythology—who invents a musical instrument while still in his cradle) as he cunningly steals his elder brother-god Apollo's cattle and boldly outfaces him is without question a superb subject for a humorist. It was also ideally suited to the requirements of satyric drama. It was *not* irreverent to dramatize this picaresque tale for presentation in the Theatre of Dionysus. Its spectators would take delight in the divine infant's talents for ingenuity and chicanery; for the Greeks, who were shrewd traders and politicians as well as inventors, appreciated resourcefulness and fast thinking in emergencies as divine traits. Apollo, who was a formidable deity in Greek mythology and religion and who generally employs in *The Searching Satyrs* the dignified language of classic tragedy, appears here as a rather sulky and petulant-character, but the situation in which he finds himself robbed of his cattle and beguiled by the impertinent little god who is his brother warrants the characterization. And the Athenian public was not unaccustomed to unflattering representations of this god, whose influential oracle at Delphi was regarded as decidedly less favorable to Athens than to its rivals and foes.

The Greek text of *The Searching Satyrs* was found on papyrus dug up in Egypt and published in 1912. Mr. Green, the translator, supplies the following comment on that manuscript and his procedure:

> It suffers from a number of small gaps in the text, and one large one; in most cases it is easy to see

---

[1] The only other possibility for audiences' relief open to the masters of tragedy was vested in romantic pieces such as Euripides' *Alcestis* and *Helena,* and it is known that the *Alcestis,* despite the appealing characterization of the self-sacrificing Alcestis and the exposé of the egotism of her husband Admetus who accepted her death as the price of his survival, actually took the place of a satyr play in a series of four plays which obtained second prize in the spring of 438 B.C.

[2] The *archon* chose a set of three tragedies and the satyr play afterpiece, gave their author a protagonist or principal actor, and assigned the mounting of the productions to a rich citizen, the *choregus.*

[3] This sense of humor is evident in the scene in *Antigone* in which a frightened sentinel from beyond the city walls reluctantly brings the news to his king, Creon, that someone scattered dust on the corpse of Antigone's slain brother, for whom Creon had forbidden burial. It is the only conclusive example of humor in the corpus of extant Greek tragedy. There is, indeed, the scene in Euripides' *Alcestis* in which the primitive hero or demigod Heracles carouses in the home of his bereaved host Admetus. But the *Alcestis* is not strictly a tragedy; it was described in the summary later appended to it as "satyrikoteron"— this is, "in the manner of a satyric piece."

708

how many lines are missing, and sometimes even to gather clues from odd words remaining as to what is lost. Two plays by Menander, recovered in much the same condition, have been superbly translated by Professor Gilbert Murray, who in doing so restored or filled in the gaps in his originals so as to present complete plays for the English reader. I have tried to do the same service to the remains of the Sophocles play, since gaps in dialogue and plot detract from most people's enjoyment—and would prevent the play from appearing on the stage.[4]

[4] "Introduction" to *Two Satyr Plays*, translated by Roger Lancelyn Green, New York: Penguin Books, 1957, p. 13.

THE SEARCHING SATYRS

By *Sophocles*

TRANSLATED BY ROGER LANCELYN GREEN

THE CHARACTERS

THE GOD PHOEBUS APOLLO
THE GOD HERMES, *son of Zeus and the nymph Maia*
KYLLENE, *nymph of the mountain so called*

SILENUS, *leader of the Satyrs*
CHORUS OF SATYRS

THE SCENE

In front of the Cave of the Nymph Kyllene *on the mountain of the same name in Arcadia in southern Greece.*

[*Enter* Apollo *full of noble rage and grief—which occasionally degenerates into petulance*]

APOLLO: I am Apollo! Hearken, all below
To what a god proclaims! For you must know,
And gods above, what great Apollo vows:
A rich reward to him who finds my cows!
My heart is racked with pain: I've lost them all!
There's not one single heifer in my stall,
Nor cow, nor smallest calf. Where they can be
Is more than this all-seeing god can see!
I really did not think that god or man
Would dare such treason, such a stealthy plan
To steal my cattle and not leave a trace!
  I have been hurrying from place to place
Since first I heard the news, and I proclaim
My loss to gods and men. All are to blame,
And here I give them warning clear and fair,
Those who pretend that they are unaware
That I have lost my cows: they tempt their fate
Who would deceive me—and I do not prate!
For I'm Apollo, I would have you know.
  Where in the world did my poor cattle go?
I've visited so many tribes of men:
I've been to Libya, and come back again,
I've been as far as Troy, and gone across
Into Epirus—always at a loss.
And now I've come from Thrace, and on the way
Touched at Euboea, glanced round Sunium bay,
Visited Athens, been to Thebes as well,
Roamed on Parnassus where the Muses dwell,
Called at my shrine in Delphi, just in case
The cows came home to their accustomed place;
But no one there had seen them, so I came
To Corinth, but my luck was just the same.
Now I come straight from Argos to the land
Of fair Arcadia. Here great mountains stand
Across my way, and first Kyllene rears
Its lofty summit. So if any hears

My voice, who dwells upon it, nymph or god,
Shepherd or farmer, or the meanest clod
That lurks among the rocks, attend to me:
Whoever finds my cows I swear shall be
Rewarded richly. Harken to my word!
I am Apollo!—and I've lost my herd!

[*Enter* Silenus *the Satyr with great haste and self-importance*]

SILENUS: Great Lord Apollo, tell me why and how
You chance to be in trouble. Though I'm now
Well gone in years, I hurried—simply ran,
As you can see—to help you. If I can
Do anything, friend Phoebus, to assist
You in your trouble, don't let me be missed
From a friend's place beside you. Undismayed,
Count now on me, I'll help you—if I'm paid.
So tell me what makes dark your shining brows.

  APOLLO: Some clever thief has stolen all my cows.
  SILENUS: I'll send my sharp-eyed sons without delay
To seek for them—provided that you pay.
  APOLLO: I praise your zeal—if you bring back my cows.
  SILENUS: Thanks for your praise—if you fulfil your vows.
  APOLLO: [*grandly*] Gold waits the finder whosoe'er it be.
  SILENUS: Gold did you say? I hope the finder's me!
  APOLLO: I'll set a wreath, besides, upon your head.
  SILENUS: No good to us. What can you give instead?
  APOLLO: I'll offer that for which all creatures seek.
  SILENUS: Go on—What is the gift of which you speak?
  APOLLO: Freedom from toil for you and all your sons.
  SILENUS: *That's* something like! I'll tell the boys at once.
    [*Shouting*] Come here, you lads, I'm on to something good,
  An easy job, with pay, well understood!
    [*Enter* Chorus of Satyrs]

FIRST SATYR: Here we are, father! Always close at hand!
An easy job, you say—with cash? How grand!
SILENUS: Both gold and freedom here Apollo vows
To us if we can find his stolen cows.
[*Exit* Apollo *with slow dignity*]
CHORUS:
Hurrah for the herdsmen of Phoebus Apollo
By misty mountain and gloomy glen!
Silenus, lead, and your sons will follow
Over the mountain from summit to hollow,
Under the mountain, and back again!

Search the wilderness, cave and cavern,
Search the cities where men abide;
Our feet shall echo in town and tavern,
Through hut and hall as we roam and raven,
Combing Hellas from side to side.

Lord Apollo be ever near to us
Follow our labors by fell and fold,
Making the quest of your cows more clear to us,
Urging us on, oh god most dear to us,
You whose wallet is lined with gold!
SILENUS: O Gods, O Fortune, and the Heavenly Guide
Show me the cows, wherever they may hide;
Be my quest short, and little labour cost
The finding of the cattle that were lost
Or stolen, plundered, looted from this god.
Here, wake up, you [*To the audience*] I say!
Don't dare to nod,
But tell me straight, has any one of you
Heard, seen, or smelt the cows? The slightest clue
Will win a gracious glance from Phoebus' eyes,
For you, his thanks and mine; for us, the prize.
So don't be shy, but come right up and tell
Where in the world—or out of it—they dwell.
CHORUS:
That would be luck, which I hope may befall
Us now. Then we'd not need to hunt at all!
A SATYR: There's someone getting up! You, down below!
SILENUS: Anyone? Someone? What, does *no* one know?
Why then, it's high time that I set to work.
Now Satyrs, to the job, don't dare to shirk!
Nose to the ground—that's right!—to catch the scent
Borne on the wind from where the cattle went.
Down on your knees, bent double, follow close
The track that leads you, or the scent that blows;
Search well and widely, do not fear to bend—
Of search and satyr let us see the end!
SATYRS: A god, a god, a god! Hip-hip-hurray!
I think we'll find them now without delay.
FIRST SATYR: A trace! A trace! Just here a cow has trod!
SECOND SATYR: Don't shout so loudly—you'll offend the god.

FIRST SATYR: Sorry I spoke! If Phoebus heard, he might
Say that our methods were not strictly right!
SECOND SATYR: You fellows over there, what have you found?
THIRD SATYR: Proof positive: some footsteps on the ground.
FOURTH SATYR: Look! Look! Some hoof-marks over there again!
FIFTH SATYR: And here another, printed clear and plain.
SATYRS: Let's scatter; if the cows are somewhere near,
Surely their lowing will reach someone's ear.
[*Sound of a lyre begins off stage very softly*]
FIRST SATYR: I still can't catch a bovine sound at all!
Would the cows come, d'you think, if I should call?
SECOND SATYR: These *are* their footsteps—we just need to hunt.
THIRD SATYR: Good gracious, look! These tracks are back to front!
Just look at that, the hoof-marks are reversed!
What can it mean? I think the cows are cursed.
What nightmare order! Front is now the rear:
These point two ways at once . . . The tracks are clear,
But sure the driver must be mad, or drunk!
[*The lyre sounds more loudly, and the Satyrs show signs of panic*]
SILENUS: I say, what's up now? Has your courage shrunk?
Running away from nothing! You'll not make
Good huntsmen, writhing there just like a snake
Flat on your bellies; what new dodge is this?
It's got no point at all, or one I miss!
Get up, you look like hedge-hogs without feet,
Crouching and crawling like an ape on heat!
It all seems daft. I only wish I knew
Who'd taught you this mad dance—explain it, do.
CHORUS:
Ou! Ou! Ou! Ah! Ah! Ou! Ah! Ou! Boo! Hoo!
SILENUS: What are you howling for? Who's scaring you?
What have you seen? It's surely not a ghost?
Why do you dance like a mad Maenad host?
I can hear nothing anywhere around—
Except a very distant scraping sound
It can't be *that!* Speak! Have you been struck dumb?
CHORUS:
Listen!
SILENUS: What should I hear, when you're all mum?
CHORUS:
Listen, I say!
SILENUS:
You're really a disgrace
Scaring yourselves, not helping in the chase.

CHORUS:
    Hush, keep still, and you will hear
      What so fills our hearts with awe;
    Drives us almost mad with fear—
      Sound no mortal heard before!
SILENUS: Why should that faint noise scare you?
  Tell me why
You stand like statues, pointing to the sky?
You worthless beasts, you see, I do declare,
Ghosts in each shadow, bogies everywhere!
You're useless, spineless, lacking in all trust,
Mere lumps of talk, and carrion, and lust:
You boast about your courage every day
And when the crisis comes, you run away.
But I, your father, I, you worthless breed,
When I was young, I was a man indeed!
The nymphs I conquered! and the deeds I did!
I *led* the battles, never went and hid;
Nor screamed when I heard cattle on a hill
Like some that I could name. My glory still
Shines bright, and you would tarnish it with fear
Because some shepherd's cunning cry you hear.
Scared like a baby by an unknown sound
You cast Apollo's riches on the ground;
Have you forgotten gold, and freedom too,
Promised by him to me as well as you?
Well, give it up then; go and hide in bed . . .
  You blethering cowards, I'll punch you on the head,
I'll make you sore and sorry if you don't
Get back to work. Now who dares say he won't?
CHORUS:
    Get in front, don't skulk behind,
      Then we'll see who's scared, who's not!
    Come and lead us, then you'll find
      That you're talking rot!
SILENUS: Never you fear, I'll come and show you
  how
A valiant hunter ought to chase a cow.
You'll dilly-dally there the whole day through;
I'll just drop in, and show you what to do!
    [SILENUS *attempts to restore order forcibly among*
    the Satyrs, who dance and sing as they try to
    avoid him]
CHORUS:
Pish! Tush! Whoop-la—and away!
    Say what is the matter with you?
Strutting and butting, and shouting and pouting,
Dancing and prancing—now really I'm doubting
    If there's one word of truth that you say
    Or one little deed that you do!
FIRST SATYR: Help me quick—he's caught me
  bending!
SECOND SATYR: Oh, he's caught you, sure enough.
FIRST SATYR: Help I say, he's tearing, rending—
SECOND SATYR: Go it, father—that's the stuff!
CHORUS:
Come now, were you really so gay,
    Old man, in the days of your youth?
Dashing and slashing, such mighty blows lavishing;
Chasing and facing, and raping and ravishing—

Just think now, and surely you'll say
    That your fancy is painting the truth!
THIRD SATYR: Help me quick—his nails are tearing!
FOURTH SATYR: Glad it isn't me, but you!
THIRD SATYR: Look, his eyes are red and glaring
FOURTH SATYR: Stop it, father—that'll do!
SILENUS: Now will you please obey me, and not
  dare
To kick your silly legs up in the air?
SATYRS: Of course we will, but what about the
  sound?
It faded when we started dancing around.
SILENUS: It never did exist, save in your head—
FIRST SATYR: Which now you've hit and made to
  buzz instead!
SECOND SATYR: Hush! Just a minute . . . There it is
  again.
Now listen, father, and you'll hear it plain.
SILENUS: I can't hear anything . . . At least I
  thought
I heard a . . . Tush, there's nothing of the sort!
FIRST SATYR: You're silent . . . Do we speak the
  truth or not?
Surely you hear it! Are you deaf, or what?
SILENUS: Shut up a moment . . . [*Sound of the*
  lyre becomes louder]
FIRST SATYR:
            What?
SILENUS:
        I mustn't stay—
Something I've got to do . . .
FIRST SATYR:
                Don't go away!
SILENUS: I really must . . . Important date . . . But
  you
Can stay and find the cows, and earn the screw
And get rich quick. I'm sorry I can't wait—
I'm wasting time . . . Goodbye . . . Important date . . .
CHORUS:
Not if we know it! Sneaking away,
    Leaving us all in the lurch like that!
Here you are, and with us you stay
    To see this through to the end—that's flat!

There's someone there, we must get him out!
    Some robber chief in a cavern lies!
Now, Silenus, suppose you shout,
    And find the cattle, and win the prize!

Louder still! Will he never come?
    Beat the ground, and bellow again:
He may be deaf, but we're far from dumb!
    One more yell, boys, with might and main!
    [*Enter the Nymph* Kyllene *from the Cave*]
KYLLENE: What rough beasts are these? What is it
  that brings,
This clamour here to frighten the wild things?
What do you seek, so changed from when, of old,
You were good subjects of Silenus' fold;
When, armed with thyrsus, clad in fawn-skin, you

Led out the dance in Dionysus' view,
Singing the chant divine amid the rout
Of revelling nymphs that follow him about?
Whence is your present madness, whence the change
That sends you screaming in a dance so strange?
I heard a call, like hunters in the wood,
Near to the lair where lies some wolfish brood,
Raised in defiant hate; and then a cry
Of thieves and rapine echoed to the sky!
'Reward', 'a proclamation', 'cows'—and then
Your words grew turgid and above my den
The stamp of feet that shook the earth around,
And one continuous roar of crazy sound.
How could I stay then in my mountain cave?
I come in fear, a harmless nymph, and crave
Protection: tell me now, what will befall
This foolish girl who has obeyed your call?

CHORUS:
    Stay your anger, stately lady,
       Not in strife and war come we
    To your bower so deep and shady,
       But your careful friends to be.

    Then assail us not with taunting,
       But the secret now disclose
    Of the music, lovely, daunting,
       That from out this hill arose.

KYLLENE: Come, that's a gentler manner than before.
Hunting like this you'll surely find much more
Than you could ever gain in violent-wise,
Scaring poor nymphs, and yelling to the skies.
Quarrels and arguments are of one breed,
So tell me calmly what it is you need.

CHORUS:
Kyllene, queen of all these mountains high,
We'll tell you what we came for by and by;
But first explain to us, this sound which quite
Sets our poor teeth on edge—but not with fright.

KYLLENE: Know first: if you reveal what I relate
Some ghastly punishment will be your fate
And bow you down with suffering and woe.
  Now for my secret: Satyrs, you must know
That Hera, Heaven's queen is swiftly stirred
To jealousy—a fact I'm sure you've heard!
Now Zeus—who likes his fling from time to time—
Sought this fair cave in the Arcadian clime,
Where Maia, child of Atlas, dwelt that day;
And in her arms all night the Thunderer lay,
Unknown to Hera. Of that union came
An only son—and Hermes is his name.
But Maia, wasted sore with labour pain,
Might not attend the baby, but was fain
To choose a nurse: that office I perform,
By day and night keeping this infant warm,
Bending above his cradle to supply
Both food and drink to him. The days go by
And every morn he grows beyond compare:
It is but six days since his mother bare
The wondrous child, and yet he grows so fast

Each day, that childhood is already past
And he begins to blossom into youth.
Such is the child I foster; and in truth
We do but hide him by his father's will.
  As for the sound that scared you from the hill,
Ringing from hands unseen, mysterious, fay—
The child invented it this very day,
Out of an upturned shell: that is as near
As I can come to name it. What you hear
Comes from an animal that lately died,
Yet still is full of music. Deep inside
The hollow cavern now the baby plays
Upon the wondrous thing; and strange amaze
Falls upon all who hear him, even as you
Were scared when harmony unknown and new
First fell upon your ears. But Maia's son
Plays happily—as if in childish fun—
Resting in the deep cave. You need not dread
A baby playing on a creature dead.

SILENUS: I can't believe that any beasts make music when they die!

KYLLENE: You must believe the words I say. A goddess does not lie.

SILENUS: So loud a voice could never swell from beast whose life was done.

KYLLENE: It's true, though: it sings loud in death, that, living, voice had none.

SILENUS: Was this same creature in its life long, curved, or fat or thin?

KYLLENE: Short like a gourd, all shrivelled up, with spots upon its skin.

SILENUS: I know! I know! It must have been a panther or a cat.

KYLLENE: Quite, quite unlike, with little legs, with body round and fat.

SILENUS: What, like a weasel, or a crab? At least its shape is plain.

KYLLENE: No, not like either in the least: you'd better guess again.

SILENUS: I know! A beetle! Such a one as Etna's slopes may boast!

KYLLENE: Well done! Well done! You've guessed at last what it resembles most.

SILENUS: But is the noise inside or out? The method of it tell.

KYLLENE: It is the crust that makes the notes, exactly like a shell.

SILENUS: What does he call it, tell us quick—this baby in the byre?

KYLLENE: He calls the beast a Tortoise, and the instrument a Lyre.

SILENUS: But tell us how a hollow shell can make a noise like that.

KYLLENE: He's covered all the hollow in, to make it smooth and flat.

SILENUS: What, you don't mean the beast's alive, imprisoned in the shell!

KYLLENE: He scraped it out, the beast is dead, as you have heard me tell.

SILENUS: Then what's he got across the crust, and
  which thing makes the sound?
KYLLENE: He stretched a skin across the shell, and
  fastened it all round.
SILENUS: And what's he used to cover it? The pelt
  of this same thing?
KYLLENE: A piece of ox-hide, newly flayed, a piece
  of gut for string.
SILENUS: Indeed this sounds a wondrous toy:
  we're very glad we came.
KYLLENE: But to disturb us as you did, I really call
  a shame.
To make this fuss about a toy, invented by a lad.
The only comfort that he has to cheer him when he's
  sad,
For you must know that he delights to sing like
  creature crazed,
And play upon the lyre and hum to tunes that he has
  raised
With subtle difference from each note. But I've been
  here too long—
And I have told you how this boy drew from the
  dead a song.
  CHORUS:
      Sweet, sweet is the voice of the lyre
        As its music floats over the land,
      Weaving fancies, string-born, that inspire
        All around, at a touch of the hand.

      Oh, granted the music's divine,
        But what I am trying to say
      Is that we have a proof and a sign
        That the thief we are hunting today

      Is this godling, whoever he be,
        Who has fashioned this exquisite toy;
      Now pray don't be angry with me!
        It's our duty, not done to annoy.
KYLLENE: Now really that's the silliest thing I've
  heard;
A charge of theft! It's rather too absurd!
SILENUS: I swear I hate to say it, lady, but—
KYLLENE: To call a god a thief! You *are* a mutt!
SILENUS: Yes, I said thief! I wish I'd been in
  time . . .
KYLLENE: To see your folly? Well, it's quite sub-
  lime!
SILENUS: To catch this trickster in the very act.
KYLLENE: The catcher would be caught, and that's
  a fact.
SILENUS: He stole the cows, and he must pay the
  cost.
KYLLENE: Really? And what besides? I feel quite
  lost . . .
SILENUS: He's killed an ox, and skinned it, don't
  you see!
KYLLENE: His brother's cow? It surely cannot be!
SILENUS: He took the herd of cattle right away—
KYLLENE: A child who hasn't seen his seventh day!
This is too much, and well I understand

That all this folly is some trick you've planned;
Some silly trick. You're full of them, I know,
But henceforth, if it really must be so,
If you enjoy buffoonery, or believe
That it will profit you, I give you leave
To laugh at me as much as you see fit—
I'll just not notice you the slightest bit!
Only I warn you, don't miscall a child
Whose sire is surely Zeus; nor make these wild
And foolish accusations against one
Who's only known six days beneath the sun!
Moreover, you can't say it comes by kind,
And he inherits vice: you will not find
Great Zeus to be a thief, nor yet the kin
Of Maia, Atlas' daughter steeped in sin.
Therefore begone, and seek your thief elsewhere
For no lean harvest tempts to thieving here,
And poverty does not invade this home.
Think of his parentage before you come
To fix a crime on him: it isn't right
Or proper. But you always have been quite
A child in your behaviour: you forget
That you're a man full grown, and you would yet
Skip like a saucy ram among the ewes,
It's wrong a bald-pate coot like you should choose
To ape the gambols of an amorous goat.
The gods bring fools to harm, I'd have you note.
  CHORUS:
      Cunning tales of double meaning
        Twisted council, clever word!
      But our judgement still is leaning
        To the verdict you have heard.

      It is he, how sure we're feeling,
        He who made the stately lyre,
      Got the cow-hide by his stealing
        Cattle from Apollo's byre.

      No more twisting, nor evasion,
        Never knit those lovely brows!
      Sure, in spite of your persuasion,
        This young Hermes stole the cows!
KYLLENE: The things you've said; the names that
  you have used!
Gods don't stand calmly by to be abused.
  SILENUS: But he's a villain, if he acts like one.
  KYLLENE: You should not dare to slander Zeus's
    son.
  SILENUS: What would you have me say, if not the
    truth?
  KYLLENE: Such words as these are foolish and un-
    couth.
  SILENUS: He stole the cattle! You cannot deny
That Hermes when he lately wished to ply
The craft of music-maker used the hide
Of a slain ox! The rest he has inside
The hollow cavern, or beneath some hill
In a wild valley that's more distant still.
I say you can't deny it: only think;
How clear the proof is; and that I would shrink

From charging gods with theft without good cause.

KYLLENE: He hasn't got a single cow indoors!

SILENUS: Why then, he's put them somewhere else instead.

KYLLENE: You'll find them straying, waiting to be fed!

SILENUS: Yes, hidden away—and Hermes knows the place!

KYLLENE: How will you prove *he* set them out to graze?

SILENUS: We've enough proof to catch the thief, I say.

KYLLENE: Villain! What thief has stolen these cows away?

SILENUS: The child you talk of—he I'm sure's the one.

KYLLENE: Again I say, don't slander Zeus's son.

SILENUS: I'll stop the moment you produce the child.

KYLLENE: You and your cattle really make me wild.

SILENUS: Suppose you send this lad you speak of here.

KYLLENE: One can't command immortals to appear.

SILENUS: Then tell him we bear news, if he would deign . . .

KYLLENE: News of what kind, I beg you to explain.

SILENUS: A message from his brother-god, who vows

Dire vengeance on the thief who stole his cows,
But rich rewards for any who can tell
Where in the world these errant cattle dwell.

KYLLENE: So Lord Apollo's hired you for this quest,

And pays you well! I really might have guessed
That such an ancient lazy thing as you,
All fat and lechery, would not pursue
This arduous duty without some good cause.

SILENUS: Fair nymph, suppose you enter by those doors

And tell the child before it is too late;
Say that Apollo calls him to the gate—
The order comes from him: now don't you see
How serious this quarrel soon may be?
Unless the boy explains, I have no doubt
That a new war in heaven will break out.

KYLLENE: I will do this. But you have been too bold:

I would not be *you* for all Phoebus' gold!

[Kyllene *goes into the Cave*]

CHORUS:
There once was a war in the heavenly halls
    In the reign of King Cronos the old;
The true gods rejoice when a Titan falls
Down, down to the brass Tartarean walls
    That round their dread prison enfold.
        What if Apollo
        Makes war, red war

With the Hermes child who has stolen his kine?
        And we must follow
        Through fresh warm gore
In danger and sorrow to peak and pine?

Oh, give us the hills where the Maenads dance
    In the train of the Bromian king;
Let us kick up our heels as we caper and prance,
As we cast on each maiden an amorous glance
    And gleefully gambol and sing!
        Would we were drinking
        The juice of the grape,
Till the earth span round and the sky came down:
        For now we are thinking
        Of some dread shape,
Some angry god with death in his frown.

        Help and protect us now,
            Good father Silenus;
        How I hate the name of cow!
        And will ever hate it, I vow.
            The god draws near in his rage;
            Unkind battle he'll wage:
        He is seeking for vengeance now!
            Why must it have been us!

[*Enter* Hermes *from the Cave, young and inno-
cent-looking, but with a merry twinkle in his
eyes*]

HERMES: As I lay sleeping in the quiet gloom
There came harsh sounds of discord and of doom
Outside the cavern, and I quaked in fear,
Not knowing what dread enemy was near.
Then came my nurse Kyllene where I lay
All swaddled in my cradle, and straightway
Bade me arise and hasten to the light
Where messengers called for me. In a fright
I sprang from bed, though but a child new-born
And hastened out into the light of morn
To see what these things were. For how am I
Even to name the creatures passing by?

CHORUS:
    A fair, tall stripling for but six days' life:
    Yet no strong thief to be the cause of strife!

SILENUS: Now look here sir, we don't want any fuss
About this business. We have called you thus
Before us to accuse you of a deed
Of dreadful villainy: you'll never speed
In your young life if you begin like this!
It happened that Apollo chanced to miss
His herd of cattle from the Doric land
Where they were left to graze. You understand
How much he loves his cows? Well now their theft
Has made him simply wild. In haste he left
The halls of heaven, and sped by land and sea
To seek them out. It chanced with us to be
Nearby on Mount Kyllene, and to hear
His proclamation; so we all drew near
The shining one—I'm an old friend of his—
And any trouble, I assured him, is

Felt just as much by me. Well, he has gone
Questing toward Tegea all alone,
Leaving us here behind to search this place
For the lost cows. Now I have chanced to trace
The theft at once to you: I've caught the thief!
Such cleverness as mine's beyond belief!

    HERMES: You strange, wild man, so hairy and so
      rough,
Do please stop talking, you've said quite enough
To puzzle my poor brain: I really can't
Imagine what on earth it is you want.

    SILENUS: We want Apollo's cows, and you know
      well
Where on the earth, or under it, they dwell.

    HERMES: What is a cow? I've only heard them
      named!
Surely you're joking: how can I be blamed,
A child of six days old—although I've grown
As well becomes a god, I'm sure you'll own.

    And why should I steal cows? I do not care
For things like that; nor wander anywhere
But in my cavern home. All I desire
Is to lie snugly down beside the fire;
Or for my nurse to bathe and cherish me,
Feed me with pap, and dandle cunningly
Until I fall asleep. It's most absurd
That I'd steal cows—of which I'd never heard
Until you mentioned them a while ago.

    But now I'll swear, if you will have it so,
A mighty oath by the Infernal Lake,
The oath that no immortal god may break—
I have not stolen things I've never seen
Called cows: my cave and conscience are both clean!

    SILENUS: Good gracious me! This youngster would
      convince
The oldest councillor, or the wisest prince!
One could believe you'd been a thief for years;
And really, to my judgement it appears
You've lied about your age! If at six days
You've done all this, it fills me with amaze
To think what deeds you'll do in time to come!
However, all true gods strike mortals dumb.

    But still, I'll swear you stole away the kine
Of great Apollo—also god divine—
And led them this way, past the cavern mouth,
And kept them here—or drove them from the south
Across this open place. The northward ground
Is rocky, and no footsteps can be found
Upon it, but they're plain enough just here;
Although confused, the main direction's clear.

    HERMES: I think you must have had a nasty dream
And don't know which things are, and which things
     seem.
You say the cows were driven to the north,
But you just said Apollo first set forth
From that direction: he'd have seen them then,
Or heard about them somewhere among men.

    CHORUS:
      There's certainly some sense in this remark,
      And, to speak truth, I'm still quite in the dark.

    SILENUS: You stole the cows, wherever they may
     be!

    HERMES: What makes you try to fix the deed on
     me?

    SILENUS: That instrument you've got beneath your
     arm . . .

    HERMES: Is called a lyre; I made it, where's the
     harm?

    SILENUS: Now tell me how you did it, with what
     art . . .

    HERMES: I used a tortoise for the lower part.

    SILENUS: Yes, and I grant you that explains the
     shell.

    HERMES: I'm pleased to find you understand so
     well.

    SILENUS: My! You were clever to devise it so!

    HERMES: Yes, I've got brains! I'm glad you fellows
     know.

    SILENUS: But what can make the hollow vessel
     sound?

    HERMES: This piece of ox-hide fastened down all
     around.

    SILENUS: Now tell me where you got that strip of
     hide!

    HERMES: The skin? I found it—picked it up inside.

    SILENUS: I don't believe it! That skin's newly
     flayed!

    HERMES: What does it mean? That funny word
     you said?

    SILENUS: We've caught you now, whatever you
     pretend.

    HERMES: I think this interview had better end.
It's really time I had a little doze.
A child needs lots of sleep—for then he grows.

    SILENUS: You've grown enough, my lad. Don't
     think to fly!
Wait here, Apollo's coming by and by!

    HERMES: I'm really not prepared for callers now:
Tell him to come again, when times allow.

    SILENUS: I've got you, and don't mean to let you
     go
Apollo will pay well for this, I know!

    HERMES: Just as you like; provided he comes soon.
And if you're quiet I'll play a little tune.
    [*He plays on the lyre*]

    CHORUS:
    [*Dancing more and more wildly*]
        When the sound of the lyre
          Gets hold of my heels,
        All my body takes fire
          Till it staggers and reels
Away and away to the madding sweet sound,
Till our bodies grow wearied and sink to the ground.

        Not the juice of the grape
          As it foams down my throat;
        Not as oft the soft shape
          Of a wood-nymph I note;
Not the fume of the wine nor the thrill of desire
Sends me mad with delight like the sound of the lyre.

Now my feet cannot cease
Nor my legs be at rest
For the wild strains increase,
And increases my zest,
I long not for love, and I crave not for wine—
Let me live, let me die with this music divine.

FIRST SATYR: Stay the wild dance! Apollo's drawing near,
And all this shady business will grow clear.
[*Enter* Apollo *eagerly*]
APOLLO: I have returned, my friends, with news indeed!
I come from Tegea now in breathless speed
Where, in a ditch, I found an ancient man
Called Battus, who revealed the villain's plan.
For he had seen, he said, a comely youth
Drawing my cows behind him from the south.
Oh wondrous cunning, insolence divine!
For this same stripling urged the frightened kine
To shamble backwards—dragged them by the tail!
Moreover as he strove his best to hale
The unwilling cows behind him, Battus said,
The youngling's feet were strangely basketed
With willow slivers and osier boughs,
That none might trace the herdsman or the cows.
And so I found the cattle: but alas,
A far more dreadful thing had come to pass,
For two of them, two of my precious cows,
Lay slain: the flesh on twelve new heaps of boughs
Burned up in offering to us gods on high.
It makes me mad to think my cows should die
Beneath this villain's hand! And now I swear
My vengeance shall be great, and wondrous rare!
[*He stops, gasping for breath, and fans himself*]
CHORUS:
To slay the lord Apollo's kine
Is really most outrageous!
We hope that you'll impose a fine,
Imprisonment—and most condign
Reproaches on the wicked thief
Whose deed, though vile beyond belief,
Is clever—we might say divine—
And really most courageous!
APOLLO: [*At his most petulant*]
I do not think it in the least
A clever trick to make a feast
Of stolen cattle—which are mine!
Impiety to gods divine
Is certain to enrage us!
CHORUS:
But see whom we have here: the villain vile
Who stole the cows, and hide them by his guile.
APOLLO: Is this the fellow? This same callow lad?
He looks too young and feeble. You are mad
To charge him with the theft. Yet stay awhile,
Just let me look . . . Yes! Something in that smile,
Those curls ambrosial . . . What *will* Hera say!
There *was* a rumour Zeus was seen to stray
Disguised down here on earth, the other day . . .
[*He chuckles to himself*]

CHORUS:
Although he has stolen your cows,
Great Phoebus Apollo,
The glory that shines from his brows
Is a proof that his birth was divine . . .
And indeed you come both of one line,
Though your father paid various vows.
(I'm sure that you follow?)
HERMES:
Oh, what's all this chatter to me?
It's as wild as the waves of the sea
That break on the shingle all day.
I'll listen no longer, but play
On my lyre, Lord Apollo.
[Hermes *plays on the lyre*]
CHORUS:
Ah, when I hear the music of the lyre
I long to dance and dance! I'm filled with fire!
APOLLO: Fair stranger, all my soul is sick with joy:
What is this witching art that you employ?
SILENUS: Hear me, good Lord Apollo, hear me quick!
Don't listen to the lyre, it's all a trick
To make you pardon him the stolen kine!
This instrument, although it seems divine,
Proves his sure guilt beyond the slightest doubt!
APOLLO: What crack-brain theory are you bringing out?
SILENUS: The lyre in his hand! Examine well.
APOLLO: A clever thing made of a tortoise shell.
SILENUS: Yes, but what else is used? Look closely please.
APOLLO: Why do you ask me questions such as these?
SILENUS: Oh do look close! What shuts the hollow in?
APOLLO: Why all this fuss about a piece of skin?
SILENUS: It's just that skin! It once was on a cow!
APOLLO: Oh, I begin to see your meaning now!
CHORUS: [*Jogging up and down excitedly*]
Forgive him, Lord Phoebus, please!
We want some more music!
There were never such tunes as these,
They give youth to our backs and our knees!
They don't, surely, make you sick?
APOLLO:
They should, but they don't! I'm on fire!
I'm enchanted! I'm fay!
Though a god, I'm enslaved—by the lyre!
Is it magic, this breathless desire
To make music all day?
SILENUS: I long to join the song and dance divine—
But, Phoebus, what about the stolen kine?
And what about the gold you promised us
If our detective work were prosperous?
APOLLO: There's truth in that! Young man, what do you say?
You stole my cows: I think you ought to pay;
Reward this person, and make up to me

The loss of those you killed so wickedly.

HERMES: Apollo, brother of the shining dart,
Why should such quarrels sever heart from heart?
Here and before you all, I swear by Styx
Never again to play Apollo tricks
Never to steal from him, nor make him cross.
    And now, as I can't quite repair his loss
(A cow once dead can scarcely graze again),
I'll see if I can soothe my brother's pain.
    Apollo, this my lyre I bestow
On you for ever. May sweet music flow
Beneath your hand eternally divine,
And high Parnassus ever be the shrine
Of all fair song. Round the Castalian spring
Notes of Apollo's lyre for ever cling!

CHORUS:
    All well and good, but what of our reward?
    Apollo, you were always a just lord!

APOLLO: You shall be free, according to my word.
And when the music of my lyre is heard,
The madness of delight, of sweet desire
Shall so possess you with its wondrous fire
That all dull things forgetting, you shall be
Swung to the fairest heights of ecstasy!
            Now hark to Apollo
                Who plays on his lyre!
            Come follow, come follow
                To seek your desire.
            With music delighting
                The children of day.

Apollo is lighting
    The world on its way.
[*Exit, playing on the lyre.*]

CHORUS:
Apollo, Apollo is speeding and leading
    The dance of my days out by valley and hill;
Sweet, sweet the desire in my heart that is breeding;
    I gasp with delight as the lyre sounds shrill:
I follow Apollo his leading, go speeding
    Away and away he is leading me still!
    [*Exeunt, dancing*]

NOTES TO *The Searching Satyrs*

The date of the *Ichneutai* is uncertain; its genuineness as a work of Sophocles is proved beyond doubt by a passage from the play quoted by Athenaeus (ii. 62). Various periods in the career of Sophocles have been put forward by scholars, but no conclusive proof is available; it may be assigned most probably to an early date, and is perhaps not much later than *Antigone*, which was produced about 440 B.C.

The scene is before a cave on Mount Kyllene in the North of the Peloponnese, and in this, as in the introduction of the nymph of that mountain in place of Maia the mother of Hermes, in the placing of the theft of the cattle before the making of the lyre, and, of course, in the introduction of the Satyrs, the play differs from the Homeric Hymn to Hermes, which it follows fairly closely in most other details. The best translation of the Hymn is that into prose by Andrew Lang (*Allen and Unwin*, 1899), whose introductory essay on the Legend and its parallels in Folklore is of considerable interest. Shelley also made a pleasant rendering of the Hymn in verse.

Euripides and The Bacchae

The masterpiece of "Dionysian drama" is also one of the major masterpieces of classic drama. Its Athenian author Euripides never wrote a finer play. Nor could a finer example be found to dictate his artistic integrity, which was often called into question by his contemporary Athenian critics, especially the comic poet Aristophanes.[1] That *The Bacchae* should have been one of three last plays written by Euripides before his death in 406 B.C., during his voluntary exile in Macedonia, is less significant than that this set of three (*Iphigenia in Aulis* and a lost *Alcmaeon at Corinth* were the other two) should have taken first prize at the City Dionysia festival when his son, Euripides the Younger,[2] brought them back to Athens. Euripides had rarely won first prize in his native city, but this belated victory was only the first of many posthumous triumphs. After the fifth century, the Greeks found Aeschylus, his predecessor in tragedy, too primitive for their taste and his rival Sophocles apparently too austere.

Although Euripides often seemed less than a careful craftsman, there can be no doubt that *The Bacchae*, even apart from its complexity of meaning, is one of the very best constructed Greek plays. The dramatic action starts quickly, the conflict between the principal characters, the young king Pentheus and Dionysius, expands and grows steadily in intensity, the dramatic interest is refreshed by reversals of situation, and the main "peripety" leads inexorably to a shattering conclusion: Pentheus' mother, Agave, arrives in the climactic scene triumphantly carrying her son's head impaled on a *thyrsus* or rod sacred to the god whose ecstatic worship has temporarily deranged her. Yet far from constituting melodrama the conflict and its horrifying resolution is profoundly tragic on several levels. There is first our interest in the family conflict of two characters, a god and a king who are not only stubborn young men but rival cousins.[3] The psychological conflict provides a second level of concern, involving not only the religious hysteria of the queen-mother Agave and the Theban bacchantes but, in the confrontation of god and man, the clash of instinctual release and repressive rationality or, in Freudian terms, *id* and *superego*. And for the Greeks there must have also been an anagogic or allegorical-mystical level of interest that cannot be easily explained but that can be deeply felt, and that takes us into the very core of the indefinable Dionysian religious experience.

"Elusive, complex and compelling," writes William Arrowsmith, "the play constantly recedes before one's grasp, advancing, not retreating, steadily into deeper chaos and larger order, coming finally to rest only god knows where—which is to say, where it matters."[4] Rationality is seen to be in conflict with instinctuality in this great tragedy, and rationalism in the case of Pentheus is shown to be blind to the god's reason-transcending reality—and therefore recklessly, and tragically, *irrational*. And involved in this extreme polarization of reason and unreason which culminates in the catastrophe are such recognizable polarities as order and disorder, law and anarchy, common and uncommon sense, the prose and poetry of life, plodding practicality and imaginative release.

It is quite apparent that Euripides remained in full possession of his Greek sense of balance as well as his dramatist's sense of character in action. He demonstrates both simultaneously by showing the human representative of Rationality as a character poised on the knife-edge of intemperate tyranny and easily toppled from his intellectual eminence when he puts on feminine attire and goes up to the mountain to spy on the ritualistic revelry of the bacchantes. The proud human representative of Rationalism is an uncommonly unreasonable proponent of Reason. He is also tragically ignorant of his own inner self. William Arrowsmith observes aptly that "it is by playing upon Pentheus' vulnerability, his deep ignorance of his own nature that the god is able to possess him, humiliate him and finally destroy him."

Finally, it becomes clear from the climactic vengeance exacted by Dionysus that the god, like any other natural force, is amoral, incapable of compassion—and inexorable. The sacred myth, or *hieros logos,* of Dionysian worship is not sweetened here by sentimentality. In dealing with Dionysus, as he had dealt earlier with the Aphrodite of his *Hippolytus*, Euripides knew he was representing a natural force that is beyond human sentiment and beyond man-made

---

[1] See *The Frogs* (pp. 71–95), especially the *agon*, the climactic scene of comic struggle, immediately before the conclusion and the *Exodus*, pp. 85–94.

[2] Also a playwright, who apparently completed his father's *Iphigenia*.

[3] Pentheus' mother, Agave, and Dionysus' fire-consumed mortal mother, Semele, were sisters. Their father Cadmus, now an aged man, is the mythical founder of the city of Thebes.

[4] See Mr. Arrowsmith's superb introduction to his translation of *The Bacchae* in *The Complete Greek Tragedies,* reprinted in volume 7 of the Modern Library edition. New York: Random House.

morality. The young Pentheus in his *hybris* of error and complacency, denied the drive of the amoral divine *Life Force,* so to speak, and was punished by it. As we might say somewhat glibly today, instinct too severely suppressed will well up from repression and become destructive. As the dreadful lesson is summed up by Moses Hadas, "it is irrational not to recognize the irrational," and "Dionysus can be heartless as well as beneficent, and men cannot choose to keep him out of their lives."

THE BACCHAE

By Euripides

TRANSLATED BY WILLIAM ARROWSMITH

CHARACTERS

DIONYSUS, *also called Bromius, Evius, and Bacchus*
CHORUS OF ASIAN BACCHAE, *followers of Dionysus*
TEIRESIAS
CADMUS
PENTHEUS

ATTENDANT
FIRST MESSENGER
SECOND MESSENGER
AGAVE
CORYPHAEUS, *chorus leader*

SCENE: *Before the royal palace at Thebes. On the left is the way to Cithaeron; on the right, to the city. In the center of the orchestra stands, still smoking, the vine-covered tomb of Semele, mother of Dionysus.*

[*Enter* Dionysus. *He is of soft, even effeminate, appearance. His face is beardless; he is dressed in a fawn-skin and carries a thyrsus (ie., a stalk of fennel tipped with ivy leaves). On his head he wears a wreath of ivy, and his long blond curls ripple down over his shoulders. Throughout the play he wears a smiling mask*]

DIONYSUS: I am Dionysus, the son of Zeus,
come back to Thebes, this land where I was born.
My mother was Cadmus' daughter, Semele by name,
midwived by fire, delivered by the lightning's
blast.
     And here I stand, a god incognito,
disguised as man, beside the stream of Dirce
and the waters of Ismenus. There before the palace
I see my lightning-married mother's grave,
and there upon the ruins of her shattered house
the living fire of Zeus still smolders on
in deathless witness of Hera's violence and rage
against my mother. But Cadmus wins my praise:
he has made this tomb a shrine, sacred to my mother.
It was I who screened her grave with the green
of the clustering vine.
     Far behind me lie
those golden-rivered lands, Lydia and Phrygia,
where my journeying began. Overland I went,
across the steppes of Persia where the sun strikes
hotly
down, through Bactrian fastness and the grim waste
of Media. Thence to rich Arabia I came;
and so, along all Asia's swarming littoral
of towered cities where Greeks and foreign nations,
mingling, live, my progress made. There
I taught my dances to the feet of living men,
establishing my mysteries and rites
that I might be revealed on earth for what I am:
a god.
     And thence to Thebes.
                         This city, first

in Hellas, now shrills and echoes to my women's
cries,
their ecstasy of joy. Here in Thebes
I bound the fawn-skin to the women's flesh and
armed
their hands with shafts of ivy. For I have come
to refute that slander spoken by my mother's sisters—
those who least had right to slander her.
They said that Dionysus was no son of Zeus,
but Semele had slept beside a man in love
and fathered off her shame on Zeus—a fraud, they
sneered,
contrived by Cadmus to protect his daughter's name.
They said she lied, and Zeus in anger at that lie
blasted her with lightning.
                         Because of that offense
I have stung them with frenzy, hounded them from
home
up to the mountains where they wander, crazed of
mind,
and compelled to wear my orgies' livery.
Every woman in Thebes—but the women only—
I drove from home, mad. There they sit,
rich and poor alike, even the daughters of Cadmus,
beneath the silver firs on the roofless rocks.
Like it or not, this city must learn its lesson:
it lacks initiation in my mysteries;
that I shall vindicate my mother Semele
and stand revealed to mortal eyes as the god
she bore to Zeus.
                         Cadmus the king has abdicated,
leaving his throne and power to his grandson Pentheus;
who now revolts against divinity, in *me;*
thrusts *me* from his offerings; forgets *my* name
in his prayers. Therefore I shall *prove* to him
and every man in Thebes that I am god
indeed. And when my worship is established here,
and all is well, then I shall go my way
and be revealed to other men in other lands.
But if the men of Thebes attempt to force
my Bacchae from the mountainside by threat of arms,
I shall marshal my Maenads and take the field.

To these ends I have laid my deity aside
and go disguised as man.
     [*He wheels and calls offstage*]
                    On, my women,
women who worship me, women whom I led
out of Asia where Tmolus heaves its rampart
over Lydia!
               On, comrades of my progress here!
Come, and with your native Phrygian drum—
Rhea's drum and mine—pound at the palace doors
of Pentheus! Let the city of Thebes behold you,
while I return among Cithaeron's forest glens
where my Bacchae wait and join their whirling
     dances.
     [*Exit* Dionysus *as the* Chorus of Asian Bacchae
     *comes dancing in from the right. They are
     dressed in fawn-skins, crowned with ivy, and
     carry thyrsi, timbrels, and flutes*]
CHORUS: Out of the land of Asia,
down from holy Tmolus,
speeding the service of god,
for Bromius we come!
Hard are the labors of god;
hard, but his service is sweet.
Sweet to serve, sweet to cry:
          Bacchus!   Evohé!

—You on the streets!
                    —You on the roads!
                                   —Make
     way!
—Let every mouth be hushed. Let no ill-omened
     words
profane your tongues.
                    —Make way! Fall back!
—Hush

—For now I raise the old, old hymn to Dionysus.

—Blessèd, blessèd are those who know the mysteries
     of god.
—Blessèd is he who hallows his life in the worship of
     god.
     he whom the spirit of god possesseth, who is one
     with those who belong to the holy body of god.

—Blessèd are the dancers and those who are purified,
     who dance on the hill in the holy dance of god.

—Blessèd are they who keep the rite of Cybele the
     Mother.
—Blessèd are the thyrsus-bearers, those who wield in
     their hands
     the holy wand of god.
—Blessèd are those who wear the crown of the ivy of
     god.
—Blessèd, blessèd are they: Dionysus is their god!

—On, Bacchae, on, you Bacchae,
     bear your god in triumph home!
     Bear on the god, son of god,

escort your Dionysus home!
     Bear him down from Phrygian hill,
     attend him through the streets of Hellas!

—So his mother bore him once
     in labor bitter; lightning-struck,
     forced by fire that flared from Zeus,
     consumed, she died, untimely torn,
     in childbed dead by blow of light!
     Of light the son was born!

—Zeus it was who saved his son;
     with speed outrunning mortal eye,
     bore him to a private place,
     bound the boy with clasps of gold;
     in his thigh as in a womb,
     concealed his son from Hera's eyes.

—And when the weaving Fates fulfilled the time,
     the bull-horned god was born of Zeus. In joy
     he crowned his son, set serpents on his head—
     wherefrom, in piety, descends to us
     the Maenad's writhing crown, her *chevelure* of
          snakes.

—O Thebes, nurse of Semele,
     crown your hair with ivy!
     Grow green with bryony!
     Redden with berries! O city,
     with boughs of oak and fir,
     come dance the dance of god!
     Fringe your skins of dappled fawn
     with tufts of twisted wool!
     Handle with holy care
     the violent wand of god!
     And let the dance begin!
     He is Bromius who runs
     to the mountain!
                    to the mountain!
     where the throng of women waits,
     driven from shuttle and loom,
     possessed by Dionysus!

—And I praise the holies of Crete,
     the caves of the dancing Curetes,
     there where Zeus was born,
     where helmed in triple tier
     around the primal drum
     the Corybantes danced. They,
     they were the first of all
     whose whirling feet kept time
     to the strict beat of the taut hide
     and the squeal of the wailing flute.
     Then from them to Rhea's hands
     the holy drum was handed down;
     but, stolen by the raving Satyrs,
     fell at last to me and now
     accompanies the dance
     which every other year
     celebrates your name:
          Dionysus!

—He is sweet upon the mountains. He drops to the
     earth from the running packs.

He wears the holy fawn-skin. He hunts the wild
    goat and kills it.
He delights in the raw flesh.
He runs to the mountains of Phrygia, to the moun-
    tains of Lydia he runs!
He is Bromius who leads us! *Evohé!*

—With milk the earth flows! It flows with wine!
It runs with the nectar of bees!

—Like frankincense in its fragrance
is the blaze of the torch he bears.
Flames float out from his trailing wand
    as he runs, as he dances,
    kindling the stragglers,
    spurring with cries,
and his long curls stream to the wind!

—And he cries, as they cry, *Evohé!*—
    On, Bacchae!
    On, Bacchae!
Follow, glory of golden Tmolus,
    hymning god
    with a rumble of drums,
with a cry, *Evohé!* to the Evian god,
with a cry of Phrygian cries,
when the holy flute like honey plays
the sacred song of those who go
to the mountain!

                to the mountain!

—Then, in ecstasy, like a colt by its grazing mother,
the Bacchante runs with flying feet, she leaps!

[*The* Chorus *remains grouped in two semicircles
about the orchestra as* Teiresias *makes his entrance. He is incongruously dressed in the bacchant's fawn-skin and is crowned with ivy. Old
and blind, he uses his thyrsus to tap his way*]

TEIRESIAS: Ho there, who keeps the gates?
                         Summon
Cadmus—
Cadmus, Agenor's son, the stranger from Sidon
who built the towers of our Thebes.
                Go, someone.
Say Teiresias wants him. He will know what errand
brings me, that agreement, age with age, we made
to deck our wands, to dress in skins of fawn
and crown our heads with ivy.

[*Enter* Cadmus *from the palace. Dressed in Dio-
nysiac costume and bent almost double with age,
he is an incongruous and pathetic figure*]

CADMUS: My old friend,
I knew it must be you when I heard your summons.
For there's a wisdom in his voice that makes
the man of wisdom known.
             But here I am,
dressed in the costume of the god, prepared to go.
Insofar as we are able, Teiresias, we must
do honor to this god, for he was born
my daughter's son, who has been revealed to men,
the god, Dionysus.
            Where shall we go, where

shall we tread the dance, tossing our white heads
in the dances of god?
                Expound to me, Teiresias.
For in such matters you are wise.
                      Surely
I could dance night and day, untiringly
beating the earth with my thyrsus! And how sweet
    it is
to forget my old age.
    TEIRESIAS: It is the same with me.
I too feel young, young enough to dance.
    CADMUS: Good. Shall we take our chariots to the
      mountain?
    TEIRESIAS: Walking would be better. It shows
      more honor
to the god.
    CADMUS: So be it. I shall lead, my old age
conducting yours.
    TEIRESIAS: The god will guide us there
with no effort on our part.
    CADMUS: Are we the only men
who will dance for Bacchus?
    TEIRESIAS: They are all blind.
Only we can see.
    CADMUS: But we delay too long.
Here, take my arm.
    TEIRESIAS: Link my hand in yours.
    CADMUS: I am a man, nothing more. I do not scoff
at heaven.
    TEIRESIAS: We do not trifle with divinity.
No, we are the heirs of customs and traditions
hallowed by age and handed down to us
by our fathers. No quibbling logic can topple *them*,
whatever subtleties this clever age invents.
People may say: "Aren't you ashamed? At your age,
going dancing, wreathing your head with ivy?"
Well, I am *not* ashamed. Did the god declare
that just the young or just the old should dance?
No, he desires his honor from all mankind.
He wants no one excluded from his worship.
    CADMUS: Because you cannot see, Teiresias, let
      me be
interpreter for you this once. Here comes
the man to whom I left my throne, Echion's son,
Pentheus, hastening toward the palace. He seems
excited and disturbed. Yes, listen to him.

[*Enter* Pentheus *from the right. He is a very young
man of athletic build, dressed in traditional
Greek dress; like* Dionysus, *he is beardless. He
enters excitedly, talking to the attendants who
accompany him*]

    PENTHEUS: I happened to be away, out of the city,
but reports reached me of some strange mischief
    here,
stories of our women leaving home to frisk
in mock ecstasies among the thickets on the moun-
    tain,
dancing in honor of the latest divinity,
a certain Dionysus, whoever he may be!
In their midst stand bowls brimming with wine.

And then, one by one, the women wander off
to hidden nooks where they serve the lusts of men.
Priestesses of Bacchus they claim they are,
but it's really Aphrodite they adore.
I have captured some of them; my jailers
have locked them away in the safety of our prison.
Those who run at large shall be hunted down
out of the mountains like the animals they are—
yes, my own mother Agave, and Ino
and Autonoë, the mother of Actaeon.
In no time at all I shall have them trapped
in iron nets and stop this obscene disorder.

I am also told a foreigner has come to Thebes
from Lydia, one of those charlatan magicians
with long yellow curls smelling of perfumes,
with flushed cheeks and the spells of Aphrodite
in his eyes. His days and nights he spends
with women and girls, dangling before them the joys
of initiation in his mysteries.
But let me bring him underneath that roof
and I'll stop his pounding with his wand and tossing
his head. By god, I'll have his head cut off!
And *this* is the man who claims that Dionysus
is a god and was sewn into the thigh of Zeus,
when, in point of fact, that same blast of lightning
consumed him and his mother both for her lie
that she had lain with Zeus in love. Whoever
this stranger is, aren't such impostures,
such unruliness, worthy of hanging?
        [*For the first time he sees* Teiresias *and* Cadmus
        in their Dionysiac costumes]
                                                What!
But this is incredible! Teiresias the seer
tricked out in a dappled fawn-skin!
                                        And *you*,
you, my own grandfather, playing at the bacchant
with a wand!
                Sir, I shrink to see your old age
so foolish. Shake that ivy off, grandfather!
Now drop that wand. Drop it, I say.
        [*He wheels on* Teiresias]
                                        Aha,
I see: this is *your* doing, Teiresias.
Yes, you want still another god revealed to men
so you can pocket the profits from burnt offerings
and bird-watching. By heaven, only your age
restrains me now from sending you to prison
with those Bacchic women for importing here to
        Thebes
these filthy mysteries. When once you see
the glint of wine shining at the feasts of women,
then you may be sure the festival is rotten.

        CORYPHAEUS: What blasphemy! Stranger, have you
                no respect
for heaven! For Cadmus who sowed the dragon
        teeth?
Will the son of Echion disgrace his house?

        TEIRESIAS: Give a wise man an honest brief to plead
and his eloquence is no remarkable achievement.
But you are glib; your phrases come rolling out

smoothly on the tongue, as though your words were
        wise
instead of foolish. The man whose glibness flows
from his conceit of speech declares the thing he is:
a worthless and a stupid citizen.
                                I tell you,
this god whom you ridicule shall someday have
enormous power and prestige throughout Hellas.
Mankind, young man, possesses two supreme bless-
        ings.
First of these is the goddess Demeter, or Earth—
whichever name you choose to call her by.
It was she who gave to man his nourishment of grain.
But after her there came the son of Semele,
who matched her present by inventing liquid wine
as his gift to man. For filled with that good gift,
suffering mankind forgets its grief; from it
comes sleep; with it oblivion of the troubles
of the day. There is no other medicine
for misery. And when we pour libations
to the gods, we pour the god of wine himself
that through his intercession man may win
the favor of heaven.
                        You sneer, do you, at that story
that Dionysus was sewed into the thigh of Zeus?
Let me teach you what that really means. When Zeus
rescued from the thunderbolt his infant son,
he brought him to Olympus. Hera, however,
plotted at heart to hurl the child from heaven.
Like the god he is, Zeus countered her. Breaking off
a tiny fragment of that ether which surrounds the
        world,
he molded from it a dummy Dionysus.
This he *showed* to Hera, but with time men garbled
the word and said that Dionysus had been *sewed*
into the thigh of Zeus. This was their story.
whereas, in fact, Zeus *showed* the dummy to Hera
and gave it as a hostage for his son.
                                        Moreover,
this is a god of prophecy. His worshippers,
like madmen, are endowed with mantic powers.
For when the god enters the body of a man
he fills him with the breath of prophecy.
                                        Besides,
he has usurped even the functions of warlike Ares.
Thus, at times, you see an army mustered under arms
stricken with panic before it lifts a spear.
This panic comes from Dionysus.
                                        Someday
you shall even see him bounding with his torches
among the crags at Delphi, leaping the pastures
that stretch between the peaks, whirling and waving
his thyrsus: great throughout Hellas.
                                        Mark my words,
Pentheus. Do not be so certain that power
is what matters in the life of man; do not mistake
for wisdom the fantasies of your sick mind.
Welcome the god to Thebes; crown your head;
pour him libations and join his revels.

        Dionysus does not, I admit, *compel* a woman

to be chaste. Always and in every case
it is her character and nature that keep
a woman chaste. But even in the rites of Dionysus,
the chaste woman will not be corrupted.
Think:
you are pleased when men stand outside your doors
and the city glorifies the name of Pentheus.
And so the god: he too delights in glory.
But Cadmus and I, whom you ridicule, will crown
our heads with ivy and join the dances of the god—
an ancient foolish pair perhaps, but dance
we must. Nothing you have said would make me
change my mind or flout the will of heaven.
You are mad, grievously mad, beyond the power
of any drugs to cure, for you are drugged
with madness.

CORYPHAEUS: Apollo would approve your words.
Wisely you honor Bromius: a great god.

CADMUS: My boy,
Teiresias advises well. Your home is here
with us, with our customs and traditions, not
outside, alone. Your mind is distracted now,
and what you think is sheer delirium.
Even if this Dionysus is no god,
as you assert, persuade yourself that he is.
The fiction is a noble one, for Semele will seem
to be the mother of a god, and this confers
no small distinction on our family.
You saw
that dreadful death your cousin Actaeon died
when those man-eating hounds he had raised himself
savaged him and tore his body limb from limb
because he boasted that his prowess in the hunt surpassed
the skill of Artemis.
Do not let his fate be yours.
Here, let me wreathe your head with leaves of ivy.
Then come with us and glorify the god.

PENTHEUS: Take your hands off me! Go worship
your Bacchus,
but do not wipe your madness off on me.
By god, I'll make him pay, the man who taught you
this folly of yours.

[He turns to his attendants]
Go, someone, this instant,
to the place where this prophet prophesies.
Pry it up with crowbars, heave it over,
upside down; demolish everything you see.
Throw his fillets out to wind and weather.
That will provoke him more than anything.
As for the rest of you, go and scour the city
for that effeminate stranger, the man who infects our
women
with this strange disease and pollutes our beds.
And when you take him, clap him in chains
and march him here. He shall die as he deserves—
by being stoned to death. He shall come to rue
his merrymaking here in Thebes.

[Exeunt Attendants]

TEIRESIAS: Reckless fool,
you do not know the consequences of your words.
You talked madness before, but this is raving
lunacy!
Cadmus, let us go and pray
for this raving fool and for this city too,
pray to the god that no awful vengeance strike
from heaven.
Take your staff and follow me.
Support me with your hands, and I shall help you too
lest we stumble and fall, a sight of shame,
two old men together.
But go we must,
acknowledging the service that we owe to god,
Bacchus, the son of Zeus.
And yet take care
lest someday your house repent of Pentheus
in its sufferings. I speak not prophecy
but fact. The words of fools finish in folly.

[Exeunt Teiresias and Cadmus. Pentheus retires
into the palace]

CHORUS: Holiness, queen of heaven,
Holiness on golden wing
who hover over earth,
do you hear what Pentheus says?
Do you hear his blasphemy
against the prince of the blessèd,
the god of garlands and banquets,
Bromius, Semele's son?
These blessings he gave:
laughter to the flute
and the loosing of cares
when the shining wine is spilled
at the feast of the gods,
and the wine-bowl casts its sleep
on feasters crowned with ivy.

—A tongue without reins,
defiance, unwisdom—
their end is disaster.
But the life of quiet good,
the wisdom that accepts—
these abide unshaken,
preserving, sustaining
the houses of men.
Far in the air of heaven,
the sons of heaven live.
But they watch the lives of men.
And what passes for wisdom is not;
unwise are those who aspire,
who outrange the limits of man.
Briefly, we live. Briefly,
then die. Wherefore, I say,
he who hunts a glory, he who tracks
some boundless, superhuman dream,
may lose his harvest here and now
and garner death. Such men are mad,
their counsels evil.

—O let me come to Cyprus,
island of Aphrodite,
homes of the loves that cast

spells on the hearts of men!
Or Paphos where the hundred-
mouthed barbarian river
brings ripeness without rain!
To Pieria, haunt of the Muses,
and the holy hill of Olympus!
O Bromius, leader, god of joy,
Bromius, take me there!
There the lovely Graces go,
and there Desire, and there
the right is mine to worship
   as I please.

—The deity, the son of Zeus,
in feast, in festival, delights.
He loves the goddess Peace,
generous of good,
preserver of the young.
To rich and poor he gives
the simple gift of wine,
the gladness of the grape.
But him who scoffs he hates,
and him who mocks his life,
the happiness of those
for whom the day is blessed
but doubly blessed the night;
whose simple wisdom shuns the thoughts
of proud, uncommon men and all
their god-encroaching dreams.
But what the common people do,
the things that simple men believe,
   I too believe and do.

[As Pentheus *reappears from the palace, enter
from the left several attendants leading* Dionysus
captive]

ATTENDANT: Pentheus, here we are; not empty-
   handed either.
We captured the quarry you sent us out to catch.
But our prey here was tame: refused to run
or hide, held out his hands as willing as you please,
completely unafraid. His ruddy cheeks were flushed
as though with wine, and he stood there smiling,
making no objection when we roped his hands
and marched him here. It made me feel ashamed.
"Listen, stranger," I said, "I am not to blame.
We act under orders from Pentheus. He ordered
your arrest."
      As for those women you clapped in
   chains
and sent to the dungeon, they're gone, clean away,
went skipping off to the fields crying on their god
Bromius. The chains on their legs snapped apart
by themselves. Untouched by any human hand,
the doors swung wide, opening of their own accord.
Sir, this stranger who has come to Thebes is full
of many miracles. I know no more than that.
The rest is your affair.
  PENTHEUS: Untie his hands.
We have him in our net. He may be quick,
but he cannot escape us now, I think.

[*While the servants untie* Dionysus' *hands,* Pentheus *attentively scrutinizes his prisoner. Then
the servants step back, leaving* Pentheus *and*
Dionysus *face to face*]
         So,
you *are* attractive, stranger, at least to women—
which explains, I think, your presence here in
   Thebes.
Your curls are long. You do not wrestle, I take it.
And what fair skin you have—you must take care
   of it—
no daylight complexion; no, it comes from the night
when you hunt Aphrodite with your beauty.
         Now then,
who are you and from where?
  DIONYSUS: It is nothing
to boast of and easily told. You have heard, I sup-
   pose,
of Mount Tmolus and her flowers?
  PENTHEUS: I know the place.
It rings the city of Sardis.
  DIONYSUS: I come from there.
My country is Lydia.
  PENTHEUS: Who is this god whose worship
you have imported into Hellas?
  DIONYSUS: Dionysus, the son of
   Zeus.
He initiated me.
  PENTHEUS: You have some local Zeus
who spawns new gods?
  DIONYSUS: He is the same as yours—
the Zeus who married Semele.
  PENTHEUS: How did he see him?
In a dream or face to face?
  DIONYSUS: Face to face.
He gave me his rites.
  PENTHEUS: What form do they take,
these mysteries of yours?
  DIONYSUS: It is forbidden
to tell the uninitiate.
  PENTHEUS: Tell me the benefits
that those who know your mysteries enjoy.
  DIONYSUS: I am forbidden to say. But they are
   worth knowing.
  PENTHEUS: Your answers are designed to make
   me curious.
  DIONYSUS: No.
our mysteries abhor an unbelieving man.
  PENTHEUS: You say you saw the god. What form
   did he assume?
  DIONYSUS: Whatever form he wished. The choice
   was his, not mine.
  PENTHEUS: You evade the question.
  DIONYSUS: Talk
   sense to a fool and he calls you foolish.
  PENTHEUS: Have you
   introduced your rites in other cities too? Or is
   Thebes the first?
  DIONYSUS: Foreigners everywhere now dance for
   Dionysus.

PENTHEUS: They are more ignorant than Greeks.

DIONYSUS: In
this matter they are not. Customs differ.

PENTHEUS: Do you
hold your rites during the day or night?

DIONYSUS: Mostly by
night.
The darkness is well suited to devotion.

PENTHEUS: Better suited to lechery and seducing
women.

DIONYSUS: You can find debauchery by daylight
too.

PENTHEUS: You shall regret these clever answers.

DIONYSUS: And you, your stupid blasphemies.

PENTHEUS: What
a bold Bacchant!
You wrestle well—when it comes to words.

DIONYSUS: Tell
me, what punishment do you propose?

PENTHEUS: First of all,
I shall cut off your girlish curls.

DIONYSUS: My hair is holy.
[Pentheus *shears away the god's curls*]
My curls belong to god.

PENTHEUS: Second, you will surrender
your wand.

DIONYSUS: *You* take it. It belongs to Dionysus.
[Pentheus *takes the thyrsus*]

PENTHEUS: Last, I shall place you under guard and
confine you in the palace.

DIONYSUS: The god himself will
set me free whenever I wish.

PENTHEUS: You will be with
your women in prison when you call on him
for help.

DIONYSUS: He is here now and sees what I endure
from you.

PENTHEUS: Where is he? I cannot see him.

DIONYSUS: With
me. Your blasphemies have made you blind.

PENTHEUS: [*To attendants*] Seize him. He is mocking me and Thebes.

DIONYSUS: I give you sober warning,
fools: place no chains on *me*.

PENTHEUS: But *I* say: chain
him. And I am the stronger here.

DIONYSUS: You do not
know the limits of your strength. You do not
know what you do. You do not know who you
are.

PENTHEUS: I am Pentheus, the son of Echion and
Agave.

DIONYSUS: Pentheus: you shall repent that name.

PENTHEUS: Off
with him.
Chain his hands; lock him in the stables by the palace.
Since he desires the darkness, give him what he
wants.
Let him dance down there in the dark.
[*As the* Attendants *bind* Dionysus' *hands, the*

Chorus *beats on the drums with increasing agitation as though to emphasize the sacrilege*]
                                As for these women,
your accomplices in making trouble here,
I shall have them sold as slaves or put to work
at my looms. That will silence their drums.
[*Exit* Pentheus]

DIONYSUS: I go,
though not to suffer, since that cannot be.
But Dionysus whom you outrage by your acts,
who you deny is god, will call you to account.
When you set chains on me, you manacle the god.
[*Exeunt* Attendants *with* Dionysus *captive*]

CHORUS: O Dirce, holy river,
child of Achelöus' water,
yours the springs that welcomed once
divinity, the son of Zeus!
For Zeus the father snatched his son
from deathless flame, crying:
Dithyrambus, come!
Enter my male womb.
I name you Bacchus and to Thebes
proclaim you by that name.
But now, O blessèd Dirce,
you banish me when to your banks I come,
crowned with ivy, bringing revels.
O Dirce, why am I rejected?
By the clustered grapes I swear,
by Dionysus' wine,
someday you shall come to know
    the name of *Bromius!*

—With fury, with fury, he rages,
Pentheus, son of Echion,
born of the breed of Earth,
spawned by the dragon, whelped by Earth!
Inhuman, a rabid beast,
a giant in wildness raging,
storming, defying the children of heaven.
He has threatened me with bonds
though my body is bound to god.
He cages my comrades with chains;
he has cast them in prison darkness.
O Lord, son of Zeus, do you see?
O Dionysus, do you see
how in shackles we are held
unbreakably, in the bonds of oppressors?
Descend from Olympus, lord!
Come, whirl your wand of gold
and quell with death this beast of blood
whose violence abuses man and god
    outrageously.

—O lord, where do you wave your wand
among the running companies of god?
There on Nysa, mother of beasts?
There on the ridges of Corycia?
Or there among the forests of Olympus
where Orpheus fingered his lyre
and mustered with music the trees,
mustered the wilderness beasts?

O Pieria, you are blessed!
Evius honors you. He comes to dance,
bringing his Bacchae, fording the race
where Axios runs, bringing his Maenads
whirling over Lydias,
generous father of rivers
and famed for his lovely waters
that fatten a land of splendid horses.

[*Thunder and lightning. The earth trembles. The Chorus is crazed with fear*]

DIONYSUS: [*From within*]
Ho!
Hear me! Ho, Bacchae!
Ho, Bacchae! Hear my cry!
CHORUS: Who cries?
Who calls me with that cry
of Evius? Where are you, lord?
DIONYSUS: Ho! Again I cry—
the son of Zeus and Semele!
CHORUS: O lord, lord Bromius!
Bromius, come to us now!
DIONYSUS: *Let the earthquake come! Shatter the floor of the world!*
CHORUS: —Look there, how the palace of Pentheus totters.
—Look, the palace is collapsing!
—Dionysus is within. Adore him!
—We adore him!
—Look there!
         —Above the pillars, how the great stones
gape and crack!
         —Listen. Bromius cries his victory!
DIONYSUS: *Launch the blazing thunderbolt of god! O lightnings, come! Consume with flame the palace of Pentheus!*
[*A burst of lightning flares across the façade of the palace and tongues of flame spurt up from the tomb of Semele. Then a great crash of thunder*]
CHORUS: Ah,
look how the fire leaps up
on the holy tomb of Semele,
   the flame of Zeus of Thunders,
his lightnings, still alive,
blazing where they fell!
Down, Maenads,
fall to the ground in awe! He walks
among the ruins he has made!
He has brought the high house low!
He comes, our god, the son of Zeus!
[*The Chorus falls to the ground in oriental fashion, bowing their heads in the direction of the palace. A hush; then Dionysus appears, lightly picking his way among the rubble. Calm and smiling still, he speaks to the Chorus with a solicitude approaching banter*]
DIONYSUS: What, women of Asia? Were you so overcome with fright

you fell to the ground? I think then you must have seen
how Bacchus jostled the palace of Pentheus. But come, rise.
Do not be afraid.
   CORYPHAEUS: O greatest light of our holy revels,
how glad I am to see your face! Without you I was lost.
   DIONYSUS: Did you despair when they led me away to cast me down
in the darkness of Pentheus' prison?
   CORYPHAEUS: What else could I do?
Where would I turn for help if something happened to you?
But how did you escape that godless man?
   DIONYSUS: With ease.
No effort was required.
   CORYPHAEUS: But the manacles on your wrists?
   DIONYSUS: There I, in turn, humiliated him, outrage for outrage.
He seemed to think that he was charming me but never once
so much as touched my hands. He fed on his desires.
Inside the stable he intended as my jail, instead of me,
he found a bull and tried to rope its knees and hooves.
He was panting desperately, biting his lips with his teeth,
his whole body drenched with sweat, while I sat nearby,
quietly watching. But at that moment Bacchus came,
shook the palace and touched his mother's grave with tongues
of fire. Imagining the palace was in flames,
Pentheus went rushing here and there, shouting to his slaves
to bring him water. Every hand was put to work: in vain.
Then, afraid I might escape, he suddenly stopped short,
drew his sword and rushed to the palace. There, it seems,
Bromius had made a shape, a phantom which resembled me,
within the court. Bursting in, Pentheus thrust and stabbed
at that thing of gleaming air as though he thought it me.
And then, once again, the god humiliated him.
He razed the palace to the ground where it lies, shattered
in utter ruin—his reward for my imprisonment.
At that bitter sight. Pentheus dropped his sword, exhausted
by the struggle. A man, a man, and nothing more,
yet he presumed to wage a war with god.
                                    For my part,

I left the palace quietly and made my way outside.
For Pentheus I care nothing.

But judging from the sound
of tramping feet inside the court, I think our man
will soon be here. What, I wonder, will he have to
say?
But let him bluster. I shall not be touched to rage.
Wise men know constraint: our passions are controlled.

[Enter Pentheus, stamping heavily, from the
ruined palace]

PENTHEUS: But this is mortifying. That stranger,
that man
I clapped in irons, has escaped.

[He catches sight of Dionysus]

What! You?
Well, what do you have to say for yourself?
How did you escape? Answer me.

DIONYSUS: Your anger
walks too heavily. Tread lightly here.

PENTHEUS: How did you escape?

DIONYSUS: Don't you remember?
Someone, I said, would set me free.

PENTHEUS   Someone?
But who? Who is this mysterious someone?

DIONYSUS: [He who makes the grape grow its
clusters for mankind]

PENTHEUS: A splendid contribution,
that.

DIONYSUS: You disparage the gift that is his
chiefest glory.

PENTHEUS: [If I catch him here, he will not escape
my anger.]
I shall order every gate in every tower
to be bolted tight.

DIONYSUS: And so? Couldn't a god
hurdle your city walls?

PENTHEUS: You are clever—very—
but not where it counts.

DIONYSUS: Where it counts the most,
there I am clever.

[Enter a Messenger, a herdsman from Mount
Cithaeron]

But hear this messenger
who brings you news from the mountain of Cithaeron.
We shall remain where we are. Do not fear:
we will not run away.

MESSENGER: Pentheus, king of Thebes,
I come from Cithaeron where the gleaming flakes of
snow
fall on and on forever—

PENTHEUS: Get to the point.
What is your message, man?

MESSENGER: Sir, I have seen
the holy Maenads, the women who ran barefoot
and crazy from the city, and I wanted to report
to you and Thebes what weird fantastic things,

what miracles and more than miracles,
these women do. But may I speak freely
in my own way and words, or make it short?
I fear the harsh impatience of your nature, sire,
too kingly and too quick to anger.

PENTHEUS: Speak freely.
You have my promise: I shall not punish you.
Displeasure with a man who speaks the truth is wrong.
However, the more terrible this tale of yours,
that much more terrible will be the punishment
I impose upon that man who taught our womenfolk
this strange new magic.

MESSENGER: About that hour
when the sun lets loose its light to warm the earth,
our grazing herds of cows had just begun to climb
the path along the mountain ridge. Suddenly
I saw three companies of dancing women,
one led by Autonoë, the second captained
by your mother Agave, while Ino led the third.
There they lay in the deep sleep of exhaustion,
some resting on boughs of fir, others sleeping
where they fell, here and there among the oak
leaves—
but all modestly and soberly, not, as you think,
drunk with wine, nor wandering, led astray
by the music of the flute, to hunt their Aphrodite
through the woods.

But your mother heard the lowing
of our horned herds and, springing to her feet,
gave a great cry to waken them from sleep.
And they too, rubbing the bloom of soft sleep
from their eyes, rose up lightly and straight—
a lovely sight to see: all as one,
the old women and the young and the unmarried girls.
First they let their hair fall loose, down
over their shoulders, and those whose straps had
slipped
fastened their skins of fawn with writhing snakes
that licked their cheeks. Breasts swollen with milk,
new mothers who had left their babies behind at
home
nestled gazelles and young wolves in their arms,
suckling them. Then they crowned their hair with
leaves,
ivy and oak and flowering bryony. One woman
struck her thyrsus against a rock and a fountain
of cool water came bubbling up. Another drove
her fennel in the ground, and where it struck the earth,
at the touch of god, a spring of wine poured out.
Those who wanted milk scratched at the soil
with bare fingers and the white milk came welling up.
Pure honey spurted, streaming, from their wands.
If you had been there and seen these wonders for
yourself,
you would have gone down on your knees and prayed
to the god you now deny.

We cowherds and shepherds
gathered in small groups, wondering and arguing
among ourselves at these fantastic things,
the awful miracles those women did.

But then a city fellow with the knack of words
rose to his feet and said: "All you who live
upon the pastures of the mountain, what do you say?
Shall we earn a little favor with King Pentheus
by hunting his mother Agave out of the revels?"
Falling in with his suggestion, we withdrew
and set ourselves in ambush, hidden by the leaves
among the undergrowth. Then at a signal
all the Bacchae whirled their wands for the revels
to begin. With one voice they cried aloud:
"*O Iacchus! Son of Zeus!*" "*O Bromius!*" they cried
until the beasts and all the mountain seemed
wild with divinity. And when they ran,
everything ran with them.

                      It happened, however,
that Agave ran near the ambush where I lay
concealed. Leaping up, I tried to seize her,
but she gave a cry: "Hounds who run with me,
men are hunting us down! Follow, follow me!
Use your wands for weapons."

                      At this we fled
and barely missed being torn to pieces by the women.
Unarmed, they swooped down upon the herds of cattle
grazing there on the green of the meadow. And then
you could have seen a single woman with bare hands
tear a fat calf, still bellowing with fright,
in two, while others clawed the heifers to pieces.
There were ribs and cloven hooves scattered every-
    where,
and scraps smeared with blood hung from the fir trees.
And bulls, their raging fury gathered in their horns,
lowered their heads to charge, then fell, stumbling
to the earth, pulled down by hordes of women
and stripped of flesh and skin more quickly, sire,
than you could blink your royal eyes. Then,
carried up by their own speed, they flew like birds
across the spreading fields along Asopus' stream
where most of all the ground is good for harvesting.
Like invaders they swooped on Hysiae
and on Erythrae in the foothills of Cithaeron.
Everything in sight they pillaged and destroyed.
They snatched the children from their homes. And
    when
they piled their plunder on their backs, it stayed in
    place,
untied. Nothing, neither bronze nor iron,
fell to the dark earth. Flames flickered
in their curls and did not burn them. Then the vil-
    lagers,
furious at what the women did, took to arms.
And *there,* sire, was something terrible to see.
For the men's spears were pointed and sharp, and yet
drew no blood, whereas the wands the women threw
inflicted wounds. And then the men *ran,*
routed by women! Some god, I say, was with them.
The Bacchae then returned where they had started,
by the springs the god had made, and washed their
    hands
while the snakes licked away the drops of blood
that dabbled their cheeks.

                 Whoever this god may be,
sire, welcome him to Thebes. For he is great
in many other ways as well. It was he,
or so they say, who gave to mortal men
the gift of lovely wine by which our suffering
is stopped. And if there is no god of wine,
there is no love, no Aphrodite either,
nor other pleasure left to men.

    [*Exit* Messenger]
    CORYPHAEUS: I tremble
to speak the words of freedom before the tyrant.
But let the truth be told: there is no god
greater than Dionysus.
    PENTHEUS: Like a blazing fire
this Bacchic violence spreads. It comes too close.
We are disgraced, humiliated in the eyes
of Hellas. This is no time for hesitation.
    [*He turns to an* Attendant]
You there. Go down quickly to the Electran gates
and order out all heavy-armored infantry;
call up the fastest troops among our cavalry,
the mobile squadrons and the archers. We march
against the Bacchae! Affairs are out of hand
when we tamely endure such conduct in our women.
    [*Exit* Attendant]
    DIONYSUS: Pentheus, you do not hear, or else you
        disregard
my words of warning. You have done me wrong,
and yet, in spite of that, I warn you once
again: do not take arms against a god.
Stay quiet here. Bromius will not let you
drive his women from their revels on the mountain.
    PENTHEUS: Don't you lecture me. You escaped
        from prison.
Or shall I punish you again?
    DIONYSUS: If I were you,
I would offer him a sacrifice, not rage
and kick against necessity, a man defying
god.
    PENTHEUS: I shall give your god the sacrifice
that he deserves. His victims will be his women.
I shall make a great slaughter in the woods of Cith-
    aeron.
    DIONYSUS: You will all be routed, shamefully de-
    feated,
when their wands of ivy turn back your shields
of bronze.
    PENTHEUS: It is hopeless to wrestle with this man.
Nothing on earth will make him hold his tongue.
    DIONYSUS: Friend,
you can still save the situation.
    PENTHEUS: How?
By accepting orders from my own slaves?
    DIONYSUS: No.
I undertake to lead the women back to Thebes.
Without bloodshed.
    PENTHEUS: This is some trap.
    DIONYSUS: A trap?
How so, if I save you by my own devices?
    PENTHEUS: I know.

You and they have conspired to establish your rites
forever.
DIONYSUS: True, I *have* conspired—with god.
PENTHEUS: Bring my armor, someone. And *you*
stop talking.
[Pentheus *strides toward the left, but when he is
almost offstage,* Dionysus *calls imperiously to
him*]
DIONYSUS: *Wait!*
Would you like to *see* their revels on the mountain?
PENTHEUS: I would pay a great sum to see that
sight.
DIONYSUS: Why are you so passionately curious?
PENTHEUS: Of
course
I'd be sorry to see them drunk—
DIONYSUS: But for all your sor-
row, you'd like very much to see them?
PENTHEUS: Yes, very
much.
I could crouch beneath the fir trees, out of sight.
DIONYSUS: But if you try to hide, they may track
you down.
PENTHEUS: Your point is well taken. I will go
openly.
DIONYSUS: Shall I lead you there now? Are you
ready to go?
PENTHEUS: The sooner the better. The loss of even
a moment would be disappointing now.
DIONYSUS: First,
however,
you must dress yourself in women's clothes.
PENTHEUS: *What?*
You want *me,* a man, to wear a woman's dress. But
why?
DIONYSUS: If they knew you were a man, they
would kill you instantly.
PENTHEUS: True. You are an old hand at cunning,
I see.
DIONYSUS: Dionysus taught me everything I know.
PENTHESUS: Your advice is to the point. What I
fail to see is what we do.
DIONYSUS: I shall go inside with
you and help you dress.
PENTHEUS: Dress? In a *woman's*
dress, you mean? I would die of shame.
DIONYSUS: Very well.
Then you no longer hanker to see the Maenads?
PENTHEUS: What is this costume I must wear?
DIONYSUS: On
your head
I shall set a wig with long curls.
PENTHEUS: And then?
DIONYSUS: Next, robes to your feet and a net for
your hair.
PENTHEUS: Yes? Go on.
DIONYSUS: Then a thyrsus for your
hand and a skin of dappled fawn.
PENTHEUS: I could not
bear it.

I cannot bring myself to dress in women's clothes.
DIONYSUS: Then you must fight the Bacchae. That
means bloodshed.
PENTHEUS: Right. First we must go and recon-
noiter.
DIONYSUS: Surely a wiser course than that of hunt-
ing bad with worse.
PENTHEUS: But how can we pass through
the city without being seen?
DIONYSUS: We shall take de-
serted streets.
I will lead the way.
PENTHEUS: Any way you like,
provided those women of Bacchus don't jeer at me.
First, however, I shall ponder your advice,
whether to go or not.
DIONYSUS: Do as you please.
I am ready, whatever you decide.
PENTHEUS: Yes.
Either I shall march with my army to the mountain
or act on your advice.
[*Exit* Pentheus *into the palace*]
DIONYSUS   Women, our prey now thrashes
in the net we threw. He shall see the Bacchae
and pay the price with death.
                              O Dionysus,
now action rests with you. And you are near.
Punish this man. But first distract his wits;
bewilder him with madness. For sane of mind
this man would never wear a woman's dress;
but obsess his soul and he will not refuse.
After those threats with which he was so fierce,
I want him made the laughingstock of Thebes,
paraded through the streets, a woman.
                                        Now
I shall go and costume Pentheus in the clothes
which he must wear to Hades when he dies, butch-
ered
by the hands of his mother. He shall come to know
Dionysus, son of Zeus, consummate god,
most terrible, and yet most gentle, to mankind.
[*Exit* Dionysus *into the palace*]
CHORUS:—When shall I dance once more
with bare feet the all-night dances,
tossing my head for joy
in the damp air, in the dew,
as a running fawn might frisk
for the green joy of the wide fields,
free from fear of the hunt,
free from the circling beaters
and the nets of woven mesh
and the hunters hallooing on
their yelping packs? And then, hard pressed,
she sprints with the quickness of wind,
bounding over the marsh, leaping
to frisk, leaping for joy,
gay with the green of the leaves,
to dance for joy in the forest,
to dance where the darkness is deepest,
    where no man is.

—What is wisdom? What gift of the gods
  is held in honor like this:
  to hold your hand victorious
  over the heads of those you hate?
  Honor is precious forever.

—Slow but unmistakable
  the might of the gods moves on.
  It punishes that man,
  infatuate of soul
  and hardened in his pride,
  who disregards the gods.
  The gods are crafty:
  they lie in ambush
  a long step of time
  to hunt the unholy.
  Beyond the old beliefs,
  no thought, no act shall go.
  Small, small is the cost
  to believe in this:
  whatever is god is strong;
  whatever long time has sanctioned,
  that is a law forever;
  the law tradition makes
  is the law of nature.

—What is wisdom? What gift of the gods
  is held in honor like this:
  to hold your hand victorious
  over the heads of those you hate?
  Honor is precious forever.

—Blessèd is he who escapes a storm at sea,
  who comes home to his harbor.
—Blessèd is he who emerges from under affliction.
—In various ways one man outraces another in the
  race for wealth and power.
—Ten thousand men possess ten thousand hopes.
—A few bear fruit in happiness; the others go awry.
—But he who garners day by day the good of life,
  he is happiest. Blessèd is he.

[*Re-enter* Dionysus *from the palace. At the
threshold he turns and calls back to* Pentheus]
  DIONYSUS: Pentheus if you are still so curious to
    see
forbidden sights, so bent on evil still,
come out. Let us see you in your woman's dress,
disguised in Maenad clothes so you may go and spy
upon your mother and her company

[*Enter* Pentheus *from the palace. He wears a
long linen dress which partially conceals his
fawn-skin. He carries a thyrsus in his hand; on
his head he wears a wig with long blond curls
bound by a snood. He is dazed and completely
in the power of the god who has now possessed
him*]
                      Why,
you look exactly like one of the daughters of
Cadmus.
  PENTHEUS: I seem to see two suns blazing in the
    heavens.

And now two Thebes, two cities, and each
with seven gates. And you—you are a bull
who walks before me there. Horns have sprouted
from your head. Have you always been a beast?
But now I see a bull.
  DIONYSUS: It is the god you see.
Though hostile formerly, he now declares a truce
and goes with us. You see what you could not
when you were blind.
  PENTHEUS: [*Coyly primping*] Do I look like any-
    one?
Like Ino or my mother Agave?
  DIONYSUS: So much alike
I almost might be seeing one of them. But look:
one of your curls has come lose from under the
    snood
where I tucked it.
  PENTHEUS: It must have worked loose
when I was dancing for joy and shaking my head.
  DIONYSUS Then let me be your maid and tuck it
    back.
Hold still.
  PENTHEUS: Arrange it. I am in your hands com-
    pletely.
    [Dionysus *tucks the curl back under the snood*]
  DIONYSUS: And now your strap has slipped. Yes,
and your robe hangs askew at the ankles.
  PENTHEUS: [*bending backward to look*] I think so.
At least on my right leg. But on the left the hem
lies straight.
  DIONYSUS: You will think me the best of friends
when you see to your surprise how chaste the Bacchae
    are.
  PENTHEUS: But to be a real Bacchante, should I
    hold
the wand in my right hand? Or this way?
  DIONYSUS   No.
In your right hand. And raise it as you raise
your right foot. I commend your change of heart.
  PENTHEUS: Could I lift Cithaeron up, do you
    think?
Shoulder the cliffs, Bacchae and all?
  DIONYSUS: If you wanted.
Your mind was once unsound, but now you think
as sane men do.
  PENTHEUS: Should we take crowbars with us?
Or should I put my shoulder to the cliffs
and heave them up?
  DIONYSUS: What? And destroy the haunts
of the nymphs, the holy groves where Pan plays
his woodland pipe?
  PENTHEUS: You are right. In any case,
women should not be mastered by brute strength.
I will hide myself beneath the firs instead.
  DIONYSUS: You will find all the ambush you de-
    serve,
creeping up to spy on the Maenads.
  PENTHEUS: Think.
I can see them already, there among the bushes,
mating like birds, caught in the toils of love.

DIONYSUS: Exactly. This is your mission: you go
  to watch.
You may surprise them—or they may surprise you.
  PENTHEUS: Then lead me through the very heart
    of Thebes,
since I, alone of all this city, dare to go.
  DIONYSUS: You and you alone will suffer for your
    city.
A great ordeal awaits you. But you are worthy
of your fate. I shall lead you safely there;
someone else shall bring you back.
  PENTHEUS: Yes, my mother.
  DIONYSUS: An example to all men.
  PENTHEUS: It is for that I go.
  DIONYSUS: You will be carried home—
  PENTHEUS: O luxury!
  DIONYSUS: cradled in your mother's arms.
  PENTHEUS: You will
    spoil me.
  DIONYSUS: I *mean* to spoil you.
  PENTHEUS: I go to my reward.
  DIONYSUS: You are an extraordinary young man,
    and you go
to an extraordinary experience. You shall win
a glory towering to heaven and usurping
god's.
  [*Exit* Pentheus]
    Agave and you daughters of Cadmus,
reach out your hands! I bring this young man
to a great ordeal. The victor? Bromius.
Bromius—and I. The rest the event shall show.
  [*Exit* Dionysus]

CHORUS:—Run to the mountain, fleet hounds of
    madness!
Run, run to the revels of Cadmus' daughters!
Sting them against the man in women's clothes,
the madman who spies on the Maenads, who peers
from behind the rocks, who spies from a vantage!
His mother shall see him first. She will cry
to the Maenads: "Who is this spy who has come
to the mountains to peer at the mountain-revels
of the women of Thebes? What bore him, Bacchae?
This man was born of no woman. Some lioness
gave him birth, some one of the Libyan gorgons!"

—O Justice, principle of order, spirit of custom,
  come! Be manifest; reveal yourself with a sword!
Stab through the throat that godless man,
  the mocker who goes, flouting custom and out-
    raging god!
O Justice, stab the evil earth-born spawn of Echion!

—Uncontrollable, the unbeliever goes,
  in spitting rage, rebellious and amok,
madly assaulting the mysteries of god,
profaning the rites of the mother of god.
Against the unassailable he runs, with rage
obsessed. Headlong he runs to death.
For death the gods exact, curbing by that bit
the mouths of men. They humble us with death
that we remember what we are who are not god,

but men. We run to death. Wherefore, I say,
  accept, accept:
humility is wise; humility is blest.
But what the world calls wise I do not want.
Elsewhere the chase. I hunt another game,
those great, those manifest, those certain goals
achieving which, our mortal lives are blest.
Let these things be the quarry of my chase:
purity; humility; an unrebellious soul,
accepting all. Let me go the customary way,
  the timeless, honored, beaten path of those who
    walk
with reverence and awe beneath the sons of heaven.

—O Justice, principle of order, spirit of custom,
  come! Be manifest; reveal yourself with a sword!
Stab through the throat that godless man,
  the mocker who goes, flouting custom and out-
    raging god!
O Justice, destroy the evil earth-born spawn of
    Echion!

—O Dionysus, reveal yourself a bull! Be manifest,
  a snake with darting heads, a lion breathing fire!
O Bacchus, come! Come with your smile!
Cast your noose about this man who hunts
your Bacchae! Bring him down, trampled
underfoot by the murderous herd of your Maenads!
  [*Enter a* Messenger *from Cithaeron*]
  MESSENGER: How prosperous in Hellas these halls
    once were,
this house founded by Cadmus, the stranger from
    Sidon
who sowed the dragon seed in the land of the snake!
I am a slave and nothing more, yet even so
I mourn the fortunes of this fallen house.
  CORYPHAEUS: What is it?
Is there news of the Bacchae?
  MESSENGER: This is my news:
Pentheus, the son of Echion, is dead.
  CORYPHAEUS: All hail to Bromius! Our god is a
    great god!
  MESSENGER: What is this you say, women? You
    dare to rejoice
at these disasters which destroy this house?
  CORYPHAEUS: I am no Greek. I hail my god
in my own way. No longer need I
shrink with fear of prison.
  MESSENGER: If you suppose this city is so short of
    men—
  CORYPHAEUS: Dionysus, Dionysus, not Thebes,
has power over me.
  MESSENGER: Your feelings might be forgiven. But
    this,
this exultation in disaster—it is not right.
  CORYPHAEUS: Tell us how the mocker died.
How was he killed?
  MESSENGER: There were three of us in all: Pentheus
    and I,
attending my master, and that stranger who volun-
    teered

his services as guide. Leaving behind us
the last outlying farms of Thebes, we forded
the Asopus and struck into the barren scrubland
of Cithaeron.

               There in a grassy glen we halted,
unmoving, silent, without a word,
so we might see but not be seen. From that vantage,
in a hollow cut from the sheer rock of the cliffs,
a place where water ran and the pines grew dense
with shade, we saw the Maenads sitting, their hands
busily moving at their happy tasks. Some
wound the stalks of their tattered wands with tendrils
of fresh ivy; others, frisking like fillies
newly freed from the painted bridles, chanted
in Bacchic songs, responsively.

                    But Pentheus—
unhappy man—could not quite see the companies
of women. "Stranger," he said, "from where I stand,
I cannot see these counterfeited Maenads.
But if I climbed that towering fir that overhangs
the banks, then I could see their shameless orgies
better."

              And now the stranger worked a miracle.
Reaching for the highest branch of a great fir,
he bent it down, down, down to the dark earth,
till it was curved the way a taut bow bends
or like a rim of wood when forced about the circle
of a wheel. Like that he forced that mountain fir
down to the ground. No mortal could have done it.
Then he seated Pentheus at the highest tip
and with his hands let the trunk rise straightly up,
slowly and gently, lest it throw its rider.
And the tree rose, towering to heaven, with my master
huddled at the top. And now the Maenads saw him
more clearly than he saw them. But barely had they
   seen,
when the stranger vanished and there came a great
   voice
out of heaven—Dionysus', it must have been—
crying: "Women, I bring you the man who has
   mocked
at you and me and at our holy mysteries.
Take vengeance upon him." And as he spoke
a flash of awful fire bound earth and heaven.
The high air hushed, and along the forest glen
the leaves hung still; you could hear no cry of beasts.
The Bacchae heard that voice but missed its words,
and leaping up, they stared, peering everywhere.
Again that voice. And now they knew his cry,
the clear command of god. And breaking loose
like startled doves, through grove and torrent,
over jagged rocks, they flew, their feet maddened
by the breath of god. And when they saw my master
perching in his tree, they climbed a great stone
that towered opposite his perch and showered him
with stones and javelins of fir, while the others
hurled their wands. And yet they missed their target,
poor Pentheus in his perch, barely out of reach
of their eager hands, treed, unable to escape.

Finally they splintered branches from the oaks
and with those bars of wood tried to lever up the tree
by prying at the roots. But every effort failed.
Then Agave cried out: "Maenads, make a circle
about the trunk and grip it with your hands.
Unless we take this climbing beast, he will reveal
the secrets of the god." With that, thousands of hands
tore the fir tree from the earth, and down, down
from his high perch fell Pentheus, tumbling
to the ground, sobbing and screaming as he fell,
for he knew his end was near. His own mother,
like a priestess with her victim, fell upon him
first. But snatching off his wig and snood
so she would recognize his face, he touched her
   cheeks,
screaming, "*No, no, Mother! I am Pentheus,
your own son, the child you bore to Echion!
Pity me, spare me, Mother! I have done a wrong,
but do not kill your own son for my offense.*"
But she was foaming at the mouth, and her crazed
   eyes
rolling with frenzy. She was mad, stark mad,
possessed by Bacchus. Ignoring his cries of pity,
she seized his left arm at the wrist; then, planting
her foot upon his chest, she pulled, wrenching away
the arm at the shoulder—not by her own strength,
for the god had put inhuman power in her hands.
Ino, meanwhile, on the other side, was scratching off
his flesh. Then Autonoë and the whole horde
of Bacchae swarmed upon him. Shouts everywhere,
he screaming with what little breath was left,
they shrieking in triumph. One tore off an arm,
another a foot still warm in its shoe. His ribs
were clawed clean of flesh and every hand
was smeared with blood as they played ball with
scraps of Pentheus' body.

               The pitiful remains lie scattered,
one piece among the sharp rocks, others
lying lost among the leaves in the depths
of the forest. His mother, picking up his head,
impaled it on her wand. She seems to think it is
some mountain lion's head which she carries in triumph
through the thick of Cithaeron. Leaving her sisters
at the Maenad dances, she is coming here, gloating
over her grisly prize. She calls upon Bacchus:
he is her "fellow-huntsman," "comrade of the chase,
crowned with victory." But all the victory
she carries home is her own grief.

                       Now,
before Agave returns, let me leave
this scene of sorrow. Humility,
a scene of reverence before the sons of heaven—
of all the prizes that a mortal man might win,
these, I say, are wisest: these are best.
   [*Exit* Messenger]

CHORUS:—We dance to the glory of Bacchus!
We dance to the death of Pentheus,
the death of the spawn of the dragon!

He dressed in woman's dress;
he took the lovely thyrsus;
it waved him down to death,
        led by a bull to Hades.
Hail, Bacchae! Hail, women of Thebes!
Your victory is fair, fair the prize,
        this famous prize of grief!
Glorious the game! To fold your child
in your arms, streaming with his blood!

CORYPHAEUS: But look: there comes Pentheus'
        mother, Agave,
running wild-eyed toward the palace.
                        —Welcome,
welcome to the reveling band of the god of joy!

[Enter Agave *with other* Bacchantes. *She is
covered with blood and carries the head of*
Pentheus *impaled upon her thyrsus*]

AGAVE: Bacchae of Asia—
CHORUS: Speak, speak.
AGAVE: We bring this branch to the palace,
this fresh-cut spray from the mountains.
Happy was the hunting.
CHORUS: I see.
I welcome our fellow-reveler of god.
AGAVE: The whelp of a wild mountain lion,
and snared by me without a noose.
Look, look at the prize I bring.
CHORUS: Where was he caught?
AGAVE: On Cithaeron—
CHORUS: On Cithaeron?
AGAVE: Our prize was killed.
CHORUS: Who killed him?
AGAVE: I struck him first.
The Maenads call me "Agave the blest."
CHORUS: And then?
AGAVE: Cadmus'—
CHORUS: Cadmus'?
AGAVE: Daughters.
After me, they reached the prey.
After me. Happy was the hunting.
CHORUS: Happy indeed.
AGAVE: Then share my glory,
share the feast.
CHORUS: Share, unhappy woman?
AGAVE: See, the whelp is young and tender.
Beneath the soft mane of its hair,
the down is blooming on the cheeks.
CHORUS: With that mane he *looks* a beast.
AGAVE: Our god is wise. Cunningly, cleverly,
Bacchus the hunter lashed the Maenads
against his prey.
CHORUS: Our king is a hunter.
AGAVE: You praise me now?
CHORUS: I praise you.
AGAVE: The men of Thebes—
CHORUS: And Pentheus, your
        son?
AGAVE: Will praise his mother. She caught
a great quarry, this lion's cub.
CHORUS: Extraordinary catch.

AGAVE: Extraordinary skill.
CHORUS: You are proud?
AGAVE: Proud and happy.
I have won the trophy of the chase,
a great prize, manifest to all.
CORYPHAEUS: Then, poor woman, show the citizens
        of Thebes
this great prize, this trophy you have won
in the hunt.

[Agave *proudly exhibits her thyrsus with the
head of* Pentheus *impaled upon the point*]

AGAVE: You citizens of this towered city,
men of Thebes, behold the trophy of your women's
hunting! *This* is the quarry of our chase, taken
not with nets nor spears of bronze but by the white
and delicate hands of women. What are they worth,
your boastings now and all that uselessness
your armor is, since we, with our bare hands,
captured this quarry and tore its bleeding body
limb from limb?
                —But where is my father Cadmus?
He should come. And my son. Where is Pentheus?
Fetch him. I will have him set his ladder up
against the wall and, there upon the beam,
nail the head of this wild lion I have killed
as a trophy of my hunt.

[Enter Cadmus, *followed by* Attendants *who bear
upon a bier the dismembered body of* Pen-
theus]

CADMUS: Follow me, attendants.
Bear your dreadful burden in and set it down,
there before the palace.

[*The* Attendants *set down the bier*]
                        This was Pentheus
whose body, after long and weary searchings
I painfully assembled from Cithaeron's glens
where it lay, scattered in shreds, dismembered
throughout the forest, no two pieces
in a single place.
                Old Teiresias and I
had returned to Thebes from the orgies on the moun-
        tain
before I learned of this atrocious crime
my daughters did. And so I hurried back
to the mountain to recover the body of this boy
murdered by the Maenads. There among the oaks
I found Aristaeus' wife, the mother of Actaeon,
Autonoë, and with her Ino, both
still stung with madness. But Agave, they said,
was on her way to Thebes, still possessed.
And what they said was true, for there she is,
and not a happy sight.
AGAVE: Now, Father,
yours can be the proudest boast of living men.
For you are now the father of the bravest daughters
in the world. All of your daughters are brave,
but I above the rest. I have left my shuttle
at the loom; I raised my sight to higher things—
to hunting animals with my bare hands.
                                You see?

Here in my hands I hold the quarry of my chase,
a trophy for our house. Take it, Father, take it.
Glory in my skill and invite your friends to share
the feast of triumph. For you are blest, Father,
by this great deed I have done.

CADMUS: This is a grief
so great it knows no size. I cannot look.
This is the awful murder your hands have done.
This, this is the noble victim you have slaughtered
to the gods. And to share a feast like this
you now invite all Thebes and me?

                              O gods,
how terribly I pity you and then myself.
Justly—too, too justly—has lord Bromius,
this god of our own blood, destroyed us all,
every one.

AGAVE: How scowling and crabbed is old age
in men. I hope my son takes after his mother
and wins, as she has done, the laurels of the chase
when he goes hunting with the younger men of
    Thebes.
But all my son can do is quarrel with god.
He should be scolded, Father, and you are the one
who should scold him. Yes, someone call him out
so he can see his mother's triumph.

CADMUS: Enough. No more.
When you realize the horror you have done,
you shall suffer terribly. But if with luck
your present madness lasts until you die,
you will seem to have, not having, happiness.

AGAVE: Why do you reproach me? Is there some-
    thing wrong?

CADMUS: First raise your eyes to the heavens.

AGAVE: There.
But why?

CADMUS: Does it look the same as it did before?
Or has it changed?

AGAVE: It seems—somehow—clearer,
brighter than it was before.

CADMUS: Do you still feel
the same flurry inside you?

AGAVE: The same—flurry?
No, I feel—somehow—calmer. I feel as though—
my mind were somehow—changing.

CADMUS: Can you still
    hear me?
Can you answer clearly?

AGAVE: No. I have forgotten
what we were saying, Father.

CADMUS: Who was your husband?

AGAVE: Echion—a man, they said, born of the
    dragon seed.

CADMUS: What was the name of the child you bore
    your husband?

AGAVE: Pentheus.

CADMUS: And whose head do you hold in
    your hands?

AGAVE: [*averting her eyes*] A lion's head—or so the
    hunters told me.

CADMUS: Look directly at it. Just a quick glance.

AGAVE: What is it? What am I holding in my
    hands?

CADMUS: Look more closely still. Study it care-
    fully.

AGAVE: *No!* O gods, I see the greatest grief there is.

CADMUS: Does it look like a lion now?

AGAVE: No, no. It is—
Pentheus' head—I hold—

CADMUS: And mourned by me
before you ever knew.

AGAVE: But *who* killed him?
Why am *I* holding him?

CADMUS: O savage truth,
what a time to come!

AGAVE: For god's sake, speak.
My heart is beating with terror.

CADMUS: *You* killed him.
You and your sisters.

AGAVE: But where was he killed?
Here at home? Where?

CADMUS: He was killed on Cithaeron,
there where the hounds tore Actaeon to pieces.

AGAVE: But why? Why had Pentheus gone to
    Cithaeron?

CADMUS: He went to your revels to mock the god.

AGAVE: But *we*—
what were we doing on the mountain?

CADMUS: You were mad.
The whole city was possessed.

AGAVE: Now, now I see:
Dionysus has destroyed us all.

CADMUS: You outraged him.
You denied that he was truly god.

AGAVE: Father,
where is my poor boy's body now?

CADMUS: There it is.
I gathered the pieces with great difficulty.

AGAVE: Is his body entire? Has he been laid out
    well?

CADMUS: [All but the head. The rest is mutilated
horribly.]

AGAVE: But why should Pentheus suffer for my
    crime?

CADMUS: He, like you, blasphemed the god. And so
the god has brought us all to ruin at one blow,
you, your sisters, and this boy. All our house
the god has utterly destroyed and, with it,
me. For I have no sons left, no male heir:
and I have lived only to see this boy,
this branch of your own body, most horribly
and foully killed.

        [*He turns and addresses the corpse*]
                    —To you my house looked up.
Child, you were the stay of my house; you were
my daughter's son. Of you this city stood in awe.
No one who once had seen your face dared outrage
the old man, or if he did, you punished him.
Now I must go, a banished and dishonored man—
I, Cadmus the great, who sowed the soldiery
of Thebes and harvested a great harvest. My son,

dearest to me of all men—for even dead,
I count you still the man I love the most—
never again will your hand touch my chin;
no more, child, will you hug me and call me
"Grandfather" and say, "Who is wronging you?
Does anyone trouble you or vex your heart, old man?
Tell me, Grandfather, and I will punish him."
No, now there is grief for me; the mourning
for you; pity for your mother; and for her sisters,
sorrow.

      If there is still any mortal man
who despises or defies the gods, let him look
on this boy's death and believe in the gods.
    CORYPHAEUS: Cadmus, I pity you. Your daughter's
      son
has died as he deserved, and yet his death
bears hard on you.

    [*At this point there is a break in the manuscript of
nearly fifty lines. The following speeches of Agave
and Coryphaeus and the first part of Dionysus'
speech have been conjecturally reconstructed from
fragments and later material which made use of the
Bacchae. Lines which can plausibly be assigned to the
lacuna are otherwise not indicated. My own inventions are designed, not to complete the speeches, but
to effect a transition between the fragments, and are
bracketed.—*TRANS.]

    AGAVE: O Father, now you can see
how everything has changed. I am in anguish now,
tormented, who walked in triumph minutes past,
exulting in my kill. And that prize I carried home
with such pride was my own curse. Upon these hands
I bear the curse of my son's blood. How then
with these accursed hands may I touch his body?
How can I, accursed with such a curse, hold him
to my breast? O gods, what dirge can I sing
[that there might be] a dirge [for every]
broken limb?

. . . .

      Where is a shroud to cover up his
    corpse?
O my child, what hands will give you proper care
unless with my own hands I lift my curse

    [*She lifts up one of* Pentheus' *limbs and asks the
help of* Cadmus *in piecing the body together.
She mourns each piece separately before replac-
ing it on the bier*]

Come, Father. We must restore his head
to this unhappy boy. As best we can, we shall make
him whole again.

        —O dearest, dearest face!
Pretty boyish mouth! Now with this veil
I shroud your head, gathering with loving care
these mangled bloody limbs, this flesh I brought
to birth

. . . .

    CORYPHAEUS: Let this scene teach those [who see
    these things:

Dionysus is the son] of Zeus
    [*Above the palace* Dionysus *appears in epiphany*]
    DIONYSUS: [I am Dionysus,
the son of Zeus, returned to Thebes, revealed,
a god to men.] But the men [of Thebes] blasphemed
    me.
They slandered me; they said I came of mortal man,
and not content with speaking blasphemies,
[they dared to threaten my person with violence.]
These crimes this people whom I cherished well
did from malice to their benefactor. Therefore,
I now disclose the sufferings in store for them.
Like [enemies], they shall be driven from this city
to other lands; there, submitting to the yoke
of slavery, they shall wear out wretched lives,
captives of war, enduring much indignity.
    [*He turns to the corpse of* Pentheus]
This man has found the death which he deserved,
torn to pieces among the jagged rocks.
You are my witnesses: he came with outrage;
he attempted to chain my hands, abusing me
[and doing what he should least of all have done.]
And therefore he has rightly perished by the hands
of those who should the least of all have murdered
    him.
What he suffers, he suffers justly.

           Upon you,
Agave, and on your sisters I pronounce this doom:
you shall leave this city in expiation
of the murder you have done. You are unclean,
and it would be a sacrilege that murderers
should remain at peace beside the graves [of those
whom they have killed].
    [*He turns to* Cadmus]

. . . .

      Next I shall disclose the trials
which await this man. You, Cadmus, shall be changed
to a serpent, and your wife, the child of Ares,
immortal Harmonia, shall undergo your doom,
a serpent too. With her, it is your fate
to go a journey in a car drawn on by oxen,
leading behind you a great barbarian host.
For thus decrees the oracle of Zeus.
With a host so huge its numbers cannot be counted,
you shall ravage many cities; but when your army
plunders the shrine of Apollo, its homecoming
shall be perilous and hard. Yet in the end
the god Ares shall save Harmonia and you
and bring you both to live among the blest.
    So say I, born of no mortal father,
Dionysus, true son of Zeus. If then,
when you would not, you had muzzled your madness,
you should have an ally now in the son of Zeus.
    CADMUS: We implore you, Dionysus. We have
      done wrong.
    DIONYSUS: Too late. When there was time, you did
      not know me.
    CADMUS: We have learned. But your sentence is
      too harsh.

DIONYSUS: I am a god. I was blasphemed by you.

CADMUS: Gods should be exempt from human passions.

DIONYSUS: Long ago my father Zeus ordained these things.

AGAVE: It is fated, Father. We must go.

DIONYSUS: Why then delay?
For you must go.

CADMUS: Child, to what dreadful end
have we all come, you and your wretched sisters
and my unhappy self. An old man, I must go
to live a stranger among barbarian peoples, doomed
to lead against Hellas a motley foreign army.
Transformed to serpents, I and my wife,
Harmonia, the child of Ares, we must captain
spearsmen against the tombs and shrines of Hellas.
Never shall my sufferings end; not even
over Acheron shall I have peace.

AGAVE: [Embracing Cadmus] O Father,
to be banished, to live without you!

CADMUS: Poor child,
like a white swan warding its weak old father,
why do you clasp those white arms about my neck?

AGAVE: But banished! Where shall I go?

CADMUS: I do not know,
my child. Your father can no longer help you.

AGAVE: Farewell, my home! City, farewell.
O bridal bed, banished I go,
in misery, I leave you now.

CADMUS: Go, poor child, seek shelter in Aristaeus'
house.

AGAVE: I pity you, Father.

CADMUS: And I pity you, my child,
and I grieve for your poor sisters. I pity them.

AGAVE: Terribly has Dionysus brought
disaster down upon this house.

DIONYSUS: I was terribly blasphemed,
my name dishonored in Thebes.

AGAVE: Farewell, Father.

CADMUS: Farewell to you, unhappy
child.
Fare well. But you shall find your faring hard.
   [Exit Cadmus]

AGAVE: Lead me, guides, where my sisters wait,
poor sisters of my exile. Let me go
where I shall never see Cithaeron more,
where that accursed hill may not see me,
where I shall find no trace of thyrsus!
   That I leave to other Bacchae.
   [Exit Agave with Attendants]

CHORUS: The gods have many shapes.
The gods bring many things
to their accomplishment.
And what was most expected
has not been accomplished.
But god has found his way
for what no man expected.
   So ends the play.

Seneca and Thyestes

Seneca was born about 4 B.C. in Cordova, Spain (then a Roman province). He was the son of a *rhetor,* or teacher of oratory of a well-to-do and distinguished family. In his infancy he was taken to Rome and later trained there for a career in oratory and politics. By the age of thirty he held the high office of *quaestor,* and during the reigns of Caligula and Claudius became a senator. He earned the more or less mad Emperor Caligula's jealousy, and in the first year of the next emperor's reign he was actually banished to Corsica on a dubious charge of adultery (he was actually a chronically sick individual and an unlikely candidate for the career of an amorist), and spent eight years in exile. In A.D. 49 he was recalled to Rome by Agrippina, Nero's mother, as tutor to her young son. Yet five years later, when Nero succeeded to the throne, he had his mother assassinated and Seneca was apparently involved in the *coup d'état.* Three years later, however, he was out of favor with his fickle master, and Nero, charging him with conspiracy against the crown in A.D. 65, ordered him to take his own life.

So, although Seneca advocated our leading a philosopher's life, he practiced a careerist's, acquiring great wealth and political influence at a considerable cost of honesty and integrity. His nondramatic career involved him both as a moralist and a pragmatist, both as a thinker who reflected on men's folly and as a man of the world who shared in their illusions and quest for power and influence. In his own time, and during the entire classic period, his fame rested on his reputation as a philosopher, essayist, wit, and rhetorician. And no single distinction became him so much as that capacity for putting a pithy style at the service of whatever he thought, felt, or imagined; an ability which made him the exemplary author of Rome's "Silver Age" of literature. Seneca's distinction as a "playwright" is mainly a creation of the Renaissance period in Italy, France, and England. But it was undoubtedly the vigor of his lines that could make his works eminently suitable for recitation. Even if they do not actually constitute plays for the stage because of a deficiency of visible action and an enormous ballast of ornate verbiage, they have the power to command attention. Well delivered, they must have drawn applause from the Roman gentry and intelligensia that was very probably Seneca's sole audience. The repartee of the characters is often especially effective. "Line-for-line dialogue in the tragedies of Seneca," writes Moses Hadas in his *History of Latin Literature,* "is like a game of battling apothegms back and forth, and the reader finds his head oscillating from one performer to the other as in a game of ping-pong."

For the Renaissance, represented for us by Shakespeare's generation, this verbal prowess was not the least of Seneca's attractions. It set an example to Elizabethan playwrights which, while undoubtedly vitiating dramatic style by making it "full of sound and fury," also encouraged verbal exertions that gave tragic dignity and poetic splendor to the villains and heroes of Renaissance drama. But the result could border on the absurd and invite the inflation of speech that Shakespeare parodies so well in *Hamlet:*

'The rugged Pyrrhus, he whose sable arms,
Black as his purpose, did the night resemble
When he lay couched in the ominous horse,
Hath now this dread and black complexion smear'd
With heraldry more dismal. Head to foot
Now is he total gules; horribly trick'd
With blood of fathers, mothers, daughters, sons,
Bak'd and impasted with the parching streets,
That lend a tyrannous and damned light
To their lord's murther. Roasted in wrath and fire,
And thus o'ersized with coagulate gore,
With eyes like carbuncles, the hellish Pyrrhus
Old grandsire Priam seeks.'

Forceful rhetoric can issue from a powerful mind or spirit and Seneca, as we've seen, was not the least of men. But for the rhetoric to mount in power, there must be an incentive in the subject matter or a justification in the state of mind of the speaker. Seneca's characters in his extant work are all tempestuous men and women caught in situations of extreme crisis and consumed by a ruling passion. If Seneca cannot be said to have written plays in the full, true sense of the term, he cannot be denied a remarkable talent for creating dramatic characters and steeping them in a dramatic atmosphere rarely less than sulphurous. He did not, it is true, invent his *dramatis personae* but drew them after the models he found in Greek tragedy and epic poetry. Most of them have for their source plays by Euripides, although they lack the latter's profundity, not to mention Sophocles' balanced dramaturgy and Aeschylus' spiritual and moral grandeur.

But there can be no question of his having made the most of his characters' passions and horrors for the purpose of dramatic effect. "Wrenching and straining and tormenting of the emotions is certainly characteristic of the tragedies of Seneca," writes Professor Hadas. If they hover, moreover, between tragedy and melodrama, they are not alone in this respect; so do many Elizabethan dramatic characters, including some of the most effective of them such as Othello's bane Iago and Gloucester's bastard son Edward. To use a term favored by Francis Fergusson, Seneca had a "histrionic imagination," although it was a transparently frustrated one as a result of the disappearance of serious drama from the Roman theatre. And to this imagination, he added a high-tragic sensibility, for he understood, as any Stoic philosopher would, that the cause of suffering lies in man's insatiable will and uncontrolled passions.

Ten extant dramas were attributed to Seneca during the Renaissance,[1] but *Thyestes* is considered the most directly influential in the English theatre. It shares with the other Senecan dramas an extremely rhetorical style, a revenge motif, a reveling in horror that seems almost gratuitous but "distanced" by the fact that the horrible deeds are not onstage events, and exhibition of extreme passions of heroic size or, as Moses Hadas has put it, a sense of character "permanently at the top pitch of emotional excitement volubly expressed." It also contains a Senecan "Ghost," the main character's guilty ancestor Tantalus. He is brought out of the pagan hell of Tartarus and urged on by a Fury to drive his descendant Atreus to commit an outrageous crime against his brother Thyestes that is the subject of Seneca's tragedy. This cannibalistic vengeance will then lead to another crime when Thyestes' son Aegisthus will connive in the murder of Atreus' famous son Agamemnon by his wife Clytemnestra, the subject of Aeschylus' tragedy Agamemnon (pages 9–29).

In *Thyestes* we also encounter a typical Senecan central character, Atreus, who in possessing an all-consuming hatred, brings a perverse grandeur to his unspeakable criminality; as do many Elizabethan and Jacobean heroes and antagonists such as the Duchess of Malfi's relentless brothers. (See pages 324–360). We also find in *Thyestes* the typically Senecan nonstrophic chorus which serves to separate the acts and

provides the conventional five-act division traced to Seneca. The Chorus is arranged solely for grandiose recitation rather than for the singing and dancing associated with Greek tragedy. Its purpose is the delivery of Stoic doctrine in the point-making aphoristic manner of the *sententiae* Seneca employed in his essays. (The Elizabethans called them "sentences" in the special sense of terse one-line generalizations consisting of well-turned sayings or apothegms.) They contain reflections on the certainty of death, the mutability of fortune, the instability of power, and the happiness of a tranquil, obscure life free from ambition.

Another Senecan figure is the Messenger, who narrates the gory events not really executed on the stage and describes them graphically. The efficient rhetoric of this personage at climactic points in the play, combined with the dialogue of the principal characters, is the very lifeblood, as well as detritus, of the work—as integral to it "as music to an operatic libretto" since "the strained language and strained emotions suit and support each other."[2]

Seneca's *Thyestes,* first translated into English in 1560 by Jasper Heywood, is almost total theatre in effect, even without the usually essential attribute of direct adaptation to stage technique. It is *theatrical* in situation and feeling as well as atmosphere, and the Elizabethan reader could find it overpowering. That in the absence of first-hand knowledge of the Greek masterpieces of Aeschylus, Sophocles, and Euripides the English authors should have turned to Seneca for example, that they tried to emulate his dialogue and monologues for better (and worse) and that they borrowed his Ghost (who plays an important role in both Thomas Kyd's *The Spanish Tragedy* and in Shakespeare's *Hamlet*) need not, therefore, surprise us.[3]

---

[1] The famous Elizabethan translations, edited by Thomas Newton, bore the title of *Seneca His Tenne Tragedies;* the versions were made by six different translators from 1559 to 1581. Among the nine now credited to his authorship, are *The Trojan Women, Medea, Phaedra, Oedipus, Agamemnon,* and *Thyestes.*

[2] Moses Hadas, "Introduction" in Seneca's *Thyestes.* New York, The Liberal Arts Press, 1950, p. vii.

[3] For Seneca's influence see especially F. L. Lucas, *Seneca and Elizabethan Tragedy.* Cambridge: Cambridge University Press, 1922, and T. S. Eliot's Introduction to *Seneca His Tenne Tragedies,* in the Tudor series, London and New York, Alfred A. Knopf, 1924.

THYESTES

By Seneca

RENDERED INTO ENGLISH VERSE BY ELLA ISABEL HARRIS; REVISED BY JOHN GASSNER

DRAMATIS PERSONÆ

ATREUS
THYESTES
THE GHOST: *Spirit of the Elder Tantalus*
PLISTHENES
TANTALUS [*Named after the ghostly grandfather Tantalus*] } *Sons of Thyestes*

A BOY
MEGÆRA [*The Fury who accompanies The Ghost*]
MESSENGER
SERVANT
CHORUS OF MEN OF MYCENÆ

SCENE—*Before the Palace of Atreus.*

ACT I. SCENE I.

Ghost: *Spirit of* Tantalus, Megæra.

SPIRIT: Who drags me from my place among the shades,
Where with dry lips I seek the flying waves?
What hostile god again shows Tantalus
His hated palace? Has some worse thing come
Than thirst amid the waters or the pangs
Of ever-gnawing hunger? Must the stone,
The slippery burden borne by Sisyphus,
Weigh down my shoulders, or Ixion's wheel
Carry my limbs around in its swift course,
Or must I fear Tityus' punishment?
Stretched in a lofty cave he feeds dun birds
Upon his vitals which they tear away,
And night renews whatever day destroyed,
And thus he offers them full feast again.
Against what evil have I been reserved?
Stern judge of Hades, whoever you are
Who mete out to the dead due penalties,
If something can be added more than pain,
Seek that at which the grim custodian
Of this dark prison must himself feel fear,
Something from which sad Acheron shall shrink,
Before whose horror I myself must fear;
For many sprung from me, who shall outsin
Their house, who, daring deeds undared by me,
Make me seem innocent, already come.
Whatever impious deed this realm may lack
My house will bring; while Pelops' line remains,
Minos shall never be unoccupied.
   MEGÆRA: Go, hated shade, and drive thy sin-
      stained home
To madness; let the sword try every crime,
And pass from hand to hand; nor let there be
Limit to rage and shame; let fury blind
Urge on their thoughts; let parents' hearts be hard
Through madness, long iniquity be heaped
Upon the children, let them never know

Leisure to hate old crimes, let new ones rise,
Many in one; let sin while punished grow;
From the proud brothers let the throne depart,
Then let it call the exiled home again.
Let the dark fortunes of a violent house
Among unstable kings be brought to naught.
Let evil fortune on the mighty fall,
The wretched come to power; let chance toss
The kingdom with an ever-changing tide
Wherever it will. Exiled because of crime,
When god would give them back their native land
Let them through crime reach home, and let them
      hate
Themselves as others hate them. Let them deem
No crime forbidden when their passions rage;
Let brother greatly fear his brother's hand,
Let parents fear their sons, and let the sons
Feel fear of parents, children wretched die,
More wretchedly be born; let wife rebel
Against her husband, wars pass over seas,
And every land be wet with blood poured forth;
Let lust, victorious, over great kings exult
And basest deeds be easy in the house;
Let right and truth and justice be no more
Between brothers. Let not heaven be immune—
Why shine the stars within the firmament
To be a source of beauty to the world?
Let night be different, day no more exist.
Overthrow thy household gods, bring hatred, death,
Wild slaughter, with thy spirit fill the house,
Deck the high portals, let the gates be green
With laurel, fires for thy advent meet
Shall glow, crimes worse than Thracian[1] shall be
      done.
Why idle lies the uncle's stern right hand?
Thyestes has not yet bewept his sons;
When will they be destroyed? Now, even now
Upon the fire the brazen pot shall boil,
The members shall be broken into parts,
The father's hearth with children's blood be wet,—
The feast shall be prepared. Thou wilt not come

---

[1] The crimes perpetrated in the barbaric northern region of Greece, Thrace.

741

Guest at a feast whose crime is new to thee:
To-day we give thee freedom; satisfy
Thy hunger at those tables, end thy fast.
Blood mixed with wine shall in thy sight be drunk,
Food have I found that even thou wouldst shun.
Stay! Whither dost thou rush?
    SPIRIT: To stagnant pools,
Rivers and waters ever slipping by,
To the fell trees that will not give me food.
Let me go hence to my dark prison-house,
Let me, if all too little seems my woe,
Seek other shores; within thy channels' midst
And by thy floods of fire hemmed about,
O Phlegethon, permit me to be left.
O ye who suffer by the fates' decree
Sharp penalties, O thou who, filled with fear,
Within the hallowed cave dost wait the fall
Of the impending mountain, thou who dreadst
The ravening lion's open jaws, the hand
Of cruel Furies that encompass thee,
Thou who, half burned, dost feel their torch applied,
Hear ye the voice of Tantalus who knows:
Love ye your penalties! Ah, woe is me,
When shall I be allowed to flee to hell?
    MEGÆRA: First into dread confusion throw thy
        house,
Bring with thee battle and the sword and love,
Strike thou the king's wild heart with frantic rage.
    SPIRIT: It is right that I should suffer punishment,
But not that I myself be punishment.
Like a death-dealing vapor must I go
Out of the riven earth, or like a plague
Most grievous to the people, or a pest
Widespread, I bring my children's children crime.
Great father of the gods, our father too—
However much our sonship cause thee shame—
Although my too loquacious tongue should pay
Due punishment for sin, yet will I speak:
Stain not, my kinsmen, holy hands with blood;
The altars with unholy sacrifice
Pollute not. I will stay and ward off crime.
    [To Megæra] Why dost thou terrify me with thy
        torch,
And fiercely threaten with thy writhing snakes?
Why dost thou stir the hunger in my reins?
My heart is burning with the fire of thirst,
My parched veins feel the flame.
    MEGÆRA: Through all thy house
Scatter this fury; thus shall they, too, rage,
And, mad with anger, thirst by turns to drink
Each other's blood. Thy house thy coming feels
And trembles at thy execrable touch.
It is enough; depart to hell's dark caves
And to thy well-known river. Earth is sad
And burdened by thy presence. Backward forced,
Seest thou not the waters leave the streams,
How all the banks are dry, how fiery winds
Drive the few scattered clouds? The foliage pales,
And every branch is bare, the fruits are fled.
And where the Isthmus has been wont to sound

With the near waters, roaring on each side,
And cutting off the narrow strip of land,
Far from the shore is heard the sound remote.
Now Lerna's waters have been backward drawn,
Sacred Alpheus' stream is seen no more,
Cithæron's summit stands untouched with snow,
And Argos fears again its former thirst.
Lo, Titan's self[2] is doubtful—shall he drive
His horses upward, bring again the day?
It will but rise to die.

SCENE II.

    CHORUS: If any god still cherish love for Greece,
Argos, and Pisa for her chariots famed,
If any cherishes the Isthmian realm,
And the twin havens, and the parted seas,
If any love Taygetus' bright snows
That shine afar, which northern winter lays
Upon its highest summits and the breath
Of summer trade winds welcome to the sails
Melts, let him whom Alpheus' ice-cold stream
Touches, well known for his Olympic course,
Wield the calm influence of his heavenly power,
Nor suffer crimes in constant series come.
Let not a grandson, readier for that crime
Even than his father's father, follow him,
Nor let the father's error please the sons.
Let thirsty Tantalus' base progeny,
Wearied at length, give up their fierce attempts;
Enough of crime! No more is right of worth,
And common wrongs of little moment seem;
The traitor Myrtilus betrayed his lord
And slew him—by such faith as he had shown
Himself dragged down, he gave the sea a name;
To ships on the Ægean never tale
Was better known. Met by the cruel sword,
Even while he ran to gain his father's kiss,
The little son was slain; he early fell
A victim to the hearth, by thy right hand,
O Tantalus, cut off that thou mightst spread
Such feasts before the gods. Eternal thirst
And endless famine followed on the feast;
Nor can a worthier punishment be found
For savage feast like that. With empty maw
Stands weary Tantalus, above his head
Hangs ready food, more swift to take its flight
Than Phineus' birds[3]; on every side it hangs;
The tree beneath the burden of its fruit
Bending and trembling, shuns his open mouth;
He though so eager, brooking no delay,
Yet oft deceived, neglects to touch the tree,
And drops his head and presses close his lips,
And shuts his hunger in behind clenched teeth.
The ripe fruit taunts him from the languid boughs,

---

[2] The sun itself. The reference is to Hyperion, the Titan.
[3] Phineus, blinded by Zeus for his cruelty, was further
punished by having his food snatched away by the harpies
whenever he was about to eat.

And whets his hunger till it urges him
To stretch again his hand oft stretched in vain.
Then the whole harvest of the bended boughs
Is lifted out of reach. Thirst rises then,
More hard to bear than hunger, when his blood
Is hot within him and his eyes aflame;
Wretched he stands striving to touch his lips
To the near waters, but the stream retreats,
Forsakes him when he strives to follow it,
And leaves him in dry sands; his eager lips
Drink but the dust.

ACT II. SCENE I.

[Atreus; Slave, *who enters in time to hear a part
of* Atreus' *soliloquy*]

ATREUS: [*Addressing himself*] O slothful, indolent,
    weak, unavenged
(This last I deem for tyrants greatest wrong
In great affairs), after so many crimes,
After thy brother's treachery to thee,
After the breaking of all laws of right,
Dost thou, O angry Atreus, waste the time
In idle lamentations? All the world
Should echo with the uproar of thy arms,
And either sea should bear thy ships of war;
The fields and cities should be bright with flame;
The flashing sword should everywhere be drawn;
All Greece shall with our horsemen's tread resound;
Woods shall not hide the foe nor towers built
Upon the highest summits of the hills;
Mycenæ's citizens shall leave the town
And sing the warsong; he shall die hard death
Who gives that hated head a hiding-place.
This palace even, noble Pelops' home,
Shall fall, if it must be, and bury me
If only on my brother too it fall.
Up, do a deed which none shall ever approve,
But one whose fame none shall ever cease to speak.
Some fierce and bloody crime must now be dared,
Such as my brother seeing shall wish his.
A wrong is not avenged but by worse wrong.
What deed can be so wild that's worse than his?
Does he lie humbled? Does he feel content
When fortune smiles, or tranquil when she frowns?
I know the tameless spirit of the man,
Not to be bent but broken, therefore seek
Revenge before he makes himself secure,
Renews his strength, lest he should fall on me
When I am unaware. Or kill, or die!
Crime is between us to be seized by one.
    SLAVE: Fearest thou not the people's hostile words?
    ATREUS: Herein is greatest good of royal power:
The populace not only must endure
Their master's deeds, but praise them.
    SLAVE: Fear shall make
Those hostile who were first compelled to praise;
But he who seeks the fame of true applause
Would rather by the heart than voice be praised.

ATREUS: The lowly oft enjoy praise truly meant,
The mighty never know aught but flattery.
The people oft must will what they would not.
    SLAVE: The king should wish for honesty and right;
Then there is none who does not wish with him.
    ATREUS: When he who rules must wish for right
    alone
He hardly rules, except on sufferance.
    SLAVE: When reverence is not, nor love of law,
Nor loyalty, integrity, nor truth,
The realm is insecure.
    ATREUS: Integrity,
Truth, loyalty, are private virtues; kings
Do as they will.
    SLAVE: O deem it wrong to harm
A brother, even though he be most base.
    ATREUS: No deed that is unlawful to be done
Against a brother but may lawfully
Be done against this man. What has he left
Untainted by his crime? Where has he spared
To do an impious deed? He took my wife
Adulterously, he took my realm by stealth,
The earnest of the realm he gained by fraud,
By fraud he brought confusion to my home.
There is in Pelops' stalls a noble sheep,
A magic ram, lord of the fruitful herd,
His body covered by a golden fleece.
In him each king sprung from the royal line
Of Tantalus his golden scepter holds,
Who has the ram possess too the realm,
The fortunes of the palace follow him.
As fits a sacred thing, he feeds apart,
In a safe meadow which a wall surrounds
Hiding the pasture with its fateful stones.
The faithless one, daring a matchless crime,
Stole him away and with him took my wife,
Accomplice in his sin. From this has flowed
Every disaster; exiled and in fear
I've wandered through my realm; no place is safe
From brother's plots; my wife has been defiled,
The quiet of my realm has been disturbed,
My house is troubled, and the ties of blood
Are insecure, of nothing am I sure
Unless it be my brother's enmity.
Why hesitate? At length be strong to act.
Look upon Tantalus, on Pelops look;
To deeds like theirs these hands of mine are called.
Tell me, how shall I slay that cursed one?
    SLAVE: Slain by the sword let him spew forth his
    soul.
    ATREUS: Thou tellest the end of punishment, I wish
The punishment itself. Mild tyrants slay;
Death is a longed-for favor in my realm.
    SLAVE: Hast thou no piety?
    ATREUS: If ever it dwelt
Within our home, let piety depart.
Let the grim company of Furies come,
Jarring Erinnys and Megæra dread
Shaking their torches twain. My breast burns not

With anger hot enough. I fain would feel
Worse horrors.

SLAVE: What new exile dost thou plot
In this mad rage?

ATREUS: No deed that keeps the bounds
Of former evils, I will leave no crime
Untried, and none is great enough for me.

SLAVE: The sword?

ATREUS: Is too poor.

SLAVE: Or fire?

ATREUS: Is not enough.

SLAVE: What weapon then shall arm such hate as
thine?

ATREUS: Thyestes' self.

SLAVE: This ill is worse than hate.

ATREUS: I admit it. In my breast a tumult reigns;
It rages deep within, and I am urged
I know not whither, yet it urges me.
Earth from its lowest depths sends forth a groan,
It thunders though the daylight is serene,
The whole house shakes as though the house were
rent,
The trembling Lares turn away their face.
This shall be done, this evil shall be done,
Which, gods, ye fear.

SLAVE: What is it thou wilt do?

ATREUS: I know not what great passion in my
heart,
Wilder than I have known, beyond the bounds
Of human nature, rises, urges on
My slothful hands. I know not what it is,
Yet something great. Yet be it what it may,
Make haste, my soul! Fit for Thyestes' hand
This crime would be; and worthy of Atreus, too,
And both shall do it. Tereus' house has seen
Such shocking feasts. I own the crime is great,
And yet it has been done; some greater crime
Let grief invent. Inspire thou my soul
O Daulian Procne, thou wast sister too;
Our cause is like, assist, impel my hand.
The father, hungrily, with joy shall tear
His children and shall eat their very flesh;
Very well, it is enough. This punishment
Is so far pleasing. But where can he be?
And why is Atreus so long innocent?
Already all the sacrifice I see,
As in a picture, see the morsels placed
Within the father's mouth. Wherefore, my soul,
Art thou afraid? Why fail before the deed?
Forward! It must be done. Himself shall do
What is in such a deed the greater crime.

SLAVE: But captured by what wiles, will he consent
To put his feet within our toils? He knows
That all are hostile.

ATREUS: It were not possible
To capture him but that he'd capture me.
He hopes to gain my kindom; through this hope
He will make haste to meet the thunderbolts
Of threatening Jove, in this hope will endure
The swelling whirlpool's threats, and dare to go

Within the Lybian Syrtes' doubtful shoals,
To see again his brother, last and worst
Of evils deemed; this hope shall lead him on.

SLAVE: Who shall persuade him he may come in
peace?
Whose word will he believe?

ATREUS: Malicious hope
Is credulous, yet I will give my sons
A message they shall to their uncle bear:
'The wandering exile, leaving chance abodes,
May for a kingdom change his misery,
May reign in Argos, sharer of my throne.'
But if Thyestes sternly spurn my prayers,
His artless children, wearied by their woes
And easily persuaded, with their plea
Will overcome him; his old thirst for rule,
Beside sad poverty and heavy toil,
With weight of evil, will subdue his soul
However hard it be.

SLAVE: Time will have made
His sorrow light.

ATREUS: Not so! The sense of ills
Increases daily. To endure distress
Is easy, but to bear it to the end
Is hard.

SLAVE: Choose others for your messengers
In this dread plan.

ATREUS: Youth freely dares the worst.

SLAVE: What now you teach them to do in enmity
Against their uncle, they may later apply
Against their father; evil deeds return
Often upon their author.

ATREUS: If they learned
The way of treachery and crime from none,
Possession of the throne would teach it them.
Art thou afraid their natures will grow base?
So were they born. That which you call now wild
And cruel, and deem hardly to be done,
Ruthless, now showing honor for god's laws,
Perchance is even now against ourselves
Attempted.

SLAVE: Shall your sons know what they do?

ATREUS: Discretion is not found with so few years.
They might perhaps disclose all the guile;
Silence is learned through long and evil years.

SLAVE: The very ones through whom you would
deceive
Another will you deceive?

ATREUS: That they themselves
May be exempt from crime or fault of mine;
Why should I mix my children in my sins?
My hatred shall unfold itself in me.
Yet be not cowardly, my soul;
If thine thou sparest, thou sparest also his.
My minister shall Agamemnon be,
And know my plan, and Menelaus too
Shall know his father's plans and further them.
Through this crime will I prove if they be mine;
If they refuse the contest nor consent
To my revenge, but call him uncle, then

I'll know he is their father. It shall be!
Yet oft a frightened look lays bare the heart,
Great plans may be unwillingly betrayed;
They must not know the great affair they aid.
You must conceal my undertaking.
SLAVE: No need
That I should be admonished; in my breast
Both fear and loyalty will keep it hid,—
Especially my loyalty!

SCENE II.

CHORUS: The ancient race of royal Inachus
At last has laid aside fraternal threats.
What madness drove you, that by turns you shed
Each other's blood and sought to mount the throne
By crime? You know not, eager for high place,
What kingly station means. It is not wealth
That makes the king, nor robes of Tyrian dye,
It is not the crown upon the royal brow,
Nor gates made bright with gold; a king is he
Whose hard heart has forgotten fear and pain,
Whom impotent ambition does not move,
Nor the inconstant favor of the crowd,
Who covets nothing that the west affords,
Nor aught that Tagus' golden waves wash up
From its bright channels, nor the grain thrashed out
Upon the glowing Libyan threshing-floors,
Who neither fears the falling thunderbolt,
Nor Eurus stirring all the sea to wrath,
Nor windy Adriatic's swelling rage;
Who is not conquered by a soldier's lance,
Nor the drawn sword; who seated on safe heights,
Sees everything beneath him; who makes haste
Freely to meet his fate, nor grieves to die.
Let kings who vex the scattered Scythians come,
Who hold the Red Sea's shore, the pearl-filled sea,
Or who intrenched upon the Caspian range
To bold Sarmatians close the way, who breast
The Danube's waves, or those who dare pursue
And spoil the noble Seres wherever they dwell.
The mind a kingdom is: there is no need
Of horse, or weapon, or the coward dart
Which from afar the Parthian hurls and flees—
Or seems to flee, no need to overthrow
Cities with engines that hurl stones afar,
When one possesses in himself his realm.
Whoever will may on the slippery heights
Of empire stand, but I with sweet repose
Am satisfied, rejoice in gentle ease,
And, to my fellow citizens unknown,
My life shall flow in calm obscurity,
And when, untouched by storm, my days have
     passed,
Then will I die, a common citizen,
In good old age. Death so heavy on him
Who dies but too well known to all the world,
Yet knowing not himself.

ACT III. SCENE I.

Thyestes, *his young sons* Plisthenes *and* Tantalus,
    and A Boy.
THYESTES: [*To himself*] The longed-for dwelling of
     my native land
And, to the wretched exile greatest boon,
Rich Argos and a stretch of native soil,
And, if there yet be gods, my country's gods
I see at last; the Cyclop's sacred towers,
Of greater beauty than the work of man;
The celebrated race-course of my youth
Where, so often, I drove my father's car
And carried off the palm. Argos will come
To meet me, and the people come in crowds,
Perhaps my brother Atreus too will come!
Rather return to exile in the woods
And mountain pastures, live the life of brutes
Among them! This bright splendor of the realm
With its false glitter shall not blind my eyes.
Look on the giver, not the gift alone.
In fortunes which the world deemed hard I lived
Joyous and brave, now am I forced to fear,
My courage fails me, gladly would I retreat,
Unwillingly I go.
TANTALUS: [*Aside*] What is this that
With hesitating step my father goes?
He seems uncertain, turns away his head.
THYESTES: [*Still to himself*] Why doubt, my soul?
     or why so long revolve
Deliberations easy to conclude?
In most uncertain things should I confide
And in my brother's realm? Why stand in fear
Of ills already conquered and found mild?
Why leave an exile's lot I've learned to bear?
Now to be wretched with the shades were joy.
Turn back, my soul, while there is time.
TANTALUS: [*To his father*]   Why turn away
From thy loved country? Why deny thyself
So much of happiness? His wrath renounced,
Thy brother gives thee back the kingdom's half
And to the jarring members of his house
Brings peace, restoring thee once more to thyself.
THYESTES: You ask me why I fear? I do not know.
I see nothing to fear and yet I fear.
Gladly would I go and yet with heavy feet
I waver and am borne unwillingly
Whither I would not; as a ship propelled
By oar and sail is driven from its course
By the opposing tide.
TANTALUS: Whatever thwarts
Or hinders overcome; see what rewards
Await thy return. Thou can yet be king.
THYESTES: And I can die.
TANTALUS: The very highest power—
THYESTES: Is naught, if one has come to wish for
     naught.
TANTALUS: Thy sons shall wear a crown.

THYESTES: No realm
can have
Two kings.

TANTALUS: Does one who might be happy choose
Unhappiness?

THYESTES: Believe me, with false name
Does power deceive; and vain it is to fear
Laborious fortunes. High in place, I feared,
Yes, feared the very sword upon my side.
How good it is to be the foe of none,
To lie upon the ground, in safety eat.
Crime enters not the cottage; without fear
May food be eaten at the humble board.
Poison is drunk from gold. I speak known truth—
Ill fortune is to be preferred to good.
No humble citizen fears to visit my house:
It is not on any mountain summit placed,
Its ceilings do not shine with ivory;
No watchman guards my sleep; we do not fish
With great fleets, nor drive the ocean from its bed
With massive walls, nor feed vile gluttony
With tribute from all nations; not for me
Are harvested the fields beyond the Getes
And Parthians; men do not honor me
With incense, nor are altars built for me
Instead of Jove; upon my palace roofs
No forests nod, no hot pools steam for me;
Day is not spent in sleep nor night in crime
And watching. No one fears me and my home,
Although without a weapon, is secure.
Great peace attends on humble circumstance;
He has a kingdom who can be content
Without a kingdom.

TANTALUS: If a favoring god
Give thee a realm, it should not be refused,
Even if not desired. A brother begs
You to share his throne.

THYESTES: Begs? Then I must surely fear.
He seeks some means whereby he may betray me

TANTALUS: Full often loyalty that was withdrawn
Is given back, and then affection gains
Redoubled strength.

THYESTES: And shall his brother love
Thyestes? Rather shall the ocean wet
The northern Bear, and the rapacious tides
Of the Sicilian waters stay their waves,
The harvest ripen in Ionian seas,
And black night give the earth the light of day;
Rather shall flame with water, life with death,
The winds with ocean join in faithful pact.

TANTALUS: What frauds dost thou still fear?

THYESTES: All.
There's no end
To fear! His hatred is as great as his power.

TANTALUS: What power has he to harm you?

THYESTES: For
myself
I do not fear; for you, my sons, I dread
My brother Atreus.

TANTALUS: Dost thou fear deceit?

THYESTES: It is too late to seek security
When one is in the very midst of ill.
Let us go on. This one thing I affirm:
I follow you, not lead.

TANTALUS: God will behold
With favor our course; let us boldly advance.

SCENE II.

[Atreus, Thyestes, Plisthenes, Tantalus, A boy.]

ATREUS: [Aside] At last the wild beast is within my
net,
For I behold him with his hated brood.
My vengeance now is sure, into my hands
Thyestes has completely fallen; my joy
I scarce can temper, scarcely curb my wrath.
Thus when the cunning Umbrian hound is held
In leash, and tracks his prey, with lowered nose
Searching the ground, when from afar he scents
By slightest clue the bear, he silently
Explores the place, submitting to be held,
But when the prey is nearer, then he fights
To free himself, and with impatient voice
Calls the slow huntsman, straining at the leash.
When passion hopes for blood it will not stand
Restraint; and yet my wrath must be restrained!
See how his heavy, unkempt hair conceals
His face, how loathsome lies his beard. Ah, well!
Faith shall be kept. [To Thyestes] To see my broth-
er's face
How glad I am! All former wrath is past.
From this day loyalty to family ties
Shall be maintained, from this day let all hate
Be banished from our hearts.

THYESTES: [Aside] O wert thou not
Such as thou art, all could be put aside.
[To Atreus] Atreus, I own, I own that I have done
All thou believest; this day's loyalty
Makes me seem truly base: he sins indeed
Who sins against a brother good as thou.
Tears must wash out my guilt. See at thy feet
These hands are clasped to plead that never before
Entreated anyone. Let all anger cease,
Let swelling rage forever be dispelled;
Receive my children, pledges of my faith.

ATREUS: No longer clasp my knees, but rather seek
My warm embrace. Ye, too, the props of age,
So young, my children, cling about my neck.
And thou, put off thy raiment mean and coarse;
Oh, spare my sight, put on these royal robes
Like mine, and gladly share a brother's realm.
This greater glory shall at last be mine:
To my illustrious brother I give back
His heritage. One holds a throne by chance,
To give it up is noble.

THYESTES: May the gods
Give thee, my brother, fair return for all
Thy benefits. Alas, my wretchedness
Forbids me to accept the royal crown,

My guilty hand shrinks from the scepter's weight;
Let me in lesser rank unnoted live.
ATREUS: This realm recovers its two kings.
THYESTES: I hold,
O brother, all of thine the same as mine.
ATREUS: Who would refuse the gifts that fortune
gives?
THYESTES: He who has learned how swiftly they
depart.
ATREUS: Refuse not thy brother the renown of
mercy.
THYESTES: Thy glory is achieved, but mine is not,
Firm is my resolution to refuse
The kingdom.
ATREUS: I relinquish all my power
Unless thou hast thy part.
THYESTES: I take it then.
I'll wear the name of king, but law and arms
And I shall be thy slaves for evermore.
ATREUS: [*Placing a crown on his head*] Wear then
upon thy head the royal crown.
And now a sacrifice unto the gods! [*They leave the
stage*]

SCENE III.

CHORUS: Who would believe it? Atreus, fierce and
wild,
Savage and tameless, shrank and was amazed
When he beheld his brother. Stronger bonds
Than nature's laws exist not. Wars may last
With foreign foes, but true love still will bind
Those whom it once has bound. When wrath, aroused
By some great quarrel, has disservered friends
And called to arms, when the light cavalry
Advance with ringing bridles, here and there
Shines the swift sword which, seeking fresh-shed
blood,
The raging war-god wields with frequent blows;
But love and loyalty subdue the sword,
And in great peace unite reluctant hearts.
What god gave sudden peace from so great war?
Throughout Mycenæ rang the crash of arms
Of late in civil strife, pale mothers held
Their children to their bosoms, and the wife
Feared for her steel-armed husband, when the sword,
Stained with the rust acquired in long peace,
Unwillingly obeyed his hand. Some sped
To strengthen falling walls, to build again
The tottering towers, to make fast the gates
With iron bars; and on the battlements
The pale watch waked throughout the anxious night.
Terror of war is worse than war itself.
But threatenings of the cruel sword have ceased,
The trumpet's deep-toned voice at last is stilled,
The braying of the strident horn is hushed,
And to the joyous city peace returns.
So when the northwest wind beats up the sea
And from the deep the swelling waves roll in,

Scylla from out her smitten caverns roars
And sailors in the havens fear the flood
That ravening Charybdis vomits forth,
And the fierce Cyclops, dwelling on the top
Of fiery Ætna, dreads his father's rage,
Lest whelmed beneath the waves, the fires that roar
Within his immemorial chimney's throat
Should be profaned, and poor Laertes thinks,
Since Ithaca is shaken, that his realm
May be submerged; then, if the winds subside,
More quiet than a pool the ocean lies,
Scattered on every side gay little skiffs
Stretch the fair canvas of their spreading sails
Upon the sea which, late, ships feared to cut;
And there where, shaken by the hurricane,
The Cyclades were fearful of the deep,
The fishes play. No fortune long endures:
Sorrows and pleasures each in turn depart,
But pleasure soonest; from the fairest heights
An hour may plunge one to the lowest depths;
He who upon his forehead wears a crown,
Who nods and Medians lay aside the sword,
Indians, too, near neighbors of the sun,
And Dacians that assail the Parthian horse,
He holds his scepter with an anxious hand,
Foresees the overthrow of all his joy,
And fears uncertain time and fickle chance.
Ye whom the ruler of the earth and sea
Has given power over life and death,
Be not so proud, a stronger threatens you
With whatsoever ills the weaker fears
From you; each realm is by a greater ruled.
Him whom the rising sun beholds in power
The setting sees laid low. Let none confide
Too much in happiness, let none despair
When he has fallen from his high estate,
For Clotho blends the evil with the good;
She turns about all fortunes on her wheel;
None may abide. Such favoring deities
No one has ever found that he may trust
To-morrow; on his flying wheel a god
Spins our swift changing fortunes.

ACT IV. SCENE I.

Messenger, Chorus.
MESSENGER: Oh, who will bear me headlong
through the air,
Like a swift wind, and hide me in thick cloud
That I no longer may behold such crime?
O house dishonored, whose base deeds disgrace
Pelops and Tantalus!
CHORUS: What news is thine?
MESSENGER: What region can it be that I behold?
Argos and Sparta to which fate assigned
Such loving brothers? Corinth or the shores
Of the two seas? The Danube that compels
The fierce Alani frequently to flee?
Hyrcania underneath eternal snows?

Is it the wandering Scythians' changing home?
What land is this that knows such monstrous deeds?
   CHORUS: Speak and declare the ill whate'er it be.
   MESSENGER: If I have courage, if cold fear relax
Its hold upon my members. Still I see
Accomplished slaughter. Bear me far from hence,
O driving whirlwind; whither day is borne
Bear me, torn hence!
   CHORUS: Control thy fear, wrung heart,
What is the deed that makes thee quake with fear?
Speak and declare its author, I ask not
Who it may be, but which. Now quickly tell.
   MESSENGER: Upon the heights a part of Pelops'
     house
Faces the south; the further side of this
Lifts itself upward like a mountain top
And overlooks the city; thence their kings
May hold the stubborn people 'neath their sway.
Here shines the great hall that might well contain
An army, vari-colored columns bear
Its golden architraves; behind the room
Known to the vulgar, where the people come,
Stretch chambers rich and wide, and far within
Lies the arcana of the royal house,
The sacred penetralia; here no tree
Of brilliant foliage grows, and none is trimmed;
But yews and cypress and black ilex trees
Bend in the gloomy wood, an ancient oak
Rises above the grove and, eminent
Over the other trees, looks down on all
From its great height. Here the Tantalides
Are consecrated kings, and here they seek
Aid in uncertain or untoward events
Here hang their votive offerings, clear-toned trumps,
And broken chariots, wreckage of the sea,
And wheels that fell a prey to treachery,
And evidence of every crime the race
Has done. Here Trojan Pelops' crown is hung,
Here the embroidered robe from barbarous foes
Won. In the shade trickles a sluggish rill
That in the black swamp lingers lazily,
Like the unsightly waters of black Styx
By which the gods make oath. It is said that here
The gods of the infernal regions sigh
Through all the dark night, that the place resounds
With rattling chains, and spirits of the dead
Go wailing up and down. Here may be seen
All dreadful things; here wanders the great throng
Of spirits of the ancient dead sent forth
From antique tombs, and monsters fill the place
Greater than have been known, and oft the wood
With threefold baying echoes, oftentimes
The house is terrible with mighty forms.
Nor does the daylight put an end to fear,
Night is eternal in the grove, and here
The sanctity of the infernal world
Reigns in the midst of day. Here sure response
Is given those who seek the oracle;
From the adytum with a thundering noise
The fatal utterance finds a passage out,

And all the grot reëchoes the god's voice.
Here raging Atreus entered, dragging in
His brother's sons; the altars were adorned—
Ah, who can tell the tale? The noble youths
Have their hands bound behind them and their brows
Bound with the purple fillet; incense too
Is there, and wine to Bacchus consecrate,
And sacrificial knife, and salted meal;
All things are done in order, lest such crime
Should be accomplished without fitting rites.
   CHORUS: Whose hand took up the sword?
   MESSENGER: He is him-
   self
The priest: He sang himself with boisterous lips
The sacrificial song, those given to death
He placed, he took the sword and wielded it;
Nothing was lacking to the sacrifice.
Earth trembled, all the grove bent down its head,
The palace nodded, doubtful where to fling
Its mighty weight, and from the left there shot
A star from heaven, drawing a black train.
The wine poured forth upon the fire was changed
And flowed red blood; the royal diadem
Fell twice, yea thrice; within the temple walls
The ivory statues wept: all things were moved
At such a deed; himself alone unmoved,
Atreus stood firm and faced the threatening gods.
And now delay at last was put aside;
He stood before the altar, sidelong, fierce
In gaze. As by the Ganges, in the woods,
The hungry tiger stands between two bulls,
Uncertain which one first shall feel his teeth—
Eager for both, now here now there he turns
His eyes and in such doubt is hungry still—
So cruel Atreus gazes on the heads
Devoted sacrifices to his rage:
He hesitates which one shall first be slain,
And which be immolated afterward;
It matters not and yet he hesitates,
And in the order of his cruel crime
Takes pleasure.
   CHORUS: Which is first to feel the sword?
   MESSENGER: Lest he should seem to fail in loyalty
First place is given to his ancestor—
The boy named Tantalus is first to fall.
   CHORUS: What courage showed the youth? How
    bore he death?
   MESSENGER: He stood unmoved, no useless prayers
    were heard.
That cruel one hid in the wound the sword,
Pressing it deep within the victim's neck,
Then drew it forth; the corpse was upright still;
It hesitated long which way to fall,
Then fell against the uncle. Atreus then,
Dragging before the altar Plisthenes,
Hurried him to his brother: with one blow
He cut away the head; the lifeless trunk
Fell prone and with a whispered sound the head
Rolled downward.
   CHORUS: Double murder this complete,

What did he then? Spared he the other boy?
Or did he heap up crime on crime?
 MESSENGER: Alas!
As crested lion in Armenian woods
Attacks the herd, nor lays aside his wrath
Though sated, but with jaws that drip with blood
Follows the bulls, and satisfied with food
Threatens the calves but languidly; so storms
Atreus, so swells his wrath, and holding still
The sword with double murder wet, forgets
Whom he attacks; with direful hand he drives
Right through the body and the sword, received
Within the breast, passes straight through the back.
He falls and with his blood puts out the fires;
By double wound he dies.
 CHORUS: O savage crime!
 MESSENGER: Are you horrified? If there the work
  had ceased,
It had been pious.
 CHORUS: Could a greater crime
Or more atrocious be by nature borne?
 MESSENGER: And dost thou think this was the end
  of crime?
It was its beginning.
 CHORUS: What more could there be?
Perchance he threw the bodies to wild beasts
That they might tear them, kept from funeral fire?
 MESSENGER: Would he had kept, would that no
  grave might hide
The dead, no fire burn them, would the birds
And savage beasts might feast on such sad food!
That which were torment else is wished for here.
Would father's eyes unburied sons might see!
O crime incredible to every age!
O crime which future ages shall deny!
The entrails taken from the living breast
Tremble, the lungs still breathe, the timid heart
Throbs, but he tears its fibre, ponders well
What it foretells and notes its still warm veins.
When he at last satisfied himself
About the victims, of his brother's feast
He makes secure. The mangled forms he cuts,
And from the trunk he separates the arms
As far as the broad shoulders, savagely
Lays bare the joints and cleaves apart the bones;
The heads he spares and the right hands they gave
In such good faith. He puts the severed limbs
Upon the spits and roasts them by slow fire:
The other parts into the glowing pot
He throws to boil them. From the food the fire
Leaps back, is twice, yea thrice, replaced and forced
At last reluctantly to do its work.
The liver on the spit emits shrill cries,
I cannot tell whether the flesh or flame
Most deeply groaned. The troubled fire smoked,
The smoke itself, a dark and heavy cloud,
Rose not in air nor scattered readily;
The ugly cloud obscured the household gods.
O patient Phœbus, thou hast backward fled
And, breaking off the light of day at noon,

Submerged the day, but thou didst set too late.
The father mangles his own sons, and eats
Flesh of his flesh, with sin polluted lips;
His locks are wet and shine with glowing oil;
Heavy is he with wine; the morsels stick
Between his lips. Thyestes, this one good
Amid thy evil fortunes still remains:
Thou knowest it not. But this good too shall die.
Let Titan, turning backward on his path,
Lead back his chariot and with darkness hide
This foul new crime, let blackest night arise
At midday, yet the deed must come to light.
All will be manifest.

SCENE II.

 CHORUS: Oh, whither, father of the earth and sky,
Whose rising puts the glory of the night
To flight, oh, whither dost thou turn thy path,
That light has fled at midday? Phœbus, why
Hast thou withdrawn thy beams? The evening star,
The messenger of darkness, has not yet
Called forth the constellations of the night,
Not yet the westward turning course commands
To free thy horses that have done their work,
The trumpet has not yet its third call given,
The signal of declining day, new night.
The plowman is amazed at the swift fall
Of supper-time, his oxen by the plow
Are yet unwearied; from thy path in heaven
What drives thee, O Apollo? What the cause
That forces from their wonted way thy steeds?
Though conquered, do the giants strive again
In war, hell's prison being opened wide?
Or does Tityus in his wounded breast
Renew his ancient wrath? The mountains rent,
Does Titan's son, Typhœus, stretch again
His giant body? Is a pathway built
By Macedonian giants to the sky,
On Thracian Ossa is Mount Pelion piled?
The ancient order of the universe
Has perished! sunrise and sunset will not be!
Eos, the dewy mother of the dawn,
Wont to the god of day to give the reins,
Sees with amaze her kingdom overthrown,
She knows not how to bathe the wearied steeds,
Nor dip the smoking horses in the sea.
The setting sun himself, amazed, beholds
Aurora, and commands the darkness rise
Ere night is ready, the bright stars rise not,
Nor do the heavens show the faintest light,
Nor does the morn dissolve the heavy shades.
Whatever come, would it were only night!
Shaken with mighty fear my bosom quakes,
Lest all the world to ruin should be hurled,
And formless chaos cover gods and men,
And nature once again enfold and hide
The land and sea and starry firmament.
With the upspringing of its deathless torch

Bringing the seasons, never more shall come
The king of stars and give the waiting world
Changes of summer and of winter's cold;
No more shall Luna meet the sun's bright flame
And take away the terror of the night,
And running through a briefer circuit pass
His brother's car; into one gulf shall fall
The heaped-up throng of gods.
The zodiac, pathway of the sacred stars,
Which cuts the zones obliquely, shall behold
The falling stars and fall itself from heaven.
Aries, who comes again in early spring
And with warm zephyr swells the sails, shall fall
Headlong into the sea through which he bore
Timorous Hella; and the Bull, that wears
The Hyades upon its shining brow,
Shall with himself drag down the starry Twins
And Cancer's claws; the Lion,[4] glowing hot,
That Hercules once conquered, shall again
Fall from the skies; and to the earth she left
The Virgin too shall fall, and the just Scales,
And with them drag the churlish Scorpion.
Old Chiron, who holds fixed the feathered dart
In the Thessalian bow, shall loose his shaft
From the snapped bowstring, and cold Capricorn
Who brings the winter's cold shall fall, and break
For thee, whoe'er thou art, thy water-jug,
Thou Water-bearer; with thee too shall fall
The Fishes, last of stars; and Charles's Wain,
That never yet has sunk below the sea,
Falling shall plunge beneath the ocean wave.
The slippery Dragon, that between the Bears
Winds like a winding river, shall descend;
And, with the Dragon joined, the Lesser Bear
So icy cold, and slow Boötes too,
Already tottering to his overthrow,
Shall fall from heaven with his heavy wain.
Out of so many do we seem alone
Worthy to be beneath the universe
Buried, when heaven itself is overthrown?
In our day has the end of all things come?
Created were we for a bitter fate,
Whether we've banished or destroyed the sun.
Let lamentation cease; depart base fear;
Eager for life is he who would not die
Even though with him all the world should fall.

ACT V. SCENE I.

ATREUS: High above all and equal to the stars
I move, my proud head touches heaven itself;
At last I hold the crown, at last I hold
My father's throne. Now I abandon you,
Ye gods, for I have touched the highest point
Of glory possible. It is enough.
Even I am satisfied. Why satisfied?
No shame withholds me, day has been withdrawn;
Act while the sky is dark. Would I might keep

[4] The constellation Leo

The gods from flight, and drag them back by force
That all might see the feast that gives revenge.
It is enough the father shall behold.
Though daylight be unwilling to abide,
Yet will I take from thee the dark that hides
Thy miseries; too long with merry look
Thou liest at thy feast: enough of wine,
Enough of food, Thyestes. There is need,
In this thy crowning ill, thou be not drunk
With wine. Slaves, open wide the temple doors,
And let the house of feasting open lie.
I long to see his color when he sees
His dead sons' heads, to hear his words that flow
With the first shock of sorrow, to behold
How, stricken dumb, he sits with rigid form.
This is the recompense of all my toil.
I do not wish to see his wretchedness
Save as it grows upon him. The wide hall
Is bright with many a torch; supine he lies
On gold and purple, his left hand supports
His head that is so heavy now with wine;
He vomits. Mightiest of the gods am I,
And king of kings! my wish has been excelled!
Full is he, in the silver cup he lifts
The wine. Spare not to drink, there still remains
Some of the victims' blood, the old wine's red
Conceals it; with this cup the feast shall end.
His children's blood mixed with the wine he drinks;
He would have drunken mine. And now he *sings*,
Sings festal songs, his mind is dimmed with wine.

SCENE II.

Atreus, Thyestes.

THYESTES: By long grief dulled, put by thy cares,
    my heart,
Let fear and sorrow fly and bitter need,
Companion of thy timorous banishment,
And shame, hard burden of afflicted souls.
Whence thou hast fallen profits more to know
Than whither; great is he who with firm step
Moves on the plain when fallen from the height;
He who, oppressed by sorrows numberless
And driven from his realm, with unbent neck
Carries his burdens, not degenerate
Or conquered, who stands firm beneath the weight
Of all his burdens, he is great indeed.
Now scatter all the clouds of bitter fate,
Put by all signs of thy unhappy days,
In happy fortunes show a happy face,
Forget the old Thyestes. Ah, this vice
Still follows misery: never to trust
In happy days; though better fortunes come,
Those who have borne afflictions find it hard
To joy in better days. What holds me back,
Forbids me celebrate the festal tide?
What cause of grief, arising causelessly,
Bids me to weep? What art thou that forbids

That I should crown my head with festal wreath?
It does forbid, forbid! Upon my head
The roses languish, and my hair that drips
With ointment rises as with sudden fear,
My face is wet and showers of tears that fall
Unwillingly, and groans break off my song.
Grief loves accustomed tears, the wretched feel
That they must weep. I would be glad to make
Most bitter lamentation, and to wail,
And rend this robe with Tyrian purple dyed.
My mind gives warning of some coming grief,
Presages future ills. The storm that smites
When all the sea is calm weighs heavily
Upon the sailor. Fool! What grief, what storm,
Dost thou conceive? Believe thy brother now.
Be what it may, thou fearest now too late,
Or causelessly. I do not wish to be
Unhappy, but vague terror smites my breast?
No cause is evident and yet my eyes
O'erflow with sudden tears. What can it be,
Or grief, or fear? Or has great pleasure tears?

SCENE III.

Atreus, Thyestes.

ATREUS: Brother, let us together celebrate
This festal day: this day it is which makes
My scepter firm, which binds the deathless pact
Of certain peace.
THYESTES: Enough of food and wine!
This only could augment my happiness,
If with my own I might enjoy my bliss.
ATREUS: Believe thy sons are here in thy embrace.
Here are they and shall be, no single part
Of thy loved offspring shall be lost to thee.
Ask and whate'er thou wishes I will give,
I'll satisfy the father with his sons;
Fear not, thou shalt be more than satisfied.
Now with my own thy young sons lengthen out
The joyous feast: they shall be sent for; drink
The wine, it is an heirloom of our house.
THYESTES: I take my brother's gift. Wine shall be
    poured
First to our fathers' gods, then shall be drunk.
But what is this? My hands refuse to lift
The cup, its weight increases and hold down
My right hand, from my lips the wine retreats,
Around my mouth it flows and will not pass
Within my lips, and from the trembling earth
The tables leap, the fire scarce gives light,
The air is heavy and the light is dim
As between day and darkness. What is this?
The arch of heaven trembles more and more,
To the dense shadows ever thicker mist
Is added, night withdraws in blacker night,
The constellations flee. Whatever it is,
I pray thee spare my sons, let all the storm
Break over my vile head. Give back my sons!

ATREUS: Yes. I will give them back, and never
    more
Shalt thou be parted from them.   [Exit.]

SCENE IV.

THYESTES: What distress
Seizes my reins? Why shake my inward parts?
I feel a burden that will forth, my breast
Groans with a groaning that is not my own.
Come, children, your unhappy father calls;
Come, might I see you all this woe would flee.
Whence come these voices?

SCENE V.

[Atreus, Thyestes, Slave bearing a covered
charger]

ATREUS: Father, spread wide thy arms, they come,
    they come.
Dost thou indeed now recognize thy sons?
    [The charger is uncovered.]
THYESTES: I recognize my brother: Canst thou
    bear
Such deeds, O earth? O Styx, wilt thou not break
Thy banks and whelm in everlasting night
Both king and kingdom, bearing them away
By a dread path to chaos' awful void?
And, plucking down thy houses, fallest thou not,
O city of Mycenæ, to the ground?
We should already be with Tantalus!
Earth, open thy prisons wide on every side;
If under Tartarus, below the place
Where dwell our kinsmen, rests a lower deep,
Within thy bosom let a chasm yawn
Thitherward, under all of Acheron
Hide us; let guilty souls roam o'er our heads
Let Phlegethon that bears its fiery sands
Down through its glowing channels, flow over me!
Yet earth unmoved lies, a mere heavy weight,
The gods have fled.
ATREUS: Take, rather, willingly
Those whom thou hast so long desired to see;
Thy brother does not hinder thee. Rejoice;
Kiss them, divide thy love between thy sons.
THYESTES: This is thy compact? This thy brother's
    faith?
Is this thy favor? Layst thou thus aside
Thy hate? I do not ask to see my sons
Unharmed; what wickedness and deathless hate
May give, a brother asks: grant to my sons
Burial; give them back, thou shalt behold
Straightway their burning.[5] I ask for nothing
I can keep but only for what I must lose.
ATREUS: All that remains of them is thine to keep.

[5] Corpses were burnt in ancient Greek burial rites.

THYESTES: Oh, do they furnish food for savage birds?
Are they destroyed by monsters, fed to beasts?
ATREUS: Thyself hast banqueted upon thy sons,
An impious feast.
THYESTES: It is this that shamed the gods!
This backward drove the daylight whence it came!
Oh my misery! What cry shall I make,
What wailing? What words will suffice for my woe?
I see the severed heads, the hands cut off,
Greedy and hungry, these I did not eat!
I feel their flesh within my bowels move;
Prisoned, the dread thing struggles, tries to flee,
But has no passage forth; give me the sword,
Brother, it has already drunk my blood:
The sword shall give a pathway to my sons.
It is denied? Then rending blows shall sound
Upon my breast. Unhappy one, restrain
Thy hand and spare the dead! Who has beheld
Such hideous crime? Not wandering tribes that dwell
On the unkindly Caucasus' rough cliffs,
Or fierce Procrustes, dread of Attica.
Behold, the father feasts upon his sons,
The sons lie heavy in him—is there found
No limit to such base and impious deeds?
ATREUS: Crime finds a limit when the crime is done,
Not when avenged. Even this is not enough.
Into thy mouth I should have poured the blood
Warm from the wounds; thou shouldst have drunk the blood
Of living sons. My hate betrayed itself
Through too much haste. I smote them with the sword,
I slew them at the altar, sacrificed
A votive offering to the household gods,
From the dead trunks I cut away the heads,
And into tiniest pieces tore the limbs;
Some in the boiling pot I plunged, and some
I bade should be before a slow flame placed;
I cut the flesh from the still living limbs,
I saw it roar upon the slender spit,
And with my own right hand I plied the fire.
All this the father might have better done:
All of my vengeance falls in nothingness!
He ate his sons with impious lips indeed,
But, alas, nor he nor they knew what he did!
THYESTES: Hear, O ye seas, stayed by inconstant shores;
Ye too, ye gods, wherever ye have fled,
Hear what a deed is done! Hear, gods of Hell,
Hear, Earth, and heavy Tartarean night
Dark with thick cloud! Oh, listen to my cry!
Thine am I, Night, thou only seest my woe,
Without a single star. I do not make
Presumptuous prayer, naught for myself I ask—
What could be granted me? I make my prayer
For you, my sons. Oh ruler of the heavens,

Almighty king of the ethereal courts,
Cover the universe with horrid clouds,
Let winds contend on every side, send forth
Thy thunders everywhere; not with light hand,
As when thou smitest with thy lesser darts
Innocent homes; but as when mountains fell
And with their threefold ruin overwhelmed
The Giants—use such power, send forth such fires,
Avenge the banished day, where light has fled
Fill up the darkness with thy thunderbolts.
Each one is evil,—do not hesitate—
Yet if not both, I sure am base; seek me
With triple dart, through this breast send this brand:
If I would give my sons a funeral pyre
And burial, let me give myself to the flames.
If nothing moves the gods, if none will send
His darts against my sinful head, let night
Remain forever and hide this gruesome crime
In everlasting shadows. If thou, Sun,
No longer shinest, I have naught to ask.
ATREUS: Now in my work I glory, now at last
I hold the victor's palm. I would have lost
My crime's reward unless I made you suffer so!
I can now believe my sons are truly mine—
Now may I trust again in a chaste bed.
THYESTES: What evil had my children done to thee?
ATREUS: Enough that they were thine.
THYESTES: But children fed to their sire—
ATREUS: Precisely; and it is this that makes me glad.
THYESTES: I call upon the gods who guard the right
To witness.
ATREUS: Why not call upon the gods
Who guard the marriage-bed you stained?[6]
THYESTES: Who punishes
A crime with crime?
ATREUS: I know what makes thee grieve:
That another first accomplished the grim deed,
For this thou mournest; thou art not distressed
Because of the dread feast, your grief is so keen
That no such feast was prepared for me.
Your thought in this was the same: to provide like food
For an unconscious brother, after seizing
My children with their mother's aid. One thing
Alone deterred thee—the thought that they were thine.
THYESTES: Avenging gods will come and punish thee;
To them my prayers commit thee.
ATREUS: To thy sons
I give thee over for *thy* punishment.

---

[6] The adultery, now avenged, committed by Thyestes with his brother Atreus' wife.

Christian Drama:
Saint and Miracle Plays

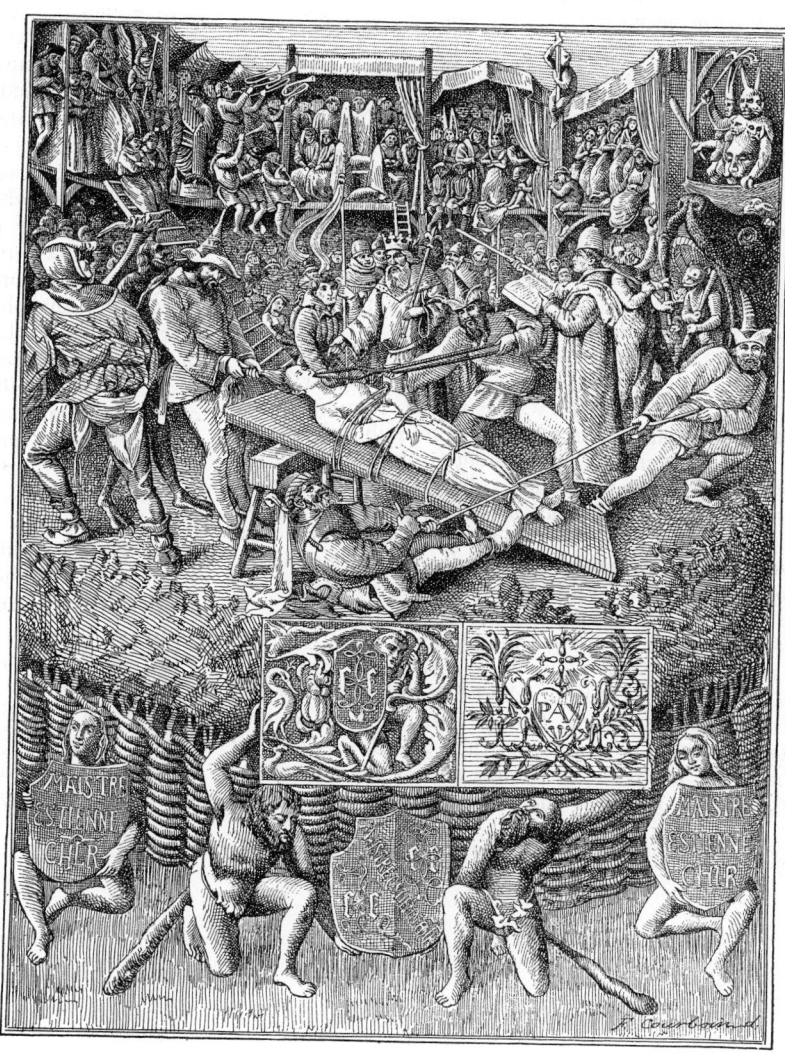

The Medieval stage. *The Martyrdom of St. Appollonia,* miniature by Jean Fouquet (1415–1483), shows the use of *mansions* set in a semicircle—occupied by saints, angels, and devils—while the main action is centered on the forestage. From Edith J. R. Isaacs and Robert M. MacGregor, *Stages of the World,* copyright 1949 by Theatre Arts Books, New York. Courtesy of the publishers.

Christian Drama: Saint and Miracle Plays

Roman comedy was influential even earlier than was Senecan tragedy, and the comedies of Terence, stylistically more refined than those of Plautus, were well regarded during the Middle Ages and were translated from the Latin into French and German before 1500. Terence influenced the monks who taught Latin before the tenth century, and the tenth-century Saxon nun Hrotsvitha went about writing Latin plays, some but not all of them comic, with the intent of celebrating Christian martyrdom and morality. Today there is a society in the United States to promote the examination of her work, and a study of this religious playwright by Sister Mary Marguerite Butler, *Hrotsvitha: The Theatricality of Her Plays,* was published in New York by the Philosophical Library in 1960. But her little drama *Paphnutius* is presented here (pages 756–762) for a different reason than to show that Terence exerted an influence even in the Dark Ages. *Paphnutius* is a very early example of a genre of medieval drama, rarely available to the student who reads only English —namely the so-called saint play. It is seldom realized how extensively saint plays were presented and how elaborately they were staged in the Middle Ages.

Two plays in middle-English, *The Conversion of St. Paul* and *Saint Mary Magdalene,* remain within the biblical canon, but when later nonbiblical characters—the latter-day saints—enter the theatre, the medieval penchant for martyrology and miracles runs riot. Thus in one Nicholas drama, produced on St. Nicholas Day, the saint provides dowries and husbands for the daughters of a worthy but economically ruined gentleman; and in another play he performs his favorite Father Christmas role as the patron of little children by solving a kidnapping case.

Miracle or *Saint* plays were particularly abundant in France, where the miracles of the Virgin Mary and of postbiblical saintly figures actually formed dramatic cycles. The popularity they gained was at least partly due to the attractiveness and excitement of the productions given in the town squares on multiple little stages or *mansions* simultaneously shown. A famous fifteenth-century production, represented on a miniature by the painter Jean Fouquet, shows an extraordinarily busy scene representing the martyrdom of St. Apollonia. Considered the "patroness against toothache," Apollonia is lying bound on an inclined plank and is having her teeth pulled out with an extraordinarily long pair of pincers by an executioner or professional torturer while busy scenes are being enacted at the booths in the background. The legend of her martyrdom tells us that "all her beautiful teeth were pulled out, one by one, with a pair of pincers; then a fire was kindled, and as she persisted in the faith, she was flung into it, and gave up her soul to God, being carried into Heaven by his angels."

The story of the hermit Paphnutius and the notorious Alexandrian courtesan Thais whom he converted is treated with a considerably greater restraint by Hrotsvitha, who probably envisioned at most a distinctly austere production in the cloister of her convent in Saxony. But later saint plays, some of which tended to incorporate *Morality Play* elements (as did the English *Mary Magdalene*), were apt to be fanciful rather than severe, replete with the embroidery of storytelling rather than moralistic, devoid of doctrinal significance, and independent not only of biblical material but also of early church history.

Saint plays were, however, part of a persuasive orientation toward drama of wonder and miracles in the Middle Ages. Even the *Passion Play* cycles or so-called Mystery Plays often loosely called Miracle Plays, reflected this interest; and none so remarkably so as the little-known Cornish cycle. *The Death of Pilate,* adapted from the *Cornish Passion cycle,* is a gemlike product of medieval Celtic imagination which well illustrates this drama of wonder and the Celtic people's tendency toward fantasy. It is included in the section that follows.[1]

[1] This imaginative streak is also apparent in the Arthurian romances such as the Welsh tales collected under the title of *The Manibogian.*

Hrotsvitha and Paphnutius

There is no external evidence that the six plays written by Hrotsvitha or Hrowitha, the tenth-century Saxon nun, were ever performed in her time, although several of them were staged in our own century; two by the present translator, Sister Mary Marguerite, at Mercy College.[1] Resolved to counteract an interest in pagan authors and eager to serve Christianity with examples of piety, chastity, and martyrdom, Hrotsvitha wrote more or less didactic saint plays. But taking Terence as her model, this evidently well-educated Benedictine canoness utilized characterization, dramatic conflict, and various degrees of humor and emotional interest. Yet it is entirely possible that she intended her plays for the stage and may have actually seen them performed at Gandersheim. If so, the stage might well have consisted of the cloister walk, with the arcades providing the background. In any case, Sister Marguerite has now proved these short plays to be entirely stageworthy, with perhaps the exception of scenes of torture, such as boiling the martyrs in oil; but these do not actually have to be presented to the audience and were very probably never intended to be shown.

Gandersheim, the site of Hrotsvitha's convent, was an important cultural center in northern Saxony and was administered by abbesses of noble rank. Hrotsvitha herself (c. 935–1001) was evidently of noble birth and had more access to the world than most Benedictine nuns were likely to have; as a canoness she was not wholly set apart from the world by her vows. It is not surprising, therefore, that Hrotsvitha, in addition to composing eight sacred legends and two historical poems in Latin, should have revealed an interest in the artistry of Terence, the last of the distinguished writers of Roman comedy, who is believed to have died about 159 B.C. Since her work also reflects the theatrical tradition of the wandering players, or mimes, whose improvisatory comic art survived from the debris of the Western Roman Empire despite the disapprobation of the Church, she was also distinctly aware of the mainstream of what little popular theatre was discernible during the so-called Dark Middle Ages. She wrote, moreover, at a time when a new Christian type of drama was starting in the tropes, the little dramatic or semidramatic compositions that were being introduced into the wordless sequences of the Mass at Christmas and Easter. It may be said, therefore, that her dramatic work is related to three streams of actual or potential dramatic and theatrical development—the classical influence, the vogue of the mimes and jongleurs who provided popular entertainment, and the evolving liturgical drama in church Latin.

Although her themes and sentiments are inviolably Christian, Hrotsvitha has wit, humor, and theatricality in her work. In the case of one of her light plays, Dulcitius, about a pagan Governor's attempt to seduce three Christian maidens, she also employed the farcical elements of popular theatre.

Paphnutius, which follows, provided an early version of the Thais story, dealing with the conversion of a courtesan by a pious hermit who comes to her disguised as a would-be lover. Paphnutius is a precursor of a genre of medieval drama which has been designated as the Saint Play. Extant examples of this type of drama in England are few and not particularly distinguished. The best-known specimens are The Conversion of Saint Paul, a longish late-fifteenth century work written in East Midland speech, apparently intended for production in a village on three stations, or platform stages, and a lengthy Mary Magdalene, also from the Midland section of England and intended for production on little platforms arranged in a circle.

Paphnutius, however, is not simply an archaic predecessor of this type of drama, but perhaps the most poignant example. The conversion of the courtesan Thais, her confinement in a narrow cell, and her death make Hrotsvitha's little scenes, conceived in such simplicity of faith, strangely moving. It should not be forgotten that a marionette production of Paphnutius inspired Anatole France to write his once widely read novel Thais, which in turn was the inspiration for Massenet's opera.

NOTE: A later publication was published in 1965 by The Hroswitha Club: Hroswitha of Gandersheim: Her Life, Times and Works, edited by Anne Lyon Haight. This volume also contains a record up to 1965 of the known stage performances of the plays.

[1] See Hrotsvitha: The Theatricality of Her Plays, by Sister Mary Marguerite Butler. New York: Philosophical Library, 1960.

PAPHNUTIUS

By Hrotsvitha

TRANSLATED BY SISTER MARY MARGUERITE BUTLER R.S.M.

THE ARGUMENT

The Conversion of Thais by the Hermit, Paphnutius.

Dressed in the disguise of a lover, the hermit Paphnutius goes in search of Thais, a harlot, that he may recall her from her evil ways. Moved by his pleading, Thais is converted. Paphnutius imposes a penance which confines her to a narrow cell for five [sic] years.

Thais, by this worthy expiation, is reconciled to God, and fifteen days after the completion of her penance, she goes to sleep in Christ.

CHARACTERS

PAPHNUTIUS, *the Hermit*
THE DISCIPLES OF PAPHNUTIUS
THAIS, *the Courtesan*

YOUNG MEN, *Lovers of Thais*
ANTHONY *and* PAUL, *Hermits*
AN ABBESS

SCENE I.[1]

DISCIPLES: Why are you so unhappy, why not the serene countenance to which we are accustomed, Father Paphnutius?

PAPHNUTIUS: He whose heart is sad wears a sorrowful countenance.

DISCIPLES: Why are you so sad?

PAPHNUTIUS: Because of the ingratitude shown to my Creator.

DISCIPLES: What is this ingratitude of which you speak.

PAPHNUTIUS: That which He suffers from His own creatures, creatures made to His image and likeness.

DISCIPLES: You frighten us by your words.

PAPHNUTIUS: It is understood that the eternal majesty of God cannot be injured by any wrong, nevertheless, if it were permitted to transfer by a metaphor the weakness of our frail nature to God, what greater wrong could be conceived than this—that while the greater part of the world is subject to His will, one part rebels against His law?

DISCIPLES: Which part rebels?

PAPHNUTIUS: Man.

DISCIPLES: Man?

PAPHNUTIUS: Yes.

DISCIPLES: What man?

PAPHNUTIUS: All men.

DISCIPLES: How can this be?

PAPHNUTIUS: It so pleases our Creator.

DISCIPLES: We do not understand.

PAPHNUTIUS: All of us do not understand.

DISCIPLES: Do explain it to us.

PAPHNUTIUS: Listen then, to what I say.

DISCIPLES: We are listening.

PAPHNUTIUS: Accordingly, the greater part of the world is made up of four contrary elements, but by the will of the Creator, the contraries are adjusted according to harmonious rule, and man possesses not only these same elements, but has more varying components.

DISCIPLES: And what then is more varying than the elements?

PAPHNUTIUS: The body and the soul, because one can understand that they are contrary, yet they are both in one person; the soul is not mortal like the body, and the body is not spiritual like the soul.

DISCIPLES: So!

PAPHNUTIUS: If, moreover, we follow the logicians, we will not admit these to be contrary.

DISCIPLES: And who can deny it?

PAPHNUTIUS: He who can argue logically; because nothing is contrary to Essence, for she is the receptacle of all contraries.

DISCIPLES: What did you mean when you said "according to harmonious rule"?

PAPHNUTIUS: I meant that, as low and high sounds are joined together harmoniously to make a certain music, thus discordant elements, being brought together harmoniously, make one world.[2]

* * *

DISCIPLES: Where did you acquire all this knowledge with which you have just wearied us?

PAPHNUTIUS: I wish to share with you the small drop of knowledge which flowed from the full well of learning; this I found, passing by chance rather than by seeking it.

DISCIPLES: We appreciate your goodness, but we

[1] The place of the action of each scene is indicated in the dialogue and action of each scene. But the rapid changes of scene suggest that the author did not have any realistic scenery in mind but an essentially neutral acting area.

[2] Here follows a lengthy theological discussion which does not contribute to the dramatic development and is therefore omitted.

are terrified by the word of the Apostle saying: "God chooses the foolish of the world to confound the wise."

PAPHNUTIUS: Whether a foolish man or a wise man does wrong, he deserves punishment from God.

DISCIPLES: Indeed he does.

PAPHNUTIUS: Knowledge does not offend God, but the wrong doing of him who has knowledge offends Him.

DISCIPLES: True, indeed!

PAPHNUTIUS: To whom may the knowledge of the arts be more worthily and rightly referred than to Him who made things which are knowable and gave us the capacity to understand them?

DISCIPLES: To none other.

PAPHNUTIUS: The more man sees by what marvelous law God has arranged all things by number, by measure, and by weight, the more intensely he will love Him.

DISCIPLES: And rightly so!

PAPHNUTIUS: But why do I dwell upon these things which afford so little pleasure?

DISCIPLES: Tell us the cause of your grief, that we may no longer be burdened by the weight of our curiosity.

PAPHNUTIUS: If ever you find it out, you will not be happy in that knowledge.

DISCIPLES: A man is often sadder when he has satisfied his curiosity, yet he is unable to overcome this fault because it is a part of our weak nature.

PAPHNUTIUS: A certain infamous woman lives in this neighborhood.

DISCIPLES: This is dangerous to the people.

PAPHNUTIUS: Her beauty is unsurpassed, her wickedness is unspeakable.

DISCIPLES: Horrible! What is her name?

PAPHNUTIUS: Thais.

DISCIPLES: That harlot!

PAPHNUTIUS: Yes, that one.

DISCIPLES: Her wickedness is known to everyone.

PAPHNUTIUS: And no wonder, because she is not satisfied to go to destruction with a few, but she is ready to ensnare all men by the enticements of her beauty and to drag them to ruin with her.

DISCIPLES: How tragic!

PAPHNUTIUS: Not only do wastrels squander their substance by wooing her, but even respectable citizens lay their wealth at her feet, enriching her to their own undoing.

DISCIPLES: Terrible to hear!

PAPHNUTIUS: Crowds of lovers flock to her.

DISCIPLES: They destroy themselves.

PAPHNUTIUS: These lovers, in blindness of heart, quarrel and fight for access to her.

DISCIPLES: One vice begets another.

PAPHNUTIUS: When the struggle begins, sometimes fist fights result in broken noses and jaws; other times they attack with weapons so shamelessly that the threshold of the vile house is drenched with blood.

DISCIPLES: O detestable sin!

PAPHNUTIUS: This is the insult to the Creator which I mourn; this is the cause of my grief.

DISCIPLES: We do not doubt that you rightly grieve aloud about this; and that the heavenly citizens mourn with you.

PAPHNUTIUS: What if I were to approach her in the disguise of a lover; might she by chance turn from her wayward life?

DISCIPLES: He Who has inspired you with this idea is able to bring about its fulfillment.

PAPHNUTIUS: Support me, meanwhile, with your fervent prayers that I may not be overcome by the wiles of the wicked serpent.

DISCIPLES: May He Who laid low the king of darkness give you victory against the enemy!

SCENE II.

PAPHNUTIUS: Look at the young men in the market place. I shall go to them first and inquire where I may find the woman for whom I am looking.

YOUTHS: Look, a stranger is coming toward us. Let us find out what he wants.

PAPHNUTIUS: Hello! Young men, who are you?

YOUTHS: We are citizens of this city.

PAPHNUTIUS: Greetings!

YOUNG MEN: And the same to you; whether a native of this country or a stranger.

PAPHNUTIUS: A stranger, for I have just now arrived.

YOUNG MEN: Why do you come? What do you seek?

PAPHNUTIUS: I cannot say.

YOUNG MEN: Why not?

PAPHNUTIUS: Because I cannot reveal it.

YOUNG MEN: It is better that you reveal it, because if you are a stranger, it will be difficult to transact any business with us citizens.

PAPHNUTIUS: What if I did tell you and in the telling I should raise some obstacle for myself?

YOUNG MEN: Not from us.

PAPHNUTIUS: I take you at your word, trusting your loyalty; I'll tell you my secret.

YOUNG MEN: There will be no disloyalty on our part, no harm shall come to you.

PAPHNUTIUS: I have learned from reports of certain persons that a woman, sweet and gracious to all, and loved by all, lives among you.

YOUNG MEN: Do you know her name?

PAPHNUTIUS: Yes, I do know it.

YOUNG MEN: Won't you tell us?

PAPHNUTIUS: Thais.

YOUNG MEN: Thais! She is the harlot.

PAPHNUTIUS: They say she is the most beautiful and most exquisite of all women.

YOUNG MEN: Those who told you this have not deceived you.

PAPHNUTIUS: For her sake, I undertook the difficulty of a long journey; I came to see her.

YOUNG MEN: There is nothing to keep you from seeing her.

PAPHNUTIUS: Where does she stay?

YOUNG MEN: In that house near by.

PAPHNUTIUS: That one to which you are pointing?

YOUNG MEN: Yes, that one.

PAPHNUTIUS: I shall go there.

YOUNG MEN: If you wish, we shall go with you.

PAPHNUTIUS: I prefer to go alone.

YOUNG MEN: As you prefer.

SCENE III.

PAPHNUTIUS: Thais, are you there? I am looking for you.

THAIS: Who is this stranger who calls on me?

PAPHNUTIUS: Your lover.

THAIS: Whoever woos me in love receives from me an equal return of love.

PAPHNUTIUS: Oh Thais, Thais! How many miles have I traveled that I might be able to speak with you and that I might be able to see your face.

THAIS: I shall not withdraw nor refuse my company.

PAPHNUTIUS: The secrecy of our conversation demands the protection of a more secluded spot.

THAIS: Here is a well-furnished room, a pleasant place.

PAPHNUTIUS: Is there not some place more secluded than this, where we can converse more secretly?

THAIS: There is another place so hidden, so secret that it is known to no one but me and God.

PAPHNUTIUS: What God?

THAIS: The true God.

PAPHNUTIUS: Do you believe that He knows everything?

THAIS: I know nothing is hidden from Him.

PAPHNUTIUS: Do you believe that He is unmindful of the deeds of the wicked or that He does not guard His justice?

THAIS: I believe that He weighs the merits of every man in the balance of His justice and that every man will be rewarded or punished according to his deeds.

PAPHNUTIUS: O Christ! How wonderful is the goodness of Your patience toward us, for You see men wilfully sinning and yet You delay to punish them.

THAIS: Why do you turn pale? Why do you weep?

PAPHNUTIUS: I tremble at your presumption. I weep over your sinfulness because, knowing such things, you have dragged so many souls to ruin.

THAIS: Alas, alas! I am unhappy.

PAPHNUTIUS: All the more justly you shall be damned, the more presumptuously you have knowingly offended the majesty of Divinity.

THAIS: Oh, no! What are you doing? Why do you threaten wretched me?

PAPHNUTIUS: The punishment of hellfire hangs over you if you persist in sin.

THAIS: The severity of your correction has shaken me to the very depths of my heart.

PAPHNUTIUS: Oh, would that you might be shaken to the depths of your heart by fear, that you might no longer consent to dangerous passion.

THAIS: What place can be left in my heart for sinful pleasure where only the bitterness of inward grief and the new dread of an awakened conscience prevail?

PAPHNUTIUS: This is my desire: when the thorns of sin have been rooted from your heart, the tears of repentance may flow.

THAIS: Oh, if you could believe, oh, if you could hope that I, stained with thousands and thousands of defilements, could ever be purified, or by any act of contrition merit pardon!

PAPHNUTIUS: There is no sin so grievous, no fault so great that cannot be atoned for by the tears of repentance, if followed by good deeds.

THAIS: My Father, I beg you to show me by the performance of what good deeds I can merit the gift of reconciliation.

PAPHNUTIUS: Despise the world. Flee the companionship of your dissolute lovers.

THAIS: And then what will I do?

PAPHNUTIUS: Retire to some secluded place where, examining yourself, you will mourn the enormity of your sinfulness.

THAIS: If you know this will be effective, I will go without a moment's delay.

PAPHNUTIUS: I am certain that it will be effective.

THAIS: Give me a moment's time, that I may collect the wealth which I have gained by evil means and have hoarded for a long time.

PAPHNUTIUS: Do not worry about that. There will be plenty of men who will find it and use it.

THAIS: I am not concerned to keep it for myself, nor do I wish to give it to my friends. Furthermore, I will not try to give it to the poor, because I do not think the price of sin to be suitable for good works.

PAPHNUTIUS: You think rightly, but what do you plan to do with your possessions?

THAIS: I would cast them to the flames and reduce them to ashes.

PAPHNUTIUS: Why?

THAIS: That those things which I have acquired by evil deeds may not remain in the world as an insult to the Creator of the world.

PAPHNUTIUS: How changed you are from what you were when you burned with sinful passion and desired only riches!

THAIS: Perhaps I shall change still more, God willing.

PAPHNUTIUS: It is not difficult for His unchangeable substance to change things as He wills.

THAIS: I shall go and carry out what I have planned.

PAPHNUTIUS: Go in peace, and return to me quickly.

SCENE IV.

THAIS: Come together, hasten, my wicked lovers.

LOVERS: The voice of Thais is calling us; let us hasten to go to her lest we offend her by being late.

THAIS: Hurry, come to me that I may speak with you.

LOVERS: O Thais, Thais! Why do you wish a funeral pyre for yourself? What are you building? Why do you heap your many and precious treasures near the flames?

THAIS: You ask?

LOVERS: We wonder greatly.

THAIS: I shall explain quickly.

LOVERS: Please do.

THAIS: Behold!

LOVERS: Stop, stop Thais. What are you doing? Are you insane?

THAIS: I am not insane; I am in my right mind.

LOVERS: But why waste four hundred pounds of gold and many other riches?

THAIS: All which I unjustly extorted from you, I would burn that you may have no spark of hope that I may yield any more to your love.

LOVERS: Stop! Delay a little and tell us the cause of your worry.

THAIS: I will not delay and I will not speak with you.

LOVERS: Why do you scorn us by your disdain? Do you accuse us of any unfaithfulness? Have we not always satisfied your wishes? But you, without cause, treat us with unjust hatred.

THAIS: Go away. Do not clutch and tear my garments. It is enough that, in the past, I have yielded to you in sinning. The end of sinning is at hand. It is time for my departure.

LOVERS: Where is she going?

THAIS: Where none of you will ever see me.

LOVERS: Indeed! What marvel is this that Thais, our delight, who always strove for wealth, who never withdrew her heart from pleasure, who gave herself completely to desire, has now destroyed so much gold and gems and has spurned us, her lovers, with insults and suddenly disappears?

SCENE V.

THAIS: Father Paphnutius, I am here, ready to follow you.

PAPHNUTIUS: Because you delayed in coming. I was very worried, thinking you were again involved in worldly affairs.

THAIS: Do not fear, because I would not change my mind. Now, I have taken care of my affairs as I wished, and I have publicly renounced my lovers.

PAPHNUTIUS: Because you have renounced them, you may now be united to your heavenly Spouse.

THAIS: Then you ought to point out to me, as with your rod, what I should do.

PAPHNUTIUS: Follow me.

THAIS: I shall follow in your footsteps, oh, would that I might also follow in your way of life.

SCENE VI.

PAPHNUTIUS: Here is a convent where lives a community of holy virgins. Here I wish you to remain during the time of your penance.

THAIS: That I will do. I have no objections.

PAPHNUTIUS: I will go inside and persuade the abbess, the superior of the nuns, to receive you.

THAIS: What do you wish me to do in the meantime?

PAPHNUTIUS: Come in with me.

THAIS: As you direct.

PAPHNUTIUS: Look, the abbess is coming. I wonder who told her so quickly that we were here.

THAIS: Rumor, which spreads very quickly.

SCENE VII.

PAPHNUTIUS: You come opportunely, Venerable Abbess, I was just coming to see you.

ABBESS: You are welcome, Reverend Father Paphnutius; beloved of God, may your coming be blessed!

PAPHNUTIUS: May the grace of the Father of all shed upon you the peace of His eternal blessing!

ABBESS: What brings Your Holiness to visit my humble lodging?

PAPHNUTIUS: I need your help in an urgent crisis.

ABBESS: Only tell me what you desire and I shall do all in my power to comply with your wishes.

PAPHNUTIUS: I have brought a half-dead kid, recently snatched from the fangs of the wolves, whom I wish to be cherished in your pity and healed by your care until she has cast aside the rough goatskin and put on the soft fleece of the lamb.

ABBESS: Explain what you mean more clearly.

PAPHNUTIUS: This woman whom you see led the life of a harlot.

ABBESS: What a pity!

PAPHNUTIUS: She gave herself entirely to lust.

ABBESS: She has brought ruin upon herself.

PAPHNUTIUS: And now, with my encouragement and with the help of Christ, the vanities which she followed she now rejects in hatred, and she embraces chastity.

ABBESS: Thanks be to the Author of this change.

PAPHNUTIUS: Because illness of the soul, like illness of the body, must be cured by contrary remedies, it follows that she must be withdrawn from the common cares of the world and be cloistered in a narrow cell where she can more freely meditate on her own sins.

ABBESS: Indeed, this is very necessary.

PAPHNUTIUS: Command that a cell be prepared as soon as possible.

ABBESS: It will be done immediately.

PAPHNUTIUS: Let there be no entrance, no access but a small window through which she may receive a portion of food which you must give her sparingly on certain days at specified hours.

ABBESS: I am afraid that the weakness of her delicate constitution can hardly endure the difficulty of so great a trial.

PAPHNUTIUS: There is no need to fear, for a grievous fault demands a severe remedy.

ABBESS: Yes, indeed!

PAPHNUTIUS: Further delay concerns me because she may be corrupted by the visit of her former lovers.

ABBESS: There is no need for delay. You can enclose her at once. The cell which you wish is ready.

PAPHNUTIUS: Good! Enter, Thais, a dwelling well-suited for atonement of your sins.

THAIS: How narrow, how dark, and how uncomfortable a dwelling for a weak woman!

PAPHNUTIUS: Why do you dislike the dwelling? Why do you shrink from entering? It is fitting that one who was wayward and undisciplined should now suffer the confinements of a narrow cell.

THAIS: A heart accustomed to lust or passion rarely welcomes a more rigid life.

PAPHNUTIUS: Therefore, such a heart should be bound by the reins of strict discipline until it no longer struggles against it.

THAIS: Whatever your fatherly goodness orders, my weakness shall not refuse to undergo, but there is a certain inconvenience in this dwelling which my frailty finds it difficult to accept.

PAPHNUTIUS: What is this inconvenience?

THAIS: I blush to mention it.

PAPHNUTIUS: Do not blush, be honest about it.

ABBESS: What could be more inconvenient, what more difficult than to be forced to take care of all the needs of the body in one place? Without a doubt the cell will soon become uninhabitable.

PAPHNUTIUS: Fear the bitterness of hellfire and do not be afraid of transitory things.

THAIS: My weakness compels me to fear.

PAPHNUTIUS: It is fitting that the sweetness of falsely flattering delight should be atoned for by bitterness.

THAIS: I do not refuse, I do not deny that I, who am stained by sin, deserve to live in a foul and loathsome place, but what grieves me more intensely and religiously call upon the name of the Divine Majesty.

PAPHNUTIUS: But are you confident that with your defiled lips you can invoke the name of the Divine Purity?

THAIS: But from whom can I hope for pardon? Or by whose Mercy can I be saved if I am forbidden to invoke Him against Whom I have sinned, and to Whom alone the offering of our prayers must be made?

PAPHNUTIUS: You ought to pray, not only in words, but in tears; not only in the sound of your musical voice, but in the moaning of a contrite heart.

THAIS: But if I am forbidden to pray to God in words, how can I hope for pardon?

PAPHNUTIUS: The more perfectly you humble yourself, the sooner will you merit pardon. Say only this: "You Who have created me, have mercy on me!"

THAIS: I need His mercy lest I be overcome in the doubtful struggle.

PAPHNUTIUS: Struggle bravely that you may be able to win the victory joyfully.

THAIS: You must pray for me that I may merit the palm of victory.

PAPHNUTIUS: There is no need to tell me that. It is now time for me to return to my beloved solitude and to see my dear disciples. Therefore to your care, to your goodness, Venerable Abbess, I entrust this captive, that you may nourish her weak body with the necessities of life and generously refresh her soul with wise counsel.

ABBESS: Do not be concerned about her. I will cherish her with motherly affection.

PAPHNUTIUS: Then I shall go.

ABBESS: May you go in peace!

SCENE VIII.

DISCIPLES: Who knocks at our door?

PAPHNUTIUS: It is I.

DISCIPLES: It is the voice of our Father Paphnutius.

PAPHNUTIUS: Unbolt the door.

DISCIPLES: Greetings, good Father!

PAPHNUTIUS: Greetings to you!

DISCIPLES: We missed you greatly in your long absence.

PAPHNUTIUS: I am glad I went away.

DISCIPLES: What has become of Thais?

PAPHNUTIUS: That which I desired.

DISCIPLES: Where is she staying?

PAPHNUTIUS: In a narrow cell where she mourns her sins.

DISCIPLES: Praise to the Exalted Trinity!

PAPHNUTIUS: And blessed be His awful Name now and forever!

DISCIPLES: Amen.

SCENE IX.

PAPHNUTIUS: Behold, three years of Thais' penance have passed, and I do not know whether or not atonement has been acceptable to God. I will arise and go to my Brother Anthony, that by his help I may learn the truth about her.

SCENE X.

ANTHONY: What unexpected pleasure is mine? What new happiness comes my way? Is this not my brother and fellow hermit, Paphnutius? Indeed, it is he.

PAPHNUTIUS: Yes, indeed it is I.

ANTHONY: It is well, Brother, you have come. You have delighted me with this coming.

PAPHNUTIUS: I am as delighted to see you as you are to see me.

ANTHONY: What is this happy occasion, so pleasing to us both, which brings you to our hermitage?

PAPHNUTIUS: I will explain.

ANTHONY: Yes, do.

PAPHNUTIUS: Three years ago, there lived some distance away a harlot by the name of Thais, who not only gave herself over to destruction, but even was wont to draw many with her to ruin.

ANTHONY: Alas! A pitiable way for a woman to live.

PAPHNUTIUS: I went to her disguised as a lover. At first I soothed her passionate heart with gentle exhortations; later I put fear into this same heart with sharper reproof.

ANTHONY: Such remedies were necessary for her passionate temperament.

PAPHNUTIUS: Finally she yielded, and despising her evil ways, she chose chastity and consented to be confined in a very narrow cell.

ANTHONY: I am so relieved to hear this that my whole being rejoices.

PAPHNUTIUS: This is in keeping with your sanctity, and I indeed greatly rejoice at her conversion; yet, nevertheless, I am somewhat concerned, because I fear that her wickedness can hardly bear the long trial.

ANTHONY: Where there is true love, there is holy compassion.

PAPHNUTIUS: Therefore, I beg your love that you and your disciples will wish to continue with me in fervent prayer until a sign from heaven will be given to us whether the mercy of Divine Providence has pardoned her because of her repentant tears.

ANTHONY: We gladly grant your request.

PAPHNUTIUS: I do not doubt but that God will very soon hear your prayers.

SCENE XI.

ANTHONY: Behold! The gospel's promise is fulfilled in us.

PAPHNUTIUS: What is this promise?

ANTHONY: Truly this, that they who pray together are able to gain all things.

PAPHNUTIUS: What do you mean?

ANTHONY: A certain vision has been revealed to Paul, my disciple.

PAPHNUTIUS: Summon him.

ANTHONY: Come here, Paul, and tell Paphnutius what you have seen.

PAUL: In a vision, I saw a magnificent couch in heaven spread with a snow-white coverlet; near it stood four shining virgins as if guarding it, and as I was gazing at the wondrous brightness, I said to myself, "This glory is fit for my father and Lord Anthony."

ANTHONY: I am not worthy of such honor.

PAUL: When I was thus speaking, a Divine Voice said, "This glory is not for Anthony as you hope, but it must be kept for Thais, the harlot."

PAPHNUTIUS: Praise to the sweetness of Your mercy, O Christ, the only begotten Son of God, because You have been so graciously pleased to comfort my sorrow.

ANTHONY: Christ deserves such praise.

PAPHNUTIUS: I shall go at once and visit my captive.

ANTHONY: It is time that you promise her the hope of pardon and the solace of eternal beatitude.

SCENE XII.

PAPHNUTIUS: Thais, my daughter, open the window and let me see you.

THAIS: Who speaks?

PAPHNUTIUS: Paphnutius, your father.

THAIS: How is it that I merit such happiness, that you deign to visit me, a sinner?

PAPHNUTIUS: Although absent from you in body for three years, nevertheless I was greatly concerned for your welfare.

THAIS: I do not doubt that.

PAPHNUTIUS: Tell me the story of your conversion, the manner of your repentance.

THAIS: I am able to tell you this, that I know I have done nothing acceptable to God.

PAPHNUTIUS: If God counts iniquities, which one of us would be saved?

THAIS: If you wish to know what I did: I gathered the multitude of my sins before my conscience as if they were a great bundle, and I kept them before my mind so that, even as I was always aware of the offensiveness of this place, so also the fear of hellfire was always in my heart.

PAPHNUTIUS: You have atoned for your sins by penance, therefore you have merited pardon.

THAIS: Oh, would that it were true!

PAPHNUTIUS: Give me your hand that I may lead you away.

THAIS: Do not, Reverend Father, do not take me away from this wretched cell, but let me stay in this place suited to my deserts.

PAPHNUTIUS: It is time, your fears allayed, that you begin to hope for life because your penance is acceptable to God.

THAIS: May all the angels praise His mercy because He has not despised the humility of a contrite heart.

PAPHNUTIUS: Be steadfast in the fear of the Lord and abide in His love, for after fifteen days, by the grace of heavenly fervor, you will be in Paradise.

THAIS: Oh, would that I deserved to escape punishment or at least to be burned in a less intense fire, for not by my own merits do I deserve everlasting happiness.

PAPHNUTIUS: God's free gift does not take into consideration man's merit, because were it given for merit, it would not be called grace.

THAIS: Therefore let all the heavenly company, and all the universe, and also all species of animals, and all surging waters praise Him who not only endures sinners, but ever freely bestows rewards upon penitents.

PAPHNUTIUS: From the beginning this was His wont, to have mercy rather than to destroy.

SCENE XIII.[3]

THAIS: Venerable Father, do not leave me, but stay with me and console me in this hour of my death.

PAPHNUTIUS: I will not leave you, I will not go away until your soul enters heaven, and I shall lay your body in the grave.

THAIS: Lo! Death is approaching.

PAPHNUTIUS: Now is the time to pray.

THAIS: You who created me, have mercy upon me! Grant that the soul which you created return to You.

PAPHNUTIUS: Oh, uncreated Being, truly form without matter, Who created man: man who is not that which is, but consists of diverse elements, grant that the various parts of this mortal may happily be united with the source of its origin by which the soul, endowed with immortality, may share in the celestial joys, and the body peacefully rest in the gentle embrace of its native earth until the dust of her ashes be gathered again and the breath of life return to her reawakened body. This same Thais may rise again in a perfect body as she was, and be at home among the snow-white lambs and be led into the joys of Eternity. Grant this, Thou above Who art what Thou art, Who in the Unity of the Trinity lives and reigns world without end.

[3] Fifteen days later, as suggested in the fifth speech from the end of the preceding scene. Thais is obviously in her cell, probably lying on a cot with Paphnutius standing or kneeling beside it.

A Cornish Miracle Play

In Cornwall, where Passion plays were staged on stationary platforms arranged in a circle rather than on pageant wagons, realism such as we find in the English cycles was not a distinctive feature. In the Cornish plays having their basis in the Bible, Celtic fantasy plays an important part. A fertile imagination or a considerable degree of symbolism informs the writing. Thus as Adam, exiled from Eden after his sin of disobedience, tries to dig the soil for the first time, the earth cries out in protest and resists him; God has to come down from heaven to rebuke the earth before Adam can till it. Thus, too, when Adam is about to die, his son Seth goes to Paradise and brings back from Eden three seeds of the apple Adam bit into before he was expelled. He places the seeds on his father's tongue, and three "rods" or shoots from the grave. They have mystical significance, for they ultimately figure in the Crucifixion as the "rood" or the cross on which Christ redeems fallen mankind.

Not all the Cornish plays are remarkable for the fanciful quality of the writing: thus a Noah play is quite ordinary except for providing Noah with a foil and opponent in the person of Tubal Cain, the son of Lamech; and a King David play (*David and Bathsheba*) is noteworthy not for any freely invented episode, but for the direct power of the treatment of David's lust and Bathsheba's ready response to his illicit wooing. But a poet's mystical imagination, no doubt drawing upon folklore, enriches the story of even so historical a character as David. One treatment of David relates him to the Cornish "Legend of the Rood" by making him bring the rods from which the cross will be made to Jerusalem. God sends the angel Gabriel to the king to order him to fetch from "Mount Tabor in arid Arabia" the three mystic shoots planted there by Moses! David locates them

and is amazed to find them so *green,* while his Counsellor notes that they are indeed "rods of grace" because they have such a rare fragrance. Brought to Palestine, they instantly prove their mystic power in healing one petitioner of his blindness and another of his lameness. David, finally, is just about to go to plant them in the ground when he learns that they have already mysteriously planted themselves, as it were: a miracle took place in the night while the king was asleep, for the rods are not only rooted in the earth "but all the three are joined in one," a detail that plainly symbolizes the Trinity. David is, of course, associated with the redemption of man on the Cross because Joseph is of the house of David, who was the son of Jesse. It was, moreover, predicted by Isaiah that the Messiah would come out of the "stem of Jesse" (*Isaiah 11:1*). "And there shall come forth a rod out of the stem of Jesse/ and a branch shall grow out of his roots," (King James Version); or "There shall come forth a shoot from the stump of Jesse,/ and a branch shall grow out of his roots." (Revised Standard Version, 1952); or "And there shall come forth a rod out of the root of Jesse: and a flower shall rise up out of his root" (Douay Version based on St. Jerome's Latin translation known as The Vulgate, the only translation with which the authors of the Cornish drama would have been familiar).

A dire fate awaits Pontius Pilate after the Crucifixion which he ordered, and his fantastic end is the substance of one of the plays of this Cornish Passion Play or cycle, *The Death of Pilate,* which follows.[1]

[1] A two-volume edition of the extant Cornish plays was published in an English translation (*The Ancient Cornish Drama,* edited by A. Norris) in 1859. For other Celtic material, see W. S. Clark, *The Early Irish Stage,* Oxford, 1955.

THE DEATH OF PILATE

ADAPTED BY JOHN GASSNER[2]

CHARACTERS

TIBERIUS CAESAR

COUNSELLOR

MESSENGER

PILATE

VERONICA

FOUR EXECUTIONERS

JAILER

SERVANT

TRAVELER

DEVILS

GENERAL SCENE: *A Playing Circle with a raised platform in the center.*

SCENE I.

TIBERIUS CAESAR: [*Seated on a throne in the center*]
I am above all people of the world, indeed,
But great is my sadness and need:
A leper I have become!
What is the best to be done?
COUNSELLOR: Lord, send word to Pilate
That he send forthwith at thy news
Christ, King of the Jews.

He can cure every malady
As He is the very Deity,
The Lord of heaven and earth,
Most truly.
EMPEROR: [*To a* Messenger]
Light-of-foot, my messenger,
Thou must go
To him immediately!
MESSENGER: [*Kneeling*] Lord Tiberius,
What do you want of me?
EMPEROR: Go to Pilate forthwith;
Pray him that he send me at thy news
Christ, King of the Jews,
God without equal, savior,
That he may have favor.
MESSENGER: Dear Lord, with all fervor,
I will do this errand;
Farewell, I say to thee.
[*He goes out bowing*]

SCENE II.

Pilate's "House" in Jerusalem.[3]

MESSENGER: Sir Pilate
Through me thou are greeted by our Emperor

To send Christ to his palace door,
Christ, the flower of all healers.
PILATE: [*Craftily*] Messenger, pray go
Into the country and seek a while;
If he be in the land, I will go
And seek also myself.
[*The* Messenger *departs*]

SCENE III.

[*As the* Messenger *walks about "in the country,"*
Veronica, *a saintly woman, meets him*]
VERONICA: Sweet young man who wanders here,
Whom seekest thou so dear?
Tell me!
MESSENGER: What is that to thee?
Surely, thou canst not help me!
To seek help the Emperor hath sent me,
For he suffers from leprosy
And finds no doctor to make him well.—
Where Jesus is I pray thee tell.
VERONICA: Jesus who was our Lord, in fay,*   faith
Is dead and gone to clay
Slain by Pilate.
Were he alive yet
You would have no need to roam.
MESSENGER: [*Grieving*] Alas, that I ever came so
far from home,
Alas that I know not where to go
Or where I shall set foot!
VERONICA: I am one of his women, lo!
And will to the emperor with thee go.
And in His name, by my word,
Shall be made a remedy
To cure his leprosy,
If he believes Christ to be heaven's Lord.
MESSENGER: Let us then hasten to my Lord,
If he can be healed by thee,
Thou shalt have gold for guerdon:*   reward
And ever shall thy will be done.
[*They go off together*]

---

2 Adapted from the literal translation by A. Norris in *The Ancient Cornish Drama*, Oxford, 1859.
3 Located at some convenient point in one of the quadrants of the playing circle, in a "theater-in-the-round" production.

SCENE IV.

The Palace.

MESSENGER: My Lord, be at ease!
That same prophet thou didst seek
Has been slain in crucifixion.
But a woman is with me, if it please,
Who, through Him, will cure thy affliction.
    EMPEROR: Alas, I will eat no meat,
Because the prophet is dead now.
But woman, what sayest thou?
    VERONICA: [*Holding out a handkerchief*] Believe in
        Christ, I advise thee.
The print of His face I will show thee,
As He gave it to me on this kerchief of lace:
As soon as thou seest His face
He will heal thee, without other salve.
    EMPEROR: What wilt thou have?
Thou wilt find much favor,
Thou shalt be made a lady
Over much land, truly.
    VERONICA: Veronica is my name,
The face of Jesus is with me,
In the likeness made by His sweat:
Whoever sees it yet,
And believes in His godhead
He needs must be healed.

In Christ believe, that He is Lord,
And salvation for the people of the world.
Then thou shalt surely be healed
Of thy leprosy.
    EMPEROR: [*Kneeling*] To Him with a full heart I
        will pray.
As thou art true God and great in grace,
Help me swiftly
As thou art Savior.
    [*Pointing to the kerchief*]
Show it to me, I pray—
That such a thing should be
Is great wonder to me.
Come near as thou lovest me,
For I would speak with thee further
Before parting.
    VERONICA: Look at it, and in the little time now
Shalt thou be cured of thy sorrow.
Believe Him to be the God of all
And Savior of all soul.
    [*She shows him the kerchief, and he kneels*]
    EMPEROR: Jesus, full of pity,
Thy dear face I will kiss—
    [*He kisses the kerchief*]
I know that thou will cure me
Of all leprosy;
Lord Christ of heaven and earth, for this
Glory be to thee always!
    [*He is healed of his leprosy*]
I am healed now.

Blessed be thou,
Who was the Lord of breath
And was done to death.
There is no Lord above thee,
God without an equal!
    VERONICA: Since thou art healed now
Know this well
There is no other God than He,
Yet Pilate killed Him.
Vengeance for Him take thou
That was Christ and hath now saved thee.
    EMPEROR: Sweet Veronica, I will do as you tell,
For through Him,
Cured of malady, I am well.
If Pilate be still in this world,
He shall go to death, most truly,
He and all his company!
    [*Shouting*]
Executioners, come to me!
    [*Enter the* Executioners]
    FIRST EXECUTIONER: My lord, here we be:
You cried out so mightily
We feared your breath!
    EMPEROR: Go, find Pilate for me.
Bring him with might to Rome
To be put to death!
    SECOND EXECUTIONER: Let us go to his home,
In Jerusalem is he to be sought.
    THIRD EXECUTIONER: [*To the* Emperor] To you he
        shall be brought.
However he be perilous
He shall not withstand us.
    [*They go to seek* Pilate]

SCENE V.

In front of Pilate's *Palace.*

FOURTH EXECUTIONER: Thou, Pilate, come to my
    Lord!
Thou must certainly go
At thy master's word,
Despite thy mother's son,
Or thou wilt be undone.
    PILATE: [*Following him with suspiciously hearty
        confidence . . .*] I will gladly go to my lord,
Tiberius Caesar, meekly,
For gentle he is to every one,
And in my heart I love him dearly.
    [*They go off together*]

SCENE VI.

In Caesar's *Palace.*

[Tiberius *is seated on a high throne as* Pilate
and the First Executioner *enter*]
    FIRST EXECUTIONER: Lord, see the fellow here.

As you have heard it,
He condemned the prophet
To be put upon the rood-tree.
And upon it Jesus died;
On His body He suffered dear
To save the race of the sons of men.—

[*The* Emperor *leaps down from his throne an-grily; but he seems strangely affected and instead of scolding* Pilate, *embraces him warmly*]

EMPEROR: Pilate, thou art most welcome,
As God is my witness, to my home,
For I love thee
As soon as I see thee;
I have no wish to harm thee,
And never shall.

PILATE: [*Smoothly*] O Lord, great thanks to you so dear!
To you surely I have shown among all lords
How much I love thee who on the earth hast no peer.
Gentle art of words,
And art a man without a peer.

SECOND EXECUTIONER: Is it for this we brought him here?
Thou, fellow, thou shalt come out with us below.

[*The* Executioners *seize* Pilate]

THIRD EXECUTIONER: Out thou shalt go!
A charm thou must have with thee.
Art thou a sorcerer
Whom no man can do injury?
Answer without ado!

[*The* Executioner *and* Pilate *are now at some distance from the* Emperor *when the latter is suddenly seized with illness again and cries out, whereupon they go no further.* Veronica *also enters to minister to him*]

EMPEROR: [*Becoming remorseful*] Out! harrow, harrow!
If Pilate be not slain
I know not what I shall do;
My heart has so much pain.

When the foul fellow came forward, so trim,
To give way, I was fain.*   glad
And in his answer I found, oh sorrow!,
No cause to punish him.

Tell me, Veronica, dear,
What to do here.

VERONICA: If he comes into your sight,
From injury he will be free
As long as there is wound about him
The garment of Jesus,
It is his undermost garment.
Bring him here again to you
And strip it from him—
There is only this to do!

[*She retires*]

EMPEROR: My blessings fall on you!

[*Calling out sternly*]

Executioners, bring him back

That my heart grow light and I prove true.

[*Three* Executioners *approach the* Emperor, *who is still somewhat distracted*]

FIRST EXECUTIONER: Lord, behold us near to you.
To serve your heart's desire.

EMPEROR: Bring Pilate again. Of wit bereaved,
Careless in my dealing with him,
I was deceived.

SECOND EXECUTIONER: [*Doubtfully*]
I will bring him to you without delay,
Whom we have not dared to slay,
For to look upon him is to love him for aye.

THIRD EXECUTIONER: [*Whimsically*] However much we may love him,
I don't mind killing him;
Never shall he sing in choir
One note higher.

[*He seizes* Pilate *and begins to drag him to the* Emperor *in the center of the stage*]

PILATE: [*Still confident*] I go to him joyfully.

[*They go up to the* Emperor]

FOURTH EXECUTIONER: Lord, beware the fellow's charm.
When you see him before you
You will not be able to do him harm. . . .

EMPEROR: Now, Pilate, I tell thee, by grace,
I'll have that robe without seam
Which is about thee.

PILATE: You are a lord, I deem
The robe I am wearing below
Will not do for you;
It is not clean, but soiled with grime;
It has not been washed a long time;
Do not desire it, I pray thee so,
At this time.

EMPEROR: I am not ashamed, Pilate,
Of wearing the garment Jesus wore.
I am anxious to have it,
I pray thee take it off; I say no more!

PILATE: [*Hedging*] Lord, now if I remove it
Before you naked I should be;
It would not be respectful to thee.

EMPEROR: I must have it!
Seek not to parley with me.

PILATE: Alas, since you must have it,
Henceforth no peace for me,
I know truly;

[*He takes the garment off*]

I do not see now
How my life to hold—
Except with much gold.

EMPEROR: Out on thee,
Thou hast killed Jesus, our Lord.

[*To an* Executioner]

Reach me my sword,
That I may slay him as quick as a word.

VERONICA: Lord, that you shall not, but call
On others to seek out the most cruel death
He may have while he has breath;
For the villain hath caused to die

That same Son who made us all,
Sea, and earth, and sky.
    EMPEROR: Into prison he shall go;
A cruel death and trim
I will ordain for him,
And no man shall save him!
Ho, jailer, take him forth.
      [Enter the Jailer *and a* Servant]
Loiter not now; let no one be afraid—
My commands must be obeyed!
    JAILER: Lord, we are ready,
To do whatever it be.
    EMPEROR: Put this fellow into dungeon to rot
And let him have no light at all;
He is a sorcerer and see he must not.
And the most cruel death I ordain for him
Who slew Jesus the Savior of all.
    SERVANT: Put him in the lowest pit we shall
Among the vermin unkind;
And a sprightly fellow is "Whip-behind."
      [He whips Pilate *away]*
    JAILER: *[Following]* Do not spare him, though you
      hear him roar.
He shall not for all his cunning stray
Without some harm befalling him!
    SERVANT: *[Thrusting him toward "prison"]* Now
      until flesh rot
Shalt thou in prison stay
And a hard death thou hast in store.
    PILATE: *[Stopping—then cannily]* Pray tell me
What death you have decreed for me,
I know well I shall die; great is my anxiety.
    JAILER: The cruelest men have ever bore:
In this world trust thou no more!
    PILATE: From that preserve myself yet I may.
      [He stabs himself]
Oh! alas and well-a-way.
      [He dies]

SCENE VII.

At the Court, in the central area where the Emperor's *throne is situated.*

      [Enter the Jailer *and the* Servant]
    EMPEROR: In what plight is Pilate
In the place where he is?
Tell me truly.
    JAILER: My lord, that man is dead:
Through pain and sorrow led,
With his knife wondrous suddenly
He smote himself to the heart.
    EMPEROR: A more cruel death on land
Than to kill himself with his own hand
No man may find, I think.
Take him by the two feet right smart
And in deep ground his carcass sink,
For I right well believe that here
Men of this body will have fear.

SCENE VIII.

Outside the City.

    JAILER: *[To his* Servant] Whip-behind, take his
      head;
By his feet I will drag him dead
Into the grave then.
    SERVANT: I will, by my rear; Amen!
      [They drop Pilate *into a grave. But he is at once*
      thrown out of the earth with an explosion. They
      leap back]
    SERVANT: *[Who is the first man to come back]* O
      master, by my soul,
This is a devil foul,
For out of the earth he has jumped, the slave!
    JAILER: When he leapt from the grave
I took fright at the noise;
But he surely could not move himself,
Shut in as he was.
    SERVANT: Boldly let us take him at once
And put him into the grave again.
I believe he will in it bide
If he be on Heaven's side—
Or else he is a devil.
      [Looking down at Pilate's *face, doubtfully]*
Black indeed is his hue!
    JAILER: If he be not on God's side,
It would take all the parish too
To lay him in the grave.
Let us put him in the earth without more ado!
      [They put him back in the ground, but the body
      is thrown up again]
    SERVANT: By my faith, he is a devil hound!
He will not stay a moment under ground!
He is a wicked slave!
    JAILER: Let us go and tell Caesar, knave.
      [They go off.]

SCENE IX.

At the Emperor's *court again.*

    JAILER: *[Approaching the* Emperor] Sir Caesar,
      lord high,
The fellow will never lie
Beneath the ground.
    EMPEROR: *[Frightened]* Come not nigh!
He was a devil before he died.
And a worse devil now, I fear.
    SERVANT: Sir, Earth parted over him
Threw him out with a sigh
So mighty it was dreadful to hear.
    EMPEROR: *[Crying out, so that* Veronica *enters at*
      his cry] Oh, what shall I do well-a-way?
Against this devil I have found
No defense in any way.
The stench of this corpse will slay

All in my kingdom's bound.
    VERONICA: My lord, in a box of iron
In the river Tiber let him sink.
From there most certainly it is
He will not come up again, I think.
    EMPEROR: O Veronica, good counsel this
Thou hast given me.
Executioners, come hither quickly!
    [*Impatiently*]
I almost get my death, I do,
With waiting for you.
    [*Enter the* Executioners]
    FIRST EXECUTIONER: Lord, coming from Spain,
I was in the middle of Germany,[4]
When I was called amain:*   quickly
Make known thy will, I pray thee.
    SECOND EXECUTIONER: If there is sorrow in thy
      heart and pain,
Thy will shall be done speedily.
    EMPEROR: Take the body of this freak
Which is stinking with a tang
That is accursed, and—
Cast it, in a box of iron, in some creek.
    [First Executioner *goes out at once*]
    THIRD EXECUTIONER: At once in a trunk of iron
      shall he be cast
In deepest water.
    FOURTH EXECUTIONER: [*Doubtfully*] The water will
      not assuredly
Be willing to contain
This bedevilled body.
May fire of the great devil burn it,
So it come no more into this country.
    FIRST EXECUTIONER: [*Returning with assistants*]
      See, I have the iron chest!
And to the water let us run with it.
    SECOND EXECUTIONER: Devil carry him to his
      place!
Let us go with great speed
To put him into green water without grace.

SCENE X.

    [*They carry* Pilate*'s body in a box to the Tiber*]
    FOURTH EXECUTIONER: Go, thou cursed Pilate!
To the bottom of it!
Surely thou shalt fall,
And with thee go the curses of all
For sentencing the Son of God
And Son of Mary.
    [*The body is thrown into the water; the* Execu-
    tioners *go off*]
    A TRAVELER: [*Entering*] I shall go and wash my
      hands
Straightway in this water
That they be white and free.

[4] The quaint freedom taken with geography by the medieval imagination is deliberately retained in this adaptation.

[*He washes his hands, and is immediately seized
    with mortal sickness*]
Alas, Death surely is come for me.
The water has done that for me!
    [*He dies*]

SCENE XI.

    MESSENGER: My lord, bring the good wise woman
      hither,
For no man goes over Tiber river
Without Pilate's body slay.
We must put Pilate away,
For Jesus' sake, to another place.
    [Veronica *enters*]
    EMPEROR: [*To Her*] Out, out! what shall I do,
I have no one to help me.
That body is accursed surely.
Give me counsel, again.
    VERONICA: Let him be sent to sea
In a boat's hold
Whatever the cost in silver or gold.
The boat shall carry him to hell,
My lord, I warrant it surely.
    EMPEROR: Blessings on thee.—
My Executioners, come at once to me!
    [*Enter the* Executioners]
Drag Pilate out of Tiber's stream
And send him in a boat out to sea.
    [*The* Executioners *bow and leave*]

SCENE XII.

By the banks of the Tiber.

    [*The four* Executioners *are seen dragging the
    river for the body*]
    FIRST EXECUTIONER: To draw it from this creek
Let drop a grappling iron on the corpse.
    SECOND EXECUTIONER: I have cast two grappling
      irons here.
Out of the water shall the body be won
Though it be heavy as a great stone.
    [*Straining hard*]
Now *haul* ye men without a fear,
    But have a care!
    THIRD EXECUTIONER: See the hateful carcass rising
      fast
Let us drag it onto the grass.
    [*They drag the body toward the sea*]

SCENE XIII.

By the sea.

    [*The* Executioners *have drawn the body to the
    seashore*]

FIRST EXECUTIONER: Without further delay now
Let us put the body into a boat for hell
With the curse of God, His Angels, and saints as well.
[*They do so*]
SECOND EXECUTIONER: Go, hoist at once the sail
That he shall go with the wind without fail
And with him the curse of God above.
[*They hoist sail*]
THIRD EXECUTIONER: Now let us shove her off!
[*A terrifying noise is heard as the boat floats out
to sea and strikes a rock*]
Hear the hideous roar
From the rock in the sea.
At his coming the water grows rough;
To my knowledge, certain many devils
Are carrying him off.
FOURTH EXECUTIONER: Let us hasten from devils
coming for their spoil;
I hear them shout so gleefully
I fear their toil!
[*The* Executioners *run off. Enter* Devils *carrying*
Pilate's *body*]
LUCIFER: My devils, all together,
I pray you come without fear
To fetch, along with his soul so dear,
The body of Pilate.
In roaring fire he is to remain,
And in torment ceaselessly,
So his song shall be "O woe is me,
That I was born into this world of pain!"
BEELZEBUB: This body accursed falls to us;
Not fit to be in earth, nor in water, nor in brine,
It is surely mine.

Ship never passed around
This way that was not drowned;
He deserved no bliss,
But to be overwhelmed with fire.
LUCIFER: From the water raised he is
Brought ashore again,
To go down with us in the abyss.
SATAN: [*Boasting, gleefully*] Mast and sail made
ready for him,
Upon a rock he was cast for me plain
And fell into my toils.
BEELZEBUB: That rock opened with fear:
There we received him neat,
His voice horrible to hear.
In fire and smoke and great heat,
In that rock he shall ever remain.
Upon a rock he was cast for me plain.
Monstrously grimacing devils
He will find, with us pent,
And all kinds of torment.
BEELZEBUB: Now everyone lend a hand
To float him in this same beer.
While thou, devil Tulfric, a plain-chant sing!
TULFRIC: [*Singing with devilish obscenity*] Yah,
kiss my rear!
Its end is out here
So long behind.
Beelzebub and Satan kind,
You sing the great drone bass
While I sing a fine treble
To please any devil
And bring Pilate to his place.

Teatro Olimpico, Vicenza. Built between 1580 and 1584 by Vincenzo Scamozzi from a basic design by Andrea Palladio. Photo: L. Chiovato, Vincenza. *Above* (left): A view from the stage of the central arch and two side arches through which actors made their entrances and exits. Note the permanent scenery behind each arch and the elaborate perspective created. Photo: Alinari. *Opposite page:* Jean Antoine Watteau, *Italian Comedians,* that is, the actors of the *commedia dell' arte*. Courtesy National Gallery of Art, Washington, D.C., Samuel H. Kress Collection.

Renaissance Forms

Renaissance Forms

As could well be expected there arose a considerable proliferation of dramatic forms during the Renaissance when individualism and traditionalism met in a fruitful symbiosis, and when national literatures grew up side by side with the pursuit of universal forms of art and literature. Some major developments have already been represented in the earlier section on the Renaissance (pages 214–283), but attention should be given here to several other dramatic forms.

One early form is the pastoral genre, which takes the reader back as far as the Hellenistic poetry of Theocritus in third-century, B.C., Sicily and brings him forward to Renaissance pastoral romances, in which shepherds and shepherdesses disported themselves in romantic situations with, despite their natural countryside environs, considerable preciosity of manners and speech. The most celebrated of these exercises were the Neapolitan Sannazaro's *Arcadia* (1504), the Portuguese Montemajor's *Diana* (1558), and Sir Philip Sidney's *Arcadia* (1590). Considerably more reputable than mere literary exercises were the pastoral plays of Torquato Tasso (*Aminta*, 1573) and Battista Guarini (*Il Pastor fido* or *The Faithful Shepherd* (1585), both celebrants of a fictive "golden age." Since, however, the masterpiece of this genre, as well as its least artificial example, is undoubtedly Shakespeare's *As You Like It* (1599–1600), the English reader is already somewhat familiar with this dramatic form.

Related to the pastoral is early music-drama or opera. This is first fully represented by Ottavio Rinuccini's *Dafne* (1594) with a score by Jacopo Peri. But since the words of early opera soon became overshadowed by the music, beginning with the great composer Claudio Monteverdi's *Orfeo* and *Arianna* in 1607 and 1608, this development falls essentially outside the province of the spoken drama.

COMMEDIA DELL' ARTE

Another Renaissance type of theatrical diversion that takes us back to the classical world is that of the *commedia dell' arte,* so named because the actors were not amateurs such as those who performed now and then at the court theatres, but professional masters of the *art* of acting—"dell' arte." Its comic and romantic characters can be traced back to the lovers, parents, and servants of fourth-century, B.C., Greek "New Comedy," whose Roman adapters and imitators were Plautus and Terence. Some scholars, however, see its origin in popular nonliterary drama, such as the Atellan farces and the mimes of Roman times as well as the professional wandering players, *jongleurs* and mimes, of the Middle Ages. Specifically, it was these species of entertainment that anticipated the kind of plays presented by such professional act-

ing companies of the Renaissance as the Confidenti, the Fedeli, and the famous Gelosi, first in Venice and then in other Italian cities. They performed as a rule, until they gained aristocratic or royal patronage, on improvised stages in market places and courtyards, displaying a variety of masked stock characters and comic situations with the help of set speeches (*concetti*) memorized by the actors, and stock stage business or tricks (*lazzi*) invented or elaborated by gifted clowns and rehearsed by their successors. An example of a *lazzo* is the apparently deftly managed "lazzo of tearing the wings from a fly." The number of such bits of pantomime, passed on from one generation of clowns to another, multiplied and grew in finesse.

Among the characters who could be counted on to convey any number of recognizable situations and disguises of servants were two old men, the Venetian-merchant Pantalone and the scholarly character or pedant from the University town of Bologna known as the Dottore or Doctor. The cast would also include a swaggering and vainglorious military man (often a Spaniard) who may have descended from the *miles gloriosus* of Plautus, and was known in Italian as the Capitano. Other colorful character types were the servant girl Colombina, (Columbine), and the servants and clowns called *zanni* in Italian. They were best known by the names of Pedrolino, Scaramouche, Pulcinella and Arlecchino (Harlequin), though they could bear one of several other names. All these characters wore characteristic masks. But the romantic leads, the lovers who were the amoroso and amorosa of the play, were unmasked and were known by individual, personal, names.

By the end of the sixteenth century the *commedia* actors had successfully invaded France and, within half a century, Molière and his semi-amateur company of the Illustre Théâtre were to encounter their stiff competition and also to learn from them. Moving into an age of ultrarefinement, France, writes Allardyce Nicoll in his *World Drama*, "created the pathetic Pierrot out of Pedrolino, and refined the early rough Colombina into the dainty Columbine."[1] And on the English stage, which reflected the *commedia dell' arte* in Shakespeare's own day (Gremio in *The Taming of the Shrew* is called a "pantalowne"), Pulcinella became Punch, and the pantomime-clown was born of the Italian *zanni.* Nicoll sums up the dispersion of Italian popular comedy by concluding that "For nearly two hundred years the *commedia dell' arte*

[1] The change which ultimately romanticized *commedia* in later times and even suffused it with romantic melancholia is reflected in Paul Verlaine's *Fêtes Galantes* (1869) in the lines:

Votre âme est un paysage choisi
Que vont charmant masques et bergamesques
Jouant du luth, et dansant, et quasi
Tristes sous leurs dèguisement fantasques.

was the most popular form of dramatic performance in most countries of the Continent" (page 197). But, in time the hard satiric outlines of many a Renaissance *commedia dell' arte* character became softened, and as interest in individual character came into vogue in the eighteenth century, dissatisfaction with the conventional masked characterizations mounted. The great Molière, who created such notably individualized characters as the religious hypocrite Tartuffe and the misanthropic gentleman Alceste, discarded them for the most part. His eighteenth-century Italian successor, Carlo Goldoni (*The Mistress of the Inn, The Fan*, and so on), who started out writing for the *commedia dell' arte* theatre after joining one of its companies in Verona and becoming its chief playwright in residence, renounced his allegiance to masked comedy. Goldoni (1707–1792) maintained that the mask of the actor "must always be very prejudicial to the action of the performer either in joy or sorrow; whether he be in love, cross, or good-humored, the same features are always exhibited; and however he may gesticulate and vary the tone of his delivery, he can never convey by the countenance, which is the interpreter of the heart, the different passions. . . ." The performer in the new age must "possess a soul" whereas "the soul under a mask is like a fire under ashes."[2] Nevertheless, the characteristics of the Renaissance *commedia dell' arte* were not forgotten by these and other playwrights, nor have they been dismissed by actors, especially by such great clowns of the twentieth century as Charles Chaplin, Ed Wynn, and Bert Lahr, and a great mime —Marcel Marceau—who have all worn a clown's white make-up. And *commedia dell' arte* conventions survived in the drama not only in musical comedy and opera (such as Mascagni's *I Pagliacci,* 1887), but in such straight plays as Jacinto Benavente's *The Bonds of Interest* and Edna St. Vincent Millay's noteworthy one-acter, *Aria da Capo,* originally produced by the pioneering Provincetown Players in New York.

There is just one difficulty in obtaining the real dramatic bouquet of the *commedia dell' arte* playwriting. It had no text other than a scenario, or *soggeto,* which is a mere plot outline. But even these scenarios are now little known. We provide one example, *The Portrait,* on pages 778–781, but since much of the vitality of these scenarios lay in their performance, a knowledge of the kind of theatre they represent will immeasurably increase one's enjoyment of it.[3]

[2] A. M. Nagler, *Sources of Theatrical History.* New York: Dover Publications, 1959.

[3] Among works to be consulted are the following: Maurice Sand, *The History of Harlequinade,* 2 volumes, London, 1915; K. M. Lea, *Italian Popular Comedy* (2 volumes), Oxford, Oxford University Press, 1934); Winifred Smith, *The Commedia dell'Arte,* New York: Columbia University Press, 1912, and *Italian Actors of The Renaissance.* New York: Coward-McCann, 1940; Pierre Louis Ducharte, *Italian Comedy. . . . ,* New York: John Day, 1929.

THE MASQUE

Another Renaissance dramatic form, the *masque,* was the polar opposite of the *commedia* scenarios in that it constituted highly refined writing intended for courtly entertainment, though the successful *commedia dell' arte* companies were also wont to perform at ducal and princely courts from time to time. The acting, the proud achievement of the *commedia,* was apt to be inconsequential in the masques, in which the performers were courtly amateurs. And the scenery became increasingly lavish and ingenious whereas the *commedia* companies made do for the greater part with platforms curtained off at the back for the actors to make conventional entrances and exits, the curtains painted to represent houses and a street. (It became customary in later indoor stages to use flats set on the stage in receding perspective.) The subject matter of the masques consisted of fancied and mythical, idyllic or pastoral matter rather than comic intrigue, and the treatment was likely to be allusive. It could also possess some moral and spiritual as well as generally poetic quality. This was notably the case in John Milton's poetic masterpiece *Comus,* "A Masque, presented at Ludlow Castle; 1634, before the Earl of Bridgewater, Lord President of Wales." *Comus* also can qualify as a pastoral play.

Masques, also spelled *masks,* may be defined as entertainments in dramatic form in which spectacles, dances, and disguises or masquerades supplemented the dialogue and the plot and usually exceeded them in importance. They were much favored in Italian courts where they acquired increasingly ingenious scenic effects and required the services of the gifted architects and painters of the Renaissance. In England masques gained considerable vogue during the sixteenth and seventeenth centuries, and attracted the services of leading playwrights such as Middleton, Chapman, Francis Beaumont, and Ben Jonson, who supplemented his own vigorously "realistic" comedies of humours with some of the best-written masques in the language.[1]

Developed in the courts of Renaissance Italy and imported from there by Henry VIII, the masque was at first a simple diversion, mostly a matter of mumming and dancing by fantastically costumed lords and ladies at banquets; their main feature at first was, in fact, the masquerade. Then scenery became an important element, and the performers came to be wheeled in on a pageant car carrying with them some set stage pieces. This essentially medieval mode of staging was later elaborated in Elizabethan times by means of prepared stationary scenery placed at the four corners of the banquet hall or side by side on a raised platform in the manner of the medieval *man-*

[1] Jonson was associated in these enterprises with the famous artist Inigo Jones (1573–1652), who had learned the art of producing perspective settings while spending eight years in Italy.

sion setting. Starting in January 1605 with *The Masque of Blackness,* for which Ben Jonson wrote the text, the medieval kind of setting was supplanted by the illusionistic settings Inigo Jones had observed in Italy—that is, by scenes created through the use of painted flats or *wings* arranged in receding perspective at the right and left sides of the stage with the space between them closed by a painted backdrop or *shutter.*

The Masque of Blackness had a front curtain behind a proscenium arch providing a seascape, and the masquers seemed to move on the waves. In the next masque by Jones and Jonson, a "turning machine" was employed and the performers were revealed on a rotating shell representing the globe. A number of such devices for "stage motions" were used in such subsequently staged entertainments as *The Masque of Beauty* and *The Hue and Cry after Cupid* in 1608. Then in February 1609 came Jones' production of Jonson's *The Masque of Queens* at the palace of Whitehall. Here a vividly staged hell scene which was replete with fire and smoke was suddenly transformed into a celestial "house of fame" to the accompaniment of music. Thus, England at last became acquainted with the technique of effecting the scene changes and the transformation scenes popular at Italian court theatres. It is not too much to say that the masque and the comic or comparatively gross "antimasque" (such as the hell scene with which *The Masque of Queens* began) inaugurated a new age in the English stage; just as masques and other courtly entertainments, especially opera, did in Italy and later in France, introducing the proscenium arch, the front curtain, the perspective settings, and finally the moving scenery of the illusionistic stage. Even the prim republican age of England under the Puritan Commonwealth ruled by Cromwell did not stop the trend toward elaborate (and expensive) stage illusionism, which by the late sixteen-thirties had invaded the theatre as well as the court. William D'Avenant produced in 1656 the first English opera with music by Henry Lawes, *The Siege of Rhodes,* a "heroic play" written by Dr. Charles Coleman and George Hudson, billed as an entertainment in the manner of the ancients. When the Commonwealth collapsed four years later and Charles II was restored to the throne of England, the theatres that had been padlocked by the Puritans reopened. But the sole remaining open-air theatre, the Red Bull playhouse, which like the Fortune and Globe before it had persisted in maintaining an Elizabethan platform stage, could not hold its own against the illusionistic proscenium-arch stage for more than a few years.[2]

[2] Useful material on the masque will be found in the following books: R. Brotanek, *Die Englische Masken-spiele,* 1902; L. B. Campbell, *Scenes and Machines on the English Stage During the Renaissance,* New York: Macmillan, 1923; H. A. Evans, *English Masques,* 1897; W. W. Greg, *A List of Masques, Pageants . . . ,* 1902; A. Nicoll, *Stuart Masques and the Renaissance Stage,*

SPANISH *GOLDEN AGE* DRAMATIC FORMS

That courtly refinements of staging and writing constituted only a very small portion of the energies of the Renaissance was particularly evident in the popular open-air theatres of Elizabethan England and the *corrales* of the Golden Age of Spain, whose leading playwrights were, respectively, Shakespeare and Lope de Vega. But there is a multiplicity of dramatic forms that fall between those of the non-literary *commedia dell' arte* and the overly literary court masques that is not fully represented by the five plays of our first Renaissance section on pages 214–381. Two other dramatic forms are presented in the present section—the *Interlude,* represented here by Cervantes' delightful farce *The Cave of Salamanca,* and baroque Morality drama of the Spanish stages as exemplified by Calderón's famous play *Life Is a Dream.* The presence of these two stage works will also extend our representation of the Spanish stage during the so-called Golden Age since the three most widely recognized authors of that period are Lope de Vega (see pages 361–381), Miguel de Cervantes, and Pedro Calderón de la Barca. Perhaps nothing, however, serves better to set the outermost limits of the classic theatre of Spain than a juxtaposition of Cervantes' little play and Calderón's somber masterpiece.

The former and earlier piece reflects the entire genre of farce or farce-comedy which started in the Middle Ages. The transitional fifteenth century *Maître Pierre Pathelin* in France is typical, as are the transitional *Interludes* of the Tudor period in England. Among the latter an early example is the Canterbury chaplain Henry Medwall's *Fulgens and Lucres* (c. 1497), in which two lovers vie for the love of a Roman senator's daughter while their clowning servants compete for the favor of her maid. But the most effective of the English interludes are the work of the actor-playwright John Heywood (?1497–1578?), who was, like Cervantes, connected with the nobility (he was related by marriage to Sir Thomas More), an educated man, and a critic of his times. His interlude masterpiece is *The Four P's* which employs a comic debate or, rather, lying match between four more or less realistically drawn and satirically heightened characters: a widely traveled Palmer, a Pardoner, a "Poticary" (an apothecary and quack physician), and a Pedlar. For all its satirical afflatus, it is clever vaudeville rather than a preachment or lesson, and is completely free from allegory.

This is also true of Cervantes' eight highly farcical Interludes, among which *The Cave of Salamanca* is one of the most successful and best known. The form of interlude he employed consists of a brief incident

London: Harrap, 1938; P. Reyer, *Les Masques Anglais,* 1909; M. Sullivan, *Court Masques of James I,* New York: Putnam, 1913; E. Welsford, *The Court Masque,* New York: Macmillan, 1927.

intended to be performed for the entertainment of a restless audience between the acts of a full-length play, and for that reason called an *entremés*. (This was not the case when the English interludes were staged, since they were given in banquet halls and not in the open-air Tudor or Elizabethan public playhouses.) As in the case of other short entertainments of this sort, the characters were likely to be stock, the piquant situations blithely contrived, and the conclusion briskly congenial. These farces were the outgrowth of performances by medieval minstrels called *juglares* in Spain, amplified with *commedia dell' arte* plots. Cervantes' racy little seventeenth-century plays, the *entreméses*, are the most distinguished examples of a general form of popular or folk theatre known under various other names such as *auto*, *sainete*, and *genero chico*.

Calderón's moralistic plays also reflect a widely diffused genre, but one that had its beginning in medieval sermons and in plays known as Moralities and Allegories. Although Calderón wrote other kinds of plays, including characteristically Spanish "cape and sword" dramas of intrigue, he sounded the depths of religious and moral feeling in a series of plays in which there was a rewarding union of medieval spirituality and Renaissance elaboration and poetic refinement. Frequently encountered in Spanish Golden Age literature and art, this combination of qualities attained an intensity and amplitude or even extravagance usually associated with baroque art. *Life Is a Dream* is the profoundest realization of Spanish baroque drama. Its author was long considered the leading Spanish playwright, and his work made an especially strong impression in Catholic countries. Representative of both the Counter-Reformation and the romantic afflatus of the age of the Conquistadores and masters of large portions of Europe, it became the best-known Spanish play. It juts out, along with a small number of other full-length works of this seventeenth-century author (he was born in 1600), from the religious and moral writings known as *autos sacramentales* that bear a strong resemblance to the *mystery* and *morality* plays of medieval England and France. These testify to the persistance of medievalism in the ambivalent Spanish Renaissance we call the Golden Age.

Flaminio Scala and The Portrait

Over eight hundred *commedia dell' arte* scenarios or *soggesti* (also called *scenari*) survived from the sixteenth, seventeenth, and eighteenth centuries. The British scholar Allardyce Nicoll[1] surmises that these must have been only a small portion of the plots employed by the traveling companies that dispensed popular theatre in Italy, France, Germany, and other European countries. He reminds us, however, that there was great duplication of themes and plots and that a single acting company probably made do with "only a dozen or a score." The largely extemporaneous dialogue must have followed conventional expressions of sentiment and attitude, and the plots had fairly standardized patterns of intrigue and complication. But both dialogue and plot plainly possessed a liveliness absent in the early, learned comedy, the *comedia erudita,* of humanistic and courtly literature (not to mention the static Senecan tragedies and the only slightly less torpid imitations of Greek drama[2]), although a lively art of literary comedy had emerged in a few works written for the stage by Ariosto, Aretino, Giordano Bruno, and Machiavelli, particularly in the latter's highly risqué *Mandragola* (*c.* 1514).

Samples of *dell' arte* dialogue were set down in 1607 in a volume, *Le bravure del Capitan Spavento della valle inferna*[3] by the actor Francesco Andreini, who made a specialty of braggart soldier or Capitano roles. They illustrate the *commedia's* verbal vivacity: The Captain tells his servant that he is "resolved to take a wife, not to say, a consort, which signifies a mate of the same quality and honors." Boasting of his prowess in lovemaking (which may recall for us the "thousand and three" conquests attributed to Don Giovanni in Mozart's opera), Andreini's braggart declares "In a single night Hercules got fifty damsels with child and in half a night I got two hundred"; whereupon the servant Trappola, who has been egging him on, exclaims with feigned admiration, "How many nurses it was necessary to find, how many swaddling clothes, how many clouts, how much milk and pap to feed them."[4]

[1] Allardyce Nicoll, *World Drama.* . . . London: Harrap, 1949, pp. 194–99.
[2] See John Gassner, *Masters of the Drama.* New York: Dover, 1954, Chapter X, pp. 163–66. The next five paragraphs in the present introductions are borrowed by me from my pp. 170–71.
[3] "The Braveries of Captain Fear of Hell Valley." For similar stock figures in English we may observe the conduct of Don Armado in *Love Labour's Lost* and Pistol in *Henry IV.*
[4] Marion T. Herrick, *Italian Comedy in the Renaissance.* Urbana: University of Illinois, 1960, pp. 214–15.

The quality of the plays is no mystery. They contain vivid descriptions of character types and contemporary manners suspended on plots of farcical intrigue. Old men are satirized as fools, and endless changes are rung on the theme of cuckoldry. Unlike the comedies of Terence which were imitated by the humanists, these plays pay scant attention to long-lost relatives, and the humor is far less kindly and conventional.

Fifty synopses of the actor-playwright Flaminio Scala, collected in his *Theatre for Fifty Days* exemplify a type of drama that frolicked mischievously. *The Portrait,* which stems from the third quarter of the sixteenth century, is a representative synopsis: Isabella, the wife of the rich merchant Pantalone, enjoys a liaison with a cavalier Oratio and gives him her portrait, which he places in a locket. The actress Vittoria, whom the young man visits, removes the portrait, and Pantalone, also calling upon her, is surprised to find his wife's portrait in her possession. Upon being upbraided by her good husband, Isabella quarrels with Oratio and demands the return of the portrait. Oratio's attempt to recover it from the actress, the wooing of the latter by Pantalone and by another old man Gratiano, the betrayal of Gratiano by his wife Flaminia with another cavalier Flavio, the romantic attachment of young Silvia to the braggart Captain—these, as well as subordinate intrigues by the servants, provide a story that bristles with action, surprise, and salacious humor.

Pantalone, the gulled old man who appears sometimes as husband and sometimes as father, could be endowed with a variety of characteristics descriptive of grasping or doting old age. The Dottore, sometimes given a personal name such as Gratiano in *The Portrait,* exemplified pedantry in its various guises. Arlecchino was the servant who invariably got his orders confused, and variants of this type could be presented as buffoons or as shrewd satirists of their time. Brighella, another servant, who had a close cousin in Scapino ("Scapin" in Molière), was often distinguished by his roguery. The Capitano, descended from the *miles gloriosus* or vainglorious soldier of Roman comedy, was satirically suggestive of the *condottiere* of Italy or of Spanish *bravos* in the Spanish-owned parts of Italy. Pulcinella—the Punch of our puppet shows—was an older, more sophisticated, and more pugnacious Brighella. Cruel, malicious and egotistic, he represented the sinister element of life.

These dubious characters and the none too scrupulous lovers and their ladies, who were rarely encumbered with virtue, comprised a rogue's gallery of considerable dimensions. Typed though they were, they could nevertheless be strongly individualized as to speech and dialect. Taken together they comprised a cross-section of middle- and lower-class society the like of which is found only in early picaresque or rogue novels like the Spanish *Lazarillo de Tormes* and the Elizabethan Thomas Nashe's *Unfortunate Traveler*. A slice of life on a figured platter, the plays are in some respects close to the amoral naturalistic comedies of the late nineteenth century known as *comédies rosses*.

It is not surprising that the *commedia dell' arte* enjoyed great popularity and exerted a marked influence on later playwrights, including Molière. Performing in hundreds of market places on crudely constructed platforms and using curtains for backgrounds and as few props as possible until, as sometimes happened, they received a permanent theatre, the actors supplied standardized amusement for the masses. Since, moreover, they counted many accomplished performers and beautiful actresses among their number, they also attracted the favor of the nobility, even when the Church thundered against them. Nor were they wholly committed to playmaking and buffoonery. The star actress of the *Gelosi* troupe, Isabella Andreini, and her husband, Francesco, had enough learning to put many a scholar to shame. They knew several languages and were accomplished musicians. They, too, were in a sense humanists.

The scenario that follows will be instructive to students because it bears, in outline, a resemblance to innumerable farces and comedies upon which the popular theatre has nourished throughout the Western world. But it must be read with imagination, since it is only a plot synopsis of something acted out, mimed, and spoken by players who brought it to life with their skills in poses, gestures, movements (acrobatics if need be), comic intonations and inflections, localizing and characterizing dialogue, time-honored and newly invented jests. The dialogue was spiced with witty repartee and innuendoes, and it was probably never the same in different performances. The over-all effect, moreover, could vary distinctly with different actors. Thus, the celebrated early *commedia* actor, Tristano Martinelli, who performed in Italy between 1588 and 1599 before captivating Parisians with his talent in pantomime, created an Arlecchino who was a coarse and blundering servant in behavior and speech. But a successor in the role, Biancolleli (1640–1688), altered the role with his lively move-

ments as a dancer and his acrobatic capability. Consequently, Arlecchino was no longer a dull-witted and boorish *zanni*, but rather, like the traditional Harlequin of pantomimes, "a boyish innocent, whose skillful, athletic, and for the most part silent escapes from danger were an unending source of amusement."[5]

To Flaminio Scala, who was active as a player, stage director, and playwright during the second half of the sixteenth century and the first two decades of the next century (he died around 1622), we owe numerous *sogetti*, of which some forty are comedies. He published these in 1611 after considerable association with a *commedia* acting company, which he may have directed. It is certain that he enjoyed the prestigious friendship of the famous *commedia* acting couple Isabella and Francesco Andreini for the latter contributed an introduction to Scala's collection. Little is known of Scala's life. He directed one *commedia* company in 1597 and appeared in another troupe in 1600–1601 while it played in France at the invitation of its royal ruler Henry IV. He published a comedy, performed in Mantua at the ducal palace in 1606, left Mantua in 1611 to take service with Giovanni de Medici in Florence and assume the direction of the company of the *Confidenti*, and in 1620 he performed in Venice. This is the last time he left any record of his activities. His lasting monument is his collection of *scenari* entitled *Il teatro delle favole rappresentative overro La Ricreazione comica, boscherreccia e tragica*, "The Theatre of the Performed Tales, or Comic, Pastoral, and Tragic Entertainments," divided into fifty "days" for which reason the collection has been known as "The Theatre for Fifty Days." Whether original in the sense of being invented or based on tales and scandals, or drawn for the most part from literary plays and novels, these *soggeti* are the source of virtually all we know about the plays of this vivacious form of theatre. The rest was left to improvisation in speech and pantomime. For this reason, and because it was possible to rely on the actors, who were thoroughly dedicated to the playing of a single stock part, or "mask," which they constantly elaborated upon or varied, the *soggeti* are also often referred to as "improvised comedy."

[5] Gassner, John and Ralph G. Allen, *Theatre and Drama in the Making*. Boston: Houghton Mifflin, 1964, p. 220.

THE PORTRAIT

A Commedia dell'Arte Scenario

By Flaminio Scala

TRANSLATED FROM THE FRENCH BY GARRETT H. LEVERTON

CHARACTERS

VITTORIA	FLAVIO
PIOMBINO	PEDROLINO
PANTALONE	ARLECCHINO
GRATIANO	CAPTAIN SPAVENTO
ISABELLA	LESBINO, *later Silvia*
FLAMINIA	A ROGUE
ORATIO	NOBLES AND CIVILIANS

PLACE: *Parma.*
TIME: Mid-Sixteenth Century.

A troupe of actors were performing in Parma. According to the custom, the principal actress received many visitors, one of whom was a cavalier of the city named Oratio. During his visit the cavalier exhibited a locket in which was hidden the portrait of the very beautiful woman who had given him this locket. During the course of the conversation, the actress—Vittoria, by name—subtly removed the portrait from the locket before returning it, at the close of his visit. A few days later the husband of the beautiful woman came to see the actress. Vittoria, not knowing who he was, chanced to show him the portrait of his wife. The husband, Pantalone, was very much surprised, and at great length tried to persuade the actress to tell him the name of the man who had given her this portrait. Pantalone concealed the reason for his interest in the affair and returned to his home in a fury to inflict exemplary chastisement on his culpable wife. However, on arriving there, the wife gave so many good excuses in support of her innocence that she succeeded in appeasing his anger.

The persons concerned in working out this situation are the actress, Vittoria, and her comrade Piombino; the two old men Pantalone and Gratiano; their wives, Isabella and Flaminia; and the wives's lovers, Oratio and Flavio. Pedrolino is valet to Pantalone, and Arlecchino to Captain Spavento. A young Milanese girl, disguised as a page, comes under the name of Lesbino to offer her services to the Captain, whom she loves.

ACT ONE. SCENE I.

After the quarrel between ISABELLA and PANTALONE, her husband, over the portrait which was last seen in the hands of VITTORIA, ISABELLA begins to doubt ORATIO's love for her. She orders PEDROLINO to go to ORATIO and to demand from him the portrait which she had given him some time previously.

SCENE II.

CAPTAIN SPAVENTO tells ARLECCHINO how through being obliged to assist in the play, he has fallen in love with the actress, VITTORIA. ARLECCHINO tells him he is wasting time.

SCENE III.

Later, the CAPTAIN consents to take LESBINO as his page, after asking him many foolish questions about his bravery and his military talents.

SCENE IV.

From her window, FLAMINIA calls to ARLECCHINO and asks him to carry a letter to a cavalier named FLAVIO, whom she will meet at the place where she conducts her rendezvous with gentlemen. ARLECCHINO takes the letter and promises to deliver it to the one to whom it is addressed. FLAMINIA gives him some money and withdraws. ARLECCHINO regards FLAMINIA's window knowingly.

SCENE V.

Doctor GRATIANO, the husband of FLAMINIA, seeing ARLECCHINO with a letter in his hand and gazing at his wife's window, becomes suspicious, and demands to know what he is doing there and for whom the letter is intended. ARLECCHINO replies that a man named FLAVIO gave it to him to deliver to a lady. The DOCTOR takes the letter and raps ARLECCHINO with his cane.

SCENES VI TO X.

PANTALONE comes between the DOCTOR and ARLEC-CHINO. FLAVIO presents himself. GRATIANO, furiously angry, returns the letter to him. FLAVIO receives it with profound humility. The others depart and FLAVIO reads the letter in which FLAMINIA begs him to frequent the theatre no longer.

SCENE XI.

When PEDROLINO asks the return of the portrait of ISABELLA, ORATIO explains that it is impossible to return it to him because the locket is being repaired at the jeweler's. PEDROLINO smiles and asks him how long it has been since he has gone to the theatre, questions him about all the actors, and finally about the SIGNORA VITTORIA.

SCENE XII.

At this moment ISABELLA arrives. She dissembles at first, then asks for the return of the portrait. But ORATIO repeats the same story he had already told PEDROLINO. She calls him a traitor and tells him she knows about his love for the actress to whom he has given her portrait. In her anger, she commands PEDROLINO to follow her and he leaves refusing to listen to ORATIO. ORATIO bemoans his ill luck and blames the presence of the actors as the reason for all his trouble. He is particularly discourteous in expressing his opinion of VITTORIA who has tricked him so deceitfully.

SCENE XIII.

The CAPTAIN, hearing what ORATIO says about the actors, and particularly VITTORIA, comes to their defense. He argues that the theatre is a noble diversion and that the SIGNORA VITTORIA is an honorable lady. ORATIO, furious, calls him a liar and reaches for his sword. At this the CAPTAIN asks ORATIO if he wishes to fight a duel with him. ORATIO replies that he is ready. Then the CAPTAIN says he goes to write a letter which will remove from ORATIO the responsibility for his death in case he is killed, and will prevent the officers of justice from regarding him as an adversary. He asks ORATIO to do the same for him. Then he departs. ARLECCHINO observes that his master has the appearance of wishing to escape the affair. Thus ends the first act.

ACT TWO. SCENE I.

VITTORIA, richly dressed, with gold necklaces and pearl bracelets, with diamonds and rubies on her fingers, engages herself through PIOMBINO to the DUKE OF PARMA, recalling the many courtesies which she was constantly receiving from the Parmesan nobility.

SCENES II TO V.

PEDROLINO praises his master PANTALONE to VITTORIA. PANTALONE appears but he does not dare to approach the actress because he sees his wife at the window. PEDROLINO persuades PANTALONE that the actress is in love with him. PANTALONE, flattered, expresses the intention of giving her a present.

SCENE VI.

While ORATIO recounts to his friend FLAVIO the unfortunate history of the portrait, ARLECCHINO brings him the CAPTAIN's letter of remission from blame. ORATIO strikes him with his fist and rushes off to the theatre.

SCENES VII TO XII.

FLAVIO and PEDROLINO, and then FLAMINIA attempt to reconcile ISABELLA and ORATIO. ISABELLA softens but she declares that ORATIO shall get nothing from her so long as he does not return the portrait, and she forbids him, moreover, to go, himself, to negotiate for its return. PEDROLINO informs them how the two old men, PANTALONE and GRATIANO, are paying attention to the actress.

SCENE XIII.

Now the DOCTOR arrives. PEDROLINO pretends to be arguing with FLAMINIA and is saying: "How do I know whether your husband goes to the theatre or not?" FLAMINIA, entering into the deception, pretends to be jealous of her husband. When she has withdrawn, PEDROLINO tells the DOCTOR of his visit to the SIGNORA VITTORIA and of how she is in love with the DOCTOR. GRATIANO is enchanted.

SCENE XIV.

PIOMBINO greets the DOCTOR in behalf of SIGNORA VITTORIA. He begs him to take to the actress a silver pitcher and vase which she needs for a play which she is going to present. The DOCTOR replies that he will send these by PEDROLINO. PIOMBINO assures him that the actress is in love with him, and that because of him, she rejects the attentions of all the gentlemen who call on her at home or at the theatre. The DOCTOR is overjoyed and promises a reward to PIOMBINO.

SCENE XV.

The CAPTAIN talks with his page, LESBINO, about the passion which the actress inspires in him. LESBINO tries to turn him away from this passion which he cannot make honorable. He asks him if he has never had another love. The CAPTAIN replies that he had been in love, in Milan, with a very beautiful young girl named SILVIA.

SCENE XVI.

ARLECCHINO interrupts his master to tell him that VITTORIA is waiting for him at a nearby jeweler's. LESBINO, desperate, seeks to persuade ARLECCHINO that he ought to kill him, LESBINO, because he has conceived the intention of killing his master. ARLECCHINO beats and injures the page. FLAMINIA and ISABELLA intervene.

SCENE XVII.

Suspecting that LESBINO is a woman in spite of her male attire, they take her to the residence of FLAMINIA. Thus ends the second act.

ACT THREE. SCENE I.

VITTORIA and PIOMBINO go to dine at the house of a rich gentleman who gives them magnificent presents. They congratulate themselves because of the custom of making gifts to actors, a common custom in Italian cities and one which is seldom neglected by persons of distinguished rank. VITTORIA confesses that she laughs at all lovers who are not generous with her. PIOMBINO promises to provide well for her old age.

SCENES II AND III.

PANTALONE comes to call on VITTORIA. She thanks him for the presents he has brought to her and invites him to be present at the theatre for the opening of her play. PANTALONE promises to be there. Presently FLAVIO arrives and the actress detains him with engaging conversation.

SCENE IV.

But FLAMINIA sees them from her window. She is so angry that she goes out and slaps FLAVIO in the face and then returns to her house. FLAVIO, putting his hand to his smarting cheek, goes without saying a word. VITTORIA laughs heartily.

SCENE V.

PANTALONE who has been a witness to this *coup de théâtre* blames FLAMINIA for her effrontery. He congratulates himself that he has such a modest and well-bred wife. After these musings, he exchanges compliments with the actress. But ISABELLA appears.

SCENE VI.

She reproaches her husband for being gallant with other women while neglecting her. She lays all the facts before him and then adds that he does not deserve a wife like her. Finally, as her anger increases, she attacks him and puts him to flight. She turns to VITTORIA and tells her that if his honor does not prevent him from compromising himself with an actress, then he will have to be taught how to behave. ISABELLA then returns to her home. VITTORIA laughs and says that wherever one finds a troupe of actors, there also will be found married women with sour dispositions.

SCENE VII.

GRATIANO now arrives. "Behold, the other pigeon waiting to have his feathers plucked," says PIOMBINO. The actress flirts with the DOCTOR. PIOMBINO reminds him of the silver pitcher and vase which he has promised her. GRATIANO joyfully takes PEDROLINO with him in order to bring back these presents. The actors ridicule his stupidity.

SCENE VIII.

ORATIO arrives and greets VITTORIA. He demands the portrait of ISABELLA. She replies, with a laugh, that she hasn't the slightest idea what he is talking about. Then she departs with PIOMBINO.

SCENE IX.

ISABELLA has seen ORATIO talking with the actress; she reproaches him for not keeping his promise. ARLECCHINO tells ORATIO that ISABELLA and FLAMINIA have taken his master's page away with them to their home, and are holding him there against his will. ISABELLA seizes the occasion to spite ORATIO and calls FLAMINIA, telling her to bring her new lover to the window. LESBINO appears and says to ISABELLA, "What do you wish of me, Signora?" ORATIO becomes enraged at the sight of this unknown person and withdraws, cursing ISABELLA.

SCENE X.

PANTALONE asks the reason for all this noise. ISABELLA says that ORATIO wished to take her page away from her. "And what do you want with this page?" PANTALONE asks angrily. Then ISABELLA tells the story of SILVIA, the Milanese girl. She then urges PANTALONE to go to the theatre, find the CAPTAIN and bring him back if possible. PANTALONE sees at once that this is the chance he himself needed in order to get to go to the theatre.

SCENES XI TO XVII.

The lovers begin to quarrel again. PEDROLINO observes that quarreling is a waste of time. Since their husbands are at the play which lasts for six hours, they could, therefore, use their time to much better advantage than quarreling. The lovers see the good sense in this remark and become reconciled. The valets try to decide on the best means to restore SILVIA to the CAPTAIN's good graces. The CAPTAIN appears.

SCENE XVIII.

PEDROLINO tells the CAPTAIN that he will find VITTORIA at the home of PANTALONE. The CAPTAIN enters through the basement of the house where he comes upon SILVIA divested of her male attire.

SCENE XIX.

The two valets, PEDROLINO and ARLECCHINO, are alone in the theatre. They sit on the floor and decide what they would say if the two old men were to return suddenly. At this moment in the scene there is some amusing pantomime. A rogue, carrying a lantern, sees the two valets. With many tears, he bemoans the fact that he has lost much money at cards. He does not have more than a dozen pieces of money left. The valets invite him to play with them. They play. The rogue wins the money and also the clothes of PEDROLINO and ARLECCHINO. He leaves them sitting on the floor in their shirts. The valets are very despondent.

SCENE XX.

A great tumult arises in the theatre. PANTALONE, GRATIANO and PIOMBINO rush in carrying VITTORIA. She begs them to protect her from the dangers of a brawl which has broken out because of her. These gentlemen brawlers—the *bravi*—pour in, their swords bared. They see VITTORIA, they seize her, and carry her out. PIOMBINO follows them with gestures of despair.

SCENE XXI.

PANTALONE and GRATIANO find themselves face to face with the valets who are clad only in their shirts. They ask them to explain what has happened. The valets invent an explanation and say that the crowd which just left the theatre, robbed them of their money and clothes. They add, philosophically, that although the theatre brings pleasure, it is also the source of numerous scandals. While they are indulging in these wise reflections, ISABELLA and FLAMINIA come in and ask their husbands why the play ended so soon.

SCENE XXII.

PANTALONE replies that a brawl interrupted it and that he has not seen the CAPTAIN. ISABELLA tells how they informed the CAPTAIN that he would find VITTORIA in the basement of their house, and that it is SILVIA instead of the actress who is waiting there for him. Fearing however, that the CAPTAIN, thus deceived might commit violence, they had asked ORATIO and FLAVIO to take the trouble to stay with them. PANTALONE and GRATIANO approve.

SCENE XXIII.

The CAPTAIN leaves the house swearing he has been betrayed. ORATIO and FLAVIO endeavor to calm him. PANTALONE and all the others intercede in behalf of SILVIA. The CAPTAIN listens. He admits that SILVIA is honorably born; that she is the daughter of a rich Milanese merchant; and that he loves her. This diabolical actress had so far bewitched him that he had forgotten poor SILVIA. But he returns to her and consents to marry her.

SCENE XXIV.

They bring in SILVIA and she learns that her lover returns her affection.

ISABELLA and FLAMINIA urge their husbands to stay away from the theatre, and instead to watch over their homes and the conduct of their wives. They reply that henceforth they will do as their wives ask. Everybody now goes to PANTALONE's home to celebrate the wedding of SILVIA and the CAPTAIN, and it is thus that the comedy of *The Portrait* ends.

Ben Jonson and His Masques

Benjamin Jonson (1572–1637), whose prowess as a writer of comedies was discussed in the introduction to Volpone (pages 283–284), acquired during the reign of James I a second and rather profitable reputation as a writer of masques "on order." Like other Elizabethans, Jonson was familiar with the special entertainments favored by Elizabeth and her court: the pageants, processions, tableaux, pastoral performances, and masques that attended her tours to the towns and the country estates of noblemen whom she complimented and at times impoverished with her visits. Elizabeth had a special Master of Revels to attend to such affairs and money was lavished on Italianate illusionist scenic effects of clouds, grottoes, painted perspective, and architectural pieces. Masque performances were so popular during this time that they even became customary additions to the plays presented at the Globe and Blackfriars theatres owned by Shakespeare's acting company. And Shakespeare himself responded to this contemporary interest. Its influence can be seen in the very structure and style of The Tempest[1] and in the fourth act there is a complete little pastoral masque put on for the diversion of the young lovers Ferdinand and Miranda.

Jonson wrote over thirty masques, starting with The Masque of Blackness presented on Twelfth Night, 1605. In association with architect-designer Inigo Jones, he brought this esoteric dramatic form to its greatest elaboration and applied to it his exquisite lyric talent, with which he produced some of the finest short poems in the English language.

It was precisely his interest in language that finally brought to a head the inevitable conflict between poetry and scenery that caused, in 1631, his ultimate quarrel with Inigo Jones, whom he called a "maker of [stage] properties" and whom he satirized in The Tale of a Tub. But Jonson himself realized that his masques could not be divorced from their stage effects without misrepresentation of their intent and purpose. He admitted that "Painting and carpentry are the soul of a masque," although it depended considerably more on these scenic effects than he was later willing to acknowledge. In The Masque of Blackness, performed in the banquet hall at Whitehall, "there was a great engine at the lower end of the room which had motion, and in it were the images of sea horses, with other terrible fishes which were ridden by the Moors." In The Masque of Queens, "part of the scene which first presented itself was an ugly Hell; which flaming beneath, smoked

unto the top of the roof." Then, with a sudden blare of music, this hell disappeared and the scene was transformed into "a glorious and magnificent building . . . in the top of which was [sic] discovered the twelve Masques, sitting upon a throne triumphal, erected in form of a pyramid and circled with all store of light."[2] By the time Hymenaei, a Twelfth Night masque in honor of a noble match, was performed, Jonson's words were decidedly secondary to the scenery which revealed a huge globe to the audience. They had, in fact, become of secondary importance even to the costuming, which included "persick crowns, that were with scroles of gold-plate turn'd outward, . . . white cloth of silver, . . . "silver Greaves," and so on.[3]

Against Inigo Jones's spectacles and costuming, how could poetry prevail? That it did in some of Jonson's masques, in Oberon, The Fairy Prince (1611), The Fortunate Isles and Their Union (1625), and the short masque The Vision of Delight (1617), which follows, is undoubtedly a tribute to Jonson's poetic power. He could not, however, although he tried determinedly, make the form yield any considerable degree of drama. Most of the characters in the masque were expected to be mythological or allegorical, such as personifications of Reason and Splendor, or of Neptune and Diana. Their formal speech requirements could have been little more than a finger exercise for the creator of Volpone (see pages 285–323) and altogether alien to the pungent dialogue that he was accustomed to distribute throughout his comedies. But Jonson performed everything that was required of him. He managed, moreover, to indulge his penchant for realism as much as possible in the comic antimasques or prefatory grotesque pieces such as the scene that opened the Masque of Queens with hell and its hags. Besides his concern for the literary content of the theatrical masques, Jonson also considered it important to establish a central idea or some moral principle to which all other elements or "devices" were to be subordinated. Thus, he endeavored to provide some progression from order to disorder in The Fairy Prince, in which the satyrs of its opening antimasque were foils to the fairies of the main masque. For Jonson these masque characters were symbolic rather than dramatic figures and represented the ruling idea of the play. He considered it the function of the spectacle to identify the characters and display the royal magnificence of the play. But he expected

---

[1] A good brief discussion will be found in the Introduction of the Arden Edition of The Tempest, edited by Frank Kermode. New York: Random House, 1964, pp. lxxi–lxxvi.

[2] Kenneth Magowan and William Melnitz, The Golden Ages of The Theatre. Englewood Cliffs, N.J.: Prentice-Hall, 1959.

[3] Nagler, A. M., A Source Book in Theatrical History: New York: Dover Publications, 1959, pp. 143–144.

the poetry to express the point or "soul" of the piece. He wanted spectacle and verbal poetry to cooperate completely in the production of the masque; although without intending to infringe on the spectacle he made it his special duty to safeguard the soul. And, by doing this, he put himself squarely in the midst of the numerous men of the Renaissance who "took for granted the ultimately moral purpose of all literature."[4]

[4] Dolora Cunningham, "The Jonsonian Masque as a Literary Form," in *Ben Jonson: A Collection of Critical Essays,* edited by Jonas A. Barish (Twentieth Century Views, Spectrum Books). Englewood Cliffs, N.J.: Prentice-Hall, 1963, pp. 160–174.

THE VISION OF DELIGHT

By Ben Jonson
A Masque

Presented at Court in Christmas, 1617

THE SCENE

A street in perspective of fair building discovered.

[Delight *is seen to come as afar off, accompanied
with* Grace, Love, Harmony, Revel, Sport,
Laughter; Wonder *following*]

DELIGHT: [*Spake in song (stilo recitativo)*]
Let us play and dance and sing,
    Let us now turn every sort
O' the pleasures of the spring
    To the graces of a court;
From air, from cloud, from dreams, from toys,
To sounds, to sense, to love, to joys;

Let your shows be new as strange,
    Let them oft and sweetly vary;
Let them haste so to their change,
    As the seers may not tarry;
Too long t' expect the pleasing'st sight
Doth take away from the delight.

    [*Here the first* Antimasque *entered*]
    [*A she-monster delivered of six* Burratines, *that
    danced with six* Pantaloons; *which done,*]

DELIGHT: [*Spake again*] Yet hear what your De-
    light doth pray:
All sour and sullen looks away,
    That are the servants of the day;
Our sports are of the humorous Night,
    Who feeds the stars that give her light,
    And useth, than her wont more bright,
    To help the vision of Delight.

    [*Here the* Night *rose and took her chariot be-
    spangled with stars*]

DELIGHT: [*Proceeds*]
See, see, her sceptre and her crown
    Are all of flame, and from her gown
    A train of light comes waving down.
This night, in dew she will not steep
    The brain, nor lock the sense in sleep;
    But all awake with phantoms keep,
    And those to make delight more deep.

    [*By this time the* Night *and* Moon *being both
    risen,* Night, *hovering over the place, sang*]

NIGHT: Break, Fancy, from thy cave of cloud,
        And spread thy purple wings;
           Now all thy figures are allowed,
        And various shapes of things.
           Create of airy forms a stream,
        It must have blood, and naught of phlegm;
           And though it be a waking dream——

THE CHOIR: Yet let it like an odour rise
           To all the senses here,
        And fall like sleep upon their eyes,
           Or music in their ear.

[*The Scene here changed to cloud, and*]

FANCY: [*Breaking forth, spake*]
Bright Night, I obey thee, and am come at thy call,
But it is no one dream that can please these all;
Wherefore I would know what dreams would de-
    light 'em;
For never was Fancy more loath to affright 'em.
And Fancy, I tell you, has dreams that have wings,
And dreams that have honey, and dreams that have
    stings;
Dreams of the maker, and dreams of the teller,
Dreams of the kitchen, and dreams of the cellar;
Some that are tall, and some that are dwarfs,
Some that were haltered, and some that wear scarfs;
Some that are proper, and signify o' thing,
And some another, and some that are nothing.
For say the French farthingale and the French hood
Were here to dispute—must it be understood
A feather for a wisp were a fit moderator?
Your ostrich, believe it, 's no faithful translator
Of perfect Utopian. And then it were an odd piece.
To see the conclusion peep forth at a cod-piece.
    The politic pudding hath still his two ends,
Though the bellows and bagpipe were ne'er so good
    friends;
And who can report what offence it would be
For the squirrel to see a dog climb a tree?
If a dream should come in now to make you afeard,
With a windmill on 's head and bells at his beard,
Would you straight wear your spectacles here at your
    toes,
And your boots o' your brows, and your spurs o'
    your nose?
Your whale he will swallow a hogshead for a pill;
But the maker o' the mousetrap is he that hath skill.
And the nature of the onion is to draw tears,
As well as the mustard. Peace, pitchers have ears,
And shuttlecocks wings: these things do not mind
    'em.
If the bell have any sides, the clapper will find 'em.
There's twice so much music in beating the tabour
As i' the stockfish, and somewhat less labour.
Yet all this while, no proportion is boasted
'Twixt an egg and an ox, though both have been
    roasted;

For grant the most barbers can lay o' the cittern,[1]
Is it requisite a lawyer should plead to a gittern?[2]
    You will say now the morris-bells were but bribes
To make the heel forget that e'er it had kibes;
I say let the wine make ne'er so good jelly,
The conscience o' the bottle is much i' the belly.
For why? do but take common counsel i' your way,
And tell me who'll then set a bottle of hay
Before the old usurer, and to his horse
A slice of salt butter, perverting the course
Of civil society? Open that gap,
And out skip your fleas, four and twenty at a clap,
With a chain and a trundle-bed following at th' heels,
And will they not cry then, the world runs a-wheels?
As for example, a belly and no face,
With the bill of a shoveller may here come in place;
The haunches of a drum, with the feet of a pot,
And the tail of a Kentishman to it—why not?
Yet would I take the stars to be cruel
If the crab and the rope-maker ever fight duel,
On any dependence, be it right, be it wrong;
But mum! a thread may be drawn out too long.
    [*Here the second* Antimasque *of* Phantasms
    came forth, which danced]
    FANCY: [*Proceeded*] Why, this you will say was
        fantastical now,
As the cock and the bull, the whale and the cow;
But vanish away! I have change to present you,
And such as I hope will more truly content you.—
    Behold the gold-haired Hour descending here,
    That keeps the gate of Heaven, and turns the year!
    Already with her sight how she does cheer
    And makes another face of things appear!
    [*Here one of the* Hours *descending, the whole
    scene changed to the bower of* Zephyrus, *whilst
    Peace sang as followeth*]
PEACE: Why look you so, and all turn dumb,
        To see the opener of the New Year come?
            My presence rather should invite,
        And aid, and urge, and call, to your de-
            light;
            The many pleasures that I bring
        Are all of youth, of heat, of life and spring,
            And were prepared to warm your blood,
        Not fix it thus, as if you statues stood.
THE CHOIR: We see, we hear, we feel, we taste,
            We smell the change in every
                flower;
            We only wish that all could last,
                And be as new still as the hour.
    [*The Song ended*]
    WONDER: [*Spake*] Wonder must speak or break:
        what is this? grows
The wealth of Nature here, or Art? it shows
As if Favonius, father of the spring,
Who in the verdant meads doth reign sole king,
Had roused him here, and shook his feathers, wet

[1] A lutelike instrument.
[2] A wire-strung guitarlike instrument.

With purple swelling nectar; and had let
The sweet and fruitful dew fall on the ground
To force out all the flowers that might be found;
    Or a Minerva with her needle had
Th' enamoured earth with all her riches clad,
And made the downy Zephyr, as he flew,
Still to be followed with the spring's best hue.
    The gaudy peacock boasts not in his train
So many lights and shadows, nor the rain-
Resolving Iris, when the Sun doth court her,
Nor purple pheasant while his aunt doth sport her
To hear him crow, and with a perchèd pride
Wave his discoloured neck and purple side.
    I have not seen the place could more surprise;
It looks, methinks, like one of Nature's eyes,
Or her whole body set in Art. Behold!
How the blue bindweed doth itself enfold
With honeysuckle, and both these entwine
Themselves with bryony and jessamine,
To cast a kind and odoriferous shade.
    FANCY: How better than they are, are all things
        made
By Wonder! But awhile refresh thine eye;
I'll put thee to thy oftener what and why.
    [*Here, to a loud music, the bower opens, and the*
    Masquers *are discovered as the glories of the
    spring*]
    WONDER: [*Again spake*] Thou wilt indeed. What
        better change appears?
Whence is it that the air so sudden clears,
And all things in a moment turn so mild?
Whose breath or beams have got proud earth with
    child
Of all the treasure that great Nature's worth,
And makes her every minute to bring forth?
How comes it winter is so quite forced hence,
And locked up under ground? that every sense
Hath several objects? trees have got their heads,
The fields their coats? that now the shining meads
Do boast the paunce, the lily, and the rose;
And every flower doth laugh as Zephyr blows?
That seas are now more even than the land?
The rivers run as smoothèd by his hand;
Only their heads are crispèd by his stroke?
How plays the yearling with his brow scarce broke
Now in the open grass? and frisking lambs
Make wanton salts about their dry-sucked dams,
Who to repair their bags do rob the fields?
    How is't each bough a several music yields?
The lusty throstle, early nightingale,
Accord in tune, though vary in their tale?
    The chirping swallow called forth by the sun,
And crested lark doth his division run?
The yellow bees the air with murmur fill?
The finches carol, and the turtles[3] bill?
Whose power is this? what god?
    FANCY: Behold a king,

[3] Doves.

Whose presence maketh this perpetual spring,
The glories of which spring grow in that bower,
And are the marks and beauties of his power.
    [*To which the* Choir *answered:*]
    'Tis he, 'tis he, and no power else,
    That makes all this what Fancy tells;
    The founts, the flowers, the birds, the bees,
    The herds, the flocks, the grass, the trees,
    Do all confess him; but most these
    Who call him Lord of the Four Seas,
    King of the Less and Greater Isles,[4]
    And all those happy when he smiles.
Advance, his favour calls you to advance,
And do your this night's homage in a dance.
    [*Here they danced their* Entry, *after which they
    sang again*]
      Again! again! you cannot be
      Of such a true delight too free,
        Which, who once saw, would ever see;
      And if they could the object prize,
      Would, while it lasts, not think to rise,
        But wish their bodies all were eyes.
    [*Here they danced their* Main Dance, *after which
    they sang*]
  CHOIR: In curious knots and mazes so

4 The king of England

The Spring at first was taught to go;
And Zephyr, when he came to woo
  His Flora, had his motions too;
    And thence did Venus learn to lead
    Th' Idalian brawls, and so to tread
As if the wind, not she, did walk;
  Nor pressed a flower, nor bowed a stalk.
[*They danced with* Ladies *and the whole* Revels
followed; after which Aurora *appeared, the*
Night *and* Moon *being descended*]
And this EPILOGUE *followed:*
I was not wearier where I lay
By frozen Tithon's[5] side tonight,
Than I am willing now to say
And be a part of your delight.
But I am urged by the Day,
Against my will, to bid you come away.
THE CHOIR:
  They yield to time, and so must all.
As night to sport, day doth to action call;
  Which they the rather do obey
Because the Morn with roses strews the way.
  [*Here they danced their going off and ended*]

5 Tithonus, Aurora's (Dawn's) aged lover (hence,
"frozen") who was granted immortality, but was not
given youth.

Cervantes and His Interludes

Miguel de Cervantes Saavedra (1547–1616) is best known as the author of *Don Quixote,* one of the masterpieces of world literature. His checkered life need not detain us here except for the fact that his varied career must have contributed to the lively realism of his interludes, which were as brisk as they were brief. We cannot discount, for instance, his life as a lively student at Salamanca and Madrid, and as a soldier for five years in the Spanish army based in Italy; he lost the use of a hand in the naval battle of Lepanto, was captured by Algerian pirates, sold into slavery, and, after being ransomed, joined a Spanish expedition against the Azores. He did not turn to writing until his thirty-seventh year when he retired from military life and married.

In 1585 he published a pastoral romance, the *Galatea,* and also began to write plays, the most serious and distinguished of which is *The Siege of Numantia* (1585), based on an episode in the history of Spain during Roman times. He also held a position as government collector of grain and later of taxes, and was at least twice imprisoned for inaccuracies in his accounts. He suffered from poverty even after the publication of the first part of *Don Quixote* (1615), originally written as a burlesque of the artificial romances of chivalry that had been widely disseminated in Spain.

Don Quixote was received with indifference at first, although it soon gained considerable popularity. But another lull in fortunes followed Cervantes' success and he did not complete the second part until he published it hurriedly in 1615 because a spurious sequel had been published in 1614. He published "Twelve Instructive or Moral Tales," or *Exemplary Novels,* without much success in 1613 and "Eight Comedies," *Ocho Comedias,* in 1615. He died of dropsy in 1616, and was buried by the Franciscans, whose order he had joined.

Cervantes had hoped in later years to return to the theatre he had abandoned for some thirty years but, although he was by then famous, the managers were disinterested. He said to himself, he reports, "Either I have changed and become another person or the times have improved immensely—which is generally the other way around, since people always praise the days gone by."[1] As a result, tired of waiting for stage productions, he accepted an offer of publication for his interludes, "glad" as he put it, "not to dicker with actors." They have been performed since then and have greater vitality than almost anything he wrote except *Don Quixote.* This is hardly surprising since they deal with the underworld and with lower-class characters, and they revolve around unsavory but undeniably popular beliefs and activities.

The interludes are held in high esteem today for their vividness, the concentration of their action, and the vivacity and individuality of their characters. In one interlude, *The Divorce-Court Judge,* we encounter a quarreling couple that apparently enjoys its squabbling; in *Choosing a Councilman in Daganzo,* a group of quarrelsome rustics; in *The Hawk-Eyed Sentinel,* a quixotically persistent poor soldier who loses his favorite kitchen maid to a well-fixed sacristan. In *Trampagos, the Pimp Who Lost His Moll,* Cervantes dramatized the seedy life of prostitutes and their protectors, and in *The Jealous Old Husband* and *The Cave of Salamanca* the domestic world of a betrayed husband and an adulterous wife. A veritable rogues' gallery enlivens these little plays, but one that is replete with varicolored life and with the typical human situations of lust, seduction, delusion, and folly, theatrically thrust home and comically exaggerated. Only the endings are perfunctory, but they are embroidered with clever doggerel verses that call for lively dances.

The interludes were intended to be treated as broad farce, though they are never slanted against the characters. It is plain that their author liked his roguish students and vividly drawn underworld characters, and that he enjoyed their follies and even their petty villainy. Although he launched into verse and song at times[2] in these short pieces, it was the actual world of prose, dialect, and reveling that he fancied. In Cervantes' Interludes, as in his *Don Quixote,* all is *life,* even if nearly all of it is also, as in *The Jealous Old Husband* and the conclusion of *The Cave of Salamanca,* illusion.

[1] Foreword by Edwin Honig in *Interludes by Miguel de Cervantes.* New York: New American Library 1964.

[2] This is less apparent in translation than in the original, but there is an excellent edition, published by the Princeton University Press in 1948, in which the student will find both the Spanish text and a translation into English by S. Griswold Morley.

THE CAVE OF SALAMANCA

(*La Cueva de Salamanca*)

By Miguel de Cervantes

TRANSLATED BY EDWIN HONIG

CAST

PANCRACIO
STUDENT, Carraolano
SACRISTAN, Reponce
BARBER, Nicholas

LEONISO, *friend of* Pancracio
LEONARDA, *wife of* Pancracio
CRISTINA, *housemaid*

[*Enter* Pancracio, Leonarda *and* Cristina]

PANCRACIO: Mistress, dry those tears and stop your sighing. Remember, I'll be away four days, not centuries. On the fifth day, at the latest, I'll be back, God preserve me. But if it upsets you so, just say the word and I'll break my promise and give up the trip altogether. Surely my sister can get married there without me.

LEONARDA: Pancracio, dear lord and master, I don't want you to be discourteous because of me. Go now, God speed you, and meet your obligation, since the matter is so pressing. My grief I'll keep to myself and spend the lonely hours as best I can. Only, I beg you to come back and not stay any longer than you promised. Oh, help me, Cristina, I've a pain in my heart!

[Leonarda *faints*]

CRISTINA: Ah, weddings and holidays—such dreadful things! Indeed, sir, if I were you, I'd never go there.

PANCRACIO: Run inside, girl, and get me a glass of water to throw in her face. No, wait, I know a few magic words I'll whisper in her ear; they can revive people who faint.

[*He speaks the words and* Leonarda *recovers, saying*]

LEONARDA: Enough. It can't be helped. I must be patient. My dear, the more you linger, the longer you delay my happiness. Your friend Leoniso should be waiting for you in the carriage. God be with you and bring you back as quickly and safely as I could wish.

PANCRACIO: If you want me to stay, my angel, I'll be like a statue and not budge an inch.

LEONARDA: No, no, sweet comfort. Your wish is my desire, which means you must leave and not stay here, for your honor and mine are one and the same.

CRISTINA: Oh, mirror of matrimony! If all wives cherished their husbands as my mistress loves hers, they'd sing a different tune.

LEONARDA: Go get my shawl, Cristina. I must see your master safely off in his carriage.

PANCRACIO: No, I beg you. Kiss me, but stay here, please. Cristina, be sure and cheer up your mistress, and I'll get you a pair of shoes when I return.

CRISTINA: On your way, sir, and don't you worry about my mistress. I'll see to it we both enjoy ourselves so she won't miss your absence.

LEONARDA: Enjoy myself? Me? What a fantastic idea! Without my love beside me, I can know no bliss or joy, only grief and sorrow.

PANCRACIO: I cannot bear this any longer. Ah, light of my eyes, farewell; I'll see nothing to delight me till I gaze upon you once again.

[*Exit* Pancracio]

LEONARDA: Good-bye, and good riddance to you! Go, and don't come back! Vanish, go up like smoke in thin air! Good God, this time all your bluster and squeamishness don't move me a bit!

CRISTINA: And I was afraid your sweet nothings would keep him here and spoil our fun.

LEONARDA: Do you think our guests will really come tonight?

CRISTINA: And why not? I've been in touch with them, and they're just dying to come. This afternoon they had the washerwoman, our confidante, bring a hamper that's full of gifts and goodies, disguised as laundry. It's like one of those huge baskets the King distributes to his beggars on Maundy Thursday, except this one's an Easter basket with pies, cold meats, blancmange, and two capons that haven't even been plucked yet, together with all sorts of fresh fruits too. And last but not least, a huge, four-gallon skin of wine that smells absolutely divine!

LEONARDA: That's my Reponce, generous as ever, my sweet sacristan, the darling of my heart.

CRISTINA: And what about my Nicholas? He's the barber of my heart, the razor that whisks away my troubles, so that when I'm with him it's as though I never had a care in the world.

LEONARDA: Did you put the hamper away safely?

CRISTINA: It's in the kitchen, covered by a straining cloth to hide it.

[*The* Student, Carraolano, *knocks at the door and then walks right in*]

THE CAVE OF SALAMANCA

LEONARDA: Cristina, see who it is.

STUDENT: Ladies, it's me, a poor student.

CRISTINA: It's quite clear you're poor and a student —first by the rags you wear, and second by your nerve. The idea that every beggar nowadays can't wait for alms in the doorway but must march right into a house and sniff around in the corners without caring if he wakes anybody up or not!

STUDENT: I expected a gentler reply from one so gracious as yourself—especially since I neither wished nor expected anything more than a loft and a bit of straw to wrap myself in tonight against the inclemencies of Heaven, which, as far as I can observe, now seem to threaten earth with the greatest severities.

LEONARDA: And where do you hail from, my friend?

STUDENT: I am a Salamantine, my lady. That is, I am a native of Salamanca. I was on the way to Rome with an uncle, who died on the road in the heart of France. Then, being alone, I decided to return home. But I was robbed in Catalonia by the lackeys or henchmen of Roque Guinarde, who was not himself present at the time. Had he been there, he would never have permitted me to be so insulted, for he is most courteous and gracious, and generous besides. Night overtook me at these sacred portals, as I regard them, and now I throw myself upon your mercy.

LEONARDA: Really, Cristina, this student moves me. I pity him.

CRISTINA: He tears my heart to pieces. Let's keep him here tonight—surely the peasantry can live on the castle's leftovers; I mean, his hunger will find enough relics to prey on in what's left of the food. And besides, he can help me pluck the poultry in the basket.

LEONARDA: What's this, Cristina, are we going to fill the house with witnesses to our little revel?

CRISTINA: He looks like the sort of fellow who'd rather stay mum than go hungry. Come here, friend. Do you know anything about plucking?

STUDENT: Do I know anything about plucking? I don't know what you mean unless you want to make fun of me because I was stripped of my money. But there's no need for that, since I readily admit it: I'm the most cleanly plucked person alive.

CRISTINA: I didn't mean that; I was only asking if you could pluck a few capons.

STUDENT: What I'd like to say to that is that I am, my dear ladies, by the grace of God, a bachelor of arts from Salamanca, and I can't say——

LEONARDA: Of course in that case you can pluck not only capons but also geese and wild turkeys. Now, how good are you at keeping a secret? Or are you the sort who itches to tell all he sees, thinks, or feels?

STUDENT: You could kill more men right in front of me than sheep in a slaughterhouse and I'd never breathe a word.

CRISTINA: Well, see to it that you keep your mouth shut tight, stitch up both ends of your tongue with a lachet, sharpen your teeth, and join us. You'll see mysteries and dine on marvels, and then you can measure your length for a cozy sleep in the straw.

STUDENT: Seven feet is all I need; I'm not in the least greedy or particular.

[Enter Sacristan Reponce and the Barber]

SACRISTAN: Hail, ye Achillean charioteers, helmsmen of our pleasures, light beams in our darkness, ye two reciprocating loves who, as pedestals and pillars, serve the amorous manufactory of our desires!

LEONARDA: That's the one thing wrong with him. Reponce dear, please speak plainly, so that I can understand, and don't go flying up so high I can't follow you.

BARBER: That's where I come in. I speak plainer than the sole of your shoe. I can call a spade a club or a club a spade—or whatever it is.

SACRISTAN: Yes, and there ought to be a difference between a sacristan who knows Latin and a plain barber who knows one tune.

CRISTINA: As for me and what I want of him, my barber knows as much Latin as Erasmus, if not more. But let's not talk about learning or learn about talking now; everyone speaks as he can, if not as he should. So let's go in and get to work; there's lots to do yet.

STUDENT: And lots to pluck.

SACRISTAN: Who is this fine fellow?

LEONARDA: A poor Salamancan student who begged to be put up overnight.

SACRISTAN: I'll give him something for bed and supper, and let him be on his way.

STUDENT: My dear Sacristan Reponce: I cheerfully accept your charity, thank you. But though I'm sworn to silence and a plucking job to oblige the young lady who invited me here, I'm no dumbwaiter, and I'll be damned if I leave this house tonight, no matter who says so! Blast you, can't you trust a man of my ability who's willing to sleep in a hayloft? And if you're so touchy about your capons, get the Devil to pluck them for you and gobble them up yourself till you burst a gut!

BARBER: This fellow sounds more like a rogue than a beggar. He looks like someone who'd rob you blind and walk away.

CRISTINA: I'll be robbed and plundered, but I like his spirit. Now let's go in and get things organized while our beggar boy plucks away, silent as a church mouse at Mass.

STUDENT: At vespers, more likely.

SACRISTAN: That miserable student scares me; I'll bet he knows more Latin than I do.

LEONARDA: That's just where he gets his spirit— from knowing so much Latin. But don't regret your charity to him, my dear; remember, charity "is the greatest of all things."

[Exeunt omnes]

[Enter Pancracio and his friend Leoniso]

FRIEND: I knew that wheel was about to collapse, but there's no one so stubborn as a coachman. If he'd just taken a short detour around the ditch, we'd have been two leagues on our way by now.

PANCRACIO: I'm not worried a bit. I'd rather go back and spend the night with my wife, Leonarda, than stay at the inn. When I left her this afternoon, she was more dead than alive at my going.

FRIEND: A wonderful woman! Heaven's been good to you, my friend. You should be grateful.

PANCRACIO: I'm as grateful as can be, but that's still not enough. Why, there's no Lucretia as chaste, no Portia as wise as she is. She is virtue and devotion rolled into one.

FRIEND: If my wife weren't so jealous, I'd have no complaints. My house is closer down this street; go that way, my friend, and you'll be home quickly. So, till tomorrow, when I find us another carriage, goodbye!

PANCRACIO: Good-bye!

[*Exeunt* Pancracio *and* Friend]

[*The* Sacristan *and the* Barber *enter with their guitars;* Leonarda, Cristina, *and the* Student. *Enter the* Sacristan, *with his cassock pulled up and tied around his waist, dancing to the music of his own guitar, and with every caper he shouts these words:*]

SACRISTAN: Marvelous night, marvelous time, marvelous supper, marvelous love!

CRISTINA: Dear Sacristan Reponce, now's not the time for dancing. Eating our supper comes first, and then the other things; so leave off dancing till the time comes.

SACRISTAN: Wonderful night, wonderful time, wonderful supper, wonderful love!

LEONARDA: Let him be, Cristina. I love to watch his nimble feet.

[Pancracio *knocks at the door*]

PANCRACIO: Are you asleep in there? Don't you hear me? What's this? You've bolted the door so early? Oh, my Leonarda, she's so terribly cautious.

LEONARDA: Ah, worse luck! I know that voice and that knock. It's my husband, Pancracio. Something must have happened to bring him back. Go hide in the coal bin—I mean in the garret, where we keep the charcoal. Run, Cristina, and show them where. Meanwhile, I'll put him off and give you time to get away.

STUDENT: Horrible night, terrible time, impossible supper, miserable love!

CRISTINA: Stormy weather ahead, no doubt of it. Come on, all of you!

PANCRACIO: What in the world is this? Here, here, open up, sleepyheads!

STUDENT: That settles it. I'm not getting involved with those fellows. Let them hide where they like—show me the way to the hayloft, and if I'm found there, at least I'll be taken for a beggar, not an adulterer.

CRISTINA: Hurry, before he batters the house down!

SACRISTAN: My heart's in my mouth.

BARBER: And mine's in my shoes.

[*Exeunt omnes, except* Leonarda, *who peers through the window*]

LEONARDA: Who's out there? Who's knocking?

PANCRACIO: It's your husband, Leonarda dear. Open up, I've been pounding at this door for half an hour.

LEONARDA: Your voice does sound like my darling Pancracio's: But one cock crows like another, so I can't be sure.

PANCRACIO: Ah, the caution, the amazing honesty of that woman! My dear, it's me, your husband, Pancracio. Don't be afraid, it's quite safe to open the door for me.

LEONARDA: Come closer, and I'll see about that. What was it I did when Pancracio left this afternoon?

PANCRACIO: You sighed, you wept, and then you fainted.

LEONARDA: That's right. But tell me now: What are the marks I have on one of my shoulders?

PANCRACIO: On your left shoulder there's a birthmark the size of a small coin; it's got three hairs on it like fine gold threads.

LEONARDA: That's right. But now tell me, what's the maid's name here?

PANCRACIO: Come on, pet, don't be tiresome. Her name is Cristina. Anything else?

LEONARDA: Cristina, Cristina! It's your master! Let him in, dear girl.

CRISTINA: I'm coming, madam. He'll be ever so welcome! What's wrong, dear master? What brings you home so soon?

LEONARDA: Oh, my darling! I am afraid something terrible has happened. Tell us quickly or I shall faint.

PANCRACIO: It was only that the coach cracked a wheel in the ditch, so my friend and I decided to come home instead of spending the night out. Tomorrow we'll find some way to go—there's plenty of time. But what's all that shouting?

[*Offstage, and as though far off, the* Student *shouts:*]

STUDENT: Open up, somebody, I'm suffocating!

PANCRACIO: Is that in the house or out on the street?

CRISTINA: I'll be tied if it isn't that poor student I locked in the hayloft for the night.

PANCRACIO: A student in my house while I was away? Hm, sounds bad! Now, madam, if I weren't so sure of your good character, I'd begin to suspect something's behind this locking-up business. But go, Cristina, and let him out. All that hay must have tumbled down on him.

CRISTINA: I'm going.

LEONARDA: Dear, it's just a poor Salamancan boy who begged us in God's name for a night's lodging, even if it were only in the hayloft. And you know how I am, unable to refuse anybody anything when

I'm asked. So we shut him in. But here he comes, and you can see for yourself.

[*Enter the* Student *and* Cristina; *his clothes, his head, and his beard are all covered with straw*]

STUDENT: If I were bolder and had fewer scruples, I could have avoided the risk of suffocating in straw; I'd have dined better and had a softer and safer bed.

PANCRACIO: Who, my friend, would have given you a better supper and a better bed?

STUDENT: Who? Why, my own ingenuity—if fear of the law hadn't tied my hands.

PANCRACIO: A dangerous sort of ingenuity, if it makes you fear the law!

STUDENT: If I could only use the science I learned in the Cave of Salamanca (my native town] without fear of the Holy Inquisition, I'd be able to eat and stuff myself, regardless of expense. And yet, perhaps I might use the science this once, when necessity compels and excuses me, though I don't know if the ladies can keep a secret as well as I did.

PANCRACIO: Never mind about them, my friend. Do what you want, and I'll see to it they keep quiet. I must certainly see something of the things they say are taught in the Cave of Salamanca.

STUDENT: Would you like me now to conjure up two demons in human form carrying in a hamper full of cold meats and delicacies?

PANCRACIO: Demons in this house, before my very eyes?

LEONARDA: [*Aside*] Gracious me! Heaven preserve me from the likes of them, or else I'm lost!

CRISTINA: [*Aside*] The very devil's got into that student! Pray God be kind to us now. My poor heart's pounding in my throat!

PANCRACIO: Well, now, if it can be done safely and not frighten anybody, I'd enjoy seeing those gentlemen demons and the hamper full of cold meats; but I warn you again, the demons mustn't scare us.

STUDENT: I say they shall appear in the shapes of the sacristan of this parish and of his friend the barber.

CRISTINA: You don't mean Sacristan Reponce and Master Nicholas, our own barber? Poor fellows, to find themselves turned into devils! But tell me, brother, will they be baptized devils?

STUDENT: What a notion! Where the devil would you find baptized devils, and why would devils be baptized anyway? But maybe these are baptized, for there's no rule without an exception. Now stand back; you're about to see wonders.

LEONARDA: [*Aside*] The jig's up! Here's where it all comes out! Here's where our sins walk out in the open! Here's where I die of shame.

CRISTINA: [*Aside*] Courage, madam. A stout heart overcomes any misfortune.

STUDENT: Hear me, you miserable creatures, come out
Of that coal bin, you're in disgrace.
Be quick, and make sure you've the grace
To bring that hamper of cold meats out.
Don't try to provoke me, I can conjure less
Gently; don't dally, I say. Come out!
Because if you don't, I've no case
And my magical purpose falls on its face.

All right, then. I know just how to treat these half-human little devils. I'll go in there myself and cast such a powerful spell over them that they'll come flying out—though by the looks of the poor devils, they'll take plain coaxing better than spellbinding.

[*Exit the* Student]

PANCRACIO: I tell you, if it all turns out as this fellow says, it will be the most astonishing thing on earth.

LEONARDA: Of course he'll do it, why not? How can he possibly deceive us?

CRISTINA: There's a commotion inside. I'll bet he flushes them out. See how he drives those demons, and look at that wraith of a hamper they're carrying!

[*Enter the* Student, *the* Sacristan, *and the* Barber]

LEONARDA: Good Lord! See how much they resemble Sacristan Reponce and the town barber!

CRISTINA: Madam, take care. You mustn't say the Lord's name in front of demons.

SACRISTAN: Say whatever you wish; we're like the blacksmith's dogs, who fall asleep to the banging hammer: nothing frightens or upsets us.

LEONARDA: Bring them closer so I can eat out of their hamper—and you eat too.

STUDENT: I'll try it first, and begin with the wine. [*Drinks*] An excellent wine—and from Esquivias, Mr. Sacri—demon?

SACRISTAN: It *is* from Esquivias, I swear to——

STUDENT: Hold on there, blast you! Don't you dare say another word! I know all about you blasphemous demons! Little demon, little demon, we haven't come here to commit mortal sin, but to while away an hour or so, chatting and eating, and then be on our way.

CRISTINA: And these fellows, must they eat with us?

PANCRACIO: Surely demons don't eat.

BARBER: Some do and some don't, but we're some who do.

CRISTINA: Oh, Master, oh, Mistress! Do let the poor devils join us, since it was they who brought the supper. It wouldn't be polite to let them go off dying of hunger. Besides, they seem to be such decent, well-behaved little devils.

LEONARDA: If they're not going to frighten us, and if my husband is willing, they're entirely welcome.

PANCRACIO: Let them stay. I'd like to see a thing or two that I never saw before.

BARBER: Pray God repay you for your generosity, good people.

CRISTINA: Oh, how well-bred, how courteous they

are! I'll be robbed and plundered, but if all devils are like these, then devils are my friends from now on.

SACRISTAN: Now everybody listen to this, then you'll really fall in love with us.

[*The* Sacristan *plays and sings, and the* Barber *joins him only in the last line of each stanza*]

SACRISTAN: Hear me, you who know so little,
And I'll tell you somewhat more
Of the knowledge that's essential

BARBER: *In the Cave of Salamanca.*

SACRISTAN: First listen to what's been inscribed
By that college man Two-Tanker
On his mare's or filly's hide,
But more especially upon
The backside such a creature raises.
On this, of course, he sang the praises

BARBER: *Of the Cave of Salamanca.*

SACRISTAN: There you know that side by side
The beggar studies with the banker,
And the narrower the mind
On starting, the broader it departs.
Professors sitting down to lecture
Find they're stuck to pitch and tar.
One expects such lively starts

BARBER: *In the Cave of Salamanca.*

SACRISTAN: Occidental Moors get lessons
In discretion at this college
Where one hears the dumbest students
Burst with scientific knowledge.
Once a man gets in, with rank or
Not, nothing more can faze him; so
Hip-hip-hurray, and hi-di-ho,

BARBER: *Dear old Cave of Salamanca.*

SACRISTAN: And if our student conjurer
Hails from grapevine country, let
All his vineyards grow and prosper
With luscious grapes both red and
white.
Any devil with the rancor
To deny this will be cudgeled
And externally expelled

BARBER: *From the Cave of Salamanca.*

CRISTINA: Enough. Must devils be poets too?

BARBER: Just as sure as all poets are devils.

PANCRACIO: Tell me, my good man, since you devils know everything, where did they start all those dances we call the Saraband, the Sambapalo, the I'm-So-Sorry Fling, and now this Escarramán, the latest thing?

BARBER: Where? In Hell, of course—wholly and solely in Hell.

PANCRACIO: Yes, that's what I think.

LEONARDA: But really, though I'm quite fond of it, I don't dare do the Escarramán—people would call me a hussy!

SACRISTAN: Ah, but if I taught you a few new steps every day, you'd be a first-rate dancer in a week. In fact, I can tell you—you're quite good at it already.

STUDENT: All that can wait. First let's go in and dine; that's the important thing now.

PANCRACIO: Yes, let's go in. I want to find out if devils eat or not, and a hundred thousand other things I've heard said about them. And, for pity's sake, don't leave my house till you've taught me all the arts and sciences you've learned in the Cave of Salamanca.

Calderón and Life Is a Dream

Lope de Vega (see pages 361–362) had numerous prolific colleagues and followers, and the number of plays written by them is staggering. But none of these ever attained the distinction or exerted the influence of Pedro Calderón de la Barca (1600–1681). Before he died, Calderón had to his credit one hundred eleven regular plays and seventy short plays, or *autos*.

Like Cervantes and Lope de Vega, Calderón joined a military expedition, and like the latter he enjoyed contributing "total theatre" to his time, participating in the staging and physical elaboration of plays. For the pageantry connected with one of his fantastic plays involving mythological figures, *Love, the Greatest Enchantment,* he received the distinguished Order of Santiago from his king, Philip IV, who also appointed him court poet after Lope's death in 1635. It was an honor fully earned not merely by his assiduity but the stylistic refinement and careful craftsmanship of his work, which has been contrasted with Lope's vivacious and theatrically effective, but rather carelessly written, stage pieces. The year 1635 is especially memorable, too, for in it he also completed *La vida es sueño,* or *Life Is a Dream,* the work in which he displayed to greatest advantage his reflective bent and philosophical, though essentially conventional, inclinations.

He gave many indications of the religious disposition which made him spend his last thirty years in holy orders and leave his possessions to the Church—chiefly in his numerous *autos* and miracle plays about saints.[1] These are distinctly more refined as literature than those of medieval times, which were for the most part folk pieces rather than the polished work of a professional writer.

Attesting his moral earnestness and the religious zeal of the Counter Reformation, which reached baroque intensity in seventeenth-century Spain, Calderón also wrote plays that resemble the allegories of the Middle Ages, of which the English masterpiece is *Everyman.* Calderón's master work in this genre is *The Great Theatre of the World,*[2] in which the "Author," who is also God, summons representatives of mankind such as Rich Man and Beggar to his throne and lets them all play a part in a Morality Play. Even when Calderón turned to writing some works in the vein of Lope's *Fuente Ovejuna* (see pages 363–381), most notably *The Mayor of Za-*

lamea (*El alcalde de Zalamea*) around 1640, he was fundamentally a moral rigorist. In *The Mayor* a farmer who has been elected mayor or magistrate of his village executes a young nobleman who seduced his daughter. He stands by his right to have done so even when he faces the king himself; and the king, recognizing the justice of his case, appoints him *alcalde* for life. And his *Physician of His Own Honor* (*El médico du su honra*), whose hero has his wife bled to death by a surgeon because of his suspicion of her adultery, confirms the playwright as an uncompromising moralist who reflected the extravagant Spanish regard for honor (*pundonor*) prevalent in his age. It should be recognized too, however, that Calderón was also capable of mocking the *pundonor* convention and the extreme caste system, as is ably demonstrated by his charming pastoral comedy *The Phantom Lady* (*La Dama Duende*).

Many threads of a high-minded view of life went into the making of *Life Is a Dream,* not the least of these being a concern with personal uprightness and just government. But, as in the case of other masterpieces, there is art as well as substance in the work. This is apparent both in Calderón's imaginative use of the dream device in the dramatic action and in his formal poetic style. *Life Is a Dream* is not wholly convincing in its psychology, but it does follow a logic of didactic narration. The interest of Segismundo's drama is to be gauged not by its adherence to strict probability and psychological motivation, but by its power of suggestion and its reflective fantasy. Calderón's verse, besides, is equal to the demands of this philosophical fable; it is marred only by passages that followed the then fashionable stylistic affectations known as euphuism in England and Gongorism in Spain.

That this play and other works by Calderón should have continued to exert a fascination on the minds of Europeans in search of an imaginative sense of human life and ideals was to be expected. The famous Victorian translator of the *Rubaiyats* of *Omar Khayyam,* Edward Fitzgerald, rendered eight of Calderón's plays into English, and *Life Is a Dream* has attracted the attention of two of the twentieth century's most romantic yet artistically disciplined poets, Roy Campbell from South Africa, who translated it, and Hofmannsthal in Austria, who adapted it twice under the title of *Der Turm,* or *The Tower.* To the romantic sensibility, indeed, few seventeenth-century writers appealed as powerfully, and the famous German romantic critic Schlegel's tribute is characteristically fervid.

If feeling of religion, a loyal heroism, honour, and love, be the foundation of romantic poetry, it could not fail to attain to its highest development in Spain, where its birth and growth were cherished

---

[1] Among the best known of these are *The Wonder-Working Magician* (El magico prodigioso, 1567) and the somewhat earlier written *Devotion of the Cross* (La devocion de la cruz).

[2] A German version, *Das Grosse Salzburger Welttheater,* by the Austrian poet Hugo von Hofmannsthal was impressively staged in the nineteen-twenties by the great impresario Max Reinhardt at the festival town of Salzburg, Mozart's birthplace.)

by the most friendly auspices. The fancy of the Spaniards, like their active powers, was bold and venturesome; no mental adventure seemed too hazardous for it to essay. The popular predilection for marvels had already shown itself in its romances of chivalry. And so they wished also to see the wonderful on the stage; when, therefore, their poets, standing on the lofty eminence of a highly polished state of art and society, gave it the requisite form, breathed into it a musical soul, and refined its beautiful hues and fragrance from all corporeal grossness, there arose, from the very contrast of the matter and the form, an irresistible fascination. Amid the harmony of the most varied metre, the elegance of fanciful allusions, and that splendour of imagery and simile which no other language than their own could hope to furnish, combined with inventions ever new, and almost always pre-eminently ingenious, the spectators perceived in imagination a faint refulgence of the former greatness of their nation which had measured the whole world with its victories. . . . On the dominions of this poetry, as on that of Charles V, the sun may truly be said never to set. . . . Religion is his peculiar love, the heart of his heart. For religion alone he excites the most over-powering emotions, which penetrate into the inmost recesses of the soul. He did not wish, it would seem, to do the same for mere worldly events. . . . Blessed man! he had escaped from the wild labyrinths of doubt into the stronghold of belief; from thence, with undisturbed tranquility of soul, he beheld and depicted the storms of the world; to him human life was no longer a dark riddle.[3]

[3] August Wilhelm Schlegel, *Lectures on Dramatic Art and Literature,* 1809. Translation by John Black, in Bohn's Standard Library, slightly modified. London.

NOTE: Because little is known about the work of Calderón by most Americans, attention should be called to the following special books, in addition to several volumes of his plays translated by Denis McCarthy in the Victorian period, Edward Fitzgerald's free translations entitled *Eight Dramas of Calderón* (1906), and *Calderón de la Barca: Five Plays* an excellent version by the American poet Edwin Honig. New York: Hill and Wang, 1961: G. H. Lewes, *The Spanish Drama: Lope de Vega and Calderón,* London, 1846; Richard Cheneux Trench, *Calderón, His Life and Genius,* New York, 1856; A. A. Parker, *The Allegorical Drama of Calderón,* Oxford, 1943; and Albert E. Sloman, *The Dramatic Craftsmanship of Calderón,* Oxford, 1958.

LIFE IS A DREAM

(*La vida es sueño*)

By Pedro Calderón de la Barca

TRANSLATED BY EDWARD AND ELIZABETH HUBERMAN

CHARACTERS

BASILIO, *King of Poland*
SEGISMUNDO, *the Prince*
ASTOLFO, *Duke of Muscovy*
CLOTALDO, *an old man, tutor of Segismundo*
CLARIN, *a talkative clown*

ESTRELLA, *a princess*
ROSAURA, *a lady*
SOLDIERS, GUARDS, MUSICIANS,
ATTENDANTS, SERVANTS, AND LADIES

SCENE: *In the Polish court, in a fortress a short distance away, and in the country.*

ACT I. SCENE I.

On one side a craggy mountain; on the other a tower whose lower section serves as a prison for Segismundo. The door facing the audience is half open. The action begins at nightfall.

[Rosaura, *in man's clothing, appears high up on the rocks, and comes down to the plain.* Clarin *follows her.*]

ROSAURA: Wild hippogriff,[1] running swift as the wind, flash without flame, bird without color, fish without scales, unnatural beast, where are you wildly rushing in the intricate labyrinth of these bare rocks? Stay here on this mountain, so that the beasts may have their Phaëthon. For I, taking the only path the laws of destiny allow me, blind and hopeless descend through the jagged tangles of this high hill, which wrinkles the frowning forehead of the sun.
Unkindly, O Poland, do you receive a stranger; for you inscribe her arrival in your land with blood; and hardly does she arrive, but she comes to grief. My fate will testify to this; but where did an unhappy person ever find pity?

CLARIN: Make it two unhappy people, and don't forget me when you complain. It was two of us who left our country to seek adventures, two of us who passed through misfortunes and madness to reach this place, and again two of us who have fallen down the mountain; shouldn't I grieve if I shared in the trouble, but not in the telling of it?

ROSAURA: I do not share my complaints with you, Clarin, because I do not wish to deprive you of your right to be consoled by weeping about your own problems. For there's so much pleasure in complaining, some philosopher once said, that troubles should be sought just for the sake of complaining about them.

[1] A mythological creature, half-horse, half-griffin.

CLARIN: That philosopher was a wretched drunkard. Oh, if someone had only punched him a thousand times or more! Then he would have something to complain of! But what are we to do señora, on foot, alone, and lost on a deserted mountain at this hour when the sun is leaving for another horizon?

ROSAURA: Whoever has seen such strange events? If my sight is not suffering the deceptions of fancy, it seems to me that in what remains of twilight I can see a building.

CLARIN: Either my desire is lying to me, or I can make out the signs myself.

ROSAURA: Here amid bare rocks rises a rustic palace, so small it scarcely dares to look at the sun. It's built with such crude skill that, at the base of so many sun-touching rocks and crags, it seems itself like some huge rock that must have tumbled from the summit.

CLARIN: Let's go nearer. While this is fine to see, señora, it would be finer if the people who live here would be kind enough to let us in.

ROSAURA: The door, or rather, the dismal mouth, is open, and from its center the night itself is born, engendered in that darkness.

[*The noise of chains is heard within.*]

CLARIN: Heavens, what do I hear?

ROSAURA: I can't move! I'm fire and ice!

CLARIN: Is a chain making that noise? May they kill me, if that isn't a galley slave being punished. My fear tells me that it is.

SEGISMUNDO: [*Within the tower*] Alas, wretched me! How unhappy I am!

ROSAURA: What sad voice do I hear? Now I must face new pains and anguish.

CLARIN: And I new fear . . .

ROSAURA: Clarin . . .

CLARIN: Señora . . .

ROSAURA: Let us run away from the dangers of this enchanted tower.

CLARIN: When it comes to that, I have no mind to flee.

ROSAURA: Isn't that faint exhalation, that pallid star, a sort of light? It trembles, fades, flares, and flashes, and makes this dim room darker with its doubtful glow. Yes, it is! For by its beams I can make out, even from afar, a gloomy prison room, the grave of a living corpse. Stranger still, dressed in the skins of beasts, and loaded with chains, a man lies on the floor, with no company but this light.

Since we can't run away, let's listen from here to his complaints; let's learn what he says.

[*The doors swing open, and* Segismundo *is seen, chained and clad in skins. There is a light in the tower.*]

SEGISMUNDO: Oh, wretch that I am! Oh, unfortunate! I try, oh heavens, to understand, since you treat me so, what crime I committed against you when I was born . . . but, since I *was* born, I understand my crime. Your cruel justice has had sufficient cause. For man's greatest crime is to have been born at all. Still, I should like to know, to ease my anxiety—leaving aside, ye gods, the sin of being born—in what way I could offend you more, to deserve more punishment? Were not all other men born too? If so, why do they have blessings that I never enjoyed?

The bird is born, with the gaudy plumage that gives it unrivalled beauty; and scarcely is it formed, like a flower of feathers or a winged branch, when it swiftly cuts the vaulted air, refusing the calm shelter of its nest. But I, with more soul, have less liberty!

The beast is born, too, with skin beautifully marked, like a cluster of stars—thanks to Nature's skilled brush; then stern necessity, cruel and savage, teaches it to be cruel also, and it reigns a monster in its labyrinth. Yet I, with better instincts, have less liberty!

The fish is born, unbreathing, a creature of spawn and seaweed, and scarcely is it seen—a scaly vessel in the waves—when it darts in all directions, measuring the vastness of the cold and deep. And I, with more free will, have less liberty!

The stream is born, a snake uncoiling among the flowers, and scarcely does this serpent of silver break through the blossoms, when it celebrates their grace with music, and with music takes its passage through the majesty of the open plain. Yet I, who have more life, have less liberty!

As I reach this pitch of anger, like a volcano, an Aetna, I could tear pieces of my heart from my own breast. What law, justice, or reason, can deny to man so sweet a privilege, so elementary a freedom, as God has given to a brook, a fish, a beast, and a bird?

ROSAURA: His words make me feel pity and fear.

SEGISMUNDO: Who's been listening to me? Clotaldo?

CLARIN: [*Aside, to* Rosaura] Say yes!

ROSAURA: It's only a sad wanderer—alas!—who heard your moans in these cold vaults.

SEGISMUNDO: Then I shall kill you here [*He seizes her*], so that you may not know my weakness. My strong arms seize you, to tear you to pieces, only because you have heard me.

CLARIN: I'm deaf; I couldn't hear you.

ROSAURA: If you were born a human being, throwing myself at your feet should be enough to make you let me go.

SEGISMUNDO: Your voice has calmed me, your presence stopped me, and the respect I feel for you disturbs me. Who are you? For even though I know so little of the world, inasmuch as this tower has been cradle and tomb for me; and even though, since I was born—if this is to be born—I have seen only this wilderness where I live in misery, a living skeleton, a moving corpse; and even though I have seen and talked to only one man here who pities my distress, and who has taught me all I know of earth and heaven; and although here—to astonish you more, and make you call me a human monster—here among terrors and fearful fancies, I am a man among wild beasts, and a beast among men; and although in my grave misfortunes I have studied politics, been instructed by the beasts and advised by the birds, and have measured the circles of the smooth-slipping stars, you only, only you have calmed my anger, brought wonder to my eyes, and astonishment to my ears.

Each time I look at you, I feel new admiration; the more I look at you, the more I want to look. My eyes must have the dropsy, I believe, for though it's death to drink, they drink even more. And thus, although I see that seeing brings me death, I still must see. But let me look at you, and die. For if seeing you kills me, I do not know, your victim that I am, what not seeing you would do to me. It would be worse than fierce death, worse than rage, madness, and terrible grief. It would be life. And of this fate I have taken the measure, for to grant life to an unhappy man is the same as to slay a happy one.

ROSAURA: Amazed to look at you, and filled with wonder to hear you, I do not know what to tell you, nor what to ask. I can only say that heaven has guided me here today to console me, if it can be the consolation of one unlucky being to see another more unlucky still. They tell the story of a wise man who was so poor and wretched that he survived only by eating the herbs he gathered. "Can there be anyone else," he said to himself, "poorer and sadder than I?" And when he turned his head, he found the answer, for he saw another wise man gathering the leaves which he had thrown away.

I lived in this world complaining of my fortune, and when I asked myself: "Can there be some other person plagued by worse luck than I?" mercifully, you answered me. For when I think things over, I find that you have gathered my pains and made joys of them.

If then, by chance, my troubles can in any way relieve you, listen to them carefully, and take what I have left over. I am . . .

CLOTALDO: [*Within*] Guards of the tower! Afraid or asleep, you let two people break into the prison.

ROSAURA: Still more trouble!

SEGISMUNDO: That's Clotaldo, my warden. My misfortunes are not over yet!

CLOTALDO: [Within] Come here, be careful! Capture them or kill them, before they can defend themselves!

VOICES: [Within] Treason!

CLARIN: Guards of the tower, who let us enter here, since you give us a choice, capturing us is easier.

[Clotaldo and Soldiers enter, the former with a pistol and all with faces covered]

CLOTALDO: [Aside to the Soldiers, as they enter] All of you cover your faces. It is important, while we are here, to be careful no one recognizes us.

CLARIN: Is this a masquerade?

CLOTALDO: You there! You who in ignorance passed the limits and boundary of this forbidden place, contrary to the decree of the King, who commands that no one dare look upon the prodigy hidden among these crags, surrender your arms and yourselves, or this pistol, this metal asp, will spit out the penetrating poison of its two bullets, with a blast that will shock the air.

SEGISMUNDO: Before you hurt them, oh tyrant master, my life will be the spoil of these miserable chains, for, God help me, I would sooner tear myself to pieces, with my hands, with my teeth, among these rocks, than permit any misfortune to occur to them or have to lament an outrage done to them.

CLOTALDO: Since you know, Segismundo, that your misfortunes are so enormous that before birth you died by heaven's law; since you know that these prison walls are a rein to check your proud fury, and a bridle to halt it, why talk like such a braggart? [To the soldiers.] Shut the door of this narrow cell! Hide him in it!

SEGISMUNDO: O heavens! How well you do to take away my freedom! For I would assault you like a giant, piling mountains of jasper on foundations of stone to break the glassy crystals of the sun!

CLOTALDO: Perhaps the punishment you suffer today will prevent you from building such piles!

[Several Soldiers take Segismundo away, and shut him in his prison]

ROSAURA: Now that I have seen you so much offended by pride, it would be stupid of me not to be humble, and fall at your feet to beg my life. May you be moved by pity toward me, for it would be extraordinary harshness, indeed, if neither pride nor humility found favor with you.

CLARIN: And if you can be influenced by neither Humility nor Pride, characters which a thousand morality plays have set in motion and shifted about, then I, neither humble nor proud, but a mixture of half and half, I beg that you help and succor us.

CLOTALDO: Ho there!

SOLDIERS: Sir?

CLOTALDO: Disarm both of them, and bind their eyes, so that they may not see how or where they leave.

ROSAURA: Here is my sword, which must be yielded to you only, because you are the chief of all here; it cannot be given to any lesser person.

CLARIN: [To a Soldier] Mine is the sort that can be given to the meanest; here, you, take it!

ROSAURA: And if I must die, I wish to leave you, in consideration of your pity, a pledge that could be truly valued by its owner, who one day girded it on. Guard it, I charge you, for although I do not know of what secret it may hint, I do know that this golden sword is the key to great mysteries. Trusting only in it, I have come to Poland to revenge an injury.

CLOTALDO: [Aside] Blessed heavens! What is this? Now my worries and bewilderment, my anxiety and my griefs, are all compounded. Who gave this to you?

ROSAURA: A woman.

CLOTALDO: What is her name?

ROSAURA: It is forbidden me to tell it.

CLOTALDO: What were you implying just now, or how do you know there is a secret in this sword?

ROSAURA: She who gave it to me said: "Go to Poland, and by trick or art or study, arrange for the leaders and nobles to see this sword in your possession, for I know that some one of them will favor and protect you." But who that was she did not wish to say, in case he might be dead.

CLOTALDO: [Aside] Heaven preserve me! What do I hear? I still cannot determine if these happenings are illusion or reality. This is the sword I left with the beautiful Violante as a pledge that I would treat him who wore it girded on his belt as if he were my son; and as a father, I would help him. But what must I do—alas!—in such a quandary, if he who carries it to gain my favor, carries it for his own death, since sentenced to death he comes to my feet? What a strange confusion! What an unhappy destiny! What inconstant luck! This is my son; the signs agree with the signals of my heart which calls from my breast when it sees him, and beats its wings. And because it cannot break the locks, it does what a man would do who was shut in and heard a noise in the street— he looks out the window; likewise my heart, since it knows not what goes on, and hears the noise, comes to my eyes, which are the windows of the heart, to look out. And from thence it flows out in tears. What must I do? Heaven help me! What am I to do? To take him to the King is to take him—too sad to think of—to his death. Yet hide him from the King I cannot, because of my oath of allegiance. On one side love for my own, and loyalty on the other; I am torn apart. But why do I hesitate? Does not loyalty to the King come before life and honor? Then let the King prevail, and life yield place. Besides, now I remember, he said he comes here to avenge an insult. A man who has been insulted is infamous. He is not my son, not my son, he does not bear my noble blood. But what if some danger, some accident occurred, from which no one escaped—for honor is such a fragile substance that a single touch may break it, or the very breeze injure it—what more, then, can he who is noble do in his own behalf than to come, at great risk, to seek his honor again? He *is* my son; his blood is mine, since he has such valor. And thus, between one doubt and another, the most important step is to go to the King and tell him that this is my son, and that he must kill him. Perhaps the very concern I have for my honor may move the King in my behalf; and if my merit wins my son's life, I'll help him to avenge that insult. But if the King, unbending in his harshness, condemns him to death, he will die without knowing I am his father.

[*To* ROSAURA *and* CLARIN] Come with me, strangers. Do not fear that you lack company in your misfortunes, for in this doubt of life or death, I know not whose misery is greatest.

[*Exeunt*]

SCENE II.

Hall of the royal palace in the Court.

[*Enter* Astolfo *and* Soldiers *on one side, and on the other, the* Infanta Estrella *and her* Ladies. *Military music within, and salvos*]

ASTOLFO: At the sight of your bright and peerless eyes, flashing like comets, the drums and trumpets, birds and fountains mingle their varied salutes; marveling at your heavenly appearance, they blend in similar music, as trumpets made of feathers, or as birds of metal. And thus, señora, the guns salute you as their queen; the birds greet you as Aurora; the trumpets, as Pallas; and the flowers, as Flora. For you mock the day, now exiled by night, and appear like Aurora in joy, Flora in peace, Pallas in war, and sovereign in my heart.

ESTRELLA: If words are to be measured by actions, you have done ill in speaking such elegant niceties when all that martial display against which I boldly fight may prove you a liar; for the flatteries I hear from you do not agree, I fear, with the terrors that I see. Mark well: it is an ignoble act, fitting only for a wild beast, the source of deceit and treachery, to flatter with the tongue while planning to kill.

ASTOLFO: You are badly informed, Estrella, to doubt the faith of my tender words; and I beg you to hear my cause, to see if I can tell it correctly. When Eustorgio the Third, King of Poland, died, he left Basilio as his heir, and two daughters, from whom you and I were born. I do not wish to tire you with what has no place here. Clorilene, your mother and my aunt, who now, beneath a canopy of stars, rules in a better kingdom, was the elder. You are her daughter. The younger, my mother and your aunt, was the graceful Recisunda, whom God preserve for a thousand years. She married in Muscovy, and of her I was born.

Now let us return to the beginning: Basilio, who now, señora, yields to the common scorn of time, is more inclined to studies than to women, and is a childless widower. You and I aspire to his throne. You argue that you are the elder sister's daughter; I, that I was born a man, and though a child of the younger sister, I ought to be preferred to you. We have related your aim and mine to our uncle. He has answered that he wishes to reconcile us, and with that in mind we appointed this place and this day. With this purpose I left Muscovy and my native land; for this reason I came here, not to make war on you, but for you to war on me. Oh, may Love, wise God, be willing that the people, sure astrologers, today conclude this agreement for us, that you may be queen, but queen by my free will. And for greater honor, our uncle will give you his crown, your own valor will give you triumphs, and your empire will be my love.

ESTRELLA: To such gracious gallantry my heart replies in kind, for I should be glad if the imperial throne were mine, only to make it yours. Still my love is not quite satisfied that you are to be trusted, for I suspect that portrait hanging at your breast gives the lie to all you say to me.

ASTOLFO: I shall try to satisfy you about that . . . But no occasion is left us. [*Drums sound.*] That sonorous instrument informs us that king and parliament now approach.

[King Basilio *enters with his following*]

ESTRELLA: Wise Thales . . .

ASTOLFO: Learned Euclid . . .

ESTRELLA: Who among signs . . .

ASTOLFO: Who among stars . . .

ESTRELLA: Today rules . . .

ASTOLFO: Today dwells . . .

ESTRELLA: And their paths . . .

ASTOLFO: And footsteps . . .

ESTRELLA: Describes . . .

ASTOLFO: Measures and marks . . .

ESTRELLA: Permit me, humbly twining . . .

ASTOLFO: Allow me, with tender embraces . . .

ESTRELLA: Like ivy to surround this trunk.

ASTOLFO: To sink in supplication at your feet.

BASILIO: My nephew and my niece, embrace me. Believe me, since you come with such affection, obedient to my loving command, neither of you will have cause to complain; both shall be treated equally. And thus, when I confess myself overcome by the tedious weight of years, I ask only for your silence; the event itself will strike you with amazement.

You already know—attend me well, my beloved niece and nephew, illustrious court of Poland, vassals, kinsmen, friends—you already know that because of my learning I have won in the world the title of Learned: for, despite time and forgetfulness, Thimantes' brushes and Lysippus' marbles proclaim me throughout the globe, Basilio the Great. You know too that the science I most study and esteem is subtle mathematics, by which I steal from Time, by which I tear from fame the province and the office of revealing what each day shall be. For when, in my calculations, I behold the events of coming centuries as if they were present, I win Time's thanks, who then has only to tell what I have told already.

These circles of snow, these canopies of glass, lighted by the sun's rays and divided by the circuits of the moon; these diamond orbs, these crystal globes which the stars adorn, and where the signs of the Zodiac are set, these are the major study of my years. These are the books where, on diamond pages, in sapphire note-books, and in golden lines of clearest letters, heaven writes our fates, whether adverse or benign. These I read so swiftly that with my spirit I follow their rapid movements, their roads and courses. Would it had pleased heaven, before my skill became a marginal commentary and an index of these pages, that my life had been first destroyed by their rages, and that therein had been all my tragedy! For to the unfortunate, even merit is a knife; he whom knowledge harms, murders himself! This I tell you now, even though my history will say it better; and to wonder at this, once more I ask your silence.

By Clorilene, my wife, I was given an unhappy son, at whose birth the heavens were consumed by prodigies. Before the living sepulchre of her womb—for birth and death are much alike—delivered him to the light of the sun, his mother numberless times, half in fancy, half in the visions of dreams, saw a rude monster in man's form tear through her entrails. Stained with her blood, he took her life, thus becoming at birth the human viper of the century. The day of birth arrived, the omens were fulfilled (for seldom or never do those that presage evil err). He was born with such a horoscope that the sun, dyed with blood, dueled furiously with the moon. With the earth as battleground, the two divine lamps struggled, not arm to arm, but light to light. This was the greatest, the most terrifying eclipse the sun has suffered since with its blood it wept the death of Christ. For the orb, flooded with living fire, seemed to be sustaining its final paroxysm; the heavens darkened; buildings shook; the clouds rained stones; the rivers ran blood. And in that frenzy, that delirium of the son, was Segismundo born, indicating his nature at once by killing his mother. With that cruel act he seemed to say: "I am a man, since I now begin to repay kindnesses with evil."

Turning to my studies, I saw in them and in everything that Segismundo would be the most insolent man, the cruelest prince, the most impious monarch, by whose hand the kingdom would be shattered and divided, a school for treason, an academy for vice. And he, borne on by his fury, among crimes and terrors, was to set his feet upon me; and I, to see myself a suppliant before him (with what shame I speak it!) the white hairs of my head a rug beneath his heel. Who does not easily believe evil, particularly the evil he has seen in his own study, where self-love fortifies the argument? So I believed the fates that with foreknowledge prophesied danger in their fatal oracles, and I determined to lock up the wild beast that had been born, to see if the sage could hold

mastery over the stars. It was announced that the infant was born dead, and, forewarned, I ordered a tower, its entrance guarded by rough obelisks, to be built among the rocks and crags of those mountains, where the light scarcely finds its way. Severe penalties and laws, publicly proclaimed, declaring that no one might enter the forbidden area of the mountain, grew out of the reasons I have told you.

There lives Segismundo, wretched, poor and captive, where only Clotaldo has talked with him, dealt with him, and seen him. Clotaldo has taught him the sciences, has instructed him in the law of the church, has been the sole witness of his misery.

Here now are three considerations: first, that I love thee, Poland, so much that I desire to free thee from oppression and servitude under a tyrant king. For he would not be a kind lord who would put his country and his realm in such danger. Second: if I deprive my own child of the right accorded by law, both human and divine, it is not Christian charity, since no law states that because I keep another from being an insolent tyrant, I may myself become one; nor that, if my son is a tyrant, I may commit crimes to prevent him from committing them. The last and third consideration is this: to see how great an error it is to believe too easily in predictions. For although his inclination may dictate rash acts, perhaps they will not overcome him; because the sternest fate, the most violent inclination, the most nefarious planet, merely influence the free will; they do not force it. And so, vacillating and thinking of one argument and another, I hit upon such a remedy as will astound your senses. Tomorrow I intend to place Segismundo—for that is his name—without his knowing that he is my son and your king, under my canopy, on my throne, and indeed, in my place where he may govern and command you, and where all of you as subjects will swear him obedience. For with this act I achieve three results with which I answer the three considerations of which I told you. First is this: if he is prudent, discreet, and benevolent, giving the lie in every way to what fate predicted for him, you will enjoy your natural prince, who has been a courtier of the mountains, and a neighbor of wild beasts. The second is this: that if, arrogant, high-mettled, insolent, and cruel, he runs unchecked the field of his vices, then will I piously have complied with my duty; and then, in dispossessing him, I shall act as king infallible, since returning him to prison will not be cruelty but punishment. And the third result is this: should the prince prove as I describe him, I shall give you, because I love you, rulers more worthy of the crown and scepter. They will be my niece and nephew, who, with their rights joined in one and cemented by a pledge of marriage, will have what they deserve. This as king I command you; this as a father I beg you; this as a sage I urge you; this as an old man I tell you; and if, as Spanish Seneca said, a king is the humble slave of his republic, then as a slave I beseech you.

ASTOLFO: If it is my place to respond, as he whose interests are most concerned here, in the name of all I say, let Segismundo appear. It is enough that he is your son.

ALL: Give us our prince, whom now we ask for king.

BASILIO: Vassals, that courtesy I value and I thank you for it. Conduct my niece and nephew, my two supporting pillars, to their rooms. Tomorrow you shall see the prince.

ALL: Long live great King Basilio!

[*Exeunt all, accompanying* Estrella *and* Astolfo; *the* King *remains*]

[Clotaldo *enters with* Rosaura *and* Clarin]

CLOTALDO: [*To the* King] May I speak to you?

BASILIO: Ah, Clotaldo, you are very welcome!

CLOTALDO: Although I ought to be welcome when I fall at your feet, my lord, this time harsh, sad fate breaks the privilege of the law and the pattern of custom.

BASILIO: What's the matter?

CLOTALDO: A misfortune, sire, has descended upon me; in other circumstances I should consider it the greatest joy.

BASILIO: Continue . . .

CLOTALDO: This handsome youth, daring or careless, entered the tower, Sire, where he saw the prince. And he is . . .

BASILIO: Do not worry, Clotaldo. If this had happened at another time, I confess I should have been incensed. But now I have told the secret, and it does not matter that he knows it. Attend me later, because I have many things to tell you, and many tasks that you must do for me. For you must be, I warn you, the instrument of the most tremendous event the world has seen. As for these prisoners, so that you will not think I am punishing your carelessness, I pardon them.

[*Exit*]

CLOTALDO: May you live, great Sire, a thousand centuries [*Aside*] Heaven has changed our luck for the better. I shall not say now that he is my son, since I can avoid it. [*Aloud*] Wandering strangers, you are free.

ROSAURA: I kiss your feet a thousand times.

CLARIN: And I *miss* them.—Two friends don't worry about one letter more or less.

ROSAURA: Since you have given me my life, señor, I live because of you. Eternally I shall be your slave.

CLOTALDO: It is not life I have given you, because a man well born does not live if his honor has been stained. Since you have come to avenge yourself for an insult, as you yourself have told me, I have not given you life, because you have not brought it with you. A dishonorable life is no life at all. [*Aside*] Those words will spur him on!

ROSAURA: I confess I do not possess it, even though I receive it from you. But by vengeance I shall leave my honor so clean that then my life, overcoming all dangers, can well appear your gift.

CLOTALDO: Take the burnished steel you brought. I know that it will be enough, dyed in the blood of your enemy, to avenge you. For steel that was mine (I refer to the little while I held the sword in my possession) will know how to take vengeance.

ROSAURA: In your name, a second time I gird it on, and on it I swear my vengeance, however powerful my enemy.

CLOTALDO: Is he so powerful?

ROSAURA: So much so that I shall not tell you of it. Not because I do not trust your prudence in greater things, but so that the wondrous favor of your mercy will not turn against me.

CLOTALDO: First you should gain my help by telling me, for that would prevent me from aiding your enemy. [*Aside*] Oh, if I only knew who he is!

ROSAURA: So that you will not think I hold your trust in low esteem, know that my adversary is no less than Astolfo, Duke of Muscovy.

CLOTALDO: [*Aside*] Ill can I withstand this sorrow, for it is graver when known than I had imagined. [*Aloud*] Let us clarify the matter further. If you were born a Muscovite, he who is your natural lord can hardly have been able to insult you. Return, then, to your fatherland, and leave the burning valor that drives you.

ROSAURA: I know that although he was my prince, he was able to injure me.

CLOTALDO: He could not, even though he rudely struck your cheek with his hand.

ROSAURA: Oh heaven, my injury was greater!

CLOTALDO: Tell me now, since you cannot say more than I imagine.

ROSAURA: Yes, I shall tell you; but I do not know, with such respect I regard you, with such affection I venerate you, with such esteem I look upon you, how I shall dare to tell you that this outward clothing is a riddle, since it is not whose it appears. Judge wisely, if I am not what I seem, and if Astolfo has come to marry Estrella, whether he may injure me. I have said enough.

[*Exeunt* Rosaura *and* Clarin]

CLOTALDO: Listen! Beware! Wait! What a confused labyrinth is this, where reason cannot find the thread. It is my honor that is smirched. The enemy is powerful, I a vassal, she a woman. Reveal the way, oh heaven; but I know not if heaven can. In such a confused hell, the whole sky's a dreadful omen, and the whole world a prodigy.

ACT II. SCENE I.

The palace.

[*Enter* Basilio, Clotaldo]

CLOTALDO: Everything has been done, just as you ordered.

BASILIO: Tell me, Clotaldo, how it happened.

CLOTALDO: Thus, Sire: with the tranquilizing drink

you ordered prepared, full of ingredients combining the virtues of certain herbs, the sovereign force and secret power of which suspend, steal, and alienate the human reason and leave a man a living corpse; the violence of which takes from him, while he sleeps, his senses and his powers. We need not argue if this be possible, since experience has so often told us, Sire, that it is. For it is certain that medicine is full of natural secrets, and there is neither animal, plant, nor stone which does not have its distinct property. Moreover, if our human malice can find a thousand poisons which bring death, how much more likely is it that, once the violence of these fatal poisons be tempered, they should bring sleep? Let us leave them aside, then, the question of whether this could possibly happen, since evidence and reason have already proved it. Well, with that drink, composed of opium, henbane, and the drowsy poppy, I went down to Segismundo's narrow cell. I talked with him a while of the humanities, wherein mute Nature, with her hills and heavens, has instructed him. In her divine school he learned the rhetoric of birds and beasts. To raise his spirit further toward the enterprise you desire, I took as subject the speed of a mighty eagle, which, scorning the sphere of the wind, passed on to soar in the supreme regions of fire, like a feathered flame or a strayed comet. I acclaimed its lofty flight, saying: "You, Eagle, are King of the Birds, and thus it is right that you excel them all." Further urging was not necessary. Eagerly, proudly, he explained his views on royalty, for, in fact, his blood incites him, stirs and moves him toward great deeds. "So," said he, "even in the noisy commonwealth of the birds there is one who makes them swear obedience. While I reason thus, my misfortunes console me, for if I am subdued, at least it is only by force. Voluntarily I would submit to no man."
Seeing him now enraged by this, which has been the theme of all his suffering, I offered him the potion. Scarcely had the liquid passed to his throat from the cup, when sleep overcame him. A cold sweat ran through all his limbs and veins, so that, if I had not known his death was feigned, I should have doubted of his life. Just then the people to whom you trusted the outcome of this experiment arrived. Putting him into a carriage, they brought him to his room, which had been prepared with all the majesty and elegance worthy of his person. On your bed they laid him, and when the lethargy has spent its force, they will serve him as they would you. For so, Sire, you commanded. And if having obeyed you merits a reward, I would only ask (pardon the liberty I take) that you tell me what your purpose is in bringing Segismundo in this way to the palace?

BASILIO: Clotaldo, the doubt you have is very reasonable, and I wish to satisfy you concerning it. The influence of the stars (well do you know this) threatens my son Segismundo with a thousand misfortunes and tragedies. I wish to test whether heaven, which cannot lie and which has given us so many proofs of harshness in his cruel nature, still may not mitigate, or at least temper, its decrees, and won over by valor and prudence, retract its doom. For man is master of the stars. This I wish to put to trial by bringing him where he may know he is my son, and where he may make proof of his nature. If magnanimity prevails in him, he shall reign; but if he shows himself cruel and tyrannical, I shall return him to his chains. Now you will ask why, for this test, was it necessary to have him carried here asleep in this way? I want to satisfy you, to give a reply to every question. If he knew today that he is my son, and tomorrow saw himself a second time reduced to miserable captivity, it is certain he would despair of his condition. For knowing who he is, what consolation can he have? Therefore I have intended to leave a way out of this danger: to tell him he only dreamed what he saw. Thus two things may be tried out: first, his nature, for when he wakens, he will act as thought and imagination dictate; and second, a means of consolation; for even though he now may be master and later is returned to his prison, he will be able to believe he dreamed. And he will be right in so believing, Clotaldo, for all of us who live in the world are dreaming.

CLOTALDO: I should not lack reasons to prove your course in error, but now it's too late for that. By all signs, it seems he has awakened and approaches us.

BASILIO: I wish to withdraw. You, as his tutor, remain, and by telling him the truth relieve him of the confusion that surrounds him.

CLOTALDO: You mean, you give me license to tell him his history?

BASILIO: Yes, for it may be, if he knows the truth, that the danger, once recognized, may more easily be overcome.

[Exit Basilio]

CLARIN: [Entering, aside] Since getting here cost me four blows from a redheaded guard, who grew a beard to match his livery, I have to see what's happening. Well, there's no window better than what a man carries with him, without appealing to a ticket agent, since, stripped or strapped, one can always get a peep at a show by pure effrontery.

CLOTALDO: [Aside] This is Clarin, the servant of that girl (oh, heavens!) that dealer in misfortune who has brought to Poland an insult for me. [Aloud] Clarin, what news?

CLARIN: Why, the news is, my lord, that your great mercy, disposed to avenge Rosaura's wrongs, counsels her to put on her proper dress.

CLOTALDO: And that is well, to keep her from appearing improper.

CLARIN: More news is this: by changing her name and discreetly taking that of your niece, she now grows so rapidly in honor that she lives in the palace as lady-in-waiting to the one and only Estrella.

CLOTALDO: It is well, too, that for once she should gain honor through me.

CLARIN: More news yet: she is hoping the time

and occasion will arrive for you to defend her honor.

CLOTALDO: This is a sure forecast: that in the end time will take care of these problems.

CLARIN: And here's a final bulletin: while she is regaled and served like a queen, as your niece, here am I, who came with her, dying of hunger, and nobody notices me. But after all, I am Clarin, and if this clarion sounds off, it may tell what's going on to the King, to Astolfo and Estrella. For a clarion and a servant are two things which keep a secret very ill. And perhaps, if the silence her hand has imposed on me were lifted, I might be singing these words:

> The Clarion that at daybreak blows
> Loud shall tell what Clarin knows.

CLOTALDO: Your complaint is justified, and I'll satisfy it. Meanwhile, be my servant.

CLARIN: Here comes Segismundo!

[*Enter* Musicians, *singing, and* Servants *attiring* Segismundo, *who seems dumbfounded*]

SEGISMUNDO: Heaven help me, what do I see! Heaven help me, what do I gaze upon! I wonder at it with some fear; I believe it, yet with much doubt. I, in a sumptuous palace? I, among silks and brocades? I, surrounded by servants so brave and splendid? I, awakened from sleep in so excellent a bed? I, in the midst of so many people who help me to dress? To say I am dreaming is not true; I know well that I am awake. Am I not Segismundo? Grant, oh heavens, that I may be freed from illusion! Tell me, what could have happened in my fancy while I slept that I now see myself here? But be that as it may, who will make me argue about it? I wish to continue being served, and let come what will come.

FIRST SERVANT: [*Aside to* Second Servant *and to* Clarin] How melancholy he is!

SECOND SERVANT: Who wouldn't be if such a thing happened to him?

CLARIN: I.

SECOND SERVANT: Now he's going to speak to him.

FIRST SERVANT [*To* Segismundo] Shall they sing again?

SEGISMUNDO: No, I don't want them to sing any more.

SECOND SERVANT: Since you are so filled with amazement, I wanted to amuse you.

SEGISMUNDO: I have no need to soothe my sorrows with their voices; martial music alone has pleased my ear.

CLOTALDO: Your highness, great Sire, give me your hand to kiss, for I must be the first to give you this token of allegiance.

SEGISMUNDO: [*Aside*] It's Clotaldo; how can he who treated me so badly in prison now address me with such respect? What is happening to me?

CLOTALDO: In the great confusion which your new estate causes you, your mind and reason must suffer a thousand doubts. But now I want to free you of all these, if possible, because you must know, Sire, that you are the Crown Prince of Poland. If you have been withdrawn and hidden, it has been in obedience to the cruelty of fate, which promises a thousand tragedies to this kingdom when its sovereign laurel crowns your august head. But in the trust that your good will may overcome the stars—for it is possible that a noble man may triumph over them—you have been brought, while overcome by sleep, to this palace from the tower where you lived. Your father, the King, my lord, will come to see you, and from him, Segismundo, you will learn the rest.

SEGISMUNDO: You vile and infamous traitor, what more do I have to know, now that I know who I am, to show from this day on my pride and power? How have you committed such treason against your country, that against right and reason you hid me and denied me this estate?

CLOTALDO: Ah, woe is me!

SEGISMUNDO: You were a traitor to the law, a flatterer to the King, and cruel to me. And thus the King, the law, and I, all victims of these wicked misdeeds, condemn you to death at my hands.

SECOND SERVANT: Sire . . .

SEGISMUNDO: Let no one interfere; it is useless to try. By the living God, if you put yourselves in the way, I'll throw you out the window!

SECOND SERVANT: Flee, Clotaldo!

CLOTALDO: Alas for you! What arrogance you display, not knowing that you are only dreaming!

[*Exit* Clotaldo]

SECOND SERVANT: Remember . . .

SEGISMUNDO: Get out of here!

SECOND SERVANT: . . . that he obeyed his king.

SEGISMUNDO: Inasmuch as the law was not just, he was not bound to obey the King; and I was his prince.

SECOND SERVANT: He had no right to question whether the law was good or bad.

SEGISMUNDO: I suspect you don't care about your life, since you persist in talking back to me.

CLARIN: What the prince says is right, and you are wrong.

SECOND SERVANT: Who gave you leave to talk?

CLARIN: I took it.

SEGISMUNDO: Who are you, pray tell?

CLARIN: A meddler, and the chief of that calling, for I'm the greatest busybody ever known.

SEGISMUNDO: In these new worlds where I move, only you have pleased me.

CLARIN: Sire, I make a habit of pleasing all the Segismundos.

ASTOLFO: [*Entering*] Happy a thousand times, O Prince, the day when you, the sun of Poland, show yourself and fill the sky, from horizon to horizon, with a divinely crimson flush of joy and splendor. For you come to us like the sun, from the bosom of the mountains! Rise, then, and although the laurel wreath that crowns your brow has come so late, long may it remain, and late wither.

SEGISMUNDO: May God keep you.

ASTOLFO: Only because you did not know me I forgive you for paying me no further honor. I am

Astolfo, born Duke of Muscovy, and your cousin. We are peers.

SEGISMUNDO: If I say, "May God keep you," do I not show you sufficient courtesy? But since you complain of this, and because you boast of who you are, the next time you see me I shall say, "May God not keep you."

SECOND SERVANT: [*To* Astolfo] Your highness must consider that since he was born in the mountains he behaves this way with everyone. [*To* Segismundo] Astolfo, Sire, prefers . . .

SEGISMUNDO: He tired me, the way he came to speak to me so solemnly. And the first thing he did was put on his hat.

SECOND SERVANT: He is a grandee.[2]

SEGISMUNDO: I am even grander.

SECOND SERVANT: Yet it is fitting that there should be more respect between you two than among others.

SEGISMUNDO: And who set you onto me?

ESTRELLA: [*Entering*] Many times welcome, Sire, to this canopied throne, which gratefully receives and desires you! And may you reign, august and lofty, despite deceit, not for years but for centuries!

SEGISMUNDO: [*To* Clarin] You, tell me now, who is this sovereign beauty? Who is this human goddess, at whose divine feet heaven's radiance lies prostrate? Who is this lovely woman?

CLARIN: She is, Sire, your cousin Estrella.

SEGISMUNDO: Estrella—that means star. Better you should say "the sun." [*To* Estrella] Although it is well that you congratulate me on my good fortune, only because I have seen you today will I accept your compliment. So, since I find myself with a blessing I don't deserve, I thank you for your courtesy, Estrella, that you could dawn and give the light of gladness to the brightest star. When you rise with the day, my lady, what is left for the sun to do? Give me your hand to kiss, from whose snowy cup the breeze drinks purity.

ESTRELLA: You are gallant, but be more restrained.

ASTOLFO: If he takes her hand, I am lost.

SECOND SERVANT: [*Aside*] I understand Astolfo's grief, and I'll interrupt. [*To* Segismundo] Remember, Sire, it is not right to be so insolent. And since Astolfo . . .

SEGISMUNDO: Didn't I tell you not to meddle with me?

SECOND SERVANT: I say only what is right.

SEGISMUNDO: All that annoys me. Nothing seems right to me which isn't to my taste.

SECOND SERVANT: Well, Sire, I've heard from you yourself that it is proper to obey and serve what is right.

SEGISMUNDO: You have also heard me say that I would throw anyone who crossed me off the balcony.

SECOND SERVANT: With men like me, that can't be done.

---

[2] Only a grandee could wear a hat in the presence of royalty.

SEGISMUNDO: No? By God! Then I'll have to prove it!

[*Seizes him in his arms and exits. All follow and enter again immediately*]

ASTOLFO: What is this I've just seen?

ESTRELLA: Go all of you to hold him back!

[*Exit*]

SEGISMUNDO: [*Returning*] He fell from the balcony into the water! By the living God, it could be done!

ASTOLFO: Measure more wisely, then, your violent actions, for the difference between men and beasts is equal to that between a mountain and a palace.

SEGISMUNDO: If you go on talking so much, you may be left without a head to put your hat on!

[*Exit* Astolfo]

BASILIO: [*Entering*] What has happened?

SEGISMUNDO: Nothing has happened. I tossed a man who tired me from the balcony.

CLARIN: [*To* Segismundo] Be careful: that's the King!

BASILIO: Your coming cost a life so quickly, the very first day?

SEGISMUNDO: He told me it couldn't be done, and I won the wager.

BASILIO: It grieves me much, Prince, that, when hoping foreknowledge would enable you to triumph over stars and fates, I come at last to see you, I find you so pitiless, so cruel. Yes, your very first deed has been a foul murder. With what love can I now offer you my arms if I know that your haughty embrace gives death? Who would not fear, that saw the naked dagger which dealt a mortal wound? Who would not feel it, that saw the bloody place where another man was slaughtered? In the strongest, this would be a natural response. So I, who behold in your arms the instrument of this death and see before me the bloody spot, I withdraw from your arms. And although I hoped to encircle your neck with loving embraces, I shall retire without them, for I am afraid of your arms.

SEGISMUNDO: I can do without them, as I have done without them until now. For it's of little importance that such a father should not embrace me— a father who could use such harshness against me, whose cruelty kept me from his side and brought me up like a beast; yea, who treated me like a monster, sought my death, and robbed me of the very nature of a man.

BASILIO: Would to heaven and God that I had never given you that nature! Then I never would have heard your voice, nor seen your insolence.

SEGISMUNDO: If you had never given it to me, I would not reproach you. But once you gave it, yes, I do reproach you for taking it away. For even though to give is the most noble and distinguished action, to give and then take away is the lowest.

BASILIO: This is fine thanks for my changing you from a poor, humble prisoner into a prince!

SEGISMUNDO: Why should I thank you for that? You have been a tyrant over my will, and now that you are old and weak and dying, what do you give me? Do you give me more than is mine? You are my father and my king; therefore nature gives me all this grandeur by right of law. And therefore, too, although my state be great, I'm not beholden to you, and I can call you to account for the time you've robbed me of liberty, life, and honor. Therefore you should thank me, that I do not claim my due from you, for you are my debtor.

BASILIO: Barbarous, rash man! Heaven has fulfilled its word; and to that very Heaven I appeal, that it may see your pride and vanity. And although you know who you are, free at last of all deceptions; although you may see yourself in a place where all defer to you, still take heed of my warning: Be gentle and humble, for perhaps you are dreaming, although you seem to be awake.

[Exit]

SEGISMUNDO: Perhaps I'm dreaming, although I seem awake? I do not dream, for I touch, I feel, and I believe what I have been and what I am. Now you may repent, but you have little remedy. I know who I am, and you cannot, with all your sighs and regrets, annul the fact that I was born heir to this crown. If at first I was bound in prison, that was because I did not know who I was. But now I have been taught who I am, and I know that I'm a mixture of man and beast.

[Enter Rosaura, dressed as a woman]

ROSAURA [Aside] I come to find Estrella, but I am most fearful of finding Astolfo. For Clotaldo wishes him not to know who I am, nor to see me, because, so Clotaldo says, it is important to my honor. I trust Clotaldo's intent, for to him I owe, most gratefully, the protection I have found here for my life and honor.

CLARIN: [To Segismundo] What has pleased you most of all you have seen and admired here?

SEGISMUNDO: Nothing has astonished me; everything has been as I expected; but if I had to admire something in the world, it would be woman's beauty. I read once, in the books I had, that the creation to which God gave his greatest art was man, because man is a whole world in small compass. But now I suspect that artful creation was rather woman, since she is a whole heaven, and is as far superior to man in beauty as heaven is to earth. And farther still if she be this one whom I see.

ROSAURA: [Aside] The prince is here; I'll withdraw.

SEGISMUNDO: Wait, woman! Wait and listen! Do not make the sun set just as it rises, by fleeing at your first step hither: for if dawn and sunset, light and cold shade, should merge, the very day would be cut short. But what is this I see?

ROSAURA: I doubt I've seen the same before; yet I believe I have.

SEGISMUNDO: [Aside] I have seen this beauty before.

ROSAURA: [Aside] And I have seen this pomp and grandeur held fast in a narrow cell!

SEGISMUNDO: [Aside] Here I have found my life! [To Rosaura] Woman, for that name is the tenderest endearment man can use: who are you? For even without my having seen you, you owe me worship, and luckily I have a faith which binds you closer yet, for I am sure that I have seen you somewhere else! Who are you, lovely woman?

ROSAURA: [Aside] I must pretend. [To Segismundo] I am an unlucky lady in Estrella's train.

SEGISMUNDO: Do not say that. Say you are the sun, in whose flame that star, Estrella, lives, since from your rays she receives splendor. I saw a kingdom all of colors, where, among troops of flowers, the divine rose reigned; and she owed her empire to her loveliness. Among precious gems, in the deep academy of the mines, I saw the diamond preferred, and hailed as emperor for its brilliance. In these beautiful courts of the restless republic of the stars, I have seen the morning star take first place, as the king. And, in the perfect spheres, where the sun calls the planet to his parliament, I have seen that he is sovereign, as the chief oracle of day. How then, if among flowers, stars, stones, signs, and planets the most beautiful take precedence, how have you served one of less beauty, you who have been, for loveliness and grace, the sun, the morning star, the diamond, the planet, and the rose?

CLOTALDO: [Entering, aside] I'd like to be the one to cut this Segismundo down to size, for after all, I brought him up. But what do I see?

ROSAURA: I respect your favor. For me, the rhetoric of silence must answer. When reason itself stumbles, Sire, he speaks best who is most quiet.

SEGISMUNDO: Wait, you need not leave. Why do you wish to leave my meaning in the dark?

ROSAURA: I beg this liberty of your highness.

SEGISMUNDO: To run away so impetuously is not to beg liberty, but to seize it.

ROSAURA: But if you won't give it to me, I'll have to take it.

SEGISMUNDO: You will change my courtesy to rudeness, because resistance is a poison that kills my patience.

ROSAURA: Although that poison, full of fury, rage, and harshness, conquers your patience, it still would not dare, nor could it conquer your respect for me.

SEGISMUNDO: You'll make me, just to see if I could, lose that fear I have of your beauty. For I am much inclined to risk the impossible. Today I threw from this balcony a man who said I couldn't do it. In the same way, to see if I could do it, it would be very easy for me to throw your honor out the window!

CLOTALDO: [Aside] He is growing most insistent! Heavens, what can I do, when, because of an insane lust, I see my honor risked a second time?

ROSAURA: Not false, surely, was the prophecy which foretold the crimes, the treachery, the wrath, the murders, which your tyranny would bring to this unhappy kingdom. But what else could be expected of a man who had no human quality except the name? A man ruthless, inhuman, cruel, proud, and barbarous, born among beasts?

SEGISMUNDO: So that you would not heap insults on me, I showed myself so courteous to you in the hope that this would win you. But if, in speaking courteously, I am all the things you say I am, then by God! you shall have good cause to call me those names. You there! Leave us alone! Close that door and let no one enter!

[Clarin *and* Servants *leave*]

ROSAURA: I am lost! Take care! . . .

SEGISMUNDO: I am a tyrant, and now in vain will you try to overthrow me!

CLOTALDO: [*Aside*] Oh, what a terrible predicament! I'll intervene, even though he kills me for it!

SEGISMUNDO: A second time you provoke me to anger, you feeble, foolish old man. Do you set so little value on my rage and fury? How did you get here?

CLOTALDO: Summoned by the accents of that voice, I came to warn you to calm your violence if you wish to reign here as king. Do not be cruel, just because you seem to be master of everything, for perhaps it is all a dream.

SEGISMUNDO: You drive me to madness, when you talk of illusions. I'll see, by killing you, whether this is dream or reality!

[*As he pulls out his dagger,* Clotaldo *seizes it and kneels before him*]

CLOTALDO: In this way, I hope to save my life.

SEGISMUNDO: Take your rash hand from the blade!

CLOTALDO: Until someone comes to check your wrath and rashness, I'll not let go.

ROSAURA: Oh, God!

SEGISMUNDO: Let go, I say, you weak and foolish, old and barbarous enemy, or you'll be crushed dead between my two arms! [*They struggle*]

ROSAURA: Come, everyone, quickly! Clotaldo is being murdered!

[*Exit* Rosaura]

[Astolfo *enters,* Clotaldo *falls at his feet, and* Astolfo *steps between him and* Segismundo]

ASTOLFO: Why, what goes on here, noble prince? Is such bright steel to be stained in an old man's frozen blood? Return that shining blade into its sheath.

SEGISMUNDO: When I see it colored with that vile blood.

ASTOLFO: His life has taken refuge now at my feet; that he has reached sanctuary should be of some profit to him.

SEGISMUNDO: May death be your profit, for in this way I shall also be able to take vengeance, by your death, for that annoyance you caused me before.

ASTOLFO: I fight in self-defense; in this there lies no offense to your majesty.

[Astolfo *draws his sword, and they fight*]

CLOTALDO: Do not harm him, my lord.

[Basilio *enters with* Estrella, *and* Attendants]

BASILIO: What, swords here?

ESTRELLA: [*Aside*] Alas! It is Astolfo, in a furious rage!

BASILIO: What has happened?

ASTOLFO: Nothing, Sire, since you have arrived.[3]

[*They sheath their swords*]

SEGISMUNDO: Much, Sire, although you have come. I tried to kill that old man.

BASILIO: Have you no respect for these white hairs?

CLOTALDO: Sire, behold, the hairs are mine; the matter is not important, you will see.

SEGISMUNDO: It's vain to expect *me* to respect white hairs! For even yours [*to the* King] may some day be seen at my very feet. I have not yet taken vengeance for your injustice in the way you brought me up.

[*Exit* Segismundo]

BASILIO: Before you see that happen, you will return to sleep where you will believe that all that has happened to you, however real it was, was only dreaming.

[*The* King, Clotaldo, *and* Attendants *leave*]

ASTOLFO: How seldom fate lies when it fortells misfortunes! Predicting evil is as certain as predicting good is doubtful! What an excellent astrologer he would be who foresaw only unhappy events, for there's no doubt but that they'd always prove true! This may be proved by me and Segismundo, Estrella, for both of us bear different signs. For him the signs prophesied harshness, arrogance, misfortune, death; and in all this they told the truth, because all this is happening. But for me, when I saw, señora, those surpassing eyes, of which the sun was only a shadow and the sky an intimation, the fates were foretelling happiness, trophies, wealth, applause; and then they spoke both truth and falsehood. For the fact is that the stars are right only when they promise favors and perform misfortunes.

ESTRELLA: I have no doubt that those fine words are meant sincerely, but meant for another woman —her whose portrait you wore hanging at your neck, Astolfo, when you first came here to see me. Since this is so, those endearments belong only to her. Run to her to receive payment for them, for neither courtesy nor faith owed to other ladies and other kings is good currency in the court of love.

ROSAURA: [*Entering, aside*] Thank God, that now my cruel misfortunes have come to an end, for whoever sees this fears nothing more!

ASTOLFO: I shall tear that picture from my breast to make way for the image of your beauty. Where Estrella enters, shadow has no place, nor a star where the sun shines. I'll go get that portrait. [*Aside*] Pardon, lovely Rosaura, for this injury; when absent from each other, men and women never keep better faith than this.

[*Exit* Astolfo]

---

[3] Dueling had to cease when a king entered, and the affair was considered to be honorably ended.

ROSAURA: [*Aside*] For fear of being seen, I couldn't hear a word.

ESTRELLA: Astrea!

ROSAURA: My lady.

ESTRELLA: I'm so pleased it's you who came, for to you only would I entrust a secret.

ROSAURA: Your honor, señora, one who obeys you.

ESTRELLA: In the short time that I have known you, Astrea, you have gained the keys of my heart. For that reason, and for your own sake, I dare to tell you what I have often hidden from myself.

ROSAURA: I am your slave.

ESTRELLA: To make it brief, then, my cousin Astolfo (calling him cousin is enough, for there are things that are spoken just by thinking them) is to marry me if fortune pleases to cancel so many misfortunes with one great happiness. It bothered me that the first day I saw him he had a portrait of a lady hung 'round his neck. I spoke about it courteously; he is gallant and loves me well, and he has gone to get it, and will bring it here. I should be embarrassed if he gave it to me. Therefore you stay here, and when he comes, tell him to give it to you. I shall say no more. You are discreet and beautiful, and you know well what love is.

[*Exit* Estrella]

ROSAURA: Would that I did not know! Heaven help me! Who could be wise enough to know what to do now, in such a difficulty? Can there be anyone else in the world whom merciless heaven surrounds with more sorrows, attacks with more misfortunes? What shall I do, confused as I am, when it seems impossible to find a means of help, nor any help that could comfort me? From my first misfortune, I've experienced nothing except further misfortunes; each succeeds the other, and inherits its qualities. Like the Phoenix, each is born from the other; each lives from that which dies, and becomes the warm, live tomb of its own ashes. Once a wise man said that cares were cowards, for it seemed that they never came singly. But I say they are brave, for they always advance and never turn their backs. He with whom they travel may dare everything, for never is there danger that they will leave him. I can well say this, for so many troubles have come to me in my life, I've never found myself without them, nor will they tire of me until they see me, mortally wounded by my fortune, in the arms of death. Ah me! What must I do now? If I tell who I am, Clotaldo, to whom I owe my life's honor and protection, may be offended with me; for he tells me that by keeping silent I may expect both honor and reparation. If I don't tell Astolfo who I am, and he sees me, how shall I dissimulate? For even though my voice, my tongue, and my eyes may seek to deceive him, my heart will tell him they are lying. What shall I do? But why do I worry about what to do, since it's clear that however much one worries, thinks, and prepares, when the time comes there's nothing to do except what pain demands? For no one has power over his sorrows. And since my soul dare not determine what's to be done, let grief today come to its end, and pain to its extremity, and let me escape at last from doubts and deceptions. But until then, help me, Heaven, help me!

[Astolfo *enters carrying the portrait*]

ASTOLFO: This, señora, is the portrait; but . . . God!

ROSAURA: Why is your highness amazed? . . . At what do you wonder?

ASTOLFO: To hear you, Rosaura, and to see you.

ROSAURA: I, Rosaura? Your highness must be deceived, if you take me for another lady. I am Astrea, and my humble station does not deserve the good fortune to cause you that agitation.

ASTOLFO: Enough, Rosaura, that's enough pretending. For the soul never lies, and although I look at you as Astrea, I love you as Rosaura.

ROSAURA: I have not understood your highness, and therefore I do not know how to answer you. All I shall say is that Estrella (who might be the star of Venus, since Estrella means star) commanded me to wait for you here, and to tell you in her behalf to give me that portrait—a very reasonable request— and I shall take it to her. So Estrella desires, and even her least commands, though they may be hard for me, must be complied with if she so wishes.

ASTOLFO: Oh Rosaura, how ill you deceive, however hard you try! Tell your eyes to tune their music with your voice, because it's necessary to gainsay and give the lie to such a jarring instrument, which seeks to adjust and measure the lies you speak with the truth you feel.

ROSAURA: I tell you, I am waiting only for the portrait.

ASTOLFO: Since you wish to carry on the deception, I'll answer in deception's terms: Say, Astrea, to the Princess, that I esteem her so that when she seeks a portrait of me, it seems a small favor to send it to her. And therefore, because I esteem and prize her, I am sending her the original; and you may take it to her, since you carry it with you as you carry yourself.

ROSAURA: When a bold man, proud and brave, resolves to carry out an enterprise, even though he may by agreement be offered something worth much more, he still feels foolish and slighted if he doesn't attain his goal. I come for a portrait, and although I might own the more valuable original, without the copy I shall feel slighted. Therefore give me that portrait, your highness, since without it I shall not return.

ASTOLFO: How are you going to take it if I don't give it to you?

ROSAURA: This way. Let it go, you ingrate! [*She tries to seize it from him*]

ASTOLFO: It's no use.

ROSAURA: As God lives, this isn't going to fall into another woman's hands!

ASTOLFO: You are a fury!

ROSAURA: And you are unfaithful!

ASTOLFO: That's enough, my Rosaura!

ROSAURA: I, yours? You lie, villain!

[*Both are grasping the portrait*]

ESTRELLA: [*Entering*] Astrea, Astolfo, what is this?

ASTOLFO: [*Aside*] There's Estrella.

ROSAURA: [*Aside*] Let love give me skill to recover my portrait. [*To* Estrella] If you wish to know what has happened, señora, I'll tell you.

ASTOLFO: [*Aside to* Rosaura] What are you trying to do?

ROSAURA: You commanded me to wait here for Astolfo, and on your behalf to ask him for a portrait. I remained alone, and as one's thoughts travel easily from one subject to another, since you had spoken of portraits, the memory of that reminded me that I had one of my own in my sleeve. I wished to see it, for someone all alone amuses herself with foolish things. It fell from my hand to the floor. Astolfo, who came to give you the portrait of another woman, picked it up, and so unwilling is he to give you what you ask, that instead of giving one, he wishes to take another; for even with pleas and persuasion I still could not regain my own. Then, angry and impatient, I tried to take it from him. That one he has in his hand is mine, you will see, for you can see it looks like me.

ESTRELLA: Astolfo, let go of the picture.

[*She takes it from his hand*]

ASTOLFO: Señora . . .

ESTRELLA: The colors, in truth, are not unflattering.

ROSAURA: Is it not mine?

ESTRELLA: What doubt is there?

ROSAURA: Now tell him to give you the other one.

ESTRELLA: Take your picture, and go.

ROSAURA: [*Aside*] I have my portrait; now let come what will!

[*Exit*]

ESTRELLA: Now give me that portrait of yours which I asked for. Although I do not intend to see or talk to you again, I do not want you to retain it, no, if only because I so foolishly desired it of you.

ASTOLFO: [*Aside*] How can I get out of such a predicament? Although I wish, beauteous Estrella, to serve and obey you, I cannot give you the portrait you seek, because . . .

ESTRELLA: You are a coarse and clownish lover. I don't want you to give it to me; for neither do I want, by taking it, to make you remember that I asked for it!

[*Exit*]

ASTOLFO: Hear me! Listen! Look! I'll explain! Oh, curses on you, Rosaura! Whence, how, by what fortune did you come to Poland today, to destroy me and to destroy yourself?

SCENE II.

The Prince's *prison in the tower.*

[Segismundo, *as in the beginning, wearing skins* and chains, lying on the ground; Clotaldo, two Servants, and Clarin]

CLOTALDO: Here you must leave him, for today his pride ends just where it began.

SERVANT: Just as it was, I shall fasten the chain once more.

CLARIN: Don't wake too soon, Segismundo, for you will find yourself lost, your luck completely changed, and your glory only imaginary—a shadow of life, a flame of death.

CLOTALDO: For one who talks so much, it would be wise to prepare a place where he may have plenty of room to argue. [*To the* Servants] This is the man you are to seize, and that's the cell in which to lock him up. [*Pointing to the next room*]

CLARIN: Why me?

CLOTALDO: Because a noisy clarion like you, who knows secrets, needs to be locked up tight in prison, where he can't sound off.

CLARIN: Did I by chance try to kill my father? No. Did I throw a lesser Icarus off the balcony? Am I dreaming, or am I sleeping? Why do they lock me up?

CLOTALDO: Because you are Clarin, a noisy trumpet.

CLARIN: Well now I say I shall be a cornet, which is a vile instrument, and so I shall remain silent.

[*They take him away, and* Clotaldo *remains alone. Enter* Basilio, *masked*]

BASILIO: Clotaldo.

CLOTALDO: Sire! Your Majesty comes here in disguise?

BASILIO: A foolish curiosity, alas! to see what's happening to Segismundo has brought me here in this condition.

CLOTALDO: Look at him there, reduced again to misery.

BASILIO: Alas, unhappy prince, born at a sad conjunction of the stars. Come, wake him up, for the opium he drank has robbed him of his strength and vigor.

CLOTALDO: Sire, he is restless, and he mutters.

BASILIO: What is he dreaming now? Let's listen!

SEGISMUNDO: [*Talking in his sleep*] A merciful prince is one who punishes tyrants. May Clotaldo die at my hands! May my father kiss my feet!

CLOTALDO: He's threatening me with death!

BASILIO: And me with harshness and insult!

CLOTALDO: He intends to take my life.

BASILIO: And to humiliate me.

SEGISMUNDO: [*In his sleep*] Let my peerless valor enter on the wide stage of the great theater of the world. So that my vengeance may be fitting, let all see Prince Segismundo triumph over his father. [*He awakes*] But alas! Where am I?

BASILIO: [*To* Clotaldo] He must not see me. You know what you are to do. I'll listen from over there. [*Withdraws*]

SEGISMUNDO: Can this be me? Do I, captive and in chains, see myself in such a state? Oh tower, are you not still my tomb? Yes! Oh God, how many things I've dreamed!

CLOTALDO: [*Aside*] Now it is my turn to come in and to pretend.

SEGISMUNDO: Isn't it time to wake up?

CLOTALDO: Yes, it is time. Will you spend the whole day sleeping? Since I followed that eagle which flew by on slow wings, and you stayed here, have you not wakened once?

SEGISMUNDO: No, nor have I now awakened. For, as I understand, Clotaldo, I'm still sleeping. And I am not deceived, because if I dreamed what I really saw and felt, then what I see now must be unreal. I see, being asleep, that when awake one dreams.

CLOTALDO: Tell me what you dreamed.

SEGISMUNDO: Supposing that it *was* a dream. No, I shall not tell you what I dreamed, but what I *saw*, Clotaldo. I awoke and found myself in a bed which might have been, such were its hues and colors, the cradle of the flowers woven by Spring. Here a thousand bowing nobles called me their prince, and bestowed on me finery, jewels, and rich robes. Then you yourself whirled me into rapture when you told me my good fortune: that, regardless of my present state, I was Prince in Póland.

CLOTALDO: For bringing you that news I must have had a good reward!

SEGISMUNDO: Not very. Twice, boldly and bravely, I tried to kill you, because you were a traitor.

CLOTALDO: Such harsh treatment for me?

SEGISMUNDO: I was lord of all, and on all I took my vengeance. Only one I loved, one woman . . . That, I believe, was true. For all the rest has vanished away, and this alone remains.

[*Exit the* King]

CLOTALDO: [*Aside*] What the King has heard has moved him. [*To* Segismundo] Because we were talking of that eagle, while you slept your dream was one of empire. But in your dreams it might be well to give honor to the one who cared for you so faithfully; for even in dreams, Segismundo, one should not cease to do good.

[*Exit*]

SEGISMUNDO: That's true. Then let us restrain this fierceness, this fury, this ambition, in case some time we dream again. And dream we will, for we are in so odd a world that just to live is to dream. Experience teaches me that each man who lives dreams what he is, until he wakes. The king dreams he is a king, and in this deception spends his days, commanding, governing, disposing. But this renown he receives is written on the wind. At the touch of death—oh dread misfortune—it turns to ashes. Can there be any who would want to reign, seeing that each king must wake in the dream of death? The rich man dreams of his riches, which only bring him greater care. The poor man dreams that he suffers misery and want. He who is beginning to prosper dreams it; he who pushes and presses ahead dreams it; he who commits injuries and offenses dreams it.

And to conclude, through the whole world, though no man knows it, all men dream the lives they lead. I dream that I am here, weighed down with chains, and I dreamed that I was in another, happier state. What is life? A madness. What is life? An illusion, a shadow, a story. And the greatest good is little enough: for all life is a dream, and dreams themselves are only dreams.

ACT III. SCENE I.

The tower.

CLARIN: Well here I am, it seems, a prisoner in an enchanted tower. What can they do to me for what I don't know, if they've killed me for what I do? O, that so hungry a man should have to die this living death! I pity myself. Everyone will say "I certainly believe it"; and well may it be believed, since this silence does not at all agree with my name, Clarin, and I cannot keep quiet. My companions here, if I guess right, are mice and spiders. What sweet songbirds they are! My last night's dreams have made my poor head ring with a thousand clarinets, trumpets, and delusions; with processions, crosses, and flagellants; some of them rise, others descend. Some faint when they see the blood that smears the others. But as for me, the truth is that I faint because I haven't eaten. I see that I am in a jail where daily I read the philosophy of no meals, and nightly, that of no suppers. If they call silence saintly, as in the new calendar, Saint Secret is for me, because I fast for him, and never feast. Still, the punishment I suffer is well deserved, since, although I am a servant, I held my tongue, and that, for a servant, is a major sacrilege.

[*Drums and bugles sound. Voices offstage*]

FIRST SOLDIER: [*Offstage*] This is the tower he's in. Smash the door to the ground! Everybody rush inside!

CLARIN: God does live! They must be looking for me, since they say I'm here! What can they want of me?

FIRST SOLDIER: [*Offstage*] Everybody go inside.

[*Enter several* Soldiers]

SECOND SOLDIER: Here he is.

CLARIN: He's not.

SOLDIERS: [*All together*] Sire . . .

CLARIN: [*Aside*] Surely they're drunk!

FIRST SOLDIER: You are our prince. We neither desire nor will we tolerate any but our native lord; we want no foreign prince. Give us your feet to kiss.

SOLDIERS: Long live our great prince!

CLARIN: [*Aside*] Surely they're drunk! Good God, they really mean it! Is it the custom in this kingdom to take somebody every day, make him a prince, and then send him back to the tower? Yes, since I see it happen every day. Now I must play my rôle.

SOLDIERS: Give us your feet.

CLARIN: I cannot, because I need them for myself.

A prince without feet would be pretty funny.

SECOND SOLDIER: We all told your father himself that we recognized only you as prince, and not that fellow from Muscovy.

CLARIN: Have you lost all respect for my father? You are worthless fellows.

SECOND SOLDIER: It was our heartfelt loyalty.

CLARIN: If it was loyalty, I pardon you.

SECOND SOLDIER: Come out and regain your empire. Viva Segismundo!

ALL: Viva!

CLARIN: [Aside] Is it Segismundo they say? Good: they call all counterfeit princes Segismundos.

SEGISMUNDO: [Entering] Who here calls Segismundo?

CLARIN: [Aside] Now I'm certainly a hollow prince!

FIRST SOLDIER: Which one is Segismundo?

SEGISMUNDO: I am he.

SECOND SOLDIER: [To CLARIN]: You insolent, foolish fellow, how dare you pose as Segismundo?

CLARIN: I Segismundo? I deny that. You were the ones who turned me into Segismundo; yours was the only insolence, the only foolishness.

FIRST SOLDIER: Great Prince Segismundo (for yours is the bearing of the prince we seek, and now by faith we hail you as our lord), your father, great King Basilio, fearful that heaven may fulfill a prophecy which says he is to see himself prostrate at your feet, conquered by you, is trying to rob you of your claim and title, and give them to Astolfo, Duke of Muscovy. To accomplish this he convened his Court, but the people, knowing that they have a native king, want no foreigner to come and rule over them. And thus, nobly scorning that harsh prophecy, they have sought you out where you live imprisoned, so that, helped by their arms, you may leave this tower, regain your imperial crown and scepter, and wrest them from the tyrant. Come out, then; for in this wasteland a large army of outlaws and commoners acclaims you. Liberty awaits you; hearken to its voice.

VOICES: [Offstage] Hail, all hail Segismundo!

SEGISMUNDO: What is this, O heavens? Again do you want me to dream of greatness which time must destroy? Do you wish me again to see, through uncertain shadows, that majesty and pomp which must disappear in the wind? Do you wish me once more to feel disillusion, once more to undertake the risk to which all human power lives exposed? It must not be! I must not see myself again subjected to my fate. And since I know that this whole life is a dream, go, you shadows which feign body and voice to my numbed senses while the truth is that you have neither voice nor body. For I want no pretended majesty, no fantastic pomp, illusions which at the slightest gust of air must disappear, just as the flowering almond tree which blossoms too early, without warning, wilts at the first breath. At the first breath, the rosy buds fade and lose the splendor of their light and beauty. Oh, I know you, indeed I know you, and I know you play the same cheat with anyone who sleeps. For me there's no more pretending. I've learned my lesson, and I know well that life is a dream.

SECOND SOLDIER: If you think we are deceiving you, turn your eyes toward those proud mountains where you may see the people waiting to obey you.

SEGISMUNDO: Once before, I saw the same, as clearly and distinctly as I see it now, and it was all a dream.

SECOND SOLDIER: Great events, great lord, always bring their omens; and this would be an omen, if you dreamt it first.

SEGISMUNDO: You say well, it was an omen; and in case it be true, since life is so short, let us dream, my soul, let us dream again; but it must be with prudence and the knowledge that we must awaken from this pleasure when the pleasure's greatest. Knowing disillusionment must come, we'll be less disillusioned when it does come. For to anticipate the remedy is to make mock of the hurt. With this forewarning, then, that even when it's most assured, all power is borrowed and must return to its owner, let us dare all. Vassals, I thank you for your loyalty. In me you have a leader who with daring and skill will free you from foreign slavery. Sound the call to arms, so that you may soon see my great va!or! I shall endeavor to take arms against my father and confirm the prediction of the stars. Soon I shall see him at my feet . . . [Aside.] But if I awake before then, will it not be better to say nothing of it, especially if I am not to accomplish it?

ALL: Hail, all hail Segismundo!

CLOTALDO: [Entering] Heavens, what is this uproar?

SEGISMUNDO: Clotaldo.

CLOTALDO: My lord . . . [Aside] He's trying his harshness out on me.

CLARIN: [Aside] I'll bet he throws him down the mountain.

[Exit Clarin.]

CLOTALDO: I come, I know, to die at your royal feet.

SEGISMUNDO. Rise, father, rise from the ground; for you must be polestar and guide in whom I may entrust my better deeds. I know I owe my upbringing to your great loyalty. Come, embrace me!

CLOTALDO: What are you saying?

SEGISMUNDO: That I am dreaming, and that I wish to do well, since good deeds are not lost, even in dreams.

CLOTALDO: Well, my lord, if doing good is now your motto, then I am sure it won't offend you that I attempt today to do the same. Must you make war on your father? I can neither advise you nor be of use to you against my king. Here I am at your feet. Kill me!

SEGISMUNDO: Worthless fellow! Traitor! Ingrate! [Aside] Oh heavens, I should control myself, for I still do not know if I am waking. Clotaldo, I envy you your courage and I thank you for it. Go serve the King, and let us meet on the field. You there, sound to arms!

CLOTALDO: A thousand times I kiss your feet.

[*Exit* Clotaldo.]

SEGISMUNDO: O fortune, we are going to reign. If I am sleeping, do not wake me; and if this is true, do not put me to sleep. But whether it be dream or truth, to do well is what matters. If it be truth, for truth's sake. If not, then to gain friends for the time when we awaken.

[*Exeunt. Drums beat*]

SCENE II.

Hall in the royal palace.

[Basilio *and* Astolfo]

BASILIO: Who, Astolfo, has the skill to check a wild stallion's fury? Who can hold back the current of a river, as it races proud and headlong to the sea? Who can boldly stop a great boulder as it falls, torn from a mountaintop? Yet all these seem easier to tame than the angry passion of a mob. Proclaim to them some partisan rumor, and at once from the depths of the mountains the repeated echo resounds: "Astolfo!" some shout, and others, "Segismundo!" The royal throne, reduced to a different function, to a horror, has become a bloody stage where troublesome Fortune acts out tragedies.

ASTOLFO: Sire, let all joy today be held in check. Cancel the praise and the soft pleasure promised me by your great hand. For if Poland (which I aspire to rule) today resists me, it is so that I may first earn her allegiance. Give me a horse, and as my shield boasts thunder, so may I proudly strike like lightning.

[*Exit*]

BASILIO: Against the inevitable there's small protection, and great danger lies in what has been foretold. If it must happen, defense is impossible; and he who most avoids it only brings it closer. Harsh law! Remorseless fate! Oh horror, horror! to meet the peril, when one intends to flee it! Because of what I have kept in hiding, I have lost myself, and I, I myself, have brought my country to destruction.

ESTRELLA: [*Entering*] O great king, if by your presence you do not try to check the tumult spreading from one faction to another through all the streets and public squares, you'll see your kingdom bathed in waves of scarlet, dyed in the purple of its own blood. For now, alas! all is misfortune, all is tragedy. So great is the ruin of your empire, and so fierce the power of rough and bloody violence, that to see it causes wonder, to hear it, terror. The sun darkens and the wind's obstructed. Each stone becomes a pyramid, and each flower a monument. Each building is a living sepulcher, and each soldier, though alive, a skeleton.

CLOTALDO: [*Entering*] Thank God that I have reached your feet alive!

BASILIO: Clotaldo, how is it with Segismundo?

CLOTALDO: The mob, a blind, headlong monster, broke into the tower, and from its depths set free the Prince. When he saw his grandeur restored to him a second time, he showed himself valiant, crying fiercely that he would draw the truth from heaven.

BASILIO: Give me a horse! I must in person boldly subdue that ingrate son. And in defense of my crown, may steel succeed where knowledge failed!

[*Exit*]

ESTRELLA: Then I, beside the Sun, shall be Bellona, and next to his I hope to place my name; for I must fly on wide extended wings, if I would rival Pallas' deity.

[*Exit; a call to arms is sounded.*]

[*Enter* Rosaura, *who detains* Clotaldo.]

ROSAURA: Even though the valor in your breast calls you to battle, listen awhile to me, for war, I know, is everywhere. And you well know that when I came to Poland poor, humble, and unhappy, I was protected by your valor; in you I found pity. You ordered me (ah heavens!) to live disguised in the palace and to try, hiding my jealousy, to conceal myself from Astolfo. Finally he did see me, and so much does he still tread upon my honor that, even though he recognized me, he continues to talk by night to Estrella in the garden. I have the key to it, and I can provide an opportunity for you to enter and put an end to my care. Thus, daring, strong, and haughty, you can defend my honor, since you are resolved to avenge me with his death.

CLOTALDO: It is true, Rosaura, that from the moment I saw you, I was inclined to do for you all that I could. Your tears were witness. First I besought you to discard the man's clothing you were wearing, so that if by chance Astolfo saw you, it might be in your own proper dress; nor would he judge as lightness a mad rashness which abuses honor. At the same time I planned what might be done to regain your lost honor, even (so much that honor swayed me) if it had to be by killing Astolfo. What senile madness! Yet since he's not my king, this deed's not one to amaze me, nor dismay me. I had thought then of killing him. But when Segismundo tried to murder me, Astolfo came to my defense. He ignored his own danger and showed a good will and a rashness surpassing courage. Now how can I, whose soul is grateful to him, kill this man who saved my life? And thus, with my affection and care divided between the two of you, since I have given life to you and received it from him, I do not know which of you to help; I do not know which of you to support. If I am bound to you because of what I gave you, I am likewise bound to him for what I have received from him. In this action, hence, there's nothing that satisfies my love because I must both do the deed, and suffer for it.

ROSAURA: It is not for me to tell so great a man that to give is noble, while to receive is base. Once you accept this principle, you need not be grateful to him. For if it is he who has given life to you, and you to me, it's clear that he forced your nobleness to commit a mean act, while I prompted you to a generous one. Therefore you are offended by him, and obliged to me, since you have given to me what you received from him. And thus you should defend my honor in so great a peril, for my case is stronger than his, by so much as giving is better than receiving.

CLOTALDO: Although nobility comes with giving, gratitude comes with receiving. And since I have known how to give, I have the name of a generous man as well as an honorable one. Leave me the name of a grateful man too, then, since to attain it I need only be grateful as well as generous; for there is as much honor in giving as in receiving.

ROSAURA: From you I received life, and you yourself told me, when you gave it to me, that a life with injured honor was no life at all. Then I have received nothing from you, since the life your hand gave me has not been a life. And if you'd rather be a creditor than a debtor (as I have heard from you yourself), I hope you will bestow that life on me, which you have not yet given. And because to give is more ennobling, if you are generous first, you will be grateful afterward.

CLOTALDO: Convinced by your argument, I shall first of all be liberal. Rosaura, I shall give you my fortune, and you must enter a convent. The proposal I offer is well thought out: in fleeing from a crime you will find yourself a sanctuary. And I, of noble birth, shall not be the one to intensify the misfortunes of our divided kingdom. When I choose this remedy, I am loyal to the kingdom, generous with you, and grateful to Astolfo. Take this course, then, which best suits you, and let the matter rest between us two. Heaven knows I could not do more if I were your father.

ROSAURA: If you were my father, I would endure this injury. But since you are not, I will not suffer it.

CLOTALDO: Then what do you intend to do?

ROSAURA: Kill the Duke.

CLOTALDO: A woman who never knew her father has so much courage?

ROSAURA: Yes.

CLOTALDO: What's driving you on?

ROSAURA: My reputation.

CLOTALDO: Observe that you must see in Astolfo . . .

ROSAURA: He who tramples all my honor underfoot!

CLOTALDO: Your king, the husband of Estrella.

ROSAURA: By the living God, he will not be that!

CLOTALDO: It's madness.

ROSAURA: So I see.

CLOTALDO: Then conquer it.

ROSAURA: I cannot.

CLOTALDO: Then you will lose . . .

ROSAURA: I know it.

CLOTALDO: Life and honor.

ROSAURA: Well do I believe it!

CLOTALDO: What are you after?

ROSAURA: My death.

CLOTALDO: That's merely spite.

ROSAURA: It's honor.

CLOTALDO: It's madness.

ROSAURA: No. It's courage.

CLOTALDO: Call it frenzy.

ROSAURA: It's rage and wrath.

CLOTALDO: Is there no way to restrain your blind passion?

ROSAURA: No.

CLOTALDO: Who will help you?

ROSAURA: I myself.

CLOTALDO: Is there no remedy?

ROSAURA: None.

CLOTALDO: Just think. Is there some other way?

ROSAURA: Only some other way to be lost.

[Exit]

CLOTALDO: Then if you must be lost, my daughter, wait, and let us both be lost together.

[Exit]

SCENE III.

A field.

[Segismundo, *clothed in skins. Soldiers marching.* Clarin. *Drums are beating*]

SEGISMUNDO: If Rome in the triumphs of her golden age could see me this day, how she would rejoice to behold so strange a sight—armies led by a wild animal, for whose high vigor heaven itself would be a minor conquest! But oh my soul, let us beat back that flight. Not in that way do we make light of this unstable applause, which will grieve me when I awake if I have won it and then lost it; no, the less it means to me, the less I'll mourn if I should lose it.

[A trumpet sounds.]

CLARIN: On a swift steed (pardon me, for I have a compulsion to exaggerate when I tell a story), on whom a map seems drawn, since his body is the earth and fire is the spirit in his breast; his foam is the sea, his breath the air—in all, a confusion where chaos may be glimpsed, for in his spirit, foam, body, and breath, he is a very monster of fire, earth, water, and wind; on such a steed, then, dappled silvery gray, and spurred on by a rider under whom he does not run, but flies—on such a steed there comes a graceful woman to your presence.

SEGISMUNDO: Her light blinds me.

CLARIN: As God lives, it's Rosaura! [He withdraws.]

SEGISMUNDO: Heaven has restored her to me.

[Enter Rosaura in a loose jacket, wearing sword and dagger]

ROSAURA: Generous Segismundo, whose heroic majesty rises from a night of shadows into a day of deeds and dawns like the sun which, in the arms of

Aurora, returns shining to plants and roses, over mountains and seas. Crowned with flashing rays of light, it shines forth, bathing the hilltops with brilliance, painting the edges of the foam. So may you, O radiant sun of Poland, dawn on the world as on this unhappy woman, who today throws herself at your feet. Give her your aid because she is a woman, and unfortunate: two reasons, either of which is enough, and more than enough to obligate a man who boasts of his chivalry. Three times have you seen me, without knowing who I am, for each time I was dressed in different clothing. At first you thought me a man, in that rough prison where your life made my misfortunes seem a pleasure. The second time you saw me as a woman, when your pomp and majesty were only a dream, a vision, a shadow. The third time is today, when, like a monstrosity of both the sexes, I bear the weapons of a warrior, though I wear a woman's dress. And, so that pity may the better dispose you to grant me protection, hear, I pray, the story of my tragic fortunes. In the Court of Muscovy I was born of a noble mother, who, since she was unhappy, must have been very beautiful. On her a traitor cast his eyes. I do not name him because I do not know him, and yet I know that he was valiant; my own valor tells me this. Since I am his offspring, I am sorry now not to have been born a pagan, so that I might fondly persuade myself he was a god, like one of those who in metamorphosis rained showers of gold on Danaë, or came as swan or bull to Leda or Europa.

I thought I was stretching out my tale too long, with these stories of perfidy, but now I find that I have told you all in these few words: my mother, lovelier than any woman, but unhappy as all of us, was persuaded, alas, to love more passionately than wisely. That foolish excuse, that promise of marriage, so carried her away that even today she weeps to think of it. As Aeneas when he fled Troy, so this tyrant when he fled my mother left his sword. Its blade is sheathed here, but I will bare it before this story ends. From this imperfect knot which neither ties nor binds, this marriage, or this crime, for it's all one, was I then born, so like my mother that I was a portrait of her, a true copy, not indeed of her beauty, but of her fortunes and misfortunes. Thus I need not say that as heiress of unhappiness, I have met a fate like hers. The most I can tell you about myself is that the man who robbed the spoils, the trophies of my honor . . . is Astolfo! Alas! When I name him—quite naturally, since he is my enemy—my heart fills with rage and passion. Astolfo was that ingrate, then, who forgot all our delights (since even the memory of a love that is over will fade), and came here to Poland, called from his notorious conquest, to marry Estrella, a star rising against my setting sun. Who will believe that since a star brought two lovers together, a star —Estrella—would separate them now?

I was hurt and mocked, I was crazed, grieved, and almost dead. I was indeed my ill-starred self, with all the confusion of Hell enclosed within my mind. But I kept silent, for there are pains and anxieties which the feelings express better than the tongue, and I told my troubles wordlessly until one day, when we were alone, my mother, Violante, broke open the prison of my woes. Then in troops they surged out of my breast, stumbling over one another. It did not embarrass me to tell her, for when one knows that the person in whom she confides her weaknesses has erred herself, it seems that this provides a balm and ease from pain; and thus at times a bad example has a use.

She listened sympathetically to my sorrows, and wanted to console me with her own. How easily can a judge who has sinned pardon sin in others! Having learned by her own experience that neither idleness nor lapse of time brought remedy to her lost honor, my mother decided on another course for me. Her best advice was that I follow him and compel him, by unrelenting effort, to repay his debt of honor. To accomplish this more easily, it was my fate to dress myself in man's clothing. My mother took down an ancient sword, which I now wear. Now is the time its blade should be unsheathed, as I promised her when, trusting in its sign, she said to me: "Go to Poland, and arrange for this sword you are wearing to be seen in your possession by the highest nobles. For it may be that in one of them your fortunes may find a merciful reception, and your woes some consolation."

I did arrive in Poland. Let us pass over, since it is not important, and you already know, the fact that a wild horse brought me to your cave, where you were amazed to see me. Let us pass over, too, the fact that there Clotaldo, passionately taking my part, begged the King for my life, which the King granted; that when Clotaldo learned who I was, he persuaded me to put on my own clothing and to serve Estrella. There ingeniously I obstructed Astolfo's love and marriage to Estrella. Nor do we need to mention the fact that, once more confused, you saw me here again, this time in woman's dress, and by these changes you were quite confounded. But let us come to the fact that Clotaldo, persuaded that it was important to him that Astolfo and the fair Estrella marry and rule the kingdom, advised me, against my honor, to lay aside my claim.

Therefore, since it is your turn, O valiant Segismundo, to take vengeance today—for heaven wishes you to break through the barriers of this rustic prison where your body has been a wild beast to feeling, a rock to suffering—and since your sword is lifted against your father and your country, I come to help you. On me the armor of Pallas is covered with the rich robes of Diana; I wear both cloth and steel. For both of us, then, great leader, it is important to impede and destroy these planned nuptials; for me, to keep him who is my husband from marrying another; and for you, to prevent the joining of their states, with increased power and strength, from placing our victory in doubt. As a woman, I come to persuade you to give aid to my honor, and as a man I come to encourage you to recover your crown. As a woman, I come to move you to pity when I throw myself at your feet, and as a man I come to serve you with my sword and with my person. And bear in mind that if today you court me as a woman, as a man I shall kill you in honorable defense of my honor. For I must be, in this war of love, a woman to tell you my complaints, and a man to gain honor.

SEGISMUNDO: [Aside] If it is true, O heavens, that I'm dreaming, suspend my memory, for it is not possible for so many things to fit into one dream. Would to God that I might either escape from all these difficulties or think of none of them! Who ever saw such troublesome uncertainties? If I merely dreamed of that grandeur in which I saw myself, how can this woman now relate such apparent proof to me? Then it was true, and not a dream. And if it was true, which would be more, not less confusing, how can my life be called a dream? Then are glories so much like dreams that the true ones are taken for false, and the false for true? There is so little difference between them that it's doubtful one can know whether what one sees or tastes is false or true! Is the copy so similar to the original that there is doubt in knowing which is real? If it is thus, and the grandeur and power, pomp and majesty are to vanish among shadows, then let us take advantage of the moment allotted to us, for in that moment we enjoy only what we can snatch between dreams.

Rosaura is in my power; my heart adores her beauty. Then let us profit from this occasion; let love break the laws of chivalry and of the trust with which she prostrates herself at my feet. This is a dream; and since it is, let us dream happiness now, for sorrows will come later. But again I convince myself with my own reasoning! If this is a dream, if this is mere vanity, then who for human vanity would lose a heavenly glory? What past blessedness is not a dream? Who has had great happiness who would not say to himself, when he recalls it in memory: "Beyond a doubt, all that I saw was just a dream." Then if this will bring me disappointment, if I know that pleasure is only a splendid flame reduced to ashes by any wind that blows, let us turn to the eternal, which is ever-living fame, where happiness does not sleep nor greatness rest. Rosaura is without honor; but a prince should give honor, not take it away. As God lives, I must win back her honor, before my crown! Let us flee from this temptation, then, for it is very strong! [To a soldier.] Sound arms! For today I must give battle before the shadows of darkness bury the day's golden light in the dark green waves.

ROSAURA: My lord, why do you withdraw so? Do not my worry and my anxiety merit even a single word from you? How is it possible, Sire, for you neither to look at me nor to hear me? Won't you even turn your face toward me?

SEGISMUNDO: Rosaura, for your honor's sake, if I am to be merciful to you, I must be cruel now. My voice does not answer you, in order that my honor may. I do not speak to you, because I wish my deeds to speak to you for me. Neither do I look at you, for it's necessary, in this moment of pain, that he who must look to your honor should not look at your beauty.

[Exit Segismundo, with the Soldiers.]

ROSAURA: Oh heavens, what are these riddles? After so much agony, I'm still left in doubt with these ambiguous replies!

CLARIN: Señora, is this a good time to see you?

ROSAURA: Ah, Clarin! Where have you been?

CLARIN: Locked up in a tower, checking a hand at cards to see whether or not death is going to strike me. The face card that turned up seemed to mean that my life was at stake. But I was on the point of bursting.

ROSAURA: Why?

CLARIN: Because I know the secret of who you are. Indeed, Clotaldo . . . But what is that noise?

[Sound of drums]

ROSAURA: What can it be?

CLARIN: An armed squadron, coming out of the besieged palace, to oppose or conquer the forces of fierce Segismundo.

ROSAURA: How cowardly I am, not to be at his side, the wonder of the world, when such cruelty hems us in with lawlessness and disorder.

[Exit]

SOME VOICES: Long live our unconquerable king!

OTHER VOICES: Long live our liberty!

CLARIN: May liberty and king both have long life! And welcome too! But to me it makes no difference whose side I'm on. For today, in the midst of all this hubbub, I'll play the role of Nero, who grieved at nothing. If I must grieve about something, let it be about myself. Well hidden here, I can see all the merriment. This spot, among these rocks, is strong and secret. Here death will not find me, so—two figs for death! [He hides; the sound of drums and arms.]

[Enter Basilio, Clotaldo and Astolfo, fleeing]

BASILIO: Is there anywhere a more unhappy king, or a father more beset?

CLOTALDO: Your conquered army runs away in full disorder.

ASTOLFO: The traitors, winning, hold the field.

BASILIO: In such battles those who win are loyal; the losers, traitors. Then let us fly, Clotaldo, from the inhuman cruelty of a tyrant son.

[Shots are heard offstage; Clarin falls wounded from his hiding-place]

BASILIO: Heaven help me!

ASTOLFO: Who is this unhappy bloodstained soldier, who has fallen at our feet?

CLARIN: I am an unlucky man who, in trying to keep myself away from death, found it. Fleeing from it, I met it, for there is no place secret from death. A clear argument, this, that he who runs from it most is the one who first reaches it. Turn back, therefore, into the bloody battle; for in the midst of arms and firing there is more safety than in the most hidden mountain. There is no path secure against the might of destiny and inclement Fate. And thus, although you seek to free yourself from death by fleeing, behold that you will die when it is God's will that you die.

[*He falls*]

BASILIO: "When it's God's will that you die!" How well, oh heavens, does this corpse, which speaks to us through the mouth of a wound, guide our error and our ignorance to greater knowledge! This bloody tongue teaches us that all man's diligence is useless when it opposes a higher power. So it is with me. For, intending to save my country from murders and sedition, I delivered it over to the very evils from which I tried to save it.

CLOTALDO: Sire, although fate knows all the roads, and finds the man it seeks even among the mountain thickets, it is not a Christian judgment to say there is no refuge from its rage. For there is; and a prudent man can attain a victory over fate. If you are not already exempted from pain and misfortune, do what you can to find yourself a shelter.

ASTOLFO: Clotaldo, Sire, speaks to you as a prudent man who has reached mature age; I, as a valiant youth: in the thick undergrowth of this mountain there is a horse, a swift monster born of the wind. Flee on it, and I, meanwhile, shall guard your flight.

BASILIO: If it is God's will that I should die, or if death awaits me here, then today I wish to find him, and meet him face to face. [*Call to arms*]

[*Enter* Segismundo, Estrella, Rosaura, Soldiers, Attendants.]

SOLDIER: In the tangles of this mountain, among its thick branches, the King is hiding.

SEGISMUNDO: Follow him! Let no tree remain on these heights which you have not carefully searched, trunk by trunk and branch by branch.

CLOTALDO: Flee, Sire!

BASILIO: Why?

ASTOLFO: What is your intention?

BASILIO: Withdraw, Astolfo.

CLOTALDO: What do you wish?

BASILIO: To take a remedy, Clotaldo, that I need. [*To* Segismundo] If it is me you seek, prince, here at your feet I am. [*Kneeling*] Let these snowy hairs of mine be a white rug under your feet. Step on my neck and tread upon my crown. Humble my dignity and drag my reverence in the dust. Take vengeance on my honor, and use me as a slave. After all I have done to prevent this, let Fate now demand its due; let heaven fulfill its prophecy.

SEGISMUNDO: Illustrious Court of Poland, you who have witnessed so many wonders, give ear, for now your prince speaks to you. What Heaven has determined and God's finger has written on the sky's blue tablet, whose ciphers and printed figures are so many sheets of azure adorned with gilded letters, never

deceives, never lies. No, he who lies and deceives is he who attempts to penetrate and unfathom these mysteries to make evil use of them. My father, here at my feet, to free himself from the rage of my nature, made of me a brute, a human beast; so that even if I, because of my inborn nobility, my honorable blood, and my gallant nature, had been born mild and gentle, this way of living, this kind of upbringing would have been enough to transform me into a beast. What a strange way to keep me from becoming one! If a man were told, "A wild animal is going to kill you," would it be wise for him to wake that creature from its sleep? If he were warned, "This sword you're wearing will kill you," to pull it from its sheath and point it as his breast would be a foolish way to evade the doom. Or if he were told, "Great seas of water, with monuments of silver foam, will be your burying place," he would do wrong to plunge into the proud sea while it raised curled hills of snow and angry steeps of crystal water. And as that man who wakes from sleep the wild beast that threatens him; or he who, fearing a sword, unsheathes it; or he who challenges the waves of a storm, so is my father. And though—listen to me—my fierceness were a sleeping beast, my wrath a tempered sword, my rage a calm and quiet sea, injustice and vengeance would never ward off the fate predicted, but rather urge it on. And thus, whoever hopes to control his fate must do it with prudence and with moderation. Not before a harm arrives can he who foresees it save himself from it. By humility, he may protect himself from it, but only after it occurs; there is no way to prevent it. Let this rare spectacle, this strange wonder, this horror, this prodigy serve as an example. Never was there a greater one than this, that in spite of so many efforts to prevent it, my father should lie conquered at my feet, a king trampled on. It was a judgment of heaven; however much he sought to stop it, he could not. And can I, younger than he in age, lesser in courage and in wisdom, conquer it? Sire, arise. [*To the* King] Give me your hand. For now that heaven has made clear to you your error in the way you opposed its decree, humbly my neck awaits your vengeance. I yield myself at your feet.

BASILIO: Oh son, so noble an action gives you new birth in my heart. You are the Prince. To you belong the laurel and the palm. You have conquered! Your deeds crown you!

ALL: Long live Segismundo!

SEGISMUNDO: Though my valor hopes to make great conquests, today the greatest must be a victory over myself. Astolfo, give your hand now to Rosaura, for it is a debt of honor, and I must retrieve it for her.

ASTOLFO: Although it's true I owe a debt to her, consider that she knows not who she is. It would be base and dishonorable for me to marry a woman who . . .

CLOTALDO: Wait! Go no further! Rosaura is as noble as you, Astolfo, and my sword will defend her in mortal combat. She's my daughter, and that should suffice.

ASTOLFO: What are you saying?

CLOTALDO: That I did not wish to make known her identity until I saw her nobly and honorably married. This makes too long a story, but the sum is brief: that she's my daughter.

ASTOLFO: Since this is so, I will fulfill my promise.

SEGISMUNDO: So that Estrella will not be left disconsolate, by losing such a valiant and glorious prince, with my own hand I shall marry her to a husband who, if he does not exceed, at least equals him in merit and in fortune. Give me your hand.

ESTRELLA: I gain in deserving such good fortune.

SEGISMUNDO: As for Clotaldo, who loyally served my father, my arms await him with the thanks that whatever he wishes shall be given him.

SOLDIER: If in this way you honor one who has not served you, then how about me? I started the great uproar in the kingdom, and I freed you from the tower in which you were imprisoned. What will you give me?

SEGISMUNDO: The very same tower. And so that you will never leave it till your death, you will be kept there under guard. The treason past, the traitor is no longer needed.

BASILIO: Your wisdom fills us all with wonder.

ASTOLFO: How changed his character!

ROSAURA: How wise and prudent!

SEGISMUNDO: What makes you wonder? What surprises you, if a dream taught me this wisdom, and if I still fear I may wake up and find myself once more confined in prison? And even if this should not happen, merely to dream it is enough. For this I have come to know, that all human happiness finally ceases, like a dream.

And now I wish to profit from the time that remains to me by asking pardon for our faults; for to noble hearts, it is natural and right to grant forgiveness.

The stage of the Teatro Farnese, with a single proscenium arch, as in modern *"picture-frame"* stages (in contrast to the three vistas of the earlier Teatro Olimpico). The theatre was built in 1618 as part of the ducal palace at Parma. From A. Streit, *Das Theater,* Vienna, 1903.

Neoclassic Variants

Painted perspective, created for an opera, in a sumptuous architectural design of 1719 by Guiseppe Galli de Bibiena. Courtesy the Metropolitan Museum of Art, Dick Fund, 1931.

Neoclassic Variants

The neoclassic theatre is often imagined to be so fixed in the molds of reason, rationality, strict order, unity of tone as well as time and place, and economy of action, that it is a surprise to find that the less well-known styles of the seventeenth- and eighteenth-century drama were varied and lively. Two noteworthy examples will occur to the historian, one at the start of the period, Corneille's *The Cid* (1636), and one during the latter part of the Neo-classic period, John Gay's irrepressibly irreverent *Beggar's Opera* (1728). Between these plays lie the alpine heights of neoclassic tragedy and comedy as represented by the masterpieces of Racine[1] and Molière respectively (see pages 389–429).

But at the beginning of the Neoclassic era, the strenuous career of Corneille illustrates the struggle to attain optimal results within the fetters of neo-classic drama. What Fergusson says of Racine and of baroque art in general, that they "show signs of strain, as though the rigid forms could not quite contain the life which they were supposed to," applies especially to the work of Corneille. And toward the closing phase of that period, Gay's decidedly less strenuous labors in the theatre show comedy issuing in virtually complete detachment in a more satirical stance than that adopted by Molière for *Tartuffe* and *The Misanthrope* (see pages 389–410) and a more cynical amoralism than Restoration comedy usually manifests in any respect other than adultery. Even Congreve's *The Way of the World* (see pages 430–462) and Wycherley's *The Country Wife* do not constitute so thorough a transvaluation or so bland a reversal of social values as does Gay's work. Certainly none of the comedies that follow *The Beggar's Opera* (a work sufficiently antiheroic to become the basis of Bertolt Brecht's *Three-Penny Opera* a decade after the close of World War I) do. Not even Sheridan's *The School for Scandal* (see pages 463–498), in which comedy of manners is somewhat sweetened with sentimentality, or Beaumarchais' *The Marriage of Figaro*, which ends on a note of moral

victory when Figaro defends his matrimonial Eden against the encroachments of a lecherous master.

When Pierre Corneille, barrister and author of a number of comedies, startled the French theatre with his masterpiece *The Cid* late in 1636, England was approaching an upheaval that would strike the death-blow to absolute monarchy in Britain.[2] In France, on the contrary, monarchy was just approaching its peak. Henry IV of France, in 1593, gave his country its greatly needed unity and enabled his minister Sully to lay the economic foundations of its greatness. Under the astute statesmanship of Louis XIII's minister, Cardinal Richelieu, the political power of the feudal nobility shrank appreciably while middle-class appointees took over the government of the provinces, a process which continued under Louis XIV. These commonplace facts are indispensable background for an understanding of the formal nature and philosophy of French neoclassicism that affected all dramatists of the day.

Corneille, born of the middle class in 1606, was and up-and-coming bourgeois dedicated to the law, the profession pursued by his father, who was the king's avocate in Rouen. Although legal practice and promotion came easily to Pierre Corneille, he was also endowed with a strong literary gift and a love of the theatre. A strolling troupe headed by the successful actor Mondori appeared at Rouen, and Corneille added the comedy *Mélite* to its repertory. This work was followed by *Clitandre,* composed in the spirit of bravado characteristic of this pugnacious playwright.[3]

NEOCLASSIC TRAGICOMEDY

Corneille then composed another comedy and his first tragedy, the classic imitation *Médée,* and retired to Rouen to resume his legal practice. But he did not remain in retirement for long. Stimulated by his acquaintance with a former secretary of Queen Marie de Medici who urged him to write something worthy of his talents, Corneille applied himself to the study of the Spanish theatre which was then at its zenith. One of its products, Guillen de Castro's *Las mocedades del Cid,* attracted him with its exciting account of the exploits of Spain's most popular hero. The

---

[1] Anyone concerned with this subject can do no better than study chapter II of Francis Fergusson's *The Idea of a Theatre.* Princeton, N.J.: Princeton University Press, 1949. He will find there a somewhat difficult but extremely illuminating treatment of the nature of neoclassic tragedy and its realization in the dramatic art of Racine as "a rationalized series of incidents intended to satisfy the discursive reason," both in the relatively standard form of his *Phèdre* (p. 59) and its variant form, of which the extreme example is *Bérénice.* See also the Appendix in this penetrating study by Fergusson on the conventionality of many details in the work of Racine and Corneille. The best explanation for Racinian dramatic form is Fergusson's statement that "Because Racine is interested only in one moment of psychic life, he replaces all the rest with purely illustrative conventional signs" (p. 56).

[2] The following comments on Corneille's career are excerpted, with alterations, from Chapter XV from John Gassner's *Masters of the Drama.* New York: Dover, 1954.

[3] He had been told that his first comedy was not written in accordance with the highly touted classic rules, that a play must transpire within twenty-four hours, and must be elevated in style. Resenting the censure of fellow-playwrights, Corneille resolved to write something that would conform to the rules and be, as he put it, "generally worthless." He succeeded only too well.

result of this attraction was the tragicomedy *The Cid,* one of the masterpieces of French drama. "Beautiful as *Le Cid*" became a proverbial expression. Town and court alike acclaimed the play, the author, and Richelieu's niece, to whom he had dedicated the work. Louis XIII and his queen complimented Corneille and granted his father a patent of nobility, ostensibly as a reward for his services but actually as a compliment to the son.

No play by Corneille bears the stamp of his early genius as distinctly as *The Cid,* although to understand its significance fully one must regard it as a transitional work, as Corneille himself was a transitional figure. It should be noted, too, that unlike most serious neoclassic plays, it is not strictly tragedy. Although he respected the new autocratic France, he was an independent spirit and not yet the complete courtier who was the ideal of the age. *The Cid* paid tribute to the ideals of honor and duty, and to this extent it reflected the new age, which set social responsibility above personal impulse. The individualism glorified by the Renaissance was now required to submit to "law" or "decorum." But in *The Cid* Corneille still celebrated the claims of individuality with the hard heroic quality, and strong feeling with little outward show of tenderness, that he assigned to his characters.

In structure and style the play was likewise something less than a rigid observance of the neoclassical regulations that were now being imposed on the drama by scholars and critics in the name of Aristotle. It is true that Corneille adhered formally to the principle that the action of a play must take place in a single locality and during a single day. But the stormy events of *The Cid* violate the spirit of these laws, for in twenty-four hours, "Roderick declares his love, fights his first duel, kills his sweetheart's father, repels in a tremendous battle a national invasion, wins a trial by combat, and in the course of all this loses and regains the favor of his king and the lady of his heart."[4] Even unity of action is imperiled in a story that embraces so many events, although the play successfully avoids the secondary plots that so frequently clutter up the work of the Elizabethans.

In vigorous, exalted dramatic verse, unequaled by anything previously written in the French language, the play told a storm-swept tale in which love and honor contended for victory. Since the characters are dominated by the Spanish code of honor, they may easily strike us as somewhat stilted, argumentative, and extravagant. Nevertheless, the emotions are obviously genuine, and their eddies are traced faithfully and with notable sensitivity. Much of the bright cynicism of our own day would be wasted on this play. The lovers are pathetically young and live in a feudal and warlike world. The code of honor that dominates them was intensely real in its own day, and even if we are inclined to sneer at it we should

not forget that at heart the heroine herself also revolts against it.

The Cid was Corneille's last tribute to individuality. His age demanded something else. A cabal against him, inspired by Richelieu, caused his temporary retirement, and when he emerged from seclusion he appeared in the theatre with his wings clipped. His later plays adhered to a stricter interpretation of the dramatic unities. He spent the second half of his life in a world that respected him but had little use for his impassioned but severe work. His splendid "crash of sound" and his strident affirmations of the heroic spirit seemed wearisome or a trifle barbaric to an age of increasing refinement and ornateness. The spirit of French neoclassicism favored a softer and more courtly kind of tragedy than Corneille could provide with his austere Roman dramas *Horace* and *Cinna.* Only farce and to some degree comedy could liberate itself from the age of elegance, and only the comic genius of Molière (see pages 389–410) could administer corrective satire to it in France.

Corneille's problem of maintaining dramatic effect within the restrictive limits of neoclassic criticism and practice was variously apparent in the work of all his seventeenth- and eighteenth-century successors except Racine. Their decidedly weaker dramatic and poetic talents resulted in a lean harvest when they applied themselves to the formidable art of tragedy. In a general study of the drama, their very names are likely to be unremembered (unless they also acquired reputations outside the theatre) while their plays are unread except by specialists. In France, we may remember Corneille's brother Thomas (*Timocrate,* 1655) and later Voltaire (*Oedipus,* 1718; *Brutus,* 1730; *Zaïre,* 1732); in England, Dryden and other writers of Restoration "heroic drama",[5] Nicholas Rowe (*The Fair Penitent,* 1703; *Jane Shore,* 1714), Joseph Addison (*Cato,* 1713), and Samuel Johnson (*Irene,* 1749); in Germany, Johann Christian Gottsched (*The Dying Cato,* 1732); in Italy, Francesco Scipione di Maffei (*Merope,* 1713) and, rather notably, the late-eighteenth century Vittorio Alfieri (*Oreste,* 1776; *Saul,* 1782; *Antigone,* 1783).

The playwrights of the neoclassic seventeenth and eighteenth centuries were decidedly more successful in the exercise of comic talent. In England, we have the Restoration playwrights, from Etherege and Dryden to Congreve and Wycherley and a little later Vanbrugh and Farquhar (*The Recruiting Officer,* 1706; *The Beaux Stratagem,* 1707); and in the

---

[4] Paul Landis in his Introduction to *Six Plays by Corneille and Racine.* New York: Modern Library, 1931.

[5] There was a mixture of Elizabethan romantic and French neoclassic elements in the best tragic writing of the Restoration period, as in John Dryden's *All for Love* (1677), his neoclassic adaptation of Shakespeare's *Antony and Cleopatra,* and Thomas Otway's *Venice Preserved* (1682). A fine chapter on Dryden's work in the genre of heroic drama will be found in Eugene M. Waith's *The Herculean Hero.* New York: Columbia University Press, 1962, pp. 152–201.

eighteenth-century from Fielding and Gay to Goldsmith, and Sheridan (see pages 430–462). In Italy, we have Carlo Gozzi (*Turandot,* 1762) and Goldoni (*La Locandiera,* or *The Mistress of the Inn,* 1753); and in France, Jean-François Regnard (*The Residuary Legatee,* 1708), Le Sage (*Turcaret,* 1709), Marivaux (*The Game of Love and Chance,* 1730), and Beaumarchais (*The Barber of Seville,* 1775; *The Marriage of Figaro,* 1784).

Several forms of comedy other than Molière's and the Restoration writers' "comedy of manners" also developed in the neoclassic theatre. One interesting form is the literary satire or *rehearsal play;* the best known examples are Molière's *The Impromptu of Versailles,* The Duke of Buckingham's *The Rehearsal,* and Sheridan's *The Critic.* Another, allied, form is the literary burlesque as written with some success by Henry Fielding, the supreme English novelist of the eighteenth century. And a remarkable English genre is "ballad-opera."

Corneille and The Cid

Pierre Corneille (1606–1684) stands at the threshold of neoclassicism, just as his junior contemporary Racine stands at its artistic zenith and Voltaire, once highly regarded as a playwright as well as *philosophe,* at its nadir. Elements of medieval romanticism and Renaissance vein appear, and not without reason, in the work of a vigorous man born at the beginning of the seventeenth century before neoclassicism had established itself in French thought and style. He had a strong moralizing bent and a rigidity of both manner and principle in a period that became increasingly an age of elegance and sophistication. In his major plays there is always a problem of conscience or principle with which the main characters must reckon. His verse is masculine, his style rhetorical, his language somewhat archaic.

His writing generally has clarity and strong definition rather than subtlety and refinement. His serious plays express a heroic strain regardless of changing subject matter and milieu: medieval Spain in *The Cid,* the Roman Republic in *Horace,* the Roman empire in *Cinna,* and the period of early Christianity in *Polyeucte.* For him, in fact, serious drama reflects a historical world of values, which his characters incorporate even while struggling against them. Some of the most dramatic situations arise and have to be resolved precisely because principle dictates one kind of decision while attachment or love inclines a character in an opposite direction. If psychological stress is often evident in this conflict of inclinations, it intensifies the action and enriches the characterization. But somehow or other Corneille always sees to it that principle is not compromised in the dénouement of the action or the conduct of a principal character. Duty is never compromised; honor is never besmirched.

Tragedy in Corneille's best work is predicated upon man's *free will* regardless of the constraints of society and decorum. Therefore his main characters are, in one respect or another, passionate and active; they have not only freedom but *power* of will. Their intentions and beliefs are clearly argued and forcefully, at times indeed *harshly,* asserted. He is a master of the *tirade,* or the extended eloquent speech, at one extreme, and of crisp summation by apothegms, on the other. It is not easy to love Corneille, but it is not difficult to admire him. *Admiration* was in fact the prime reaction he desired to evoke from his audience for his principal characters; for him it took precedence over the Aristotelian elements of "pity and terror" as the cardinal criterion of tragedy. Corneille was also austerely disinclined to allow the experience of drama to dissolve into mere feeling. In this respect, far more than in his somewhat awkward efforts to adhere to the neoclassic unities of time, place, and action, he was a genuine neoclassic playwright. The famous nineteenth-century French critic Sainte-Beuve rightly observed that Corneille's intellect, "open and clear, never cloudy and misty . . . resembles the austere mind of Descartes, who was *Le Cid's* great contemporary."[1]

At the same time, it must be noted that *The Cid* is "less abstract than Corneille's subsequent plays. If we are more for the brilliant Rodrique (Rodrigo) than for Corneille's other heroes, it is because there is more life in him, more fire and flash."[2] The touch of romanticism, borrowed at least in part from Corneille's Spanish source (*Las mocedades del Cid* by Guillen de Castro, which was in turn based on a famous medieval Spanish romance), undoubtedly helped secure the first important neoclassical playwright the greatest success he ever enjoyed in the theatre despite the enmity it aroused in contemporary literary circles. That this element of romanticism appeared in a neoclassic matrix and exists in a tension with it only makes the play more viable and more genuinely exciting.

From the vantage point of the early nineteenth-century Romantic movement in Germany, its leading critic August Wilhelm Schlegel correctly concluded concerning Corneille's dramatic aims that "It was by no means so much his object to exite our terror and compassion as our admiration for the characters and astonishment at the situation of his heroes." Schlegel concluded that "The rapturous applause, which, on its first appearance universally welcomed a piece like this (in the year 1636) which, without the admixture of any ignoble incentive, founded its attraction altogether on the represented conflict between the purest feelings of love, honour, and filial duty is a strong proof that the romantic spirit was not yet extinct among spectators who were still open to such natural impressions."[3] The admixture of romanticism and classicism in the work, finally, is attested, as the author himself realized, by the very genre into which it falls—that is, the mixed genre of *tragicomedy.* And in this respect, too, Corneille escaped the strict restrictions of the start of the French neoclassical theatre. This is an important aspect of what Victor Hugo, the leader of French modern romanticism

[1] Sainte-Beuve: *Selected Essays.* Translated by Frances Steegmuller and Norbert Guterman. New York: Anchor Books, 1964, p. 34.
[2] *Ibid.*
[3] Schlegel, *Lectures on Dramatic Art and Literature,* London, 1904, pp. 274–284.

two centuries later, rhapsodically acclaimed when he wrote of "the miracle of *The Cid* as "the natural work of an entirely modern genius."[4]

Corneille's concern with moral imperatives accounts for part of the stiffness in plays such as *Horace* and *Cinna* and for some strained motivation. But his vigor provides relief from addiction to private sensibility and "love interest" in the French theatre, against which Racine reacted toward the close of his literary career in writing his great biblical drama *Athalie* (*Athaliah*). It was with Corneille, more than with any other classic dramatist, that twentieth-century Existentialist playwrights, especially Sartre (in *No Exit* and *The Flies* particularly) could identify. This is the stern Corneille who was once referred to as "the same old Corneille, firmly frozen in the ice of honor and duty."[5] There were indeed *two* Corneilles, one of them a romantic *persona* and the other a classic one, of whom one modern scholar, Borgerhoff, can write that "there is in him somewhere a deep fissure, some kind of gap that never closed" which helps to explain why he was a controversial and contradictory figure during his career. As this scholar goes on to say, "For some he represents the surrender of French drama to the supposed absolutism of the classic system. For others he is a kind of Seventeenth Century romantic. . . . Corneille has been made to represent what is most undying and what is most dead in French serious drama." One thing is certain: He was more sensitive to theatrical possibilities than to philosophical generalities; and was emotionally disposed to admiration of what he called "*grandeur d'âme*," greatness of soul as exemplified by strength of will or character. Corneille's interest was dramatic rather than analytical: "He was not interested in philosophy or in theology. He was interested in magic."[6]

[4] "*Le merveille du Cid . . . le produit naturel d'un génie tout moderne*" in his famous preface to *Cromwell* (1827).

[5] E.B.O. Borgerhoff, *The Freedom of French Classicism*. Princeton, N.J.: Princeton University Press, 1950, pages 46 ff. The chapter in this book entitled "The Liberalism of Pierre Corneille" is a masterly discussion of the divided nature of this transitional dramatist.

[6] E. B. O. Borgerhoff, *Ibid.*

THE CID

By Pierre Corneille

TRANSLATED BY WALLACE FOWLIE

CHARACTERS

DON FERDINAND, *King of Castille*
THE INFANTA, *his daughter*
DON DIEGUE, *father of Don Rodrigue*
COUNT GOMES, *father of Chimene*
DON RODRIGUE, *in love with Chimene*
DON SANCHE, *in love with Chimene*

DON ARIAS, *noble*
DON ALONSO, *noble*
CHIMENE[1]
LEONOR, *confidante of the Infanta*
ELVIRE, *confidante of Chimene*
A PAGE

SCENE: Seville. The King's palace, Chimene's house, a street in Seville.

ACT I. SCENE I.

Chimene *and* Elvire.

CHIMENE: Are you telling me the truth, Elvire?
Have you kept back any of my father's words?
ELVIRE: I am still under the spell of those words.
He respects Rodrigue as much as you love him,
and if I am not mistaken in my reading of his heart,
he will command you to accept Rodrigue's love.
CHIMENE: Please tell me once again
what makes you feel he approves of my choice.
Tell me once more what hope I may cherish.
You cannot repeat such joyous news too often.
Keep promising, to the passion of our love,
the sweet privilege of its being revealed.
What did he say about the intrigue
in which Don Sanche and Don Rodrigue have involved you?
Did you not show too clearly the choice I have made
between my two suitors?

ELVIRE: No, I described your heart as indifferent,
neither raising nor quelling the hope of either one,
looking upon them neither severely nor with favor,
and waiting your father's order to choose a husband.
He loved your respect. His words and countenance
gave instant testimony to it.
And since you want me to repeat the story,
this is what he said, in haste, about you and about
them:
"She is dutiful. Both men are worthy of her.
Both come from a noble lineage that is strong and
sure,
both young, but with eyes that reveal
the dazzling virtue of their brave ancestors.

[1] The French name Chimène is spelled Chimene
throughout, but the French pronunciation should be used.

Every expression on Rodrigue's face
displays the true image of a courageous man.
His family is so endowed with warriors
that they seem to have been born with laurel leaves.
The valor of his father, who was without peer in his
day,
was looked upon as miraculous.
His prowess is now engraved in the creases of his
brow,
marking for us the sign of his past deeds.
What the father accomplished I look for in the son,
and if my daughter loves him, she pleases me
thereby."
He was late for the council when I saw him
and had to cut short his speech,
but in those few words I can tell
he is not hesitating between your two suitors.
The King has to choose a tutor for his son,
and your father is the obvious choice for this honor.
There is no doubt, for his exceptional valor
allows no rival to be feared.
His lofty exploits have no parallel,
and for so well-deserved a hope there is no competition.
Don Rodrigue has convinced his father
to make this proposal at the end of the council.
You may be sure he will choose the right moment,
and all your desires will soon be realized.

CHIMENE: Yet my soul is troubled.
It refuses this joy and is bewildered.
One moment may give different masks to the same
fate,
and in my great happiness I fear a great reversal.
ELVIRE: This fear of yours will end in good fortune.

CHIMENE: Come with we while we await the outcome.

823

SCENE II.

Infanta, Leonor, Page.

INFANTA: Page, go find Chimene and tell her
that today she has delayed her visit too long,
and that my love for her complains of her absence.
   [*Exit* Page]
   LEONOR: Your Highness, each day the same desire
     compels you.
Each day she comes to you and I hear you ask
how far her love for Rodrigue has developed.
   INFANTA: It is not without motive. I have almost
     forced her
to welcome the arrows which wound her.
She loves Rodrigue and it was I who gave him to her.
Thanks to me he overcame her scorn.
Since I created the love which binds these lovers,
I am eager to see an end to their torment.
   LEONOR: But your Highness, this happy outcome
stirs excessive sorrow in you.
Does this love which crowns them with joy,
transform your heart to sadness?
Does the great interest you have in them
make you wretched when they are happy?
But I presume too much and am indiscreet.
   INFANTA: My sadness grows stronger when it is
     secret.
Listen now to the struggle I have waged.
Let me tell you of the attacks made on my virtue.
Love is a tyrant who spares no one.
I am in love with this knight, with this lover
I have given away.
   LEONOR: You are in love!
   INFANTA: If you put your hand
on my heart, you would see how it beats at the name
of its conqueror.
   LEONOR: I apologize
if I seem disrespectful in censuring this love.
How can a princess forget her birth
and allow her heart to love a simple knight?
What would the King say? And Castille?
Have you forgotten whose daughter you are?
   INFANTA: I remember so well that I would take my
     life
before stooping to belie my rank.
I could answer that in a well-born soul
merit alone has the right to incite love;
and that if my passion sought an excuse,
a hundred famous examples might serve as prece-
     dents.
I will not go where my honor may be endangered.
The flaring of my senses will not affect my courage;
and I still tell myself that being the daughter of a
     king,
no man save a monarch is worthy of my name.
When I saw that my heart could not protect itself,
I gave what I did not dare take.

Rather than myself, I led Chimene into the bonds of
     love.
I ignited their flame in order to extinguish mine.
Do not be amazed if my troubled soul
now waits impatiently for their marriage.
Today my peace of mind depends on it.
If love lives on hope, it dies with the death of hope.
It is a fire that goes out when there is nothing left to
     feed it.
Despite the trial of my sad adventure,
when Chimene has taken Rodrigue as husband,
my hope will be dead, my torment over.
But meanwhile the anguish of my suffering continues.
Until that marriage, I will love Rodrigue.
I am doing all I can to lose him though I cannot bear
     losing him.
This is the pattern of my secret sorrow.
It is hopelessly clear that love is forcing me
to long for the man I must avoid.
My mind is split in two.
My courage is strong, but my heart is in flames.
This marriage is my death: I both want it and fear it.
All I can hope for is an imperfect joy.
My honor and my love have such power
that I will die with this marriage, and die if there is
     no marriage.
   LEONOR: Your Highness, there is nothing for me
     to say,
except that I join you in your lament.
If I blamed you once, I now pity you.
But since your honor resists the charm and the power
of so sweet and painful a grief,
repulses the attack and rejects the allure,
it will restore peace to your bewildered mind.
Place all your hope in it and in the passage of time.
Place your hope in God whose justice
will not allow your honor to suffer too long.
   INFANTA: My sweetest hope is to lose hope.
     [Page *enters*]
   PAGE: At your Highness' order, Chimene is here.
   INFANTA: Go speak to her outside.
   LEONOR: Do you wish to be alone with your
     thoughts?
   INFANTA: No, but I need a few minutes
in which to recover my composure.
Then I will join you.
     [Leonor *and* Page *leave*]
                         O God, whose help I need,
Put an end to the suffering that has hold of me.
Grant me rest and preserve my honor.
I seek happiness in the happiness of someone else.
This marriage has meaning for all three of us.
Make it come about more swiftly or make my soul
     stronger.
If these two are joined in the bonds of marriage,
then my bonds will be broken and my torment over.
Chimene is waiting. I must go to her
and let her words lessen my pain.

SCENE III.

The Count, Don Diegue

COUNT: So it is you who win, and the King's favor,
in making you tutor to the Prince of Castille,
raises you to a rank which was due me.

DIEGUE: This mark of honor he bestows on my
  family
proves to all he is just and willing
to reward past services.

COUNT: Whatever their power may be, kings are
  human like all of us
and may make a mistake like other men.
This choice demonstrates to all courtiers
that kings give small recompenses for present services.

DIEGUE: Let's have no more words about this
  choice which so upsets you.
Favor may have caused it as much as merit.
But we owe to his divine right the respect
of questioning nothing when it is the will of a king.
To the honor he has paid me, add one more.
Let us join in a sacred bond my house and yours.
You have but one daughter, and I one son.
Their marriage will make us something more than
  friends.
Grant us this grace and accept my son as yours.

COUNT: Your handsome son should aim higher
  now.
The new brilliance of his honor
must swell his heart with further vanity.
Exercise your honor, Diegue, and teach the prince.
Show him how a province must be ruled,
how the people must tremble under his law,
how the good must be filled with love and the wicked
  with terror.
Join to these the virtues of a captain.
Show him how he must toughen himself in work
and surpass everyone else in soldiery,
how he must spend days and nights on horseback,
sleep in his armor, storm a wall,
and win a battle by his own prowess.
Be his model and make him perfect,
explaining your lessons to him by accomplishments.

DIEGUE: To learn in this way, by examples,
he will merely read the story of my life.
There, in a long series of noble actions,
he will see how nations are conquered,
how a city square is attacked and an army organized,
and how one's fame is built on great exploits.

COUNT: Living examples have a better effect.
A prince ill learns his duty from books.
What did your many years accomplish
which one of my days cannot equal?
If you were valiant once, I am valiant today,
and my arm is the strongest support of the kingdom.
Granada and Aragon tremble at the flash of my
  sword,
my name is a rampart for all of Castile.

If I were not here, you would soon be under other
  laws
and your enemies would be your kings.
To heighten my honor, each day and each moment
piles laurels on laurels, and victory on victory.
At my side, the prince, in battle, would
test his courage under the shadow of my arm.
He would learn how to conquer by watching me,
and to give swift answer to his noble spirit,
he would see . . .

DIEGUE: I know this. You serve your king well.
I have seen you fight and command under me.
When age sent its icy coldness through my veins,
your exceptional valor took over my place.
To cut short these unnecessary words,
you are today what I was in earlier years.
Yet you see that in this rivalry
the monarch does establish a difference between us.

COUNT: All that I deserved, you have won.

DIEGUE: The man who triumphed over you deserved it.

COUNT: He who can train the prince is the worthier man.

DIEGUE: But to be refused is not a good sign.

COUNT: The old courtier in you won this by intrigue.

DIEGUE: My only spokesman was the fame of my
  past deeds.

COUNT: Let us be clear: the King pays honor to
  your age.

DIEGUE: If so, the King measures it by my courage.

COUNT: And thereby this honor should have come
  to me.

DIEGUE: He who did not get it did not deserve it.

COUNT: Did not deserve it? You mean me?

DIEGUE: You.

COUNT: Your impudence
and your presumption deserve this.
  [*He gives him a slap*]

DIEGUE: [*Drawing his sword*]
Come, take my life after such an insult.
I am the first of my family to blush with shame.

COUNT: And what do you plan to do in your impotence?

DIEGUE: Oh God, my weakened strength is of no
  use now.

COUNT: Your sword is mine, but you would be too
  vain
if my hand took this shameful trophy.
Adieu. In spite of envy, let the prince
read, for his lesson, the story of your life.
This just punishment for your insolent words
will not become a small episode for his amusement.

SCENE IV.

Don Diegue.

DIEGUE: My years are my enemy!
Have I lived this long only to know such infamy?

Has my hair turned white in the labor of battles
to see all my laurels wither in one day?
My arm, once acclaimed by all Spain,
my arm which saved the empire countless times,
and so often supported the throne of its king
now betrays my quarrel and leaves me helpless.
Now the memory of my honored life is cruel
and the labor of so many days is wiped out in one
    day.
A new honor comes and destroys my happiness.
A high precipice from which my name is hurled
    down!
Must I see this count triumph over my honor,
and die unavenged or live in shame?
Let the count now be the governor of my prince:
such a rank is not permitted a dishonored man.
The daring insult from his jealous pride
has made me unworthy, in spite of the King's choice.
You, once glorious instrument of my battles,
now useless ornament for a body grown cold,
sword that was once feared, but which in this offense
served me as a decoration, not as a defense,
leave me, the least of men,
and pass into better hands for my revenge.

SCENE V.

Don Diegue, Don Rodrigue.

DIEGUE: Rodrigue, have you courage?

RODRIGUE: Any man save my father
could test it at this moment.

DIEGUE: Righteous anger!
Your noble feeling is sweet to my pain.
I recognize my blood in your fine wrath.
My youth lives again in your swift zeal.
My son who are my blood, will you make amends for
    my shame?
Will you avenge me?

RODRIGUE: For what?

DIEGUE: For so harsh an insult
that it bears a mortal blow to the honor of us both:
for a hand that struck my face! The wretch would
    have died,
but my age tricked my high-minded desire;
this sword which my arm can no longer support,
I hand over to you for vengeance and punishment.
Test your courage against a proud man's.
Such an outrage is settled only with blood.
Die or kill. Moreover—I must not mislead you—
I am giving you as adversary a much-feared man.
I have seen him, covered with blood and dust,
bring terror to an entire army.
I have seen a hundred squadrons routed by his
    strength,
and—to tell you one more thing about him—
more than being a brave soldier and a great captain,
this man is . . .

RODRIGUE: In God's name, tell me.

DIEGUE: The father of Chimene.

RODRIGUE: The . . .

DIEGUE: Don't try to answer. I know
    your love.
But an infamous man is not worthy to live.
The dearer the offender, the greater is the offense.
Well, you know the insult and you hold the instru-
    ment of vengeance.
I will say nothing further. Avenge me and avenge
    yourself.
Show that the son is worthy of his father.
Bowed down with the woes of destiny,
I must withdraw, but you, rush with speed to venge-
    ance.

SCENE VI.

Don Rodrigue.

RODRIGUE: My heart is pierced with this word,
as unexpected as it is mortal,
I stand unable to move,
wretched avenger in a just cause,
sad victim of unjust rigor,
and my soul yields to this killing blow.
So close to seeing my love rewarded!
Oh God! what a strange plight!
In this insult, my father is offended,
and the offender, the father of Chimene.
    A bitter fight is being waged in me
where my love takes sides against my honor.
I have to avenge a father and lose my betrothed.
One incites my anger, and the other holds back my
    arm.
My sad choice is to betray my love
or live in infamy.
Either way my suffering is endless.
Oh God! what strange punishment!
Must I leave this insult unpunished?
Must I punish the father of Chimene?
My father or my betrothed, my honor or my love.
Harsh constraint or pleasing tyranny.
Either my joy is over or my honor stained.
One makes me wretched, and the other unworthy of
    life.
Cherished and cruel hope of a noble soul
which is at the same time in love.
Worthy enemy of my greatest happiness,
sword which creates my pain,
were you given me to avenge my honor,
were you given me to lose my Chimene?
    It is better to die.
I owe my life to my betrothed as well as to my father.
By avenging myself, I will earn her hate and wrath;
not avenging myself, I will earn his scorn.
To my sweetest hope, one makes me unfaithful,
and the other makes me unworthy of her.
My pain grows as I yearn to cure it.
Everything increases my suffering.

Come, Rodrigue, since I must die,
at least let me die without offending Chimene.
   Die without obtaining satisfaction?
Seek a death so fatal to my honor?
Allow Spain to ascribe to my memory
the refusal to defend the honor of my house?
Respect a love whose collapse
my dazed mind knows is certain?
I must stop thinking of that enticing image
which only increases my suffering.
Come! At least I will save my honor,
since in either outcome I will lose Chimene.
Yes, my mind was deceived.
I owe all to my father before my betrothed.
Whether I die in combat or die from sorrow,
I will shed my blood as pure as I received it.
I have delayed too long
and must rush to vengeance.
I am ashamed of having hesitated this much.
Let my suffering be over,
since today my father is insulted,
even if the offender is the father of Chimene.

ACT II. SCENE I.

Don Arias, *the* Count.

COUNT: I acknowledge it. My anger was too strong
and over one word it mounted to violence.
But since it is done, the deed cannot be repaired.
   ARIAS: Let your great courage bend to the King's
     will.
He has an interest in this affair, and his irritation
will go against you with all the weight of his au-
   thority.
You have no valid defense.
The rank of the offended man and the magnitude of
   the offense
demand duties and submissions
which exceed ordinary reparations.
   COUNT: At his will, the King may dispose of my
    life.
   ARIAS: An excess of anger follows hard on your
    mistake.
The King still loves you. Appease his wrath.
He said: "I wish it thus." Will you disobey?
   COUNT: But considering all the esteem in which
    I am held,
a slight disobedience is not so great a crime.
And however great it is, my services today
are more than enough to efface it.
   ARIAS: However illustrious and important the serv-
    ice be,
a king is never indebted to his subject.
You deceive yourself, for you must know
that who serves his king well, does only his duty.
You will bring disaster if you persist in your
   belief.
   COUNT: I will believe you after the test.

   ARIAS: You should fear the power of a king.
   COUNT: A single day does not wipe out a man like
    myself.
Let him in all his greatness prepare for my punish-
   ment.
The entire state will perish if I perish.
   ARIAS: So, you fear sovereign power so little . . .
   COUNT: A scepter which would drop from his hand
    without me?
My life has too much value for him.
If my head fell, his crown would follow.
   ARIAS: Let reason soothe your spirits.
Listen to good advice.
   COUNT: My decision is made.
   ARIAS: What shall I say then? I have to bring him
    word.
   COUNT: That I will in no way consent to my
    shame.
   ARIAS: But remember that kings are absolute.
   COUNT: The die is cast. There is no need for
    further talk.
   ARIAS: I take leave then, since I cannot change
    your mind.
With all your laurels, you should still fear divine
   wrath.
   COUNT: I will wait without fear.
   ARIAS   But not without result.
   COUNT: In that case Diegue will have satisfaction.
    [Don Arias *goes out*]
He who has no fear of death has no fear of threats.
My courage is stronger than the harshest disgrace.
I can be forced to live without happiness
but I cannot be forced to live without honor.

SCENE II.

The Count, Rodrigue.

   RODRIGUE: A word with you, Count.
   COUNT: Speak.
   RODRIGUE: Dispel my doubts.
Do you know Don Diegue?
   COUNT: Yes.
   RODRIGUE: Listen carefully.
Did you know that my father was the virtue,
the valor and the power of his time? Did you know
   that?
   COUNT: Perhaps I did.
   RODRIGUE: Do you know that the ardor
in my eyes comes from him? Do you know that?
   COUNT: It is not my concern.
   RODRIGUE: It will be your concern a few paces
    from here.
   COUNT: Presumption of youth!
   RODRIGUE: Don't let emotion color your words.
It is true I am young, but in the well-born,
valor does not wait for age.
   COUNT: What vanity puts you in my class?
You have never carried arms into battle.

RODRIGUE: Men like me need no second test to
　　show their valor.
Their trial stroke is also their master stroke.
　　COUNT: Do you know who I am?
　　RODRIGUE: 　　　　　　　　Yes. Any other man
at the sound of your name would tremble with fear.
The victory wreaths that have crowned your head
would seem to bear the sign of my defeat.
I am rashly attacking a man who has always con-
　　quered.
But my courage will give me great strength.
Nothing is impossible for a son avenging his father.
You are unconquered but not invincible.
　　COUNT: That very courage which shows forth in
　　　　your words,
I have seen in your eyes day after day,
and believing I had found in you the honor of
　　Castille,
I was pleased to think of you as a future son.
I know of your love and I am gratified to see
all of its power yield to the power of duty.
Your passion has not weakened your noble ardor,
and your virtue justifies my esteem.
In wanting a perfect warrior for a son,
I was not wrong in choosing you.
But now my pity is involved in what I feel for you.
I admire your courage and I pity your youth.
Do not attempt a trial duel that would be fatal.
Spare me an uneven fight.
No honor would accompany such a victory.
In winning without danger, a man triumphs without
　　glory.
All would know you were defeated without effort,
and I would be left with sorrow for your death.
　　RODRIGUE: Such unworthy pity follows fast on
　　　　your boldness.
So, the man who takes my honor fears taking my life?
　　COUNT: Leave this place.
　　RODRIGUE: 　　　Let's go together without more talk.
　　COUNT: Are you tired of living?
　　RODRIGUE: 　　　　　　Are you afraid of dying?
　　COUNT: So be it! Do your duty. The son degen-
　　　　erates
who for one moment survives the honor of his father.

SCENE III.

Infanta, Chimene, Leonor

INFANTA: Chimene, your suffering will lessen,
and your strength will overcome this blow.
Peace will return after this slight storm.
If your joy is covered now by a few clouds,
you will lose nothing by having it delayed.
　　CHIMENE: There is no more hope in my vexed and
　　　　outraged heart.
So swift a storm upsetting a smooth sea
brings the sign of certain catastrophe.

I cannot doubt it, and I am perishing in the harbor.
I loved, I was loved, and our fathers had consented.
I was telling you this joyous news
at the fatal moment of their quarrel.
That wretched story, as soon as it was told to you,
violated my sweet expectations.
Oh! accursed ambition and hateful wrath
whose tyranny sways the noblest men!
This honor so pitiless to my dearest desires
will cost me the tears and sighs of a lifetime.
　　INFANTA: You have no reason to fear anything
　　　　from this quarrel.
It sprang up in a moment, and it will be over in a
　　moment.
It has caused too much uproar not to be put down,
and already the King plans to pacify them.
And you know that I, who am sensitive to your
　　affliction,
will do the impossible to eradicate its source.
　　CHIMENE: Compromises will have no effect at this
　　　　point.
Such mortal insults are not forgiven.
It is futile to use force and prudence.
If the evil is cured, it will only be in appearance.
The hate which is preserved by the heart within
feeds passion that is hidden, but all the more ardent
　　for that.
　　INFANTA: The holy bond which will join Rodrigue
　　　　and Chimene
will disperse the hate between the enemy fathers,
and we shall soon see your stronger love
stifle this discord in a happy marriage.
　　CHIMENE: I long for this more than I hope for it.
Don Diegue is too proud and I know my father.
The tears I want to hold back are beginning to flow.
The past is my torment and the future my fear.
　　INFANTA: What do you fear? The impotence of an
　　　　old man?
　　CHIMENE: Rodrigue is courageous.
　　INFANTA: 　　　　　　　He is too young.
　　CHIMENE: Such men are valiant in their first duel.
　　INFANTA: There is no need to fear for him.
He is too much in love to will your displeasure,
and two words from you will arrest his anger.
　　CHIMENE: If he does not obey me, what suffering
　　　　lies ahead?
And if he obeys, what will they say of him?
How can he, of such birth, bear such an outrage?
If he accepts or resists the love which binds us,
I shall be either ashamed of his respect
or bewildered by his refusal.
　　INFANTA: You have a noble soul, and although it
　　　　is deeply distressed,
it will not allow a base thought.
If I made this perfect lover my prisoner
until the day of reconciliation,
and thus prevented any sign of his courage,
would your loving spirit take offense?
　　CHIMENE: If you do this, my worry is over.

SCENE IV.

Infanta, Chimene, Leonor, Page.

INFANTA: Page, seek out Rodrigue and bring him
   here.
PAGE: The Count Gomes and he . . .
CHIMENE: Oh! it is too late!
INFANTA: Speak!
PAGE: . . . left the palace together.
CHIMENE: Alone?
PAGE: Alone! They were arguing in a low
   voice.
CHIMENE: They are already fighting, and it's use-
   less to speak further.
Your Highness, forgive them for this haste.

SCENE V.

Infanta, Leonor.

INFANTA: A new conflict rises up in my mind.
I am sorry for her suffering, and I still love Rodrigue.
There is no peace in my mind, for my love is re-
   kindled.
What separates Rodrigue from Chimene
brings back to life my hope and my pain.
Their estrangement grieves me
and creates a secret pleasure in my bewitched mind.
   LEONOR: Does the lofty virtue of your soul
give over this quickly to an unworthy love?
   INFANTA: Do not call it unworthy; within me
it is now a strong triumphant law.
Pay it respect since it is dear to me.
My virtue fights it, but I hope in spite of myself.
My ill-protected heart, full of so mad a hope,
flies to the lover whom Chimene has lost.
   LEONOR: Are you allowing your honorable courage
      to collapse,
and is reason losing its sway over you?
   INFANTA: Reason speaks with little effect
when the heart is reached by such spell-binding poi-
   son!
When the sick man loves his sickness,
he will not allow any remedy to be administered.
   LEONOR: Your hope has changed you and your
      sickness is sweet,
but Rodrigue is unworthy of you.
   INFANTA: I know it too well. But if my virtue
      yields,
learn how love soothes a heart it possesss.
If this one time Rodrigue is victor,
if this great warrior falls under his valor,
I may esteem him, I may love him without shame.
If he wins over the Count, what will he not do?
I can imagine that at his most inconspicuous feats,
entire kingdoms will submit to his law.
My flattering love already persuades me
that I see him seated on the throne of Granada,

with the subjugated Moors trembling as they kneel,
with Aragon welcoming the new conqueror,
and Portugal submitting, and all his noble days
bearing beyond the seas his great mission,
and the blood of Africa watering his laurels.
Everything that is said of famous warriors,
I expect of Rodrigue after this victory,
and out of his love I will make a cause for my own
   honor.
   LEONOR: Your Highness, see how far you have led
      him
from a duel which perhaps will not take place.
   INFANTA: Rodrigue is insulted. The Count is the
      offender. They have gone off together. What
more is needed?
   LEONOR: Well, if you insist, let them have their
      fight,
but will Rodrigue go as far as you have imagined?
   INFANTA: You are right! I have lost my mind.
You can see the disasters my love creates.
Come with me and help me with your words.
Do not leave me in my bewildered state.

SCENE VI.

The King, Don Arias, Don Sanche.

KING: So, the Count is that vain and that unreason-
   able!
Does he still believe his crime can be pardoned?
   ARIAS: I spoke to him at some length in your name.
I did my best, Sire, with no result.
   KING: Can it be that a presumptuous subject
has so little respect and so little desire to please me?
He insults Don Diegue and scorns his king!
Before my court he lays down the law.
He is a brave warrior and a great captain,
but I have the means to quell such a proud spirit.
Were he valor itself and the god of war,
he will see what it means to disobey.
Despite all that such violence deserved,
I had decided first to treat him gently.
But since he goes so far, arrest him today
whether he makes resistance or not.
   SANCHE: A little time, perhaps, would temper his
      rebellion.
He was caught still angry from his quarrel.
In the heat of a first impulse, Sire,
so noble a heart submits with difficulty.
He understands he is wrong, but his pride
will not allow him to confess his guilt at once.
   KING: Be silent, Don Sanche, and know
that to take his side is criminal.
   SANCHE: I obey and I will be silent, but I entreat
      you, Sire, one further word in his defense.
   KING: What
      can you say?
   SANCHE: That a spirit accustomed to great deeds
cannot bend to submission.
Every form of submission will be shameful.

Only this act did the Count resist.
He found in this duty too much harshness,
and would obey you if he had less heart.
Command that his arm, so strengthened in battle,
repair this insult with the point of his sword.
He will give satisfaction, Sire.

KING: Your respect for me diminishes, but I pardon your age,
and excuse the ardor of your youthful courage.
A king whose prudence has a better goal
is a better steward of his subjects' blood.
I watch over my people; my care protects them,
just as the head needs the members which serve it.
So your reason is not reason for me.
You speak as a soldier; I must act as a king.
Despite what you say and what he believes,
the Count in obeying me cannot lose his honor.
Moreover this insult affects me. He dishonored
the man whom I had made governor of my son.
To attack my choice is to attack me,
and to belittle my sovereign power.
But no more of this. Ten vessels of our old enemy
have been sighted raising their flags.
They have dared approach the mouth of the river.

ARIAS: The Moors know you by the strength of your army,
and, conquered so often, have lost the courage
to risk themselves against so great a conquerer.

KING: Yet they will never regard without jealousy
my scepter ruling Andalusia.
This noble country which they owned too long
is always looked upon with envy.
This is the one reason that has forced me for ten years
to place the throne of Castille in Seville,
in order to see them at closer range, and, with a swifter order
overturn at once whatever they undertook.

ARIAS: At the expense of their best leaders
they know your presence assures your victory.
You have nothing to fear.

KING: And nothing to neglect.
Overconfidence attracts danger.
You know what a simple thing it is
for the rising tide to bring them here.
Yet I would be wrong, since the information is uncertain,
to spread panic in the hearts of my people.
The terror which a useless alarm would produce
would disturb the city too much tonight.
Double the guard at the walls and the harbor.
That is enough for now.

SCENE VII.

The King, Don Sanche, Don Alonso.

ALONSO: Sire, the Count is dead.
Don Diegue, through his son, has been avenged.

KING: As soon as I learned of this affront, I foresaw the vengeance,
and I tried at once to prevent calamity.

ALONSO: Chimeme is bringing her grief into your presence.
Tearfully she comes to plead for justice.

KING: Although I share in her affliction,
the Count fully deserved
this penalty for his rashness.
Yet however justified his punishment,
I cannot without regret lose such a captain.
After a long service to his country,
after the countless wounds he received for me,
whatever resentment his pride imposes on me,
his loss weakens us and his death grieves us.

SCENE VIII.

The King, Diegue, Chimene, Sanche, Arias, Alonso.

CHIMENE: Sire! Give me justice!
DIEGUE: Sire, listen to me!
CHIMENE: I kneel before you.
DIEGUE: I bow at your feet.
CHIMENE: I ask for justice.
DIEGUE: Heed my defense.
CHIMENE: Punish the insolence and rashness of this youth.
He has slain the support of your scepter.
He has killed my father.
DIEGUE: He has avenged his own father.
CHIMENE: A king owes justice to his subjects.
DIEGUE: For a just vengeance there can be no punishment.
KING: Rise up, both of you, and speak more deliberately.
Chimene, I share in your sorrow.
My own heart weeps with yours.
[To Don Diegue]
You will speak afterward. Do not interrupt her complaint.
CHIMENE: Sire, my father is dead. My eyes saw his blood
gush forth from his side.
It was that life-blood which preserved your ramparts
and so often won battles for you.
His blood is still angered
at being shed for someone other than yourself.
In the midst of danger, war itself could not spill his blood.
Rodrigue in your court has covered the earth with it.
Without strength or color I ran to the spot
and found him lifeless. Pardon my grief,
Sire, my voice fails me in this fatal story.
Let my tears and sobbing tell you the rest.
KING: Take courage, my child, and know that today
your king will replace your father.

CHIMENE: Sire, too great an honor follows on my woe.
I repeat, I found him lifeless.
His side was opened, and to move me even more,
his blood inscribed my duty on the dust:
or rather, his valor, reduced to such a state,
spoke to me through his wound and urged me to action.
To be heard by the most just of kings,
it borrowed my voice from that grievous opening.
Sire, do not allow such license
to reign before your very eyes.
Do not allow the bravest of your subjects
to be exposed to a rash attack,
or a proud youth to triumph with impunity over such a man's honor,
bathe in his blood and defy his memory.
The death of so valiant a soldier as he who has just been taken away
weakens the will to serve you if he is not avenged.
My father, Sire, is dead, and I want vengeance
more for your own interests than for my consolation.
You are the loser in this death of a man of his rank.
Avenge it by another. One death for one death.
Slay him, not for me, but for your crown,
for your highness, for your person.
I repeat, Sire, sacrifice for the good of the state
the man whom so lofty an assault has inflated with pride.
KING: Give answer, Don Diegue.
DIEGUE: A man is to be envied
when, on losing his strength, he also loses his life,
and when, at the end of his career, a long life
has prepared his noble spirit for a calamitous fate.
My labors in the past had brought me honors.
Victory once followed me wherever I went,
but today, because I have lived too long,
I was unable to avenge an insult.
The Count, in your court, almost before your eyes,
did what had never been done
by combat, siege, or ambush,
neither by Aragon nor Granada,
neither by your enemies nor those envious of me.
He was jealous of your choice and proud of the advantage
which the impotency of my years gave to him.
Sire, my hair, which has turned white under your armor,
my blood, often spilled in your service,
this arm, which was once dreaded by your enemies,
would have descended, covered with shame, into the tomb,
if I had not brought forth a son worthy of me,
worthy of his country and worthy of his king,
He lent me his strength and killed the Count.
He gave me back my honor and effaced my shame.
If showing courage and anger,
if avenging an insult, deserve punishment,
the wrath of the tempest should fall on me.

Whether you name the cause of our contention a crime or not,
Sire, I am the head and he is but the arm.
Chimene laments that Rodrigue killed her father, but he would never have done it, if I had been able to.
Slay rather this head which old age will soon cut down,
and save for yourself the arm which can serve.
Satisfy Chimene by shedding my blood.
I will not resist. I consent to my penalty.
Rather than complaining over so rigorous a decree,
dying without dishonor, I shall die without regret.
KING: The affair is important and the positions well considered.
It should be deliberated in open council.
Don Sanche, take Chimene back to her house.
Don Diegue will have as a prison my court and his word.
Find Rodrigue. I will mete out justice.
CHIMENE: O King, it is just that a murderer die.
KING: Take some rest, my child, and quiet your grief.
CHIMENE: To order me to rest is to increase my grief.

ACT III. SCENE I.

Rodrigue, Elvire.

ELVIRE: Rodrigue, what are you doing? Why are you here?
RODRIGUE: To carry out the sad ending of my fate.
ELVIRE: How can you have the boldness and the pride
to appear in this house which you have made a place of mourning?
Have you come to defy the body of the Count?
Didn't you kill him?
RODRIGUE: His life was my shame.
My honor demanded that deed from my hand.
ELVIRE: But a murderer does not seek refuge
in the house of death.
RODRIGUE: I know. I come to give myself up to my judge.
Don't look at me with such surprise.
I am here for my death—after giving death.
My judge is my love, my judge is Chimene.
I deserve death because I deserve her hatred.
And I have come to receive, as a sovereign good,
the decree from her lips and the sword from her hands.
ELVIRE: It is better to leave her alone and avoid her violence.
Don't stay to witness her first outburst.
Leave and don't expose yourself
to the fresh impulse of her anger.
RODRIGUE: No! I have pained her.
Let her anger be boundless for my punishment.
I will avoid a hundred deaths which await me

if by dying sooner I can redouble it.
ELVIRE: Chimene, all in tears, is in the palace,
and she will return with an escort.
Go, Rodrigue, I beg you. I will be blamed.
What will they say if you are here?
Do you want some slanderer, as a final blow,
to accuse her of seeing the assassin of her father?
She is returning. I can see her now.
At least hide, for the sake of her honor.

SCENE II.

Don Sanche, Chimene, Elvire.

SANCHE: Yes, my Lady, you must have the blood
  of the murderer.
Your anger is just and your tears justified.
I will not attempt with my words
to soften your anger or bring you consolation.
But if I am able to serve you,
use my sword to punish the guilty man.
Use my love to avenge this death.
My arm will be strong when it is directed by you.
CHIMENE: What woe there is for me!
SANCHE: Let me serve you.
CHIMENE: I would offend the King who has prom-
  ised justice.
SANCHE: The justice of the law moves slowly
and often the crime is forgotten in the passing of
  years.
Time in its slowness brings forth too much weeping.
Permit a knight to avenge you by a duel.
It is a surer way and swifter for punishment.
CHIMENE: That is for the last recourse. If I have
  to come to it,
and if you still feel pity for my plight,
I will then give you leave to avenge me.
SANCHE: It is the one happiness I yearn for.
Since you give me hope, I take my leave now.

SCENE III.

Chimene, Elvire.

CHIMENE: At last I am freed from the court
and do not have to hide my grief.
I can sigh without restraint
and open up to you my heart and my woe.
My father is dead, Elvire, and the first sword
held by Rodrigue in duel, cut off his life.
Let all my tears flow!
Half of my life put the other half into the grave,
and forces me to avenge after this fatal deed
my father's death on the life of Rodrigue.
ELVIRE: You must take some rest.
CHIMENE: "Rest" is a strange word
in the midst of such calamity.
How will my sorrow ever end

if I cannot hate the hand which caused it?
And what can I hope for—save endless pain
if I prosecute for a crime and love the criminal?
ELVIRE: He deprives you of a father, and you still
  love him?
CHIMENE: Love is not strong enough, Elvire, I
  worship him!
My passion contends with my anger.
Within my enemy I find my lover,
and I know that despite all my wrath,
Rodrigue is still fighting my father in my heart.
He attacks him, bears down, withdraws, defends him-
  self.
He is strong, then weak, then triumphant.
But in this harsh combat of anger and passion,
he tears my heart without dividing my soul.
Yet despite the power of love over me,
I do not hesitate over the way of duty.
I have followed the obligations of honor.
Rodrigue is precious to me, and I am aggrieved in his
  interest.
My heart takes his side, but that does not count.
I know what I am and that my father is dead.
ELVIRE: Do you intend to prosecute him?
CHIMENE: That unreal word!
I must prosecute him.
I must demand his head and fear obtaining it.
My death will follow his, and I must punish him.
ELVIRE: Give up this tragic plan.
Don't put yourself under so harsh a law.
CHIMENE: But my father died, almost in my arms.
Am I deaf to his blood crying for vengeance?
My heart, shamefully held by the spell of love,
believes that I owe him only useless tears.
Shall I allow a seductive love
to stifle my honor under cowardly silence?
ELVIRE: You will be excused
if you show less wrath for the man you love,
for so loved a suitor. You have done enough.
You have seen the King. Do not insist on more.
Do not persist in this strange mood.
CHIMENE: My honor is at stake. I must be avenged.
However strong the desire of my love,
a noble spirit cannot make a shameful excuse.
ELVIRE: But you love Rodrigue. He cannot offend
  you.
CHIMENE: I know that.
ELVIRE: Well then, what do you plan to do?
CHIMENE: To preserve my honor and end my sor-
  row,
I will prosecute, have him slain, and die after him.

SCENE IV.

Rodrigue, Chimene, Elvire.

RODRIGUE: There is no need to prosecute.
You will have the honor of ending my life.
CHIMENE: Where are we, Elvire? Who is this?

Is Rodrigue here? Is Rodrigue in my house?

RODRIGUE: Do not spare my blood. There is no obstacle now to my death and to your vengeance.

CHIMENE: God!

RODRIGUE: Listen to me.

CHIMENE: I cannot!

RODRIGUE: For one moment.

CHIMENE: Go, let me die.

RODRIGUE: I will be brief.

And then you can answer with this sword.

CHIMENE: It is still wet with my father's blood.

RODRIGUE: Chimene!

CHIMENE: Take it out of my sight.

It reproaches me for your crime and your life.

RODRIGUE: Look at it then and let it arouse your hate,

and bring on your anger and hasten my punishment.

CHIMENE: It is tainted with my blood.

RODRIGUE: Plunge it into mine,

and it will lose the color of yours.

CHIMENE: What cruel fate is this that in one day

kills the father by the sword and his child by the sight of the sword!

Take it away from here. I cannot bear it.

You want me to listen and you cause my death.

RODRIGUE: I will obey. I still long

to see my life end by your hand.

Do not expect from my love

any cowardly repentance for a good deed.

Your father's irreparable insult

dishonored my father and shamed me.

You know the effect of such a gesture on a noble spirit.

I was involved in this affront and I sought out the man.

I came to him, and avenged my honor and my father.

I would do it again if there were need.

At first my love fought on your behalf

against my father and myself.

You can judge of its power: even in that offense

I hesitated before taking vengeance.

Faced with displeasing you or suffering an affront,

I thought I was too quick to take the sword

and blamed myself for too much violence.

Your beauty would have been the victor,

had I not been convinced

that a man without honor was unworthy of you,

that despite the place I had in your heart,

you would hate me dishonored;

listening to your love and obeying its voice

would desecrate the choice of your love.

Let me say it again, although it is painful,

let me say it until I breathe my last breath:

I have offended you—but I had to

in order to wipe out my shame and deserve you.

But now that I have satisfied my father and my honor,

I come to satisfy you.

I am here in order to offer my life.

I did what was my obligation, and now this is my present duty.

I know that the death of a father hardens you against my crime,

and I will not rob you of a victim.

Sacrifice courageously to the blood he lost

the man whose honor was in shedding it.

CHIMENE: Rodrigue, it is true. Even if I am your enemy,

I cannot blame you for escaping infamy.

However strong my outburst of grief,

I do not accuse you and I weep for sorrow.

I know what honor, after such outrage,

demands of a noble heart.

You did your duty as a knight,

and in doing it, you taught me mine.

Your fateful valor instructs me in its victory.

It avenged your father and preserved your honor.

The same pride is before me, and, for my grief,

I must preserve my honor and avenge my father.

My love for you is my despair.

If some other cause had taken my father from me,

I would have found in the joy of seeing you

the one solace I could have hoped for.

I would have found a cure to my grief

when your loving hand dried my tears.

Now I have to destroy you after losing him.

This quelling of my love is due my honor.

And this frightful duty, whose demand is my death,

forces me to strive toward your death.

Do not expect from my love

any cowardly sentiments. In the cause of your punishment,

though our love pleads in your favor,

my soul must equal yours in nobleness.

In offending me, you became worthy of me.

In asking for your death, I will be worthy of you.

RODRIGUE: Don't put off any longer what your honor claims.

It wants my life and I give it to you.

Sacrifice it to your noble purpose.

The blow will be as welcome to me as the decree.

If after my crime you wait upon slow justice,

you will delay your honor as well as my punishment.

I will die in happiness if it is by your hand.

CHIMENE: I am your adversary. I am not your executioner.

If you offer me your hand, is it for me to take?

I have to attack your life but you have to defend it.

I must get it from someone other than from you.

I am to prosecute you but not punish you.

RODRIGUE: Whatever our love plead in my favor,

your soul must equal mine in nobleness.

To borrow someone else in order to avenge a father

is no solution, my Chimene.

My hand alone avenged my father,

your hand alone should avenge yours.

CHIMENE: Why do you insist on this cruel point?

You were avenged without help and yet you offer me help!

I will follow your example. My courage is too great
to allow my honor to be shared with you.
My father and my honor will owe nothing
to the force of your love and your despair.

RODRIGUE: Oh! the hardness of this honor! Can I
do nothing
to win this grace from you?
In the name of a dead father, in the name of our
love,
punish me through vengeance or at least through pity.
Your wretched lover will be less grieved
in dying by your hand than in living with your
shame.

CHIMENE: I do not hate you.

RODRIGUE: You should.

CHIMENE: I cannot.

RODRIGUE: Have you such little fear of blame and
slander?
When my crime is learned and your love still endures,
what will not envy and falsehood proclaim?
Force them to silence and without further speech,
preserve your fame by causing me to die.

CHIMENE: It will be more manifest if you live.
I want the voice of the blackest envy
to raise to heaven my honor and to pity my grief,
knowing that I love you and still prosecute you.
Leave me. You stand before me
as the man I love and whom I must destroy.
Conceal your departure under the shadow of night.
If you are seen leaving here, my honor may be im-
periled.
The one chance for slander
is to learn that here I allowed your presence.
Do not give it cause to attack my virtue.

RODRIGUE: Let me die!

CHIMENE: Go!

RODRIGUE: To what are you resigned?

CHIMENE: Despite my love, which thwarts my
anger,
I will do all I can to avenge my father.
And yet in the face of so cruel a duty,
my one wish is to have no power.

RODRIGUE: Miracle of love!

CHIMENE: No greater distress is possible.

RODRIGUE: Our fathers will cost us countless woes.

CHIMENE: Rodrigue, who would have believed
that our happiness which was so close could fail?

RODRIGUE: Chimene, who would have said
that so close to the harbor, against all appearances,
so swift a storm would have broken all hope?

CHIMENE: Leave now. I wish to hear no more.

RODRIGUE: Farewell. I will pursue a dying life
until your prosecution takes it from me.

CHIMENE: If I succeed in that, I pledge my word
not to live an hour after your death.
Farewell. Go now and take care no one sees you.

ELVIRE: However great our trials, heaven . . .

CHIMENE: Trouble me no further. Leave me to
myself.
For my tears I need silence and the night.

SCENE V.

Don Diegue.

DIEGUE: A perfect happiness is impossible to know.
Our happiest moments are tinged with sadness.
A few worries in every event always
disturb the purity of our satisfaction.
In the midst of happiness my soul is troubled:
I am surrounded with joy and yet tremble with fear.
I have seen the corpse of the man who insulted me,
and yet I cannot find the hand which avenged me.
I have uselessly exerted myself
in looking throughout the city—despite my age.
The meager strength my years have left me
is wasted vainly in seeking the victor.
Everywhere throughout this dark night
I thought I was embracing him but it was a shadow.
And my love, tricked by this deceptive ghost,
engenders suspicions which redouble my fears.
I can find no signs of his flight.
I fear the friends and consorts of the dead count.
Their numbers terrify my mind.
Either Rodrigue is dead or languishing in prison.
God in heaven! Is my sight again deceived,
or is this at last my one hope?
Yes, it is he, there is no doubt. My prayers are an-
swered,
my fears are over and my worry ended.

SCENE VI.

Don Diegue, Don Rodrigue.

DIEGUE: Rodrigue, at last heaven sends you to me!

RODRIGUE: Alas!

DIEGUE: Do not mingle your sighs with my joy.
Let me catch my breath before praising you.
My valor has no reason to disown you.
You emulated it and your famed daring
means the heroes of my race live again in you.
You are their descendant and you come from me.
Your first thrust of the sword equals all of mine.
Ardently your virile youth
reaches my fame in this great test.
Support of my old age, height of my happiness,
touch this white hair which you have honored,
kiss this cheek and you will see the spot
where the insult was stamped, wiped out by your
courage.

RODRIGUE: The honor was due you. I could do
nothing less,
since I had come from you and was raised by you.
I consider myself privileged and my heart is content
that my first combat pleases the author of my days.
But in your pleasure, do not be jealous
if I dare in my turn to seek satisfaction.

Allow my despair now freely to burst forth.
For too long have your words tricked it.
I am not sorry I served you,
but give me back the happiness this combat stole.
My arm, to avenge you, raised against my love,
took away my soul in that honorable fight.
Say nothing more to me. For your sake, I have lost
    everything.
What I owed you, I have paid back generously.

    DIEGUE: Raise higher than this the fruit of your
        victory.
I gave you life and you have given back honor to me.
And because honor is dearer to me than life,
I owe you all the more in return.
But you must expel from your noble heart all weak-
    ness.
We have only one honor. There are many mistresses.
Love is but a pleasure, honor is a duty.

    RODRIGUE: What are you saying to me?

    DIEGUE: What you must know.

    RODRIGUE: My offended honor is taking vengeance
        on me,
and you dare urge me to the shame of infidelity!
It is the same infamy and is equally attached
to the warrior without courage and the perfidious
    lover.
Do not mock my fidelity.
Let me be noble without being a perjurer.
My bonds are too strong to be broken thus.
Even without hope, my faith still binds me,
and unable to leave Chimene or to possess her,
the death I am seeking is my sweetest torment.

    DIEGUE: There is no time left to seek your death.
Your prince and your country need you.
The boats that were feared, already at the river,
are planning to surprise the city and pillage all about.
The Moors are on us. The tide and the night
will bring them noiselessly in one hour to our walls.
Disorder reigns in the court, and the people are
    alarmed.
All you hear are shouts and all you see are tears.
In this public disaster luck granted
my finding at my door five hundred friends,
who, knowing of my insult, and prompted by the
    same zeal,
came to offer themselves to avenge my quarrel.
You anticipated them. But their valor
can be better used against the African army.
March at their head where honor places you.
Their noble company wants you as their leader.
Go and withstand the attack of our old enemies.
If you wish to die, you will find there a worthy death.
Seize this chance, since it is offered you.
Your king will hereby owe his safety to your sacri-
    fice.
But I would rather you return with palm leaves on
    your head.
Do not limit your honor to avenging an affront.
Bear it farther. Let your valor force
our monarch to a pardon and Chimene to silence.

If you love her, know that to return victorious
is the one way of again winning her heart.
But time is too precious to be lost in words.
Let me interrupt you here and send you off.
Come, I will show you the way, and you will show
    your king
that what he loses in the Count, he recovers in you.

ACT IV. SCENE I.

Chimene, Elvire.

    CHIMENE: Isn't this a mere rumor? Are you sure,
        Elvire?

    ELVIRE: You would never believe how he is ad-
        mired by all;
how all, with one voice, raise to heaven
the glorious deeds of this young hero.
The Moors, to their shame, scattered before him.
Their landing was swift, their flight was swifter.
Three hours of combat gave to our warriors
full victory and two kings as prisoners.
Our leader's valor found no obstacle.

    CHIMENE: Did Rodrigue's hand perform those
        miracles?

    ELVIRE: The two kings are the prize of his great
        effort.
It was his hand which conquered and took them.

    CHIMENE: From whom have you learned this be-
        wildering news?

    ELVIRE: From the people who shout his praise
        everywhere.
They call him the author of their joy,
their guardian angel and their liberator.

    CHIMENE: How does the King look upon such
        valor?

    ELVIRE: Rodrigue has not yet dared to appear in
        his presence.
But Don Diegue, elated, in the name of his son
has presented him with the two crowned captives
    in chains,
and has asked of our noble prince that, as a favor,
he receive the man who saved the country.

    CHIMENE: Is he wounded?

    ELVIRE: There is no report of that.
Your color changes. Try to recover your feelings.

    CHIMENE: I must try to recover my weakened
        anger.
Through worry for him, must I forget myself?
He is praised and acclaimed, and my heart consents.
My honor is mute and my duty powerless.
Silence, my love, let my anger come forth!
He may have conquered two kings, but he killed my
    father.
This dress of black where I can see my grief
is the first result of his valor,
and no matter what is said elsewhere of his great
    heart,
here every object speaks to me of his crime.

You who give strength to my anger,
veils, crepe and dress, ornaments of woe,
pomp which his first victory enjoins on me,
sustain my honor against my passion;
and when my love is too powerful,
speak to my mind of my sad duty.
Fear nothing as you attack a triumphant man.

ELVIRE: Calm your feelings, here is the Infanta.

SCENE II.

Infanta, Chimene, Leonor, Elvire.

INFANTA: I do not come here to console you;
I come to mingle my sighs with your tears.

CHIMENE: Rather should you participate in the common joy
and delight in the fortune that heaven sends you.
No one but me has the right to lament.
The peril out of which Rodrigue has drawn us,
and the safety of the people which his valor has preserved,
allow only me to shed tears on this day.
He has saved the city and served his king.
His warrior's arm was fatal only to me.

INFANTA: It is true, Chimene, he has performed miracles.

CHIMENE: When this painful report reached my ears,
I heard him loudly called
as brave in war as he is unfortunate in love.

INFANTA: But why should this public acclaim he painful to you?
He possessed your soul and lived by your laws.
If you praise his valor, you will honor your own choice.

CHIMENE: Everyone else can praise him with justice.
But for me his praise is a new torment.
By raising him so high, you embitter my pain.
I see what I am destroying when I see what he is worth.
This is cruel vexation for the mind of a lover.
The more I learn of his valor, the more my passion grows.
Yet my duty is still the stronger,
and in spite of my love, it will seek his death.

INFANTA: You were highly esteemed yesterday for this duty.
The struggle you waged was so noble,
so worthy of a great heart, that every courtier
admired your courage and pitied your love.
Will you accept now the counsel of a faithful friend?

CHIMENE: I would be criminal not to obey you.

INFANTA: What was lawful yesterday is no longer today.
Rodrigue now is our one support.
He is the hope and the love of a jubilant people,
the prop of Castille and the terror of the Moors.
Even the King subscribes to the truth
that your father lives again in him,
and, to explain matters briefly,
in his death you pursue the destruction of us all.
To avenge a father is it permissible
to give over one's country to the enemy?
Is your prosecution fair to us?
Do we have any part in this crime?
You are not obliged to marry
the man whom a dead father obliged you to accuse.
Let me help remove this desire from your heart.
Obliterate your love but leave us his life.

CHIMENE: It is not for me to have such kindness.
The duty that embitters me is not limited.
Although my love is still involved with this conqueror,
even if the people worship him and the King flatters him,
even if he is surrounded by valiant warriors,
I will go under the cypress trees to crush his laurels.

INFANTA: It is a noble thing, when to avenge a father
our duty attacks so beloved a person,
but it is more noble and of the highest worth
to give up for the public good the interests of family.
Believe me, it is enough that you extinguish your love.
He will be punished enough if he is no longer in your heart.
Let the prosperity of the nation impose this law on you:
Besides, what can the King grant you now?

CHIMENE: He can refuse me, but I will not be silent.

INFANTA: Dear Chimene, reflect carefully on what you should do.
Adieu. You must reach your decision in solitude.

CHIMENE: After this death of my father, I have no choice.

SCENE III.

The King, Diegue, Arias, Rodrigue, Sanche.

KING: Noble heir of an illustrious family
which was always the glory and support of Castille,
race with so many ancestors famous for their valor,
whom you matched in your trial valor,
my power is too limited to reward you.
It is less than the merit you have shown.
The country, made safe from so fierce an enemy,
my scepter, firmly placed in my hand by yours,
the Moors, defeated before I could give
orders to repulse their attack—
these are not exploits which leave your king
the means or the hope of paying his debt to you.
But your two captive kings have spoken your reward.
Both of them called you their Cid in my presence.
Since in their language Cid is the equal of Lord,

I will not begrudge you this honorable title.
Henceforth you are the Cid: may all obstacles collapse before this name!
May it fill Granada and Toledo with fear,
and may it show to all who live under my law
what you mean to me and what I owe to you!
    RODRIGUE: Sire, will your Majesty spare my shame!
It values too highly a meager service,
and forces me to blush before so great a king
at deserving so poorly the honor I have received.
I know that to the welfare of your empire I owe
the blood coursing in my veins and the air I breathe,
and even if I lost them for so worthy an object,
I would merely be carrying out the duty of a subject.
    KING: All those who are bound by this duty to my service
do not satisfy their obligations with the same courage,
and when valor does not attempt the impossible,
it does not produce such extraordinary results.
Allow this praise, then, and tell me
at greater length the real tale of your victory.
    RODRIGUE: Sire, you learned that in the press of this danger,
which cast over the entire city a deep fright,
a group of friends meeting at my father's house
pleaded with my heart which was still confused . . .
But Sire, you must pardon my boldness
if I dared to use it without your authority.
The danger was coming close. Their brigade was ready.
If I had come to the court, I was risking my life,
and if I had to lose my life, it was more pleasing for me
to die when I was fighting for you.
    KING: I pardon the violence with which you avenged your insult.
The State you defended speaks in your defense.
Henceforth Chimene's plea will not be considered.
I will listen to her and console her. That is all.
Continue.
    RODRIGUE: Under my direction these men advanced,
and showed on their faces a virile confidence.
We were five hundred at first, but with a swift reinforcement,
we were three thousand when we reached the harbor;
and seeing us march, with determination in our faces,
the most terrified recovered their courage.
On arriving, I hid two-thirds of the men
in the bottom of the boats which we found there.
The rest, whose numbers increased hourly,
remained close by, devoured by impatience,
and lay on the ground, where they kept silence,
and spent a part of a magnificent night.
At my command, the guard did likewise,
and staying out of sight, they helped my stratagem.
Then I boldly pretended I had received from you
the order I announced and gave to all.
    That obscure light which falls from the stars
at last showed us, with the tide, thirty ships.

The wave swelled under them, and in a joint effort
the Moors and the sea entered the harbor.
We let them pass. Everything seemed quiet to them.
Not a soldier at the harbor, not a soldier at the city walls.
Our deep silence deceived them
and they no longer doubted they had caught us.
Fearlessly they approached, anchored, disembarked,
and rushed into the hands waiting for them.
We rose up then, and all together
uttered a thousand war cries which reached the heavens.
More of our men answered these cries from their ships.
We appeared in arms. The Moors were thrown into rout.
Terror seized them while they were still landing.
Before the fighting began, they knew they had lost.
They were bent on pillaging and they encountered battle.
We attacked by water and by land,
and caused rivers of their blood to flow
before one of them could resist.
But soon, in spite of us, their princes rallied them,
their courage came back and their terror fled.
The shame of dying without combat
stopped their confusion and reanimated their valor.
Against us they firmly drew their scimitars
and made a horrible mingling of our blood with theirs.
The land, the river, their ships, the harbor
were the sites of slaughter where death reigned.
    Countless acts and courageous deeds
were not even visible under the cover of darkness,
where each man, the only witness of his own thrusts,
could not see whom fortune was favoring.
I went everywhere encouraging our men,
making some move ahead, lending support to others,
placing those who joined with us, urging them on,
and I did not know the result until daybreak.
At last its light showed our advantage.
The Moors saw their defeat and then lost courage
when they saw reinforcements come to our help.
The hope of victory turned into the fear of death.
They reached their ships and cut the cables.
With terrible shrieks resounding everywhere,
they retreated in an uproar, without considering
whether their kings could retreat with them.
Their terror was too strong for them to heed this duty.
The incoming tide had brought them, and the ebb tide took them away
while their kings, in combat with us,
and a few of their men, wounded by our swords,
fought valiantly and sold their lives dearly.
In vain I urged them to surrender.
but they held their scimitars and refused to listen.
Then seeing all their men fall at their feet
and aware they were fighting in vain,
they asked for the leader. I came forward and they surrendered.

I sent both of them to you at the same time.
And the fighting stopped because there were no more
    fighters.
It was thus that in serving you . . .

SCENE IV.

The King, Diegue, Rodrigue, Arias, Alonso, Sanche.

ALONSO: Sire, Chimene is here asking for justice.
KING: I am sorry to hear this. Her duty is now
    oppressive.
    [*To* Rodrigue]
Leave. There is no need to force her to see you.
Rather than thanking you, I am sending you away.
But before you leave, come here, let me embrace
    you.
    [*Exit* Rodrigue]
DIEGUE: Chimene prosecutes him and yet wants to
    save him.
KING: I was told she loves him and I will now test
    her.
    [*To* Diegue]
Show more sadness on your face.

SCENE V.

The King, Diegue, Arias, Sanche, Alonso, Chimene, Elvire.

KING: You can rest now,
Chimene, because the outcome satisfies your request.
If Rodrigue won over our enemies,
he died in our presence from the wounds he received.
Offer thanks to Heaven who has avenged you.
    [*To* Diegue]
See her face, how it changes color.
DIEGUE: She is fainting, Sire, and from perfect
    love.
See all the signs in her swoon.
Her grief has betrayed the secrets of her soul.
We can no longer doubt her love.
CHIMENE: You say Rodrigue is dead?
KING: No, he lives,
and bears for you an unchanging love.
Quiet your grief which we aroused.
CHIMENE: Sire, it is possible to faint from joy as
    well as from sorrow.
Excess of happiness is able to weaken us,
and when it surprises the soul, it overcomes the
    senses.
KING: Do you want us to believe the impossible on
    your behalf?
Your grief, Chimene, was too visible.
CHIMENE: Sire, then add this climax to my woe,
and call my fainting the result of my grief.
A just anger had overcome my feelings.

His death had taken away the object of my prosecu-
    tion.
If he dies from wounds received for the good of his
    country,
my vengeance is lost and my plans betrayed.
Such a noble end is offensive to my cause.
I am asking for his death, but not a glorious death,
not one which elevates him so high in acclaim,
not on a bed of honor, but on a scaffold.
Let him die for my father, and not for his country.
Let his name be sullied and his memory tarnished.
To die for one's country is not a sad fate.
That noble death is immortality.
    Therefore I am glad for his victory, and I am un-
    ashamed.
It assures the State and gives me back my victim.
He is noble now and famous among all warriors.
He is the leader, crowned, not with flowers but with
    laurel,
and, to say in one word what I think of him: he is
worthy of being sacrificed to the shade of my father.
    Alas! the vain hope I indulged in!
Rodrigue has nothing to fear from me.
    What power could my tears, that are scorned, have
    against him?
Your whole empire is a place of refuge for him.
He will be given every freedom under your rule.
He triumphs over me as he did over his enemies.
In their spilled blood strangled justice
serves as a new trophy for the conqueror's crime.
We increase the pomp, and scorn for the law
makes us follow his chariot between two kings.
KING: My daughter, your outburst is too violent.
When justice is meted out, everything has to be
    weighed.
Your father was killed, but he was the aggressor.
Justice itself commands me to use leniency.
Before you accuse my judgment,
consult your heart. Rodrigue is its master,
and your love secretly gives thanks to your king,
whose favor protects your lover.
CHIMENE: Not my lover! My enemy! He's the ob-
    ject of my anger,
the author of my woes! the assassin of my father!
You give so little heed to my just prosecution
that you think you favor me by not listening to me!
Since you refuse my grief any justice,
Sire, allow me to have recourse to weapons.
That is the manner in which I must be avenged.
I ask all your warriors for his head.
Let one of them bring it to me, and I am his con-
    quest.
Let the combat begin, Sire, and when it is over,
if Rodrigue is punished, I will marry the conqueror.
Allow this to be published under the seal of your
    authority.
KING: This custom, long ago established here,
under the pretense of punishing an unjust assault,
weakens the State with the loss of good fighters.
Often the deplorable outcome of this abuse

crushes the innocent and defends the guilty.
I exempt Rodrigue from it. He is too valuable
to expose to the blows of a capricious fate;
and whatever crime his magnanimous heart did commit,
the Moors took away in their flight.

    DIEGUE: Sire, for him alone are you reversing a law
observed by your court many times?
What will your people believe, what will envy say,
if under your protection he runs no risk
and makes this a pretext not to appear
where men of honor seek a noble death?
Such favors would sully his honor.
Let him taste, without blushing, the fruits of his victory.
He punished the Court's rashness;
he did it as a brave man and must maintain it.

    KING: Since you wish it, I will grant him leave.
But a thousand would take the place of one conquered warrior,
and the prize which Chimene has promised the conqueror
would make of all my warriors his enemies.
To set him alone against all would be unjust.
Let him go into the lists only once.
Choose the man you wish, Chimene, and choose well.
But after this one combat, ask for nothing more.

    DIEGUE: Do not excuse thereby those who might be terrified.
Leave the lists opened. No one will enter
after Rodrigue's revelation today.
Who has enough courage to attack him?
Who would risk his life against such an adversary?

    SANCHE: Open the lists and you will find the assailant.
I am this rash man—or better, I am this valiant man.
Grant this grace to my ardor, Chimene.
You will remember your promise.

    KING: Chimene, will you put your cause into his hands?

    CHIMENE: I gave my promise, Sire.

    KING: Be ready tomorrow.

    DIEGUE: No, Sire, let there be no delay.
A courageous man is always ready.

    KING: Can he fight again so soon after the battle?

    DIEGUE: He has taken rest by telling you all that happened.

    KING: At least for one or two hours I insist that he rest.
But for fear lest such a combat become an example,
and to testify to all that regretfully I allow
this bloody proceeding which never had my favor,
he will not have the presence of myself or of my court.

    [To Arias]
Only you will judge the valor of the fighters.
See to it that both behave as honorable men,
and when the fight is over, bring the victor to me.
Whoever he be, his effort will earn the same prize.
I myself will present him to Chimene,

and he will receive her troth as a reward.

    CHIMENE: Sire, how can you impose on me so hard a ruling!

    KING: You complain, but your love, rather than confessing your complaint,
will accept it without compulsion if Rodrigue is victor.
Stop complaining about so sweet a decree.
Whichever it is of the two, I will make your husband.

ACT V. SCENE I.

Chimene, Rodrigue.

    CHIMENE: Rodrigue! You dare show yourself here in daytime!
You jeopardize my honor. Leave at once, I beg you.

    RODRIGUE: I am going to die, Chimene, and I come to you here,
before the mortal deed, to bid you my last farewell.
The unchanging love which binds me under your law
will not accept my death unless I pay you homage with it.

    CHIMENE: You are going to die!

    RODRIGUE: I am hastening to those happy moments
which will give my life over to your resentment.

    CHIMENE: You are going to die! Is Don Sanche so terrible
that he instills fear in your invincible heart?
Who has made you so weak, or who has made him so strong?
Rodrigue, about to fight, thinks he is already dead!
The man who had no fear of the Moors or of my father,
is going to fight Don Sanche, and gives up hope!
So, in time of need, your courage collapses?

    RODRIGUE: I am going to my punishment and not to a duel.
Since you want my death, my faithful love
relieves me of any desire to defend my life.
My heart is the same, but my arms are useless
when they would preserve what does not please you.
Last night would also have been mortal for me,
If I had fought solely for myself.
But in defending my king, his people and my land,
I would have been traitor had I fought badly.
My spirit does not have enough hate of life
to wish to die by faithlessness.
Now that only I am concerned,
you ask for my death and I accept your decree.
Your resentment has chosen the hand of a warrior
(I was not worthy of dying by your hand):
I will not ward off the sword thrusts of this man.
I owe respect to the one who fights for you,
and since it is your honor that is being defended,
I will uncover my chest before him

and worship in his your hand which will slay me.

CHIMENE: If the just violence of a sad duty
which forces me in spite of myself to prosecute your
    valor,
prescribes for your love so hard a law
that it makes you defenseless before the man who
    fights for me,
do not forget in this blindness
that your honor is at stake as well as your life,
and that despite the glory Rodrigue knew alive,
when he is dead, he will be looked upon as van-
    quished.
Your honor is dearer to you than I am,
since it plunged your hands into my father's blood,
and made you renounce, in spite of your passion,
the secret hope of possessing me.
Yet you esteem this so lightly
that without fighting back you ask to be vanquished.
What inconsistency is debasing your honor?
Why did you lose it, or why did you once have it?
Are you honorable only in your will to insult me?
Have you no courage except to offend me?
Did you treat my father with such harshness
so that after defeating him, you could allow a con-
    queror?
Give up wishing to die. Let me prosecute you
while you defend your honor, even if you have no
    desire to live.

RODRIGUE: After the death of the Count and the
    defeat of the Moors,
does my honor need any more exploits?
It can now scorn the need of self-defense.
It is known that my courage will undertake anything,
that my valor is strong and that nothing is precious
    to me
under Heaven after my honor.
No, believe what you wish, in this combat
Rodrigue may die without harming his honor,
without being accused of lacking courage,
without being defeated, without allowing a victor.
People will say: "He loved Chimene.
He had no desire to live and deserve her hate.
He yielded to the rigor of that fate
which forced Chimene to seek his death.
She demanded his head, and had he refused,
his generous heart would have committed a crime.
In avenging his honor, he lost his love,
in avenging his beloved, he lost his life,
preferring, more than the hope which had ruled his
    soul,
his honor to Chimene and Chimene to his life."
Thus, in this combat you will see my death
increase my honor rather than diminish it.
And this honor will follow my willful death
which in no other way could have satisfied you.

CHIMENE: Since your life and your honor are too
    weak
to keep you from rushing into death,
even if I loved you, Rodrigue,

defend yourself now as revenge, to keep me from
    Don Sanche.
Fight to release me from a condition
which gives me over to the object of my aversion.
Must I say more? think of your own defense
in order to force my duty, and impose silence on me.
If you feel your heart still in love with me,
come out victorious from a combat of which Chi-
    mene is the prize.
Farewell. These last words cover me with shame.

RODRIGUE: Does the enemy exist whom I could not
    defeat?
Appear before me: Navarese, Moors, and Castillians,
and all valorous men whom Spain has raised.
Join together and form an army
to fight a single man aroused as I am.
Join all your efforts to defeat so sweet a hope.
You would be too few to reach success.

SCENE II.

Infanta.

INFANTA: Respect for my birth, shall I heed you
    again who make a crime of my love?
Shall I listen to you, love, whose sweet power
makes my prayers revolt against this proud tyrant?
    Poor princess, to which of the two
    must you be obedient?
Rodrigue, your valor makes you worthy of my name,
but though you are valiant, you are not the son of a
    king.
Pitiless fate whose rigor separates
    my honor from my desire!
Can it be said that the choice of so rare a virtue
costs my passion such deep sorrow?
    What sighs must my heart
    be prepared to utter
if it is never able from so long a torment
to extinguish my love or accept my lover!
I have too many scruples and my reason is amazed
    at my scorn for such a worthy choice.
Although my birth gives me to monarchs alone,
I will live honorably, Rodrigue, under your law.
    Since you conquered two kings,
    could you lack a crown?
Does not the great title of Cid which you have just
    won
show clearly over whom you should reign?
He is worthy of me, but be belongs to Chimene.
    The gift I made is now my undoing.
The death of a father has put so little hate between
    them
that the duty to her family prosecutes him regretfully.
    I must hope for no result
    of his crime or of my suffering,
since, to punish me, fate has allowed
love to continue even between two enemies.

SCENE III.

Infanta, Leonor.

INFANTA: Why do you come, Leonor?
LEONOR: To rejoice, your Highness,
over the peace which your soul has found at last.
INFANTA: How could such peace come into my
    endless pain?
LEONOR: If love lives on hope, and dies with it,
Rodrigue can no longer charm your courage.
You know the fight in which Chimene engages him.
Since either he will die or become her husband,
your hope is over, and your mind is cured.
INFANTA: How far it is from being that!
LEONOR: What do you hope for?
INFANTA: Rather what hope would you forbid me?
If Rodrigue fights under these conditions,
I have many means to change the result.
Love is the author of my cruel suffering
and love teaches wiles to the minds of lovers.
LEONOR: What would your power be, since a dead
    father
could not arouse discord in their minds?
For Chimene easily shows by her conduct
that hate does not direct her prosecution.
She was granted a combat and for her fighter
she just now accepted the first one to offer himself.
She had no recourse to those noble men
who have become famous in their great exploits.
Don Sanche is all she has and he deserves her choice,
because he is fighting for the first time.
In this duel she prefers this lack of experience.
As he is without fame, she is without fear.
The ease of all this must show you
that she is seeking a combat which will fulfill her
    duty,
give Rodrigue an easy victory,
and permit her to appear appeased.
INFANTA: I have seen this, and yet my heart,
as much as Chimene's, worships this conqueror.
How can I be resigned?
LEONOR: You must remember your birth.
Heaven owes you a king, and you are in love with a
    subject!
INFANTA: My passion has changed its object.
I am not in love with Rodrigue, a mere noble.
My feelings give him another name.
I love the author of those marvelous deeds.
I love the valiant Cid, the master of two kings.
Yet I will overcome my feelings, not through fear of
    censure,
but to refrain from tormenting so beautiful a love;
and when, to suit my purpose, he is crowned,
I will not take back what I gave away.
Since his victory in such a battle is certain,
I will once again give him to Chimene.
And you who know the real suffering of my heart,
will watch me accomplish what I began.

SCENE IV.

Chimene, Elvire.

CHIMENE: Elvire, can you see my suffering and my
    plight?
Nothing can be hoped for and everything is to be
    feared.
My heart forms no prayer that is acceptable.
Each of my desires brings a quick repentance.
Two rivals for my hand are in combat,
and the happier outcome will cost me tears.
Whatever fate commands on my behalf,
my father is unavenged or my lover is dead.
ELVIRE: In either way you will be consoled.
Either you have Rodrigue or you are avenged.
And whatever fate decides for you,
it will glorify your honor and give you a husband.
CHIMENE: He will be the object of my hate or my
    anger.
The murderer of Rodrigue or my father's murderer!
In either case, I will have a husband
stained with blood I have cherished.
My soul rebels against both solutions.
More than death I fear the end of my quarrel.
Vengeance and love, bewildering me,
have no consolation at this high price.
May the prime mover of my outrageous fate
end this combat without a victor,
without making one of them a conqueror or a de-
    feated man!
ELVIRE: That would be too harsh an outcome.
The combat will be a new suffering for you
if it obliges you to ask again for justice,
to live with your worthy resentment,
and continue to seek the death of your lover.
It is better that his unusual valor
impose silence on you as it crowns his brow,
that the law of the duel stifle your sighs
and that the King force you to follow your desire.
CHIMENE: When he is victor, do you think I will
    surrender?
My duty is too strong and my loss too great.
The law of the duel and the will of the King
are not enough to make the law for me.
He can overcome Don Sanche with very little effort,
but not so easily the honor of Chimene.
And whatever a monarch has promised the victor,
my honor will make for me a thousand enemies
    more.
ELVIRE: Take care lest Heaven, to punish this
    strange pride,
allow you to be avenged at the end.
Why persist in refusing the joy
of maintaining an honorable silence?
What does your duty expect, and what does it hope
    for?
Will the death of your lover give you back your
    father?

Is one calamity so insignificant for you
that you need loss after loss and grief after grief?
Come now! In the obstinate caprice of your mind
you do not deserve the lover you are destined to
    have.
Heaven in justified anger may well
leave you Don Sanche for a husband after Rodrigue's
    death.
    CHIMENE: Elvire, I have endured enough suffering.
Do not increase it with this fatal augury.
If I can, I will avoid both men.
If I can't, my prayers are for Rodrigue in this duel.
Not that a mad passion inclines me toward him,
but if he were defeated, I would belong to Don
    Sanche.
This fear gives rise to my desire.
    [Don Sanche enters]
It is he, Elvire, all is over!

SCENE V.

Don Sanche, Chimene, Elvire.

    SANCHE: Since I have to lay this sword at your
    feet . . .
    CHIMENE: Still covered with Rodrigue's blood?
Traitor, how can you come into my presence
after taking the life of the man I loved?
Now I can speak of love, there is no need to hide it.
My father is appeased, there is no more constraint.
The same sword assured my honor,
thrust my soul into despair and released my love.
    SANCHE: With a more calm mind . . .
    CHIMENE: You still dare to speak,
and you are the hated slayer of a hero whom I love!
You killed him treacherously. So valiant a warrior
could not have succumbed to such an adversary.
Hope for nothing from me. You did not serve me.
You took life itself away when you thought
        you were avenging me.
    SANCHE: Your false impression—if only you would
    listen . . .
    CHIMENE: Do you want me to listen to you boast
    of his death,
to hear calmly the insolence with which
you depict his woe, my crime, and your bravery?

SCENE VI.

The King, Diegue, Arias, Sanche, Alonso, Chimene, Elvire.

    CHIMENE: Sire, there is no need now to conceal
    from you
what all my efforts were not able to hide.
I was in love. You knew this. But to avenge my
    father,

I was willing to proscribe my beloved.
Your Majesty, Sire, could see
how I subordinated my love to duty.
Now Rodrigue is dead, and his death has changed me
from an implacable enemy into an afflicted lover.
I owed this vengeance to the man who gave me life,
and now I owe these tears to my love.
Don Sanche destroyed me by taking my defense,
and I am the reward for the arm that destroyed me.
Sire, if pity can move a king,
I beg you to revoke so harsh a law.
As a prize for a victory in which I lost the man I
    loved,
I leave him my fortune. And I pray he leave me to
    myself.
In some sacred cloister let me weep without pause,
to the end of my life, for my father and for Rodrigue.
    DIEGUE: She is still in love, Sire, and does not be-
    lieve it a crime
to confess in words so legitimate a love.
Chimene, learn that Rodrigue is not dead.
Don Sanche was defeated and made a false report.
    SANCHE: Sire, she was deceived, in spite of my ef-
    forts, by too much ardor.
I had left the fight in order to tell her of the outcome.
The noble warrior who charms her heart
said when he disarmed me, "Have no fear.
I would rather leave the victory uncertain
than take your life which was risked for Chimene.
But since my duty calls me to the King,
go tell her for me of our combat,
and take her your sword in the name of the victor."
Sire, I went to Chimene. The sword deceived her.
On seeing me, she thought I was the victor,
and her anger at once betrayed her love
with such transport and impatience
that I could not make myself heard.
Although defeated, I look upon myself as fortunate,
and despite the anxiety of my own love,
losing infinitely much, I welcome my defeat
which ensures the noble outcome of so perfect a love.
    KING: My daughter, you must not be ashamed of
this pure love,
nor look for ways of disavowing it.
A praiseworthy shame should have no power over
    you.
Your honor is redeemed and your duty is discharged.
Your father is at peace, and you are avenged
by placing Rodrigue in danger so many times.
You see that Heaven decrees a different end.
Having done so much for your father, do something
    now for yourself.
Do not rebel against my command
which gives you a husband you have loved so dearly.

SCENE VII.

The King, Diegue, Arias, Rodrigue, Alonso,
Sanche, Infanta, Chimene, Leonor, Elvire.

INFANTA: Dry your tears, Chimene, and gladly receive
from the hands of your princess this noble conqueror.

RODRIGUE: Do not be offended, Sire, if in your presence
my loving respect bends my knees before her,
I am not here, Chimene, to demand my conquest.
I have come again to offer you my life.
My love will not exploit for myself
the law of combat or the will of the King.
If all that has been done is too little for a father,
tell me in what way you will be satisfied.
Must I fight a thousand more rivals,
extend my labors to the two extremes of the earth,
attack a camp singlehanded, rout an army,
exceed the fame of legendary heroes?
If my crime can thus be pardoned,
I will undertake and carry out any deed.
But if your proud honor is still unbending,
and will not be appeased without the death of the criminal,
do not arm the power of a man against me.
My head is here before you. Avenge yourself with your own hand.
Your hand alone has the right to overcome me.
Take this vengeance which no one else can.
But then let my death be sufficient for the punishment.
Do not banish me from your memory.
And since my death preserves your honor,
preserve my memory as you take your revenge,
and say at times as you pity my fate,
"If he had not loved me, he would not be dead."

CHIMENE: Stand up, Rodrigue. Let me speak, Sire.
I have said too much, to deny my words.
Rodrigue has a strength I cannot despise.
When a king commands, he should be obeyed.
But to whatever you have condemned me,
can you before your very eyes allow this marriage?
And even if you wish from me this dutiful effort,
can the justice of your kingship permit it?

If Rodrigue becomes so necessary to the state,
must I be the reward for what he does for you?
Must I give myself up to the eternal reproach
of having bathed my hands in the blood of my father?

KING: Often enough, time has justified
what once seemed criminal.
Rodrigue won you. You belong to him.
But although his valor conquered you today,
I would have to be an enemy of your honor
to give him now the reward of his victory.
A deferred marriage will not infringe upon a law
which promises him your faith without heed to time.
Take a year, if you wish, to dry your tears.
In the meantime, Rodrigue, you must take up arms.
After conquering the Moors on our shores,
upsetting their plans and repulsing their efforts,
go wage war on them in their own land,
command my army and pillage their cities.
They will tremble with fear at your name of Cid.
They have called you lord and will want you for a king.
But be faithful to her in all your great deeds.
Come back from there, if that is granted, still more worthy of her.
Have yourself so esteemed by your exploits
that it will be an honor then for her to marry you.

RODRIGUE: In order to marry Chimene and serve you,
I will carry out every command you give.
Whatever I have to endure in my separation from her,
Sire, to be able to hope is my great happiness.

KING: Take hope in your courage and in my promise.
And since you already possess the heart of your beloved,
to triumph over a point of honor which is against you,
rely on time and valor and on your king.

John Gay. His epitaph, written by himself, reads: "Life is a jest, and all things show it; I thought so once, but now I know it." *Opposite page: The Beggar's Opera,* Act I, Scene I. Engraving dated February 21, 1823, from a painting by G. Clint of Blanchard, Mrs. Davenport, and Miss M. Tree, as Peachum, Mrs. Peachum, and Polly. From Doran, *Their Majesties Servants, Annals of the English Stage,* Vol. I. Theatre Collection, Library and Museum of the Performing Arts at Lincoln Center.

Ballad Opera and Burlesque

Ballad Opera and Burlesque

Until the nineteen-twenties we were unfamiliar with the genre of "ballad opera" in the American theatre, although it was sufficiently familiar to us in English literature courses and the British stage had been hospitable to the *The Beggar's Opera*, the masterpiece of the genre, for a century and a half. Our ignorance, however, was replaced with delight in the 'twenties when the devotees of avantgarde theatre developed a taste for sophisticated comedies and a number of Restoration and eighteenth-century pieces received stage productions. Among these was John Gay's *The Beggar's Opera*, the classic of English ballad opera. This entrancing work, however, soon came to be taken for granted and the genre it so charmingly represented was all but forgotten in the professional theatre, until interest in the work was once more revived by *Die Dreigroschenoper*, or *The Threepenny Opera*, by the celebrated German playwright Bertolt Brecht and his gifted composer-collaborator, Kurt Weill. Although *The Threepenny Opera* had won sensational success in Central Europe in 1928, it had its first successful American production in an adaptation by Marc Blitzstein, which opened at the Greenwich Village Theatre de Lys on March 10, 1954. It had such a long run there and has been staged so frequently elsewhere in university and community theatres that it seems strange that this type of play could have escaped our attention for so long a time.

In the eighteenth century, ballad opera had a considerable vogue after the success of Gay's play, and several variant forms appeared. If we stretch the definitions of the term *ballad opera* to cover all the musical potpourris that have reached the stage anywhere, with or without benefit of a satirical frame of reference, it may be said to represent a bountiful area of entertainment. Its kinship with musical comedy and revues is certainly considerable. In possessing two such masterpieces as *The Beggar's Opera* from the year 1728 and *The Threepenny Opera* from the year 1928 (exactly two centuries later) the genre is not an inconsequential one.

A specific historical interest also pertains to ballad opera as an extension of the art of burlesque (not to be confused with mere lascivious displays of pulchritude) or dramatic caricature and parody. *The Beggar's Opera* and its sequel *Polly* burlesqued Italian opera with its elaborate resort to arias and verbal flourishes at a time when it had gained considerable vogue in England. As parodies, Gay's ballad operas belong to a tradition at least as old as Aristophanes' *The Frogs*, in which Aeschylus and Euripides poke fun at each other's dramatic style (pages 85–94). And there are examples of parody in the "Pyramus and Thisbe" performance in *A Midsummer Night's Dream*, in the first Player's scene in *Hamlet* (Act II, Scene II), and The Duke of Buckingham's *The Re-*hearsal* (1672) which half a century before *The Beggar's Opera* satirized Restoration "heroic tragedy."

After Gay, the career of literary burlesque in the English theatre acquired other noteworthy practitioners. In 1730 came Henry Fielding's lively and well-aimed satire on the inflated style of heroic tragedy, *The Tragedy of Tragedies; or The Life and Death of Tom Thumb the Great*. Fielding also succeeded with his *Welsh Opera* (1731), a ballad opera burlesquing the British royal family. Gilbert and Sullivan's comic opera *Patience* (1881), ridiculing the Victorian esthetic movement, is the best-known English musical satire. But W. S. Gilbert, writing without any collaboration with Sullivan, turned out a superb parody of *Hamlet* in 1891, entitled *Rosencrantz and Guilderstern*, in which King Claudius makes the dire confession that "Many years since—when but a headstrong lad—I wrote a five-act tragedy" but that

Ere the first act had traced one-half its course
The curtain fell, never to rise again.

Claudius adds that "The acts were five—though by five acts too long."

In France, the vogue of burlesques and so-called vaudeville was always strong. Medieval French theatre inclined toward the genre in *soties* or short topical skits on political and social matters. Molière wrote masterpieces in this vein such as *Les précieuses ridicules* and *The Learned Ladies* (*Les Femmes savantes*), although the latter is essentially a high comedy. Several of his plays were also comedy-ballets, blending dialogue and dance with music by Lulli and other composers. The assiduous Eugene Scribe, the late nineteenth-century *farceurs* Labiche, Courteline, and the extravagantly funny Feydeau often approached burlesque in their work. Toward the very end of the century came Alfred Jarry's influential extravaganza *Ubu Roi* (*King Ubu*), published in 1896 and performed in the same year at Lugne-Poë's little experimental theatre, in the Theâtre de l'Oeuvre, with the celebrated actor Firmin Gémier in the title role of the swinish mediocrity who is the embodiment of human stupidity and brutishness. And Jarry's French successors of the loosely labeled "theatre of the absurd" (they are to be found in England and America, too) have accounted for much that has passed for modernism on the avant-garde stages since World War II. The best known of these current practitioners of the "absurd," Eugene Ionesco (born in Rumania in 1912) started his ascent in the theatre with a burlesque masterpiece, *The Bald Soprano*, in 1948.

In Russia, burlesque started effectively in the nineteenth century. Gogol's *The Inspector General* (see pages 598–633) has excellent elements of burlesque,

846

and Chekhov wrote a collection of frequently performed one-act "vaudevilles" before the production of his full-length masterpieces. After the Russian Revolution, antibourgeois sentiment was a natural incitement to extravagant satirists, notably the futurist poet Mayakovsky in *The Bedbug*. And in Germany, indeed in most of Central Europe, during the first half of the twentieth century, there not only was Brecht with a variety of work in the burlesque vein, reflecting both his early Dadaist and later Marxist and anti-Nazi attitudes, but Karl Sternheim 1878–1943), who flayed the German middle class in satire after satire with expressionistic extravagance.

The American theatre, beginning in the sophisticated nineteen-twenties but continuing on into the nineteen-thirties followed suit with the farce-comedies of George S. Kaufman and his collaborators which satirized Hollywood in *Once in a Lifetime,* "tin-pan alley" popular-music business in *June Moon,* and American mass-production industry and art in the expressionistic *Beggar on Horseback.* The American theatre became very successful with its musical variant of satire, with or without parody, in musical comedies such as *Pal Joey* and *Kiss Me Kate* and in musical revues, beginning with the famous *Grand Street Follies* and the Theatre Guild's *Garrick Gaieties* by

Richard Rodgers and Lorenz Hart. The vogue of satirical revues continues, and one of their most successful techniques is parody. A recently successful musical comedy, *Little Mary Sunshine,* consisted entirely of "spoofs" on the romantic operettas of the early twentieth-century theatre. Obviously the ghost of John Gay and the spirit of his art of ballad opera has outlasted the eighteenth century, although it was specifically that century that had inspired it with its flair for deflationary humor, which even the vogue of romanticism could not completely extinguish.[1]

[1] Evidence of the persistence of satirical parody will be found in Byron's satire poetry (such as *The Vision of Judgment,* a travesty on the romantic poet Southey, who had become a conservative apologist) and Shelley's satire on Wordsworth, who had also turned conservative, *Peter Bell the Third* and the burlesque drama *Oedipus Tyrannus, or Swellfoot the Tyrant,* aimed at King George IV's matrimonial affairs. In Germany, the intensely romantic playwright Heinrich Kleist turned out an extremely amusing satiric farce *The Broken Jug* (1811), and his contemporary Ludwig Tieck several folk-tale spoofs such as *Bluebeard, Puss-in-Boots (Der gestiefelte Kater),* and *The Life and Death of Little Riding Hood,* in which Little Red Riding Hood has a rationalistic mother and the Wolf is a disenchanted idealist.

John Gay and The Beggar's Opera

A sophisticated man about town with a penchant for a mildly sybaritic existence, John Gay (1685–1732) took a suggestion from one of his distinguished acquaintances, Jonathan Swift, to write a "Newgate pastoral," as it could be "an odd pretty sort of thing." The immediate result of this frivolous enterprise in 1728 was a masterpiece which brought its author a profit of some eight hundred pounds (a goodly sum in the early eighteenth century) from the London production by John Rich, the manager of the Lincoln's Inn Fields theatre. (It also inspired the quip that The Beggar's Opera made "Gay rich and Rich gay.")

The beneficiary of this windfall, who might have also made a good profit on the successfully published sequel Polly had the Lord Chancellor not forbidden a stage production for it, started his literary career diffidently in 1708 with the publication of a poem, "Wine," in which that beverage was declared indispensable to literary creativity. Launched into society in a fashion, Gay, whose less than prosperous family had a long pedigree, acquired such distinguished friends as Lord Bolingbroke and the poet Alexander Pope. He also attained congenial employment in 1712 for two years as secretary to the Duchess of Monmouth, and in 1714 published a long poem, Rural Sports, and wrote occasional pieces for Richard Steele's periodical Guardian. A year later, his Shepherd's Week appeared; it consists of eclogues, or pastoral poems, in mock-heroic classical style that made amusing comment on the times. This was followed, after Gay's visit to the court of Hanover on a diplomatic mission, by his first play. It was a satirical afterpiece or short farce, burlesquing high-flown neoclassic drama like Joseph Addison's once acclaimed Cato; it was briskly called What d'ye Call It (1715). Next came his amusing poem on eighteenth-century manners, aptly entitled Trivia, and then, in 1717, his collaboration with other London wits, and, with the poet Alexander Pope and the essayist Thomas Arbuthnot, on a comedy called Three Hours After Marriage.

After a financial disaster caused by speculation in South Seas funds and other unlikely ventures, he found congenial shelter in the home of highly placed patrons, the Duke and Duchess of Queensbury, and continued to devote himself to writing wittily and at leisure. The delightful results appeared first in a series of Fables, which gained considerable popularity in 1727, and then The Beggar's Opera (1728) and its unproduced sequel, Polly, in both of which he excelled with ballad writing as well as general satire. He further served the musical stage with librettos for Handel's operas Acis and Galatea (1732) and Achilles (1733).

The premiere of Gay's dramatic masterpiece is charmingly described by Alexander Pope in Spenser's Anecdotes:[1]

> We were all, at the first night of it, in great uncertainty of the event; till we heard the Duke of Argyll, who sat in the next box to us, say: "It will do, it must do! I see it in the eyes of them." This was a good while before the first act was over, and gave us ease soon; for the Duke (besides his own good taste) has a particular knack, as any one now living, in discovering the taste of the public. He was quite right in this, as usual; the good nature of the audience appeared stronger and stronger every act, and ended in a clamor of applause. Never was a triumph more complete.

After an unprecedented run of sixty-three days in London, The Beggar's Opera toured the provinces. Its Polly, the young actress Lavinia Fenton, became the toast of London and later married a duke. (A parallel career awaited the Polly of the Berlin production of The Threepenny Opera, Lotte Lenya, who won celebrity overnight and later married the gifted composer of the music, Kurt Weill.) The most popular songs were painted on silk screens and ladies' fans, and the scene in which Gay's impressionable gentleman-highwayman Macheath wavers between his two loves Polly and Lucy became the subject of several paintings by Hogarth.

Although The Beggar's Opera was richly allusive and conveyed political satire, leveled particularly at England's first prime minister, Sir William Walpole, this comedy transcends topicality. It sparkles almost continually as a result of Gay's aptitude for reversing accepted values of glamor, romance, love and marriage, on the one hand, and morality, political integrity and honorable business enterprise, on the other. Its hero is a highwayman whose opponent is an informer and a receiver of stolen goods. There is a truly dadaist inversion and dissociation of morals in the work. The world it pictures is that of laissez faire, of social Darwinism before the time of Darwin, and of all-pervading hypocrisy in public and private relationships and in romantic situations. At the same time, it is not to be forgotten that Gay's theatrical tour de force was primarily intended for ironic en-

[1] Quoted in Representative English Dramas from John Dryden to Sheridan. Edited by Frederick Tupper and James W. Tupper. New York: Oxford University Press, 1934, p. 475.

tertainment. This effect is uppermost when Polly's mother, Mrs. Peachum, for example, is outraged that her daughter would marry for love and exclaims, "I thought the girl had been better bred!" and when she asks her somewhat earlier "Can you support the expense of a husband . . . have you money enough to carry on the daily quarrels of man and wife about who shall squander most?" while Mr. Peachum expostulates, "Do you think your mother and I should have lived comfortably so long together if ever we had been married? Baggage!" Mrs. Peachum is also upset that her highwayman son-in-law Macheath gambles with gentlemen: "What business hath he to keep company with lords and gentlemen? he should leave them to prey upon one another." The talents fused in the making of *The Beggar's Opera* are Gay's genius for comic characterization and dialogue and his talent for composing lyrics to popular old tunes such as "Greensleeves," "Lillebullero," and "Over the Hills and Far Away." They are delightful, as a rule, whether they are as irreverent as the first song coming to the conclusion "All professions be-rogue one another" or as hearty as

Were I laid on Greenland's coast
And in my arms embrac'd my lass:
Warm amidst eternal frost,
Too soon the half year's night would pass.

One thing remains to be noted about *The Beggar's Opera* that no discussion of its genre alone can cover —namely, the special grace that is its *style,* in the full sense of the term. No one has written more pointedly about it than the English essayist William Hazlitt:

He chose a very unpromising ground to work upon, and he has prided himself in adorning it with all the graces, the precision and brilliancy of style. It is a vulgar error to call this a vulgar play. So far from it that we do not scruple to declare our opinion that it is one of the most refined productions in the language. The elegance of the composition is in exact proportion to the coarseness of the materials: by "happy alchemy of mind," the author has extracted an essence of refinement from the dregs of human life, and turns its very dross into gold. The scenes, characters, and incidents are, in themselves, of the lowest and most disgusting kind: but, by the sentiments and reflections which are put into the mouths of highwaymen, turnkeys, their mistresses, wives, or daughters, he has converted this motley group into a set of fine gentlemen and ladies, satirists and philosophers.[1]

[1] William Hazlitt, *The Round Table and Characters of Shakespeare's Plays,* In Everyman's Library, No. 65. London and New York: Dutton, p. 65.

THE BEGGAR'S OPERA

By John Gay

CHARACTERS

PEACHUM
LOCKIT
MACHEATH
FILCH
JEMMY TWITCHER ⎫
CROOK-FINGER'D JACK ⎪
WAT DREARY ⎪
ROBIN OF BAGSHOT ⎬ *Macheath's Gang*
NIMMING NED ⎪
HARRY PADINGTON ⎪
MATT OF THE MINT ⎭
BEN BUDGE
BEGGAR

PLAYER
MRS. PEACHUM
POLLY PEACHUM
LUCY LOCKIT
DIANA TRAPES
MRS. COAXER ⎫
DOLLY TRULL ⎪
MRS. VIXEN ⎪
BETTY DOXY ⎪
JENNY DIVER ⎬ *Women of the Town*
MRS. SLAMMEKIN ⎪
SUKY TAWDRY ⎪
MOLLY BRAZEN ⎭
CONSTABLES, DRAWER, TURNKEY, &c.

INTRODUCTION*

Beggar, Player.

BEGGAR: If Poverty be a Title to Poetry, I am sure No-body can dispute mine. I own myself of the Company of Beggars; and I make one at their Weekly Festivals at St. Giles. I have a small Yearly Salary for my Catches, and am welcome to a Dinner there whenever I please, which is more than most Poets can say.

PLAYER: As we live by the Muses, 'tis but Gratitude in us to encourage Poetical Merit where-ever we find it. The Muses, contrary to all other Ladies, pay no Distinction to Dress, and never partially mistake the Pertness of Embroidery for Wit, nor the Modesty of Want for Dullness. Be the Author who he will, we push his Play as far as it will go. So (though you are in Want) I wish you Success heartily.

BEGGAR: This Piece I own was originally writ for the celebrating the Marriage of James Chanter and Moll Lay, two most excellent Ballad-Singers. I have introduc'd the Similes that are in all your celebrated Operas: The Swallow, the Moth, the Bee, the Ship, the Flower, &c. Besides, I have a Prison Scene which the Ladies always reckon charmingly pathetick. As to the Parts, I have observ'd such a nice Impartiality to our two Ladies, that it is impossible for either of them to take Offence. I hope I may be forgiven, that I have not made my Opera throughout unnatural, like those in vogue; for I have no Recitative: Excepting this, as I have consented to have neither Prologue nor Epilogue, it must be allow'd an Opera in all its forms. The Piece indeed hath been heretofore frequently represented by our selves in our great Room at St.

* The Eighteenth-century capitalization has been retained because it accentuates humor and innuendo.

Giles's, so that I cannot too often acknowledge your Charity in bringing it now on the Stage.

PLAYER: But I see 'tis time for us to withdraw; the Actors are preparing to begin. Play away the Overture. [*Exeunt*]

ACT I. SCENE I.

Peachum's *House*.

PEACHUM: [*Sitting at a table with a large book of accounts before him*]

AIR

Through all the Employments of Life
Each Neighbour abuses his Brother;
Whore and Rogue they call Husband and Wife:
All Professions be-rogue one another.
The Priest calls the Lawyer a Cheat,
The Lawyer be-knaves the Divine;
And the Statesman, because he's so great,
Thinks his Trade as honest as mine.

A Lawyer is an honest Employment, so is mine. Like me too he acts in a double Capacity, both against Rogues and for 'em; for 'tis but fitting that we should protect and encourage Cheats, since we live by them.

SCENE II.

Peachum, Filch.

FILCH: Sir, Black Moll hath sent word her Tryal comes on in the Afternoon, and she hopes you will order Matters so as to bring her off.

PEACHUM: Why, she may plead her Belly[1] at worst; to my Knowledge she hath taken care of that Security. But as the Wench is very active and industrious, you may satisfy her that I'll soften the Evidence.

FILCH: Tom Gagg, Sir, is found guilty.

PEACHUM: A lazy Dog! When I took him the time before, I told him what he would come to if he did not mend his Hand. This is Death without Reprieve. I may venture to Book him. [Writes] For Tom Gagg, forty Pounds. Let Betty Sly know that I'll save her from Transportation, for I can get more by her staying in England.

FILCH: Betty hath brought more Goods into our Lock[2] to-year than any five of the Gang; and in truth, 'tis a pity to lose so good a Customer.

PEACHUM: If none of the Gang take her off, she may, in the common course of Business, live a Twelve-month longer. I love to let Women scape. A good Sportsman always lets the Hen Partridges fly, because the breed of the Game depends upon them. Besides, here the Law allows us no Reward; there is nothing to be got by the Death of Women—except our Wives.

FILCH: Without dispute, she is a fine Woman! 'Twas to her I was oblig'd for my Education, and (to say a bold Word) she hath train'd up more young Fellows to the Business than the Gaming-table.

PEACHUM: Truly, Filch, thy Observation is right. We and the Surgeons are more beholden to Women than all the Professions besides.

AIR

FILCH: *'Tis Woman that seduces all Mankind,*
By her we first were taught the wheedling Arts:
Her very Eyes can cheat; when most she's kind,
She tricks us of our Money with our Hearts.
For her, like Wolves by night we roam for Prey,
And practise ev'ry Fraud to bribe her Charms;
For Suits of Love, like Law, are won by Pay,
And Beauty must be fee'd into our Arms.

PEACHUM: But make haste to Newgate, Boy, and let my Friends know what I intend; for I love to make them easy one way or another.

FILCH: When a Gentleman is long kept in suspence, Penitence may break his Spirit ever after. Besides, Certainty gives a Man a good Air upon his Tryal, and makes him risque another without Fear or Scruple. But I'll away, for 'tis a Pleasure to be the Messenger of Comfort to Friends in Affliction.

SCENE III.

PEACHUM: But 'tis now high time to look about me for a decent Execution against next Sessions. I hate

[1] Pregnant women were exempted from execution.
[2] A warehouse where stolen goods were hidden away; "to-year," this year.

a lazy Rogue, by whom one can get nothing 'til he is hang'd. A Register of the Gang, [Reading] "Crook-finger'd Jack." A Year and a half in the Service; Let me see how much the Stock owes to his Industry; one, two, three, four, five Gold Watches, and seven Silver ones. A mighty clean-handed Fellow! Sixteen Snuff-boxes, five of them of true Gold. Six dozen of Handkerchiefs, four silver-hilted Swords, half a dozen of Shirts, three Tye-Perriwigs, and a Piece of Broad Cloth. Considering these are only the Fruits of his leisure Hours, I don't know a prettier Fellow, for no Man alive hath a more engaging Presence of Mind upon the Road. "Wat Dreary, alias Brown Will," an irregular Dog, who hath an underhand way of disposing of his Goods. I'll try him only for a Sessions or two longer upon his good Behaviour. "Harry Padington," a poor petty-larceny Rascal, without the least Genius; that Fellow, though he were to live these six Months, will never come to the Gallows with any Credit. "Slippery Sam;" he goes off the next Sessions, for the Villain hath the Impudence to have views of following his Trade as a Taylor, which he calls an honest Employment. "Mat of the Mint;" listed not above a Month ago, a promising sturdy Fellow, and diligent in his way; somewhat too bold and hasty, and may raise good Contributions on the Publick, if he does not cut himself short by Murder. "Tom Tipple" a guzzling soaking Sot, who is always too drunk to stand himself, or to make others stand. A Cart is absolutely necessary for him. "Robin of Bagshot, alias Gorgon, alias Bluff Bob, alias Carbuncle, alias Bob Booty."

SCENE IV.

Peachum, Mrs. Peachum.

MRS. PEACHUM: What of Bob Booty, Husband? I hope nothing bad hath betided him. You know, my Dear, he's a favourite Customer of mine. 'Twas he made me a Present of this Ring.

PEACHUM: I have set his Name down in the Black-List, that's all, my Dear; he spends his Life among Women, and as soon as his Money is gone, one or other of the Ladies will hang him for the Reward, and there's forty Pound lost to us for-ever.

MRS. PEACHUM: You know, my Dear, I never meddle in matters of Death; I always leave those Affairs to you. Women indeed are bitter bad Judges in these cases, for they are so partial to the Brave that they think every Man handsome who is going to the Camp or the Gallows.

AIR

If any Wench Venus's Girdle wear,
Though she be never so ugly;
Lillys and Roses will quickly appear,
And her Face look wond'rous smuggly.

Beaneath the left Ear so fit but a Cord,
(A Rope so charming a Zone is!)
The Youth in his Cart[3] *hath the Air of a Lord,*
And we cry, There dies an Adonis!

But really, Husband, you should not be too hard-hearted, for you never had a finer, braver set of Men than at present. We have not had a Murder among them all, these seven Months. And truly, my Dear, that is a great Blessing.

PEACHUM: What a dickens is the Woman always a whimpring about Murder for? No Gentleman is ever look'd upon the worse for killing a Man in his own Defence; and if Business cannot be carried on without it, what would you have a Gentleman do?

MRS. PEACHUM: If I am in the wrong, my Dear, you must excuse me, for No-body can help the Frailty of an overscrupulous Conscience.

PEACHUM: Murder is as fashionable a Crime as a Man can be guilty of. How many fine Gentlemen have we in Newgate every Year, purely upon that Article! If they have wherewithal to persuade the Jury to bring it in Manslaughter, what are the worse for it? So, my Dear, have done upon this Subject. Was Captain Macheath here this Morning, for the Bank-notes he left with you last Week?

MRS. PEACHUM: Yes, my Dear; and though the Bank hath stopt Payment, he was so cheerful and so agreeable! Sure there is not a finer Gentleman upon the Road than the Captain! If he comes from Bagshot at any reasonable Hour he hath promis'd to make one this Evening with Polly and me, and Bob Booty, at a Party of Quadrille. Pray, my Dear, is the Captain rich?

PEACHUM: The Captain keeps too good Company ever to grow rich. Marybone[4] and the Chocolate-houses are his undoing. The Man that proposes to get Money by Play should have the Education of a fine Gentleman, and be train'd up to it from his Youth.

MRS. PEACHUM: Really, I am sorry upon Polly's Account the Captain hath not more Discretion. What business hath he to keep Company with Lords and Gentlemen? he should leave them to prey upon one another.

PEACHUM: Upon Polly's Account! What, a Plague, does the Woman mean?—Upon Polly's Account!

MRS. PEACHUM: Captain Macheath is very fond of the Girl.

PEACHUM: And what then?

MRS. PEACHUM: If I have any Skill in the Ways of Women, I am sure Polly thinks him a very pretty Man.

PEACHUM: And what then? You would not be so mad to have the Wench marry him! Gamesters and Highwaymen are generally very good to their Whores, but they are very Devils to their Wives.

MRS. PEACHUM: But if Polly should be in love,

[3] The cart in which condemned are taken to the gallows.

[4] A London gambling resort.

how should we help her, or how can she help herself? Poor Girl, I am in the utmost Concern about her.

AIR

If Love the Virgin's Heart invade,
How, like a Moth, the simple Maid
Still plays about the Flame!
If soon she be not made a Wife,
Her Honour's sing'd, and then for Life,
She's—what I dare not name.

PEACHUM: Look ye, Wife. A handsome Wench in our way of Business is as profitable as at the Bar of a Temple Coffee-House, who looks upon it as her livelihood to grant every Liberty but one. You see I would indulge the Girl as far as prudently we can. In any thing, but Marriage! After that, my Dear, how shall we be safe? Are we not then in her Husband's Power? For a Husband hath the absolute Power over all a Wife's Secrets but her own. If the Girl had the Discretion of a Court Lady, who can have a dozen young Fellows at her Ear without complying with one, I should not matter it; but Polly is Tinder, and a Spark will at once set her on a Flame. Married! If the Wench does not know her own Profit, sure she knows her own Pleasure better than to make herself a Property! My Daughter to me should be, like a Court Lady to a Minister of State, a Key to the whole Gang. Married! If the Affair is not already done, I'll terrify her from it, by the Example of our Neighbours.

MRS. PEACHUM: May-hap, my Dear, you may injure the Girl. She loves to imitate the fine Ladies, and she may only allow the Captain Liberties in the View of Interest.

PEACHUM: But 'tis your Duty, my Dear, to warn the Girl against her Ruin, and to instruct her how to make the most of her Beauty. I'll go to her this moment, and sift her. In the mean time, Wife, rip out the Coronets and Marks of these dozen of Cambric Handkerchiefs, for I can dispose of them this Afternoon to a Chap in the City. ·

SCENE V.

MRS. PEACHUM: Never was a Man more out of the way in an Argument than my Husband! Why must our Polly, forsooth, differ from her Sex, and love only her Husband? And why must Polly's Marriage, contrary to all Observation, make her the less followed by other Men? All Men are Thieves in Love, and like a Woman the better for being another's Property.

AIR

A Maid is like the golden Oar,
Which hath Guineas intrinsical in't,
Whose Worth is never known before

It is try'd and imprest in the Mint.
  A Wife's like a Guinea in Gold,
Stampt with the Name of her Spouse;
  Now here, now there; is bought, or is sold;
And is current in every House.

SCENE VI.

Mrs. Peachum, Filch.

MRS. PEACHUM: Come hither, Filch. I am as fond of this Child, as though my Mind misgave me he were my own. He hath as fine a Hand at picking a Pocket as a Woman, and is as nimble-finger'd as a Juggler. If an unlucky Session does not cut the Rope of thy Life, I pronounce, Boy, thou wilt be a great Man in History. Where was your Post last Night, my Boy?

FILCH: I ply'd at the Opera, Madam; and considering 'twas neither dark nor rainy, so that there was no great Hurry in getting Chairs and Coaches, made a tolerable hand on't. These seven Handkerchiefs, Madam.

MRS. PEACHUM: Colour'd ones, I see. They are of sure Sale from our Warehouse at Redress among the Seamen.

FILCH: And this Snuff-box.

MRS. PEACHUM: Set in Gold! A pretty Encouragement this to a young Beginner.

FILCH: I had a fair tug at a charming Gold Watch. Pox take the Taylors for making the Fobs so deep and narrow! It stuck by the way, and I was forc'd to make my Escape under a Coach. Really, Madam, I fear I shall be cut off in the Flower of my Youth, so that every now and then (since I was pumpt) I have thoughts of taking up and going to Sea.

MRS. PEACHUM: You should go to Hockley in the Hole, and to Marybone, Child, to learn Valour. These are the Schools that have bred so many brave Men. I thought, Boy, by this time, thou hadst lost Fear as well as Shame. Poor Lad! how little does he know as yet of the Old-Bailey! For the first Fact I'll insure thee from being hang'd; and going to Sea, Filch, will come time enough upon a Sentence of Transportation. But now, since you have nothing better to do, ev'n go to your Book, and learn your Catechism; for really a Man makes but an ill Figure in the Ordinary's[4] Paper, who cannot give a satisfactory Answer to his Questions. But, hark you, my Lad. Don't tell me a Lye; for you know I hate a Lyar. Do you know of any thing that hath past between Captain Macheath and our Polly?

FILCH: I beg you, Madam, don't ask me; for I must either tell a Lye to you or to Miss Polly; for I promis'd her I would not tell.

MRS. PEACHUM: But when the Honour of our Family is concern'd—

FILCH: I shall lead a sad Life with Miss Polly, if

ever she come to know that I told you. Besides, I would not willingly forfeit my own Honour by betraying any body.

MRS. PEACHUM: Yonder comes my Husband and Polly. Come, Filch, you shall go with me into my own Room, and tell me the whole Story. I'll give thee a glass of a most delicious Cordial that I keep for my own drinking.

SCENE VII.

Peachum, Polly.

POLLY: I know as well as any of the fine Ladies how to make the most of my self and of my Man too. A Woman knows how to be mercenary, though she hath never been in a Court or at an Assembly. We have it in our Natures, Papa. If I allow Captain Macheath some trifling Liberties, I have this Watch and other visible Marks of his Favour to show for it. A Girl who cannot grant some Things, and refuse what is most material, will make but a poor hand of her Beauty, and soon be thrown upon the Common.

AIR

Virgins are like the fair Flower in its Lustre,
Which in the Garden enamels the Ground;
Near it the Bees in Play flutter and cluster,
And gaudy Butterflies frolick around.
But, when once pluck'd, 'tis no longer alluring,
To Covent-Garden 'tis sent (as yet sweet).
There fades, and shrinks, and grows past all enduring,
Rots, stinks, and dies, and is trod under feet.

PEACHUM: You know, Polly, I am not against your toying and trifling with a Customer in the way of Business, or to get out a Secret, or so. But if I find out that you have play'd the fool and are married, you Jade you, I'll cut your Throat, Hussy. Now you know my Mind.

SCENE VIII.

Peachum, Polly, Mrs. Peachum.

MRS. PEACHUM: [*In a very great Passion*]

AIR

Our Polly is a sad Slut! nor heeds what we taught her.
I wonder any Man alive will ever rear a Daughter!
For she must have both Hoods and Gowns, and
  Hoops to swell her Pride.
With Scarfs and Stays, and Gloves and Lace; and she
  will have Men beside;

And when she's drest with Care and Cost, all-tempting, fine and gay,
As Men should serve a Cowcumber, she flings herself away.
Our Polly is a sad Slut, &c.

You Baggage! you Hussy! you inconsiderate Jade! had you been hang'd, it would not have vex'd me, for that might have been your Misfortune; but to do such a mad thing by Choice! The Wench is married, Husband.

PEACHUM: Married! The Captain is a bold man, and will risque any thing for Money; to be sure he believes her a Fortune. Do you think your Mother and I should have liv'd comfortably so long together, if ever we had been married? Baggage!

MRS. PEACHUM: I knew she was always a proud slut; and now the Wench hath play'd the Fool and married, because forsooth she would do like the Gentry. Can you support the expence of a Husband, Hussy, in gaming, drinking and whoring? have you Money enough to carry on the daily Quarrels of Man and Wife about who shall squander most? There are not many Husbands and Wifes, who can bear the Charges of plaguing one another in a handsome way. If you must be married, could you introduce no-body into our Family but a Highwayman? Why, thou foolish Jade, thou wilt be as ill-us'd, and as much neglected, as if thou hadst married a Lord!

PEACHUM: Let not your Anger, my Dear, break through the Rules of Decency, for the Captain looks upon himself in the Military Capacity, as a Gentleman by his Profession. Besides what he hath already, I know he is in a fair way of getting, or of dying; and both these ways, let me tell you, are most excellent Chances for a Wife. Tell me, Hussy, are you ruin'd or no?

MRS. PEACHUM: With Polly's Fortune, she might very well have gone off to a Person of Distinction. Yes, that you might, you pouting Slut!

PEACHUM: What, is the Wench dumb? Speak, or I'll make you plead by squeezing out an Answer from you. Are you really bound Wife to him, or are you only upon liking? [*Pinches her*]

POLLY: Oh! [*Screaming*]

MRS. PEACHUM: How the Mother is to be pitied who hath handsome Daughters! Locks, Bolts, Bars, and Lectures of Morality are nothing to them: They break through them all. They have as much Pleasure in cheating a Father and Mother, as in cheating at Cards.

PEACHUM: Why, Polly, I shall soon know if you are married, by Macheath's keeping from our House.

AIR

POLLY: *Can Love be controul'd by Advice?*
Will Cupid our Mothers obey?
Though my Heart were as frozen as Ice,
At his Flame 'twould have melted away.

When he kist me so closely he prest,
'Twas so sweet that I must have comply'd:
So I thought it both safest and best
To marry, for fear you should chide.

MRS. PEACHUM: Then all the Hopes of our Family are gone for ever and ever!

PEACHUM: And Macheath may hang his Father and Mother-in-Law, in hope to get into their Daughter's Fortune.

POLLY: I did not marry him (as 'tis the Fashion) cooly and deliberately for Honour or Money. But, I love him.

MRS. PEACHUM: Love him! worse and worse! I thought the Girl had been better bred. Oh Husband, Husband! her Folly makes me mad! my Head swims! I'm distracted! I can't support myself—Oh! [*Faints*]

PEACHUM: See, Wench, to what a Condition you have reduc'd your poor Mother! a Glass of Cordial, this instant. How the poor woman takes it to Heart!

[*Polly goes out, and returns with it*]

Ah, Hussy, now this is the only Comfort your Mother has left!

POLLY: Give her another Glass, Sir; my Mama drinks double the Quantity whenever she is out of Order. This, you see, fetches her.

MRS. PEACHUM: The Girl shows such a Readiness, and so much Concern, that I could almost find in my Heart to forgive her.

AIR

O Polly, you might have toy'd and kist.
By keeping Men off, you keep them on.
POLLY: *But he so teaz'd me,*
And he so pleas'd me,
What I did you must have done.

MRS. PEACHUM: Not with a Highwayman.—You sorry Slut!

PEACHUM: A Word with you, Wife. 'Tis no new thing for a Wench to take a Man without consent of Parents. You know 'tis the Frailty of Woman, my Dear.

MRS. PEACHUM: Yes, indeed, the Sex is frail. But the first time a Woman is frail, she should be somewhat nice methinks, for then or never is the time to make her Fortune. After that, she hath nothing to do but to guard herself from being found out, and she may do what she pleases.

PEACHUM: Make your self a little easy; I have a Thought shall soon set all Matters again to rights. Why so melancholy, Polly? since what is done cannot be undone, we must all endeavour to make the best of it.

MRS. PEACHUM: Well, Polly; as far as one woman can forgive another, I forgive thee.—Your Father is too fond of you, Hussy.

POLLY: Then all my Sorrows are at an end.

MRS. PEACHUM: A mighty likely Speech in troth, for a Wench who is just married!

AIR

POLLY: *I, like a Ship in Storms, was tost;*
Yet afraid to put into Land;
For seiz'd in the Port the Vessel's lost,
Whose Treasure is contreband.
    The Waves are laid,
    My Duty's paid.
O Joy beyond Expression!
    Thus, safe a-shore,
    I ask no more,
My All is in my Possession.

PEACHUM: I hear Customers in t'other Room; Go, talk with 'em, Polly; but come to us again, as soon as they are gone.—But, heark ye, Child, if 'tis the Gentleman who was here Yesterday about the Repeating-Watch; say, you believe we can't get Intelligence of it, till to-morrow. For I lent it to Suky Straddle, to make a Figure with it to-night at a Tavern in Drury-Lane. If t'other Gentleman calls for the Silver-hilted Sword; you know Beetle-brow'd Jemmy hath it on, and he doth not come from Tunbridge till Tuesday Night; so that it cannot be had till then.

SCENE IX.

Peachum, Mrs. Peachum.

PEACHUM: Dear Wife, be a little pacified. Don't let your Passion run away with your Senses. Polly, I grant you, hath done a rash thing.

MRS. PEACHUM: If she had had only an Intrigue with the Fellow, why the very best Families have excus'd and huddled up a Frailty of that sort. 'Tis Marriage, Husband, that makes it a blemish.

PEACHUM: But Money, Wife, is the true Fuller's Earth for Reputations, there is not a Spot or a Stain but what it can take out. A rich Rogue now-a-days is fit Company for any Gentleman; and the World, my Dear, hath not such a Contempt for Roguery as you imagine. I tell you, Wife, I can make this Match turn to our Advantage.

MRS. PEACHUM: I am very sensible, Husband, that Captain Macheath is worth Money, but I am in doubt whether he hath not two or three Wives already, and then if he should dye in a Session or two, Polly's Dower would come into Dispute.

PEACHUM: That, indeed, is a Point which ought to be consider'd.

AIR

A Fox may steal your Hens, Sir,
A Whore your Health and Pence, Sir,
Your Daughter rob your Chest, Sir,
Your Wife may steal your Rest, Sir,
A Thief your Goods and Plate.
But this is all but picking;
With Rest, Pence, Chest and Chicken,
It ever was decreed, Sir,
If Lawyer's Hand is fee'd, Sir,
He steals your whole Estate.

The Lawyers are bitter Enemies to those in our Way. They don't care that any Body should get a Clandestine Livelihood but themselves.

SCENE X.

Mrs. Peachum, Peachum, Polly.

POLLY: 'Twas only Nimming Ned. He brought in a Damask Window-Curtain, a Hoop-Petticoat, a Pair of Silver Candle-sticks, a Perriwig, and one Silk Stocking, from the Fire that happen'd last Night.

PEACHUM: There is not a Fellow that is cleverer in his way, and saves more Goods out of the Fire than Ned. But now, Polly, to your Affair; for Matters must not be left as they are. You are married then, it seems?

POLLY: Yes, Sir.

PEACHUM: And how do you propose to live, Child?

POLLY: Like other Women, Sir, upon the Industry of my Husband.

MRS. PEACHUM: What, is the Wench turn'd Fool? A Highwayman's Wife, like a Soldier's, hath as little of his Pay, as of his Company.

PEACHUM: And had not you the common Views of a Gentlewoman in your Marriage, Polly?

POLLY: I don't know what you mean, Sir.

PEACHUM: Of a Jointure, and of being a Widow.

POLLY: But I love him, Sir: how then could I have Thoughts of parting with him?

PEACHUM: Parting with him! Why, that is the whole Scheme and Intention of all Marriage Articles. The comfortable Estate of Widow-hood, is the only hope that keeps up a Wife's Spirits. Where is the Woman who would scruple to be a Wife, if she had it in her Power to be a widow whenever she pleas'd? If you have any Views of this sort, Polly, I shall think the Match not so very unreasonable.

POLLY: How I dread to hear your Advice! Yet I must beg you to explain yourself.

PEACHUM: Secure what he hath got, have him peach'd the next Sessions, and then at once you are made a rich Widow.

POLLY: What, murder the Man I love! The Blood runs cold at my Heart with the very Thought of it.

PEACHUM: Fye, Polly! What hath Murder to do in the Affair? Since the thing sooner or later must happen, I dare say, the Captain himself would like that we should get the Reward for his Death sooner than a Stranger. Why, Polly, the Captain knows, that as 'tis his Employment to rob, so 'tis ours to take

Robbers; every Man in his Business. So that there is no Malice in the Case.

MRS. PEACHUM: Ay, Husband, now you have nick'd the Matter. To have him peach'd is the only thing could ever make me forgive her.

AIR

POLLY: *Oh, ponder well! be not severe;*
So save a wretched Wife!
For on the Rope that hangs my Dear
Depends poor Polly's Life.

MRS. PEACHUM: But your Duty to your Parents, Hussy, obliges you to hang him. What would many a Wife give for such an Opportunity!

POLLY: What is a Jointure, what is Widow-hood to me? I know my Heart. I cannot survive him.

AIR

The Turtle thus with plaintive crying
Her Lover dying,
The Turtle thus with plaintive crying
Laments her Dove.
Down she drops quite spent with sighing,
Pair'd in Death, as pair'd in Love.

Thus, Sir, it will happen to your poor Polly.

MRS. PEACHUM: What, is the Fool in love in earnest then? I hate thee for being particular: Why, Wench, thou art a Shame to thy very Sex.

POLLY: But hear me, Mother.—If you ever lov'd—

MRS. PEACHUM: Those cursed Playbooks she reads have been her Ruin. One Word more, Hussy, and I shall knock your Brains out, if you have any.

PEACHUM: Keep out of the way, Polly, for fear of Mischief, and consider of what is propos'd to you.

MRS. PEACHUM: Away, Hussy. Hang your Hus-band, and be dutiful.

SCENE XI.

Mrs. Peachum, Peachum, Polly *listening.*

MRS. PEACHUM: The Thing, Husband, must and shall be done. For the sake of Intelligence we must take other Measures, and have him peach'd the next Session without her Consent. If she will not know her Duty, we know ours.

PEACHUM: But really, my Dear, it grieves one's Heart to take off a great Man. When I consider his Personal Bravery, his fine Stratagem, how much we have already got by him, and how much more we may get, methinks I can't find in my Heart to have a Hand in his Death. I wish you could have made Polly undertake it.

MRS. PEACHUM: But in a Case of Necessity—our own Lives are in danger.

PEACHUM: Then, indeed, we must comply with the Customs of the World, and make Gratitude give way to Interest.—He shall be taken off.

MRS. PEACHUM: I'll undertake to manage Polly.

PEACHUM: And I'll prepare Matters for the Old-Bailey.

SCENE XII.

POLLY: Now I'm a Wretch, indeed.—Methinks I see him already in the Cart, sweeter and more lovely than the Nosegay in his Hand!—I hear the Crowd extolling his Resolution and Intrepidity!—What Vollies of Sighs are sent from the Windows of Holborn, that so comely a Youth should be bought to disgrace!—I see him at the Tree! The whole Circle are in Tears! —even Butchers weep!—Jack Ketch himself hesitates to perform his Duty, and would be glad to lose his Fee, by a Reprieve. What then will become of Polly! —As yet I may inform him of their Design, and aid him in his Escape.—It shall be so.—But then he flies, absents himself, and I bar my self from his dear, dear Conversation! That too will distract me.—If he keep out of the way, my Papa and Mama may in time relent, and we may be happy.—If he stays, he is hang'd, and then he is lost for ever!—He intended to lye conceal'd in my Room, 'till the Dusk of the Evening: If they are abroad, I'll this Instant let him out, lest some Accident should prevent him. [*Exit, and returns*]

SCENE XIII.

Polly, Macheath.

AIR

MACHEATH: *Pretty Polly, say,*
When I was away,
Did your Fancy never stray
To some newer Lover?
POLLY: *Without Disguise,*
Heaving Sighs,
Doating Eyes,
My constant Heart discover.
Fondly let me loll!
MACHEATH: *O pretty, pretty Poll.*

POLLY: And are *you* as fond as ever, my Dear?

MACHEATH: Suspect my Honour, my Courage, suspect any thing but my Love.—May my Pistols miss Fire, and my Mare slip her shoulder while I am pursu'd, if I ever forsake thee!

POLLY: Nay, my Dear, I have no Reason to doubt you, for I find in the Romance you lent me, none of the great Heroes were ever false in Love.

AIR

MACHEATH: *My Heart was so free,*
It rov'd like the Bee,
'Till Polly my Passion requited;
I sipt each Flower,
I chang'd ev'ry Hour,
But here ev'ry Flower is United.

POLLY: Were you sentenc'd to Transportation, sure, my Dear, you could not leave me behind you—could you?

MACHEATH: Is there any Power, any Force that could tear me from thee? You might sooner tear a Pension out of the Hands of a Courtier, a Fee from a Lawyer, a pretty Woman from a Looking-glass, or any Woman from Quadrille.—But to tear me from thee is impossible!

AIR

Were I laid on Greenland's Coast
And in my Arms embrac'd my Lass,
Warm amidst eternal Frost
Too soon the Half Year's Night would pass.
   POLLY: *Were I sold on Indian Soil,*
Soon as the burning Day was clos'd,
I could mock the sultry Toil
When on my Charmer's Breast repos'd.

MACHEATH: *And I would love you all the Day,*
POLLY: *Every Night would kiss and play,*
MACHEATH: *If with me you'd fondly stray*
POLLY: *Over the Hills and far away:*

POLLY: Yes, I would go with thee. But oh!—how shall I speak it? I must be torn from thee. We must part.

MACHEATH: How! Part!

POLLY: We must, we must.—My Papa and Mama are set against thy Life. They now, even now are in Search after thee. They are preparing Evidence against thee. Thy Life depends upon a Moment.

AIR

O what Pain it is to part!
Can I leave thee, can I leave thee?
O what Pain it is to part!
Can thy Polly ever leave thee?
But lest Death my Love should thwart,
And bring thee to the fatal Cart,
Thus I tear thee from my bleeding Heart!
   Fly hence, and let me leave thee.

One Kiss and then—one Kiss—begone—farewell.

MACHEATH: My Hand, my Heart, my Dear, is so rivited to thine, that I cannot unloose my Hold.

POLLY: But my Papa may intercept thee, and then I should lose the very glimmering of Hope. A few Weeks, perhaps, may reconcile us all. Shall thy Polly hear from thee?

MACHEATH: Must I then go?

POLLY: And will not Absence change your Love?

MACHEATH: If you doubt it, let me stay—and be hang'd.

POLLY: O how I fear! how I tremble!—Go—but when Safety will give you leave, you will be sure to see me again; for 'till then Polly is wretched.

AIR

[Parting, and looking back at each other with fondness; he at one Door, she at the other]
MACHEATH: *The Miser thus a Shilling sees,*
Which he's oblig'd to pay,
With Sighs resigns it by degrees
And fears 'tis gone for aye.
POLLY: *The Boy, thus, when his Sparrow's flown,*
The Bird in Silence eyes;
But soon as out of Sight 'tis gone,
Whines, whimpers, sobs and cries.

ACT II. SCENE I.

A Tavern near Newgate.

[Jemmy Twitcher, Crook-Finger'd Jack, Wat Dreary, Robin of Bagshot, Nimming Ned, Henry Paddington, Matt of the Mint, Ben Budge, and the rest of the Gang, *at the Table, with Wine, Brandy and Tobacco*]

BEN: But pr'ythee, Matt, what is become of thy Brother Tom? I have not seen him since my Return from Transportation.

MATT: Poor Brother Tom had an Accident this time Twelve-month, and so clever a made Fellow he was, that I could not save him from those fleaing Rascals the Surgeons; and now, poor Man, he is among the Anatomies at Surgeon's Hall.

BEN: So it seems, his Time was come.

JEMMY: But the present Time is ours, and no Body alive hath more. Why are the Laws levell'd at us? are we more dishonest than the rest of Mankind? What we win, Gentlemen, is our own by the Law of Arms, and the Right of Conquest.

JACK: Where shall we find such another Set of practical Philosophers, who to a Man are above the Fear of Death?

WAT: Sound Men, and true!

ROBIN: Of try'd Courage, and indefatigable Industry!

NED: Who is there here that would not dye for his Friend?

HARRY: Who is there here that would betray him for his Interest?

MATT: Show me a Gang of Courtiers that can say as much.

BEN: We are for a just Partition of the World, for every Man hath a Right to enjoy Life.

MATT: We retrench the Superfluities of Mankind. The World is avaritious, and I hate Avarice. A covetous fellow, like a Jackdaw, steals what he was never made to enjoy, for the sake of hiding it. These are the Robbers of Mankind, for Money was made for the Free-hearted and Generous, and where is the injury of taking from another, what he hath not the Heart to make use of?

JEMMY: Our several Stations for the Day are fixt. Good luck attend us all. Fill the Glasses.

AIR

MATT: *Fill ev'ry Glass, for Wine inspires us,*
And fires us
With Courage, Love and Joy.
Women and Wine should Life employ.
Is there ought else on Earth desirous?
CHORUS: *Fill ev'ry Glass, &c.*

SCENE II.

To them enter Macheath.

MACHEATH: Gentlemen, well met. My Heart hath been with you this Hour; but an unexpected Affair hath detain'd me. No Ceremony, I beg you.

MATT: We were just breaking up to go upon Duty. Am I to have the Honour of taking the Air with you, Sir, this Evening upon the Heath? I drink a Dram now and then with the Stage-Coachmen in the way of Friendship and Intelligence; and I know that about this Time there will be Passengers upon the Western Road, who are worth speaking with.

MACHEATH: I was to have been of that Party—but—

MATT: But what, Sir?

MACHEATH: Is there any man who suspects my Courage?

MATT: We have all been witnesses of it.

MACHEATH: My Honour and Truth to the Gang?

MATT: I'll be answerable for it.

MACHEATH: In the Division of our Booty, have I ever shown the least Marks of Avarice or Injustice?

MATT: By these Questions something seems to have ruffled you. Are any of us suspected?

MACHEATH: I have a fixt Confidence, Gentlemen, in you all, as Men of Honour, and as such I value and respect you. Peachum is a Man that is useful to us.

MATT: Is he about to play us any foul Play? I'll shoot him through the Head.

MACHEATH: I beg you, Gentlemen, act with Conduct and Discretion. A Pistol is your last resort.

MATT: He knows nothing of this Meeting.

MACHEATH: Business cannot go on without him. He is a Man who knows the World, and is a necessary Agent to us. We have had a slight Difference, and till it is accommodated I shall be oblig'd to keep out of his way. Any private Dispute of mine shall be of no ill consequence to my Friends. You must continue to act under his Direction, for the moment we break loose from him, our Gang is ruin'd.

MATT: As a Bawd to a Whore, I grant you, he is to us of great Convenience.

MACHEATH: Make him believe I have quitted the Gang, which I can never do but with Life. At our private Quarters I will continue to meet you. A Week or so will probably reconcile us.

MATT: Your Instructions shall be observ'd. 'Tis now high time for us to repair to our several Duties; so till the Evening at our Quarters in Moor-fields we bid you farewell.

MACHEATH: I shall wish my self with you. Success attend you.

[*Sits down melancholy at the Table*]

AIR

MATT: *Let us take the Road.*
Hark! I hear the sound of Coaches!
The hour of Attack approaches,
To your Arms, brave Boys, and load.
See the Ball I hold!
Let the Chymists toil like Asses,
Our fire their fire surpasses
And turns all our Lead to Gold.

[*The Gang, rang'd in the Front of the Stage, load their Pistols, and stick them under their Girdles; then go off singing the first Part in Chorus*]

SCENE III.

Macheath, Drawer.

MACHEATH: What a Fool is a fond Wench! Polly is most confoundedly bit.—I love the Sex. And a Man who loves Money, might as well be contented with one Guinea, as I with one Woman. The Town perhaps hath been as much oblig'd to me, for recruiting it with free-hearted Ladies, as to any Recruiting Officer in the Army. If it were not for us and the other Gentlemen of the Sword, Drury-Lane would be uninhabited.

AIR

If the Heart of a Man is deprest with Cares,
The Mist is dispell'd when a Woman appears;
Like the Notes of a Fiddle, she sweetly, sweetly
Raises the Spirits, and charms our Ears.
Roses and Lillies her Cheeks disclose,
But her ripe Lips are more sweet than those.
Press her,
Caress her
With Blisses,
Her Kisses
Dissolve us in Pleasure, and soft Repose.

I must have Women. There is nothing unbends the Mind like them. Money is not so strong a Cordial for the Time. Drawer!

[*Enter* Drawer]

Is the Porter gone for all the Ladies, according to my directions?

DRAWER: I expect him back every Minute. But you know, Sir, you sent him as far as Hockley in the Hole, for three of the Ladies, for one in Vinegar Yard, and for the rest of them somewhere about Lewkner's Lane. Sure some of them are below, for I hear the Barr Bell. As they come I will show them up. Coming, coming.

SCENE IV.

Macheath, Mrs. Coaxer, Dolly Trull, Mrs. Vixen, Betty Doxy, Jenny Diver, Mrs. Slammekin, Suky Tawdry, *and* Molly Brazen.

MACHEATH: Dear Mrs. Coaxer, you are welcome. You look charmingly to-day. I hope you don't want the Repairs of Quality, and lay on Paint.—Dolly Trull! kiss me, you Slut; are you as amorous as ever, Hussy? You are always so taken up with stealing Hearts, that you don't allow your self Time to steal any thing else.—Ah Dolly, thou wilt ever be a Coquette!—Mrs. Vixen, I'm yours, I always lov'd a Woman of Wit and Spirit; they make charming Mistresses, but plaguy Wives.—Betty Doxy! Come hither, Hussy. Do you drink as hard as ever? You had better stick to good Wholesome Beer; for in troth, Betty, Strong-Waters will in time ruin your Constitution. You should leave those to your Betters.—What! and my pretty Jenny Diver too! As prim and demure as ever! There is not any Prude, though ever so high bred, hath a more sanctify'd Look, with a more mischievous Heart. Ah! thou art a dear artful Hypocrite. —Mrs. Slammekin! as careless and genteel as ever! all you fine Ladies, who know your own Beauty, affect an Undress.—But see, here's Suky Tawdry come to contradict what I was saying. Everything she gets one way she lays out upon her Back. Why Suky, you must keep at least a dozen Tallymen. Molly Brazen! [*She kisses him*] That's well done. I love a free-hearted Wench. Thou hast a most agreeable Assurance, Girl, and art as willing as a Turtle.—But hark! I hear musick. The Harper is at the Door. If Musick be the Food of Love, play on. E'er you seat your selves, Ladies, what think you of a Dance? Come in.

[*Enter* Harper]

Play the French Tune, that Mrs. Slammekin was so fond of.

[*A Dance á la ronde in the French Manner; near the End of it this Song and Chorus*]

AIR

Youth's the Season made for Joys,
  Love is then our Duty,
She alone who that employs,
  Well deserves her Beauty.
    Let's be gay,
    While we may,
    Beauty's a Flower, despis'd in decay.
Youth's the Season, &c.

Let us drink and sport to-day,
  Ours is not to-morrow.
Love with Youth flies swift away,
  Age is nought but Sorrow.
    Dance and sing,
    Time's on the Wing,
Life never knows the return of Spring.
CHORUS: *Let us drink, &c.*

MACHEATH: Now, pray Ladies, take your Places. Here Fellow [*Plays the* Harper], Bid the Drawer bring bring us more Wine. [*Exit* Harper] If any of the Ladies chuse Ginn, I hope they will be so free to call for it.

JENNY: You look as if you meant me. Wine is strong enough for me. Indeed, Sir, I never drink Strong-Waters, but when I have the Cholic.

MACHEATH: Just the Excuse of the fine Ladies! Why, a Lady of Quality is never without the Cholic. I hope, Mrs. Coaxer, you have had good Success of late in your Visits among the Mercers.

MRS. COAXER: We have so many Interlopers—Yet with Industry, one may still have a little Picking. I carried a silver flower'd Lute-string, and a Piece of black Padesoy to Mr. Peachum's Lock but last Week.

MRS. VIXEN: There's Molly Brazen hath the Ogle of a Rattle-Snake. She rivetted a Linnen-draper's Eye so fast upon her, that he was nick'd of three Pieces of Cambric before he could look off.

BRAZEN: Oh dear Madam!—But sure nothing can come up to your handling of Laces! And then you have such a sweet deluding Tongue! To cheat a Man is nothing; but the Woman must have fine Parts indeed who cheats a Woman!

MRS. VIXEN: Lace, Madam, lyes in a small Compass, and is of easy Conveyance. But you are apt, Madam, to think too well of your Friends.

MRS. COAXER: If any Woman hath more Art than another, to be sure, 'tis Jenny Diver. Though her Fellow be never so agreeable, she can pick his Pocket as cooly, as if Money were her only Pleasure. Now that is a Command of the Passions uncommon in a Woman!

JENNY: I never go to the Tavern with a Man, but in the View of Business. I have other Hours, and other sort of Men for my Pleasure. But had I your Address, Madam—

MACHEATH: Have done with your Compliments, Ladies; and drink about: You are not so fond of me, Jenny, as you use to be.

JENNY: 'Tis not convenient, Sir, to show my Fondness among so many Rivals. 'Tis your own Choice, and not the warmth of my Inclination that will determine you.

AIR

Before the Barn-door crowing,
  The Cock by Hens attended,
His Eyes around him throwing,
  Stands for a while suspended.
Then One he singles from the Crew,
  And cheers the happy Hen;
With how do you do, and how do you do,
  And how do you do again.

MACHEATH: Ah Jenny! thou art a dear Slut.

TRULL: Pray, Madam, were you ever in keeping?

TAWDRY: I hope, Madam, I ha'n been so long upon the Town, but I have met with some good Fortune as well as my Neighbours.

TRULL: Pardon me, Madam, I meant no harm by the Question; 'twas only in the way of Conversation.

TAWDRY: Indeed, Madam, if I had not been a Fool, I might have liv'd very handsomely with my last Friend. But upon his missing five Guineas, he turn'd me off. Now I never suspected he had counted them.

MRS. SLAMMEKIN: Who do you look upon, Madam, as your best sort of Keepers?

TRULL: That, Madam, is thereafter as they be.

MRS. SLAMMEKIN: I, Madam, was once kept by a Jew; and bating their Religion, to Women they are a good sort of People.

TAWDRY: Now for my part, I own I like an old Fellow: for we always make them pay for what they can't do.

MRS. VIXEN: A spruce Prentice, let me tell you, Ladies, is no ill thing, they bleed freely. I have sent at least two or three dozen of them in my time to the Plantations.

JENNY: But to be sure, Sir, with so much good Fortune as you have had upon the Road, you must be grown immensely rich.

MACHEATH: The Road, indeed, hath done me justice, but the Gaming-Table hath been my ruin.

AIR

JENNY: *The Gamesters and Lawyers are Jugglers alike,*
If they meddle your All is in danger.
Like Gypsies, if once they can finger a Souse,
Your Pockets they pick, and they pilfer your House,
  And give your Estate to a Stranger.

These are the Tools of a Man of Honour. Cards and Dice are only fit for cowardly Cheats, who prey upon their Friends. [*She takes up his Pistol.* Tawdry *takes up the other*]

TAWDRY: This, Sir, is fitter for your Hand. Besides your Loss of Money, 'tis a Loss to the Ladies. Gaming takes you off from Women. How fond could I be of you! but before Company, 'tis ill bred.

MACHEATH: Wanton Hussies!

JENNY: I must and will have a Kiss to give my Wine a zest.

[*They take him about the Neck, and make Signs to* Peachum *and* Constables, *who rush in upon him*]

SCENE V.

[*To them*, Peachum *and* Constables]

PEACHUM: I seize you, Sir, as my Prisoner.

MACHEATH: Was this well done, Jenny?—Women are Decoy Ducks; who can trust them! Beasts, Jades, Jilts, Harpies, Furies, Whores!

PEACHUM: Your case, Mr. Macheath, is not particular. The greatest Heroes have been ruin'd by Women. But, to do them justice, I must own they are a pretty sort of Creatures, if we could trust them. You must now, Sir, take your leave of the Ladies, and if they have a Mind to make you a Visit, they will be sure to find you at home. The Gentleman, Ladies, lodges in Newgate. Constables, wait upon the Captain to his Lodgings.

AIR

MACHEATH: *At the Tree I shall suffer with pleasure,*
At the Tree I shall suffer with pleasure,
  Let me go where I will,
  In all kinds of Ill,

PEACHUM: Ladies, I'll take care the Reckoning shall be discharg'd.

I shall find no such Furies as these are.

[*Exit* Macheath, *guarded with* Peachum *and* Constables]

SCENE VI.

[The Women *remain*]

MRS. VIXEN: Look ye, Mrs. Jenny, though Mr. Peachum may have made a private Bargain with you and Suky Tawdry for betraying the Captain, as we were all assisting, we ought all to share alike.

MRS. COAXER: I think Mr. Peachum, after so long an acquaintance, might have trusted me as well as Jenny Diver.

MRS. SLAMMEKIN: I am sure at least three Men of his hanging, and in a Year's time too (if he did me justice) should be set down to my account.

TRULL: Mrs. Slammekin, that is not fair. For you know one of them was taken in Bed with me.

JENNY: As far as a Bowl of Punch or a Treat, I believe Mrs. Suky will join with me.—As for any thing else, Ladies, you cannot in conscience expect it.

MRS. SLAMMEKIN: Dear Madam—

TRULL: I would not for the World—

MRS. SLAMMEKIN: 'Tis impossible for me—

TRULL: As I hope to be sav'd, Madam—

MRS. SLAMMEKIN: Nay, then I must stay here all Night—

TRULL: Since you command me.

[*Exeunt with great Ceremony*]

SCENE VII.

Newgate.

Lockit, Turnkeys, Macheath, Constables

LOCKIT: Noble Captain, you are welcome. You have not been a Lodger of mine this Year and half. You know the custom, Sir. Garnish, Captain, Garnish.[5] Hand me down those Fetters there.

MACHEATH: Those, Mr. Lockit, seem to be the heaviest of the whole sett. With your leave, I should like the further pair better.

LOCKIT: Look ye, Captain, we know what is fittest for our Prisoners. When a Gentleman uses me with Civility, I always do the best I can to please him. —Hand them down I say.—We have them of all Prices, from one Guinea to ten, and 'tis fitting every Gentleman should please himself.

MACHEATH: I understand you, Sir. [*Gives Money*] The Fees here are so many, and so exorbitant, that few Fortunes can bear the Expense of getting off handsomly, or of dying like a Gentleman.

LOCKIT: Those, I see, will fit the Captain better. —Take down the further Pair. Do but examine them, Sir.—Never was better work.—How genteely they are made!—They will fit as easy as a Glove, and the richest Man in England might not be asham'd to wear them. [*He puts on the Chains*] If I had the best Gentleman in the Land in my Custody I could not equip him more handsomly. And so, Sir—I now leave you to your private Meditations.

SCENE VIII.

Macheath.

AIR

Man may escape from Rope and Gun,
Nay, some have out-liv'd the Doctor's Pill;
Who takes a Woman must be undone,
    That Basilisk is sure to kill.
The Fly that sips Treacle is lost in the Sweets,
So he that tastes Woman, Woman, Woman,
    He that tastes Woman, Ruin meets.

To what a woful plight have I brought my self! Here must I (all day long, 'till I am hang'd) be confin'd to hear the Reproaches of a Wench who lays her Ruin

[5] Bribe me, Captain, bribe me.

at my Door.—I am in the Custody of her Father, and to be sure if he knows of the matter, I shall have a fine time on't betwixt this and my Execution.—But I promis'd the Wench Marriage.—What signifies a Promise to a Woman? Does not Man in Marriage itself promise a hundred things that he never means to perform? Do all we can, Women will believe us; for they look upon a Promise as an Excuse for following their own Inclinations.—But here comes Lucy, and I cannot get from her.—Wou'd I were deaf!

SCENE IX.

Macheath, Lucy.

LUCY: You base Man you,—how can you look me in the Face after what hath past between us?—See here, perfidious Wretch, how I am forc'd to bear about the load of Infamy you have laid upon me. —O Macheath! thou hast robb'd me of my Quiet— to see thee tortur'd would give me pleasure.

AIR

Thus when a good Husewife sees a Rat
    In her Trap in the Morning taken,
With pleasure her Heart goes pit a pat
    In Revenge for her loss of Bacon.
        Then she throws him
        To the Dog or Cat,
To be worried, crush'd and shaken.

MACHEATH: Have you no Bowels, no Tenderness, my dear Lucy, to see a Husband in these Circumstances?

LUCY: A Husband!

MACHEATH: In ev'ry respect but the Form, and that, my Dear, may be said over us at any time. —Friends should not insist upon Ceremonies. From a Man of honour, his Word is as good as his Bond.

LUCY: 'Tis the pleasure of all you fine Men to insult the Women you have ruin'd.

AIR

How cruel are the Traytors,
    Who lye and swear in jest,
To cheat unguarded Creatures
    Of Virtue, Fame, and Rest!
Whoever steals a Shilling,
    Through shame the Guilt conceals:
In Love the perjur'd Villain
    With Boasts the Theft reveals.

MACHEATH: The very first opportunity, my Dear, (have but patience) you shall be my Wife in whatever manner you please.

LUCY: Insinuating Monster! And so you think I know nothing of the Affair of Miss Polly Peachum. I could tear thy Eyes out!

MACHEATH: Sure Lucy, you can't be such a Fool as to be jealous of Polly!

LUCY: Are you not married to her, you Brute, you?

MACHEATH: Married! Very good. The Wench gives it out only to vex thee, and to ruin me in thy good Opinion. 'Tis true, I go to the House; I chat with the Girl, I kiss her, I say a thousand things to her (as all Gentlemen do) that mean nothing, to divert my self; and now the silly Jade hath set it about that I am married to her, to let me know what she would be at. Indeed, my dear Lucy, these violent Passions may be of ill consequence to a Woman in your condition.

LUCY: Come, come, Captain, for all your Assurance, you know that Miss Polly hath put it out of your power to do me the Justice you promis'd me.

MACHEATH: A jealous Woman believes ev'ry thing her Passion suggests. To convince you of my Sincerity, if we can find the Ordinary, I shall have no scruples of making you my Wife; and I know the consequence of having two at a time.

LUCY: That you are only to be hang'd, and so get rid of them both.

MACHEATH: I am ready, my dear Lucy, to give you satisfaction—if you think there is any in Marriage. —What can a Man of Honour say more?

LUCY: So then it seems, you are not married to Miss Polly.

MACHEATH: You know, Lucy, the Girl is prodigiously conceited. No Man can say a civil thing to her, but (like other fine Ladies) her Vanity makes her think he's her own for ever and ever.

AIR

The first time at the Looking-glass
The Mother sets her Daughter,
The Image strikes the smiling Lass
With Self-love ever after.
Each time she looks, she, fonder grown,
Thinks ev'ry Charm grows stronger.
But alas, vain Maid, all Eyes but your own
Can see you are not younger.

When Women consider their own Beauties, they are all alike unreasonable in their demands; for they expect their Lovers should like them as long as they like themselves.

LUCY: Yonder is my Father—perhaps this way we may light upon the Ordinary, who shall try if you will be as good as your Word.—For I long to be made an honest Woman.

SCENE X.

[Peachum, Lockit *with an Account-Book*]

LOCKIT: In this last Affair, Brother Peachum, we are agreed. You have consented to go halves in Macheath.

PEACHUM: We shall never fall out about an Execution.—But as to that Article, pray how stands our last Year's account?

LOCKIT: If you will run your Eye over it, you'll find 'tis fair and clearly stated.

PEACHUM: This long Arrear of the Government is very hard upon us! Can it be expected that we should hang our Acquaintance for nothing, when our Betters will hardly save theirs without being paid for it? Unless the People in employment pay better, I promise them for the future, I shall let other Rogues live besides their own.

LOCKIT: Perhaps, Brother, they are afraid these matters may be carried too far. We are treated too by them with Contempt, as if our Profession were not reputable.

PEACHUM: In one respect indeed, our Employment may be reckon'd dishonest, because, like Great Statesmen, we encourage those who betray their Friends.

LOCKIT: Such Language, Brother, any where else, might turn to your prejudice. Learn to be more guarded, I beg you.

AIR

When you censure the Age,
Be cautious and sage,
Lest the Courtiers offended should be:
If you mention Vice or Bribe
'Tis so pat to all the Tribe;
Each crys—That was levell'd at me.

PEACHUM: Here's poor Ned Clincher's Name, I see. Sure, Brother Lockit, there was a little unfair proceeding in Ned's case: for he told me in the Condemn'd Hold, that for Value receiv'd you had promis'd him a Session or two longer without Molestation.

LOCKIT: Mr. Peachum—This is the first time my Honour was ever call'd in Question.

PEACHUM: Business is at an end—if once we act dishonourably.

LOCKIT: Who accuses me?

PEACHUM: You are warm, Brother.

LOCKIT: He that attacks my Honour, attacks my Livelyhood.—And this Usage—Sir—is not to be born.

PEACHUM: Since you provoke me to speak—I must tell you too, that Mrs. Coaxer charges you with defrauding her of her Information-Money, for the apprehending of curl-pated Hugh. Indeed, indeed, Brother, we must punctually pay our Spies, or we shall have no Information.

LOCKIT: Is this Language to me, Sirrah—who have sav'd you from the Gallows, Sirrah! [*Collaring each other*]

PEACHUM: If I am hang'd, it shall be for ridding the World of an arrant Rascal.

LOCKIT: This Hand shall do the office of the Halter you deserve, and throttle you—you Dog!—

PEACHUM: Brother, Brother—We are both in the Wrong—We shall be both Losers in the Dispute—for you know we have it in our Power to hang each other. You should not be so passionate.

LOCKIT: Nor you so provoking.

PEACHUM: 'Tis our mutual Interest; 'tis for the Interest of the World we should agree. If I said any thing, Brother, to the Prejudice of your Character, I ask pardon.

LOCKIT: Brother Peachum—I can forgive as well as resent.—Give me your Hand. Suspicion does not become a Friend.

PEACHUM: I only meant to give you occasion to justifie yourself: But I must now step home, for I expect the Gentleman about this Snuff-box, that Filch nimm'd two Nights ago in the Park. I appointed him at this hour.

SCENE XI.

Lockit, Lucy.

LOCKIT: Whence come you, Hussy?

LUCY: My Tears might answer that Question.

LOCKIT: You have then been whimpering and fondling, like a Spaniel, over the Fellow that hath abus'd you.

LUCY: One can't help Love; one can't cure it. 'Tis not in my Power to obey you and hate him.

LOCKIT: Learn to bear your Husband's Death like a reasonable Woman. 'Tis not the fashion, now-a-days, so much as to affect Sorrow upon these Occasions. No Woman would ever marry, if she had not the Chance of Mortality for a Release. Act like a Woman of Spirit, Hussy, and thank your Father for what he is doing.

AIR

LUCY: *Is then his Fate decreed, Sir?*
Such a Man can I think of quitting?
When first we met, so moves me yet,
O see how my Heart is splitting!

LOCKIT: Look ye, Lucy—There is no saving him.—So, I think you must ev'n do like other Widows—Buy your self Weeds, and be cheerful.

AIR

You'll think e'er many Days ensue
This Sentence not severe;
I hang your Husband, Child, 'tis true,
But with him hang your Care.
Twang dang dillo dee.

Like a good Wife, go moan over your dying Husband. That, Child, is your Duty—Consider, Girl, you can't have the Man and the Money too—so make yourself as easy as you can by getting all you can from him.

SCENE XII.

Lucy, Macheath.

LUCY: Though the Ordinary was out of the way to-day I hope, my Dear, you will, upon the first opportunity, quiet my Scruples—Oh Sir!—my Father's hard Heart is not to be soften'd, and I am in the utmost Despair.

MACHEATH: But if I could raise a small Sum—Would not twenty Guineas, think you, move him?—Of all the Arguments in the way of Business, the Perquisite is the most prevailing.—Your Father's Perquisites for the Escape of Prisoners must amount to a considerable Sum in the Year. Money well tim'd, and properly apply'd, will do any thing.

AIR

If you at an Office solicit your Due,
And would not have Matters neglected,
You must quicken the Clerk with the perquisite, too,
To do what his Duty directed.
Or would you the Frowns of a Lady prevent,
She too has this palpable Failing
The Perquisite softens her into Consent;
That Reason with all is prevailing.

LUCY: What Love or Money can do shall be done: for all my Comfort depends upon your Safety.

SCENE XIII.

Lucy, Macheath, Polly.

POLLY: Where is my dear Husband?—Was a Rope ever intended for this Neck!—O let me throw my Arms about it, and throttle thee with Love!—Why dost thou turn away from me?—'Tis thy Polly—'Tis thy Wife.

MACHEATH: Was ever such an unfortunate Rascal as I am!

LUCY: Was there ever such another Villain!

POLLY: O Macheath! was it for this we parted? Taken! Imprison'd! Try'd! Hang'd!—cruel Reflection! I'll stay with thee 'till Death—no Force shall tear thy dear Wife from thee now.—What means my Love?—Not one kind Word! not one kind Look! think what thy Polly suffers to see thee in this Condition.

AIR

Thus when the Swallow, seeking Prey,
   Within the Sash is closely pent,
His Consort, with bemoaning Lay,
   Without sits pining for th' Event.
Her chatt'ring Lovers all around her skim;
She heeds them not (poor Bird!) her Soul's with him.

MACHEATH: I must disown her. [*Aside*] The Wench is distracted.

LUCY: Am I then bilk'd of my Virtue? Can I have no Reparation? Sure Men were born to lye, and Women to believe them! O Villain! Villain!

POLLY: Am I not thy Wife—Thy Neglect of me, thy Aversion to me too severely proves it.—Look on me.—Tell me, am I not thy Wife?

LUCY: Perfidious Wretch!

POLLY: Barbarous Husband!

LUCY: Hadst thou been hang'd five Months ago, I had been happy.

POLLY: And I too—If you had been kind to me 'till Death, it would not have vex'd me. And that's no very unreasonable Request (though from a Wife) to a Man who hath not above seven or eight Days to live.

LUCY: Art thou then married to another? Hast thou two Wives, Monster?

MACHEATH: If Women's Tongues can cease for an Answer—hear me.

LUCY: I won't.—Flesh and Blood can't bear my Usage.

POLLY: Shall I not claim my own? Justice bids me speak.

AIR

MACHEATH: *How happy could I be with either,*
Were t'other dear Charmer away!
But while you thus teaze me together,
To neither a Word will I say;
   But tol de rol, &c.

POLLY: Sure, my Dear, there ought to be some Preference shown to a Wife! At least she may claim the Appearance of it. He must be distracted with his Misfortunes, or he could not use me thus!

LUCY: O Villain, Villain! thou hast deceiv'd me— I could even inform against thee with Pleasure. Not a Prude wishes more heartily to have Facts against her intimate Acquaintance, than I now wish to have Facts against thee. I would have her Satisfaction, and they should all out.

AIR

POLLY: *I'm bubbled.*[6]
LUCY: *. . . I'm bubbled.*
POLLY: *Oh how I am troubled!*
LUCY: *Bamboozled, and bit!*

[6] Deceived.

POLLY: *. . . My Distresses are doubled.*
LUCY: *When you come to the Tree, should the*
    Hangman refuse,
These Fingers, with Pleasure, could fasten the Noose.
POLLY: *I'm bubbled, &c.*

MACHEATH: Be pacified, my dear Lucy—This is all a Fetch of Polly's, to make me desperate with you in case I get off. If I am hang'd, she would fain have the Credit of being thought my Widow—Really, Polly, this is no time for a Dispute of this sort; for whenever you are talking of Marriage, I am thinking of Hanging.

POLLY: And hast thou the Heart to persist in disowning me?

MACHEATH: And hast thou the Heart to persist in persuading me that I am married? Why Polly, dost thou seek to aggravate my Misfortunes?

LUCY: Really, Miss Peachum, you but expose yourself. Besides, 'tis barbarous in you to worry a Gentleman in his Circumstances.

AIR

POLLY: *Cease your Funning;*
   Force or Cunning
   Never shall my Heart trapan.[7]
   All these Sallies
   Are but Malice
To seduce my constant Man.
   'Tis most certain,
   By their flirting
Women oft' have Envy shown;
   Pleas'd, to ruin
   Others wooing;
Never happy in their own!

POLLY: Decency, Madam, methinks might teach you to behave yourself with some Reserve with the Husband, while his Wife is present.

MACHEATH: But seriously, Polly, this is carrying the Joke a little too far.

LUCY: If you are determin'd, Madam, to raise a Disturbance in the Prison, I shall be oblig'd to send for the Turnkey to show you the Door. I am sorry, Madam, you force me to be so ill-bred.

POLLY: Give me leave to tell you, Madam: These forward Airs don't become you in the least, Madam. And my Duty, Madam, obliges me to stay with my Husband, Madam.

AIR

LUCY: *Why how now, Madam Flirt?*
   If you thus must chatter;
   And are for flinging Dirt,
   Let's try for best can spatter;
     Madam Flirt!

[7] Seduce.

POLLY: *Why how now, saucy Jade;*
Sure the Wench is Tipsy!
How can you see me made [To him]
The Scoff of such a Gipsy?
              Saucy Jade! [To her]

SCENE XIV.

Lucy, Macheath, Polly, Peachum.

PEACHUM: Where's my Wench? Ah Hussy! Hussy! —Come you home, you Slut; and when your Fellow is hang'd, hang yourself, to make your Family some amends.

POLLY: Dear, dear Father, do not tear me from him—I must speak; I have more to say to him—Oh! twist they Fetters about me, that he may not haul me from thee!

PEACHUM: Sure all Women are alike! If ever they commit the Folly, they are sure to commit another by exposing themselves—Away—Not a Word more —You are my Prisoner now, Hussy.

AIR

POLLY: *No Power on Earth can e'er divide*
The Knot that Sacred Love hath ty'd.
When Parents draw against our Mind,
The True-love's Knot they faster bind.
Oh, oh ray, oh Amborah—oh, oh, &c.
(*Holding* MACHEATH, PEACHUM *pulling her.*)

SCENE XV.

Lucy, Macheath.

MACHEATH: I am naturally compassionate, Wife: so that I could not use the Wench as she deserv'd; which made you at first suspect there was something in what she said.

LUCY: Indeed, my Dear, I was strangely puzzled.

MACHEATH: If that had been the Case, her Father would never have brought me into this Circumstance —No, Lucy,—I had rather dye than be false to thee.

LUCY: How happy am I, if you say this from your Heart! For I love thee so, that I could sooner bear to see thee hang'd than in the Arms of another.

MACHEATH: But couldst thou bear to see me hang'd?

LUCY: O Macheath, I can never live to see that Day.

MACHEATH: You see, Lucy, in the Account of Love you are in my debt, and you must now be convinc'd that I rather chuse to die than be another's. —Make me, if possible, love thee more, and let me owe my Life to thee—If you refuse to assist me, Peachum and your Father will immediately put me beyond all means of Escape.

LUCY: My Father, I know, hath been drinking hard with the Prisoners: and I fancy he is now taking his Nap in his own Room—if I can procure the Keys, shall I go off with thee, my Dear?

MACHEATH: If we are together, 'twill be impossible to lye conceal'd. As soon as the Search begins to be a little cool, I will send to thee—'Till then my Heart is thy Prisoner.

LUCY: Come then, my dear Husband—owe thy Life to me—and though you love me not—be grateful—But that Polly runs in my Head strangely.

MACHEATH: A Moment of time may make us unhappy for-ever.

AIR

LUCY: *I like the Fox shall grieve,*
Whose Mate hath left her side,
Whom Hounds, from Morn to Eve,
Chase o'er the Country wide.
Where can my Lover hide?
Where cheat the weary Pack?
If Love be not his Guide,
He never will come back!

ACT III. SCENE I.

Newgate [Prison].

Lockit, Lucy

LOCKIT: To be sure, Wench, you must have been aiding and abetting to help him to this Escape.

LUCY: Sir, here hath been Peachum and his Daughter Polly, and to be sure they know the Ways of Newgate as well as if they had been born and bred in the Place all their Lives. Why must all your Suspicion light on me?

LOCKIT: Lucy, Lucy, I will have none of these shuffling Answers.

LUCY: Well then—If I know any Thing of him I wish I may be burnt!

LOCKIT: Keep your Temper, Lucy, or I shall pronounce you guilty.

LUCY: Keep yours, Sir,—I do wish I may be burnt. I do—And what can I say more to convince you?

LOCKIT: Did he tip handsomely?—How much did he come down with? Come Hussy, don't cheat your Father; and I shall not be angry with you—Perhaps, you have made a better Bargain with him than I could have done—How much, my good Girl?

LUCY: You know, Sir, I am fond of him, and would have given Money to have kept him with me.

LOCKIT: Ah Lucy! thy Education might have put thee more upon thy Guard; for a Girl in the Bar of an Alehouse is always besieg'd.

LUCY: Dear Sir, mention not my Education—for 'twas to that I owe my Ruin.

AIR

When young at the Bar you first taught me to score,
And bid me be free of my Lips, and no more;
I was kiss'd by the Parson, the Squire, and the Sot.
When the Guest was departed, the Kiss was forgot.
But his Kiss was so sweet, and so closely he prest,
That I languish'd and pin'd till I granted the rest.

If you can forgive me, Sir, I will make a fair Confession, for to be sure he hath been a most barbarous Villain to me.

LOCKIT: And so you have let him escape, Hussy—Have you?

LUCY: When a Woman loves, a kind Look, a tender Word can persuade her to anything—And I could ask no other Bribe.

LOCKIT: Thou wilt always be a vulgar Slut, Lucy.—If you would not be look'd upon as a Fool, you should never do any thing but upon the Foot of Interest. Those that act otherwise are their own Bubbles.

LUCY: But Love, Sir, is a Misfortune that may happen to the most discreet Woman, and in Love we are all Fools alike.—Notwithstanding all he swore, I am now fully convinc'd that Polly Peachum is actually his Wife.—Did I let him escape, (Fool that I was!) to go to her?—Polly will wheedle herself into his Money, and then Peachum will hang him, and cheat us both.

LOCKIT: So I am to be ruin'd, because forsooth, you must be in Love!—a very pretty Excuse!

LUCY: I could murder that impudent happy Strumpet:—I gave him his Life, and that Creature enjoys the Sweets of it.—Ungrateful Macheath!

AIR

My Love is all Madness and Folly,
*   Alone I lye,*
*   Toss, tumble, and cry,*
What a happy Creature is Polly!
Was e'er such a Wretch as I!
With Rage I redden like Scarlet,
That my dear inconstant Varlet,
*   Stark blind to my Charms,*
*   Is lost in the Arms*
Of that Jilt, that inveigling Harlot!
*   Stark blind to my Charms,*
*   Is lost in the Arms*
Of that Jilt, that inveigling Harlot!
This, this my Resentment alarms.

LOCKIT: And so, after all this Mischief, I must stay here to be entertain'd with your catterwauling, Mistress Puss!—Out of my sight, wanton Strumpet! you shall fast and mortify yourself into Reason, with now and then a little handsome Discipline to bring you to your Senses.—Go.

SCENE II.

LOCKIT: Peachum then intends to outwit me in this Affair; but I'll be even with him—The Dog is leaky in his Liquor, so I'll ply him that way, get the Secret from him, and turn this Affair to my own Advantage.—Lions, Wolves, and Vulturs don't live together in Herds, Droves or Flocks.—Of all Animals of Prey, Man is the only sociable one. Every one of us preys upon his Neighbour, and yet we herd together.—Peachum is my Companion, my Friend—According to the Custom of the World, indeed, he may quote thousands of Precedents for cheating me—And shall not I make use of the Privilege of Friendship to make him a return?

AIR

Thus Gamesters united in Friendship are found,
Though they know that their Industry all is a Cheat;
They flock to their Prey at the Dice-Box's Sound,
And join to promote one another's Deceit.
*   But if by mishap*
*   They fail of a Chap,*
To keep in their Hands, they each other entrap.
Like Pikes, lank with Hunger, who miss of their Ends,
They bite their Companions, and prey on their
*   Friends.*

Now, Peachum, you and I, like honest Tradesmen, are to have a fair Tryal which of us two can overreach the other.—Lucy.

[*Enter* Lucy]

Are there any of Peachum's People now in the House?

LUCY: Filch, Sir, is drinking a Quartern of Strong-Waters in the next Room with Black Moll.

LOCKIT: Bid him come to me.

SCENE III.

Lockit, Filch.

LOCKIT: Why, Boy, thou lookest as if thou wert half starv'd; like a shotten Herring.

FILCH: One had need have the Constitution of a Horse to go through the Business.—Since the favourite Child-getter was disabled by a Mis-hap, I have pick'd up a little Money by helping the Ladies to a Pregnancy against their being call'd down to Sentence.—But if a Man cannot get an honest Livelyhood any easier way, I am sure, 'tis what I can't undertake for another Session.

LOCKIT: Truly, if that great Man should tip off, 'twould be an irreparable Loss. The Vigour and Prowess of a Knight Errant never sav'd half the Ladies in Distress that he hath done.—But, Boy, can'st thou tell me where thy Master is to be found?

FILCH: At his Lock, Sir, at the Crooked Billet.

LOCKIT: Very well.—I have nothing more with you. [*Exit* Filch] I'll go to him there, for I have many important Affairs to settle with him; and in the way of those Transactions, I'll artfully get into his Secret. —So that Macheath shall not remain a Day longer out of my Clutches.

SCENE IV.

[Macheath *in a fine tarnish'd Coat*, Ben Budge, Matt of the Mint]

MACHEATH: I am sorry, Gentlemen, the Road was so barren of Money. When my Friends are in Difficulties, I am always glad that my Fortune can be serviceable to them. [*Gives them Money*] You see, Gentlemen, I am not a mere Court Friend, who professes every thing and will do nothing.

AIR

The Modes of the Court so common are grown,
    That a true Friend can hardly be met;
Friendship for Interest is but a Loan,
    Which they let out for what they can get.
        'Tis true, you find
        Some Friends so kind,
Who will give you good Counsel themselves to defend.
        In sorrowful Ditty,
        They promise, they pity,
But shift you for Money from Friend to Friend.

But we, Gentlemen, have still Honour enough to break through the Corruptions of the World.—And while I can serve you, you may command me.

BEN: It grieves my Heart that so generous a Man should be involv'd in such Difficulties, as oblige him to live with such ill Company, and herd with Gamesters.

MATT: See the Partiality of Mankind!—One Man may steal a Horse, better than another look over a Hedge—Of all Mechanics, of all servile Handy-craftsmen, a Gamester is the vilest. But yet, as many of the Quality are of the Profession, he is admitted amongst the politest Company. I wonder we are not more respected.

MACHEATH: There will be deep Play to-night at Marybone, and consequently Money may be pick'd up upon the Road. Meet me there, and I'll give you the Hint who is worth Setting.[8]

MATT: The Fellow with a brown Coat with a narrow Gold Binding, I am told, is never without Money.

MACHEATH: What do you mean, Matt?—Sure you will not think of meddling with him!—He's a good honest kind of a Fellow, and one of us.

[8] The references are to gambling at the Marybone establishment.

BEN: To be sure, Sir, we will put our selves under your Direction.

MACHEATH: Have an Eye upon the Money-Lenders. —A Rouleau,[9] or two, would prove a pretty sort of an Expedition. I hate Extortion.

MATT: Those Rouleaus are very pretty Things.—I hate your Bank Bills.—There is such a Hazard in putting them off.

MACHEATH: There is a certain Man of Distinction, who in his Time hath nick'd me out of a great deal of the Ready. He is in my Cash, Ben;—I'll point him out to you this Evening, and you shall draw upon him for the Debt.—The Company are met; I hear the Dice-box in the other Room. So, Gentlemen, your Servant. You'll meet me at Marybone.

SCENE V.

Peachum's *Lock: A Table with Wine, Brandy, Pipes and Tobacco.*

[Peachum, Lockit]

LOCKIT: The Coronation Account,[10] Brother Peachum, is of so intricate a Nature, that I believe it will never be settled.

PEACHUM: It consists indeed of a great Variety of Articles.—It was worth to our People, in Fees of different Kinds, above ten Instalments—This is part of the Account, Brother, that lies open before us.

LOCKIT: A Lady's Tail of rich Brocade—that, I see, is dispos'd of.

PEACHUM: To Mrs. Diana Trapes, the Tallywoman, and she will make a good Hand on't in Shoes and Slippers, to trick out young Ladies, upon their going into Keeping.—

LOCKIT: But I don't see any Article of the Jewels.

PEACHUM: Those are so well known, that they must be sent abroad—You'll find them enter'd under the Article of Exportation.—As for the Snuff-Boxes, Watches, Swords, &c.—I thought it best to enter them under their several Heads.

LOCKIT: Seven and twenty Women's Pockets compleat; with the several things therein contain'd; all Seal'd, Number'd, and enter'd.

PEACHUM: But, Brother, it is impossible for us now to enter upon this Affair.—We should have the whole Day before us.—Besides, the Account on the last Half Year's Plate is in a Book by it self, which lies at the other Office.

LOCKIT: Bring us then more Liquor.—To-day shall be for Pleasure—To-morrow for Business.—Ah Brother, those Daughters of ours are two slippery Hussies—Keep a watchful Eye upon Polly, and Macheath in a Day or two shall be our own again.

[9] Gold coins, easier to dispose of than bank bills.
[10] Things stolen from the crowd celebrating George II's coronation. The "take" was worth more than the thefts at ten installations of Lord Mayors of London.

AIR

LOCKIT: *What Gudgeons are we Men!*
Ev'ry Woman's easy Prey.
Though we have felt the Hook, again
We bite and they betray.
The Bird that hath been trapt,
When he hears his calling Mate,
To her he flies, again he's clapt
Within the wiry Grate.

PEACHUM: But what signifies catching the Bird, if your Daughter Lucy will set open the Door of the Cage?

LOCKIT: If Men were answerable for the Follies and Frailties of their Wives and Daughters, no Friends could keep a good Correspondence together for two Days.—This is unkind of you, Brother; for among good Friends, what they say or do goes for nothing.

[*Enter a* Servant]

SERVANT: Sir, here's Mrs. Diana Trapes wants to speak with you.

PEACHUM: Shall we admit her, Brother Lockit?

LOCKIT: By all means—She's a good Customer, and a fine-spoken Woman—And a Woman who drinks and talks so freely, will enliven the Conversation.

PEACHUM: Desire her to walk in. [*Exit* Servant]

SCENE VI.

Peachum, Lockit, Mrs. Trapes.

PEACHUM: Dear Mrs. Dye, your Servant—One may know by your Kiss, that your Ginn is excellent.

MRS. TRAPES: I was always very curious[11] in my Liquors.

LOCKIT: There is no prefum'd Breath like it—I have been long acquainted with the Flavour of those Lips —Han't I, Mrs. Dye?

MRS. TRAPES: Fill it up.—I take as large Draughts of Liquor, as I did of Love.—I hate a Flincher in either.

AIR

In the Days of my Youth I could bill like a Dove, fa,
*   la, la, &c.*
Like a Sparrow at all times was ready for Love, fa
*   la, la, &c.*
The Life of all Mortals in Kissing should pass,
Lip to Lip while we're young—then the Lip to the
*   Glass, fa, &c.*

But now, Mr. Peachum, to our Business.—If you have Blacks of any kind, brought in of late, Mantoes —Velvet Scarfs—Petticoats—Let it be what it will—

11 Choosy.

I am your Chap—for all my Ladies are very fond of Mourning.

PEACHUM: Why, look ye, Mrs. Dye—you deal so hard with us, that we can afford to give the Gentlemen, who venture their Lives for the Goods, little or nothing.

MRS. TRAPES: The hard Times oblige me to go very near in my Dealing.—To be sure, of late Years I have been a great Sufferer by the Parliament.— Three thousand Pounds would hardly make me amends.—The Act for destroying the Mint,[12] was a severe Cut upon our Business—'Till then, if a Customer stept out of the way—we knew where to have her—No doubt you know Mrs. Coaxer—there's a Wench now ('till to-day) with a good Suit of Cloaths of mine upon her Back, and I could never set Eyes upon her for three Months together.—Since the Act too against Imprisonment for small Sums, my Loss there too hath been very considerable, and it must be so, when a Lady can borrow a handsome Petticoat, or a clean Gown, and I not have the least Hank[13] upon her! And, o' my conscience, now-a-days most Ladies take a Delight in cheating, when they can do it with Safety.

PEACHUM: Madam, you had a handsome Gold Watch of us t'other Day for seven Guineas.—Considering we must have our Profit—To a Gentleman upon the Road, a Gold Watch will be scarce worth the taking.

MRS. TRAPES: Consider, Mr. Peachum, that Watch was remarkable, and not of very safe Sale.—If you have any black Velvet Scarfs—they are a handsome Winter-wear; and take with most Gentlemen who deal with my Customers.—'Tis I that put the Ladies upon a good Foot. 'Tis not Youth or Beauty that fixes their Price. The Gentlemen always pay according to their Dress, from half a Crown to two Guineas; and yet those Hussies make nothing of bilking of me.— Then, too, allowing for Accidents.—I have eleven fine Customers now down under the Surgeon's Hands,—what with Fees and other Expences, there are great Goings-out, and no Comings-in, and not a Farthing to pay for at least a Month's cloathing.— We run great Risques—great Risques indeed.

PEACHUM: As I remember, you said something just now of Mrs. Coaxer.

MRS. TRAPES: Yes, Sir.—To be sure I stript her of a Suit of my own Cloaths about two hours ago; and have left her as she should be, in her Shift, with a Lover of hers at my House. She call'd him up Stairs, as he was going to Marybone in a Hackney Coach.— And I hope, for her own sake and mine, she will perswade the Captain to redeem her, for the Captain is very generous to the Ladies.

LOCKIT: What Captain?

MRS. TRAPES: He thought I did not know him—

12 Where debtors could be safe from arrest.
13 No hold upon her.

An intimate Acquaintance of yours, Mr. Peachum—Only Captain Macheath—as fine as a Lord.

PEACHUM: To-morrow, dear Mrs. Dye, you shall set your own Price upon any of the Goods you like—We have at least half a dozen Velvet Scarfs, and all at your service. Will you give me leave to make you a Present of this Suit of Night-cloaths for your own wearing?—But are you sure it is Captain Macheath?

MRS. TRAPES: Though he thinks I have forgot him, no Body knows him better. I have taken a great deal of the Captain's Money in my Time at second-hand, for he always lov'd to have his Ladies well drest.

PEACHUM: Mr. Lockit and I have a little business with the Captain;—You understand me—and we will satisfye you for Mrs. Coaxer's Debt.

LOCKIT: Depend upon it—we will deal like Men of Honour.

MRS. TRAPES: I don't enquire after your Affairs—so whatever happens, I wash my Hands on't.—It hath always been my Maxim, that one Friend should assist another—But if you please—I'll take one of the Scarfs home with me. 'Tis always good to have something in Hand.

SCENE VII.

Newgate.

LUCY: Jealousy, Rage, Love and Fear are at once tearing me to pieces. How I am weather-beaten and shatter'd with distresses!

AIR

I'm like a Skiff on the Ocean tost,
   Now high, now low, with each Billow born,
With her Rudder broke, and her Anchor lost,
   Deserted and all forlorn.
While thus I lye rolling and tossing all Night,
That Polly lyes sporting on Seas of Delight!
Revenge, Revenge, Revenge,
Shall appease my restless Sprite.

I have the Rats-bane ready—I run no Risque; for I can lay her Death upon the Ginn, and so many dye of that naturally that I shall never be call'd in Question.—But say, I were to be hang'd—I never could be hang'd for any thing that would give me greater Comfort, than the poysoning that Slut.

[*Enter* Filch]

FILCH: Madam, here's our Miss Polly come to wait upon you.

LUCY: Show her in.

SCENE VIII.

Lucy, Polly.

LUCY: Dear Madam, your Servant.—I hope you will pardon my Passion, when I was so happy to see you last.—I was so overrun with the Spleen, that I was perfectly out of my self. And really when one hath the Spleen, every thing is to be excus'd by a Friend.

AIR

When a Wife's in her Pout
(As she's sometimes, no doubt)
   The good Husband as meek as a Lamb,
   Her Vapours to still
   First grants her her Will,
And the quieting Draught is a Dram.
Poor Man! And the quieting Draught is a Dram.

—I wish all our Quarrels might have so comfortable a Reconciliation.

POLLY: I have no Excuse for my own Behaviour, Madam, but my Misfortunes.—And really, Madam, I suffer too upon your Account.

LUCY: But, Miss Polly—in the way of Friendship, will you give me leave to propose a Glass of Cordial to you?

POLLY: Strong-Waters are apt to give me the Head-ache—I hope, Madam, you will excuse me.

LUCY: Not the greatest Lady in the Land could have better in her Closet, for her own private drinking.—You seem mighty low in Spirits, my Dear.

POLLY: I am sorry, Madam, my Health will not allow me to accept of your Offer.—I should not have left you in the rude Manner I did when we met last, Madam, had not my Papa haul'd me away so unexpectedly—I was indeed somewhat provok'd, and perhaps might use some Expressions that were disrespectful.—But really, Madam, the Captain treated me with so much Contempt and Cruelty, that I deserv'd your Pity, rather than your Resentment.

LUCY: But since his Escape, no doubt all Matters are made up again.—Ah Polly! Polly! 'tis I am the unhappy Wife; and he loves you as if you were only his Mistress.

POLLY: Sure, Madam, you cannot think me so happy as to be the Object of your Jealousy.—A Man is always afraid of a Woman who loves him too well—so that I must expect to be neglected and avoided.

LUCY: Then our Cases, my dear Polly, are exactly alike. Both of us indeed have been too fond.

AIR

POLLY: *A Curse attends that Woman's Love,*
Who always would be pleasing.
LUCY: *The Pertness of the billing Dove,*
Like tickling, is but teazing.
POLLY: *What then in Love can Woman do?*
LUCY: *If we grow fond, they shun us.*
POLLY: *And when we fly them, they pursue.*
LUCY: *But leave us when they've won us.*

LUCY: Love is so very whimsical in both Sexes, that it is impossible to be lasting.—But my Heart is particular, and contradicts my own Observation.

POLLY: But really, Mistress Lucy, by his last Behaviour, I think I ought to envy you.—When I was forc'd from him, he did not shew the least Tenderness.—But perhaps, he hath a Heart not capable of it.

AIR

Among the Men, Coquets we find,
Who Court by turns all Woman-kind;
And we grant all their Hearts desir'd,
When they are flatter'd, and admir'd.

The Coquets of both Sexes are Self-lovers, and that is a Love no other whatever can dispossess. I fear, my dear Lucy, our Husband is one of those.

LUCY: Away with these melancholy Reflections,—indeed, my dear Polly, we are both of us a Cup too low.—Let me prevail upon you, to accept of my Offer.

AIR

Come, sweet Lass,
Let's banish Sorrow
'Till To-morrow;
Come, sweet Lass,
Let's take a chirping Glass.
Wine can clear
The Vapours of Despair;
And make us light as Air;
Then drink, and banish Care.

I can't bear, Child, to see you in such low Spirits.—And I must persuade you to what I know will do you good.—I shall now soon be even with the hypocritical Strumpet. [*Aside*]

SCENE IX.

Polly.

POLLY: All this wheedling of Lucy cannot be for nothing.—At this time too! when I know she hates me!—The Dissembling of a Woman is always the Fore-runner of Mischief.—By pouring Strong-Waters down my Throat, she thinks to pump some Secrets out of me—I'll be upon my Guard, and won't taste a Drop of her Liquor, I'm resolv'd.

SCENE X.

[Lucy, *with Strong-Waters;* Polly]
LUCY: Come, Miss Polly.

POLLY: Indeed, Child, you have given yourself trouble to no purpose.—You must, my Dear, excuse me.

LUCY: Really, Miss Polly, you are so squeamishly affected about taking a Cup of Strong-Waters as a Lady before Company. I vow, Polly, I shall take it

monstrously ill if you refuse me.—Brandy and Men (though Women love them never so well) are always taken by us with some Reluctance—unless 'tis in private.

POLLY: I protest, Madam, it goes against me.—What do I see! Macheath again in Custody!—Now every glimm'ring of Happiness is lost. [*Drops the Glass of Liquor on the Ground*]

LUCY: Since things are thus, I'm glad the Wench hath escap'd: for by this Event, 'tis plain, she was not happy enough to deserve to be poison'd. [*Aside*]

SCENE XI.

Lockit, Macheath, Peachum, Lucy, Polly.

LOCKIT: Set your Heart to rest, Captain.—You have neither the Chance of Love or Money for another Escape,—for you are order'd to be call'd down upon your Tryal immediately.

PEACHUM: Away, Hussies!—This is not a time for a Man to be hamper'd with his Wives.—You see, the Gentleman is in Chains already.

LUCY: O Husband, Husband, my heart long'd to see thee; but to see thee thus distracts me!

POLLY: Will not my dear Husband look upon his Polly? Why hadst thou not flown to me for Protection? With me thou hadst been safe.

AIR

POLLY: *Hither, dear Husband, turn your Eyes.*
LUCY: *Bestow one Glance to cheer me.*
POLLY: *Think with that Look, thy Polly dyes.*
LUCY: *O shun me not—but hear me.*
POLLY: *'Tis Polly sues.*
LUCY: *. . . 'Tis Lucy speaks.*
POLLY: *Is thus true Love requited?*
LUCY: *My Heart is bursting.*
POLLY: *. . . Mine too breaks.*
LUCY: *Must I*
POLLY: *. . . Must I be slighted?*

MACHEATH: What would you have me say, Ladies?—You see, this Affair will soon be at an end, without my disobliging either of you.

PEACHUM: But the settling this Point, Captain, might prevent a Law-suit between your two Widows.

AIR

MACHEATH: *Which way shall I turn me?—How*
can I decide?
Wives, the Day of our Death, are as fond as a Bride.
One Wife is too much for most Husbands to hear,
But two at a time there's no Mortal can bear.
This way, and that way, and which way I will,

What would comfort the one, t'other Wife would take ill.

POLLY: But if his own Misfortunes have made him insensible to mine—A Father sure will be more compassionate.—Dear, dear Sir, sink the material Evidence, and bring him off at his Tryal—Polly upon her Knees begs it of you.

AIR

When my Hero in Court appears,
   And stands arraign'd for his Life,
Then think of poor Polly's Tears;
   For Ah! Poor Polly's his Wife.
Like the Sailor he holds up his Hand,
   Distrest on the dashing Wave.
To die a dry Death at Land,
   Is as bad as a watry Grave.
   And alas, poor Polly!
   Alack, and well-a-day!
   Before I was in Love,
   Oh! every Month was May.

LUCY: If Peachum's Heart is harden'd, sure you, Sir, will have more Compassion on a Daughter.—I know the Evidence is in your Power.—How then can you be a Tyrant to me?
   [*Kneeling*]

AIR

When he holds up his Hand arraign'd for his Life,
O think of your Daughter, and think I'm his Wife!
What are Cannons, or Bombs, or clashing of Swords?
For Death is more certain by Witnesses' Words.
Then nail up their Lips; that dread Thunder allay;
And each Month of my Life will hereafter be May.

LOCKIT: Macheath's time is come, Lucy.—We know our own Affairs, therefore let us have no more Whimpering or Whining.

PEACHUM: Set your Heart at rest, Polly.—Your Husband is to dye to-day.—Therefore, if you are not already provided, 'tis high time to look about for another. There's Comfort for you, you Slut.

LOCKIT: We are ready, Sir, to conduct you to the Old-Baily.

AIR

MACHEATH: *The Charge is prepar'd; The Lawyers are met,*
   The Judges all rang'd (a terrible Show!)
   I go, undismay'd.—For Death is a Debt,
   A Debt on demand.—So, take what I owe.
     Then farewell, my Love—Dear Charmers, adieu.
   Contented I die—'Tis the better for you.
   Here ends all Dispute the rest of our Lives.
   For this way at once I please all my Wives.

Now, Gentlemen, I am ready to attend you.

SCENE XII.

Lucy, Polly, Filch.

POLLY: Follow them, Filch, to the Court. And when the Tryal is over, bring me a particular Account of his Behaviour, and of every thing that happen'd.—You'll find me here with Miss Lucy. [*Exit Filch*] But why is all this Musick?

LUCY: The Prisoners, whose Tryals are put off till next Session, are diverting themselves.

POLLY: Sure there is nothing so charming as Musick! I'm fond of it to distraction!—But alas!—now, all Mirth seems an Insult upon my Affliction.—Let us retire, my dear Lucy, and indulge our Sorrows.—The noisy Crew, you see, are coming upon us. [*Exeunt*]

[*A Dance of Prisoners in Chains, &c.*]

SCENE XIII.

The Condemn'd Hold

MACHEATH: [*In a melancholy Posture*]

AIR

O cruel, cruel, cruel Case!
Must I suffer this Disgrace?

AIR

Of all the Friends in time of Grief,
When threatning Death looks grimmer,
Not one so sure can bring Relief
As this best Friend, a Brimmer. [Drinks]

AIR

Since I must swing,—I scorn, I scorn to wince or whine. [Rises]

AIR

But now again my Spirits sink;
I'll raise them high with Wine. [Drinks a Glass of Wine]

AIR

But Valour the stronger grows,
The stronger Liquor we're drinking.
And how can we feel our Woes,
When we've lost the Trouble of Thinking? [Drinks]

AIR

If thus—A Man can die
Much bolder with Brandy. [Pours out a Bumper of Brandy]

AIR

*So I drink off this Bumper.—And now I can stand
the Test.
And my Comrades shall see, that I die as brave as the
Best.* [Drinks]

AIR

*But can I leave my pretty Hussies,
Without one Tear, or tender Sigh?*

AIR

*Their Eyes, their Lips, their Busses
Recall my Love.—Ah, must I die?*

AIR

*Since Laws were made for ev'ry Degree,
To curb Vice in others, as well as me,
I wonder we han't better Company
    Upon Tyburn Tree!
But Gold from Law can take out the Sting;
And if rich Men like us were to swing,
'Twould thin the Land, such Numbers to string
    Upon Tyburn Tree!*

JAILOR: Some Friends of yours, Captain, desire to
be admitted.—I leave you together.

SCENE XIV.

Macheath, Ben Budge, Matt of the Mint.

MACHEATH: For my having broke Prison, you see,
Gentlemen, I am order'd immediate Execution.—The
Sheriffs Officers, I believe, are now at the Door.—
That Jemmy Twitcher should peach me, I own surpriz'd me!—'Tis a plain Proof that the World is all
alike, and that even our Gang can no more trust one
another than other People. Therefore, I beg you,
Gentlemen, look well to yourselves, for in all proba-
bility you may live some Months longer.
MATT: We are heartily sorry, Captain, for your
Misfortune.—But 'tis what we must all come to.
MACHEATH: Peachum and Lockit, you know, are
infamous Scoundrels. Their Lives are as much in
your Power, as yours are in theirs.—Remember your
dying Friend!—'Tis my last Request.—Bring those
Villains to the Gallows before you, and I am satisfied.
MATT: We'll do't.
JAILOR: Miss Polly and Miss Lucy intreat a Word
with you.
MACHEATH: Gentlemen, Adieu.

SCENE XV.

Lucy, Macheath, Polly.

MACHEATH: My dear Lucy—My dear Polly—
Whatsoever hath past between us is now at an end.—

If you are fond of marrying again, the best Advice I
can give you is to Ship yourselves off for the West-
Indies, where you'll have a fair chance of getting a
Husband a-piece, or by good Luck, two or three, as
you like best.
POLLY: How can I support this Sight!
LUCY: There is nothing moves one so much as a
great Man in Distress.

AIR

LUCY: *Would I might be hang'd!*
POLLY: *. . . And I would so too!*
LUCY: *To be hang'd with you.*
POLLY: *. . . My Dear, with you.*
MACHEATH: *O Leave me to Thought! I fear! I
doubt! I tremble! I droop!—See, my Courage is out.*
[Turns up the empty Bottle]
POLLY: *No token of Love?*
MACHEATH: *. . . See, my Courage is out.* [Turns
up the empty Pot]
LUCY: *No token of Love?*
POLLY: *. . . Adieu.*
LUCY: *. . . Farewell.*
MACHEATH: *But hark! I hear the Toll of the Bell.*
CHORUS: *Tol de rol lol, &c.*

JAILOR: Four Women more, Captain, with a Child
a-piece! See, here they come.
[*Enter* Women *and* Children]
MACHEATH: What—four Wives more!—This is too
much.—Here—tell the Sheriffs Officers I am ready.
[*Exit* Macheath *guarded*]

SCENE XVI.

[*To them, Enter* Player *and* Beggar]
PLAYER: But, honest Friend, I hope you don't intend that Macheath shall be really executed.
BEGGAR: Most certainly, Sir.—To make the Piece
perfect, I was for doing strict poetical Justice.—Macheath is to be hang'd; and for the other Personages of
the Drama, the Audience must have suppos'd they
were all either hang'd or transported.
PLAYER: Why then, Friend, this is a down-right
deep Tragedy. The Catastrophe is manifestly wrong,
for an Opera must end happily.
BEGGAR: Your Objection, Sir, is very just; and is
easily remov'd. For you must allow, that in this kind
of Drama, 'tis no matter how absurdly things are
brought about.—So—you Rabble there—run and cry
a Reprieve—let the Prisoner be brought back to his
Wives in Triumph.
PLAYER: All this we must do, to comply with the
Taste of the Town.
BEGGAR: Through the whole Piece you may observe such a similitude of Manners in high and low
Life that it is difficult to determine whether (in the
fashionable Vices) the fine Gentlemen imitate the
Gentlemen of the Road, or the Gentlemen of the

Road the fine Gentlemen.—Had the Play remain'd as I at first intended, it would have carried a most excellent Moral. 'Twould have shown that the lower Sort of People have their Vices in a degree as well as the Rich: And that they are punish'd for them.

SCENE XVII.

[*To them,* Macheath *with* Rabble, &c.]

MACHEATH: So, it seems, I am not left to my Choice, but must have a Wife at last.—Look ye, my Dears, we will have no Controversie now. Let us give this Day to Mirth, and I am sure she who thinks herself my Wife will testifie her Joy by a Dance.

ALL: Come, a Dance—a Dance.

MACHEATH: Ladies, I hope you will give me leave to present a Partner to each of you. And (if I may without Offence) for this time, I take Polly for mine. —And for Life, you Slut,—for we were really marry'd.—As for the rest—But at present keep your own Secret. [*To* Polly]

[A Dance]

AIR

Thus I stand like the Turk, *with his Doxies around;*
From all Sides their Glances his Passion confound;
For black, brown, and fair, his Inconstancy burns,
And the different Beauties subdue him by turns:
Each calls forth her Charms, to provoke his Desires:
Though willing to all, with but one he retires.
But think of this Maxim, and put off your Sorrow,
The Wretch of To-day may be happy To-morrow.

CHORUS: *But think of this Maxim, &c.*

Victor Hugo. *Above* (center): Friedrich von Schiller. From Lewes, *On Actors and the Art of Acting. Right:* Michelot as Don Carlos in *Hernani. Opposite page:* Talma as Leicester and Mlle. Duchesnois as the Queen of Scotland in *Mary Stuart.* From *Theatre, Comedie Française,* Vol. II. Theatre Collection, New York Public Library.

Romantic Forms of Drama

Romantic Forms of Drama

The major romantic form of drama is amply illustrated by Goethe's *Faust* (see pages 505–555), especially when read in its entirety as a two-part drama. We have in this work an essentially Shakespearian freedom of form and complete disregard of the neoclassical unities of place, time, and action. We confront in it the free play of fancy so necessary to the romantic imagination. We find here a rich variety of style; the juxtaposition of grave and gay matter, grandeur and levity, tragedy and comedy, the ideal and the grotesque, universality and specificity of time and place, and a general abundance of both observation and imagination. We observe great metrical variety in the use of verse forms ranging from discursive blank verse to ballad meter (as in Gretchen's famous spinning song),[1] and a general *mélange des genres* that inevitably culminates in Wagnerian "music-drama" or opera. With all this, moreover, we find in *Faust* a veritable *summa* of romantic optimism, the reaching out toward maximum human possibilities of feeling and thought of Doctor Faust's struggle for knowledge, power, and practical accomplishment. At the opposite extreme, we encounter in Georg Buchner's *Danton's Death*, a drama about the French Revolution written but a few years after the completion of *Faust* and the death of Goethe in 1832, a work in form almost as "free" or "Shakespearian" (as well as modern and "expressionistic") but in content a severe historical delimitation of human possibilities and expectations from social action. (See pages 570–597.)

The ideality favored by proponents of romanticism was apt to be undermined by self-indulgent individuality as well as tumid fervency of rebellious sentiment or revolutionary zeal. This was variously the case during the period that extended from about 1780 to about 1837. It was especially unfortunate in its effect on dramatic writing, during the early period noted for the youthful excesses of Goethe in *Goetz von Berlichingen* and Schiller in *The Robbers,* not to mention the violent work of minor playwrights of the *Sturm und Drang* movement in Germany before 1800. The extravagances of romanticism also vitiated the plays written in the next four decades by fervent poets such as Byron and Shelley in England and Victor Hugo in France as well as by purveyors of marketable melodrama such as the popular Kotzebue and his imitators in Europe and America. But ideality managed to be preserved and indeed refined by Germany's greatest poets, Goethe and Schiller, as they matured under the influence of classic art. In the second half of the eighteenth century classic art had become idealized in Germany under the influence of leading critics of art and literature such as Winckelmann and Lessing, and this sense of form in art and discipline in life was asserted in the work of Goethe

[1] See page 538.

and Schiller. If they never really expelled the romantic artist in their constitution and their work they imposed restraints on both that justify the appelation "classicism" or, rather, quasi-classicism. This provocative and here and there highly productive tension is apparent not only in the plays of Goethe and Schiller but in the work of the gifted, though regrettably short-lived, Heinrich von Kleist, the author of the powerful dramas of psychological tension *Penthesilea* and *The Prince of Homburg.*

Of romantic idealism the purest representative was Friedrich von Schiller (1759–1805). Perhaps the best summation of his ingrained idealism will be found in his view of tragic art, as exemplified in *Mary Stuart,* that "tragedy is the *poetic* imitation of an action," that "it lets us see *"man suffering,"* that "the very idea of man suffering implies a *man in the full sense of the term,"* and that the final aim of tragedy is to "excite *pity"* or "awaken *sympathy."*

Schiller's mature plays were in part the product of a deliberate effort by Goethe and himself to temper the "storm and stress" run-away type of romanticism which they had helped to launch in Germany in the seventeen-seventies and seventeen-eighties. Only a new classicism would be able to correct this emotional and dramatic anarchy. Goethe, who had become the artistic head of the state theatre at Weimar in 1791, made it the center of this endeavor to purify and idealize the drama and the stage, and he enlisted his gifted friend Schiller in this enterprise, which came to be known as Weimar classicism. From it, Goethe boasted "All that was morbid, weak, lachrymose, and sentimental, as well as all that was frightful, horrible and offensive to decorum was utterly excluded. . . ." He "educated" the actors, dedicated them to the "perpetual exercise of excellence," and went out of his way to elevate their social status by introducing the most talented of them into his own intellectual and aristocratic circles. Schiller, he was pleased to acknowledge, "proceeded in the same spirit as myself." Cultivation of mind and the social graces, as well as good elocution, was considered essential to the kind of actor Weimar classicism favored. Since Goethe and Schiller were devoted to the writing of poetic rather than realistic prose drama, their instrument, the actor, was carefully instructed to serve the ideality of art. Goethe even set down numerous rules for the actor, who was to acquaint himself with classic sculptures in order to fix in his mind "the natural grace of their sitting, standing, and walking," and was to study the best ancient and modern authors.[2]

[2] A number of these instructions are given in chapter XI on Weimar Classicism, pages 425–444 in Alois Nagler's *Sources of Theatrical Theatre,* New York: Theatre Annual, 1952 (reprinted in 1959 by Dover Publications). The fragmentary quotations above are from this book.

In Schiller's work, Weimar classicism was combined with an acute sense of history as the battlefield of ideas and ideals on which man defines himself and discovers his potentiality for the good. *Ideal* drama in Schiller was therefore *idealistic* drama. In *Mary Stuart,* for example, the Stuart queen arrives through error and suffering at some measure of self-understanding and self-denial, and a resignation to fate but trust in a merciful and forgiving God. Dramatic art, for which Schiller had a natural endowment, was confined in his case with an aspiring spirit and an inquiring, but believing rather than disenchanted, intellect.

Victor Lange, the Princeton scholar-critic, sums up this poet's inclinations aptly when he writes that "he was unremittingly preoccupied with the possibility of justifying life, which in its natural state seemed chaotic and meaningless, by transforming it into an achievement of ideal coherence." And it was Schiller's ambition "that the emerging German stage should be fascinating by the seriousness of his message as well as the spectacular power of its theatrical illusions and serve as a 'moral' institution."[3]

Between the polarities represented by the classically controlled mature plays of Schiller, and Victor Hugo's ultra-romantic dramatic work in *Hernani* (see pages 928–957) and several of his later plays, will be found a number of dramatic forms to which romanticism provided a stimulus. One much favored type of play was historical and biographical tragedy, represented in the present section by Schiller's *Mary Stuart* (see pages 882–925), one of a half dozen noteworthy examples of the genre he produced. Another, and indeed equally noteworthy, example is the great Russian poet Pushkin's chronicle tragedy *Boris Godunov,* completed in 1825. What helped to make romantic tragedy a well-regarded genre was that a variety of ideas or themes could be impacted in it—the struggle against social injustice, for instance, present in Schiller's *Fiesco,* Goethe's *Egmont,* Byron's Venetian tragedies *Marino Faliero* and *The Two Foscari,* and Shelley's *The Cenci,* which combines domestic tragedy with an attack on the church and state in Renaissance Italy. (Beatrice, the heroine of this remarkable if not perfectly stageworthy drama, goes to her death for the murder of her incestuously inclined father crying out, "What a world we make, the oppressor and the oppressed!") Characteristically, Schiller combined a drama of romantic passion with a theme of liberal idealism in *Don Carlos,* and wrote a Joan of Arc play, though a sadly sentimentalized one with a flagrantly unhistorical conclusion. Even Browning and Tennyson tried their wings in the theatre of historical drama. The latter wrote a turgid *Beckett,* thus anticipating T. S. Eliot's distinctly sharper treatment of the conflict between church and state in *Murder in the Cathedral.*

Another product of the romantic theatre, often more commodity than art, is *melodrama;* in its most glaring manifestations of perfervid emotionalism and violent action it is a product of romanticism in the theatre. Its prose form, often accompanied by music (hence the term *melo-drama*) in the stage production, became one of the staples of the popular stage in nineteenth century Europe and America. But melodrama also had some literary as well as popular success. Victor Hugo, in particular, did amazing things in his few verse melodramas, one of which—*Hernani* —approached tragic elevation with its language. Victor Hugo's success with *Hernani* in 1830, moreover, set a seal of approval on romantic principles of dramatic composition, announced three years earlier with the publication of a preface to his youthful prose play, *Cromwell.* It struck a blow for freedom of dramatic form and style that proved applicable to both romantic and naturalistic drama throughout the rest of the century.

In his fervid *Préface,*[4] Hugo called upon the theatre to abandon neoclassicism and accept the validity and dramatic interest of ugliness, distortion, and the element of the *grotesque,* for which this author evinced a special fondness in a number of his plays as well as novels such as his *Nôtre Dame de Paris* or *The Hunchback of Notre Dame.*

I—The "Grotesque"

Christianity leads poetry to the truth. Like it, the modern muse will see things in a higher and broader light. It will realize that everything in creation is not humanely *beautiful,* that the ugly exists beside the beautiful, the unshapely beside the graceful, the grotesque on the reverse of the sublime, evil with good, darkness with light. It will ask itself if the narrow and relative sense of the artist should prevail over the infinite, absolute sense of the Creator; if it is for man to correct God; if a mutilated nature will be the more beautiful for the mutilation; if art has not the right to duplicate, so to speak, man, life, creation; if things will progress better when their muscles and their vigor have been taken from them; if, in short, to be incomplete [in excluding whatever is not beautiful or exalted, as was the case in the neoclassic tragedies of France up to Hugo's time] is the best way to be harmonious. . . .

In the idea of men of modern times, the grotesque plays an enormous part. It is found everywhere; on the one hand it creates the abnormal and the horrible, on the other the comic and the burlesque. . . . It is the grotesque which scatters lavishly, in air, water, earth, fire, those myriads of intermediary creatures which we find all alive in the popular traditions of the Middle Ages; it is the grotesque which impels the ghastly antics

---

[3] Victor Lange, "Introduction." *Classical German Drama,* New York, Bantam Books 1963 (pp. 15–16).

[4] For the complete preface consult the French text; for a larger selection in English than the paragraphs that follow, Barrett Clark's *European Theories of the Drama,* Revised Edition by Henry Popkin. New York: Crown, 1965, pp. 357–370.

of the witches' revels, which gives Satan his horns, his cloven foot and his bat's wings. It is the grotesque, still the grotesque, which now casts into the Christian hell the frightful faces which the severe genius of Dante and Milton will evoke, and again peoples it with those laughter-moving figures amid which Callot, the burlesque Michelangelo, will disport himself. If it passes from the world of imagination to the real world, it unfolds an inexhaustible supply of parodies of mankind. Creations of its fantasy are the Scaramouches, Crispins and Harlequins, grinning silhouettes of man, types altogether unknown to serious-minded antiquity, although they originated in classic Italy. It is the grotesque, lastly, which, coloring the same drama with the fancies of the North and of the South in turn, exhibits Sganarelle capering about Don Juan and Mephistopheles crawling about Faust. . . .

Thanks to it, there is no thought of monotony. Sometimes it injects laughter, sometimes horror, into tragedy. It will bring Romeo face to face with the apothecary, Macbeth with the witches, Hamlet with the grave-diggers. Sometimes it may, without discord, as in the scene between King Lear and his jester, mingle its shrill voice with the most sublime, the most dismal, the dreamiest [manifestations] of the soul.

II—"The Unities"

We see how quickly the arbitrary distinction between the species of poetry vanishes before common sense and taste. No less easily one might demolish the alleged rule of the two unities.[5] We say *two* and not *three* unities, because unity of plot or of *ensemble,* the only true and well-founded one, was long ago removed from the sphere of discussion. . . .

Where did any one ever see a porch or peristyle of that sort? What could be more opposed—we will not say to the truth, for the scholastics hold it very cheap, but to probability? The result is that everything that is too characteristic, too intimate, too local, to happen in the antechamber or on the street-corner—that is to say the whole drama—takes place [out of sight] in the wings. We see on the stage only the elbows of the plot, so to speak; its hands are somewhere else. Instead of scenes, we have narrative; instead of tableaux, descriptions.

People are beginning to understand in our day that *exact localization* is one of the first elements of reality. The speaking or acting characters are not the only ones who engrave on the minds of the spectators a faithful representation of the facts. The place where this or that catastrophe took place becomes a terrible and inseparable witness thereof;

5 Place and time.

and the absence of silent "characters" of this sort would make the greatest scenes of history incomplete in the drama.

Unity of time rests on no firmer foundation than unity of place. A plot forcibly confined within twenty-four hours is as absurd as one confined within a peristyle. Every plot has its proper duration as well as its appropriate place. Think of administering the same dose of time to all events! of applying the same measure to everything! . . . Let us say, rather, that everything will die in the operation, and so the dogmatic mutilators reach their ordinary result; what was alive in the chronicles is dead in [neoclassic] tragedy. . . .

A final argument, taken from the very bowels of the art, would of itself suffice to show the absurdity of the rule of the two unities. It is the existence of the third unity, unity of plot—the only one that is universally admitted, because it results from a fact; neither the human eye nor the human mind can grasp more than one *ensemble* at one time. This one is as essential as the other two are useless. It is the one which fixes the viewpoint of the drama; and, by this very fact, it excludes the other two. There can no more be three unities in the drama than three horizons in a picture. But let us be careful not to confound unity with simplicity of plot. The former does not in any way exclude the secondary plots on which the principal plot may depend. It is necessary only that these parts, being skillfully subordinated to the general play, shall tend constantly toward the central plot and group themselves about it at the various stages, or rather on the various levels, of the drama. Unity of plot is the stage law of perspective. . . .

III—Art and Nature

It is a grand and beautiful sight to see this broad development of a drama wherein art powerfully seconds nature; of a drama wherein the plot moves on to the conclusion with a firm and unembarrassed step, without diffuseness and [but also] without undue compression; of a drama wherein the poet abundantly fulfills the multifold object of art, which is to open to the spectator a double prospect, to illuminate at the same time the interior and the exterior of mankind. . . .

It will readily be imagined that, for a work of this kind, if the poet must *choose* (and he must, he should choose) not the *beautiful,* but the *characteristic.* Not that it is advisable to "make local color," as they say today; that is, to add as an afterthought a few discordant touches here and there to a work that is at best utterly conventional and false. The local color should not be on the surface of the drama, but in its substance, in the very heart of the work, whence it spreads . . . naturally and evenly, and . . . into every corner of the drama, as the sap ascends from the root to the tree's topmost leaf. . . .

In this tableau of the stage, each figure must be held down to its most prominent, most individual, most precisely defined characteristic. Even the vulgar and the trivial should have an accent of their own.

That "art" should not be in conflict with "nature" was a central thesis in the celebrated Preface to *Cromwell* which is excerpted above. That society, with its pretences and prejudices, should not be in conflict with nature and should not suppress or pervert healthy human instinct was parallel romantic doctrine in social thought, educational philosophy, and "psychology" from the time of Rousseau's vogue in late eighteenth-century Europe. But the best treatment of this viewpoint in the dramatic form did not come from Hugo but from that refined, rather than thunderous, poet of romantic sensibility Alfred de Musset, whose masterpiece the reader will have encountered in the first part of this book (pages 551–569). Unlike Hugo, Musset provided no program for the theatre either before or after *No Trifling with Love,* but he became a master of romantic and dramatic irony, thus providing another genre of romantic playwriting in his *comédies proverbes,* (or, *proverbes dramatiques,* p. 552). Hugo, however, must occupy an extremely important place in the history of the Romantic Theatre as its latter-day prophet and champion in theory and attempted practice.

Schiller and Mary Stuart

Friedrich von Schiller (1759–1805) is the ideal representative of German romanticism and of the "classicism" at which he and his great friend and fellow-poet Goethe arrived after renouncing their youthful *Sturm und Drang* (Storm and Stress) extravagances. Idealism is the keystone of the arch of his philosophical and political thinking and it pulsates in his historical works, his writing on esthetics, and his poetry as well as his plays.

Schiller's emotional liberalism was heightened by his early experiences. Born in 1759 in the little duchy of Würtemberg, he tasted the irksomeness of parental discipline from a tyrannical father who served as a captain in the Duke's two-by-four army. Since he inherited his mother's sensitivity along with her blue eyes and blond hair, he was first intended for the clergy. Nevertheless, he soon entered a Prussianized military academy at the Duke's command. At sixteen he was allowed to substitute medicine for military science, and he actually became a regimental surgeon at Stuttgart in 1780.

Schiller began to flutter his artistic wings first in morbidly sentimental and pessimistic poems, and a year after his appointment to the army his first play, *The Robbers*, appeared. It was full of romantic rebellion and gloom, and it contrasted the extreme nobility of its idealistic hero, Karl Moor, with the utter villainy of a designing brother who piles evil upon evil in a world that favors hypocrisy. The hero of this energetic but adolescent tragedy takes to the forests, where he plays Robin Hood to a band of outlaws whose morals are superior to those of the Philistines who hug their pelf under the protection of the law. When the play was produced at Mannheim in January 1782, its effect was electrifying. Years, later, the French Republic made the author an honorary citizen in recognition of his services to the revolutionary cause, although his own ardor for revolutions had subsided considerably by then.

Defying his duke's order to write no more without permission and to correspond with no one abroad, Schiller escaped from Würtemberg in a closed carriage. He spent some time in Mannheim under a false name, but found himself without means there when the intimidated director of its theatre rejected his new work, *Fiesco*. This play, another and a somewhat better constructed paean to rebellion, set in Renaissance Italy, was published by a courageous bookseller. A noble lady, Frau von Wolzogen, gave the refugee shelter in her country house near Meiningen, and he spent half a year there preparing his next bombshell *Intrigue and Love* (*Kabale und Liebe*), a domestic tragedy patterned after Lessing's *Emilia Galotti*.

Fortunately, Schiller was soon able to overcome the scruples of the Mannheim director, Dalberg, and became his "theatre poet." *Fiesco* was produced next

year and *Intrigue and Love* followed soon after. Schiller then founded a literary journal, wrote criticism, and published the first act of his next play *Don Carlos* with which he won the favor of the "German Maecenas" Duke Karl August of Weimar.

Removing to Leipzig and living happily among generous literary friends, Schiller became a calmer spirit. Here he wrote lyrics like the famous *Hymn to Joy,* engaged in historical studies, and completed the play *Don Carlos,* which was based on them. It was his first drama in verse, and despite its zealous liberalism it revealed the poet transferring his faith from revolution to evolution. Schiller deplored the corruption of the Spanish court of Philip II and honored the revolutionary idealism of the ill-starred Don Carlos. But the moral emphasis was on the noble figure of the latter's friend the Marquis de Posa, who held that man could be redeemed by reasonableness and proved the point by converting Philip, although not soon enough to save Don Carlos. This play, which for all its sprawling character has been a favorite in Schiller's homeland, is in fact an epitome of Schilleresque romanticism.

Through Goethe's influence, he soon received a professorship in history at the famous University of Jena, and it was in connection with this position that he completed his book *The Revolt of the Netherlands* and turned out the popular *History of the Thirty Years' War,* which gave him material for his next play, the *Wallenstein* trilogy. After traveling for his health, Schiller finally settled in Weimar and basked in the friendship of Goethe. And it was here he wrote his final chapter in the German theatre, along with his best poems.

Wallenstein's Camp, a vivid picture of military life, appeared in 1788, and eleven years later came its sequels, the two related plays, *The Piccolimini* and *Wallenstein's Death,* generally considered his best work and accorded the accolade of translation by Coleridge. The trilogy dramatizes in human terms the tragedy of the Catholic generalissimo of the Thirty Years' War who, upon losing favor with the Holy Roman Emperor and developing doubts concerning the righteousness of the war, plans to make peace with the Protestants and establish an independent kingdom in Bohemia. He is assassinated before he can do so, having been betrayed by his closest friend, Piccolimini, whose idealistic son Max is betrothed to Wallenstein's daughter. *The Piccolimini* is wearying, but *Wallenstein's Death,* except for Schiller's characteristic overidealization of the lovers, is a poetic tragedy of noble proportions.

Schiller lapsed indeed into intellectual softness in some of the works that followed; he chose sentimental themes, idealized his characters, and substituted fervor for thought. But his *Mary Stuart,* in 1800, still disclosed considerable grasp of the realities in

880

presenting Mary as a crime-stained, if exalted, heroine who, in addition, loses her temper in the crucial
scene with Elizabeth and may be said to have hastened her own end. Leicester, Mary's vacillating
lover, and Queen Elizabeth also possess some gristle.
Only Schiller's somewhat sentimental treatment of
his heroine in the conclusion keeps the well-con-
structed and classically tempered tragedy distinctly in
the milieu of romantic theatre.

Schiller, in fact, had difficulty in maintaining a
strictly classical orientation. His *Mary Stuart* was followed in 1801 by the extremely romantic *Maid of
Orleans,* in which he idealized Joan of Arc perfer-
vidly, sentimentalized her story, and took many liberties with it; at the end she performs the miracle of
breaking her chains with her hands, hastens to save
the French king, and dies on the battlefield instead
of allowing herself to be burned at the stake. He
endeavored to write one classical drama two years
later, *The Bride of Messina* (*Die Braut von Messina*), which contains beautifully written choruses
and rhymed dialogue. But the fratricidal rivalry of
two brothers over a girl who turns out to be their
sister produces a remote "fate" drama and Schiller's
customary romanticization of life is present behind
the classic façade. Schiller's last play, the familiar
Wilhelm Tell, written in 1804, is an epitome of its
author's virtues and faults. It is a stirring evocation of
the liberty-loving Swiss who rise up against their oppressor, and it revels in an unforced lyric splendor.
Yet its elementary division of goats from sheep, of
the noble Wilhelm Tell from the melodramatic
Austrian tyrant Gessler, reflects Schiller's characteristic defects.

On the ninth of May, 1805, at forty-six, Schiller
succumbed to his tuberculosis. Racing against time,
he wrote at night and immersed his feet in cold water
in order to stay awake. When he died, he was
mourned by all who knew him, for he was one of
those lovable poets who win every heart. Madame de
Staël's impression, when she visited Weimar, of "his
sweet and gentle character," his tall, slender figure,
and his "exquisitely chiseled" mouth and Roman
nose is the picture of a matinee idol and makes a
suitably romantic symbol. His idealizing imagination
and dream of the good and the beautiful, combined
with a showman's instinctive feeling for theatre, made
him the favorite playwright of the German people.

Although many have considered the third play
of the Wallenstein series, *The Death of Wallenstein*
(*Wallenstein's Tod*) Schiller's most impressive work,
the play now usually considered his best, in the
American theatre, is the historical tragedy *Mary
Stuart*. This beautifully written and carefully designed (if somewhat wordy) work, rich in action and
twists of irony (as when Leicester's plan to reconcile
Elizabeth and Mary misfires because of an unfortunate clash of personalities), was completed by Schiller in 1800 under the influence of both Racine and
Goethe. Their strong interest in psychological drama
is evident in Schiller's effective characterization of
the rival queens Elizabeth and Mary Stuart, Leicester,
and several other dramatic personages. Without blinking at Mary's faults and errors, moreover, Schiller
enables the heroine to grow in moral stature, a
development essential to tragedy as well as to the
chastened and "classical" romanticism of the author.
He achieves this effect, moreover, without depriving
Mary of a highly dramatic flare-up when taunted by
her rival and captor in the climax, giving us one of
the finest scenes in romantic dramatic literature.

MARY STUART

A Tragedy

By *Friedrich von Schiller*

TRANSLATED BY THEODORE H. LUSTIG

CHARACTERS

ELIZABETH, *Queen of England*

MARY STUART, *Queen of Scotland, a prisoner in England*

ROBERT DUDLEY, *Earl of Leicester*

TALBOT, *Earl of Shrewsbury, Lord Privy Seal*

LORD BURLEIGH, *Lord High Treasurer*

THE EARL OF KENT

SIR WILLIAM DAVISON, *Secretary to Queen Elizabeth*

SIR AMIAS PAULET, *Mary Stuart's keeper*

MORTIMER, *his nephew*

COUNT AUBESPINE, *French Ambassador*

COUNT BELLIEVRE, *Extraordinary Emissary from France*

O'KELLY, *Mortimer's friend*

SIR DRUGEON DRURY, *Paulet's assistant*

MELVIL, *Mary's former steward*

BURGOYNE, *her physician*

HANNAH KENNEDY, *her nurse*

MARGARETA CURL, *her chambermaid*

THE SHERIFF, *English and French* NOBLES, GUARDS, LACKEYS *of the Queen of England,* MALE *and* FEMALE SERVANTS *of the Queen of Scotland*

ACT I. SCENE I.

A room in Fotheringhay Castle

[Hannah Kennedy, *nurse of the Queen of Scotland, in a violent quarrel with* Paulet, *who is about to force open a cupboard.* Drugeon Drury, *his assistant, is busy with a wrecking bar*]

HANNAH: What are you doing, sir? What new impertinence
Is this? Do not disturb this cabinet.

PAULET: Whence came those jewels? They were thrown
From windows on this floor to bribe our gardener!
My curse on women's tricks! Despite my vigilance
And all my searching for your valuables,
You still have hidden treasures in this room.
    [*He begins to search the cupboard*]
Where that was secreted there will be more.

HANNAH: Away! What insolence! This is the place
Where all my lady's secrets are.

PAULET: Precisely those I hope to find.
    [*He pulls out some writings*]

HANNAH: Those papers are of no importance,
They're only exercises that were written
To drive away the gloom of this sad jail.

PAULET: When wicked minds are idle—they create.

HANNAH: Those papers are in French.

PAULET: So much the worse. That is the language
Of England's enemies.

HANNAH: They're merely drafts
For letters to the English Queen.

PAULET: I shall deliver them. But look—what's this?
    [*He has touched a secret spring and now takes some jewelry from a hidden compartment*]
A royal diadem, encrusted richly
With precious stones, embellished with—
The lilies of the Kings of France!
    [*He gives it to* Drury]
You keep it, Drury. Put it with the rest.
    [Drury *leaves*]

HANNAH: Oh, shameful force which we must suffer!

PAULET: While she still has possessions she is dangerous.
In her hand everything becomes a weapon.

HANNAH: Have pity, sir! Do not deprive our lives
Of these last jewels. In her misery,
The sight of former glory brings her joy.
Now you have taken everything from her.

PAULET: It's in good hands and, in good time,
Will be restored to her.

HANNAH: Would anyone imagine that a queen
Resides within these barren walls?
No canopy above her seat! She is obliged
To put her tender foot that has been used
To gentle softness on these rough and common floors.
She finds her table set with tin, the likes of which
The meanest noblewoman would disdain.

PAULET: That's how, at Sterlyn, she had set her husband's table,
While with her lover she drank wine from golden cups.

HANNAH: She even lacks the small convenience of a mirror.

PAULET: As long as vainly she regards her image
She will not cease to hope and plot.

HANNAH: She has no books to entertain her mind.

PAULET: She has the Bible to improve her heart.

HANNAH: They even took her lute.

PAULET: Because she played on it lascivious melodies.

HANNAH: What fate for her, brought up with
    gentleness,
A queen already in her cradle,
And at the Medici's luxurious court
Grown up amidst its lavish pleasures!
Do not begrudge her these poor baubles.
A noble heart learns, in the end, to bear
A great misfortune, but it's hard to forego
The trifles which embellish life.
    PAULET: They only make a woman vain;
She ought to contemplate and ask forgiveness.
Humiliation, want—that is the price
One has to pay for luxury and vice.
    HANNAH: If, in her tender years, she sinned,
She must make peace with God and with her heart.
No one in England can presume to be her judge.
    PAULET: She will be judged where she did wrong.
    HANNAH: Her fetters are too strong for any evil-
    doing.
    PAULET: And yet her fetters were not strong
    enough.
She reached into the world and flung the brand
Of civil war into the realm, she armed
The bands of killers whom she sent against
Our Queen, whom God may long preserve.
She was within these walls when she spurred Parry,
That evil man, and Babington
To try their cursed hands at regicide!
These iron gates were not enough to hold her back
When she snared Norfolk's noble heart!
A sacrifice to her, his head, the best
Upon this isle, fell to the executioner's ax.
And even that most pitiable sight
Did not restrain those raving maniacs
Who still compete to throw themselves
Into the abyss for her sake.
For her sake, in a never-ending stream,
Men mount the scaffold's steps to die.
And that will never end until she, too,
The real criminal, is sacrificed.
The day be cursed on which these English shores
Hospitably received this Helen.
    HANNAH: Hospitably, you say, she was received?
Poor woman! On the day she set her foot
Upon this soil, expelled, a suppliant,
And asked protection from her relatives,
She was imprisoned and she has been forced,
In bold defiance of the Law of Nations
And of her royal dignity, to mourn
The lovely years of youth in narrow prison walls.
Now she has tasted all the bitterness
That prisons hold, but that is not enough!
You drag her like a common criminal
Before the bars of justice—her, a queen—
And shamefully indict her upon pain of death.
    PAULET: She came to England as a murderess,
Chased by her people, driven from the throne
Which she had sullied by her monstrous crime.
Sworn to destroy the happiness of England,
She came with the intention of restoring

The bloody era of the Spanish Mary,
To make all England Catholic again
And to betray her to the French.
Why did she scorn to sign the treaty
Of Edinburgh? Why not renounce her claim
To England and unlock her prison doors
With one stroke of her pen? No, she prefers
Captivity, prefers ill treatment
To giving up her pompous, empty title.
And why? Because she still has faith in wily schemes,
She trusts the evil art of sly conspiracy.
She hopes, by spinning wickedness, to conquer
All of this island from a prison cell.
    HANNAH: You mock her, sir. You are not only
    hard,
You now add bitter ridicule.
She harbor dreams like those? Immured alive,
No word of solace, not a word from friends
In her beloved country ever reaches her.
She never sees a human face, except
Her jailers' gloomy countenances.
She only recently was given yet
Another coarse-grained guard, your relative.
More bars than ever fence her in.
    PAULET: No iron bars protect against her cunning.
Perhaps these bars have been filed through, these
    walls,
This floor, which seem so solid, hollowed out
To let a traitor enter while I sleep.
I've been assigned to cursed office,
To guard a wily woman bent on mischief.
Fear does not let me sleep in peace,
I walk by night like a tormented ghost,
I try the locks, I test the guards,
And trembling I await each morning—
My fears may have come true!
But, fortunately, there is hope that soon
All this will end. I would prefer to guard
The gates of hell, the legions of the damned,
Than guard this scheming queen.
    HANNAH: Here she is now.
    PAULET: The Christ she carries in her hand,
Conceit and worldly pleasures in her heart.

SCENE II.

[Hannah *and* Paulet; Mary *enters, veiled, with a
    crucifix in her hand*]
HANNAH: [*Rushing toward* Mary]
My Queen! They put their feet upon our necks.
There is no limit to their tyranny
And to their ruthlessness. Each day they heap
New sorrows and new shame upon your head.
    MARY: Now, calm yourself and tell me what has
    happened.
    HANNAH: Look! He has forced your secretary and
    has seized
Your letters and the only treasure, saved
With so much difficulty, that was left,
The only piece of all the bridal jewelry

That you received from France. No regal souvenir
Remains. The robbery is now complete.

MARY: Don't worry, Hannah. Baubles do not make
A queen. If they can treat us meanly,
They cannot demean us. I've become
Accustomed to so many things in England
That I can easily forget this, too.
You, Sir Amias, took by force
What I already had resolved
To give you voluntarily today.
Among those papers is a letter which
I have intended for the Queen, my royal sister.
Give me your word of honor that you will
Deliver it to her in person, you yourself,
And not into Lord Burleigh's faithless hands.

PAULET: I shall reflect upon what I must do.

MARY: I want you to have knowledge of its contents, sir.
I'm asking her for an important favor,
An audience with her whom I have never seen.
They've summoned me before a court of men
Whom I cannot and will not recognize
As equals, and in whom I have no confidence.
Elizabeth is of my blood, my rank,
My sex. To her, a woman and a queen,
To her, my sister, I can bare my heart.

PAULET: My Lady, you have often put
Your honor and your fate into the hands
Of men less worthy of your confidence.

MARY: I'm asking for a second favor
Which it would be inhuman to deny.
For many years now I have been
Without the consolation of my Church,
The blessing of the sacraments.
Though she has robbed me of my crown and freedom,
Although she threatens now my life, she cannot want
To bar the doors of heaven to my soul.

PAULET: Whenever you desire, the village dean—

MARY: [Interrupts him violently]
I do not want a dean, I want a priest
Of my own church. I furthermore demand
Some clerks and notaries to make my will.
My sorrows and the long confinement sap
My strength, I feel my days are numbered.
I am a dying woman.

PAULET: Now, these are fitting thoughts for you.

MARY: The slow effect of grief may well be hastened
By one quick blow. I can't be certain.
I therefore wish to make my testament
And to dispose of my possessions.

PAULET: That is your privilege. The Queen of
England
Will not enrich herself by robbing you.

MARY: I have been separated from my faithful
ladies
And from my servants. Where are they?
I can well do without their services
But I would like to be assured that they,
For being faithful, do not want or suffer.

PAULET: Your servants have been cared for. [He
turns to go]

MARY: You're going, sir? You leave me once again
Without a word to soothe the torturing
Uncertainty of my alarmed and troubled heart?
Thanks to the vigilance of your informers,
I have been kept apart from all the world;
No message reaches me across these prison walls.
My fate is in the hands of enemies.
One month, painfully long, has passed
Since your forty commissioners intruded here,
Set up their court and, in unseemly haste,
Put me, quite unprepared and without aid
Of counsel, before this quite unheard-of jury;
Stunned and surprised, from memory, I was obliged
To answer grave and cleverly concocted charges.
Like ghosts they came and left again. Since then,
All have been silent, and I try in vain
To read upon your face who won, my innocence,
The fervor of my friends, or the nefarious advice
Of enemies. Now—break your silence. Let me know
What I must fear, what I may hope.

PAULET: [After a silence] Make up your reckoning
with God.

MARY: I hope for heaven's mercy—and I also hope
For justice from my judges here on earth.

PAULET: You need not doubt that justice will be
done.

MARY: Has a decision been announced?

PAULET: I do not know.

MARY: Then—have I been condemned?

PAULET: My Lady, I know nothing.

MARY: In England, one is fond of acting with dispatch.
Will murderers surprise me, as the judges did?

PAULET: Assume in any case that it is so.
Thus death will find you better armed than justice did.

MARY: No, nothing would surprise me, sir.
I can imagine how a court in Westminster,
Led on by Burleigh's hate and Hutton's zeal,
Will dare to judge, for I know all too well
How England's Queen may dare to act.

PAULET: For England's rulers there is no restraint
But Parliament and their own conscience.
What justice has decreed, before the world
And fearlessly their might will execute.

SCENE III.

The same.

[Mortimer, *Paulet's nephew, enters and speaks to*
Paulet; *he takes no notice of the* Queen]

MORTIMER: We have been looking for you, Uncle.
[*He leaves, again seemingly unaware of the*
Queen's *presence. Angrily she turns to* Paulet
who is about to follow Mortimer]

MARY: One more request, sir. When you wish to
tell me something—

I honor your old age—from you I will accept it.
But this young man's impertinence I will not stand.
Spare me the sight of his uncouth comportment.

PAULET: I value what makes him unbearable to
you.
No, he is not one of those gentle fools
Who melt when women shed deceitful tears.
He has returned from Paris and from Rheims
But has brought back his faithful English heart.
Your wiles, my Lady, will be lost on him. [He leaves]

SCENE IV.

[Mary and Hannah]

HANNAH: How does he dare, the brute, to tell you
that
Right to your face! Oh, it is hard!

MARY: [Musing] In those lost days of glorious hap-
piness
We often lent our ear too willingly
To flatterers. It's therefore just that now
We should be forced to listen to the graver sounds
Of reprimands.

HANNAH: So humble, my dear Lady?
Why so discouraged? You have always been so gay,
And it was you who used to comfort me.
I had more cause to scold you for your giddiness
Than for despondency.

MARY: I recognize him.
It is King Darnley's bloody shadow
That, wrathful, rises from his burial vault,
And he will never make his peace with me
Until misfortune fills my cup.

HANNAH: What thoughts—

MARY: You, Hannah, can forget.
My memory is accurate: today
Another anniversary
Of the horrendous deed has come around,
For me a day of penitence and fasting.

HANNAH: No, you must put to rest this wretched
ghost.
You have atoned for what you did with your re-
morse,
With all these years of agony.
The Church, which has the key to absolution,
And heaven have forgiven you.

MARY: Bleeding anew, the long forgiven guilt
Arises from its lightly covered grave.
No sacristan with tinkling bell, no priest
With host in hand, can send
My husband's vengeful ghost back to his tomb.

HANNAH: It was not you who murdered him! The
others did.

MARY: I knew about it, and I let it happen,
With flattery I lured him to his death.

HANNAH: You were so young. Your tender youth
Must mitigate your guilt.

MARY: So tender, yes—

I weighed my youth with such enormous guilt.

HANNAH: He had provoked you with his insults,
His insolence—that man whom you had raised
From his obscurity by love, as with a goddess' hand,
Whom you led through your bridal chamber to the
throne,
Whom you enthralled both with your youthful bloom
And with the crown you had inherited.
Could he forget that it had been your love
And generosity which raised him to his height?
Unworthy man, he did forget!
His mean suspicion and his boorish conduct
Insulted your devoted tenderness.
Thus he became repulsive to your eyes,
The spell with which he had deceived you faded,
And you, infuriated, fled from his embrace,
Abandoning the shameless man to scorn.
And he? Instead of trying to regain
Your favor, falling at your feet
To beg forgiveness and to vow reform,
The execrable man defied you!
Your creature, he presumed to be your king!
Before your eyes he had the handsome Rizzio,
Your favorite singer, run through with a sword.
That bloody deed you bloodily avenged.

MARY: And bloody will be the revenge it wreaks
on me.
Your words of solace are my condemnation.

HANNAH: When you permitted them to murder him,
You were not your own master, not yourself.
The blinding madness of a burning love
Held you enslaved to Bothwell; wretched man
And terrible seducer, he ruled you
With willful arrogance. With magic potions,
With hellish artifices he confused your mind
And fanned the flames—

MARY: He used no artifice,
He used my weakness and his strength.

HANNAH: No, it was more! In order to succeed
In blinding all your senses with his cloak,
He had to call to aid the spirits of damnation.
The warning voices of your friends
No longer reached your ear, your eyes
No longer recognized the road of decency.
No longer were you sensitive and gentle,
Your cheeks no longer blushed with modesty.
Your face was burning with the searing flames of lust.
You threw away the veil of secrecy,
Your reticence was overcome
By Bothwell's bold display of vice, and brazenly,
For all to see, you flaunted your own shame.
You let that man, a murderer pursued
By all the people's curses, carry
The royal sword of Scotland through the streets
Of Edinburgh triumphantly ahead of you.
At last, you ringed your Parliament with arms,
And there, where Justice has her temple,
You forced the judges to take part
In an outrageous farce, to free the murderer,
Ignore his crime and to absolve him from his guilt.

You went still further—God!

MARY: Go on!

Before God's altar I gave him my hand.

HANNAH: Enough! Let silence cover what you did.
It was revolting, horrible, the deed
Of a lost soul. But your soul is not lost,
I know you, it is I who brought you up.
Your heart is gentle, full of modesty;
Your only vice is recklessness.
There are bad spirits, I repeat, which suddenly possess
An unsuspecting heart and quickly do
Their heinous deed; then, fleeing back to hell,
They leave a horrified and sullied heart behind.
Since that first crime which blackens your whole life
You never have committed any vicious act.
I am witness to your change of heart.
Take courage and make peace within yourself.
Whatever you may wish to see undone,
In England you are blameless. Neither Parliament
Nor Queen Elizabeth have any right to judge you.
It's force which here oppresses you. Before
That arrogant and righteous court you may appear
With all the boldness of your innocence.

MARY: Is someone coming?

[Mortimer *appears in the door*]

HANNAH: It is the nephew. Leave me with him.

SCENE V.

The same.

[Mortimer *enters hesitantly*]

MORTIMER: [*To* Hannah] Leave us alone and guard
the door. I must talk to the Queen.

MARY: [*With authority*] Hannah, you stay!

MORTIMER: You need not fear, my Lady. You will
come to know me.

[*He hands her a letter*]

MARY: [*Looks at it; in consternation*] Lord! What
is this?

MORTIMER: [*To* Hannah]   Go, Hannah, and
make sure
That we are not surprised here by my uncle.

MARY: [*To* Hannah, *who hesitates and looks ques-
tioningly at the* Queen] Go, go, do as he says.

[Hannah *leaves, obviously perplexed*]

SCENE VI.

[Mary *and* Mortimer]

MARY: A letter from my uncle, from the Cardinal!

[*She reads*] "Have confidence in Mortimer who brings
you this.
He is your truest friend in England."

[*She looks at* Mortimer *in great surprise*]

It cannot be! Is this a ruse?
I find a friend close by while I believed
That I was all alone, forsaken by the world,

And this one friend—the nephew of my jailer
Upon whom I had looked as my worst enemy!

MORTIMER: [*Throws himself at her feet*]

Forgive me, Queen, for having worn that hateful
mask
Which I despise and never used without revulsion,
But which gave me the opportunity
To come to you and offer help and rescue.

MARY: Arise, sir—please—you come upon me un-
awares.
It's difficult to leap from deepest misery
To hope. Please, tell me more, explain,
So I may find my fortune credible.

MORTIMER: [*Arises*] There's not much time. My
uncle may be here
At any moment—and with him a hateful man.
Before their frightful message takes you by surprise,
Learn how your rescue was devised in heaven.

MARY: A miracle worked by His omnipotence.

MORTIMER: Permit that first I speak about myself.

MARY: Please, speak!

MORTIMER: My lady, I was raised in strict
Obedience to my duties and was nursed
With sullen hatred for the Pope until,
When I was twenty years, an irrepressible
Desire to see the Continent drove me from home.
I left the Puritans and all their musty meeting rooms
Behind and quickly made my way through France
In ardent search of Italy—the land of promise.
It was the time then of the Church's great feast,
The roads were crowded with the host of pilgrims,
A wreath around each crucifix; it seemed
As if all mankind had begun a pilgrimage,
With heaven's kingdom as their goal.
The surging current of the faithful multitude
Soon swept me up and carried me
Into the heart of Rome. Oh, how I felt
When columns and triumphal arches
Magnificently rose before my eyes,
When suddenly the Colosseum's splendor
Held my astonished gaze, and when I sensed
The lofty spirit of creation
In the serene domain of man-made marvels!
I'd never known the power of the arts.
The church that brought me up abhors
All sensual delight, condones no image.
The disembodied word alone is held in reverence.
Ah, how I felt when I stepped into churches
Where music floated down from heaven.
Where an entire new world of images
Extravagantly gushed from walls and ceiling,
Where the Magnificent and the Supreme
Had come to life, enthralled the senses.
I saw them now, the holy figures,
The message of the angel and the birth of Christ,
Transfiguration in a glowing light,
The Holy Mother, Trinity descending.
I saw the Pope, resplendent, celebrating Mass
And blessing all the people of this earth.
Oh, what are gold and dazzling jewels

With which the kings of earth adorn themselves
Compared to him who's bathed in godliness?
His house is truly heaven's kingdom,
Because those forms are of another world.

   MARY: Have pity! Stop! Don't spread the glowing
     carpet
Of life too temptingly before me.
I am a wretched prisoner.

   MORTIMER: I, too, have been a prisoner, your
     Majesty.
My prison doors sprang open, and at once
My spirit soared to meet the shining day of life.
I swore undying hatred to the narrow, musty Book,
And jubilant, a wreath of flowers on my brow,
I vowed to share the company of joyous men.
My friends were many noble Scots,
The lively companies of Frenchmen.
They took me to your noble uncle,
The Cardinal of Guise. Oh, what a sure
And clear and manly man he is!
A leader born; the model of a royal priest,
A prince and churchman as I've never seen before.

   MARY: You've seen him, then! You've seen his
     face, so dear
To me, beloved and revered by multitudes,
The man who was my guide when I was young.
Oh, tell me more about him! Does he still
Remember me? Does Fortune love him still?
Has life preserved him in his flower?
Does he still guard, a solid rock, our Church?

   MORTIMER: Oh yes! He condescended to explain
     to me
The venerable doctrines of our faith
And he dispelled my few remaining doubts.
He showed me that man's ever-searching reason
Leads him astray and that our eyes must see
What we expect our heart to understand,
That it is necessary for the Church
To have a head that all can clearly see,
That truth presided at the councils of the fathers.
Thus soon my childish misconceptions
Evaporated in the heat of his triumphant mind
And his persuasive tongue, and I returned
Into the lap of our beloved Church.
Into his hands I disavowed my errors.

   MARY: So you are one among the thousands
Whom he has led to their salvation,
Moved with his eloquence, a gift from heaven,
As once the reverend Preacher of the Mountain did.

   MORTIMER: Soon afterward the duties of his office
     called
Him back to France, and he sent me to Rheims
Where the Society of Jesus piously
Prepares the priests for England's Church.
That noble Scotsman, Morgan, I met there
And Lessley, your devoted, scholarly
Bishop of Rosse, who spend their hapless days
Of banishment in France. I spent much time
With both these venerable men and strengthened

My new-found faith. One day, while in the bishop's
    study,
A strangely moving portrait of a lady caught
My eye. I stood before the picture, deeply stirred,
Unable to control my powerful emotions.
You may well stand before this picture, moved,
The bishop said to me, she's the most beautiful
Of living women, she also has the saddest fate.
She suffers for our faith, and England is
The country where she suffers.

   MARY: Not all is lost while upright men like he
Stand by me in my misery.

   MORTIMER: He told me then, so eloquently that it
    broke
My heart, the story of your martyrdom
And of your enemies' bloodthirsty plans.
He also told me of your family
And demonstrated your direct descent
From the exalted House of Tudor.
He thus persuaded me that you alone
Are worthy to be England's ruler—not that woman
Who masquerades as queen, who was conceived
In an adulterous bed, whom her own father, Henry,
Repudiated as a bastard daughter.
His testimony, though, was not enough.
I asked advice from legal scholars,
Consulted ancient books of heraldry,
And all who are conversant with the facts
Confirm the justice of your claim.
I am convinced now that your crime
Consists but in your just right to the throne,
That you are held, a guiltless prisoner,
In England, which is yours by right.

   MARY: That fateful, hateful right! It is
The only source of all my woes.

   MORTIMER: It was about that time when news
    arrived
That you had been removed from Talbot's castle
And handed over to my uncle's care.
I saw in that event the hand of God,
Miraculously pointing to your rescue.
I heard the clarion call of destiny
Which had selected me to bring you freedom.
The plans were quickly made, and I returned
To England where, as you already know,
I landed just ten days ago.
    [He pauses]
Then I saw you, my Queen—I saw yourself,
And not a picture. Ah, what treasure holds this castle!
This is no prison—it's a sacred hall,
More splendid than the royal court of England!
Blessed the man who is allowed to breathe
The air which you are breathing. Ah, how right
She was to bury you so deep!
For all the youth of England would rise up,
Unsheathe their swords, and with its giant head
Held high, revolt would stride across this peaceful
    island,
If Britons ever saw their Queen!

MARY: Luck would be hers if every Briton looked
Upon her with your eyes.
    MORTIMER: They would if they, like me, saw how
    you suffer,
And saw the gentleness and the composure
With which you bear indignities.
From all your trials you emerge as Queen,
No prison can deprive your beauty of its sheen.
You lack the meanest ornament, yet life
And light surround you with their glow.
Each time I cross this threshold torments tear my
    heart,
But each time I'm enchanted by your sight.
Now, terribly, the moment of decision looms,
The danger grows with every hour, I can delay
No longer, can no longer hide the frightful news—
    MARY: Has sentence been pronounced? Feel free to
    speak.
I'll bear it.
    MORTIMER: Yes—it has. The forty-two,
Your judges, have pronounced you guilty—more,
The House of Lords, the Commons and the City
Of London are insistent that the sentence
Be swiftly carried out. The Queen alone
Still hesitates—not from a feeling, to be sure,
Of human kindness or of mercy, but waiting
Cunningly to be prevailed upon.
    MARY: [Calmly] Sir Mortimer, I'm not surprised
    nor frightened.
I've long expected this. I know my judges.
The treatment which I have been made to suffer
Made it quite clear that they would never set me free.
I know what they intend—to keep me prisoner
In perpetuity, to bury me
Together with my vengeance and my rightful claims.
    MORTIMER: No, no, your Majesty! They do not
    stop at that!
No tyranny can be content with leaving things
Half-done. As long as you're alive, her fears will live.
There is no dungeon deep enough to bury you.
Your death alone can guarantee her throne.
    MARY: She would not dare to put the crowned
    head of a queen
Upon the executioner's block.
    MORTIMER: She will! Don't doubt that she will
    dare.
    MARY: She cannot wish to pull into the dust
Her majesty and that of every king.
Does she not fear the vengeance of the French?
    MORTIMER: She is concluding an eternal pact with
    France;
She's offering the Duke of Anjou hand and throne.
    MARY: The King of Spain would surely rush to
    arms.
    MORTIMER: She does not fear a world in arms
While she's at peace at home, in England.
    MARY: Would she present this spectacle to Eng-
    land, then?
    MORTIMER: This country has in recent years seen
    more than one

Crowned lady leave the throne to mount the scaffold.
Her mother went that way and Catherine Howard,
A crown wore Lady Grey before she died.
    MARY: [After a pause] No, Mortimer. Your fear is
    blinding you.
It is your loyalty that makes you apprehensive
And lets you see imaginary horrors.
I do not fear the scaffold, sir.
Elizabeth has other and less noisome means
To still my claims and give her peace.
Much sooner than a hangman she could find
A murderer to do her bidding.
That is what makes me tremble, sir.
Each time I put a goblet to my lips
I shudder thinking that my royal sister
May well have filled it with her love for me.
    MORTIMER: No murder, open or in secret, shall
    succeed.
You need not fear, all is in readiness.
Twelve noble youths, men of this country, are
In league with me; this morning they received
The sacrament and swore, by force of arms,
To aid in your abduction from this castle.
Count Aubespine, the French ambassador,
Has knowledge of our league, has offered help,
And at his palace we shall meet.
    MARY: You make me tremble, sir—but not with
    happiness.
I feel an ill foreboding. Have you weighed well
What you are undertaking? Are you not deterred
By Babington's and Tichburn's bloody heads,
Impaled as warning upon London Bridge?
Nor by the fate of all those countless men
Who met their death in similar adventures
And made my chains still heavier?
Unfortunate, misguided man, escape!
Take flight while there's still time—unless, of course,
Lord Burleigh knows about you and has planted
A traitor in your midst. Be quick and flee the realm!
Luck does not smile on those who fight for Mary
    Stuart.
    MORTIMER: Not Babington's and Tichburn's bloody
    heads,
Impaled on London Bridge as warning,
Nor the destruction of those countless men
Who lost their lives in similar adventures frighten
    me.
Their death brought them eternal glory.
To die for you is happiness.
    MARY: It is in vain. No force, no ruse can rescue
    me.
The enemy is vigilant and powerful.
Not only Paulet and his throng of jailers,
All England guards my prison door.
Elizabeth alone, of her free will,
Can open it.
    MORTIMER: There is no hope of that.
    MARY: There is one man who might succeed.
    MORTIMER: Who is?
    MARY: The Earl of Leicester.

MORTIMER: Leicester? He? The man
Who raves against you more than anyone—
The favorite of Elizabeth . . . through him—
MARY: If anyone can save me it is he.
And I want you to go to him. Speak frankly.
As proof that I am sending you, bring him
This letter. It contains my portrait.

[*She draws an envelope from her bosom.* Mortimer *steps back, hesitates to take it*]

Accept it. I have carried it upon
My person since I wrote it long ago.
Your uncle's vigilance and strictness
Had blocked all means of reaching him. But now,
My guardian angel sent me—you.
MORTIMER: Your Majesty . . . this riddle . . .
please explain.
MARY: The Earl of Leicester, I am sure, will solve
it.
Trust him, he will trust you. Who's there?
HANNAH: [*Hurries in, busily*] Sir Paulet with some
gentleman from court.
MORTIMER: That is Lord Burleigh. Hear him out
With equanimity. Rest calm, your Majesty.

[*He leaves by a side door, followed by* Hannah]

SCENE VII.

Mary, Lord Burleigh *and* Paulet.

PAULET: You asked to know your fate for certain.
Now—
His Lordship brings you certainty. This is
Lord Burleigh. Hear his message humbly.
MARY: With dignity, I hope, as befits my inno-
cence.
BURLEIGH: I come as emissary from the court.
MARY: My Lord, you eagerly accept serving the
court,
Whose mind you were, now also as a mouthpiece.
PAULET: You speak as if you knew the verdict.
MARY: I know a message that Lord Burleigh brings
Before he speaks. But to the point, my Lord.
BURLEIGH: Your Majesty, you did accept
The jurisdiction of the forty-two—
MARY: Excuse me if I interrupt at once, my Lord.
Accepted jurisdiction of the forty-two?
I never did. I never could accept
Yielding so much, my rank, the dignity
Of son and people and of every king.
Does English law not give to an accused
The right of judgment by his peers?
Which of the jurors is my peer?
My peers are kings!
BURLEIGH: You listened to the articles
Of the indictment, submitted to examination by the
court—
MARY: I was misled by Hutton's cunning false-
hoods.
To guard my honor, and with confidence

In the persuasive power of my arguments,
I did agree to listen to the charges
And to explain their origin—no more.
I did so also out of the esteem
In which I hold the worthy Lords as persons, not
In their capacity. That I repudiate.
BURLEIGH: Whether you recognize their jurisdic-
tion,
Or whether you object is but an empty gesture.
It cannot influence the course of justice.
You do breathe England's air, enjoy
Her laws' protection and their benefits,
And you are therefore subject to their power.
MARY: Yes, I am breathing England's air—in
prison.
Is that what you call living in your country?
Is that enjoying your laws' benefits?
I hardly know your laws. Nor did I ever swear
Obedience to them. I'm not a citizen
Of England's realm. I am a foreign queen—and free.
BURLEIGH: Do you believe that carrying a royal
name
Implies the right of sowing discord
In foreign countries with impunity?
How safe would any kingdom be
If Themis' righteous sword were not so long
That it could reach a culpable, though royal guest
As easily as any beggar?
MARY: I am not trying to evade your justice.
The judges who dispense it I reject.
BURLEIGH: The judges! Why, my Lady? Why? Are
they
Perhaps some nameless outcasts picked
At random from the rabble, shameless blabberers
To whom truth and justice are but goods for sale?
Or who would willingly become
The hired servants of tyrannical oppression?
Are not these judges the most noble men
In England, free enough to speak the truth,
Men who stand far above the fear of kings
And miserable bribery? These are
The very men who govern a great people
In justice and in freedom, men whose names
Alone suffice to silence any doubt
And all suspicion. At their head,
The pious shepherd, Archbishop of Canterbury,
Then come the Earl of Shrewsbury, our wise
Lord Privy Seal; the valiant Howard, the Lord Ad-
miral—
Now, please—could England's ruler have done more
Than choose from all her kingdom the most noble
men
As judges in this royal suit?
And even though among them may be some
Who could be swayed by partisan dislikes,
Could forty carefully selected men
Unite in a decision based on private passion?
MARY: [*After a silence*] I listen in amazement to
your eloquence
Which always has been my misfortune.

And how can I, an unlearned woman,
Compete with such a skillful orator?
Well!—If these Lords were really
As you describe them, I could say no more;
My cause would be hopelessly lost if they condemned.
But all those names which you so highly praise,
Which are to crush me by their weight—my Lord,
I see their bearers play a different role in England's history.
I see your high nobility, your realm's
Majestic senate, flattering the whims
Of my great-uncle, Henry the Eighth,
As eunuchs fawn at the seraglio's master.
I see this noble House of Lords,
Just as subserviently as the venal Commons,
Make laws and abrogate them, close a marriage
And soon dissolve it—as their master bids;
See them brand English princesses as bastards
Or disinherit them—tomorrow crown them queens.
I see these worthy peers so true to their
Convictions that, to suit four governments,
They change their faith four times—
    BURLEIGH: You claim to be a stranger to our laws
But you're well versed in England's weaknesses.
    MARY: Those men then are my judges! You, my Lord—
I will be just in judging you, I hope
You will be just with me. I'm told
You have your Queen's, your country's interest
At heart, that you are always vigilant,
Untiring, incorruptible.
I will believe it. You do what is best
For Queen and country, do not count your own
Advantage. That is why you must be on your guard:
Do not mistake your country's interest for justice.
I do not doubt that there are other men
As honorable as yourself among my judges.
But they are Protestants, fanatic partisans
Of England's welfare who judge me—
A Papist and the Queen of Scots!
No Briton ever judged a Scotsman justly.
That is an age-old saying and is why
It has been custom since our fathers' ancient times
That Englishmen may never testify before the law
Against a Scot, nor Scots against an Englishman.
Necessity created this odd rule,
But wisdom speaks in old traditions,
And we should honor them, my Lord.
Two fiery nations Nature threw upon
This floating board, this isle, gave them unequal shares
And ordered them to fight for its possession.
The narrow river Tweed alone divides
These boisterous neighbors, and their blood
Has often mingled with its waves.
Thus, hand on hilt, they've threateningly stared
From either bank across the Tweed for a thousand years.
No enemy has ever crowded England

To whom the Scot would not extend a helping hand.
No civil war has ever burned the towns of Scotland,
For which the Briton did not carry tinder.
This hatred will not die until at last
One Parliament unites the fighting brothers,
One scepter reigns this isle.
    BURLEIGH: And you, a Stuart, meant
To bring that happy fortune to our realm?
    MARY: Why not admit it? Yes, I nourished hopes,
I hoped to bring together these proud nations
Beneath the olive tree, both free and happy.
I never thought that I would at once become
The victim of their rivalry and hate.
I hoped to bank the fires of age-old discord,
Of their eternal jealousy,
And, as my ancestor, the Duke of Richmond, tied
Together the two Roses after bloody wars,
My hope was to unite the crowns
Of England and of Scotland in a peaceful marriage.
    BURLEIGH: You chose an evil way to reach that goal
When you inflamed the realm and sought to climb
The throne across the raging fires of civil war.
    MARY: I never wanted that! Good God, whenever
Did I want that? Where is your proof?
    BURLEIGH: I did not come to argue. This no longer is
A matter to be fought with words.
With forty voices against two, the jury found
That you have violated the decree
Which Parliament last year enacted,
That you are guilty under law. The act reads thus:
"If there arise disturbances within the Kingdom,
In name or fact of benefit to anyone
Pretending to the Crown, that person shall
Be prosecuted under law and punished unto death."
Now, since it's proven—
    MARY: Yes, my Lord!
No doubt, a law expressly made for me,
Conceived to ruin me, can now be used against me.
Beware, poor victim, when the mouth that gives the law
And that which passes sentence is the same.
Can you deny, my Lord, that this law aimed
At my destruction?
    BURLEIGH: It was meant to warn you.
It was you who changed it to a trap.
You saw the abyss yawning at your feet,
Were duly warned, and still plunged into it.
You were in league with Babington, that traitor,
With all his hired assassins, knew their plans,
And from your prison guided the conspiracy.
    MARY: When did I do all that? Show me the documents!
    BURLEIGH: You saw them recently in court.
    MARY: Those copies written by I don't know whom?
Bring proof that I dictated them myself,
That I dictated them as they were read.

BURLEIGH: Sir Babington, before he died, acknowl-
edged them
To be the documents which you had given him.
MARY: Why was I not confronted with him then
While he was still alive? Why the unseemly haste
In sending him into the other world
Before I had a chance to see him face to face?
BURLEIGH: Your clerks, too, Curl and Nau, swore
that those letters
Were written in their hand as you dictated them.
MARY: Thus on the testimony of my servants
Am I condemned? Upon the word of men
Who could betray their Queen, betrayed their trust
The moment they agreed to testify against me?
BURLEIGH: You used to praise that Scotsman, Curl,
yourself
As virtuous and most dependable.
MARY: That's how I knew him. But the character
of men
Is proven only in the hour of danger.
Perhaps the torture frightened him,
And he confessed and testified to lies.
Perhaps he thought that he could save himself
By his false testimony and cause me,
His Queen, no harm.
BURLEIGH: He swore to it on his free oath.
MARY: Not in my presence. Why, my Lord—two
witnesses,
Those two, are still alive! Why may I not confront
them?
Let them repeat their testimony to my face.
Do you deny a favor, no, a right to me
Which you would not refuse a murderer?
I know from Talbot, when he guarded me,
That under this, the present government
An act was passed that guarantees the right
To an accused to face the person who accuses him.
Is that not true? Am I mistaken? Paulet!
I've always looked upon you as an honorable man;
Now—prove it! Tell me, is that not the truth?
Is there not such a law in England?
PAULET: There is, my Lady. That's the law in Eng-
land.
I must tell you the truth.
MARY: Well, then, my Lord! If you inflict the full
severity
Of English law upon me when it harms,
Why circumvent that very law
When it may benefit me? Answer that.
Why was I not confronted, eye to eye,
With Babington, according to the law?
Why not with my domestics who are still alive?
BURLEIGH: Do not excite yourself, my Lady. Your
accord
With Babington is not the only charge—
MARY: It is the only accusation which exposes me
To legal prosecution and the only one
From which I have to clear myself.
Keep to the point, my Lord! Do not evade the issue!

BURLEIGH: We also have the proof of negotiations
with His Spanish Majesty's ambassador—
MARY: [Agitated] Keep to the point, my Lord!
BURLEIGH: And that you had designs on over-
throwing
The state's religion, that you schemed
To form a league of all the kings in Europe
For waging war against the Queen—
MARY: Suppose I did? I did not, but suppose I
did?
I am held prisoner against the Law of Nations.
I did not come here, sword in hand; I came,
A supplicant who claimed the ancient right
Of hospitality, I came to throw myself
Into the arms of Queen Elizabeth, my relative.
But I was seized by force and chained by those
Whom I beseeched for help. My Lord,
In conscience, what do I owe England?
Do I have duties here? To search for ways
Of breaking these intolerable bonds,
To counter might with might, and to incite
And summon all the countries of the continent—
All that is nothing but my sacred right
Of self-defense. I am entitled to conduct
This war by all means that are fair and chivalrous.
My conscience and my pride will not admit
That I use foul and secret means, that I use murder.
For murder would dishonor me and soil my hands.
I say, dishonor—not subject me to your laws,
And surely not condemn me. No, what counts
Between myself and England is not right, but might.
BURLEIGH: [Ominously] Do not invoke the fright-
ful right of force.
It does not favor prisoners, my Lady.
MARY: Elizabeth is powerful, and I am weak.
Well, let her use her power, let her kill me.
Let my death be the sacrifice she brings
To guarantee her safety. If she does,
She must admit she exercises force, not justice.
The sword used to remove her hated enemy
Cannot be borrowed from the law.
She cannot veil the brutish force
Of her blood-red audacity in sacred garments.
Such travesty would not deceive the world.
To murder me, she has the power—not to judge me.
Let her abandon any thought of harvesting
The fruits of crime, while she parades her virtue.
May she have courage to appear as what she is.
    [She leaves]

SCENE VIII.

Lord Burleigh and Paulet.

BURLEIGH: Defiance! And she will keep on defying
us
Up to the scaffold's steps. Unbreakable
Is her proud heart. Was she surprised

About the verdict? Did she weep?
She did not even blanch, nor ask for sympathy.
She knows too well that England's Queen
Is torn by doubts. Our fears make her courageous.

PAULET: My Lord, her vain defiance feeds, if I
    may say so,
On flaws which obviously mar the legal process.
Remove those flaws, and her defiance will soon vanish.
She should have been allowed to face
That Babington and Tichburn and her servants.

BURLEIGH: [Quickly] No, Sir Amias, never that!
    We could not dare.
Her power over people is too great,
So are her tears, the weapon of a woman.
If Curl, her clerk, had ever faced her to repeat
The words which spell her death, he would have
    turned,
Intimidated, and recanted his confession.

PAULET: But now, the enemies of England soon
Will fill the world with hateful rumors,
And the elaborate proceedings of the trial
Will seem but an audacious farce.

BURLEIGH: Precisely that is what disturbs our
    Queen.
Would that this mischief-maker had expired
Before she ever set her foot on English soil!

PAULET: To that I say Amen.

BURLEIGH: Or that she had succumbed to illness in
    her prison!

PAULET: That would have spared this country great
    misfortune.

BURLEIGH: But even if an accident of nature
Had put an end to her, we still would be
Her murderers.

PAULET: Quite true. One can never
Prevent the world from thinking what it wants.

BURLEIGH: It could never be proven, and the noise
Would not be quite so shrill—

PAULET: Oh, never mind the noise. Reproaches
    only hurt
When they are just, not when they're loud.

BURLEIGH: Not even heaven's justice can escape
Its human censors. People always sympathize
With the unfortunate, and envy is the lot
Of the victorious. The judge's sword adorns
A man, but it is hated in a woman's hand.
The world does not believe in women's justice,
When any other woman is the victim.
It was in vain that we, as judges, followed
Our conscience. She now has the royal right
Of clemency, and she must use it.
To countenance that justice take its course
Is inconceivable.

PAULET: And so—

BURLEIGH: [Quickly interrupting him] And so
We let her live? Oh no. She must not live.
This it is that frightens the Queen,
That is why sleep avoids her bed.
I read her inner battle in her eyes,

Her mouth would never dare to speak her wish,
But full of meaning, silently, her gaze demands:
Is there not one among my servants
Who would relieve me of this fateful choice,
To tremble on my throne in endless fear,
Or callously to let a queen, my relative,
Become a victim of the executioner's ax?

PAULET: That is the choice, and nothing can be
    done about it.

BURLEIGH: It could be different, the Queen must
    think,
If only she had more attentive servants.

PAULET: Attentive?

BURLEIGH: Yes, men who can interpret silent or-
    ders.

PAULET: Silent orders!

BURLEIGH: Men who, if given poisonous snakes to
    guard,
Would not protect this enemy entrusted to
Their care as thoughtfully as precious gems.

PAULET: [Firmly] The Queen's good name and
    blameless reputation
Are precious gems, indeed. One cannot be
Too careful with them, sir.

BURLEIGH: When Mary was removed from Shrews-
    bury's domain
And Sir Amias Paulet was assigned
To guard the lady—why, one thought—

PAULET: I hope, my Lord, one thought that the
    most difficult
Assignment should be put into the cleanest hands.
By God, I never would have lent myself
To playing bailiff, had I not been firm
In my belief that no man but the best
In England was required for it.
Do not suggest, my Lord, that I owe my appointment
To anything other than my spotless reputation.

BURLEIGH: The rumor could be spread that she
    was ill,
That she was getting weaker, finally,
That she had peacefully succumbed.
She thus would fade from people's memories—
Your reputation still untarnished.

PAULET: But not my conscience!

BURLEIGH: If you don't choose to lend your hand,
You surely would not stop another man—

PAULET: [Interrupts him] No murderer will cross
    her threshold while
She is protected by my household gods.
To me her life is sacred—just as sacred as
The head of Queen Elizabeth.
You are the judges. Judge her then. Condemn her.
When it is time to have the carpenter
Come with his ax and saw to build the scaffold,
I will not bar the way to executioner or sheriff.
For now, she is entrusted to my care.
You may be sure that I will keep her safe,
So she will neither cause nor suffer harm.
    [Both leave]

ACT II. SCENE I.

The Palace at Westminster.

[The Earl *of* Kent *and* Sir William Davison *encounter each other*]

DAVISON: You here, my Lord? Is all the jousting finished,
Since you return so soon from the display?
KENT: Did you not, too, attend the tournament?
DAVISON: My office kept me here.
KENT: You missed a beautiful performance, sir.
It was most tastefully designed, and executed
With great nobility. It was a play
In which Desire attacked the citadel of Chastity
And Beauty, which the Lord Chief Justice,
The Marshal and the Lord High Steward
Defended with ten other knights.
The cavaliers from France were the attackers.
At first, a herald came who, in a madrigal,
Demanded the surrender of the fortress.
Then, from the wall, the Chancellor replied.
The turn then came for the artillery,
The dainty cannons firing flowers
And precious aromatic essences.
It was in vain! Repelled were their attacks,
Desire was forced into an ignominious retreat.
DAVISON: An inauspicious omen for the courtship
of the French.
KENT: I hardly think so. It was all in fun.
When things get serious, the fortress will,
I think, surrender in the end.
DAVISON: Do you believe so? I have given up all
hope.
KENT: Why, the most complicated articles
Have been agreed, the French have given in.
Monsieur will be content to worship in his way
Behind locked doors, while publicly he will accord
Respect and give protection to the state religion.
You should have seen the jubilation of the crowds
When that news spread! For what the country feared
Was that the Queen might die without an heir
And thus surrender England once again
To Papist slavery in the event
That Mary followed her upon the throne.
DAVISON: Of that fear they can be relieved—
Into her bridal chamber steps the Queen,
While Mary Stuart mounts the scaffold's steps.
KENT: Here comes the Queen.

SCENE II.

The Same.

[Elizabeth *enters on the arm of the* Earl *of*
Leicester. Count Aubespine, Count Bellievre,
the Earl *of* Shrewsbury, Lord Burleigh *and other
French and English nobles follow them*]

ELIZABETH: [*To* Aubespine] I do feel sorry, Count,
for all these gentlemen
Whom their most gallant eagerness to cross
The sea brought here, and who are forced to miss
The splendor of the court of St. Germain.
I am not able to invent amusements
As elegant as those the French Queen Mother offers.
A well-behaved and happy people, apt
To crowd round my chair each time I show myself
In public—that's the only spectacle
That I can proudly show my foreign visitors.
The glitter of such noble ladies
As blossom forth in Catherine's flower garden
Would but obscure me and my dull accomplishments.
AUBESPINE: The Court of Westminster displays
one lady only
To the admiring eyes of foreigners,
But in this one example they will see
Embodied all the charms of her alluring sisters.
BELLIEVRE: Your Majesty, permit us now to take
our leave.
The long-awaited happy tidings will delight
Monsieur, our royal master, whom his great
Impatience would not let remain in Paris.
He waits in Amiens, his runners spread
From there up to Calais, so that your Yes,
As quickly as your Majesty pronounces it,
May reach his ear on eagle's wings
And make him drunk with happiness.
ELIZABETH: Count Bellievre, do not press me further.
The time is not well-suited, I repeat,
To light the merry wedding torches.
The sky is black above this land,
And it behoves me more to wear deep mourning
Than sparkling bridal gowns. My heart
And my whole house are threatened by a cruel blow.
BELLIEVRE: Give us your promise, then, your
Majesty,
Redeem it when the time is more propitious.
ELIZABETH: Kings are but slaves of their exalted
rank.
They never may pursue the dictates of their hearts.
I've always wished to die unmarried,
I would have traded all my fame, so that
One day upon my tombstone one would read:
"Here lies the Virgin Queen." My subjects, though,
Are of a different mind; they busily
Think of the time—already now—when I am gone.
They are not satisfied to count the blessings
Which now make England such a happy place,
No, for their future, too, I am to sacrifice myself.
I am to offer up what is most dear to me,
The freedom of a virgin, to my people.
They force me to accept a master—and
Thereby give me to understand
That I am but a woman. I had thought
That I had ruled like any man and like a king.
I know full well that one does not serve God
By flouting all the rules of nature.

Praise be to them who sat upon this throne before me
For opening the monasteries and returning
To nature's duties all those thousands
Who had been victims of misguided piety.
A queen, however, does not waste her days
In idle contemplation; cheerfully
And tirelessly she performs the hardest task
Of all, and she should be exempt from nature's law
Which makes one-half of mankind servants of the
    other.
    AUBESPINE: Your Majesty, you've glorified upon
      your throne
All virtues—except one: to set all womanhood,
Whose pride you have become, in their own sphere
A proud example. It is true,
No man on earth deserves that you give up
Your freedom for his sake. But if there is
One mortal man whom birth, exalted station,
Heroic virtue and manly beauty
Make worthy of that honor, then—
    ELIZABETH: The marriage with a royal son of
      France
Would greatly honor me, my dear Ambassador;
There is no doubt of that, and, I admit it frankly,
If it must be, if there is nothing I can do
But yield to the insistence of my people—
And they'll be stronger, I'm afraid, than I—
I cannot think of any prince in Europe
To whom I would with less reluctance sacrifice
My greatest treasure, freedom. Now—
Let this confession be enough.
    BELLIEVRE: To have this hope is priceless; still,
It's only hope. My master wished for more . . .
    ELIZABETH: What does he want?
      [*She takes a ring from her finger and looks at it
      reflectively*]
A queen is, after all, not very different
From any burgher's wife. The symbols are the same,
So are the duties and the servitude
Which they imply. A ring makes marriages,
And rings make chains. Take this, it is
A present for his Highness. It's not yet a chain,
It does not bind me yet, although in time
It may become a circlet that does bind me.
    BELLIEVRE: [*Kneels before her to receive the ring*]
Kneeling before you, I accept
This present in his name, and in his stead
I press this kiss of homage on my monarch's hand.
    ELIZABETH: [*To* Leicester, *at whom she has gazed
      steadily during the foregoing speech*] Permit me,
      my Lord.
      [*She takes the blue ribbon from his neck and
      hangs it around that of* Bellievre]
Pass on this decoration to his Highness,
As I now decorate you and accept you
Into the duties of my order.
Honi soit qui mal y pense!
May all suspicion fade between our nations,
And may a bond of trust henceforth unite
The crowns of England and of France.

    AUBESPINE: Illustrious Queen! This is a day of joy.
May all regard it so, may there not be
A single sufferer upon this isle
Who mourns today. Oh, that a glimmer of that
    radiance
Which mercy's light has spread upon your features
May fall upon that most unhappy queen
Whose fate so intimately touches both our nations!
    ELIZABETH: No more, Count Aubespine! Let us
    not mingle
Two matters which are incompatible.
If France desires our union earnestly,
She must share our concerns and not befriend our
    foes.
    AUBESPINE: In your own eyes, she would act cow-
    ardly
If she forgot, because of our alliance,
The hapless woman, widow of her king
And sister in the faith. If nothing else,
Compassion, honor would demand—
    ELIZABETH: In that sense I accept your master's
    intercession
And shall appraise it at its worth.
France does her duty as a friend;
With your permission, I shall act as Queen.
    [*She inclines her head toward the French nobles
    who, with the other lords, respectfully withdraw*]

SCENE III.

Elizabeth, Leicester, Burleigh *and* Shrewsbury.

[*The* Queen *sits down*]
    BURLEIGH: Most glorious Majesty! Today you
    grant
Your people's ardent wishes. Only now
Can we enjoy the blessed days which you bestow
On us, now that we need no longer tremble
When we direct our gaze into a stormy future.
One sacrifice the people still demand from you.
Grant it, and England's welfare will forever rest
On the foundation laid today.
    ELIZABETH: What do my people ask, my Lord?
    BURLEIGH: They ask for Mary Stuart's head. If you
Desire to make secure the precious gift
Of freedom and the hard-won light of truth,
She must not live. The enemy must perish
Lest we always tremble for your life.
As you well know, not all your Britons think alike.
The Roman idol-worship still
Has many secret followers in England,
And all of them hatch hostile thoughts.
They have their hearts set on this Stuart,
They're allies of the brothers from Lorraine,
Whose hate for you is unremitting.
These furious partisans are sworn to fight
Their bitter war against you to the death,
A war which they pursue with hellish weapons.

They have their armory at Rheims, the Cardinal's
    See,
And there they fashion lightning bolts, teach regicide,
And busily dispatch to England missions
Of disciplined fanatics, well-disguised
In fanciful array. Three murderers
Already have been sent from there. That pit
Is inexhaustible and procreates
Forever secret enemies.
The Atē of this never-ending war
Sits quietly at Fotheringhay
And with the torch of love inflames the realm.
Our youths, in whom she sparks with flattery false
    hopes,
Risk gladly certain death for her.
Their watchword is to set her free,
Their aim to put her on your throne.
Lorraine will never recognize your sacred right,
To them you are a rank usurper of the throne,
Whom Fortune crowned. These are the men
Who viciously persuaded the deluded woman
To call herself the Queen of England!
There is no peace with her and all her tribe.
You have to strike—or else be struck.
Her life—your death; her death—your life!

ELIZABETH: My Lord, you are the advocate of
    gloom.
I know your zeal rests on the purest motives,
I know the wisdom of your words is unalloyed.
But wisdom which commands that blood be spilled
I hate with all my soul. Think of more lenient
    counsel.
My Lord of Shrewsbury, you give me your opinion.

SHREWSBURY: You gave the fervor which moves
    loyal Burleigh
The praise which it deserves. Though I can never
    speak
With equal eloquence, my heart is no less honest.
Long live my Queen, to be her people's joy
And to prolong their happy peace!
This isle has never seen more pleasant days
Since her own princes governed her.
May England never purchase happiness
With her good name. But if she does, at least,
I hope that Talbot's eyes no longer see.

ELIZABETH: May God forbid that we befoul her
    fame.

SHREWSBURY: Then you will think of other ways
    to save the realm.
To execute the Stuart is illegal;
You have no right to try her, for she's not your
    subject.

ELIZABETH: My Privy Council, then, my Parlia-
    ment are wrong
And all the courts of justice are in error,
For all of them advised me that I have that right.

SHREWSBURY: Majority decisions are no proof
Of legal rights. England is not the world,
Her parliament does not include all men.
The England of today is not

The England that will be—or that once was.
Upon the waves of changeable opinion
The verdict of the court is tossed about.
Don't say that you are forced, that you obey
Necessity and the insistence of your people.
For you can prove at any moment, if you will,
That you are free to act the way you please.
Try it! Declare that you loathe bloodshed
And that you *wish* to save your sister's life.
Show openly your royal indignation
To those who want to give you other counsel—
Soon the necessity will disappear
And right will quickly change to wrong.
You must decide yourself, you cannot lean
Upon this feeble, swaying reed.
Obey your heart's advice, be merciful.
God did not put severity
Into a woman's heart. This nation's founders,
Who gave the reins of government to women, too,
Showed thereby clearly that severity
Was not to be a virtue of the English kings.

ELIZABETH: You are a most devoted advocate for
    her,
The enemy of England and—my own.
I do prefer a councillor
Who has my interests at heart.

SHREWSBURY: She was refused an advocate, and no
    one dares
To speak for her and thus incur your wrath.
Give your permission, then, to an old man,
Who, close to death, is no longer enticed
By worldly hopes, to be her advocate.
It never shall be said that in your council
The sounds of passion and selfishness were loud,
But that compassion did not dare to speak.
All is in league against her. You yourself
Have never seen her face to face,
She strikes no chords of friendship in your heart.
I am not trying to excuse her guilt. They say
That she allowed her husband to be murdered,
And it is true she married his assassin.
That is a heinous crime. But it was done
In an unhappy, dark epoch,
Amid the pressing fears of civil war.
Then she, weak and surrounded by a host
Of importuning vassals, threw herself
Into the arms of that most powerful
And brazen man, succumbing to who knows
What wily, evil forces. Yes,
A fragile thing, indeed, is woman.

ELIZABETH: No, women are not weak. There are
    strong souls
Among the female sex. Do not
Speak in my presence of their weakness.

SHREWSBURY: Misfortune taught *you* many lessons,
Life had no smiles for you. You saw no throne
That beckoned in the distance—only graves
That yawned before your feet.
At Woodstock, in the Tower's gloomy night,
The gracious father of the country brought

Your duties home to you by raising you
In misery. The flatterer's seductive chatter
Was far from you, the futile noises of the world
Did not distract you. There, your mind could con-
      centrate
And meditate upon life's genuine values.
No God saved that poor woman! At a tender age,
She was transplanted to French soil and to a court
Where nothing but frivolity and thoughtless gaiety
Surrounded her. Inebriated by unending feasts,
And blinded by the glitter of their vices,
She never heard the sober voice of truth.
The torrent of corruption carried her away.
And she was beautiful. Her bloom outshone
All other women, and that vain possession
No less than her exalted birth—
      ELIZABETH: Collect yourself, Lord Shrewsbury!
Remember that we are engaged in serious council.
Her charms, indeed, must be extraordinary,
If they can fan such flames in old men's hearts!
My Lord of Leicester, you alone are silent.
Does what makes Lord Shrewsbury wag his tongue,
Tie yours?
      LEICESTER: Your Majesty,
I have been silent in astonishment,
Amazed that one makes bold to fill your ear
With horror stories, fairy tales that strike
The gullible and foolish rabble on the streets
With fear. Now they are being seriously argued
In your exalted council by wise men.
I'm speechless, I admit, that Mary, Queen of Scots
Without a country, who could not maintain herself
On her own little throne, whom her own vassals
      mock,
An outcast, should become so dangerous to you
Now that she is in prison. What, in heaven's name,
Makes her so terrible? Her claim on England?
Is it because the House of Guise
Refuses to acknowledge you as Queen?
Can their objections weaken rights
Which you possess by birth, and which have been
      confirmed
By Parliament? Did Henry's testament
Not tacitly refute her claims? And will
The English, happy in their new-found light,
Now throw themselves into a Papist's arms?
Would they desert their Queen, whom they adore,
To follow Darnley's murderess?
What do these people want who so impatiently
Torment you, while you're still alive, about an heir,
Who cannot wed you soon enough because,
They say, you must save state and church?
You stand before us in the bloom of youth,
She fades, a little closer to her grave each day.
I hope, by God, that you will walk for many years
Upon her grave. There is no need for you
To push her into it.
      BURLEIGH: My Lord, that has not always been
      your judgment.
      LEICESTER: As member of a court of law, it's true,

I voted for her death; but I speak differently
As member of the Privy Council.
Here, law is not the issue, only interest.
Is this the time to be afraid of her,
Now that she's been abandoned by her last
Protector, France; now that you are about
To give your hand to a delighted prince;
Now that there's hope of seeing soon
A newly founded family of English kings again?
Why kill her when she is already dead?
Contempt kills most effectively. Watch out
Lest she be resurrected by compassion.
My counsel therefore is to leave the sentence,
By which she is condemned to die, in full effect,
To let her live—but live beneath
The executioner's upraised ax, and let it drop
If one man lifts his sword for her.
      ELIZABETH: [Rises] I've heard your views, my
      Lords.
I am most grateful for your zeal.
Now, with the aid of God, who lights the way of
      kings,
I shall examine your opinions
And choose what I believe is best.

SCENE IV.

The same.

      [Paulet *and* Mortimer *enter*]
      ELIZABETH: Here comes Amias Paulet. Sir Amias,
What news have you for us?
      PAULET: Most gracious Majesty! My nephew,
But recently returned from far-flung travels,
Has come to kneel and pay you homage.
May he find favor in your eyes
And may the sun of your affection warm him.
      MORTIMER: [Kneels before the Queen].
Long live my gracious Queen.
May happiness and glory crown her head.
      ELIZABETH: Arise. I welcome you to England, sir.
Your travels, I am told, took you to France,
You were in Rheims and stayed in Rome.
Tell me what plots our enemies are hatching.
      MORTIMER: May God confound them and reverse
Against the archers' breasts the arrows' flight
They aim at you, my gracious Queen.
      ELIZABETH: Did you see Morgan and that spinner
      of intrigues,
The Archbishop of Rosse?
      MORTIMER: I came to know all Scottish exiles who
      at Rheims
Forge their conspiracies against this isle.
I wormed my way into their confidence
In order to discover their intrigues.
      PAULET: They even trusted him with secret letters,
Addressed in code to Mary, Queen of Scots,
Which loyally he handed us.
      ELIZABETH: What are their latest schemes?

MORTIMER: The news that France abandons them,
Allies herself with England, hit them like a thunder-
  bolt.
They now set all their hopes in Spain.
  ELIZABETH: That is what Walsingham reports to
  me.
  MORTIMER: The Papal Bull, which recently Pope
  Sixtus flung
Against you from the Vatican, arrived
As I was leaving Rheims. It will be brought
To England by the ship from France.
  LEICESTER: Such weapons do not frighten England
  any more.
  BURLEIGH: Used by fanatics, they are terrible.
  ELIZABETH: [Looking searchingly at Mortimer]
Some have accused you of attending schools
At Rheims and of abjuring your religion.
  MORTIMER: I don't deny it, but it was pretense.
My eagerness to serve you went so far.
  ELIZABETH: [To Paulet, who holds a paper out to
  her]
What is that paper?
  PAULET: It is a letter from the Queen of Scots.
  BURLEIGH: [Quickly reaching for it] Give it to me.
  PAULET: [Handing it to the Queen]
I beg your pardon, Lord High Treasurer,
She asked me to remit it to the Queen.
Although she thinks that I'm her enemy,
I only hate her vice; what I can reconcile
With my responsibilities, I'll do for her.
  [The Queen has taken the letter. While she reads
  it, Mortimer and Leicester secretly exchange a
  few words]
  BURLEIGH: [To Paulet] What can it be but mean-
  ingless complaints
Which we should not impose upon the Queen's kind
  heart.
  PAULET: She did not hide from me what it contains.
She asks a favor—she desires to see the Queen.
  BURLEIGH: [Quickly] Never.
  SHREWSBURY: Why not? That would not be im-
  proper.
  BURLEIGH: She's forfeited the right to see the
  Queen.
She thirsts for blood, has instigated murder!
A loyal servant of the Queen
Would never give such treacherous advice.
  SHREWSBURY: But if the Queen desires to grant
  that favor,
Would you attempt to check that gentle impulse?
  BURLEIGH: She is condemned, her head is on the
  block.
It is not fitting for a queen's exalted eyes
To look upon a woman doomed to die.
Once she's admitted to the presence of the Queen,
The sentence never can be carried out.
The royal presence means a royal pardon.
  ELIZABETH: [Has finished reading the letter and is
  drying her tears]
Oh, what is Man? And what is worldly happiness?

To what point has this Queen been brought,
Who started out with such high hopes,
Whom destiny put on the oldest throne
In Christendom, who in her dreams already saw
A triple crown upon her head!
How different the language she speaks now from that
She used when she adopted England's coat of arms
And had her courtiers flatter her
As Queen of both Britannic isles!
Excuse me, gentlemen, it rends my heart,
My soul is bleeding, sadness seizes me,
As I perceive the instability
Of all that's human, and how close
The frightful fate of humans passed by me.
  SHREWSBURY: God touched your heart, your
  Majesty.
Obey this heavenly command. Her guilt
Is terrible, but she has paid a fearful price.
The time has come to end her trials.
Descend into her dungeon's gloomy tomb,
The radiant apparition of an angel,
Reach out to lift the deeply fallen woman—
  BURLEIGH: Be steadfast, Majesty. Do not let senti-
  ment,
However praiseworthy, misguide your action.
Do not deprive yourself of your prerogative
To do what surely will be necessary.
You cannot save, you cannot pardon her.
Do not invite the odious reproach
That you, in cruel mocking triumph,
Had gloated at your victim's agony.
  LEICESTER: My Lords, let us not go beyond our
  competence.
The Queen is wise and has no need of us
In choosing what her dignity requires of her.
A private audience in no way would affect
The course of justice. Mary was condemned
By English law, not by the Queen's decree.
It would be worthy of her noble soul
For Queen Elizabeth to heed
The dictate of her gentle heart,
If she does not obstruct the law's severity.
  ELIZABETH: Leave us, my Lords. We shall find
  ways to do
What mercy and necessity impose on us.
  [The Lords leave. As Mortimer reaches the door,
  the Queen calls him back]
Sir Mortimer, a word with you.

SCENE V.

Elizabeth and Mortimer.

  ELIZABETH: [After gazing at Mortimer for a few
  moments]
You have great courage and possess
A rare degree of self-control for one so young.
One who has mastered the demanding art
Of subterfuge so early has reached manhood

Before his time and shortens his apprenticeship.
Your destiny calls you along the path of greatness.
It's fortunate for you that I, your oracle,
Can also make my prophecy come true.

MORTIMER: My gracious Queen, my person and
  abilities
Will be devoted to your service.

ELIZABETH: You've come to know the enemies of
  England.
You know how unrelentingly they hate her Queen,
Their inexhaustible supply of bloody schemes.
To this day, God Almighty has protected me,
But never will the crown upon my head be firm
As long as she still lives who is their hope
And serves as pretext for their zeal.

MORTIMER: Command it, and she dies.

ELIZABETH: I thought that I had reached my goal,
But now, alas, I am no further than I was
In the beginning. Yes, I meant to leave
The matter to the law and not to soil my hands.
The law has enacted now—what have I gained?
The sentence must be carried out,
And it is I who must command that it be done.
The hateful deed will come upon *my* head,
I must acknowledge it, I cannot veil it.
That is the worst.

MORTIMER: Why be concerned about the light
In which an honest cause appears?

ELIZABETH: You do not know the world, Sir
  Mortimer.
What one appears to be is judged by all,
But no one judges what one is.
No one will be persuaded of my right,
And I must therefore seek to leave
The part I played in Mary's death in doubt.
When deeds have such ambiguous complexion,
Our only safeguard is obscurity.
The fateful step is that which one admits.
What one does not reveal, one has not lost.

MORTIMER: It would perhaps be best then—

ELIZABETH: Certainly
That would be best. Oh, my good angel speaks
Through you. Continue, sir, go on,
You are a serious man, you think things through,
You're very different from your uncle—

MORTIMER: [*Taken aback*] Did you uncover your
  desire to him?

ELIZABETH: I did, I now regret it.

MORTIMER: He is old.
Forgive him, for his years make him too cautious.
A daring deed needs youthful recklessness.

ELIZABETH: [*Quickly*] May I—

MORTIMER: I lend my hand to you, but you
Must judge how you can save your reputation.

ELIZABETH: Ah, if one morning you would wake
  me with the news:
Your hated enemy, the Queen of Scots,
Expired last night!

MORTIMER: You may rely on me.

ELIZABETH: When will my head rest peacefully at
  night?

MORTIMER: The next new moon will end your
  fears.

ELIZABETH: Farewell, Sir Mortimer. Do not feel
  grieved
That my great gratitude will have to wear
The cloak of night—but silence is the god
Of happiness. The strongest and most tender bonds
Are tied by secrets held in common.
  [*She leaves*]

SCENE VI.

Mortimer *alone*.

MORTIMER: Go, queen of treachery and falsehood!
As you deceive the world, so you will be deceived.
Betraying you, indeed, is right, a noble deed.
Do I look like a murderer? Did you
See in my eyes the baseness of a villain?
Yes, trust my arm—hold back your own.
Yes, show the world your pious, lying face of mercy,
While secretly you count on me to murder her.
Ah, that will give us time to rescue her.
You want to elevate me, show me in the distance,
Allusively, a far more precious prize?
Are you that prize, your favors and your love?
Poor woman, what have you to offer me?
Vainglorious fame and honors do not tempt me.
She is the only one who makes my life worth living.
The gods of grace and youthful eagerness
Perform around her their eternal dance of joy,
At her breast—heaven's happiness.
Your gifts are dead. The greatest prize,
The shining ornament of life,
A heart that gives itself in sweet forgetfulness,
Enchanted and enchanting, to a kindred heart,
That crown of womanhood you never have possessed,
No man has ever been exalted by your love—
I must wait for the Earl, give him her letter.
A hateful errand. I don't trust this courtier.
No one but I can save her. Mine shall be
The danger and the fame, and mine shall be the
  prize.
  [*As he turns to leave,* Paulet *enters*]

SCENE VII.

Mortimer *and* Paulet.

PAULET: What did the Queen desire of you?

MORTIMER: Oh, nothing, sir.

PAULET: [*Regarding him sternly*] The ground on
  which you now
Are venturing is slippery, my nephew.
The favors princes have to offer may well tempt
A youth, for youth loves honors. You, I hope,

Will not allow ambition to divert your step.
    MORTIMER: You brought me here.
    PAULET: I wish that I had not.
The court is not the ground on which our family
Collected honors. Nephew, stand your ground!
Don't pay too high a price, don't go against
Your conscience.
    MORTIMER: Why? What notions!
    PAULET: Mistrust her flattery, no matter what
She promises. She will not hesitate
To disavow you if you do as she commands,
And to avenge the bloody deed she hatched herself,
So that her name may not be stained.
    MORTIMER: The bloody deed? What do you mean?
    PAULET: No more pretense. I know exactly what
         the Queen
Has planned and asked of you. She hopes that you,
Young, eager and ambitious, will be more
Inclined to lend a willing ear—and hand—
Than I, an obstinate old man. Did you say yes?
    MORTIMER: But Uncle!
    PAULET: If you agreed, I curse and I disown you
         . . . I—
    [Leicester *enters*]
    LEICESTER: Distinguished knight, permit me to ex-
         change
A word with this young man. The Queen, it seems,
Has graciously received him and desires
That he from now on be entrusted with
The full responsibility of guarding Mary Stuart,
She trusts his honesty—
    PAULET: His honesty—I see.
    LEICESTER: I beg your pardon?
    PAULET: The Queen trusts him, I said, my Lord,
         and I
Rely upon myself and on my open eyes. [*He leaves*]

SCENE VIII.

Leicester *and* Mortimer.

    LEICESTER: [*Perplexed*] Is something wrong with
         Sir Amias?
    MORTIMER: I don't know.
Perhaps this unexpected confidence . . .
    LEICESTER: [*Giving him a searching look*]
I wonder . . . Do you merit confidence?
    MORTIMER: [*In the same manner*]
That very question I ask you, my Lord.
    LEICESTER: You wished to speak with me in
         private.
    MORTIMER: Give me assurance that I safely may.
    LEICESTER: What proof have I that I can safely
         talk to you?
Don't take offense at my apparent lack
Of confidence. You show two faces here
At court. One must be false—but which?
    MORTIMER: I'm in the same predicament, my Lord.

    LEICESTER: Who then will be the first to drop his
         guard?
    MORTIMER:The one who has the least to lose.
    LEICESTER: Well, that is you, of course.
    MORTIMER: Oh no. That's you. One word from
         you, my Lord,
Armed with your influence and power, easily
Could be my end. But nothing I could say
Would count against your rank and royal favor.
    LEICESTER: You are mistaken. I am powerful
In every way, but in that tender point
Which I am to lay open to your view.
I'm weak, the weakest man at court.
The meanest witness could destroy me.
    MORTIMER: When the all-powerful Lord Leicester
         stoops
To make me such a confidence, I may
Be justified in thinking higher of myself.
Then I will set a generous example.
    LEICESTER: Precede me on the road of confidence,
And I shall follow.
    MORTIMER: [*Quickly produces the letter*]
The Queen of Scotland sends you this.
    LEICESTER: [*Terrified, quickly grabs the letter*]
Speak softly, sir. What is it? Ah, her picture!
    [*He kisses it and stares at it in silent enchantment*]
    MORTIMER: [*Has watched him attentively while he
         was reading the letter*]
My Lord, I trust you now.
    LEICESTER: [*Has quickly run through the letter*]
Do you know what this letter is about?
    MORTIMER: No, I do not.
    LEICESTER: She must have told you, surely—
    MORTIMER: She told me nothing. You, she said,
         would clear
The mystery. To me it is a mystery how you,
The favorite of Elizabeth and Mary's enemy,
One of her judges, could yet be the man
On whom she counts to rescue her. And still,
It must be so. Your eyes betray
Too clearly what you feel for her.
    LEICESTER: Before I speak, explain to me why you
Take such a fervent interest in her.
What made her put her trust in you?
    MORTIMER: My Lord, that's easily explained. I
         changed
My faith in Rome, I'm now in league
With Cardinal de Guise; the Archbishop
Of Rheims gave me a letter to the Queen.
    LEICESTER: I heard of your conversion. That awoke
My confidence in you. Give me your hand!
Forgive me for my hesitation,
But I can't be too cautious. Walsingham
And Burleigh hate me, lie in wait for me;
You might have been their creature and the bait
That was to lure me to their net.
    MORTIMER: How carefully the great at court must
         step!
I sympathize with you, my Lord.

LEICESTER: What joy that I can now embrace a trusted friend
And throw aside the strictures which I bore so long.
You are surprised, you say, to find
My feelings toward Mary changed.
The truth is that I never hated her.
By force of circumstance alone I joined
The ranks of her oppressors. As you know,
She had been promised me before she married Darnley,
When she still stood amid the smiles of grandeur.
Unmoved, I pushed my happiness away,
But now that she's a prisoner and at the gates
Of death—I seek her out and risk my life.

MORTIMER: That's generous, indeed, my Lord.

LEICESTER: Things have a different aspect now, Sir Mortimer.
Ambition, then, made me insensitive
To youth and beauty; Mary's hand, I thought,
Was far too small a prize for me, I hoped
To win the Queen of England!

MORTIMER: Yes, the world well knew
That she preferred you to all other men.

LEICESTER: Yes, so it seemed, but now—now that ten years
Have passed in unrelenting wooing
And hateful obligations—now my heart is overfilled.
I must give vent to my resentment, long concealed.
They call me fortunate. If they but knew
That what they envy are my chains!
For ten long, bitter years I made my sacrifices
Before the idol of her vanity,
Endured the despotism of her changing moods
With slavish meekness, a toy of her capricious whims,
One minute coddled by her tenderness,
The next repulsed by prudish pride,
Tormented equally by kindness and disdain,
Watched like a prisoner with sharp-eyed jealousy,
Called to account like any little boy
And scolded like a servant—oh, there are
No words to paint that hell!

MORTIMER: I pity you, my Lord.

LEICESTER: And now, so near the goal, the prize eludes my grasp.
Now someone else arrives to cheat me of the fruit
Of all my pains. I lose my long-held rights
To this young man, the husband of her choice.
I am to leave the stage on which I played
So long the hero, I risk losing her,
And not alone her hand, her favor, too.
She is a woman—he a charming man.

MORTIMER: He is the son of Catherine. There is
No better school to learn the art of flattery.

LEICESTER: Thus all my hopes are ruined, and my eyes
Search the horizon for a plank that might
Yet save me from the shipwreck of my fortunes and—
Return to her, my first and fairest hope.
Her image stood before me suddenly,

Her radiant charm, her beauty and her youth
I saw anew—and in their proper light.
Not cold ambition but the heart compared,
And now I knew that I had lost a pearl.
With horror I perceived her plunged
Into the deepest misery—and through my fault.
My hopes aroused, I thought that there might still
Be time to rescue her, to make her yet my own.
Helped by a loyal friend I reached her ear,
Revealed my change of heart to her.
This letter which you brought from her
Gives me assurance that she pardons me,
That she will give herself to me as prize—
If I will rescue her.

MORTIMER: But you've done nothing!
Without a word, you let them sentence her,
You even voted for her death.
It took a miracle. The light of truth
First had to fall upon her keeper's nephew,
And far away, in Rome, God's providence
Had to prepare an unexpected ally,
Before she even found her way to you.

LEICESTER: The thought of it has been a constant torment.
Just then, she was removed from Talbot's care,
Transferred to Fotheringhay, and there
Confided to your uncle's watchful guard.
All roads were blocked, and I had to continue
To play before the world the role of persecutor.
But do not think that I would let her die
A painful death. I hoped, and I still hope
To stave off that extremity, to gain
The time and find the means to rescue her.

MORTIMER: You have the means! Your noble confidence, my Lord,
Deserves to be returned. I want to free the Queen,
That's why I'm here. The preparations have been made.
Your powerful support assures success.

LEICESTER: What's that? You frighten me. You mean—

MORTIMER: I want to force her prison. I have friends,
All is in readiness—

LEICESTER: You have accomplices and confidants?
God help me! Don't make me a partner to your recklessness.
Do all your friends know of *my* secret, too?

MORTIMER: Don't be alarmed. Our plans were laid without
Your help, and so they would be carried out,
If she did not insist that you deliver her.

LEICESTER: Can you assure me that my name
Has not been mentioned in your league?

MORTIMER: Yes, rest assured. But why so cautious now,
My Lord, that you find help? You said you mean
To save and to possess the Queen, but now,
The moment you discover unexpected friends,
The moment that the means to do so drop

Into your lap from heaven, you appear
Embarrassed more than overjoyed.
    LEICESTER: It can't be done by force. That is too
      risky.
    MORTIMER: So is delay.
    LEICESTER: I tell you, sir, it is too dangerous.
    MORTIMER: For you who wish to possess the
      Queen!
We only want to save her—but are not so timid.
    LEICESTER: You are too rash, young man, in such
      a dangerous
And difficult affair.
    MORTIMER: You are too hesitant in matters of
      your honor.
    LEICESTER: I see the traps which are around us on
      all sides.
    MORTIMER: I feel the courage to demolish them.
    LEICESTER: Your courage—it's audacity, it's mad-
      ness.
    MORTIMER: Your prudence—is that courage, sir?
    LEICESTER: Are you so keen to end like Babington?
    MORTIMER: You don't seem keen to rival Norfolk's
      generosity.
    LEICESTER: Norfolk did not bring home his bride.
    MORTIMER: He proved that he deserved her,
      though.
    LEICESTER: If we should fail, we'll pull her down
      with us.
    MORTIMER: If we are squeamish, she will not be
      saved.
    LEICESTER: You do not think, you do not listen,
Impetuous and blind, you will destroy
What had been well along its hopeful way.
    MORTIMER: Along a way which you had smoothed?
Have you done anything to rescue her?
Suppose I had been knave enough to murder her,
As I have been commanded by the Queen—
And as she even now expects of me—
Tell me, what have you done to guard her life?
    LEICESTER: The Queen gave that command to you?
    MORTIMER: Elizabeth misjudged me just as Mary
Misjudged the Earl of Leicester.
    LEICESTER: But you agreed to carry out her order?
    MORTIMER: In order to be sure she would not buy
Another pair of hands, I offered mine.
    LEICESTER: Well done! That gives us elbow room.
      While she
Relies on you to render her this bloody service,
The sentence can't be carried out—and we gain time.
    MORTIMER: [Impatiently] No, we will squander
      precious time.
    LEICESTER: She counts on you. She therefore will
      not hesitate
To show the world how merciful she is.
Perhaps, with cunning, I'll persuade her
To meet her adversary face to face,
And that would tie her hands. Burleigh is right.
Once she has seen her, she can never have
The sentence carried out. Yes, I shall try with all—

    MORTIMER: What good is that? When she finds
      out that I
Deceived her and that Mary does not die,
Is then not everything exactly as it was?
She'll never free her. Life imprisonment
Would be the mildest fate for Mary.
If thus you must act boldly in the end,
Why not begin by being bold?
You hold the power in your hands, you could
Easily raise by arming the nobility
Who live upon your property and castles!
Mary has many secret friends, yes—even now.
There are still many heroes left among
The Percys and the Howards, though the heads
Of all these noble families have tumbled.
They only wait that one of England's great
May set them an example. Yes, act openly!
Enough pretense! Guard your beloved like a knight,
Do battle, fight for her the noble fight!
You can be master of the Queen of England's person
At any time you choose. Entice her then
Where she has often followed you, to one of your
    castles.
Show her that you are man enough to talk
To her as master, hold her there—
Till she sets Mary free.
    LEICESTER: I am aghast, you frighten me. How far
Will your insanity yet carry you?
Do you know where you are? And do you know
What things are like at court, how men
Are suffocated by this woman's regimen?
Go on, look for the heroism here,
The spirit that one used to find in England!
All is servility, and everyone
Now clings to apron strings. The springs
Of courage are unwound. Let me direct your steps.
Consider well the risks. Someone is coming! Go!
    MORTIMER: Mary still hopes. Must I return with
      empty sympathy?
    LEICESTER: Bring her the vows of my eternal love.
    MORTIMER: Take them yourself to her. I offered
      help
In saving her, not as a messenger of love.
    [He leaves]

SCENE IX.

Elizabeth *and* Leicester.

    ELIZABETH: Who was that? Someone left, I heard
      you talking.
    LEICESTER: [Startled, quickly turns around]
That was Sir Mortimer.
    ELIZABETH: Is something wrong? You seem per-
      turbed, my Lord.
    LEICESTER: [Takes hold of himself]
To see you thus before me—yes, indeed,
I never saw you looking so enchanting.
I'm blinded by your beauty. Ah, my God!

ELIZABETH: Why do you sigh?

LEICESTER: Do I not have sufficient reason? As my eyes
Behold your charm the nameless pain
Of my impending loss renews itself.

ELIZABETH: What will you lose?

LEICESTER: Your heart, your lovely self.
The youthful arms of your impassioned husband
Will soon bring happiness to you,
And he will own your undivided heart.
He of royal blood, that I am not.
But no man on this earth adores you more
Than I. The Duc d'Anjou has never seen you yet,
He only loves your image and your fame—
But I love you. If you were but the poorest shepherdess
And I born to the highest throne on earth,
I would descend to where you are
And lay my crown in homage at your feet.

ELIZABETH: Commiserate with me instead of scolding me.
I may not ask my heart. It would choose otherwise.
Oh, how I envy other women
Who are allowed to choose the man they love.
I'm not so fortunate as to have the right
To put the crown on that man's head who is
Most dear to me. The Stuart had that privilege.
She gave her hand to whom she gave her heart,
Took every liberty and drained
The well-filled cup of pleasure.

LEICESTER: She now drinks from the cup of sorrow.

ELIZABETH: For her, the world's opinion was of no account.
She chose the easy life and never bore
The yoke which I took on my shoulders.
I could have made the same demands, to taste
And to enjoy my life and earthly pleasure.
But I preferred the burden of my royal duties.
Yet she became the favorite of men,
Was courted by both young and old because—
Her one ambition was to be a woman.
Yes, such are men. Voluptuous adulterers!
In their pursuit of frivolous and passing joys,
They do not value what they should revere.
Why, did not even Talbot seem rejuvenated
When he began to talk about her charms?

LEICESTER: You must forgive him. He was once her keeper,
The wily woman caught him with her flatteries.

ELIZABETH: But is it true? Is she so beautiful?
I've had to listen to them rave about that face
So often that I'm curious how much of it is true.
Paintings can flatter and descriptions lie,
I only trust my eyes. Why do you look
At me with such a strange expression?

LEICESTER: I put you next to Mary in my thoughts.
I must confess I would enjoy, provided that
It could be done in secret, to confront

You with her. Only then would you at last
Enjoy the fullest flavor of your victory.
That shame I wish her, that with her own eyes—
And envy has sharp eyes—she could convince
Herself that you are her superior
In dignity and stature just as much
As in all other virtues of a queen.

ELIZABETH: In years she is much younger than I am.

LEICESTER: In years! To look at her, one could not tell.
Of course, she's suffered much, and that
May well have made her age before her time.
It would be still more vexing for the lady
If she saw you as bride. Those lovely hopes
Of life to come lie far behind her now,
And she would see you walking toward happiness,
What's more, about to wed the Prince of France.
For her who always made so much and was so proud
Of her French marriage, and who even now
Insists that mighty France will rescue her,
That would indeed be bitter.

ELIZABETH: [Offhand] I'm being pressed to grant an interview.

LEICESTER: What she requests as favor, grant as punishment.
The scaffold would not pain her more
Than being overshadowed by your beauty.
That is the way to murder her, as once
She meant to murder you. For when she sees
Your beauty, guarded by your honor and enhanced
By an untarnished reputation—
Her own thrown carelessly and shamelessly away—
Exalted by the splendor of your crown,
Embellished now by tender hopes of marriage,
The hour of death has struck for her.
Yes, when I look upon you now,
You never have been better armed for victory
By beauty. When you entered here, a while ago,
I felt myself bathed in blinding rays
From an ethereal luminescence.
If you faced her this moment, as you are,
You would not live to see a finer hour.

ELIZABETH: Now? No—not now—no, Leicester—no.
I have to give it thought, and talk to Burleigh—

LEICESTER: [Interrupting] To Burleigh! He can think of nothing but
The welfare of the country. But your womanhood
Also has rights, a subtle point
Which you have to decide and not a statesman.
Yet statecraft, too, demands that you should see her,
That by your generosity you win the public mind.
Deal later with your enemy, as you see fit.

ELIZABETH: I could not, properly and decently,
Confront a relative in want and shame.
I'm told that her surroundings are not regal.
To see her in distress, I would feel as reproach.

LEICESTER: You need not cross her threshold. Hear my counsel.

It happens that today the hunt takes place,
The way will lead past Fotheringhay, and there
She could be walking in the park,
When you, as if by chance, come by. Of course,
It must not seem deliberate, and if
You do not wish you need not even speak to her.

ELIZABETH: If this is foolishness, the foolishness
Is yours, not mine. Today I cannot look askance
At anything you might desire, Lord Leicester,
Because today I hurt you more than anyone.

[*With a tender glance at him*]
Even if this is just a whim of yours,
Affection shows itself by being pleased
To grant a thing—yes, even though it may be wrong.

[Leicester *throws himself at her feet*]

ACT III. SCENE I.

*The Park of Fotheringhay, many trees in the fore-
ground, a wide view in the background.*

[Mary, *running, comes from behind a group of
trees.* Hannah *follows her slowly*]

HANNAH: You're running as if wings assisted you,
I cannot follow you so fast. Please wait.

MARY:[1]
*Let me delight in my precious new freedom,
Let me again be a child and rejoice
Testing the hurrying, light-footed step
On the green meadows' resilient carpet.
Have I escaped the gloom of my prison?
Am I released from my sorrowful tomb?
Let me then drink in long, thirsty draughts
Freedom's heady, heavenly air.*

HANNAH: Oh my dear Lady, your old prison
Has only been enlarged, its walls are still
Around us, even though the trees and shrubs
May for the moment shield them from our view.

MARY: Oh, thank you, thank you, friendly trees,
Your kind green arms blot out my prison walls.
I want to dream that I am free and happy,
Why, Hannah, wake me from my sweet illusion?
I am surrounded by the vast, blue sky,
Free and unfettered my eye sweeps
Across the limitless expanse.
There where you see the clouds' grey mountains rise,
There is the boundary of my domain, my glance
Accompanies the clouds where southward lies
The goal they search beyond the ocean; France!
*Hurrying clouds, ships of the sky!
That I could sail with you, that I could fly!
Take my love to the land of my youth.
I am a prisoner, I am in chains,
You be the messenger of my pains.
Freely you course in the infinite air,
No one your master, no queen your despair.*

HANNAH: Oh dearest Lady, you're beside yourself,

---

[1] The indented, italic, passages are rhymed in the original German, thus emphasizing the lyrical effect.—J.G.

The air of freedom, missed so long, makes you extravagant.

MARY:
*There is a fisherman tying his boat!
Frail as it is, it could be a tool,
To take me to lands under more friendly rule.
Scarce is the food that he catches afloat.
I would load up his boat with the richest of treasure,
Such fish he hauled never, try as he may,
In his nets he would find good luck without measure,
If his rescuing bark would take me away.*

HANNAH: A forlorn hope! Do you not see the spies
Who in the distance follow us?
A dismal, cruel order chases
All sympathetic creatures from our path.

MARY: No, Hannah. No, believe me, not in vain
Have they thrown open now my prison doors.
This little favor must announce
Still greater happiness. I can't be wrong.
I see a loving hand at work,
The Earl of Leicester's mighty arm.
Yes, bit by bit they will expand the walls,
Preparing me with small for greater things
Until at last I stand before the man
Who will release me from my chains forever.

HANNAH: I see no rhyme or reason in all this:
It was but yesterday that they announced
That you must die, and now, today, this privilege.
I've also heard it said that those
May benefit from slight concessions
Whom their eternal liberty awaits.

MARY:
*Listen! The hunting horn! Did you hear
Its mighty call across meadow and forest?
Oh, how I wish I could mount my brave steed
To be part of the chase!
Again it sounds! How well I know its voice,
Full of memories, painful and sweet!
Often it filled my ear with delight
On the hilly heath of the highlands,
When the boisterous hunters approached.*

SCENE II.

[Mary *and* Hannah. Paulet *enters*]

PAULET: My Lady, have I pleased you now, at
last?
Do I, for once, deserve your gratitude?

MARY: You sir? Did you obtain this favor for me?
You?

PAULET: And why not I? I gave the Queen your
letter—

MARY: You did? The freedom which I now enjoy
Is the result of what I wrote the Queen?

PAULET: [*Significantly*] And not the only one. Prepare yourself
For even greater favors.

MARY: For greater favors, sir? What do you mean?

PAULET: You must have heard the hunting horn.

MARY: [*Shrinking back with a sudden suspicion*]
You frighten me.

PAULET: The Queen is hunting in this neighborhood—

MARY: The Queen—

PAULET: —and any moment she may stand before you.

HANNAH: [*Hurries to* Mary *who, trembling, seems about to faint*]
What is it, my dear Lady? You look pale.

PAULET: Again displeased? Is this not what you asked?
The favor has been granted sooner than you thought.
You've always had a lively tongue—now use it well.
Now is the time to speak.

MARY: Why have I not been warned?
I'm not prepared for it, I am not ready now.
What I requested as the greatest favor,
Terrifies me now—it makes me shudder.
Dear Hannah, take me to my rooms, I must
Collect myself.

PAULET: Stay here. This is
Where you must wait for her. I'm not surprised
That you are terrified to stand before your judge.

SCENE III.

The same.

[*The* Earl of Shrewsbury *enters*]

MARY: That's not the reason. I feel strange—
Ah, noble Shrewsbury, you come as my
Good angel, sent from heaven—no, my Lord,
I cannot see her now, I cannot bear
To see the hated woman, save me, please!

SHREWSBURY: Compose yourself. This is the fateful hour.
Now you must be courageous.

MARY: How I've waited!
For years I have prepared myself, repeated to myself
What I would say, engraved it in my memory,
So I would surely move her. Now, at last,
The moment has arrived and now—I have forgotten.
Now I feel nothing but my burning sense
Of suffering, my heart is turned against her,
In raging hatred, all kind of thoughts have fled,
Appalling shapes from hell, shaking their Gorgon's heads,
Surround me on all sides.

SHREWSBURY: Restrain your boiling blood, my Lady; conquer
The bitterness that fills your heart. No good
Can come of hatred meeting hatred in
This interview. Although you may rebel,
You must obey this moment's special law.
Humble yourself—she has the power.

MARY: To her? I can't!

SHREWSBURY: You must. Speak calmly to the Queen,
Respectfully, address her generosity,
And don't stand on your rights—not now.

MARY: Ah, what I prayed for now becomes my ruin,
I'm cursed because my pleas were heard.
We should not look upon each other, never,
No good will come of it, now now—not ever.
It is more probable that fire and water
Will lovingly embrace, more likely that
The lamb will kiss the tiger—no, she's wounded me,
She has insulted me too deeply—
We never can be reconciled.

SHREWSBURY: Wait till you see her face to face.
I saw how much your letter touched her heart.
Her eyes were filled with tears, she is not heartless.
Have confidence. That's why I hurried here,
To help you calm yourself and to prepare you.

MARY: [*Seizes his hands*] Oh, Talbot, you have always been my friend.
Why did they move me from your gentle prison!
Since then I've met with much adversity.

SHREWSBURY: Don't think of that. Think only that you must
Be humble when you meet the Queen.

MARY: Is Burleigh with her, my dark angel?

SHREWSBURY: No one is with her but the Earl of Leicester.

MARY: Leicester!

SHREWSBURY: You need not be afraid of him.
He's not your enemy. It is his doing
That she agreed to see you here.

MARY: I thought so!

SHREWSBURY: What did you say, my Lady?

PAULET: Here is the Queen.

ELIZABETH: [*To* Leicester] What is the name of this estate?

[*All step aside, only* Mary *remains where she stands, leaning on* Hannah]

SCENE IV.

The same.

[Elizabeth, Leicester *and* Attendants *enter*]

LEICESTER: It's Fotheringhay.

ELIZABETH: [*To* Shrewsbury] Our hunting party is to go ahead to London.
The people push too closely on the streets.
We seek protection in this peaceful park.
[Shrewsbury *sends the* Attendants *away.* Elizabeth, *although now addressing* Paulet, *keeps her eyes fixed on* Mary]
My people love me far too much, their joy
Is too extravagant, they idolize me.
That is the way to honor God, but not a mortal queen.

MARY: [*Has been leaning on* Hannah *during the foregoing exchange; she was close to fainting; now she straightens up and meets* Elizabeth's *steady gaze.*

Trembling she shrinks back, hiding her face at Hannah's *shoulder*]

Oh God! A woman with such features has no heart.

ELIZABETH: Who is the lady?

[*General silence*]

LEICESTER: You are at Fotheringhay, your Majesty.

ELIZABETH: [*Pretends surprise and glowers at* Leicester]

Who dared to bring me here, Lord Leicester?

LEICESTER: Your Majesty, it's happened. Now that heaven

Has guided your steps here, let generosity

And pity govern you.

SHREWSBURY: Please your Majesty

To look upon this most unfortunate of women,

Who withers at your sight.

[Mary *calms herself, takes a few steps toward* Elizabeth *but stops again, shuddering. Her gestures express a terrible inner battle*]

ELIZABETH: Who was it, gentlemen, who told me to expect

A woman deeply bowed? This is a woman full

Of pride, untractable for all her suffering.

MARY: So be it. I'll submit to this supreme

Indignity, I shall renounce my pride,

Forget that I'm a queen and what I suffered.

I'll throw myself upon her mercy—hers

Who pushed me into this disgrace.

[*She turns toward the Queen*]

The heavens have decided in your favor, sister,

The victor's crown is on your happy brow.

My prayers rise to God who has exalted you.

[*She throws herself on the ground before* Elizabeth]

My sister, now you, too, be generous.

Don't let me lie here, shamefully,

Before you in the dust. Extend your hand

To raise me up from my abysmal fall.

ELIZABETH: [*Taking a step backward*]

You are where you belong, my Lady.

And I praise God and thank Him for His mercy

That He has not seen fit to let me lie

At your feet as you're lying now at mine.

MARY: [*With growing passion*]

Do not forget how changeable our human fortunes are.

The gods still live who will avenge false pride.

Respect and fear those terrifying powers

Which brought me to my knees and at your feet,

Before these witnesses, honor in me yourself,

Do not disgrace and vilify the Tudor blood

Which flows in my veins as it does in yours.

Merciful God! Do not stand there before me,

As blunt and inaccessible as cliffs

Are to a drowning swimmer's vainly grasping hands.

All that is mine, my life, my fate, depend

Upon the power of my words and tears.

Relieve my heart so that I can reach yours.

When you regard me with that icy stare,

My heart contracts, my tears dry up,

Cold horror freezes on my tongue my words.

ELIZABETH: [*Cold and severe*] What do you wish to tell me, Lady Stuart?

You wished to speak with me. I will forget

That I am Queen, that you have gravely wronged me,

And I will do my duty as a sister.

I offer you the consolation of my presence.

I yield to impulse and my generosity,

Expose myself to justified reproaches

Of having stooped too low, for—you remember—

You had plans for my assassination.

MARY: How shall I start? How shall I cleverly

Compose my words so they will move but will not hurt you?

Oh God, give power to my words,

Let them be without sting to wound her.

For I cannot defend my cause without

Accusing you, and that I do not want.

You treated me unjustly. I am a queen,

Like you, but you made me your prisoner.

I came to you as supplicant, but you,

Mocking the sacred rules of hospitality

And in defiance of the Law of Nations,

Entombed me in a dungeon, tore my friends

And servants from my side, degraded me,

Exposed me to disgraceful want,

Arraigned me, finally, before an ignominious court—

No more of that! Oblivion may forever cover

The cruelties you made me suffer.

I'm willing to ascribe all that to fate.

You are not guilty, but I too am free of guilt.

An evil spirit rose from its abysmal pit

And threw the firebrand of hate into our hearts,

Divided even when we both were children.

As we grew up, so grew our hatred,

And wicked people fanned its ugly flames,

Fanatic madmen furnished swords and daggers

To arm the hands of willing interlopers—

That is the curse which fate called down on kings

That they, divided, tear the world asunder,

Set loose the storming furies of contention.

No stranger stands between us now,

[*Confidently she steps closer to* Elizabeth *and continues in endearing tones*]

Now we stand face to face. Now, sister, speak.

Of what crime am I guilty? I shall answer you.

If you had only listened earlier

When I so urgently prayed for your presence!

It never would have come to this,

We would not have met at this dismal place

For this unfortunate and sad encounter.

ELIZABETH: Good fortune saved me from the fate

Of nurturing a serpent at my breast.

Not destiny, your own black heart, the wild

Ambition of your family is guilty.

No enmity had been between us when your uncle,

That proud and power-hungry priest

Who reaches with his brazen hand for crowns,

Flung down the gauntlet, beguiled you to adopt

My coat of arms, to claim my royal titles,
And to engage me in a fight of life and death.
Whom did he not incite against me!
The words of priests, the arms of nations,
The dreadful weapon of religious frenzy.
And even here, in my own peaceful realm,
He fanned the flames of insurrection.
But God was on my side, the haughty priest
Did not prevail. My head was threatened—yours will
    fall.

MARY: My life is in God's hand. You would not
    dare
To stretch your power over life and death—

ELIZABETH: Who could prevent me? Why should I
Not follow the example which your uncle set?
He showed the monarchs of the world
The way to pacify one's enemies.
I'll take the night of St. Bartholomew as guide.
You speak of blood relationship,
The Law of Nations—what are they to me?
The Church cuts all the bonds of duty,
It sanctifies disloyalty and regicide.
I only do what your priests preach.
What warrant would you offer me to vouch for you,
If I were generous enough to set you free?
St. Peter's key fits any lock
That I might use to guard your loyalty.
My safety lies in force alone,
One cannot make a pact with vipers.

MARY: Oh, now your bitter, dark suspicion speaks
    again.
You always have considered me an enemy
And stranger. Yet, had you but named me your suc-
    cessor,
As was my right, my love and gratitude
Then would have made of me a loyal friend, your
    sister.

ELIZABETH: Abroad you have your friends, my
    Lady.
Your home—the Vatican; your brothers—monks.
Name you successor! You! What cunning trickery!
Let you, a sly Armida,[2] while I'm still alive,
Seduce my people and ensnare
The noble youth of England cleverly
Into the net of your adultery,
Wait till your rising sun attracts all eyes, while I—

MARY: Ah, reign in peace! I gladly will renounce
All claims that I have ever made upon your throne.
The wings on which my spirit used to soar
Are limp now, greatness tempts no more.
You have succeeded—only Mary's shadow lives,
Her courage shattered by the endless shame of prison.
You've done your worst, you have destroyed me in
    my bloom.
Now, sister, make an end of it! Now say
The word which you have come to let me hear,
For I cannot believe you came to taste
Your power, cruelly to mock your victim.
Say: "Mary, you are free. I've taught you to respect

2 The sorceress in Tasso's epic, *Jerusalem Delivered*.

My strength, now learn that I am generous."
Say that, and gladly I'll receive
My life and freedom from your hand.
One word, and all the past will be undone.
I'm waiting—do not make me wait too long.
If you don't speak those words, then woe betide you!
Unless you part from me as a magnificent
And bounteous goddess, then—oh, sister—then
Not for the prize of this whole wealthy island,
Not for the crown of all the kingdoms of this earth,
Would I want to face you as you then would face me.

ELIZABETH: Do you admit at last that you're de-
    feated?
Is this the end of your intrigues?
Are no more murderers abroad? Have all
Adventurers renounced their vain intent to risk
Their sorry chivalry for you?
Yes, it is finished, Lady Stuart.
No more seductions now. The world
Has other things to think about.
Not one man lusts to be the fourth,
For you're as deadly to your suitors as to husbands.

MARY: [Flares up] Sister, sister! God, grant me re-
    straint!

ELIZABETH: [Looks at her with haughty disdain]
So these are the bewitching charms, Lord Leicester,
which no man can behold unscathed.
This is the woman next to whom
No other woman dares to show herself.
Indeed! That fame was won at no great cost,
To be acclaimed as an uncommon beauty is not hard
If one becomes a beauty common to all men.

MARY: This is too much!

ELIZABETH: [With a derisive laugh]
There—that is your true face; till now
You've only shown a mask.

MARY: [Flushed with rage, but with dignity]
I made mistakes, but they were human errors;
And I was young, my power tempted me.
I did not hide them, I disdained to cover them
With false appearances, I was a forthright queen.
The world has known the worst about me, and—
I think that I am better than my fame.
Beware if once the cloak of rectitude
That hides the secret of your burning appetites
Is torn away. It's not respectability
That from your mother you inherited.
We know what virtues brought Anne Boleyn to the
    scaffold.

SHREWSBURY: [Steps between the Queens]
Merciful God! Why did it have to come to this?
Is this your moderation, your humility?

MARY: Humility! I have submitted to as much
As anyone can bear. This is enough!
The placid lamb is dead, long-suffering patience dead!
My anger breaks its chains at last,
Emerges growling from its cave and speaks.
And you who gave the basilisk the eye that kills,

Give me a poisoned arrow that my tongue can
    shoot—
    SHREWSBURY: She is beside herself. Forgive the
    raving woman.
    [Elizabeth *is speechless with rage and looks at*
    Mary *with a furious expression*]
    LEICESTER: [*Greatly upset, tries to lead* Elizabeth
    away]
Don't listen to her madness, come away
From this ill-favored place.
    MARY: A bastard desecrates the throne of England
And dupes its noble people
With cunning trickery.
If justice reigned the world, it would be you
Who crawled before me in the dust.
For I'm your Queen.
    [Elizabeth *hurries off; her gentlemen follow her*
    in utter consternation]

SCENE V.

[Mary *and* Hannah]
HANNAH: What have you done! You have infuri-
    ated her.
Now everything is lost, all hope is gone.
    MARY: [*Still in great agitation*]
Enraged she leaves, and death is in her heart.
    [*She embraces* Hannah]
How well I feel! At last, at last! The years
Of suffering and humiliation are avenged,
This moment of my triumph wipes them out.
The weight of mountains lifted from my heart
When deep into her breast I plunged the knife.
    HANNAH: Your madness carried you away to
    wound
Your mortal enemy. She is the Queen,
Hers is the thunder, and you derided her
Before her lover.
    MARY: I humbled her before the eyes of Leicester,
He saw it, he was witness to my victory.
As I struck out to tumble her from her pedestal,
He stood and looked; his presence gave me strength.

SCENE VI.

The same.

[Mortimer]
HANNAH: Sir Mortimer, now everything—
MORTIMER: I heard it all.
    [*He signals to* Hannah *to go back to her look-*
    out post and steps closer to Mary. *His behavior*
    and expression betray his violent emotions]
You conquered her. You stamped her down into the
    dust.
You were the Queen, and she the criminal.
Your courage thrills me, I adore you as you stand
Before me now, a great and radiant goddess.
    MARY: You talked to Leicester, handed him

My letter and my present? Tell me, please.
    MORTIMER: [*Looking at her ardently*]
Your noble wrath was like an aureole
Around you, it transfigured you. No woman is
More beautiful than you in all the world.
    MARY: Oh please, sir. I'm impatient to discover—
What did he say, what can I hope from him?
    MORTIMER: Who? He? That miserable coward!
Hope nothing of him—ah, despise, forget him.
    MARY: What are you saying?
    MORTIMER: He save you and possess you? Let him
    dare!
He first would have to fight me for the privilege.
    MARY: Then you did not give him my letter? Oh,
    I'm lost.
    MORTIMER: The coward loves his life too much.
    A man
Who wants to save you and to call you his
Must be prepared to welcome death, too, with
A warm embrace.
    MARY: He will do nothing for me?
    MORTIMER: Ah, enough of him.
What can he do? What do you want of him?
I'll rescue you myself.
    MARY: What can you do?
    MORTIMER: Do not deceive yourself. Today
Is different from yesterday. Her mood
When she left you, the turn your conversation took,
Rules out a pardon. From the Queen no help will
    come.
Now is the time for action, boldness will
Decide, the stakes are high and high the gain.
You shall be free before the morning dawns.
    MARY: What's that? Tonight? How is that possible?
    MORTIMER: This is our plan. I summoned my com-
    panions
In secret to a chapel where a priest
Heard our confessions, gave us absolution
For all the sins we had committed
And in advance for trespasses to come.
We then received the sacrament, the last,
And now we're ready for our final journey.
    MARY: What frightful preparations!
    MORTIMER: The castle will be seized tonight. I
    have the keys.
We kill the guards, abduct you from your room
By force, and every living soul must die;
Not one must live who may betray the raid.
    MARY: And Drury? Sir Amias? They will spill
The last drop of their blood before—
    MORTIMER: They'll be the first my dagger stabs.
    MARY: Your uncle who to you has been a second
    father?
    MORTIMER: Killed by my hand, he'll fall.
    MARY: Outrageous crime!
    MORTIMER: All sins have been forgiven in ad-
    vance.
I am prepared to do the worst—I'll do it.
    MARY: How awful!

MORTIMER: And if I have to slay the Queen,
I've sworn upon the Host that I won't waver.
MARY: No, Mortimer. Before the blood begins
To run in rivers for my sake—
MORTIMER: What is my life compared to you and
to my love!
Let all the bonds that hold the world together break,
Let with its rushing waves another deluge come
To swallow every living thing on earth—
I do not care. The world will see
Its day of doom approach before I shall renounce
you.
MARY: [Steps back] My God! What language, sir—
what glances!
You frighten me.
MORTIMER: [With a strange look in his eyes and
an expression of quiet madness]
Our lives last but a moment, so does death.
Let them drag me to Tyburn and pull limb
From limb with red-hot iron tongs—
[With wide-open arms he takes a few quick steps
toward Mary]
When I embrace you, my beloved—
MARY: [Stepping back] You're mad! Away
from me!
MORTIMER: Ah, at this breast, from this mouth,
breathing love—
MARY: Away, sir! Let me go!
MORTIMER: He would be mad indeed who did not
hold
Good fortune in unbreakable embrace
When God presents it to his grasping hands.
You will be rescued, I shall rescue you,
No matter if it costs a thousand lives.
Yes, rescue you I will but—by the living God
I swear—I also will possess you.
MARY: Is there no God, no angel to protect me?
Terrible destiny that thrusts me cruelly
From terror on to other terrors.
Is it my fate to waken only fury?
Do hate and love conspire to frighten me?
MORTIMER: Yes, burning as their hatred is my
love.
This lovely head they yearn to sever, cut
This neck, this gleaming whiteness, with an ax—
Oh, consecrate to life and happiness
What you must sacrifice to hate.
Why not bring ecstasy to your enchanted lover
With charms which are no longer yours?
This silken hair, these shining tresses,
Already forfeit to the King of Death,
Use them to bind your slave forever.
MARY: No more! If you do not respect the queen,
Hold sacred my misfortune and my suffering.
MORTIMER: The crown has tumbled from your
head,
All traces of your earthly majesty are gone.
Try it, command your servants, call your friends,
And see how many rescuers will come.
Nothing is left but your celestial beauty,

Its power to enthrall and stir the heart;
It gives me strength to dare and to accomplish,
It drives me forward to the scaffold's steps.
MARY: Will no one come to save me from his fury!
MORTIMER: Audacious service merits bold rewards.
Why does a man of courage spill his blood?
To live is life's supreme reward,
And mad the man who wastes it aimlessly.
First let me rest at life's most warming hearth—
[He embraces her passionately]
MARY: Must I call out for help against my rescuer?
MORTIMER: No, you are not insensitive; the world
Does not charge you with cold severity.
A lover's fervent plea can move you.
The singer Rizzio enjoyed your love,
And Bothwell was permitted to abduct you.
MARY: What impudence!
MORTIMER: He was your tyrant;
He made you tremble—but you loved the man.
If it takes terror to seduce you, then—
By all the gods of hell—
MARY: You are insane. Let go of me.
MORTIMER: I, too, will make you tremble.
HANNAH: [Rushes in] They're coming. They're al-
ready close.
Armed men are spreading through the park.
MORTIMER: [Quickly reaching for his sword]
I shall protect you.
MARY: Hannah, save me from this man.
Where shall I now find refuge? To which saint
Shall I pray now? Where shall I turn?
Here it is violence, inside the house it's murder.
[She flees toward the castle, Hannah follows]

SCENE VII.

[Mortimer; Paulet and Drury enter in great ex-
citement. Men of their retinue rush across the
stage]
PAULET: Lock all the gates. Draw up the bridges.
MORTIMER: What's happened, Uncle?
PAULET: Where is the murderess? Throw her
Into the deepest dungeon.
MORTIMER: What is it? What has happened?
PAULET: The Queen! What devilish audacity!
My curse on them!
MORTIMER: The Queen! Which queen?
PAULET: The Queen of England. She was killed
On her return to London.
[He hurries toward the castle, Drury follows]

SCENE VIII.

[Mortimer and, after a moment, O'Kelly]
MORTIMER: Am I delirious? Did someone pass just
now
And shout, "The Queen was killed"? No, no.
It cannot be. I must have dreamed.

A feverish illusion must present
As true and real to my mind
The horrible ideas I have nourished.
Who is it? Ah, O'Kelly—and he looks
As if the furies persecuted him.

O'KELLY: [*Rushes in*] Flee, Mortimer, flee. All is
  lost.

MORTIMER: But what is lost?

O'KELLY: Don't waste your time with questions.
  Flee.

MORTIMER: But what has happened?

O'KELLY: Sauvage, that madman, struck the blow.

MORTIMER: It's true then?

O'KELLY: Yes, yes, it's true. Quick, save yourself.

MORTIMER: She's dead, and Mary Queen of England.

O'KELLY: Dead? Who told you that?

MORTIMER: You did yourself.

O'KELLY: She is alive, but you and I, we all are
  dead.

MORTIMER: She is alive!

O'KELLY: He missed. A mantle caught his thrust,
And Shrewsbury disarmed the murderer.

MORTIMER: She is alive!

O'KELLY: It was the Barnabite, come from Toulon.
You saw him in the chapel, sitting lost in thought,
While the Black Friar was expounding the anathema
With which the Pope has cursed the Queen.
He wanted to use any means, take any steps
To liberate the Church of God
And gain the crown of martyrdom.
Confiding only in the priest, he planned the deed,
It was accomplished on the road to London.

MORTIMER: [*After a pause*] Oh, most unfortunate
  of women,
A grimly raging fate pursues you. Yes,
Now you must die, your downfall caused by me,
Who was to be your helping angel.

O'KELLY: Where will you flee? I shall hide out
Somewhere far in the northern forests.

MORTIMER: Flee, flee—may God direct your steps.
I stay. One more attempt to save her life;
If not, I'll die upon her coffin.

[*They leave in opposite directions*]

ACT IV. SCENE I.

An Antechamber.

[Aubespine, Leicester *and* Kent]

AUBESPINE: How is her Majesty? My Lords,
I am beside myself, I'm horrified.
How did it happen? And how could it happen
In the midst of all her faithful subjects?

LEICESTER: It was not one of them who struck the
  blow.
A subject of your King, a Frenchman, did it.

AUBESPINE: A madman, without doubt.

KENT: A Papist certainly, Count Aubespine.

SCENE II.

The same.

[Burleigh *enters, in conversation with* Davison]

BURLEIGH: The orders for her execution must be
  drafted
Immediately and sealed. As soon as that is done,
Submit the paper to her Majesty
For signature.

DAVISON: It will be done, my Lord.

AUBESPINE: [*Takes a few steps toward* Burleigh]
My Lord, I share this island's happiness
With all my heart. Thanked be the Lord
Who fended off the blow and saved her life.

BURLEIGH: Praise be to him who thwarted the
  despicable
Designs of England's enemies.

AUBESPINE: God's curse on him who dared commit
So dastardly a crime!

BURLEIGH: On him—and on the man who planned
  the foul attack!

AUBESPINE: [*To* Kent] My dear Earl Marshal, may
  it please your Lordship
To bring me to her Majesty
So that I may duly convey to her
The greetings of my King and master.

BURLEIGH: You need not take the trouble, Count.

AUBESPINE: [*Very formally*] My Lord, I'm well
  aware of what is fitting.

BURLEIGH: For you it will be fitting, Count,
To leave this island—now.

AUBESPINE: What does that mean?

BURLEIGH: Today the sacred privileges still
Protect your life, not so tomorrow.

AUBESPINE: And of what crime am I accused?

BURLEIGH: Once mentioned, it becomes unpardonable.

AUBESPINE: I hope, my Lord, the right of an ambassador—

BURLEIGH: Will not protect a traitor to the realm.

LEICESTER and KENT: What's that?

AUBESPINE: My Lord, have you considered
  well . . .

BURLEIGH: A passport, written by your hand, was
  found
Upon the person of the murderer.

KENT: How is that possible?

AUBESPINE: I issue many passports and cannot
  divine
The private thoughts of every man.

BURLEIGH: The murderer went to confession in
  your house.

AUBESPINE: My house is open.

BURLEIGH: Yes, to all our enemies.

AUBESPINE: Hold an inquiry. I demand it.

BURLEIGH: You ought to fear it, Count.

AUBESPINE: That is an insult to my sovereign.
He will tear up the treaty we have signed.

BURLEIGH: The Queen already tore it up,
England will not wed France.
My Lord of Kent will you be good enough to escort
Count Aubespine in safety to the sea.
Enraged, the people have already stormed
His residence and found an arsenal
Of weapons. They will tear him limb from limb
If he should show himself. Conceal the Count
Until their rage subsides. You are responsible.
    AUBESPINE: And I am glad to leave a country
Where pacts are toys, and where the Law of Nations
Is trampled on. My sovereign will seek
Bloody revenge.
    BURLEIGH: Let him come here and take it.
    [Kent *and* Aubespine *leave*]

SCENE III.

Leicester *and* Burleigh.

    LEICESTER: So you dissolve the union now yourself
Which without warrant but with fervor you have
    sought.
That will not earn you England's gratitude,
My Lord, you might have saved yourself much trou-
    ble.
    BURLEIGH: My purposes were honest. God decreed
That it was not to be. Happy the man
Who need not charge himself with worse offense.
    LEICESTER: I see that secretive expression on your
    face,
The well-known sign that you hunt traitors.
This is a most propitious time for you,
My Lord. A monstrous crime has been committed
And mystery still shrouds the criminal.
A court of inquisition now will be
Installed where every word and glance are weighed
And even thoughts arraigned before the bar.
You'll be the all-important man,
An Atlas of the state upon whose shoulders
The entire weight of England rests.
    BURLEIGH: My Lord, I recognize you as my
    master;
Your eloquence has won a victory
Such as my own has never yet achieved.
    LEICESTER: What do you mean, my Lord?
    BURLEIGH: Was it not you who cleverly enticed
The Queen to Fotheringhay, behind my back?
    LEICESTER: Behind your back, indeed! I've never
    tried
To hide my actions from your scrutiny.
    BURLEIGH: You lead the Queen to Fotheringhay?
    Oh no!
You did not lead the Queen, it was the Queen
Who graciously agreed to guide you there.
    LEICESTER: What are you driving at?
    BURLEIGH: That noble personage whom you let
    play the Queen
At Fotheringhay; and at the glorious triumph

You thoughtfully prepared for her
Who trusted you implicitly. Poor Queen!
How shamelessly you have been mocked,
How mercilessly you were sacrificed!
So that's the magnanimity, the tolerance
Which in the Council overwhelmed you suddenly.
That is why Mary Stuart was so weak
And so contemptible an enemy
That killing her would be too great an honor.
A clever plan! How finely honed! Too bad,
It was too finely honed—the point snapped off.
    LEICESTER: What impudence! Come with me to
    the Queen at once,
Repeat your accusations at her throne.
    BURLEIGH: I'll meet you there. Make sure, my
    Lord,
That you have all your eloquence at your disposal.
    [*He leaves*]

SCENE IV.

Leicester *alone; shortly,* Mortimer.

    LEICESTER: The veil is lifted. I'm found out. How
    did
The spying scoundrel find my tracks?
If he has proof, I'm lost. My God,
How can I face the Queen if she discovers
That Mary and myself had understandings?
How treacherous my counsel must appear,
My urging that she go to Fotheringhay!
She must believe that I intended
The insults and the mockery, that I
Betrayed her to her hated enemy.
That she will not forget and not forgive.
Now everything must seem premeditated,
The bitter turn their conversation took,
The triumph and derisive laughter of her foe,
Even down to the murderous attempt
Upon her life, an unexpected stroke of fate,
Which now she must believe I instigated.
There is no hope, no help, no rescue.
    MORTIMER: [*Enters in a state of great excitement
    and looks all around, suspiciously*]
My Lord, thank God it's you. Are we alone?
    LEICESTER: Away from here, unhappy man. What
    brings you here?
    MORTIMER: They're after us—and you. Watch out.
    LEICESTER: Away from here, away.
    MORTIMER: They know that there were secret
    meetings,
They know we were at Aubespine's—
    LEICESTER: What do I care!
    MORTIMER: They know that the assassin was
    among us—
    LEICESTER: That's your concern. Do you make
    bold
To implicate me in your murderous schemes?
Defend your wicked enterprise yourself.

MORTIMER: But listen to me—
LEICESTER: Go to hell.
Why do you, like an evil spirit, cling to me?
Begone. I do not know your name or face.
I don't keep company with common cutthroats.
MORTIMER: I've come to warn you, listen—won't
   you hear?
Your dealings, too, have been betrayed—
LEICESTER: What?
MORTIMER: Lord Burleigh was in Fotheringhay
Soon after the attack. He searched the Queen's
Apartment and he found—
LEICESTER: What did he find?
MORTIMER: A letter which the Queen had just
   begun,
Addressed to you—
LEICESTER: Good Lord!
MORTIMER: Exhorting you
To keep your word, repeating that she promised you
Her hand and mentioning the portrait which—
LEICESTER: Hell and damnation!
MORTIMER: And he has the letter.
LEICESTER: That seals my death.
   [In utter despair, he walks restlessly up and down
   while Mortimer speaks the following]
MORTIMER: There's still a chance. Anticipate his
   move.
You still can save yourself and her.
Think of excuses, swear a thousand oaths,
Prevent the worst. Myself, I now can do no more.
Our league is torn assunder, my companions
Are scattered, I am on my way to Scotland. There
I hope to find new friends. It's up to you,
Now show what your prestige, what a bold front
   can do.
LEICESTER: [Stands still, suddenly determined]
That is what I shall do.
   [He steps to the door, opens it and calls]
Hey, guard!
   [To the Officer who enters with guards]
Arrest this traitor, guard him well.
An infamous conspiracy has been discovered.
I will inform the Queen myself.
   [He leaves]
MORTIMER: [At first stunned, soon recovers; with a
   look of utter contempt in Leicester's direction]
The scoundrel! I deserve it, though.
Why did I give that wretch my confidence?
He steps on me and blithely walks away,
My body is his stepping stone to safety.
Go, save yourself. My mouth is closed.
I shall not drag you with me to perdition,
Not even dying do I want your company.
The wicked only have one thing to lose, their life.
   [To the Officer of the Guard, who steps forward
   to arrest him]
What do you want, you venal slave of tyranny?
I do not fear you, I am free.
   [He draws a dagger]
OFFICER: He's armed, quick, get his dagger.

   [The soldiers charge him, but he fends them off]
MORTIMER: Free in this dying moment of my life,
I finally can bare my heart and speak.
May death strike you and may damnation be your
   lot,
You who betrayed your God and your true Queen,
Who turned your backs on Mary, Queen of Scots
As faithlessly as on the Mary who is Queen of
   Heaven.
You are the servants of a bastard queen—
OFFICER: Seize the blasphemer! At him, quick!
MORTIMER: Beloved Mary, I have failed,
Your life I could not save. All I can do
Is set you an example by my death.
Saint Mary, pray for me and take me unto you,
So I may live forever in your heaven.
   [He plunges the dagger into his heart and falls
   into the arms of the Guards]

SCENE V.

The Queen's chamber.

   [Elizabeth, holding a letter in her hand, and
   Burleigh]
ELIZABETH: To lure me there and have his fun
   with me!
In triumph to parade his Queen before his paramour!
No woman ever was so shabbily betrayed.
BURLEIGH: I cannot understand how he succeeded.
What did he do, what powers did he use,
What magic craft, to trick my prudent Queen?
ELIZABETH: I die of shame. He must have gloated
   at my weakness.
To humble her was my intent, instead
I was the object of her mockery.
BURLEIGH: Now you believe that I gave sound
   advice.
ELIZABETH: I was severely punished for not follow-
   ing
Your prudent counsel, but why should I not trust
   him?
How could I dream that he concealed a trap
Behind his oaths of loyalty and love?
Whom can I trust when he betrays me?
He whom I made the greatest of the great,
He who has always been the closest to my heart,
Whom I permitted to behave as master at my court,
To play the part of King?
BURLEIGH: And all the time,
He was betraying you to that false Queen of Scots.
ELIZABETH: She'll die for it! Have you prepared
   the orders?
BURLEIGH: They're ready for your signature, your
   Majesty,
As you commanded.
ELIZABETH: Yes, she will die for it.
He'll watch her die and follow her to death.
I have expelled him from my heart,

My love is gone, and hatred is my master.
High as his rise has been as deep
And ignominious be his downfall.
He shall be a memorial to my severity,
As his aggrandizement has proved my weakness.
Let him be taken to the Tower!
I shall appoint the peers to be his judges
And let the law's full rigor deal with him.
  BURLEIGH: He will attempt to speak to you
And to defend himself—
  ELIZABETH: How could he dare?
Is not the letter testimony to his guilt?
His crime is clear as day.
  BURLEIGH: But you are lenient.
Your kindness, at his sight . . . his mighty presence—
  ELIZABETH: I do not wish to see him, now or ever
    more.
Did you convey my order to refuse
Him entry if he comes?
  BURLEIGH: I did, your Majesty.
    [A Page enters]
PAGE: The Earl of Leicester.
  ELIZABETH: Oh, the audacity! I will not see him.
    Tell him that.
PAGE: I do not dare to tell that to my Lord,
And he would not believe me if I did.
  ELIZABETH: So high I raised him that my servants
    tremble at
His sight, they fear him more than they fear me.
  BURLEIGH: [To the Page] The Queen forbids him
    to come near.
    [Hesitantly, the Page leaves]
  ELIZABETH: [After a pause] And still, it may be
    possible—
If he were able to explain—
Could it not be a trap that Mary set
To separate me from my dearest friend?
She is a vicious viper. If—suppose
She wrote the letter only to imbed
The poison of suspicion in my heart,
To plunge the man she hates into the abyss—
  BURLEIGH: Your Majesty, weigh well—

SCENE VI.

The same.

[Leicester]
LEICESTER: [*Flings the door open and enters with
    the bearing of a master*]
What insolence! I want to see the man
Who dares to bar this door to me.
  ELIZABETH: Oh, the audacity!
  LEICESTER: To turn me away! If a Lord Burleigh
    is allowed
To enter here, then so am I.
  BURLEIGH: You're very bold, my Lord, to enter
    here
Without the Queen's permission.

LEICESTER: And you, my Lord, presume too much
    to speak.
Permission! There is no one at this court
From whom the Earl of Leicester will accept
Permission or refusal—except—
    [*Humbly approaching* Elizabeth]
                              —my Queen.
  ELIZABETH: [*Without looking at him*] Out of my
    sight, you traitor!
  LEICESTER: The voice is yours, my kind Elizabeth,
But yours, Lord Burleigh, are the words—
My enemy's ungracious words. I wish to speak
To my Elizabeth. You lent your ear to him,
I now demand the same.
  ELIZABETH: Speak then! Deny your crime and
    make it worse.
  LEICESTER: Let this superfluous attendant leave
Before I speak. Leave us alone, my Lord.
What I'm about to tell my Queen
Does not require a witness. Go.
  ELIZABETH: [*To* Burleigh] Stay! I command it.
  LEICESTER: Why let a third one come between us
    two?
When I speak to my worshiped Queen,
I shall uphold the rights of my position.
They're sacred rights, and I insist that you,
Lord Burleigh, now leave us alone.
  ELIZABETH: Your arrogance befits you well.
  LEICESTER: It does, indeed. For I'm the happy man
On whom you graciously bestowed your favor.
That sets me above him and everyone.
Your heart raised me to this exalted rank,
And what your love gave me, that I shall guard,
That I'll defend, by God, to my last breath.
Let him be off, and it will not be long
Before we understand each other.
  ELIZABETH: Vain is your hope that cunningly you
    will
Deceive me once again with pretty speeches.
  LEICESTER: He tricked you with malicious gossip.
I want to talk straight to your heart.
Within the knowledge of your love I did,
I will defend before your heart;
I recognize no other court.
  ELIZABETH: That is the court that first condemned
    you, brazen man.
My Lord, show him the letter.
  BURLEIGH: Read it! Here!
  LEICESTER: [*Quickly scans the letter, without losing
    his composure*]
It's Mary Stuart's writing.
  ELIZABETH: Read, and say no more.
  LEICESTER: [*Reads the letter; calmly*]
Appearances condemn me, but I hope
That I will not be judged by specious evidence.
  ELIZABETH: Can you deny your secret dealings
    with her,
Deny that you received her portrait or deny
That you held out the hope of liberation?

LEICESTER: If I felt any guilt, it would be easy to reject
This testimony of an enemy.
But as it is, my conscience is quite clear,
So I admit that what she writes is true.

ELIZABETH: Well then?

BURLEIGH: He stands condemned by his own words.

ELIZABETH: Out of my sight and to the Tower, traitor.

LEICESTER: That I am not. It was perhaps not right
To keep you in the dark about my plans,
But I was honest in my purpose,
To learn her schemes, the better to defeat her.

ELIZABETH: A lame excuse, my Lord.

BURLEIGH: Do you believe—

LEICESTER: I played a risky game, I know, and at this court
No one but Leicester could have dared to play it.
The world knows well enough how I hate Mary.
My rank, the confidence with which the Queen
Has honored me, will readily refute
The least suspicion of my loyalty.
The man whom your affection has distinguished more
Than any other man must have the privilege
To walk his own bold path in doing what he must.

BURLEIGH: Why, if your purpose was so pure, keep it a secret?

LEICESTER: You like to wag your tongue before you act, my Lord.
You trumpet your accomplishments. That is
Your way. Mine is to act before I speak.

BURLEIGH: And now you speak because you must.

LEICESTER: [Looking him up and down disdainfully]
You are so proud of having saved your Queen,
You have performed a wondrously enormous feat
In sniffing out a traitor, you know everything
And nothing can escape your eagle eye.
Poor braggart! Mary Stuart would be free today,
If I had not prevented it.

BURLEIGH: You did—

LEICESTER: Yes, I, my Lord. The Queen confided in Sir Mortimer,
Confided him her secret hopes and went so far
As to charge him with a bloody mission against Mary
Because his uncle had refused with horror
A similar request. It that not true?
[The Queen and Burleigh look at each other in consternation]

BURLEIGH: How did you find that out?

LEICESTER: Is it not true? Well then, my Lord. Where were
Your thousand spying eyes that you did not
Become aware of Mortimer's deception?
That he, a furious Papist, was a tool
Of Cardinal de Guise, a creature of the Stuart,
A purposeful and bold fanatic who came back

To see her free and kill the Queen?

ELIZABETH: Sir Mortimer?

LEICESTER: He was the one who carried messages
Between myself and Mary. That is how we met.
Today she was to be abducted from her prison,
As he told me himself just now.
I called the guard and, desperate
At the frustration of his plans and his
Exposure, Mortimer took his own life.

ELIZABETH: Oh, I have been imposed upon most shamelessly.

BURLEIGH: That happened now, just after I had left you?

LEICESTER: For my sake, I regret exceedingly
That he so ended, for his testimony,
If he were still alive, would totally
Absolve me, clear me of the last suspicion.
That's why I wished to see him in the hands
Of Justice. I was sure that I could prove
Before a court of law, before the world
That I am innocent.

BURLEIGH: You said he killed himself.
You're sure he did? It was not you who killed him?

LEICESTER: What reprehensible suspicion!
The officer to whom I handed him may speak.
[He opens the door and calls the Officer of the Guard, who enters promptly]
Make your report, so that her Majesty
May know the details of Sir Mortimer's demise.

OFFICER: I guarded with my men the antechamber,
When suddenly the door flew open and my Lord
Gave me the order to arrest the knight
As traitor to the Crown. He flew into a rage,
Drew out his dagger, screaming calumnies
Against the Queen, and plunged it deep into his breast.
Before we could prevent it, he fell dead—

LEICESTER: The Queen has heard enough, sir; you may go.
[The Officer leaves]

ELIZABETH: What an abyss of abominations!

LEICESTER: Who was it then that saved you? Burleigh?
Did Burleigh know what dangers threatened you?
Did he avert them? Your good angel was—
The Earl of Leicester.

BURLEIGH: This Mortimer died most conveniently, my Lord.

ELIZABETH: I don't know what to say. I do believe you and—
I don't. I think that you are guilty and—
That you are not. That cursed woman is
The cause of all my sorrow.

LEICESTER: Now she has to die.
Now I, too, vote in favor of her death.
I counseled you to leave the sentence in suspense
Until someone would lift his arm for her.
That's happened now, and I insist

On carrying the sentence out at once.

BURLEIGH: That's your advice?

LEICESTER: I am appalled by extreme measures,
But I am now convinced the welfare of the Queen
Requires this sacrifice. I therefore ask
That orders for her execution
Be instantly prepared.

BURLEIGH: [*To the* Queen] My Lord seems so sin-
cere and serious,
That I propose he be appointed
To have the sentence carried out.

LEICESTER: I.

BURLEIGH: You. There is no better way to lay at
rest
All lingering suspicion than that you,
Who's been accused of having loved her,
Be named to supervise her execution.

ELIZABETH: [*Fixing her gaze on* Leicester]
My Lord's advice is good. So be it.

LEICESTER: My rank should properly excuse me
From missions of so sad a nature,
Which are in every way more suitable
For a Lord Burleigh. Someone who's as close
To his beloved Queen as I should not
Take part in such unhappy tasks.
However, I shall prove my eagerness
And do all that my Queen may ask of me.
I waive the privileges of my rank,
I'll undertake this hateful duty.

ELIZABETH: You'll share your task with my Lord
Burleigh.
[*To* Burleigh]
See that the orders are prepared at once.
[Burleigh *leaves. Tumultuous voices are heard
outside*]

SCENE VII.

The same.

[*The* Earl *of* Kent *enters*]

ELIZABETH: What is this uproar in the streets, my
Lord?

KENT: Your Majesty, the people are beleaguering
Your palace, clamoring to see their Queen.

ELIZABETH: What do my people want?

KENT: They're terrified by rumors spreading
through
The streets of London that your life is threatened,
That murderers are still abroad sent by the Pope,
That there's a vast conspiracy of Catholics
To force the Stuart's prison, free her and—
Proclaim her Queen. The mob believes these tales
And is enraged. Nothing will pacify
Their fury but the Stuart's head—today.

ELIZABETH: Am I to be compelled to act?

KENT: They are determined to maintain their siege
Until the sentence is confirmed and signed.

SCENE VIII.

The same.

[Burleigh *and* Davison *enter with a document*]

ELIZABETH: What do you bring me, Davison?

DAVISON: [*Solemnly approaches the* Queen] Your
Majesty commanded—

ELIZABETH: What is it?
[*As she moves to take the document, she recoils
with a shudder*]
Oh, my God!

BURLEIGH: Obey the people's voice, it is the voice
of God.

ELIZABETH: [*Struggling with her emotions, un-
decided*]
My Lords, how can I know that this is really
The voice of all my people and of all the world,
That a different voice will not rise tomorrow
If I obey what is the people's wish today?
Precisely those who urge me now to act
May well severely blame me when the deed is done.

SCENE IX.

The same.

[Shrewsbury *enters*]

SHREWSBURY: [*Enters in great agitation*]
They want to hurry you, your Majesty,
Stand fast.
[*He notices the document in* Davison's *hand*]
Am I too late? Has it been done?
That is a fateful paper. It must not be put
Before her Majesty just now—not now.

ELIZABETH: Lord Shrewsbury, they would compel
me—

SHREWSBURY: Who could compel you? You are
Queen.
Now is the time to show them your authority.
Command those vulgar voices to be silent
That insolently try to force your hand
And to be masters of your will.
Blind fear and wild emotions rule the crowd,
You are upset yourself, grievously hurt,
And you are human. Now you cannot justly judge.

BURLEIGH: She has been judged. The judgment
that has been
Pronounced needs only to be executed.

KENT: [*Who had left at* Shrewsbury's *entrance,
returns*]
The crowd is growing. It's impossible
To hold the mob in check.

ELIZABETH: [*To* Shrewsbury]
You see, I am compelled.

SHREWSBURY: I only plead postponement. Your
life,
Your happiness and peace, will be decided

By this one stroke your pen will make.
For years you have been weighing what to do,
Let not one stormy moment now decide
On your behalf. A short postponement only,
Collect yourself, await a calmer hour.
    BURLEIGH: Wait, hesitate, delay until at last
The realm will be ablaze, until she finally
Succeeds with her foul plans of murder.
God has averted an assassin's blow three times,
Today it almost found its mark. To hope
For one more miracle would be to tempt your fate.
    SHREWSBURY: That God who held His saving hand
Above your head four times, who gave today
An old man's trembling hand the force to overcome
A madman, that God does deserve your trust.
I will not raise the voice of justice now,
There will be time for that. But think of this:
You tremble now before the living Mary.
You need not fear her while she lives,
Mary beheaded, Mary dead—that is the danger.
Arising from her grave, she will, a goddess of dissen-
    sion,
Sow discord in your people's hearts,
A Spirit of Revenge, she'll stalk your realm
Until your people turn away from you.
Because they fear her now, they hate her,
When she is dead, they will avenge her.
They will no longer look
Upon her as an enemy of their religion,
But mourn her as the daughter of their kings,
A victim of your hate and jealousy.
You'll quickly note the change. Walk through the
    streets
Of London, once her blood is spilled,
And show yourself among your people
Who used to crowd around you, cheering you;
You'll see another England and another people.
No longer will the aureole of justice,
Which conquered every heart, adorn you. Fear,
That dreadful mate of tyranny, will roam the streets,
Precede you on your path, and where you go
Deserted streets will lie before your eyes.
If her head falls, the worst will have been done,
For if a queen's life is not sacred,
Whose life then is secure?
    ELIZABETH: Oh, Shrewsbury, you saved my life
    today,
You fended off the murder sword,
Why did you not allow the blow to fall?
It would have ended all my battles.
Relieved of all my doubts, unsoiled by guilt
And peaceful, I would lie in my still grave.
I'm tired of life, I'm tired of ruling lives.
If one of us, the rival queens, must die
So that the other one may live—
And I do recognize that this is so—
Why cannot I give way? My people may decide,
I give them back their sovereignty.
God is my witness that I lived my life
Not for myself, but for my people's welfare.

If they expect that fawning Mary,
The younger queen, to bring them greater happiness,
I'll gladly leave my throne to her, return
To Woodstock and its quiet solitude.
That is where unpretentiously I spent my youth
And where I found, far from the vain ambitions of
    the world,
Nobility within myself.
I am not made to rule. A ruler must be capable
Of being hard; my heart is soft.
For many years I've ruled this island happily
Because I needed only give it happiness.
But now the harsher side of royal office faces me,
And now I feel my weakness.
    BURLEIGH: When I must hear my Queen speak
    such unqueenly words,
I would betray my duty and the realm
Were I to listen and be silent.
You say you love your people most,
More than yourself. Now is the time to prove it.
You cannot choose to be at peace yourself
And let the country flounder on the stormy waves.
Think of the Church! Are all the old,
Discarded superstitions to return
With Mary Stuart? Are the monks to rule again?
Are Roman emissaries to be given franchise
To come and lock our churches, to dethrone our
    kings?
From you I now demand the souls of all your sub-
    jects.
As you act now, they will be lost or saved.
This is no time for softness and compassion,
Your supreme duty is the country's weal.
Your life was saved by Shrewsbury today,
I want to save the life of England. That is more.
    ELIZABETH: I wish to be alone, my Lords. No man
Can offer comfort or advice in such
An important matter. I'll consult a higher judge.
As He instructs me, I shall act. For now,
Leave me alone, my Lords.
    [*To* Davison]
               You, sir, please stay nearby.

SCENE X.

Elizabeth *alone.*

    ELIZABETH: It's slavery to serve the people, shame-
    ful servitude.
I'm tired of flattering this idol
Which, deep within myself, I do despise.
Will ever I be free upon my throne?
Public opinion must be pleased, I must
Debase myself to win the rabble's praise,
Do what the mob that only loves a fool
May think is right. He is not truly king
Who has to please the world. He only is
Who need ask no man's approbation when he acts.
I've hated arbitrary power all my life,

I have been just, and thus I've tied my hands
For this inevitable act of violence.
The standard which I set myself condemns me now.
But had I been a tyrant like the Spanish Mary,[3]
My predecessor on the throne, I now
Could shed the blood of kings without reproach.
Was it by my own choice that I was just?
All-powerful necessity, which bends
The will of kings as it controls all men,
Decreed that justice be my foremost virtue.
Surrounded on all sides by enemies,
The people's will alone has kept me on the throne.
All powers of the Continent seek to destroy me;
Implacable, the Pope hurls his anathema
Against me; France betrays me with a Judas kiss,
The Spaniards arm for furious warfare on the seas.
Thus I must fight against a world, alone,
An unarmed woman. I've been forced to use
Imposing virtue to conceal my threadbare rights,
The stain upon my royal birth
With which I was disgraced by my own father.
In vain I've tried to cover it.
The furious hatred of my enemies
Exposed it to the world and pitted Mary,
A frightening and unrelenting specter,
Against me. No, this fear must end.
Her head must fall. At last, I want my peace.
She is the Fury of my life, a vengeful sprite
Which fate glued to my heels to torture me.
Wherever I plant hope or happiness,
This hellish serpent coils before me in the grass.
She tears my lover from my arms, she steals
My bridegroom. Mary Stuart—that's the name
By which I call all my misfortune.
Once she is extirpated, I am free as mountain air.
      [*After a silence*]
With what contempt she looked upon me,
As if to grind me with her eyes into the dust!
But you are powerless, I have the better weapons.
Their blow is mortal—and you are no more.
      [*She steps quickly to the table and takes the pen*]
You call me bastard? Fool! I am
A bastard only while you breathe, all doubts
About my royal birth will be erased
As soon as I have crushed you.
When Britons have no other choice but me,
I'll be at once a child of holy wedlock.
      [*She signs the document with quick, firm strokes;
      then, with an expression of terror, she drops the
      pen and steps back. After a while, she rings the
      bell*]

SCENE XI.

[Elizabeth *and* Davison]
ELIZABETH: Where are the other lords?
DAVISON: They went outside

[3] Elizabeth's elder sister Queen Mary Tudor, daughter of Henry VIII's first, Spanish-born, wife Katharine of Aragon.

To calm the raging crowd. The uproar died,
Indeed, at once when they saw Shrewsbury.
"That's he! It's he," a hundred voices roared,
"He is the one who saved the Queen. He is
The bravest man in England. Hear his words."
He spoke to them and in his gentle, forceful manner
Rebuked them for their violence and soon
Persuaded them. Calm was restored, and quietly
They slunk away.
      ELIZABETH: The vacillating crowd
That changes with the wind. Beware the man
Who leans upon this slender reed.
Thank you, you may withdraw.
      [*As he turns to leave*]
Oh yes, this sheet.
I give it back to you, it's in your trust.
      DAVISON [*Glances at the document, shrinks back*]
Your Majesty, your name—have you decided then?
      ELIZABETH: I was to sign—I did. A piece of paper
Does not decide. It bears my name, but names don't
      kill.
      DAVISON: Your name, your Majesty, upon this
      document
Decides and kills. It's like a bolt of lightning
That strikes and kills in a single flash.
This paper orders both commissioners
And sheriff to proceed at once to Fotheringhay,
There to announce her death to Mary Stuart,
And with the rising light of morn to have
The sentence executed. There is no doubt,
There will be no delay. The Queen of Scotland
Will be dead as I pass on this document.
      ELIZABETH: Quite true, sir. God has put, you see,
Into your feeble hands a matter fraught with destiny.
Implore Him to enlighten you with wisdom.
I leave you to your duties. I must go.
      [*She turns to go*]
      DAVISON: [*Steps quickly in front of her*]
No, no, your Majesty, you cannot leave
Without informing me of your desire.
Can there be any other wisdom here
Than to obey your orders to the letter?
You put this sheet into my hands, I presume,
So that I may pass it on at once for action?
      ELIZABETH: If, in your wisdom, you—
      DAVISON: [*Interrupts her, terrified*]
Not in my wisdom! God forbid! Obeying you
Is all my wisdom. Nothing must be left
For me, your servant, to decide.
A small mistake might lead to regicide,
To unforeseeable disaster.
Let me remain your willing tool, without a will.
Put your intentions into crystal words—
What shall I do with this death warrant?
      ELIZABETH: That is precisely what it is.
      DAVISON: That means—you wish it carried out at
      once?
      ELIZABETH: [*Hesitatingly*] I didn't say that, and I
      shudder at the thought.

DAVISON: You wish me to withhold it, then?

ELIZABETH: [*Quickly*]
At your own risk. You'll be responsible for the results.

DAVISON: At my risk? God! Please it your Majesty
To tell me—what do you desire?

ELIZABETH: [*Impatiently*] It's my desire that this
unfortunate affair
Be now forgotten, that I finally
Be rid of it—for good, that I have peace.

DAVISON: One word is all I ask. Please say it!
Command what's to become of this.

ELIZABETH: I told you. Don't torment me further.

DAVISON: You told me? But you told me nothing.
Please,
Your Majesty, remember!

ELIZABETH: [*Stamps her foot*]
                            This is intolerable.

DAVISON: Have patience with me, please! I've come
Into this office only recently.
I don't yet understand the words of kings.
I have grown up in simple customs. Please,
Be patient with your servant, don't begrudge
Me the one word that makes my duty clear.
[*He approaches her in an attitude of supplica-
tion; she turns her back. He stands in silent de-
spair, then says with great determination*]
Take back this document. Please, take it back.
It turns to fire, it burns my hands.
Do not choose me to serve you in this fearful task.

ELIZABETH: Discharge the duties of your office.
[*She leaves*]

SCENE XII

[Davison; *shortly,* Burleigh]

DAVISON: She goes. And I stand here, perplexed
and full of doubts,
This frightful paper in my hand.
What am I now to do? Withhold it? Pass it on?
[*To* Burleigh, *who enters*]
Good, good that you have come, my Lord!
You introduced me to my office, now
Relieve me of my duties. I was unaware
Of the responsibilities I would assume.
Let me return to the obscurity
From which I came. The court is not for me.

BURLEIGH: What happened to you, sir? Compose
yourself.
The Queen called you. Where is the warrant?

DAVISON: She left me, in a rage. Advise me, help
me, please!
Release me from this hell of doubt and fear.
Here is the sentence, it is signed.

BURLEIGH: [*Quickly*] She signed? Give it to me!

DAVISON: I cannot do that.

BURLEIGH: What?

DAVISON: She has not told me clearly what she
wants.

BURLEIGH: Not clearly! She has signed it. Let me
have the sheet!

DAVISON: I am to have it carried out—and I am
not—
Oh God, who knows what I must do!

BURLEIGH: [*Increasingly insistent*]
At once, this instant you're to have it executed.
Give it to me, you're lost if you delay.

DAVISON: I'm lost if I'm too hasty.

BURLEIGH: You're a fool.
You must be mad. Give me the document!
[*He snatches the paper from* Davison's *hands
and hurries out*]

DAVISON: [*Follows him quickly*]
What are you doing? Stay! You'll ruin me!

ACT V. SCENE I.

The scene is the same as in Act I.

[Hannah Kennedy, *in deep mourning, is seen
sealing packages and letters. Her eyes are tear-
swollen, her face expresses deep but quiet grief.
Overcome, she frequently interrupts her task to
immerse herself in silent prayer.*
Paulet *and* Drury *enter, also dressed in black.
They are followed by a great number of servants
who carry in silver vessels, mirrors, paintings
and other precious objects which they deposit in
the background, almost filling that part of the
room.* Paulet *hands Hannah a small jewel box
and a paper, indicating to her by gestures that it
constitutes an inventory of the objects brought
into the room. At the sight of the treasures,*
Hannah *is again overcome by grief. She sinks
into deep mourning, as the others leave the
room.* Melvil *enters*]

HANNAH: [*Calls out as she notices* Melvil]
You, Melvil! It is you! Oh, to see you again!

MELVIL: Yes, loyal Hannah, here we meet again.

HANNAH: It's been so long, a long and painful
separation.

MELVIL: And now it is a cruel, sad reunion.

HANNAH: Oh God, you've come—

MELVIL: To bid my Queen a last farewell.

HANNAH: Now finally, the morning of her death,
She is allowed to have her long-missed friends
Around her. I won't ask how you, good sir,
Haved fared, nor tell you how the Queen has suffered
Since you were taken from our side. Some day,
Alas, there may be time for that. Oh, Melvil,
Why did we have to live so long
That we must see the dawn of such a day!

MELVIL: Let us not weaken one another. I shall
weep
As long as there is life in me. My face
Shall never brighten with a smile again,
And I shall never shed these gloomy garments.
I'll mourn forever, but today
I will be resolute. You too must promise me

That you will check your tears although the others
May yield to their inconsolable grief.
Let us be her example, nobly poised,
So she may lean upon us as she walks to death.
    HANNAH: You are mistaken, Melvil, if you think
The Queen needs our support to help her face
Her fate unflinchingly. She is the one
Who sets us an example with her noble poise.
No, have no fear! The Queen will die a queen.
    MELVIL: Did she take calmly the announcement of
    her death?
I heard she was quite unprepared.
    HANNAH: She was, but other horrors frightened her.
Not death, her liberator made her tremble.
She had been promised freedom. Mortimer
Had vowed that he would take us this last night
Away from here, and torn between her fears and
    hope,
Not sure if she could really entrust
Her honor and her person to the bold young man,
She waited for the day to break.
Then a great uproar burst upon the castle,
Our ears were frightened by the noise of pounding,
The sound of many hammers, and we thought
We heard our rescuers. Hope beckoned sweetly,
Irresistibly the will to live
Once more awoke in her. Then suddenly,
The door is opened, Sir Amias comes
To tell us that, below, the carpenters—
Have started to erect—the scaffold.
    [*Overcome by grief, she averts her face*]
    MELVIL: Merciful God! How did she take that ter-
    rifying news?
    HANNAH: [*After a pause, during which she has
    calmed herself*]
One does not shed one's life in little pieces.
In one swift movement the transition
From life on earth to life eternal must be made.
God granted her, in that decisive moment,
The strength to thrust all earthly hope aside
And resolutely to embrace eternity.
No sign of fear, no blanching, no complaint
Dishonored her. Not till she heard the news
Of Leicester's shameful treason, of the sacrifice
The noble youth had brought her by his death,
Not till she saw his uncle's tragic grief,
Whose last hope now had died because of her,
Then only flowed her tears. Not her fate, no,
The grief of others made her weep.
    MELVIL: Where is she now? Can you conduct me
    to her?
    HANNAH: She spent the time that still remained
    before the dawn
Awake, she prayed, wrote letters to her friends
And signed her testament. Now she is resting.
May her last sleep on earth refresh my Lady.
    MELVIL: Is anybody with her now?
    HANNAH: Burgoyne, her personal physician, and
    her women.

SCENE II.

The same.

    [Margareta Curl *enters*]
    HANNAH: What news? Is she awake?
    MARGARETA: [*Drying her tears*]   She is already
    dressed.
She wants you.
    HANNAH: I shall go at once.
    [*To* Melvil, *who is about to follow her*]
Not yet. First let me warn her of your coming.
    [*She goes into the next room*]
    MARGARETA: Oh, Melvil! Our old steward!
    MELVIL: Yes, I'm he.
    MARGARETA: This house no longer needs a steward.
You come from London, Melvil; have you news
For me about my husband?
    MELVIL: He will be freed, I hear, as soon—
    MARGARETA: As soon as our beloved Queen is dead!
The coward, the abominable traitor!
He is the murderer of our dear Lady,
His testimony, I am told, condemned her.
    MELVIL: That's so.
    MARGARETA: His soul be damned to hell. He lied!
    MELVIL: Now, Margareta, watch what you are
    saying!
    MARGARETA: I'll swear to it before the bars of
    justice,
I will repeat it to his face, I'll fill
The world with it: he lied, and she is innocent!
    MELVIL: So help us God.

SCENE III.

The same.

    [Burgoyne *enters; shortly,* Hannah]
    BURGOYNE: [*Discovering* Melvil] Melvil!
    MELVIL: Burgoyne!
    BURGOYNE: [*To* Margareta]   Quick, get a cup of
    wine.
    MELVIL: Why? Is the Queen not well?
    BURGOYNE: Oh, she feels strong.
Her courage gives her a deceptive strength,
And thus she does not feel the need to eat,
But she still has a cruel test before her.
Her enemies shall have no cause to boast
That she was pale from fear of death,
When only nature's weakness blanched her cheeks.
    MELVIL: [*To* Hannah, *who enters*]
She will come presently herself.
You seem to look around, surprised; your eyes
Demand: why all this splendor in a room
Where death has come to dwell? Oh, Melvil,
We suffered want while there was life and hope,
Abundance has returned to us with death.

SCENE IV.

The same.

[*Two of* Mary's *chambermaids enter, also in mourning. At the sight of* Melvil, *they break out in tears and lamentations*]

MELVIL: Oh, that I must see you again—like this! Gertrude and Rosamond!

SECOND CHAMBERMAID: She sent us out.
She wants to be alone to talk to God.

[*Two more servants enter, in mourning like the others, and express their grief by silent gestures*]

SCENE V.

The same.

[Margareta *comes back carrying a golden cup filled with wine. She puts it on a table and, pale and trembling, holds on to a chair*]

MELVIL: What is it? What has frightened you?

MARGARETA: Oh God!

MELVIL: What is the matter?

MARGARETA: Oh, I saw—

MELVIL: Please, calm yourself and tell us what it is.

MARGARETA: As I came up the stairs to bring this cup
I passed the lower hall, the door was open,
I looked in—and saw—oh God!

MELVIL: What did you see? Compose yourself.

MARGARETA: The walls were draped in black, a giant scaffold,
All covered with black cloth, rose from the floor
And on its top, right in the middle, a dark block,
A pillow and beside it gleamed a well-honed ax.
The hall was filled with people crowding round
The scaffold, in their eyes hot lust of blood.

CHAMBERMAIDS: May God have mercy on our Queen!

MELVIL: Be calm now! Here she comes.

SCENE VI.

The same.

[Mary *enters, dressed in a white, festive gown; a chain made of small beads, from which an Agnus Dei is suspended, hangs around her neck; a rosary is fastened to her belt; she carries a crucifix. Her head is adorned with a tiara, her long, black veil is thrown back. As she enters, all step aside with expressions of their grief. In an instinctive gesture,* Melvil *drops to his knees*]

MARY: [*Looking all around with calm dignity*]
Why do you grieve? Why do you weep? You should
Rejoice with me that I am near the end

Of all my trials, that my chains will drop,
My prison open and my joyous soul
Will float on angels' wings to its eternal freedom.
While I was in the power of my haughty foe
And suffered such indignities
As no queen should be made to suffer,
Then was the time to weep for me.
Soothing and healing, death comes closer now,
My solemn friend. His great, black wings will cloak
My shame. When man has seen the bottom of the pit,
He finds a new nobility in this encounter.
I feel the crown upon my head again,
And in my soul the proud serenity I used to know.
     [*She advances a few steps*]
You here, Sir Melvil? Not like this, dear sir.
Arise! You have not come to see the death,
You're here to see the triumph of your Queen.
It is an unexpected happiness for me
That you, a friend who shares my faith,
Will be a witness when I die, for how I die
Will thus be known not only to my enemies.
Tell me, Sir Melvil, how have you been treated
In this barbarian, hostile land since I lost sight
Of you? Your fate has often troubled me.

MELVIL: What weighed upon me was not want, it was
My grief for you, the knowledge of my helplessness.

MARY: What has become of Didier, my chamberlain?
The loyal man has probably been in his grave
For many years now; he was very old.

MELVIL: That mercy God did not bestow on him.
He is alive and now must bury his young Queen.

MARY: How I have wished that I, before my death,
Could once more have embraced my dearest relatives.
But I must be content to die among
You, friendly strangers, and to see you weep for me.
To you, my loyal Melvil, I entrust
My last farewell to all my family.
I bless my husband's brother, the most Christian King
Of France and all the royal family.
I bless the Cardinal, my uncle, and Henri de Guise,
My cousin. I also bless the Pope,
The Holy Vicar of Christ, who blesses me, I know,
And give my blessing to that Catholic King
Who nobly offered rescue and revenge.
My testament lists all their names,
And they will not, I hope, despise the gifts
I leave them, poor as they may be.
     [*She turns to her servants*]
The King of France, my royal brother,
To whom I've recommended all of you,
Will care for you and give you once again a home.
Accept this last request of mine:
Do not remain in England, do not let
The overbearing Britons gloat at your misfortune,
Do not allow them to humiliate
A single one because he served me faithfully.
Give me your promise on this crucifix

That you will leave this wretched land when I am
    gone.
    MELVIL: [*His hand on the crucifix*] I swear for all
    of us.
    MARY: What I, poor woman who was robbed so
    viciously,
Possess and can dispose of at my will,
I have distributed for you to share.
I hope my testament will be respected.
This, too, all that I wear upon my walk to death,
Is yours. Do not begrudge me this last use
Of worldly splendor on my way to heaven.
    [*To her* Chambermaids]
To you, dear Alix, Gertrude, Rosamond,
I give my pearls and garments. You are still so
    young,
You will enjoy this finery.
You, Margareta, are the next who has a claim
Upon my generosity, for you will be
The most unhappy one of all I leave behind.
My will shows that I don't take my revenge
On you for what your husband did.
You, faithful Hannah, are not tempted
By gleaming gold and sparkling stones, the memories
You have of me will be your greatest treasure. Still,
This shawl is yours; I have embroidered it
For you myself, and all the tears I've wept
Are part of its design. Use it to blindfold me—
When that time comes. That service is the last
That I shall ask of you, dear Hannah.
    HANNAH: I cannot bear it, Melvil!
    MARY: Come now,
Come, all of you, and let me say good-bye.
    [*She holds out her hands, and one after the other
    kneels before her and, weeping, kisses her hand*]
Farewell, my Margareta—farewell, Alix—
Thank you for all you did for me, Burgoyne—
Your mouth is hot, Gertrude. I have been hated
    much,
But many, too, have loved me. May a noble man
Make you, my Gertrude, happy, for your burning
    heart
Needs love—You, Bertha, chose the better part,
You want to be the virgin bride of heaven.
Do hurry to complete your vows!
All worldly goods are so deceptive,
That lesson you may learn from me. Enough!
Farewell! Good-bye! Farewell forever!
    [*She quickly turns away; all her attendants, ex-
    cept* Melvil, *leave*]

SCENE VII.

Mary *and* Melvil.

    MARY: All the affairs of this world I have ordered,
I hope that I depart this life
A debtor to no living soul.

But one thing, Melvil, still prevents my troubled soul
From soaring, free and joyous, heavenward.
    MELVIL: I am your old and trusted friend. To me
Reveal your troubles; ease your burden.
    MARY: I stand upon the threshold of eternity
And soon must step before my Supreme Judge,
But I am not yet reconciled with God.
I am denied a priest, the presence of my Church,
And I refuse the Holy Sacrament
Presented to me by their own, false priests.
I wish to die without surrendering my faith,
For it alone can bring salvation.
    MELVIL: Rest calm, for God accepts a fervent,
    pious wish
In place of actions. Tyranny can only tie
Your hands, your heart's devotion reaches God.
The word is dead, the faith gives life.
    MARY: No, Melvil, that is not enough. Faith does
    not need
Itself alone, it needs a token to assure
Possession of the supreme grace.
That is why God became a man, that is why He
Mysteriously enshrined the gifts of heaven,
Not visible to us, in His substantial body.
It is the Church, our Holy Church, that builds
For us a ladder to eternity.
We call our Church the Catholic, the all-embracing
    Church,
Because the faith of the community
Strengthens the faith in each of us.
When thousands worship, thousands pray together,
The embers of our faith flare up in searing flames,
Bewinged, our spirit soars to heaven.
Oh, happy those who joyously assemble
For common prayer in a house of God!
The altar splendidly bedecked, the candles glow,
The fragrance of the incense—then the bell,
The bishop in his shining vestments
Holds up the chalice, blesses it, announces
The miracle of the transfiguration,
And in the presence of their living God,
The faithful fall upon their knees—
Oh, I alone am barred, the benediction
Does not reach me forsaken in my prison cell.
    MELVIL: It reaches you! It is close by. Have faith
In omnipotent God. The driest branch
May yet sprout leaves if only we have faith.
The One who could release a spring from solid rock
Can also build an altar in your prison,
Transform this cup, the worldly food that it contains,
Into a sacred vessel and eternal nurture.
    [*He takes the cup from the table and holds it up*]
    MARY: Oh, Melvil—it is hard to comprehend—
But yes—I understand! There is no priest, no church,
No Host, but our Redeemer said: "Where there are
    two
Who come together in my name,
There I am present in their midst."
What is the consecration of a priest?
What gives him power to proclaim the Word?

His blameless heart, his spotless life.
Thus you can be, for me, a priest,
Albeit unconsecrated, and a messenger
Of God to bring me peace. To you, then, I shall
      make
My last confession and from you
I will receive my absolution.
    MELVIL: Since faith drives you so powerfully, learn
That God has worked a miracle to comfort you.
You say there is no priest here and no Host,
No church? You are mistaken! Here's the priest,
And he has brought the body of our Lord.
    [*With these words, he uncovers his head and
    shows her the Host in a golden bowl*]
I am the priest. So that I might receive
Your last confession and bring peace to you
As you walk to your death, I have received
The seven consecrations, and I bring
This Host to you, sent by the Holy Father;
It has been consecrated by His Holiness.
    MARY: Heavenly joy that comes to me,
Now even at the gates of death!
As an immortal God descends to earth
On golden clouds, as once the angel broke
The prison chains that fettered the apostle—
Not sentries' swords nor iron bars can hinder him
As he strides mightily through walls and doors—
A messenger from heaven now surprises me,
I stand in awe before his glory,
Now that all human rescuers have failed.
And you who once served me are now God's servant,
His holy words come to me through your mouth.
As you once bent your knee before your Queen,
Thus I now lie before you in the dust.
    [*She falls on her knees*]
    MELVIL: [*Makes the sign of the cross over her
    head*]
In the name of God the Father, God the Son
And of the Holy Ghost! Queen Mary, did you search
Your heart, and do you vow and swear that you will
      speak
The truth before the God who is the Truth?
    MARY: My heart lies open before Him and you.
    MELVIL: Of what sins does your conscience blame
    you, sins
Committed since you last propitiated God?
    MARY: My heart was filled with jealousy and hate,
The thought of vengeance raged within my mind.
I who had sinned and prayed forgiveness
Did not have strength enough to pardon her
Who was my enemy.
    MELVIL: Do you repent,
And is it now your firm resolve
To pass from life, at peace with her?
    MARY: As truly as I hope for God's forgiveness.
    MELVIL: And of what other sins do you accuse
    yourself?
    MARY: Oh, even more than by my hate I have
    affronted God
By sinful love. My heart was vain,

It was attracted by the man
Who faithlessly deserted me.
    MELVIL: Do you regret your failing? Has your
    heart
Returned to God from the false idols it adored?
    MARY: It was the hardest fight I had to win,
The last of all my earthly bonds is torn.
    MELVIL: Is there another sin with which your con-
    science charges you?
    MARY: A deed of blood, committed long ago
And long ago confessed, returns to me
With doubled terror in this hour of final reckoning,
And black it looms between me and the gate of
    heaven.
I had the King, my husband, murdered,
I gave my heart and hand to the seducer.
I did atone for it with all the penalties
The Church imposed, but in my soul
The viper lives and will not let me sleep.
    MELVIL: Are there no other sins, not yet confessed
And not yet expiated, which oppress your heart?
    MARY: I've told you all that weighed upon my
    heart.
    MELVIL: Remember the proximity of the Omnis-
    cient,
Think of the penalties the Church decrees
For incomplete confession! That sin means
Eternal death, it outrages the Holy Ghost.
    MARY: May heaven's everlasting mercy grant me
    victory
In my last struggle, I hide nothing knowingly.
    MELVIL: What? Do you hide from God the crime
Of which the world accuses you?
You tell me nothing of your share in Babington's
And Perry's treacherous offense?
For that crime you will lose your life on earth,
Do you intend to forfeit life eternal, too?
    MARY: I'm now prepared to face my Supreme
    Judge.
It will be only minutes till I stand
Before His throne, and I repeat,
I've made complete confession.
    MELVIL: Weigh your words!
The mind deceives. Perhaps you did avoid,
With cunning ambiguity, the word
That would condemn, but shared the crime by willing
    it.
But juggler's tricks will not deceive
The flaming eye that looks into your heart.
    MARY: I summoned all the princes of the Con-
    tinent
To free me from demeaning bonds,
But never did I touch, in thought or deed,
The life of my opponent.
    MELVIL: The testimony of your clerks then was a
    lie?
    MARY: It is as I have said. God be the judge
Of what they testified.
    MELVIL: Convinced, then, of your innocence you
    mount the scaffold?

MARY: God has seen fit to let me expiate
My early crime by dying innocently.
    MELVIL: [*Makes the sign of the cross over her*]
Go then, and by your death atone for it,
Put down your life as sacrifice before the altar.
Blood can redeem a deed of blood.
Your crime was but a woman's frailty,
And mortal weakness stays behind
When our transfigured souls ascend to heaven.
By virtue of the power to unite
And to dissolve, which has been given me,
I now absolve you from all sin.
As you believed, thus be done unto you.
    [*He gives her the Host*]
This is the body that was sacrificed for you.
    [*He takes the cup from the table, consecrates the
    wine with a silent prayer, then offers it to her.
    She hesitates and refuses the cup with a gesture
    of her hand*]
Accept the blood which Jesus shed for you.
Accept it, for the Pope grants you this favor.
The noblest right of kings, the sacerdotal right,
It shall be yours unto your death.
    [*She accepts the cup*]
And as your God is now mysteriously joined
With you in this, your earthly shell,
Thus you shall be united with your God
In all eternity, to live,
A blessed angel, in His joyous realm
Where neither guilt nor tears exist.
    [*He puts down the cup. Hearing a noise, he
    covers his head and steps to the door. Mary re-
    mains on her knees, in silent prayer*]
    MELVIL: [*Returning from the door*]
One painful struggle still remains for you.
Do you feel strong enough to vanquish
All bitterness or hate that you may feel?
    MARY: I'm not afraid of their return. I've sacrificed
My hate and all my love to God.
    MELVIL: Prepare yourself, then, to receive
The Earl of Leicester and Lord Burleigh. They are
    here.

SCENE VIII.

The same.

    [Burleigh, Leicester, *and* Paulet *enter.* Leicester
    stands far back and does not raise his eyes.
    Burleigh, *noticing his behavior, steps between
    him and* Mary]
    BURLEIGH: I come, my Lady, to receive your last
      commands.
    MARY: Thank you, my Lord.
    BURLEIGH: My Queen desires
That any fair request be granted you.
    MARY: My testament contains my final wishes.
I've given it to Sir Amias, and I hope

That it be executed faithfully.
    BURLEIGH: You may rely on that.
    MARY: I also ask that you allow my servants
To leave for France or Scotland without hindrance,
Wherever they themselves may wish to go.
    BURLEIGH: It will be done as you desire.
    MARY: And since my body may not rest in con-
      secrated ground,
I ask that you permit this loyal servant
To take my heart to France. There it has always been.
    BURLEIGH: So be it. Is there any other wish—
    MARY: Take to the Queen of England my sincere
And sisterly regard. Tell her
That in my hour of death I pardon her
With all my heart, and that I ask of her
Forgiveness for my violence of yesterday.
May God preserve her and grant her a happy reign.
    BURLEIGH: Have you not reconsidered? Do you
      still refuse
The consolations of the dean?
    MARY: I've made my peace with God. Oh, Sir
      Amias,
I've caused you, much against my wish, great pain.
I've robbed you of the comfort and support
Of your old age. Please, let me hope
That you won't hate my memory.
    PAULET: [*Takes her hand*] Go peacefully, and God
      be with you!

SCENE IX.

    [Hannah *and the other women of* Mary's *retinue
    return, visibly terrified; they are followed by the*
    Sheriff *who carries a white staff. Behind him,
    armed men are seen through the open door*]
    MARY: What is it, Hannah? Yes, the time has come.
Here is the sheriff who will lead us to our death.
Now we must part. Farewell! Farewell!
    [*Her women cling to her; to* Melvil]
You, sir, and Hannah shall accompany
My last steps in this world. Lord Burleigh,
You will not deny me this last favor.
    BURLEIGH: I've no authority to grant it.
    MARY: You would refuse me this one small re-
      quest?
Do you have no respect for women?
Who, then, shall render me the final service?
It cannot be my sister's wish
That you insult, in me, all womanhood,
That men shall touch me with their uncouth hands!
    BURLEIGH: No woman is allowed to mount the
      scaffold's steps
With you. Her screams and lamentations would—
    MARY: Hannah will not lament. She will be calm
And strong, I warrant you. Be kind, my Lord!
Don't separate me from my faithful nurse
In this last hour. On her arms I was carried
Into life, let her guide me to death

With gentle hands.

PAULET: [*To* Burleigh] Grant her request.

BURLEIGH: So be it, then.

MARY: Now I have finished with this world.

[*She kisses the crucifix*]

My Savior and Redeemer, as your arms
Were stretched upon the cross, now spread them
            wide
To welcome me!

[*As she turns to go, her eyes fall upon* Leicester *who had, startled by her departure, roused himself and looked at her. At his sight,* Mary *begins to tremble, falters and is about to fall;* Leicester *catches her in his arms. For a moment, she gazes at him, silently and solemnly; he averts his eyes. Finally, she speaks*]

                You keep your promise, Leicester.
You vowed to lead me from my prison on your arm,
And now you do.

[*He stands in silence, crushed by her words. She continues in a soft voice*]

                Yes, Leicester, I expected
Not only freedom from your hands,
You were to make my freedom dear to me.
I hoped that on your arm, rejoicing in your love,
I would begin a new, delicious life.
Now that I am about to leave this world
And to become a blessed spirit
Whom worldly love no longer tempts,
Now I admit that weakness without blushing.
Farewell and, if you can, live happily!
You had the privilege to woo two queens:
You scorned the tender, loving heart of one,
To win the proud heart of the other.
Kneel, then, before Elizabeth!
I hope your prize will not become your punishment.
Farewell! Now I have finished with this earth.

[*She leaves, preceded by the* Sheriff, *at her side* Melvil *and* Hannah. Burleigh *and* Paulet *follow, while the others stare after her in silent grief until she is out of sight. Then they leave by the other two doors*]

SCENE X.

Leicester *alone.*

LEICESTER: I'm still alive? How can I bear to live?
Why does this roof not fall and crush me with its
            weight?
Why does no abyss open up to swallow me?
What have I lost! What jewel have I thrown away!
The bliss of heaven I have squandered.
She goes, already a transfigured spirit,
And I remain to suffer the despair of hell.
What happened to my firm resolve to choke
My senses and to suffocate my heart,

Unfeelingly to watch her die?
Is it the sight of her that reawakened
My shame which I had killed? Does she,
Even in death, ensnare me with the bonds of love?
I am abominable and I have no right
To melt in womanly commiseration.
The happiness of love does not lie on my path,
I must protect my breast with iron armor, be a rock.
Proceed! I must complete the infamy that I began
Lest I be cheated of its fair reward.
Compassion—die! Eyes—turn to stone!
I shall be witness, I shall see her die.

[*He takes a few determined steps toward the door through which* Mary *left the room; before reaching it, he stops*]

In vain! In vain! Hell's horror grips my soul
I cannot face the terrifying sight,
I cannot see her die. Ah! What was that?
They are already in the hall,
The ghastly work proceeds below my feet.
Now I hear voices—no! Away! Away
From this abode of death and horror!

[*He tries to escape through another door but finds it locked. He recoils in terror*]

What? Does a vengeful God encage me here?
Am I compelled to hear what I don't dare to see?
The deacon's voice—he cautions her—
She interrupts—there—now she prays aloud—
Her voice is firm—now she is quiet—all is still—
So still—there is no sound but that
Of weeping women and of sobs—
Now they undress her—there—they move the stool—
She kneels upon the pillow—now she puts her head—

[*He has spoken the last lines with steadily mounting terror; then, suddenly his body twitches and he falls to the floor, unconscious. At the same moment, the dull roar of many voices is heard from below and continues for some time*]

SCENE XI.

The Queen's *chamber. This is the same room as in the second part of Act IV.*

[Elizabeth *enters through a side door; her movements indicate her extreme agitation*]

ELIZABETH: No one here yet—no messenger! Will
            night not fall
Today? The sun stands still in its celestial course.
How long am I to suffer torture waiting for
The long-awaiting news? Has it been done
Or has it not? I shudder at the thought of both.
I dare not ask. No sign of Leicester or of Burleigh,
Whom I have named to carry out the sentence.
If they left London, it has happened.
The arrow has been shot, it flies, it finds its mark.
Not for my kingdom could I stop it now. Who's
            there?

SCENE XII.

Elizabeth *and a* Page.

ELIZABETH: You come alone? Where are the lords?
PAGE: The Earl of Leicester and Lord Burleigh—
ELIZABETH: [*With bated breath*] Where are they?
PAGE: They're not in London.
ELIZABETH: They're not? Where are they, then?
PAGE: No one could tell me, but it seems they left
The city before dawn in haste and secrecy.
ELIZABETH: [*Bursts out*] Then—I am Queen of
     England!
     [*She paces up and down in great agitation*]
Go—call—no, stay! She's dead! She's dead.
At last there is room enough for me on earth.
Why do I tremble? Why am I afraid?
My fear lies in her grave, and who can say
I did it? I shall not lack tears to mourn her death.
     [*To the* Page]
Are you still here? I want my secretary,
Davison, to come at once. Send for
The Earl of Shrewsbury. Ah, here he is.
     [*The* Page *leaves*]

SCENE XIII.

Elizabeth *and* Shrewsbury.

ELIZABETH: Welcome, my Lord. What news have
     you?
It must be an important matter that directs
Your steps to me so late at night.
SHREWSBURY: Your Majesty, today my troubled
     heart
And fear for your good name impelled me to the
     Tower,
Once more to test the truthfulness of Curl and Nau,
The Stuart's clerks, who are imprisoned there.
Embarrassed, the Lieutenant of the Tower
At first refused to let me see the prisoners.
My threats, at last, gained me admittance.
God, what a sight my eyes beheld!
Unkempt, a wild look in his eye, the Scotsman, Curl,
Lay on his bed as if pursued by Furies;
No sooner did he recognize my face,
The wretch fell on his knees before me, clutched
My legs and, twisting like a worm and screaming,
Implored and begged of me to tell him Mary's fate.
A rumor, so it seems, that she had been condemned
To death had penetrated to the Tower's depth.
When I confirmed that this was true and said
Moreover that his testimony was
The reason of her death, the man sprang to his feet
And in a rage attacked his fellow prisoner;
He pushed him down, and with a madman's strength
He tried to strangle him. We barely managed
To tear the man from his infuriated grip.

But now he turned his rage against himself
Clawed at his breast with his fierce hands and cursed
Himself and his companion to eternal hell.
His testimony had been false, he cried,
The letters to Sir Babington which he had sworn
Were true had been a forgery, the words
Which he had written were not those
That Mary had dictated. Nau
Had talked him into this treachery.
With that, he ran and tore the window open
And screamed into the street, where people quickly
     gathered,
That he was Mary Stuart's clerk, the fiend
Who had accused her falsely and that now,
As a false witness, he was damned.
ELIZABETH: You said yourself that he was mad.
The words that madmen speak prove nothing.
SHREWSBURY: His madness, by itself, proves all the
     more.
Your Majesty, I do implore you not to act
Too hastily. Command a new inquiry.
ELIZABETH: That I shall do—because you ask, my
     Lord,
And not because I can believe my peers
Have judged the matter hastily.
Yes, to appease your conscience I command
That the investigation be renewed.
Good that there is still time. There shall not be
The faintest doubt to cast a shadow on our royal
     honor.

SCENE XIV.

The same.

     [Davison *enters*]
ELIZABETH: Where is the sentence, sir, which I put
     in your hands?
Where is it?
DAVISON: [*Perplexed*] What? The sentence?
ELIZABETH: Yes, the
     document
I gave you yesterday to keep—
DAVISON: To keep!
ELIZABETH: The crowd insisted that I sign, I had
To grant their wish, and so I did.
I was compelled to sign, and to gain time,
I put the document into your hands,
And you remember what I told you. Well?
I want it back.
SHREWSBURY: Please, sir, return it. Things
Are different now. A new inquiry will be made.
ELIZABETH: Do not waste time. Where is the
     paper?
DAVISON: Oh, I am lost! This is my death!
ELIZABETH: [*Quickly*] I hope you did not—
DAVISON: I do not have it any more—I'm ruined!
ELIZABETH: What did you say?
SHREWSBURY: Merciful God!

DAVISON: Lord Burleigh has the document—since
  yesterday.
  ELIZABETH: You wretch! Is that how you obey my
    orders!
It was my strict command that you retain it.
  DAVISON: No, that, your Majesty, was not your
    order.
  ELIZABETH: Do you propose to make a liar of me,
    scoundrel?
When did I say to give the sheet to Burleigh?
  DAVISON: Not in so many words—not clearly—
    but—
  ELIZABETH: Do you, then, dare interpret my com-
    mands
And give them the unholy meaning you pretend
To see in them? If a misfortune should result
From what you did on your, and only your,
Authority, you'll pay for it. I'll have your life!
Oh, Shrewsbury, you see how they misuse my name!
  SHREWSBURY: I see it clearly. Oh, my God!
  ELIZABETH: What
    did you say?
  SHREWSBURY: If this man did presume to act
At his own risk and without your approval,
He must be tried before his peers for having made
Your name repulsive for all time.

SCENE XV.

The same.
Burleigh; *at the end,* Kent.

  BURLEIGH: [*Enters and kneels before the Queen*]
Long live my Queen! May all the enemies
Of England end as Mary Stuart ended!
    [Shrewsbury *covers his face;* Davison *wrings his
    hands in despair*]
  ELIZABETH: Tell me, my Lord, did you receive
    from me
The order for her death?
  BURLEIGH: No, I did not, your Majesty.
I had it from this gentleman.
  ELIZABETH: Did Davison give you the order in my
    name?
  BURLEIGH: No, not exactly—
  ELIZABETH: But you were quick to execute it with-
    out first

Confirming my desire? Just was the sentence,
The world cannot find fault with us.
But to forestall my clemency you had no right.
Therefore you're banished from my presence.
    [*To* Davison]
You may expect a stricter judgment,
For you have overstepped your competence
And with impertinence abused a sacred trust.
Conduct him to the Tower! It is my desire
That he be tried on pain of death.
You, Noble Talbot, I have found to be
The only one among my councillors
Who has been just. You be my friend and counsel.
  SHREWSBURY: Don't banish your most faithful
    friends,
Do not imprison those who acted in your stead
And now are silent for your sake.
I, gracious Majesty, ask your permission
To put again into your hands the seal
With which for twelve years you have trusted me.
  ELIZABETH: [*Taken aback*] No, Shrewsbury, you
    cannot leave me now—
  SHREWSBURY: Forgive me, I'm too old and this
    straight hand
Too stiff to seal your novel[4] actions.
  ELIZABETH: The man who saved my life would
    now abandon me?
  SHREWSBURY: What I did was not much. The
    nobler part of you
I could not save. Live long, reign happily!
Your enemy is dead. You now need have
No fear and no respect for anything.[5]
    [*He leaves*]
  ELIZABETH: [*To* Kent *who enters*]
I wish to see the Earl of Leicester
  KENT: The Earl of Leicester asks to be excused.
He has embarked for France.
    [Elizabeth *controls herself and remains calm and
    composed*]

CURTAIN

[4] Literally "new" actions or acts, but implying that these
could also be reprehensible.—J.G.
[5] In German this reads "[*du*]*brauchst nichts mehr zu
achten,*" meaning "you don't have to be on guard against
anymore" but also, ambiguously, "you don't have to consider [or 'respect'] anything anymore"—an implied reproof
to Elizabeth for her unscrupulousness.—J.G.

Victor Hugo and Hernani

The most popular and versatile of French nine-teenth-century poets, Victor Hugo (1802–1885), the son of one of Napoleon the Great's generals, was also one of the most considerable French dramatists during the first half of his century. He performed the important task of breaking the stranglehold neo-classicism had continued to have on the theatre in Paris. If he was not its most distinguished romantic writer—the superiority of Alfred de Musset is now generally acknowledged (see pages 551–569)—he was its most torrential force. And if the great victory he won over entrenched neoclassicists in 1830 with the production of *Hernani* did not eventuate in a harvest of distinguished romantic dramas, in routing neoclassic conservatism from the stage he did pre-pare the way for modern French drama.

Although he had such noteworthy associates as Alexander Dumas, Alfred de Vigny and Alfred de Musset in his assault on the theatre, the distinction of opening its portals to romantic drama devolved mainly on Hugo. He had announced as early as 1827 a program for doing away with the rigidities of the unities of time, place, and action as well as the rules of decorum that forbade the mingling of comedy and tragedy or of the beautiful and the ugly in the same play.

In 1829 came his *Marion Delorme,* an early senti-mentalization of the eternal courtesan. Then in 1830 the main assault started with his *Hernani,* a wildly romantic treatment of love and honor in the Spanish manner. Hernani, the outlaw, and Don Carlos, the heir-apparent to the Spanish throne, are rivals for the ward of an old Spanish nobleman, who intends to marry her himself. Hernani joins a conspiracy against Don Carlos, who is now the king of Spain; but the latter, having also been elected Emperor of the Holy Roman Empire, exercises regal magnanim-ity. He restores Hernani to his title and lands and bestows the heroine upon him. Then at the height of the young lovers' ecstasy the old Count asserts a claim upon his life, and Hernani honorably fol-lows the Count's horn which calls him to death. The play is operatic in its sentiments and survives now chiefly as Verdi's opera. But *Hernani* became the occasion of a pitched battle between old-guard con-servatives and avant-garde French romanticists. The latter won the day, and Hugo's services in clearing the way for modern French realism cannot be dis-missed lightly.

Hugo's later plays followed the same pyrotechnic formula. *The King Amuses Himself* (*Le Roi s'Amuse*) in 1832 dramatized the vengeance of the king's jester against the profligate master who has seduced his daughter. Although the play, which was prohibited by the government for daring to criticize royalty, plainly revels in excitement, it can now be endured only in its suitable reincarnation as Verdi's *Rigoletto.*

Then Hugo, who had given these early works the benefit of his genuine though overblown poetic gifts, took another step toward liberating French tragedy by writing the prose dramas *Lucrèce Borgia* (turned into an opera by Donizetti), *Mary Tudor,* and *Angelo.* Finally, he returned to the grand style with *Ruy Blas* (also converted into an opera), another Spanish tragedy even more romantic than *Hernani,* and with a trilogic fiasco entitled *The Burgraves.*

Hugo labored like a Titan, and because such thumping birth pangs are theatrically impressive, he remains a ponderable figure in the theatre's annals. But the dramatic work of this poet who has been aptly called a "Michelangelo in terra cotta" is more grandiose than substantial. He dissipated, it is true, the formal recitative technique of French classicism, and he helped to prepare the theatre for the reception of any kind of experiment on the principle that there should be "no more formulas, no standards of any sort." But the uses to which he put the new freedoms were themselves artificial, and his exotic art was, therefore, a quickly extinguished blaze. Even in the heyday of his success he shared his popularity with Eugene Scribe (1791–1861), who wooed the large prosaic world of the middle classes, and the advent of realistic drama was soon to leave France's thunderous romanticist far behind.

After 1850 Hugo's energies went into affairs of the heart; into politics when he came to oppose the political ambitions of Louis Napoleon, who became Napoleon III; into voluminous verse; and into the writing of such famous novels as *Les Misérables* and *Nôtre Dame de Paris.*

A sturdy "classicist" such as Harvard's Irving Babbitt writing about a century after the success of Hugo's dramatic masterpiece, could say summarily that "the total impression *Hernani* produces is that of a parvenu melodrama," *parvenu* because it is decked out in verse and literary fireworks but is, like so many earlier and contemporary romantic plays, melodramatic in action and characterization. Hugo's characters are extravagant in daring, courtesy, pas-sion, and principle. We may note, too, how neatly Hernani's rival in love, Don Carlos, turns magnani-mous the moment he learns that he has become King of Spain and Holy Roman Emperor. Coldly con-sidered, the plot does seem greatly contrived and somewhat jejune; and the characters may well be considered ancestors of Hollywood heroes of costume drama. Nevertheless, the theatrical pulse of the play, made appropriate by its Spanish background and theme of honor, was strong enough to keep Parisian audiences coming to applaud or deride it for some hundred consecutive performances. It was the high-water mark of French romanticism and poetic melo-drama in the nineteenth century.

After Hugo's pyrotechnical displays it was time

for the sober theatre of realism or at least pseudo-realism to establish its claims, which it did in plays by Hebbel, Turgenev, Ostrovsky, Dumas *fils,* Augier, and Ibsen. Hugo himself, however, continued to be a symbol of all that was noble and exalting in public life and art. He returned from self-imposed exile during the reign of Napoleon III and was received jubilantly in Paris after the monarchy collapsed as a result of the defeat of France in the Franco-Prussian War (1870). He arrived one day after the proclamation of the Third French Republic. Many honors were heaped upon him, and when he died he was accorded a state funeral in Paris and his body interred in the Pantheon, which shelters the tombs of some of the most illustrious heroes of France.

HERNANI

By Victor Hugo
ENGLISH VERSION BY LINDA ASHER

CHARACTERS

HERNANI
DON CARLOS
DON RUY GOMEZ DE SILVA
DOÑA SOL DE SILVA
DUKE OF BAVARIA
DUKE OF GOTHA
DUKE OF LUTZELBURG
DON SANCHO
DON MATIAS
DON RICARDO
DON GARCI SUAREZ

DON FRANCISCO
DON JUAN DE HARO
DON GIL TELLEZ GIRON
FIRST CONSPIRATOR
A MOUNTAINEER
IAQUEZ
DOÑA JOSEFA DUARTE
A LADY
OTHER CONSPIRATORS, MOUNTAINEERS, LORD, SOLDIERS, PAGES, *etc.*

The action of the play takes place in Spain, in 1519.

ACT I. THE KING. SCENE I.

Saragossa: a bedchamber. It is night. A lamp on the table.

[Doña Josefa Duarte, *an old woman in black, with the bodice of her gown ornamented in jet, in the style of Isabella the Catholic; she draws the crimson window drapes and arranges a few chairs. There is a knock at a small hidden door on the right. She listens; there is a second knock*] DOÑA JOSEFA: Has he arrived already? [*Another knock*] It *is* from the secret stairway, no doubt of that. [*A fourth knock*] Quick, then—I must open it. [*She opens the covered door. Don Carlos enters, his cloak across his lower face, and his hat low over his eyes*] Good evening to you, sir. [*She leads him in. He opens his cloak and reveals a rich outfit of velvet and silk, in the fashion of Castile in 1519. She looks at him more closely, and draws back, astonished*] What? Señor Hernani—but it is not you! Help! Guards!

DON CARLOS: [*Gripping her arm*] Two more words out of you, old woman, and you die! [*He stares hard at her; she subsides into terrified silence*] Is this the apartment that belongs to Doña Sol? They tell me she is promised to her uncle, the old duke—a gracious lord, proud, venerable, and decrepit. They say this beauty spurns all other men, but that she loves a smooth-faced youth, and every night she meets this young lover—without whiskers or mustache—beneath the very nose of the old man. Is this all true? [*She is silent; he shakes her arm*] Well? Will you answer me?

DOÑA JOSEFA: You forbade me to speak even two words, my lord.

DON CARLOS: I asked for only one—a yes or no. Doña Sol de Silva *is* your mistress? Speak.

DOÑA JOSEFA: Yes. Why?

DON CARLOS: No matter. And her old fiancé, the duke—he is out at present?

DOÑA JOSEFA: Yes.

DON CARLOS: She must be awaiting her young man, then?

DOÑA JOSEFA: Yes.

DON CARLOS: Oh, I could die!

DOÑA JOSEFA: Yes.

DON CARLOS: Duenna—is this where they meet?

DOÑA JOSEFA: Yes.

DON CARLOS: Hide me here somehow!

DOÑA JOSEFA: Hide you!

DON CARLOS: Yes.

DOÑA JOSEFA: But why?

DON CARLOS: No matter why.

DOÑA JOSEFA: You're asking me to hide you?

DON CARLOS: Yes—somewhere here.

DOÑA JOSEFA: Never!

DON CARLOS: [*Drawing a knife and a purse at once from his sash*] Madame, do me the honor of choosing —this purse or else this blade.

DOÑA JOSEFA: [*Taking the purse*] You must be the devil.

DON CARLOS: Yes, I am.

DOÑA JOSEFA: [*Opening a narrow closet in the wall*] Come in here.

DON CARLOS: [*Looking in*] This box?

DOÑA JOSEFA: [*Closing it*] If it does not suit you, leave.

DON CARLOS: [*Opening it again and examining it*] It will do perfectly. [*With another glance inside*] Is this the stable where you keep your broomstick between rides? [*He cramps himself into it with difficulty*] Ouff!

DOÑA JOSEFA: [*Clasping her hands in horror*] A man—here in this room!

DON CARLOS: [*From the still-open closet*] Oh, then your lady was expecting a woman?

DOÑA JOSEFA: Good heavens—I hear her coming now—please, my lord, close the door, quickly! [*She pushes the door shut*]

DON CARLOS: [*From inside*] Remember, duenna—say one word, and you shall die.

DOÑA JOSEFA: [*Alone*] Who is this man, Good Jesus! Shall I call for help? But whom can I call? Except my lady and myself, all the palace is asleep. Well, the other one will be arriving soon, and this is his affair—he has a good sword. May the Lord save us from perdition! [*Weighs the purse in her hand*] After all, it's not as though he were a common thief.

[Doña Sol *enters, in white;* Doña Josefa *hides the purse*]

SCENE II.

DOÑA SOL: Josefa!

DOÑA JOSEFA: My lady?

DOÑA SOL: I am afraid—Hernani should be here by now. [*Sound of steps at the small door*] Listen—I hear him now on the stair. Open before he knocks—and be quick—hurry!

[Josefa *opens the tiny door.* Hernani *enters, in a great cloak and broad hat. Underneath he is dressed as an Aragonese mountaineer, in gray, with a leather jerkin; a sword, a dagger, and a horn are at his waist*]

DOÑA SOL: [*Running to him*] Hernani!

HERNANI: Doña Sol! At last you stand before me, and the voice I hear is yours! Ah, why must fate set my path so far from yours? I need you to help me forget the rest of this unhappy life.

DOÑA SOL: Your cloak is drenched! Is it raining so hard?

HERNANI: I do not know.

DOÑA SOL: You must be chilled.

HERNANI: It is nothing.

DOÑA SOL: Take off that cloak.

HERNANI: Doña Sol, my beloved, tell me this—when you fall to rest at night, all calm, and innocent and pure—when a happy sleep half opens your fresh lips, and when its finger closes your dark eyes—does some angel come and tell you how dear a thing you are to me, a man deserted and rebuffed by all the world?

DOÑA SOL: You are so late, my lord! But tell me, are you cold?

HERNANI: Beside you I only burn! When a fierce love rages in my head, when my heart swells with its own swirling tempests—then how can I feel nature's cloud outside, with all its flash and storming?

DOÑA SOL: [*Unfastening his cloak*] Come—give me your cape. And your sword too.

HERNANI: No—this is another friend, as innocent and loyal as you. Doña Sol, the old duke, your uncle, your promised husband—is he away?

DOÑA SOL: Yes, this hour belongs to us.

HERNANI: This hour, and nothing more! No more than just an hour for our love! And afterwards, I must forget, or die. My angel, one hour with you when I would ask for all of life and all eternity!

DOÑA SOL: My Hernani!

HERNANI: [*Bitterly*] How fortunate I am, that the duke has left the palace! Like a miserable thief I force the door—I creep within and see you, and steal an hour of your sweet song and gaze from the old man. And I am lucky, and others envy me for stealing an hour from him, while he steals my whole life.

DOÑA SOL: Please, Hernani. [*Handing the cloak to the old woman*] Josefa, dry his cloak. [Josefa *goes out.* Doña Sol *sits down, and gestures to* Hernani *to come closer.*] Come here by me.

HERNANI: [*Not hearing her*] So the duke is away from the castle. . . .

DOÑA SOL: [*Smilingly*] How tall you are!

HERNANI: He is gone awhile—

DOÑA SOL: Dear Hernani, let us not think about the duke.

HERNANI: But we must think about him! That old man loves you, and will marry you. . . . He took a kiss from you the other day—not think about him!

DOÑA SOL: [*Laughing*] Is that what's thrown you into such despair? An uncle's kiss—and on the brow besides! Almost a fatherly caress. . . .

HERNANI: No; a lover's kiss, a husband's—the kiss of a jealous man. Oh, my lady, you will soon belong to him! Do you realize that? The foolish, stooped old man, he needs a wife to end his journey and complete his day—and so the chilly specter takes himself a young girl! The mad old man! Does he not see that while he marries you with one hand, death weds him by the other? He comes so heedlessly to thrust himself into our love—when he should instead be measuring himself for the gravedigger! Doña Sol, who made this match? You were forced to it, I hope?

DOÑA SOL: The king desires it, they say.

HERNANI: The king! the king! My father died upon the gallows, condemned by his! And though we have grown older since that day, my hatred is still fresh toward the old king's ghost, his widow, and his son—toward all his flesh. He is dead, he counts no more; but when I was a child I made a vow to avenge my father on his son. Carlos, king of the Castiles—I have sought you everywhere, for the loathing between our houses does not die! Our fathers struggled without pity or remorse for thirty years; now, with our fathers dead, nothing has changed. They died in vain, for their enmity lives on; peace has not yet come to them, for their sons still stand, and still pursue the duel. So it is you, Carlos, who made this shameful match! So much the better. I sought for you, and here you are astride my path.

DOÑA SOL: You frighten me.

HERNANI: I have sworn to carry out a curse, and I must frighten even myself. Listen. The man they have betrothed you to, Don Ruy de Silva, is duke of Pastraña; he is a nobleman of Aragon, a count and grandee of Castile. He cannot give you youth, my sweet young girl; but in its place he offers you such gold, such jewels and gems that your brow will shine among the glittering crowns of royalty. His duchess will hold such power and pride, splendor and wealth, that many a queen could envy her. Such is the duke. While I—I am poor; as a child I had nothing but the forests where I roamed barefoot. I too may own some glowing coat of arms, hid now by clotted blood; I too may have rights that now are cloaked in the folds and shadows of a black gallows-cloth; unless my waiting be in vain, perhaps one day those rights will flash out from this sheath again as I draw my sword. Meanwhile, a jealous heaven has granted me nothing but air, and light, and water—no more than the dowry it offers every man. Let me free you now from one of us, the duke or me. You must choose between us: marry him, or come with me.

DOÑA SOL: I shall go with you.

HERNANI: To live among my rough companions? They are outlaws, whose names the hangman already knows, men whose blades never grow blunt, nor their hearts tender—each of them with some blood vengeance that whips him on. Would you come and be the queen of such a band? For I never told you this—I am an outlaw! When I was hunted through the land of Spain, only old Catalonia welcomed me like a mother into her forests, her harsh mountains, her rough rocks where only the soaring eagle peers. Among her highlanders, her solemn, poor, free men, I grew to manhood; and tomorrow if I sound this horn, three thousand of them will come. . . . You shiver—think again. Would you follow me into the trees, over the hills, along the river's edge? To the land of men who look like the devils in your dreams? And live in doubt, suspecting everything—eyes, voices, footfalls, rustlings—and sleep on the bare grass, and drink from the stream; and as you nurse some waking child at night, to hear musket balls go hissing by your ear?

Would you be an outlawed wanderer with me, and if need be, follow me to where I shall follow my father—onto the scaffold?

DOÑA SOL: I will follow you.

HERNANI: The duke is prosperous and powerful—his life is good. There is no stain on his old family name. The duke can do what he will. He offers you not just his hand, but treasure, titles, and contentment.

DOÑA SOL: We will leave tomorrow. Hernani, do not condemn me for my new boldness. Are you my demon or my angel? I cannot tell—but I am your slave. Wherever you go I will go. Stay, or depart—I belong to you. Why? I cannot say. I need to see you, and must have you near, and have you all the time. When the sound of your step fades, then I think that my heart has stopped its beat; you are gone, and I am gone from myself. But no sooner does that beloved footfall sound in my ear again, then I remember life and feel my soul come back to me!

HERNANI: [*Taking her in his arms*] My love!

DOÑA SOL: At midnight, then, tomorrow. Bring your men to my window, and clap your hands three times. You will see—I will be strong and brave.

HERNANI: Do you realize now what I am?

DOÑA SOL: My lord, what does it matter? I am going with you.

HERNANI: No—since you want to follow me, impulsive woman, you must learn what name, what rank, what soul, what destiny is hidden in this rough Hernani. You would take a brigand; but would you have a banished man?

DON CARLOS: [*Clattering the cupboard door open*] Will you never finish telling her your tale? Do you suppose it's pleasant, cramped into this closet?

[Hernani *starts back, astonished.* Doña Sol *cries out and flies into his arms, staring fearfully at* Don Carlos]

HERNANI: [*His hand on his sword hilt*] Who is this man?

DOÑA SOL: Great heavens! Help! Help, guards!

HERNANI: Quiet, Doña Sol! You'll waken angry eyes! When I am with you, please, whatever comes, never call for any hand but mine to aid you. [*To* Don Carlos] What were you doing there?

DON CARLOS: I can hardly claim I was out for a gallop through the woods.

HERNANI: When a man banters after he offends, only his heir is likely to enjoy the joke.

DON CARLOS: One good line deserves another. Sir, let us speak frankly. You love this lady; you come to watch your eyes in hers each night: very good. I love her too, and want to know who it is I have seen so often entering by the window while I stay at the door.

HERNANI: I swear you shall leave the way I enter, sir.

DON CARLOS: We shall see. So then, I offer my lady my love too. Let us share her, shall we? I've seen such goodness in her soul, so much tender feeling, that I should think she had enough for two lovers. And so, tonight, I thought to bring my plans to fruit. I was mistaken for you, and slipped in by surprise; I hid, I listened—you see how frank I am—but in this slot I hardly heard a word, and nearly suffocated. Besides, my French vest was crumpling badly. I am coming out.

HERNANI: My dagger is uneasy in its hiding place too, and eager to come out.

DON CARLOS: [*Acknowledging the challenge*] As you like, sir.

HERNANI: [*Drawing his sword*] En garde!

[Don Carlos *draws his own*]

DOÑA SOL: [*Throwing herself between them*] Hernani! No!

DON CARLOS: Peace, señora.

HERNANI: Tell me your name.

DON CARLOS: Tell me your own!

HERNANI: I am keeping it a deadly secret for another man—one day he will lie beneath my conquering knee and feel my name in his ear, and my knife at his heart.

DON CARLOS: Then what is that man's name?

HERNANI: What can it mean to you? On guard! Defend yourself!

[*They cross swords. Doña Sol falls trembling onto a chair. Knocking at the main door*]

DOÑA SOL: [*Rising in alarm*] Someone is at the door! [*The duel stops. Josefa enters through the small door, highly agitated*]

HERNANI: [*To Josefa*] Who is knocking there?

DOÑA JOSEFA: [*To Doña Sol*] My lady, a terrible thing! The duke has just returned!

DOÑA SOL: [*Wringing her hands*] The duke! Then there is no hope. . . .

DOÑA JOSEFA: [*Glancing about her*] Gracious Lord—the stranger, and these swords—they're battling! This is a fine affair!

[*The two adversaries slip their swords back into the sheaths. Don Carlos wraps himself in his cloak and pulls his hat down over his eyes. The knock is heard again*]

HERNANI: What shall we do?

[*Another knock*]

A VOICE OUTSIDE: Doña Sol, open the door. It is I. [*Doña Josefa takes a step toward the door, but Hernani stops her*]

HERNANI: No.

DOÑA JOSEFA: [*Fingering her rosary*] Good Saint James, help us through this trial!

[*More knocking*]

HERNANI: We must hide. [*He points to the closet*]

DON CARLOS: In that closet again?

HERNANI: [*Opening its door*] Go on in, yes; it will hold the two of us.

DON CARLOS: Lord no, it's far too small.

HERNANI: Let us leave then, through the secret door.

DON CARLOS: Good night. I shall stay here.

HERNANI: You will pay for this! [*To Doña Sol*] Can I barricade the door?

DON CARLOS: [*To Josefa*] Open it.

HERNANI: What is he saying?

DON CARLOS: Open it, I say! [*She is standing bewildered. The knocking is repeated.* Doña Josefa *goes trembling to answer it*]

DOÑA SOL: Lord in heaven, help me!

SCENE III.

DON RUY GOMEZ DE SILVA: [*White-haired, white-bearded, dressed in black*] Men at this hour in my niece's room! Guards, come closer—this calls for brighter light! [*To Doña Sol*] By Saint John of Avila, there are three of us here—two more than should be,

madam! [*To the young men*] You young cavaliers, what business have you here? When the Cid lived, and in Bernardo's day, those two giants of Spain and of the world moved through the Castiles doing honor to the aged and granting women the safeguard of their shields. Those were powerful men—their iron and their steel rode lighter on their shoulders than your velvet does on you. Those men respected a gray beard; they brought their love to consecration in the church and betrayed no man, and their reason was that they must keep the honor of their line. When they desired a woman, they wed her unsullied and in full daylight before the eyes of all, and with their sword, or halberd, or lance firmly in hand. But these criminals who skulk by dark, trusting only the night with their shameful deeds—who steal a woman's honor behind her husband's back—I tell you that the Cid, the ancestor of us all, would have named them vile and forced them to their knees. He would degrade their rank, for they are mere usurpers of nobility; he would deface their coat of arms with a slap of his sword.

Ah, what regret I feel as I think of it—how those men of other times would deal with men today!

Why are you here? To tell me I am an old man, at whom the young shall sneer? Will they laugh at me, who fought at Zamora? When I pass by, white-headed, will they laugh? Not you—no, you at least will not be there to laugh!

HERNANI: Duke—

DON RUY: Silence! . . . You have your swords, your daggers, your lances; you have hunting, and banquets, festivals, and falcons; songs to sing at evening under a balcony, plumes in your hats, and cloaks of silk, and balls and tournaments, and youth, and joy—and yet you children weary of all that! You must have a new plaything; you cast about and pick an old man for it—and now, you have smashed the toy! But God willing, the pieces will spring up whole again and burst in your very teeth! Come out with me!

HERNANI: My lord duke—

DON RUY: Come out with me! Draw your swords! Gentlemen, was this only a whim? Was it? There is a treasure in my house—a young girl's honor, the honor of a woman and of a whole family. I love this girl; she is my niece, and soon she will exchange her ring for the one I wear. I believe her to be chaste and pure, and sacred to all men. It happens that I leave the house an hour, and a thief slips in through the door to steal my honor. Wash off your hands, you soulless men—by no more than a touch you taint our women. Or better—have I still something more for you? [*He pulls off his gold collar of knighthood*] Here, take and trample this, my Golden Fleece! [*Throws off his hat*] Wrench out my hair, make it a lowly thing, and tomorrow go and boast throughout the town that never in their shameless games have scoundrels defiled a nobler head, nor whiter hairs.

DOÑA SOL: My lord—

DON RUY: [*To his servants*] Guards—my hatchet, and my knife, and my Toledo blade. And you two, come out with me now!

DON CARLOS: [*Stepping forward*] Duke, there is more pressing business first. I came to tell you of Maximilian, emperor of Germany: he is dead. [*He throws off his cloak, and uncovers his face*]

DON RUY: Are you joking? . . . God, it is the king!

DOÑA SOL: The king!

HERNANI: [*His eyes flaring*] The king of Spain!

DON CARLOS: Yes, Carlos of Spain. My lord duke, then, do you understand? My grandsire the emperor has died; I heard this only now, and hastened here in person to tell you of the news, as a loyal and beloved subject. I came by dark, and incognito, to ask your guidance—all quite simple, and yet see what confusion you arouse!

[*Don Ruy sends his servants away with a sign. He draws closer to* Don Carlos, *whom* Doña Sol *watches in fear and surprise.* Hernani *gazes attentively on, from his corner*]

DON RUY GOMEZ: But why that long delay before the door was opened?

DON CARLOS: With good reason—you come with a whole escort. When a state secret brings me to your house, am I expected to confide in all your men?

DON RUY: Highness, forgive me! Appearances—

DON CARLOS: Good father, I named you governor of the Figueras castle. Now who will govern you?

DON RUY: Forgive me—

DON CARLOS: Enough. We'll talk no more of it, my lord. Well. The emperor is dead.

DON RUY: Your highness' grandfather—he is dead?

DON CARLOS: I stand before you now heavy with grief.

DON RUY: Who will succeed him?

DON CARLOS: A Saxon duke, perhaps; or Francis the First of France, who is one of the contenders.

DON RUY: Where will the electors meet?

DON CARLOS: At Aix-la-Chapelle, I think, or Spires or Frankfurt.

DON RUY: And our own Spanish king, whose days God guard, has he never considered the throne of empire for himself?

DON CARLOS: Incessantly.

DON RUY: It goes to you by right.

DON CARLOS: I know it.

DON RUY: Your father was archduke of Austria; and I hope the electors will recall that the man who has just fallen from the imperial purple to the shroud was your ancestor.

DON CARLOS: Besides, I am a citizen of Ghent.

DON RUY: I saw your grandfather once when I was young—alas, I am the last survivor of a whole century; everyone else has died now. He was a superb, a mighty emperor.

DON CARLOS: Rome is on my side.

DON RUY: Valiant, firm—and yet no tyrant—that head well suited the old Germanic body! [*He bends to kiss the king's hands*] I pity you—so young and made to know so terrible a grief.

DON CARLOS: Sicily belongs to me; the pope wants it back again. An emperor cannot own Sicily; thus he makes me emperor; and I, the docile son, give Naples over. Let us first win the eagle and then we'll see whether I let his wings be clipped.

DON RUY: What joy that old ruler would feel to see your already broad brow assume his crown. My lord, we weep with you for that very great and good and Christian emperor!

DON CARLOS: The holy father is nimble. What is Sicily, after all: an island dangling from my realm; a ragged tag, a remnant that hangs off Spain and trails along beside her. He will say this: "What use have you, my son, for that misshapen shred of land that clings by a mere thread to the imperial world? Your empire is badly shaped. Quick now, the shears, and let us cut it off."

Most holy Father, thanks! For if fortune is good to me, I shall expect to stitch a couple of those pieces back again onto the holy empire; and if some few strips are missing here and there, I'll patch my estates together again with duchies and with islands!

DON RUY: May you find consolation. There is an empire of just men where the dead are found again, still holier and grander than they were in life.

DON CARLOS: This King Francis the First is an ambitious man. No sooner does the emperor die than he ogles the throne! He already has his France—a fine piece of Christian land, and well worth holding to. My grandfather the emperor used to say to King Louis, "If I were God the Father, and I had two sons, I should make the elder God, and the other king of France." [*To the duke*] Do you suppose that Francis has a chance?

DON RUY: He has a habit of success.

DON CARLOS: Everything would have to be amended. The Golden Bull forbids a foreigner to reign.

DON RUY: But in that respect, Your Highness, you are king of Spain.

DON CARLOS: But I am a citizen of Ghent.

DON RUY: His latest campaign has made King Francis very strong.

DON CARLOS: The eagle who may hatch upon my crest can spread his wings wide too.

DON RUY: Does Your Highness know Latin?

DON CARLOS: Only poorly.

DON RUY: That is a pity. The German nobles like to be addressed in Latin.

DON CARLOS: They will be satisfied with a noble Spanish. For mark my words, it makes small difference what tongue a voice may speak, if it speaks strongly enough.

I am setting out for Flanders. Your king, dear Silva, must return to you as emperor. The king of France will do all that he can to win his way; I must overtake him. I shall go shortly.

DON RUY: Will you leave us, sire, with Aragon still

unpurged of these new bandits who raise their brazen heads throughout our mountainland?

DON CARLOS: I shall leave orders with the Duke of Arcos to wipe them out.

DON RUY: And will you also command their leader to let himself be taken?

DON CARLOS: Who is their leader—his name?

DON RUY: I do not know it. But he is said to be a formidable man.

DON CARLOS: Nonsense. I know that just now he is hidden in Galicia, and can be taken with a few militia troops.

DON RUY: Then the rumors are false that say he is nearby?

DON CARLOS: Completely false. . . . You will give me a bed for the night.

DON RUY: [*Bowing to the floor*] Thank you, sire. [*Calling his servants*] All of you, do honor to the king, my guest.

[*The servants bring torches, and the duke orders them into two rows to the door in rear. Meanwhile* Doña Sol *draws imperceptibly closer to* Hernani; *the king watches the pair of them*]

DOÑA SOL: [*Low to* Hernani] Tomorrow at midnight, beneath my window—do not fail. And clap three times.

HERNANI: [*Softly*] Tomorrow night . . .

DON CARLOS: [*To himself*] Tomorrow! [*And aloud to* Doña Sol, *toward whom he moves with courtly gesture*] Allow me to escort you. [*He leads her to the door; she exits*]

HERNANI: [*His hand inside his breast, on the pommel of his dagger*] My faithful blade! . . .

DON CARLOS: [*Returning, aside*] Our friend has the expression of a man who is trapped. [*He draws* Hernani *aside*] I did you the honor, sir, of touching your sword. I could mistrust you for a hundred different reasons—but King Carlos has no taste for betrayals. Go. I am willing to protect you in your flight.

DON RUY: [*Coming closer and indicating* Hernani] Who is this gentleman?

DON CARLOS: One of my followers. He is leaving now.

[*They go out with the servants and the torches, the duke ahead of the king, with a candle in his hand*]

SCENE IV.

HERNANI: [*Alone*] One of your followers—yes, King! Your follower, true! Night and day, and step by step, I follow you. A knife in my fist I go, my eye fixed on your trail—my race in me pursues your race in you. And now besides, you are become my rival. For a moment I hung hesitant between love and hatred; my heart was not large enough to hold both you and her. In loving her I forgot the hatred for you that weighs on me; but since you wish it, since you

yourself come to remind me, good! I remember! My love bends the uncertain scales, and falls now wholly to the side of hatred. Yes, I am one of your followers. No courtier dancing in your accursed halls, no noble lord kissing your shadow, no steward denying his own man's heart for your heart's whim, no palace dog trained to slink at the king's heel, will dog your step more diligently than I! All that those Castilian grandees want of you is some pointless title, some shiny trinket, some golden sheep to hang about their throats; I'm not so foolish as to yearn so small! What I want from you is no vain favor—it is your body's soul, your vein's blood; I want what a fuming, conquering knife can dredge out from a heart's dark root. Lead on before me! I shall follow you. My vengeance is alert, it moves with me and speaks into my ear. Lead! I am here, I watch and I listen; my step seeks yours soundlessly, pursues it, and draws close. By day, my king, you'll never turn your head but you shall find me motionless and dark amid your celebration. But night you shall not turn your eyes, my king, but you shall see my burning eyes glow hot behind you! [*He goes out the small door*]

ACT II.   THE BANDIT.   SCENE I.

Saragossa. A patio in the Silva palace. At left, the palace's high walls, with a balconied window. Beneath the window is a small door. At right and rear are houses and streets. It is night. Here and there in the buildings a few windows are still showing light.

[Don Carlos, Don Sancho Sanchez de Zuñiga, Don Matias Centurion, Don Ricardo de Roxas, *all four arrive onstage, with* Don Carlos *at their head. Their hats are pulled low and they are enveloped in long cloaks whose lower edges are lifted by their spears*]

DON CARLOS: [*Surveying the balcony*] There is the balcony, and the door, just as she said. . . . My blood is boiling hot. [*Pointing to the unlit window*] No light there yet! [*His eyes rove over the other lighted casements*] Lights everywhere that are no use to me, and none where I would see one!

DON SANCHO: That traitor; my lord—you simply let him leave?

DON CARLOS: Yes.

DON MATIAS: And he may have been the bandit general!

DON CARLOS: He might have been their general or their drummer boy, but no sceptered king ever bore himself more nobly.

DON SANCHO: What was his name, my lord?

DON CARLOS: [*His eyes on the casement window*] Muñoz— . . . Fernan— . . . [*He suddenly remembers something*] A name that ends in i.

DON SANCHO: Hernani, possibly?

DON CARLOS: Yes.

DON MATIAS: Hernani? Then it *was* the chief!

DON SANCHO: [*To the king*] Do you remember anything of what he said?

DON CARLOS: [*Who has not taken his eyes from the window*] I could not hear a thing in their damned closet.

DON SANCHO: But why let him go when he was in your hands?

DON CARLOS: [*Turning slowly and staring at him*] Count of Monterey, do you question me? [*The two lords draw back and are silent*] Besides, that is not what concerns me now. I want his mistress, not his head. I want her black eyes, friends! The loveliest in the world! Two mirrors! Two black beams of light, two dark torches! I heard nothing of their babble but these few words: "Tomorrow, come at midnight"— but they are the important ones. A perfect arrangement, gentlemen, I think you will agree: while this winsome bandit dallies at some murder or other, or digging someone's grave, I come at my ease and make off with his dove.

DON RICARDO: Your Highness, it were more decisive to take the dove by killing off the vulture.

DON CARLOS: [*To Don Ricardo*] A valuable suggestion, Count! Your hand is quick!

DON RICARDO: [*Bowing deeply*] By what title does the king please to name me count?

DON SANCHO: [*Angrily*] That was an error!

DON RICARDO: [*To Don Sancho*] The king called me count.

DON CARLOS: That's enough. [*To Don Ricardo*] I dropped that title. Pick it up.

DON RICARDO: [*Bowing again*] Thank you, Highness.

DON SANCHO: [*To Don Matias*]: A fine count—a count by accident!

[*The king walks about stage rear, looking at the lighted windows impatiently. The two noblemen converse in the foreground*]

DON MATIAS: [*To Don Sancho*] But what will the king do, once he has the woman?

DON SANCHO: [*Watching Ricardo out of the corner of his eye*] Make her a countess, and then a lady in waiting; then, if he has a son by her, it will be king.

DON MATIAS: Oh, come now. A bastard? Count, even a king can never draw a king out of a countess.

DON SANCHO: He'll make her a marquise then, my dear marquis.

DON MATIAS: Bastards are brought up to be the viceroys of conquered countries—that is how they are used.

[Don Carlos *comes back*]

DON CARLOS: [*Looking about at all the lighted windows*] They are watching us like dozens of jealous eyes. . . . Well, finally—two have just gone out. Now for the rest of them! Gentlemen, how long these waiting minutes! Who can make the time move faster?

DON SANCHO: We often wonder in Your Highness' court.

DON CARLOS: And meanwhile my people are say-ing it of you [*The last bright window dims*] The last of them is out! [*He turns toward the balcony of* Doña Sol's *room; it is still dark*] You damned glass, when will you turn light? This night is very dark. Doña Sol, come shine like a star in all this blackness! [*To Don Ricardo*] What time is it?

DON RICARDO: Nearly midnight.

DON CARLOS: This business must be done with soon—the other one may come at any moment!

[Doña Sol's *window brightens. Her shadow is visible on the lighted panes*] Friends—a torch—her shadow at the window! No dawn was ever more beautiful to me than this one. I must be quick: give the signal she is waiting for, and clap my hands three times. In an instant, friends, you'll see her! . . . But our number will frighten her, perhaps—go, the three of you, into the shadow there, and watch for him. We'll share the loving pair among us—I take the lady, and you three the brigand.

DON RICARDO: A thousand thanks.

DON CARLOS: If he comes, get to him quickly and stun him with your swords. Then, while he is still unconscious, I'll go off with the girl; we shall meet later. But be sure not to kill him. He is a valiant man, and a man's death is a serious thing.

[*The two noblemen bow and leave.* Don Carlos *waits till they disappear then claps twice. At the second, the window opens, and* Doña Sol *appears on the balony*]

SCENE II.

DOÑA SOL: [*From the balcony*] Is it you, Hernani?

DON CARLOS: [*To himself*] I must not speak! [*He claps his hands once more*]

DOÑA SOL: I shall come down.

[*She closes the window, and the light goes out. A moment later, the small door opens and she emerges, a lantern in her hand and a cloak over her shoulders*]

DOÑA SOL: Hernani! [Don Carlos *pulls his hat low over his face, and hurries to her*] That is not his step! [*She turns to go back.* Don Carlos *runs to her and holes her by the arm*]

DON CARLOS: Doña Sol!

DOÑA SOL: And not his voice!

DON CARLOS: What more adoring voice could you desire? It is still a lover's voice, and a royal lover's besides.

DOÑA SOL: The king!

DON CARLOS: Wish or command—a kingdom is yours to have! For the man whose gentle grasp you would break is the king your lord, and Carlos is your slave!

DOÑA SOL: [*Struggling to free herself*] Hernani, help me!

DON CARLOS: You fear the wrong man—this is not your bandit holding you; it is the king!

DOÑA SOL: No. *You* are the bandit! Do you feel no

shame? I blush with it for you. Are these the exploits for a king to boast? To come by night and take a woman by force? My bandit is worth a thousand of you! If a man's birth matched his nobility—if God gave rank according to men's hearts, then he would be the king, and you the criminal!

DON CARLOS: [*Trying to draw her with him*] Madame—

DOÑA SOL: Have you forgotten that my father was a count?

DON CARLOS: I shall make you a duchess.

DOÑA SOL: [*Pushing him away*] Shame! [*She draws back a few steps*] There can be nothing of the sort between us, Don Carlos. My aged father poured out his blood for you. I am a noblewoman, I come from that proud blood—too haughty for a concubine, and too lowly for a bride.

DON CARLOS: Princess!

DOÑA SOL: Go offer your love games to common girls, King Carlos; else, if you dare to treat me in such disgraceful manner, I can show you quite clearly that I am a lady and a woman both.

DON CARLOS: Well then, come share my throne and my name too. Come—you shall be queen, and empress besides—

DOÑA SOL: No. That is a ruse. Besides, Your Highness, I must speak honestly—no matter if you were another man, I would rather wander with Hernani, my own king; rather live outside the world, and the law, in hunger, and thirst, forever hunted and in flight, rather share his sorry destiny from day to day, share his solitude, his battles and his exile, his grief, his poverty, his fear—I would rather all that than be empress to any emperor.

DON CARLOS: How fortunate he is!

DOÑA SOL: He is a pitiful exile!

DON CARLOS: But fortunate even so, for he is loved. I am alone, and an angel walks with him. Do you loathe me?

DOÑA SOL: I do not love you.

DON CARLOS: [*Seizing her violently*] Whether you love me or not can make no difference—you will come! My hand is stronger than yours—you will come. I want you! We shall soon see if I am king of Spain and of the Indies for nothing.

DOÑA SOL: [*Struggling*] Have pity on me, my lord! You are king! You are royal! You have but to select a duchess, a marquise, or a countess. The loyal ladies of the court can always find a love that's ready made to answer yours. But my exiled beloved, what did the miserly heavens ever grant to him? You have Castile, Aragon, and Navarre; and Murcia and León; ten other realms, and Flanders; you have India with all its golden mines! You own an empire vast beyond any other king's, a domain so wide it never sees a setting sun! And with all of this, could you, the king, take a poor girl from him who has nothing else? [*She throws herself to her knees. He tries to draw her away*]

DON CARLOS: Come! I do not hear your words.

Come, and if you will, I give you any four of my Spains. Which will you have? Come, choose them! [*She struggles in his arms*]

DOÑA SOL: For my honor's sake, I want nothing of you but this dagger, sir! [*She wrenches the knife from his belt. He releases her and falls back*] Come forward now! Take a single step!

DON CARLOS: So that is how she plays! I do not wonder now that she should love a rebel! [*He moves to take a step; she raises the dagger*]

DOÑA SOL: One step and I kill you and myself. [*He draws back again. She turns away and cries loudly*] Hernani! Hernani!

DON CARLOS: Quiet!

DOÑA SOL: [*The knife ready*] One step, and all is over!

DON CARLOS: Madam! Now you have gone too far; I can be gentle no longer. I have three men here to force you . . .

HERNANI: [*Springing from behind him*] There is one you did not count!

[*The king turns and sees* Hernani *poised behind him in the shadows, his arms crossed under his long cloak, and the broad border of his hat raised.* Doña Sol *cries out, runs to* Hernani, *and throws her arms around him*]

SCENE III.

HERNANI: [*Motionless, his arms still crossed and his glittering eyes set on the king*] As God is my witness, I did not want to confront you now, nor here.

DOÑA SOL: Hernani, save me from him!

HERNANI: Be calm, my love.

DON CARLOS: What are my men doing in the town to have let this gypsy chieftain pass? Monterey! [*He calls*]

HERNANI: Your men are in the hands of mine— no use to cry out for their powerless swords. For any three that came to your call, sixty would run to mine. Sixty, and every one of them worth four of yours. So . . . we shall settle our quarrel between the two of us. You raised your hand against this girl! It was an unwise move, my lord king of Castile; a coward's act.

DON CARLOS: [*Smiling disdainfully*] My lord bandit, let there be no reproach from you to me.

HERNANI: He laughs! I am no king; but when a king insults me, and then scoffs, my rage springs up and lifts me to his height. Beware, for when I am offended, men fear my angry brow more than any kingly crest! You are mad if you have some illusion of hope. [*He seizes the king*] Do you know whose hand grips you now? Listen. Your father sentenced mine to death. For that I hate you. You took my title and my estate. For that I hate you. We love the same woman, both of us. For that I hate you, I hate you for everything—I hate you from my soul!

DON CARLOS: Very well.

HERNANI: And yet this evening my hatred seemed

far away. I felt only one desire, one heat, one need —Doña Sol! I hastened here, full of love—and I find you in this vile attempt on her! I had forgotten you, but you are set across my path! You are mad, Don Carlos! You are caught in your own snare without help, or hope of escape. I have you in my hand! You are alone, surrounded by furious enemies. What will you do?

DON CARLOS: [*Proudly*] You dare to question me!

HERNANI: I will not have you struck down by some strange hand—my vengeance must not elude me now. No one but I shall touch you; defend yourself. [*He draws his sword*]

DON CARLOS: I am the king, your master. Strike; but I will not duel with you.

HERNANI: If you recall, only yesterday you crossed your blade with mine.

DON CARLOS: Yesterday it still could be. I did not know your name, nor you my rank. Today you know who I am and I know you.

HERNANI: Perhaps.

DON CARLOS: No duel, then. Assassinate me.

HERNANI: Do you suppose that kings are sacred to me? Draw your sword!

DON CARLOS: You ´must murder me. [Hernani *draws back.* Don Carlos *sets his eagle eyes on him*] Do you believe your bandit gangs can roam through our towns at will? Striped with gore and stained with murder as you are, do you believe that you can still strut and pose as noble men, and expect that we should dignify your knives by striking ours against them? Are we such gullible victims? No, crime holds you in its grip; it trails you where you go. And we—are we to duel with you? Never. Murder me.

HERNANI: [*Brooding and thoughtful, stands for a few seconds gripping and releasing the hilt of his sword; then he turns abruptly back to the king, and snaps the swordblade against the flagstones*] Then leave here. [*The king half turns back toward him, and stares haughtily at him*] Go.

DON CARLOS: Very well, sir. In a few hours I shall return. My first concern will be to call for the prosecutor. Is there a price already set upon your head?

HERNANI: Yes.

DON CARLOS: From this day forward you shall be considered a traitor and a rebel. I warn you of this; I shall pursue you everywhere. I hereby place you under the ban of the kingdom.

HERNANI: I am already banished.

DON CARLOS: Good.

HERNANI: But France is close by Spain; it will be a haven.

DON CARLOS: I shall be emperor. I set you under the ban of all the empire.

HERNANI: As you will. I have the rest of the world to defy you from. There are many other lands where your power cannot reach me.

DON CARLOS: And when I have the world?

HERNANI: Then I shall have my grave.

DON CARLOS: I will put an end to your insolent activities.

HERNANI: Revenge is lame; it comes with halting steps—but it does come.

DON CARLOS: [*Half laughing, disdainful*] That I should touch the woman this outlaw loves!

HERNANI: [*His eyes blazing again*] Have you forgotten you are still within my grasp? You would-be Roman Caesar, do not remind me that you lie frail and small in my hand's cup; that if I were to clench this too-honorable fist, I should crush the imperial eagle in the egg!

DON CARLOS: Then do so.

HERNANI: Go! Leave this place! [*He takes off his mantle and throws it over the king's shoulders*] Take my cloak, and go; without it you could not pass alive among my men. [*The king wraps himself in the cloak*] You may leave in safety now. My thirsting rage will let no hand but mine cut off your life.

DON CARLOS: Remember how you spoke to me tonight, and ask no mercy of me when we meet again. [*He goes out*]

SCENE IV.

DOÑA SOL: [*Seizing* Hernani's hand] Let us go now quickly!

HERNANI: [*Holding her away, with gentle gravity*] My love, you have determined to join more firmly in my misery each day; to hold to it always, and to share my days without reserve until they end. Your scheme is a noble one, and one that is worthy of so steadfast a heart. But Lord God, you can see it is too late now to accept so much of her, and heedlessly to carry off to my lair this beauteous gem a king wants for his own; to have my Doña Sol follow me and to own her, to take her life and wed it to my own, to lead her off with no shame or remorse—there is no time! The scaffold looms too near!

DOÑA SOL: What are you saying?

HERNANI: I defied the king to his face, and he will punish me for having dared to free him. He is gone; perhaps already in his palace, gathering his men, his soldiers, and his noblemen; calling his executioners . . .

DOÑA SOL: Hernani! I am frightened! Then hurry —we must leave now together!

HERNANI: Together . . . no. No. The time for that is past. Doña Sol, when first you revealed yourself to me, so good, and kind enough to love me with a willing love, I dared to offer you everything I have: my mountain, my woods, my stream. Your sympathy emboldened me; I offered you my outlaw's bread, and half the green and tufted bed the forest gives me. But to offer you half my gallows—oh no, my Doña Sol— the gallows is mine alone.

DOÑA SOL: Yet you promised to share everything.

HERNANI: [*Falling to his knees*] My saint! At this moment when death perhaps is near, when my dark destiny draws to a dark close, I must tell you this: banished, and burdened by a solemn mission born in a bloody cradle; and as black as is the grief that shades my life—I am a happy man, and call upon all men to envy me! For you have loved me, for you have told me so, for you have leaned and blessed my cursed brow!

DOÑA SOL: [*Bending over him*] Hernani!

HERNANI: How kind is the fate that set this flower at the chasm's edge for me! [*He rises*] And I speak not for your sake; I speak for the listening heavens, and for God.

DOÑA SOL: Let me go with you.

HERNANI: It would be a crime to wrench out the flower as I fall into the abyss! No, I have breathed its perfume, and that is enough. Go link the life I've troubled to another man's. Marry the old duke. I myself unbind you. I return into my night. And you—be happy, and forget!

DOÑA SOL: No, I shall come with you. I want my share of your shroud! I shall go where you go!

HERNANI: [*Grasping her in his arms*] Ah, let me go alone! [*He turns from her with a convulsive movement*]

DOÑA SOL: [*Mournfully, and clasping her hands*] Hernani, you would go from me! So, foolish woman, you give your life and see it turned away; and after so much love, and so much pain, you do not earn even the joy of dying by his side.

HERNANI: I am a banished man! I am outlawed! I bring misfortune!

DOÑA SOL: You are a thankless man.

HERNANI: [*Turning back to her*] Then no! no, I shall stay. You desire it—then I am here. Come . . . oh come into my arms! I shall stay, and for as long as you shall want me. Let us forget the others. We shall stay here. [*He seats her on a bench*] Sit here on this stone. [*He settles at her feet*] Flames from your eyes wash over my lids; sing me some song as you used to sing at evening, with tears in your dark eyes. Let us be happy! And drink, for the cup is filled, for this hour is ours, and all the rest is madness. Speak to me, sing, and say: Is it not sweet to love and to know you are adored? To be true? To be alone? And is it not sweet to speak our love at night, when all's at rest? . . . Oh let me sleep and dream upon your breast. Doña Sol! My love, my beauty!

[*Sound of alarm bells in the distance*]

DOÑA SOL: [*Rising, frightened*] The alarm! Do you hear it? The alarm!

HERNANI: [*Still on his knees*] No . . . they are tolling our marriage. [*The sound of bells grows louder. There are cries, torches, and lights at all the windows, on all the roofs, in every street*]

DOÑA SOL: Hernani, flee! Almighty God! All Saragossa is alight!

HERNANI: [*Half rising*] Our wedding shall be lit by torches!

DOÑA SOL: A deathly wedding! A marriage of the tomb!

[*Sound of swords and cries*]

HERNANI: [*Reclining again on the stone bench*] Come lie here in my arms!

[*A mountaineer runs in, his sword in hand*]

MOUNTAINEER: Sir, long columns of militia and police are entering the square! Be quick, my lord! [Hernani *rises*]

DOÑA SOL: [*Pale*] You were right; he did prepare this.

MOUNTAINEER: Men—to the rescue!

HERNANI: [*To the* Mountaineer] I am ready. All is well. [*Cries offstage:* "Death to the bandit!"] Your sword. [*To Doña Sol*] Then farewell!

DOÑA SOL: You are lost through my doing! Where will you go? [*Pointing to the small door*] Come this way! We can leave by that open door.

HERNANI: Abandon my comrades? What are you saying?

DOÑA SOL: This clamor stabs my heart. [*She holds* Hernani] Remember that if you die, I die!

HERNANI: [*Holding her close*] One kiss!

DOÑA SOL: My husband! My Hernani! Oh, my master!

HERNANI: [*Kissing her brow*] Alas—it is our first.

DOÑA SOL: It is perhaps our last.

[*He leaves. She falls to the bench*]

ACT III.   THE OLD MAN.   SCENE I.

The Silva Castle, in the mountains of Aragon. The portrait gallery of the Silva family: a large hall in which the portraits form the decor, in rich frames with ducal coronets and golden blazons. In rear, a tall gothic door. Between every two portraits stands a full panoply of armor, a suit representing each of the different centuries.

[Doña Sol, *pale, standing by a table;* Don Ruy Gomez de Silva, *seated in his great ducal chair of oak*]

DON RUY GOMEZ: At last! Today, within an hour, you shall be my duchess, and I no longer an uncle. And you will embrace me—but have you forgiven me? I was wrong, I know; I caused you shame, and made your cheek turn pale. My doubts surged up too soon; I should not have condemned you thus before I heard you. How false appearances can be—how unjust we are! Two fine young men were there indeed with you; still, I should not have believed my eyes. But what can you expect, my poor child, from an old man like me?

DOÑA SOL: [*Motionless and grave*] You still return to that. Who has blamed you for it?

DON RUY GOMEZ: I myself! I was wrong. I should have known a Doña Sol would allow no lovers courting—not such a woman as you, nor one whose heart is flushed with good Spanish blood.

DOÑA SOL: It is good and pure blood indeed, my lord; perhaps it will soon be seen.

DON RUY GOMEZ: [*Rising and going toward her*] Understand, a man is not master over himself, when he loves as I love you, and when he is old. Why might a man be jealous, and even cruel? Because he is old. Because grace and fairness, youth in another man all make for fear, all threaten him. Because he is envious of others, and ashamed of himself. What a mockery is this limping love—it brings a drunken fire back to the heart, it makes the soul young again, but it forgets the body! Often when some young shepherd goes by—ah yes, it's come to that—as we pass, he singing and I musing, he to his green pasture, I to my dark halls, often I murmur low beneath my breath "How gladly I would give my battlements, my ancient ducal keep; and I would give my fields and forestlands, and the vast herds that browse upon my hills, my ancient name, my title, and all my ruins, and all my old forbears who soon will welcome me among them—I would give it all for his new-thatched cottage and for his youthful brow!" His hair is black, his eye gleams like your own; you might see him and say "A young man!" And then think of me who am old. I know this. I bear the Silva name, but it is no longer enough. And my mind is ever running on this theme. You see how great a love I bear you. I would give all I have to be young and fair as you. But what am I dreaming of, I young and fair? I who must go so long before you to the grave!

DOÑA SOL: Who can tell?

DON RUY GOMEZ: But believe me, Doña Sol; such gay gallants as those can give no love more lasting than fine phrases. Let a girl love and give her faith to such a man, she may die of it and he will laugh. All those young cockerels, with their bright wings and with their languid song—their love molts like their plumage. The aged ones, whose tone and tints are muted by the years, have a more trusty wing and they are better, though less fair to see. We love well. Our steps may be heavy, our eyes dull, perhaps, and our brows deep-lined—but the heart does not show the crease of age. Alas! When an old man loves, one must go gently; the heart is always young, and it still can bleed. My love is no crystal toy that gleams and trembles; it is a stern and solid love—deep, sure, paternal, friendly, carved of the same oak as my ducal throne. See then how I love you—and I love you too a hundred other ways, as one loves the dawn, as one loves flowers, and as one loves the skies. To know that I shall see you every day—you with your graceful step and your pure brow, the rich fire in your proud eye—I laugh, and in my soul I feel an endless joy.

DOÑA SOL: Alas!

DON RUY GOMEZ: And then, you know, when a man is waning limb by limb, when he stumbles against the marble of the tomb—the world thinks well of the woman watching over him; an innocent dove, an angel sheltering him and suffering a useless antique good only for death. It is a sacred work, and they are right to praise it, when a devoted heart performs this crowning good—to console a dying man until he ends his day—and even perhaps without love, has all the look of love.

Ah, you shall be my woman-hearted angel, who still sweetens the soul of a pitiful old man, and helps to bear the weight of his last years—a daughter in respect, a sister in compassion.

DOÑA SOL: Far from preceding me, you may well follow, my lord. Youth is not reason enough for living. Often the old ones linger, the younger go before; suddenly their eyelids drop like an open tomb whose stone falls back to place.

DON RUY GOMEZ: What mournful talk! I must scold you, my child—a day like this is holy and joyful. But the hour is late; how is it you are not ready for the chapel? Hurry then, and dress yourself. I shall count every second. Put on your wedding gown!

DOÑA SOL: There still is time.

DON RUY GOMEZ: Not much of it. [*A page enters*] What does Iaquez want of us?

PAGE: My lord, a man—a pilgrim or a beggar—is at the door and asks you for asylum.

DON RUY GOMEZ: Whatever he may be, good fortune enters with the stranger. Let him come. Has there been a report from the outside? What do they say of the treacherous bandit who fills our forests with his rebel acts?

PAGE: Hernani is done for; the mountain lion is finished.

DOÑA SOL: [*Aside*] Oh God!

DON RUY GOMEZ: What?

PAGE: The band has been destroyed. They say the king himself set after them. Hernani's head is worth a thousand crowns; but I have heard he is dead.

DOÑA SOL: [*Aside*] Without me, Hernani!

DON RUY GOMEZ: Thanks be to heaven! the rebel's dead! Now, my dear, we can truly rejoice. Go and prepare yourself, my love, my pride! Today's a double holiday!

DOÑA SOL: [*Aside*] . . . A wedding dress for widow's weeds! . . . [*She goes out*]

DON RUY GOMEZ: [*To the page*] Send her the jewel case I prepared for her. [*He sits down again in his armchair*] I want to see her adorned like a madonna; I want her gentle eyes and all my jewels to make her so beautiful a pilgrim would fall upon his knees at sight of her. Oh—and the one who has begged shelter of us, tell him to enter, and ask his pardon. Quickly. [*The page salutes and goes out*] Leaving a guest to linger at the door! A shameful thing.

[*The rear door opens. Hernani appears, disguised as a pilgrim. The duke rises and goes toward him*]

SCENE II.

HERNANI: [*Stopping on the threshold*] My lord, peace and happiness!

DON RUY GOMEZ: [*Saluting him with a gesture of his hand*] Peace and happiness to you, my guest! [Hernani *enters. The duke sits again*] You are a pilgrim?

HERNANI: Yes. [*He bows*]

DON RUY GOMEZ: You come from Armillas?

HERNANI: No. I took another road. There was fighting there.

DON RUY GOMEZ: The outlaw's men?

HERNANI: I do not know.

DON RUY GOMEZ: And Hernani, their leader—what of him? Do you know?

HERNANI: Who is this man, my lord?

DON RUY GOMEZ: You do not know him? A pity, then you shall not win the bounty for him. Hernani is a rebel who has gone too long unpunished. If you go to Madrid, you still may see him hang.

HERNANI: I am not going there.

DON RUY GOMEZ: The reward goes to whatever man can take him.

HERNANI: [*Aside*] Let them come!

DON RUY GOMEZ: Where are you bound for, good pilgrim?

HERNANI: My lord, I go to Saragossa.

DON RUY GOMEZ: For a vow made to some saint? to Our Lady?

HERNANI: Yes, Duke—to Our Lady.

DON RUY GOMEZ: Of Pilar?

HERNANI: Of Pilar.

DON RUY GOMEZ: It would be an empty soul that did not fulfill the vows made to the saints. But when you have accomplished yours, have you no further plans? To see the Lady of the Pillar is all you want?

HERNANI: Yes, I want to see the torches and the candles burn; to see Our Lady glowing in her brilliant shrine, with all her golden vestments, and then turn home again.

DON RUY GOMEZ: Very good. Your name, my brother? I am Ruy de Silva.

HERNANI: [*Hesitating*] My name . . . ?

DON RUY GOMEZ: You need not pronounce it, if you so choose. None has the right to demand it here. Have you not come to ask asylum?

HERNANI: Yes, Duke.

DON RUY GOMEZ: Thank you. Be welcome; stay here, my friend, and want for nothing. As for your name, you are called my guest. Whoever you be, it is well. I'd welcome Satan himself with peace of mind, if God sent him to me.

[*The double door at rear opens.* Doña Sol *enters dressed in Castilion wedding costume of the period. Behind her are pages and attendants; two women carry upon a velvet cushion a chiseled silver box which they place upon a table. It holds a rich array of jewels, a duchess' coronet, bracelets, collars, necklaces, pearls, and diamonds in a tumbled heap. Hernani, breathless and startled, his eyes burning, stares at* Doña Sol *without listening to the duke*]

SCENE III.

DON RUY GOMEZ: [*Continuing*] Here is my own holy lady. A prayer to her will bring you good fortune. [*He goes to offer his hand to* Doña Sol, *who is still pale and grave*] My lovely bride, come forward. What? You wear no ring, and still no coronet?

HERNANI: [*In a thunderous voice*] Who here would earn a thousand crowns? [*All turn toward him, astonished. He rips off his pilgrim's robe, throws it to the door, and appears in his mountaineer's outfit*] I am Hernani.

DOÑA SOL: [*Aside, joyfully*] He is alive!

HERNANI: [*To the valets*] I am the man they seek. [*To the duke*] You asked if I were called—what, Perez, or Diego? No, I am named Hernani. It is a name much greater, an exile's name, an outlaw's name! You see this head? It is worth enough to pay for your whole feast! [*To the attendants*] I offer it to all of you. You will be well rewarded! Take it! Tie my hands, and bind my feet—bind them! No, that is needless; there is a chain that holds me and that I shall never break!

[*Horror on* Doña Sol's *part*]

DON RUY GOMEZ: Madness—my guest is a madman!

HERNANI: Your guest is a bandit.

DOÑA SOL: Do not listen to him!

HERNANI: I have said what I have said.

DON RUY GOMEZ: A thousand golden crowns! Sir, the sum is a high one, and I cannot be sure of all my men.

HERNANI: What does it matter? So much the better if there is one among them who will do it. [*To the attendants*] Give me up! Sell me!

DON RUY GOMEZ: [*Trying to quiet him*] Be still! Someone may take you at your word.

HERNANI: My friends, it is a matchless opportunity! I tell you I am the criminal, the rebel—I am Hernani!

DON RUY GOMEZ: Quiet!

HERNANI: Hernani!

DOÑA SOL: [*Her voice faint, in his ear*] Oh be still, my love!

HERNANI: [*Half turning toward her*] There is a wedding here! and I shall share in it! My bride awaits me too. [*To the duke*] She is less lovely than your own, my lord, but no less faithful. Her name is Death. [*To the servants*] Not one of you steps forward?

DOÑA SOL: [*Low*] Have pity on me!

HERNANI: [*To the servants*] Hernani! A thousand crowns in gold!

DON RUY GOMEZ: It is the devil himself!

HERNANI: [*To the young servant*] Come, you there; you can win the bounty; you shall be rich, and from a servant become a man again. [*To the other unmoving men*] And you, you tremble too! Oh, have I not misery enough!

DON RUY GOMEZ: Brother, in touching your head they risk their own. Were you Hernani, were you a thousand times worse; if the reward for your head were more than gold, were it a whole empire, I still must protect you in this house against the king himself, for as my guest you are here by will of God. May I die if a single hair falls from your brow. [*To Doña Sol*] My niece, within the hour you shall be my wife. Go to your rooms. I must order the castle armed, and bar the door. [*He goes out, and the servants follow him*]

HERNANI: [*Glancing despairingly at his weaponless sash*] Not even a knife!

[*When the duke has gone,* Doña Sol *starts to follow her ladies off, then stops. When they have disappeared, she comes anxiously back to* Hernani]

SCENE IV.

[Hernani *gazes coldly at the nuptial jewel casket on the table, and seems almost unaware of her. Then he raises his head abruptly, and his eyes flare*]

HERNANI: I compliment you! You cannot imagine how thoroughly charming I find your ornaments . . . Enchanting; really, quite admirable. [*He moves to the casket*] The ring is most tasteful; I like the coronet; the necklace is lovely work, the bracelet quite rare— but a hundred, a hundred times less so than the woman who can hide such perfidy behind so pure a brow! [*He examines the box again*] And what have you paid for all of this? A little of your love? Why, excellent! That is nothing at all. Good God! To so betray, to feel no shame, and still live on! [*Looking through the jewel box*] But perhaps though, after all, these are no more than painted pearls, and copper that seems gold, and glass and lead; unreal diamonds, false sapphires, false gems and glittering stones! If that is so, then your heart is false as well. Duchess— false as these ornaments, and you are only gilt! [*He goes back to the case*] But no. No. It is all real, all good, and every piece is fine. He would not dare to cheat, so near the grave. There is nothing lacking. [*He takes one piece after another from the case*] Necklets, brilliants, ear pendants . . . a ducal coronet, a ring of gold—marvelous! A fitting thanks to steadfast, true, and deepest love—the precious jewel case!

DOÑA SOL: [*Going to the casket; she reaches beneath the jewels, and draws out a dagger*] You have not reached deep enough. Here is the knife I took from King Carlos with my holy Lady's help, when he was offering me a throne; and I refused, for you who vilify me.

HERNANI: [*Dropping to her feet*] Oh—I beg from my knees—let me wipe those bitter beloved tears out from your sorrowing eyes. Take my blood for your tears!

DOÑA SOL: [*Softened*] Hernani! I love you and forgive you. I feel only love for you.

HERNANI: She has forgiven me, and loves me! But how can I forgive and love myself again, after what I have said? My heavenly angel, show me where you have walked, and let me kiss the pavement where it was.

DOÑA SOL: My love!

HERNANI: No, I cannot be but hateful to my eyes! Listen, say to me: "I love you!" Assure a doubtful heart, and tell me. Often a woman's lips have healed many pains with those few words.

DOÑA SOL: [*Absorbed, unhearing*] How could he think my love so short of memory? That lusterless men could shrink a heart wherein his name has entered down to the size of other loves, however noble the world might think them!

HERNANI: I have blasphemed! Doña Sol, if I were in your stead, I should have had enough; I should be weary of this wild fool, of this brooding, senseless man who knows not how to kiss till he has wounded. I should tell him "Go." Turn me away, you must! And I shall only bless you, for you were good, and kind; for you have borne me far too long already, for I am evil—I would darken your days with my black nights.

It is too much—your spirit is high and good and pure; if I am bad, why should you suffer for it? Wed the old duke, he is a good man, and noble; he owns Olmedo from his mother, Alcala from his father. Once more I bid you, be rich with him; be happy! Do you know what splendid gifts my own generous hand can offer you? A dowry of sorrow. A choice between blood and tears. Exile, chains, death, the constant fear around me—there is your golden necklace, and your handsome crown, and never has proud husband offered his bride a richer treasure chest of pain and mourning! Marry the old man, I tell you. He deserves you. Who would ever match my doomed head with your clear brow? Who ever, seeing the two of us—you calm and fair, me violent and perilous, you tranquil and blossoming like a shaded flower, me storm-tossed against a thousand different reefs—who would think to say our fates are joined by a single law? No. God, who determines good things, did not make you for me. I have no heaven-sent right to you. I am resigned. I have your heart, but I have it by theft. I hand it to another, worthier man. Heaven has never consented to our love. When I told you it was your destiny, I lied. And in any case, farewell to all revenge and love! My day is done. I'll go then, futile, with my double dream, unable either to win love or to punish. I should have been built to hate, but I can only love! Forgive me, and flee! These prayers are all I ask; do not refuse them, for they are my last. You live, and I am dead. You must not wall yourself into my tomb with me.

DOÑA SOL: Ungrateful love!

HERNANI: Mountains of Aragon! Galicia, Estremadura! I bring misfortune to all who join with me. I have taken your best sons to serve my claims; relentless, I have sent them into battle, and they are dead of it. They were the most valiant in all of valiant

Spain. And they are dead. They have fallen in the mountains, all of them upon their backs as brave men do, before God; if they were to open their eyes again, they would see the blue heavens. And this is what I do to all who join me. Is this a destiny that you should want to share? Doña Sol, take the duke—take hell itself, take the king! Anyone is better! There is not one friend left who thinks of me; everything else has gone, and now your turn has come to leave me too, for I must live alone. Flee my contamination; do not make a religion of love. Oh, have mercy on yourself, and flee! . . . Perhaps you think me a man like all the rest, a rational thing who first perceives his goal and then will move straight toward it. Do not be fooled—I am not such a man. I am a resistless energy—the blind and deafened agent of doleful mysteries, a soul of sorrows bound together with darkness. Where am I bound? I cannot say. But yet I feel myself hurled on by some impulsive gale, some wild determination. I fall, and fall, and never do I rest. . . . If once, gasping for breath, I dare to turn my head, a voice commands "Go on!"; and the chasm is a deep one, and the depth of it is red with blood or flame! And meanwhile, along my headlong course, all things are crushed, or die. Woe to him who comes close to me! Oh, flee! Turn from my fated path. Against my will I'll do you injury!

DOÑA SOL: Oh God!

HERNANI: My devil is a fearsome one—the single miracle he cannot work is my happiness. And you are happiness! So you are not meant for me; seek out another man. Heaven has rejected me; if ever it should smile upon my fate, do not believe in it! It would only be in irony. Marry the duke.

DOÑA SOL: It still was not enough—you tore my heart and now you crush it. You do not love me now.

HERNANI: You are my heart, my soul! The glowing hearth that warms me by its flames is you! Do not hate me that I flee, my love.

DOÑA SOL: I do not hate you. But I shall die of it.

HERNANI: Die? For whom? For me? Could you die for so little?

DOÑA SOL: [Letting her tears come] It is all!

HERNANI: [Sitting beside her] You weep, and once more through my doing. And who will punish me? For you, I know, will pardon me again. Can you ever know what pain I feel when even a single tear drowns the radiance in your eyes? For their brightness is my joy. Oh, my friends are dead! I am a fool. Forgive me. I want to love, but I do not know the way—and yet I love so deeply! Weep no more—let's rather die. If I owned a world I would give it to you. What misery this is!

DOÑA SOL: [Throwing herself at his neck] Oh my proud, my noble lion! I love you.

HERNANI: How supreme a blessing love would be, if one could die of loving too well!

DOÑA SOL: I love you, my lord! I love you and I am wholly yours!

HERNANI: [Dropping his head onto her shoulder]

How sweet a dagger blow would be from you. . . .

DOÑA SOL: [Imploring] Have you no fear that God will punish you for words like those?

HERNANI: [Still leaning on her breast] Let him unite us then! . . . You wish it—let it be! I have fought against it!

[They gaze ecstatically at one another in an embrace, hearing nothing, seeing nothing else, and totally absorbed in their own gaze. Don Ruy Gomez enters by the door at rear. He sees them and stops frozen on the doorsill]

SCENE V.

DON RUY GOMEZ: [Motionless, his arms crossed, on the threshold] Then this is hospitality's reward!

DOÑA SOL: It is the duke! [The two turn as if shocked awake]

DON RUY GOMEZ: [Still unmoving] Are these my wages, guest? Run, my lord host, and see if the wall is high enough, if the gate is strongly barred and the archer in his tower; go look once, and once again, about your castle for our sake. Look through your arsenal for armor that will fit—try on your battle trappings again at sixty years! And here's our kind of loyalty in payment for your good faith. You do that for us; we shall do this for you. Saints in heaven! I have lived more than sixty years, and seen a hundred bandits, with lawless and untrammeled soul; often, as I drew my dagger from its sheath, I have flushed the hangman's game where I walked. I have seen murderers, forgers, traitors; and faithless grooms serve poison to their masters. I have seen men die without the cross, and without prayer. I saw Sforza, and Borgia; I see Luther now—but never have I seen evil so great as to betray one's host in the face of heaven's thunder! I come from other times. So black a treason petrifies an old man on the threshold of his home; the aging master, as he waits to fall, takes on the aura of a statue carved for his own tomb. Moors and Castilians! Tell me, what is this man? [He raises his eyes and runs them over the portraits that circle the hall] Oh all ye Silvas who hear me now, forgive me if I say this to you—forgive me if my wrath pronounces hospitality a poor adviser!

HERNANI: [Rising] Duke—

DON RUY: Silence! [He takes three or four slow steps into the hall, and again looks about him at the Silva portraits on the walls] Sacred departed ones! My ancestors! Men of iron! You who see all that comes from heaven and hell—tell me, my lords, tell me—what is this man? He is not Hernani, no; his name is Judas! Oh strain to speak, and tell me who he is! [Crossing his arms] Have you ever in your times seen such a thing? No!

HERNANI: My lord duke—

DON RUY GOMEZ: [Still to the portraits] Do you see this? The villain wants to speak! But you can read better in his soul than I. Oh do not hear him, he is a knave! He will tell you he sees that my own hand longs to drench my house with blood; that perhaps my heart is brewing some revenge amid its storm, some vengeance like the feast of the Seven Heads.[1] He will declare he is an exile, and that the name of Silva will ring with all the horror of the Lara name. He will say he is my guest, and yours as well. . . . My fathers, oh my sires, say, am I to blame? Judge now between us!

HERNANI: Ruy Gomez de Silva, if ever a noble brow was raised to heaven, if ever there was fine heart, or lofty soul, they are yours, my lord! I who speak to you am guilty; I have nothing more to say than that I am most surely damned. Yes, I desired to take your bride from you; I did wish to soil your marriage bed, and that is infamous. I have life and blood in me—you have the right to spill it, then wipe your sword, and think no more of it.

DOÑA SOL: My lord, the fault is mine, not his! Strike me instead!

HERNANI: Be silent, Doña Sol. This moment is supreme; this time belongs to me, and it is all I own. Then let me talk to the duke. Sir, believe these last words from my lips: I swear that I am guilty, but be at peace, for she is innocent. That is the whole tale— I guilty and she pure. Your good faith must go to her, and the thrust of a sword or knife to me. Then toss the body away and wash the floor if you wish; it matters not.

DOÑA SOL: No! I alone have done it all! Because I love him. [Don Ruy *starts at this word, and turns a terrible gaze on* Doña Sol. *She throws herself to her knees*] Yes, forgive me. I love him, my lord.

DON RUY GOMEZ: You love him! [*To* Hernani] Then tremble! [*A blare of trumpets outside. The page enters. To the page*] What is that sound?

PAGE: It is the king himself, my lord, with a troop of archers, and his herald.

DOÑA SOL: The king! A final stab of fate!

PAGE: [*To the duke*] He demands to know the reason why the gate is closed, and wants it opened.

DON RUY GOMEZ: Open to the king. [*The page bows and leaves*]

DOÑA SOL: He is lost!

[Don Ruy *goes to one of the paintings, which is his own portrait, the last on the left; he touches a spring, the portrait turns out like a door, and shows a hiding place in the wall. He turns to* Hernani]

DON RUY GOMEZ: Step in here, sir.

HERNANI: My life belongs to you. Surrender it, my lord; I hold it ready. I am your prisoner.

[*He steps into the hiding place. Don Ruy touches the spring again, and the painting moves back into place*]

PAGE: [*Returning*] His Highness the King. [Doña Sol *quickly lowers her veil. The double door opens.*

---

[1] The heads of his seven children were served up to their father at table by their uncle, Ruy Velasquez de Lara.

Don Carlos *enters outfitted for war, followed by a crowd of gentlemen armed as he is, and halberdiers, arquebusiers, and crossbowmen*]

SCENE VI.

[Don Carlos *advances slowly, his left hand on the hilt of his sword, his right inside his bosom, and stares at the duke in anger. The duke steps before the king and bows deeply. Silence. Suspense and fear in the atmosphere. Finally the king, reaching the duke, lifts his own head abruptly*]

DON CARLOS: How is that today, my cousin, your gate is so firmly locked? By the very saints, I had thought your blade more rusty by now! I should not have imagined it would be so quick to flash in your fist again when we should come to see you. [Don Ruy Gomez *attempts to speak, but the king continues, with an imperious gesture*] It is a little late to play the young man! Do we wear a turban? Are we named Boabdil, or Mohammed, and not Carlos— answer!—that you should lower the portcullis or raise the bridge before us?

DON RUY GOMEZ: [*Bowing*]: Highness—

DON CARLOS: [*To his men*] Take the keys and seize the gates. [*Two officers go out. Several others arrange the soldiers into triple file in the hall, from the king to the main door.* Don Carlos *turns again toward the duke*] So, you yearn to awaken dead mutinies: God in heaven—if you dukes assume such airs with me, the king will act the king! I shall go about among the lofty mountain peaks and crush their lordships in their battlemented nests with my own warring hands!

DON RUY GOMEZ: [*Straightening*] Highness, the Silvas are loyal—

DON CARLOS: [*Interrupting him*] Answer me without guile, Duke, or I shall have your eleven towers razed to earth. A spark still glows from the extinguished blaze; from all the slaughtered bandits, their chief survives. Who is concealing him? It is you! This Hernani, this vicious rebel—you are hiding him here within your castle now!

DON RUY GOMEZ: My lord, it is true.

DON CARLOS: Very well. I want his head—or else your own, you understand, my cousin?

DON RUY GOMEZ: [*Bowing*] You shall be satisfied.

[Doña Sol *hides her face in her hands and falls into a chair*]

DON CARLOS: [*Softening*] Ah, you improve. Now give me my prisoner.

[*The duke crosses his arms, lowers his head, and remains thoughtful for a few moments. The king and* Doña Sol *watch him in silence, and with contrary emotions. Finally the duke raises his head, goes to the king, takes his hand, and leads him slowly up to the oldest of the portraits, the one starting the row at the spectator's right*]

DON RUY GOMEZ: [*Showing the portrait to the king*]

This is the oldest of the Silvas, the forefather, the ancestor, the great man! Don Silvius, who three times was Roman consul. [*Moving to the next portrait*] Here is Don Galceran de Silva, the other Cid. At Toro, near Valladolid, there is a golden case that holds his remains, and a thousand candles burn around the shrine. He liberated León from the tribute of the hundred virgins.[2] [*He passes to another*] Don Blas, who by his own decision and his conscience placed himself in exile, for having given the king poor counsel. [*At another*] Christoval. At the battle of Escalona, the king Don Sancho was forced to flee on foot, and the furious blows fell harshest around his royal white plume. He cried out "Christoval!" Christoval took on the plume and gave his horse. [*At the next*] Don Jorge, who paid the ransom for Ramirez, king of Aragon.

DON CARLOS: [*Crossing his arms and looking at* Don Ruy *from head to toe*] Don Ruy, by God, I wonder at you! I want my prisoner now!

DON RUY: [*Moving to another portrait*] This is Ruy Gomez de Silva; he was named Grand Master of Saint James and of Calatrava.[3] His giant armor would far surpass our size. He took three hundred flags, won thirty battles; he conquered Motril for the king, and Antequera, Suez, and Nijar, and died a pauper. Highness, salute them. [*He himself bows and uncovers his head, then goes on to another. The king listens to him with growing impatience and anger*] Beside him, Gil his son, beloved by noble hearts. His hand upon an oath was worth a king's. [*At another*] Don Gaspard, the glory of Mendoza and of Silva! Every noble house has some alliance with the Silvas, Highness. The house of Sandoval dreads and weds us in alternation; Manrico's line is envious, the Laras jealous, and Alencastro hates us. Our feet touch all the dukes at once, and our foreheads all the kings.

DON CARLOS: [*Annoyed*] Do you make sport of us?

DON RUY: [*Going to other portraits*] Here is Don Vasquez, called the Wise; and Don Jaime, called the Strong. One day as he went by he stopped Zamet and a hundred Moors alone. I shall pass over others, some better still! [*As the king makes an angry gesture, he moves past a great many of the paintings, and stops at the last three portraits at the spectator's left*] My noble grandfather. He lived for sixty years, keeping his promised word even to Jews. [*At the next-to-last*] This old man, this holy face—this is my father. He was a great man, although he came the last. The Moors at Granada had taken prisoner Count Alvar Giron, his friend. But my father gathered six hundred soldiers to find and free him. He had a Count Alvar Giron carved out in stone, and carried the statue with him, swearing by his patron saint that never would he turn back until the stony count itself should turn about and seek retreat. He battled, reached the count, and saved him.

[2] A yearly levy extorted by the victorious Moors there.
[3] Orders of chivalry.

DON CARLOS: My prisoner, Duke!

DON RUY GOMEZ: He was a Gomez de Silva. When in this house one sees the portraits of these heroes, this is what one says—

DON CARLOS: My prisoner, and instantly!

[Don Ruy Gomez *bows deeply before the king, takes his hand and leads him to the last portrait, the one behind which he has hidden* Hernani. Doña Sol *watches him anxiously, and the others are silent and attentive.*]

DON RUY GOMEZ: This portrait is my own. And I thank you, King Carlos; for what you ask is that on seeing it, all men should say "This last one, the son of such heroic race—he was a traitor that sold his guest away."

[*Joy on* Doña Sol's *face; a murmur of astonishment among the others present. The king, disconcerted, moves off in a fury, and keeps silence for several moments, his lips trembling and eyes blazing*]

DON CARLOS: Duke, your castle is in my way, and I shall throw it down!

DON RUY GOMEZ: For you would indeed pay me for his head, Your Highness, would you not?

DON CARLOS: For such defiance as this, I shall level all its towers, and order nettles sown where once it stood.

DON RUY GOMEZ: Better that nettles grow where my towers rose, than that a stain should mark the Silva name. [*To the portraits*] Is that not so, my fathers?

DON CARLOS: Duke, his head is ours, and you had promised me—

DON RUY GOMEZ: I promised one or the other. [*To the portraits*] Is that not so, my sires? [*Touching his own head; to the king*] I give you this one. Take it.

DON CARLOS: Duke, his head is ours, and you had promised me—

DON RUY GOMEZ: I promised one or the other. [*To the portraits*] Is that not so, my sires? [*Touching his own head; to the king*] I give you this one. Take it.

DON CARLOS: I thank you, Duke—but I lose by this arrangement. The head I need is young; once severed, it must be lifted by the hair before the people. But yours! What use have I for it? The headsman would seek in vain to grasp its hair. You have not even enough to fill the hand!

DON RUY GOMEZ: Highness, do not insult me! My head is still a good one, and easily worth a rebel's thatch, I think. You disdain a Silva head?

DON CARLOS: Give us Hernani!

DON RUY GOMEZ: My lord, I have spoken.

DON CARLOS: [*To his men*] Search everywhere! In every wing, in every cellar and tower—

DON RUY GOMEZ: My dungeon is as faithful as myself. Alone it knows the secret that I know, and both of us will guard it well.

DON CARLOS: I am the king.

DON RUY GOMEZ: Unless they build my tomb up, stone by stone, from my demolished castle, they will find nothing.

DON CARLOS: Pleas and threats are all in vain! Give me the bandit, Duke, or I will demolish head and castle both!

DON RUY GOMEZ: I have spoken.

DON CARLOS: Well then, instead of one, I shall take two heads. [*To the* Duke of Alcala] Jorge, arrest the duke.

DOÑA SOL: [*Tearing off her veil and throwing herself between the duke and the guards*] Carlos, you are an evil king!

DON CARLOS: Good Lord, what is this? Doña Sol!

DOÑA SOL: Highness, you have not a Spaniard's heart!

DON CARLOS: [*Disturbed and hesitant*] Madam, you are too harsh toward the king. [*He approaches* Doña Sol, *and speaks low to her*] You yourself have put this fury in my heart. A man turns saint or monster by your touch. How quickly one grows evil when one is loathed! I was already great; if you had wished it, perhaps I might have been the lion of Castile! You have made me its tiger with your rage. And now that tiger roars. Be silent, then. [Doña Sol *looks at him. He bows*] However, I'll obey. [*He turns back to the duke*] My cousin, I respect you. Your scruples after all have something worthy in them. Be loyal to your guest, and disloyal to your king. Very well, I pardon you and am the better man. I shall only take your niece with me as hostage.

DON RUY GOMEZ: Only!

DOÑA SOL: [*Shocked and frightened*] Take me, my lord?

DON CARLOS: Yes, you!

DON RUY GOMEZ: So you exact no more than that of me? Oh, what splendid clemency! Oh, generous victor, to spare the head and torture the heart instead! Fine mercy, this!

DON CARLOS: Make your choice—Doña Sol or the traitor. I must have one of them.

DON RUY GOMEZ: Ah, you are the master!

[Don Carlos *approaches* Doña Sol *to take her away. She retreats toward* Don Ruy Gomez]

DOÑA SOL: Save me, my lord! [*She stops; then, to herself*] But I must! My uncle's head or his—no, sooner myself. [*To the king*] I go with you.

DON CARLOS: [*Aside*] By all the saints! What an excellent idea this was! You shall have to soften finally, my girl! [Doña Sol *moves with deliberate step toward the box that holds the jewels; she opens it and takes the dagger out, hiding it in her bosom.* Don Carlos *comes up beside her and offers her his hand*] What have you there?

DOÑA SOL: Nothing.

DON CARLOS: Some precious jewel?

DOÑA SOL: Yes.

DON CARLOS: [*Smiling*] Let us see it.

DOÑA SOL: Later you shall. [*She gives him her hand and prepares to go with him.* Don Ruy Gomez, who has remained motionless and deeply absorbed in thought, turns and takes a few steps, shouting*]

DON RUY GOMEZ: Doña Sol! Heaven and earth, my Doña Sol! . . . Since this man has no heart in him —castle, come to my aid! Crumble, you weapons and fortress walls, fall in upon us all! [*He runs to the king*] Leave me my child! I have nothing but her, my king!

DON CARLOS: [*Dropping* Doña Sol's *hand*] My prisoner, then!

[*The duke drops his head, and seems caught by a tortured hesitation; then he raises his eyes and gazes at the portraits, clasping and stretching his hands toward them imploringly*]

DON RUY GOMEZ: Have pity on me, my fathers! [*He takes a step toward the hiding place;* Doña Sol's *eyes follow him in anguish. He turns back toward the portraits; to them*] Oh, hide your eyes—your gaze will hold me back! [*He advances falteringly as far as his portrait, then turns back to the king again*] It is your will?

DON CARLOS: Yes.

[*The duke raises his trembling hand toward the spring*]

DOÑA SOL: God in heaven!

DON RUY GOMEZ: No! [*He throws himself at the king's feet*] Have pity, take my head!

DON CARLOS: Your niece!

DON RUY GOMEZ: [*Rising*] Then take her! And leave me my honor.

DON CARLOS: [*Gripping* Doña Sol's *trembling hand*] Farewell, Duke.

DON RUY GOMEZ: Until we meet again. [*His eyes follow the king, who moves slowly off with* Doña Sol; *then he puts his hand to his dagger*] God protect you, Highness! [*He comes forward again, and stands motionless, hearing and seeing nothing; his gaze is fixed, his arms crossed on his chest, which rises and falls in a convulsive rhythm. Meanwhile, the king goes out with* Doña Sol, *and all the courtiers go gravely after him, two by two, each in order of his rank. They speak low among themselves*]

DON RUY: [*To himself*] King, as you leave my home rejoicing, my ancient loyalty leaves my weeping heart. [*He raises his eyes, looks about him, and sees that he is alone. He dashes to the wall, takes down two swords from a display there, compares and examines them, and sets them on a table. This done, he goes to the portrait, pushes the spring, and opens the secret door*]

SCENE VII.

DON RUY: Come out. [Hernani *appears at the doorway of the hiding place.* Don Ruy *points to the two swords on the table*] Choose one of them. Don Carlos has left my house; now you must settle with me. Choose, and do it swiftly. . . . Come now! Your hand is trembling!

HERNANI: A duel! Old man, we cannot fight one another.

DON RUY GOMEZ: And why not? Are you afraid? Or is it that you are not noble? Damnation! Noble or not, any man who injures me is gentleman enough to cross his sword with mine!

HERNANI: Old man—

DON RUY GOMEZ: Kill me, or die yourself.

HERNANI: Die—yes. You have saved me despite my will, and so my life is yours to take.

DON RUY GOMEZ: That is your wish? [To the portraits] You see that he asks it. [To Hernani] Very well; then say your prayer.

HERNANI: I make my last to you, my lord.

DON RUY GOMEZ: Address the other Lord.

HERNANI: No—no, to you! Old man, strike me, with anything, knife, dagger, sword! But grant me this last joy, in pity's name—Duke, before I die, let me see her!

DON RUY GOMEZ: See her!

HERNANI: Or at least let me her her voice once more—only one last time!

DON RUY GOMEZ: Hear her voice!

HERNANI: My lord, I understand your jealousy; but death already clutches at my young life—forgive me. Tell me that I may hear her voice again, even if it must be without the sight of her. And I shall die tonight. Only to hear her! Fill my last longing—how contented I should breathe out my life, if you would let my soul look into hers again, into her eyes, before I fly to heaven! I shall not speak to her—you will be there, my father. And take me afterwards!

DON RUY GOMEZ: [Looking amazed at the open door of the cupboard] Can that closet be so deep, so tightly sealed, that he heard nothing?

HERNANI: I heard nothing at all.

DON RUY GOMEZ: I was forced to yield him Doña Sol, or you.

HERNANI: Yield her to whom?

DON RUY GOMEZ: The king.

HERNANI: You fool! He loves her!

DON RUY GOMEZ: Loves her!

HERNANI: He has stolen her from us! He is our rival!

DON RUY GOMEZ: My God! . . . Men! To your horses, your horses! We must go after the abductor!

HERNANI: Listen. Vengeance that is well planned makes far less noise as it comes. I belong to you; you have the right to kill me. But do you wish to use me first, to avenge your niece and her honor? Let me share in your revenge! Ah, grant me that share—if I must fall and kiss your feet, I do it, but let us both pursue the king! Come, I shall be your striking arm —I shall avenge you, Duke. And afterwards you can slay me.

DON RUY GOMEZ: And then, just as today, you will give yourself up to death?

HERNANI: Yes, Duke.

DON RUY GOMEZ: How do you swear it?

HERNANI: Upon my father's head.

DON RUY GOMEZ: And will you swear to recall the vow yourself?

HERNANI: [Handing him the horn he takes from his belt] Take this horn. Whatever may happen, when you wish it, lord, and in whatever place, when you feel that it is time for me to die, then sound this trumpet, nothing more. It shall be done.

DON RUY GOMEZ: [Offering him his hand] Your hand. [They clasp hands. Then, to the portraits] And you, my fathers—you all are witness to it!

ACT IV.   **THE TOMB.**   SCENE I.

Aix-la-Chapelle: the underground crypt that holds the tomb of Charlemagne. The great vaults of Lombard architecture, arches, massive low pillars, their capitals carved with birds and flowers. To the right, Charlemagne's tomb with a small bronze door, low and arched. A single lamp hung from the height of an arch picks out its inscription: Carolus Magnus. It is dark. The far end of the cavern cannot be seen; it is lost among the arcades, the stairs and pillars that merge and disappear into the dimness.

[Don Carlos *and* Don Ricardo de Roxas, *with a lantern in his hand. Full cloaks, hatbrims pulled low*]

DON RICARDO: [His hat in his hand] This is the place.

DON CARLOS: It is here that the conspiracy will meet—and I shall have them all in the hollow of my hand! My Lord Elector of Treves, this is the place and you have lent it to them. . . . It is an admirable choice—a black plot flourishes in the air of catacombs, and tombstones are good for sharpening stilettos. And yet the game is crucial—a life is at stake, my lords assassins. We shall see. Well, they are wise indeed to choose a sepulcher for such a conference; they will have less distance to go. [To Don Ricardo] Do these caverns stretch far beneath the ground?

DON RICARDO: Down to the castle-fort.

DON CARLOS: More space than I shall need.

DON RICARDO: Others on this side go as far as the monastery of Altenheim. . . .

DON CARLOS: Where Rudolph killed Lothair. Good —now once again, Count, recite me all the names and grievances: where, why, and how.

DON RICARDO: Gotha—

DON CARLOS: I know why that good duke would plot with them: he wants a German emperor for Germany.

DON RICARDO: Hohenburg—

DON CARLOS: Hohenburg, I think, would rather choose hell with Francis at its head, than heaven itself with me.

DON RICARDO: Don Gil Tellez Giron—

DON CARLOS: Saint Mary and Castile! So he is in revolt against his king, the traitor!

DON RICARDO: They say he found you with Lady Giron, the evening of the day you made him baron. He would avenge the honor of his sweet wife.

DON CARLOS: And thus turns rebel against Spain? . . . Who else is there?

DON RICARDO: The Reverend Vasquez, the bishop of Avila, is said to be among them.

DON CARLOS: Is that to avenge his wife's dishonor too?

DON RICARDO: Then Guzman de Lara is discontent; he wants the collar of your knighthood.

DON CARLOS: Ah! Guzman de Lara—if he wants only a collar, he will have it.

DON RICARDO: The duke of Lutzelburg. As for his intentions—

DON CARLOS: The duke of Lutzelburg stands just a head too tall.

DON RICARDO: And Juan de Haro, who wants Astorga.

DON CARLOS: Those Haros have always earned the headsman twice his wages.

DON RICARDO: That is the list.

DON CARLOS: You have named only seven, Count, and I had been warned of more.

DON RICARDO: There are some bandits besides, engaged by Treves, or France. . . .

DON CARLOS: Men without a true allegiance, whose everready knives turn toward the fattest purse like compass needles toward the pole.

DON RICARDO: I did make out two more conspirators both of them newly arrived. One young, one old.

DON CARLOS: Their names? [Don Ricardo shrugs his shoulders; he does not know] Their ages then?

DON RICARDO: The younger one seems twenty.

DON CARLOS: What a pity!

DON RICARDO: The elder, sixty at least.

DON CARLOS: The one is too young, the other too old. Too bad; I shall take care of them. The headsman can count upon my help when it is needed. My sword will not be kind to treachery, and I shall lend it when his ax grows dull; and if the scaffold cloth should prove too small, I shall stitch my imperial purple onto it. But shall I indeed be emperor?

DON RICARDO: The college of electors is gathered now to vote.

DON CARLOS: I cannot tell—they will name Francis the First, or else their Saxon, their Frederick the Wise—ah, Luther is right, Europe is in bad times! Fine men to choose a sacred majesty, reasons of gold alone can sway their mood. A Saxon heretic! An imbecilic count palatine, and a primate of Treves who is a libertine! The Bohemian king will vote for me. But Hessian princes even smaller than their fiefs— young idiots and debauched old men. Oh, crowns —there are many crowns, but heads? only try to find one! Dwarfs all of them, that laughable council, whom I could carry off like Hercules draped in my lionskin. Without their purple mantles, they would

none of them have a skull as large as Triboulet's![4] . . . I lack three voices, Ricardo! And lacking them, I shall lack everything! Oh, I would give Toledo, Ghent, and Salamanca or any three cities they could wish, for three more votes! For those three voices —mark thee, Count, I would give up three cities in Castile or in Flanders! For I could take them back another time. [Don Ricardo bows deeply to the king, and puts his hat on his head] You cover your head before me?

DON RICARDO: My lord, you called me "thou"; [He bows again] thus I am made a grandee.

DON CARLOS: [Aside]: Ah, you pitiful things, so ambitious for a pittance! A self-seeking breed of animals, who follow their single strand of purpose through our own concerns! This is a shabby barnyard where they beg shamelessly of the king, and he dispenses scraps of greatness to all these famished beasts. [Reflectively] Only God and the emperor are great—and the holy father. The rest, the kings and dukes—what are they?

DON RICARDO: Indeed, I hope they will select Your Highness for the throne.

DON CARLOS: [Aside] Highness! Am I still only highness? Must misfortune follow me? If I should remain only king . . .

DON RICARDO: [Aside] Enough—emperor or not, I am now a grandee of Spain.

DON CARLOS: How will they announce his name when they elect the German emperor?

DON RICARDO: If it is the duke of Saxony, a single cannon shot. Two for the king of France, and three if it is Your Highness.

DON CARLOS: And then Doña Sol! Everything has joined to irritate and wound me! Count, if fortune falls my way and makes me emperor, quickly bring her here. Perhaps she will find a Caesar more to her taste.

DON RICARDO: [Smiling] Your Highness is most generous.

DON CARLOS: [Interrupting him haughtily] Silence, upon that subject! I have not yet said what I wish opinion to be. When will we know the council's choice?

DON RICARDO: Within the hour at latest, I think.

DON CARLOS: Three voices more! Only three. . . . But first we must crush this plotting rabble here, and afterwards see who will have the empire. [He counts on his fingers and stamps his foot] Still three votes too few! The others have it! Yet that Cornelius Agrippa predicted them—he saw thirteen stars in the celestial sea come sailing swiftly toward my northern one. I'll have the empire then! . . . But on the other hand, they say that Abbé Jean Trithème prophesied for Francis. I should have helped the auguries along by military means, for then fate would be clear! Predictions by the best of sorcerers come best to birth

---

[4] Fool at the courts of Louis XII and Francis I; main character in Hugo's Le roi s'amuse (1832), which play Verdi later adapted for Rigoletto.

when a good army serves as midwife; an army with its cannon and its pikes, with soldiers, horsemen and with marching tunes will lead a wavering fate in the right direction. Which of the two is better, Cornelius Agrippa or Jean Trithème? The one with regiments behind his words; the one who makes his points with iron lance, who underlines them with troops and mercenaries; their swords can set imperfect fortune straight, and mold the event according to the prophet.

They are poor fools who aim to have the empire of the world, who with proud eye and brow declare "It is my right!" They have a thousand cannon stretched in rows, whose hot breath could melt cities; they've vassals, soldiers, horses, and one assumes that they will march to their goal over the conquered peoples. . . . But no! When they have reached the great crossroads of human destiny, where many paths lead to the pit and one leads to the throne, they hardly take three steps but stop in indecision; wondering, they try in vain to read the book of fate; they hesitate, uncertain of themselves; and, caught by doubt, go running to the neighboring necromancer, to ask their way!

[To Don Ricardo] Leave me now; the traitors' league will soon be here. Oh—and the key to the tomb?

DON RICARDO: [Handing it to him] My lord, you will remember the Count of Limburg, the guardian here? He gave me the key, and he does all that's in his power for your sake.

DON CARLOS: [Dismissing him] Do everything as I have ordered you. Everything!

DON RICARDO: [Bowing] I go at once, Your Highness.

DON CARLOS: I need three cannon shots, you said? [Don Ricardo bows and leaves. Don Carlos, left alone, falls into a deep reverie. His arms cross, his head falls to his chest; then he lifts it and turns toward the tomb]

SCENE II.

DON CARLOS: Charlemagne, forgive me! These silent vaults should not reverberate with any but solemn words. You must be indignant at hearing our ambition hum about your monument. . . . Charlemagne is here! You somber sepulcher, how can you hold so great a spirit and yet not burst? Are you truly there, giant creator of a world? And can you stretch your length within those walls? . . . It is a spectacle to astound the mind, as it was before he came, and as he later made it! A vast structure with two men at its top, elected lords to whom each king is subject. Each state and duchy, military fief, kingdom, and march—almost all are hereditary reigns; yet the people sometimes have their pope or Caesar. The mechanism works, and one chance corrects another; so equilibrium comes, and order triumphs. Electors in cloth of gold, and scarlet cardinals—the sacred double senate that stirs the earth—are but display, and God will have His will. An idea may rise one day born of the times; it grows, and burns, and spreads, and mingles with all things; takes human form, grips hearts, and carves a furrow; many a king will trample it underfoot, or gag its voice. But if one day it penetrates the diet, or the papal conclave, then suddenly the kings will see the once-enslaved idea loom up, with globe in hand or the tiara on its brow, and bow their royal heads beneath its feet.

The pope and emperor are everything. Nothing is on earth but for or by them. A sublime mystery dwells in them, and heaven, from which they hold their privilege, endows them with a feast of peoples and of kings; heaven keeps them underneath its thunderous canopy of cloud, seated alone at table where God serves them up the world. Side by side, they sit to rule and sentence, arranging the universe as a reaper does his field. All that is occurs between those two. The kings stand at the door, breathing the savory steam of dishes carried past, staring through the window, watchful, agitated, and rising on their toes to see. Beneath them the world falls into ranks and groups. They do and they undo. One absolves, the other cuts. The one is truth, the other might. Their purpose is contained within them; they are because they are. When they emerge from the sanctuary, both equal, the one in purple, the other in his white soutane, the dazzled universe in terror regards these two halves of God, the pope and the emperor.

Emperor! To be emperor—oh fury, not to be, and to feel one's heart filled with courage! How fortunate was he who sleeps within this tomb; how great was he! And it was still finer in his time. The pope and the emperor: they were more than two men. Peter and Caesar—in themselves the two Romes were joined, each fertilized the other by mystic marriage, giving new form and soul to human kind; melding peoples and kingdoms as they wished to form a new Europe, and both of them by their hands refashioning the bronze that still remained of the old Roman world. A lofty fate—and yet, this tomb in his. Is all so trivial then, that this is where it ends? To have been prince, and king, and emperor—to have been the sword and been the law . . . a giant, with Germany for his pedestal, with Caesar for his title, and Charlemagne for name! To have been greater than Hannibal, or than Attila, as great as all the world—and this is where it ends!

Then scheme for empire, and see the dust an emperor leaves! Cover the earth entire with fanfare and with tumult; raise and build your endless empire; slash and carve out an enormous edifice—do you know what will remain one day? Ah, lunacy—this stone! And of the title and the triumphal name? A few letters, that serve to teach a child his spelling! However high the goal your pride envisions, here is the last limit! Oh empire! I do not care—I touch at it, and find it to my liking. Something tells me: "You shall have it." It shall be mine . . . if it only were!

Oh heaven, to be what is beginning! Alone, upright, atop the enormous spiral; to be the keystone in the arch of all the states arranged one on the other, to see beneath one all the many kings, and wipe one's sandals on them.

To see beneath the kings the feudal houses, margraves and cardinals, doges, and dukes with floral seals; then bishops, abbots, heads of clans, great barons! Then priests and soldiers next; then in the shadow, far below the peak whereon we stand—deep within the chasm—are men!

Men—a mass, a sea, great rumbling, tears and cries, sometimes a bitter laugh—a whole lament that wakes the startled earth, and through a hundred thousand echoes reaches us as a skirl of trumpets! Men! . . .. Cities, towers, a vast swarm of high church belfries to ring their gongs! (*Musingly.*) A base of human nations, bearing on their shoulders the enormous pyramid that leans on the two poles; living waves that grasp it always in their hollows, and float it pitching on their vast swells; waves that shift everything about, and at its upper reaches topple thrones like footstools, so that all kings cease their vain disputes and raise their eyes to heaven.

Kings! Look down beneath you! Ah, the people—that ocean—that never-resting wave, where nought can be cast in but stirs the whole! A swell that may crush a throne or rock a tomb! Mirror wherein a king will rarely find a handsome image of himself. If he should sometimes gaze into that dark swell, he'd see at bottom numberless empires, great shipwrecked vessels swaying in its ebb and flow—empires that had disturbed the ocean's stream and now exist no more!

To think of ruling over all of that! To mount up to that pinnacle if the electors call—to climb there, conscious that one is but a man! To see the chasm below! If only I do not at that same moment grow dazed with vertigo—oh, shifting pyramid of kings and countries, your summit is so narrow! Woe to the fearful foot! By whom should I hold steady? Suppose I stumble at feeling the world shudder beneath my feet! At feeling the earth live, and surge, and pulse! Or when I have that globe between my hands, what then? Shall I be capable of carrying it? What is there in me? Emperor, my God! to fill the role of king was hard for me! Surely the man is rare whose soul can stretch with fortune. But I—who shall make me great? Who will be my guide and give me counsel?

[*He falls to his knees before the tomb*] Charlemagne—you shall! Since God, before whom all obstacles fall back, has taken our two majesties and set them face to face, then from the depths of this your grave imbue my heart with something sublime! Ah, show me all things from their every aspect, show me that the world is small, for I dare not lay my hand on it. Show me that within this tower of Babel, rising from shepherd to Caesar to the skies, each man at his own rank delights himself, admires what he is, observes the man beneath him and cannot help but

mock. Teach me your secrets of conquest and of rule, and tell me that it is better to punish than forgive—is this not so? If it is true that sometimes the world's clatter wakes a great shadow in his lonely resting place; if it is true his wide bright tomb can open suddenly, and throw the world a flare in its dark night—if these things are true, emperor of Germany, then tell me, what can a man do when he comes after Charlemagne?

Speak! Though it mean your sovereign breath in speaking must crack this bronze door across my brow! Or rather let me enter alone within your sanctuary, and see your face in death—do not repulse me by an icy breath but raise yourself upon your bed of stone, and let us talk. Yes, even though you should tell me, in your fateful voice, of matters that darken the eye and pale the brow! Speak, and do not blind your fearful son, for your tomb must be so full with light! Or else, if you will say nothing, let me study that deeply peaceful head, as if it were a world; let me measure you carefully, oh giant, for nothing here below is great as is thy dust! Let the ashes guide me if the spirit would not.

[*He puts the key to the lock*] We shall go in. [*He draws back*] But what if he should speak to me indeed? if he is there, awake and upright, walking with slow steps! And I should reappear with my hair white! Still—I shall enter. [*Sound of footsteps*] Someone is approaching. Who but I could dare to come here at this hour, and rouse the home of such a corpse? Who is it? [*The noise is closer*] Ah, I had forgotten—it is my murderers. Let us go in then.

[*He opens the door to the tomb and closes it behind him. Several men come on, with muffled steps, hidden in their cloaks and hats*]

SCENE III.

[*The conspirators; they move about among themselves, clasping hands and exchanging a few words in low voices*]

FIRST CONSPIRATOR: [*Who alone carries a lighted torch*] *Ad augusta.*

SECOND CONSPIRATOR: *Per angusta.*

FIRST: May the saints protect us.

THIRD: May the dead serve us.

FIRST: God keep us.

[*Sounds of steps in the darkness*]

SECOND: Who goes there?

VOICE: *Ad augusta.*

SECOND: *Per angusta.*

[*Other conspirators appear. Sound of footsteps again*]

FIRST CONSPIRATOR: [*To the* Third] Look there, another's coming.

THIRD: Who goes there?

VOICE IN SHADOWS: *Ad augusta.*

THIRD: *Per angusta.*

[*Still others appear, with signs of greeting*]

FIRST: Good, we are all here. Gotha, give us your report. My friends, the dark await the light.

[*All the conspirators seat themselves on tombs in a half circle. The first conspirator passes among them, and from his torch each lights a candle and holds it in his hand. Then the first conspirator takes a seat silently upon a tomb at the center of the circle and higher than the others*]

DUKE OF GOTHA: [*Rising*] Friends, this Charles of Spain, a foreigner through his mother, lays claim to the Holy Empire.

FIRST CONSPIRATOR: He shall have the grave instead.

GOTHA: [*Throwing his torch to the ground and grinding it out with his foot*] May his skull be as this flame!

ALL: May it be!

FIRST: Death to him!

GOTHA: May he die!

ALL: May he be slain!

DON JUAN DE HARO: His father was a German.

DUKE OF LUTZELBURG: His mother was Spanish.

GOTHA: He is Spanish no longer, and not a German. Death!

ONE OF THE CONSPIRATORS: What if the electors were to name him emperor at this moment?

FIRST: They name him? Never!

DON GIL TELLEZ GIRON: What does that matter, friends! If we strike the head, the crown will die with it.

FIRST: Whatever he may be, if he wins the Holy Empire, he becomes mighty and august, and only God can touch him.

GOTHA: The surest way is to act before he gains that state.

FIRST: He shall not be elected.

ALL: He shall not have the Empire!

FIRST: How many hands are needed to wind him in his shroud?

ALL: Only one.

FIRST: How many strokes to the heart?

ALL: Only one!

FIRST: Who will do it?

ALL: All of us!

FIRST: Our victim is a traitor. They are choosing an emperor; let us make a high priest. We shall draw lots.

[*All the conspirators write their names on their tablets, tear off the sheet, roll it up, and go one after the other to drop it into the urn on one of the tombs*]

FIRST CONSPIRATOR: Let us pray. [*They all kneel. The* First *rises*] May the chosen one put his faith in God, strike like a Roman, and die like a Hebrew! He must brave the wheel and pincers, sing at the rack, and laugh at the fiery brand; he must do all to kill and die in resignation! [*He draws one of the parchment sheets from the urn*]

ALL: What name is it?

FIRST: [*Loudly*] Hernani.

HERNANI: [*Emerging from the group*] I've won! Ah revenge, I have you now, you whom I have pursued so long!

DON RUY GOMEZ: [*Moving through the crowd and taking* Hernani *aside*] Let me take your place!

HERNANI: No, upon my life! My lord, do not grudge me my fortune! It is the first time that luck has come to me!

DON RUY: You have nothing. Then listen—I give you my fiefs, my castles, and my vasalages—a hundred thousand peasants in my three hundred villages—I give them all to you, my friend, for the right to strike that blow!

HERNANI: No!

GOTHA: Your weaker arm would strike with less effect, old man.

DON RUY GOMEZ: Silence! If not the arm, I have the spirit for it! Do not judge the blade by the rust that coats its scabbard [*To* Hernani] You belong to me.

HERNANI: My life is yours, yes. But his belongs to me!

DON RUY GOMEZ: [*Drawing the horn from his waist*] Listen, my friend: I give you back this horn.

HERNANI: [*Shaken*] What? My life? Ah, what does it mean to me? My vengeance is at hand! God is with me in this. I have my father to avenge, and more perhaps! Would you give *her* to me?

DON RUY GOMEZ: Never! But I yield up this horn!

HERNANI: No.

DON RUY GOMEZ: Reflect upon it, boy!

HERNANI: Duke, leave me my prey.

DON RUY: Then be accursed for denying me that joy. [*He replaces the horn in his belt*]

FIRST CONSPIRATOR: [*To* Hernani] Brother, before they can elect him, it would be well to watch for Carlos on this very night—

HERNANI: Fear not! I know how to put a man into his grave.

FIRST: May any treason fall back upon the traitor, and God be with us! And if he should fall without having slain, then, counts and barons, we shall continue it! Let us swear to strike, each of us in turn, without evasion—for Carlos must die.

ALL: We swear it!

GOTHA: [*To the* First Conspirator] Upon-what, my brother?

DON RUY GOMEZ: [*Upending his sword, taking it by the tip and raising it over his head*] Let us swear upon this cross!

ALL: [*Raising their swords*] May he die unrepentant.

[*A far-off cannon shot is heard. They all stop, silent. The door to the tomb opens slightly; Don Carlos appears on the threshold. Pale, he listens. A second shot. A third. He opens the door wide, but without stepping forward; he stands motionless on the doorsill*]

SCENE IV.

DON CARLOS: Go on, my lords! The emperor is listening. [*All the torches go out at once. Deep silence. He moves a step in the shadows, so dark that the mute and motionless conspirators are scarcely visible*] Silence and darkness! the swarm emerges from the black, and now returns there. Do you believe somehow that all of this will seem a dream, and that because you have put out your flares, I shall take you all for stone figures seated on their tombs? But a moment since, my statues, your voices were still loud! Come now! raise up your lowered heads, for Charles the Fifth is here! Strike me now—take even a step. Let us see it, do you dare? No, you dare not. Your torches flamed like blood beneath these vaults; and my breath alone sufficed to put them out. But look, turn your quavering eyes—I did extinguish many, but I light many more. [*He strikes the iron key on the bronze door of the tomb; at the sound, the depths of the cavern fill with soldiers bearing torches and halberds. At their head are the* Duke of Alcala *and the* Marquis of Almuñan] Come here, my falcons! I have the nest, and I have the prey! [*To the* Conspirators] Now I bring light in my turn. Look, the sepulcher's aflame. [*To the soldiers*] Come forward, all of you; this is a flagrant crime.

HERNANI: [*Looking at the soldiers*] That is better now. Alone, he seemed too large. At first I thought that it was Charlemagne; it is only Charles the Fifth.

DON CARLOS: [*To the* Duke of Alcala] Constable of Spain! [*To the* Marquis of Almuñan] Admiral of Castile, come forward! Disarm them all. [*The plotters are surrounded and disarmed*]

DON RICARDO: [*Running up and bowing to the ground*] Majesty!

DON CARLOS: I name thee alcalde of the palace.

DON RICARDO: [*Bowing again*] Two electors are come to congratulate Your Sacred Majesty, in the name of the Golden Chamber.

DON CARLOS: Let them come in. [*Low, to* Ricardo] Doña Sol.

[Ricardo *salutes and leaves. The* King of Bohemia *and the* Duke of Bavaria *enter with torches and trumpet flourishes; both are clothed in their gold-embroidered mantles, with crowns on their heads. A large cortege follows them, made up of German lords carrying the imperial banner—the two-headed eagle with the Spanish shield at its center. The soldiers form an aisle to the emperor for the two electors. They salute him deeply and he returns it by raising his hat*]

DUKE OF BAVARIA: Charles, King of the Romans, Most Sacred Majesty, Emperor! The world is now within your hands, for the Empire is yours. Yours, the throne that every monarch covets! Frederick, Duke of Saxony, was first elected; but he judged you more worthy of it, and declined. Come then, receive this crown and take the globe. The Holy Empire, King, invests you with its purple robe; it arms you with its sword, and you are great.

DON CARLOS: I shall thank the council on my return. Go now, my lords. Thank you, my brother Bohemia, and my cousin Bavaria. Go now—and I myself must leave.

KING OF BOHEMIA: Charles, our ancestors were friends; my father loved your father, and their sires too loved each other. Charles, you are so young a man to face disturbing fortunes—tell me, would you wish that I should be your brother among brothers? I knew you as a child, and I cannot forget—

DON CARLOS: [*Interrupting him*] King of Bohemia, you are most familiar! [*He presents his hand for the* King *to kiss, and to the* Duke of Bavaria, *then dismisses the two electors, who bow deeply*] Go now. [*They leave with their suites*]

CROWD: Long live the emperor!

DON CARLOS: [*Aside*] I am emperor! And everything has made way for me. Emperor! through the refusal, though, of Frederick the Wise!

[Doña Sol *enters, led by* Ricardo]

DOÑA SOL: Soldiers! and the emperor—oh God, I did not expect this! Hernani!

HERNANI: Doña Sol!

DON RUY: [*Beside* Hernani, *to himself*] She does not even see me!

[DOÑA SOL: *runs to* Hernani; *his defiant stare stops her*]

HERNANI: My lady!

DOÑA SOL: [*Drawing the knife from her bodice*] I have his dagger still.

HERNANI: My beloved!

DON CARLOS: Silence, all of you. [*To the plotters*] Have you recovered your determination? It is fitting that I show the world a lesson here. Lara the Castilian, and Saxon Gotha—all of you—what did you come here to do? Speak!

HERNANI: [*Stepping forward*] Sire, it is a simple thing, and we call tell you of it: we were writing the sentence upon Balthazar's wall. [*He draws his knife and brandishes it*] We render unto Caesar what is Caesar's.

DON CARLOS: I see. [*To* Don Ruy Gomez] And you, Silva— a traitor!

DON RUY GOMEZ: Which of us two is traitor, sire?

HERNANI: [*Turning to the other* Conspirators] He has what he desires—our heads and empire both! [*To the* Emperor] A king's blue robe could hinder your steps. This purple suits you better: it does not show blood.

DON CARLOS: [*To* Don Ruy Gomez] My cousin Silva—this is crime enough to strike your barony from your coat of arms. It is high treason, Don Ruy; consider that well.

DON RUY GOMEZ: Count Julians are made by King Rodrigos.[5]

---

[5] This Visigoth king defiled the count's daughter, and was killed by him.

DON CARLOS: [*To the* Duke of Alcala] Take only the dukes or counts. The rest—

[Don Ruy Gomez, *the* Duke of Lutzelburg, *the* Duke of Gotha, Don Juan de Haro, Don Guzman de Lara, Don Gil Tellez Giron, *and the* Baron of Hohenburg *step out of the group;* Hernani *remains with it. The* Duke of Alcala *surrounds the lords with guards*]

DOÑA SOL: [*Aside*] He is safe!

HERNANI: [*Stepping forward*] I claim my place among these others! [*To* Don Carlos] Since this is a matter of the ax; since Hernani the humble peasant would slip beneath your feet unpunished; since his brow is no longer worthy of your sword; since one must be a nobleman to die, I rise. God who awards the scepter and who gave it you, God made me Duke of Segorbia and Cardona, the Marquis of Monroy, Count Albatera and Viscount of Gor— and lord of lands whose number or whose names I cannot count. I am Juan of Aragon, grand master of Avis, born in exile—the banished son of a father slaughtered by your father's word, King Carlos of Castile! Murder is a family affair between us. You have the scaffold; we have the knife. Thus, heaven made me a duke, and exile a mountaineer. I have whetted my sword against the hills and tempered it in rushing streams; but since all my preparation must come to nothing—[*He puts on his hat, and says to the other conspirators*]—cover your heads, all you grandees of Spain! [*All the nobles do so. To* Don Carlos] Yes, King—our heads have the right to fall before you covered! [*To the prisoners*] Silva, Haro, Lara—men of title and of race—open your ranks to Juan of Aragon! Dukes and counts, give me my place! [*To the courtiers and guards*] I am Juan of Aragon, king, headsmen and grooms. And if your scaffolds are too small, change them for others! [*He joins the group of captured lords*]

DOÑA SOL: Why did he speak?

DON CARLOS: True, I had forgotten that whole story.

HERNANI: The man whose flesh has bled remembers better. And the wrong forgotten by the offender lives on still active in the injured heart.

DON CARLOS: Then I am the son of men who felled your fathers' heads—that is title enough for me.

DOÑA SOL: [*Throwing herself to her knees before the emperor*] Sire, pardon! Pity, sire—be merciful! Or else then kill us both by the same stroke, for he is my beloved, my husband! I live in him alone. Oh, I tremble, sire; find the compassion to kill the two of us together! Majesty, I lie at your sainted feet! I love him! He is mine, as the empire is yours! Oh mercy! [*Don Carlos watches her, impassive*] What dark idea absorbs you now?

DON CARLOS: Rise, Duchess of Segorbia, Countess Albatera, Marchioness of Monroy. . . . [*To* Hernani] What are your other names, Don Juan?

HERNANI: Who is it says these things? The king?

DON CARLOS: No, the emperor.

DOÑA SOL: [*Rising*] Great heavens!

DON CARLOS: [*Indicating her to* Hernani] Duke, here is your wife.

HERNANI: [*His eyes raised to heaven, and* Doña Sol *in his arms*] God of justice!

DON CARLOS: [*To* Don Ruy Gomez] Cousin, you are jealous and proud in your nobility, I know. But an Aragon may wed a Silva.

DON RUY GOMEZ: [*Darkly*] It is not for my nobility.

HERNANI: [*Gazing lovingly at* Doña Sol, *and holding her close*] Ah, I feel my hatred vanishing. . . . [*He throws down his dagger*]

DON RUY GOMEZ: [*Watching the pair*] Shall my rage burst from me? Oh no—senseless love, and senseless grief. . . . They would pity your old Spanish head. Burn flameless, old man—love and suffer secretly. Let your heart be consumed, but not a cry, for they would laugh.

DOÑA SOL: [*Still in* Hernani's *arms*] My duke!

HERNANI: I have nothing left in my heart but love.

DOÑA SOL: What happiness . . .

DON CARLOS: [*Aside, his hand upon his breast*] Quiet, my heart that still is young and full of love! Let intellect rule now, for too long you have had your way. Henceforward all your loves, and alas, your only mistresses are Germany and Flanders and old Spain. [*He eyes his banner*] The emperor is like the eagle, his companion: in the heart's stead there hangs only an escutcheon.

HERNANI: You are Caesar indeed!

DON CARLOS: [*To* Hernani] Your heart is worthy of your noble line, Don Juan. [*Indicating* Doña Sol] And worthy too of her. On your knees, Duke! [Hernani *kneels.* Don Carlos *takes off the collar of the Golden Fleece, and sets it around* Hernani's *neck*] Receive this collar. [Don Carlos *draws his sword and taps him three times upon the shoulder*] Be faithful. In the name of Saint Stephen, Duke, I name thee knight. [*He raises and embraces him*] But you have the best and sweetest collar yet, one I have not, and on that even the highest rank can lack: the arms of a beloved woman loving you. Ah, you shall be happy; and I, I am emperor. . . . [*To the conspirators*] I know your names no more, sirs. Hatred and anger— I would forget them all. Go then; I pardon you. This is the lesson I must give the world. It shall not be in vain that the emperor Charles the Fifth succeeds to Charles the First, the king; nor that, before a mourning, orphaned Europe, a law should change a Catholic highness into a sacred majesty.

[*The plotters fall to their knees*]

CONSPIRATORS: Glory to Carlos! Hail!

DON RUY GOMEZ: [*To* Don Carlos] And so I alone remain condemned to suffering.

DON CARLOS: And I.

DON RUY: [*Aside*] But unlike him, I have not forgiven!

HERNANI: Who is it has changed us all?

ALL: [Soldiers, Conspirators, Nobles] Long live Germany and Charles the Fifth!

DON CARLOS: [*Turning toward the tomb*] Honor to Charlemagne! Leave the two of us together now. [*All exeunt*]

SCENE V.

DON CARLOS: [*Alone; he bows before the tomb*] Are you content with me? Have I stripped away the pettiness of kings, Charlemagne, and am I indeed become another man? May I join my helmet to the Roman miter? Have I the right to bend the fortunes of the world? Have I a firm and steady foot, one that may walk upon this path, all strewn with vandal's ruins, that you have beaten out for us with your broad sandals? Have I caught your flame to kindle my own torch? And understood the voice that sounds within your tomb? Ah, I was alone and lost before an empire, a whole howling world that plots and threatens me—there is the Dane to punish, the Holy Father to pay; Venice and Suleiman; Luther, Francis the First—a thousand jealous blades already gleaming in the dark, snares and hidden reefs, and enemies unnumbered; twenty peoples, and each of them enough to frighten twenty kings—all hurry and urgent, all to do at once. And I cried out to you: "How shall I start?" And you replied: "My son, by clemency!"

ACT V.   THE WEDDING.   SCENE I.

Saragossa. A terrace of the palace of Aragon. At stage rear, a flight of stairs down into the garden. At right and left, two doors opening onto the terrace, which is enclosed by a balustrade topped by two rows of Moorish arcades; above and through them are visible the palace gardens, fountains in the shade, clumps of trees with lights moving among them, and beyond it all the Gothic and Arab lines of the brightly lit palace. It is night. We hear faraway trumpet flourishes. Persons in masks and dominoes, single or in groups, cross over the terrace here and there. In the foreground, a group of young lords, their masks in hand, are laughing and chattering noisily.

[Don Sancho Sanchez de Zuñiga, Don Matias Centurion, Don Ricardo de Roxas, Don Francisco de Sotomayor, Don Garci Suarez de Carbajal]

DON GARCI: Well, here's to joy, and long live the lovely bride!

DON MATIAS: [*Watching the balcony*] All Saragossa is hanging out of its windows tonight.

DON GARCI: And so it should! There has never been a wedding with gayer lights, nor a gentler night, nor for a handsomer pair!

DON MATIAS: The emperor is good!

DON SANCHO: Marquis, I remember a dusky night when we went out with him to try our chance. Who could have told that it would end this way?

DON RICARDO: [*Interrupting him*] I was there too. [*To the others*] Listen to this tale. Three lovers— one a bandit destined for the block, and a duke, and then a king—all three lay siege to a single woman's heart. When the battle clears, who holds it? It is the bandit.

DON FRANCISCO: But nothing is astonishing in that. In Spain as everywhere, love and luck turn on a play of loaded dice. The thief will always win!

DON RICARDO: And I, I've made my fortune by watching the course of love. First count, then grandee, then alcalde of the court; I have spent my time quite well, and none observed me.

DON SANCHO: Your secret is to hang about the king's path . . .

DON RICARDO: And turn my rights and actions to advantage.

DON GARCI: You profited by his preoccupation.

DON MATIAS: What is the old duke doing now? Having his coffin built?

DON SANCHO: Marquis, do not scoff. He is a valiant man. And he loved Doña Sol. Sixty years had turned his hair to gray, and one day made it white.

DON GARCI: He has not appeared again in Saragossa, they say.

DON SANCHO: Would you have this festival send him sooner to the grave?

DON FRANCISCO: And the emperor? how is he?

DON SANCHO: The emperor is sad today; Luther distresses him.

DON RICARDO: That Luther is fine cause for worry and alarm! With three or four armed men I'd take him easily.

DON MATIAS: He is disturbed by Suleiman as well.

DON GARCI: Oh, Luther, Suleiman, Neptune, the devil, Jupiter—what are they all to me? The women are pretty, the masquerade's a good one, and I've laughed all evening long!

DON SANCHO: Those are the things that count.

DON RICARDO: Garci is right—on holidays I am no longer myself; when I pull on a mask I fully believe I have a different head entirely!

DON SANCHO: [*Low to* Matias] If only each day were a holiday!

DON FRANCISCO: [*Pointing to the door at right*] My lords, is that not the bridal apartment?

DON GARCI: [*Nodding*] They will appear in just a moment.

DON FRANCISCO: Do you think so?

DON GARCI: I am sure of it!

DON FRANCISCO: Good! The bride is so very beautiful.

DON RICARDO: How generous the emperor is—to think this rebel Hernani should have the Golden Fleece—and be wed—and pardoned too! If he had taken my advice, the emperor would have given the outlaw a bed of stone, and the lady one of down.

DON SANCHO: [*Low to* Don Matias] Ah, how my blade would love to slit his throat—that false, tinsel lord, all patched together with string! A count's doublet stuffed with a steward's soul!

DON RICARDO: [*Drawing near*] What are you saying?

DON MATIAS: [*Low to* Don Sancho] Count, let's have no quarrels here! [*Aloud to* Don Ricardo] He was singing me one of Petrarch's sonnets to his love.

DON GARCI: Gentlemen, among the flowers and the women, and all these brightly colored costumes, have you noticed that specter leaning at the parapet and dimming the feast with his black domino?

DON RICARDO: I have indeed!

DON GARCI: Who is it?

DON RICARDO: Well, from his height, his manner, it must be Don Prancasio, the admiral.

DON FRANCISCO: No.

DON GARCI: He has not taken off his mask.

DON FRANCISCO: He has been cautious not to. It is the duke of Soma, who wants to draw attention—nothing more.

DON RICARDO: No, the duke spoke to me.

DON GARCI: Who is he then? Look now, there he goes.

[*A black domino slowly crosses the terrace at the rear. All turn to watch him, without his seeming to notice*]

DON SANCHO: If the dead walk, that is their step.

DON GARCI: [*Approaching the dark figure*] Good sir! . . .

[*The figure turns and stops;* Garci *draws back*] Gentlemen, I swear, a flame gleams in his eyes!

DON SANCHO: If he is the devil, he has found the man to talk to. [*He goes to the black domino, who stands motionless*] Evil one! Have you come to us from hell?

MASKED FIGURE: I do not come; I go there. [*He continues his progress and disappears by the flight of stairs. All watch him go with a kind of horror*]

DON MATIAS: His voice comes from the grave!

DON GARCI: Enough now! what's frightening otherwise is only amusing at a ball!

DON SANCHO: It is some sorry joke!

DON GARCI: Or if it's Lucifer who's stopped to watch us dance while on his way to hell, then let us dance!

DON SANCHO: It is certainly some game.

DON MATIAS: We shall find out tomorrow.

DON SANCHO: [*To* Don Matias] Look below, I beg you. Where is he now?

DON MATIAS: [*Leaning over the balustrade*] He has gone down the staircase. I see no more of him.

DON SANCHO: A droll trick . . . [*Musingly*] it is strange. . . .

DON GARCI: [*To a lady passing by*] Marquise, shall we dance this one together? [*He bows and presents his hand*]

LADY: My dear sir, you know my husband counts the ones we dance together.

DON GARCI: Only the more reason. If he finds pleasure in that, he shall count, and we shall dance, you and I. [*The lady gives him her hand, and they go out*]

DON SANCHO: [*Thoughtfully*] It is curious, indeed.

DON MATIAS: Here is the bridal pair! Silence!

[*Enter* Hernani *and* Doña Sol *hand in hand.* Doña Sol *wears a magnificent bridal costume;* Hernani *is all in black velvet, the Golden Fleece about his neck. Behind them, a crowd of masked figures, ladies and lords forming a retinue. Two halberdiers in rich livery follow them, and four pages precede them. All present separate and bow as they pass. Fanfare*]

SCENE II.

HERNANAI: [*Saluting*] My dear friends!

DON RICARDO: [*Going up to him and bowing*] Your happiness is ours, Excellency!

DON FRANCISCO: [*Gazing at* Doña Sol] Holy Saint James! . . .

DON SANCHO: [*To* Don Matias] It is late. Shall we go now?

[*All of them move forward to greet the pair and then leave, some through the door, others by the stairway in rear*]

HERNANI: [*Moving with them*] God keep you all!

DON SANCHO: [*The last to go, grips his hand*] I wish you joy. [*He leaves*]

[Hernani *and* Doña Sol *remain alone. The sound of footsteps and voices fades and disappears completely. Throughout the beginning of the following scene, the faraway trumpets and the lights diminish gradually, and darkness and silence return*]

SCENE III.

DOÑA SOL: They all have gone, at last.

HERNANI: [*Attempting to draw her into his arms*] My dearest love!

DOÑA SOL: [*Blushing and drawing back*] It—it is late, I think.

HERNANI: My angel, it is always late for us to come together!

DOÑA SOL: All the activity was tiring me. Do you not find, my dear lord, that so much gaiety turns happiness numb?

HERNANI: It is true. Happiness is a thing of gravity. It seeks for hearts of bronze, and carves itself there slowly; pleasure startles it away by tossing flowers to it. Joy's smile is much more close to tears than it is to laughter.

DOÑA SOL: In your eyes, that smile is daybreak.

[Hernani *tries to lead her toward the door. She flushes*] Soon.

HERNANI: I am your slave—yes, linger, linger! Do what you will, I ask you nothing. You know what you would have; you can do only good. I shall laugh if you desire it, or sing. My soul burns. Ah, tell the volcano to smother its flame—the volcano shall close its gaping chasms, and rim its sides with flowers and green grass. For the giant is held captive, Vesuvius is enslaved; its lava-boiling heart must not affect you. It is flowers you would have? Very well! Then the spitting volcano must do its best to burst with blossom!

DOÑA SOL: How kind you are to a poor woman, Hernani my heart!

HERNANI: What name is that, my lady? Ah, never call me by that name again, I beg of you! You remind me then of all I have forgotten. I know that once upon a time, in some dream, there lived a Hernani, whose eye glinted like a sword—a man of night and of the mountains, an outlaw who wore the word "revenge" scrawled everywhere upon him, a miserable man who trailed a curse behind him! But I do not know this Hernani. I am a man who loves the meadows, and flowers, and woods, and the nightingale's soft song; I am Juan of Aragon, and wed to Doña Sol! I am a happy man!

DOÑA SOL: I too am happy!

HARNANI: What do I care for the rags I left behind me at the door? Here I am returned to my saddened palace; an angel of the Lord awaits me on the stair. I enter, and set upright the shattered columns; I light the fire, I open wide the casements, and tear the growth from between the flagstones in the court—I am nothing now but joy, enchantment, love.

Let them return my towers, my cellars and bastilles, my crest and seat within the council of the Castiles; give me my Doña Sol, all flushed, and her brow bent low—let the two of us be left alone, and the rest is past, forgotten. I have seen nothing, said and done nothing. I begin anew, wipe everything away, forget! Be it wisdom or madness, I have you, I love you, and you are all my joy!

DOÑA SOL: [*Examining his collar*] How handsome this collar is against the velvet black!

HERNANI: You saw the king dressed thus before myself.

DOÑA SOL: I did not notice it. What is another man to me? And then besides, is it the velvet, or the satin? No, my duke, it is your throat that suits the gold so well. You are noble and proud, my lord. [*He urges her off again*] Soon! A moment yet! Look at me, do you see? This is joy, and I am weeping with it! Come look upon the lovely night! [*She goes to the balustrade*] Only a moment, my duke! Only for long enough to breathe and gaze. All is dimmed now, the flares and festive tunes. Only the night and us. Perfect delight. . . . Say then, do you not feel that dreaming nature still half watches over us with love? There is not a cloud. All is at rest, as we are. Come, breathe the rose-perfumed air with me. No torches, not a sound. All is still. A while ago the moon climbed up from the horizon, and as you spoke your voice and its trembling light both pierced my heart together. I felt myself joyful and calm, oh my beloved; I should have liked to die then.

HERNANI: Who'd not forget all things at that celestial voice? Your tones are a song that has nothing human left in it. And like a traveler carried on a stream, who slips upon the waters through a summer night, and sees a thousand flowery fields slide past him, my bewitched spirit goes wandering in your reveries. . . .

DOÑA SOL: This silence is too dark, this peace is too profound. Would you not set a star there in the sky? Or hear a night voice sing out suddenly, all tender and sweet? . . .

HERNANI: [*Smiling*] Capricious girl—only a moment since, you yearned for the light and singing to be done!

DOÑA SOL: The celebration, yes! But a bird who would sing above the meadow, a single nightingale amid the moss and shadow, or else a distant flute. . . . Such music is sweet; it brings its harmony into the soul, and sets a thousand voices singing in the heart like heavenly choirs! Oh, how lovely it would be! [*The distant sound of a horn is heard*] God! My prayer is answered!

HERNANI: [*Starting; aside*] Oh no, it cannot be!

DOÑA SOL: An angel heard my thought—your guardian angel!

HERNANI: [*Bitterly*] Yes, my guardian angel! [*The horn is heard again. Aside*] Again!

DOÑA SOL: [*Smilingly*] Don Juan, I recognize the sound of your own horn!

HERNANI: Yes.

DOÑA SOL: Have you then some part in this serenade?

HERNANI: Some part—yes.

DOÑA SOL: Unpleasant wedding feast—how much more I love the horn deep in the wood. And then besides, it is your horn, and so like your own voice.

[*Sound of the horn again*]

HERNANI: [*Aside*] The tiger is there, and howling for his prey!

DOÑA SOL: Its music fills my heart with delight, Don Juan.

HERNANI: [*Rising, in terrible fury*] Call me Hernani! Hernani! For I have not yet done with that terrible name!

DOÑA SOL: [*Trembling*] What is wrong?

HERNANI: The old man!

DOÑA SOL: My God! What horror in your eyes! What is it?

HERNANI: The old man, laughing in the dark! Can you not see him?

DOÑA SOL: What wildness is this? What old man?

HERNANI: The old man!

DOÑA SOL: [*Falling to her knees*] I beg you from

my knees, tell me, what secret tears at you? What is it?

HERNANI: I gave my oath!

DOÑA SOL: Your oath? [*She watches all his movements anxiously. He stops suddenly and wipes his hand over his brow*]

HERNANI: [*Aside*] What did I nearly tell? I must spare her. [*Aloud*] Nothing, nothing. What did I say to you?

DOÑA SOL: You said—

HERNANI: No—no. I was distressed. I am a little ill, it is nothing. . . . I did not mean to frighten you.

DOÑA SOL: Is there something you need? Tell me, I am your servant!

[*The horn begins again*]

HERNANI: [*Aside*] He demands it, and he has my pledge! [*He feels at his waist, but finds no sword, no dagger*] Nothing there! It should be done by now!

DOÑA SOL: Do you suffer such pain?

HERNANI: An old wound, one I thought had healed. It has reopened. [*Aside*] She must be sent away. [*Aloud*] Doña Sol, beloved, listen. The box I carried with me always in less happy days—

DOÑA SOL: I know the one you mean—what do you want of it?

HERNANI: There is a vial inside; it holds a remedy to end the pain I feel. Go!

DOÑA SOL: I go, my lord. [*She leaves by the door of the marriage chamber*]

SCENE IV.

HERNANI: [*Alone*] So this is what he would make of my good fortune! This is the fateful finger that gleams upon the wall! Oh, how sardonically fate laughs at me! [*He falls into a deep, convulsive reverie; then turns abruptly*] Well? . . . But all is still. . . . I hear nothing approach. . . . Could I have been mistaken?

[*The masked figure in its black domino appears at the head of the stairs. Hernani stops, frozen*]

SCENE V.

MASK: "Whatever may happen, when you wish it, and in whatever place—when you feel that it is time for me to die, then sound this trumpet, nothing more. It shall be done." The dead were witness to that pact. Well now, and is it done?

HERNANI: [*His voice low*] It is he!

MASK: I come now to your home, and tell you it is time. Now is the hour I choose. I find you late.

HERNANI: Very well. What is your will? What would you do with me? Speak.

MASK: You may choose—the knife or poison. I have brought both with me. We shall go together.

HERNANI: So be it.

MASK: Shall we pray?

HERNANI: What does it matter?

MASK: Which will you take?

HERNANI: The poison.

MASK: Very well. Give me your hand. [*He gives a small flask to* Hernani, *who takes it, paling*] Now drink—and let me finish it.

HERNANI: Oh, Duke, have pity! Tomorrow! Ah, if you have still a heart, or even a soul—if you are more than a specter from the flames, one of the damned dead, a phantom or a demon till eternity—if God has not yet set the hideous mark of "Never" on your brow—if you have known this highest joy, to love at twenty years of age, and to marry your beloved—if ever a cherished woman has trembled in your arms, then wait until tomorrow! Tomorrow come for me!

MASK: What a fool you are to say this! Tomorrow! Tomorrow! You must be mocking me! The bells you rang this morning tolled your end! What would become of me, this night? I should die of it, and who would come and take you afterwards? Shall I go alone to death? Young man, you must come with me!

HERNANI: No! No, you devil, I free myself from you—I shall not obey!

MASK: I suspected you would not. Very well. For after all, how did you swear this vow? On nothing so important, after all—only your father's head. That can be overlooked. Youth's vows are frivolous.

HERNANI: My father! Father! Oh, I shall go mad!

MASK: No, it is only perjury and treason.

HERNANI: Duke!

MASK: Since the sons of Spanish houses play so lightly now with pledges and denials, farewell! [*He makes as if to go*]

HERNANI: Stay!

MASK: Well then—

HERNANI: Cruel old man! [*He raises the vial*] I turn about and trace my steps back to the door of heaven!

[Doña Sol *returns, but does not see the masked figure, who stands at the rear*]

SCENE VI.

DOÑA SOL: I could not find your box—

HERNANI: [*Aside*] She has returned! And at so terrible a moment!

DOÑA SOL: I startle him, he shudders at my voice! . . . What have you in your hand? No—what have you in your hand? Answer me! [*The domino approaches and unmasks. She cries out as she recognizes* Don Ruy] It is poison!

HERNANI: Great heaven!

DOÑA SOL: [*To* Hernani] What have I done to you? What hellish mystery! You meant to betray me, Don Juan!

HERNANI: I should have hid it from you. When the duke saved me I promised him that I would die at his command. Aragon must pay its debt to Silva.

DOÑA SOL: You belong to me, and not to him. What do I care for any other of your vows? [*To Don Ruy Gomez*] Duke, love makes me strong. I shall defend him, against you and all the world.

DON RUY GOMEZ: [*Immobile*] Defend him if you can against a sworn pledge.

DOÑA SOL: What pledge?

HERNANI: I did swear it.

DOÑA SOL: No, no—nothing shall bind you! It cannot be! It is a crime! Murder! Madness!

DON RUY GOMEZ: Duke, let us proceed.

[Hernani *makes as if to obey.* Doña Sol *tries to draw him away*]

HERNANI: No, Doña Sol; I must. The Duke has my word, and my father is watching from above.

DOÑA SOL: [*To Don Ruy Gomez*] You would do better to tear their young from the tigers than the one I love from me! Do you know this Doña Sol? For a long while, compassion for your age and for your sixty years made me the docile daughter, all innocent and mild. But now you see my eyes are wet with tears of rage. [*She draws a dagger from her bodice*] And do you see this dagger? Ah, you mad old man, do you not fear the knife, when the eye has already sent its threat? Take care, Don Ruy, my uncle; I am of your line! Listen to me. Were I your very daughter, woe to you if you should lift your hand against my husband! [*She throws down the knife, and falls to her knees before the duke*] Mercy! Alas, my lord, I am only a woman! I am weak, my strength stops short within my soul. I break too easily. I fall to your feet! Ah, I implore you, have pity on us!

DON RUY GOMEZ: Doña Sol!

DOÑA SOL: Forgive! We Spaniards speak our pain in hasty words, you know that. You were not cruel before! Have pity! Uncle, you kill me in wounding him! Pity—I love him so!

DON RUY GOMEZ: [*Darkly*] You love him too well!

HERNANI: [*To Doña Sol*] Do you weep?

DOÑA SOL: No, no, my love—you must not die! No, I will not let you! [*To Don Ruy*] Be merciful today! I shall be fond of you as well!

DON RUY GOMEZ: After him! Do you think to appease the thirst that harrows me with such remnants of love—of friendship—no, even less than that! [*Points to* Hernani] He is the only one. He is everything. But I, what need have I for pity? What can I do with your affection? Oh, fury! He, he would have your heart, your love, the throne, and he would offer me the alms of a kind glance from you! And if a word were needed to calm my wild desires, he would tell you "Say this, and nothing more," cursing below his breath the avid beggar who gets the leavings in the empty cup. Shame! and mockery! No. It must be ended. Drink!

HERNANI: He has my word, and I must keep it.

DON RUY GOMEZ: Drink!

[Hernani *brings the vial to his lips.* Doña Sol *throws herself upon his arm*]

DOÑA SOL: Not yet! Both of you, ah hear me!

DON RUY GOMEZ: The grave is open, and I cannot wait.

DOÑA SOL: A moment! My lord, and my Don Juan! Ah, both of you, you are so harsh! What do I ask of them? An instant only, I ask no more! A moment to let this sorry woman speak what is in her heart! Oh let me speak!

DON RUY GOMEZ: [*To* Hernani] I cannot wait.

DOÑA SOL: My lords, you make me tremble! What have I done to you?

HERNANI: Her cry undoes me!

DOÑA SOL: [*Still clutching his arm*] You see I have a thousand things to say!

DON RUY GOMEZ: [*To* Hernani] Death is waiting.

DOÑA SOL: [*Still hanging from* Hernani's *arm*] Don Juan, when I have spoken, you shall do what you will. [*She snatches the vial from him*] I have it now! [*She raises the vial to the gaze of* Hernani *and the astonished old man*]

DON RUY GOMEZ: Since I must deal here with two women, Don Juan, I shall go elsewhere to seek souls. You make fine vows upon the blood you spring from; I shall go now among the dead and speak of it to your father. Farewell. [*He takes a few steps away.* Hernani *holds him back*]

HERNANI: Duke, stop! [*To Doña Sol*] Alas, I implore you, would you see me a man of false word, a felon, a perjurer? Would you have me go about the world with treason written on my brow? For pity's sake, give me back that poison! by our love, by our immortal souls. . . !

DOÑA SOL: [*Somberly*] You wish it? [*She drinks*] Here, take it now.

DON RUY GOMEZ: [*Aside*] Then it was meant for her!

DOÑA SOL: [*Handing* Hernani *the half-empty vial*] Take it, I tell you!

HERNANI: [*To Don Ruy*] You see this, vile old man!

DOÑA SOL: Do not be angry with me; I saved your share for you.

HERNANI: [*Taking the vial*] Lord God!

DOÑA SOL: You would not have left mine for me. You! You have not the heart a Christian wife has. You cannot love as a Silva loves. But I have drunk first and am at peace. Go on! Drink if you wish!

HERNANI: Alas, what have you done, my wretched love!

DOÑA SOL: It is you who forced me to it.

HERNANI: It is a hideous death!

DOÑA SOL: No, why should it be?

HERNANI: This potion takes us to the grave!

DOÑA SOL: Were we not to sleep together through this night? What difference in what bed?

HERNANI: My father, you have your revenge on me, for I forgot you! [*He puts the vial to his lips*]

DOÑA SOL: [*Throwing herself upon him*] Ah heaven! What unearthly agony! Ah, throw that flask far from you! My reason's wandering. Stop! Alas, my

Don Juan, this poison is a living thing! It opens out a hundred-toothed hydra in the heart that gnaws and then devours! Ah, I did not know one could feel such hideous pain! What is that thing? Pure fire! Do not drink it! You would suffer too horribly!

HERNANI: [*To* Don Ruy] Ah, your soul is wicked! Could you not choose a different way for her? [*He drinks, and throws down the vial*]

DOÑA SOL: What are you doing?

HERNANI: What have you done?

DOÑA SOL: Come, oh my young love, come to my arms. [*They sit by one another*] Is it not a terrible pain?

HERNANI: No.

DOÑA SOL: So now begins our wedding night! Am I not strangely pale for a young bride?

HERNANI: Ah!

DON RUY GOMEZ: Now destiny is done.

HERNANI: What torment! That Doña Sol should suffer, and I watch!

DOÑA SOL: Be calm. It is better now. Soon we shall open our wings together, and move toward some new brightness. Let us fly side by side toward a better world. . . . A kiss, though; only a kiss! [*They embrace*]

DON RUY GOMEZ: Oh, what pain to see them. . . .

HERNANI: [*His voice weakening*] Oh, blessed be heaven; it gave me a life hemmed in by chasms and haunted by shades; but when I wearied of so hard a road, it let me drop to sleep, with my lips pressed to your hand!

DON RUY GOMEZ: They are happy!

HERNANI: [*His voice weaker and weaker*] Come, come . . . Doña Sol . . . it is dark. Are you in pain?

DOÑA SOL: [*Her voice as faint*] Nothing, nothing now. . . .

HERNANI: Do you see flames within the shade?

DOÑA SOL: Not yet.

HERNANI: [*With a sigh*] Here . . . [*He falls*]

DON RUY GOMEZ: [*Raising his head, then dropping it*] Dead!

DOÑA SOL: [Disheveled, half rising from her bench] Dead! No, not dead! we are asleep. He sleeps. You see, he is my husband. We love one another. This is where we shall lie. It is our bridal night. [*Her voice failing*] Do not awaken him. He is weary. [*She turns* Hernani's *head to her*] Turn your face to me, my love. Nearer . . . nearer still. . . . [*She falls back*]

DON RUY GOMEZ: Dead! Oh, I am damned! [*He kills himself*]

Alexander Ostrovsky. *Opposite page:* Brereton as George Barnwell, Act III, *The London Merchant,* from an engraving published December 1, 1776. Theatre Collection, Library and Museum of the Performing Arts at Lincoln Center.

Middle Class Drama

Middle Class Drama

As important in the history of the drama as it is of special importance in the modern theatre is the type of play that has been designated middle-class drama, *drame bourgeois*. Programmatically most significant is the term *middle-class tragedy* because it reflects a surge toward social recognition or status on the part of the middle-classes which became pronounced during the eighteenth century. A parallel development in the same century's theatre was a species of middle-class comedy that came to be known in France as *comédie larmoyante* and in England, where it succeeded Restoration comedy of urbane banter and wit, as "sentimental comedy." The two middle-class genres were, as a matter of fact, not particularly distinguishable since "sentimental comedy" purveyed more sobriety than amusement and "middle-class tragedy" more sentiment than tragic exaltation.

In the field of dramatic criticism there has been much controversy whenever more than very modest claims have been advanced for a middle-class drama. Even after the American and French Revolutions of the late eighteenth century, it was difficult for formal critics and romantic writers to reconcil themselves to the trend toward a style of playwriting in which common characters and situations dominated the dramatic action. Rigorous critics have looked askance at Ibsen, the alleged father of modern drama, and they have vigorously rejected Arthur Miller's claims to have written tragedy with such plays as *Death of a Salesman* and *A View from the Bridge*. But proponents of middle-class drama have defended it as the most democratic and therefore most modern form of theatre insofar as it vested in the common man, real tragic passion and dramatic significance.

Perhaps no one in our times has pressed the claims of the ordinary citizen more forcefully and exemplified him more persuasively than did Arthur Miller. He did so first with *Death of a Salesman* in 1949 and in the prefatory comments he published immediately before its New York première in *The New York Times* under the title of "Tragedy and the Common Man." Here he wrote that "Insistence upon the rank of the tragic hero or the so-called nobility of his character, is really but a clinging to the outward forms of tragedy," adding that "surely the right of one monarch to capture the domain from another [as in many a conventional tragedy written since the Renaissance] no longer raises our passions. . . ." According to Miller, in tragedy, man, regardless of his rank in society, is driven to assert his right to self-realization and engages in a struggle or "thrust for freedom" against the confining circumstances of his existence, whether these be considered primarily psychological or "purely sociological."

Middle-class elements actually appeared in the European drama long before the nineteenth century; in the Middle Ages, when the drama began to proliferate in prosperous towns under the auspices of the municipality or the medieval guilds and during the Elizabethan period, when the middle-class grew in wealth and influence, its life was vividly treated in many a comedy, most notably in Thomas Dekker's *The Shoemaker's Holiday* (1599). Middle-class tragedy also made an effective appearance at this time and three extant plays call for special notice. The earliest is the anonymous *Arden of Feversham*, a drama of adultery and murder once attributed to the tragedian Thomas Kyd, and even to Shakespeare. The play takes into account the greed of a gentleman who has a passion for land-grabbing at a time when the enclosure of communal land for private gain was common practice. Characteristically, the unidentified author, whose main concern with the theme of adultery has no direct relation to this subject, tries to draw a moral from it. Arden, whose unfaithful wife connives in his death at the hands of hired assassins, is significantly buried in the same plot of ground that he had wrested from its owner. Heaven has evidently taken a hand in punishing him for his sin of avarice. A second Elizabethan drama, a domestic drama with a middle-class savor, Thomas Heywood's *A Woman Killed with Kindness* (1603), is a distinctly lugubrious play in which an adulteress dies of grief. Here the besetting sentimentality of middle-class drama characteristically undermines the tragic possibilities of the work by substituting pathos in large measure for tragic austerity and exhilaration.

A third and somewhat later play, *The Yorkshire Tragedy* (1608), also falsely attributed to Shakespeare, revolves around an obsessive gambler whose remorse is worse than his misconduct since it leads him to strangle the children and wound the wife he has impoverished with his weakness. This play is flawed by both melodramatic and moralizing traits, but these did not conflict with the taste of the age and were not deemed inacceptable in the then loosely defined genre of tragedy. *The Yorkshire Tragedy* belonged to a type of domestic dramas or domestic tragedies considerably in vogue and somewhat related to the medieval and Tudor moralities. Significantly these plays not only possessed much realistic detail but were, in a number of instances (such as *Arden of Feversham, A Warning to Fair Women* and *The Yorkshire Tragedy*) founded upon actual murder cases, foreshadowing in this respect journalistic tendencies in the modern realistic theatre.

Already in the sixteenth century, a claim for middle-class realism may be noted as a counterweight to the generally aristocratic bias of Elizabethan tragedy, "a reaction from the royalties, marvels, and unrealities of the contemporary tragedy," as Ashley Thorndike puts it in a book on English tragedy. This view is stated directly in the Epilogue to *Arden of Fever-*

sham in which the author requests pardon for "this naked tragedy" which has "nothing to make it gracious to the ear and eye" but claims that "simple truth is gracious enough/And needs no other point of glossing stuff." It was in the eighteenth century, however, even before the climactic advance of middle-class consciousness in the course of the American and French revolutions, that a program for middle-class tragedy came to be strongly worded if only partially achieved.

A claim for so-called serious drama or the *genre sérieux*, as contrasted with the pomp and sonorities of conventional high tragedy, was advanced by the French encyclopedist and intellectual leader Denis Diderot in an essay he provided for his drama *Le Père de Famille* (1758). He directly contended in that essay that a writer must not merely understand human nature in a general sense but be "a student of the social system and know well its function and importance, its advantages, and disadvantages." He claimed that his own play brought to the stage such matters of a directly practical and objective nature as "education, the duties of fathers toward their children, of the children to their parents, marriage, celibacy"; that his domestic drama actually treated the family as a sort of microcosm of the social system and its problems.[1]

Several years later, in an "Essay on the Serious Drama," Beaumarchais followed Diderot's example when he wrote a defense of his early middle-class play *Eugénie* in 1767. In it he contended that there could be "neither interest nor moral appeal on the stage without some sort of connection between a play and its audience," that the real relationship is always between man and man, "not between man and king," and "that the nearer the suffering man [in a play] is to my station in life the greater is his claim upon my sympathy.[2] But neither *Eugénie* nor Diderot's earlier produced play achieved any success or exerted much direct influence on the course of the theatre.

In England, a considerably earlier play, George Lillo's *The London Merchant* (1731), did. It influenced Diderot, in fact; and it contributed with Diderot's help, to the development of bourgeois drama in Germany, starting in 1755 with the critic Lessing's first major play, *Miss Sara Sampson*, which reflects Samuel Richardson's famous novel *Clarissa Harlowe*. From then on, there was a steady movement on the European continent toward social realism in the context of middle-class life, culminating in Germany in Hebbel's mid-century masterpiece *Maria Magdalena*, in Russia in the work of Ostrovsky, in France in the plays of Dumas *fils* and Augier, and in Scandinavia in the writings of Ibsen and Björnson.[3]

In England the climactic development was reached during the first two decades of the twentieth century in the social dramas of John Galsworthy (such as *Justice* and *Strife*); in the United States after 1930 in the work of Clifford Odets, most notably in *Awake and Sing* (1935). In the American theatre, Odets was succeeded by Miller, who in his 1958 introduction to *Collected Plays* contended with missionary zeal that "it matters not at all in tragedy whether his [a playwright's] hero falls from a great height or a small one, whether he is highly conscious or dimly aware of what is happening, whether his pride brings the fall or an unseen pattern written in the clouds." Despite obvious shortcomings, then, Lillo's *The London Merchant* (pages 965–987) is a milestone in dramatic history.

How far the middle-class tragedy could go later on without ceasing perhaps to be both "middle-class" and "tragedy" is exemplified by Ostrovsky's *The Thunderstorm* (pages 990–1012). Without announcing a program of *drame bourgeois*, Ostrovsky captured a Russian merchant-class environment capitally and made his dramatic action arise from it with compelling power. Moreover, writing almost a century and a half later than Lillo, the Russian author is inclined to be critical of the milieu. In this respect, Ostrovsky and many other modern playwrights part company with Lillo, who appears to have considered it his duty to exalt the mercantile world by idealizing it with its representatives, especially with George Barnwell's employer Thorowgood (whose very name proclaims his merit to the world), as well as with pronouncements on the integrity of the rising mercantile world.

Ostrovsky's dramatic technique, the result of greater experience with realistic playwrighting than anyone could have had in the early eighteenth century, is distinctly superior to Lillo's. It focuses on a central character instead of diverging from it, and it secures empathy for his middle-class heroine without sentimentality. Lillo endeavored to cajole the public into sympathizing with George Barnwell by stressing the remorse of the young criminal and the forgiveness extended to him by the worthy characters, including the uncle he stabbed to death for his money, whereas Ostrovsky could let the plight of his well-drawn Katerina speak for itself. Modern realism had sufficiently advanced by the middle of the nineteenth century to provide middle-class drama with ample individuality of characterization; the characters no longer bear any resemblance to Morality Play *personae*. The style of a modern prose drama such as *The Thunderstorm* exemplifies emancipation from

[1] See pp. 238–251 of Barrett Clark's *European Theories of the Drama*, newly revised by Henry Popkin, New York: Crown, 1965.

[2] Clark, pp. 253–259.

[3] For some special studies in this area, see especially F. O. Nolte's *Early Middle Class Drama*, Lancaster, Pa.: Lancaster Press, 1935; Artur Eloesser's *Das Bürgerliche Drama*, 1898; and Elise Dosenheimer's *Das Deutsche soziale Drama von Lessing bis Sternheim*, 1949. Beginning in the modern theatre of the eighteen-nineties there follows an offshoot of bourgeois social drama—"working-class" or "proletarian" drama, whose first masterpiece, Gerhart Hauptmann's *The Weavers*, appeared in 1892.

pseudopoetic artificiality whereas Lillo's stiff prose dialogue is often disguised blank verse. Modern writers of prose drama really learned how to write good dialogue, although they sacrificed this knowledge, not always with the least results, when Maeterlinck and others started employing poetic prose for symbolist and neoromantic drama toward the end of the century.

With the Hegelian Hebbel's middle-class midcentury tragedy *Maria Magdalena* (pages 634–653), in which a dialectical view of social realism asserts itself, we move toward the critical realist Ibsen, one of the masters of modern drama. With Turgenev's *A Month in the Country* (pages 654–699), we approach another modern master, the poetic naturalist Chekhov. With Ostrovsky we move toward the numerous playwrights of secondary rank who have filled the modern theatre with familiar middle-class environments, tensions, and problems.

With these developments in middle-class drama we stand on the threshold of the stage of ultrademocratic art—namely, the serious dramatic treatment of the common man as peasant, urban worker, slum dweller, and derelict. We cross this threshold in the late eighteen-eighties with Tolstoy in his powerful peasant tragedy *The Power of Darkness* and in the early eighteen-nineties with Gerhart Hauptmann's naturalistic account of a working class revolt in midcentury Germany, *The Weavers*. With these plays we enter the theatre of the twentieth century which gives us masterpieces by Sean O'Casey and Bertolt Brecht, such as *The Plough and the Stars*[4] and *The Good Woma of Setzuan*. Middle-class tragedy is indeed the opening wedge into an important area of modern drama.

[4] See Volume II of *A Treasury of the Theatre*.

George Lillo and The London Merchant

Little is known about George Lillo (1693–1739) except that he may have been of Flemish descent and that he was said to have been a jeweller in the City of London. Why he turned to playwriting is not known, but it is plain that he made a career of it. His first play, *Sylvia, or the Country Burial,* was performed in London with apparently no success in 1731, but his next play, *The London Merchant, or the History of George Barnwell,* produced in the same year, won instant and immense popularity. Three years later, he had a traditional neoclassic blank-verse tragedy, *The Christian Hero,* on the stage; and in 1736 a melodrama also in blank verse, *The Fatal Curiosity,* best known today in Albert Camus' Existentialist treatment, *Le Malentendu* (c. 1944), *The Misunderstanding* (translated in the United States under the title of *Cross-Purposes*), deals with the murder of a long absent son by his mother and sister, who fail to identify him when he conceals his identity from them; here the plot was used as a demonstration of the absurdity of life. A year before his death, Lillo made an unsuccessful adaptation of Shakespeare's romantic drama *Pericles,* and about the same time he wrote two posthumously produced plays, an adaptation of the anonymous early middle-class drama *Arden of Feversham* and a neoclassic blank-verse tragedy *Elmerick, or Justice Triumphant.* It is also known that he provided a masque, *Britannia and Batavia,* in 1734 for the celebration of the marriage of the Princess Royal of England with the Prince of Orange. It is evident that the ex-jeweller had become a professional, if generally hack, playwright.

Lillo's sole claim to fame in the annals of the stage is *The London Merchant,* a play written appropriately in prose, which in addition to winning success in the theatre ran through seven printings within less than a decade after the stage production. Lillo himself made claims for his *chef d'oeuvre* to which his large middle-class public could subscribe, writing in the dedicatory epistle he appended to the published work that "If Tragick Poetry be, as Mr. [John] Dryden has somewhere said, the most excellent and most useful kind of writing, the most extensively useful the moral of any tragedy is the most excellent that piece must be of its kind." He added a generalization which connects Lillo with the later French champions of middle-class drama, Diderot and Beaumarchais: "What I would infer is this, I think, evident truth: that tragedy is so far from losing its dignity by being accommodated to the circumstance of the generality of mankind that it is more truly august in proportion to the extent of its influence, and the numbers [that is, the number of people] that are properly affected

by it." He also observed that "If Princes, etc., were alone liable to misfortunes arising from vice or weakness in themselves or others, there would be good reason for confining the characters in tragedy to those of superior rank; but, since the contrary is evident, nothing can be more reasonable than to proportion the remedy to the disease." And intelligently considering himself a forerunner of a relatively new genre of playwriting rather than as its consummate master (a title reserved about a century and a half later for Henrik Ibsen), he declared that he had attempted "to enlarge the promise of the province of the graver kind of poetry and should be glad to see it carried on by some abler hand."

The early eighteenth century London public was apparently less fastidious in criticism than the author in self-appraisal. The distinct didacticism of *The London Merchant* won the unqualified approval of the middle-class which reportedly sent its young apprentices to the play for moral instruction. They were expected to draw a warning lesson from the fate of an impressionable youth ensnared into crime by an immoral woman. The play, which opened at the Drury Lane Theatre on June 22, 1731, appeared as a refreshing novelty, and accorded well with the sentiments of the theatre's growing middle-class audience.

Lillo proved to be both a skillful contriver of plot and a spokesman for middle-aspirations, especially in the characterization of George Barnwell's worthy employer Thorowgood, who intended to marry his daughter to a lord, and expected thereby to derive "status" from his thrift and mercantile assiduity. If the characters have little psychological reality and genuine individuality but bear kinship to stock morality figures, they nevertheless serve the author's intentions unmistakably—and theatrically. And if the play is apt to strike present-day readers and audiences as unmitigated melodrama, for Lillo's contemporaries it had earnestness of purpose to its credit and recommended itself to them as a genre of democratic tragedy.

This was the case not merely in England but in western Europe generally. *The London Merchant* was translated into French by 1748 and won Diderot's approbation, and became the basis of German middle-class tragedy when Lessing fell under Lillo's spell. In England it set the example for Edward Moore's *The Gamester,* presented in 1753, and became the subject of a maudlin street ballad entitled "The Ballad of George Barnwell." Lillo's play continued to be revived even as late as 1796 when the famous actor Charles Kemble played George Barnwell while his sister, the celebrated Mrs. Siddons,

963

known to her admirers as the Tragic Muse, played Millwood. And as late as the middle of the present century the prominent British editor and critic Bonamy Dobree[1] thought it still possessed vitality or "a certain rough being" as well as both literary quality and acting possibilities despite its maudlin embellishments, some artificial rhetoric, and moraliz-

ing scene conclusions in the form of rhymed couplets. In providing social causation in the case of courtesan Millwood's situation, moreover, Lillo anticipated a major characteristic of modern drama, which has tended to translate Greek concepts of fate into naturalistic terms of environment as well as of instinct and heredity.

---

[1] Introduction (1948) to an edition of *The London Merchant,* New York: Grove, 1952. See also *Understanding Drama* by Cleanth Brooks and Robert B. Heilman, New York: Holt, Rinehart and Winston, 1948, pp. 146–189. Brooks and Heilman emphasize "Lillo's muddled sense· of tragedy," failure to centralize the action and keep the main character in focus, lapses into conventional dialogue, and his "tendency to wander into the extraneous."

THE LONDON MERCHANT

OR THE HISTORY OF GEORGE BARNWELL

By George Lillo

DRAMATIS PERSONAE

THOROWGOOD	MARIA
BARNWELL, *Uncle to* George	MILLWOOD
GEORGE BARNWELL	LUCY
TRUEMAN	
BLUNT	
OFFICERS *with their* ATTENDANTS	
KEEPER	
FOOTMEN	

SCENE: *London, and an adjacent Village*

ACT I. SCENE I.

A Room in Thorowgood's *House.*

[*Enter* Thorowgood *and* Trueman]

TRUEMAN: Sir, the packet from Genoa is arriv'd. [*Gives letters*]

THOROWGOOD: Heav'n be praised, the storm that threatened our royal mistress, pure religion, liberty and laws, is for a time diverted; the haughty and revengeful Spaniard, disappointed of the loan on which he depended from Genoa, must now attend the slow return of wealth from his new world, to supply his empty coffers, e'er he can execute his purpos'd invasion of our happy island; by which means time is gain'd to make such preparations on our part as may, Heav'n concurring, prevent his malice, or turn the meditated mischief on himself.

TRUEMAN: He must be insensible indeed, who is not affected when the safety of his country is concern'd.—Sir, may I know by what means—if I am too bold—

THOROWGOOD: Your curiosity is laudable; and I gratify it with the greater pleasure, because from thence you may learn how honest merchants, as such, may sometimes contribute to the safety of their country, as they do at all times to its happiness; that if hereafter you should be tempted to any action that has the appearance of vice or meanness in it, upon reflecting on the dignity of our profession, you may with honest scorn reject whatever is unworthy of it.

TRUEMAN: Shou'd Barnwell, or I, who have the benefit of your example, by our ill conduct bring any imputation on that honourable name, we must be left without excuse.

THOROWGOOD: You compliment, young man. [Trueman *bows respectfully*] Nay, I'm not offended. As the name of merchant never degrades the gentleman, so by no means does it exclude him; only take heed not to purchase the character of complaisant at the expense of your sincerity.—But to answer your question. The bank of Genoa had agreed, at excessive interest and on good security, to advance the King of Spain a sum of money sufficient to equip his vast Armada; of which our peerless Elizabeth (more than in name, the Mother of her People) being well informed, sent Walsingham, her wise and faithful secretary, to consult the merchants of this loyal city, who all agreed to direct their several agents to influence, if possible, the Genoese to break their contract with the Spanish court. 'Tis done; the state and bank of Genoa, having maturely weigh'd and rightly judged of their true interest, prefer the friendship of the merchants of London to that of a monarch who proudly stiles himself King of both Indies.

TRUEMAN: Happy success of prudent councils! What an expence of blood and treasure is here saved! Excellent Queen! O how unlike to former princes, who made the danger of foreign enemies a pretence to oppress their subjects by taxes great and grievous to be borne.

THOROWGOOD: Not so our gracious Queen, whose richest exchequer is her people's love, as their happiness her greatest glory.

TRUEMAN: On these terms to defend us, is to make our protection a benefit worthy her who confers it, and well worth our acceptance.—Sir, have you any commands for me at this time.

THOROWGOOD: Only to look carefully over the files to see whether there are any trades-mens bills unpaid; and if there are, to send and discharge 'em. We must not let artificers lose their time, so useful to the publick and their families, in unnecessary attendance.[1]

[*Exit* Trueman]

SCENE II.

Thorowgood *and* Maria.

[*Enter* Maria]

THOROWGOOD: Well, Maria, have you given orders for the entertainment? I would have it in some measure worthy the guests. Let there be plenty, and of the best; that the courtiers, tho' they should deny us citizens politeness, may at least commend our hospitality.

MARIA: Sir, I have endeavoured not to wrong your well-known generosity by an ill-tim'd parsimony.

THOROWGOOD: Nay, 'twas a needless caution; I have no cause to doubt your prudence.

MARIA: Sir, I find myself unfit for conversation at present; I should but increase the number of the company without adding to their satisfaction.

THOROWGOOD: Nay, my child, this melancholy must not be indulged.

MARIA: Company will but increase it. I wish you would dispense with my absence; solitude best suits my present temper.

THOROWGOOD: You are not insensible that it is chiefly on your account these noble lords do me the honour so frequently to grace my board; shou'd you be absent, the disappointment may make them repent their condescension, and think their labour lost.

MARIA: He that shall think his time or honour lost in visiting you can set no real value on your daughter's company, whose only merit is that she is yours. The man of quality, who chuses to converse with a gentleman and merchant of your worth and character may confer honour by so doing, but he loses none.

THOROWGOOD: Come, come, Maria; I need not tell you that a young gentleman may prefer your conversation to mine, yet intend me no disrespect at all; for, tho' he may lose no honour in my company, 'tis very natural for him to expect more pleasure in yours. I remember the time when the company of the greatest and wisest man in the kingdom would have been insipid and tiresome to me if it had deprived me of an opportunity of enjoying your mother's.

MARIA: Your's no doubt was as agreeable to her; for generous minds know no pleasure in society but where 'tis mutual.

THOROWGOOD: Thou know'st I have no heir, no child but thee; the fruits of many years successful industry must all be thine. Now, it would give me pleasure great as my love to see on whom you would

[1] In waiting to be paid

bestow it. I am daily solicited by men of the greatest rank and merit for leave to address you; but I have hitherto declin'd it, in hopes that by observation I shou'd learn which way your inclination tends; for, as I know love to be essential to happiness in the marriage state, I had rather my approbation should confirm your choice than direct it.

MARIA: What can I say? How shall I answer, as I ought, this tenderness, so uncommon even in the best of parents? But you are without example; yet had you been less indulgent, I had been most wretched. That I look on the croud of courtiers that visit here with equal esteem, but equal indifference, you have observed, and I must needs confess; yet had you asserted your authority, and insisted on a parent's right to be obey'd, I had submitted, and to my duty sacrificed my peace.

THOROWGOOD: From your perfect obedience in every other instance, I fear'd as much; and therefore wou'd leave you without a byass in an affair wherein your happiness is so immediately concern'd.

MARIA: Whether from a want of that just ambition that wou'd become your daughter, or from some other cause, I know not; but I find high birth and titles don't recommend the man who owns them to my affections.

THOROWGOOD: I wou'd not that they shou'd, unless his merit recommends him more. A noble birth and fortune, tho' they make not a bad man good, yet they are a real advantage to a worthy one, and place his virtues in the fairest light.

MARIA: I cannot answer for my inclinations, but they shall ever be submitted to your wisdom and authority; and, as you will not compel me to marry where I cannot love, so love shall never make me act contrary to my duty. Sir, have I your permission to retire?

THOROWGOOD: I'll see you to your chamber.

[*Exeunt*]

SCENE III.

A Room in Millwood's *House.*

[Millwood *at her toilet.* Lucy, *waiting*]

MILLWOOD: How do I look to day, Lucy?

LUCY: O, killingly, madam! A little more red, and you'll be irresistible! But why this more than ordinary care of your dress and complexion? What new conquest are you aiming at?

MILLWOOD: A conquest wou'd be new indeed!

LUCY: Not to you, who make 'em every day, but to me.—Well! 'tis what I'm never to expect, unfortunate as I am. But your wit and beauty——

MILLWOOD: First made me a wretch, and still continue me so. Men, however generous or sincere to one another, are all selfish hypocrites in their affairs with us. We are no otherwise esteemed or regarded by them, but as we contribute to their satisfaction.

LUCY: You are certainly, madam, on the wrong side in this argument. Is not the expence all theirs? And I am sure it is our own fault, if we hav'n't our share of the pleasure.

MILLWOOD: We are but slaves to men.

LUCY: Nay, 'tis they that are slaves most certainly; for we lay them under contribution.

MILLWOOD: Slaves have no property; no, not even in themselves. All is the victor's.

LUCY: You are strangely arbitrary in your principles, madam.

MILLWOOD: I would have my conquests compleat, like those of the Spaniards in the New World: who first plunder'd the natives of all the wealth they had, and then condemn'd the wretches to the mines for life to work for more.

LUCY: Well, I shall never approve of your scheme of government; I should think it much more politick, as well as just, to find my subjects an easier imployment.

MILLWOOD: It's a general maxim among the knowing part of mankind, that a woman without virtue, like a man without honour or honesty, is capable of any action, tho' never so vile; and yet, what pains will they not take, what arts not use, to seduce us from our innocence, and make us contemptible and wicked, even in their own opinions! Then is it not just, the villains, to their cost, should find us so. —But guilt makes them suspicious, and keeps them on their guard; therefore we can take advantage only of the young and innocent part of the sex, who, having never injured women, apprehend no injury from them.

LUCY: Ay, they must be young indeed.

MILLWOOD: Such a one, I think, I have found.—As I've passed thro' the City, I have often observ'd him receiving and paying considerable sums of money; from thence I conclude he is employed in affairs of consequence.

LUCY: Is he handsome?

MILLWOOD: Ay, ay, the stripling is well made.

LUCY: About——

MILLWOOD: Eighteen.

LUCY: Innocent, handsome, and about eighteen. —You'll be vastly happy.—Why, if you manage well, you may keep him to your self these two or three years.

MILLWOOD: If I manage well, I shall have done with him much sooner. Having long had a design on him; and, meeting him yesterday, I made a full stop, and gazing wishfully on his face, ask'd him his name; he blush'd, and bowing very low, answer'd: 'George Barnwell'. I beg'd his pardon for the freedom I had taken, and told him that he was the person I had long wish'd to see, and to whom I had an affair of importance to communicate at a proper time and place. He named a tavern; I talk'd of honour and reputation, and invited him to my house: he swallow'd the

bait, promis'd to come, and this is the time I expect him. [*Knocking at the door*] Some body knocks— d'ye hear; I am at home to no body to day but him.
[*Exit* Lucy]

SCENE IV.

Millwood.

MILLWOOD: Less affairs must give way to those of more consequence; and I am strangely mistaken if this does not prove of great importance to me and him too, before I have done with him.—Now, after what manner shall I receive him? Let me consider —what manner of person am I to receive? He is young, innocent, and bashful; therefore I must take care not to shock him at first.—But then, if I have any skill in phisiognomy, he is amorous, and, with a little assistance, will soon get the better of his modesty.—I'll trust to nature, who does wonders in these matters.—If to seem what one is not, in order to be the better liked for what one really is; if to speak one thing, and mean the direct contrary, be art in a woman,—I know nothing of nature.

SCENE V.

[Millwood. *To her* Barnwell, *bowing very low.* Lucy *at a distance*]

MILLWOOD: Sir! the surprize and joy——

BARNWELL: Madam——

MILLWOOD: [*Advancing*] This is such a favour——

BARNWELL: [*Still advances*] Pardon me, madam——

MILLWOOD: So unhop'd for——[Barnwell *salutes her, and retires in confusion*] To see you here.—Excuse the confusion——

BARNWELL: I fear I am too bold.

MILLWOOD: Alas, sir! All my apprehensions proceed from my fears of your thinking me so.—Please, sir, to sit.—I am as much at a loss how to receive this honour as I ought, as I am surpriz'd at your goodness in confering it.

BARNWELL: I thought you had expected me—I promis'd to come.

MILLWOOD: That is the more surprizing; few men are such religious observers of their word.

BARNWELL: All who are honest are.

MILLWOOD: To one another.—But we silly women are seldom thought of consequence enough to gain a place in your remembrance.

[*Laying her hand on his, as by accident*]

BARNWELL: [*Aside*] Her disorder is so great, she don't perceive she has laid her hand on mine. Heaven! how she trembles!—What can this mean?

MILLWOOD: The interest I have in all that relates

to you (the reason of which you shall know here-after), excites my curiosity; and, were I sure you would pardon my presumption, I should desire to know your real sentiments on a very particular affair.

BARNWELL: Madam, you may command my poor thoughts on any subject; I have none that I would conceal.

MILLWOOD: You'll think me bold.

BARNWELL: No, indeed.

MILLWOOD: What then are your thoughts of love?

BARNWELL: If you mean the love of women, I have not thought of it at all.—My youth and circumstances make such thoughts improper in me yet. But if you mean the general love we owe to mankind, I think no one has more of it in his temper than my self.—I don't know that person in the world whose happiness I don't wish, and wou'dnt promote, were it in my power.—In an especial manner, I love my Uncle, and my Master, but, above all, my friend.

MILLWOOD: You have a friend then whom you love?

BARNWELL: As he does me, sincerely.

MILLWOOD: He is, no doubt, often bless'd with your company and conversation?

BARNWELL: We live in one house together, and both serve the same worthy merchant.

MILLWOOD: Happy, happy youth!—Who e'er thou art, I envy thee, and so must all, who see and know this youth.—What have I lost, by being form'd a woman! I hate my sex, my self. Had I been a man, I might, perhaps, have been as happy in your friendship as he who now enjoys it; but, as it is—Oh!

BARNWELL: [Aside] I never observ'd women before, or this is sure the most beautiful of her sex! You seem disorder'd, madam! May I know the cause?

MILLWOOD: Do not ask me,—I can never speak it, whatever is the cause.—I wish for things impossible. —I wou'd be a servant, bound to the same master as you are, to live in one house with you.

BARNWELL: [Aside] How strange, and yet how kind, her words and actions are! And the effect they have on me is as strange. I feel desires I never knew before;—I must be gone, while I have power to go. Madam, I humbly take my leave.

MILLWOOD: You will not sure leave me so soon!

BARNWELL: Indeed I must.

MILLWOOD: You cannot be so cruel!—I have prepar'd a poor supper, at which I promis'd my self your company.

BARNWELL: I am sorry I must refuse the honour that you design'd me—but my duty to my master calls me hence. I never yet neglected his service; he is so gentle, and so good a master, that, should I wrong him, tho' he might forgive me, I never should forgive my self.

MILLWOOD: Am I refus'd, by the first man, the second favour I ever stoop'd to ask?—Go then, thou proud hard-hearted youth!—But know, you are the only man that cou'd be found who would let me sue twice for greater favours.

BARNWELL: What shall I do!—How shall I go or stay!

MILLWOOD: Yet do not, do not, leave me! I wish my sex's pride wou'd meet your scorn:—But when I look upon you,—when I behold those eyes,—Oh! spare my tongue, and let my blushes speak.—This flood of tears to that will force their way, and declare —what woman's modesty should hide.

BARNWELL: Oh, heavens! she loves me, worthless as I am; her looks, her words, her flowing tears confess it;—and can I leave her then?—Oh, never, never! —Madam, dry up those tears! You shall command me always; I will stay here for ever, if you'd have me.

LUCY: [Aside] So! she has wheedled him out of his virtue of obedience already, and will strip him of all the rest of his virtues, one after another, 'till she has left him as few as her ladyship, or my self.

MILLWOOD: Now you are kind, indeed; but I mean not to detain you always. I would have you shake off all slavish obedience to your master; but you may serve him still.

LUCY: [Aside] Serve him still!—Aye, or he'll have no opportunity of fingering his cash, and then he'll not serve your end, I'll be sworn.

SCENE VI.

[To them Blunt]

BLUNT: Madam, supper's on the table.

MILLWOOD: Come, sir, you'll excuse all defects.— My thoughts were too much employ'd on my guest to observe the entertainment.

[Exeunt Millwood and Barnwell]

SCENE VII.

Lucy and Blunt.

BLUNT: What! is all this preparation, this elegant supper, variety of wines, and musick, for the entertainment of that young fellow?

LUCY: So it seems.

BLUNT: What! is our mistress turn'd fool at last? She's in love with him, I suppose.

LUCY: I suppose not; but she designs to make him in love with her, if she can.

BLUNT: What will she get by that? He seems under age, and can't be suppos'd to have much money.

LUCY: But his master has; and that's the same thing, as she'll manage it.

BLUNT: I don't like this fooling with a handsome young fellow; while she's endeavouring to ensnare him, she may be caught her self.

LUCY: Nay, were she like me, that would certainly

be the consequence; for, I confess, there is something in youth and innocence that moves me mightily.

BLUNT: Yes, so does the smoothness and plumpness of a partridge move a mighty desire in the hawk to be the destruction of it.

LUCY: Why, birds are their prey, as men are ours; though, as you observ'd, we are sometimes caught our selves; but that I dare say will never be the case with our mistress.

BLUNT: I wish it may prove so; for you know we all depend upon her. Should she trifle away her time with a young fellow, that there's nothing to be got by, we must all starve.

LUCY: There's no danger of that, for I am sure she has no view in this affair but interest.

BLUNT: Well, and what hopes are there of success in that?

LUCY: The most promising that can be. 'Tis true, the youth has his scruples; but she'll soon teach him to answer them, by stifling his conscience. O, the lad is in a hopeful way, depend upon't.

[*Exeunt*]

SCENE VIII.

Barnwell *and* Millwood *at an entertainment.*

BARNWELL: What can I answer? All that I know is that you are fair and I am miserable.

MILLWOOD: We are both so, and yet the fault is in ourselves.

BARNWELL: To ease our present anguish, by plunging into guilt, is to buy a moment's pleasure with an age of pain.

MILLWOOD: I should have thought the joys of love as lasting as they are great. If ours prove otherwise, 'tis your inconstancy must make them so.

BARNWELL: The law of Heaven will not be revers'd; and that requires us to govern our passions.

MILLWOOD: To give us sense of beauty and desires, and yet forbid us to taste and be happy, is cruelty to nature.—Have we passions only to torment us?

BARNWELL: To hear you talk, tho' in the cause of vice—to gaze upon your beauty—press your hand —and see your snow-white bosom heave and fall— enflames my wishes. My pulse beats high—my senses all are in a hurry, and I am on the rack of wild desire. Yet, for a moment's guilty pleasure, shall I lose my innocence, my peace of mind, and hopes of solid happiness.

MILLWOOD: *Chimeras all!—Come on with me and prove:*
No joy's like woman kind, nor Heav'n like love.

BARNWELL: I wou'd not, yet must on.—
Reluctant thus, the merchant quits his ease,
And trusts to rocks, and sands, and stormy seas;
In hopes some unknown golden coast to find,

Commits himself, tho' doubtful, to the wind;
Longs much for joys to come, yet mourns those left behind.

THE END OF THE FIRST ACT

ACT II. SCENE I.

A Room in Thorowgood's *House.*

[*Enter* Barnwell]

BARNWELL: How strange are all things round me! Like some thief, who treads forbidden ground, fearful I enter each apartment of this well known house. To guilty love, as if that was too little, already have I added breach of trust.—A thief!—Can I know my self that wretched thing, and look my honest friend and injured master in the face? Tho' hypocrisy may a while conceal my guilt, at length it will be known, and publick shame and ruin must ensue. In the mean time, what must be my life? Ever to speak a language foreign to my heart; hourly to add to the number of my crimes in order to conceal 'em.—Sure, such was the condition of the grand apostate, when first he lost his purity; like me, disconsolate he wander'd, and, while yet in Heaven, bore all his future Hell about him.

[*Enter* Trueman]

SCENE II.

Barnwell *and* Trueman.

TRUEMAN: Barnwell! O how I rejoice to see you safe! So will our master and his gentle daughter, who during your absence often inquir'd after you.

BARNWELL: [*Aside*] Wou'd he were gone! His officious love will pry into the secrets of my soul.

TRUEMAN: Unless you knew the pain the whole family has felt on your account, you can't conceive how much you are belov'd. But why thus cold and silent? When my heart is full of joy for your return, why do you turn away? why thus avoid me? What have I done? how am I alter'd since you saw me last? Or rather, what have you done? and why are you thus changed, for I am still the same.

BARNWELL: [*Aside*] What have I done, indeed?

TRUEMAN: Not speak nor look upon me!

BARNWELL: [*Aside*] By my face he will discover all I wou'd conceal; methinks, already I begin to hate him.

TRUEMAN: I cannot bear this usage from a friend —one whom till now I ever found so loving, whom yet I love, tho' this unkindness strikes at the root of friendship, and might destroy it in any breast but mine.

BARNWELL: [*Turning to him*] I am not well. Sleep

has been a stranger to these eyes since you beheld them last.

TRUEMAN: Heavy they look indeed, and swoln with tears;—now they o'erflow. Rightly did my sympathizing heart forbode last night, when thou wast absent, something fatal to our peace.

BARNWELL: Your friendship ingages you too far. My troubles, whate'er they are, are mine alone; you have no interest in them, nor ought your concern for me give you a moment's pain.

TRUEMAN: You speak as if you knew of friendship nothing but the name. Before I saw your grief I felt it. Since we parted last I have slept no more than you, but pensive in my chamber sat alone, and spent the tedious night in wishes for your safety and return; e'en now, tho' ignorant of the cause, your sorrow wounds me to the heart.

BARNWELL: 'Twill not be always thus. Friendship and all engagements cease, as circumstances and occasions vary; and, since you once may hate me, perhaps it might be better for us both that now you lov'd me less.

TRUEMAN: Sure, I but dream! Without a cause would Barnwell use me thus? Ungenerous and ungrateful youth, farewell!—I shall endeavour to follow your advice. [*Going*] [*Aside*] Yet stay, perhaps I am too rash, and angry when the cause demands compassion. Some unforeseen calamity may have befaln him, too great to bear.

BARNWELL: [*Aside*] What part am I reduc'd to act! 'Tis vile and base to move his temper thus—the best of friends and men!

TRUEMAN: I am to blame; prithee forgive me, Barnwell!—Try to compose your ruffled mind; and let me know the cause that thus transports you from your self: my friendly counsel may restore your peace.

BARNWELL: All that is possible for man to do for man, your generous friendship may effect; but here even that's in vain.

TRUEMAN: Something dreadful is labouring in your breast. O give it vent, and let me share your grief; 'twill ease your pain, shou'd it admit no cure, and make it lighter by the part I bear.

BARNWELL: Vain supposition! My woes increase by being observ'd; shou'd the cause be known, they wou'd exceed all bounds.

TRUEMAN: So well I know thy honest heart, guilt cannot harbour there.

BARNWELL: [*Aside*] O torture insupportable!

TRUEMAN: Then why am I excluded? Have I a thought I would conceal from you.

BARNWELL: If still you urge me on his hated subject, I'll never enter more beneath this roof, nor see your face again.

TRUEMAN: 'Tis strange—but I have done. Say but you hate me not!

BARNWELL: Hate you! I am not that monster yet.

TRUEMAN: Shall our friendship still continue?

BARNWELL: It's a blessing I never was worthy of; yet now must stand on terms, and but upon conditions can confirm it.

TRUEMAN: What are they?

BARNWELL: Never hereafter, tho' you shou'd wonder at my conduct, desire to know more than I am willing to reveal.

TRUE: 'Tis hard; but upon any conditions I must be your friend.

BARNWELL: Then, as much as one lost to himself can be another's, I am yours.

[*Embracing*]

TRUEMAN: Be ever so, and may Heav'n restore your peace!

BARNWELL: Will yesterday return? We have heard the glorious sun, that till then incessant roll'd, once stopp'd his rapid course, and once went back. The dead have risen, and parched rocks pour'd forth a liquid stream to quench a peoples thirst; the sea divided, and form'd walls of water, while a whole nation pass'd in safety thro' its sandy bosom; hungry lions have refus'd their prey, and men unhurt have walk'd amidst consuming flames. But never yet did time, once past, return.

TRUEMAN: Tho' the continued chain of time has never once been broken, nor ever will, but uninterrupted must keep on its course, till lost in eternity it ends there where it first begun: yet, as Heav'n can repair whatever evils time can bring upon us, he who trusts Heav'n ought never to despair. But business requires our attendance—business, the youth's best preservative from ill, as idleness his worst of snares. Will you go with me?

BARNWELL: I'll take a little time to reflect on what has past, and follow you.

[*Exit* Trueman]

SCENE III.

Barnwell.

BARNWELL: I might have trusted Trueman to have applied to my uncle to have repaired the wrong I have done my master,—but what of Millwood? Must I expose her too? Ungenerous and base! Then Heav'n requires it not.—But Heaven requires that I forsake her. What! never see her more! Does Heaven require that?—I hope I may see her, and Heav'n not be offended. Presumptuous hope—dearly already have I prov'd my frailty; should I once more tempt Heav'n, I may be left to fall never to rise again. Yet shall I leave her, for ever leave her, and not let her know the cause? She who loves me with such a boundless passion—can cruelty be duty? I judge of what she then must feel by what I now indure. The love of life and fear of shame, oppos'd by inclination strong as death or shame, like wind and tide in raging conflict met, when neither can prevail, keep me in doubt. How then can I determine?

SCENE IV.

Thorowgood *and* Barnwell.

[*Enter* Thorowgood]
THOROWGOOD: Without a cause assign'd, or notice given, to absent your self last night was a fault, young man, and I came to chide you for it, but hope I am prevented. That modest blush, the confusion so visible in your face, speak grief and shame. When we have offended Heaven, it requires no more; and shall man, who needs himself to be forgiven, he harder to appease? If my pardon or love be of moment to your peace, look up, secure of both.
BARNWELL: [*Aside*] This goodness has o'er come me.—O sir! you know not the nature and extent of my offence; and I shou'd abuse your mistaken bounty to receive 'em. Tho' I had rather die than speak my shame; tho' racks could not have forced the guilty secret from my breast, your kindness has.
THOROWGOOD: Enough, enough, whate'er it be, this concern shows you're convinc'd, and I am satisfied. [*Aside*] How painful is the sense of guilt to an ingenuous mind—some youthful folly which it were prudent not to enquire into.—When we consider the frail condition of humanity, it may raise our pity, not our wonder, that youth should go astray: when reason, weak at the best when oppos'd to inclination, scarce form'd, and wholly unassisted by experience, faintly contends, or willingly becomes the slave of sense. The state of youth is much to be deplored; and the more so, because they see it not: they being then to danger most expos'd, when they are least prepar'd for their defence.
BARNWELL: It will be known, and you recall your pardon and abhor me.
THOROWGOOD: I never will; so Heav'n confirm to me the pardon of my offences! Yet be upon your guard in this gay, thoughtless season of your life; now, when the sense of pleasure's quick, and passion high, the voluptuous appetites raging and fierce demand the strongest curb, take heed of a relapse: when vice becomes habitual, the very power of leaving it is lost.
BARNWELL: Hear me, then, on my knees confess——
THOROWGOOD: I will not hear a syllable more upon this subject; it were not mercy, but cruelty, to hear what must give you such torment to reveal.
BARNWELL: This generosity amazes and distracts me.
THOROWGOOD: This remorse makes thee dearer to me than if thou hadst never offended; whatever is your fault, of this I'm certain: 'twas harder for you to offend than me to pardon.
[*Exit*]

SCENE V.

Barnwell.

BARNWELL: Villain, villain, villain! basely to wrong so excellent a man! Shou'd I again return to folly—detested thought—but what of Millwood then?—Why, I renounce her;—I give her up:—the struggle's over and virtue has prevail'd. Reason may convince, but gratitude compels. This unlook'd for generosity has sav'd me from destruction.
[*Going*]

SCENE VI.

[Barnwell. *To him a* Footman]
FOOTMAN: Sir, two ladies from your uncle in the country desire to see you.
BARNWELL: [*Aside*] Who shou'd they be?—Tell them I'll wait upon 'em.
[*Exit* Footman]

SCENE VII.

Barnwell.

BARNWELL: Methinks I dread to see 'em. Guilt, what a coward hast thou made me! Now every thing alarms me.

SCENE VIII.

Another Room in Thorowgood's *House.*

[Millwood *and* Lucy, *and to them a* Footman]
FOOTMAN: Ladies, he'll wait upon you immediately.
MILLWOOD: 'Tis very well.—I thank you.
[*Exit* Footman]

SCENE IX.

Millwood *and* Lucy.

[*Enter* Barnwell]
BARNWELL: Confusion! Millwood!
MILLWOOD: That angry look tell me that here I'm an unwelcome guest. I fear'd as much—the unhappy are so everywhere.
BARNWELL: Will nothing but my utter ruin content you?
MILLWOOD: Unkind and cruel! Lost my self, your happiness is now my only care.

BARNWELL: How did you gain admission?

MILLWOOD: Saying we were desir'd by your uncle to visit and deliver a message to you, we were receiv'd by the family without suspicion, and with much respect directed here.

BARNWELL: Why did you come at all?

MILLWOOD: I never shall trouble you more; I'm come to take my leave for ever. Such is the malice of my fate. I go hopeless, despairing ever to return. This hour is all I have left me. One short hour is all I have to bestow on love and you, for whom I thought the longest life too short.

BARNWELL: Then we are met to part for ever?

MILLWOOD: It must be so—yet think not that time or absence ever shall put a period to my grief or make me love you less; tho' I must leave you, yet condemn me not!

BARNWELL: Condemn you? No, I approve your resolution, and rejoice to hear it. 'Tis just; 'tis necessary; I have well weigh'd, and found it so.

LUCY [Aside] I'm afraid the young man has more sense than she thought he had.

BARNWELL: Before you came, I had determin'd never to see you more.

MILLWOOD: [Aside] Confusion!

LUCY: [Aside] Ay! we are all out; this is a turn so unexpected, that I shall make nothing of my part; they must e'en play the scene betwixt themselves.

MILLWOOD: 'Twas some relief to think, tho' absent, you would love me still. But to find, tho' fortune had been kind, that you, more cruel and inconstant, had resolv'd to cast me off—this, as I never cou'd expect, I have not learnt to bear.

BARNWELL: I am sorry to hear you blame in me a resolution that so well becomes us both.

MILLWOOD: I have reason for what I do, but you have none.

BARNWELL: Can we want a reason for parting, who have so many to wish we never had met!

MILLWOOD: Look on me, Barnwell! Am I deform'd or old, that satiety so soon succeeds enjoyment? Nay, look again, am I not she whom yesterday you thought the fairest and the kindest of her sex? whose hand, trembling with extacy, you prest and moulded thus, while on my eyes you gazed with such delight, as if desire increas'd by being fed?

BARNWELL: No more; let me repent my former follies, if possible, without remembring what they were.

MILLWOOD: Why?

BARNWELL: Such is my frailty that 'tis dangerous.

MILLWOOD: Where is the danger, since we are to part?

BARNWELL: The thought of that already is too painful.

MILLWOOD: If it be painful to part, then I may hope at least you do not hate me?

BARNWELL: No—no—I never said I did.—O my heart!——

MILLWOOD: Perhaps you pity me?

BARNWELL: I do—I do—indeed, I do.

MILLWOOD: You'll think upon me?

BARNWELL: Doubt it not, while I can think at all!

MILLWOOD: You may judge an embrace at parting too great a favour, though it would be the last? [He draws back] A look shall then suffice—farewell for ever.

[Exit with Lucy]

SCENE X.

Barnwell.

BARNWELL: If to resolve to suffer be to conquer, I have conquer'd. Painful victory!

SCENE XI.

Barnwell, Millwood and Lucy.

[Re-enter Millwood and Lucy]

MILLWOOD: One thing I had forgot: I never must return to my own house again. This I thought proper to let you know, lest your mind shou'd change, and you shou'd seek in vain to find me there. Forgive me this second intrusion; I only came to give you this caution; and that perhaps was needless.

BARNWELL: I hope it was; yet it is kind, and I must thank you for it.

MILLWOOD: [To Lucy] My friend, your arm.—Now I am gone forever.

[Going]

BARNWELL: One thing more: sure, there's no danger in my knowing where you go?—If you think otherwise——

MILLWOOD: [Weeping] Alas!

LUCY: [Aside] We are right, I find; that's my cue. Ah; dear sir, she's going she knows not whither; but go she must.

BARNWELL: Humanity obliges me to wish you well: why will you thus expose your self to needless troubles?

LUCY: Nay, there's no help for it. She must quit the town immediately, and the kingdom as soon as possible; it was no small matter, you may be sure, that could make her resolve to leave you.

MILLWOOD: No more, my friend; since he for whose dear sake alone I suffer, and am content to suffer, is kind and pities me. Wheree'er I wander through wilds and desarts, benighted and forlorn, that thought shall give me comfort.

BARNWELL: For my sake! O tell me how; which way am I so curs'd as to bring such ruin on thee?

MILLWOOD: No matter, I am contented with my lot.

BARNWELL: Leave me not in this incertainty!

MILLWOOD: I have said too much.

BARNWELL: How, how am I the cause of your un-doing?

MILLWOOD: 'Twill but increase your troubles.

BARNWELL: My troubles can't be greater than they are.

LUCY: Well, well, sir; if she won't satisfy you, I will.

BARNWELL: I am bound to you beyond expression.

MILLWOOD: Remember, sir, that I desir'd you not to hear it.

BARNWELL: Begin, and ease my racking expectation!

LUCY: Why, you must know, my lady here was an only child; but her parents, dying while she was young, left her and her fortune (no inconsiderable one, I assure you) to the care of a gentleman who has a good estate of his own.

MILLWOOD: Ay, ay, the barbarous man is rich enough—but what are riches when compared to love?

LUCY: For a while he perform'd the office of a faithful guardian, settled her in a house, hir'd her servants—but you have seen in what manner she liv'd, so I need say no more of that.

MILLWOOD: How I shall live hereafter, Heaven knows!

LUCY: All things went on as one cou'd wish, till, some time ago, his wife dying, he fell violently in love with his charge, and wou'd fain have marry'd her. Now, the man is neither old nor ugly, but a good personable sort of a man; but I don't know how it was she cou'd never endure him. In short, her ill usage so provok'd him, that he brought in an account of his executorship, wherein he makes her debtor to him——

MILLWOOD: A trifle in itself, but more than enough to ruin me, whom, by this unjust account, he had stripp'd of all before.

LUCY: Now, she having neither money, nor friend, except me, who am as unfortunate as her self, he compell'd her to pass his account, and give bond for the sum he demanded; but still provided handsomely for her, and continued his courtship, till, being inform'd by his spies (truly I suspect some in her own family) that you were entertain'd at her house, and stay'd with her all night, he came this morning raving and storming like a madman; talks no more of marriage—so there's no hopes of making up matters that way—but vows her ruin, unless she'll allow him the same favour that he supposes she granted you.

BARNWELL: Must she be ruin'd, or find her refuge in another's arms?

MILLWOOD: He gave me but an hour to resolve in. That's happily spent with you—and now I go.

BARNWELL: To be expos'd to all the rigours of the various seasons, the summer's parching heat, and winter's cold; unhous'd to wander friendless thro' the unhospitable world, in misery and want, attended with fear and danger, and pursu'd by malice and re-venge woud'st thou endure all this for me, and can I do nothing, nothing to prevent it?

LUCY: 'Tis really a pity there can be no way found out!

BARNWELL: O where are all my resolutions now? Like early vapours, or the morning dew, chas'd by the sun's warm beams, they're vanish'd and lost, as tho' they had never been.

LUCY: Now, I advis'd her, sir, to comply with the gentleman; that wou'd not only put an end to her troubles, but make her fortune at once.

BARNWELL: Tormenting fiend, away!—I had rather perish, nay, see her perish, than have her sav'd by him; I will my self prevent her ruin, tho' with my own.—A moment's patience; I'll return immediately.

[Exit]

SCENE XII.

Millwood and Lucy.

LUCY: 'Twas well you came; or, by what I can perceive, you had lost him.

MILLWOOD: That, I must confess, was a danger I did not foresee; I was only afraid he should have come without money. You know a house of entertainment like mine is not kept with nothing.

LUCY: That's very true; but then you shou'd be reasonable in your demands; 'tis pity to discourage a young man.

SCENE XIII.

Millwood and Lucy.

[Enter Barnwell with a bag of money]

BARNWELL: [Aside] What am I about to do!—Now you, who boast your reason all-sufficient, suppose your selves in my condition, and determine for me: whether it's right to let her suffer for my faults, or, by this small addition to my guilt, prevent the ill effects of what is past.

LUCY: These young sinners think every thing in the ways of wickedness so strange; but I cou'd tell him that this is nothing but what's very common; for one vice as naturally begets another, as a father a son. But he'll find out that himself, if he lives long enough.

BARNWELL: Here, take this, and with it purchase your deliverance; return to your house, and live in peace and safety.

MILLWOOD: So I may hope to see you there again.

BARNWELL: Answer me not, but fly—lest, in the agonies of my remorse, I take again what is not mine to give, and abandon thee to want and misery!

MILLWOOD: Say but you'll come!

BARNWELL: You are my fate, my heaven, or my

hell; only leave me now, dispose of me hereafter as you please.

[*Exeunt* Millwood *and* Lucy]

SCENE XIV.

Barnwell.

BARNWELL: What have I done!—Were my resolutions founded on reason, and sincerely made—why then has Heaven suffer'd me to fall? I sought not the occasion; and, if my heart deceives me not, compassion and generosity were my motives.—Is virtue inconsistent with itself, or are vice and virtue only empty names? Or do they depend on accidents, beyond our power to produce or to prevent—wherein we have no part, and yet must be determin'd by the event? But why should I attempt to reason? All is confusion, horror, and remorse: I find I am lost, cast down from all my late erected hopes, and plung'd again in guilt, yet scarce know how or why—

Such undistinguish'd horrors make my brain,
Like Hell, the seat of darkness and of pain.

THE END OF THE SECOND ACT

ACT III. SCENE I.

A Room in Thorowgood's *House.*

[Thorowgood *and* Trueman *sitting at a table with account books*]

THOROWGOOD: Methinks, I wou'd not have you only learn the method of merchandize, and practise it hereafter, merely as a means of getting wealth. 'Twill be well worth your pains to study it as a science. See how it is founded in reason, and the nature of things; how it has promoted humanity, as it has opened and yet keeps up an intercourse between nations, far remote from one another in situation, customs and religion; promoting arts, industry, peace and plenty; by mutual benefits diffusing mutual love from pole to pole.

TRUEMAN: Something of this I have consider'd, and hope, by your assistance, to extend my thoughts much farther. I have observ'd those countries, where trade is promoted and encouraged, do not make discoveries to destroy, but to improve mankind by love and friendship; to tame the fierce and polish the most savage; to teach them the advantages of honest traffick, by taking from them, with their own consent, their useless superfluities, and giving them, in return, what, from their ignorance in manual arts, their situation, or some other accident, they stand in need of.

THOROWGOOD: 'Tis justly observ'd: the populous East, luxuriant, abounds with glittering gems, bright pearls, aromatick spices, and health-restoring drugs. The late-found Western World grows with unnum-

ber'd veins of gold and silver ore. On every climate and on every country, Heaven has bestowed some good peculiar to itself. It is the industrious merchant's business to collect the various blessings of each soil and climate, and, with the product of the whole, to enrich his native country.—Well! I have examin'd your accounts: they are not only just, as I have always found them, but regularly kept, and fairly enter'd. I commend your diligence. Method in business is the surest guide. He who neglects it frequently stumbles, and always wanders perplex'd, uncertain, and in danger.—Are Barnwell's accounts ready for my inspection? He did not use to be the last on these occasions.

TRUEMAN: Upon receiving your orders he retir'd, I thought, in some confusion. If you please, I'll go and hasten him.—I hope he hasn't been guilty of any neglect.

THOROWGOOD: I'm now going to the Exchange; let him know, at my return, I expect to find him ready.

[*Exeunt*]

SCENE II.

[*Enter* Maria *with a book; sits and reads*]

MARIA: How forcible is truth! The weakest mind, inspir'd with love of that, fix'd and collected in itself, with indifference beholds—the united force of earth and Hell opposing. Such souls are rais'd above the sense of pain, or so supported that they regard it not. The martyr cheaply purchases his heaven. Small are his sufferings, great is his reward; not so the wretch, who combats love with duty; when the mind, weaken'd and dissolved by the soft passion, feeble and hopeless opposes its own desires.—What is an hour, a day, a year of pain, to a whole life of tortures, such as these?

SCENE III.

Trueman *and* Maria.

[*Enter* Trueman]

TRUEMAN: O, Barnwell! O, my Friend, how art thou fallen!

MARIA: Ha! Barnwell! What of him! Speak, say, what of Barnwell?

TRUEMAN: 'Tis not to be conceal'd. I've news to tell of him that will afflict your generous father, your self, and all who knew him.

MARIA: Defend us, Heaven!

TRUEMAN: I cannot speak it.—See there.

[*Gives a letter. Maria reads*]

Trueman,

I know my absence will surprize my honour'd master and your self and the more, when you shall understand that the reason of my withdrawing, is my having embezzled part of the cash with which I was entrusted. After this, 'tis needless to inform you that I intend never to return again. Though this might have been known by examining my accounts, yet, to prevent that unnecessary trouble, and to cut off all fruitless expectations of my return, I have left this from the lost.

George Barnwell.

TRUEMAN: Lost indeed! Yet, how he shou'd be guilty of what he there charges himself withal, raises my wonder equal to my grief. Never had youth a higher sense of virtue; justly he thought, and as he thought he practised; never was life more regular than his; an understanding uncommon at his years—an open, generous, manliness of temper—his manners easy, unaffected and engaging.

MARIA: This and much more you might have said with truth. He was the delight of every eye, and joy of every heart that knew him.

TRUEMAN: Since such he was, and was my friend, can I support his loss?—See! the fairest and happiest maid this wealthy city boasts, kindly condescends to weep for thy unhappy fate, poor ruin'd Barnwell!

MARIA: Trueman, do you think a soul so delicate as his, so sensible of shame, can e'er submit to live a slave to vice?

TRUEMAN: Never, never! So well I know him, I'm sure this act of his, so contrary to his nature, must have been caused by some unavoidable necessity.

MARIA: Is there no means yet to preserve him?

TRUEMAN: O, that there were! But few men recover reputation lost—a merchant never. Nor wou'd he, I fear, though I shou'd find him, ever be brought to look his injur'd master in the face.

MARIA: I fear as much—and therefore wou'd never have my father know it.

TRUEMAN: That's impossible.

MARIA: What's the sum?

TRUEMAN: 'Tis considerable. I've mark'd it here, to show it, with the letter, to your father, at his return.

MARIA: If I shou'd supply the money, cou'd you so dispose of that, and the account, as to conceal this unhappy mismanagement from my father?

TRUEMAN: Nothing more easy. But can you intend it? Will you save a helpless wretch from ruin? Oh! 'twere an act worthy such exalted virtue as Maria's. Sure, Heaven, in mercy to my friend, inspired the generous thought!

MARIA: Doubt not but I wou'd purchase so great a happiness at a much dearer price.—But how shall he be found?

TRUEMAN: Trust to my diligence for that. In the mean time, I'll conceal his absence from your father, or find such excuses for it, that the real cause shall never be suspected.

MARIA: In attempting to save from shame one whom we hope may yet return to virtue, to Heaven, and you, the judges of this action, I appeal, whether I have done any thing misbecoming my sex and character.

TRUEMAN: Earth must approve the deed, and Heaven, I doubt not, will reward it.

MARIA: If Heaven succeed it, I am well rewarded. A virgin's fame is sullied by suspicion's slightest breath; and therefore as this must be a secret from my father and the world, for Barnwell's sake, for mine, let it be so to him!

[*Exeunt*]

SCENE IV.

Millwood's *House.*

[*Enter* Lucy *and* Blunt]

LUCY: Well! what do you think of Millwood's conduct now?

BLUNT: I own it is surprizing; I don't know which to admire most, her feign'd or his real passion—tho' I have sometimes been afraid that her avarice wou'd discover her. But his youth and want of experience make it the easier to impose on him.

LUCY: No, it is his love. To do him justice, notwithstanding his youth, he don't want understanding; but you men are much easier imposed on, in these affairs, than your vanity will allow you to believe. Let me see the wisest of you all as much in love with me as Barnwell is with Millwood, and I'll engage to make as great a fool of him.

BLUNT: And all circumstances consider'd, to make as much money of him too.

LUCY: I can't answer for that. Her artifice in making him rob his master at first, and the various stratagems by which she has obliged him to continue in that course, astonish even me, who know her so well.

BLUNT: But then you are to consider that the money was his master's.

LUCY: There was the difficulty of it. Had it been his own it had been nothing. Were the world his, she might have it for a smile.—But those golden days are done; he's ruin'd, and Millwood's hopes of farther profits there, are at an end.

BLUNT: That's no more than we all expected.

LUCY: Being call'd by his master to make up his accounts, he was forc'd to quit his house and service, and wisely flies to Millwood for relief and entertainment.

BLUNT: I have not heard of this before! How did she receive him?

LUCY: As you wou'd expect. She wonder'd what he meant; was astonish'd at his impudence; and, with an air of modesty peculiar to her self, swore so heartily that she never saw him before, that she put me out of countenance.

BLUNT: That's much indeed! But how did Barnwell behave?

LUCY: He griev'd, and, at length, enrag'd at this barbarous treatment, was preparing to be gone; and, making toward the door, show'd a bag of money, which he had stol'n from his master—the last he's ever like to have from thence.

BLUNT: But then, Millwood?

LUCY: Aye, she, with her usual address, return'd to her old arts of lying, swearing and dissembling. Hung on his neck, and wept, and swore 'twas meant in jest; till the easy fool, melted into tears, threw the money into her lap, and swore he had rather die than think her false.

BLUNT: Strange infatuation!

LUCY: But what follow'd was stranger still. As doubts and fears, follow'd by reconcilement, ever increase love, where the passion is sincere: so in him it caus'd so wild a transport of excessive fondness, such joy, such grief, such pleasure, and such anguish, that nature in him seem'd sinking with the weight, and the charm'd soul dispos'd to quit his breast for hers. Just then, when every passion with lawless anarchy prevail'd, and reason was in the raging tempest lost, the cruel, artful Millwood prevail'd upon the wretched youth to promise what I tremble but to think on.

BLUNT: I am amaz'd! What can it be?

LUCY: You will be more so, to hear it is to attempt the life of his nearest relation, and best benefactor.

BLUNT: His uncle, whom we have often heard him speak of as a gentleman of a large estate and fair character in the country, where he lives?

LUCY: The same. She was no sooner possess'd of the last dear purchase of his ruin, but her avarice, insatiate as the grave, demands this horrid sacrifice—Barnwell's near relation; and unsuspected virtue must give too easy means to seize the good man's treasure, whose blood must seal the dreadful secret, and prevent the terrors of her guilty fears.

BLUNT: Is it possible she cou'd perswade him to do an act like that? He is, by nature, honest, grateful, compassionate, and generous; and though his love and her artful perswasions have wrought him to practise what he most abhors; yet we all can witness for him with what reluctance he has still comply'd! So many tears he shed o'er each offence, as might, if possible, sanctify theft, and make a merit of a crime.

LUCY: 'Tis true; at the naming the murder of his uncle he started into rage, and, breaking from her arms, where she till then had held him with well dissembled love and false endearments, call'd her 'cruel monster, devil,' and told her she was born for his destruction. She thought it not for her purpose to meet his rage with rage, but affected a most passionate fit of grief—rail'd at her fate, and curs'd her wayward stars: that still her wants shou'd force her to press him to act such deeds as she must needs abhor, as well as he; but told him, necessity had no law, and love no bounds; that therefore he never truly lov'd, but meant, in her necessity, to forsake her: then kneel'd and swore, that since, by his refusal, he had given her cause to doubt his love, she never wou'd see him more—unless, to prove it true, he

robb'd his uncle to supply her wants, and murder'd him, to keep it from discovery.

BLUNT: I am astonish'd! What said he?

LUCY: Speechless he stood; but in his face you might have read that various passions tore his very soul. Oft he, in anguish, threw his eyes towards Heaven, and then as often bent their beams on her; then wept and groan'd, and beat his breast; at length, with horror, not to be express'd, he cry'd: 'Thou cursed Fair! have I not given dreadful proofs of love? What drew me from my youthful innocence, to stain my then unspotted soul, but love? What caus'd me to rob my gentle master but cursed love? What made me now a fugitive from his service, loath'd by my self, and scorn'd by all the world, but love? What fills my eyes with tears, my soul with torture, never felt on this side death before? Why, love, love, love! And why, above all, do I resolve' (for, tearing his hair, he cry'd 'I do resolve') 'to kill my uncle'?

BLUNT: Was she not mov'd? It makes me weep to hear the sad relation.

LUCY: Yes, with joy, that she had gain'd her point. She gave him no time to cool, but urg'd him to attempt it instantly. He's now gone; if he performs it, and escapes, there's more money for her; if not, he'll ne'er return, and then she's fairly rid of him.

BLUNT: 'Tis time the world was rid of such a monster.

LUCY: If we don't do our endeavours to prevent this murder, we are as bad as she.

BLUNT: I'm afraid it is too late.

LUCY: Perhaps not.—Her barbarity to Barnwell makes me hate her. We've run too great a length with her already. I did not think her or my self so wicked, as I find, upon reflection, we are.

BLUNT: 'Tis true, we have all been too much so. But there is something so horrid in murder, that all other crimes seem nothing when compared to that. I wou'd not be involv'd in the guilt of that for all the world.

LUCY: Nor I, Heaven knows; therefore, let us clear our selves by doing all that is in our power to prevent it. I have just thought of a way that, to me, seems probable. Will you join with me to detect this curs'd design?

BLUNT: With all my heart.—How else shall I clear my self? He who knows of a murder intended to be committed and does not discover it, in the eye of the law and reason is a murderer.

LUCY: Let us lose no time; I'll acquaint you with the particulars as we go.

[Exeunt]

SCENE V.

A Walk at some distance from a Country Seat.

[Enter Barnwell]

BARNWELL: A dismal gloom obscures the face of day; either the sun has slip'd behind a cloud, or journeys down the west of Heaven, with more than common speed, to avoid the sight of what I'm doom'd to act. Since I set forth on this accursed design, where'er I tread, methinks, the solid earth trembles beneath my feet.—Yonder limpid stream, whose hoary fall has made a natural cascade, as I pass'd by, in doleful accents seem'd to murmur 'Murder.' The earth, the air, and water, seem concern'd—but that's not strange: the world is punish'd, and nature feels the shock, when Providence permits a good man's fall!—Just Heaven! Then what shou'd I be! For him, that was my father's only brother, and since his death has been to me a father, who took me up an infant, and an orphan; rear'd me with tenderest care, and still indulged me with most paternal fondness— yet here I stand avow'd his destin'd murderer.—I stiffen with horror at my own impiety.—'Tis yet un- perform'd. What if I quit my bloody purpose, and fly the place! [*Going, then stops*]—But whither, O whither, shall I fly? My master's once friendly doors are ever shut against me; and without money Mill- wood will never see me more, and life is not to be endured without her. She's got such firm possession of my heart, and governs there with such despotick sway—aye, there's the cause of all my sin and sor- row! 'Tis more than love: 'tis the fever of the soul, and madness of desire. In vain does nature, reason, conscience, all oppose it; the impetuous passion bears down all before it, and (drives me on to lust, to theft and murder. Oh conscience! feeble guide to virtue, who only shows us when we go astray, but wants the power to stop us in our course.—Ha, in yonder shady walk I see my uncle. He's alone. Now for my disguise! [*Plucks out a vizor*] This is his hour of private meditation. Thus daily he prepares his soul for Heaven, whilst I—but what have I to do with Heaven? Ha! No struggles, conscience!

Hence, hence, remorse, and ev'ry thought that's good:
The storm that lust began must end in blood.

[*Puts on the vizor, draws a pistol. And exit*]

SCENE VI.

A Close Walk in a Wood.

[*Enter* Uncle]

UNCLE: If I was superstitious, I shou'd fear some danger lurk'd unseen, or death were nigh.—A heavy melancholy clouds my spirits; my imagination is fill'd with gashly forms of dreary graves and bodies chang'd by death; when the pale, lengthen'd visage attacks each weeping eye, and fills the musing soul, at once, with grief and horror, pity and aversion.—I will indulge the thought. The wise man prepares himself for death, by making it familiar to his mind. When strong reflections hold the mirror near, and the living in the dead behold their future selves,

how does each inordinate passion and desire cease, or sicken at the view? The mind scarce moves; the blood, curdling and chill'd, creeps slowly thro' the veins; fix'd, still, and motionless, like the solemn object of our thoughts, we are almost at present what we must be hereafter, 'till curiosity awakes the soul, and sets it on inquiry.

SCENE VII.

Uncle. George Barnwell *at a distance.*

UNCLE: O Death, thou strange mysterious power, —seen every day, yet never understood but by the incommunicative dead—what art thou? The extensive mind of man, that with a thought circles the earth's vast globe, sinks to the centre, or ascends above the stars; that worlds exotick finds, or thinks it finds—thy thick clouds attempts to pass in vain, lost and be- wilder'd in the horrid gloom; defeated, she returns more doubtful than before; of nothing certain but of labour lost.

[*During this speech,* Barnwell *sometimes presents the pistol and draws it back again; at last he drops it, at which his uncle starts, and draws his sword*]

BARNWELL: Oh, 'tis impossible!

UNCLE: A man so near me, arm'd and masqu'd!

BARNWELL: Nay, then there's no retreat.

[*Plucks a poniard from his bosom, and stabs him*]

UNCLE: Oh! I am slain! All-gracious Heaven re- gard the prayer of thy dying servant! Bless, with thy choicest blessings, my dearest nephew, forgive my murderer, and take my fleeting soul to endless mercy!

[Barnwell *throws off his mask, runs to him, and, kneeling by him, raises and chafes him*]

BARNWELL: Expiring saint! Oh, murder'd, martyr'd uncle! Lift up your dying eyes, and view your nephew in your murderer! O, do not look so tenderly upon me! Let indignation lighten from your eyes, and blast me e're you die!—By Heaven, he weeps in pity of my woes. Tears,—tears, for blood! The murder'd, in the agonies of death, weeps for his murderer.—Oh, speak your pious purpose—pronounce my pardon then— and take me with you!—He wou'd, but cannot. O why with such fond affection do you press my mur- dering hand!—What! will you kiss me! [*Kisses him. Uncle groans and dies*] He's gone for ever—and oh! I follow. [*Swoons away upon his uncle's dead body*] Do I still live to press the suffering bosom of the earth? Do I still breathe, and taint my infectious breath the wholesome air! Let Heaven from its high throne, in justice or in mercy, now look down on that dear murder'd saint, and me the murderer. And, if his vengeance spares, let pity strike and end my wretched being!—Murder the worst of crimes, and parricide the worst of murders, and this the worst of parri- cides! Cain, who stands on record from the birth of time, and must to its last final period, as accurs'd, slew a brother, favour'd above him. Detested Nero by another's hand dispatch'd a mother that he fear'd and hated. But I, with my own hand, have murder'd a brother, mother, father, and a friend, most loving and belov'd. This execrable act of mine's without a parallel. O may it ever stand alone—the last of murders, as it is the worst!

The rich man thus, in torment and despair,
Prefer'd his vain, but charitable prayer.
The fool, his own soul lost, wou'd fain be wise
For others good; but Heaven his suit denies.
By laws and means well known we stand or fall,
And one eternal rule remains for all.

THE END OF THE THIRD ACT

ACT IV. SCENE I.

A Room in Thorowgood's *House.*

[Maria]

MARIA: How falsely do they judge who censure or applaud as we're afflicted or rewarded here! I know I am unhappy, yet cannot charge my self with any crime, more than the common frailties of our kind, that shou'd provoke just Heaven to mark me out for sufferings so uncommon and severe. Falsely to accuse our selves, Heaven must abhor; then it is just and right that innocence should suffer, for Heaven must be just in all its ways. Perhaps by that they are kept from moral evils much worse than penal, or more improv'd in virtue; or may not the lesser ills that they sustain be the means of greater good to others? Might all the joyless days and sleepless nights that I have past but purchase peace for thee—

Thou dear, dear cause of all my grief and pain,
Small were the loss, and infinite the gain;
Tho' to the grave in secret love I pine,
So life, and fame, and happiness were thine.

SCENE II.

Trueman *and* Maria.

[*Enter* Trueman]

MARIA: What news of Barnwell?

TRUEMAN: None. I have sought him with the greatest diligence, but all in vain.

MARIA: Doth my father yet suspect the cause of his absenting himself?

TRUEMAN: All appear'd so just and fair to him, it is not possible he ever shou'd; but his absence will no longer be conceal'd. Your father's wise; and, though he seems to hearken to the friendly excuses I wou'd

make for Barnwell, yet, I am afraid, he regards 'em only as such, without suffering them to influence his judgment.

MARIA: How does the unhappy youth defeat all our designs to serve him! Yet I can never repent what we have done. Shou'd he return, 'twill make his reconciliation with my father easier, and preserve him from future reproach from a malicious, unforgiving world.

SCENE III.

[*To them* Thorowgood *and* Lucy]

THOROWGOOD: This woman here has given me a sad, and (bating some circumstances) too probable account of Barnwell's defection.

LUCY: I am sorry, sir, that my frank confession of my former unhappy course of life shou'd cause you to suspect my truth on this occasion.

THOROWGOOD: It is not that; your confession has in it all the appearance of truth. [*To them*] Among many other particulars, she informs me that Barnwell has been influenc'd to break his trust, and wrong me, at several times, of considerable sums of money; now, as I know this to be false, I wou'd fain doubt the whole of her relation, too dreadful to be willingly believ'd.

MARIA: Sir, your pardon; I find my self on a sudden so indispos'd, that I must retire.—[*Aside*] Providence opposes all attempts to save him. Poor ruin'd Barnwell! Wretched, lost Maria!

[*Exit*]

SCENE IV.

Thorowgood, Trueman *and* Lucy.

THOROWGOOD: How am I distress'd on every side? Pity for that unhappy youth, fear for the life of a much valued friend—and then my child, the only joy and hope of my declining life! Her melancholy increases hourly, and gives me painful apprehensions of her loss.—O Trueman! this person informs me that your friend, at the instigation of an impious woman, is gone to rob and murder his venerable uncle.

TRUEMAN: O execrable deed! I am blasted with the horror of the thought.

LUCY: This delay may ruin all.

THOROWGOOD: What to do or think I know not. That he ever wrong'd me, I know is false; the rest may be so too—there's all my hope.

TRUEMAN: Trust not to that; rather suppose all true than lose a moment's time. Even now the horrid deed may be a doing—dreadful imagination! Or it may be done, and we are vainly debating on the means to prevent what is already past.

THOROWGOOD: [*Aside*] This earnestness convinces

me that he knows more than he has yet discover'd.
—What ho! without there! who waits?

SCENE V.

[*To them a* Servant]

THOROWGOOD: Order the groom to saddle the swiftest horse, and prepare himself to set out with speed!—An affair of life and death demands his diligence.

[*Exit* Servant]

SCENE VI.

Thorowgood, Trueman *and* Lucy.

THOROWGOOD: For you, whose behaviour on this occasion I have no time to commend as it deserves, I must ingage your farther assistance. Return and observe this Millwood till I come. I have your directions, and will follow you as soon as possible.

[*Exit* Lucy]

SCENE VII.

Thorowgood *and* Trueman.

THOROWGOOD: Trueman, you I am sure wou'd not be idle on this occasion.

[*Exit*]

SCENE VIII.

Trueman.

TRUEMAN: He only who is a friend can judge of my distress.

[*Exit*]

SCENE IX.

Millwood's *House.*

[Millwood]

MILLWOOD: I wish I knew the event of his design: the attempt without success would ruin him.—Well! what have I to apprehend from that? I fear too much. The mischief of being only intended, his friends, in pity of his youth, turn all their rage on me. I shou'd have thought of that before.—Suppose the deed done: then, and then only, I shall be secure; or what if he returns without attempting it at all?

SCENE X.

[Millwood, *and enter* Barnwell, *bloody*]

MILLWOOD: But he is here, and I have done him wrong; his bloody hands show he has done the deed, but show he wants the prudence to conceal it.

BARNWELL: Where shall I hide me? whither shall I fly to avoid the swift, unerring hand of justice?

MILLWOOD: Dismiss those fears: tho' thousands had pursu'd you to the door, yet being enter'd here you are safe as innocence. I have such a cavern, by art so cunningly contriv'd, that the piercing eyes of jealousy and revenge may search in vain, nor find the entrance to the safe retreat. There will I hide you, if any danger's near.

BARNWELL: O hide me from my self, if it be possible; for while I bear my conscience in my bosom, tho' I were hid, where man's eye never saw, nor light e'er dawned, 'twere all in vain. For that inmate,—that impartial judge, will try, convict and sentence me for murder; and execute me with never ending torments. Behold these hands all crimson'd o'er with my dear uncle's blood! Here's a sight to make a statue start with horror, or turn a living man into a statue.

MILLWOOD: Ridiculous! Then, it seems you are afraid of your own shadow, or, what's less than a shadow, your conscience.

BARNWELL: Though to man unknown I did the accursed act, what can we hide from Heav'ns omniscient eye?

MILLWOOD: No more of this stuff! What advantage have you made of his death? or what advantage may yet be made of it? Did you secure the keys of his treasure—those no doubt were about him. What gold, what jewels, or what else of value have you brought me?

BARNWELL: Think you I added sacrilege to murder? Oh! had you seen him as his life flowed from him in a crimson flood, and heard him praying for me by the double name of nephew and of murderer —alas, alas! he knew not then that his nephew was his murderer: how wou'd you have wish'd, as I did, tho' you had a thousand years of life to come, to have given them all to have lengthen'd his one hour! But being dead, I fled the sight of what my hands had done, nor cou'd I, to have gain'd the empire of the world, have violated by theft his sacred corps.

MILLWOOD: Whining, preposterous, canting, villain, to murder your uncle, rob him of life, natures first, last, dear prerogative, after which there's no injury, then fear to take what he no longer wanted; and bring to me your penury and guilt! Do you think I'll hazard my reputation; nay, my life to entertain you?

BARNWELL: Oh! Millwood! this from thee!—but I have done—if you hate me, if you wish me dead: then are you happy—for oh! 'tis sure my grief will quickly end me.

MILLWOOD: In his madness he will discover all, and involve me in his ruin. We are on a precipice from whence there's no retreat for both—then, to preserve my self. [*Pauses*] There is no other way,—'tis dreadful; but reflection comes too late when danger's pressing, and there's no room for choice.—It must be done. [*Stamps*]

[Above speech is undoubtedly an aside—Ed.]

SCENE XI.

[*To them a* Servant]

MILLWOOD: Fetch me an officer, and seize this villain: he has confess'd himself a murderer. Shou'd I let him escape, I justly might be thought as bad as he.

[*Exit* Servant]

SCENE XII.

Millwood *and* Barnwell

BARNWELL: O Millwood! sure thou dost not, cannot mean it. Stop the messenger, upon my knees I beg you, call him back. 'Tis fit I die indeed, but not by you. I will this instant deliver myself into the hands of justice; indeed I will, for death is all I wish. But thy ingratitude so tears my wounded soul, 'tis worse ten thousand times than death with torture.

MILLWOOD: Call it what you will, I am willing to live, and live secure; which nothing but your death can warrant.

BARNWELL: If there be a pitch of wickedness that seats the author beyond the reach of vengeance, you must be secure. But what remains for me but a dismal dungeon, hard-galling fetters, an awful tryal, and ignominious death—justly to fall unpitied and abhorr'd; after death to be suspended between Heaven and earth, a dreadful spectacle, the warning and horror of a gaping croud. This I cou'd bear, nay wish not to avoid, had it come from any hand but thine.

SCENE XIII.

[Millwood, Barnwell. *Enter* Blunt, Officer *and* Attendants]

MILLWOOD: Heaven defend me! Conceal a murderer! Here, sir; take this youth into your custody. I accuse him of murder, and will appear to make good my charge.

[*They seize him*]

BARNWELL: To whom, of what, or how shall I complain? I'll not accuse her: the hand of Heav'n is in it, and this the punishment of lust and parricide. Yet Heav'n, that justly cuts me off, still suffers her to live, perhaps to punish others. Tremendous mercy! so fiends are curs'd with immortality, to be the executioners of Heaven.—

Be warn'd, ye youths, who see my sad despair,
Avoid lewd women, false as they are fair
By reason guided, honest joys pursue
The fair, to honour and to virtue true,
Just to her self, will ne'er be false to you.
By my example learn to shun my fate
(How wretched is the man who's wise too late!)
E'er innocence, and fame, and life, be lost,
Here purchase wisdom, cheaply, at my cost!

[*Exit with* Officers]

SCENE XIV.

Millwood *and* Blunt.

MILLWOOD: Where's Lucy? Why is she absent at such a time?

BLUNT: Wou'd I had been so too, thou devil!

MILLWOOD: Insolent! This to me!

BLUNT: The worst that we know of the devil is, that he first seduces to sin and then betrays to punishment.

[*Exit*]

SCENE XV.

Millwood.

MILLWOOD: They disapprove of my conduct, and mean to take this opportunity to set up for themselves. My ruin is resolv'd. I see my danger, but scorn it and them. I was not born to fall by such weak instruments.

[*Going*]

SCENE XVI.

Thorowgood *and* Millwood.

[*Enter* Thorowgood]

THOROWGOOD: Where is this scandal of her own sex, and curse of ours?

MILLWOOD: What means this insolence? Who do you seek?

THOROWGOOD: Millwood.

MILLWOOD: Well, you have found her then. I am Millwood.

THOROWGOOD: Then you are the most impious wretch that e'er the sun beheld.

MILLWOOD: From your appearance I shou'd have expected wisdom and moderation, but your manners bely your aspect.—What is your business here? I know you not.

THOROWGOOD: Hereafter you may know me better; I am Barnwell's master.

MILLWOOD: Then you are master to a villain; which, I think, is not much to your credit.

THOROWGOOD: Had he been as much above thy arts as my credit is superior to thy malice, I need not blush to own him.

MILLWOOD: My arts? I don't understand you, sir. If he has done amiss, what's that to me? Was he my servant, or yours? You shou'd have taught him better.

THOROWGOOD: Why shou'd I wonder to find such uncommon impudence in one arriv'd to such a height of wickedness? When innocence is banish'd, modesty soon follows. Know, sorceress, I'm not ignorant of any of your arts, by which you first deceiv'd the unwary youth. I know how, step by step, you've led him on, reluctant and unwilling from crime to crime, to this last horrid act, which you contriv'd, and, by your curs'd wiles, even forced him to commit—and then betray'd him.

MILLWOOD: [Aside] Ha! Lucy has got the advantage of me, and accused me first. Unless I can turn the accusation, and fix it upon her and Blunt, I am lost.

THOROWGOOD: Had I known your cruel design sooner, it had been prevented. To see you punish'd as the law directs, is all that now remains.—Poor satisfaction—for he, innocent as he is, compared to you, must suffer too. But Heaven, who knows our frame, and graciously distinguishes between frailty and presumption, will make a difference, tho' man cannot, who sees not the heart, but only judges by the outward action.

MILLWOOD: I find, sir, we are both unhappy in our servants. I was surpriz'd at such ill treatment from a gentleman of your appearance, without cause, and therefore too hastily return'd it; for which I ask your pardon. I now perceive you have been so far impos'd on as to think me engaged in a former correspondence with your servant, and, some way or other, accessary to his undoing.

THOROWGOOD: I charge you as the cause, the sole cause of all his guilt and all his suffering—of all he now endures, and must endure, till a violent and shameful death shall put a dreadful period to his life and miseries together.

MILLWOOD: 'Tis very strange! But who's secure from scandal and detraction?—So far from contributing to his ruin, I never spoke to him till since that fatal accident, which I lament as much as you. 'Tis true, I have a servant, on whose account he has of late frequented my house; if she has abus'd my good opinion of her, am I to blame? Hasn't Barnwell done the same by you?

THOROWGOOD: I hear you; pray, go on!

MILLWOOD: I have been inform'd he had a violent passion for her, and she for him; but I always thought it innocent; I know her poor, and given to expensive pleasures. Now who can tell but she may have influenced the amorous youth to commit this murder, to supply her extravagancies? It must be so; I now recollect a thousand circumstances that confirm it. I'll have her and a man-servant, that I suspect as an accomplice, secured immediately. I hope, sir, you will lay aside your ill-grounded suspicions of me, and join to punish the real contrivers of this bloody deed.

[Offers to go]

THOROWGOOD: Madam, you pass not this way! I see your design, but shall protect them from your malice.

MILLWOOD: I hope you will not use your influence, and the credit of your name, to skreen such guilty wretches. Consider, sir, the wickedness of perswading a thoughtless youth to such a crime!

THOROWGOOD: I do—and of betraying him when it was done.

MILLWOOD: That which you call betraying him, may convince you of my innocence. She who loves him, tho' she contriv'd the murder, would never have deliver'd him into the hands of justice, as I, struck with the horror of his crimes, have done.

THOROWGOOD: [Aside] How shou'd an unexperienc'd youth escape her snares? The powerful magick of her wit and form might betray the wisest to simple dotage, and fire the blood that age had froze long since. Even I, that with just prejudice came prepared, had, by her artful story, been deceiv'd, but that my strong conviction of her guilt makes even a doubt impossible.—Those whom subtilly you wou'd accuse, you know are your accusers; and, what proves unanswerably their innocence and your guilt, they accus'd you before the deed was done, and did all that was in their power to have prevented it.

MILLWOOD: Sir, you are very hard to be convinc'd; but I have such a proof, which, when produced, will silence all objections.

[Exit]

SCENE XVII.

[Thorowgood. *Enter* Lucy, Trueman, Blunt, Officers, *etc.*]

LUCY: Gentlemen, pray, place yourselves, some on one side of that door, and some on the other; watch her entrance, and act as your prudence shall direct you—this way! [*To* Thorowgood] and note her behaviour. I have observ'd her: she's driven to the last extremity, and is forming some desperate resolution. —I guess at her design.

SCENE XVIII.

[*To them* Millwood *with a pistol*. Trueman *secures her*]

TRUEMAN: Here thy power of doing mischief ends, deceitful, cruel, bloody woman!

MILLWOOD: Fool, hypocrite, villain—man! Thou can'st not call me that.

TRUEMAN: To call thee woman were to wrong the sex, thou devil!

MILLWOOD: That imaginary being is an emblem of thy cursed sex collected—a mirrour, wherein each particular man may see his own likeness, and that of all mankind.

TRUEMAN: Think not by aggravating the fault of others to extenuate thy own, of which the abuse of such uncommon perfections of mind and body is not the least!

MILLWOOD: If such I had, well may I curse your barbarous sex, who robb'd me of 'em, e'er I knew their worth, then left me, too late, to count their value by their loss. Another and another spoiler came; and all my gain was poverty and reproach. My soul disdain'd, and yet disdains, dependence and contempt. Riches, no matter by what means obtain'd, I saw, secur'd the worst of men from both; I found it therefore necessary to be rich; and, to that end, I summon'd all my arts. You call 'em wicked; be it so! They were such as my conversation with your sex had furnish'd me withal.

THOROWGOOD: Sure, none but the worst of men convers'd with thee.

MILLWOOD: Men of all degrees and all professions I have known, yet found no difference, but in their several capacities; all were alike wicked to the utmost of their power. In pride, contention, avarice, cruelty and revenge, the reverend priesthood were my unerring guides. From suburb-magistrates, who live by ruin'd reputations, as the unhospitable natives of Cornwall do by shipwrecks, I learn'd that to charge my innocent neighbours with my crimes, was to merit their protection; for to skreen the guilty is the less scandalous, when many are suspected, and detraction, like darkness and death, blackens all objects and levels all distinction. Such are your venal magistrates, who favour none but such as, by their office, they are sworn to punish. With them, not to be guilty is the worst of crimes; and large fees privately paid is every needful virtue.

THOROWGOOD: Your practice has sufficiently discover'd your contempts of laws, both human and divine; no wonder then that you shou'd hate the officers of both.

MILLWOOD: I hate you all; I know you, and expect no mercy. Nay, I ask for none; I have done nothing that I am sorry for; I follow'd my inclinations, and that the best of you does everyday. All actions are alike natural and indifferent to man and beast, who devour, or are devour'd, as they meet with others weaker or stronger than themselves.

THOROWGOOD: What pity it is, a mind so comprehensive, daring and inquisitive shou'd be a stranger to religion's sweet, but powerful charms.

MILLWOOD: I am not fool enough to be an atheist, tho' I have known enough of men's hypocrisy to make a thousand simple women so. Whatever religion is in itself—as practis'd by mankind, it has caus'd the evils you say it was design'd to cure. War, plague, and famine, has not destroy'd so many of the human race as this pretended piety has done, and with such barbarous cruelty—as if the only way to honour Heaven, were to turn the present world into Hell.

THOROWGOOD: Truth is truth, tho' from an enemy and spoke in malice. You bloody, blind, and superstitious bigots, how will you answer this?

MILLWOOD: What are your laws, of which you make your boast, but the fool's wisdom, and the coward's valour; the instrument and skreen of all your villanies, by which you punish in others what you act yourselves, or wou'd have acted, had you been in their circumstances. The judge who condemns the poor man for being a thief, had been a thief himself, had he been poor. Thus you go on deceiving, and being deceiv'd, harrassing, and plaguing, and destroying one another: but women are your universal prey.

Women, by whom you are, the source of joy,
With cruel arts you labour to destroy
A thousand ways our ruin you pursue,
Yet blame in us those arts first taught by you.
O may, from hence, each violated maid,
By flatt'ring, faithless, barb'rous man betray'd,
When robb'd of innocence, and virgin fame,
From your destruction raise a nobler name
To right their sex's wrongs devote their mind,
And future Millwoods prove, to plague mankind!

THE END OF THE FOURTH ACT

ACT V. SCENE I.

A Room in a Prison.

[Thorowgood, Blunt *and* Lucy]

THOROWGOOD: I have recommended to Barnwell a reverend divine, whose judgment and integrity I am well acquainted with. Nor has Millwood been neglected; but she, unhappy woman, still obstinate, refuses his assistance.

LUCY: This pious charity to the afflicted well becomes your character; yet pardon me, sir, if I wonder you were not at their trial.

THOROWGOOD: I knew it was impossible to save him, and I and my family bear so great a part in his distress, that to have been present wou'd have aggravated our sorrows without relieving his.

BLUNT: It was mournful indeed. Barnwell's youth and modest deportment, as he past, drew tears from every eye: when placed at the bar, and arraigned before the reverend judges, with many tears and interrupting sobs he confess'd and aggravated his offences, without accusing, or once reflecting on Millwood, the shameless author of his ruin; who dauntless and unconcern'd stood by his side, viewing with visible pride and contempt the vast assembly, who all with sympathizing sorrow wept for the wretched youth. Millwood, when called upon to answer, loudly insisted upon her innocence, and made an artful and a bold defence; but, finding all in vain, the impartial jury and the learned bench concurring to find her guilty, how she did curse herself, poor Barnwell, us, her judges, all mankind! But what cou'd that avail? She was condemn'd, and is this day to suffer with him.

THOROWGOOD: The time draws on. I am going to visit Barnwell, as you are Millwood.

LUCY: We have not wrong'd her, yet I dread this interview. She's proud, impatient, wrathful, and unforgiving. To be the branded instruments of vengeance, to suffer in her shame, and sympathize with her in all she suffers, is the tribute we must pay for our former ill-spent lives, and long confederacy with her in wickedness.

THOROWGOOD: Happy for you it ended when it did! What you have done against Millwood, I know, proceeded from a just abhorrence of her crimes, free from interest, malice, or revenge. Proselytes to virtue shou'd be encourag'd. Pursue your proposed reformation, and know me hereafter for your friend.

LUCY: This is a blessing as unhop'd for as unmerited; but Heaven, that snatched us from impending ruin, sure, intends you as its instrument to secure us from apostacy.

THOROWGOOD: With gratitude to impute your deliverance to Heaven is just. Many, less virtuously dispos'd than Barnwell was, have never fallen in the manner he has done;—may not such owe their safety rather to Providence than to themselves? With pity and compassion let us judge him! Great were his faults, but strong was the temptation. Let his ruin learn us diffidence, humanity and circumspection; for we, who wonder at his fate—perhaps, had we like him been tried, like him we had fallen too.

[Exeunt]

SCENE II.

A Dungeon. A table and lamp.

[Barnwell, *reading. Enter* Thorowgood]

THOROWGOOD: See there the bitter fruits of passion's detested reign and sensual appetite indulg'd—severe reflections, penitence and tears.

BARNWELL: My honoured, injured master, whose goodness has covered me a thousand times with shame, forgive this last unwilling disrespect! Indeed, I saw you not.

THOROWGOOD: 'Tis well; I hope you were better imploy'd in viewing of your self. Your journey's long, your time for preparation almost spent. I sent a reverend divine to teach you to improve it, and shou'd be glad to hear of his success.

BARNWELL: The word of truth, which he recommended for my constant companion in this my sad retirement, has at length remov'd the doubts I labour'd under. From thence I've learn'd the infinite extent of heavenly mercy; that my offences, tho'

great, are not unpardonable; and that 'tis not my interest only, but my duty, to believe and to rejoice in that hope: so shall Heaven receive the glory, and future penitents the profit of my example.

THOROWGOOD: Go on! How happy am I who live to see this!

BARNWELL: 'Tis wonderful that words shou'd charm despair, speak peace and pardon to a murderer's conscience! But truth and mercy flow in every sentence attended with force and energy divine. How shall I describe my present state of mind? I hope in doubt, and trembling I rejoice. I feel my grief increase, even as my fears give way. Joy and gratitude now supply more tears than the horror and anguish of despair before.

THOROWGOOD: These are the genuine signs of true repentance, the only preparatory certain way to everlasting peace.—O the joy it gives to see a soul form'd and prepar'd for Heaven! For this the faithful minister devotes himself to meditation, abstinence and prayer, shunning the vain delights of sensual joys, and daily dies, that others may live for ever. For this he turns the sacred volumes o'er, and spends his life in painful search of truth. The love of riches and the lust of power he looks on with just contempt and detestation, who only counts for wealth the souls he wins, and whose highest ambition is to serve mankind. If the reward of all his pains be to preserve one soul from wandering, or turn one from the error of his ways, how does he then rejoice, and own his little labours over paid!

BARNWELL: What do I owe for all your generous kindness? But, tho' I cannot, Heaven can and will reward you.

THOROWGOOD: To see thee thus is joy too great for words. Farewell! Heaven strengthen thee! Farewell!

BARNWELL: O, sir, there's something I cou'd say, if my sad swelling heart would give me leave.

THOROWGOOD: Give it vent a while, and try.

BARNWELL: I had a friend—'tis true I am unworthy, yet methinks your generous example might perswade—cou'd I not see him once before I go from whence there's no return?

THOROWGOOD: He's coming, and as much thy friend as ever; but I'll not anticipate his sorrow: too soon he'll see the sad effect of this contagious ruin.—[Aside] This torrent of domestick misery bears too hard upon me; I must retire to indulge a weakness I find impossible to overcome.—Much lov'd and much lamented youth, farewell! Heaven strengthen thee! Eternally farewell!

BARNWELL: The best of masters and of men, farewell! While I live, let me not want your prayers!

THOROWGOOD: Thou shalt not. Thy peace being made with Heaven, death's already vanquish'd; bear a little longer the pains that attend this transitory life, and cease from pain for ever.

[Exit]

SCENE III.

Barnwell.

BARNWELL: I find a power within that bears my soul above the fears of death, and, spight of conscious shame and guilt, gives me a taste of pleasure more than mortal.

SCENE IV.

[*To him* Trueman *and* Keeper]
KEEPER: Sir, there's the prisoner.
[*Exit*]

SCENE V.

Barnwell *and* Trueman.

BARNWELL: Trueman—my friend, whom I so wisht to see! Yet now he's here I dare not look upon him.
    [*Weeps*]
TRUEMAN: Oh Barnwell! Barnwell!
BARNWELL: Mercy, Mercy, gracious Heaven! For death, but not for this, was I prepared.
TRUEMAN: What have I suffer'd since I saw you last! What pain has absence given me!—But oh! to see thee thus!
BARNWELL: I know it is dreadful! I feel the anguish of thy generous soul—but I was born to murder all who love me.
    [*Both weep*]
TRUEMAN: I came not to reproach you; I thought to bring you comfort. But I'm deceiv'd, for I have none to give. I came to share thy sorrow, but cannot bear my own.
BARNWELL: My sense of guilt indeed you cannot know—'tis what the good and innocent, like you, can ne'er conceive. But other griefs at present I have none, but what I feel for you. In your sorrow I read you love me still. But yet methinks 'tis strange, when I consider what I am.
TRUEMAN: No more of that! I can remember nothing but thy virtues, thy honest, tender friendship, our former happy state, and present misery.—O, had you trusted me when first the fair seducer tempted you, all might have been prevented.
BARNWELL: Alas, thou know'st not what a wretch I've been! Breach of friendship was my first and least offence. So far was I lost to goodness, so devoted to the author of my ruin, that, had she insisted on my murdering thee, I think I shou'd have done it.
TRUEMAN: Prithee, aggravate thy faults no more!
BARNWELL: I think I shou'd! Thus, good and generous as you are, I shou'd have murder'd you!

TRUEMAN: We have not yet embrac'd, and may be interrupted. Come to my arms!
BARNWELL: Never, never will I taste such joys on earth; never will I so sooth my just remorse! Are those honest arms and faithful bosom fit to embrace and to support a murderer? These iron fetters only shall clasp, and flinty pavement bear me [*Throwing himself on the ground*]—even these too good for such a bloody monster.
TRUEMAN: Shall fortune sever those whom friendship join'd? Thy miseries cannot lay thee so low, but love will find thee. [*Lies down by him*] Upon this rugged couch then let us lie; for well it suits our most deplorable condition. Here will we offer to stern calamity, this earth the altar, and our selves the sacrifice! Our mutual groans shall echo to each other thro' the dreary vault. Our sighs shall number the moments as they pass, and mingling tears communicate such anguish as words were never made to express.
BARNWELL: Then be it so! Since you propose an intercourse of woe, pour all your griefs into my breast, and in exchange take mine! [*Embracing*] Where's now the anguish that you promis'd? You've taken mine, and make me no return. Sure, peace and comfort dwell within these arms, and sorrow can't approach me while I'm here! This too is the work of Heaven, who, having before spoke peace and pardon to me, now sends thee to confirm it. O take, take some of the joy that overflows my breast!
TRUEMAN: I do, I do. Almighty Power, how have you made us capable to bear, at once, the extreams of pleasure and of pain?

SCENE VI.

[*To them,* Keeper]
KEEPER: Sir!
TRUEMAN: I come.
[*Exit* Keeper]

SCENE VII.

Barnwell *and* Trueman.

BARNWELL: Must you leave me? Death would soon have parted us for ever.
TRUEMAN: O my Barnwell, there's yet another task behind; again your heart must bleed for others' woes.
BARNWELL: To meet and part with you, I thought was all I had to do on earth! What is there more for me to do or suffer?
TRUEMAN: I dread to tell thee; yet it must be known!—Maria—
BARNWELL: Our master's fair and virtuous daughter?
TRUEMAN: The same.
BARNWELL: No misfortune, I hope, has reach'd

that lovely maid! Preserve her, Heaven, from every ill, to show mankind that goodness is your care!

TRUEMAN: Thy, thy misfortunes, my unhappy friend, have reach'd her. Whatever you and I have felt, and more, if more be possible, she feels for you.

BARNWELL: [*Aside*] I know he doth abhor a lie, and would not trifle with his dying friend. This is, indeed, the bitterness of death!

TRUEMAN: You must remember, for we all observ'd it, for some time past, a heavy melancholy weigh'd her down. Disconsolate she seem'd, and pin'd and languish'd from a cause unknown;—till, hearing of your dreadful fate,—the long stifled flame blaz'd out. She wept, she wrung her hands, and tore her hair, and, in the transport of her grief, discover'd her own lost state, whilst she lamented yours.

BARNWELL: Will all the pain I feel restore thy ease, lovely unhappy maid? [*Weeping*] Why didn't you let me die and never know it?

TRUEMAN: It was impossible; she makes no secret of her passion for you, and is determin'd to see you e'er you die. She waits for me to introduce her.

[*Exit*]

SCENE VIII.

Barnwell.

BARNWELL: Vain, busy thoughts, be still! What avails it to think on what I might have been? I now am what I've made myself.

SCENE IX.

[*To him,* Trueman *and* Maria]

TRUEMAN: Madam, reluctant I lead you to this dismal scene. This is the seat of misery and guilt. Here awful justice reserves her public victims. This is the entrance to shameful death.

MARIA: To this sad place, then, no improper guest, the abandon'd, lost Maria brings despair—and see the subject and the cause of all this world of woe! Silent and motionless he stands, as if his soul had quitted her abode, and the lifeless form alone was left behind—yet that so perfect that beauty and death, ever at enmity, now seem united there.

BARNWELL: I groan, but murmur not. Just Heaven, I am your own; do with me what you please.

MARIA: Why are your streaming eyes still fix'd below, as tho' thoud'st give the greedy earth thy sorrows, and rob me of my due? Were happiness within your power, you should bestow it where you pleas'd; but in your misery I must and will partake!

BARNWELL: Oh, say not so, but fly, abhor, and leave me to my fate! Consider what you are—how vast your fortune, and how bright your fame; have pity on your youth, your beauty, and unequalled virtue, for which so many noble peers have sigh'd

in vain! Bless with your charms some honorable lord! Adorn with your beauty, and by your example improve, the English court, that justly claims such merit: so shall I quickly be to you as though I had never been.

MARIA: When I forget you, I must be so indeed. Reason, choice, virtue, all forbid it. Let women, like Millwood, if there be more such women, smile in prosperity, and in adversity forsake! Be it the pride of virtue to repair, or to partake, the ruin such have made.

TRUEMAN: Lovely, ill-fated maid! Was there ever such generous distress before? How must this pierce his grateful heart, and aggravate his woes?

BARNWELL: E'er I knew guilt or shame—when fortune smiled, and when my youthful hopes were at the highest—if then to have rais'd my thoughts to you, had been presumption in me, never to have been pardon'd: think how much beneath your self you condescend, to regard me now!

MARIA: Let her blush, who, professing love, invades the freedom of your sex's choice, and meanly sues in hopes of a return! Your inevitable fate hath render'd hope impossible as vain. Then, why shou'd I fear to avow a passion so just and so disinterested?

TRUEMAN: If any shou'd take occasion, from Millwood's crimes, to libel the best and fairest part of the creation, here let them see their error! The most distant hopes of such a tender passion from so bright a maid might add to the happiness of the most happy, and make the greatest proud. Yet here 'tis lavish'd in vain: tho' by the rich present, the generous donor is undone, he on whom it is bestow'd receives no benefit.

BARNWELL: So the aromatick spices of the East, which all the living covet and esteem, are, with unavailing kindness, wasted on the dead.

MARIA: Yes, fruitless is my love, and unavailing all my sighs and tears. Can they save thee from approaching death—from such a death? O, terrible idea! What is her misery and distress, who sees the first last object of her love, for whom alone she'd live —for whom she'd die a thousand, thousand deaths, if it were possible—expiring in her arms? Yet she is happy, when compar'd to me. Were millions of worlds mine, I'd gladly give them in exchange for her condition. The most consummate woe is light to wine. The last of curses to other miserable maids is all I ask; and that's deny'd me.

TRUEMAN: Time and reflection cure all ills.

MARIA: All but this; his dreadful catastrophe virtue herself abhors. To give a holiday to suburb slaves, and passing entertain the savage herd, who, elbowing each other for a sight, pursue and press upon him like his fate! A mind with piety and resolution arm'd may smile on death. But publick ignomy, everlasting shame,—shame, the death of souls—to die a thousand times, and yet survive even death itself, in never dying infamy—is this to be endured? Can I, who live in him, and must, each hour of my devoted life, feel all these woes renew'd, can I endure this?

TRUEMAN: Grief has impair'd her spirits; she pants as in the agonies of death.

BARNWELL: Preserve her, Heaven, and restore her peace; nor let her death be added to my crime! [*Bell tolls*] I am summon'd to my fate.

SCENE X.

[*To them,* Keeper]

KEEPER: The officers attend you, sir. Mrs. Millwood is already summon'd.

BARNWELL: Tell 'em, I'm ready.—And now, my friend, farewell! [*Embracing*] Support and comfort the best you can this mourning fair.—No more! Forget not to pray for me!—[*Turning to* Maria] Would you, bright excellence, permit me the honour of a chaste embrace, the last happiness this world cou'd give were mine. [*She inclines toward him, they embrace*] Exalted goodness! O turn your eyes from earth, and me, to Heaven, where virtue, like yours, is ever heard. Pray for the peace of my departing soul! Early my race of wickedness began, and soon has reach'd the summit. E'er nature has finish'd her work, and stamp'd me man—just at the time that others begin to stray—my course is finish'd. Tho' short my span of life, and few days, yet, count my crimes for years, and I have liv'd whole ages. Justice and mercy are in Heaven the same: its utmost severity is mercy to the whole, thereby to cure man's folly and presumption, which else wou'd render even infinite mercy vain and ineffectual. Thus justice, in compassion to mankind, cuts off a wretch like me, by one such example to secure thousands from future ruin.

If any youth, like you, in future times
Shall mourn my fate, tho' he abhor my crimes;
Or tender maid, like you, my tale shall hear,
And to my sorrows give a pitying tear;
To each such melting eye, and throbbing heart,
Would gracious Heaven this benefit impart
Never to know my guilt, nor feel my pain:
Then must you own, you ought not to complain;
Since you nor weep, nor shall I die, in vain.
[*Exeunt*]

SCENE XI.

The place of Execution. The gallows and ladders at the farther end of the stage. A crowd of spectators. Blunt *and* Lucy.

LUCY: Heavens! what a throng!

BLUNT: How terrible is death, when thus prepar'd!

LUCY: Support them, Heaven; thou only can support them; all other help is vain.

OFFICER: [*Within*] Make way there; make way, and give the prisoners room!

LUCY: They are here; observe them well! How humble and composed young Barnwell seems! But Millwood looks wild, ruffled with passion, confounded and amazed.

[*Enter* Barnwell, Millwood, Officers *and* Executioners]

BARNWELL: See, Millwood, see: our journey's at an end. Life, like a tale that's told, is past away; that short but dark and unknown passage, death, is all the space 'tween us and endless joys, or woes eternal.

MILLWOOD: Is this the end of all my flattering hopes? Were youth and beauty given me for a curse, and wisdom only to insure my ruin? They were, they were! Heaven, thou hast done thy worst. Or, if thou hast in store some untried plague—somewhat that's worse than shame, despair and death, unpitied death, confirm'd despair and soul confounding shame—something that men and angels can't describe, and only fiends, who bear it, can conceive: now pour it now on this devoted head, that I may feel the worst thou canst inflict, and bid defiance to thy utmost power!

BARNWELL: Yet, ere we pass the dreaful gulph of death—yet, ere you're plunged in everlasting woe: O bend your stubborn knees and harder heart, humbly to deprecate the wrath divine! Who knows but Heaven, in your dying moments, may bestow that grace and mercy which your life despised!

MILLWOOD: Why name you mercy to a wretch like me? Mercy's beyond my hope—almost beyond my wish. I can't repent, nor ask to be forgiven.

BARNWELL: O think what 'tis to be for ever, ever miserable; nor with vain pride oppose a Power, that's able to destroy you!

MILLWOOD: That will destroy me; I feel it will. A deluge of wrath is pouring on my soul. Chains, darkness, wheels, racks, sharp stinging scorpions, molten lead, and seas of sulphur, are light to what I feel.

BARNWELL: O! add not to your vast account despair, a sin more injurious to Heaven than all you've yet committed.

MILLWOOD: O! I have sin'd beyond the reach of mercy.

BARNWELL: O say not so; 'tis blasphemy to think it. As yon bright roof is higher than the earth, so, and much more, does Heaven's goodness pass our apprehension. O! what created being shall presume to circumscribe mercy, that knows no bounds?

MILLWOOD: This yields no hope. Tho' mercy may be boundless, yet 'tis free; and I was doom'd, before the world began, to endless pains, and thou to joys eternal.

BARNWELL: O gracious Heaven! extend thy pity to her! Let thy rich mercy flow in plenteous streams, to chase her fears and heal her wounded soul!

MILLWOOD: It will not be. Your prayers are lost

in air, or else returned, perhaps with double blessing, to your bosom; but me they help not.

BARNWELL: Yet hear me, Millwood!

MILLWOOD: Away, I will not hear thee. I tell thee, youth, I am by Heaven devoted a dreadful instance of its power to punish. [Barnwell *seems to pray*] If thou wilt pray, pray for thyself, not me! How doth his fervent soul mount with his words, and both ascend to Heaven—that Heaven whose gates are shut with adamantine bars against my prayers, had I the will to pray.—I cannot bear it! Sure, 'tis the worst of torments to behold others enjoy that bliss that we must never taste!

OFFICER: The utmost limit of your time's expired.

MILLWOOD: Incompassed with horror, whither must I go? I wou'd not live—nor die. That I cou'd cease to be, or ne'er had been!

BARNWELL: Since peace and comfort are denied her here, may she find mercy where she least expects it, and this be all her hell!—From our example may all be taught to fly the first approach of vice; but, if o'ertaken

> *By strong temptation, weakness, or surprize,*
> *Lament their guilt and by repentance rise!*
> *Th' impenitent alone die unforgiven;*
> *To sin's like man, and to forgive like Heaven.*
> [*Exeunt*]

SCENE XII.

[*Enter* Trueman *to* Blunt *and* Lucy]

LUCY: Heart-breaking sight! O wretched, wretched Millwood!

TRUEMAN: You came from her, then; how is she disposed to meet her fate?

BLUNT: Who can describe unalterable woe?

LUCY: She goes to death encompassed with horror, loathing life, and yet afraid to die; no tongue can tell her anguish and despair.

TRUEMAN: Heaven be better to her than her fears: may she prove a warning to others, a monument of mercy in her self!

LUCY: O sorrow insupportable! Break, break, my heart!

TRUEMAN: In vain

> *With bleeding hearts and weeping eyes we show*
> *A humane gen'rous sense of others' woe,*
> *Unless we mark what drew their ruin on,*
> *And, by avoiding that, prevent our own.*

FINIS

Ostrovsky and The Thunderstorm

Although Ostrovsky's masterpiece reflects its author's interest in the old Russian merchant class, the play transcends that interest through its compassion and poetic atmosphere. The masterpieces of writers not of the first rank are apt to be atypical in some respects; and there is good reason why this should be so in the case of Ostrovsky, who not only wrote a great many plays but also branched off from directly middleclass drama into several other genres. Among these are various plays depicting "folksy" peasant life, the milieu of the petty Russian government bureaucracy, fashionable Russian society (treated with special success in the often performed *Woe from Wit,* 1868), and the theatrical world. And Ostrovsky also wrote a number of historical dramas such as *The Death of Ivan the Terrible, Tsar Theodore,* and *Tsar Boris* (1866–1870), and one fairy-tale masterpiece *The Snow Maiden* (*Snegúrochka*), the source of Rimsky-Korsakov's opera of the same name.

The Thunderstorm, however, can be most meaningfully related to his main dramatic enterprise. It belongs to Ostrovsky's major, if long unrequited, studies of middle-class life. It was the life he knew best, and his intimacy with it made him the Balzac of the mid-century Russian merchant world. He identified with it but also exposed it, reproduced its main features with vivid portraits of its representative men and women but depicted its provincial backwardness, traditionalism, and repressiveness.

Alexander Ostrovsky (1823–1886) was born in the residential quarter of Moscow mercantile society to a government clerk who left the service to practice law among the merchants of the city. The son was duly sent to the University in Moscow but left after a quarrel with the authorities and became a clerk of the court that considered commercial cases. He served in the Commercial Court for a period of eight years during which he turned to literary activities and joined a group of writers. By the time he was twenty-four, he had begun to have his work published. Playwriting became his forte, and his first play was produced in 1856. His assiduity grew, although his writings could not sustain him, and he wrote over forty plays. He also translated foreign works for the Russian stage such as Cervantes' *entremeses* or interludes (see page 787) and Shakespeare's *The Taming of the Shrew.*

On the whole, Ostrovsky's realism clung to the surfaces of the life he represented. He evinced little concern with psychology and even less with philosophy. His dramatic style, for the most part, was serviceable rather than poetic and suggestive. His realism was in no way subjective as far as one can tell, and while he was often implicitly critical of the life and mores he represented, he maintained no particular consistency of viewpoint. The distinguished historian of Russian literature, Prince D. S. Mirsky could only conclude that "it is extraordinarily difficult to extract a social and political *Weltanschauung* out of Ostrovsky." In his writing, he was affected by practical considerations and strategies of dramatic effectiveness. He escaped censure from critics as a contriver of plots due to his ability to provide a sense of authenticity to his characters, and his playwriting, generally free from theatrical flamboyance and artificial ingenuity, must be disassociated in the main from the work of such arch-contrivers masquerading as realists as Scribe and Sardou, from whom even Ibsen was not entirely disassociated when he wrote *The Pillars of Society* and *A Doll's House* in the late eighteen-seventies.

Credit also accrued to Ostrovsky because he displayed the power of natural dialogue to a greater degree than most writers of serious Russian plays. The middle-class characters he drew were thoroughly individualized and at the same time fully integrated with their status and environment, even in such early plays as *The Bankrupt* (1850) and *The Poor Bride* (1852). Nevertheless Ostrovsky often had but meager success in his lifetime with many of his best plays, and he was also hampered by official censorship for his real and fancied social criticism, especially his depiction of glaring domestic tyranny and greed.

In *The Thunderstorm* all of the aforementioned qualities are more or less in evidence, and at least one prominent critic of the period, N. A. Dubrolyubov, acclaimed the work as a virtually revolutionary act. For this critic, the unfortunate Katerina's struggle for love and happiness represented the beginnings of revolt against a joylessly narrow, oppressively materialistic, and tradition-bound evironment. "Is it true," he asked, "that in Katerina vital Russian nature found its expression; is it true that the Russian background, with everything surrounding it—the need of the rising movement of Russian life is revealed in the content of the play . . . ?[1] And another commentator, M. I. Pisarev, who became a leading actor, found an appreciable degree of symbolism in its very title. He wrote that the actual thunderstorm that occurs in it "serves merely as a parallel to the still more dreadful moral storm" in Ostrovsky's miserable heroine, who is terrified by the sudden squall and expects to be struck down by the thunderstorm for her lapse into adultery. It is during this storm that Katerina is driven to make public confession of her crime and then throw herself into the river. As the English translator of this work, Andrew McAndrew, puts it, "There is a kinship between the ele-

[1] B. V. Varneke, *History of the Russian Theatre,* New York: Macmillan, 1951, p. 327.

mental force of nature and the elemental passions of Katerina."

It does not, however, follow that political interpretations of her conduct are essential. The storm and other more or less symbolic elements or tonalities in the play are primarily a part of the atmosphere of the action and of Katerina's perturbed state of mind caused by an unhappy marriage with a weak-willed young husband in a household ruled by his strong-willed and narrow-minded mother. There is, in fine, considerable poetry, not verbal but atmospheric, in *The Thunderstorm,* and this deepens the drama and enables it to attain as much tragedy as it is possible to achieve with a central character who is essentially *distrait* and pathetic. Her revolt against frustrations is entirely personal and furtive and, since she is cowed by tradition and religious fear, is quickly repented.

The Thunderstorm won for its author the coveted Uvarov Prize from the Russian Academy nine months after its publication in 1860, and he was finally appointed, shortly before his death in 1886, artistic director of Moscow's Imperial Theatres. At his best, as in *The Thunderstorm,* he exhibited an instinctive regard for the controlled spontaneity and organic structure which even dramatic realism cannot forego without risking extinction as art, and with which it became "art" after Ostrovsky's time in the prose plays of Chekhov, Synge, and O'Casey. It was not without reason that *The Thunderstorm,* whose Katerina became a favorite role for Russia's leading actresses, was staged by renowned directors such as Meyerhold and Tairov both before and after the Russian Revolution. And it was not without reason that this affecting atmospheric work attracted composers. Tchaikovsky wrote an overture for *The Thunderstorm;* one opera based on it (by V. Kashperov) was performed in Russia in 1867, and a better known one, entitled *Katya Kabanova,* was developed

from Ostrovsky's drama by the modern Czech composer, Janacek.[2]

So far as Ostrovsky's realism is concerned, it is noteworthy that even later Russian writers could not carry it further without moving into the miasmas of rank naturalism, in which only Gorky managed to survive creditably in *The Lower Depths.*[3] And Ostrovsky's theme of the spiritual bankruptcy or, at least, stalemate of the old order was soon to become a favorite subject, most notably in Chekhov's turn-of-the-century plays as well as in Gorky's masterpiece of the Soviet era, *Yegor Bulychev,* dealing with the once powerful merchant who dies of cancer at the outbreak of the Russian Revolution. With Ostrovsky's best plays we draw close to important twentieth-century Russian playwrights as well as to modern writers elsewhere who dealt with dessicated characters in constricting materialistic environments. Moreover, this playwright contributed substantially to modern realistic staging as developed by the influential Moscow Art Theatre and its leader Konstantin Stanislavsky. "The great Russian playwright," writes David Magarshack in his biography of the director, "was more than anyone responsible for building up the remarkable company of great actors of the Maly Theatre, which had contributed so greatly to Stanislavsky's artistic development and, as he himself confessed, had taught him "to see and observe the beautiful." It is not too much to say therefore that Ostrovsky is an authentic forerunner of modern drama in his native land and indirectly the rest of the Western world.

[2] For two comprehensive summaries of Ostrovsky's work, students can refer to D. S. Mirsky's *A History of Russian Literature,* Knopf 1949, and B. V. Varneke's *History of the Russian Theatre,* New York: Macmillan 1951.

[3] See Volume II of *A Treasury of the Theatre.*

THE THUNDERSTORM

A Drama in Five Acts

By Alexander Ostrovsky

TRANSLATED BY ANDREW MacANDREW

CHARACTERS

DIKOY, *a merchant and an important figure in the town*

BORIS, *his nephew, a fairly well-educated young man*

MRS. KABANOV, *a rich merchant's widow*

BARBARA, *her daughter*

TIKHON, *her son*

KATERINA, *his wife*

KULIGIN, *a self-taught watchmaker, trying to discover perpetual motion*

VANIA KUDRASH, *a young man, Dikoy's clerk*

SHAPKIN, *a tradesman*

FEKLUSHA, *a pilgrim-woman*

GLASHA, *a maid at the Kabanovs'*

A LADY, *a half-mad old woman of 70, attended by two footmen*

TOWNSPEOPLE, *of both sexes*

The action takes place in the town of Kalinov on the banks of the Volga, in summertime. There is an interval of ten days between Acts III and IV. All except Boris wear Russian-style clothes.

ACT I.

A public park atop the steep bank of the Volga. Beyond the Volga, a stretch of rural scenery. On stage, two benches and a few bushes. Kuligin is sitting on a bench gazing out across the river. Vania and Shapkin are strolling about.

KULIGIN: [*Singing*] Upon a velvet hilltop
              Among the valleys low . . .
    [*Stops singing*]
Its a real wonder, I swear. I'm telling you, Vania, I've come here to look at the Volga everyday for fifty years now and I still can't get my fill of looking.

VANIA: What d'you mean?

KULIGIN: What an incredible view! Such beauty, it makes my heart sing.

VANIA: You don't say!

KULIGIN: It's a marvel and that's all you have to say! Either you're so used to it you don't see it any more or you just have no feel for all the beauty there is in nature.

VANIA: Ah, what's the good trying to talk to you. You're a real showpiece around here, a chemist!

KULIGIN: No, an engineer, a self-taught one.

VANIA: It all comes to the same thing. [*Silence*]

KULIGIN: [*Pointing to one side*] Take a look, Vania, who's that flailing his arms about over there?

VANIA: Why, that's Dikoy bawling out his nephew.

KULIGIN: Fine place he picked!

VANIA: Doesn't make any difference to him where he does it. There's nothing to stop him. He has Boris to take it out on now and he really makes the most of it.

SHAPKIN: You won't find another bully like our Mr. Dikoy, no matter how hard you look. It don't take nothing to make him tear into a man.

VANIA: He's real mean!

SHAPKIN: And that Kabanov woman's not so hot either!

VANIA: Yes, but she at least makes out she does it because she's religious like, respectable, while this one's like a vicious dog that's broken loose.

SHAPKIN: There's no one to keep a hold on him, so he just goes storming around.

VANIA: Ah, what we need's a few more fellows like me around—we'd soon cure him of his tricks.

SHAPKIN: And what would you do?

VANIA: We'd give him a good scare.

SHAPKIN: How'd you do that?

VANIA: A bunch of four or five of us would just have a little talk with him, you know, face to face, in an alley somewhere, and he'd turn silky soft in no time. What's more, he wouldn't dare breathe a word to nobody about the lesson we'd given him and he'd keep a sharp eye out wherever he went after that.

SHAPKIN: Ah, now I see he had a point wanting to send you in the army.

VANIA: All right, he wanted to but he didn't and so I'm here. He won't send me now because he's got a feeling in his stomach that he'd not get off lightly if he tried. He may be a terror to you, but me, I know how to talk to him.

SHAPKIN: Is that so?

VANIA: What d'you mean, is that so? Everybody knows I don't take no nonsense from him or anyone else. But he still keeps me on, don't he? Must be because he needs me, then. So I've got no reason to be scared of him—let him be scared of me.

SHAPKIN: As if he didn't call you names whenever he feels like it!

VANIA: Of course he does. Swearing's like breathing to him. But I don't let him get away with it. Every word he says, I give him back ten, so he just gets disgusted and gives up. You won't catch me knuckling under to him.

KULIGIN: What's the sense following his example? I'd rather just put up with it than be like him.

VANIA: Well then, if you're so smart, you teach him manners first and then come and tell us how you done it. It's a pity those daughters of his are just kids. Ah, if only one of them was grown-up!

SHAPKIN: And what if one was?

VANIA: I'd have shown him. I know how to handle myself with dames.

[Dikoy and Boris walk past; Kuligin takes off his cap]

SHAPKIN: [To Vania] Let's make ourselves scarce or who says he won't pick on us.

[They move off]

DIKOY: So you thought you'd come here and loaf, you good-for-nothing sponger! Like hell I'll let you!

BORIS: But it's a holiday today. What's there for me to do in the house?

DIKOY: You'd find plenty to do if you looked around. I've warned you once and I've warned you twice: stay out of my way! But with you, it goes in one ear and out the other. What's the matter, isn't there enough room for you here? Wherever I go, there you are already. Ah, damn you, you fool, what're you standing there like a post for? Well, d'you hear me?

BORIS: Yes, I hear you. What more can I do?

DIKOY: [Looking at him] Get out of my sight! I don't even want to talk to a Jesuit like you. [He walks away] What did you have to come and hang around my neck for?

[Spits in disgust and exits]

KULIGIN: How can you have anything to do with him, sir? We here just can't understand it. Why d'you want to stay with him and put up with all that?

BORIS: Who's talking of wanting, Kuligin. I don't have any choice.

KULIGIN: But, if you don't mind me asking, sir, why don't you? If you can tell us why, sir, please do.

BORIS: Why shouldn't I tell you? Did you know my grandmother, Anfisa Mikhailovna?

KULIGIN: How could I help knowing her?

VANIA: We sure did.

BORIS: Well then, she quarreled with my father because he married a lady. And so my parents went to live in Moscow. My mother used to say she couldn't stand my father's family after she'd spent three days with them, they seemed such a bunch of savages to her.

KULIGIN: I'm not surprised she should've felt like that, sir. You've gotta be used to their ways, sir.

BORIS: Well, my parents gave us a good education in Moscow—they didn't grudge us a thing. They sent me to business school there and my sister to a girls' boarding school, but then they both got cholera and died suddenly, and my sister and I were left orphans. Then we heard that our grandmother here had died too, and that in her will she'd provided that our uncle should pay us our share when we came of age—on one condition.

KULIGIN: What condition, sir?

BORIS: That we treat him with respect.

KULIGIN: Well, in that case, sir, you'll never see your inheritance.

BORIS: Worse than that! First he'll vent his spite on us, insult us on the slightest pretext, and then in the end he still won't give us anything except perhaps a token payment. And even then, he'll claim he gave us that out of the kindness of his heart, that we really weren't entitled to it either.

VANIA: Well, that's the way the merchants are around here. And then, even if you do treat him with respect, what's to stop him saying you don't?

BORIS: Yes, of course. Every so often, even now, he says: "I've my own kids—why should I give money to strangers and take it away from my own flesh and blood?"

KULIGIN: So I see it's a bad business for you, sir!

BORIS: If it was just me, I wouldn't care. I'd give up the whole thing and leave. But there's my sister, you see. He sent for her to come too, but our relatives on my mother's side wouldn't let her go. They wrote back that she was sick. I wouldn't even want to think what kind of a life she'd have here.

VANIA: You're right there! A man like Mr. Dikoy sure don't know how to treat people decent.

KULIGIN: So, what's your actual position in his house, sir?

BORIS: No position whatever. "You live here," he told me, "and do what you're told to do and I'll decide what I'll pay you." That means that a year from now he'll fix whatever sum suits him.

VANIA: That's just like him! We none of us dare to say a word about our pay—he bawls our heads off if we do. "How," he says, "can you know what goes on in my mind? You think you can see right down inside me? Who knows, maybe I'll feel in the mood to pay you a whole five thousand." Just try talking to him! The trouble is, in his whole life he's never felt that way—not once.

KULIGIN: Well, what can you do, sir? You'll have to try and humor him somehow or other.

BORIS: That's just the trouble, Kuligin. It's just plain impossible. Even his own family can't humor him, so what hope do I have?

VANIA: How can anyone humor him when all he knows is abusing people? And especially when it comes to money; not one account ever gets settled without a whole lot of swearing and abuse. People'd rather give up what's their rightful due, just so he'll quiet down. And if someone steps on his toes first thing in the morning, there's hell to pay! He'll keep picking on us all for the rest of the day.

BORIS: Every morning my aunt begs us all, with tears in her eyes: "Please don't make him angry. Please try not to make him mad."

VANIA: As if you could stop him. He just has to set foot in the market and he's off. He abuses all the peasants and even if they'll settle for a loss, he still won't leave till he's sworn their heads off. And once he's started, he keeps going all day.

SHAPKIN: In fact, he's fighting mad all the time!

VANIA: And how!

BORIS: And it's terrible too, when someone he wouldn't dare tell off crosses him. Then his whole family had better watch out!

VANIA: Ah, you should have seen the time that hussar told him what he could do with himself on the Volga ferry. You should've seen the dance he did after that!

BORIS: And didn't we get it at home! For a couple of weeks afterward we had to keep ducking out of his way and hiding in the attics and storerooms.

KULIGIN: Look, are they out of evening service already?

[Several people cross backstage]

VANIA: Come on, Shapkin, let's go and get ourselves a drink. What's there to stand around here for?

[They nod to the others and exit]

BORIS: Ah, Kuligin, it's hard for me here—I'm just not used to it. They all give me such odd looks, as if I were out of place, as if I were in their way. I don't understand the local customs. I know it's all very Russian and should be familiar to me, but I just can't get used to it.

KULIGIN: And you never will get used to it, sir.

BORIS: Why d'you say that?

KULIGIN: It's a cruel life here in our town, sir, real brutal. Among the working people you'll find nothing but coarseness and naked poverty. And we don't have a chance to break our way out of the crust that covers us, because we can't ever earn more than enough for dry bread by honest labor. And those who do have money, they try to enslave the poor and force them to work for nothing to get more money yet. D'you know what your uncle told the mayor once? The workmen had complained because your uncle hadn't settled properly with a single one of them. So the mayor says to your uncle: "Look, Mr. Dikoy," he says, "pay your workmen properly! Every day I get complaints!" And your uncle slaps the mayor on the back and he says to him: "Why, Your Honor, should you and I waste our time on unimportant things? Why, in a year, I have a lot of workers coming and going. So, you understand, suppose I hold back one miserable kopek from each man—that makes thousands for me, which is just fine!" And that's how it goes, sir! And the way the well-off treat each other, sir! They undermine each others' trade and that not so much out of greed as out of jealousy. They keep fighting each other. Then they entice lawyers into their houses and feed them drinks. And you should see those lawyers! They don't even look human; they've had all the humanity crushed out of them. And for a small sum, they'll file fraudulent claims against those people's closest friends for them. So then there's a lawsuit between them, sir, and there's no end to the misery it causes. First they have a hearing here that goes on and on, then they go to the capital of the province and start all over. And there are plenty of people just waiting for them there, who'll lick their chops when they see them coming. So, to make a long story short, they haul them from court to court. And, what's more, they don't mind being dragged around like that at all; in fact, it's just what they want. "I'll pay if I must," they say, "as long as he has to fork out a pretty penny too." I'd like to put the whole thing into a poem.

BORIS: Why, can you write poetry?

KULIGIN: The kind of poetry they wrote in the old days, sir. I've read a lot of Lomonosov, Derzhavin . . . a wise man, that Lomonosov, believe me, sir, a student of nature, and yet, he was from the common people—just like me.

BORIS: You should write that poem. It'd be very interesting to see.

KULIGIN: How could I, sir? They'd eat me alive. As it is, I get it in the neck for talking too much, but I can't help it! Well, I wanted to tell you something of the family life here too, sir, but we'll have to make it another time. I'm sure you'll find it quite interesting.

[Enter Feklusha and another woman]

FEKLUSHA: Great, my dear, real great! My, it's so beautiful here! I'm telling you, you live in the promised land! Ah, those merchants of yours are a real God-fearing lot, blessed with many virtues, great generosity and much almsgiving! I'm full to the gills with happiness from it all. They haven't turned us away and so, I say, their abundance will be still further increased, especially in the Kabanov household. [They exit]

BORIS: The Kabanov household?

KULIGIN: Ah, that hypocrite! To beggars she gives, but you should see how she treats her own people. [Pauses] Ah, if only I could discover perpetual motion, sir!

BORIS: Why? What would you do then?

KULIGIN: What d'you mean, sir? Why, them English are offering a million to the one who finds it. Me, I'd spend all that money for the good of the community, sir. Working men should be given work. As it is, there are people with willing hands and there's nothing for them to do.

BORIS: And you really hope to discover perpetual motion?

KULIGIN: I sure do, sir! All I need now's a little cash to build a model. But I must be on my way now. Good-by, sir! [Exits]

BORIS: [Alone] Wonderful fellow! It'd be a shame to disillusion him! He wraps himself up in a dream and he's happy. As to me, it looks as if I'm going to have to waste my youth in this hole. Ah, I'm completely done in as it is, and now I've got this new idiocy in my head! That's all I needed, really! What do I want with love, for God's sake? Here I'm shouted at and pushed around and now I have to go and fall in love like an idiot. And with whom? With a woman I'll never even get a chance to speak to. [*Silence*] And yet I can't get her out of my head, try as I may. Oh, there she is! She's coming this way with her husband, oh, and her mother-in-law's with them too! Ah, what an idiot I am! All right I'll just steal a glance at her from round the corner and then get off home. [*Exits*]

[Mrs. Kabanov, *her daughter* Barbara, *her son* Tikhon *and his wife* Katerina *enter from the opposite side of the stage*]

MRS. KABANOV: Listen to your mother now, and when you get there, do just as I told you.

TIKHON: How could I not do as you told me, Mother?

MRS. KABANOV: Nowadays the younger generation is not that respectful of their elders.

BARBARA: [*Aside*] Just try not respecting you!

TIKHON: I don't believe, Mother, that I've ever taken a step without your consent.

MRS. KABANOV: Perhaps I'd believe that, my boy, if I'd not seen with my own eyes and heard with my own ears how children treat their parents nowadays. I wish you'd remember at least all the suffering your mother's put up with for your sake.

TIKHON: Mother, I . . .

MRS. KABANOV: Even if she who gave you birth does say something to hurt your pride, I think you ought to bear it—don't you agree?

TIKHON: But, Mother, when have I ever failed to bear anything from you?

MRS. KABANOV: Your mother's old and stupid and you young people, who're so clever, shouldn't be too demanding toward us old fools.

TIKHON: [*Sighing, aside*] Oh, good Lord! [*To his Mother*] Who'd even think of such a thing, Mother!

MRS. KABANOV: Don't you realize that if your parents are stern, it's only because they love you; it's out of love that they nag you—they're trying to teach you to act right. But children don't appreciate that nowadays and they go all around the place telling people that their mother's a nag, that she won't let them breathe, that she's poisoning their lives. And if, God forbid, the mother says a word that's not quite to the daughter-in-law's liking, then everyone starts yelling that she's pushing her straight into the grave.

TIKHON: Who's ever said anything like that, Mother?

MRS. KABANOV: Well, I must say I've never actually heard it, my boy, never. I don't want to invent things—but if I had heard something like that, I'd be talking to you quite differently now! [*Sighs*] It doesn't take long to commit a sin, my boy. Just get talking on a subject that touches you and before you know it, you've lost your temper, and that's a dreadful sin. So I'd better let you say anything you like

about me; anyway if I don't let you do so to my face, you'll say it behind my back.

TIKHON: May my tongue shrivel if I ever . . .

MRS. KABANOV: Stop it, no oaths, and lying is sinful, remember. I realized long ago that you feel closer to your wife than to your mother. Since you got married, you haven't loved me the way you used to.

TIKHON: What makes you think so, Mother?

MRS. KABANOV: Everything, my boy, everything! What a mother doesn't see with her eyes, her heart tells her; a mother's heart's a weathervane. I don't know that it is, perhaps it's your wife causing the rift.

TIKHON: What are you saying, Mother? Of course she isn't!

KATERINA: But I feel toward you just as I feel toward my own mother and I know Tikhon loves you as much as he ever did.

MRS. KABANOV: Did I ask you anything? So why don't you keep quiet, my girl? You don't have to defend Tikhon, I won't hurt him—he's my son after all, something you seem to forget. And why'd you have to jump to his defense like that? To show people how much you love your husband? Why, we all know how much you love him. In public, that is.

BARBARA: [*Aside*] Couldn't she find a better place to lecture them?

KATERINA: You're wrong about me, Mother. In public or private, I'm always the same; I never try to put on a show.

MRS. KABANOV: Ah, I didn't even want to talk about you. It just happened to come up.

KATERINA: Even so, I don't see why you have to say things like that about me.

MRS. KABANOV: You're really getting too uppity; I can't say a word without your taking offense right away.

KATERINA: Who likes to be accused without reason!

MRS. KABANOV: I know, I know what I say goes against the grain, but I can't help that. I'm no stranger and my heart bleeds for you! I noticed long ago that you wanted to live your own lives. Well, why not, you'll have a chance soon enough—when I'm no longer here. Then you'll do just as you please, without your elders around. And perhaps you'll remember me then, too.

TIKHON: But we pray night and day, Mother, that God should grant you health, happiness, and success in business.

MRS. KABANOV: Enough, enough, stop it please . . . I grant you, it's possible you did love your mother as long as you were a bachelor. But when do you have time to think of me with a young wife like yours?

TIKHON: One doesn't prevent the other: a wife is a wife, but I'll always honor and respect my mother.

MRS. KABANOV: So you'd be prepared to give up your wife for your mother? That I'll have to see to believe!

TIKHON: But what need is there to give either of you up? I love you both.

MRS. KABANOV: There you go, trying to dodge that one too! I see I'm in your way.

TIKHON: Think what you like, I can't stop you. I only know that I'm a miserable man and that whatever I do displeases you.

MRS. KABANOV: Why, you're trying to pass yourself off as a poor, stepped-on little boy! I do believe you're on the verge of tears, upon my word! What kind of a man and a husband can you be after that? Look at yourself. Do you think your wife could ever fear and respect you now?

TIKHON: Why should she fear me? She loves me and that's good enough for me.

MRS. KABANOV: What do you mean, "Why should she fear me"? Are you out of your mind or what? If your wife doesn't fear you, she certainly won't fear me either. Then what sort of order will we have in our house? Isn't she your lawful wife then? Or perhaps the law doesn't mean a thing to you? Well, and if you must talk such stuff and nonsense, at least don't do it in front of her; nor in front of your own sister, because she'll have to marry too and whoever her husband is, he won't thank you for putting such ideas into her head. You can see for yourself you don't have too much brain after all, although you keep saying that you'd like to run your own life.

TIKHON: But, Mother, I never said I wanted to run my own life. I know I couldn't manage it.

MRS. KABANOV: So you imagine you must be all kindness to your wife, never tell her off, never threaten her? Is that it?

TIKHON: But, Mother, I only . . .

MRS. KABANOV: [Heatedly] She could even take a lover if she takes it into her head, couldn't she? Perhaps that's nothing in your opinion either? Well, speak up!

TIKHON: But I swear, Mother . . .

MRS. KABANOV: [Icily] Idiot! [Sighs] What's the good of talking to a fool this way? It just makes me irritated. [A pause] I'm going home.

TIKHON: We'll be coming home too, Mother. We'll just take a little stroll along the avenue first.

MRS. KABANOV: Please yourselves, but don't be late. Remember, I don't like it!

TIKHON: No, Mother, God forbid.

MRS. KABANOV: You'd better see you're not! [Exit]

TIKHON: See, you always get me in trouble with mother. Ah, what a life!

KATERINA: It's not my fault, is it?

TIKHON: I don't know whose fault it is any more.

BARBARA: Oh, you wouldn't know, of course.

TIKHON: She used to nag me all the time. "Get married," she'd say, "if only so we can see what you'll look like as a married man." And now she nags me so because of you that I can't find a place to hide. It's all your fault!

BARBARA: As if it were her fault, really! Mother keeps attacking her and you join in. And after that you dare claim you love your wife! It makes me sick just looking at you. [Turns away]

TIKHON: It's easy for you to talk. What do you expect me to do?

BARBARA: Mind your own business and shut up if you can't do anything better. And now, why are you dancing around like that? Ah, I know what's on your mind.

TIKHON: What then?

BARBARA: You're thinking of going over to Mr. Dikoy's for a drink. Right?

TIKHON: You guessed it.

KATERINA: Take it easy and come home soon or Mother'll be angry.

BARBARA: Yes, don't be long or you know what'll happen.

TIKHON: I sure do.

BARBARA: We aren't too eager to take a lot of her ranting just because of you.

TIKHON: I won't be long. Wait for me. [Exits]

KATERINA: I see you feel sorry for me, don't you, Barbara?

BARBARA: [Looking away] Of course I do.

KATERINA: That shows you're fond of me. [Kisses her]

BARBARA: How could I help being fond of you?

KATERINA: I'm very happy you feel that way. You're so sweet yourself and I like you very much. [Pauses] You know what's just come into my head?

BARBARA: What?

KATERINA: How come people can't fly?

BARBARA: What are you talking about?

KATERINA: I mean, why is it people can't fly? Fly like birds, you know. You know, there're times when I fancy I'm a bird. When I stand on top of a hill, I have a terrible urge to take off—to take a run, lift my arms into the air and leave the ground. Shall I try now? [She is about to start running]

BARBARA: The things you think up sometimes!

KATERINA: [Sighing] Ah, I used to be full of zest once, but I've wilted in our house.

BARBARA: I know, I've noticed.

KATERINA: Yes, I used to be quite different. I lived without a care in the world, like an uncaged bird. My mother adored me, dressed me up like a doll, never made me do any work. I could do whatever came into my head. Let me tell you what my life was like before I married your brother. I'd get up early and if it was summer, I'd go out, wash myself in the stream, then bring water back with me and water all the flowers in the house. I had lots and lots of flowers. Then I'd go to church with my mother and all the pilgrim-women would come too, because our house was always full of pilgrim-women. And when we came back from church, my mother and I would sit down to some embroidery—usually gold thread on black velvet—while the pilgrim-women told us about the places they'd been to or perhaps sang psalms. And so the time would pass till dinner. Then, after the meal, the old women'd lie down for a nap and I'd go out for a walk in the garden. Then it'd be time for vespers and, later in the evening, more tales and more singing.

BARBARA: But it's very much the same in our house.

KATERINA: Yes, but in your house it's as though everything was sort of forced down your throat. Ah, I used to be crazy about going to church! I felt I was in paradise. I didn't see the people around me, and I'd forget the time and always be surprised when the service came to an end. The whole thing might've taken one second! My mother used to tell me that everyone around was staring at me, wondering what had come over me . . . And you know, on sunny days, a thick shaft of sunlight would fall from the dome with clouds of incense floating in it and I remember I sometimes fancied there were angels flying and singing in it, too. And also, when I was a girl, I'd get up during the night, kneel before an icon with a sanctuary lamp burning in front of it—ah, we had icons with lamps all over our house—and sometimes I'd stay there praying till morning. Other times, I'd run out into the garden just after sunrise, fall on my knees and pray and cry without knowing myself what I was praying and crying about, and later they'd find me there like that. And what could I have been praying for then, what could I have been asking for? Seems like I had everything I could wish. And what dreams I used to dream, Barbara, ah, what beautiful dreams! There were all kinds of gilded palaces or the most marvelous gardens and always unseen voices singing and singing, and everything around smelling of cypresses, and the mountains and the countryside beyond, not as they are in real life but just like in the icons. And at other times, I flew through the air all the time. I still have dreams sometimes, but not often and not the same.

BARBARA: Why, what sort of dreams d'you have now?

KATERINA: [After a pause] I'll die soon.

BARBARA: What are you talking about!? What nonsense!

KATERINA: No, I know I'll die soon. Ah, Barbara, something bad is happening to me. It's as if I'd started to live again or . . . I don't know myself.

BARBARA: But what's happening to you? What is it?

KATERINA: [Taking her hand] I'm in good health. It'd be better if I were sick, because as it is there's no excuse. A wish keeps creeping into my head and I just can't get away from it. I try to think of something else but I can't keep my thoughts together; I try praying, but prayers won't keep it away. My tongue keeps mumbling the words but all the time other things are going through my head. It's as if the devil were whispering in my ear and what he whispers isn't good . . . And the things I imagine, Barbara—they're so wicked I'm ashamed. What's come over me? Something dreadful's going to happen; I know it. At night I can't sleep. I keep hearing that whisper and it coos so caressingly to me, just like a

tender dove, you know. I don't dream of trees and mountains like the ones in the icons any more, Barbara, but of someone's putting his arms round me and hugging me passionately and then leading me away somewhere and I follow him on and on . . .

BARBARA: Well? Go on!

KATERINA: I shouldn't be talking to you like this, really. You aren't married.

BARBARA: [Looking around] Tell me, tell me. I'm worse than you.

KATERINA: I can't tell you. I'm ashamed.

BARBARA: You don't have to be. You can tell me.

KATERINA: I get to feeling that there's not enough air in our house and I long to run away, and I say to myself that if I had my choice, I'd be in a boat now sailing down the Volga and singing songs or driving around in a troika with his arm around me . . .

BARBARA: Not Tikhon's arm though.

KATERINA: What do you know about it?

BARBARA: How could I help knowing that?

KATERINA: Ah, Barbara, my head is so full of sinful thoughts! Believe me, I've cried and cried, and I've tried so hard but there's nothing doing, I can't get away from sin! No, there's no escape for me and it's a terrible sin. I love another man, Barbara dear. D'you understand?

BARBARA: I can't judge you. I have my own sins.

KATERINA: So what am I to do? I don't have the strength to fight it. Where can I go? I feel I'll do away with myself in my despair.

BARBARA: What are you talking about? Wait! My brother's leaving tomorrow and we'll manage something. Maybe you'll be able to see him.

KATERINA: No, no, I don't want to! God forbid!

BARBARA: But why are you so frightened?

KATERINA: If I talk to him even once, I'll run away afterward. I'd never be able to go back home, not for anything in the world.

BARBARA: Wait, we'll see when the time comes.

KATERINA: No, no, I don't even want to hear about it.

BARBARA: Why should you let yourself dry out and fade! Even if you die of despair, they won't be sorry for you, you'll see! And why should you make things even harder for yourself?

[Enter a Lady accompanied by two Footmen in tricorns]

LADY: Well, my beauties, what are you doing here? Waiting for your young men? You're enjoying yourselves, are you? You're happy because you're beautiful? Well, you know where your beauty will lead you! There! [She points to the Volga] Straight into the whirlpool! [Barbara smiles] Why are you laughing? You'll burn in everlasting fire and be boiled in molten pitch. That's where your beauty will get you!

[Exits]

KATERINA: Ah, how she scared me. I'm all ashiver. It's like a prophecy, you know.

BARBARA: She can speak for herself, the old hag!

KATERINA: What did she say? What were her words?

BARBARA: It's a lot of stupid nonsense. Why pay attention to her silly chatter? She says that to everybody. She did plenty in her youth herself—ask anyone. But now she's afraid to die and so she scares others with death. Even the streetboys duck away from her for she keeps threatening them with her cane and shouts [*Imitating the old lady*] "You'll all burn in everlasting fire, all of you!"

KATERINA: [*Half-closing her eyes as if dazzled by a bright light*] Ah, stop it, be quiet. I feel dizzy.

BARBARA: There's really nothing to be afraid of. She's just an old fool.

KATERINA: But I'm scared to death. I keep seeing her before my eyes.

BARBARA: [*After a pause, looking around*] What's Tikhon doing all this time? I think we're going to have a thunderstorm.

KATERINA: [*Sounding terrified*] A thunderstorm! Let's run home! Hurry!

BARBARA: You must really be out of your mind! How can you show yourself in the house without Tikhon?

KATERINA: No, no, I want to run home! I don't care about him!

BARBARA: But why this panic? The thunderstorm is still quite a way off.

KATERINA: Well, if it's far away, we'd better wait a little. Although I really think we should go right away. Let's go, what d'you say?

BARBARA: But you know, if something's fated to happen, hiding at home won't help.

KATERINA: Still, it's better, more reassuring, at home; and then there are the icons there and I could pray.

BARBARA: Why, I never knew you were so frightened of thunderstorms. I'm not.

KATERINA: How can you not be frightened? Everyone should fear thunderstorms. And the frightening thing about it is not that the lightning might kill you but that death might strike suddenly, when you're just as you are with all your sins and all the evil temptations. I'm not afraid to die but when I think that I might have to appear before God just as I am this minute, after all the things we've said, then I'm really scared. Ah, I'm even too frightened to name the terrible sin that's on my mind now. [*Thunder*] Ah!

[*Enter* Tikhon]

BARBARA: Here comes my brother. [*To* Tikhon] Run, hurry! [*Thunder*]

KATERINA: Oh, hurry, hurry!

CURTAIN

ACT II.

A room in the Kabanovs' house. Glasha is packing clothes. Feklusha enters.

FEKLUSHA: You always work so hard, dearie. What is it now?

GLASHA: Packing the master's things. He's going on a trip.

FEKLUSHA: Why, is he going away, the dear man?

GLASHA: Yes.

FEKLUSHA: For long?

GLASHA: No.

FEKLUSHA: Well, hope he has a nice, pleasant trip. And what d'you say, will his wife start wailing when he goes?

GLASHA: I wouldn't know.

FEKLUSHA: But does she wail sometimes—your mistress?

GLASHA: Don't know, I never heard her.

FEKLUSHA: Ah, I must confess, dearie, I love to hear a good wail, there's nothing like it. [*She pauses*] And now, let me give you a piece of advice, dearie. You'd better keep your eye on that beggar-woman or she might swipe something.

GLASHA: Who can ever tell with you people? You're a funny lot, you pilgrims—you keep saying all sorts of things about each other. It'd seem you should be quite happy in this house: you get plenty to eat and drink and all that and yet you keep bickering with each other. It's a sin for sure but it looks like you aren't scared of that.

FEKLUSHA: No one can be without sin, dearie, in the world we live in. Let me tell you this, my dear: you ordinary people, you have one devil each to lure you from the path of righteousness, while we, the saintly pilgrims, we have six devils apiece working on us all the time, and some of us even have as many as twelve. And so we have to overcome the lot of them. It isn't easy, believe me, dear girl.

GLASHA: Why is it there're so many devils attached to you people?

FEKLUSHA: It's because the chief devil specially hates us for leading such a righteous life. But I personally, I don't like to quarrel—that's not a sin I can be accused of. But I do have one failing. I know it and I don't mind admitting it. I like good food. Well, and what happens? The good Lord takes pity on my weakness and sends me to houses where I can eat.

GLASHA: And have you had to go far in your travels, Feklusha?

FEKLUSHA: No, dearie, I'm not strong enough to go far but I sure have heard a lot. I heard that there are countries in this world that aren't even ruled by Christian Tsars but by sultans instead. In one country, there's a Turkish sultan called Makhnut and in another a Persian sultan called Makhnut, and they sit on their thrones and judge people and I must tell you, my dear girl, they aren't fair in their decisions, not fair at all. You see, they just can't pass the right judgment on anything because such is their fate. Our law is the righteous law and theirs is the unrighteous and whatever our law orders, theirs orders the contrary. And all the judges in those countries are unrighteous too, so that people even write to them in their petitions: "Please judge us unfairly, your honor!" And then there are lands too where all the people have dogs' heads.

GLASHA: Why dogs' heads?

FEKLUSHA: To punish them because they're infidels. Well, I must be going now, my dear. I think I'll go and knock on some merchants' doors and see whether any of them wishes to give something to a poor pilgrim. See you later, dearie.

GLASHA: Good-by. [*Exit* Feklusha] Who would've thought there were such strange lands on earth! Ah, the miracles that exist in the world! And to think we just sit here and never hear about anything. Thank God there are some decent people who'll tell you what's going on at least, otherwise we'd stay ignorant and stupid to our dying day.

[*Enter* Katerina *and* Barbara]

BARBARA: [*To* Glasha] Go and put Mister Tikhon's things in the coach, the horses are ready. [Glasha *leaves; to* Katerina] They married you off too young. They should have given you a chance to have some fun first. It's no wonder your heart didn't have time to settle down a bit.

KATERINA: And it never will settle down.

BARBARA: Why do you say that?

KATERINA: It's the way I was born, so full of fire. Shall I tell you what I did when I was no more than six? They scolded me unfairly at home, so I ran down to the Volga, got into a boat, untied it, and the next morning they found me ten miles or so downstream.

BARBARA: And tell me, did the boys stare at you later?

KATERINA: They sure did.

BARBARA: So why . . . didn't you like any of them?

KATERINA: No, I didn't. I just laughed.

BARBARA: You've never loved Tikhon, have you, Katerina?

KATERINA: Loved him? Well, yes, I'm so sorry for him.

BARBARA: No, of course you don't love him. If you're sorry for him you certainly can't love him. And I may as well say straight out: there's no reason why you should love him. You don't have to hide it from me. I noticed long ago that you were in love with someone else.

KATERINA: [*Sounding frightened*] What did you notice?

BARBARA: You're funny really! I wasn't born yesterday, you know. As soon as you see him, your whole face changes. [Katerina *stares at her with wide-open eyes*] Ah, there are so many ways to tell . . .

KATERINA: [*Looking at the floor*] Well, who?

BARBARA: You know very well yourself. No point in my telling you his name.

KATERINA: No, tell me who! Name him!

BARBARA: Boris.

KATERINA: Yes, Barbara, it's him! But please don't . . .

BARBARA: What do you take me for? You'd better watch your own tongue.

KATERINA: I'm so bad at deceit; I can never keep anything secret.

BARBARA: But it's impossible to do without it. Just remember where you live! Our entire family is held together by deception. I wasn't born a liar either, you know, but I've learned to lie when I have to. When I went out for a walk yesterday, I met him and we had a talk.

KATERINA: [*After a brief silence, looking down*] Well, what did he say?

BARBARA: He asked me to give you his best . . . He said it's a shame there's nowhere he could meet you.

KATERINA: [*Lowering her head even further*] Yes, where? And what would be the point?

BARBARA: He looked so sad . . .

KATERINA: Don't tell me about him, please! I don't want to know anything about him! I'll always love my husband! Tikhon, darling, I won't leave you for anyone! I didn't even want to give it a thought so why do you come trying to tempt me?

BARBARA: If you don't want to give it a thought— don't; no one's forcing you.

KATERINA: Ah, you have no pity for me at all. You say "Don't think" and then you keep reminding me of him yourself. Do you think I want to think of him? I don't but what can I do, since I can't get him out of my head. Whatever I try to think about, he's always there, right before my eyes. I want to force myself to forget but I can't, however much I try. Do you know, last night the devil came to pester me again. I almost ran away from home.

BARBARA: Ah, you're so complicated, God bless you. But if you want to listen to my advice, you'll do just as you please—but just don't let anyone find out about it.

KATERINA: I don't want it that way. That's no good. I guess I'd rather try and bear things as they are as long as I can.

BARBARA: And what if you can't bear it?

KATERINA: If I can't bear it?

BARBARA: Yes, what will you do then?

KATERINA: Then I'll do just as I please.

BARBARA: Just try! They'll eat you alive here.

KATERINA: What do I care? I'll leave this place and that'll be that.

BARBARA: How can you leave? You're Tikhon's wife, remember.

KATERINA: Ah, Barbara, I see you don't know me yet. Of course, I hope it won't go so far—God forbid! But if I get to hate the whole place too much, then there'll be nothing that can hold me back, no force! I'll jump out of the window, throw myself into the Volga . . . If I don't want to live here, I won't —they can kill me if they want, that won't change a thing!

[*Silence*]

BARBARA: You know what, Katerina? While Tikhon's away, let's you and I sleep in the summerhouse in the garden.

KATERINA: Why do you want to do that, Barbara?

BARBARA: What's the difference?

KATERINA: I'm scared to sleep in an unfamiliar place.

BARBARA: What is there to be scared of? I'll have Glasha sleep there with us, too.

KATERINA: It's quite scary even with her . . . Still, if you . . .

BARBARA: I wouldn't have asked you but mother won't let me sleep there alone. And I have to do it.

KATERINA: [Looking into her eyes] And why do you have to?

BARBARA: [Laughing] We'll tell each other's fortunes there, see?

KATERINA: You're kidding!

BARBARA: Sure I am. I didn't expect you to believe that. [A pause]

KATERINA: What can Tikhon be doing all this time? Where is he?

BARBARA: What do you need him for?

KATERINA: Just wondering. But it's almost time for him to leave.

BARBARA: He's sitting with mother in her room and she's nagging him; it eats him the way rust eats iron.

KATERINA: Why? What did he do?

BARBARA: Nothing special, she's just trying to teach him wisdom. He'll be out of her sight for two whole weeks—just think of that! She'll be eating her heart out at the thought that he'll be free to come and go without asking her permission all that time. So now she's giving him instructions, each sterner than the last and when she's through, she'll make him kneel before an icon and swear he'll do exactly as she's told him.

KATERINA: She has him nicely tied even when he's free and on his own.

BARBARA: Ah, you think he's tied? No sooner is he out of her sight than he begins drinking. He's there now, letting her have her say and thinking how he can manage to get away from her quickly and be on his way.

[Enter Mrs. Kabanov and Tikhon]

MRS. KABANOV: So I hope you'll remember everything I've told you. You'd better!

TIKHON: I'll remember, Mother.

MRS. KABANOV: All right, we're all set now. The horses are waiting. Say good-by and godspeed.

TIKHON: Yes, Mother, I'd better be going.

MRS. KABANOV: Well!

TIKHON: Did you wish something else, Mother?

MRS. KABANOV: Well, don't just stand there! Do you still not know the proper ways? Tell your wife what she's to do while you're away [Katerina lowers her eyes]

TIKHON: I'm sure she knows herself.

MRS. KABANOV: Don't give me any back talk! Go on, tell her, as I said. I want to hear you give her

your orders. And when you come back, you must make her account to you for how she's obeyed.

TIKHON: Obey Mother, Katerina.

MRS. KABANOV: Tell her not to be rude to me.

TIKHON: Don't be rude.

MRS. KABANOV: Tell her to honor me as she would her own mother.

TIKHON: Honor mother as you would your own mother, Katerina.

MRS. KABANOV: Tell her not to sit around not doing any work, like some duchess.

TIKHON: Do some work while I'm away.

MRS. KABANOV: She mustn't stare out of the window all the time.

TIKHON: But, Mother, when does she . . .

MRS. KABANOV: Go on, tell her.

TIKHON: Don't look out of the windows, Katerina.

MRS. KABANOV: Tell her she mustn't make eyes at young men while you're away.

TIKHON: But really, Mother!

MRS. KABANOV: [Severely] Come, stop dilly-dallying! Do as your mother says. [Smiles] I know what I'm talking about.

TIKHON: [With embarrassment] Don't make eyes at young men [Katerina gives him a haughty look]

MRS. KABANOV: All right, now you may have a few private words if you feel like it. Come, let's go, Barbara!

[Exit Mrs. Kabanov and Barbara]

TIKHON: Katerina! [Silence] You're not angry with me, are you?

KATERINA: [After a pause, shaking her head] No.

TIKHON: Why do you look so strange? All right, I'm sorry.

KATERINA: [Looking at him absently and shaking her head] Ah, forget it! [Covers her face with her hands] That hurt, what she said!

TIKHON: If you take everything to heart like that you'll be consumptive in no time. Why pay any attention to her? You know she just has to say things like that all the time. So let her and you let it go in one ear and out the other. But I must be on my way, good-by now!

KATERINA: [Flinging her arms round his neck] Don't go, Tikhon, please! Believe me, darling, it's best if you don't go. Stay!

TIKHON: I can't, dear! How could I since it's mother who's sending me?

KATERINA: Then take me along!

TIKHON: [Getting loose from her embrace] I can't.

KATERINA: Why can't you, Tikhon?

TIKHON: Some good time I'd have dragging you along! Don't I get enough nagging from the lot of you when I'm here? I don't know how to get away from it all quick enough and here you're trying to latch on to me.

KATERINA: So you don't love me any more?

TIKHON: Oh no, I love you. It's just that, to escape my life here, I'd run away from the most beautiful wife on earth! Think for yourself: whatever else I may be, I'm still a man. And when a man is forced to live the kind of life I do, he'll run away from a wife and anything else whenever he gets a chance. Now I know that for two weeks no lightning will hit me, no thunder will roll over my head, there will be no fetters round my ankles! How can I be expected to think of my wife?

KATERINA: How can you expect me to love you when you talk like that?

TIKHON: What's wrong with the way I talk? What do you expect me to say? What are you afraid of anyway? I'm not leaving you alone, there'll be mother here to look after you.

KATERINA: Don't mention her! It breaks my heart! Ah, I'm so miserable, so miserable . . . [*Starts to cry*] I don't know where to go. I have no one to stand up for me. Ah, I'm lost!

TIKHON: Oh, stop it, Katerina!

KATERINA: [*Stepping up close to* Tikhon *and putting her arms around his neck*] Ah, Tikhon, if only you'd stay here with me or take me along with you, I'd love you so, I'd be so tender, darling . . . [*She snuggles against him*]

TIKHON: I can't understand you, Katerina: one minute I can't get a word out of you and the next you're falling all over me. I can't make you out.

KATERINA: So you're leaving me, Tikhon. I tell you there'll be trouble while you're away. Yes, there'll be trouble, trouble!

TIKHON: Well, whatever it is, I can't help it.

KATERINA: Then you know what, make me swear some terrible oath . . .

TIKHON: What oath?

KATERINA: Make me swear to you that while you're away I won't talk to any stranger whatever happens; that I won't see any man or think of any man except you.

TIKHON: But why?

KATERINA: Just to ease my mind. Do it as a favor to me, my darling.

TIKHON: How can you guarantee you won't think . . . Who knows what'll come into his head?

KATERINA: [*Kneeling. In a solemn tone*] May I never see my father and mother again, may I die without the sacrament if ever I . . .

TIKHON: [*Pulling her to her feet*] Stop it, stop it! It's a sin to say things like that. I don't even want to hear it!

[Mrs. Kabanov's *voice is heard offstage*]

MRS. KABANOV: It's time for you to go, Tikhon!

[*Enter* Mrs. Kabanov, Barbara, *and* Glasha]

MRS. KABANOV: Well, off you go, Tikhon, godspeed! [*Sits down*] But first, let's sit down for a second. [*All sit down; silence*] All right, good-by now! [*Gets up and so do all the others*]

TIKHON: [*Going up to her*] Good-by, Mother.

MRS. KABANOV: [*Pointing downward*] Down on your knees! [Tikhon *kneels, then gets up and kisses her*] Now say good-by to your wife!

TIKHON: Good-by Katerina. [Katerina *flings her arms round his neck*]

MRS. KABANOV: Come on, you shameless thing—hanging on his neck like that! You're not saying good-by to some lover of yours—he's your husband, your master! Or don't you know how to behave decently? Come, let go of him and bow low. [Katerina *bows low*]

TIKHON: Good-by, sister. [*Kisses* Barbara] 'Bye Glasha. Good-by Mother. [*Bows*]

MRS. KABANOV: Good-by, good-by, off you go now. Long partings only mean extra tears to shed.

[*Exit* Tikhon, *then* Katerina, Barbara *and* Glasha]

MRS. KABANOV: [*Alone*] Ah, the young! They make me laugh! If they weren't my own family, I wouldn't have been able to restrain myself, I'd have laughed till my sides split. They have no idea how things should be done. Don't even know how to say good-by. Lucky for them there's still a parent around to hold the household together while she's alive. But then, the fools want to live their own lives and whenever they try, they become the laughing-stock of decent people. Sure, some may take pity on them, but most'll just laugh. And how can they help laughing. If, for instance, they invite guests to their home, they don't know where to seat them properly and they're even liable to forget to invite some relative or other. Yes, it's funny but that's how the good old ways get lost. There are young people like that whose houses I won't put a foot in, or if I do, it makes me so sick I'm in a hurry to get out again. What will happen when we, the older generation, are gone, I hate to think. I can't imagine how the world will go on. Ah, the only good thing about it is that I won't be here to see it.

[*Enter* Katerina *and* Barbara]

MRS. KABANOV: Here, you, Katerina, you kept boasting about loving your husband so much but now I see how you love him. A good wife, when she's seen her husband off, goes on wailing for, I'd say, an hour and a half, rolling around on the front steps. But look at you. It doesn't seem to touch you at all!

KATERINA: What's the point of doing that? I wouldn't even know how to do it if I tried. It'd just make people laugh.

MRS. KABANOV: It's not that hard if you put your mind to it. If you loved him truly, you'd learn soon enough. And even if you couldn't do it properly, you could at least have pretended, if only for appearances' sake. But it looks as if all your love for Tikhon is just talk. Well, I'm going to say my prayers now, so you two'd better keep quiet and not disturb me.

BARBARA: I think I'll go into town, Mother.

MRS. KABANOV: [*In a friendly tone*] That's fine with me. Go on, have a good time while you can. You'll sit at home plenty once you're married!

[*Exit* Mrs. Kabanov *and* Barbara]

KATERINA: [*Alone; dreamily*] Ah, it's going to be quiet as the grave. And so boring, too! If only there were some children in this house! But, I have no children. If I had, I'd spend my time with them, playing and making them laugh. I love talking to children because they are like angels. [*Pause*] It would've been better if I'd died young. I'd be looking down from the sky now and enjoying myself. Or else I could fly wherever I wished unseen. I'd fly out into the fields and flutter from cornflower to cornflower just like a butterfly. [*Sinks into reverie*] Ah, here's what I'll do: since I promised him I'd work, I'll go to town and buy some material. Then I'll sew some clothes and give them to the poor and they'll pray for me. So Barbara and I, we'll sit down to our sewing and we won't even notice how the time passes and the next thing we know, Tikhon'll be back with us.

[*Enter* Barbara]

BARBARA: [*Putting kerchief on her head before the mirror*] I'm off to town now to have a good time. And in the meantime, Glasha will make up our beds in the summerhouse in the garden. Mother says it's all right. You know the gate in the garden, behind the raspberry bushes? Mother usually locks it and hides the key. Well, I found it and put another key in its place so she won't miss it. Here, perhaps you'll need it. [*Hands her the key*] If I meet him, I'll tell him to come to that gate.

KATERINA: [*Pushing away key in dismay*] Why? Why? I don't want it! I don't need it!

BARBARA: You may not need it, but I do. Take it anyway, keys don't bite!

KATERINA: What are you trying to do, you wicked thing? You mustn't! Have you even given it a thought? What's come over you!

BARBARA: Well, I don't like to argue and anyway I haven't much time. I'm in a hurry to go out and enjoy myself. [*Exit*]

KATERINA: [*Holding key in hand*] What's she doing? The things she thinks up! Ah, she's mad, mad! It would be the end of me! I must throw the key away, into the river, so that no one'll ever find it! It's burning my hand like a hot coal. [*Thinks a while*] Yes, that's the way a woman gets lost! Who can be happy being shut up like me? All kinds of things keep cropping up in a woman's head, when she's locked up like this. And so, when she gets the chance, she throws herself at it. But how can one do anything without thinking it over, weighing what'll come of it? It doesn't take long to get into trouble and after that you'll regret it all your life and your bondage will be even more bitter than before. [*Pause*] Ah, but it's a bitter bondage. It's bad enough as it is! People cry over being locked in, especially us women. Take me, I'm bored, I'm tormented by all sorts of things and I don't see any way out! It'll only get worse and worse with time. And now, that sinful thing . . . [*Sinks into thought*] Ah, if it wasn't for my mother-in-law! She's made me hate this house. By now I loathe the very walls. [*Looks dreamily at the key*] Shall I throw it away? Of course I must! Why am I holding it in my hand in the first place? It was given to tempt me, to

bring about my perdition. [*Listens*] Ah, someone's coming. Oh, that scared me! [*Hides key in her pocket*] No, no one's coming. Why did I have to get so frightened? Why did I hide the key? . . . Well, all right, let it stay in my pocket. I suppose my fate is written that way in the book. And anyway, what's wrong if I only glance at him from a distance? Even if I talked to him the way other people talk to each other, what'd be so bad about that? But what about the promise I made to Tikhon? But then, he didn't even want me to make that oath! And possibly I'll never get another opportunity like this in my life. Then I'll never forgive myself for having let it slip by. Well, what's the point of lying to myself? Even if I had to die, I would still see him if I could. For whose benefit am I putting all this on? Throw away the key? Not on your life! It's mine now. Whatever happens, I will see Boris! Ah, I wish it were night!

CURTAIN

ACT III. SCENE I.

A street. The gates of the Kabanovs' *house with a bench by them.* Mrs. Kabanov *and* Feklusha *sit on the bench.*

FEKLUSHA: The day of judgment is approaching, Mrs. Kabanov, everything points to it. At least in our town there's peace and quiet, but other places, it's like Sodom itself: a terrible din and mad rushing around, people darting all over the place, one running here, another there.

MRS. KABANOV: There's nothing for us to hurry over here, that's why we live quietly.

FEKLUSHA: No, Ma'am, that's not the reason. It's so quiet and peaceful here because you have so many people like you whose virtues adorn them like flowers. That's why everything in this town is so sober and respectable. Because what d'you think it means, all this shouting and rushing around, even, say, in Moscow? People there run to and fro now and no one knows what for. That's vanity for you! People are full of vanity, Mrs. Kabanov, and that's what makes them run. People imagine they're hurrying about their business. They don't recognize friends in their rush and keep imagining someone's beckoning to them, but when they get to the place they're headed for, there's nothing there and they see it was all their imagination. And so they go sadly on their way. Another man may think he's trying to catch up with someone he knows. Anyone else looking on can see very well that there's no one ahead of him, but the man keeps tearing along. That's because it's very much like a fog—vanity. Here in this town, very few people come out on a fine evening like this to sit by their gates, but in Moscow at this hour the noise is like thunder and people stroll around and have a good time. They don't even hesitate to harness fiery dragons to carriages, just to move around faster. That's how they are over there.

MRS. KABANOV: I've heard about it, my dear.

FEKLUSHA: But me, Ma'am, I've seen it with my own eyes. Of course, other people, looking through that fog of vanity, say it's engines pulling them along, but I've seen for myself that great, evil hairy paw with those spread-out claws pushing them. It looked like that. [*She fans out her fingers*] And the horrible growl the devil lets out, that can be heard by people who lead a righteous life!

MRS. KABANOV: One can call anything by any name and one machine is just as good as another. People are stupid and they're ready to believe everything. As to me, I wouldn't travel in one of those unholy things for all the gold in the world!

FEKLUSHA: Ah, may God preserve you from such a calamity, Ma'am! And now let me tell you about a vision I had in Moscow once. One day, very early in the morning, as the sun was just beginning to rise, I'm walking down a street. Suddenly I look up and lo and behold, there's someone standing on top of a very tall house and his face is all black. Well, you understand, of course, who that was. Then he makes gestures with his hands as if he's scattering something, although actually there's nothing. And so I realized he was scattering some special seeds that people would pick up without knowing it, blinded as they are by the fog of their vanity. And that's why they all rush around like that and their women are so thin. Yes, it's as if they were all running and looking for something and their faces are so sad it makes you sorry for them.

MRS. KABANOV: Everything's possible, my dear. Nothing would surprise me nowadays.

FEKLUSHA: Yes, these are hard times, Ma'am, real hard. And time itself is beginning to grow shorter.

MRS. KABANOV: What do you mean "grow shorter"?

FEKLUSHA: Yes, shorter, although we, of course, don't notice it in our hustle and bustle and vanity. But wise people now, they notice that time's getting shorter. The winter or the summer used to go on and on and we'd wonder when they'd ever come to an end but now you don't even notice how they fly by. Sure, the days and the hours are the same as before but the time in them is getting shorter, to punish us for our sins. That's what clever people say.

MRS. KABANOV: And it'll get worse yet.

FEKLUSHA: I just hope I won't live long enough to see it, Ma'am.

MRS. KABANOV: Who knows, we may yet have to see it.

[*Enter* Dikoy]

MRS. KABANOV: What are you doing out so late, dear Mr. Dikoy?

DIKOY: Any objections?

MRS. KABANOV: No, why should I object?

DIKOY: So what are you talking about? Do I have to ask permission to walk around now? What sort of damned nonsense is that?

MRS. KABANOV: You'd better take it easy with me, my good man! Go and find someone else to abuse for nothing like that, because, me, I won't let you get off lightly. Now, be on your way, back where you came from. Come, let's go home, Feklusha.

[*Rises*]

DIKOY: Wait, Mrs. Kabanov, wait a minute. You've plenty of time to get home since your home is right here, right behind your back.

MRS. KABANOV: If you're here on business don't holler the way you did just now, just state sensibly what it is.

DIKOY: I have no business, I'm just drunk, see what I mean?

MRS. KABANOV: And what do you want me to do then—congratulate you?

DIKOY: No, don't congratulate me but don't abuse me, either. I'm drunk and that's all there is to it. Until I've slept it off, there'll be no putting it right.

MRS. KABANOV: So go and sleep it off.

DIKOY: Where shall I go?

MRS. KABANOV: Home, of course, where else?

DIKOY: And what if I don't want to go home?

MRS. KABANOV: And why don't you want to go home, may I ask?

DIKOY: Because I have a war going on there.

MRS. KABANOV: Who can be at war with you? You're the only warrior there.

DIKOY: All right, I'm a warrior. So what?

MRS. KABANOV: Nothing. But I must say you don't gain much honor in your wars, because you always wage them against women only.

DIKOY: That's because they won't submit to my will. Why, you don't think I should submit to theirs, do you?

MRS. KABANOV: Well, let me tell you, I've been watching you for a long time, marveling: there are so many people in your house and none of them can do a thing right according to you.

DIKOY: And what about you?

MRS. KABANOV: Now tell me, what do you want of me?

DIKOY: I'll tell you what: talk to me, take the load off my heart. You're the only one who can do that.

MRS. KABANOV: Go in, Feklusha, and order them to prepare a snack and something to drink. [Feklusha *goes into the house*]

MRS. KABANOV: Come in then, Mr. Dikoy.

DIKOY: No, I won't go inside. It's worse in there.

MRS. KABANOV: Tell me then, what have they done to make you so angry?

DIKOY: Ah, it's been going on since morning.

MRS. KABANOV: They must've asked you for money.

DIKOY: As if they'd agreed to drive me mad: one after the other, they kept pestering me all day long!

MRS. KABANOV: They must've wanted something very badly to pester you like that.

DIKOY: I can understand that myself, but what do you expect me to do about it with a heart like mine? Sure, I know I should pay them, but I can't make myself do it of my own free will. You're my friend, for instance, but if you came to me and claimed something I owed you, I wouldn't be able to contain myself and I'd start abusing you. I'd pay you, but I'd abuse you first! Because as soon as one mentions money in my presence, all my innards begin burning and then I start swearing at people about nothing.

MRS. KABANOV: It's because you have no one wiser than you in your house and so you go around bullying everyone.

DIKOY: No, you wait, my dear woman, you listen to me! This is the sort of thing that happened to me during Lent: As I was fasting, the devil sent me a peasant to claim the money I owed him—he had carted my logs for me. So, sure I sinned. I abused him something awful. In fact, I almost took a punch at him. That's the kind of temper I have. After that I asked for forgiveness, bowed low to him, like this, see. Yes, I tell you, I bowed to that stupid peasant! I stood in the mud in the courtyard and bowed to him! That's where my terrible temper can lead me!

MRS. KABANOV: But why are you purposely working yourself into a lather, friend. That's bad, you know!

DIKOY: Why do you say "purposely"?

MRS. KABANOV: I've seen you do it before and I know what I'm talking about. Whenever you see someone is about to ask you for something, you immediately find something to pick on and work yourself into a state because you're sure that then they won't ask you for anything. That's how you work it, my friend.

[Enter Glasha]

GLASHA: The refreshments are served, Ma'am.

MRS. KABANOV: Well, what d'you say, Mr. Dikoy, come in and have something, whatever God has sent us.

DIKOY: Don't mind if I do.

MRS. KABANOV: Please come in then. [She lets Dikoy into the house and follows him Glasha stands with her arms akimbo by the gate.]

GLASHA: That looks like Mr. Boris coming. Has he come to fetch his uncle and take him home? Or is he just out for a stroll? I think he's just out for a walk.

[Enter Boris]

BORIS: Is my uncle here, by any chance?

GLASHA: He is, sir. You wish to see him?

BORIS: They sent me from home to find out where he was and since he's in your house, let him stay there. Who d'you think wants him? Everyone at home is very happy that he's out.

GLASHA: Ah, I wish my mistress was married to him—it wouldn't take her long to tame him! But what am I doing, standing here chatting with you, Mr. Boris? Good-by now.

[Exits]

BORIS: Oh Lord, if only I could steal one glimpse of her! I can't just walk into the house without being invited. What a life! We live in the same town but I hardly ever see her more than once a week, in church, unless I chance to come across her in the street. In this town, when a girl gets married she really gets buried. [Pause] It would be better if I never saw her at all. I only see her now and then and there are always people around and hundreds of eyes staring at you. It just breaks my heart. And then, I can't control myself: whenever I go for a walk, somehow I always find myself near this house. Why do I have to come here, since I know I can't see her anyway? It'll only make people talk and get her into trouble. Ah, what a lousy little town! [Starts walking. Kuligin approaches from the opposite side]

KULIGIN: Out for a walk, sir?

BORIS: Yes, the weather was so nice, I thought I'd go for a stroll.

KULIGIN: It's very nice out at this hour, sir, it's so quiet and there's not a cloud in the sky. The air is so fresh and the breeze from across the Volga carries the scent of the wild flowers over here.

A star-filled abyss black the sky does rend,
The stars are myriad—chasm without an end.

Let's go over the square, sir, there's no one there at this hour.

BORIS: All right, let's go.

KULIGIN: That's the sort of town we have, sir: they've built a public square but no one goes there except on holidays and even then, they only pretend that they've come out for a walk or for the fresh air—really they go there to show off their clothes. The only person we're liable to meet there is some drunken clerk on his way home from a tavern. The poor haven't much time to go out, sir. They work day and night and get only about three hours sleep. You might think the rich at least would go out all the time to breathe the fresh air. But no! The gates of their houses are locked early and vicious dogs are let loose in their courtyards. Now you may think that they're busy doing something at home or saying their prayers, perhaps? Nothing of the sort, sir: all they do is bully their families and if they let their dogs loose, it's not to keep thieves out but so that people won't see or hear the tears and cries coming from their houses. I don't have to tell you, sir. You know yourself what goes on behind those locked doors—all that horrible debauchery, those drunken orgies! And it's all kept covered up and secret! But we know about those secrets that make only one person happy while the others must wail with pain. And is it really a secret? Who doesn't know it? Robbing orphans, nephews, thrashing members of their households so they won't dare to let out a squeak about what's going on in the house—that's all there is to their secrets. Ah, why bother with them! I think only girls and their young men go out in this town, to try to steal an hour or so before they go to bed. Look, here comes a couple.

[Vania and Barbara come into sight; they stop and kiss]

BORIS: They're kissing.

KULIGIN: Nothing wrong with that, sir.

[*Exit* Vania. Barbara *walks up to the gate and beckons to Boris. He goes up to her*]

KULIGIN: I think I'll go to the square, sir. I don't want to be in your way. I'll wait for you there.

BORIS: All right, I'll join you there.

[*Exit* Kuligin]

BARBARA: [*Hiding her face in her kerchief*] Do you know the ravine behind the garden?

BORIS: I do.

BARBARA: Be there later tonight.

BORIS: What for?

BARBARA: You're really very stupid. Come and you'll find out. Go now, your friend is waiting for you. [*Exit* Boris] He didn't recognize me! Well, let him guess. I'm sure Katerina won't hold out—she'll rush to meet him. [*Disappears through the gate*]

SCENE II.

Night. A bushy ravine. At the top of the bank, the fence of the Kabanov's garden with a gate in it. A path leads down from the gate.

VANIA: [*Entering with guitar*] No one around. What can be keeping her? Well, never mind. I can sit here and wait. [*Sits down on a stone*] I'll sing something just to kill time. [*Sings*]

*Oh, there was a Don Cossack led his horse out to
    drink,
And now here he stands at the gate, straight and still.
As he stands at the gate, a thought he does think.
He thinks as he stands there, his wife he must kill.
But his wife, yes his wife, does her husband implore,
And hastily bows to him low to the floor:
"Oh, husband, my heart's friend, my loved one, my
    pet,
Do not beat me now, do not kill me yet,
But wait till the darkness of midnight does fall
And sleep covers my children so dear with its pall,
My dear little children, my closest of all!"*

[*Enter* Boris]

VANIA: [*Stopping singing*] Well, well! Everybody thought you were such a quiet one, but I see you're going in for it too, now!

BORIS: Is that you, Vania?

VANIA: Sure it's me, Mr. Boris.

BORIS: What are you doing here?

VANIA: What am I doing? Well, I suppose I have business here, for if I didn't, I wouldn't be here. And what are you doing, may I ask?

BORIS: [*Looking around*] You know, Vania, I have to wait here and, if it's all the same to you, couldn't you go somewhere else?

VANIA: Oh no, sir! You're here for the first time, but I've been coming for a long time. Why, that path was trodden by me. I like you, Mr. Boris, and I'd be glad to be of any service to you, but you'd better not cross my path here or something bad may come of it. Now that's a fair warning, sir.

BORIS: What's come over you, Vania?

VANIA: What's this, Vania? What's that, Vania? Just leave me alone and be on your way! Get yourself a girl and go wherever you wish with her and no one will interfere with you. But don't touch girls who're already taken. It's not done around here and you may find yourself with a few broken ribs. And if someone tries to fool around with my girl, I'll slash his throat for him.

BORIS: What're you talking about! I never thought of trying to take your girl away from you. Anyway, I wouldn't even be here if someone hadn't asked me to come.

VANIA: And who asked you?

BORIS: I couldn't make out who, it was dark . . . Some girl stopped me in the street and asked me to come to this very spot: the ravine, she said, behind the Kabanovs' garden gate.

VANIA: Who could it've been?

BORIS: Listen, can I talk to you openly, without your going around repeating what I say?

VANIA: You don't have to worry about that. No one'll hear a word of it from me.

BORIS: I know nothing about the ways and customs you have here but here's what's happened to me . . .

VANIA: You've fallen in love?

BORIS: Yes.

VANIA: Well, there's nothing wrong with that. We're very broad-minded about that sort of thing. Our girls go around with fellows and their parents don't want to know anything about it. Only the married women sit locked in their houses.

BORIS: That's just the trouble, Vania.

VANIA: You mean you've fallen in love with a married woman?

BORIS: Yes, Vania, I have.

VANIA: You'd better forget about it, Mr. Boris.

BORIS: That's easy to say, forget it! Perhaps you can forget one and find another to take her place but, me, once I've fallen in love . . .

VANIA: But it'll be the end of her if you ever . . .

BORIS: Oh, God forbid, no! How could I want to harm her! I'd just like to see her. I don't need more more than that.

VANIA: Who can be sure of himself? And remember, the people here will get after her and they won't stop till they've nailed her coffin shut.

BORIS: Don't say that, Vania, you frighten me.

VANIA: And what about her, does she love you, too?

BORIS: I don't know.

VANIA: Have you met her? Have you spoken to her at least?

BORIS: I was in her house once with my uncle. Otherwise, I only see her in church and in the street. Ah, Vania, you should see her when she's praying! She has such a radiant smile on her face, a light seems to shine from it.

VANIA: Must be Tikhon Kabanov's wife then?

BORIS: Yes, Vania.

VANIA: Ah, congratulations!

BORIS: Why do you say that?

VANIA: Well, if you were told to come here, that must mean things are turning out fine for you.

BORIS: You mean it was she who told me . . . ?

VANIA: Who else could it've been?

BORIS: You must be joking! That's impossible! [Seizes his head]

VANIA: What's the matter with you?

BORIS: I'm so happy, it's driving me crazy.

VANIA: Some reason to go crazy! You'd better watch your step. Don't get into trouble and, above all, don't get her into a mess! I know her husband's a fool, but her mother-in-law's a real dragon, so she'd better watch out!

[Barbara comes through the gate]

BARBARA: [Singing by the gate]

My young man walking over the lea.
Beyond the swift river I can see

VANIA: [Chiming in] He's bringing a present here for me . . . [He whistles]

BARBARA: [Coming down the path, her face covered with a kerchief, and approaching Boris] You, fellow, wait a bit. It may be worth your while. [To Vania] Let's go down to the Volga, you and I.

VANIA: Why are you so late? You know I don't like waiting. [Barbara puts one arm around him and they exit]

BORIS: It's like a dream! The night, that song he sang, this date! They walk around locked in each other's arms! This is all so new, so unknown, so marvelous! And now, I'm waiting for something myself. But I don't know what exactly. All I know is that my every vein is throbbing! I can't imagine what I'll say to her; just thinking of it takes my breath away, makes my knees shake! Ah, my foolish heart! When it starts seething, there's nothing I can do to stop it. Ah, someone's coming!

[Katerina walks slowly down the path draped in a large white shawl; she looks down at her feet; a silence]

BORIS: Is that you, Katerina? [Silence] I don't even know how to thank you. [Silence] If only you knew how much I'm in love with you, Katerina! [Tries to take her hand]

KATERINA: [In a frightened voice, without raising her eyes] Don't . . . don't touch me.

BORIS: Please don't be angry with me.

KATERINA: Go away, leave me alone, you evil man. Don't you know that all the prayers in the world will never wash away this terrible sin, never! It will always weigh on my heart like a heavy stone.

BORIS: Please don't chase me away!

KATERINA: Why did you come here? Do you want to cause my perdition? You know I'm married and that I'll live with him until they nail my coffin shut.

BORIS: But you asked me to come yourself . . .

KATERINA: But don't you understand, you, my enemy—I must live with him till they lay me in my coffin!

BORIS: It would've been better if I'd never set eyes on you.

KATERINA: [Agitated] But do you realize what I am doing to myself? Don't you know where my place is?

BORIS: Please, calm yourself. Sit down. [Takes her hand]

KATERINA: Why do you want to ruin me?

BORIS: How could I want to ruin you when I love you more than anything in the world—more than myself!

KATERINA: But you are ruining me, as things are!

BORIS: Oh no, I'm not really a villain, I assure you . . .

KATERINA: You've ruined me, ruined me, ruined me!

BORIS: God save me from ruining you, Katerina. I'd rather die!

KATERINA: But if you haven't ruined me, why have I run away from my husband's house in the middle of the night and joined you here?

BORIS: But you did it of your own free will, Katerina.

KATERINA: I have no will—if I had, I wouldn't be here with you. [She raises her eyes and looks at Boris. A brief silence.] I'm ruled by your will now, can't you see that? [Throws herself on his neck]

BORIS: [Embracing her] You're my life!

KATERINA: You know what? I wish I could die now.

BORIS: Why die when it's so good to live?

KATERINA: No, living is not for me, I know that.

BORIS: Oh, don't say that! I can't stand it!

KATERINA: Oh, it's all right for you to talk, you're free, but I . . .

BORIS: But no one will find out about our love. Don't you trust me to keep it secret?

KATERINA: Ah, why should you? I've asked for it, so go ahead and ruin me! Let them all know, let them all see what I'm up to! [Embraces him] Don't you understand that if I weren't too afraid of the sin in coming to you, I can't fear the judgment of men? They even say that it's better if you suffer for your sins on earth. It makes it easier later.

BORIS: Why think of all that now? Let's just be happy.

KATERINA: You're right, I'll have plenty of time to think of it and cry.

BORIS: You scared me at first—I thought you were going to chase me away.

KATERINA: [Smiling] Chase you away? How could I? The way I feel. I believe that if you hadn't come, I'd have gone to you myself.

BORIS: I never suspected you loved me.

KATERINA: I've loved you for a long time. It's as if you'd come here just on purpose to lead me into sin. Once I'd seen you, I was never the same again. I think if you'd beckoned to me the very first time, I'd have followed you. If you'd gone to the edge of the world, I'd have gone with you without ever looking back.

BORIS: How long is your husband going to be away?

KATERINA: Two weeks.

BORIS: Oh, we'll have a great time. It's a long time, two weeks.

KATERINA: Yes, we'll have a great time and then . . . [*Sinks into thought*] Then they'll lock me in and it will be death. But if I have half a chance, I'll always find a way to you!

[*Enter* Vania *and* Barbara]

BARBARA: Well, how are you getting along, you two?

BORIS: We're getting along fine.

BARBARA: Why don't you go for a walk now and we'll wait here. Vania will call out if anything happens.

[*Exit* Boris *and* Katerina; Vania *and* Barbara *sit down on a stone*]

VANIA: You sure started a big thing with that garden gate. It's very handy.

BARBARA: You see how clever I am.

VANIA: I know you're clever, but what about your mother? Won't she find out?

BARBARA: It'll never even occur to her.

VANIA: But just imagine, what if she . . .

BARBARA: She sleeps very soundly at the beginning of the night. It's only toward morning that she keeps waking up.

VANIA: But who can ever be sure? What if some evil force suddenly wakes her?

BARBARA: Well, what of it? I locked the gate behind me, so she'll knock on it for a while and then, I guess, she'll just walk away. And in the morning we'll tell her that we were asleep and never heard a thing. And then, Glasha is looking out for us. If something goes wrong, she'll sing out. I've taken every precaution, to be sure not to get into trouble. [Vania *strums on his guitar.* Barbara *leans on his shoulder. He goes on playing.*]

BARBARA: [*Yawning*] How can we find out what time it is?

VANIA: It's just after twelve.

BARBARA: How do you know?

VANIA: I heard the night-watchman bang his gong.

BARBARA: [*Yawning*] It's time they came back. Give the signal. Tomorrow we'll come earlier so we'll have more time.

VANIA: [*Whistling and singing out loudly*]
Home, home, all go home.
But I want to stay and roam!

BORIS' VOICE: [*Off-stage*] I hear!

BARBARA: [*Getting up*] Good-by then! [*Yawns and gives* Vania *a cool kiss, as to an old acquaintance*] Mind you come a bit earlier tomorrow! [*Looks to the side on which* Boris *and* Katerina *went out.*] You've said good-by to each other for long enough. You aren't parting for ever, remember. You'll probably

see each other tomorrow. [*Yawns and stretches herself*]

[Katerina *comes running in, followed by* Boris]

KATERINA: [*To* Barbara] Well, let's go, it's time! [*They go up the path.* Katerina *looks back*] Good-by!

BORIS: See you tomorrow!

KATERINA: Yes, tomorrow! Remember your dreams and tell me! [*Reaches gate*]

BORIS: I will.

VANIA [*Singing and accompanying himself on the guitar*]
Sing, my girl, dance and play,
Till the night replaces day . . .

BARBARA: [*By the gate, singing*]
But after the sunset red,
A nice girl is home in bed! [*Exits*]

VANIA: [*Singing*]
When the night is black and deep,
There my girl is, fast asleep . . .

CURTAIN

ACT IV.

Front stage, a narrow, vaulted gallery in an old building that is falling into decay. In places, tufts of grass and bushes. The Volga can be seen through the arches. Several people of both sexes, out for a stroll, pass behind the arches.

FIRST MAN: It's beginning to rain! I hope we won't get a thunderstorm.

SECOND MAN: We'll get one all right.

FIRST MAN: At least we've a shelter here.

A WOMAN: Look at all those people out for a stroll on the square, and the merchants' wives in their Sunday clothes!

FIRST MAN: They'll find some place to get out of the rain.

SECOND MAN: It'll be crowded here in no time!

FIRST MAN: [*Examining the walls*] Look, these walls were covered with frescoes once. One can still see them in places.

SECOND MAN: Sure they used to be covered with frescoes. The building was abandoned after the fire. They never bothered to repair it and now it's all dilapidated and grown over. Of course, you don't remember the fire. It happened forty years ago.

FIRST MAN: What'd you say this is a picture of? Difficult to make out, isn't it?

SECOND MAN: Why, it's a burning pit.

FIRST MAN: So that's what it is!

SECOND MAN: And here, you see, are all the people being thrown into it.

FIRST MAN: Oh, I see now.

SECOND MAN: And they come from all stations of life, rich and poor.

FIRST MAN: Some of them are Negroes, aren't they?

SECOND MAN: Yes, Negroes are being thrown in, too.

FIRST MAN: And what's that over there?

SECOND MAN: That's the rout of the Lithuanians. It's a battle, see. Our people are giving the Lithuanians hell.

FIRST MAN: And what did they want here, them, Lithuanians?

SECOND MAN: Well, that's Lithuanians for you.

FIRST MAN: Yes, I heard they dropped on us out of the blue.

SECOND MAN: That, I can't tell you. Could be.

THE WOMAN: I can tell you for sure—that's where they dropped from and, what's more, that's why there are those funeral mounds at the place where that battle was fought.

[Enter Dikoy followed by Kuligin, hat in hand. All bow and assume respectful attitudes]

DIKOY: Ah, damn it, I'm soaked through! [To Kuligin] You leave me alone, you hear! [Losing his temper] Ah, you stupid fool!

KULIGIN: But, Mr. Dikoy, please, just think—it would benefit everybody.

DIKOY: Go away! What benefit? Who needs benefits?

KULIGIN: But wouldn't you like it yourself, Mr. Dikoy? What would you think of having it put in a spot that'd been specially cleared for it? And it won't cost much either! What could it come to? A small stone pillar [Showing with his hands the size of each item he mentions], a round brass plate about like that, and a style, just a straight one, like that, you know, the most ordinary kind. As for the rest, I'll fix it all up and even engrave the figures myself. After that, you, sir, when you take a stroll in the square here, as well as all the other people who come, will always know what time it is. For it's such a beautiful spot here, yet somehow it always looks as if there were something missing. And then there are the travelers from out of town who come to see the sights and really, it would make the whole place more pleasing to the eye.

DIKOY: But why do you have to pester me with all this bunk? Did you ask me, in the first place, whether I wanted to talk to you at all? You should always find out first whether I'm in a mood to listen to a fool or not. Do you imagine, by any chance, that we're equals, a couple of pals or something? Ah, is that your important business that you think entitles you to push your snout into my face?!

KULIGIN: If I'd come to you with something that was just for myself, you'd be absolutely right saying that, sir. But it's for the general good, Mr. Dikoy! What can a matter of about ten rubles mean to you, if it's for the good of the whole town? It won't come to more than that, I'm sure, sir.

DIKOY: And who can guarantee you don't intend to steal the money?

KULIGIN: But since I'm offering my labor for nothing, how could I steal, sir? And everyone in this town knows me and can tell you I'd never do a thing like that.

DIKOY: So let them know you if they want. As for me, I don't wish to know you.

KULIGIN: But why do you have to be so insulting to an honest man, sir?

DIKOY: And now you imagine perhaps that I have to account to you for that, too! I don't account to people, not even if they're ten times more important than you. I think and say just what I please about people. Now if you seem honest to others, to me you're a thief and that's all there is to it. Is that what you wanted me to say? All right, so now you have it. So I say you're a crook. Perhaps you want to make something of it, you worm? Now remember: if I decide to forgive you, I'll forgive you and if I decide to step on you, I'll crush you.

KULIGIN: God forgive you, Mr. Dikoy. I know I'm a humble man and it wouldn't be too hard for you to push me around. But let me tell you this, sir: virtue is respectable even in beggar's tatters.

DIKOY: Don't you dare be rude to me! I'll show you!

KULIGIN: I certainly didn't mean to be rude, sir. I simply thought maybe you'd want to do something for our town. You're a very powerful man, sir, and you could do a great deal of good if you wanted to. Look, for instance—we have a lot of thunderstorms in this part of the country, but there are hardly any lightning rods in our town.

DIKOY: [Haughtily] Oh, they're useless!

KULIGIN: How can you say that, sir? Experiments have proved what lightning rods do.

DIKOY: What kind of lightning rods are you talking about?

KULIGIN: Steel ones.

DIKOY: [Impatiently] Well, what else is there to them?

KULIGIN: They're rods, sir, rods made of steel.

DIKOY: [Working himself up into a temper] I know what a rod is, you damned idiot, I'm asking you what else there is to them! Don't go on repeating "rods, rods, rods."

KULIGIN: That's all there is to them, sir.

DIKOY: And what is a thunderstorm in your opinion, eh? Come on, answer me that! Speak up, man!

KULIGIN: Electricity.

DIKOY: [Stamping his foot] What are you talking about! Electricity—shmectricity! And after that, go and claim you aren't a crook! Everyone knows that thunderstorms are sent us as a punishment, to make us feel the Lord's anger, and you want to protect yourself with some sort of rods and poles! What are you, a Moslem or something? Come, admit you're a Tartar infidel—right?

KULIGIN: But Mr. Dikoy, remember, our great Russian poet Derzhavin said:

While my body to dust will decay,
My mind over lightning will hold sway.

DIKOY: I could hand you over to the police chief

for those words and he'd throw you in jail. Hey, people, listen to what he's saying, this man!

KULIGIN: I guess there's nothing doing, so I might just as well give up. When I get my own million rubles, I'll come back to it.

[*Shrugs and walks away*]

DIKOY: Where'll you get the money? Steal it somewhere? Ah, the thief! Stop thief! You have to watch out with that kind! [*To the crowd*] And you, you damned rotten bunch, you'd drive anyone into sin! I didn't want to lose my temper this morning, but that man made me lose it on purpose. May hell swallow him up! [*Gruffly*] Isn't the rain over yet?

A MAN: I think it's stopped, sir.

DIKOY: You don't have to think, you fool, go and look.

THE MAN: [*Walking out from under the arches*] It's stopped.

[*Dikoy exits, the others follow him. For a few moments the stage is empty, then* Barbara *enters hurriedly and hides in a corner under an archway. She peeks out from there, apparently watching for someone*]

BARBARA: I think that's him now! [Boris *passes in the background*] Psssst! [Boris *turns his head*] Hey, come over here! [*Beckons to him;* Boris *approaches*] Tell me now, what shall we do with Katerina?

BORIS: Why?

BARBARA: It's terrible, her husband's come back. We didn't expect him so soon but he's come just the same. Hadn't you heard?

BORIS: No.

BARBARA: She's simply gone out of her mind.

BORIS: It looks as if I've had my share of happiness—ten days, and now my whole life seems to be over. I won't see her again.

BARBARA: Ah, that's all you're worried about! Wait, listen to me: she's shivering as if she had a great fever. She's terribly pale and tears about the house like a wild thing, as if she were looking for something. And her eyes are like a madwoman's. This morning she started crying and she's been crying and sobbing and won't stop. Ah, my God, what am I to do with her?

BORIS: Perhaps . . . perhaps she'll get over it in time.

BARBARA: Not likely. She daren't look her husband in the face. Mother has noticed it and she keeps watching her and she looks at her with snake's eyes and that makes it even worse for poor Katerina. It breaks my heart to see her like that. And then, I'm afraid.

BORIS: What are you afraid of?

BARBARA: You don't know her—she's a strange one, she could do anything. She could cause so much trouble that . . .

BORIS: Oh, good Lord, what are we to do then? You ought to try and reason with her a bit. Won't she really listen to reason?

BARBARA: I've tried already but she won't listen. Looks as if it's better if I stay away.

BORIS: But what do you think she'll do?

BARBARA: What? She could, for instance, go down on her knees to her husband and blurt out everything to him. That's what I'm afraid she'll do.

BORIS: [*Frightened*] Could she really do that?

BARBARA: You can expect anything from her.

BORIS: Where is she now?

BARBARA: She's out in the square with Tikhon. Mother's with them, too. You can go and see for yourself. Although no, you'd better not. She's liable to lose her head completely if she sees you. [*Thunder in the distance*] Looks like a thunderstorm. [*Looks outside*] Yes, it's started raining again. Ah, and now there are people running this way for shelter. Hide yourself and I'll stand here in full view so that no one will suspect anything.

[*Enter several people of both sexes, then* Kuligin]

FIRST MAN: That little lady seems to be really afraid of the lightning. Look how she's running for shelter!

A WOMAN: No shelter will help her if it's written in her fate that lightning is to get her.

KATERINA: [*Rushing in*] Ah, Barbara! [*Catches hold of* Barbara's *hand and holds it*]

BARBARA: Come, take it easy. What's the matter with you?

KATERINA: I'm going to die!

BARBARA: Come, pull yourself together. Stop that nonsense!

KATERINA: No, I can't, I can't! It hurts too much!

MRS. KABANOV: [*Walking in, followed by* Tikhon] Well, that's why people must always live decently, so as to be ready to die at any moment. They wouldn't be afraid then.

TIKHON: But what kind of sin could she have committed? There's nothing special about her sins, they're just like anyone else's. She's just fearful by nature, that's all.

MRS. KABANOV: What do you know about her? Another person's soul is as much of a mystery to us as the blackest night.

TIKHON: [*Jokingly*] Unless something happened while I was away, because when I'm here, I know she's not all that sinful.

MRS. KABANOV: Well, it could be, then, that she did something while you were away.

TIKHON: [*Jokingly*] All right, Katerina, my girl, you'd better confess if you've sinned, for you have no chance of keeping it a secret from me. Not on your life! I know everything about you!

KATERINA: [*Looking straight into his eyes*] Ah, Tikhon, my dear . . .

BARBARA: [*To* Tikhon] Why don't you leave her alone? Can't you see it's hard enough for her as it is!

[Boris *comes out of his hiding place and bows to the* Kabanovs]

KATERINA: [*Suppressing a scream*] Ah!

TIKHON: What are you so frightened of? She

must've thought you were a stranger. Come, we know him, Katerina. How's your uncle, Boris?

BORIS: He's fine, thank you.

KATERINA: [*To* Barbara] What does he want of me now? Isn't it enough for him to have made me suffer so? [*Buries her face in* Barbara's *shoulder and sobs*]

BARBARA: [*Aloud so that* Mrs. Kabanov *will hear*] We are at our wits' end trying to think what to do with her and it's really too much when strangers come and meddle! [*She makes a sign to* Boris *and he walks off to the entrance at the farthermost end of the stage*]

KULIGIN: [*Stepping from the crowd into the center of the stage and addressing all*] Well, what are you afraid of? Tell me! Every blade of grass, every flower is glad, while we hide here as if the thunderstorm were a disaster. You're afraid the thunderstorm'll kill you! Why should it? Why don't you understand that it's not a calamity but a good thing? Anyway, you're afraid of everything: you're even afraid of the northern lights and you run indoors instead of looking at the sky and admiring them. "From midnight lands the dawn cometh"—and you are panicky and keep wondering whether it's a sign announcing war or pestilence. If a comet appears in the sky, one would expect a man to be reluctant to take his eye from such beauty, because while the eye becomes accustomed to the stars, a comet is something unusual and bright . . . But you, you're even afraid to look up into the sky and just stand there trembling with fear. Ah, all the bogies you folks have invented for yourselves! Me, I'm not afraid! Come, Mr. Boris, let's go out!

BORIS: Yes, let's go, it's more frightening in here!

[Kuligin *and* Boris *exit*]

MRS. KABANOV: What speeches! Ever hear anything like it? The times we live in! What's he trying to teach us? If he were a youngster it'd be one thing, but he's an old man! Ah, what're we coming to?

A WOMAN: Look at the sky, the clouds are so thick they cover it like a fur hat.

FIRST MAN: Look at that cloud rolling along, just like a hedgehog, and it looks as if there's a live thing inside it and it's about to come at us any moment.

SECOND MAN: Mark my word, fellow, we won't get off lightly with this thunderstorm. I know. It'll either kill someone or set a house on fire. You'll see. Look at the color of the sky!

KATERINA: [*Listening*]: What are they saying? They said it'd kill someone.

TIKHON: They come out with the first bit of nonsense that goes through their heads.

MRS. KABANOV: Don't judge your elders. They've more experience than you have. Old people know all the signs. They don't just talk to say nothing.

KATERINA: Tikhon, I know who's to be killed.

BARBARA: [*Quietly to* Katerina]. Ah, keep quiet!

TIKHON: How can you know?

KATERINA: I'm going to be killed. Pray for me when I'm gone.

[*Enter the* Old Lady *with the* Footman. Katerina *screams and hides*]

THE LADY: Why are you hiding? It's no use. You're afraid, are you? You don't want to die? You'd like to live a little longer perhaps? I'm sure you would, pretty as you are! Ha-ha-ha! Beauty! Why, try praying to God to take away your beauty, because beauty is the cause of women's perdition. Beauty corrupts you, tempts men, and then leaves you to admire what your beauty has caused. Yes, your beauty is liable to lead many people astray. Young fools fight duels over it, slashing each other with their swords, and old fools forget to think about their impending death when they're seduced by it. And who do you think will have to answer for it all? You, you will have to. Throw your beauty into the whirlpool and hurry up about it! [Katerina *hides herself*] What's the point of hiding, silly thing. You can't run away from God. Yes, and all of you will burn in everlasting fire.

KATERINA: Ah, I'm dying!

BARBARA: Stop torturing yourself, after all. Come, step to one side and try to pray. Maybe it'll make you feel better.

KATERINA: [*Walking up to the wall, kneeling by it, then suddenly jumping up*] Ah, ah, the burning pit! [Tikhon, Mrs. Kabanov *and* Barbara *crowd round her*] Ah, my heart is all in tatters, I can't stand it any more! Mother, Tikhon, I'm guilty before God and before you! Didn't I swear to you that I wouldn't let my eyes rest on anyone while you were away! Yes, you do remember! But do you know, worthless as I am, what I did while you weren't here? The very first night I walked out of the house . . .

TIKHON: [*In tears, pulling at her sleeve*] No, don't say anything, no need . . . Don't! . . . You mustn't in front of mother.

MRS. KABANOV: [Sternly] Yes, speak! Say it! Since you've begun, finish now!

KATERINA: I went out on every one of those ten nights . . . [*Sobs.* Tikhon *makes a gesture to embrace her*]

MRS. KABANOV: Don't touch her! Who was he?

BARBARA: Don't believe her, she doesn't know what she's saying.

MRS. KABANOV: You shut up! Ah, so that's what it was. Well, what's his name?

KATERINA: Boris . . . [*A clap of thunder*] Ah! [*Faints in* Tikhon's *arms*]

MRS. KABANOV: Well, son, what do you say now? I warned you what you could expect, allowing them all that freedom, but you wouldn't listen to me. So now you have it!

CURTAIN

ACT V.

Same setting as Act I. Darkness is falling. Kuligin *sits on a bench.* Tikhon *enters, walking through the park.*

KULIGIN: [*Singing*]

The veil of night has covered the skies,
On earth the people have closed their eyes . . .

[*He catches sight of* Tikhon] Ah, good-evening, sir. Are you going far?

TIKHON: I'm on my way home. I suppose you must've heard of our troubles? Our whole family is in a real turmoil.

KULIGIN: I've heard, sir.

TIKHON: And you know I went to Moscow? Before I left home, mother kept telling me how to behave but as soon as I was out of her sight, I let myself go. I was so glad to get away from it all. And so I drank all through the trip to Moscow, and I drank when I got there . . . I was trying to make up for lost time and fill myself so full it'd take me a year to sober up. I never thought about home once. And even if I had thought of it, I never would've guessed what was going on here. And have you heard what was going on?

KULIGIN: Yes, I've heard.

TIKHON: I'm a miserable, broken man! I'm lost and I don't know what I've done to deserve it.

KULIGIN: If you don't mind my saying so, sir, I think your mother's a bit rough.

TIKHON: Sure she is and, in fact, it's mostly her fault what happened. But why did it have to happen to me? What have I done to deserve it? Just now, I went over to Dikoy's and we had a few drinks. I hoped it'd make me feel better but if anything, it's made me feel worse. Ah, what my wife did to me! There can't be anything worse than that, Kuligin.

KULIGIN: It's hard to judge, sir, who's to blame for it all.

TIKHON: What are you talking about? What can be worse than what she did? I say killing her for it isn't enough! Mother says she ought to be buried alive to make her pay for it. But me, I love her, and I couldn't really hurt her. I did hit her a little but it was only because my mother made me. It breaks my heart just to look at her. Do you understand that, Kuligin? My mother keeps after her all the time, but she walks around like a dumb shadow. She does nothing but cry all the time and she's just melting away like wax. And it about kills me just to look at her.

KULIGIN: You ought to settle it all in a friendly way, I think. Perhaps you could forgive her and never mention what she did again? Why shouldn't you—I'm sure you yourself also have a few sins on your conscience, haven't you?

TIKHON: Oh, sure I have.

KULIGIN: But you should see you don't reproach her with it, even when you're drunk, and no matter how drunk. I'm sure, sir, she'd be as good a wife as you could wish for.

TIKHON: But don't you understand, Kuligin, that if it was only up to me, I'm sure I'd have forgotten the whole thing, but there's my mother, remember, and you surely don't think she'd listen to that sort of thing, do you?

KULIGIN: If I may say so, sir, I think it's high time you used your own judgment and lived your own life.

TIKHON: What d'you want me to do—tear myself in two? I'm told I haven't enough sense to live by my own judgment, so I must follow someone else's. All I'm good for is to spend my last kopek on drink, and after that I'd have to go back to my mother anyway and she'd take care of her stupid son.

KULIGIN: Ah, what a business! But tell me, what about Boris?

TIKHON: Ah, him, the rat! His uncle's sending him to Tyakhta—that's a small place on the Chinese border—to work in an office there for three years.

KULIGIN: How did he take it? Do you know?

TIKHON: Ah, he's in a state, too! He rushes all over the place, crying all the time. Just now, his uncle and I, we set on him. We abused and berated him for quite some time but he never answered back, not a word. It's as if he'd gone completely helpless all of a sudden. Do just as you please with me, he says. Just don't harm her. Because he feels terribly sorry for her too, you see.

KULIGIN: He's a nice man, Boris.

TIKHON: He's ready for his journey now and even the horses are waiting. He's miserable—something terrible! I can see that he'd give anything to say good-by to her. But why should I care? He's my enemy, after all, isn't he? He should really be tortured to death for what he's done . . .

KULIGIN: We must forgive our enemies, sir.

TIKHON: Go and tell that to mother and see what she says. So you see, friend, my family is all broken up. We're no longer like a family but like enemies to each other. My mother nagged my sister Barbara so much that finally the poor girl couldn't take any more of it and walked out on us.

KULIGIN: Where did she go?

TIKHON: Who knows? Some stay she left with Vania because he's vanished, too. Now, in that, there's no doubt it was mother's fault, because she began to bully Barbara and to lock her up. Barbara said "Don't lock me in, Mother, I warn you," but mother wouldn't listen and, sure enough, Barbara ran away. So tell me, Kuligin, what am I to do now and how can I go on living? I can't bear the sight of our house. I can't look people straight in the face, and if I try to work at something, I find my hands are like wood. Now, for instance, I'm on my way home and, believe me, the mere thought of going back there sickens me.

[*Enter* Glasha]

GLASHA: Mr. Tikhon, sir!

TIKHON: What is it now?

GLASHA: There's trouble at home, sir.

TIKHON: Oh God, one thing after another. What is it? Tell me.

GLASHA: Your wife, sir . . .

TIKHON: Well what? Is she dead or what?

GLASHA: Oh, no sir, but she's gone. We've looked for her everywhere, but we can't find her.

TIKHON: I'd better run and look for her, Kuligin. I'm afraid she may try to kill herself, she's in such a state. Ah, she's heartbroken—I can't even tell you—and it breaks my own heart just looking at her. You sure she's not somewhere in the house, Glasha? How long ago did you miss her?

GLASHA: Not long, sir. It's our fault. We should've kept a sharper eye on her. But how could we keep track of her every second, sir. It can't be done.

TIKHON: Well, don't just stand here! Run, keep looking for her! [Exit Glasha] Come, Kuligin, let's go too. [They exit]

[For some time the stage is empty. From the opposite side, Katerina enters and walks slowly across the stage]

KATERINA: [Alone, speaking as if in a daze] He's nowhere . . . What can he be doing now? If only I could say good-by to him, then. . . then I wouldn't mind dying. Why, why did I have to bring it all down on him? I'm worse off than before now. . . . Ah, I wish only my life had been ruined. Now, I'm ruined, he's ruined—I am dishonored and he will always be blamed for it. [Pause] I wish I could remember his words. Ah, how he worried about me, how sorry he was for me. [Clutches her head] I can't remember. I've forgotten everything . . . my nights are so painful: other people just go to sleep but for me it is like going into the grave and it's so frightening, the dark in there. I hear sounds and people singing as if they were burying someone, and all that is going on in the distance. . . . I'm so happy when daybreak comes. But I don't want to get up for I know I will only see the same faces, hear the same words, go through the same torments. Why do people look at me like that? Why don't they kill the likes of me any more these days? Why have they changed that? I hear they used to kill them. I wish they'd take me and throw me in the Volga. They say that if you're put to death, it removes the sin from you, but if you live on you must go on paying for it by suffering. But haven't I suffered enough? How much longer will I have to go on with it? What's the good of my living now? I don't want anything, nothing moves me, there's nothing for me in all God's world—but still, death won't come. I keep calling death but it won't come. All the things I see and hear can only hurt me here. [Points to her heart] If I could've lived with him now, at least, I would perhaps have still found some joy in life. . . . Yes, what difference would it make now, when I've lost my soul anyway. Ah, how I miss him! If only I could hear his voice, even without seeing him, even from afar. Oh, you wild, wild winds, carry him news of my sadness and my sorrow! I miss him so! [Goes to the bank of the Volga and calls out loudly] Oh, you, my happiness! You, my life! You, my soul! I love you! Answer me! [Starts to cry]

[Enter Boris]

BORIS: [Not seeing her] God, but it was her voice! Where is she? [Looks around]

KATERINA: [Running to him and flinging her arms around his neck] Ah, I've found you! [Cries on his bosom. Silence]

BORIS: Well, at least God has allowed us to cry a little together.

KATERINA: You haven't forgotten me!

BORIS: How could I ever forget you!

KATERINA: No, no, that's not what I meant. Are you angry with me?

BORIS: Why should I be angry?

KATERINA: Anyway, forgive me. I didn't want to harm you, but I couldn't stop myself. I said things, did things, like in a dream.

BORIS: Don't say that! How can you say such things?

KATERINA: But you, how do you feel about it all now?

BORIS: I'm going away.

KATERINA: Where?

BORIS: I'm going far away, Katerina. To Siberia.

KATERINA: Take me with you.

BORIS: I can't take you, Katerina—I'm not going of my own free will. My uncle is sending me off. I must go at once. The horses are waiting. I just got my uncle to let me go out for a little stroll before leaving because I wanted at least to see once more the place where we used to meet.

KATERINA: Then God go with you, Boris, and don't worry about me. You may miss me a little at first but later you'll get over it and forget.

BORIS: Ah, whatever happens to me, I'm free at least, Katerina, but what about you? What about your mother-in-law?

KATERINA: Well, she keeps after me, locks me in. . . . She tells everyone, Tikhon too, that they shouldn't believe a thing I say, that I am false through and through. She keeps following me around all day long and sometimes she laughs right in my face. She keeps bringing you up every minute.

BORIS: And what does Tikhon say?

KATERINA: Tikhon? Sometimes he's nice, at others —nasty, but, all the time, he keeps drinking. But I've come to loathe him now and when he tries to be tender, it's harder on me than if he beat me.

BORIS: It must be awful for you, Katerina!

KATERINA: Yes, it's awful. I wish I were dead.

BORIS: Who would've thought we'd have to pay so dearly for our love. I should have fled from here before anything happened.

KATERINA: Yes, meeting you was my undoing, my darling. I've had little happiness from you and so much sorrow! And there's much more to come still. But why think of the future? At least I've seen you now and no one can take that away from me. Now, I don't need anything else. To see you once more was all I wanted. I kept thinking that you were angry and cursing me . . .

BORIS: How could you think that? Why?

KATERINA: No, that's not really what I was trying to say. I simply missed you terribly, and now I've seen you.

BORIS: I hope they don't find us together now. That'd be the end . . .

KATERINA: Wait, wait, I wanted to tell you something else. . . . Ah, I've forgotten! I'm all mixed up. I can't remember what it was.

BORIS: I must be going now, Katerina.

KATERINA: Wait, wait!

BORIS: What was it you wanted to say?

KATERINA: I'll tell you in a second. [Stops and thinks] Ah, yes, if on your way there you come across beggars, give something to each of them and ask them to pray for my sinful soul.

BORIS: If only those who are forcing us to part knew how terrible this is for me! I only wish they could feel for one day what I feel now! Good-by, Katerina! [Embraces her and wants to go] Ah, you freaks, you monsters! I wish I were strong enough to show you!

KATERINA: Wait! Let me look at you once more, for the last time. [Looks into his eyes] Now that's enough, God be with you! Well, go now, go quickly, hurry!

BORIS: [Walks away a few steps, then stops] I feel there's something wrong, Katerina. Perhaps you're thinking of doing something terrible? I'll worry myself to death during the journey.

KATERINA: No, no, nothing, go, good luck to you! [Boris wants to return to her] Go now, that's enough.

BORIS: [Sobbing] Well, God be with you, Katerina. [To himself] I can only pray God to send her death soon, to end her suffering. [To Katerina] Good-by, Katerina!

KATERINA: Good-by, Boris!

[Exit Boris. Katerina follows him with her eyes, remaining silent and lost in thought for some time]

KATERINA: [Alone] Where can I go now? Home? No, to me home is just like the grave. No, it'd be better for me in the grave. A little grave under a tree, with the sun shining on it, the rain washing it, with soft, soft grass growing around it in the spring. . . . Birds would come and sing in the tree and hatch their young . . . little flowers would grow—red ones, yellow ones, blue ones, all sorts . . . [Dreams in silence] Everything's so quiet and nice. Ah, I think I feel better now. And I don't want to think any more about life. Must I really go on living? No, no, I don't want to . . . Life is bad. I don't like people, I don't like my home—I loathe it all. No, I won't go back there! No, no, no! If I went back, they'd want to talk to me, but why should I? It's all dark now and the singing has begun again. Where? What are they singing? I can't make it out. . . It would be so nice to die now! What are they singing? What's the difference whether death comes by itself or whether I myself— All I know is I can't go on living. But it's a sin! They won't pray over me! Well, those who love me will pray anyway . . . They fold people's hands when they put them in the coffin . . . I just happened to

remember that. If they catch me, they'll take me back home by force. Ah, quick, quick! [Walks up to the bank. In a loud voice] My dearest! My beloved! Farewell!

[Enter Mrs. Kabanov, Tikhon, Kuligin and Workers carrying lanterns]

KULIGIN: They say they saw her here.

TIKHON: You sure?

KULIGIN: Yes, that's what they said.

TIKHON: Well, thank God, at least they saw her alive!

MRS. KABANOV: And you were so scared and even crying already! Don't worry, we'll have to suffer her for a long time yet!

TIKHON: Who would've thought she'd try to hide in such a place! People keep coming past here all the time.

MRS. KABANOV: Can't you see what she's up to? She's still trying to have her way with you!

[From every side people arrive with lanterns]

A MAN WITH A LANTERN: Found her?

MRS. KABANOV: Not yet. She seems to have vanished.

SEVERAL VOICES: Strange! Where could she have gone? There's something wrong!

A VOICE: She'll turn up!

ANOTHER VOICE: Sure, they'll find her in the end!

THIRD VOICE: I bet she'll come home by herself.

A VOICE OFFSTAGE: Hey, get a boat!

KULIGIN: [Shouting in the direction of the voice] Who's calling? What is it?

A VOICE: A woman's jumped into the river!

[Kuligin, followed by several men, exits running]

TIKHON: Oh God, I'm sure it's her! [Wants to run off; his mother holds him back by the arm] Mother, please let me go! I'll get her out of the river or . . . or I myself . . . I can't live without her!

MRS. KABANOV: No, I won't let you. You're not going to risk your life for her. She's not worth it. As if she hadn't brought enough disgrace down on our house!

TIKHON: Let me go!

MRS. KABANOV: There are plenty of people to get her out without you. I'll curse you, if you go!

TIKHON: [Going down on his knees] Let me just look at her once!

MRS. KABANOV: You'll look at her when they've fished her out.

TIKHON: [Standing up, to the men] Well, fellows, did you see anything?

A MAN: It's too dark, can't see nothing. [Noise offstage]

SECOND MAN: They're shouting something over there but I can't make out what they're saying.

FIRST MAN: They're coming this way. Yes, and I can see now. They're carrying her.

[Some men enter]

ONE OF THEM: You have to hand it to Kuligin: he found her. She was very close to the bank, in a whirlpool. You can see quite far out over the water with a lantern. So he saw her dress and fished her out.

TIKHON: Is she alive?

ANOTHER MAN: Alive? How could she be? She threw herself from the steep bank and she must have hit her head against a mooring, the poor thing! But she looks as if she were alive—just a little wound on her temple and a few drops of blood.

[Tikhon *rushes forward, then stops;* Kuligin *and some* Men *enter carrying the dead* Katerina]

KULIGIN: Here's your wife. Do with her as you please. That is, you can have only her body, her soul is now facing a much more merciful Judge than you! [*Deposits body on the ground, exits running*]

TIKHON: [*Falling on the body*] Katerina! Katerina!

MRS. KABANOV: Stop it! That'll do! It's sinful to cry for her.

TIKHON: Mother, it was you who killed her! It was you, you, you!

MRS. KABANOV: What! You're out of your mind! You forget you're talking to your mother!

TIKHON: You killed her! Yes, you, you!

MRS. KABANOV: Wait until we're home, we'll have a little talk about this still! [*To the* Men, *bowing low*] Thank you kindly, good people, for your help! [*They bow to her*]

TIKHON: Ah, Katerina, you're all right now! But I, I must go on living and suffering. Why? . . . [*Falls on* Katerina's *body*]

CURTAIN

Epilogue

WITH HEBBEL'S AND TURGENEV'S two mid-century masterpieces we have approached the modern age of the drama. But only prematurely so. Another quarter of a century was to elapse before the theatre began to veer more or less steadily in the modern direction. Although the prose play became the dominant dramatic form, it was generally contrived with a view to effecting theatrical sensations (*coups de théâtre*). It had prose; it did not yet have life. And, although an increasing number of plays revolved around social problems, these plays did not yet penetrate to the fundamental private and social issues inherent in the problems. As a matter of fact, the spirit of inquiry and the critical intellect were more apparent in such formally romantic plays as Ibsen's early masterworks *Brand* and *Peer Gynt* than in the cut and dried realism and conventional moralism of an Augier or a Dumas *fils*. A modernist such as Shaw would have noted that these "problem plays" still did not constitute "drama of ideas." The third quarter of the nineteenth century was primarily an interlude in the theatre.

In the fourth quarter of the century, the new dispensation foreshadowed by Hebbel and Turgenev became well defined in European drama. From Becque and Ibsen to Chekhov, playwrights opened the sluices of naturalness to make prose drama something more than a concession to the commonplace world. And realism became a means for probing that world, proving that the problem play could be more provocative than a Sunday-school lesson. Western drama began to front reality —and to live it. The loss of poetic drama entailed by the prevalence of prose dialogue could then be compensated by a charged vitality of content and expression. Moreover, it was not long before modern realism could even recover a certain degree of poetry, without the formalism of verse, as in the plays of a Synge or an O'Casey.

Once insurgent realism had discredited romantic pomp and flamboyance, poetic drama, both in prose and verse, could return to the stage. It returned purged and chastened, as well as invigorated, by the detachment—the irony or the disenchantment—that marks mature realizations. There is a difference of sophistication between the idealism of the young Schiller and the idealism of a T. S. Eliot or Lorca. Even Rostand, for all his heat and glitter, was not impervious to the ironies in *Cyrano de Bergerac* and *Chantecler*. There is also a difference between the hidalgo heroics of a Victor Hugo in *Hernani* and the worldly, not infrequently acrid romanticism of a Jean Giraudoux or Jean Anouilh. An even wider rift between the pre-Ibsen and post-Ibsen drama was to occur when fantastication reappeared on the modern stage in expressionism and surrealism. Fancy became hallucination; fables became nightmares.

Availing themselves of the steadily infiltrating scientism, political consciousness, and psychological advances of the age, playwrights employing modern styles evolved a drama—*and a theatre*—disconcerting in variety, piquancy, and provocativeness. This fact will be found recorded in the essays and illustrated by the plays in the second volume of *A Treasury of the Theatre,* which presents European playwriting from Ibsen to Sartre and English-American playwriting from Wilde to Miller. The stage became subject to the law of acceleration that Henry Adams predicated for modern history. A world in transition could hardly be expected to sustain an invariable and unchanging art. Changes of dramatic style and of attitude

1013

were rapid, although these did not occur simultaneously or to the same degree in all countries. Style displaced style, attitude supplanted attitude, and one vogue trod on the heels of the next. It becomes even more apparent that "literary history is no more orderly than any other history," as Allen Tate has declared, when the "literary history" is theatre history.

The changes in theatrical art were so rapid (although realism managed to weather most of them) that a commingling of styles was inevitable. The pervasive feature of the contemporary Western stage is its eclecticism. In a single season in New York, London, or Paris, the plays and stage productions have usually varied greatly. And even a single play may hold in solution several theoretically distinct kinds of drama, such as realism, symbolism, and expressionism. Imaginative and resourceful playwrights—playwrights as dissimilar as Molnár, O'Neill, O'Casey, Pirandello, Lorca, Brecht, Miller, and Williams, among others—made it plain in their practice that dramatic forms and styles might be merged to provide a new mode of expression. (O'Neill and Miller, for example, did not hesitate to move from naturalistic to expressionistic scenes in *The Hairy Ape* and *Death of a Salesman*, respectively.) The modern theatre has long stood on shifting sands. Only an extremely complacent or exceptionally obtuse observer can claim fixity for it.

A REPRESENTATIVE LIST OF PLAYS TO 1875

THE FOLLOWING APPENDIX is intended to supplement this anthology with a selected list of historically important plays written before 1875, or, more accurately, before the appearance of Zola's naturalistic drama *Thérèse Raquin,* in 1873. To some slight degree it may serve as a skeletal review of the history of the drama covered in the present volume. Many of these titles have already been mentioned or discussed in the introductions, but they are repeated here for the convenience of the reader. The editor makes no claim of completeness for this list, and the informed reader, the student, and his instructor will undoubtedly want to add their own preferences.

It should be noted that there are many plays in foreign languages that are esteemed in the countries in which they were written but that have not made an equally strong impression in the theatre of other lands. The perspective of selection in this list, as well as in the anthology, is English and American, although, I trust, not narrowly so.

The dates given for many plays written before the seventeenth century are necessarily approximate. In some cases, no date can be given.

CLASSIC DRAMA

AESCHYLUS: *Prometheus Bound* (479 B.C.). A drama of the struggle between Prometheus and Zeus, revolving about the question of divine beneficence and justice, demonstrating Aeschylus' concern with moral and cosmic problems. (Shelley's dramatic poem *Prometheus Unbound* is a romantic treatment of the same theme.)

The Seven Against Thebes (467 B.C.). Deals with the tragic rivalry between the sons of Oedipus. The first fully developed Greek play.

Agamemnon (458 B.C.). See page 9.

The Libation Pourers (*Choephoroe*) (458 B.C.). The second part of the Oresteian trilogy; a play of revenge and matricide.

Eumenides (458 B.C.). The third part of the Oresteian trilogy; a drama of guilt and conscience. (For a modern treatment of the Oresteian trilogy the reader is referred to Eugene O'Neill's *Mourning Becomes Electra.*)

SOPHOCLES: *Antigone* (441 B.C.). The famous tragedy of Antigone's burial of her brother in defiance of a royal decree; a notable treatment of the conflict between private conscience and the state.

Ajax (c. 440 B.C.). A tragedy of ambition that culminates in madness and suicide. A Greek psychological drama.

Oedipus the King (after 441 B.C., perhaps about 430). See page 30.

Electra (410 B.C.). An austere treatment of matricide, dealing with the murder of Clytemnestra by her children. (Compare with Aeschylus' *Choephoroe* and Euripides' *Electra.*)

Philoctetes (409 B.C.). An idyllic drama of the conflict between unscrupulous statesmanship and the generous impulses of youth. One of the most graceful of classic plays.

Oedipus at Colonus (405 B.C.). A serene lyrical and mystical conclusion of the tragic saga of Oedipus.

EURIPIDES: *Alcestis* (438 B.C.). A miracle fantasy play dealing with the legendary self-sacrifice of Alcestis, who dies to save her husband from the doom of death. Combines fantasy with realistic psychology.

Medea (431 B.C.). A notable dramatic treatment of the theme of jealousy, full of insight into the conflict of the sexes.

Hippolytus (428 B.C.). A psychological tragedy of sexual repression and its consequences.

Hecuba (426 B.C.). An antimilitaristic play concerning the brutalizing effects of war.

The Trojan Women (415 B.C.). See page 52.

Electra (413 B.C.). A realistic treatment of the murder of Clytemnestra by her children.

The Bacchae (406 B.C.). A psychological tragedy of the conflict between instinct and reason and of the danger of repression. One of the most powerful classic tragedies, notable for its subtlety and its symbolic treatment of the myth of Dionysus. See page 721.

Iphigenia in Aulis (405 B.C.). A powerful indictment of militarism and superstition, dealing with the legendary sacrifice of Iphigenia, Agamemnon's daughter. Finished, probably, by another dramatist.

ARISTOPHANES: *The Acharnians* (425 B.C.). An imaginative satire on militarism.

The Knights (424 B.C.). A satire on demagogues and militarists, notable for its invectives against prominent contemporaries.

The Clouds (423 B.C.). A satire on the absurdities of moral sophistry, in which Socrates is the scapegoat.

The Peace (421 B.C.). A fantastic antimilitaristic comedy.

The Birds (414 B.C.). A good-natured fantasy set in Cloudcuckooland, the kingdom of the birds.

Lysistrata (411 B.C.). Famous comedy in which Athenian women stage a "sex strike" in order to put an end to war.

The Frogs (405 B.C.). See page 71.

The Ecclesiazusae (392 B.C.). A rollicking satire on Hellenic feminism and utopianism.

MEANDER: *Arbitration* (300? B.C.). The first extant domestic comedy; incomplete. It concerns a man's suspicions that his wife has been unfaithful.

PLAUTUS: *The Menaechmi*. See page 96.

The Captives (late 3rd century B.C.). A comedy in which an old man recovers two lost sons, one of whom he has unknowingly had in his service as a slave and been punishing for recalcitrance.

The Crock of Gold (194? B.C.). A comedy about miserliness. (Molière's *The Miser* is a later version.)

TERENCE: *Phormio* (161 B.C.). A comedy of love intrigue revolving about such standard comic characters as a parasite and an intriguing servant.

The Eunuch (161 B.C.). A comedy of love and intrigue in which a lover impersonates a eunuch.

The Brothers (160 B.C.). See page 118.

SENECA: *Thyestes* (c. 4 B.C.). See page 741.

ORIENTAL DRAMA

SHUDRAKA: *The Little Clay Cart* (4th century). A fantastic Hindu comedy of personal romance and political intrigue, attributed by tradition to King Shudraka.

KALIDASA: *Shakuntala* (5th century). See page 140.

AUTHOR UNKNOWN: *The Circle of Chalk* (13th or 14th century). A Chinese play on crime, political corruption, and the final triumph of justice.

KWANAMI KIYOTSUGU: *Sotoba Komachi* (14th century). See page 179.

SEAMI MOTOKIYO: *Atsumori* (15th century). A Japanese Noh play on the death of a hero.

Tsunemasa (15th century). A Noh play on the death of a noble flute player slain in battle.

Kagekiyo (15th century). A Noh play on the meeting between a ghostly warrior and his daughter.

ZEMBO MOTOYASU: *Ikuta* (15th or early 16th century). A Noh play on the meeting between a ghostly warrior and his son.

MEDIEVAL EUROPEAN DRAMA

HROTSVITHA: *Paphnutius* (10th century). See page 756.

AUTHOR UNKNOWN: *Adam* (middle of 12th century). Probably the first play in medieval French. A "miracle" or "mystery" drama dealing with the fall of man.

AUTHOR UNKNOWN: The Brome *Abraham and Issac* (15th-century transcription of a 14th-century play). See page 189.

AUTHOR UNKNOWN: *The Death of Pilate* (14th or 15th century). See page 764.

AUTHOR UNKNOWN: *The Second Shepherds' Play* (1st half of 14th century). See page 194.

AUTHOR UNKNOWN: *The Coventry Nativity Play* (15th century?). A miracle play dealing with the Nativity; it contains the famous ranting Herod referred to in *Hamlet*.

AUTHOR UNKNOWN: *Everyman* (end of 15th century). See page 204.

TUDOR AND STUART DRAMA*

HENRY MEDWALL: *Fulgens and Lucrece* (1497). An advance over the medieval *débat,* or disputation. Deals with the Renaissance question of what makes a gentleman, with Lucrece choosing a virtuous commoner instead of a highborn but worthless patrician. Considered the first English secular play.

JOHN HEYWOOD: *The Four P's* (1520–22). A comic "interlude"; an advance over the medieval *débat* in that it has no moralistic purpose, only a comic intention. Crisply compounded of popular humor and character types, such as a pardoner, a pilgrim, and an apothecary.

NICHOLAS UDALL: *Ralph Roister Doister* (1550–1553). The first notable example of Roman comedy of manners thoroughly domesticated. The hero, Ralph, is an English version of the classic "braggart soldier" (*miles gloriosus*) stock character; his crony Merrygreek is a variant of the classic parasite or hanger-on. (See Terence's *Phormio*.)

THOMAS NORTON and THOMAS SACKVILLE: *Gorboduc, or Ferrex and Porrex* (first acted in 1561). The first English drama written in blank verse. A melodrama of political rivalry, civil war, and murder, showing the influence of Senecan tragedy of revenge.

WILLIAM STEVENSON: *Gammer Gurton's Needle* (1552–1563). A realistic comedy of English rustic life; patterned after Roman comedy.

GEORGE GASCOIGNE: *The Supposes* (1566). An adaptation of Ariosto's *I Suppositi,* itself an Italian Renaissance adaptation of the Roman comedies *The Captives* by Plautus and *The Eunuch* by Terence. Noteworthy for introducing Italian comedy into the Elizabethan theatre and for being the first English comedy written entirely in prose.

JOHN LYLY: *Alexander and Campaspe* (1580–1584). An early court play that helped to inaugurate the vogue of Elizabethan romantic comedy; written in more or less witty and elaborate ("euphuistic") prose.

* Often loosely called "Elizabethan Drama."

GEORGE PEELE: *The Arraignment of Paris* (1581–1584). Notable for helping to introduce the fashion of pastoral drama, of which *As You Like It* is the most famous example.

THOMAS KYD: *The Spanish Tragedy* (written between 1584 and 1588 or 1589; first published in 1592). An adaptation of Senecan tragedy. The first powerful revenge tragedy or melodrama of the Elizabethan stage, it was popular throughout the Elizabethan period. A father wreaks ingenious and sanguinary revenge upon his son's murderers, employing the device of staging a play. (*Hamlet,* also a "revenge play," reverses the situation by having a son avenge his father's death.)

CHRISTOPHER MARLOWE: *Tamburlaine* (1587–1592?). A heroic tragedy dealing with the rise of an Oriental conqueror who represents the active will-to-power and desire for glory celebrated in Renaissance Europe. Notable for Marlowe's "mighty line" of blank verse dialogue and soliloquy.

The Tragical History of Doctor Faustus (1592?) See page 219.

Edward II (1592; published in 1594). The first distinguished chronicle play, revolving about Edward II's tragic infatuation for an upstart and the revolt against him. The best pre-Shakespearian tragedy.

ROBERT GREENE: *James IV* (*c.* 1590; published 1598). A pseudo-historical comedy or tragicomedy, notable for its winning heroine, Dorothea, who foreshadows Shakespeare's charming heroines.

AUTHOR UNKNOWN: *Arden of Feversham* (1585–1592). The first domestic tragedy in the Elizabethan theatre; also the first middle-class tragedy, since it revolves around the murder of a landowner and land dealer by his unfaithful wife and her lover. Based on a contemporary crime, it is, in a sense, a journalistic drama. (Attributed to Thomas Kyd.)

William Shakespeare: Complete List of Plays

The chronology is largely conjectured even in the most scrupulous Shakespearean scholarship, and so, in some instances, is the attribution to Shakespeare. Records of first productions are extremely meager. Publication dates and dates of registration in the files of the equivalent of a copyright office, the Stationer's Company, are inconclusive. It was not customary in Shakespeare's time to publish plays before or immediately after the first stage production. Credit for authorship was not so strictly recorded as it is today. Texts were often pirated and for this, as well as other, reasons they are often corrupt, and readings in different early editions differ in some respects. Considerable scholarship has been expended since Shakespeare's death upon the effort to establish satisfactory and authentic texts, and there are still disagreements over some words and phrases.

The sequence of Shakespeare's plays in the first collection, the First Folio, published in 1623, divided them into three comprehensive groups—comedies, histories, and tragedies. Although this order is still retained in some editions, it has no chronological validity whatsoever, and it provides no clue to Shakespeare's development as a dramatist and response to theatrical fashion as a showman.

The chronology here represents the consensus of contemporary scholarship, but is influenced to some slight degree by the editor's conjectures. In conveying indebtedness to sources, these notes may suggest something about the working habits of the playwright.

THE EARLIEST COMEDIES

The Comedy of Errors (about 1589, but perhaps later). A farce directly or indirectly based on the Roman farce *The Menaechmi*, by Plautus. (See page 96.) Probably Shakespeare's first play, although he may well have done some adapting or doctoring of plays before then.

The Two Gentlemen of Verona (about 1592). Possibly based on a lost play. Directly or indirectly affected by Italian models. Shows the influence of John Lyly in the style and of Robert Greene in the dramatic formula. Shakespeare's first romantic comedy, it shows an interest in female characters and a deepening of emotional interest.

Love's Labour's Lost (about 1593, but perhaps earlier). Shows interest in wit play and in country life, with humor at the expense of preciosity and artificiality. Shakespeare appears to have invented the plot and to have used topical events as a source.

EARLY CHRONICLE OR HISTORY PLAYS

Henry VI, Parts I, II, and III (1590–1592). Authorship in dispute; Shakespeare is credited with only a small portion of this chronicle. Probably the three parts are revisions of older plays by Marlowe, George Peele, and Shakespeare. A rhetorical, moralistic, and episodic historical panorama with some striking scenes.

Richard III (1593–1594). A melodramatic "chronicle." Marlowe may have collaborated on the writing and undoubtedly influenced it. Its story is a sequel to *Henry VI, Part III*. Richard III is Shakespeare's first fully realized and dominant "Machiavellian" figure.

A FIRST "TRAGEDY"

Titus Andronicus (1593–1594). A labored and extravagantly melodramatic revenge play, written in the Senecan style. Shakespeare's authorship of it has been long questioned, although it was published under his name in 1594. He may have hastily reworked an older play.

LATER CHRONICLE PLAYS

Richard II (about 1595). Based largely upon the main Elizabethan historical source book, Holinshed's *Chronicles*. The sequence of episodes follows the source rather closely. (Probably influenced by Marlowe's *Edward II*.) Notable less for dramatic action than for its characterization and for the poetic distinction of the writing.

King John (1594–1596). A recasting and improvement but still a poorly organized version of an older play possibly written by Shakespeare himself. One character, Faulconbridge, is more or less a prototype of Falstaff.

Henry IV, Parts I and II (1597–1598). Based, in the serious parts, largely upon Holinshed's *Chronicles* and, possibly, also on an older play. Famous for its verse, characterization (especially the creation of Falstaff), and mingling of rich humor with historical events. Mingles poetry and prose and is episodic, although it may be considered unified under the theme of the education of a national hero (See *Henry V*).

Henry V (1598–1599). Based upon Holinshed's *Chronicles* and on an older play. Inferior to *Henry IV* and less rich in characterization, but notable for its exciting action and fervid nationalism.

THE EARLY TRAGEDIES

Romeo and Juliet (1596–1597). Based on an Elizabethan poem (Arthur Brooke's *The Tragical History of Romeus and Juliet*, 1592) and on a prose redaction in Painter's *Palace of Pleasure* (1567). Possibly also a rewritten version of an earlier play by Shakespeare.

Julius Caesar (1598–1599). Based on Plutarch's *Lives*. Possibly also a revision of an older play. The first of three tragedies based on Roman history, the other two being *Antony and Cleopatra* and *Coriolanus*. Shaw called the play "the most splendidly written political melodrama we possess."

THE EARLY ROMANTIC COMEDIES

A Midsummer Night's Dream (about 1595). The first of the two Shakespearean fairy plays, the other being *The Tempest*. Possibly infused with topical satire, now long forgotten; essentially a happy mingling of rustic comedy with fancy.

The Merchant of Venice (about 1595). A play that marks an advance in characterization and humanitarian feeling, even though it reflects traditional anti-Semitism; a combination of the tragicomic Shylock theme with romantic elements.

FARCE COMEDIES

The Taming of the Shrew (probably 1594–1597). A "play within the play" farce comedy. Based possibly upon a comedy by Ariosto or its English adaptation (Gascoigne's *The Supposes*), and probably also upon an earlier anonymous piece, *The Taming of a Shrew*, which has an epilogue describing what happened to the intoxicated Christopher Sly after the performance of the play.

The Merry Wives of Windsor (about 1599). Probably largely invented by Shakespeare; his only comedy—or, rather, farce comedy—of middle-class manners.

HIGH ROMANTIC COMEDIES OF THE MIDDLE PERIOD

Much Ado About Nothing (1598–1600). Based in part on an Italian *novella*, or short tale, via Belleforest's *Histoires Tragiques*. Of Shakespeare's invention are the Dogberry matter and, probably, the Benedick and Beatrice plot. The first of the so-called "joyous" romantic comedies, in spite of the tragicomic Claudio-and-Hero plot.

As You Like It (1599–1600). The plot follows the lines of Sir Thomas Lodge's pastoral romance *Rosalynde* and was possibly influenced by the Robin Hood ballads and folk plays. But Jaques, Touchstone, and Audrey, among other minor characters, were invented by Shakespeare. We find here Shakespeare's most thorough use of the pastoral convention of Renaissance drama.

Twelfth Night, or What You Will (1599–1601). Source in *Riche in Farewell to Military Profession* by Barnaby Rich, itself based on Italian stories and (or) a redaction of them in Belleforest's *Histoires Tragiques*. The Malvolio plot is probably entirely of Shakespeare's invention.

"DARK COMEDIES" OR "PROBLEM PLAYS"

All's Well That Ends Well (1601–1603). Probably a revision of an earlier play (about 1596) by Shakespeare, based in large part on a story by Boccaccio as retold in Painter's

Palace of Pleasure. Helena, daughter of a physician, is Shakespeare's only middle-class romantic heroine. The play is generally considered Shakespeare's least attractive romantic comedy.

Troilus and Cressida (1601–1603). Based on Chaucer's *Troilus and Criseyde* (1372–1384), accounts of Troy by Caxton and perhaps Lydgate, and George Chapman's famous Elizabethan translation of the *Iliad*. An ironical, antiheroic treatment of romantic and epic material.

Measure for Measure (1603–1604). Founded on an earlier play, *History of Promos and Cassandra,* itself based on the sixteenth-century Italian story collection *Hecatommithi* (Part 8, Story 5), by Cinthio.

THE LATE TRAGEDIES

Hamlet, Prince of Denmark (1600–1601). Probably based on an earlier, lost "revenge play," Thomas Kyd's *Hamlet,* which is believed to have also formed the basis of an extant German play, *Der bestrafte Brudermord: oder Prinz Hamlet aus Dänemark* (*Fratricide Punished: or Prince Hamlet of Denmark*), 1710. (To the Kyd version may be attributed much of the machinery of the play: the ghost—a Senecan device; the "play within the play" device; and the fencing match.) The outline of the story, to which there are some references from the tenth to the thirteenth centuries, appears in Saxo Grammaticus' Danish history *Historia Danica,* about 1200; and a version of Saxo Grammaticus' story of Hamlet appears in the fifth book of Belleforest's *Histoires Tragiques,* 1570. See page 238.

Othello, The Moor of Venice (1604–1605). Based mainly on *Il Moro di Venezia,* the seventh story of the third division of Cinthio's *Hecatommithi* (1565), no doubt itself based on older sources. Historical material may have been drawn upon; for example, a Christofalo Moro was the Venetian Republic's Lord-Lieutenant of Cyprus at the beginning of the sixteenth century. Much of the treatment is original, although the main incidents and the characters appear in Cinthio's *novella.*

King Lear (1605–1606). The legend of Lear appeared early—in Geoffrey of Monmouth's early-twelfth-century *Historia Regum Brittanniae* ("History of the Kings of Britain")

—and was frequently retold. The immediate sources were the fifth and sixth chapters of Holinshed's *Chronicles.* The subplot of Gloucester and his sons may have been derived from Sidney's prose romance *Arcadia.* The tragedy may also have been based on an earlier anonymous play, *The most famous Chronicle history of Lear king of England and his Three Daughters* (1594), a crude melodrama with a happy ending. In everything that makes *King Lear* a literary masterpiece, however, the work is original.

Macbeth (1604–1606). Based on Holinshed's *Chronicles* and possibly influenced by James I's treatment of witchcraft in his *Daemonologie* (1597) and by Reginald Scot's *Discourse of Witchcraft* (1584).

Antony and Cleopatra (1607–1608). Based on Plutarch's *Lives* in the famous Elizabethan translation by North.

Timon of Athens (1605–1608; very little evidence for dating this play). Based on material in Plutarch's *Lives* and other accounts and possibly on an earlier play. May have been a revision by Shakespeare that was completed by someone else— Chapman or Middleton.

Pericles, Prince of Tyre (1607–1608). Based on Gower's medieval poem (a collection of stories) *Confessio Amantis* and a later source. The story is ultimately derived from a lost Greek romance and was retold in Latin works. The play was probably a collaboration, with Shakespeare writing or rewriting the last three acts.

Coriolanus (1608–1610). Based on Plutarch's *Lives.*

TRAGICOMEDIES OR ROMANCES

Cymbeline (1609–1610). Based in part on a tale in Boccaccio's *Decameron,* with the political background and the name "Cymbeline" provided by Holinshed's *Chronicles.*

The Winter's Tale (1610–1611). Based on Robert Greene's story *Pandosto.* The first part (the first three acts) is tragic; the second part is romantic comedy.

The Tempest (1611–1612). There are many possible sources for the play, but none has been established strongly enough to win the argument. Gonzalo's second-act description of an ideal society was probably derived from the Elizabethan (Florio) translation of Montaigne's essay *Of the Cannibals.*

OTHER PLAYS

Henry VIII (1612–1613). Based mainly on Holinshed's *Chronicles;* Act V based on Foxe's *Acts and Monuments,* Hall's *Chronicle,* and George Cavendish's *Life of Cardinal Wolsey.* A collaboration with John Fletcher. Act I, Scenes I and II; Act II, Scenes III and IV; the first 200 lines of Act III, Scene II; and Act V, Scene I, are attributed to Shakespeare.

The Two Noble Kinsmen (1613, but first published in 1634). A Shakespearean tragi-comedy based, in the main, on Chaucer's *The Knight's Tale* in *The Canterbury Tales.* A collaboration with Fletcher. The first scene of Act I, the third scene of Act III, and the first scene of Act V are attributed to Shakespeare.

Sir Thomas More (date of writing undeterminable; first published in 1844). A revision of Anthony Munday's play *Sir Thomas More.* By five writers, among whom was Shakespeare, if the handwriting evidence is correct. His contribution to this play must have been very slight.

(Other plays were once attributed, at least in part, to Shakespeare.)

BEN JONSON: *Every Man in His Humour* (1598). A comedy of manners and intrigue. A satire on idiosyncrasies, or "humours."

Volpone (1606). See page 283.

Epicoene, or The Silent Woman (1609). A farcical comedy of eccentricity and intrigue revolving around a curmudgeon who is obsessed with a fear of noise.

The Alchemist (1610). A satire on human credulity and greed, based on the contemporary belief in alchemy.

Bartholomew Fair (1614). A robust satirical comedy of roguery and hypocrisy in London.

THOMAS DEKKER: *The Shoemaker's Holiday* (1599). A spirited romantic comedy of middle-class life in the time of Queen Elizabeth, containing the famous character Simon Eyre, the shoemaker who became Lord Mayor of London.

THOMAS HEYWOOD: *A Woman Killed with Kindness* (1603). A psychological drama of marital infidelity and its punishment, revolving around the country gentry and distinguished by genuine pathos rather than by the high tragic afflatus of most serious Elizabethan plays. (Charles Lamb called Heywood "a sort of prose Shakespeare.") Unusual is the fact that the husband forgives his erring wife, who is destroyed by her own grief over her guilt rather than by an act of vengeance on the part of the wronged man. His kindness toward her is the worst punishment, since it intensifies her pangs of conscience.

JOHN MARSTON: *The Malcontent* (1604). A mordant melodrama of scheming, evil, and revenge, most notable for its spirit of disenchantment and cynicism.

GEORGE CHAPMAN: *Bussy d'Ambois* (1600–1604). The drama of an unregenerate Renaissance individualist, full of hyperbolic assertions of egotism; interesting as a representation of the Renaissance glorification of the individual's self-esteem and independence and his tendency to be ruthless in the pursuit of self-realization. (See also the sequel, *The Revenge of Bussy D'Ambois,* 1607–1612, in which the avenger is a Hamlet-like figure and a stoic.)

GEORGE CHAPMAN, BEN JONSON, and JOHN MARSTON: *Eastward Ho!* (1605). A bustling, satirical picture of London life—of prodigals, rascals, adventurers, tradesmen, apprentices, wanton and good women, and other types. The action revolves around two apprentices—one worthy and prudent, who marries his employer's modest daughter, and the other a dissipated lout. (For a slur on the Scotch, which was construed as a slur on James I, the authors were imprisoned as disloyal to the new, Stuart regime.)

THOMAS MIDDLETON: *A Trick to Catch the Old One* (1604–1607). A brilliant comedy of manners revolving around a greedy and unscrupulous man who is outsmarted by his nephew, whom he has cheated out of his estate; the nephew is aided by a courtesan whom the nephew palms off on the old man as a wealthy widow.

GEORGE WILKINS: *A Yorkshire Tragedy* (1605–1608). The drama of a gambler who ruins himself and his family; based upon a contemporary crime case. Another early example of journalistic "middle-class" tragedy.

CYRIL TOURNEUR: *The Revenger's Tragedy* (1606–1607). An extravagant and morbid revenge play, replete with the melodrama and cynicism that became pronounced in Stuart drama. (See also Tourneur's *The Atheist's Tragedy,* 1607–1611.)

JOHN WEBSTER: *The White Devil* (probably acted in 1609; published in 1612). An intense tragedy of illicit passion and revenge, notable for its characterization of a demonic woman and her Machiavellian brother.

    The Duchess of Malfi (probably acted in 1612; published in 1623). See page 324.

FRANCIS BEAUMONT: *The Knight of the Burning Pestle* (1607–1610). A mock-heroic comedy and a satire on the popular theatre and its naïve audiences, as well as a parody of romantic literature; enriched with amusing bourgeois character types.

FRANCIS BEAUMONT and JOHN FLETCHER: *The Maid's Tragedy* (1608–1611). A famous drama of lust and revenge, revolving around the sordid affair of a king and his mistress, whom he marries to a member of his court in order to conceal his immoral relationship.

THOMAS MIDDLETON and WILLIAM ROWLEY: *The Changeling* (1622). A powerful psychological tragedy of an ugly and morbid but passionate man's love for a highborn girl, for whose sake he commits murder; and of the girl's subjection to him after the crime.

PHILIP MASSINGER: *A New Way to Pay Old Debts* (probably acted in 1626; published in 1633). A moral comedy of intrigue directed against a notorious "extortioner" and expropriator of men's property, Sir Giles Overreach, by the nephew he has fleeced.

JOHN FORD: *'Tis Pity She's A Whore* (acted and published in 1633). A powerful tragedy of incestuous passion between a brother and sister.

SPANISH DRAMA

AUTHOR UNKNOWN: *The Star of Seville* (early 17th century). A typical Spanish "cape and sword" romantic drama of love and honor.

CERVANTES: *The Cave of Salamanca* (c. 1615). See page 788.

LOPE DE VEGA: *Fuente Ovejuna* (*The Sheep Well*). See page 361.

    The Gardener's Dog (c. 1615). A comedy revolving around social pride and the ease with which it is circumvented for the sake of the love that a highborn lady feels for a commoner.

    The King the Greatest Alcalde (published in 1635). A democratic drama in which a feudal overlord abducts a peasant's bride and is punished with death by a righteous king.

TIRSO DE MOLINA: *The Deceiver of Seville and the Stone Guest* (published in 1630). The first dramatic treatment of the story of Don Juan. (See Molière's *Don Juan,* Lorenzo da Ponte's libretto for Mozart's great opera *Don Giovanni,* and Rostand's *The Last Night of Don Juan.*)

PEDRO CALDERÓN DE LA BARCA: *The Physician of His Own Honor* (1635). A typical Spanish drama of the "Golden Age," revolving around a jealous husband's sadistic revenge on his unfaithful wife.

    Life Is a Dream (c. 1636). A philosophical play in which an heir to the throne is purged of his evil passions and taught moderation by the psychological treatment of being led to believe that his misconduct had not actually taken place but had been dreamt by him. See page 795.

    The Wonder-Working Magician (1637). A religious drama of St. Cyprian's conversion from paganism to Christianity, his final victory over the Devil, who tempts him with love after being defeated by him in argument.

    The Mayor of Zalamea (c. 1640). Deals with the vengeance of a peasant, the mayor of his village, when his daughter is violated by a nobleman.

    The Great Theatre of the World (c. 1645). An example of a philosophical allegorical religious play, or *auto,* prevalent in Spain; demonstrates God's "law of grace," which is for men to do well.

NEOCLASSIC FRENCH DRAMA

PIERRE CORNEILLE: *The Cid* (1636). A "heroic drama" based on Spanish legend, representing the conflict between duty and love in the case of a young woman whose father was killed by her lover in a duel. The first effort to adhere to the principle of the unities of time, place, and action according to neo-classic prescriptions. See page 823.

Polyeucte (*c.* 1642). A heroic tragedy of a woman's sense of honor, which takes the form of a sense of loyalty to her husband. Set against the conflict between Christianity and paganism in Roman times. The Roman heroine, who loves a pagan, learns to admire her Christian husband's virtues, becomes a Christian herself, and shares his martyrdom.

MOLIÈRE: *The School for Husbands* (1661). A defense of young love against possessive old age. (A delightful modernized version of this play by Arthur Guiterman and Lawrence Langner was produced in New York in 1933–1934 by the Theatre Guild.)

The School for Wives (1662). An ingenious comedy satirizing crabbed old age and championing young love. It contains the delightful ingénue Agnes, whose conduct demonstrates that ignorance is not innocence.

Tartuffe (first three acts produced privately for Louis XIV in 1664; prohibited for five years; first produced in its entirety in 1669). A satire on religious hypocrisy, containing the inimitable archhypocrite Tartuffe.

Don Juan (1665). A thoughtful and scintillating comedy based on the famous Spanish legend of Don Juan, which has been the sub-ject of plays, poems, and music.

The Misanthrope (1666). See page 389.

Georges Dandin (1668). A comedy of domestic infidelity, notable for its sharp picture of shoddy aristocracy.

The Miser (1668). A satire on avarice.

The Would-be Gentleman (1669). A farcical satire on pretentiousness and social aspirations, containing the famous bourgeois who discovers that he has been speaking "prose" all his life.

The Learned Ladies (1672). A brilliant satire on pretentious learning and affectation.

The Imaginary Invalid (1672). A comedy of hypochondria and an Aristophanic satire on the medical profession of Molière's time.

JEAN RACINE: *Andromache* (1667). A tragedy of love and jealousy, distinguished by its char-:cterization of Andromache.

Britannicus (1669). A tragedy dealing with the rivalry between Nero and his brother, showing the deterioration of Nero into a tyrant.

Bérénice (1670). A tragic treatment of conflict between love and duty and of renunciation of passion.

Iphigenia (1674). A treatment of Euripides' *Iphigenia in Aulis,* with pathological additions.

Phaedra (1677). See page 411.

Athalia (1691). A great choral tragedy, based on Biblical history.

RESTORATION DRAMA

WILLIAM WYCHERLEY: *The Country Wife* (1672–1674; published in 1675). A comedy of domestic infidelity revolving about a resourceful ingénue. Based on Molière's *School for Husbands* and *School for Wives.*

The Plain Dealer (1674; published about 1676). A slashing adaptation of Molière's *The Misanthrope,* lacking the latter play's subtlety but possessing a power of its own.

JOHN DRYDEN: *All for Love* (1678). An effective adaptation of Shakespeare's *Antony and Cleopatra,* more unified than the Elizabethan play, but lacking its poetic power. The best and most notable of Shakespearean adaptations.

THOMAS OTWAY: *Venice Restored* (1682). A blank-verse drama of the conflict between love and honor, treated in a Shakespearean manner. For a long time a favorite English tragedy.

WILLIAM CONGREVE: *Love for Love* (1695). A spirited comedy of dalliance and intrigue in Congreve's dazzling and impeccable manner.

The Way of the World (1700). See page 430.

SIR JOHN VANBRUGH: *The Relapse* (1696). A satire on affectation and foppishness.

EIGHTEENTH-CENTURY DRAMA

GEORGE FARQUHAR: *The Recruiting Officer* (1706). A pleasant, slightly sentimental comedy of love.

The Beaux' Stratagem (1707). Another pleasant comedy of love, containing a discussion of the ethics of divorce. Both these plays exemplify a change of taste in favor of sentimental as opposed to satiric comedy.

JOHN GAY: *The Beggar's Opera* (1728). Famous rogue's comedy and satire on political chicanery. See page 850.

OLIVER GOLDSMITH: *She Stoops to Conquer* (1773). A farce comedy of amusing situations, noted for its zest and sentiment.

RICHARD BRINSLEY SHERIDAN: *The Rivals* (1775). A comedy of manners, love, and intrigue, famous for its caricatures, such as Miss Lydia Languish and Mrs. Malaprop.

The School for Scandal (1777). See page 463.

LUDWIG HOLBERG: *Erasmus Montanus* (1731). A rustic comedy written in the manner of Molière, satirizing pedantry. The first important Scandinavian (Danish) play.

CARLO GOLDONI: *The Mistress of the Inn* (1752). A gay Italian comedy of character and situation.

ALAIN-RENÉ LE SAGE: *Turcaret* (1709). A brilliant satire on avarice and social corruption in prerevolutionary France.

BEAUMARCHAIS: *The Barber of Seville* (1775). A celebrated comedy of love and intrigue, containing the delightful comic figure Figaro.

The Marriage of Figaro (1784). The robust sequel to *The Barber of Seville;* notable for its zest and its democratic sympathies.

GOTTHOLD EPHRAIM LESSING: *Minna von Barnhelm* (1765). A comedy of love and sentiment, notable for its idealism and its Germanic character types.

Emilia Galotti (1771). A tragedy dealing with the tyranny of petty princes and the nobility of the common man. A "bourgeois tragedy," since the girl seduced by the prince is a middle-class girl, whose father kills her to save her honor and his own.

Nathan the Wise (published in 1779; produced in 1783). A romantic drama, notable for its gospel of humanitarianism and religious tolerance. Lessing's play reflects the social idealism of the eighteenth-century "Enlightenment."

ROMANTICISM

JOHANN WOLFGANG VON GOETHE: *Goetz von Berlichingen* (1773). A semihistorical tragedy celebrating the medieval baron who fought church and state, championing individual freedom; a typical "Storm and Stress" drama.

Egmont (1787). A historical tragedy dealing with Count Egmont, one of the leaders of the revolt of the Netherlands; notable for its psychological treatment of a historical character.

Faust (Part One published in 1808; Part Two completed in 1831, published in 1833). See page 504.

FRIEDRICH VON SCHILLER: *Don Carlos* (1787). A romantic historical tragedy dealing with the struggle for liberty in Spain and the Netherlands.

Wallenstein (1799). A historical trilogy on the Napoleonic ambitions and death of the famous military figure of the Thirty Years' War.

Mary Stuart (1800). A tragedy of the trial and death of Mary Stuart; an idealization. (The reader may find it interesting to compare this play with Maxwell Anderson's *Mary of Scotland,* 1933.) See page 882.

The Maid of Orleans (1801). The tragedy of Joan of Arc. (The reader would do well to read this extremely romantic play along with Shaw's twentieth-century treatment, *Saint Joan.*)

HEINRICH VON KLEIST: *Penthesilea* (1808). A pathological drama of inverted love, revolving around an Amazon queen's murder of Achilles when she finds herself drawn to him with a passion contrary to the antiromantic Amazonian precepts by which she had hitherto lived.

Das Kätzchen von Heilbronn (1810). A romantic and psychological treatment of a young woman's masochistic readiness to endure every humiliation imposed on her by her lover.

The Prince of Homburg (1811). A psychological study of heroism and cowardice, combined with a Prussian conception of military discipline.

FRANZ GRILLPARZER: *Sappho* (1819). A romantic retelling of the Sappho and Phaon legend. The lover discovers that he had been infatuated with Sappho's talent rather than with her physical attractions, and she commits suicide when he falls in love with a young girl.

The Golden Fleece (1822). A romantic trilogy

which retells the Medea legend. Deals with Medea's love for Jason and her sufferings when he proves disloyal to her once they are in Greece after the search for the golden fleece.

The Jewess of Toledo (1837). The tragedy of a king's passion for a Jewess from whom his statesman cannot separate him; a work of strong psychological interest.

GEORG BÜCHNER: *Danton's Death* (1835). See page 570.

Woyzeck (written about 1836; first published in 1879). A naturalistic tragedy revolving around the infidelity of a conscript's common-law wife, his humiliations and jealousies, his murder of his wife, and his suicide. Remarkable for its study of the operations of blind instinct, natural law, and psychopathological tensions and for its mordant irony.

KARL GUTZKOW: *Uriel Acosta* (1846). A liberal romantic drama revolving around the struggles and destruction of a Jewish freethinker who revolts against the orthodox religion. The most famous literary product of the revolutionary, democratic "Young Germany" movement.

FRIEDRICH HEBBEL: *Gyges and His Ring* (1854). Deals with the vengeance of a woman when her husband, king of Lydia, exposes her body to another man's eyes. A historical drama with philosophical significance.

FERDINAND RAIMUND: *The Spendthrift* (*Der Verschwender*) (1834). A romantic fairy drama with middle-class sentiments. Revolves around a prodigal aristocrat, the fairy who loves him, and the good servant who helps him after he has exhausted his fortune. A popular example of the *Zauberpossen,* or fairy-tale style of comedy or folk tale, developed by Raimund and Johann Nestroy in the Viennese theatre.

ALEXANDER PUSHKIN: *Boris Godunov* (1825). A Shakespearean tragedy about a conscience-burdened usurper of the throne of the Czars. After murdering the legitimate heir, he is threatened with the rise of another pretender to the throne. An interesting character study and a surging, if diffuse, drama, in which the common people are involved. (The basis for the famous Moussorgsky opera.)

ZYGMUNT KRASINSKI: *The Undivine Comedy* (1830–1840). A symbolic, romantic representation of the struggles between the feudal aristocracy and the peasantry. The most famous Polish play.

IMRE MADÁCH: *The Tragedy of Man* (1862). A symbolic, romantic account of the corruption and failure of humanity through the ages as a result of Satan's influence; inspired by Goethe's *Faust* but presenting a pessimistic point of view. The most famous premodern Hungarian play.

PERCY BYSSHE SHELLEY: *The Cenci* (published in 1820). The most impressive drama written by the English romantic poets; a story of incestuous passion, tyranny, and injustice, permeated with Shelley's liberal idealism. Based on a famous Italian trial.

JAMES SHERIDAN KNOWLES: *William Tell* (1825). The most stageworthy of the poetic historical plays of the English romantic theatre.

EDWARD BULWER-LYTTON: *The Lady of Lyons* (1838). The popular English romantic melodrama and perhaps the best example of the melodramas that romanticism introduced into the English theatre. The vogue of melodrama continued throughout the nineteenth century. (A famous later example is the Sir Henry Irving success *The Bells,* 1871; a still later one is *The Prisoner of Zenda,* 1895.)

VICTOR HUGO: *Hernani* (1830). The most famous example of French romantic drama, marking the break with French classicism— that is, violating the unities of time and place and the restraint of action by neoclassic rules. Here Hugo also discarded the precision of Racine's poetry for the "grand" or turgid style of romanticism. In the "Battle of Hernani," the romanticists won the victory and the way was prepared for modern drama in France. The play revolves around the rivalry of a king (later Emperor Charles V) and a noble outlaw for the affections of an elderly nobleman's young wife. The theme of Spanish "honor" dominates the story and the sentiments. See page 928.

The King Amuses Himself (or *The King Takes His Pleasure—Le roi s'amuse*) (1832). A court jester, Triboulet, avenges himself for his king's seduction of his daughter. A revolutionary amplification of "grotesque" romantic drama. (This play provided the matter of Verdi's opera *Rigoletto.*)

ALFRED DE MUSSET: *The Follies of Marianne* (1833). A comedy with a "tragic ending." Revolves around the capriciousness of a married woman who makes the wrong choice of a lover.

Fantasio (1833). A "grotesque" comedy in

which a disenchanted Byronic character turns court fool and saves a princess from an unhappy state marriage.

No Trifling with Love (1834). See page 551.

The Chandler (or *The Decoy*) (1835). A brilliant comedy in which a romantic young man chosen to act as a decoy to a betrayed husband wins the affections of the wife and supplants her lover, a dragoon, in her affections; the tables are turned and the dragoon now serves as the decoy.

A Door Should Be Open or Shut (1845). A clever miniature comedy in which a nobleman who comes only to pay a lady a social call ends by proposing marriage to her. Like *No Trifling with Love* (literally, "One Does Not Trifle with Love"), this playlet is a good example of a *comédie-proverbe*.

HENRIK IBSEN: *Love's Comedy* (1862). An unconventional treatment of sex relations and a satire on conventional society, exposing its marriages as failures. Also contains romantic affirmations by a poet who goes off to freedom and adventure.

The Pretenders (1864). A philosophical and psychological historical play revolving around the unification of Norway. Contrasts two rulers, one sure of his goal, the other visionary but weak.

Brand (1866). Famous verse play about an uncompromising idealist's struggle against opportunistic middle-class life, petty materialism, and perfunctory piety.

Peer Gynt (1867). Ibsen's masterpiece in the romantic style. It employs lyricism, folklore, and fantasy in a loose chronicle, but is actually a satire on shallow romanticism and false individualism.

Emperor and Galilean (1873). A historical, philosophical treatment of Julian the Apostate's visionary paganism and defeat by the forces of Christianity, expounding the need for a "Third Kingdom" which would fuse the best of paganism with the best of Christianity.

GEORGE HENRY BOKER: *Francesca da Rimini* (1855). A poetic treatment of the famous Paolo and Francesca love affair. The first American play to possess some literary distinction, it best exemplifies the spread of romantic drama to America.

EARLY REALISM

VASILI KAPNIST: *Chicane* (*Chicanery*) (1798). An early Russian social satire on judicial corruption, replete with realistic touches.

ALEXANDER GRIBOYEDOV: *Woe from Wit* (1821–1831). A satirical exposition of Russian society as seen and opposed by an idealist, Chatsky, whose criticism deprives him of the girl he loves.

NIKOLAI GOGOL: *The Inspector* (*Revizor, The Inspector General, The Government Inspector*) (1836). See page 598.

IVAN TURGENEV: *A Month in the Country* (1849). See page 654.

ALEXANDER OSTROVSKY: *The Thunderstorm* (1860). The tragedy of a young wife frustrated in the rigid merchant-class society of Russia. See page 990.

FRIEDRICH HEBBEL: *Maria Magdalena* (1844). See page 634.

OTTO LUDWIG: *The Forester* (*Der Erbförster*) (1850). A grimly realistic account of the feud between a hereditary forester, who insists upon his hereditary rights, and the owner of the land.

ALEXANDRE DUMAS *fils*: *The Lady of the Camellias* (or *Camille*) (1852). The famous sentimental drama of the courtesan Marguerite Gautier, who dies after renouncing her lover for his sake. The first-act picture of the background of her decline presents realistic elements, and the idea of the "noble courtesan" and her renunciation of the only real love in her life are the sentimental, romantic elements.

The Outer Edge of Society (1855). A picture of not quite respectable French society and an exposé of a designing woman.

The Illegitimate Son (1858). The first of Dumas' "problem" or "thesis" plays; a sermonizing example of this type of drama which has been prevalent in the realistic theatre to the present day. The illegitimate hero refuses to acknowledge his father after becoming famous and takes his mother's name.

ÉMILE AUGIER: *The Marriage of Olympia* (1855). A realistic treatment of the role of courtesans in French society—an objective counterpart to *The Lady of the Camellias*, revolving around a family's effort to save an impressionable son from a grasping demi-mondaine.

ÉMILE AUGIER and JULES SANDEAU: *The Son-in-law of Monsieur Poirier* (1854). A social comedy which contrasts middle-class practicality and aristocratic shiftlessness in the complications that arise when the daughter of a businessman marries a young nobleman.

T. W. ("TOM") ROBERTSON: *Caste* (1867). A picture of English snobbery. The earliest semirealistic social drama of the English theatre by a playwright who also promoted realistic stagecraft.

BIBLIOGRAPHY

SOME GENERAL STUDIES

ARCHER, WILLIAM: *Play-Making: A Manual of Craftsmanship.* Introduction by John Gassner. New York: Dover Publications, 1960.

ARISTOTLE: *See* Butcher.

BATES, ALFRED (editor): *The Drama,* 22 volumes. London: Atheneum Society, 1903.

BENTLEY, ERIC: *The Life of the Drama.* New York: Atheneum Publishers, 1964.

BROOKS, CLEANTH and HEILMAN, ROBERT B.: *Understanding Drama.* New York: Holt, Rinehart and Winston, 1948.

BUSSE, BRUNO: *Das Drama,* 4 volumes. Leipzig: B. G. Teubner, 1922.

BUTCHER, S. H.: *Aristotle's Theory of Poetry and Fine Art.* Introduction by John Gassner. New York: Dover Publications, 1951.

CHENEY, SHELDON: *The Theatre.* New York: Longman's, 1930. Revised edition. New York: David McKay Co., 1959.

CLARK, BARRETT H.: *European Theories of the Drama* (with an American Supplement) Newly Revised by Henry .Popkin. New York: Crown Publishers, 1965.

CORRIGAN, ROBERT W. (editor): *Comedy: Meaning and Form.* San Francisco: Chandler Publishing Co., 1965.

————*Tragedy: Vision and Form.* San Francisco: Chandler Publishing Co., 1965.

DREW, ELIZABETH: *Discovering Drama.* London: Jonathan Cape, 1937.

DUBECH, LUCIEN: *Histoire générale du Théâtre,* 5 volumes. Paris: Librairie de France, 1931–34.

ELLIS–FERMOR, UNA: *The Frontiers of Drama.* London: Methuen & Co., 1946.

Enciclopedia dello Spettacolo, 9 volumes; more to follow. Rome, 1955–.

FERGUSSON, FRANCIS: *The Idea of a Theatre.* Princeton: Princeton University Press, 1949.

FREEDLEY, GEORGE and JOHN A. REEVES: *A History of the Theatre,* Crown Publishers, 1941 (and later editions).

GASSNER, JOHN: *Masters of the Drama.* New York: Dover Publications, 1954 (and later edition, when available).

———— and RALPH ALLEN: *Theatre and Drama in the Making.* Boston: Houghton Mifflin Company, 1964.

GORELIK, MORDECAI: *New Theatres for Old.* New York: Samuel French, 1941.

GREGOR, JOSEF: *Weltgeschichte des Theaters.* Zürich: Phaidon, 1933.

HARTNOLL, PHYLLIS (editor): *The Oxford Companion to the Theatre.* London: Oxford University Press, 1951. (And later editions.)

HERRICK, MARVIN: *Tragicomedy.* Urbana: University of Illinois Press, 1955.

HOY, CYRUS: *The Hyacinth Room: An Investigation into the Nature of Comedy, Tragedy and Tragicomedy.* New York: Alfred A. Knopf, 1964.

KINDERMANN, HEINZ: *Theatergeschichte Europas,* 7 volumes: Salzburg: Otto Müller Verlag, 1957–.

MAGOWAN, KENNETH and WILLIAM MELNITZ: *The Living Theatre.* Englewood Cliffs, N.J.: Prentice-Hall, 1955.

MANTZIUS, KARL: *A History of Theatrical Art in Ancient and Modern Times,* 6 volumes. London: Duckworth, 1903–1921.

MILLETT, FRED G. and GERALD E. BENTLEY: *The Art of the Drama.* New York: Appleton-Century, 1935.

NAGLER, ALOIS: *A Source Book in Theatrical History,* New York: Dover Publications, 1959.

NICOLL, ALLARDYCE: *The Development of the Theatre.* New York: Harcourt, Brace & World, 1948.

————*World Drama,* New York: Harcourt, Brace & World, 1950.

SIMONSON, LEE: *The Stage Is Set.* New York: Harcourt, Brace & World, 1932. (And later editions.)

SOBEL, BERNARD: *The Theatre Handbook and Digest of Plays.* New York: Crown, 1940 (and later editions).

SOUTHERN, RICHARD: *The Seven Ages of the Theatre.* New York: Hill and Wang, 1961.

STAUFFER, RUTH M.: *The Progress of Drama Through the Centuries.* New York: Macmillan, 1928.

STYAN, J. L.: *The Elements of Drama*. Cambridge: University Press, 1963.

STUART, DONALD CLIVE: *The Development of Dramatic Art*. New York: Appleton-Century, 1928 (reprinted by Dover Publications).

THOMPSON, ALAN R.: *The Anatomy of Drama*. Berkeley: University of California Press, 1946.

WEALES, GERALD: *A Play and Its Parts*. New York: Basic Books, 1964.

SOME SPECIAL STUDIES

For Classic Drama

BEARE, W.: *The Roman Stage*. Cambridge: Harvard University Press, 1951.

BIEBER, MARGARETE: *The History of the Greek and Roman Theatre*. Princeton: Princeton University Press, 1938 (and later editions).

CUNLIFFE, JOHN W.: *The Influence of Seneca on Elizabethan Tragedy*, (1893). New York: G. E. Stechert, 1925.

DUCKWORTH, GEORGE: *The Complete Roman Drama*. New York: Random House, 1942.

ELSE, GERALD F.: *The Origin and Early Form of Greek Tragedy*. Cambridge: Harvard University Press, 1965.

FLICKINGINGER, R. S.: *The Greek Theatre and its Drama*. Chicago: University of Chicago Press, 1926.

GREENE, DAVID and RICHMOND LATTIMORE, *The Complete Greek Tragedies*, 4 volumes, Chicago: University of Chicago Press, 1957.

GRUBE, G.M.A.: *The Drama of Euripides* (1941). New York: Barnes & Nobles, 1961.

HARSCH, PHILIP WHALEY: *A Handbook of Classical Drama*. Stanford: Stanford University Press, 1944.

KITTO, H.D.F.: *Greek Tragedy, A Literary Study* (1939). New York: Doubleday & Company (Anchor Books), 1954.

NORTON, GILBERT: *Greek Comedy* (1931). New York: Hill and Wang. n.d.

————*Greek Tragedy* (1920). New York: Hill and Wang. n.d.

OATES, WHITNEY J. and EUGENE O'NEILL, Jr.: *The Complete Greek Drama*, 2 volumes. New York: Random House, 1938.

PICKARD-CAMBRIDGE, A. W.: *Dithyramb, Tragedy and Comedy*. Oxford: The Clarendon Press, 1927.

WHITMAN, CEDRIC: *Sophocles: A Study of Heroic Humanism*. Cambridge: Harvard University Press, 1951.

WOODART, THOMAS: *Sophocles. A Collection of Critical Essays*. Englewood Cliffs: Prentice Hall, 1966.

For Oriental Drama

BOWERS, FAUBION: *Japanese Theatre*. New York: Hill and Wang, 1952.

BUSS, KATE: *Studies in the Chinese Drama*. Boston: Four Seas Co., 1922.

GARGI, BALWANT: *Theatre in India*. New York: Theatre Arts Books, 1962.

KEITH, A. BERNEDALE: *The Sanskrit Drama*. Oxford: The Clarendon Press, 1924.

LOMBARD, FRANK A.: *An Outline History of the Japanese Drama*. London: Allen & Unwin, 1928.

MURRAY, GILBERT: *Euripides and His Age*. New York: Holt, 1913.

WALEY, ARTHUR.: *The Noh Plays of Japan*. New York. Alfred A. Knopf, 1922.

WELLS, HENRY WILLIS: *Classical Drama of India*. Bombay: Asia Publishing House, 1963.

————*Classical Drama of the Orient*. N.Y.: Asia Publishing House, 1965.

YAJNIK, R. K.: *The Indian Theatre*. London: Allen & Unwin, 1933.

For Medieval Drama

BORCHERT, H. H.: *Das Europäische Theater im Mittelalter u.i. der Renaissance*. Leipzig: J. J. Weber, 1935.

CHAMBERS, E. K.: *The Medieval Stage*, 2 volumes. Oxford: Clarendon Press, 1903.

COHEN, GUSTAVE: *Le Théâtre en France au Moyen Age*. Paris: Universitaires de France, 1948. (Original edition, 1928.)

CRAIG, HARDIN: *English Religious Drama of the Middle Ages.* Oxford: The Clarendon Press, 1955.

FARNHAM, WILLARD: *The Medieval Heritage of Elizabethan Tragedy.* Oxford: Basil Blackwell, 1956.

WILLIAMS, ARNOLD: *The Drama of Medieval England.* Lansing: Michigan State University Press, 1961.

YOUNG, KARL: *The Drama of the Medieval Church,* 2 volumes. Oxford: The Clarendon Press, 1933.

For Renaissance Drama

BARISH, JONAS: *Ben Jonson: A Collection of Critical Essays.* Englewood Cliffs: Prentice Hall, 1963.

BECKERMAN, BERNARD: *Shakespeare at the Globe.* New York: The Macmillan Company, 1962

BENTLEY, G. E.: *Jacobean and Caroline Stage,* 5 volumes. Oxford: Clarendon Press, 1941–56.

BOAS, F. S.: *An Introduction to Tudor Drama.* London: Oxford University Press, 1938.

———*An Introduction to Stuart Drama.* London: Oxford University Press, 1946.

BRADLEY, A. C.: *Shakespearian Tragedy.* London: Macmillan, 1904 (and later editions).

CHAMBERS, E. K.: *The Elizabethan Stage,* 4 volumes. Oxford: The Clarendon Press, 1923.

CRAIG, HARDIN: *An Interpretation of Shakespeare.* New York: Dryden Press, 1948.

DEAN, LEONARD F.: *Shakespeare: Modern Essays in Criticism.* New York: Oxford University Press, 1957.

ELIOT, T. S.: *Selected Essays,* London: Faber & Faber, 1934.

FLUCHÈRE, HENRI: *Shakespeare and the Elizabethans.* New York: Hill and Wang, 1956.

GRANVILLE-BARKER, HARLEY: *Prefaces to Shakespeare,* 2 volumes. Princeton: Princeton University Press, 1946, 1947.

HARBAGE, ALFRED: *Shakespeare: The Tragedies. A Collection of Critical Essays.* Englewood Cliffs: Prentice Hall, 1964.

HERRICK, MARVIN T.: *Italian Comedy in the Renaissance.* Urbana: University of Illinois Press, 1960.

KERNODLE, GEO. R.: *From Art to Theatre.* Chicago: University of Chicago Press, 1944.

KOTT, JAN: *Shakespeare Our Contemporary.* New York: Doubleday & Company, 1964.

LEVIN, HARRY: *The Overreacher: A Study of Christopher Marlowe.* Cambridge: Harvard University Press, 1952.

NAGLER, A. M.: *Theatre Festivals of the Medici, 1539–1637.* New Haven, Yale University Press, 1964.

NICOLL, ALLARDYCE: *Stuart Masques and the Renaissance Stage.* New York: Harcourt Brace & World, 1938.

PARROTT, THOMAS MARC and ROBERT HAMILTON BALL: *A Short View of Elizabethan Drama.* New York: Charles Scribner's Sons, 1943.

RIBNER, IRVING: *Patterns in Shakespearian Tragedy.* London: Methuen & Co., 1960.

SPENCER, THEODORE: *Shakespeare and the Nature of Man.* New York: The Macmillan Company, 1949.

SPRAGUE, ARTHUR COLBY: *Shakespeare and the Actors.* Cambridge: Harvard University Press, 1945.

VAN DOREN, MARK: *Shakespeare.* New York: Holt Rinehart and Winston, 1943.

WAITH, EUGENE M.: *Shakespeare: The Histories. A Collection of Critical Essays.* Englewood Cliffs: Prentice Hall, 1965.

WEBSTER, MARGARET: *Shakespeare without Tears.* New York: Whittlesey House, 1942.

WELLS, HENRY W.: *Elizabethan and Jacobean Playwrights.* New York: Columbia University Press, 1935.

For Neoclassic 17th and 18th Century Drama

BARTHÉS, ROLAND: *On Racine.* New York: Hill and Wang, 1964.

BORGERHOFF, E.B.O.: *The Freedom of French Classicism.* Princeton: Princeton University Press, 1950.

CLARK, A.F.G.: *Jean Racine.* Cambridge: Harvard University Press, 1939.

DOBREE, BONAMY: *Restoration Tragedy, 1660–*

1720. London: Oxford University Press, 1929.

FUJIMÚRA, THOMAS H.: *The Restoration Comedy of Wit.* Princeton: Princeton University Press, 1952.

KRUTCH, JOSEPH WOOD: *Comedy and Conscience After the Restoration.* New York: Columbia University Press, 1949.

LANCASTER, H. CARRINGTON: *A History of French Dramatic Literature.* Baltimore: Johns Hopkins University Press, 1935.

LOFTIS, JOHN: *Comedy and Society from Congreve to Fielding.* Stanford: Stanford University Press, 1959.

MOORE, W. G.: *Molière, a New Criticism.* New York: Oxford University Press, 1950.

NETTLETON, GEORGE HENRY: *English Drama of the Restoration and Eighteenth Century, 1642–1780.* New York: The Macmillan Company, 1914.

NICOLL, ALLARDYCE: *A History of the Restoration Drama, 1660–1700.* London: Cambridge University Press, 1923.

PALMER, JOHN: *Molière.* New York: Brown & Warren, 1930.

PERRY, HENRY TEN EYCK: *Masters of Dramatic Comedy and Their Social Themes.* Cambridge: Harvard University Press, 1939.

SUMMERS, MONTAGUE: *The Restoration Theatre.* New York: The Macmillan Company, 1934.

TURNELL, MARTIN: *The Classical Moment.* New York: New Directions, 1946.

For Romantic Drama

ARVIN, N. C.: *Eugene Scribe and the French Theatre, 1815–1860.* Cambridge: Harvard University Press, 1924.

BERTAULT, JULES: *L'époque romantique.* Paris: Editions Jules Tallandier, 1949.

Lancaster. (*Vide supra.*)

LEWES, GEORGE HENRY: *The Life and Works of Goethe.* London, 1875.

NEVINSON, HENRY W.: *Life of Schiller.* New York: Thomas Whittaker Co., 1889.

PASCAL, ROY: *The German "Sturm und Drang."* New York: Philosophical Library, 1953.

PEACOCK, RONALD: *Goethe's Major Plays.* New York: Hill and Wang, 1959.

ROBERTSON, JOHN G.: *The Romantic Spirit Exhibited.* London: Routledge & Kegan Paul, 1927.

VIËTOR, KARL: *Georg Büchner.* Bern: A Francke, 1949.

For Middle-Class and Early Realistic Drama

Arvin, N. C.: (*Vide supra.*)

DOSENHEIMER, ELISE: *Das deutsche soziale Drama von Lessing bis Sternheim.* Konstanz: Südverlag, 1949.

Lancaster: (*Vide supra.*)

MIRSKY, PRINCE D. S.: *A History of Russian Literature.* London: Routledge & Keegan Paul, 1927.

SLONIM, MARC: *Russian Theatre from the Empire to the Soviet.* Cleveland: World Publishing Company, 1961.

VARNECKE, B. V.: *History of the Russian Theatre.* New York: The Macmillan Company, 1951.

WATSON, ERNEST BRADLEE: *Sheridan to Robertson, a Study of the Nineteenth-Century Stage.* Cambridge: Harvard University Press, 1926.

WITKOWSKI, GEORG: *German Drama of the 19th Century.* New York: Holt, 1909.

ABOUT THE EDITOR

JOHN GASSNER *has been acclaimed as "the greatest authority on the drama living in America" by* Commonweal *and as "the American theatre's official anthologist-in-chief" by* Theatre Arts. *He has also been well known as a drama critic, having written play reviews for a number of periodicals, and been a member of the New York Drama Critics Circle since 1936. His articles have been translated into many languages and his books have been used all over the world. As a practical man of the theatre, Mr. Gassner was for two decades chairman of the Theatre Guild's Play Department and executive head of Columbia Pictures' Play Department, in addition to operating subsequently as an independent Broadway producer. Throughout an extraordinarily busy career, which has included adapting plays for the stage and for educational television, he has also found time to be a lecturer, radio commentator, and teacher; and many of the best-known younger playwrights have been at one time or another his students or protégés. He became in 1956 Sterling Professor of Playwriting and Dramatic Literature at the School of Drama of Yale University. In addition to having had several play adaptations produced, Mr. Gassner has published more than forty books on drama, theatrical art, motion pictures, and comparative literature. Among the best known of these are his* Masters of the Drama, Producing the Play, The Theatre in Our Times, Directions in Modern Theatre and Drama, *and* Our Heritage of World Literature. *Mr. Gassner was educated at Columbia University and was awarded university and Guggenheim Fellowships and other distinctions including directorships and honorary degrees.*

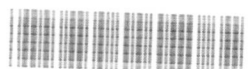
DATE DUE			
			ALESCO